W9-BRH-271

Random House
LATIN-AMERICAN SPANISH
DICTIONARY
SPANISH-ENGLISH
ENGLISH-SPANISH

Random House
LATIN-AMERICAN
SPANISH DICTIONARY
SPANISH-ENGLISH
ENGLISH-SPANISH

BALLANTINE BOOKS • NEW YORK

Revised and edited by David L. Gold

A Ballantine Book
Published by The Ballantine Publishing Group
Copyright © 1996 by Random House, Inc.

http://www.randomhouse.com

Library of Congress Catalog Card Number: 96-96203

ISBN 0-345-40546-3

Manufactured in the United States of America

First Ballantine Books Edition: August 1996

OPM 18 17 16 15 14 13 12 11 10

Contents

Preface

Selection of Vocabulary

The aim of this dictionary is to cover as much current vocabulary as possible, as well as certain items found in standard works of modern Spanish and English literature.

This dictionary includes items often omitted in other bilingual dictionaries—road and street signs, for example—though few things could be as frustrating (and, sometimes, as dangerous) as seeing such signs but not knowing what they mean (in this dictionary, all kinds of public notices are enclosed by the symbols « » in Spanish and by double quotation marks in English). Also, many vocabulary items consisting of more than one word have been treated here (see for instance **do** in the English-Spanish section).

For lack of space, however, not every current or useful item could be included, and a selection of material was necessary.

Spanish Spelling and Alphabetization

On January 1, 1959, the Spanish language academies changed certain spelling rules and on April 27, 1994, they eliminated **ch** and **ll** as separate letters of the alphabet. Thus, whereas words like **chico** and **chocolate** were formerly alphabetized under their own letter (**ch**, which came between **c** and **d**) and words like **llamar** and **llegar** were formerly alphabetized under their own letter (**ll**, which came between **l** and **m**), words containing **ch** or **ll**, in whatever part of the word they may appear, are now alphabetized as they would be in English (**chico** therefore now appears under **c** and **llegar** under **l**).

Field Labels

Only essential field labels are given in this dictionary. For example, the label *medicine* or *pathology* is unnecessary at **flebitis** 'phlebitis' (in the Spanish-English section) because both the Spanish and the English words refer only to the pathological condition so called in those languages.

In contrast to that entry, we do need a label at **foca** 'seal' (in the Spanish-English section) because English **seal** has several meanings and only the zoological one is intended here. Anglophones looking up **foca** thus need the label *zoology* (hispanophones need no label because they know that **foca** is the name of an animal, hence they will correctly assume that **seal** is intended only in its zoological sense).

Spatial Labels for Spanish

Spatial variation in Spanish ranges from nil to extreme. On one hand, the words for 'flower' and 'mother-in-law', for example, are everywhere **flor** and **suegra** respectively. On the other hand, the language has many words for 'bus' and 'ballpoint pen' (see the

English-Spanish section of this dictionary).

Little of what has been written on how Spanish differs from place to place is reliable. For example, the Spanish-English section of one dictionary offers **alborotos** *Central America* 'popcorn,' **cabritos** *Chile* 'popcorn,' and **palomitas** 'popcorn,' but the English-Spanish section of the very same dictionary has **popcorn** 'alborotos' *the River Plate region and Peru,* 'cabritas,' and 'palomitas de maíz.'

In the absence of trustworthy sources, spatial labels are best dispensed with, though some are given in this dictionary when I have been able to ascertain at first hand that a less than universal usage is found in a certain area.

In general, this dictionary emphasizes Spanish of the Western Hemisphere. In particular, it tries to convey some of the spatial variation that may be found from country to country within that area. Therefore, certain usages are labeled *Latin America* (if they are used in at least many Western Hemispheric countries) and others are given more restricted labels, like *Argentina* and *Mexico* (if they appear to be limited to just certain countries).

Spatial characterizations in this dictionary should be interpreted in a minimal way. For instance, *Mexican* means that the usage so labeled is found in Mexico but it says nothing about whether that usage is present or absent elsewhere (something that only further research could determine).

Subentries

If a main-entry head is repeated in a subentry in exactly the same form, it is abbreviated to its first letter (for instance, at **fin** in the Spanish-English section we find **a f. de**, which stands for **a fin de**). If the main entry head appears in any other form, the full form is given in the subentry (thus, at **fin,** the subentry head **a fines de** is spelled without abbreviation).

Irregular Spanish Verbs and the Direction "See . . ."

If a Spanish verb is irregular, it has been treated in one of two ways: either its principal parts are shown (see for example the end of the entry for **caber**) or you are referred to an analogous irregular verb for guidance (see for example the end of the entry for **comparecer,** where you are directed to **conocer**). Thus, since the irregular form **conozco,** is shown at **conocer** (it being irregular in the sense that it has a **z**), you may infer that **comparecer** has the irregular form **comparezco.**

One of the consequences of the changes in Spanish spelling of January 1, 1959, is that a new kind of orthographically irregular verb has come into existence (for example **ahijar, ahincar, ahitar, ahuchar, ahumar, ahusar, cohibir, prohijar, rehilar, rehusar, sahumar, sobrehilar,** and **trashumar**).

If "See . . ." is all you find at an entry, you are being directed to a synonym. Thus, "**descompasarse** See **descomedirse**" means that the translations of **descomedirse** are those of **descompasarse** too.

The Basics of Standard Spanish Pronunciation

As may be expected of a language that has been used for many centuries, over a vast area, and by diverse people, Spanish is now pronounced in various ways. Of the many current pronunciations, two are offered as most suitable for speakers of Spanish as a second language. The two standards are identical to a large extent, differing chiefly with respect to the pronunciation of **c** before **e**; **c** before **i**; **z** in any position; and, optionally, **ll** in any position.

To the extent that the two standards differ, features belonging to just one of them are labeled either *Standard 1* or *Standard 2* below.

Features labeled *Standard 1* are accepted as standard in Spain but not in the Western Hemisphere. Features labeled *Standard 2* are accepted as standard in the Western Hemisphere but not in Spain. If you speak Spanish mostly with Spaniards or mostly with people in or from the Western Hemisphere, your choice of standard will thus be straightforward. If you speak with people from both areas, you can either try to master both standards or, if you want to follow just one of them no matter to whom you speak, pick Standard 2.

In the Western Hemisphere, features labeled *Standard 1* are often either erroneously admired as being "the correct pronunciation of the language" or, quite the opposite, disdained as highfalutin (which are precisely the same reactions to British English frequently heard in English-speaking areas outside Europe). Neither standard, however, is intrinsically better than the other.

If possible, review the material given here with a speaker of Standard Spanish and hear how the sample words, phrases, and sentences are pronounced.

a is pronounced /a/, which is similar to the second vowel of the English interjection **aha!** and the vowel of the English interjection **ah,** although much shorter in duration.

See also "Diphthongs and Triphthongs" below.

b has three pronunciations. At the beginning of an utterance, after [m] (whether represented by **m** or by **n**), or after [n] (whether represented by **n** or by **m**), the letter **b** is pronounced [b], which is similar to the pronunciation of the first consonant of English **beach, broth,** etc. For example, in the sentence **Bulgaria envió a ambos embajadores en un barco japonés,** each of the four instances of **b** (and the one instance of **v**) is so pronounced.

Before /č/, /f/, /t/, /k/, /s/, /x/, or /θ/ in the same word (see **ch** [under **c**], **f, t, c, g,** and **c** respectively for interpreting those symbols), **b** is pronounced [p] (see **p** for interpreting that symbol), as in **subtítulo, absceso, subjefe,** and, in Standard 1, **subcentral.** That rule also holds before [p] in the same word (with the further result that [p] + [p] is reduced to [p]; hence the first two syllables of **subproducto,** for example, are [supro]) and for [p] before /s/ in the same word (with the further result that [ps] may be reduced to [s.] In certain words, nonpronunciation of **b** became so widespread that the only spelling now used is without that letter, for instance **ofuscar** and its derivatives (contrast English **obfuscate, obfuscation,** etc.).

At the end of a word, more than one pronunciation of **b** may be heard. For example, **club** may be [klub], [kluβ], or [klu]. Its plural (**clubs**) may be [klups], [klus], and possibly [kluβs] (unless the plural **clubes** is used, whose universal pronunciation is [kluβɛs] (see the next paragraph for interpreting [β] and **e** for interpreting [ɛ]). All of the foregoing holds for compounds of **club**, like **aeroclub. In esnob** ~ snob, the final **b** is pronounced [b].

In all other positions (for example, **habas, hablar,** and **habré**), **b** is pronounced [β], a sound absent in English, which is made by bringing the lips close together without letting them touch each other (as if you were blowing dust away or blowing out a match or candle), expelling air through the mouth, and vibrating the vocal cords. This sound is thus similar to /v/ (as in English **very** and **vowel**), except that the latter is made by making the lower lip touch the upper teeth. English-speakers should not mistake Spanish [β] for English /v/.

c has several pronunciations. If it is followed by **e** or **i**, the letter **c** is pronounced /θ/ in Standard 1 and [s] in Standard 2. The pronunciation of /θ/ in Spanish is similar to that of **th** in English **thatch, think,** etc., but made with somewhat more protrusion of the tongue. The sound [s] is similar to the pronunciation of **s** in English **say, simple,** etc., though in northern Spain [s] is often produced with the tip of the tongue higher in the mouth than in other varieties of Spanish, the result being that this sound has a hushing quality there (similar to Modern Greek /s/), which English-speakers should not mistake for /š/, which is the pronunciation of **sh** in English **shall, should,** etc.

Although Standard 1 has /θ/ for **c** before **e** or **i**, people who use that pronunciation will not be put off if they hear you pronounce the **c** as [s], because the latter is widespread (though not standard) in Spain. In the Western Hemisphere, **c** before **e** or **i** is always pronounced [s] and never /θ/. Speakers of Western Hemispheric Spanish will react to /θ/ either as "the correct pronunciation" ("though we don't use it") or as a highfalutin pronunciation (unless it comes from people who are to the manner born, i.e., many Spaniards). Thus, whereas it is desirable though not obligatory that you use Standard 1 in Spain, you would be well advised to use only Standard 2 in the Western Hemisphere, where /θ/ is bound to elicit a sharp reaction of one kind or another (as sharp as British **drawing pin, lorry,** or **trunk call** instead of **thumbtack, truck, long-distance call** would probably elicit in the United States).

If **c** ends a syllable that is not the last syllable in the word and the next syllable begins with /t/, it is pronounced /k/ in most words (like **actor** and **actriz**) and in at least one you may pronounce it /k/ or not pronounce it at all (**coctel** (**coctel** ~ **cocteles**). In the place name **Vitoria** the absence of /k/ has been universal for so long that that is now its only spelling (in contrast to the female given name **Victoria** and the common noun **victoria**).

If **c** or **k** ends the last syllable of the word, that letter is pronounced /k/ at least in **cinc** ~ **zinc, clac, copec, frac, Nueva York,** and **tictac,** whereas in **biftec, bistec,** and **coñac** many speakers do not pronounce it (likewise in the plural of the last word, **coñacs**).

In all other cases (as in **aclarar, acoplar, acreditar, capaz, chucruta, claro,** and **creer**), **c** is pronounced /k/.

d has several pronunciations. At the beginning of an utterance, after [n], or after /l/, this letter is pronounced [d], which is similar to the pronunciation of **d** in English **dear, dust,** etc., with this difference: in the production of Spanish [d], the tongue touches the lower edge of the upper front incisors.

When between two vowels, when preceded by a vowel and followed by **r,** or when at the end of a word and not preceded by **r** (as in **pedir, Pedro,** and **liber-** **tad**), the letter **d** is pronounced [ð], which is similar to the pronunciation of **th** in English **that, there,** etc., but less interdental than English [ð] (in the production of the Spanish sound, the tip of the tongue touches the lower edge of the upper incisors).

If **d** is at the end of a word and it is preceded by **r** (as in **lord, milord**), it is silent. In the plurals, no matter how they are spelled, **d** is never present, hence never pronounced: **lores, milores.**

e has two pronunciations. The instruction given in some books that **e** is pronounced [e] when stressed and [ɛ] when unstressed does not hold true for today's Spanish and may never have been an accurate description of its pronunciation in any variety of the language.

Here are better guidelines for **e** (except when it is part of a diphthong or triphthong):

If **e** is found in a syllable ending in a consonant (see "Syllabification" below), it is pronounced [ɛ], which is similar to the pronunciation of **è** in French or to the vowel of **bet, let, met,** etc., as pronounced in Standard English, that is, with considerable lowering of the jaw. For example, **embaldosar, fresco, hablen,** and **mestizo.**

If **e** ends a syllable and the next one begins with **r, rr,** or **t,** it is pronounced [ɛ]. For instance, **pero, caballete** (the first **e**), **cerrar,** and **jinete.**

Otherwise, **e** is pronounced [e], which is similar to the pronunciation of **é** in French, that is, the jaw is lowered only minimally (the closest English comes to having a sound like [e] is probably the vowel of **ache, rake, stake,** etc.). For example, **caballete** (the second **e**), **hablé, mesa,** and **poeta. Caballete** thus has both renditions of **e,** though the plural of that word, **caballetes,** has only [ɛ], because here the last syllable ends in a consonant.

f is pronounced /f/, which is similar to the pronunciation of **f** in English **fate, feet,** etc. For example, **afectar, fecha, golf, golfo, iufl.**

See also **h.**

g has several pronunciations. At the beginning of an utterance and when followed by **a, o, u,** or a consonant letter except **n** (as in **gato, goma, gusto, glaciar,** or **grave**), **g** is pronounced [g], which is similar to the pronunciation of **g** in English **get, go, gumption,** etc.

At the beginning of a word and when followed by **n,** the letter **g** is silent (as in **gnomo**). That pronunciation is in fact so widespread and reputable that a **g**-less spelling is now acceptable and is in fact preferred in this dictionary (see "Miscellaneous" below).

When **g** is preceded by **n** and is followed in the next syllable of the same word by **a, o, u, ü,** or a consonant letter (as in **angosto, ángulo, ungüento, englobar,** and **engrasar**), it is pronounced [g].

When **g** occurs at the end of a syllable and is preceded by **n,** it is silent, as in **bumerang.** In older borrowings from other languages, that **g** was systematically or sometimes omitted, as in **sterling** > **esterlina, pudding** > **pudín.**

Before **e** or **i** (as in **gemir** and **gigante**), except if it comes at the end of a word, the letter **g** is pronounced /x/, which is absent in most varieties of current English. This sound is similar to the pronunciation of **ch** in German **Bach,** that of **ch** in Israeli Hebrew **zecher,** and that of **ch** in Scots English **loch, Lochaber,** etc. Press the back of the tongue against the soft palate, expel air (as if coughing), and do not vibrate the vocal chords.

If **g** ends a syllable that is not the last syllable of the word (as in **dogma** and the first syllable of **zigzag**), this letter is pronounced [g]. In such cases, the next syllable always begins with a consonant.

Otherwise, **g** is pronounced [ɣ], a sound absent in English, which is made by bringing the back of the tongue close to the soft palate (without letting them touch), expelling air through the mouth, and vibrating the vocal chords. Examples are **hago** and **hígado.**

h is silent. In older Spanish, this letter was pronounced /h/ (a sound similar to the first consonant of **here, how,** and **huddle** in Standard English), which has remained in a few words in the guise of /x/ (see **g** for interpreting that symbol). In such cases, **h** has been replaced by **j** (**cante jondo,** from older **cante hondo.** In at least four words, both spellings remain standard: **halar ~ jalar, halón ~ jalón, holgorio ~ jolgorio, ¡hopo!** and **¡jopo!** (in the first variant of each pair, the **h** is not now pronounced). To at least some

Spanish ears, the variants with /x/ are more emphatic or affective than those without it.

i has two pronunciations. When representing a full vowel, it is pronounced [i], which is similar to the vowel of English **beet, feet, sheen,** etc., but shorter (for instance, **dicho, isla,** and **cursi**). When bearing a dieresis, this letter is likewise pronounced [i], as in **pïada** (were the dieresis absent, **ia** here would represent a diphthong).

When **i** represents part of a diphthong or a triphthong (see "Diphthongs and Triphthongs" below), it is pronounced [y], which is similar to the pronunciation of **y** in English **year, yes,** or **yolk**. Thus, **miel** and **tiesto** are pronounced [myɛl] and [tyɛsto].

See also **y**.

j is almost always pronounced /x/ (see **g** for interpreting that symbol). A notable exception is **reloj,** which many speakers pronounce [re'lo]. That pronunciation of **reloj** is so widespread that **reló** is an alternate spelling of the singular form, but only in informal writing. In the plural, everyone pronounces /x/ and therefore writes the **j: relojes**.

See **x**.

k, which is now found only in recent borrowings from other languages, is pronounced /k/ (see **c** for interpreting that symbol). The letter combination **ck** (as in **crack, flashback, shock, snack, stock**) is pronounced /k/.

l when not doubled is pronounced /l/, which is formed by putting the tip of the tongue against the sockets of the upper incisors, the remainder of the tongue lying flat. Spanish /l/ thus does not have the hollow sound of English /l/, in whose formation the back of the tongue rises toward the palate.

The letter combination **ll** (which always begins a syllable) has two pronunciations in Standard Spanish: /ʎ/ (which is similar to the pronunciation of **lli** in English **million** or that of **li** in **vermilion**) and [y], which is similar to the pronunciation of **y** in English **year, yes,** or **yolk**. Since English words like **million** and **vermilion** actually have [ly] rather than /ʎ/, that is, [l] ends one syllable of those English words and [y] begins the next one (whereas Spanish **ll,** except at the end of a word, always begins a syllable), English-speakers should be careful not to misinterpret /ʎ/ as [ly]. To achieve a good rendition of Spanish /ʎ/, pronounce **million** as if it did not contain **mi-,** that is, as if it were ***llion**. Good practice words are those beginning with **ll** (like **llamar, llegar,** and **llorar**) since here you are forced to pronounce /ʎ/ at the beginning of a syllable. See also **ñ** and "Syllabification" below.

In Spain, although /ʎ/ is still prestigious, it has been going out of use for decades as more and more people switch to [y] (in the unvarnished pronunciation of Madrid, for example, /ʎ/ has disappeared entirely). Spaniards now using /ʎ/ natively are mostly from northern Spain or, if not from that part of the country, they first learned [y] and later intentionally replaced that sound by the more prestigious /ʎ/. You may thus use either pronunciation in speaking to Spaniards, but [y] has a cachet in Spain that /ʎ/ lacks. Standard 1 therefore has /ʎ/.

In the Western Hemisphere, **ll** is pronounced /ʎ/, [y], /ž/, or /š/, according to area or speaker (/ž/ is similar to the pronunciation of **z** in English **azure** and of **zs** in the name **Zsa Zsa;** /š/ is similar to the pronunciation of **sh** in English **shall, should,** etc.). You may want to pick the sound your interlocutors use or, if you want to choose a SINGLE pronunciation that most speakers of Western Hemispheric Spanish will find acceptable (whatever they themselves use), take /ʎ/ or [y] (though /ʎ/ might sound a tad highfalutin to certain Spanish-speakers in the Western Hemisphere who do not use it themselves).

m: Traditionally, Spanish does not have [m] at the end of a word when it is pronounced in isolation. Consequently, in many words borrowed from other languages ending in that sound, it was replaced by [n] (see the next section for interpreting that symbol) and the word was re-spelled accordingly (for example, **harén, ínterin, Jerusalén, macadán, querubín, ron, serafín**). However, a few words (all learned borrowings from Latin and recent borrowings from other languages) end in **m** (for example, **álbum, factótum, ídem, médium, memorándum, ultimátum,** and **vademécum**) and that letter also appears in the Spanish names of many places outside Spanish-speaking areas, like **Bírming-**

ham, Búckingham, Siam, and **Vietnam.**

n has several pronunciations. If immediately followed by a labial consonant (represented by **b, f, m, p,** or **v**), whether in the same word or in the next one, it is pronounced [m] (as in the words **anfitrión, inmediato, anverso** or the sentences **insiste en bucear, insiste en pelear,** and **en muchos casos hay más**). Since [m] + [m] is reduced to a single [m], **en muchos casos** actually has just one [m].

However, [n] + [m] (as in **insomne**) is not reduced.

Before /k/ or [g] (as in **aunque** and **angosto**), **n** is pronounced [ŋ], which is similar to the final consonant of **long, sing,** and **song** as pronounced in Standard English.

In all other positions (as in **Anatolia, andan** and **nombrar**), **n** is pronounced [n], which is similar to the pronunciation of **n** in English **hand, near,** etc.

ñ is pronounced /ɲ/, which is similar to the pronunciation of **ny** in English **canyon** or **ni** in English **onion.** Since English words like those two actually have [ny] rather than /ɲ/ (that is, [n] ends one syllable and [y] begins the next one), English-speakers should be careful not to misinterpret /ɲ/ as [ny]. To achieve a good rendition of Spanish /ɲ/ (which always begins a syllable), pronounce **canyon** as if it did not contain **ca-,** that is, as if it were **nyon,** or **onion** as if it were **nion.** Good practice words are those beginning with **ñ** (like **ñiquiñaque** and **ñoño**) since here you are forced to pronounce /ɲ/ at the beginning of a syllable.

o has two pronunciations, neither of which can easily be described with reference to English. In a syllable ending in a consonant (see "Syllabification" below), this letter is pronounced somewhat like the **o** of English **port** or **short** (for instance **pondré** and **sondear**). Otherwise (that is, when **o** ends the syllable), it is pronounced somewhat like the **o** of English **coke** or **tote** (for instance, **codo** and **lodo**). The words **costo** and **zonzo** thus contain an example of each kind of **o**. The two kinds of /o/ are similar to the closed and open /o/ of Italian.

p, where it is pronounced, stands for [p], which is similar to the pronunciation of **p** in English **space, spear, spook,** etc., but different from that of **p** in English **pike, peak, poke,** etc. To achieve a good rendition of Spanish [p], hold your open palm in front of your mouth and pronounce first **pike, peak, poke,** then **space, spear, spook.** When pronouncing the first three words, you felt a noticeable puff of air on your palm, but in the last three words you felt almost no puff at all. A noticeable puff of air accompanying a speech sound is called *aspiration;* sounds pronounced with aspiration are *aspirated;* and those pronounced without it are *unaspirated.* Spanish [p] (like Spanish /k/ and /t/) is always unaspirated, wherever it occurs.

Spanish **ps** at the beginning of a word is pronounced [s]. Some pretentious Spanish-speakers may tell you that the "correct" pronunciation is [ps], but that would be as artificial as pronouncing English **psyche, psychology,** etc., in that way. In fact, nonpronunciation of **p** in the combination **ps** at the beginning of a word is so entrenched in Spanish that the preferred spelling is now **s**.

q is always followed by **ue** or **ui.** The sequence **que** is pronounced either [kɛ] or [ke] and **qui** is pronounced [ki] (for example, **quince**) or [ky] (for instance, **quien**) (see "Diphthongs and Triphthongs" below). To represent the sound sequences [kwe], [kwɛ], and [kwi], Spanish has **cue, cue,** and **cui** respectively (as in **cueva, cuestión,** and **cuidar**). Because **q** is always followed by **u,** if Spanish-speakers borrow words containing just **q** from other languages, that letter is changed to **k.** Thus, the Spanish names of Iraq and Qatar, for example, are **Irak** and **Katar.**

r has two pronunciations. At the beginning of a word or when it comes after **l, n,** or **s** (for example, **reir, alrededor, enrojecer,** and **Israel**), this letter has the same pronunciation as **rr** (see below). If **b** ends one syllable and **r** begins the next one in the same word (see "Syllabification" below), **r** is pronounced exactly like **rr** (for example **subrayar** if syllabified **sub-ra-yar**). If **b** + **r** belong to the same syllable (for instance **bramar** and **lubricar**), **r** is pronounced with one flip of the upper front part of the tongue against the sockets of the upper incisors (for instance

subrayar if syllabified **su-bra-yar**). See "Syllabification" below on the alternative now permitted in words beginning with the prefix **sub-**.

In all other positions, **r** is likewise pronounced with one flip of the upper front part of the tongue against the sockets of the upper incisors (for instance, **leer, para, pera, pero, tercero,** and **treinta**).

rr is pronounced with a trill (several flips) of the upper front part of the tongue against the sockets of the upper incisors (for instance, **parra, perra, perro,** and **sierra**). Thus, **para** and **parra** are different words, with different pronunciations and different meanings. The same applies to **caro** and **carro, pera** and **perra, pero** and **perro, torero** and **torrero,** and other pairs of words.

s has several pronunciations. When it represents the plural ending of nouns recently borrowed from other languages, it is silent in certain words, like **cabarets, carnets, complots, conforts, superávits, tíckets, trusts, vermuts.**

Before the letters **b, v, d, g** (but only when this letter is not followed by **e** or **i**), **l, m, n,** or **r** (whether any of those eight letters appear in the same word as **s** or they appear in the next word), you have an alternative (in both standards) if **s** is not the last letter of the word: it may be pronounced [z] (a sound similar to the pronunciation of **z** in English **zebra, zoo,** etc.) or [s] (see **c** for interpreting that symbol): **esbelto, esdrújulo, esgrimir, isla, esmalte, Israel, los** **baúles, los varones, los dedos, los guantes, los lagos, los maestros, los nervios, los ratones,** etc. If **s** is the last letter, only [s] is found (for instance, in the family name **Pons**).

If **s** is followed by **r** (whether in the same word or in the next one), besides the two pronunciations suggested above [s] or [z]), a third possibility is not to pronounce the **s** at all and, as a compensation, trill the **r** more. The word **Israel** (and its derivatives) thus has three pronunciations: [isrraɛl], [izrraɛl], and [irrraɛl].

Otherwise, **s** is pronounced [s] (as in **ese, especial, hablas, hasta, insistir, seco**).

If **s** is followed by **h,** the foregoing paragraph applies, except in the case of Spanish words recently borrowed from other languages or words modeled on such recently borrowed words, in which **sh** constitutes a unit, to be pronounced /š/ (a sound similar to the pronunciation of **sh** in English **shall, sheet, should,** etc.). Thus, in **deshacer,** an old Spanish word not recently borrowed from another language, the instructions about **s** apply and the **h** is silent (hence the first two syllables of that word are [desa]), whereas in **riksha** and **yídish, sh** is pronounced /š/.

t, except before **l** in the same word, is pronounced [t], which is similar to the pronunciation of **t** in English **stake, steer, stoop,** etc., but different from that of **t** in English **take, teak, took,** etc. To achieve a good rendition of Spanish /t/, hold your open palm in front of your mouth and pronounce first **take, teak, took,** then **stake, steer, stoop.** When pronouncing the first three words, you felt a noticeable puff of air on your palm, but in the last three words you felt almost no puff at all. A noticeable puff of air is called *aspiration;* sounds pronounced with aspiration are *aspirated;* and those pronounced without it are *unaspirated.* Spanish /t/ (like Spanish /k/ and /p/) is always unaspirated, wherever it occurs.

In three positions, **t** may not be pronounced as described above. First, before **l** or **m** in the same word (as in **atleta, aritmético,** and **ritmo**) you have an alternative: **t** may be pronounced as described or it may be pronounced [ð] (see **d** for interpreting that symbol).

Second, the **t** of the prefix **post-** is not pronounced if it is followed by any pronounced consonant letter except **r,** so much so that alternate spellings without **t** are also found and they are in fact the preferable ones, for instance, **posguerra** and posmeridiano. (but also **postergar,** etc.).

Third, **t** at the end of a word may be silent, as in **cabaret, carnet, complot, tícket, trust,** and **vermut,** which are pronounced as if written ***cabaré, *carné, *compló, *tique, *trus,** and ***vermú** (the plurals are pronounced identically to their singulars. In still other words you have an alternative: **confort** is pronounced either [kom'for] or [kom'fort] (the plural **conforts** has both variants too).

u has several pronunciations. In the combinations **gue, gui, que,** and **qui,** the letter **u** is silent. For example, **guedeja** [geðexa] ~ [ɣeðexa], **quedar** [keðar], and **quien** [kyen] (see **q** and **e** on the pronunciation of those letters).

When **u** represents part of a diphthong or a triphthong (see "Diphthongs and Triphthongs" below), it is pronounced [w], which is similar to the first sound of English **win** and **won.** Thus, **puesto** and **seudónimo,** for example, are pronounced [pwɛsto] and [sewðonimo].

If a **u** bears a dieresis, it is pronounced [w]. Thus, **lingüista** is pronounced [lingwista].

In all other cases, **u** is pronounced [u], which is similar to the vowel of English **coot** or **toot,** although in the production of the Spanish sound the lips are more rounded and the vowel is of shorter duration than in the production of the English one. For example, **ducha, hubo, u, Unamuno,** and **uno.**

v has two pronunciations. At the beginning of an utterance or after **n** (which in this position is pronounced [m]), the letter **v** is pronounced [b], which is similar to the first consonant of English **beach, broth,** etc. In all other positions, this letter is pronounced [β] (see **b** for interpreting that symbol). For example, in the sentence **¿Verdad que en el anverso de la medalla se ve un pavo real?,** the first and fifth words have [b] and the tenth and twelfth have [β].

w, which is found only in borrowings from Germanic languages and French, has several pronunciations. In several words, it is pronounced as if it were **b** or **v** and in such cases alternate spellings with **v** are found too: **wagneriano ~ vagneriano, Westfalia ~ Vestfalia.** The forms with **v** are preferable.

In at least a few words, **w** is pronounced [w] (a sound similar to the first sound of English **win** and **won**) and for one of them an alternate spelling with **u** exists: **Malawi, Taiwán, Zimbabwe.**

In **whisky,** the letter combination **wh** is pronounced [w] by those who want to show off their knowledge of English and [gw] or [ɣw] by those who speak normally (the choice of [gw] or [ɣw] depends on the position of the word in the utterance; see the instructions for **g**).

Whereas **Trans World Airlines** is shortened to the initialism **TWA** in English, in Spanish it is shortened to the acronym **la TWA,** which is pronounced /la'tua/.

x has several pronunciations. If **x** occurs before a consonant (as in **experiencia, extremidad** and **mixto**), pronounce it [s]. That pronunciation is probably most frequent in words beginning with the prefix **ex-** followed by a consonant, for example **excelente,** widely pronounced [ɛsθelɛnte] or [ɛselɛnte]. In the latter pronunciation, [s] + [s] becomes a single [s], though an effect of the double [s] remains: the preceding **e** is pronounced [ɛ], not [e], that is, as if the first syllable ended in a consonant, i.e., as if it ended in the first [s].

If **x** occurs between vowels, you have an alternative in certain words (**examen** and **exiguo,** for example, may be pronounced with [ks], [gz], or [s]) but not in others (for instance, all Spanish-speakers, it seems, now pronounce **sexo** with [ks]).

At the end of a word, the pronunciation of **x** is in flux. In **ántrax, Benelux, dux, fénix, látex,** and **tórax,** [ks] seems to be most frequent if not universal today, whereas in **clímax** and **flux,** [s] may now be more frequent.

y has several pronunciations. In the word **y,** it is pronounced [i] (see **i** for interpreting that symbol).

When it represents the first or last segment of a diphthong or triphthong (see "Diphthongs and Triphthongs" below), as in **ya, yegua, yunque, ley, rey, soy,** and **Paraguay,** the letter **y** is pronounced [y] (see **ll** [under **l**] for interpreting that symbol).

In certain varieties of Spanish, [y] is pronounced with more occlusion, so that it has come to be close to [ž] if not actually that sound (see **ll** [under **l**] for interpreting the latter symbol); and in still other varieties it is pronounced with so much occlusion that it has come to be close to [ǰ] if not actually that (ǰ) is similar to the first consonant of English **Jacob, Jerusalem, Jew,** etc.). Both Standard 1 and Standard 2 have [y] rather than [ž] or [ǰ], except in the emphatic pronunciation of **yo** (as in **iyo, y yo sólo, soy el dueño aquí!**), for which [ǰo] is a widespread rendition acceptable in both standards.

Certain family names have two spelling variants, an archaic one with **y** and one spelled in modern fashion with **i** (like **Yglesias**

~ **Iglesias**). Here, **y** is pro-
nóunced /i/, that is, just like **i.**

z has several pronunciations.
In Standard 1, you have an alternative:
(1) In all positions, pronounce it
[θ] (see **c** for interpreting that
symbol). Or,
(2) Before the letters **b, v, d, g, l,
m, n,** or **r** (whether in the
same word or in the next
one), pronounce it [ð] (see **d**
for interpreting that symbol)
and in all other positions pronounce it [θ] (see **c** for interpreting that symbol).
In Standard 2, you have an alternative:
(3) In all positions, pronounce it
[s] (see **s** for interpreting that
symbol). Or,
(4) Before the letters **b, v, d, g, l,
m, n,** or **r** (whether in the
same word or in the next
one), pronounce it [z] and in
all other positions pronounce
it [s] (see **s** for interpreting
that symbol).

That is to say, if you pro-
nounce **c** before **e** or **i** as [θ],
you must follow instruction
(1) or (2) above. If you pronounce **c** before **e** or **i** as [s],
you must follow instruction
(3) or (4) above.

Furthermore, if you choose
to pronounce **s** as [s] before
b, v, d, g, l, m, n, or **r,** you
must pronounce **z** before any
of those eight letters as [θ] (=
Standard 1) or as [s] (= Standard 2); if you choose to pronounce **s** as [z], you must
pronounce **z** before any of
those eight letters as [ð] (=
Standard 1) or [z] (= Standard 2).

Thus, in the phrase **César,
el hazmerreír de toda la**

isla, for example, you have
these choices for the **c** of the
first word, the **z** of the third
word, and the **s** of the seventh word:

c [θ] + **z** [θ] + **s** [s] (= Standard 1)
c [θ] + **z** [ð] + **s** [z] (= Standard 1)
c [s] + **z** [s] + **s** [s] (= Standard 2)
c [s] + **z** [z] + **s** [z] (= Standard 2)
The same restrictions apply
to any individual word. Thus,
civilización, for example,
must be pronounced either
[θiβiliθaθyon] (= Standard 1)
or [siβilisasyon] (= Standard
2).

Diphthongs and Triphthongs

Spanish has fifteen diph-
thongs and six triphthongs.

Eight of the diphthongs begin
with a semivowel:
ia [ya] is spelled **ya** at the beginning of a word, e.g.,
desahuciar, yámbico.
ua [wa] (e.g., **guardar**).
ie [ye] or [yɛ] is spelled **ye** at the
beginning of a word, e.g.,
**agüero, bien, higiene,
siete, yema.** The rules for
choosing [e] or [ɛ] (see **e**)
apply to [ye] and [yɛ] too.
ue [we] or [wɛ] is spelled **üe**
after **g** that is not pronounced [x], e.g., **huelga,
hueste, huevo, vergüenza.**
The rules for choosing [e] or
[ɛ] (see **e**) apply to [we] or
[wɛ] too.
io and **yo** [yo], e.g. **soslayar,
yo.** The spelling **io** at the beginning of a word is an imitation of Greek.
uo [wo] (e.g., **arduo**).

iu [yu] is spelled **yu** at the beginning of a word, e.g., **triunfo, yugo.**

ui [wi] (spelled **uy** in **muy**), e.g., **cuidar, muy.** For uy representing [uy], see **uy** in the next section.

Take care to pronounce diphthongs beginning with a semi-vowel as diphthongs and not as two syllables. Thus, whereas English **barrio** has three syllables, Spanish **barrio** has two (**ba-rrio**), pronounced [barryo].

Six of the diphthongs end in a semivowel:

ai [ay] is spelled **ay** at the end of most words; rarely, **ay** is found in the middle of a word (e.g., **aimará ~ aymará, hay, Raimundo, Seychelles**). If **ay** occurs before a vowel in the same word, it represents not a diphthong but /a/ + /y/ and each of those sounds belongs to a different syllable (thus, **aya** and **haya** for example are syllabified **a-ya** and **ha-ya**).

au [aw] (e.g., **caudillo**).

ei is almost always pronounced [ey] and is almost always spelled **ey** at the end of a word, e.g., **reina, rey.** A pronunciation exception is **reir,** which is pronounced as if spelled *reír. If **ey** occurs before a vowel in the same word, it represents not a diphthong but /e/ + /y/ and each of those sounds belongs to a different syllable (thus, **reyes** and **leyenda,** for instance, are syllabified **re-yes** and **le-yen-da**).

eu [ew] (e.g., **seudónimo**).

oi is almost always pronounced [oy] and is spelled **oy** at the end of a word (e.g., **hoy**) and in certain family names in other positions too (like **Goytisolo**). A pronunciation exception is **oir,** which is pronounced as if spelled *oír. If **oy** occurs before a vowel in the same word, it represents not a diphthong but /o/ + /y/ and each of those sounds belongs to a different syllable (thus, **Goya** is syllabified **Go-ya**).

uy, which always occurs at the end of a word, is almost always pronounced [uy] (as in **¡huy!, Jujuy**). The exception is **muy,** whose pronunciation is given in the previous section. If **uy** occurs before a vowel in the same word, it represents not a diphthong but /u/ + /y/ and each of those sounds belongs to a different syllable (thus, **cuyo** and **tuyas** are syllabified **cu-yo** and **tu-yas**).

The triphthongs are:

iai [yay] (e.g., **despreciáis**).
iau [yaw] (e.g., **miau**).
iei [yey] (e.g., **despreciéis**).
uai [way] (spelled **uay** at the end of a word), e.g., **evaluáis, Uruguay.**
uau [waw] (e.g., **guau**).
uei [wey] (spelled **uey** at the end of a word), e.g., **evaluéis, buey.**

Syllabification

Spanish is a consonant-vowel language, that is, syllables preferably end in a vowel (though many exceptions are found). Therefore, a single consonant and the vowel following it usually form a syllable or, expressed otherwise, a single consonant between two vowels usually goes with the following vowel (thus, **ba-jo, a-dhe-sión**). Since **ch, ll, ñ,** and **rr** represent a single consonant, the syllabification is, for example, **mu-cha-cho, ha-llar, ni-ño, ba-rrio,** and **haz-me-rreír.**

The consonant clusters **bl, cl, dl, fl, gl, pl, tl, br, cr, dr, fr, gr, pr,** and **tr** form a syllable with the following vowel, for instance, **ha-blar, a-cla-rar, a-flo-jar, a-glo-me-rar, a-pla-zar, a-tle-ta, a-bra-zar, a-cre-di-tar, a-drede, a-fran-ce-sar, a-gre-gar,** and **a-pren-der.**

When representing /š/, **sh** is not divided, whereas if a consonant letter + **h** is found in the middle of a word and the **h** is silent, the **h** begins a new syllable: **al-ha-ra-ca, clor-hi-dra-to, des-hi-dra-tar, in-hu-ma-ción.**

Stress

Most Spanish words have only one primary stress, which can be determined from the spelling according to these rules:

(1) If a word is spelled with a stress mark, stress the syllable in which it is found (like **águila, bíceps, fórceps, hablarán, Martínez**), the only exception being **ó,** which is not stressed (this is the form taken by the conjunction **o** when it appears between two Arabic numerals, the purpose of the mark being solely to prevent misinterpreta-tion of the conjunction as the Arabic numeral for zero; thus, **6 ó 7,** for instance, means '6 or 7').

(2) If a word contains no stress mark:

   [2.A] Stress the last syllable if the word ends in:

      [2.A.i] a vowel letter + **y** (like **convoy, Uruguay, vir-rey**),

      [2.A.ii] a consonant letter other than **n** or **s** (like **con-sentir, David, lateral**),

      [2.A.iii] **n** not preceded by a vowel letter (like **Isern**),

      [2.A.iv] **s** not preceded by a vowel letter (like **Fonta-nals, Casals**).

   [2.B] Stress the next-to-last syllable if the word ends in:

      [2.B.i] a vowel letter other than **y** (like **casi, habla, hable, hablo, fatuo, patria, sitio**),

      [2.B.ii] a vowel letter + **n** (like **con-sienten, ha-blan**),

      [2.B.iii] a vowel letter + **s** (like **con-sientes, ha-blas**).

Spanish Irregular Verbs

Infinitive	Present	Future	Preterit	Past Part.
andar	ando	andaré	anduve	andado
caber	quepo	cabré	cupe	cabido
caer	caigo	caeré	caí	caído
conducir	conduzco	conduciré	conduje	conducido
dar	doy	daré	di	dado
decir	digo	diré	dije	dicho
estar	estoy	estaré	estuve	estado
haber	he	habré	hube	habido
hacer	hago	haré	hice	hecho
ir	voy	iré	fui	ido
jugar	juego	jugaré	jugué	jugado
morir	muero	moriré	morí	muerto
oir	oigo	oiré	oí	oído
poder	puedo	podré	pude	podido
poner	pongo	pondré	puse	puesto
querer	quiero	querré	quise	querido
saber	sé	sabré	supe	sabido
salir	salgo	saldré	salí	salido
ser	soy	seré	fui	sido
tener	tengo	tendré	tuve	tenido
traer	traigo	traeré	traje	traído
valer	valgo	valdré	valí	valido
venir	vengo	vendré	vine	venido
ver	veo	veré	vi	visto

Las Formas del Verbo Inglés

1. Se forma la 3ª persona singular del tiempo presente exactamente al igual que el plural de los sustantivos, añadiendo **-es** o **-s** a la forma sencilla según las mismas reglas, así:

(1)	teach	pass	wish	fix	buzz		
	teaches	passes	wishes	fixes	buzzes		
(2)	place	change	judge	please	freeze		
	places	changes	judges	pleases	freezes		
(3a)	find	sell	clean	hear	love	buy	know
	finds	sells	cleans	hears	loves	buys	knows
(3b)	think	like	laugh	stop	hope	meet	want
	thinks	likes	laughs	stops	hopes	meets	wants
(4)	cry	try	dry	carry	deny		
	cries	tries	dries	carries	denies		

Cinco verbos muy comunes tienen 3ª persona singular irregular:

(5)	go	do	say	have	be
	goes	does	says	has	is

2. Se forman el tiempo pasado y el participio de modo igual, añadiendo a la forma sencilla la terminación **-ed** o **-d** según las reglas que siguen:

(1) Si la forma sencilla termina en **-d** o **-t**, se le pone **-ed** como sílaba aparte:

end	fold	need	load	want	feast	wait	light
ended	folded	needed	loaded	wanted	feasted	waited	lighted

(2) Si la forma sencilla termina en cualquier otra consonante, se añade también **-ed** pero sin hacer sílaba aparte:

(2a)	bang	sail	seem	harm	earn	weigh
	banged	sailed	seemed	harmed	earned	weighed

(2b)	lunch	work	look	laugh	help	pass
	lunched	worked	looked	laughed	helped	passed

(3) Si la forma sencilla termina en **-e**, se le pone sólo **-d**:

(3a)	hate	taste	waste	guide	fade	trade
	hated	tasted	wasted	guided	faded	traded

(3b)	free	judge	rule	name	dine	scare
	freed	judged	ruled	named	dined	scared

(3c)	place	force	knife	like	hope	base
	placed	forced	knifed	liked	hoped	based

(4) Una **-y** final que sigue a cualquier consonante se cambia en **-ie** al añadir la **-d** del pasado/participio:

cry	try	dry	carry	deny
cried	tried	dried	carried	denied

3. Varios verbos muy comunes forman el tiempo pasado y el participio de manera irregular. Pertenecen a tres grupos.

(1) Los que tienen una sola forma irregular para tiempo pasado y participio, como los siguientes:

bend	bleed	bring	build	buy	catch	creep	deal
bent	bled	brought	built	bought	caught	crept	dealt

dig	feed	feel	fight	find	flee	get	hang
dug	fed	felt	fought	found	fled	got	hung

have	hear	hold	keep	lead	leave	lend	lose
had	heard	held	kept	led	left	lent	lost

make	mean	meet	say	seek	sell	send	shine
made	meant	met	said	sought	sold	sent	shone

shoot	sit	sleep	spend	stand	strike	sweep	teach
shot	sat	slept	spent	stood	struck	swept	taught

(2) Los que tienen una forma irregular para el tiempo pasado y otra forma irregular para el participio, como los siguientes:

be	beat	become	begin	bite
was	beat	became	began	bit
been	beaten	become	begun	bitten
blow	break	choose	come	do
blew	broke	chose	came	did
blown	broken	chosen	come	done
draw	drink	drive	eat	fall
drew	drank	drove	ate	fell
drawn	drunk	driven	eaten	fallen
fly	forget	freeze	give	go
flew	forgot	froze	gave	went
flown	forgotten	frozen	given	gone
grow	hide	know	ride	ring
grew	hid	knew	rode	rang
grown	hidden	known	ridden	rung
rise	run	see	shake	shrink
rose	ran	saw	shook	shrank
risen	run	seen	shaken	shrunk
sing	sink	speak	steal	swear
sang	sank	spoke	stole	swore
sung	sunk	spoken	stolen	sworn
swim	tear	throw	wear	write
swam	tore	threw	wore	wrote
swum	torn	thrown	worn	written

(3) Los que no varían del todo, la forma sencilla funcionando también como pasado/ participio; entre éstos son de mayor frecuencia:

bet	burst	cast	cost	cut
hit	hurt	let	put	quit
read	set	shed	shut	slit
spit	split	spread	thrust	wet

El Plural del Sustantivo Inglés

A la forma singular se añade la terminación **-es** o **-s** de acuerdo con las reglas siguientes.

(1) Si el singular termina en **-ch, -s, -sh, -x** o **-z**, se le pone **-es** como sílaba aparte:

match	glass	dish	box	buzz
matches	glasses	dishes	boxes	buzzes

(2) Si el singular termina en **-ce, -ge, -se** o **-ze**, se le pone una **-s** que con la vocal precedente forma sílaba aparte:

face	page	house	size
faces	pages	houses	sizes

(3) Una -**y** final que sigue a cualquier consonante se cambia en -**ie** a ponérsele la -**s** del plural:

sky	city	lady	ferry	penny
skies	cities	ladies	ferries	pennies

(4) Los siguientes sustantivos comunes tienen plural irregular:

man	woman	child	foot	mouse	goose
men	women	children	feet	mice	geese

wife	knife	life	half	leaf	deer
wives	knives	lives	halves	leaves	deer

List of Abbreviations Used in this Dictionary

a adjective
abb abbreviation
acc accusative
adv adverb
aer aeronautics
agr agriculture
anat anatomy
ant antiquated
arch architecture
archeol archeology
art. article
art art
ast astronomy
astrol astrology
aut automobiles
aux auxiliary
biol biology
bot botany
cards card games
carp carpentry
chem chemistry
com commerce
comp comparative
condit conditional
conjunc conjunction
cul culinary
dance dancing
dat dative
dim diminutive
ecc ecclesiastical
elec electricity
eng engineering
ent entomology
euphem euphemism
f feminine
fig figurative
fig inf used figuratively in
    informal speech or
    writing
fut future
gen generally; genitive
geog geography

geol geology
geom geometry
gram grammar
gym gymnastics
her heraldry
hist history
icht ichthyology
imperf imperfect
impers impersonal
ind indicative
indef art. indefinite
    article
inf informal
infin infinitive
insep inseparable
interj interjection,
    exclamation
interr interrogative
iron ironical
irr irregular
Lat. Am. Latin America
law law
ling linguistics
lit literature
m masculine
mas masonry
math mathematics
mech mechanics
med medical
met metallurgy
mf masculine or
    feminine
mil military
min mineralogy
mus music
myth mythology
n noun
naut nautical
nav naval
neut neuter
opt optics
orn ornithology

part participle
pers personal; person
pharm pharmacy
phil philosophy
phon phonetics
phot photography
phys physics
physiol physiology
pl plural
poet poetic
pol political
pol econ political
    economy
poss possessive
prep preposition
pres present
print printing
pron pronoun
psy psychology
rad radio
rw railway
s substantive, noun
sew sewing
sing singular
spirit spiritualism
sport sports
subjunc subjunctive
sup superlative
surg surgery
surv surveying
tan tanning
theat theater
theol theology
univ university
v aux auxiliary verb
vi intransitive verb
vr reflexive verb
vt transitive verb
WH Western Hemispheric
    Spanish
zool zoology

SPANISH-ENGLISH
Dictionary

A

a *f*, name of the letter A

a *prep* to; at; on; by; in, into; up to; according to; if, etc. 1. Denotes the direct complement of verb before objects representing specified persons or animals, personified nouns, pronouns referring to specific persons (**alguien, entrambos, cualquiera,** etc.), demonstrative or relative pronouns, collective nouns representing persons (**el público, la muchedumbre,** etc.), names of countries, cities, rivers, etc., except where these invariably take the def. art., e.g. **Dejé a Varsovia,** I left Warsaw, *but* **Dejé el Perú,** I left Peru. 2. Introduces indirect obj. when this is a noun governed by a verb implying motion, or an emphatic pers. pron., e.g. **Nos conviene a ti y a mí,** It suits both you and me. It is also used before indirect obj. to avoid ambiguity when there is both an indirect and direct obj. 3. Denotes the complement of verb when this is an infin., e.g. **Enseñó a pintar a María,** He taught Mary to paint. 4. Indicates direction or destination, e.g. **Vamos a Edimburgo,** We are going to Edinburgh. 5. Signifies location, or point of time when action takes place, e.g. **Vinieron a las doce.** They came at twelve o'clock. 6. Describes position of persons or things, e.g. **Se sentaron a la puerta,** They sat down at the door. **La casa queda a la derecha,** The house is on the right. 7. Denotes interval of time or place between one thing and another, e.g. **de tres a cinco de la tarde,** from three to five in the afternoon, **de calle a calle,** from street to street. 8. Expresses manner of action, e.g. **a la francesa,** in the French way, **bordado a mano,** embroidered by hand. 9. Indicates rate or price, e.g. **a cuatro pesetas la libra,** at four pesetas the lb. 10. Indicates difference or comparison, e.g. **Va mucho de querer a hacer,** There's a difference between wishing and doing. 11. Sometimes is synonymous with **hasta, según, hacia** and governs almost all parts of speech. Has many idiomatic uses. 12. Before infin. sometimes has conditional sense, e.g. **A haber sabido las noticias no lo hubiéramos hecho,** If we had heard the news we would not have done it. 13. With certain nouns, adjectives, and infinitives forms adverbial phrases, e.g. **poco a poco,** little by little, **a veces,** sometimes, **a ciegas,** blindly, etc. **la veri** let's see!; *Colombia* hello! (on telephone). **A +** def. art. becomes **al,** e.g. **al rey,** to the king. **Al +** infin. means when or on, e.g. **al marcharme yo,** when I left (on my leaving); *Lat. Am.* **al año** a year later; *Lat. Am.* **a la semana** a week later; *Lat. Am.* **al mes** a month later

abacería *f*, grocery shop

abacero (-ra) *n* grocer

ábaco *m*, *arch* abacus; counting frame

abajo *adv* under; underneath; below; down. Used immediately after noun in adverbial phrases, e.g. **cuesta a., escalera a.,** downhill, downstairs. *interj* Down with! e.g., **¡A. el rey!** Down with the king! **venirse a.,** to fall down; *fig* collapse

abalanzar *vt* to balance; impel violently; *vr* throw oneself upon; attack, rush upon; *(with prep* a*)* rush into, risk. **Se abalanzó hacia ellos,** He rushed toward them

abalear *vt*, *Lat. Am.* to shoot at

abalorio *m*, glass bead; bead work

abanderado *m*, standardbearer; (Argentina) valedictorian

abanderizar *vt* to organize in groups; *vr* band together

abandonado *a* deserted; forlorn; helpless; indolent, careless; slovenly

abandonamiento *m*, desertion; forlornness; helplessness; carelessness; slovenliness

abandonar *vt* to forsake, desert; neglect; leave; give up; renounce; *vr* neglect oneself; grow discouraged; *(with prep* a*)* give oneself over to

abandono *m*, abandonment; defencelessness; forlornness; dilapidation; renunciation; neglect; slovenliness; debauchery

abanicar *vt* to fan

abanico *m*, fan; anything fan-shaped; *inf* sword; railway signal; *naut* derrick. **en a.,** fan-shaped

abaniqueo *m*, fanning; swinging, oscillation; gesticulation

abarcador(-ra) *n* one who clasps or embraces; monopolist

abarcadura *f*, **abarcamiento** *m*, inclusion; scope

abarcar *vt* to clasp, encircle; include; comprise; undertake, attempt; monopolize

abarrancadero *m*, rough road; ravine; precipice; *fig* difficult situation

abarrancar *vt* to ditch; make a ravine; *vr* fall into a pit; stick (in the mud, etc.); get into difficulties; *naut* run aground

abarrotería *f*, *Mexico* grocery store, grocery, grocer's

abarrotero, -a *mf Lat. Am.* grocer

abarrotes *m pl*, *Lat. Am.* groceries

abastar see **abastecer**

abastecedor (-ra) *a* provisioning, supplying. *n* provider; purveyor, supplier; caterer

abastecer *vt irr* to supply, provide; purvey. See **conocer**

abastecimiento *m*, providing; supply, provision; catering; supplies

abasto *m*, provisions, food; *com* supply. *adv* plentifully, abundantly

abatido *a* dejected, depressed; spiritless;

discouraged; crushed, humbled; *com* depreciated

abatimiento *m*, dejection, depression; humiliation; discouragement; falling; lowering; (*aer naut*) drift

abatir *vt* to knock down; overthrow; demolish; lower, take down; droop; humiliate; discourage; *naut* dismantle; *vi* (*naut aer*) drift; *vr* be despondent, despair; humble oneself; swoop down (of birds). **a. el vuelo,** to fly down

ABC *m*, ABCs (e.g. **el ABC de la física,** the ABCs of physics)

abdicación *f*, abdication

abdicar *vt* to abdicate; revoke, cancel; give up (rights, opinions)

abdomen *m*, abdomen

abdominal *a* abdominal

abecé *m*, ABCs

abecedario *m*, ABC, alphabet; reading book, primer

abeja *f*, bee. **a. maestra,** queen bee. **a. obrera,** worker

abejar *m*, beehive

abejero (**-ra**) *n* beekeeper

aberración *f*, deviation; error, lapse; (*ast phys biol*) aberration

abertura *f*, opening; aperture, gap, hole; fissure, cleft; mountain pass; naturalness, frankness

abierto *a* free, unobstructed; open, not enclosed; open, full-blown (flowers); frank, sincere. *adv* openly

abigarrado *a* variegated; varied; speckled

abigarrar *vt* to variegate; vary; speckle; fleck; spot; dapple

abintestato *a law* intestate

abismal *a* abysmal

abismar *vt* to plunge into an abyss; depress, sadden; *vr* despair; be plunged in thought, be abstracted; be amazed

abismo *m*, chasm, abyss, gulf; hell

abjurar *vt* to forswear, retract

ablactar *vt* to wean

ablandamiento *m*, softening; placating

ablandante *a* softening; placatory

ablandar *vt* to soften; appease, placate; loosen; relax; *vi* and be softened; be appeased; grow less stormy; (elements) decrease in force

ablandecer *vt irr* to soften. See **conocer**

abnegación *f*, abnegation, self-sacrifice

abnegado *a* self-sacrificing

abnegarse *vr irr* to deprive oneself, sacrifice oneself. See **cegar**

abobado *a* bewildered; foolish-looking, silly

abobar *vt* to daze, bewilder; make stupid

abocado *a* full-flavoured, pleasant (of wine)

abocar *vt* to seize with the mouth; bring nearer; transfer (contents of one jug to

another); *vr* meet, assemble; *vi naut* enter (a channel, port, etc.). **abocarse (con . . .),** to contact (. . .), get in touch (with . . .)

abochornado *a* flushed (of the face); ashamed; embarrassed

abochornar *vt* to overheat, make flushed; shame; embarrass; *vr* (plants) dry up

abofetear *vt* to slap, hit; buffet

abogacía *f*, legal profession; practice of law; advocacy

abogaderas, abogaderías *f pl Lat. Am.* hair-splitting, specious arguments, legalistics

abogado (**-da**) *n* lawyer

abogar *vi* to defend at law; intercede for; advocate, champion

abolengo *m*, lineage, descent, family; inheritance .

abolición *f*, abolition

abolir *vt* to abolish; cancel; annul

abollar *vt* to bruise; dent

abombar *vt* to make convex; *inf* deafen, bewilder; *vr* begin to putrefy; get intoxicated; *Mexico* become tight, get tight (tipsy)

abominable *a* abominable

abominación *f*, abomination; loathing, detestation

abominar *vt* to abominate, loathe, detest

abonado (**-da**) *a* trustworthy, reliable; ready, prepared, inclined. *n* subscriber; season ticket holder (for concerts, etc.)

abonanzar *vi impers* to clear up, be fine (weather)

abonar *vt* to guarantee; go surety for; improve, better; manure; ratify, confirm; pay; *com* place to the credit of; *vr* subscribe, become a subscriber; take out (season tickets, etc.)

abonaré *m*, *com* due bill; promissory note, I.O.U.

abono *m*, subscription; voucher; guarantee; manure. **a. verde,** leaf mold. **en a. de,** in payment of; in support of

aboquillado *a* tipped (of cigarettes)

abordar *vt naut* to board a ship; *naut* collide, run into; accost, tackle; undertake; *vi naut* put into port

aborigen *a* aboriginal

aborígenes *m pl*, aborigines

aborrachado *a* bright red; highly colored; flushed

aborrecedor (**-ra**) *a* a hateful. *n* hater, loather

aborrecer *vt irr* to hate, loathe; desert offspring (animals, birds). See **conocer**

aborrecible *a* hateful, detestable

aborrecimiento *m*, hate, detestation; dislike

abortar *vt* to abort; foil (a plot); *vi med* miscarry; fail, go awry

abortivo *a* abortive

aborto *m*, abortion; miscarriage; monster; failure

abotonar *vt* to button; *vi* bud, sprout

abra *f*, cove, small bay; narrow gorge; fissure, cleft; *Argentina* clearing (in a forest)

abrasador a burning, flaming

abrasamiento *m*, burning; ardour, heat

abrasar *vt* to burn; dry up, parch (plants); squander, waste; shame; *vi* burn; *vr* be very hot, glow; burn with passion

abrasivo a and *m*, abrasive

abrazadera *f*, clasp; clamp

abrazamiento *m*, embracing

abrazar *vt* to embrace, clasp in one's arms; follow, adopt; engage in; seize, take advantage of; comprise, include; surround; take in hand; clamp; clasp. **abrazarse a,** to clutch, hang on to

abrazo *m*, embrace

abrelatas *m*, can opener

abreviación *f*, abbreviation, shortening; summary; hastening

abreviar *vt* to abbreviate, shorten; hasten, accelerate; condense, abridge. **a. tiempo,** to save time. **Y para a. . . . ,** And, to cut a long story short . . .

abridor *m*, opener; ear-ring (for keeping holes in ears open). **a. de guantes,** glove-stretcher. **a. de láminas,** engraving needle. **a. de latas,** can opener

abridura *f*, (act of) opening (e.g. of a trunk)

abrigada *f*, **abrigadero** *m*, sheltered place

abrigar *vt* to shelter, protect (against the cold, etc.); defend, help; hold (opinions); nurse (a hope, etc.); cover; *vr* take shelter; wrap oneself up

abrigo *m*, shelter; defence; protection; help; sheltered place; wrap, coat; *naut* haven

abril *m*, April; youth; *pl poet* years

abrillantar *vt* to cut in facets like a diamond; polish, burnish; cause to shine; *fig* improve, add lustre to

abrir *vt* to open; reveal; unlock; slide the bolt of; extend, spread out; cleave; engrave; clear (the way, etc.); begin; head, lead; separate; dig; inaugurate. *vi* unfold (flowers); expand; **en un abrir y cerrar de ojos,** in the twinkling of an eye, in the wink of an eye; *vr* open; expand; *(with con)* confide in. **a. el camino (a . . .),** to pave the way (for . . .). **abrirse camino,** to make one's way; **abrirse paso a codazos,** to elbow one's way out, (or through)

abrochar *vt* to button; fasten, clasp; hook up (a dress, etc.); buckle; *Lat. Am.* **abrocharse (con . . .)** struggle (with . . .), wrestle (with . . .)

abrogación *f*, repeal, annulment

abrogar *vt* to repeal, annul

abroncar *vt inf* to bore, annoy

abrumador a burdensome, crushing, oppressive; troublesome, tiresome; exhausting

abrumar *vt* to weigh down; overwhelm, oppress; weary, exhaust; *vr* grow misty

abrupto a steep; rough, broken (ground); rugged

absceso *m*, abscess

absentismo *m*, absenteeism

absolución *f*, *(ecc and law)* absolution; remission, pardon

absoluta *f*, *mil* discharge

absoluto a absolute; categorical; *inf* despotic. **en a.,** absolutely

absolver *vt irr* to absolve; acquit (of a charge). *law* **a. de la instancia,** to dismiss the case. See **mover**

absorbente a and *m*, absorbent

absorber *vt* to absorb; consume, use up; attract, hold (the attention, etc.); imbibe

absorción *f*, absorption

absortar *vt* to amaze, dumbfound

absorto a amazed, astounded; abstracted, lost in thought

abstemio a abstemious

abstención *f*, abstention

abstenerse *vr irr* to refrain; abstain. See **tener**

abstinencia *f*, abstinence; fasting

abstinente a abstemious; temperate

abstracción *f*, abstraction; preoccupation; absent-mindedness

abstracto a abstract. **en a.,** in the abstract

abstraer *vt irr* to abstract; consider separately; *vi (with de)* do without, exclude; *vr* be preoccupied; let one's thoughts wander. See **traer**

abstraído a retired, recluse; preoccupied; absent-minded

abstruso a abstruse

absurdidad *f*, absurdity; folly, nonsense

absurdo a ridiculous, absurd. *m*, piece of folly, nonsense

abuchear *vt vi* to boo, hoot, jeer

abuela *f*, grandmother; old woman, dame

abuelo *m*, grandfather; ancestor *gen pl* old man; *pl* grandparents

abulia *f*, lack of will-power, abulia

abultado a bulky, large; voluminous; exaggerated

abultamiento *m*, bulkiness; enlargement, increase; mound; exaggeration

abultar *vt* to enlarge, increase; exaggerate; model in rough (sculpture); *vi* be bulky; be large

abundancia *f*, abundance, plenty

abundante a abundant, plentiful; abounding (in)

abundar *vi* to be plentiful, abound

aburrido a boring, tedious, dull; tired, weary

aburrimiento *m*, boredom; dullness; wearisomeness, tediousness

aburrir *vt* to bore; *inf* spend (time, money); (birds) desert the nest; *vr* grow bored; be weary

¡abusado! *Mexico* careful!, look out!, watch out!

abusar *vi* to abuse; exceed one's rights, go too far; (*with de*) take advantage of

abusivo *a* abusive

abuso *m*, abuse. **a. de confianza,** abuse of trust

abyección *f*, degradation, misery; abjectness, servility

abyecto *a* abject, wretched; servile

acá *adv* hither, here; at this time, now. **a. y acullá,** hither and thither. **desde ayer a.,** from yesterday until now

acabable *a* terminable, finishable; achievable

acabado *a* complete; perfect; expert, consummate; old, worn out; ill, infirm. *m*, finish

acabamiento *m*, finishing, completion; end; death, decease

acabar *vt* to end, terminate; finish; complete, perfect; kill; (*with con*) destroy, finish off; suppress; squander; *vi* end; die; be destroyed; (*with de + infin*) to have just (e.g. **Acaba de salir,** He has just gone out); *vr* end, be exhausted, run out of (e.g. **Se le acabó el dinero,** His money ran out); fade, grow weak; be destroyed. **Se les acabaron las dudas,** Their doubts were cleared up. **a. de desconcertar,** to nonplus completely; **a. de decidirse,** to come to a decision; **a. de saber,** to finally learn

academia *f*, academy

académico (**-ca**) *a* academic. *n* academician. **a. de la lengua,** member of the Royal Spanish Academy

acaecer *vi irr* to happen, occur. See **conocer**

acaecimiento *m*, happening, occurrence, event

acalambrarse (**muscle**) **to contract with cramps. Estar acalambrado,** to have cramps

acallar *vt* to quieten, hush; soothe, appease

acalorado *a* hot; fervent; *fig* heated

acaloramiento *m*, excitement, agitation, vehemence; ardour

acalorar *vt* to warm; aid, encourage; excite, stimulate; stir, move (to enthusiasm); inflame, rouse; tire (by exercise); *vr* grow hot; become agitated or excited; become heated (arguments)

acamar *vt* to lay flat (plants by the wind); *vr* be flattened (plants); lie down (animals); go rotten (fruit)

acampar *vi* and *vt* to encamp

acantilado *a* steep, precipitous; shelving (ocean-bed). *m*, cliff

acantonar *vt* to billet or quarter troops

acaparador (**-ra**) *n* monopolist

acaparar *vt com* to monopolize, corner; seize, take possession of

acápite *m*, *WH* new paragraph

acarear *vt* to face; face up to, meet with courage

acariciador (**-ra**) *a* caressing, loving. *n* fondler

acariciar *vt* to caress; brush, touch lightly; cherish, treat affectionately; toy with (a suggestion)

acarraladura *f*, *Lat. Am.* run (in a stocking)

acarreamiento, acarreo *m*, cartage, carting; transport, carriage; occasioning

acarrear *vt* to cart, transport; occasion, bring (gen. evil). **La guerra acarreó la carestía,** The war brought scarcity

acaso *m*, chance. *adv* by chance; perhaps, perchance. **por si a.,** in case (e.g. **Por si a. venga,** In case he comes)

acatable *a* venerable, worthy

acatamiento *m*, respect; reverence; observance

acatar *vt* to treat with respect, honor, revere; observe

acatarrar *vt*, *Lat. Am.* to annoy, bother, pester

acatarrarse *vr* to catch a cold; *Argentina* booze up, tank up

acaudalado *a* wealthy, well-to-do

acaudalar *vt* to make money; hoard up wealth; acquire (learning, etc.)

acceder *vi* (*with prep* a) to concede, grant; accede to, agree to

accesibilidad *f*, accessibility; approachableness

accesible *a* accessible; approachable

accesión *f*, agreement, acquiescence; accession; accessory; feverish attack

acceso *m*, access; paroxysm, outburst; *med* attack

accesorio *a* accessory

accesorios *m pl*, accessories; *theat* properties

accidentado *a* rough, uneven; stormy, troubled (life, etc.)

accidentar *vt* to cause (someone) an accident; *vr* be the victim of an accident; be seized by a fit

accidente *m*, chance; accident, mishap; illness, indisposition; *med* fit; *gram* accidence; *mus* accidental. **a. del trabajo,** accident at work. **por a.,** by chance, accidentally

acción *f*, action; battle; skirmish; *mech* drive; *com* share; gesture; lawsuit; *lit* action (of play, etc.); *art* posture, pose. **a. de gracias,** thanksgiving; *com* **a. liberada,** paid-up share. **a. privilegiada,** preference share

accionar *vi* to gesture, gesticulate; *Lat. Am.* act, be active

accionista *mf com* shareholder

acechar *vt* to spy upon, watch; lie in ambush for

acecho *m*, spying upon, watch; waylaying, ambush. **al a.,** in ambush; on the watch

acecinar *vt* to salt and dry (meat); *vr* (persons) wither, dry up

acedar *vt* to make bitter, sour; embitter, displease; *vr* turn sour; wither (plants)

aceitar *vt* to oil, lubricate; rub with oil

aceite *m*, olive oil; oil. **a. de hígado de bacalao**, cod-liver oil. **a. de linaza**, linseed oil. **a. de ricino**, castor-oil. **a. de trementina**, oil of turpentine

aceitera *f*, woman who sells oil; oil can; oil bottle; *pl* cruet

aceitoso *a* oily

aceituna *f*, *bot* olive

aceitunero (-ra) *n* olive picker; olive seller. *m*, warehouse for storing olives

aceituno *m*, olive tree; *a*, *Lat. Am.* olive-colored

aceleración *f*, speed, haste; acceleration

acelerador *a* accelerating. *m*, hastener; *aut* accelerator

acelerar *vt* to hasten, speed up; accelerate

acendrado *a* pure, unblemished, spotless

acendrar *vt* to refine (metals); purify, make spotless

acento *m*, accent; tone, inflection; *poet* voice, words. **a. agudo**, acute accent. **a. circunflejo**, circumflex accent. **a. grave**, grave accent. **a. ortográfico**, graphic accent, written accent. **a. tónico**, tonic accent

acentuación *f*, accentuation, stress; emphasis

acentuar *vt* to accent; stress, emphasize; *vr* become evident, become marked, be noticeable

acepción *f*, meaning, significance, acceptation. **a. de personas**, partiality, preference

acepilladura *f*, sweeping, brushing; planing; wood-shaving

acepillar *vt* to sweep, brush; plane; *inf* brush up, polish up

aceptabilidad *f*, acceptability

aceptable *a* acceptable

aceptación *f*, acceptance; popularity; approval

aceptador (-ra) *a* accepting. *n* acceptor

aceptar *vt* to accept; approve; accept a challenge; *com* honor

acequia *f*, ditch, trench; irrigation channel

acera *f*, sidewalk, pavement. **a. del sol**, sunny side of the street

acerado *a* steel; steel-like; strong, tough; mordant, incisive

acerar *vt* to steel; treat (liquids) with steel; harden, make obdurate

acerbidad *f*, bitterness, acerbity; sourness; harshness, cruelty

acerbo *a* sour, tart, bitter; cruel, harsh

acerca de *adv* about, concerning

acercamiento *m*, approach

acercar *vt* to bring nearer; *vr* be near at hand, draw near; (*with prep a*) approach

acero *m*, steel; blade, sword; *pl* bravery, spirit; *inf* good appetite. **a. inoxidable**, stainless steel

acérrimo *a sup* extremely strong, mighty; most harsh; most resolute, unflinching; very strong (taste, smell)

acerrojar *vt* to lock, padlock; bolt

acertado *a* well-aimed; fitting, suitable; wise; successful

acertar *vt irr* to hit the mark; find, come across; succeed (in), achieve; guess, find out; **No acertaba a explicármelo**, I couldn't quite understand it. **a. por chambra**, to make a lucky guess; (*with prep a* + *infin*) happen, occur, come to pass. *Pres. Ind.* **acierto, aciertas, acierta, aciertan.** *Pres. Subjunc.* **acierte, aciertes, acierte, acierten**

acertijo *m*, riddle

acervo *m*, pile, heap; *fig* storehouse, wealth (e.g. of words)

acetato *m*, acetate

achacar *vt* to attribute, impute, assign. **achacable a**, imputable to

achacoso *a* ailing, ill, sickly

achantarse *vr inf* to hide from danger; put up with, bear

achaparrado *a* stocky

achaque *m*, ailment, illness (permanent); *inf* period, menstruation; pregnancy; matter, affair; pretext; failing, bad habit. **En a. de . . . ,** Re . . . , concerning . . .

achatar *vt* to flatten, make flat

achicar *vt* to make smaller, diminish; drain, bail out; depreciate, belittle

achicarse *inf* to sing small

achicharrar *vt cul* to overcook; overheat; annoy, importune

achicoria *f*, chicory

achispado *a inf* tipsy

achuchar *vt inf* to squeeze, hug; jostle, push against

achuchón *m*, *inf* shove, push; hug, squeeze

achulado *a inf* brazen, tough

aciago *a* unhappy, ill-omened; fateful

acibarar *vt* to add bitter aloes to; embitter, sadden

acicalado *a* polished; neat; well-groomed. *m*, polishing, burnishing (of weapons)

acicalador (-ra) *a* polishing. *n* polisher. *m*, burnisher (machine)

acicalar *vt* to burnish (weapons); adorn, deck; *vr* dress oneself with care

acicate *m*, Moorish spur; incitement, stimulus

acicatear *vt* to induce, spur on. **a. la curiosidad,** arouse curiosity

acidez *f*, acidity, bitterness

acidia *f*, indolence; sluggishness

ácido a acid; sour; harsh. *m*, acid. **a. fénico,** carbolic acid. **a. graso,** fatty acid

acierto *m*, good hit, bull's-eye; success; achievement; cleverness; dexterity, skill; wisdom, sense; tact

aclamación *f*, acclamation; shout of acclamation. **por a.,** unanimously

aclamador (-ra) a acclaiming. *n* applauder, acclaimer

aclamar *vt* to acclaim; applaud

aclaración *f*, explanation; elucidation

aclarado *m*, rinse; rinsing

aclarador, aclaratorio a explanatory

aclarar *vt* to clarify, purify; clear; rinse (clothes); explain; thin; *vi* clear; (sky) clear up; dawn

aclimatación *f*, acclimatization; *Lat. Am.* air-conditioning

aclimatar *vt* to acclimatize

acné *m*, acne

acobardar *vt* to intimidate, frighten

acocil *m*, *Mexico* freshwater shrimp

acodiciar *vt* to yearn for, covet, desire

acogedizo a gathered haphazardly

acogedor (-ra) a welcoming, friendly; inviting (e.g. a chair or room); *n* protector

acoger *vt* to receive, welcome, admit; protect, harbour; *vr* take refuge; (*with prep* a) make use of, resort to; **acogerse a sagrado,** seek sanctuary

acogida *f*, reception, welcome; protection, shelter; meeting place; confluence (of waters). **tener buena a.,** to be well received

acogollar *vt* to protect, cover (plants); *vi* sprout, shoot

acogotar *vt* to fell by a blow on the neck; *inf* knock out

acolada *f*, accolade

acólito *m*, acolyte

acomedido, -a *Lat. Am.* helpful, obliging

acometedor (-ra) a capable, enterprising; aggressive. *n* aggressor, attacker

acometer *vt* to attack furiously; undertake; take in hand; overcome (of sleep, etc.)

acometida *f*, **acometimiento** *m*, assault, onrush; undertaking

acomodable a easily arranged

acomodación *f*, adjustment; adaptation; accommodation

acomodadizo a accommodating, easygoing

acomodado a suitable; convenient; wealthy, well-off; comfort-loving; moderate, low (of price)

acomodador (-ra) *n* theater attendant, usher

acomodamiento *m*, agreement, transaction; accommodation

acomodar *vt* to arrange, adjust, accommodate; adapt; appoint; place; reconcile; employ, take on; equip, provide; lodge; *vi* suit, be convenient; *vr* compromise, agree

acomodaticio a accommodating

acomodo *m*, post, employment; arrangement; settlement

acompañamiento *m*, accompaniment; following, retinue; *mus* accompaniment; *theat* crowd, chorus

acompañanta *f*, chaperon; maid, servant

acompañante *m*, *mus* accompanist

acompañar *vt* to accompany; follow, escort; enclose (a letter, etc.); *mus* accompany

acompasado a rhythmic; deliberate, slow

acondicionado a conditioned; (*with* **bien** or **mal**) in good or bad condition; of good or bad quality; good- or ill-natured. **reflejo acondicionado** *med* conditioned reflex

acondicionar *vt* to prepare; mend, repair; *vr* condition oneself

acongojar *vt* to sadden, grieve; oppress

aconsejable a advisable

aconsejar *vt* to advise; *vr* (*with con*) consult, ask advice of

acontecer *vi* *irr impers* to happen. See **conocer**

acontecimiento *m*, event, occurrence

acopio *m*, collection, store; accumulation, gathering

acopladura *f*, **acoplamiento** *m*, (*carp. mech*) joint; coupling; yoking; mating (of animals)

acoplar *vt* to join, couple; yoke; mate (animals); reconcile (opinions); *vr* *inf* fall in love

acoquinar *vt* *inf* to intimidate, terrify

acorcharse *vr* to dry up, shrivel; go numb (limbs)

acordadamente *adv* by common consent, unanimously; deliberately; after due thought

acordar *vt* *irr* to decide unanimously; resolve; remind; tune; harmonize (colors); *vi* agree; *vr* remember; come to an agreement. **Si mal no me acuerdo,** If memory serves me right. *Pres. Ind.* **acuerdo, acuerdas, acuerda, acuerdan.** *Pres. Subjunc.* **acuerde, acuerdes, acuerde, acuerden**

acorde a agreed; in harmony; in agreement. *m*, *mus* chord; harmony

acordeón *m*, accordion; (slang) crib sheet

acordonar *vt* to lace; cordon off, surround; mill (coins)

acorralamiento *m*, corralling, penning

acorralar *vt* to corral, pen; confine; corner, silence (in argument); frighten; harass

acorrer *vt* to aid, assist; *vi* run, hasten; *vr* take refuge

acortamiento *m*, shortening

acortar *vt* to shorten; *vr* be speechless, be shy. **a. las velas,** to take in sail

acosador (-ra) *a* persecuting. *n* persecutor

acosamiento *m*, persecution

acosar *vt* to persecute relentlessly; annoy, harass

acostado *a* in bed; stretched out; *her* couchant

acostar *vt irr* to lay down, stretch out; put to bed; *vi* lean, tilt; *vr* lie down; go to bed; *naut* come alongside. See **contar**

acostumbrado *a* accustomed, usual

acostumbrar *vt* to habituate, accustom; *vi* be in the habit of (e.g. **Acostumbramos ir a la playa en el verano,** We generally go to the seashore in summer); *vr* (*with prep* **a**) become used to

acotación *f*, noting; marginal note; stage direction; ordnance survey number

acotar *vt* to annotate; mark out boundaries; fix, establish; accept; *inf* choose; testify; fill in elevation figures (on a map); *vr* seek refuge

acotejar *vt*, *Lat. Am.* to arrange, put in order

acre *a* bitter, sour; harsh; biting, mordant. *m*, acre (land measure)

acrecencia *f*, **acrecentamiento** *m*, increase; addition

acrecentar *vt irr* to increase; augment; promote, prefer. See **acertar**

acrecer *vt irr* to increase; augment. See **conocer**

acreditado *a* accredited, well-reputed; respected

acreditar *vt* to prove; verify; accredit; recommend; sanction, authorize; vouch for, guarantee; *com* credit

acreedor (-ra) *n* creditor; claimant. *a* deserving. **a. hipotecario,** mortgagee

acreencia *f*, debt; *com* claim

acribillar *vt* to riddle with holes; wound repeatedly; pelt; torment; *inf* pester, harass

acriminar *vt* to accuse, charge

acrimonia *f*, acrimony

acriollarse *vr*, *Lat. Am.* to adopt local customs, go native

acrisolar *vt* to refine, purify (metals); perfect; clarify, elucidate

acrobacia *f*, acrobatics

acróbata *mf* acrobat

acrobático *a* acrobatic

acta *f*, minutes, record; certificate of election (as deputy to Cortes, etc.); *pl* deeds (of a martyr). **a. matrimonial,** marriage register

actitud *f*, attitude

activar *vt* to stimulate, make active; accelerate, hasten

actividad *f*, activity; movement, bustle. **en a.,** in action; at work

activo *a* active. *m*, *com* assets

acto *m*, act, deed, action; act, law; act (of a play); public ceremony; *pl* minutes (of a meeting), proceedings (of a conference). **a. continuo** *or* **a. seguido,** immediately afterwards. **a. vandálico,** act of vandalism. **los Actos de los Apóstoles,** Acts of the Apostles. **en a.,** in the act (of doing). **en el a.,** in the act; immediately

actor *m*, actor; *law* plaintiff

actriz *f*, actress

actuación *f*, operation, functioning; action; *pl* legal functions, judicial acts

actual *a* present; contemporary

actualidad *f*, present, present time; topic of interest. **actualidades,** current events. **en la a.,** at the present time

actuar *vt* to operate, set in motion; *vi* act; exercise legal functions

actuario (de seguros) *m*, actuary

acuarela *f*, water-color painting

acuarelista *mf* water-colorist

acuario *m*, aquarium; Aquarius

acuartelamiento *m*, billeting (of troops); billet, quarters

acuartelar *vt* to billet

acuático, acuátil *a* aquatic

acuatizar *vi*, *Lat. Am.* to land on water, touch down on water

acuchillar *vt* to hack, cut about; stab, put to the sword; slash (sleeves, etc.); *vr* fight with swords, daggers

acucia *f*, fervor, zeal; yearning, longing

acuciar *vt* to incite; goad; stimulate; encourage

acuciosidad *f*, eagerness, fervor, zeal

acucioso *a* eager, fervent, keen, zealous

acuclillarse *vr* to squat, crouch

acudir *vi* to go, repair (to); come; go or come to the aid of; attend, be present; **No me acude ningún ejemplo a la memoria,** No example comes to mind; resort (to), seek protection; reply, respond

acueducto *m*, aqueduct

acuerdo *m*, motion, resolution; decision; harmony, agreement; opinion, belief; remembrance; report; meeting (of members of a tribunal); *art* harmony (of colors). **de a.,** in agreement, in conformity; unanimously. **estar de a. (con),** to agree (with). **estar de acuerdo en (+ inf.),** to agree to (+ inf.) **ponerse de a.,** to come to an understanding

acuilmarse *vr* Central America to get depressed, get the blues

acumulación *f*, accumulation, collection

acumulador (-ra) *a* accumulative. *m*, accumulator, storage battery. *n* collector, accumulator

acumular *vt* to accumulate, amass, collect; accuse, charge with

acuñación *f*, minting, coining; wedging

acuñador (**-ra**) *n* coiner, stamper; wedge. *m*, coining machine.

acuñar *vt* to mint, stamp, coin; wedge

acuoso *a* aqueous, watery

acurrucarse *vr* to huddle; curl up; crouch

acusación *f*, accusation; *law* charge; *law* prosecution

acusado (**-da**) *a* accused; prominent; well-defined; *n* accused; *law* defendant

acusador (**-ra**) *a* accusing. *n* accuser; *law* prosecutor

acusar *vt* to accuse; blame; denounce; *com* acknowledge receipt; *law* prosecute; *law* charge. **acusarle a uno las cuarenta**, *inf* to give someone a piece of one's mind

acusatorio *a* accusatory

acusón (**-ona**) *n* *inf* telltale, sneak, informer

acústica *f*, acoustics

acústico *a* acoustic

adagio *m*, adage; *mus* adagio

adaptar *vt* to adapt, make suitable; *vr* adapt oneself

adarme *m*, tittle, jot. **por adarmes**, in bits and pieces, in drabs and driblets

adecentar *vt* to make decent; tidy up; *vr* tidy oneself

adecuación *f*, adequacy; suitability

adecuado *a* adequate; suitable

adecuar *vt* to proportion, fit; *fig* tailor

adefesio *m*, *inf* folly, absurdity (gen. *pl*); extravagant attire; guy, sight

adelantado *a* precocious; forward, pert; fast (clocks); early (of fruit); excellent; capable, proficient. **por a.**, in advance

adelantamiento *m*, promotion, furtherance; progress, advancement; betterment, improvement; *ant* office of **adelantado**; anticipation

adelantar *vt* to advance, move on; hasten; forestall; overtake; put on (the hands of clocks); improve, better; beat, excel; place in front; *vi* progress, advance; be fast (clocks); grow, develop; *vr* come forward

adelante *adv* on, forward; further on; straight ahead. **¡A.!** Onward!; Come in! **de hoy en a.**, henceforth, from today

adelanto *m*, anticipation; progress; *com* payment in advance. **el a. de la hora**, moving the clock forward

adelgazamiento *m*, loss of weight; slenderness; thinness

adelgazar *vt* to make slender or thin; *fig* split hairs; whittle, taper; *vi* grow slender or thin

ademán *m*, posture, attitude; gesture; *pl* behaviour, manners

además *adv* besides, in addition; moreover. **a. de**, as well as

adentro *adv* inside, within

adentros *m* *pl*, private thoughts (e.g. **Pensé para mis adentros**, I thought to myself). *interj* **¡Adentro!** Come in!; Go in!

adepto *a* affiliated; adept, proficient

aderezamiento *m*, dressing; seasoning; embellishment

aderezar *vt* to deck, embellish; cook; *cul* season; *cul* dress; prepare; repair, mend; guide, direct; dress (cloth)

aderezo *m*, dressing, adornment; beautifying; finery, ornament; preparation; seasoning; set of jewels; horse's trappings; gum starch (for dressing cloth); equipment

adeudar *vt* to owe; be dutiable (goods); *com* debit; *vi* become related (by marriage); *vr* run into debt

adeudo *m*, debt; customs duty; *com* debit

adherente *a* adhesive; connected, attached. *mf* adherent, follower; *m* *pl*. **adherentes**, accessories, requisites

adherirse *vr irr* to adhere, stick; follow; believe (in). See **herir**

adhesivo *a* adhesive

adición *f*, addition; *Argentina* check (in a restaurant)

adicional *a* additional, extra

adicionar *vt* to add up; add to

adicto (**-ta**) *a* addicted, fond; joint. *n* addict; follower, disciple; *Lat. Am.* (drug) addict

adiestrador (**-ra**) *n* trainer, coach; guide, teacher

adiestrar *vt* to train, coach; guide, teach; lead; *vr* practise, perfect oneself

adifés *adv*, *Central America* deliberately, on purpose

adinerado *a* wealthy, well-off, rich

adiós *interj* Good-bye!; Hello, God be with you! (used as greeting). *m*, farewell

aditamento *m*, addition

adivinanza *f*, divination; riddle; puzzle. **adivinanzas**, guessing games. **no estar para jugar a las a.**, to be in no mood for guessing games

adivinar *vt* to prophesy, foretell; divine, guess; solve, guess (riddles, etc.)

adjetivo *a* adjectival. *m*, adjective

adjudicación *f*, adjudication, award

adjudicar *vt* to adjudge; award; *vr* appropriate

adjuntar *vt* to enclose (with a letter, etc.)

adjunto *a* attached; enclosed, accompanying; assistant, deputy; adjectival. *m*, addition, supplement

administración *f*, administration; direction, control; administratorship

administrador (**-ra**) *a* administrative. *n* administrator. **a. de correos**, postmaster

administrar *vt* to control, manage; provide, supply; administer. **administrarse el tiempo,** to budget one's time

administrativo a administrative, executive

admiración f, amazement; admiration; wonder; exclamation mark

admirador (-ra) a admiring. n admirer

admirar vt to admire; surprise, amaze (e.g. **Me admira su acción,** His action surprises me); to see (e.g. **Desde la colina se pueden admirar varios edificios de la ciudad,** From the hill several buildings in the city can be seen); vr (with de) be surprised at or by

admirativo a admiring; admirable, excellent

admisibilidad f, allowability, permissibility

admisible a admissible; permissible

admisión f, admission; acceptance; allowance

admitir vt to admit; receive, accept; tolerate, brook; allow, permit

admonición f, admonition, warning; reprimand

adobar vt to prepare; cul garnish; pickle (meat); cook; dress (hides)

adobo m, repairing; dressing (for cloth, leather); cul savory sauce; pickling sauce; make-up, cosmetic

adoctrinar vt to instruct

adolecer vi irr to fall ill; (with de) suffer from (diseases, defects); vr be sorry for, regret. See **conocer**

adolescencia f, adolescence

adolescente a and mf adolescent

adonde adv (interr a dónde) where to, whither (e.g. **¿A dónde fuiste?** Where did you go to?)

adondequiera adv wherever

adopción f, adoption

adoptador (-ra) a adopting. n adopter

adoptar vt to adopt (children); make one's own, embrace (opinions); take (decisions)

adoptivo a adoptive

adoquín m, cobble-stone; fig blockhead

adoquinado m, cobbling, paving. m, cobbled pavement

adoración f, worship, adoration. **A. de los Reyes,** Adoration of the Magi; Epiphany

adorador (-ra) a adoring. n adorer

adorar vt to adore; worship; (with en) dote on; vi pray

adormecedor a soporific, drowsy

adormecer vt irr to make drowsy; soothe, lull; hush to sleep; vr go to sleep; (limbs); fall asleep; (with en) persist in. See **conocer**

adormecimiento m, sleepiness; lulling asleep; numbness

adormitarse vr to doze, take a nap, snooze

adornamiento m, adornment, decoration

adornar vt to deck, beautify; decorate; trim, embellish; adorn (of virtues, etc.)

adorno m, decoration, adornment; ornament; trimming. **de a.,** ornamental; flowering (shrubs)

adquiridor (-ra) a acquiring. n acquirer

adquirir vt irr to acquire, get; achieve, obtain. Pres. Ind. **adquiero, adquieres, adquiere, adquieren.** Pres. Subjunc. **adquiera, adquieras, adquiera, adquieran**

adquisición f, acquirement; acquisition. **poder de a.,** purchasing power

adquisidor (-ra) a acquiring. n acquirer, obtainer

adquisitivo a acquisitive

adrede adv on purpose, intentionally

adrenalina f, adrenaline

adscribir vt to ascribe, attribute; appoint (to a post, etc.)

adscripción f, ascription, attribution; appointment

aduana f, customs house, customs. **pasar por la a.,** to go through customs

aduanero a customs. m, customs officer

aducir vt irr to adduce, allege, cite; add. See **conducir**

adueñarse (-de) vr to appropriate, take possession (of)

adulación f, adulation, flattery

adulador (-ra) a fawning. n flatterer

adular vt to flatter, fawn upon, adulate

adulonería f, Lat. Am. flattery, fawning

adulteración f, adulteration; falsification

adulterador (-ra) a adulterant. n adulterator; falsifier; coiner

adulterar vi to commit adultery; vt adulterate; falsify

adulterio m, adultery

adúltero (-ra) a adulterous; corrupt. n adulterer

adulto (-ta) a and n adult

adusto a extremely hot (of climate); grave, austere; standoffish, reserved

advenedizo a foreign, alien; strange, unknown; upstart; newly rich; Lat. Am. novice, tyro

advenimiento m, advent, arrival; ascension (to the throne)

advenir vi irr to come, arrive; happen, befall. See **venir**

adventicio a casual, accidental; bot adventitious

adversario (-ia) n adversary, rival; opponent

adversidad f, adversity, misfortune, sorrow

adverso a unfavorable, contrary, adverse; opposite

advertencia f, warning; introduction, preface; remark

advertido a capable, clever; experienced; expert

advertir vt irr to observe, notice; warn; advise; feel, be conscious of; point out, indicate; inform; discover. See **sentir**

adyacencia f, Argentina nearness, proximity

adyacente a adjacent, near-by, neighboring

aéreo a aerial; airborne; airy; air; aeronautic; unsubstantial, fantastic. **correo a.,** airmail. **línea aérea** airline

aerobismo m, aerobics

aerodinámica f, aerodynamics

aeromozo, -a mf, Lat. Am. flight attendant

aeronauta mf aeronaut, balloonist

aeronáutica f, aeronautics

aeronáutico a aeronautic

aeropuerto m, airport

afabilidad f, affability, geniality, friendliness

afable a affable, genial, pleasant

afamado a famous, well-known

afán m, effort; manual labor; desire, anxiety **a. de mando,** thirst for power

afanar vt to press, urge on; filch; vr toil, labor; (with por) work hard to, try to

afanoso a hard, laborious; hard-working, painstaking; eager, anxious

afear vt to make ugly; distort, deform; blame; criticize

afección f, fondness, affection; complaint, ailment, trouble

afectación f, affectation

afectado a affected

afectar vt to feign, assume; affect; move, touch; law encumber; Lat. Am. damage, hurt, injure

afectivo a affective

afecto a fond, affectionate; law encumbered; (with prep a) addicted to. m, emotion, sentiment; affection

afectuoso a affectionate, fond

afeitada f, shave, shaving

afeitar vt to shave; make up (one's face); adorn, beautify

afeite m, cosmetic; make-up (for the complexion)

afelpado a velvet-like, plushy

afeminado a effeminate

afeminar vt to make effeminate; weaken; vr grow effeminate

aferradamente adv tenaciously, persistently, obstinately

aferramiento m, seizing, clutching; naut furling; naut grappling; mooring, anchoring; obstinacy

aferrar vt to seize, clutch; naut take in, furl; naut grapple; vi naut anchor; vr (with con, en, a) persist in, insist on

afianzamiento m, fastening, fixing; propping; grasping; guarantee, security

afianzar vt to fasten, fix; prop; consolidate (e.g. one's power); guarantee, be security for; grasp

afición f, propensity, inclination; fondness. **tomar a. (a),** to take a liking to

aficionado (-da) a amateur. n amateur, fan, enthusiast. **ser a a.,** to be fond of, have a liking for

aficionar vt to inspire liking or affection; vr (with prep a) take a liking to, grow fond of; become an enthusiast of

afiladera f, whetstone, grindstone

afilado a sharp, keen (of edges)

afilador m, grinder (of scissors, etc.); razor strop

afilalápices m, pencil sharpener

afilar vt to sharpen; grind, whet; taper; Lat. Am. flatter; Lat. Am. court, woo; vr grow thin; taper

afiliación f, affiliation

afiliar vt (with prep a) to affiliate with; vr (with prep a) become affiliated with; join, become a member of

afiligranado a filigree; delicate, fine; slender

afilón m, steel, knife sharpener; razor-strop

afín a nearby, contiguous; similar, related. mf relative by marriage

afinador m, tuning key; tuner (of pianos, etc.)

afinar vt to finish, perfect; fig polish, refine; tune (musical instruments); vi sing in tune; vr grow refined

afinidad f, affinity, analogy; relationship (by marriage); chem affinity

afirmación f, affirmation, statement

afirmar vt to make firm; fix, fasten; affirm; vr steady oneself; hold on to

afirmativa f, affirmative

afirmativo a affirmative

aflicción f, affliction, grief

aflictivo a sorrowful, grievous

afligir vt to sadden; afflict, trouble; vr lament, mourn

aflojamiento m, slackening; loosening; diminution

aflojar vt to slacken; loosen; vi relax, weaken; abate, diminish. **a. el paso,** to slow down

afluencia f, crowd, concourse; eloquence, fluency

afluente a fluent, eloquent. m, tributary (river)

afluir vi irr to crowd, swarm; flow (into). See **huir**

afonía f, med aphonia, loss of voice; hoarseness

afónico a hoarse

aforrador (-ra) n one who lines jackets, etc.

aforrar vt to line (clothes, etc.); vr wrap oneself up; inf gormandize

afortunado a lucky, fortunate; happy; stormy

afortunar vt to bring luck to, make happy

afrancesamiento m, adoption of the French way of life; servile imitation of everything French

afrancesar vt to make French, gallicize; Frenchify; vr become a Francophile

afrenta f, insult, affront; disgrace

afrentar vt to insult; vr be ashamed

afrentoso a insulting, outrageous; disgraceful

África Africa

africano -na a and n African

afrodisíaco a and m, aphrodisiac

afrontar vt to place opposite; confront; face (danger, etc.)

afuera adv outside, out.

afueras f pl, suburbs, outskirts

afusilar vt, Lat. Am. to shoot

agachada f, crouch, duck; jerk

agachar vt inf bend, bow; vr inf crouch down; lie low, hide

agalla f, oak-apple; tonsil (gen. pl); zool gill; inf gall, cheek

agalludo, -a a, Argentina mean, stingy, tight; bold, daring

ágape m, agape; banquet, feast

agarrada f, inf brawl, scuffle

agarradero m, handle; heft; inf influence, pull

agarrado a inf tight-fisted, mean

agarrar vt to grip, grasp; seize, take; inf nab (jobs); vr grip, hold on

agarro m, hold; grip, grasp

agarrotar vt to garrotte; tighten (ropes, etc.); press, squeeze; vr (limbs) go numb

agasajar vt to indulge, spoil, pet; receive kindly; entertain; caress

agasajo m, indulgence, kindness; affability, geniality; entertainment; gift, offering

agazapar vt inf to nab, catch; vr inf squat, crouch

agencia f, influence, agency

agenciar vt to negotiate, arrange; procure, manage

agenda f, notebook; agenda

agente m, agent. **a. de bolsa** or **a. de cambio,** bill broker. **a. de negocios,** business agent. **a. de policía,** police officer. **a. fiscal,** revenue officer

agestado a used generally with advs. **bien** or **mal,** well or ill-featured

agigantado a enormous, gigantic; outstanding, extraordinary

ágil a agile, nimble; easy to use (e.g. **un libro ágil,** a book easy to use)

agilidad f, agility, nimbleness

agilizar vt to make agile, limber; refresh one's knowledge of (e.g. **Quiero agilizar mi español,** I want to refresh my knowledge of Spanish); to enable; vr limber up

agitación f, shaking; agitation, excitement

agitador (-ra) a stirring; agitating. n agitator. m, stirrer, stirring rod

agitar vt to stir; shake; agitate, excite **a. una cuestión,** raise a question; discuss a question

aglomeración f, agglomeration

aglomerar vt to agglomerate, amass

agnóstico (-ca) a and n agnostic

agobiar vt to bow, bend down; fig weigh down, oppress; vr bend (beneath a weight)

agobio m, bowing, bending down; oppression, burden, weight

agolparse vr to rush, crowd, swarm

agonía f, agony, anguish

agonizante a dying

agonizar vt to attend a dying person; inf pester, annoy; vi be dying (gen. **estar agonizando**)

agorar vt to prophesy, foretell

agorero (-ra) a prophetic; ill-boding. n seer, augur

agosto m, August; harvest. inf **hacer su a.,** to make hay while the sun shines

agotado a exhausted; out of print (of books)

agotador a exhausting; exhaustive

agotar vt to drain off (water); empty (a glass); exhaust; run through (money); study thoroughly, examine closely (a subject)

agraciado a graceful; pretty

agraciar vt to lend grace to; make pretty; favor

agradable a agreeable, pleasant

agradar vi to be pleasing, like, please (e.g. **Me agrada su sinceridad,** I like his sincerity)

agradecer vt irr to be grateful for; thank for; fig repay, requite. See **conocer**

agradecido a grateful; thankful

agradecimiento m, gratitude; thankfulness

agrado m, pleasure; desire, liking; amiability, affability

agrario a agrarian

agrarismo m, Mexico farmers' movement, peasant movement

agravación f, **agravamiento** m, aggravation, worsening

agravador a aggravating; worsening; increasing

agravar vt to aggravate, increase; oppress (taxes, responsibilities); make worse; exaggerate; vr grow worse

agraviador -ra a offensive. n offender

agraviar vt to offend; wrong; vr take offence, be insulted

agravio m, offence, insult; wrong, injury

agraz m, unripened grape; verjuice; fig bitterness

agredir *vt* to attack

agregación *f*, association, aggregation; total, collection, aggregate

agregado *m*, aggregate; assistant; attaché; *Lat. Am.* sharecropper

agregar *vt* to add; collect, amass; appoint (to a post). **agregarse a . . . ,** to join . . . (e.g. an association)

agresión *f*, aggression

agresivo *a* aggressive

agresor (-ra) *a* and *n* aggressor

agreste *a* rural, rustic; wild; uncouth, rude

agriar *vt* to make bitter or sour; exasperate, provoke

agrícola *a* agricultural; *mf* agriculturalist, farmer

agricultura *f*, agriculture

agridulce *a* bitter-sweet

agrietarse *vr* to crack, split

agrimensor *m*, surveyor

agrio *a* bitter, sour; rough, uneven (ground); brittle; sharp (of color contrast); unsociable; disagreeable

agronomía *f*, agronomy

agrónomo *a* agronomic. *m*, agronomist

agrupación *f*, congregation, assembly; group; crowd; crowding, grouping

agrupar *vt* to assemble, group; *vr* crowd, cluster

agrura *f*, bitterness; sourness; asperity

agua *f*, water; rain; slope of a roof; *pl* shot or watered effect on silks, etc.; medicinal waters; waves; water (of precious stones). **a. abajo,** down-stream. **a. arriba,** upstream. **a. bendita,** holy water. **a. cruda,** hard water. **a. de colonia,** eau de Cologne. **a. dulce,** fresh water. **a. fresca,** cold water. **a. nieve,** sleet. **a. oxigenada,** hydrogen peroxide. *fig inf* **estar con el a. al cuello,** to be in low water. *fig inf* **estar entre dos aguas,** to be between two fires. *naut* **hacer a.,** to leak. **Todo eso es ya a. pasada,** That's all water under the bridge

aguacate *m*, *Mexico* alligator pear

aguacero *m*, heavy rainfall, shower

aguada *f*, water supply on board ship; flood (in mines); watering station; *art* water color

aguado *a* watery; abstemious; watered

aguador (-ra) *n* water carrier, water seller; drawer (of water)

aguafiestas *mf fig inf* wet blanket

aguafuerte *f*, etching

aguaje *m*, tide, waves; sea current; water supply (on board ship); wake (of a ship)

aguamanil *m*, washstand; pitcher, ewer

aguamarina *f*, aquamarine

aguantable *a* tolerable, bearable

aguantar *vt* to bear, tolerate, endure; restrain, resist, oppose; *vr* bear in silence, keep quiet

aguante *m*, patience, endurance; resistance

aguar *vt* to water down (wine, etc.); spoil (fun, etc.); *vr* be filled with water; be flooded; become watery or thin

aguardar *vt* to await; expect; allow time to (debtors)

aguardentoso *a* spirituous, containing **aguardiente;** hoarse, husky (of the voice)

aguardiente *m*, liquor. **a. de caña,** rum

aguarrás *m*, oil of turpentine

aguatinta *f*, aquatint

aguatocha *f*, pump (for water, etc.)

agudeza *f*, sharpness; keenness; distinctness; alertness, cleverness; witty sally, repartee; wit; swiftness

agudo *a* sharp; alert, clever; (*geom med*) acute; fine, keen; rapid; high-pitched; strong (of scents, etc.)

agüero *m*, omen, sign; prophecy, prediction

aguerrir *vt defective* to harden to war; toughen

aguijada *f*, goad, spur

aguijar *vt* to prick (with a goad); urge on, encourage (animals); incite, instigate; spur on; *vi* walk swiftly

aguijón *m*, goad; sting; thorn, prickle; spur; incitement, stimulus. **tener aguijones,** to be on pins and needles

aguijonazo *m*, prick (with a goad)

águila *f*, eagle; master mind. **a. caudal** or **a. real,** royal eagle. **á. o sol,** *Mexico* heads or tails

aguileño *a* aquiline

aguinaldo *m*, Christmas present; New Year's gift

aguja *f*, needle; hand, pointer; hatpin; engraver's burin; switch; *rw* point; *rw* rail; obelisk; spire; bodkin; knitting needle; crochet hook; (compass) needle. *pl bot* plumelet. **a. capotera, a. de zurcir,** darning needle. **a. de marear** *naut*, binnacle; mariner's compass. **a. de media,** knitting needle. **a. espartera,** packing needle

agujerear *vt* to perforate, make holes in

agujero *m*, hole, aperture; needle maker or seller; needle case

agujeta *f*, lace (for shoes, etc.); *pl* muscular pains, aches; tip, gratuity

aguzar *vt* to sharpen; grind, whet; stimulate, encourage; urge on, incite

aherrojar *vt* to put (a prisoner) in irons; oppress

aherrumbrar *vt* to give the color or taste of iron to; *vr* taste or look like iron; go rusty

ahí *adv* there; over there. **de a.,** thus, so. **por a.,** somewhere about, near at hand.

ahijado (-da) *n* godchild; protégé

ahijar *vt* to adopt (children); mother (animals); attribute, impute; *vi* bring forth offspring; *bot* sprout. See **prohibir**

ahincado *a* earnest, eager

ahincar *vt* to urge, press; *vr* hurry, hasten. See **prohibir**

ahínco *m*, earnestness, eagerness

ahitar *vt* to stuff with food; bore, disgust. See **prohibir**

ahíto *a* full of food; *fig* fed up. *m*, indigestion

ahogado (-da) *a* drowned; suffocated; stuffy, unventilated; stifling. *n* drowned person; victim of suffocation

ahogamiento *m*, drowning; suffocation

ahogar *vt* to drown; suffocate; put out (the fire); stifle (yawns, etc.); suppress, extinguish; tire; overwater (plants); *vr* *naut* sink, founder; drown; suffocate

ahogo *m*, anxiety, grief; difficulty in breathing, oppression; asthma; embarrassment; suffocation; straitened circumstances

ahondamiento *m*, in-depth treatment (e.g. **el a. de un problema,** in-depth treatment of a problem)

ahondar *vt* to deepen; excavate, dig; go into thoroughly; go deep into, penetrate; *vr* (earth) subside

ahora *adv* now; very soon; just now, a short time ago. *conjunc* whether; now. **a. bien,** well now, given that. **a. mismo,** immediately, at once; **por a.,** for the present

ahorcar *vt* to execute by hanging, hang. *inf* **a. los hábitos,** to leave the priesthood, cease to be an ecclesiastic

ahorita *adv, Mexico* right away, right now

ahormar *vt* to adjust, shape; break in (new shoes); make (a person) see reason

ahorquillar *vt* to prop up (trees) with forks; *vr* grow forked

ahorrar *vt* to free (slaves); save, economize; avoid, eschew; *vr* avoid; remove clothing

ahorro *m*, economy, thrift; *pl* savings

ahuciar *vt* take possession of (a house)

ahuecar *vt* to hollow out; loosen; shake out; puff out, inflate; put on a solemn voice; hoe, dig; *inf* *vr* puff oneself up; put on airs

ahumado *a* smoked; smoky

ahumar *vt* to smoke (herrings, etc.); fill with smoke; *vi* smoke, burn; *vr* be full of smoke; taste smoked; *inf* get drunk. See **desahuciar**

ahuyentar *vt* to frighten off; drive away; dismiss, banish (anxiety, etc.); *vr* flee

airado *a* angry

airar *vt* to annoy, anger; *vr* grow annoyed

aire *m*, air; atmosphere (sometimes *pl*); breeze, wind; bearing, appearance; vanity; (horse's) gait; futility, frivolity; grace, charm; gracefulness; *mus* air; *mus* tempo. **a. popular,** popular tune. **al a. libre,** in the open air, outdoors. *inf* **beber los aires (por),** to yearn (for)

airear *vt* to air; ventilate; aerate; *vr* take the air; catch a chill

airecito *m*, *Lat. Am.* breeze, gentle wind

airosidad *f*, gracefulness; jauntiness

airoso *a* airy, open; windy, breezy; fresh; graceful; handsome; jaunty; victorious, successful

aislacionamismo *m*, *pol* isolationism

aislacionista *mf pol* isolationist

aislado *a* isolated; remote; individual; single; *elec* insulated

aislador *m*, *phys* insulator

aislamiento *m*, isolation; *phys* insulation

aislante *a* isolating; insulating

aislar *vt* to isolate; *elec* insulate; *vr* become a recluse; become isolated

¡ajá! *interj inf* Aha! Good!

ajar *vt* to crease, crumple, spoil; humiliate; *vr* fade, wither (flowers)

ajedrecista *mf* chess player

ajedrez *m*, chess

ajeno *a* alien; belonging to another; various, diverse; free, exempt; unsuitable; irrelevant

ajetrear *vt* to tire out, exhaust; *vr* be overtired

ajetreo *m*, exhaustion, fatigue

ají *m*, *Lat. Am.* chili, red pepper; chili sauce; **estar hecho un ají** to be hopping mad, be fuming

ajo *m*, garlic; *inf* make up, paint; disreputable affair, shady business; curse, oath. *inf* **revolver el a.,** to stir up trouble

ajornalar *vt* to hire by the day

ajuar *m*, trousseau; household equipment

ajustado *a* exact; tight-fitting; trim

ajustador (-ra) *a* adjusting. *n* adjuster. *m*, tight-fitting jacket

ajustamiento *m*, adjustment; agreement

ajustar *vt* to adjust; fit; arrange; make an agreement about; reconcile; settle (accounts); engage, employ; retain (a barrister); regulate; tune up (a motor); *vi* fit; *vr* adapt oneself. *inf* **a. cuentas viejas,** to settle old accounts

ajuste *m*, fitting; adjustment; agreement; arrangement; *print* make-up. reconciliation; settlement; regulation; engagement, appointment

ajusticiar *vt* to put to death

al (contraction of *a* + *el*). 1. *prep a* + *m. def. art.,* to the, e.g. **Han ido al mar,** They have gone to the sea. 2. *prep a* + *el* used as *dem. pron* to that, to the one, e.g. **Mi sombrero se parece mucho al que tiene Vd.,** My hat is very similar to the one you have. *al* + *infin.* means when, as, at the same time as, e.g. **Al llamar a la puerta la vi en el jardín,** As I was knocking at the door, I saw her in the garden

ala *f*, *zool* wing; row, line; brim (of a hat);

eaves; (*arch aer mil bot*) wing; blade (of propeller); fin (of fish); *pl* courage. **a. del corazón**, *anat* auricle. **arrastrar el a.**, to woo, flirt with. *fig* **cortar** (*or* **quebrar**) **las alas (a)**, to clip a person's wings

alabanza *f*, praise; eulogy

alabar *vt* to praise; *vr* brag, boast

alabastro *m*, alabaster

alacena *f*, cupboard; recess; closet; safe (for food)

alacrán *m*, scorpion

alacre *a*, *Mexico* agile, nimble

alacridad *f*, alacrity, eagerness; *Mexico* agility, nimbleness

alado *a* winged; feathered; *fig* soaring

alambicado *a* sparing, frugal; subtle; euphuistic

alambicar *vt* to distil; examine carefully, scrutinise; make over-subtle or euphuistic (of style)

alambique *m*, still

alambre *m*, wire; sheep bells. **a. espinoso**, barbed wire

alambrera *f*, wire fence; wire-netting; wire cover

alambrista *mf* tight-rope walker; (Mexico) wetback

alameda *f*, poplar wood or grove; avenue of poplars

álamo *m*, poplar. **a. temblón**, aspen tree

alarde *m*, *mil* parade; display, ostentation. **hacer a. de**, to brag about

alargamiento *m*, lengthening; stretching

alargar *vt* to lengthen; prolong; pass, hand (things); pay out (ropes, etc.); increase; *vr* go away, depart; be wordy, spread oneself; lengthen

alarido *m*, yell, shout; shriek, scream; howl; yelp; cry (of a seagull)

alarma *f*, alarm. **a. aérea**, air-raid warning

alarmante *a* alarming

alarmar *vt* to give the alarm; frighten; *vr* be alarmed

alarmista *mf* alarmist

alazán *a* sorrel-colored. *m*, sorrel horse

alazo *m*, flap or stroke of the wings

alba *f*, dawn; *ecc* alb, vestment. **al a.**, at dawn

albacea *mf* executor, executrix; testator

albañil *m*, mason, bricklayer

albañilería *f*, masonry; bricklaying

albaricoque *m*, apricot

albaricoquero *m*, apricot tree

albarrada *f*, stone wall; mud fence

albear *vi* to become white, whiten

albedrío *m*, free will; fancy, caprice

alberca *f*, reservoir, tank; vat; artificial lake; *Lat. Am.* (swimming) pool

albergar *vt* to shelter; nourish, harbor; *vi* and *vr* take refuge or shelter; lodge

albergue *m*, shelter, refuge; den, lair; hospitality; lodging; asylum

albóndiga *f*, forced meat ball, rissole

albor *m*, whiteness; dawnlight, dawn. **a. de la vida**, life's dawning, childhood

alborada *f*, dawn; reveille; *mil* dawn attack; *mus* aubade

alborear *vi* to grow light, dawn

albornoz *m*, burnouse

alborotado *a* impulsive; turbulent; noisy; excitable

alborotar *vt* to disturb; *vi* make a noise; be gay; *vr* riot; grow rough (sea)

alboroto *m*, noise; confusion; tumult, riot; rejoicing, gaiety

alborotos *mpl*, *Argentina*, *Central America*, *Peru* popcorn

alborozar *vt* to overjoy, gladden; *vr* rejoice, be glad

alborozo *m*, gladness, rejoicing, joy

albricias *f pl*, reward for bringer of good tidings. *interj* **¡A.!** Joy! Congratulations!

álbum *m*, album

albúmina *f*, albumin

albur *m*, *icht* dace; chance, risk. **al a. de**, at the risk of

alcachofa *f*, artichoke

alcahuete *m*, procurer, go-between; pimp, pander; *fig inf* protector, screen; *inf* scandalmonger

alcahuetear *vt* to procure, act as a go-between for; *vi* be a pimp or a procuress

alcalde *m*, mayor; magistrate. *inf* **tener el padre a.**, to have a friend at court

alcaldesa *f*, mayoress

alcaldía *f*, office or authority of an alcalde

alcance *m*, reaching, attainment; range (of firearms, etc.); scope; arm's length or reach; pursuit; stop press *or* extra edition (newspapers); *com* deficit; importance; *pl* talent; capacity. **al a. de la voz**, within call. **hombre de cortos alcances**, a limited, dull man. **poner al a. de**, to make available to; make intelligible to

alcancía *f*, money-box; coin bank, piggy bank

alcanfor *m*, camphor

alcantarilla *f*, little bridge; sewer; culvert; bed for electric cable

alcantarillado *m*, sewage system; main sewer

alcanzable *a* obtainable; attainable

alcanzadizo *a* attainable, easily reached

alcanzar *vt* to overtake; reach; range (of guns, etc.); attain, achieve; understand; *fig* equal (in attainments); live at the same time as, be contemporaneous with; be capable of, be able; *vi* reach; share, participate in; be enough

alcaucil *m*, (in most places) wild artichoke; (in some places) cultivated artichoke

alcazaba *f*, fortress (within a walled town or city), casbah

alcázar *m*, fortress; royal residence, castle; *naut* quarterdeck

alcista *mf* speculator (on Stock Exchange)

alcoba *f*, bedroom; alcove, recess; Moorish flute

alcohol *m*, alcohol; galena; eye black (cosmetic); spirits of wine. **a. desnaturalizado,** industrial alcohol, methylated spirit. **a. metílico,** wood alcohol

alcohólico *a* alcoholic

alcoholismo *m*, alcoholism

Alcorán *m*, Koran

alcornoque *m*, cork tree; dunderhead, dolt

alcorza *f*, *cul* icing, sugar-paste

alcorzar *vt cul* to ice, cover with sugar; decorate, adorn

alcurnia *f*, lineage, family, descent

aldaba *f*, door knocker; bolt, latch; *pl* protectors, influential helpers. *inf* **tener buenas aldabas,** to have plenty of pull

aldabada *f*, rap with the knocker; sudden shock

aldea *f*, village

aldeano (-na) *a* village; country, ignorant. *n* villager; countryman, peasant

aleación *f*, alloy

alear *vi* to flutter, beat the wings; flap one's arms; recuperate, grow well; *vt* alloy

aleatorio *a* accidental, fortuitous

aleccionamiento *m*, teaching, training, coaching

aleccionar *vt* to teach, train, coach

aledaño *a* adjoining; border. *m*, boundary, border

alegación *f*, allegation, statement

alegar *vt* to allege, state; cite; *vi law* bring forward, adduce

alegato *m*, *law* speech (for the prosecution or defence)

alegoría *f*, allegory

alegórico *a* allegorical

alegorizar *vt* to interpret allegorically, treat as an allegory

alegrar *vt* to make happy, gladden, rejoice; adorn, beautify; stir (fires); *vr* be glad, rejoice; *inf* be merry (tipsy)

alegre *a* joyful, glad; cheerful, gay; bright (colors, etc.); pretty, attractive; *inf* risqué; *inf* flirtatious, light

alegría *f*, joy, gladness; cheerfulness, gaiety; *pl* public rejoicings

alegrón *m*, sudden unexpected joy; *inf* flash of light. *a inf* flirtatious

alejamiento *m*, placing at a distance, removal; withdrawal

Alejandría Alexandria

alejar *vt* to place at a distance, remove; withdraw; ward off (dangers, etc.); *vr* depart, go away; withdraw. **alejarse de,** to

abandon (a belief, custom, superstition, etc.)

alelar *vt* to make silly or stupid

aleluya *mf*, alleluia. *m*, Eastertide. *f*, small Easter cake; *inf* daub, poor painting; *inf* doggerel; joy, rejoicing

alemán (-ana) *a* and *n* German. *m*, German language.

Alemania Germany

alentada *f*, deep breath

alentado *a* valiant, spirited; proud; *Argentina* strong, vigorous

alentador *a* encouraging, inspiring, stimulating

alentar *vi irr* to breathe; *vt* encourage, inspire; *vr* be encouraged. See **sentar**

alergia *f*, allergy

alergólogo *m*, allergist

alero *m*, projecting roof; splashboard (of carriages); eaves; gable end

alerta *adv* watchfully. *interj* Take care! Look out! **estar ojo a.,** to be on the watch

alerto *a* watchful, alert

aletargado *a* lethargic; comatose

aletargamiento *m*, lethargy

aletargar *vt* to cause lethargy; *vr* become lethargic

aletazo *m*, flapping, beating (of wings); *inf* theft

aletear *vi* to flap the wings, flutter; move the arms up and down; become convalescent

aleteo *m*, fluttering, flapping of wings; beating, palpitation (of heart)

aleve *a* See **alevoso**

alevosía *f*, *law* malice; treachery

alevoso *a law* malicious; treacherous

alfabético *a* alphabetical

alfabetización *f*, literacy work

alfabetizador *m*, literacy worker

alfabeto *m*, alphabet. **a. manual,** sign language

alfandoque *m*, *Lat. Am.* cheesecake; maraca

alfanje *m* cutlass; *Mexico* machete

alfar *m*, potter's workshop; pottery, earthenware

alfarería *f*, pottery shop; potter's workshop; potter's craft

alfarero *m*, potter

alfeñique *m*, *cul* icing, sugarpaste; *inf* affectation

alfil *m*, bishop (in chess)

alfiler *m*, pin; brooch with a pin; tiepin; *pl* pin-money, dress-allowance; *fig inf* **no estar uno con sus alfileres,** to have a slate loose. *inf* **vestido de veinticinco alfileres,** dressed to the nines

alfombra *f*, carpet; rug

alfombrado *m*, carpeting

alfombrar *vt* to carpet

alfombrilla eléctrica *f*, electric pad or blanket

alfombrista *m*, carpet merchant; layer of carpets

alforja *f*, saddle-bag; *mil* knapsack

alforza *f*, *sew* tuck; *inf* scar

alforzar *vt sew* to tuck

alga *f*, alga, seaweed

algarabía *f*, Arabic; *inf* gibberish; din of voices, uproar

algarada *f*, troop of horse; uproar, hubbub; outcry

algarroba *f*, *bot* carob bean

algazara *f*, Moorish war cry; rejoicing, merriment; noise, clamor

álgebra *f*, algebra; art of bone setting

algo *indef pron* some, something (e.g. **Se ve que hay a. que le molesta,** You can see that something is irritating him). *adv* somewhat, a bit. **en a.,** in some way

algodón *m*, cotton plant; cotton flower; cotton fabric; candy floss (UK), cotton candy (USA). **a. en rama,** cotton-wool. **a. hidró-filo,** absorbent cotton wool. **a. pólvora,** nitrocellulose

alguacil *m*, policeman, constable; *ant* city governor; short-legged spider

alguien *indef pron* someone, somebody, e.g. **Dime si viene a.,** Tell me if anyone comes

algún *abb* of **alguno** bef. *m sing* noun, e.g. **a. libro**

alguno *a* (*abb* **algún** bef. *m, sing*) some, any. *indef pron* someone, somebody; *pl* some, some people. **alguno que otro,** a few

alhaja *f*, jewel; ornament; treasure, precious object; *inf* gem, excellent person (also ironic, e.g. **Es una a.,** He's a fine fellow)

alhajar *vt* to adorn with jewels, bejewel; furnish, equip

alharaca *f*, vehemence, demonstration, fuss (gen. *pl*)

aliado (**-da**) *a* allied. *n* ally

alianza *f*, alliance; pact, agreement; relationship (by marriage); sum total, whole (of factors, etc.); wedding-ring

aliarse *vr* to join together, become allies; be associated

alicaído *a* drooping; *inf* weak, exhausted; discouraged, downhearted; come down in the world

alicates *m pl*, pincers, pliers

aliciente *m*, attraction, inducement

alienación *f*, alienation

alienado *a* insane, mad

alienar *vt* See **enajenar**

aliento *m*, breathing; breath; courage, spirit; encouragement. **el posterior a.,** one's last breath. **cobrar a.,** to regain one's breath; take heart. **de un a.,** in one breath; without stopping

aligación *f*, binding together, alligation

aligeramiento *m*, lightening, reduction in weight

aligerar *vt* to lighten, make less heavy; quicken, hasten; ease, alleviate; moderate; shorten, abbreviate

alimaña *f*, destructive animal

alimentación *f*, nourishment; feeding

alimentar *vt* to feed; nourish; encourage, foment; assist, aid; keep, support

alimenticio *a* nourishing; feeding

alimento *m*, food, nourishment; stimulus, encouragement; *pl* alimony; allowance

alindar *vt* to mark the boundary of; beautify, adorn; *vi* border, be contiguous

alineación *f*, alignment

alinear *vt* to align, range in line; dress (troops); *vr* fall into line

aliñar *vt* to decorate, adorn; *cul* season; prepare; set (bones)

aliño *m*, decoration, ornament; preparation; condiment, seasoning; setting (bones)

aliquebrado *a* broken-winged; *inf* down in the mouth

alisador (**-ra**) *a* smoothing; polishing. *n* polisher

alisar *vt* to smooth; polish; sleek; plane; comb lightly

alisios *m pl*, trade winds

aliso *m*, alder tree and wood

alistador *m*, enroller

alistamiento *m*, enlistment; conscription; enrolment

alistar *vt* to enrol, list; enlist; conscript; prepare, get ready; *vr* enrol; *mil* enlist; get ready

alitranca *f*, *Chile, Peru* brake

aliviar *vt* to lighten; alleviate, mitigate; relieve; ease; quicken (one's step); hasten, speed up; steal

alivio *m*, lightening; relief; alleviation; ease

aljófar *m*, small irregular shaped pearl; dew-drop, raindrop, tear drop

allá *adv* there; to that place. **más a.,** farther on, beyond. Used in conjunction with phrases of time, indicates remoteness, e.g. **a. en tiempos de los Reyes Católicos,** long ago in the time of the Catholic Monarchs. **a. por 1900,** way back in 1900

allanamiento *m*, leveling, flattening; condescension, affability; (police) raid, (police) search acceptance of a judicial finding

allanar *vt* to level, flatten; overcome (difficulties); soothe; break into (a house, etc.); give entrance to the police; *vr* collapse (buildings, etc.); abide by, adapt oneself (to); condescend, be affable. **a. el camino (a . . .),** to pave the way (for . . .)

allegado (**-da**) *a* near, allied; related. *n* follower, ally

allegar *vt* to gather, collect; draw nearer; *agr* reap; add; *vi* arrive

allende *adv* beyond; besides. **de a. el mar,** from beyond the sea

allí *adv* there; to that place, thereto; thereupon, then. **por a.,** through there; that way

alma *f,* soul; living person; essence, core; vivacity, animation; energy, vitality; spirit, ghost; core (of a rope). **a. de cántaro,** fool, ninny. **a. de Dios,** simple soul, kind person. **a. en pena,** soul in purgatory. **¡A. mía!** My darling! **con todo el a.,** with all my heart. **Lo siento en el a.,** I feel it deeply

almacén *m,* warehouse; store, shop

almacenaje *m,* cost of storage

almacenar *vt* to store; put in store; hoard

almacenero *m,* warehouseman, store-keeper

almacenista *mf* owner of a store; assistant, salesman (saleswoman)

almanaque *m,* calendar, almanac

almeja *f, icht* clam

almendra *f,* almond; kernel; crystal drop (of chandeliers, etc.); cocoon; bean (of cocoa tree, etc.). **a. garapiñada,** sugar almond

almendro *m,* almond tree

almíbar *m,* sugar syrup; nectar

almibarar *vt* to coat with sugar; preserve (fruit) in syrup; flatter with sweet words

almidón *m,* starch

almidonado *a* starched; *fig inf* stiff, unbending; prim, starchy

almidonar *vt* to starch

alminar *m,* minaret (of mosque)

almirantazgo *m,* Admiralty; admiralship; Admiralty Court

almirante *m,* admiral

almohada *f,* pillow; pillowcase; cushion. *inf* **aconsejarse** *or* **consultar con la a.,** to think over (a matter) carefully, sleep on it

almohadilla *f, dim* small cushion; lace or sewing cushion; pin cushion

almohadillado *a* cushioned; padded

almoneda *f,* auction; furniture sale

almonedear *vt* to auction; sell off (furniture)

almorranas *f pl,* hemorrhoids

almorzar *vi irr* to lunch; breakfast. See **forzar**

almuercería *f, Mexico* lunch counter, luncheonette

almuecín, almuédano *m,* muezzin

almuerzo *m,* luncheon; breakfast (not so usual)

alocado *a* feather-brained, reckless; crazy, wild

alocución *f,* allocution, address, harangue

áloe *m, bot* aloe

alojado (**-da**) *m,* billeted soldier. *n* lodger, guest

alojamiento *m,* lodging; dwelling; *mil* billeting; *naut* steerage; camp, encampment

alojar *vt* to lodge; billet, quarter (troops); insert, introduce; *vi* and *vr* lodge; live, dwell

alpaca *f,* alpaca (animal and fabric); nickel silver

alpargata *f,* sandal with hemp sole

alpargatero (**-ra**) *n* manufacturer or seller of alpargatas

Alpes, los the Alps

alpestre *a* Alpine; rock (of plants); mountainous, lofty

alpinismo *m,* mountaineering

alpinista *mf* mountaineer, climber

alpino *a* Alpine

alpro *f,* (Alianza para el Progreso)

alquería *f,* farmstead

alquiladizo *a* rentable, hirable

alquilador (**-ra**) *n* hirer

alquilamiento *m,* See **alquiler**

alquilar *vt* to rent; hire out; hire; *vr* hire oneself out, serve on a wage basis

alquiler *m,* hiring out; renting; rental; hire; wages. **de a.,** for hire, on hire

alquitrán *m,* tar, pitch. **a. mineral,** coal tar

alquitranado *a* tarred. *m, naut* tarpaulin

alrededor *adv* around, round about. **a. de,** around; approximately, about (e.g. **a. de cinco dólares,** about $5)

alrededores *m pl,* environs, surrounding country

alta *f,* certificate of discharge from hospital

altanería *f,* hawking; haughtiness, disdain; superciliousness

altanero *a* soaring, high-flying (of birds); supercilious; haughty, disdainful

altar *m,* altar. **a. mayor,** high altar

altavoz *m,* loudspeaker; megaphone

altearse *vr* to rise, grow steep (of land)

alterabilidad *f,* alterability, changeability

alteración *f,* alteration, change; debasement (of coinage); agitation

alterar *vt* to change, alter; debase (coinage); disturb, agitate; *vr* grow angry; become excited

altercación, *f.* **altercado** *m,* altercation, quarrel

altercar(se) *vi* and *vr* to quarrel, dispute, altercate

alternación *f,* alternation

alternado *a* alternate

alternador *a* alternating. *m, elec* alternator

alternante *a* alternating

alternar *vt* to alternate; make one's debut as a **matador;** *vi* alternate; (*with* **con**) have dealings with, know

alternativa f, alternative, option; service performed by turns; alternation

alternativo a alternative

alterno a alternative; bot alternate

alteza f, altitude, height; sublimity, perfection; **(A.)** Highness (title)

altibajo m, embossed velvet; pl inf rough ground; inf vicissitudes of fortune

altillo m, hillock, eminence; garret, attic

altímetro m, aer altimeter

altiplano m plateau; **el A.** the High Andes, the high Andean plateau

altiplanicie f, plateau; highland

altisonante a sonorous; sublime; high-flown, pompous

altitud f, altitude, height

altivez f, arrogance, haughtiness

altivo a arrogant, haughty

alto a high; tall; difficult, arduous; sublime; deep; most serious (of crimes, etc.); dear (of price); small, early (hours). m, height; eminence, hill; story, floor; mil halt; red light (traffic light). adv up, above, on high; loudly. interj **¡A.!** mil Halt! mil **A. Mando,** High Command. **las altas horas de la noche,** the small (or early) hours. **en alta voz,** in a loud voice. **en alto,** on high; up above. **hacer alto,** to halt, stop

altozano m, mound, hillock; viewpoint, open space

altruismo m, altruism

altruista a altruistic. mf altruist

altura f, height; altitude; geom altitude or height; top, peak; sublimity; tallness

alucinación f, **alucinamiento,** m, hallucination

alucinado m, person suffering from hallucinations

alucinador a hallucinatory, deceptive

alucinar vt to dazzle, fascinate; deceive

alud m, avalanche

aludir vi to allude (to); refer (to), cite

alumbrado m, lighting; pl illuminati

alumbramiento m, lighting, supply of light; childbirth

alumbrar vt to light, illuminate; give sight to the blind; instruct, teach; inflict (blows); hoe vine roots; vi give birth to a child; vr inf grow tipsy

aluminio m, aluminum

alumno (-na) n ward, adopted child; pupil. **a. externo,** day pupil. **a. interno,** boarder

alunizar vi to land on the moon

alunizaje m, landing on the moon, moon-landing

alusión f, allusion

alusivo a allusive, suggestive; hinting

aluvión m, alluvium. **de a.,** alluvial

alverjana f, Lat. Am. pea

alza f, rise (of temperature, etc.); increase (in price); front sight (of guns)

alzada f, horse's stature; mountain pasture; law appeal

alzado a fraudulent (of bankruptcy); fixed (of price); Mexico haughty, proud m, theft; Lat. Am. wild; insolent; rebellious; arch front elevation

alzamiento m, raising, lifting; higher bid (at auction); rising, rebellion; fraudulent bankruptcy

alzaprima f, lever; wedge; bridge (of string instruments)

alzar vt to raise; lift up; elevate (the Host); steal, remove; hide; gather in the harvest; build, construct; naut heave; or raise (of temperature, mercury, price, etc.); make a fraudulent bankruptcy; law appeal; (with con) run off with, steal. naut **a. la vela,** to set sail

ama f, mistress of the house; owner; housekeeper; wet nurse. **a. de casa,** housemaker, housewife. **a. de leche,** foster-mother. **a. de llaves** or **a. de gobierno,** housekeeper. **a. seca,** children's nurse

amabilidad f, lovableness; kindness; niceness, goodness, helpfulness

amable a lovable; kind; nice, good, helpful

amador (-ra) a loving. n lover, admirer

amadrigar vt to welcome, receive well; vr go into a burrow or lair; go into seclusion

amaestrar vt to train, instruct; tame; break in (horses)

amagar vt and vi to threaten; vt show signs of (diseases, etc.); vr inf hide

amago (contra . . .), threat (to . . .), menace (to . . .)

amainar vt naut to take in the sails; vi drop (of the wind); vi and vt relax (efforts, etc.)

amalgama f, chem amalgam

amalgamación f, amalgamation

amalgamar vt to amalgamate; vr be amalgamated

amamantamiento m, suckling, nursling

amamantar vt to suckle

amancillar vt to discredit, dishonor; tarnish; stain

amanecer vi irr to dawn; arrive or be somewhere or be doing, at dawn (e.g. **Amanecimos en el barco,** Dawn came while we were on the ship. **Amanecimos escribiendo la carta,** The day broke as we were writing the letter); appear at daybreak; begin to appear. m, dawn, daybreak. See **conocer**

amanerado a mannered; affected

amaneramiento m, manneredness; mannerism

amanerarse vr to acquire mannerisms or tricks of style; become affected

amansador (-ra) a soothing, calming. n appeaser

amansar *vt* to tame; appease, moderate; soothe, pacify; break in (horses)

amante *a* loving. *mf* lover

amanuense *mf* amanuensis, secretary, clerk

amañar *vt* to execute with skill; *vr* grow skilful

amaño *m*, skill, dexterity; *pl* schemes, intrigues; tools, equipment

amapola *f*, poppy

amar *vt* to love

amarar *vi* to alight on the water (of hydroplanes)

amarchantarse con *vr*, *Lat. Am.* deal regularly with, do business with

amargar *vi* to taste or be bitter; *vt* make bitter; embitter

amargo *a* bitter; embittered; grievous, sad. *m*, bitterness; *pl* bitters

amargor *m*, **amargura,** *f*, bitter taste, bitterness; trouble, affliction, pain

amarillear *vi* to look yellow; turn yellow; tend to yellow

amarillento *a* yellowish, turning yellow

amarillo *a* and *m*, yellow

amarilloso *a*, *Lat. Am.* yellowish, turning yellow

amarradero *m*, *naut* mooring berth; mooring-post; hitchingpost or ring

amarrar *vt* to tie up, hitch; moor

amarre *m*, mooring; hitching

amartelar *vt* to make jealous; court, woo, make love to; *vr* be jealous; fall madly in love

amartillar *vt* to hammer, knock; cock (firearms)

amasador (-ra) *a* kneading. *n* kneader

amasar *vt* to knead; massage; scheme, plot

amasijo *m*, *cul* dough; kneading; portion of plaster or mortar; *inf* hotchpotch, mixture; scheme, plot

amatista *f*, amethyst

amazacotado *a* heavy, dense; *fig* stodgy (of writings, etc.)

amazona *f*, Amazon; independent woman; woman rider; woman's riding habit

ambages *m pl*, maze, intricate paths; circumlocutions

ámbar *m*, amber. **a. gris,** ambergris

ambición *f*, ambition

ambicionar *vt* to long for; desire eagerly; be ambitious to

ambicioso *a* ambitious; eager, desirous

ambidextro *a* ambidextrous

ambiente *a* ambient, surrounding. *m*, air, atmosphere; environment

ambigú *m*, cold buffet; buffet (in theaters, etc.)

ambigüedad *f*, ambiguity

ambiguo *a* ambiguous

ámbito *m*, precincts; boundary, limit; compass, scope

ambos, *a m pl*, **ambas** *a f pl*, both, e.g. **ambas casas,** both houses

ambulancia *f*, ambulance. **a. de correos,** railway post office. **a. fija,** field-hospital

ambulante *a* walking; traveling, wandering

amedrentar *vt* to frighten, scare; intimidate

ameliorar *vt* to better, improve

amén *m*, amen, so be it. **a. de,** besides, in addition to. *inf* **en un decir a.,** in a trice

amenaza *f*, threat

amenazador, **amenazante** *a* menacing, threatening

amenazar *vt* to threaten; *vt* and *vi* presage, be pending

amenguamiento *m*, lessening, diminution; discredit; loss of prestige

amenguar *vt* to lessen, decrease; dishonor, discredit

amenidad *f*, amenity; agreeableness

amenizar *vt* to make pleasant or attractive

ameno *a* pleasant; entertaining; agreeable, delightful

América America

América del Norte North America

América del Sur South America

americana *f*, (man's) jacket

americanismo *m*, usage typical of Western-Hemisphere Spanish

americano (-na) *a* a Western Hemispheric; *mf* native of the Western Hemisphere; resident of the Western Hemisphere

ameritar *vt* WH to deserve, merit

ametrallador *m*, machine-gunner

ametralladora *f*, machine-gun

amianto *m*, *min* amianthus, asbestos

amiba *f*, *zool* ameba

amiga *f*, woman friend; mistress, lover; dame, schoolmistress; dame school

amigabilidad *f*, friendliness, amicability

amigable *a* friendly, amicable; harmonious; suitable

amígdala *f*, tonsil

amigdalitis *f*, tonsillitis

amigo (-ga) *a* friendly; fond, addicted. *n* friend. *m*, lover. *inf* **ser muy a. de,** to be very friendly with; be very keen on or fond of

amilanar *vt* to terrify, intimidate; *vr* grow discouraged

aminorar *vt* to diminish, lessen

amistad *f*, friendship; liaison; favor; *pl* acquaintances, friends

amistar *vt* to introduce, make known to each other; bring about a reconciliation between or with

amistoso *a* friendly

amnesia *f*, amnesia

amnistía *f*, amnesty

amnistiar *vt* to concede an amnesty, pardon

amo *m*, head of the house; master; owner; overlord; overseer. **a. de huéspedes,** keeper of a boarding house. **Nuestro A.** Our Lord. *inf* **ser el a. del cotarro,** to rule the roost

amoblado *m*, *Central America, Mexico* furniture

amodorramiento *m*, stupor, deep sleep

amodorrarse *vr* to fall into a stupor; fall into a heavy sleep

amoladera *f*, whetstone

amolador *m*, scissors grinder; knife grinder; sharpener

amoladura *f*, grinding, whetting, sharpening

amolar *vt irr* to grind, sharpen; *inf* pester, annoy. See **colar**

amoldar *vt* to mold; adjust; *vr* adapt oneself

amonestación *f*, warning; advice. **correr las amonestaciones,** to publish banns of marriage

amonestador (-ra) *a* warning, admonitory. *n* admonisher

amonestar *vt* to warn; advise; rebuke; *ecc* publish bans of marriage

amoníaco *m*, ammonia

amontillado *m*, kind of pale, dry sherry

amontonamiento *m*, accumulation; gathering, collection; piling up, heaping

amontonar *vt* to pile up, heap; gather; collect; accumulate; *vr inf* fly into a rage

amor *m*, love; beloved; willingness, pleasure; *pl* love affairs; caresses. **a. propio,** self-esteem; vanity. *inf* **con mil amores,** with great pleasure. **por a. de,** for love of; for the sake of

amoral *a* amoral

amoratado *a* livid, bluish

amorcillo *m*, *dim.* little love; unimportant love affair; Cupid

amordazar *vt* to muzzle; gag; prevent speaking

amorfo *a* amorphous

amorío *m*, *inf* wooing, love making; *pl* love affairs

amoroso *a* loving; gentle; mild, balmy

amorrar *vi inf* to hang one's head; sulk, be sullen

amortajar *vt* to wrap in a shroud; enshroud

amortiguador *m*, *mech* shock absorber. *aut* **a. de los muelles,** shock-absorber

amortiguamiento *m*, softening, deadening; mitigation, lessening

amortiguar *vt* to soften, deaden; absorb (shocks); moderate, mitigate; soften (colors)

amortización *f*, amortization

amortizar *vt* to amortize; recover, redeem; suppress, abolish (posts)

amoscarse *vr inf* to be piqued or annoyed; become agitated

amostazar *vt inf* to annoy; *vi* become peeved

amotinador (-ra) *a* mutinous, rebellious. *n* rebel, mutineer; rioter

amotinar *vt* to incite to rebellion; unbalance, unhinge (mind); *vr* rebel; riot; *fig* be unhinged

amovible *a* movable, removable; removable (of officials, etc.)

amparador (-ra) *a* protective; sheltering. *n* protector, defender, helper; shelterer

amparar *vt* to protect, favor, help; shelter; *vr* take refuge, take shelter; defend oneself

amparo *m*, shelter, refuge; protection, favor, help; defense

amper *m*, *elec* ampere

amperímetro *m*, *elec* ammeter

amperio *m*, *elec* ampere

ampliable *a* amplifiable

ampliación *f*, enlargement, increase, extension; *phot* enlargement

ampliador (-ra) *a* enlarging. *n* enlarger

ampliadora *f*, *phot* enlarger

ampliar *vt* to extend, enlarge, increase; *phot* enlarge

amplificación *f*, extension, amplification; *phot* enlargement

amplificar *vt* to enlarge; extend; increase; amplify, expatiate upon

amplio *a* wide; extensive; roomy, ample; prolix

amplitud *f*, extension; width; spaciousness, amplitude

ampolla *f*, blister; ampoule; bubble; *elec* bulb

amputación *f*, amputation

amputar *vt* to amputate

amuchachado *a* boyish

amueblar *vt* to furnish; provide with furniture

amuinar *vt*, *Mexico* to anger, make angry

amuleto *m*, amulet, charm

amurallar *vt* to surround with a wall, wall

amurrarse *vr*, *Lat. Am.* get depressed, get the blues

amusgar *vt* and *vi* to flatten the ears (animals); *vt* screw up the eyes (to see better)

anacardo *m*, cashew (nut)

anacrónico *a* anachronous

anacronismo *m*, anachronism

ánade *mf* duck

anafrodisíaco *a* anaphrodisiac

anagrama *m*, anagram

anales *m*, *pl* annals

analfabetismo *m*, illiteracy

analfabeto (-ta) *a* and *n* illiterate

analgesia *f*, analgesia

analgésico *a* and *m*, *med* analgesic

análisis *m*, analysis; *gram* parsing

analista *mf* analyst

analizar *vt* to analyse

analogía *f*, analogy

analógico, análogo *a* analogous

ananás *m*, pineapple

anaquel *m*, shelf, ledge

anaranjado *a* and *m*, orange (color)

anarquía *f*, anarchy

anárquico *a* anarchical

anatema *mf*, anathema

anatomía *f*, anatomy

anatómico *a* anatomical

ancianidad *f*, old age; seniority; oldness

anciano (-na) *a* old; ancient. *n* old person

ancla *f*, anchor. **a. de la esperanza,** sheet anchor. **echar anclas,** to anchor

anclar *vi* to anchor

ancón *m*, cove, *Mexico* corner

áncora *f*, anchor; refuge, haven

ancho *a* wide, broad. *m*, width, breadth. *inf* **a mis (tus, sus,** etc.) **anchas** *or* **anchos,** at my (your, his, etc.) ease, with complete freedom

anchoa *f*, anchovy

anchura *f*, width, breadth; ease, freedom; extent

anchuroso *a* very wide; extensive; spacious

andada *f*, wandering, roving; hard bread roll; pasture; *pl* trail, tracks. *fig inf* **volver a las andadas,** to return to one's old tricks

andaderas *f pl*, go-cart (for learning to walk)

andador *a* walking; swift walking; wandering. *m*, walker; garden path; *pl* leading-strings, reins

andadura *f*, walk, gait; pace, step

Andalucía Andalusia

andaluz (-za) *a* and *n* Andalusian

andaluzada *f*, *inf* exaggeration, tall story

andamio *m*, scaffolding; stand, platform

andanada *f*, *naut* broadside; cheapest priced seat in a bullring; *inf* dressing-down, scolding

andante *a* walking, strolling; errant (of knights). *a* and *m*, *mus* andante

andanza *f*, happening, occurrence; *pl* doings, deeds. **buena a.,** good fortune

andar *vi irr* to walk; move; work, operate, run (machines, etc.); progress, get along (negotiations, etc.); be, feel; elapse (of time); be occupied; behave; (*with prep a*) administer (blows, etc.); (*with en*) upset, turn over (papers, etc.); ride in or on (cars, bicycles, etc.); be engaged in; (*with con*) use, handle; *vt* traverse. *m*, gait, walk. **a. por los cuarenta,** to be in one's forties. **a. con paños tibios,** not to be firm. **a. con pies de plomo,** to be extremely cautious. **a. tras,** to follow, go after; persecute; desire ardently (things). **andarse a la flor del berro,** to sow one's

wild oats. *fig inf* **andarse por las ramas,** to beat about the bush. **¡Anda!** Get along with you!; Hurry up!; You don't say so! **¡Andando!** Let's get going!, Let's get a move on it! *Preterite* **anduve,** etc. *Imperf subjunc* **anduviese,** etc.

andariego *a* swift walking; wandering, vagrant

andarín (-ina) *n* good walker; professional walker

andas *f pl*, kind of stretcher; bier

andén *m*, railway platform; *Lat. Am.* sidewalk

andinismo *m*, *Lat. Am.* mountain climbing **andinista** *mf Lat. Am.* mountain climber

andino *a* Andean

andrajo *m*, rag, wisp of cloth, tatter

andrajoso *a* ragged, tattered

andurriales *m pl*, byways, unfrequented paths; remote places

anécdota *f*, anecdote

anegación *f*, drowning; flooding, inundation

anegar *vt* to drown; inundate; shipwreck; *vr* drown; be flooded

anejo *a* attached, annexed. *m*, annexed borough

anemia *f*, anemia

anémico *a* anemic

anémona, anémone *f*, anemone. **anémona de mar,** sea-anemone

anestesia *f*, anesthesia

anestesiador (-ra) *n* anesthetist

anestesiar *vt* to anesthetize

anestésico *a* and *m*, anesthetic

aneurisma *mf med* aneurism

anexar *vt* to annex

anexión *f*, annexation

anexo *a* attached, joined. *m*, annex

anfibio *a* amphibious. *m*, amphibian

anfiteatro *m*, amphitheater; operating theater; dissecting room; morgue; *theat* dress-circle

anfitrión *m*, *inf* host, one who entertains guests

angarillas *f pl*, hand barrow; table cruet; yoke and panniers

ángel *m*, angel; *Lat. Am.* (hand) microphone **á. de la guarda,** guardian angel. **estar con los ángeles,** to be in Heaven (euphem. for 'to be dead')

angelical, angélico *a* angelic; divine, excellent

angina *f*, *med* angina, tonsillitis. **a. de pecho,** angina pectoris

anglicismo *m*, anglicism

angostar *vi* and *vt* to narrow; tighten

angosto *a* narrow; tight

angostura *f*, narrowness; tightness; narrow pass; strait; *fig* tight corner, fix

anguila *f*, *icht* eel; *pl naut* slipway, slips

ángulo *m*, angle. **á. inferior izquierdo,**

lower lefthand corner. **á. inferior derecho,** lower righthand corner. **á. superior izquierdo,** upper lefthand corner. **á. superior derecho,** upper righthand corner. **á. recto,** right angle

anguloso a angulate; angular, gaunt; cornered

angustia f, anguish, grief

angustiante a distressing

angustiar vt to grieve; afflict; vr be full of anguish

anhelación f, panting, hard breathing; yearning, longing

anhelar vi to pant, breathe with difficulty; vi and vt long for, yearn for, desire

anhélito m, pant, hard breathing

anhelo (de) m, longing (for), desire (for), yearning (for)

anheloso a difficult, labored (of breathing); anxious, longing

anidar vi to nest (birds); swell; vt shelter, protect; vr nest; dwell; nestle

anilla f, curtain ring; pl gymnastic rings

anillo m, finger ring; small ring; coil (of serpents and ropes) **a. de compromiso** Mexico engagement ring inf **venir como a. al dedo,** to fit like a glove; come just at the right moment

ánima f, soul, spirit; soul in purgatory; bore (of firearms); pl prayer bell for the souls of the departed

animación f, liveliness, gaiety; animation, vivacity; bustle, movement

animal m, animal; inf dolt, brute. a animal; inf brutish, doltish

animalada f, inf stupidity, foolishness

animalidad f, animalism

animar vt to animate; encourage, incite; invigorate, enliven; make gay, cheer up; make attractive, adorn; vr take heart; make up one's mind; cheer up; grow gay

animismo m, animism

ánimo m, soul, spirit; courage; endurance, fortitude; will, intention; mind. **con ánimo de + inf.,** with the intention of + ger. **1Á.!** Courage!

animosidad f, hatred, animosity, dislike

animoso a spirited, lively; valiant

aniñado a childlike, childish

aniquilación f, destruction, annihilation; suppression; decay

aniquilador (-ra) a destructive, annihilating. n destroyer

aniquilamiento m, See **aniquilación**

aniquilar vt to annihilate, destroy completely; vr waste away, decay

anís m, aniseed, anise; anisette (liqueur)

aniversario a annual. m, anniversary

ano m, anus

anoche adv last night; the previous night

anochecer vi irr to grow night; become dark; be in a place or be doing something at nightfall (e.g. **Anochecimos en Lérida,** We were in Lerida at nightfall). vr

poet be obscured or darkened. m, nightfall, dusk. See **conocer**

anochecida f, dusk, late twilight

anodino a med anodyne; ineffective, useless; inoffensive. m, anodyne

anomalía f, anomaly, inconstancy, irregularity; ast anomaly

anómalo a anomalous, abnormal, unusual

anonadación, f. anonadamiento m, destruction, annihilation; despair, melancholy; suppression

anonadar vt to destroy, annihilate; suppress; fig overwhelm, depress; humble

anónimo a anonymous. m, anonymity; anonymous letter; unsigned literary work

anormal a abnormal; irregular, unusual. mf abnormal person

anormalidad f, abnormality; irregularity, inconsistency

anotación f, annotation; Lat. Am. score (in sports)

anotador (-ra) n annotator

anotar vt to annotate; note down

anquilostoma m, med hookworm

ansia (de) f, anxiety, trouble; grief; longing (for), yearning (for); greed

ansiar vt to long for, yearn for; covet, desire

ansiedad f, anxiety, anguish, worry

ansión f, intense desire

ansioso a anxious; grievous, painful; eager, desirous; greedy

antagónico a antagonistic

antagonismo m, antagonism

antagonista mf antagonist, adversary

antaño adv last year, yesteryear; long ago

ante m, zool elk; suede; buffalo

ante prep in the presence of, before; regarding, in the face of (e.g. **a. deber tan alto,** in the face of so noble a duty)

anteanoche adv the night before last

anteayer adv the day before yesterday

antebrazo m, forearm

antecedente a, antecedent. **antecedentes** m pl background (of a case, situation, etc.)

anteceder vt to precede

antecesor (-ra) a previous. n predecessor. m, forebear, ancestor

antecoger vt to carry in front, lead before; pick too soon

antecomedor m, breakfast nook, breakfast room

antedatar vt to antedate

antedicho a aforementioned, aforesaid

antelación f, advance, anticipationz

antellevar vt, Mexico to knock down, run over

antemano, de adv in advance, beforehand

antemeridiano a antemeridian, forenoon

antena f, antenna; rad aerial

antenacido a born prematurely

antenombre m, title (placed before name)

anteojo m, spy-glass, small telescope; pl horse's blinkers; eyeglasses, glasses; spectacles; goggles

antepagar vt to pay in advance

antepasado a previous, past. m, ancestor (gen. pl)

antepecho m, parapet; windowsill; railing, balustrade; front (of a theater box, etc.); naut bulwark

antepenúltimo a antepenultimate, second from the last

anteponer vt irr to place before; prefer, favor. See **poner**

anteproyecto m, first sketch, preliminary work or plan

anterior a previous, former; anterior; aforementioned, preceding

anteriormente adv beforehand, previously

antes adv before; rather, on the contrary; previously. **a. bien**, rather, sooner. **a. con a.** or **cuanto a.**, as soon as possible

antesala f, antechamber

antevíspera f, two days previously

antiaéreo a antiaircraft. m pl. **(cañones) antiaéreos**, A.A. guns

anticipación f, anticipation; advance

anticipada f, foul thrust (in fencing, etc.)

anticipadamente adv in advance; prematurely

anticipado a in advance; premature

anticipador a anticipatory

anticipar vt to anticipate; foresee; forestall; advance (money); lend; vr happen before time; (with prep a) act in advance of, anticipate; get ahead of oneself

anticipo m, anticipation, advance; advance payment; sum of money lent

anticlímax m, anticlimax

anticonstitucional a unconstitutional

anticuado a antiquated, ancient

anticuario m, antiquarian, antique dealer

antídoto m, antidote

antiespasmódico a and m, med antispasmodic

antiestético a unesthetic

antietimológico a non-etymological, unetymological

antifaz m, mask; face-covering

antiflogístico a and m, med antiphlogistic

antigramatical a ungrammatical

antigualla f, antique; ancient custom; anything out-of-date

antiguamente adv in time past, formerly

antiguamiento m, seniority

antigüedad f, antiquity; ancients; length of service (in an employment); pl antiquities

antiguo a ancient, very old; antique; senior (in an employment); former. m, senior member (of a community, etc.). m pl, ancients. **A. Testamento**, Old Testament. **de a.**, from ancient times. **en lo antiguo**, in ancient times; in former times, in days of yore

antillano (-na) a and n of or from the Antilles

Antillas, las the Antilles

antílope m, antelope

antipalúdico a antimalarial

antipara f, screen, shield

antiparras f pl, inf spectacles, eyeglasses, glasses

antipatía f, antipathy

antipático a disagreeable; unattractive

antipatriótico a unpatriotic

antípoda a and m, or f, antipode

antiquísimo a sup, **antiguo**, most ancient

antisemita a anti-Semitic. mf anti-Semite

antisemitismo m, anti-Semitism

antiséptico a and m, antiseptic

antisifilítico a med anti-syphilitic

antisocial a antisocial

antítesis f, antithesis

antitético a antithetic, contrasted

antojadizo a capricious, fanciful, whimsical

antojarse vr to have a fancy for, want (e.g. **Se me antoja marcharme al campo**, I have a yen to go to the country); suspect, imagine

antojito m, Mexico typical Mexican dish (of food)

antojo m, caprice, fancy, whim; desire, will; pl birthmark

antología f, anthology

antólogo m, anthologist

antonomasia f, antonomasia. **por a.**, by analogy, by transference

antorcha f, torch, flambeau

antracita f, anthracite

ántrax m, med anthrax

antro m, cave, cavern; anat antrum

antropología f, anthropology

antropológico a anthropological

antropólogo m, anthropologist

antruejo m, three days of carnival before Lent

anual a yearly, annual

anualidad f, annuity

anuario m, directory, yearbook, handbook

anubarrado a covered with clouds, cloudy

anublado a lowering, overcast; clouded

anublar vt to cloud; darken, obscure; blight (plants); vr cloud over; become blighted or mildewed

anudar vt to knot; tie, fasten; join; continue; **a. amistad de,** to strike up a friendship with. **a. la corbata,** to put on one's tie, tie one's tie; vr grow stunted

anulable a annullable, voidable

anulación f, annulment, abrogation

anular a annular, ring-shaped. vt to annul; math cancel out

anuloso a annulate, formed of rings

anunciación f, ecc Annunciation; announcement

anunciador (-ra), n **anunciante** mf announcer; advertiser

anunciar vt to announce; publish, proclaim; advertise; foretell, presage. **Anuncian lluvia,** The forecast calls for rain

anuncio m, announcement; publication; proclamation; advertisement; presage, omen. **a. luminoso,** sky-sign

anzuelo m, fish-hook; cul fritter; inf attraction, inducement

añadido m, hair-switch; make-weight

añadidura f, addition; make-weight, extra

añadir vt to add; increase

añejo a very old

añicos m pl, fragments, small pieces. **hacer a.,** to break into fragments

añil m, indigo; indigo blue

año m, year; pl birthday. **a. bisiesto,** leap-year. **a. económico,** fiscal year. **A. Nuevo,** New Year. **tener (siete) años,** to be (seven) years old.

añoranza f, homesickness, loneliness; nostalgia

añorar vi to be homesick or lonely

añoso a very old, full of years

añublo m, mildew

aojar vt to bewitch, place under a spell; spoil, frustrate

aojo m, evil eye; magic spell

aorta f, anat aorta

apabullante a crushing, flattening

apacentadero m, grazing land, pasture

apacentamiento m, pasturage; grazing

apacentar vt irr to put out to grass; teach, instruct; satisfy (one's desires); vr graze (cattle). See **acertar**

apachurar vt, Mexico to press (button, etc.)

apacibilidad f, agreeableness; mildness; peaceableness

apacible a agreeable; mild; peaceable; calm, peaceful

apaciguamiento m, appeasement, soothing, pacification

apaciguar vt to appease, pacify; calm

apadrinar vt to act as godfather to; be

best man to (at a wedding); act as a second for (in a duel); sponsor; favor

apagable a extinguishable

apagado a timid, nervous; pale (of colors); dull, lusterless

apagador (-ra) a quenching. n extinguisher. m, candle-snuffer; damper (of a piano)

apagaincendios m, ship's fire-extinguisher

apagamiento m, quenching, extinguishment

apagar vt to extinguish, put out; fig quench, moderate; slake (lime); art tone down (colors); shut off (engines)

apagarrisas mf crapehanger, killjoy, wet blanket

apalabrar vt to make an appointment with; discuss, consider

apaleamiento m, beating, thrashing

apalear vt to beat, thrash; knock down with a stick

apañar vt to take away, remove; seize; steal; dress, get ready; inf wrap up; patch, repair; vr inf grow skilful

apaño m, dexterity, skill; craft, guile

aparador m, sideboard; workshop; ecc credence (table); Mexico (shop) window

aparato m, apparatus; equipment, utensils; pomp, ostentation; symptoms; sign, circumstance, token. **a. digestivo,** digestive system; digestive tract. **a. fonador,** speech apparatus

aparatoso a showy, ostentatious. **incendio. a.,** conflagration, large fire

aparear vt to match, make equal; pair; mate (animals); vr form up in pairs

aparecer(se) vi and vr irr to appear; seem; be. See **conocer**

aparecido m, apparition, specter

aparejador m, overseer, foreman; naut rigger

aparejar vt to prepare, make ready; saddle (horses); prime, size; rig (a ship)

aparejo m, preparation, arrangement; harness, trappings; naut rigging; naut gear; priming, sizing; mech tackle; pl equipment

aparentar vt to pretend, simulate

aparente a seeming, apparent; obvious, visible; suitable, proper

aparición f, appearance, arrival; apparition, phantom

apariencia f, appearance, looks, probability, likelihood; outward semblance; pl theat scenery

apartadero m, passing place for cars; railway siding; grass verge. **a. ferroviario,** railway marshaling yard

apartado a distant, far off; secluded; different. m, post-office box; secluded room; smelting house; sorting of cattle; selection of bulls for a bullfight

apartamento m *Lat. Am.* (*except Argentina*) apartment

apartamiento m, separation; withdrawal, retiral; seclusion; apartment, flat; *law* withdrawal of an action

apartar vt to separate; remove (e.g. an obstacle), take away; rw shunt; dissuade; sort; vr obtain a divorce; *law* withdraw an action. **apartarse de la tradición,** to depart from tradition

aparte adv aside, on one side; separately; *theat* aside; besides; beyond. m, *theat* aside; paragraph; space between words. **¡Aparte!** Move to one side!

apartidario a non-partisan

apasionado (**-da**) a impassioned; fervent, devoted; passionate; enthusiastic. n admirer, lover; enthusiast

apasionamiento m, passion

apasionar vt to arouse to passion; pain; vr (*with por*) grow passionately fond of; become enthusiastic for

apatía f, apathy

apático a apathetic

apear vt to dismount; hobble (horse); survey, map out; fell a tree; *fig* overcome (difficulties); *inf* dissuade; prop; remove, bring down; scotch (a wheel); vr dismount; alight, step off

apechugar vi to push with the breast; *inf* put up with reluctantly

apedazar vt to tear; break; mend, repair

apedrear vt to stone; stone to death; vi *impers* hail; vr be damaged by hail (crops)

apegarse vr to grow fond (of), become attached (to)

apego m, fondness, inclination; affection, attachment

apelación f, *law* appeal; *inf* doctor's consultation

apelante a and mf *law* appellant

apelar vi *law* to appeal; (*with prep a*) have recourse to; vi be of the same color (horses)

apellidar vt to name, call; acclaim; call to arms; vr be named

apellido m, surname; nickname; call to arms; clamor; name

apenar vt to grieve, afflict; cause sorrow

apenarse vr *Lat. Am.* to be ashamed

apenas adv scarcely; immediately, as soon as; with trouble or difficulty

apéndice m, appendix, supplement; *anat* appendix

apendicitis f, appendicitis

apeo m, survey; scaffolding; prop, support

apercibimiento m, preparation; provision; warning; *law* summons

apercibir vt to prepare, furnish; warn; *law* summon

apergaminarse vr *inf* to shrivel, dry up (with old age, etc.)

aperitivo a aperitive. m, aperient; aperitive, appetiser

apertura f, opening; inauguration; reading (of a will)

apesadumbrar vt to sadden, afflict, grieve

apestar vt to infect with the plague; catch the plague; *fig* corrupt; *inf* pester, annoy; vi stink

apestoso a stinking, putrid

apetecer vt *irr* to want, desire; attract. See **conocer**

apetecible a attractive, desirable

apetencia f, appetite; desire

apetito m, appetite

apetitoso a appetising; tasty, savory; attractive

apiadarse vr (*with de*) to have compassion on, be sorry for

ápice m, apex; peak, summit, top; orthographic accent; iota, tittle; crux (of a problem)

apicultor (**-ra**) n apiarist, beekeeper

apicultura f, apiculture, beekeeping

apilar vt to pile, heap

apimplado, -a a, *Lat. Am.* boozed up, drunk

apiñado a crowded, serried

apiñar vt to group together, crowd; vr crowd

apio m, celery

apisonar vt to roll, stamp, flatten, ram down; tamp, pack down (e.g. tobacco in a pipe)

aplacable a appeasable, placable

aplacamiento m, appeasement

aplacar vt to appease, calm; moderate, mitigate

aplacible a agreeable, pleasant

aplanacalles mf, *Lat. Am.* idler, lay about, lazybones

aplanar vt to flatten, level; roll (pastry); *inf* dumbfound, overwhelm; vr collapse (buildings); lose heart

aplastar vt to flatten, squash, crush; *inf* squash flat, floor

aplaudir vt to applaud, clap; praise, commend, approve

aplauso m, applause; clapping, plaudit; approbation, commendation

aplazamiento m, postponement; appointment, summons

aplazar vt to summon, arrange a meeting; postpone; adjourn

aplicación f, application; diligence, assiduity; appliqué, ornamentation

aplicado a diligent, hardworking; appliqué

aplicar vt to apply; impute; intend, destine (for processions); *law* adjudge; vr engage in; apply oneself. **a. el oído,** to listen intently. **a. sanciones,** *pol* to impose sanctions

aplomado *a* self-possessed, dignified; leaden, lead-colored

aplomo *m*, self-possession, dignity; sang-froid

apocado *a* spiritless, timid; base, mean

apocamiento *m*, timidity, pusillanimity; depression, discouragement; shyness; baseness, meanness

apocar *vt* to diminish, reduce; humiliate, scorn

apoderado *a* authorized. *m*, attorney; deputy; proxy

apoderar *vt* to authorize; grant powers of attorney to; *vr* (*with de*) seize, take possession of

apodo *m*, nickname

apogeo *m*, *ast* apogee; *fig* zenith, peak (of fame, etc.)

apolillar *vt* to eat clothes (moths); *vr* be moth-eaten

apologista *mf* apologist

apólogo *m*, apologue, moral fable

apoplejía *f*, apoplexy

aporrear *vt* to beat, cudgel; *vr* work hard, slog away

aportación *f*, contribution; occasionment

aportar *vt* to cause, occasion; contribute; *vi naut* reach port; **El buque aportó a Nueva York,** The ship reached New York, The ship sailed into New York harbor; arrive at an unexpected place

aposentar *vt* to lodge, give hospitality to; *vr* lodge, settle down

aposento *m*, room; suite, apartments; lodging, accommodation; *theat* box

apósito *m*, poultice, external application; (medical) dressing

apostar *vt irr* to bet; station (soldiers); *vi* compete, rival. See **contar**

apostilla *f*, marginal note, gloss

apóstol *m*, apostle

apóstrofe *m*, or *f*, apostrophe, hortatory exclamation

apóstrofo *m*, *gram* apostrophe

apostura *f*, neatness, spruceness

apoteosis *f*, apotheosis

apoyar *vt* (*with en*) to lean against; rest upon; *vt* uphold, favor; confirm, bear out; droop the head (horses); second (a motion); *vi* (*with en*) rest on; lean against; *vr* (*with en*) rest on; lean against; **apoyarse de codos,** to lean on one's elbows; be upheld by; *fig* be founded on; *fig* depend on, lean on

apoyo *m*, support, prop; windowsill, sill; assistance; backing, support

apreciable *a* appreciable; estimable; important

apreciación *f*, appreciation; valuation, estimate

apreciador (**-ra**) *a* appreciatory. *n* appreciator

apreciar *vt* to estimate (values); appreciate; like, esteem, have a regard for

apreciativo *a* appreciative

aprecio *m*, valuation; appreciation, regard

aprehender *vt* to apprehend, catch; seize (contraband); understand, grasp

aprehensión *f*, seizure, apprehension

apremiador, apremiante *a* urgent, pressing

apremiar *vt* to hurry; urge, press; force, oblige; burden, oppress (with taxes)

apremio *m*, insistence, pressure; compulsion; demand note

aprender *vt* to learn. **a. de memoria,** to learn by heart

aprendiz (**-za**) *n* apprentice

aprendizaje *m*, apprenticeship. **hacer el a.,** to serve an apprenticeship

aprensión *f*, capture; fear, apprehension; suspicion, fancy; prejudice, scruple

aprensivo *a* apprehensive, nervous, fearful

apresar *vt* to nab, catch; capture (a ship); imprison; fetter

apresurar *vt* to quicken; *vr* hasten, be quick

apretado *a* difficult, dangerous; tight; crabbed (of handwriting); clustered (e.g. **casas apretadas alrededor de la sinagoga,** houses clustered around the synagogue). *inf* mean, close-fisted. *m*, small close handwriting

apretar *vt irr* to tighten; compress; urge on, press; harass, vex; trouble, worry; speed up; squeeze; press (bells, gun triggers, etc.); *vi* increase, grow worse (storms, heat, etc.); pinch, hurt (shoes). **a. los pasos,** to quicken one's pace. *inf* **a. a correr,** to take to one's heels. **¡Aprieta!** *inf* Nonsense! It can't be! See **acertar**

apretón *m*, squeeze, grip, pressure; *inf* sprint, spurt; *inf* fix, pickle. **a. de manos,** handshake

apretujar *vt inf* to squeeze, hug

aprieto *m*, crowd, crush; urgency; *inf* jam, trouble, fix

aprisa *adv* quickly, in a hurry

aprisionar *vt* to imprison; bind, fetter; tie

aprobación *f*, approbation, approval, commendation; ratification (of a bill); pass (in an examination)

aprobado *m*, pass certificate (in examinations)

aprobar *vt irr* to approve; pass (in an examination). See **contar**

aprontar *vt*, *Lat. Am.* to pay in advance, prepay

apropiación *f*, appropriation; application; adaptation

apropiado *a* appropriate, suitable, proper

apropiar *vt* to appropriate; adapt, fit; *vr* appropriate, take possession

aprovechable a usable, available

aprovechado a advantageous; assiduous, conscientious; capable; thrifty

aprovechador a self-seeking

aprovechamiento *m*, utilization, employment; exploitation; profitable use

aprovechar *vi* to be advantageous or useful; be beneficial; make progress (in studies, etc.); *vt* use; profit by; *vr* take advantage of, make use of. **¡Que aproveche!** May it do you good! (said to anyone eating)

aprovisionar *vt* to provision, supply

aproximación *f*, approximation; consolation prize (in a lottery)

aproximar *vt* to bring or draw nearer; *vr* approach; be almost, be approximately; draw closer

aptitud *f*, aptitude, ability; fitness; propensity

apto a suitable, fitting; competent. **no apta para menores,** not suitable for children (of films, etc.)

apuesta *f*, bet, wager; competition

apuestas benéficas de fútbol football pools

apuesto a elegant; handsome; well set-up

apuntador (-ra) *n* note-taker; observer. *m, theat* prompter; *theat* stage-manager

apuntalar *vt* to prop, prop up, underpin, bolster

apuntar *vt* to aim (a gun, etc.); point to, indicate; note down; mark; sketch; sharpen; bet (at cards); fasten temporarily; *inf* mend; *theat* prompt; suggest, hint (e.g. **La fecha está apuntada en varios manuscritos,** The date is hinted at in various manuscripts); *vi* begin to appear. *inf* **a. y no dar,** to promise and do nothing

apunte *m*, abstract; note; annotation; sketch; *theat* prompt *or* prompter *or* prompt book *or* cue; stake in a card game

apuñalar *vt* to stab, attack with a dagger

apurado a poor, needy; dangerous; difficult; accurate, exact; hurried

apurar *vt* to purify; drain; exhaust; finish, conclude; examine closely, scrutinize (e.g. **apurar una materia,** to exhaust a subject, examine a subject thoroughly); irritate, make impatient; urge on, hasten; *vr* be anxious, fret; *Lat. Am.* hurry, hurry up

apuro *m*, difficulty, fix; poverty, want; anxiety, worry. **pasar apuros,** to have a hard time

aquejar *vt* to afflict; weary, beset, harass; *vr* complain; hurry

aquel, a *m* **aquella, a** *f* **aquellos, a** *m pl* **aquellas** *a f pl,* that, those; that or those over there (farther off than **ese**)

aquel *m*, charm, attraction, it

aquél, aquélla, aquéllos, aquéllas *dem pron m, f,* sing. and pl., that, the

one, those, those ones; the former. e.g. **La casa que ve usted a lo lejos aquélla es la vivienda de mi tío,** The house that you see in the distance, that is my uncle's dwelling. **Éste no me gusta pero aquél sí,** I do not like the latter, but I like the former

aquello *dem pron neut* that; the fact; the matter, the affair, the former (remark, idea, etc.). e.g. **Todo a. por fin acabó,** All that came to an end at last. **a. de,** the fact that

aquí *adv* here. **de a.,** hence the fact that. **¡He a.!** Behold!

aquietar *vt* to calm, soothe

aquilatar *vt* to assay; scrutinize; examine, weigh up (persons)

aquistar *vt* to attain, acquire

ara *f*, altar; **en aras de,** in honor of; for the sake of

árabe a Arab, Arabic. *mf* Arab. *m*, Arabic (language)

arabesco a Arabic. *m, art* arabesque

Arabia Saudita Saudi Arabia

arado *m*, plow

arador a plowing. *m*, plowman. **a. de la sarna,** *ent* scabies mite

aragonés (-esa) a and *n* Aragonese

araguato *m, Lat. Am.* howler monkey

arahuaco a and *n* Arawak, Arawakian

arancel *m*, tariff, duty, tax

arancelar to charge tuition for (e.g. **a. la universidad,** charge tuition for college studies)

arancelario a tariff, tax; customs

arándano *m, bot* bilberry

arandela *f*, candle-dripper; *mech* washer; wall candelabrum

araña *f*, spider; chandelier; *Lat. Am.* whore

arañacielos *m*, skyscraper

arañar *vt* to scratch; *inf* scrape together, hoard

arañazo *m*, scratch

arar *vt* to plough. **a. en el mar,** to labor in vain

arbitrador (-ra) *n* arbitrator

arbitraje *m*, arbitration; arbitrament, decision

arbitrar *vt* to judge freely; *law* arbitrate, mediate; devise; invent; marshal (money, resources, etc.); draft (a law) *vr* make shift, contrive

arbitrariedad *f*, arbitrariness

arbitrario a arbitral, mediatory; arbitrary, capricious

arbitrio *m*, free will; arbitration; means, way; discretion; arbitrament, judgment; *pl* rates, municipal taxes

árbitro (-ra) a arbitrary. *n* arbiter. *m, sport* umpire; referee

árbol *m*, tree; *mech* shaft; *naut* mast; axis of a winding stair. **a. de amor** or **a. de Judas,** Judas tree. **a. de la ciencia (del**

bien y del mal), Tree of Knowledge (of good and evil). **a. de levas,** mech camshaft. **a. del pan,** breadfruit tree. naut **a. mayor,** mainmast. **a. motor** mech, drivingshaft

arbolado a tree-covered, wooded. m, copse, woodland

arboladura f, naut masts and spars

arbolar vt to hoist (flags); naut fit with masts; place upright; vr rear, prance (horses)

arboleda f, copse, grove, spinney

arbusto m, shrub, woody plant

arca f, chest; money-box, coffer; ark; pl (treasury) vaults. **a. de agua,** water-tower. **a. de la alianza.** or **a. del testamento,** Ark of the Covenant (Bible). **a. de Noé,** Noah's Ark; lumber box

arcada f, arcade; series of arches; pl sickness, nausea

arcaico a archaic

arcaísmo m, archaism

arcano a secret. m, mystery, arcanum

arce m, bot maple tree

archifeliz a extremely happy, in bliss

archimillonario (-ia) a and n multimillionaire

archipiélago m, archipelago

Archipiélago de Colón m, Galapagos Islands

archivar vt to place in an archive; file (papers)

archivero m, archivist, keeper of the archives; librarian; registrar; (Mexico) file cabinet, filing cabinet

archivista mf archivist; file clerk, filing clerk

archivo m, archives

arcilla f, clay

arcilloso a clayey, like or full of clay

arco m, geom arc; mil bow; bow (of a stringed instrument); hoop (of casks, etc.); arch arch; Lat. Am. goal (in sports). **a. del cielo** or **a. de San Martín** or **a. iris,** rainbow. **a. voltaico,** electric arc. mus **para a.,** for strings

arder vi to burn; shine, gleam; fig burn (with passion, etc.); vt to set alight, burn

ardid a crafty. m, trick, stratagem

ardiente a burning; ardent, passionate; vehement; enthusiastic; flame-colored; fiery-red

ardilla f, squirrel; Lat. Am. wheeler-dealer

ardite m, ancient Spanish coin of little value; fig farthing, fig, straw. **no valer un a.,** to be not worth a straw

ardor m, great heat; zeal, earnestness; passion, ardor; courage

ardoroso a ardorous

arduo a arduous

área f, area; small plot of ground; common threshing floor; arc (surface measure)

arena f, sand; arena; grit, gravel. **a. movediza,** quicksand

arenal m, quicksand; sand pit; sandy place

arenga f, harangue, discourse Argentina argument, fight, quarrel

arenisca f, sandstone

arenisco a sandy

arenque m, herring

arete m, earring

argamasa f, mortar

argayo m, landslide; (Asturias) **a. de nieve,** avalanche

Árgel Algiers

Argelia Algeria

argelino (-na) a and n Algerian

argentado a silvered; silvery

argentífero a silver-yielding

argentino (-na) a silvery. a and n Argentinian. m, Argentinian gold coin

argento m, silver. **a. vivo,** mercury

argolla f, thick metal ring (for hitching, etc.); croquet (game); stocks, pillory; hoop, iron arch; Lat. Am. wedding ring

argucia f, sophism, quibble; subtlety

argüir vt irr to deduce, imply; prove; reveal, manifest; accuse; vi argue, debate; dispute, oppose. See **huir**

argumentador (-ra) a argumentative. n arguer

argumentar vi to argue; dispute; oppose

argumento m, contention, case; theme (of a book, etc.); argument, discussion

aridez f, aridity, dryness; drought; sterility, barrenness; dullness, lack of interest

árido a dry, arid; sterile, barren; uninteresting, dull

arisco a unsociable, surly; wild, shy (animals)

aristocracia f, aristocracy

aristócrata mf aristocrat

aristocrático a aristocratic

aritmética f, arithmetic

aritmético (-ca) a arithmetical. n arithmetician

arlequín m, harlequin; inf fool, buffoon; Neapolitan ice-cream

arma f, weapon; mil arm, branch; bull's horn; pl troops, army; means, way; arms, coat of arms. **a. arrojadiza,** missile. **a. blanca,** steel weapon. **a. de fuego,** firearm. ¡**Armas al hombro!** Shoulder Arms! **armas portátiles,** small arms. inf **de armas tomar,** belligerent; resolute. **pasar por las armas,** mil to shoot. **presentar las armas,** mil to present arms. **ser a. de dos filos,** fig to cut both ways

armada f, navy, armada; fleet, squadron; Argentina lasso

armadía f, raft, pontoon

armador (-ra) n supplier, outfitter. m,

shipowner; pirate; privateer; jacket; assembler, fitter

armadura f, armature, armor; frame, framework; skeleton (of a building); skeleton (of vertebrates); *phys* armature; plate armor (of persons)

armamento m, *mil* armament; arms, military equipment

armar vt to arm; *mech* mount; man (guns); put together, assemble; roll (a cigaret); reinforce (concrete); *inf* arrange, prepare; *inf* occasion (quarrels); *inf* outfit; *naut* equip; commission (a ship); vr prepare oneself, arm oneself. **a. caballero,** to knight. **a. los remos,** to ship the oars. *inf* **armarla,** to cause a row or quarrel

armario m, cupboard; wardrobe. **a. de luna,** wardrobe with a mirror

armatoste m, unwieldy piece of furniture; *fig inf* dead weight, clumsy person; snare

armazón f, frame, framework; ship's hulk. m, *anat* skeleton

armenio (-ia) a and n Armenian. m, Armenian language

armería f, armory; heraldry; gunsmith's craft or shop

armisticio m, armistice

armonía f, harmony; friendship, concord; *mus* harmony

armónica (de boca) f, mouth-organ

armónico a harmonious. a and m, *mus* harmonic

armonio m, harmonium

armonioso a harmonious

armonización f, *mus* harmonization

armonizar vt to bring into harmony; *mus* harmonize

arnero m, *Lat. Am.* sieve

arnés m, armor; harness; *pl* horse trappings; *inf* equipment, tools

aro m, hoop; rim (of wheel, etc.); napkinring; croquet hoop; *bot* wild arum; child's hoop; *Lat. Am.* earring **a. de empaquetadura,** *mech* gasket

aroma m, aroma, fragrance; balsam; sweet-smelling herb

aromático a aromatic

arpa f, harp. **a. eolia,** Eolian harp

arpar vt to scratch, claw; tear, rend

arpía f, harpy

arpicordio m, harpsichord

arpista mf harpist, harp player

arquear vt to arch; bend; beat (wool); gauge (ship's capacity); vt retch

arqueo m, arching; bending, curving; *naut* tonnage; gauging (of ship's capacity); *com* examination of deposits and contents of safe

arqueología f, archeology

arqueológico a archeological

arqueólogo m, archeologist

arquero m, *com* cashier, treasurer; *mil* archer

arquitecto m, architect. **a. de jardines,** landscape gardener

arquitectura f, architecture

arrabal m, suburb, district; *pl* outskirts

arracimarse vr to cluster; group

arracimadamente adv deeply, firmly

arraigado a deep-rooted; firm; convinced

arraigar vi to take root; vi and vr *fig* become established, take hold; vr settle; take up residence

arraigo m, rooting; settlement, establishment; landed property

arrancadero m, *sport* starting-point

arrancar vt to uproot; pull out; wrench; tear off; extirpate; obtain by threats; clear one's throat; vt and vi *naut* put on speed; vi start (a race); *inf* leave, quit; derive, originate **¡Arranca!** And they're off! (races)

arrancarse vr, *Lat. Am.* to kick the bucket, pop off

arranque m, uprooting; extirpation; wrenching, pulling, seizing; stimulus (of passion); sudden impulse; *mech* start; *mech* starter. **a. automático,** self-starter

arras f *pl*, dowry; coins given by bridegroom to his bride; earnest money, token

arrasamiento m, demolition, destruction; leveling

arrasar vt to demolish, destroy; level; fill to the brim; vi and vr clear up (sky). **ojos arrasados de lágrimas,** eyes brimming with tears

arrastrado a *inf* poverty-stricken, wretched; *inf* knavish; unhappy, unfortunate

arrastrar vt to drag; trail; convince; haul; vi trail along or touch the ground; trump (at cards); vr crawl, creep; shuffle along; humble oneself

¡arre! *interj* Gee up! Get along!

arrebañar vt to pick clean, clear; eat or drink up

arrebatado a precipitate, headlong; rash; flushed, red

arrebatador a overwhelming; violent; bewitching, captivating; delightful

arrebatamiento m, abduction; seizure; fury; ecstasy

arrebatar vt to abduct, carry off; seize, grab; attract, charm; grip (the attention); vr be overcome with rage

arrebato m, fit (gen. of anger); ecstasy, rapture

arrebozar vt to muffle; envelop

arrebujarse vr to huddle; wrap oneself up

arreciar vi to increase in intensity; vr grow strong

arrecife m, reef (in the sea); stone-paved road

arregazar(se) vt and vr to tuck up one's skirts

arreglado a regular; regulated; ordered; methodical

arreglar vt to regulate; arrange; adjust, put right; tidy; make up (the face); vr (with prep a) conform to; (with con) reach an agreement with. **Me voy a a.,** I am going to make myself presentable. inf **arreglárselas,** to shift for oneself

arreglo m, arrangement; rule; regulation; method, order; agreement; adjustment; compromise

arrellanarse vr to settle comfortably in one's chair; be happy in one's work

arremangar vt to roll up (sleeves, trousers, etc.); vr inf make a decision

arremetedor (-ra) n attacker, assailant

arremeter vt to attack, assail; vi launch oneself (at); fig spoil the view, shock the eye

arremetida f, attack, assault

arremolinarse vr to crowd, cluster, group

arrendador (-ra) n landlord; renter; hirer; tenant

arrendamiento m, letting, renting; hiring; rental; agreement, lease

arrendar vt irr to let, lease; hire; rent (as a tenant); train (horses); tie up (horses); restrain; mimic, imitate. See **recomendar**

arrendatario (-ia) a rent, lease. n tenant; lessee; hirer. **a. de contribuciones,** tax farmer

arreo m, ornament; apparel; pl horse trappings; appurtenances, equipment

¡Arrepa! But look!, Hold on!, Hold your horses!, Not so fast!

arrepentimiento m, repentance

arrepentirse vr irr to repent. See **sentir**

arrestado a courageous, audacious, bold

arrestar vt to arrest, detain; vr be bold, dare

arresto m, arrest; detention; imprisonment; audacity, boldness

arriada f, lowering (of a boat); taking in (of sail)

arriar vt naut to strike (colors); take in (sail); pay out (ropes, etc.); lower (boats); flood, inundate

arriate m, garden border; avenue, walk; trellis (for plants)

arriba adv up, above; overhead; upstairs; earlier, before; upwards (with prices). interj **iA.!** Up with!; Long live! **de a. abajo,** from head to foot, from one end to the other; completely, wholly

arribada f, naut arrival. **de a.,** emergency (port)

arribar vi naut to arrive; put into an emergency port; reach, arrive at; inf convalesce; attain; naut drift

arribista mf social climber

arriesgado a dangerous, risky; rash, daring

arriesgar vt to risk; vr run into danger; dare, risk

arrimado m, Mexico parasite

arrimar vt to bring or draw near; abandon (professions, etc.); lay aside, discard; inf administer (blows); naut stow (cargo); vr (with prep a) lean against, rest on; join, go with; seek the protection of. **Cada cual se arrima a su cada cual,** Birds of a feather flock together

arrimo m, bringing or placing near; leaning or resting against; abandonment, giving up; protection; staff, support

arrinconado a remote, secluded; forgotten, neglected

arrinconar vt to discard, lay aside; corner, besiege; set aside, dismiss; forsake; vr go into retirement, withdraw

arriscado a craggy, rugged; bold, resolute; sprightly, handsome

arriscarse vr Lat. Am. to dress to kill, dress to the nines

arrobamiento m, ecstasy, rapture; trance

arrobar vt to charm, entrance; vr be enraptured; be in ecstasy

arrodillar vt to cause to kneel down; vi and vr kneel down

arrogancia f, arrogance; courage; majesty, pride

arrogante a arrogant, haughty; courageous; proud, majestic

arrogar vt to adopt (as a son); vr usurp, appropriate

arrojadizo a easily cast or hurled; projectile

arrojado a bold, determined; rash

arrojar vt to throw, hurl, cast; shed (light, etc.; e.g. **La cuenta arroja un total de cien dólares,** The bill shows a total of a hundred dollars); com show (a balance, etc.); put out (sprouts); dismiss, send away; vr cast oneself; (with prep a) hurl oneself against or upon; undertake, venture upon. **a. de sí (a),** to get rid of, dismiss

arrojo m, daring, intrepidity; boldness

arrollar vt to roll; make into a roll, roll up; defeat (the enemy); silence, confound; rock to sleep; bear along, carry off

arrostrar vt to confront, defy, face up to; vr fight hand to hand. **a. las consecuencias,** fig to face the music

arroyo m, stream, brook; street gutter; road, street; fig flood, plenty

arroz m, rice

arruga f, wrinkle; fold, pleat; crease

arrugamiento m, wrinkling; fold, pleating; crumpling, creasing; corrugation

arrugar vt to wrinkle; pleat; corrugate; crumple, crease. **a. el ceño,** to knit one's brow, scowl

arruinamiento m, ruin, decay, decline

arruinar vt to ruin; destroy, damage severely

arrullar vt to bill and coo (doves); lull to sleep; inf whisper sweet words to, make love to

arrumaco m, inf embrace, caress (gen. pl); ornament in bad taste

arrumaje m, naut stowage; clouds on the horizon

arsenal m, dockyard; arsenal; fig store (of information, etc.)

arsénico m, arsenic

arte mf, art; skill; ability, talent; guile, craftiness. **las bellas artes,** fine arts. inf **no tener a. ni parte en,** to have nothing to do with, have no part in

artefacto m, machine, mechanism, apparatus; device, appliance. **a. atómico,** atomic bomb

arteria f, med artery; main line (of communication)

artería f, craftiness, guile

arterial a arterial

artesano (-na) n artisan; mechanic

ártico a Arctic

articulación f, joint, articulation; jointing; enunciation, pronunciation

articular vt to joint, articulate; enunciate, pronounce clearly

artículo m, finger knuckle; heading; article; anat joint; gram article; pl goods, things. **a. de fondo,** leading article (in a newspaper). **a. de primera necesidad,** prime necessity, essential

artífice mf craftsman, artificer; author, creator; forger

artificial a artificial

artificio m, skill, art; appliance, contraption, mechanism; trick, cunning device; guile, craftiness

artificioso a skilful; artificial; crafty, cunning

artillería f, artillery. **a. de costa,** coastal guns. **a. ligera, a. montada, a. rodada** or **a. volante,** field artillery

artillero m, gunner

artimaña f, trick, ruse, stratagem

artista mf artist; performer

artístico a artistic

artrítico a med arthritic

artritis f, med arthritis

arzobispo m, archbishop

as m, Roman copper coin; ace (aer cards, etc.)

asa f, handle; pretext, excuse

asadero m, Mexico cottage cheese

asado m, cul roast

asador m, cul roasting-spit; roaster

asadura f, cul chitterlings; offal

asaltador (-ra) a attacking. n assailant, attacker

asaltar vt to storm, besiege; assault, attack; occur to (ideas); come on suddenly (illness)

asalto m, storming, besieging; assault, attack; bout (in fencing, boxing, wrestling); round (in a fight)

asamblea f, congregation, assembly; meeting; legislative assembly; mil assembly (bugle call)

asambleísta mf member of an assembly

asar vt cul to roast; grill; vr be burning-hot; fig burn (with enthusiasm)

asaz adv sufficiently, enough; very; in abundance. a sufficient; many

asbesto m, asbestos

ascalonia f, bot shallot

ascendencia f, lineage, ancestry, origin

ascender vi irr to ascend, climb; be promoted; (with prep a) amount to (bills, etc.); vt promote. See **entender**

ascendiente mf ancestor, forbear. m, influence, ascendancy

ascensión f, ascension; promotion; ast exaltation

ascenso m, ascent; promotion, preferment

ascensor m, lift, elevator

ascensorista mf elevator operator

asceta mf ascetic

ascético a ascetic

asco m, nausea; repugnance, loathing; revolting thing. inf **Me da a.,** It sickens me

ascua f, live coal, ember. **estar como una a. de oro,** to be as bright as a new pin. **estar en ascuas,** fig to be on pins

aseado a clean, tidy

asear vt to tidy, make neat; clean up; decorate, adorn

asechanza f, ambush; trick, snare, stratagem

asechar vt to ambush, waylay; fig lay snares for

asediar vt to besiege; pester, importune

asedio m, siege; importunity

asegurado (-da) a insured. n insured person

asegurador (-ra) a insuring. n insurer

asegurar vt to fasten, make secure; pinion, grip; reassure, soothe; assert, state; com insure; guarantee; ensure, secure; vr com insure oneself; (with de) make sure of

asemejar vt to imitate, copy; make similar to; vr (with prep a) be like, be similar to

asenso m, assent. **dar a.,** to believe, give credence (to)

asentaderas f pl, inf buttocks, seat

asentado a prudent, circumspect; permanent, stable

asentamiento m, seating; settlement, residence; prudence, judgment

asentar vt irr to seat; place; fasten, fix; found; plant (flags); pitch (a tent); establish, make firm; smooth; hone (razors); estimate, budget, arrange, set forth; note down; affirm, believe; com enter (in an account); *vi* fit (clothes); *vr* seat oneself; alight (birds); settle (liquids); *arch* settle, subside; to be located (e.g. **El edificio se asienta en una esquina,** The building is located on a corner). **a. la mano en,** to strike hard. See **acertar**

asentimiento *m,* assent; consent, approval

asentir *vi irr* to assent, agree; (*with en*) consent to. See **sentir**

aseñorado *a* refined, gentlemanly; ladylike; presumptuous

aseo *m,* cleanliness, neatness

asequible *a* attainable; obtainable

aserción *f,* assertion

aserrar *vt irr* to saw. See **acertar**

aserrín *m,* sawdust

aserruchar *vt, Lat. Am.* to saw

aserto *m,* assertion

asesinar *vt* to assassinate, murder

asesinato *m,* assassination, murder

asesino *mf* assassin, murderer; murderess

asesor (-ra) *n* assessor

asesorar *vt* to give advice; *vr* take legal advice; seek advice

asestar *vt* to aim (firearms); fire; deal (a blow)

aseveración *f,* assertion, statement

aseveradamente *adv* affirmatively

aseverar *vt* to affirm, assert

asfaltado *m,* asphalting; asphalt pavement

asfaltar *vt* to asphalt

asfalto *m,* asphalt

asfixia *f, med* asphyxia

asfixiante *a* asphyxiating

asfixiar *vt* to asphyxiate

así *adv* thus, so, in this way; like this (e.g. **en días a.,** on days like this); even if; so that, therefore. **a. a.,** middling, so-so. **a. como a.,** as well as; as soon as. **a. las cosas,** that being the case, **a. que,** as soon as, immediately; consequently, thus

asiático (-ca) *a* and *n* Asiatic

asidero *m,* hold, grasp; handle, haft; pretext, excuse

asiduo *a* assiduous

asiento *m,* seat; place; position; site; base (of a vase, etc.); lees, sediment; indigestion; *arch* subsidence, settling; treaty, pact; contract; note, reminder; *com* entry; permanence, stability; prudence; bit (of a bridle); *pl* buttocks, seat. **estar de a.,** to be established (in a place)

asignación *f,* assignation; appropriation (of money); salary; portion, share

asignar *vt* to assign; apportion; destine, intend; appoint

asignatario, -a *mf Lat. Am.* heir, heiress, legatee

asignatura *f,* subject (of study in schools, etc.)

asilar *vt* to give shelter to, receive; put into an institution

asilo *m,* shelter, refuge; sanctuary, asylum; *fig* protection, defence; home, institution

asimetría *f,* asymmetry

asimétrico *a* asymmetrical

asimiento *m,* hold, grasp; attachment, affection

asimilar *vt* to compare, liken; (*bot zool gram*) assimilate; *vi* resemble, be like; *fig* assimilate, digest (ideas)

asimismo *adv* similarly, likewise

asir *vt irr* to grasp, take hold of; seize; *vi* take root (plants); *vr* (*with de*) lay hold of; take advantage of; make an excuse to. *Pres. Ind.* **asgo, ases,** etc. *Pres. Subjunc.* **asga,** etc.

asirio (-ia) *a* and *n* Assyrian. *m,* Assyrian language

asistencia *f,* presence, attendance; minimal attendance required (e.g. **Los alumnos tienen que completar una a.,** Pupils must attend a certain number of classes) assistance, help; service, attendance; medical treatment; remuneration; *pl* allowance. **a. pública,** Public Assistance. **a. social,** social work

asistenta *f,* daily maid; waiting-maid

asistente *m,* assistant; *mil* orderly

asistir *vt* to accompany; assist, help; attend, treat; (*with de*) act as; *vi* (*with prep a*) be present at, attend; follow suit (in cards)

asma *f,* asthma

asmático (-ca) *a* asthmatic. *n* asthma sufferer

asno *m,* ass

asociación *f,* association; company, partnership; society, fellowship

asociado (-da) *n* associate; member; partner

asociar *vt* to associate; *vr* associate oneself; join together; form a partnership

asolar *vt irr* to destroy, devastate, lay flat; *vr* wither; settle (liquids). See **contar**

asolear *vt* to expose to the sun; *vr* sun oneself; become sunburnt

asomada *f,* brief appearance; vantage point

asomar *vt* to show, allow to appear, put forth; *vi* begin to show; *vr* show oneself, appear; *inf* be flushed (with wine); (*with prep a, por*) look out of. **asomarse a la ventana,** to show oneself at, or look out of, the window

asombrar *vt* to shade, shadow; darken (a color); terrify; amaze

asombro *m,* fright, terror; amazement; wonder, marvel

asombroso *a* amazing; marvellous, wonderful

asorocharse *vr, Peru* to come down with altitude sickness, get altitude sickness

aspa f, cross; sail of a windmill

aspaviento m, exaggerated display of emotion; gesture (of horror, etc.); **hacer aspavientos,** to make a fuss

aspecto m, look, appearance; aspect, outlook

aspereza f, roughness, harshness; ruggedness, rockiness; severity, asperity

áspero a rough, harsh; uneven, rocky; jarring, grating; hard, severe

aspersión f, ecc aspersion; sprinkling

aspiración f, breath; breathing; aspiration, desire; mus pause

aspirador (de polvo) m, vacuum cleaner

aspirante m, aspirant, novice; office-seeker; applicant

aspirar vt to breathe in, inhale; gram aspirate; (with prep a) aspire to, desire

aspirina f, aspirin

asquear vi and vt to hate, loathe

asquerosidad f, filthiness, loathsomeness; vileness, hatefulness

asqueroso a nauseating; loathsome, revolting; vile, hateful

asta f, lance, spear, pike; horn (of bull); antler; flagstaff; shaft. **a media a.,** at half-mast

asterisco m, asterisk

astigmático a astigmatic

astil m, handle, pole, shaft; bar of a balance; beam feather

astilla f, splinter

astillero m, shipyard; rack for lances and pikes

astilloso a splintery, fragile

astringente a astringent

astringir vt to tighten up; compress; constrain

astro m, heavenly body

astrología f, astrology

astrólogo (-ga) n astrologist

astronauta m, astronaut

astronomía f, astronomy

astronómico a astronomical

astrónomo m, astronomer

astucia f, astuteness, guile, craftiness

astuto a guileful, crafty, astute

asueto m, day's holiday

asumir vt to assume; adopt, appropriate

asunción f, assumption

asunto m, matter, theme, subject; business, affair

asustadizo a timid, nervous, easily frightened

asustar vt to frighten; **que asusta,** terribly (e.g. **Es de una ñoñería que asusta,** It's a terribly timid thing to do) vr be frightened

atacador (-ra) a attacking. n aggressor, attacker

atacar vt to attack; fasten, button; fit (clothes); ram (guns); fig press hard, corner (persons). **a. a los nervios,** to jar on the nerves

ataché m. Central America (paper) clip

atadero m, rope, tie, cord; hook, ring, etc. (for hitching); hindrance, impediment; hitching or fastening point

atadura f, tying, stringing, fastening, tie; knot; connection

atajar vi to take a short cut; vt intercept, cut off; screen off, divide; impede, stop; interrupt (people); **atajarle la palabra a uno,** to cut somebody off, interrupt vr be overcome (by fear, shame, etc.)

atajo m, short cut, quick way; cutting, abbreviation; division. inf **echar por el a.,** to go to the root of (a matter)

atalaya f, look out, watch tower; observation point. m, lookout

atalón m, atoll, coral island

atañadero: en lo atañadero a with regard to, with respect to

atañer vi impers to concern, affect; belong, pertain

ataque m, (mil med) attack; quarrel, fight

atar vt to tie; fasten; lace; stop, paralyse; vr get in a fix; confine oneself. **a. cabos,** to put two and two together

atardecer vi irr impers to grow dusk. See **conocer**

atardecer m, dusk, evening

atarear vt to set to work, assign work to; vr work hard

atarugar vt to wedge; stop up; plug; block; inf silence, shut up; stuff, cram; vr fig inf lose one's head

atasajar vt to cut up, jerk (beef, etc.)

atascadero m, deep rut, boggy place; impediment, obstacle

atascar vt to plug; block up; stop (a leak); hinder, obstruct; vr stick in the mud; be held up or delayed; inf get stuck in a speech

atasco m, obstruction, block

ataúd m, coffin

ataviar vt to deck, apparel, adorn

atavío m, get-up, dress, apparel; pl ornaments

ate m, Mexico kind of Turkish delight

ateísmo m, atheism

atejonarse vr Mexico to hide

atelaje m, team, yoke (of horses); trappings, harness; inf trousseau

atemperar vt to moderate, mitigate; adapt, adjust; temper, cool. **atemperarse a la realidad,** to adjust to reality

Atenas Athens

atenazar vt to grip, grasp; torture

atención f, attention; solicitude, kindness; courtesy, civility; pl business affairs. interj ¡A.¡ Take care! Look out!; mil Attention! en a., (a), taking into consideration. **estar en a.,** (patient) to be under treatment

atender vt irr to await, expect; take care

of, look after; *vi* (*with prep* a) attend to, listen to; *vi* remember. See **entender**

atenerse *vr irr* (*with prep* a) to abide by; resort to, rely on. See **tener**

atentado *a* prudent, sensible; secret, silent. *m*, infringement, violation; attempt (on a person's life); crime

atentar *vt irr* to do illegally; attempt a crime; *vr* proceed cautiously; restrain oneself. See **acertar**

atento *a* attentive; courteous, civil. *adv* taking into consideration. **su atenta** (**atta**), *com* your favor

atenuación *f*, attenuation, diminution

atenuante *a* attenuating; extenuating (of circumstances)

atenuar *vt* to attenuate, diminish; extenuate

ateo (**-ea**) *a* atheistic. *n* atheist

aterirse *vr defective* to grow stiff with cold

aterramiento *m*, horror, terror; terrorization; *naut* landing; ruin, demolition

aterrar *vt irr* to demolish; discourage; cover with earth; *vi* land; *vr naut* draw near to land. See **acertar**

aterrizaje *m*, *aer* landing. **a. forzoso**, forced landing. **campo de a.**, landing field

aterrizar *vi aer* to land, touch down

aterrorizar *vt* to terrify; terrorize

atesar *vt Lat. Am.* to tighten (up)

atesorar *vt* to hoard, treasure up

atestación *f*, attestation; affidavit

atestar *vt irr* to stuff, cram; insert; *inf* stuff with food; crowd, fill with people. See **acertar**

atestar *vt* to attest, testify

atestiguación *f*, deposition, testimony

atestiguar *vt* to testify, attest

atetar *vt* to suckle; *vi* suck

atezado *a* bronzed, sunburnt; black

atiesar *vt* to stiffen

atildar *vt* to place a tilde over; blame, criticize; decorate, ornament

atinado *a* pertinent, relevant

atinar *vi* to find by touch; discover by chance; guess; hit the mark

atinente a . . . concerning . . .

atingencia *f*, *Lat. Am.* connection, relationship

atingir *vt*, *Lat. Am.* to concern, relate to

atisbar *vt* to spy upon, watch

atisbo *m*, prying, watching; suspicion, hint

atisbón *a* penetrating (mind, vision)

atizador *m*, poker (for the fire)

atizar *vt* to poke (the fire); dowse, snuff; trim (lamps); excite, rouse; *inf* slap, wallop

atlántico *a* Atlantic. *m*, Atlantic Ocean

atleta *m*, athlete

atlético *a* athletic

atletismo *m*, athletics

atmósfera *f*, atmosphere

atmosférico *a* atmospheric

atolladero *m*, rut; mud; bog

atolón *m*, atoll, coral island

atolondrado *a* scatter-brained, flighty

atolondramiento *m*, rashness, recklessness; bewilderment

atolondrar *vt* to bewilder, confuse

atómico *a* atomic

átomo *m*, atom; speck, particle

atónito *a* amazed, astounded

atontar *vt* to confuse, daze; make stupid; stun

atormentador (**-ra**) *a* torturing. *n* tormentor; torturer

atormentar *vt* to torment; torture; grieve, harass

atorrante *a* and *mf* (Argentina) good-for-nothing

atracadero *m*, jetty, landingstage

atracar *vt inf* to stuff with food; *naut* tie up, moor; hold up, rob; *vi naut* moor, stop; *vr inf* guzzle, gorge

atracción *f*, attraction

atraco (**a**) *m*, hold up (of), ambush (of)

atractivo *a* attractive. *m*, attraction, charm

atraer *vt irr* to attract; charm, enchant. See **traer**

atragantarse *vr* to choke; *inf* be at a loss, dry up (in conversation)

atrancar *vt* to bar the door; obstruct; block; hinder; *vi inf* stride; skip (in reading)

atrapar *vt inf* grab, seize, catch; net, obtain; deceive

atrás *adv* behind, back; past; previously. ¡**A!** Back! **años a.**, years ago

atrasado *a* slow (of clocks); backward; old-fashioned; hard-up, poor. **a. mental**, retarded person

atrasar *vt* to delay, retard; fix a later date than the true one; put back (clocks). *vi* be slow (clocks); *vr* be late; be left behind

atraso *m*, delay; backwardness, dullness; slowness (clocks); lateness; *pl* arrears. **El reloj lleva cinco minutos de a.**, The watch is five minutes slow

atravesado *a* slightly squint-eyed; mongrel, crossbreed; half-caste; ill-intentioned

atravesar *vt irr* to lay across, put athwart; cross, traverse; pierce; obstruct; *naut* lie to; *vr* be among, mingle (with); interrupt; interfere, take part; quarrel; occur, arise. See **confesar**

atrayente *a* attractive

atreverse *vr* to dare, risk, venture; be overbold or insolent

atrevido *a* bold, audacious; hazardous, dangerous; brazen, impudent

atribuible *a* attributable

atribución *f*, attribution; perquisite, attribute

atribuir *vt irr* to impute, attribute; assign, turn over to; *vr* take upon oneself, assume. See **huir**

atributo *m*, attribute, quality

atril *m*, lectern, reading desk; music stand

atrincherar *vt* to protect with entrenchments; *vr* entrench oneself

atrio *m*, atrium; hall, vestibule; *arch* parvis

atrocidad *f*, atrocity, cruelty; *inf* terrific amount; enormity, crime

atrofia *f*, atrophy

atrojarse *vr Mexico* to be stumped, be stuck (for an answer)

atronar *vt irr* to deafen, stun with noise; confuse, daze. See **tronar**

atropellado *a* rash, foolhardy

atropellar *vt* to trample upon; thrust out of the way; knock down; disregard, violate (feelings); insult, abuse; transgress; do hastily; *vr* act rashly

atropello *m*, trampling; road accident; knocking over; upsetting; violation; outrage

atroz *a* atrocious, savage; monstrous, outrageous; *inf* terrific, enormous

atún *m*, tunny fish

aturdido *a* reckless, scatterbrained, silly; thoughtless; stunned

aturdimiento *m*, daze; confusion, bewilderment

aturdir *vt* to daze; confuse, bewilder; amaze; stun

atusar *vt* to trim (hair, beard); *agr* prune; smooth down (hair); *vr* dress over-carefully

audacia *f*, audacity

audaz *a* audacious, daring

audibilidad *f*, audibility

audición *f*, audition

audiencia *f*, audience, hearing; *law* audience; audience chamber

audífono *m*, hearing aid

audioteca *f*, audio library

auditorio *a* auditory. *m*, audience

auge *m*, *fig* zenith, height; *ast* apogee

aula *f*, lecture or class room; *poet* palace

aullar *vi* to howl; bay

aullido *m*, howl; baying

aumentar(se) *vt vi vr* to increase, augment

aumentativo *a* *gram* augmentative

aumento *m*, increase; progress; enlargement; *Mexico* postscript **ir en a.**, to increase; advance, progress; prosper

aun *adv* even. **A. los que viven lejos han de oíros,** Even those who live far must hear you. **a. así** *or* **a. siendo así,** even so. **a. ayer,** only yesterday. **a. cuando,** even if. **más a.,** even more. **ni a. si,** not even if.

aún *adv* still, yet. **A. no te creen** *or* **No te creen a.,** They still don't believe you **¿A. se lo darás?** *or* **¿Se lo darás a.?** Will you still give it to her?

aunque *conjunc* although, even if, even though. It takes the Indicative referring to statement of fact and Subjunctive referring to a hypothesis, e.g. **A. vino, no lo hizo,** Although he came, he did not do it. **A. él cantase yo no iría allí,** Even though he sang (were to sing), I should not go there

auricular *a* auricular. *m*, little finger; receiver, ear-piece (of a telephone); earphone (radio)

aurora *f*, dawn; genesis, beginnings. **a. boreal,** aurora borealis, Northern Lights

auscultar *vt med* to auscultate

ausencia *f*, absence. **en ausencia de,** in the absence of

ausentar *vt* to send away; *vr* absent oneself

ausente *a* absent. *mf* absent person

auspicio *m*, augury, prediction; favor, patronage; *pl* auspices

austeridad *f*, austerity; mortification of the flesh

austero *a* austere, ascetic; severe, harsh; honest, upright

australiano (-na) *a* and *n* Australian

austríaco (-ca) *a* and *n* Austrian

autenticación *f*, authentication

autenticar *vt* to authenticate, attest; prove genuine

autenticidad *f*, authenticity

auténtico *a* authentic

autero, -a *mf, Lat. Am.* car thief

auto *m*, *law* sentence, decision; *theat* one-act allegory (gen. religious); *pl* proceedings. **a. de fe,** auto-da-fé. **a. de reconocimiento,** search-warrant. **a. sacramental,** one-act religious drama on theme of mystery of the Eucharist. **hacer a. de fe de,** to burn

autobiografía *f*, autobiography

autobús *m*, motor bus, bus

autocitarse *vr* to quote from one's own works

autoclave *m*, pressure cooker

autocracia *f*, autocracy

autócrata *mf* autocrat

autocrático *a* autocratic

autodescubrimiento *m*, self-discovery

autodidacto *a* autodidactic; self-educated, self-taught

autógeno *a* autogenous, self-generating

autografía f, autography

autográfico a autographic, in lithographic reproduction

autógrafo a autographical. m, autograph

autoinducción f, self-induction

autómata m, automaton

automático a automatic. m, sew press stud

automatismo m, automatism

automejoramiento m, self-improvement

automóvil m, automobile, motor car. a automatic

automovilismo m, motoring

automovilista mf motorist

autonombrarse vr to call oneself, go by the name of

autonomía f, autonomy

autónomo a autonomous

autopista f, motor road

autopsia f, med autopsy, post-mortem

autor (-ra) n agent, originator; author; inventor; law perpetrator

autoridad f, authority; pomp, show

autoritario a authoritarian; authoritative

autorización f, authorization

autorizado a approved, authorized, responsible

autorizar vt to authorize; law attest, testify; cite, prove by reference; approve; exalt

autorretrato m, self-portrait

autostopista mf hitchhiker (Spain)

autosugestión f, autosuggestion

auxiliador (-ra) a assistant; helpful. n helper, assistant

auxiliar vt to help, aid; attend (the dying). m, univ lecturer. a assisting

auxilio m, help, aid, assistance

aval m, com endorsement; voucher

avalar vt to enhance. **avalado por la tradición,** hallowed by tradition

avalentado a boastful, bragging

avalorar vt to value, estimate; put spirit into, encourage

avance m, advance; advance payment; balance sheet; attack

avanzada f, mil advance guard

avanzado a advanced, progressive

avanzar vt to advance; promote; vi advance; attack; grow late (time)

avanzo m, balance sheet; price estimate

avaricia f, greed, avarice

avaricioso, avariento a avaricious, greedy

avaro (-ra) a miserly; greedy. n miser

avasallador a dominating; fig overwhelming; enslaving

avasallar vt to subdue, dominate; vr become a vassal; surrender, yield

ave f, bird. **a. de paso,** migratory bird; flg bird of passage. **a. de rapiña,** bird of prey. **a. fría,** orn plover. **ave cantora,** songbird

avecinarse vr to be approaching (e.g. **el año que avecina,** the coming year)

avellana f, hazel nut

avellano m, bot hazel

avemaría f, Hail Mary (prayer); Angelus; rosary bead. Inf **en un a.,** in a trice

avena f, oats; poet oaten pipe. **a. loca,** wild oats

avenar vt to drain (land); drain off (liquids)

avenencia f, agreement, arrangement; transaction; conformity, harmony

avenida f, flood, spate; avenue; abundance; way, approach (to a place)

avenido a (with bien or mal) well or ill-suited

avenidor (-ra) n arbitrator, mediator

avenir vt to reconcile; vi happen (used in infinitive and third singular and plural); vr be reconciled; agree; compromise, give way; harmonize (things); (with con) get on with, agree with. See **venir**

aventador m, agr winnower; pitchfork

aventajado a outstanding, talented; advantageous. m, mil private who enjoys extra pay

aventajar vt to improve, better; promote, prefer; excel; vr (with prep a) surpass, excel. **Te aventajo en diez años,** I'm ten years older than you

aventón m, Mexico hitch, lift, ride

aventura f, adventure; chance, luck; risk, danger

aventurar vt to risk, hazard

aventurero (-ra) a adventurous; unscrupulous, intriguing; undisciplined (of troops). n adventurer

avergonzar vt irr to shame; make shy, abash; vr be ashamed; be shy or sheepish. Pres. Ind. **avergüenzo, avergüenzas, avergüenza, avergüenzan.** Pres. Subjunc. **avergüence, avergüences, avergüence, avergüencen**

avería f, aviary; damage (to merchandise); loss, harm; elec fault; breakdown. **a. gruesa,** general average (marine insurance)

averiarse vr to be damaged; deteriorate; break down

averiguable a examinable, investigable; discoverable

averiguación f, inquiry, investigation; discovery

averiguar vt to investigate, inquire into; discover, ascertain. **laverígüelo Vargas!** Beats me!, Search me!

averigüetas mf, Lat. Am. snoopers, nosy parker

averío *m*, flock of birds

aversión *f*, aversion, repugnance

avestruz *m*, ostrich

avezar *vt* to accustom; *vr* grow accustomed (to)

aviación *f*, aviation

aviador *m*, aviator

aviar *vt* to outfit, equip; prepare, make ready; *inf* speed up; caulk (ship). *fig inf* **estar aviado,** to be in a mess

avidez *f*, avidity, greed; longing, desire

ávido *a* avid, greedy

avieso *a* twisted, crooked; ill-natured; sinister; *m Colombia* abortion

avillanado *a* countrified; gross, vulgar; boorish

avío *m*, preparation, provision; picnic lunch; money advanced (to miners or laborers); *pl inf* equipment, tools. **avíos de pesca,** fishing tackle

avión *m*, airplane; *orn* martin or swift. **a. de bombardeo,** bomber. **a. de caza,** fighter plane. **a. de combate nocturno,** night fighter. **a. de hostigamiento,** interceptor. **a. de reacción,** jet airplane. **a. de transporte,** *aer* transport. **a. en picado,** dive-bomber. **a. taxi,** air taxi. **por a.,** by airmail «**Avión**» "Airmail"

avioneta *f*, light airplane, small airplane

avisado *a* shrewd, sensible. **mal a.,** ill-advised, imprudent

avisar *vt* to inform, acquaint; warn; advise

aviso *m*, notice, announcement; warning; advice; care, caution; attention; shrewdness, prudence. **estar sobre a.,** to be on call; be on the alert

avispa *f*, wasp

avispado *a inf* smart, clever, quick; wide-awake

avispar *vt* to goad, prick; *inf* rouse, incite; *vr* be uneasy, fret

avispero *m*, wasp's nest; swarm of wasps; *fig inf* hornet's nest

avistar *vt* to descry, sight, spot; *vr* **avistarse con,** to interview

avituallar *vt* to victual, supply with food

avivar *vt* to enliven; stimulate, encourage; stir (fire); trim (wicks); brighten (colors); inflame; vivify, invigorate; *vi* revive, recover

avizor *m*, watcher, spy. *a* watchful, vigilant

avizorar *vt* to watch, spy upon

axila *f*, *bot* axil; *anat* axilla, armpit

axioma *m*, axiom

axiomático *a* axiomatic

¡ay! *interj* Alas! Woe is me! *m*, complaint, sigh

ayer *adv* yesterday; a short while ago; in the past. *m*, past

ayllu *m*, *Peru* Native American commune

ayo *m*, tutor

ayote *m*, *Mexico, Central America* pumpkin

ayuda *f*, help, assistance; enema; clyster; watch dog. *m*, **a. de cámara,** valet

ayudador (-ra) *a* helping, assisting. *n* helper

ayudante *m*, assistant; teaching assistant; *mil* adjutant. **a. a cátedra,** *univ* assistant lecturer. **a. de plaza,** post adjutant

ayudar *vt* to assist; help, aid; *vr* make an effort; avail oneself of another's help

ayunador (-ra) *a* fasting. *n* faster; abstainer

ayunar *vi* to fast

ayuno *m*, fast. *a* fasting; ignorant, unaware. **en a.** *or* **en ayunas,** before breakfast, fasting; *inf* ignorant, unaware

ayuntamiento *m*, meeting, assembly; municipal government; town hall; sexual union

azabache *m*, *min* jet

azada *f*, *agr* spade; hoe

azafata *f*, queen's waiting-maid *ant*; flight attendant

azafate *m*, flat basket; small tray

azafrán *m*, *bot* saffron; crocus

azahar *m*, flower of orange, lemon or sweet lime tree

azar *m*, chance, hazard; unexpected misfortune; losing card or throw of dice

azararse *vr* to go wrong, fail (negotiations, etc.); grow nervous; become confused; blush

azaroso *a* unlucky, ill-omened; hazardous

ázimo *a* unleavened (bread)

ázoe *m*, nitrogen

azogar *vt* to silver (mirrors, etc.); slake lime; *vr* suffer from mercury poisoning; *inf* grow uneasy, be agitated

azogue *m*, *min* mercury, quick-silver; market-place

azolve *m*, silt

azoramiento *m*, alarm, terror; confusion, stupefaction; incitement

azorar *vt* to alarm, terrify; confuse, stun, dumbfound; excite, stimulate; encourage

azotacalles *mf inf* idler, street loafer

azotar *vt* to whip, beat, flog; acourge, ravage; knock against or strike repeatedly

azote *m*, whip; scourge; lash, blow with a whip; spank, slap; misfortune, disaster. *inf* **azotes y galeras,** monotonous diet

azotea *f*, flat terrace roof

azotera *f*, *Lat. Am.* beating, thrashing

azozador party whip, whip

azteca *a* and *mf* Aztec

azúcar *m*, sugar. **a. blanco** or **a. de flor,** white sugar. **a. de pilón,** loaf sugar. **a. moreno,** brown sugar. **a. quebrado,** brown sugar. **a. y canela,** sorrel gray (of horses)

azucarado *a* sugary; sugared, sugar-coated; *inf* honeyed, flattering

azucarar *vt* to coat with sugar; sweeten; *inf* soften, mitigate; *vr* crystallize; go sugary (jam)

azucarero *a* sugar-producing (e.g. province)

azucarillo *m*, *cul* bar made of white of egg and sugar for sweetening water

azufre *m*, sulphur

azul *a* and *m*, blue. **a. celeste,** sky blue, azure. **a. de mar** or **a. marino,** navy blue. **a. de ultramar,** ultramarine. **a. turquí,** indigo

azulejo *m*, ornamental glazed tile

azurumbado *m*, *Central America* dumb, silly, stupid; boozed up, drunk

azuzar *vt* to set on (dogs); irritate, provoke; incite, urge

B

baba f, saliva; secretion (of snails, etc.); viscous fluid (of plants). *inf* **caérsele (a uno) la b.,** to ooze satisfaction; be dumb-founded

babador, babero m, bib, feeder

babear *vi* to dribble, slaver; *fig inf* slobber over, be sloppy

babel m, babel

babélico a Babelian, Babel-like confused; unintelligible

Babia, estar en to be daydreaming

bable m, Asturian (language)

babor m, *naut* larboard, port

babosa f, slug; young onion

baboso a slavering; *fig inf* "sloppy"; *inf* incompetent, useless; *Lat. Am.* dumb, stupid

babucha f, heelless slipper, babouche

babuino m, *zool* baboon

baca f, luggage carrier (on roof of bus, etc.)

bacalao m, codfish

baceta f, pool (in card games)

bache m, rut (in road); pothole

bacheo m, repairing of streets

bachiller mf high-school graduate m, *inf* babbler. f. **bachillera**, *inf* blue-stocking; garrulous woman

bachillerarse *vr* to graduate as a bachelor

bachillerato m, baccalaureate, bachelor's degree

bacho m, *Peru* fib, tall tale

bacía f, bowl; barber's circular shaving-dish; barber's trade sign

bacilo m, bacillus

bacterial, bacteriano a bacterial

báculo m, staff; walking-stick; *fig* support. **b. episcopal,** bishop's crozier

badajo m, clapper (of a bell); chatterbox, gossip

badana f, cured sheepskin, chamois leather, washleather; sweat band; *inf* **zurrar (a uno) la b.,** to take the hide off; insult

badén m, channel made by rain, furrow; conduit

badulaque m, *inf* good-for-nothing

bagaje m, *mil* baggage; beast of burden, transport animal; luggage

bagatela f, trifle, oddment, bagatelle

bagazo m, oilcake, bagasse

bagual a *WH* untamed, wild; doltish, dull. m, untamed horse, wild horse

bahía f, bay, harbor

bailable a dance (of music). m, *theat* dance number

bailador (-ra) n dancer

bailar *vi* to dance; spin round. **b. al son que le toca,** to adapt oneself to circumstances

bailarín a dancing. m, professional dancer. **b. de cuerda, bailarín de la cuerda floja,** tightrope dancer

bailarina f, ballerina

baile m, dance; ball; ballet. **b. de máscaras, b. de trajes,** fancy-dress ball. **b. de San Vito,** St. Vitus' dance. **b. ruso,** ballet

bailotear *vi* to jig about; dance

baja f, drop, diminution; fall (in price, etc.); *mil* casualty; discharge. *inf* **darse de b.,** to leave an employment

bajada f, descent, fall; slope, incline; hollow, depression. **b. de aguas,** roof gutter

bajamar f, low tide

bajar *vi* to descend; go down; get off; drop; fall, decrease; *vt* lower, take down, bring down; let down; dismount, alight, bend, droop; drop; reduce (price); *fig* lower (voices); humiliate, humble; **b. a tierra,** to step ashore; **b. la cabeza ante,** to submit to (e.g. a judgment) *vr* alight, dismount; humble oneself

bajeza f, base action; meanness; *fig* humble estate, lowliness. **b. de ánimo,** timorousness

bajío m, *naut* shallows, shoal; depression, hollow

bajista mf speculator, bear (Stock Exchange)

bajo a low; short, not tall; downcast; under; subordinate; pale (of colors); humble (origin); base; coarse, vulgar; cheap (price); low (sounds). m, depth; shoal, sand bank; *mus* bass; *pl* petticoats, skirts; horses' hoofs. adv beneath, below. prep under, beneath. **b. juramento,** upon oath. **bajo relieve,** bas relief. **en voz baja,** in a low voice. **planta baja,** ground floor. **por lo b.,** in a whisper; in secret, on the sly

bajón m, *mus* bassoon; bassoon player; *fig inf* downfall

bajonista mf bassoon player

bala f, bullet, ball; bale. **b. fría,** spent bullet. **b. luminosa,** tracer bullet. **b. perdida,** stray bullet. *inf* **como una b.,** like a shot

balacear *vt*, *Central America, Mexico* to shoot (at)

balada f, ballad, song

baladí a worthless, insignificant

baladro m, yell, outcry, shout

baladrón a braggart

baladronada f, bravado, bragging

balagar m, straw rick

balance m, balance; swinging, oscillation; rolling, rocking (of a ship, etc.); doubt, insecurity, *com* balance; com balance sheet **b. de situación** *Lat. Am.* balance sheet

balancear *vi* to swing; oscillate; vacillate,

hesitate; *vt* balance; *vr* balance oneself; rock or swing oneself

balanceo *m*, balancing; rocking; swinging; rolling (of a ship, etc.)

balancín *m*, swing-bar; whipple-tree; balance beam; tight-rope dancer's pole; minting-mill; yoke (for carrying pails); *pl naut* lifts

balandra *f*, *naut* sloop, cutter

balanza *f*, balance; scale; judgment; comparison. **b. de comercio**, balance of trade. **en balanzas**, in doubt or danger, in the balance

balar *vi* to bleat (sheep)

balasto *m*, *rw* ballast

balaustrada *f*, balustrade

balaustre *m*, baluster

balazo *m*, shot; bullet wound

balbuceo *m*, stammering; babbling; lisping; **balbuceos** *fig* beginnings, early stages (e.g. **los b. de la literatura yídica**, the beginnings of Yiddish literature)

balbuciente *a* stammering; babbling; lisping

balbucir *vi irr defective* to stammer; lisp; babble; read hesitantly. See **lucir**

Balcanes, los the Balkans

balcón *m*, balcony

baldaquín *m*, canopy, baldachin

baldar *vt* to cripple; impede, obstruct

balde *m*, bucket

balde (en) *adv* in vain. **de b.**, gratis, free of charge

baldear *vt naut* to wash the decks

baldío *a* untilled; fallow; useless, worthless; vagrant

baldón *m*, insult; dishonor

baldonar *vt* to insult

baldosa *f*, paving stone; tile

Baleares, las Islas the Balearic Islands

baleárico *a* Balearic

baliza *f*, *naut* buoy, beacon

balizamiento *m*, marking with beacons, marking with buoys; traffic signs and signals

ballena *f*, whale; whalebone

balneario *a* pertaining to public baths; bathing; holiday; spa. *m*, watering place, spa

balompié *m*, football (game)

balón *m*, large ball; football; *chem* balloon; bundle; bale. **b. de ensayo**, *fig* feeler

baloncesto *m*, *sport* basket ball

balota *f*, ballot

balotaje *m*, balloting; run-off election

balotar *vi* to ballot

balsa *f*, pond; raft

balsadera *f*, ferry

bálsamo *m*, balm

balsero *m*, ferryman; rafter (person fleeing a country by raft, rowboat, etc.)

báltico *a* Baltic. **el Mar Báltico** the Baltic Sea

baluarte *m*, bulwark; bastion; protection, defence

bambolearse *vr* to sway; swing; totter; be shaky; stagger

bamboleo *m*, rocking; swinging; tottering; staggering; reeling

bambolla *f*, *inf* ostentation, swank

bambú *m*, bamboo

banal *a* banal, commonplace

banana *f*, banana

banasta *f*, big basket

banca *f*, bench; card game; stall; *com* banking

bancada *f*, rowing seat

bancal *m*, oblong garden plot; terrace

bancario *a* banking, bank

bancarrota *f*, bankruptcy. **hacer b.,** to go bankrupt

banco *m*, form, bench; rowing seat; settle; seat; *carp* bench; *com* bank; *naut* bar, shoal; school (of fish). **b. azul**, government benches in Spanish Parliament. **b. de arena**, sand-bank. **b. de descuento**, discount bank. **b. de emisión, banco emisor,** bank of issue. **b. de hielo**, iceberg. **b. de nivel**, benchmark

banda *f*, wide ribbon; sash; ribbon, insignia; strip; border; party, group; gang; flock (of birds); zone, belt; side (of ship); *mus* band; cushion (billiards); *her* bar, bend. **b. elástica**, rubber band. *naut* **dar a la b.,** to lie along

bandada *f*, flock (of birds)

bandeja *f*, tray, salver

bandera *f*, banner, flag; colors, standard. **b. de popa**, ensign. **jurar la b.,** (*mil nav*) to take the oath of allegiance

banderilla *f*, banderilla (bullfighting)

banderillero *m*, man who puts banderillas on bulls

banderín *m*, *dim* small flag; recruiting post

banderizo *a* factious; vehement, excitable

banderola *f*, banderole, pennon; bannerole

bandido (-da) *a* and *n* outlaw, fugitive. *m*, bandit; highwayman; rogue, desperado

bando *m*, proclamation, order; faction, group, party

bandolerismo *m*, brigandage

bandolero *m*, robber, footpad, brigand

bandolín *m*, mandolin

bandurria *f*, *mus* mandolin

banjo *m*, banjo

banquero *m*, banker

banqueta *f*, three-legged stool; seat; footstool; *Mexico* sidewalk

banquete *m*, banquet, feast

banquetear *vt* and *vi* to banquet

banqueteo *m*, banqueting, feasting

bañadera *f*, *Argentina* bathtub

bañado *m*, chamber pot; *WH* marshy land, marsh; **bañados** *pl* marsh

bañador (**-ra**) *a* bathing. *n* bather. *m*, bathing dress; bath, vat

bañar *vt* to bathe; coat, cover; dip; lave, wash; *fig* bathe (of sunlight, etc.). *vr* take a bath; bathe

bañera *f*, bath attendant; bathtub

bañista *mf* bather; one who takes spa waters

baño *m*, bathing; bath; bathroom; bathtub; bagnio, Turkish prison; covering, coat; *pl* mineral baths, spa. **b. de China** *Argentina* shower bath, shower **b. de mar**, sea bath. **b. de María**, double saucepan. **b. de sol**, sunbath. **casa de baños**, public baths. **cuarto de b.**, bathroom

baptisterio *m*, baptistery; *ecc* font

baquelita *f*, bakelite

baqueta *f*, ramrod; *pl* drumsticks; *mil* gauntlet

bar *m*, bar; café

barahúnda *f*, See **baraúnda**

baraja *f*, pack (of cards); game of cards

barajar *vt* to shuffle (cards); jumble, mix; *vi* quarrel

baranda *f*, handrail, banister; cushion (of billiard table)

barandilla *f*, *dim* railing

barata *f*, *Mexico* bargain sale, sale

baratija *f*, (gen. *pl*) trifle, oddment

baratillo *m*, second-hand article, frippery; second-hand shop or stall; bargain counter

barato *a* cheap; easy. *m*, bargain sale. *adv* cheaply

baratura *f*, cheapness

baraúnda *f*, uproar, confusion

barba *f*, chin; beard; whiskers; fin; barb (of a feather); *m*, actor who plays old men. *f pl*, fibers of plants. **b. bien poblada**, a thick beard. **barbas de ballena**, whalebone. *fig inf* **echar a las barbas**, to throw in a person's face. **en la barba, en las barbas**, to ones face (e.g. **Me lo dijeron en las barbas.** They told me so to my face). **hacer la b.**, to shave; *inf* annoy

barbacoa *f*, *WH* barbecue; trellis (for climbing plants)

barbado *a* bearded. *m*, shoot; sucker; transplanted plant

barbárico *a* barbarian; barbaric

barbaridad *f*, barbarity; blunder; atrocity; outrage; *inf* huge amount. **¡Qué b.!** How awful! You don't say so!

barbarie *f*, barbarism; barbarity, cruelty

barbarismo *m*, barbarism; cruelty; barbarians

bárbaro (**-ra**) *a* and *n* barbarian. *a* fierce; headstrong; uncivilized. **como un b.**, like

crazy (e.g. **estudiar como un b.**, to study like crazy)

barbechar *vt* to plow; leave fallow

barbecho *m*, *agr* fallow; first plowing

barbería *f*, barber shop

barbero *m*, barber; *Guatemala, Mexico* flatterer

barbihecho *a* fresh-shaved

barbilampiño *a* smooth-faced, beardless, clean-shaven

barbilindo *a* dandified, dappy; *m*, dandy

barbilla *f*, point of the chin; chin. **acariciar la b.** (**de**), to chuck under the chin

barbiquejo *m*, *naut* bobstay; hat-guard

barbudo *a* a heavily bearded

barbulla *f*, *inf* babble, chatter, murmur of voices

barca *f*, small boat, bark; barge. **b. de pasaje**, ferryboat. **b. plantaminas** minelayer

barcada *f*, boat-load; ferry crossing

barcaza *f*, *naut* lighter; barge. **b. de desembarco**, landingcraft

barco *m*, boat; ship; hollow, rut. **b. barredero**, trawler. **b. siembraminas**, minelayer

barda *f*, horse armor; thatch; *carp* shingle; (Mexico) cement fence, cement wall

bardal *m*, thatched wall; mud wall

bardar *vt* to thatch

bario *m*, barium

barítono *m*, baritone

barlovento *m*, *naut* windward

barnacla *m*, barnacle

barniz *m*, varnish; glaze; smattering, veneer

barnizar *vt* to varnish; glaze

barométrico *a* barometric

barómetro *m*, barometer

barquero *m*, boatman; bargee; *ent* water-boatman

barquillo *m*, wafer, cornet

barra *f*, bar; ingot; railing (in courtroom); sandbank; fault (in cloth); lever, crossbar; (in cricket) bail; *mus* bar. **b. de jabón de afeitar**, shaving-stick. **a barras derechas**, without deceit

barraca *f*, cabin, hut; stall; sideshow; *Latin Am.* barracks **b. de tiro**, shooting gallery

barranca, *f*, **barranco** *m*, furrow, channel, rut; gorge; difficulty, fix

barredor (**-ra**) *n* sweeper

barredura *f*, sweeping; *pl* sweepings; rubbish

barrena *f*, borer, gimlet, drill, auger. *aer* **b. de cola**, tail-spin

barrenar *vt* to drill, bore; blast (in quarries)

barrenero *m*, driller; blaster

barreno *m*, blast hole; bore, drill; vanity; *Lat. Am.* mania, pet peeve

barrer *vt* to sweep; *fig* clear, make a clean sweep

barrera *f*, barrier; barricade; *fig* obstacle. **b. de golpe,** automatic gate (at level crossings, etc.). **b. de minas,** minefield

barriada *f*, district; quarter (of a city); *Peru* slum, shanty town

barricada *f*, barricade

barriga *f*, *inf* belly

barrigón, barrigudo a pot-bellied

barril *m*, barrel; cask; water-butt

barrilero *m*, cooper

barrio *m*, district; quarter; suburb. **barrios bajos,** slums, back streets. **el otro b.,** the other world, Eternity

barrizal *m*, muddy place; claypit

barro *m*, mud; clay; earthenware drinking vessel; *inf* money

barroco a baroque

barrote *m*, thick iron bar; stave, bond

barruntar *vt* to conjecture; suspect

barrunto *m*, conjecture; indication, sign

bártulos *m pl*, household goods; *fig* means, wherewithal

barullo *m*, *inf* confusion, disorder; mob

basar *vt* to base, place on a base; *fig* found, base; *vr* (*with en*) rely upon, base oneself on

basca *f*, (gen. *pl*) nausea; retching; wave of anger

báscula *f*, weighing-machine, platform-scale; weigh-bridge

base *f*, base; (*chem geom mil*) base; basis; *arch* pedestal; *mus* root. **sin b.,** baseless

básico a basic

Basilea Basel, Basle

basílica *f*, palace; church, basilica

basquear *vi* to retch; feel squeamish

bastante a sufficient, enough. *adv* sufficiently; enough; fairly; a good deal; somewhat. **Hace b. calor,** It is quite hot. **Tengo b.,** I have enough. **Tenemos b. tiempo,** We have sufficient time

bastar *vi* to suffice. ¡Basta! Enough! No more! Stop! ¡Basta de . . . ! Enough of . . . ! **Basta decir que . . . ,** Suffice it to say that . . .

bastardía *f*, bastardy, illegitimacy; baseness, meanness

bastardilla *f*, *print* italics

bastardo (-da) a bastard; spurious. *n* bastard

bastear *vt sew* to baste

bastidor *m*, embroidery frame; *art* stretcher (for canvas); *theat* wing; *mech* underframe; chassis, carriage; frame (of a window). *fig* **entre bastidores,** behind the scenes

bastilla *f*, *sew* hem; bastille

bastimentar *vt* to provision; supply

bastimento *m*, supplies; provisioning

bastión *m*, bastion

basto *m*, pack-saddle; ace of clubs; clubs (cards). a rude; tough; *fig* unpolished, rough

bastón *m*, cane, walking-stick; rod (of office); truncheon. **b. de junquillo,** Malacca cane. **empuñar el b.,** to take control, take over. **meter el b.,** to mediate

basura *f*, rubbish, refuse; dung; sweepings

basural *m*, *Lat. Am.* garbage dump

basurero *m*, dustman; dunghill, rubbish dump; kitchen middens; dust-bin

bata *f*, dressing-gown; smoking-jacket; old-fashioned dress; overall, smock

batacazo *m*, bump, noise of a fall; *pol* dark horse

batahola *f*, *inf* hurly-burly, hubbub

batalla *f*, battle; *fig* struggle, conflict; tournament; *art* battle-piece. **b. campal,** pitched battle

batallador a fighting, warlike

batallar *vi* to battle, fight; dispute, argue; hesitate

batallón *m*, battalion

batata *f*, sweet potato, yam

batea *f*, wooden tray; punt

bateador, -a *mf*, *Lat. Am.* batter

batear *vt*, *Lat. Am.* to bat

batería *f*, (*mil elec naut*) battery. **b. de cocina,** kitchen utensils. **b. de pilas secas,** dry battery. **b. de teatro,** stage lights. **b. eléctrica,** electric battery

batida *f*, game drive; attack; *met* beating

batido a beaten (of metals); shot (of silk); trodden, worn (roads, etc.). *m*, *cul* batter; hunting party

batidor *m*, beater; scout; outrider; hair comb; *cul* whisk. **b. de oro** (*or* **de plata**), gold (*or* silver) beater

batiente *m*, jamb (of door, etc.); damper (piano); leaf (of door); place where sea beats against cliffs, etc.

batihoja *m*, gold beater; metal worker

batimiento *m*, beating

batín *m*, smoking-jacket; man's dressing-gown

batir *vt* to beat, slap; demolish; dismantle, take down (stall, etc.); hammer, flatten; batter; *fig* beat (of sun, etc.); stir; pound; churn; comb (hair); vanquish, defeat; coin; reconnoiter; beat; throw down or drop; *vr* fight; swoop (birds of prey). **b. palmas,** to clap, applaud

batista *f*, cambric, batiste

baturrillo *m*, hotchpotch (gen. food); *inf* farrago, medley

batuta *f*, baton, conductor's wand. **llevar la b.,** *inf* boss the show, call the music, be in charge, to rule the roost

baúl *m*, trunk; *inf* belly; *Lat. Am. also* trunk (of a car) **b. escaparate** *or* **b. mundo,** wardrobe trunk

bausán (-ana) n guy, strawman; puppet; fool, idiot; lazybones

bautismo m, baptism

bautista m, baptizer, baptist. **San Juan B.,** St. John the Baptist

bautisterio m, baptistery

bautizar vt to baptize, christen; inf nickname; inf water (wine); accidentally shower with water

bautizo m, baptism; christening party

baya f, berry

bayeta f, baize; flannel

bayo (-ya) a bay (of horses)

bayoneta f, bayonet. **b. calada,** fixed bayonet

bayonetazo m, bayonet thrust

baza f, tricks taken (playing cards). fig inf **meter b.,** to stick one's oar in

bazar m, bazaar; shop, store; department store

bazo m, anat spleen. a yellow-brown

bazucar, bazuquear vt to shake or stir (liquids)

bazuqueo m, shaking or stirring of liquids

be f, letter B. m, baa

beata f, devout woman; inf pious hypocrite, prude; Sister of Mercy; over-religious woman

beatería f, sanctimoniousness; bigotry

beatificación f, beatification

beatificar vt to make happy; sanctify; beatify

beatitud f, blessedness, beatitude; happiness

beato (-ta) a happy; blessed, beatified; devout; prudish. n devout person; over-pious person

beba f, Argentina baby (girl)

bebé m, baby

bebedero a drinkable. m, drinking trough or place

bebedizo a drinkable. m, draught of medicine; love-potion; poisonous drink

bebedor (-ra) a drinkable. n drinker; toper

beber vt to drink; absorb; vi toast, drink to the health (of); tipple. m, drinking; drink

bebida f, drink; beverage; alcoholic liquor

beca f, academic scarf or sash; scholarship, exhibition

becado, becario m, exhibitioner, scholarship holder

becerro m, bullock; bull calf; calf-skin. **b. marino,** zool seal

bedel m, beadle; servitor, university porter

befar vt to mock, ridicule

befo a thick-lipped; knock-kneed. m, animal's lip

bejín m, bot puff-ball; spoilt child

beldad f, beauty; belle

beldar vt agr to winnow

Belén Bethlehem

belén m, nativity; manager; inf bedlam; inf gossip

belfo a thick-lipped

belga a and mf Belgian

Bélgica Belgium

bélgico a Belgian

Belice Belize

belicista adj war, militaristic; mf warmonger

bélico a warlike, military

belicoso a bellicose, aggressive; warlike

beligerancia f, belligerency

beligerante a and mf belligerent

belitre a inf knavish, cunning

bellaco (-ca) a artful, cunning. n knave; Lat. Am. untamed horse

bellaquería f, roguery, knavery, cunning

bellasombra f, umbra tree

belleza f, beauty, loveliness, fairness

bello a beautiful

bellota f, acorn; carnation bud; ornamental button, knob

bemol a and m, mus flat. inf **tener bemoles,** to be thorny, be difficult

bencina f, benzine; petrol, gasoline, gas

bendecir vt irr to praise, extol; bless; dedicate, consecrate. See **decir**

bendición f, benediction; blessing; consecration; pl marriage ceremony. **b. de la mesa,** grace before meals

bendito a holy, blessed; fortunate; simple. **ser un b.,** to be a simpleton; be a good soul. **¡Benditos los ojos que te ven!** It's so nice to see you!

beneficencia f, beneficence; charitable institutions

beneficiación f, benefaction

beneficiado (-da) n beneficiary. m, incumbent of a benefice

beneficiador (-ra) n benefactor

beneficiar vt to benefit; improve; cultivate (land); exploit (mine); purchase (directorship, etc.); sell at a loss (bonds, etc.)

beneficiario (-ia) n beneficiary

beneficiencia f, beneficence, charity

beneficio m, benefit; profit; cultivation (land, etc.); working (mine); ecc benefice; theat benefit

beneficioso a beneficial; useful

benéfico a beneficent; kind, helpful; charitable

benemérito a benemeritus, worthy, meritorious

beneplácito m, approbation; consent

benevolencia f, benevolence, goodwill

benévolo a benevolent, kind

benignidad f, kindness; mildness (of the weather, etc.)

benigno a kind; benign; mild; balmy

beodo (-da) a drunk, intoxicated. n drunkard

berbén m, Mexico scurvy

berenjena f, eggplant

bergante m, rascal, rogue

Berlín Berlin

berlinés (-esa) a and n of or from Berlin

bermejear vi to be or look reddish

bermejo a reddish; red; redgold; carroty (of hair)

bermellón m, vermilion

bernardina f, lie; boast; gibberish

bernardo (-da) a and n ecc Bernardine (Order of St. Bernard)

berquelio m, berkelium

berrear vi to low, bellow; yell, squall; shriek; vr reveal, confess

berrido m, lowing, bellowing; inf yell

berrinche m, inf tantrum, fit, fit of sulks

berro m, watercress

berroqueña f, granite

berza f, cabbage

besamanos m, ceremony of kissing royal hand, levee; kissing fingers (in salute)

besar vt to kiss; inf brush against, touch (of things); vr kiss one another; inf bang into, knock against one another

beso m, kiss; knock, collision

bestia f, quadruped (especially horses or mules); beast. mf inf nasty piece of work. **b. de carga**, beast of burden. **como una b.**, like a dog (e.g. **Trabajo como una b.** I work like a dog)

bestial a bestial; brutal; beastly

bestialidad f, brutality; bestiality; beastliness

bestialismo m, bestiality (sexual orientation)

besuquear vt inf to cover with kisses; vr inf spoon, make love

besuqueo m, inf kissing and spooning

betabel m, Mexico beetroot

betún m, bitumen; shoe blacking; kind of cement. **b. de Judea** or **b. judaico**, asphalt

bezo m, blubber lip; proud flesh (of a wound)

bezudo a thick-lipped

biberón m, feeding bottle

Biblia f, Bible

bíblico a biblical

bibliófilo m, bibliophile

bibliografía f, bibliography

bibliográfico a bibliographical

biblioteca f, library; book series. **b. por subscripción**, circulating library

bibliotecario (-ia) n librarian

bibliotecnia, bibliotecología, biblioteconomía f, library science

bicarbonato m, bicarbonate

bíceps m, biceps

bicherío m, Lat. Am. bugs, insects

bicho m, any small animal or reptile; quadruped; fighting bull; scarecrow, sight. **b. viviente**, inf living soul. **mal b.**, rogue

bicicleta f, bicycle, bike. **ir** (or **andar** or **montar) en b.**, to bicycle, bike, go by bicycle, go by bike

bicoca f, inf trifle, bagatelle

bicolor a bicolored

bidé m, bidet

bien m, ideal goodness, perfection; benefit, advantage; welfare; pl property, wealth. adv well; willingly; happily; perfectly; easily; enough, sufficient; all right! very well! **b. que**, although. **b. de equipo**, capital good. **bienes muebles**, movables, goods and chattels. **bienes raíces**, real estate. **el B. y el Mal**, Good and Evil. **¡Está b.!** All right! **no b.**, scarcely, as soon as. **si b.**, although, even if. **¿Y b.?** And so what? Well, then; What next?

bienal a biennial

bienamado a dearly beloved

bienandante a prosperous; happy

bienandanza f, happiness, welfare; prosperity

bienaventurado a blessed, holy; happy; inf over-simple, innocent, foolish

bienaventuranza f, blessedness

bienestar m, wellbeing; ease; comfort

bienhablado a well-spoken; civil, polite

bienhadado a fortunate, happy

bienhechor (-ra) a kind, helpful. n benefactor

bienintencionado a well-meaning

bienio m, biennium, space of two years, period of two years

bienquisto a respected; generally esteemed

bienvenida f, safe or happy arrival; welcome. **dar la b.**, to welcome

bienvivir vi to live comfortably; live decently or uprightly

bies m, bias, cross; slant

bife m Argentina beefsteak, steak

biftec m, beefsteak, steak

bifurcación f, bifurcation; fork, branch, junction

bifurcarse vr to fork, branch

bigamia f, bigamy

bígamo (-ma) a bigamous. n bigamist

bigote m, moustache; pl whiskers

bigotudo a moustached, whiskered

bikini m, bikini

bilateral a bilateral

bilingüe a bilingual

bilioso a bilious

bilis f, bile

billar m, billiards; billiard table

billete m, note, short letter; ticket; banknote. **b. circular**, excursion ticket. **b. de**

abono, season ticket. **b. de andén,** platform ticket. **b. de banco,** banknote. **b. de favor,** free ticket. **b. de ida y vuelta,** round trip ticket. **b. entero,** full fare. **b. kilométrico,** tourist ticket. **b. sencillo,** one-way. **medio b.,** half-fare

billón *m*, billion

bimestral a bimonthly

bimestre a bimonthly. *m*, two months' duration; money paid or received at two-monthly intervals

bimotor a two-motor. *m*, twin-engined aircraft

binario a binary

bincha *f*, *Lat. Am.* hairband

binóculo *m*, opera glasses

biofísica *f*, biophysics

biografía *f*, biography

biográfico a biographical

biógrafo (-fa) *n* biographer; (Chile) movie theater (e.g. **¡Vamos al biógrafo!** Let's go to the movies!)

biología *f*, biology

biológico a biological

biólogo *m*, biologist

biombo *m*, screen

bioquímica *f*, biochemistry

bioquímico *m*, biochemist

bipartido a bipartite

biplano *m*, biplane

biplaza a two-seater

birlar *vt* to bowl from where the bowl stopped; *inf* knock down; snatch away; *inf* rob

Birmania Burma

birmano (-na) a and *n* Burmese

bis *adv* twice; repeat; encore. a duplicate; **B** (in addresses, e.g., **Calle de Alcalá 18bis,** 18b Alcalá St.)

bisabuela *f*, great-grandmother

bisabuelo *m*, great-grandfather

bisagra *f*, hinge; shoemaker's polisher

bisbis *m*, game of chance

bisbisar *vt inf* to mutter; whisper

bisbiseo *m*, *inf* muttering; murmuring; whispering

bisecar *vt* to bisect

bisectriz *f*, bisector

bisel *m*, bevel, chamfer

bisiesto a leap and *m*, leap (year)

bisnieto (-ta) *n* great-grandchild

bisonte *m*, bison

bisoño (-ña) a inexperienced, raw. *n* recruit; *inf* greenhorn

bistec *m*, beef steak

bisturí *m*, surgical knife

bisunto a grubby, greasy

bisutería *f*, imitation jewelry

bizarría *f*, handsomeness; dash; verve; gallantry, courage; magnificence; liberality; whim, caprice

bizarro a handsome; dashing; gallant, courageous; liberal; splendid; magnificent

bizco a squint-eyed, cross-eyed

bizcocho *m*, biscuit; spongecake; bisque

bizma *f*, poultice. **poner bizmas,** to poultice

biznieto *n* See **bisnieto**

blanca *f*, old Spanish coin; *inf* penny; *mus* minim. **sin b.,** penniless

blanco a white; fair-skinned; blank, vacant; *inf* cowardly. *m*, target; blank left in writing; white person; interval. **b. de España,** whiting. **b. de la uña,** half-moon of the nail. **dar en el b.,** to hit the mark. **en b.,** blank, unused; *inf* in vain; uncomprehendingly; (of nights) sleepless

blancor, *m.* **blancura** *f*, whiteness; fairness (of skin)

blandear *vt* to moderate, soothe; brandish; *vi fig* give way, yield

blandir *vt* to brandish, wield, flourish

blando a soft; mild (weather); delicate; kind; peaceable; delicate, effeminate; *inf* cowardly

blandón *m*, wax taper

blandura *f*, softness; poultice; blandishment, compliment; mildness (of weather); gentleness, affability; luxury

blanquear *vt* to bleach; whitewash; whiten; *vi* appear white; show white

blanquecino a whitish

blanqueo *m*, whitening; whitewashing; bleaching

blanquillo *m*, *Central America, Mexico* egg; *Chile, Peru,* white peach

blasfemador (-ra) a blaspheming. *n* blasphemer

blasfemar *vi* to blaspheme; curse, swear

blasfemia *f*, blasphemy; insult

blasfemo (-ma) *n* blasphemer. a blasphemous

blasón *m*, heraldry; escutcheon; glory, honor. **una familia con antiguos blasones,** a family of ancient lineage

blasonar *vt* to blazon; *vi* boast, brag, blazon abroad

bledo *m*, blade, leaf. **no importar un b.,** not to matter a straw

blindado a *nav* armored, ironclad

blindaje *m*, *nav* armor-plating; *mil* blindage

blindar *vt* to plate with armor, to case with steel

blofista *mf*, *Lat. Am.* bluffer

blondo a fair, blond, flaxen-haired

bloque *m*, block, slab

bloquear *vt* to blockade; besiege

bloqueo *m*, blockade; siege; blocking; freezing (of assets). **violar el b.,** to run the blockade

blusa *f*, blouse

boa *f*, boa, large snake. *m*, boa (fur)

boato *m*, outward show, ostentation

bobería *f*, foolishness, stupidity

bóbilis, bóbilis (de) *adv inf* free of charge; without effort

bobina *f*, bobbin, spool, reel; *elec* coil; spool (of fishing rod)

bobo (-ba) a stupid, idiotic; simple, innocent. *n* fool. *m*, clown, jester

boca *f*, mouth; pincers (of crustaceans); entrance or exit; mouth (of a river), gulf, inlet; orifice, opening; muzzle (of guns); cutting edge (of tools); taste (of wine, etc.). **b. abajo,** face down, prone. **b. arriba,** on one's back, face up, supine. **b. del estómago,** pit of the stomach. **b. rasgada,** large mouth. **a b.,** verbally. **a b. de jarro,** point-blank. **a pedir de b.,** just as one would wish. **de b.,** by word of mouth. *inf* **sin decir esta b. es mía,** without a word, in silence

bocacalle *f*, entrance (to a street); street junction

bocadillo *m*, narrow ribbon; sandwich

bocado *m*, mouthful. **b. de reyes,** delicacy, exquisite dish (of food); snack; bite; (horse's) bit; bridle; *pl* preserved fruit cut up

bocamanga *f*, wrist (of sleeve)

bocana *f*, *Lat. Am.* estuary

bocanada *f*, mouthful (of liquid); cloud (of smoke). **b. de aire,** gust of wind

boceto *m*, sketch; outline; rough-cast model

bocha *f*, *sport* bowl; *pl* bowls

bochorno *m*, sultry weather; heat, stuffiness; blush, hot flush; shame

bochornoso a sultry; shameful

bocina *f*, trumpet; megaphone; foghorn; hooter; *aut* horn; horn (of gramophone); *ast* Ursa Minor

bocio *m*, *med* goiter

boda *f*, wedding, marriage. **bodas de oro,** fiftieth (golden) anniversary. **bodas de plata,** silver wedding anniversary

bodega *f*, wine-cellar; storeroom; stockroom; granary; *Puerto Rico* grocery store; *naut* hold (of ship)

bodegón *m*, eating-house; tavern; *art* still-life; genre picture

bofes *m pl*, lungs, lights. *inf* **echar los b.,** to work oneself to death

bofetada *f*, **bofetón** *m*, blow, slap; box on the ear

boga *f*, rowing; fashion, vogue; *mech* bogie. *mf* oarsman, rower. **estar en b.,** to be fashionable

bogador (-ra) *n* rower, oarsman

bogar *vi* to row

bogavante *m*, lobster

bohemio (-ia) a and *n* gipsy; bohemian; Bohemian. *m*, archer's short cloak

bohío *m*, *Lat. Am.* hut

boicotear *vt* to boycott

boicot, boicoteo *m*, boycott

boina *f*, Basque cap; beret

bola *f*, globe; ball; *sport* bowl; *arch* balloon; *inf* trick, lie; (Cuba) rumor; *Mexico* shoeshine, shine. **b. de nieves,** snowball. *inf* **dejar rodar la b.,** to let things slide

bolea *f*, (tennis) volley; throw

bolera *f*, bowling alley

bolero *m*, bolero; dancer; *inf* top hat; *Mexico* bootblack

boleta *f*, admission ticket; billet ticket; warrant, voucher; summons, ticket, traffic ticket

boletería *f*. *Lat. Am.* ticket office, box office

boleto *m*. *Lat. Am.* ticket

boletín *m*, bulletin; admission ticket; pay warrant; *com* price list; learned periodical. **b. de noticias,** news bulletin. **b. meteorológico,** weather report

boliche *m*, jack (in bowls); cup-and-ball toy; small oven (for charcoal); dragnet; *Mexico* bowling **juego de b.,** bowls

bólido *m*, *ast* bolide, meteor

boliviano(-na) a and *n* Bolivian. *m*, silver coin

bollo *m*, bread roll; bun; bulge, bruise (in metal); *med* lump

bollón *m*, round-headed or brass-headed nail; *bot* bud (especially vines)

bolo *m*, skittle, ninepin; pillow (for lace making); Cuban coin; *med* large pill; *fig* *inf* blockhead; *pl* skittles (game of)

bolsa *f*, purse; bag; footmuff; fold, pucker; pouch; exchange, stock exchange, capital, money; prize money; *med* sac; *min* pocket. **b. de estudio,** scholarship grant. **b. de trabajo,** labor exchange. **b. de valores,** stock exchange. **bajar (or subir) la b.,** to fall (or rise) (of stock exchange quotations). **jugar a la b.,** to speculate on the stock exchange

bolsillo *m*, pocket; purse; money

bolsista *mf* stock-broker; speculator (on the stock exchange)

bomba *f*, *mech* pump; pumping engine; bomb; *mil* shell; lamp globe; *inf* improvised verses; *inf* drinking bout. **¡B.!** Listen! Here goes! **b. de incendios,** fire-engine. **b. marina,** waterspout. **b. de mecha atrasada,** time bomb. **b. volante,** flying-bomb. **a prueba de b.,** bombproof. **arrojar bombas,** to bomb. *inf* **caer como una b.,** to be a bombshell

bombachos a baggy, loose-fitting; *m pl*, plus fours

bombardear *vt* to bombard; bomb; shell

bombardeo *m*, bombardment, bombing; shelling

bombástico a bombastic, high sounding

bombazo *m*, bombshell; bomb crater; noise of an exploding bomb

bombear *vt* to pump; bombard, shell; praise

bombero *m*, worker of a pressure pump; fireman; mortar, howitzer

bombilla *f*, *naut* lantern; (*elec phys*) bulb; small pump; straw for drinking maté *WH*

bombillo *m*, w.c. siphon; handpump

bombo *m*, big drum or player of it; *naut* barge, ferry; ballot box; exaggerated praise

bombón *m*, bonbon, sweet

bombonera *f*, box for toffee, etc.

bonachón *a inf* genial, good-natured

bonaerense *a* and *mf* of or from the Province of Buenos Aires

bonancible *a* calm (of weather, sea)

bonanza *f*, fair weather; prosperity

bondad *f*, goodness; kindness, helpfulness. **Tenga la b. de . . . ,** Be good enough to . . . , Please . . .

bondadoso *a* good, kind

bonete *m*, academic cap; *zool* reticulum (ruminants); *ecc* biretta. **gran b.,** important person. *inf* **a tente b.,** insistently

boniato *m*, *Lat. Am.* sweet potato, yam

bonificación *f*, bonus; allowance, discount

bonísimo, *a sup* **bueno** extremely good

bonito *a* pretty; graceful; (ironical) fine. *m*, *icht* striped tunny

bono *m*, voucher; *com* bond, certificate. **b. postal,** postal money order. **bono del gobierno,** government bond

boñiga *f*, cow-dung, animal manure

boqueada *f*, gasp, opening of the mouth. **dar las boqueadas, estar en las últimas boqueadas,** to be at the last gasp

boquear *vi* to gasp; be dying; *inf* be at last gasp (of things); *vt* say, utter

boquerón *m*, large opening; *icht* anchovy (fish); whitebait

boquete *m*, narrow entrance, aperture; gap, breach; hole

boquiabierto *a* open-mouthed; amazed

boquiancho *a* wide-mouthed

boquiasombrado *a* gaping

boquilla *f*, *dim* small mouth; mouthpiece (of wind instruments, etc.); cigar- or cigarette-holder; gas-burner; nozzle; tip (of cigarettes)

boquirroto *a inf* loquacious, indiscreet

borbollar *vi* to bubble, foam, froth

borbollón, borbotón *m*, gushing, bubbling, welling up. **a borbollones,** in a torrent; hastily, impetuously

borbotar *vi* to gush out, well up

bordado *m*, embroidery

bordador (-ra) *n* embroiderer

bordar *vt* to embroider; *fig* perform perfectly

borde *m*, edge; fringe; verge; rim; mount (of a picture); brim (of a hat); side (of ship). *a* wild (of plants); illegitimate. **estar**

lleno hasta los bordes, to be full to the brim

bordear *vt* to border, trim with a bordear; line (a street, e.g. **Diez mil personas bordearon las calles durante el desfile,** Ten thousand people lined the streets during the parade)

bordillo *m*, curbstone, curb.

bordo *m*, side (of ships); border, edge. **a b.,** on board

bordón *m*, pilgrim's staff; monotonous repetition; refrain; *mus* bass string; *fig* guide, stay

borgoña *m*, Burgundy wine

bórico *a* boric

boricua *a*, **borinqueño, -a** *a*, *mf* Puerto Rican

borla *f*, tassel; puff (for powder). *fig* **tomar la b.,** to take one's doctorate, graduate

bornear *vt* to bend, twist; *arch* hoist into position; *vr* warp (wood)

borra *f*, yearling ewe; thickest wool; wadstuffing; lees, sediment; fluff, dust; *inf* trash. **b. de algodón,** cotton-waste

borrachera *f*, drunkenness; orgy, carousal; *inf* blunder

borrachín (-ina) *n* tippler, toper

borrachito *a* high (on liquor), tipsy

borracho (de) *a* drunk (on), intoxicated (with); *inf* blind (with rage, etc.). *n* tippler, drunkard

borrador *m*, rough draft. **en borrador,** in the works (e.g. **Tiene dos ensayos en borrador,** She has two essays in the works). **estar en borrador,** to be in the works

borradura *f*, erasure

borrajear *vt* to scribble

borrar *vt* to erase; cross out; blot out; *fig* obliterate

borrasca *f*, storm, tempest; peril, danger; *inf* orgy

borrascoso *a* stormy; disordered, turbulent

borrego (-ga) *n* lamb; *inf* nincompoop, simpleton; *m pl*, fleecy clouds; white horses (waves)

borrico (-ca) *n* donkey; fool. *m*, *carp* sawing-horse

borrón *m*, blot; rough draft; defect; *fig* stigma

borroso *a* blurred, indistinct; full of dregs, muddy

bosque *m*, wood, forest

bosquejar *vt art* to sketch; sketch out, draft; model in rough (sculpture); outline

bosquejo *m*, outline, sketch; rough plan or idea; unfinished work. **en bosquejo,** grosso modo

bostar *m*, ox barn

bostezar *vi* to yawn

bostezo *m*, yawning; yawn

bota *f*, small wineskin; barrel, butt; boot.

b. de montar, riding boot. **botas de campaña,** top-boots. **botas de vadear,** waders

botada, botadura f, launching (of a ship)

botador m, thrower; boating-pole; *carp* nail-puller

botana f, *Lat. Am.* bite (to eat), snack

botánica f, botany

botánico (-ca) a botanical. n botanist

botar vt to fling; launch (boat); *Lat. Am.* to discard, throw away, throw out *naut* shift the helm; vi jump; bounce, rebound; rear, prance (horses)

botarate m, *inf* madcap, devil-may-care

botarel, botarete m, *arch* abutment, buttress, flying buttress

bote m, thrust (with lance, etc.); rearing (of horse); rebound; *aer* bump; open boat; small bottle, jar. **b. salvavidas,** lifeboat. *inf* **de b. en b.,** chockfull

botella f, bottle; bottleful; flask

botica f, chemist's shop; medicines, remedies; physic; store, shop; medicine chest

boticario m, apothecary, chemist

botija f, earthen jug; *slang* chunky person

botijo m, earthenware jar with spout and handle

botillería f, ice-cream bar

botín m, gaiter; buskin; booty

botiquín m, first-aid kit; medicine chest

botón m, bud; button; knob, handle; switch (electric); press button (bell); *bot* center; button (on a foil); *mech* stud

bóveda f, *arch* vault, arch; crypt; cavern. **b. celeste,** sky

boxeador m, boxer

boxear vi *sport* to box

boxeo m, *sport* boxing

boya f, *naut* buoy; float

boyante a floating; light, buoyant; prosperous

boyar vi *naut* to float

boyero m, cowherd

boza f, painter (of a boat)

bozal m, muzzle; nosebag; harness bells. *mf inf* greenhorn; a wild, untamed (horses)

bozo m, down which precedes beard; muzzle; headstall; lips, snout

bracero m, one who offers his arm (to a lady); day laborer; strong man. **de b.,** arm-in-arm

bracete m, small arm. **de b.,** arm-in-arm

braga f, (gen. *pl*) breeches; knickerbockers; hoist or pulley rope

bragazas m, *inf* weak-willed, fellow, soft specimen

braguero m, *med* truss

bragueta f, fly (of breeches)

bramante a roaring. m, twine, packthread

bramar vi to roar; rage; *fig* howl (of the wind, etc.)

bramido m, bellowing; roaring; yell of rage; *fig* howling (wind, sea, etc.)

brancada f, drag net

branquia f, (gen. *pl*) *icht* gill

brasa f, live coal. **estar como en brasas,** to be like a cat on hot bricks

brasero m, brazier; *Mexico* fireplace

Brasil Brazil

brasileño (-ña) a and n Brazilian

bravata f, bravado; threat

braveza f, ferocity, savageness; valor; violence, fury (of elements)

bravío a savage, untamed; wild (plants); uncultured

bravo a valiant; surly, rude; independent, strong-minded, good, excellent; savage (animals); stormy (sea); rough, rugged; violent, angry; *inf* sumptuous, magnificent.

bravura f, ferocity (animals); courage (persons); boastful threat

braza f, *naut* fathom; stroke (in swimming)

brazado m, armful

brazal m, armlet, brassard

brazalete m, bracelet; brassard

brazo m, arm; upper arm; front paw; *mech* arm; branch (of chandelier, etc.); bough; arm (of chair); power, courage; *pl* protectors; workmen, hands. **b. de mar,** firth, arm of the sea. **a b. partido,** in unarmed fight, man to man. **con los brazos abiertos,** welcomingly; willingly, gladly. **dar los brazos (a),** to embrace. *inf* **hecho un b. de mar,** dressed up to the nines

brea f, pitch, tar; sacking, canvas

brebaje m, beverage; unpleasant drink; *naut* draught (of beer, grog, etc.)

brecha f, *mil* breach; opening; *fig* impression (on mind). **morir en la b.,** to fight to the last ditch; die in harness

brécol m, *bot* broccoli

brega f, fight; quarrel; disappointment; trick. **andar a la b.,** to work hard. **dar b.,** to play a trick

bregar vi to fight; work hard; *fig* struggle; **bregarse con,** to tackle (a problem)

breña f, rough ground, bramble patch

breñoso a rugged, rocky

brete m, fetters, shackles; *fig* fix, squeeze, tight spot, tight squeeze (e.g. **Estoy en un brete.** I'm in a tight spot)

breva f, early fig; early acorn; *fig* advantage, "plum"; *inf* peach (girl); *inf* windfall, piece of luck; Havana cigar

breve a brief; concise. m, papal brief. f, *mus* breve. **en b.,** shortly, concisely; in a short while, soon

brevedad f, brevity **a la mayor brevedad** *Lat. Am.* as soon as possible

breviario *m*, breviary

brezal *m*, heath, moor

brezo *m*, *bot* heath

bribón (-ona) *n* rogue, ruffian. a knavish, dishonest; lazy

bribonada *f*, knavery, mischievous trick

bribonear *vi* to idle; play tricks, be a rogue

bribonería *f*, rascality, vagrant life

brida *f*, bridle

brigada *f*, *mil* brigade; *naut* division of fleet; beasts of burden. **brigada millonaria**, (Castroist Cuba) team of thirty sugarcane cutters who cut a million or more arrobas in one harvest

brillante a sparkling, brilliant; *fig* outstanding. *m*, diamond

brillantez *f*, brightness, luster; fame; *fig* brilliance

brillantina *f*, brilliantine

brillar *vi* to shine, sparkle, gleam, glisten; *fig* be brilliant or outstanding

brillo *m*, brilliancy, brightness, shine; fame, glory; distinction, brilliance, splendour

brincar *vi* to spring, leap, skip, frisk; *fig* *inf* skip, omit; *inf* grow angry; *vt* jump a child up and down

brinco *m*, leap, spring; skip, frolicking

brindar *vi* to invite, provoke (of things); *(with prep a or por)* drink the health of, toast; *vt* and *vi* give, present; offer; *vr* offer one's services

brindis *m*, toast (drink)

brío *m*, vigor; spirit, courage; gusto, verve

brioso a vigorous, enterprising; spirited, courageous; dashing, lively

briqueta *f*, briquette

brisa *f*, breeze; grape pressings

británico a British

brizna *f*, shred, paring; blade (grass); filament, fiber; string (of bean-pod, etc.); splinter, chip

briznar *vi*, *Lat. Am.* to drizzle

brocado *m*, brocade. a brocade or embroidered like brocade

brocal *m*, puteal (of a well); mouthpiece (of wineskin); metal ring (of sword-sheath)

brocha *f*, brush. **b. de afeitar,** shaving brush. **de b. gorda,** crudely painted. **pintor de b. gorda,** decorator

brochada *f*, stroke (of the brush)

broche *m*, clasp, fastening; brooch; hooks and eyes; *Lat. Am.* (paper) clip

broma *f*, merriment; joke, jest; shipworm. **b. literaria,** literary hoax

bromear(se) *vi* and *vr* to joke, make fun

bromista a joking, jesting; mischievous. *mf* genial person; prankster, tease

bronca *f*, *inf* shindy

bronce *m*, bronze; brass; *poet* gun, bell, trumpet; bronze statue; sunburn

bronceado a bronzed; sunburnt. *m*, sunburn

broncear *vt* to bronze; sunburn

bronco a rough, coarse; brittle; (of metals); harsh (voice, musical instruments); rigid, stiff; surly

bronconeumonía *f*, bronchopneumonia

bronquial a bronchial

bronquio *m*, (gen. *pl*) bronchi

bronquitis *f*, bronchitis

broquel *m*, shield; *fig* protection

broqueta *f*, skewer

brotadura *f*, budding

brotar *vi* to germinate, sprout; gush forth (water); issue forth, burst out; *fig* appear (of rash); *fig* begin to appear; *vt* to bring forth; produce (of earth)

brote *m*, bud, sprout; *fig* germ, genesis; iota, jot, atom

broza *f*, garden rubbish; debris; thicket

bruces (a *or* **de)** *adv* face downwards. **caer de b.,** to fall flat. Also with other verbs: *dar, echarse,* etc.

bruja *f*, witch; owl; *inf* hag

brujería *f*, witchcraft

brujo *m*, magician, wizard

brújula *f*, magnetic needle; compass; mariner's compass. **b. de bolsillo,** pocket compass. **b. giroscópica,** gyro-compass

brumoso a misty, hazy

bruno a dark brown

bruñidor (-ra) a polishing. *n* burnisher. *m*, polisher (instrument)

bruñir *vt* to polish, burnish; *inf* apply make up

brusco a brusque, rude; blunt; sudden, unexpected; sharp (of bends)

Bruselas Brussels

brusquedad *f*, brusquerie, rudeness; bluntness; suddenness, unexpectedness; sharpness (of a bend)

brutal a brutal

brutalidad *f*, brutality; *fig* brutishness; viciousness

bruto a stupid, unreasonable; vicious; unpolished, rough. *m*, animal (gen. quadruped). **en b.,** in the rough; *com* in bulk. **diamante en b.,** an uncut diamond

bruza *f*, strong brush; scrubbing brush

Bs. As. abbrev. of Buenos Aires

bu *m*, *inf* bogey man

buba *f*, pustule; *pl* buboes

bubónico a bubonic

buceador *m*, diver

bucear *vi* to work as a diver; swim under water; *fig* investigate

buceo *m*, diving; dive; *fig* investigation

buchaca *f*, *Lat. Am.* saddlebag; billiard pocket

buche *m*, craw or crop; mouthful; wrinkle, pleat; *inf* stomach, belly. *fig inf* inmost heart

bucle *m*, ringlet, curl

bucólico a bucolic

budismo *m*, Buddhism

budista a and *mf* Buddhist

budín *m*, pudding

buen a *abb* of **bueno**, good. Used before *m*, singular nouns and infinitives used as nouns, e.g. **un b. libro**, a good book. **el b. cantar**, good singing

buenaventura *f*, good luck; fortune told from hand

bueno (see **buen**) a good; kind; useful; convenient; pleasant; healthy; large (drink, etc.); simple, innocent; suitable; sufficient; opportune. **IB.!** Good!; Enough!; *Mexico* Hello! (on telephone); All right! **a buenas**, willingly. **de buenas a primeras**, at first sight, from the beginning. **hacer bueno**, to prove, justify (a claim)

buey *m*, ox. **b. suelto**, *inf* freelance; bachelor

búfalo (**-la**) *n* buffalo

bufanda *f*, scarf

bufar *vi* to bellow; snort; *inf* snort with rage

bufete *m*, desk, writing table; lawyer's office or practice; sideboard

bufo a comic. *m*, clown, buffoon

bufón *m*, buffoon, clown; jester. a comical, clownish

bufonada *f*, buffoonery, clowning; raillery, taunt

bufonear(se) *vr* and *vi* to joke, jest, parody

bufonería. See **bufonada**

buhardilla *f*, garret; skylight

búho *m*, owl; *inf* hermit, unsociable person

buhonería *f*, pedling, hawking; pedler's wares

buhonero *m*, pedler

buido a sharp-pointed; sharp

buitre *m*, vulture

bujía *f*, candle; candlestick; *elec* candle-power; *aut* sparking plug

bulbo *m*, *bot* bulb. **b. dentario**, pulp (of teeth)

bulevar *m*, boulevard, promenade

bulla *f*, noise; bustle; confusion; fuss. *inf* **meter a b.**, to throw into great confusion

bullente *adj* boiling, bubbling; frothey (beer); swarming, teeming. **b. de sol**, drenched in sunlight, sun-drenched

bullebulle *mf* busybody; madcap

bullicio *m*, noise, bustle; rioting; uproar

bullicioso a noisy, merry, boisterous; rebellious; lively, restless

bullir *vi* to boil; foam, bubble; *fig* seethe; *fig* swarm (insects); bustle; *vt* move, stir; *vr* stir, give signs of life

bulto *m*, bulk, mass, size; form of person, etc., seen indistinctly; swelling; bust, statue; bundle, package, piece of luggage; pillowcase. *fig inf* **poner de b.**, to put clearly, emphasize. **ser de b.**, to be obvious

bumerang *m*, boomerang

buñuelo *m*, bun; waffle, fritter; *fig* botch

buque *m*, ship, vessel; capacity of ship; ship's hull. **b. barreminas**, minesweeper. **b. de guerra**, battleship, man-of-war. **b. de vapor**, steamer. **b. de vela**, sailing ship. **b. escuela**, trainingship. **b. mercante**, merchant vessel. **b. submarino**, submarine. **b. transbordador**, train-ferry

burbuja *f*, bubble

burbujear *vi* to bubble

burdel *m*, brothel; *inf* untidy, noisy place. a lascivious

burdo a coarse, tough

burgo *m*, borough, burgh

burgués (**-esa**) a and *n* bourgeois

burguesía *f*, bourgeoisie

buriel a dark red

buril *m*, burin, engraver's tool

burla *f*, mockery; joke, jest; trick. **b. burlando**, without effort; negligently. **de burlas**, in fun. **entre burlas y veras**, half-jokingly

burlador a mocking. *m*, libertine, rake; deceiver

burlar *vt* to play a trick on; deceive; disappoint; *vr* and *vi* (*with de*) make fun of, laugh at, ridicule

burlesco a jocular, comic, burlesque

burlón (**-ona**) a joking; mocking, scoffing. *n* joker; scoffer

buró *m*, bureau, writing-desk; *Mexico* night table

burocracia *f*, bureaucracy

burócrata *mf* bureaucrat

burocrático a bureaucratic

burocratismo *m*, bureaucracy, red tape

burrajo *m*, dry stable dung used as fuel

burro *m*, ass, donkey; sawing-horse; card game

bursátil a *com* relating to the stock exchange; financial

busca *f*, search; hunting party; research; pursuit

buscado *adj* deliberate, intentional (negligence, etc.)

buscador (**-ra**) *n* searcher; investigator. *m*, finder (of a camera, etc.)

buscapié *m*, hint or suggestion; *fig* feeler

buscapiés *m*, squib, cracker, firecracker

buscapleitos *mf Lat. Am.* troublemaker

buscar *vt* to search, look for; pursue. **ir a b.**, to go to look for, go and get; bring, fetch

buscarruidos *mf inf* quarrel maker

buscavidas *mf inf* busybody; *inf* go-getter

buscón (-ona) *n* searcher; pickpocket, thief, swindler, rogue

buscona *f*, prostitute

busilis *m*, *inf* knotty problem, snag; **ahí está el b.,** there's the rub; core, main point

búsqueda (de) *f*, search (for)

busto *m*, *art* bust, head and shoulders

butaca *f*, armchair; *theat* orchestra stall; seat (in movies, etc.)

buzo *m*, diver

buzón *m*, mailbox; letter-box; canal, channel; sluice

C

cabal a just, exact; perfect; complete; faultless. *interj* Exactly! **por sus cabales,** according to plan; perfectly

cábala *f,* cabala; divination; *inf* intrigue. **hacer cábalas,** to venture a guess

cabalgar *vi* to ride a horse; ride in procession

caballa *f,* mackerel

caballeresco a gentlemanly; knightly; chivalrous

caballería *f,* riding animal; cavalry; knightly deed or quest; any of Spanish Military Orders; knight-errantry; knighthood; chivalry; share of the spoils of war; horsemanship. **c. andante,** knight-errantry. **c. ligera,** *mil* light horse. **c. mayor,** horses, mares, mules. **c. menor,** asses, donkeys

caballeriza *f,* stable; stud of horses; staff of a stable

caballerizo *m,* head stable-groom. **c. mayor del rey,** Master of the King's Horse

caballero *m,* gentleman; cavalier; knight. **c. andante,** knight-errant. *inf* **c. de industria,** adventurer, sharper. **el C. de la Mancha,** the Knight of La Mancha. **el C. Sin Miedo y Sin Tacha,** the Seigneur de Bayart. **c. del hábito,** knight of one of the Spanish Military Orders. **c. novel,** untried knight. **armar c.,** to dub a knight

caballerosidad *f,* gentlemanliness; nobility; generosity; chivalry

caballeroso a gentlemanly; noble; generous; chivalrous

caballete *m,* ridge (of a roof); *mil* wooden horse; brake (for flax and hemp); *agr* furrow; easel; sawing-frame; trestle; bridge (of the nose)

caballito *m, dim* little horse; *pl* merry-go-round; automatic horse gambling game; circus equestrian act. **c. del diablo,** dragonfly

caballo *m,* horse; (chess) knight; (Spanish cards) queen; sawing-frame; *pl* cavalry. **c. balancín,** rocking horse. **c. de batalla,** war-horse; *fig* hobby-horse; forte; crux. **c. de cartón,** hobby-horse; rocking horse. **c. de carrera,** racehorse. **c. de tiro,** draft-horse. **c. de vapor,** horsepower. **c. marino,** sea-horse. **a c.,** on horseback. **A c. regalado no le mires el diente,** Never look a gift horse in the mouth. **caer bien a c.,** to have a good seat (on a horse). **ser un c. loco en una cacharrería,** to be like a bull in a china shop

cabaña *f,* hut, cabin, cottage; flock (of sheep); drove (of mules); *Argentina* cattle ranch; *art* pastoral scene; balk (billiards)

cabaret *m,* cabaret, nightclub

cabaretero *m,* nightclub owner

cabeceada *f, Lat. Am.* nod (of the head)

cabecear *vi* to nod; shake the head in disapproval; move the head from side to side; toss the head (horses); (*aer naut*) pitch; sway (of a carriage); lean; *vt* refoot (socks); head (wine)

cabeceo *m,* nod, shake (of head); (*naut aer*) pitching; lurching (of a carriage, etc.); bight (of river)

cabecera *f,* top, upper portion, head; seat of honor; bed-head; river source; capital (country or county); illustrated chapter heading; pillow; inscription, heading

cabellera *f,* head of long hair; hair-switch; tail (of comet)

cabello *m,* hair; head of hair; silk (of maize). *fig inf* **asirse de un c.,** to clutch at a straw

cabelludo a hairy; *bot* fibrous

caber *vi irr* to be room for, contain; fit into, go into (e.g. **No cabemos todos en este coche,** There isn't room for all of us in this car); happen, befall, have (e.g. **No les cupo tal suerte,** They did not have such luck—Such luck did not befall them); be possible (e.g. **Todo cabe en Dios,** All things are possible with God). **No cabe más,** There's no room for anything else; *fig* That's the limit. *fig* **no c. en sí,** to be beyond oneself (with joy, pride, etc.). **No cabe duda de que,** There's no doubt that. *Pres. Ind.* **quepo, cabes,** etc. *Fut.* **cabré,** etc. *Conditional* **cabría,** etc. *Preterite* **cupe, cupiste,** etc. *Pres. Subjunc.* **quepa, quepas,** etc. *Imperf. Subjunc.* **cupiese,** etc.

cabestrillo *m,* sling; thin chain (for ornament). **en c.,** in a sling (e.g. **Tenía el brazo en c.,** His arm was in a sling)

cabeza *f,* head; top; upper end; nail-head; brain; mind; judgment; self-control; edge (of book); peak, summit; source, origin; individual, person; head of cattle; capital city. *m,* leader, chief, head. *mech* **c. de biela,** big-end. *inf* **c. de chorlito,** scatterbrain (person). **c. de hierro,** blockhead. *mil* **c. de puente,** bridgehead. **c. de partido,** principal town of a region. **c. de turco,** scapegoat. **irse la c. (a alguien),** to feel giddy. *fig inf* **meter a uno en la c.,** to put into someone's head. *inf* **quebrarse la c.,** to rack one's brains. *inf* **quitar a uno de la c. (una cosa),** to dissuade; get an idea out of someone's head

cabezada *f,* blow with or on the head; nod; headshake; headstall; *naut* pitching. **dar cabezadas,** to nod, go to sleep

cabezal *m,* small head pillow; *surg* pad; bolster; narrow mattress; *mech* head

cabezudo a large-headed; *inf* obstinate; *inf* heady (of wine). *m,* carnival grotesque

cabida *f,* space, capacity; extent, area

cabildear *vi* to canvass votes, lobby

cabildo *m, ecc* chapter; municipal council; meeting, or meeting place of council. **c. abierto,** town meeting

cabina *f*, cabin. **c. telefónica** phone booth

cabinero, -a *mf*, *Lat. Am.* flight attendant

cabizbajo *a* crestfallen; pensive, melancholy

cable *m*, cable; string (of bridge); cable's length; **c. aéreo**, overhead cable. **c. alimentario**, feed line. **c. eléctrico**, electric cable

cabo *m*, end, extremity; stump, stub; handle, shaft, haft; leader; *geog* cape; end, conclusion; *naut* rope; ply (of wool, etc.); *mil* corporal; *pl* accessories (clothes); horse's tail and mane. **c. de maestranza**, foreman. **c. de mar**, naval quartermaster. **c. furriel**, *mil* quartermaster. **al c.**, in the end. **llevar a c.**, to finish

Cabo de Hornos Cape Horn

cabra *f*, nanny-goat; goat. **c. montesa**, wild goat

cabrerizo (-za) *a* goatish. *m*, goatherd

cabrero (-ra) *m*, goatherd; *a Argentina* bad-tempered, cantankerous

cabria *f*, winch, hoist

cabrilla *f*, *carp* saw-horse; *pl ast* Pleiades; burn marks on legs from sitting too near fire; white crests (of waves)

cabrillear *vi* to foam, froth (the sea)

cabrío *a* goatish. *m*, herd of goats. **macho c.**, male goat, he-goat

cabriola *f*, fouetté (in dancing); spin in the air (acrobats); curvet (horses); caper

cabriolar *vi* to curvet; caper, skip

cabritilla *f*, dressed kid; lambskin, etc.

cabrito *m*, *zool* kid; *pl* toasted maize, popcorn

cabrón *m*, billy goat, buck, he-goat; *inf* complaisant husband, cuckhold; *Chile* owner or operator of a brothel

cabrona *f*, *Chile* bawd, madam

cabujón *m*, *min* uncut gem; unpolished ruby; *pl* vignettes

cacahuete *m*, *bot* peanut, monkey nut

cacao *m*, *bot* cacao tree; cacaonut

cacarear *vi* to crow, cackle; *vt inf* boast

cacatúa *f*, cockatoo

cacería *f*, hunting party; hunting bag, booty; *art* hunting scene

cacerola *f*, stew-pot, casserole

cachalote *m*, sperm whale

cachar *vt* to break in fragments; split (wood)

cacharro *m*, coarse earthenware vessel; *inf* decrepit, worthless object

cachazudo *a* phlegmatic, slow

cachear *vt* to search (a person) for weapons

cachemira *f*, cashmere

cacheo *m*, search (of persons) for weapons

cachetada *f*, *Lat. Am.* slap (in the face)

cachete *m*, blow on the head or face with one's fist; cheek (especially fat one)

cachimba *f*, *Lat. Am.* pipe (for smoking)

cachiporra *f*, club, bludgeon

cachivache *m*, *inf* (gen. *pl*) trash; pots, pans, utensils

cacho *m*, small slice (gen. of bread or fruit)

cachón *m*, breaker, wave; small waterfall

cachorro (-rra) *n* puppy; cub. *m*, small pistol

cacillo *m*, ladle; basting spoon

cacique *m*, Indian chief, cacique; *inf* political "boss"

caciquismo *m*, political "bossism"

caco *m*, pickpocket, thief; *inf* poltroon

cacofonía *f*, cacophony

cacografía *f*, cacography

cacto *m*, cactus

cacumen *m*, *inf* brains, acumen

cada *a* every, each. **c. cual**, each. **c. que**, whenever; every time that. **c. y cuando que**, whenever

cadalso *m*, scaffold; platform, stand

cadáver *m*, corpse

cadena *f*, chain; link, tie; *fig* bond; *fig* sequence (of events); *law* imprisonment; *arch* buttress; grand chain (dancing); **c. de montañas**, range of mountains. **c. perpetua**, life imprisonment

cadencia *f*, cadence; rhythm; *mus* measure, time; *mus* cadenza

cadencioso *a* rhythmic

cadente *a* falling, declining; decaying, dying; rhythmic

cadera *f*, hip; flank

cadete *m*, *mil* cadet

cadi *mf* caddy

caducar *vi* to become senile; become invalid, be annulled; expire, lapse; *fig* be worn out

caducidad *f*, decrepitude; lapse, expiry

caduco *a* senile; decrepit; perishable; lapsed; obsolete

caduquez *f*, senility

caedizo *a* ready to fall; timid, cowardly, weak

caer *vi irr* to fall, drop; drop out or off; suit, fit, become; fall; fade (colors); *fig* drop (voice); (*with sobre*) attack, fall upon; (*with en*) fall in or on to; decay, collapse; understand; (*with preps. a, hacia*) *fig* look on to, face; (*with por, en*) *fig* fall on, occur on; *vr aer* crash; fly off (buttons, etc.). **c. de cabeza**, to fall head foremost. **c. en conflicto (con)**, to come into conflict (with) **c. en las manos de uno**, to come into somebody's possession (come to be owned by somebody). **c. en gracia**, to make a good impression, arouse affection. **caerse de suyo**, to be self-evident. **c. por tierra**, (plan, etc.) to fall through. **Cayó enfermo**, He was taken ill. **cayendo y levantado**, dying *Pres. Ind.* **caigo, caes**, etc. *Pres. Part.* **cayendo**.

Preterite **cayó cayeron.** *Pres. Subjunc.* **caiga,** etc.

café *m,* coffee (tree, berry, drink); café; coffeehouse. **c. con leche,** café au lait. **c. negro** *Lat. Am. (except Columbia)* black coffee. **c. solo** *Spain* black coffee. **c. tinto** *Colombia* black coffee

cafeína *f,* caffeine

cafetal *m,* coffee plantation

cafetera *f,* coffeepot; *Peru* cab, taxi

cafeto *m,* coffee tree

cafiche *m, Argentina, Chile* pimp

caficultor *m,* coffee-grower

caficultura *f,* coffee-growing

cafúa *f, Argentina* clink, slammer

cagar(se) *vi vt vr* to evacuate (bowels); *vt inf* spoil, make a botch of

cagarruta *f,* dung of sheep, deer, rabbits, etc.

caída *f,* falling; fall; ruin; failure; close (of day); *fig* falling off; hanging (curtains, etc.); diminution; incline; *pl* coarse wool; *inf* repartee. **a la c. de la tarde,** at the end of the afternoon. **a la c. del sol,** at sunset

caído (-da) a debilitated, languid; lapsed; (of a shoulder) sloping. **los caídos,** the fallen, the dead (in war, etc.)

caimán *m,* alligator; *inf* shark, astute person

caite *m, Central America* sandal

caja *f,* box; safe, cash box; coffin; (of a vehicle) body; *mus* drum; case (of piano, watch, etc.); cavity; well (of a stair); *com* cash; cash-desk; cashier's office; *bot* sheath. **c. de ahorros,** savings bank. **c. de caudales,** strong-box. *print* **c. de imprenta,** type case. **c. de música,** musical box. **c. de reclutamiento,** recruiting office. **c. de velocidades,** gearbox. **c. registradora,** cash register. **c. torácica,** rib cage, thoracic cage

cajero (-ra) *m,* boxmaker; *n com* cashier; pedler **c. automático,** automatic teller, automatic teller machine, bank machine, money machine

cajetilla *f,* packet (cigarettes, etc.)

cajón *m,* chest, locker, case; drawer. **c. de municiones,** ammunition-box

cal *f,* lime. **c. muerta,** slaked lime. **c. viva,** quicklime. *fig inf* **de c. y canto,** tough, strong

cala *f,* sample slice (of fruit); *naut* hold; *surg* probe; cove, small bay; *bot* iris

calabacera *f, bot* pumpkin or gourd plant

calabaza *f, bot* pumpkin (plant and fruit); gourd; *inf* dolt. **dar calabazas,** to refuse (suitor); flunk (an examinee). *inf* **llevar calabazas,** to get the sack; be jilted

calabobos *m, inf* drizzle

calabozo *m,* dungeon; prison cell; pruning knife

calada *f,* soaking, wetting through; flight of bird of prey; swoop. **dar una c.,** *fig inf* to dress down

calado a soaked, wet through. *m, sew* open-work; fretwork; *naut* draught of a ship; water level; *pl* lace. **c. hasta los huesos,** soaked to the skin; madly in love

calador *m,* one who does open or fretwork; caulking iron; borer; *surg* probe

calafatear *vt naut* to caulk

calamaco *m, Mexico* kidney bean

calamar *m, zool* squid, calamary

calambre *m,* cramp. **c. del escribiente,** writer's cramp

calamidad *f,* misfortune, calamity

calamina *f, min* calamine

calamitoso a calamitous; unfortunate, unhappy

cálamo *m,* ancient flute; stalk (of grass); *poet* pen

calandria *f, orn* calender, lark; *mech* calender; treadmill. *mf inf* malingerer

calaña *f,* sample; model; pattern; kind, quality; temperament; cheap fan

calar *vt* to permeate, soak through; pierce; do openwork (in cloth, paper, metal); cut a sample slice from fruit; pull (hat, etc.) well down on head; put down (an eyeshade or visor); fix (bayonets, etc.); *inf* understand (persons); *inf* guess, realize; *naut* let down; *vi naut* draw (water); *vr* be drenched, wet through; swoop (birds of prey); *inf* sneak in. a calcareous

calatear *vt, Peru* to undress

calato, -a a, *Peru* naked, nude; broke, penniless

calavera *f,* skull. *m,* dare-devil, madcap; roué; *Mexico* taillight

calaverada *f, inf* dare-devilment, foolishness; escapade

calcañar *m,* heel (of foot)

calcar *vt* to trace (drawing); press with foot; copy servilely, imitate

calce *m,* rim of a wheel; wedge; tyre

calceta *f,* stocking; fetter. *inf* **hacer c.,** to knit

calcetería *f,* hosiery shop; hosiery trade

calcetero (-ra) *n* hosier; hose maker or darner

calcetín *m,* sock

calcificación *f, med* calcification

calcio *m,* calcium

calco *m,* tracing (drawing)

calcografiar *vt* to transfer; make chalcographies of

calcomanía *f,* transfer

calculación *f,* calculation

calculado a calculated

calculador a calculating. *m,* calculating machine, comptometer

calcular *vt* to calculate

cálculo *m,* calculation; *math* estimate; investigation; conjecture; (math med) calculus. **c. hepático,** *med* gallstone

calda *f,* heating; *pl* hot mineral baths

caldear vt to heat

caldeo m, heating

caldera f, cauldron; cauldron full; WH teapot; eng boiler. **c. de vapor**, steam-boiler

calderería f, coppersmith's trade and shop

calderero m, boiler maker; coppersmith; tinker

calderilla f, holy water stoup; any copper coin

caldero m, small cauldron; casserole; kettle

calderón m, large cauldron; mus rest; mus trill; pause

caldo m, broth; salad dressing; pl agr oil, wine, vegetable juices

calefacción f, heating. **c. central**, central heating

calendario m, calendar. **c. deportivo**, fixture card. **c. gregoriano**, Gregorian calendar

calendas f pl, calends. **en las c. griegas**, at the Greek calends

caléndula f, marigold

calentador a heating, warming. m, heater; warming-pan

calentamiento m, heating, warming

calentar vt irr to heat, warm; rev-up (an engine); hasten; inf spank; vr warm oneself; be in heat (animals); grow excited. See **acertar**

calentura f, fever

calera f, lime-pit; lime-kiln; fishing smack

calesa f, calash, calèche, chaise (two-wheeled carriage)

calesita f, Lat. Am. merry-go-round

caleta f, cove, creek

caletre m, inf discernment, head, sense

calibrar vt to calibrate; gauge

calibre m, mech gauge; bore, caliber; diameter (tubes, pipes, etc.)

calidad f, quality; role; character, temperament; condition, requisite; importance, gravity; personal particulars; nobility; pl qualities of the mind. **c. originaria**, rank and birth. **c. de oficio**, justification for action. **en c. de**, in the capacity of

cálido a warm, hot; warming, heating; vehement, ardent; art warm

calidoscopio m, kaleidoscope

calientalibros mf, bookworm (person)

calientapiés m, footwarmer

calientaplatos m, hot plate, platewarmer

caliente a warm, hot; excited; art warm

calientito a piping hot

calificable a classifiable; qualifiable

calificación f, classification; qualification; judgment; mark, place (examinations)

calificar vt to class; authorize; judge (qualities); fig ennoble; vr prove noble descent

californio (-ia) a and n Californian

caliginoso a murky, dark

caligrafía f, calligraphy

calígrafo m, calligraphist

calistenia f, callisthenics

caliza f, limestone

callado a silent; reserved; secret

callar(se) vi and vr to say nothing, keep silent; stop speaking; stop making any sound (persons, animals, things); vt conceal, keep secret; omit, leave out; inf interj **¡Calle!** You don't say so! **Quien calla otorga**, Silence gives consent

calle f, street. **c. de un sentido**, **c. de una corrida** Mexico one-way street. **c. de una sola mano** Argentina one-way street inf **abrir c.**, to clear the way. inf **dejar en la c.**, to leave destitute. inf **echar a la c.**, put out of the house, to throw out of the house; make known, publish. **ponerse en la c.**, to go out

calleja, **callejuela** f, small street, alley, side street

callejear vi to walk the streets, wander about the streets, loaf around the streets

callejero a fond of gadding. m, street directory

callejón m, alley, lane. **c. sin salida**, cul-de-sac; fig impasse

callicida m, corn cure

callista mf chiropodist

callo m, corn, callosity; med callus; pl tripe

calloso a callous, horny

calma f, calm, airlessness; serenity; composure; quiet, tranquillity, peace. **c. chicha**, dead calm. **en c.**, at peace; tranquil; calm (of the sea)

calmante a calming, soothing. med a and m, sedative, tranquilizer

calmar vt to soothe, calm; moderate, mitigate; pacify; quench (thirst); vi grow calm; moderate; be becalmed

calmoso a calm, tranquil; inf sluggish, lazy; imperturbable

calor m, heat; ardor, vehemence; cordiality; fig heat (of battle); excitement

caloría f, phys calorie

calórico a phys caloric, thermic

calorífero a heat-giving. m, heater, radiator

calumnia f, calumny; law slander

calumniador (-ra) a slandering. n calumniator, slanderer

calumniar vt to calumniate; law slander

calumnioso a calumnious, slanderous

caluroso a hot, warm; cordial, friendly; enthusiastic; ardent, impassioned; excited

calva f, bald patch on head; worn place (cloth, etc.); bare spot, clearing (trees, etc.)

Calvario m, Calvary; inf series of disasters; inf debts

calvicie f, baldness

calvo a bald; bare, barren (land); worn (cloth, etc.)

calza f, breeches (gen. pl); wedge; inf stocking. inf **tomar calzas,** to beat it

calzada f, roadway. **c. romana,** Roman road

calzado m, footwear, shoes

calzador m, shoehorn

calzadura f, wedging (of a wheel); act of putting on shoes; felloe of a wheel

calzar vt to put on shoes; wear (spurs, gloves, etc.); wedge, block (wheel); scotch (a wheel). fig inf **c. el coturno,** don the buskin; write in the sublime style; write a tragedy, write tragedies. **calzarse a una persona,** to have a person in one's pocket

calzón m, breeches (gen. pl). fig inf **ponerse los calzones,** to wear the breeches (of a woman)

calzonazos m, inf weak-willed, easily led fellow

calzoncillos m pl, drawers, pants

calzoneras fpl, Mexico pants buttoned down the sides

cama f, bed; bedstead; bedhanging; lair, form; floor (of a cart); check (of bridle) (gen. pl). **c. de campaña,** camp bed. **c. de matrimonio,** double bed. **c. de monja,** single bed. **c. de operaciones,** operating table. **c. turca,** settee-bed. **guardar c.,** to stay in bed

camafeo m, cameo

camaleón m, chameleon; inf changeable person

cámara f, chamber; hall; house (of deputies); granary; naut state room; chamber (firearms, mines); phys camera; human excrement; aut inner tube. **c. acorazada,** strong-room. **c. alta,** Upper House, **c. baja** or **c. de los comunes,** lower house, house of commons. **c. de comercio,** chamber of commerce. **c. oscura,** (optics) dark room

camarada mf pal, companion, comrade

camaradería f, comradeship, companionship

camarera f, waiting-maid; waitress; chambermaid; stewardess

camarero m, waiter; papal chamberlain; chamberlain; steward; valet. **c. mayor,** lord chamberlain

camarilla f, palace or other clique, coterie; inf back-scratch

camarín m, theat dressing-room; closet; boudoir; cage (of a lift); niche

camarón m, prawn, shrimp; tip, reward

camarote m, cabin; berth

cambalachear vt inf to barter

cambalache m, Lat. Am. secondhand shop; exchange

cambiable a exchangeable; changeable

cambiante a exchanging; changing. m, sheen, luster (gen. pl); money changer

cambiar vt to exchange; convert. vt and vi change, alter; vi and vr to veer (wind). **c. de aguas,** poet to move (change one's residence). **c. de aire,** get a change of scenery. **c. de frente,** to face about; fig change front

cambio m, exchange; change; com rate of exchange; money change; com premium on bills of exchange. **a c. de, en c. de,** in exchange for; instead of. **en c.,** instead, on the other hand. **c. de velocidad,** aut gear-changing. **letra de c.,** bill of exchange. **libre c.,** free trade

cambista mf money changer. m, banker

cambullón m, Lat. Am. swindle

cambur m, Venezuela banana

camelar vt inf to woo; seduce

camello m, camel. **c. pardal,** giraffe

camellón m, furrow; drinking trough; Mexico island, traffic island, median strip

camilla f, couch; small round skirted table with brazier underneath; stretcher, litter

caminador a in the habit of walking a great deal

caminante mf walker, traveler

caminar vi to travel; walk; fig move on, go (inanimate things). fig inf **c. derecho,** to walk uprightly

caminata f, long, tiring walk; excursion

caminejo m, worn path

camino m, road; route; journey; way, means; **c. de hierro,** railway. **c. de mesa,** table-runner. **c. de sirga,** towpath. **c. real,** highway, main road. **de c.,** on the way, in passing. **ponerse en c.,** to set out

camión m, truck. **c. de volteo, c. volquete** dump truck; Mexico bus; truck

camionera f, Mexico bus station

camioneta f, light truck, pick-up truck; WH station wagon

camisa f, shirt, stiff shirt; thin skin (of fruit); sloughed skin of snakes; coat (of whitewash, etc.); mech jacket; mantle (gas). **c. de fuerza,** straitjacket. **dejar sin c.,** inf to leave penniless

camisería f, shirt shop or factory

camiseta f, undershirt, T-shirt. **c. de fútbol,** soccer player's jersey

camisón m, large wide shirt; night shirt

camomila f, chamomile

camorra f, inf brawl, shindy. **armar c.,** to start a row

camote m, Lat. Am. sweet potato

campamento m, camping; mil encampment; camp; jamboree

campana f, bell; anything bell-shaped; church, parish. **c. de chimenea,** mantelpiece. **c. de hogar,** hood, shutter (of a fireplace)

campanario m, belfry, bell tower

campaneo m, bell-ringing; chime

campanilla f, hand-bell; bubble; any bell-shaped flower

campante a outstanding; inf proud, satisfied

campanudo a bell-shaped; sonorous (of words); pompous (of speech)

campaña f, level country; campaign. naut voyage, cruise. **correr la c.**, to reconnoiter. **la C. del Desierto**, the War against the Gauchos (in Argentina)

campar vi to camp. inf **c. por sus respetos**, to stand on one's own feet

campeador a mighty in battle

campear vi to go out to graze; grow green (crops); excel; mil be engaged in a campaign, reconnoiter

campechano a inf hearty; frank; cheerful; generous

campeón m, champion; advocate, defender

campeonato m, championship

campesino (**-na**) a rural, rustic. n country dweller

campestre a rural

campiña f, expanse of cultivated land; countryside, landscape

campo m, country (as opposed to urban areas); field; fig sphere, province; (phys her mil) field; art ground; mil camp, army; plain ground (of silks, etc.). «**C. Abierto**», "Miscellaneous" (e.g. as the title of a section in a book catalog). **c. de aterrizaje**, aer landing-field. **c. de batalla**, battlefield. **c. de concentración**, concentration camp. **c. de experimentación**, testing ground. **c. de golf**, golf course. **c. de prisioneros** mil prison camp. **c. de tiro**, rifle-range. **c. santo**, graveyard. **c. visual**, field of vision. **a c. abierto**, in the open air. **a c. travieso**, cross-country

camuflaje m, camouflage

camuflar vt to camouflage

cana f, gray hair

Canadá Canada

canadiense a and mf Canadian

canal m, canal. mf, geol subterranean waterway; channel; anat canal, duct; defile, narrow valley; gutter; drinking trough; animal carcass. **abrir en c.**, to open up, split open

canalera f, roof gutter

canaleta f, (wooden) trough; gutter (on roof)

canalete m, paddle

canalización f, canalization; elec main, mains; piping, tubing

canalizar vt to make canals or channels; regulate waters of rivers, etc.; canalize

canalón m, gutter, spout; shovel hat; pantile

canalla f, inf mob, rabble. m, inf scoundrel

canallesco a scoundrelly, knavish; despicable

canapé m, sofa

canario (**-ia**) m, canary. a and n pertaining to or native of the Canary Islands.

canasta f, hamper, basket; card game

canastilla f, small basket; layette

canastillo m, basket-work tray

cáncamo m, ring-bolt

cancamusa f, inf trick, deception

cancel m, draftscreen; ecc screen

cancela f, wrought-iron door

cancelación f, cancellation; expunging

cancelar vt to cancel; expunge, annul; abolish, blot out; pay off, clear (a mortgage)

cáncer m, cancer

cancerar vt to consume; weaken; mortify; vr suffer from cancer; become cancerous

canceroso a cancerous

cancha f, sport fronton; (tennis) court; cockpit; yard; hippodrome; widest part of a river; road; toasted maize. **cancha** Argentina, Chile to be in one's element. **tener cancha** Argentina to be experienced; Venezuela have charisma, charm, allure

canciller m, chancellor; foreign minister; assistant vice-consul

cancillería f, chancellorship; chancellery; foreign ministry

canción f, song; lyric poem; musical accompaniment; old name for any poetical composition. **volver a la misma c.,** fig to be always harping on the same theme

cancionero m, collection of songs and verses; songbook

cancionista mf singer; song writer

candado m, padlock; earring

candela f, candle; horse-chestnut flower; candlestick; inf fire. **en c.,** naut vertical (of masts, etc.)

candelabro m, candelabrum

candelero m, candlestick; lamp; candle maker or seller; naut stanchion

candente a candescent, red-hot

candidatear vi to run (for office)

candidato (**-ta**) n candidate

candidatura f, candidature

candidez f, simplicity, ingenuousness; candidness

cándido a white; simple, ingenuous; candid, frank

candil m, oil lamp; Greek lamp; tips of stag's horns; inf cock of a hat

candileja f, oil reservoir of lamp; pl footlights, floats

candor m, extreme whiteness; sincerity; candor; simplicity, innocence

candoroso a candid, open; simple, honest

canela f, bot cinnamon; fig anything exquisitely perfect

canelo *m*, cinnamon tree. a cinnamon-colored

cangilón *m*, pitcher, jar; bucket (for water); dredging bucket

cangreja *f*, *naut* gaffsail. **c. de mesana,** *naut* jigger

cangrejo *m*, crab. **c. de mar,** sea-crab. **c. ermitaño,** hermit crab

canguro *m*, kangaroo

caníbal a and *mf* cannibal

canibalismo *m*, cannibalism

canica *f*, marble (for playing with)

canícula *f*, dog days; *ast* Dog star

caniculares *m pl* dog days

canijo a *inf* delicate, sickly; anemic, stunted

canilla *f*, long bone of leg or arm; any principal bones in bird's wing; tap, faucet; spool, reel; fault (in cloth)

canillera *f*, *Lat. Am.* cowardice; fear

canillito, -a *mf*, *Lat. Am.* newsboy, newsgirl

canino a canine

canje *m*, (diplomacy, *mil.*, *com.*) exchange, substitution. **c. de prisioneros,** exchange of prisoners

canjear *vt* to exchange

cano a white-haired, hoary; ancient; *poet* white

canoa *f*, canoe; launch. **c. automóvil,** motor launch

canoero (-ra) *n* canoeist

canon *m*, rule; (*ecc print*) canon; catalog; part of the Mass; *mus* canon, catch; *tax. pl* canon law

canonizar *vt* to canonize; extol, exalt; approve, acclaim

canoso a white-haired, hoary

cansado (-da) a tired; weary; exhausted; decadent; tiresome; *inf* fed up. *n* bore, tedious person

cansancio *m*, fatigue, weariness

cansar *vt* to tire, weary; *agr* exhaust soil; bore; badger, annoy; *vr* be tired; grow weary

cantante a singing. *mf* professional singer

cantar *vi* to sing; twitter, chirp; extol; *inf* squeak, creak; *fig* call (cards); *inf* squeal, confess. *m*, song. **C. de los Cantares,** Song of Songs. **cantarlas claras,** to call a spade a spade

cántara *f*, pitcher, jug

cantárida *f*, Spanish fly

cántaro *m*, pitcher, jug; jugful; varying wine measure; ballot box; tax on spirits and oil

cantata *f*, cantata

cantatriz *f*, singer, prima donna

cante *m*, song; singing

cantera *f*, *min* quarry; capacity, talent

cantería *f*, stone-cutting; quarrying; building made of hewn stone

cantidad *f*, quantity; large part; portion; sum of money; quantity (prosody). **c. llovida,** rainfall

cantil *m*, cliff; steep rock

cantimplora *f*, water cooler; canteen (of water); siphon

cantina *f*, wine cellar; canteen; refreshment room

cantinero *m*, sutler; owner of a canteen

canto *m*, singing; song; canto; epic or other poem; end, rim, edge; non-cutting edge (knives, swords); pebble, stone; angle (of a building). *mus* **c. llano,** plainsong. **al c. del gallo,** at cockcrow. **de c.,** on edge

cantón *m*, province, region; corner (of a street); cantonment; *her* canton, quartering

cantonera *f*, corner-piece (books, furniture, etc., as ornament); angle-iron; bracket, small shelf

cantor (-ra) a singing. *n* singer; songbird

cantuja *f*, *Peru* underworld slang

canturía *f*, singing exercise; vocal music; monotonous song; droning; *mus* execution, technique

canturreo, *m*, **canturria** *f*, humming, droning

canturriar *vi inf* to hum, sing under one's breath

caña *f*, stalk; reed; bone of arm or leg; leg (of a trouser, stocking, boot, etc.); marrow; *bot* cane; tumbler, glass; wine measure; gallery (of mine); *pl* mock joust on horseback using **cañas** as spears. **c. de azúcar,** sugar-cane. **c. de pescar,** fishing rod. **c. del timón,** tiller *naut*

cañada *f*, glen, gulch, gully, hollow, ravine, vale, cattle path; *WH* brook, cattle track

cañamazo *m*, hempen canvas; embroidery canvas; embroidered canvas

cáñamo *m*, hemp; *Lat. Am.* marijuana

cañar *m*, canebrake; growth of reeds; fishgarth made of reeds

cañavalera *f*, canefield

cañaveral *m*, cane-brake; *WH* bamboo field

cañazo *m*, blow with a cane

cañería *f*, conduit; pipe; piping

cañero *m*, pipe layer

caño *m*, pipe, tube, sewer; organ pipe; jet (of water); mine gallery

cañón *m*, pipe, cylindrical tube; flue; quill (of birds); cannon; soft down; *arch* shaft (of column); stack (of a chimney). **c. antiaéreo,** A.A. gun. **c. antitanque,** anti-tank gun. **c. de escalera,** well of a staircase; *slang* terrific-looking, absolutely gorgeous (e.g. mujer cañón)

cañonazo *m*, cannon shot; roar of a cannon

cañonería *f*, *mil* group of cannon; *mus* set of organ pipes

cañonero *m*, gunboat

cañuto *m*, *bot* internode; small pipe or tube; *inf* tale-bearer

caoba *f*, *bot* mahogany

caos *m*, chaos; confusion

caótico *a* chaotic

capa *f*, cloak; cape; *ecc* cope; coating; layer; cover; coat (animals); *fig* cloak, disguise; *geol* stratum. **la c. del cielo,** the canopy of heaven. *fig inf* **echar la c. al toro,** to throw one's cap over the windmill. *naut* **estarse** (*or* **ponerse**) **a la c.,** to lie to

capacete *m*, helmet

capacha *f* basket; *Argentina, Chile* clink, jug (jail)

capacidad *f*, capacity; extension, space; mental capacity, talent; opportunity, means; *law* capacity. **c. de compra,** buying power, purchasing power. **c. de producción,** output

capacitación *f*, qualification, (act of) qualifying; (act of) training

capacitar *vt* to capacitate, qualify, enable

capar *vt* to castrate, geld; *inf* diminish, reduce

caparazón *m*, caparison, horse blanket; waterproof cover; hood (of carriages); nosebag; shell (insects, crustaceans)

capataz *m*, foreman, steward; overseer

capaz *a* capacious; large, spacious; capable, competent; *law* able

capcioso *a* deceitful, artful; captious, carping

capear *vt* to steal a cape; play the bull with a cape (bullfighting); *inf* put off with excuses, deceive; *naut* lie to

capellán *m*, chaplain; any ecclesiastic

capeo *m*, playing the bull with a cape (bullfighting)

caperuza *f*, hood, pointed cap; *arch* coping-stone

capigorrón *a inf* loafing. *m*, loafer, idler

capilar *a* capillary

capilla *f*, cowl, hood; chapel; *ecc* chapter; *ecc* choir. **c. ardiente,** chapelle ardente. **estar en c.,** to await execution (criminals); *inf* be in suspense, await anxiously

capillo *m*, baby's bonnet; cocoon of silkworm; flowerbud

capirote *m*, academic hood and cap; hood (falconry); tall pointed cap. **ser tonto de c.,** *inf* to be a complete fool

capitación *f*, poll-tax, capitation

capital *a* relating to the head; capital (sins, etc.); main, principal. *m*, capital, patrimony; *com* capital stock. *f*, capital (city). **c. pagado,** paid-in capital stock

capitalino, -a *Lat. Am. a* of the capital; *n* native of the capital; resident of the capital

capitalismo *m*, capitalism

capitalista *a* capitalistic. *mf* capitalist

capitalización *f*, capitalization

capitalizar *vt* to capitalize

capitán *m*, captain, skipper; chief, leader; ringleader. *aer* **c. de aviación,** group captain. **c. de fragata,** *nav* commander. **c. de puerto,** harbor master. **c. general de ejército,** field-marshal

capitana *f*, admiral's ship; *inf* captain's wife

capitanear *vt* to captain, command; *fig* guide, lead

capitolio *m*, dignified building; *arch* acropolis; Capitol

capitulación *f*, agreement, pact; capitulation; *pl* marriage articles

capitular *a* capitulary, belonging to a Chapter. *m*, capitular, member of a Chapter. *vi* to make an agreement; capitulate; sing prayers; arrange order

capítulo *m*, *ecc* Chapter; meeting of town council, etc.; chapter (of book); item (in a budget); determination, decision

capó *m*, *aut* hood

capón *a* castrated; gelded. *m*, capon; bundle of firewood or vines

caponera *f*, coop for fattening capons; *inf* gaol; *inf* place where one lives well free of charge

capota *f*, *bot* head of teasel; bonnet; hood (of vehicles)

capote *m*, short, brightly colored cape (used by bullfighters); cape coat; (cards) slam; *inf* scowl

capricho *m*, caprice, fancy; strong desire

caprichoso *a* capricious; whimsical

cápsula *f*, cartridge-case; bottlecap; (*bot med chem zool*) capsule

captar *vt* gain, attract (goodwill, attention, etc.); *mech* collect; monitor (foreign broadcasts)

captor *m*, capturer

captura *f*, *law* capture; seizing, arrest

capturar *vt* to capture; arrest, apprehend

capucha *f*, hood; cowl; *print* circumflex accent

capullo *m*, cocoon; flower bud; acorn cup; *anat* prepuce

caqui *m*, khaki; khaki color

cara *f*, face; likeness, aspect; façade; front; surface; side (of metal, etc.); mien. **c. a c.,** face to face; frankly; openly. *inf* **c. de juez,** severe face. *inf* **c. de pascua,** smiling face. *inf* **c. de vinagre,** sour face. **c. o cruz,** heads or tails. **c. o sello** *Argentina, Chile,* heads or tails **de c.,** opposite. **hacer a dos caras,** to be deceitful, be two-faced. **hacer c. (a),** to stand up to

caraba *f*, *slang* 25-centimo coin

carabina *f*, carbine; rifle

caracol *m*, snail; snail's shell; cure; *zool* cochlea; winding stair. **c. marino,** periwinkle. **¡Caracoles!** Fancy!

caracola *f*, conch shell used as a horn

caracolear *vi* to prance from side to side (horses)

carácter m, sign, mark; character, writing (gen. pl); style of writing; brand (animals); nature, temperament; character, individuality, strong-mindedness, energy, firmness; condition, state, capacity. **comedia de c.,** psychological play. **en su c. de,** as in one's capacity as. **caracteres de imprenta,** printing types

característica f, quality, characteristic; math characteristic; actress who plays the part of an old woman

característico a characteristic, distinctive. m, actor who plays roles of old men

caracterización f, characterization; theat make-up

caracterizar vt to characterize; confer an office, honor, dignity, on; theat create a character; vr theat to make up, dress as, a character

¡caramba! interj gosh!; blast!

carámbano m, icicle

carambola f, cannon (billiards); inf double effect; inf trick, deception

caramelo m, caramel; toffee

caramillo m, flageolet; small flute, pipe; gossip, intrigue

carancho m, Argentina vulture; Peru owl

carapacho m, carapace, shell

carátula f, mask; fig dramatic art, the theater

caravana f, caravan, group of traders, pilgrims, etc. (especially in East); inf crowd of excursionists, picnickers, etc.

¡caray! interj blast!; gosh!

carbón m, coal; charcoal; black chalk, crayon. **c. bituminoso,** soft coal. **c. de coque,** coke. **c. de leña,** charcoal. **c. mineral,** coal, anthracite. **mina de c.,** coal-mine

carbonada f, Lat. Am. meat stew

carbonear vt to turn into charcoal; naut coal

carboneo m, coaling

carbonera f, coal-cellar, coal-house, etc.; coal-scuttle; woman who sells charcoal or coal; charcoal burner

carbonería f, coal or charcoal merchant's office

carbonero a relating to coal or charcoal. m, collier; charcoal maker; coal merchant; naut coal ship

carbónico a chem carbonic

carbonizar vt to carbonize

carbono m, chem carbon

carbunco m, med carbuncle

carbúnculo m, carbuncle, ruby

carburador m, carburetor

carcaj m, quiver (for arrows); Mexico rifle case

carcajada f, burst of laughter, guffaw. **reírse a carcajadas,** to roar with laughter

carcajearse vi to guffaw

carcamal m, inf dotard

cárcel f, prison, jail

carcelario a prison, jail

carcelero (-ra) a jail. n jailer

cárcola f, treadle (of a loom)

carcoma f, wood-worm; dry rot; fig gnawing care; spendthrift

carcomer vt to gnaw wood (worms); fig undermine (health, etc.); vr be wormeaten

carda f, card, carding; teasel head; card brush; inf reprimand

cardador (-ra) n carder, comber

cardadura f, carding; carding frame

cardar vt to card, tease; brush up (felt, etc.)

cardenal m, cardinal; cardinal bird; bruise

cárdeno a livid

cardíaco a med cardiac

cardinal a principal; cardinal (point); gram cardinal (number)

cardiógrafo m, med cardiograph

cardiograma m, med cardiogram

cardo m, bot thistle

carear vt to confront; compare; vi turn towards, face; vr meet; come together

carecer vi irr to be short; lack, need (e.g. **Carece de las condiciones necesarias,** It lacks the necessary conditions). See **conocer**

carencia f, shortage, lack

carestía f, shortage, scarcity; famine; dearness, high price

careta f, mask; beekeeper's veil; fencing mask. fig **quitar la c.** (a), to unmask

carey m, zool shell turtle; tortoise-shell

carga f, loading; elec charging, charge; load; burden, weight; cargo; explosive charge; fig imposition; tax; duty, obligation. naut **c. de profundidad,** depth charge

cargadero m, place where goods are loaded or unloaded

cargado a loaded; heavy, sultry; strong (tea, coffee). **c. de cadenas,** (prisoner, etc.) in chains. **c. de espaldas,** round-shouldered

cargador m, loader; porter; dockhand; pitchfork; rammer; mech stoker; elec charger

cargamento m, naut cargo, freight, shipload

cargar vt to load; charge (guns, etc.); stoke; overburden; tax, impose; blame for, charge with; inf annoy, bore; Argentina inf to kid, tease; com charge, book; mil attack; (football) tackle; vi tip, slope; (with con) carry away; be loaded with (fruit); assume responsibility; (with sobre) importune, urge; lean against; vr turn (head, etc.); lower, grow darker (sky); (with de) be abundant (in or with); load oneself with

cargazón f, cargo; loading; heaviness; darkness (of the sky)

cargo m, loading; load, weight; post, office; duty, obligation; management, charge; care; *com* debit; accusation. **com el c. y la data,** debit and credit. **hacerse c. de,** to take charge of; understand; consider carefully. **ser en c. (a),** to be debtor (to)

cargosear vt, Lat. Am. to annoy, pester

cargoso, -a a, Lat. Am. annoying, pestering

cariarse vr to become carious

caribe a Caribbean. *mf* cannibal, savage

caricatura f, caricature

caricaturista mf caricaturist

caricaturizar vt to caricature

caricia f, caress

caridad f, charity; charitableness; alms

caries f, caries

carilargo a *inf* long-faced

carilleno a *inf* plump-faced, round-faced

cariño m, affection; love; caress affectionately (gen. pl); fondness, inclination. **con c.,** affectionately

cariñoso a affectionate; loving; kind

carioca a of Rio de Janeiro; n native of Rio de Janeiro; resident of Rio de Janeiro

carismático a charismatic

caritativo a charitable

cariz m, appearance of the sky; look, face; aspect; *inf* outlook (for a business deal, etc.)

carmen m, country house and garden (Granada); song; poem

carmesí a crimson. m, crimson color; cramoisy

carmín m, red, carmine color; red wild rose-tree and flower

carnada f, bait

carnaje m, salted meat

carnal a carnal; lascivious; materialistic, worldly; related by blood

carnaval m, carnival. **martes de c.,** Shrove Tuesday

carnavalesco a carnival

carne f, flesh; meat; pulpy part of fruit; carnality, la. **c. concentrada,** meat extract. **c. congelada,** frozen meat. **c. de gallina** *fig* gooseflesh. **c. de membrillo,** quince cheese or conserve. **c. y hueso,** *fig* flesh and blood. *inf* **cobrar carnes,** to put on weight. **poner toda la c. en el asador,** *inf* to put all one's eggs in one basket

carné de conductor Argentina driver's license

carnero m, sheep; mutton; mortuary; charnel-house; family burial vault. **c. marino,** zool seal

carnet m, notebook, diary; identity card; membership card, pass. **c. de chófer,** driver's license

carnicería f, butcher's shop; carnage, slaughter

carnicero a carnivorous; inhuman, cruel. m, butcher

carnívoro a carnivorous. m, carnivore

carnosidad f, proud flesh; local fat; fatness

carnoso a a meaty; fleshy; full of marrow; *bot* pulpy, juicy

caro a beloved; expensive; dear. *adv* expensively; dear

carótida f, carotid artery

carpa f, *icht* carp. **c. dorada,** goldfish; Lat. Am. tent; awning

carpanta f, *inf* violent hunger; *Mexico* gang

carpeta f, table or chest cover, doily; writing case; portfolio; docket, letter file

carpetazo, dar vt to shelve (a project, etc.)

carpintear vi to carpenter

carpintería f, carpenter's shop; carpentry

carpintero m, carpenter, joiner; *theat* scene-shifter. **c. de carretas,** wheelwright. **c. de ribera,** shipwright

carraca f, rattle; ratchet-drill

carraspear vi to clear one's throat, cough

carraspera f, *inf* hoarseness

carrera f, run; race; racing; racecourse; *ast* course; high road; route; *mas* layer, course; line, row; *fig* ladder (in stockings, etc.); course; duration (of life); career, profession; conduct; girder. **c. de fondo,** long-distance race. **c. de relevos, c. de equipos,** relay race. **a c. abierta, a c. tendida,** at full speed

carrerista mf racing enthusiast; professional racer

carreta f, long, narrow two-wheeled cart; wagon; tumbril

carretada f, cart-load; *inf* great deal, mass

carretaje m, cartage; carriage, transport

carrete m, spool, reel, bobbin; fishing reel; *elec* coil; *phot* film spool

carretera f, high road; highway

carretería f, number of carts; carting trade; cartwright's yard

carretero m, cartwright; carter, driver

carretilla f, wheelbarrow; hand cart; railway truck; squib. **de c.,** *inf* mechanically, without thought; (with saber, repetir, etc.) by rote

carretón m, truck, trolley; hand cart

carril m, wheel mark; furrow, rut; cart road, narrow road; rail (railways, etc.)

carrillera f, jaw (of some animals); chin strap; *pl* bonnet strings, etc.

carrillo m, cheek; jowl

carriola f, truckle bed; curricle

carro m, cart; cartload; car, chariot; carriage (of a typewriter, etc.); chassis; *ast* Plow, Great Bear; Lat. Am. automobile, auto, car; *mil* **c. blindado,** armored car.

mil **c. de asalto,** tank. **c. de mudanzas,** moving van. **c. de regar,** watercart

carrocería *f*, place where carriages are made, sold, repaired; *aut* coachwork, body shop

carrocha *f*, eggs (of insects)

carromato *m*, road wagon; covered wagon

carroña *f*, putrid flesh, carrion

carroza *f*, elegant coach; state coach; carriage; float (for tableaux, etc.); *naut* awning

carruaje *m*, carriage; any vehicle

carta *f*, letter; charter; royal order; playing card; chart, map. **c. certificada,** registered letter. **c. de amparo,** safe-conduct. **c. de crédito,** *com* letter of credit. **c. de marear,** sea chart. **c. de naturaleza,** naturalization papers. **c. de pésame,** letter of condolence. **c. de venta,** *com* bill of sale. **c. ejecutoria de hidalguía,** letters patent of nobility. **carta-poder,** letter of proxy, proxy. **cartas rusas,** (game of) consequences. **poner las cartas boca arriba,** *fig* to lay one's cards on the table

cartabón *m*, set-square; shoemaker's slide; quadrant

cartaginés (-esa) a and *n* Carthaginian

cartapacio *m*, note-book; schoolbag, satchel; file, batch of papers

cartear *vi* cards to play low; *vr* to correspond by letter

cartel *m*, placard, poster; cartel; pasquinade, lampoon. **fijar carteles,** to placard

cartela *f*, tablet (for writing); slip (of paper, etc.); *arch* console, bracket

cartelera *f*, billboard

cartelero *m*, billpaster, billsticker

carteo *m*, correspondence (by letter)

cartera *f*, pocketbook; wallet; dispatch-case; portfolio; notebook; pocket flap; office of a cabinet minister; *com* shares

cartería *f*, sorting room (in a post-office)

carterista *mf* pickpocket

cartero *m*, mail carrier, postman

Cartesio Descartes

carteta *f*, lansquenet (card game)

cartilaginoso a cartilaginous

cartílago *m*, cartilage

cartilla *f*, first reading book; primer; certificate of ordination; note-book; liturgical calendar. **c. de racionamiento,** ration book

cartógrafo *m*, map maker

cartón *m*, pasteboard, cardboard; *arch* bracket; *art* cartoon, design

cartucho *m*, cartridge; paper cone

cartuja *f*, Carthusian Order or monastery

cartujo *m*, Carthusian monk; *inf* taciturn, reserved man

cartulina *f*, Bristol board, oaktag, pasteboard, card

carúncula *f*, caruncle, comb of cock, etc.

casa *f*, house; home; household; residence, dwelling; family house; *com* firm. **c. consistorial,** town hall. **c. cuna,** crèche. **c. de campo,** country-house. **c. de empeño,** pawnshop. **c. de huéspedes,** boarding house, lodging-house. **c. de los sustos,** haunted house (at amusement park). **c. de moneda,** mint. **c. de socorro,** First Aid Post. **c. de vecindad,** tenement. **c. mala,** house of ill repute. **c. solar** or **c. solariega,** family seat. **en c.,** at home (also sport usage). **poner c.,** to set up house

casaca *f*, dress coat. **volver la c.,** to become a turncoat, change one's allegiance

casación *f*, *law* cassation

casadero a marriageable

casadoro *m*, *Costa Rica* bore

casamiento *m*, marriage; wedding

casar *vt* to marry (of a priest); *law* repeal; *inf* marry off; join; match, harmonize; *vi* and *vr* (*with con*) to get married

casar *m*, group of houses

casca *f*, grape skin; tan (bark); shell, peel, rind

cascabel *m*, small bell (for harness, etc.). **serpiente de c.,** rattlesnake. *inf* **ser un c.,** to be feather-brained

cascabeleo *m*, jingling of bells

cascabillo *m*, husk (of cereals)

cascada *f*, cascade; waterfall

cascadura *f*, cracking, crack

cascajo *m*, gravel, shingle; *inf* broken, old things, junk; nuts

cascanueces *m*, nutcrackers

cascar *vt* to crack, split, break; *inf* beat; *fig inf* break down (of health); *vi inf* talk, chatter

cáscara *f*, shell; peel, rind; bark. *med* **c. sagrada,** cascara

cascarón *m*, eggshell; *arch* vault

cascarrabias *mf inf* spitfire

cascarriento, -a *Argentina* filthy; greasy

casco *m*, cranium; broken fragment of china, glass, etc.; crown of hat; helmet; tree of saddle; bottle; tank, pipe; barrel; *naut* hull; hoof; quarter (of fruit); *pl inf* head. **c. colonial,** sun-helmet. **c. respiratorio,** smoke-helmet

caserío *m*, group of houses; country house

casero a home made; home bred; familiar; *informa; inf* domesticated, home-loving; domestic. *m*, landlord; caretaker; tenant

caserón *m*, large tumbledown house, mansion, hall

caseta *f*, hut; cottage; booth, stall. **c. de baños,** bathing van

casi *adv* almost, nearly. **c. c.,** very nearly

casilla *f*, hut; cabin; lodge; ticket office;

pigeon-hole; *Argentina, Chile* post-office box *aer* **c. del piloto,** cockpit

casillero *m,* file cabinet, filing cabinet; locker (as in a locker room); set of pigeonholes; *sports* scoreboard; *rw* crossing guard

casino *m,* casino; club

caso *m,* happening, event; chance, hazard; occasion, opportunity; case, matter; *(med gram)* case. **en el c. de,** in a position to (e.g. **No estamos en el c. de pagar tanto dinero.** We are in no position to pay so much money). **en tal c.,** in such a case. **en todo c.,** in any case. **no hacer c. de,** to take no notice of. **venir al c.,** to be opportune

caspa *f,* dandruff; scab

casquillo *m,* tip, cap, ferrule; socket; arrow-head; metal cartridge-case

casta *f,* race; caste; breed (animals); kind, species, quality. **de buena c.,** pedigree (e.g. **perros de buena c.,** pedigree dogs)

castaña *f, bot* chestnut; knot, bun (of hair)

castañar *m,* chestnut plantation or grove

castañetear *vi* to play the castanets; snap one's fingers; chatter (of teeth); knock together (of knees)

castaño a chestnut-colored. *m,* chestnut tree; chestnut wood. **c. de Indias,** horse-chestnut tree

castañuela *f,* castanet. **tocar las castañuelas,** to play the castanets

castellano (**-na**) *n* Castilian; Spaniard. *m,* Spanish (language); castellan. *a* Castilian; Spanish

casticismo *m,* purity (of language); Spanish spirit; traditionalism

castidad *f,* chastity

castigador *a* punishing. *m,* punisher; *inf* lady-killer

castigadora *f, inf* man-hunter

castigar *vt* to punish; chastise; chasten, advise; pain, grieve; correct, edit; decrease (expenses); *com* allow a discount

castigo *m,* punishment; emendation, correction

Castilla Castile

castillo *m,* castle; howdah. **c. de naipes,** house of cards. **c. de proa,** *naut* forecastle. **c. fuerte,** fortified castle. *inf* **hacer castillos en el aire,** to build castles in the air or in Spain

castizo a pure-blooded; prolific; pure (of language); typically Spanish; traditional

casto a chaste; pure, unsullied

castor *m, zool* beaver (animal and fur); soft, woollen cloth

castración *f,* castration, gelding

castrar *vt* to castrate, geld; prune; remove honeycomb from hives; weaken

castrense a military

castrista *v* and *mf* Castroite

casual a accidental, casual

casualidad *f,* chance, coincidence. **por c.,** by chance. **ser mucha c. que . . . ,** to be too much of a coincidence that . . .

casucha *f, inf* tumbledown hut

casuista a casuistic. *mf* casuist

cata *f,* tasting; taste, sample; *Lat. Am.* parrot

catabolismo *m,* catabolism

cataclismo *m,* cataclysm

catacumbas *f pl,* catacombs

catador *m,* taster, sampler

catadura *f,* tasting; look, countenance (gen. qualified)

catafalco *m,* catafalque

catalán (**-ana**) a and *n* Catalan, Catalonian. *m,* Catalan (language)

cataléptico a cataleptic

catalogar *vt* to catalogue, list

catálogo *m,* catalogue, list

Cataluña Catalonia

cataplasma *f,* cataplasm

catapulta *f,* catapult

catar *vt* to taste, sample; see, examine; inspect; regard

catarata *f,* cataract, waterfall; *med* cataract (of the eyes)

catarral a catarrhal

catarro *m,* catarrh; common cold

catástrofe *f, lit* tragic climax; catastrophe

catastrófico a catastrophic

catavinos *mf,* professional wine taster; *inf* tippler, tavern haunter

catecismo *m,* catechism

cátedra *f,* university chair; chair in a Spanish **instituto**; professorship; university lecture room; subject taught by professor; reading desk, lectern; *ecc* throne; *ecc* see. **c. del espíritu santo,** pulpit. **c. de San Pedro,** Holy See

catedral *f,* and a cathedral

catedrático (**-ca**) *n* professor

categoría *f, phil* category; class, rank

categórico a categorical, downright

cateo *m, WH* sampling; prospecting; house search (by the police)

catequismo *m,* catechism; question and answer method of teaching

catequista *mf* catechist

catequizar *vt* to catechize; persuade, induce

caterva *f,* crowd, throng; jumble, collection

catéter *m, surg* probe; catheter

catoche *m, Lat. Am.* bad temper

catódico a *elec* cathodic

cátodo *m,* cathode

catolicismo *m,* Catholicism

católico (**-ca**) a universal, catholic; infallible. a and *n* Catholic (by religion)

catorce a fourteen; fourteenth. *m,* number fourteen; fourteenth (of days of month)

catre *m*, camp-bed; truckle-bed; cot

Cáucaso, el the Caucasus

cauce *m*, river or stream bed; ditch, irrigation canal

cauchal *m*, rubber plantation

cauchera *f*, rubber tree

caucho *m*, caoutchouc, rubber; *Lat. Am.* tire

caución *f*, caution, precaution; surety; security

caucional *a* See **libertad**

caudal *m*, wealth, capital; flow, volume (of water); plenty, abundance (e.g. **un c. de conocimientos,** a wealth of knowledge)

caudaloso *a* carrying much water; wealthy; abundant

caudillo *m*, head, leader; chieftain. **el C.,** (title of Francisco Franco)

causa *f*, cause; reason, motive; lawsuit; *law* trial. **c. final,** *phil* final cause. **c. pública,** public welfare. **ser c. bastante para . . . ,** to be reason enough to . . .

causador (**-ra**) *a* a motivating. *n* occasioner, originator

causalidad *f*, causality

causante a causative, causing. *m*, *law* principal; *Mexico* taxpayer

causar *vt* to cause; occasion

causticidad *f*, causticity; mordacity

cáustico *a* burning, caustic; scathing; mordant; *surg* caustic

cautela *f*, caution; astuteness, cunning

cauteloso *a* cautious; cunning

cauterio *m*, cautery

cauterización *f*, cauterization

cauterizar *vt* to cauterize

cautivar *vt* to capture; captivate, charm; attract; *vi* become a prisoner

cautiverio *m*, captivity

cautivo (**-va**) *a* and *n* captive

cauto *a* cautious; prudent; sly

cava *f*, digging (especially vines); wine cellar in royal palaces

cavador (**-ra**) *n* digger, hoer

cavadura *f*, digging, hoeing; sinking (wells)

cavar *vt* to dig, hoe; sink (wells); *vi* hollow; *fig* go deeply into a thing

caverna *f*, cavern, cave; *med* cavity (generally in the lung)

cavernícola a cave. **hombre c.,** caveman

cavernoso *a* cavernous; caverned; *fig* hollow (cough, etc.); deaf

cavidad *f*, cavity; sinus; cell

cavilación *f*, caviling

cavilar *vt* to cavil; criticize

caviloso *a* captious

caza *f*, hunting; hunt, chase; game. *m*, *aer* fighter. **aer c. lanzacohetes,** rocket-launching aircraft. **c. nocturno,** night fighter. *naut* **dar c.,** to pursue

cazaautógrafos *mf*, autograph hunter

cazadero *m*, hunting ground

cazador a hunting. *m*, *mil* chasseur; huntsman

cazadora *f*, huntress; jacket; forage cap

cazafortunas *mf* fortune hunter

cazar *vt* to hunt, chase; *fig inf* run to earth; *fig inf* catch out; *inf* overcome by flattery

cazo *m*, ladle; dipper

cazoleta *f*, small pan; bowl (of pipe, etc.); sword guard; boss of a shield; pan (of a firelock)

cazuela *f*, earthenware cooking dish; stew-pot; part of theater formerly reserved for women; *theat* gallery

cazurro *a inf* unsociable; surly, boorish

ce *f*, name of the letter C. *interj* Look! Chist! **ce por be,** in detail

cebada *f*, barley (plant and grain). **c. perlada,** pearl barley

cebado *a* on the prowl; having tasted human flesh (animal)

cebar *vt* to feed or fatten (animals); fuel, feed (furnace, etc.); prime, charge (firearms, etc.); start up (machines); bait (fish hook); stimulate (passion, etc.); *vi* stick in, penetrate (nails, screws, etc.); *vr* put one's mind to; grow angry. **cebarse en vanas esperanzas,** to nurture vain hopes

cebo *m*, fodder; detonator; encouragement, food; bait

cebolla *f*, onion; onion bulb; any bulbous stem; oil bulb (of lamp). **c. escalonia,** shallot

cebollana *f*, chive

cebollero (**-ra**) *n* onion seller

cebolleta *f*, leek; young onion

cebollino *m*, onion seed; onion bed; chive

cebra *f*, zebra

ceca *f*, mint (for coining money); name of mosque in Cordova. **de C. en Meca,** from pillar to post, hither and thither

cecear *vi* to lisp

ceceo *m*, lisping

cedazo *m*, sieve, strainer

ceder *vt* to cede, give up; transfer; *vi* give in, yield; diminish, decrease (fever, storm, etc.); fail, end; happen, turn out; sag, give, stretch. **No c. la fama a,** to be no less famous than

cedro *m*, cedar tree; cedar wood. **c. dulce,** red cedar

cédula *f*, document, certificate, card. *ecc* **c. de comunión,** Communion card. **c. personal,** identity card. **c. real,** royal letters patent

céfiro *m*, west wind; *poet* zephyr

cegajoso *a* blear-eyed

cegar *vi irr* to become blind; *vt* to put out the eyes; *fig* blind; wall up, close up, stop up; infatuate. *Pres. Ind.* **ciego, ciegas,**

ciega, ciegan. *Pres. Subjunc.* **ciegue, ciegues, ciegue, cieguen**

cegato a *inf* short-sighted

ceguedad, ceguera f, blindness; delusion; ignorance

ceja f, eyebrow; cloud cap; mountain peak; *mus* bridge (of stringed instruments). *fig* **quemarse las cejas,** to burn the midnight oil

cejar *vi* to go backwards; give way, hesitate

cejijunto a having eyebrows that almost meet, beetle-browed

cejo m, river mist

cejudo a having long thick eyebrows

celada f, helmet; ambush; fraud, trick

celador (-ra) a watchful, zealous. *n* supervisor; caretaker; guard (at a museum, etc.)

celaje m, sky with scudding clouds (gen. *pl*); skylight, window; promising sign, presage

celar *vt* to be zealous in discharge of duties; spy upon; watch; oversee, superintend; conceal; engrave

celda f, cell

celebración f, celebration; applause

celebrador (-ra) n celebrator; applauder

celebrante a celebrating. m, *ecc* celebrant

celebrar *vt* to celebrate; applaud; praise; venerate; hold, conduct; **c. que** + *subj,* to be happy that, be glad that. *vt* and *vi ecc* officiate; *vr* take place

célebre a famous

celebridad f, fame, celebrity; magnificence, show, pomp

celeridad f, celerity

celeste a celestial, heavenly

celestial a celestial, heavenly; perfect, delightful; *inf* foolish (ironical)

celestina f, procuress (allusion to *Tragicomedia de Calixto y Melibea*)

celibato m, celibacy; *inf* bachelor

célibe a celibate, unmarried. *mf* unmarried person

celo m, enthusiasm, ardor; religious zeal; devotion; jealousy; heat, rut; *pl* jealousy, suspicion. **dar celos (a),** to make jealous

celosía f, lattice; Venetian blind

celoso a zealous; jealous; suspicious

célula f, cell

celulosa f, cellulose

cementar *vt* to cement

cementerio m, cemetery

cemento m, cement

cena f, evening meal; supper; Last Supper

cenáculo m, cenacle

cenador m, diner out; arbor, pergola

cenagal m, quagmire; *fig* impasse

cenar *vi* to dine, sup; *vt* eat for evening meal, sup off

cenceño a slim, thin

cencerrada f, noisy mock serenade given to widows or widowers on the first night of their new marriage

cencerrear *vi* to jingle; *inf* play out of tune; bang in the wind, rattle; squeak

cencerreo m, jingling; jangle; rattling; squeaking

cencerro m, cow-bell

cendal m, gauze; *ecc* stole; barbs of a feather

cenicero m, ash-pan; ash-pit; ash-tray

ceniciento a ash colored, ashen. **la Cenicienta,** Cinderella

cenit m, *ast* zenith; *fig* peak, summit

ceniza f, ash, cinders

cenotafio m, cenotaph

cenote m, Central America, Mexico cenote (deep natural well or sinkhole)

censo m, census; agreement for settlement of an annuity; annual ground rent; leasehold

censor m, censor; censorious person; *univ* proctor

censual a pertaining to census, annuity, rents

censualista *mf* annuitant

censura f, censorship; criticism; blame, reproach; scandal, gossip; *psy* censorship

censurable a reprehensible; censorable

censurar *vt* to judge; censure; criticize

centauro m, *myth* centaur

centavo m, hundredth part; cent; *Lat. Am.* centavo

centella f, lightning; spark; flash; *fig* spark (of anger, affection, etc.)

centellear *vi* to flash; twinkle; sparkle

centelleo m, scintillation; sparkle; flash

centén m, Spanish gold coin once worth 100 reals and later 25 pesetas

centena f, hundred

centenal, centenar m, hundred; centenary; rye field. **a centenares,** by the hundred, in crowds

centenario (-ia) a centenary. *n* centenarian. m, centenary

centeno m, *bot* rye

centésimo a and m, hundredth

centígrado a centigrade

centigramo m, centigram

centilitro m, centiliter

centímetro m, centimeter. **c. cúbico,** cubic centimeter, milliliter

céntimo a hundredth. m, centime (coin)

centinela *mf mil* sentry, sentinel; person on watch. **estar de c.,** to be on sentry duty; be on guard

central a central; centric. f, head office; central depot; mother house. **c. de fuerza,** power-house. **c. telefónica,** telephone exchange

centralilla, centralita f, local exchange, private exchange

centralización f, centralization

centralizador a centralizing

centralizar vt to centralize

centrar vt to center

céntrico a central, centric; centrally located; downtown

centrífugo a centrifugal

centrípeto a centripetal

centro m, center; headquarters, meeting place, club; center, hub; middle; core (of a rope); fig focus. phys **c. de gravedad,** center of gravity. **c. de mesa,** table center-piece. anat **centro nervioso,** nerve center

Centroamérica f. Central America

centroamericano (-na) a and n Central American

ceñidamente tightly (e.g. un argumento c. organizado, a tightly organized plot)

ceñido a thrifty; wasp-waisted, slender waisted; fitting (of garments)

ceñir vt irr to girdle; surround; shorten, abbreviate; vr be moderate (speech, expenditure, etc.); conform, confine oneself (to). **ceñirse a las reglas,** to abide by the rules. Pres. Ind. **ciño, ciñes, ciñen.** Pres. Part. **ciñendo.** Preterite **ciñó, ciñeron.** Pres. Subjunc. **ciña,** etc. Imperf. Subjunc. **ciñese,** etc.

ceño m, band, hoop; frown; fig dark outlook

ceñudo a frowning

cepillar vt to brush; plane; smooth

cepa f, stump; vine-stock; root (tails, antlers, etc.); fig origin, trunk (of a family); biol strain. **de la más pura c.,** of the best quality

cepillo m, brush; carp plane; poor-box, offertory-box. **c. para los dientes,** toothbrush. **c. para ropa,** clothes-brush. **c. para el suelo,** scrubbing-brush. **c. para las uñas,** nail-brush

cepo m, bough; wooden stocks; snare; trap; poor-box; collecting-box

cera f, beeswax; wax; wax candles, etc., used at a function. inf **ser como una c.,** to be like wax (in the hands of)

cerador m, floor waxer (person)

ceradora f, floor waxer (machine)

cerámica f, ceramics; ceramic art, pottery

cerámico a ceramic

cerbatana f, blow-pipe, popgun; pea-shooter; ear-trumpet

cerca f, fence, wall

cerca adv near. **c. de,** near to; almost, nearly (e.g. **c. de las once,** nearly eleven o'clock)

cercado m, enclosure, fenced in place; fence

cercanía f, nearness, proximity; (gen. pl) outskirts, surroundings

cercano a near, neighboring; impending, early

cercar vt to enclose; build a wall or fence round; to lay siege to; crowd round; mil surround

cercenamiento (a) m, curtailment (of)

cercenar vt to lop off the ends, clip; curtail, diminish; abridge; whittle

cerciorar vt to assure, confirm; vr make sure

cerco m, ring, hoop; fence; siege; small conversational circle; spin, circling; halo (sun, moon); frame; sash (of a window). **poner c. (a),** to lay siege to, blockade

cerda f, sow; bristle

Cerdeña Sardinia

cerdo m, pig, hog

cereal a and m, cereal

cerebelo m, anat cerebellum

cerebro m, cerebrum; brain; intelligence

ceremonia f, ceremony; function, display; formality. **de c.,** ceremonial; formally. **por c.,** for politeness' sake

ceremonial a ceremonial. m, ceremony; rite; protocol (rules of behavior)

ceremonioso a ceremonious; formal, over-courteous

cereza f, cherry

cerezal m, cherry orchard

cerezo m, cherry tree; cherry wood

cerilla f, wax taper; match; ear wax

cerillo m, Mexico match

cerner vt irr to sieve; watch, observe; fig sift, clarify; vi bolt (of plants); drizzle; vr waddle; hover; threaten (of evil, etc.). Pres. Ind. **cierno, ciernes, cierne, ciernen.** Pres. Subjunc. **cierna, ciernas, cierna, ciernan**

cernidillo m, drizzle; teetering walk

cernido m, sifting, sieving; sifted flour

cerniduras f pl, siftings

cero m, math zero; naught; (tennis) love. fig inf **ser un c.,** to be a mere cipher

cerote m, cobbler's wax. inf fear

cerquita adv very near, hard by

cerradero, m, **cerradera,** f, bolt staple; catch of a lock; clasp or strings of a purse

cerradizo a closable, lockable

cerrado a closed; compact; incomprehensible, obscure; overcast, cloudy; inf taciturn; secretive. m, enclosure

cerradura f, fastening, lock; closing, locking

cerraja f, lock (of a door); bolt

cerrajería f, locksmith's craft; locksmith's workshop or shop

cerrajero m, locksmith

cerramiento m, closing, locking up; fence; enclosure, shooting preserve; partition wall

cerrar vt irr to close; lock, fasten, bolt; shut up; mech shut off, turn off; fold up; block or stop up; seal (letters, etc.); close down; terminate; obstruct; (with con) attack; vi close; close in (of night, etc.); vr heal up (wounds); close (flowers); *rad* close down; crowd together; *fig* stand firm. *inf* **cerrarse la espuela,** to take a nightcap, have a last drink. **c. la marcha,** to bring up the rear. **al c. la edición,** stop press. See **acertar**

cerrazón *f*, dark, overcast sky heralding a storm

cerril a rough, rocky; wild, untamed (cattle, horses); *inf* boorish

cerro *m*, neck of an animal; spine, backbone; hill. *fig* **irse por los cerros de Úbeda,** to go off the track, indulge in irrelevancies

cerrojo *m*, bolt (of a door, etc.); lock (of a door, gun, etc.)

certamen *m*, contest; competition; match

certero a well-aimed; sure, well-timed; knowledgeable, sure

certeza, certidumbre *f*, certitude, assurance

certificación *f*, certification; certificate; affidavit

certificado a certified; registered. *m*, registered letter; certificate

certificar *vt* to certify; register (letter, etc.)

certificatorio a certifying or serving to certify

certísimo a learned form of the superlative of **cierto** (see **certísimo**)

certitud *f*, certitude

cervantino a Cervantine

cervecería *f*, brewery; ale-house

cervecero (-ra) *n* brewer; beer seller

cerveza *f*, beer, ale. **c. negra,** stout

cerviz *f*, cervix, nape (of neck). **doblar** (*or* **bajar**) **la c.,** to humble oneself

cesación *f*, cessation, stopping

cesante a dismissed; pensioned off. **declarar c.** (**a**)**,** to dismiss (a person from a post). **estar c.,** to be out of a job

cesantía *f*, status of dismissed or retired official; retirement pension

cesar *vi* to cease, stop, end; leave an employment; desist; retire

cesáreo a Cesarean; imperial

cese *m*, stopping of payment for an employment

cesión *f*, cession; transfer; resignation; *law* release

césped *m*, grass, sward; sod, lawn

cesta *f*, basket, hamper; *sport* racket; cradle (for a wine bottle)

cestada *f*, basketful

cestería *f*, basketmaking, basketweaving; basket factory; basket shop; basketwork

cestero (-ra) *n* basket maker or seller

cesto *m*, basket, hamper, skip

cesura *f*, cesura

cetrino a greenish-yellow; sallow; citrine; melancholy; reserved, aloof

cetro *m*, scepter; verge; reign

chabacanería *f*, bad taste; vulgarity

chabacano a vulgar, common; rude, uncouth

chacal *m*, *zool* jackal

cháchara *f*, *inf* empty chatter; verbiage

chacharear *vi* to chatter; gabble, cackle

chacharero a *inf* chattering; talkative

chacolotear *vi* to clatter, clink (loose horseshoe)

chacota *f*, merriment, mirth

chacotear *vi inf* to be merry, have fun

chacotón a of a boisterous humor

chacra *f*, *Lat. Am.* small farm, small holding

chafado a taken aback; disappointed

chafallar *vt inf* to mend carelessly, botch

chafar *vt* to flatten; crumple, crease (clothes); *inf* heckle

chagüe *m*, *Central America* bog, marsh, swamp

chal *m*, shawl

chalanear *vt* to bargain; indulge in sharp practice

chalar *vt* to drive mad; enamour

chaleco *m*, waistcoat; cardigan

chalequear *vt*, *Mexico* to pilfer, swipe

Chalo pet form of the male given name *Carlos* 'Charles', hence = English *Chuck, Bud, Mac* (in direct address to a male whose name one does not know)

chalote *m*, shallot

chalupa *f*, shallop; launch; canoe; long boat, ship's boat

chamar *vt inf* to palm off, barter

chamarasca *f*, brushwood, tinder

chamarilero (-ra) *n* secondhand dealer

chamarreta *f*, sheepskin jacket; *Mexico* jacket

chambón a *inf* awkward, clumsy; lucky

chambonada *f*, *inf* blunder; fluke, chance

chambra *f*, dressing-jacket, peignoir, negligee

chamicera *f*, piece of scorched earth (woodland, etc.)

chamorro a close-cropped, shorn (hair)

champán *m*, champagne. **c. obrero,** *humorous* cider

champaña *m*, champagne

champar *vt inf* to cast in a person's face, remind

champú *m*, shampoo

chamuscar *vt* to scorch; singe

chanada *f*, *inf* trick, mischievous act

chancaca *f*, *Lat. Am.* syrup cake

chancada *f*, *Lat. Am.* dirty trick

chancearse *vr* to joke

chancero a joking, facetious

chancho, -a *mf*, *Lat. Am.* pig

chanchollada *f*, dirty trick, foul play, trick

chanchullo *m*, *inf* fraud

chanciller *m*, chancellor

chancillería *f*, chancery

chancla *f*, down at heel shoe; heelless slipper

chancleta *f*, heelless slipper, babouche. *mf inf* ninny

chanclo *m*, overshoe; Wellington

chanfaina *f*, *cul* savory fricassee

chanflón a tough, coarse; ungainly

changador *m*. *Argentina* porter

chantaje *m*, blackmail

chantajista *mf* blackmailer

chantar *vt* to put on, clothe; *inf* tell plainly. *inf* **c. sus verdades,** to tell hometruths

chanza *f*, joke, jest

¡chao! *Argentina, Chile* bye!

chapa *f*, plate, sheet; veneer; clasp; *inf* prudence, common sense; rouge. **c. de hierro,** sheet-iron. **c. de identidad,** number plate

chapado a la antigua a old-fashioned

chapalear *vi* to dabble in water; splash; clatter (of a horseshoe)

chapaleo *m*, dabbling, paddling; splash; clattering, clink (of a horseshoe)

chapaleteo *m*, lapping of water; splashing (of rain)

chaparrear *vi* to pour with rain

chaparrón *m*, heavy shower of rain, downpour

chapear *vt* to veneer; *vi* clatter (loose horseshoe)

chaperón *m*, hood

chapeta *f*, *dim* clasp; red flush or spot on cheek

chapetón (-ona) *n* WH recently arrived European, especially Spaniard

chapino a and *m*, *Mexico contemptuous* Guatemalan

chapodar *vt* to prune, lóp off branches; cut down, reduce

chapotear *vt* to sponge, moisten, damp; *vi* paddle, splash; dabble or trail the hands (in water)

chapoteo *m*, moistening, sponging; paddling, splashing; dabbling

chapucear *vt* to botch, do badly; bungle

chapuceramente *adv* awkwardly. **hablar el japonés c.,** to speak broken Japanese

chapucería *f*, roughness, poor workmanship; botch

chapucero a rough, badly finished; bungling, clumsy, awkward

chapurrado a broken (e.g. **hablar un italiano c.,** to speak broken Italian)

chapurrar, chapurrear *vt* to speak badly (a language); jabber; *inf* mix (drinks)

chapuz *m*, ducking, submerging; plunge; unimportant job; clumsiness

chapuzar *vt* to duck, submerge; plunge

chaqueta *f*, jacket; *mech* casing

chaquetilla *f*, short jacket; coatee; blazer

chaquetón *m*, short coat. **c. de piloto,** aer pea-jacket

charamusca *f*, *Lat. Am.* firewood, kindling

charca *f*, pond, pool; reservoir

charco *m*, puddle; *inf* sea

charla *f*, *inf* chatter; conversation; talk, informal lecture

charlar *vi inf* to prattle, chatter; chat, converse; give a talk (on)

charlatán (-ana) a loquacious, garrulous; indiscreet; fraudulent, false. *n* charlatan; chatterer

charlatanería *f*, loquacity, garrulity; quackery

charlatanismo *m*, charlatanism, quackery

charnela *f*, hinge; hinged joint

charol *m*, japan, varnish; patent leather

charolar *vt* to japan, varnish

charpa *f*, pistol-belt; sling

charrán (-ana) *n* rogue, trickster

charranada *f*, roguery, knavery

charrería *f*, tawdriness; gaudiness

charro a churlish, coarse; flashy, tawdry

chasca *f*, brushwood, firewood

chascar *vi* to creak, crack; clack (the tongue); swallow

chascarrillo *m*, *inf* amusing anecdote, good story

chasco *m*, trick, practical joke; disappointment. **llevarse un c.,** to meet with a disappointment

chasis *m*, *aut* chassis; *phot* plate-holder; *mech* underframe

chasquear *vt* to play a trick on; wag (one's tongue); crack (a whip, one's knuckles); break a promise, disappoint; *vi* creak, crack; meet with a disappointment

chasquido *m*, crack (of whip); creaking (of wood); click (of the tongue)

chatarra *f*, scrap iron; junk

chato a flat-nosed; flat

chauvinismo *m*, chauvinism

chaval a *inf* young. *m*, lad

chaveta *f*, *mech* bolt, pin, peg, cotter, key

checo (-ca) a and *n* Czech. Czech (language)

Chejov Chekov

Chengis-Jan Genghis Khan

chepa *f*, *inf* hunch (back); hump

cheque *m*, check. **c. cruzado,** crossed check

chica *f*, girl; *inf* dear

chicana *f*, chicanery

chicano (-na) a and *n* Chicano, American of Mexican ancestry

chicha *f*, *Lat. Am.* corn liquor

chícharo *m*, pea

chicharrón *m, cul* crackling; burnt meat; *inf* sunburnt person

chichón *m,* bruise, bump

chichonera *f,* child's protective hat (something like a straw crash-helmet)

chicle *m,* chewing gum

chico a little, small; young. *m,* little boy; youth; *inf* old boy, dear. **Es un buen c.,** He's a good fellow

chicoleo *m, inf* compliment

chicote *mf* sturdy child. *m, inf* cigar; *Lat. Am.* whip

chifla *f,* whistling, whistle; tanner's paring knife

chiflado a *inf* cracked, daft; crack-brained

chifladura *f,* whistling; *inf* whim, mania, hobby

chiflar *vi* to whistle; *vt* to make fun of, hiss; pare or scrape leather; *inf* swill, tipple; *vr inf* have a slate loose; be slightly mad; *inf* lose one's head over, adore

chifle *m,* whistle, whistling; decoy call (birds)

chiflón *m, Lat. Am.* draft (of air)

chile *m, bot* red pepper, chilli

chileno (**-na**) a and *n* Chilean

chilla *f, Argentina* fox

chillador a screaming, shrieking

chillar *vi* to scream, shriek; creak; squeak; jabber (monkeys, etc.); *art* be strident (of colors)

chillería *f,* shrieking, screaming

chillido *m,* scream, shriek; squeak (of mice, etc.); jabber (of monkeys, etc.)

chillón a *inf* screaming, yelling; strident, piercing; crude, loud (colors)

chimenea *f,* chimney; funnel; fireplace; kitchen range

chimpancé *m,* chimpanzee

china *f,* pebble; porcelain, china; Chinese silk

chinche *f,* bedbug; thumbtack, drawing-pin. *mf inf* bore

chinchona *f,* quinine

chinchorrería *f, inf* impertinence, tediousness; gossip

chinero *m,* china cupboard

chingana *f, Lat. Am.* bar

chino (**-na**) a and *n* Chinese. *m,* Chinese (language)

Chipre Cyprus

chiquillada *f,* childishness, puerility

chiquillería *f, inf* crowd of children

chiquillo (**-lla**) *n* small boy

chiquito (**-ta**) a *dim* **chico,** tiny, very small. *n* little one, small boy

chiripa *f,* (billiards) fluke; *inf* happy coincidence, stroke of luck; lucky guess

chirlar *vi inf* to gabble, talk loudly

chirlo *m,* knife wound, sabre cut; knife scar

chirona *f, inf* jail

chirriador a sizzling, crackling; creaking, squeaking

chirriar *vi* to sizzle, crackle; creak, squeak; squawk; *inf* croak, sing out of tune

chirrido *m,* squawk; croaking; noise of grasshoppers; squeaking; creaking, creak

¡chis! *interj* Shh! Silence!

chisme *m,* gossip, tale; *inf* small household utensil, trifle

chismear *vt* to tell tales, gossip

chismero (**-ra**), **chismoso** (**-sa**) a gossiping, talebearing. *n* gossip, tale bearer

chispa *f,* spark; ember; *elec* spark; tiny diamond; small particle; wit; quickwittedness; *inf* drunkenness. **c. del encendido,** ignition spark

chispazo *m,* flying out of a spark, sparking; damage done by spark; *inf* gossip, rumor

chispeante a sparking; sparkling; *fig* scintillating (with wit etc.)

chispear *vi* to throw out sparks, spark; sparkle, gleam; *fig* scintillate; drizzle gently

chisporrotear *vi inf* to sputter; fizz

chisposo a sputtering, throwing out sparks

chistar *vi* to speak, break silence (gen. used negatively)

chiste *m,* witticism, bon mot; amusing incident; joke

chistera *f,* creel (for fish); *inf* top-hat, tile

chistoso a joking; amusing, funny

chiticallando *adv* quietly, stealthily; *inf* on the quiet, in secret

¡chito! ¡chitón! *interj* Hush! Sh!

chiva *f, Colombia, Panama* bus; *Venezuela* beard, goatee; **chivas** *f, Venezuela* hand-me-downs

chivo *n zool* kid. **c. expiatorio,** scapegoat

chocante a colliding; provoking; shocking; surprising

chocar *vi* to collide; strike (against); run into; fight, clash; *vt* clink (glasses); provoke, annoy; surprise, shock. **¡Choca cinco!** Clasp five!, Gimme five!, Put it there!, Give some skin! (invitation to shake hands)

chocarrería *f,* coarse joke

chochear *vi* to be senile; *fig inf* dote (on)

chocho a senile; *fig inf* doting

choco *m,* small hump, hunchback

chocolate *m,* chocolate; drinking chocolate. **c. a la española,** thick chocolate. **c. a la francesa,** French drinking chocolate

chófer *m,* chauffeur; driver

chompa *f, Lat. Am.* jumper, pullover

chonta *f, Lat. Am.* palm tree

choque *m,* collision; shock; jar; *med* concussion; fight; clink (of glasses); clash; *mil* skirmish

choricera *f*, sausage-making machine

choricero (-ra) *n* sausage maker

chorizo *m*, kind of pork sausage; counterweight

chorrear *vi* to spout, jet; drip; *fig inf* trickle, arrive slowly

chorreo *m*, drip, dripping; spouting, gushing

chorrera *f*, spout; drip; jabot, lace front

chorro *m*, jet; stream (of water, etc.); *fig* shower. **a chorros**, in a stream; in abundance, plentifully

choza *f*, hut, cabin; cottage

chubasco *m*, squall, downpour; storm; transitory misfortune

chuchería *f*, gewgaw, trinket; savory tidbit; snaring, trapping

chucruta *f*, sauerkraut

chueca *f*, round head of a bone; small ball; game like shinty; *inf* practical joke

chueco *a Mexico* bent, crooked, twisted

chufa *f*, *bot* chufa; *inf* joke, trick

chufería *f*, place where drink made of **chufas** is sold

chufla *f*, flippant remark

chufleta *f*, *inf* joke; taunt

chulada *f*, mean trick, base action; drollery

chulería *f*, drollness; attractive personality

chuleta *f*, *cul* cutlet, chop; mutton-chop; *inf* slap

chulo *a* droll, amusing; attractive. *m*, slaughterhouse worker; bullfighter's assistant; pimp; rogue

chumbera *f*, prickly pear; Indian fig

chupada *f*, sucking; suck; suction

chupado de cara, c. de mofletes *a* lantern-jawed

chupador *a* sucking. *m*, baby's comforter or dummy

chupar *vt* to suck; absorb (of plants); *fig inf* drain, rob; *vr* grow thin. **chuparse los dedos**, *inf* to lick one's lips; be delighted

churdón *m*, raspberry cane; raspberry; raspberry vinegar

churrigueresco *a* Churrigueresque

churro *a* coarse (of wool). *m*, *cul* a kind of fritter eaten with chocolate, coffee, etc.

churumbela *f*, *mus* pipe; reed for drinking mate *WH*

chusma *f*, galley hands, crew; rabble, mob

chuzón *a* wily, suspicious, cunning

cianuro *m*, cyanide

ciar *vi* to go backwards; *naut* row backwards; *fig* make no headway (negotiations)

ciática *f*, sciatica

ciático *a* sciatic

cicatero *a* avaricious, niggardly, mean

cicatriz *f*, cicatrice; *fig* scar, mark, impression

cicatrizar *vt* to cicatrize, heal; *vr* scar over

cíclico *a* cyclic, cyclical

ciclismo *m*, bicycling

ciclista *mf* cyclist

ciclo *m*, cycle (of time). **c. artúrico, c. de Artús**, Arthurian Cycle. **c. de conferencias**, series of lectures

ciclón *m*, cyclone

ciclópeo *a* cyclopean

cicuta *f*, hemlock

cidra *f*, citron

cidro *m*, citron tree

ciego *a* blind; dazed, blinded; choked up. *m*, blind man; *anat* cæcum. **a ciegas**, blindly; heedlessly

cielo *m*, sky, firmament; atmosphere; climate; paradise; Providence; bliss, glory; roof, canopy; *inf* darling. **a c. abierto**, in the open air. **parecer un c.**, to be heavenly

ciempiés *m*, centipede

cien *a abb.* **ciento**, hundred. Used always before substantives (e.g. **c. hombres**, 100 men)

ciénaga *f*, swamp; morass

ciencia *f*, science; knowledge; erudition, ability. **ciencias naturales**, natural science. **a c. cierta**, for certain, without doubt (gen. with *saber*)

cieno *m*, slime, mud; silt

científico *a* scientific. *m*, scientist

ciento (cf. **cien**) a hundred; hundredth. *m*, hundred. **por c.**, per cent.

cierne, en c. in flower; *fig* in the early stages, in embryo

cierre *m*, closing, shutting; closing time of shops, etc.; fastening; fastener; clasp (of a necklace, handbag, etc.). **c. cremallera**, zip fastener. **c. metálico**, doorshutter

ciertamente *adv* certainly; undoubtedly; indeed

cierto *a* certain, sure; true; particular (e.g. **c. hombre**, a certain man (note no *def. art.*)). **un c. sabor**, a special flavor. **una cosa cierta**, something certain. **no, por c.**, no, certainly not. **por c.**, truly, indeed

cierva *f*, hind

ciervo *m*, stag. **c. volante**, stagbeetle

cifra *f*, number; figure; sum total; cipher, code; monogram; abbreviation

cifrar *vt* to write in cipher; summarize, abridge; (*with en*) be dependent on; depend on

cigarra *f*, *ent* cicada, harvest fly

cigarral *m*, (Toledo) countryhouse and garden or orchard

cigarrera *f*, woman who makes or sells cigars; cigar-cabinet; cigar-case

cigarrería *f*, *Lat. Am.* tobacco shop

cigarrillo *m*, cigarette

cigarro *m*, cigar; *Lat. Am.* cigarette

cigüeña *f*, *orn* stork; *mech* crank

cilindrero *m*, organ grinder

cilíndrico *a* cylindrical

cilindro *m*, cylinder; roller

cima *f*, summit; top of trees; apex; *arch* coping; head (thistle, etc.); *fig* aim, goal, end

cimbalero (-ra) *n* cymbalist

címbalo *m*, cymbal

cimborrio *m*, *arch* cupola; cimborium

cimbrar, cimbrear *vt* to bend; brandish; *vr* sway (in walking)

cimbreño *a* graceful, lithe, willowy

cimbreo *m*, swaying, bending

cimbrón *m*, Lat. Am. vibration

cimentar *vt irr* to lay foundations; refine (gold, metals, etc.); found; *fig* ground (in virtue, etc.). See **acertar**

cimera *f*, crest of helmet

cimiento *m*, foundation (of a building); bottom; groundwork; origin, base. **abrir los cimientos,** to lay the foundations

cinc *m*, zinc

cincel *m*, chisel; burin, engraver

cincelador (-ra) *n* engraver; chiseler

cincelar *vt* to chisel; carve; engrave

cincha *f*, girth of a saddle

cincho *m*, belt, girdle; iron hoop

cinco *a* and *m*, five; fifth. **a las c.,** at five o'clock

cincuenta *a* and *m*, fifty; fiftieth

cincuentavo *a* fiftieth

cincuentenario *m*, fiftieth anniversary

cincuentón (-ona) *a* and *n* fifty years old (person)

cine, cinema *m*, cinema, movies. **c. sonoro,** sound film

cinemática *f*, *phys* kinematics

cinematografía *f*, cinematography

cinematográfico *a* cinematographic

cinematógrafo *m*, cinematograph; cinema

cínico *a* cynical; impudent; untidy. *m*, cynic

cinismo *m*, cynicism

cinta *f*, ribbon; tape; strip; film (cinematograph). **c. métrica,** tape-measure

cintillo *m*, hatband; small ring set with gems

cinto *m*, belt, girdle. **c. de pistolas,** pistol-belt

cintoteca *f*, tape library

cintura *f*, waist; belt, girdle

cinturón *m*, large waist; belt girdle; sword-belt; that which encircles or surrounds. **c. de seguridad,** seat belt

ciprés *m*, *bot* cypress tree or wood

circo *m*, circus; amphitheater

circón *m*, zircon

circuir *vt. irr* to surround, encircle. See **huir**

circuito *m*, periphery; contour; (*elec phys*) circuit. **corto c.,** short circuit

circulación *f*, circulation; traffic. **c. de la sangre,** circulation of the blood. **calle de gran c.,** busy street

circular *a* circular. *f*, circular. *vt* to pass round; *vi* circle; circulate; move in a circle; move about; run, travel (traffic)

circulatorio *a* circulatory

círculo *m*, circle; circumference; circuit; casino, social club

circuncidar *vt* to circumcise; modify, reduce

circuncisión *f*, circumcision

circunciso *a* circumcised

circundar *vt* to surround

circunferencia *f*, circumference

circunflejo *a* circumflex. **acento c.,** circumflex accent

circunnavegación *f*, circumnavigation

circunnavegar *vt* to circumnavigate

circunscribir *vt* to circumscribe. *Past Part.* **circunscrito**

circunscripción *f*, circumscription

circunspección *f*, circumspection; seriousness, dignity

circunspecto *a* circumspect; serious, dignified

circunstancia *f*, circumstance; incident, detail; condition. **c. agravante,** aggravating circumstance. **c. atenuante,** extenuating circumstance. **bajo las circunstancias,** in the circumstances. **de circunstancias,** occasional (e.g. **poesías de circunstancias,** occasional verse). **estar al nivel de las circunstancias,** to rise to the occasion

circunstanciado *a* circumstantiated, detailed

circunstancial *a* circumstantial; occasional (e.g. **poesías circunstanciales,** occasional verse)

circunstante *a* surrounding; present. *mf* person present, bystander

circunvecino *a* adjacent, neighboring

cirial *m*, processional candlestick

cirio *m*, wax candle

cirrosis *f*, cirrhosis

ciruela *f*, plum; prune. **c. claudia, c. veidal,** greengage. **c. damascena,** damson

ciruelo *m*, plum tree

cirugía *f*, surgery

cirujano *m*, surgeon

cisma *m*, or *f*, schism; disagreement, discord. **el C. de Occidente,** the Western Schism

cismático *a* schismatic; discordant, inharmonious

cisne *m*, swan

cisterna *f*, water-tank, cistern

cístico *a* cystic

cita *f*, appointment; quotation, citation

citación *f*, quotation; *law* summons

citar *vt* to make an appointment; cite,

quote; *law* summon. **c. en comparecencia,** to summon to appear in court

cítara *f. mus* zither

citatorio *m,* summons

citerior a hither, nearer

cítrico a citric

ciudad *f,* city; municipal body. **la c. señorial,** the Aristocratic City (Ponce, Puerto Rico)

ciudadanía *f,* citizenship

ciudadano (-na) a city; civic, born in or belonging to a city. *n* citizen; burgess; bourgeois. **c. de honor,** freeman (of a city)

ciudadela *f,* citadel

cívico a civic; patriotic; *Lat. Am.* police officer

civicultura *f,* raising of civets

civil a civil; civilian; polite

civilidad *f,* politeness, civility

civilización *f,* civilization

civilizador a civilizing

civilizar *vt* to civilize; educate; *vr* grow civilized; be educated

civismo *m,* civism; patriotism; civics

cizalla *f,* shears, shearing machine; metal filings

cizaña *f, bot* darnel, tare; vice, evil; dissension, discord (gen. with *meter* and *sembrar*)

clamar *vi* to cry out; *fig* demand (of inanimate things); vociferate; speak solemnly

clamor *m,* outcry, shouting; shriek, complaint; knell, tolling of bells

clamorear *vt* to implore, clamor (for); *vi* toll (of bells)

clamoroso a noisy, clamorous

clandestino a clandestine, secret

clara *f,* white of egg; bald patch (in fur); *inf* fair interval on a rainy day

claraboya *f,* skylight; *arch* clerestory

clarear *vt* to clear; give light to; *vi* to dawn; grow light; *vr* be transparent; *inf* reveal secrets unwittingly

clarete *m,* claret (wine); claret color. a claret; claret-colored

claridad *f,* clearness; transparency; lightness, brightness; distinctness; clarity; good reputation, renown; plain truth, home truth (gen. *pl*)

clarificación *f,* clarification; purifying, refining

clarificar *vt* to illuminate; clarify, purify; refine (sugar, etc.)

clarín *m,* bugle; clarion; organ stop; bugler

clarinete *m,* clarinet; clarinet player

clarión *m,* white chalk, crayon

clarividencia *f,* perspicuity, clear-sightedness

clarividente a perspicacious, clear-sighted

claro a clear; light, bright; distinct; pure, clean; transparent, translucent; light (of colors); easily understood; evident, obvious; frank; cloudless; shrewd, quick-thinking; famous. *m,* skylight; space between words; break in a speech; space in procession, etc.; *art* (gen. *pl*) high lights. *interj* **¡C.!** or **¡C. está!** Of course! **a las claras,** openly, frankly

claroscuro *m,* chiaroscuro; monochrome

clase *f,* class, group; kind, sort, quality; class (school, university); lecture room; lecture, lesson; order, family. **c. dirigente,** ruling class. **c. media,** middle class. **c. social,** social class

clasicismo *m,* classicism

clasicista a and *mf* classicist

clásico a classic; notable; classical. *m,* classic

clasificación *f,* classification

clasificador (-ra) *n* classifier. **c. de billetes,** ticket-punch

clasificar *vt* to classify, arrange. **c. correspondencia,** to file letters

claudicación *f,* limping; negligence; hesitancy, weakness; backing down

claudicar *vi* to limp; be negligent; hesitate, give way

claustro *m,* cloister; council, faculty, senate (of university); monastic rule

claustrofobia *f,* claustrophobia

cláusula *f,* clause. **c. de negación implícita,** contrary-to-fact clause. **c. principal,** main clause. **c. subordinada,** dependent clause, subordinate clause. **c. sustantiva,** noun clause

clausura *f,* sanctum of convent; claustration; solemn ending ceremony of tribunal, etc. **la vida de c.,** monastic or conventual life

clava *f,* club, truncheon; *naut* scupper

clavadizo a nail-studded (doors, etc.)

clavar *vt* to nail; fasten with nails; pierce, prick; set gems (jeweler); spike (cannon, gum); *fig* fix (eyes, attention, etc.); *inf* cheat

clave *m,* clavichord. *f,* code, key; *mus* clef; *arch* keystone; plug (telephones); **c. (de),** key to. *mus* **c. de sol,** treble clef

clavel *m, bot* carnation plant and flower

clavetear *vt* to stud with nails; *fig* round off (business affairs)

clavicordio *m,* clavichord

clavícula *f,* clavicle

clavija *f,* peg, pin; plug; peg of stringed instrument; axle-pin

clavo *m,* nail, spike, peg; corn (on foot); anguish. **c. de especia,** clove. **c. de herradura,** hob-nail

clemencia *f,* mildness; clemency; mercy

clemente a mild; clement; merciful

cleptomanía *f,* kleptomania

cleptómano (-na) a and *n* kleptomaniac

clerecía *f,* clergy

clerical a belonging to the clergy; clerical

clericalismo m, clericalism

clérigo m, cleric, clergyman; clerk (in Middle Ages)

clero m, clergy

cliente mf client, customer; protégé, ward

clientela f, patronage, protection; clientele

clima m, climate, clime

clímax m, climax

clínica f, clinic, nursing home; department of medicine or surgery

clínico a clinical

cloaca f, sewer, drain; zool cloaca

cloquear vi to go broody (hen); cluck

cloqueo m, cluck, clucking

clorato m, chlorate

cloro m, chlorine

cloroformizar vt to chloroform

cloroformo m, chloroform

club m, club

clueca f, broody hen

clueco a broody (hens); inf doddering

C.N.T. initialism of Confederación Nacional de Trabajo

coacción f, coercion

coactivo a coercive

coadjutor m, co-worker, assistant

coadunar vt to join or mingle together

coagulación f, coagulation

coagular vt to coagulate; clot; curdle

coágulo m, clot; coagulation; congealed blood

coalición f, coalition

coartada f, alibi. **probar la c.,** to prove an alibi

coartar vt to limit, restrict

cobarde a cowardly; irresolute. m, coward

cobardía f, cowardice

cobayo m, guinea-pig

cobertera f, lid, cover

cobertizo m, overhanging roof; shack, shed, hut. **c. de aeroplanos,** aer hangar

cobertura f, covering; coverlet; wrapping

cobija f, imbrex tile; cover; Lat. Am. blanket

cobijar vt to cover; shelter

cobra f, zool cobra; rope or thong for yoking oxen; retrieval (of game)

cobradero a that which can be collected, recoverable

cobrador m, collector, receiver. a collecting. **c. de tranvía,** tram conductor

cobranza f, receiving, collecting; collection of fruit or money

cobrar vt to collect (what is owed); charge; earn; regain, recover; feel, experience (emotions); wind, pull in (ropes, etc.); gain, acquire; retrieve (game); vr recuperate. **c. ánimo,** to take courage. **c.**

cariño (a), to grow fond of. **c. fuerzas,** to gather strength. **c. importancia,** to gain importance. **¿Cuánto cobra Vd.?** How much do you charge?; How much do you earn?

cobre m, min copper; copper kitchen utensils; pl mus brass; Lat. Am. (copper) cent, centavo

cobrizo a containing copper; copper-colored

cocacolonizar vt (United States) to gain economic control of . . . and introduce into its pop culture

cocacolonización f, economic domination by the United States and introduction of its pop culture

cocaína f, cocaine

coceador a inclined to kick; kicking (animals)

coceadura f, kicking

cocear vi to kick; inf kick against, oppose

cocedero a easily cooked

cocer vt. irr to boil; cook; bake (bricks, etc.); digest; surg suppurate; vi boil (of a liquid); ferment; vr suffer pain or inconvenience over a long period. Pres. Ind. **cuezo, cueces, cuece, cuecen.** Pres. Subjunc. **cueza, cuezas, cueza, cuezan**

cochayuyo m, Lat. Am. edible seaweed

coche m, carriage, car. **c. camas,** sleeping car. **c. -camioneta,** station wagon. **c. cerrado,** aut sedan. **c. de muchos caballos,** high-powered car. **c. de plaza,** hackney-carriage. **c. fúnebre,** hearse. **c. -línea,** intercity bus. f, Ecuador puddle

cochera f, coach house; tramway depot

cochero m, coachman; driver. a easily cooked

cochina f, sow

cochinería f, inf filthiness; mean trick

cochinilla f, wood louse; cochineal insect; cochineal

cochinillo m, sucking-pig. **c. de Indias,** guinea-pig

cochino m, pig; inf filthy person. a filthy

cocido a boiled, cooked, baked. m, dish of stewed meat, pork, chicken, with peas, etc.

cociente m, quotient

cocimiento m, cooking; decoction

cocina f, kitchen; pottage; broth; cookery. **c. de campaña,** field-kitchen. **c. económica,** cooking range

cocinar vt to cook; vi inf meddle, interfere

cocinería f, naut galley

cocinero (-ra) n cook, chef

cocinilla f, spirit-stove

coco m, bot coconut tree and fruit; coconut shell; grub, maggot; bogeyman; hobgoblin; inf grimace. inf **ser un c.,** to be hideously ugly

cocacolismo n inf economic dependence on the United States and adoption of its pop culture

cocodrilo m, crocodile

cócora mf inf bore, nosy Parker

cocotero m, coconut palm

coctel m, cocktail

cocuyo m, firefly

codal a cubital. m, shoot of a vine; prop, strut; frame of a hand-saw

codazo m, blow or nudge of the elbow. **dar codazos,** to elbow, shoulder out of the way

codear vi to jostle; elbow, nudge; vr be on terms of equality with

codeína f, codeine

codelincuente mf partner in crime, accomplice

codera f, elbow rash; elbow-piece or patch

códice m, codex

codicia f, covetousness; greed

codiciar vt to covet

codicilo m, codicil

codicioso (-sa) a covetous; inf hardworking. n covetous person

codificación f, codification

codificar vt to codify, compile

código m, code of laws. **c. civil,** civil laws. **c. de la circulación, c. de la vía pública,** highway code, traffic code. naut **c. de señales,** signal code. **c. penal,** criminal laws. **c. postal,** zip code

codillo m, knee (of quadrupeds); shaft (of branch); bend (pipe, tube); stirrup

codo m, elbow; angle, bend (pipe, tube); cubit. inf **hablar por los codos,** to chatter

codorniz f, orn quail

coeficiente m, coefficient

coercer vt to restrain, coerce

coercitivo a coercive

coetáneo (-ea) a contemporaneous. n contemporary

coevo a coeval

coexistencia f, co-existence

coexistir vi to co-exist

cofradía f, confraternity, brotherhood or sisterhood **c. de gastronomía,** eating club (US); dining society (UK)

cofre m, trunk, chest (for clothes); coffer

cogedor (-ra) m, collector, gatherer; dustpan; coal-shovel

coger vt to seize, hold; catch; take, collect, gather; have room for; take up or occupy space; find; catch in the act; attack, surprise; reach; **c. un berrinche,** have a fit, have a tantrum. vi have room, fit

cogida f, gathering, picking; inf fruit harvest; toss (bullfighting)

cogido m, pleat, fold; crease. **estar c. de tiempo** to be pressed for time.

cogitabundo a very pensive

cognación f, cognation; kinship

cogollo m, heart (of lettuce, etc.); shoot; topmost branches of pine tree

cogote m, nape (of neck)

cohabitación f, cohabitation

cohabitar vt to cohabit

cohechar vt to bribe, corrupt, suborn

cohecho m, bribing; bribe

coherencia f, coherence, connection

coherente a coherent

cohesión f, cohesion

cohesivo a cohesive

cohete m, rocket

cohibir vt to restrain; repress. See **Prohibir**.

cohombro m, cucumber

cohonestar vt fig to gloss over, cover up; make appear decent (actions, etc.)

cohorte f, cohort

coima f, Lat. Am. bribe

coincidencia f, coincidence

coincidir vt to coincide; (two or more people) be in the same place at the same time. **c. con que . . .** to agree that . . .

coito m, coitus

cojear vi to limp; wobble, be unsteady (of furniture); fig inf go wrong or astray; inf suffer from (vice, bad habit)

cojera f, lameness, limp

cojijoso a peevish

cojín m, cushion; pad; pillow (for lacemaking)

cojinete m, small cushion; mech bearing. **c. de bolas,** ball-bearing

cojo a lame; unsteady, wobbly (of furniture, etc.)

col f, cabbage. **c. de Bruselas,** Brussels sprouts

cola f, tail; train (of gown); shank (of a button); queue; tailpiece (of a violin, etc.); appendage; glue. **c. de milano,** carp dovetail. **c. de pescado,** isinglass. **formar c.,** to line up, queue up

colaboración f, collaboration. **en c.,** joint (e.g. **obra en colaboración,** joint work)

colaboracionista mf collaborationist

colaborador (-ra) n collaborator

colaborar vt to collaborate

colación f, conferment of a degree; collation (of texts); light repast; cold supper; area of a parish

colada f, wash; bleaching; mountain path; met casting; inf trusty sword (allusion to name of one of the Cid's swords)

coladero m, colander, sieve, strainer; narrow path

colador m, colander

coladura f, straining, filtration; inf untruth; inf howler, mistake

colapso m, med prostration, collapse

colar vt irr to filter, strain; bleach; met cast; vi go through a narrow place; inf drink wine; vr thread one's way; inf enter by stealth, steal in; inf tell untruths. Pres.

Ind. **cuelo, cuelas, cuela, cuelan.** *Pres.*
Subjunc. **cuele, cueles, cuele, cuelen**

colcha *f,* bedspread, counterpane, quilt

colchadura *f,* quilting

colchón *m,* mattress. **c. de muelles,**
spring-mattress. **c. de viento,** air-bed

colección *f,* collection

coleccionador (-ra) *n* collector

coleccionar *vt* to collect

coleccionista *mf* collector

colecta *f,* assessment; collection (of donations); *ecc* collect; voluntary offering

colectivero *m,* bus driver

colectividad *f,* collectivity; body of people

colectivismo *m,* collectivism

colectivo *a* collective; *Argentina* (local)
bus

colector *m,* gatherer; collector; tax-collector; water-pipe; water-conduit; *elec*
commutator, collector

colega *m,* colleague

colegial (-la) *a* college, collegiate. *n* student; pupil; *fig inf* novice.

colegiarse *vr* to meet as an association
(professional, etc.)

colegiata *f,* college church

colegiatura *f,* scholarship, fellowship
(money granted a student); tuition (fee
paid by a student), tuition fee, tuition fees

colegio *m,* college; school; academy; association (professional); council, convocation; college or school buildings. **c. de
abogados,** bar association. **c. de car-
denales,** College of Cardinals. **c. electoral,** polling-booth. **c. militar,** military
academy

colegir *vt irr* to collect, gather; deduce,
infer. See **elegir**

cólera *f,* bile, anger. *m,* cholera. **montar
en c.,** to fly into a rage

colérico *a* angry; choleric; suffering from
cholera

colesterina *f, chem* cholesterol

coletazo *m,* blow with one's tail, lash with
one's tail; lash of a dying fish; *fig* last hurrah

colgadero *a* able to be hung up. *m,* coat-
hanger, hook

colgadizo *a* hanging. *m,* overhanging
roof

colgadura *f,* hangings, drapery, tapestries. **c. de cama,** bedhangings

colgajo *m,* tatter; bunch (of grapes, etc.);
surg skin lap

colgar *vt irr* to hang up; decorate with
hangings; *inf* hang, kill; *vi* hang, be suspended; *fig* be dependent. See **contar**

colibrí *m,* hummingbird

cólico *m,* colic

coliflor *f,* cauliflower

coligarse *vr* to confederate, unite

colilla *f,* stub (of a cigar or cigarette)

colina *f,* hill; cabbage seed; *chem* choline

colindante *a* adjacent, contiguous

coliseo *m,* coliseum; theater

colisión *f,* collision; abrasion, bruise; *fig*
clash (of ideas)

colitis *f,* colitis

collado *m,* hill, hillock

collar *m,* necklace; chain of office or
honor; collar (dogs, etc.)

collerón *m,* horse collar

colmado *a* abundant. *m,* provision shop

colmar *vt* to fill to overflowing; bestow
generously, heap upon

colmena *f,* beehive

colmenero (-ra) *n* beekeeper

colmillo *m,* canine tooth; tusk; fang

colmo *m,* overflow; highest point; completion, limit, end. **ser el c.,** *inf* to be the
last straw. **el c. de los colmos,** the absolute limit

colocación *f,* placing, putting; situation,
place; employment; *sport* placing; order,
arrangement; *ling* collocation

colocar *vt* to place, put, arrange; place in
employment. **c. bajo banderas,** to draft
(into the armed forces). *vr* place oneself

colocho *m, Guatemala* (naturally) curly
hair

colofonia *f,* solid resin (for bows of
stringed instruments, etc.)

colombiano (-na) *a* and *n* Colombian

colonia *f,* colony; plantation

coloniaje *m, Lat. Am.* colonial period; colonial government

colonial *a* colonial

colonización *f,* colonization

colonizador (-ra) *a* colonizing. *n* colo-
nizer

colonizar *vt* to colonize; settle

colono *m,* settler, colonist; farmer

coloquio *m,* colloquy, conversation, talk;
colloquium

color *m,* color; dye; paint; rouge; coloring; pretext, excuse; character, individuality; *pl* natural colors. **c. estable, c.
sólido,** fast color. **mudar de c.,** to
change color. **de c.,** colored. **so c.,** under
the pretext. **ver las cosas de c. de rosa,** to
see things through rose-colored glasses

colorado *a* colored. *WH* red, reddish; *inf*
blue, obscene; specious

colorante *a* coloring. *m,* dyestuff; coloring (substance)

colorar *vt* to color; dye

colorear *vt* to color; pretext; *fig* whitewash, excuse; *vi* show color; be reddish;
grow red, ripe (tomatoes, cherries, etc.)

colorete *m,* rouge

colorido *m,* coloring, color

colosal *a* colossal, enormous; extraordinary, excellent

coloso *m,* colossus; *fig* outstanding person or thing; giant; **el C. del Norte, el**

Gran C. del Norte, (contemptuous epithet for the United States of America)

columbrar vt to discern in the distance, glimpse; conjecture, guess

columna f, mil arch print column; fig protection, shelter; naut stanchion. **c. cerrada,** mil etc. mass formation. **c. de los suspiros,** agony column (in a newspaper)

columnata f, colonnade

columpiar vt to swing; dangle (one's feet); vr inf sway in walking; swing

columpio m, swing

colusión f, collusion

coma f, gram comma. m, med coma

comadre f, midwife; inf procuress, go-between; inf pal, gossip

comadrear vi inf to gossip

comadrón m, accoucheur

comadrona f, midwife

comandancia f, mil command; commandant's H.Q.

comandante m, commandant; commander; major; squadron-leader. a mil commanding. **c. en jefe,** commanding officer

comandita f, com sleeping partnership; private company

comando m, mil commando

comarca f, district, region

comatoso a comatose

comba f, bend, warping; jump rope, skipping-rope; camber (of road)

combadura f, curvature; warping; camber (of a road)

combar vt to bend; twist; warp; camber (of a road)

combate m, fight, combat; mental strife; contradiction, opposition. **c. judicial,** trial by combat. **dejar fuera de c.,** (a) (boxing) to knock out

combatiente m, combatant, soldier

combatir vi to fight; vt attack; struggle against (winds, water, etc.); contradict, oppose; fig disturb, trouble (emotions)

combi m, Mexico minibus

combinación f, combination; list of words beginning with same letter; project; concurrence; underskirt, petticoat. **estar en c. (con),** to be in cahoots (with), connive (with)

combinar vt to combine; (mil nav) join forces; arrange, plan; chem combine; **combinar para + inf.** (two or more people) to make arrangements to + inf.

combustible a combustible. m, fuel

combustión f, combustion. **c. activa,** rapid combustion. **c. espontánea,** spontaneous combustion

comedia f, comedy; play; theater; comic incident; fig play-acting, theatricalism. **c. alta,** art theater. **c. de costumbres,** comedy of manners. **c. de enredo,** play with very involved plot. inf **hacer la c.,** to play-act, pretend

comediante m, actor; inf dissembler.

comedianta f, actress

comedido a courteous; prudent; moderate

comedimiento m, courtesy; moderation; prudence

comedir vt ir to prepare, premeditate; vr restrain oneself, be moderate; offer one's services. See **pedir**

comedor a voracious. m, dining-room

comensal mf table companion

comentador (-ra) n commentator

comentar vt explain (document); inf comment

comentario (a) m, commentary (on)

comento m, comment; commentary

comenzante mf beginner, novice. a initial

comenzar vt vi irr to begin, commence. See **empezar**

comer m, eating; food. vi to eat; feed; dine. vt eat; inf enjoy an income; waste (patrimony); consume, exhaust; fade (of colors); vr be troubled, uneasy, remorseful. **ser de buen c.,** to have a good appetite; taste good. **tener que c.,** to be obliged to eat; have to eat; have enough to eat

comerciable a marketable; sociable, pleasant (of persons)

comercial a commercial

comerciante a trading. mf merchant, trader

comerciar vt to trade; have dealings (with)

comercio m, trade, commerce; intercourse, traffic; illicit sexual intercourse; shop, store; tradesmen; commercial quarter of town

comestible a edible, eatable. m, (gen. pl) provisions

cometa m, ast comet. f, kite (toy). **c. celular,** box-kite

cometer vt to entrust, hand over to; commit (crime, sins, etc.); com order

cometido m, charge, commission; moral obligation; function

comezón f, itching, irritation; hankering, longing

cómico a comic; funny, comical. m, actor; comedian. **c. de la legua,** strolling player

comida f, food; meal; dinner; eating. **c. corrida** Mexico table d'hôte **c. de gala,** state banquet. **c. de prueba,** med test meal

comienzo m, beginning, origin

comilón (-ona) a inf gluttonous. n glutton

comillas f pl, gram inverted commas

comisar vt to confiscate, sequestrate

comisaría f, commissaryship; commissariat. **c. de policía,** police station

comisario m, deputy, agent; commissary, head of police; commissioner; Ar-

gentina, purser. **alto c.,** high commis-sioner. **c. propietario,** stockholders' representative

comisión *f,* perpetration, committal; commission; committee; *com* commis-sion

comisionado (-da) a commissioned. *m,* commissary

comisionar *vt* to commission

comité *m,* committee

comitiva *f,* retinue, following

como *adv* like, as; in the same way; thus, accordingly; in the capacity of; so that; since. *conjunc* if *(followed by subjunc.);* because. **c. no,** unless. **¿Cómo?** How? In what way? Why? Pardon? What did you say? *interj* **¡Cómo!** What! You don't say! **¡Cómo no!** Why not! Of course! Surely! **¿Cómo que . . . ?** What do you mean that . . . ?

cómo *m,* the wherefore. **no saber el porqué ni el c.,** not to know the why or wherefore

cómoda *f,* chest of drawers

comodidad *f,* comfort; convenience; ad-vantage; utility, interest

comodín *m,* (in cards) joker

cómodo a comfortable; convenient; op-portune

comoquiera que *adv* by any means that, anyway; whereas, given that

compacto a compact, dense; close (type)

compadecer *vt irr* to pity; *vr (with* **de)** sympathize with; pity; harmonize, agree with. See **conocer**

compadre *m, inf* pal; *Argentina* bully

compaginar *vt* to fit together; join, put in order; harmonize, square (e.g. **compag-iné una cuenta con la otra,** I squared one account with the other); *print* make up

compañero (-ra) *n* companion, com-rade; fellow-member; partner (games); *fig* pair, fellow, mate (things). **c. de armas,** brother-in-arms, companion-at-arms. **c. de cabina,** boothmate. **c. de ex-ilio,** companion in exile, fellow exile. **c. de generación,** contemporary, person of the same generation.

compañía *f,* company; society, associa-tion; theatrical company; *(com mil)* com-pany. **C. de Jesús,** Order of Jesus. **c. de la zarza,** guild of guards and woodcutters for autos de fe. **c. de navegación,** ship-ping company. **c. por acciones,** joint stock company

comparación *f,* comparison

comparar *vt* to compare; collate

comparativo a comparative

comparecencia *f,* (gen. *law)* appearance

comparecer *vi law* to appear (before tribunal, etc.); present oneself. See **cono-cer**

comparendo *m, law* summons

comparsa *f,* retinue; *theat* chorus; troop

of carnival revelers dressed alike. *mf theat* supernumerary actor

compartimiento *m,* share, division; railway carriage. *naut* **c. estanco,** com-partment

compartir *vt* to share out, divide; partici-pate

compás *m,* compasses; callipers; size; compass, time; range of voice; *(naut min)* compass; *mus* time, rhythm, bar, mark-ing time. **c. de mar,** mariner's compass. **c. de puntas,** dividers, callipers. **fuera de c.,** *mus* out of time; out of joint (of the times). *mus* **llevar el c.,** to beat time

compasar *vt* to measure with com-passes; arrange or apportion accurately; *mus* put into bars

compasivo a compassionate; tender-hearted

compatibilidad *f,* compatibility

compatriota *mf* compatriot

compeler *vt* to compel, force

compendiar *vt* to abridge, summarize

compendio *m,* compendium. **en c.,** briefly

compendioso a summary, condensed; compendious

compenetración *f,* co-penetration; in-termingling

compenetrado (de) a thoroughly con-vinced (of)

compenetrarse *vr* to co-penetrate; in-termingle

compensación *f,* compensating; com-pensation

compensar *vt* to equalize, counterbal-ance; compensate

compensatorio a compensatory; equal-izing

competencia *f,* competition, contest; ri-valry; competence; aptitude; *law* jurisdic-tion

competente a adequate, opportune; rightful, correct; apt, suitable; learned, competent

competer *vi irr* to belong to; devolve on; concern. See **pedir**

competición *f,* competition

competidor (-ra) *n* competitor

competir *vi irr* to compete, contest; be equal (to), vie (with). See **pedir**

compilar *vt* to compile

compinche *mf inf* pal, chum

complacencia *f,* satisfaction, pleasure

complacer *vt irr* to oblige, humor; *vr (with* **en)** be pleased or satisfied with; de-light in, like to. See **nacer**

complaciente a pleasing; obliging, help-ful

complejo a complex; intricate. *m,* com-plex. **c. de inferioridad,** inferiority com-plex

complemento *m,* complement (all meanings)

completar vt to complete; perfect

completo a full; finished; perfect

complexión f, physical constitution

complexo a complex; intricate

complicación f, complication

complicar vt to complicate; muddle, confuse; vr be complicated; be muddled or confused

cómplice mf accomplice

complot m, inf conspiracy, plot, intrigue

componedor (-ra) n repairer; arbitrator; bone-setter; mus composer; writer, author, compiler; print compositor

componenda f, mending, repair; inf settlement; compromise, arbitration; inf shady business

componente a and m, component

componer vt irr to construct, form; mech resolve; compose, create; print compose; prepare, concoct, mend, repair; settle (differences); remedy; trim; correct, adjust; lit mus compose; add up to, amount to; vi write (verses); mus compose; vr dress oneself up. **c. el semblante,** to compose one's features; inf **componérselas,** to fix matters, use one's wits. See **poner**

componible a reparable, mendable; able to be arranged or adjusted

comportamiento m, conduct; deportment

comportar vt to tolerate; vr behave, comport oneself

composición f, composition; repair; arrangement, compromise; print composition; gram compound; chem constitution; mech resolution

compositor (-ra) n mus composer; print compositor

compostura f, composition, structure; repair; neatness (of person); adulteration; arrangement, agreement; discretion, modesty

compota f, fruit preserve, compote; thick sauce

compra f, buying; marketing, shopping; purchase. **estar de compras,** euphem to be in the family way. **ir de compras,** to go shopping

comprador (-ra) a purchasing. n purchaser; buyer; shopper

comprar vt to buy; bribe

comprender vt to encircle, surround; include, comprise, contain; understand

comprensible a comprehensible

comprensión f, comprehension, understanding

comprensivo a understanding; comprehensive

compresa f, med compress, swab; pack (for the face, etc.)

compresión f, compression; squeeze

compresivo a compressive

compresor m, compressor; aut aer supercharger

comprimido m, tablet, pill

comprimir vt to compress; squeeze; restrain; vr restrain oneself

comprobación f, verification; checking; proof

comprobante a verifying; confirmatory

comprobar vt irr to verify, check; confirm, prove. See **probar**

comprobatorio a confirmatory; verifying; testing

comprometedor a inf compromising; jeopardizing

comprometer vt to submit to arbitration; compromise; imperil, jeopardize; vr pledge oneself; inf compromise oneself

comprometido a awkward, embarrassing; (e.g. literature of a writer) committed, engagé

compromiso m, compromise, agreement, arbitration, commitment, obligation; appointment, engagement; jeopardy; difficulty

compuesto a and past part made-up, built-up; composite; circumspect; bot gram compound. m, composite; preparation, compound

compulsar vt to collate; law make a transcript of

compulsivo a compelling

compunción f, compunction

compungir vt to cause remorse or pity; vr repent; sympathize with, pity

computación f, **cómputo** m, calculation, computation

computador (-ra) n computer

computar vt to compute

cómputo m, computation; estimate

comulgar vt to administer Holy Communion; vi receive Holy Communion

comulgatorio m, communion rail, altar rail

común a general, customary, ordinary; public, communal; universal, common; vulgar, low. m, community, population; water-closet. **en c.,** in common; generally. **por lo c.,** generally. **sentido c.,** common sense

comuna f, Lat. Am. district

comunicable a communicable; communicative, sociable

comunicación f, communication; (telephone) call, message; letter (to the press); mil communiqué; pl lines of communication, transport

comunicado m, official communication, communiqué; letter (to the press)

comunicar vt to communicate; transmit; impart, share; vr **comunicarse con,** (door) to open onto (e.g. **Esta puerta se comunica con el jardín.** This door opens onto the garden); communicate, converse, correspond with each other

comunidad f, the common people; community; generality, majority; pl hist Commune

comunión f, communion; intercourse, fellowship; ecc Communion

comunismo m, communism

comunista a and mf communist

con prep with; by means of; in the company of; towards, to; although (followed by infin., but generally translated by an inflected verb, e.g. **C. ser almirante, no le gusta el mar,** Although he is an admiral, he doesn't like the sea); by (followed by infin. and generally translated by a gerund, e.g. **c. hacer todo esto,** by doing all this). **c. bien,** safe and sound, safely (e.g. **Llegamos con bien.** We arrived safely.) **c. cuentagotas,** sparingly; stingily. **c. que,** so, then. **c. tal que,** provided that, on condition that. **c. todo,** nevertheless. **¿Con . . . ?** Is this . . . ? (on the telephone, e.g. **¿Con el Sr. Piñangos?** Is this Mr. Piñangos?)

conato m, effort, endeavor; tendency; law attempted crime

concatenación f, concatenation

concavidad f, concavity; hollow

cóncavo a concave. m, concavity; hollow

concebible a conceivable

concedente a conceding

conceder vt to confer, grant; concede; agree to

concejal m, councillor; alderman

concejo m, town council; town hall; council meeting

concentración f, concentration

concentrado a concentrated; (of persons) reserved

concentrar vt to concentrate

concéntrico a concentric

concepción f, conception; idea, concept; ecc Immaculate Conception

concepto m, idea, concept; epigram; opinion. **en mi c.,** in my opinion; judgment. **por c. de,** in payment of

conceptuar vt to judge, take to be; believe; imagine

conceptuoso a witty, ingenious

concernencia f, respect, relation

concerniente a concerning

concernir vi irr defective to concern. See **discernir**

concertadamente adv methodically, orderly; by arrangement, or agreement

concertar vt irr to arrange, settle, adjust; bargain; conclude (business deal); harmonize; compare, correlate; tune instruments; vi reach an agreement. See **acertar**

concertina f, concertina

concertista mf mus performer, soloist; mus manager. **c. de piano,** concert pianist

concesión f, conceding, grant; concession; lease

concesionario m, law concessionaire, leaseholder

concho m, Lat. Am. dregs, sediment

conciencia f, consciousness; conscience; conscientiousness. **c. doble,** dual personality. **ancho de c.,** broad-minded. **a c.,** conscientiously

concienzudo a of a delicate conscience, scrupulous; conscientious

concierto m, methodical arrangement; agreement; mus concert; mus concerto. **de c.,** by common consent

conciliábulo m, conclave, private meeting; secret meeting

conciliación f, conciliation; similarity, affinity; protection, favor

conciliador a conciliatory

conciliar m, councilor. vt to conciliate; fig reconcile (opposing theories, etc.). **c. el sueño,** to induce sleep, woo sleep. vr win liking (or sometimes dislike)

concilio m, council; ecc assembly; conciliary decree; findings of council

concisión f, conciseness, brevity

conciso a concise

concitar vt to stir up, foment

conciudadano (-na) n fellow citizen; fellow countryman

cónclave m, conclave; meeting

concluir vt irr to conclude, finish; come to a conclusion, decide; infer, deduce; convince by reasoning; law close legal proceedings; vr expire, terminate. **c. con,** to put an end to. See **huir**

conclusión f, finish, end; decision; close, denouement; theory, proposition (gen. pl); deduction, inference; law close. **en c.,** in conclusion

conclusivo a final; conclusive

concluyente a concluding; convincing; conclusive

concomer vi inf to give a shrug, shrug one's shoulders; fidget with an itch. **c. de placer,** to itch with pleasure

concomitante a and m, concomitant

concordador (-ra) a peacemaking. n peacemaker

concordancia f, harmony, agreement; (mus gram) concord; pl concordance

concordar vt irr to bring to agreement; vi agree. See **acordar**

concorde a agreeing; harmonious

concordia f, concord, agreement, harmony; written agreement

concreción f, concretion

concretar vt to combine, bring together; make concise; resume; vr fig confine oneself (to a subject) to hammer out, work out (an agreement)

concreto a concrete, real, not abstract. **en c.,** in definite terms; finally, to sum up

concubina f, concubine, mistress

conculcar *vt* to trample under foot, tread on; break, violate

concupiscente *a* concupiscent, lustful; greedy

concurrencia *f*, assembly; coincidence; attendance; help, influence

concurrido *a* crowded; busy; frequented

concurrir *vi* to coincide; contribute; meet together; agree, be of same opinion; compete (in an examination, etc.)

concurso *m*, crowd, concourse; conjunction, coincidence; help; competition; (tennis) tournament; competitive examination; invitation to offer tenders. **c. de acreedores,** creditors' meeting. **c. interno,** competitive examination for a position open to staff members only

concusión *f*, concussion; shock; extortion

concha *f*, shell; turtle-shell; prompter's box; cove, creek; anything shell-shaped. *fig* **meterse en su c.,** to retire into one's shell. *inf* **tener más conchas que un galápago,** to be very cunning

condado *m*, earldom; county

condecir (con) *vi* to agree (with)

condecoración *f*, conferment of an honor, decoration; medal

condecorar *vt* to confer a decoration or medal

condena *f*, *law* sentence; punishment; penalty

condenable *a* culpable, guilty; worthy of damnation

condenado (-da) *a* damned; wicked, harmful. *n law* convicted criminal

condenador *a* condemning; incriminating; blaming

condenar *vt law* to pronounce sentence (on), convict; condemn; disapprove; wall or block or close up. **c. a galeras,** to condemn to the gallies. *vr* blame oneself; be eternally damned

condenatorio *a* condemnatory; incriminating

condensación *f*, condensation

condensador *a* condensing. *m*, (*elec mech chem*) condenser

condensante *a* condensing

condensar *vt* to condense; thicken; abridge

condescendencia *f*, affability, graciousness

condescender *vi irr* to be obliging, helpful, agreeable. See **entender**

condescendiente *a* affable, gracious

condestable *m*, *hist* constable, commander-in-chief

condición *f*, condition; quality; temperament, character; (social) position; rank, family; nobility; circumstance; stipulation, condition, requirement. **estar en condiciones de,** to be in a position to. **no estar en condiciones de,** to be in no condition to

condicional *a* conditional

condicionar *vi* to come to an agreement, arrange; *vt* impose conditions

condimentación *f*, *cul* seasoning

condimentar *vt* to flavor, season (food)

condimento *m*, condiment, flavoring

condiscípulo *m*, schoolfellow

condolencia *f*, compassion; condolence

condolerse *vr* (*with de*) to sympathize with, be sorry for. See **doler**

condonar *vt* to condone

conducción *f*. **conducencia,** *f*, transport, conveyance; carriage; guiding; direction, management; *phys* conduction; *mech* control-gear. *aut* **c. a izquierda,** left-hand drive

conducente *a* conducting, conducive

conducir *vt irr* to transport, convey, carry; *phys* conduct; guide, lead; manage, direct; *aut* drive; conduce; *vi* be suitable; *vr* behave, conduct oneself. *Pres. Ind.* **conduzco, conduces,** etc. *Preterite* **conduje, condujiste,** etc. *Pres. Subjunc.* **conduzca, conduzcas,** etc. *Imperf. Subjunc.* **condujese,** etc.

conducta *f*, transport, conveyance; management, conduct, direction; behavior

conductivo *a* conductive

conducto *m*, pipe, conduit, drain, duct; *fig* channel, means; *anat* tube

conductor (-ra) *n* guide; leader; driver (vehicles); *m*, *phys* conductor. **c. de caballos,** teamster. **c. de entrada,** *rad* lead-in. **c. del calor,** heat-conductor. **c. eléctrico,** electric wire or cable

conectar *vt elec* to connect, switch on; couple; attach, join

conejillo de Indias *m*, guineapig

conejo *m*, rabbit

conexión *f*, connection; *elec* switching on, connection; joint; joining; *pl* friends, connections; *elec* wiring

conexo *a* connected

confabulación *f*, confabulation, conspiracy

confabular *vi* to confer; *vr* scheme, plot

confalón *m*, standard, banner

confección *f*, making; confection; making-up; concoction, remedy; ready-made garment

confeccionador (-ra) *n* maker (of clothes, etc.)

confeccionar *vt* to make; prepare; make up (pharmaceuticals)

confederación *f*, alliance, pact; confederacy, federation

confederarse *vr* to confederate, be allied

conferencia *f*, conference, meeting; lecture; (telephone) long-distance call (US), trunk call (UK)

conferenciante *mf* lecturer

conferencista *mf*, *Lat. Am.* lecturer

conferenciar *vi* to confer

conferir *vt irr* to grant, concede; consider, discuss; compare, correlate. See **herir**

confesable *a* acknowledgeable, avowable

confesar *vt irr* to avow, declare; acknowledge, admit; *ecc* hear confession; *vr ecc* confess. *Pres. Ind.* **confieso, confiesas, confiesa, confiesan.** *Pres. Subjunc.* **confiese, confieses, confiese, confiesen**

confesión *f,* confession

confesionario, confesonario, confesorio *m, ecc* confessional

confesor *m,* confessor

confeti *m,* confetti

confianza *f,* confidence, trust; assurance, courage; over-confidence, conceit; intimacy; familiarity. **de c.,** reliable (e.g. **persona de c.,** reliable person); informal (e.g. **reunión de c.,** informal meeting). **en c.,** in confidence, confidentially

confianzudo *a inf* overconfident

confiar *vi (with en)* to trust in, hope; *vt (with prep a or en)* entrust, commit to the care of; confide in

confidencia *f,* trust; confidence; confidential information

confidente (-ta) a trustworthy, true. *m,* seat for two. *n* confidant(e); spy

configuración *f,* configuration, form, lie

configurar *vt* to shape

confín *m,* boundary, frontier; limit. *a* boundary

confinar *vi (with con)* to be bounded by, contiguous to; *vt* banish; place in confinement

confirmación *f,* corroboration; *ecc* confirmation

confirmar *vt* to corroborate; uphold; *ecc* confirm

confiscación *f,* confiscation

confiscar *vt* to confiscate

confitar *vt* to candy, crystallize or preserve (fruit, etc.); *fig* sweeten

confite *m,* bonbon, sugared almond, etc.

confitería *f,* confectionery

confitura *f,* preserve, jam

conflagración *f,* conflagration, blaze; uprising, rebellion

conflicto *m,* strife, struggle; spiritual conflict; *fig* difficult situation

confluencia *f,* confluence; crowd

confluir *vi irr* to meet, flow together (rivers); run together (roads); crowd. See **huir**

conformación *f,* conformation; make-up, structure (e.g. of an organization)

conformar *vt* to fit, adjust; *vr* agree, be of the same opinion; submit, comply; to make up (e.g. **los grupos sociales que conforman este país,** the social groups who make up this country)

conforme *a* similar, alike; consistent; in agreement; long-suffering, resigned. *adv* according (to), in proportion (to)

conformidad *f,* conformity; similarity; resignation; agreement, harmony; proportion, symmetry. **de c.,** by common consent. **en c.,** according to

confort *m,* comfort

confortante *a* comfort;ng; consoling; strengthening (of beverages)

confortar *vt* to comfort, reassure; encourage; console

confrontación *f,* confrontment; comparison (of texts, etc.)

confrontar *vt* to bring face to face; compare, correlate; *vi* face; *(with con)* be contiguous to, border on

confundir *vt* to mix, confuse; jumble together; mistake; *fig* confound (in argument); humble; bewilder, perplex; *vr* be mixed together; mistake, confuse; be ashamed; be bewildered

confusión *f,* confusion; perplexity; shame; jumble

confuso *a* mixed, upset; jumbled; obscure; indistinct; blurred; bewildered

confutar *vt* to confute

congelación *f,* freezing; congealment. **punto de c.,** freezing point

congelar *vt* to congeal; freeze

congénito *a* congenital

congestión *f, med* congestion

congestionar *vt* to congest; *vr med* be overcharged (with blood)

conglomeración *f,* conglomeration

conglomerar *vt* to conglomerate

congoja *f,* anguish, anxiety, grief

congraciarse (con), *vr* to ingratiate oneself (with), get into the good graces (of)

congratulación *f,* congratulation

congratular *vt* to congratulate; *vr* congratulate oneself

congratulatorio *a* congratulatory

congregación *f,* gathering, meeting, congregation; brotherhood, guild

congregar(se) *vt* and *vr* to meet, assemble

congreso *m,* congress; conference, meeting; sexual intercourse

congrio *m,* conger eel

congruencia *f,* suitability, convenience; *math* congruence

congruente *a* convenient, opportune; *math* congruent

cónico *a* conical, tapering *math* conic

conjetura *f,* conjecture

conjeturar *vt* to conjecture surmise

conjugación *f,* conjugation

conjugar *vt* to conjugate

conjunción *f,* connection, union association; *(ast gram)* conjunction

conjuntivitis *f,* conjunctivitis

conjunto *a* united, associated adjoining; mingled, mixed (with) bound, affiliated.

m, whole; combo, ensemble (of musicians). **c. habitacional,** housing complex, housing project

conjura, conjuración *f,* conspiracy, plot

conjurador (-ra) *n* conspirator, plotter; exorcist

conjurar *vi* to conspire, plot *vt* swear, take an oath; exorcise; implore, beg; ward off (danger)

conjuro *m,* plot, conspiracy, spell, incantation; entreaty

conllevar *vt* to share (troubles) bear, put up with; endure

conmemoración *f,* commemoration

conmemorar *vt* to commemorate

conmemorativo *a* commemorative

conmensurable *a* commensurable

conmigo *pers. pron* 1st pers. sing. *mf* with myself, with me

conminar *vt* to threaten

conmiseración *f,* commiseration, compassion, pity

conmoción *f,* disturbance (mind or body); upheaval, commotion. **c. eléctrica,** electric shock

conmovedor *a* moving, pitiful; stirring, thrilling

conmover *vt irr* to perturb, stir; move to pity. **c. los cimientos de,** to shake the foundations of; *vr* be emotionally moved. See **mover**

conmutador *m, elec* commutator; change-over switch

conmutar *vt* to commute; *elec* switch, convert

connato *a* contemporary

connatural *a* innate, inborn

connivencia *f,* connivance

connotado, -a *a, Lat. Am.* well-known

connotar *vt* to connote

cono *m, (geom bot)* cone. **el C. Sur,** the Southern Cone

conocedor (-ra) *n* one who knows; connoisseur; expert

conocer *vt irr* to know; understand; observe, perceive; be acquainted (with); conjecture; confess, acknowledge; know carnally; *vr* know oneself; know one another. **conocerle a uno la voz,** to recognize somebody's voice (e.g. **Le conozco la voz.** I recognize her by her voice.) **conocerle a uno en su manera de andar,** to recognize somebody by his gait, recognize somebody by his walk. *Pres. Ind.* **conozco, conoces,** etc. *Pres. Subjunc.* **conozca,** etc.

conocido (-da) *a* illustrious, distinguished. *n* acquaintance

conocimiento *m,* knowledge; understanding; intelligence; acquaintance (*not* friend); consciousness; *com* bill of lading; *pl* knowledge, learning

conque *conjunc* so, so that (e.g. ¿C. Juan se va? So John's going away?)

conquista *f,* conquest

conquistar *vt* to conquer; *fig* captivate, win

consagración *f,* consecration; dedication

consagrar *vt* to consecrate; dedicate, devote; deify; *vr (with prep* a) dedicate oneself to, engage in

consciente *a* conscious; aware; sane. *m, psy* conscious

conscripción *f,* conscription

conscripto *m,* conscript

consecuencia *f,* consequence, outcome; logical consequence, conclusion; importance; consistence (of people)

consecuente *a* consequent, resultant; consistent. **c. consigo mismo,** self-consistent *m,* consequence; *math* consequent

consecutivo *a* consecutive, successive

conseguir *vt irr* to obtain, achieve. See **seguir**

consejero (-ra) *n* adviser; member of council. *m.* **c. de estado,** counselor of state

consejo *m,* advice; council, commission, board; council chamber or building. **c. de administración,** board of directors. **c. de guerra,** council of war. **c. del reino,** council of the realm. **c. privado,** privy council

consenso *m,* consensus of opinion, unanimity

consentido *a* complaisant (of husband); spoilt, over-indulged

consentimiento *m,* consent; assent

consentir *vt irr* to permit, allow; believe; tolerate, put up with; over-indulge, spoil; *vr* crack, give way (furniture, etc.). **c. en,** to consent to; to agree to. See **sentir**

conserje *m,* concierge, porter; warden or keeper (of castle, etc.)

conserjería *f,* conciergerie, porter's lodge; warden's dwelling (in castles, etc.)

conserva *f,* jam; preserve; pickles; *naut* convoy. **en c.,** preserved, tinned

conservación *f,* upkeep; preservation, maintenance; *cul* preserving; conservation. **c. refrigerada,** coldstorage

conservador (-ra) *a* keeping, preserving. *a* and *n* preserver; *pol* conservative; traditionalist. *m,* curator

conservadurismo *m,* conservatism

conservar *vt* to keep, maintain, preserve; keep up (custom, etc.); guard; *cul* preserve. **c. en buen estado,** to keep in repair

conservatorio *m,* conservatoire; academy; *Lat. Am.* greenhouse. **c. de música,** academy of music, conservatoire

considerable *a* considerable; worthy of consideration, powerful; numerous; large; important

consideración *f,* consideration, attention; reflection, thought; civility; importance. **en c. de,** considering

considerado a considerate; prudent; distinguished; important

considerar *vt* to consider, reflect upon; treat with consideration (persons); judge, estimate, feel (e.g. **Considero que . . .** I feel that . . .)

consigna *f*, *mil* watchword; left luggage office

consignar *vt* to assign, lay aside; deposit; *com* consign; entrust, commit; put in writing; *law* deposit in trust; book (a suspect)

consignatario *m*, *law* trustee; mortgagee; *com* consignee. **c. de buques,** shipping agent

consigo *pers. pron* 3rd sing. and pl. *mf* with himself, herself, oneself, yourself, yourselves, themselves

consiguiente a consequent, resulting. *m*, consequence. **por c.,** in consequence

consistencia *f*, solidity; consistence, density; consistency, congruity, relevance

consistente a of a certain consistency; solid

consistir *vi* (*with en*) to consist in; be comprised of; be the result of

consola *f*, console table; piertable; *mech* bracket

cónsola *f*, radio cabinet

consolador (**-ra**) *n* comforter, consoler

consolar *vt irr* to comfort, console. **consolarse de + inf.,** to console oneself for + *pp*. See **contar**

consolidación *f*, consolidation; stiffening

consolidar *vt* to consolidate; strengthen; combine, unite; *vr law* unite

consomé *m*, consommé

consonancia *f*, harmony; agreement

consonante a consonant, consistent. *m*, rhyme. *f*, *gram* consonant

consorcio *m*, partnership; trust; intimacy, common life

consorte *mf* consort; companion, associate, partner; spouse

conspicuo a outstanding, distinguished; conspicuous

conspiración *f*, conspiracy

conspirador (**-ra**) *n* conspirator

conspirar *vi* to conspire; plot, scheme; tend, combine

constancia *f*, constancy, steadfastness; stability, steadiness; transcript (of grades); *Lat. Am. law* deposition. **c. de estudios,** transcript (of grades)

constante a constant; durable; *mech* steady, non-oscillating. *m*, constant

constar *vi* to be evident, be clear; (*with de*) be composed of, consist of, comprise

constelación *f*, *ast* constellation; climate

consternación *f*, dismay, alarm

consternarse *vr* to be dismayed or alarmed

constipado *m*, *med* cold; chill

constiparse *vr* to catch a cold or chill

constitución *f*, constitution; composition, make-up (e.g. **la c. del suelo,** the make-up of the soil)

constituir *vt irr* to constitute, form; found, establish; (*with en*) appoint, nominate; *fig* place in (a difficult situation, etc.); *vr* (*with en* or *por*) be appointed or authorized; be under (an obligation). See **huir**

constituyente, constitutivo a and *m*, constituent

constreñir *vt irr* to constrain, oblige; constrict; constipate. See **ceñir**

constricción *f*, constriction; contraction, shrinkage

construcción *f*, construction; art or process of construction; fabric, structure; *gram* construction; building, erection. **c. de caminos,** road making. **c. naval,** shipbuilding

constructor (**-ra**) a building, constructive. *n* builder; constructor

construir *vt irr* to construct; build, make; *gram* construct. See **huir**

consuelo *m*, consolation; comfort, solace; joy, delight

cónsul *m*, consul

consulado *m*, consulate. **c. general,** consulate general

consulta *f*, deliberation, consideration; advice; reference; conference, consultation

consultar *vt* to discuss, consider; seek advice, consult. **consultarlo con la almohada,** *fig* to sleep on it, think it over, mull it over

consultor (**-ra**) a consultative, advisory; consulting. *n* consultant; adviser. **c. externo,** outside consultant

consultorio *m*, *med* consulting rooms; surgery; technical information bureau

consumación *f*, consummation; completion, attainment; extinction, end

consumar *vt* to consummate; complete, accomplish, perfect

consumido a *inf* emaciated, wasted away; timid, spiritless

consumidor (**-ra**) a consuming. *n* consumer, user

consumir *vt* to destroy; consume, use; waste away, wear away; *ecc* take communion; *inf* grieve; *vr* be destroyed; *inf* be consumed with grief

consumo *m*, consumption; demand. **c. de combustible,** fuel consumption

contabilidad *f*, bookkeeping; accounts; accounting

contable *m*, bookkeeper

contacto *m*, contact (also *elec mil*). **en c.,** in common (e.g. **Los dos libros ti-**

enen mucho en c. The two books have much in common.)

contado a few; infrequent; rare. **al c., com** cash down. **por de c.,** presumably; of course, naturally

contador a counting. m, accountant; law auditor; counter (in banks); elec meter, counter; naut purser. **c. oficial,** Argentina certified public accountant. **c. público titulado,** certified public accountant

contagiar vt to infect; corrupt, pervert; vr (with con, de or por) be infected by or through

contagio m, infection; contagious disease; fig contagion, perversion, corruption

contagioso a infectious; fig catching, contagious

contaminación f, contamination, pollution

contaminar vt to pollute, contaminate; infect; fig corrupt

contante a ready (of money)

contar vt irr to count; recount, tell; place to account; include, count among; vi calculate, compute. **contarle a uno las cuarenta,** inf to give someone a piece of one's mind. **c. con,** to rely upon; reckon upon. Pres. Ind. **cuento, cuentas, cuenta, cuentan.** Pres. Subjunc. **cuente, cuentes, cuente, cuenten**

contemplación f, meditation, contemplation; consideration

contemplar vt to consider, reflect upon; look at, contemplate; indulge, please

contemporáneo (de) a contemporaneous (to or with) n contemporary

contemporizar vi to temporize, gain time

contencioso a contentious, argumentative; law litigious

contender vi irr to contain; restrain, hold back; comprise; vr control oneself. See **entender**

contendiente mf contestant

contener vt irr to contain; include; comprise; hold back; restrain; check, repress; hold down, subdue; suppress, put down; vr contain oneself; keep one's temper; keep quiet; refrain. See **tener**

contenido m, contents. a contained; fig restrained; reserved (of persons)

contentar vt to satisfy, please; com endorse; vr be pleased or satisfied

contento a happy; content; satisfied; pleased. m, pleasure; contentment. **no caber de c.,** to be overjoyed

contestación f, reply, answer; discussion, argument, dispute

contestar vt to reply, answer; confirm, attest; vi accord, harmonize

contexto m, context

contienda f, struggle, fight; quarrel, dispute; discussion

contigo pers. pron 2nd sing. mf with thee, with you

contiguo a adjacent, near

continencia f, moderation, self-restraint; continence; chastity; containing

continental a continental. m, express messenger service; Puerto Rico person from the mainland United States

continente a continent. m, container; demeanor, bearing; geog continent; mainland

contingente a incidental; fortuitous; dependent; m, mil taskforce, contingent

continuación f, continuation; prolongation; sequel (of a story, etc.)

continuar vt to continue; vi continue; last, remain, go on; vr be prolonged

continuidad f, continuity

continuo a continuous, steady, uninterrupted; persevering, tenacious; persistent, lasting, unremitting. m, a united whole. **de c.,** continuously

contonearse vr to swing the hips (in walking); strut

contorno m, contour, outline; (gen. pl) environs, surrounding district

contra prep against, counter, athwart; opposed to, hostile to; in front of, opposite; towards. m, opposite view or opinion. f, inf difficulty, trouble. **c. la corriente,** upstream. **el pro y el c.,** the pros and cons. **en c.,** in opposition, against

contrabalancear vt to counterbalance; fig compensate

contrabandista a smuggling. mf smuggler

contrabando m, contraband; smuggling

contracción f, contraction; shrinkage; abridgment; abbreviation

contradanza f, square dance

contradecir vt irr to contradict; vr contradict oneself. See **decir**

contradicción f, contradiction

contradictorio a contradictory

contraer vt irr to shrink, reduce in size, shorten; abridge; contract (matrimony, obligations); fig acquire (diseases, habits); vr shorten, contract, shrink. See **traer**

contrahacer vt irr to forge, counterfeit; mimic; imitate. See **hacer**

contrahecho a deformed

contralto m, contralto (voice)

contramarcha f, retrogression; mil countermarch

contramedida f, counter-measure

contraorden f, countermand

contrapedalear vi to backpedal

contrapelo a adv the wrong way of the hair, against the grain; inf reluctantly, distastefully

contrapeso m, counterpoise, counterweight; balancing-pole (acrobats); fig counterbalance; makeweight

contraponer *vt irr* to compare; place opposite; oppose. See **poner**

contraproducente *a* counteractive, counterproductive, unproductive, self-deceiving; self-defeating

contrapuesto *a* opposing, divergent

contrapunto *m*, counterpoint

contrariar *vt* to counter, oppose; impede; vex, annoy

contrariedad *f*, contrariety, opposition; obstacle; vexation, trouble

contrario (-ia) *a* opposite; hostile, opposed; harmful; adverse, contrary. *n* adversary; opponent. *m*, obstacle. *f*, **contraria**, contrary, opposite. **al contrario,** on the contrary. **llevar la contraria (a),** to oppose; contradict

contrasentido *m*, wrong sense, opposite sense (of words); contradiction of initial premise; self-contradiction; nonsense

contraseña *f*, countersign; *mil* password

contrastar *vt* to contrast; oppose, resist; check (weights and measures); assay; *mech* calibrate, gauge; *vi* contrast

contraste *m*, contrast; opposition, difference; weights and measures inspector; dispute, clash. **en c. a,** in contrast to

contrata *f*, **contrato,** *m*, contract. **contrato de arrendamiento,** lease

contratación *f*, hiring; *com* transaction; commerce, trade

contratar *vt* to contract, enter into an agreement; make a bargain (with), deal (with); hire, contract

contratiempo *m*, mishap, accident

contratista *mf* contractor

contravención *f*, contravention; violation. **en c. a,** in violation of

contraveneno *m*, *med* antidote; remedy, precaution

contravenir *vt irr* to infringe, contravene. See **venir**

contraventana *f*, shutter (for windows)

contravidriera *f*, storm window

contrayente *a* contracting. *mf* contracting party (used of matrimony)

contribución *f*, contribution; tax. **c. sobre la propiedad,** property tax

contribuir *vt irr* to pay (taxes); contribute. See **huir**

contribuyente *a* contributing; contributory. *mf* contributor; taxpayer

contrincante *m*, competitor, candidate (public examinations); rival, opponent

control *m*, control; checking. **c. de precios,** price control

controlar *vt* to control

controversia *f*, controversy

controvertir *vi* and *vt irr* to dispute, argue against, deny. See **sentir**

contumacia *f*, obstinacy; *law* contumacy

contumaz *a* stubborn; impenitent; *law* contumacious; *med* obstinate, resistant (to cure)

conturbar *vt* to perturb, make anxious, disturb; *vr* be perturbed

contuso *a* contused, bruised

convalecencia *f*, convalescence; convalescent home

convalecer *vi irr* to convalesce, get better; *fig* recover, regain (influence, etc.). See **conocer**

convaleciente *a* and *mf* convalescent

convalidar *vt* to ratify, confirm

convencer *vt* to convince; prove beyond doubt, demonstrate to (persons); be convincing (e.g. **No convence,** It's not convincing; **He's not convincing.**) *vr* be convinced

convencimiento *m*, conviction, belief, assurance

convención *f*, pact, formal agreement; harmony, conformity; convention

convencionalismo *m*, conventionality

convenido *a* agreed

conveniencia *f*, conformity, harmony, adjustment; experience, suitability, convenience; advantage; agreement, pact; post as domestic; ease, comfort; *pl* income; social conventions

conveniente *a* convenient, opportune; suitable, fitting; profitable; useful; decorous. **tener por c. + inf,** to think it fitting to + *inf*; find it appropriate to + *inf*

convenio *m*, pact, treaty; *com* agreement, contract

convenir *vi irr* to agree; assemble, congregate; belong; be suitable; *vr* agree; suit oneself. **No me conviene salir esta tarde,** It does not suit me to go out this afternoon. **Me convendría pasar un mes allí,** It would be a good idea (or a wise thing) for me to spend a month there. See **venir**

conventillo *m*, *Lat. Am.* tenement

convento *m*, convent; monastery; religious community

conventual *a* conventual; monastic. *m*, *ecc* conventual

convergencia *f*, convergence

convergir *vi* to converge; *fig* coincide (views, etc.)

conversación *f*, conversation; intercourse, company; *law* criminal conversation

conversar *vi* to converse; chat; live with others; know socially

conversión *f*, conversion; change, transformation; *com* conversion; *mil* wheel; wheeling

convertible *a* convertible

convertir *vt irr* to change, transform; convert; reform; *vr* be transformed; be converted; be reformed. See **sentir**

convexo *a* convex

convicción *f*, conviction; certitude; *law* conviction

convicto (-ta) *a* and *n law* convict

convidado (-da) n guest

convidar vt to invite (persons); encourage, provoke; entice, attract; vr invite oneself; offer one's services

convincente a convincing

convite m, invitation; banquet; party

convivencia f, coexistence, common life, life together. **c. pacífica,** peaceful coexistence

convivir vi to live together, live under the same roof

convocación f, convocation

convocar vt to convene, convoke

convoy m, convoy; escort; following; cruet-stand

convulsión f, convulsion

convulsivo a convulsive

conyugal a conjugal

cónyuge mf husband or (and) wife (used gen. in pl)

coñac m, brandy

coñete a, Chile, Peru mean, stingy

cooperación f, cooperation

cooperador (-ra) a cooperative. n cooperator, collaborator

cooperar vt to cooperate

cooperativa f, cooperative society

cooperativo a cooperative

coordenada f, coordinate

coordinación f, coordination

coordinar vt to coordinate, classify

copa f, wineglass, goblet; glassful; top branches (of trees); crown (of hat); cards heart; gill (liquid measure); inf drink, glass; pl cards hearts (in Spanish pack, goblets)

copal m, Central America, Mexico resin

copartícipe mf co-partner, partaker, participant

copec m, kopeck

Copenhague Copenhagen

copero m, cupbearer; sideboard; cocktail cabinet

copete m, lock, tress (hair); tuft, crest; forelock (horses); head, top (ice-cream, drinks); inf **de alto c.,** aristocratic; socially prominent

copetudo, -a a, Lat. Am. tufted, crested; haughty, stuck-up

copia f, abundance, plenty; copy, reproduction; transcript; imitation

copiador (-ra) a copying. n copier; transcriber. m, copybook

copiar vt to copy

copioso a abundant, plentiful

copla f, couplet; popular four-line poem; couple, pair; pl inf verses

coplero (-ra) n balladmonger; poetaster

copo m, cop (of a spindle); snowflake

copón m, large goblet; ecc ciborium, chalice

cópula f, connection; coupling; joining; copulation

copularse vr to copulate

coque m, coke

coqueluche f, whooping cough

coqueta f, coquette, flirt

coquetear vi to flirt

coqueteo m, coquetry; flirtation

coquetería f, coquetry

coquetón a coquettish

coraje m, courage, valor; anger

coral m, coral. f, coral snake. m, bot coral tree; pl coral beads

coral a choral

coraza f, cuirass; shell (of tortoise); armor-plate, armor (ships, etc.)

corazón m, heart; courage, spirit; love, tenderness; goodwill, benevolence; core (of a fruit); fig pith. **de c.,** sincerely. **tener el c. en la mano,** to wear one's heart on one's sleeve

corazonada f, feeling, instinct; presentiment, apprehension

corbata f, necktie; scarf; ribbon (insignia)

corbatería f, necktie shop

corbatero m, necktie maker; necktie dealer; tie rack

corchea f, mus quaver

corchete m, sew hook and eye; hook

corcho m, bot cork, cork bark; stopper, cork; cork mat; bee hive

corcova f, hump, abnormal protuberance

corcovado (-da) a hunchbacked, crooked. n hunchback

cordaje m, naut cordage, tackling, rope

cordel m, cord; naut line. **a c.,** in a straight line

corderillano, -a a, Argentina, Chile Andean

cordero m, lamb; dressed lambskin; peaceable, mild man; Jesus (gen. **Divino C.**)

cordial a warming, invigorating; affectionate, loving, friendly. m, med cordial

cordialidad f, cordiality, friendliness

cordillera f, mountain range

cordobán m, cured goatskin; Cordovan leather, Spanish leather

cordobés (-esa) a and n Cordovan

cordón m, cord; cordon; ecc rope girdle; arch string-course

cordoncillo m, rib (in cloth); ridge, milling (of coins); sew piping

cordura f, good sense, prudence

Corea Korea

coreografía f, choreography; art of dancing

coreógrafo m, choreographer

corista m, ecc chorister. mf theat member of the chorus

cornada f, horn thrust or wound (bulls, etc.)

córnea f, cornea

corneja f, carrion or black crow

córneo a horny, corneous

corneta f, mus bugle; mus cornet; swineherd's horn; mil pennon. m, bugler; mil cornet. **c. de monte,** hunting horn

cornetín m, dim **corneta,** mus cornet; cornet player

cornezuelo m, dim little horn; med ergot; bot variety of olive

cornisa f, cornice

cornucopia f, cornucopia, horn of plenty; sconce; mirror

cornudo a horned. m, cuckold. **el C.,** the Devil

coro m, choir; chorus; arch choir. **hacer c. (a),** to listen to, support. **saber de c.,** to know by heart

corolario m, corollary

corona f, garland, wreath; halo; (ast arch) corona; crown (of tooth); crown (of head); tonsure; crown (coin); royal power; kingdom; triumph; reward; summit, height, peak; circlet (for candles)

coronación f, coronation; coping stone

coronamiento m, coronation; coping stone; fig crowning touch; naut taffrail

coronar vt to crown; crown (in draughts); complete, round off; vr be crowned; crown oneself; be tipped or capped

coronel m, colonel

coronela f, inf colonel's wife

coronelía f, colonelcy

coronilla f, dim small crown; crown of head; fig inf **estar hasta la c.,** to be fed up

coroza f, dunce's cap

corpiño m, bodice

corporación f, corporation, body, association

corporal a and m, ecc corporal

corporativo a corporate, corporative

corpóreo a corporeal

corporizar vt to embody

corpulento a corpulent, stout

Corpus m, Corpus Christi

corpúsculo m, corpuscle

corral m, yard; pen, enclosure, corral; old-time theater. **c. de madera,** timber yard. inf **hacer corrales,** to play truant

correa f, leather strap or thong; flexibility; mech belt, band

corrección f, correction; correctness; punishment; emendation. **c. de pruebas,** proofreading, proofing, reading proof

correccional a correctional. m, reformatory

correcto a correct; well-bred; unexceptionable, irreproachable; regular (of features)

corredera f, link (engines); mech slide; naut log; racecourse; inf procuress

corredizo a easy to untie; running (of knots); sliding

corredor (-ra) n runner. m, com broker; corridor; inf meddler; inf procurer, pimp. a running. **c. de bolsa,** stockbroker

corregible a corrigible

corregir vt irr to correct; scold, punish; moderate, counteract; mech adjust; vr mend one's ways. **c. pruebas,** to read proof. Pres. Ind. **corrijo, corriges, corrige, corrigen.** Pres. Part. **corrigiendo.** Pres. Subjunc. **corrija, corrijas,** etc. Imperf. Subjunc. **corrigiese,** etc.

correligionario (-ia) n coreligionist; fellow-supporter or believer

correlón, -ona a Mexico, Venezuela cowardly

correntada f, Argentina rapids

correo m, courier; mail; post-office; letters. **c. aéreo,** air-mail. **c. certificado,** registered mail. **a vuelta de c.,** by return of mail. **tren c.,** mail train

correr vi to run; race; sail, steam; flow; blow; flood; extend, stretch; pass (of time); fall due (salary, etc.); be current or general; (with con) be in charge of or responsible for; vt run (a horse); fasten, slide (bolts, etc.); draw (curtains); undergo, suffer; sell, auction; inf steal; fig embarrass; spread (a rumor, etc.); catch, make (bus, train, etc.); vr slide, glide, slip; run (of colors); inf spread oneself, talk too much. **c. cañas,** to participate in a mock joust using reeds as spears

correspondencia f, relationship, connection; intercourse, communication; correspondence, letters; equivalence, exact translation

corresponder vi to requite, repay; be grateful; belong to, concern; devolve upon, fall to; suit, harmonize (with); fit; vr correspond by letters; like or love each other

correspondiente a suitable; proportionate; corresponding. mf correspondent

corresponsal mf correspondent (especially professional); com agent

correveidile mf inf tale-bearer, gossip

corrida f, race, run; aer taxying; bull fight (abb. for **c. de toros**)

corrido a extra, over (of weight); embarrassed; experienced

corriente a current, present; well-known; usual, customary; fluent (style); ordinary, average; easy. f, flow, stream; fig course (of events, etc.); elec current. adv quite, exactly. elec **c. alterna,** alternating current. **c. continua,** direct current. **c. de aire,** draught. **estar al c.,** to be informed (of something)

Corriente del Golfo Gulf Stream

corro m, circle, group; ring (for children's games)

corroboración f, corroboration, confirmation

corroborar vt to fortify; corroborate, support

corroer vt irr to corrode, waste away; fig gnaw. See **roer**

corromper vt to rot; mar; spoil, ruin; seduce; corrupt (texts); bribe; fig contaminate, corrupt; vi stink; vr putrefy, rot; be spoilt; fig be corrupted

corrosión f, corrosion

corrosivo a corrosive

corrugación f, corrugation, wrinkling

corrupción f, rot, putrefaction; corruption, depravity; decay; stink; bribery; falsification (of texts); corruption (of language, etc.)

corrupto a corrupt

corruptor (-ra) n corrupter

corsé m, corset

corsetería f, corset shop or manufactory

cortacircuitos m, elec circuit breaker, cut-out; disconnecting switch

cortado a fitting, proportioned; disjointed (style); confused, shamefaced

cortador m, cutter; cutter-out (dresses, etc.); butcher

cortadura f, cut, wound; cutting (from periodicals); defile; pl clippings, cuttings

cortalápices m, pencil sharpener

cortante a cutting; sharp; piercing (of wind, etc.); trenchant; m, Argentina scissors pl.

cortapapel m, paper-knife

cortapisa f, condition, stipulation

cortaplumas m, penknife

cortar vt to cut; cut out (dresses, etc.); switch off, shut off (water, electricity, etc.); cleave, divide; cut (cards); pierce (wind, etc.); interrupt, impede; omit, cut; fig interrupt (conversation); decide, determine; vr be confused or shamefaced; curdle, turn sour (e.g. **Se cortó la leche,** The milk turned sour); split, fray; chap

cortavidrios m, diamond, glasscutter

corte f, court (royal); retinue; yard; pl Spanish parliament. m, cutting, cut; blade, cutting edge; cutting out, dressmaking; length, material required for garment, shoes, etc.; cut, fit; style; book edge; arch section; means, expedient; counting of money (in a till). **c. de caja,** counting of money (in a till). **c. trasversal,** side view

cortedad f, shortness, brevity; smallness; stupidity, dullness; timidity, shyness. **c. de fuerzas,** lack of strength

cortejar vt to accompany, escort; woo, court

cortejo m, courtship, wooing; suite, accompaniment; gift, present; homage, attention; inf lover, beau

cortés a polite, attentive, courteous, civil

cortesía f, politeness, courtesy; attentiveness; civility; gift, present; favor. **c. internacional,** courtesy of nations. **c. de boca mucho vale y poco cuesta.** Courtesy is worth much and costs little

corteza f, bot bark; anat cortex; skin, peel, crust; aspect, appearance; roughness. **c. terrestre,** Earth's crust, crust of the Earth. **de c.,** superficial (e.g. explanation)

cortijo m, farmhouse and land

cortina f, curtain; fig veil; inf heel taps; mil curtain, screen. **c. de fuego de artillería,** anti-aircraft barrage. **c. de globos de intercepción,** balloon barrage. **c. de humo,** smoke screen. **c. metálica,** metal shutter

corto a short, brief; timid, bashful; concise; defective; stupid, dull; tongue-tied, inarticulate. **c. circuito,** elec short-circuit. **c. de alcances,** dull-witted. **c. de vista,** short-sighted

coruscar vi to glitter, shine

corvadura f, bend; curvature

cosa f, thing. **c. rara,** strange to relate; an extraordinary thing. **como si tal c.,** as though nothing had happened. inf **poquita c.,** a person of no account

cosecha f, harvest; harvest time; reaping, gathering, lifting; yield, produce; crop, shower (of honors, etc.). **c. de vino,** vintage

cosechar vi and vt to harvest, reap

coseno m, cosine

coser vt to sew, stitch; join, unite; press together (lips, etc.). **c. a puñaladas,** to stab repeatedly

cosmético a and m, cosmetic

cósmico a cosmic

cosmografía f, cosmography

cosmonave f, spaceship

cosmopolita a and mf cosmopolitan

cosmopolitismo m, cosmopolitanism

cosmos m, cosmos

cospel m, blank (from which to stamp coins); to ken; subway to ken

cosquillas f pl, tickling. **hacer c. (a),** to tickle

cosquillear vt to tickle

cosquilleo m, tickle, tickling

cosquilloso a ticklish; hypersensitive, touchy

costa f, cost; expense; coast; pl law costs. **a c. de,** by dint of; at the cost of. **a toda c.,** at all costs

Costa de Marfil Ivory Coast

costado m, anat side; mil flank; side; pl line of descent, genealogy. naut **dar el c.,** to be broadside on

costal m, sack, bag

costanero a sloping; coast, coastal

costar vi irr to cost; cause. See **contar**

costarriqueño (-ña) a and n Costa Rican

coste m, cost, price

costear vt to pay for, defray the expense of; naut coast; Argentina pasture; vr pay (for itself)

costilla f, (anat aer naut arch) rib; fig inf better half, wife; pl inf back, behind

costillaje, costillar m, anat ribs; naut ship's frame

costoso a expensive, costly; valuable; dear, costly, difficult

costra f, crust; scab; rind (of cheese)

costumbre f, habit; custom

costumbrista mf writer on everyday life and customs. a (of literary work) dealing with life and customs

costura f, sewing; seam; needlework; carp joint; riveting

costurar, costurear vi, Lat. Am. to sew

costurera f, seamstress

cota f, surv elevation, height; coat (of mail); quota. **c. de malla,** chain-mail

cotangente f, cotangent

cotejar vt to compare; collate

cotejo m, comparison; collation

cótel m, cocktail, drink

cotelera f, cocktail shaker

cotidiano a daily

cotizable a valued at; (of prices, shares) quoted

cotización f, com quotation; com rate. **boletín de c.,** price list (of shares, etc.)

cotizar vt com to quote (prices, rates)

coto m, enclosed ground; boundary stone; preserve, covert; hand's breadth; end, stop, limit. **c. de caza,** game preserve

cotorra f, small green parrot; magpie; inf chatterbox

coyote m, coyote, prairie wolf; Mexico fixer (anyone who can pull strings to cut red tape or achieve something illegally); smuggler (of goods or people)

coyuntura f, anat joint; juncture, occasion

coz f, kick, recoil (of gun); butt (of a rifle); inf slap in the face, unprovoked rudeness. **dar coces,** to kick

cranearse vr, Chile to burn the midnight oil

cráneo m, cranium, skull

crápula f, drunkenness; depravity, immorality, debauchery

craso a fat, greasy; thick; unpardonable, crass (often with ignorancia). m, fatness; ignorance

creación f, creation; universe, world; foundation, establishment; appointment (dignitaries)

creador (-ra) n creator, originator. m, God. a creative

crear vt to create; found, institute, establish; make, appoint

crecer vi irr to grow; grow up; increase in size; grow longer; wax (moon); come in (of the tide); increase in value (money); vr become more sure of oneself; swell with pride; grow in authority. See **nacer**

creces f pl, increase, interest. **con c.,** fully, amply. **pagar con c.,** fig to pay with interest

crecida f, swollen river or stream; food; rising (of the tide)

crecido a grown up; considerable; abundant, plentiful; large; full; serious, important

crecidos m pl, widening stitches (knitting)

creciente a growing; rising (of the tide); crescent (moon). m, her crescent. f, rising of the tide; crescent moon

crecimiento m, growing; growth, development; increase (in value, money); waxing (of moon)

credenciales f pl, credentials

credibilidad f, credibility

crédito m, belief, credence; assent, acquiescence; reputation, name; favor, popularity, acceptance; com credit; com letter of credit. **créditos activos,** assets. **créditos pasivos,** liabilities. **a c.,** on credit

credo m, creed. inf **en un c.,** in a jiffy

credulidad f, credulity

crédulo a credulous

creencia f, belief; religion, sect, faith

creer vt irr to believe; think, consider, opine; think likely or probable. **¡Ya lo creo!** I should just think so! Rather! **creerse la divina garza,** Mexico to think one is God's gift to the world. **creerse descender del sobaco de Jesucristo,** to think one is God's gift to the world. Pres. Part. **creyendo.** Preterite **creyó, creyeron.** Imperf. Subjunc. **creyese,** etc.

creíble a credible

creído, -a a, Lat. Am. credulous, trusting

crema f, cream (off milk); custard mold, cream, shape; face cream; cold cream; elect, flower (of society, etc.)

cremallera f, mech rack, ratch; zip fastener. **colgar la c.,** to give a housewarming

crematorio m, crematorium. a burning; cremating

cremoso a creamy

crencha f, parting (of the hair); each side of parting

crepitación f, crackling, sputtering; hissing; roar (of a fire); med crepitation

crepitar vi to crackle; sputter; hiss; roar (of a fire); med crepitate

crepuscular a twilight

crepúsculo m, twilight, half light

Creso Croesus

crespo a curly, frizzy (hair); rough (of animal's fur); curled (leaves); artificial, involved (style)

crespón m, crape

cresta f, comb (of cock, etc.); tuft, topknot (birds); plume; summit, top (of mountains); crest (of a wave); her crest

creta f, chalk

creyente a believing; religious. mf believer

cría f, rearing; bringing up; nursing; suckling; breeding; brood; litter

criada f, servant, maid

criadero m, min vein, deposit; tree nursery, plantation; breeding farm or place. a prolific

criado m, servant. a bred, brought up (used with bien or mal, well or badly brought up)

criador (-ra) n breeder, keeper, raiser. a creating; rearing; creative; fertile, rich

criandera f. Lat. Am. nursemaid, wet nurse

crianza f, feeding, suckling; lactation; manners. **buena** (or **mala**) **c., good** (or **bad**) **breeding or upbringing**

criar vt to create; procreate; rear, educate, bring up; feed, nurse, suckle; raise (birds, animals); inspire, give rise to. **Me crié raquítico,** I grew up delicate

criatura f, being, creature; man, human being; infant; small child; fetus; fig puppet, tool

criba f, sieve, cribble

cribar vt to sieve; riddle (earth, etc.)

crimen m, crime. **c. pasional,** crime of passion

criminal a and m, criminal

criminalidad f, guilt; crime ratio; delinquency

criminalista mf criminal lawyer; criminologist

criminología f, criminology

crin f, horsehair; (gen. pl) mane

crinolina f, crinoline

crío m, inf kid, brat

criollo (-lla) a and n creole. a indigenous, native

cripta f, crypt

criptografía f, cryptography

crisis f, crisis. **c. de desarrollo,** growing pains. **c. de vivienda,** housing shortage

crisma m, or f, chrism

crisol m, crucible; melting pot

crispado a stiffened

crispar vt to cause to contract or twitch; vr twitch. inf **Se me crispan los nervios,** My nerves are all on edge

cristal m, crystal; glass; windowpane; mirror; water. **c. tallado,** cut glass

cristalería f, glassware; glass manufacture; glass panes; glass and china shop

cristalino a crystalline. m, lens (of the eye)

cristalización f, crystallization

cristalizar vi to crystallize; fig take shape; vt cause to crystallize

cristalografía f, crystallography

cristiandad f, Christendom

cristianismo m, Christianity; Christendom

cristianizar vt to convert to Christianity, christianize

cristiano (-na) a and n Christian. a inf watered (of wine). m, inf Spanish (contrasted with other languages); inf soul, person

cristo m, Christ; crucifix. inf **donde C. dio las tres voces,** in the middle of nowhere

cristus m, Christ-cross; alphabet. **no saber el c.,** to be extremely ignorant

criterio m, criterion, standard; judgment, discernment; opinion. **a c. de,** in the opinion of. **según mi c.,** in my opinion

crítica (a) f, criticism (of)

criticar vt to criticize; censure, find fault with, blame

crítico a critical; censorious; dangerous, difficult; med critical. m, critic; fault-finder

criticón (-ona) a censorious, hyper-critical. n fault-finder

Croacia Croatia

croar vi (frog) to croak

croata a and mf Croatian

croché m, crochet work

cromado a chromium-plated

crónica f, chronicle; diary of events

crónico a chronic; inveterate

cronología f, chronology

cronológico a chronological

cronómetro m, stop-watch

croqueta f, croquette

croquis m, sketch, outline, drawing. **c. de nivel,** (optical) foresight

crótalo m, rattlesnake; snapper (kind of castanet)

cruce m, crossing; point of intersection; crossroads

crucero m, ecc cross-bearer; crossroads; arch transept; ast Cross; naut cruiser

crucificar vt to crucify; fig inf torment, torture

crucifijo m, crucifix

crucifixión f, crucifixion

crucigrama m, crossword puzzle

cruda f, Mexico hangover

crudeza f, rawness, uncookedness; unripeness; rawness (silk, etc.); crudeness; harshness; inf boasting

crudo a uncooked, raw; green, unripe; indigestible; raw, natural, unbleached; harsh, cruel; cold, raw; inf boastful. **crudos de petróleo,** m pl crude oil

crueldad f, cruelty; harshness

cruento a bloody

crujía f, passage, corridor; naut midship gangway

crujidero a crackling; creaking; crispy; clattering; rustling; chattering

crujido m, creak, crack, crackling, rustle

crujir vi to creak, crackle, rustle

crup m, croup

crustáceo a and m, crustacean

cruz f, cross; tails (of coin); withers (of animals); insignia, decoration; affliction, trouble; *ast* Southern Cross; *print* dagger, obelisk, obelus. **c. doble,** diesis, double dagger. **c. de mayo,** May cross. **c. gamada,** swastika. *inf* **IC. y raya!** An end to this! **en c.,** in the shape of a cross. *inf* **hacerse cruces,** to be left speechless, be dumbfounded

cruza *f, Lat. Am.* intersection

cruzada *f,* crusade; crossroads; campaign

cruzado *a* cross; double-breasted (of coats). *m,* crusader; member of military order

cruzamiento *m,* crossing; intersection

cruzar *vt* to cross; intersect; interbreed; bestow a cross upon; *naut* cruise; *Chile, Peru* quarrel with; *vr* take part in a crusade; cross one another; coincide; *geom* intersect

cu *f,* name of the letter Q

cuaco *m, Lat. Am.* horse

cuaderna *f, naut* ship's frame, timber; double fours (backgammon)

cuaderno *m,* notebook, jotter, account book; *inf* card pack. *naut* **c. de bitácora,** logbook

cuadra *f,* stable; ward, dormitory; hall, large room; quarter of a mile; *Lat. Am.* block (of houses)

cuadrado *a* square; perfect, exact. *m,* square; (*carp mil math*) square; windowframe; clock (of a stocking)

cuadragésima *f,* Quadragesima

cuadrángulo *m,* quadrangle

cuadrante *m,* quadrant; dial, face

cuadrar *vt* (*math carp*) to square; make square; *vi* correspond, tally; fit, be appropriate. *vr mil* stand at attention; *fig inf* dig one's heels in

cuadrática *f,* quadratic equation

cuadrático *a* quadratic

cuadratura *f,* squareness; (*math ast*) quadrature

cuadrilátero *m,* quadrilateral; boxing ring. *a* quadrilateral

cuadrilla *f,* gang; company, band, group; police patrol; quadrille (dance); matadors and their assistants (at a bull fight). **c. carrillana,** track gang

cuadro *m,* square; picture-frame; frame (of bicycle); flowerbed; *theat* scene; spectacle, sight; board (of instruments); description (in novel, etc.); *mil* command, officers; square (of troops). **c. de distribución,** *elec* main switchboard. **c. enrejado,** play pen. **cuadro de costumbres,** word-picture of everyday life and customs. **cuadro vivo,** tableau vivant. **a cuadros,** checked, in squares

cuadrúpedo (**-da**) *a* and *n* quadruped

cuádruple *a* quadruple

cuajada *f,* curd (of milk)

cuajar *m,* maw (of a ruminant)

cuajar *vt* to coagulate; curdle; *vi inf* achieve, get away with; *vr* be coagulated

or curdled; *inf* be packed or chock full; get stuck (e.g. a piece of food in one's throat)

cuajarón *m,* clot (of blood, etc.)

cuajo *m,* rennet; coagulation; curdling; *anat* abomasum

cual *rel. pron* sing. *mf* and *neut. pl* **cuales,** which; who; such as (e.g. **Le detuvieron sucesos cuales suelen ocurrir,** He was detained by events such as usually happen). **a c. mas,** vying (with) (e.g. **Los dos canónigos a c. más grueso,** The two canons each fatter (vying in fatness) than the other). **c.** is used with *def. art* **el** (**la, lo, los, las**) **cual(es),** who; which, when the antecedent is a noun (e.g. **Juan saltó en el barco, el c. zarpó en seguida,** John jumped into the boat which sailed at once). **por lo c.,** for which reason. *adv* like (gen. literary or poet.). **¿cuál?** *interr. pron* (no article) which? what? e.g. **Aquí tienes dos cuadros, ¿cuál de ellos te gusta?** Here are two pictures, which one do you like? Also expresses an implicit question, e.g. **No sé cuál te guste,** I don't know which one you like. **¡cuál!** *adv* how! **c. . . . . c.** *indef pron* some . . . some

cualesquier *a pl* of **cualquier**

cualesquiera *a pl* of **cualquiera**

cualidad *f,* quality; characteristic; talent

cualitativo *a* qualitative

cualquier *abb* of **cualquiera,** any; *pl* **cualesquier.** Only used as abb. *before noun*

cualquiera *a mf* any, e.g. **una canción c.,** any song. *pron* anybody, each, anyone whatsoever, whoever (e.g. **IC. diría que no te gusta!** Anyone would say you don't like it!) *inf* **un c.,** a nobody

cuán *adv* how (e.g. **IC. bello es!** How beautiful it is). Used only before a or *adv*. Abb. of **cuánto**

cuando *adv* when; if. *interr* **¿cuándo?** *conjunc* although; since; sometimes; *prep* during (e.g. **c. la guerra,** during the war) **c. más,** at most, at best. **c. menos,** at the least. **c. no,** if not (e.g. **Es agnóstica cuando no atea,** She's an agnostic, if not an atheist) **de c. en c.,** from time to time

cuandoquiera *adv* whenever

cuantía *f,* quantity, amount; importance, rank, distinction

cuantiar *vt* to value, estimate; tax

cuantioso *a* large, considerable; numerous; plentiful, abundant

cuantitativo *a* quantitative

cuanto *a* as much as, all the; *pl* as many as, all the (e.g. **Te daré cuantas muñecas veas allí,** I'll give you all the dolls you see there). *a. correlative* the . . . the, as . . . as (e.g. **C. más tanto, mejor,** The more the better). **cuánto,** *a* and *pron interr* and *interj* how much!; *pl* how many (e.g. **¡Cuánto tiempo sin verla!** How long without seeing her!) *pron neut* **cuanto,** as much as, all that (e.g. **Te daré c. quieras,** I shall give you all that you wish). *adv* **cuanto,** as soon as. **c. antes,** as soon as possible. **c. a** or **en c. a,** concerning. *adv* and *conjunc* **c. más,** all the more (e.g. **Se lo diré c. más que tenía esa intención,** I shall tell him all the more because I meant to do so). *adv* **en c.,** as soon as, immediately (e.g. **Lo haré en c. venga,** I shall do it immediately he comes). **en c. a,** with regard to. **por c.,** inasmuch, for this reason. *adv interr* **¿Cuánto?** How much? How long? *adv interj* How! How much! (e.g. **¡Cuánto me gustaría ir!** How much I should like to go!)

cuáquero (-ra) *n* Quaker

cuarenta *a* and *m,* forty; fortieth. **esas son otras cuarenta** *Argentina, Peru* that's a different story, that's a horse of another color

cuarentena *f,* fortieth; period of forty days, months or years; Lent; quarantine

cuarentón (-ona) *n* person forty years old

cuaresma *f,* Lent

cuarta *f,* quarter, fourth; hand's breadth; *mus* fourth; *ast* quadrant

cuartear *vt* to quarter, divide into quarters; cut or divide into pieces

cuartel *m,* barracks; *naut* hatch; quarter, fourth; her quarter; district, ward; flower-bed; *inf* house, accommodation; *mil* quarter, mercy; *mil* billet, station. *mil* **c. general,** general headquarters

cuartelada *f, naut* quarter; military rebellion, military uprising, mutiny

cuartelazo *m,* military rebellion, military uprising, mutiny

cuarto *m,* room; quarter, fourth; point (of compass); watch (on battleships); *ast* quarter, phase; portion, quarter; joint (of meat); *pl* quarters (of animals); *inf* penny, farthing. *a* quarter, fourth. **c. creciente,** first phase (of moon). **c. de hora,** quarter of an hour. **c. doble** *Mexico* double room. **c. sencillo** *Mexico* single room. **en c.,** *print* in quarto. *inf* **no tener un c.,** to be broke

cuarzo *m,* quartz

cuasidelito *m, law* technical offence

cuatrillón *m,* quadrillion

cuatrimestre *a* of four months' duration. *m,* space of four months

cuatrimotor *m, aer* four-engine airplane

cuatrisílabo *a* quadrisyllabic

cuatro *a* four; fourth. *m,* figure four; fourth (of days of months); playing-card with four spots; *mus* quartet. **el c. de mayo,** the fourth of May. **Son las c.,** It is four o'clock

cuatrocientos *a* four hundred; four hundredth.

cuba *f,* barrel, cask; tub, vat; *inf* pot-bellied person; *inf* drunkard, toper

cubano (-na) *a* and *n* Cuban

cubería *f,* cooperage

cubeta *f, dim* keg, small cask; bucket, pail; *phot* developing dish

cubicar *vt math* to cube; *geom* measure the volume of

cúbico *a* cubic

cubículo *m,* cubicle

cubierta *f,* cover; envelope; casing; deck (of ship); tire cover; book-jacket; pretext, excuse. **c. de escotilla,** *naut* companion-hatch. **c. de paseo,** promenade deck

cubierto *m,* cover, place at table; course (of a meal); table d'hôte, complete meal; roof. **un c. de doscientas pesetas,** a two hundred peseta meal

cubil *m,* lair, den (of animals)

cubilete *m, cul* mold; dice box; conjurer's cup

cubismo *m,* cubism

cubista *mf* cubist. *a* cubistic

cubo *m,* bucket, pail; *mech* socket; *math* cube; hub (of a wheel); mill-pond

cubrecama *m,* bedspread

cubrir *vt* to cover; *mil* defend; spread over, extend over; conceal, hide; *com* cover; dissemble; *arch* roof; cover one's head; pay, meet (debts, etc.); cover or protect oneself (by insurance, etc.). *Past Part.* **cubierto**

cucaracha *f,* cockroach

cuchara *f,* spoon; ladle; *naut* boat scoop; scoop, dipper. *fig meter* **c.,** to stick one's oar in

cucharada *f,* spoonful; ladleful

cuchí *m, Peru* hog

cúchi *a inf, Venezuela* cute, sweet

cuchichear *vi* to whisper

cuchicheo *m,* whisper; whispering; murmur

cuchillada *f,* knife thrust or wound; *pl* (in sleeves, etc.) slashes; fight, blows

cuchillo *m,* knife; *sew* gore, gusset (gen. *pl*); authority, power; anything triangular in shape. **pasar a c.,** to put to the sword

cuclillas, en *adv* in a squatting position

cuculla *f,* cowl, hood

cucurucho *m,* paper cornet

cueca *f, chile* cueca (Chilean dance)

cuello *m, anat* neck; neck (of bottle, etc.); *sew* neck; collar; necklet (of fur, etc.)

cuenca *f,* socket (of eye); *geog* catchment-basin; gorge, deep valley. **c. de un río,** river-basin

cuenta *f,* count, counting; calculation; account; bead; charge, responsibility; reckoning; explanation, reason; *com* bill. **c. a cero, c. a la inversa, c. atrás,** count-down. **c. corriente,** current account. **cuentas alegres, cuentas galanas,** *inf* idle dreams, illusions. **c. pendiente,** outstanding account. *inf* **caer en la c.,** to tumble to, realize. **llevar la c.,** to reckon, keep account. **sin c.,** countless. **tener en c.,** to bear in mind

cuentacorrentista *mf* one who has a bank account

cuentagotas *m*, dropper, dropping tube

cuentakilómetros *m*, speedometer

cuentapasos *m*, pedometer

cuentista *mf* storyteller; *inf* gossip

cuento *m*, story, tale; narrative; calculation; *inf* gossip, fairytale; *math* million. **c. de viejas,** old wives' tale. *fig inf* **dejarse de cuentos,** to go straight to the point. *inf* **Va de c.,** it is told, they say

cuerda *f*, rope; cord; string; *geom* chord; *mus* string; catgut; chain (of clock); *mus* chord; vocal range. **dar c. (a),** to wind up (a watch); lead on, make talk. **de cuerdas cruzadas,** overstrung (of a piano)

cuerdo *a* sane; prudent; levelheaded

cuerno *m*, *anat* horn; feeler, antenna; *mus* horn; horn (of the moon). **c. de abundancia,** horn of plenty. *inf* **poner en los cuernos de la luna,** to praise to the skies

cuero *m*, hide, pelt; leather. **c. charolado,** patent leather. **en cueros,** stark naked

cuerpo *m*, *anat* body or trunk; flesh (as opposed to spirit); bodice; volume, book; main portion; collection; size, volume; physical appearance; corpse; group, assembly; corporation, association; *geom* solid; *chem* element; thickness, density; *mil* corps. **c. de bomberos,** fire brigade. **c. de guardia,** guardhouse. **c. de la vida,** staff of life; *inf* **dar con el c. en tierra,** to fall flat. **de c. entero,** *art* full-length (portrait). **en c.,** without a coat, lightly clad. **un c. a c.,** a clinch (in wrestling)

cuervo *m*, raven; crow

cuesta *f*, slope, incline, gradient. **c. abajo (arriba),** down (up) hill. **a cuestas,** on one's back; having the responsibility of

cuestión *f*, problem, question; quarrel, disagreement; affair, matter; torture

cuestionar *vt* to discuss, debate

cuestionario *m*, questionnaire

cueva *f*, cave, cavern; basement, cellar. *fig* **c. de ladrones,** den of thieves

cui *m*, *Lat. Am.* guinea pig

cuico, -a *mf*, *Argentina, Chile* foreigner, outsider; *Mexico, informal* cop (police officer)

cuidado *m*, carefulness, pains; attention; charge, care, responsibility; anxiety, fear. *interj* **IC.I** Careful! Look out! **Me tiene sin c. su opinión,** I am not interested in his (your) opinion. *inf* **estar al c. de,** to be under the direction of. **estar de c.,** to be dangerously ill

cuidadoso (de) *a* careful (about or with); anxious (about); concerned (with); watchful; conscientious

cuidar *vt* to care for; tend; take care of, look after; mind, be careful of; *vr* look after oneself

cuita *f*, misfortune, anxiety, trouble

cuitado *a* unfortunate, worried; timid, bashful, humble

cuitla *f*, *Mexico* poultry manure

culata *f*, *anat* haunch; butt (of fire-arms); back, rear; *aut* sump

culebra *f*, snake; *inf* trick, joke; *inf* sudden uproar. **hacer c.,** to stagger along

culebrear *vi* to wriggle; grovel; meander, wind

culí *m*, coolie

culinario *a* culinary

culminación *f*, culmination, peak; *ast* zenith

culminante *a* culminating; *fig* outstanding

culminar *vi* to culminate (in)

culo *m*, buttocks, seat; rump; anus; base, bottom. **c. de lámpara,** *arch* pendant; print tail-piece

culpa *f*, fault; blame. **echar la c. (a),** to blame. **por c. de,** through the fault of. **tener la c.,** to be to blame

culpabilidad *f*, guilt

culpable *a* culpable

culpado (-da) *n* culprit

culpar *vt* to blame, accuse; criticize, censure

cultígeno *m*, cultigen

cultivación *f*, cultivation; culture

cultivador (-ra) *n* cultivator; planter

cultivar *vt* to cultivate; develop; exercise, practise (professions); culture (bacteriology)

cultivo *m*, cultivation; farming; culture (bacteriological)

culto *a* cultivated; educated; cultured; elegant, artificial (style). *m*, worship; cult; religion, creed; homage

cultura *f*, cultivation; culture. **de c. universitaria,** college-educated

cultural *a* cultural

cumbre *f*, peak, crest, summit; *fig* zenith, acme

cumpleaños *m*, birthday

cumplido *a* complete; thorough; long; plentiful; courteous, punctilious; fulfilled. *m*, courtesy, attention; formality. **gastar cumplidos,** to stand on ceremony; be formal

cumplimentar *vt* to congratulate; perform, carry out

cumplimentero *a* over-complimentary; *inf* gushing

cumplimiento *m*, fulfilment, performance; courtesy, formality; completion; complement

cumplir *vt* to perform, carry into effect; reach (of age); keep (promises). **c. su palabra,** to keep one's word; *vi* perform a duty; expire, fall due; serve the required term of military service; be necessary, behove; *vr* be fulfilled, come true. **por c.,** as a matter of form

cumulativo a cumulative

cúmulo *m,* heap, pile; great many, host, mass, myriad; (cloud) cumulus; thunderhead

cuna *f,* cradle; foundling hospital; birthplace; origin, genesis; *pl* cat's cradle (game)

cundir *vi* to extend, spread (gen. liquids); be diffused (news); expand, grow

cuneco, -a *mf Venezuela* baby of the family

cuneiforme a wedge-shaped, cuneiform

cuña *f,* wedge; *mech* quoin. *mil* **practicar una c.,** to make a wedge

cuñada *f,* sister-in-law

cuñado *m,* brother-in-law

cuño *m,* die, stamp; *fig* impression; mark on silver, hallmark. **de viejo c.,** old-guard (e.g. socialites)

cuota *f,* quota; share; subscription; fee

Cupido *m,* Cupid; philanderer

cupo *m,* quota; share; tax rate; *mil* contingent

cupón *m,* coupon

cúpula *f, arch* dome, cupola; *bot* cup

cura *m,* parish priest; *inf* Roman Catholic priest. *f,* cure (e.g. **La enfermedad tiene c.,** The illness can be cured); healing; remedy. **c. de almas,** cure of souls. **primera c.,** first aid. *inf* **c. de misa y olla,** ignorant priest

curación *f,* cure, remedy; healing

curador (-ra) *n* curer, salter. *m,* (*Scots law*) curator. a curing; healing

curaduría *f, law* guardianship

curanderismo *m,* quackery, charlatanism; quack medicine

curandero (-ra) *n* quack doctor; charlatan

curar *vi* to heal, cure; (*with de*) take care of; care about, mind; *vt* cure, salt; treat medically (bandage, give medicines, etc.); cure (leather); bleach (cloth); season (timber); *fig* remedy (an evil)

curativo a curative

curato *m, ecc* parish, cure

Curazao Curaçao

curia *f, law* bar; tribunal; *ecc* curia; care, attention

curiana *f,* cockroach

curiosear *vi* to pry; be curious (about); meddle, be a busybody

curiosidad *f,* curiosity; inquisitiveness, meddlesomeness; neatness; carefulness, conscientiousness; curio

curioso a curious; inquisitive; interesting, odd; neat, clean; conscientious, careful

Curita *f, trademark* Band-Aid

cursado a experienced, versed

cursante *m,* student

cursar *vt* to frequent, visit; do repeatedly; study, attend classes, take courses (e.g. **¿En qué escuela cursan?** At what school are you studying?); expedite (public admin.)

cursi a *inf* vulgar, in bad taste; loud, crude

cursilería *f, inf* vulgarity, bad taste

cursillo *m,* minicourse, short course; short series of lectures

cursiva *f,* italics. **en c.,** in italics, italicized

cursivo a cursive

curso *m,* course, direction; duration, passage (time); progress; route; course of study; academic year; succession, series; *com* tender

curtido *m,* tanning; leather; tanned leather (gen. *pl*)

curtidor *m,* tanner

curtiduría *f,* tannery

curtimiento *m,* tanning; effect of weather on the complexion; toughening-up; hardening

curtir *vt* to tan; *fig* bronze (complexions); make hardy, harden up; *vr* be weather-beaten; be hardy. *inf* **estar curtido en,** to be experienced in; be expert at

curul a **curule** *m,* seat (in parliament)

curva *f,* curve; bend. *surv* **c. de nivel,** contour line

curvatura, curvidad *f,* curvature

curvo a curved; bent. *m,* curve

cusma *f, Lat. Am.* sleeveless shirt, tunic

custodia *f,* custody; guardianship, care; *ecc* monstrance; custodian, keeper; guardian; guard

custodiar *vt* to watch, guard; look after, care for; *naut* convoy

custodio a guardian; guarding; custodial. *m,* custodian; guard. **angel c.,** guardian angel

cutama *f, Argentina* blanket; *Chile* bag, sack

cutáneo a cutaneous, skin

cutícula *f,* cuticle

cutis *m,* complexion; skin (sometimes *f*)

cuyo (cuya, cuyos, cuyas) *rel pron poss* whose, of which (e.g. **el viejo cuya barba era más blanca que la nieve,** the old man whose beard was whiter than snow). *interr* **¿Cúyo?** Whose? (e.g. **¿Cúyos son estos lápices?** Whose pencils are these?) (gen. **de quién** or **de quiénes** is used rather than **cúyo**). *m,* beau, lover

D

dable a practicable, possible

daca Give me!

dadista mf, Mexico gambler

dádiva f, gift, present

dadivoso a generous, liberal

dado m, die; arch dado. conjunc **d. que,** given that, supposing that. **cargar los dados,** to load the dice

dador (-ra) n giver, donor. m, com bearer; com drawer (of a bill of exchange)

daguerrotipo m, daguerreotype

¡dale! interj Stop! No more about . . . !

dalia f, bot dahlia

dallar vt to scythe (grass)

dalle m, scythe

dalmática f, dalmatic, loose tunic or vestment

daltoniano a color-blind

daltonismo m, color-blindness

dama f, lady; noblewoman; lady-in-waiting; lady-love; mistress, concubine; queen (chess); king (checkers); theat **d. primera,** leading lady

damas f pl, checkers (game)

Damasco Damascus

damería f, prudery, affectation

damnificar vt to injure

danés (-esa) a Danish. n Dane. m, Danish (language)

danta f, zool tapir

Danubio, el the Danube

danza f, dance; set (of dancers); fig inf dirty business. **d. de arcos,** dance of the arches. **d. de cintas,** maypole dance. **d. de monos,** amusing spectacle

danzador (-ra) n dancer; a dancing

danzar vt and vi to dance; vi jump up and down, rattle; inf interfere, meddle

danzarín (-ina) n good dancer; inf meddler; inf playboy

danzón m, Cuban dance

dañado a evil, perverse; damned; spoiled, damaged

dañador (-ra) a harmful. n injurer, offender

dañar vt to hurt, harm; damage, spoil; vr spoil, deteriorate

dañino a destructive (often of animals); hurtful, harmful. **animales dañinos,** vermin, pests

daño m, hurt; damage; loss. law **daños y perjuicios,** damages. **hacerse d.,** to hurt oneself

dañoso a hurtful, harmful

dar vt irr to give; wish, express (congratulations, etc.); hand over; concede, grant; inspire; produce, yield; cause, create; sacrifice; propose, put forward; take (a walk); believe, consider; deliver (blows, etc.); administer (medicine); provide with; apply, coat with; occasion; perform (plays); propose (a toast); give forth, emit; set (norms), render (thanks, etc.); hold (banquets, etc.); proffer, hold out; vi to strike (clocks); (with prep a) overlook, look on to (e.g. **Su ventana da a la calle,** His window looks on to the street); (with con) find, meet (things, persons); (with de) fall on, fall down (e.g. **Dio de cabeza,** He fell head first. **Dio de espaldas,** He fell on his back); (with en) fall into, incur; insist on or persist in (doing something); acquire the habit of (e.g. **Dieron en no venir a vernos,** They took to not coming to see us); solve, guess (riddles, etc.); strike, wound, hurt (e.g. **La bala le dio en el brazo,** The bullet struck him in the arm); (with por) decide on (e.g. **Di por no hacerlo,** I decided not to do it). vr to yield, give in; (with prep a) engage in, devote oneself to; (with por) think or consider oneself (e.g. **Me di por muerto,** I gave myself up for dead). **d. alas a,** to propagate, spread (a belief). **darse a la vela,** to set sail. **darse la mano,** to shake hands. **darse por buenos,** to make up a quarrel, be friends. **darse prisa,** to hurry up, make haste. **darse uno a conocer,** to make oneself known. **darse uno por entendido,** to show that one understands; be grateful. **No se me da un bledo,** I don't care a straw. **d. abajo,** to fall down. **d. bien por mal,** to return good for evil. **d. a conocer,** to make known. **d. a entender,** to suggest, hint. **d. a luz,** to give birth; publish, issue. **d. cuenta de,** to give an account of. **d. de baja,** mil to muster out, discharge. **d. de comer,** to feed. **d. de sí,** to stretch, expand; produce, yield; give of itself (oneself, himself, themselves) (either in good or bad sense). **d. diente con diente,** to chatter (of teeth), shiver. **d. el pésame,** to tender condolences. **d. en cara,** fig inf to throw in one's face. **d. en el clavo,** fig to hit the mark. **d. en qué pensar,** to make suspicious, cause to think. **d. fe,** to certify, attest. **d. fiado,** to give on credit. **d. fianza,** to give security. **d. fin a,** to finish. **d. licencia,** to permit, allow. **d. los buenos días,** to wish good day or good morning. **d. mal,** to have bad luck at cards. **d. parte de,** to announce; issue a communiqué about (e.g. **Dieron parte de la pérdida del buque,** They announced the loss of the ship). **d. prestado,** to lend. **d. qué decir,** to cause a scandal. **d. qué hacer,** to cause trouble. **d. razón de,** to give an account of. **d. sobre uno,** to assault a person. **d. un abrazo,** to embrace. **d. voces,** to shriek; call out. inf **Donde las dan las toman,** It's only tit-for-tat. inf **No me da la real gana,** I darn well don't want to. Pres. Ind. **doy, das,** etc. Preterite **di, diste,** etc. Pres. Subjunc. **dé,** etc. Imperf. Subjunc. **diese,** etc.

dardo *m,* (*mil sport*) dart; *icht* dace; lampoon

dares y tomares *m, pl* give and take; *inf* back-chat. Generally used with *andar,* *haber* or *tener*

dársena *f, naut* dock

data *f,* date (calendar); *com* credit

datar *vt* to date; *vi* (*with de*) date from; *vr* *com* credit

dátil *m, bot* date

dato *m,* datum; basis, fact

de *f,* name of letter D. *prep* of (possessive) (e.g. **Este cuadro es de Vd.,** This picture is yours); from (place and time) (e.g. **Vengo de Madrid,** I come from Madrid. **de vez en cuando,** from time to time); with, of, from, as the result of (e.g. **Lloraban de miedo,** They were crying with fright. **Murió de un ataque del corazón,** He died from a heart attack); for, to (e.g. **Es hora de marchar,** It is time to leave); with (of characteristics) (e.g. **el señor de los lentes,** the gentleman with the eyeglasses. **el cuarto de la alfombra azul,** the room with the blue carpet); when, as (e.g. **De niños nos gustaban los juguetes,** When we were children we liked toys); by (e.g. **Es un ensayo del mismo autor,** It is an essay by the same author. **Fue amado de todos,** He was loved by all. **Es hidalgo de nacimiento,** He is a gentleman by birth). Indicates the material of which a thing is made (e.g. **La mesa es de mármol,** The table is marble). Indicates contents of a thing (e.g. **un vaso de leche,** a glass of milk). Shows manner in which an action is performed (e.g. **Lo hizo de prisa,** He did it hurriedly). Shows the use to which an article is put (e.g. **una mesa de escribir,** a writing-table. **una máquina de coser,** a sewing-machine. **un caballo de batalla,** a war-horse). Sometimes used for emphasis (e.g. **El tonto de tu secretario,** That fool of a secretary of yours). Used by Spanish married women before husband's family name (e.g. **Señora Martínez de Cabra,** Mrs. Cabra (née Martínez)). Used after many adverbs (generally of time or place) to form prepositional phrases (e.g. **detrás de,** behind. **enfrente de,** opposite to; in front of. **de acá para allá,** here and there. **de allí a poco,** shortly afterward. **de allí a pocos días,** a few days later. **de bamba,** by chance. **de cabo a rabo,** from cover to cover. **además de,** besides, etc.). Used at beginning of various adverbial phrases (e.g. **de noche,** at night. **de día,** by day. **de antemano,** previously, **la persona de mi derecha** the person at my right, etc.). Used partitively before nouns, pronouns, adjectives (e.g. **Estas historias tienen algo de verdad,** These stories have some truth in them. **¿Qué hay de nuevo?** What's the news?) Forms many compound words (e.g. **deponer, dene-**

gar, etc.). With **"uno"** means "at" (e.g. **Lo cogió de un salto,** He caught it at one bound). **de a** is used before expressions of price, weight, etc. (e.g. **un libro de a cinco pesetas,** a five-peseta book)

debajo *adv* underneath; below

debate *m,* discussion, debate; dispute

debatible *a* debatable

debatir *vt* to discuss, debate, argue

debe *m, com* debtor

debelar *vt* to conquer, overthrow

deber *vt* to owe (e.g. **Le debo mil pesetas,** I owe him one thousand pesetas). Used as auxiliary verb followed by infinitive, ought to, be obliged to (e.g. **Debía haberlo hecho,** I ought to have done it. **Deberá hacerlo,** He will have to do it); be destined to (e.g. **La princesa que más tarde debió ser reina,** The princess who later was destined to be queen); be essential, must (e.g. **La cuestión debe ser resuelta,** The question must be settled); (*with de* + *infin.*) be probable (indicates supposition) (e.g. **Debe de tener cincuenta años,** He is probably about fifty. **Debía de sufrir del corazón,** He probably suffered from heart trouble); (preceded by a negative *with de* + *infin.*) be impossible (e.g. **No debe de ser verdad,** It can't be true)

deber *m,* duty, obligation; debt. **hacer su d.,** to do one's duty

debidamente *adv* justly, rightly; duly

debido *a* correct, due. **d. a,** owing to, because of

débil *a* weak; *fig* spineless; frail

debilidad *f,* weakness; feebleness

debilitación *f,* debilitation

debilitante *a* weakening

debilitar *vt* to weaken; *vr* become weak

débito *m,* debit, debt; duty

debutar *vi* to appear for the first time, make one's début

decadencia *f,* decadence, decline

decadente *a* decadent, decaying

decaer *vi irr* to fail (persons); decay, decline. See **caer**

decagramo *m,* decagram

decaimiento *m,* decadence; *med* prostration

decalaje *m,* aer stagger

decalitro *m,* decaliter

decálogo *m,* decalogue, the Ten Commandments

decampar *vi mil* to decamp

decano *m,* senior member; *univ* dean

decantación *f,* decantation

decantar *vt* to decant (wines); praise

decapitación *f,* decapitation

decapitar *vt* to decapitate, behead

decena *f,* ten; *mus* tenth

decenario *m,* decade

decencia *f*, propriety, decency; decorum, modesty

decenio *m*, decade

deceno a tenth

decentar *vt irr* to begin, cut (loaves, etc.); *fig* undermine (health, etc.); *vr* suffer from bedsores. See **acertar**

decente a decent, honest; respectable; suitable; tidy

decepción *f*, disillusionment, disappointment

dechado *m*, model, ideal; *sew* sampler; exemplar, ideal

decible a expressible

decidero a that which can be safely said

decidido a decided; resolute, determined

decidir *vt* to resolve, decide; *vr* make up one's mind

decidor (**-ra**) a talkative, fluent, eloquent. *n* good talker

decimal a decimal; pertaining to tithes. **sistema d.**, metric system

décimo a tenth. *m*, tenth part; tenth of a lottery ticket

decimoctavo a eighteenth

decimocuarto a fourteenth

decimonono a nineteenth

decimoquinto a fifteenth

decimoséptimo a and *m*, seventeenth

decimosexto a sixteenth

decimotercio a thirteenth

decir *vt irr* to say; name; indicate; show; tell. **d. bien,** to go with, suit; speak the truth; be eloquent. **d. entre** (*or* **para**) **sí,** to say to oneself. *inf* **d. nones,** to refuse. **¡Diga!** Hello! (telephone). *inf* **el que dirán,** public opinion (what will people say!). **Es d.,** That is to say. **Se dice,** It is said, people say. *Pres. Ind.* **digo, dices,** etc. *Pres. Part.* **diciendo.** *Past Part.* **dicho.** *Fut.* **diré,** etc. *Condit.* **diría,** etc. *Preterite* **dije,** etc. *Pres. Subjunc.* **diga,** etc. *Imperf. Subjunc.* **dijese,** etc.

decir *m*, saying, saw; maxim, witticism (often *pl.*)

decisión *f*, decision, resolution; *law* judgment; firmness, strength (of character)

decisivo a decisive

declamación *f*, declamation, oration; *theat* delivery; recitation

declamar *vi* to make a speech, declaim; recite

declamatorio a declamatory, rhetorical

declaración *f*, declaration; exposition, explanation; confession; statement; *law* deposition. **d. jurada,** affidavit, sworn statement

declaradamente *adv* avowedly

declarante a declaring. *mf law* deponent

declarar *vt* to declare; make clear, explain; *law* find; *vi law* give evidence; *vr* avow, confess (one's sentiments, etc.); show, reveal itself

declinación *f*, fall, descent; decadence,

decay; *ast* declination; *gram* declension. *inf* **no saber las declinaciones,** not to know one's ABC, be very ignorant

declinar *vi* to slope; diminish, fall; decline, deteriorate; *fig* near the end; *vt gram* decline

declive, *m*. **declividad** *f*, slope, incline; gradient

decomisar *vt* to confiscate, seize

decoración *f*, decoration; ornament, embellishment; *theat* scenery

decorado *m*, *theat* scenery, décor

decorador *m*, decorator

decorar *vt* to adorn, ornament; *poet* decorate, honor

decorativo a decorative

decoro *m*, respect, reverence; prudence, circumspection; decorum, propriety; integrity, decency; *arch* decoration

decoroso a decorous, honorable, decent

decrecer *vi irr* to decrease, grow less. See **conocer**

decreciente a decreasing

decrépito a decrepit

decretar *vt* to decree, decide; *law* give a judgment (in a suit)

decreto *m*, decree, order; judicial decree

decuplar, decuplicar *vt* to multiply by ten

decurso *m*, course, lapse (of time)

dedada *f*, thimbleful, finger; pinch

dedal *m*, thimble; finger-stall

dédalo *m*, labyrinth

dedeo *m*, *mus* touch

dedicación *f*, dedication (all meanings)

dedicar *vt* to dedicate; devote; consecrate; *vr* (*with prep a*) dedicate oneself to, engage in

dedicatoria *f*, dedication (of a book, etc.)

dedicatorio a dedicatory

dedillo, saber al *fig* to have at one's fingertips, know perfectly

dedo *m*, finger; toe; finger's breadth. **d. anular,** third (ring) finger. **d. de en medio** *or* **del corazón,** middle finger. **d. índice,** forefinger. **d. meñique,** little finger. **d. pulgar,** thumb or big toe. *fig inf a* **dos dedos de,** within an inch of. *fig inf* **chuparse los dedos,** to smack one's lips over. *inf* **estar unidos como los dedos de la mano,** to be as thick as thieves

deducción *f*, inference, deduction; derivation; (*mus math*) progression

deducir *vt irr* to deduce, infer; deduct, subtract; *law* plead, allege in pleading. See **conducir**

defecación *f*, purification; defecation

defecar *vt* to clarify, purify; defecate

defección *f*, defection

defectible a deficient; imperfect

defecto *m*, defect, fault; imperfection

defectuoso a imperfect, defective

defender *vt irr* to defend, protect; maintain, uphold; forbid; hinder; *vr* defend oneself. See **entender**

defendible *a* defensible

defensa *f*, defence; protection; (hockey) pad; *law* defense; *sport* back; *pl mil* defenses; *naut* fenders. **d. química,** chemical warfare. **mil defensas costeras,** coastal defenses

defensiva *f*, defensive

defensivo *a* defensive. *m*, safeguard

defensor (-ra) *n* defender. *m, law* counsel for the defense

deferencia *f*, deference

deferente *a* deferential

deferir *vi irr* to defer, yield; *vt* delegate. *Pres. Ind.* **defiero, defieres, defiere, defieren.** *Pres. Part.* **defiriendo.** *Preterite* **defirió, defirieron.** *Pres. Subjunc.* **defiera,** etc. *Imperf. Subjunc.* **defiriese,** etc.

deficiencia *f*, defect, deficiency

deficiente *a* faulty, deficient

déficit *m*, deficit

definible *a* definable

definición *f*, definition; decision

definido *a* definite

definir *vt* to define; decide

definitivo *a* definitive. **en definitiva,** definitely; in short

deflagración *f*, sudden blaze, deflagration

deflagrar *vi* to go up in flames

deformado *a* deformed; misshapen

deformador (-ra) *a* disfiguring, deforming. *n* disfigurer

deformar *vt* to deform; *vr* become deformed or misshapen

deformidad *f*, deformity; gross error; vice, lapse

defraudación *f*, defrauding; deceit

defraudador (-ra) *n* defrauder

defraudar *vt* to defraud; usurp; frustrate, disappoint; impede

defunción *f*, decease, death

degeneración *f*, degeneration. **d. grasienta,** fatty degeneration

degenerado (-da) *a* and *n* degenerate

degenerar *vi* to degenerate

deglución *f*, swallowing, deglutition

deglutir *vi* and *vt* to swallow

degollación *f*, decollation, throat slitting

degolladero *m*, slaughterhouse; execution block

degollar *vt irr* to behead; slit the throat; *fig* destroy; (*fig theat*) murder; *inf* annoy, bore. *Pres. Ind.* **degüello, degüellas, degüella, degüellan.** *Pres. Subjunc.* **degüelle, degüelles, degüelle, degüellen**

degradación *f*, degradation; humiliation, debasement; *art* gradation, shading (colors, light)

degradante *a* degrading, humiliating

degradar *vt* to degrade; humiliate; *art* grade, blend; *vr* degrade oneself

degustación *f*, act of tasting or sampling

dehesa *f*, pasture, meadow

deificación *f*, deification

deificar *vt* to deify; overpraise

dejadez *f*, slovenliness; neglect; laziness; carelessness

dejado *a* lazy; neglectful; slovenly; discouraged, depressed

dejamiento *m*, relinquishment; negligence; lowness of spirits; indifference

dejar *vt* to leave; omit, forget, allow, permit (e.g. **Déjame salir,** Let me go out); yield, produce, entrust, leave in charge; believe, consider; intend, appoint; cease, stop; forsake, desert; renounce, relinquish; bequeath; give away; *vr* neglect oneself; engage (in); lay oneself open to, allow oneself; abandon oneself (to), fling oneself (into); *fig* be depressed or languid; (*with de +* infin.) cease to (e.g. **Se dejó de hacerlo,** He stopped doing it); *vi* (*with de +* adjective) be none the less, be rather (e.g. **No deja de ser sorprendente,** It isn't any the less surprising). **d. aparte,** to omit, leave out. **d. atrás,** to overtake; *fig* leave behind, beat. **d. caer,** to let fall. **dejarse caer,** to let oneself fall; *fig inf* to let fall, utter; appear suddenly. **dejarse vencer,** to give way, allow oneself to be persuaded

dejo *m*, relinquishment; end; accent (of persons); savor, after-taste; negligence; *fig* touch, flavor

del contraction of **de + el,** (*déf. art. m.*) of the (e.g. **del perro,** of the dog)

delación *f*, accusation, denunciation

delantal *m*, apron

delante *adv* before, in front, in the presence (of)

delantera *f*, front, front portion; *theat* orchestra stall, front seat; front (of garment). **tomar la d.,** to take the lead; *inf* steal a march on

delantero *a* fore, front. *m*, postilion; *sport* forward. **d. centro,** *sport* centerforward

delatable *a* impeachable; blameworthy

delatar *vt* to inform against, accuse; impeach

delator (-ra) *a* denunciatory, accusing. *n* denouncer, informer

delegación *f*, delegation; proxy

delegado (-da) *n* delegate; proxy

delegar *vt* to delegate

deleitable *a* delightful

deleitar *vt* to delight, charm, please; *vr* delight (in)

deleite *m*, delight; pleasure

deleitoso *a* delightful, pleasant

deletrear *vi* to spell; *fig* decipher

deletreo *m*, spelling; *fig* decipherment

deleznable a fragile, brittle; slippery; brief, fugitive, transitory

delfín m, (*icht ast*) dolphin; dauphin

delgadez f, thinness; slenderness; leanness

delgado a slim; thin; scanty; poor (of land); sharp, perspicacious

delgaducho a slenderish, somewhat thin

deliberación f, deliberation; consideration; discussion

deliberadamente adv deliberately

deliberante a deliberative, considering

deliberar vi to deliberate, consider; vt decide after reflection; discuss

delicadez f, weakness; delicacy; hypersensitiveness; amiability

delicadeza f, delicacy; fastidiousness; refinement, subtlety; sensitiveness; consideration, tact; scrupulosity

delicado a courteous; tactful; fastidious; weak, delicate; fragile, perishable; delicious, tasty; exquisite; difficult, embarrassing; refined, discriminating, sensitive; scrupulous; subtle; hypersensitive, suspicious. **d. de salud,** in poor health

delicia f, pleasure, delight; sensual pleasure

delicioso a delightful, agreeable, pleasant

delincuencia f, delinquency

delincuente a and mf delinquent

delineación f, delineation; diagram, design, plan

delineador (-ra), n **delineante** m, draftsman, designer

delineamiento m, delineation

delinear vt to delineate; sketch; describe

delirante a delirious

delirar vi to be delirious; act or speak foolishly

delirio m, delirium; frenzy; foolishness, nonsense. **d. de grandezas,** illusions of grandeur

delito m, delict, offense against the law, crime

delta f, fourth letter of Greek alphabet. m, delta (of a river)

delusorio a deceptive

demacrado a emaciated

demacrarse vr to become emaciated

demagogia f, demagogy

demagogo (-ga) n demagogue

demanda f, petition, request; collecting (for charity); collecting box; want ad; question; search; undertaking; com order or demand; law claim

demandadero (-ra) n convent or prison messenger; errandboy

demandado (-da) n law defendant; law respondent

demandante mf law plaintiff

demandar vt to ask, request; desire, yearn for; question; law claim

demarcar vt to fix boundaries, demarcate

demás a other. adv besides. **lo d.,** the rest. **los (las) d.,** the others. **por d.,** useless; superfluous. **por lo d.,** otherwise; for the rest

demasía f, excess; daring; insolence; guilt, crime. **en d.,** excessively

demasiado a too; too many; too much. adv excessively

demencia f, madness, insanity

demencial a insane

dementar vt to render insane; vr become insane

demente a insane, mad. mf lunatic

demérito m, demerit, fault

demisión f, submission, acquiescence

democracia f, democracy

demócrata mf democrat

democrático a democratic

democratizar vt to make democratic

demoledor (-ra) a demolition. n demolisher

demoler vt irr to demolish, destroy, dismantle. See **moler**

demolición f, demolition, destruction, dismantling

demoníaco a devilish; possessed by a demon

demonio m, devil; evil spirit. interj **¡Demonios!** Deuce take it! inf **tener el d. en el cuerpo,** to be always on the move, be very energetic

demora f, delay; naut bearing; com demurrage

demorar vt to delay; vi stay, remain, tarry; naut bear

demorón, -ona a, Lat. Am. slow

demostración f, demonstration; proof

demostrador (-ra) a demonstrating. n demonstrator

demostrar vt irr to demonstrate, explain; prove; teach. See **mostrar**

demostrativo a demonstrative. gram **pronombre d.,** demonstrative pronoun

demudación f, change; alteration

demudar vt to change, vary; alter, transform; vr change suddenly (color, facial expression, etc.); grow angry

denario a denary. m, denarius

denegación f, denial; refusal

denegar vt irr to deny, refuse. See **acertar**

dengue m, affectation, faddiness, fastidiousness

denigrable a odious

denigración f, slander, defamation (of character)

denigrante a slanderous

denigrar vt to slander; insult

denodado a valiant, daring

denominar vt to name, designate

denostar vt irr to revile, insult. See **acordar**

denotar *vt* to denote, indicate

densidad *f*, density; closeness, denseness; *phys* specific gravity; obscurity

denso *a* compact, close; thick, dense; crowded; dark, confused

dentado *a* toothed; pronged; dentate

dentadura *f*, set of teeth (real or false). **d. de rumiante,** teeth like an ox. **d. postiza,** false teeth

dental *a* dental

dentar *vt irr* to provide with teeth, prongs, etc.; *vi* cut teeth. See **sentar**

dentellada *f*, gnashing or chattering of teeth; bite; toothmark

dentellar *vt* to chatter, grind, gnash (teeth)

dentellear *vt* to bite, sink the teeth into

dentera *f*, **(dar)** to set one's teeth on edge; *fig inf* make one's mouth water

dentición *f*, teething, dentition

dentífrico *m*, toothpaste

dentista *mf* dentist

dentro *adv* within, inside. **d. de poco,** soon, shortly. **por d.,** from the inside; on the inside

denudación *f*, denudation; *geol* erosion

denudar *vt* to denude

denuesto *m*, insult

denuncia *f*, denunciation, accusation

denunciante *a* accusing. *mf law* denouncer

denunciar *vt* to give notice, inform; herald, presage; declare, proclaim; denounce; *law* accuse

denunciatorio *a* denunciatory

deparar *vt* to furnish, offer, present

departamental *a* departmental

departamento *m*, department; compartment (railway); branch, section; *Argentina* apartment. **d. de lactantes,** nursery (in a hospital)

depauperar *vt* to impoverish; *vr med* grow weak, become emaciated

dependencia *f*, dependence; subordination; dependency; *com* branch; firm, agency; business affair; kinship or affinity; *pl arch* offices; *com* staff; accessories

depender *vi* (*with de*) to be subordinate to; depend on; be dependent on, need

dependiente **(-ta)** *a* and *n* dependent, subordinate. *m*, employee; shop assistant

depilar *vt* to depilate

depilatorio *m*, depilatory

deplorar *vt* to deplore, lament

deponente *a* deposing; affirming. *mf* deponent. *gram* **verbo d.,** deponent verb

deponer *vt irr* to lay aside; depose, oust; affirm, testify; remove, take from its place; *law* depose; *Central America, Mexico* throw up, vomit. See **poner**

deportación *f*, deportation

deportar *vt* to exile; deport

deporte *m*, sport; *pl* games. **d. de vela,** sailing; boating

deportismo *m*, sport

deportista *a* sporting. *mf* sportsman (sportswoman)

deportivo *a* sporting

deposición *f*, affirmation, statement; *law* deposition; degradation, removal (from office, etc.)

depositador **(-ra)** *a* depositing. *n* depositor

depositar *vt* to deposit; place in safety; entrust; lay aside, put away; *vr chem* settle

depositario **(-ia)** *a* pertaining to a depository. *n* depositary, trustee

depósito *m*, deposit; depository; *com* depot, warehouse; *chem* deposit, sediment; tank, reservoir; *mil* depot. **d. de bencina, d. de gasolina,** gas tank; service station. **d. de municiones,** munitions dump. *com* **en d.,** in bond. **Queda hecho el d. que marca la ley,** Copyright reserved

depravación *f*, depravity

depravar *vt* to deprave, corrupt; *vr* become depraved

deprecación *f*, supplication, petition; deprecation

deprecar *vt* to supplicate, petition; deprecate

depreciación *f*, depreciation, fall in value

depreciar *vt* to depreciate, reduce the value (of)

depredar *vt* to pillage

depresión *f*, depression. **d. nerviosa,** nervous breakdown

deprimir *vt* to depress, compress, press down; depreciate, belittle; *vr* be compressed

depuración *f*, cleansing, purification; *pol* purge

depurar *vt* to cleanse, purify; *pol* purge

derecha *f*, right hand; *pol* (gen. *pl*) Right. *mil* **¡D.!** Right Turn! **a la d.,** on the right

derechamente *adv* straight, directly; prudently, justly; openly, frankly

derechista *mf pol* rightist

derecho *a* straight; upright; right (not left); just, reasonable; *sport* forehand. *adv* straightaway. *m*, right; law; just claim; privilege; justice, reason; exemption; right side (cloth, etc.); *pl* dues, taxes; fees. **d. a la vía,** right of way. **d. de apelación,** right to appeal. **d. de visita,** (international law) right of search. **derechos de aduana,** customhouse duties. **derechos de entrada,** import duties. **según d.,** according to law. **usar de su d.,** to exercise one's right

derechura *f*, directness, straightness; uprightness; *Lat. Am.* good luck

derivación *f*, origin, derivation; inference, consequence; *gram* derivation

derivar vi to originate; naut drift; vt conduct, lead; gram derive; elec tap

dermatología f, dermatology

derogación f, repeal, annulment; deterioration

derogar vt to annul, repeal; destroy, suppress

derramado a extravagant, wasteful

derramamiento m, pouring out; spilling; scattering

derramar vt to pour out; spill; scatter; apportion (taxes); publish abroad, spread; vr be scattered; overflow

derrame m, spilling; leakage; overflow; scattering; slope

derredor m, circumference. **al** (or **en**) **d.**, round about

derrelicto a abandoned; derelict. m, naut derelict

derrengado a crooked; crippled

derretimiento m, melting; thaw; liquefaction; inf burning passion

derretir vt irr to melt, liquefy; waste, dissipate; vr be very much in love; inf be susceptible (to love); inf long, be impatient. See **pedir**

derribar vt to demolish; knock down; fell; throw down; aer shoot down; throw (in wrestling); fig overthrow; demolish, explode (a myth); control (emotions); vr fall down; prostrate oneself; throw oneself down. **d. el chapeo**, humorous to doff one's hat

derribo m, demolition; debris, rubble; throw (in wrestling)

derrocadero m, rocky precipice

derrocar vt to throw down from a rock; demolish (buildings); overthrow, oust

derrochador (-ra) a wasteful, extravagant. n spendthrift

derrochar vt to waste, squander

derrota f, road; route, path; naut course; mil defeat

derrotar vt to squander; destroy, harm; mil defeat; vr naut drift, lose course

derrotero m, naut course; naut ship's itinerary; number of sea charts; means to an end, course of action

derrotista mf defeatist

derruir vt irr to demolish (a building). See **huir**

derrumbadero m, precipice; risk, danger

derrumbar vt to precipitate; vr throw oneself down, collapse, tumble down (buildings, etc.)

derrumbe m, collapse; subsidence

desabarrancar vt to pull out of a ditch or rut; extricate (from a difficulty)

desabor m, insipidity

desabotonar vt to unbutton; vi open (flowers)

desabrido a insipid, poor-tasting; in-clement (weather); disagreeable; unsociable; homely, plain (woman)

desabrigar vt to uncover; leave without shelter

desabrigo m, want of clothing or shelter; poverty, destitution

desabrimiento m, insipidity; harshness, disagreeableness; melancholy, depression

desabrir vt to give a bad taste (to food); annoy, trouble

desabrochar vt to unbutton, untie; open; vr inf confide, open up

desacatar vt to behave disrespectfully (towards); lack reverence

desacato m, irreverence; disrespect

desacertar vi irr to be wrong; act imprudently. See **acertar**

desacierto m, mistake, miscalculation, blunder

desacomodado a lacking means of subsistence; poor; unemployed (servants); troublesome

desacomodar vt to incommode, make uncomfortable, inconvenience; dismiss, discharge

desaconsejar vt to advise against, dissuade

desacoplar vt to disconnect

desacordar vt irr mus to put out of tune; vr (with de) forget. See **acordar**

desacostumbrado a unaccustomed; unusual

desacotar vt to remove (fences); refuse, deny; vi withdraw (from agreement, etc.)

desacreditar vt to discredit

desacuerdo m, disagreement, discord; mistake; forgetfulness; swoon, loss of consciousness

desadornar vt to denude of ornaments

desadorno m, lack of ornaments; bareness

desafecto a disaffected; hostile. m, disaffection

desaferrar vt irr to untie, unfasten; fig wean from; naut weigh anchor. See **acertar**

desafiador (-ra) a challenging. n challenger. m, duelist

desafiar vt to challenge; compete with; oppose; Mexico fight

desafinar vi mus to go out of tune; fig inf speak out of turn

desafío m, challenge; competition; duel

desaforado a lawless; outrageous; enormous

desaforar vt to infringe (laws, etc.); vr be disorderly

desaforrar vt to remove the lining of or from

desafortunado a unfortunate

desagarrar vt inf to release, loosen; unhook

desagraciado a ugly, unsightly

desagraciar *vt* to disfigure, make ugly

desagradable *a* disagreeable; unpleasant

desagradar *vi* to be disagreeable, displease (e.g. **Me desagrada su voz,** I find his voice unpleasant)

desagradecer *vt irr* to be ungrateful (for). See **conocer**

desagradecido *a* ungrateful

desagrado *m*, displeasure, dislike, dissatisfaction

desagraviar *vt* to make amends, apologize; indemnify

desagravio *m*, satisfaction, reparation; compensation

desagregar(se) *vt* and *vr* to separate

desaguar *vt* to drain off; dissipate; *vi* flow (into sea, etc.)

desagüe *m*, drainage; outlet, drain; catchment

desaguisado *a* outrageous, lawless. *m*, offense, insult

desahogado *a* brazen, insolent; clear, unencumbered; in comfortable circumstances

desahogar *vt* to ease, relieve; *vr* unburden oneself; recover (from illness, heat, etc.); get out of debt; speak one's mind

desahogo *m*, relief, alleviation; ease; comfort, convenience; freedom, frankness; unburdening (of one's mind). *inf* **vivir con d.,** to be comfortably off

desahuciar *vt* to banish all hope; give up, despair of the life of; put out (tenants); *Chile* dismiss

desahúcio *m*, ejection, dispossession (of tenants); *Chile* dismissal

desahumar *vt* to clear of smoke

desairado *a* unattractive, graceless, ugly; unsuccessful, crestfallen; slighted

desairar *vt* to disdain, slight, disregard; underrate (things)

desaire *m*, gracelessness, ugliness; insult, slight

desalabanza *f*, disparagement; criticism

desalación *f*, desalinization

desalado *a* anxious, precipitate, hasty

desalar *vt* to remove the salt from; take off wings; *vr* walk or run at great speed; long for, yearn

desalentar *vt irr* to make breathing difficult (work, fatigue); discourage; *vr* be depressed or sad. See **sentar**

desaliento *m*, depression, discouragement, dismay

desalinear *vt* to throw out of the straight

desaliñar *vt* to disarrange, make untidy, crumple

desaliño *m*, untidiness, slovenliness; negligence, carelessness

desalmado *a* soulless, conscienceless; cruel

desalmamiento *m*, inhumanity, consciencelessness; cruelty

desalmidonar *vt* to remove starch from

desalojamiento *m*, dislodgement, ejection

desalojar *vt* to dislodge, remove, eject; *vi* move out, remove

desalquilado *a* untenanted, vacant

desalquilar *vt* to leave, or cause to leave, rented premises

desalterar *vt* to soothe, calm

desamarrar *vt* to untie; separate; *naut* unmoor

desamor *m*, indifference; lack of sentiment or affection; hatred

desamotinarse *vr* to cease from rebellion; submit

desamparar *vt* to abandon, forsake; leave (a place)

desamparo *m*, desertion; need

desamueblado *a* unfurnished

desamueblar *vt* to empty of furniture

desangrar *vt med* to bleed; drain (lake, etc.); impoverish, bleed; *vr* lose much blood

desangre *m*, *Lat. Am.* bleeding, loss of blood

desanidar *vi* to leave the nest; *vt* eject, expel

desanimado *a* downhearted; (of places) dull, quiet

desanimar *vt* to discourage, depress

desanublar, *vt* **desanublarse** *vr* to clear up (weather)

desanudar *vt* to untie; disentangle

desapacibilidad *f*, disagreeableness, unpleasantness

desapacible *a* disagreeable; unpleasant; unsociable

desaparecer *vt irr* to cause to disappear; *vi* and *vr* disappear. See **conocer**

desaparecido *a* late (deceased); *mil* missing

desaparejar *vt* to unharness

desaparición *f*, disappearance

desapegar *vt* to unstick, undo; *vr* be indifferent, cast off a love or affection

desapego *m*, lack of affection or interest, coolness

desapercibido *a* unnoticed; unprovided, unprepared

desapiadado *a* merciless

desaplicación *f*, laziness, lack of application; carelessness, negligence

desaplicado *a* lazy; careless

desapoderado *a* precipitate, uncontrolled; furious, violent

desapoderar *vt* to dispossess, rob; remove from office

desapolillar *vt* to free from moths; *vr inf* take an airing

desaposentar *vt* to evict; drive away

desapreciar *vt* to scorn

desaprensivo *a* unscrupulous

desapretar(se) *vt* and *vr irr* to slacken. See **acertar**

desaprisionar *vt* to release from prison

desaprobación *f*, disapproval

desaprobar *vt irr* to disapprove; disagree with. See **probar**

desapropiamiento *m*, renunciation or transfer of property

desapropiarse *vr* to renounce or transfer (property)

desaprovechado *a* unprofitable; backward; unintelligent

desaprovechar *vt* to take no advantage of, waste; *vi fig* lose ground, lose what one has gained

desarmador *m*, *Mexico* screwdriver

desarmar *vt* to disarm; dismantle, dismount; appease

desarme *m*, disarming; disarmament

desarraigar *vt* to pull up by root (plants); extirpate, suppress; eradicate (opinion, etc.); exile

desarraigo *m*, uprooting; extirpation; eradication; exile

desarreglado *a* disarranged; untidy; intemperate, immoderate

desarreglar *vt* to disarrange

desarreglo *m*, disorder; disarrangement; irregularity

desarrendar *vt irr* to unbridle a horse; end a tenancy or lease. See **recomendar**

desarrollar *vt* to unroll; increase, develop, grow, unfold; explain (theory); *vr* develop, grow

desarrollo *m*, unrolling; development, growth; explanation

desarropar *vt* to uncover, remove the covers, etc. from

desarticular *vt* to disarticulate; *mech* disconnect

desaseado *a* dirty; unkempt, slovenly

desaseo *m*, dirtiness; slovenliness

desasosegar *vt irr* to disturb, make anxious. See **cegar**

desasosiego *m*, uneasiness, disquiet

desastre *m*, disaster, calamity

desastroso *a* unfortunate, calamitous

desatacar *vt* to unfasten, undo, unbutton

desatadura *f*, untying

desatar *vt* to untie; melt; dissolve; elucidate, explain; *vr* loosen the tongue; lose self control; lose all reserve; unbosom oneself

desatascar *vt* to pull out of the mud; free from obstruction; extricate from difficulties

desatavío *m*, carelessness in dress, slovenliness

desatención *f*, inattention, abstraction; incivility

desatender *vt irr* to pay no attention to; disregard, ignore. See **entender**

desatentado *a* imprudent, ill-advised; excessive, immoderate

desatento *a* inattentive, abstracted; discourteous

desatinado *a* foolish, imprudent, wild

desatinar *vt* to bewilder; *vi* behave foolishly; lose one's bearings

desatino *m*, folly, foolishness, imprudence, rashness; blunder, faux pas, mistake

desatrancar *vt* to unbar the door; remove obstacles

desaturdir *vt* to rouse (from torpor, etc.)

desautorizar *vt* to remove from authority; discredit

desavenencia *f*, disharmony, disagreement

desavenido *a* disagreeing, discordant

desavenir *vt irr* to upset. See **venir**

desaventajado *a* disadvantageous; unfavorable, inferior

desaviar *vt* to lead astray; deprive of a necessity; *vr* lose one's way

desayunador *m*, breakfast nook

desavisado *a* unaware, unprepared

desavisar *vt* to take back one's previous advice

desayunarse *vr* to have breakfast, eat breakfast

desayuno *m*, breakfast

desazón *f*, insipidity, lack of flavor; poorness (soil); anxiety, trouble; vexation

desazonar *vt* to make insipid; make anxious, worry; vex; *vr* feel out of sorts

desbandada *f*, dispersal, rout. **a la d.,** in confusion or disorder

desbandarse *vr* to disband, retreat in disorder; *mil* desert

desbaratado *a inf* corrupt, vicious

desbaratar *vt* to spoil, destroy; dissipate, waste; foil, thwart (a plot); *mil* rout; *vi* talk foolishly; *vr* go too far, behave badly

desbastar *vt carp* to plane, dress; polish, refine, civilize

desbocar *vt* to break the spout or neck (of jars, etc.); *vi* run (into) (of streets, etc.); *vr* bolt (horses); curse, swear

desboquillar *vt* to remove or break a stem or mouthpiece

desbordamiento *m*, overflowing, flood

desbordarse *vr* to overflow; lose self-control. **d. en alabanzas para,** to heap praise on

desbravar *vt* to break in (horses, etc.); *vi* grow less savage; lose force, decrease

descabalgadura *f*, alighting (from horses, etc.)

descabalgar *vi* to alight (from horse); *vt* dismantle (gun)

descabellado *a* disheveled; ridiculous, foolish

descabellar *vt* to disarrange, ruffle (hair)

descabezado a headless; rash, impetuous

descabezar vt to behead; cut the top off (trees, etc.); fig inf break the back of (work); vi abut, join; vr (with con or en) rack one's brains about

descacharrado, -a a, Central America dirty, filthy, slovenly

descalabazarse vr inf to rack one's brains

descalabradura f, head wound or scar

descalabrar vt to wound in the head; wound; harm

descalabro m, misfortune, mishap

descalzar vt to remove the shoes and stockings; undermine; vr remove one's shoes and stockings; lose a shoe (horses)

descalzo a barefoot

descaminar vt to lead astray; pervert, corrupt

descamisado (-da) a inf shirtless; ragged, poor. n inf down and out, outcast; vagabond

descansado a rested, refreshed; tranquil

descansar vi to rest, repose oneself; have relief (from anxiety, etc.); sleep; agr lie fallow; sleep in death; (with en) trust, have confidence in; (with sobre) lean on or upon; vt (with sobre) rest (a thing) on another. **¡Que en paz descanse!** May he rest in peace!

descanso m, rest, repose; relief (from care); landing of stairs; mech bench, support; mil stand easy

descarado a impudent, brazen

descararse vr to behave impudently

descarga f, unloading; naut discharge of cargo; elec discharge; mil volley. **d. cerrada**, dense volley, fusillade

descargadero m, wharf

descargador m, unloader, docker; elec discharger

descargar vt to unload; mil fire; unload (fire-arms); elec discharge; rain (blows) upon; fig free, exonerate; vi disembogue (of rivers); burst (clouds); vr relinquish (employment); shirk responsibility; law clear oneself

descargo m, unloading; com acquittance; law answer to an impeachment

descargue m, unloading

descarnado a fleshless; scraggy; spare, lean

descarnador m, dental scraper; tanner's scraper

descarnar vt to scrape off flesh; corrode; inspire indifference to earthly things

descaro m, impudence

descarriar vt to lead astray; vr be lost, be separated (from others); fig go astray

descarrilamiento m, derailment

descarrilar vi to run off the track, be derailed

descarrío m, losing one's way

descartar vt to put aside; vr discard (cards); shirk, make excuses

descascarar vt to peel; shell; vr peel off

descendencia f, descendants, offspring; lineage, descent

descender vi irr to descend; flow (liquids); (with de) descend from, derive from; vt lower, let down. See **entender**

descendiente mf descendant, offspring. a descending

descenso m, descent; lowering, letting down; degradation

descentralizar vt to decentralize

desceñir(se) vt and vr irr to ungird, remove a girdle, etc. See **ceñir**

descepar vt to tear up by the roots; fig extirpate

descercado a unfenced, open

descifrable a decipherable

descifrador m, decipherer, decoder

descifrar vt to decipher; decode

descinchar vt to loosen or remove girths (of horse)

desclavar vt to remove nails; unnail, unfasten

descoagular vt to liquefy, dissolve, melt

descocado a inf brazen, saucy

descogollar vt to prune a tree of shoots; remove hearts (of lettuces, etc.)

descolar vt irr to cut off or dock an animal's tail; Mexico slight, snub. See **colar**

descolgar vt irr to unhang; lower; vr lower oneself (by rope, etc.); come down, descend; inf come out (with), utter. See **volcar**

descoloramiento m, discoloration

descolorar vt to discolor; vr be discolored

descolorido a discolored; pale-colored; pallid

descollar vi irr to excel, be outstanding. See **degollar**

descomedido a excessive, disproportionate; rude

descomedimiento m, disrespect, lack of moderation, rudeness

descomedirse vr irr to be disrespectful or rude. See **pedir**

descomponer vt irr to disorder, disarrange; chem decompose; unsettle; vr go out of order; rot, putrefy; be ailing; lose one's temper. See **poner**

descomposición f, disorder, confusion; discomposure; chem decomposition; putrefaction

descompostura f, decomposition; slovenliness, dirtiness, untidiness; impudence, rudeness

descompuesto a rude, impudent; Lat. Am. tipsy; Venezuela ill, sick

descomunal a enormous, extraordinary

desconcertar vt irr to disorder, disarrange; dislocate (bones); disconcert, embarrass; *vr* disagree; be impudent. See **acertar**

desconcierto *m*, disorder, disarrangement; dislocation; embarrassment; disagreement; impudence

desconectar *vt* to disconnect; switch off

desconfianza *f*, lack of confidence

desconfiar *vi* to lack confidence

desconocer *vt irr* to forget; be unaware of; deny, disown; pretend ignorance; not to understand (persons, etc.). See **conocer**

desconocido (-da) *a* unknown; ungrateful. *n* stranger; ingrate

desconocimiento *m*, unawareness; ignorance; ingratitude

desconsiderado *a* inconsiderate; discourteous; rash

desconsolación *f*, affliction, trouble

desconsolar *vt irr* to afflict, make disconsolate; *vr* grieve, despair. See **colar**

desconsuelo *m*, anguish, affliction, despair

descontar *vt irr com* to make a discount; ignore, discount; take for granted, leave aside. See **contar**

descontentadizo *a* discontented, difficult to please; fastidious, finicky

descontentar *vt* to displease; *vr* be dissatisfied

descontento *m*, discontent, dissatisfaction

descontextualizar *vt* to take out of context

descontrolarse *vr* to lose control, lose control of oneself.

desconveniencia *f*, inconvenience, unsuitability, disagreement

desconvenir *vi irr* to disagree; be unsuitable, unsightly or odd (things). See **venir**

descorazonamiento *m*, depression, despair

descorazonar *vt* to tear out the heart; depress, discourage

descorchar *vt* to take the cork from cork tree; draw a cork (bottles); force, break into (safes)

descorrer *vt* to re-run (race, etc.); draw back (curtains, etc.); *vi* run, flow (liquids)

descortés *a* impolite

descortesía *f*, impoliteness, discourtesy

descoser *vt sew* to unpick; *vr* be unpicked; be indiscreet or tactless

descosido *a* tactless, talkative; *fig* disjointed; desultory; unsewn. *m*, *sew* rent, hole

descoyuntamiento *m*, dislocation (bones); irritation, bore; ache, pain

descoyuntar *vt* to dislocate (bones); bore, annoy; *vr* be dislocated

descrédito *m*, fall in value (things); discredit (persons)

descreer *vt irr* to disbelieve; depreciate, disparage (persons). See **creer**

descreído (-da) *a* unbelieving. *n* unbeliever; infidel

descremar *vt*, *Lat. Am.* to skim (milk)

describir *vt* to describe; outline, sketch. *Past Part.* **descrito**

descripción *f*, description; *law* inventory

descuajar *vt* to liquefy; *inf* discourage; *agr* pull up by the root

descuartizar *vt* to quarter; joint (meat); *inf* carve, cut into pieces, break up

descubierto *a* bareheaded; exposed. *m*, deficit. **al d.,** openly; in the open, without shelter. **girar en d.,** to overdraw (a bank account)

descubridor (-ra) *n* discoverer; inventor; explorer. *m*, *mil* scout

descubrimiento *m*, find; discovery; revelation; newly discovered territory

descubrir *vt* to reveal; show; discover; learn; unveil (memorials, etc.); *vr* remove one's hat; show oneself, reveal one's whereabouts. *Past Part.* **descubierto**

descuento *m*, reduction; *com* rebate, discount

descuidado *a* negligent; careless; untidy; unprepared

descuidar *vt* to relieve (of responsibility, etc.); distract, occupy (attention, etc.); *vi* and *vr* be careless; *vr* (*with de* or *en*) neglect

descuido *m*, carelessness, negligence; oversight, mistake; incivility; forgetfulness; shameful act

desde *prep* since, from (time or space); after (e.g. **d. hoy,** from today). **d. la ventana,** from the window. **d. allá,** from the other world. **d. aquella época,** since that time

desdecir *vi irr* (*with de*) to degenerate, be less good than; be discordant, clash; be unworthy of; *vr* unsay one's words, retract. See **decir**

desdén *m*, indifference, coldness; disdain, scorn

desdeñar *vt* to scorn; *vr* (*with de*) dislike, be reluctant

desdeñoso *a* disdainful, scornful

desdibujado *a* badly drawn; blurred, confused

desdicha *f*, misfortune; extreme poverty, misery. **por d.,** unfortunately

desdichado *a* unfortunate; *inf* timid, weak-kneed

desdicharse *vr* to bewail one's fate

desdinerarse una fortuna *vr* to spend a fortune

desdoblar *vt* to unfold

desdoro *m*, discredit, dishonor

deseable *a* desirable

desear *vt* to desire; yearn or long for

desechar *vt* to reject, refuse; scorn; cast out, expel; put away (thoughts, etc.); cast off (old clothes); turn (key); give up

desecho *m*, residue, rest, remains; cast-off; scorn; *Lat. Am.* shortcut

desembalar *vt* to unpack

desembarazar *vt* to clear of obstruction; disembarrass, free; vacate; *vr fig* rid oneself of obstacles

desembarazo *m*, freedom, insouciance, naturalness

desembarcadero *m*, landing-stage

desembarcar *vt* to unload; *vi* disembark; alight from vehicle

desembarco *m*, disembarkation, landing; staircase landing

desembargar *vt* to free of obstacles or impediments; *law* remove an embargo

desembargo *m*, *law* removal of an embargo

desembarque *m*, disembarkation, landing

desembocadero *m*, exit, way out; mouth (rivers, etc.)

desembocadura *f*, mouth (rivers, etc.); street opening

desembocar *vi* (*with en*) to lead to, end in; flow into (rivers)

desembolsar *vt* to take out of a purse; pay, spend

desembolso *m*, disbursement; expenditure

desemboscarse *vr* to get out of the wood; extricate oneself from an ambush

desembozo *m*, uncovering of the face

desembragar *vt mech* to disengage (the clutch, etc.)

desembravecer *vt irr* to tame, domesticate. See **conocer**

desembriagar(se) *vt* and *vr* to sober up (after a drinking bout)

desembrollar *vt inf* to disentangle, unravel

desemejanza *f*, unlikeness

desemejar *vi* to be unlike; *vt* disfigure, deform

desempacar *vt* to unpack

desempapelar *vt* to unwrap, remove the paper from; remove wallpaper

desempaquetar *vt* to unpack

desemparentado *a* without relatives

desempedrar *vt irr* to take up the flags (of a pavement). See **acertar**

desempeñar *vt* to redeem (pledges); free from debt; fulfil (obligations, etc.); take out of pawn; hold, fill (an office); extricate (from difficulties, etc.); perform, carry out; *theat* act

desempeño *m*, redemption of a pledge; fulfilment (of an obligation, etc.); performance, accomplishment; *theat* acting of a part

desempolvar *vt* to free from dust, dust

desencadenar *vt* to unchain, unfetter; *fig* unleash, let loose; *vr fig* break loose

desencajamiento *m*, disjointedness,

dislocation; ricketiness, broken-down appearance

desencajar *vt* to disconnect, disjoint; dislocate; *vr* be out of joint; be contorted (of the face); be tired looking

desencantar *vt* to disenchant

desencanto *m*, disenchantment; disillusionment

desencerrar *vt irr* to set at liberty; unlock; disclose, reveal. See **acertar**

desenchufar *vt* to disconnect, unplug (electric plugs, etc.)

desenclavijar *vt* to remove the pegs or pins; disconnect, disjoint

desencolerizar *vt* to placate; *vr* lose one's anger, grow calm

desenconar *vt* to reduce (inflammation); appease (anger, etc.); *vr* become calm

desencono *m*, reduction of inflammation; appeasement (of anger, etc.)

desenfadado *a* expeditious; natural, at ease; gay; forward, bold; wide, spacious

desenfadar *vt* to appease, make anger disappear

desenfado *m*, freedom; ease; unconcern, frankness

desenfrailar *vi* to leave the cloister, become secularized; *inf* emancipate oneself

desenfrenar *vt* to unbridle (horses); *vr* give rein to one's passions, etc.; break loose (storms, etc.)

desenfreno *m*, license, lasciviousness; complete freedom from restraint

desenganchar *vt* to unhook; uncouple; unfasten; unharness

desengañador *a* undeceiving

desengañar *vt* to undeceive, disillusion

desengaño *m*, undeceiving, disabuse; disillusionment

desengarzar *vt* to loosen from its setting; unlink, unhook, unclasp

desengastar *vt* to remove from its setting (jewelry, etc.)

desengrasar *vt* to remove the grease from, clean; *vi inf* grow thin

desenlace *m*, loosening, untying; *lit* denouement, climax (of play, etc.)

desenlatar *vt*, *Lat. Am.* to open (canned food)

desenlazar *vt* to untie, unloose; *lit* unravel (a plot)

desenmarañar *vt* to disentangle; *fig* straighten out

desenmascarar *vt* to remove the mask from; *fig* unmask

desenmudecer *vi irr* to be freed of a speech impediment; break silence, speak. See **conocer**

desenojar *vt* to soothe, appease; *vr* distract oneself, amuse oneself

desenredar *vt* to disentangle; *fig* set right; straighten out; *vr* extricate oneself, get out of a difficulty

desenredo m, disentanglement; *lit* climax

desenroscar vt Lat. Am. to unscrew

desentablar vt to tear up planks or boards; disorder, disrupt

desentenderse vr irr (with de) to pretend to be ignorant of; take no part in. See **entender**

desenterramiento m, disinterment; *fig* unearthing, recollection

desenterrar vt irr to unbury, disinter; rummage out; *fig* unearth, bring up, recall. See **acertar**

desentoldar vt to take away an awning; *fig* strip of ornament

desentonar vt to humiliate; vi mus be out of tune; speak rudely; vr be inharmonious; raise the voice (anger, etc.), behave badly

desentono m, bad behavior, rudeness; mus discord; grating quality or harshness (of voice)

desentorpecer vt irr to restore feeling to (numbed limbs); free from torpor; vr become bright and intelligent. See **conocer**

desentramparse vr inf free oneself from debt

desentrañar vt to disembowel; *fig* unravel, penetrate; vr give away one's all

desentumecer vt irr to free from numbness (limbs); vr be. restored to feeling (numb limbs). See **conocer**

desenvainar vt to unsheath; *inf* reveal, bring into the open

desenvoltura f, naturalness, ease, freedom; eloquence, facility (of speech); effrontery, audacity, shamelessness (especially in women)

desenvolver vt irr to unravel; unfold; *fig* unravel, explain; *fig* develop, work out (theories, etc.); vr unroll; unfold; lose one's timidity, blossom out; be over-bold; extricate oneself (from a difficulty). See **resolver**

desenvuelto a natural, easy; impudent, bold

deseo m, desire, will, wish

deseoso a desirous, wishful

desequilibrar(se) vt and vr to unbalance

desequilibrio m, lack of balance; confusion, disorder; mental instability

deserción f, mil desertion. **d. estudiantil**, school dropout

desertar vt mil to desert; *inf* quit

desertor m, mil deserter; *inf* quitter

desesperación f, desperation, despair; frenzy, violence

desesperado a desperate, hopeless; frenzied

desesperanza f, despair; hopelessness

desesperanzar vt to render hopeless; vr despair, lose hope

desesperar vt to make hopeless; *inf* annoy, make furious; vr lose hope, despair; be frenzied

desestimación f, disrespect, lack of esteem; rejection

desestimar vt to scorn; reject

desfachatado a inf impudent, brazen

desfachatez f, inf effrontery, cheek

desfalcador (-ra) a embezzling. n embezzler

desfalcar vt to remove a part of; embezzle

desfalco m, diminution, reduction; embezzlement

desfallecer vt irr to weaken; vi grow weak; faint, swoon. See **conocer**

desfallecimiento m, weakness, languor; depression, discouragement; faint, swoon

desfavorable a unfavorable; hostile, contrary

desfavorecer vt irr to withdraw one's favor, scorn; disfavor; oppose. See **conocer**

desfiguración f, deformation; disfigurement

desfigurar vt to deform, misshape; disfigure; *fig* disguise, mask; obscure, darken; distort, misrepresent; vr be disfigured (by rage, etc.)

desfiladero m, defile, gully

desfilar vi to walk in file; *inf* file out; mil file or march past

desfile m, mil march past; parade; walk past; procession

desflorar vt to tarnish, stain; deflower, violate; *fig* touch upon, deal lightly with

desfortalecer vt irr mil to dismantle a fortress. See **conocer**

desgaire m, untidiness, slovenliness; affectation of carelessness (in dress); scornful gesture. **al d.**, with an affectation of carelessness, negligently

desgajar vt to tear off a tree branch; break; vr break off; dissociate oneself (from)

desgana f, lack of appetite; lack of interest, indifference; reluctance

desganar vt to dissuade; vr lose one's appetite; become bored or indifferent, lose interest

desgarbado a slovenly, slatternly; gawky, graceless

desgarrado a dissolute, vicious; impudent, brazen

desgarrar vt to tear; vr leave, tear oneself away

desgarro m, tearing; rent, breach; boastfulness, impudence, effrontery; Lat. Am. phlegm

desgastar vt to corrode, wear away; spoil, corrupt; vr lose one's vigor, grow weak; wear away

desgaste m, attrition; wearing down or away; corrosion; wear and tear

desgobernar *vt irr* to upset or rise against the government; dislocate (bones); *naut* neglect the tiller; *vr* affect exaggerated movements in dancing. See **recomendar**

desgobierno *m*, misgovernment; mismanagement; maladministration; disorder, tumult

desgoznar *vt* to unhinge; *vr fig* lose one's self-control

desgracia *f*, misfortune, adversity; mishap, piece of bad luck; disgrace, disfavor; disagreeableness, brusqueness; ungraciousness. **por d.,** unhappily, unfortunately

desgraciado *a* unfortunate, unhappy; unlucky; dull, boring; disagreeable

desgraciar *vt* to displease; spoil the development (of), destroy; maim; *vr* fall out of friendship; be out of favor; turn out badly, fail; be destroyed or spoiled; be maimed

desgranar *vt agr* to thresh, flail; *vr* break (string of beads, etc.)

desgrasante *m*, grease remover

desgreñar *vt* to dishevel the hair; *vr inf* pull each other's hair, come to blows

desguarnecer *vt irr* to strip of trimming; *mil* demilitarize; *mil* disarm; dismantle; unharness. See **conocer**

deshabitado *a* uninhabited, empty

deshabituar *vt* to disaccustom; *vr* lose the habit, become unaccustomed

deshacer *vt irr* to undo; destroy; *mil* rout, defeat; take to pieces; melt; pulp (paper); untie (knots, etc.); open (parcels); diminish, decrease; break in pieces, smash; *fig* obstruct, spoil; *vr* be wasted or spoiled; be full of anxiety; vanish; try or work very hard; injure oneself; be emaciated, grow extremely thin; (*with de*) part with. **d. agravios,** to right wrongs. See **hacer**

desharrapado *a* tattered, shabby

deshebillar *vt* to unbuckle

deshecha *f*, pretense, evasion; courteous farewell; obligatory departure

deshelar *vt irr* to thaw, melt. See **acertar**

desherbar *vt irr* to pull up weeds. See **acertar**

desheredar *vt* disinherit; *vr fig* lower oneself

desherrar *vt irr* to unfetter, unchain; strike off horseshoes; *vr* lose a shoe (horses). See **acertar**

deshidratación *f*, dehydration

deshidratar *vt* to dehydrate

deshielo *m*, thaw

deshilado *a* in single file. *m, sew* drawn-thread work (gen. *pl*). **a la deshilada,** *mil* in file formation; secretly

deshiladura *f*, unraveling

deshilar *vt* to unravel; *sew* draw threads; *cul* shred, grate

deshilvanado *a fig* disjointed, disconnected

deshilvanar *vt sew* to remove the tacking threads

deshincar *vt* to pull out, remove, draw out

deshinchar *vt* to remove a swelling; deflate; lessen the anger of; *vr* decrease, subside (swellings); deflate; *inf* grow humble

deshollejar *vt* to skin, peel (fruit); shell (peas, etc.)

deshollinador *m*, chimney-sweep; wall-brush; chemical chimney cleaner

deshollinar *vt* to sweep chimneys; clean down walls; *inf* examine closely

deshonestidad *f*, immodesty, shamelessness; indecency

deshonesto *a* shameless, immodest; dissolute, vicious; indecent

deshonor *m*, dishonor; disgrace, insult

deshonrabuenos *mf inf* slanderer; degenerate

deshonrador (-ra) *a* dishonorable. *n* dishonorer

deshonrar *vt* to dishonor; insult; seduce (women)

deshonroso *a* dishonorable, insulting, indecent

deshora *f*, inconvenient time. **a d.,** or **a deshoras,** at an inconvenient time, unseasonably; extempore

deshuesar *vt* to bone, remove the bone (from meat); stone (fruit)

deshumedecer *vt irr* to dry; *vr* become dry. See **conocer**

desidia *f*, negligence; laziness

desidioso *a* negligent; lazy

desierto *a* deserted, uninhabited, solitary. *m*, desert; wilderness

designación *f*, designation; appointment

designar *vt* to plan, intend; designate; appoint

designio *m*, intention, idea

desigual *a* unequal; uneven (ground); rough; arduous, difficult; changeable

desigualar *vt* to make unequal; *vr* prosper

desigualdad *f*, inequality; unevenness, rockiness; *fig* changeability; variability

desilusión *f*, disillusionment; disappointment

desilusionar *vt* to disillusion; *vr* become disillusioned; be undeceived

desinclinar *vt* to dissuade

desinfectante *a* and *m*, disinfectant

desinfectar *vt* to disinfect

desinflar *vt* to deflate

desinterés *m*, disinterestedness

desinteresado *a* disinterested; generous

desinteresarse *vr* to lose interest, grow indifferent

desistencia, f, **desistimiento** m, desistance, ceasing

desistir vi to desist; cease; law renounce

desjuntar(se) vt and vr to separate; divide

deslavar vt to wash superficially; spoil by washing, take away the body of (cloth, etc.)

desleal a disloyal, treacherous

deslealtad f, disloyalty

deslenguado a shameless, foulmouthed

desliar vt to untie, undo, unloose

desligadura f, untying, loosening

desligar vt to unfasten, unbind; fig solve, unravel; relieve of an obligation; mus play staccato; vr come unfastened, grow loose. **desligarse de,** to weasel out of, wiggle out of (a promise)

deslindar vt to fix the boundaries (of); limit, circumscribe

desliz m, slipping, slip, slide; skid; indiscretion, slip; peccadillo, trifling fault

deslizadizo a slippery

deslizar vt to slip, slide; skid; vr commit an indiscretion; speak or act unwisely; escape, slip away; slip; skid

deslucido a fruitless, vain; stupid, clumsy, awkward; discolored; tarnished, dull; unsuccessful

deslucimiento m, clumsiness, gracelessness; failure, lack of success

deslucir vt irr to fade; discolor, stain; tarnish; spoil; sully the reputation of; vr do a thing badly, fail at. See **lucir**

deslumbrador a dazzling

deslumbrar vt to dazzle; confuse, bewilder; fig daze (with magnificence)

deslustrar vt to dull, dim, tarnish; frost (glass); discredit, sully (reputation)

deslustre m, dullness, tarnish; frosting (of glass); disgrace, stigma

deslustroso a ugly, unsuitable, unbecoming

desmadejar vt to debilitate, enervate

desmalezar vt, Lat. Am. to clear the underbrush from; weed

desmán m, outrageous behavior; disaster, misfortune

desmandado a disobedient

desmandar vt to cancel, revoke (orders); withdraw (an offer). vr behave badly; stray

desmantelado a dismantled, dilapidated

desmantelamiento m, dismantling; dilapidation

desmantelar vt to dismantle; abandon, forsake

desmaña f, lack of dexterity, clumsiness, awkwardness

desmañado a clumsy, awkward, unhandy

desmayar vt to cause to faint; vi grow discouraged, lose heart; vr swoon, faint

desmayo m, depression, discouragement; faint, swoon

desmedido a disproportionate; excessive

desmedirse vr to misbehave, go too far

desmedrado a thin, emaciated; deteriorated, spoiled

desmedrar vt to spoil, ruin; vi deteriorate; decline

desmedro m, impairment; decline, deterioration. **en d. de,** to the detriment of

desmejorar vt to spoil, impair, cause to deteriorate; vr deteriorate; vi and vr decline in health; lose one's beauty

desmelenar vt to ruffle or dishevel the hair

desmembrar vt to dismember; separate, divide

desmentida f, action of giving the lie to

desmentir vt irr to give the lie to; contradict, deny; lower oneself; behave unworthily; vi deviate (from right direction, etc.). See **sentir**

desmenuzar vt to crumble, break into small pieces; fig examine in detail; vr be broken up

desmerecedor a unworthy

desmerecer vt irr to become undeserving of; vi deteriorate; be inferior to. See **conocer**

desmesura f, insolence; disproportion; excess

desmesurado a disproportionate; excessive, enormous; insolent, uncivil

desmesurar vt to disarrange, disorder; vr be insolent

desmigajar(se) vt and vr to crumble

desmilitarizar vt to demilitarize

desmonetización f, demonetization; conversion of coin into bullion

desmontable a movable; sectional

desmontadura f, clearing; deforestation; leveling; demounting, dismounting

desmontar vt to clear wholly or partly of trees or shrubs; clear up (rubbish); level (ground); dismantle; dismount; uncock (firearms); vi and vr dismount (from horse, etc.)

desmonte m, clearing of trees and shrubs; clearing, cleared ground; timber remaining

desmoralización f, demoralization, corruption

desmoralizador a demoralizing

desmoralizar vt to demoralize, corrupt

desmoronamiento m, crumbling; decay, ruin

desmoronar vt to destroy, decay; crumble; vr crumble away, fall into ruin; decline, decay; wane, fade (power, etc.)

desmovilizar vt to demobilize

desnacificación f, denazification

desnatar *vt* to skim; *fig* take the cream or best

desnaturalización *f*, denaturalization

desnaturalizar *vt* to denaturalize; exile; deform, disfigure, pervert; *vr* give up one's country

desnivel *m*, unevenness; slope, drop

desnivelar(se) *vi* and *vr* to become uneven

desnudar *vt* to undress; *fig* despoil, strip, denude; *vr* undress oneself; deprive oneself

desnudez *f*, nudity; nakedness; bareness; plainness

desnudo *a* nude; ill-clad; bare, naked; clear, patent; *fig* destitute (of grace, etc.). *m*, *art* nude

desnutrición *f*, malnutrition

desobedecer *vt irr* to disobey. See **conocer**

desobediencia *f*, disobedience

desobediente *a* disobedient

desobligar *vt* to free from obligation; offend, hurt

desocupación *f*, lack of occupation; leisure

desocupado *a* idle; vacant, unoccupied

desocupar *vt* to empty; vacate; *vr* give up an employment or occupation

desodorante *a* and *m*, deodorant

desojar *vt* to break the eye of (needles, etc.); *vr* gaze intently

desolación *f*, destruction, desolation; affliction

desolador *a* desolate; grievous

desolar *vt irr* to lay waste, destroy; *vr* grieve, be disconsolate. See **contar**

desollado *a inf* impertinent, barefaced. *m*, carcass

desolladura *f*, flaying, skinning; *inf* slander

desollar *vt irr* to flay, skin; harm, discredit. **d. vivo,** *inf* to extort an exorbitant price; slander. See **contar**

desopinado *a* discredited

desopinar *vt* to discredit, defame

desorden *m*, disorder, disarray; confusion; excess

desordenado *a* disordered; vicious; licentious

desordenar *vt* to disorder; confuse; *vr* go beyond the just limits; behave badly; be impertinent

desorganización *f*, disorganization

desorientación *f*, disorientation, loss of bearings; lack of method, confusion

desorientar *vt* to disorient; perplex, confuse; *vr* lose one's way; be disoriented

desove *m*, spawning; spawning season

desovillar *vt* to unwind; uncoil; uncurl; explain, clarify

despabilado *a* alert, wide-awake; watchful, vigilant

despabilar *vt* to snuff (a candle); trim (lamps); hasten, expedite; finish quickly; steal, rob; *fig* quicken (intelligence, etc.); *inf* kill; *vr* rouse oneself, wake up

despachador (**-ra**) *n* dispatcher, sender

despachar *vt* to expedite; dispatch, conclude; forward, send; attend to correspondence; sell; dismiss; *inf* serve in a shop; *inf* kill; *vi* hasten; carry letters to be signed (in offices, etc.); *vr* get rid of

despachero, -a *mf Chile* shopkeeper, storekeeper

despacho *m*, transaction, execution; study; office, room; department; booking-office; dispatch, shipment; expedient; commission, warrant; dispatch (diplomatic); telegram; telephone message. **d. particular,** private office

despachurrar *vt inf* to crush, squash; recount in a muddled fashion; *fig* squash flat, confound

despacio *adv* slowly, little by little; deliberately, leisurely. *interj* Careful! Gently now!

despacito *adv inf* very slowly

despampanar *vt agr* to prune vines; *inf* amaze, stun, astound; *vi inf* relieve one's feelings; *vr inf* receive a serious injury (through falling)

desparpajar *vt* to spoil; *vi inf* chatter

desparpajo *m*, *inf* loquaciousness, pertness; disorder, muddle

desparramar *vt* to disperse, scatter; squander, waste (money, etc.); *vr* amuse oneself; be dissipated

despavorido *a* terrified, panicstricken

despechar *vt* to anger; make despair; *inf* wean; *vr* be angry; be in despair

despecho *m*, rancor, malice; despair. **a d. de,** in spite of

despechugar *vt* to cut off the breast (fowls); *vr inf* show the bosom

despectivo *a* contemptuous, depreciatory

despedazar *vt* to cut or break into pieces; *fig* break (heart, etc.)

despedida *f*, dismissal, discharge; seeing off (a visitor, etc.); farewell, good-by

despedir *vt irr* to throw out, emit, cast up; dismiss, discharge; see off (on a journey or after a visit); banish (from the mind); get rid of; *vr* say good-by; leave (employment). See **pedir**

despegado *a inf* indifferent, unconcerned, cold

despegar *vt* to unstick; unglue; separate, detach; *vr* become estranged; come apart or unstuck; *vi aer* take off. **sin d. los labios,** without saying a word

despegue *m*, *aer* take-off

despeinar *vt* to disarrange the hair; undo the coiffure

despejado *a* lively, sprightly; logical, clear-cut; cloudless; spacious, unobstructed, clear

despejar *vt* to clear, free of obstacles; **d. el camino de,** to clear the way for; *fig* elucidate, solve; *math* find the value of; *vr* smarten up, grow gay; amuse oneself; clear up (weather, sky, etc.); improve (a patient)

despejo *m*, freeing of obstacles; smartness, gaiety; grace, elegance; perkiness; clear-sightedness, intelligence

despeluzar *vt* to disorder the hair; cause the hair to stand on end; horrify; *vr* stand on end (hair); be horrified or terrified

despeluznante *a* hair-raising, terrifying

despender *vt* to spend; waste

despensa *f*, larder, pantry; store (of food); *naut* steward's room; stewardship

despeñadero *m*, precipice, crag; dangerous undertaking, risk. a steep, precipitous

despeñar *vt* to precipitate, fling down from a height, hurl down; *vr* fling oneself headlong; throw oneself into (vices, etc.)

despeño *m*, precipitation; headlong fall; *fig* collapse, ruin

desperdiciador (**-ra**) *a* a squandering, wasting. *n* squanderer

desperdiciar *vt* to squander; *fig* misspend, waste

desperdicio *m*, waste; remains, leftovers (gen. *pl*)

desperdigar *vt* to separate, sever; scatter

desperecerse *vr irr* to crave, yearn (for). See **conocer**

desperezarse *vr* to stretch oneself

desperfecto *m*, imperfection, flaw; slight deterioration

despernado *a* a weary, footsore

despertador (**-ra**) *a* a awakening. *n* awakener. *m*, alarm clock; incentive, stimulus

despertar *vt irr* to awaken; bring to mind, recall; incite, stimulate; *vi* waken; *fig* wake up, become more intelligent. See **acertar**

despiadado *a* a cruel, merciless

despicar *vt* to satisfy, content; *vr* revenge oneself

despierto *a* a wide-awake, clever

despilfarrar *vt* to squander, waste

despilfarro *m*, slovenliness; waste, extravagance; mismanagement, maladministration

despintar *vt* to paint out; wash off the paint; efface, blot out; disfigure, deform; *vi* be unlike or unworthy (of); *vr* fade (colors); forget

despiojar *vt* to remove lice, delouse; *inf* rescue from misery

despique *m*, vengeance, revenge

despistar *vt* to throw off the scent; mislead

desplacer *vt irr* to displease. *m*, disgust, displeasure, sorrow. See **placer**

desplantar(se) *vt* and *vr* to deviate from the vertical

desplazamiento *m*, *naut* displacement

desplegadura *f*, unfolding

desplegar *vt irr* to unfold; spread open; *fig* reveal, disclose, explain; evince, display; *mil* deploy troops; *vr* unfold, open (flowers, etc.); *mil* deploy. See **cegar**

despliegue *m*, unfolding; spreading out; evincing, demonstration; *mil* deployment

desplomar *vt* to put out of the straight, cause to lean (walls, buildings); *vr* lean, tilt (buildings); topple, fall down (walls, etc.); collapse (people); be ruined

desplome *m*, collapse

despoblación *f*, depopulation. **d. forestal,** deforestation

despoblado *m*, wilderness; deserted place

despojar *vt* to plunder, despoil; dispossess; *vr* (*with de*) remove (garments, etc.); relinquish, give up

despojo *m*, pillaging, spoliation; booty, plunder; butcher's offal; *pl* remains, leavings; debris, rubble; corpse

despolvorear *vt* to remove dust; *fig* shake off

desposado *a* a recently married; fettered, handcuffed. **los desposados,** the newly-weds

desposeer *vt* to dispossess; *vr* renounce one's possessions. See **creer**

desposorio *m*, betrothal, promise of marriage; (gen. *pl*) wedding, marriage

déspota *m*, despot, tyrant

despótico *a* a tyrannical

despotricarse *vr* to rave (against), rail (against)

despreciable *a* a worthless, contemptible

despreciar *vt* to scorn, despise; *vr* despise oneself

despreciativo *a* a contemptuous, scornful

desprecio *m*, contempt, scorn

desprender *vt* to loosen, remove, unfix; give off (gases, etc.); *vr* work loose, give way; deduce, infer; give away, deprive oneself (of)

desprendido *a* a disinterested; generous

desprendimiento *m*, loosening; removal, separation; emission; indifference, lack of interest; generosity; impartiality

despreocupación *f*, fair mindedness, impartiality; lack of interest

despreocupado *a* a unprejudiced, broad-minded; indifferent, uninterested

despreocuparse *vr* to shake off prejudice; (*with de*) pay no attention to; set aside

desprestigiar *vt* to discredit; *vr* lose prestige; lose caste

desprestigio *m*, loss of prestige, discredit

desprevenido a unprepared, improvident

desproporción f, disproportion

desproporcionado a disproportionate; out of proportion

despropósito m, nonsense, absurdity

después adv afterwards, after, next (of time and place) (e.g. **Vendrá d. de Pascua,** He will come after Easter. **Zaragoza viene d. de Madrid,** Saragossa comes after Madrid)

despuntar vt to blunt the point; naut double, sail round; vi show green, sprout; appear (the dawn); grow clever; fig stand out, excel

desquiciamiento m, unhinging; disconnecting; fig upsetting, throwing out of gear; downfall, fall from favor

desquiciar vt to unhinge; disconnect; fig throw out of gear, upset; banish from favor; vr become unhinged; fig be disordered; upset

desquitar(se) vt and vr to retrieve a loss; take revenge, retaliate

desquite m, compensation; revenge

desrielar vt, Lat. Am. to derail

destacamento m, mil detachment

destacar vt mil to detach; vr excel; be prominent; be conspicuous; art stand out

destajista mf pieceworker; jobber (worker)

destajo m, piecework; job. **a d.,** quickly and diligently. inf **hablar a d.,** to chatter, talk too much

destapar vt to remove the cover or lid; reveal, uncover; vr be uncovered; reveal oneself. **no destaparse,** to keep quiet, be mum

destartalado a tumble-down, rickety; poverty-stricken

destello m, gleam, sparkle, brilliance; flash, beam, ray; fig gleam (of talent)

destemplado a out of tune; inharmonious; intemperate; art inharmonious; inf out of sorts, indisposed

destemplanza f, inclemency, rigor (weather); intemperance, excess, abuse; inf indisposition; lack of moderation (actions, speech)

destemplar vt to disturb, upset, alter; mus put out of tune; put to confusion; vr be unwell; fig go too far, behave badly; lose temper (metals)

destemple m, mus being out of tune; med indisposition; uncertainty (weather); lack of temper (metals); disturbance, disorder; intemperance, excess, confusion

desternillarse de risa to shake with laughter

desterrado (-da) a exiled. n exile

desterrar vt irr to exile; shake off the soil; fig discard, lay aside; extirpate (an error). See **recomendar**

destetar vt to wean

destiempo, a adv untimely, inopportunely

destierro m, banishment, exile; place of exile; remote place

destilación f, distillation

destilador (-ra) n distiller. m, still

destilar vt to distil; filter; vi to drip

destilatorio a distilling. m, distillery; still

destilería f, distillery

destinar vt to destine; appoint; assign

destino m, fate, destiny; post, appointment; destination. **con d. a,** going to, bound for

destitución f, destitution; discharge, dismissal

destituir vt irr (with de) to dismiss or discharge from (employment); deprive of. See **huir**

destorcer vt irr to untwist; straighten out; vr naut drift. See **torcer**

destornillado a reckless; fig inf with a screw loose

destornillador m, screwdriver

destornillar vt to unscrew; vr act rashly

destrenzar vt to unplait. **destrenzarse las cintas,** to unlace one's shoes

destreza f, dexterity; agility

destrón m, blind person's guide

destronamiento m, dethronement

destronar vt to dethrone, depose; oust

destroncamiento m, detruncation

destroncar vt to lop, detruncate (trees); dislocate, disjoint; mutilate; fig ruin, seriously harm; tire out; Lat. Am. uproot vr be exhausted or tired

destrozar vt to destroy; break in pieces, shatter; mil wipe out, annihilate; squander, dissipate

destrozo m, destruction, ruin; shattering; mil rout; dissipation, waste

destrozón a hard on wearing apparel, shoes, etc.

destrucción f, destruction; ruin, irreparable loss

destructor (-ra) a destructive. n destroyer. m, nav destroyer

destruir vt irr to destroy, ruin, annihilate; frustrate, blast, disappoint; deprive of means of subsistence; squander, waste; vr math cancel. See **huir**

desuello m, flaying, skinning; forwardness, impertinence; extortion, fleecing. fig inf **¡Es un d.!** It's highway robbery!

desunión f, disunion, separation; fig discord, disharmony

desunir vt to disunite, separate; fig cause discord or disharmony

desvaído a gaunt, lanky; pale, faded, dull (of colors)

desvalido a unprotected, helpless

desvalimiento m, defenselessness, lack of protection; lack of favor; desertion, abandonment

desvalorización f, devaluation

desván m, garret

desvanecer vt irr to cause to disappear; disintegrate; make vain; remove; vr evaporate; faint, swoon; grow vain or conceited. See **conocer**

desvanecimiento m, faintness, loss of consciousness; vanity, conceit

desvariar vi to be delirious; rave, talk wildly

desvarío m, foolish action, absurdity; delirium; monstrosity; whim, caprice

desvelar vt to keep awake; vr be sleepless; (with por) take great care over

desvelo m, sleeplessness, vigil; care, attention, vigilance; anxiety. **con d.,** watchfully

desvencijar vt to loosen, disconnect, disjoint; vr work loose, become disjointed

desventaja f, disadvantage. **estar en d.,** to be at a disadvantage

desventajoso a disadvantageous

desventura f, misfortune

desventurado a unfortunate; timid, faint-hearted; miserly

desvergonzado a shameless, brazen, impudent

desvergonzarse vr irr to be brazen, be impudent. See **avergonzar**

desvergüenza f, insolence; shamelessness

desvestir(se) vt and vr irr to undress. See **pedir**

desviación f, deviation, deflection

desviar vt to divert, deflect; dissuade

desvío m, deviation; indifference, coldness; repugnance

desvirtuar vt to decrease in strength or merit

desvivirse vr (with por) to adore, love dearly; yearn for, be dying to; do one's best to please, (e.g. **Juan se desvive por servirme,** John does his best to help me)

detallar vt to tell in detail; relate

detalle m, detailed account; detail, particular

detallismo m, meticulous attention to details

detective mf detective

detector m, detector; rad catwhisker

detención f, stop, halt; delay; prolixity; arrest, detention. **con d.,** carefully, meticulously

detener vt irr to detain, stop; arrest; retain, keep; vr go slowly; tarry; halt, stop; (with en) pause over, stop at. See **tener**

detenido a timid, irresolute; miserable, mean

deterioración f, deterioration

deteriorar(se) vt and vr to deteriorate

determinación f, determination; daring; decision

determinado a resolute, determined

determinar vt to determine, limit; discern, distinguish; specify, appoint; decide, resolve; law define, judge; vr make up one's mind

detersorio a and m, detergent

detestable a detestable

detestar vt to abominate, detest

detonación f, detonation

detonar vi to detonate

detractor (-ra) a slandering n detractor, slanderer

detraer vt irr to detract, take away; separate; slander. See **traer**

detrás adv behind, after (place). **por d.,** in the rear; fig behind one's back

detrimento m, detriment; moral harm. **en d. de,** to the detriment of

deuda f, debt; fault, offence; sin. **d. exterior,** foreign debt. **estar en d. con,** to be indebted to. **Perdónanos nuestras deudas,** Forgive us our trespasses

deudo m, relative, kinsman; kinship, relationship

deudor (-ra) a indebted. n debtor. **d. hipotecario,** mortgagor

devanadera f, bobbin, reel, spool; winder (machine)

devanador (-ra) n winder (person). m, spool, bobbin

devanar vt to reel, wind. inf **devanarse los sesos,** to rack one's brains

devanear vi to rave, talk nonsense

devaneo m, delirium; foolishness, nonsense; dissipation; love affair

devastación f, devastation

devastar vt to devastate, lay waste; fig destroy, ruin

develador m, betrayer

devengar vt to have a right to, earn (salary, interest, etc.)

devoción f, piety; affection, love; pious custom; prayer

devocionario m, prayer book

devolver vt irr to restore to original state; return, give back; repay; **devolverse** vr Lat. Am. to come back, go back, return. See **resolver**

devorador (-ra) a devouring. n devourer

devorar vt to devour; destroy, consume

devoto (-ta) a devout, pious; devoted, fond. n devotee. m, object of devotion

día m, day; daylight; pl name or saint's day; birthday (e.g. **Hoy son los días de María,** This is Mary's saint's day (or birthday)). **d. de Año Nuevo,** New Year's Day. **d. de asueto,** day off. **d. de ayuno** or **de vigilia,** fast day. **d. del cura,** humorous wedding day. **d. del juicio,** Day of Judgment. **d. de los difuntos,** All Souls' Day. **d. de recibo,** at home day. **d. de Reyes,** Epiphany (when Spanish children receive their Christmas presents). **d. de trabajo** or **d. laborable,** working day. **d. por medio,** every other day. **días canicu-**

lares, dog days. **d. por d.**, day by day. **al d.**, up to date; per day. **al otro d.**, next day. **¡Buenos días!** Good morning! Good day! **de d.**, by day. **de d. en d.**, from day to day. **de un d. a otro**, any time now, very soon. **el d. de mañana**, tomorrow, the near future. **un d. sí y otro no**, every other day. **vivir al d.**, to live up to one's income

diabético a diabetic

diablo m, devil; Satan; *fig* fiend. *inf* **d. cojuelo**, mischievous devil; *fig inf* imp. *inf* **Anda el d. suelto**, The Devil's abroad, there's trouble. *inf* **tener el d. en el cuerpo**, to be as clever as the Devil; be mischievous

diablura f, mischief, prank; devilry

diabólico a diabolical, devilish; *inf* fiendish, iniquitous

diadema f, diadem; crown; tiara

diafanidad f, transparency

diáfano a transparent, diaphanous

diafragma m, *anat mech* diaphragm; sound-box (of a phonograph)

diagnosticar vt *med* to diagnose

diagnóstico a diagnostic. m, diagnosis. **d. precoz**, early diagnosis

diagonal a diagonal; oblique

diagrama m, diagram

diagramación f, layout (of a publication)

dialecto m, dialect

dialogar vi to hold dialogue, converse; vt write dialogue

diálogo m, dialogue

diamante m, diamond; miner's lamp; glass-cutting diamond. **d. bruto**, rough diamond

diamantista mf diamond-cutter; diamond merchant

diámetro m, diameter

diana f, mil reveille; bull's-eye (of a target); the moon

¡diantre! interj inf the deuce!

diapasón m, mus tuning fork; diapason; neck (of violins, etc.). **d. normal**, tuning fork. **d. vocal**, pitch-pipe

diapositiva f, phot diapositive; (lantern) slide

diario a daily. m, diary; daily paper; daily expenses. **d. de navegación**, ship's log. **d. de viaje**, travel diary, trip journal

diarismo m, *Lat. Am.* journalism

diarrea f, diarrhea

diatriba f, diatribe

dibujante m, sketcher; draftsman; designer

dibujar vt *art* to draw; describe, depict; vr appear, be revealed; be outlined, stand out

dibujo m, drawing; sketch, design, pattern; depiction, description. **d. a la pluma**, pen-and-ink drawing. **d. a pulso**, freehand drawing. **d. del natural**, drawing from life

dicción f, word; diction, language, style

diccionario m, dictionary

díceres m pl WH news

diciembre m, December

dictado m, title of honor; dictation; pl promptings (of heart, etc.). **escribir al d.**, to write to dictation

dictador m, dictator

dictadura f, dictatorship

dictamen m, judgment, opinion

dictaminar vi to give judgment or opinion

dictar vt to dictate; suggest, inspire; *Lat. Am.* give (a lecture). **dictar fallo**, to hand down a decision, render judgment

dictatorial, dictatorio a dictatorial

dicterio m, taunt, insult

dicha f, happiness; good fortune. **por d.**, by chance; fortunately

dicharacho m, inf vulgar expression, slangy expression

dicho m, saying, phrase, expression; witty remark; law declaration; inf insult. a said, aforementioned. past part **decir**, "said." **D. y hecho**, No sooner said than done. **Del d. al hecho hay muy gran trecho**, There's many a slip 'twixt the cup and the lip. **Lo d. d.**, The agreement stands

dichoso a happy; lucky; inf blessed, wretched, darn

didáctica f, didactics

didáctico a didactic

diecinueve a and m, nineteen

dieciocho a and m, eighteen

dieciséis a and m, sixteen

diecisiete a and m, seventeen

diente m, tooth; tooth (of saw, etc.); tusk; cog (of wheel); prong (of fork); tongue (of a buckle). **d. de leche**, milk-tooth. *bot* **d. de león**, dandelion. **d. de perro**, *sew* feather-stitch. *inf* **dar d. con d.**, to chatter (teeth). *fig inf* **enseñar** (or **mostrar**) **los dientes**, to show one's teeth; threaten. *inf* **estar a d.**, to be famished. **hablar entre dientes**, to mutter; fume, grumble. *inf* **tener buen d.**, to have a good appetite. **traer a uno entre dientes**, to loathe someone; speak scandal of

diestra f, right hand; protection

diestro a right (hand); skilful, dextrous; shrewd; astute, cunning; favorable, happy. m, expert fencer; bullfighter; halter; bridle

dieta f, med diet; inf fast, abstinence; legislative assembly; travel allowance (gen. pl); day's journey of ten leagues; daily fee (gen. pl)

dietario m, household accounts' book

dietética f, dietetics

dietista mf dietician

diez a ten; tenth. m, ten; decade of rosary

diezmar vt to tithe; decimate; punish every tenth person

diezmillo m, *Mexico* sirloin

diezmo m, ten per cent tax; tithe

difamación f, defamation, libel

difamador (-ra) a libeling. n libeler

difamar vt to libel; denigrate

difamatorio a libelous, defamatory

diferencia f, unlikeness, dissimilarity; *math* difference; dissension, disagreement. **a d. de**, unlike; in contrast to

diferenciación f, differentiation. **d. del trabajo**, division of labor

diferencial a differential

diferenciar vt to differentiate; change the function (of); vi dissent, disagree; vr be different, differ; distinguish oneself

diferente a different, various

diferir vt irr to delay, retard; postpone; suspend, interrupt; vi be different. See **discernir**

difícil a difficult

dificultad f, difficulty; impediment, obstacle; objection

dificultar vt to raise difficulties; put obstacles in the way; vi think difficult (of achievements)

dificultoso a difficult; *inf* ugly (face, figure, etc.)

difidencia f, mistrust; lack of faith, doubt

difidente a mistrustful

difracción f, diffraction

difteria f, diphtheria

difundir vt to diffuse (fluids); spread, publish, divulge; *rad* broadcast

difunto (-ta) a and n deceased. m, corpse

difusión f, diffusion; prolixity; *rad* broadcasting

difusivo a diffusive

difuso a widespread, diffuse; prolix, wordy

digerible a digestible

digerir vt irr to digest; bear patiently; consider carefully; *chem* digest. See **sentir**

digestivo a digestive

digitación f, *mus* fingering

digital a digital. f, *bot* foxglove, digitalis

dígito a digital. m, (*ast math*) digit

dignarse vr to deign, condescend

dignatario m, dignitary

dignidad f, dignity, stateliness; serenity, loftiness; high office or rank; high repute, honor; *ecc* dignitary

dignificar vt to dignify

digno a worthy, deserving; upright, honorable; fitting, suitable, appropriate

digresión f, digression

dije m, charm; trinket, any small piece of jewelry; *inf* person of excellent qualities, jewel

dilacerar vt to lacerate, tear flesh; *fig* discredit

dilación f, delay

dilapidación f, waste, dissipation, squandering

dilapidar vt to waste, squander

dilatación f, expansion; enlargement, widening; prolongation; *surg* dilatation; respite (in trouble)

dilatar vt to dilate, enlarge; expand; delay, postpone; spread, publish abroad; prolong; vr expand; be prolix, spread oneself; *Lat. Am.* to be slow, take a long time

dilatorio a procrastinating, dilatory

dilección f, affection, love

dilema m, dilemma

diletantismo m, dilettantism

diligencia f, care, conscientiousness, industry; haste, briskness; diligence (coach); *inf* business, occupation. **hacer sus diligencias**, to try one's best

diligenciar vt to set on foot, put into motion

diligente a diligent, conscientious, industrious; speedy, prompt

dilucidación f, elucidation, clarification

dilucidar vt to elucidate, clarify

dilución f, dilution

diluir vt irr to dilute. See **huir**

diluviar vi to teem with rain

diluvio m, flood, inundation; *inf* very heavy rain, deluge; overabundance

dimanación f, emanation, source

dimanar vi (*with de*) to rise in (rivers); proceed from, originate in

dimensión f, dimension; size, extent

dimes y diretes m pl, *inf* back-chat

diminuto a defective, incomplete; minute, very small

dimisión f, resignation (of office, etc.)

dimisorias f pl, *ecc* letter dimissory. *inf* **dar d. a uno**, to give a person his marching orders, dismiss

dimitente a resigning; retiring. mf resigner (of a post)

dimitir vt to resign (office, post, etc.)

Dinamarca Denmark

dinamarqués (-esa) a Danish. n Dane

dinámica f, dynamics

dinámico a dynamic

dinamita f, dynamite

dínamo f, dynamo

dinastía f, dynasty

dineral m, large amount of money, fortune

dinero m, money; Peruvian coin; wealth, fortune; currency. **d. contante, d. junto**, ready cash. **Poderoso caballero es Don D.**, Money talks

dinosauro m, dinosaur

dintel m, lintel; *Lat. Am.* threshold

diocesano a diocesan

diócesis f, diocese

Dios m, God; deity. **¡D. le guarde!** God keep you! **¡D. lo quiera!** God grant it! **D.**

mediante, God willing (D.V.). **ID. míol** Good gracious! **De menos nos hizo D.,** Nothing is impossible, Never say die. *inf* **haber** (or **armarse**) **la de D. es Cristo,** to be the deuce of a row. **INo lo quiera D.I** God forbid! **IPlegue a D.I** Please God! **IPor D.I** For goodness sake! Heavens! **IVálgame D.I** Bless me! **IVaya Vd. con D.I** Goodbye! Off with you! Depart! **IVive D.I** By God!

diosa *f,* goddess

diploma *m,* license, bull; diploma. **d. de suficiencia,** general diploma

diplomacia *f,* diplomacy; tactfulness; *inf* astuteness

diplomarse *vr,* Lat. Am. to get one's degree, receive one's degree

diplomático *a* diplomatic; tactful; *inf* astute. *m,* diplomat. **cuerpo d.,** diplomatic corps

dipsomanía *f,* dipsomania

diputación *f,* deputation; mission

diputado (**-da**) *n* deputy, delegate. **d. a Cortes,** member of the Spanish Parliament, congressman

diputar *vt* to appoint, depute; delegate; empower

dique *m,* dike; dam; dry dock; *fig* bulwark, check; **d. flotante,** floating dock

dirección *f,* direction; management, control, guidance; directorate; instruction; information; order, wish, command; editorial board; directorship, managership; (postal) address; managerial office. **d. cablegráfica,** cable address. **d. particular,** home address

directiva *f,* board, governing body

directivo *a* directive, control, ling, guiding, managing

directo *a* direct; straight

director (**-ra**) *a* directing, controlling. *n* director; manager; principal, head (schools, etc.); editor. **d. del ceremonial,** chief of protocol. **d. de escena,** stagemanager. **d. espiritual,** *ecc* father confessor. **d. gerente,** managing director

directorio *a* directory, advising. *m,* directory; directorate, board of directors

dirigir *vt* to direct; regulate; govern; supervise; guide; *mus* conduct; address (an envelope, etc.); keep (a shop, etc.); edit; put (a question); point (a gun); cast (a glance); *vr* go; wend one's way. **d. la palabra** (**a**), to speak to, address. **d. la vista a,** to look towards, look in the direction of, turn towards, turn in the direction of. **dirigirse a,** to go towards; make one's way to

dirimir *vt* to annul, make void; break, dissolve; settle (disputes, etc.)

discernimiento *m,* discernment; judgment; discrimination

discernir *vt irr* to discern, distinguish. *Pres. Ind.* **discierno, disciernes, dis-**

cierne, disciernen. *Pres. Subjunc.* **discierna, disciernas, discierna, disciernan**

disciplina *f,* discipline; system, philosophy, education; submission, obedience; subject (arts or science); *pl* scourge

disciplinar *vt* to train; educate; scourge, beat; discipline; *vr* scourge oneself

disciplinario *a* disciplinary

discipulado *m,* pupilship, studentship; education, teaching; discipleship; body of pupils (of a school, etc.)

discípulo (**-la**) *n* pupil, student; disciple, follower

disco *m,* discus; disk; phonograph record; *ast* disk. **d. de señales,** railway signal. **d. giratorio,** turntable (of a phonograph)

discontinuo *a* intermittent, discontinuous

discordancia *f,* discord, disagreement

discordar *vi* to be discordant; disagree; *mus* be out of tune

discreción *f,* discretion; circumspection; prudence, good sense; shrewdness; pithy or clever saying. **a d.,** at discretion; at will; voluntarily. *mil* **darse** (or **entregarse**) **a d.,** to surrender unconditionally

discrecional *a* optional, voluntary

discrepancia *f,* discrepancy; disagreement

discrepar *vi* to be discrepant; differ; disagree

discreto *a* discreet; ingenious, witty

disculpa *f,* excuse

disculpable *a* excusable

disculpar *vt* to excuse; forgive, pardon; *vr* apologize; excuse oneself

discurrir *vi* to wander, roam; flow, run (rivers, etc.); (*with en*) consider, think about; (*with sobre*) discourse on; *vt* invent; conjecture

discursivo *a* discursive; thoughtful, reflective

discurso *m,* reasoning power; oration, discourse; consideration, reflection; speech, conversation; dissertation. **d. aceptatorio,** acceptance speech

discusión *f,* discussion

discutible *a* debatable; disputable

discutir *vt* to discuss, debate, consider

disecar *vt anat* to dissect; stuff animals; mount plants

diseminación *f,* dissemination

diseminar *vt* to disseminate; spread

disensión *f,* dissension

disentería *f,* dysentery

disentimiento *m,* dissent

diseñador *m,* delineator, drawer

diseñar *vt* to outline, sketch

diseño *m,* outline, sketch; plan; description

disertación *f,* dissertation

disertar *vi* (*with* sobre) to discourse on, discuss, treat of

disfavor *m*, disfavor, discourtesy, slight

disforme *a* deformed; ugly; enormous

disfraz *m*, disguise; mask; fancy dress; pretence

disfrazar *vt* to disguise; dissemble, misrepresent; *vr* disguise oneself; wear fancy dress

disfrutar *vt* to enjoy (health, comfort, friendship, etc.); reap the benefit of; *vi* take pleasure in, enjoy

disfrute *m*, enjoyment, use, benefit

disgustado *a* annoyed; discontented, dissatisfied; melancholy, depressed

disgustar *vt* to displease, dissatisfy; annoy; *fig* depress; *vr* quarrel, fall out. **Me disgusta la idea de marcharme,** I don't like the idea of going away

disgusto *m*, displeasure, dissatisfaction; discontent; annoyance; affliction, sorrow, trouble; quarrel; boredom; repugnance

disidente *a* dissenting. *mf* dissenter, nonconformist

disímil *a* dissimilar, different, unlike

disimulación *f*, dissimulation, pretence

disimulado *a* feigned, pretended

disimular *vt* to dissemble; pretend, feign; put up with, tolerate; misrepresent, misinterpret

disimulo *m*, pretence, dissimulation; tolerance, patience

disipación *f*, dispersion; dissipation, frivolity; immorality

disipado *a* spendthrift; dissipated, frivolous

disipar *vt* to disperse; squander; *vr* evaporate; vanish, fade, disappear

dislate *m*, absurdity, nonsense

dislocar *vt* to dislocate; *vr* dislocate; sprain

disminución *f*, diminution. **Ir (una cosa) en d.,** to diminish, decrease; taper, grow to a point

disminuido físico *m*, physically impaired person, physically handicapped person

disminuir *vt* and *vi irr* to diminish, decrease. See **huir**

disociación *f*, dissociation. **d. nuclear,** nuclear fission

disociar *vt* to dissociate, separate; *chem* dissociate

disolución *f*, dissolution; immorality, laxity; disintegration; loosening, relaxation

disoluto *a* dissolute, vicious

disolvente *m*, dissolvent, solvent

disolver *vt irr* to loosen, undo; *chem* dissolve; separate, disintegrate; annul. See **resolver**

disonancia *f*, dissonance; disagreement; *mus* dissonant

disonante *a* dissonant; discordant, inharmonious

disonar *vi irr* to be inharmonious; disagree. See **sonar**

dispar *a* unequal; unlike, different

disparador *m*, shooter, firer; trigger (of firearms); ratchet (of watch); *a, Mexico* lavish

disparar *vt* to shoot, fire; throw or discharge with violence; *vr* run precipitately; rush (towards); bolt (horses); race (of a machine); explode, go off; *inf* go too far, misbehave; *Mexico* spend lavishly

disparatado *a* foolish; absurd, unreasonable

disparatar *vi* to act or speak foolishly

disparate *m*, foolishness, nonsense

disparidad *f*, disparity, dissimilarity

disparo *m*, shooting; explosion; racing (of an engine); discharge; foolishness

dispendio *m*, squandering, extravagance

dispensa *f*, dispensation; privilege

dispensación *f*, dispensation; exemption

dispensar *vt* to grant, concede, distribute; exempt; excuse, forgive

dispepsia *f*, dyspepsia

dispersar *vt* to disperse, scatter, separate; *mil* rout

dispersión *f*, dispersion

disperso *a* dispersed, scattered; *mil* separated from regiment

displicencia *f*, disagreeableness, coldness; hesitation, lack of enthusiasm

displicente *a* unpleasant, disagreeable; difficult, peevish

disponer *vt irr* to arrange, dispose; direct, order; decide; prepare, get ready; *vi* (*with* de) make free with; possess; have at one's disposal; *vr* prepare oneself to die; make one's will; get ready. See **poner**

disponible *a* disposable; available

disposición *f*, arrangement; order, instruction; decision; preparation; aptitude, talent; disposal; condition of health; temperament; grace of bearing; promptitude, competence; measure, step, preliminary; *arch* plan; proviso, stipulation; symmetry. **A la d. de Vd,** I (am, he, it, etc.) am at your disposal. **hallarse en d. de hacer una cosa,** to be ready to do something. **última d.,** last will and testament

dispuesto *a* ready, prepared; handsome, gallant; clever, wide-awake. **bien d.,** well-disposed; well, healthy. **mal d.,** ill-disposed; disinclined; out of sorts, indisposed

disputa *f*, dispute. **sin d.,** undoubtedly

disputar *vt* to argue, debate; dispute, question; *fig* fight for

distancia *f*, distance; interval of time; difference, dissimilarity; unfriendliness, coolness

distanciar *vt* to separate, place farther apart

distante *a* separated; distant; far off

distar *vi* to be distant (time and place); be different, unlike

distender(se) *vt* and *vr med* to distend, swell

distinción *f*, distinction, differentiation; difference, individuality; privilege, honor; clarity, order; distinction (of bearing or mind). **a d. de,** unlike, different from

distinguible *a* distinguishable

distinguido *a* distinguished, illustrious

distinguir *vt* to distinguish, discern; differentiate; characterize; esteem, honor, respect; discriminate; see with difficulty; make out; *vr* be different; excel, distinguish oneself

distintivo *a* distinguishing; distinctive. *m*, distinguishing mark

distinto *a* different; distinct; clear

distracción *f*, distraction; abstraction, heedlessness, absentmindedness; pleasure, amusement; licentiousness

distraer *vt irr* to lead astray; distract (attention); influence for bad; amuse. *vr* be absentminded; amuse oneself. See **traer**

distraído *a* abstracted, absentminded; inattentive; licentious *Lat. Am.* slovenly

distribución *f*, distribution; (gen. *pl*) share

distribuidor (-ra) *a* distributing. *n* distributor

distribuir *vt irr* to distribute; share out, divide. See **huir**

distributivo *a* distributive

distrito *m*, district

disturbio *m*, disturbance

disuadir *vt* to dissuade

disuasión *f*, dissuasion

disuasivo *a* dissuasive

dita *f*, *Lat. Am.* debt

diurético *a* diuretic

divagación *f*, wandering, roaming; digression

divagar *vi* to wander, roam; digress

diván *m*, divan (Turkish supreme council); divan, sofa; collection of Arabic, Persian or Turkish poems

divergencia *f*, divergence; disagreement

divergente *a* divergent; conflicting, dissentient

divergir *vi* to diverge; dissent

diversidad *f*, diversity, unlikeness, difference; variety

diversificar *vt* to differentiate; vary

diversión *f*, pastime, amusement; *mil* diversion

diverso *a* diverse, unlike; *pl* various, many

divertido *a* amusing, funny, entertaining

divertir *vt irr* to lead astray, turn aside; entertain; *mil* create a diversion. *vr* amuse oneself. See **sentir**

dividendo *m*, dividend. *com* **d. activo,** dividend

dividir *vt* to divide; distribute; stir up discord; *vr* (*with de*) part company with, leave

divieso *m*, *med* boil

divinamente *adv* divinely; excellently, admirably, perfectly

divinidad *f*, divinity, Godhead; person or thing of great beauty

divino *a* divine; excellent; admirable, superb

divisa *f*, badge, emblem; *her* motto

divisar *vt* to glimpse, descry

división *f*, division, partition; discord; (*math mil*) division; hyphen; apportionment; district, ward

divisor (-ra) *a* dividing, separating. *m*, *math* divisor. *n* divider, separator

divisoria *f*, dividing line

divorciar *vt* to divorce; separate; *vr* be divorced, be separated

divorcio *m*, divorce

divulgación *f*, spreading, publication, propagation

divulgar(se) *vt* and *vr* to spread abroad, publish

dobladillo *m*, *sew* hem; turn-up (of a trouser)

doblado *a* stocky, thickset, sturdy; rocky, rough, uneven; dissembling. *m*, garret

dobladura *f*, fold, crease; crease mark

doblamiento *m*, doubling; folding

doblar *vt* to double, multiply by two; fold, double; bend; persuade, induce; *naut* double, sail round; turn, walk round; *vi* *ecc* ring the passing bell; *theat* double a role; *vr* fold, double; bend; bow; stoop; allow oneself to be persuaded

doble *a* double, twofold; duplicate; insincere, false; thick (cloth); *bot* double (flowers); hardy, robust. *m*, fold, crease; *ecc* passing-bell; Spanish dance step. *adv* double, twice. *ecc* **rito d.,** full rites

doblegar *vt* to fold; bend; brandish; dissuade in favor of another proposition; *vr* submit, give way, acquiesce

doblete *a* of medium thickness. *m*, imitation jewel

doblez *m*, fold, crease; fold mark. *mf*, double dealing, treachery

doce *a* twelve. *m*, twelve; twelfth (of the month). **las d.,** twelve o'clock

docena *f*, dozen. **la d. del fraile,** baker's dozen

docente *a* teaching

dócil *a* docile; obedient; flexible, easily worked (metals, etc.)

docilidad *f*, docility; obedience; flexibility

docto *a* learned, erudite

doctor (-ra) *n* doctor; physician; teacher. *f*, *inf* blue-stocking

doctorado *m*, doctorate

doctorarse *vr* to get one's doctorate

doctrina *f*, doctrine; instruction, teaching; theory, conception; *ecc* sermon

documentación *f*, documentation; collection of documents, papers

documental *a* documental. *m*, documentary film

documentar *vt* to document

dogal *m*, halter; noose; slipknot. *fig* **estar con el d. a la garganta,** to be in a fix

dogma *m*, dogma

dogmático *a* dogmatic

dólar *m*, dollar

dolencia *f*, ailment; pain; ache

doler *vi irr* to be in pain; be reluctant; *vr* be sorry, regretful; grieve; sympathize, be compassionate; complain. *Pres. Ind.* **duelo, dueles, duele, duelen.** *Pres. Subjunc.* **duela, duelas, duela, duelan**

doliente *a* suffering; ill; afflicted, sad. *mf* sufferer, ill person. *m*, chief mourner

dolo *m*, fraud; deception; deceit; *law* premeditation

dolor *m*, pain, ache; mental suffering. **d. sordo,** dull pain

dolorido *a* painful; afflicted, sad

doloroso *a* sad, regrettable; mournful, sorrowful; pitiful; painful

doloso *a* deceitful, fraudulent

domable *a* tamable; controllable

domadura *f*, taming, breaking in; controlling (emotions)

domar *vt* to tame, break in; control, repress (emotions)

domesticable *a* tamable; domesticable

domesticar *vt* to tame; domesticate; *vr* grow tame; become domesticated

doméstico (-ca) *a* domestic, domesticated; tame. *n* domestic worker

domiciliar *vt* to domicile; *vr* become domiciled, settle down; *Mexico* address (a piece of mail)

domicilio *m*, domicile; house

dominación *f*, domination; power, authority; command (of a military position, etc.); *mil* high ground; *pl* dominions, angels

dominador *a* dominating; overbearing

dominante *a* dominating; overbearing, domineering; dominant. *f*, *mus* dominant

dominar *vt* to dominate; repress, subdue; *fig* master (branch of knowledge); *vi* stand out; *vr* control oneself

domingo *m*, Sunday. **d. de Cuasimodo,** Low Sunday. **d. de Pentecostés,** Whitsuntide Sunday. **d. de Ramos,** Palm Sunday. **d. de Resurrección,** Easter Sunday

dominicano (-na) *a* and *n* Dominican; native of Santo Domingo

dominio *m*, authority, power; rule, sovereignty; dominion (country); domain

dominó *m*, domino; game of dominoes

don *m*, gift; quality, characteristic; talent. **d. de gentes,** the human touch; charm

don *m*, title of respect equivalent to English Mr. or Esquire. Used only before

given name and *not* before a family name, e.g. **don Juan Martínez,** *or* **don Juan**

donación *f*, donation, gift, grant

donador (-ra) *a* donating. *n* donor

donaire *m*, discretion, wit; witticism; gracefulness, elegance

donar *vt* to bestow, give; transfer; grant

donde *adv* where, wherein. Sometimes used as relative pronoun "in which" (e.g. **La casa d. estaba,** The house in which I was); *Lat. Am.* at the house of, at . . .'s; to the house of, to . . .'s (e.g. **Mi tía está donde mis abuelos** My aunt is at my grandparents' **Mi tío no fue donde mis primos** My uncle did not go to my cousins') *interrog* **¿dónde? ¿A dónde va Vd.?** Where are you going to? **¿De dónde viene Vd.?** Where do you come from? **¿Por dónde se va a Madrid?** Which is the way to Madrid?

dondequiera *adv* wherever, anywhere, everywhere

donoso *a* witty; graceful

donosura *f*, wit; grace; dash, verve

doña *f*, feminine equivalent of **don** (e.g. **D. Catalina Palacios)**

dorado *a* golden, gilded; fortunate, happy. *m*, gilding

dorador *m*, gilder

doradura *f*, gilding

dorar *vt* to gild; make golden; *fig* gild the pill; *cul* toast lightly; *vr* become golden

dormidero *a* soporiferous, narcotic; *m*, *Lat. Am.* roost (of chickens)

dormilón (-ona) *a inf* sleepy. *n* sleepyhead

dormir *vi irr* to sleep; spend the night; *fig* grow calm; sleep (tops); (*with sobre*) sleep on, consider; *vt* put to sleep; *vr* go to sleep; go slow over, neglect; be dormant; go numb (limbs). **d. como un lirón,** to sleep like a top. *inf* **d. la mona,** to sleep oneself sober. **entre duerme y vela,** half-awake. *Pres. Ind.* **duermo, duermes, duerme, duermen.** *Pres. Part.* **durmiendo.** *Preterite* **durmió, durmieron.** *Pres. Subjunc.* **duerma, duermas, duerma, duerman**

dormitar *vi* to doze

dormitivo *a* and *m*, sedative

dormitorio *m*, dormitory; bedroom

dorso *m*, back; dorsum

dos *a* two. *m*, two; second (of the month). **las d.,** two o'clock. **d. a d.,** two against two. **de d. en d.,** two by two. *inf* **en un d. por tres,** in a twinkling

doscientos *a* and *m*, two hundred; two hundredth

dosel *m*, canopy; dais

dosis *f*, dose; quantity

dotación *f*, endowment; *naut* crew; staff, workers; equipment

dotar *vt* to give as dowry; endow, found;

fig endow (with talents, etc.); equip; apportion (salary)

dote *mf*, dowry. *f*, (gen. *pl*) gifts, talents. **dotes de mando,** capacity for leadership

draga *f*, dredger

dragado *m*, dredging

dragaminas *m*, *nav* minesweeper

dragar *vt* to dredge

dragón *m*, dragon; *bot* snapdragon; *mil* dragoon; *zool* dragon, giant lizard; *ast* Draco

dragona *f*, female dragon; *mil* shoulder-strap

dragonear *vi*, Lat. Am. to boast, brag

drama *m*, play; drama. **d. lírico,** opera

dramática *f*, dramatic art

dramático a dramatic; vivid, unexpected, moving

dramaturgo *m*, dramatist, playwright

drenaje *m*, drainage (of land and wounds)

dril *m*, drill, cotton cloth

droga *f*, drug; falsehood, deception; nuisance

droguería *f*, chemist's shop; drug trade

droguero (**-ra**) *n* chemist, druggist

ducado *m*, dukedom; duchy; ducat

ducha *f*, shower-bath; douche; stripe in cloth; furrow

ducho a experienced, skilful

dúctil a ductile (metals); adaptable, docile, flexible

ductilidad *f*, ductility; adaptability

duda *f*, doubt, hesitation; problem. **sin d.,** doubtless

dudable a doubtful

dudar *vi* to be in doubt; *vt* doubt, disbelieve

dudoso a doubtful; uncertain, not probable

duela *f*, hoop, stave

duelista *mf* dueler; duelist

duelo *m*, sorrow, grief; mourning; mourners; duel; (gen. *pl*) troubles, trials. **duelos y quebrantos,** *cul* fried offal. **sin d.,** in abundance

duende *m*, imp, elf, sprite, ghost

dueña *f*, owner, proprietress, mistress; duenna; married lady *ant*

dueño *m*, owner, proprietor; master (of servants). **d. de sí mismo,** self-controlled

dula *f*, common pasture ground or herds

dulce a sweet; fresh, pure; fresh, not salty; fragrant; melodious; pleasant, agreeable; tender, gentle; soft (metals). *m*, sweetmeat, bonbon. **d. de almíbar,** preserved fruit.

dulcedumbre *f*, sweetness; softness

dulcémele *m*, dulcimer

dulcera *f*, preserve dish, fruit dish

dulcería *f*, See **confitería**

dulcificar *vt* to make sweet; alleviate, sweeten

dulcinea *f*, *inf* sweetheart; ideal

dulzaina *f*, *mus* flageolet

dulzura *f*, sweetness; gentleness; pleasure; meekness; agreeableness

duna *f*, (gen. *pl*) sand dune

dúo *m*, *mus* duet

duodécimo a twelfth

duodeno a twelfth. *m*, *anat* duodenum

duplicación *f*, duplication

duplicado *m*, duplicate

duplicar *vt* to duplicate; double

duplicidad *f*, duplicity, falseness

duque *m*, duke

duquesa *f*, duchess

duración *f*, duration; durability

duradero a lasting; durable

durante *adv* during

durar *vi* to continue; endure, last

dureza *f*, hardness; *med* callosity; severity, harshness

durmiente a sleeping. *mf* sleeper; *m*, *arch* dormant

duro a hard; firm, unyielding; vigorous, robust; severe, inclement; exacting, cruel; *mus* metallic, harsh; *art* crude, too sharply defined; miserly, avaricious; obstinate; self-opinionated; unbearable, intolerable; merciless, hard; harsh (style). *m*, Spanish coin worth five pesetas

E

e *f*, letter E. *conjunc* used instead of *y* (and) before words beginning with *i* or *hi*, provided this last is not followed by a diphthong (e.g. **e invierno, e hijos,** *but* **y hierro)**

¡ea! *interj* Well!; Come on!; Let's see! (often used with **pues)**

ebanista *mf* cabinetmaker

ebanistería *f*, cabinetmaker's shop; cabinetmaking or work

ébano *m*, ebony

ebrio *a* intoxicated, inebriated

ebullición *f*, boiling, ebullition

echada *f*, throw, cast; pitch; fling; length of a man

echador (-ra) *n* thrower. *m, inf* chucker-out

echadura *f*, sitting on eggs to hatch them; (gen. *pl*) gleanings

echamiento *m*, throw, fling; throwing, casting; rejection

echar *vt* to throw, fling; eject, drive away; cast out, expel; put forth, sprout; emit, give forth; cut (teeth); dismiss, discharge; couple (animals); pour (liquids); place, apply; put into, fill; turn (keys, locks); impute; attribute; impose (penalty, taxes, etc.); play (game); try one's luck; distribute; publish, make known; perform (plays); *(with por)* go in direction of; *(with prep a + infin.)* begin to **(e. a andar,** to begin to walk); *vr* throw oneself down, lie down; sit on eggs (birds); abate, calm (wind); apply oneself, concentrate on; rush (towards); fling oneself (upon). **e. abajo,** to overthrow; demolish. **e. aceite al fuego,** to add fuel to the flames. **e. a perder,** to spoil, deteriorate. *naut* **e. a pique,** to sink. **e. a vuelo,** to ring (bells). **e. carnes,** to put on weight, grow fat. **e. cuentas,** to reckon up. **e. de menos,** to miss; mourn absence of. **e. de ver,** to notice. *fig* **e. en cara,** to throw in one's face, reproach. **echarla de majo,** to play the gallant. **e. las cartas al correo,** to post the letters. **e. las cartas,** to tell fortunes. **e. el pie atrás,** *fig* to climb down; *fig* back out. **e. raíces,** to take root; **e. las bases de, e. los cimientos de,** to lay the foundation of, lay the foundation for. *fig* become established. **e. rayos por la boca,** to fly into a rage. **e. suertes,** to draw lots. **echarlo todo a rodar,** to spoil everything. **e. una mano,** to lend a hand. **echar un volado** *Mexico* to toss a coin

ecléctico *a* and *n* eclectic

eclesiástico *a* ecclesiastical. *m*, ecclesiastic, clergyman; Ecclesiasticus

eclipsar *vt ast* to eclipse; surpass, outvie; *vr ast* be in eclipse; disappear

eclipse *m, ast* eclipse; retirement, withdrawal

eco *m*, echo; verse-echo; muffled sound; slavish imitation or imitator

economato *m*, trusteeship; cooperative store

economía *f*, economy, thrift; structure, organization; poverty, shortage; saving (of time, labor, etc.); *pl* savings. **e. dirigida,** planned economy. **e. doméstica,** domestic economy. **e. política,** political economy

económico *a* economic; thrifty; avaricious; cheap

economista *mf* economist

economizar *vt* to economize; save

ecónomo *m*, trustee, guardian

ecuación *f*, (*math* and *ast*) equation. **e. personal,** personal equation

ecuador *m*, equator

ecuánime *a* calm, unruffled; impartial

ecuanimidad *f*, calmness, serenity; impartiality

ecuatorial *a* equatorial

ecuatoriano (-na) *a* and *n* Ecuadorian

ecuestre *a* equestrian

ecuménico *a* ecumenical

eczema *m*, eczema

edad *f*, age; epoch; period. **e. de piedra,** Stone Age. **e. media,** Middle Ages. **de cierta e.,** middle-aged. **ser mayor de e.,** to have attained one's majority. **ser menor de e.,** to be a minor

edema *m*, edema

Edén *m*, Eden; *fig* paradise

edición *f*, edition. **e. diamante,** miniature edition. **e. príncipe,** first edition

edicto *m*, edict, decree; public notice

edificación *f*, building, construction; edification

edificador (-ra) *a* uplifting, edifying; building. *n* builder

edificar *vt* to build, construct; edify

edificio *m*, building, structure, fabric

editar *vt* (of a publisher) to publish; edit

editor (-ra) *n* publisher; editor

editorial *a* publishing; editorial. *m*, editorial, leading article

edredón *m*, down of an eiderduck; eiderdown, quilt

educación *f*, upbringing; education; good breeding, good manners

educado *a* educated. **ser mal e.,** to be badly brought up; be ill-mannered

educador (-ra) *a* educating. *n* educator

educar *vt* to educate; bring up, train, teach, develop

educativo *a* educational, educative

efe *f*, name of letter F

efectivo *a* effective; real. *m*, cash. **hacer e.,** to put into effect

efecto *m*, effect, result; purpose, intent;

impression; *pl* assets; goods, chattels. **efectos de escritorio**, stationery. **efectos públicos**, public securities. **en e.**, in fact, actually. **llevar a e.**, to put into effect; make effective

efectuación *f*, accomplishment, execution

efectuar *vt* to accomplish, effect; make (a payment); *vr* be effected; happen, take place

eferente *a* efferent

efervescencia *f*, effervescence; excitement, enthusiasm

efervescente *a* effervescent

eficacia *f*, efficacy; effectiveness

eficaz *a* efficacious; effective

eficiencia *f*, efficiency

eficiente *a* efficient, effective

efigie *f*, effigy; image, representation, symbol

efímero *a* ephemeral; brief

eflorescencia *f*, *chem* efflorescence

efusión *f*, effusion; *fig* spate (of words, etc.)

efusivo *a* effusive, expansive

Egeo, Mar Aegean Sea

égida *f*, shield; egis, protection

egipcíaco (-ca), egipcio (-ia) *a* and *n* Egyptian

Egipto Egypt

egoísmo *m*, egoism

egoísta *a* egoistic. *mf* egoist

egotismo *m*, egotism

egotista *a* egotistical. *mf* egotist

egregio *a* distinguished, celebrated

egresado *m*, graduate. (of a certain school)

egresar (de . . .) *vi*, *Lat. Am.* to go out (of . . .), leave (. . .); be graduated (from . . .)

egreso *m*, *Lat. Am.* departure, leaving; graduation

eje *m*, axis; axle-tree; shaft; pivot, fundamental idea. **e. trasero**, rear-axle

ejecución *f*, accomplishment, performance; execution, technique; death penalty

ejecutable *a* feasible, practicable

ejecutante *mf mus* executant, performer

ejecutar *vt* to discharge, perform; put to death; (*art mus*) execute; serve (a warrant, etc.); *law* seize (property)

ejecutivo *a* executive; urgent

ejecutor *m*, executor

ejecutoria *f*, letters patent of nobility; *law* judgment, sentence

ejemplar *a* exemplary. *m*, copy, specimen; precedent; example; warning

ejemplificar *vt* to exemplify

ejemplo *m*, example, precedent; illustration, instance; specimen. **dar e.**, to set an example. **por e.**, for example

ejercer *vt* to practise (a profession); perform, fulfil; exercise, use

ejercicio *m*, exercise; practice; performance; exertion, effort; *mil* exercises (gen. *pl*). **ejercicios espirituales**, spiritual exercises. **ejercicios físicos**, physical training

ejercitar *vt* to exercise; train, teach; *vr* exercise; practice

ejército *m*, army

ejote *m*, *Central America, Mexico* string bean

el *def art. m*, *sing* the

él *pers pron sing m*, he; it (*f*. **ella**. *neut* **ello**) (e.g. **Lo hizo él,** He did it). Also used with prep. (e.g. **Lo hicimos por él,** We did it for him)

elaboración *f*, elaboration, working out

elaborado *a* elaborate

elaborar *vt* to elaborate; produce, work out

elasticidad *f*, elasticity; adaptability

elástico *a* elastic; adaptable. *m*, elastic tape; elastic material

ele *f*, name of letter L

elección *f*, choice; election; selection; discrimination

electivo *a* elective

elector (-ra) *n* elector, voter. *m*, German prince *ant*

electorado *m*, electorate

electoral *a* electoral

electricidad *f*, electricity

electricista *mf* electrician

eléctrico *a* electric; electrical

electrificar *vt* to electrify

electrizar *vt* to electrify; startle; *vr* be electrified

electrocución *f*, electrocution

electrocutar *vt* to electrocute

electroimán *m*, electromagnet

electrólisis *f*, electrolysis

electromotriz *a* electromotive. **fuerza e.,** electromotive force

electrón *m*, electron

electrotecnia *f*, electrical engineering

electroterapia *f*, *med* electrotherapy

elefante (-ta) *n* elephant

elefantino *a* elephantine

elegancia *f*, elegance, grace; fashionableness; *lit* beauty of style

elegante *a* elegant; graceful, lovely; fashionable, stylish

elegantoso, -a *a*, *Lat. Am.* = **elegante**

elegía *f*, elegy

elegibilidad *f*, eligibility

elegible *a* eligible

elegir *vt irr* to select, prefer; elect. *Pres. Ind.* **elijo, eliges, elige, eligen.** *Pres. Part.* **eligiendo.** *Preterite* **eligió, eligieron.** *Pres. Subj.* **elija,** etc.

elemental *a* elemental; fundamental; elementary

elemento *m*, element; component, con-

stituent; *elec* element; *pl* rudiments. *mil*
elementos de choque, shock troops

elenco *m*, Lat. Am. cast (of characters)

elevación *f*, lifting, raising; height, high
ground; elevation; altitude; *fig* eminence;
elevation, advancement; ecstasy; raising
(of the voice)

elevado *a* sublime, lofty

elevar *vt* to raise, lift; *fig* exalt; *vr* be in
ecstasy, be transported. **elevarse de
categoría,** to rise in status

elfo *m*, elf

eliminación *f*, elimination

eliminador *a* eliminatory. *m*, eliminator

eliminar *vt* to eliminate

elíptico *a* elliptic

elíseo *m*, Elysium. *a* Elysian. **campos
elíseos,** Elysian fields

elocución *f*, elocution; style of speech

elocuencia *f*, eloquence

elocuente *a* eloquent

elogiador (**-ra**) *a* eulogistic. *n* eulogist

elogiar *vt* to eulogize, praise

elogio *m*, eulogy, praise. «**Elogio de la
Locura**», "In Praise of Folly"

elote *m*, Central America, Mexico corn

elucidar *vt* to elucidate, clarify

eludible *a* escapable, avoidable

eludir *vt* to elude, avoid

elusivo, -a *a*, Lat. Am. evasive, tricky

ella *pers. pron 3rd sing. f* she; it. See **él**

ello *pers. pron 3rd sing. neut* that, the
fact, it. **Ello es que . . . ,** The fact is that
. . . **No tengo tiempo para ello,** I have
no time for that

ellos, ellas *pers. pron 3rd pl. m* and *f*,
they. See **él**

emaciación *f*, emaciation

emanación *f*, emanation; effluvium

emanar *vi* to emanate (from), originate
(in)

emancipación *f*, emancipation; enfranchisement

emancipador (**-ra**) *a* emancipatory. *n*
emancipator

emancipar *vt* to emancipate, free; enfranchise; *vr* emancipate oneself;
become independent; free oneself

emascular *vt* to emasculate

embadurnar *vt* to smear, smudge, daub

embajada *f*, embassy; ambassadorship;
embassy building; *inf* message

embajador *m*, ambassador; emissary

embajadora *f*, wife of ambassador;
woman ambassador

embalaje *m*, packing; bale; wrapper;
packing charge

embalar *vt* to pack

embaldosado *m*, tiled pavement or floor

embaldosar *vt* to tile, pave with tiles

embalsamar *vt* to embalm; perfume

embalse *m*, dam; damming, impounding
(of water)

embanastar *vt* to place in a basket;
crowd, squeeze

embarazada *a f*, pregnant

embarazar *vt* to impede, hinder, embarrass; *vr* be hindered or embarrassed; be
pregnant

embarazo *m*, difficulty, impediment;
pregnancy; timidity, embarrassment

embarazoso *a* embarrassing; inconvenient; difficult, troublesome

embarcación *f*, ship, vessel; embarkation

embarcadero *m*, wharf, dock; quay; pier;
jetty

embarcar *vt* to embark, ship; board
(boat, train, etc.); *vr* embark; board

embarco *m*, embarking, embarkation

embargar *vt* to obstruct, impede; *law*
seize; suspend, paralyse

embargo *m*, *law* seizure; embargo. **sin
e.,** nevertheless, however

embarque *m*, loading, embarkation
(goods)

embarrancar *vi naut* to run aground; *vr
naut* be stuck on a reef or in the mud

embarrilar *vt* to barrel

embarullar *vt inf* to mix up, muddle; do
hastily and badly

embastar *vt sew* to baste; tack

embaste *m*, *sew* basting; tacking stitch

embate *m*, beating of the waves; sudden
attack; unexpected misfortune

embaucar *vt* to deceive, hoodwink

embaular *vt* to pack in a trunk; *inf* stuff
with food

embazar *vt* to dye brown; hinder; amaze;
vr be amazed; be tired or bored; be satiated

embebecer *vt irr* to entertain, amuse;
engross, fascinate; *vr* be dumbfounded.
See **conocer**

embebecimiento *m*, astonishment; absorption, engrossment

embeber *vt* to absorb; contain; shrink,
contract; saturate; insert, introduce; incorporate; *vi* shrink; *vr* be amazed; master or absorb (a subject). **embebido en
sus pensamientos,** absorbed in thought

embelecar *vt* to dupe, deceive, trick

embelesar *vt* to astonish; fascinate, enchant; *vr* be astonished or fascinated

embeleso *m*, astonishment; fascination;
charm

embellecer *vt irr* to embellish; *vr* beautify oneself. See **conocer**

embellecimiento *m*, beautifying, embellishment

embestida *f*, assault, attack, onrush; *inf*
importunity

embestir *vt irr* to rush upon, assault; *inf*

importune, be a nuisance to; *vi fig inf* clash, be inharmonious. See **pedir**

emblema *m*, emblem; symbol; badge

emblemático *a* emblematic; symbolical

embobar *vt* to entertain, fascinate; *vr* be dumbfounded

embobecer *vt irr* to make stupid. See **conocer**

embocadero *m*, narrow entrance, bottleneck; mouth of a channel

embocadura *f*, entrance by a narrow passage; *mus* mouthpiece; flavor (of wine); estuary, mouth of a river; *theat* proscenium

embocar *vt* to put in the mouth; go through a narrow passage; deceive; *inf* devour, wolf; initiate a business deal

embolador, -a *mf*, *Lat. Am.* bootblack

embolia *f*, embolism

émbolo *m*, *mech* piston, plunger

embolsar *vt* to place money in a purse; collect (a debt, etc.)

emborrachar *vt* to intoxicate; daze, stupefy; *vr* become intoxicated; run (of dyes)

emborrascarse *vr* to be furious; become stormy (weather); *fig* go downhill (business concern)

emborronar *vt* to blot; scribble, write hastily

emboscar *vt mil* to set an ambush; *vr* lie in ambush

embotar *vt* to blunt (cutting edge); *vi fig* weaken; *vr* become blunt

embotellado *m*, bottling; *fig* bottleneck

embotellador (-ra) *n* bottler. *f*. **embotelladora,** bottling outfit

embotellar *vt* to bottle; bottle up, prevent from escaping

embozar *vt fig* to cloak, dissemble; muffle; *vr* muffle oneself up

embozo *m*, anything used to cover or muffle the face; pretense, pretext; facings (gen. *pl*); yashmak

embullo *m*, *Central America* noise; excitement; revelry

embragar *vt* to sling, lift; *mech* let in the clutch

embrague *m*, hoisting, slinging; *mech* clutch

embravecer *vt irr* to infuriate; *vr* be enraged; be boisterous (sea). See **conocer**

embrazadura *f*, grasping, clasping; handle, clasp

embrear *vt* to tar, paint with pitch

embriagador *a* intoxicating

embriagar *vt* to intoxicate; enrapture; *vr* become inebriated

embriaguez *f*, intoxication, inebriation; rapture

embrión *m*, embryo; germ, rough idea

embrionario *a* embryonic

embrollar *vt* to entangle; embroil

embrollo *m*, tangle; falsehood; difficult situation

embromar *vt* to tease, chaff; trick, deceive; waste the time of; annoy; harm

embrujar *vt* to bewitch

embrutecer *vt irr* to make brutish or stupid; *vr* become brutish. See **conocer**

embudo *m*, *chem* funnel

embuste *m*, lie, fraud; *pl* trinkets

embustero (-ra) *a* deceitful, knavish. *n* liar, cheat, trickster

embutido *m*, inlaid work; *cul* sausage

embutir *vt* to inlay; stuff full, cram; *vt* and *vr inf* stuff with food

eme *f*, name of letter M

emergencia *f*, emergence; accident, emergency

emerger *vi* to emerge; have its source (rivers, etc.)

emérito *a* emeritus

emético *a* and *m*, emetic

emigración *f*, emigration; migration; number of emigrants

emigrado *m*, emigrant, emigré

emigrante *a* and *mf* emigrant

emigrar *vi* to emigrate; migrate

eminencia *f*, highland; importance, prominence; outstanding personality, genius; title given to cardinals

eminente *a* high, elevated; prominent, illustrious

emisión *f*, emission; *rad* broadcast; *com* issue (bonds, etc.); floating (of a loan)

emisor *m*, *elec* transmitter.

emisora *f*, *rad* broadcasting station

emitir *vt* to emit; *rad* broadcast; *com* issue (bonds, paper money, etc.); utter, give voice to

emoción *f*, emotion

emocional *a* emotional; emotive

emocionante *a* moving, causing emotion; thrilling

emocionar *vt* to cause emotion, move; *vr* be stirred by emotion; be thrilled

emolumento *m*, emolument (gen. *pl*)

empachado *a* awkward, clumsy

empachar *vt* to hinder, impede; disguise, dissemble; *vr* overeat, stuff; be bashful

empacho *m*, bashfulness, timidity; embarrassment, impediment; indigestion, satiety

empadronamiento *m*, census

empadronar *vt* to take the census

empalagoso *a* sickly, oversweet; cloying; *fig* sugary, honeyed

empalar *vt* to impale

empalizada *f*, stockade, fencing

empalmar *vt* to dovetail; splice (ropes); clamp; *fig* combine (plans, actions, etc.); *vi* join (railroad lines); couple (railroad trains); *vr* palm (as in conjuring)

empalme *m*, connection; splicing; *fig*

combination (of plans, etc.); railroad junction; continuation; palming, secreting

empanada f, savory turnover or pie; secret negotiations, intrigue

empanar vt to bread; cul cover with breadcrumbs; agr sow grain

empañar vt to swaddle; tarnish, dim; blur; fig sully (fame, etc.)

empapar vt to saturate; absorb; impregnate; vr be saturated; absorb; fig be imbued

empapelador m, paperhanger

empapelar vt to wrap in paper; paper (a room, etc.)

empaque m, packing; paneling; inf mien, air; pomposity

empaquetador (-ra) n packer

empaquetar vt to pack; make up parcels or packages; overcrowd

emparedado (-da) a a cloistered, reclusive. n recluse. m, cul sandwich

emparejar vt to pair, match; equalize, make level; vi come abreast (of); be equal

emparentar vi irr to become related by marriage. See **acertar**

empastadura f, filling (of teeth)

empastar vt to cover with glue or paste; bind in boards (books); fill (teeth). **empastado en tela**, clothbound

empaste m, pasting; gluing; filling (teeth)

empatar vt to equal, tie with

empate m, tie, draw; dead heat

empavonarse vr, Central America to dress to the nines

empecatado a willful; evil-minded, wicked; incorrigible, impenitent; extremely unlucky

empecer vt irr to harm, damage; vi hinder. See **conocer**

empecinado, -a a, Lat. Am. pigheaded, stubborn

empedernido a stony-hearted, cruel

empedrado a dappled (horses); fig flecked (with clouds). m, paving; pavement

empedrar vt irr to pave with stones. See **acertar**

empegar vt to coat with pitch; mark with pitch (sheep)

empeine m, groin; instep

empellar vt to push, jostle

empellón m, hard push. inf **a empellones**, by pushing and shoving

empeñado a violent, heated (of disputes)

empeñar vt to pledge, leave as surety; pawn; oblige, compel; appoint as mediator; vr bind oneself, be under an obligation; (with en) insist on; persist in; vr intercede; mediate; mil begin (a battle). **empeñado en**, determined to, intent on

empeño m, pledge, surety; obligation,

engagement; fervent desire; purpose, intention; determination, resolve; guarantor; inf influence, favor

empeoramiento m, worsening; deterioration

empeorar vt to make worse; vi and vr deteriorate, grow worse

empequeñecer vt irr to diminish, lessen; make smaller; belittle. See **conocer**

emperador m, emperor

emperatriz f, empress

emperezar vt to obstruct, hinder; vr be lazy

empezar vt irr to begin, commence; initiate; vi begin. Pres. Ind. **empiezo, empiezas, empieza, empiezan**. Preterite **empecé, empezaste**, etc. Pres. Subjunc. **empiece, empieces, empiece, empecemos, empecéis, empiecen**

empiezo m, Lat. Am. beginning

empilonar vt, Lat. Am. to pile up

empinado a steep; lofty; arrogant; exalted

empinar vt to raise; tip, tilt (drinking vessels); vr stand on tiptoe; rear, prance; tower, rise; aer zoom, climb steeply. inf **e. el codo**, to lift the elbow, tipple

empírico (-ca) a empiric. n quack, charlatan

empizarrado m, slate roof

emplastar vt med to apply plasters; make up; paint; inf hinder, obstruct; vr be smeared

emplasto m, med plaster; poultice; inf put-up job, fraud

emplazamiento m, placing, location; site; law summons; naut berth

emplazar vt to convene, arrange a meeting; law summon

empleado (-da) n employee; clerk. **e. público**, civil servant

emplear vt to employ; lay out, invest (money); use; vr be employed or occupied

empleo m, employment; investment, laying out (of money); occupation; post, office

emplomar vt to lead, solder or cover with lead; affix lead seals on or to; weight (a stick, etc.); Argentina fill (a tooth)

emplumecer vi irr to fledge, grow feathers. See **conocer**

empobrecer vt irr to impoverish; vi and vr become poor; decay. See **conocer**

empobrecimiento m, impoverishment

empollar vt to hatch; vi produce a brood (of bees); inf brood on, consider; inf grind, cram, swot (of students)

empollón (-ona) n inf plodder, grind, swot

empolvar vt to cover with dust; powder

emponzoñar vt to poison; pervert, corrupt

emporio *m*, emporium

empotrar *vt* to embed, implant; fix down

emprendedor *a* capable, efficient, enterprising

emprender *vt* to undertake; (*with prep a or con*) *inf* accost, tackle, buttonhole

empresa *f*, undertaking, task; motto, device; intention, design; management, firm; enterprise, deal

empresarial *a* entrepreneurial

empresario *m*, contractor; theatrical manager

empréstito *m*, loan

empujar *vt* to push; *fig* exert pressure, influence

empuje *m*, push; *arch* pressure; energy; power, influence

empujón *m*, violent thrust or push. *inf* a **empujones**, by pushing and shoving; intermittently

empuñar *vt* to grasp; grip; clutch

empurrarse *vr*, *Central America* to get angry

emulación *f*, emulation, competition, rivalry

emulador *a* emulative

emular *vt* to emulate, rival, compete with

émulo (**-la**) *a* emulative, rival. *n* competitor, rival

en *prep* in; into; on, upon; at; by. **en Madrid**, in Madrid. **en junio**, in June. **Se echó en un sillón**, He threw himself into an armchair. **Se transformó en mariposa**, It turned into a butterfly. **Hay un libro en la mesa**, There is a book on the table. **María está en casa**, Mary is at home. **en un precio muy alto**, at a very high price. **El número de candidatos ha disminuido en un treinta por ciento**, The number of candidates has decreased by thirty percent. **En** appears in a number of adverbial phrases, e.g. **en particular**, in particular, **en secreto**, in secret, **en seguida**, immediately. When it is used with a gerund, it means after, as soon as, when, e.g. **En llegando a la puerta llamó**, When he arrived at the door, he knocked. **En todas partes se cuecen habas**, That happens everywhere; It happens in the best of families

enaceitar *vt*, *Argentina* to oil

enagua *f*, slip, crinoline, petticoat

enajenación *f*, transference, alienation (property); abstraction, absent-mindedness. **e. mental**, lunacy

enajenar *vt* to transfer (property)

enaltecer *vt irr* to elevate, raise; exalt. See **conocer**

enamoradizo *a* susceptible, easily enamoured; fickle

enamorado *a* in love, lovesick; easily enamoured

enamorar *vt* to arouse love in; court,

make love to; *vr* fall in love; (with *de*) become fond of (things)

enano (**-na**) *a* small, dwarf. *n* dwarf

enarbolar *vt* to hoist (flags); *vr* prance (horses); become angry

enardecer *vt irr* to kindle, stimulate (passion, quarrel, etc.); *vr* be afire (with passion); *med* be inflamed. See **conocer**

encabestrarse *vr*, *Lat. Am.* to dig one's heels in

encabezamiento *m*, census taking; tax register; tax assessment; heading, inscription, running head

encabezar *vt* to take the census of; put on the tax register; open a subscription list; put a heading or title to; lead, head; *vr* compound, settle by agreement (taxes, etc.)

encadenamiento *m*, fettering, chaining; connection, link, relation

encadenar *vt* to chain, fetter; *fig* link up, connect; *fig* paralyze. **encadenar el interés de**, to capture the interest of

encajar *vt* to insert, fit one thing inside another; force in; fit tightly; *inf* be opportune, fit in (often with *bien*); *vr* squeeze or crowd in; *inf* butt in, interfere

encaje *m*, fitting, insertion; socket, groove; joining; lace; inlay, mosaic

encajero, -a *mf*, lace maker; lace seller

encalar *vt* to whitewash

encalvecer *vi irr* to grow bald. See **conocer**

encallar *vi naut* to run aground; *fig* be held up (negotiations, etc.)

encamado *a* bedridden, confined to one's bed; *m*, person confined to his bed

encamarse *vr* to go to bed (gen. illness); be laid flat (grain, etc.); crouch

encaminadura *f*, **encaminamiento** *m*, directing, forwarding, routing

encaminar *vt* to guide; direct; regulate; manage; promote, advance; *vr* (with *prep a*) make for, go in the direction of

encandecer *vt irr* to make incandescent. See **conocer**

encandilar *vt* to dazzle; mislead; *inf* poke (the fire); *vr* be bloodshot (eyes)

encanecer *vi irr* to grow gray- or white-haired; grow mold; grow old. See **conocer**

encanijar *vt* to make weak, sickly (gen. of babies); *vr* be delicate or ailing

encantado *a inf* daydreaming, abstracted; haunted; rambling (of houses)

encantador *a* captivating, bewitching, delightful. *m*, sorcerer, magician. **e. de serpientes**, snake charmer

encantamiento *m*, enchantment, spell; charm

encantar *vt* to enchant, weave a spell; delight, captivate, charm

encañada *f*, gorge, ravine

encañado *m*, trellis; pipeline

encañar vt to run water through a pipe; stake plants; wind thread on a spool

encañonar vt to run into pipes; pleat, fold

encapotarse vr to muffle oneself in a cloak; scowl; be overcast; lower (sky)

encapricharse vr to take a fancy (to); insist on having one's own way, be stubborn

encaramar vt to raise, lift; climb; praise, extol. **e. al poder,** to put in power (e.g. a dictator). **encaramarse por,** to climb up

encarar vt to place face to face; aim (at); vt and vr face; come face to face

encarcelación f, incarceration

encarcelar vt to imprison, jail; carp clamp

encarecer vt irr to raise the price; overpraise, exaggerate; recommend strongly; vi and vr increase in price. See **conocer**

encarecimiento m, increase (in price); enhancement; exaggeration. **con e.,** insistently, earnestly

encargado m, person in charge; manager; agent, representative. **e. de negocios,** chargé d'affaires

encargar vt to enjoin; commission; recommend; advise; com order

encargo m, charge, commission; order; office, employ; responsibility

encariñarse (con), vi to become fond (of)

encarnación f, incarnation

encarnar vi to incarnate; pierce the flesh; fig leave a strong impression; vt symbolize, personify; vr mingle, blend

encarnizado a bloodshot (eyes); flesh-colored; bloody, cruel (gen. of battles)

encarnizamiento m, cruelty, fury

encarnizar vt to infuriate; vr devour flesh (animals); persecute, ill-treat

encarrilar vt to set on the track or rails (vehicles); fig put right, set on the right track

encartar vt to proscribe, outlaw; place on the tax register; law summon, cite

encartonar vt to cover with cardboard; bind in boards (books)

encasar vt surg to set (a bone)

encasquetar(se) vt and vr to pull a hat well down on the head; vr get a fixed idea

encasquillador, -a mf, Lat. Am. blacksmith

encastillar vt to fortify with castles; vr retire to a castle; be headstrong, obstinate

encauzar vt to channel; fig direct, guide

encefalitis f, encephalitis. **e. letárgica,** encephalitis lethargica, sleeping sickness. **enceguedor** a blinding, dazzling

encendedor a lighting. m, lighter. **e. de bolsillo,** pocket lighter

encender vt irr to light; switch on; set fire to, kindle; arouse (emotions); inflame, incite; vr blush. See **entender**

encendido a high-colored; inflamed; ardent. m, aut ignition

encerado a wax-colored. m, oilskin; sticking plaster; blackboard; tarpaulin

encerar vt to wax, varnish with wax; stain with wax; inspissate (lime)

encercar vt, Lat. Am. to encircle

encerrar vt irr to shut up, imprison; include, contain; vr go into seclusion. See **acertar**

enchilada f, Mexico rolled-up tortilla filled with meat or cheese and covered with sauce or cream

enchufar vt to connect tubes; fig combine (jobs, etc.); elec plug, connect

enchufe m, joint, fitting together (of tubes); elec wall socket, plug; part-time post; inf cushy job. **e. de reducción,** elec adapter

encía f, gum (of the mouth)

enciclopedia f, encyclopedia

enciclopédico a encyclopedic

encierro m, act of closing or shutting up; prison; retreat, confinement

encima adv over; above; at the top; besides; (with de) on, on top of. **por e. de esto,** over and above this, besides this

encinta a f, pregnant

encintar vt to decorate with ribbons

enclavar vt to nail; pierce; embed; inf deceive

enclenque a ailing, weak; puny, anemic

encoger vt to shrink, contract, recoil; discourage; vi shrink (wood, cloth, etc.); vr shrink from, recoil; be discouraged; be timid or bashful

encogimiento m, shrinkage; contraction; depression, discouragement; timidity; bashfulness

encolerizar vt to anger; vr be angry

encomendar vt irr to charge with, entrust; recommend, commend; vr (with prep a) put one's trust in; send greetings to. See **acertar**

encomiar vt to eulogize, praise

encomienda f, commission, charge; knight commandership; insignia of knight commander; land formerly granted in America to conquistadores; recommendation, commendation; protection, defense; pl greetings, compliments, messages

encomio m, eulogy; strong recommendation

enconar vt to irritate, exasperate; vr med be inflamed; be exasperated; (with en) burden one's conscience with

encono m, rancor, resentment, ill will

encontrado a facing, opposite, in front; hostile, inimical, opposed (to)

encontrar vt irr to meet; find; vi meet; encounter unexpectedly; (with con) run into, collide with; vr be antagonistic; find; feel, be; differ, disagree (opinions); (with con) meet, come across. **e. eco,** to strike a responsive chord. **encontrarse con el cura de su pueblo,** to find someone who knows all about, meet someone who knows all about. **¿Cómo se encuentra Vd?** How are you? *Pres. Ind.* **encuentro,** etc. *Pres. Subjunc.* **encuentre,** etc.

encontrón *m,* collision, violent impact

encopetado *a* conceited, proud; of noble descent; prominent, important

encorajar *vt* to encourage, inspire, hearten; *vr* be angry

encorvadura *f,* bending, curving

encorvar *vt* to bend, curve; *vr* have a leaning toward, favor

encostrar *vt* to cover with a crust; *vr* form a crust

encrespar *vt* to curl (hair); enrage; *vr* be curly (hair); stand on end (hair, feathers, from fright); be angry; grow rough (sea); become complicated, entangled

encrestado *a* crested; haughty, arrogant

encrestarse *vr* to stiffen the comb or crest (birds)

encrucijada *f,* crossroad, intersection; ambush

encrudecer *vt irr* to make raw-looking; annoy; *vr* be annoyed. See **conocer**

encuadernación *f,* bookbinding; binding (of a book); bookbinder's workshop. **e. en tela,** cloth binding

encuadernador (-ra) *n* bookbinder

encuadernar *vt* to bind (a book)

encuadrar *vt* to frame; fit one thing into another, insert; limit; *mil* enlist

encubierto *a* concealed; secret

encubridor (-ra) *a* a concealing, hiding. *n* hider; harborer; accomplice; receiver (of stolen goods); *law* accessory after the fact

encubrimiento *m,* hiding, concealment; *law* accessory before (after) the fact; receiving (of stolen goods)

encubrir *vt* to conceal; receive (stolen goods); *law* prosecute as an accessory. *Past. Part.* **encubierto**

encuentro *m,* collision; meeting, encounter; opposition, hostility; *mil* fight, skirmish; *arch* angle. **ir al e. de,** to go in search of. **salir al e. (de),** to go to meet; resist

encuerado, -a *a, Lat. Am.* naked, nude, in the buff

encuesta *f,* investigation, examination

encumbrado *a* elevated, high

encumbramiento *m,* act of elevating; height; aggrandizement, advancement

encumbrar *vt* to raise, elevate; exalt, promote; ascend, climb to the top; *vr* be proud; be lofty, tower

encurtir *vt* to pickle

ende *adv ant* there. **por e.,** therefore

endeble *a* weak, frail

endeblez *f,* weakness

endémico *a med* endemic

endemoniado *a* a devil-possessed; *inf* fiendish, malevolent

endemoniar *vt* to possess with a devil; *inf* enrage

endentar *vt irr mech* to cut the cogs (of a wheel); engage, interlock (gears, wheels, etc.). See **regimentar**

endentecer *vi irr* to cut teeth. See **conocer**

enderezamiento *m,* straightening; directing, guiding; putting right, correction

enderezar *vt* to straighten; direct, guide; put right, correct; *vi* take the right road; *vr* straighten oneself; prepare to

endeudarse *vr* to contract debts; be under an obligation

endiablado *a* ugly, monstrous; *inf* fiendish

endiosar *vt* to deify; *vr* be puffed up with pride; be abstracted or lost in ecstasy

enditarse *vr, Lat. Am.* to go into debt

endomingarse *vr* to put on one's Sunday best

endosante *m,* endorser

endosar *vt com* to endorse; transfer, pass on

endoso *m, com* endorsement

endrogarse *vr, Mexico* = **enditarse**

endulzar *vt* to sweeten; soften, mitigate

endurecer *vt irr* to harden; toughen; inure; make severe or cruel; *vr* grow hard; become hardened or robust; be harsh or cruel. **endurecerse al trabajo,** to become hardened to work. See **conocer**

endurecimiento *m,* hardness; obstinacy, tenacity

ene *f,* name of letter Ñ

enemigo (-ga) *a* hostile. *n* enemy; antagonist. *m,* devil

enemistad *f,* enmity, hostility

enemistar *vt* to make enemies of; *vr* (*with con*) become an enemy of; cease to be friendly with

energético, -a *a, Lat. Am.* = **enérgico**

energía *f,* energy, vigor

enérgico *a* energetic, vigorous

enero *m,* January

enervar *vt* to enervate, weaken; *fig* take the force out of (reasons, etc.)

enfadar *vt* to make angry; *vr* become angry; *Lat. Am.* to get bored

enfado *m,* anger; annoyance; trouble, toil

enfadoso *a* vexatious; troublesome, wearisome

enfaldar *vt* to tuck up the skirts; lop off lower branches (of trees)

enfangarse *vr* to cover oneself with mud; *inf* dirty one's hands, sully one's reputation; wallow in vice

énfasis *m,* or *f,* emphasis

enfático *a* emphatic

enfermar *vi* to fall ill; *vt* cause illness; *fig* weaken. **Enfermó del corazón,** He fell ill with heart trouble.

enfermedad *f*, illness; *flg* malady, distemper. **e. del sueño,** sleeping sickness

enfermería *f*, infirmary; hospital; first-aid station

enfermero, -a *mf* nurse

enfermizo *a* ailing, delicate; unhealthy, unwholesome

enfermo (**-ma**) *a* ill; *flg* corrupt, diseased; delicate, sickly. *n* patient. **e. venéreo,** person with a venereal disease

enfilar *vt* to place in line; string; *mil* enfilade

enflaquecer *vt irr* to make thin; weaken, enervate; *vi* grow thin; lose heart. See **conocer**

enfocar *vt* to focus; envisage

enfoque *m*, focus

enfoscado *a* ill-humored; immersed in business matters

enfrascar *vt* to bottle; *vr* (*with en*) plunge into, entangle oneself in (undergrowth, etc.); become engrossed or absorbed in

enfrenar *vt* to bridle; curb (a horse); restrain, repress; check

enfrente *adv* in front, opposite, facing; in opposition

enfriadero *m*, cooling place, cold cellar, root cellar

enfriar *vt* to cool; *flg* chill, make indifferent; *vr* grow cold; *flg* grow stormy (weather)

enfurecer *vt irr* to enrage. See **conocer**

enfurruñarse *vr inf* to fume, be angry; be disgruntled

engalanar *vt* to decorate, embellish. **engalanado como nunca,** dressed to the nines, dressed to kill

enganchar *vt* to hook; couple; connect; hitch, harness, yoke; *inf* seduce, hook; *mil* bribe into army; *vr* be hooked or caught on a hook; *mil* enlist

enganche *m*, hooking; coupling (of railroad trains, etc.); connection; yoke, harness; hook; *inf* enticement; *mil* enlistment; *Mexico* down payment

engañadizo *a* easily deceived, simple

engañador (**-ra**) *a* deceiving; deceptive. *n* deceiver, impostor

engañar *vt* to deceive; defraud, cheat; beguile, while away; hoax, humbug; *vr* be mistaken; deceive oneself. **e. como a un chino,** *inf* to pull the wool over a person's eyes. **Las apariencias engañan,** Appearances are deceptive

engañifa *f*, *inf* swindle, fraud

engaño *m*, deceit; deception, illusion; fraud; falsehood

engañoso *a* deceitful, false; fraudulent; deceptive, misleading

engaratusar *vt*, *inf*, *Lat. Am.* = **engatusar**

engarce *m*, hooking; coupling; setting (of jewels)

engarzar *vt* to link, couple, enchain; hook; curl; set (jewels)

engastar *vt* to set (jewels)

engaste *m*, setting (of jewels)

engatusar *vt inf* to wheedle, coax, flatter

engendrar *vt* to procreate; engender, produce, cause

engendro *m*, fetus; abnormal embryo; literary monstrosity

engestarse *vr*, *Mexico* to make a wry face

englobar *vt* to include, comprise, embrace

engolfarse *vr* to sail out to sea; (*with en*) *flg* be absorbed in

engomar *vt* to gum

engordar *vt* to fatten; *vi* grow fat; *inf* prosper, grow rich

engorrar *vt*, *Lat. Am.* to annoy, needle

engorro *m*, impediment, obstacle, difficulty

engorroso *a* difficult, troublesome

engranaje *m*, *mech* gearing, gear; *flg* connection, link

engrandecer *vt irr* to enlarge; augment; eulogize; promote, exalt. See **conocer**

engrandecimiento *m*, enlargement; increase; exaggeration, eulogization; advancement, promotion

engrasar *vt* to grease; lubricate, oil; manure; stain with grease

engreír *vt irr* to make conceited; *vr* become vain or conceited. See **reír**

engrescar(**se**) *vt* and *vr* to start a quarrel

engrosar *vt irr* to fatten, thicken; *flg* increase, swell; manure; *vi* put on weight, grow fat. See **contar**

engrudar *vt* to paste, glue

engullir *vt* to gobble, swallow

enhebrar *vt* to thread (needles); string

enhestar *vt irr* to erect; set upright; *vr* rise; rear up; straighten oneself up. See **acertar**

enhiesto *a* upright, erect

enhorabuena *f*, congratulation. *adv* well and good. **dar la e.,** to congratulate

enhoramala *adv* in an evil hour. *inf* **¡Vete e.!** Go to the devil!

enhorquetado *a* in the saddle

enigma *m*, enigma

enigmático *a* enigmatical

enjabonar *vt* to soap; *inf* soap down, flatter

enjalbegar *vt* to whitewash

enjambrar *vt* to hive bees; *vi* multiply, increase

enjambre *m*, swarm (of bees); crowd

enjaular *vt* to cage; *inf* jail

enjoyar vt to adorn with jewels; beautify; set with precious stones

enjuagadura f, rinsing (the mouth); rinse water; mouthwash

enjuagar vt to rinse; vr rinse the mouth

enjuague m, rinse; rinsing; mouthwash; tooth mug; scheme, plan

enjugar vt to dry; cancel, write off; wipe, mop (perspiration, tears, etc.); vr. grow lean

enjuiciar vt to submit a matter to arbitration; law prosecute; law render judgment; law adjudicate (a case)

enjundia f, animal fat or grease; fig substance, meat; strength, vigor; constitution, temperament

enjuto a dry; lean. m pl, brushwood; cul canapés, savories

enlace m, connection; link; tie; chem bond; alliance, relationship; marriage

enlazar vt to tie, bind; join, link; lasso; vr marry; be allied, related. **e. con,** to connect with (of trains); link up with

enlentecerse vr to decelerate, go slow, slow down

enlodar vt to muddy; fig smirch, sully

enloquecer vt irr to drive insane; vi go mad. See **conocer**

enlosado m, tile floor

enlozar vt, Lat. Am. to enamel, glaze

enlucir vt irr to plaster (walls); polish (metals). See **lucir**

enlutar vt to put in mourning, drape with crepe; darken, obscure; sadden; vr go into mourning; become dark

enmarañar vt to tangle, disorder (hair, etc.); complicate, confuse; vr be tangled; be sprinkled with clouds

enmascarar vt to mask; disguise, dissemble; vr be masked

enmendar vt irr to correct, improve; reform; compensate, indemnify; law repeal; vr be improved or corrected; mend one's ways. See **acertar**

enmienda f, correction; reform; indemnity; compensation; amendment; pl agr fertilizers

enmohecer vt irr to rust; vr become moldy. See **conocer**

enmudecer vt irr to silence; vi become dumb; be silent. See **conocer**

enmugrecer vt irr to cover with grime; vr be grimy, dirty. See **conocer**

enmugrentar vt, Chile = **enmugrecer**

ennegrecer vt irr to dye black; make black; vr become black; become dark or cloudy. See **conocer**

ennoblecer vt irr to ennoble; enrich, embellish; adorn, befit. See **conocer**

ennoblecimiento m, ennoblement; enrichment

enojadizo a irritable, peevish

enojar vt to anger; annoy, irritate; vr be angry; rage, be rough (wind, sea)

enojo m, anger; resentment; vexations, troubles, trials (gen. pl). **con gran e. de,** much to the annoyance of

enojoso a annoying; troublesome, tiresome

enorgullecer vt irr to make proud; vr be proud. See **conocer**

enorme a enormous, huge; monstrous, heinous

enormidad f, hugeness; enormity; wickedness

enramar vt to intertwine branches; embower; vi branch (trees)

enrarecer vt irr to rarefy; vr become rarefied; grow rare. See **conocer**

enredador (-ra) a mischievous, willful; intriguing, scheming; inf gossiping, meddlesome. n intriguer; inf meddler

enredar vt to catch in a net; put down nets or snares; entangle; sow discord; compromise, involve (in difficulties); vi be mischievous; vr be entangled; be involved (in difficulties)

enredo m, tangle; mischief, prank; intrigue, malicious falsehood; difficult situation; plot

enredoso a tangled; fraught with difficulties

enrejado m, railing, paling; trellis or latticework; sew openwork

enriquecer vt irr to enrich; exalt, aggrandize; vi grow rich; prosper, flourish. See **conocer**

enriscado a craggy, rocky

enrojecer vt irr to redden; make blush; vr grow red; blush. See **conocer**

enroscar vt to twist, twine; vr turn (screw); twist; coil

ensaimada f, Spanish pastry cake

ensalada f, salad; hodgepodge

ensaladera f, salad bowl

ensalmo m, spell, charm. **por e.,** as if by magic, rapidly

ensalzar vt to exalt, promote; praise

ensamblador m, joiner, assembler

ensambladura f, assemblage, joinery; joining; dovetailing

ensamblar vt to assemble; join, dovetail, mortise

ensanchador, -a mf, glove stretcher

ensanchar vt to widen, enlarge, extend; sew let out, stretch; vr put on airs

ensanche m, dilatation, widening; stretch; extension; sew turnings, letting out; (city) extension

ensangrentar vt irr to stain with blood; vr be bloodstained; be overhasty. See **regimentar**

ensañar vt to irritate, infuriate; vr be merciless (with vanquished)

ensartar vt to string (beads); thread (needles); spit, pierce; tell a string (of falsehoods)

ensayar *vt* to try out; *chem* test; *theat* rehearse; assay

ensayista *mf* essayist

ensayo *m*, test, trial; *lit* essay; assay; experiment; rehearsal. **e. general,** dress rehearsal

ensenada *f*, cove, inlet

enseñanza *f*, teaching; education; example, experience. **e. primaria,** elementary education. **e. secundaria,** secondary education. **e. superior,** higher education

enseñar *vt* to teach, instruct; train; point out; exhibit, show; *vr* become accustomed. **e. la oreja,** *fig* to show the cloven hoof

enseñorearse *vr* to take possession (of)

enseres *m pl*, household goods; utensils; equipment

ensillar *vt* to saddle

ensimismarse *vr* to be lost in thought; *Lat. Am.* to become conceited

ensoberbecer *vt irr* to make haughty; *vr* become arrogant; grow rough (sea). See **conocer**

ensordecedor *a* deafening

ensordecer *vt irr* to deafen; *vi* become deaf; keep silent, refuse to reply. See **conocer**

ensuciar *vt* to soil, dirty; *fig* sully; *vr* be dirty; *inf* accept bribes

ensueño *m*, dream; illusion, fancy

entabicar *vt*, *Lat. Am.* to partition off

entablado *m*, stage, dais; wooden floor; planking

entablar *vt* to plank, floor with boards; board up; *surg* splint; undertake, initiate (negotiations, etc.); begin (conversations, etc.); *vr* settle (winds). **e. acción judicial,** to take legal action

entalladura *f*, carving; sculpture; *carp* mortise, notch

entallar *vt* to carve; sculpture; engrave; notch, groove; tap (trees); fit (well or ill) at the waist

entallecer *vi irr* to sprout (plants). See **conocer**

entapizar *vt* to hang with tapestry; upholster; *fig* cover, carpet

entarimado *m*, wooden floor; dais

ente *m*, entity, being; *inf* object, individual

entechar *vt*, *Lat. Am.* to roof, to put a roof on

enteco *a* sickly, ailing, delicate

entendederas *f pl*, *inf* understanding

entendedor **(-ra)** *a* understanding, comprehending. *n* one who understands. **A buen e. pocas palabras,** A word to the wise is sufficient

entender *vt irr* to comprehend, understand; know; deduce, infer; intend; believe; (*with de*) be familiar with or knowledgeable about; (*with en*) have as a profession or trade; be engaged in; have

authority in; *vr* understand oneself; have a reason (for behavior); understand each other; have an amatory understanding; be meant, signify; (*with con*) have an understanding with. **a mi e.,** in my opinion, as I see it. *Pres. Ind.* **entiendo, entiendes, entiende, entienden.** *Pres. Subjunc.* **entienda, entiendas, entienda, entiendan**

entendido *a* learned, knowledgeable

entendimiento *m*, understanding; mind, reason, intelligence

enteramente *adv* completely, entirely, wholly

enterar *vt* to inform, advise

entereza *f*, entirety; completeness; impartiality, integrity; fortitude, constancy; strictness, rigour

enternecer *vt irr* to soften, make tender; move to pity; *vr* be touched by compassion. See **conocer**

enternecimiento *m*, compassion, pity; tenderness

entero *a* entire; whole; robust, healthy; upright, just; constant, loyal; virgin; pure; *inf* strong, tough (cloth); *math* integral; *Lat. Am.* payment

enterrador *m*, gravedigger

enterrar *vt irr* to inter; outlive; bury, forget. See **acertar**

entibiar *vt* to make lukewarm; *fig* cool, temper

entidad *f*, entity; value, importance

entierro *m*, interment, burial; grave; funeral; buried treasure

entoldar *vt* to cover with an awning; hang with tapestry, etc., drape; cover (sky, clouds)

entonación *f*, intonation; modulation (voice); conceit

entonado *m*, haughty, conceited

entonar *vt* to modulate (voice); intone; blow (organ bellows); lead (song); *med* tone up; *art* harmonize; *vr* become conceited; *com* improve, harden (stock, etc.)

entonces *adv* then, at that time; in that case, that being so

entontecer *vt irr* to make stupid or foolish; *vr* become stupid. See **conocer**

entornar *vt* to leave ajar; half-close; upset, turn upside down

entorpecer *vt irr* to numb, make torpid; confuse, daze; obstruct, delay; *vr* go numb; be confused. See **conocer**

entorpecimiento *m*, numbness, torpidity; stupidity, dullness; delay, obstruction

entrada *f*, entrance; door, gate; admission; *cul* entree; admission ticket; *theat* house; takings, gate; *mil* entry; beginnings (of month, etc.); intimacy; right of entry. **entradas y salidas,** comings and goings; collusion; *com* ingoing and outgoing

entrampar *vt* to trap (animals); swindle;

fig inf entangle (business affairs); *inf* load with debts; *vr* be bogged down; *inf* be in debt

entrante a incoming, entrant; next, coming (month)

entraña *f*, entrail; *pl* heart; *fig* center, core; humaneness; temperament. *inf* **no tener entrañas**, to be heartless, be without feeling

entrañable a intimate; dearly loved

entrar *vi* (*with* en) to enter, go into, come in; flow into; *fig* have access to; join, become a member; *fig* be taken by (fever, panic, etc.); *mil* enter; be an ingredient of; (*with por, en*) penetrate, pierce; (*with de*) embrace (professions, etc.); (*with prep a* + *infin*) begin to; (*with en* + *noun*) begin to be (e.g. **e. en calor,** begin to be hot) or begin to take part in (e.g. **e. en lucha,** begin to fight); *vt* introduce, make enter; *mil* (*with* en) occupy; *vr* (*with* en) squeeze in. **e. en apetito,** to work up an appetite, get an appetite. *inf* **no e. ni salir en,** to take no part in. *inf* **No me entra,** I don't understand it

entre *prep* between; among; to. **e. joyas,** among jewels. **E. las dos se escribió la carta,** Between them, they wrote the letter. **Dije e. mí,** I said to myself. **los días de e. semana,** weekdays. **e. tanto,** in the meanwhile.

entreabrir *vt* to leave ajar; half-open. *Past Part.* **entreabierto**

entreacto *m*, interval, entr'acte; small cigar

entrecerrar *vt*, *Lat. Am* to close halfway, half-close; leave ajar

entrecoger *vt* to intercept, catch; constrain, compel

entrecortado a intermittent (sounds); faltering, broken (voice)

entredicho *m*, prohibition; *ecc* interdiction

entredós *m*, *sew* insertion

entrefino a middling, fairly fine

entrega *f*, handing over; delivery; *lit* part, serial; installment. **por entregas,** as a serial, serial (of stories)

entregar *vt* to hand over; deliver; surrender; *vr* give oneself up; surrender; submit; (*with prep a*) engage in, be absorbed in; (*with prep a or en*) give oneself over to (vice, etc.)

entreguista *mf* defeatist

entrelazar *vt* tó interlace, intertwine; interweave

entrelistado a striped

entrelucir *vi irr* to show through, be glimpsed. See **lucir**

entremedias *adv* in between, halfway; in the meantime

entremés *m*, hors d'oeuvres (gen. *pl*); interlude, one-act farce

entremeter *vt* to place between or among; *vr* intrude; meddle, pry

entremetido (**-da**) a meddlesome. *n* busybody, meddler

entremetimiento *m*, meddlesomeness

entremezclar *vt* to intermingle

entrenador (**-ra**) *n* trainer; *sport* coach

entrenamiento *m*, training, exercise

entrenar(se) *vt* and *vr* to train; exercise; *sport* coach

entreoír *vt* to overhear; hear imperfectly

entrepaño *m*, arch panel; pier (between windows, etc.)

entrepiernas *f pl*, crotch

entresacar *vt* to choose or pick out; thin out (plants); thin (hair)

entresuelo *m*, mezzanine, entresol; ground floor

entresueño *m*, daydream

entretejer *vt* to interweave; interlace; *lit* insert

entretela *f*, *sew* interlining

entretener *vt irr* to keep waiting; make more bearable; amuse; entertain; delay, postpone; maintain, upkeep; *vr* amuse oneself. See **tener**

entretenido a amusing, entertaining

entretenimiento *m*, amusement; pastime, diversion; upkeep, maintenance

entretiempo *m*, between seasons, spring or autumn

entreverar *vt* to intermingle

entrevista *f*, meeting, interview

entristecer *vt irr* to sadden; *vr* grieve. See **conocer**

entromparse *vt*, *Lat. Am.* to get angry

entroncar *vt* to prove descent; *vi* be related, or become related (by marriage)

entronque *m*, blood relationship, cognation; junction

entrucharse *vr*, *Mexico* to meddle into other people's business

entumecer *vt irr* to numb; *vr* go numb; swell, rise (sea, etc.). See **conocer**

enturbiar *vt* to make turbid or cloudy; confuse, disorder; *vr* become turbid; be in disorder

entusiasmar *vt* to inspire enthusiasm; *vr* be enthusiastic

entusiasmo *m*, enthusiasm

entusiasta a enthusiastic. *mf* enthusiast

enumerar *vt* to enumerate

enunciación *f*, statement, declaration, enunciation

enunciar *vt* to state clearly, enunciate

envalentonamiento *m*, boldness; braggadocio, bravado

envalentonar *vt* to make bold (gen. in a bad sense); *vr* strut, brag; take courage

envanecer *vt irr* to make vain or conceited; *vr* be vain; be conceited

envanecimiento *m*, conceit, vanity

envasador (**-ra**) *n* packer. *m*, funnel

envasar *vt* to bottle; barrel; sack (grain,

etc.); pack in any container; pierce (with sword)

envase *m*, bottling; filling; container; packing

envejecer *vt irr* to make old, wear out; *vi* grow old. See **conocer**

envenenamiento *m*, poisoning

envenenar *vt* to poison; corrupt, pervert; put a malicious interpretation on; embitter; *vr* take poison

envergadura *f*, wingspan

envés *m*, wrong side of anything; *inf* back. **al e.**, wrong side out

enviado *m*, messenger; envoy. **e. extraordinario**, special envoy

enviar *vt* to send, dispatch

enviciar *vt* to corrupt, make vicious; *vr* (with **con, en**) take to (drink, etc.)

envidia *f*, envy; emulation; desire (to possess)

envidiable *a* enviable

envidiar *vt* to envy, grudge; emulate

envidioso *a* envious

envilecer *vt irr* to debase; *vr* degrade oneself. See **conocer**

envinarse *vr*, *Mexico* to get drunk (on wine)

envío *m*, *com* remittance; consignment

enviudar *vi* to become a widow or widower

envoltura *f*, swaddling clothes; covering; wrapping

envolver *vt irr* to enfold; envelop; wrap up, parcel; *fig* contain, enshrine; swaddle, swathe; roll into a ball; confound (in argument); *mil* outflank; implicate (person). See **mover**

enyesado *m*, plastering; stucco

enyesar *vt* to plaster; *surg* apply a plaster bandage

enzarzar *vt* to fill or cover with brambles; *vr* be caught on brambles; set one person against another; get in difficulties; quarrel

eñe *f*, name of the letter Ñ

épica *f*, epic

épico *a* epic

epicúreo (**-ea**) *a* epicurean; sensual, voluptuous. *n* epicure

epidemia *f*, epidemic

epidémico *a* epidemic

epifanía *f*, Epiphany, Twelfth Night

epiglotis *f*, epiglottis

epígrafe *m*, epigraph, inscription; title, motto

epigrama *m*, inscription; epigram

epilepsia *f*, epilepsy

epiléptico (**-ca**) *a* and *n* epileptic

epílogo *m*, recapitulation; summary, digest; epilogue

episodio *m*, episode; digression

epitafio *m*, epitaph

epíteto *m*, epithet

epítome *m*, epitome; summary, abstract

época *f*, epoch, period; space of time. **é. de celo**, mating season. **é. de lluvias**, rainy season. **é. de secas**, dry season. **en aquella é.**, at that time

epopeya *f*, epic poem; *fig* epic

equidad *f*, fairness; reasonableness; equity

equidistante *a* equidistant

equilibrar *vt* to balance; *fig* maintain in equilibrium, counterbalance

equilibrio *m*, equilibrium; equanimity; *fig* balance

equilibrista *mf* equilibrist, tightrope walker

equipaje *m*, luggage, baggage; *naut* crew

equipar *vt* to equip, furnish

equipo *m*, outfitting, furnishing; equipment; team; trousseau

equis *f*, name of the letter X

equitación *f*, horsemanship, riding

equitativo *a* equitable, just, fair

equivalencia *f*, equivalence, equality

equivalente *a* equivalent

equivaler *vi irr* to be equivalent; *geom* be equal. See **valer**

equivocación *f*, error, mistake

equivocadamente *adv* mistakenly, by mistake

equivocar *vt* to mistake; *vr* be mistaken or make a mistake. **equivocarse de medio a medio**, to be off by a long shot

equívoco *a* equivocal, ambiguous. *m*, equivocation

era *f*, era; threshing floor; vegetable or flower bed

erario *m*, public treasury, exchequer

erección *f*, raising; erection, elevation; foundation, institution

erguir *vt irr* to raise; straighten; lift up; *vr* straighten up; tower; grow proud. *Pres. Ind.* **irgo** (or **yergo**), **irgues**, **irguen**. *Pres. Part.* **irguiendo**. *Preterite* **irguió**, **irguieron**. *Pres. Subjunc.* **irga** or **yerga**, etc.

erial *m*, uncultivated land

erigir *vt* to found, establish; promote, exalt. **erigirse contra**, to rise up against

erisipela *f*, erysipelas

erizado *a* standing on end (of hair); prickly, covered with bristles or quills. **e. de espinas**, bristling with thorns; covered with bristles or quills

erizar *vt* to set on end (hair); beset with difficulties; *vr* stand on end, bristle (hair, quills, etc.)

erizo *m*, hedgehog; husk (of some fruits); *inf* touch-me-not, unsociable person; *mech* sprocket wheel. **e. de mar**, sea urchin

ermitaño *m*, hermit

erogación f, *Lat. Am.* expenditure

erosión f, erosion

erótico a erotic

errabundo a wandering, errant, vagrant

erradamente adv erroneously

erradicable a eradicable

erradicación f, eradication

erradicar vt to eradicate

errante a wandering; erring; errant

errar vi irr to err, fail; rove, roam; wander (attention, etc.); vr be mistaken. **aut e. el encendido,** to misfire. *Pres. Ind.* **yerro, yerras, yerra, yerran.** *Pres. Subjunc.* **yerre, yerres, yerre, yerren**

errata f, misprint

errático a wandering, vagrant; *med* erratic

erre f, name of the letter R

erróneo a erroneous, mistaken

error m, error. **error de más,** an overestimate. **error de menos,** an underestimate

eructar vi to eructate, belch

erudición f, erudition

erudito a learned, erudite. m, scholar. **e. a la violeta,** pseudo-learned

erupción f, *med* rash; eruption

es irr *3rd pers. sing Pres. Ind.* of ser, is

esa f, *dem* a that. **ésa,** f, *dem. pron* that one; the former; the town in which you are (e.g. **Iré a é. mañana,** I shall come to your town tomorrow). Used generally in letters. See **ése**

esbeltez f, slenderness

esbelto a tall and slim and graceful, willowy

esbozar vt to sketch, outline

esbozo m, sketch; outline, rough plan, first draft

escabechar vt to pickle; dye (the hair, etc.); *inf* kill in anger; *inf* fail (an examination)

escabeche m, *cul* pickle; hair dye

escabechina f, *inf* heavy failure (in an examination)

escabel m, footstool; small backless chair; *fig* steppingstone

escabioso a scabby, scabious

escabro m, scab, mange

escabroso a rough; rocky; uneven; rude, unpolished, uncivil; risqué, improper

escabullirse vr irr to escape; run away; slip out unnoticed. See **mullir**

escafandra f, diving suit, diving outfit

escala f, ladder; (*mus math*) scale; dial (of machines); proportion, ratio; stage, stopping place; measuring rule; *naut* port of call. **e. de toldilla,** companion ladder. *mus* **e. mayor,** major scale. **e. menor,** minor scale. *naut* **hacer e. en un puerto,** to call at a port

escalada f, escalade

escalafón m, salary scale; roll, list

escalamiento m, scaling, climbing; storming

escalar vt to scale; climb, ascend; storm, assail, enter or leave violently

escaldadura f, scalding; scald

escaldar vt to scald; make red-hot; vr scald or burn oneself. **Gato escaldado del agua fría huye,** Once bitten, twice shy

escalera f, staircase; stair. **e. abajo,** below stairs. **e. de caracol,** spiral staircase. **e. de mano,** ladder. **e. de tijera,** stepladder. **e. móvil,** escalator

escalfar vt to poach (eggs); burn (bread)

escalinata f, outside staircase or flight of steps, perron

escalofrío m, (gen. pl) shiver, shudder

escalón m, step, stair; rung (of a ladder); *fig* steppingstone; grade, rank. **en escalones,** in steps

escalpar vt to scalp

escalpelo m, scalpel

escama f, *zool* scale; anything scale-shaped; flake; suspicion, resentment

escamar vt to scale (fish); make suspicious. vr *inf* be suspicious or disillusioned

escamoso a scaly

escamotear vt to make disappear; palm (in conjuring); steal

escamoteo m, disappearance; stealing

escampada f, *inf* clear interval on a rainy day

escampar vi to cease raining; clear up (of the weather, sky); stop (work, etc.)

escandalizar vt to shock, scandalize; disturb with noise; vr be vexed or irritated

escándalo m, scandal; commotion, uproar; bad example; viciousness; astonishment

escandaloso a disgraceful, scandalous; turbulent

Escandinavia Scandinavia

escandinavo (-va) a and n Scandinavian

escantillón m, template, pattern; rule

escaño m, bench with a back

escapada f, escape; escapade

escapar vt to spur on (a horse); vi escape; flee; avoid, evade; vr escape; leak (gas, etc.). **Se me escapó su nombre,** His name escaped me. **e. por un pelo,** to have a narrow escape

escaparate m, showcase, cabinet; shop window

escapatoria f, escape, flight; *inf* way out, loophole

escape m, flight; evasion; escape (gas, etc.); *aut* exhaust. **a e.,** at full speed

escápula f, scapula

escara f, scar

escarabajo m, beetle, scarab; *fig inf* dwarf; *pl inf* scrawl

escaramuza f, skirmish

escaramuzar vi to skirmish

escarapela f, cockade, rosette; brawl

escarbadientes m, toothpick

escarbar vt to scratch, scrabble (fowls); rootle, dig; rake out (the fire); inquire into

escarcha f, hoarfrost

escarchar vt cul to frost, ice; spread with frosting; vi freeze lightly

escardar vt to weed; fig separate good from bad

escarlata f, scarlet; scarlet cloth

escarlatina f, scarlet fever

escarmentar vt irr to reprehend or punish severely; vi learn from experience, be warned. See **acertar**

escarmiento m, disillusionment, experience; warning; punishment, fine

escarnecedor (-ra) a mocking. n mocker

escarnecer vt irr to mock. See **conocer**

escarnio m, gibe, jeer

escarola f, endive; frilled ruff

escarpa f, steep slope, declivity; escarpment; Mexico pavement

escasear vt to dole out, give grudgingly; save, husband; vi be scarce or short; grow less

escasez f, meanness, frugality; want; shortage, scarcity

escaso a scarce; short; bare; parsimonious

escatimar vt to cut down, curtail

escatimoso a malicious, guileful

escayola f, plaster of Paris

escena f, theat stage; scene; scenery; theater, drama; spectacle, sight; episode, incident. **director de e.,** producer. **poner en e.,** theat to produce

escenario m, theat stage; scenario

escénico a scenic

escenografía f, scenography

escepticismo m, scepticism

escéptico (-ca) a sceptical. n sceptic

escindir vt to split

escisión f, cleavage, split; splitting; schism; disagreement

esclarecer vt irr to illuminate; ennoble, make illustrious; fig enlighten; elucidate; vi dawn. See **conocer**

esclarecido a distinguished, illustrious

esclavitud f, slavery; fraternity

esclavizar vt to enslave

esclavo (-va) n slave; member of a brotherhood. a enslaved. f, slave bracelet; ID bracelet

esclerosis f, sclerosis

esclerótica f, sclerotic

esclusa f, lock; sluice gate; weir

escoba f, broom, brush; bot yellow broom

escobada f, sweep, stroke (of a broom)

escobar vt to sweep with a broom

escocer vi irr to smart; fig sear; vr hurt, smart; be chafed. See **mover**

escocés (-esa) a Scots, Scottish. n Scot

Escocia Scotland

escofina f, rasp, file

escoger vt to choose, select

escogido a choice, select

escolar a school; pupil. m, pupil

escoleta f, Mexico amateur band

escollera f, breakwater, sea wall, jetty

escollo m, reef; danger, risk; difficulty, obstacle

escolta f, escort, guard

escoltar vt to escort; guard, conduct

escombrar vt to remove obstacles, free of rubbish; fig clean up

escombro m, debris, rubble, rubbish; mackerel

esconder vt to hide, conceal; fig contain, embrace; vr hide

escondidas, a adv secretly

escondite, escondrijo m, hiding place. **jugar al escondite,** to play hide-and-seek

escopeta f, shotgun. **e. de aire comprimido,** air gun, popgun. **e. de pistón,** repercussion gun. **e. de viento,** air gun

escopetazo m, gunshot; gunshot wound; fig bombshell

escopetear vt to shoot repeatedly

escopetero m, musketeer; gunsmith; man with a gun

escoplo m, chisel

escorbuto m, scurvy

escoria f, dross, slag; scoria, volcanic ash; fig dregs

escorial m, slag heap

escorpión m, scorpion; Scorpio

escorzo m, art foreshortening

escotado a low-cut (of dresses)

escotadura f, a low neck (of a dress); piece cut out of something; theat large trapdoor; recess

escotar vt to cut low in the neck (of dresses); pay one's share (of expenses)

escote m, low neck (of a dress); shortness (of sleeves); share (of expenses); lace yoke

escotilla f, naut hatch

escozor m, smart, pricking pain; irritation, prickle; heartache

escriba m, (Jewish hist.) scribe

escribanía f, secretaryship; notaryship; bureau, office; writing case; inkstand

escribano m, notary public; secretary

escribiente mf clerk

escribir vt to write; vr enlist; enroll; correspond by writing. Past Part. **escrito**

escrito m, writing, manuscript; literary or scientific work; law writ. **por e.,** in writing

escritor (-ra) n writer, author

escritorio m, escritoire; office

escritura f, writing; handwriting; law

deed; literary work. **Sagrada E.,** Holy Scripture

escrófula f, scrofula

escroto m, scrotum

escrúpulo m, scruple, qualm; conscientiousness; scruple (pharmacy)

escrupulosidad f, conscientiousness, scrupulousness

escrupuloso a scrupulous; exact, accurate

escrutador (-ra) n scrutinizer. a examining, inspecting

escrutar vt to scrutinize, examine; count (votes)

escrutinio m, scrutiny, examination; count (votes)

escuadra f, carpenter's square; architect's square; nav fleet; aer squadron; mil squad. **e. de agrimensor,** surv cross-staff

escuadrar vt (carp and mas) to square

escuadrilla f, squadron (airplanes, small ships)

escuálido a filthy, squalid; sordid; thin

escucha f, listening; peephole; mil sentinel

escuchar vt to listen; attend to, heed; vr like the sound of one's own voice

escudero m, squire, page; gentleman; shield maker

escudete m, escutcheon; shield; gusset; white water lily

escudilla f, bowl

escudo m, shield; escudo; escutcheon; protection, defense; ward (of a keyhole)

escudriñador (-ra) a searching; curious, prying. n scrutinizer; pryer

escudriñar vt to scrutinize; scan; investigate; pry into

escuela f, school; school building; style; (lit and art) school. **e. de artes y oficios,** industrial school. **e. industrial,** technical school. **e. normal,** normal school

escuelante m, Mexico schoolmaster

escueto a dry, bare, unadorned; simple, exact; unencumbered

escuincle mf, Mexico child

esculpir vt to sculpture; engrave

escultor (-ra) n sculptor

escultura f, sculpture; carving; modeling

escupir vi to expectorate; vt fig spit out; cast away, throw out

escurreplatos m, dishrack, draining rack

escurrido a narrow-hipped; skintight (of skirts)

escurridor m, colander, sieve; dishrack; drainingboard

escurriduras f pl, lees, dregs

escurrir vt to drain to the dregs; wring, press out, drain; vi trickle, drip; slip, slide; vr slip away, edge away; escape, slip out; skid

esdrújulo a gram of words where the

stress falls on the antepenultimate syllable

ese f, name of letter S; S-shaped link (in a chain). *inf* **andar haciendo eses,** to reel about drunkenly

ese m, dem a (f, **esa.** pl **esos, esas**) that; those. **ése,** m, dem pron (f, **ésa.** neut **eso.** pl **ésos, ésas**) that one; the former (e.g. **Me gusta éste, pero ése no me gusta,** I like this one, but I do not like that one

esencia f, essence, nature, character; extract; chem essence

esencial a essential

esfera f, geom sphere, globe, ball; sky; rank; face, dial; province, scope

esférico a spherical

esfinge f, sphinx

esforzado a valiant, courageous; spirited

esforzar vt irr to encourage; invigorate; vr make an effort. See **contar**

esfuerzo m, effort; courage; spirit; vigor; exertion, strain; mech stress. **sin e.,** effortless

esfumar vt art shade; art stump; dim; vr disappear

esgrima f, (art of) fencing

esgrimidor m, fencer, swordsman

esgrimir vt to fence; fend off

esguince m, dodging, twist; expression or gesture of repugnance; med sprain

eslabón m, link (in a chain); steel for producing fire. **e. perdido,** fig missing link

eslabonar vt to link; connect, unite

eslavo (-va) a Slavic. n Slav

esmaltar vt to enamel; decorate, adorn

esmalte m, enamel; enamelwork; smalt; brilliance

esmerado a careful, painstaking

esmeralda f, emerald

esmerar vt to polish; vr (with en) take great pains with (or to)

esmeril m, emery

esmero m, great care, conscientiousness

esnob a snobbish. mf snob

eso neut dem pron that; the fact that; that idea, affair, etc.; about (of time) (e.g. **Vendrá a e. de las nueve,** He will come about nine o'clock). **Eso** refers to an abstraction, never to one definite object. **No me gusta e.,** I don't like that kind of thing. **e. es,** that's it. **por e.,** therefore, for that reason

esófago m, esophagus

esotérico a esoteric

espaciar vt to space; print lead; vr spread oneself, enlarge (upon)

espacio m, space; capacity; interval, duration; slowness; print lead

espada f, sword; matador; swordsman; (cards) spade. **entre la e. y la pared,** fig between a rock and a hard place; between undesirable alternatives.

espadachín *m*, good swordsman; bully, quarrelsome fellow

espalda *f*, *anat* back (often *pl*); *pl* rear, back portion; *mil* rear guard. **de espaldas,** with one's (its, his, etc.) back turned; on one's (its, etc.) back

espaldar *m*, backpiece of a cuirass; back (of chair); garden trellis, espalier

espaldarazo *m*, accolade

espaldera *f*, espalier, trellis

espantadizo a easily frightened

espantapájaros *m*, scarecrow

espantar *vt* to frighten, terrify; chase off; *vr* be amazed; be scared

espanto *m*,.terror, panic; dismay; amazement; threat

espantoso a horrible, terrifying, awesome; amazing

España Spain

español (-la) a Spanish. *n* Spaniard. *m*, Spanish (language). **a la española,** in Spanish fashion

españolía *f*, Spanish colony, Spanish community (outside Spain)

españolismo *m*, love of things Spanish; Hispanism

españolizar *vt* to hispanize; *vr* adopt Spanish customs

esparadrapo *m*, court plaster

esparcimiento *m*, scattering; naturalness, frankness; geniality

esparcir *vt* to scatter, sprinkle, disperse; spread, publish abroad; entertain; *vr* be scattered; amuse oneself

espárrago *m*, asparagus

esparraguera *f*, asparagus plant; asparagus bed; asparagus dish

Esparta Sparta

espartano (-na) a and *n* Spartan

esparto *m*, esparto grass

espasmo *m*, spasm

espasmódico a spasmodic

espátula *f*, spatula; palette knife

especia *f*, spice. **nuez de e.,** nutmeg

especial a special; particular

especialidad *f*, speciality; branch (of learning)

especialista *mf* specialist

especialización *f*, specialization

especializarse *vr* to specialize

especie *f*, class, kind; species; affair, matter, case; idea, image; news; pretext, appearance

especiería *f*, spice trade; spice shop

especiero (-ra) *n* spice merchant; spice rack

especificación *f*, specification. **e. normalizada,** standard specification

especificar *vt* to specify, particularize

específico a and *m*, specific patent medicine

espécimen *m*, specimen, sample

especioso a lovely, perfect; specious

espectacular a spectacular

espectáculo *m*, spectacle, sight; show, display

espectador (-ra) *n* spectator

espectral a spectral; faint, dim

espectro *m*, phantom, specter; *phys* spectrum

especulación *f*, conjecture; *com* speculation

especulador (-ra) *n* speculator

especular *vt* to examine, look at; (*with en*) reflect on, consider; *vi com* speculate

especulativo a speculative; thoughtful, meditative

espejismo *m*, mirage; illusion

espejo *m*, mirror; *fig* model. **e. de cuerpo entero,** full-length mirror. **e. retrovisor,** rearview mirror

espejuelo *m*, small mirror; *min* selenite; *min* sheet of talc; *pl* lenses, eyeglasses

espeluznante a hair-raising

espeluznar *vt* to dishevel; untidy (hair, etc.); *vr* stand on end (hair)

espera *f*, waiting; expectation; *law* adjournment; caution, restraint; *law* respite

esperantista *mf* Esperantist

esperanto *m*, Esperanto

esperanza *f*, hope

esperanzar *vt* to inspire hope in

esperar *vt* to hope; expect; await; (*with en*) have faith in. **e. sentado,** *fig inf* to whistle for

esperma *f*, sperm, semen. **e. de ballena,** spermaceti

esperpento *m*, *inf* scarecrow, grotesque; folly, madness; fantastic dramatic composition

espesar *vt* to thicken; make closer; tighten (fabrics); *vr* thicken; grow denser or thicker

espeso a thick; dense; greasy, dirty

espesor *m*, thickness; density

espesura *f*, thickness; density; thicket; filth

espetar *vt cul* to spit, skewer; pierce; *inf* utter, give; *vr* be stiff or affected; *inf* push oneself in, intrude

espía *mf* spy. *f*, *naut* warp

espiar *vt* to spy upon, watch; *vi naut* warp

espiga *f*, *bot* spike, ear; sprig; *carp* peg; tang, shank (of sword); *carp* tenon, dowel; *naut* masthead; *her* garb

espigar *vt* to glean; *carp* tenon; *vi bot* begin to show the ear or spike; *vr bot* bolt; shoot up, grow (persons)

espigón *m*, sting; sharp point; breakwater; bearded spike (corn, etc.)

espigueo *m*, gleaning

espiguero *m*, *Mexico* granary

espín *m*, porcupine

espina *f*, thorn; prickle; splinter; fish bone; *anat* spine; suspicion, doubt

espinaca f, spinach

espinal a spinal

espinar m, thorn brake; fig awkward position. vt to prick, wound, hurt

espinazo m, backbone

espinilla f, shinbone; blackhead

espinoso a thorny; difficult, intricate

espionaje m, espionage; spying

espira f, (geom arch) helix; turn, twist (of winding stairs); whorl (of a shell)

espiración f, expiration; respiration

espiral a spiral. f, geom spiral; spiral watchspring

espirar vt to exhale, breathe out; inspire; encourage; vi breathe; breathe out; poet blow (wind)

espiritismo m, spiritualism

espiritista a spiritualist. mf spiritualist

espiritoso a lively, active, spirited; spirituous

espíritu m, spirit; apparition, specter; soul; intelligence, mind; mood, temper, outlook; underlying principle, spirit; devil (gen. pl) vigor, ardor, vivacity; chem essence; chem spirits; turn of mind. **E. Santo**, Holy Ghost

espiritual a spiritual

espiritualidad f, spirituality

esplendidez f, liberality, abundance; splendor, pomp

espléndido a magnificent; liberal; resplendent (gen. pl)

esplendor m, splendor, brilliance; distinction, nobility

esplendoroso a splendid, brilliant, radiant

espliego m, lavender

esplín m, spleen, melancholy

espolear vt to prick with the spur; encourage, stimulate

espoleta f, fuse (of explosives); breastbone (of fowls); wishbone. **e. de tiempo, e. graduada,** time fuse. **e. de seguridad,** safety fuse

espolón m, spur (of a bird or mountain range); naut ram; breakwater; buttress; naut fender

espolvorear vt to sprinkle with powder

esponja f, sponge

esponjadura f, sponging

esponjar vt to make spongy; sponge; vr swell with pride; inf bloom with health

esponjoso a spongy, porous

esponsales m pl, betrothal; marriage contract

espontaneidad f, spontaneity

espontáneo a spontaneous

espora f, spore

esporádico a sporadic

esposa f, wife; pl handcuffs

esposo m, husband; pl husband and wife

espuela f, spur; stimulus; (orn bot) spur. **e. de caballero,** larkspur

espuelar vt, Lat. Am. to spur, spur on

espulgar vt to delouse; examine carefully

espuma f, froth, foam; cul scum; fig the best of anything, flower; fig inf **crecer como la e.,** to flourish like weeds

espumadera f, skimming ladle

espumajear vi to foam at the mouth

espumajoso a frothy, foaming

espumar vt to skim (soup, etc.); vi foam; increase rapidly

espumilla f, Lat. Am. meringue

espumoso a frothy, foaming

espurio a bastard; spurious

esputo m, sputum

esquela f, note; (printed) card

esqueleto m, skeleton; Mexico, blank, form (to be filled out) inf skinny person; framework

esquema f, diagram, layout sketch; scheme, plan. **e. de una máquina,** drawing of a machine

esquemático a schematic; diagrammatic

esquematizar vt to plan, outline

esquí m, ski, snowshoe

esquiador, -a mf, skier

esquiar vi to ski

esquila f, cattle bell; small bell, hand bell; sheep shearing; (icht bot) squill

esquiladora f, shearing machine

esquilar vt to shear, clip (sheep, etc.)

esquilmar vt to harvest; impoverish

esquimal a and mf Eskimo

esquina f, corner; Lat. Am. corner shop; village shop

esquinado a having corners; fig difficult to approach (people)

esquirol m, inf strikebreaker, blackleg

esquivada f, Lat. Am. evasion

esquivar vt to avoid; vr slip away, disappear; excuse oneself

esquivez f, unsociableness; unfriendliness, aloofness

esquivo a unsociable, elusive, aloof

estabilidad f, stability; fastness (of colors)

estabilizar vt to stabilize

estable a stable; fast (of colors)

establecer vt irr to establish, found, institute; decree; vr take up residence; open (a business firm). See **conocer**

establecimiento m, law, statute; foundation, institution; establishment

establo m, stable

estaca f, stake, pole; agr cutting; cudgel

estacada f, fence; mil palisade; place fixed for a duel

estacar vt to stake; fence; tie to a stake; vr fig be as still as a post

estación f, position, situation; season;

station (railroad, etc.); depot; time, period; stop, halt; building, headquarters; *bot* habitat; (*surv geom ecc*) station

estacionamiento *m*, stationing; *aut* parking

estacionar *vt* to station, place; *aut* park (a car); *vr* remain stationary; place oneself

estacionario a motionless; *ast* stationary. *m*, stationer

estacionómetro *m*, Mexico parking meter

estadía *f*, stay, sojourn; *art* sitting (of a model)

estadio *m*, racetrack; stadium; furlong

estadista *mf*. statistician; statesman, stateswoman

estadística *f*, statistics

estadístico a statistical

estadizo a stagnant

estado *m*, state; condition; rank, position; *pol* state; profession; status; *com* statement. **e. de guerra**, state of war; martial law. **e. mayor central,** (*nav mil*) general staff. **e. tapón,** *pol* buffer state. **tomar e.,** to marry; *ecc* profess; be ordained a priest

Estados Unidos de América United States of America

estadounidense a United States

estafa *f*, swindle

estafador (-ra) *n* swindler

estafar *vt* to swindle

estafeta *f*, courier, messenger; branch post office; diplomatic pouch

estagnación *f*, stagnation

estallar *vi* to explode; burst; *fig* break out

estallido *m*, explosion, report; crash, crack; *fig* outbreak; *aut* **e. de un neumático,** blowout (of a tire)

estambre *m*, woolen yarn, worsted; stamen

estameña *f*, serge

estampa *f*, illustration, picture; print; aspect; printing press; track, step; *met* boss, stud

estampación *f*, stamping; printing; imprinting. **e. en seco,** tooling (of a book)

estampado a printed (of textiles). *m*, textile printing; printed fabric

estampar *vt* to print, stamp; leave the print (of); bestow, imprint. **e. en relieve,** to emboss. **e. en seco,** to tool (a book)

estampería *f*, print or picture shop; trade in prints

estampero *m*, print dealer, picture dealer

estampido *m*, report, bang, detonation; crash

estampilla *f*, rubber stamp; seal; *Lat. Am* (except Mexico), (postage) stamp

estampillar *vt* to stamp, imprint

estancado a stagnant; blocked, held up

estancar *vt* to check, stem; set up a monopoly; *flg* hold up (negotiations, etc.); *vr* be stagnant

estancia *f*, stay, residence; dwelling; lounge, livingroom; stanza; *WH* farm; ranch

estanciero *m*, *WH* farmer; rancher

estanco a *naut* watertight. *m*, monopoly; shop selling government monopoly goods; archive

estandarte *m*, standard, flag. **e. real,** royal standard

estanque *m*, tank; pool; reservoir

estanquero (-ra) *n* seller of government monopoly goods (tobacco, matches, etc.)

estante a present; extant; permanent. *m*, shelf; bookcase; bin (for wine)

estantería *f*, shelving; shelves, bookcase

estañar *vt* to tin; solder

estaño *m*, tin

estaquilla *f*, peg, cleat

estar *vi irr* to be. Indicates: 1. Position or place (e.g. **Está a la puerta,** He is at the door). 2. State (e.g. **Las flores están marchitas,** The flowers are faded). 3. Used to form the continuous or progressive tense (e.g. **Siempre está (estaba) escribiendo,** He is (was) always writing). 4. In contrast to verb ser, indicates impermanency (e.g. **Está enfermo,** He is ill). 5. **Estar** forms an apparent passive where no action is implied (e.g. **El cuadro está pintado al óleo,** The picture is painted in oils). 6. Used in some impersonal expressions (e.g. **¡Bien está!** All right! **¡Claro está!** Of course! etc.). **e. de,** to be in, or on, or acting as (e.g. **e. de prisa,** to be in a hurry. **e. de capitán,** to be acting as a captain). **e. para,** to be on the point of; to be nearly; to be in the mood for. **e. para llover,** to be on the point of raining. **e. por,** to remain to be done; have a mind to (e.g. **La historia está por escribir,** The story remains to be written). **e. a mano (con . . .)** *Lat. Am.* to be even (with . . .), be quits (with . . .) **e. bien,** to be well (healthy). *mech* **e. bajo presión,** to have the steam up. *pol* **e. en el poder,** to be in office. **e. en una cuenca,** *Dominican Republic* to be broke. **¿A cómo** (or **A cuántos**) **estamos?** What is the date? *Pres. Ind.* **estoy, estás, está, estamos, estáis, están.** *Preterite* **estuve,** etc. *Pres. Subjunc.* **esté, estés, esté, estén.** *Imperf. Subjunc.* **estuviese,** etc.

estatal a state

estático a static

estatizar *vt*, *Lat. Am.* to nationalize

estatua *f*, statue

estatuaria *f*, statuary

estatuir *vt irr* to establish, order. See **huir**

estatura *f*, stature, height (of persons)

estatuto *m*, statute, law

este *m*, east

este *m, dem* a this (*f*, **esta**, *pl* **estos**, **estas**, these). **éste**, *m, dem pron* this one; the latter. (*f*, **ésta**, *neut* **esto**, *pl* **éstos**, **éstas**, these ones; the latter) (e.g. **Aquel cuadro no es tan hermoso como éste**, That picture is not as beautiful as this one)

estela *f*, wake, track (of a ship)

estenografía *f*, shorthand

estentóreo a stentorian

estepa *f*, steppe, arid plain

estera *f*, matting

esterar *vt* to cover with matting; *vi inf* muffle oneself up

estercolar *vt* to manure

estercolero *m*, manure pile; driver of a dung cart

estereoscopio *m*, stereoscope

estéril a sterile, barren; unfruitful, unproductive

esterilidad *f*, sterility; barrenness, unfruitfulness

esterilización *f*, sterilization

esterilizador a sterilizing. *m*, sterilizer

esterilizar *vt* to make barren; *med* sterilize

esterilla *f*, mat, matting

esterlina a *f*, sterling. **libra e.,** pound sterling

esternón *m*, sternum

estertor *m*, stertorous breathing, rattle

estética *f*, aesthetics. a aesthete

estético a aesthetic *m*, aesthete

estetoscopio *m*, stethoscope

esteva *f*, plow handle

estevado a bandy-legged

estibador *m*, stevedore, dock worker

estibar *vt naut* to stow

estiércol *m*, dung; manure

estigio a Stygian; (*fig poet*) infernal

estigma *m*, stigma

estigmatizar *vt* to brand; stigmatize; insult

estilar *vi* to be accustomed; *vt* draw up (document)

estilete *m*, stiletto, dagger; needle, hand, pointer; *med* stylet

estilista *mf* stylist

estilística *f*, stylism, stylistics

estilo *m*, (*art arch lit*) style, writing instrument; gnomon, pointer; manner, way; *bot* style. **por el e.,** in some such way, like that

estilográfico a stylographic. **pluma estilográfica,** fountain pen

estima *f*, appreciation, esteem, consideration

estimable a estimable

estimación *f*, valuation, estimate; regard, esteem. **e. prudente,** conservative estimate

estimar *vt* to value, estimate; esteem, judge

estimulante *m, med* stimulant, a stimulating

estimular *vt* to stimulate, excite; goad on, encourage, incite

estímulo *m*, stimulus; incitement, encouragement

estío *m*, summer

estipendio *m*, stipend, pay, remuneration

estipulación *f*, stipulation; *law* clause, condition

estipular *vt* to stipulate; arrange terms; *law* covenant

estirado a stretched out; tight, stiff; wire-drawn (metals); stiff, pompous; parsimonious

estirar *vt* to stretch; iron roughly (clothes); *met* wire-draw; dole out (money); *fig* stretch, go beyond the permissible; *vr* stretch oneself

estirpe *f*, race, stock, lineage

esto *dem pron neut* this, this matter, this idea, etc. Always refers to abstractions, never to a definite object. **e. de,** the matter of. **e. es,** that's it; namely. **por e.,** for this reason. **a todo e.,** meanwhile

Estocolmo Stockholm

estofa *f, sew* quilting; kind, quality

estofado *m*, stew. a *sew* quilted; stewed

estofar *vt sew* to quilt; make a stew

estoicismo *m*, stoicism

estoico (**-ca**) *n* stoic. a stoical

estólido (**-da**) a idiotic. a idiot

estomacal a stomach

estómago *m*, stomach

estomático a pertaining to the mouth, oral

estomatitis *f*, stomatitis

estonio (**-ia**) a and *n* Estonian. *m*, Estonian (language)

estopa *f*, tow; oakum

estopilla *f*, batiste, lawn; calico, cotton cloth

estopín *m, mil* quick march

estoque *m*, rapier; narrow sword

estoquear *vt* to wound or kill with a rapier

estorbador (**-ra**) a obstructive. *n* obstructer

estorbar *vt* to obstruct, impede; hinder

estorbo *m*, obstruction; hindrance, nuisance

estornudar *vi* to sneeze

estornudo *m*, sneezing; sneeze

estrabismo *m, med* strabismus, squint, cast

estrada *f*, road, highway

estrado *m*, dais

estrafalario a *inf* slovenly, untidy; *inf* eccentric, odd estragar *vt* to corrupt, spoil, vitiate; ruin, destroy

estrago *m*, devastation, destruction, ruin, havoc

estrambólico, -a *Lat. Am.* = estrambótico

estrambótico *a inf* eccentric, odd, outlandish

estrangulación *f*, strangulation; *aut* throttling

estrangulador (-ra) *a* strangling. *n* strangler. *m*, *aut* throttle

estrangular *vt* to strangle

estraperlista *mf* black marketeer

estraperlo *m*, black market

estratagema *f*, stratagem, trick

estrategia *f*, strategy

estratégico *a* strategic

estratego *m*, strategist

estrato *m*, *geol* stratum

estratosfera *f*, stratosphere

estrechar *vt* to make narrower, tighten; hold tightly, clasp; compel, oblige; *vr* tighten oneself up; reduce one's expenses; *fig* tighten the bonds (of friendship, etc.). **e. la mano**, to shake hands

estrechez *f*, narrowness; tightness; scantiness; poverty, want. **e. de miras**, narrowmindedness

estrecho *a* narrow; tight; intimate, close; austere, rigid; meanspirited. *m*, *geog* strait

estregar *vt irr* to rub, scour, scrub, scrape, scratch. See **cegar**

estrella *f*, star; fortune, fate; anything star-shaped; *fig* star. **e. de la pantalla**, movie star. **e. de mar**, starfish. **e. de rabo**, comet. **e. fugaz**, shooting star. **tener e.**, to be born under a lucky star

estrellado *a* star-shaped; full of stars, starry; shattered, broken; fried (eggs)

estrellamar *f*, starfish

estrellar *vt inf* to shatter, break into fragments; fry (eggs); *vr* be starry or sprinkled with stars; be dashed against; fail in, come up against

estrellón *m*, large, artificial star (painted or otherwise); star-like firework; *Lat. Am.* crash

estremecer *vt irr* to cause to tremble; perturb; *vr* shudder, tremble. See **conocer**

estremecimiento *m*, shudder, trembling; agitation

estrenar *vt* to use or do for the first time; inaugurate; give the first performance of (plays, etc.); *vr* do for the first time; *com* make the first sale of the day

estreno *m*, commencement, inauguration; first appearance; *theat* first performance, opening night, premiere

estrenuo *a* strong, energetic, agile

estreñimiento *m*, constipation

estreñir *vt* to constipate

estrépito *m*, clamor, din, great noise; fuss, show

estrepitoso *a* noisy, clamorous

estreptomicina *f*, streptomycin

estribar *vi* (*with en*) to lean on, rest on, be supported by; *fig* be based on

estribillo *m*, refrain

estribo *m*, stirrup; footboard, step, running board (of vehicles); *arch* buttress or pier; *fig* stay, support; *anat* stapes; *mech carp* stirrup piece. **perder los estribos**, to lose patience, forget oneself

estribor *m*, starboard

estricnina *f*, strychnine

estricto *a* strict, exact; unbending, severe

estridente *a* strident, shrill

estridor *m*, strident or harsh sound; screech; creak

estro *m*, inspiration

estrofa *f*, strophe; verse, stanza

estropajo *m*, scourer, dishcloth; worthless person or thing

estropajoso *a inf* indistinct, stammering; dirty and ragged; tough (meat, etc.)

estropear *vt* to spoil, damage; ruin, undo, spoil (plans, effects, etc.); ill-treat, maim; *vr* hurt oneself, be maimed; spoil, deteriorate

estructura *f*, fabric, structure; *fig* construction

estructural *a* structural

estruendo *m*, din, clatter; clamor, noise; ostentation

estruendoso *a* noisy

estrujar *vt* to squeeze, crush (fruit); hold tightly, press, squeeze, bruise; *fig inf* squeeze dry

estrujón *m*, squeeze, pressure; final pressing (grapes)

estuario *m*, estuary

estuco *m*, stucco; plaster

estuche *m*, case; casket, box; cover; sheath

estudiantado *m*, *Lat. Am.* student body, students

estudiante *mf* student

estudiantil *a inf* student

estudiantina *f*, strolling band of students playing and singing, generally in aid of charity

estudiar *vt* to study. **e. de**, study to be a (e.g. **e. de rabino**, study to be a rabbi); learn; *art* copy

estudio *m*, study; sketch; disquisition, dissertation; studio; diligence; *art* study; reading room, den

estudiosidad *f*, studiousness

estudioso *a* studious

estufa *f*, heating stove; hothouse; hot room (in bathhouses); drying chamber; *elec* heater

estufador *m*, stewpot or casserole

estulto a foolish

estupefacción f, stupefaction

estupefacto a stupefied, stunned, amazed

estupendo a wonderful, marvelous

estupidez f, stupidity

estúpido a stupid

estupor m, med stupor; astonishment

estupro m, law rape

estuque m, stucco

estuquería f, stuccowork

esturión m, sturgeon

esvástica f, swastika

etapa f, mil field ration; mil halt, camp; stage, juncture. **a pequeñas etapas,** by easy stages (of a journey)

etcétera etcetera

éter m, ether; poet sky

eternidad f, eternity

eternizar vt to drag out, prolong; eternize, perpetuate

eterno a eternal, everlasting; lasting, enduring

ética f, ethics

ético a ethical. m, moralist

etimología f, etymology

etimológico a etymological

etiología f, etiology

etíope a and mf Ethiopian

Etiopía Ethiopia

etiqueta f, etiquette; label

etiquetero a ceremonious, stiff; prim

étnico a ethnic; heathen

etrusco (**-ca**) a and n Etruscan

eucalipto m, eucalyptus

Eucaristía f, Eucharist

eufemismo m, euphemism

eufonía f, euphony

eufónico a euphonious

euforia f, resistance to disease; buoyancy, well-being

eunuco m, eunuch

Europa Europe

europeo (**-ea**) a and n European

éuscaro a Basque. m, Basque (language)

evacuación f, evacuation

evacuar vt to vacate; evacuate, empty; finish, conclude (a business deal, etc.)

evadir vt to avoid, elude; vr escape; elope

evaluación f, valuation; estimation

evaluar vt to evaluate, estimate; gauge; value

evangélico a evangelical

evangelio m, Gospel; Christianity; inf indisputable truth

evangelizar vt to evangelize

evaporación f, evaporation

evaporar(se) vt and vr to evaporate; disappear, vanish

evasión, evasiva f, subterfuge, evasion; flight, escape

evasivo a evasive

evento m, happening, event; contingency

eventual a possible, fortuitous; accidental (expenses); extra (emoluments)

eventualidad f, eventuality

evicción f, law eviction

evidencia f, proof, evidence. **ponerse en e.,** to put oneself forward

evidenciar vt to show, make obvious

evidente a obvious, evident

evitable a avoidable

evitación f, avoidance

evitar vt to avoid; shun, eschew

evocación f, evocation

evocador a evocative

evocar vt to evoke

evolución f, evolution; development; (mil nav) maneuver; change; geom involution

evolucionar vi to evolve; (nav mil) maneuver; change, alter

evolutivo a evolutional

exacerbación f, exacerbation

exacerbar vt to exasperate; exacerbate

exactitud f, exactitude; correctness; punctuality

exacto a exact; correct; punctual

exageración f, exaggeration

exagerador (**-ra**) a given to exaggerating. n exaggerater

exagerar vt to exaggerate

exaltación f, exaltation

exaltar vt to exalt, elevate; extol; vr grow excited or agitated

exalumna f, Lat. Am. alumna, graduate

exalumno m, Lat. Am. alumnus, graduate

examen m, inquiry; investigation, research; examination; geol survey. **e. parcial,** quiz (at school)

examinador (**-ra**) n examiner

examinando (**-da**) n candidate, examinee

examinar vt to inquire into; investigate; inspect; examine; vr take an examination

exangüe a bloodless, pale; exhausted, weak; dead

exánime a lifeless; spiritless, weak

exasperación f, exasperation

exasperador, exasperante a exasperating

exasperar vt to exasperate; irritate, annoy

excarcelar vt to release from jail

excavación f, excavation

excavador (**-ra**) n excavator. f, mech excavator

excavar vt to hollow; excavate; agr hoe (roots of plants)

excedente a exceeding; excessive; surplus

exceder *vt* to exceed; *vr* forget oneself, go too far

excelencia *f*, excellence, superiority; Excellency (title)

excelso *a* lofty, high; eminent, mighty; sublime

excentricidad *f*, eccentricity

excéntrico *a* unconventional; erratic; *geom* eccentric

excepción *f*, exception

exceptuar *vt* to except

excerpta, excerta *f*, excerpt, extract

excesivo *a* excessive

exceso *m*, excess; *com* surplus; *pl* crimes, excesses. **e. de peso** or **e. de equipaje**, excess baggage

excisión *f*, excision

excitable *a* excitable, high-strung

excitación *f*, excitation; excitement

excitador *a* exciting, stimulating. *m*, *phys* exciter

excitar *vt* to excite, stimulate, provoke; *elec* energize; *vr* become agitated or excited

exclamación *f*, exclamation, interjection

exclamar *vi* to exclaim

excluir *vt irr* to exclude, keep out; reject, bar. See **huir**

exclusiva *f*, exclusion; special privilege, sole right

exclusive *adv* exclusively; excluded

exclusivo *a* exclusive

excomulgado (**-da**) *a* and *n ecc* excommunicate; *inf* wicked (person)

excomulgar *vt* to excommunicate

excomunión *f*, excommunication

excoriar *vt* to flay, excoriate; *vr* graze oneself

excremento *m*, excrement

excretar *vi* to excrete

exculpación *f*, exoneration

exculpar(se) *vt* and *vr* to exonerate

excursión *f*, excursion, outing, trip; *mil* incursion

excursionarse *vr*, *Lat. Am.* to go on a trip, go on an outing, go on an excursion

excursionismo *m*, sightseeing; hiking

excursionista *mf* excursionist; hiker

excusa *f*, excuse

excusado *a* excused; exempt; unnecessary, superfluous; reserved, private. *m*, lavatory, toilet

excusar *vt* to excuse; avoid, ward off, prevent; exempt; *vr* excuse oneself

execración *f*, execration

execrar *vt* to execrate; denounce; loathe

exención *f*, exemption

exentar *vt* to exempt

exento *a* exempt; free, liberated; open (of buildings, etc.)

exequias *f pl*, obsequies

exhalación *f*, exhalation; shooting star; lightning; emanation, effluvium

exhalar *vt* to exhale, give off; *fig* give vent to

exhibición *f*, exhibition

exhibicionismo *m*, exhibitionism

exhibicionista *mf* exhibitionist

exhibir *vt* to exhibit, show

exhortación *f*, exhortation

exhortar *vt* to exhort

exhumar *vt* to exhume, disinter

exigencia *f*, exigency; demand

exigente *a* exigent

exigir *vt* to exact, collect; need, require; demand

exiguo *a* exiguous, meager

exliado, -a *Lat. Am.* a exiled, in exile; *mf* exile

eximio *a* most excellent; illustrious

eximir *vt* to exempt

existencia *f*, existence; *pl com* stock on hand

existir *vi* to exist, be; live

éxito *m*, success; result, conclusion

exitoso, -a *a*, *Lat. Am.* successful

éxodo *m*, Exodus; exodus, emigration. **é. rural**, rural depopulation

exoneración *f*, exoneration

exonerar *vt* to exonerate; discharge (from employment)

exorbitancia *f*, exorbitance

exorbitante *a* exorbitant, excessive

exorcista *m*, exorcist

exorcizar *vt* to exorcize

exornar *vt* to adorn; embellish (*lit* style)

exótico *a* exotic, rare

expandir *vt* to expand

expansión *f*, expansion; recreation, hobby

expansivo *a* expansive; communicative, frank

expatriación *f*, expatriation

expatriarse *vr* to emigrate, leave one's country

expectante *a* expectant

expectativa *f*, expectancy; expectation

expectoración *f*, expectoration

expectorar *vt* to expectorate

expedición *f*, expedition; speed, promptness; *ecc* bull, dispensation; excursion; forwarding, dispatch

expediente *m*, *law* proceedings; file of documents; expedient, device, means; expedition, promptness; motive, reason; provision

expedir *vt irr* to expedite; forward, send, ship; issue, make out (checks, receipts, etc.); draw up (documents); dispatch, deal with. See **pedir**

expedito *a* expeditious, speedy

expeler *vt* to expel, discharge, emit

expendedor (**-ra**) *a* spending. *n* spender; agent; retailer; seller; *law* **e. de moneda falsa,** distributor of counterfeit money

expendeduría *f,* shop where government monopoly goods are sold (tobacco, stamps, etc.)

expender *vt* to spend (money); *com* retail; *com* sell on commission; *law* distribute counterfeit money

expendio *m, Lat. Am.* tobacco shop

expensas *f pl,* costs, charges

experiencia *f,* experience; practice, experiment

experimentación *f,* experiencing

experimentar *vt* to test, try; experience; feel

experimento *m,* experiment

experto (**-ta**) *a* practiced, expert. *n* expert

expiación *f,* expiation

expiar *vt* to expiate, atone for; pay the penalty of; *fig* purify

expiatorio *a* expiatory

expiración *f,* expiration

expirar *vi* to die; *fig* expire; die down; exhale, expire

explanación *f,* leveling; explanation, elucidation

explanar *vt* to level; explain

explayar *vt* to extend, enlarge; *vr* spread oneself, enlarge (upon); enjoy an outing; confide (in)

explicación *f,* explanation; elucidation

explicar *vt* to explain; expound; interpret, elucidate; *vr* explain oneself

explicativo *a* explanatory

explícito *a* explicit, clear

exploración *f,* exploration

explorador *a* exploring. *m,* explorer; prospector; boy scout; *mil* scout

explorar *vt* to explore; investigate; *med* probe

exploratorio *a* exploratory

explosión *f,* explosion; outburst, outbreak. **hacer falsas explosiones,** *mech* to misfire

explosivo *a* and *m,* explosive. **e. violento,** high explosive

explotación *f,* development, exploitation

explotar *vt* to work (mines); *fig* exploit

expoliación *f,* spoliation

expoliar *vt* to despoil

exponente *a* and *mf* exponent. *m, math* index

exponer *vt irr* to show, expose; expound; interpret; risk, jeopardize; abandon (child). See **poner**

exportación *f,* exportation; export

exportador (**-ra**) *a* export. *n* exporter

exportar *vt* to export

exposición *f,* exposition, demonstration; petition; exhibition; *lit* exposition; *phot* exposure; orientation, position

expósito (**-ra**) *a* and *n* foundling

expositor (**-ra**) *a* and *n* exponent. *n* exhibitor

exprés *a* express. *m,* messenger or delivery service; express train; transport office

expresar *vt* to express (all meanings)

expresión *f,* statement, utterance; phrase, wording; expression; presentation; manifestation; gift, present; squeezing; pressing (of fruits, etc.)

expresivo *a* expressive; affectionate

expreso *a* express; clear, obvious. *m,* courier, messenger

exprimir *vt* to squeeze, press (fruit); press, hold tightly; express, utter

expropiación *f,* expropriation

expropiar *vt* to expropriate; commandeer

expugnar *vt mil* to take by storm

expulsar *vt* to expel, eject, dismiss

expulsión *f,* expulsion

expurgar *vt* to cleanse, purify; expurgate

exquisito *a* exquisite, choice; delicate, delicious

extasiarse *vr* to fall into ecstasy; marvel (at), delight (in)

éxtasis *m,* ecstasy; rapture

extático *a* ecstatic

extemporáneo *a* untimely; inopportune, inconvenient

extender *vt irr* to spread; reach, extend; elongate; enlarge, amplify; unfold, open out, stretch; draw up (documents); make out (checks, etc.); *vr* stretch out; lie down; spread, be generalized; extend; last (of time); record; stretch, open out. **extenderse en,** to expatiate on. See **entender**

extensión *f,* extension; expanse; length; extent; duration; extension (logic)

extensivo *a* extensive, spacious; extensible

extenso *a* extensive, vast

extensor *a* extensor. *m,* chest expander

extenuación *f,* emaciation, weakness; extenuation

extenuar *vt* to exhaust, weaken; *vr* become weak

exterior *a* external; foreign (trade, etc.). *m,* outside, exterior; outward appearance

exterioridad *f,* outward appearance; outside, externality; *pl* ceremonies, forms; ostentation

exteriorizar *vt* to exteriorize, reveal

exterminador (**-ra**) *a* exterminating. *n* exterminator

exterminar *vt* to exterminate; devastate

exterminio *m,* extermination; devastation

externado *m,* day school

externo (**-na**) *a* external. *n* day

extinción f, extinction; extinguishment; abolition, cancellation

extinguir vt to extinguish; destroy

extintor m, fire extinguisher

extirpación f, extirpation

extirpador (-ra) a extirpating. n extirpator

extirpar vt to extirpate; fig eradicate

extorsión f, extortion

extorsionar vt to extort

extra prefix outside, without, beyond. prep besides. a extremely, most. m, inf extra

extracción f, extraction; drawing (lottery); origin, lineage; exportation

extractar vt to abstract, summarize

extracto m, abstract, summary; chem extract

extractor a extracting. m, extractor

extradición f, extradition

extraer vt irr to extract; draw out; export; chem extract. See **traer**

extranjero (-ra) a alien, foreign. n foreigner. m, abroad, foreign country

extrañar vt to exile; alienate, estrange; wonder at; miss, feel the loss of; vr be exiled; be estranged; be amazed (by); refuse (to do a thing)

extrañeza f, strangeness; estrangement; surprise

extraño a strange, unusual; foreign, extraneous

extraoficial a unofficial

extraordinario a extraordinary; special. m, cul extra course

extraterrenal, extraterreno a, Lat. Am. extraterrestrial, unearthly

extravagancia f, eccentricity; queerness; folly

extravagante a eccentric; queer, strange; absurd

extravertido m, extrovert

extraviar vt to mislead; mislay; vr lose one's way; be lost (of things); fig go astray

extravío m, deviation, divergence; error; aberration, lapse

extremado a extreme

extremar vt to take to extremes; vr do one's best

extremidad f, end; extremity; remotest part; edge; limit; pl extremities

extremista a and mf extremist

extremo a last, ultimate; extreme; furthest; great, exceptional; utmost. m, end, extreme; highest degree; extreme care; pl excessive emotional display

extremoso a immoderate, exaggerated; very affectionate

exuberante a abundant, copious; exuberant

exudar vi and vt to exude

exultación f, exultation; rejoicing

exultar vi to exult

fa *m*, *mus* fa, F

fabada *f*, dish of broad beans with pork, sausage or bacon

fábrica *f*, manufacture; making; factory, works; fabric, structure, building; creation; invention. **f. de papel,** paper mill. **marca de f.,** trademark

fabricación *f*, make; making; construction. **f. en serie,** mass production

fabricador (**-ra**) *a* creative, inventive. *n* fabricator; maker

fabricante *a* manufacturing. *m*, manufacturer; maker

fabricar *vt* to manufacture; make; construct, build; devise; invent, create

fabril *a* manufacturing

fábula *f*, rumor, gossip; fiction; fable; story, plot; mythology; myth; laughing-stock; falsehood.

fabuloso *a* fabulous; fictitious; incredible, amazing

faca *f*, jackknife

facción *f*, rebellion; faction, party, band; feature (of the face) (gen. *pl*); military exploit; any routine military duty

faceta *f*, facet (gems); aspect, view

facha *f*, *inf* countenance, look, face; guy, scarecrow. *naut* **ponerse en f.,** to lie to

fachada *f*, facade, front (of a building, ship, etc.); *inf* build, presence (of a person); frontispiece (of a book)

fachenda *f*, *inf* boastfulness, vanity

fachinal *m*, *Argentina* swamp

fachoso, -a *a*, *Lat. Am.* elegant, smart

fácil *a* easy; probable; easily led; docile; of easy virtue (women). *adv* easy

facilidad *f*, easiness; facility, aptitude; ready compliance; opportunity

facilitar *vt* to facilitate; expedite; provide, deliver

facineroso *a* criminal, delinquent. *m*, criminal; villain

facsímile *m*, facsimile

factible *a* feasible, practicable

facticio *a* factitious, artificial

factor *m*, *com* factor, agent; *math* factor; element; consideration

factótum *m*, *inf* factotum, handyman; *inf* busybody; confidential agent or deputy

factura *f*, *com* invoice, bill, account; *art* execution; workmanship; making

facturar *vt com* to invoice; register (luggage on a railroad)

facultad *f*, faculty; mental or physical aptitude, capability; authority, right; science, art; *univ* faculty; license

facultar *vt* to authorize, permit

facultativo *a* belonging to a faculty; optional, permissive. *m*, physician

facundia *f*, eloquence

facundo *a* eloquent

faena *f*, manual labor; mental work; business affairs (gen. *pl*)

fagot *m*, bassoon

fagotista *mf* bassoon player

faisán (**-ana**) *orn* cock (hen) pheasant

faja *f*, belt; sash, scarf; corset; girdle; *geog* zone; newspaper wrapper; *arch* fascia; swathing band

fajar *vt* to swathe; swaddle (a child)

fajero *m*, swaddling band

fajín *m*, ceremonial ribbon or sash worn by generals, etc.

fajina *f*, stack; brushwood; (*fort*.) fascine; *Mexico* lunch

fajo *m*, bundle, sheaf; *pl* swaddling clothes

falacia *f*, fraud, deceit; deceitfulness; fallacy

falange *f*, *mil* phalanx; *anat* phalange; (*Spanish pol*.) Falange

falaz *a* deceitful; fallacious

falda *f*, skirt; lap, flap, panel (of a dress); slope (of a hill); the lap; loin (of beef, etc.); brim of a hat; *pl inf* petticoats, women. **f. escocesa,** kilt. **f.-pantalón,** divided skirt, culottes.

faldero *a* lap (dog); fond of the company of women

faldón *m*, long, flowing skirt; shirttail; coattail

falibilidad *f*, fallibility

falible *a* fallible

falla *f*, deficiency, defect; failure; *geol* displacement; bonfire (Valencia); *min* slide

fallar *vt law* to pass sentence; *vi* be deficient

fallecer *vi irr* to die; fail. See **conocer**

fallecimiento *m*, death, decease

fallido *a* frustrated; bankrupt

fallo *m*, *law* verdict; judgment

falsario *a* falsifying, forging, counterfeiting; deceiving, lying. *m*, falsifier, forger, counterfeiter

falseamiento *m*, falsifying; forging

falsear *vt* to falsify; forge; counterfeit; penetrate; *vi* weaken; *mus* be out of tune (strings)

falsedad *f*, falseness; falsehood

falsete *m*, spigot; *mus* falsetto voice

falsificación *f*, falsification; forgery

falsificador *a* falsifying; forging. *m*, falsifier; forger

falsificar *vt* to forge, counterfeit; falsify

falso *a* false; forged, counterfeit; treacherous, untrue, deceitful; incorrect; sham; vicious (horses). **de f.,** falsely; deceitfully

falta *f*, lack, shortage; defect; mistake; *sport* fault; shortcoming; nonappearance, absence; deficiency in legal weight of coin; *law* offense. **f. de éxito**, failure. **hacer f.**, to be necessary. **sin f.**, without fail

faltar *vi* to be lacking; fail; die; fall short; be absent from an appointment; not to fulfill one's obligations. **f. a**, to be unfaithful to, break (e.g. **Faltó a su palabra**, He broke his promise). *inf* **¡No faltaba más!** I should think not!; That's the limit!

falto *a* lacking, wanting; defective; wretched, mean, timid. **f. de personal**, short-handed

faltriquera *f*, pocket; hip pocket

fama *f*, rumor, report; reputation; fame

famélico *a* ravenous

familia *f*, family; household; kindred. **ser de f.**, to run in the family

familiar *a* family; familiar; well known; unceremonious; plain, simple; colloquial (language). *m, ecc* familiar; servant; intimate friend; familiar spirit

familiaridad *f*, familiarity

familiarizar *vt* to familiarize; *vr* become familiar; accustom oneself

familiarmente *adv* familiarly

famoso *a* famous; notorious; *inf* excellent, perfect; *inf* conspicuous

fámula *f*, *inf* female servant

fámulo *m*, servant of a college; *inf* servant

fanal *m*, lantern (of a lighthouse); *naut* poop lantern; lantern; lamp glass

fanático (-ca) *a* fanatical. *n* fanatic; *inf* fan, enthusiast

fanatismo *m*, fanaticism

fanatizar *vt* to make fanatical; turn into a fanatic

fandango *m*, lively Andalusian dance; *Lat. Am.* rowdy party

fanega *f*, grain measure about the weight of 1.60 bushel; land measure (about $1\frac{1}{2}$ acres)

fanfarrón (-ona) *a inf* boastful; swaggering. *n* swashbuckler; boaster

fanfarronear *vi* to swagger; brag

fanfarronería *f*, bragging

fango *m*, mud, mire; degradation

fangoso *a* muddy, miry

fantasear *vi* to let one's fancy roam; boast

fantasía *f*, fancy, imagination; fantasy; caprice; fiction; *inf* presumption; *mus* fantasia

fantasma *m*, ghost, phantom; vision; image, impression; presumptuous person. *f*, *inf* scarecrow; apparition

fantasmagórico *a* phantasmagoric

fantástico *a* fanciful, imaginary; fantastic, imaginative; presumptuous, conceited

fantoche *m*, puppet; *inf* yes-man, mediocrity

faquín *m*, porter, carrier

farabute *mf*, *Argentina* rogue

faramallear *vi*, *Lat. Am.* to boast, brag

farándula *f*, profession of low comedian; troupe of strolling players; cunning trick

fardel *m*, bag, knapsack; bundle

fardo *m*, bundle, bale, package

farfulla *f*, *inf* mumbling; gibbering. *mf inf* mumbler

farfullar *vt inf* to mumble; gibber; *inf* act in haste

faringe *f*, pharynx

faringitis *f*, pharyngitis

farmacéutico *a* pharmaceutical. *m*, pharmacist

farmacia *f*, pharmacy

farmacólogo *m*, pharmacologist

faro *m*, lighthouse; beacon, guide; *aut* headlight

farol *m*, lantern, lamp; streetlamp; cresset

farola *f*, lamppost (generally with several branches); lantern

farolero *m*, lantern maker; lamplighter; lamp tender. *a inf* swaggering, braggart

fárrago *m*, hodgepodge

farruto, -a *a*, *Lat. Am.* sickly, weak

farsa *f*, old name for a play; farce; theatrical company; poor, badly constructed play; sham, trick, deception

farsante *m*, comedian; *ant* actor; *fig inf* humbug

fascinación *f*, evil eye; enchantment, fascination

fascinador (-ra) *a* bewitching; fascinating. *n* charmer

fascinante *a* fascinating

fascinar *vt* to bewitch, place under a spell; deceive, impose upon; attract, fascinate

fascismo *m*, fascism

fascista *a* and *mf* fascist

fase *f*, phase; aspect

fastidiar *vt* to disgust, bore; annoy; *vr* be bored

fastidio *m*, sickness, squeamishness; annoyance, boredom, dislike, repugnance

fastidioso *a* disgusting, sickening; annoying; boring, tiresome

fastuoso *a* ostentatious; pompous

fatal *a* fatal, mortal; predetermined, inevitable; ill-fated, unhappy, disastrous; evil

fatalidad *f*, fatality; inevitability; disaster, ill-fatedness

fatalista *a* fatalistic. *mf* fatalist

fatalmente *adv* inevitably, unavoidably; unhappily, unfortunately; extremely badly

fatídico *a* prophetic (gen. of evil)

fatiga *f*, fatigue; toil; difficult breathing; hardship, troubles (gen. *pl.*)

fatigar *vt* to tire; annoy; *vr* be tired

fatigoso *a* tired; tiring; tiresome, annoying

fatuidad *f,* fatuousness, inanity, foolishness; conceit; priggishness

fatuo *a* fatuous, foolish; conceited; priggish. *m,* self-satisfied fool. **fuego f.,** will-o'-the-wisp

fauces *f pl,* gullet

faul *m, Lat. Am.* foul

faulear *vt, Lat. Am.* to foul

fauna *f,* fauna

fausto *m,* pomp, magnificence, ostentation. *a* fortunate, happy

fautor *m,* protector, helper; accomplice. **f. de guerra,** warmonger

favor *m,* aid, protection, support; favor, honor, service; love favor, sign of favor. **a f. de,** in favor of; on behalf of

favorable *a* kind, helpful; favorable

favorecedor (-ra) *a* favoring, helping. *n* helper; protector

favorecer *vt irr* to aid, protect, support; favor; do a service, grant a favor. See **conocer**

favorito (-ta) *a* and *n* favorite

fayenza *f,* faience

faz *f,* face; external surface of a thing, side; frontage

fe *f,* faith; confidence, trust, good opinion; belief; solemn promise; assertion; certificate, attestation; faithfulness. **f. de erratas,** *print* errata. **dar f.,** *law* to testify. **de buena f.,** in good faith. **en f.,** in proof

fealdad *f,* ugliness; base action

febrero *m,* February

febril *a* feverish; ardent, violent; passionate

fecundar *vt* to fertilize; fecundate

fecundizar *vt* to fertilize; make fruitful

fecundo *a* fertile, fecund, prolific; abundant

fecha *f,* date. **a la f.,** at present, now. **hasta la f.,** up to the present (day)

fechar *vt* to date, write the date

federación *f,* federation, league

federal *a* federal. *mf* federalist

fehaciente *a law* authentic, attested

felicidad *f,* happiness; contentment, satisfaction; good fortune

felicitación *f,* congratulation

felicitar *vt* to congratulate; wish well; *vr* congratulate oneself

feligrés (-esa) *n* parishioner

feligresía *f,* parish

feliz *a* happy; fortunate; skillful, felicitous (of phrases, etc.)

felón (-ona) *n* felon

felonía *f,* felony

felpa *f,* plush; *inf* drubbing, beating

felpudo *a* plush

femenino *a* feminine; female; *fig* weak

fementido *a* sly, false, treacherous, unfaithful

feminismo *m,* feminism

feminista *a* feminist. *mf* feminist

fémur *m,* femur, thigh bone

fenecer *vt irr* to conclude, finish; *vi* die; be ended. See **conocer**

fenecimiento *m,* end; death

fenomenal *a* phenomenal; *inf* terrific

fenómeno *m,* phenomenon; *inf* something of great size

feo *a* ugly; alarming, horrid; evil. *m, inf* slight, insult

feraz *a* fruitful, fertile

féretro *m,* coffin; bier

feria *f,* fair, market; workday; holiday; rest

feriar *vt* to buy at a fair; bargain. *vi* cease work, take a holiday

fermentación *f,* fermentation

fermentar *vi* to ferment; be agitated; *vt* cause to ferment

fermento *m,* ferment; leaven; *chem* enzyme

ferocidad *f,* ferocity, cruelty

feroz *a* ferocious, cruel; *Lat. Am.* ugly

férreo *a* ferrous; hard, tenacious. **línea férrea,** railroad

ferretería *f,* ironworks; ironmonger's shop; ironware, hardware

ferrocarril *m,* railroad, railway; railroad train. **f. de cremallera,** rack railroad. **f. funicular,** funicular railway

ferroviario *a* railroad, railway. *m,* railroad employee

fértil *a* fertile; fruitful, productive

fertilidad *f,* fertility

fertilizar *vt* to fertilize, make fruitful

férula *f,* ferule; *surg* splint; *fig* yoke, rule

fervor *m,* intense heat; fervor, devotion; zeal

fervoroso *a* fervent, zealous, devoted

festejar *vt* to feast, entertain; woo; celebrate; *vr* amuse oneself; *Mexico* to thrash

festejo *m,* feast, entertainment; courtship, wooing; *pl* public celebrations

festín *m,* private dinner or party; sumptuous banquet

festival *m,* musical festival; festival

festividad *f,* festivity; *ecc* celebration, solemnity; witticism

festivo *a* a joking, witty; happy, gay; solemn, worthy of celebration. **día f.,** holiday

festón *m,* garland, wreath; festoon; border; scalloped edging

festonear *vt* to garland, festoon; border

fetal *a* fetal

fetiche *m,* fetish

fétido *a* stinking, fetid

feto *m,* fetus

feudal *a* feudal; despotic

fiado, al *adv* on credit. **en f.,** on bail

fiador (-ra) *n* guarantor; bail. *m,* fastener, loop (of a coat, clock, etc.); safety catch, bolt. **salir f.,** to be surety (for); post bail

fiambre m, cold meat, cold dish; *inf* stale, out-of-date news, etc.; *inf* corpse

fiambrera f, lunchbox, lunchpail

fiambrería f delicatessen

fianza f, guarantee, bail; surety; security. *law* **dar f.,** to guarantee; post bail

fiar vt to go surety for, post bail; sell on credit; trust; confide; vr (*with de*) confide in; trust

fibra f, fiber; filament; energy, strength; *mln* vein; grain (of wood)

fibroso a fibrous; fibroid

ficción f, falsehood; invention; fiction, imaginative creation; pretense

ficha f, chip, counter; domino; index card, filing card. **f. antropométrica,** personal particulars card

fichar vt to record personal particulars on a filing card; file, index

fichero m, filing cabinet; card catalog

ficticio a fictitious

fidedigno a trustworthy, bona fide

fidelidad f, fidelity, honesty; loyalty; punctiliousness

fideos m pl, vermicelli. m, *inf* scraggy person

fiduciario a *law* fiduciary. m, *law* trustee

fiebre f, fever; great agitation, excitement. **f. de oro,** gold fever. **f. palúdica,** malarial fever. **f. puerperal,** puerperal fever. **f. tifoidea,** typhoid fever

fiel a faithful, loyal; true, exact. m, axis; pointer (of a scale or balance)

fieltro m, felt

fiera f, wild beast; cruel person

fiereza f, savageness, wildness; cruelty, fierceness; deformity

fiero a wild, savage; ugly; huge, enormous; horrible, alarming; haughty

fiesta f, merriment, gaiety; entertainment, feast; *inf* joke; festivity, celebration; public holiday; caress, cajolery (gen. pl); pl holidays. **f. fija** ecc immovable feast. *inf* **estar de f.,** to be making merry. **hacer f.,** to take a holiday. *inf* **Se acabó la f.,** It's all over and done with

fifiriche a, *Central America, Mexico* sickly, weak

figón m, eating house, diner

figura f, shape, form; face; *art* image, figure; *law* form; court card; *mus* note; *theat* character, role; (*geom gram dancing*) figure. **f. de nieve,** snowman. *naut* **f. de proa,** figurehead. *flg* **f. decorativa,** figurehead. *flg* **hacer f.,** to cut a figure

figurado a figurative; rhetorical

figurar vt to shape, mold; simulate, pretend; represent; vi be numbered among; cut a figure; vr imagine

figurilla mf *inf* ridiculous, dwarfish figure. f, *art* statuette

figurín m, fashion plate or model

figuroso, -a a, *Lat. Am.* flashy, loud, showy

fijación f, fixing; nailing; sticking, posting; attention, fixity; *chem* fixation; firmness, stability

fijador m, (*med phot*) fixative; setting lotion; *art* varnish. a fixing

fijamente adv firmly; attentively

fijar vt to fix; glue, stick; nail; make firm; settle, appoint (a date); fix, concentrate (attention, gaze); (*phot med*) fix; vr decide; notice (e.g. **No me había fijado,** I hadn't noticed). **f. anuncios,** to post bills

fijeza f, fixedness; firmness, stability; constancy, steadfastness

fijo a firm; fixed; stable; steadfast; permanent; exact. **de f.,** certainly, without doubt

fila f, line, row; *mil* rank; antipathy, hatred. **en f.,** in a line

filacteria f, phylactery

filamento m, filament

filantropía f, philanthropy

filantrópico a philanthropic

filántropo m, philanthropist

filarmónico a philharmonic

filatelia f, philately, stamp collecting

filatélico a philatelic

filatelista mf philatelist, stamp collector

filete m, *arch* filet; *cul* small spit; filet (of meat or fish); thread of a screw; *sew* hem

filiación f, filiation; affiliation, relationship; *mil* regimental register

filial a filial; affiliated

filibustero m, filibuster

filigrana f, filigree; watermark (of paper); *flg* delicate creation

Filipinas, las the Philippines

filipino (-na) a and n Philippine

filmar vt to film

filo m, cutting edge; dividing line

filólogo m, philologist

filón m, *mln* vein, lode; *flg* gold mine

filoso, -a a, *Lat. Am.* sharp

filosofar vi to philosophize

filosofía f, philosophy. **f. moral,** moral philosophy. **f. natural,** natural philosophy

filosófico a philosophic

filósofo m, philosopher. a philosophic

filtrar vt to filter; vi filter through, percolate; vr *flg* disappear (of money, etc.)

filtro m, filter, strainer; love potion, philter

filudo, -a a, *Lat. Am.* = **filoso**

fin m, finish, end, conclusion; purpose, goal, aim; limit, extent. **a f. de,** in order to, so that. **a fines de,** toward the end of (with months, years, etc.) (e.g. **a fines de octubre,** toward the end of October). **en f.,** at last; in fine; well then! **por f.,** finally

finado (-da) n deceased, dead person

final a final. m, end, finish; *sport* final (gen. pl)

finalidad *f*, finality; purpose

finalista *mf sport* finalist

finalizar *vt* to conclude, finish; *vi* be finished; close (stock exchange)

financiar *vt* to finance

financiero *a* financial. *m*, financier

finanzas *f pl*, finance

finar *vi* to die; *vr* desire, long for a thing

finca *f*, land, real estate; house property, country house, ranch

fineza *f*, fineness; excellence, goodness; kindness, expression of affection; good turn, friendly act; gift; beauty, delicacy

fingido *a* pretended; assumed; feigned; sham

fingimiento *m*, pretense; affectation, assumption

fingir *vt* to pretend, feign; imagine

finiquitar *vt* to close and pay up an account; *inf* end

finiquito *m*, closing of an account; final receipt, quittance; quietus

finito *a* finite

finlandés (-esa) *a* Finnish. *n* Finn. *m*, Finnish (language)

fino *a* fine; excellent, good; slim, slender, thin; delicate, subtle; dainty (of people); cultured, polished; constant, loving; sagacious, shrewd; *min* refined

finura *f*, fineness; excellence; delicacy; courtesy

fiordo *m*, fjord

firma *f*, signature; act of signing; *com* firm name, firm

firmamento *m*, firmament

firmante *a* signing. *mf* signatory

firmar *vt* to sign

firme *a* firm; hard; steady, solid; constant, resolute, loyal. *m*, foundation, base. *mil* ¡Firmes! Attention! **batir de f.,** to strike hard

firmeza *f*, stability, firmness; constancy, resoluteness, loyalty

fiscal *a* fiscal. *m*, attorney general; public prosecutor; meddler. **f. de quiebras,** official receiver

fiscalizar *vt* to prosecute; pry into; meddle with; censure, criticize

fisco *m*, national treasury, exchequer, revenue

fisgar *vt* to harpoon; pry; *vi* mock, make fun of

fisgón (-ona) *a* prying; mocking. *n* pryer; mocker; eavesdropper

fisgoneo *m*, prying; eavesdropping

física *f*, physics

físico *a* physical. *m*, physicist; physician; physique

fisioterapia *f*, physiotherapy

fisonomía *f*, physiognomy

fistol *m*, *Mexico* tie pin; crafty person, sly person

fístula *f*, pipe, conduit; *mus* pipe; *surg* fistula

fisura *f*, fissure

fláccido *a* flaccid, soft, flabby

flaco *a* thin; weak, feeble; *fig* weak-minded; dispirited. *m*, failing, weakness. *inf* **hacer un f. servicio,** to do an ill turn. **estar f. de memoria,** to have a weak memory

flagelar *vt* to scourge; *fig* lash

flagelo *m*, whip, scourge

flagrante *a poet* refulgent; present; actual. **en f.,** in the very act, flagrante delicto

flagrar *vi poet* to blaze, be refulgent

flamante *a* resplendent; brand-new; fresh, spick-and-span

flamenco (-ca) *m*, *orn* flamingo. *a and n* Flemish. *a* Andalusian; gypsy; buxom, fresh

flan *m*, baked custard, creme caramel. **estar como un f.,** to shake like a leaf, be nervous

flanco *m*, side; *mil* flank

flanquear *vt mil* to flank

flanqueo *m*, *mil* outflanking

flaquear *vi* to grow weak; weaken; totter (buildings, etc.); be disheartened, flag

flaqueza *f*, weakness; thinness; faintness, feebleness; frailty, fault; loss of zeal

flato *m*, flatulence, gas

flatulento *a* flatulent, gassy

flauta *f*, flute

flautín *m*, piccolo

flautista *mf* flutist

flebitis *f*, phlebitis

flecha *f*, arrow, dart

flechar *vt* to shoot an arrow or dart; wound or kill with arrows; *inf* inspire love; *vi* bend a bow to shoot

flechazo *m*, wound with an arrow; *inf* love at first sight

flechero *m*, archer; arrow maker

fleco *m*, fringe; fringe (of hair)

flema *f*, phlegm; sluggishness

flemático *a* phlegmatic; sluggish

flemón *m*, gumboil; abscess

flequero, -a *a*, *Lat. Am.* dishonest, tricky

flequillo *m*, fringe (of hair)

fletamento *m*, chartering (a ship)

fletar *vt* to charter a ship; embark merchandise or people

flete *m*, freightage; cargo, freight

flexibilidad *f*, flexibility; suppleness, adaptability

flexible *a* pliant, supple; flexible, adaptable. *m*, *elec* flex

flirtear *vi* to flirt

flirteo *m*, flirtation

flojedad *f*, flabbiness; weakness, feebleness; laziness, negligence

flojo a flabby; slack, loose; weak, feeble; lazy, slothful; poor (of a literary work, etc.)

floqueado a fringed

flor f, flower; best (of anything); bloom (on fruit); virginity; grain (of leather); compliment (gen. pl); menstruation (gen. pl). **f. de especia**, mace. **f. de la edad**, prime, youth. **f. del cuclillo**, mayflower. **f. del estudiante**, French marigold. **flores de mano**, artificial flowers. **flores de oblón**, hops. **a f. de**, on the surface of, level with. **andarse en flores**, fig to beat about the bush. **echar flores**, to pay compliments. **en f.**, in bloom

flora f, flora

floral a floral. **juegos florales**, poetry contest

florear vt to adorn with flowers; vi execute a flourish on the guitar

florecer vi irr to flower, bloom; flourish, prosper; vr grow mold (of cheese, etc.). See **conocer**

floreciente a flowering; prosperous

florecimiento m, flowering; prosperity

floreo m, witty conversation; flourish (on the guitar or in fencing)

florero m, vase; flower pot; art flower piece

florescencia f, flowering; flowering season, florescence

floresta f, grove, wooded park, woodland; fig collector of beautiful things; anthology

florido a flowery; best, most select; florid, ornate

florilegio m, anthology, collection

florista mf artificial-flower maker; florist; flower seller

florón m, large flower; arch fleuron; honorable deed

flota f, fleet of merchant ships. **f. aérea**, air force

flotación f, floating. naut **línea de f.**, water line

flotador a floating. m, float

flotamiento m, floating

flotante a floating

flotar vi to float on water or in air

flote m, floating. **a f.**, afloat; independent, solvent

flotilla f, flotilla; fleet of small ships. **f. aérea**, air fleet

fluctuación f, fluctuation; hesitation, vacillation

fluctuante a fluctuating

fluctuar vi to fluctuate; be in danger (things); vacillate, hesitate; undulate; oscillate

fluidez f, fluidity

flúido a fluid; fluent. m, fluid; elec current

fluir vi irr to flow. See **huir**

flujo m, flow, flux; rising tide. **f. de sangre**, hemorrhage

fluminense formal a of Rio de Janeiro;

mf native of Rio de Janeiro; resident of Rio de Janeiro

fluorescente a fluorescent

flus m, Colombia, Venezuela suit (of clothes)

flux m, flush (in cards)

foca f, zool seal

foco m, focus; center; origin; source; theat spotlight; core (of an abscess)

fofo a spongy, soft; flabby

fogata f, bonfire

fogón m, fire, cooking area, kitchen range, kitchen stove; furnace of a steam-boiler; vent of a firearm

fogonazo m, powder flash

fogonero m, stoker

fogosidad f, enthusiasm; vehemence; ardor

fogoso a ardent; vehement; enthusiastic

folclórico a pertaining to folklore

folclorista mf folklorist

folículo m, follicle

folio m, leaf of a book or manuscript, folio. **en f.**, in folio

follaje m, foliage; leafy ornamentation; crude, unnecessary decoration; verbosity

folletín m, feuilleton, literary article; serial story; inf dime novel, potboiler

folleto m, pamphlet, leaflet

follisca f, Lat. Am. brawl

follón a lazy; caddish; craven

fomentación f, med fomentation, poultice

fomentador a fomenting. m, fomenter

fomentar vt to warm, foment; incite, instigate; med apply poultices

fomento m, heat, shelter; fuel; protection, encouragement; med fomentation

fonda f, inn; restaurant

fondear vt naut to sound; search a ship; examine carefully; vi naut anchor; vr, Lat. Am. get rich

fondillos m pl, seat (of the trousers)

fondista mf owner of an inn or restaurant

fondo m, bottom (of a well, etc.); bed (of the sea, etc.); depth; rear, portion at the back; ground (of fabrics); background; com capital; com stock; fig fund (of humor, etc.); character, nature; temperament; fig substance, core, essence; naut bottom; pl com resources, funds. **f. de amortización**, sinking fund. **f. doble** or **f. secreto**, false bottom. **f. muerto**, **f. perdido** or **f. vitalicio**, life annuity. com **fondos inactivos**, idle capital. **a fondo**, completely, thoroughly. **artículo de f.**, editorial, lead article. sport **carrera de f.**, long-distance race. naut **irse a f.**, to sink, founder

fonética f, phonetics

fonético a phonetic

fontanero m, pipe layer; plumber

forajido (-da) a fugitive, outlawed. n robber, fugitive

foramen m, *Lat. Am.* hole

forastero (-ra) a strange, foreign; alien, exotic. n stranger

forcejear vi to struggle; try, strive; oppose, contradict

forcejo m, struggle; endeavor; opposition, hostility

forense a forensic

forillo m, *theat* backdrop

forja f, forge

forjador m, smith, ironworker

forjar vt to forge; fabricate; create; counterfeit

forma f, shape, form; arrangement; method; style; manifestation, expression; formula, formulary; ceremonial; *print* form; manner; means, way; mold, matrix; style of handwriting. *law* **en debida f.,** in due form

formación f, formation; form, contour, shape; (*mil geol*) formation. **f. del censo,** census taking

formador a forming, shaping

formal a apparent, formal; serious, punctilious, steady; truthful, reliable; sedate; orderly, regular, methodical

formaldehído m, formaldehyde

formalidad f, orderliness, propriety; formality; requirement, requisite; ceremony; seriousness, sedateness; punctiliousness

formalismo m, formalism; bureaucracy, red tape

formalizar vt to put into final form; legalize; formulate, enunciate; vr take seriously (a joke)

formar vt to shape; form; educate; mold; *mil* form. **formarle causa a uno,** to bring charges against someone. vr develop, grow; *Mexico* get in line

formato m, *print* format; *chem* formate

formidable a formidable, awe-inspiring; huge, enormous

fórmula f, formula; prescription; mode of expression. (*math chem*) **f. clásica,** standard formula

formular vt to formulate; prescribe

formulario m, *law* formulary; handbook

formulismo m, formulism; bureaucracy, red tape

fornicador (-ra) a and n fornicator

fornicar vi to fornicate

fornido a stalwart, muscular, strong

foro m, forum; law courts; law, bar, legal profession; *theat* back scenery; leasehold

forraje m, forage, fodder; foraging

forrajear vt to gather forage, go foraging

forrar vt *sew* to line; cover, encase, make a cover for

forro m, lining, inner covering; cover (of a book); *Argentina* condom; *Lat. Am.* fraud, swindle

fortalecedor a fortifying

fortalecer vt irr to fortify. See **conocer**

fortaleza f, vigor; fortitude; fortress; natural defense; *Lat. Am.* stench, stink. **aer f. volante,** flying fortress

fortificación f, fortification

fortificador a fortifying

fortificar vt to fortify

fortísimo a *sup* **fuerte** extremely strong

fortuito a fortuitous, chance

fortuna f, fate, destiny; fortune, capital, estate; tempest. **por f.,** fortunately. **probar f.,** to try one's luck

forzado a forced, obliged. m, convict condemned to the galleys

forzador m, violator, seducer

forzar vt irr to force, break open; take by force; rape, ravish; oblige, compel. *Pres. Ind.* **fuerzo, fuerzas, fuerza, fuerzan.** *Preterite* **forcé, forzaste,** etc. *Pres. Subjunc.* **fuerce, fuerces, fuerce, forcemos, forcéis, fuercen**

forzoso a obligatory, unavoidable, necessary

forzudo a brawny, stalwart

fosa f, grave; socket (of a joint). **f. común,** potter's field.

fosar vt to undermine; dig a trench around

fosforecer vi irr to phosphoresce. See **conocer**

fosforera f, matchbox

fosforescente a phosphorescent

fósforo m, phosphorus; match; morning star

fósil a and m, fossil; *inf* antique

foso m, hole, hollow, pit; trench; pit (in garages); *theat* room under the stage.

foto f, snapshot, photo

fotocopia f, photocopy

fotogénico a photogenic

fotograbado m, photogravure

fotografía f, photography; photograph

fotografiar vt to photograph

fotográfico a photographic

fotógrafo m, photographer

fotostato m, photostat

frac m, tail coat

fracasar vi to break, crumble, be shattered; collapse (of plans, etc.); fail; be disappointed

fracaso m, shattering; collapse (of plans, etc.); disaster; failure, disappointment, downfall

fracción f, division into parts; fraction. **f. impropia,** *math* improper fraction

fractura f, fracture. **f. conminuta,** compound fracture

fracturar vt to fracture

fragancia f, fragrance, perfume; renown, good name

fragante a fragrant; perfumed; flagrant

frágil a fragile, brittle; perishable, frail; weak, sinful

fragilidad f, fragility; frailty, sinfulness

fragmentario a fragmentary

fragmento m, fragment

fragor m, noise, crash

fragosidad f, roughness, rockiness, unevenness

fragoso a craggy, rocky; rough; noisy, clamorous

fragua f, forge

fraguar vt to forge, work; plot, scheme; vi set (concrete, etc.)

fraile m, friar, monk. inf **f. de misa y olla,** ignorant friar

frambuesa f, raspberry

francachela f, inf binge

francés (-esa) a French. n Frenchman (-woman). m, French (language). **a la francesa,** in French fashion

francesilla f, cul French roll

Francia France

francmasón (-ona) n Freemason

francmasonería f, freemasonry

franco a generous, liberal; exempt; sincere, genuine, frank; duty-free; Frank; Franco (in compound words). m, franc (coin). **f. de porte,** post-free; prepaid

francotirador m, sharpshooter, franc tireur

franela f, flannel; Lat. Am. undershirt; T-shirt

frangir vt to divide, quarter

frangollar vt to scamp, skimp (work); botch, bungle

franja f, fringe; border, trimming; stripe. rad **f. undosa,** wave band

franjar vt sew to fringe, trim

franqueadora f, postage meter

franquear vt to exempt; make free, make a gift of; clear the way; stamp, prepay; free (slaves); vr fall in easily with others' plans; make confidences

franqueo m, exemption; bestowal, making free; postage, stamping; enfranchisement (of slaves)

franqueza f, exemption, freedom; generosity, liberality; sincerity, frankness

franquicia f, exemption from excise duties

frasco m, bottle, flask; powder flask or horn. **f. cuentagotas,** drop bottle

frase f, sentence; phrase; epigram; idiom, style. **f. hecha,** cliché

fraseología f, phraseology; wording

fraternal a brotherly

fraternidad f, fraternity, brotherhood

fraternizar vi to fraternize

fraude m, fraud, deception

fraudulento a a fraudulent

fray m, abb **fraile.** Always followed by a proper name

frazada f, blanket

frecuencia f, frequency. **f. radioeléctrica,** radiofrequency

frecuentación f, frequenting, visiting

frecuentador (-ra) n frequenter

frecuentar vt to frequent

frecuente a frequent

fregada f, Lat. Am. bother, hassle, nuisance

fregadero m, kitchen sink

fregado m, scrubbing; rubbing; scouring; washing; inf murky business

fregador m, kitchen sink; scrub brush; dishcloth. **f. mecánico de platos,** dishwasher

fregandera f, Mexico charwoman, cleaning woman

fregar vt irr to rub; scour; wash (dishes). See **cegar**

fregotear vt inf to clean or scour inefficiently

freír vt irr cul to fry. See **reír**

fréjol m, kidney bean

frenar vt to restrain, hold back; bridle, check; mech brake

frenesí m, madness, frenzy; vehemence, exaltation

frenético a mad, frenzied; vehement, exalted

freno m, bridle; mech brake; restraint, check. **f. de pedal,** foot brake. **f. neumático,** vacuum brake, pneumatic brake

frente f, brow, forehead; front portion; countenance; head; heading; beginning (of a letter, etc.). m, mil front. mf facade; front; obverse (of coins). adv in front, opposite. **f. a f.,** face to face. **con la f. levantada,** with head held high; proudly; insolently. **de f.,** abreast

fresa f, strawberry plant and fruit (especially small or wild varieties); mech milling cutter, miller

fresadora f, milling machine

fresal m, strawberry bed

fresca f, cool air; fresh air; inf home truth

fresco a cool; fresh, new; recent; buxom; fresh-colored; calm, serene; inf impudent, cheeky, bold; thin (clothes). m, coolness; fresh air; art fresco. **al f.,** in the open air. **hacer f.,** to be cool or fresh

frescote a inf ruddy and corpulent

frescura f, coolness; freshness; pleasant verdure and fertility; inf cheek, nerve; piece of insolence; unconcern, indifference; calmness, serenity

fresón m, strawberry (large, cultivated varieties)

fresquera f, meat locker; cool place

fresquería f, Mexico refreshment stand

fresquista mf fresco painter

friable a brittle; friable, powdery

frialdad f, coldness, chilliness; med frigidity; indifference, lack of interest; foolishness; negligence

fríamente adv coldly; coolly, with indifference; dully, flatly

fricción f, friction

friccionar vt to rub; give a massage

friega f, friction, massage

frigidez f, See **frialdad**

frígido a frigid

frigorífico a refrigerative. m, refrigerator, cold-storage locker

frijol m, bean; bot kidney bean

frijoles refritos con queso mpl, Mexico twice fried Mexican beans with cheese

frío a cold; med frigid; indifferent, uninterested; dull, uninteresting; inefficient. m, coldness, chill; cold

friolero a sensitive to cold

frisa f, frieze cloth

frisar vt to frizz, curl (cloth); scrub, rub; vi approach, be nearly (e.g. **Frisa en los setenta años,** He's nearly seventy)

friso m, frieze; dado, border

fritada f, cul fry, fried food

frito a fried

fritura f, frying; fried food

frivolidad f, frivolity

frivolité m, sew tatting

frívolo a frivolous, superficial; futile, unconvincing

fronda f, bot leaf; frond (of ferns); pl foliage

frondoso a leafy

frontera f, frontier; facade

fronterizo a frontier; facing, opposite

frontero a facing, opposite. m, (ant mil) frontier commander

frontispicio m, frontispiece; facade; fig inf face, dial

frontón m, pelota court; jai alai court; arch pediment; Mexico jai alai

frotamiento, frote m, rubbing, friction

frotar vt to rub

frotis m, med smear

fructífero a fruitful, fructiferous

fructuoso a fruitful, fertile; useful

frufrú m, rustle (of silk, etc.)

frugal a frugal; saving, economical

frugalidad f, frugality, abstemiousness, moderation

fruición f, enjoyment; fruition; satisfaction

fruir vi irr to enjoy what one has long desired. See **huir**

frunce m, sew shirring; gather; ruffling; tuck; pucker; wrinkle

fruncimiento m, wrinkling; puckering; sew shirring

fruncir vt to frown; purse (the lips); pucker; sew shirr, pleat, gather; reduce in size; conceal the truth; vr pretend to be prudish. **f. el ceño,** to knit one's brow, scowl

fruslería f, trifle, nothing

frustración f, frustration

frustrar vt to disappoint; frustrate, thwart

fruta f, fruit; inf consequence, result. **f. bomba** Cuba papaya **f. de hueso,** stone fruit. cul **f. de sartén,** fritter

frutal a fruit-bearing. m, fruit tree

frutería f, fruit

frutero (-ra) a fruit. n fruit seller. m, fruit dish; art painting of fruit; basket of imitation fruit

fruticultura f, fruit farming

fruto m, fruit; product, result; profit, proceeds; agr grain

fu spitting (of cats). interj expression of scorn. inf **ni f. ni fa,** neither one thing nor the other

fuego m, fire; conflagration; firing (of firearms); beacon; hearth, home; rash; ardor; heat (of an argument, etc.); interj ¡F.! mil Fire! **fuegos artificiales,** fireworks. **a sangre y f.,** by fire and sword. mil **hacer f.,** to fire (a weapon). **pegar f.,** to set on fire

fuelle m, bellows; bag (of a bagpipe); sew pucker, wrinkle; hood (of a carriage, etc.); wind cloud; inf talebearer. **f. de pie,** foot pump

fuente f, stream, spring; fountain; meat dish; genesis, origin; source, headwaters; tap

fuera adv outside, out. interj get out! **f. de,** besides, in addition to. **f. de alcance,** out of reach. **f. de sí,** beside oneself (with rage, etc.). **de f.,** from the outside. **por f.,** on the outside, externally

fuereño, -a mf, Mexico foreigner

fuero m, municipal charter; jurisdiction; compilation of laws; legal right or privilege; pl inf arrogance. **los fueros de León,** the laws of León

fuerte a strong, resistant; robust; spirited, vigorous; hard (of diamonds, etc.); rough, uneven; impregnable; terrible, tremendous; overweight (of coins); active; efficacious, effective; expert, knowledgeable; gram strong; intense; loud; tough. m, fort; talent, strong point; mus forte. adv strongly; excessively. **tener genio f.,** to be quick-tempered

fuerza f, strength; power, might; force; efficacy; fortress; sew stiffening; mech power; violence; toughness, durability, solidity; potency; authority; courage; vigor; pl fig inf livewires, influential people. **a f. de,** by means of, by dint of. **a la f.,** forcibly. **en f. de,** because of, on account of. **por f. mayor,** by main force. **ser f.,** to be necessary

fuga f, flight, escape, running away; leak (gas, etc.); elopement; mus fugue; ardor, strength. **f. de cerebros,** brain drain

fugarse vr to run away; elope; escape

fugaz a fugitive; fleeting, brief

fugitivo (-va) a fugitive; runaway, escaping; transient. n fugitive

fulano (**-na**) n so-and-so, such a person **f., zutano, y mengano,** inf Tom, Dick, and Harry

fulcro m, fulcrum

fulgente, fúlgido a brilliant, shining

fulgor m, brilliance, brightness

fulminante a med fulminant; fulminating; thundering. m, percussion cap

fulminar vt to fulminate (all meanings)

fulmíneo, fulminoso a fulminous, pertaining to lightning

fullero (**-ra**) a cheating; crafty, astute. n cheat, cardsharper

fumadero m, smoking room

fumador (**-ra**) a smoking. n smoker. «No fumadores», "Nonsmoking" (area)

fumar vi to smoke; vr inf dissipate, waste

fumigación f, fumigation

fumigador (**-ra**) n fumigator

fumigar vt to fumigate

funámbulo n tightrope walker, acrobat

función f, function; working, operation; theat performance; activity, duty; ceremony; celebration; math function; mil battle

funcional a functional

funcionamiento m, functioning

funcionar vi to function, work. «No funciona», "Out of order"

funcionario m, functionary, official; civil servant

funda f, case, cover, sheath; hold-all. **f. de almohada,** pillowcase

fundación f, foundation

fundadamente adv with reason, on good evidence

fundador (**-ra**) n founder, creator; originator

fundamental a fundamental

fundamento m, mas foundation; basis; basic principle, reason; origin, root

fundar vt to build, erect; base; found, institute; create, establish; vr (with en) found, base upon. **f. una compañía,** com to float a company

fundición f, foundry; smelting, founding, casting; cast iron; print font

fundido fotográfico m, composite photograph

fundidor m, founder, smelter.

fundir vt to melt; found, smelt; cast (metals); vr join together, unite; elec blow (fuses)

fúnebre a funeral; dismal, lugubrious, mournful

funerales m pl, funeral; ecc memorial masses

funeraria f, funeral home, undertaker

funestidad f, Mexico calamity, catastrophe

funesto a unlucky, unfortunate; mournful, melancholy, sad

fungoso a spongy, fungous

furgón m, wagon; van; guard's van, baggage car, luggage cart. **f. postal,** mail truck

furia f, myth fury; rage, wrath; fit of madness; raging, violence (of the elements); speed, haste

furibundo a frantic, furious; raging

fúrico a stark raving mad

furioso a furious, enraged; mad, insane; violent, terrible; enormous, excessive

furor m, fury, rage; poetic frenzy; violence; furor

furtivo a furtive; covert, clandestine; pirate (editions)

fuselado a streamlined

fuselaje m, fuselage

fusible a fusible. m, elec fuse; fuse wire

fusil m, rifle

fusilamiento m, execution by shooting

fusilar vt to execute by shooting; inf plagiarize

fusilazo m, rifle shot

fusión f, melting, liquefying; fusion, blending; mixture, union; com merger, amalgamation

fusionar vt to blend, fuse, merge; vr com combine, form a merger

fusta f, brushwood; whip

fustán m Lat. Am. skirt

fuste m, wood, timber; poet saddle; fig core, essence; importance, substance; shaft of a lance; arch shaft. **hombre de buen f.,** a man with a good (physical) constitution

fustigar vt to whip, lash; rebuke harshly

fútbol m, football; soccer

futbolista mf football player; soccer player

fútil a futile, ineffectual, worthless

futilidad f, futility, worthlessness

futura f, law reversion (of offices); inf fiancée

futurista mf futurist

futuro (**-ra**) a future. m, future. n inf betrothed

gabacho (-cha) *a* and *n* (*inf* scornful) Frenchman

gabán *m*, overcoat; cloak

gabardina *f*, gabardine; weatherproof coat

gabarro *m*, flaw (in cloth); knot (in stone); snag, drawback; slip, error (in accounts)

gabinete *m*, study, library; sitting room; den; *pol* cabinet; collection, museum, gallery; laboratory; boudoir; studio; display cabinet. **g. de lectura,** reading room

gacel, *m*. **gacela** *f*, gazelle

gaceta *f*, bulletin, review, record; newspaper; gazette (official Spanish government organ); *inf* newshound

gacetero (-ra) *n* newsdealer. *m*, news reporter

gacetilla *f*, news in brief, miscellany column; society news; gossip column; *inf* newshound

gacha *f*, unglazed crock; *pl* pap; porridge

gaché *m*, (among the Romany) Andalusian; *inf* fellow

gacho *a* drooping, bent downward; slouch (hat); (of ears) lop; *Mexico* unpleasant

gachón *a inf* attractive, charming

gafar *vt* to claw; seize with a hook, hook; mend with a bracket (pottery)

gafas *f pl*, spectacles; goggles; spectacle earhooks; grapplehooks

gafete *m*, hook and eye; clasp

gaita *f*, bagpipe; hand organ; kind of clarinet; *inf* neck. **g. gallega,** bagpipe

gaitería *f*, crude, gaudy garment or ornament

gaitero *a inf* overmerry; loud, crude. *m*, piper

gajes *m pl*, salary; emoluments; perquisites

gajo *m*, branch, bough (gen. cut); little cluster (of grapes); bunch (of fruit); quarter (of oranges, etc.); prong (of forks, etc.)

gala *f*, evening or full dress; grace, wit; flower, cream, best; gala; *pl* finery, trappings; wedding presents. **de g.,** full dress. **hacer g. de,** to glory in, boast of

galán *m*, handsome, well-made man; lover, wooer, gallant; *theat* leading man or one of leading male roles

galancete *m*, handsome little man; *theat* male juvenile lead

galano *a* smart, well-dressed; agreeable, pleasing; beautiful; ornamented; *fig* elegant (speech, style, etc.)

galante *a* gallant, courtly, attentive; flirtatious (of women); licentious

galanteador *a* flirtatious. *m*, philanderer; wooer

galantear *vt* to court; flirt with; make love to; *fig* procure assiduously

galanteo *m*, courtship; flirtation; lovemaking; wooing

galantería *f*, courtesy; attention, compliment; elegance, grace; gallantry; generosity, liberality

galanura *f*, showiness, gorgeousness; elegance, grace; prettiness

galápago *m*, freshwater tortoise; cleat

galardón *m*, reward, recompense, prize

galardonar *vt* to reward, recompense

galbanoso *a inf* slothful

galera *f*, van, wagon, cart; *naut* galley; prison for women; *print* galley; *Central America, Mexico* shed. **echar a galeras,** to condemn to the galleys

galerada *f*, galley proof

galería *f*, gallery; corridor, passage; collection of paintings; *min* gallery, drift; *theat* gallery

galerna *f*, tempestuous northwest wind (gen. on Spanish north coast)

Gales Wales

galés (-esa) *a* a Welsh. *n* Welshman. *m*, Welsh (language)

galga *f*, boulder, rolling stone; greyhound bitch

galgo *m*, greyhound. **g. ruso,** borzoi

gálibo *m*, *naut* mold; elegance

galicado *a* gallicized

galicismo *m*, gallicism

gálico *m*, syphilis. *a* gallic

Galilea Galilee

galimatías *m*, *inf* gibberish, nonsense

gallardear *vi* to behave with ease and grace

gallardete *m*, pennant; bunting

gallardía *f*, grace, dignity; spirit, dash; courage; liveliness

gallardo *a* handsome, upstanding; gallant; spirited; fine, noble; lively

gallear *vi inf* to put on airs; be a bully; shout, bawl (with anger, etc.); *fig inf* stand out

gallego (-ga) *a* and *n* Galician. *m*, Galician (language)

galleta *f*, biscuit; *inf* slap; anthracite, lump coal; small jar or vessel

gallina *f*, hen. *mf inf* coward. **g. ciega,** blindman's buff. *inf* **acostarse con las gallinas,** to go to bed early

gallinaza *f*, hen dung

gallinero (-ra) *n* poultry dealer. *m*, henhouse; brood of hens; *theat* gallery; babel, noisy place

gallito *m*, small cock; cock of the walk; bully

gallo *m*, *orn* cock; *inf* false note (in singing); *inf* boss, chief. **g. de viento,** weathercock. *inf* **alzar el g.,** to put on airs, boast. **Cada g. canta en su muladar,** Every man is boss in his own house. *inf*

G

Otro g. nos cantara, Our lot (or fate) would have been very different

galón *m,* galloon, braid; *mil* stripe; gallon (measure)

galoneadura *f,* braiding, trimming

galonear *vt* to trim with braid

galopante *a* galloping (of consumption, etc.)

galopar *vi* to gallop; *mech* wobble

galope *m,* gallop. **a or de g.,** at the gallop; on the run, quickly. **andar a g. corto,** to canter

galopín *m,* ragamuffin, urchin; rogue, knave; *inf* clever rogue; *naut* cabin boy

galvanizar *vt elec* to galvanize; electroplate; *fig* shock into life

gama *f, mus* scale; gamut, range; doe

gambado *a Lat. Am.* knock-kneed

gambito *m,* gambit (in chess)

gamella *f,* trough (for washing, feeding animals, etc.)

gamo *m,* buck (of the fallow deer)

gamuza *f,* chamois; chamois leather

gana *f,* appetite; wish, desire. **de buena g.,** willingly. **de mala g.,** reluctantly. **tener g. (de),** to wish, desire, want. **no tener g.,** to have no appetite, not be hungry. **No me da la g.,** I don't want (to), I won't

ganable *a* attainable; earnable

ganadería *f,* livestock; strain (of cattle); cattle raising; stock farm; cattle dealing

ganadero *m,* cattle raiser or dealer; herdsman

ganado *m,* livestock, herd; flock; hive (of bees); *inf* mob. **g. mayor,** cattle, mules, horses. **g. menor,** sheep, goats, etc. **g. moreno,** hogs, swine. **g. vacuno,** cattle

ganador (-ra) *a* winning. *n* winner

ganancia *f,* winning; gain, profit

ganancial, ganancioso *a* gainful, profitable; lucrative

ganapán *m,* laborer; porter; *inf* boor

ganar *vt* to gain; win; conquer; arrive at; earn; surpass, beat; achieve; acquire; *vi* prosper

ganchero *m,* lumberjack

ganchillo *m,* crochet hook; crochet. **hacer g.,** to crochet

gancho *m,* hook; stump (of a branch); shepherd's crook; crochet hook; *inf* trickster, pimp; *inf* scribble

ganchoso *a* hooked; bent; curved

gandujar *vt sew* to pleat, tuck, shirr

gandul (-la) *a inf* lazy. *n* lazybones, loafer

ganga *f, min* gangue, matrix; bargain, cinch

ganglio *m,* ganglion

gangoso *a* nasal; with a twang (of speech)

gangrena *f,* gangrene

gangrenoso *a* gangrenous

ganoso *a* wishful, desirous, anxious

gansada *f, inf* impertinence, foolishness

ganso (-sa) *n* goose, gander; slow-moving person; yokel, bumpkin

ganzúa *f,* skeleton key; *inf* picklock, burglar; *inf* pumper, inquisitive person

gañán *m,* farm worker; day laborer; brawny fellow

gañir *vi irr* to yowl, yelp, howl (of dogs, etc.); crow, croak; *inf* talk hoarsely. See **mullir**

garabatear *vi* to hook, catch with hooks; scribble; *fig inf* beat around the bush

garabato *m,* hook; *agr* weed clearer; scrawl, scribble; *inf* charm, sex appeal; pothook; boat hook; *pl* gestures, movements (with the hands)

garaje *m,* garage

garante *mf* guarantor; reference (person). *a* responsible, guaranteeing

garantía *f,* guarantee; security, pledge; *law* warranty

garantir *vt* to guarantee; warrant, vouch for

garañón *m Lat. Am.* stallion

garapiñar *vt* to ice, freeze (drinks, syrups, etc.); *cul* candy, coat with sugar

garbanzo *m,* chickpea. **g. negro,** *fig* black sheep

garbo *m,* jaunty air; grace, elegance; frankness; generosity, liberality

garboso *a* attractive; handsome, sprightly, gay; graceful; munificent

garduño (-ña) *n inf* sneak thief

garete (ir or irse al) *naut* to be adrift

garfear *vi* to catch with a hook, hook

garfio *m,* grappling iron, hook, drag hook, cramp; gaff

gargajear *vi* to expectorate

gargajo *m,* phlegm

garganta *f,* throat; gullet; instep; defile; neck, shaft, narrowest part

gargantear *vi* to warble, trill

gárgara *f,* gargling (gen. *pl*). **hacer gárgaras,** to gargle

gargarismo *m,* gargling; gargle

gárgol *a* rotten (eggs). *m,* groove, mortise

garita *f,* sentry box; porter's lodge; hut; cabin. **g. de señales,** (railroad) signal box

garitero *m,* gambling house keeper; gambler

garito *m,* gambling house; profits of a gambling house

garra *f,* paw with claws; talon; hand; *mech* clamp, claw. *fig* **caer en las garras de,** to fall into the clutches (of)

garrafa *f,* decanter, carafe; carboy

garrapata *f, ent* tick

garrapatear *vi* to scribble

garrapaticida *m, Lat. Am.* insecticide

garrapato *m,* scribble, scrawl

garrido *a* handsome; gallant; elegant; graceful

garroba f, carob bean

garrocha f, goad. **salto a la g.,** pole jumping

garrotazo m, blow with a truncheon or cudgel. **dar garrotazos de ciego,** to lay about one

garrote m, truncheon, club; *med* tourniquet; *garrote*. **dar g. (a),** to strangle

garrotillo m, croup

garrucha f, pulley; *mech* gin block

garrulidad f, garrulity, loquaciousness

gárrulo a twittering, chirping (birds); garrulous; murmuring, babbling (wind, water, etc.)

ganuar vi *Lat. Am.* to drizzle

garza f, heron

garzo a blue (gen. of eyes)

gas m, gas; fumes. **g. asfixiante,** poison gas. **cámara de g.,** gasbag, gas chamber

gasa f, gauze. **tira de g.,** black mourning band

gaseosa f, aerated water

gaseoso a gaseous

gasista mf gas fitter; gasman

gasolina f, gasoline, petrol

gasómetro m, gas meter; gasometer

gastado a worn; worn-out; exhausted

gastador (-ra) a extravagant, wasteful. n spendthrift. m, *mil* sapper; convict condemned to hard labor

gastar vt to spend (money); wear out; exhaust; ruin, destroy; display or have habitually; possess, use, wear; vr wear out; run down (of a battery)

gasto m, spending; expenditure; consumption (of gas, etc.); expense, cost, charge; wear (and tear). **g. suplementario,** extra charge

gástrico a gastric

gastritis f, gastritis

gastronomía f, gastronomy

gastrónomo (-ma) n gastronome

gata f, she-cat; wreath of mist; *inf* Madrilenian woman. **a gatas,** on all fours

gatear vi to climb like a cat; *inf* crawl on all fours; vt *inf* scratch (of a cat); steal, pinch

gatillo m, *dim* small cat; dental forceps; trigger (of gun); *inf* juvenile petty thief

gato m, cat; tomcat; moneybag or its contents; *mech* jack; mousetrap; *inf* cat burglar, sneak thief; *inf* Madrilenian; *carp* clamp. **g. atigrado,** tiger cat. **g. de algalia,** civet cat. **g. de Angora,** Persian cat. **g. montés,** wildcat. **g. romano,** tabby cat. **dar g. por liebre,** to serve cat for hare, to deceive; misrepresent. *inf* **Hay g. encerrado,** There's more to this than meets the eye

gaucho (-cha) n gaucho; cowboy, rider

gaveta f, drawer (of a desk)

gavia f, main topsail; pl topsails; crow's-nest

gavilla f, sheaf (of corn, etc.); gang, rabble

gaviota f, seagull

gazapo m, young rabbit; *inf* cunning fellow; fib, lie; slip, blunder

gazmoñería f, prudery, priggish affectation

gazmoño a hypocritical, prudish, priggish

gaznápiro (-ra) n ninny, simpleton

gaznate m, windpipe

gazpacho m, cold soup containing bread, onions, vinegar, olive oil, garlic, etc.

ge f, name of the letter G

gehena m, gehenna, hell

géiser m, geyser

gelatina f, gelatin. **g. incendiaria,** napalm. **g. seca,** cooking gelatin

gelatinoso a gelatinous

gemelo (-la) a and n twin. m pl, field or opera glasses, binoculars; cuff links; *ast* Gemini

gemido m, groan, lament, moan

gemidor a groaning, moaning; wailing (of the wind, etc.)

gemir vi *irr* to moan, groan, lament; *fig* wail, howl. See **pedir**

gene m, gene

genealogía f, genealogy

genealógico a genealogical

genealogista mf genealogist

generación f, generation, reproduction; species; generation

generador a generative. m, *mech* generator

general a general; universal; widespread; common, usual. m, (*mil ecc*) general. **g. de división,** *mil* major general. **en or por lo g.,** generally

generalidad f, majority, bulk; generality

generalísimo m, generalissimo, commander in chief

generalización f, generalization

generalizar vt to generalize; vr become widespread or general

generar vt to generate

genérico a generic

género m, kind; class; way, mode; *com* goods; species, genus; *gram* gender; cloth, material. **g. chico,** short theatrical pieces (gen. one act). **g. humano,** humankind

generosidad f, hereditary nobility; generosity, magnanimity; liberality, munificence; courage

generoso a noble (by birth); magnanimous; generous (of wine); munificent; courageous; excellent

genésico a genetic

génesis m, Genesis. f, beginning, origin

genial a of genius; highly talented; brilliant; characteristic, individual; pleasant; cheerful

genialidad *f*, genius; talent; brilliance; eccentricity, oddity

genio *m*, nature, individuality, temperament; temper; character; talent; genius; genie, spirit. **corto de g.,** unintelligent. **mal g.,** bad temper

genital *a* genital. *m*, testicle (gen. *pl*)

genitivo *a* reproductive, generative. *m*, *gram* genitive

Génova Genoa

gente *f*, people, a crowd; nation; army; *inf* family; followers, adherents. **g. baja,** rabble. **g. de bien,** honest folk; respectable people. **g. de paz,** friends (reply to sentinel's challenge). **g. fina,** nice, cultured people. **g. menuda,** children, small fry

gentecilla *f*, *dim inf* rabble; contemptible people

gentil *a* pagan, idolatrous; spirited, dashing, handsome; notable, extraordinary; graceful, charming

gentileza *f*, grace; elegance; beauty; verve, sprightliness; courtesy; show, ostentation

gentilhombre *m*, gentleman; handsome man; kind sir! **gentileshombres de cámara,** gentlemen-in-waiting

gentilicio *a* national; family

gentilidad *f*, idolatry, paganism; heathendom

gentío *m*, crowd, throng

gentualla, gentuza *f*, canaille, rabble

genuflexión *f*, genuflection

genuino *a* pure; authentic, genuine; *Colombia* great, wonderful

geografía *f*, geography

geográfico *a* geographical

geógrafo *m*, geographer

geología *f*, geology

geológico *a* geological

geólogo *m*, geologist

geometría *f*, geometry. **g. del espacio,** solid geometry

geométrico *a* geometrical

geranio *m*, geranium

gerencia *f*, *com* managership; manager's office; management

gerente *m*, *com* manager

germanía *f*, thieves' slang; association of thieves; sixteenth-century political brotherhood

germen *m*, germ, sprout; *bot* embryo; genesis, origin

germinación *f*, germination

germinar *vi* to germinate, sprout; develop, grow

gerundio *m*, *gram* gerund; *inf* pompous ass; *inf* tub-thumper

gesta *f*, heroic deed. **cantar de g.,** epic or heroic poem

gestación *f*, gestation

gestear *vi* to gesture, grimace

gesticulación *f*, gesticulation; grimace

gesticular *vi* to grimace, gesticulate. *a* gesticulatory

gestión *f*, negotiation; management, conduct; effort, exertion; measure

gestionar *vt* to negotiate; conduct; undertake; take steps to attain

gesto *m*, gesture; facial expression; grimace; face, visage

gestor (-ra) *n* manager; partner; promoter. *a* managing

Getsemaní Gethsemane

giba *f*, hump, hunchback; *inf* nuisance, inconvenience

gibón *m*, gibbon

giboso *a* hunchbacked

gibraltareño *a* Gibraltarian

gigante *a* gigantic. *m*, giant.

giganta *f*, giantess

gigantesco *a* a giant, gigantic; *fig* outstanding

gigantez *f*, gigantic size

gigantón (-ona) *n* enormous giant; carnival grotesque

gimnasia *f*, gymnastics

gimnasio *m*, gymnasium; school, academy

gimnasta *mf* gymnast

gimnástico *a* gymnastic

gimotear *vi* *inf* to whine (often used scornfully)

gimoteo *m*, *inf* whining, whimpering

ginebra *f*, gin (drink); confusion; babble, din

ginecología *f*, gynecology

ginecológico *a* gynecological

ginecólogo (-ga) *n* gynecologist

girado *m*, *com* drawee

girador *m*, *com* drawer

giralda *f*, weathercock in the shape of a person or animal; tower at Seville

girar *vi* to revolve; deal (with), concern; turn, branch (streets, etc.); *com* trade; *mech* turn on, revolve; *vt* and *vi com* draw, cash. **g. en descubierto,** *com* to overdraw

girasol *m*, sunflower

giratorio *a* revolving, gyrating; swiveling

giro *m*, revolution, turn; revolving; trend; course (of affairs); style, turn (of phrase); threat; knife gash; *com* draft, drawing; *com* line of business, speciality. **g. postal,** postal order

giroscopio *m*, gyroscope

gis *m* Lat. Am. chalk; *Mexico also* pulque

gitanería *f*, cajolery, wheedling; gypsies; gypsy saying or action

gitanesco *a* gypsy, gypsy-like

gitano (-na) *a* gypsy; gypsy-like; seductive, attractive; sly. *n* gypsy

glaciar *m*, glacier

glándula f, gland

glanco a Lat. Am. light green

glicerina f, glycerin, glycerol

globo m, geom sphere; globe, world; globe (elec gas); balloon. **g. aeroestático,** air balloon. **g. terrestre,** world; geographical globe

glóbulo m, globule.

gloria f, heavenly bliss; fame, glory; delight, pleasure; magnificence, splendor; art apotheosis, glory. m, ecc doxology

gloriar vt to praise; vr (with de or en) boast about; be proud of, rejoice in

glorieta f, bower, arbor; open space in a garden; street square

glorificación f, glorification

glorificador a glorifying

glorificar vt to exalt, raise up; glorify, extol; vr (with de or en) be proud of; glory in; boast of

glorioso a glorious; ecc blessed; boastful, bragging

glosa f, gloss; explanation, note

glosar vt lit to gloss

glosario m, glossary

glosopeda f, foot-and-mouth disease

glotón (-**ona**) a greedy, gluttonous. n glutton

glotonería f, gluttony, greed

glucosa f, glucose

gn- For words so beginning, see spellings without g.

gobernación f, government; governor's office or building; ministry of the interior, home office (abb. for ministerio de G.)

gobernador (-**ra**) a governing. n governor

gobernalle m, helm

gobernante a governing. m, inf self-appointed director or manager

gobernar vt irr to govern, rule; lead, conduct; manage; steer; control; vi govern; naut obey the tiller. See **recomendar**

gobierno m, government (all meanings); naut helm; control (of machines, business, etc.)

goce m, enjoyment; possession

gol m, sport goal

gola f, throat; gullet; gorget; tucker, bib

golf m, golf. **palo de g.,** golf club

golfear vi to loaf

golfería f, loafing; vagabondage; loafers

golfo (-**fa**) m, geog gulf; sea, ocean. n ragamuffin, urchin. m, inf loafer; lounge lizard, wastrel

golilla f, ruff; Lat. Am. scarf; m, inf magistrate

gollería f, dainty, tidbit; inf affectation, persnicketiness

gollete m, gullet; neck (of a bottle, etc.); mech nozzle

golondrina f, orn swallow; Chile moving van. **g. de mar,** tern

golosina f, tidbit, delicacy; desire, caprice; pleasant useless thing

goloso a fond of sweet things; greedy, desirous; appetizing

golpe m, blow, knock; pull (at the oars); ring (of a bell); mech stroke; crowd; fall (of rain, etc.); mass, torrent; misfortune; shock, collision; spring lock; beating (of the heart); flap (of a pocket); sew passementerie; surprise; point, wit; bet. **g. de estado,** coup d'état. **g. de fortuna,** stroke of fortune. **g. de mano,** rising, insurrection. **g. en vago,** blow in the air; disappointment. **g. franco,** sport free kick. **de g.,** suddenly; quickly

golpeadura f. **golpeo** m, knocking, striking; beating, throbbing

golpear vt and vi to knock, strike; beat, throb

goma f, gum, rubber; India rubber; rubber band

gomería f, tire store

gomero a gum; rubber. m, WH rubber planter

gomoso a gummy; gum

góndola f, gondola

gondolero m, gondolier

gonorrea f, gonorrhea

gordo a fat, stout; greasy, oily; thick (thread, etc.). m, animal fat, suet. inf **ganar el g.,** to win first prize (in a lottery, etc.)

gorgojo m, weevil; fig dwarf

gorgoritear vi inf to trill, quaver

gorgorito m, inf quaver, tremolo, trill (gen. pl)

gorgoteo m, gurgle

gorjear vi to trill, warble; twitter; vr crow (of a baby)

gorjeo m, trill, shake; warbling, twitter; crowing, lisping (of a child)

gorra f, cap; bonnet; mil busby; hunting cap. **vivir de g.,** inf to sponge

gorrista mf inf parasite; sponger

gorro m, cap; bonnet

gorrón m, smooth, round pebble; mech pivot, gudgeon; sponger, waster. a parasitical

gota f, drop (of liquid); gout

gotear vi to drop, trickle, drip; leak; drizzle; give or receive in driblets

gotero m Lat. Am. (medicine) dropper

gótico a Gothic; noble, illustrious

gotoso (-**sa**) a gouty. n sufferer from gout

gozar vt to enjoy, have; take pleasure (in), delight (in); know carnally; vi (with de) enjoy; have, possess

gozne m, hinge

gozo m, enjoyment, possession; gladness, joy; pl couplets in honor of the Virgin Mary or a saint. inf **iMi g. en el pozo!** I'm sunk! All is lost!

gozoso a glad, happy. adv gladly; with pleasure

grabado m, engraver's art; engraving; illustration, picture. **g. al agua fuerte,** etching. **g. al agua tinta,** aquatint

grabador (-ra) n engraver

grabar vt to engrave; fig leave a deep impression

gracejo m, humor, wit; cheerfulness

gracia f, grace; attraction, grace; favor; kindness; jest, witticism; pardon, mercy; pleasant manner; obligingness, willingness; pl thanks, thank you. **gracias a,** thanks to. **¡Gracias a Dios!** Thank God! Thank goodness! **las Gracias,** the Three Graces

grácil a slender; small

graciosidad f, beauty, perfection, grace

gracioso (-sa) a attractive, graceful, elegant; witty, humorous; free, gratis. n theat comic role; m, theat fool

grada f, step, stair; gradin, seat; stand, gallery; agr harrow; naut runway; pl perron, flight of stairs

gradación f, gradation; climax

grado m, step, stair; degree (of relationship); university degree; grade, class (in schools); (fig geom phys) degree; will, desire. **de buen g.,** willingly. **en sumo g.,** in the highest degree

graduación f, graduation; mil rank; rating (of a ship's company). **g. de oficial,** mil commission

graduado a graded; mil brevet. m, graduate

gradual a gradual

graduar vt to classify; mil grade; confer a degree on; measure; test; com standardize; mech calibrate; vr graduate, receive a degree. **g. la vista,** to test the eyes. **graduarse de oficial,** mil to get one's commission

gráfica f, graph

gráfico a graphic; vivid

grafología f, graphology

grajear vi to caw; gurgle, burble (of infants)

grajo m, orn rook

grama f, Dominican Republic, Venezuela grass, lawn

gramática f, grammar. inf **g. parda,** horse sense

gramático a grammatical. m, grammarian

gramo m, gram

gran a abb See **grande.** Used before a singular noun. big; great; grand

grana f, grain, seed; seed time; cochineal; kermes; red

granada f, mil grenade, shell; pomegranate

granadero m, grenadier; inf very tall person; Lat. Am. riot policeman

granar vi agr to seed; run to seed

granate m, garnet; dark red

Gran Bretaña Great Britain

grande a big, large; great, illustrious; grand. m, great man; grandee. **en g.,** in a large size; as a whole; in style, lavishly

grandeza f, largeness; greatness, magnificence; grandeeship; vastness, magnitude

grandílocuo a grandiloquent

grandioso a grandiose, magnificent

grandor m, size

granear vt agr to sow; grain (of leather)

granero m, granary; grain-producing country

granito m, dim small grain; granite; small pimple

granizar vi to hail, sleet; vi and vt fig shower down, deluge

granizo m, hail, sleet; hailstorm; fig shower, deluge

granja f, farm; farmhouse; dairy farm, dairy

granjear vt to trade, profit, earn; obtain, acquire; vr gain, win

granjería f, farming; agricultural profits; earnings, profits

granjero (-ra) n farmer

grano m, agr grain; seed; bean (coffee, etc.); particle; markings, grain (of wood, etc.); pimple; grain (measure). fig inf **ir al g.,** to go to the root of the matter; come to the point

granuja f, grape pit. m, inf urchin, scamp; knave, rogue

granujiento a pimply

gránulo m, granule

granuloso a granulous

grapa f, cramp, dowel, clamp; block hook; elec cleat; staple

grasa f, fat; grease; oil; dripping, suet

grasiento a greasy; grubby, dirty

gratificación f, monetary reward; fee, remuneration; gratuity

gratificar vt to recompense; please, gratify

gratis a and adv gratis

gratitud f, gratitude

grato a pleasing, agreeable; free, gratuitous; Lat. Am. appreciative, grateful

gratuito a gratuitous, free; baseless, unfounded

gravamen m, obligation; burden; tax

gravar vt to burden, weigh upon; tax

grave a heavy; important, momentous; grave; dignified, serious; sedate; tiresome; low-pitched, low; gram grave accent

gravedad f, phys gravity

gravitación f, phys gravitation; seriousness; sedateness; importance; enormity, gravity

gravitar vi to gravitate; lean or rest (upon)

gravoso a grievous, oppressive; onerous; costly

graznar *vi* to caw; cackle; quack; croak; sing stridently, screech

Grecia Greece

gregario a gregarious

gregüescos *m pl*, wide breeches (sixteenth and seventeenth centuries)

gremial a pertaining to a guild, union, or association. *m*, member of a guild, union, or association

gremio *m*, guild, corporation, union; society, association; (univ.) general council

greña *f*, tangled lock (of hair) (gen. *pl*); tangle, confused mass

gresca *f*, uproar, tumult; fight, row

grey *f*, flock, drove, herd; *ecc* flock, company; people, nation

griego (-ga) a and *n* Greek. *m*, Greek (language); *inf* gibberish

grieta *f*, fissure; crevice; chink; split; flaw; vein (in stone, etc.); *mech* leak

grifo *m*, griffin; tap; cock

grillo *m*, cricket; *bot* shoot; *pl* fetters, irons, chains; *fig* shackles

grima *f*, revulsion, horror

gringo (-ga) *n inf* foreigner (scornful)

gripe *f*, influenza; grippe

gris a and *m*, gray

grisú *m*, firedamp

gritador (-ra) a shouting. *n* shouter

gritar *vi* to shout, yell, scream; howl down; hoot

gritería *f*, shouting, yelling, clamor

grito *m*, shout, yell, shriek, scream. *inf* **poner el g. en el cielo**, to cry to high heaven, complain. **el Grito de Dolores** the Proclamation of Mexican Independence (1810)

Groenlandia Greenland

grosería *f*, rudeness; roughness (of workmanship); ignorance; rusticity

grosero a coarse; rough; thick; unpolished, rude

grotesco a grotesque, absurd

grúa *f*, *mech* crane, hoist, derrick. **g. de pescante**, jib crane. **g. móvil**, traveling crane

gruesa *f*, twelve dozen, gross

grueso a stout, corpulent; large. *m*, bulk, body; major portion, majority; thick stroke (of a letter); thickness, density. **en g.**, in bulk

grulla *f*, *orn* crane

grumo *m*, clot; heart (of vegetables); bunch, cluster; bud

gruñido *m*, grunt; growl

gruñir *vi* to grunt; growl; grumble; squeak, creak (doors, etc.). *Pres. Part.* **gruñendo**. *Pres. Ind.* **gruño, gruñes**, etc.

grupo *m*, knot, cluster; band, group; *art* group; *mech* set

gruta *f*, cavern, grotto

guacamayo *m*, macaw

guadamecí *m*, embossed decorated leather

guadaña *f*, scythe

guagua, *f Caribbean* bus

gualdo a yellow, golden

gualdrapa *f*, saddlecloth, trappings; *inf* tatter, rag

guante *m*, glove. **g. con puño**, gauntlet glove. **g. de boxeo**, boxing glove. **g. de cabritilla**, kid glove. **arrojar el g.**, to throw down the gauntlet; challenge, defy

guapear *vi inf* to make the best of a bad job; *inf* pride oneself on being well dressed

guapeza *f*, prettiness; *inf* resolution, courage; *inf* smartness or showiness of dress; boastful act or behavior

guapo a pretty; handsome; *inf* daring, enterprising; *inf* smart, well-dressed, foppish; *inf* handsome. *m*, braggart, brawler; beau, lover; *inf* fine fellow, son of a gun

guaracha *f*, *Cuba, Puerto Rico* guaracha (vigorous dance in triple meter; music for this dance)

guarda *mf* keeper, guard. *f*, guarding, keeping, custodianship, preservation; guardianship; observance, fulfilment; flyleaf, end page (books); warder (of locks or keys); *mech* guard; guard (of a fan)

guardabarrera *mf* gatekeeper at a level crossing (railroad)

guardabarro *m*, mudguard

guardabosque *mf* gamekeeper

guardabrisa *m*, *aut* windshield; glass candle shield

guardacostas *m*, coast guard; *naut* revenue cutter

guardalmacén *mf* storekeeper

guardameta *mf* goalkeeper

guardamuebles *m*, furniture warehouse

guardapolvo *m*, dustcover; light overcoat; inner case of a pocket watch

guardar *vt* to keep; preserve, retain; maintain, observe; save, put aside, lay away; defend, protect; guard; *vr (with de)* avoid, guard against. **g. compás con**, to be in tune with. **guardarse mucho**, to think twice before. **g. silencio**, to keep silent. **¡Guarda!** Take care! **¡Guárdate del agua mansa!** Still waters run deep!

guardarropa *m*, cloakroom. *mf* cloakroom attendant; keeper of the wardrobe. *m*, wardrobe, clothes closet

guardarropía *f*, theatrical wardrobe

guardería *f*, day nursery, day-care center

guardia *f*, guard, escort; protection; (*mil naut*) watch; regiment, body (of troops); guard (fencing). *m*, guardsman; policeman. **g. de asalto**, armed police. **g. de corps**, royal bodyguard. **g. civil**, civil guard. **g. marina**, midshipman. **g. municipal**, city police. *mil* **montar la g.**, to mount guard

guardián (-ana) *n* keeper; custodian; warden. *m*, watchman; jailer

guardilla f, attic, garret

guarecer vt irr to shelter, protect, aid; preserve, keep; cure; vr take shelter. See **conocer**

guarida f, lair, den; refuge, shelter; haunt, resort

guarismo m, math figure; number, numeral

guarnecer vt irr to decorate, adorn; sew trim, face, border; mil garrison; mas plaster. See **conocer**

guarnecido m, mas plastering

guarnición f, sew trimming, ornament, border, fringe; mech packing; mil garrison; setting (of jewels); guard (of a sword, etc.); pl harness; fittings

guasa f, inf dullness, boringness; joke. **de g.,** jokingly

guasón a inf dull, tedious; humorous, jocose

guatemalteco (-ca) a and n Guatemalan

guayaba f, guava; guava jelly; Lat. Am. also hoax

Guayana Guiana

gubernamental a governmental

gubernativo a governmental; administrative

guedeja f, long tress or lock of hair; forelock; lion's mane

guerra f, war; struggle, fight; fig hostility. inf **dar g.,** to give trouble, annoy. **en g. con,** at war with. **la g. de Cuba,** the Spanish-American War

guerrear vi to make war, fight; oppose

guerrero (-ra) a war, martial; warrior; inf troublesome, annoying. n fighter. m, warrior, soldier

guerrillear vi to wage guerrilla warfare; fight as a guerrilla

guerrillero m, guerrilla fighter

guía mf guide, conductor; adviser, director. f, guide, aid; guidebook; mech guide, slide; directory; signpost. **g. de ferrocarriles,** train schedule, railroad timetable. **g. de teléfonos,** telephone directory

guiar vt to guide; lead, conduct; mech work, control; aut drive; pilot; teach, direct, govern

guija f, pebble

guijarro m, smooth, round pebble; boulder; cobblestone

guijarroso a pebbly, cobbled

guijo m, gravel; granite chips; pebble

guillotina f, guillotine; paper-cutting machine

guillotinar vt to guillotine, decapitate

guinga f, gingham

guiñada f, wink; blink; naut yaw

guiñapo m, rag, tatter; sloven, ragamuffin

guiñar vt to wink; blink; naut yaw; vr wink at each other

guiño m, wink

guión m, royal standard; banner; summary; leader of a dance; gram hyphen; subtitle (in films). **g. mayor,** gram dash

guirigay m, inf gibberish; uproar, babble

guirnalda f, garland, wreath

guisa f, way, manner; will, desire. **a g. de,** in the manner or fashion of

guisado m, cul stew; cooked dish

guisante m, agr pea; pea plant. **g. de olor,** sweetpea

guisar vt to cook; stew; cul prepare, dress; adjust, arrange

guiso m, cooked dish

güisquisoda f Spain highball

guitarra f, guitar

guitarrista mf guitar player

guito a vicious (horses, mules)

gula f, greed, gluttony

gusaniento a worm-eaten; maggoty

gusano m, worm; caterpillar; maggot; meek, downtrodden person. **g. de seda,** silkworm

gusanoso a wormy

gustar vt to taste, savor; try; vi be pleasing, give pleasure; like. **Me gusta el libro,** I like the book. **La película no me gustó,** I didn't like the film. **g. de,** to like, is used only when a person is the subject

gusto m, taste; flavor, savor; pleasure, delight; will, desire; discrimination, taste, style, fashion, manner; whim, caprice. **a g.,** to taste; according to taste. **con mucho g.,** with great pleasure. **dar g.,** to please. **de buen g.,** in good taste

gustoso a savory, palatable; willingly, with pleasure; pleasant, agreeable

haba *f*, broad bean; bean (coffee, cocoa, etc.). **h. de las Indias**, sweetpea. **Esas son habas contadas**, That's a certainty

Habana, la Havana

habanero (-ra), habano (-na) *a* and *n* Havanese, from Havana. *m*. **habano**, Havana cigar

haber *m*, estate, property (gen. *pl*); income; *com* credit balance. **h. monedado**, specie

haber *vt irr* to have; catch, lay hands on (e.g. **El reo fue habido**, The criminal was caught). *v aux* (e.g. **Hemos escrito la carta**, We have written the letter). *v impers* to happen, take place; be. *3rd pers. sing Pres. Ind.* **ha** is replaced by **hay**, meaning there is or there are (e.g. **No hay naranjas en las tiendas**, There are no oranges in the shops). In certain weather expressions, **hay** means it is (e.g. **Hay luna**, It is moonlight). Used of expressions of time, **haber** means to elapse and **ha** (*3rd pers. sing Pres. Ind.*) has adverbial force of 'ago' (e.g. **muchos días ha**, many days ago). **h. de**, to be necessary (less strong than **h. que**) (e.g. **Hemos de verle mañana**, We must see him tomorrow. **He de hacer el papel de Manolo**, I am to play the part of Manolo). **h. que**, to be unavoidable, be essential. With this construction the form **hay** is used (e.g. **Hay que darse prisa**, We (or one) must hurry. **No hay que enojarse**, There's no need to get annoyed. **no h., más que pedir**, to leave nothing to be desired. **no h. tal**, to be no such thing. *inf* **habérselas con**, to quarrel or fall out with. **Hubo una vez . . .** , Once upon a time . . . **¡No hay de qué!**, Don't mention it! Not at all! You're welcome! **No hay para que . . .** , There's no point in. . . . **poco tiempo ha**, a little while ago. **¿Qué hay?** What's the matter? What's new? **¿Qué hay de nuevo?** What's new? *Pres. Ind.* **he, has, ha, hemos, habéis, han.** *Fut.* **habré,** etc. *Condit.* **habría,** etc. *Preterite* **hube, hubiste, hubo, hubimos, hubisteis, hubieron.** *Pres. Subjunc.* **haya,** etc. *Imperf. Subjunc.* **hubiese,** etc.

habichuela *f*, kidney bean

hábil *a* clever; skillful; able; lawful

habilidad *f*, ability; skill; accomplishment; craftsmanship, workmanship

habilidoso *a* accomplished; able; skillful

habilitación *f*, habilitation; paymastership; equipment; furnishing

habilitar *vt* to qualify; equip; furnish; habilitate; enable; *com* capitalize

habitable *a* habitable

habitación *f*, habitation, dwelling; room in a house; residence; (*bot zool*) habitat; caretaking

habitante *m*, inhabitant

hábito *m*, attire; *ecc* habit; use, custom; skill, facility; *pl* vestments; gown, robe. **tomar el h.**, to become a monk or nun

H

habitual *a* habitual, usual

habituar *vt* to accustom; *vr* accustom oneself; grow used (to)

habitud *f*, habit, custom; connection, relationship

habla *f*, speech; language; dialect; discourse. **al h.**, within speaking distance

hablado *a* spoken. **bien h.**, well-spoken; courteous. **mal h.**, ill-spoken; rude

hablador (-ra) *a* talkative; gossipy; *Mexico also* boastful. *n* chatterbox; gossip

habladuría *f*, gossip; impertinent chatter

hablanchín *a inf* chattering, gossiping

hablar *vi* to speak; converse; express oneself; arrange; (*with de*) speak about, discuss; gossip about, criticize; (*with por*) intercede on behalf of; *vt* speak (a language); say, speak; *vr* speak to one another. **no hablarse**, to not be on speaking terms. **h. a gritos**, to shout. **h. alto**, to speak loudly or in strong terms. **h. bien** (or **mal**), to be well- (or ill-) spoken; be polite (or rude). **h. claro**, to speak frankly. **h. consigo** or **h. entre sí**, to talk to oneself. *inf* **h. cristiano, h. en cristiano**, to speak clearly or intelligibly; speak frankly. **hablarlo todo**, to talk too much. **h. por h.**, to talk for talking's sake. *inf* **h. por los codos**, to chatter. **h. sin ton ni son**, to speak foolishly

hablilla *f*, rumor, tittletattle, gossip

hacecillo *m*, small sheaf; small bundle; *bot* fascicle; beam (of light)

hacedero *a* feasible, practicable

hacedor *m*, maker; steward, manager; Creator

hacendado (-da) *a* landed. *n* landowner; *WH* cattle rancher

hacendoso *a* diligent, hard-working

hacer *vt irr* to make; fashion, form, construct; do, perform; cause, effect; arrange, put right; contain; accustom, harden; pack (luggage); imagine, invent, create; improve, perfect; compel, oblige; deliver (speeches); compose; earn; *math* add up to; suppose, imagine (e.g. **Sus padres hacían a María en casa**, Her parents imagined that Mary was at home); put into practice, execute; play the part of or act like (e.g. **h. el gracioso**, to play the buffoon); shed, cast (e.g. **El roble hace sombra**, The oak casts a shadow); assemble, convoke (meetings, gatherings); give off, produce (e.g. **La chimenea hace humo**, The chimney is smoking); perform (plays); (*with el, la, lo, and some nouns*) pretend to be (e.g. **Se hizo el desconocido**, He pretended to be ignorant). (**h.** followed by infin. is sometimes translated by a past participle in English (e.g. **Lo hice h.**, I had it done).) *vi* to matter, be important, signify (e.g. **Su llegada no hace nada al caso,** His arrival makes no difference to the case. **Se me hace muy poco . . . ,** It matters to me very little . . .); be fitting or suitable; concern, be pertinent; match, go with; agree, be in harmony; (*with de*) act as, discharge duties of temporarily (e.g. **h. de camarero,** to be a temporary waiter); (*with por*) try to, attempt to (e.g. **Haremos por decírselo,** We shall try to tell him). *vi impers* 1. lapse of time. English uses the verb 'to be' in both cases, e.g.:

1. **hace buen** (*or* **mal**) **tiempo,** it is fine (or bad) weather. **hace mucho frío,** it is very cold. **hace sol,** it is sunny. **hace viento,** it is windy. **¿Qué tiempo hace?** What is the weather like?

2. **hace** + an expression of time is followed by **que** introducing a clause (e.g. **Hace dos horas que llegamos,** It is two hours since we arrived) or **hace** + an expression of time may be followed by **desde** + a noun (e.g. **Hace dos años desde aquel día,** It is two years since that day)

When an action or state that has begun in the past is still continuing in the present, the Spanish verb is in the Pres. Ind., whereas the English verb is in the Perfect (e.g. **Hace un mes que la veo todos los días,** I have been seeing her every day for a month). This rule holds good with other tenses. English Pluperfect, Future Perfect, Conditional Perfect become in Spanish Imperfect, Future, Conditional, respectively. *naut* **h. agua,** to leak. **h. aguas,** to pass water, urinate. **h. alarde de,** to boast of. **h. América,** to strike it rich. **h. el amor a,** to make love to, court, woo. **h. autoridad,** to be authoritative. **h. a todo,** to have many uses; be adaptable. **h. bancarrota,** to go bankrupt. **h. un berrinche, hacerse un berrinche,** to have a fit, have a tantrum. *fig inf* **h. buena,** to justify. **h. calceta,** to knit. **h. cara** *or* **frente a,** to face; resist. **h. caso,** to take notice, mind (e.g. **¡No hagas caso!** Never mind!). **h. causas,** to bring charges, institute proceedings. **h. cuentas,** to reckon up. **h. daño,** to harm. *inf* **h. de las suyas,** to behave in his usual manner or play one of his usual tricks. **h. diligencias por,** to endeavor to. **h. fiesta,** to take a holiday. **h. fuerza,** to struggle. **h. fuerza a,** *fig* to do violence to (e.g. **Hizo fuerza a sus creencias,** He did violence to his beliefs). **h. h.,** to cause to be made (e.g. **He hecho hacer un vestido,** I have had a dress made). **h. juego,** to make a set, match (e.g. **El sombrero hace juego con el traje,** The hat goes with the dress). **h. la corte (a),** to court, woo. *fig inf* **h. la vista gorda,** to turn a blind eye. **h. la vida del claustro,** to lead a cloistered existence. **h. mal,** to do wrong; be harmful (food, etc.). **h. pedazos,** to break. **h. pinos** (*or* **pinitos**)

to totter; toddle; stagger. *aer* **h. rizos,** to loop the loop. **h. saber,** to make known; notify. **h. seguir,** to forward (letters). **h. señas,** to make signs (wave, beckon, etc.). *inf* **h. una que sea sonada,** to cause a big scandal. **¡Hágame el favor!** Please! *Pres. Ind.* **hago, haces,** etc. *Fut.* **haré,** etc. *Condit.* **haría,** etc. *Imperat.* **haz, haga, hagamos, haced, hagan.** *Preterite* **hice, hiciste, hizo, hicimos, hicisteis, hicieron.** *Pres. Subjunc.* **haga,** etc. *Imperf. Subjunc.* **hiciese,** etc.

hacerse *vr irr* to become (e.g. **Se ha hecho muy importante,** It (or he) has become very important); grow up (e.g. **Miguel se ha hecho hombre,** Michael has grown up (become a man)); develop, mature; pass oneself off as, pretend to be; (*with prep* a) become accustomed to or used to (e.g. **Me haré a este clima,** I shall grow used to this climate); withdraw or retire to (of places); (*with de or con*) provide oneself with. **h. a la vela,** to set sail. **h. a (uno),** to seem (e.g. **Eso que me cuentas se me hace increíble,** What you tell me seems incredible). *inf* **h. chiquito,** to be modest. **h. tarde,** to grow late; *fig* be too late. See **hacer**

hacia *prep* toward, near, about. **h. adelante,** forward, onward

hacienda *f,* country estate, land; property; *pl* domestic tasks; cattle. **h. pública,** public funds. **ministerio de h.,** national treasury, exchequer

hacina *f, agr* stack; heap, pile

hacinamiento *m,* stacking, piling; accumulation

hacinar *vt agr* to stack sheaves; accumulate, amass; pile up, heap

hacha *f,* large candle; torch; ax. **h. pequeña,** hatchet

hachazo *m,* stroke of an ax

hache *f,* name of the letter H

hada *f,* fairy

hado *m,* fate; destiny

Haití Haiti

haitiano (**-na**) *a* and *n* Haitian

halagar *vt* to caress; flatter; coax; please, delight

halago *m,* flattery; coaxing; caress; source of pleasure, delight

halagüeño *a* flattering; pleasing; caressing; hopeful, promising

hálito *m,* breath; vapor; *poet* breeze

hallado *a* and *Past Part.* found, met. **bien h.,** welcome; happy, contented. **mal h.,** unwelcome; uneasy, discontented

hallar *vt* to find; meet; observe; discover; find out; *vr* be present; be, find oneself

hallazgo *m,* finding; thing found; finder's reward

halo *m,* halo

halterofilia *f,* weightlifting

hamaca *f,* hammock

hambre f, hunger; famine; desire, yearning. **tener h.**, to be hungry

hambriento a hungry; famished; *fig* starved (of affection, etc.)

hamo m, fishhook

hampa f, rogue's life; gang of rogues; underworld, slum

hangar m, hangar

haragán (-ana) a lazy, idle. n idler, lazybones

harapiento a ragged

harapo m, tatter, rag

harina f, flour; powder; farina. *inf* **ser h. de otro costal**, to be a horse of another color

harnear vt Lat. Am. to sieve, sift

harnero m, sieve

harón a slothful, slow; lazy, idle

harpillera f, sackcloth, sacking

hartar vt to satiate; tire, annoy; satisfy the appetite; shower (with blows, etc.)

hartazgo m, satiety

harto a satiated; tired (of), adv enough

hartón a Central America, Mexico gluttonous

hartura f, satiety; abundance

hasta prep until; as far as; down or up to. conjunc also, even. **h. la vista**, See you! Ciao! Au revoir! **h. mañana**, until tomorrow

hastío m, loathing; distaste; nausea

hato m, personal clothing; herd of cattle; gang (of suspicious characters); crowd, mob; *inf* group, party. *inf* **liar el h.**, to pack up

hay there is; there are. See haber

haz m, bundle, sheaf; *mil* file; *pl* fasces. f, visage; surface, face. **h. de la tierra**, face of the earth. **h. de luz**, beam of light. *fig* **ser de dos haces**, to be two-faced

haz 2nd pers Imperat **hacer**

hazaña f, exploit, prowess

hazmerreír m, *inf* laughingstock

he *interj* and adv Hallo! Hist! Behold! **Heme aquí!** Here I am. **he aquí**, here is ...

hebilla f, buckle

hebra f, thread; fiber; flesh; *min* vein, streak; filament (textiles); grain (of wood); *pl poet* hair. *inf* **pegar la h.**, to start a conversation

hebreo (-ea) a Hebraic, Jewish. n Jew. m, Hebrew (language)

hechicería f, sorcery; spell, enchantment

hechicero a bewitching, magic; charming, attractive

hechizar vt to bewitch; charm, attract, delight

hechizo m, magic spell; fascination, charm; delight, pleasure; a Lat. Am. homemade, produced locally, locally produced

hecho a developed, mature; accustomed,

used; perfected, finished; ready-made. **h. una furia**, like a fury, very angry. **bien h.**, well-made, well-proportioned; well or rightly done

hecho m, deed, action; fact; happening, event. **los Hechos de los Apóstoles**, the Acts of the Apostles

hechura f, making, make; creation; form; figure, statue; *lit* composition; build (of body); *fig* puppet, creature; *pl* price paid for work done. **de h. sastre**, a tailormade

hectárea f, hectare

heder vi irr to stink; be intolerable. See **entender**

hediondez f, stink, stench

hediondo a stinking; intolerable, pestilential; obscene

hegemonía f, hegemony

helada f, frost. **h. blanca,** hoarfrost

heladera f, refrigerator

helado a frozen; ice-cold; astounded, disdainful. m, iced drink; sherbet, ice cream

helar vt irr to freeze; ice, chill; astound; discourage; vr become iced; freeze; become ice-cold. v impers to freeze. See **acertar**

helecho m, fern

hélice f, spiral, helical line; screw, propeller; *geom* helix; *ast* Ursa Major

helicóptero m, aer helicopter

helio m, helium

helvecio (-ia) a and n Helvetian

hembra f, female; *inf* woman; nut of a screw; eye of a hook. *inf* **una real h.,** a fine figure of a woman

hemiciclo m, hemicycle; floor (of a legislative building)

hemisférico a hemispherical

hemisferio m, hemisphere

hemofilia f, hemophilia.

hemoglobina f, hemoglobin

hemorragia f, hemorrhage

hemorroides f, hemorrhoids

henchido a swollen

henchimiento m, swelling; inflation; filling

henchir vt irr to fill; stuff; swell. *Pres. Ind.* **hincho, hinches, hinche, hinchen.** *Pres. Part.* **hinchiendo.** *Pres. Subjunc.* **hincha,** etc. *Imperf. Subjunc.* **hinchiese,** etc. *Imperat.* **hinche, hincha, hinchamos, henchid, hinchan**

hendedura f, fissure; rift

hender vt irr to split, crack; *fig* cleave (air, water, etc.); make one's way through. See **entender**

hendidura f, split, fissure, crack, chink

hendija f, Lat. Am. crack, crevice

heno m, hay

hepático a hepatic

heráldica f, heraldry

heraldo m, herald; harbinger

herbaje m, herbage; pasture, grass; thick woolen cloth

herbario m, herbalist, botanist; herbarium. a herbal

herbívoro a herbivorous

hercúleo a herculean

heredad f, landed property; country estate

heredar vt to inherit; make a deed of gift to; inherit characteristics, etc.; take as heir

heredera f, heiress

heredero m, heir; inheritor. **h. aparente,** heir apparent. **presunto h.,** heir presumptive

hereditario a hereditary

hereje mf heretic

herejía f, heresy

herencia f, inheritance; heredity; heritage

herético a heretical

herida f, wound; insult; anguish. **h. contusa,** contusion. **h. penetrante,** deep wound

herir vt irr to wound; strike, harm; fig pierce (of sun's rays); fig pluck (strings of a musical instrument); impress (the senses); affect (the emotions); offend (gen. of words). Pres. Part. **hiriendo.** Pres. Ind. **hiero, hieres, hiere, hieren.** Preterite **hirió, hirieron.** Pres. Subjunc. **hiera, hieras, hiera, hiramos, hiráis, hieran.** Imperf. Subjunc. **hiriese,** etc.

hermafrodita a and mf hermaphrodite

hermana f, sister; twin, pair (of things). **h. de leche,** foster sister. **h. política,** sister-in-law

hermanar vt to join; mate; harmonize; Chile to pair (like socks); vt and vr be the spiritual brother of, be compatible

hermanastra f, stepsister

hermanastro m, stepbrother

hermandad f, brotherhood; friendship, intimacy; relationship (of one thing to another); confraternity. **Santa H.,** Spanish rural police force instituted in the fifteenth century

hermano m, brother; pair, twin (of things); ecc brother. **h. de raza,** member of the same race. **h. político,** brother-in-law

hermético a hermetic

hermosear vt to embellish, beautify, adorn

hermoso a beautiful; shapely; handsome; fine, wonderful (weather, view, etc.)

hermosura f, beauty; pleasantness, attractiveness, perfection of form; belle

hernia f, hernia

héroe m, hero

heroicidad f, heroism

heroico a heroic

heroína f, heroine

heroismo m, heroism

herpes m pl, or f pl, herpes

herrada f, pail

herrador m, blacksmith

herradura f, horseshoe

herraje m, ironwork; Lat. Am. horseshoe

herramienta f, tool; set of tools

herrar vt irr to shoe horses; brand (cattle); decorate with iron. See **acertar**

herrería f, forge; ironworks; blacksmith's shop; clamor, tumult, confusion

herrero m, smith

herrete m, ferrule, tag

herrumbre f, rust; taste of iron

herrumbroso a rusty

hervidero m, boiling, bubbling; fig ebullition; swarm, crowd

hervir vi irr to boil; foam and froth (sea); seethe (emotions); surge (crowds); (with en) abound in, swarm with. See **sentir**

hervor m, boiling; ebullition, vigor, zest; seething, agitation

hesitación f, hesitation, doubt, uncertainty

hesitar vi to hesitate, vacillate

heterodina a f, rad heterodyne

heterodoxia f, heterodoxy

heterodoxo a heterodox

heterogeneidad f, heterogeneity

heterogéneo a heterogeneous

hético a hectic, consumptive

hexagonal a hexagonal

hexágono m, hexagon

hez f, (gen. pl **heces**) lees, dregs

hiato m, hiatus

hibridación f, hybridization

híbrido a and m, hybrid

hidalgo (**-ga**) n noble, aristocrat. a noble; illustrious; generous

hidalguía f, nobility; generosity, nobility of spirit

hidrato m, hydrate. **h. de carbono,** carbohydrate

hidráulica f, hydraulics

hidráulico a hydraulic

hidroavión m, flying boat

hidrocéfalo a hydrocephalic

hidrodinámica f, hydrodynamics

hidroeléctrico a hydroelectric

hidrofobia f, hydrophobia; rabies

hidrógeno m, hydrogen

hidropesía f, dropsy

hidroplano m, seaplane

hidroterapia f, hydrotherapy

hiedra f, ivy

hiel f, gall, bile, bitterness, affliction; pl troubles

hielo m, ice, frost; freezing, icing; stupefaction; indifference, coldness. inf **estar hecho un h.,** to be as cold as ice

hiena f, hyena

hierba *f,* grass; small plant; herb. **h. cana,** groundsel. **mala h.,** weed

hierbabuena *f, bot* mint

hierra *f,* branding time

hierro *m,* iron; brand with hot iron; iron or steel head of a lance, etc.; instrument or shape made of iron; weapon of war. *pl* fetters. **h. colado,** cast iron. **h. dulce,** wrought iron. **h. en planchas,** sheet iron. **h. viejo,** scrap iron

hígado *m,* liver; courage; *Central America, Mexico also* nuisance

higiene *f,* hygiene; cleanliness, neatness. **h. privada,** personal hygiene. **h. pública,** public health

higiénico *a* hygienic

higo *m,* fig. **h. chumbo,** prickly pear

higuera *f,* fig tree

hija *f,* daughter; native of a place; offspring

hijastro (-ra) *n* stepchild

hijo *m,* son; child; native of a place; offspring; shoot, sprout; *pl* descendants. **h. de la cuna,** foundling. **h. de leche,** foster child. **h. natural,** natural child. **h. político,** son-in-law

hijuela *f,* little daughter; small mattress; small drain; side road; accessory, subordinate thing; piece of material for widening a garment; *law* part of an inheritance; *Lat. Am.* rural property

hila *f,* row, line; gut; *surg* lint (gen. *pl*)

hilacha *f,* thread raveled from cloth; fiber, filament. **h. de vidrio,** spun glass

hilado *m,* spinning; thread, yarn

hilandería *f,* spinning; spinning mill; mill. **h. de algodón,** cotton mill

hilandero (-ra) *n* spinner

hilar *vt* to spin; reason, infer, discourse

hilaridad *f,* hilarity; quiet happiness

hilaza *f,* yarn

hilera *f,* line, file, row; fine yarn; *mil* file, rank; *met* wire drawer; *mas* course (of bricks)

hilo *m,* thread; linen; wire; mesh (spiders, silkworm's web, etc.); edge (of a blade); thin stream (of liquid); thread (of discourse)

hilván *m, sew* basting; tack

hilvanar *vt sew* to baste

himen *m,* hymen

himeneo *m,* marriage, wedding

himno *m,* hymn

hin *m,* whinny, neigh

hincapié *m,* foothold. **hacer h.,** to insist, make a stand

hincar *vt* to thrust in; drive in, sink; *vr* kneel. **h. el diente,** to bite. **h. la uña,** to scratch. **hincarse de rodillas,** to kneel down

hinchado *a* puffed up, vain; pompous, high-flown, redundant (style)

hinchar *vt* to inflate; puff out (the chest);

swell (of a river, etc.); exaggerate (events); *vr* swell; grow vain, be puffed up

hinchazón *f,* swelling; vanity, presumption; pomposity, euphuism (style)

hinojo *m, bot* fennel; knee. **de hinojos,** on bended knee

hipar *vi* to hiccup; pant (of dogs); be overanxious; be overtired; sob, cry

hipérbole *f,* hyperbole

hiperbólico *a* hyperbolical

hipertrofiarse *vr* to hypertrophy

hipnosis *f,* hypnosis

hipnótico *a* hypnotic. *m,* hypnotic drug

hipnotismo *m,* hypnotism

hipnotización *f,* hypnotization

hipnotizar *vt* to hypnotize

hipo *m,* hiccup; sob; longing, desire; dislike, disgust

hipocondría *f,* hypochondria

hipocondríaco (-ca) *a* hypochondriacal. *n* hypochondriac

hipocresía *f,* hypocrisy

hipócrita *a* hypocritical. *mf* hypocrite

hipodérmico *a* hypodermic

hipódromo *m,* hippodrome, racetrack

hipopótamo *m,* hippopotamus

hipoteca *f,* mortgage

hipotecable *a* mortgageable

hipotecar *vt* to mortgage

hipótesis *f,* hypothesis

hipotético *a* hypothetical

hirsuto *a* hirsute, hairy

hirviente *a* boiling

hispánico *a* Spanish

hispanismo *m,* Hispanism

hispanista *mf* Hispanist

hispanoamericano (-na) *a* and *n* Spanish-American, Hispano-American

histeria *f,* hysteria

histérico *a* hysterical; hysteric

histerismo *m, med* hysteria

historia *f,* history; narrative, story; tale; *inf* gossip (gen. *pl*); *art* historical piece. **h. natural,** natural history. **h. sagrada,** biblical history. *fig inf* **dejarse de historias,** to stop beating around the bush

historiador (-ra) *n* historian

historiar *vt* to narrate, relate; record, chronicle

histórico *a* historical; historic

historieta *f,* short story; anecdote

historiografía *f,* historiography

histriónico *a* histrionic

hitlerismo *m,* Hitlerism

hito *m,* milestone; boundary mark; *fig* mark, target. **de h. en h.,** from head to foot

hocico *m,* snout; *inf* face, mug; *inf* angry gesture; *naut* prow. **meter el h.,** to stick one's nose into other people's business

hogaño *adv inf* during this year; at the present time

hogar m, hearth, fireplace; home, house; family life; firebox (of a locomotive)

hoguera f, bonfire

hoja f, bot leaf; petal; sheet (metal, paper, etc.); leaf (door, window); sword. **h. de servicios,** service or professional record. **h. de tocino,** side of bacon. **h. extraordinaria,** extra, special edition (of a newspaper). **h. volante,** handbill, supplement. **volver la h.,** to turn over (pages); change one's opinion; turn the conversation

hojalata f, tin plate

hojalatería f, tinware; tin shop

hojalatero m, tinsmith

hojalda, hojalde m = **hojaldre**

hojaldre m, or f, puff pastry

hojarasca f, withered leaves; excessive foliage; rubbish, trash

hojear vt to turn the leaves of a book; skip, skim, read quickly; vi exfoliate

hojuela f, dim little leaf; bot leaflet; pancake

¡hola! interj Hallo! Goodness!

Holanda Holland

holandés (**-esa**) a and n Dutchman (-woman) m, Dutch (language)

holgado a leisured, free; loose, wide; comfortable; well-off, rich

holganza f, repose, leisure, ease; idleness; pleasure

holgar vi irr to rest; be idle; be glad; be unused or unnecessary (things). vr enjoy oneself, amuse oneself; be glad. See **contar**

holgazán (**-ana**) a idle. n idler

holgazanería f, idleness, sloth

holgorio m, rejoicing, festivity, merriment

holgura f, enjoyment, merrymaking; width; comfort, ease; mech free play

hollar vt irr to trample under foot; humiliate. See **degollar**

hollejo m, peel, thin skin (of fruit); agr chaff

hollín m, soot

holocausto m, holocaust. **el H.** the Holocaust

hológrafo m, holograph

hombradía f, manliness; courage

hombre m, man; adult; omber (cards). interj **¡h.!** inf Old fellow! You don't say so! **¡h. al agua!** Man overboard! **h. de bien,** honest, honorable man. **h. de estado,** statesman. **h. de muchos oficios,** jack-of-all-trades. **h. de negocios,** businessman; man of affairs. **h. de pro,** worthy man; famous man. **ser muy h.,** to be a real man, be very manly

hombrera f, epaulette; shoulderpad

hombro m, shoulder. **echar al h.,** to shoulder; undertake, take the responsibility of. **encogerse de hombros,** to

shrug one's shoulders; be indifferent or uninterested

hombruno a inf mannish (of a woman)

homenaje m, allegiance; homage; veneration, respect

homeópata a homeopathic. mf homeopath

homicida a murderous, homicidal. mf murderer (-ess)

homicidio m, homicide (act)

homilía f, homily

homogéneo a homogeneous

homónimo a homonymous. m, homonym

homosexual a and mf homosexual

honda f, sling, catapult, slingshot

hondear vt naut to sound, plumb; naut unload; Lat. Am. to hit with a slingshot

hondo a deep; low; fig profound; deep, intense (emotion). m, depth

hondón m, depth, recess

hondonada f, hollow; glen; valley

hondura f, depth

hondureño (**-ña**) a and n Honduran

honestidad f, honorableness; virtue; respectability; modesty; courtesy

honesto a honorable, virtuous; modest; honest, just

hongo m, fungus; toadstool; bowler hat

honor m, honor; fame; reputation (women); modesty (women); praise; pl rank, position; honors

honorable a honorable

honorario a honorary. m, honorarium, fee

honorífico a honorary; honorable

honra f, self-respect, honor, personal dignity; reputation; chastity and modesty (women); pl obsequies

honradez f, honesty; honorableness; integrity; respectability

honrado a honest; honorable

honrar vt to respect; honor; vr to be honored

honroso a honor-giving, honorable

¡hopa! interj Argentina cut it out!, stop it!

hora f, hour; opportune moment; pl book of hours. **horas hábiles,** working hours. **horas muertas,** wee hours; wasted time. **a última h.,** at the last minute. **dar la h.,** to strike the hour. **¿Qué h. es?** What time is it?

horadar vt to bore, pierce

horario a hourly. m, timetable; hour hand of a clock; watch

horca f, gibbet, gallows; agr pitchfork; fork; prop for trees

horcajadas (a) adv astride

horcajadura f, crotch

horchata f, drink made of chufas or crushed almonds

horda f, horde

horizontal a horizontal

horizonte *m*, horizon. **nuevos horizontes,** new opportunities

horma *f*, mold; cobbler's last; stone wall. *fig inf* **hallar la h. de su zapato,** to find what suits one; meet one's match

hormiga *f*, ant

hormigón *m*, concrete. **h. armado,** ferro-concrete

hormiguear *vi* to itch; crowd, swarm

hormiguero *m*, anthill; crowd, swarm

hormona *f*, hormone

hornero (-ra) *n* baker

horno *m*, oven; furnace; kiln; bakery. **h. alfarero,** firing oven (for pottery). **h. de cocina,** kitchen stove. **h. de cuba,** blast furnace. **h. de ladrillo,** brick kiln. **alto h.,** iron-smelting furnace

horóscopo *m*, horoscope

horquilla *f*, forked stick; hairpin; hatpin; *agr* fork; hook. **viraje en h.,** hairpin turn

horrendo *a* horrible, frightful

horrible *a* horrible

horrífico *a* horrific

horripilante *a* hair-raising, horrifying

horrisono *a poet* horrid-sounding, terrifying

horror *m*, horror; horribleness; atrocity, enormity

horrorizar *vt* to horrify; *vr* be horrified, be terrified

horroroso *a* dreadful, horrible; horrid; *inf* hideous, most ugly

hortaliza *f*, green vegetable, garden produce

hortelano *m*, market gardener

horticultura *f*, horticulture

hosco *a* dark brown; unsociable, sullen; crabbed

hospedaje *m*, lodging; board, payment

hospedar *vt* to lodge, receive as a guest; *vr* and *vi* lodge, stay

hospicio *m*, hospice; almshouse, workhouse; lodging; orphanage

hospital *m*, hospital; hospice. **h. de sangre,** field hospital

hospitalario *a* hospitable

hospitalidad *f*, hospitality; hospitableness; hospital

hostelero (-ra) *n* innkeeper

hostería *f*, hostelry; inn

hostia *f*, ecc wafer, Host; sacrificial victim

hostigamiento *m*, harassment. **h. sexual,** sexual harassment

hostigar *vt* to chastise; harass; tease, annoy

hostil *a* hostile

hostilidad *f*, hostility

hotel *m*, hotel; villa

hotelero (-ra) *n* hotelkeeper

hoy *adv* today; at present. **h. día** *or* **h. en día,** today. **h. por h.,** day by day; at the present time. **de h. en adelante,** from today forward

hoya *f*, hole; grave; valley, glen; bed (of a river)

hoyo *m*, hole; pockmark; grave; hollow

hoyuelo *m*, *dim* little hole; dimple

hoz *f*, sickle; defile

hozar *vt* to root (pigs, etc.)

hucha *f*, large chest; strongbox; savings

hueco *a* empty; hollow; vain; hollow (sound); pompous (style); spongy, soft; inflated. *m*, hollow; interval of time or place; *inf* vacancy; gap in a wall, etc.

huelga *f*, strike; leisure; lying fallow; merrymaking. **h. de brazos caídos,** sit-down strike. **h. patronal,** lockout strike

huelguista *mf* striker

huella *f*, footprint, track; footstep; tread (of stairs); *print* impression; vestige, trace. **h. digital,** fingerprint

huérfano (-na) *n* orphan. *a* unprotected, uncared for

huero *a* addled; empty, hollow

huerta *f*, kitchen garden; orchard; irrigation land

huerto *m*, orchard; kitchen garden

hueso *m*, bone; stone (of fruit); kernel, core; drudgery; cheap, useless thing of poor quality. *inf* **no dejar un h. sano,** to tear (a person) to pieces. **tener los huesos molidos,** to be tired out; be bruised

huésped (-da) *n* guest; host; innkeeper

hueste *f*, (gen. *pl*) army on the march; host; party, supporters

huesudo *a* bony

huevo *m*, egg. **h. duro,** hard-boiled egg. **h. estrellado,** fried egg. **h. pasado por agua,** soft-boiled egg. **huevos revueltos,** scrambled eggs

huida *f*, flight, escape; bolting (of a horse); outlet

huir *vi irr* to flee; fly (of time); elope; run away, bolt; (*with de*) avoid. *Pres. Part.* **huyendo.** *Pres. Ind.* **huyo, huyes, huyen.** *Preterite* **huyó, huyeron.** *Pres. Subjunc.* **huya,** etc. *Imperf. Subjunc.* **huyese,** etc.

hule *m*, oilcloth; rubber; *Central America, Mexico* rubber tree

hulla *f*, coal mine, coal, soft coal

hullera *f*, colliery, coal mine

humanidad *f*, humanity; human nature; human weakness; compassion; affability; *inf* stoutness; *pl* study of humanities

humanismo *m*, humanism

humanista *mf* humanist. *a* humanistic

humanitario *a* humanitarian

humanizar *vt* to humanize

humano *a* human; understanding, sympathetic. *m*, human being

humareda *f*, cloud of smoke

humear *vi* to give forth smoke; give one-self airs; *Lat. Am.* fumigate; beat, thrash

humedad *f,* humidity; dampness; mois-ture

humedecer *vt irr* to moisten, wet, damp; *vr* grow moist. See **conocer**

húmedo *a* humid; damp; wet

humildad *f,* humility; lowliness; humble-ness

humilde *a* meek; lowly; humble

humillación *f,* humiliation

humillante *a* humiliating; debasing; mortifying

humillar *vt* to humble; humiliate; *vr* humble oneself

humo *m,* smoke; vapor, fume; vanity, airs

humor *m, med* humor; temperament, disposition; mood. **de buen h.,** good-tempered. **de mal h.,** ill-tempered

humorada *f,* humorous saying, extrava-gance, witticism

humorista *mf* humorist

humorístico *a* humorous

humoso *a* smoky, reeky

hundible *a* sinkable

hundido *a* sunken (of cheeks, etc.); hol-low, deep-set (of eyes)

hundimiento *m,* sinking; collapse; sub-sidence (of earth)

hundir *vt* to sink; oppress; confound; de-stroy, ruin; *vr* collapse (building); sink; *fig inf* disappear

húngaro (**-ra**) *a* and *n* Hungarian. *m,* Hungarian (language)

Hungría Hungary

huracán *m,* hurricane

huraña *f,* shyness, unsociableness; diffi-dence; wildness (of animals, etc.)

huraño *a* shy, unsociable; diffident; wild (of animals, etc.)

hurgar *vt* to stir; poke, rake; touch; rouse, incite. *vr* pick one's nose

hurgón *m,* fire rake, poker; *inf* sword

hurgonada *f,* raking (of the fire, etc.)

hurguete *mf, Argentina* busybody, nosy parker

hurón (**-ona**) *n* ferret. *a* shy, unsociable

¡hurra! *interj* Hurrah!

hurtadillas (**a**) *adv* by stealth, secretly

hurtar *vt* to steal; encroach (sea, river); plagiarize; *vr* hide oneself

hurto *m,* theft. **coger con el h. en las manos,** *fig* to catch red-handed

husmear *vt* to sniff out; *inf* pry; *vi* smell bad (of meat)

huso *m,* spindle; bobbin

¡huy! *interj* (denoting pain or surprise) Oh!

ibérico a Iberian

ibero (-ra) a and n Iberian

icnografía f, ichnography

icnográfico a ichnographical

icono m, icon

iconoclasta a iconoclastic. mf iconoclast

iconografía f, iconography

ictericia f, jaundice

ida f, setting out, departure, going; impetuous action; precipitancy; track, trail (of animals). **de i. y vuelta,** round trip (of tickets)

idea f, idea. inf **¡Qué ideas tienes!** What (odd) ideas you have!

ideal a ideal; perfect. m, model; ideal

idealidad f, ideality

idealismo m, idealism

idealista a idealistic. mf idealist

idealización f, idealization

idealizar vt to idealize

idear vt to imagine; devise; plan; design; draft, draw up

ideático, -a a, Lat. Am. eccentric

ídem adv idem

idéntico a identical

identidad f, identity

identificable a identifiable

identificación f, identification

identificar vt to identify; recognize; vr (with con) identify oneself with

ideología f, ideology. **i. racista,** racial ideology

ideológico a ideological

ideólogo (-ga) n ideologist; dreamer, planner

idioma m, language, tongue

idiomático a idiomatic

idiosincrásico a idiosyncratic

idiota a idiot; idiotic. mf idiot

idiotez f, idiocy

idiotismo m, gram idiom; ignorance

idiotizar vt, Lat. Am. to drive crazy, drive insane.

idólatra a idolatrous; adoring. mf idolater, heathen

idolatrar vt to idolize; worship, love excessively

idolatría f, idolatry; adoration, idolization

ídolo m, idol

idóneo a suitable; competent, fit

iglesia f, church. **i. colegial,** collegiate church. **cumplir con la i.,** to discharge one's religious duties. **llevar a una mujer a la i.,** to lead a woman to the altar

ignición f, ignition

ignominioso a ignominious

ignorancia f, ignorance. **pretender i.,** to plead ignorance

ignorante a ignorant; unaware, uninformed. mf ignoramus

ignorar vt to be unaware of, not to know

ignoto a unknown, undiscovered

igual a equal; level; even, smooth; very similar; alike; uniform; proportionate; unchanging; constant; indifferent; same. mf equal. m, math equal sign. **al i.,** equally. **sin i.,** peerless, without equal. **Me es completamente i.,** It's all the same to me

igualación f, equalization; leveling; arrangement; agreement; matching; math equation

igualar vt to equalize, make equal; match; pair; level, flatten; smooth; adjust; arrange, agree upon; weigh, consider; math equate; vi be equal

igualdad f, equality; uniformity, harmony; evenness; smoothness; identity; sameness. **i. de ánimo,** equability, equanimity

igualmente adv equally; the same, likewise

ijada f, side, flank; pain in the side

ilación f, connection, reference

ilegal a illegal

ilegalidad f, illegality

ilegible a illegible, unreadable

ilegítimo a illegitimate; false

ileso a unharmed, unhurt

iletrado a unlettered, uncultured

iliberal a illiberal; narrow-minded

iliberalidad f, illiberality; narrow-mindedness

ilícito a illicit

ilimitado a unlimited, boundless

iliterato a illiterate, uncultured

ilógico a illogical

iluminación f, illumination; lighting. **i. intensiva,** floodlighting

iluminador (-ra) a lighting; illuminating. n art illuminator

iluminar vt to illuminate; light; art illuminate; enlighten; vr. Lat. Am. get drunk

ilusión f, illusion; illusoriness; hope; dream

ilusionarse vr to harbor illusions

ilusivo a deceptive, illusive

iluso a deceived, deluded; dreamy; visionary

ilusorio a illusory; deceptive; null

ilustración f, illustration, picture; enlightenment; explanation; illustrated newspaper or magazine; erudition, knowledge; example, illustration

ilustrado a erudite, learned; knowledgeable, well-informed

ilustrador (-ra) a illustrative. n illustrator

ilustrar vt to explain, illustrate; enlighten, instruct; illustrate (books); make illustrious; inspire with divine light

ilustrativo a illustrative

ilustre a illustrious, distinguished

imagen f, image; effigy, statue; idea; metaphor, simile. **i. nítida,** sharp image

imaginable a imaginable

imaginación f, imagination

imaginar vi to imagine; vt to suppose, conjecture; discover, invent; imagine. **¡Imagínese!** Just imagine!

imaginario a imaginary

imaginativa f, imagination; common sense

imaginativo a imaginative

imaginería f, imagery

imán m, magnet; attraction, charm; imam

imanar vt to magnetize

imbécil a imbecile; stupid, idiotic. mf imbecile

imbecilidad f, imbecility; folly, stupidity

imberbe a beardless. inf **joven i.,** stripling

imborrable a ineffaceable

imbuir vt irr to imbue. See **huir**

imitable a imitable

imitación f, imitation; reproduction, copy

imitado a imitation; imitated

imitador (**-ra**) a imitation; imitative. n imitator

imitar vt to imitate; counterfeit

imitativo a imitative

impacción f, impact

impaciencia f, impatience

impacientar vt to make impatient, annoy; vr grow impatient

impaciente a impatient

impacto m, impact. **i. de lleno,** direct hit

impago, -a Lat. Am. remaining to be paid, still to be paid, unpaid; m non-payment

impalpable a impalpable

impar a odd; unpaired; single, uneven. **número impar,** odd number

imparcial a impartial

imparcialidad f, impartiality

impartible a indivisible

impasibilidad f, impassivity, indifference

impasible a impassive

impavidez f dauntlessness; serenity in the face of danger; Lat. Am. cheek, cheekiness, effrontery

impávido a dauntless; calm, composed, imperturbable; Lat. Am. cheeky, fresh

impecabilidad f, impeccability, perfection

impecable a impeccable, perfect

impedido a disabled

impedimento m, obstacle; hindrance; law impediment

impedir vt irr to impede; obstruct; prevent; thwart; disable; delay; poet amaze. See **pedir**

impeler vt to push; incite; drive; urge

impender vt to spend money

impenetrabilidad f, impenetrability; imperviousness; obscurity, difficulty

impenetrable a impenetrable, dense; impervious; fig unfathomable; obscure

impenitencia f, impenitence

impenitente a impenitent

impensado a unexpected, unforeseen

imperante a ruling, dominant

imperar vi to rule; command

imperativo a commanding. a and m, gram imperative

imperdible m, safety pin

imperdonable a unpardonable, inexcusable

imperecedero a undying, eternal, everlasting

imperfección f, imperfection, inadequacy; fault, blemish; weakness

imperfecto a imperfect; inadequate; faulty. a and m, gram imperfect

imperial a imperial. f, upper deck of a bus or streetcar

impericia f, inexpertness; unskillfulness; unhandiness

imperio m, empire; rule, reign; command, sway; imperial dignity; arrogance, haughtiness. fig inf **valer un i.,** to be priceless

imperioso a imperious

imperito a inexpert; clumsy, unskilled

impermeabilizar vt to waterproof

impermeable a watertight, impermeable; impervious. m, raincoat, mackintosh

impertérrito a unafraid, dauntless

impertinencia f, impertinence, insolence; peevishness; fancy, whim; overexactness, meticulousness; interference, intrusion

impertinente a impertinent; irrelevant; inopportune; officious, interfering

imperturbabilidad f, imperturbability

imperturbable a calm, imperturbable

impetrar vt to obtain by entreaty; implore

ímpetu m, impetus, momentum; speed, swiftness; violence

impetuosidad f, impetuosity

impetuoso a impetuous; precipitate

impiedad f, cruelty, harshness; irreligion

impío a impious, wicked; irreverent, irreligious

implacabilidad f, implacability, relentless

implantación f, inculcation, implantation

implantar vt to inculcate, implant (ideas, etc.)

implicación f, implication; contradiction (in terms); complicity

implicar vt to implicate; imply, infer; involve, entangle; vi imply contradiction (gen. with negatives)

implicatorio a contradictory; implicated (in crime)

implícito a implicit; implied

implorante a imploring

implorar vt to implore, entreat

impolítico a impolitic; unwise, inexpedient; tactless

imponderable a imponderable, immeasurable; most excellent

imponencia f. Lat. Am. impressiveness

imponente a imposing, impressive; awe-inspiring

imponer vt irr to exact, impressive; impose; malign, accuse falsely; instruct, acquaint; fig impress (with respect, etc.); invest or deposit (money); print impose; give, bestow (a name). vr assert oneself. See **poner**

imponible a taxable; ratable

impopular a unpopular

importación f, com importation; import

importador (-ra) a import, importing. n importer

importancia f, importance; magnitude

importante a important

importar vi to matter; be important; concern, interest; vt amount to; import; include, comprise. ¡No importa! It doesn't matter! Never mind!

importe m, amount; value, cost. i. bruto, gross or total amount. i. líquido or neto, net amount

importunación f, importuning; importunity

importunadamente adv importunately

importunar vt to importune, pester

importunidad (also **importunación**) f, importunity

importuno a importunate, inopportune, ill-timed; persistent; tedious

imposibilidad f, impossibility

imposibilitado a disabled, crippled; incapable, unable

imposibilitar vt to disable; render unable; make impossible

imposible a impossible

imposición f, imposition; exaction; tax, duty, tribute; print makeup **i. de manos,** ecc laying on of hands

impostor (-ra) n impostor

impostura f, swindle, imposture; aspersion, slur, imputation

impotable a undrinkable

impotencia f, impotence

impotente a impotent; powerless

impracticable a impracticable; impossible; impassable (roads, etc.)

imprecar vt to imprecate, curse

impregnación f, impregnation, permeation, saturation

impregnar vt impregnate; to permeate; vr become impregnated

impremeditado a unpremeditated

imprenta f, printing; printing house or office; print; letterpress

impreparación f, unpreparedness

imprescindible a indispensable, essential

impresión f, printing; impression; effect; influence; imprint, stamp; print impression; print. **impresión digital,** fingerprint

impresionable a impressionable, susceptible

impresionante a imposing; moving, affecting

impresionar vt to impress; affect; fix in the mind; fig move deeply, stir; (rad cinema) record

impreso m, (gen. pl) printed matter

impresor m, printer

imprevisión f, lack of foresight; improvidence

imprevisto a unforeseen, unexpected, sudden

imprevistos m pl, incidental expenses

imprimar vt to prime (of paint)

imprimir vt to print; stamp; impress upon (the mind)

improbable a improbable

improbo a vicious, corrupt, dishonest; hard, arduous

improductivo a unproductive; unprofitable, fruitless

impronta f, art cast, mold

impronunciable a unpronounceable; ineffable

improperio m, insult, affront

impropiedad f, inappropriateness; unsuitableness; impropriety

impropio a unsuitable; inappropriate; inadequate; improper

improporcionado a disproportionate, out of proportion

impróvido a improvident, heedless

improvisación f, improvisation

improvisador (-ra) n improviser

improvisamente adv unexpectedly, suddenly

improvisar vt to improvise

improviso, improvisto a unexpected, unforeseen. **al** (or **de**) **improviso,** unexpectedly

imprudencia f, imprudence, rashness, indiscretion

imprudente a imprudent, unwise, rash

impúbero a below the age of puberty

impudencia f, impudence, impertinence

impudente a brazen, impudent

impudicia f, immodesty, brazenness

impúdico a immodest, brazen

impuesto m, tax; duty. **i. de utilidades,** income tax. **i. sucesorio,** inheritance tax

impugnable a impugnable, refutable

impugnación f, refutation; contradiction

impugnar vt to refute, contradict; oppose; criticize

impulsar vt to impel; prompt, cause; drive, operate, propel

impulsión f, impulse; impetus; mech operation, driving; propulsion

impulsivo a impulsive; irreflexive, precipitate

impulso m, stimulus, incitement; impulse, desire; mech drive, impulse

impulsor (-ra) a driving, impelling. n driver, operator

impune a unpunished

impunemente adv with impunity

impureza f, impurity; lack of chastity; obscenity, indecency

impurificar vt to defile; make impure; adulterate

impuro a impure; adulterated; polluted; immoral, unchaste

imputar vt to impute; attribute

inacabable a endless, interminable, ceaseless; wearisome

inaccesible a inaccessible; incomprehensible

inacción f, inaction

inaceptable a unacceptable

inactivo a inactive; idle; unemployed; naut laid-up

inadecuado a inadequate, insufficient

inadvertencia f, inadvertence; oversight, mistake, slip

inadvertido a unnoticed; inattentive; inadvertent, unintentional; negligent

inafectado a unaffected, natural

inagotable a inexhaustible, unfailing; abundant

inaguantable a unbearable, intolerable

inajenable a inalienable

inalterable a unalterable

inamovibilidad f, immovability

inamovible a immovable

inanición f, inanition

inanimado a inanimate

inapagable a inextinguishable

inapelable a unappealable; irremediable, inevitable

inapetencia f, lack of appetite

inaplazable a undeferable, unable to be postponed

inaplicación f, laziness, inattention, negligence

inaplicado a lazy; inattentive; careless

inapreciable a inappreciable; invaluable

inarticulado a inarticulate

inasequible a unattainable; out of reach

inaudito a unheard of, unprecedented; extraordinary, strange

inauguración f, inauguration; induction; inception, commencement

inaugurar vt to inaugurate; induct

inaveriguable a unascertainable

inca mf Inca

incaico a Incan

incalificable a indescribable, unclassable; vile

incandescencia f, incandescence, white heat

incandescente a incandescent

incansable a indefatigable; unflagging; unwearying

incapacidad f, incapacity; incompetence

incapacitar vt to incapacitate; disable

incapaz a incapable, incompetent; inefficient

incasable a unmarriageable; antimarriage

incásico, -a a, Lat. Am. Inca

incautarse vr to seize, take possession (of)

incauto a incautious; unwary

incendiar vt to set on fire, set alight

incendiario (-ia) a and n incendiary

incendio m, conflagration, fire; consuming passion

incensar vt irr ecc to cense, incense; flatter. See **acertar**

incensario m, incense burner, incensory

incentivo m, incentive; encouragement

incertidumbre f, uncertainty, incertitude

incesable, incesante a incessant, continuous

incesto m, incest

incestuoso a incestuous

incidencia f, incidence

incidente a incidental. m, incident, event, occurrence

incidir vi (with en) to incur, fall into (e.g. **Incidió en el pecado**, He fell into sin)

incienso m, incense; flattery

incierto a untrue, false; uncertain; unknown

incinerador m, incinerator

incinerar vt incinerate, reduce to ashes

incipiente a incipient

incircunciso a uncircumcised

incisión f, incision

incisivo a sharp, keen; incisive, sarcastic, caustic

inciso m, clause; comma

incitación f, incitement; fig spur, stimulus

incitar vt to incite; stimulate, encourage

incivil a rude, discourteous, uncivil

incivilidad f, rudeness, incivility

inclasificable a unclassifiable

inclemencia f, harshness, severity; inclemency (of the weather). **a la i.,** at the mercy of the elements

inclemente a inclement

inclinación f, inclination; slope; slant;

tendency, propensity; predilection, fondness; bow (in greeting); *geom* inclination

inclinar *vt* to incline, tilt, slant; bow; bend; influence; persuade; *vi* resemble; *vr* lean; stoop; tilt; tend, incline (to), view favorably (e.g. **Me inclino a creerlo,** I am inclined to believe it)

ínclito a famous, celebrated

incluir *vt irr* to comprise, embrace, contain; include, take into account. See **huir**

inclusa *f*, foundling home

inclusión *f*, inclusion; relationship, intercourse, friendship

inclusive *adv* including

inclusivo a inclusive

incluso *adv* including, inclusive. *prep* even

incoar *vt* to begin (especially lawsuits)

incobrable a irrecoverable; irredeemable

incógnita *f*, *math* X; unknown quantity; secret motive; unknown lady

incógnito a unknown. *m*, incognito, assumed name, disguise

incoherente a incoherent, disconnected, illogical

íncola *mf* resident, dweller, inhabitant

incoloro a colorless, uncolored

incólume a unharmed, unscathed; untouched, undamaged

incombustibilidad *f*, incombustibility

incomodar *vt* to disturb, incommode, inconvenience; annoy; *vr* disturb oneself, put oneself out; grow angry. **INo se incomode!** Please don't move!; Please don't be angry!

incomodidad *f*, discomfort; inconvenience; trouble, upset; annoyance

incómodo a uncomfortable; inconvenient; troublesome, tiresome; *Argentina, Chile* fed up *m*, discomfort; inconvenience

incompartible a indivisible

incompasivo a unsympathetic, hard

incompetencia *f*, incompetence

incomplejo, incomplexo a noncomplex, simple

incomponible a unrepairable, unmendable

incomprensible a incomprehensible

incomprensión *f*, incomprehension

incomunicado a in solitary confinement (of a prisoner)

incomunicar *vt* to sentence to solitary confinement; isolate, deprive of means of communication; *vr* become a recluse

inconcebible a inconceivable

inconciliable a irreconcilable

incondicional a unconditional; *Lat. Am.* fawning, servile

inconexión *f*, disconnectedness

inconexo a unconnected; incoherent

inconfeso a unconfessed

incongruencia *f*, incongruity

incongruente a incongruous, inappropriate

inconmovible a immovable; unflinching, unshakable

inconmutable a unalterable, immutable, unchangeable

inconquistable a unconquerable; *fig* resolute, inflexible

inconsciencia *f*, unconsciousness; subconscious

inconsciente a unconscious, involuntary; subconscious

inconsecuencia *f*, inconsequence; inconsistency

inconsecuente a inconsequential; inconsistent

inconsideración *f*, thoughtlessness

inconsiderado a thoughtless; heedless, selfish

inconsiguiente a illogical, inconsistent

inconsistente a inconsistent

inconstancia *f*, inconstancy, infidelity

inconstante a inconstant, fickle

inconstitucional a unconstitutional

incontaminado a uncontaminated

incontestable a undeniable, unquestionable

incontinencia *f*, incontinence

incontinente a incontinent

incontrastable a insuperable, invincible; undeniable, unanswerable; *fig* unshakable, inconvincible

incontrovertible a undeniable, incontrovertible

inconvencible a inconvincible

inconveniencia *f*, discomfort; inconvenience; unsuitability

inconveniente a awkward, inconvenient; uncomfortable; inappropriate. *m*, inconvenience; obstacle, impediment; disadvantage

incorporar *vt* to incorporate; cause to sit up, lift up; *vr* sit up, raise oneself; become a member, join (associations); be incorporated; blend, mix

incorpóreo a incorporeal; immaterial

incorrección *f*, incorrectness; indecorum, impropriety

incorrecto a incorrect; indecorous, unbecoming, improper

incorregible a incorrigible

incorrupción *f*, incorruption; purity; integrity; wholesomeness

incorrupto a incorrupt; pure; chaste

incredulidad *f*, incredulity, scepticism

incrédulo (-la) a incredulous; atheistic. *n* atheist; unbeliever, sceptic

increíble a incredible; marvelous, extraordinary

incremento *m*, increment, increase

increpación *f*, scolding, harsh rebuke

increpar *vt* to scold, rebuke harshly

incriminante a incriminating

incriminar vt to incriminate, accuse; exaggerate (a charge, etc.)

incrustación f, incrustation; art inlay

incubación f, hatching; med incubation

incubadora f, incubator (for chickens)

incubar vi to sit on eggs (of hens); vt hatch; med incubate

inculcar vt to press one thing against another; instill, inculcate; vr grow more fixed in one's views

inculpable a blameless, innocent

inculpar vt to blame; accuse

incultivable a uncultivatable; untillable

inculto a uncultivated, untilled; uncultured; uncivilized

incultura f, lack of cultivation; lack of culture

incumbencia f, obligation, moral responsibility, duty

incumbir vi to be incumbent on; concern

incurable a incurable; inveterate, hopeless

incuria f, negligence, carelessness

incurrir vi (with en) to fall into (error, etc.); incur (dislike, etc.)

incursión f, incursion; inroad

indagación f, investigation, inquiry

indagar vt to investigate, examine; inquire. **i. precios,** to inquire about prices

indebido a undue, immoderate improper; illegal, illicit

indecencia f, indecency; obscenity; impropriety

indecente a indecent; obscene; improper

indecible a unutterable, ineffable, unspeakable

indeciso a undecided; hesitant, irresolute; vague; noncommittal

indeclinable a obligatory; unavoidable; gram indeclinable, uninflected

indecoro m, impropriety, indecorum

indecoroso a indecorous, unbecoming; base, mean

indefectible a unfailing; perfect

indefectiblemente adv invariably

indefendible a indefensible

indefenso a unprotected, defenseless

indefinible a indefinable, vague; indescribable

indefinido a indefinite, vague; undefined; gram indefinite

indeleble a indelible

indeliberado a unpremeditated; unconsidered

indemme a unharmed, undamaged

indemnidad f, indemnity

indemnización f, compensation, indemnification; indemnity

indemnizar vt to indemnify, compensate

indemostrable a indemonstrable, incapable of demonstration

independencia f, independence

independiente a independent; self-contained

indescifrable a undecipherable; illegible

indeterminado a indeterminate; vague, doubtful, uncertain; hesitant, irresolute; math indeterminate

indiano (-na) a and n Indian; East Indian; West Indian. m, nouveau riche, one who returns rich from the Western Hemisphere

indicación f, indication; sign, evidence; intimation, hint

indicador a indicative. m, indicator. **i. del nivel de gasolina,** gas gauge

indicar vt to indicate; show; point out; simply, suggest; intimate

indicativo a indicative. a and m, gram indicative

índice m, index; indication, sign; library catalogue; catalogue room; hand (of a clock); pointer, needle (of instruments); gnomon (of a sundial); math index; forefinger. **I. expurgatorio,** the Index

indicio m, indication; sign; evidence. **indicios vehementes,** circumstantial evidence

indiferencia f, indifference

indiferente a indifferent

indígena a native, indigenous. mf native

indigencia f, destitution, indigence; impecuniosity

indigenismo m, Lat. Am. Native American movement

indigente a destitute, indigent; impecunious

indigestión f, indigestion

indigesto a indigestible; lit muddled, confused; unsociable, brusque

indignación f, indignation, anger

indignado a indignant

indignar vt to anger, make indignant; vr grow angry

indignidad f, unworthiness; indignity; personal affront

indigno a unworthy; base, despicable

indio (-ia) a Indian; blue. n Indian. m, indium

indirecta f, hint, covert suggestion, innuendo. inf **i. del padre Cobos,** strong hint

indirecto a indirect

indisciplinado a undisciplined

indiscreción f, indiscretion

indiscreto a indiscreet

indiscutible a unquestionable, undeniable

indisoluble a indissoluble

indispensable a indispensable

indisponer vt irr to make unfit or incapable; indispose, make ill; (with con or contra) set against, make trouble with; vr be indisposed; (*with con or contra*) quarrel with. See **poner**

indisposición *f*, reluctance, disinclination; indisposition, brief illness

indistinguible *a* undistinguishable

indistinto *a* indistinct; indeterminate; vague

individual *a* individual; peculiar, characteristic. *m*, (tennis) single

individuo (-**ua**) *a* individual; indivisible. *m*, individual; member, associate; *inf* self. *n inf* person

indiviso *a* undivided

indócil *a* unmanageable; disobedient; brittle, unpliable (of metals)

indocilidad *f*, indocility; disobedience; brittleness (of metals)

índole *f*, temperament, nature; kind, sort

indolencia *f*, idleness, indolence

indolente *a* nonpainful; indifferent, insensible; idle, indolent

indoloro *a* painless

indomable *a* untamable; invincible; indomitable; ungovernable, unmanageable

indómito *a* untamed; untamable; unmanageable, unruly; indomitable

indubitable *a* unquestionable

inducción *f*, persuasion; *phys* induction

inducir *vt irr* to persuade, prevail upon; induce; infer, conclude. See **conducir**

indudable *a* indubitable

indulgente *a* indulgent, tender; tolerant

indultar *vt* to pardon; exempt

indulto *m*, amnesty; exemption; forgiveness; *ecc* indult

indumentaria *f*, clothing; outfit (of clothes)

industria *f*, assiduity, industriousness; pains, effort, ingenuity; industry. **i. pesada**, heavy industry. **i. cárnica**, meat industry. **i. extractivos**, mining industry

industrial *a* industrial. *m*, industrialist

industrialismo *m*, industrialism

industriar *vt* to teach, train; *vr* find a way, manage, succeed in

industrioso *a* industrious; diligent, assiduous

inédito *a* unpublished; unedited

inefable *a* ineffable

ineficacia *f*, inefficiency; ineffectiveness

ineficaz *a* ineffective; inefficient

ineludible *a* unavoidable

ineptitud *f*, ineptitude

inepto *a* inept, incompetent; unfit, unsuitable

inequívoco *a* unequivocal

inercia *f*, inertia

inerme *a* defenseless, unprotected; (*bot zool*) unarmed

inerte *a* inert

inescrutable *a* inscrutable, unfathomable

inesperado *a* unexpected, sudden

inestable *a* unstable

inestimable *a* inestimable

inevitable *a* inevitable

inexactitud *f*, inexactitude, inaccuracy; error, mistake

inexacto *a* inexact, inaccurate; erroneous

inexcusable *a* inexcusable, unforgivable; indispensable

inexhausto *a* inexhaustible

inexistente *a* nonexistent

inexorable *a* inexorable

inexperiencia *f*, inexperience

inexperto *a* inexperienced; inexpert

inexplorado *a* unexplored

inexplosible *a* inexplosive

inexpresivo *a* inexpressive; reticent

inexpugnable *a* impregnable; *fig* unshakable, firm; obstinate

inextinguible *a* inextinguishable; everlasting, perpetual

infalibilidad *f*, infallibility

infalible *a* infallible

infamación *f*, defamation

infamador (-**ra**) *a* slandering. *n* slanderer

infamar *vt* to defame, slander

infame *a* infamous, vile

infamia *f*, infamy; baseness, vileness

infancia *f*, infancy, babyhood; childhood

infantería *f*, infantry

infantil *a* infantile, babyish; innocent, candid

infatigable *a* unwearying, indefatigable

infatuación *f*, infatuation

infatuar *vt* to infatuate; *vr* become infatuated

infausto *a* unlucky, unfortunate

infección *f*, infection

infeccioso *a* infectious

infectar *vt* to infect; corrupt, pervert; *vr* become infected; be corrupted

infecto *a* infected; corrupt, perverted; tainted

infecundo *a* sterile, barren

infelice *a poet* unhappy, unfortunate

infelicidad *f*, unhappiness

infeliz *a* unhappy; unfortunate; *inf* simple, good-hearted

inferencia *f*, inference, connection

inferior *a* inferior; lower; second-rate; subordinate. *mf* inferior, subordinate

inferioridad *f*, inferiority

inferir *vt irr* to infer, deduce; involve, imply; occasion; inflict. See **sentir**

infernáculo *m*, hopscotch

infernal *a* infernal; devilish, fiendish; wicked, inhuman; *inf* confounded

inferno *a poet* infernal

infértil *a* infertile

infestación f, infestation

infestar vt to infest, swarm in; infect; injure, damage

infesto a poet harmful, dangerous

inficionar vt to infect; pervert, corrupt

infidelidad f, faithlessness, infidelity; disbelief in Christian religion; unbelievers, infidels

infidencia f, disloyalty, faithlessness

infiel a unfaithful, disloyal; inaccurate, incorrect; infidel, unbelieving. mf infidel, nonbeliever

infierno m, hell; hades (gen. pl); fig inf inferno. **en el quinto i.,** very far off, at the end of the world. **en los quintos infiernos,** at the end of nowhere

infiltración f, infiltration; inculcation, implantation

infiltrar vt to infiltrate; imbue, inculcate

ínfimo a lowest; meanest, vilest, most base; cheapest, poorest (in quality)

infinidad f, infinity; infinitude; great number

infinitivo a and m, gram infinitive

infinito a infinite; endless; boundless; countless. m, math infinite. adv excessively, immensely

inflación f, inflation; distension; pride, vanity

inflador m. Lat. Am. bicycle pump

inflamable a inflammable

inflamación f, inflammation; eng ignition

inflamador a inflammatory

inflamar vt to set on fire; fig inflame, excite; vr take fire; med become inflamed; grow hot or excited

inflamatorio a med inflammatory

inflar vt to inflate; blow up, distend; throw out (one's chest); exaggerate; make haughty or vain; vr be swollen or inflated; be puffed up with pride

inflexibilidad f, inflexibility; rigidity; immovability, constancy

inflexión f, bending, flexion; diffraction (optics); inflection

infligir vt to impose, inflict (penalties)

influencia f, influence; power, authority; elec charge

influir vt irr to influence; affect; (with en) cooperate in, assist with. See **huir**

influjo m, influence; flux, inflow of the tide

influyente a influential

información f, information; legal inquiry; report; research, investigation

informador (-ra) a informing, acquainting. n informant

informal a informal, irregular; unreliable (of persons); unconventional

informalidad f, irregularity; unconventionality; unreliability

informar vt to inform, acquaint with; vi

law plead; vr (with de, en, or sobre) find out about, investigate

informática f, information sciences

informativo a informative

informe a formless, shapeless. m, report, statement; information; law plea; pl data, particulars; references

infortificable a unfortifiable

infortuna f, astrol evil influence

infortunado a unfortunate

infortunio m, misfortune; unhappiness, adversity; mischance, ill luck

infracción f, transgression, infringement

infracto a imperturbable

infrangible a unbreakable

infranqueable a insuperable, unsurmountable

infrarrojo a infrared

infrascrito a undersigned; undermentioned

infringir vt to infringe, transgress, break

infructífero a unfruitful; worthless, useless

infructuosidad f, unfruitfulness; worthlessness, uselessness

infructuoso a fruitless; useless, worthless

infundado a unfounded, groundless

infundio m, inf nonsense, untruth

infundir vt to infuse, imbue with

infusión f, infusion

ingeniar vt to devise, concoct, plan; vr contrive, find a way, manage

ingeniería f, engineering

ingeniero m, engineer. **i. agrónomo,** agricultural engineer. **i. de caminos, canales y puertos,** civil engineer. **i. radiotelegrafista,** radio engineer. **cuerpo de ingenieros,** royal engineers

ingenio m, mind; inventive capacity; imaginative talent; man of genius; talent, cleverness; ingeniousness; machine; guillotine (bookbinding)

ingeniosidad f, ingeniousness; witticism, clever remark

ingenioso a talented, clever; ingenious

ingénito a unengendered, unconceived; innate, inborn

ingente a huge, enormous

ingenuidad f, ingenuousness, naiveté

ingenuo a ingenuous, naive, artless, unaffected

Inglaterra England

ingle f, groin

inglés (-esa) a English; British. n Englishman; Briton. m, English (language); inf creditor. **a la inglesa,** in English fashion. **marcharse a la inglesa,** inf to take French leave

ingobernable a ungovernable, unruly

ingratitud f, ingratitude

ingrato a ungrateful; irksome, thankless; disagreeable

ingrávido a light weight

ingrediente m, ingredient; *Argentina* appetizer

ingresar vi to return, come in (money); (*with* en) join, become a member of, enter

ingreso m, joining, entering, admission; *com* money received; opening, commencement; *pl* earnings, takings, revenue

inhábil a unskillful; unpracticed; incompetent, unfit; unsuitable, ill-chosen

inhabilidad f, unskillfulness; incompetence; unsuitability; inability

inhabilitación f, incapacitation; disqualification; disablement

inhabilitar vt to make ineligible; disqualify; incapacitate, make unfit; vr become ineligible; be incapacitated

inhabitable a uninhabitable

inhabitado a uninhabited, deserted

inhalación f, inhalation

inhalador m, *med* inhaler

inhalar vt to inhale

inhallable a nowhere to be found, unfindable

inheredltable a uninheritable

inherencia f, inherency

inherente a inherent, innate

inhestar vt *irr* to raise, lift up; erect. See **acertar**

inhibición f, inhibition

inhibir vt *law* to inhibit; vr inhibit or restrain oneself. See **prohibir**

inhibitorio a *law* inhibitory

inhonesto a indecent, obscene; immodest

inhospedable, inhospitalario a inhospitable; bleak, uninviting; exposed

inhospitalidad f, inhospitality

inhumación f, inhumation, burial

inhumadora f, crematory

inhumanidad f, inhumanity; brutality

inhumano a inhuman; brutal, barbarous

inhumar vt to bury, inter

iniciación f, initiation

iniciador (-ra) a initiating; n initiator

inicial a and f, initial

iniciar vt to initiate; admit, introduce; originate; vr be initiated; *ecc* take minor or first orders

iniciativa f, initiative

inicuo a iniquitous, most unjust, wicked

inimaginable a inconceivable

inimicísimo a *sup* **enemigo** most hostile

ininteligible a unintelligible

iniquidad f, iniquity, wickedness

injerir vt *irr* to insert, place within, introduce; interpolate; vr meddle. See **sentir**

injertar vt *agr* to graft

injerto m, *agr* graft; grafting; grafted plant, briar, or tree

injuria f, insult; slander; outrage; wrong, injustice; harm, damage

injuriador (-ra) a insulting. n offender, persecutor

injuriar vt to insult; slander; outrage; wrong, persecute; harm, damage

injurioso a insulting; slanderous; offensive, abusive; harmful

injusticia f, injustice; lack of justice; unjust action

injustificable a unjustifiable

injustificado a unjustified

injusto a unjust; unrighteous

inllevable a unbearable, intolerable

inmaculado a immaculate, pure

inmarcesible, inmarchitable a unfading, imperishable

inmaterial a incorporeal; immaterial

inmaturo a immature; unripe

inmediación f, nearness, proximity; contact; *pl* outskirts, neighborhood, environs

inmediatamente adv near; immediately, at once

inmediato a adjoining, close, nearby; immediate, prompt

inmejorable a unsurpassable, unbeatable

inmemorable, inmemorial a immemorial

inmensidad f, vastness, huge extent; infinity; infinite space; immensity; huge number

inmenso a vast; infinite; immense; innumerable

inmensurable a immeasurable, incalculable

inmerecido a undeserved, unmerited

inmérito a wrongful, unjust

inmeritorio a unmeritorious, unpraiseworthy

inmersión f, immersion; dip

inmigración f, immigration

inmigrante a and *mf* immigrant

inmigrar vi to immigrate

inminente a imminent

inmiscuir vt to mix; vr meddle. May be conjugated regularly or like **huir**

inmobiliario a concerning real estate

inmoble a immovable; motionless, immobile, stationary; *fig* unshakable, unflinching

inmoderación f, immoderateness, excess

inmoderado a immoderate; unrestrained, excessive

inmodestia f, immodesty

inmodesto a immodest

inmolar vt to immolate; *fig* sacrifice, give up; vr *fig* sacrifice oneself

inmoral a immoral

inmortal a immortal

inmortalizar vt to immortalize

inmotivado a unfounded, without reason

inmoto a motionless, stationary

inmóvil a immovable, fixed; motionless; steadfast, constant

inmovilizar vt to immobilize

inmueble m, law immovable estate

inmundicia f, filth, nastiness; dirt; rubbish, refuse; obscenity, indecency

inmundo a dirty, filthy; obscene, indecent; unclean

inmune a exempt; med immune

inmunidad f, exemption; immunity

inmunizar vt to immunize

inmutable a immutable, unchangeable; imperturbable

inmutación f, change, alteration, difference

inmutar vt to change, alter, vary; vr change one's expression (through fear, etc.)

innato a innate; inherent; instinctive, inborn

innatural a unnatural

innavegable a unnavigable; unseaworthy (of ships)

innecesario a unnecessary,

innegable a undeniable; indisputable, irrefutable

innocuo a harmless, innocuous

innovación f, innovation

innovador (-ra) a innovatory. n innovator

innovar vt to introduce innovations

innumerable a innumerable, countless

innúmero a countless, innumerable

inobediente a disobedient

inobjetable a, Lat. Am. unobjectionable

inobservable a unobservable

inobservancia f, inobservance

inobservante a unobservant

inocencia f, innocence; simplicity, candor; harmlessness

inocentada f, inf naïve remark or action; fool's trap; practical joke

inocente a innocent; candid, simple; harmless; easily deceived

inocentón a inf extremely credulous and easily taken in

inoculación f, inoculation

inoculador m, inoculator

inocular vt to inoculate; pervert, corrupt; contaminate

inodoro a odorless. m, toilet, lavatory

inofensivo a inoffensive, harmless

inolvidable a unforgettable

inoperable a inoperable

inopia f, poverty; scarcity

inopinado a unexpected, sudden

inoportunidad f, inopportuneness, unseasonableness; unsuitability

inoportuno a inopportune, untimely

inorgánico a inorganic

inoxidable a rustless

inquebrantable a unbreakable; final, irrevocable

inquietador (-ra) a disturbing. n disturber

inquietar vt to disturb; trouble, make anxious, worry; vr be disquieted, worry

inquieto a restless; unquiet; fidgety; disturbed, anxious, worried, uneasy

inquietud f, restlessness; uneasiness; worry; trouble, care, anxiety

inquilinato m, tenancy; rent; law lease; (rental) rates

inquilino (-na) n tenant; lessee; Chile tenant farmer

inquina f, dislike, grudge

inquinar vt to contaminate, corrupt, infect

inquiridor (-ra) a inquiring, examining. n investigator

inquirir vt irr to inquire; examine, look into. See **adquirir**

inquisición f, inquiry, investigation; ecc Inquisition

inquisidor (-ra) a inquiring, investigating. n investigator. m, ecc inquisitor; judge

insaciable a insatiable

insalubre a unhealthy

insanable a incurable

insania f, insanity

insano a insane, mad

inscribir vt to inscribe; record; enter (a name on a list, etc.), register, enroll; engrave; geom inscribe. Past Part. **inscrito**

inscripción f, inscription; record, enrollment; registration; government bond

insecticida a insecticide

insecto m, insect

inseguridad f, insecurity

inseguro a insecure; unsafe; uncertain

insensatez f, folly, foolishness

insensato a foolish, stupid, mad

insensibilidad f, insensibility; imperception; callousness, hard-heartedness

insensibilizar vt to make insensible (to sensations)

insensible a insensible; imperceptive, insensitive; unconscious, senseless; imperceptible, inappreciable; callous

inserción f, insertion; interpolation; grafting

insertar vt to insert; introduce; interpolate; vr (bot zool) become attached

inservible a useless; unfit; unsuitable

insidia f, insidiousness; snare, ambush

insidiar vt to waylay, ambush; set a trap for; scheme against

insidioso a insidious; treacherous; scheming, guileful

insigne a illustrious, famous; distinguished

insignia f, symbol; badge; token; banner, standard; *naut* pennant; *pl* insignia

insignificancia f, meaninglessness; unimportance, triviality; insignificance, insufficiency

insignificante a meaningless; unimportant; insignificant, small

insinuación f, insinuation; hint; implication; suggestion

insinuador a insinuating; suggestive, implicative

insinuar vt to insinuate; suggest, hint; vr ingratiate oneself; creep in

insipidez f, tastelessness, insipidity; *fig* dullness

insípido a tasteless, insipid; dull, uninteresting, boring

insistencia f, insistence

insistente a insistent

insistir vi (*with en or sobre*) to lay stress upon, insist on; persist in

ínsito a inherent, innate

insociable a unsociable

insolación f, insolation, exposure to the sun; sunstroke

insolar vt to expose to the sun's rays; vr contract sunstroke

insolencia f, insolence; impudence, impertinence

insolentarse vr to grow insolent; be impudent

insolente a insolent; impudent, impertinent

insólito a unaccustomed; infrequent; unusual; unexpected

insoluble a insoluble

insoluto a unpaid, outstanding

insolvente a insolvent

insomne a sleepless

insomnio m, insomnia

insondable a unfathomable, bottomless; inscrutable, secret

insoportable a intolerable, unbearable

insostenible a indefensible; arbitrary, baseless

inspección f, inspection; supervision; examination; inspectorship; inspector's office

inspeccionar vt to inspect; survey, examine. **i. una casa,** to view a house

inspector (**-ra**) a inspecting, examining. n supervisor. m, inspector; surveyor

inspiración f, inspiration; inhalation

inspirador (**-ra**) a inspiring. n inspirer

inspirar vt to breathe in, inhale; blow (of the wind); inspire; vr be inspired; (*with en*) find inspiration in, imitate

instabilidad f, instability; unsteadiness; shakiness; unreliability, inconstancy

instable a unstable

instalación f, plant, apparatus; erection; fitting; induction; installment, settling in

instalador (**-ra**) n fitter; one who installs (electricity, etc.)

instalar vt to appoint, induct; erect (a plant, etc.); install, put in; lay on; *elec* wire; vr install oneself, settle down

instancia f, instance; argument; suggestion; supplication; request; formal petition. **de primera i.,** in the first instance, firstly

instantánea f, *phot* snapshot

instantáneo a instantaneous

instante a urgent. m, second; instant, moment. **a cada i.,** every minute; frequently. **al i.,** at once, immediately. **por instantes,** continually; immediately

instar vt to press; persuade; insist upon; vi be urgent, press

instauración f, restoration; renewal; renovation; *Lat. Am.* establishment

instaurador (**-ra**) a renovating, renewing. n restorer, renovator

instaurar vt to restore; repair; renovate, renew; *Lat. Am.* establish, set up

instigación f, instigation, incitement

instigar vt to instigate, incite; induce

instilación f, instillment, pouring drop by drop; inculcation, implantation

instintivo a instinctive

instinto m, instinct. **por i.,** by instinct, naturally

institución f, setting up, establishment; institution; teaching, instruction; *pl* institutes, digest

instituir vt *irr* to found, establish; institute; instruct, teach. See **huir**

instituto m, institute; secondary school. **i. de belleza,** beauty parlor, beauty salon

instrucción f, teaching, instruction; knowledge, learning; education; *pl* orders; rules; instruction. **i. primaria,** primary education. **i. pública,** public education

instructivo a instructive

instructor (**-ra**) a instructive. n instructor

instruido a cultured, well-educated; knowledgeable

instruir vt *irr* to teach, instruct; train; inform, acquaint with; *law* formulate. See **huir**

instrumentista mf *mus* instrumentalist; instrument maker

instrumento m, tool, implement; machine, apparatus; *mus* instrument; means, medium; legal document. **i. de cuerda,** string instrument. **i. de percusión,** percussion instrument. **i. de viento,** wind instrument

insuave a unpleasant (to the senses); rough

insubordinación f, insubordination, rebellion

insubordinado a insubordinate, unruly

insubordinar vt to rouse to rebellion; vr become insubordinate, rebel

insubsistente a unstable; groundless, unfounded

insubstancial a insubstantial, unreal, illusory; pointless, worthless, superficial

insubstancialidad f, superficiality, worthlessness

insuficiencia f, insufficiency, shortage; incompetence, inefficiency

insuficiente a insufficient, scarce, inadequate

insufrible a insufferable, unbearable, intolerable

insulina f, insulin

insulsez f, insipidity, tastelessness; dullness; tediousness

insulso a insipid, tasteless; tedious; dull

insultante a insulting

insultar vt to insult; call names; vr take offense

insulto m, insult; sudden attack; sudden illness, fit; *Argentina* fit of fainting; *Mexico* indigestion

insumable a incalculable; excessive, exorbitant

insumergible a unsinkable

insumiso a rebellious

insurgente a insurgent, rebellious. m, rebel

insurrección f, insurrection

insurreccionar vt to incite to rebellion; vr rise in rebellion

insurrecto (-ta) n rebel

insustituible a indispensable

intacto a untouched; intact, uninjured; whole, entire; complete; pure

intachable a irreproachable; impeccable, perfect

integración f, integration

integrar vt to integrate; *com* repay

integridad f, wholeness; completeness; integrity, probity, honesty; virginity

íntegro a integral, whole; upright, honest

integumento m, integument; pretense, simulation

intelectiva f, understanding

intelecto m, intellect

intelectual a intellectual

intelectualidad f, understanding, intellectuality; intelligentsia

inteligencia f, intelligence; intellect; mental alertness; mind; meaning, sense; experience, skill; understanding, secret agreement; information, knowledge; Intelligence, Secret Service

inteligente a intelligent; clever; skillful; capable, competent

inteligible a intelligible; understandable; able to be heard

intemperancia f, intemperance, lack of moderation

intemperante a intemperate

intemperie f, stormy weather. **a la i.,** at the mercy of the elements; in the open air

intempestivo a inopportune, ill-timed

intención f, intention; determination, purpose; viciousness (of animals); caution. *inf* **con segunda i.,** with a double meaning, slyly

intencionado a intentioned, disposed

intencional a intentional, designed, premeditated

intendencia f, management; supervision; administration; *pol* intendancy; *Argentina* mayoralty. *mil* **cuerpo de i.,** quartermaster corps, army supply corps

intensar vt to intensify

intensidad f, intensity; ardor; vehemence

intensificar vt to intensify

intensivo a intensive

intenso a intense; ardent; fervent, vehement

intentar vt to intend, mean; propose; try, endeavor; initiate. **i. fortuna,** to try one's luck

intento m, intention, determination; purpose. **de i.,** on purpose; knowingly

interacción f, interaction; reciprocal effect; *chem* reaction

intercalar vt to intercalate; interpolate; include, insert

intercambiable a interchangeable

intercambio m, interchange

interceder vi to intercede, plead for

interceptación f, interception

interceptar vt to intercept; interrupt; hinder

intercesor (-ra) a interceding. n intercessor

intercutáneo a intercutaneous

interdecir vt irr to forbid, prohibit. See **decir**

interdicción f, interdiction, prohibition

interdicto m, interdict

interés m, interest; yield, profit; advantage; *com* interest; inclination, fondness; attraction, fascination; *pl* money matters. **i. compuesto,** compound interest. **intereses creados,** bonds of interest; vested interests

interesado a involved, concerned; biased; selfish

interesante a interesting

interesar(se) vi and vr to be interested; vt *com* invest; interest

interfecto (-ta) n *law* victim (of murder)

interferencia f, *phys* interference

ínterin m, interim. adv meanwhile, in the meantime

interinamente adv in the interim; provisionally

interinar vt to discharge (duties) provisionally, act temporarily as

interino a acting, provisional, temporary

interior a interior; inner; inside; indoor; inland; internal, domestic (policies, etc.);

inward, spiritual. *m*, interior, inside; mind, soul; *pl* entrails

interiorizar *vt*, *Lat. Am.* to investigate closely, look into, scrutinize

interjección *f*, *gram* interjection, exclamation

interlocución *f*, dialogue, conversation

interlocutorio *a law* interlocutory

intérlope *a* interloping. *mf* interloper

interludio *m*, interlude

intermediario (**-ia**) *a* and *n* intermediary. *m*, *com* middleman

intermedio *a* intermediate. *m*, interim; *theat* interval. **por i. de,** through, by the mediation of

intermisión *f*, intermission, interval

intermitente *a* intermittent

intermitir *vt* to interrupt, suspend, discontinue

internación *f*, going inside; penetration; taking into

internacional *a* international

internado *m*, boarding school

internamiento *m*, internment

internar *vt* to take or send inland; *vi* penetrate; *vr* (*with en*) go into the interior of (a country); get into the confidence of; study deeply (a subject)

interno (**-na**) *a* interior; internal; inner; inside; boarding (student). *n* boarding school student; *med* intern

interpelación *f*, *law* interpellation; appeal

interpelar *vt law* to interpellate; appeal to, ask protection from

interpolación *f*, interpolation, insertion; interruption

interpolar *vt* to interpolate; interject

interponer *vt irr* to interpose, insert, intervene; designate as an arbitrator; *vr* intervene. See **poner**

interposición *f*, interposition; intervention; mediation, arbitration

interpretación *f*, interpretation; translation

interpretador (**-ra**) *a* interpretative. *n* interpreter

interpretar *vt* to interpret; translate; attribute; expound, explain. **i. mal,** to misconstrue; translate wrongly

intérprete *mf* interpreter

interregno *m*, interregnum; *Lat. Am.* interim. **i. parlamentario,** parliamentary recess

interrogación *f*, interrogation, question; *gram* question mark

interrogador (**-ra**) *n* questioner

interrogante *a* interrogating. *m*, *print* question mark

interrogar *vt* to interrogate, question

interrogativo *a* interrogative

interrumpir *vt* to interrupt; hinder, obstruct; *elec* break contact

interrupción *f*, interruption; stoppage (of work); *elec* break

interruptor (**-ra**) *a* interrupting. *n* interrupter. *m*, *elec* switch, interruptor. **i. de dos direcciones,** *elec* two-way switch

intersticio *m*, interstice, crack, crevice; interval, intervening space

intervalo *m*, interval

intervención *f*, intervention; mediation, intercession; auditing (of accounts)

intervenir *vi irr* to take part (in); intervene, interfere; arbitrate, mediate; happen, occur; *vt com* audit. See **venir**

interventor (**-ra**) *a* intervening. *n* one who intervenes. *m*, auditor; inspector

intestado (**-da**) *a* and *n law* intestate

intestino *a* intestinal. *m*, intestine

íntima, intimación *f*, intimation, notification

intimar *vt* to intimate; inform, notify; *vr* penetrate; *vr* and *vi* become intimate or friendly

intimidación *f*, intimidation, terrorization

intimidad *f*, intimacy

intimidar *vt* to intimidate, terrorize, cow

íntimo *a* intimate; deep-seated, inward; private, personal

intitular *vt* to give a title to, entitle, call; *vr* call oneself

intolerable *a* intolerable; unbearable

intolerancia *f*, narrow-mindedness, intolerance, bigotry

intolerante *a* narrow-minded, illiberal; *med* intolerant

intonso *a* long-haired, unshorn; boorish, ignorant

intoxicación *f*, poisoning

intoxicar *vt* to poison

intraducible *a* untranslatable

intramuros *adv* within the town walls, within the city

intranquilizar *vt* to disquiet, make uneasy, worry

intranquilo *a* uneasy, anxious

intransferible *a* untransferable, not transferable

intransigencia *f*, intolerance, intransigence

intransigente *a* intolerant, intransigent

intransitable *a* impassable; unsurmountable

intransitivo *a* intransitive

intrascendente *a*, *Lat. Am.* unimportant

intratable *a* intractable; impassable; rough; unsociable, difficult

intrauterino *a* intrauterine

intravenoso *a* intravenous

intrepidez *f*, intrepidity, dauntlessness, gallantry

intrépido *a* intrepid, dauntless, gallant

intriga *f*, scheme, intrigue; entanglement; *lit* plot

intrigante *mf* intriguer, schemer

intrigar *vi* to intrigue, scheme, plot; **intrigarse** *Lat. Am.* to be intrigued, be puzzled

intrincación *f*, intricacy

intrincado *a* intricate

intrincar *vt* to complicate; obscure, confuse

intríngulis *m*, *inf* ulterior motive

intrínseco *a* intrinsic, inherent; essential

introducción *f*, introduction

introducir *vt irr* to introduce; insert; fit in; drive in; present, introduce; bring into use; cause, occasion; show in, bring in; *vr* interfere, meddle; enter. See **conducir**

intromisión *f*, intromission; interference; *geol* intrusion

introspección *f*, introspection

introverso *a* introvert

intruso (-sa) *a* intruding, intrusive. *n* intruder

intuición *f*, intuition

intuir *vt irr* to know by intuition. See **huir**

intuitivo *a* intuitive

intuito *m*, glance, look, view

inundación *f*, flood; flooding; excess, superabundance

inundar *vt* to flood; swamp; *fig* inundate, overwhelm

inurbano *a* discourteous, uncivil, impolite

inusitado *a* unusual, unaccustomed; rare

inútil *a* useless

inutilidad *f*, uselessness

inutilizar *vt* to render useless; disable, incapacitate; spoil, damage

invadir *vt* to invade

invalidación *f*, invalidation

invalidar *vt* to invalidate

invalidez *f*, invalidity; disablement; infirmity

inválido (-da) *a* weak, infirm; invalid, null; disabled. *n* invalid; disabled soldier

invariable *a* invariable

invariación *f*, invariableness

invariante *m*, invariant

invasión *f*, invasion, encroachment, incursion

invasor (-ra) *a* invading; *med* attacking. *n* invader

invectiva *f*, invective

invencible *a* invincible

invención *f*, invention, discovery; deception, fabrication, lie; creative imagination; finding (e.g. **i. de la Santa Cruz,** Invention of the Holy Cross)

invendible *a* unsalable

inventar *vt* to invent; create; imagine; concoct, fabricate (lies, etc.)

inventariar *vt* to make an inventory of; *com* take stock of

inventario *m*, inventory; *com* stock taking

inventiva *f*, inventiveness, ingenuity; creativeness

inventivo *a* inventive

invento *m*, See **invención**

inventor (-ra) *n* inventor, discoverer; liar, storyteller

inverecundo *a* shameless, brazen

inverisímil *a* See **inverosímil**

invernáculo *m*, greenhouse; conservatory

invernadero *m*, winter quarters; greenhouse

invernal *a* wintry; winter

invernar *vi irr* to winter; hibernate; be wintertime. See **acertar**

inverosímil *a* unlikely, improbable

inverosimilitud *f*, improbability

inverso *a* inverse; inverted

inversor, -a *mf*, *Lat. Am.* invester

invertebrado *a* and *m*, invertebrate

invertir *vt irr* to invert, transpose; reverse; *com* invest; spend (time). See **sentir**

investigación *f*, investigation, examination; research; inquiry

investigador (-ra) *a* investigating. *n* investigator; researcher

investigar *vt* to investigate, examine; research on

investir *vt irr* to confer upon, decorate with; invest, appoint. See **pedir**

inveterado *a* inveterate

invicto *a* invincible; unconquered

invierno *m*, winter; rainy season

inviolabilidad *f*, inviolability. **i. parlamentaria,** parliamentary immunity

inviolable *a* inviolable; infallible

inviolado *a* inviolate

invisibilidad *f*, invisibility

invisible *a* invisible; *m*, *Argentina* hairpin; *Mexico* hairnet

invitación *f*, invitation

invitado (-da) *n* guest

invitar *vt* to invite; urge, request; allure, attract

invocación *f*, invocation

invocador (-ra) *n* invoker

invocar *vt* to invoke

involuntario *a* involuntary

invulnerable *a* invulnerable

inyección *f*, injection

inyectado *a* bloodshot (of eyes)

inyectar *vt* to inject

ir *vi irr* to go; bet (e.g. **Van cinco pesetas que no lo hace,** I bet five pesetas he doesn't do it); be different, be changed (e.g. **¡Qué diferencia va entre esto y aquello!** What a difference there is between this and that!); suit, be becoming, fit (e.g. **El vestido no te va bien,** The dress doesn't suit you); extend; lead, go in the direction of (e.g. **Este camino va a Lérida,** This road leads to Lerida); get along, do, proceed, be (e.g. **¿Cómo te va estos días?** How are you getting along these days?); come (e.g. **Ahora voy,** I'm coming now); *math* carry (e.g. **siete y van cuatro,** seven, and four to carry); *math* leave (e.g. **De quince a seis van nueve,** Six from fifteen leaves nine). With a gerund, **ir** indicates the continuance of the action, or may mean to become or to grow (e.g. **Iremos andando hacia el mar,** We shall go on walking toward the sea, or **Entre tanto iba amaneciendo,** In the meanwhile it was growing light). With a past participle, **ir** means 'to be' (e.g. **Voy encantado de lo que he visto,** I am delighted with what I have seen). With *prep a* + *infin,* **ir** means to prepare (to do) or to intend (to do) or to be on the point of doing (e.g. **Van a cantar la canción que te gusta,** They are going (or preparing) to sing the song you like). With *prep a* + *noun,* **ir** indicates destination (e.g. **Voy al cine,** I'm going to the cinema. **¿A dónde vamos?** Where are we going to?). **ir** + *con* means to go in the company of, or to do a thing in a certain manner (e.g. **Hemos de ir con cuidado,** We must go carefully). **ir** + *en* means to concern, interest (e.g. **¿Qué le va a él en este asunto?** What has this affair to do with him?). **ir** + *por* means to follow the career of, become (e.g. **Juan va por abogado,** John is going to be a lawyer). It also means to go and bring, or to go for (e.g. **Iré por agua,** I shall go and bring (or for) water). *vr* to go away, leave, depart; die; leak (of liquids); evaporate; overbalance, slip (e.g. **Se le fueron las pies,** He slipped (and lost his balance)); be worn out, grow old, deteriorate; be incontinent; *fig inf* **írsele a uno una cosa,** not to notice or not to understand a thing. *naut* **irse a pique,** to founder, sink. **Se le fueron los ojos tras María,** He couldn't keep his eyes off Mary. **i. a caballo,** to ride, go on horseback. **i. adelante,** to go on ahead, lead; *fig inf* forge ahead, go ahead. **i. al cuartel,** to go into the army. **i. a una,** to cooperate in. **i. bien** *fig inf* to go on well; be well. **i. de brazo,** to walk arm in arm. **i. de compras,** to go shopping. **i. de juerga** *inf* to go on a binge. **i. de bicicleta** *or* **en coche,** to go by bicycle or to ride (in a car or carriage). **i. por,** to do things in order, take one thing at a time. *fig inf* **i. tirando,** to carry on, manage. **¿Cómo le va?** How are things with you? How are you getting along? *inf* **no irle ni venirle a uno nada en un asunto,** to be not in the least concerned in (an affair). **¡Qué va!** Rubbish! Nothing of the sort! **¿Quién va?** *mil* Who goes there? **Vamos,** Let's go (also used as an exclamation: Good gracious! You don't say so! Well!) **Vamos a ver . . . ,** Let's see. **. . . ¡Vaya!** What a . . . !; Come now! Never mind! **¡Vaya a paseo!** *or* **¡Vaya con su música a otra parte!** Take yourself off! Get out! **¡Vaya con Dios!** God keep you! Good-bye! *Pres. Ind.* **voy, vas, va, vamos, váis, van.** *Pres. Part.* **yendo.** *Preterite* **fui, fuiste, fue, fuimos, fuisteis, fueron.** *Imperf.* **iba,** etc. *Pres. Subjunc.* **vaya,** etc. *Imperf. Subjunc.* **fuese,** etc. *Imperat.* **vé**

ira *f,* wrath, anger; vengeance; raging, fury (of elements); *pl* cruelties, acts of vengeance

iracundia *f,* irascibility, irritability; anger

iracundo *a* irascible, irritable, choleric; angry; raging, tempestuous

iranio (-ia) *a* and *n* Iranian

irascibilidad *f,* irascibility; petulance

iridiscencia *f,* iridescence

iridiscente *a* iridescent

iris *m,* rainbow; *anat* iris (of the eye)

irlandés (-esa) *a* and *n* Irishman (woman)

Irlanda Ireland

ironía *f,* irony

irónico *a* ironical

irracional *a* irrational; illogical, unreasonable; *math* irrational, absurd

irradiación *f,* radiation, irradiation

irradiar *vt* to radiate, irradiate

irrazonable *a* unreasonable

irreal *a* unreal

irrealidad *f,* unreality

irrealizable *a* unachievable, unattainable

irrebatible *a* irrefutable, evident

irreconciliable *a* irreconcilable, intransigent

irrecuperable *a* irretrievable

irredimible *a* irredeemable

irreemplazable *a* irreplaceable

irreflexivo *a* thoughtless; rash, impetuous

irreformable *a* unreformable

irrefragable *a* indisputable, unquestionable

irrefrenable *a* unmanageable, uncontrollable

irrefutable *a* irrefutable

irregular *a* irregular; infrequent, rare

irregularidad *f,* irregularity; abnormality; *inf* moral lapse

irreligión *f,* irreligion

irreligiosidad *f,* impiety, godlessness

irreligioso *a* irreligious, impious

irremediable *a* irremediable

irremediablemente *adv* unavoidably; hopelessly

irremisible *a* unpardonable, inexcusable

irremunerado *a* unremunerated, gratuitous

irreparable *a* irreparable

irreprensible a blameless, unexceptionable

irreprochable a irreproachable

irresistible a irresistible; ravishing

irresolución f, vacillation, indecision

irresoluto a hesitant, irresolute

irrespetuoso a disrespectful

irresponsabilidad f, irresponsibility

irresponsable a irresponsible

irreverencia f, irreverence

irreverente a irreverent

irrevocabilidad f, irrevocability, finality

irrevocable a irrevocable

irrigación f, irrigation

irrigador m, spray, sprinkler; med syringe, spray

irrigar vt (med agr) to irrigate

irrisible a ridiculous, laughable, absurd

irrisión f, derision; laughingstock

irrisorio a ridiculous; derisive

irritabilidad f, irritability, petulance, irascibility

irritable a irritable

irritación f, med irritation; petulance, exasperation

irritador a irritating; exasperating. m, irritant

irritante a irritating; exasperating

irritar vt to exasperate, annoy; provoke, inflame; (med law) irritate

írrito a law null, void

irrogar vt to occasion (damage, harm)

irrompible a unbreakable

irrumpir vi to enter violently, break in

irrupción f, irruption, incursion, invasion

irruptor a invading, attacking

isabelino a Isabelline (pertaining to Spanish Queen Isabella II (reigned 1830–68)); bay (of horses)

isla f, island; block (of houses)

islámico a Islamic

islamismo m, Islam

islandés (**-esa**), **islándico** (**-ca**) a Icelandic. n Icelander. m, Icelandic (language)

Islandia Iceland

isleño (**-ña**) a island. n islander; native of the Canary Islands

isleta f, islet

islote m, barren islet

isoca f, Argentina caterpillar

isótope, isótopo m, isotope

israelita mf Israelite. a Israeli

ístmico a isthmian

istmo m, isthmus

Italia Italy

italiano (**-na**) a and n Italian. m, Italian (language)

itálico a italic

iteración f, iteration, repetition

iterar vt to repeat, reiterate

iterativo a iterative, repetitive

itinerario a and m, itinerary

izar vt naut to hoist

izquierda f, left, left-hand side; pol left. **II.I** mil Left face! **a la i.,** on the left

izquierdo a left, left-hand; left-handed; bent, twisted, crooked

jaba f, Lat. Am. basket; Mexico crate

jabalí m, wild boar

jabalina f, sow of wild boar; javelin

jabón m, soap. **j. blando,** soft soap. **j. de olor** or **j. de tocador,** toilet soap. **j. de sastre,** French chalk, steatite

jabonadura f, soaping; pl soapsuds, lather

jabonar vt to soap; wash; inf dress down, scold

jabonera f, soapdish or box; soapwort

jabonoso a soapy

jaca f, pony; filly

jacal m, Mexico hut, shack

jácara f, gay, roguish ballad; song and dance

jacinto m, hyacinth; jacinth. **j. de ceilán,** zircon. **j. occidental,** topaz. **j. oriental,** ruby

jaco m, short coat of mail; hack, jade

jactancia f, bragging, boasting

jactancioso (-sa) a boastful. n braggart

jactarse vr to brag, boast

jaculatoria f, ejaculatory prayer

jade m, min jade

jadeante a panting

jadear vi to pant

jadeo m, pant; panting; hard breathing

jaez m, harness (gen. pl); kind, sort; pl trappings

jaguar m, jaguar

jaiba f, Lat. Am. crab

jáibol m, Lat. Am. highball

jáilaif m, Lat. Am. high life

¡ja, ja, ja! interj Ha! ha! ha!

jalbegar vt to whitewash; make up the face

jalbegue m, whitewash

jalde a bright yellow

jalea f, jelly. **j. de membrillo,** quince jelly

jalear vt to encourage, urge on (by shouts, etc.)

jaleo m, act of encouraging dancers by clapping, shouting, etc.; Andalusian song and dance, inf uproar

jamaicano (-na) a and n Jamaican

jamás adv never. **nunca j.,** never. **por siempre j.,** for always, forever

jamba f, jamb (of a door or window)

jambarse vr, Lat. Am. to overeat

jamón m, ham

jamona f, inf plumpish middle-aged woman

Japón Japan

japonés (-esa) a and n Japanese. m, Japanese (language)

jaque m, check (in chess); braggart. **j. mate,** checkmate. **en j.,** at bay

jaquear vt to check (in chess); mil harass the enemy

jaqueca f, migraine, sick headache. inf **dar una j.,** to annoy

jarabe m, syrup. **j. tapatío,** Mexican hat dance

jarana f, roundhouse; inf revelry; fight, roughhouse; trick, deception

jarcia f, equipment; naut tackle, rigging (gen. pl); fishing tackle; inf heap, mixture, medley

jardín m, garden

jardinar vt to landscape

jardinera f, plant stand, jardiniere; open streetcar

jardinería f, gardening

jardinero (-ra) n gardener

jareta f, sew running hem; naut netting

jarra f, jar, jug. **en jarras,** arms akimbo

jarrete m, calf (of the leg)

jarretera f, garter. **Orden de la J.,** Order of the Garter

jarro m, pitcher; jug; jar; vase

jarrón m, garden urn; vase

jaspe m, jasper

jaspeado a marbled, mottled; dappled; frosted (of glass)

jauja f, fig paradise, land of milk and honey

jaula f, cage; crate; miner's cage

jazmín m, jasmine. **j. amarillo,** yellow jasmine. **j. de la India,** gardenia

jefa f, forewoman; manager; leader, head

jefatura f, chieftainship; managership; leadership. **J. de policía,** police station or headquarters

jefe m, chief; head, leader; manager; mil commanding officer. **mil j. de estado mayor,** chief of staff. **j. del tren,** railroad guard

jengibre m, ginger

jeque m, sheik

jerarca m, hierarch

jerarquía f, hierarchy

jerárquico a hierarchical

jerez m, sherry

jerga f, thick frieze cloth; jargon

jergón m, straw or hay mattress, pallet; misfit (garments); inf fat, lazy person

Jericó Jericho

jerigonza f, jargon; gibberish

jeringa f, syringe

jeringar vt to inject; syringe; inf annoy

jeringuilla f, small syringe; mock orange

jeroglífico a hieroglyphic. m, hieroglyph

jersey m, jersey, sweater

Jerusalén Jerusalem

jesuita m, Jesuit

Jesús m, Jesus. interj Goodness!; Bless you! (said to someone after sneezing). **¡ay J.!** Alas! inf **en un decir J.,** in a trice

jeta f, hog's snout; blubber lip; *inf* face, mug

jícama f, *Central America* sweet turnip

jicote m, *Lat. Am.* wasp

jinete m, horseman, rider; horse soldier, cavalryman

jip m, jeep

jipijapa f, very fine straw. **sombrero de j.,** panama hat

jira f, strip of cloth; picnic; tour

jirafa f, giraffe

jirón m, rag; piece of a dress, etc.; portion of a whole

jitomate, m, *Mexico* tomato. See **tomate**

jocosidad f, pleasantry, jocularity; joke

jocoso a waggish; jocose, joyous

jocundidad f, jocundity

jocundo a jocund

jofaina f, washbowl

Jordán Jordan (river)

jornada f, day's journey; journey, trip; *mil* expedition; duration of a working day; opportunity; span of life; act of a drama. **a grandes jornadas,** by forced marches, rapidly

jornal m, day's wages or labor

jornalear vi to work by the day

jornalero (-ra) n day laborer; wage earner

joroba f, hump; *inf* impertinence, nuisance

jorobado (-da) a humpbacked. n hunchback

jota f, name of letter J; popular Spanish dance; jot, tittle (always used negatively). **no saber j.,** to be completely ignorant

joven a young. *mf* young man or woman

jovenzuelo (-la) n youngster, boy

jovialidad f, joviality, cheerfulness

joya f, jewel; present; *arch* astragal; *fig* a jewel of a person

joyería f, jeweler's shop or workshop

joyero m, jeweler; jewel box

juanete m, bunion; prominent cheekbone; *naut* topgallant sail

jubilación f, retirement; pensioning off; pension

jubilado a retired

jubilar vt to pension off; excuse from certain duties; *inf* put aside as useless (things); vr rejoice; retire or be pensioned off

jubileo m, jubilee

júbilo m, rejoicing, merriment. **j. de vivir,** joie de vivre

jubiloso a jubilant, happy

judaísmo m, Judaism

judería f, Jewry

judesmo m, Judezmo (Romance language of Jews)

judía f, Jew (female); Jewish quarter, Jewish neighborhood; haricot bean. **judías verdes,** string beans

judicatura f, judicature; judgeship; judiciary

judío (-ía) a Jewish. n Jew. **j. errante,** wandering Jew

juego m, play, sport; gambling; hand (of cards); set; suite; *mech* play, working. **j. de café,** coffee set. **j. de los cientos,** piquet. **j. de manos,** sleight of hand, conjuring. **j. de naipes,** game of cards. **j. limpio,** fair play. **j. sencillo,** single (at tennis). **j. sucio,** foul play. **juegos florales,** floral games, poetry contest. **juegos malabares,** juggling. **en j.,** in operation; at stake. **entrar en j.,** to come into play. **hacer j.,** to match. **hacer juegos malabares,** to juggle

juerga f, *inf* spree, binge. **ir de j.,** *inf* to go on a binge

jueves m, Thursday. **¡No es cosa del otro j.!** *inf* It's no great shakes! It's nothing to write home about!

juez m, judge. **j. arbitrador,** arbitrator; referee. **j. municipal,** magistrate

jugada f, play; playing; move, throw; *fig* bad turn

jugador (-ra) a gambling; playing. n gambler; player. **j. de manos,** conjurer

jugar vi irr to play; frolic; take part in a game; gamble; make a move (in a game); *mech* work; handle (a weapon); com intervene; vt play (a match); bet; handle (a weapon); risk. **j. el lance,** *fig* to play one's cards well. **j. limpio,** to play fair; *fig inf* be straightforward. **j. sucio,** to play foul. **jugarse el todo por el todo,** to stake everything. Pres. Ind. **juego, juegas, juega, juegan.** Pres. Subjunc. **juegue, juegues, juegue, jueguen**

juglar m, entertainer; buffoon, juggler; minstrel

juglaresco a pertaining to minstrels

jugo m, sap; juice; *fig* essence. **j. de muñeca,** elbow grease

jugosidad f, juiciness, succulence; *fig* pithiness

jugoso a juicy, succulent; *fig* pithy

juguete m, toy; plaything; *fig* puppet

juguetear vi to frolic, gambol

jugueteo m, gamboling; play, dalliance

juguetería f, toy trade; toy shop

juguetón a playful

juicio m, judgment; wisdom, prudence; sanity, right mind; opinion; horoscope. **j. final,** Last Judgment. **j. sano,** right mind. **asentar el j.,** to settle down, become sensible. **estar fuera de j.,** to be insane. **pedir en j.,** to sue at law

juicioso a judicious; prudent

julepear vt, *Lat. Am.* to get scared, be terrified

julio m, July; *elec* joule

jumento m, ass; beast of burden

junco m, bot rush, reed; naut junk

junio m, June

junta f, joint; assembly, council; committee; union, association; session, sitting; entirety, whole; board, management. **j. de comercio,** board of trade. **j. directiva,** managerial board

juntar vt to join, unite (with prep a or con); couple; assemble; amass; leave ajar (door); vr (with con) frequent company of; meet; join; copulate

junto a united, together. adv (with prep a) near; adv together, simultaneously. **en j.,** altogether, in all

jura f, solemn oath; swearing

jurado m, jury; jury

juramentar vt to swear in; vr take an oath

juramento m, oath; curse, imprecation. **j. falso,** perjury, **prestar j.,** to take an oath

jurar vt to swear an oath; swear allegiance; vi curse, be profane

jurídico a juridical, legal

jurisconsulto m, jurisconsult

jurisdicción f, law jurisdiction; boundary; authority

jurisprudencia f, jurisprudence

jurista mf jurist

justar vi to joust

justicia f, justice; equity, right; penalty, punishment; righteousness; court of justice; inf death penalty, execution. **administrar j.,** to dispense justice

justiciero a just

justificable a justifiable

justificación f, justification, impartiality, fairness; convincing proof

justificar vt to justify, vindicate; adjust, regulate; prove innocent; vr justify oneself; prove one's innocence

justipreciar vt to appraise, value

justiprecio m, appraisement, valuation

justo a just; righteous, virtuous; exact, accurate; tight-fitting, close. adv justly; exactly; tightly

juvenil a young

juventud f, youthfulness, youth; younger generation

juzgado m, court of law; jurisdiction; judgeship

juzgar vt to judge, pass sentence on; decide, consider

K

ka *f*, name of the letter K

kerosén *m*, kerosene

kilo *prefix* meaning a thousand. *m*, *abb* kilogram

kilogramo *m*, kilogram (2.17 lb.)

kilometraje *m*, number of kilometers; mileage

kilométrico *a* kilometric. **billete k.,** tourist ticket

kilómetro *m*, kilometer (about $\frac{5}{8}$ mile)

kilovatio *m*, *elec* kilowatt

kiosco *m*, kiosk

klaxon *m*, *Mexico* horn

L

la *def art. f, sing* the (e.g. **la mesa,** the table). **la** is replaced by **el** *m, sing* before feminine nouns beginning with stressed *a* or *ha* (e.g. **el hambre,** hunger). **la** is sometimes used before names of famous women (e.g. **la Juana de Arco, la Melba** (Joan of Arc, Melba)) and is generally not translated. *pers pron acc f sing* her; it (e.g. **La veo venir,** I see her coming). *dem. pron* followed by *de,* or by *que* introducing relative clause, that of, that which, the one that, she who (e.g. **La casa está lejos de la en que escribo,** The house is far from the one in which I write). **la de** is used familiarly for Mrs. (e.g. **la de Jiménez,** Mrs. Jimenez). **la** means some, any, one, as substitution for noun already given (e.g. **Su hija lo haría si la tuviera,** Her daughter would do it if she had one)

laberinto *m,* labyrinth; *fig* tangle, complication; *anat* labyrinth of the ear

labia *f, inf* blarney, gab

labihendido *a* harelipped

labio *m,* lip; rim, edge. **l. leporino,** harelip. **cerrar los labios,** to close one's lips; keep silent

labor *f,* work, toil; sewing; needlework; husbandry, farming; silkworm egg; *min* working; trimming; plowing, harrowing; *Central America* small farm

laborable *a* workable; cultivable, tillable. **día l.,** workday

laborar *vt* to work; till; plow; construct; *vi* scheme, plot, plan; *Central America* work

laboratorio *m,* laboratory

laborear *vt* to work; till, cultivate; *naut* reeve

laboreo *m,* tilling, cultivation; working, development (of mines, etc.)

laborioso *a* industrious, diligent; laborious, tedious, hard

laborista *a* and *mf* belonging to the Labor Party

labra *f,* stonecutting; carving or working (metal, stone, or wood)

labrada *f,* fallow land ready for sowing

labradero *a* workable; cultivable, tillable

labrado *a* and *past part* worked; fashioned; carved; embroidered; figured, patterned. *m,* (gen. *pl*) cultivated ground

labrador *m,* laborer, worker; farmer; peasant

labradora *f,* peasant girl; farm girl

labrandera *f,* seamstress

labrantío *a* tillable, cultivable. *m,* farming

labranza *f,* tillage, cultivation; farm; farmland; farming; employment, work

labrar *vt* to work, do; carve; fashion, construct, make; *agr* cultivate, till; plow; embroider; sew; bring about, cause; *vi fig* impress deeply, leave a strong impression

labriego (**-ga**) *n* agricultural laborer; peasant

laca *f,* lac; lacquer, varnish; *art* lake (pigment)

lacayo *m,* groom; lackey, footman

lacear *vt sew* to trim with bows; tie, lace; snare, trap; *Lat. Am.* lasso

laceración *f,* laceration

lacerado *a* unhappy, unfortunate; leprous

lacerar *vt* to lacerate, mangle, tear; distress, wound the feelings of

lacería *f,* poverty, misery; toil, drudgery; trouble, affliction

lacero *m,* cowboy, one who uses a lasso; poacher

lacio *a* drooping, limp; withered, faded; straight (hair)

lacónico *a* laconic, concise; Laconian

lacra *f,* aftereffect, trace (of illness); vice; fault; *Lat. Am.* sore, ulcer

lacrar *vt* to impair the health; infect with an illness; injure, prejudice (the interests, etc.); seal with sealing wax

lacre *m,* sealing wax. *a* red

lacrimoso *a* tearful, lachrymose

lactancia *f,* lactation

lactar *vt* to suckle; feed with milk; *vi* take or drink milk

lácteo *a* lacteal; milky

ladear *vt* to incline; tilt; turn aside, twist; skirt, pass close to; reach by a roundabout way, go indirectly to; *vr* tilt; be in favor of, incline to; be equal to

ladeo *m,* tilt; sloping; turning aside

ladera *f,* slope, incline; hillside

ladería *f,* terrace on a hillside

ladero *a* lateral; *Argentina* helper

ladilla *f,* crab louse

ladino *a* eloquent; versatile linguistically; wily, crafty; *m,* Ladino (variety of Judezmo)

lado *m,* side; edge, margin; slope, declivity; faction, party; side, flank; face (of a coin); *fig* aspect, view; line of descent; means, way; favor, protection; *pl* helpers, protectors; advisers. **al l.,** near at hand. *inf* **dar de l.** (**a**), to cool off, fall out with. **dejar a un l.** (**una cosa**), to omit, pass over (a thing). **mirar de l.** or **de medio l.,** to look upon with disapproval; steal a look at

ladrar *vi* to bark; *inf* threaten without hurting

ladrido *m,* bark, barking; slander, gossip

ladrillar *vt* to floor or pave with bricks. *m,* brickyard; brickkiln

ladrillo *m,* brick; tile

ladrón (**-ona**) *a* robbing, thieving. *n* thief, robber; burglar. *m.* **l. de corazones,** ladykiller

ladronera f, thieves' den; thieving, pilfering; strongbox

lagar m, wine or olive press

lagarta f, female lizard; *inf* she-serpent, cunning female

lagartija f, wall lizard, small lizard

lagarto m, lizard; *inf* sly, artful person, fox

lago m, lake

lagotear vi *inf* to wheedle, play up to

lagotería f, wheedling, coaxing, flattery

lágrima f, tear; drop (of liquid); exudation, ozzing (from trees)

lagrimal a lachrymal

lagrimear vi to shed tears

lagrimeo m, weeping, crying; watering of the eyes

lagrimoso a tearful; watery (of eyes); sad, tragic

laguna f, small lake, lagoon; lacuna; gap, hiatus

laicismo m, secularism

laico a lay, secular

laja f, *Lat. Am.* flagstone, slab

lama f, ooze, slime. m, lama, Buddhist priest

lambioche a, *Mexico* cringing, fawning

lameculos mf *inf* toady

lamedura f, licking; lapping

lamentable a lamentable

lamentación f, lamentation; lament

lamentador (-ra) a lamenting, wailing. n wailer, mourner

lamentar vt to mourn, lament, bewail; vr bemoan, bewail

lamento m, lament

lamentoso a lamenting, afflicted; lamentable

lamer vt to lick; pass the tongue over; touch lightly; lap

lámina f, sheet (of metal); lamina; engraving; illustration; picture; engraving plate

laminación f, lamination, rolling (of metals)

laminar a laminate; laminated. vt to roll (metals); laminate; lick

lampa f, *Chile, Peru* hoe

lámpara f, lamp; radiance, light, luminous body; grease spot. **l. de los mineros** or **l. de seguridad,** safety lamp. **l. de soldar,** blowpipe. **l. termiónica,** *rad* thermionic valve. **atizar la l.,** to trim the lamp; *inf* refill drinking glasses

lampazo m, *Lat. Am.* (floor) mop

lampiño a beardless, clean-shaven; smooth-faced; *bot* nonhirsute

lana f, wool; fleece; woolen garments or cloth; woolen trade (gen. pl)

lanar a wool; wool-bearing. **ganado l.,** sheep

lance m, throw, cast; casting a fishing line; catch of fish; crisis, difficult moment;

lit episode; quarrel; move (in a game). *fig* **l. apretado,** difficult position, tight corner. **l. de fortuna,** chance, fate. **l. de honor,** affair of honor; duel

lancear vt to wound with a lance; lance

lanceta f, lancet; *Lat. Am.* goad

lancha f, *naut* launch; lighter; ship's boat; small boat; flagstone. **l. bombardera** or **l. cañonera,** gunboat. **l. de salvamento,** ship's lifeboat. **l. escampavía,** patrol boat

landa f, lande

lanero a woolen. m, wool merchant; wool warehouse

langosta f, locust; lobster. **l. migratoria,** locust

langostín m, crayfish

languidecer vi *irr* to languish, pine. See **conocer**

languidez f, lassitude, inertia; languor

lánguido a listless, weak, languid; half-hearted; languishing, languorous

lanolina f, lanolin

lanosidad f, woolliness; down (on leaves, etc.)

lanoso, lanudo a woolly

lanza f, lance, spear; lancer; nozzle (of a hosepipe). **correr lanzas,** to joust (in a tournament). **estar con la l. en ristre,** to have the lance in rest; be prepared or ready. *inf* **ser una l.,** to be very clever

lanzadera f, weaver's shuttle; sewing machine shuttle. *inf* **parecer una l.,** to be constantly on the go

lanzallamas m, flamethrower

lanzamiento m, throwing; cast, throw; *law* dispossession; *naut* launching

lanzaminas m, minelayer

lanzar vt to throw, cast, hurl; *naut* launch; vomit; *law* dispossess; *agr* take root; vr hurl oneself, rush; take (to), embark (upon)

lanzatorpedos (tubo) m, torpedo tube

lañar vt to clamp; clean fish (for salting)

lapa f, barnacle, limpet; *Mexico* scrounger

lapicera f, *Argentina* ballpoint (pen)

lapicero m, pencil holder, pencil case; mechanical pencil

lápida f, memorial tablet; gravestone

lapidar vt to stone, lapidate; throw stones at

lapislázuli m, lapis lazuli

lápiz m, graphite; pencil; crayon. **l. para los labios,** lipstick

lapizar m, graphite mine. vt to pencil

lapón (-ona) a Lappish. n Laplander. m, Sami (language)

lapso m, lapse, period, passage; slip, error, failure

laquear vt to lacquer, paint

lardear vt *cul* to baste

lardo m, lard; animal fat

lardoso a greasy; fat; oily

larga f, longest billiard cue; delay (gen. pl). **a la l.,** in the long run

largamente adv fully, at length; generously; widely, extensively; comfortably

largar vt to slacken, loosen; naut unfurl; set at liberty; fig inf let fly (oaths, etc.); administer (blows, etc.); vr inf quit, leave (in a hurry or secretly); naut set sail

largo a long; generous, liberal; abundant, plentiful; protracted; prolonged; expeditious; pl many long (e.g. **por largos años,** for many long years). m, mus largo; length. inf **¡L. de aquí!** Get out! **a la larga,** in length; eventually, finally; slowly; with many digressions. **a lo l.,** lengthwise; along the length (of); in the distance, far off; along the length (of). fig **ponerse de l.,** to make one's debut in society; come of age

largor m, **largura** f, length

largucho, -a a, Lat. Am. lanky

largueza f, length; generosity, munificence

largura f, length

laringe f, larynx

laringitis f, laryngitis

larva f, larva; worm, grub; specter, phantom

las def art. f pl, of **la** the. pers pron acc f pl, of **la,** them

lascivia f, lasciviousness

lascivo a lascivious, lewd; wanton

lasitud f, lassitude, weariness, exhaustion

laso a weary, exhausted; weak; untwisted (of silk, etc.)

lástima f, compassion, pity; pitiful sight; complaint, lamentation. **dar l.,** to cause pity. **Es l.,** It's a pity. **tener l. (a** or **de)** to be sorry for (persons)

lastimador a harmful, injurious; painful

lastimadura f, Lat. Am. injury, wound

lastimar vt to hurt, harm, injure; pity; fig wound, distress; vr (with de) be sorry for or about; complain, lament

lastimero a pitiful; mournful; injurious, harmful

lastimoso a pitiful, heartbreaking; mournful

lastre m, ballast; good sense, prudence

lata f, can, tin; tin plate; can of food. **en l.,** canned, tinned (of food). inf **Es una l.,** It's a bore, It's an awful nuisance

latamente adv extensively, at length; broadly

latente a latent

lateral a lateral

látex m, latex

latido m, yelp, bark; beat; throb; palpitation

latifundios m pl, latifundia (large agricultural estates)

latigazo m, lash; crack of a whip; sudden

blow of fate; inf draft (of wine, etc.); harsh scolding; naut jerk or flapping (of sails)

látigo m, whip, lash; cinch, girth of a saddle

latín m, Latin. **bajo l.,** low Latin. inf **saber l.,** to know the score; be smart

latinajo m, inf bad Latin

latinizar vt to latinize; vi inf use Latin phrases

latino a Latin; lateen sail

latinoamericano (-na) a and n Latin-American

latir vi to yelp, howl; bark; throb, palpitate, beat **me late que . . .** Mexico, I have a hunch that . . .

latitud f, latitude; area, extent; breadth

latitudinario a latitudinarian

lato a extensive; large; broad (of word meanings)

latón m, brass

latoso a boring, troublesome, annoying

latrocinio m, larceny

latvio (-ia) a and n Latvian

laúd m, lute

laudable a praiseworthy, laudable

laudatorio a laudatory

laurear vt to crown with laurel; honor, reward

laurel m, bay tree. **l. cerezo,** laurel. **l. rosa,** rosebay, oleander

láureo a laurel

lauréola f, laurel wreath

lauro m, bay tree; glory, triumph

lava f, lava

lavable a washable

lavabo m, washstand; cloakroom, lavatory

lavada f, load of wash, load

lavadedos m, fingerbowl

lavadero m, washing place; laundry

lavado m, washing; cleaning; wash. **l. al seco,** dry cleaning

lavadura f, washing

lavamanos m, washstand; lavatory

lavamiento m, washing, cleansing, ablution

lavanda f, lavender

lavandera f, laundress; washerwoman

lavandería f, laundry

lavandero m, laundry; laundryman

lavaplatos m, dishwasher; Chile, Mexico (kitchen) sink

lavar vt to wash; fig wipe out, purify; paint in watercolors. **l. al seco,** to dry-clean

lavativa f, enema; syringe; clyster; inf nuisance, bore

lavatorio m, washing, lavation; ecc lavabo; lavatory, washing place; ecc maundy

lavazas f pl, dirty soapy water

laxante a and m, laxative

laxar vt to loosen, relax; soften

laxitud *f*, laxity

laxo *a* lax; slack

lazar *vt* to lasso

lazarillo *m*, boy who guides a blind person

lazo *m*, bow; knot of ribbons; tie; ornamental tree; figure (in dancing); lasso; rope, bond; lace (of a shoe); *fig* trap, snare; bond, obligation; slipknot. **l. corredizo**, running knot. *fig inf* **armar l.,** to set a trap. *inf* **caer en el l.,** to fall into the trap, be deceived

le *pers pron dat m*, or *f*, *3rd pers sing* to him, to her, to it, to you (e.g. **María le dio el perro,** Mary gave him (her, you) the dog). Clarity may require the addition of a **él, a ella, a usted** (e.g. **Le dio el perro a ella,** etc.). *pers pron acc m*, *3rd pers sing* him (e.g. **Le mandé a casa,** I sent him home)

leal *a* loyal; faithful (animals)

lealtad *f*, loyalty; faithfulness; sincerity, truth

lección *f*, reading; lesson; oral test; warning, example. **l. práctica,** object lesson. **dar l.,** to give a lesson. **tomar la l.,** to hear a lesson

lechas *f pl*, soft roe; milt

leche *f*, milk; milky fluid of some plants and seeds; *Lat. Am.* good luck. *inf* **estar con la l. en los labios,** to be young and inexperienced

lechera *f*, milkmaid; milk can or jug; *Lat. Am.* cow

lechería *f*, dairy; dairy shop; *Lat. Am.* meanness

lechero (-ra) *a* dairy, milk; milky; milch, milk-giving. *n* milk seller. **industria lechera,** dairy farming

lecho *m*, bed; couch; animal's bed, litter; riverbed; bottom of the sea; layer; *geol* stratum

lechón *m*, suckling pig; hog; *inf* slovenly man

lechosa *f*, *Dominican Republic, Venezuela* papaya

lechoso *a* milky

lechudo, -a *a*, *Lat. Am.* lucky

lechuga *f*, lettuce; frill, flounce. *inf* **como una l.,** as fresh as a daisy

lechuguina *f*, *inf* affected, overdressed young woman

lechuguino *m*, lettuce plant; *inf* young blood, gallant; *inf* foppish young man

lechuza *f*, barn owl

lector (-ra) *n* reader; lecturer

lectura *f*, reading; lecture; culture, knowledge

ledo *a* happy, content

leer *vt irr* to read; explain, interpret; teach; take part in an oral test. See **creer**

legación *f*, *ecc* legateship; legation

legado *m*, legacy; legate

legajo *m*, bundle, docket; file

legal *a* legal; legitimate; upright, trustworthy

legalidad *f*, legality

legalizar *vt* to legalize

legamente *adv* ignorantly, stupidly

légamo *m*, mud, slime

legañoso *a* bleary-eyed

legar *vt* to bequeath; send as a legate

legatario (-ia) *n* legatee, one to whom a legacy is bequeathed

legendario *a* legendary

legible *a* legible

legión *f*, legion

legionario *a* and *m*, legionary

legislación *f*, legislation

legislador (-ra) *a* legislative. *n* legislator

legislar *vi* to legislate

legislativo *a* legislative

legislatura *f*, legislature

legista *mf* jurist; student of law

legítima *f*, portion of a married man's estate that cannot be willed away from his wife and children

legitimación *f*, legitimation

legitimar *vt* to legitimize

legitimidad *f*, legitimacy

legítimo *a* legitimate; real, true

lego *a* lay, secular. *m*, layman

legua *f*, league (approximately 5.573 meters). **a la l., de cien leguas, desde media l.,** from afar

legumbre *f*, pulse; vegetable

leída *f*, *Lat. Am.* reading. **de una leída** in one reading, at one go

leído *a* well-read

lejanía *f*, distance

lejano *a* distant, remote, far off

lejía *f*, lye; bleaching solution; *inf* dressing-down, scolding

lejos *adv* far off, far, distant. *m*, perspective, view from afar; *art* background. **a lo l.,** far off, in the distance. **de** or **desde l.,** from afar, from a distance

lelo *a* stupid; fatuous, inane

lema *m*, chapter heading; argument, summary; motto; theme, subject

lencería *f*, linen goods; linen merchant's shop; linen closet

lene *a* smooth, soft; kind, sweet, gentle; lightweight

lengua *f*, *anat* tongue; mother tongue, language; clapper of a bell; information. *mf* spokes. **l. de escorpión** or **mala l.,** scandalmonger, backbiter. **l. de fuego,** *ecc* tongue of fire, flame. **l. del agua,** waterline, tidemark. **l. de oc,** langue d'oc. **l. de oil,** langue d'oil. **l. de tierra,** neck of land, promontory. **l. viva,** modern language. *inf* **andar en lenguas,** to be on every lip, be famous. *inf* **hacerse lenguas de,** to praise to the skies. *inf* **irse (a uno) la l.,** to be indiscreet, talk too much. **poner l.** or **lenguas en,** to gossip about.

inf **tener mucha l.,** to be very talkative.
tomar l. *or* **lenguas,** to find out about, inform oneself on

lenguado *m, icht* sole

lenguaje *m,* language; style; speech, idiom. **l. vulgar,** common speech

lengüeta *f, dim* little tongue; *mus* tongue (of wind instruments); barb (of an arrow); needle (of a balance)

lengüeterías *Lat. Am.* gossip

lenitivo a lenitive; soothing. *m, med* lenitive; *fig* balm (of sorrow, etc.)

lente *m,* lens; *pl* eyeglasses. **l. de aumento,** magnifying glass

lenteja *f,* lentil; lentil plant

lentejuela *f,* sequin

lentitud *f,* lentitude; slowness, deliberation

lento a slow, deliberate; sluggish, heavy; *med* glutinous, adhesive

leña *f,* firewood; *inf* beating, birching. *fig* **echar l. al fuego,** to add fuel to the flame. *fig* **llevar l. al monte,** to carry coals to Newcastle

leñador (-ra) *n* woodcutter; firewood dealer

leñera *f,* woodpile; woodshed

leño *m,* wooden log; wood, timber; *poet* ship; *inf* blockhead

leñoso a woody, ligneous

león *m,* lion. *ast* Leo; valiant man; *Lat. Am.* puma. **l. marino,** sea lion

leona *f,* lioness; *Chile* confusion, mixup

leonés (-esa) a and *n* Leonese

leopardo *m,* leopard

leperada *f, Central America, Mexico* coarse remark

lepra *f,* leprosy

leproso a leprous

lerdo a slow, lumbering (gen. horses); stupid, slow-witted, dull

les *pers pron dat 3rd pers pl mf,* to them (e.g. **Les dimos las flores,** We gave them flowers. **Les hablé del asunto,** I spoke to them about the matter)

lesbio (-ia) a and *n* lesbian

lesión *f,* lesion, wound; *fig* injury

lesionar *vt* to wound; *fig* injure

leso a wounded, hurt; offensive, injurious; *fig* unbalanced, perturbed (of the mind); *Lat. Am.* dumb, stupid. **crimen de lesa majestad,** crime of lèse-majesté

letal a lethal; deadly

letanía *f,* ecc litany

letargia *f, med* lethargy

letárgico a lethargic

letargo *m,* lethargy; indifference, apathy

letra *f,* letter (of alphabet); *print* type; penmanship, hand; *fig* letter, literal meaning; words (of a song); inscription; *com* bill, draft; cunning, shrewdness; *pl* learning, knowledge. **l. abierta,** *com* open credit. **l. de cambio,** *com* bill of ex-

change. **l. gótica,** Gothic characters. **l. itálica,** italics. **l. mayúscula,** capital letter. **l. paladial,** palatal. **facultad de letras,** faculty of arts. **La l. con sangre entra,** Learning is acquired with pain. **primeras letras,** early education, first letters

letrado a learned, educated; *inf* presumptuous; pedantic. *m,* lawyer

letrero *m,* label; inscription; poster, bill; sign, indicator. **l. luminoso,** illuminated sign

letrilla *f,* short poem, often set to music

letrina *f,* latrine

leva *f, naut* weighing anchor; *mil* levy, forced enrolment; tappet; *mech* lever; *mech* cam; *inf* **irse a l. y a monte,** to flee, beat it, quit

levadizo a able to be raised or lowered (bridges). **puente l.,** drawbridge

levadura *f,* leaven, yeast; rising (of bread)

levantada *f,* act of rising from bed

levantamiento *m,* raising, lifting; rebellion, revolt; ennoblement, elevation; settlement of accounts

levantar *vt* to raise, lift; pick up; build, construct; cancel, remove; encourage, rouse; recruit, enlist; cut (cards); leave, abandon; survey; disturb (game); produce, raise (a swelling); found, institute; increase (prices); raise (the voice); *fig* ennoble, elevate; cause, occasion; libel, accuse falsely; *vr* rise; get up; stand up; stand out, be prominent; rebel; leave one's bed after an illness. **l. bandera,** to rebel. **l. el campo,** to break camp. **levantarse del izquierdo,** *inf* to get out of bed on the wrong side

levante *m,* east; Levant; east wind

levar *vt naut* to weigh anchor; *vr* set sail

leve a light (in weight); unimportant, trifling

levedad *f,* lightness (in weight); unimportance, levity, flippancy

levita *m,* Levite; deacon. *f,* frock coat

levitación *f,* levitation

levítico a Levitical. *m,* Leviticus

levitón *m,* frock coat

léxico *m,* lexicon

ley *f,* law; precept; regulation; rule; doctrine; loyalty, faithfulness; affection, love; legal standard (weights, measures, quality); ratio of gold or silver in coins, jewelry; statute, ordinance; *pl* the Law. **l. de préstamo y arriendo,** Lend-Lease Act. **ley suntuaria,** sumptuary law. *inf* **a la l.,** with care and decorum. **a l. de caballero,** on the word of a gentleman. **de buena l.,** a excellent; *adv* genuinely; in good faith. **de mala l.,** a disreputable, base; *adv* in bad faith

leyenda *f,* legend; inscription; story, tale

leyente a reading. *mf* reader

lezna *f,* awl

lía *f,* plaited esparto rope; *pl* lees, dregs

liar *vt* to fasten or tie up; wrap up, parcel; roll (a cigarette); *inf* entangle, embroil; *vr* take a lover, enter on a liaison. *inf* **liarlas,** to quit, sneak off; *inf* kick the bucket, die

Líbano, el Lebanon

libar *vt* to suck; perform a libation; sip, taste; sacrifice

libelo *m,* libel; *law* petition

libélula *f,* dragonfly

liberación *f,* liberation, freeing; receipt, quittance; *law* reconveyance (of mortgages)

liberador (-ra) *a* liberating, freeing. *n* liberator

liberal *a* generous, openhanded; liberal, tolerant; learned (of professions). *a* and *mf pol* liberal

liberalidad *f,* generosity, magnanimity

liberalismo *m,* liberalism

liberalizar *vt* to liberalize, make liberal

liberar *vt* to liberate

libertad *f,* liberty, freedom; independence; privilege, right (gen. *pl*); exemption; licentiousness; forwardness, familiarity; naturalness, ease of manner; facility, capacity; immunity. **l. caucional,** freedom on bail, release on bail. **l. de cultos,** freedom of worship; religious toleration. **l. vigilada,** *law* probation. **poner en l.,** to set at liberty; *(with de) fig* free from

libertador (-ra) *a* liberating, freeing. *n* liberator, deliverer

libertinaje *m,* libertinage, licentiousness

libertino (-na) *a* a debauched, licentious. *m,* libertine. *n* child of a freed slave

libídine *f,* lust

libidinoso *a* libidinous, lustful

libra *f,* pound (measure, coinage); *ast* Libra. **l. esterlina,** pound sterling. **l. medicinal,** pound troy

librador (-ra) *a* a freeing, liberating. *n* deliverer, liberator. *m,* *com* drawer (of bill of exchange, etc.)

libramiento *m,* liberation, deliverance; *com* delivery; order of payment

libranza *f,* *com* draft. **l. de correos, l. postal** *Lat. Am.* (postal) money order

librar *vt* to liberate, free; protect (from misfortune); *com* draw (a draft); *com* deliver; place confidence in; issue, enact; *vi* bring forth children; *vr* *(with de)* escape from; get rid of

libre *a* free; at liberty, disengaged; unhampered, untrammeled; independent; bold, brazen; dissolute, vicious; exempt; vacant, unoccupied; unmarried; clear, free; mutinous, rebellious; isolated, remote; innocent; unharmed; *Mexico, Venezuela* taxi. **l. cambio,** free trade

librea *f,* livery

librecambio *m,* free trade

librepensador (-ra) *a* freethinking. *n* freethinker

librera *f, Lat. Am.* bookcase

librería *f,* bookshop; book trade, bookselling; bookcase

librero *m,* bookseller; *Lat. Am.* bookcase. **l. anticuario,** antiquarian bookseller; rare-book dealer

libreta *f, cul* 1-lb. loaf; notebook; passbook, bankbook

libretista *mf* librettist

libreto *m,* libretto

libro *m,* book; *mus* libretto; *zool* omasum. **l. copiador,** *com* letter book. **l. de actas,** minute book. **l. de caja,** *com* cash book. **l. de cheques,** checkbook. **l. de facturas,** *com* invoice book. **l. de reclamaciones,** complaint book. **l. de texto,** textbook. **l. diario,** *com* daybook. **l. mayor,** ledger. **l. talonario,** receipt book. *fig inf* **hacer l. nuevo,** to turn over a new leaf; introduce innovations

licencia *f,* permission, license; licentiousness; boldness, insolence; *univ* bachelor's degree, licentiate. **l. absoluta,** *mil* discharge. **l. de manejar** *Lat. Am.* driver's license

licenciado (-da) *a* pedantic; free, exempt; licensed. *n univ* bachelor; licentiate. *m,* discharged soldier

licenciar *vt* to allow, permit; license; dismiss, discharge; confer degree of bachelor or licentiate; *mil* discharge; *vr* become licentious; receive bachelor's degree or licentiate

licenciatura *f,* degree of licentiate or bachelor; graduation as such; licentiate course of study

licencioso *a* licentious, dissolute

liceo *m,* lyceum; *Lat. Am.* secondary school, high school

licitación *f,* bidding (at auction)

licitador *m,* bidder (at auction); *Lat. Am.* auctioneer

licitar *vt* to bid for (at auction)

lícito *a* permissible, lawful

licor *m,* liquor, alcoholic drink; liquid

licuadora *f,* blender

licuar *vt* to liquefy

lid *f,* combat, fight; dispute, controversy. **en buena l.,** in fair fight; by fair means

líder *m,* leader; chief

lidia *f,* fighting; bullfight

lidiador (-ra) *n* combatant, fighter

lidiar *vi* to fight; *fig* struggle; *(with contra* or *con)* oppose, fight against; *vt* fight (a bull). **¡Cuánto tienen que l. con . . . !** *fig* What a struggle they have with . . . !

liebre *f,* hare

liendre *f,* nit

lienza *f,* narrow strip (of cloth)

lienzo *m,* linen; cotton; cambric; hemp cloth; *art* canvas

liga *f,* garter; bandage; birdlime; mixture, blend; *met* alloy; alliance, coalition; league (football, etc.)

ligación f, tying; binding; union

ligado m, mus legato; mus tie

ligadura f, bond, tie; binding, fastening; fig shackle, link; (surg mus) ligature; naut lashing

ligamento m, tie, bond; mixture; anat ligament

ligar vt to tie, bind; met alloy; join, connect; render impotent by sorcery; mus slur (notes); vr ally, join together; fig bind oneself. **l. cabos**, to put two and two together

ligereza f, lightness (of weight); swiftness, nimbleness; fickleness; tactless remark, indiscretion

ligero a light (in weight); swift, nimble; light (sleep); unimportant, insignificant; easily digested (food); thin (fabrics, etc.); fickle, changeable. **l. de cascos**, frivolous, gay. **a la ligera**, lightly; quickly; without fuss. **de l.**, impetuously, thoughtlessly; easily, with ease

lija f, dogfish; sandpaper

lila f, lilac bush and flower; lilac color. a inf foolish, vain

lima f, sweet lime, citron fruit; lime tree; file (tool); filing, polishing

limadura f, filing; polishing; pl filings

limar vt to file, smooth with a file; fig touch up, polish

limazo m, slime, viscosity (especially of snails, etc.)

limbo m, limbo; edge, hem; (ast bot) limb; limb (of a quadrant, etc.). inf **estar en el l.**, to be bewildered or abstracted

limeño (**-ña**) a and n native of or belonging to Lima (Peru)

limitación f, limitation; limit, extent; bound; district, area

limitar vt to limit; curb, restrict; bound

límite m, limit, extent; boundary, border; end, confine

limítrofe a bordering, contiguous

limo m, mud, mire, slime; Lat. Am. lime tree

limón m, lemon; lemon tree

limonada f, lemonade. **l. seca**, lemonade powder

limonar m, lemon grove

limonero (**-ra**) n lemon seller. m, lemon tree

limosna f, alms

limosnear vi to beg, ask alms

limoso a slimy, muddy

limpiabotas m, bootblack (person)

limpiador (**-ra**) a cleaning. n cleaner

limpiadura f, cleaning; pl rubbish

limpiamanos m, Central America, Mexico towel

limpiamente adv cleanly; dexterously, neatly; sincerely, candidly; generously, charitably

limpiaparabrisas m, windshield wiper

limpiapipas m, pipe cleaner

limpiar vt to clean; fig cleanse, clear; empty, free (from); agr thin out; inf steal, pinch; inf win (gambling); vr clean oneself

limpiauñas m, orange stick (for fingernails)

limpidez f, poet limpidity

límpido a poet limpid

limpieza f, cleanliness; cleaning; chastity; purity; altruism; uprightness, integrity; neatness, tidiness; dexterity, skill, precision; fair play

limpio a clean; pure, unalloyed, unmixed; neat, tidy; pure-blooded; unharmed, free. **en l.**, in substance; as a fair copy; clearly; com net

linaje m, lineage, family; offspring; kind; sort, quality

linajudo (**-da**) a highborn. n noble, aristocrat; one who alleges his noble descent

linaza f, linseed

lince m, lynx; Mexico wild cat; fig. fox, crafty person

linchamiento m, lynching

linchar vt to lynch

lindar vi to run together, be contiguous

linde mf limit, extent; boundary

lindero a bordering, contiguous. m, boundary. inf **con linderos y arrabales**, with many digressions

lindeza f, beauty, loveliness; witticism; pl (inf ironical) insults

lindo a lovely, beautiful; perfect, exquisite. m, inf fop (gen. **lindo don Diego**)

línea f, line; kind, class; ancestry, lineage; limit, extent; mil file; equator. **l. aérea**, airline. naut **l. de flotación**, waterline. **l. de toque**, touchline (in soccer). **l. recta**, direct line (of descent)

linear a linear. vt to line, mark with lines; art sketch

linfa f, med lymph; vaccine; poet water

linfático a lymphatic

lingote m, ingot; bar (of iron). **l. de fundición**, pig iron

lino m, bot flax; linen; poet ship's sail, canvas

linóleo m, linoleum

linterna f, lantern; lighthouse; lamp. **l. sorda**, dark lantern

lío m, bundle; inf muddle, imbroglio; inf liaison, amour. inf **armar un l.**, to make a muddle, cause trouble. inf **hacerse un l.**, to get in a fix; get in a muddle

liquidable a liquefiable

liquidación f, liquefaction; com clearance, sale; com settlement

liquidar vt to liquefy; com settle; com liquidate; finish; vr liquefy

liquidez f, liquidness

líquido a liquid; com net. m, liquid; com net profit

lira f, mus lyre; ast Lyra; lira (coin)

lírica f, lyrical verse, lyric

lírico a lyrical

lirio m, lily. **l. cárdeno,** yellow flag (iris). **l. de los valles,** lily of the valley

Lisboa Lisbon

lisiado a lame, crippled

lisiar vt to cripple, lame; vr be disabled; be lame

liso a smooth; sleek; unadorned, plain; unicolored

lisonja f, flattery, adulation

lisonjear vt to flatter; fawn upon; fig delight (the ear). **lisonjearse de . . . ,** to flatter oneself on . . .

lisonjero (-ra) a flattering; sweet, pleasant (sounds). n flatterer

lista f, strip of cloth; streak; rib; stripe; catalog, list. **l. de correos,** general delivery, poste restante. **l. de platos,** bill of fare; Mexico **l. de raya** payroll. **pasar l.,** to call the roll; check the list

listado a streaked; striped; ribbed

listo a clever; expeditious, diligent; ready, prepared

listón m, ribbon; strip (of wood)

lisura f, smoothness; sleekness; flatness; sincerity

lisurero, -a, a, Peru cheeky, impudent

litera f, litter; naut berth

literal a literal

literario a literary

literato (-ta) a literary. n writer, litterateur

literatura f, literature

litigación f, litigation

litigante mf litigant

litigar vt to litigate; vi dispute, argue

litigio m, lawsuit; dispute, argument

litigioso a litigious; quarrelsome, disputatious

litisexpensas f pl, law costs of a suit; legal expenses

litoral a and m, littoral

litro m, liter; Chile coarse woolen cloth

Lituania Lithuania

liturgia f, liturgy

litúrgico a liturgical

liviandad f, lightness (of weight); fickleness; unimportance; frivolity; lewdness; act of folly, indiscretion

liviano a light weight; fickle; unimportant, trifling, frivolous; lascivious

lívido a livid; Lat. Am. pale, pallid

llaga f, ulcer; sore; grief, affliction; fig thorn in the flesh

llagar vt to ulcerate; make or produce sores; fig wound; vr be covered with sores

llama f, flame; ardor, vehemence; marsh; zool llama

llamada f, call; mil call-to-arms, call. **l. molestosa,** annoyance call, nuisance call

llamado a called; so-called

llamador (-ra) n caller. m, door knocker; doorbell

llamamiento m, calling; call; divine summons, inspiration; invocation, appeal; summons, convocation

llamar vt to call; invoke, call upon; summon, convoke; name; attract; vi knock (at a door); ring (a bell); vr be named, be called; naut veer (wind). **Se llama Pedro,** His name is Peter

llamarada f, flame, flash; blaze, flare (of anger, etc.)

llamativo a striking, showy; provocative

llamear vi to throw out flames, blaze

llampo m, Lat. Am. ore

llana f, mason's trowel; plain; surface of a page

llanada f, plain

llanamente adv frankly, plainly; naturally, simply; candidly, sincerely

llanero (-ra) n plain dweller

llaneza f, naturalness; candor; familiarity; simplicity (of style)

llano a flat, level; smooth, even; shallow (of receptacles); unaffected, homely, natural; plain (of dresses); manifest, evident; easy; straightforward, candid; informal; simple (of style). m, plain; level stretch of ground

llanta f, aut tire; rim, felloe. **l. de refacción** Mexico spare tire **l. de rueda,** wheel, rim

llanto m, weeping, flood of tears

llanura f, smoothness, evenness, levelness; plain

llave (de) f, key (to); spigot (of), faucet (of), tap (of); spanner, wrench; elec switch; clock winder; mus key, clef; arch keystone; print brace; mech wrench; lock (of a gun); tuning key; piston (of musical instruments); lock (in wrestling); fig key (of a problem or a study). **l. de transmisión,** sender (telegraphy). **l. inglesa,** monkey-wrench, spanner. **l. maestra,** master key, skeleton key. **echar la l.,** to lock. **torcer la l.,** to turn the key

llavero (-ra) n keeper of the keys. m, key ring. **l. de cárcel,** turnkey

llegada f, arrival, advent

llegar vi to arrive; last, endure; reach; achieve a purpose; be sufficient, suffice; amount (to); make; vt bring near, draw near; gather; vr come near, approach; adhere. **l. a ser,** to become. **l. a un punto muerto,** to reach a deadlock. **l. hasta . . . ,** to stretch as far as . . .

llena f, spate, overflow

llenar vt to fill; occupy (a post); satisfy, please; fulfill; satiate; pervade; fill up (a form); vi be full (of the moon); vr inf stuff, overeat; fig inf be fed-up

lleno a full; replete; abundant; complete. m, full moon; theat full house; inf glut, abundance; perfection. **de l., de l. en l.,** entirely, completely

llevadero a tolerable, bearable

llevar vt to carry, transport; charge (a price); yield, produce; carry off, take away; endure, bear; persuade; guide, take; direct; wear (clothes); carry (a handbag, etc.); introduce, present; gain, achieve; manage (a horse); pass, spend (of time) (with past part) have (e.g. **Llevo escrita la carta,** I have written the letter); math carry; (with prep. a) surpass, excel. **l. a cabo,** to accomplish. **l. a cuestas,** to carry on one's back; support. **l. la correspondencia,** to look after the correspondence. **l. la delantera,** to take the lead. **l. luto,** to be in mourning. **l. por delante** Argentina, Chile to run over (e.g., a pedestrian) **llevarse bien,** to get on well, agree

llorar vi to weep, cry; drip; water (eyes); vt lament, mourn; bewail one's troubles

lloriquear vi to whine, snivel

lloriqueo m, whining, sniveling

llorón a weeping; sniveling, whining. m, long plume. **niño llorón,** crybaby

lloroso a tearful; grievous, sad; sorrowful

llover vi impers irr to rain; come in abundance (of troubles, etc.); vr leak (roofs, etc.). **l. a cántaros,** to rain in torrents, rain cats and dogs. **l. sobre mojado,** to add insult to injury. **como llovido,** unexpectedly. See **mover**

llovida f, Lat. Am. rain, shower

llovizna f, drizzle, fine rain

lloviznar vi to drizzle

lluvia f, rain; rainwater; fig shower; rose (of watering can) Chile, Nicaragua shower bath, shower

lluvioso a rainy, showery

lo def art. neut the thing, part, fact, what, that which. Used before adjectives, past participles, sometimes before nouns and adverbs (e.g. **Lo barato es caro,** Cheap things are dear (in the long run).) **Lo mío es mío, pero lo tuyo es de ambos,** What's mine is mine, but what is yours belongs to both of us. **Juan siente mucho lo ocurrido,** John is very sorry for what has happened. **a lo lejos,** in the distance). **lo . . . que,** how (e.g. **No sabes lo bueno que es,** You don't know how good he is). pers pron acc m, or neut him, it; that, it (e.g. **Lo harán mañana,** They will do it tomorrow). Means some, any, one, as substitute for noun already mentioned (e.g. **Carecemos de azúcar; no lo hay,** We are short of sugar; there isn't any). **Lo cortés no quita lo valiente,** One can be courteous and still insistent

loa f, praise, eulogy; theat prologue; short dramatic piece; ant; dramatic eulogy

loable a praiseworthy

loar vt to praise; commend

lobo (-ba) n wolf. m, (bot anat) lobe; inf drinking fit. **l. marino,** zool seal. inf **pillar un l.,** to get drunk

lóbrego a murky, dark; dismal; mournful, lugubrious

lobreguez f, obscurity, gloom, darkness

lóbulo m, lobe

local a local. m, premises; place, spot, scene

localidad f, location; locality; place, spot; seat (in theaters, etc.)

localización f, localization, placing; place

localizar vt to localize

loción f, lotion

loco (-ca) a insane, mad; rash, foolish, crazy; excessive, enormous; amazing; extraordinary; infatuated. n lunatic; rash person. fig inf **Es un l. de atar,** He's completely crazy!

locomoción f, locomotion

locomotor a locomotive

locomotora f, locomotive

locro m, Lat. Am. meat-and-vegetable stew

locuaz a loquacious

locución f, style of speech; phrase, idiom; gram locution

locura f, insanity, lunacy; madness, fury; folly, foolishness

locutor (-ra) n (radio) announcer; commentator

locutorio m, locutory; phone booth

lodo m, mud

lodoso a muddy

logarítmico a logarithmic

logaritmo m, logarithm

logia f, (Freemason's) lodge

lógica f, logic. inf **l. parda,** common sense

lógico (-ca) a logical. n logician

logística f, logistics

lograr vt to achieve, attain, obtain; enjoy; (with infin) succeed in; vr succeed in, achieve; reach perfection

logro m, achievement, attainment; profit, gain; usury, money-lending

loma f, knoll, hill

lombarda f, red cabbage

lombardo (-da) a of or from Lombardy. n native of Lombardy (Italy). m, mortgage bank

lombriciento, -a a, Lat. Am. having worms, suffering from worms

lombriz f, earthworm, common worm. **l. intestinal,** intestinal worm. **l. solitaria,** tapeworm

lomo m, loin, back of a book; ridge between furrows; pl ribs; loins

lona f, canvas, sailcloth

lonchería f, Lat. Am. luncheonette, lunch counter, snack bar

Londres London

longanimidad f, longanimity, fortitude

longaniza f, cul pork sausage

longevidad f, longevity

longitud f, length; longitude. **l. de onda,** rad wavelength

lonja f, slice, rasher; com exchange; market; grocery store; woolen warehouse

lonjista mf provision merchant, grocer

lontananza f, distance (also art). **en l.,** in the distance, far off

loor m, praise

loquear vi to play the fool; romp

loro m, orn parrot

los def art. m pl, (the. g. **l. sombreros,** the hats). pers. pron acc 3rd pers m pl, them. **Tus cigarrillos no están sobre la mesa; los tengo en mi bolsillo,** Your cigarettes are not on the table; I have them in my pocket. Means some, any, ones, as substitution for noun already stated (e.g. **Los cigarros están en la caja si los hay,** The cigars are in the box, if there are any). Used demonstratively followed by de or que introducing relative clause, those of (those which, those who; the ones that (who) (e.g. **Estaba leyendo algunos libros de los que tienes en tu cuarto,** I was reading some books from among those which you have in your room)

losa f, flagstone; slab; tombstone

lote m, lot, portion, share

lotería f, lottery; lotto (game); lottery office

lotero (-ra) n seller of lottery tickets

loto m, lotus; lotus flower or fruit

loza f, porcelain, china

lozanía f, luxuriance (of vegetation); vigor, lustiness; arrogance

lozano a luxuriant, exuberant; vigorous, lusty; arrogant

lubricación f, lubrication

lubricante a lubricant

lubricar vt to lubricate

lúbrico a slippery, smooth; lascivious, lustful

lucera f, skylight

lucerna f, large chandelier; skylight

lucero m, evening star; any bright star; white star (on a horse's head); brilliance, radiance; pl poet eyes, orbs. **l. del alba,** morning star

lucha f, fight; struggle; wrestling match; argument, disagreement. **l. grecorromana,** wrestling. **l. igualada,** close fight. **l. libre,** catch-as-catch-can

luchador (-ra) n fighter; struggler

luchar vi to fight hand to hand; wrestle; fight; struggle; argue

lucidez f, brilliance, shine; lucidity, clarity

lucido a splendid, brilliant; sumptuous; fine, elegant

lúcido a poet brilliant; lucid; clear

luciente a bright, shining

lucimiento m, brilliance, luster; success, triumph; elegance; display, ostentation

lucir vi irr to shine, scintillate; excel, outshine; be successful; vt illuminate; display, show off; show; vr dress elegantly; be successful; excel, be brilliant. Pres. Ind. **luzco, luces,** etc. Pres. Subjunc. **luzca,** etc.

lucrativo a lucrative

lucro m, gain, profit

luctuoso a lugubrious, mournful

lucubración f, lucubration

ludibrio m, mockery, ridicule

luego adv immediately; afterward, later; then; soon, presently. conjunc therefore. **l. que,** as soon as. **desde l.,** immediately, at once; of course, naturally; in the first place. **hasta l.,** au revoir, good-by for the present

lueguito adv Lat. Am. at once, right away, right now; Central America, Chile, Mexico near, nearby

luengo a long

lugar m, place; spot; village, town, city; region, locality; office, post; passage, text; opportunity, occasion; cause, motive; place on a list; room, space; seat. **l. común,** commonplace. **en l. de,** instead of. **en primer l.,** firstly, in the first place. **hacer l.,** to make room, make way. law **No ha l.,** The petition is refused. **tener l.,** to take place; have the time or opportunity (to)

lugareño (-ña) a peasant, regional. n villager, peasant

lugarteniente m, lieutenant; substitute, deputy

lúgubre a lugubrious, dismal, mournful

lujo m, luxury; abundance, profusion. **artículos de l.,** luxury goods

lujoso a luxurious; abundant, profuse

lujuria f, lasciviousness; excess, intemperance

lujuriante a luxuriant, abundant, profuse

lujurioso a lascivious, voluptuous

lumbago m, lumbago

lumbre f, fire; light; splendor, lustre; transom window, opening, skylight; pl tinderbox

lumbrera f, luminary; skylight; dormer window; eminent authorit; Mexico box (in a theater or bullring)

luminar m, luminary (also fig)

luminaria f, illumination; fairy lamp, small light; lamp burning before the Sacrament in Catholic churches

luminosidad f, luminosity

luminoso a luminous; bright

luna f, moon; mirror; satellite; sheet of plate glass. **l. creciente,** new or rising moon. **l. de miel,** honeymoon. **l. llena,** full moon. **l. menguante,** waning moon. **media l.,** crescent moon

lunado a half-moon, crescent

lunar m, beauty spot; fig stain, blot (on reputation, etc.); blemish, slight imperfection. a lunar

lunático (-ca) a and n lunatic

lunes m, Monday

luneta f, lens (of eyeglasses), *theat* orchestra stall; (*arch mil*) lunette

lupa f, magnifying glass

lupanar m, brothel

lustrador m, polisher; *Lat. Am.* bootblack. **l. de piso,** floor polisher

lustrar vt to lustrate, purify; polish, burnish; roam, journey

lustre m, polish, sheen, gloss; glory, luster

lustro m, lustrum, period of five years; chandelier

lustroso a shining, glossy; brilliant; glorious, noble

luterano (-na) a and n Lutheran

luto m, mourning; grief, affliction; *pl* mourning draperies. **estar de l.,** to be in mourning

luxación f, *surg* luxation, dislocation

luz f, light; glow; brightness, brilliance; information, news; *fig* luminary; day, daylight; *pl* culture, learning; windows. **luces de estacionamiento,** parking lights. **a buena l.,** in a good light; in a favorable light; after due consideration. **a primera l.,** at dawn. **dar a l.,** to publish (a book); bring forth (children); reveal. **entre dos luces,** in the dawn light; in the twilight; *inf* tipsy. **media l.,** half-light, twilight

M

maca *f*, bruise or blemish on fruit; defect, flaw; *inf* fraud, swindle

macabro *a* macabre

macadán *m*, macadam

macagua *f*, *orn* macaw

macanudo *a* (*inf WH*) extraordinary; enormous; robust; fine, excellent

macarrones *m pl*, macaroni; *naut* stanchions

macarrrónico *a* macaronic, recondite, stylized

macarse *vr* to go bad, rot (fruit)

maceración *f*, maceration; steeping, soaking; mortification of the flesh

macerar *vt* to macerate; steep, soak; mortify

maceta *f*, *dim* small mace; handle, haft (of tools); stonecutter's hammer; flowerpot; *Lat. Am.* bouquet, bunch (of flowers)

machaca *f*, pestle; pulverizer. *mf inf* bore, tedious person

machacador (-ra) *a* crushing, pounding. *n* beater, crusher, pounder

machacar *vt* to crush, pound; *vi* importune; harp on a subject

machacón *a* tiresome, prolix

machado *m*, hatchet, ax

machete *m* machete

macho *m*, male; male animal (he-goat, stallion, etc.); male plant (he-goat, hook and eye); screw; *met* core; tap (tool); *inf* dunderhead, fool; *arch* buttress. *a* male; stupid, ignorant; vigorous, strong. **m. cabrío**, he-goat

machucadura *f*, **machucamiento** *m*, pounding, crushing; bruising

machucar *vt* to crush, pound; bruise

machucho *a* prudent, sensible; adult, mature

macicez *f*, solidity; massiveness; thickness

macilento *a* thin, lean, emaciated

macizar *vt* to block up, fill up

macizo *a* massive; compact, solid; *fig* well-founded, unassailable; thick; strong. *m*, solidity, compactness; bulk; volume; flowered; solid tire

macrocosmo *m*, macrocosm

macuco, -a *a*, *Lat. Am.* crafty, cunning, sly

mácula *f*, stain, spot; *fig* blot, blemish; *inf* trick, deception; *ast* macula

madeja *f*, skein, hank; lock of hair; *inf* dummy, useless person

madera *f*, wood; timber; *inf* kind, sort; *mus* wind instruments. **m. contrachapada**, plywood. **m. de construcción**, timber. **maderas de sierra**, lumber wood. *inf* **ser de mala m.**, to be a ne'er-do-well

maderada *f*, lumber wood

maderaje *m*, woodwork, timber work

maderero *m*, timber merchant; lumber-jack; carpenter

madería *f*, timber yard

madero *m*, wooden beam; log, piece of lumber; ship, vessel; *inf* blockhead or insensible person

madrastra *f*, stepmother; anything unpleasant

madraza *f*, *inf* overindulgent mother

madre *f*, mother; matron; cause, genesis; *inf* dame, mother; riverbed; dam; womb; main sewer; chief irrigation channel. **m. de familia**, mother; housewife. **m. de leche**, wet nurse. **m. política**, mother-in-law; stepmother. *inf* **sacar de m. (a)**, to provoke, irritate (a person)

madreperla *f*, mother-of-pearl

madreselva *f*, honeysuckle

madrigado *a* twice-married (women); *inf* experienced, wide-awake

madrina *f*, godmother; matron of honor or bridesmaid; sponsor; patroness; prop; stanchion

madrugada *f*, dawn, daybreak; early rising. **de m.**, at dawn

madrugador (-ra) *a* early rising. *n* early riser

madrugar *vi* to get up early; gain time; anticipate, be beforehand

maduración *f*, ripening; mellowing; preparation; ripeness; maturity

madurador *a* ripening; maturing

maduramente *adv* maturely; sensibly

madurar *vt* to ripen; mature; think out; *vi* ripen; grow mature, learn wisdom

madurez *f*, ripeness; maturity; mellowness; wisdom

maduro *a* ripe; mature; mellow; adult; wise

maestra *f*, schoolmistress; teacher, instructor; queen bee; guide, model

maestral *a* referring to the grand master of one of the Spanish military orders; teaching, pedagogic. *m*, mistral (wind); cell of a queen bee

maestranza *f*, *Lat. Am.* machine shop

maestrear *vt* to direct, control, manage; prune vines; *vi inf* bully, domineer

maestría *f*, mastery, skill; *univ* master's degree

maestro *a* masterly; excellent; chief; main; midship. *m*, master; expert; teacher; instructor; master craftsman; *univ* master; *mus* composer; *naut* mainmast. **m. de armas**, fencing master. **m. de capilla**, *ecc* choirmaster. **m. de obras**, building contractor; master builder. **El ejercicio hace m.**, Practice makes perfect

Magallanes, Estrecho de Straits of Magellan

magdalena *f*, madeleine (cake); magdalen, penitent. *inf* **estar hecha una M.,** to be inconsolable

magia *f*, magic

mágica *f*, magic; enchantress, sorceress

mágico *a* magic; marvelous, wonderful. *m*, magician; enchanter, wizard

magín *m*, *inf* imagination; head, mind

magisterio *m*, teaching profession; teaching diploma; teaching post; pedantry, pompousness. **ejercer su m. en,** to be employed as a teacher in

magistrado *m*, magistrate; magistracy

magistral *a* magistral; authoritative, magisterial; pedantic, pompous

magnanimidad *f*, magnanimity; generosity, liberality

magnánimo *a* magnanimous, generous, noble

magnate *m*, magnate

magnavoz *m*, *Mexico* loudspeaker

magnesia *f*, magnesia

magnesio *m*, magnesium

magnético *a* magnetic

magnetizar *vt* to magnetize; mesmerize

magneto *m*, magneto

magnificar *vt* to magnify, enlarge; praise, extol

magnificencia *f*, magnificence, pomp, splendor

magnífico *a* magnificent; splendid, wonderful, fine; excellent

magnitud *f*, magnitude; quantity; importance

magno *a* great; famous. **Alejandro M.,** Alexander the Great

magnolia *f*, magnolia

mago *m*, magician; *pl* magi

magro *a* lean; scraggy. *m*, *inf* lean pork

magullar *vt* to bruise

magullón *m*, *Lat. Am.* bruise

mahonesa *f*, mayonnaise

maíz *m*, corn

maja *f*, belle

majada *f*, sheepfold; dung

majaderear *vt*, *Lat. Am.* to nag, pester

majadería *f*, impertinence, insolence

majadero *a* persistent, tedious. *m*, bobbin (for lace making); pestle. *n* fool, bore

majador *m*, pestle

majar *vt* to pound, crush; *inf* importune, annoy

majestad *f*, majesty (title); dignity; stateliness

majestuosidad *f*, majesty; dignity

majestuoso *a* majestic; stately; dignified

majo *a* arrogant, aggressive; gaudily attired, smart; dashing, handsome; attractive, pretty; elegant, well-dressed. *m*, beau, gallant, man about town

majuelo *m*, new vine; species of white hawthorn

mal *a* *abb* **malo.** Used only before *m sing*

nouns (e.g. **un m. cuarto de hora,** a bad quarter of an hour). *m*, evil; damage; harm; misfortune; illness, disease; trouble (e.g. **El m. es,** The trouble is). **m. de altura,** air sickness. **m. de ojo,** evil eye. **m. de piedra,** lithiasis, stone. **m. francés,** syphilis. **el m. menor,** the lesser of two evils. **interj IM. haya!** A curse upon! **echar a m.,** to scorn (things); waste, squander. **llevar a m. (una cosa),** to take (a thing) badly, complain. **No hay m. que por bien no venga,** It's an ill wind that blows no one any good, Every cloud has a silver lining. **parar en m.,** to come to a bad end

mal *adv* badly; unfavorably; wrongly; wickedly; with difficulty; scarcely, barely. **m. que bien,** willingly or unwillingly; rightly or wrongly. **de m. en peor,** from bad to worse

malabarista *mf* juggler

malaconsejado *a* ill-advised; imprudent

malacostumbrado *a* badly trained, spoiled; having bad habits

malandanza *f*, evildoing; misfortune, misery; poverty

malandrín *a* wicked, ill-disposed. *m*, scoundrel, miscreant

malanga *f*, *Central America* kind of tuber resembling a sweet potato

malaria *f*, malaria

malaventura *f*, misfortune, adversity, bad luck

malaventurado *a* unfortunate, unlucky

malbaratador (-ra) *a* wasteful, spendthrift. *n* squanderer, spendthrift

malbaratar *vt* to squander, waste; sell at a loss

malcasado *a* adulterous, unfaithful

malcasar(se) *vt* and *vr* to marry badly

malcomido *a* underfed

malcontento (-ta) *a* dissatisfied, discontented; rebellious. *n* malcontent, rebel

malcriado *a* badly brought up; ill-bred; spoiled, peevish

maldad *f*, badness; depravity; wickedness

maldecidor (-ra) *a* slanderous. *n* scandalmonger, slanderer

maldecir *vt irr* to curse; *vt* and *vi* slander, backbite. See **decir**

maldiciente *a* defamatory, slanderous; cursing, reviling. *m*, slanderer; curser

maldición *f*, malediction; curse, imprecation

maldispuesto *a* indisposed, ill; reluctant

maldita *f*, *inf* tongue. *inf* **soltar la m.,** to say too much, go too far

maldito *a* accursed; wicked; damned; poor (of quality); *inf* not a . . .

maleabilidad *f*, malleability, flexibility

maleable *a* malleable, flexible

maleante *a* rascally, villainous. *mf* evildoer

malecón *m*, breakwater

maledicencia *f*, slander, abuse, backbiting; cursing

maleficencia *f*, wrongdoing

maleficio *m*, (magic) curse; spell; charm

maléfico *a* malefic, harmful. *m*, sorcerer

malestar *m*, indisposition, slight illness; discomfort

maleta *f*, suitcase, valise, grip; *m*, *inf* clumsy matador; duffer (at games, etc.). **hacer la m.,** to pack a suitcase; *inf* prepare for a journey, get ready to leave

maletín *m*, small suitcase or valise

malevolencia *f*, malevolence, hatred, malice

malévolo *a* malevolent, malicious

maleza *f*, weeds; undergrowth; thicket

malgastador (**-ra**) *a* a thriftless, wasteful. *n* squanderer

malgastar *vt* to waste (time); squander, throw away (money)

malhablado a foul-tongued, indecent

malhadado a ill-fated, unhappy

malhecho a deformed, twisted (persons). *m*, evil deed, wrongdoing

malhechor (**-ra**) *n* malefactor; evildoer

malhumorado a ill-humored, bad-tempered

malicia *f*, wickedness, evil; malice, maliciousness; acuteness, subtlety, shrewdness; craftiness, guile; *inf* suspicion

maliciar *vt* to suspect; spoil, damage; hurt, harm

malicioso a malicious; vindictive; wicked; shrewd, clever; *inf* suspicious; artful

malignidad *f*, malignancy, spite, ill will

maligno a malignant, spiteful; wicked; *med* malignant

malintencionado a ill-intentioned, badly disposed

malla *f*, mesh (of a net); coat of mail; *pl theat* tights. **m. de alambre,** wire netting. **cota de m.,** coat of mail

Mallorca Majorca

malmandado a disobedient; reluctant, unwilling

malo a bad; wicked; evil; injurious; harmful; illicit; licentious; ill; difficult; troublesome, annoying; *inf* mischievous; knavish; rotten, decaying. *interj* ¡M.! That's bad!; You shouldn't have done that!; That's a bad sign! **de malas,** unluckily, unhappily. **el M.,** the Evil One, the Devil. **estar m.,** to be ill. **Lo m. es,** The trouble is, The worst of it is. **por malas o por buenas,** willy-nilly, willingly or unwillingly. **ser m.,** to be wicked; be evil; behave badly (children)

malograr *vt* to lose (time); waste, throw away (opportunities); *vr* fall through, fail; wither, fade; die early, come to an untimely end

malogro *m*, loss, waste (time, opportu-

nity); frustration; decline, fading; untimely death

malparar *vt* to ill-treat; damage. **quedar malparado,** to get the worst of

malparir *vt med* to miscarry

malparto *m*, miscarriage; abortion

malquerencia *f*, ill will, aversion, dislike

malquistar *vt* to stir up trouble; make unpopular; estrange; *vr* make oneself disliked

malquisto a unpopular, disliked

malsano a unhealthy

malta *m*, malt

maltraer *vt irr* to ill-treat; insult. See **traer**

maltraído, -a *a*, *Lat. Am.* shabby

maltratamiento *m*, abuse, ill usage; damage, deterioration

maltratar *vt* to ill-treat; abuse, insult; misuse, spoil, damage

maltrato *m*, maltreatment; misuse

maltrecho a ill-treated, bruised; abused, insulted; damaged

malucho a *inf* off-color, below par, not well

malva *f*, mallow. **m. real, m. rosa,** or **m. loca,** hollyhock. **ser como una m.,** *fig inf* to be a clinging vine

malvado a evil, malevolent, fiendish. *n* villain, fiend

malvavisco *m*, *bot* marshmallow

malversación *f*, malversation, maladministration; misappropriation (of funds)

malversador (**-ra**) *n* bad or corrupt administrator

malversar *vt* to misappropriate (funds)

Malvinas, las *fpl* the Falkland Islands

mamá *f*, mamma

mamado, -a *a*, *Lat. Am.* drunk, tipsy

mamar *vt* to suck (the breast); *inf* wolf, swallow; learn from an early age; enjoy, obtain unfairly; *vr* get drunk

mamarracho *m*, *inf* scarecrow, dummy; anything grotesque looking

mamífero a mammalian. *m*, mammal

mamotreto *m*, notebook, memorandum; *inf* large book or bulky file of papers

mampara *f*, folding screen; screen; partition

mamparo *m*, bulkhead

mampostería *f*, masonry, stonemasonry

maná *m*, manna

manada *f*, handful; herd, flock; group, drove, crowd

manadero *m*, herdsman, drover; spring, stream

manantial *m*, fountain, source, spring; head (of a river)

manar *vi* to flow, stream; be plentiful

manatí *m*, sea cow, manatee

mancar *vt* to injure, maim; *vi* grow calm (elements)

manceba *f*, concubine; girl

mancebo *m*, youth, stripling; bachelor; shop assistant

mancha *f*, spot, smear, stain; blotch; plot of ground; patch of vegetation; stigma, disgrace

manchar *vt* to stain; smear; spot; speckle; disgrace; tarnish

mancilla *f*, stain; slur

mancillar *vt* to stain; *fig* smirch

manco (-ca) *a* maimed, disabled; one-handed; one-armed; armless; handless; incomplete, faulty. *n* disabled person

mancomunidad *f*, association, society; community, union; commonwealth; regional legislative assembly

mancorna, *f*, *Colombia* cuff link **man-cuerna**, **mancuernilla** *f*, *Central America* cuff link

manda *f*, offer, suggestion, proposition; legacy

mandadero (-ra) *n* convent or prison messenger; errand boy (girl)

mandado *m*, order, command; errand

mandamiento *m*, order, command; *ecc* commandment; *law* writ; *pl inf* one's five fingers

mandar *vt* to order, command; bequeath, will; send; control, drive; promise, offer; order (e.g. **Mandó hacerse un traje**, He ordered a suit to be made); *vr* walk unaided (convalescents, etc.); lead into one another (rooms, etc.); **¿Quién manda aquí?** Who is in charge here?

mandarina *f*, mandarin (classical Chinese); mandarin orange

mandato *m*, mandate; command; *ecc* maundy. *pol* mandate. **cuarto m.**, fourth term (of President, Governor, etc.)

mandíbula *f*, jaw; jawbone, mandible

mandilón *m*, *inf* coward, nincompoop

mandioca *f*, manioc, cassava; tapioca

mando *m*, authority, power; (*mil nav*) command; *eng* regulation; controls (of a machine, etc.). **m. a distancia**, remote control. **aer m. de dos pilotos**, dual-controlled. **mandos gemelos**, dual control. **al m. de**, under the command of; under the direction of

mandolín *m*. **mandolina** *f*, mandolin

mandón a domineering, bossy

manear *vt* to hobble (a horse); manage, control

manecilla *f*, *dim* little hand; hand of a clock; *print* fist

manejable a manageable, controllable

manejar *vt* to handle; use, wield; control; manage, direct; ride (horses); *vr* manage to move around (after an accident, illness)

manejo *m*, handling; use, wielding; control; management, direction; horsemanship; intrigue

maneota *f*, hobble, shackle

manera *f*, manner, way, means; behavior;

style (gen. *pl*); class (of people); *art* style; manner. **a la m. de**, like, in the style of. **de esa m.**, in that way; according to that, in that case. **de m. que**, so that. **en gran m.**, to a great extent. **sobre m.**, exceedingly

manga *f*, sleeve; bag; grip; handle; pipe (of a hose); strainer; waterspout; body of troops; beam, breadth of a ship; *pl* profits. **m. de viento**, whirlwind. **echar de m. a**, to make use of a person. *inf* **estar de m.**, to be in league. **tener m. ancha**, to be broad-minded. *fig inf* **traer (una cosa) en la m.**, to have (something) up one's sleeve

mangana *f*, lasso

manganilla *f*, sleight of hand; hoax, trick

mangle *m*, mangrove tree

mango *m*, handle, haft, stock; mango. **m. de cuchillo**, knife handle

mangonear *vi inf* to loaf, roam about; interfere, meddle

mangonero *a inf* meddlesome

mangosta *f*, mongoose

mangote *m*, *inf* long, wide sleeve; black oversleeve

manguera *f*, hose; sleeve, tube; airshaft; waterspout

manguito *m*, muff; black oversleeve; wristlet, cuff; *mech* bush, sleeve

manía *f*, mania, obsession; whim, fancy

maniabierto, -a *a*, *Lat. Am.* generous, giving, open-handed

maníaco (-ca) *a* maniacal; capricious, extravagant. *n* maniac

maniático (-ca) *a* maniacal; capricious; faddy, fussy. *n* crank

manicomio *m*, insane asylum, mental hospital

manicura *f*, manicure

manicuro (-ra) *n* manicurist

manida *f*, lair, den; dwelling, habitation

manifestación *f*, declaration, statement; exhibition; demonstration; *ecc* exposition (of the Blessed Sacrament)

manifestante *mf* demonstrator

manifestar *vt irr* to declare, make known, state; exhibit, show; *ecc* to expose (the Blessed Sacrament). See **acertar**

manifiesto *a* obvious, evident. *m*, manifesto; *naut* manifest; *ecc* exposition of the Blessed Sacrament. **poner de m.**, to show; make public; reveal

manija *f*, handle, stock, haft; hand lever; clamp; tether (for horses, etc.)

manilla *f*, bracelet; handcuff, manacle

maniobra *f*, operation, process; *mil* maneuver; intrigue; tackle, gear; handling, management; *naut* working of a ship; *pl* shunting (trains)

maniobrar *vi mil* to maneuver; *naut* handle, work (ships)

manipulación *f*, handling; manipulation; control, management

manipulador *a* manipulative. *m*, sending key (telegraphy)

manipular *vt* to handle; manipulate; manage, direct

maniquí *m*, mannequin; dummy; *inf* puppet, weak person

manirroto (-ta) *a* wasteful, extravagant. *n* spendthrift

manivela *f*, *mech* crank, lever; *Lat. Am.* handle

manjar *m*, dish, food; pastime, recreation, pleasure. **m. blanco,** blancmange; *Lat. Am.* fudge

mano *f*, hand; coat, coating; quire (of paper); front paw (animals); elephant's trunk; side, hand; hand (of a clock); game (of cards, etc.); lead (at cards); way, means; ability; power; protection, favor; compassion; aid, help; scolding; *mus* scale; pestle; workers. *inf* editing, correction of a literary work (gen. by a person more skilled than the author). **m. de mortero,** pestle. **m. de obra,** (manual) labor. **manos muertas,** *law* mortmain. **m. sobre m.,** with folded hands; lazily, indolently. **a la m.,** at hand, nearby; within one's grasp. **a manos llenas,** in abundance, abundantly. **bajo m.,** in an underhand manner, secretly. **buenas manos,** cleverness, ability; dexterity. **de primera m.,** first-hand, new. **estar dejado de la m. de Dios,** to be very unlucky; be very foolish. **poner la m. en,** to ill-treat; slap, buffet. **Si a m. viene . . . ,** If by chance . . . **tender la m.,** to put out one's hand, shake hands. **traer entre manos,** to have on hand, be engaged in

manojo *m*, bunch, handful. **a manojos,** in handfuls; plentifully, in abundance

manosear *vt* to handle; paw, touch repeatedly; finger

manoseo *m*, handling; fingering; *inf* pawing, feeling

manotada *f*, slap, cuff

manotear *vt* to slap, cuff; *vi* gesticulate, gesture with the hands

manoteo *m*, gesticulation with the hands

mansalva (a) *adv* without danger

mansedumbre *f*, meekness; kindness; gentleness

mansión *f*, stay, visit; dwelling, abode; mansion

manso *a* soft, gentle; meek, mild; tame; peaceable, amiable; calm

manta *f*, blanket; horse blanket; traveling rug; *inf* hiding, thrashing. **m. de viaje,** traveling rug. *inf* **a m. de Dios,** in abundance. **dar una m.,** to toss in a blanket. *fig inf* **tirar de la m.,** to let the cat out of the bag

mantear *vt* to toss in a blanket

manteca *f*, lard; cooking fat; grease; *Argentina* butter. **como m.,** as mild as milk, as soft as butter

mantecada *f*, buttered toast

mantecoso *a* greasy

mantel *m*, tablecloth; altar cloth

mantelería *f*, table linen

mantener *vt irr* to maintain; keep, feed; support; continue, persevere with; uphold, affirm; keep up; *vr* support oneself; remain in a place; (*with en*) continue to uphold (views, etc.), persevere in. **mantenerse firme,** *fig* to stand one's ground. See **tener**

mantenimiento *m*, maintenance; support; sustenance, nourishment; affirmation; upkeep; livelihood

mantequera *f*, churn; dairymaid; butter dish

mantequero *m*, dairyman; butter dish

mantequilla *f*, butter

mantilla *f*, mantilla; saddlecloth. *pl* baby's long clothes. **estar en mantillas,** to be in swaddling clothes; *fig* be in early infancy

manto *m*, cloak; cover, disguise; *zool* mantle; *min* layer

mantón *m*, shawl. **m. de Manila,** Manila shawl

manuable *a* easy to handle or use, handy

manual *a* manual; handy, easy to use; docile, peaceable. *m*, manual, textbook; *ecc* book of ritual; notebook

manubrio *m*, handle, crank; *Lat. Am.* handlebars

manufactura *f*, manufacture; manufactured article; factory

manufacturar *vt* to manufacture

manufacturero *a* manufacturing

manuscrito *a* and *m*, manuscript

manutención *f*, maintenance; upkeep; protection

manzana *f*, apple; block (of houses); city square; Adam's apple; *Argentina* 2.5 acres; *Central America* 1.75 acres

manzanal *m*, apple orchard; apple tree

manzanar *m*, apple orchard

manzanilla *f*, white sherry wine; *bot* chamomile; chamomile tea; knob, ball (on furniture); pad (on an animal's foot)

manzano *m*, apple tree

maña *f*, skill, dexterity; craftiness, guile; vice, bad habit (gen. *pl*). **darse m. para,** to contrive to

mañana *f*, morning; tomorrow. *m*, future, tomorrow. *adv* tomorrow; in time to come; soon. **¡M.!** Tomorrow! Another day! Not now! (generally to beggars). **de m.,** early in the morning. **muy de m.,** very early in the morning. **pasado m.,** the day after tomorrow

mañanica *f*, early morning

mañear *vt* to arrange cleverly; *vi* behave shrewdly

mañero a shrewd, clever; easily worked; handy

mañoso a clever, skillful; crafty; vicious, with bad habits

mañuela f, low guile

mapa m, map; card. **m. en relieve,** relief map. **m. del estado mayor,** ordnance map. inf **no estar en el m.,** to be off the map; be most unusual (of things)

mapache m, raccoon

maqueta f, (art arch) model

maquiavélico a Machiavellian

maquiladora f, maquiladora (factory run by a U.S. company in Mexico to take advantage of cheap labor and lax regulation)

maquillaje m, makeup, cosmetics; making up (of the face)

maquillar (**se**) vt and vr to make up (the face, etc.)

máquina f, machine, mechanism; engine; apparatus; plan, scheme; machine, puppet; inf mansion, palace; plenty; locomotive; fantasy, product of the imagination. **m. de vapor,** steam engine. **m. de arrastre,** traction engine; tractor. **m. de coser,** sewing machine. **m. de escribir,** typewriter. **m. fotográfica,** camera. **m. de impresionar,** movie camera. **m. de imprimir,** printing machine. **m. herramienta,** machine tool. **m. neumática,** air pump

maquinación f, intrigue, machination

maquinador (-ra) n intriguer, schemer

maquinar vt to intrigue, scheme, plot

maquinaria f, machinery; applied mechanics; mechanism

maquinista mf driver, engineer; mechanic; machinist; locomotive driver

mar mf sea; great many, abundance. **m. bonanza** or **m. en calma,** calm sea. **m. de fondo** or **m. de leva,** swell. **alta m.,** high seas. **a mares,** plentifully. **arar en el m.,** to labor in vain. naut **hacerse a la m.,** to put out to sea. **la m. de historias,** a great number of stories

maraña f, undergrowth; tangle; fig difficult position; intrigue; silk waste

marasmo m, med marasmus, atrophy; inactivity, paralysis

maravilla f, marvel, wonder; admiration; amazement; marigold. **a m.,** wonderfully. **a las mil maravillas,** to perfection, excellently. **por m.,** by chance; occasionally

maravillar vt to amaze, cause admiration; vr (with de) marvel at, admire; be amazed by

maravilloso a marvelous, wonderful

marbete m, label, tag; edge, border

marca f, mark, sign; brand; frontier zone, border country; standard, norm (of size); make, brand; measuring rule; sport record. **m. de fábrica,** brand, trademark. **m. de ley,** hallmark. **m. registrada,** reg-

istered name. **de m.,** excellent, of excellent quality

marcado a marked; pronounced; strong (of accents)

marcador a marking. m, marker; scoreboard; bookmark

marcar vt to mark; brand; embroider initials on linen; tell the time (watches); show the amount (cash register, etc.); dial (telephone); sport score (a goal); notice, observe; set aside, earmark; vr naut check the course. **m. el compás** to beat time

marcha f, departure; running, working; mil march; speed (of trains, ships, etc.); mus march; progress, course (of events). **m. atrás,** backing, reversing. **m. de ensayo,** trial run. **m. forzada,** mil forced march. **a largas marchas,** with all speed. **a toda m.,** at top speed; full speed ahead; by forced marches; mil **batir la m.,** to strike up a march. **en m.,** underway; working; in operation

marchante, -a mf Lat. Am. client, customer; dealer, merchant; pedlar

marchar vi to run; work; function; go; leave, depart; progress, proceed; mil march; go (clocks); vr leave, go away

marchitable a perishable, fragile

marchitar vt to wither, fade; blight, spoil; weaken; vr wither; be blighted

marchito a withered; faded; blighted, frustrated

marcial a martial; courageous, militant

marcialidad f, war-like spirit, militancy

marco m, mark (German coin); boundary mark; frame (of a picture, etc.). **m. de ventana,** window frame

marea f, tide; strand, water's edge; light breeze; drizzle; dew; street dirt. **m. creciente,** flood tide. **m. menguante,** ebb tide. **m. muerta,** neap tide

mareaje m, seamanship; ship's course

marear vt to navigate; sell; sell publicly; inf annoy; vr be seasick; feel faint; feel giddy; be damaged at sea (goods)

marejada f, surge, swell; high sea; tidal wave; commotion, uproar

mareo m, seasickness; nausea, dizziness; inf irritation, tediousness

mareta f, movement of the waves; sound, noise (of a crowd)

marfil m, ivory

marfileño a ivory; ivory-like

marfuz a spurned, rejected; deceitful

margarina f, margarine

margarita f, pearl; marguerite, oxeye daisy; daisy; periwinkle

margen mf edge, fringe, border, verge; margin (of a book); opportunity; marginal note. **dar m. para,** to provide an opportunity for; give rise to

marginal a marginal

margoso a loamy, marly

marica *f*, magpie. *m*, (*offensive*) homosexual; milksop

maricón *m*, (*offensive*) homosexual

maridable *a* marital, matrimonial

maridaje *m*, conjugal union and harmony; intimate relationship (between things)

maridar *vi* to get married; mate, live as husband and wife; *vt* unite, link, join together

marido *m*, husband

marihuana *f*, marijuana

marimacho *m*, *inf* mannish woman

marina *f*, coast, seashore; *art* seascape; seamanship; navy, fleet. **m. de guerra**, navy. **m. mercante**, merchant navy

marinera *f*, sailor's blouse

marinería *f*, profession of a sailor; seamanship; crew of a ship; sailors (as a class)

marinero *m*, sailor, seaman. **m. de agua dulce**, freshwater sailor (a novice). **m. práctico**, able seaman. **a la marinera**, in a seaman-like fashion

marinesco *a* seamanly

marino *a* marine, sea; seafaring; shipping. *m*, sailor, mariner

marioneta *f*, marionette, puppet

mariposa *f*, butterfly; night-light

mariposear *vi* to flutter, flit, fly about; flirt, be fickle; follow about, dance attendance on

mariquita *f*, *ent* ladybird; parakeet.

marisabidilla *f*, *inf* blue-stocking, know-it-all

mariscal *m*, *mil* marshal; field marshal; blacksmith

marisco *m*, shellfish

marisma *f*, bog, morass, swamp

marital *a* marital

marítimo *a* maritime, sea

marmita *f*, stewpot; copper, boiler; *Mexico* kettle

mármol *m*, marble; work executed in marble

marmóreo *a* marble; *poet* marmoreal

marmota *f*, *zool* marmot; sleepyhead, dormouse

Mar Muerto Dead Sea

maromero, -a *mf*, *Lat. Am.* acrobat, tightrope walker; opportunist

marquesina *f*, marquee

marquetería *f*, marquetry

marrana *f*, sow; *inf* slattern, slut

marrano *m*, pig, hog; Marrano

marras (de) *adv* long ago, in the dim past

marrasquino *m*, maraschino liqueur

marro *m*, tick, tag (game)

marrón *a* maroon; brown. *m*, brown color; maroon color; quoit

marroquí *a* and *mf* Moroccan. *m*, Morocco leather

Marruecos Morocco

marrullería *f*, flattery, cajolery

marrullero (-ra) *a* a wheedling, flattering. *n* wheedler, cajoler

marsopa *f*, porpoise

marta *f*, sable; marten

martajar *vt*, *Lat. Am.* to grind, pound

Marte *m*, Mars

martes *m*, Tuesday. **m. de carnaval**, mardi gras

martillar *vt* to hammer; oppress

martillazo *m*, hammer blow

martilleo *m*, hammering; noise of the hammer; clink, clatter

martillero, -a *mf*, *Lat. Am.* auctioneer

martillo *m*, hammer; oppressor, tyrant; auction rooms. **a m.**, by hammering. **de m.**, wrought (of metals)

martín pescador *m*, kingfisher

martinete *m*, hammer (of a pianoforte); pile driver; drop hammer. **m. de báscula**, tilt hammer

Martinica Martinique

mártir *mf* martyr

martirio *m*, martyrdom

martirizar *vt* to martyr; torture, torment, martyrize; tease, annoy

marzo *m*, March

mas *conjunc* but; yet

más *adv comp* more; in addition, besides; rather, preferably. *math* plus. **el (la**, etc.) **más**, *adv sup* the most, etc. **m. bien**, more; rather; preferably. **m. que**, only; but; more than; although, even if. **a lo m.**, at the most; at the worst. **a m.**, besides, in addition. **de m.**, superfluous, unnecessary, unwanted. **no. . . . m. que**, only. **por m. que**, however; even if. **sin m. ni m.**, without further ado. **M. vale un mal arreglo que un buen pleito**, A bad peace is better than a good war

masa *f*, mass; dough; whole, aggregate; majority (of people); mortar. **en la m. de la sangre**, *fig* in the blood, in a person's nature

masada *f*, farmhouse and stock

masaje *m*, massage

masajista *mf* masseur; masseuse

masato *m*, *Lat. Am.* drink made from bananas, fermented corn, yucca, etc.

mascar *vt* to chew; masticate; *inf* mumble, mutter

máscara *f*, mask; fancy dress; pretext, excuse. *mf* masquerader, reveler; *pl* masquerade. **m. para gases**, gas mask

mascarada *f*, masquerade; company of revelers

mascarón *m*, large mask; *arch* gargoyle. **m. de proa**, *naut* figurehead

mascota *f*, mascot

masculinidad *f*, masculinity

masculino *a* masculine; male; manly, vigorous

mascullar *vt inf* to chew; mutter, mumble

masera *f*, kneading bowl; cloth for covering dough

masilla *f*, mastic, putty

masón (-ona) *n* Freemason

masonería *f*, freemasonry

masónico *a* masonic

masoquismo *m*, masochism

masticación *f*, mastication

masticar *vt* to masticate, eat; *inf* chew upon, consider

mástil *m*, *naut* mast; upright, stanchion; pole (of a tent); stem, trunk; neck (of a guitar, etc.)

mastín *m*, mastiff

mastodonte *m*, mastodon

mastoides *a* mastoid

mastuerzo *m*, watercress; fool, blockhead

masturbación *f*, masturbation

masturbarse *vr* to masturbate

mata *f*, plant, shrub; stalk, sprig; grove, copse. **m. de pelo,** mat of hair

matachín *m*, mummer; butcher; *inf* swashbuckler

matadero *m*, slaughterhouse, abattoir; *Lat. Am.* brothel

matafuego *m*, fire extinguisher; fireman

matalotaje *m*, ship's supplies, stores; *inf* hodgepodge

matamoros *a* swashbuckling, swaggering

matamoscas *m*, fly swatter

matanza *f*, killing, massacre, slaughter; butchery (animals); *inf* persistence, determination

matar *vt* to kill; quench (thirst); put out (fire, light); slake (lime); tarnish (metal); bevel (corners, etc.); pester, importune; suppress; compel; *art* tone down; *vr* kill oneself; be disappointed, grieve; overwork. **estar a m.,** to be at daggers drawn. **matarse por,** to try hard to; work hard for

matasanos *m*, *inf* quack (doctor); bad doctor

matasellos *m*, cancellation, postmark

mate *a* matte, unpolished, dull. *m*, checkmate (chess); maté, Paraguayan tea; gourd; vessel made from gourd, coconut, etc.

maté *m*, maté, Paraguayan tea

matemáticas *f pl*, mathematics. **m. prácticas,** applied mathematics. **m. teóricas,** pure mathematics

matemático *a* mathematical; exact. *m*, mathematician

materia *f*, matter; theme, subject matter; subject (of study); matter, stuff, substance; pus, matter; question, subject; reason, occasion. **m. colorante,** dye. **materias plásticas,** plastics. **materias primas,** raw materials. **en m. de,** concerning; in the matter of

material *a* material; dull, stupid, limited. *m*, material; ingredient; plant, factory; equipment. **m. móvil ferroviario,** rolling stock (railroads)

materialista a materialistic. *mf* materialist; *Mexico* truckdriver

materializar *vt* to materialize; *vr* materialize; grow materialistic, grow less spiritual

maternidad *f*, maternity, motherhood

materno *a* maternal

matiz *m*, combination of colors; tone, hue; shade (of meaning, etc.)

matizar *vt* to combine, harmonize (colors); tint, shade; tinge (words, etc.)

matojo *m*, shrub, bush

matorral *m*, thicket, bush, undergrowth

matraca *f*, rattle; *inf* scolding, dressing-down; insistence, importunity

matraquear *vi* to make a noise with a rattle; *inf* scold

matriarcado *m*, matriarchy

matrícula *f*, list, register; matriculation; registration number (of a car, etc.). **m. de buques,** maritime register. **m. de mar,** mariner's register; maritime register

matriculación *f*, matriculation; registration

matricular *vt* to matriculate; enrol; *naut* register; *vr* matriculate; enroll, register

matrimonial *a* matrimonial

matrimonio *m*, marriage, matrimony; married couple. **m. a yuras,** secret marriage. **m. de la mano izquierda** or **m. morganático,** morganatic marriage. **contraer m.,** to get married

matritense *a* and *mf* Madrilenian

matriz *f*, uterus, womb; matrix, mold; *min* matrix; nut, female screw

matrona *f*, married woman; matron; midwife; female customs officer

matusalén *m*, Methuselah, very old man

matute *m*, smuggling; contraband; gambling den

matutero (-ra) *n* smuggler, contrabandist

matutino *a* matutinal, morning

maula *f*, trash; remnant; deception, fraud, trick. *mf inf* good-for-nothing; lazybones. *inf* **ser buena m.,** to be a trickster or a fraud

maulería *f*, remnant stall; trickery

maullar *vi* to meow, mew (cats)

mausoleo *m*, mausoleum

maxilar *a* maxillary. *m*, jaw

máxima *f*, maxim, rule, precept, principle

máxime *adv* principally, chiefly

máximo *a sup* **grande** greatest, maximum, top. *m*, maximum

maya *f*, common daisy; May queen

mayo *m*, May; maypole; bouquet, wreath of flowers; *pl* festivities on eve of May Day

mayonesa *f*, mayonnaise

mayor *a comp* **grande** bigger; greater; elder; main, principal; older; high (mass, etc.); *mus* major. *mf* major (of full age). *a sup* **grande. el, la, lo mayor, los (las) mayores,** the biggest, greatest; eldest; chief, principal. **por m.,** in short, briefly; *com* wholesale

mayor *m*, head, director; chief clerk; *mil* major; *pl* ancestors

mayoral *m*, head shepherd; coachman, driver; foreman, overseer, supervisor, steward

mayorazgo *m*, *law* entail; entailed estate; heir (to an entail); eldest son; right of primogeniture

mayoreo *m*, *Lat. Am.* wholesale

mayoría *f*, majority

mayormente *adv* chiefly; especially

mayúscula *f*, capital letter, upper-case letter

mayúsculo *a* large; capital (letters). **letra mayúscula,** capital letter, upper-case letter

maza *f*, mallet; club, bludgeon; mace; bass drum stick; pile driver; bone, stick, etc., tied to dog's tail in carnival; *inf* pedant, bore; important person, authority; *Lat. Am.* hub (of a wheel). **m. de polo,** polo mallet

mazamorra *f*, dish made of cornmeal; biscuit crumbs; broken fragments, remains

mazapán *m*, marzipan

mazmorra *f*, dungeon

mazo *m*, mallet; bundle, bunch; importunate person; clapper (of a bell); *Argentina,* deck (of cards)

mazonería *f*, stonemasonry

mazonero *m*, stonemason

mazorca *f*, spindleful; spike, ear (of corn); cocoa berry; camarilla, group

me *pers pron acc or dat 1st sing mf* me; to me

meandro *m*, meandering, twisting, winding; wandering

mecánica *f*, mechanics; mechanism, machinery; *inf* worthless thing; mean action

mecánico *a* mechanical; power-operated; base, ill-bred. *m*, engineer; mechanic

mecanismo *m*, mechanism; works, machinery

mecanizar *vt* to mechanize

mecanografía *f*, typewriting

mecanografiar *vt* to typewrite, type

mecanografista *mf* **mecanógrafo (-fa)** *n* typist

mecate *m*, *Lat. Am.* twine; coarse person

mecedor *a* rocking, swaying. *m*, swing; *Lat. Am.* rocking chair

mecedora *f*, rocking chair

mecenas *m*, Maecenas, patron

mecer *vt* to stir, mix; shake; rock; swing

mecha *f*, wick; bit, drill; fuse (of explosives); match (for cannon, etc.); fat bacon (for basting); lock of hair; skein, twist; *Lat. Am.* fright, scare

mechar *vt cul* to baste, lard

mechero *m*, gas burner; pocket lighter; socket of a candlestick

medalla *f*, medal; medallion; plaque, round panel; *inf* piece of eight (coin)

medallón *m*, large medal; medallion; locket

media *f*, stocking

mediación *f*, mediation, arbitration; intercession

mediado *a* half-full. **a mediados (del mes,** etc.**),** toward the middle (of the month, etc.)

mediador (-ra) *n* mediator, arbitrator; intercessor

medianamente *adv* moderately; passably, fairly well

medianero (-ra) *a* middle; intervening, intermediate; mediatory. *n* mediator. *m*, owner of a semidetached house or of one in a row

mediano *a* medium, average; moderate; *inf* middling, passable, fair

medianoche *f*, midnight

mediante *a* mediatory. *adv* by means of, by, through

mediar *vi* to reach the middle; get halfway; elapse half a given time; intercede; mediate; arbitrate; be in between or in the middle; intervene, take part

medicación *f*, medication

medicamento *m*, medicament, medicine, remedy

medicastro *m*, unskilled physician; quack, charlatan

medicina *f*, medicine; medicament

medicinar *vt* to attend; treat (patients)

médico (-ca) *a* medical. *n* doctor of medicine. **m. de cabecera,** family doctor. **m. general,** general practitioner

medida *f*, measurement; measuring stick; measure, precaution (gen. with *tomar, adoptar,* etc.); gauge; judgment, wisdom; meter; standard. **a m. que,** while, at the same time as. **tomar las medidas (a),** *fig* to take a person's measure, sum him up. **tomar sus medidas,** to take his (their) measurements; take the necessary measures. **un traje hecho a m.,** a suit made to measure

medidor *m Lat. Am.* gauge, meter. **m. de aqua** water meter. **m. de gas** gas meter

medio *a* half; middle; intermediate; halfway. *m*, half; middle; *art* medium; spiritualist medium; proceeding, measure, precaution; environment, medium; middle way, mean; *sport* halfback. **m. galope,** canter. **m. tiempo,** *sport* halftime. **a medias,** by halves; half, partly. **de por m.,** by halves; in between; in the way. **estar de por m.,** to be in the way; take part in. *inf* **quitar de en m.,** to get rid of.

inf **quitarse de en m.,** to go away, remove oneself

mediocre *a* mediocre

mediodía *m*, noon, meridian; south

mediopelo *m*, lower middle class

medir *vt irr* to measure; (metrics) scan; survey (land); compare; *vr* measure one's words; act with restraint. See **pedir**

meditabundo *a* pensive, meditative, thoughtful

meditación *f*, meditation; consideration, reflection

meditador *a* meditative, thoughtful

meditar *vt* to meditate, consider, muse

mediterráneo *a* mediterranean; inland, landlocked

medra *f*, progress; improvement, betterment; growth; prosperity

medrar *vi* to flourish, grow; become prosperous or improve one's position

medro *m*, improvement, progress. See **medra**

medroso *a* timid, frightened; frightful, horrible

médula *f*, marrow; *bot* pith; *fig* essence, core

medusa *f*, jellyfish

megáfono *m*, megaphone

megalómano (-na) *n* megalomaniac

mejicano (-na) *a* and *n* Mexican

Méjico Mexico

mejilla *f*, *anat* cheek

mejor *a comp* bueno better. *adv* better; rather; sooner; preferably. *a sup* **bueno. el, la, lo mejor; los, las mejores,** the best; most preferable. **m. que m.,** better and better. *inf* **a lo m.,** probably, in all probability. **tanto m.,** so much the better

mejora *f*, improvement; bettering; progress; higher bid (at auctions)

mejorable *a* improvable

mejoramiento *m*, betterment, improvement

mejorar *vt* to improve; better; outbid; *vi* grow better (in health); improve (weather); make progress; rally (of markets). **Mejorando lo presente,** Present company excepted

mejoría *f*, improvement, progress; betterment; superiority; advantage, profit

mejunje *m*, *inf* brew, potion, cure-all, stuff; *Lat. Am.* mess

melancolía *f*, melancholia; sadness, depression, melancholy

melancólico *a* melancholy, sad; depressing

melaza *f*, molasses

melena *f*, long side whiskers; loose, flowing hair (in women); overlong hair (in men); lion's mane. *inf* **andar a la m.,** to start a fight or quarrel. *inf* **traer a la m.,** to drag by the hair, force

melifluo *a* mellifluous, sweet-voiced; honeyed

melindre *m*, honey fritter; affectation, scruple, fastidiousness; narrow ribbon

melindroso *a* overfastidious, affected, prudish

mella *f*, nick, notch; dent; gap; harm, damage (to reputation, etc.). **hacer m.,** *fig* to make an impression (on the mind); *mil* breach, drive a wedge

mellar *vt* to nick, notch; dent; damage

mellizo (-za) *a* and *n* twin

melocotón *m*, peach; peach tree

melodía *f*, melody, tune; melodiousness

melódico *a* melodic, melodious

melodioso *a* melodious, tuneful, sweet-sounding

melodrama *m*, melodrama

melodramático *a* melodramatic

melón *m*, melon

meloso *a* honeyed; sweet; gentle; mellifluous

membrana *f*, membrane

membrete *m*, note, memorandum; note or card of invitation; superscription, heading; address (of person)

membrillo *m*, quince tree; quince; quince jelly

membrudo *a* brawny, strong, muscular

memo *a* silly, stupid

memorándum *m*, notebook, jotter; memorandum

memorar(se) *vt* and *vr* to remember, recall

memoria *f*, memory; remembrance, recollection; monument; memorial; report; essay, article; codicil; memorandum; record, chronicle; *pl* regards, compliments, greetings; memoirs; memoranda. *inf* **m. de grillo,** poor memory. **de m.,** by heart. **flaco de m.,** forgetful. **hacer m.,** to remember

memorial *m*, notebook; memorial, petition

memorioso *a* mindful, unforgetful

mención *f*, mention. **m. honorífica,** honorable mention. **hacer m. de,** to mention

mencionar *vt* to mention

mendacidad *f*, mendacity, untruthfulness

mendaz *a* mendacious, untruthful

mendicante *a* begging; *ecc* mendicant. *mf* beggar

mendigar *vt* to beg for alms; entreat, supplicate

mendigo (-ga) *n* beggar

mendoso *a* mendacious, untruthful; mistaken

mendrugo *m*, crust of bread

menear *vt* to sway, move; wag; shake; manage, control, direct; *vr inf* get a move on; sway, move; wriggle

meneo *m*, swaying movement; wagging;

shaking; wriggling; management, direction; *aer* bump; *inf* spanking

menester *m*, lack, shortage; necessity; occupation, employment; *pl* physical necessities; *inf* tools, implements, equipment. **haber m.**, to need, require. **ser m.**, to be necessary or requisite

menesteroso *a* indigent, poverty-stricken, needy

menestra *f*, vegetable soup; dried vegetable (gen. *pl*)

mengano (-na) *n* so-and-so (used instead of the name of the person)

mengua *f*, decrease; lack, shortage; waning (of the moon, etc.); dishonor, disgrace; poverty

menguado (-da) *a* timid, cowardly; silly, stupid; mean, avaricious. *n* coward; fool; skinflint. *m*, narrowing stitch when knitting socks

menguante *a* ebb; waning; decreasing. *f*, ebb tide; decadence, decline. **m. de la luna**, waning of the moon

menguar *vi* to decrease; decline, decay; wane; ebb; narrow (socks); *vt* diminish; disgrace, discredit

menopausia *f*, menopause

menor *a comp* less, smaller; younger, minor; *mus* minor. *m*, minor. *f*, (logic) minor. *a sup* **el, la, lo m.; los, las menores**, the least; smallest; youngest. **m. de edad**, minor (in age). **por m.**, at retail; in detail

menoría *f*, subordination, dependence; inferiority; minority (underage); childhood, youth

menorista *Lat. Am.*, a retail; *mf* retailer

menos *adv* less; minus; least; except. **m. de** *or* **m. que**, less than. **al m., por lo m.**, at least. **a m. que**, unless. **De m. nos hizo Dios**, Never say die, Nothing is impossible. **poco más o m.**, more or less, about

menoscabar *vt* to lessen, diminish, decrease; deteriorate, damage; disgrace, discredit

menoscabo *m*, decrease, diminishment; harm, damage, loss

menospreciable *a* despicable, contemptible

menospreciador (-ra) *a* scornful. *n* scorner, despiser

menospreciar *vt* to despise, scorn; underestimate, have a poor opinion of

menosprecio *m*, scorn, derision; underestimation

mensaje *m*, message; official communication

mensajería *f*, carrier service; steamship line

mensajero (-ra) *n* messenger; errand boy

menso, -a *a*, *Mexico* dumb, silly, stupid

menstruación *f*, menstruation

menstruar *vi* to menstruate

mensual *a* monthly

mensualidad *f*, monthly salary, monthly payment

mensurar *vt* to measure

menta *f*, menthe, mint; peppermint

mentado *a* celebrated, distinguished, famous

mental *a* mental

mentalidad *f*, mentality

mentar *vt irr* to mention. See **sentar**

mentas *fpl*, *Argentina* reputation, gossip

mente *f*, mind; intelligence, understanding; will, intention

mentecatería *f*, folly, stupidity

mentecato (-ta) *a* foolish, silly; feeble-minded, simple. *n* fool, idiot

mentir *vi irr* to lie, be untruthful; deceive, mislead; falsify; *poet* belie; disagree, be incompatible; *vt* break a promise, disappoint. **m. como un bellaco**, to lie like a trooper See **sentir**

mentira *f*, lie, falsehood; error (in writing); *inf* white spot (on a fingernail); cracking (of fingerjoints). **m. oficiosa**, white lie. **Parece m.**, It seems incredible

mentiroso *a* lying, false; full of errors (literary works); deceptive

mentís *m*, giving the lie (literally, you lie); proof, demonstration (of error)

mentol *m*, menthol

menú *m*, menu

menudamente *adv* minutely; in detail, circumstantially

menudear *vt* to do frequently; do repeatedly; *vi* happen frequently; describe in detail; *com* sell by retail

menudencia *f*, minuteness, smallness; exactness, care, accuracy; trifle, worthless object; small matter; *pl* offal; pork sausages

menudeo *m*, repetition; description in detail; *com* retail. **al m.**, at retail

menudillos *m pl*, giblets; offal

menudo *a* minute, tiny; despicable; thin; small; vulgar; meticulous, exact; small (money). *m*, small coal; *m pl*, offal, entrails; small change (money). **a m.**, often, frequently. **por m.**, in detail, carefully; *com* in small lots

meñique *a inf* very small. *m*, little finger (in full, **dedo m.**)

meollo *m*, brain; *anat* marrow; *fig* essence, core, substance; understanding; *inf* **no tener m. (una cosa)**, to be worthless, unsubstantial (things)

mequetrefe *m*, *inf* coxcomb, whippersnapper

mercadeo *m*, marketing (study of markets)

mercader *m*, dealer, merchant, trader. **m. de grueso**, wholesaler

mercado *m*, market; marketplace

mercancía *f*, goods, merchandise; commerce, trade, traffic

mercante a trading; commercial. *m*, merchant, dealer, trader

mercantil a mercantile, commercial

merced *f*, salary, remuneration; favor, benefit, kindness; will, desire, pleasure; mercy, grace; courtesy title given to untitled person (e.g. **vuestra m.**, your honor. Has now become **usted** and is universally used). **m. a**, thanks to. **estar uno a m. de**, to live at someone else's expense, be dependent on

mercenario (**-ia**) *n ecc* member of the Order of la Merced. *m*, *mil* mercenary; day laborer. a mercenary

mercería *f*, haberdashery, mercery

mercerizar *vt* to mercerize

mercero *m*, haberdasher, mercer

mercurio *m*, mercury, quicksilver; *ast* Mercury

merecedor a deserving, worthy

merecer *vt irr* to deserve, be worthy of; attain, achieve; be worth; *vi* deserve, be deserving. **m. bien de,** to deserve well of; have a claim on the gratitude of. See **conocer**

merecido *m*, due reward

merecimiento *m*, desert; merit

merendar *vi irr* to have lunch; pry into another's affairs; *vt* have (a certain food) for lunch. *inf* **merendarse** (**una cosa**), to obtain (a thing), have it in one's pocket. See **recomendar**

merendero *m*, lunchroom; tearoom

merengue *m*, *cul* meringue

meridiana *f*, daybed, chaise longue; siesta

meridiano a meridian. *m*, meridian. **a la meridiana**, at noon

meridional a meridional, southern

merienda *f*, tea, snack; lunch; *inf* hunchback. *inf* **juntar meriendas**, to join forces, combine interests

merino a merino. *m*, merino wool; shepherd of merino sheep

mérito *m*, merit; desert; worth, excellence. **de m.,** excellent, notable. **hacer m. de,** to mention

meritorio a meritorious. *m*, unpaid worker, learner

merluza *f*, hake; *inf* drinking bout. *inf* **pescar una m.,** to get drunk

merma *f*, decrease, drop; loss, waste, reduction; leakage

mermar *vi* to diminish, waste away, decrease; evaporate; leak; *vt* filch, pilfer; reduce, decrease

mermelada *f*, conserve, preserve; jam; marmalade

mero a mere; simple; plain

merodear *vi* to maraud, raid; *Mexico* make money illegally

merodeo *m*, raiding, marauding

mes *m*, month; menses, menstruation

mesa *f*, table; board, directorate; meseta,

tableland; staircase landing; flat (of a sword, etc.); game of billiards. **m. de batalla,** post office sorting table. **m. de caballete,** trestle table. **m. de noche,** bedside table. **m. de tenis,** *Mexico* tennis court. **m. de tijeras,** folding table. **m. giratoria,** turntable. **alzar** (*or* **levantar**) **la m.,** to clear the table. **cubrir** (*or* **poner**) **la m.,** to set the table

mesada *f*, monthly wages, monthly payment

mesera *f Mexico* waitress

mesero *m Mexico* waiter

meseta *f*, staircase landing; plateau, tableland

mesiánico a Messianic

Mesías *m*, Messiah

mesilla *f*, small table; laughing admonition; landing (of a stair)

mesón *m*, inn, tavern

mesonero (**-ra**) *n* innkeeper; *Venezuela* waiter, waitress

mesta *f*, ancient order of sheep farmers; *pl* confluence, meeting (of rivers)

mester *m*, craft, occupation. **m. de clerecía,** learned poetic meter of the Spanish Middle Ages. **m. de juglaría,** popular poetry and troubadour songs

mestizo a half-breed; hybrid; cross-breed

mesura *f*, sedateness; dignity; courtesy; moderation

mesurado a sedate; dignified; moderate, restrained, temperate

meta *f*, goalpost *fig* aim, end; goal; goalkeeper

metabolismo *m*, metabolism

metáfora *f*, metaphor

metafórico a metaphorical

metal *m*, metal; brass; timbre of the voice; state, condition; quality, substance; *her* gold or silver; *mus* brass (instruments)

metálico a metallic. *m*, metalworker; coin, specie; bullion

metalizar *vt* to metallize, make metallic; *vr* become metallized; grow greedy for money

metalurgia *f*, metallurgy

metalúrgico a metallurgical. *m*, metallurgist

metamorfosis *f*, metamorphosis

metate *m*, *Central America, Mexico* flat stone for grinding and pounding

metedor (**-ra**) *n* placer, inserter; smuggler, contrabandist

metelón, -ona a, *Mexico* meddling, meddlesome

metemuertos *inf* meddler, Nosy Parker

meteórico a meteoric

meteorito *m*, meteorite

meteoro *m*, meteor

meteorología *f*, meteorology

meteorologista *mf* meteorologist; weather forecaster

meter *vt* to place; put; introduce, insert; stake (gambling); smuggle; cause, occasion; place close together; persuade to take part in; *sew* take in fullness; deceive, humbug; cram in, pack tightly; *naut* take in sail; *vr* interfere, butt in; meddle (with); take up, follow (occupations); be over-familiar; disembogue, empty itself (rivers, etc.); attack with the sword; (*with prep* a) follow (occupations); become, turn (e.g. **meterse a predicar,** to turn preacher); (*with con*) pick a quarrel with. **meterse en precisiones,** to go into details. *inf* **meterse en todo,** to be very meddlesome

metesillas y sacamuertos *m*, scene shifter, stagehand

metiche *a, Mexico* = **metellón**

meticulosidad *f*, meticulosity; timorousness

meticuloso *a* meticulous, fussy; timid, nervous

metido *a* tight; crowded; crabbed (of handwriting). *m, sew* material for letting out (seams). **m. en años,** quite old (person)

metimiento *m*, insertion, introduction; influence, sway

metódico *a* methodical

método *m*, method

metodología *f*, methodology

metralla *f, mil* grapeshot, shrapnel

métrico *a* metric; metrical

metro *m*, (verse) meter; meter (measurement); subway, underground railway

metrónomo *m*, metronome

metrópoli *f*, metropolis, capital; see of a metropolitan bishop; mother country

metropolitano *a* metropolitan. *m*, metropolitan bishop

mexicano *Lat. Am.* = **mejicano México** *Lat. Am.* = **Méjico**

mezcla *f*, mixture; blend, combination; mixed cloth, tweed; mortar

mezclar *vt* to mix, blend, combine; *vr* mix, mingle; take part; interfere, meddle; intermarry

mezcolanza *f, inf* hodgepodge

mezquindad *f*, poverty; indigence; miserliness; paltriness; meanness, poorness

mezquino *a* needy, impoverished; miserly, stingy; small, diminutive; unhappy; mean, paltry

mezquita *f*, mosque

mi *poss pron* my. *m, mus* mi, E

mí *pers pron acc gen dat 1st pers sing* me. Used only after prepositions (e.g. **Lo hicieron por mí,** They did it for me)

miaja *f*, See **migaja**

mica *f, min* mica; coquette, flirt

micho (-**cha**) *n inf* puss, pussycat

micra *f*, micron, thousandth part of a millimeter

micro *m, Chile, Peru* (large, express) bus; *elsewhere in Lat. Am.* minibus

microbio *m*, microbe

microbiología *f*, microbiology

microbrigada *f*, team of volunteer workers (in Castroist Cuba)

microcosmo *m*, microcosm

micrófono *m*, microphone

microonda *f*, microwave

microscópico *a* microscopic

microscopio *m*, microscope

miedo *m*, fear, apprehension, terror. **m. al público,** stagefright. **tener m.,** to be afraid

miedoso *a inf* fearful, nervous

miel *f*, honey. **m. de caña,** sugarcane syrup. *inf* **quedarse a media m.,** to see one's pleasure snatched away. *inf* **ser de mieles,** to be most pleasant or agreeable

mielitis *f*, myelitis

miembro *m, anat* limb; penis; member, associate; part, portion, section; *math* member

miente *f*, thought, imagination, mind. **parar** *or* **poner mientes en,** to consider, think about. **venírsele a las mientes,** to occur to one's mind

mientras *adv* while. **m. más . . .,** the more . . . . **m. que,** while (e.g. **m. que esperaba en el jardín,** while he was waiting in the garden). **m. tanto,** in the meanwhile

miércoles *m*, Wednesday. **m. de ceniza,** Ash Wednesday

mierda *f*, (*vulgar*) shit; *inf* filth

mies *f*, cereal plant, grain; harvest time; *pl* grain fields

miga *f*, breadcrumb; crumb; *inf* essence, core; substance; bit, scrap; *pl* fried breadcrumbs. *inf* **hacer buenas** (*or* **malas**) **migas,** to get on well (or badly) together

migaja *f*, breadcrumb; bit, scrap; trifle, mere nothing; *pl* crumbs (from the table); remains, remnants

migajón *m*, crumb (of a loaf); *fig inf* essence, substance, core

migración *f*, migration; emigration

migraña *f*, migraine

migratorio *a* migratory

mijo *m*, millet; maize

mil *a* thousand; thousandth; many, large number. *m*, thousand; thousandth. *inf* **Son las m. y quinientas,** It's extremely late (of the hour)

milagrero *a inf* miraculous

milagro *m*, miracle; marvel, wonder. **¡M.! ¡**Amazing! Just fancy!

milagroso *a* miraculous; marvelous, wonderful

mildeu *m*, mildew

milenario *a* millenary; millennial. *m*, millenary; millennium

milésimo a thousandth

milicia f, militia; military; art of war; military profession

milico m, Lat. Am., derogatory soldier

miligramo m, milligram

mililitro m, milliliter

milímetro m, millimeter

militante a militant

militar a military. m, soldier. vi to fight in the army; struggle (for a cause); fig militate (e.g. **Las circunstancias militan en favor de** (or **contra**) **sus ideas,** Circumstances militate against his ideas)

militarismo m, militarism

militarista a militaristic. mf militarist

militarizar vt to militarize; make war-like

milla f, mile

millar m, thousand; vast number (gen. pl)

millón m, million

millonario (-ia) a and n millionaire

milpa f, Central America, Mexico corn field

milpero, -a mf, Lat. Am. corn grower

mimar vt to spoil, overindulge; caress, fondle

mimbre mf osier; willow tree. m, wicker

mimbrear vi to sway, bend

mimbrera f, osier; osier bed; willow

mímica f, mimicry; mime

mímico a mimic

mimo m, mimic, buffoon; mime; caress, expression of affection, tenderness; overindulgence

mimoso a affectionate, demonstrative

mina f, mine; excavation, mining; underground passage; lead (in a pencil); (mil nav) mine; fig gold mine. mil **m. terrestre,** landmine

minador m, excavator; nav minelayer; mil sapper

minar vt to excavate, mine; fig undermine; (mil nav) mine; work hard for

minarete m, minaret

mineral a and m, mineral

mineralogía f, mineralogy

mineralógico a mineralogical

minería f, mining, mineworking; mineworkers

minero a mining. m, miner, mineworker; source, origin

minga f, Lat. Am. voluntary communal labor

miniatura f, miniature

miniaturista mf miniaturist

mínima f, mus minim; very small thing or portion

mínimo a sup **pequeño** smallest; minimum; meticulous, precise. m, minimum; (meteorological) trough

ministerial a ministerial

ministerio m, office, post; pol cabinet; ministry; government office; government department.

ministrar vt and vi to fill; administer (an office); vt minister to; give, provide

ministro m, instrument, agency; minister of state, cabinet minister; clergyman, minister; minister plenipotentiary; policeman. **m. de estado,** secretary of state. **m. de gobernación,** secretary of the interior. **m. de hacienda,** treasurer. **m. de relaciones extranjeras,** foreign secretary. **primer m.** prime minister

minorar vt to diminish, decrease

minoría f, minority, smaller number; minority (of age)

minoridad f, minority (of age)

minorista mf, Lat. Am. retailer

minucia f, smallness; morsel, mite; pl details, trifles, minutiae

minucioso a meticulous, precise, minute

minúsculo a minute, very small

minuta f, memorandum, minute; note; list, catalogue

minutero m, minute hand (of a clock)

minuto a minute, very small. m, minute

mío m. **mía,** f, (m pl. **míos,** f pl. **mías**) poss pron mine (e.g. **Las flores son mías,** The flowers are mine). **Mi** is used before nouns, not **mío.** Also used with article (e.g. **Este sombrero no es el mío,** This hat is not mine (my one)). **de mío,** by myself, without help. inf **¡Esta es la mía!** This is my chance!

miope a myopic. mf myopic person

miopía f, shortsightedness

mira f, sight (optical instruments, guns); intention, design; mil watchtower; care, precaution. **andar, estar** or **quedar a la m.,** to be vigilant, be on the lookout

mirada f, look; gaze. **lanzar miradas de carnero degollado (a),** to cast sheep's eyes at

miradero m, object of attention, cynosure; observation post, lookout

mirador (-ra) n spectator. m, arch oriel; enclosed balcony; observatory

miramiento m, observation, gazing; scruple, consideration; precaution, care; thoughtfulness

mirar vt to look at, gaze at; observe, behold; watch; consider, look after; value, appreciate; concern; believe, think; (with prep a) overlook, look on to; face; (with por) care for, protect; look after, consider. **m. contra el gobierno,** inf to be squint-eyed. **m. de hito en hito,** to look over, stare at. **mirarse en (una cosa),** to consider (a matter) carefully

miríada f, myriad, huge number

mirilla f, peephole

miriñaque m, trinket, ornament; crinoline

mirlarse vr inf to give oneself airs

mirón a inquisitive, curious

mirto *m*, myrtle

misa *f*, (*ecc mus*) mass. **m. de difuntos**, requiem mass. **m. del gallo**, midnight mass. **m. mayor**, high mass. **m. rezada**, low mass. **como en m.**, in profound silence. **oír m.**, to attend mass

misal *m*, missal

misantropía *f*, misanthropy

misantrópico *a* misanthropic

miscelánea *f*, medley, assortment, miscellany

misceláneo *a* assorted, miscellaneous, mixed

miserable *a* miserable, unhappy; timid, pusillanimous; miserly, mean; despicable

miseria *f*, misery; poverty, destitution; avarice, miserliness; *inf* poor thing, trifle

misericordia *f*, mercy, compassion

misericordioso *a* merciful, compassionate

mísero *a inf* fond of churchgoing

misión *f*, mission; vocation; commission, duty, errand

misionar *vi* to missionize, act as a missionary; *ecc* conduct a mission

misionero *m*, missioner; missionary

mismo *a* same; similar; self (e.g. **ellos mismos**, they themselves); very, same (e.g. **Ahora m. voy**, I'm going this very minute). **Me da lo m.**, It makes no difference to me. **por lo m.**, for that selfsame reason

misógino *m*, misogynist

misterio *m*, mystery

misterioso *a* mysterious

mística *f*, **misticismo** *m*, mysticism

místico *a* mystic

mistificación *f*, mystification; mystery; deception

mistificar *vt* to mystify; deceive

mitad *f*, half; middle, center. *fig inf* **cara m.**, better half. *inf* **mentir por la m. de la barba**, to lie barefacedly

mítico *a* mythical

mitigación *f*, mitigation

mitigar *vt* to mitigate, moderate, alleviate; appease

mitin *m*, mass meeting

mito *m*, myth

mitología *f*, mythology

mitológico *a* mythological

mitón *m*, mitten

mixto *a* mixed, blended; hybrid; composite; mongrel. *m*, mixed train (carrying freight and passengers); sulphur match

mixtura *f*, mixture, blend; compound; mixture (medicine)

¡miz, miz! puss, puss!

mobiliario *a* movable (goods). *m*, furniture

moblaje *m*, household goods and furniture

mocasín *m*, moccasin

mocedad *f*, youth, adolescence; mischief, prank. *fig inf* **correr sus mocedades**, to sow one's wild oats

mochila *f*, knapsack; nosebag; military rations for a march

mocho *a* blunted, topless, lopped; *inf* shorn, cropped. *m*, butt, butt end

moción *f*, motion, movement; impulse, tendency; divine inspiration; motion (of a debate)

moco *m*, mucus; candle drips; snuff of a candle. *inf* **caérsele el m.**, to be very simple, be easily deceived

mocoso (**-sa**) *a* running of the nose, sniffling; unimportant, insignificant. *n* coxcomb, stripling; *Lat. Am.* child

moda *f*, fashion. **estar** *or* **ser de m.**, to be fashionable, be in fashion. **la última m.**, the latest fashion

modales *m pl*, manners, behavior

modalidad *f*, form, nature; *mus* modality

modelado *m*, art modeling

modelar *vt art* to model; *vr* model oneself (on), copy

modelo *m*, example, pattern; model. *mf art* life model

moderación *f*, moderation; restraint, temperance, equability

moderado *a* moderate; restrained, temperate

moderador (**-ra**) *a* moderating. *n* moderator

moderar *vt* to moderate; temper, restrain; *vr* regain one's self-control; behave with moderation

modernista *a* modernistic; modern. *mf* modernist

modernización *f*, modernization

modernizar *vt* to modernize

moderno *a* modern. *m*, modern. **a la moderna**, in modern fashion

modestia *f*, modesty

modesto *a* modest

módico *a* moderate (of prices, etc.)

modificable *a* modifiable

modificación *f*, modification

modificador, modificante *a* modifying, moderating

modificar *vt* to modify; moderate

modismo *m*, idiom, idiomatic expression

modista *mf* dressmaker; couturier; milliner

modo *m*, mode, method, style; manner, way; moderation, restraint; civility, politeness (often *pl*); *mus* mode; *gram* mood. **m. de ser**, nature, temperament. **de m. que**, so that. **de ningún m.**, not at all, by no means. **de todos modos**, in any case

modorra *f*, deep sleep, stupor

modorro *a* drowsy, heavy

modoso *a* demure; well-behaved

modulación *f*, modulation

modulador (-ra) a modulative. n modulator, m, mus modulator

modular vt and vi to modulate

mofa f, mockery, ridicule, jeering

mofador (-ra) a jeering. n scoffer, mocker

mofarse vr (with de) to make fun of, jeer at

mofeta f, noxious gas; damp (gas); zool skunk

moflete m, inf plump cheek

mofletudo a plump-cheeked

mohín m, grimace

mohína f, grudge, rancor; sullenness; sulkiness

mohíno a depressed, gloomy; sulky; black or black-nosed (of animals)

moho m, mold, fungoid growth; moldiness; moss. inf **no criar m.,** to be always on the move

mohoso a mossy; moldy

mojada f, wetting; inf stab; sop of bread

mojador (-ra) n wetter. m, stamp moistener

mojar vt to wet; moisten; inf stab, wound with a dagger; vi take part in; meddle, interfere; vr get wet

mojicón m, kind of spongecake; inf slap in the face

mojiganga f, masquerade, mummer's show; farce; funny sight, figure of fun

mojigatería f, hypocrisy; sanctimoniousness; prudery

mojigato (-ta) a hypocritical; sanctimonious; prudish. n hypocrite; bigot; prude

mojón m, boundary marker; milestone; heap. **m. kilométrico,** milestone

molar a molar

molde m, mold, matrix; fig model, pattern. **de m.,** printed; suitable, conveniently; perfectly. **letra de m.,** printed letters, print

moldear vt to mold, cast

moldura f, molding

moldurar vt carp to mold

molécula f, molecule

mole f mass, bulk

mole de guajolote m, Mexico turkey served with a heavy dark sauce made of different kinds of chiles, spices, etc.

moler vt irr to grind, crush; tire, exhaust; ill-treat; pester, annoy. **m. a palos,** to beat black and blue. Pres. Ind. **muelo, mueles, muele, muelen.** Pres. Subjunc. **muela, muelas, muela, muelan**

molestia f, inconvenience, trouble; annoyance; discomfort, pain; bore, nuisance. **Es una m.,** It's a nuisance

molesto a inconvenient, troublesome; annoying; painful; uncomfortable; boring, tedious

molestoso, -a a, Lat. Am. annoying, bothersome

moletón m, flannelet

molicie f, softness, smoothness; effeminacy, weakness

molienda f, milling; grinding; mill; portion ground at one time; inf exhaustion, fatigue; inf nuisance

molificar vt to mollify, appease

molimiento m, milling; grinding; exhaustion, fatigue

molinero a mill. m, miller

molinillo m, hand mill, small grinder; mincing machine; beater. **m. de café,** coffee mill

molino m, mill; harum-scarum, rowdy; bore, tedious person; inf mouth. **m. de rueda de escalones,** treadmill. **m. de viento,** windmill

molleja f, gizzard

mollera f, crown of the head; brains, sense. inf **ser duro de m.,** to be obstinate; be stupid

molusco m, mollusk

momentáneo a momentary, brief; instantaneous, immediate

momento m, moment, minute; importance; mech moment. **al m.,** immediately. **a cada m.,** all the time; frequently. **por momentos,** continually; intermittently

momería f, mummery

momero (-ra) n mummer

momia f, mummy

momificar vt to mummify; vr become mummified

mona f, female monkey; inf imitator; drinking bout; drunk. inf **Aunque la m. se vista de seda, m. se queda,** Breeding will tell. inf **ser la última m.,** to be of no account, be unimportant

monacillo m, ecc acolyte

monada f, mischievous prank; affected gesture or grimace; small, pretty thing; childish cleverness; flattery; rash act; pl monkey shines

monaguillo m, ecc acolyte

monarca mf monarch

monarquía f, monarchy

monasterio m, monastery; convent

monástico a monastic

mondadientes m, toothpick

mondar vt to skin, peel; agr prune; cut the hair; cleanse; free of rubbish; inf deprive of possessions; Lat. Am. to beat, beat up, thrash vr pick one's teeth

mondo a simple, plain; bare; unadulterated, pure

mondongo m, Lat. Am. tripe

moneda f, coin, piece of money; coinage; inf wealth; cash. **m. corriente,** currency. **m. metálica,** specie. **pagar en buena**

m., to give entire satisfaction. **pagar en la misma m.,** to pay back in the same coin, return like for like. *inf* **ser m. corriente,** to be usual or very frequent

monedero *m*, coiner, minter; handbag; purse

monería *f*, mischievous trick; unimportant trifle; pretty thing; childish cleverness, pretty ways

monetario a monetary. *m*, collection of coins and medals

monigote *m*, *inf* boor; grotesque, puppet

monitor *m*, monitor

monja *f*, nun; *pl* sparks

monje *m*, monk

monjil a nun-like. *m*, nun's habit

mono a *inf* pretty, attractive; amusing, funny. *m*, monkey; person given to grimacing; rash youth; coverall. *inf* **estar de monos,** to be on bad terms

monogamia *f*, monogamy

monógamo a monogamous. *n* monogamist

monografía *f*, monograph

monograma *m*, monogram

monolítico a monolithic

monolito *m*, monolith

monólogo *m*, monologue

monomaníaco (-ca) *n* monomaniac

monopatín *m*, scooter

monoplano *m*, monoplane

monopolio *m*, monopoly

monopolista *mf* monopolist

monopolizar *vt* to monopolize

monoteísmo *m*, monotheism

monoteísta *mf* monotheist

monotonía *f*, monotony; monotone

monótono a monotonous

monroísmo *m*, Monroe doctrine

monseñor *m*, monsignor

monserga *f*, *inf* rigmarole; jargon

monstruo *m*, monster; freak, monstrosity; cruel person; hideous person or thing

monstruosidad *f*, monstrousness, monstrosity

monstruoso a monstrous, abnormal; enormous; extraordinary; atrocious, outrageous

monta *f*, mounting a horse; total; *mil* mounting signal; breeding station (horses)

montacargas *m*, hoist, lift; freight elevator

montador *m*, mounter; mounting block

montadura *f*, mounting; mount, setting (of jewels)

montaje *m*, assembling, setting up (machines); presentation (of a book); (cinema) montage

montano a hilly, mountainous

montante *m*, upright, stanchion; tent pole

montaña *f*, mountain; mountainous country. **montañas rusas,** roller coaster (at an amusement park)

montañés (-esa) a mountain. *n* mountain dweller; native of Santander

montañoso a mountainous; hilly

montar *vi* to ascend, climb up, get on top; mount (a horse); ride (a horse); be important; *vt* get on top of; ride (a horse); total, amount to; set up (apparatus, machinery); *naut* sail around, double; set, mount (gems); cock (firearms); fine for trespassing; wind (a clock); command (a ship); *naut* carry, be fitted with (guns, etc.). **m. a horcajadas en,** to mount astride; straddle. **montarse en cólera,** to fly into a rage

montaraz a mountain-dwelling; wild, savage; rude, uncivilized, uncouth. *m*, gamekeeper, forester

monte *m*, mount, hill; woodland; obstacle, impediment. **m. de piedad,** pawnshop. **m. pío,** savings fund

montepío *m*, *Lat. Am.* pawnshop

montería *f*, hunt, chase; art of hunting

montés a wild, savage, untamed

montículo *m*, mound, hill

montón *m*, heap, pile; *inf* abundance, lot. *inf* **a, de** or **en m.,** all jumbled up together. **a montones,** in abundance

montonero, -a *mf* domineering, overbearing

montuoso a mountainous

montura *f*, riding animal, mount; horse trappings; setting up, mounting (artillery, etc.)

monumento *m*, monument; document, record; tomb

monzón *mf*, monsoon

moña *f*, doll; dressmaker's model; bow for the hair; bullfighter's black bow; baby's bonnet; *inf* drinking bout

moño *m*, bun, chignon; topknot (birds); bunch of ribbons; *pl* tawdry trimmings

moquete *m*, slap in the face

mora *f*, blackberry; mulberry; bramble; Moorish girl, Moorish woman

morada *f*, dwelling, abode; sojourn, stay

morado a purple

morador (-ra) *n* dweller; sojourner

moral a moral, ethical. *f*, morality, ethics; morale. *m*, blackberry bush

moraleja *f*, moral, lesson

moralidad *f*, morality

moralista *mf* moralist

moralización *f*, moralization

moralizador (-ra) a moralizing. *n* moralizer

moralizar *vt* to reform, correct; *vi* moralize

moratoria f, moratorium

morbidez f, art morbidezza; softness

mórbido a morbid, diseased; art delicate (of flesh tones); soft

morbo m, illness. **m. gálico,** syphilis

morboso a ill; morbid, unhealthy

morcilla f, cul black pudding; (inf theat) gag

morcillero (-ra) n seller of black puddings; (inf theat) actor who gags

mordacidad f, corrosiveness; mordacity, sarcasm; cul piquancy

mordaz a corrosive; sarcastic, caustic, mordant; cul piquant

mordaza f, gag

mordedor a biting; scandalmongering

mordedura f, bite, biting

mordelón, -ona mf, Central America, Mexico given to taking bribes

morder vt irr to bite; nibble, nip; seize, grasp; corrode, eat away; slander; etch. Pres. Ind. **muerdo, muerdes, muerde, muerden.** Pres. Subjunc. **muerda, muerdas, muerda, muerdan**

mordida f, Lat. Am. bite; Central America, Mexico also bribe

mordiente m, fixative (for dyeing); mordant. a mordant (of acid)

mordiscar vt to nibble, bite gently; bite

mordisco m, nibble; nibbling; bite; biting; piece bitten off

moreno (-na) a dark brown; swarthy complexioned; dark (of people). n inf negro, mulatto

morfina f, morphine

morfinómano (-na) n morphine addict

moribundo (-da) a moribund, dying. n dying person

morillo m, andiron, fire-dog

morir vi irr to die; fade, wither; decline, decay; disappear; yearn (for); long (to); go out (lights, fire); vr die; go numb (limbs); (with por) adore, be mad about. inf **m. vestido,** to die a violent death. ¡Muera! Down with! Past Part. **muerto.** For other tenses see **dormir**

morisco (-ca) a Moorish. n Morisco, Moor converted to Christianity

mormón (-ona) n Mormon

moro (-ra) a Moorish. n Moor; Mohammedan. inf **haber moros y cristianos,** to be the deuce of a row. inf **Hay moros en la costa,** The coast is not clear; There's trouble in the offing

moronga f, Central America, Mexico blood sausage

morosidad f, slowness, delay; sluggishness, sloth

moroso a slow, dilatory; sluggish, lazy

morra f, crown of the head

morral m, nose-bag; knapsack; game-bag; inf lout

morriña f, cattle plague, murrain; inf depression, blues; homesickness

morro m, anything round; hummock, hillock; round pebble; headland, cliff

morrón m, Lat. Am. hot red pepper

morsa f, walrus

mortaja f, shroud, winding sheet

mortal a mortal; fatal, deadly; on the point of death; great, tremendous; certain, sure. mf mortal

mortalidad f, humanity, human race; mortality, death-rate

mortandad f, mortality, number of deaths

mortecino a dead from natural causes (animals); weak; fading; dull, dead (of eyes); flickering; on the point of death or extinction

mortero m, mortar (for building); mil mortar; pounding mortar

mortífero a deadly, mortal

mortificación f, med gangrene; humiliation, wounding; mortification (of the flesh)

mortificar vt med to mortify; humiliate, wound, hurt; mortify (the flesh); vr become gangrenous

mortuorio a mortuary. m, funeral, obsequies

mosaico a and m, mosaic

mosca f, fly; inf nuisance; bore, pest; cash; pl sparks. inf **m. muerta,** underhanded person. inf **papar moscas,** to gape, be dumbfounded. inf **soltar la m.,** to give or spend money unwillingly

moscardón m, gadfly

moscatel a muscatel. m, muscatel (grapes and wine); inf pest, tedious person

Moscú Moscow

mosquear vt to drive off flies; reply crossly; whip; vr be exasperated; brush aside obstacles

mosquero m, flypaper

mosquitero m, mosquito net

mosquito m, mosquito; midge, gnat; inf tippler, drunkard

mostacho m, mustache, whiskers; inf smudge on the face

mostaza f, mustard plant or seed; cul mustard

mostrador (-ra) n one who shows, exhibitor. m, shop counter; face of a watch

mostrar vt irr to show; indicate, point out; demonstrate, prove; manifest, reveal; vr show oneself, be (e.g. **Se mostró bondadoso,** He showed himself to be kind). Pres. Ind. **muestro, muestras, muestra, muestran.** Pres. Subjunc. **muestre, muestres, muestre, muestren**

mostrenco a inf stray, vagrant, homeless; inf dull, ignorant; inf fat, heavy

mota f, fault in cloth; mote, defect, fault; mound, hill; thread of cotton, speck of dust, etc.; fleck (of the sun, etc.); spot

mote m, maxim, saying; motto, device; catchword, slogan; nickname; *Lat. Am.* boiled corn

motejar vt to nickname, call names, dub

motete m, motet

motín m, mutiny; riot

motivar vt to motivate, cause; explain one's reasons

motivo a motive. m, cause, motive; *mus* motif. **con m. de,** on account of, because of. **de m. propio,** of one's own free will

motocicleta f, motorcycle

motociclista mf motorcyclist

motor (**-ra**) a motive, driving. m, motor, engine. n (person) mover, motive force. **m. de combustión interna,** internal combustion engine. **m. de retroacción,** jet engine

motorista mf motorist, driver

movedizo a movable; insecure, unsteady; shaky; changeable, vacillating

mover vt irr to move; operate, drive; sway; wag; persuade, induce; excite; move (to pity, etc.); (*with prep* a) cause; vi sprout (plants); vr move. *Pres. Ind.* **muevo, mueves, mueve, mueven.** *Pres. Subjunc.* **mueva, muevas, mueva, muevan**

movible a movable; insecure, shaky. m, motive, cause, incentive

movilizar vt to mobilize

movimiento m, movement; perturbation, excitement; *mus* movement; *lit* fire, spirit; *mech* motion, movement. **mil m. envolvente,** encircling movement

moza f, maid; girl; waitress. **m. de partido,** party girl, prostitute. **buena m.,** fine, upstanding young woman

mozo a young, unmarried. m, boy, youth; bachelor; waiter; porter. **m. de cordel** or **m. de esquina,** street porter, message boy. **m. de estación,** railroad porter. **buen m.,** fine, upstanding young man

muaré m, moiré silk

mucama f, *Argentina* chambermaid

muceta f, *univ* hood, short cape (of a graduate's gown)

muchacha f, girl, lass; female servant

muchachada f, childish prank

muchachez f, boyhood; girlhood

muchachil a boyish; girlish

muchacho m, boy, youth; male servant

muchedumbre f, abundance, plenty; crowd, multitude; mass, mob

muchísimo a *sup* very much. adv very great deal, very much

mucho a much; plenty of; very; long (time); *pl* many, numerous. adv a great deal; much; very much; yes, certainly; frequently, often; very (e.g. **Me alegro m.,** I am very glad); to a great extent; long (time). **con m.,** by far, easily. **ni con m.,** nor anything like it, very far from it. **ni m. menos,** and much less. **por m. que,** however much

mucílago m, mucilage, gum

muda f, change, transformation; change of clothes; molting season; molt, sloughing of skin (snakes, etc.); change of voice (in boys)

mudable a changeable, inconstant

mudanza f, change; furniture removal; step, figure (in dancing); changeability, inconstancy

mudar vt to change; alter, transform; exchange; remove; dismiss (from employment); molt; slough the skin (snakes, etc.); change the voice (boys); vr alter one's behavior; change one's clothes; change one's residence, move; change one's expression; *inf* go away, depart

mudéjar m, *arch* style containing Moorish and Christian elements. mf Moor who remained in Spain under Christian rule

mudez f, dumbness; silence, muteness

mudo a dumb; silent, mute, quiet

mueblaje m, household goods and furniture

mueble m, piece of furniture; furnishing

mueblería f, furniture store or factory

mueca f, grimace

muela f, grindstone; molar (tooth); millstone; flat-topped hill. **m. del juicio,** wisdom tooth. **dolor de muelas,** toothache

muelle a soft, smooth; voluptuous, sensuous; luxurious. m, spring (of a watch, etc.); wharf, quay; freight platform (railroad). **m. real,** mainspring (of a watch). **m. del volante,** hairspring.

muérdago m, mistletoe

muerte f, death; destruction, annihilation; end, decline. *inf* **una m. chiquita,** a nervous shudder. **a m.,** to the death, with no quarter. **de m.,** implacably, inexorably (of hatred); very seriously (of being ill). **dar m. (a),** to kill. **estar a la m.,** to be on the point of death. **a cada m. de un obispo,** once in a blue moon

muerto (**-ta**) a dead; slaked (lime); *mech* neutral; faded, dull (colors); languid, indifferent. **m.** is used in familiar speech as *past part* **matar** (e.g. **Le ha muerto,** He has killed him). n corpse. *inf* **desenterrar los muertos,** to speak ill of the dead. *inf* **echarle a uno el m.,** to pass the buck. *inf* **estar m. por,** to be dying, yearning for. **ser el m.,** to be dummy (at cards)

muesca f, notch, mortise, groove

muestra f, shop sign; sample, specimen; pattern, model; demeanor; watch or clock face; sign, indication; poster, placard; *mil* muster roll. **hacer m.,** to show

mugido m, mooing or lowing (of cattle)

mugir *vi* to low or moo (cattle); bellow, shout; rage (elements)

mugre *f*, grease, grime, dirt

mugriento *a* grimy, greasy

mujer *f*, woman; wife. **m. de la vida airada** *or* **m. del partido** *or* **m. pública**, prostitute. **m. de la luna**, man in the moon. **m. de su casa**, good housewife. **tomar m.**, to take a wife

mujerero, -a *a*, *Lat. Am.* fond of women

mujeriego *a* womanly, feminine; (of men) dissolute, given to philandering. **cabalgar a mujeriegas**, to ride sidesaddle

mujeril *a* womanly, feminine

mula *f*, female mule; mule (heelless slipper); *Colombia* dope smuggler; *Mexico* junk, trash. *inf* **Se me fue la m.**, My tongue ran away with me

muladar *m*, refuse heap, junkpile, dunghill

mular *a* mule; mulish

mulato (-ta) *a* and *n* mulatto

muleta *f*, crutch; bullfighter's red flag; support, prop

mullir *vt irr* to make soft, shake out (wool, down, etc.); *fig* prepare the way; *agr* hoe the roots (of vines, etc.). *Pres. Part.* **mullendo.** *Preterite* **mulló, mulleron.** *Imperf. Subjunc.* **mullese,** etc.

mulo *m*, mule

multa *f*, fine

multar *vt* to impose a fine on

multicolor *a* multicolored

multilátero *a* multilateral

multimillonario (-ia) *a* and *n* multimillionaire

multiplicación *f*, multiplication

multiplicador (-ra) *n* multiplier. *m*, *math* multiplier

multiplicar((se) *vt* and *vr* to multiply; reproduce

multisecular *a* age-old, many centuries old

multitud *f*, multitude, great number; crowd; rabble, masses, mob

mundanal, mundano *a* worldly, mundane

mundial *a* world, worldwide

mundo *m*, world, universe; human race; earth; human society; world (of letters, science, etc.); secular life; *ecc* vanities of the flesh; geographical globe. **echar al m.**, to give birth to; produce, bring forth. **el Nuevo M.**, the New World, America. *inf* **medio m.**, half the earth, a great crowd. *inf* **ponerse el m. por montera**, to treat the world as one's oyster. **ser hombre del m.**, to be a man of the world. *inf* **tener m.** *or* **mucho m.**, to be very experienced, know the world. **todo el m.**, everyone. **venir al m.**, to be born. **ver m.**, to travel, see the world

mundología *f*, worldliness, experience of the world

munición *f*, *mil* munition; small shot. *mil* **m. de boca,** fodder and food supplies

municipal *a* municipal. *m*, policeman

municipalidad *f*, municipality

municipio *m*, municipality, town council

munificencia *f*, munificence, generosity

munífico *a* munificent, generous

muñeca *f*, *anat* wrist; doll; puppet; dressmaker's dummy; polishing pad; mannequin; boundary marker; *inf* flighty young woman

muñeco *m*, boy doll; puppet; *inf* playboy

muñir *vt irr* to summon, convoke; arrange, dispose. See **mullir**

mural a mural

muralla *f*, town wall; rampart, fortification

murar *vt* to surround with a wall, wall in

murciélago *m*, *zool* bat

murmullo *m*, whisper; whispering; rustling; purling, lapping, splashing; mumbling, muttering

murmuración *f*, slander, backbiting, gossip

murmurador (-ra) *a* gossiping, slanderous. *n* gossip, backbiter

murmurar *vi* to rustle (leaves, etc.); purl, lap, splash (water); whisper; mumble, mutter; *vi* and *vt inf* slander, backbite

murmurio *m*, rustling; lapping (of water); whispering; murmur; *inf* slander

muro *m*, wall; defensive wall, rampart

musaraña *f*, *zool* shrew; any small animal; *inf* ridiculous effigy, guy. *inf* **mirar a las musarañas,** to be absent-minded

musculatura *f*, musculature

músculo *m*, muscle; strength, brawn

musculoso *a* muscular; strong, brawny

muselina *f*, muslin

museo *m*, museum. **m. de pintura,** art gallery, picture gallery

musgo *m*, moss

música *f*, music; melody, harmony; musical performance; musical composition; group of musicians; sheet music. *inf* **m. celestial,** vain words, moonshine. *inf* **m. ratonera,** badly played music. *inf* **¡Vaya con su m. a otra parte!** Get out! Go to hell!

musical *a* musical

músico (-ca) *a* music. *n* musician. **m. ambulante,** strolling musician. **m. mayor,** bandleader

musitar *vi* to mutter, mumble

muslo *m*, thigh

mustango *m*, *Lat. Am.* mustang

musulmán (-ana) *a* and *n* Muslim

mutación *f*, change, mutation; sudden change in the weather; *theat* change of scene

mutilación *f*, mutilation; damage; defacement

mutilar *vt* to mutilate; spoil, deface, damage; cut short; reduce

mutis *m, theat* exit. **hacer m.** *theat* to exit; keep quiet, say nothing

mutismo *m*, mutism, dumbness; silence, speechlessness

mutualidad *f*, reciprocity, mutuality, interdependence; principle of mutual aid; mutual aid society

mutualista *mf* member of a mutual aid society

mutuo *a* reciprocal, mutual, interdependent

muy *adv* very; very much; much. Used to form absolute superlative (e.g. **m. rápidamente,** very quickly). Can modify adjectives, nouns used adjectivally, adverbs, participles (e.g. **María es m. mujer,** Mary is very much a woman (very womanly)). **m. temprano,** very early. **M. señor mío,** Dear Sir (in letters)

naba *f*, swede, turnip

nabo *m*, turnip; turnip root; any root stem; *naut* mast; stock (of a horse's tail)

nácar *m*, mother-of-pearl

nacer *vi irr* to be born; rise (rivers, etc.); sprout; grow (plumage, fur, leaves, etc.); descend (lineage); appear (stars, etc.); originate; *fig* issue forth; appear suddenly; (*with prep a or para*) be destined for, have a natural leaning toward. **n. con pajitas de oro en la cuna**, to be born with a silver spoon in one's mouth. *vr* grow; sprout; *sew* split at the seams. *Pres. Ind.* **nazco, naces**, etc. *Pres. Subjunc.* **nazca**, etc.

nacido *a* and *past part* born; suitable, fit. *m*, (gen. *pl*) the living and the dead. **bien n.**, noble, well-born; well-bred. **mal n.**, base-born; ill-bred

naciente *a* growing; nascent. *m*, east

nacimiento *m*, birth; source (of rivers, etc.); birthplace; origin; lineage; *ast* rising; nativity crib, manger. **de n.**, from birth; by birth; born

nación *f*, nation; country; *inf* birth

nacional *a* national; native. *mf* citizen, national

nacionalidad *f*, nationality

nacionalismo *m*, nationalism

nacionalización *f*, naturalization; nationalization; acclimatization

nacionalizar *vt* to naturalize; nationalize

nada *f*, void, nothingness. *pron indef* nothing. *adv* by no means. **casi n.**, very little, practically nothing. **¡De n.!** Not at all! Don't mention it! You're welcome! **No vale para n.**, He (it, she) is of no use

nadaderas *f pl*, water wings (for swimming)

nadador (-ra) *n* swimmer. *a* swimming

nadar *vi* to swim; float; have an abundance (of); *inf* be too large (of garments, etc.). **n. y guardar la ropa**, *fig* to sit on the fence

nadería *f*, trifle

nadie *pron indef* no one. *m*, *fig* a nobody

nadir *m*, nadir

nado *a* by swimming; afloat

nafta *f*, naphtha; *Argentina* gas, gasoline

naftalina *f*, naphthalene

naipe *m*, playing card; pack of cards

nalga *f*, (gen. *pl*) buttock(s)

nana *f*, *inf* grandma; lullaby; *Mexico* wet nurse; nurserymaid

nao *f*, ship

napoleónico *a* Napoleonic

Nápoles Naples

napolitano (-na) *a* and *n* Neapolitan

naranja *f*, orange. **n. dulce**, blood orange. **n. mandarina**, tangerine. *inf* **media n.**, better half

naranjada *f*, orangeade

naranjo *m*, orange tree; *inf* lout, blockhead

narciso *m*, narcissus; dandy, fop. **n. trompón**, daffodil

narcótico *a* and *m*, narcotic

narcotraficante *mf* drug dealer

nardo *m*, tuberose, spikenard, nard

narigudo *a* large-nosed; nose-shaped

nariz *f*, nose; nostril; snout; nozzle; sense of smell; bouquet (of wine). **n. perfilada**, well-shaped nose. **n. respingona**, snub nose. *inf* **meter las narices**, to meddle, interfere

narración *f*, narration, account

narrador (-ra) *a* narrative. *n* narrator

narrar *vt* to narrate, tell, relate

narrativa *f*, narrative; account; narrative skill

narrativo, narratorio *a* narrative

nata *f*, cream; *fig* the flower, elite; *pl* whipped cream with sugar

natación *f*, swimming. **n. a la marinera**, trudgen stroke

natal *a* natal; native. *m*, birth; birthday

natalicio *a* natal. *a* and *m*, birthday

natalidad *f*, birth rate

natatorio *a* swimming. *m*, swimming pool

natillas *f pl*, custard

natividad *f*, nativity; birth; Christmas

nativo *a* indigenous; native; innate

nato *a* born; inherent; ex officio

natura *f*, nature; *mus* major scale

natural *a* natural; native; indigenous; spontaneous; sincere, candid; physical; usual, ordinary; *mus* natural; unadulterated, pure; *her* proper. *mf* native, citizen. *m*, temperament; disposition; instinct (of animals); natural inclination. **al n.**, naturally, without art. **del n.**, *art* from life

naturaleza *f*, nature; character; disposition; instinct; temperament; nationality; origin; naturalization; kind, class; constitution, physique. **n. humana**, humankind. **n. muerta**, *art* still life

naturalizar *vt* to naturalize; acclimatize; *vr* become naturalized; become acclimatized

naufragar *vi* to be shipwrecked; fail, be unsuccessful

naufragio *m*, shipwreck; disaster, loss

náufrago (-ga) *n* shipwrecked person. *m*, shark

náusea *f*, nausea (*pl* more usual); repugnance

nauseabundo, nauseoso *a* nauseous; nauseating, repugnant

náutica *f*, navigation; yachting; seamanship

náutico *a* nautical

navaja *f*, razor; clasp knife; boar tusk; sting; *inf* slanderous tongue. **n. de afeitar**, (shaving) razor

navajada *f*, slash with a razor

naval *a* naval

navarro (-ra) *a* and *n* Navarrese

nave *f*, ship; *arch* nave. **n. aérea**, airship. *arch* **n. lateral**, aisle. **n. principal**, *arch* nave

navegable *a* navigable

navegación *f*, navigation; sea voyage

navegante *a* voyaging; navigating. *m*, navigator

navegar *vi* to navigate; sail; fly

navidad *f*, nativity; Christmas; *pl* Christmastime

naviero *a* shipping. *m*, ship owner

navío *m*, warship; ship. **n. de transporte**, transport. **n. de tres puentes**, three-decker

nazismo *m*, nazism

neblina *f*, fog; mist

nebuloso *a* foggy; misty; cloudy; somber, melancholy; confused, nebulous

necedad *f*, silliness

necesario *a* necessary; unavoidable

neceser *m*, dressing case. *sew* **n. de costura**, workbox

necesidad *f*, necessity; poverty, want; shortage, need; emergency. **de n.**, necessarily

necesitado (-da) *a* needy, poor. *n* poor person

necesitar *vt* to necessitate; compel, oblige; *vi* be necessary, need

necio *a* stupid; senseless; unreasonable

necrología *f*, necrology, obituary

neerlandés *a* Dutch

nefando *a* iniquitous

nefario *a* nefarious

nefasto *a* disastrous, ill-omened

nefritis *f*, nephritis

negable *a* deniable

negación *f*, negation; privation; negative; nay; *gram* negative particle; *law* traverse

negado *a* inept, unfitted; stupid

negar *vt irr* to deny; refuse; prohibit; disclaim; dissemble; disown; *law* traverse; *vr* refuse, avoid; decline (to receive visitors). See **acertar**

negativa *f*, denial; refusal; *phot* negative

negativo *a* negative

negligencia *f*, negligence; omission; carelessness; forgetfulness

negligente *a* negligent; careless; neglectful

negociable *a* negotiable

negociación *f*, negotiation; business affair, deal

negociado *m*, department, section (of a ministry, etc.); business; *Chile* shop, store; *elsewhere in Lat. Am.* shady deal

negociante *m*, businessman. *a* negotiating; trading

negociar *vi* to trade, traffic; negotiate

negocio *m*, occupation; trade; business; employment; transaction; *Argentina* shop, store; *pl* business affairs. **hombre de negocios**, businessman

negra *f*, black girl, black woman; *inf* honey, *WH* sweetheart

negro *a* black; dark; melancholy; disastrous; *her* sable. *m*, black; black (color). **n. de humo**, lampblack

negruzco *a* blackish

neme *m*, *Colombia* asphalt

nemotécnica *f*, mnemonics

nene (-na) *n inf* baby; darling

nenúfar *m*, white water lily

neo *m*, neon

neófito (-ta) *n* neophyte

neoyorquino (-na) *a* New York. *n* New Yorker

nepotismo *m*, nepotism

Neptuno *m*, *ast* Neptune; *poet* sea

nervio *m*, nerve; sinew; *bot* vein; vigor; *mus* string. **n. ciático**, sciatic nerve

nervioso *a* nervous; overwrought, agitated; vigorous; neural; sinewy; jerky (of style, etc.)

nervosidad *f*, nervousness; nervosity; flexibility (metals); jerkiness (of style, etc.); force, efficacy

nervudo *a* strong-nerved, vigorous

nesga *f*, *sew* gore

neto *a* neat; clean; pure; *com* net. *m*, *arch* dado

neumático *a* pneumatic. *m*, rubber tire

neumococo *m*, pneumococcus

neurálgico *a* neuralgic

neurastenia *f*, neurasthenia

neurasténico (-ca) *a* and *n* neurasthenic

neurólogo *m*, neurologist

neurosis *f*, neurosis. **n. de guerra**, war neurosis; shell shock

neurótico (-ca) *a* and *n* neurotic

neutral *a* neutral; indifferent

neutralidad *f*, neutrality; impartiality; indifference

neutralizar *vt* to neutralize; counteract, mitigate

neutro *a* neuter; *chem* neutral; *mech* neuter; sexless

nevada *f*, snowfall

nevado *m*, *Lat. Am.* snow-capped mountain

nevar *vi irr impers* to snow. *Pres. Ind.* **nieva**. *Pres. Subjunc.* **nieve**

nevazón *f*, *Lat. Am.* blizzard, snowstorm

nevera *f*, refrigerator; icehouse

nevoso *a* snowy

nexo *m*, nexus; connection; union

ni *conjunc* neither, nor. **ni bien ni mal,**

neither good nor bad. **ni siquiera,** not even. ¡Ni crea!, ¡Ni creas! Nonsense!

niara f, haystack, rick

nicaragüeño (-ña) a and n Nicaraguan

nicho m, niche; recess (in a wall)

nicotina f, nicotine

nidada f, nest full of eggs; brood, clutch

nidal m, nest; nest egg; haunt; cause, foundation

nido m, nest; den; hole; dwelling; haunt. **n. de ametralladoras,** mil pillbox

niebla f, fog; mist; cloud; mildew; haze

nieto (-ta) n grandchild; descendant

nieve f, snow; whiteness. **deportes de n.,** winter sports

Nilo, el the Nile

nimbo m, halo, nimbus

nimiedad f, prolixity; inf fussiness; fastidiousness, delicacy

nimio a prolix; inf fussy; fastidious; inf parsimonious

ninfa f, nymph; ent chrysalis

ningún a abb of **ninguno. De n. modo,** In no way! Certainly not!

niña f, girl. **n. del ojo,** pupil (of the eye). **n. de los ojos,** apple of one's eye, darling

niñada f, childishness, foolish act

niñera f, nursemaid

niñería f, childish act; trifle; childishness, folly

niñez f, childhood; beginning, early days; fig cradle

niño (-ña) a childish; young; inexperienced; imprudent. n child; young or inexperienced person. **n. de la doctrina,** charity child. **n. terrible,** enfant terrible. **desde n.,** from childhood

nipón (-ona) a and n Japanese

níquel m, chem nickel

niquelar vt to chrome-plate

niquelera f, Colombia purse, change purse

nirvana m, nirvana

níspero m, medlar tree; medlar

níspola f, medlar

nitidez f, brightness, neatness, cleanliness

nítido a bright, neat, clean (often poet.)

nitrato m, nitrate

nítrico a nitric

nitrógeno m, nitrogen

nivel m, level; levelness. **n. de albañil,** plummet. **n. de burbuja,** spirit level. **a n.,** on the level. **estar al n. de las circunstancias,** to rise to the occasion; save the day

nivelación f, leveling

nivelador (-ra) a leveling. n leveler

nivelar vt to level; fig make equal

níveo a snowy; snow-white

no adv no; not. **no bien,** no sooner. **no sea que,** unless. **no tal,** no such thing

noble a noble, illustrious; generous; outstanding, excellent; aristocratic. mf nobleman (-woman)

nobleza f, nobility

noche f, night; darkness; confusion, obscurity. inf **n. toledana,** restless night. ¡Buenas noches! Good night! **de n.,** by night. **esta n.,** tonight

nochebuena f, Christmas Eve

nochebueno m, yule log; Christmas cake

nochote m, Mexico cactus beer

noción f, notion, idea; pl elementary knowledge

nocividad f, noxiousness

nocivo a noxious

nocturno a nocturnal; melancholy. m, mus nocturne

nodriza f, wet nurse

nogal m, walnut tree; walnut wood

nómada a nomadic

nombradía f, renown

nombramiento m, naming; appointment; nomination

nombrar vt to name; nominate; appoint; mention (in dispatches, etc.)

nombre m, name; title; reputation; proxy; gram noun; mil password. **n. de pila,** Christian name. **por n.,** called; by name. **Su n. anda puesto en el cuerno de la Luna,** He (she) is praised to the skies

nomenclatura f, nomenclature

nómina f, list, register; payroll; amulet

nominación f, nomination, appointment

nominador (-ra) a nominating. n nominator

nominal a nominal

nomo m, gnome

non a odd (of numbers)

nonada f, nothing, practically nothing

nonagenario (-ia) a and n nonagenarian

nones m, pl certainly not, definitely not, nope

nopal m, nopal, prickly pear tree

noquear vt (boxing) to knock out, K.O.

norabuena f, congratulation

nordeste m, northeast

nórdico (-ca) a and n Nordic

noria f, water well; chain pump; inf hard, monotonous work

norma f, square (used by builders, etc.); fig norm, standard, model

normal a normal, usual; standard, average. f, normal school, teacher's college (also **escuela n.**)

normalidad f, normality

normalista mf student at a teacher's college

normalización f, normalization; standardization

normalizar vt to make normal; standardize

noroeste *m*, northwest

norte *m*, north pole; north; north wind; polestar; *fig* guide

norteamericano (-na) *a* and *n* North American; (*U.S.A.*) American

norteño *a* northerly, northern

Noruega Norway

noruego (-ga) *a* and *n* Norwegian. *m*, Norwegian (language)

nos *pers pron pl mf acc* and *dat* (direct and indirect object) of **nosotros**, us; to us (e.g. **Nos lo dio,** He gave it to us)

nosotros, nosotras *pers pron pl mf* we; us. Also used with preposition (e.g. **Lo hicieron por nosotros,** They did it for us)

nostalgia *f*, nostalgia

nostálgico *a* nostalgic; melancholy; homesick

nota *f*, mark, sign; annotation, comment; *mus* note; memorandum; *com* bill, account; criticism, imputation; mark (in exams); repute, renown; note (diplomatic)

notable *a* notable, remarkable; outstanding, prominent; with distinction (examination mark). *m pl*, notabilities

notación *f*, (*mus math*) notation; annotation

notar *vt* to mark, indicate; observe, notice; note down; annotate; dictate, read out; criticize, reproach; discredit

notaría *f*, profession of a notary; notary's office

notarial *a* notarial

notario *m*, notary public

noticia *f*, rudiment, elementary knowledge; information; news (gen. *pl*); *pl* knowledge. **atrasado de noticias,** *fig* behind the times

noticiar *vt* to inform, give notice

noticiario *m*, news bulletin, newsreel.

noticiero *m*, newspaper

noticioso *a* informed; learned; newsy

notificación *f*, *law* notification. **n. de reclutamiento,** draft notice

notificar *vt* to notify officially; inform; warn

noto *a* known. *m*, south wind

notoriedad *f*, notoriety, publicity; flagrancy; fame, renown

notorio *a* well-known; notorious, obvious; flagrant

novatada *f*, *inf* ragging (of a freshman); blunder

novato (-ta) *a* new, inexperienced. *n* novice, beginner

novecientos *a* and *m*, nine hundred

novedad *f*, newness, novelty; change, alteration; latest news; surprise; *pl* novelties. **sin n.,** no change; all well (or as usual); safely, without incident

novel *a* new; inexperienced

novela *f*, novel; tale; falsehood. **n. caballista,** western, cowboy story. **n. por entregas,** serial (story)

novelero (-ra) *a* fond of novelty and change; fond of novels; fickle. *n* newshound, gossip

novelesco *a* novelistic; imaginary

novelista *mf* novelist

novelística *f*, art of novel writing

novena *f*, *ecc* novena, religious services spread over nine days

noveno *a* and *m*, ninth

noventa *a* and *m*, ninety; ninetieth

novia *f*, bride; fiancée

noviar con *vi*, *Argentina* to court, woo

noviazgo *m*, engagement, betrothal

novicio (-ia) *n ecc* novice; beginner, apprentice; unassuming person

noviembre *m*, November

novillo *m*, bullock. **hacer novillos,** to play truant

novio *m*, bridegroom; fiancé; novice, beginner

nubada *f*, cloudburst, rainstorm; abundance, plenty

nubarrón *m*, dense, lowering cloud, storm cloud

nube *f*, cloud; *fig* screen, impediment. **n. de verano,** summer cloud; passing annoyance

nublado *a* cloudy; overcast. *m*, storm cloud; menace, threat; multitude, crowd

nublarse *vr* to cloud over

nubloso *a* cloudy; unfortunate, unhappy

nuca *f*, nape

núcleo *m*, kernel; stone, pip (of fruit); nucleus; *fig* core, essence

nudillo *m*, knuckle; *mas* plug

nudo *m*, knot; (*bot med*) node; joint; *naut* knot; *fig* bond, tie; *fig* crux, knotty point. **n. al revés,** granny knot. **n. de comunicaciones,** communication center. **n. de marino,** reef knot. **n. de tejedor,** sheet bend (knot). **n. en la garganta,** *fig* lump in the throat (from emotion)

nudoso *a* knotted, knotty; gnarled

nuera *f*, daughter-in-law

nuestro, nuestra *poss pron 1st pers pl mf* our; ours. **los nuestros,** our friends, supporters, party, profession, etc.

nueva *f*, news

nuevamente *adv* again

Nueva Orleans New Orleans

Nueva York New York

Nueva Zelanda, Nueva Zelandia New Zealand

nueve *a* nine; ninth. *m*, number nine; ninth (of the month) (e.g. **el nueve de marzo,** March 9th). **a las nueve,** at nine o'clock

nuevo *a* new; fresh; newly arrived; inexperienced; unused; scarcely worn. **de n.,** again. **¿Qué hay de n.?** What's the news? What's new?

Nuevo México *m* New Mexico

nuez *f*, walnut; *anat* Adam's apple. **n. moscada,** nutmeg

nulidad *f*, nullity; incompetence, ineptitude; worthlessness

nulo *a* null, void; incapable; worthless

numeración *f*, calculation; numbering

numerar *vt* to number; enumerate; calculate

numerario *a* numerary. *m*, cash

numérico *a* numerical

número *m*, number; figure; numeral; size (of gloves, etc.); quantity; issue, copy; rhythm; *gram* number; item (of a program); *pl ecc* Numbers. **n. del distrito postal,** ZIP code. **n. quebrado,** *math* fraction. **sin n.,** numberless

numeroso *a* numerous; harmonious

numismática *f*, numismatics

nunca *adv* never. **n. jamás,** nevermore. **N. digas «De esta agua no beberé!»** Never say "Never!"

nuncio *m*, messenger; papal nuncio; *fig* harbinger

nupcial *a* nuptial

nupcialidad *f*, marriage rate

nupcias *f pl*, nuptials, marriage

nutrición *f*, nourishment; nutrition

nutrido *a* abundant; numerous

nutrimento *m*, nutriment; nourishment; nutrition; *fig* food, encouragement

nutrir *vt* to nourish; encourage; *fig* fill

nutritivo *a* nourishing, nutritive

Ñ

ñácara *f, Central America* sore, ulcer

ñaña *f, Lat. Am.* wet nurse; nursemaid; elder sister

ñaques *m pl,* odds and ends, rubbish

ñiquiñaque *m, inf* good-for-nothing, wastrel; *inf* trash

ñoco, -a *a, Lat. Am.* one-handed; missing a finger

ñoñería *f, inf* drivel; folly, stupidity

ñoño (-ña) *a inf* sentimental; foolish, idiotic. *n* fool.

o f, letter O. *conjunc* or, either. **o** becomes **u** before words beginning with **o** or **ho** (e.g. **gloria u honor**)

oasis m, oasis; *fig* refuge, haven

obduración f, obstinacy, stubbornness, obduracy

obedecer vt *irr* to obey; *fig* respond; bend, yield (metals, etc.); vi result (from), arise (from). See **conocer**

obedecimiento m, **obediencia** f, obedience

obediente a obedient; docile

obertura f, *mus* overture

obeso a obese

óbice m, obstacle, impediment

obispo m, bishop. **o. sufragáneo,** suffragan bishop

óbito m, death, demise

obituario m, obituary; obituary column

objeción f, objection

objetar vt to object to, oppose

objetivar vt to view objectively

objetividad f, objectivity

objetivo a objective. m, *opt* eyepiece; object finder; aim, goal

objeto m, object; subject, theme; purpose; aim, goal. **sin o.,** without object; aimlessly

oblicuo a slanting, oblique

obligación f, obligation; *com* bond; *com* debenture; *pl* responsibilities; *com* liabilities

obligacionista mf *com* bond holder, debenture holder

obligado m, contractor (to a borough, etc.); *mus* obbligato

obligar vt to compel, oblige, constrain; lay under an obligation; *law* mortgage; vr bind oneself, promise

obligatorio a obligatory

oboe m, oboe; oboe player, oboist

óbolo m, obol, ancient Greek coin

obra f, work; anything made; literary, artistic, scientific production; structure, construction; repair, alteration (to buildings, etc.); means, influence, power; labor, or time spent; action, behavior. **o. de caridad,** charitable act. **o. maestra,** masterpiece. **obras públicas,** public works. **poner por o.,** to put into effect; to set to work on. **o. de,** about, approximately

obrar vt to work; make, do; execute, perform; affect; construct, build; vi be; exist (things); act, behave. **o. mal,** to behave badly, do wrong

obrero (-ra) a working. n worker; *pl* workers

obscenidad f, obscenity

obsceno a obscene

obsequiar vt to entertain, be attentive (to); give presents (to); court, make love to. **Me obsequia con un reloj,** He is presenting me with a watch

O

obsequio m, attention; gift; deference. **en o. de,** as a tribute to

obsequioso a obliging, courteous, attentive

observable a observable

observación f, observation; remark

observador (-ra) a observing. n observer

observancia f, observance; respect, reverence

observar vt to notice; inspect, examine; fulfill; remark; watch, spy upon; *ast* observe

observatorio m, observatory

obsesión f, obsession

obsesionar vt to obsess

obseso a obsessed

obsolecer vi to obsolesce, become obsolete

obsoleto a obsolete

obstáculo m, impediment; obstacle

obstante, no adv in spite of; nevertheless

obstar vi to impede, hinder

obstetra mf obstetrician

obstetricia f, obstetrics

obstinación f, obstinacy

obstinado a obstinate, stubborn

obstinarse vr (*with en*) to persist in, insist on, be stubborn about

obstinaz a obstinate

obstrucción f, obstruction

obstruccionar vt, *Lat. Am.* to obstruct, stonewall

obstruir vt *irr* to obstruct; block; hinder; vr become choked or stopped up (pipes, etc.). See **huir**

obtención f, obtainment; attainment, realization

obtener vt *irr* to obtain; attain; maintain, preserve. See **tener**

obturador m, stopper; shutter (of a camera)

obturar vt to stopper, plug; block, obstruct

obtuso a blunt, dull; (*geom* and *fig*) obtuse

obviar vt to obviate

obvio a obvious, evident, apparent

ocasión f, occasion; opportunity; motive, cause; danger, risk; *inf* **asir la o. por la melena,** to take time by the forelock. **de o.,** second-hand

ocasional a chance, fortuitous; occasional

ocasionar vt to cause, occasion; excite, provoke; risk, endanger

ocaso m, sunset; west; dusk; decadence, decline

occidental a Western

occidente m, West, Occident

occiso a murdered; killed

oceánico a oceanic

océano m, ocean; immensity, abundance

ochenta a and m, eighty; eightieth

ochentón (-ona) n octogenarian

ocho a eight; eighth. m, figure eight; playing card with eight pips; eight; eighth day (of the month). **las o.,** eight o'clock

ochocientos a and m, eight hundred; eight-hundredth

ocio m, leisure, idleness; pl pastimes; leisure time

ociosidad f, idleness, laziness; leisure

ocioso (-sa) a idle; useless, worthless; unprofitable, fruitless. n idle fellow

ocozoal m, Mexico rattlesnake

octava f, octave

octavo a eighth. m, eighth. **en o.,** in octavo

octogenario (-ia) a and n octogenarian

octubre m, October

ocular a ocular. m, eyepiece

oculista mf oculist

ocultación f, hiding, concealment

ocultar vt to hide, conceal; disguise; keep secret

oculto a hidden; secret; occult. **en o.,** secretly, quietly

ocupación f, occupancy; occupation, pursuit; employment, office, trade

ocupado a occupied; busy

ocupante m, occupant

ocupar vt to take possession of; obtain or hold (job); occupy, fill; inhabit; employ; hinder, embarrass; hold the attention (of); vr (with en) be engaged in, be occupied with; (with con) concentrate on (a business affair, etc.)

ocurrencia f, occurrence, incident; bright idea; witty remark

ocurrir vi to anticipate; happen, take place; occur, strike (ideas)

oda f, ode

odiar vt to hate; Chile annoy, irk

odio m, hatred; malevolence

odioso a hateful, odious; Argentina, Chile, Peru annoying, irksome

odisea f, odyssey

odorífero a odoriferous, fragrant

odre m, goatskin, wineskin; inf wine bibber

oeste m, west

ofender vt to ill-treat, hurt; offend, insult; anger, annoy; vr be offended

ofendido a offended; resentful

ofensa f, injury, harm; offense, crime

ofensiva f, mil offensive. **tomar la o.,** to take the offensive

ofensivo a offensive

ofensor (-ra) n offender

oferta f, offer; gift; proposal; com tender. **o. y demanda,** supply and demand

oficial a official. m, official; officer; clerk; executioner; worker

oficiala f, trained female worker

oficialidad f, officialdom; officers

oficiar vt ecc to celebrate or serve (mass); communicate officially, inform; inf (with de) act as

oficina f, workshop; office; pharmaceutical laboratory; pl cellars, basement (of a house)

oficinesco a bureaucratic, red-tape

oficinista mf clerk, office employee, office worker

oficio m, occupation, employment; office, function, capacity; craft; operation; trade, business; official communication; office, bureau; ecc office. **Santo O.,** Holy Office. fig **buenos oficios,** good offices

oficiosidad f, diligence, conscientiousness; helpfulness, friendliness; officiousness

oficioso a conscientious; helpful, useful; officious; meddlesome; unofficial, informal

ofrecer vt irr to offer; present; exhibit; consecrate, dedicate; vr occur, suggest itself; volunteer. **¿Qué se le ofrece?** What do you require? What would you like? See **conocer**

ofrecimiento m, offer, offering

ofrenda f, ecc offering; gift, present

oftalmología f, ophthalmology

oftalmólogo m, oculist, ophthalmologist

ofuscación f. **ofuscamiento** m, obfuscation, dazzle, dimness of sight; mental confusion, bewilderment

ofuscar vt to dazzle, daze; dim, obfuscate; confuse, bewilder

ogro m, ogre

oídas, de adv by hearsay

oído m, sense of hearing; ear. **de o.,** by ear. **decir al o.,** to whisper in a person's ear. mus **duro de o.,** hard of hearing; having a bad ear (for music). **estar sordo de un o.,** to be deaf in one ear

oidor m, hearer; judge, ant magistrate

oír vt irr to hear; give ear to, listen; understand. Pres. Part. **oyendo.** Pres. Ind. **oigo, oyes, oye, oyen.** Preterite **oyó, oyeron.** Pres. Subjunc. **oiga,** etc. Imperf. Subjunc. **oyese,** etc.

ojal m, buttonhole; slit, hole

¡ojalá! interj If only that were so! God grant!

ojeada f, glance

ojear vt to look at, stare at; bewitch; scare, startle

ojera f, dark shadow (under the eye); eye bath

ojeriza f, ill-will, spite

ojeroso a having dark shadows under the eyes, wan, haggard

ojete m, eyelet

ojo m, eye; hole; slit; socket; keyhole; eye (of a needle); span (of a bridge); core (of a corn); attention, care; mesh; spring, stream; well (of a staircase); pl darling. **¡Ojo!** Take care! **o. avizor,** sharp watch; lynx eye. **Ojos que no ven, corazón que no siente,** Out of sight, out of mind. **o. saltón,** prominent, bulging eye. **o. vivo,** bright eye. **a o. de buen cubero,** at a guess. **a ojos vistas,** visibly; patently

ojota f, Chile, sandal

ola f, billow; wave (atmospheric)

¡olé! interj Bravo!

oleada f, big wave, breaker; swell (of the sea); fig surge (of a crowd)

oleaje m, swell, surge, billowing

olear vt to administer extreme unction

óleo m, oil; ecc holy oil (gen. pl). **al ó.,** in oils

oleoducto m, oil pipeline

oler vt irr to smell; guess, discover; pry, smell out; vi smell; (with prep a) smell of; smack of, be reminiscent of. Pres. Ind. **huelo, hueles, huele, huelen.** Pres. Subjunc. **huela, huelas, huela, huelan**

olfatear vt to sniff, snuff, smell; inf pry into

olfativo, olfatorio a olfactory

olfato m, sense of smell; shrewdness

olfatorio a olfactory

oliente (mal) a evil-smelling

oligárquico a oligarchic

olímpico a Olympic; Olympian

olisco, -a a, Lat. Am. spoiled, tainted (meat)

oliva f, olive tree; olive; barn owl; peace

olivar m, olive grove

olivo m, olive tree

olmo m, elm tree

olor m, odor, scent, smell; hope, promise; suspicion, hint; reputation. **o. de santidad,** odor of sanctity

oloroso a fragrant, perfumed

olvidadizo a forgetful

olvidar(se) vt and vr to forget; neglect, desert. **Se me olvidó el libro,** I forgot the book. **Me olvidé de lo pasado,** I forgot the past

olvido m, forgetfulness; indifference, neglect; oblivion

olla f, stew pot; Spanish stew; whirlpool. **o. podrida,** rich Spanish stew containing bacon, fowl, meat, vegetables, ham, etc. **las ollas de Egipto,** the fleshpots of Egypt

ombligo m, navel; fig core, center

ominoso a ominous

omisión f, omission; carelessness, negligence; neglect

omiso a omitted; remiss; careless. **hacer caso o. de,** to set aside, ignore

omitir vt to omit

ómnibus m, bus

omnímodo a all-embracing

omnipotencia f, omnipotence

omnipotente a omnipotent, all-powerful

omnisciencia f, omniscience

omniscio a omniscient

omnívoro a omnivorous

omoplato m, scapula, shoulder blade

once a eleven; eleventh. m, eleven; eleventh (of the month). **las o.,** eleven o'clock

onceno a eleventh

onda f, wave; fig flicker (of flames); sew scallop; phys wave; ripple; pl waves (in hair). rad **o. corta,** short wave. **o. etérea,** ether wave. **o. sonora,** sound wave

ondeante a waving; flowing

ondear vi to wave; ripple; undulate; roll (of the sea); float, flutter, stream; sew scallop; vr swing, sway

ondeo m, waving; undulation

ondulación f, undulation; wave; wriggling; twisting. **o. permanente,** permanent wave, perm

ondulado a wavy; undulating; scalloped

ondular vi to writhe, squirm, wriggle; twist; coil; vt wave (in hair)

oneroso a onerous, heavy; troublesome

ónice m, onyx

onomástico a onomastic. **día o.,** saint's day

onza f, ounce. **por onzas,** by ounces; sparingly

onzavo a and m, eleventh

opacidad f, opacity; obscurity; gloom

opaco a opaque; dark; gloomy, sad

ópalo m, opal

opción f, option; choice, selection; law option

ópera f, opera

operación f, surg operation; execution, performance; com transaction

operar vt surg to operate; vi act, have an effect; operate, control; com transact

operario (-ia) n worker, hand; operator; mechanic

opereta f, operetta, light opera

opinar vi to have or form an opinion, think; judge, estimate

opinión f, opinion, view; reputation

opio m, opium. **fumadero de o.,** opium den

opíparo a magnificent, sumptuous (banquets, etc.)

oponer vt irr to oppose; resist, withstand; protest against; vr oppose; be contrary or hostile (to); face, be opposite; object (to); set oneself against; compete (in public exams.). See **poner**

oporto m, port (wine)

oportunidad f, opportunity, occasion

oportunista a and *mf* opportunist

oportuno a opportune, timely

oposición *f*, opposition; resistance; antagonism; public competitive exam for a post; (*ast pol*) opposition

opositor (**-ra**) *n* opponent; competitor

opresión *f*, oppression; hardship; pressure. **o. de pecho**, difficulty in breathing

opresor (**-ra**) a oppressive. *n* oppressor

oprimir *vt* to oppress; treat harshly; press, crush; choke

oprobio *m*, opprobrium

optar *vt* to take possession of; (*with por*) choose

óptica *f*, *phys* optics; peepshow

óptico a optic, optical. *m*, optician

optimismo *m*, optimism

optimista *mf* optimist. a optimistic

óptimo a *sup* **bueno** best, optimal, optimum

opugnar *vt* to resist violently; *mil* assault, attack; impugn, challenge

opulencia *f*, opulence, riches; excess, superabundance

opulento a opulent, rich

opúsculo *m*, monograph, opuscule

oración *f*, oration, speech; prayer; *gram* sentence

oráculo *m*, oracle

orador (**-ra**) *n* orator; speech maker. *m*, preacher

oral a oral; verbal; buccal

orar *vi* to harangue, make an oration; pray; *vt* request, beg

orate *mf* lunatic

oratoria *f*, oratory, eloquence

oratorio a oratorical. *m*, oratory, chapel; *mus* oratorio

órbita *f*, *ast* orbit; *fig* sphere; *anat* orbit, eye socket

orden *mf* order, mode of arrangement; succession, sequence; group; system; orderliness, neatness; coherence, plan; *ecc* order, brotherhood; (*zool bot*) group, class; *arch* order; *math* degree. *f*, precept, command; *com* order; *pl ecc* ordination. (*mil naut*) **o. de batalla**, battle array. **o. de caballería**, order of knighthood. **o. del día**, order of the day. *ecc* **dar órdenes**, to ordain. **en o.**, in order; with regard (to). **por su o.**, in its turn; successively

ordenación *f*, order, orderly arrangement, disposition; ordinance, precept; *ecc* ordination

ordenador *m Spain* computer

ordenancista *mf mil* martinet; disciplinarian

ordenanza *f*, order, method; command, instruction; ordinance, regulation (gen. pl). *m*, *mil* orderly

ordenar *vt* to put in order, arrange; command, give instructions to; decree; direct,

regulate; *ecc* ordain; *vr* (*with de*) *ecc* be ordained as

ordeñar *vt* to milk

ordinal a ordinal. *m*, ordinal number

ordinario a ordinary, usual; vulgar, coarse, uncultured; rude; commonplace, average, mediocre. *m*, *ecc* ordinary; carrier; courier. **de o.**, usually, ordinarily

orégano *m*, wild marjoram

oreja *f*, external ear; lug; tab, flap; tongue (of a shoe). *inf* **con las orejas caídas**, down in the mouth, depressed

orejera *f*, earflap; mold board (of a plow)

orejudo a large- or long-eared

oreo *m*, zephyr; ventilation; airing

orfanato *m*, orphanage, orphan asylum

orfandad *f*, orphanhood; defenselessness, lack of protection

orfebre *mf* gold- or silversmith

orfebrería *f*, gold- or silverwork

orfeón *m*, choral society

organdí *m*, organdy

orgánico a organic; harmonious; *fig* organized

organillero (**-ra**) *n* organ grinder

organillo *m*, barrel organ

organismo *m*, organism; organization, association

organista *mf* organist

organización *f*, organization; order, arrangement

organizador (**-ra**) a organizing. *n* organizer

organizar *vt* to organize; regulate; constitute

órgano *m*, *mus* organ; (*anat bot*) organ; means, agency. **o. de manubrio**, barrel organ

orgasmo *m*, orgasm

orgía *f*, orgy

orgullo *m*, pride; arrogance

orgulloso a proud; haughty

orientación *f*, orientation; exposure, prospect; bearings

oriental a Oriental, Eastern. *mf* Oriental; *Argentina* Uruguayan

orientar *vt* to orientate; *vr* find one's bearings; familiarize oneself (with)

oriente *m*, Orient, the East; luster (of pearls); youth, childhood; origin, source

origen *m*, origin, source; root; stock, extraction; reason, genesis. **dar o. a**, to give rise to. **país de o.**, native land

original a original; earliest, primitive; new, first-hand; novel, fresh; inventive, creative; eccentric; quaint. *m*, original manuscript; original; sitter (for portraits); eccentric

originalidad *f*, originality

originar *vt* to cause, originate; invent; *vr* spring from, originate (in)

originario a original, primary; primitive; native (of)

orilla *f*, limit, edge; hem, border; selvage; shore, margin; bank (of a river, etc.); sidewalk; brink, edge. **a la o.,** on the brink; nearly

orillar *vt* to settle, arrange, conclude; *vi* reach the shore or bank; *sew* leave a hem; *sew* border; leave a selvage on cloth

orín *m*, rust; *pl* urine

orinar *vi* to urinate

oriundo *a* native (of); derived (from)

orla *f*, border, fringe; selvage (of cloth, garments); ornamental border (on diplomas, etc.)

orlar *vt* to border; edge, trim

ornamentación *f*, ornamentation

ornamental *a* ornamental

ornamentar *vt* to ornament; embellish

ornamento *m*, ornament; decoration; gift, virtue, talent; *pl ecc* vestments

ornar *vt* to ornament, adorn, embellish

ornato *m*, decoration, ornament

oro *m*, gold; gold coins or jewelery; *fig* riches; *pl* diamonds (cards). **o. batido,** gold leaf. **o. en polvo,** gold dust. *fig* **como un o.,** shining with cleanliness. **el as de oros,** the ace of diamonds

orondo *a* hollow; *inf* pompous; *inf* swollen, spongy

oropel *m*, brass foil; showy, cheap thing; trinket; tinsel

orquesta *f*, orchestra

orquestación *f*, orchestration

orquestal *a* orchestral

orquestar *vt* to orchestrate

orquídea *f*, orchid

ortiga *f*, *bot* nettle

orto *m*, rising (of sun, stars)

ortodoxia *f*, orthodoxy

ortodoxo *a* orthodox

ortografía *f*, orthography

ortográfico *a* orthographical

ortopedia *f*, orthopedics

ortopédico **(-ca)** *a* orthopedic. *n* orthopedist

ortopedista *mf* orthopedist

oruga *f*, caterpillar

orzuelo *m*, *med* sty; trap (for wild animals)

os *pers pron 2nd pl mf dat* and *acc* of **vos** and **vosotros** you, to you

osa *f*, she-bear; *ast* **O. mayor,** Big Bear; **O. menor,** Little Bear

osadía *f*, boldness, audacity

osado *a* daring, bold

osamenta *f*, skeleton; bones (of a skeleton)

osar *vi* to dare; risk, venture

oscilante *a* oscillating

oscilar *vi* to oscillate, sway; hesitate, vacillate

ósculo *m*, kiss, osculation

oscurear *Mexico* = oscurecer

oscurecer *vt irr* to darken; *fig* tarnish, dim, sully; confuse, bewilder; express obscurely; *art* shade; *vn* grow dark; *vr* cloud over (sky); *inf* disappear (things, gen. by theft). See **conocer**

oscuridad *f*, darkness; gloom, blackness; humbleness, obscurity, abstruseness

oscuro *a* dark; humble, unknown; abstruse, involved; obscure; uncertain, dangerous. **a oscuras,** in the dark; ignorant

osificarse *vr* to ossify

ósmosis *f*, osmosis

oso *m*, bear. **o. blanco,** polar bear

ostensible *a* ostensible; obvious

ostensión *f*, show, display, manifestation

ostensivo *a* ostensive

ostentación *f*, manifestation; ostentation

ostentar *vt* to exhibit, show; boast, show off

ostentoso *a* magnificent, showy, ostentatious

osteópata *mf* osteopath

osteopatía *f*, osteopathy

ostión, *m*, *Mexico* oyster

ostra *f*, oyster. **vivero de ostras,** oyster bed

ostracismo *m*, ostracism

otear *vt* to observe; look on at

otero *m*, hill, height, eminence

otomana *f*, ottoman, couch

otomano *a* Ottoman

otoñal *a* autumnal, autumn, fall

otoño *m*, autumn, fall

otorgamiento *m*, granting; consent, approval; license, award

otorgar *vt* to grant; concede, approve; *law* grant, stipulate, execute

otro **(-ra)** *a* other, another. *n* another one

otrosí *adv* besides, moreover

ovación *f*, ovation, triumph; applause

ovacionar *vt* to applaud

oval *a* oval

óvalo *m*, oval

ovario *m*, ovary

oveja *f*, ewe

overol *m* *Lat. Am.* overalls

ovillar *vi* to wind thread into a ball; *vr* curl up; huddle

OVNI *m*, UFO

ovulación *f*, ovulation

óxido *m*, oxide. **ó. de carbono,** carbon monoxide. **ó. de cinc,** zinc oxide

oxígeno *m*, oxygen

oyente *mf* hearer; *pl* audience

ozono *m*, ozone

P

pabellón *m*, pavilion; colors, flag; bell tent. **p. británico,** Union Jack. **p. de reposo,** rest home. **en p.,** stacked (of arms)

pábulo *m*, food; *fig* pabulum

pacedero *a agr* grazing, meadow

pacer *vi irr agr* to graze; *vt* nibble away; eat away. See **nacer**

paciencia *f*, patience

paciente *a* patient; long-suffering; complacent. *mf med* patient

pacienzudo *a* extremely patient or long-suffering

pacificación *f*, pacification; serenity, peace of mind

pacificador (-ra) *a* peace making; pacifying. *n* peace maker

pacificar *vt* to pacify; *vi* make peace; *vr* grow quiet, become calm (sea, etc.)

pacífico *a* pacific, meek, mild; peace-loving, peaceful. **el Océano P.,** the Pacific Ocean

pacifista *a* and *mf* pacifist

pacotilla *f*, goods. *inf* **hacer su p.,** to make one's packet or fortune. **ser de p.,** to be poor stuff; be jerry-built (of houses)

pactar *vt* to stipulate, arrange; contract

pacto *m*, agreement, contract; pact

padecer *vt irr* to suffer; feel keenly; experience, undergo; tolerate. **p. desnudez,** to go unclothed. **p. hambre,** to go hungry. See **conocer**

padrastro *m*, stepfather; cruel father; *fig* impediment, obstacle; hangnail

padrazo *m*, *inf* indulgent father

padre *m*, father; stallion; head (of the family, etc.); *ecc* father; genesis, source; author, creator; *pl* parents; ancestors. **p. adoptivo,** foster father. **p. de familia,** paterfamilias. **P. Eterno,** Eternal Father. **p. nuestro,** Lord's Prayer. **P. Santo,** Holy Father, the Pope

padrear *vi* to take after one's father; *zool* reproduce, breed

padrejón *m*, *Argentina* stallion

padrino *m*, godfather; sponsor; second (in duels, etc.); patron; best man

padrón *m*, census; pattern, model; memorial stone

paella *f*, *cul* savory rice dish of shellfish, chicken, and meat

paga *f*, payment; amends, restitution; pay; payment of fine; reciprocity (in love, etc.)

pagadero *a* payable. *m*, date and place when payment is due

pagador (-ra) *n* payer. *m*, teller; wages clerk; paymaster

pagaduría *f*, pay office

pagano (-na) *a* and *n* pagan; heathen

pagar *vt* to pay; make restitution, expiate; return, requite (love, etc.); *vr* (*with de*) become fond of; be proud of. **p. adelantado,** to prepay. *com* **p. al contado,** to pay cash. **p. la casa,** to pay the rent (for one's residence)

pagaré *m*, *com* promissory note, I.O.U.

página *f*, page (of a book); episode, occurrence

paginar *vt* to paginate

pago *m*, payment; recompense, reward; region of vineyards, olive groves, etc.; *Argentina* area, region

país *m*, country, nation; region; *art* landscape. **del p.,** typical of the country of origin (gen. of food)

paisaje *m*, countryside; landscape, scenery

paisajista, paisista *mf* landscape painter

paisano (-na) *n* compatriot; peasant; civilian

Países Bajos, los the Low Countries, the Netherlands

paja *f*, straw; chaff; trash; *fig* padding. **ver la p. en el ojo del vecino y no la viga en el nuestro,** to see the mote in our neighbor's eye and not the beam in our own

pájara *f*, hen (bird); kite (toy); *inf* jay; prostitute. **p. pinta,** game of forfeits

pajarear *vt* to snare birds; loaf, idle about

pajarero *m*, bird catcher or seller. *a inf* frivolous, giddy; *inf* gaudy (colors); *Lat. Am.* skittish (horse)

pajarita *f*, bow tie

pájaro *m*, bird. **p. bobo,** penguin. **p. carpintero,** woodpecker. *fig inf* **p. gordo,** big gun. **p. mosca,** hummingbird

paje *m*, page; *naut* cabin boy

pajizo *a* made of straw; covered or thatched with straw; strawcolored

pala *f*, paddle; blade (of an oar); shovel; spade; baker's peel (long-handled shovel); cutting edge of a spade, hoe, etc.; *sport* racket; vamp, upper (of a shoe); pelota or jai alai racket; tanner's knife; *inf* guile, cunning; cleverness, dexterity. **p. de hélice,** propeller blade. **p. para pescado,** fish server. *inf* **corta p.,** ignoramus; blockhead

palabra *f*, word; power of speech; eloquence; offer, promise; *inf* magic formula, spell. **p. de clave,** code word. **p. de matrimonio,** promise of marriage. **p. de rey,** inviolable promise. **palabras cruzadas,** crossword puzzle. **bajo p. de,** under promise of. **cuatro palabras,** a few words; short conversation. **de p.,** verbally, by word of mouth. **dirigir la p. a,** to address, speak to. **faltar a su p.,** to break one's promise. **llevar la p.,** to be spokesperson. **medias palabras,** half-words; hint, insinuation. **su p. empeñada,** one's solemn word. **tener la p.,** to have the right to speak (in meetings, etc.) (e.g. **El señor Martínez tiene la p.**, Mr. Martinez has the floor)

palabrería f, verbosity, wordiness

palabrota f, *inf* coarse language; long word

palaciego (-ga) a pertaining to palaces; *fig* courtesan. n courtier

palacio m, palace; mansion

paladar m, *anat* palate; taste; discernment, sensibility

paladear vt to taste with pleasure, savor; enjoy, relish

paladino a public, clear, open

palanca f, *mech* lever; handle; bar; (high) diving board. **p. de arranque**, starting gear. **p. de cambio de velocidad**, gear-changing lever. **p. de mando**, control stick

palangana f, washbasin

palanganear vi, *Lat. Am.* to show off

palanganero m, washstand

palastro m, sheet iron or steel

palazón f, woodwork

palco m, *theat* box; stand, raised platform, enclosure. **p. de platea**, orchestra

palenque m, enclosure; stand; platform; palisade

paleografía f, paleography

paleógrafo m, paleographer

paleta f, *dim* little shovel; trowel; *art* palette; fireplace shovel; mason's trowel; *anat* shoulder blade; blade (of a propeller, ventilator, etc.); *chem* spatula

paliacate m, *Mexico* kerchief

paliación f, palliation; excuse

paliar vt to dissemble, excuse; palliate, mitigate

paliativo a palliative; extenuating

palidecer vi irr to turn pale. See **conocer**

palidez f, pallor, paleness

pálido a pale, pallid

palillo m, *dim* small stick; toothpick; bobbin (for lacemaking); drumstick; *fig* chatter; *pl* castanets

palinodia f, *lit* palinode. **cantar la p.**, to eat one's words, recant

palio m, Greek mantle; cape; *ecc* pallium; canopy, awning

palique m, *inf* chat. **estar de p.**, to be having a chat

paliquear vi to chat

paliza f, caning, beating

palizada f, paling, fence; palisade, stockade. **p. de tablas**, hoarding

palma f, palm tree; palm leaf; date palm; palm (of the hand); hand; triumph. **llevarse la p.**, to bear away the palm; take the cake

palmada f, slap; *pl* hand-clapping

palmado a web (of feet); palmy

palmar a palmaceous; palmar; clear, obvious. m, palm grove

palmatoria f, ferule, ruler; candlestick

palmear vi to clap hands

palmeta f, ferrule, ruler

palmetazo m, slap on the hand with a ruler; *fig* slap in the face

palmo m, span; hand's breadth. **p. a p.**, inch by inch, piecemeal

palmotear vt to applaud; clap

palo m, stick; rod; pole; timber; wood; wooden log; *naut* mast; blow with a stick; execution by hanging; suit (of playing cards); fruit stalk; *her* pale. **p. de Campeche**, logwood. **p. de hule**, rubber tree. **p. de rosa**, tulipwood. *naut* **p. mayor**, mainmast. *naut* **a p. seco**, under bare poles. **de tal p., tal astilla**, a chip off the old block; like father like son. **estar del mismo p.**, to be of the same mind, agree

paloma f, dove; pigeon; gentle person; *pl naut* white horses. **p. buchona**, pouter pigeon. **p. mensajera**, carrier pigeon. **p. torcaz**, wood pigeon

palomar m, dovecote; pigeon loft

palomero (-ra) n pigeon fancier; pigeon dealer

palomino m, young pigeon

palomo m, male pigeon; wood pigeon

palotes m pl, drumsticks; pothooks (in writing)

palpabilidad f, palpability

palpable a palpable, tangible

palpar vt to palpate, examine by touch; grope, walk by touch; *fig* see clearly

palpitación f, beating (of a heart); *med* palpitation; convulsive movement

palpitante a palpitating; quivering; beating; (of a question) burning

palpitar vi to beat (heart); throb, palpitate; shudder, move convulsively; *fig* manifest itself (passions, etc.)

me palpita que . . . *Argentina*, I have a hunch that . . .

palpo m, palp, feeler

palta f, *Lat. Am.* avocado (pear)

palúdico a marshy, swampy; malarial

paludismo m, malaria; paludism

palurdo (-da) a *inf* gross, rude, boorish. n boor

palustre m, mason's trowel. a marshy, swampy

pamela f, wide-brimmed straw sailor (woman's hat)

pamema f, *inf* unimportant trifle; *inf* caress

pampa f, pampa, treeless plain

pamplina f, *inf* nonsense, rubbish

pan m, bread; loaf; *cul* piecrust; *fig* food; wheat; gold leaf; *pl* cereals. **p. ázimo**, unleavened bread. **p. de oro**, gold leaf. **llamar al p. p. y al vino vino**, to call a spade a spade. **venderse como p. bendito**, to sell like hot cakes

pana f, velveteen, velours

panacea f, panacea; cure-all

panadería f, bakery trade or shop; bakery

panadero (-ra) n baker. m pl, Spanish dance

panadizo m, med whitlow; inf ailing person, crock

panal m, honeycomb; wasp's nest

Panamá Panama

panamá m, Lat. Am. Panama hat

panameño (-ña) a and n Panamanian

panamericanismo m, pan-Americanism

panarra m, inf simpleton

páncreas m, pancreas

pancreático a pancreatic

panda f, gallery of a cloister. mf zool panda

pandereta f, tambourine

pandero m, tambourine; inf windbag

pandilla f, league, group; gang (of burglars, etc.); party, crowd, band

pane f, breakdown

panecillo m, dim roll (of bread)

panegírico a and m, panegyric

panel m, panel

panetela f, panada

pánfilo (-la) a sluggish, phlegmatic, slow-moving. n sluggard

panfleto m, pamphlet

paniaguado m, servant; favorite, protégé

pánico a and m, panic

panoli a inf doltish, stupid

panorama m, panorama; view

panorámico a panoramic

pantalón m, pant, trouser (gen. pl); knickers. **p. de corte**, striped trousers. **pantalones bombachos**, plus fours

pantalla f, lampshade; face screen; movie screen; shade, reflector

pantano m, marsh, swamp; impediment; artificial pool

pantanoso a marshy, swampy; fig awkward, full of pitfalls

panteón m, pantheon; Mexico cemetery

pantera f, panther; Venezuela jaguar, ocelot

pantomima f, pantomime; mime

pantorrilla f, calf (of the leg)

pantuflo m, house slipper

panza f, paunch, stomach; belly (of jugs, etc.). inf **un cielo de p. de burra**, a dark gray sky. **p. mojada** Mexico wetback

pañal m, diaper; shirttail; pl long clothes, swaddling clothes; infancy

pañería f, drapery stores; drapery

paño m, woolen material; cloth, fabric; drapery, hanging; tapestry; linen, bandage; tarnish or other mark; naut canvas; sew breadth, width (of cloth); panel (in a dress); floor cloth, duster; livid mark on the face; pl garments. **p. de lágrimas**, consoler, sympathizer. **p. mortuorio**, pall (on a coffin). **paños menores**, underwear. **p. verde**, gambling table. **al p.**, theat from the wings, from without. inf **poner el p. al púlpito**, to hold forth, spread oneself

pañoleta f, kerchief, triangular scarf; fichu

pañuelo m, kerchief; handkerchief

papa m, pope; inf papa, daddy. f, inf potato; stupid rumor; nonsense; pl pap; cul sop; food

papá m, inf papa, daddy

papada f, double chin; dewlap

papado m, papacy

papagayo m, parrot

papal m, Lat. Am. potato field

papanatas m, inf simpleton

papar vt to sip, take soft food; inf eat; neglect, be careless about

papel m, paper; document; manuscript; theat role, part; pamphlet; sheet of paper; paper, monograph, essay; guise, role; theat character. **p. carbón, p. carbónico**, carbon paper. **p. celofán**, cellophane. **p. cuadriculado**, graph paper, cartridge paper. **p. de calcar**, carbon paper; tracing paper. **p. de escribir**, writing paper. **p. de estaño**, tinfoil. **p. de estraza**, brown paper. **p. de fumar**, cigarette paper. **p. de lija**, emery- or sandpaper. **p. de paja de arroz**, rice paper. **p. de seda**, tissue paper. **p. de tornasol**, litmus paper. **p. del estado**, government bonds. **p. higiénico**, toilet paper. **p. moneda**, paper money. **p. pintado**, wallpaper. **p. secante**, blotting paper. **p. sellado**, official stamped paper. **hacer buen (mal) p.**, to do well (badly). **hacer el p. (de)**, theat to act the part (of); feign, pretend

papelear vi to turn over papers, search among them; inf cut a dash

papeleo m, bureaucracy, red tape

papelera f, mass of papers; desk (for keeping papers)

papelería f, heap of papers; stationer's shop; stationery

papelero (-ra) a paper, stationery. n paper maker; stationer

papeleta f, slip or scrap of paper

papelista mf paper maker; stationer; paperhanger

papelucho m, old or dirty piece of paper; trash, worthless writing; inf rag (newspaper)

papera f, mumps

papilla f, pap; guile, wiliness

papiro m, papyrus

papo m, dewlap; gizzard (of a bird); goiter. **p. de cardo**, thistledown

paquete m, packet; parcel, package

par a equal; alike; corresponding. m, pair,

couple; team (of oxen, mules); peer (title); rafter (of a roof); *mech* torque, couple; *elec* cell. *f*, par. **a la p.,** jointly; simultaneously; *com* at par. **a pares,** two by two. **de p. en p.,** wide-open (doors, etc.). **sin p.,** peerless, excellent

para *prep* in order to; for; to; for the sake of (e.g. **Lo hice p. ella,** I did it for her sake); enough to (gen. with *bastante,* etc.); in the direction of, toward; about to, on the point of (e.g. **Está p. salir,** He is on the point of going out). Expresses:

1. *Purpose* (e.g. **La educan p. bailarina,** They are bringing her up to be a dancer. **Lo dije p. ver lo que harías,** I said it to (in order to) see what you would do)

2. *Destination* (e.g. **Salió p. Londres,** He left for London)

3. *Use* (e.g. **seda p. medias,** silk for stockings. **un vaso p. flores,** a vase for flowers)

4. *An appointed time* (e.g. **Lo pagaré p. Navidad,** I will pay it at Christmas)

p. con, toward (a person) (e.g. **Ha obrado muy bien p. con mi hermano,** He has behaved very well toward my brother)

p. coneretar, to be exact, to wit

p. que, in order to, so that (e.g. **Lo puse en la mesa p. que lo vieses,** I put it on the table so that you would see it) **¿P. qué?** Why? For what reason?

p. siempre, forever. **decir p. sí,** to say to oneself. **sin qué ni p. qué,** without rhyme or reason

parábola *f*, parable; *geom* parabola

parabrisas *m*, windshield

paracaídas *m*, parachute

paracaidista *mf* parachutist

parada *f*, stopping, halting; stop; stoppage, suspension; halt; *mil* review; interval, pause; cattle stall; dam; gambling stakes; parry (in fencing); relay (of horses). **p. de coches,** taxi rank. **p. de tranvía,** streetcar stop. **p. discrecional,** request stop (buses, etc.)

paradear (con . . .) *vi, Argentina* to brag (about . . .)

paradero *m*, railroad station; stopping place; end, conclusion; whereabouts

parado a still; indolent, lazy; unoccupied, leisured; silent, reserved; timid; unemployed

paradoja *f*, paradox

paradójico a paradoxical

parador *m*, inn, tavern, hostelry

paráfrasis *f*, paraphrase

paraguas *m*, umbrella

paraguayo (-ya) a and *n* Paraguayan

paraíso *m*, paradise; garden of Eden; heaven; (*inf theat*) gallery, gods

paraje *m*, place, locality, spot; state, condition

paralela *f*, *mil* parallel; *pl* parallel bars (for gymnastic exercises)

paralelo a parallel; analogous; similar. *m*, parallel, similarity; *geog* parallel

parálisis *f*, paralysis

paralítico (-ca) a and *n* paralytic

paralización *f*, paralysis; cessation; *com* dullness, quietness

paralizar *vt* to paralyze; stop

paramento *m*, ornament; trappings (of a horse); face (of a wall); facing (of a building). **paramentos sacerdotales,** liturgical vestments or ornaments

páramo *m*, paramo, treeless plain; desert, wilderness

parangón *m*, comparison; similarity

parangonar *vt* to compare

paraninfo *m*, *arch* paranymph, university hall; best man (weddings); messenger of good

paranoico *m*, paranoiac

parapetarse *vr* to shelter behind a parapet; take refuge behind

parapoco *mf inf* ninny, numskull

parar *vi* to stop, halt; end, finish; lodge; come into the hands of; *vt* stop; detain; prepare; bet, stake; point (hunting dogs); parry (fencing); *vr* halt; be interrupted; *Lat. Am.* to get up, stand up **p. mientes en,** to notice; consider. **sin p.,** immediately, at once; without stopping

pararrayos *m*, lightning conductor

parasitario, parasítico a parasitic

parásito *m*, parasite; *fig* sponger; *pl rad* interference. a parasitic

parasol *m*, sunshade; *bot* umbel

paratifoidea *f*, paratyphoid

parca *f*, Fate; *poet* death. **las Parcas,** the Three Fates

parcela *f*, plot, parcel (of land); atom, particle

parchar *vt*, *Lat. Am.* to mend, patch, patch up

parche *m*, *med* plaster; *aut* patch; drum; drumhead, parchment of drum; patch, mend

parcial a partial, incomplete; biased, prejudiced; factional, party; participatory

parcialidad *f*, partiality, bias, prejudice; party, faction, group; intimacy, friendship

parco a scarce, scanty; temperate, moderate; frugal

parcómetro *m Lat. Am.* (*except Argentina and Mexico*) parking meter

pardo a brown; gray, drab, dun-colored; cloudy, dark; husky (voices). *m*, leopard

parear *vt* to pair, match; put in pairs; compare

parecer *vi irr* to appear; look, seem; turn up (be found). *impers* believe, think (e.g. **me parece,** it seems to me, I think, my opinion is); *vr* look alike, resemble one another. See **conocer**

parecer m, opinion, belief; appearance; looks

parecido a (with bien or mal) good- or bad-looking. m, resemblance

pared f, wall; partition wall; side, face. **p. maestra**, main wall. **p. medianera**, party wall. **Las paredes oyen**, The walls have ears. inf **pegado a la p.**, confused, taken aback

pareja f, pair; dance partner; couple. **p. desparejada**, mismatched pair. **parejas mixtas**, mixed doubles (in tennis). **correr parejas** or **correr a las parejas**, to be equal; go together, happen simultaneously; be on a par

parejo a equal; similar; smooth, flat; even, regular

parentela f, relatives, kindred; parentage

parentesco m, kinship; relationship; affinity; inf connection, link

paréntesis m, parenthesis; digression. **entre p.**, incidentally

paria mf pariah; outcast

parida a f, newly delivered of a child

paridad f, parity; analogy, similarity

pariente (-ta) n relative, relation; inf husband (wife)

parir vt to give birth to; fig bring forth; reveal, publish; vi lay eggs

París Paris

parla f, speech; loquaciousness, eloquence; verbiage

parlamentar vi to converse; discuss (contracts, etc.); mil parley

parlamento m, legislative assembly; parliament; discourse, speech; theat long speech; mil parley

parlanchín a inf talkative, chattering, loquacious

parlar vt and vi to speak freely or easily; chatter; reveal, speak indiscreetly; babble (of streams, etc.)

parlero a talkative; gossiping, indiscreet; talking (birds); fig expressive (eyes, etc.); prattling, babbling (brook, etc.)

parlotear vi inf to chatter, gossip

paro m, inf work stoppage; lockout; orn tit. **p. forzoso**, unemployment

parodia f, parody

parótida f, parotid gland; parotitis; mumps

parotiditis f, parotitis, mumps

paroxismo m, med paroxysm; frenzy, ecstasy, fit

parpadear vi to blink

párpado m, eyelid

parque m, park; depot, park; paddock, pen. **p. de atracciones**, pleasure ground. **p. de** (or **para**) **automóviles**, car park, parking lot

parquear vt, vi, Lat. Am. to park

parquedad f, scarcity; moderation, temperance; parsimony, frugality

parquímetro m Spain, Venezuela parking meter

parra f, vine. **hoja de p.**, fig fig leaf

párrafo m, paragraph; gram paragraph sign. **p. aparte**, new paragraph. **echar un p.**, to chat, gossip

parranda f, inf binge; strolling band of musicians. **ir de p.**, to go on a binge

parrilla f, cul griller, broiler; grill, gridiron; eng grate. **cul a la p.**, grilled

párroco m, parish priest; parson

parroquia f, parish church; clergy of a parish; clientele, customers

parroquiano (-na) a parochial. n parishioner; client, customer

parsimonia f, frugality, thrift; prudence, moderation

parsimonioso a parsimonious

parte f, part; share; place; portion; side, faction; law party; theat part, role. m, communication, message; telegraph or telephone message; (mil nav) communiqué. f pl, parts, talents. **p. actora**, law prosecution. **p. de la oración**, part of speech. **partes litigantes**, law contending parties. **dar p.**, to notify; (mil naut) report; give a share (in a transaction). **de algún tiempo a esta p.**, for some time past. **de p. de**, in the name of, from. **en p.**, partly. **por todas partes**, on all sides, everywhere. **ser p. a** or **ser p. para que**, to contribute to. **tener de su p. (a)**, to count on the favor of. **la quinta p.**, one-fifth, etc.

partera f, midwife

partero m, accoucheur

partición f, partition, distribution; (aer naut) accommodation

participación f, participation; notice, warning; announcement (of an engagement, etc.); com share

participante a and mf participant

participar vi to participate, take part (in); share; vt inform; announce (an engagement, etc.)

partícipe a sharing. mf participant

participio m, participle

partícula f, particle, grain; gram particle

particular a private; peculiar; special, particular; unusual; individual. mf private individual. m, matter, subject. **en p.**, especially; privately

particularidad f, individuality; speciality; rareness, unusualness; detail, circumstance; intimacy, friendship

particularizar vt to detail, particularize; single out, choose; vr (with en) be characterized by

partida f, departure; entry, record (of birth, etc.); certificate (of marriage, etc.); com item; com lot, allowance; mil guerrilla; armed band; expedition, excursion; game (of cards, etc.); rubber (at bridge, etc.); inf conduct, behavior; place, locality; death. com **p. doble**, double entry.

Las siete Partidas, code of Spanish laws compiled by Alfonso X (1252–84)

partidarismo *m,* partisanship

partidario (-ia) *a* partisan. *n* adherent, disciple. *m,* partisan, guerrilla

partido *m,* party, group, faction; profit; *sport* match; team; agreement, pact. **p. conservador,** *pol* conservative party. **p. obrero** or **p. laborista,** *pol* labor party. **buen p.,** *fig* good match, catch. **sacar p. de,** to take advantage of, make the most of. **tomar p.,** to enlist; join, become a supporter (of)

partidor *m,* divider, apportioner; cleaver, chopper; hewer

partir *vt* to divide; split; crack, break; separate; *math* divide; *vi* go, depart; start (from). **p. como el rayo,** be off like a flash. *vr* disagree, become divided; leave, depart

partitura *f, mus* score

parto *m,* parturition, birth; newborn child; *fig* creation, offspring; important event

parturienta *a f,* parturient

parva *f,* light breakfast; threshed or unthreshed grain; heap, mass

parvedad *f,* smallness; scarcity; light breakfast (taken on fast days)

parvo *a* little, small

párvulo (-la) *n* child. *a* small; innocent, simple; lowly, humble

pasa *f,* raisin; *naut* channel; passage, flight (of birds). **p. de Corinto,** currant

pasada *f,* passing, passage; money sufficient to live on; passage, corridor. **dar p.,** to let pass, put up with. *inf* **mala p.,** bad turn, dirty trick

pasadero *a* passable, traversable; fair (health); tolerable, passable. *m,* steppingstone

pasadizo *m,* narrow corridor or passage; alley, narrow street; *naut* alleyway

pasado *m,* past; *pl* ancestors. **Lo p., p.,** What's past is past. **p. de moda,** out of fashion, unfashionable

pasador *m,* bolt, fastener; *mech* pin, coupler; pin (of brooches, etc.); colander; *naut* marlin spike; shirt stud

pasaje *m,* passing; passage; fare; passage money; *naut* complement of passengers; channel, strait; (*mus lit*) passage; *mus* modulation, transition (of voice); voyage; passage; covered way; road; *Lat. Am.* dead-end street

pasajero (-ra) *a* crowded public (thoroughfare); transitory, fugitive; passing; temporary. *n* passenger

pasamanería *f,* passementerie work, industry or shop

pasamano *m,* passementerie; banister, handrail; *naut* gangway

pasante *a her* passant. *m,* student teacher; articled clerk; apprentice; student. **p. de pluma,** law clerk

pasaporte *m,* passport; license, permission. **dar el p. (a),** *inf* to give the sack (to)

pasar *vt* to pass; carry, transport; cross over; send; go beyond, overstep; run through, pierce; upset; overtake; transfer; suffer, undergo; sieve; study; dry (grapes, etc.); smuggle; surpass; omit; swallow (food); approve; dissemble; transform; spend (time); *vi* pass; be transferred; be infectious; have enough to live on; cease; last; pass away; pass (at cards); be transformed; be current (money); be salable (goods); (*with prep a* + *infin*) begin to; (*with por*) pass as; have a reputation as; visit; (*with sin*) do without. *impers* happen, occur. *vr* end; go over to another party; forget; go stale or bad; *fig* go too far, overstep the mark; permeate. **p. contrato,** to draw up a contract; sign a contract. **p. la voz,** to pass the word along. **p. por alto (de),** to omit, overlook. **p. de largo,** to go by without stopping. **pasarse de listo,** to be too clever. **¡No pases cuidado!** Don't worry!

pasarela *f,* gangplank

pasatiempo *m,* pastime, hobby, amusement

pascua *f,* Passover; Easter; Christmas; Twelfth Night; Pentecost; *pl* twelve days of Christmas. **P. florida,** Easter Sunday. **dar las pascuas,** to wish a merry Christmas. **¡Felices pascuas!** Merry Christmas!

pase *m,* pass (with the hands and in football, etc.); safe conduct; free pass; thrust (in fencing)

paseante *mf* stroller, promenader, passerby

pasear *vt* to take a walk; parade up and down, display; *vi* take a walk; go for a drive; go for a ride (on horseback, etc.); stroll up and down; *vr* touch upon lightly, pass over; loaf, be idle; drift; float

paseo *m,* walk, stroll; drive; outing, expedition; promenade; boulevard. **p. a caballo,** ride on horseback

pasillo *m,* gallery; corridor; lobby; railway corridor; *sew* basting stitch

pasión *f,* suffering; passivity; passion; desire; *ecc* passion. **con p.,** passionately

pasivo *a* passive; inactive; *com* sleeping (partner); *gram* passive. *m, com* liabilities

pasmar *vt* to freeze to death (plants); dumbfound, amaze, stun; chill; *vr* be stunned or amazed

pasmo *m,* amazement, astonishment; wonder, marvel; *med* tetanus, lockjaw

pasmoso *a* astounding, amazing; wonderful

paso *a* dried (of fruit)

paso *m,* step; pace; passage, passing; way; footstep; progress, advancement; passage (in a book); *sew* tacking stitch; occurrence, event; *theat* short play; gait, walk; strait, channel; migratory flight (birds); *mech* pitch; event or scene from the Passion; armed combat; death; *Lat. Am.* ford. *pl* measures, steps. *adv* softly, in a low voice; gently. **p. a nivel,** level crossing. **p. a p.,** step by step. **p. doble,** quick march; Spanish dance. **p. volante,** (gymnastics) giant stride. **a cada p.,** at every step; often. **al p.,** without stopping; on the way, in passing. **ceder el p.,** to allow to pass. **de p.,** in passing; incidentally. **llevar el p.,** to keep in step. **marcar el p.,** to mark time. **salir al p. (a),** to waylay, confront; oppose. **seguir los pasos (a),** to follow; spy upon

paspa *f, Peru* chapped skin

paspadura *f, Argentina* = **paspa**

pasparse *vr, Lat. Am.* to chap, crack

pasta *f, cul* dough; paste; pastry; pie-crust; batter; *cul* noodle paste; paper pulp; board (bookbinding). **ser de buena p.,** to be good-natured

pastar *vt* to take to pasture; *vi* graze, pasture

pastel *m,* cake; *art* pastel; pie; *inf* plot, secret understanding; cheating (at cards); *print* pie; *inf* fat, stocky person

pastelear *vi inf* to indulge in shady business (especially in politics)

pastelería *f,* cake bakery; cake shop; confectioner's art; confectionery

pastelillo *m, cul* turnover

pastelón *m,* meat or game pie

pasteurizar *vt* to pasteurize

pastilla *f,* tablet, cake; lozenge; pastille, drop; tread (of a tire)

pasto *m,* grazing land, pasture; fodder; *fig* fuel, food; spiritual food. **a p.,** in plenty, abundantly. **de p.,** of daily use

pastor (-ra) *n* shepherd. *m, ecc* pastor

pastoral *a* rustic, country; *ecc* pastoral, *f,* pastoral poem; *ecc* pastoral letter

pastorear *vt* to graze, put to grass

pastoso *a* doughy; mealy; pasty; mellow

pata *f,* paw and leg (animals); foot (of table, etc.); duck; *inf* leg. **p. de gallo,** blunder; crow's-foot; wrinkle. **meter la p.,** to interfere, put one's foot in it. *inf* **tener mala p.,** to be unlucky

patada *f,* kick, stamp; *inf* step, pace

patagón (-ona) *a* and *n* Patagonian

patalear *vi* to stamp (with the feet)

pataleo *m,* kicking; stamping

patán *m, inf* yokel; boor, churl

patanería *f, inf* boorishness, churlishness

patata *f,* potato

patatús *m, inf* petty worry; mishap; *med* stroke, fit

patear *vt inf* to stamp; *fig* walk on, treat badly; *vi inf* stamp the feet; be furiously angry; (*golf*) putt

patena *f,* engraved medal worn by country women; *ecc* paten

patentar *vt* to issue a patent; take out a patent, patent

patente *a* obvious, patent; *f,* patent; warrant, commission; letters patent. **p. de invención,** patent. **p. de sanidad,** clean bill of health

patentizar *vt* to make evident

paternidad *f,* paternity

paterno *a* paternal

patético *a* pitiable; pathetic, moving

patibulario *a* heartrending, harrowing

patíbulo *m,* scaffold

paticojo *a inf* lame; wobbly; unsteady

patilla *f,* side whisker (gen. *pl*); *pl* old Nick, the Devil

patín *m,* skate; runner (of a sled); (*aer* and of vehicles) skid; *mech* shoe. **p. del diablo,** scooter. **p. de ruedas,** roller skate

patinador (-ra) *n* skater

patinar *vi* to skate; slip, lose one's footing; skid (vehicles and planes)

patinazo *m,* skid (of a vehicle)

patinete *m,* child's scooter

patio *m,* courtyard; *theat* pit; *Mexico* shunting yard

patitieso *a inf* paralyzed in the hands or feet; open-mouthed, amazed; stiff, unbending, proud

patituerto *a* crooked-legged; pigeon-toed; *inf* lopsided

pato *m,* duck; *inf* **pagar el p.,** to be a scapegoat

patojo *a* waddling

patología *f,* pathology

patoso *a fig* heavy, pedestrian, tedious

patraña *f,* nonsense, rubbish, fairy tale

patria *f,* motherland, native country; native place. **p. chica,** native region

patriarca *m,* patriarch

patricio (-ia) *a* and *n* patrician

patrimonio *m,* patrimony

patriota *mf* patriot

patriótico *a* patriotic

patriotismo *m,* patriotism

patrocinar *vt* to protect, defend; favor, sponsor; patronize

patrocinio *m,* protection, defense; sponsorship; patronage

patrón (-ona) *n* patron, sponsor; patron saint; landlord; employer. *m,* coxswain; *naut* master, skipper; pattern, model; standard. **p. de oro,** gold standard

patronato *m,* patronage, protection; employers' association; charitable foundation. **p. de turismo,** tourist bureau

patrono (-na) *n* protector; sponsor; patron; patron saint; employer

patrulla *f, mil* patrol; group, band

patrullar *vi mil* patrol; march about

pauperismo *m,* destitution, pauperism

pausa *f,* pause, interruption; delay; *mus* rest; *mus* pause. **a pausas,** intermittently

pausado *a* deliberate, slow. *adv* slowly, deliberately

pausar vi to pause

pauta f, standard, norm, design; fig guide, model

pava f, Argentina kettle; Venezuela broad-brimmed straw hat, inf bad luck

pavada f, flock of turkeys

pavana f, pavane, stately dance

pavero (**-ra**) a vain; strutting. n turkey keeper or vendor. m, broad-brimmed Andalusian hat; mf, Chile, Peru practical joker

pavimentación f, paving, flagging

pavimento m, pavement

pavo (**-va**) n orn turkey. **p. real**, peacock. inf **pelar la pava**, to serenade, court

pavón m, orn peacock; peacock butterfly; preservative paint (for steel, etc.); gunmetal

pavonear vi to strut, peacock (also vr); inf hoodwink, dazzle

pavor m, terror, panic

pavoroso a fearful, awesome, dreadful

payador m, Argentina, Chile gaucho minstrel

payasada f, clowning, practical joke; clown's patter

payasear vi, Lat. Am. to clown around

payaso m, clown

paz f, peace; harmony, concord; peaceableness. **¡P. sea en esta casa!** Peace be upon this house! (salutation). **estar en p.**, to be at peace; be quits, be even. **poner** (or **meter**) **p.**, to make peace (between dissentients). **venir de p.**, to come with peaceful intentions

pazguato (**-ta**) n simpleton, booby

pe f, name of the letter P. inf **de pe a pa**, from A to Z, from beginning to end

peaje m, toll (on bridges, roads, etc.)

peatón m, pedestrian; walker; country postman

peca f, mole, freckle

pecado m, sin; fault; excess; defect; inf the Devil. **p. capital**, mortal sin

pecador a sinful. m, sinner. **¡P. de mí!** Poor me!

pecadora f, sinner; inf prostitute

pecaminoso a sinful

pecar vi to sin; trespass, transgress; (with de) be too . . . (e.g. **El libro peca de largo**, The book is too long)

peceño a pitch-black (horses, etc.); tasting of pitch

pechera f, shirt front; chest protector; bib, tucker; shirt frill; inf bosom

pecho m, anat chest; breast; bosom; mind, conscience; courage, endurance; mus quality (of voice); incline, slope. **p. arriba**, uphill. **abrir su p. a** (or **con**), to unbosom oneself to. **dar el p.** (**a**), to suckle. **de pechos**, leaning on. **echar el p. al agua**, fig to embark courageously

upon. **tomar a pechos** (**una cosa**), to take (a thing) very seriously; take to heart

pechuga f, breast (of a bird); inf breast, bosom; slope, incline

pecoso a freckled; spotted (with warts)

pecuario a agr stock; cattle

peculiar a peculiar, individual

peculiaridad f, peculiarity

peculio m, private money or property

pecunia f, inf cash

pedagogía f, education, pedagogy

pedagogo m, schoolmaster; educationalist; fig mentor

pedal m, mech treadle, lever, mus pedal; mus sustained harmony. aut **p. de embrague**, clutch pedal

pedalear vi to pedal

pedante a pedantic. mf pedant

pedantería f, pedantry

pedazo m, bit, piece; lump; fragment, portion. inf **p. del alma**, **p. del corazón**, **p. de las entrañas**, loved one, dear one. **a pedazos** or **en pedazos**, in pieces, in bits. **hacer pedazos**, to break into fragments

pedernal m, flint; anything very hard

pedestal m, pedestal; base; stand; fig foundation

pedestre a pedestrian; dull, uninspired

pediatra mf pediatrician

pedicuro m, chiropodist

pedido m, com order; request, petition

pedigüeño a importunate, insistent

pedimento m, petition, demand; law claim; law motion

pedir vt irr to ask, request; com order; demand; necessitate; desire; ask in marriage. **p. aventón** Mexico to hitch a ride **p. en juicio**, law to bring an action against. inf **pedírselo** (**a uno**) **el cuerpo**, to desire (something) ardently. **a p. de boca**, according to one's wish. Pres. Part. **pidiendo**. Pres. Ind. **pido, pides, pide, piden**. Preterite **pidió, pidieron**. Pres. Subjunc. **pida**, etc. Imperf. Subjunc. **pidiese**, etc.

pedo m, fart

pedrada f, casting a stone; blow with a stone; innuendo

pedrea f, stone throwing; fight with stones; shower of hailstones

pedregal m, stony ground, rocky ground

pedrería f, precious stones

pedrisco m, hailstone; shower of stones; pile of stones

pega f, sticking; cementing; joining; pitch; varnish; inf joke; beating; orn magpie

pegadizo a sticky, gummy, adhesive; detachable, removable; fig clinging, importunate (of people)

pegado m, sticking plaster; patch

pegajoso a sticky, gluey; viscid; contagious, catching; *inf* oily, unctuous; *fig inf* cadging, sponging

pegar *vt* to stick; cement; join, fasten; press (against); infect with (diseases); hit, strike; give (a shout, jump, etc.); patch; *vi* spread, catch (fire, etc.); *fig* make an impression, have influence; be opportune; *vr cul* stick, burn; meddle; become enthusiastic about; take root in the mind. **p. un tiro (a)**, to shoot

pegote *m*, sticking plaster; *fig inf* sponger; *inf* patch

peinado *m*, hairdressing or style; headdress. *a inf* effeminate, overelegant (men); overcareful (style). **un p. al agua**, a finger wave

peinador (-ra) *m*, peignoir, dressing gown; *Lat. Am.* dressing table. *n* hairdresser

peinadura *f*, brushing or combing of hair; *pl* hair combings

peinar *vt* to comb, dress the hair; card (wool); cut away (rock)

peine *m*, comb; *mech* hackle, reed; instep; *inf* crafty person

peladilla *f*, sugared almond; smooth, small pebble

pelado *a* plucked; bare, unadorned; needy, poor; hairless; skinned; peeled; without shell; treeless

peladura *f*, peeling; shelling; skinning; plucking (feathers)

pelafustán *m*, *inf* good-for-nothing, scamp

pelagra *f*, pellagra

pelaje *m*, fur, wool

pelamesa *f*, brawl, fight; lock, tuft (of hair)

pelapatatas *m*, potato peeler

pelar *vt* to tear out or cut the hair; pluck; skin; peel; shell; rob, fleece; *vr* lose one's hair

peldaño *m*, step, stair; tread, rung

pelea *f*, battle; quarrel, dispute; fight (among animals); effort, exertion; *fig* struggle

peleador *a* fighting; quarrelsome, aggressive

pelear *vi* to fight; quarrel; struggle, strive. **p. como perro y gato**, to fight like cat and mouse. *vr* come to blows; fall out, become enemies

pelechar *vi* to get a new coat (of animals); grow new feathers (of birds); *inf* prosper, flourish; grow well

pelele *m*, effigy; *inf* nincompoop

peletería *f*, furrier; fur shop

pelícano *m*, pelican

película *f*, film. **p. fotográfica,** roll of film. **p. sonora,** sound film

peligrar *vi* to be in danger

peligro *m*, danger, peril. **correr p.** or **estar en p.,** to be in danger

peligroso *a* dangerous, perilous, risky

pelirrojo *a* red-haired

pelleja *f*, hide, skin (of animals); sheepskin

pellejo *m*, hide; pelt; skin; wineskin; *inf* drunkard; peel, skin (of fruit)

pelliza *f*, fur or fur-trimmed coat

pellizcar *vt* to pinch, tweak, nip; pilfer

pellizco *m*, pinch, nip, tweak; pilfering, pinching; bit, pinch

pelmazo *m*, squashed mass; *inf* idler, sluggard; *inf* bore

pelo *m*, hair; down (on birds and fruit); fiber, filament; hair trigger (firearms); hairspring (watches); kiss (in billiards); nap (of cloth), grain (of wood); flaw (in gems); raw silk. **p. chino,** *Mexico* (naturally) curly hair **p. de camello,** camel's hair. **a p.,** in the nude; without a hat; opportunely. **en p.,** bareback (of horses). **hacerse el p.,** to do one's hair; have one's hair cut. *inf* **no tener p. de tonto,** to be smart, clever. *inf* **no tener pelos en la lengua,** to be outspoken. *inf* **tomar el p. (a),** to pull a person's leg. **venir a p.,** to be apposite; come opportunely

pelón *a* hairless; *fig inf* broke, fleeced

pelonería *f*, *inf* poverty, misery

pelota *f*, ball; ball game. **p. base,** baseball. **p. vasca,** pelota. **en p.,** stark naked

pelotari *m*, professional pelota player

pelotazo *m*, knock or blow with a ball

pelotear *vt* to audit accounts; *vi* play ball; throw, cast; quarrel, argue

pelotera *f*, *inf* brawl

pelotón *m*, big ball; lump of hair; crowd, multitude; *mil* platoon. **p. de ejecución,** firing squad

peluca *f*, wig; periwig; *inf* scolding

peludo *a* hairy. *m*, long-haired rug

peluquería *f*, hairdressing establishment; hairdressing trade

peluquero (-ra) *n* hairdresser; barber

pelusa *f*, down, soft hair; fluff, nap

pena *f*, punishment, penalty; grief, pain, suffering; difficulty, trouble; mourning veil; hardship; anxiety; embarrassment; tail feather. **p. capital** or **p. de la vida,** capital punishment. **a duras penas,** with great difficulty. **so p. de,** under penalty of. **valer** (*or* **merecer) la p.,** to be worth while

penable *a* punishable

penacho *m*, topknot, crest (of birds); plume, panache; *inf* pride, arrogance

penado (-da) *a* difficult, laborious; painful, troubled, afflicted. *n* convict

penal *a* penal; punitive

penalidad *f*, trouble, labor, difficulty; *law* penalty

penar *vt* to penalize; punish; *vi* suffer; undergo purgatorial pains; *vr* suffer anguish. **p. por,** to long for

pendejo *m*, pubic hair; *inf* coward; jerk

pendencia *f*, fight; quarrel

pendenciar *vi* to fight; quarrel

pendenciero a quarrelsome, aggressive

pender *vi* to hang; depend; be pending

pendiente a pending; hanging; *com* outstanding. *m*, earring; pendant. *f*, slope, incline; gradient

péndola *f*, feather, plume; quill pen; pendulum (of a clock)

pendón *m*, pennon, banner; *bot* shoot; *inf* lanky, slatternly woman; *pl* reins

péndulo a pendulous, hanging. *m*, pendulum

pene *m*, penis

peneque, *m*, *Mexico* roll of maize dough filled with cheese

penetración *f*, penetration; understanding, perspicuity; sagacity, shrewdness

penetrador a penetrating, perspicacious; sagacious, acute

penetrante a penetrating; deep; piercing (of sounds); acute, shrewd

penetrar *vt* to penetrate; permeate; master, comprehend; (*with en*) enter

penicilina *f*, penicillin

península *f*, peninsula. **la P.** the Iberian Peninsula

Península Ibérica, la the Iberian Peninsula

penique *m*, penny

penitencia *f*, penitence, repentance; penance

penitenciaría *f*, penitentiary

penitente a penitent, repentant. *mf* penitent

penoso a laborious, difficult; grievous; painful; troublesome; *inf* foppish; *Lat. Am.* shy, timid

pensado a premeditated, deliberate. **de p.**, intentionally. **mal p.**, malicious, evil-minded

pensador a thinking; pensive. *m*, thinker

pensamiento *m*, mind; thought; idea; suspicion, doubt; heartsease pansy; maxim; intention, project

pensar *vt irr* to think; purpose, intend; (*with en, sobre*) reflect upon; think about; *vt* feed (animals). **p. entre sí, p. para consigo** or **p. para sí,** to think to oneself. See **acertar**

pensativo a reflective, pensive

pensión *f*, pension, allowance; boarding house, private hotel; scholarship grant; cost of board; trouble, drudgery

pensionado (-da) a pensioned; retired. *n* scholarship holder. *m*, boarding school

pensionar *vt* to pension, grant a pension to; charge a pension on

pensionista *mf* pensioner; boarder

pentágono *m*, pentagon. a pentagonal

Pentateuco *m*, Pentateuch

Pentecostés *m*, Pentecost, Whitsuntide

penúltimo a next to the last, penultimate

penuria *f*, scarcity; want, penury

peña *f*, crag, rock; boulder; group of friends; club. **ser una p.,** to be stony-hearted

peñasco *m*, craggy peak

peñón *m*, rock; cliff; peak

peón *m*, pedestrian; laborer; *South America* farmhand; top (toy); piece (chess, checkers); *mech* axle; infantryman. **p. caminero,** road mender. **p. de ajedrez,** pawn (in chess)

peonar *vi*, *Argentina* to do manual labor

peonza *f*, top; teetotum

peor a *comp* **malo** worse. adv *comp* **mal,** worse. a *sup* **el (la, lo) peor; los (las) peores,** the worst. **p. que p.,** worse and worse. **tanto p.,** so much the worse

pepino *m*, cucumber plant; cucumber; *fig* pin, straw

pepita *f*, *min* nugget; pip, seed (of fruit)

péptico a peptic

pequeñez *f*, littleness, smallness; pettiness; childhood; infancy; trifle, insignificant thing; meanness, baseness

pequeño a little, small; petty; very young; short, brief; humble, lowly

pequero, -a *mf*, *Argentina* cardsharp

pera *f*, pear; goatee; *fig* plum, sinecure

perca *f*, *icht* perch

percal *m*, percale, calico

percalina *f*, percaline, binding cloth

percance *m*, perquisite, attribute (gen. *pl*); disaster, mischance

percepción *f*, perception; idea, conception

perceptible a perceptible

perceptivo a perceptive

perceptor (-ra) a perceptive. *n* observer

percha *f*, stake, pole; coat hanger; perch (for birds); rack (for hay); hall stand, coat and hat stand, coatrack

perchero *m*, hall stand; clothes rack; row of perches (for fowl, etc.)

percibir *vt* to collect, draw, receive; perceive; understand, grasp

percibo *m*, perceiving; collecting, drawing, receiving

percolador *m*, percolator (coffee)

percusión *f*, percussion; shock, vibration

percutir *vt* to percuss, strike

perdedor (-ra) a losing. *n* loser

perder *vt* to lose; throw away, squander; spoil, destroy; *vi* fade (of colors); *vr* lose one's way, be lost; be confused or perplexed; be shipwrecked; take to vice, become dissolute; be spoiled or destroyed; disappear; love madly. **p. la chaveta (por),** to go out of one's head (for), be wild (about). **p. la ocasión,** to let the chance slip. **p. los estribos,** to lose patience. **p. terreno,** to lose ground. **perderse de vista,** to be lost to sight. **echarse a p.,** to spoil, be damaged. See **entender**

perdición f, loss; perdition, ruin; damnation; depravity, viciousness

pérdida f, loss; waste. **p. cuantiosa,** heavy losses

perdidamente adv ardently, desperately; uselessly

perdigón m, young partridge; decoy partridge; hailstone, pellet, shot

perdiz f, partridge. **p. blanca,** ptarmigan

perdón m, pardon, forgiveness; remission. **con p.,** with your permission; excuse me

perdonable a pardonable, excusable

perdonar vt to pardon, forgive; remit, excuse; exempt; waste, lose; give up (a privilege)

perdulario a careless, negligent; slovenly; vicious, depraved

perdurable a perpetual, everlasting; enduring, lasting

perdurar vi to last, endure

perecedero a brief, fugitive, transient; perishable. m, inf poverty, want

perecer vi irr to end, finish; perish, die; suffer (damage, grief, etc.); be destitute; vr (with por) long for, crave; desire ardently. See **conocer**

peregrinación f, journey, peregrination; pilgrimage

peregrinamente adv rarely, not often; beautifully, perfectly

peregrino (-na) a and n pilgrim. a migratory (birds); rare, unusual; extraordinary, strange; beautiful, perfect

perejil m, parsley; inf ornament or apparel (gen. pl); pl honors, titles

perengano (-na) n so-and-so, such a one

perenne a incessant, constant; bot perennial

perentorio a peremptory; conclusive, decisive; urgent, pressing

pereza f, laziness; languor, inertia; slowness, deliberateness

perezoso a lazy; languid; slothful; slow, deliberate. m, zool sloth

perfección f, perfection; perfecting, perfect thing, virtue, grace

perfeccionamiento m, perfecting; progress, improvement

perfeccionar vt to perfect; complete

perfecto a perfect; excellent, very good; complete; whole; gram perfect

perfidia f, perfidy, treachery

pérfido a perfidious, treacherous

perfil m, ornament, decoration; outline, contour; profile; section (of metal); fine stroke (of letters); pl finishing touches; politeness, attention, courtesy. **de p.,** in profile; sideways

perfilado a long, elongated (of faces, etc.)

perfilar vt to draw in profile; outline; vr place oneself sideways, show one's profile; inf dress up, titivate

perforación f, perforation, boring; hole

perforador a perforating, boring. m, mech drill

perforar vt to perforate, pierce; bore, drill, make a hole in

perfumador (-ra) a perfuming. n perfumer. m, perfume burner

perfumar vt to perfume; vi give off perfume

perfume m, perfume; scent, fragrance

perfumería f, scent factory; perfumery; perfume shop

perfunctorio a perfunctory

pergamino m, parchment, vellum; document; diploma; pl aristocratic descent

pericia f, expertness; skilled workmanship

pericial a expert, skillful

perico m, parakeet; giant asparagus

periferia f, periphery

periférico a peripheral

perilla f, pear-shaped ornament; goatee; imperial. **p. de la oreja,** lobe of the ear. **venir de p.,** to be most opportune

perímetro m, perimeter; precincts

perínclito a distinguished, illustrious; heroic

periodicidad f, periodicity

periódico a periodic. m, newspaper; periodical publication

periodicucho m, rag (bad newspaper)

periodismo m, journalism

periodista mf journalist

periodístico a journalistic

período m, period; phys cycle; menstruation period; gram clause; age, era

peripatético a peripatetic

peripecia f, sudden change of fortune, vicissitude

peripuesto a inf overelegant, spruce, too well-dressed; smart

periquete m, inf jiffy, trice

periquito m, parakeet; budgerigar

periscopio m, periscope

perito (-ta) a expert; skillful, experienced. n expert

perjudicador (-ra) a injurious, prejudicial. n injurer

perjudicar vt to harm, damage, injure; prejudice

perjudicial a injurious, noxious, harmful; prejudicial

perjuicio m, injury, damage; harm; law prejudice

perjurador (-ra) n perjurer

perjurar vi to perjure oneself, commit perjury; swear; curse

perjurio m, perjury

perjuro (-ra) a perjured, forsworn. n perjurer

perla *f*, pearl; *arch* bead; *fig* treasure, jewel, dear. **de perlas,** excellent; exactly right

perlero a pearl

perlesía *f*, paralysis; palsy

permanecer *vi irr* to stay, remain. **p. en posición de firme,** to stand at attention. See **conocer**

permanencia *f*, stay, sojourn; permanence

permanente a permanent; lasting, enduring

permisible a permissible, allowable

permisivo a permissive

permiso *m*, permission, leave; permit; (*mil* etc.) pass. **¡Con p.!** Excuse me! Allow me!

permitir *vt* to permit, allow

permuta *f*, exchange

permutación *f*, permutation, interchange

permutar *vt* to exchange

pernear *vi* to kick; *inf* bustle; fret, be impatient

pernetas, en *adv* barelegged

perniciosidad *f*, perniciousness

pernicioso a pernicious

pernil *m*, *anat* hock; ham; leg of pork; leg (of trousers)

pernio *m*, hinge (of doors, windows)

perniquebrar *vt irr* to break the legs of. See **quebrar**

perno *m*, bolt, pin, spike

pernoctar *vi* to spend the night (away from home)

pero *conjunc* but. *m*, *inf* defect; difficulty, snag

perogrullada *f*, *inf* truism

perol *m*, *cul* pan

peronista a, *mf* Peronist

peroración *f*, peroration

perorar *vi* to make a speech; *inf* speak pompously; ask insistently

peróxido *m*, peroxide

perpendicular a perpendicular. *f*, perpendicular

perpetración *f*, perpetration

perpetrar *vt* to perpetrate

perpetua *f*, *bot* immortelle, everlasting

perpetuación *f*, perpetuation

perpetuar *vt* to perpetuate; *vr* last, endure

perpetuo a everlasting; lifelong

perplejidad *f*, perplexity, bewilderment, doubt

perplejo a perplexed, bewildered, doubtful

perquirir *vt irr* to search carefully. See **adquirir**

perra *f*, bitch; *inf* sot, drunkard; tantrums. **p. chica,** five-cent coin. **p. gorda,** ten-cent coin

perrada *f*, pack of dogs; *inf* dirty trick

perramus *m*, *Argentina* raincoat

perrera *f*, dog kennel; useless toil; *inf* tantrums

perrería *f*, pack of dogs; *inf* dirty trick; fit of anger

perro *m*, dog. **p. caliente** hot dog. **p. danés,** Great Dane. **p. de aguas,** poodle; spaniel. **p. de casta,** thoroughbred dog. **p. de lanas** poodle. **p. de muestra,** pointer. **p. de presa,** bulldog. **p. de San Bernardo,** St. Bernard (dog). **p. de Terranova,** Newfoundland (dog). **p. del hortelano,** dog in the manger. **p. dogo** bulldog. **p. esquimal** husky. **p. faldero,** lap dog. **p. lobo,** wolfhound. **p. pachón,** dachshund. **p. pastor alemán** or **p. policía,** German shepherd. **p. pequinés,** Pekingese. **p. perdiguero,** retriever. **p. pomerano,** spitz, Pomeranian (dog). **p. sabueso español,** spaniel. **p. zorrero,** foxhound. *inf* **A p. viejo no hay tus tus,** You can't fool an old dog. **vivir como perros y gatos,** *inf* to live like cat and dog

persa a and *mf* Persian. *m*, Persian (language)

persecución *f*, pursuit; persecution; annoyance, importuning

perseguidor (-ra) a pursuing; tormenting. *n* pursuer; tormentor, persecutor

perseguimiento *m*, pursuit

perseguir *vi irr* to pursue; persecute, torment; importune. See **seguir**

perseverancia *f*, perseverance

perseverante a persevering; constant

perseverar *vi* to persevere; last, endure

persiana *f*, Venetian blind; flowered silk material

persignar *vt* to sign; make the sign of the cross over; *vr* cross oneself

persistencia *f*, persistence

persistente a persistent

persistir *vi* to persist

persona *f*, person; personage; character (in a play, etc.); (*gram ecc*) person. **de p. a p.,** in private, face to face

personaje *m*, important person, personage; character (in a play, etc.)

personal a personal. *m*, staff, personnel

personalidad *f*, personality

personalismo *m*, personality; personal question

personalizar *vt* to become personal, be offensive

personarse *vr* to present oneself, call, appear

personificar *vt* to personify

perspectiva *f*, perspective; view; outlook; aspect, appearance. **p. aérea,** bird's-eye view

perspicacia *f*, perspicacity, shrewdness

perspicaz a perspicacious, clear-sighted

perspicuo a lucid, clear

persuadir vt to persuade

persuasible a persuadable

persuasión f, persuasion; belief, conviction, opinion

persuasivo a persuasive

pertenecer vi irr to belong; relate, concern. See **conocer**

perteneciente a belonging (to); pertaining (to)

pertenencia f, ownership, proprietorship; property, accessory

pértiga f, long rod; pole. **salto de p.**, pole vaulting

pertinacia f, pertinacity, doggedness

pertinaz a pertinacious, stubborn, dogged

pertinencia f, relevance, appropriateness

pertinente a relevant, apposite; appropriate

pertrechar vt to supply, equip; prepare, make ready

pertrechos m pl, mil armaments, stores; equipment, appliances

perturbación f, disturbance; agitation

perturbar vt to disturb; agitate

Perú m Peru

peruano (-na) a and n Peruvian

perversidad f, wickedness, depravity

perversión f, perversion; wickedness, evil

perverso a wicked, iniquitous, depraved

pervertir vt irr to pervert, corrupt; distort. See **sentir**

pesa f, weight; clock weight; gymnast's weight. **pesas y medidas**, weights and measures

pesacartas m, letter scale, letter balance

pesadez f, heaviness; obesity; tediousness, tiresomeness; slowness; fatigue

pesadilla f, nightmare

pesado a heavy; obese; deep (of sleep); oppressive (of weather); slow; unwieldy; tedious; impertinent; dull, boring; offensive

pesadumbre f, heaviness; grief, sorrow; trouble, anxiety

pésame m, expression of condolence. **dar el p.**, to present one's condolences

pesantez f, weight, heaviness; seriousness, gravity

pesar m, grief, sorrow; remorse. **a p. de**, in spite of

pesar vi to weigh; be heavy; be important; grieve, cause regret (e.g. **Me pesa mucho**, I am very sorry); influence, affect; vt to consider. **Mal que me** (**te**, etc.) **pese . . .**, Much as I regret . . .

pesaroso a regretful, remorseful; sorrowful

pesca f, fishery; angling, fishing; catch of fish. **p. a la rastra**, trawling. **p. depor-**

tiva sport fishing. **p. mayor**, deep-sea fishing

pescadería f, fishery; fish store; fish market

pescado m, fish (out of the water); salt cod

pescador (-ra) n fisherman; angler

pescar vt to fish; inf catch in the act; acquire. **p. a la rastra**, to trawl

pescuezo m, neck; throat; haughtiness, arrogance. **torcer el p.**, to wring the neck (of chickens, etc.)

pesebre m, manger, stable; feeding trough

pesero m, Mexico jitney, jitney taxi

pesimismo m, pessimism

pesimista a pessimistic. mf pessimist

pésimo a sup **malo** extremely bad

peso m, weighing; weight; heaviness; gravity; importance; influence; load; peso (money); scale, balance. **p. bruto**, gross weight. **p. de joyería**, troy weight. **p. específico**, phys specific gravity. **p. pluma**, (boxing) featherweight

pespunte m, backstitch

pesquera f, fishing ground, fishery

pesquería f, fishing, angling; fisherman's trade; fishing ground, fishery

pesquisa f, investigation, examination; search

pesquisar vt to investigate, look into; search

pestaña f, eyelash; sew edging, fringe; ear, lug; naut fluke

pestañear vi to wink; blink; flutter one's eyelashes

peste f, plague, pestilence; nauseous smell; epidemic; pest; vice; Chile smallpox; pl oaths, curses. **p. bubónica**, bubonic plague. **p. roja** syphilis. **p. de las abejas**, foul brood. **echar pestes**, to swear; fume

pestífero a noxious

pestilencia f, plague, pestilence

pestilente a pestilential

pestillo m, latch; lock bolt. **p. de golpe**, safety latch

petaca f, cigarette or cigar case; tobacco pouch; Mexico suitcase.

pétalo m, petal

petardo m, detonator; torpedo; firecracker; fraud

petición f, petition, request

peticionar vt, Lat. Am. to petition

petimetra f, stylish and affected young woman

petimetre m, fop

petitorio a petitionary. m, inf importunity

peto m, breastplate; front (of a shirt); bib

pétreo a petrous

petrificación f, petrifaction

petrificar vt to petrify; vr become petrified

petróleo *m*, petroleum; oil, mineral oil. **p. bruto,** crude oil. **p. de lámpara,** kerosene

petrolero (-ra) a oil, petroleum. *n* petroleum seller; incendiarist. *m*, oil tanker

petrolífero a oil-bearing

petulancia *f*, insolence; vanity

petulante a insolent; vain

pez *m*, fish; *pl* Pisces. *f*, *chem* pitch. **p. sierra,** swordfish

pezón *m*, *bot* stalk; nipple; axle pivot; point (of land, etc.)

piadoso a compassionate; kind, pitiful; pious, religious

piafar *vi* to stamp, paw the ground (horses)

pianista *mf* piano maker; piano dealer; pianist

piano *m*, pianoforte. **p. de cola,** grand piano. **p. de media cola,** baby grand. **p. vertical,** upright piano

piante a chirping, twittering

piar *vi* to chirp, twitter

piara *f*, herd of swine; pack (of horses, etc.)

pibe, -a *mf*, Argentina kid, child

pica *f*, *mil* pike; bullfighter's goad; pike soldier; stonecutter's hammer. **a p. seca,** in vain. **pasar por las picas,** to suffer hardship. **poner una p. en Flandes,** to triumph over great difficulties

picada *f*, prick; bite; peck; *aer* dive

picado a *sew* pinked. *m*, *cul* hash

picador *m*, horse trainer; meat chopper; horseman armed with a goad (bullfights)

picadura *f*, puncture; prick; sting; *sew* pinking; peck (of birds); cut tobacco; black tobacco; beginning of caries in teeth

picajoso a hypersensitive, touchy, peevish

picanear *vt*, *Lat. Am.* to goad on, spur on

picante a piquant; mordant; hot, highly seasoned. *m*, mordancy; pungency

picantería *f*, *Lat. Am.* restaurant specializing in spicy foods

picapleitos *m*, *inf* shady lawyer, pettifogger

picaporte *m*, latch, door catch; door knocker

picar *vt* to prick; sting; peck; bite; chop fine; mince; nibble (of fishing); irritate (the skin); *sew* pink; burn (the tongue); eat (grapes); goad; spur; stipple (walls); stimulate, encourage; split, cleave; *mil* harass; vex; *mus* play staccato; *vi* burn (of the sun); smart (of cuts, etc.); *aut* knock; (*with en*) knock at (doors, etc.); *vr* be moth-eaten; go rotten (fruit, etc.); grow choppy (of the sea); be piqued; boast

picardear *vi* to play the rogue; behave mischievously

picardía *f*, knavery, roguery; mischievousness; practical joke; wantonness

picaresco a roguish, picaresque, knavish

pícaro (-ra) a knavish; base, vile; astute; mischievous. *n* rogue

picatoste *m*, kind of fritter

picazo *m*, blow with a pike or anything pointed; peck, tap with a beak (of birds); sting

picazón *f*, itch, irritation; annoyance

pichincha *f*, Argentina bargain

pichón (-ona) *m*, male pigeon. *n inf* darling

pico *m*, beak (of birds); peak; woodpecker; odd amount (e.g. **treinta y p.,** thirty-odd); sharp point; spout (of a jug, etc.); *inf* mouth; blarney, gab. **p. de cigüeña,** crane's-bill. **p. de oro,** silver-tongued orator

picor *m*, burning sensation in the mouth; smarting; itching, irritation

picoso a pitted, marked by smallpox; *Mexico* hot, spicy (food)

picota *f*, pillory; peak; spire

picotazo *m*, peck; dab; sting, bite

picotear *vt* to peck (of a bird); *vi* toss the head (of horses); *inf* chatter senselessly; *vr inf* slang each other

picotero a *inf* chattering, talkative; indiscreet

pictórico a pictorial

picudo a pointed, peaked; having a spout; *inf* chattering; *Mexico* clever, crafty, sly

pie *m*, foot; stand, support; stem (of a glass, etc.); standard (of a lamp); *bot* trunk, stem; sapling; lees, sediment; *theat* cue; foot (measure); custom; (metrics) foot; motive, cause; pretext; (metrics) meter. **p. de cabra,** crowbar. **p. de imprenta,** printer's mark, printer's imprint. **p. de piña,** clubfoot. **p. de rey,** caliper. **p. palmado,** webfoot. **al p. de la letra,** punctiliously. *inf* **andar con pies de plomo,** to walk warily. **a p.,** on foot. **a p. firme,** without budging; steadfastly. *inf* **buscar tres pies al gato,** to look for something that isn't there; twist a person's words. **de a p.,** on foot. **en p. de guerra,** on a wartime footing. *inf* **poner pies en polvorosa,** to quit

piedad *f*, piety; pity, compassion; *art* pietà

piedra *f*, stone; tablet; *med* gravel. **p. de amolar,** whetstone, grindstone. **p. angular,** cornerstone (also *fig*). **p. caliza,** limestone. **p. clave,** keystone. **p. de construcción,** building stone; child's block. **p. de toque,** touchstone, test. **p. filosofal,** philosopher's stone. **p. fundamental,** foundation stone. **p. miliaria,** milestone. **p. mortuoria,** tombstone. *fig inf* **no dejar p. sin remover,** to leave no stone unturned. **no dejar p. sobre p.,** to demolish, destroy completely

piel f, skin; fur; hide; leather; peel (of some fruits); rind (of bacon). **p. de gallina,** fig goose flesh. **p. de rata,** horse blanket. **p. de Rusia,** Russian leather.

piélago m, high seas; sea, ocean; glut, superabundance

pienso m, agr fodder

pierna f, anat leg; mech shank; leg of a compass. inf **a p. suelta,** at one's ease. **en piernas,** barelegged

pietista a pietistic. mf pietist

pieza f, portion; piece; component part; room; theat play; roll (of cloth); piece (in chess, etc.); coin; piece (of music). **p. de recambio** or **p. de repuesto,** spare part. **p. de recibo,** reception room. inf **quedarse en una p.,** to be struck dumb

pigmentación f, pigmentation

pigmento m, pigment

pignoración f, hypothecation; pawning; mortgage

pignorar vt to hypothecate; pawn; mortgage

pigre a lazy; negligent, careless

pigricia f, laziness; negligence Chile, Peru trifle

pijama m, pajamas

pila f, trough, basin; heap, pile; elec battery; ecc parish; pier, pile; phys cell. **p. atómica,** atomic pile. **p. bautismal,** ecc font

pilar m, fountain basin; milestone; pillar

pilastra f, pier, pile; pilaster

pilche m, Lat. Am. calabash, gourd

píldora f, med pill; inf disagreeable news

pileta (de natación) f, Argentina, (swimming) pool

pillador (-ra) a pillaging, plundering. n plunderer

pillaje m, pillaging, looting; robbery, theft

pillar vt to pillage; steal, rob; seize, snatch; inf surprise, find out (in a lie, etc.). **pillarse el dedo,** to get one's finger caught (in a door, etc.)

pillería f, inf gang of rogues; inf rogue's trick

pillo m, rogue, knave

pilón m, fountain basin; pestle; loaf sugar; pylon; Mexico, Venezuela gratuity, tip

pilotar vt to pilot

pilotear vt to pilot

piloto m, pilot; mate (in merchant ships). **p. de pruebas,** test pilo

pilsen m, Chile beer

pimentero m, pepper plant; pepper shaker

pimentón m, red pepper, cayenne

pimienta f, pepper. **p. húngara,** paprika. inf **ser como una p.,** to be sharp as a needle

pimiento m, pimento; capsicum; red

pepper; pepper plant. **p. de cornetilla,** chili pepper

pina f, conical stone; felloe (of a wheel)

pinacoteca f, art gallery, picture gallery

pináculo m, pinnacle, summit; climax, culmination; arch finial

pincel m, paintbrush; artist, painter; painting technique. **p. para las cejas,** eyebrow pencil

pincelada f, brushstroke. **dar la última p.,** to add the finishing touch

pincelero (-ra) n seller or maker of paintbrushes; brush box

pinchadura f, prick, puncture, piercing; sting; nipping, biting

pinchar vt to prick; puncture; pierce; sting; nip, bite. **no p. ni cortar,** to be ineffective (of persons)

pinchazo m, prick; puncture; sting; incitement

pinche m, scullion, kitchen boy; Argentina minor office clerk; a, Mexico damn

pineda f, pinewood

pingajo m, inf tatter, rag

pingo m, inf tatter, rag; pl inf cheap clothes

pingüe a fat, greasy; fertile, rich

pingüino m, penguin

pino a steep. m, bot pine, deal; poet ship. **p. de tea,** pitch pine. **p. silvestre,** red fir

pinta f, spot; marking; mark; fleck; look, appearance; pint (measure); drop, drip; spot ball (in billiards)

pintamonas mf inf dauber

pintar vt to paint; describe; picture; exaggerate; vi show, manifest itself; vr make up (one's face). inf **pintarse solo para,** to be very good at, excel at

pintiparado a most similar, very alike; fitting, apposite

pintiparar vt inf to compare

pintor (-ra) n painter, artist. **p. callejero,** sidewalk artist, pavement artist. **p. de brocha gorda,** house painter

pintoresco a picturesque, quaint, pretty

pintorrear vt inf to daub, paint badly

pintura f, painting; paint, pigment; picture, painting; description. **p. a la aguada,** watercolor painting. **p. al fresco,** fresco. **p. al látex,** latex paint. **p. al óleo,** oil painting. **p. al pastel,** pastel drawing

pinturero a inf affected, conceited; dandified, overdressed

pinza f, clamp. **p. de la ropa,** clothes peg

pinzas f pl, pincers; pliers; tweezers; forceps. **p. hemostáticas,** arterial forceps

piña f, pineapple; cluster, knot (of people, etc.); pinecone

piñón m, pine nut; mech pinion, chain wheel

pío a pious; compassionate; good; piebald. m, chirping, cheep; inf longing

piocha *f, Lat. Am.* pickax

piojo *m,* louse

piojoso *a* lousy; avaricious, stingy

piola *f, Lat. Am.* cord, string; rope; tether

pionero *m,* pioneer

pipa *f,* barrel, cask; tobacco pipe; pip (of fruits)

pipar *vi* to smoke a pipe

pipiar *vi* to chirp, twitter

pique *m,* pique, resentment. **a p. de,** on the verge of, about to. **echar a p.,** *naut* to sink; destroy. **irse a p.,** to sink, founder

piquete *m,* puncture, small wound; *mil* picket; pole, stake; small hole (in garments); picket (in strikes)

pira *f,* funeral pyre; bonfire

piragua *f,* piragua, canoe

pirámide *f,* pyramid

piraña *f* piranha

pirarse *vr inf* to slip away

pirata *a* piratical *mf* pirate; savage, cruel person

piratear *vi* to play the pirate

piratería *f,* piracy; plunder, robbery

pirático *a* piratical

pirca *f, Lat. Am.* dry-stone wall

pirenaico, pirineo *a* Pyrenean

Pirineos, los the Pyrenees

piropear *vt inf* to pay compliments to

piropo *m,* carbuncle; *inf* compliment. **echar piropos,** to pay compliments

pirotécnico *a* pyrotechnical. *m,* pyrotechnist

pirrarse *vr inf* to desire ardently

pírrico *a* Pyrrhic

pirueta *f,* pirouette, twirl

pisada *f,* treading, stepping; footprint, footstep; stepping on a person's foot. **seguir las pisadas de alguien,** *fig* to follow in someone's footsteps, imitate someone

pisapapeles *m,* paperweight

pisar *vt* to tread upon; trample upon; crush; *mus* press (strings); trespass upon; *vr, Argentina* to be mistaken

pisaverde *m, inf* fop, dandy

piscicultura *f,* pisciculture, fish farming

piscina *f,* fishpond; swimming pool; *ecc* piscina

piscolabis *m, inf* snack, light meal

piso *m,* treading, trampling; story, floor; flooring; apartment. **p. bajo,** ground floor

pisón *m,* rammer, ram

pisotear *vt* to trample; crush under foot; tread on; step on; humiliate, treat inconsiderately

pisoteo *m,* trampling under foot; treading

pista *f,* track, trail (of animals); circus ring; racetrack, racecourse. **p. de pati-**nar, skating rink. **p. de vuelo,** *aer* landing field. *inf* **seguir la p. a,** to spy upon

pistacho *m,* pistachio

pistar *va* to pestle, pound

pistero *m,* feeding cup

pistilo *m,* pistil

pisto, *m, Central America, slang* dough (money)

pistola *f,* pistol. **p. ametralladora,** machine gun.

pistolera *f,* holster; pistol case

pistolero *m,* gangster

pistoletazo *m,* pistol shot; pistol wound

pistón *m, mus* piston; *mil* percussion cap; *mech* piston

pitada *f,* blast on a whistle, whistling; impertinence

pitanza *f,* alms, charity; *inf* daily food; pittance, scanty remuneration

pitar *vi* to play the whistle; *vt* pay (debts); smoke; give alms to

pitido *m,* blast on a whistle; whistling (of birds)

pitillera *f,* cigarette case; female cigarette maker

pito *m,* whistle; *mus* fife. *inf* **Cuando pitos flautas, cuando flautas pitos,** It's always the unexpected that happens. *inf* **no valer un p.,** to be not worth a straw

pitoflero (-ra) *n* mediocre performer (gen. on a wind instrument); *inf* talebearer, gossip

pitón *m, zool* python; nascent horn (of goats, etc.); spout; protuberance; *bot* sprout

pitorrearse *vr* to ridicule, mock

pivote *m,* pivot, swivel, gudgeon

piyama *m,* pajamas

pizarra *f,* slate; blackboard

pizarrín *m,* slate pencil

pizca *f, inf* atom, speck, crumb; jot, whit. **¡Ni p.!** Not a scrap!

pizpireta *a f, inf* coquettish; smart; dressed up

placa *f,* plate, disk; *art* plaque; *phot* plate; star (insignia). **p. recordatorio,** commemorative plaque

pláceme *m,* congratulation

placentero *a* agreeable, pleasant

placer *vt irr* to please, give pleasure to, gratify. *m, naut* reef, sandbank; pleasure; wish, desire; permission, consent; entertainment, diversion. **a p.,** at one's convenience; at leisure. *Pres. Ind.* **plazco, places,** etc. *Preterite* **plugo, pluguieron.** *Pres. Subjunc.* **plazca,** etc. *Imperf. Subjunc.* **pluguiese,** etc.

placible *a* agreeable, pleasant

plácido *a* a placid, calm, serene

placiente *a* a pleasing, attractive

plácito *m,* decision, judgment, opinion

plaga *f,* plague; disaster, calamity; epidemic; glut; pest; grief

plagar *vt (with de)* to infect with; *vr (with de)* be covered with; be overrun by; be infested with

plagiar *vt* to plagiarize, copy; kidnap, hold for ransom

plagiario (-ia) *n* plagiarist; *Lat. Am.* kidnapper

plagio *m,* plagiary; kidnapping

plan *m,* plan; scheme; plane. **p. quinquenal,** five-year plan

plana *f,* sheet, page; mason's trowel; plain. **p. mayor,** *(mil nav)* staff

planadora *f,* steamroller

plancha *f,* sheet, slab, plate; flatiron; horizontal suspension (in gymnastics); *naut* gangway, gangplank; *inf* howler

planchado *m,* ironing; ironing to be done or already finished

planchador (-ra) *n* ironer

planchar *vt* to iron, press with an iron

planeador *m, aer* glider

planear *vt* to plan out; make plans for; *vi aer* glide

planeta *m,* planet

planetario *a* planetary. *m,* planetarium

planicie *f,* levelness, evenness; plain

planilla *f, Lat. Am.* application, application form, blank; payroll; list; ballot

plano *a* flat, level; plane. *m, geom* plane; plan, map; *aer* aileron, wing

planta *f, bot* plant; sole (of the foot); plantation; layout, plan; position of the feet (in dancing, fencing); scheme, project. **p. baja,** ground floor. **p. vivaz,** perennial plant. *inf* **buena p.,** good appearance

plantación *f,* planting; plantation; nursery

plantador (-ra) *n* planter. *m, agr* dibble. *f,* **plantadora,** mechanical planter

plantar *vt* to plant; erect; place; found, set up; pose (a problem); raise (a question, etc.); *inf* leave in the lurch; *vr* take up one's position; jib (of horses); oppose

planteamiento *m,* execution; putting into practice; planning; statement (of problems)

plantel *m,* nursery garden; training school; nursery

plantilla *f,* young plant; insole (of shoes); *mech* template, jig

plantío *m,* plantation, afforestation; planting. *a* planted or ready for planting (ground)

plantón *m,* plant or sapling ready for transplanting; *bot* cutting; doorkeeper, porter. **dar un p. (a),** to keep (a person) waiting a long time

plañidero *a* mournful, piteous, anguished

plañido *m,* lament, weeping, wailing

plañir *vi* and *vt irr* to lament, wail, weep. See **tañer**

plasma *m,* plasma

plasmar *vt* to mold, throw (pottery)

plástica *f,* art of clay modeling; plastic

plástico *a* plastic; flexible, malleable, soft

plata *f,* silver; silver (coins); *Lat. Am.* money; white. **p. labrada,** silverware

plataforma *f,* platform; running board (of a train); *rw* turntable

platal *m, Lat. Am.* wealth

plátano *m,* banana tree, banana; plantain; plane tree

platea *f, theat* pit. **butaca de p.,** pit stall

plateado *a* silvered; silver-plated; silvery

platear *vt* to electroplate, silver

platería *f,* silversmith's art or trade; silversmith's shop or workshop

platero *m,* silversmith; jeweler

plática *f,* conversation; exhortation, sermon; address, discourse

platicar *vt* and *vi* to converse (about)

platillo *m,* saucer; kitty (in card games); pan (of a scale); *pl* cymbals

platinado *m,* plating

platino *m,* platinum

platívolo *m,* flying saucer

plato *m,* plate; dish; *cul* course, dish; pan (of a scale). **p. sopero,** soup plate. **p. trinchero,** meat dish. *inf* **comer en un mismo p.,** to be on intimate terms. **nada entre dos platos,** much ado about nothing

platónico *a* Platonic

platudo, -a *mf,* rich, wealthy, well-heeled

plausible *a* plausible, reasonable; commendable

playa *f,* beach, seashore, strand

plaza *f,* square (in a town, etc.); marketplace; fortified town; space; duration; employment, post.; *com* market. **p. de armas,** garrison town; military camp. **p. de toros,** bullring. **p. fuerte,** strong place, fortress. **sentar p.,** to enlist in the army

plazo *m,* term, duration; expiration of term, date of payment; installment. **a plazos,** *com* by installments, on the installment system

plazoleta *f,* small square (in gardens, etc.)

pleamar *f, naut* high water

plebe *f,* common people; rabble, mob

plebeyo (-ya) *a* plebeian. *n* commoner, plebeian

plebiscito *m,* plebiscite

plegable *a* foldable

plegadera *f,* folder; folding knife; paper folder

plegadizo *a* folding; collapsible; jointed

plegado *m,* pleating; folding

plegador *a* folding. *m,* folding machine

plegadura *f,* folding, doubling; fold, pleat

plegar *vt irr* to fold; pleat; *sew* gather; *vr* submit, give in. See **acertar**

plegaria *f*, fervent prayer

pleitear *vt* to go to court about; indulge in litigation

pleitista *a* quarrelsome, litigious

pleito *m*, action, lawsuit; dispute, quarrel; litigation. **p. de familia,** family squabble. **ver el p.,** *law* to try a case

plenario *a* full, complete; *law* plenary

plenipotencia *f*, full powers (diplomatic, etc.)

plenipotenciario *a* and *m*, plenipotentiary

plenitud *f*, fullness, completeness; plenitude, abundance

pleno *a* full. *m*, general meeting

pleuresía *f*, pleurisy

pliego *m*, sheet (of paper); letter, packet of papers

pliegue *m*, fold, pleat; *sew* gather

plisar *vt* to pleat; fold

plomada *f*, plummet; sounding lead; plumb, lead

plomería *f*, plumbing; plumbing business; lead roofing

plomero *m*, plumber

plomizo *a* lead-like; lead-colored, gray

plomo *m*, lead (metal); plummet; bullet; *inf* bore, tedious person

pluma *f*, feather; pen; plumage; quill; penmanship; writer; writing profession. **p. estilográfica,** fountain pen. **a vuela p.,** as the pen writes, written in a hurry

plumado *a* feathered

pluma fuente *f*, *Lat. Am.* fountain pen

plumaje *m*, plumage, feathers; plume

plúmeo *a* feathered, plumed

plumero *m*, feather duster; plume, feather; plumage

plumón *m*, down; feather bed *Lat. Am.* felt-tipped pen

plural *a* and *m*, plural

pluralidad *f*, plurality; multitude, number

plurilingüe *a* multilingual

plusmarquista *mf sport* recordholder

plutocracia *f*, plutocracy

plutócrata *mf* plutocrat

pluviómetro *m*, rain gauge

poblacho *m*, miserable town or village

población *f*, peopling; population; town

poblado *m*, inhabited place; town; village

poblador (-ra) *a* populating. *n* colonist, settler

poblar *vt irr* to colonize; people, populate; breed fast; stock, supply; *vr* put forth leaves (of trees). See **contar**

pobre *a* poor; indigent, needy; mediocre; unfortunate; humble, meek. *mf* beggar, pauper, needy person. *inf* **ser p. de solemnidad,** to be down and out

pobretón *a* extremely needy

pobreza *f*, poverty, need; shortage; timidity; *mín* baseness; poorness (of soil, etc.)

pocilga *f*, pigsty; *inf* filthy place

poción *f*, potion, drink; mixture, dose

poco *a* little, scanty; *pl* few. *m*, small amount, a little. *adv* little; shortly, in a little while. **p. a p.,** by degrees, little by little; slowly. **p. más o menos,** more or less, approximately. **por p.,** almost, nearly (always used with the present tense, e.g. **Por p. me caigo,** I almost fell). **tener en p.** (a), to have a poor opinion of; undervalue

podadera *f*, pruning knife

podar *vt agr* to prune, trim

poder *m*, power; authority, jurisdiction; *law* power of attorney; strength; ability; proxy; efficacy; possession; *pl* authority; power of attorney. **los poderes constituidos,** the established authorities; the powers that be. **p. de adquisición,** purchasing power. **casarse por poderes,** to be married by proxy

poder *vt irr* to be able to (e.g. **Podemos comprar estas naranjas,** We can (are able to) buy these oranges). **Dice que la calamidad podía haberse evitado,** He says that the disaster could have been averted). **p.** also expresses possibility (e.g. **Pueden haber ido a la ciudad,** They may have gone to the city. **¡Qué distinta pudo haber sido su vida!** How different his life might have been!). *impers* be possible. **a más no p.,** of necessity, without being able to help it; to the utmost. **no p. con,** to be unable to control or manage. **no p. hacer más,** to have no alternative; have to; be unable to do more. **no p. menos de,** to be obliged to, have no alternative but. **no p. contener su emoción,** to be overcome with emotion. **no p. ver a,** to hate (persons). *impers* **Puede que venga esta tarde,** He may come (perhaps he will come) this afternoon. *Pres. Part.* **pudiendo.** *Pres. Ind.* **puedo, puedes, puede, pueden.** *Fut.* **podré,** etc. *Condit.* **podría,** etc. *Preterite* **pude, pudiste,** etc. *Pres. Subjunc.* **pueda, puedas, pueda, puedan.** *Imperf. Subjunc.* **pudiese,** etc.

poderío *m*, power, authority; sway, rule; dominion; wealth

poderoso *a* powerful; opulent; effective, efficacious; mighty, magnificent

podredumbre *f*, decay; pus; *fig* canker, anguish

podredura, podrición *f*, putrefaction; decay

podrido *a* rotten; putrid; corrupt; decayed

podrir *vt* See **pudrir**

poema *m*, poem. **p. sinfónico,** tone poem

poesía *f*, poetry, verse; lyric, poem

poeta *m*, poet

poética f, poetics

poético a poetical

poetisa f, poetess

poetizar vi to write verses; vt poeticize

polaco (-ca) a Polish. n Pole. m, Polish (language)

polainas f pl, leggings, puttees, gaiters

polar a polar

polarización f, polarization

polarizar vt to polarize

polca f, polka

polea f, pulley; naut block

polémica f, polemic, controversy, dispute

polémico a polemical

polemista mf disputant, controversialist

polen m, pollen

polichinela m, Punchinello

policía f, police; government, polity, administration; civility, courtesy; cleanliness, tidiness. m, policeman. **p. urbana**, city police

policíaco a police; detective

policial a police; m, Lat. Am. police officer

polifacético a many-sided

polifónico a polyphonic

poligamia f, polygamy

polígamo (-ma) a polygamous. n polygamist

polígloto (-ta) n polyglot. f, polyglot Bible

polígono a polygonal. m, polygon

polilla f, moth; moth grub; destroyer, ravager

polinesio (-ia) a and n Polynesian

polinización f, pollination

poliomielitis f, poliomyelitis, polio

pólipo m, zool polyp; octopus; med polyp

polista mf polo player

politécnico a polytechnic

politeísta a polytheistic. mf polytheist

política f, politics; civility, courtesy; diplomacy; tact; policy

politicastro m, corrupt politician

político a political; civil, courteous; in-law, by marriage (relationships). m, politician

politiquear vi inf to dabble in politics, talk politics

póliza f, com policy; com draft; share certificate; revenue stamp; admission ticket; lampoon. **p. a prima fija**, fixed-premium policy. **p. de seguros**, insurance policy. **p. dotal**, endowment policy

polizón m, loafer, tramp; stowaway; bustle (of a dress)

polla f, pullet; inf flapper, young woman

pollastre (-ra) n pullet.

pollera f, female poultry breeder or seller; chicken coop; go-cart; Argentina, Chile skirt

pollería f, poultry market or shop

pollero n poultry breeder; poulterer. m, hen coop; Lat. Am. gambler

pollo m, chicken; inf youth, stripling; fig inf downy bird. inf **p. pera**, young blood, lad. **sacar pollos**, to hatch chickens

polo m, pole (all meanings); fig support; popular Andalusian song; sport polo. **de p. a p.**, from pole to pole

polonés (-esa) a Polish. n Pole

Polonia Poland

poltrón a lazy, idle

poltronear vi to loaf about

poltronería f, idleness, laziness

polución f, med ejaculation

polvareda f, dust cloud; storm, agitation

polvera f, powder bowl; powder puff; powder compact

polvillo m, Lat. Am. blight

polvo m, dust; powder; pinch (of snuff, etc.); pl face or dusting powder. **Se hizo como por polvos de la madre celestina**, It was done as if by magic. inf **limpio de p. y paja**, gratis, for nothing; net (of profit)

pólvora f, gunpowder; bad temper. **p. de algodón**, guncotton.

polvoriento a dusty; powdery, covered with powder

polvorín m, very fine powder; powder magazine; powder flask

pomada f, pomade; salve, ointment

pómez f, pumice stone (**piedra p.**)

pomo m, bot pome; pomander; nosegay; pommel, hilt (of a sword); handle; rose (of watering can)

pompa f, pomp, splendor; ceremonial procession; air bubble; peacock's out-spread tail; naut pump; billowing of clothes in the wind

Pompeya Pompeii

pomposo a stately, ostentatious, magnificent; inflated, pompous; florid, bombastic

pómulo m, cheekbone

ponchada f Lat. Am. great deal, large amount

ponche m, punch, toddy

ponchera f, punch bowl

poncho a lazy, negligent. m, military cloak; poncho, cape

ponderación f, weighing; reflection, consideration; exaggeration

ponderador a reflective, deliberate; exaggerated

ponderar vt to weigh; consider, ponder; exaggerate; overpraise

ponderoso a heavy; ponderous; circumspect

ponencia f, clause, section; office of referee or arbitrator; report, referendum

poner vt irr to place, put; arrange; set (the table); bet, stake; appoint (to an office);

call, name; lay (eggs); set down (in writing); calculate, count; suppose; leave to a person's judgment; risk; contribute; prepare; need, take; cause, inspire (emotions); make, cause; adapt; add; cause to become (angry, etc.); insult; praise; (*with prep a + infin*) begin to. **p. a contribución,** to lay under contribution, turn to account, utilize. **ponerle el cascabel al gato or el collar al gato,** to bell the cat. **p. los cuernos (a),** to cuckold. **p. al corriente,** to bring up to date, inform. **p. a prueba,** to test. **p. casa,** to set up house. *inf* **p. colorado a,** to make blush. **p. coto a,** to put a stop to, check. **p. en comparación,** to compare. **p. conato en,** to put a great deal of effort into. **p. en cotejo,** to collate. **p. en limpio,** to make a fair copy (of). **p. en marcha,** to start, set in motion. **p. en práctica,** to put into effect. **p. por caso,** to take as an example (e.g. **Pongamos por caso . . .** For example, . . .). **p. por encima (de),** to prefer. *vr* to place oneself; become; put on (garments, etc.); dirty or stain oneself; set (of the sun, stars); oppose; deck oneself, dress oneself up; arrive; (*with prep a + infin*) begin to. **ponerse al corriente,** to bring oneself up to date. **ponerse bien,** to improve; get better (in health). **ponerse colorado,** to blush, flush. **p. una base racional a la fe,** to give faith a rational foundation. **p. los cimientos de,** lay the foundation of, lay the foundations for. **p. una conferencia,** to make a long-distance call. *Pres. Ind.* **pongo, pones,** etc. *Fut.* **pondré,** etc. *Condit.* **pondría,** etc. *Imperat.* **pon.** *Past Part.* **puesto.** *Preterite* **puse, pusiste,** etc. *Pres. Subjunc.* **ponga,** etc. *Imperf. Subjunc.* **pusiese,** etc.

pongo *m Bolivia, Peru* Native American serf

pongueaje *m Bolivia, Peru* Native American serfdom

poniente *m,* west; west wind

pontazgo *m,* bridge toll

pontificado *m,* pontificate, papacy

pontífice *m,* pontifex; pope, pontiff; archbishop; bishop

ponzoña *f,* poison, venom

ponzoñoso *a* poisonous, venomous; noxious; harmful

popa *f, naut* stern, poop. **en p.,** abaft, astern, aft

popote *m, Mexico* (drinking) straw

populachería *f,* cheap popularity with the rabble

populachero *a* a mob, vulgar

populacho *m,* mob, rabble

popular *a* popular

popularidad *f,* popularity

popularizar *vt* to popularize; *vr* grow popular

populoso *a* populous, crowded

popurrí *m, cul* stew; potpourri; miscellany

poquedad *f,* paucity, scarcity; timidity, cowardice; trifle, mere nothing

poquísimo *a sup* **poco** very little

poquito *m,* very little

por *prep* for; by; through, along; during; because, as (e.g. **Lo desecharon p. viejo,** They threw it away because it was old); however (e.g. **p. bonito que sea,** however pretty it is); during; in order to (e.g. **Lo hice p. no ofenderla,** I did it in order not to offend her); toward, in favor of, for; for the sake of; on account of, by reason of (e.g. **No pudo venir p. estar enfermo,** He could not come on account of his illness); via, by (e.g. **p. correo aéreo,** by airmail); as for (e.g. **P. mí, lo rechazo,** As for me, I refuse it. **p. mi cuenta,** to my way of thinking; on my own); in exchange for (e.g. **Me vendió dos libros p. seis dólares,** He sold me two books for six dollars); in the name of; as a substitute for, instead of (e.g. **Hace mi trabajo p. mí,** He is doing my work for me); per. **Por** has several uses: 1. Introduces the agent after a passive (e.g. **La novela fue escrita p. él,** The novel was written by him). 2. Expresses movement through, along or about (e.g. **Andaban p. la calle,** They were walking along (or down) the street). 3. Denotes time at or during which an action occurs (e.g. **Ocurrió p. entonces un acontecimiento de importancia,** About that time an important event occurred). 4. Expresses rate or proportion (e.g. **seis por ciento,** six percent). 5. With certain verbs, means 'to be' and expresses vague futurity (e.g. **El libro queda p. escribir,** The book remains to be written). **p. cortesía,** by courtesy, out of politeness. **p. cortesía de,** by courtesy of. **p. escrito,** in writing. **p. fas or p. nefas,** by fair means or foul; at any cost. **p. mucho que,** however great, however much; in spite of, notwithstanding. **¿P. qué?** Why? **p. si acaso,** in case, if by chance. **estar p.,** to be about to; be inclined to. **P. un clavo se pierde la herradura,** For want of a nail, the shoe was lost.

porcelana *f,* porcelain, china; chinaware

porcentaje *m,* percentage

porción *f,* portion; *com* share; *inf* crowd; allowance, pittance

porcionista *mf* shareholder; sharer; boarding school student

pordiosear *vi* to ask alms, beg

pordioseo *m,* asking alms, begging

pordiosero (-ra) *a* begging. *n* beggar

porfía *f,* obstinacy; importunity; tenacity. **a p.,** in competition

porfiado *a* obstinate, obdurate, persistent

porfiar *vi* to be obstinate, insist; persist

pórfido *m,* porphyry

pormenor *m*, particular, detail (gen. *pl*); secondary matter

pormenorizar *vt* to describe in detail

pornografía *f*, pornography

pornográfico a pornographic, obscene

poro *m*, pore; *Lat. Am. also* leek

porongo *m*, *Lat. Am.* calabash, gourd

poroso a porous, leaky

poroto *m*, *Lat. Am.* bean; *Chile* child, kid

porque *conjunc* because, for; in order that

porqué *m*, reason, wherefore, why; *inf* money. **el cómo y el p.,** the why and the wherefore

porquería *f*, *inf* filth, nastiness; dirty trick; rudeness, gross act; trifle, thing of no account

porra *f*, club, bludgeon; last player (in children's games); *inf* vanity, boastfulness; bore, tedious person

porrada *f*, blow with a club; buffet, knock, fall; *inf* folly; glut, abundance

porrazo *m*, blow with a club; buffet, knock, fall

porrear *vi inf* to insist, harp on

porrería *f*, *inf* folly; obduracy, persistence

porreta *f*, green leaves of leeks, onions, and cereals. *inf* **en p.,** stark-naked

porsiacaso *m*, *Argentina, Venezuela* knapsack

portaaviones *m*, aircraft carrier

portachuelo *m*, defile, narrow mountain pass

portada *f*, front, facade; frontispiece; title page; portal, doorway

portado (bien or **mal)** a well- or ill-dressed or behaved

portador (-ra) *n* carrier. *m*, *com* bearer; *mech* carrier

portaestandarte *m*, standard-bearer

portafolio *m*, portfolio; *Lat. Am. also* briefcase

portafusil *m*, rifle sling

portal *m*, entrance, porch; portico; city gate

portalámpara *f*, lamp holder; *elec* socket

portalibros *m*, bookstrap

portalón *m*, gangway

portamanteo *m*, traveling bag

portamonedas *m*, pocketbook; handbag, purse

portanuevas *mf* bringer of news, newsmonger

portaobjetos *m*, stage (of a microscope)

portar *vt* to retrieve (of dogs); carry (arms); *vr* behave (well or badly); bear oneself, act; be well, or ill (in health)

portátil a portable

portavoz *m*, megaphone; spokesman, mouthpiece

portazgo *m*, toll; tollbooth

portazguero *m*, toll collector

portazo *m*, bang of the door; slamming the door in a person's face

porte *m*, transport; *com* carriage; postage; freight, transport cost; porterage; behavior, conduct; bearing, looks; capacity, volume; size, dimension; nobility (of descent); *naut* tonnage. **p. pagado,** charges prepaid

porteador *m*, carrier; porter; carter

portear *vt* to carry, transport; *vr* migrate (of birds)

portento *m*, marvel, prodigy, portent

portentoso a marvelous, portentous

porteño, -a a of Buenos Aires; native of Buenos Aires; resident of Buenos Aires

portería *f*, porter's lodge; porter's employment; *sport* goal

portero (-ra) *n* doorman, doorkeeper; porter; concierge; janitor; *sport* goalkeeper. **p. eléctrico,** door buzzer

portezuela *f*, *dim* small door; carriage door; pocket flap

pórtico *m*, portico, piazza; porch; vestibule, hall

portillo *m*, breach, opening; defile, narrow pass; *fig* loophole

portón *m*, hall door, inner door; *Chile* back door

portorriqueño (-ña) a and *n* Puerto Rican

portuario a dock, port

portugués (-esa) a and *n* Portuguese. *m*, Portuguese (language)

portuguesada *f*, exaggeration

porvenir *m*, future time

¡pórvida! *interj* By the saints! By the Almighty!

pos *prefix* after; behind. Also *adv* **en p.,** with the same meanings

posa *f*, tolling bell; *pl* buttocks

posada *f*, dwelling; inn, tavern; lodging; hospitality

posaderas *f pl*, buttocks

posadero (-ra) *n* innkeeper; boarding-house keeper

posar *vi* to lodge, live; rest; alight, perch; *vt* set down (a burden); *vr* settle (liquids); (*with en* or *sobre*) perch upon

posdata *f*, P.S., postscript

pose *f*, *phot* time exposure; *inf* pose

poseedor (-ra) *n* possessor, holder

poseer *vt irr* to own, possess; know (a language, etc.); *vr* restrain oneself. **estar poseído por,** to be possessed by (passion, etc.); be thoroughly convinced of. See **creer**

posesión *f*, ownership, occupancy; possession; property, territory (often *pl*)

posesionarse *vr* to take possession; lay hold (of)

posesor (-ra) *n* owner, possessor

posfecha *f*, postdate

posguerra f, postwar period

posibilidad f, possibility; probability; opportunity, means, chance; pl property, wealth

posibilitar vt to make possible, facilitate

posible a possible. m pl, property, personal wealth. **hacer lo p.** or **hacer todo lo p.**, to do everything possible; do one's best

posición f, placing; position; situation; status

positivo a positive; certain, definite; (math elec) plus; true, real

posma f, inf sluggishness, sloth

poso m, sediment; lees, dregs; repose, quietness

posponer vt irr (with prep a) to place after; make subordinate to; value less than. See **poner**

posta f, post horse; stage, ·post; stake (cards)

postal a postal. f, postcard, postal card

poste m, post, stake

postema f, tumor, abscess; bore, tedious person

postergación f, delay; delaying; relegation; disregard of seniority (in promotion)

postergar vt to delay; disregard a senior claim to promotion

posteridad f, descendants; posterity

posterior a back, rear; hind; subsequent

posteriormente adv later, subsequently

postigo m, secret door; grating, hatch; postern; shutter (of a window)

postizo a false, artificial, not natural. m, switch of false hair

postor m, bidder (at an auction)

postración f, prostration; exhaustion; depression, distress

postrar vt to cast down, demolish; prostrate, exhaust; vr kneel down; be prostrated or exhausted

postre a last (in order). m, cul dessert. **a la p.**, at last, finally

postrero a last (in order); rearmost, hindmost

postrimeramente adv lastly, finally

postulación f, entreaty, request

postulado m, assumption; supposition; working hypothesis; geom postulate

postulante (-ta) n ecc postulant, applicant, candidate

postular vt to postulate; Lat. Am. nominate

póstumo a posthumous

postura f, posture, bearing; laying (of an egg); bid (at an auction); position; agreement, pact; bet, stake; planting; transplanted tree. **p. de vida,** way of life

potable a drinkable. **agua p.,** drinking water

potaje m, stew, potage; dried vegetables; mixed drink; hotchpotch

potasa f, potash

potasio m, potassium

pote m, pot; jar; flowerpot; cul cauldron; cul stew

potencia f, power; potency; mech performance, capacity; strength, force; math power; rule, dominion

potencial a potential

potente a potent; powerful; inf enormous

potestad f, authority, power; podesta, Italian magistrate; potentate; math power; pl angelic powers

potestativo a law facultative

potingue m, inf brew; mixture; lotion; medicine; filthy place, pigsty

poto m, Lat. Am. calabash, gourd; backside

potra f, filly

potrear vt inf to tease, annoy

potro m, colt, foal; rack (for torture); vaulting horse. **p. mesteño,** mustang

pozo m, well; shaft (in a mine). aut **p. colector,** crankcase

pozole, m, Mexico stew of pork, corn, chile, etc.

práctica f, practice; custom, habit; method; exercise

practicabilidad f, feasibility

practicable a feasible, practicable

practicante m, medical practitioner; medical student; med intern; first-aid practitioner

practicar vt to execute, perform; practice; make

práctico a practical; experienced, expert; workable. m, naut pilot

pradera f, meadow, field; lawn

prado m, meadow; grassland; field; lawn; walk (in cities)

Praga Prague

pragmatista a pragmatic. mf pragmatist

pravedad f, wickedness, immorality, depravity

pravo a wicked, immoral, depraved

pre m, mil daily pay. prep insep pre-

preámbulo m, preamble, preface; importunate digression

precario a precarious, uncertain, insecure

precaución f, precaution, safeguard

precaucionarse vr to take precautions, safeguard oneself

precautelar vt to forewarn; take precautions

precaver vt to prevent, avoid; vr (with de or contra) guard against

precavido a cautious, forewarned

precedencia f, priority, precedence; superiority; preference, precedence

precedente a preceding. m, antecedent; precedent

preceder vt to precede; have precedence over, be superior to

preceptivo a a preceptive; didactic

precepto m, precept; order, injunction; rule, commandment. **de p.,** obligatory

preceptor (**-ra**) n teacher, instructor, tutor, preceptor

preciado a excellent, esteemed, precious; boastful

preciar vt to esteem, value; valuate, price; vr boast

precintar vt to seal; rope, string, tie up

precinto m, sealing; roping, tying up; strap

precio m, price, cost; recompense, reward; premium; rate; reputation, importance; esteem. **p. de tasa,** controlled price

preciosidad f, preciousness; exquisiteness, fineness; richness; wittiness; inf loveliness, beauty; thing of beauty

precioso a precious; exquisite, fine, rare; rich; witty; inf lovely, delicious, attractive

preciosuna f, Lat. Am. thing of beauty

precipicio m, precipice; heavy fall; ruin, disaster

precipitación f, precipitancy, haste; rashness; chem precipitation

precipitadamente adv precipitately, in haste; rashly, foolishly

precipitado a precipitate; rash, thoughtless. m, chem precipitate

precipitar vt to precipitate, hurl headlong; hasten; chem precipitate; vr hurl oneself headlong; hasten, rush

precipitoso a precipitous; rash, heedless

precisamente adv exactly, precisely, just; necessarily. **Y p. en aquel instante llegó,** And just at that moment he arrived

precisar vt to fix, arrange; set forth, draw up, state; compel, force, oblige

precisión f, accuracy, precision; necessity, conciseness, clarity; compulsion, obligation

preciso a necessary, unavoidable; concise, clear; precise, exact

precitado a aforementioned

preclaro a illustrious, distinguished, celebrated

precocidad f, precocity

precognición f, foreknowledge

precolombino, -a a pre-Columbian

preconcebido a preconceived

preconcepto m, preconceived idea, preconceived notion

preconizar vt to eulogize, praise publicly

preconocer vt irr to know beforehand; foresee. See **conocer**

precoz a precocious

precursor (**-ra**) a precursory; preceding, previous. n precursor

predecesor (**-ra**) n predecessor

predecir vt irr to foretell, prophesy. See **decir**

predestinación f, predestination

predestinado (**-da**) a predestined; fore-ordained. n one of the predestined

predestinar vt to predestine, foreordain

prédica f, inf (contemptuous) sermon

predicación f, preaching; homily, sermon

predicador (**-ra**) a preaching. n preacher

predicamento m, predicament; reputation

predicar vt to publish; manifest; preach; vi overpraise; inf lecture, scold. **p. en el desierto,** to preach to the wind

predicción f, prediction, prophecy

predilección f, predilection, preference, partiality

predilecto a favorite, preferred

predisponer vt irr to predispose. See **poner**

predisposición f, predisposition; tendency, prejudice

predominación f, predominance

predominante a predominant; prevailing

predominar vi and vt to predominate; prevail; tower above; overlook

predominio m, predominance, ascendancy, preponderance

preeminencia f, preeminence

preeminente a preeminent

preexistente a preexistent

preexistir vi to preexist, exist before

prefacio m, introduction, preface, prologue; ecc preface

prefecto m, prefect

preferencia f, preference; superiority. **de p.,** preferred, favorite; preferably

preferente a preferable; preferential; preferred (of stock)

preferible a preferable

preferir vt irr to prefer; excel, exceed. Pres. Part. **prefiriendo.** Pres. Ind. **prefiero, prefieres, prefiere, prefieren.** Preterite **prefirió, prefirieron.** Pres. Subjunc. **prefiera, prefieras, prefiera, prefieran.** Imperf. Subjunc. **prefiriese,** etc.

prefijo m, prefix

pregón m, public proclamation; marriage banns

pregonar vt to proclaim publicly; cry one's wares; publish abroad; eulogize, praise; proscribe, outlaw. **p. a los cuatro vientos,** to shout from the rooftops

preguerra f, prewar period

pregunta f, question; com inquiry; questionnaire, interrogation. inf **andar** (or **estar**) **a la cuarta p.,** to be very hard up, be on the rocks. **hacer una p.,** to ask a question

preguntador (-ra) a questioning; inquisitive. *n* questioner; inquisitive person

preguntar *vt* to question, ask; (*with por*) inquire for; *vr* ask oneself, wonder

prehistoria *f*, prehistory

prehistórico a prehistoric

prejuicio *m*, prejudice

prejuzgar *vt* to prejudge, judge hastily

prelación *f*, preference

preliminar a preliminary, prefatory. *m*, preliminary

preludiar *vi* and *vt mus* to play a prelude (to); *vt* prepare, initiate

preludio *m*, introduction, prologue; *mus* prelude; *mus* overture

prematuro a premature, untimely; unseasonable; immature, unripe

premeditar *vt* to premeditate, plan in advance

premiador (-ra) a rewarding. *n* rewarder

premiar *vt* to reward, requite

premio *m*, prize; reward; premium; *com* interest. **p. en metálico,** cash prize. *inf* **p. gordo,** first prize (in a lottery)

premioso a tight; troublesome, annoying; stern, strict; slow-moving; burdensome, hard; labored (of speech or style)

premisa *f*, premise; sign, indication

premonitorio a premonitory

premura *f*, urgency, haste

prenda *f*, pledge; token, sign; jewel; article of clothing; talent, gift; loved one; *pl* game of forfeits

prendar *vt* to pawn; charm, delight; *vr* (*with de*) take a liking to

prender *vt* to seize; arrest; capture, catch. *vi* take root (plants); catch fire; be infectious

prendería *f*, second-hand shop

prenombre *m*, given name, praenomen

prensa *f*, press; printing press; newspapers, the press. **dar a la p.,** to publish

prensado *m*, **prensadura** *f*, pressing; flattening; squeezing

preñado a pregnant; bulging, sagging (walls, etc.); swollen. *m*, pregnancy

preñez *f*, pregnancy; suspense

preocupación *f*, anxiety, preoccupation; prejudice

preocupar *vt* to preoccupy; make anxious; bias, prejudice; *vr* be anxious; be prejudiced

preordinar *vt ecc* to predestine

preparación *f*, preparation; treatment; compound, specific

preparado a ready, prepared. *m*, preparation, patent food, etc.

preparar *vt* to prepare; *vr* prepare oneself; qualify

preparativo a preparatory. *m*, preparation

preparatorio a preparatory

preponderancia *f*, preponderance

preponderante a preponderant; dominant

preponderar *vi* to preponderate; dominate; outweigh

preposición *f*, preposition

prepósito *m*, chairman, head, president; *ecc* provost

prerrogativa *f*, prerogative

presa *f*, hold, grasp; seizure, capture; booty; dam; lock (on rivers, canals); weir; ditch, trench; embankment; slice, bit. **hacer p.,** to seize; take advantage of (circumstances)

presagiar *vt* to prophesy, presage, bode

presagio *m*, presage, sign; presentiment, foreboding

présbita a long-sighted, farsighted

presbiteriano (-na) a and n Presbyterian

presciencia *f*, prescience, foresight

presciente a prescient, farsighted

prescindible a nonessential, able to be dispensed with

prescindir *vi* (*with de*) to pass over, omit; do without. **Prescindiendo de esto . . . ,** Leaving this aside. . . .

prescribir *vt* to prescribe, order

prescripción *f*, prescription

presencia *f*, presence, attendance; appearance, looks; ostentation. **p. de ánimo,** presence of mind

presenciar *vt* to be present at; witness, behold

presentación *f*, presentation; introduction; *Lat. Am. also* petition

presentar *vt* to show; present, make a gift of; introduce (persons); *vr* occur; present oneself; offer one's services

presente a present. *m*, gift; present time. *law* **Por estas presentes . . . ,** By these presents . . . . **tener p.,** to remember

presentimiento *m*, presentiment, apprehension

presentir *vt irr* to have a presentiment of. See **sentir**

preservación *f*, preservation, protection, saving

preservar *vt* to preserve, protect, save

preservativo a preservative. *m*, preservative, safeguard, protection

presidencia *f*, presidency; chairmanship; presidential seat or residence

presidencial a presidential

presidenta *f*, female president; president's wife; chairwoman

presidente *m*, president; chairman; head, director; presiding judge

presidiar *vt* to garrison

presidiario *m*, convict

presidio *m*, garrison; garrison town; fortress; penitentiary; imprisonment; *law* hard labor; assistance, protection

presidir *vt* to preside over; act as chairperson for; influence, determine

presión f, pressure

preso (-sa) n prisoner, captive; convict

prestador (-ra) a lending, loan. n lender

prestamista mf moneylender; pawnbroker

préstamo m, loan; lending. **casa de préstamos,** pawnshop

prestar vt to lend; assist; pay (attention); give; Lat. Am.' to borrow; vi be useful; give, expand; vr be suitable; lend itself; offer oneself. **tomar prestado,** to borrow

presteza f, speed; promptness, dispatch

prestidigitador (-ra) n juggler, conjurer

prestigio m, magic spell, sorcery; trick, illusion (of conjurers, etc.); influence, prestige

prestigioso a illusory; influential

presumido a conceited, vain; presumptuous

presumir vt to suppose, presume; vi be conceited

presunción f, supposition, presumption; vanity, presumptuousness

presuntuoso a presumptuous, vain

presuponer vt irr to presuppose, assume; budget, estimate. See **poner**

presuposición f, presupposition

presupuesto m, motive, reason; supposition, assumption; estimate; com tender; national budget

presuroso a swift, speedy

pretencioso a pretentious, vain

pretender vt to seek, solicit; claim; apply for; attempt, try; woo, court

pretendiente (-ta) n pretender; candidate; petitioner; suitor

pretensión f, pretension; claim; pl ambitions

pretérito a past. m, preterite

pretextar vt to allege as a pretext or excuse

pretexto m, pretext, excuse

prevalecer vi irr to prevail; be dominant; take root (plants). See **conocer**

prevaleciente a prevailing; prevalent

prevaricador (-ra) n prevaricator

prevaricar vi to prevaricate

prevención f, prevention; precaution; prejudice; police station; mil guard room; foresight, prevision; preparation. **de p.,** as a precaution

prevenido a prepared; cautious, forewarned

prevenir vt irr to prepare; prevent, avoid; warn; prejudice; occur, happen; fig overcome (obstacles); vr be ready; be forewarned. See **venir**

preventivo a preventive

prever vt irr to foresee, forecast, anticipate. See **ver**

previamente adv previously, in advance

previo a previous, advance.

previsión f, forecast; foresight, prevision; prescience. **p. social,** social insurance

previsor a farsighted, provident

prieto a almost black, blackish; tight; mean, avaricious; Lat. Am. dark-skinned, swarthy

prima f, ecc prime; com premium; female cousin

primacía f, supremacy, preeminence; primacy; primateship

primada f, inf act of sponging on, taking advantage of

primario a primary. m, professor who gives the first lecture of the day

primavera f, springtime; primrose; figured silk material; beautifully colored thing; youth; prime

primerizo (-za) n novice; beginner; apprentice; firstborn

primero a first; former; excellent, first-rate. adv first; in the first place. **primera enseñanza,** primary education. **primera materia,** raw material. **primer plano,** art foreground. **primera cura,** first aid. **de buenas a primeras,** all at once, suddenly

primicia f, first fruits; offering of first fruits; pl first effects

primitivo a original, early; primitive

primo (-ma) a first; excellent, fine. n cousin; inf simpleton; inf pigeon, dupe. **p. carnal,** first cousin. inf **hacer el p.,** to be a dupe. inf **ser prima hermana de,** to be the twin of (of things)

primogénito (-ta) a and n firstborn

primor m, exquisite care; beauty, loveliness; thing of beauty

primoroso a beautiful; exquisitely done; dexterous, skillful

princesa f, princess

principal a chief, principal; illustrious; fundamental, first. m, head, principal (of a firm); com capital, principal; first floor

principalmente adv principally, chiefly

príncipe m, leader; prince. **p. de Asturias,** prince of Asturias. **p. de la sangre,** prince of the blood royal

principiante (-ta) n beginner, novice; apprentice

principiar vt to begin, commence

principio m, beginning; principle; genesis, origin; rudiment; axiom; constituent. **al p.,** at first. **a principios,** at the beginning (of the month, year, etc.). **en p.,** in principle

pringar vt cul to soak in fat; stain with grease; inf wound; take part in a business deal; slander; vr inf appropriate, misuse (funds, etc.)

pringo m, Lat. Am. drop (of a liquid)

pringoso a greasy

pringue mf, animal fat, lard; grease spot

prioridad f, priority

prisa f, haste, speed; skirmish, foray. **a**

toda p., with all speed. **correr p.,** to be urgent. **dar p.,** to hasten, speed up. **darse** (*or* **estar de**) **p.,** to hurry

prisión *f,* prison, jail; seizure; captivity, imprisonment; *fig* bond; obstacle, shackle; *pl* fetters

prisonero (-ra) *n* prisoner; *fig* victim (of passion, etc.)

prisma *m,* prism

prismáticos *m pl,* field glasses

pristino *a* pristine

privación *f,* privation; lack, shortage; deprivation; degradation

privada *f,* toilet, privy, water closet

privadamente *adv* privately; individually, separately

privado *a* private; individual, personal. *m,* favorite; confidant

privar *vt* to deprive; dismiss (from office); interdict, forbid; *vi* prevail, be in favor; *vr* swoon; deprive oneself

privilegiar *vt* to privilege; bestow a favor on

privilegio *m,* privilege; prerogative; concession; copyright; patent

pro *mf* advantage, benefit. **el p. y el contra,** the pros and cons. **en p.,** in favor

proa *f,* prow, bow

probabilidad *f,* probability

probable *a* probable; likely; provable

probación *f,* proof, test; novitiate, probation

probado *a* tried, tested, proved

probar *vt irr* to prove; test; taste; try on (clothes); *vi* suit; (*with prep a +* infin) try to. **p. fortuna,** to try one's luck. *Pres. Ind.* **pruebo, pruebas, prueba, prueban.** *Pres. Subjunc.* **pruebe, pruebes, prueben**

probidad *f,* probity, trustworthiness, honesty

problema *m,* problem

problemático *a* problematical, uncertain

probo *a* honest, trustworthy

procaz *a* insolent, pert, brazen

procedencia *f,* origin, source; parentage, descent; port of sailing or call

procedente *a* arriving or coming from

proceder *vi* to proceed; behave; originate, arise; continue, go on; act. *law* **p. contra,** to proceed against (a person)

procedimiento *m,* proceeding, advancement; procedure; legal practice; process

proceloso *a* tempestuous

prócer *a* exalted, eminent; lofty. *m,* exalted personage

procesado (-da) *n* defendant

procesar *vt law* to proceed against, sue

procesión *f,* proceeding, emanating; procession; *inf* train, string. **andar** (*or* **ir**)

por dentro la p., to feel keenly without betraying one's emotion

proceso *m,* process; progress, advancement; lapse of time; lawsuit

proclamación *f,* proclamation; acclaim, applause

proclamar *vt* to proclaim; acclaim; publish abroad; reveal, show

proclividad *f,* proclivity, tendency

procreación *f,* procreation

procreador (-ra) *a* procreative. *n* procreator

procrear *vt* to procreate, beget, engender

procuración *f,* procurement; assiduity, care; *law* power of attorney; *law* attorneyship

procurador (-ra) *m,* proxy; *law* attorney; proctor. *n* procurer

procurar *vt* to try, attempt; procure, get; exercise the profession of a lawyer

prodigalidad *f,* prodigality, lavishness, waste, extravagance

prodigar *vt* to waste, squander; lavish, bestow freely; *vr* make oneself cheap

prodigio *m,* marvel, wonder; prodigy; monster; miracle

prodigioso *a* wonderful; prodigious; monstrous; miraculous

pródigo (-ga) *a* wasteful, extravagant; lavish, generous. *n* spendthrift, wastrel, prodigal

producción *f,* production; output, yield; generation (of heat, etc.); crop

producir *vt irr* to produce; generate; yield, give; cause, occasion; publish; *vr* explain oneself; arise, appear, be produced. **p. efecto,** to have effect; take effect. See **conducir**

productividad *f,* productivity

productivo *a* productive; fertile; profitable

producto *m,* produce; product; profit; yield, gain; *math* product. *chem* **p. derivado,** by-product

productor (-ra) *a* productive. *n* producer

proeza *f,* prowess, gallantry; skill; *Lat. Am.* boast

profanación *f,* profanation

profanar *vt* to profane

profano *a* profane; dissolute; pleasure-loving, worldly; immodest; lay, ignorant

profecía *f,* prophecy; *ecc* Book of the Prophets; opinion, view

proferir *vt irr* to utter, pronounce. See **herir**

profesar *vt* to exercise, practice (professions); *ecc* profess; believe in; teach

profesión *f,* profession; trade, occupation; avowal, admission

profesional *a* professional

profeso (-sa) *a ecc* professed. *n* professed monk

profesor (-ra) *n* teacher; professor

profesorado *m,* teaching staff; teaching profession; professorship; professorate

profeta *m,* prophet; seer

profetisa *f,* prophetess

profetizar *vt* to prophesy; imagine, suppose

proficiente *a* proficient

profiláctico *a* and *m,* prophylactic

prófugo ·(**-ga**) *a* and *n* fugitive from justice. *m, mil* one who evades military service

profundidad *f,* depth; profundity, obscurity; *geom* depth; concavity; intensity (of feeling); vastness (of knowledge, etc.)

profundizar *vt* to deepen; hollow out; *fig* go into deeply, fathom

profundo *a* deep; low; *fig* intense, acute; abstruse, profound; *fig* vast, extensive; high. *m,* depth, profundity; *poet* ocean, the deep; *poet* hell

profuso *a* profuse, abundant; extravagant, wasteful

progenie *f,* descendants

prognosis *f,* prognosis; forecast

programa *m,* program; edict, public notice; plan, scheme; *univ* calendar; syllabus; timetable

progresar *vt* and *vi* to make progress; progress, advance

progresión *f,* progression; advancement, progress

progresista *a pol* progressive. *mf* progressive

progresivo *a* progressive; advancing

progreso *m,* progress, advancement; growth; improvement, development

prohibición *f,* forbidding, prohibition

prohibir *vt* to forbid, prohibit. «**Prohibido el paso,**» ''No thoroughfare''

prohijamiento *m,* child adoption; fathering (of a bill, etc.)

prohijar *vt* to adopt (children, ideas); *fig* father

prohombre *m,* master of a guild; respected, wellliked man

prójimo *m,* fellow man, brother, neighbor.

prole *f,* progeny, young offspring

proletariado *m,* proletariat

proletario *a* poor; common, vulgar. *m,* plebeian; pauper; proletarian

prolífico *a* prolific; abundant, fertile

prolijo *a* verbose, prolix; fussy, fastidious; tedious, importunate; *Argentina* indefatigable, untiring

prologar *vt* to prologue; provide with a preface

prólogo *m,* preface; prologue; introduction

prolongación *f,* lengthening; prolongation, protraction; extension

prolongar *vt* to lengthen; *geom* produce; prolong, spin out

promediar *vt* to distribute or divide into two equal portions; average; *vi* arbitrate; place oneself between two people; reach half-time

promedio *m,* average; middle, center

promesa *f,* promise; augury, favorable sign

prometer *vt* to promise; attest, certify; *vi* promise well, look hopeful; *vr* devote oneself to service of God; anticipate confidently, expect; become engaged (marriage). *inf* **prometérselas muy felices,** to have high hopes

prometido (-da) *n* betrothed. *m,* promise

prominencia *f,* prominence, protuberance; eminence, hill

prominente *a* prominent, protuberant; eminent, elevated

promiscuar *vi* to eat meat and fish on fast days

promiscuo *a* indiscriminate, haphazard, promiscuous; ambiguous

promoción *f,* promotion; batch, class, year (of recruits, students, etc.)

promontorio *m,* headland; promontory; cumbersome object

promotor (-ra) *a* promotive. *n* promoter; supporter

promover *vt irr* to promote, further, advance; promote (a person). **p. un proceso (a),** to bring a suit (against). See **mover**

promulgación *f,* promulgation

promulgar *vt* to publish officially, proclaim; promulgate. *law* **p. sentencia,** to pass judgment

pronombre *m,* pronoun

pronosticar *vt* to prognosticate, forecast; presage

pronóstico *m,* omen, prediction; almanac; prognosis; sign, indication. **p. del tiempo,** weather forecast

prontitud *f,* quickness, promptness; quick-wittedness; *fig* sharpness, liveliness; celerity, dispatch

pronto *a* quick, speedy; prompt; ready, prepared. *m, inf* sudden decision. *adv* immediately; with all speed; soon. **de p.,** suddenly; without thinking. **por lo p.,** temporarily, provisionally

prontuario *m,* compendium, handbook; summary

pronunciación *f,* pronunciation

pronunciamiento *m,* military uprising; political manifesto; *law* pronouncement of sentence

pronunciar *vt* to pronounce, articulate; decide, determine; *law* pronounce judgment; give or make (a speech)

propagación *f,* propagation; dissemination; transmission

propaganda f, propaganda organization; propaganda

propagandista mf propagandist

propagar vt to reproduce; propagate, disseminate; vr reproduce, multiply; propagate, spread

propalar vt to disseminate, spread abroad

propasarse vr to go too far, forget oneself; overstep one's authority

propender vi to be inclined, have a leaning toward

propensión f, propensity, inclination; tendency

propenso a inclined, disposed; liable

propiciación f, propitiation

propiciar vt to propitiate, appease

propicio a propitious, auspicious; kind, favorable

propiedad f, estate, property; ownership; landed property; attribute, quality, property; art resemblance, naturalness

propietario (-ia) a proprietary. n proprietor, owner

propina f, gratuity, tip. inf **de p.,** in addition, extra

propinar vt to treat to a drink; administer (medicine); inf give (slaps, etc.)

propincuo a near, contiguous, adjacent

propio a own, one's own; typical, characteristic; individual, peculiar; suitable, apt; natural, real; same. m, messenger; pl public lands

proponente a proposing. m, proposer; com tenderer

proponer vt irr to propose, suggest; make a proposition; propose (for a post, office, etc.); math state; vr intend, purpose. **proponerse para un empleo,** to apply for a post. See **poner**

proporción f, proportion; chance, opportunity; size; math proportion

proporcionado a fit, suitable; proportionate; symmetrical

proporcionar vt to allot, proportion; supply, provide, give; adapt

proposición f, proposition; motion (in a debate)

propósito m, proposal; intention, aim; subject, question, matter. **a p.,** suitable, apropos; by the way, incidentally. **de p.,** with the intention, proposing. **fuera de p.,** irrelevant

propuesta f, proposal, tender

propugnar vt to defend, protect

propulsar vt to repulse, throw back; propel, drive

propulsión f, repulse; propulsion

prorrata f, quota, share, apportionment. **a p.,** in proportion

prorratear vt to apportion, distribute proportionately, prorate

prorrogación f, prorogation, adjournment; extension (of time); renewal (of a lease, etc.)

prorrogar vt to extend, prolong; defer, suspend, prorogue; renew (leases, etc.)

prorrumpir vt (with en) to burst out; utter, give vent to, burst into

prosa f, prose; prosaism, prosaic style; inf dull verbosity; monotony, tediousness; Lat. Am. pomposity

prosaico a prosaic; prosy; monotonous, tedious; matter-of-fact

prosapia f, family, lineage, descent

proscribir vt to proscribe, outlaw; forbid, prohibit. Past Part. **proscrito**

proscrito (-ta) n outlaw, exile

prosecución f, prosecution, performance; pursuit

proseguir vt irr to continue, proceed with. See **pedir**

prosélito m, convert, proselyte

prosista mf prose writer

prospecto m, prospectus

prosperar vt to prosper; protect; vi flourish, prosper

prosperidad f, prosperity; wealth; success

próspero a favorable, propitious, fortunate; prosperous

próstata f, prostate

prostitución f, prostitution

prostituir vt irr to prostitute; vr become a prostitute; sell oneself, debase oneself. See **huir**

prostituta f, prostitute

protagonista mf hero or heroine, principal character; leading figure, protagonist

protección f, protection, defense; favor, aid

protector a protective. m, protector; guard

protectorado m, protectorate

protectriz f, protectress

proteger vt to protect, defend; favor, assist

protegido (-da) n protégé

proteína f, protein

protervia f, depravity, perversity

protervo a depraved, perverse

protesta, protestación f, protest; protestation, declaration

protestante a and mf Protestant

protestantismo m, Protestantism

protestar vt to declare, attest; (with contra) protest against; (with de) affirm vigorously

protesto m, com protest; objection

protocolo m, protocol

prototipo m, model, prototype

protuberancia f, protuberance, projection, swelling

provecto a ancient, venerable; mature, experienced

provecho m, gain, benefit; profit; advantage; progress, proficiency. **¡Buen p.!** Enjoy your food! Enjoy your meal! **ser de p.,** to be advantageous or useful

provechoso a beneficial; profitable; advantageous; useful

proveer vt irr to provide; furnish; supply; confer (an honor or office); transact, arrange. **p. de,** to furnish or supply with; fit with. See **creer**

provenir vi irr (with de) to originate in, proceed from. See **venir**

proverbio m, proverb; omen; pl Book of Proverbs

providencia f, precaution, foresight; provision, furnishing; measure, preparation. **la Divina P.,** Providence

próvido a provident, thrifty, careful; kind, favorable

provincia f, province; fig sphere

provincial a provincial. m, ecc provincial

provinciano (-na) a provincial. n provincial, rustic, countryman; native of Biscay

provisión f, stock, store; provision; supply; food supply (gen. pl); catering; means, way

provisional a temporary, provisional

provisor m, purveyor, supplier; ecc vicar general

provisorio, -a a, Lat. Am. = **provisional**

provocador (-ra) a provocative. n provoker; instigator

provocar vt to provoke; incite; irritate; help, assist; inf vomit; Lat. Am. **¿te provoca ir al cine?** Would you like to go to the movies?

provocativo a provocative

próximamente adv proximately; soon; approximately

proximidad f, nearness, proximity (in time or space)

próximo a near, neighboring; next; not distant (of time)

proyección f, projection (all meanings)

proyectar vt to throw, cast; plan, contrive; design; project; vr jut out; be cast (a shadow, etc.)

proyectil m, projectile

proyecto a placed in perspective. m, project, plan, scheme; planning; intention, idea

proyector (-ra) n designer, planner. m, searchlight; spotlight; projector

prudencia f, prudence, sagacity, caution; moderation

prudencial a prudent, discreet; safe

prudente a prudent, cautious; provident

prueba f, proof; test; testing; trial; fitting (of garments); sample; taste; law evidence; (phot print) proof. law **p. de indicios** or **p. indiciaria,** circumstantial evidence. phot **p. negativa,** negative.

com a p., on approval; on trial; up to standard, perfect. **a p. de,** proof against (water, etc.). **poner a p.,** to put to the test, try out

prurito m, pruritus; desire, longing

ps- For words so beginning (e.g. psicología, psiquiatría), see spellings without **p**

púa f, prong; tooth (of a comb); quill (of a porcupine); agr graft; plectrum (for playing the mandolin, etc.); anxiety, grief; pine needle; inf crafty person

pubertad f, puberty

púbico a pubic

publicación f, publication; announcement, proclamation; revelation; publishing of marriage banns

publicador (-ra) a publishing. n publisher; announcer

publicar vt to publish; reveal; announce, proclaim; publish (marriage banns)

publicidad f, publicity; advertising, propaganda

publicista mf publicist; publicity agent

público a well-known, universal; common, general; public. m, public; audience; gathering, attendance. **dar al p.** or **sacar al p.,** to publish

puchero m, cul kind of stew; stew pot; inf daily food; puckering of the face preceding tears

pudicia f, modesty; bashfulness; chastity

púdico a modest; bashful; chaste

pudiente a rich, wealthy; powerful

pudín m, pudding

pudor m, modesty; bashfulness, shyness

pudoroso a modest; shy

pudrir vt to rot, putrefy; irritate, worry, provoke; vi rot in the grave; vr rot; be consumed with anxiety

puebla f, town; population; gardener's seed setting

pueblada f, Lat. Am. riot; rebellion, revolt, uprising

pueblo m, town; village, hamlet; people, population, inhabitants; common people; working classes; nation

puente mf bridge; mus bridge (of stringed instruments); naut bridge; carp crossbeam, transom. **p. colgante,** suspension bridge. **p. levadizo,** drawbridge. **hacer p. de plata (a),** to remove obstacles for, make plain sailing

puerco m, pig; wild boar. a filthy; rough, rude; low, mean. **p. espín** or **p. espino,** porcupine. **p. marino,** dolphin. **p. montés** or **p. salvaje,** wild boar

puericultura f, child care

pueril a childish, puerile; foolish, silly; trivial

puerilidad f, puerility; foolishness; triviality

puerro m, leek

puerta f, door; gate; goal (football, soccer, hockey); means, way. **p. batiente,** swinging door. **p. caediza,** trapdoor. **p. corrediza,** sliding door. **p. de servicio,** tradesman's entrance. **p. falsa** or **p. secreta,** secret door; side door. **p. trasera,** back door. **a p. cerrada,** in camera; in secret. *inf* **dar con la p. en las narices (de),** to slam the door in a person's face; offend, insult. **llamar a la p.,** to knock at the door; be on the verge of happening. **tomar la p.,** to depart, go away

puerto m, harbor; port; defile, narrow pass; refuge, haven. **p. franco,** free port. **tomar p.,** to put into port; take refuge

Puerto Rico m Puerto Rico

puertorriqueño, -a a and mf Puerto Rican

pues conjunc then; since, as; for, because; well. adv yes, certainly. conjunc **p. que,** since, as

puesta f, ast setting, sinking; stake (in gambling). **p. al día,** aggiornamento, updating; modernization. **p. de largo,** coming of age; coming-out party. **p. del sol,** sunset

puesto m, post, job; booth, stall; beat, pitch; place, position; state, condition; mil encampment, barracks; office, position. **p. de los testigos,** witness box. **p. de mando,** command, position of authority.

puesto a (with bien or mal) well-or badly dressed. conjunc **p. que,** since, as; although

pugilista mf boxer

pugna f, fight, struggle; rivalry, conflict

pugnante a hostile, conflicting, rival

pugnar vi to fight; quarrel; (with con, contra) struggle against, oppose; (with por, para) strive to

pugnaz a pugnacious

puja f, outbidding (at an auction); higher bid; push, thrust

pujador (-ra) n bidder or outbidder (at an auction)

pujante a strong, powerful, vigorous

pujanza f, strength, vigor

pujar vt to push on; bid or outbid (at an auction); vi to stutter; hesitate, falter; inf show signs of weeping

pujo m, irresistible impulse; desire; will; purpose, intention

pulcritud f, beauty, loveliness, delicacy; fastidiousness, subtlety

pulcro a beautiful, lovely; delicate, fine; fastidious, subtle

pulga f, flea; small top (toy). **el juego de la p.,** tiddlywinks. inf **tener malas pulgas,** to be irritable

pulgada f, inch

pulgar m, thumb

pulguiento a, Lat. Am. = **pulgoso**

pulidez f, elegance, fineness; polish, smoothness; neatness

pulido a elegant, fine; polished, smooth; neat

pulimentar vt to polish, burnish

pulir vt to polish, burnish; give the finishing touch to; beautify, decorate; fig polish up, civilize; vr beautify oneself; become polished and polite

pulmón m, lung

pulmonía f, pneumonia

pulpa f, fleshy part of fruit; anat pulp; wood pulp

pulpería f, WH grocery, grocery store, general store; bar, tavern

púlpito m, pulpit

pulpo m, octopus. inf **poner como un p.,** to beat to a pulp

pulposo a pulpy, pulpous

pulsación f, pulsation; throb, beat

pulsar vt to touch, feel; take the pulse of; fig explore (a possibility); vi beat (the heart, etc.)

pulsera f, bracelet; wrist bandage. **p. de pedida,** betrothal bracelet

pulso m, pulse; steadiness of hand; tact, diplomacy, circumspection. **a p.,** freehand (drawing). **tomar a p. (una cosa),** to try a thing's weight. **tomar el p. (a),** to take a person's pulse

pulular vi to pullulate, sprout; abound, be plentiful; swarm, teem; multiply (of insects)

pulverización f, pulverization; atomization

pulverizador m, atomizer, sprayer; scent spray

pulverizar vt to pulverize, grind, make into powder; atomize; spray

pulla f, lewd remark; strong hint; witty comment

pundonor m, (**punto de honor**) point of honor, sense of honor

pundonoroso a careful of one's honor; honorable, punctilious

pungir vt to prick, pierce; revive an old sorrow; fig wound, sting (passions)

punitivo a punitive, punitory

punta f, sharp end, point; butt (of a cigarette); end, point, tip; cape, headland; trace, touch, suspicion; nib (of a pen); pointing (pointer dogs); her point; pl point lace. **p. de París,** wire nail. **p. seca,** drypoint, engraving needle. **sacar p.,** to sharpen; inf twist (a remark)

puntada f, sew stitch; innuendo, hint

puntal m, naut draft, depth; stanchion, prop, brace, pile; fig basis, foundation; Lat. Am. bite (to eat), snack

puntapié m, kick

punteado m, plucking the strings of a guitar, etc.; sewing

puntear *vt* to make dots; *mus* pluck the strings of; play the güitar; sew; *art* stipple; *vi naut* tack

puntera *f.* mend in the toe of a stocking; toe cap; new piece on the toe of shoe; *inf* kick

puntería *f.* aiming (of a firearm); aim, sight (of a firearm); marksmanship

puntiagudo *a* pointed, sharp-pointed

puntilla *f.* narrow lace edging; headless nail, wire nail; brad, tack. **de puntillas,** on tiptoe

puntilloso *a* punctilious; overfastidious, fussy

punto *m.;* dot; point; pen nib; gun sight; *sew* stitch; dropped stitch, hole; weaving stitch, mesh; *gram* full stop, period; hole (in belts for adjustment); place, spot; point, mark; subject matter; *mech* cog; degree, extent; taxi stand; instant; infinitesimal amount; opportunity, chance; vacation, recess; aim, goal; point of honor. **p. de congelación,** freezing point. **p. de ebullición,** boiling point. **p. de fuga,** vanishing point. **p. de fusión,** melting point. **p. de partida,** starting point. **p. de vista,** point of view. **p. final,** *gram* period, full stop. **p. interrogante,** question mark. **p. menos,** a little less. **p. y coma,** semicolon. **p. cardinal,** cardinal point. **p. suspensivo,** *gram* ellipsis point, suspension point, leader, dot. **a p.,** in readiness; immediately. **en p.,** sharp, prompt (e.g. **a las seis en p.,** at six o'-clock sharp)

puntuación *f.* punctuation; *sport* score

puntual *a* punctual; punctilious; certain, indubitable; suitable, convenient

puntualidad *f.* punctuality; punctiliousness; certainty; exactitude, accuracy

puntualizar *vt* to describe in detail; give the finishing touch to, perfect; impress on the mind

puntuar *vt* to punctuate

puntudo *a,* *Lat. Am.* = **puntiagudo**

punzada *f.* prick, sting; puncture, piercing; sudden pain, twinge, stitch; *fig* anguish, pain

punzar *vt* to pierce, puncture; prick; punch, perforate; *vi* revive, make itself felt (pain or sorrow)

puñado *m.* handful; a few, some, a small quantity. **a puñados,** in handfuls; liberally, lavishly

puñal *m.* dagger

puñalada *f.* dagger thrust; stab, wound; *fig* unexpected blow (of fate). **p. por la espalda,** stab in the back

puñetazo *m.* blow with the fist

puño *m.* fist; handful; cuff (of a sleeve); wristband; handle, head, haft; hilt (of a sword); *pl inf* guts, courage. **p. de amura,** *naut* tack. **p. de un manillar,** handlebar grip. *inf* **meter en un p.,** tooverawe. *inf* **ser como un p.,** to be tightfisted; be small (in stature)

pupila *f.* female child ward; *anat* pupil; *inf* cleverness, talent

pupilaje *m.* pupilage, minority; boarding house, guesthouse; boarding school; price of board residence; dependence, bondage

pupilo (-la) *n* ward, minor; boarder; boarding school student; *Lat. Am.* prostitute, whore

pupitre *m.* desk, school desk

puquío *m Lat. Am.* spring (of water)

pureza *f.* purity; perfection, excellence; chastity; disinterestedness, genuineness; clearness

purga *f.* laxative, purge; waste product

purgación *f.* purging; menstruation; gonorrhea

purgante *a* purgative. *m,* purge, cathartic

purgar *vt* to cleanse, purify; expiate, atone for; (*med law*) purge; suffer purgatorial pains; clarify, refine; *vr* rid oneself, purge oneself

purgatorio *m.* purgatory. *a* purgatorial

puridad *f.* purity; secrecy, privacy. **en p.,** openly, without dissembling; secretly, in private

purificación *f.* purification; cleansing

purificar *vt* to purify; cleanse; *vr* be purified

puritano (-na) *a* puritanical. *n* Puritan

puro *a* pure; undiluted; unalloyed; unmixed; disinterested, honest; virgin; absolute, sheer; mere, simple. *m,* cigar. **de p.,** by sheer . . . , by dint of

púrpura *f.* purple; *poet* blood; purpura; *her* purpure; purple (cloth); dignity of an emperor, cardinal, consul

purpurear *vi* to look like purple; be tinged with purple

purpurina *f Lat. Am.* metallic paint

pus *m,* pus, matter

pusilánime *a* pusillanimous, timid, cowardly

pústula *f.* pustule

putativo *a* putative

puto, -a *mf* prostitute

putrefacto *a* rotten, decayed

pútrido *a* putrid, rotten

puyar *vt Lat. Am.* to jab, prick, stick; *fig* needle

putrefacción *f.* putrefaction; rottenness, putrescence

que *pron. rel* all genders sing. and pl. who; which; that; whom; when (e.g. **Un poema en que habla de su juventud,** A poem in which he speaks of his youth. **El libro que tengo aquí,** The book (that) I have here. **No es oro todo lo que reluce,** All that glitters is not gold. **Un día que nos vimos,** One day when we met. *interr* **¿qué?** what? *interj* what a ———! what! how! (e.g. **¿Qué hay?** What's the matter? **¡Qué día más hermoso!** What a lovely day! **¿qué de . . . ?** how many? **¿qué tal?** how? *inf* **¿Qué tal estás hoy?** How are you today? **¿qué tanto?** how much?) **¿a qué?** why? for what reason? (e.g. **¿A qué negarlo?** Why deny it?). *conjunc* that (e.g. **Me dijo que vendría,** He said (that) he would come). Means 'so that,' 'that,' 'for,' in commands (e.g. **Mandó que le trajesen el libro,** He ordered that they bring him the book (He ordered them to bring him the book)). Note that the translation of **que** is often omitted in English.

In compound tenses where the participle is placed first, **que** means 'when' (e.g. **llegado que hube,** when I had arrived). In comparisons, **que** means 'than' (e.g. **más joven que yo,** younger than I).

With subjunctives and expressing commands or wishes, **que** means 'let' (e.g. **¡Que venga!** Let him come!) Preceding a subjunctive, **que** is generally translated by 'to' (e.g. **Quiero, que venga or que llueva,** I want him to come or I want it to rain). Also means 'may' (e.g. **¡Que lo pase bien!** May you enjoy yourself! (I hope you . . .)). **es (era) que,** the fact is (was) that . . . **que . . . que,** whether . . . or . . .

quebrada *f,* mountain gorge, ravine; *com* bankruptcy; *Lat. Am.* brook, stream

quebradizo *a* brittle, fragile; ailing, infirm; delicate, frail

quebrado (-da) *m, math* fraction; *n com* bankrupt. *a* rough, uneven (ground); *med* ruptured; bankrupt; ailing, broken-down

quebradura *f,* snap, breaking; gap, crevice; hernia

quebrantamiento *m,* crushing; splitting, cleaving; fracture, rupture; profanation, desecration; burglary; violation, breaking, infringement; fatigue; *law* annulment; exhaustion

quebrantanueces *m,* nutcrackers

quebrantar *vt* to break, shatter; crush, pound, transgress, infringe; break out, force; tone down, soften; moderate, lessen; bore, exhaust; move to pity; *inf* break in (horses); profane; overcome (difficulties); assuage, placate; *law* revoke (wills); *vr* be shaken or bruised; suffer from aftereffects

quebranto *m,* breaking, shattering; crushing, pounding; infringement; breaking out (from prison); weakness, exhaus-

tion; compassion, pity; loss, damage; pain, suffering

quebrar *vt irr* to break, shatter; crush; impede, hinder; make pale (color, gen. of complexion); mitigate, moderate; bend, twist; overcome (difficulties); *vi* break off (a friendship); weaken, give way; go bankrupt; *vr med* suffer from hernia; be interrupted (of mountain ranges). **quebrarse los ojos,** to strain one's eyes. *Pres. Ind.* **quiebro, quiebras, quiebra, quiebran.** *Pres. Subjunc.* **quiebre, quiebres, quiebre, quiebren**

queda *f,* curfew; curfew bell

quedada *f,* stay, sojourn

quedar *vi* to stay, sojourn; remain; be left over; *(with por + infin.)* remain to be (e.g. **Queda por escribir,** It remains to be written); *(with por)* be won by or be knocked down to; be, remain in a place; end, cease; *(with en)* reach an agreement (e.g. **Quedamos en no ir,** We have decided not to go). **q. en esta alternativa . . . ,** to face this alternative: . . . *vr* remain; abate (wind); grow calm (sea); *(with con)* keep, retain possession of. **q. bien o mal,** to behave well or badly, come off well or badly (in business affairs, etc.). **quedarse muerto,** to be astounded

quedo *a* still, motionless; quiet, tranquil. *adv* in a low voice; quietly, noiselessly. **de q.,** slowly, gradually. *interj* **¡Q.!** Quiet!

quehacer *m,* odd job; task; business (gen. *pl*)

queja *f,* lamentation, grief; complaint, grudge; quarrel

quejarse *vr* to lament; complain, grumble; *law* lodge an accusation (against)

quejido *m,* complaint, moan

quejoso *a* querulous, complaining

quejumbre *f,* complaint, whine; querulousness

quelite *m, Central America, Mexico* vegetables

quema *f,* burn; burning; fire, conflagration

quemado *m,* burned patch of forest; *inf* anything burned or burning

quemador (-ra) *m,* jet, burner. *n* incendiary

quemadura *f,* burn; scald; burning

quemajoso *a* a smarting, burning, pricking

quemar *vt* to burn; dry up, parch; scorch; tan, bronze; scald; throw away, sell at a loss; *vi* burn, be excessively hot; *vr* be very hot; be dried up with the heat; burn with (passions); *inf* be near the attainment of a desired end. **quemarse las**

cejas, to burn the midnight oil, study too hard

quemazón f, burning; conflagration; intense heat; inf smarting; inf hurtful remark; inf vexation, soreness

quena f kind of Native American flute

querella f, complaint; quarrel, fight

querellarse vr to complain; lament, bemoan; law lodge an accusation; law contest a will

querelloso a complaining, grumbling, querulous

querencia f, love, affection; homing instinct; lair; natural inclination or desire

querer vt irr to desire, wish; want, will; attempt, endeavor; (with a) love. impers be on the point of. **q. decir,** to mean. **¿Qué quiere decir esto?** What does this mean? **sin q.,** unintentionally. See **entender**

querer m, affection, love

querido (-da) n lover; beloved; darling. a dear

querub, querube poet **querubín** m, cherub

quesadillas, fpl, Mexico maize dough with beans or cheese fried like a turnover

quesera f, dairymaid; dairy; cheese vat; cheese board; cheese dish

queso m, cheese. **q. de bola,** Dutch cheese. **q. rallado,** grated cheese

¡quia! interj inf You don't say so!

quianti inf, chianti

quicio m, threshold; hinge; mech bushing. **fuera de q.,** out of order; unhinged. **sacar de q.,** to displace (things); annoy, irritate; drive crazy

quiebra f, breach, crack; rut, fissure; loss; bankruptcy

quiebro m, twisting of the body, dodging; mus trill

quien rel pron mf pl **quienes.** interr **quién, quiénes** who; whom; he (she, etc.) who, anyone who, whoever; which; whichever (e.g. **mis padres a quienes respeto,** my parents whom I respect. **Quien te quiere te hará llorar,** Whoever (he, those, who) love(s) you will make you weep. **¿Quién está a la puerta?** Who is at the door? **¿De quién es?** Whose is it? To whom does it belong?). indef pron one (pl some)

quienquiera indef pron mf pl **quienesquiera,** whosoever, whichever, whomsoever

quietador (-ra) a tranquilizing, soothing. n soother

quieto a quiet, still; peaceful, tranquil; virtuous, respectable

quietud f, stillness, repose; peacefulness; rest, quietness

quijada f, jawbone, jaw; mech jaw

quijotada f, quixotic action, quixotism

quijote m, cuisse; thigh guard; quixotic person

quijotesco a quixotic

quilate m, carat; degree of excellence (gen. pl). inf **por quilates,** in small bits, parsimoniously

quillotrar vt inf to encourage, incite; woo, make love to; consider; vr inf fall in love; dress up; whine, complain

quillotro m, inf incentive; indication, sign; love affair; puzzle, knotty point; compliment; dressing up

quimera f, chimera; fancy, vision; quarrel, dispute

quimérico a chimerical, fanciful

química f, chemistry

químico a chemical. m, chemist. **productos químicos,** chemicals

quimono m, kimono

quina f, cinchona; quinine; pl Arms of Portugal. inf **tragar q.,** to suffer in patience, put up with

quinario m, Argentina mud hut

quincalla f, cheap jewelry; fancy goods

quincallería f, cheap jewelery shop; hardware factory or industry; cheap jewelry; fancy goods

quince a and m, fifteen; fifteenth

quinceañero f, sweet sixteen party, sweet sixteen (in Spanish-speaking areas, held at age fifteen)

quincena f, fortnight, two weeks; bimonthly pay; mus fifteenth

quincenal a fortnightly; lasting a fortnight, lasting two weeks

quinceno a fifteenth

quinientos a five hundred; five-hundredth. m, five hundred

quinina f, quinine

quinqué m, oil lamp, student's lamp, table lamp; perspicuity, talent

quinquenio m, period of five years, lustrum

quinta f, country house; mus fifth; conscripting men into army by drawing lots; mil draft

quintaesencia f, quintessence

quintar vt to draw one out of every five; draw lots for conscription into the army; vi reach the fifth (day, etc., gen. of the moon)

quintería f, farm

quintero m, farmer; farmworker

quinteto m, quintet

Quintín, San. armarse (or **haber) la de San Q.** to quarrel, make trouble; be a row

quinto a a fifth. m, one-fifth; mil conscript; duty of twenty percent; law fifth part of an estate. **quinta columna,** fifth column. **quinta esencia,** quintessence

quintuplicar vt to quintuplicate

quíntuplo a fivefold, quintuple

quiñón *m*, share of land owned jointly, share of the profits

quiosco *m*, kiosk, stand; pavilion, pagoda. **q. de música,** bandstand

quipo *m* quipu (Native American rope writing in Peru)

quiquiriquí *m*, cock-a-doodle-doo; *fig inf* cock of the walk

quiromancia *f*, chiromancy, palmistry

quiromántico (-ca) *n* chiromancer, palmist

quirúrgico *a* surgical

quirurgo *m*, surgeon

quisicosa *f*, *inf* riddle, puzzle, enigma

quisquilla *f*, trifle, quibble, scruple; prawn, shrimp

quisquilloso *a* quibbling, overscrupulous, fastidious; hypersensitive; irascible, touchy

quistarse *vr* to make oneself well-liked or loved

quiste *m*, *med* cyst

quita *f*, *law* discharge (of part of a debt)

quitaesmalte *m*, nail polish remover (for fingernails)

quitamanchas *mf*, dry cleaner, clothes cleaner

quitamotas *mf inf* flatterer, adulator

quitanieve *m*, snowplow

quitanza *f*, quittance; quietus

quitapesares *m*, *inf* consolation, solace, comfort

quitar *vt* to remove; take off or away; clear (the table); rob, steal; prevent, impede; parry (in fencing); separate; redeem (pledges); forbid; annul, repeal (laws, etc.); free from (obligations); *vr* shed, take off, remove; get rid of; leave, quit. **quitarse de encima (a),** to get rid of someone or something. **q. el polvo,** to dust. **de quita y pon,** detachable, removable; adjustable

quitasol *m*, parasol, sunshade

quitasueño *m*, *inf* sleep banisher, anxiety

quite *m*, hindering, impeding; obstruction; parry (in fencing). **estar al q.,** to be ready to protect someone

quizá, quizás *adv* perhaps. **q. y sin q.,** without doubt, certainly

R

rabadilla f, rump, croup

rábano m, radish. **r. picante,** horseradish

rabel m, mus rebec; inf backside, seat

rabera f, tail-end; chaff, siftings

rabí m, rabbi

rabia f, rabies, hydrophobia; anger, fury. inf **tener r. (a),** to hate

rabiar vi to suffer from hydrophobia; groan with pain; be furious; (with por) yearn for, desire. **a r.,** excessively

rabieta f, inf tantrum

rabínico a rabbinical

rabinismo m, rabbinism

rabino m, rabbi. **gran r.,** chief rabbi

rabioso a rabid; furious, angry; vehement. **perro r.,** mad dog

rabo m, tail; bot stalk; inf train (of a dress); shank (of a button). **r. del ojo,** corner of the eye. fig inf **ir r. entre piernas,** to have one's tail between one's legs

rabón a tailless, docked; bobtailed

rabonear vi, Lat. Am. to play hookey

rabudo a big-tailed

racimo m, bunch (of grapes or other fruits); cluster; raceme

raciocinar vi to reason

raciocinio m, reasoning; ratiocination; discourse, speech

ración f, ration; portion (in a restaurant); meal allowance; ecc prebendary. inf **r. de hambre,** starvation diet; pittance, starvation wages

racional a reasonable, logical; rational

racionalidad f, reasonableness; rationality

racionamiento m, rationing. f. **cartilla de r.,** ration book

racionar vt to ration

rada f, bay, cove; naut road, roadstead

radar m, radar

radiación f, radiation; rad broadcasting

radiactividad f, radioactivity

radiactivo a radioactive

radiador m, radiator (for heating); aut radiator

radiante a phys radiating; brilliant, shining; fig beaming (with satisfaction)

radiar vi phys to radiate; vt broadcast (by radio); Lat. Am. to cross off, delete, erase

radical a a radical; fundamental; pol radical. m, gram root; (math chem) radical. mf pol radical

radicar(se) vi and vr to take root. **r. una solicitud,** file an application, submit an application. vi be (in a place)

radio m, (geom anat) radius; radium. f, radio

radioaficionado (-da) n radio amateur; inf ham, wireless fan or enthusiast

radioaudición f, radio broadcast

radiocomunicación f, radio transmission

radiodifundir vt rad to broadcast

radiodifusión, radioemisión f, rad broadcast; broadcasting

radiodifusora f, Lat. Am. = **radioemisora**

radioemisora f, radio station; (radio) transmitter

radioescucha mf radio listener

radiofotografía f, radiophotography; x-ray photograph. **tomar una r. de,** to x-ray

radiografía f, radiography

radiografiar vt to x-ray, radiograph

radiología f, radiology

radiólogo mf radiologist

radiorreceptor m, receiver, wireless set

radioscopia f, radioscopy

radioyente mf radio listener

radioterapia f, radiotherapy, radiotherapeutics

radiotransmisor m, (radio) transmitter

raedera f, scraper

raedor a scraping; abrasive

raedura f, scraping; rubbing; fraying

raer vt irr to scrape; abrade; fray; fig extirpate. See **caer**

ráfaga f, gust or blast of wind; light cloud; flash (of light)

rafe m, eaves

rafia f, raffia

raicear vi, Lat. Am. to take root

raído a frayed, threadbare; brazen, barefaced

raíz f, root. **r. amarga,** horseradish. **r. cuadrada (cúbica),** square (cubed) root. **r. pivotante,** tap root. **r. fuerte,** Mexico horseradish **a r.,** close to the root, closely. **a r. de,** as a result of; after. **de r.,** from the root, entirely. **echar raíces,** to take root

raja f, split, crack; chip, splinter (of wood); slice (of fruit, etc.)

rajadura f, splitting; crack, split, crevice; geol break

rajar vt to crack, split; slice; vi inf boast; chatter; vr crack, split; inf take back one's words

ralea f, kind, quality; (inf scornful) race, lineage

ralear vi to grow thin (cloth, etc.); behave true to type (gen. in a bad sense)

rallador m, cul grater

rallar vt cul to grate; inf bother, annoy

rallo m, cul grater; rasp

ralo a sparse, thin

rama f, bough, branch; fig branch (of family). fig inf **andarse por las ramas,** to beat around the bush. **en r.,** com raw; unbound (of books)

ramaje *m*, thickness of branches, denseness of foliage

ramal *m*, strand (of rope); halter; branch line (of a railroad); fork (of a road, etc.); ramification, division

ramalazo *m*, blow with a rope; mark left by this; bruise

rambla *f*, bed, channel, course; avenue, boulevard (in Catalonia)

ramera *f*, whore

ramificación *f*, ramification; *anat* bifurcation

ramificarse *vr* to branch, fork; *fig* spread

ramillete *m*, bouquet; table centerpiece; *bot* cluster

ramo *m*, *bot* branch; twig; spray; bouquet, bunch; wreath; *fig* branch (of learning, etc.); *com* line (of business); *fig* touch, slight attack. **Domingo de Ramos**, Palm Sunday

ramoso a branchy, thick with branches

rampa *f*, gradient, incline; *mil* ramp; launching site

ramplón a stout, heavy (of shoes); coarse; vulgar; bombastic

rana *f*, frog. **r. de San Antonio**, tree frog

ranchero *m*, *mil* cook; small farmer; *WH* rancher

rancho *m*, mess, rations; settlement, camp; hut, cabin; *inf* group, huddle; *WH* ranch; *naut* gang. **hacer r.**, *inf* to make room

rancidez *f*, rancidness; staleness; rankness; antiquity

ranciedad *f*, rancidness; antiquity, oldness; mustiness

rancio a rancid, rank; mellow (of wine); ancient; traditional; musty

rancotán *adv*, *Lat. Am.* in cash

rango *m*, grade, class; range; (*mil nav* and social) rank; file, line

ranura *f*, groove; rabbet; slot, notch

rapacidad *f*, rapacity, avidity, greed

rapador a scraping. *m*, *inf* barber

rapapolvo *m*, *inf* severe scolding, dressing-down

rapar(se) *vt* and *vr* to shave; *vt* crop, cut close (hair); *inf* steal, pinch

rapaz a rapacious. *m*, young boy. **ave r.**, bird of prey

rapaza *f*, young girl

rape *m*, *inf* hasty shave or haircut. **al r.**, close-cropped

rapidez *f*, speed, swiftness, rapidity

rápido a quick, swift; express (trains). *m*, torrent, rapid; express train

rapiña *f*, robbery, plundering, sacking

rapiñar *vt* *inf* to steal, pinch

raposa *f*, vixen, fox; *inf* wily person

raposo *m*, (male) fox

rapsodia *f*, rhapsody

raptar *vt* to abduct; rob

rapto *m*, abduction, rape; snatching, seizing; ecstasy, trance; *med* loss of consciousness

raptor *m*, kidnapper, abductor

raqueta *f*, racket (tennis, badminton, squash rackets); croupier's rake. **r. de nieve**, snowshoe

raquítico a *med* rachitic; small, minute; weak, feeble; rickety

raquitismo *m*, rickets

rarefacer(se) *vt* and *vr* to rarefy. See **satisfacer**

rareza *f*, rareness, unusualness; eccentricity, whim; oddity, curio

raridad *f*, rarity; thinness; scarcity

raro a rare, unusual, uncommon; notable, outstanding; odd, eccentric, queer; rarefied (gases, etc.). **rara vez**, seldom. **lo r. de**, the strange thing about (e.g. **Lo r. del caso es . . .**, the strange thing about the case is . . .)

ras *m*, level. **a r.**, flush (with), nearly touching

rasa *f*, worn place in cloth; clearing, glade

rasar *vt* to level with a strickle; graze, brush, touch lightly; *vr* grow clear (of the sky, etc.)

rascacielos *m*, skyscraper

rascadura *f*, scraping; scratching

rascar *vt* to scratch; claw; scrape; twang (a guitar, etc.). *inf* **¡Que se rasque!** Let him put up with it! Let him lump it!

rascón a sour, tart

rasgado, -a a, *Lat. Am.* outspoken

rasgadura *f*, tearing; tear, rip, rent

rasgar(se) *vt* and *vr* to tear, rip; *vt* strum the guitar

rasgo *m*, flourish (of the pen); felicitous expression; characteristic, quality; *Lat. Am.* irrigation channel; *pl* features (of the face)

rasgón *m*, rip, tear

rasguear *vt* to strum, twang (the guitar); *vi* write with a flourish

rasgueo *m*, flourish (on a guitar); scratch (of a pen)

rasguñar *vt* to scratch, scrape; claw; *art* sketch

rasguño *m*, scratch; *art* sketch, outline

raso a flat; free of obstacles; glossy; clear (sky, etc.); plain; undistinguished; backless (chairs). *m*, satin. **al r.**, in the open air

raspa *f*, *bot* beard (of cereals); fishbone; bunch of grapes; *bot* husk; *carp* scraper

raspador *m*, eraser; scraper, rasp

raspadura *f*, scraping; erasing; shavings, filings; *Lat. Am.* brown sugar

raspar *vt* to scrape; erase; rob, steal; burn, bite (wine, etc.); *Lat. Am.* scold; to fail (student), fire (employee)

rastra *f*, trace, sign; sled; string of onions, etc.; anything dragging; *agr* harrow; *agr* rake. **a la r.**, dragging; reluctantly. **pescar a la r.**, to trawl

rastrear vt to trace, trail; drag, trawl; surmise, conjecture, investigate; vi agr rake; fly low

rastrero a dragging, trailing; low-flying; servile, abject; bot creeping. m, slaughterhouse employee

rastrillar vt to rake; dress, comb (flax)

rastrillo m, agr rake; hackle; portcullis; agr rack

rastro m, agr rake; track, trail; wholesale meat market; slaughterhouse; trace, vestige; second-hand market (in Madrid)

rasurar(se) vt and vr to shave

rata f, rat. m, inf pickpocket. **r. almizclera,** muskrat. inf **más pobre que las ratas,** poorer than a church mouse

ratear vt to rebate pro rata; apportion; thieve on a small scale, filch; vi crawl, creep

ratería f, filching, petty theft, picking pockets; meanness, parsimony

ratero (-ra) n pilferer, petty thief, pickpocket

ratificación f, ratification

ratificar vt to ratify

rato m, short interval of time, while. **buen (mal) r.,** pleasant (unpleasant) time. **r. perdido,** leisure moment. **a ratos,** sometimes, occasionally. **de r. en r.,** from time to time. **pasar el r.,** inf to while away the time

ratón (-ona) n mouse

ratonera f, mousetrap; mousehole; mouse nest; Lat. Am. hovel. fig **caer en la r.,** to fall into a trap

raudal m, torrent, cascade; fig flood, abundance

raudo a swift, rapid

ravioles m pl, ravioli

raya f, stripe, streak; limit, end; part (of the hair); boundary; gram dash; score (some games). m, icht ray. **pasar de r.,** to go too far; misbehave

rayadillo m, striped cotton

rayano a neighboring; border; almost identical, very similar

rayar vt to draw lines; streak; stripe; cross out; underline; rifle (a gun); vi verge (on), border (on); appear (of dawn, daylight); excel; be similar. **Raya en los catorce años,** He is about fourteen

rayo m, phys beam, ray; thunderbolt; flash of lightning; spoke; quick-witted person; capable, energetic person; sudden pain; disaster, catastrophe. **r. de sol,** sunbeam. **r. catódico,** cathode ray. **r. x,** x-ray. fig **echar rayos,** to breathe forth fury

rayón m, rayon

raza f, race; breed; lineage, family; kind, class; crack, crevice. **de r.,** purebred

razón f, reason; reasoning; word, expression; speech, argument; motive, cause; order, method; justice, equity; right, authority; explanation; math ratio, proportion. **r. de estado,** raison d'état, reasons of state. com **r. social,** firm, trade name. **a r. de,** at a rate of. **dar la r. (a),** to agree with. **estar puesto en r.,** to stand to reason. **tener r.,** to be in the right

razonable a reasonable; moderate

razonamiento m, reasoning

razonar vi to reason; speak; vt attest, confirm

razzia f, foray; pillaging, sacking; police raid

re m, mus re, D

reabsorción f, reabsorption

reacción f, reaction. **r. de Bayardo,** quick reaction of someone always ready to help those in distress

reaccionar vi to react

reaccionario (-ia) a and n reactionary

reacio a recalcitrant

reactivo m, reagent. a reactive; reacting

readmitir vt to readmit

reajustar vt to readjust

real a actual, real; kingly; royal; royalist; fig regal; inf fine, handsome. m, silver coin, real; m pl, encampment, camp. **alzar el r.,** mil to strike camp. **asentar el r.,** mil to encamp. **r. decreto,** royal decree. **sitio r.,** royal residence. **un r. sobre otro,** inf cash in full

realce m, raised or embossed work; renown, glory; art high light

realeza f, royalty, royal majesty

realidad f, reality; sincerity, truth. **en r.,** in fact, actually

realismo m, realism; regalism; royalism

realista a realistic; royalist. mf realist; royalist; regalist

realizable a realizable; practicable

realización f, realization; performance, execution

realizar vt to perform, execute, carry out; com realize. **r. beneficio,** to make a profit

realmente adv really, truly; actually

realzar vt to heighten, raise; emboss; exalt; enhance; art intensify (colors, etc.)

reanimar vt to reanimate; revive, restore, resuscitate; encourage

reanudación f, resumption, renewal

reanudar vt to resume, continue

reaparecer vi irr to reappear. See **conocer**

rearmar vi to rearm

reaseguro m, reinsurance, underwriting

reata f, string of horses or mules. **de r.,** in single file; inf blindly, unquestioningly; inf at once

rebaja f, diminution; com discount, rebate; remission

rebajar vt to lower; curtail, lessen; remit; com reduce in price; mech file; elec step down; humble, humiliate; vr cringe, humble oneself

rebanada f, slice, piece (of bread, etc.)

rebanar vt to cut into slices; split

rebaño m, flock, drove, herd; ecc flock

rebasar vt to exceed, go beyond; mil bypass

rebate m, altercation, dispute, quarrel

rebatir vt to repulse, repel; fight again; fight hard; oppose, resist; com deduct; refuse, reject

rebato m, alarm, tocsin; mil surprise attack; panic, dismay

rebeca f, cardigan, jersey

rebelarse vr to mutiny, rebel; oppose, resist

rebelde a mutinous, rebellious; wilful, disobedient; stubborn. mf rebel

rebeldía f, rebelliousness; willfulness; stubbornness; law nonappearance

rebelión f, insurrection, revolt

rebenque m, Lat. Am. whip

reblandecer vt irr to soften; vr become soft. See **conocer**

reblandecimiento m, softening; med flabbiness

reborde m, rim, edge; mech flange. **r. de acera,** curb

rebordear vt to flange

rebosar vi to overflow, run over; fig abound in; express one's feelings

rebotar vi to rebound; clinch (nails, etc.); refuse; vr change color; inf be vexed

rebote m, rebounding; rebound

rebozar vt to muffle up; coat with batter

rebozo m, muffling up, hiding the face; head shawl; pretense, excuse. fig **sin r.,** openly

rebueno a inf extremely good, fine

rebullir vi to stir, show signs of movement; fig swarm, seethe

rebusca f, close search; gleaning; remains

rebuscado a affected, unnatural (of style)

rebuznar vi to bray

recadero (-ra) n messenger, errand boy

recado m, message; greeting, note; gift, present; daily marketing; outfit, implements; precaution, safeguard

recaer vi irr to fall again; med relapse; lapse, backslide; devolve, fall upon. See **caer**

recaída f, falling again; med relapse; lapse

recalar vt to impregnate; naut call at (a port), come within sight of land

recalcada f, pressing down, squeezing; emphasis; naut list

recalcar vt to press down; squeeze; pack tight; stress, emphasize; vi naut list; vr inf say over and over, savor one's words

recalcitrante a obdurate, recalcitrant

recalentar vt irr to overheat; superheat; reheat. See **sentar**

recamado m, raised embroidery

recámara f, dressing room; explosives chamber; breech of a gun; inf caution

recamarera f, Mexico chambermaid

recambio m, spare, spare part; com reexchange

recapacitar vi to search one's memory; think over

recapitulación f, summary, résumé

recapitular vt to recapitulate, summarize

recargar vt to recharge; load again; reaccuse; overcharge; overdress or overdecorate; vr med become more feverish. **r. acumuladores,** to recharge batteries

recargo m, charge; new load; law new accusation; overcharge, extra cost; med temperature increase

recatado a prudent, discreet, circumspect; modest, shy

recatar vt to hide, conceal; vr be prudent or cautious

recato m, caution, prudence; modesty, shyness, reserve

recauchutar vt to retread (tires)

recaudación f, collecting; collection (of taxes, etc.); tax collector's office

recaudador m, tax collector

recaudar vt to collect, recover (taxes, debts, etc.); deposit, place in custody

recaudo m, collecting; collection (of taxes, etc.); precaution, safeguard; law surety; Lat. Am. daily supply of vegetables

recelar vt to suspect, fear, mistrust; vr (with de) be afraid or suspicious of

recelo m, suspicion, mistrust, doubt, fear

receloso a suspicious, distrustful, doubtful

recepción f, receiving, reception; admission, acceptance; reception, party; law cross-examination

receptáculo m, receptacle, container; fig refuge; bot receptacle

receptador (-ra) n receiver (of stolen goods); accomplice

receptor (-ra) a receiving. n recipient. m, elec receiver; wireless set. **r. de galena,** crystal set. **r. telefónico,** telephone receiver

receta f, med prescription; cul recipe

recetar vt med to prescribe; inf demand

rechapear vt to replate

rechazar vt to repulse; resist; refuse; oppose, deny (the truth of); contradict

rechazo m, recoil; rebound; refusal

rechinamiento, rechino m, squeaking, creaking; gnashing (of teeth)

rechinar vi to squeak, creak; gnash (teeth); chatter (teeth); do with a bad grace

rechoncho a squat, stocky, thickset

recibí m, com receipt

recibidor (-ra) a receiving. n recipient. m, reception room

recibimiento *m*, reception; welcome; greeting; reception room, waiting room; hall, vestibule

recibir *vt* to obtain, receive; support, bear; suffer, experience (attack, injury); approve; accept, receive; entertain; stand up to (attack); *vr (with de)* graduate as, take office as

recibo *m*, reception; *com* receipt; reception room, waiting room; hall, vestibule. *com* **acusar r.**, to acknowledge receipt

recidiva *f*, *med* relapse

recién *adv* recently, newly. Shortened form of **reciente** before a past participle (e.g. **r. llegado**, newly arrived)

reciente *a* recent; new; fresh

recinto *m*, precincts; neighborhood; premises, place

recio *a* strong; robust; bulky, thick; rough, uncouth; grievous, hard; severe (weather); impetuous, precipitate

recipiente *a* receiving. *m*, receptacle, container, vessel

reciprocar *vt* to reciprocate

recíproco *a* reciprocal

recitación *f*, recitation

recitar *vt* to recite, declaim

reclamación *f*, reclamation; objection, opposition; *com* claim

reclamar *vi* to oppose, object to; *poet* resound; *vt* call repeatedly; *com* claim; decoy (birds)

reclamo *m*, decoy bird; enticement, allurement; *law* reclamation; advertisement. **objeto de r.**, advertising sample. **venta de r.**, bargain sale

recluir *vt irr* to immure, shut up; detain, arrest. See **huir**

reclusión *f*, confinement, seclusion; prison

recluso (-sa) *n* recluse

recluta *f*, recruiting. *mf mil* recruit

reclutamiento *m*, recruiting

reclutar *vt* to enlist recruits, recruit; *Argentina* round up

recobrar *vt* to recover, regain; *vr* recuperate; regain consciousness

recobro *m*, recovery; *mech* pick-up

recocer *vt irr* to reboil; recook; overboil; overcook; anneal (metals); *vr fig* be tormented (by emotion), be all burned up. See **cocer**

recodo *m*, bend, turn, loop

recogedor *a* sheltering. *m*, *agr* gleaner

recoger *vt* to gather, pick; pick up; retake; collect (letters from a mailbox, etc.); amass; shrink, narrow; keep; hoard; shelter; reap, pick; *vr* withdraw, retire; go home; go to bed; retrench, economize; give oneself to meditation

recogida *f*, collection (of letters from a mailbox); withdrawal; retirement; harvest

recogido *a* recluse; cloistered, confined

recogimiento *m*, gathering, picking; collection, accumulation; seclusion; shelter; women's reformatory

recolección *f*, summary, résumé; harvest; collection (of taxes, etc.); *ecc* convent of a reformed order; mystic ecstasy

recomendación *f*, recommendation (all meanings)

recomendar *vt irr* to recommend (all meanings); entrust, commend. *Pres. Ind.* **recomiendo, recomiendas, recomienda, recomiendan.** *Pres. Subjunc.* **recomiende, recomiendes, recomiende, recomienden**

recompensa *f*, compensation; recompense, reward

recompensar *vt* to compensate; requite; reward, recompense

recomposición *f*, recomposition

recomprar *vt* to repurchase

reconcentrar *vt* to concentrate; dissemble; *vr* withdraw into oneself, meditate

reconciliable *a* reconcilable

reconciliación *f*, reconciliation

reconciliar *vt* to reconcile; *ecc* reconsecrate; *ecc* hear a short confession; *vr* become reconciled; *ecc* make an additional confession

recondicionar *vt* to rebuild, overhaul, recondition

recóndito *a* recondite

reconocer *vt irr* to examine, inspect; recognize; admit, acknowledge; own, confess; search; *pol* recognize; *mil* reconnoiter; *(with por)* adopt as (a son, etc.); recognize as; *vr* be seen, show; acknowledge, confess; know oneself. **Bien se reconoce que no está aquí,** It's easy to see he's not here. See **conocer**

reconocido *a* grateful

reconocimiento *m*, examination, inspection; recognition; acknowledgement, admission; search; *mil* reconnoitering; adoption; gratitude

reconstruir *vt irr* to reconstruct, rebuild; recreate. See **huir**

reconvención *f*, rebuke, reproof; recrimination; *law* countercharge

recopilación *f*, summary, compendium; collection (of writings); digest (of laws)

recopilar *vt* to compile, collect

recordar *vt irr* to cause to remember, remind; remember; *vi* remember; awake. See **acordar**

recordatorio *m*, reminder. *a* commemorative (e.g. a plaque)

recorrer *vt* to travel over; pass through; wander around; examine, inspect; read hastily; overhaul, renovate

recorrido *m*, journey, run; *mech* stroke; overhaul. **r. de despegue,** *aer* take-off run

recortar *vt* to clip, trim, pare; cut out; *art* outline; *vr* stand out (against), be outlined (against)

recorte *m*, clipping, paring; cutting; cut-out; *art* outline; *pl* snippets, clippings. **r. de periódico,** newspaper cutting, newspaper clipping

recostar *vt irr* (*with en or contra*) to lean, rest against; *vr* (*with en or contra*) lean against, rest on; lean back; recline. See **contar**

recreación *f,* recreation, hobby

recrear *vt* to entertain, amuse; *vr* amuse oneself; delight (in), enjoy

recreo *m,* recreation, hobby; playtime, recess (in schools); place of amusement. **salón de r.,** recreation room

recriminador a recriminatory

recriminar *vt* to recriminate

recrudecer(se) *vi* and *vr irr* to recur, return. See **conocer**

rectángulo *m,* rectangle. a rectangular

rectificable a rectifiable

rectificación *f,* rectification; *mech* grinding

rectificar *vt* to rectify; *mech* grind; *vr* mend one's ways; *mil* **r. el frente,** to straighten the line

rectitud *f,* straightness; rectitude, integrity; exactness; righteousness

recto a straight; upright; erect; literal (meaning); just, fair; single-breasted (of coats); *m,* right angle; rectum

rector (**-ra**) *n* director; principal, headmaster. *m, ecc* rector

rectorado *m,* principalship, headmaster- (mistress-) ship, directorship; *ecc* rectorship

recua *f,* drove of beasts of burden; *inf* string or line (of things)

recubrir *vt* to re-cover; coat; plate. *Past Part.* **recubierto**

recuento *m,* calculation; recount; inventory

recuerdo *m,* memory, remembrance; memento; *pl* greetings, regards

recular *vi* to recoil, draw back; *inf* go back on, give up

recuperable a recoverable, recuperable

recuperación *f,* recovery, recuperation; *chem* recovery

recurrir *vi* to recur; (*with prep a*) have recourse to; appeal to

recurso *m,* recourse, resort; choice, option; reversion; petition; *law* appeal; *pl* means of livelihood; *fig* way out, last hope

recusar *vt* to refuse; challenge the authority (of)

red *f,* net; network; hairnet; railing, grating; *fig* snare; system (of communications, etc.); *fig* combination (of events, etc.); *elec* mains. **r. de arrastre,** trawl net. *fig inf* **caer en la r.,** to fall into the trap

redacción *f,* phrasing; editorial office; editing; editorial board

redactar *vt* to write, phrase; draw up; edit

redactor (**-ra**) a editorial. *n* editor

redención *f,* redemption; ransom; deliverance, salvation; redeeming, paying off (a mortgage, etc.)

redentor (**-ra**) a redeeming, redemptive. *n* redeemer

redil *m,* sheepfold

redimible a redeemable

redimir *vt* to ransom; redeem, buy back; pay off (a mortgage, etc.); deliver, free; *ecc* redeem

rédito *m, com* income, revenue, interest, profit

redoblamiento *m,* redoubling; bending back (of nails, etc.); rolling (of a drum)

redoblar *vt* to redouble; repeat; bend back (nails, etc.); *vi* roll (a drum)

redoble *m,* doubling; redoubling; repetition; roll (of a drum)

redonda *f,* district; pasture ground; *naut* square sail; *mus* semibreve. **a la r.,** around

redondear *vt* to make round; round; free (from debt, etc.); *vr* acquire a fortune; clear oneself (of debts, etc.)

redondel *m,* traffic circle, rotary, roundabout

redondo a round; circular; unequivocal, plain. *m,* round, circle; *inf* cash

reducción *f,* reduction; *mil* defeat, conquest; decrease; *com* rebate; (*math chem*) reduction

reducir *vt irr* to reduce; decrease, cut down; break up; *art* scale down; *elec* step down; subdue; (*chem math surg*) reduce; exchange; divide into small fragments; persuade; *vr* be obliged to, have to; live moderately. See **conducir**

redundancia *f,* redundance

redundante a redundant

redundar *vi* to overflow; be excessive or superfluous; (*with en*) redound to

reduplicar *vt* to reduplicate

ree For words so beginning (e.g. *reeditar, reexportar*), see spellings with one **e**

refacción *f,* refection, light meal; compensation, reparation

refaccionar *vt, Lat. Am.* to fix, repair

refajo *m,* skirt, underskirt; *Colombia* mild drink consisting of champagne, soda and beer

refección *f,* refection, light meal

refectorio *m,* refectory

referencia *f,* report, account; allusion; regard, relation; *com* reference (gen. *pl*); consideration

referente a concerning, related (to)

referir *vt irr* to narrate; describe; direct, guide; relate, refer, concern; *vr* allude (to); refer (to); concern. See **sentir**

refinación *f,* refining

refinado a refined; polished, cultured; crafty

refinamiento *m,* refinement, subtlety, care

refinar vt to refine, purify; polish, perfect

refinería f, refinery

reflector a reflecting. m, reflector; searchlight; shade (for lamps, etc.)

reflejar vi phys to reflect; vt consider; show, mirror; vr fig be reflected, be seen

reflejo m, reflection; image; glare. a reflex; considered, judicious

reflexión f, phys reflection; consideration, thought

reflexionar vt (with en or sobre) to consider, reflect upon

reflexivo a phys reflective; thoughtful

reflorecer vi irr to flower again; return to favor (ideas, etc.). See **conocer**

reflujo m, reflux, refluence; ebb tide

refocilar vt to warm up, brace up; give pleasure to; vr enjoy oneself

reforma f, reform; improvement; reformation; hist Reformation

reformación f, reform, improvement

reformador (**-ra**) a reformatory, reforming. n reformer

reformar vt to remake; reshape; repair, mend, restore; improve, correct; ecc reform; reorganize; vr mend one's ways, improve; control oneself

reformatorio m, reformatory. a reforming, reformatory

reformista mf reformist, reformer. a reformatory

reforzador m, phot reinforcing bath; elec booster

reforzamiento m, stiffening, reinforcing

reforzar vt irr to reinforce, strengthen, stiffen; encourage, inspirit. See **forzar**

refractar vt to refract

refractario a stubborn; (phys chem) refractory; unmanageable, unruly; fireproof

refrán m, proverb

refranero m, collection of proverbs

refregar vt irr to rub; scrub, scour; fig inf rub in, insist on. See **cegar**

refrenar vt to curb, check (horses); control, restrain

refrendar vt to countersign, endorse, legalize

refrescante a refreshing, cooling

refrescar vt to cool, chill; repeat; fig brush up, revise; vi be rested or refreshed; grow cooler; take the air; freshen (wind); take a cool drink; vr grow cooler; take the air; take a cool drink

refresco m, refreshment; cool drink; Lat. Am. soft drink, soda, pop

refresquería f, Lat. Am. refreshment stand

refriega f, affray, scuffle, rough-and-tumble

refrigeración f, refrigeration

refrigerador m, refrigerator

refrigerante a refrigerative; chilling; cooling. m, cooling chamber, cooler

refrigerar vt to chill; cool; freeze, refrigerate; refresh

refrigerio m, coolness; consolation; refreshment, food

refuerzo m, reinforcement, strengthening; aid, help

refugiado (**-da**) a and n refugee

refugiar vt to protect, shelter; vr take refuge

refugio m, refuge, shelter, protection; traffic island. **r. antiaéreo,** air raid shelter. **r. para peatones,** traffic island

refulgencia f, resplendence, splendor, brilliance

refulgente a resplendent, refulgent, dazzling

refulgir vi to shine, be dazzling

refundición f, recasting (of metals); adaptation; rehash, refurbishing

refundir vt to recast (metals); include, comprise; adapt; rehash, refurbish; vi fig promote, contribute to

refunfuñador a grumbling, fuming

refunfuñar vi to grumble, growl, fume

refunfuño m, grumble, fuming; snort

refutar vt to refute

regadera f, watering can; irrigation canal; sprinkler; Lat. Am. shower bath, shower

regadío m, irrigated land; irrigation, watering. a irrigated

regajal, regajo m, pool, puddle; stream, brook

regalado a delicate, highly bred; luxurious, delightful

regalar vt to make a gift of, give; caress, fondle; indulge, cherish; entertain, regale; vr live in luxury

regalía f, royal privilege; right, exemption; perquisite, emolument

regaliz m, **regaliza** f, licorice

regalo m, gift, present; satisfaction, pleasure; entertainment, regalement; luxury, comfort

regalón a inf pampered

regalonear vt, Lat. Am. to pamper, spoil

regañadientes, a adv unwillingly, grumblingly

regañar vi to snarl (dogs); crack (skin of fruits); grumble, mutter; inf quarrel; vt inf scold

regaño m, angry look or gesture; inf scolding

regañón (**-ona**) a inf grumbling, complaining; scolding. n inf grumbler

regar vt irr to water, sprinkle with water; flow through, irrigate; spray; fig shower (with), strew. See **cegar**

regata f, regatta; small irrigation channel (for gardens, etc.)

regate m, twist of the body, sidestep; dribbling; (in soccer); inf dodging, evasion

regatear vt to haggle over, beat down

(prices); resell, retail; dribble (a ball); *fig inf* dodge, avoid; *vi* bargain, haggle; *naut* take part in a regatta, race

regateo *m*, haggling, bargaining

regatero (**-ra**) a retail. *n* retailer

regatón (**-ona**) *m*, ferrule, tip. a . haggling, bargaining. *n* haggler; retailer

regatonear *vt* to resell at retail

regazo *m*, lap, knees; *flg* heart, bosom

regenerador (**-ra**) *n* regenerator. a regenerative, reforming

regenerar *vt* to regenerate, reform

regenta *f*, wife of the president of a court of session

regentar *vt* to fill temporarily (offices); rule, govern; manage, run (businesses)

regente a ruling. *mf* regent. *m*, president of a court of session; manager

regidor a ruling, governing. *m*, magistrate, alderman

régimen *m*, administration, management; regime; (*med gram*) regimen; *mech* rating

regimentación *f*, regimentation

regimentar *vt irr* to form into regiments; regiment. *Pres. Ind.* **regimiento, regimientas, regimienta, regimientan. Pres. Subjunc. regimiente, regimientes, regimiente, regimienten**

regimiento *m*, *mil* regiment; administration, rule; *Lat. Am.* crowd (of people)

regio a royal; magnificent, regal. **iregio! great!, wonderful!**

región *f*, region, country; area, tract, space. **r. industrial,** industrial area

regir *vt irr* to govern, rule; administer; conduct; *gram* govern; *vi* be in force (laws, etc.); work, function; *naut* obey the helm. See **pedir**

registrador a recording. *m*, registrar, keeper of records; recorder. **caja (registradora),** (cash) register

registrar *vt* to examine, inspect; search; copy, record; mark the place (in a book); observe, note; (of thermometers, etc.) record, show; look on to (houses, etc.); *vr* register (hotels, etc.)

registro *m*, search; registration, entry; record; recording; reading (of a thermometer, etc.); *mech* damper; registry; register (book); *mus* range, compass (voice); *mus* register (organ); (*mech print*) register; bookmark. **r. civil,** register of births, marriages, and deaths

regla *f*, ruler, measuring stick; rule, principle, guide, precept; system, policy; *med* period; moderation; method, order. **r. de cálculo,** slide rule. **r. T,** T-square. **en r.,** in due form. **por r.,** general, generally, as a rule

reglamentación *f*, regulation; rules and regulations

reglamento *m*, bylaw; regulation, ordinance

reglar *vt* to rule (lines); regulate; govern;

control; *vr* restrain oneself, mend one's ways

regocijar *vt* to cheer, delight; *vr* enjoy oneself, rejoice

regocijo *m*, happiness, joy; cheer, merriment

regordete a *inf* chubby

regresar *vi* to return

regresión *f*, return; retrogression; regression

regreso *m*, return

reguera *f*, irrigation channel, ditch

regulación *f*, regulation; *mech* control, timing

regulador *m*, *mech* governor, regulator. a regulating, controlling

regular *vt* to adjust, regulate; *mech* govern. a methodical, ordered; moderate; average, medium; (*ecc mil geom gram*) regular; so-so, not bad; probable. **por lo r.,** generally

regularidad *f*, regularity

regularizar *vt* to regularize; regulate

regurgitar *vi* to regurgitate

rehabilitación *f*, rehabilitation

rehabilitar *vt* to rehabilitate; *vr* rehabilitate oneself

rehacer *vt irr* to remake; repair, mend; *vr* recover one's strength; control one's emotions; *mil* rally. See **hacer**

rehén *m*, hostage (gen. *pl*); *mil* pledge, security

rehenchir *vt irr* to restuff; refill, recharge. See **henchir**

reherir *vt irr* to repulse. See **herir**

rehilar *vt* to spin too much or twist the yarn; *vi* totter, stagger; whizz (arrows, etc.). See **prohibir**

reimponer *vt irr* to reimpose. See **poner**

reimpresión *f*, reprint

reimprimir *vt* to reprint

reina *f*, queen; queen (in chess); queen bee; peerless beauty, belle

reinado *m*, reign; heyday, fashion

reinante a reigning; prevalent

reinar *vi* to reign; influence; endure, prevail

reincidencia *f*, relapse (into crime, etc.), recidivism

reincidente *mf* backslider

reincidir *vi* to relapse (into crime, etc.)

reincorporar *vt* to reincorporate; *vr* join again, become a member again

reino *m*, kingdom

reinstalación *f*, reinstatement

reinstalar *vt* to reinstate; *vr* be reinstalled

reintegrar *vt* to reintegrate; *vr* be reinstated, recuperate, recover

reir *vi irr* to laugh; sneer, jeer; *flg* smile (nature); *vt* laugh at; *vr inf* (*with de*) scorn. **reírse a carcajadas,** to shout with laughter. *Pres. Part.* **riendo.** *Pres. Ind.*

río, ríes, ríe, ríen. *Preterite* **rió, rieron.** *Pres. Subjunc.* **ría,** etc. *Imperf. Subjunc.* **riese,** etc.

reiteración f, reiteration, repetition

reiteradamente adv repeatedly, reiteratively

reiterar vt to reiterate, repeat

reivindicar vt law to recover

reja f, colter, plowshare; plowing, tilling; grating, grille; Lat. Am. jail, prison

rejado m, railing, grating

rejilla f, grating; grille, lattice; luggage rack (in a train); cane (for chairs, seats, etc.); wire mesh; small brazier; elec grid; mech grate

rejo m, Lat. Am. whip

rejuntar vt to point (a wall)

rejuvenecer vt irr to rejuvenate; fig revive; bring up to date; vi and vr be rejuvenated, grow young again, rejuvenesce. See **conocer**

relación f, relation; connection (of ideas); report, statement; narrative, account; math ratio; law brief; intercourse, association, dealings (gen. pl); list; analogy, relation. **tener relaciones con,** to have dealings with; be engaged or betrothed to; woo, court

relacionar vt to recount, narrate, report; connect, relate; vr be connected

relajación f, relaxation; recreation; laxity, dissoluteness

relajar vt to relax; recreate, amuse; make less rigorous; law remit; vr become relaxed; be dissolute, lax, or vicious

relamer vt to lick again; vr lick one's lips; fig overpaint, make up too much; ooze satisfaction, brag

relamido a overdressed; affected

relámpago m, lightning; flash, gleam; streak of lightning (of quick persons or things); flash of wit, witticism

relampaguear vi to lighten (of lightning); flash, gleam

relapso a relapsed, lapsed (into error, vice)

relativo a relevant, pertinent; relative, comparative; gram relative

relato m, narration, account, report

relator (-ra) a narrating. n narrator. m, law reporter

relección f, reelection

releer vt irr to reread; revise. See **creer**

relegar vt to banish; relegate, set aside

relegir vt irr to reelect. See **elegir**

relente m, night dew, dampness; inf cheek, impudence

relevación f, art relief; release; remission, exemption

relevar vt art to work in relief; emboss; relieve, free; dismiss; excuse, pardon; aid, succor; fig aggrandize; mil relieve; vi carve in relief

relevo m, relay; mil relief

relieve m, art relief; pl leftovers, remains (of food). **alto r.,** high relief. **bajo r.,** low relief

religar vt to retie, fasten again; fasten more securely; solder

religión f, religion; creed, faith, philosophy; devotion, religious practice. **r. reformada,** Protestantism. **entrar en r.,** ecc to profess

religiosidad f, religiosity; religiousness; conscientiousness, punctiliousness

religioso (-sa) a religious; punctilious, conscientious; moderate. n religious

relinchar vi to whinny, neigh

reliquia f, residue (gen. pl); ecc relic; vestige, remnant, memento; permanent disability or ailment

rellanar vt to make level again; vr stretch oneself at full length

rellano m, landing (of a staircase); level stretch (of ground)

rellenar vt to refill, replenish; fill up; mas plug, point; cul stuff; inf cram with food (gen. vr)

relleno m, cul stuffing; replenishing; filling; fig padding (of speeches, etc.)

reloj m, clock; watch. **r. de arena,** hourglass. **r. de bolsillo,** watch. **r. de la muerte,** deathwatch beetle. **r. de péndulo,** grandfather clock. **r. de pulsera,** wristwatch. **r. de repetición,** repeater. **r. de sol** or **r. solar,** sundial

relojería f, watch or clock making; jeweler, watch maker's shop

relojero (-ra) n watch maker, watch repairer

reluciente a shining, sparkling; shiny

relucir vi irr to glitter, sparkle, gleam; fig shine, excel. See **lucir**

relumbrar vi to be resplendent, shine, glitter

remache m, riveting; rivet

remaduro, -a a, Lat. Am. overripe

remanso m, backwater; stagnant water; sloth, dilatoriness

remar vi to row, paddle, scull; toil, strive

rematadamente adv completely, entirely, absolutely

rematado a beyond hope, extremely ill; utterly lost; law convicted

rematar vt to end, finish; finish off, kill; knock down at auction; sew finish; vi end; vr be ruined or spoiled

remate m, end, conclusion; extremity; arch coping; arch terminal; highest bid; auction. **de r.,** utterly hopeless

rematista mf, Lat. Am. auctioneer

rembarcar vt to reembark, reship

rembolsable a repayable

rembolsar vt to recover (money); refund, return (money)

rembolso m, repayment. **contra r.,** cash on delivery, C.O.D.

remedar vt to copy, imitate; mimic

remediar vt to remedy; aid, help; save from danger; prevent (trouble)

remedio m, remedy; emendation, correction; help; refuge, protection; med remedy. **No hay más r.,** There's nothing else to do, It's the only way open. **no tener más r.,** to be unable to help (doing something), be obliged to

remedo m, imitation; poor copy

remendar vt irr to mend, patch; darn; repair; correct. See **recomendar**

remendón (-ona) n cobbler; mender of old clothes

remero (-ra) n oarsman, rower; sculler

remesa f, remittance; consignment, shipment

remezón m, Lat. Am. (earth) tremor

remiendo m, sew patch; mend, darn; emendation; inf insignia of one of the Spanish military orders. **a remiendos,** inf piecemeal

remilgo m, affectation; mannerism; prudery, squeamishness

reminiscencia f, reminiscence; memory, recollection

remirado a wary, cautious, prudent, circumspect

remirar vt to revise, go over again; vr take great care over; behold with pleasure

remisión f, sending; remission; pardon, forgiveness; foregoing, relinquishment; abatement, diminution; lit reference, allusion

remise m, Argentina limousine, hired taxi

remiso a timid, spiritless; languid, slow

remitente mf sender. a sending

remitir vt to remit, send; pardon, forgive; defer, postpone; abate, diminish; relinquish, forgo; lit refer; vr remit, submit, consult; refer (to), cite

remo m, oar, scull, paddle; arm or leg (of men or animals, gen. pl); wing (gen. pl); hard, continuous toil; galleys. **al r.,** by dint of rowing; inf struggling with hardships

remojar vt to soak, steep; celebrate by drinking

remolacha f, beet

remolcador m, naut tow, tug. a naut towing

remolcar vt (naut aut) to tow; fig press into service, use

remoler vi, Lat. Am. to live it up, live the life of Riley

remolino m, whirlwind; eddy, swirl; whirlpool; crowd, throng, swarm; disturbance, riot

remolonear vi inf to loiter, lag; avoid work; be lax or dilatory

remolque m, towage, towing; towline; barge; aut trailer. **a r.,** on tow

remontar vt to scare off (game); mil supply with fresh horses; resole (shoes); fig

rise to great heights (of oratory, etc.); vr soar (of birds); (with prep a) date from, go back to; originate in

remoquete m, blow with the fist; witticism; inf flirtation, courtship

remorder vt irr to bite again or repeatedly; fig gnaw, nag, cause uneasiness or remorse; vr show one's feelings. See **morder**

remordimiento m, remorse

remoto a distant, remote; unlikely, improbable

remover vt irr to remove, move; stir; turn over; dismiss, discharge. See **mover**

remozar vt to cause to appear young; freshen up, bring up to date; vr look young

remplazar vt to replace; exchange, substitute; succeed, take the place of

remplazo m, replacement; exchange, substitute; successor; mil replacement

remudar vt to replace

remuneración f, remuneration; reward

remunerador (-ra) a remunerative, recompensing. n remunerator

remunerar vt to recompense, reward

remusgar vi to suspect, imagine

renacer vi irr to be reborn. See **nacer**

renacimiento m, rebirth; Renaissance

renacuajo m, tadpole; mech frog; inf twerp

rencarnación f, reincarnation

rencarnar(se) vi and vr to be reincarnated

rencilla f, grudge, grievance, resentment

rencilloso a peevish, easily offended, touchy

rencor m, rancor, spite, old grudge. **guardar r.,** to bear malice

rencoroso a rancorous, malicious, spiteful

rencuentro m, collision; mil encounter, clash

rendición f, surrender; yield, profit

rendido a submissive, obsequious

rendija f, crevice, cleft, crack, fissure

rendimiento m, weariness, fatigue; submissiveness, obsequiousness; yield, profit; mech efficiency

rendir vt irr mil to cause to surrender; defeat; overcome, conquer; give back, return; yield, provide; tire, exhaust; vomit; pay, render; vr be exhausted, be worn out; surrender. **mil r. el puesto,** to retire from or give up a post. See **pedir**

renegado (-da) n renegade, apostate; turncoat; inf malignant person. a renegade

renegador (-ra) n blasphemer; foul-mouthed person

renegar vt irr to deny, disown; loathe, hate; vi (with de) apostatize; blaspheme; inf curse. See **cegar**

renganchar(se) vt and vr mil to reenlist

renganche *m, mil* reenlistment

renglón *m, print* line; *pl* writing, composition

renguear *vi, Lat. Am.* to limp

renguera *f, Lat. Am.* limp

reniego *m,* blasphemy; *inf* foul language, cursing

renitencia *f,* repugnance

renombrado *a* illustrious, famous

renombre *m,* surname; renown, reputation, fame

renovable *a* renewable, replaceable

renovación *f,* replacement; renewal; renovation; transformation, reform

renovador (-ra) *n* reformer; renovator. *a* renovating; reforming

renovar *vt irr* to renew; renovate; replace; exchange; reiterate, repeat. See **contar**

renta *f,* yield, profit; income; revenue; government securities; rent; tax

rentero (-ra) *n* tenant farmer. *m,* one who farms out land

rentista *mf* financier; bondholder; person who lives on a private income, rentier

renuente *a* refractory, willful

renuncia, renunciación *f,* renunciation; resignation; abandonment, relinquishment

renunciar *vt* to renounce; refuse; scorn; abandon, relinquish; resign; revoke (at cards). **r. a,** to give up

renuncio *m,* revoke (cards); *inf* falsehood

reñidamente *adv* strongly, stubbornly, fiercely

reñir *vi irr* to quarrel, dispute; fight; be on bad terms, fall out; *vt* scold; fight (battles, etc.). See **ceñir**

reo *mf* criminal; offender, guilty party; *law* defendant

reojo *m,* (**mirar de**) to look out of the corner of the eye; *fig* look askance

reóstato *m,* rheostat

repantigarse *vr* to stretch out one's legs, make oneself comfortable

reparable *a* remediable, reparable; worthy of note

reparación *f,* repair, mending; reparation, satisfaction; indemnity, compensation

reparador *a* repairing, mending; fault-finding; restoring; satisfying, compensating

reparar *vt* to repair; restore; consider; correct, remedy; atone for, expiate; indemnify; hold up, detain; protect, guard; (*with en*) notice; *Lat. Am.* to ape, imitate, mimic; *vi* halt, be detained; *vr* control oneself

reparo *m,* repair; restoration; remedy; note, reflection; warning; doubt, scruple; guard, protection; parry (at fencing)

repartición *f,* distribution

repartidor (-ra) *a* distributing. *n* distributor; tax assessor

repartimiento *m,* distribution, allotment; assessment

repartir *vt* to distribute; share out; allot; deal (cards); assess; *com* deliver

reparto *m,* distribution; assessment; delivery (of letters, etc.); *theat* cast; deal (at cards); *Lat. Am.* building site, construction site

repasador *m, Lat. Am.* dish cloth, dishrag

repasar *vt* to pass by again; peruse, reexamine; brush up, revise; skim, glance over; mend, repair (garments); edit, revise; hone

repaso *m,* second passage through; reexamination, perusal; revision, editing; brushing up, revision; repair, mending; *inf* dressing-down, scolding

repatriado (-da) *n* repatriate

repatriar *vt* to repatriate; *vi* and *vr* return to one's own country

repecho *m,* steep slope. **a r.,** uphill

repelar *vt* to pull by the hair; put through its paces (of a horse); clip, cut; remove, diminish

repeler *vt* to repel, throw back; reject, refute

repelo *m,* anything against the grain; *inf* skirmish; reluctance, repugnance

repente *m, inf* sudden or unexpected movement. **de r.,** suddenly

repentino *a* sudden, unexpected

repentizar *vi mus* to sight-read

repercusión *f,* repercussion; vibration

repercutir *vi* to recoil, rebound; *vr* reverberate; reecho; *fig* have repercussions; *vt med* repel

repertorio *m,* repertory

repetición *f,* repetition; *art* replica, copy; repeater (in clocks); recital

repetidamente *adv* repeatedly

repetir *vt irr* to repeat, do over again; reiterate; *art* copy, make a replica of; recite. See **pedir**

repicar *vt* to chop, mince; peal (of bells); prick again; *vr* pride oneself (on), boast

repique *m,* chopping, mincing; peal, pealing (of bells); disagreement, grievance

repisa *f, arch* bracket; ledge; shelf. **r. de chimenea,** mantelpiece

replegar *vt irr* to refold, fold many times; *vr mil* retreat in good order. See **cegar**

repleto *a* replete

réplica *f,* reply, answer; replica

replicar *vi* to contradict, dispute; answer, reply. **¡No me repliques!** *inf* Don't answer back!

repliegue *m,* double fold, crease; doubling, folding; *mil* withdrawal

repoblación *f,* repeopling, repopulation

repoblar *vt* to repeople, repopulate

repollo *m*, white cabbage; heart (of lettuce, etc.)

reponer *vt irr* to replace; reinstate; restore; reply; *vr* recover, regain (possessions); grow well again; grow calm. See **poner**

reportación *f*, serenity, moderation

reportaje *m*, journalistic report

reportar *vt* to restrain, moderate; achieve, obtain; carry; bring; *vr* control oneself

reporte *m*, report, news; rumor

reportero (-ra) *a* news, report. *n* reporter

reposado a quiet, peaceful, tranquil

reposar *vi* to rest, repose oneself; sleep, doze; lie in the grave; settle (liquids); rest (on)

reposición *f*, replacement; restoration; renewal; recovery (of health); *theat* revival

repositorio *m*, repository

reposo *m*, rest, repose; peace, tranquility; sleep

repostada *f*, *Lat. Am.* cheeky reply, saucy retort

repostería *f*, confectioner's shop; pantry; butler's pantry

repostero *m*, confectioner, pastry cook

repreguntar *vt* to cross-examine

reprender *vt* to scold, reprimand, rebuke

reprensible a reprehensible, censurable

reprensión *f*, scolding, reprimand, rebuke

represa *f*, damming, holding back (water); dam, lock; restraining, controlling

represalia *f*, reprisal (gen. *pl*); retaliation

represar *vt* to dam, harness (water); *naut* retake, recapture; *fig* restrain, control

representación *f*, representation; *theat* performance; authority; dignity; *com* agency; portrait, image; depiction, expression; petition

representante a representative. *mf* representative; actor; performer

representar *vt* to represent; *theat* perform; depict, express; describe, portray; *vr* imagine, picture to oneself

representativo a representative

represión *f*, repression; recapture

represivo a repressive

reprimenda *f*, rebuke, reprimand

reprimir *vt* to repress, restrain, control; *vr* restrain oneself

reprobación *f*, censure; reprobation

reprobar *vt irr* to reprove; censure; fail (in an exam). See **probar**

reproche *m*, reproaching; rebuke, reproach

reproducción *f*, reproduction. **r. a gran escala**, large-scale model

reproducir *vt irr* to reproduce. See **conducir**

reproductor (-ra) *a* reproductive. *n* breeding animal

reps *m*, rep (fabric)

reptil a reptilian; crawling. *m*, reptile

república *f*, republic; state, commonwealth. **la r. de las letras**, the republic of letters

República Dominicana Dominican Republic

republicano (-na) a and *n* republican

repudiación *f*, repudiation

repudiar *vt* to cast off (a wife); repudiate, renounce

repuesto a retired, hidden. *m*, stock, provision; serving table; pantry; stake (at cards, etc.). **de r.**, spare, extra

repugnancia *f*, inconsistency, contradiction; aversion, dislike; reluctance; repugnance

repugnante a repugnant, loathsome

repugnar *vt* to contradict, be inconsistent with; hate, be averse to (e.g. **La idea me repugna,** I hate the idea)

repujar *vt* to work in repoussé

repulir *vt* to repolish, reburnish; *vt* and *vr* make up too much, overdress

repulsa *f*, snub, rebuff; rejection; repulse

repulsar *vt* to decline, reject; repulse; deny, refuse; rebuff

repulsión *f*, repulsion; rebuff; aversion, dislike

repulsivo a repellent

reputación *f*, reputation

reputar *vt* to believe, consider (e.g. **Le reputo por honrado,** I believe him to be an honorable man); appreciate, esteem

requebrar *vt irr* to break into smaller pieces; make love to, woo; compliment, flatter. See **quebrar**

requemar *vt* to burn again; overcook; dry up, parch (of plants, etc.); burn (the mouth) (of spicy foods, etc.); *vr fig* suffer inwardly

requerir *vt irr* to inform, notify; examine; need, necessitate; require; summon; woo; persuade. See **sentir**

requesón *m*, cream cheese; curd

requetebién *adv inf* exceedingly well

requiebro *m*, compliment, expression of love; wooing, flirtation

requintar *vt*, *Lat. Am.* to tighten

requisito *m*, requisite

res *f*, animal, beast; head of cattle; *Lat. Am.* steak

resabiar *vt* to make vicious, cause bad habits; *vr* contract bad habits or vices; be discontented; relish

resabio *m*, disagreeable aftertaste; bad habit, vice

resaca *f*, surf, undertow, surge; *com* redraft

resacar *vt* to distil

resalado a *inf* very witty; most attractive

resaltar *vi* to rebound; project, jut out; grow loose, fall out; *fig* stand out, be prominent

resalto *m*, rebound; projection

resbaladizo *a* slippery; difficult, delicate (of a situation)

resbalar *vi* to slip; slide; skid; err, fall into sin

resbalón *m*, slip; slide; skid; temptation, error

rescatador (-ra) *n* ransomer; rescuer

rescatar *vt* to ransom; redeem, buy back; barter; free, rescue; *fig* redeem (time, etc.)

rescate *m*, ransom; redemption; barter; amount of ransom

rescoldo *m*, ember, cinder; scruple, qualm, doubt

resentimiento *m*, deterioration, impairment; animosity, resentment

resentirse *vr irr* to deteriorate, be impaired; be hurt or offended. See **sentir**

reseña *f*, *mil* review; short description; review (of a book)

reseñar *vt mil* to review; describe briefly, outline

reserva *f*, store, stock; exception, qualification; reticence; restraint, moderation; (*ecc law*) reservation; (*mil naut*) reserve. **sin r.,** frankly, without reserve

reservación *f*, reservation; scruple

reservado *a* reserved, reticent; prudent, moderate; kept, reserved. *m*, reserved compartment; private apartment, private garden, etc.

reservar *vt* to keep, hold; postpone; reserve (rooms, etc.); exempt; keep secret; withhold (information); *ecc* reserve; *vr* await a better opportunity; be cautious

reservista *a* (*mil nav*) reserved. *mf* reservist

resfriado *m*, *med* cold, chill

resfriar *vt* to chill; *fig* cool, moderate; *vi* grow cold; *vr* catch a cold; *fig* cool off (of love, etc.)

resguardar *vt* to protect; shelter; *vr* take refuge; (*with de*) guard against; (*with con*) shelter by

resguardo *m*, protection, guard; *com* guarantee, security; *com* voucher; preservation; vigilance (to prevent smuggling, etc.); contraband guards

residencia *f*, stay, residence; home, domicile; *ecc* residence

residencial *a* residential; resident, residentiary

residente *a* resident. *mf* inhabitant. *m*, resident, minister resident (diplomatic)

residir *vi* to live, inhabit; reside officially; be found, be, exist

residuo *m*, residuum, remainder; *math* remainder; *chem* residue

resignación *f*, resignation; fortitude, submission

resignar *vt* to resign, relinquish; *vr* submit, resign oneself

resina *f*, resin

resistencia *f*, resistance, opposition; endurance; (*phys mech psy*) resistance

resistente *a* resistant; tough; hardy (of plants)

resistir *vi* to resist, oppose; reject; *vt* endure, bear; resist; *vr* fight, resist

resolución *f*, decision; boldness, daring; determination, resolution; decree

resoluto *a* resolute, bold; brief, concise; able, expert

resolver *vt irr* to determine, decide; summarize; solve; dissolve; analyze; (*phys med*) resolve; *vr* decide, determine; be reduced to, become; *med* resolve. *Pres. Ind.* **resuelvo, resuelves, resuelve, resuelven.** *Past Part.* **resuelto.** *Pres. Subjunc.* **resuelva, resuelvas, resuelva, resuelvan**

resonancia *f*, resonance, sonority, ring; fame, reputation

resonante *a* resonant; resounding

resonar *vi irr* to resound, echo. See **tronar**

resoplido, resoplo *m*, heavy breathing, pant, snort

resorte *m*, *mech* spring; elasticity; *fig* means, instrument; *Lat. Am.* rubber band

respaldo *m*, back (of chairs, etc.); reverse side (of a piece of paper)

respecto *m*, relation, regard, reference. **con r. a,** or **r. a,** with regard to, with respect to, concerning

respetabilidad *f*, respectability; worthiness

respetable *a* worthy of respect; respectable; *fig* considerable, large

respetar *vt* to respect, revere

respeto *m*, respect, honor; consideration, reason. **de r.,** spare, extra; special, ceremonial

respetuoso *a* venerable, worthy of honor; respectful, courteous

respingo *m*, wincing; jerk, shake; *inf* gesture of reluctance or dislike

respiración *f*, breathing, respiration; ventilation

respirador *a* breathing; respiratory. *m*, respirator

respirar *vi* to breathe; exhale, give off; take courage; have a breathing space, rest; *inf* speak. **sin r.,** continuously, without stopping for breath

respiratorio *a* respiratory

respiro *m*, breathing; breathing space, respite

resplandecer *vi irr* to glitter, gleam; shine, excel. See **conocer**

resplandeciente *a* glittering, resplendent, shining

resplandor *m*, radiance, brilliance; glitter, gleam; majesty, splendor

responder *vt* to reply; satisfy, answer; *vi* reecho; requite, return; produce, provide; *fig* answer, have the desired effect; *com* (*with de*) answer for, guarantee; *com* correspond

respondón *a inf* pert, impudent, cheeky, given to answering back

responsabilidad *f*, responsibility

responsable *a* responsible

respuesta *f*, answer, reply; response; refutation; repartee

resquebrajarse *vr* to crack, split

resquicio *m*, crack, chink, slit; opportunity; *Lat. Am.* sign, trace, vestige

restablecer *vt irr* to reestablish; restore; *vr* recover one's health; reestablish oneself. See **conocer**

restablecimiento *m*, reestablishment; restoration

restar *vt math* to subtract; deduct; return (a ball); *vi* remain. **No me resta más que decir adiós,** It only remains for me to say good-by

restauración *f*, restoration; renovation

restaurante *m*, restaurant

restaurantero *m*, restaurant operator; restaurant owner; restaurateur

restaurar *vt* to recover, recuperate; renovate, repair; restore

restaurativo *a* and *m*, restorative

restitución *f*, restitution

restituible *a* returnable, replaceable

restituir *vt irr* to return, give back; restore; reestablish; *vr* return to one's place of departure. See **huir**

resto *m*, rest, balance; *math* remainder; *pl* remains

restorán *m*, restaurant

restricción *f*, limitation, restriction

restrictivo *a* restrictive; restraining

restringir *vt* to limit, restrict; contract

resucitar *vt* to raise from the dead; *fig inf* revive; *vi* resuscitate

resuelto *a* audacious, daring; resolute, capable

resuello *m*, breathing; panting, hard breathing

resulta *f*, consequence, result; decision, resolution; vacant post. **de resultas de,** as the result of; in consequence of

resultado *m*, result, consequence, outcome

resultar *vi* to result, follow; turn out, happen; result (in); *inf* turn out well. **El vestido no me resulta,** The dress isn't a success on me

resumen *m*, summary. **en r.,** in short

resumir *vt* to summarize, abridge; sum up, recapitulate; *vr* be contained, be included

resurgimiento *m*, resurgence, revival

resurgir *vi* to reappear, rise again; revive; resuscitate

resurrección *f*, resurrection

retablo *m*, *arch* altarpiece, retable; frieze; series of pictures

retador, -a *mf*, *Lat. Am.* challenger

retaguardia *f*, rear guard. **a r.,** in the rear. **picar la r.,** to harass the rear guard

retajar *vt* to cut in the round; circumcise

retama *f*, *bot* broom. **r. común** or **r. de olor,** Spanish broom. **r. de escobas,** common broom

retar *vt* to challenge; *inf* reproach, accuse

retardar *vt* to retard, delay

retardo *m*, delay, retardment

retazo *m*, remnant, cutting; excerpt, fragment

retemplar *vt*, *Lat. Am.* to cheer up

retén *m*, stock, reserve, provision; *mil* reserve

retención *f*, retention

retener *vt irr* to keep, retain; recollect, remember; keep back; *law* detain; deduct. See **tener**

retentiva *f*, retentiveness, memory

retentivo *a* retentive

reticencia *f*, reticence

reticente *a* reticent

retina *f*, retina

retintín *m*, ringing; tinkling; *inf* sarcastic tone

retiñir *vi* to tinkle, clink; jingle

retirada *f*, withdrawal; retirement; seclusion, refuge; *mil* retreat

retirado *a* remote, secluded; *mil* retired

retirar *vt* to withdraw; remove; repel, throw back; hide, put aside; *vr* withdraw; retire; *mil* retreat

retiro *m*, withdrawal; removal; seclusion, privacy; *mil* retreat; retirement; *ecc* retreat. **dar el r. (a),** to place on the retired list

reto *m*, challenge; threat

retocar *vt* to touch again or repeatedly; *phot* retouch; restore (pictures); *fig* put the finishing touch to

retoñar *vi* to sprout, shoot; *fig* revive, resuscitate

retoño *m*, sprout, shoot

retoque *m*, frequent touching; finishing touch; touch, slight attack

retorcer *vt irr* to twist; contort; confound with one's own argument; misconstrue, distort; *vr* contort; writhe. See **torcer**

retórica *f*, rhetoric; *pl inf* quibbling

retórico (-ca) *a* rhetorical. *n* rhetorician

retornar *vt* to return, give back; turn, twist; turn back; *vi* and *vr* return, go back

retorno *m*, return, going back; recompense, repayment; exchange; return journey

retortijón *m*, twisting, curling. **r. de tripas,** stomachache

retozar *vi* to skip, frisk, frolic, gambol; romp; *fig* be aroused (passions)

retracción f, drawing back, retraction

retractar vt to retract, recant, withdraw

retráctil a retractile

retraer vt irr to bring back again; dissuade; buy back, redeem; vr take refuge; retire; withdraw; go into seclusion. See **traer**

retraído a fugitive, refugee; retired, solitary; timid, nervous, unsociable

retranca f, Lat. Am. brake

retrancar vt, Lat. Am. to brake

retrasar vt to postpone, delay; turn back (the clock); vi be slow (of clocks); vr be behind time, be late; be backward (persons)

retraso m, lateness; delay, dilatoriness; loss of time (clocks); setting back (of the clock) **El reloj lleva cinco minutos de r.**, The clock is five minutes slow)

retratar vt to paint or draw the portrait of; portray, describe; photograph; copy, imitate

retratería f, Lat. Am. photographer's studio

retrato m, portrait; portrayal; fig image, likeness

retrechería f, inf craftiness, evasiveness

retrete m, toilet, water closet

retribución f, recompense, reward

retribuir vt irr to recompense, reward. See **huir**

retroactivo a retroactive

retroceder vi to withdraw, move back, draw back; recede

retroceso m, retrocedence, withdrawal; med retrogression

retrogradación f, retrogression

retrógrado a retrogressive, retrograde; pol reactionary

retronar vi irr to bang, thunder, resound with noise. See **tronar**

retrospectivo a retrospective

retruécano m, antithesis; play on words, pun

retumbante a resounding; pompous, high-flown

retumbar vi to resound, echo, reverberate; roll (of thunder); roar (of a cannon)

retumbo m, reverberation, echo; rumble; roll (of thunder); roar (of a cannon, etc.)

reumático a rheumatic

reumatismo m, rheumatism

reunión f, reunion, union; meeting; assembly, gathering

reunir vt to reunite; unite; join; gather, assemble; vr meet, assemble; unite

revacunar vt to revaccinate

revalidación f, ratification, confirmation

revalidar vt to ratify, confirm; vr pass a final examination

revejido a prematurely old

revelación f, revelation; phot developing

revelador a revealing. m, phot developer

revelar vt to reveal; phot develop

revendedor (-ra) a reselling, retail. n retailer

revender vt to resell; retail (goods)

reventa f, resale; retail

reventar vi irr to burst, explode; break in foam (waves); burst forth; fig burst (with impatience, etc.); inf explode (with anger, etc.); vt break, crush; fig wear out, exhaust; inf irritate, vex; vr burst; fig be exhausted. See **sentar**

reventón a bursting. m, explosion, bursting; steep hill; hole, fix, difficulty; uphill work, heavy toil

reverberación f, reflection (of light); reverberation, resounding

reverberar vi to reflect; resound, reverberate

reverbero m, reverberation; reflector; Lat. Am. small stove

reverdecer vi irr to grow green again; revive, acquire new vigor. See **conocer**

reverencia f, respect, veneration; bow; curtsy; ecc reverence (title)

reverencial a reverential, respectful

reverenciar vt to revere; honor; respect

reverendo a reverend; venerable; inf overprudent

reversión f, reversion

reverso m, wrong side, back; reverse side (of coins)

reverter vi irr to overflow. See **entender**

revertir vi law to revert

revés m, wrong side, back, reverse; cuff, slap; backhand (in ballgames); check, setback, reverse; disaster, misfortune. **al r.**, on the contrary; wrong side out. **de r.**, from left to right, counterclockwise

revesado a complicated, difficult; willful

revestimiento m, mas lining, coating

revestir vt to dress; mas coat, line; fig cover, clothe; vr be dressed or dress oneself; fig be captivated (by an idea); become haughty or full of oneself; rise to the occasion, develop qualities necessary. See **pedir**

reviejo a very old. m, dead branch (of trees)

revisar vt to revise; examine

revisión f, revision; reexamination; law retrial

revisor a revising, examining. m, reviser; ticket inspector

revista f, reexamination, revision; review, periodical; theat revue; reinspection; review (of a book, etc.); law new trial; mil review. **pasar r.**, to inspect; review

revivir vi to resuscitate; revive

revocación f, revocation, cancellation, annulment

revocar vt to revoke, annul; dissuade; repel, throw back; wash (walls); law discharge

revolcar *vt irr* to knock down, trample underfoot; lay flat (in an argument); *vr* wallow; dig one's heels in, be obstinate. See **volcar**

revolotear *vi* to flutter, fly around; twirl; *vt* hurl, toss

revoltillo *m*, jumble, hodgepodge; confusion, tangle; *Venezuela* scrambled eggs

revoltoso *a* rebellious; mischievous, willful; intricate

revoltura *f, Mexico* dish of eggs and vegetables

revolución *f*, turn, revolution; rebellion, uprising; revolution

revolucionar *vt* to revolutionize

revolucionario (**-ia**) *a* and *n* revolutionary

revolver *vt irr* to turn over; turn upside down; wrap up; revolve; stir; reflect upon, consider; upset, cause disharmony; search through, disorder (papers, etc.); *vr* move from side to side; change (in the weather). See **resolver**

revólver *m*, revolver

revuelco *m*, wallowing

revuelo *m*, second flight (of birds); irregular course of flight; disturbance, upset

revuelta *f*, second turn or revolution; revolt, rebellion; quarrel, fight; turning point; change of direction, turn; change (of opinions, posts, etc.)

revueltamente *adv* in confusion, higgledy-piggledy

revulsión *f*, revulsion

rexaminar *vt* to reexamine

rexpedir *vt* to forward, send on

rexportación *f*, reexport

rexportar *vt com* to reexport

rey *m*, king (in cards, chess); queen bee; *inf* swineherd; *fig* king, chief. **her r. de armas**, king-of-arms. **reyes magos**, magi. **día de Reyes**, Twelfth Night. **servir al r.**, to fight for the king

reyerta *f*, quarrel, row, rumpus

rezagar *vt* to leave behind; postpone, delay; *vr* lag behind, straggle

rezar *vt* to pray, say prayers; say mass; *inf* state, say; *vi* pray; *inf* fume, grumble. **El edicto reza así**, The edict runs like this, The edict reads like this

rezo *m*, prayer; devotions

rezongar *vi* to grouse, grumble

rezumar(se) *vr* and *vi* to percolate, ooze through; *inf* leak out, be known

ría *f*, estuary, river mouth, firth

riachuelo *m*, rivulet, stream

ribaldería *f*, ribaldry

ribaldo *a* ribald. *m*, knave

ribazo *m*, slope, incline

ribera *f*, bank, margin, shore, strand; *Lat. Am.* slum

ribereño (**-ña**) *a* and *n* riparian

ribete *m*, binding, border, trimming; stripe; increase, addition; dramatic touch, exaggeration; *pl* indications, signs

ribetear *vt sew* to bind, trim, edge

ricacho (**-cha**) *n inf* newly rich person, nouveau riche

ricamente *adv* richly, opulently; beautifully, splendidly; luxuriously

ricino *m*, castor oil plant

rico *a* wealthy, rich; abundant; magnificent, splendid; delicious. **r. como Creso,** rich as Croesus

ricura *f, inf* richness, wealth

ridiculez *f*, absurd action or remark; ridiculousness; affectation; folly

ridículo *a* ridiculous, absurd; grotesque; preposterous, outrageous. *m*, reticule

riego *m*, watering, spraying; irrigation

riel *m*, ingot; rail (of a train or streetcar)

rienda *f*, rein (gen. *pl*); restraint; *pl* administration, government. **a r. suelta,** swiftly; without restraint

riesgo *m*, risk, danger

riesgoso, -a *a, Lat. Am.* dangerous, risky

rifa *f*, raffle; quarrel, disagreement

rifar *vt* to raffle; *vi* quarrel, fall out

rifle *m*, rifle

rigidez *f*, stiffness; rigidity; harshness

rígido *a* stiff; rigid; inflexible; severe, harsh

rigor *m*, severity, sternness; rigor; hardness; inflexibility; *med* rigor. **en r.,** strictly speaking. **ser de r.,** to be essential, be indispensable

rigorista *mf* martinet

riguroso *a* rigorous; harsh, cruel; austere, rigid; strict, exact, scrupulous

rijoso *a* quarrelsome; lascivious

rima *f*, rhyme, rime; heap; *pl* lyrics

rimador (**-ra**) *a* rhyming, rimer. *n* rhymer, rimer

rimar *vi* to compose verses; *vi* and *vt* rhyme, rime

rimbombo *m*, reverberation (of a sound)

rimero *m*, heap, pile

Rin, el the Rhine

rincón *m*, corner, angle; retreat, hiding place; *inf* home, nest, nook

rinconera *f*, corner cupboard; corner table

ringlera *f*, file, line, row

ringlero *m*, guiding line for writing

ringorrangos *m pl, inf* exaggerated flourishes in writing; *inf* unnecessary frills or ornaments

ringueletear *vi, Lat. Am.* to wander through the streets

rinoceronte *m*, rhinoceros

riñón *m*, kidney; *fig* center, heart; *pl anat* back

río *m*, river; *fig* stream, flood

rioja *m*, red wine from Rioja

rioplatense *a* of the River Plate area; *mf*

native of the River Plate area; resident of the River Plate area

ripio m, remains, rest; debris, rubbish; *lit* padding; verbiage, prolixity. **no perder r.,** to lose no occasion or opportunity

riqueza f, riches, wealth; abundance; richness, magnificence

risa f, laugh; laughter; cause of amusement, joke

risco m, crag

riscoso a craggy

risible a laughable

risoles m pl, rissoles

risotada f, loud laugh

ristra f, string (of onions, etc.); file, line, row

risueño a smiling; cheerful; pleasant, agreeable; favorable, hopeful

rítmico a rhythmic

ritmo m, rhythm

rito m, rite

rivalidad f, rivalry, competition; hostility

rivalizar vi to compete, rival

rizado m, curling; pleating; crimping; rippling, ruffling

rizar vt to curl (hair); ripple, ruffle (of water); pleat, crimp; vr be naturally wavy (of hair)

rizo m, curl, ringlet; cut velvet. **aer hacer el r.,** to loop the loop; *naut* to take in reefs

rizoso a naturally curly or wavy (hair)

robador (-ra) a robbing. n robber, thief. m, abductor

robar vt to rob; abduct; wash away, eat away (rivers, sea); remove honey from the hive; draw (in cards, dominoes); *fig* capture (love, etc.)

roblar vt to reinforce, strengthen; clinch

roble m, oak tree; oak; *fig* bulwark, tower of strength

roblón m, rivet

robo m, theft, robbery; booty

robustecer vt irr to strengthen. See **conocer**

robustez f, strength, robustness

robusto a vigorous, robust, hearty, strong

roca f, rock; *fig* tower of strength

roce m, rubbing, brushing, touching, friction; social intercourse

rociada f, dewing; sprinkling; dew-wet grass given as medicine to horses and mules; *fig* shower; general slander; harsh rebuke

rociar vi to fall as dew; drizzle; vt sprinkle, spray; *fig* shower (with)

rocín m, sorry nag; hack; *inf* ignoramus, boor

rocinante m, poor nag (alluding to Don Quixote's horse)

rocío m, dew; dewdrop; drizzle, light shower; *fig* sprinkling, spray

rocoso a rocky

rodaballo m, turbot; *inf* crafty man

rodada f, wheel mark or track

rodado a dappled (of horses)

rodaje m, wheeling; shooting (of a film)

rodante a rolling

rodar vi to roll; revolve, turn; run on wheels; wander, roam; be moved about; be plentiful, abound; happen successively; (*with* por) fall down, roll down

rodear vi to walk around; go by a roundabout way; *fig* beat around the bush; vt encircle, surround; besiege; *WH* round up (cattle)

rodeno a red (of rocks, earth, etc.)

rodeo m, encirclement; indirect and longer way; trick to evade pursuit; *WH* rodeo, roundup; stockyard, cattle enclosure; *fig* beating around the bush; evasive reply

rodera f, rail, track, line; cart rut or track

rodilla f, knee; floor cloth. **de rodillas,** on one's knees. **ponerse de rodillas,** or **hincar las rodillas,** to kneel down

rodillera f, kneecap, kneepad; mend at the knee of garments; bagginess of trouser knees

rodillo m, roller; traction engine; *print* inking roller; garden roller. **r. de pastas,** *cul* rolling pin

rododendro m, rhododendron

rodrigón m, stake, prop (for plants); *inf* old retainer who serves as a ladies' escort

roedor a gnawing; *fig* nagging; biting. a and m, rodent

roedura f, biting, gnawing; corrosion

roer vt irr to gnaw, nibble, eat; corrode, wear away; trouble, afflict. *Pres. Ind.* **roigo, roes,** etc. *Preterite* **royó, royeron.** *Imperf. Subjunc.* **royese,** etc.

rogación f, request, supplication, entreaty; *ecc* rogation

rogar vt irr to request; beseech, beg. See **contar**

rogativo a supplicatory, petitioning

roído a gnawed, eaten; *inf* miserable, stingy

rojal a red (of soil, etc.). m, red earth

rojear vi to appear red; be reddish

rojete m, rouge

rojez f, redness

rojizo a reddish

rojo a red; fair; red-gold (of hair); *pol* radical, red

rol m, roll, list

roldana f, pulley wheel

rollizo a round; plump, sturdy. m, log

rollo m, roll; rolling pin; log; town cross or pillar; anything rolled (paper, etc.); twist (of tobacco)

Roma Rome

romance a and m, romance (language). m, Spanish; ballad; romance of chivalry;

pl fig fairy tales, excuses. **en buen r.,** *fig* in plain words

romano (-na) a and *n* Roman. **a la romana,** in the Roman way. **cabello a la romana,** *inf* bobbed hair

romántico (-ca) a romantic; emotional; fanciful. *n* romantic; romanticist

romería *f,* pilgrimage; excursion, picnic (made on a saint's day)

romero (-ra) *m,* rosemary. *n* pilgrim

romo a blunt, dull, unsharpened; flat (of noses); *m. Lat. Am.* rum

rompecabezas *m,* bludgeon; knuckleduster; *inf* teaser, puzzle, riddle; jigsaw puzzle

rompeimágenes *mf* iconoclast

rompeolas *m,* jetty, breakwater

romper *vt* to break; shatter, break into fragments; spoil, ruin; break up, plow; *fig* cut, divide (of water, etc.); *fig* end, break; interrupt; infringe, break; *vi* break; break (of waves); sprout, flower; (*with prep* a) begin to. **Rompió a hablar,** He broke into speech. *Past Part.* **roto**

rompiente a breaking. *m,* reef, shoal

rompimiento *m,* break, rupture; crack, split; breakage; infringement; plowing up; *fig* dividing (water, etc.); spoiling, ruining; opening (of buds, etc.)

ron *m,* rum

roncar *vi* to snore; *fig* roar, howl (of the sea, wind, etc.); *inf* brag

roncear *vi* to be dilatory or unwilling; *inf* flatter, cajole; *naut* lag behind, sail slowly

roncero a dilatory, slow; grumbling, complaining; cajoling, flattering; *Lat. Am.* sly

roncha *f,* wheal; bruise; bump; *inf* money lost through trickery; thin, round slice

ronco a hoarse, husky

ronda *f,* round, beat, patrol; serenading party; *inf* round (of drinks)

rondador *m,* watchman; roundsman; serenader; night wanderer

rondalla *f,* tale, fairy tale

rondar *vi* to patrol, police; walk the streets by night; serenade; *vt* haunt; hover about; *inf* overcome (of sleep, etc.)

ronquear *vi* to be hoarse

ronquera *f,* hoarseness

ronquido *m,* snore; hoarse sound

ronronear *vi* to purr (of cats)

ronzar *vt* to munch, crack with the teeth

roña *f,* mange (in sheep); grime, filth; mold; moral corruption; *inf* stinginess; *inf* trick, deception

roñería *f, inf* meanness, stinginess

roñoso a scabby; filthy; rusty; *inf* mean, stingy

ropa *f,* fabric, material, stuff; clothes, wearing apparel; garment, outfit; robe (of office). **r. blanca,** underclothes; (domestic) linen. **r. hecha,** ready-made clothing. **r. talar,** long gown; cassock

ropaje *m,* clothes, garments; vestments; drapery; *fig* form, outline

ropavejería *f,* old-clothes shop

ropavejero (-ra) *n* old-clothes dealer

ropería *f,* clothier's shop or trade; wardrobe; cloakroom

ropero (-ra) *n* clothier; keeper of the wardrobe. *m,* wardrobe; charitable organization

ropón *m,* a loose-fitting gown generally worn over clothes

roque *m,* rook (in chess)

roqueño a rocky; hard as rock

rorro *m, inf* infant, baby

rosa *f,* rose; anything rose-shaped; artificial rose; red spot on the body; *arch* rose window; *pl* rosettes. *m,* rose color. **r. de los vientos,** mariner's compass. **r. laurel,** oleander

rosado a rose-colored; rose; rosé (wines)

rosal *m,* rose tree. **r. de tallo,** standard rose tree

rosaleda, rosalera *f,* rose garden

rosario *m,* rosary; *fig* string; chain pump; *inf* backbone

rosbif *m,* roast beef

rosca *f,* screw and nut; *cul* twist (of bread or cake); spiral

roscado a twisted, spiral

rosear *vi* to turn to rose, become rose-colored

róseo a rose-colored

roseta *f, dim* small rose; rosette; rose of a watering can; rosette copper; *pl* toasted maize. **r. de fiebre,** rush of fever

rosetón *m,* large rosette; *arch* rose window

roso a bald, worn; red

rosquete *m, Lat. Am.* bun

rosquilla *f,* ring-shaped cake

rostro *m,* bird's beak; face, visage. **conocer de r.,** to know by sight. **dar en r.,** *fig* to throw in one's face

rotación *f,* rotation. **r. de cultivos,** rotation of crops

rotativo a rotary

rotisería *f, Lat. Am.* steakhouse; grillroom

roto a shabby, ragged; vicious, debauched

rotonda *f,* rotunda

rótula *f,* rotula, patella

rotular *vt* to label; give a title or heading to

rótulo *m,* title; poster; placard; label

rotundamente *adv* tersely, roundly, plainly

rotundidad *f,* rotundity; roundness; finality (of words, etc.)

rotundo a round; rotund; sonorous; final, plain (of words, etc.)

rotura *f,* breaking, shattering; plowing up; breakage; rupture

roya f, rust, mildew; tobacco

roza f, agr clearing (of weeds, etc.); ground ready for sowing. **de r. abierta**, open cast (of mining)

rozador m, Lat. Am. machete

rozadura f, rubbing, friction; abrasion, chafing

rozagante a long and elaborate (dresses); upstanding; handsome; strapping, fine

rozamiento m, grazing, brushing, rubbing; discord, disharmony, disagreement; mech friction

rozar vt agr to clear of weeds; crop, nibble; scrape; brush against, touch; vi brush, rub, touch; vr have dealings with, know; stammer; be like, resemble

rubeola f, rubella

rubí m, ruby; jewel (of a watch)

rubia f, bot madder; blonde (girl, woman)

rubicundez f, rubicundity, ruddiness, redness

rubicundo a red-gold; ruddy-complexioned; reddish

rubio a red-gold, gold; fair, blond

rubor m, blush, flush; bashfulness

ruborizarse vr to blush; be shamefaced

ruboroso a shamefaced; blushing

rúbrica f, rubric; personal mark, flourish added to one's signature

rubricar vt to sign and seal; sign with an X or other symbol; sign with a flourish

rucio a fawn, light-gray (of animals); inf going gray, gray-haired

rudamente adv rudely, abruptly, churlishly; roughly

rudeza f, roughness; rudeness, uncouthness; stupidity

rudimentario a rudimentary

rudimento m, embryo; pl rudiments

rudo a rough; unfinished; uncouth, boorish, rude; stupid

rueca f, distaff (in spinning); spinning wheel; curve, twist

rueda f, wheel; group, circle; spread of a peacock's tail; roller, castor; round piece or slice; turn, chance; succession (of events); wheel (used for torture). **r. libre**, freewheeling. inf **hacer la r. (a)**, to flatter, make a fuss of

ruedo m, turning, rotation; circumference; lined hem of a cassock; circuit

ruego m, request, entreaty

rufián m, ruffian; pimp

rufo a fair; red-haired; curly-haired

rugido m, roaring, roar; creaking; gnashing; rumbling

rugir vi to roar; squeak, creak; gnash (the teeth)

ruibarbo m, rhubarb

ruido m, noise, din; disturbance; rumor. **hacer (or meter) r.**, to cause a sensation. inf **ser más el r. que las nueces**, to be much ado about nothing

ruidoso a noisy; notable

ruin a base, vile; despicable; mean; puny

ruina f, ruin, downfall; financial ruin; fall, decline; pl ruins

ruinar vt to ruin

ruindad f, baseness; meanness; pettiness, unworthiness; mean trick, despicable action

ruinoso a half-ruined; ruinous; useless, worthless

ruiseñor m, nightingale

ruleta f, roulette

rumano (**-na**) a and n Romanian. m, Romanian (language)

rumba f rumba; Lat. Am. party (celebration)

rumbo m, naut course, way, route; direction; inf swank; Lat. Am. party (celebration) **con r. a**, headed for, in the direction of. **hacer r. a**, to sail for; make for

rumboso a inf pompous, dignified; open-handed, generous

rumia f, rumination; cud

rumiante a and mf zool ruminant. a inf reflective, meditative

rumiar vt zool to ruminate; inf reflect upon, chew on; inf fume, rage

rumor m, noise; rumor; murmur, babble; dull sound

rúnico a runic

rupia f, rupee

ruptura f, fig rupture; surg hernia

rural a rustic, rural

Rusia Russia

ruso (**-sa**) a and n Russian. m, Russian (language)

rusticar vi to rusticate

rusticidad f, rusticity; boorishness, coarseness

rústico a rustic, country; boorish, uncouth. m, countryman; yokel; peasant. **en rústica**, in paper covers (of books)

ruta f, route; fig way. **r. de evitación**, bypass, detour

rutilante a poet sparkling, glowing

rutilar vi poet to gleam, sparkle

rutina f, routine

rutinario a routine

rutinero (**-ra**) a routinistic. n routinist

S

sábado *m*, Saturday; Jewish sabbath. **s. de gloria,** Easter Saturday

sábalo *m*, *icht* shad

sabana *f*, savannah

sábana *f*, bed sheet; altar cloth. *inf* **pegársele (a uno) las sábanas,** to be tied to the bed, get up late

sabandija *f*, any unpleasant insect or reptile; *fig* vermin

sabanero (-ra) *n* savannah dweller. *a* savannah

sabanilla *f*, small piece of linen (kerchief, towel, etc.); altar cloth

sabático *a* sabbatical

sabedor *a* aware; knowledgeable, knowing

sabelotodo *mf inf* know-it-all

saber *m*, learning; wisdom

saber *vt irr* to know; be able to, know how; *vi* know; be shrewd, be well aware of; (*with prep a*) taste of; be like or similar to. **s. al dedillo,** *fig* to have at one's fingertips. **a s.,** viz., namely. *inf* **no s. cuántas son cinco,** not to know how many beans make five. **no s. dónde meterse,** to be overcome by shame; have the jitters. **No sé cuántos,** I don't know how many. **No sé quién,** I don't know who (which person). **No sé qué,** I don't know what. **un no sé qué,** a certain something; a touch (of). **¡Quién sabe!** Who knows!; Time will tell. *Pres. Ind.* **sé, sabes,** etc. *Fut.* **sabré,** etc. *Condit.* **sabría,** etc. *Preterite* **supe,** etc. *Pres. Subjunc.* **sepa,** etc. *Imperf. Subjunc.* **supiese,** etc.

sabidillo (-lla) *a and n inf* know-it-all

sabiduría *f*, prudence, wisdom; erudition, learning; knowledge, awareness. **Libro de la S. de Salomón,** Book of Wisdom

sabiendas, a *adv* knowingly, consciously

sabihondo (-da) *n inf* know-it-all

sabio (-ia) *a* wise; learned, erudite; prudent, sagacious; knowing (of animals); performing (of animals). *n* wise person; scholar, erudite person

sablazo *m*, saber thrust or wound; *inf* sponging, taking advantage of. **dar un s. (a),** *inf* to sponge on; touch for money

sable *m*, saber; *her* sable; *inf* talent for sponging on people. *a her* sable

sablear *vi inf* to touch for invitations, loans, etc.; cadge

sablista *mf inf* sponger, cadger

saboneta *f*, hunting case watch, hunter

sabor *m*, taste, flavor; impression, effect. **a s.,** to taste; at pleasure

saboreamiento *m*, savoring; relishing; enjoyment

saborear *vt* to flavor, season; relish, savor; appreciate, enjoy; *vr* relish, savor; enjoy

saboreo *m*, tasting; savoring; relishing

sabotaje *m*, sabotage

saboteador *m*, saboteur

sabroso *a* tasty, savory, well-seasoned; delightful, delicious; *inf* piquant, racy; *Lat. Am.* garrulous, talkative

sabueso *m*, cocker spaniel. **s. de artois,** hound

saburra *f*, fur (on the tongue)

saca *f*, drawing out, removing; export, transport, shipping; removal, extraction; legal copy (of a document). **estar de s.,** to be on sale; *inf* be marriageable (of women)

sacabocados *m*, punch (tool); *inf* cinch, easy matter

sacabuche *m*, *mus* sackbut; sackbut player; *inf* insignificant little man; *naut* hand pump

sacacorchos *m*, corkscrew

sacacuartos *m*, *inf* catchpenny

sacada *f*, territory cut off from a province

sacamanchas *mf*. See **quitamanchas**

sacamiento *m*, removing, taking out

sacamuelas *mf* dentist; charlatan, quack; *inf* windbag

sacapotras *m*, *inf* unskilled surgeon

sacar *vt* to draw out; extract; pull out; take out; remove; dispossess, turn out; free from, relieve; examine, investigate; extort (the truth); extract (sugar, etc.); win (prizes, games); copy; discover, find out; elect by ballot; obtain, achieve; exclude; show, exhibit; quote, mention; produce, invent; manufacture; note down; put forth; unsheath (swords); bowl (in cricket); serve (in tennis). **s. a bailar,** to invite to dance. **s. a luz,** to publish, print; reveal, bring out. **s. a paseo,** to take for a walk. **s. de pila,** to be a godfather or godmother to. **s. en claro** or **s. en limpio,** to copy; conclude, infer, gather. **sacarse en conclusión que . . . ,** the conclusion is that . . .

sacarina *f*, saccharine

sacasillas *mf*, *inf theat* stagehand

sacerdocio *m*, priesthood

sacerdotal *a* priestly

sacerdote *m*, priest

sacerdotisa *f*, priestess. **sumo s.,** high priestess

saciable *a* satiable

sachar *vt* to weed

saciar *vt* to satisfy; satiate; *vr* be satiated

saciedad *f*, satiety, surfeit

saco *m*, handbag; sack, bag; sackful; sack coat; *biol* sac; *mil* sack, plundering. **s. de noche,** dressing case, weekend case. *inf* **no echar en s. roto,** not to forget, to remember

sacramentalmente *adv* sacramentally; in confession

sacramentar *vt* to consecrate; administer the Blessed Sacrament; hide, conceal

sacramentario (**-ia**) *n* sacramentalist; sacramentarian

sacramento *m*, sacrament; *ecc* Host; *ecc* mystery. **s. del altar,** Eucharist. **con todos los sacramentos,** with all the sacraments; done in order, complete with all formalities. **recibir los sacramentos,** to receive the last sacraments

sacrificador (**-ra**) *a* sacrificing. *n* sacrificer

sacrificar *vt* to sacrifice; slaughter; *vr* consecrate oneself to God; sacrifice oneself; devote or dedicate oneself (to)

sacrificio *m*, sacrifice; offering, dedication; surrendering, forgoing; compliance, submission. **s. del altar,** sacrifice of the mass

sacrilegio *m*, sacrilege

sacrílego *a* sacrilegious

sacristán *m*, sacristan; sexton; hoop (for dresses). *inf* **s. de amén,** yes-man. *inf* **ser gran s.,** to be very crafty

sacristana *f*, wife of a sacristan or sexton; nun in charge of a convent sacristy

sacristanía *f*, office of a sacristan or sexton

sacristía *f*, sacristy; vestry; office of a sacristan or sexton

sacro *a* sacred; *anat* sacral

sacrosanto *a* sacrosanct

sacudida *f*, shake, shaking; jerk, jar, jolt; twitch, pull; *aer* bump

sacudido *a* unsociable; difficult, wayward; determined, bold

sacudidor (**-ra**) *a* shaking; jerking. *n* shaker. *m*, carpet beater; duster

sacudidura *f*, shaking (especially to remove dust); jerking

sacudimiento *m*, shake, shaking; jerk; twitch, pull; jolt

sacudir *vt* to shake; flap, wave; jerk, twitch; beat, bang; shake off; *vr* shake off, avoid

sadismo *m*, sadism

sadista *mf* sadist

sadístico *a* sadistic

saeta *f*, arrow, dart; clock hand, watch hand; magnetic needle; short sung expression of religious ecstasy; *ast* Sagitta

saga *f*, saga

sagacidad *f*, sagacity

sagaz *a* sagacious, shrewd; farseeing; quick on the scent (dogs)

sagrado *a* sacred; holy; sacrosanct, venerable; accursed, detestable. *m*, sanctuary, refuge; haven

Sáhara, el the Sahara

sahornarse *vr* to chafe, grow sore

sahorno *m*, chafing, abrasion

sahumado *a* improved, rendered more excellent; perfumed; fumigated

sahumador *m*, perfumer; fumigating vessel

sahumar *vt* to perfume; fumigate. See **desahuciar**

sahumerio *m*, perfuming; fumigation; fume, smoke

saín *m*, fat, grease; sardine oil (for lamps); grease spot (on clothes)

sainar *vt* to fatten up (animals)

sainete *m*, *cul* sauce; *theat* one-act parody or burlesque; farce; delicacy, tidbit; delicate taste (of food)

sainetero *m*, writer of sainetes

sajar *vt* *surg* to scarify

sal *f*, salt; wit; grace, gracefulness. **s. de cocina,** common kitchen salt. **s. de la Higuera,** Epsom salts. **s. gema,** rock salt. **s. marina,** sea salt. **sales inglesas,** smelling salts. *inf* **estar hecho de s.,** to be full of wit. *inf* **hacerse s. y agua,** to melt away, disappear (of riches, etc.)

sala *f*, drawing room; large room; hall; *law* courtroom; *law* bench; **s. de apelación,** court of appeal. **s. de hospital,** hospital ward. **s. de justicia,** court of justice. **s. de lectura,** reading room. *law* **guardar s.,** to respect the court

salacidad *f*, lewdness, salaciousness

saladero *m*, salting or curing place; *WH* meat packing factory

saladillo *m*, salt pork

salado *a* salty, briny; brackish; witty; attractive, amusing

salador (**-ra**) *a* salting, curing. *n* salter, curer. *m*, curing place

saladura *f*, salting, curing

salamandra *f*, salamander; fire sprite

salar *vt* to salt; season with salt; oversalt; cure, pickle (meat, etc.); *m*, *Lat. Am.* salt marsh

salario *m*, salary

salaz *a* lewd, lecherous

salazón *f*, salting, curing; salt meat or fish trade

salazonero *a* salting, curing

salchicha *f*, sausage

salchichería *f*, sausage shop

salchichón *m*, *cul* salami, kind of sausage

saldar *vt* *com* to settle, pay in full; sell out cheap; balance

saldo *m*, *com* balance; closing of an account; bargain sale. **s. acreedor,** credit balance. **s. deudor,** debit balance. **s. líquido,** net balance

salero *m*, saltshaker, saltcellar; salt storage warehouse; *inf* wit

salida *f*, going out; leaving; departure; sailing; exit, way out; projection, protrusion; *fig* escape, way out; outcome, result; witty remark; *mil* sally; *com* outlay, expense; *com* opening, sale, salability; environs, outskirts; *Argentina* bathrobe **s. de dólares,** dollar drain. **s. de tono,** *inf* an impertinent remark. **dar s.**, *com* to enter on the credit side

salidero a fond of going out; *m*, exit, way out

salidizo *m*, *arch* projection. a projecting

saliente a outgoing; salient; projecting. *m*, east; projection; salient. **s. continental**, continental shelf

salina *f*, salt mine; saltworks

salinero *m*, salt merchant; salter; salt worker

salino a saline. *m*, *med* saline

salir *vi irr* to go out; depart, leave; succeed in getting out; escape; appear (of the sun, etc.); sprout, show green; fade, come out (of stains); project, stand out; grow, develop; turn out, result; happen, take place; cost; sail; end (of seasons, time); lead off, start (some games); be published (books); do (well or badly), succeed or fail; appear, show oneself; be drawn, win (lottery tickets); balance, come out right (accounts); be elected; become; give up (posts); lead to (of streets, etc.); *naut* overtake; (*with prep a*) guarantee, be surety for; resemble, be like; (*with con*) utter, come out with; commit, do inopportunely; succeed in, achieve (e.g. **Salió con la suya,** He got his own way); (*with de*) originate in; break away from (traditions, conventions); get rid of; (*with por*) stand up for, protect; go surety for, guarantee. *vr* leak; boil over; overflow; (*with con*) achieve, get; (*with de*) *fig* break away from. *theat* **s. a la escena,** to enter, come on to the stage. **s. de,** to recover from (an illness). **no acabar de s. de,** to not be completely recovered from. **s. del apuro,** to get out of trouble. **s. de estampía,** to stampede (of animals). **s. pitando,** *inf* to get out in a hurry. **Esta idea no salió de Juan,** This wasn't John's idea. **salga lo que saliere,** *inf* come what may. . . . *Pres. Ind.* **salgo, sales,** etc. *Fut.* **saldré,** etc. *Condit.* **saldría,** etc. *Pres. Subjunc.* **salga,** etc.

salitre *m*, saltpeter

saliva *f*, saliva. *inf* **tragar s.,** to put up with; be unable to speak through emotion

salivación *f*, salivation

salivar *vi* to salivate; spit

salmear *vi* to intone psalms

salmista *mf* psalmist; psalmodist, psalm chanter

salmo *m*, psalm

salmodia *f*, psalmody; *inf* drone; psalter

salmodiar *vi* to chant psalms; *vt* drone

salmón *m*, salmon

salmonete *m*, red mullet

salmuera *f*, brine

salobre a salt, salty; brackish

salón *m*, drawing room; large room or hall; reception room; salon, reception, social gathering. **s. de muestras,** showroom

salpicadura *f*, sprinkling, spattering, splashing

salpicar *vt* to sprinkle, scatter; bespatter, splash

salpicón *m*, *cul* kind of salmagundi; *inf* hodgepodge; spattering

salpimentar *vt irr* to season with pepper and salt; sprinkle; *fig* leaven, enliven (a speech, etc.). See **regimentar**

salpullido *m*, rash, skin eruption

salsa *f*, sauce; gravy. **s. mahonesa** or **s. mayonesa,** mayonnaise sauce. **s. mayordoma,** sauce maître d'hôtel

salsera *f*, sauce boat, gravy boat

saltabanco *m*, mountebank; street entertainer, juggler

saltabarrancos *mf inf* madcap, harumscarum

saltador (-ra) a jumping. *n* jumper; acrobat. *m*, jump rope, skip rope

saltamontes *m*, grasshopper

saltaparedes *mf inf* madcap, romp

saltar *vi* to jump, leap, spring; prance; frisk, gambol; rebound; blow up; burst, break asunder; pop (of corks); fly off, come off (buttons, etc.); gush out, shoot up (liquids); break apart, be shattered; be obvious, stand out; come to mind, suggest itself; show anger; *fig* let slip, come out with (remarks); *vt* leap or jump over; poke out (eyes); cover (the female); omit, pass over; blow up, explode. **s. a la cuerda,** to jump rope, play with a skip rope. **s. a la vista,** to be obvious, leap to the eye. **s. diciendo,** *inf* to come out with, say

saltarín (-ina) a dancing. *n* dancer

saltatriz *f*, ballet dancer, female acrobat

saltatumbas *m*, (*inf* contemptuous) cleric who makes his living off funerals

salteador *m*, highwayman

salteamiento *m*, highway robbery, holdup; assault, attack

saltear *vt* to hold up and rob; assault, attack; jump from one thing to another, do intermittently; forestall; surprise, amaze

salterio *m*, psaltery

saltimbanco, saltimbanqui *m*, *inf*. See **saltabanco**

salto *m*, jump, leap, bound; leapfrog (game); precipice, ravine; waterfall; assault; important promotion; omission (of words). **s. de agua,** waterfall. **s. de cama,** peignoir, bathrobe. **s. de campana,** overturning. *inf* **s. de mal año,** sudden improvement in circumstances. **s. de mata,** flight, escape. **s. mortal,** leap of death; somersault. **s. de pie,** spillway. **dar un s.,** to leap. **en un s.,** at one jump; swiftly

saltón a jumping, leaping; prominent (teeth, eyes). *m*, grasshopper

salubre a salubrious, healthful

salubridad *f*, healthfulness

salud *f*, health; salvation; welfare, well-being; *ecc* state of grace; *pl* civilities, greetings. **¡S. y pesetas!** Here's to your good health and prosperity! (on drinking). **gastar s.,** to enjoy good health. *inf* **vender** (*or* **verter**) **s.,** to look full of health

saludable *a* healthy, wholesome

saludador (**-ra**) *a* greeting, saluting. *n* greeter. *m*, charlatan, quack

saludar *vt* to greet, salute; hail (as king, etc.); send greetings to; bow; *mil* fire a salute

saludo *m*, greeting, salutation; bow; (*mil nav*) salute

salutación *f*, greeting, salutation; Ave Maria

salva *f*, salutation, greeting; (*mil nav*) salvo, volley; salute (of guns); salver; ordeal (to establish innocence); solemn assurance, oath; sampling, tasting (of food, drink). **s. de veintiún cañonazos,** twenty-one-gun salute

salvación *f*, liberation, deliverance; salvation

salvado *m*, bran

salvador (**-ra**) *a* saving, redeeming. *n* deliverer. *m*, redeemer

salvadoreño (**-ña**) *a* and *n* Salvadorean

salvaguardia *m*, guard, watch. *f*, safeguard; protection, defense; safe conduct, passport

salvajada *f*, savagery, brutal action

salvaje *a* wild (plants, animals); rough, uncultivated; uncultured, uncivilized. *mf* savage

salvajismo *m*, savagery

salvamano, a *adv* safely

salvamente *adv* safely, securely

salvamento *m*, salvation; deliverance, security, safety; place of safety; salvage

salvante *adv inf* except, save

salvar *vt* to save; *ecc* redeem; avoid (difficulty, danger); exclude, except; leap, jump; pass over, clear; *law* prove innocent; *naut* salve. **s. la diferencia,** to bridge the gap. *vi* taste, sample (food, drink); *vr* be saved from danger; *ecc* be redeemed

salvavidas *m*, life belt; safety belt; life preserver; traffic island

salvedad *f*, qualification, reservation

salvo *a* safe, unharmed; excepting, omitting. *adv* except. **a s.,** safely, without harm. **a su s.,** to his (her, their) satisfaction; at his (her, etc.) pleasure. **dejar a s.,** to exclude, leave aside. **en s.,** in safety

salvoconducto *m*, safe conduct, pass

sallar *vt* to weed

samarita *a* and *mf* **samaritano** (**-na**) *a* and *n* Samaritan

samba *f* samba

sambenito *m*, penitent's gown (Inquisition); disgrace, dishonor

sambubia *f*, *Mexico* pineapple drink

san *a abb* of **santo.** Used before masculine singular names of saints except **Santos Tomás** (*or* **Tomé**), **Domingo, Toribio**

sanable *a* curable

sanador (**-ra**) *a* healing, curing. *n* healer

sanalotodo *m*, *inf* cure-all, universal remedy

sanar *vt* to cure, heal; *vi* recover, get well; heal

sanatorio *m*, sanatorium; convalescent home

sanción *f*, authorization, consent; sanction; penalty

sancionable *a* sanctionable

sancionar *vt* to authorize, approve; sanction

sancochar *vt cul* to parboil, half-cook

sancocho *m*, parboiled meat

sandalia *f*, sandal

sandez *f*, foolishness, stupidity; folly

sandía *f*, watermelon

sandio *a* foolish, inane

sandunga *f*, *inf* attractiveness, winsomeness, grace; *Lat. Am.* carousing

sandunguero *a inf* attractive, appealing, winsome

saneado *a* unencumbered, nontaxable, free

saneamiento *m*, guarantee, security; indemnity; stabilization (of currency); drainage

sanear *vt com* to guarantee, secure; indemnify; stabilize (currency); drain (land, etc.)

Sanedrín *m*, Sanhedrin

sangradura *f*, inner bend of the arm; *surg* bleeding; draining off

sangrar *vt surg* to bleed; drain off; *inf* extort money, bleed; *print* indent; draw off resin (from pines, etc.); *vi* bleed; *vr* bleed; have oneself bled; run (of colors)

sangre *f*, blood; lineage, family. **s. fría,** sang-froid. **a s. fría,** in cold blood, premeditated. **a s. y fuego,** by fire and sword, without quarter. *inf* **bullir la s.,** to have youthful blood in one's veins. **llevar en la s.,** *fig* to be in the blood. **subírsele la s. a la cabeza,** to grow excited. *fig inf* **tener s. de horchata,** to have milk and water in one's veins

sangría *f*, *surg* bloodletting; resin cut (on pines, etc.)

sangriento *a* bloody, bloodstained; bloodthirsty, cruel; mortal (insults, etc.); *poet* blood-colored

sangüesa *f*, raspberry

sanguijuela *f*, leech; *fig inf* sponger

sanguinario *a* vengeful, bloody, cruel

sanguíneo *a* blood; sanguineous; sanguine, fresh-complexioned; blood-colored

sanidad f, safety, security; healthiness; health department. **s. interior,** Public Health. **S. militar,** army medical corps

sanitario a sanitary, hygienic. m, mil medical officer

sano a healthy; safe, secure; healthful, wholesome; unhurt, unharmed; upright, honest; sincere; inf entire, undamaged; sane. **s. y salvo,** safe and sound. inf **cortar por lo s.,** to cut one's losses

San Pablo São Paulo

santa f, female saint

santamente adv in a saintly manner; simply

santero (-ra) a given to image worship. n accomplice (of a burglar); caretaker (of a hermitage); beggar

santiamén m, inf trice, twinkling

santidad f, sanctity; saintliness; godliness. **Su S.,** His Holiness

santificador (-ra) a sanctifying. n sanctifier

santificar vt to sanctify, make holy; consecrate; dedicate; keep (feast days)

santiguada f, crossing oneself; rough treatment, harsh reproof

santiguar vt to make the sign of the cross over; inf beat, rain blows on; vr cross oneself; inf be dumbfounded

santo a holy; saintly; saint (see **san**); consecrated; inviolate, sacred; inf simple, sincere, ingenuous. m, saint; image of a saint; saint's day, name day (of a person); mil password. **Santa Hermandad,** Holy Brotherhood (former name of the Spanish rural police force). **S. Oficio,** Holy Office, Inquisition. **S. y bueno,** Well and good, All right! inf **alzarse con el s. y la limosna,** to take the lot, make off with everything. **llegar y besar el s.,** to do in a trice. inf **No es s. de mi devoción,** I'm not very keen on him. inf **todo el s. día,** the whole blessed day

santón m, dervish, santon. inf hypocrite, sham saint

santoral m, book of saints; calendar of saints; choir book

santuario m, sanctuary

santurrón (-ona) a sanctimonious; hypocritical; prudish. n hypocrite

santurronería f, sanctimoniousness

saña f, fury, blind rage; lust for revenge, cruelty

sañoso, sañudo a furious, blind with rage; cruel

sapidez f, flavor, sapidity

sápido a tasty, savory

sapiencia f, wisdom; knowledge; erudition

sapo m, toad

saque m, sport serve, service; service or bowling line; sport server; sport bowler; bowling (in cricket)

saqueador (-ra) a looting, pillaging. n pillager, plunderer

saquear vt to pillage, plunder, sack

saqueo m, plundering, pillage, sacking

sarampión m, measles

sarape, m, Mexico woolen shawl or blanket worn by males

sarasa m, (inf and contemptuous) pansy, faggot

sarcasmo m, sarcasm

sarcástico a sarcastic

sarcia f, load, cargo

sarcófago m, sarcophagus

sarda f, mackerel

sardana f, traditional Catalonian dance

sardina f, sardine. **s. arenque,** herring. **como sardinas en banasta,** fig packed like sardines

sardinero (-ra) a sardine. n sardine seller or dealer. m, famous district of Santander

sardónico a sardonic

sarga f, (silk) serge; willow

sargenta f, sergeant's wife; inf mannish, overbearing woman

sargentear vt to be in charge as a sergeant; command, captain; inf boss

sargento m, sergeant

sarita f, Peru straw hat

sarna f, scabies. **s. perruna,** mange. **más viejo que la s.,** inf older than the plague

sarnoso a itchy; mangy

sarraceno (-na) a Saracen. n Saracen; Moor

sarracina f, scuffle

sarro m, furry encrustation, scale; film; tartar (on teeth)

sarta f, string, link (of pearls, etc.); file, line

sartén f, frying pan. **tener la s. por el mango,** inf to be top dog

sastra f, female tailor; tailor's wife

sastre m, tailor. **ser buen s.,** inf to be an expert (in)

sastrería f, tailoring; tailor's shop

Satanás m, Satan; devil

satánico a satanic

satélite m, satellite; follower, admirer, sycophant

satén m, sateen

satinar vt to calender; glaze; satin (paper)

sátira f, satire

satírico a satiric

satisfacción f, settlement, payment; atonement, expiation; satisfaction; gratification; amends; complacency, conceit; contentment; apology. **tomar s.,** to avenge oneself

satisfacer vt irr to pay, settle; atone for, expiate; gratify; quench; fulfill, observe; compensate, indemnify; discharge; meet; convince, persuade; allay, relieve; reward; explain; answer, satisfy; vr avenge oneself; satisfy oneself. Pres. Ind. **satis-**

fago, satisfaces, etc. *Fut.* **satisfaré,** etc. *Condit.* **satisfaría,** etc. *Preterite* **satisfice,** etc. *Past Part.* **satisfecho.** *Pres. Subjunc.* **satisfaga,** etc. *Imperf. Subjunc.* **satisficiese,** etc.

satisfactorio a satisfactory

satisfecho a self-satisfied, complacent; happy, contented

saturar *vt* to satiate, fill; saturate

saturnino a saturnine, melancholy, morose

Saturno m, Saturn

sauce m, willow. **s. llorón,** weeping willow

savia f, sap; energy, zest

saxófono *or* **saxofón** m, saxophone

saya f, skirt; long tunic

sayal m, thick woolen material

sayo m, loose smock; *inf* any garment. **cortar un s. (a),** *inf* to gossip behind a person's back

sayón m, executioner; *inf* hideous-looking man

sazón f, ripeness, maturity; season; perfection, excellence; opportunity; taste, flavor; seasoning. **a la s.,** at that time, then. **en s.,** in season; opportunely

sazonador (-ra) a seasoning. n seasoner

sazonar *vt cul* to season; mature; *vr* mature, ripen

se *object pron reflexive 3rd sing and pl mf* 1. Used as accusative (direct object) himself, herself, yourself, themselves, yourselves (e.g. **Juan se ha cortado,** John has cut himself). 2. Used as dative or indirect object to himself, at himself, herself, themselves, etc. (e.g. **María se mira al espejo,** Mary looks at herself in the mirror). Reciprocity is also expressed by reflexive (e.g. **No se hablan,** They do not speak to one another). When a direct object pron. (accusative) and an indirect object pron., both in the 3rd pers. (sing. or pl.), are used together, the indirect object pron. becomes **se** (instead of **le** or **les**) (e.g. **Se lo doy,** I give it to him). Many Spanish reflexive verbs have English equivalents that are not reflexive (e.g. **desayunarse,** to breakfast, **arrepentirse,** to repent, **quejarse,** to complain). Some intransitive (neuter) verbs have a modified meaning when used reflexively (e.g. **marcharse,** to go away, **dormirse,** to fall asleep). The passive may be formed by using **se** + 3rd pers. sing. of verb (e.g. **se dice,** it is said, people say). A number of impersonal phrases are also formed in this way (e.g. «**Se alquila,**» "To Let," «**Se vende,**» "For Sale"). The imperative is used in the same way (e.g. **Véase la página dos,** See page two)

sebáceo a sebaceous

sebo m, tallow; candle grease; fat, grease

seboso a tallowy; fat, greasy

seca f, drought; *naut* unsubmerged sandbank

secadora f, dryer, drying machine, clothesdryer. **s. de cabello,** hairdryer

secamente *adv* tersely, brusquely, curtly; dryly

secamiento m, drying

secano m, nonirrigated land; *naut* unsubmerged sandbank; anything very dry

secante a drying. a and f, *geom* secant. **papel s.,** blotting paper

secar *vt* to dry; desiccate; annoy, bore; *vr* dry; dry up (of streams, etc.); wilt, fade (of plants); become parched; grow thin, become emaciated; be very thirsty; become hard-hearted

sección f, act of cutting; section, part, portion; *geom mil* section. **s. cónica,** conic section. **s. de amenidades,** entertainment section (of a newspaper). **s. de reserva,** mil reserve list

seccionar *vt* to divide into sections, section

secesión f, secession

seco a dry; dried up, parched; faded, wilted; dead (plants) dried (fruits); thin, emaciated; unadorned; barren, arid; brusque, curt; severe, strict; indifferent, unenthusiastic; sharp (sounds); dry (wines). **a secas,** only; solely; simply, just. **en s.,** on dry land; curtly. *inf* **dejar s. (a),** to dumbfound, petrify

secreción f, segregation, separation; *med* secretion

secretaría f, secretaryship; secretary's office, secretariat

secretario (-ia) n secretary; amanuensis, clerk. m, actuary; registrar. **s. de asuntos exteriores** *or* **s. de asuntos extranjeros,** foreign secretary. **s. particular,** private secretary

secretear *vi inf* to whisper, have secrets

secreto m, secret; secrecy, silence; confidential information; mystery; secret drawer. a secret; private, confidential. **en s.,** in secret, confidentially. **s. a voces,** open secret

secta f, sect

sectario (-ia) a and n sectarian. n fanatical believer

sector m, sector

secuaz mf follower, disciple

secuela f, sequel, result

secuencia f, *ecc* sequence; (cinema) sequence

secuestrador (-ra) a sequestrating. n sequestrator

secuestrar *vt* to sequester; kidnap

secuestro m, sequestration; kidnapping; *surg* sequestrum

secular a secular, lay; centennial; age-old, ancient; *ecc* secular

secularizar *vt* to secularize; *vr* become secularized

secundar *vt* to second, aid

secundario *a* secondary; accessory, subordinate; *geol* mesozoic

sed *f*, thirst; desire, yearning, appetite. **apagar** (*or* **matar**) **la s.,** to quench one's thirst. **tener s.,** to be thirsty

seda *f*, silk; bristle (boar, etc.). **s. cordelada,** twist silk. **s. ocal,** floss silk. **s. vegetal** *or* **s. artificial,** artificial silk. *inf* **como una s.,** as smooth as silk; sweet-tempered; achieved without any trouble

sedación *f*, calming, soothing

sedar *vt* to soothe, calm

sedativo *a and m, med* sedative

sede *f, ecc* see; bishop's throne; *fig* seat (of government, etc.); Holy See (also **Santa S.**)

sedentario *a* sedentary

sedición *f*, sedition

sedicioso *a* seditious

sediento *a* thirsty; parched, dry (land); eager (for), desirous (of)

sedimentación *f*, sedimentation

sedimentar *vt* to leave a sediment; *vr* settle, form a sediment

sedimento *m*, sediment; dregs, lees; scale (on boilers)

sedoso *a* silky, silk-like

seducción *f*, seduction; temptation, blandishment, wile; charm, allurement

seducir *vt irr* to seduce; tempt, lead astray; charm, attract; corrupt, bribe. See **conducir**

seductivo *a* tempting; seductive, charming

seductor (**-ra**) *a* tempting; charming. *n* seducer; charming person

sefardí *mf* Iberian Jew or Jewess; *pl* Sephardim. *a* Sephardic

segadera *f*, sickle

segador *m*, reaper, harvester

segadora *f*, mowing machine, harvester; woman harvester

segar *vt irr* to scythe, cut down; reap, harvest; mow. See **cegar**

seglar *a* secular, lay. *mf* layman

segmento *m*, segment; *geom* segment. **s. de émbolo,** piston ring

segoviano (**-na**) *a and n* Segovian

segregación *f*, segregation

segregar *vt* to segregate, separate; *med* secrete

seguida *f*, continuation, prolongation. **de s.,** continuously; immediately. **en s.,** at once, immediately

seguidamente *adv* continuously; immediately

seguidilla *f*, popular Spanish tune and dance and verse sung to them; *inf* diarrhea

seguido *a* continuous, successive; direct, straight

seguidor (**-ra**) *a* following. *n* follower, disciple

seguimiento *m*, following, pursuit; continuation, resumption

seguir *vt irr* to follow; go after, pursue; prosecute, execute; continue, go on; accompany, go with; exercise (a profession); subscribe to, believe in; agree with; persecute; pester, annoy; imitate; *law* institute (a suit); handle, manage; *vr* result, follow as a consequence; follow in order, happen by turn; originate. *Pres. Part.* **siguiendo.** *Pres. Ind.* **sigo, sigues, sigue, siguen.** *Pres. Subjunc.* **siga,** etc. *Imperf. Subjunc.* **siguiese**

según *adv* according to; as. **s. parece,** as it seems. **s. y como,** as, according to

segundar *vt* to repeat, do again; *vi* be second, follow the first

segundero *a agr* of the second flowering or fruiting. *m*, second hand (of a watch)

segundo *a* second. *m*, second in command, deputy head; *ast geom* second. **segunda intención,** double meaning. **segunda velocidad,** *aut* second gear. **de segunda mano,** second-hand. **sin s.,** without peer or equal

segundogénito (**-ta**) *a and n* second-born

segurador *m*, surety, security (person)

seguramente *adv* securely, safely; surely, of course, naturally

seguridad *f*, security; safety; certainty; trustworthiness; *com* surety; *Mexico* clasp, lock (of a suitcase, trunk, etc) **con toda s.,** with complete safety, surely, absolutely. **de s.,** a safety

seguro *a* secure; safe; certain, sure; firm, fixed; reliable, trustworthy; unfailing. *m*, certainty; haven, place of safety; *com* insurance; permit; *mech* ratchet. **s. contra incendio, accidentes, robo,** fire, accident, burglary insurance. **s. sobre la vida,** life insurance. **de s.,** surely, certainly. **en s.,** in safety. **s. social** *Lat. Am.* social security

seis *a* six; sixth. *m*, six; sixth (of the month); playing card or domino with six spots. **Son las s.,** It is six o'clock

seiscientos *a* six hundred; six-hundredth. *m*, six hundred

selección *f*, selection, choice. **s. natural,** natural selection

selectivo *a* selective

selecto *a* choice, select, excellent

sellado *m, Argentina* postage

sellar *vt* to seal; stamp; end, conclude; close

sello *m*, seal; stamp. **s. fiscal,** stamp duty. **s. postal,** postage stamp. **s. y cruz** *Colombia,* heads or tails

selva *f*, forest, wood; jungle

selvático *a* sylvan, wood, forest; wild

selvoso *a* wooded, sylvan

semáforo *m*, semaphore, traffic light.

semana f, week; week's salary. **S. Mayor** or **S. Santa,** Holy Week. **entre s.,** during the week, on weekdays; weekdays

semanal a weekly; of a week's duration

semanario a weekly. m, weekly periodical

semanero, -a a employed by the week; paid by the week; person employed by the week; person paid by the week

semblante m, facial expression, countenance; face; appearance, look, aspect. **componer el s.,** to pull oneself together, straighten one's face. **mudar de s.,** to change color, change one's expression; alter (of circumstances)

semblanza f, biographical sketch. **s. literaria,** short literary biography

sembrado m, sown land

sembrador (-ra) a sowing. n sower

sembradura f, agr sowing

sembrar vt irr agr to sow; scatter, sprinkle; spread, disseminate. See **sentar**

semeja f, resemblance, similarity; indication, sign (gen. pl)

semejante a like, similar; such a; math similar. m, similarity, imitation. mf fellow man

semejanza f, similarity, likeness. **a s. de,** in the likeness of; like

semejar(se) vi and vr to resemble

semen m, semen; bot seed

semental a agr seed; breeding (of male animals). m, stallion

sementera f, agr sowing; sown land; seedbed; seedtime; fig hotbed, nursery, genesis

semestral a biannual, half-yearly; lasting six months

semestre a biannual. m, half-year, period of six months; six months' salary; semester

semicírculo m, semicircle

semidifunto a half-dead

semidormido a half-asleep

semilla f, bot seed; fig germ, genesis

semillero m, seedbed; nursery; fig hotbed, origin

seminario m, seedbed; nursery; genesis, origin; seminary; tutorial. **s. conciliar,** theological seminary

seminarista mf seminarist

semiótica f, med symptomatology; semiotics

semita mf Semite. a Semitic

semítico a Semitic

semivivo a half-alive

sémola f, semolina

sempiterna f, everlasting flower; thick woolen material

sempiterno a eternal

Sena, el the Seine

senado m, senate; senate house; any grave assembly

senador m, senator

senario a senary

senatorio a senatorial

sencillez f, simplicity; naturalness; easiness; ingenuousness, candor

sencillo a simple; unmixed; natural; thin, light (fabric); easy; ingenuous, candid; unadorned, plain; single; sincere

senda f, path, footpath; way; means

senderear vt to conduct along a path; make a pathway; vi attain by tortuous means

sendero m, footpath, path

sendos, sendas a m, and f pl, one each (e.g. **Les dio sendos lápices,** He gave them each a pencil)

senectud f, old age

senil a senile

senilidad f, senility

seno m, hollow; hole; concavity; bosom, breast; chest; uterus, womb; any internal cavity of the body; bay, cove; lap (of a woman); interior (of anything); heart; gulf; math sine; anat sinus

sensación f, sensation

sensacional a sensational

sensacionalista a sensationalist

sensatez f, prudence, good sense

sensato a prudent, wise

sensibilidad f, sensibility

sensibilizar vt phot to sensitize

sensible a sensible, sensitive; tender, feeling; perceptible; noticeable, definite; sensitive; sad, regrettable

sensiblemente adv appreciably; perceptibly; painfully, sadly

sensiblería f, sentimentality, sentimentalism

sensiblero a oversentimental

sensitivo a sensuous; sensitive, sensible

sensorio a sensory. m, sensorium

sensual a sensual; sensitive, sensible; carnal, voluptuous

sensualidad f, sensuality; sensualism

sensualismo m, sensualism; phil sensationalism

sensualista mf phil sensationalist; sensualist

sentadera f, Lat. Am. seat (of a chair)

sentadero m, resting place, improvised seat

sentado a prudent, circumspect

sentar vt irr to seat; vi inf suit, agree with (e.g. **No me sienta este clima (este plato),** This climate (dish) doesn't suit me); fit, become; inf please, satisfy, be agreeable to; vr sit down; inf leave a mark on the skin. Pres. Ind. **siento, sientas, sienta, sientan.** Pres. Subjunc. **siente, sientes, siente, sienten**

sentencia f, opinion, belief; maxim; law verdict, sentence; decision, judgment.

law **fulminar** (*or* **pronunciar**) **la s.,** to pass sentence

sentenciador *a law* sentencing

sentenciar *vt law* to sentence; *inf* destine, intend

sentencioso *a* sententious

sentidamente *adv* feelingly; sadly, regretfully

sentido *m*, sense (hearing, seeing, touch, smell, taste); understanding, sense; meaning, interpretation, signification; perception, discrimination; judgment; direction, way. *a* and *past part* felt; expressive; hypersensitive, touchy. **s. común,** common sense. **costar un s.,** *fig inf* to cost a fortune. **perder el s.,** to lose consciousness

sentimental *a* emotional; sentimental; romantic

sentimentalismo *m*, emotional quality; sentimentalism

sentimiento *m*, feeling, sentiment; sensation, impression; grief, sorrow. **Le acompaño a usted en su s.,** I sympathize with you in your sorrow (bereavement)

sentina *f*, well (of a ship); *naut* bilge; cesspool; sink of iniquity

sentir *vt irr* to feel, experience; hear; appreciate; grieve, regret; believe, consider; envisage, foresee; *vr* complain; suffer; think or consider oneself; crack; feel, be; go rotten, decay (gen. with *estar + past part.*). *m*, view, opinion; feeling. **sin s.,** without feeling; without noticing. *Pres. Part.* **sintiendo.** *Pres. Ind.* **siento, sientes, siente, sienten.** *Preterite* **sintió, sintieron.** *Pres. Subjunc.* **sienta, sientas, sienta, sintamos, sintáis, sientan.** *Imperf. Subjunc.* **sintiese,** etc.

seña *f*, sign, mark; gesture; *mil* password; signal; *pl* address, domicile. **s. mortal,** definite or unmistakable sign. **dar señas,** to show signs, manifest. **hablar por señas,** to converse by signs

señal *f*, mark, sign; boundary stone; landmark; scar; signal; trace, vestige; indication, symptom; token; symbol, sign; image, representation; prodigy, marvel; deposit, advance payment. **s. de aterrizaje,** *aer* landing signal. **s. de niebla,** fog signal. **señales horarias,** *rad* time signal. **en s.,** as a sign, in proof of. **s. luminosa de la circulación,** traffic light, traffic robot

señaladamente *adv* especially, particularly, notably

señalado *a* famous, distinguished; important, notable

señalador *m, Argentina* bookmark

señalamiento *m*, marking; pointing out; appointment, designation

señalar *vt* to mark; indicate, point out; fix, arrange; wound; signal; stamp; appoint (to office); *vr* excel

señero *a* solitary, isolated

señor *a inf* gentlemanly. *m*, owner, master; mister, esquire; **(S.)** the Lord; lord, sire. **s. de horca y cuchillo,** feudal lord, lord of life and death

señora *f*, lady; owner, mistress; madam; wife. **s. de compañía,** chaperon; lady companion. **Nuestra S.,** Our Lady

señorear *vt* to control, run, manage; master; domineer; appropriate, seize; dominate, overlook; restrain (emotions); *vr* behave with dignity

señoría *f*, lordship (title and person); lordship, jurisdiction; area, territory; control, restraint

señoría *f*, dignity, sedateness; self-control

señorial *a* manorial; noble, dignified, lordly

señoril *a* lordly, noble, aristocratic

señorío *m*, lordship; jurisdiction; dominion

señorita *f*, young lady; miss; *inf* mistress of the house •

señorito *m*, young gentleman; *inf* master of the house; master (address); *inf* young man about town

señuelo *m*, decoy; bait; allurement, attraction. **caer en el s.,** *fig inf* to fall into the trap

sepancuantos *m, inf* scolding, rebuke; spanking

separación *f*, separation

separado *a* separate

separador (**-ra**) *a* separating. *n* separator. *m*, filter. **s. de aceite,** oil filter

separar *vt* to separate; divide; dismiss (from a post); lay aside; *vr* retire, resign; separate

separatismo *m*, separatism

separatista *a* and *mf* separatist

septentrión *m, ast* Great Bear; north

septentrional *a* north; northern

septicemia *f*, septicemia

séptico *a* septic

septiembre *m*, September

séptimo *a* and *m*, seventh

septuagenario (**-ia**) *a* and *n* septuagenarian

sepulcro *m*, sepulcher

sepultador (**-ra**) *a* burying. *n* gravedigger; burier

sepultar *vt* to inter, bury; hide, cover up

sepultura *f*, interment; grave; tomb

sepulturero *m*, gravedigger

sequedad *f*, dryness, barrenness; acerbity, sharpness

sequía *f*, drought

séquito *m*, following, suite, retinue; general approval, popularity

ser *m*, essence, nature; being; existence, life. **El S. Supremo,** The Supreme Being, God

ser *vi irr* to be (e.g. **El sombrero es azul,**

The hat is blue). **Ser** may agree with either subject or complement, though when latter is *pl* the verb tends to be so too (e.g. **Son las once,** (**horas**), It is eleven o'clock. **Cien libras son poco dinero,** A hundred pounds is a small amount). If verbal complement is pers. pron., **ser** agrees with it both in number and person (e.g. **Son ellos,** It is they. **Soy yo,** It is I). In impers. phrases the pron. is not expressed (e.g. **Es difícil,** It is difficult. **Es sorprendente,** It is surprising). **ser** means to exist (e.g. **Pienso luego soy,** I think, therefore I am). **ser** (also **ser de** with nouns or obj. prons.) means to belong to, be the property of (e.g. **Este gato es mío,** This cat is mine. **El libro es de Juan,** The book belongs to John). Signifies to happen, occur (e.g. **¿Cómo fue eso?** How did that happen?). Means to be suitable or fitting (e.g. **Este vestido no es para una señora mayor,** This dress is not suitable for an elderly lady). Expresses price, to be worth (e.g. **¿A cuánto es la libra?** How much is it a pound?; How much is the pound (sterling) worth?). Means to be a member of, belong to (e.g. **Es de la Academia Española,** He is a member of the Spanish Academy). Means to be of use, be useful for (e.g. **Esta casa no es para una familia numerosa,** This house is no use for a large family). **Ser** expresses nationality (e.g. **Son francesas,** They are French. **Somos de Londres,** We are from London). *Auxiliary verb* used to form passive tense (e.g. **Esta historia ha sido leída por muchos,** This story has been read by many. **Fueron mandados al Japón,** They were sent to Japan. **s. de ver,** to be worth seeing. **s. para poco,** to be of little use, amount to little. **s. testigo de,** to witness. **¡Cómo es eso!** How can that be! Surely not! **¡Cómo ha de s.!** How should it be!; One must resign oneself. **Érase una vez** or **que érase,** Once upon a time. **es a saber,** viz., that is to say. **un sí es no es,** a touch of, a suspicion of. *Pres. Part.* **siendo.** *Pres. Ind.* **soy, eres, es,´ somos, sois, son.** *Fut.* **seré,** etc. *Condit.* **sería,** etc. *Preterite* **fui, fuiste, fue, fuimos, fuisteis, fueron.** *Imperf.* **era,** etc. *Past Part.* **sido.** *Pres. Subjunc.* **sea,** etc. *Imperf. Subjunc.* **fuese,** etc. *Imperat.* **sé**

seráfico *a* seraphic

serafín *m,* seraphim

serenar *vt* to calm; soothe; clear; *vr* grow calm; clear up (weather); clear (liquids); be soothed or pacified

serenata *f,* serenade

serenidad *f,* serenity, composure, tranquility; Serene Highness (title)

sereno *a* cloudless, fair; composed, serene. *m,* dew; night watchman

serie *f,* series, sequence, succession;

math progression; (*biol elec*) series; break (in billiards)

seriedad *f,* seriousness, earnestness; gravity; austerity; sternness; importance; sincerity; solemnity

serigrafía *f,* silkscreen printing

serio *a* serious, earnest; grave; austere; stern; important; sincere, genuine; solemn. **en s.,** seriously

sermón *m,* sermon; scolding. **dar un s.,** to give a sermon; scold

sermonear *vi* to preach sermons; *vt* scold

serpear *vi* to wind, twist; wriggle, squirm; coil

serpentear *vi* to wind, twist, meander; stagger along; wriggle; coil; *aer* yaw

serpenteo *m,* winding, twisting; wriggling; coiling; *aer* yaw

serpentina *f, min* serpentine; paper streamer

serpentino *a* serpentine; *poet* winding, sinuous

serpiente *f,* snake, serpent; Satan, the Devil; *ast* Serpent. **s. de anteojos,** cobra. **s. de cascabel,** rattlesnake

serranía *f,* mountainous territory

serrano (-na) *a* mountain, highland. *n* highlander, mountain dweller

serruchar *vt, Lat. Am.* to saw, saw off

serrucho *m,* handsaw. **s. de calar,** fretsaw

Servia Serbia

servible *a* serviceable; useful

servicial *a* useful, serviceable; obliging, obsequious

servicio *m,* service; domestic service; cult, devotion; care, attendance; military service; set, service; department, section; present of money; cover (cutlery, etc., at table); domestic staff, servants. **s. informativo,** news service. **s. nocturno permanente,** all-night service. **hacer un flaco s. (a),** *inf* to do someone an ill turn. **prestar servicios,** to render service, serve

servidor (-ra) *n* servant, domestic; name by which one refers to oneself (e.g. **Un s. lo hará con mucho gusto,** I (your servant) will do it with much pleasure). *m,* wooer, lover; bowler (in cricket). **los servidores de una ametralladora,** the crew (of a gun). **Quedo de Vd. atento y seguro s.,** I remain your obedient servant (in letters), Yours faithfully

servidumbre *f,* serfdom; servitude; servants, domestic staff; obligation, duty; enslavement (by passions); right of way; use, service

servil *a* servile; humble

servilismo *m,* servility; abjectness; absolutism (Spanish history)

servilleta *f,* table napkin. **s. higiénica,** sanitary napkin

servio (-ia) *a* and *n* Serbian

servir *vi irr* to be employed (by), be in the service (of); serve (as), perform the duties (of); be of use; wait (on), be subject to. *mil* serve in the armed forces; wait at table; be suitable or favorable; *sport* serve; perform a service; follow the lead (cards); (*with de*) act as, be a deputy for; be a substitute for; *vt* serve; worship; do a favor to; woo, court; serve (food, drink); *vr* be pleased or willing, deign; help oneself to (food); (*with de*) make use of. **no s. para nada,** to be good for nothing, be useless. **No sirves para tales cosas,** You are no good at this sort of thing. **Para s. a Vd,** At your service. **¡Sírvase de . . . !** (followed by infin.), Please! **s. de,** to serve as (e.g. **s. de base a,** to serve as a basis for). See **pedir**

sésamo *m,* sesame

sesenta *a and m,* sixty; sixtieth

sesentón (-ona) *n inf* person of sixty

sesga *f, sew* gore

sesgado *a* oblique, slanting

sesgar *vt sew* to cut on the bias; slant, slope; place askew, twist to one side

sesgo *a* slanting, oblique; serious-faced. *m,* slope, slant, obliquity; compromise, middle way. **al s.,** on the slant

sesión *f,* session, meeting; conference, consultation; *law* sitting; term. **abrir la s.,** to open the meeting. **levantar la s.,** to adjourn the meeting

seso *m,* brain; prudence; *pl* brains. **perder el s.,** to go mad; *fig* lose one's head

sestear *vi* to take an afternoon nap; rest; settle

sesteo *m, Lat. Am.* nap, siesta

sesudez *f,* prudence, shrewdness

sesudo *a* sensible, prudent

seta *f,* mushroom. **s. venenosa,** poisonous toadstool

setal *m,* mushroom bed, patch, or field

setecientos *a and m,* seven hundred; seven-hundredth

setenta *a and m,* seventy; seventieth

setentón (-ona) *n* septuagenarian

seter *m,* setter (dog)

setiembre *m.* See **septiembre**

seto *m,* fence; hedge

seudo *a* pseudo

seudónimo *m,* pseudonym

severidad *f,* severity; harshness; strictness, rigor; austerity, seriousness

severo *a* severe; harsh; strict, rigid, scrupulous, exact; austere, serious

sevillano (-na) *a and n* of or from Seville, Sevillian

sexagenario (-ia) *n* sexagenarian

sexo *m,* sex; (sexual) organ

sexología *f,* sexology

sexólogo (-ga) *n* sexologist

sexto *a* sixth

sexualidad *f,* sexuality

si *m, mus* B, seventh note of the scale. *conjunc* if; whether; even if, although. In conditional clause, **si,** meaning if, is followed by indicative tense unless statement be contrary to fact (e.g. **Si pierdes el tren, volverás a casa,** If you miss your train you will return home, *but* **Si hubieran venido habríamos ido al campo,** If they had come (but they didn't) we would have gone to the country). **Si** is used at the beginning of a clause to make expressions of doubt, desire, or affirmation more emphatic (e.g. **¡Si lo sabrá él, con toda su experiencia!** Of course he knows it, with all his experience. **¿Si será falsa la noticia?** Can the news be false?) **Si** also means whether (e.g. **Me preguntaron si era médico o militar,** They asked me whether I was a doctor or a soldier). Sometimes means even if, although (e.g. **Si viniesen no lo harían,** Even if they came they would not do it. **como si,** as if. **por si acaso,** in case, in the event of. **si bien,** although.

sí *pers pron reflexive 3rd pers m, and f, sing and pl* himself, herself, itself, themselves. Always used with prep. (e.g. **para sí,** for himself, herself, etc. **de por sí,** separately, on its own. **decir para sí,** to say to oneself

sí *adv* yes. **sí** or **sí que** is frequently used to emphasize a verb generally in contrast to a previous negative (e.g. **Ellos no lo harán, pero yo sí,** They won't do it but I will). Often translated by 'did' (e.g. **No lo vi todo, pero lo que sí vi,** I didn't see it all, but what I did see . . .), assent; yes; consent. **dar el sí,** to say yes; agree; accept an offer of marriage

siberiano (-na) *a and n* Siberian

sicario *m,* paid assassin

Sicilia Sicily

siciliano (-na) *a and n* Sicilian

sicoanálisis *m,* psychoanalysis

sicoanalista *mf* psychoanalyst

sicoanalizar *vt* to psychoanalyze

sicofanta, sicofante *m,* sycophant

sicología *f,* psychology

sicológico *a* psychological

sicólogo (-ga) *n* psychologist

sicomoro *m,* sycamore

sicopático *a* psychopathic

sicosis *f, med* psychosis

sicoterapia *f,* psychotherapy

SIDA *m,* AIDS

sidra *f,* cider

siega *f,* reaping, harvesting; harvest time; harvest, crop

siembra *f, agr* sowing; seedtime; sown field

siempre *adv* always. **s. que,** provided that; whenever. **para s.,** forever. **por s. jamás,** for always, for ever and ever

siempreviva *f, bot* everlasting flower. **s. mayor,** houseleek

sien f, anat temple

sierpe f, serpent, snake; anything that wriggles; kite (toy); bot sucker; hideous person

sierra f, carp saw; ridge of mountains; sawfish; slope; hillside. **s. de cerrojero,** hacksaw. **s. de cinta,** handsaw

siervo (-va) n slave; servant; serf

siesta f, noonday heat; afternoon nap

siete a seven; seventh. m, seven; seventh (days of the month); playing card with seven spots; number seven. **las s.,** seven o'clock. inf **más que s.,** more than somewhat, extremely

sífilis f, syphilis

sifilítico (-ca) a and n syphilitic

sifón m, siphon; siphon bottle; soda water; mech trap

sigilo m, seal; secrecy, concealment; silence, reserve

sigiloso a secret, silent

sigla f, acronym

siglo m, century; long time, age; social intercourse, society, world. **s. de oro,** golden age. **en** or **por los siglos de los siglos,** for ever and ever

signar vt to sign; make the sign of the cross over; vr cross oneself

signatura f, print signature; mark, sign; mus signature

significación f, **significado** m, meaning; importance, significance

significar vt to signify, indicate; mean; publish, make known; vi represent, mean; be worth

significativo a significant

signo m, sign, indication, token; sign, character; math symbol; sign of the zodiac; mus sign; med symptom; ecc gesture of benediction; destiny, fate

siguiente a following; next, subsequent. **el día s.,** the next day

sílaba f, syllable

silabear vi and vt to pronounce by syllables, syllabize

silabeo m, pronouncing syllable by syllable, syllabication

sílabo m, syllabus, list

silba f, hissing (as a sign of disapproval)

silbador (-ra) a whistling; hissing. n whistler; one who hisses

silbar vi to whistle; whizz, rush through the air; vi and vt theat hiss

silbato m, whistle; air hole

silbido, silbo m, whistle, whistling; hiss, hissing

silenciar vt to silence; keep secret

silencio m, silence; noiselessness, quietness; omission, disregard; mus rest. **en s.,** in silence; quietly; uncomplainingly. **pasar en s. (una cosa),** to pass over (something) in silence, omit. **s. de muerte,** deathly silence

silencioso a silent; noiseless; tranquil, quiet. m, (aut firearms) silencer

silla f, chair; riding saddle; mech rest, saddle; ecc see. **s. de manos,** sedan chair. **s. de montar,** riding saddle. **s. de posta,** post chaise. **s. de ruedas,** wheelchair. **s. de tijera,** deck chair; campstool. **s. giratoria,** swivel chair. **s. poltrona,** easy chair. inf **pegársele la s.,** to overstay one's welcome

sillar m, ashlar, quarry stone; horseback

sillería f, set of chairs; pew, choir stalls; chair factory; shop where chairs are sold; chair making; mas ashlar masonry

silleta f, bedpan; fireman's lift

sillín m, light riding saddle; seat, saddle (of bicycles, etc.)

sillón m, armchair; sidesaddle; Lat. Am. rocking chair. **s.-cama,** reclining chair. **s. de mimbres,** cane chair

silo m, agr silo; dark cavern, dark cave

silogismo m, syllogism

silueta f, silhouette; figure

siluro m, catfish; nav self-propelling torpedo

silva f, literary miscellany; metrical form

silvestre a bot wild; sylvan; uncultivated; savage

silvicultor m, forester

silvicultura f, forestry

sima f, abyss, chasm

simbiosis f, symbiosis

simbólico a symbolical

simbolismo m, symbolism

simbolista mf symbolist

simbolizar vt to symbolize, represent

símbolo m, symbol. **s. de la fe,** ecc Creed

simetría f, symmetry

simétrico a symmetric; symmetrical

simetrizar vt to make symmetrical

simiente f, seed; semen; germ, genesis, origin

simiesco a apish, ape-like

símil a similar. m, comparison; simile

similar a similar

similitud f, similarity

simio (-ia) n ape

simpatía f, liking, understanding, affection; fellow feeling; sympathy

simpático a friendly, nice, decent, congenial; sympathetic. **gran s.,** anat sympathetic

simpatizar vi to get on well, be congenial

simple a simple; single, not double; insipid; easy; plain, unadorned; stupid, silly; pure, unmixed; easily deceived, simple; naïve, ingenuous; mere; mild, meek. mf simpleton; fool

simpleza f, foolishness, stupidity; simplicity

simplicidad f, simplicity; candour, ingenuousness

simplicísimo *a sup* most simple, exceedingly simple

simplificable *a* simplifiable

simplificación *f*, simplification, simplifying

simplificador *a* simplifying

simplificar *vt* to simplify

simplista *mf* herbalist

simulación *f*, pretense, simulation

simulacro *m*, image, simulacrum; vision, fancy; *mil* mock battle

simuladamente *adv* pretendedly

simulador (**-ra**) *a* feigned. *n* dissembler

simular *vt* to feign, pretend

simultanear *vt* to perform simultaneously

simultaneidad *f*, simultaneousness

simultáneo *a* simultaneous

simún *m*, sandstorm

sin *prep* without (e.g. **Lo hizo s. hablar,** He did it without speaking). **s. embargo,** nevertheless. **s. fin,** endless. **s. hilos,** radio, wireless

sinagoga *f*, synagogue

sinapismo *m*, *med* mustard plaster; *inf* pest, bore

sincerarse *vr* to justify oneself; vindicate one's actions

sinceridad *f*, sincerity

sincero *a* sincere

síncope *m*, syncope

sincronizar *vt* to synchronize; *rad* tune in

sindéresis *f*, discretion, good sense

sindicación *f*, syndication

sindicado *m*, syndicate

sindical *a* syndical

sindicalismo *m*, syndicalism, trade unionism

sindicalista *mf* syndicalist, trade unionist. *a* syndicalistic, trade unionist

sindicar *vt* to accuse, charge; censure; syndicate

sindicato *m*, syndicate; trade union. **s. gremial,** trade union. **S. Internacional de Trabajadoras de la Aguja,** International Ladies' Garment Workers' Union

sindicatura *f*, (official) receivership

síndico *m*, *com* receiver, trustee

síndrome *m*, syndrome. **síndrome de inmunidad deficiente adquirida** acquired immunity deficiency syndrome

sinecura *f*, sinecure

sinergia *f*, synergy

sinfín *m*, countless number

sinfonía *f*, symphony

sinfónico *a* symphonic

sinfonista *mf* composer of symphonies, player in a symphony orchestra

sinfonola *f*, jukebox

singladura *f*, *naut* day's sailing; nautical twenty-four hours (beginning at midday)

singlar *vi naut* to sail a given course

singular *a* singular, single; individual; extraordinary, remarkable. *a* and *m*, *gram* singular

singularidad *f*, individuality, peculiarity; strangeness, remarkableness; oddness, eccentricity

singularizar *vt* to particularize, single out; *gram* make singular, singularize; *vr* distinguish oneself, stand out; be distinguished (by)

sinhueso *f*, *inf* tongue (organ of speech)

siniestra *f*, left, lefthand

siniestro *a* left (side); vicious, perverse; sinister; unlucky. *m*, viciousness, depravity (gen. *pl*); shipwreck, sinking; disaster, catastrophe; *com* damage, loss

sinnúmero *m*, countless number

sino *m*, fate, destiny. *conjunc* but; except (e.g. **No lo hicieron ellos s. yo,** They didn't do it, I did. **no . . . s.,** not . . . , but); only (e.g. **No sólo lo dijo él s. ella,** Not only he said it, but she did too)

sinónimo *a* synonymous. *m*, synonym

sinopsis *f*, synopsis

sinóptico *a* synoptic

sinrazón *f*, injustice, wrong

sinsabor *m*, unpleasantness, trouble; grief, anxiety

sintaxis *f*, syntax

síntesis *f*, synthesis

sintético *a* synthetic

sintetizar *vt* to synthesize

síntoma *m*, symptom

sintomático *a* symptomatic

sintonización *f*, *rad* tuning in

sintonizador *m*, *rad* tuner

sintonizar *vt rad* to tune in

sinuosidad *f*, sinuosity

sinuoso *a* sinuous, winding

sinvergüenza *mf* rascal, knave, rogue

sinvergüenzada *f*, *Lat. Am.* dirty thing (to do)

Sión Zion

sionismo *m*, Zionism

sionista *a* and *mf* Zionist

siquiatra *m*, psychiatrist

siquiatría *f*, psychiatry

síquico *a* psychic

siquiera *conjunc* although, even if. **s. . . . s.,** whether . . . or. *adv* at least; even (e.g. **Hay que pedir mucho para tener s. la mitad,** One must ask a great deal to get even half). **ni s.,** not even (e.g. **No había nadie, ni s. un perro,** There was no one, not even a dog)

Siracusa Syracuse

sirena *f*, mermaid, siren; siren; foghorn

sirga *f*, towline

Siria Syria

sirio (**-ia**) *a* and *n* Syrian. *m*, Sirius

sirte *f*, sandbank, submerged rock

sirvienta *f*, female servant

sirviente a serving. *m*, servant

sisa *f*, pilfering; *sew* dart. **s. dorada,** gold lacquer

sisador (-ra) *n* filcher, pilferer

sisar *vt* to pilfer, filch, steal; *sew* take in, make darts in

sisear *vi* and *vt* to hiss (disapproval); sizzle

sísmico a seismic

sismógrafo *m*, seismograph

sismología *f*, seismology

sismológico a seismological

sistema *m*, system. **s. ferroviario,** railroad system. **s. métrico,** metric system

sistemático a systematic

sistematizar *vt* to systematize

sístole *f*, systole

sitiador a besieging. *m*, besieger

sitiar *vt mil* to lay siege to; surround, besiege

sitio *m*, place, spot; room, space; site; locality; *mil* siege, blockade; *Lat. Am.* taxi stand **No hay s.,** There's no room

sito *past part* situated, located

situación *f*, situation; position; circumstances; condition, state; location

situado *past part* situated, placed. *m*, income, interest

situar *vt* to situate, locate, place; assign funds; *vr* place oneself

smoking *m*, tuxedo, tux, dinner jacket

snobismo *m*, snobbery

so *prep* under (used only with **color, pena, pretexto, capa**) (e.g. **so color de,** under the pretext of). *interj* **¡So!** Whoa! (to horses); *Lat. Am.* Hush!

soba *f*, rubbing; kneading; massaging; drubbing, beating; handling, touching

sobaco *m*, armpit; *bot* axil

sobajar *vt* to squeeze, press

sobaquera *f*, *sew* armhole; dress shield

sobar *vt* to rub; knead; massage; beat, thrash; handle, touch, paw (persons); soften

soberanear *vi* to tyrannize, domineer

soberanía *f*, sovereignty; dominance, sway, rule; dignity, majesty

soberano (-na) a sovereign; superb; regal, majestic. *n* ruler, lord. *m*, sovereign (coin)

soberbia *f*, arrogance, haughtiness; conceit, presumption; ostentation, pomp; rage, anger

soberbio a haughty, arrogant; conceited; superb, magnificent; lofty, soaring; spirited (of horses)

sobón a *inf* overdemonstrative, mushy; *inf* lazy

sobordo *m*, *naut* manifest, freight list

sobornador (-ra) a bribing. *n* briber

sobornar *vt* to bribe

soborno *m*, bribing; bribe; inducement

sobra *f*, excess, surplus; insult, outrage;

pl leftovers (from a meal); remains, residue; rubbish, trash. **de s.,** in abundance; in excess, surplus; unnecessary, superfluous; too well

sobradamente *adv* abundantly; in excess

sobrado a excessive; brazen, bold; wealthy, rich. *m*, garret

sobrante a surplus, leftover, remaining. *m*, remainder, surplus, excess

sobrar *vt* to exceed; have too much of (e.g. **Me sobran mantas,** I have too many blankets); *vi* be superfluous; remain, be left. *inf* **Aquí sobro yo,** I am in the way here, My presence is superfluous

sobrasada *f*, spicy sausage

sobre *prep* upon, on; above, over; concerning, about; apart from, besides; about (e.g. **s. las nueve,** at about nine o'clock) (indicates approximation); toward; after. *m*, envelope; address, superscription. **s. cero,** above freezing (Fahrenheit); above zero (Centigrade). **s. el nivel del mar,** above sea level. **s. manera,** excessively, extremely. **s. todo,** especially

sobreabundancia *f*, superabundance, excess

sobreabundante a superabundant

sobreabundar *vi* to be superabundant

sobrealiento *m*, heavy, painful breathing

sobrealimentación *f*, overfeeding; *aut* supercharge

sobrealimentar *vt aut* to supercharge

sobrecama *f*, bedspread, quilt

sobrecarga *f*, overload; rope, etc., for securing bales and packs; additional trouble or anxiety

sobrecargar *vt* to overload; weigh down; *sew* oversew, fell

sobrecargo *m*, *naut* purser; flight attendant

sobrecejo *m*, frown

sobrecoger *vt* to take by surprise; *vr* frightened or apprehensive

sobrecogimiento *m*, fright, apprehension

sobrecomida *f*, dessert

sobrecoser *vt sew* to oversew, whip

sobrecrecer *vi irr* to grow too much. See **conocer**

sobrecubierta *f*, second lid or cover; dust jacket (of a book); *naut* upper deck

sobrecuello *m*, overcollar; loose collar

sobredicho a aforementioned, aforesaid

sobreexcitar *vt* to overexcite

sobrefaz *f*, surface, exterior

sobreganar *vt* to make an excess profit

sobreguarda *m*, head guard; extra or second guard

sobrehilar *vt* to oversew or overcast. See **prohibir**

sobrehumano a superhuman

sobrellevar vt to help in the carrying of a burden; endure, bear; make excuses for, overlook; help

sobremesa f, tablecloth; after-dinner conversation. **de s.,** fig at the dinner table

sobrenatural a supernatural; extraordinary, singular

sobrenombre m, additional surname; nickname

sobrentender vt irr to take for granted, understand as a matter of course; vr go without saying. See **entender**

sobrepaga f, overpayment; extra pay

sobreparto m, time after parturition; afterbirth

sobrepasar vt to exceed; outdo, excel

sobreponer vt irr to place over; overlap; vr rise above (circumstances); dominate (persons). See **poner**

sobreprecio m, extra charge, rise in price

sobreproducción f, overproduction

sobrepujar vt to excel, surpass, outdo

sobrerrealista a and mf surrealist

sobrerrealismo m, surrealism

sobresaliente a overhanging; projecting; distinctive, outstanding; excellent, remarkable. m, "excellent" (mark in examinations). mf theat understudy

sobresalir vi irr to overhang, project; stand out; be conspicuous or noticeable; excel; distinguish oneself. See **salir**

sobresaltar vt to assail, rush upon; startle, frighten suddenly; vi art stand out, be striking; vr be startled or frightened

sobresalto m, sudden attack; unexpected shock; agitation; sudden fear. **de s.,** unexpectedly

sobresanar vt to heal superficially but not deeply; conceal, dissemble

sobrescribir vt to label; address, superscribe. Past Part. **sobrescrito**

sobrescrito m, address, superscription

sobrestante m, overseer; supervisor; foreman; inspector

sobresueldo m, additional salary, bonus

sobretarde f, early evening, late afternoon

sobretodo m, overcoat

sobrevenida f, sudden arrival

sobrevenir vi irr occur, take place; supervene. See **venir**

sobrevidriera f, storm window; wire-mesh window guard

sobrevienta f, gust of wind; fury, violence; shock, surprise. **a s.,** suddenly

sobreviviente a surviving. mf survivor

sobrevivir vi to survive

sobriedad f, sobriety, moderation

sobrina f, niece

sobrino m, nephew

sobrio a sober, moderate, temperate

socaliña f, cunning, craft

socaliñero (-ra) a cunning. n trickster

socapa f, blind, pretext. **a s.,** secretly; cautiously

socarra f, scorching, singeing; craftiness

socarrón a cunning, deceitful; malicious, sly (of humor, etc.)

socarronería f, cunning, craftiness; slyness (of humor, etc.); knavish action

socava f, undermining; agr hoeing round tree roots

socavar vt to undermine

sociabilidad f, sociability

sociable a sociable; social

social a social

socialismo m, socialism

socialista mf socialist. a socialistic

sociedad f, society; association; com partnership; com company. com **s. anónima,** incorporated company, limited company. **S. de las Naciones,** League of Nations. **s. de socorros mutuos,** mutual aid society, **s. en comandita,** private company

socio (-ia) n associate, partner; member. **s. comanditario,** com silent partner

sociología f, sociology

sociológico a sociological

sociólogo (-ga) n sociologist

socolor m, pretext. adv (also **so c.**) under pretext

socorredor (-ra) a aiding, succoring. n helper

socorrer vt to aid, succor, assist; pay on account

socorrido a helpful, generous, prompt to assist; well-equipped, well-furnished; well-supplied

socorro m, aid, help, assistance; payment on account; mil relief (provisions or arms)

socrático a socratic

sodio m, sodium

sodomía f, sodomy

sodomita mf sodomite. a sodomitic

soez a base, vile; vulgar

sofá m, sofa, couch

sofisma m, sophism, fallacy

sofista a sophistic. mf sophist, quibbler

sofistería f, sophistry

sofístico a sophistic, fallacious

soflama f, thin flame; glow; flush, blush; specious promise, deception

soflamar vt to shame, make blush; promise with intent to deceive, swindle; vr cul burn

sofocación f, suffocation, smothering; shame; anger

sofocador, sofocante a suffocating; stifling

sofocar vt to suffocate, smother; extinguish; dominate, oppress; pester, importune; shame, make blush, make angry; agitate; vr be ashamed; be angry

sofoco *m*, mortification, chagrin; shame; anger; suffocation, smothering; hot flush

sofrenada *f*, sudden check, pulling up short (of horses); harsh scolding; moral restraint

sofrenar *vt* to pull up, check suddenly (horses); scold harshly; restrain, repress (emotions)

soga *f*, rope; land measure (varies in length). *m*, *inf* rogue, knave

soja *f*, soybean

sojuzgador (-ra) *a* conquering, oppressive. *n* conqueror, oppressor

sojuzgar *vt* to conquer, oppress, subdue

sol *m*, sun; sunlight; day; Peruvian coin; *mus* G, fifth note of the scale, sol. **de s. a s.,** from sunrise to sunset. **hacer s.,** to be sunny. **morir uno sin s. sin luz y sin moscas,** *inf* to die abandoned by all. **no dejar a s. ni a sombra,** *inf* to follow everywhere; pester constantly. **tomar el s.,** to bask in the sun

solado *m*, paving; tile floor

solamente *adv* only; exclusively; merely, solely. **s. que,** only that; nothing but

solana *f*, sunny corner; Solarium

solanera *f*, sunburn; sunny spot

solapa *f*, lapel; excuse, pretext. **de s.,** *inf* secretly

solapado *a* cunning, sly

solapar *vt* *sew* to provide with lapels; *sew* cause to overlap; dissemble; *vi* *sew* overlap

solapo *m*, lapel; *inf* slap, buffet. **a s.,** *inf* secretly, slyly

solar *vt* *irr* to pave; sole (shoes). *m*, family seat, manor house; building site; lineage, family. *a* solar. See **colar**

solariego *a* a memorial; of an old and noble family

solas, a *adv* alone, in private

solaz *m*, consolation; pleasure; relief, relaxation. **a s.,** enjoyably, pleasantly

solazar *vt* to solace, comfort; amuse, entertain; rest; *vr* be comforted; find pleasure (in)

soldada *f*, salary, wages, emoluments; (*nav mil*) pay

soldadesca *f*, soldiering, military profession; troops. **a la s.,** in a soldier-like way

soldadesco *a* military, soldier

soldado *m*, soldier; defender, partisan. **s. raso,** *mil* private

soldador *m*, solderer, welder; soldering iron

soldadura *f*, welding, soldering; correction, emendation

soldar *vt* *irr* to weld; mend by welding; correct, put right; *mil* wipe out, liquidate. See **contar**

solecismo *m*, solecism

soledad *f*, solitude; loneliness; homesickness; *pl* melancholy Andalusian song and dance (also *f pl.* **soleares**)

solemne *a* solemn; magnificent; formal; serious, grave, important; pompous; *inf* downright, complete

solemnidad *f*, solemnity; magnificence; formality; gravity, seriousness; solemn ceremony; religious ceremony; legal formality

solemnización *f*, solemnization

solemnizar *vt* to solemnize, celebrate; extol

soler *vi* *irr defective* to be in the habit, be used; happen frequently (e.g. **Solía hacerlo los lunes,** I generally did it on Mondays. **Suele llover mucho aquí,** It rains a great deal here). See **moler**

solercia *f*, shrewdness, ability, astuteness

solevantado *a* agitated; restless

solevantar *vt* to raise, push up; incite to rebellion. **s. con gatos,** *mech* to jack up

solfeo *m*, *mus* sol-fa; *inf* spanking, drubbing

solicitación *f*, request; application; solicitation; wooing; search (for a post); attraction, inducement

solicitador (-ra) *a* soliciting. *n* solicitor. *m*, agent; applicant

solicitante *mf* applicant, candidate

solicitar *vt* to solicit; request; apply for; make love to, court; seek (posts, etc.); try to, attempt to; manage (business affairs); *phys* attract; appeal to

solícito *a* a solicitous; conscientious; careful

solicitud *f*, diligence, conscientiousness; solicitude; request; application; appeal, entreaty; petition; *com* demand. **a s.,** on request

solidaridad *f*, solidarity

solidario *a law* jointly responsible or liable

solidez *f*, solidity; *fig* force, weight (of arguments, etc.)

solidificar(se) *vt* and *vr* to solidify

sólido *a* compact, solid; thick; fast or lasting (of colors); indisputable, convincing. *m*, (*geom phys*) solid; solidus (ancient coin)

soliloquiar *vi* *inf* to soliloquize, talk to oneself

soliloquio *m*, soliloquy

solista *mf* soloist

solitario (-ia) *a* abandoned, deserted; solitary; secluded; solitude-loving. *n* recluse. *m*, solitaire diamond; hermit; solitaire (card game). **hacer solitarios,** to play solitaire (card game)

sólito *a* accustomed, wonted; customary, habitual

soliviantar *vt* to rouse, incite, excite

soliviar *vt* to help to lift up; *vr* half get up, raise oneself

sollastre *m*, scullion; brazen rogue

sollozante *a* sobbing

sollozar *vi* to sob

sollozo *m*, sob

solo *a* sole, only; alone; lonely; deserted, forsaken. *m*, solo performance; (cards) solo; solitaire (card game). **a solas**, alone; without help, unaided

sólo *or* **solo** *adv* only; merely, solely; exclusively

solomillo *m*, sirloin; filet (of meat)

solsticio *m*, solstice. **s. hiemal**, winter solstice. **s. vernal**, summer solstice

soltar *vt irr* to loosen; let go; disengage; untie; release; let drop; let out (a laugh, etc.); solve; *inf* utter; turn on (taps); set free; *vr* work loose; grow skillful; (*with prep.* a + *infin.*) begin to do (something). See **contar**

soltera *f*, spinster

soltería *f*, bachelorhood; spinsterhood

soltero *a* unmarried, single. *m*, bachelor

solterón *m*, confirmed bachelor

solterona *f*, confirmed old maid

soltura *f*, loosening; untying; freedom from restraint; ease, independence; impudence; immorality, viciousness; facility of speech; *law* release

soluble *a* soluble, dissolvable; solvable

solución *f*, dissolution, loosening; (*math chem*) solution; answer, solution; payment, satisfaction; *lit* climax; conclusion, end (of negotiations)

solucionar *vt* to solve, find a solution for

solvencia *f*, *com* solvency

solventar *vt* to pay or settle accounts; solve (problems, difficulties)

solvente *a com* solvent

somático *a* somatic, corporeal

sombra *f*, shadow; shade; darkness, dimness; specter, phantom; defense, refuge, protection; resemblance, likeness; defect; *inf* luck; gaiety, charm; trace, vestige; *art* shading, shadow. **sombras chinescas**, shadow show. **a la s.**, in the shade; *inf* in jail. **hacer s.**, to shade; *fig* stand in the light, be an obstacle; protect. **ni por s.**, by no means; without warning. **no tener s. de**, to have not a trace of. **. . . tener buena s.**, *inf* to be witty or amusing and agreeable. **tener mala s.**, *inf* to bring bad luck, exert an evil influence upon; be dull and disagreeable

sombrear *vt* to shadow, shade; *art* shade; *vi* begin to show (of mustaches, beards)

sombrerera *f*, milliner; hatbox

sombrero *m*, hat; *mech* cap, cowl; sounding board; head (of mushrooms, toadstools). **s. calañés**, Andalusian hat. **s. chambergo**, broad-brimmed plumed hat. **s. de canal** *or* **teja**, shovel hat (worn by clergymen). **s. de copa**, top hat. **s. de jipijapa**, Panama hat. *Lat. Am.* top hat. **s. de pelo** *Lat. Am.* top hat. **s. de tres picos**, three-cornered hat, cocked hat. **s. flexible**, soft felt hat. **s. hongo**, bowler (hat)

sombría *f*, shady spot

sombrilla *f*, sunshade

sombrío *a* dark; shadowy; overcast; *art* shaded; gloomy, melancholy

someramente *adv* superficially; briefly, summarily

somero *a* superficial, shallow; summary, rudimentary, brief

someter *vt* to put down, defeat; submit, place before; subject. **s. a votación**, to put to a vote. *vr* yield, surrender; (*with prep* a) undergo

sometimiento *m*, defeat; submission (to arbitration, etc.); subjection

somnambulismo *m*, somnambulism, sleepwalking

somnámbulo (-la) *a* somnambulistic. *n* somnambulist

son *m*, sound; rumor; reason, motive; means, way; guise, manner. **al s. de**, to the sound of; to the music of. **en s. de**, in the manner of, as, like, under pretext of

sonado *a* famous; much admired or talked of. **hacer una que sea sonada**, *inf* to cause a great scandal; do something noteworthy

sonaja *f*, metal jingles on a tambourine; baby's rattle

sonajero *m*, baby's rattle

sonar *vi irr* to sound; be quoted, be mentioned; ring; *inf* be familiar, remember (e.g. **No me suena el nombre,** I don't remember the name); (*with prep* a) be reminiscent of; *vt* sound; ring; play on; clink; *vr* be rumored, be reported; blow one's nose. *Pres. Ind.* **sueno, suenas, suena, suenan.** *Pres. Subjunc.* **suene, suenes, suene, suenen**

sonata *f*, sonata

sonda *f*, *naut* taking of soundings, heaving the lead; sound, plummet, lead; dragrope; probe, sound

sondar *vt naut* to take soundings; probe; *inf* sound, try to find out; bore, drill

sondeo *m*, *naut* sounding; *min* drilling; probing

soneto *m*, sonnet

sonido *m*, sound; literal meaning; rumor, report

sonoro *a* sounding; resonant, loud; sonorous

sonreir, sonereírse *vi and vr irr* to smile; *vi* look pleasant (landscape, etc.); look favorable (of circumstances). **sonreir tras la barba,** to laugh to oneself. See **reir**

sonriente *a* smiling

sonrisa *f*, smile

sonrojar *vt* to cause to blush; *vr* blush

sonrosado *a* rosy, rose-colored, pink

sonrosar *vt* to make rose-colored; *vr* blush, flush

sonroseo *m*, blush, flush

sonsaca *f*, removal by stealth; pilfering;

enticement; *fig* pumping (of a person for information)

sonsacar *vt* to remove by stealth; steal, pilfer; entice away; *fig* pump (a person for information), draw out

sonsonete *m*, rhythmic tapping or drumming; monotonous sound (gen. unpleasant); sarcastic tone of voice

soñador (**-ra**) *a* dreamy, sleepy. *n* dreamer

soñar *vt* to dream; imagine, conjure up; (*with con*) dream of; (*with prep a*) fear (of persons)

soñoliento *a* sleepy, drowsy; soothing; slow, leisurely

sopa *f*, sop, piece of bread; soup. **s. boba**, beggar's portion; life of ease at others' expense. **andar a la s.**, to beg one's way. **hecho una s.**, *inf* wet through

sopera *f*, soup tureen

sopero *m*, soup plate, soup bowl. *a* fond of soup

sopesar *vt* to try the weight of

sopetón *m*, blow, cuff. **de s.**, suddenly

soplada *f*, puff of wind

soplado *a inf* overelegant; haughty, stiff. *m*, fissure, chasm

soplador (**-ra**) *a* instigatory. *m*, blower, fan. *n* instigator; blower

soplar *vi* to blow; *vt* blow; blow away; inflate, blow up; filch, steal; instigate, inspire; accuse; fan; prompt, help out; *vr inf* eat and drink too much; *inf* be puffed up, grow haughty. *interj* **¡Sopla!** *inf* You don't say so!

soplo *m*, blow; blowing; instant, trice; *inf* hint, tip; *inf* accusation; *inf* tale-bearer; puff, breath (of wind)

soplón (**-ona**) *a inf* tale-bearing, backbiting. *n* tale-bearer. *m*, *aut* scavenger

soponcio *m*, *inf* fainting fit

sopor *m*, stupor; deep sleep

soporífero *a* soporiferous

soportable *a* bearable

soportar *vt* to bear; carry, support; put up with, tolerate

soporte *m*, rest, support; *mech* bearing; *mech* bracket, support; backup (of a computer file)

sorbedor (**-ra**) *a* supping, sipping. *n* sipper

sorber *vt* to suck; imbibe; swallow; *fig* absorb eagerly (ideas); sip

sorbete *m*, sherbet, iced drink; French ice cream

sorbo *m*, sucking; imbibition; swallow; sip; mouthful, gulp

sordamente *adv* secretly, quietly

sordera *f*, deafness

sórdido *a* dirty, squalid; mean, niggardly; sordid

sordina *f*, *mus* sordine, mute; *mus* damper. **a la s.**, on the quiet, in secret

sordo *a* deaf; silent, quiet; dull, muted (of

sounds); insensible, inanimate; obdurate, uncompliant. **a la sorda** *or* **a lo s.** *or* **a sordas**, in silence, quietly

sordomudez *f*, deaf-muteness, deaf-mutism

sordomudo (**-da**) *a* and *n* deaf-mute

sorna *f*, slowness, sluggishness; craftiness, guile, knavery; malice

soroche *m*, *Peru* altitude sickness, mountain sickness

sorprendente *a* surprising, amazing

sorprender *vt* to surprise, amaze

sorpresa *f*, surprise; amazement; shock

sorpresivo, -a *a*, *Lat. Am.* sudden, unexpected; surprising

sortear *vt* to raffle; draw lots for; avoid artfully (difficulties, etc.); fight (bulls)

sorteo *m*, raffle; casting lots

sortija *f*, ring (for a finger); ring (for a curtain, etc.); curl

sortilegio *m*, sorcery, magic

sortílego (**-ga**) *a* magic. *n* sorcerer, fortuneteller

sosa *f*, sodium carbonate, soda ash. **s. cáustica**, sodiumhydroxide, caustic soda, soda

sosegado *a* tranquil, peaceful, calm

sosegador (**-ra**) *a* soothing, calming. *n* appeaser, soother

sosegar *vt irr* to soothe, quiet; reassure; appease, moderate; *vi* grow still; rest, sleep; *vr* grow quiet; calm down, be appeased; grow still. See **cegar**

sosia *m*, double, exact likeness (of persons)

sosiego *m*, calm; peace, tranquility

soslayar *vt* to slant, place in an oblique position; *fig* go around (a difficulty)

soslayo *a* slanting. **al s.**, obliquely, on the slant; askance

soso *a* saltless, insipid; dull, uninteresting; heavy (of people)

sospecha *f*, suspicion

sospechar *vt* and *vi* to suspect

sospechoso *a* suspicious. *m*, suspect

sostén *m*, support; *mech* stand, support; brassiere, bra, bustier; steadiness (of a ship)

sostenedor (**-ra**) *a* supporting. *n* supporter

sostener *vt irr* to support; defend, uphold; bear, tolerate; help, aid; maintain, support. **s. una conversación,** to carry on a conversation. See **tener**

sostenido *a mus* sostenuto, sustained. *a* and *m*, *mus* sharp

sostenimiento *m*, support; defense; toleration, endurance; maintenance, sustenance

sota *f*, jack, knave (in cards); *inf* baggage, hussy. *m*, foreman, supervisor. *prep* deputy, substitute (e.g. **sotamontero,** deputy huntsman)

sótano *m*, basement, cellar

sotavento *m*, leeward. **a s.,** on the lee

sotechado *m*, hut, shed

soterrar *vt irr* to bury in the ground; hide, conceal. See **acertar**

sotileza *f*, fine cord for fishing (in Santander province)

soto *m*, thicket, grove, copse

soviético a soviet

sovoz, a *adv* in a low voice

su, sus *poss pron 3rd pers mf sing* and *pl* his, her, its, one's, your, their

suasorio a suasive, persuasive

suave a soft, smooth; sweet; pleasant, harmonious, quiet; slow, gentle; meek; delicate, subtle

suavidad *f*, softness, smoothness; sweetness; pleasantness; quietness; gentleness; meekness; delicacy

suavizador a softening, smoothing; soothing, quietening. *m*, razor strop

suavizar *vt* to soften; smooth; strop (a razor); moderate, temper; *mech* steady; quieten; ease

subalternar *vt* to put down, subdue

subalterno a subordinate. *m*, subordinate; *mil* subaltern

subarrendar *vt irr* to sublet. See **recomendar**

subarrendatario (-ia) *n* sublessee

subarriendo *m*, sublease, sublet

subasta *f*, auction sale. **sacar a pública s.,** to sell by auction

subastar *vt* to auction

subcentral *f*, substation

subclase *f*, subclass

subcomisión *f*, subcommittee

subconsciencia *f*, subconscious

subcutáneo a subcutaneous

subdirector (-ra) *n* deputy, assistant director

súbdito (-ta) a dependent, subject. *n* subject (of a state)

subdividir *vt* to subdivide

subgobernador *m*, deputy governor, lieutenant governor

subibaja *f*, seesaw, teetertotter

subida *f*, ascension, ascent; upgrade; rise; carrying up; raising (of a theater curtain)

subidero *m*, uphill road; mounting block; way up (to a higher level)

subido a strong (of scents); deep (of colors); expensive, high-priced; best, finest

subidor *m*, porter, carrier; elevator

subintendente *m*, deputy or assistant intendant

subir *vi* to ascend, climb, go up; mount; rise; *com* amount (to); reach; prosper, advance, be promoted; grow more acute (of illnesses); intensify; *mus* raise the pitch (of an instrument or voice); *vt* ascend, climb; pick up, take up; raise up; place higher; build up, make taller;

straighten up, place in a vertical position; increase, raise (in price or value); *vr* ascend, climb. **s. a caballo,** to mount a horse. **subirse a la cabeza,** *inf* to go to one's head (of alcohol, etc.)

subitáneo a sudden

súbito a unexpected, unforeseen; sudden; precipitate, impulsive. *adv* suddenly (also **de s.**)

subjefe *m*, deputy chief, second in command

subjetivo a subjective

subjuntivo a and *m*, subjunctive

sublevación *f*, **sublevamiento** *m*, rebellion, mutiny, uprising

sublévar *vt* to rouse to rebellion; excite (indignation, etc.); *vr* rebel

sublimación *f*, sublimation

sublimado *m*, *chem* sublimate

sublimar *vt* to exalt, raise up; *chem* sublimate

sublime a sublime

sublimidad *f*, sublimity, majesty, nobility

submarino a submarine. *m*, submarine. **s. de bolsillo** or **s. enano,** midget submarine

suboficial *m*, *mil* subaltern; *nav* petty officer

subordinación *f*, dependence, subordination

subordinado (-da) a and *n* subordinate

subordinar *vt* to subordinate

subproducto *m*, by-product

subrayar *vt* to underline; emphasize

subrepción *f*, underhand dealing; *law* subreption

subrepticio a surreptitious; clandestine

subrogar *vt law* to surrogate, elect as a substitute

subs—For words so beginning not found here, see sus—

subsanar *vt* to make excuses for; remedy, put right; indemnify

subscriptor (-ra) *n* subscriber

subsecretario (-ia) *n* assistant secretary

subsecuente a subsequent

subsidiario a subsidized; subsidiary

subsidio *m*, subsidy

subsiguiente a subsequent; next

subsistencia *f*, permanence; stability; subsistence, maintenance; livelihood

subsistir *vi* to last, endure; subsist, live; make a livelihood

subsuelo *m*, subsoil, substratum

subte *m*, *Argentina,* informal subway

subterfugio *m*, subterfuge, trick

subterráneo a underground, subterranean. *m*, subterranean place

subtítulo *m*, subtitle; caption

suburbano (-na) a suburban. *n* suburbanite

suburbio *m*, suburb

subvención f, subsidy, subvention, grant

subvencionar vt to subsidize

subvenir vt irr to help, succor; subsidize. See **venir**

subversivo a subversive

subvertir vt irr to subvert, overturn, ruin. See **sentir**

subyugación f, subjugation

subyugador (-ra) a subjugating. n conqueror

subyugar vt to subjugate, overcome

succión f, suction

suceder vi to follow, come after; inherit, succeed. *impers* happen, occur

sucedido m, inf event, occurrence

sucesión f, succession; series; offspring, descendants; law estate

sucesivo a successive. **en lo s.,** in future

suceso m, happening, occurrence; course (of time); outcome, result

sucesor (-ra) a succeeding. n successor

suciedad f, dirt; filth, nastiness; obscenity

sucinto a succinct, brief, concise

sucio a dirty, unclean; stained; easily soiled; fig sullied, spotted; obscene; dirty (of colors); fig tainted, infected. **jugar s.,** sport to play in an unsporting manner

suco m, juice

sucoso a juicy

sucre m sucre (monetary unit of Ecuador)

suculencia f, succulence; juiciness

suculento a succulent; juicy

sucumbir vi to yield, give in; die, succumb; lose a lawsuit

sucursal a branch. f, com branch (of a firm)

sud m, south (gen. **sur**). Used in combinations like **sudamericano**

sudadero m, horse blanket; sudatorium, sweating bath

sudafricano (-na) a and n South African

Sudamérica f South America

sudamericano (-na) a and n South American

sudante a sweating, perspiring

sudar vi and vt to perspire, sweat; ooze; vi inf toil; vt bathe in sweat; inf give reluctantly. **s. frío,** to break out in a cold sweat. **s. la gota gorda,** fig inf to be in a stew

sudario m, shroud

sudeste m, southeast; southeast wind

sudoeste m, southwest; southwest wind

sudor m, sweat, perspiration; toil; juice, moisture, sap, gum

sudoroso a sweaty

Suecia Sweden

sueco (-ca) a Swedish. n Swede. m, Swedish (language)

suegra f, mother-in-law

suegro m, father-in-law

suela f, sole (of a shoe); icht sole; tanned leather; base. **no llegarle a uno a la s. del zapato,** inf to be not fit to hold a candle to.

sueldo m, salary, wages; ant Spanish coin. **a s.,** for a salary, salaried

suelo m, ground, earth; soil; bottom, base; sediment, dregs; site, plot; floor; flooring; story; land, territory; hoof (of horses); earth, world; pl chaff of grain. **s. natal,** native land; **besar el s.,** inf to fall flat. **dar consigo en el s.,** to fall down. **dar en el s. con,** to throw down; damage, spoil. inf **estar (una cosa) por los suelos,** to be dirt cheap

suelta f, loosening, unfastening; hobble (for horses); relay of oxen. **dar s. a,** to let loose, allow to go out for a time

sueltista mf, Lat. Am. freelance journalist, stringer

suelto a swift; competent, efficient; odd, separate; licentious; flowing, easy (style); loose, unbound. m, single copy (of a newspaper); loose change; newspaper paragraph

sueño m, dream; sleep; drowsiness, desire for sleep; vision, fancy. **s. pesado,** deep sleep. **conciliar el s.,** to court sleep. **echar un s.,** inf to take a nap. **en sueños,** in a dream; while asleep. **entre sueños,** between sleeping and waking. **¡Ni por sueño!** inf Certainly not! I wouldn't dream of it!

suero m, serum. **s. de la leche,** whey

suerte f, chance, luck; good luck; destiny, fate; condition, state; kind, species, sort; way, manner; bullfighter's maneuver; parcel of land. **de s. que,** so that; as a result. **echar suertes,** to draw lots. **tener buena s.,** to be lucky

suéter m, sweater

suficiencia f, sufficiency; talent, aptitude; pedantry. **a s.,** enough

suficiente a sufficient, enough; suitable

sufijo m, suffix

sufragar vt to assist, aid; favor; pay, defray

sufragio m, aid, assistance; ecc suffragium, pious offering; vote; suffrage

sufragista f, suffragette

sufrible a bearable, endurable

sufrido a long-suffering, resigned; complaisant (of husbands); dirt-resistant (colors)

sufrimiento m, suffering, pain; affliction; tolerance

sufrir vt to suffer, undergo, experience; bear, endure; tolerate, put up with; allow, permit; resist, oppose; expiate; vi suffer

sugerir vt irr to suggest. See **sentir**

sugestión f, suggestion

sugestionable a easily influenced, open to suggestion

sugestionador a suggestive

sugestionar *vt* to suggest hypnotically; dominate, influence

sugestivo a suggestive, stimulating

suicida a suicidal, fatal. *mf* suicide (person)

suicidarse *vr* to commit suicide

suicidio *m*, suicide (act)

Suiza Switzerland

suizo (-za) a and *n* Swiss

sujeción *f*, subjection, domination; fastening, fixture; obedience, conformity

sujetador *m*, clamp; clip

sujetar *vt* to fasten, fix; hold down; grasp, clutch; subdue; *vr (with prep* a) conform to, obey. **s. con alfileres,** to pin up. **s. con tornillos,** to screw down

sujeto a liable, subject. *m*, topic, subject; person, individual; *gram phil* subject

sulfurar *vt* to sulphurate; *vr* grow irritated, become angry

sulfúrico a sulphuric

sultán *m*, sultan

suma *f*, total; amount, sum; *math* addition; summary, digest; computation. **en s.,** in brief, in short, finally

sumador (-ra) *n* summarizer; computator, adder

sumamente *adv* extremely, most

sumar *vt* to sum up, summarize; *math* add up

sumaria *f*, written indictment

sumariamente *adv* concisely, in brief; *law* summarily

sumario a brief, concise, abridged; *law* summary. *m*, summary, résumé, digest

sumergible a sinkable; submergible. *m*, submarine

sumergir *vt* to dip, immerse, sink, submerge; *fig* overwhelm (with grief, etc.); *vr* sink; dive; be submerged

sumersión *f*, immersion, dive, submersion

sumidero *m*, cesspool; drain; sink; pit, gully

suministrar *vt* to purvey, supply, provide

suministro *m*, purveyance; provision; supply

sumir *vt* to sink; submerge; *ecc* consummate; *fig* overwhelm (with grief, etc.); *vr* fall in, become sunken (of cheeks, etc.); sink; be submerged; *Lat. Am.* cower, cringe

sumisión *f*, submission, obedience; *com* estimate, tender

sumiso a submissive, docile

sumista *mf* quick reckoner, computator. *m*, condenser, summarizer, abridger

sumo a supreme; high; tremendous, extraordinary. **a lo s.,** at the most; even if, although. **en s. grado,** in the highest degree

suntuoso a magnificent, luxurious, sumptuous

supeditar *vt* to oppress; overcome, conquer; subordinate

superabundante a superabundant, excessive

superádito a superadded

superar *vt* to overcome, conquer; surpass; do better than

superávit *m*, *com* balance, surplus

superchería *f*, trickery, guile

supereminencia *f*, supereminence, greatest eminence

supereminente a supereminent

superentender *vt irr* to supervise, superintend. See **entender**

superestructura *f*, superstructure

superficial a surface, shallow; superficial, rudimentary; futile

superficialidad *f*, superficiality; futility; shallowness

superficie *f*, area; surface; outside, exterior. **s. de rodadura,** tire tread

superfino a superfine

superfluo a superfluous, redundant

superhombre *m*, superman

superintendencia *f*, supervision; superintendentship; higher administration

superintendente *mf* superintendent; supervisor

superior a higher, upper; excellent, fine; superior; higher (education, etc.). *m*, head, director; superior

superiora *f*, mother superior

superioridad *f*, superiority

superlativo a and *m*, superlative

superproducción *f*, overproduction; superproduction

superrealismo *m*, surrealism

superrealista a surrealist

superstición *f*, superstition

supersticioso a superstitious

supervigilancia *f*, *Lat. Am.* supervision

supervivencia *f*, survival

superviviente a surviving. *mf* survivor

supino a supine; foolish, stupid. *m*, *gram* supine

suplantación *f*, supplanting

suplantar *vt* to forge, alter (documents); supplant

suplefaltas *mf inf* scapegoat

suplementario a supplementary, additional

suplemento *m*, supplement; supply, supplying; newspaper supplement; *geom* supplement

suplente *m*, substitute, proxy; *fig* makeweight

súplica *f*, supplication, prayer; request

suplicación *f*, entreaty, supplication; *law* petition

suplicante a supplicatory; *law* petitioning. *mf* supplicator; *law* petitioner

suplicar vt to beg, supplicate; request; law appeal

suplicio m, torment, torture; execution; place of torture or execution; affliction, anguish. **último s.,** capital punishment

suplir vt to supply, furnish; substitute, take the place of; overlook, forgive

suponer vt irr to suppose, take for granted; simulate; comprise, include; vi carry weight, wield authority. See **poner**

suposición f, supposition; conjecture, assumption; distinction, talent, importance; falsity, falsehood

supositorio m, suppository

supremacía f, supremacy

supremo a supreme; matchless, incomparable; last

supresión f, suppression; destruction, eradication; omission

suprimir vt to suppress; destroy, eradicate; omit, leave out. **s. una calle al tráfico,** to close a street to traffic, ban traffic from a street

supuesto a supposed; so-called; reputed. m, supposition, hypothesis. **por s.,** presumably; doubtless

supurar vi to suppurate

sur m, south; south wind

surcar vt to plow furrows; furrow, line; cut, cleave (water, etc.)

surco m, furrow; wrinkle, line; groove, channel; rut

surgidero m, naut road, roadstead

surgir vi to spout, gush, spurt; naut anchor; appear, show itself; come forth, turn up

surrealismo m, surrealism

surrealista a and mf surrealist

surtida f, hidden exit; false door; naut slipway

surtidero m, outlet, drain; jet, fountain

surtido a mixed, assorted. m, variety, assortment; stock, range. **de s.,** in everyday use

surtidor (-ra) n purveyor, supplier. m, fountain, jet. **s. de gasolina,** gasoline pump, gas pump

surtimiento m, assortment; stock

surtir vt to provide, supply, furnish; vi spurt, gush

surto a calm, reposeful; naut anchored

susceptibilidad f, susceptibility

susceptible a susceptible, open to; touchy, oversensitive

suscitar vt to cause, originate; provoke, incite; vr arise, take place

suscribir vt to sign; agree to; vr subscribe, contribute; take out a subscription (to a periodical, etc.). Past Part. **suscrito**

suscripción f, subscription; agreement, accession

susodicho a aforesaid

suspender vt to suspend, hang up; postpone, defer, stop; amaze, dumbfound; suspend (from employment); fail (an exam); adjourn (meetings); vr rear (of horses)

suspensión f, suspension; postponement, stoppage, deferment; amazement; failure (in an exam); adjournment (of a meeting); springs (of a car). com **s. de pagos,** suspension of payments. **con mala s.,** badly sprung (of a car)

suspensivos m, pl suspension points, ellipsis points

suspenso a amazed, bewildered. m, failure slip (in an exam). **en s.,** in suspense

suspensor m, Lat. Am. suspender (for pants)

suspicacia f, suspiciousness; mistrust, uneasiness

suspicaz a suspicious, mistrustful

suspirado a eagerly desired, longed for

suspirar vt and vi to sigh. **s. por,** to long for

suspiro m, sigh; breath; glass whistle; mus brief pause, pause sign. **último s.,** inf last kick, end

sustancia f, substance, juice, extract, essence; fig core, pith; fig meat; wealth, estate; worth, importance; nutritive part; inf common sense. anat **s. gris,** gray matter. **en s.,** in short

sustanciación f, substantiation

sustancial a substantial, real; important, essential; nutritive; solid

sustanciar vt to substantiate; summarize, extract, abridge

sustancioso a substantial; nutritive

sustantivo a and m, gram substantive, noun

sustentable a arguable, defensible

sustentación f, maintenance; defense

sustentar vt to sustain, keep; support, bear; nourish, feed; uphold, advocate. **s. un ciclo de conferencias,** to give a series of lectures

sustento m, maintenance, preservation; nourishment, sustenance; support

sustitución f, substitution

sustituible a substitutive, replaceable

sustituir vt irr to substitute. See **huir**

sustituto (-ta) n substitute

susto m, fright, shock; apprehension. **dar un s. (a),** to scare

sustracción f, subtraction

sustraer vt irr to remove, separate; rob, steal; math subtract; vr depart, remove oneself; avoid. See **traer**

susurrador (-ra) a whispering; murmuring; rustling. n whisperer

susurrante a whispering; murmuring; rustling

susurrar vi to whisper; murmur; rustle; babble, purl, prattle (of water); vi and vr be whispered abroad

susurro *m*, whispering, whisper; murmur; rustle; lapping

sutil a fine, thin; penetrating, subtle, keen

sutileza, sutilidad *f*, fineness, thinness; subtlety, penetration. **sutileza de manos,** dexterity; light-fingeredness; sleight of hand

sutilizaciones *f, pl* casuistry, hairsplitting, quibbling

sutilizar *vt* to make thin, refine; *fig* finish, perfect; *fig* split hairs, make subtle distinctions

sutura *f*, suture

suyo, suya *m*, and *f*, *pl* **suyos, suyas,** *poss pron* and *a 3rd pers* his; hers; its; yours; theirs; of his, of hers, etc. (e.g. **Este libro es suyo,** This book is his (hers, yours, theirs). **Este libro es uno de los suyos,** This book is one of his (hers, etc.). (**suyo** is often used with def. art. **el, la,** etc.) **los suyos,** his (hers, yours, etc.) family, following, adherents, etc. **de suyo,** of its very nature, of itself; spontaneously. **salirse con la suya,** to get one's own way. *inf* **ver la suyo,** to see one's opportunity

T

tabacó *m*, tobacco plant, tobacco leaf; tobacco; cigar. **t. de pipa,** pipe tobacco. **t. flojo,** mild tobacco. **t. rubio,** Virginia tobacco

tabalear(se) *vt* and *vr* to rock, sway, swing; *vi* drum with the fingers

tabaleo *m*, swaying, rocking; drumming with the fingers

tábano *m*, *ent* horsefly

tabanque *m*, potter's wheel

tabaque *m*, small osier basket (for fruit, sewing, etc.); large tack

tabaquera *f*, tobacco jar, tobacco tin; bowl of pipe tobacco; tobacco pouch; snuffbox

tabaquería *f*, tobacconist's shop

tabaquero (-ra) *n* tobacco grower; tobacco merchant; tobacco factory worker; tobacconist

tabardillo *m*, fever. **t. de tripas,** typhoid. **t. pintado,** typhus

taberna *f*, public house, tavern

tabernáculo *m*, tabernacle

tabicar *vt* to wall or board up; hide, cover up

tabique *m*, partition wall, inside wall; thin wall

tabla *f*, plank of wood, board; *met* plate; slab; flat side, face (of wood); *sew* box pleat; table (of contents, etc.); *art* panel; vegetable garden; butcher's slab; butcher's stall; *pl* tablets (for writing); (*math* etc.) tables; stalemate (chess, checkers); draw (in an election); *theat* boards, stage. **t. de armonía,** sounding board (of musical instruments). **t. de lavar,** washboard. **t. de materias,** table of contents. **t. de multiplicación,** multiplication table. **t. rasa,** clean sheet (of paper, etc.); complete ignorance. **T. Redonda,** Round Table (of King Arthur). **escapar** *or* **salvarse en una t.,** to have a narrow escape, escape in the nick of time

tablado *m*, flooring; platform; *theat* stage; scaffold, gibbet. **sacar al t.,** to produce, put on the stage; to make known, publish

tablear *vt* to saw into planks; *sew* make box pleats in; hammer iron into sheets

tablero *m*, board (of wood); paneling, boarding; slab; shop counter; board (checkers, chess). **t. de instrumentos,** dashboard; instrument panel

tableta *f*, tablet; pastille; lozenge

tablilla *f*, small board; tablet; bulletin board, notice board

tablón *m*, thick plank; wooden beam; *inf* drinking bout

tabú *m*, taboo

taburete *m*, stool; tabouret

tacañería *f*, miserliness, niggardliness; craftiness

tacaño a miserly, niggardly; crafty

tacha *f*, imperfection, defect; spot, stain; fault; large tack. **poner t.,** to criticize, object to

tachable a censurable, blameworthy

tachar *vt* to criticize, blame; cross out, erase; charge, accuse

tacho de basura *m*, *Argentina* garbage can

tachón *m*, round-headed ornamental nail; *sew* gold or silver studs, trimming; crossing out, erasure

tachonar *vt* to stud with round-headed nails; *sew* trim with gold or silver studs or trimming

tachoso a imperfect, defective, faulty; spotted, stained

tachuela *f*, *carp* tack

tácito a silent, unexpressed; tacit, implied

taciturno a taciturn; reserved; dismal, gloomy, melancholy

taco *m*, stopper, plug; billiard cue; rammer; wad, wadding (in a gun); pop gun; taco (filled tortilla); tear-off calendar; *Argentina*, heel (of a shoe) *inf* snack; obscenity, oath. **t. de papel,** writing tablet

tacón *m*, heel (of a shoe)

taconear *vi* to stamp with one's heels; walk heavily on one's heels; walk arrogantly

táctica *f*, method, technique; *mil* tactics; policy, way, means

táctico a tactical. *m*, *mil* tactician

táctil a tactile

tacto *m*, sense of touch; touch, feel; touching; skill; tact

tafetán *m*, taffeta; *pl* flags, standards. **t. de heridas** *or* **t. inglés,** court plaster

tafilete *m*, morocco leather

tahúr *m*, gambler; cardsharper

Tailandia Thailand

taimado a knavish, crafty; obstinate, headstrong

taimería *f*, cunning, craftiness

taita *m*, daddy

taja *f*, cut, cutting; slice; washboard

tajada *f*, slice; strip, portion; steak, filet; *inf* cough; drinking bout; hoarseness

tajadera *f*, cheese knife; chisel; *pl* sluice gate

tajado a steep, sheer (of cliffs, etc.)

tajadura *f*, cutting, dividing, dissection

tajar *vt* to cut, chop; sharpen, trim (quill pens)

tajear *vt*, *Lat. Am.* to cut up

Tajo, el the Tagus

tajo *m*, cut, incision; task; cutting (in a mountain, etc.); cut, thrust (of sword); executioner's block; chopping board; washboard; steep cliff, precipice

tajón *m,* butcher block; chopping board

tal *a pl* **tales,** such; said (e.g. **el t. Don Juan,** the said Don Juan). **tal** is always used before nouns and (except when meaning 'the said') without def. art. **un t.,** a certain (e.g. **un t. hombre,** a certain man). *pron* some, some people; someone; such a thing. *adv* so, thus. **t. para cual,** two of a kind, a well-matched pair; tit for tat. **con t. que,** *conjunc* on condition that, provided that. **No hay t.,** There is no such thing. *inf* **¿Qué t.?** How are you? What's the news? What's new?

tala *f,* felling or cutting down (of trees); cropping of grass (ruminants)

talador (-ra) *a* felling, cutting; destructive. *n* feller, cutter; destroyer

taladrar *vt* to drill, bore, gouge holes; pierce, perforate; punch (a ticket); assail or hurt the ear (sounds); *fig* go into deeply (a subject)

taladro *m,* drill, gimlet, gouge; drill hole, bore; puncher (for tickets, etc.)

tálamo *m,* marriage bed; *(bot anat)* thalamus

talante *m,* mode of execution, technique; personal appearance, mien; disposition, temperament; wish, desire; aspect, appearance. **de buen (mal) t.,** willingly (unwillingly)

talar *a* full-length, long (of gowns, robes, etc.)

talar *vt* to fell, chop down (trees); ravage, lay waste; prune (gen. olive trees)

talco *m, min* talc; sequin; tinsel

talcualillo *a inf* not too bad, fairly good; slightly better (of health)

taled *m,* prayer shawl, tales, tallit

talega *f,* sack, bag; sackful; money bag; *pl inf* cash wealth

talego *m,* narrow sack; *inf* dumpy person

talento *m,* talent (Greek coin); talent, gift, quality; intelligence, understanding; cleverness

talentoso *a* talented

talión *m,* **(ley de)** law of retaliation

talismán *m,* talisman

talla *f,* carving (especially wood); cutting (of gems); reward for apprehension of a criminal; ransom; stature, height, size; height measuring rod

tallado *a* **bien** (or **mal**), well (or badly) carved; well (or badly) proportioned, of a good (or bad) figure

tallado *m,* carving

tallador *m,* metal engraver; die sinker

tallar *vt art* to carve; engrave; cut (gems); value, estimate; measure height (of persons)

tallarín *m,* (gen. *pl*) *cul* noodle

talle *m,* figure, physique; waist; fit (of clothes); appearance, aspect. *inf* **largo de t.,** long-waisted; long drawn out, overlong. **tener buen t.,** to have a good figure

taller *m,* workshop; factory; mill; workroom, atelier; industrial school; school of arts and crafts; studio

tallista *mf* engraver; wood carver; sculptor

tallo *m, bot* stalk; shoot; slice of preserved fruit; cabbage. **t. rastrero,** *bot* runner

talludo *a* long-stalked; lanky, overgrown; no longer young, aging (of women); habit-ridden

talmúdico *a* Talmudic

talón *m,* heel; heel (of a shoe); *com* counterfoil; luggage receipt; *com* sight draft; coupon; heel (of a violin bow). *inf* **apretar los talones,** to take to one's heels. *inf* **pisarle (a uno) los talones,** to follow on a person's heels; rival successfully

talonario *m,* stub book

tamaño *a comp* so big; so small (e.g. **La conocí tamaña,** I knew her when she was so high) (indicating her size with a gesture)); so great, so large (e.g. **tamaña empresa,** so great an undertaking). *m,* size

tamarindo *m,* tamarind

tambalear(se) *vi* and *vr* to totter, sway, shake; reel, stagger

tambaleo *m,* swaying; tottering; rocking; shaking; staggering, reeling

también *adv* also, too; in addition, as well

tambor *m, mus* drum; drummer; embroidery frame; *mech* drum, cylinder; roaster (for coffee, chestnuts, etc.). **t. mayor,** drum major. **a t.** (or **con t.**) **batiente,** with drums beating; triumphantly, with colors flying

tamborear *vi* to totter, sway; stagger, reel

tamboril *m,* tabor

tamborilear *vi* to play the tabor; *vt* eulogize, extol

tamborín *m,* tabor

Támesis, el the Thames

tamiz *m,* sieve

tamizar *vt* to sieve

tampoco *adv* neither, not . . . either, nor . . . either; no more (e.g. **No lo ha hecho María t.,** Mary hasn't done it either)

tampón *m,* stamp moistener; *surg* tampon

tan *adv abb* **tanto** so, as. Used before adjectives and adverbs, excepting **más, mejor, menos, peor,** which need **tanto. t. . . . como,** as . . . as. **t. siquiera,** even (see **siquiera**). **t. sólo,** only, solely (e.g. **No vengo t. sólo para saludarte,** I do not come merely to greet you). **qué . . . t.,** what a . . . (e.g. **¡Qué día t. hermoso!** What a lovely day!)

tanda *f,* turn; opportunity; task; shift; relay; game (of billiards); bad habit; collection, batch, group; round (of a game); *(dance)* set

tándem m, tandem

tandeo m, allowance of irrigation water, turn for using water

tangente a and f, geom tangent

tanque m, mil tank; cistern, tank, reservoir; ladle, dipper

tanteador m, sport scorer, marker; scoreboard

tantear vt to measure, compare; consider fully; test, try out; flg probe, pump (persons); estimate roughly; art sketch, block in; vt and vi sport keep the score of

tanteo m, measurement, comparison; test; rough estimate; sport score

tanto a so much; as much; very great; as great; pl **tantos**, so many; as many (e.g. **Tienen tantas flores como nosotros**, They have as many flowers as we). In comparisons **tanto** is used before **más, mejor, menos, peor**, but generally **tan** is used before adjectives and adverbs (e.g. **¡Tanto peor!** So much the worse!). pron dem that (e.g. **por lo t.**, therefore, on that account). m, so much, a certain amount; copy of a document; man, piece (in games); point (score in games); com rate (e.g. **el t. por ciento**, the percentage, the rate); pl approximation, odd (e.g. **Llegaron cien hombres y tantos**, A hundred-odd men arrived). adv so much; as much; so, in such a way. **t. . . . como**, the same as, as much as. **t. . . . cuanto**, as much as. **t. más**, the more. **t. menos**, the less (e.g. **Cuanto más (menos) dinero tiene t. más (menos) quiere**, The more (less) money he has, the more (less) he wants). **t. más (menos) . . . cuanto que**, all the more (less) . . . because. **algún t.**, a certain amount, somewhat. **al t. de (una cosa)**, aware of, acquainted with (a thing). **en t. or entre t.**, meanwhile. **las tantas**, inf late hour, wee hours. **No es para t.**, inf It's not as bad as that, there's no need to make such a fuss; he (she, it) isn't equal to it. **otro t.**, the same; as much; as much more. **un t.**, a bit, somewhat

tañedor (-ra) n mus player

tañer vt irr mus to play; vi sway, swing. **t. la occisa**, to sound the death (in hunting). Pres. Part. **tañendo**. Preterite **tañó, tañeron**. Imperf. Subjunc. **tañese**, etc.

tañido m, tune, sound, note; toll, peal; ring

tapa f, lid; cover; cover (of books)

tapaboca m, blow on the mouth; f, scarf, muffler; inf remark that silences someone

tapada f, veiled woman, one whose face is hidden

tapadera f, loose lid, top, cover

tapadero m, stopper

tapado m, Argentina coat, overcoat

tapador (-ra) a covering. n coverer. m, stopper; lid; cover

tapagujeros m, inf unskilled mason or bricklayer; flg inf stopgap (person)

tapar vt to cover; cover with a lid; muffle up, veil; hide, keep secret; close up, stop up

taparrabo m, loincloth; swimming trunks

tapete m, rug; tablecover. inf **t. verde**, gaming table. flg **estar sobre el t.**, to be on the carpet, be under consideration

tapia f, adobe; mud wall; fence. inf **más sordo que una t.**, as deaf as a post

tapiar vt to wall up; put a fence around, fence in

tapicería f, set of tapestries; tapestry work; art of tapestry making; upholstery; tapestry storehouse or shop

tapicero m, tapestry weaver or maker; upholsterer; carpet layer; furnisher

tapisca f Central America, Mexico corn harvest

tapiz m, tapestry; carpet

tapizar vt to cover with tapestry; cover, clothe; upholster; carpet; hang with tapestry; furnish with hangings or drapes

tapón m, stopper; cork (of a bottle); plug; surg tampon

taponar vt to stopper, cork; plug; surg tampon; mil seal off

tapujarse vr to wrap oneself up, muffle oneself

tapujo m, scarf, muffler, face covering; disguise; inf pretense, subterfuge

taquera f, rack (for billiard cues)

taquería f, taco stand

taquígrafo (-fa) n shorthand writer, stenographer

taquilla f, booking office; box office; grille, window (in banks, etc.); rolltop desk, cupboard for papers; theat takings, cash

tara f, tally stick; com tare

taracea f, inlaid work, marquetry

taracear vt to inlay

tarambana mf inf madcap

tarántula f, tarantula

tararear vt to hum a tune

tarareo m, humming, singing under one's breath

tarasca f, figure of a dragon (carried in Corpus Christi processions); inf hag, trollop

tarascada f, bite, nip; inf insolent reply

tarascar vt to bite; wound with the teeth

tardanza f, delay, tardiness; slowness

tardar vi to delay; be tardy, arrive late; take a long time. **a más t.**, at the latest

tarde f, afternoon. adv late. **¡Buenas tardes!** Good afternoon! **de t. en t.**, from time to time, sometimes. **hacerse t.**, to grow late. **Más vale t. que nunca**, Better late than never

tardecer vi impers irr to grow dusk. See **conocer**

tardecica, tardecita f, dusk, late afternoon

tardíamente *adv* late; too late

tardío *a* late; backward; behind; slow, deliberate

tardo *a* slow, slothful, tardy; late; dilatory; stupid, slow-witted; badly spoken, inarticulate

tarea *f*, task, work

tarifa *f*, price list; tariff

tarifar *vt* to put a tariff on

tarima *f*, stand, raised platform

tarín barín *adv inf* more or less, about

tarja *f*, large shield; ancient coin; tally stick. *inf* **beber sobre t.,** to drink on credit

tarjar *vt* to reckon by tally; *Lat. Am.* cross out, erase

tarjeta *f*, buckler, small shield; *arch* tablet bearing an inscription; title (of maps and charts); visiting card; invitation (card). **t. de visita,** visiting card. **t. postal,** postcard, postal card

tárraga *f*, old Spanish dance

tarro *m*, jar, pot; *Lat. Am.* top hat

tarso *m*, *anat* tarsus, ankle; *zool* hock; *orn* shank

tarta *f*, cake pan; cake; tart

tártago *m*, spurge; *inf* misfortune, disappointment

tartajear *vi* to stammer; stutter

tartajeo *m*, stammering; stutter

tartajoso (-sa) *a* stammering; stuttering. *n* stutterer

tartalear *vi inf* to stagger, totter; be speechless, be dumbfounded

tartamudear *vi* to stammer, stutter

tartamudeo *m*. **tartamudez** *f*, stammering; stuttering

tártaro (-ra) *m*, cream of tartar; tartar (on teeth); *poet* hell, hades. *a* and *n* Tartar

tartufo *m*, hypocrite

tarugo *m*, thick wooden peg; stopper; wooden block; *a Lat. Am.* dumb, stupid

tasa *f*, assessment, valuation; valuation certificate; fixed price; standard rate; measure, rule

tasación *f*, valuation; assessment

tasador *m*, public assessor; valuer

tasajo *m*, salt meat; piece of meat

tasar *vt* to value; price; fix remuneration; tax; regulate; rate; dole out sparingly

tasca *f*, gambling den; tavern

tascar *vt* to dress (hemp, etc.); graze, crop the grass

tasquera *f*, *inf* quarrel, row, rumpus

tasquil *m*, wood splinter, chip

tata *m*, *inf WH* daddy

tatarabuela *f*, great-great-grandmother

tatarabuelo *m*, great-great-grandfather

tataranieta *f*, great-great-granddaughter

tataranieto *m*, great-great-grandson

tatas, andar a *vt* to walk on all fours

¡tate! *interj* Stop!; Be careful!; Go slowly!; Now I understand!, Of course!

tatuaje *m*, tattooing

tatuar *vt* to tattoo

taumaturgo *m*, thaumaturge, magician

taurino *a* taurine; pertaining to bullfights

tauromaquia *f*, bullfighting, tauromachy

tautología *f*, tautology

taxi *m*, taxi

taxista *m*, taxi driver

taz a taz *adv* in exchange, without payment; even

taza *f*, cup; cupful; basin (of a fountain)

tazar(se) *vt* and *vr* to fray (of cloth)

tazón *m*, large cup; bowl

te *f*, name of the letter T. *mf* dat. and acc. of *pers pron* 2nd *pers sing* thee; you; to thee, to you. Never used with a preposition

té *m*, tea

tea *f*, torch; firebrand

teatral *a* theatrical

teatro *m*, theater; stage; dramatic works; dramatic art; drama, plays. **t. de variedades,** music hall. **t. por horas,** theater where short, one-act plays are staged hourly

teca *f*, teak

techado *m*, ceiling; roof

techador *m*, roofer

techar *vt* to roof

techo *m*, roof; ceiling; dwelling, habitation

techumbre *f*, ceiling; roof

tecla *f*, key (of keyed instruments); typewriter, linotype, or calculating machine key; *fig* difficult or delicate point. *inf* **dar en la t.,** to hit on the right way of doing a thing

teclado *m*, keyboard

teclear *vi* to finger the keyboard; run one's fingers over the keyboard; *inf* drum or tap with the fingers; *vt* tap (the keys, etc.); *inf* try out various schemes

tecleo *m*, fingering the keys; *inf* drumming with the fingers; scheme, means

técnica *f*, technique

tecnicismo *m*, technical jargon; technicality, technical term

técnico *a* technical. *m*, technician

tecnicolor *m*, technicolor

tecnología *f*, technology

tecnológico *a* technological

tecnólogo *m*, technologist

tecolote *m*, *Central America, Mexico* owl; *Mexico* cop (police officer)

tedio *m*, tedium, boredom, ennui

tedioso *a* tedious, boring

teja *f*, tile, slate. *inf* **de tejas abajo,** in the normal way; in the world of men. **de tejas arriba,** in a supernatural way; in heaven

tejado *m*, roof

tejano, -a a and ms Texan. **tejanos** jeans

tejar m, tile works. vt to roof with tiles

Tejas m Texas

tejavana f, penthouse, open shed

tejedor (-ra) a weaving; inf scheming. n weaver; inf schemer

tejedura f, weaving; fabric; texture

tejemaneje m, inf cleverness, knack

tejer vt to weave; plait; spin a cocoon; arrange, regulate; concoct, hatch (schemes); wind in and out (in dancing)

tejido m, texture, weaving; textile; anat tissue; fabric, material

tejo m, quoit, discus; metal disk; yew tree

tela f, fabric, material, cloth; membrane; film (on liquids); spiderweb, cobweb; inner skin (of fruit, vegetables); film over the eye; matter, subject; scheme, plot. **t. metálica**, wire gauze. **en t. de juicio**, under consideration, in doubt. **llegarle a uno a las telas del corazón**, to hurt deeply, cut to the quick

telar m, loom, weaving machine; theat gridiron

telaraña f, cobweb; mere trifle, bagatelle. inf **mirar las telarañas**, to be absent-minded

telarañoso a cobwebby

telecomunicación f, telecommunication

telefonear vt to telephone, call

telefonía f, telephony. **t. sin hilos**, wireless telephony, broadcasting

telefónico a telephonic

telefonista mf telephone operator

teléfono m, telephone. **t. automático**, dial telephone. **llamar por t. (a)**, to telephone, call, ring up

telefundir vt to telecast

telegrafía f, telegraphy. **t. sin hilos**, wireless telegraphy

telegrafiar vt to telegraph

telegráfico a telegraphic

telegrafista mf telegraph operator

telégrafo m, telegraph. **t. sin hilos**, wireless telegraph. inf **hacer telégrafos**, to talk by signs

telegrama m, telegram

telepatía f, telepathy

telepático a telepathic

telescópico a telescopic

telescopio m, telescope

telespectador m, TV viewer, member of the television audience

televisión f, television

telilla f, film (on liquids); thin fabric

telón m, theat curtain; drop scene. **t. contra incendios, t. de seguridad,** theat safety curtain. **t. de boca,** drop curtain. **t. de foro,** drop scene

∙∙∙a m, theme, subject; mus motif, **∙∙∙e**; thesis, argument. f, obstinacy;

obsession, mania; hostility, grudge, rancor

temático a thematic; pigheaded, obstinate

temblador (-ra) a trembling, shaking. n Quaker

temblante a shaking; quivering. m, bracelet

temblar vi irr to tremble, shake; wave, quiver; shiver with fear. See **acertar**

temblequear, tembletear vi inf tremble; shake with fear

temblón a inf trembling, shaking. m, inf aspen

temblor m, shake, trembling, shiver. **temblor (de tierra)** earthquake

tembloroso, tembloso a trembling, shaking, shivering, quivering

temedero a fearsome, dread

temer vt to fear, dread; suspect, imagine; vi be afraid

temerario a reckless, impetuous; thoughtless, hasty

temeridad f, recklessness, impetuosity, temerity; thoughtlessness; act of folly; rash judgment

temerón a inf swaggering, bombastic

temeroso a frightening, dread; fearful, timid; afraid, suspicious

temible a dread, awesome

temor m, fear

temoso a obstinate, headstrong

témpano m, tabor; drumhead; block, flat piece; side of bacon. **t. de hielo,** iceberg, ice floe

temperación f, tempering

temperamento m, temperament, nature; compromise, agreement

temperar vt to temper; Lat. Am. spend the summer

temperatura f, temperature

temperie f, weather conditions

tempestad f, storm

tempestivo a opportune, seasonable

tempestuoso a stormy

templa f, tempera; pl anat temples

templado a moderate; temperate (of regions); lukewarm; mus in tune; restrained (of style); inf brave, long-suffering. **estar bien** (or **mal**) **templado,** inf to be well (or badly) tuned (of musical instruments); be in a good (or bad) temper; be good- (or ill-) natured

templanza f, moderation; sobriety; mildness of climate

templar vt to tune; met temper; moderate; warm; allay, appease; anneal; art harmonize, blend; naut trim the sails; or control oneself; be moderate; vi grow warm

temple m, weather conditions; temperature; temper (of metals, etc.); nature, disposition; bravery; mean, average; mus tuning. **al t.,** in tempera

templete m, dim shrine; niche (for statues); kiosk, pavilion

templo m, temple

temporada f, space of time, season, while. **de t.**, seasonal; temporary. **estar de t.**, to be out of town, on holiday

temporal a temporal; temporary; secular, lay; transient, fugitive. m, storm, tempest; rainy period; seasonal laborer

temporáneo, temporario a temporary, impermanent, fleeting

temporejar vt naut to lie to in a storm

temporizar vi to while away the time; temporize

tempranear vi, Lat. Am. to get up early

tempranero a early

temprano a early. adv in the early hours; prematurely, too soon

temulento a intoxicated, drunken

ten con ten m, inf tact, diplomacy

tenacidad f, adhesiveness; resistance; toughness; obstinacy, tenacity

tenacillas f pl, dim small tongs; candle snuffers; sugar tongs; curling irons; tweezers

tenaz a adhesive; hard, resistant, unyielding; tenacious, obstinate

tenaza f, claw (of a lobster, etc.); pl tongs; pincers; pliers; dental forceps

tenazada f, seizing with tongs; strong bite, snap; rattle of tongs

tenazón (a or **de)** adv without taking aim, wildly; unexpectedly

tención f, retention, holding; grip

tendencia f, tendency

tendencioso a tendentious, biased

tender vt irr to hang out; unfold, spread out; extend, hold out; mas plaster; vi tend, incline; vr lie down at full length; place one's cards on the table; gallop hard (of horses). See **entender**

tendero (-ra) n shopkeeper; retailer. m, tent maker

tendido m, row of seats in a bullfight arena; clothes hung out to dry; clear sky; mas plaster

tendón m, tendon

tenebroso a dark, gloomy

tenedor m, table fork; possessor, retainer; com holder; payee. **t. de libros,** bookkeeper

teneduría f, employment of a bookkeeper. **t. de libros,** bookkeeping

tenencia f, possession; tenancy; occupation; lieutenancy

tener vt irr to have; hold; grasp; possess, own; uphold, maintain; contain; include; hold fast, grip; stop; keep (promises); lodge, accommodate; (with en) value, estimate (e.g. **Le tengo en poco,** I have a poor opinion of him); (with para) be of the opinion that (e.g. **tengo para mí,** my opinion is); (with por) believe, consider; vi be wealthy; vr steady oneself; hold on

to; lean (on); rest (on); defend oneself; uphold; rely on; (with por) consider oneself as. **tener** is used to express: 1. Age (e.g. **¿Cuántos años tiene Vd?** How old are you?). 2. Possession (e.g. **Tenemos muchos sombreros,** We have a great many hats). 3. Measurements (e.g. **El cuarto tiene dieciocho metros de largo,** The room is eighteen meters long). Translated by 'be' when describing some physical and mental states (e.g. **Tenemos miedo,** We are afraid. **Tengo sueño,** I am sleepy. **Tienen frío (calor),** They are cold (hot)). Used as auxiliary verb replacing **haber** in compound tenses of transitive verbs (e.g. **Tengo escritas las cartas,** I have written the letters). **t. a bien,** to think fit, please, judge convenient. **t. algo en cuenta a uno,** to hold something against someone. **t. a menos de hacer (una cosa),** to scorn to do (a thing). **t. cruda,** to have a hangover. **t. curiosidad por,** to be curious about. **t. curiosidad por que** + subj to be interested that. **t. en aprecio,** to appreciate, esteem, value. **t. en cuenta,** to bear in mind. **t. en menos (a),** to despise (a person). **t. gana,** to want, wish; feel disposed; have an appetite. **t. lugar,** to take place, occur. **t. muchas partes cruzadas,** to be well-traveled. **t. mucho colegio** to be well-educated. **t. muy en cuenta,** to certainly bear in mind. **t. poco colegio,** to have had little education. **t. presente,** to remember. **t. que,** to have to (e.g. **tengo que hacerlo,** I must do it). **t. que ver (con),** to have something to do (with), be related to. **no tenerlas todas consigo,** inf to have the jitters. Pres. Ind. **tengo, tienes, tiene, tenemos, tenéis, tienen.** Preterite **tuve,** etc. Fut. **tendré,** etc. Condit. **tendría,** etc. Pres. Subjunc. **tenga,** etc. Imperf. Subjunc. **tuviese,** etc.

tenguerengue, en adv inf rickety, insecure

tenia f, tapeworm; arch fillet, narrow molding

teniente a owning, holding; unripe (of fruit); inf slightly deaf; stingy, mean. m, deputy, substitute; mil first lieutenant, lieutenant. **t. coronel,** lieutenant colonel. **t. de navío,** naval lieutenant. **t. general,** mil lieutenant general. **t. general de aviación,** air marshal

tenis m, tennis

tenor m, import, contents (of a letter, etc.); constitution, composition; mus tenor

tenorio m, rake, Don Juan, philanderer

tensión f, tautness; tension; strain, stress; elec tension

tenso a taut; tight; tense

tentación f, temptation; attraction, inducement

tentáculo m, tentacle; feeler

tentadero *m*, yard for trying out young bulls for bullfighting

tentador (-ra) a tempting; attractive. *n* tempter. *m*, the Devil

tentalear *vt* to examine by touch

tentar *vt irr* to touch, feel; examine by touch; incite, encourage; try, endeavor; test; tempt; *surg* probe. See **sentar**

tentativa *f*, endeavor, attempt; preliminary exam (at some univs.)

tentempié *m*, *inf* snack, bite

tenue a thin; slender, delicate; trivial, worthless, insignificant; pale; faint

tenuidad *f*, slenderness; delicacy; triviality, insignificance; paleness; faintness

teñir *vt irr* to dye; *art* darken; color, tinge; *vr* be dyed; be tinged or colored. See **ceñir**

teocracia *f*, theocracy

teocrático a theocratic

teologal a theological

teología *f*, theology, divinity

teológico a theological

teólogo a theological. *m*, theologian, divine; student of theology

teorema *m*, theorem

teoría *f*, theory

teórica *f*, theory

teórico a theoretical, speculative. *m*, theorist

teorizar *vt* to consider theoretically, theorize about

teoso a resinous, gummy

teosofía *f*, theosophy

tepe *m*, sod, cut turf

tequila *f*. *Mexico* tequila, maguey brandy

terapéutico a therapeutic

terapia *f*, therapy

tercer a *abb* of **tercero** third. Used before *m*, *sing* nouns

tercera *f*, procuress; *mus* third

tercería *f*, arbitration, mediation; temporary occupation of a fortress, etc.

tercero (-ra) a third; mediatory. *n* third; mediator. *m*, pimp; *ecc* tertiary; tithes collector; third person. ¡A la tercera va la vencida! Third time lucky!

terceto *m*, tercet, triplet

tercia *f*, one-third; *ecc* tierce, third hour; storehouse for tithes. **tercias reales,** royal share of ecclesiastical tithes

terciana *f*, tertian fever

terciar *vt* to slant; sling sideways; divide into three; equalize weight (on beasts of burden); plow or dig for the third time; *agr* prune; *vr* be opportune, come at the right time. *vi* mediate, arbitrate; make up a number (for cards, etc.); reach the third day (of the moon); take part, participate

tercio a third. *m*, one-third; *mil* infantry regiment; *ant*, body of foreign volunteers; fishermen's association; *pl* brawny limbs of a man. **hacer t.,** to take part in; make

up the number of. **hacer buen** (or **mal**) **t. a alguien,** to do someone a good (or bad) turn

terciopelo *m*, velvet; velveteen

terco a pigheaded, obstinate; hard, tough

tergiversación *f*, tergiversation, vacillation

tergiversar *vt* to tergiversate, shuffle, vacillate

termal a thermal

termas *f pl*, thermal springs, hot mineral baths; thermal

térmico a thermic

terminación *f*, conclusion, termination; end, finish; ending of a word; *gram* termination

terminador (-ra) a concluding. *n* finisher

terminal a terminal; final. *m*, *elec* terminal. **t. de carga,** cargo terminal

terminante a conclusive, definite; categorical

terminar *vt* to end, conclude; complete; *vr* and *vi* end

término *m*, limit, end; term, expression; boundary marker; district, suburb; space, period; state, condition; boundary; object, aim; appearance, demeanor, behavior (gen. *pl*); completion; *mus* tone; (*math law logic*) term. **t. medio,** *math* average; medium; compromise, middle way. **correr el t.,** to lapse (of time). **en primer t.,** *art* in the foreground. **medios términos,** evasions, excuses. **primer t.,** (cinema) closeup

terminología *f*, terminology

termita *f*, termite. *m*, termite

termodinámica *f*, thermodynamics

termómetro *m*, thermometer

termos *m*, thermos, vacuum bottle

termóstato *m*, thermostat

terna *f*, triad, trio; set of dice

terne a *inf* bullying, braggartly; persistent, obstinate; robust. *mf* bully

ternera *f*, female calf; veal

ternero *m*, male calf

terneza *f*, tenderness, kindness; softness; softheartedness; endearment, caress, compliment (gen. *pl*)

ternilla *f*, cartilage, gristle

ternísimo a *sup* **tierno** most tender

terno *m*, triad; suit of clothes, three-piece suit; oath, curse

ternura *f*, softness; softheartedness; tenderness, kindness, sweetness

terquedad, terquería, terqueza *f*, obstinacy, obduracy

terracota *f*, terra cotta

terrado *m*, flat roof

Terranova Newfoundland

terraplén *m*, embankment; *mil* terreplein

terraplenar *vt* to fill up with earth; fill in

(a hollow); make into an embankment; terrace

terrateniente *mf* landowner

terraza *f*, terrace; flat roof; flower border (of a garden)

terregoso a lumpy, full of clods (of soil)

terremoto *m*, earthquake

terrenal a terrestrial

terreno a terrestrial. *m*, ground, land; *fig* sphere; region; soil; plot of land. **ganar t.**, *fig* to win ground, make progress. **medir el t.**, *fig* to feel one's way

térreo a earthy

terrero a earthly; low-flying, almost touching the ground; humble. *m*, flat roof; pile or mound of earth; deposit of earth, alluvium; target; mineral refuse

terrestre a terrestrial, earthly

terrezuela *f*, poor soil

terribilidad *f*, terribleness, horribleness; rudeness

terribilísimo a *sup* most terrible

terrible a terrible, horrible; rude, unsociable, ill-humored; enormous, huge

terrífico a terrible, frightful

territorial a territorial

territorialidad *f*, territoriality

territorio *m*, territory; jurisdiction. **t. bajo mandato,** mandated territory

terrizo a earthen

terrón *m*, clod (of earth); lump; *pl* lands, landed property. **t. de azúcar,** lump of sugar

terrorismo *m*, terrorism

terrorista *mf* terrorist

terrosidad *f*, earthiness

terroso a earthy; earthen

terruño *m*, plot of ground; native earth; country; soil

terso a smooth, shiny, glossy; *lit* elegant, polished (style)

tersura *f*, smoothness, glossiness; elegance (of style)

tertulia *f*, regular social meeting (gen. in cafés); conversational group; party; part of Spanish cafés set apart for players of chess, etc. **hacer t.,** to meet for conversation

tertuliano (-na) *n* **tertuliante,** *mf* **tertulio (-ia),** *n* member of a tertulia

tesar *vt naut* to make taut; *vi* step backward, back (oxen)

tesela *f*, tessera, square used in mosaic work

tesina *f*, master's essay, thesis

tesis *f*, thesis

teso a tight, taut, tense. *m*, hilltop; bulge; lump

tesón *m*, persistence, obstinacy, tenacity

tesorería *f*, treasury; treasuryship

tesorero (-ra) *n* treasurer

tesoro *m*, treasure; public treasury;

hoard; *fig* gem, excellent person; thesaurus. **t. de duende,** fairy gold

testa *f*, head; face, front; *inf* sense, acumen. **t. coronada,** crowned head

testación *f*, erasure, crossing out

testado a testate

testador (-ra) *n* testator

testaferro *m*, *fig* figurehead, proxy

testamentar *vt* to bequeath

testamentaria *f*, execution of a will; *law* estate; executors' meeting

testamentario a testamental, testamentary

testamento *m*, *law* will; testament. **Antiguo T.,** Old Testament. **ordenar (or otorgar) su t.,** to make one's will

testar *vi* to make a will; *vt* erase, cross out

testarrón a *inf* pigheaded

testarudez *f*, obstinacy, obduracy

testarudo a stubborn, obstinate

testera *f*, front, face; front seat (in a vehicle); upper half of an animal's face; tester, canopy

testículo *m*, testicle

testificar *vt* to testify; affirm, assert; attest, prove

testigo *mf* witness. *m*, proof, evidence. *law* **t. de cargo,** witness for the prosecution. *law* **t. de descargo,** witness for the defense. **t. de vista,** eyewitness. *law* **hacer testigos,** to bring forward witnesses

testimonial a confirmatory, proven

testimoniar *vt* to attest, confirm, bear witness to

testimoniero (-ra) a slanderous; hypocritical. *n* slanderer, hypocrite

testimonio *m*, testimony, proof; slander; affidavit

testuz *m*, front of the head (of some animals); nape (of animals)

teta *f*, mammary gland, breast; teat, dug, udder. **dar la t. (a),** to suckle

tétano, tétanos *m*, tetanus

tetera *f*, teapot; teakettle; *Lat. Am.* (feeding) bottle

tetilla *f*, *dim* rudimentary teat or nipple; nipple (of a nursing bottle)

tétrico a gloomy; somber

textil a and *m*, textile

texto *m*, text; quotation, citation; textbook

textura *f*, texture; weaving; structure (of a novel, etc.); animal structure

tez *f*, complexion, skin

ti *pers pron 2nd sing mf dat acc abl* thee, you. Always used with prep. (e.g. **por ti,** by thee (you))

tía *f*, aunt; *inf* wife, mother, dame; *inf* coarse creature. **t. abuela,** grandaunt, great-aunt. *inf* **quedarse para t.,** to be left an old maid

tianguis *m, Central America, Mexico* open-air market

tiara *f,* ancient Persian headdress; papal tiara; coronet; dignity and power of the papacy

tibetano (-na) *a* and *n* Tibetan. *m,* Tibetan (language)

tibia *f,* flute; tibia

tibieza *f,* tepidity; indifference, lack of enthusiasm

tibio *a* tepid, warm; indifferent, unenthusiastic

tiburón *m,* shark

ticket *m,* ticket; pass, membership card

tico, -a *mf inf* Costa Rican

tictac *m,* ticktock (of a clock)

tiempo *m,* time; season; epoch, period; chance, opportunity; leisure, free time; weather; *mus* tempo; *gram* tense; *naut* storm. **t. ha,** many years ago, long ago. **t. medio** *or* **medio t.,** *sport* halftime. **abrir el t.,** to clear up (of the weather). **ajustar los tiempos,** to fix the date (chronology). **a largo t.,** after a long time. **andando el t.,** in the course of time. **a su t.,** in due course, at the proper time. **a t.,** in time, at the right time. **a un t.,** simultaneously, at the same time. **cargarse el t.,** to cloud over (of the sky). **con t.,** in advance, with time; in time. **correr el t.,** to pass, move on (of time). **de t. en t.,** from time to time. **engañar** (*or* **entretener**) **el t.,** to kill time, while away the hours. *inf* **en t., de Maricastaña** *or* **del rey Perico,** long, long ago. **fuera de t.,** unseasonably, inopportunely; out of season. **ganar t.,** to gain time; *inf* hurry. **hacer t.,** to wait, cool one's heels; *fig* mark time. **perder el t.,** to waste time; misspend or lose time. **sentarse el t.,** to clear up (of the weather). **tomarse t. (para),** to postpone, take time for (or to)

tienda *f,* tent; *naut* awning, canopy; shop, store. **t. de abarrotes** *Lat. Am.* grocery store, grocery, grocer's **t. de antigüedades,** antique shop. **t. de campaña,** bell tent, pavilion. **t. oxígena,** oxygen tent

tienta *f,* astuteness; cleverness; *surg* probe; trying out young bulls for the bullring. **a tientas,** by touch, gropingly

tiento *m,* touching, feeling; touch, feel; blind person's cane; tightrope walker's pole; manual control, steady hand; caution, care, tact; *mus* preliminary flourish; *inf* slap buffet; tentacle. **a t.,** by touch; unsurely, gropingly

tierno *a* soft; tender; kind; sweet; delicate; softhearted; fresh, recent; affectionate

tierra *f,* world, planet; earth; soil; ground; cultivated ground, land; homeland, native land; region; district, territory. **t. adentro,** inland. **t. de batán,** fuller's earth. **t. de Promisión,** Promised Land. **t. de Siena,** sienna. **besar la t.,** *inf* to fall

down. **dar en t. con,** to throw down; demolish. **echar en t.,** *naut* to put ashore, land. **echar por t.,** *fig* to overthrow, destroy. **echar t. a,** *fig* to bury, forget. *inf* **la t. de María Santísima,** Andalusia. **por t.,** overland. **saltar en t.,** to land, disembark. **venir** (*or* **venirse**) **a t.,** to fall down, topple over

Tierra Santa Holy Land

tieso *a* hard, rigid, stiff; healthy, robust; taut; spirited, courageous; obstinate, stiff-necked; distant, formal. *adv* firmly, strongly

tiesto *m,* flowerpot; broken piece of earthenware

tiesura *f,* hardness, rigidity, stiffness; physical fitness; courageousness; obstinacy; formality, stiffness

tifoidea *f,* typhoid

tifón *m,* typhoon

tifus *m,* typhus. **t. exantemático,** trench fever

tigre *m,* tiger; ferocious person; *Lat. Am.* jaguar

tijera *f,* scissors (gen. *pl*); any scissor-shaped instrument; shears; drainage channel; carpenter's horse; scandalmonger, gossip

tijeretear *vt* to cut with scissors; *inf* interfere arbitrarily

tijereteo *m,* scissor cut; click of the scissors

tila *f,* lime tree or flower; linden tree or flower; infusion made of lime flowers

tildar *vt* to cross out, erase; stigmatize; place a tilde over a letter

tilde *mf,* bad reputation; tilde; *f,* jot, iota

timar *vt* to swindle, cheat, deceive; *vr inf* exchange looks or winks

timba *f, inf* casino, gambling den; game of chance

timbal *m,* kettledrum

timbalero *m,* kettledrum player

timbrador *m,* stamper; stamping machine; rubber stamp

timbrar *vt* to stamp; place the crest over a coat of arms

timbre *m,* postage stamp; heraldic crest; excise stamp; bell, push-button; *mus* timbre; noble deed; personal merit; *Mexico* (postage) stamp; *Lat. Am.* description (of a person or goods)

timidez *f,* timidity, nervousness

tímido *a* timid, nervous

timo *m, inf* swindling, trick; thymus

timón *m, naut* helm; rudder; management, direction; stick of a rocket. **t. de dirección,** *aer* tailfin

timonear *vi naut* to steer

timonel, timonero *m,* helmsman, coxswain

timorato *a* godfearing; timid, vacillating

tímpano *m, anat* eardrum, tympanum;

mus kettledrum; *arch* tympanum; *print* tympan

tina *f*, vat; flour bin; large earthenware jar; wooden tub; bath

tinaco *m*, *Mexico* (water) tank

tinaja *f*, large earthenware jar; jarful

tinglado *m*, overhanging roof; open shed; penthouse; intrigue

tiniebla *f*, gloom, darkness (gen. *pl*); *pl* profound ignorance; confusion of mind; *ecc* tenebrae

tino *m*, skilled sense of touch; good eye, accurate aim; judgment, shrewdness; vat. **sacar de t. (a),** to bewilder, confuse; irritate, exasperate. **sin t.,** without limit, excessively

tinta *f*, color, tint; ink; staining, dyeing; dye, stain; *pl* shades, colors; *art* mixed colors ready for painting. **t. china,** India ink. **t. simpática,** invisible ink. **recargar las tintas,** *fig* to overpaint, lay the colors on too thick. *inf* **saber de buena t. (una cosa),** to learn (a thing) from a reliable source

tintar *vt* to dye; color, tinge, stain

tinte *m*, dyeing, staining; color; dye; stain; dye house; pretext, disguise

tintero *m*, inkwell. *inf* **dejar** (or **quedársele a uno) en el t.,** to forget, omit (to say, write)

tintín *m*, ring, peal; clink; chink

tintinar *vi* to ring, tinkle; clink; jingle

tintineo *m*, ringing, tinkling; clinking; jingle

tinto *a* red (of wine). *m*, red wine; dark red

tintorera *f*, *Lat. Am.* shark

tintorería *f*, dyeing industry; dyeing and dry-cleaning shop

tintorero (-ra) *n* dyer; dry cleaner

tintura *f*, dyeing, staining; color, tint; dye; stain; tincture; smattering, slight knowledge

tinturar *vt* to dye; color, tinge, stain; give a superficial notion of

tiña *f*, ringworm; *inf* meanness, stinginess

tiñoso *a* mangy; afflicted with ringworm; *inf* mean, stingy

tío *m*, uncle; gaffer; fellow, chap; fool; stepfather; father-in-law. **t. abuelo,** granduncle, great-uncle

tiovivo *m*, merry-go-round

típico *a* typical

tiple *m*, soprano or treble voice. *mf* soprano

tipo *m*, model, pattern; type; print, type; species, group (of animals, etc.); *inf* guy, chap

tipografía *f*, typography

típula *f*, daddy-longlegs

tiquismiquis *m pl*, ridiculous scruples; affected courtesies. *a inf* faddy, fussy

tira *f*, strip, band, ribbon; stripe, rib. **t. cómica,** comic strip

tirabotas *m*, buttonhook

tirada *f*, throwing; drawing, pulling; cast, throw; distance, space; *print* edition, issue; circulation (of a newspaper, etc.); stroke (in golf); lapse, interval (of time). **t. aparte,** reprint (of an article, etc.)

tirado *a inf* dirt-cheap. *m*, wire drawing

tirador (-ra) *n* thrower, caster; drawer, puller; marksman. *m*, handle, knob; *mech* trigger; bell rope, bell pull; *print* pressman. **t. de bota,** boot tag. **t. de gomas,** catapult. **t. de oro,** gold wire drawer

tiramiento *m*, pulling; stretching

tiramira *f*, long, narrow mountain range; long line of persons or things; distance

tiranía *f*, tyranny, despotism

tiránico *a* tyrannical

tiranizar *vt* to tyrannize over

tirano (-na) *a* tyrannous, tyrannical; *fig* overwhelming, dominating. *n* tyrant

tirante *a* taut; tense, strained. *m*, trace (of a harness); shoulderstrap; suspender (gen. *pl*); *arch* tie

tirantez *f*, tautness; tension, strain; straight distance between two points. **estado de t.,** *pol* strained relations

tiranuelo *m*, petty tyrant

tirar *vt* to throw, cast; fling, aim, toss; throw down, overthrow; pull; draw; discharge, shoot; stretch, pull out; rule, draw (lines); squander, waste; *print* print; *vi* attract; pull; (*with prep* a) turn to, turn in the direction of; incline, tend to; incline toward, have a tinge of (colors); try, aspire to; (*with de*) wield, unsheath, draw out (firearms, arms); *vr* cast oneself, precipitate oneself; throw oneself on. *inf* **ir tirando,** to carry on, get along somehow

tirilla *f*, *sew* shirt neckband

tiritaña *f*, thin silk material; *inf* mere nothing, trifle

tiritar *vi* to shiver with cold

tiritón *m*, shiver, shudder

tiro *m*, throwing; throw, cast; toss, fling; try (in football); shooting; piece of artillery; report, shot (of a gun); discharge (firearms); shooting range or gallery; team (of horses); range (of firearms, etc.); hoisting cable; flight (of stairs); *min* shaft; *inf* trick; robbery, theft; innuendo, insinuation; grave harm or injury; *pl* sword belt. **t. de pichón,** pigeon shooting. **t. par,** four-in-hand. **a t.,** within firing range; within reach. **de tiros largos,** *inf* in full regalia

tiroides *f*, thyroid gland

tirón *m*, novice, beginner; pull, tug, heave. **de un t.,** with one tug; at one stroke, at one blow

tiroriro *m*, *inf* sound of a wind instrument; *pl* wind instruments

tirotearse *vr mil* to exchange fire; indulge in repartee

tiroteo *m*, shooting, exchange of shots; crackle (of rifle fire)

tirria f, *inf* hostility, grudge, dislike

tirulato a dumbfounded, stupefied

tisana f, tisane

tísico (**-ca**) a tuberculous. n sufferer from tuberculosis, consumptive

tisis f, tuberculosis

tisú m, silver or gold tissue

titánico a titanesque; colossal, huge

títere m, puppet; *fig inf* dummy, grotesque; *inf* fool; obsession, fixed idea; *pl inf* circus; Punch and Judy show. *inf* **echar los títeres a rodar,** to upset the whole show; quarrel, fall out with. *inf* **no dejar t. con cabeza,** to destroy entirely, smash up completely; leave no one

titerero (**-ra**), **titiritero** (**-ra**), n **titerista** mf puppet showman; acrobat; juggler

titilación f, quiver, tremor; twinkling, winking, gleam

titilador, titilante a quivering, trembling; twinkling

titilar vi to quiver, tremble; twinkle

titiritaina f, *inf* muffled strains of musical instruments; merrymaking; uproar

titiritar vi to tremble, shiver, shudder

titubear vi to totter, sway, rock; stutter, stammer; toddle; hesitate, vacillate

titubeo m, tottering, swaying; stuttering; hesitation

titulado m, titled person; one who holds an academic title

titular a titular. vt to entitle, call; vi obtain a title (of nobility); vr style oneself, call oneself

título m, title; heading; inscription; pretext, excuse; diploma, certificate; claim, right; noble title and its owner; section, clause; (univ.) degree; com stock certificate, bond; com title; caption; qualification, right, merit; basis of a claim or privilege; *pl com* securities, stocks. **t. de la columna,** *print* running title. **títulos de propiedad,** title deeds. **t. del reino,** title of nobility. **a t.,** under pretext

tiza f, chalk; whiting; calcined stag's antler

tiznar vt to make sooty; dirty, stain, begrime; *fig* sully, tarnish

tizne m, (sometimes f) soot; charcoal; stain (on one's honor, etc.); *agr* blight

tizón m, firebrand; *agr* blight; *fig* stain (on one's honor, etc.)

tizona f, *inf* sword (by allusion to name of that of the Cid)

tizonear vi to poke or rake the fire

toalla f, towel. **t. continua,** roller towel. **t. rusa,** Turkish towel

tobillera f, *inf* girl, flapper

tobillo m, ankle

tobogán m, toboggan; chute (in apartment buildings or amusement parks)

toca f, headdress; toque; wimple; coif

tocable a touchable

tocado a *fig* touched, half-crazy. m, headdress; coiffure; hairdressing

tocador (**-ra**) n *mus* player. m, dressing table; kerchief; boudoir; cloakroom; dressing room; dressing case

tocamiento m, touching, feeling; touch; *fig* inspiration

tocante a touching. **t. a,** concerning, with regard to

tocar vt to touch, feel; *mus* play; knock, rap; summon; ring, peal; brush against; discover by experience; persuade, inspire; mention, touch upon; *naut* touch bottom; *art* retouch, touch up. vi belong; stop (at), touch at; be one's turn; concern, interest; be one's lot; adjoin, be near to; be opportune; be allied or closely related to; find the scent (of dogs). **t. en un puerto,** *naut* to touch at a port. **Ahora me toca a mí,** Now it's my turn. **Es un problema que me toca de cerca,** It is a problem that touches me very nearly. **a toca teja,** *inf* in ready cash

tocayo (**-ya**) n namesake

tocho a boorish, loutish, countrified. m, iron bar

tocino m, bacon; salt pork

tocón m, stump (of a tree or an amputated limb)

todavía adv still; even; nevertheless; yet. **No han venido t.,** They have not come yet. **Queda mucho que hacer t.,** There is still much to be done.

todo a all; whole, entire; every, each. m, whole, entirety; whole word (in charades); all; *pl* all; everyone. adv wholly, entirely. **t. lo posible,** everything possible; all one can, one's best. **t. lo que,** all that which. **ante t.,** in the first place; especially, particularly. **así y t.,** nevertheless. **a t. esto,** in the meanwhile. **con t.** or **con t. esto** or **con t. y esto,** nevertheless, in spite of this. **del t.,** wholly, completely. **jugar el t. por el t.,** to risk everything on the outcome. **sobre t.,** especially. **y t.,** in addition, as well. **Todos somos hijos de Adán y Eva, sino que nos diferencia la lana y la seda,** We are all equal, but some of us are more equal than others

todopoderoso a all-powerful, almighty. m, the Almighty, God

toga f, toga; robe, gown

tolda f canvas; tent; shelter

toldadura f, awning; canopy; hanging, curtain

toldillo m, covered litter or sedan chair; *WH* mosquito net

toldo m, awning; canopy; pomp, show

tole m, outcry, uproar, tumult

tolerable a bearable, tolerable

tolerancia f, tolerance, forbearance; permission

tolerante a tolerant, broad-minded

tolerantismo m, religious toleration

tolerar vt to put up with, bear, tolerate; overlook, allow, forgive

tolla f, marsh, bog

tollina f, inf spanking, whipping

tolmo m, tor

tolondro a stupid, heedless, reckless. m, bump, bruise

tolva f, chute (for grain, etc.)

toma f, taking; receiving; conquest, capture; dose (of medicine)

tomadura f, taking; receiving; dose (of medicine). inf **t. de pelo**, leg-pull, joke

tomar vt to take; pick up; conquer; eat; drink; adopt, employ; contract (habits); engage (employees); rent; understand; steal; remove; buy; suffer; fig overcome (by laughter, sleep, etc.); choose; possess physically; vi (with por) go in the direction of; vr grow rusty; go moldy; (with con) quarrel with. **t. a chacota**, to take as a joke. **t. a pechos**, to take to heart. **t. el fresco**, to take the air. **tomarla con**, to contradict, oppose; bear a grudge. **t. la delantera**, to take the lead; excel, beat. **t. las de Villadiego**, inf to quit; show one's heels. **t. por su cuenta**, to undertake, take charge of; take upon oneself. **t. su desquite con**, to get even with. **Más vale un toma que dos te daré**, A little help is worth a lot of promises. **¡Toma!** inf Fancy! You don't say!; Of course! There's nothing new about that!

tomate m, tomato; tomato plant; Mexico small green tomato; inf hole, potato (in stockings, etc.)

tomatera f, tomato plant

tómbola f, raffle (gen. for charity); jumble sale

tomillo m, thyme

tomo m, volume, book; importance, worth

ton m, abb **tono. sin t. ni son**, inf without rhyme or reason

tonada f, words of a song and its tune

tonadilla f, dim short song; comic song; theat musical interlude ant

tonalidad f, tonality

tonar vi poet to thunder or lightning

tonel m, barrel; cask; butt

tonelada f, ton

tonga, tongada f, layer, stratum; inf task

tónico a tonic. m, med tonic; pick-me-up

tonificador, tonificante a strengthening, invigorating tonic

tonillo m, dim monotonous singsong voice; regional accent

tonina f, tuna; dolphin

tono m, inflection, modulation; (mus med art) tone; pitch, resonance; energy, strength; style; manner, behavior; mus key; mode of speech. **bajar el t.**, fig inf to change one's tune. inf **darse t.**, to put on side, give oneself airs. **de buen (mal) t.**, in good (bad) taste

tonsila f, tonsil

tonsilitis f, tonsillitis

tonsura f, shearing; hair cutting; ecc tonsure

tonsurar vt to shear, clip; cut the hair off; ecc tonsure

tontaina mf inf ninny, fool

tontear vi to behave foolishly; play the fool

tontería f, foolishness, stupidity; piece of folly; trifle, bagatelle

tontiloco a inf crazy, daft

tontivano a vain, conceited

tonto (-ta) a silly, stupid, simple; foolish, absurd. n fool, idiot. m, short coat, stroller. **t. de capirote**, inf an utter fool. **a tontas y a locas**, without rhyme or reason, topsy-turvy. **volver t. (a)**, fig inf to drive crazy

topacio m, topaz

topar vt (with con) to run into, collide with, hit; meet unexpectedly; come across, find; vi butt (of horned animals); take a bet (in cards); consist in (of obstacles); meet with (difficulties); inf be successful

tope m, projection, part that juts out; obstacle, impediment; collision, bump; crux, difficult point; quarrel, fight; mech stop; naut masthead; rw buffer; Mexico speed bump. **hasta el t.**, completely full, full to the brim

topetada f, butt (of horned animals); inf knock, bang

topetar vt and vi to butt (of horned animals); vt meet, run into

topetón m, butt; collision, impact, bump; blow on the head

tópico a topical. m, topic, theme

topo m, zool mole; inf clumsy or short-sighted person; dolt, ninny

topografía f, topography

toque m, touch, touching; pealing, ringing (of bells); crux, essence; test, proof; touchstone; met assay; warning; inf tap (on the shoulder, etc.); art touch. **t. de luz**, art light (in a picture). **t. de obscuro**, art shade (in a picture). **t. de queda**, curfew. **t. de tambor**, beating of a drum. **dar un t. a**, inf to put to the test; pump (for information)

toquetear vt to keep touching, handle repeatedly

toquilla f, hatband, hat trimming; kerchief; small shawl

torácico a thoracic

toral a principal, chief, main

tórax m, thorax

torbellino m, whirlwind; spate of things; inf madcap

torcedero a twisted, crooked

torcedor a twisting. m, twister; cause of continual anxiety

torcedura f, twisting; sprain, wrench

torcer vt irr to twist; bend; turn, bear (of roads, etc.); slant, slope, incline; misconstrue, pervert; dissuade; wrench, sprain (muscles); corrupt (justice). **t. el gesto,** to make a wry face. *vr* turn sour (of wine, milk); *fig* go astray; turn out badly (of negotiations). *Pres. Ind.* **tuerzo, tuerces,** etc. *Pres. Subjunc.* **tuerza, tuerzas, tuerza, tuerzan**

torcido a bent, crooked, sloping, inclined; curved; dishonest, tortuous. *m,* silk twist

torcijón *m,* stomachache

torcimiento *m,* twisting; twist, turn; circumlocution; digression

toreador *m,* bullfighter

torear *vi* and *vt* to fight bulls; *vt* ridicule; exasperate, provoke; *inf* string along, deceive

toreo *m,* bullfighting

torera *f,* bullfighter's jacket

torero a *inf* bullfighting. *m,* bullfighter

torete *m, dim* small bull; *inf* problem, difficult question; engrossing topic of conversation

tormenta *f,* storm; misfortune, calamity; indignation, agitation

tormento *m,* torment; torture; pain; anxiety, anguish. **dar t. (a),** to torture; inflict pain (on)

tormentoso a stormy, tempestuous; *naut* pitching, rolling

torna *f,* return; restitution; backwater

tornaboda *f,* day after a wedding; rejoicings of this day

tornada *f,* return home; return visit, revisit; *poet* envoy

tornadizo (-za) a *inf* changeable. *n* turncoat

tornamiento *m,* return; change, transformation

tornar *vt* to return; give back; change, transform; *vi* return, go back; continue

tornasol *m,* sunflower; sheen, changing light; *chem* litmus

tornasolar *vt* to look iridescent; change the color of, cause to appear variegated

tornátil a turned (in a lathe); inconstant, changeable; *poet* spinning, revolving

tornavoz *m,* soundboard, sounding board

torneador *m,* turner; jouster, fighter in a tournament

tornear *vt sport* to put a spin on (balls); turn in a lathe; *vi* turn around, spin; fight in a tournament; turn over in the mind

torneo *m,* tournament

tornillero *m,* (*inf mil*) deserter

tornillo *m,* screw; (*inf mil*) desertion

torniquete *m,* turnstile; tourniquet. **dar t. (a),** to pervert, misinterpret (meanings)

torniscón *m, inf* slap, buffet, blow; pinch

torno *m,* lathe; turntable (of a convent, etc.); turn, rotation; windlass; dumbwaiter; axletree; spinning wheel; bend,

loop (in a river). **en t.,** round about, around; in exchange

toro *m,* bull; Taurus; *pl* bullfight. *inf* **t. corrido,** tough nut to crack, wise guy. *inf* **Ciertos son los toros,** So it's true (gen. of bad news)

toronja *f,* grapefruit

toroso a strong, vigorous, robust

torpe a heavy, slow, encumbered; torpid; clumsy, unskilled; stupid, dull-witted; obscene, indecent; base, infamous; ugly

torpedear *vt* to torpedo

torpedero *m,* torpedo boat

torpedo *m, icht* torpedo fish, electric ray; torpedo; sports car. **t. automóvil,** self-propelling torpedo

torpeza *f,* slowness, heaviness; torpidity; stupidity; lack of skill, clumsiness; indecency; ugliness; baseness, infamy

tórpido a torpid

torrar *vt* to toast, brown

torre *f,* tower; belfry, steeple; turret; rook (in chess); *naut* gun turret; stack, pile (of chairs, etc.); country house with a garden. **t. del tráfico,** traffic light. **t. de viento,** castle in the air, castle in Spain

torrefacción *f,* toasting (of coffee, etc.)

torrencial a torrential, rushing

torrente *m,* torrent; *fig* spate, rush; crowd

torrentoso, -a a, *Lat. Am.* = **torrencial**

torreznero (-ra) *n inf* lazybones, idler

tórrido a torrid

torsión *f,* twisting, torsion

torta *f,* cake; pastry, tart; *inf* slap. **t. de reyes,** traditional Twelfth Night cake

tortada *f,* meat pie, game pie

tortera *f,* cake pan; baking dish; whorl (of a spindle)

tortícolis *m,* crick (in the neck)

tortilla *f,* omelet; *Central America, Mexico* tortilla (corn pancake) **t. a la española,** potato omelet. **hacer t.,** to smash to atoms. **Se volvió la t.,** *inf* The tables are turned

tortillero, -a *mf Central America, Mexico* tortilla vendor

tórtolo *m,* male turtledove; *inf* devoted lover

tortuga *f,* turtle; tortoise. **a paso de t.,** at a snail's pace

tortuosidad *f,* tortuousness; winding; indirectness; deceitfulness

tortuoso a tortuous; winding; disingenuous, deceitful

tortura *f,* twistedness; torture, torment; anguish, grief. **una t. china,** excruciating torture

torturar *vt* to torture

torva *f,* squall of rain or snow

tos *f,* cough. **t. ferina,** whooping cough

tosco a rough, unpolished; coarse; boorish, uncouth

toser *vi* to cough

tósigo *m*, poison, venom; anguish; affliction

tosigoso *a* poisoned, venomous

tosquedad *f*, roughness, lack of polish; coarseness; boorishness, uncouthness

tostada *f*, *cul* toast

tostado *a* golden brown, tanned. *m*, roasting (of coffee, etc.)

tostador (-ra) *n* toaster (of peanuts, etc.). *m*, toaster (utensil); coffee or peanut roaster

tostadura *f*, toasting; roasting (of coffee, etc.)

tostón *m*, buttered toast; anything overtoasted; roast pig; *inf* nuisance, bore

total *a* total, entire, whole; general. *m*, total. *adv* in short; so, therefore

totalidad *f*, whole; aggregate, entirety

totalitario *a* totalitarian

tótem *m*, totem

tóxico *a* toxic. *m*, toxic substance

toxicología *f*, toxicology

tozo *a* dwarfish, small

tozudo *a* obstinate, obdurate

tozuelo *m*, scruff, fat nape (of animals)

traba *f*, setting (of a saw's teeth); tether (for horses); difficulty, obstacle; fastening; bond, tie; shackle; *law* distraint

trabacuenta *f*, mistake in accounts; argument, difference of opinion

trabajado *a* and *past part* wrought; fashioned; labored, exhausted, weary

trabajador (-ra) *a* working; conscientious. *n* worker

trabajar *vi* to work; function; stand the strain, resist (of machines, etc.); exert oneself, strive; toil, labor; operate, work; produce, yield (the earth fruits, etc.); *vt* work; till, cultivate; exercise (a horse); worry, annoy, weary; operate, drive; *vr* make every effort, work hard

trabajo *m*, work; toil, labor; operation, working; difficulty, obstacle; literary work; hardship, trouble; process; *pl* poverty; hardship. **t. a destajo**, piecework. **t. al ralentí**, go-slow tactics. **trabajos forzados** (or **forzosos**), *law* hard labor. **pasar trabajos**, to undergo hardships

trabajosamente *adv* painstakingly

trabajoso *a* difficult, hard; ailing, delicate; needy; afflicted

trabalenguas *m*, *inf* tongue twister, jaw-breaker

trabamiento *m*, joining, fastening; uniting; initiation, commencement; shackling; hobbling (of horses)

trabar *vt* to join, unite, fasten; grasp, seize; set the teeth (of a saw); thicken; begin, initiate; hobble (of horses); reconcile, bring together, harmonize; shackle; *law* distrain; *vr* speak with an impediment; stutter, hesitate. **t. amistad**, to make friends. **t. conversación**, to get into conversation. **Se me trabó la lengua**, I began to stutter

trabazón *f*, join, union, fastening; connection; thickness, consistency

trabilla *f*, vest strap; dropped stitch (in knitting)

trabuca *f*, squib, Chinese firecracker, riprap

trabucar *vt* to turn upside down, upset; confuse, bewilder; mix up, confuse (news, etc.); pronounce or write incorrectly

trabucazo *m*, shot or report of a blunderbuss; *inf* calamity, unexpected misfortune

trabuco *m*, *mil* catapult; blunderbuss

trabuquete *m*, catapult

tracalada *f*, *Lat. Am.* crowd (of people); lot (large amount)

tracamundana *f*, *inf* barter, exchange of trash; hubbub, uproar

tracción *f*, pulling; traction

tracoma *f*, trachoma

tracto *m*, tract, area, expanse; lapse of time

tractor *m*, tractor. **t. de orugas**, caterpillar tractor

tradición *f*, tradition

tradicional *a* traditional

traducción *f*, translation; interpretation, explanation

traducible *a* translatable

traducir *vt irr* to translate; interpret, explain; express. See **conducir**

traductor (-ra) *n* translator; interpreter

traedizo *a* portable, movable

traer *vt irr* to bring; attract; cause, occasion; wear, have on; quote, cite (as proof); compel, force; persuade; conduct, lead (persons); be engaged in; *vr* dress (well or badly). **t. consigo**, to bring with it; have or carry or bring with one. **t. entre manos**, to have on hand. *Pres. Ind.* **traigo, traes**, etc. *Pres. Part.* **trayendo**. *Preterite* **traje, trajiste**, etc. *Pres. Subjunc.* **traiga**, etc. *Imperf. Subjunc.* **trajese**, etc.

trafagador *m*, dealer, trafficker, merchant

tráfago *m*, traffic, trade; toil, drudgery

trafalmejas *a* *inf* rowdy, crazy, *mf* *inf* rowdy

traficante *mf* dealer, merchant, trader

traficar *vi* to trade; travel

tráfico *m*, traffic; trade, commerce

tragaderas *f pl*, throat, gullet. *inf* **tener buenas t.**, to be very credulous; be tolerant (of evil)

tragadero *m*, throat, gullet; sink, drain; hole, plug

tragador (-ra) *n* glutton, guzzler

tragahombres *mf* *inf* braggart, bully

tragaleguas *mf* *inf* fast walker

tragaluz *m*, skylight; fan light

tragantón (-ona) *a inf* guzzling, greedy. *n* glutton

tragantona *f, inf* spread, large meal; swallowing with difficulty; *fig inf* hard pill to swallow

tragaperras *m, inf* vending machine, catchpenny

tragar *vt* to swallow; eat ravenously, devour; engulf, swallow up; believe, take in; tolerate, put up with; dissemble; consume, absorb

tragedia *f,* tragedy

trágico (-ca) *a* tragic. *n* tragedian; writer of tragedies

tragicómico *a* tragicomic

trago *m,* swallow, gulp, draft; *fig inf* bitter pill. **a tragos,** *inf* little by little, slowly

tragón (-ona) *a inf* greedy, gluttonous. *n* glutton

tragonear *vt inf* to devour, eat avidly

traición *f,* treason, treachery. **a t.,** treacherously

traicionar *vt* to betray

traicionero (-ra) *a* treacherous. *n* traitor

traída *f,* conduction. **t. de aguas,** water supply

traidor (-ra) *a* treacherous. *n* traitor

traílla *f,* lead, leash (for animals)

traje *m,* dress, apparel; outfit, costume; suit. **t. de americana,** lounge suit. **t. de ceremonia** *or* **t. de etiqueta,** full-dress uniform; evening dress (men). **t. de luces,** bullfighter's gala outfit. **t. de montar,** riding habit. **t. de noche,** evening dress (women). **t. paisano,** civilian dress; lounge suit

trajín *m,* carriage, transport; busyness, moving around; bustle; clatter

trajinar *vt* to carry, transport; *Argentina* cheat, swindle; *vi* be busy, go about one's business

tralla *f,* rope, cord; lash (of a whip); whip

trama *f,* woof, texture of cloth); twisted silk; intrigue, scheme; *lit* plot; olive flower

tramar *vt* to weave; prepare, hatch (plots); *fig* prepare the way for; *vi* flower (of trees, especially olive)

tramitación *f,* transaction, conduct; procedure, method

tramitar *vt* to transact, conduct, settle

trámite *m,* transit; negotiation, phase of a business deal; requirement, condition

tramo *m,* plot of ground; flight of stairs, staircase; stretch, expanse, reach, tract

tramontana *f,* north wind; arrogance, haughtiness

tramoya *f, theat* stage machinery; trick, deception, hoax

tramoyista *mf* stage carpenter; stagehand; scene-shifter; trickster, impostor, swindler

trampa *f,* trap, snare; trapdoor; flap of a shop counter; trouser fly; trick, swindle; overdue debt. *fig inf* **caer en la t.,** to fall

into the trap. *inf* **coger en la t.,** to catch in a trap; catch in the act

trampantojo *m, inf* optical illusion, swindle

trampeador *a inf* swindling. *n* trickster, swindler

trampear *vi inf* to obtain money on false pretenses; struggle on (against illness, etc.); keep oneself alive, make shift; *vt* defraud, swindle

trampolín *m,* springboard; diving board; *fig* jumping-off place

tramposo (-sa) *n* debtor; cardsharper; swindler

tranca *f,* thick stick, cudgel; bar (of a window, etc.)

trancada *f,* stride

trancar *vt* to bar the door; *vi* oppose, resist; *vr, Lat. Am.* be constipated

trancazo *m,* blow with a stick; influenza, flu

trance *m,* crisis, difficult juncture; danger, peril. **t. de armas,** armed combat. **a todo t.,** at all costs, without hesitation

tranco *m,* stride; threshold. *inf* **en dos trancos,** in a trice

tranquilar *vt com* to check off

tranquilidad *f,* tranquility, peace, quietness; composure, serenity

tranquilizador *a* tranquilizing, soothing

tranquilizar *vt* to calm, quiet; soothe

tranquilo *a* tranquil, quiet, peaceful; serene, composed

tranquiza *f, Mexico* beating, thrashing

transacción *f,* compromise, arrangement; transaction, negotiation, deal

transandino *a* transandean

transatlántico *a* transatlantic. *m,* (transatlantic) liner

transbordar *vt* to transship; transfer, remove goods from one vehicle to another

transbordo *m,* transshipment, transshipping; transfer, removal

transcendencia *f* See **trascendencia**

transcendental *a.* See **trascendental**

transcribir *vt* to transcribe; copy. *Past Part.* **transcrito**

transcripción *f,* transcription; copy, transcript

transcurrir *vi* to elapse, pass (time)

transcurso *m,* passage, lapse, course (of time)

transepto *m,* transept

transeúnte *a* transient, temporary. *mf* passerby; visitor, sojourner

transferencia *f,* transfer (from one place to another); *law* conveyance, transference. **t. bancaria,** bank draft

transferidor (-ra) *a* transferring. *n* transferrer; *law* transferor

transferir *vt irr* to transfer, move from one place to another; *law* convey (property, etc.); postpone. See **sentir**

transfigurar *vt* to transfigure

transfijo *a* transfixed

transformación *f*, transformation

transformador *a* transformative. *m*, *elec* transformer

transformar *vt* to transform; reform (persons); *vr* be transformed; reform, mend one's ways

tránsfuga *mf* **tránsfugo** *m*, fugitive; political turncoat

transfusor *a* transfusive

transgredir *vt* to transgress, infringe

transgresión *f*, infringement, violation, transgression

transgresor (-ra) *a* infringing. *n* transgressor, violator

transición *f*, transition, change

transido *a* exhausted, worn-out, spent; niggardly, mean

transigencia *f*, tolerance, forbearance, indulgence

transigente *a* tolerant, forbearing

transigir *vi* to be tolerant; be broad-minded. *vt* put up with, tolerate

transitable *a* passable, traversable

transitar *vi* to cross, pass through; travel

tránsito *m*, passage, crossing; transit; stopping place; transition, change; gallery of a cloister; *ecc* holy death. **de t.,** temporarily; in transit (of goods). **hacer tránsitos,** to break one's journey, stop

transitorio *a* transitory, fugitive, fleeting

tránslimitación *f*, trespass; bad behavior; armed intervention in a neighboring state

translimitar *vt* to overstep the boundaries (of a state, etc.); overstep the limits (of decency, etc.)

translúcido *a* translucent, semitransparent

transmigrar *vi* to migrate; transmigrate (of the soul)

transmisión *f*, transmission. **t. del pensamiento,** thought transference

transmisor *a* transmitting. *m*, *elec* transmitter, sender

transmitir *vt* to transmit; *mech* drive

transoceánico *a* transoceanic

transparencia *f*, transparency; obviousness

transparentarse *vr* to be transparent; show through; *fig* reveal; give away (secrets)

transparente *a* transparent; translucent; evident, obvious. *m*, windowshade, blind

transpiración *f*, transpiration; perspiration

transpirar *vi* to perspire; transpire

transponer *vt* *irr* to move, transfer; transplant; transpose; *vr* hide behind; sink behind the horizon (of the sun, stars); be half-asleep. See **poner**

transportador (-ra) *a* transport. *n* transporter. *m*, *geom* protractor

transportar *vt* to transport; *mus* transpose; carry; *vr* *fig* be carried away by (anger, rapture)

transporte *m*, transport, carriage; cartage; *naut* transport; strong emotion, transport, ecstasy

transversal, transverso *a* transverse

tranvía *m*, street railway; streetcar. **t. de sangre,** horse-drawn streetcar.

trapacear *vi* to cheat, swindle

trapacete *m*, *com* daybook

trapacista *mf* trickster, swindler, knave

trapajoso *a* ragged, shabby, tattered

trápala *f*, noise, confusion, hubbub; noise of horse's hoofs, gallop; *inf* trick, swindle; prattling, babbling. *mf* *inf* babbler, prattler; trickster

trapalear *vi* to walk noisily, tramp; *inf* chatter, babble

trapatiesta *f*, *inf* brawl, row, quarrel

trapaza *f*, hoax, swindle

trapeador *m*, *Lat. Am.* (floor) mop

trapear *vt*, *Lat. Am.* to mop (the floor)

trapecio *m*, trapeze; *geom* trapezium, trapezoid

trapería *f*, old-clothes shop; old clothes, rags, trash, frippery

trapero (-ra) *n* old-clothes seller; rag merchant; ragpicker

trapezoide *m*, trapezium, trapezoid

trapichear *vi* *inf* to make shift, endeavor

trapiento *a* ragged, shabby

trapillo *m*, *inf* poverty-stricken lover; nest egg, savings. *inf* **de t.,** in a state of undress, in négligé

trapío *m*, *inf* spirit of a fighting bull; verve, dash, independent air (of women)

trapisonda *f*, *inf* uproar, brawl; hubbub, bustle; snare, fix

trapisondear *vi* *inf* to be given to brawling; scheme, intrigue

trapisondista *mf* brawler; schemer, trickster

trapo *m*, rag; *naut* canvas; bullfighter's cape; *pl* garments, bits and pieces. *inf* **poner como un t. (a),** to dress down, scold. *inf* **soltar el t.,** to burst out crying or laughing

trapujo *m*, *inf* trick; subterfuge

traque *m*, report, bang (of a rocket, etc.); fuse (of a firework)

tráquea *f*, trachea

traqueotomía *f*, tracheotomy

traquetear *vi* to crack, bang, go off with a report; rattle; jolt (of trains, etc.). *vt* shake, stir; *inf* paw, handle too much

traqueteo *m*, banging (of fireworks); creaking; rattling; jolting (of trains, etc.)

traquido *m*, report (of a gun); crack (of a whip); creak

tras *prep* after; behind; following, in pursuit of; trans- (in compounds). *m, inf* buttock; sound of a blow, bang, bump. **t. t.,** knocking (at a door); banging

trasalcoba *f*, dressing room

trasbarrás *m*, bang, bump, noise

trasbocar *vt, Lat. Am.* to vomit

trascendencia *f*, transcendence, excellence; consequence, result

trascendental a transcendental; important, farreaching

trascender *vi irr* to spread to, influence; become known, leak out; exhale a scent; *vt* investigate, discover. See **entender**

trascolar *vt irr* to filter, strain; cross over, traverse. See **colar**

trascordarse *vr irr* to mix up, make a muddle of, forget. See **acordar**

trasechar *vt* to ambush, waylay

trasegar *vt irr* to upset, turn upside down; transfer, move from one place to another; empty, pour out, upset (liquids). See **cegar**

traseñalar *vt* to re-mark, mark again

trasera *f*, rear, back, rear portion

trasero a rear, back. *m*, hindquarters, rump; buttocks, seat; *pl inf* ancestors

trasgo *m*, imp, sprite, puck

trashumar *vi* to go from winter to summer pasture (or vice versa) (of flocks)

trasiego *m*, emptying, pouring out, upsetting (of liquids); decanting (of wines)

traslación *f*, removal, transfer; alteration (of the date for a meeting); metaphor

trasladable a removable, movable, transferable

trasladar *vt* to remove, transfer; move from one place to another; alter (the date of a meeting); translate; copy, transcribe; *vr* remove (from a place)

traslado *m*, removal; transfer; transcription

traslapar *vt* to cover, overlap

traslapo *m*, overlap, overlapping

traslucirse *vr irr* to be transparent or translucent; shine through; come out (of secrets); infer, gather. See **lucir**

traslumbramiento *m*, dazzle, glare, brilliance

traslumbrar *vt* to dazzle; *vr* flicker, glimmer; fade quickly, disappear

trasluz *m*, reflected light. **al t.,** against the light

trasminar *vt* to undermine, excavate; *vi* percolate, ooze; penetrate, spread

trasnochada *f*, previous night, last night; night's vigil; sleepless night; *mil* night attack

trasnochado a stale, old; weary; hackneyed; drawn, pinched

trasnochador (-ra) *n* one who watches by night or stays up all night; *inf* night owl, reveler

trasnochar *vi* to stay up all night; watch

through the night; spend the night; *vt* sleep on, leave for the following day

trasnoche, trasnocho *m, inf* night out; night vigil

trasoir *vt irr* to hear incorrectly, misunderstand. See **oir**

trasojado a haggard, tired-eyed

trasoñar *vt irr* to imagine, mistake a dream for reality. See **contar**

traspalar *vt* to fork (grain); shovel; transfer, move

trasparencia *f*. See **transparencia**

traspasar *vt* to transfer, move; cross; *law* convey, make over to; pierce; transgress, flout; exceed one's authority; *fig* go too far; reexamine, go over again; give intolerable pain (of illness, grief). **se traspasa,** to be disposed of (houses, etc.)

traspaso *m*, transport, transfer; *law* conveyance; property transferred; price agreed upon

traspatio *m, Lat. Am.* backyard

traspié *m*, slip, catching of the foot, stumble; heel of the foot. **dar traspiés,** *inf* to blunder

trasplantación *f*, **trasplante** *m*, transplantation; emigration

trasplantar *vt agr* to transplant; *vr* emigrate

trasplante *m*, planting out

traspuesta *f*, transposition; back quarters; rear (of a house); back yard

trasquilar *vt* to cut the hair unevenly; shear (sheep); *inf* cut down, diminish

trastada *f, inf* dirty trick, mean act

traste *m*, fret (of stringed instruments); tasting cup. **dar al t. con,** to spoil, upset, damage. *inf* **sin trastes,** topsy-turvy, without method

trastear *vt* to play well (on the mandolin, etc.); *inf* manage tactfully; *vi* move around, change (furniture, etc.); discuss excitedly

trastejar *vt* to repair the roof; renew slates; overhaul

trastienda *f*, back of a shop; room behind a shop; *inf* wariness, caution

trasto *m*, piece of furniture; (household) utensil; lumber, useless furniture; *theat* wing or set piece; *inf* useless person, ne'er-do-well; oddment, thing; *pl* implements, equipment

trastornable a easily overturned or upset; easily agitated

trastornar *vt* to turn upside down; perturb, disturb; *fig* overpower (of scents, etc.); disorder, upset; dissuade; make mad; derange the mind

trastorno *m*, upset; perturbation, anxiety; disorder; mental derangement; confusion (of the senses)

trastrabillar *vi* to stumble, slip; totter, sway; hesitate; stutter, be tongue-tied

trastrocamiento *m*, alteration, change; disarrangement

trastrocar *vt irr* to alter, change, disarrange; change the order of. See **contar**

trasudar *vt* to perspire

trasuntar *vt* to copy, transcribe; summarize

trasunto *m,* copy, transcript; imitation

trasver *vt irr* to see through or between, glimpse; see incorrectly. See **ver**

trata *f,* slave trade. **t. de blancas,** white slave traffic

tratable *a* easily accessible, sociable, unpretentious

tratadista *mf* writer of a treatise; expert, writer on special subjects

tratado *m,* pact, agreement; treaty; treatise

tratador (-ra) *n* arbitrator

tratamiento *m,* treatment; courtesy title; address, style; *med* treatment; process

tratante *m,* merchant, dealer

tratar *vt* to handle, use; conduct, manage; have dealings with, meet, know (e.g. **Yo no le trato,** I don't know him); behave well or badly toward; care for, treat; discuss, deal with (e.g. **¿De qué trata el libro?** What is the book about?); propose, suggest; *chem* treat; *(with de)* address as, call; *vi* have amorous relations; *(with de)* try to, endeavor to; *(with en)* trade in; *vr* look after oneself, treat oneself; conduct oneself

trato *m,* use, handling; management; conduct, behavior; manner, demeanor; appellation, title; commerce, traffic; dealings, intercourse; treatment; agreement; arrangement. **t. colectivo,** collective bargaining

traumático *a* traumatic

través *m,* slant, slope; mishap; *(mil arch)* traverse. **a t. or al t.,** across; through. **de t.,** athwart; crossway

travesaño *m,* crossbar; bolster; rung (of a ladder); *carp* traverse

travesear *vi* to run about, romp, be mischievous; lead a vicious life; speak wittily; move ceaselessly (of water, etc.)

travesía *f,* crossing; traverse; crossroad; side road or street; distance, space; sea crossing; crosswise position; stretch of road within a town

travestido *a* disguised, dressed up

travesura *f,* romping, frolic; mischief; prank; quick-wittedness

traviesa *f,* sleeping car, sleeper (railroad); *arch* rafter; distance between two points

travieso *a* transverse, crosswise; mischievous, willful; debauched; clever, subtle; ever-moving (of streams, etc.)

trayecto *m,* run, distance, journey; stretch, expanse, tract; fare stage

trayectoria *f,* trajectory; journey

traza *f,* plan, design, draft; scheme, project; idea, proposal; aspect, appearance;

means, manner. **Hombre pobre todo es trazas,** A poor man is full of schemes (for bettering himself)

trazado *m,* designing, drawing; design, draft, model, plan; course, direction (of a canal, etc.)

trazar *vt* to plan, draft, design; make a drawing of; trace; describe; map out, arrange

trazo *m,* line, stroke; outline, contour, form, line; *art* fold in drapery; stroke of the pen

trebejar *vi* to frolic, skip, play

trebejo *m,* chessman, chess piece; utensil, article (gen. *pl*); plaything

trébol *m,* clover

trece *a* and *m,* thirteen, thirteenth. *m,* thirteenth (day of the month)

trecho *m,* distance, space; interval (of time). **a trechos,** at intervals. **de t. en t.,** from time to time

trefe *a* pliable, flexible; light; spurious (of coins)

tregua *f,* truce, respite, rest. **dar treguas,** to afford relief, give a respite; give time

treinta *a* and *m,* thirty; thirtieth. *m,* thirtieth (day of the month)

tremebundo *a* fearsome, dread

tremedal *m,* bog; quagmire

tremendo *a* fearful, formidable; awesome; *inf* tremendous, enormous

trementina *f,* turpentine

tremolar *vt* and *vi* to wave, fly (of banners); *fig* make a show of

tremolina *f,* noise of the wind; *inf* hubbub, confusion

trémulo *a* trembling, tremulous

tren *m,* supply, provision; outfit; equipment; pomp, show; railroad train; following, train; *Mexico also* streetcar, trolley car, trolley. **t. ascendente,** up train (from coast to interior). *inf* **t. botijo,** excursion train. **t. con coches corridos,** corridor train. **t. correo,** mail train. **t. descendente,** down train (from interior to coast). **t. mixto,** train carrying passengers and freight. **t. ómnibus,** accommodation train, slow, stopping train. **t. rápido,** express

trencilla *f,* braid, trimming

trenza *f,* plait, braid; plait of hair; bread twist; *Lat. Am.* string (of onions). **en t.,** in plaits, plaited (of hair)

trenzar *vt* to plait, braid; *vi* curvet, prance *Lat. Am.* **trenzarse (en . . .)** get involved (in . . .), e.g. **trenzarse en una disputa** get involved in a dispute

trepa *f,* perforation, boring, piercing; climbing; creeping; *inf* half-somersault; grain, surface (of wood); craftiness, slyness; deception, fraud; beating, drubbing

trepador *a* climbing; crawling; *bot* creeping, climbing. *m,* climbing place

trepanación *f,* trepanning . . .

trepanar *vt* to trepan

trepante *a* creeping; *bot* twining, climbing

trepar *vi* to climb, ascend; *bot* climb or creep; bore, perforate

trepatrepa *m*, jungle gym, monkey bars

trepidación *f*, trepidation, dread; vibration; jarring; shaking

trepidar *vi* to shiver, shudder; vibrate; shake; jar; *Lat. Am.* hesitate

trépido *a* a shuddering, shivering; vibrating

tres *a* a three; third. *m*, figure three; third (day of the month); three (of playing cards); trio. *inf* **como t. y dos son cinco,** as sure as two and two make four

trescientos *a* and *m*, three hundred; three-hundredth

treta *f*, scheme; trick, hoax; feint (in fencing)

tría *f*, selection, choice; worn place (in cloth)

triangulación *f*, triangulation

triángulo *a* triangular. *m*, (*geom mus*) triangle. **t. acutángulo,** acute triangle. **t. obtusángulo,** obtuse triangle. **t. rectángulo,** right-angled triangle

triar *vt* to select, pick out; *vi* fly in and out of the hive (of bees); *vr* grow threadbare, become worn

tribu *f*, tribe; species, family

tribulación *f*, tribulation, suffering

tribuna *f*, tribune; platform, rostrum, pulpit; spectators' gallery; stand. **t. de la prensa,** press gallery. **t. del jurado,** jury box. **t. del órgano,** organ loft

tribunado *m*, tribunate

tribunal *m*, law court; *law* bench; judgment seat; tribunal; board of examiners. **t. de menores,** children's court, juvenile court. *naut* **t. de presas,** prize court. **t. de primera instancia,** *law* petty sessions. **t. militar,** court-martial

tribuno *m*, tribune; political speaker

tributar *vt* to pay taxes; offer, render (thanks, homage, etc.)

tributario (**-ia**) *a* a tributary; tax-paying, contributive. *n* taxpayer. *m*, tributary (of a river)

tributo *m*, contribution; tax; tribute, homage; census

triciclo *m*, tricycle

tricolor *a* a three-colored

tricorne *a poet* three-cornered, three-horned

tricornio *a* a three-cornered. *m*, three-cornered hat

tricotomía *f*, trichotomy, division into three

tridente *a* tridentate, three-pronged. *m*, trident

trienio *m*, space of three years

trigo *m*, wheat plant; ear of wheat; wheat field (gen. *pl*); wealth, money. **t. sar-**

raceno, buckwheat. **t. tremés** *or* **t. trechel** *or* **t. tremesino** *or* **t. de marzo,** summer wheat

trigonometría *f*, trigonometry

trigueño *a* a brunette, dark

triguero *a* a wheat; wheat-growing. *m*, grain sieve; grain merchant

trilátero *a* a three-sided, trilateral

trilingüe *a* a trilingual

trilla *f*, red mullet; *agr* harrow; threshing; threshing season

trillado *a* a frequented, trodden, worn (of paths); hackneyed

trilladora *f*, threshing machine

trillar *vt* to thresh; *inf* frequent; ill-treat

trillo *m*, threshing machine; harrow

trillón *m*, trillion

trilogía *f*, trilogy

trimestral *a* a quarterly; terminal (in schools, etc.)

trimestre *a* a quarterly; terminal. *m*, quarter, three months; term (in schools, etc.); quarterly payment; quarterly rent

trinado *m*, *mus* trill; twittering, shrilling (of birds)

trinar *vi mus* to trill; twitter, shrill; *inf* get in a temper, be furious

trincapiñones *m*, *inf* scatterbrained youth

trincar *vt* to fasten securely; tie tightly; pinion; *naut* lash, make fast; cut up, chop; *inf* tipple; *vi naut* sail close to the wind

trincha *f*, vest strap

trinchante *m*, table carver; carving fork; stonecutter's hammer

trinchar *vt* to carve (at table); *inf* decide, dispose

trinche *m Mexico* pitchfork; *elsewhere in Lat. Am.* fork

trinchera *f*, *mil* trench; cutting (for roads, etc.); trench coat

trinchero *m*, platter, trencher; serving table, side table

trineo *m*, sledge, sleigh

trinidad *f*, trinity

trinomio *m*, trinomial

trinquete *m*, *naut* mainmast; mainsail; *sport* rackets; *mech* ratchet

trinquis *m*, *inf* draft, drink

trío *m*, trio

tripa *f*, entrail, gut; *inf* belly; inside (of some fruits). *inf* **hacer de tripas corazón,** *inf* to take heart, buck up. **revolver las tripas (a),** *fig inf* to make one sick

tripartición *f*, tripartition

tripartito *a* a tripartite

tripicallos *m pl*, *cul* tripe

triple *a* a triple; three-ply (of yarn)

triplicar *vt* to treble

trípode *m*, (sometimes *f*) three-legged stool or table; tripod; trivet

tripulación *f*, crew (ships and aircraft)

tripulante *m*, crew member

tripular *vt* to provide with a crew, man; equip, furnish; serve in, work as the crew of

trique *m*, crack, creak. *inf* **a cada t.,** at every moment

triquiñuela *f*, *inf* evasion, subterfuge

triquitraque *m*, tap, rap; crack; firework

tris *m*, crack, noise of glass, etc., cracking; *inf* instant, trice. **estar en un t. (de),** to be on the verge (of), within an inch (of)

trisar *vt* to crack, break, splinter (of glass); *vi* chirp, twitter (especially of swallows)

trisca *f*, cracking, crushing, crackling (of nuts, etc.); noise, tumult

triscar *vi* to make a noise with the feet; gambol, frolic; creak, crack; *vt* blend, mingle; set the teeth of a saw

trisecar *vt* to trisect

trisemanal *a* three times weekly; every three weeks

trisílabo *a* trisyllabic

trismo *m*, lockjaw, trismus

triste *a* unhappy, sorrowful; melancholy, gloomy; sad;·piteous, unfortunate; useless, worthless; *m*, *Lat. Am.* sad love song

tristeza, tristura *f*, unhappiness; melancholy, gloom; sadness; piteousness

tritón *m*, merman

triturar *vt* to crumble, crush; chew; masticate; ill-treat, bruise; refute, contradict

triunfada *f*, trumping (at cards)

triunfador (-ra) *a* triumphant. *n* victor

triunfal *a* triumphal

triunfante *a* triumphant

triunfar *vi* to triumph; be victorious, win; trump (at cards); spend ostentatiously

triunfo *m*, triumph; victory; trump card; success; booty, spoils of war; conquest

trivial *a* well-known, hackneyed; frequented, trodden; commonplace, mediocre; trivial, unimportant

trivialidad *f*, banality, triteness; mediocrity; triviality

trivio *m*, road junction

triza *f*, fragment, bit; *naut* rope. **hacer trizas,** to smash to bits

trizar *vt* to smash up, destroy

trocada, a la *adv* contrariwise; in exchange

trocar *vt* *irr* to exchange; vomit; distort, misconstrue, mistake; *vr* change, alter one's behavior; change places with another; be transferred. See **contar**

trocha *f*, short cut; trail, path, track

trochemoche, a *adv* *inf* without rhyme or reason, pell-mell

trocear *vt* to divide into pieces

trofeo *m*, trophy; victory; military booty

troglodita *a* and *mf* troglodyte. *m*, *fig* savage, barbarian. *mf* glutton

troj *f*, granary

trola *f*, *inf* lie, nonsense, hoax

trole *m*, trolley

trolebús *m*, trolley car

trolero *a* *inf* deceiving, lying

tromba *f*, waterspout

trombón *m*, trombone; trombone player. **¡Trombones y platillos!** Great Scot!

trombosis *f*, thrombosis

trompa *f*, elephant's trunk; *mus* horn; proboscis (of insects); waterspout; humming top. **t. de Falopio,** fallopian tube

trompada *f*, *inf* bang, bump; blow, buffet, slap; collision

trompazo *m*, heavy blow, knock, bang

trompear *vi* to play with a top; *vt* knock about

trompero *m*, top maker. *a* deceiving, swindling

trompeta *f*, trumpet; bugle. *m*, trumpeter; bugler; *inf* ninny. **t. de amor,** sunflower

trompetada *f*, *inf* stupid remark, piece of nonsense

trompetazo *m*, bray of a trumpet; bugle blast; *inf* stupid remark

trompetear *vi* *inf* to play the trumpet or bugle

trompeteo *m*, trumpeting, trumpet call; sound of the bugle

trompetería *f*, collection of trumpets; metal organ pipes

trompetero *m*, trumpet or bugle maker or player

trompetilla *f*, *dim* little trumpet; ear trumpet

trompicar *vt* to make stumble, trip. *vi* stumble, trip up

trompo *m*, humming or spinning top; *inf* dolt, idiot

tronada *f*, thunderstorm

tronado *a* worn-out; threadbare, old; poor, poverty-stricken; down at the heels

tronar *v* *impers* *irr* to growl, roar (of guns); *inf* go bankrupt, be ruined; *inf* protest against, attack; *Central America, Mexico* execute, shoot; (*with con*) quarrel with. *Pres. Ind.* **trueno, truenas, truena, truenan.** *Pres. Subjunc.* **truene, truenes, truene, truenen**

troncal *a* trunk; main, principal

troncha *f*, *Lat. Am.* piece; slice

tronchar *vt* to break off, lop off (branches)

troncho *m*, *bot* stem, stalk, branch

tronco *m*, *anat* *bot* trunk; main body or line (of communications); trunk line; common origin, stock; *fig* blockhead, dolt; callous person. *fig* **estar hecho un t.,** to lie like a log; sleep like a log

tronera *f*, *naut* porthole; embrasure; slit window; pocket of a billiards table. *mf* *inf* madcap, harumscarum

trono *m*, throne; *ecc* tabernacle; shrine;

kingly might; *pl* thrones, hierarchy of angels

tronzador *m*, two-handled saw

tronzar *vt* to smash, break into bits; *sew* pleat; exhaust, overtire

tropa *f*, crowd (of people); troops, military; *mil* call to arms; *pl* army. **t. de línea,** regiment of the line. **tropas de asalto,** storm troopers. **tropas de refresco,** fresh troops. **en t.,** in a crowd; in groups

tropel *m*, rush, surge (of crowds, etc.); bustle, confusion; crowd, multitude; heap, jumble (of things). **en t.,** in a rush; in a crowd

tropelía *f*, rush, dash; violence; outrage

tropezar *vi irr* to stumble, slip; (*with con*) meet unexpectedly or accidentally come up against, be faced with (difficulties); quarrel with or oppose; fall into (bad habits). See **empezar**

tropezón *m*, stumbling, slipping; stumbling block, obstacle. **a tropezones,** *inf* stumblingly; by fits and starts

tropical *a* tropical

trópicos *m pl*, tropics

tropiezo *m*, stumble; stumbling block, obstacle; hitch; impediment; slip, peccadillo, fault; difficulty, embarrassment; fight, skirmish; quarrel

tropo *m*, trope, figure of speech

troquel *m*, die, mold

trotamundos *mf, inf* globetrotter

trotar *vi* to trot; *inf* hurry, get a move on

trote *m*, trot; toil, drudgery. **t. corto,** jogtrot. **al t.,** with all speed

trotón (-ona) *a* trotting. *m*, horse. *f*, chaperone

trova *f*, verse; song, lay, ballad; love song

trovador (-ra) *m*, troubadour, minstrel. *n* poet

trovadoresco *a* pertaining to minstrels, troubadour

trovar *vi* to compose verses; write ballads; misconstrue, misinterpret

trozo *m*, part, fragment; piece, portion; *lit* selection. **t. de abordaje,** *nav* landing party

trucha *f*, trout. **t. asalmonada,** salmon trout

truco *m*, trick, deception

truculencia *f*, harshness, cruelty, truculence

truculento *a* fierce, harsh, truculent

trueco *m*, exchange. **a t. de,** in exchange for; on condition that

trueno *m*, thunder; report, noise (of firearms); *inf* rake, scapegrace

trueque *m*, exchange. **a. (or en) t.,** in exchange

trufa *f*, *bot* truffle; nonsense, idle talk

trufar *vt cul* to stuff with truffles; *vi inf* lie, tell fibs

truhán (-ana) *a* knavish, roguish, comic. *n* knave, rogue; clown, buffoon

truhanería *f*, knavery, act of a rogue; clowning, buffoonery; collection of rogues

trujar *vt* to partition off

trulla *f*, uproar, tumult; crowd, throng

truncar *vt* to shorten, truncate; decapitate, mutilate; omit, cut out (words, etc.); curtail, abridge; mutilate, deform (texts, etc.)

tú *pers pron 2nd sing mf* thou, you. **tratar de t. (a),** to address familiarly; be on intimate terms with

tu *poss pron mf* thy, your. Used only before nouns

tubería *f*, piping, tubing; pipe system; pipe factory

tubo *m*, pipe, tube; lamp chimney; flue; *anat* duct, canal. **t. acústico,** speaking tube. **t. de ensayo,** test tube. **t. de escape,** exhaust pipe. **t. lanzatorpedos,** torpedo tube. **t. termiónico,** *rad* thermionic valve

tucán, tucano *m* toucan

tuerca *f*, nut (of a screw)

tuerto *a* one-eyed. *m*, *law* tort; *pl* afterpains. **a t.,** unjustly

tueste *m*, toasting

tuétano *m*, marrow. *inf* **hasta los tuétanos,** to the depths of one's being

tufillas *mf inf* easily irritated person

tufo *m*, strong smell, poisonous vapor; *inf* stink; side, airs, conceit (often *pl*); lock of hair over the ears

tugurio *m*, shepherd's hut; miserable little room; *inf* haunt, low dive

tulipán *m*, tulip

tullido *a* partially paralyzed; maimed, crippled

tullir *vt irr* to maim, cripple; paralyze; *vr* become paralyzed; be crippled. See **mullir**

tumba *f*, tomb; tumble, overbalancing; somersault; Catherine wheel

tumbar *vt* to knock down; kill, drop; *inf* overpower, overcome (of odors, wine). *vi* fall down; *naut* run aground; *vr inf* lie down, stretch oneself out

tumbo *m*, tumble, overbalancing; undulation (of ground); rise and fall of sea waves; imminent danger; book containing deeds and privileges of monasteries and churches

tumbón *a inf* crafty, sly; idle, lazy. *m*, trunk with an arched lid

tumefacción *f*, swelling

tumefacto, túmido *a* swollen

tumor *m*, tumor

tumulto *m*, riot, uprising; tumult, commotion, disturbance

tumultuario, tumultuoso *a* noisy, tumultuous, confused

tuna *f*, prickly pear tree or fruit; vagrant

life; strolling student musicians (playing to raise money for charity)

tunante a rascally, roguish. *mf* rascal, scoundrel

tunantuelo (-la) *n inf* imp, little rascal

tunda *f*, shearing of cloth; *inf* sound beating, hiding

tundear *vt* to beat, drub, buffet

tundidora *f*, woman who shears cloth; cloth-shearing machine; lawn mower

tundir *vt* to shear (cloth); mow (grass); *inf* beat, wallop

túnel *m*, tunnel

túnica *f*, tunic, chiton; tunicle; robe

tuno (-na) a knavish, rascally. *n* rascal, scoundrel

tupición *f*, *Lat. Am.* blockage, obstruction; cold (in the head)

tupido a thick, dense; obtuse, dull, stupid; *Lat. Am.* blocked up, obstructed

tupir *vt* to thicken, make dense; press tightly; *vr* stuff oneself with food or drink

turba *f*, crowd, multitude; peat

turbación *f*, disturbance; upset;`perturbation; bewilderment, confusion; embarrassment

turbador (-ra) a disturbing, upsetting. *n* disturber, upsetter

turbamulta *f*, *inf* mob, rabble

turbante a upsetting, perturbing. *m*, turban

turbar *vt* to disturb, upset; make turbid, muddy; bewilder, confuse; embarrass

turbina *f*, turbine

turbio a turbid, muddy; troublous; turbulent, disturbed; obscure, confused (style); indistinct, blurred, *m pl*, lees, sediment (of oil)

turbión *m*, brief storm, squall; *fig* shower, rush

turbulencia *f*, turbidity, muddiness; turbulence, commotion; disturbance, confusion

turbulento a muddy, turbid; turbulent, disturbed; confused

turca *f*, *inf* drinking bout

turco (-ca) a Turkish. *n* Turk. *m*, Turkish (language)

turgencia *f*, swelling, turgidity

turgente a *med* turgescent; *poet* turgid, prominent, swollen

turismo *m*, touring, tourist industry. **coche de t.,** touring car

turista *mf* tourist

turno *m*, turn. **por t.,** in turn

turquesa *f*, turquoise

Turquía Turkey

turrón *m*, kind of nougat; almond paste; *inf* soft job, sinecure; civil service job

turulato a *inf* dumbfounded, speechless, inarticulate

¡tus! *interj* word for calling dogs. **sin decir t. ni mus,** *inf* without saying anything

tusa *f*, *Central America* corncob; whore; *Argentina* mane (of a horse)

tutear *vt* to address as tú (instead of the formal usted); treat familiarly

tutela *f*, guardianship; tutelage; protection, defense

tuteo *m*, the use in speaking to a person of the familiar tú instead of the formal usted

tutor (-ra) *n* guardian. *m*, stake (for plants); protector, defender

tuyo, tuya, tuyos, tuyas *poss pron 2nd sing* and *pl mf* thine, yours. Used sometimes with def. art. (e.g. **Este sombrero es el tuyo,** This hat is yours)

U

u *f*, letter U. *conjunc* Used instead of **o** or before words beginning with **o** or **ho** (e.g. **fragante u oloroso**)

ubérrimo *a sup* most fruitful; very abundant

ubicación *f*, situation, position, location

ubicar *vt* to place, situate; *vi* and *vr* be situated

ubicuo *a* omnipresent; ubiquitous

ubre *f*, udder

Ucrania Ukraine

ucranio (-ia) *a* and *n* Ukrainian

ucelele *m*, ukulele

¡uf! *interj* ugh!

ufanarse *vr* to pride oneself, put on airs

ufanía *f*, pride, conceit

ufano *a* conceited, vain; satisfied, pleased; expeditious, masterly

ujier *m*, usher

úlcera *f*, ulcer

ulcerar(se) *vt* and *vr* to ulcerate

ulpo *m*, *Chile*, *Peru* corn gruel

ulterior *a* farther, ulterior; subsequent

ulteriormente *adv* subsequently, later

ultimación *f*, ending, finishing

ultimar *vt* to end, conclude

ultimátum *m*, ultimatum

último *a* last; farthermost; ultimate; top; final, definitive; most valuable; best; latter; recent. **«Última Hora.»** "Stop Press." **a última hora**, *fig* at the eleventh hour. **en estos últimos años**, in recent years. **a últimos de mes**, towards the end of the month. **el ú. piso**, the top floor. **por ú.**, finally. *Inf* **estar en las últimas**, to be at the end, be finishing

ultra, *adv* besides; (with words like *mar*) beyond; (as prefix) excessively

ultrajar *vt* to insult; scorn, despise

ultraje *m*, insult, outrage

ultrajoso *a* offensive, insulting, abusive

ultramar *m*, overseas, abroad

ultramarino *a* oversea; ultramarine. *m*, foreign produce (gen. *pl*)

ultrarrojo *a* infrared

ultratumba *adv* beyond the grave

ultravioleta *a* ultraviolet

ululación *f*, screech, howl; hoot of an owl

ulular *vi* to howl, shriek, screech; hoot (of an owl)

umbral *m*, threshold; *fig* starting point; *arch* lintel. **atravesar (or pisar) los umbrales**, to cross the threshold

umbría *f*, shady place

umbrío *a* shady, dark

umbroso *a* shady

un *abb* of **uno, a,** one. Used before *m*, *sing f*, **una**, *indef art*. a, an; a; one

unánime *a* unanimous

unanimidad *f*, unanimity. **por u.**, unanimously

unción *f*, anointing; *ecc* Extreme Unction; unction, fervor

undécimo *a* eleventh

undulación *f*, undulation; *phys* wave

undular *vi* to undulate; wriggle; float, wave (flags, etc.)

undulatorio *a* undulatory

ungir *vt* to anoint

ungüento *m*, ointment; lotion; *fig* balm, unguent

único *a* unique; sole, solitary, only. **Lo ú. que se puede hacer es . . .,** The only thing one can do is . . .

unicolor *a* of one color

unidad *f*, unity; unit; *(math mil)* unit. **u. de bagaje,** piece of baggage. (of drama) **u. de lugar,** unity of place. **u. de tiempo,** unity of time

unidamente *adv* jointly; harmoniously

unificación *f*, unification

unificar(se) *vt* and *vr* to unify, unite

uniformación *f*, standardization

uniformar *vt* to make uniform, standardize; put into uniform; *vr* become uniform

uniforme *a* uniform; same, similar. *m*, uniform

uniformidad *f*, uniformity

unilateral *a* one-sided, unilateral

unión *f*, union; correspondence, conformity; agreement; marriage; alliance, federation; composition, mixture; combination; proximity, nearness; (mystic) union

unionista *mf pol* unionist

unir *vt* to unite, join; mix, combine; bind, fasten; connect, couple; bring together; marry; *fig* harmonize, conciliate; *vr* join together, unite; be combined; marry; *(with prep* **a** *or con)* be near to; associate with

unísono *a* unisonant. **al u.,** in unison; unanimously

universal *a* universal; well-informed; widespread

universidad *f*, university; universality; universe

universitario *a* university

universo *a* universal. *m*, universe

uno (f, una) *a* a, one; single, only; same; *pl* some; about, nearly. *m*, one (number). **Tiene unos doce años,** He is about twelve. **unas pocas manzanas,** a few apples. *pron* someone; one thing, same thing; *pl* some people. **No sabe uno qué creer,** One doesn't know what to believe. **Unos dicen que no, otros que sí,** Some (people) say no, others yes. **Juan no tiene libros y le voy a dar uno,** John has no books and I am going to give him one. **Todo es uno,** It's all the same. **u. a u.,** one by one. **u. que otro,** a few. **u. y otro,**

both. **unos cuantos,** a few, some. **Es la una,** It is one o'clock

untar *vt* to anoint; grease, oil; *inf* bribe; *vr* smear oneself with grease or similar thing; *fig inf* line one's pockets. **u. el carro,** *fig* to grease the wheels

unto *m,* grease; animal fat; *fig* balm; *Chile* shoe polish

untuoso *a* fat, greasy

uña *f,* nail (of fingers or toes); hoof, trotter, claw; stinging tail of scorpion; thorn; stump of tree branch; *naut* fluke; *fig inf* light fingers (gen. *pl*). **afilarse las uñas,** to sharpen one's claws, prepare for trouble. **comerse las uñas,** to bite one's nails. **caer en las uñas de,** to fall into the clutches of. **hincar la u. (en),** to stick the claws into; to defraud, overcharge. **ser u. y carne,** to be devoted friends

uñero *m,* ingrowing nail, ingrown nail

¡upa! *interj* Up you get! Up you go! Upsy daisy! (gen. to children)

uranio *m,* uranium

urbanidad *f,* civility, good manners, urbanity

urbanismo *m,* town planning; housing scheme

urbanizar *vt* to civilize, polish; urbanize

urbano *a* urban, city; urbane

urbe *f,* city, metropolis

urbícola *mf* city dweller

urdemalas *mf,* schemer, intriguer

urdidera *f,* warping-frame

urdimbre *f,* warp; scheming, plotting

urdir *vt* to warp; weave; scheme, intrigue

uretra *f,* urethra

urgencia *f,* urgency; necessity; compulsion

urgente *a* urgent

urgir *vi* to be urgent; be valid, be in force (laws)

urinario *a* urinary. *m,* urinal

urna *f,* urn; ballot box; glass case

urraca *f,* magpie

Uruguay *m* Uruguay

uruguayo (-ya) *a* and *n* Uruguayan

usado *a* worn out; accustomed, efficient. *com* **al u.,** in the usual form. **ropa usada,** second-hand clothing, worn clothing

usanza *f,* custom, usage

usar *vt* to use; wear, make use of; follow (trade, occupation); *vi* be accustomed

usina *f, Argentina* power plant

uso *m,* use; custom; fashion; habit; wear and tear. **al u.,** according to custom. **al u. de,** in the manner of

usted *mf* you. *pl* **ustedes.** Often abbreviated to **Vd, V, Vds, VV or Ud, Uds**

usual *a* usual; general, customary; sociable

usufructo *m, law* usufruct; life-interest; profit

usura *f,* usury; profiteering. **pagar con u.,** to pay back a thousandfold

usurario *a* usurious

usurear *vi* to lend or borrow with usury; profiteer, make excess profits

usurero (-ra) *n* usurer; profiteer

usurpador (-ra) *a* usurping. *n* usurper

usurpar *vt* to usurp

utensilio *m,* utensil; tool, implement (gen. *pl*)

uterino *a* uterine

útero *m,* uterus

útil *a* useful; profitable; *law* lawful (of days, etc.). *m,* usefulness, profit; *pl* **útiles,** utensils, tools

utilidad *f,* utility; usefulness; profit

utilitario *a* utilitarian

utilizar *vt* to utilize

utillaje *m,* machinery

utópico *a* Utopian

uva *f,* grape. **u. espina,** kind of gooseberry. **u. moscatel,** muscatel grape. *inf* **hecho una u.,** dead-drunk

uvero (-ra) *a* pertaining or relating to grapes, grape. *n* grape seller

V

v f, letter V. **v doble** or **doble v,** letter W. **V** or **Vd, VV,** abbs **vuestra(s) merced(es),** mf sing and pl you

vaca f, cow. **v. de San Antón,** ent ladybug

vacación f, vacation, holiday (gen. pl); vacancy; act of vacating (employment). **vacaciones retribuídas,** paid vacation

vacada f, herd of cows

vacancia f, vacancy

vacante a vacant. f, vacancy

vacar vi to be vacant; take a holiday; retire temporarily; (with prep a) dedicate oneself to, engage in

vaciado m, plaster cast; arch excavation

vaciamiento m, emptying; molding, casting; depletion

vaciar vt to empty; drain, drink; mold, cast; arch excavate; hone; copy; vi flow (into) (rivers); vr inf blurt out

vaciedad f, emptiness; foolishness, inanity

vacilación f, swaying; tottering; staggering; hesitation, perplexity

vacilada Mexico, f joke, trick (played on someone)

vacilante a swaying; tottering; staggering; hesitating, vacillating

vacilar vi to sway; totter; stagger; flicker; hesitate

vacío a empty, void; fruitless, vain; unoccupied, vacant, deserted; imperfect; hollow, empty; conceited, immature. m, hollow; anat flank; vacancy; shortage; phys vacuum. **v. de aire,** airpocket. **de v.,** unloaded (carts, etc.). **en v.,** in vacuo. inf **hacer el v. (a),** to send to Coventry

vacuidad f, emptiness; vacuity

vacuna f, cowpox; vaccine. **v. antivariolosa,** smallpox vaccine

vacunación f, vaccination

vacunar vt to vaccinate; inoculate

vacuo a empty; vacant. m, void; vacuum

vadeable a fordable (rivers, etc.); fig surmountable

vadear vt to ford, wade; fig overcome (obstacles); fig sound, find out the opinion (of); vr behave

vademécum m, vade mecum; school satchel

vado m, ford; expedient, help

vagabundear vi to wander, roam, loiter

vagabundeo m, vagabondage

vagabundo (-da) a roving, wandering; vagrant. n tramp, vagabond

vagar m, leisure; interval, pause. vi be idle or at leisure; wander, roam

vagido m, cry, wail (infants)

vago (-ga) a vagrant, idle; vague; art in-

definite, blurred. n idler. m, tramp; loafer. **en v.,** unsuccessfully, vainly

vagón m, wagon; (railway) coach. **v. comedor,** dining car

vagoneta f, open truck (railways, mines, etc.)

vaguear vi to roam, wander; loaf

vaguedad f, vagueness; vague remark

vaharada f, whiff, exhalation

vahído m, vertigo, dizzy spell

vaho m, vapor, fume

vaina f, scabbard; bot sheath, pod; case (scissors, etc.); Colombia hassle. **¡Qué vaina!** What a hassle!

vainilla f, bot vanilla; sew drawn-thread work

vaivén m, swing, sway, seesaw; instability, fluctuation

vajilla f, china; dinner service

vale m, com bond, I.O.U., promissory note; voucher; valediction; Lat. Am. buddy, pal

valedero a valid, binding

valedor (-ra) n protector, sponsor

valentía f, bravery; heroic deed; boast; (art lit) dash, imagination, fire; superhuman effort

valentón a boastful, blustering

valer vt irr to protect; defend; produce (income, etc.); vi be worth; deserve; have power or authority; be of importance or worth; be a protection; be current (money); be valid; vr (with de) make use of. m, value, worth. **v. la pena,** to be worthwhile. **v. tanto como cualquiera,** to be as good as the next guy, be as good as the next fellow. **¡Válgame Dios!** Heavens! Bless me! **Más vale así,** It's better thus. **Vale más ser cola de león que cabeza de ratón.** Better a big frog in a small puddle than a small frog in a big puddle. Pres. Ind. **valgo, vales,** etc. Fut. **valdré,** etc. Condit. **valdría,** etc. Pres. Subjunc. **valga,** etc.

valeroso a active, energetic; courageous; powerful

valía f, value, price; influence, worth; faction, party. **a las valías,** at the highest price

validación f, validation; force, soundness

validar vt to make strong; validate

validez f, validity

valido a favorite, esteemed. m, court favorite; prime minister

válido a firm, sound, valid; strong, robust

valiente a strong, robust; courageous; active; excellent; excessive, enormous (gen. iron); boastful

valija f, valise, suitcase, grip; mail bag; mail

valimiento m, value; favor; protection; influence

valioso a valuable; powerful; wealthy

valisoletano (-na) *a* and *n* of or from Valladolid

valla *f,* barricade, paling; stockade; *fig* obstacle. **v. publicitaria,** billboard

vallado *m,* stockade; enclosure; *Mexico* deep ditch

valle *m,* valley; vale; river-basin

valor *m,* worth, value; price; courage; validity; power; yield, income; insolence; *pl com* securities

valoración *f,* valuation; appraisement

valorar *vt* to value; appraise

valorización *f,* valuation

vals *m,* waltz

valsar *vi* to waltz

valuación *f.* See **valoración**

valuar *vt* to value; appraise; assess

válvula *f, mech* valve. *aut* **v. de cámara (del neumático),** tire-valve. **v. de seguridad,** safety-valve

vampiro *m,* vampire; *fig* bloodsucker

vanagloria *f,* vaingloriousness, conceit

vanagloriarse *vr* to be conceited

vanaglorioso (-sa) *a* conceited. *n* boaster

vanamente *adv* vainly; without foundation; superstitiously; arrogantly

vandalismo *m,* vandalism; destructiveness

vanguardia *f,* vanguard; *pl* outerworks. **a v.,** in the forefront

vanidad *f,* vanity; ostentation; empty words; illusion. *inf* **ajar la v. de,** to take (a person) down a peg

vanidoso (-sa) *a* vain; ostentatious. *n* conceited person

vano *a* vain; hollow, empty; useless, ineffectual; unsubstantial, illusory. *m,* span (bridge). **v. único,** single span. **en v.,** uselessly, in vain

vapor *m,* steam, vapor; fainting fit; steamboat; *pl* hysterics. **v. de ruedas, v. de paleta,** paddle steamer. **v. volandero,** tramp steamer. **al v.,** full steam ahead; *inf* with all speed

vaporación *f,* evaporation

vaporización *f,* vaporization

vaporizador *m,* vaporizer; spray, sprayer

vaporizar *vt* to vaporize; spray

vaporoso *a* vaporous; ethereal; gauzy

vapular *vt* to whip

vapuleo *m,* whipping, spanking

vaquería *f,* herd of cattle; dairy; dairy farm

vaquero (-ra) *n* cowboy; **vaqueros,** *m, pl* jeans

vara *f,* staff; rod; wand (of authority); vara (2.8 feet); shaft (of cart). **v. de aforar,** water gauge

varar *vi naut* to run aground; *fig* be held up (negotiations, etc.); *vt naut* put in dry dock

varear *vt* to knock down (fruit from tree);

beat (with a rod); measure with a rod; sell by the rod; *vr* grow thin

variabilidad *f,* variableness

variable *a* variable; changeable, inconsistent

variación *f,* variation

variado *a* varied; variegated

variante *a* varying. *f,* variant; discrepancy

variar *vt* to vary; change; *vi* change; be different

varicela *f,* chicken pox

varicoso *a* varicose

variedad *f,* variety; change; inconstancy, instability; alteration; variation; *biol* variety

varilla *f, dim* rod; rib (fan, umbrella). **v. de virtudes,** conjurer's wand. *mech* **v. percusora,** tappet rod

vario *a* different, diverse; inconstant, changeable; variegated; *pl* some, a few

varón *m,* male; man

varonil *a* male; manly

Varsovia Warsaw

vasallaje *m,* vassalage; dependence; tribute money

vasallo (-lla) *n* vassal. *a* vassal; dependent

vasco (-ca), vascongado (-da) *a* and *n* Basque

vascuence *m,* Basque (language); *inf* gibberish

vaselina *f,* vaseline

vasija *f,* vessel, receptacle, jar

vaso *m,* receptacle; glass, tankard, mug; glassful; (*naut anat bot*) vessel; garden-urn; vase

vástago *m,* stem, shoot; offspring, descendant; piston rod

vastedad *f,* extensiveness, largeness, vastness

vasto *a* vast, extensive

vate *m,* bard; seer

vaticano *a* and *m,* Vatican

vaticinar *vt* to prophesy, foretell

vaticinio *m,* prediction

vatio *m,* watt. **v. hora,** watt hour

ve *f,* name of the letter V. **v. doble** or **doble v.,** name of the letter W

vecinal *a* neighboring, adjacent

vecindad *f,* neighborhood; *Lat. Am.* slum. **buena v.,** good neighborliness. **hacer mala v.,** to be a nuisance to one's neighbors

vecindario *m,* neighborhood; population of a district

vecino (-na) *a* neighboring; near; similar. *n* neighbor; citizen; inhabitant

vector *m,* carrier (of disease)

veda *f,* close season; prohibition

vedamiento *m,* prohibition

vedar *vt* to forbid; prevent

vedija *f,* tangled lock of hair; piece of matted wool; curl (of smoke)

vega f, fertile lowland plain; meadow

vegada f. See **vez**

vegetal a vegetal; plant. m, vegetable, plant

vegetar vi to flourish, grow (plants); fig vegetate

vegetariano (-na) a and n vegetarian

vehemencia f, vehemence

vehemente a vehement; vivid

vehículo m, vehicle; means, instrument

veinte a and m, twenty; twentieth

veintena f, a score

veinticinco a and m, twenty-five; twenty-fifth

veinticuatro a and m, twenty-four; twenty-fourth

veintidós a and m, twenty-two; twenty-second

veintinueve a and m, twenty-nine; twenty-ninth

veintiocho a and m, twenty-eight; twenty-eighth

veintiséis a and m, twenty-six; twenty-sixth

veintisiete a and m, twenty-seven; twenty-seventh

veintitrés a and m, twenty-three; twenty-third

veintiuno a and m, twenty-one; twenty-first. Abbreviates to **veintiún** before a noun (even if one or more adjectives intervene)

vejación f, ill-treatment, persecution

vejamen m, irritation, provocation; taunt; lampoon

vejar vt to ill-treat, persecute; plague

vejatorio a vexing, annoying

vejete m, inf silly old man

vejez f, oldness; old age; platitude. **vejeces,** pl ailments of old age. inf **a la v., viruelas,** the older the madder

vejiga f, bladder; blister. **v. natatoria,** float (of a fish)

vela f, vigil; watch; pilgrimage; sentinel, watchman; candle; naut sail; awning; night work, overtime. **v. de cangreja,** boom sail. **v. de mesana,** mizzen sail. **v. de trinquete,** foresail. **v. latina,** lateen sail. **a toda v.,** with all speed. **alzar velas,** to hoist sail. **en v.,** wakeful, without sleep. inf **estar entre dos velas,** to be tipsy

velación f, vigil; watch; marriage ceremony of veiling (gen. pl)

velada f, vigil; watch; evening party

velado a veiled; dim; (of voice) thick, indistinct

velador (-ra) a watchful; vigilant. m, candlestick; small round table; Mexico lampshade. n watcher, guard

velar vi to watch, be wakeful; work overtime or at night; ecc watch; fig (with por) watch over, defend; vt veil; conceal; phot

blur; (with prep a) wake (corpse); sit with (patient at night)

veleidad f, velleity; fickleness

veleidoso a inconstant, changeable

velero (-ra) m, sailing ship; sailmaker. n candlemaker

veleta f, weathercock; float, quill (fishing). mf changeable person

velís m, Mexico suitcase.

vello m, down, soft hair

vellocino m, wool; fleece

vellón m, fleece; copper and silver alloy formerly used in sense of 'sterling'; ant copper coin

vellosidad f, downiness, hairiness

velloso a downy, hairy

velludo a hairy, downy. m, plush, velvet

velo m, veil; curtain; ecc humeral veil; excuse, pretext; zool velum. **v. del paladar,** soft palate. **correr el v.,** to disclose a secret. **tomar el v.,** to take the veil, become a nun

velocidad f, speed; mech velocity. aer **v. ascensional,** rate of climb. mech **v. del choque,** speed of impact. **en gran v.,** by passenger train. **en pequeña v.,** by goods train

velocímetro m, Mexico speedometer

velódromo m, velodrome

velón m, oil lamp

velorio m, Lat. Am. (funeral) wake; dull party

veloz a swift; quick-thinking or acting

vena f, (bot anat) vein; streak, veining (in wood or stone); min seam; underground spring; inspiration. **estar de v.,** to be in the mood; be inspired

venablo m, javelin

venado m, venison; deer

venal a venous; saleable; venal

venalidad f, saleableness; venality

vencedor (-ra) a conquering. n conqueror

vencer vt to conquer; defeat; overcome, rise above; outdo, excel; restrain, control (emotions); convince, persuade; vi succeed, triumph; com fall due, mature; com expire; vr control oneself; twist, incline; Argentina wear out

vencible a conquerable; superable

vencimiento m, defeat; conquest, victory; bend, twist (of things); com expiration; com maturity (of a bill)

venda f, bandage; fillet. **tener una v. en los ojos,** to be blind (to the truth)

vendaje m, bandage

vendar vt to bandage; fig blind (generally passions)

vendaval m, strong wind

vendedor (-ra) a selling. n seller

vender vt to sell; betray; vr sell oneself; be sold; risk all (for someone); fig give away (secret); (with por) sell under false pretenses. **v. al contado,** to sell for cash. **v. al por mayor,** to sell wholesale. **v. al por menor,** to sell retail. **venderse caro,** to be unsociable

vendí m, com certificate of sale

vendible a purchasable; saleable

vendimia f, vintage; profit, fruits

vendimiar vt to harvest the grapes; take advantage of; inf kill

veneno m, poison; venom; danger (to health or soul); evil passion

venenoso a poisonous, venomous

venera f, scallop-shell (pilgrim's badge); badge, decoration

veneración f, respect, veneration

venerador (-ra) a venerating. n venerator, respector

venerar vt to venerate; worship

venéreo a venereal

venero m, spring of water; horary line on sundial; origin, genesis; min bed

venezolano (-na) a and n Venezuelan

vengador (-ra) a avenging. n avenger

venganza f, revenge

vengar vt to avenge; vr avenge oneself

vengativo a vindictive

venia f, pardon, forgiveness; permission; inclination of head (in greeting); law license issued to minors to manage their own estate

venial a venial

venialidad f, veniality

venida f, arrival, coming; return; attack (fencing); precipitancy

venidero a future

venideros m pl, successors; posterity

venir vi irr to come; arrive; turn up (at cards); fit, suit; consent, agree; agr grow; follow, come after, succeed; result, originate; occur (to the mind); feel, experience; (with prep a + infin.) happen finally, come to pass; (with en) decide, resolve; vr ferment. **v. a menos,** to deteriorate, decline; come upon evil days. **v. a pelo,** to come opportunely, be just right. **v. a ser,** to become. **venirse abajo,** to fall, collapse. **¿A qué viene este viaje?** What is the purpose of this journey? **el mes que viene,** next month. **El vestido te viene muy ancho,** The dress is too wide for you. **Me vino la idea de marcharme,** It occurred to me to leave. **en lo por venir,** in the future. Pres. Ind. **vengo, vienes, viene, venimos, venís, vienen.** Pres. Part. **viniendo.** Fut. **vendré,** etc. Condit. **vendría,** etc. Preterite **vine, viniste, vino, vinimos, vinisteis, vinieron.** Pres. Subjunc. **venga,** etc. Imperf. Subjunc. **viniese,** etc.

venta f, selling; sale; inn; inf wilderness; pl com turnover. **v. pública,** auction. **a la v.,** on sale. **la V. de la Mesilla,** the Gadsden Purchase

ventada f, gust of wind

ventaja f, advantage; profit

ventajoso a advantageous; Lat. Am. unscrupulous

ventana f, window. **v. de guillotina,** sash window. **v. salediza,** bay window. **echar algo por la v.,** to waste a thing

ventanal m, large window

ventanilla f, small window (as in railway compartments); grill (ticket office, bank, etc.); nostril

ventarrón m, high wind

ventear v impers to blow (of the wind); vt sniff air (animals); air, dry; investigate; Lat. Am. brand (an animal); vr be spoiled by air (tobacco, etc.)

ventero (-ra) n innkeeper

ventilación f, ventilation; ventilator; current of air

ventilador m, ventilating fan; ventilator

ventilar vt to ventilate; shake, winnow; air; discuss

ventisca f, snowstorm

ventiscar, ventisquear v impers to snow with a high wind

ventisquero m, glacier; snowfield, snowdrift; snowstorm

ventolera f, gust of wind; inf boastfulness; whim, caprice

ventolina f, Lat. Am. sudden gust (of wind)

ventor (-ra) n pointer (dog)

ventosa f, vent (pipes, etc.); zool sucker; surg cupping glass

ventoso a windy; flatulent

ventrículo m, ventricle

ventrílocuo (-ua) a ventriloquial. n ventriloquist

ventriloquia f, ventriloquism

ventrudo a big-bellied

ventura f, happiness; chance, hazard; risk, danger. **a la v.,** at a venture. **buena v.,** good luck. **por v.,** perhaps; by chance; fortunately

venturoso a fortunate

Venus m, Venus. f, beautiful woman, beauty

ver vt irr to see; witness, behold; visit; inspect, examine; consider; observe; know, understand; Lat. Am. look at, watch (television, etc.) (with de + infin.) try to; vr be seen; show oneself, appear; experience, find oneself; exchange visits; meet. **v. mundo,** to travel. **V. y creer,** Seeing is believing. **A mi v.,** In my opinion. **¡A v.!** Let's see! Wait and see! **no tener nada que v. con,** to have no connection with, nothing to do with. **Veremos,** Time will tell. **Verse en la casa,** to be a stay-at-home. **Ya se ve,** Of course, Naturally. Pres. Ind. **veo, ves,** etc. Imperf. **veía,** etc. Past Part. **visto.** Pres. Subjunc. **vea,** etc. Imperf. Subjunc. **viese,** etc.

vera f, edge; border; shore. **a la v.,** on the edge, on the verge

veracidad f, truthfulness, veracity

veraneante mf summer resident, summer vacationist, holiday-maker

veranear vi to spend the summer

veraneo m, summer vacation, summer holidays, summering

veraniego a summer; light, unimportant

verano m, summer; dry season WH

veras f pl, reality, truth; fervor, earnestness. **de v.,** really; in earnest

veraz a truthful, veracious

verbal a verbal; oral

verbena f, bot verbena, vervain; fair held on eve of a saint's day

verbigracia adv for instance. m, example

verbo m, word; vow; gram verb. **v. activo** or **v. transitivo,** active or transitive verb. **v. auxiliar,** auxiliary verb. **v. intransitivo** or **v. neutro,** intransitive or neuter verb. **v. reflexivo** or **v. recíproco,** reflexive verb

verbosidad f, verbosity

verboso a verbose, prolix

verdad f, truth, veracity; reality. **a la v.,** indeed; without doubt. **en v.,** in truth; indeed. **cantar cuatro verdades a alguien,** to tell someone a few home truths. **la pura v.,** the plain truth

verdadero a true; real; sincere; truthful

verdal a green. **ciruela v.,** greengage

verde a green; unripe; fresh (vegetables); youthful; immature, undeveloped; obscene, dissolute. m, green (color); verdure, foliage

verdear vi to look green; be greenish; grow green

verdecer vi irr to grow green, be verdant. See **conocer**

verdín m, verdure; mold; verdigris

verdinegro a dark green

verdor m, verdure; greenness; strength; youth (also pl)

verdoso a greenish

verdugo m, hangman, executioner; wale, mark; shoot of tree; switch; whip; fig scourge; tyrant

verdulera f, greengrocer; market woman; inf harridan

verdulería f, greengrocer's shop

verdulero m, greengrocer

verdura f, verdure; green garden produce, vegetables (gen. pl); art foliage; obscenity

verecundo a bashful

vereda f, footpath; sheep track; Argentina, Chile, Peru sidewalk

veredicto m, law verdict; judgment, considered opinion

verga f, steel bow of crossbow; naut yard; inf penis

vergel m, orchard

vergonzoso (-sa) a shameful; bashful, shamefaced. n shy person

vergüenza f, shame; self-respect; bashfulness, timidity; shameful act; public punishment

vericueto m, narrow, stony path

verídico a veracious; true, exact

verificación f, verification, checking; law **v. de un testamento,** probate

verificador (-ra) a verifying, checking. n inspector, checker

verificar vt to prove; verify; vr take place, happen; check; come true. elec **v. las conexiones,** to check the connections

verisímil a credible, probable

verja f, grating, grill; railing

vermut m, vermouth

vernáculo a native, vernacular

verosímil a credible, probable

verosimilitud f, verisimilitude, probability

verruga f, med wart; inf bore; defect

versar vi to revolve; (with sobre) concern, deal with (book, etc.); vr become versed (in)

versátil a zool versatile; changeable; fickle

versatilidad f, zool versatility; changeableness; fickleness

versículo m, versicle; verse (of the Bible)

versificar vi to write verses; vt put into verse, versify

versión f, translation; version; account

verso m, poetry, verse; stanza; line (of a poem). **v. suelto,** blank verse

vertedor m, drain, sewer; chute

verter vt irr to pour, spill; empty; translate; vi flow. See **entender**

vertical a and f, vertical

vértice m, vertex

vertiente a emptying. mf, slope, incline; watershed; Lat. Am. also spring (of water)

vertiginoso a giddy; vertiginous

vértigo m, giddiness, faintness

vesícula f, blister; (anat bot) vesicle

vespertino a evening

vestíbulo m, hall, vestibule foyer

vestido m, dress; clothes; Panama, Peru suit

vestidura f, garment; pl vestments

vestigio m, footprint; trace, mark; remains; fig vestige

vestir vt irr to clothe, dress; adorn; embellish (ideas); fig disguise (truth); simulate, pretend; vi be dressed; vr dress oneself; fig be covered. See **pedir**

vestuario m, clothing, dress; theat wardrobe or dressing room; ecc vestry; mil uniform

veta f, vein; stripe, rib (fabric)

veterano (-na) a and n veteran

veterinaria f, veterinary science

veterinario a veterinary. m, veterinary surgeon

veto m, veto; prohibition

vetusto a ancient, very old

vez f, time, occasion; turn; pl proxy, deputy, substitute. **a la v.,** simultaneously. **alguna v.,** sometime. **a su v.,** in its (her, his, their) turn. **a veces,** sometimes. **de una v.,** at the one time. **de v. en cuando,** from time to time. **en v. de,** instead of. **hacer las veces de,** to be a substitute for. **otra v.,** again. **Su cuarto es dos veces más grande que éste,** His room is twice as large as this one

vía f, way; road; railway track or gauge; anat tract; (mystic) way; route; conduct; pl procedure. **v. ancha,** broad-gauge (railway). **v. angosta,** narrow gauge. **v. de agua,** naut leak. law **v. ejecutiva,** seizure, attachment. **v. férrea,** railway. **v. láctea,** Milky Way. **v. muerta,** railway siding. **v. principal,** main line. **v. pública,** public thoroughfare. **v. romana,** Roman road. **v. secundaria,** rw side line. **por v. aérea,** by air, by airplane

viable a viable; practicable; workable; passable

viaducto m, viaduct

viajante mf traveling salesman, commercial traveler

viajar vi to travel, journey, voyage

viaje m, journey; voyage; water-supply; travel journal; naut **v. de ensayo,** trial trip. **v. redondo,** circular tour. **¡Buen v.!** Have a good trip! Bon voyage!

viajero (-ra) a traveling. n traveler; passenger

víbora f, viper; Lat. Am. poisonous snake

vibración f, vibration; jar, jolt; thrill

vibrante a shaking; vibrant; thrilling

vibrar vt to shake, oscillate; vi vibrate; jar, jolt; quiver, thrill

vibratorio a vibratory, vibrative

vicario a vicarious. m, vicar; curate; deputy

vicepresidente (-ta) n vice president

viciar vt to corrupt; adulterate; forge; annul; interpret maliciously, misconstrue; vr become vicious

vicio m, vice; defect; error, fraud; bad habit; excess, exaggerated desire; viciousness (animals); overgrowth (plants); peevishness (children). **tener el v. de,** to have the bad habit of. **el v. del juego,** fondness for gambling

vicioso a vicious; vigorous, overgrown; abundant; inf spoilt (children)

vicisitud f, vicissitude

víctima f, victim

victimar vt, Lat. Am. to murder

victimario, -a mf, Lat. Am. killer, murderer

¡víctor! interj Victor!; Long live!; Hurrah!

victoria f, victory, triumph; victoria

victoriano (-na) a and n Victorian

victorioso a victorious

vicuña f vicuna

vid f, vine

vida f, life; livelihood; human being; biography; vivacity. **v. airada,** dissolute life. **la v. allende la muerte,** life after death. **de por v.,** for life. **darse buena v.,** to live comfortably; enjoy one's life. **dar mala v.,** to ill-treat. **en la v.,** in life; never. **ganarse la v.,** to make one's living

vidente m, clairvoyant; seer

videograbación f, videotape

vidriar vt to glaze (earthenware)

vidriera f, glass window (gen. stained or colored)

vidriero m, glazier. a made of glass

vidrio m, glass; anything made of glass; fragile thing; touchy person. **v. inastillable,** safety-glass. **v. jaspeado,** frosted glass. **v. pintado** or **v. de color,** stained-glass. **v. plano,** plate glass. **v. soplado,** blown glass

vidrioso a brittle; slippery; fragile; hypersensitive; fig glazed (eyes)

vieja f, old woman

viejo a old; ancient; former; old-fashioned; worn out. m, old man

Viena Vienna

vienés (-esa) a and n Viennese

viento m, wind; scent (of game, etc.); guy (rope); upheaval; vanity. **v. en popa,** naut following wind; without a hitch, prosperously. **vientos alisios,** trade-winds. **v. terral,** land wind. **a los cuatro vientos,** in all directions. **contra v. y marea,** fig against all obstacles. **correr malos vientos,** to be unfavorable (of circumstances). **refrescar el v.,** to stiffen (of the breeze)

vientre m, stomach; belly; vitals; law venter

viernes m, Friday. **V. Santo,** Good Friday

viga f, beam, rafter; girder; joist; mill beam. **v. maestra,** main beam or girder

vigente a in force (laws, customs)

vigésimo a twentieth

vigía f, watch tower; (gen. m) look-out, watch

vigilancia f, watchfulness, vigilance; watch patrol

vigilante a watchful. m, watcher; watchman. **v. escolar,** truant officer

vigilar vt to watch over; supervise

vigilia f, vigil; wakefulness; night study; ecc vigil, eve; wake; mil watch. **día de v.,** fast-day

vigor m, strength; activity; vigor, efficiency; validity

vigorizar vt to invigorate; exhilarate; encourage

vigoroso a strong, vigorous

vihuela f, lute

vil a vile, infamous; base; despicable; untrustworthy

vileza f, baseness; vileness, infamy

vilipendiar vt to revile

vilipendio *m*, vilification; contempt

villa *f*, villa; country house; town. **v. miseria** *Argentina* slum

villancico *m*, carol

villanesco *a* peasant; rustic, country

villanía *f*, humbleness of birth; vileness; villainy

villano (**-na**) *n* peasant. a rustic, country; boorish; base

vilote *mf*, *Lat. Am.* chicken, coward

vinagre *m*, vinegar

vinagreta *f*, vinegar sauce

vinagroso *a* vinegary; *inf* bad-tempered, acid

vincular *vt law* to entail; *fig* base; *vr* perpetuate. a *law* entail

vínculo *m*, tie, bond; *law* entail

vindicación *f*, vindication; justification; excuse

vindicador (**-ra**) *n* vindicator. a vindicative

vindicar *vt* to avenge; vindicate; justify; excuse

vindicativo *a* avenging; vindicatory

vinería *f*, *Lat. Am.* wineshop

vinícola *a* wine-growing; wine

vinicultor (**-ra**) *n* wine grower, viniculturalist

vinicultura *f*, wine-growing, viniculture

vino *m*, wine; fermented fruit juice. **v. de Oporto,** port wine. **v. generoso,** well-matured wine. **v. tinto,** red wine

vinoso *a* vinous; fond of wine

viña *f*, vineyard

viñador *m*, vineyard-keeper; vine-cultivator

viñedo *m*, vineyard

viñeta *f*, vignette

viola *f*, *mus* viola; *bot* viola, pansy. *mf* viola player

violación *f*, violation; infringement

violado *a* violet

violador (**-ra**) *n* violator. *m*, seducer

violar *vt* to violate; infringe; rape; spoil, harm

violencia *f*, violence; outrage; rape

violentar *vt* to force; falsify, misinterpret; force an entrance; *vr* force oneself

violento *a* violent; repugnant; impetuous, hasty-tempered; unnatural, false; unreasonable

violeta *f*, *bot* violet. *m*, violet color. **v. de febrero,** snowdrop

violín *m*, violin

violinista *mf* violinist

violón *m*, double-bass, bass viol; double-bass player

violoncelista *mf* cellist

violoncelo *m*, cello

vira *f*, welt (of a shoe); dart

viraje *m*, *aut* change of direction; bend, turn

virar *vt naut* to put about; *phot* tone; *vi naut* tack; *aut* change direction. **v. de bordo,** *naut* to lay off

virgen *mf* virgin. *f*, *ast* Virgo

virginal *a* virginal; pure, unspotted

virginidad *f*, virginity

virgulilla *f*, comma; cedilla; accent; apostrophe; fine line

viril *a* manly, virile. *m*, clear glass screen

virilidad *f*, virility

virote *m*, arrow; shaft; *inf* young blood; *Mexico* roll (bread)

virrey *m*, viceroy

virtual *a* virtual; implicit

virtualidad *f*, virtuality

virtualmente *adv* virtually; tacitly

virtud *f*, virtue; power; strength, courage; efficacy. **en v. de,** in virtue of

virtuosidad *f*, virtuosity

virtuoso *a* virtuous; powerful, efficacious. *m*, virtuoso, artist

viruela *f*, smallpox (gen. *pl*)

virulencia *f*, virulence

virulento *a* virulent

virus *m*, virus

viruta *f*, wood-shaving

vis cómica *f*, the comic spirit

visa *f*, *Lat. Am.* visa

visado *m*, *Spain* visa

visaje *m*, grimace

visar *vt* to visa; endorse

viscoso *a* viscous, sticky

visera *f*, visor; eye-shade; peak (of a cap)

visibilidad *f*, visibility

visillo *m*, window-blind

visión *f*, seeing, sight; queer sight; vision; hallucination; *inf* scarecrow, sight

visionario (**-ia**) *a* and *n* visionary

visir *m*, vizier. **gran v.,** grand vizier

visita *f*, visit; visitor; inspection. **v. de cumplido,** formal call. **v. de sanidad,** health inspection. **hacer una v.,** to pay a call

visitación *f*, visitation; visit

visitador (**-ra**) *n* regular visitor. *m*, inspector. a visiting; inspecting

visitar *vt* to visit; inspect; *med* attend; *ecc* examine. **v. los monumentos,** to see the sights, go sightseeing

visiteo *m*, receiving or paying of visits

vislumbrar *vt* to glimpse; surmise, conjecture

vislumbre *f*, glimmer, glimpse; surmise, glimmering (gen. *pl*); semblance, appearance

viso *m*, view point, elevation; glare; shimmer, gleam; colored slip under transparent dress; semblance. **de v.,** prominent (persons)

visón *m*, mink

víspera *f*, eve; *ecc* day before festival;

prelude, preliminary. *pl ecc* vespers. **en vísperas de,** on the eve of

vista *f,* vision, sight; view; eyes; eyesight; meeting, interview; *law* hearing (of a case); apparition; picture of a view; clear idea; connection (of things); proposition, intention; glance; *pl* window, door, skylight, opening for light. **v. corta,** short sight. **v. de lince,** sharp eyes. **a primera v.,** at first sight. **a v. de,** in sight of; in the presence of. **conocer de v.,** to know by sight. **dar una v.,** to take a look. **doble v.,** second sight; clairvoyance. **en v. de,** in view of, considering. **estar a la v.,** to be evident. *inf* **hacer la v. gorda,** to turn a blind eye. **¡Hasta la v.!** Good-bye! **perder de v. (a),** to lose sight of

vistazo *m,* glance. **echar un v.,** to cast a glance

visto *past part irr* **ver.** *law* whereas. **bien v.,** approved. **mal v.,** disapproved. **V. Bueno** (**V° B°**) Approved, Passed. **v. que,** since, inasmuch as

vistoso *a* showy, gaudy; beautiful

visual *a* visual

vital *a* vital; essential

vitalicio *a* lifelong. *m,* life-insurance

vitalidad *f,* vitality

vitamina *f,* vitamin

vitando *a* odious; bad; vital

vitela *f,* vellum

vitícola *a* viticultural. *mf* viticulturist

viticultura *f,* viticulture

¡vítor! *interj* Victor!; Hurrah!; Long live!

vitorear *vt* to cheer; applaud, acclaim

vítreo *a* glassy, vitreous

vitrina *f,* show-case; display cabinet; *Argentina, Chile, Venezuela* (shop) window

vitriólico *a* vitriolic

vitriolo *m,* vitriol

vitualla *f,* (gen. *pl*) victuals, provisions

vituperable *a* blameworthy, vituperable

vituperar *vt* to censure, blame, vituperate

vituperio *m,* vituperation

viuda *f,* widow

viudo *m,* widower

¡viva! *interj* Long live!; Hurrah!

vivacidad *f,* vivacity, gaiety; ardor, warmth; brightness

vivamente *adv* quickly, lively

vivaque *m,* bivouac

vivar *m,* warren; aquarium; breeding ground; well (of a fishing boat); *vt, Lat. Am.* to cheer, shout hurrah (for . . .)

vivaracho *a inf* sprightly, cheery, lively

vivaz *a* vigorous; quick-witted; sprightly; *bot* perennial; vivid, bright

víveres *m pl,* provisions; *mil* stores

vivero *m, bot* nursery; vivarium; small marsh

viveza *f,* quickness, briskness; vehemence; perspicuity; witticism; resem-

blance; brightness (eyes, colors); thoughtless word or act

vividero *a* habitable

vívido *a poet* vivid

vividor (**-ra**) *a* frugal, thrifty; dissolute. *n* liver; long-liver; libertine, rake

vivienda *f,* dwelling

viviente *a* living

vivificar *vt* to vivify; comfort

vivir *vi* to be alive, live; last, endure; (*with en*) inhabit. *m,* life. **¿Quién vive?** *mil* Who goes there? **v. a costillas ajenas,** to live at someone else's expense, live off someone else

vivisección *f,* vivisection

vivo *a* alive; intense, strong; bright; *mil* active; subtle, ingenious; precipitate; *fig* lasting, enduring; diligent; hasty; persuasive, expressive. *m,* edge. **al v., a lo v.,** to the life; vividly

vizcaíno (**-na**) *a* and *n* Biscayan

Vizcaya, el Golfo de the Bay of Biscay

vocablo *m,* word

vocabulario *m,* vocabulary

vocación *f,* vocation; trade, profession

vocal *a* vocal; oral. *f, gram* vowel. *mf* voting member

voceador, -a *mf, Lat. Am.* newsvendor

vocear *vi* to cry out, shout; *vt* proclaim; call for; acclaim

vocerío *m,* shouting; clamor, outcry

vociferación *f,* vociferation, outcry

vociferar *vt* to boast (of); *vi* shout, vociferate

voclinglería *f,* clamor; babble, chatter

vocinglero *a* vociferous; prattling, babbling

vodca *m,* vodka

volada *f,* short flight; *Mexico* flat tire, flat. *mech* **v. de grúa,** jib

voladura *f,* explosion; blasting

volandas (en), volandillas (en) *adv* in the air, as though flying; *inf* in a trice

volante *a* flying; wandering, restless. *m,* frill, flounce; screen; fan (of a windmill); *mech* flywheel; *mech* balance wheel (watches); coiner's stamp mill; shuttlecock. *aut* **v. de dirección,** steering-wheel

volantón (**-ona**) *n* fledgeling

volar *vi irr* to fly (birds, insects, aviation); float in the air; hurry; disappear suddenly; burst, explode; jut out (buttresses, etc.); cleave (air) (arrows, etc.); *fig* spread (rumors); *vt* explode; blast; anger. See **contar**

volatería *f,* fowling; fowls; poultry; flock of birds; *fig* crowd (of ideas)

volátil *a* volatile; inconstant

volcán *m,* volcano; violent passion. **v. extinto,** extinct volcano

volcar *vt irr* to overturn, capsize; make dizzy; cause a change (of opinion); annoy;

vi overturn. *Pres. Ind.* **vuelco, vuelcas, vuelca, vuelcan.** *Preterite* **volqué, volcaste,** etc. *Pres. Subjunc.* **vuelque, vuelques, vuelque, vuelquen**

volear *vt* to strike in the air, volley; *agr* sow broadcast

voleo *m*, volley (tennis, etc.); high kick; straight punch

volición *f*, volition

volquete *m*, tip-cart

voltaje *m*, voltage

voltario *a* versatile; capricious, headstrong

voltear *vt* to whirl, turn; overturn; change place (of); *arch* construct an arch or vault; *vi* revolve; tumble, twirl (acrobats)

volteo *m*, turning, revolution; whirl; overturning; twirling; *elec* voltage

voltereta *f*, somersault

voltio *m*, volt

volubilidad *f*, inconstancy, fickleness

voluble *a* easily turned; inconstant, changeable; *bot* twining

volumen *m*, bulk, size; volume, book

voluminoso *a* voluminous, bulky

voluntad *f*, will, volition; wish; decree; free will; intention; affection; free choice; consent. **a v.**, at will; by choice. **de buena v.**, of good will; willingly, with pleasure. **de su propia v.**, of one's own free will. **mala v.**, hostility, ill-will

voluntario (**-ia**) *a* voluntary; strong-willed. *n* volunteer

voluntarioso *a* self-willed

voluptuoso *a* voluptuous

volver *vt irr* to turn; turn over; return; pay back; direct, aim; translate; restore; change, alter; close (doors, etc.); vomit; reflect, reverberate; *vi* come back; continue (speech, etc.); bend, turn (roads); (*with prep a* + *infin.*) do something again (e.g. **v. a leer,** to read over again); (*with por* + *noun*) protect; *vr* become; go sour; turn. **v. a las filas,** *mil* to reduce to the ranks. **v. en sí,** to regain consciousness. **v. la cabeza,** to turn one's head. **volverse atrás,** *fig* to back out. **volverse loco,** to go mad. See **resolver**

vomitar *vt* to vomit; *fig* vomit forth; *fig* spit out (curses, etc.); *inf* burst into confidences

vomitivo *a* and *m*, emetic

vómito *m*, vomit

vorágine *f*, vortex, whirlpool

voraz *a* voracious; *Mexico* bold

vórtice *m*, whirlpool; *fig* vortex

vortiginoso *a* vortical

vos *pers pron 2nd pers sing* and *pl* you.

vosear *vt* to use the pronoun *vos*; address (someone) as *vos*

vosotros, vosotras *pers pron 2nd pers pl mf* you

votación *f*, voting

votador (**-ra**) *n* voter; swearer

votar *vi* and *vt* to vote; make a vow; curse, swear. **v. una proposición de confianza,** to pass a vote of confidence

votivo *a* votive

voto *m*, vote; vow; voter; prayer; curse; desire; opinion. **v. de calidad,** casting vote. **v. de confianza,** vote of confidence

voz *f*, voice; sound, noise; cry, shout (gen. *pl*); word; expression; *mus* singer or voice; *gram* mood; vote; rumor; instruction, order. **v. común,** general opinion. **a voces,** in a shout, loudly. **llevar la v. cantante,** *inf* to have the chief say

vuelco *m*, overturning

vuelo *m*, flight; wing; *sew* skirt-fullness; ruffle, frill; *arch* buttress. **v. a ciegas,** *aer* blind flying. **v. de distancia,** long-distance flight. **v. de patrulla,** patrol or reconnaissance flight. **v. de reconocimiento,** reconnaissance flight. **v. nocturno,** *aer* night flying. **v. sin parar,** nonstop flight. **al v.,** on the wing; in passing; quickly. **alzar** (*or* **levantar**) **el v.,** to take flight

vuelta *f*, revolution, turn; bend, curve; return; restitution; recompense; repetition; wrong side; beating; *sew* facing, cuff; change (money); conning (lessons, etc.); stroll, walk; change; vault, ceiling; *sport* round; *mech* **vueltas por minuto,** revolutions per minute. **a v. de correo,** by return mail, by return of post. **a la v.,** on returning; overleaf. **dar la v.,** to turn round, make a détour. **dar una v.,** to take a stroll. **dar vueltas,** to revolve; search (for); consider. **media v.,** half turn

vuelto *m, Lat. Am.* change (money returned)

vuestro, vuestra, vuestros, vuestras *poss pron 2nd pl mf* your, yours

vulgar *a* popular; general, common; vernacular; mediocre

vulgaridad *f*, vulgarity

vulgarismo *m*, vulgarism

vulgarización *f*, vulgarization; popularization

vulgarizar *vt* to vulgarize; popularize; translate into the vernacular; *vr* grow vulgar

vulgo *m*, mob

vulnerable *a* vulnerable

wagneriano a Wagnerian

wáter m, toilet, water-closet

whisky m, whiskey

xenofobia f, xenophobia, hatred of foreigners

xilófono m, xylophone

ya adv already; formerly; soon; now; finally; immediately; well, yes, quite. Used of past, present and future time, and in various idiomatic ways. **Ha venido ya,** He has already come. **¡Ya caerá!** His time will come! He will get his comeuppance! **Ya vendrá,** He will come soon. **¡Ya voy!** Coming! **¡Ya lo creo!** Of course!; I should think so! **¡Ya!** Quite!; I understand. **ya no,** no longer. **ya que,** since

yacaré m, Lat. Am. alligator

yacente a recumbent, reclining (statues, etc.)

yacer vi irr to be lying at full length; lie (in the grave); be situated, be; lie (with), sleep (with); graze by night. Pres. Ind. **yazgo** or **yazco, yaces,** etc. Pres. Subjunc. **yazga** or **yazca,** etc.

yacija f, bed; couch; tomb

yacimiento m, geol bed, deposit

yanqui a and mf contemptuous and offensive North American (gen. U.S.A.)

yarda f, yard (English measure)

yate m, naut yacht

ye f, name of the letter Y

yegua f, mare

yelmo m, helmet

yema f, bud; yolk (of egg); sweetmeat; fig best of anything. **y. del dedo,** finger-tip

yerba mate m mate (drink)

yermo a uninhabited, deserted; uncultivated. m, wilderness, desert

yerno m, son-in-law

yerro m, error; mistake; fault

yerto a stiff, rigid

yesca f, tinder; fuel, stimulus

yeso m, gypsum, calcium sulphate; plaster; plaster cast

yesquero m, Lat. Am. (cigaret) lighter

yídish n and a Yiddish

yip m jeep

yo pers pron 1st sing mf I. **el yo,** the ego

yodo m, iodine

yuca f, yucca

yucateco (-ca) a and n Yucatecan

yugo m, yoke; nuptial tie; oppression; naut transom; fig **sacudir el y.,** to throw off the yoke

yugular a anat jugular. m, jugular vein

yunque m, anvil; patient, undaunted person; hard worker; anat incus

yunta f, yoke (of oxen, etc.)

yute m, jute fiber or fabric

yuxtaponer vt irr to juxtapose. See **poner**

yuxtaposición f, juxtaposition

zafadura f, Lat. Am. dislocation, sprain

W, X, Y, Z

zafar vt to embellish, garnish, adorn; naut lighten (a ship); vr escape, hide oneself; (with de) excuse oneself, avoid; get rid of

zafarrancho m, naut clearing the decks; inf damage; inf scuffle

zafiedad f, rudeness, ignorance, boorishness

zafio a rude, unlettered, boorish

zafiro m, sapphire

zafra f, olive oil container; sugar crop or factory; min waste

zaga f, rear. m, last player. **en z.,** behind. inf **no quedarse en z.,** not to be left behind; be not inferior

zagal m, youth; strong, handsome lad; young shepherd; full skirt

zagala f, maiden, girl; young shepherdess

zagual m, paddle

zaguán m, entrance hall; vestibule

zaguero a loitering, straggling. m, sport back

zahareño a untamable, wild (birds); unsociable, disdainful

zaherir vt irr to upbraid, reprehend; nag. See **herir**

zahorí m, soothsayer; waterfinder; sagacious person

zahúrda f, pigsty

zaino a treacherous; vicious (horses); chestnut (horses); black (cows)

zalagarda f, ambush; skirmish; snare, trap; inf trick, ruse; inf mock battle

zalamería f, adulation, flattery

zalamero (-ra) a wheedling, flattering. n flatterer

zalea f, sheepskin

zamacuco m, inf oaf, dolt; inf drinking bout

zamarra f, sheepskin jacket

zamarrear vt to worry, shake (prey); fig inf beat up; inf floor, confound

zambo a knock-kneed

zambullida f, plunge, submersion; thrust (in fencing)

zambullir vt to plunge in water, submerge; vr dive; hide oneself, cover oneself

zampar vt to conceal (one thing in another); eat greedily; (with en) arrive suddenly

zampatortas mf inf glutton

zampoña f, rustic flute; inf unimportant work

zanahoria f, carrot

zanca f, long leg (birds); inf long thin leg; arch stringboard (of stairs)

zancada f, swift stride

zancadilla f, trip (wrestling); *inf* trick, deceit. **echar la z. (a)**, to trip up

zancajear *vi* to stride about

zancajo m, heel-bone; torn heel (stocking, shoe); *inf* ill-shaped person. *inf* **no llegarle al z.**, to be immensely inferior to someone

zancajoso a flatfooted; slovenly

zanco m, stilt. *fig inf* **andar** (or **estar**) **en zancos**, to have gone up in the world

zancudo a long-legged

zangandungo (**-ga**) n *inf* loafer

zanganear *vi inf* to loaf

zángano m, *ent* drone; *inf* idler, parasite

zangolotear *vt inf* to shake violently; *vi* fuss about, bustle; *vr* rattle (windows, etc.)

zangoloteo m, shaking; rattling

zanguango m, *inf* lazybones

zanja f, trench, ditch; drain; furrow

zanjar *vt* to excavate; *fig* remove (obstacles)

zapa f, shovel, spade; *mil* sap; sandpaper

zapador m, *mil* sapper

zapapico m, pick-ax; mattock

zapaquilda f, *inf* she-cat

zapar *vi mil* to sap

zaparrastrar *vi inf* to trail along the floor (dresses)

zapata f, half-boot; piece of leather used to stop creaking of a hinge; *arch* lintel; (*naut mech*) shoe

zapatazo m, blow with a shoe; fall, thud; stamping (horses); flap (of sail)

zapateado m, dance in which rhythmic drumming of heels plays important part

zapatear *vt* to hit with a shoe; stamp feet; drum heels (in dancing); *inf* ill-treat; thump ground (rabbits); *vi* stamp (horses); *naut* flap (sails); *vr fig* stand one's ground

zapateo m, stamping; rhythmic drumming of heels

zapatera f, cobbler's wife; woman who makes or sells shoes

zapatería f, shoemaking; shoe shop

zapatero m, shoemaker; shoe seller. **z. remendón**, cobbler

zapatilla f, slipper; trotter; hoof

zapato m, shoe. **z. de hule** *Mexico*, galosh, rubber

zapatón m, *Lat. Am.* galosh, overshoe

¡zape! *interj inf* shoo! Used for frightening away cats; exclamation of surprise or warning

zapear *vt* to scare away cats; *inf* frighten off

zaque m, leather bottle, wineskin; *inf* drunkard, sot

zaquizamí m, garret; dirty little house or room

zarabanda f, saraband; *inf* racket, row

zaragata f, *inf* fight, brawl

Zaragoza Saragossa

zaragüelles m, pl wide pleated breeches

zaranda f, sieve, strainer, colander

zarandajas f, pl *inf* odds and ends

zarandar *vt* to sieve (grapes, grain); strain; *inf* pick out the best; *vr inf* move quickly

zarandillo m, small sieve, strainer; *inf* a live wire, energetic person; Spanish dance

zaraza f, chintz

zarcillo m, earring; *bot* tendril; *agr* trowel

zarco a light blue (generally eyes or water)

zarpa f, *naut* weighing anchor; paw

zarpada f, blow with a paw

zarpar *vt* and *vi naut* to weigh anchor, sail

zarza f, *bot* bramble, blackberry bush

zarzal m, bramble patch

zarzamora f, blackberry

zarzo m, hurdle; wattle

zarzoso a brambly

zarzuela f, comic opera; musical comedy

¡zas! m, sound of a bang or blow

zascandil m, *inf* busybody

zatara f, raft

zeda f, name of the letter Z

zenit m. See **cenit**

zeta f. See **zeda**

zigzag m, zigzag

zigzaguear *vi* to zigzag

zinc m, zinc

zipizape m, *inf* row, quarrel

zoca f, square

Zócalo, el m, the Main Square (of Mexico City)

zoclo m, clog, sabot

zoco m, square; market; clog, sabot

zodiaco m, zodiac

zona f, girdle, band; strip (of land); zone; *med* shingles. **z. de depresión**, air pocket. **z. templada**, temperate zone. **z. tórrida**, torrid zone

zonal a zonal

zoncear *vi, Lat. Am.* to behave stupidly

zonzo, -a a, *Lat. Am.* silly, stupid

zoología f, zoology

zopenco a *inf* oafish

zopo a maimed, deformed (hands, feet)

zoquete m, *carp* block; dowel; hunk of bread; *inf* short, ugly man; *inf* dunderhead

zorcico m, Basque song and dance

zorra f, vixen; fox; *inf* cunning person; *inf* prostitute; *inf* drinking bout; truck, dray

zorrera f, foxhole

zorro m, fox; fox-skin; *inf* knave

zóster f, *med* shingles

zote a dull, ignorant

zozobra f, *naut* foundering, capsizing; anxiety

zozobrar *vi naut* to founder, sink; *naut* plunge, shiver; be anxious, vacillate

zueco *m*, sabot; juice; clog

zulú *a* and *mf* Zulu

zumbar *vi* to buzz, hum; ring (of the ears); whizz; twang (of a guitar, etc.); *fig inf* be on the brink

zumbido *m*, buzzing, humming; ringing (in the ears); whizz; twanging (of a guitar, etc.); *inf* slap, blow

zumbón *a* waggish, jocose

zumo *m*, sap; juice; profit, advantage

zumoso *a* succulent, juicy

zurcido *m*, *sew* darn; mend

zurcidor (-ra) *n* darner, mender. **z. de voluntades**, *humorous* pimp

zurcidura *f*, darning; mending; darn

zurcir *vt* to darn; mend, repair; join; *fig* concoct, weave

zurdo *a* left-handed

zurra *f*, *tan* currying; *inf* spanking; *inf* quarrel

zurrapa *f*, (gen. *pl*) sediment, lees, dregs

zurrar *vt* to curry (leather); *inf* spank; *inf* dress down, scold

zurriago *m*, whip

zurribanda *f*, *inf* whipping; fight, quarrel

zurriburri *m*, *inf* ragamuffin; mob; uproar

zurrido *m*, *inf* blow; dull noise

zurrir *vi* to have a confused sound, hum, rattle

zurrón *m*, shepherd's pouch; leather bag; *bot* husk

zutano (-na) *n inf* so-and-so, such a one

ENGLISH-SPANISH
Dictionary

A

a n (letter) a, f; *mus* la, m. **symphony in A major,** sinfonía en la mayor, f. **A1,** de primera clase; de primera calidad, excelente

a, an *indef art.* (one) un, m; una, f; (with weights, quantities) el, m; la, f; (with weeks, months, years, etc.) por, al, m; a la, f. The indef. art. is omitted in Spanish before nouns expressing nationality, profession, rank, and generally before a noun in apposition. It is omitted also before certain words such as **mil, ciento, otro, semejante, medio,** etc. Not translated in book titles, e.g., **A History of Spain,** Historia de España. *prep* a. In phrases such as **to go hunting,** ir a cazar. As prefix, see **abed, ashore,** etc. **Madrid, a Spanish city,** Madrid, ciudad de España. **three times a month,** tres veces al mes. **ten dollars an hour,** diez dólares por hora. **thirty miles an hour,** treinta millas por hora. **a certain Mrs. Brown,** una tal Sra. Brown. **a thousand soldiers,** mil soldados. **half an hour later,** media hora después

aback *adv naut* en facha; *fig* sorprendido, desconcertado. **to take a.,** desconcertar, coger desprevenido (a)

abandon *vt* abandonar; dejar; desertar, desamparar; renunciar; entregar. *n* entusiasmo, fervor, m; naturalidad, f. **to a. oneself to,** (despair, vice, etc.) entregarse a

abandonment n abandono, m; renunciación, f; deserción, f

abase *vt* humillar; degradar; abatir

abasement n humillación, degradación, f; abatimiento, m

abash *vt* avergonzar; confundir; desconcertar

abate *vt* disminuir, reducir; (a price) rebajar; (suppress) suprimir, abolir; (remit) condonar, remitir; (annul) anular; (moderate) moderar; (of pride, etc.) humillar; (of pain) aliviar. *vi* disminuir; moderarse; (of the wind and *fig*) amainar; cesar; apaciguarse, calmarse

abatement n disminución, f; reducción, f; mitigación, f; (of price) rebaja, f; supresión, f; remisión, f; (annulment) anulación, f; (of pride) humillación, f; (of the wind and of enthusiasm, etc.) amaine, m; (of pain, etc.) alivio, m

abbreviate *vt* abreviar; condensar, resumir

abbreviation n abreviación, f; resumen, m, condensación, f; (of a word) abreviatura, f

abdicate *vt* renunciar; (a throne) abdicar

abdication n renuncia, f; abdicación, f

abdomen n abdomen, m

abduct *vt* raptar, secuestrar

abduction n rapto, m; (*anat phil*) abducción, f

aberration n aberración (also *ast phys biol*), f

abet *vt* ayudar, apoyar, favorecer; incitar, alentar; (in bad sense) ser cómplice de

abeyance n suspensión, f; expectativa, esperanza, f. **in a.,** en suspenso; vacante; latente

abhor *vt* detestar, odiar, aborrecer; repugnar

abhorrence n detestación, f, odio, aborrecimiento, m; repugnancia, f

abhorrent a detestable, odioso, aborrecible; repugnante

abide *vi* morar, quedar. *vt* aguardar; *inf* aguantar, sufrir. **to a. by,** atenerse a, cumplir; sostener

abiding a permanente, constante, perenne

ability n habilidad, facultad, f, poder, m; talento, m, capacidad, f. **to the best of my a.,** lo mejor que yo pueda

abject a abyecto, miserable; despreciable, vil; servil

abjure *vt* abjurar; renunciar; retractar

ablaze *adv* en llamas, ardiendo. a brillante; (with, of anger, etc.) dominado por

able a capaz (de); (clever) hábil; competente; en estado (de); *law* apto legalmente, capaz; bueno, excelente. **to be able to,** poder; ser capaz de; (know how) saber. **a.-bodied,** fuerte, fornido. **a.-bodied seaman,** marinero práctico, m

ably *adv* hábilmente; competentemente

abnormal a anormal; irregular

aboard *adv* a bordo. *prep* a bordo de. **to go a.,** embarcarse, ir a bordo. **All a.!** ¡Viajeros a bordo!; (a train) ¡Viajeros al tren!

abode n morada, habitación, f; residencia, f; (stay) estancia, f

abolish *vt* abolir, suprimir, anular

abominable a abominable, aborrecible; repugnante, execrable; *inf* horrible

abominate *vt* abominar, aborrecer, detestar

abomination n abominación, f; aborrecimiento, m; horror, m

aboriginal a aborigen; primitivo

aborigines n pl aborígenes, m pl

abort *vi* abortar, malparir; *fig* malograrse

abortion n aborto, Columbia avieso m; *fig* fracaso, malogro, m

abound *vi* abundar (en)

about *adv* (around) alrededor; (round about) a la redonda, en torno; (all over) por todas partes; (up and down) acá y acullá; por aquí, por ahí; en alguna parte; por aquí; (in circumference) en circunferencia; (almost) casi, aproximadamente; (by turns) por turnos, en rotación. *prep* alrededor de; en torno; por; (near to) cerca de; (on one's person) sobre; (on the subject of) sobre; (concerning) acerca de; (over) por, a causa de; en; (of) de; (with time by the clock) a eso de, sobre; (towards) hacia; (engaged in) ocupado en; (on the point of) a punto de. **a. here**, por aquí. **a. nothing**, por nada. **a. supper time**, hacia la hora de cenar. **a. three o'clock**, a eso de las tres. **A. turn!** ¡Media vuelta! (a la izquierda or a la derecha). **He wandered a. the streets**, Vagaba por las calles. **somewhere a.**, en alguna parte. **to be a. to**, estar para, estar a punto de. **to bring a.**, ocasionar. **to come a.**, suceder. **to know a.**, saber de. **to set a.**, empezar, iniciar; (a person) acometer. **What are you thinking a.?** ¿En qué piensas?

above *adv* arriba; en lo alto; encima; (superior) superior; (earlier) antes; (higher up on a page, etc.) más arriba; (in heaven) en el cielo. *prep* encima de; por encima de; sobre; (beyond) fuera de; fuera del alcance de; (superior to) superior a; (more than) más de; (too proud to) demasiado orgulloso para; (too good to) demasiado bueno para; (in addition to) además de, en adición a; (with degrees of temperature) sobre. a anterior; (with past participles) antes. **from a.**, desde arriba. **a. all**, sobre todo. **over and a.**, además de. **a. board**, *adv* abiertamente, con las cartas boca arriba. a franco y abierto. **a. mentioned**, supradicho, susodicho, antes citado

abrasion *n* abrasión, *f*; rozadura, *f*; *geol* denudación, *f*

abreast *adv* de frente, al lado uno de otro; *naut* por el través. **to keep a. of the times**, mantenerse al día. **to ride six a.**, cabalgar a seis de frente. **a. with**, al nivel de, a la altura de

abridge *vt* abreviar; resumir, condensar, compendiar; disminuir; reducir

abridgment *n* abreviación, *f*; resumen, *m*, sinopsis, *f*; disminución, *f*; reducción, *f*

abroad *adv* (out) fuera, afuera; (gone out) salido; ausente; (everywhere) en todas partes; (in foreign lands) en el extranjero. **to go a.**, salir de casa, echarse a la calle; ir al extranjero; (of rumors, etc.) propagarse, rumorearse

abrogation *n* abrogación, anulación, *f*

abrupt *a* (precipitous) escarpado, precipitado, abrupto; (unexpected) repentino, inesperado; (of persons) brusco, descortés; (of style) seco

abscess *n* absceso, *m*

abscond *vi* evadirse; huir, escaparse; (with money) desfalcar

absence *n* ausencia, *f*; alejamiento, *m*; (of mind) abstracción, *f*, ensimismamiento, *m*; (lack) falta, *f*. **leave of a.**, permiso

para ausentarse, *m*; *mil* licencia, *f*, permiso, *m*

absent *a* ausente; alejado (de); (in mind) abstraído, ensimismado, distraído. *vt* ausentarse; alejarse. **the a.**, los ausentes. **a.-mindedness**, ensimismamiento, *m*, abstracción, *f*

absentee *n* ausente, *mf*

absently *adv* distraídamente

absolute *a* absoluto; perfecto; puro; (unconditional) incondicional; (downright) categórico; completo; (true) verdadero; (unlimited) ilimitado. **the a.**, lo absoluto

absolve *vt* absolver; (free) exentar, eximir; librar; exculpar

absorb *vt* absorber; (drink) beber; (use) gastar; (of shocks) amortiguar; (*fig* digest) asimilar; (engross) ocupar (el pensamiento, etc.). **to be absorbed in**, *fig* enfrascarse en, engolfarse en, estar entregado a

absorbent *a* and *n* absorbente, *m*. **a. cotton**, algodón hidrófilo, *m*

absorbing *a* absorbente; *fig* sumamente interesante

absorption *n* absorción, *f*; (*fig* digestion) asimilación, *f*; (engrossment) enfrascamiento, *m*, preocupación, abstracción, *f*

abstain *vi* abstenerse (de); evitar

abstemious *a* abstemio, abstinente; sobrio; moderado

abstention *n* abstención, *f*; abstinencia, *f*; privación, *f*

abstinence *n* abstinencia, *f*. **day of a.**, día de ayuno, *m*

abstract *a* abstracto. *n* extracto, resumen, *m*; abstracción, *f*. *vt* abstraer; separar; extraer; (précis) resumir; (steal) substraer. **in the a.**, en abstracto

abstracted *a* distraído, desatento, absorto, ensimismado

abstraction *n* abstracción, *f*; (of mind) preocupación, desatención, *f*; (stealing) substracción, *f*

abstruse *a* abstruso, ininteligible; obscuro; recóndito

absurd *a* absurdo, grotesco; ridículo, disparatado; cómico

absurdity *n* absurdidad, ridiculez, *f*; disparate, *m*, tontería, *f*

abundance *n* abundancia, copia, *f*; muchedumbre (de), multitud (de), *f*; riqueza, *f*; prosperidad, *f*

abundant *a* abundante, copioso; rico. **to be a. in**, abundar en

abuse *n* abuso, *m*; (bad language) insulto, *m*, injuria, *f*. *vt* (ill-use) maltratar; (misuse) abusar (de); (revile) insultar, injuriar; (deceive) engañar

abuser *n* abusador (-ra); injuriador (-ra); (defamer) denigrante, *mf*

abusive *a* abusivo; (scurrilous) insultante, injurioso, ofensivo

abut (on) *vi* lindar con; terminar en; estar adosado a

abysmal *a* abismal

abyss *n* abismo, *m*, sima, *f*; (hell) infierno, *m*

academic *a* académico

academy *n* academia, *f*; conservatorio, *m*; (school) colegio, *m*; (of riding, etc.) escuela, *f*. **A. of Music,** Conservatorio de Música, *m*

accede *vi* (to a throne) ascender (al trono); tomar posesión (de); (join) hacerse miembro (de); aceptar; (agree) acceder (a), consentir (en), convenir (en)

accelerate *vt* acelerar; apresurar; (shorten) abreviar

accelerator *n* (of a vehicle) acelerador, *m*

accent *n* acento (all meanings), *m*. *vt* acentuar

accentuate *vt* acentuar; dar énfasis a

accept *vt* aceptar; (believe) creer; recibir; admitir; (welcome) acoger

acceptability *n* aceptabilidad, *f*; mérito, *m*

acceptable *a* aceptable; admisible; agradable; (welcome) bien acogido

acceptably *adv* aceptablemente; agradablemente

acceptance *n* aceptación, *f*. **a. speech** discurso aceptatorio; (approval) aprobación, *f*; (welcome) buena acogida, *f*; *com* aceptación, *f*

access *n* acceso, *m*; entrada, *f*; (way) camino, *m*; *med* ataque, *m*; (fit) transporte, *m*; (advance) avance, *m*. **easy of a.,** accesible; fácil de encontrar

accessible *a* accesible; asequible

accession *n* (to the throne, etc.) advenimiento, *m*; aumento, *m*; (acquisition) adición, *f*; adquisición, *f*; *law* accesión, *f*

accessory *a* accesorio; secundario; suplementario, adicional. *n* accesorio, *m*; *law* cómplice, *mf*. **a. before the fact,** instigador (-ra). **a. after the fact,** encubridor (-ra)

accident *n* accidente, *m*; (chance) casualidad, *f*; (mishap) contratiempo, *m*. **by a.,** por casualidad, accidentalmente. **a. insurance,** seguro contra accidentes de

accidental *a* accidental, casual, fortuito. *n* *mus* accidente, *m*

accidentally *adv* accidentalmente; por casualidad; sin querer

acclaim *vt* aclamar; proclamar; vitorear, aplaudir

acclamation *n* aclamación, *f*; aplauso, vítor, *m*

acclimatize *vt* aclimatar

accolade *n* acolada, *f*, espaldarazo, *m*

accommodate *vt* acomodar; ajustar; adaptar; (reconcile) reconciliar; (provide) proveer, proporcionar; (oblige) complacer; (fit) poner, instalar; (lodge) hospedar; (lend) prestar; (hold) tener espacio

para, contener; (give a seat to) dar un sitio a. **to a. oneself to,** adaptarse a

accommodating *a* acomodadizo; (obliging) servicial

accommodation *n* acomodación, *f*; ajuste, *m*; adaptación, *f*; (arrangement) arreglo, *m*; (reconciliation) reconciliación, *f*; (lodging) alojamiento, *m*; (aer naut) partición, *f*; (space, room or seat) sitio, *m*; (loan) préstamo, *m*. **We found the accommodations good in this hotel,** Estuvimos muy bien en este hotel. **a. ladder,** escalera real, *f*

accompaniment *n* acompañamiento, *m*

accompanist *n* acompañante (-ta)

accompany *vt* acompañar

accompanying *a* anexo *n* acompañamiento, *m*

accomplice *n* cómplice, comparte, *mf*

accomplish *vt* llevar a cabo, efectuar; terminar; (fulfil) cumplir; perfeccionar; (achieve) conseguir, lograr

accomplished *a* consumado; perfecto; culto; (talented) talentoso

accomplishment *n* efectuación, *f*; realización, *f*, logro, *m*; (fulfilment) cumplimiento, *m*; (gift) prenda, *f*, talento, *m*; *pl* **accomplishments,** partes, dotes, *f pl*; conocimientos, *m pl*

accord *n* acuerdo, *m*; unión, *f*; consentimiento, *m*; concierto, *m*, concordia, *f*; voluntad, *f*. *vt* otorgar, conceder. *vi* estar de acuerdo (con); armonizar (con). **of one's own a.,** espontáneamente. **with one a.,** unánimemente

accordance *n* acuerdo, *m*, conformidad, *f*; arreglo, *m*. **in a. with,** de acuerdo con, según, con arreglo a

according *adv* según, conforme. **a. as,** conforme a, a medida que. **a. to,** según

accordingly *adv* en consecuencia, por consiguiente; pues

accordion *n* acordeón, *m*. **to a.-pleat,** *vt* plisar

accost *vt* abordar, acercarse a; dirigirse a, hablar

account *vt* (judge) considerar, creer, juzgar, tener por. *vi* (for) explicar; (understand) comprender; (be responsible) responder de, dar razón de; justificar

account *n* (bill) cuenta, *f*; factura, *f*; (narrative) narración, relación, *f*; (description) descripción, *f*; historia, *f*; versión, *f*; (list) enumeración, *f*; (reason) motivo, *m*, causa, *f*; (importance) importancia, *f*; (weight) peso, *m*; (news) noticias, *f pl*; (advantage) provecho, *m*, ventaja, *f*. **by all accounts,** según lo que se oye, según voz pública. **current a.;** cuenta corriente, *f*. **outstanding a.,** cuenta pendiente, *f*. **on a.,** a cuenta. **on a. of,** a causa de, por motivo de. **on no a.,** de ninguna manera. **on that a.,** por lo tanto. **to be of no a.,** ser insignificante; ser de poca importancia; *inf* ser la última mona. **to give an a.,** contar, hacer una relación (de). **to**

give an a. of oneself, explicarse. **to keep a.,** llevar la cuenta. **to settle accounts,** ajustar cuentas. **to take into a.,** considerar. **to turn to a.,** sacar provecho de. **a. book,** libro de cuentas, *m*

accountability *n* responsabilidad, *f*

accountable *a* responsable

accountancy *n* contabilidad, *f*

accountant *n* contador, *m*. **chartered a.,** contador autorizado, *m*. **accountant's office,** contaduría, *f*

accouterment *n* atavío, *m*; equipo, *m*

accredit *vt* acreditar

accretion *n* acrecentamiento, aumento, *m*; *law* accesión, *f*

accrue *vi* resultar (de); proceder (de); originarse (en); aumentar

accumulate *vt* acumular; amontonar, atesorar. *vi* acumularse; aumentarse, crecer

accumulation *n* acumulación, *f*; amontonamiento, *m*

accumulative *a* acumulador; adquisitivo, ahorrador

accuracy *n* exactitud, corrección

accurate *a* exacto, correcto, fiel; (of persons) exacto, minucioso; (of apparatus) de precisión

accurately *adv* con exactitud, correctamente; con precisión

accursed *a* maldito.

accusation *n* acusación, *f*. **to lodge an a.,** querellarse ante el juez

accusatory *a* acusatorio

accuse *vt* acusar

accused *n law* acusado (-da)

accuser *n* acusador (-ra)

accustom *vt* acostumbrar (a), habituar (a)

accustomed *a* acostumbrado, usual; general; característico

ace *n* as, *m*; *fig* pelo, *m*. **to be within an ace of,** estar a dos dedos de

acerbity *n* acerbidad, *f*; *fig* aspereza, *f*; severidad, *f*; sequedad, *f*

acetylene *n* acetileno, *m*. **a. lamp,** lámpara de acetileno, *f*

ache *n* dolor, *m*; pena, *f*. *vi* doler. **My head aches,** Me duele la cabeza, Tengo dolor de cabeza

achievable *a* alcanzable, asequible; factible

achieve *vt* conseguir, lograr; (reach) alcanzar; (obtain) obtener, ganar

achievement *n* logro, *m*, realización, *f*; obtención, *f*; (deed) hazaña, *f*; (work) obra, *f*; (success) éxito, *m*; (discovery) descubrimiento, *m*; (victory) victoria, *f*

aching *n* dolor, *m*; pena, angustia, *f*. a doliente; afligido

acid *a* and *n* ácido, *m*. **fatty a.,** ácido graso, *m*

acknowledge *vt* reconocer; confesar;

(reply to) contestar a; (appreciate) agradecer. **to a. receipt,** *com* acusar recibo

acknowledgment *n* reconocimiento, *m*; confesión, *f*; (appreciation) agradecimiento, *m*; (reward) recompensa, *f*; (of a letter) acuse de recibo, *m*

acme *n* cumbre, *f*; *fig* auge, apogeo, *m*

acne *n* acné, *m*.

acolyte *n* acólito, monacillo (male) *m*, acólita, monacilla *f*, (female)

acorn *n* bellota, *f*. **a. cup,** capullo de bellota, *m*. **a.-shaped,** en forma de bellota, abellotado

acoustic *a* acústico

acoustics *n pl* acústica, *f*

acquaint *vt* dar a conocer, comunicar, informar (de), dar parte (de); familiarizar (con). **to be acquainted with,** conocer; saber. **to make oneself acquainted with,** familiarizarse con; entablar amistad con

acquaintance *n* conocimiento, *m*; (person) conocido (-da); *pl* **acquaintances,** amistades, *f pl*. **to make their a.,** conocer (a), llegar a conocer (a)

acquiesce *vi* asentir (en), consentir (a)

acquiescence *n* acquiescencia, *f*, consentimiento, *m*

acquire *vt* adquirir, obtener; (diseases, habits) contraer; ganar; (learn) aprender

Acquired Immune Deficiency Syndrome *n* el síndrome de Inmunodeficiencia Adquirida, *m*

acquirement *n* adquisición, *f*; (learning) conocimiento, *m*; (talent) talento, *m*

acquisition *n* adquisición, *f*

acquisitive *a* adquisitivo

acquit *vt* (a debt) pagar; exonerar; *law* absolver; (a duty) cumplir. **to a. oneself well (badly),** portarse bien (mal); salir bien (mal)

acquittal *n* (of a debt) pago, *m*; *law* absolución, *f*; (of a duty) cumplimiento, *m*

acre *n* (measure) acre, *m*; *pl* **acres,** terrenos, campos, *m pl*. **1.75 acres** *Central America* manzana *f*. **2.5 acres** *Argentina* manzana *f*

acreage *n* acres, *m pl*

acrimonious *a* acrimonioso, áspero; mordaz, sarcástico

acrobat *n* acróbata. *Lat. Am. also* maromero (-ra) *mf*

acrobatic *a* acrobático

acronym *n* sigla, *f*

across *adv* a través, de través, transversalmente; (on the other side) al otro lado; de una parte a otra; (of the arms, etc.) cruzados, *m pl*. *prep* a través de; al otro lado de; (upon) sobre; por. **He went a. the road,** Cruzó la calle. **to run a.,** correr por; tropezar con; dar con. **a. country,** a campo travieso. **a. the way,** en frente

act *n* acción, obra, *f*, hecho, *m*; acto, *m*; *law* ley, *f*; *theat* acto, *m*. **in the act,** en el acto. **in the act (of doing),** en acto de

(hacer algo). **in the very act,** en flagrante. **the Acts of the Apostles,** los
Actos de los Apóstoles. **act of God,**
fuerza mayor, *f.* **act of indemnity,** bill de
indemnidad, *m*

act *vt* (a play) representar, hacer; (a part)
desempeñar, hacer (un papel); (pretend)
simular, fingir. *vi* obrar, actuar, *Lat. Am.*
accionar; (behave) portarse, conducirse;
(function) funcionar; producir su efecto;
(feign) fingir; (as a profession) ser actor.
to act as, hacer de; cumplir las funciones
de. **to act as a second,** (in a duel) apadrinar. **to act for,** representar; ser el representante de. **to act upon,** obrar
sobre; afectar; influir en

acting *n* (of a play) representación (de
una comedia), *f;* (of an actor) interpretación (de un papel), *f;* (as a hobby) el hacer
comedia; (dramatic art) arte dramática, *f.*
a interino, suplente; comanditario. **He is
a. captain,** Está de capitán. **a. partner,**
socio (-ia) comanditario (-ia)

action *n* acción, *f;* función, *f;* operación, *f;*
(movement) movimiento, *m;* (effect)
efecto, *m;* influencia, *f; law* proceso, *m;*
mil batalla, acción, *f; lit* acción, *f.* **in a.,** en
actividad; en operación; *mil* en el campo
de batalla. **man of a.,** hombre de acción,
m. **to be killed in a.,** morir en el campo
de batalla. **to bring an a. against,** pedir
en juicio, entablar un pleito contra. **to
put into a.,** hacer funcionar; introducir.
to take a., tomar medidas (para). **to
take a. against,** prevenirse contra; *law*
proceder contra

actionable a procesable, punible

active a activo; ágil; diligente; *mil* vivo;
enérgico; *gram* activo. **be a.** *Lat. Am.* accionar. **to make a.,** activar, estimular

activity *n* actividad, *f*

actor *n* actor, *m;* (in comedy) comediante,
m

actress *n* actriz, *f;* (in comedy) comediante, *f*

actual a actual, existente; real, verdadero

actuality *n* realidad, *f*

actually *adv* en efecto, realmente, en
realidad

actuary *n* actuario de seguros, *m*

actuate *vt* mover, animar, excitar

acumen *n* cacumen, *m,* agudeza, sagacidad, *f*

acute a agudo; (shrewd) perspicaz; (of a
situation) crítico. **a. accent,** acento
agudo, *m.* **a.-angled,** acutángulo

acuteness *n* agudeza, *f;* (shrewdness)
perspicacia, penetración, *f*

ad *n* anuncio, *m.* See **advertisement**

Adam *n* Adán, *m.* **Adam's apple,** nuez de
la garganta, *f*

adamant a firme, duro, inexorable

adapt *vt* adaptar; ajustar, acomodar; aplicar; (a play, etc.) refundir, arreglar; *mus*
arreglar

adaptability *n* adaptabilidad, *f*

adaptable a adaptable

adaptation *n* adaptación, *f;* (of a play,
etc.) refundición, *f;* (*mus* etc.) arreglo, *m*

adapter *n* (of a play, etc.) refundidor (-ra);
elec enchufe de reducción, *m*

add *vt* añadir; juntar; (up) sumar. **add insult to injury,** al mojado echarle agua,
añadir a una ofensa otra mayor. **to add
to,** añadir a; (increase) aumentar, acrecentar. **to add up,** sumar. **to add up to,**
subir a; (mean) querer decir.

adder *n* víbora, serpiente, *f*

addict *n* adicto (-ta). **to a. oneself to,**
dedicarse a, entregarse a

addicted a aficionado (a), amigo (de),
dado (a); adicto (a)

addiction *n* afición, propensión, *f;* adic-
ción, *f*

addition *n* añadidura, *f; math* adición,
suma, *f.* **in a. (to),** además (de), también

address *n* (on a letter) sobrescrito, *m;* (of
a person) dirección, *f,* señas, *f pl;*
(speech) discurso, *m;* (petition) memorial, *m,* petición, *f;* (dedication) dedicatoria, *f;* (invocation) invocación, *f;* (deportment) presencia, *f;* (tact) diplomacia,
habilidad, *f; pl* **addresses,** corte, *f. vt* (a
ball) golpear; (a letter) dirigir, poner el
sobrescrito a, *Mexico* domiciliar; (words,
prayers) dirigir (a); hablar, hacer un discurso. **to a. oneself to a task,** dedicarse
a (or entregarse a or emprender) una
tarea. **to deliver an a.,** pronunciar un
discurso. **to pay one's addresses to,**
cortejar, hacer la corte (a), galantear

addressee *n* destinatario (-ia)

adduce *vt* aducir, alegar; aportar

adenoids *n pl* amígdalas, *f pl*

adept a adepto, versado, consumado. *n*
adepto, *m*

adequacy *n* adecuación, *f;* suficiencia, *f;*
competencia, *f*

adequate a adecuado; proporcionado;
suficiente; competente; a la altura (de)

adhere *vi* adherirse; pegarse; ser fiel (a);
persistir (en)

adherence *n fig* adhesión, *f*

adherent *n* partidario (-ia)

adhesion *n* adherencia, *f;* (to a party,
etc.) adhesión, *f*

adhesive a adhesivo; (sticky) pegajoso.
a. tape, esparadrapo, *m; elec* cinta aisladora adherente, *f*

adjacent a próximo, contiguo, adyacente, vecino

adjective *n* adjetivo, *m*

adjoin *vt* estar contiguo a, lindar con;
juntar. *vi* colindar

adjoining a vecino, de al lado, adyacente; cercano

adjourn *vt* aplazar, diferir; (a meeting,
etc.) suspender, levantar. *vi* retirarse.
The debate was adjourned, Se suspen-

dió el debate. **to a. a meeting,** levantar la sesión

adjournment n aplazamiento, m; (of a meeting) suspensión (de la sesión), f

adjudicate vt adjudicar; law declarar; juzgar. vi ejercer las funciones del juez; fallar, dictar sentencia

adjudication n adjudicación, f; law fallo, m, sentencia, f; (of bankruptcy) declaración (de quiebra), f; concesión, f, otorgamiento, m

adjunct n atributo, m; accesorio, m; adjunto, m; gram adjunto, m

adjure vt conjurar; rogar encarecidamente

adjust vt ajustar; regular; arreglar; (correct) corregir; adaptar

adjustable a ajustable; regulable; desmontable; de quita y pon

adjustment n ajuste, m; regulación, f; arreglo, m; (correction) corrección, f; adaptación, f; com prorrateo, m

administer vt administrar; (laws) aplicar; (blows, etc.) dar; (an office) ejercer; (govern) regir, gobernar; (provide) suministrar; (an oath) tomar; (justice) hacer; (the sacraments) administrar; (with to) contribuir a. **to a. an oath,** tomar juramento (a)

administration n administración, f; (government) gobierno, m; dirección, f; (of laws) aplicación, f; distribución, f

administrative a administrativo; gubernativo

administrator n administrador, m

admirable a admirable

admiral n almirante, m. **A. of the Fleet,** almirante supremo, m. **admiral's ship,** capitana, f

admiration n admiración, f

admire vt sentir admiración por; (love) amar; (like) gustar; (respect) respetar

admirer n admirador (-ra); (amateur) aficionado (-da), apasionado (-da); (partisan) satélite, m; (lover) enamorado, amante, m

admiring a admirativo, de admiración

admissible a admisible; aceptable; lícito, permitido

admission n admisión, f; recepción, f; entrada, f; confesión, f; reconocimiento, m. **No a.!** Entrada prohibida. **right of a.,** derecho de entrada, m. **A. free,** Entrada libre. **a. ticket,** entrada, f

admit vt admitir; recibir; dejar entrar; hacer entrar, introducir; (hold) contener; (concede) conceder; (acknowledge) reconocer, confesar. **to a. of,** permitir; sufrir

admittance n admisión, f; entrada, f. **No a.!** Prohibida la entrada. **to gain a.,** lograr entrar

admittedly adv según opinión general; sin duda

admonish vt (advise) aconsejar; amonestar, advertir; (reprimand) reprender

admonition n amonestación, f; advertencia, f; admonición, f

admonitory a amonestador

ad nauseam adv hasta la saciedad

ado n (noise) ruido, m; (trouble) trabajo, m, dificultad, f; (fuss) barahúnda, f. **much ado about nothing,** mucho ruido y pocas nueces, nada entre dos platos. **without more ado,** sin más ni más

adolescence n adolescencia, f

adolescent a and n adolescente, mf

adopt vt adoptar. **a. local customs** Lat. Am. acriollarse

adopted a adoptivo

adoption n adopción, f; (choice) elección, f

adore vt adorar

adoringly adv con adoración

adorn vt adornar, embellecer; (fig of persons) adornar con su presencia

adornment n adorno, m; ornamento, m; embellecimiento, m

adrenalin n adrenalina, f

adrift a and adv a merced de las olas; a la ventura. **to turn a.,** inf poner de patitas en la calle

adroit a hábil

adult a and n adulto (-ta)

adult education n educación de los adultos, f

adulterate vt adulterar; falsificar; contaminar. a adulterado; falsificado; impuro

adulteration n adulteración, f; falsificación, f; impureza, f; contaminación, f

adulterer n adúltero, m

adultery n adulterio, m. **to commit a.,** cometer adulterio, adulterar

advance n avance, m; (progress) progreso, adelantamiento, m; (improvement) mejora, f; (of shares) alza, f; (of price) subida, f; (loan) préstamo, m; (in rank) ascenso, m; pl **advances,** (overtures) avances, m pl; (proposals) propuestas, f pl; (of love) requerimientos amorosos, m pl. **in a.,** de antemano, con anticipación, con tiempo, previamente; (of money) por adelantado. **a. guard,** mil avanzada, f. **a. payment,** anticipo, m, paga por adelantado, f

advance vt avanzar; (suggest) sugerir, proponer; (encourage) fomentar; (a person) ascender; (improve) mejorar; (of events, dates) adelantar; (of prices, stocks) hacer subir; (money) anticipar; (of steps) tomar. vi avanzar; (progress) progresar; (in rank, studies, etc.) adelantar; (of prices) subir

advanced a avanzado; (developed) desarrollado; (mentally, of children) precoz; (course) superior. **a. research,** investigaciones superiores. **a. standing,** equivalencias, f pl. **a. views,** ideas avanzadas, f pl

advancement n adelantamiento, m; progreso, m; (encouragement) fomento, m; (in employment) promoción, f; prosperidad, f

advancing a que avanza; (of years) que pasan

advantage n ventaja, f; superioridad, f; (benefit) provecho, beneficio, m; interés, m; ocasión favorable, oportunidad, f; (tennis) ventaja, f. **to have the a. of,** tener la ventaja de. **to show to a.,** embellecer, realzar; aumentar la belleza (etc.) de. **to take a. of,** sacar ventaja de, aprovecharse de; (deceive) engañar. **to take a. of the slightest pretext,** asirse de un cabello

advantageous a ventajoso, provechoso. **to be a.,** ser de provecho

adventure n aventura, f; riesgo, m; (chance) casualidad, f; com especulación, f, vt aventurar, arriesgar. vi arriesgarse, osar

adventurer n aventurero, m; (one living by his wits) caballero de industria, m; (in commerce) especulador, m

adventuresome a de aventura

adventurous a aventurero; osado, audaz; (dangerous) peligroso, arriesgado

adversary n adversario (-ia)

adverse a adverso; hostil (a); malo; desfavorable; (opposite) opuesto

advertise vt anunciar. vi poner un anuncio; (oneself) llamar la atención

advertisement n anuncio, m; (poster) cartel, m; (to attract attention) reclamo, m. **to put an a. in the paper,** poner un anuncio en el periódico. **a. hoarding,** cartelera, f

advertiser n anunciante, mf

advertising n anuncios, m pl; publicidad, propaganda, f; medios publicitarios, m pl

advice n consejo, m; (warning) advertencia, amonestación, f; (news) noticia, f; aviso, m; com comunicación, f; (belief) parecer, m, opinión, f. **piece of a.,** consejo, m. **to follow the a. of,** seguir los consejos de. **to give a.,** dar consejos

advisable a conveniente, aconsejable; prudente

advise vt aconsejar; (inform) avisar, informar

advised a avisado; premeditado. **ill-a.,** mal aconsejado; imprudente. **well-a.,** bien aconsejado; prudente

adviser n consejero (-ra)

advocacy n defensa, f; apología, f; abogacía, intercesión, f

advocate n law abogado (-da); defensor (-ra); (champion) campeón, m. vt abogar, defender; sostener, apoyar; recomendar

aegis n égida, f; protección, f

aerial a aéreo, de aire; etéreo; fantástico. n (radio) antena, f. **indoor a.,** antena interior, f

aerobics n aerobismo m

aeronaut n aeronauta, mf

aeronautics n aeronáutica, f

afar adv a lo lejos, en la distancia. **from a.,** desde lejos

affable a afable, condescendiente

affair n asunto, m, cosa, f; cuestión, f; (business) negocio, m; (fam applied to a machine, carriage, etc.) artefacto, m; (of the heart) amorío, m. **a. of honour,** lance de honor, m

affect vt afectar; influir; med atacar; (move) impresionar, conmover; enternecer; (harm) perjudicar; (frequent) frecuentar; (like) gustar de; (love) amar; (wear) vestir; (use) gastar, usar; (feign) aparentar; (boast) hacer alarde de

affected a afectado; influido; med atacado; (moved) conmovido, impresionado; enternecido; (inclined) dispuesto, inclinado; (artificial) artificioso; amanerado, afectado; (of style) rebuscado, artificial

affection n afecto, cariño, m; amor, m; apego, m; simpatía, f; (emotion) emoción, f, sentimiento, m; med afección, enfermedad, f

affectionate a afectuoso, cariñoso; mimoso; (tender) tierno; expresivo

affectionately adv afectuosamente. **Yours a.,** tu cariñoso ..., tu ..., que te quiere

affidavit n declaración jurada, declaración jurídica f, atestiguación, f

affiliate vt afiliar; adoptar; law imputar; law legitimar

affiliation n afiliación, f; adopción, f; legitimación de un hijo, f

affirm vt afirmar, aseverar, declarar; confirmar. vi law declarar ante un juez

affirmation n afirmación, aserción, f; confirmación, f; law declaración, deposición, f

affix vt fijar; pegar; añadir; (seal, one's signature) poner.

afflict vt afligir, atormentar, aquejar

affliction n aflicción, f; tribulación, pesadumbre, f; calamidad, f; miseria, f; (ailment) achaque, m

affluence n afluencia, f; abundancia, f; riqueza, f; opulencia, f

affluent a abundante; rico; opulento

afford vt dar, proporcionar; producir; ofrecer; (bear) soportar; poder con; (financially) tener medios para; permitirse el lujo de; (be able) poder. **I could not a. to pay so much,** No puedo (podía) pagar tanto

afforestation n conversión en bosque, f; plantación de un bosque, f

affront n afrenta, f; insulto, agravio, m. vt insultar; ultrajar, afrentar; (offend) ofender

afield adv en el campo; lejos. **to go far a.,** ir muy lejos

afire *adv* en fuego, en llamas; *fig* ardiendo

aflame *adv* en llamas; *fig* encendido

afloat *adv* a flote; *naut* a bordo; (solvent) solvente; en circulación; (floating) flotante; (swamped) inundado; (in full swing) en marcha, en movimiento

afoot *adv* a pie; en marcha, en movimiento; en preparación. **to set a.,** iniciar, poner en marcha

aforesaid a consabido, dicho, susodicho

afraid a espantado; temeroso, miedoso. **I'm a. that . . . ,** Me temo que. . . . **to be a.,** tener miedo. **to make a.,** dar miedo (a)

afresh *adv* de nuevo, otra vez

African a and *n* africano (-na)

aft *adv* en popa; a popa. **fore and aft,** de proa a popa

after *prep* (of place) detrás de; (of time) después de; (behind) en pos de; (following) tras; (in spite of) a pesar de; (in consequence of) después de, a consecuencia de; (in accordance with) según; (in the style of) al estilo de, en imitación de. *adv* (later) después, más tarde; (subsequently) después (que); (when) cuando. a futuro, venidero. **day a. day,** día tras día. **on the day a.,** al día siguiente. **soon a.,** poco después. **to look a.,** cuidar de. **to go a.,** ir a buscar; seguir. **the day a. tomorrow,** pasado mañana. **What are you a.?** ¿Qué buscas? **a. all,** después de todo. **a. the manner of,** a la moda de, según la moda de; al estilo de. **a.-dinner conversation,** conversación de sobremesa, *f.* **a. glow,** resplandor crepuscular, reflejo del sol poniente en el cielo, *m.* **a. life,** vida futura, *f.* **a. pains,** dolores de sobreparto, *m pl.* **a. taste,** dejo, resabio, *m*

afterbirth *n* placenta, *f*

aftermath *n* consecuencias, *f pl,* resultado, *m*

afternoon *n* tarde, *f.* Good a.! ¡Buenas tardes! **a. nap,** siesta, *f.* **a. tea,** el té de las cinco

afterthought *n* reflexión tardía, *f;* segunda intención, *f.* **to have an a.,** pensar en segundo lugar

afterwards *adv* después; más tarde

again *adv* (once more) otra vez, de neuvo; por segunda vez, dos veces; (on the other hand) por otra parte; (moreover) además; (likewise) también; (returned) de vuelta. Sometimes translated by prefix **re** in verbs. **as much a.,** otro tanto. **never a.,** nunca más. **not a.,** no más. **now and a.,** de vez en cuando. **to do a.,** volver a hacer, hacer de nuevo. **a. and a.,** repetidas veces

against *prep* (facing) enfrente de; contra; (in preparation for) para; (contrary to) contrario a; (opposed to) opuesto a; (near) cerca de. **to be a.,** oponer; estar enfrente de. **a. the grain,** a contrapelo

age *n* edad, *f;* (generation) generación, *f;* (epoch) siglo, período, *m;* época, *f;* (old age) vejez, *f;* (majority) mayoría de edad, *f, vi* envejecer. **at any age,** a cualquier edad. **the golden age,** la edad de oro; (in literature, etc.) el siglo de oro. **from age to age,** por los siglos de los siglos. **to be of age,** ser mayor de edad. **to be under age,** ser menor de edad. **to come of age,** llegar a la mayoría de edad. **She is six years of age,** Ella tiene seis años. **age-old,** secular

aged a de la edad de; (old) anciano, viejo. **a girl a. four,** una niña de cuatro años

ageless a siempre joven; eterno

agency *n* órgano, *m,* fuerza, *f;* acción, *f;* influencia, *f;* intervención, *f;* mediación, *f; com* agencia, *f.* **through the a. of,** por la mediación (or influencia) de

agenda *n* agenda, *f*

agent *n* agente, *m; com* representante, *mf; law* apoderado (-da). **business a.,** agente de negocios, *m*

agglomeration *n* aglomeración, *f*

aggrandizement *n* engrandecimiento, *m*

aggravate *vt* agravar, hacer peor; intensificar; (annoy) irritar, exasperar

aggravating a agravante, agravador; (tiresome) molesto; (annoying) irritante. **a. circumstance,** circunstancia agravante, *f*

aggravation *n* agravación, *f,* intensificación, *f;* (annoyance) irritación, *f*

aggregate a total. *n* agregado, conjunto, *m.* **in the a.,** en conjunto

aggression *n* agresión, *f*

aggressive a agresivo

aggrieved a afligido; ofendido; lastimero

aghast a horrorizado, espantado; (amazed) estupefacto

agile a ágil; ligero, *Mexico* alacre; vivo

agility *n* agilidad, *f;* ligereza, *f, Mexico* alacridad

agitate *vt* agitar; excitar; inquietar, perturbar; discutir. **to a. for,** luchar por; excitar la opinión pública en favor de

agitation *n* agitación, *f;* perturbación, *f;* discusión, *f*

aglow a and *adv* brillante, fulgente; encendido

ago *adv* hace. **a short while ago,** hace poco. **How long ago?** ¿Cuánto tiempo hace? **long ago,** hace mucho. **many years ago,** hace muchos años. **I last saw him ten years ago,** La última vez que le vi fue hace diez años

agog a agitado; ansioso; excitado; impaciente; curioso. *adv* con agitación; con ansia; con curiosidad

agonize *vt* atormentar. *vi* sufrir intensamente; retorcerse de dolor

agonizing a (of pain) intenso, atormentador

agony *n* agonía, *f;* angustia, *f;* paroxismo,

m. **a. column,** columna de los suspiros, *f*

agree *vi* estar de acuerdo. **Do you a. or disagree?** ¿Coincides o discrepas?; convenir (en); acordar; ponerse de acuerdo, entenderse; (suit) sentar bien, probar; (consent) consentir (en); *gram* concordar, (get on well) llevarse bien; (correspond) estar conforme (con). **to a. to,** convenir en, consentir en. **to a. with,** estar de acuerdo con, apoyar; dar la razón a; (suit) sentar bien; *gram* concordar

agreeable *a* agradable, afable, amable; (pleasant) ameno, grato; conforme; dispuesto a (hacer algo); conveniente

agreeableness *n* (of persons) afabilidad, amabilidad, *f;* amenidad, *f;* deleite, *m;* conformidad, *f*

agreeably *adv* agradablemente; de acuerdo (con), conforme (a)

agreed *a* convenido, acordado; (approved) aprobado. *interj* ¡convenido! ¡de acuerdo!

agreement *n* acuerdo, *m;* pacto, *m;* acomodamiento, concierto, *m;* contrato, *m; com* convenio, *m;* conformidad, *f;* consentimiento, *m; gram* concordancia, *f.* **in a.,** conforme. **in a. with,** de acuerdo con; según. **to reach an a.,** ponerse de acuerdo

agricultural *a* agrícola. **a. engineer,** ingeniero agrónomo, *m.* **a. laborer,** labriego, *m.* **a. show,** exposición agrícola, *f*

agriculture *n* agricultura, *f*

agronomist *n* agrónomo, *m*

agronomy *n* agronomía, *f*

aground *adv naut* varado, encallado. **running a.,** varada, *f.* **to run a.,** varar

ague *n* fiebre intermitente, *f; fig* escalofrío, *m*

ahead *adv* delante; enfrente; al frente (de); a la cabeza (de); adelante; hacia delante; *naut* por la proa. **Go a.!** ¡Adelante! **It is straight a.,** Está directamente enfrente. **to go straight a.,** ir hacia delante; seguir (haciendo algo)

aid *n* ayuda, *f;* socorro, auxilio, *m;* subsidio, *m, vt* ayudar; socorrer, auxiliar. **in aid of,** pro, en beneficio de. **first aid,** primera cura, *f.* **first aid post,** puesto de socorro, *m.* **to come or go to the aid of,** acudir en defensa de

AIDS *n* el SIDA, *m*

ail *vt* afligir, doler; pasar. *vi* estar indispuesto (or enfermo). **What ails you?** *inf* ¿Qué te pasa?

ailing *a* enfermizo, enclenque, achacoso

ailment *n* enfermedad, *f,* achaque, *m*

aim *n* (of firearms) puntería, *f;* (mark) blanco, *m; fig* objeto, fin, *m; fig* intención, *f,* propósito, *m, vt* (a gun) apuntar; dirigir; (throw) lanzar; (a blow) asestar. *vi* apuntar (a); (a remark at) decir por; aspirar (a); intentar, proponerse. **Is your remark aimed at me?** ¿Lo dices por mí?

to aim high, apuntar alto; *inf* picar alto. **to miss one's aim,** errar el tiro. **to take aim,** apuntar. **with the aim of,** con objeto de, a fin de

aimless *a* **aimlessly,** *adv* sin objeto, a la ventura

air *n* aire, *m,* (all meanings). **by air,** en avión; (of mail) por avión; (of goods) por vía aérea. **in the air,** al aire; al aire libre; (as though flying) en volandas. **in the open air,** al aire libre, al fresco, a la intemperie. **to be on the air,** *rad* hablar por radio. **to give oneself airs,** darse tono, tener humos. **to take the air,** tomar el fresco; despegar. **air balloon,** globo aerostático, *m;* (toy) globo, *m.* **air-base,** base aérea, *f.* **air-bed,** colchón de viento, *m.* **air-borne (to become),** levantar el vuelo, despegar. **air-brake,** *mech* freno neumático, *m.* **air-chamber,** cámara de aire, *f.* **air chief marshal,** general del ejército del aire, *m.* **air-cock,** válvula de escape de aire, *f.* **air commodore,** general de brigada de aviación, *m.* **air conditioning,** purificación de aire, *f. Lat. Am.* aclimatación, **air-cooled,** enfriado por aire. **air crash,** accidente de aviación, *m.* **air current,** corriente de aire, *f.* **air-cushion,** almohadilla neumática, *f.* **air-field,** campo de aviación, *m.* **air fleet,** flotilla aérea, *f.* **air force,** fuerza aérea, flota aérea, *f.* **air-gun,** escopeta de viento, *f.* **air-hole,** respiradero, *m.* **air-hostess,** azafata, *f.* **air-lift,** puente aéreo, *m.* **air-liner,** avión de pasajeros, *m.* **airline** línea aérea, aerolínea, *f.* **air-mail,** correo aéreo, *m.* **by airmail,** por avión. **air marshal,** teniente general de aviación, *m.* **air-pocket,** bolsa (or vacío, *m)* de aire, *f.* **air pollution** contaminación atmosférica, *f.* **air pump,** bomba neumática, *f.* **air raid,** bombardeo aéreo, *m.* **air-raid shelter,** refugio antiaéreo, *m.* **air-raid warning,** alarma aérea, *f.* **air-route,** vía aérea, *f.* **air-screw,** hélice de avión, *f.* **air-shaft,** respiradero de mina, *m.* **air shuttle,** puente aéreo, *m.* **air squadron,** escuadrilla aérea, *f.* **air stream,** chorro de aire, *m.* **air taxi,** avión taxi, *m.* **air-tight,** herméticamente cerrado. **air valve,** válvula de aire, *f.* **air vice-marshal,** general de división de aviación, *m*

air *vt* airear, orear; secar al aire; ventilar; *fig* sacar a lucir, emitir; *fig* ostentar

aircraft *n* aparato, avión, *m.* **a. barrage,** cortina de fuego de artillería, *f.* **a.-carrier,** porta-aviones, *m.* **a. factory,** fábrica de aeroplanos, *f*

airing *n* aireación, *f;* ventilación, *f;* secamiento, *m;* (walk) vuelta, *f,* paseo, *m.* **to take an a.,** dar una vuelta

airplane *n* aeroplano, avión, *m.* **jet-propelled a.,** aeroplano de reacción, *m.* **model a.,** aeroplano en miniatura, *m*

airport *n* aeropuerto, *m*

airsick *a* mareado en el aire, mareado

airy *a* aéreo; (breezy) airoso; ligero; vaporoso; alegre; (vain) vano; (flippant) frívolo

aisle *n* nave lateral, ala, *f*

ajar *a* entreabierto, entornado. **to leave a.**, dejar entreabierto, entornar

akimbo *adv* en jarras. **with arms a.**, con los brazos en jarras

akin *a* consanguíneo, emparentado; análogo, relacionado; semejante

alarm *n* alarma, *f*, toque de alarma, *m*; (tocsin) rebato, *m*; sobresalto, *m*, alarma, *f*. *vt* alarmar; *mll* dar la alarma (a); asustar. **to give the a.**, dar la alarma. **a. bell**, timbre de alarma, *m*. **a. clock**, despertador, *m*. **a. signal**, señal de alarma, *f*

alarming *a* alarmante

alarmingly *adv* de un modo alarmante; espantosamente

alarmist *n* alarmista, *mf*

alas! *interj* ¡ay!

albeit *conjunc* aunque, si bien; sin embargo

album *n* álbum, *m*

albumin *n* albúmina, *f*

alcohol *n* alcohol, *m*. **industrial a.**, alcohol desnaturalizado, *m*. **wood a.**, alcohol metílico, alcohol de madera, *m*

alcoholic *a* alcohólico

alcove *n* alcoba, *f*; nicho, *m*

alderman *n* concejal, *m*

ale *n* cerveza, *f*. **ale-house**, cervecería, *f*

alert *a* alerto; vigilante; despierto; vivo. *n* sirena, *f*. **to be on the a.**, estar sobre aviso; estar vigilante

alertly *adv* alertamente

alertness *n* vigilancia, *f*; viveza, *f*; prontitud, *f*

algebra *n* álgebra, *f*

algebraic *a* algebraico

Algeria Argelia, *f*

Algerian *a* and *n* argelino (-na)

alias *adv* alias, por otro nombre. *n* nombre falso, seudónimo, *m*

alibi *n* law coartada, *f*. **to prove an a.**, probar la coartada

alien *a* ajeno; (foreign) extranjero; extraño; contrario. *n* extranjero (-ra). **a. to**, ajeno a; repugnante a. **Aliens Department**, Sección de Extranjeros, *f*

alienable *a* enajenable

alienate *vt* alejar, hacer indiferente; (property) enajenar, traspasar

alienation *n* desvío, *m*; enajenación, *f*; traspaso, *m*; enajenación mental, *f*

alight *vi* apearse (de), bajar (de); desmontar (de); (of birds, etc.) posarse (sobre)

alight *a* encendido, iluminado; en llamas

align *vt* alinear

alignment *n* alineación, *f*

alike *a* semejante; igual. *adv* del mismo modo; igualmente

alimentary *a* nutritivo; alimenticio. **a. canal**, tubo digestivo, *m*

alimony *n* law alimentos, *m pl*, pensión alimenticia, *f*

alive *a* viviente; vivo; del mundo; (busy) animado, concurrido; (aware) sensible; (alert) lleno de vida, enérgico, despierto. **He is still a.**, Aún vive. **He is the best man a.**, Es el mejor hombre que existe, Es el mejor hombre del mundo. **half-a.**, semivivo. **while a.**, en vida. **a. to**, consciente de, sensible de. **a. with**, plagado de, lleno de

all *a* todo, *m*; toda, *f*; todos, *m pl*; todas, *f pl*; (in games) iguales. *adv* enteramente, completamente; del todo; absolutamente; después de todo; sin embargo. **at all**, nada; de ninguna manera; en absoluto. **fifteen all**, (tennis) quince iguales. **for good and all**, para siempre. **if that's all**, si no es más que eso. **in all**, en conjunto. **It is all one to me**, Me da igual. **not at all**, de ningún modo, nada de eso; nada; (never) jamás; (as a polite formula) No hay de qué. **once for all**, una vez por todas; por última vez. **That is all**, Eso es todo. **all along**, (of time) siempre, todo el tiempo; (of place) a lo largo de, de un extremo a otro de. **all but**, (almost) casi, por poco; (except) todo menos. **all joking aside**, fuera de burla. **all of them**, todos ellos, *m pl*; todas ellas, *f pl*. **All right!** ¡Bien! ¡Está bien! ¡Entendido! **all that**, todo eso; (as much as) cuanto. **all that which**, todo lo que. **all those who**, todos los que, *m pl*; todas las que, *f pl*. **all the more**, cuanto más. **all the same**, sin embargo, a pesar de todo. **all the worse**, tanto peor

all *n* todo, *m*; todas, *f pl*; (everyone, all men) todo el mundo. **to lose one's all**, perder todo lo que se tiene. **All is lost**, Todo se ha perdido. **all told**, en conjunto

all (in compounds) **all-absorbing**, que todo lo absorbe; sumamente interesante. **all-bountiful**, de suma bondad. **all-conquering**, invicto. **all-consuming**, que todo lo consume; irresistible; ardiente. **all-enduring**, resignado a todo. **All Fools' Day**, Día de los Inocentes, *m*, (December 28). **all-fours**, a cuatro patas; a gatas. **to go on all fours**, andar a gatas. **All hail!** ¡Salud! ¡Bienvenido! **all-important**, sumamente importante. **all-in insurance**, seguro contra todo riesgo, *m*. **all-in wrestling**, lucha libre, *f*. **all-loving**, de un amor infinito. **all-merciful**, de una compasión infinita, sumamente misericordioso. **all-powerful**, omnipotente, todo poderoso. **all-round**, completo, cabal; universal. **an all-round athlete**, un atleta completo. **All Souls' Day**, Día de las Ánimas, Día de los difuntos, *m*. **all-wise**, omniscio

allay vt calmar; (relieve) aliviar; apaciguar

allegation n alegación, f

allege vt afirmar, declarar; alegar

allegiance n lealtad, f; fidelidad, f; obediencia, f

alleluia n aleluya, mf

allergic a alérgico

allergist n alergólogo, m

allergy n alergia, f

alleviate vt aliviar

alleviation n alivio, m; mitigación, f

alley n callejuela, f, callejón, m; avenida, f; (skittle a.) pista de bolos, f. **a.-way**, naut pasadizo, m

alliance n alianza, f; parentesco, m

allied a aliado; allegado

alligator n caimán, m. **a. pear**, avocado, Mexico aguacate m

allocate vt asignar, destinar; distribuir, repartir

allocation n asignación, f; distribución, f, repartimiento, m

allotment n repartimiento, m, distribución, f; porción, f; lote, m; parcela de tierra, huerta, f

allow vt permitir; autorizar; dejar; tolerar, sufrir; (provide) dar; conceder, otorgar; (acknowledge) admitir; confesar; (discount) descontar; (a pension) hacer; deducir. **to a. for**, tener en cuenta; ser indulgente con; deducir; dejar (espacio, etc.) para

allowable a admisible, permisible; lícito, legítimo

allowance n ración, f; (discount) descuento, m; pensión, f; concesión, f; excusa, f; (subsidy) subsidio, m; (bonus) abono, m; (monthly) mesada, f. **to make a. for**, tener presente; hacer excusas para, ser indulgente con

alloy n aleación, f; liga, f; mezcla, f. vt alear, ligar; mezclar

all-star game n juego de estrellas, m

allude vi aludir (a), referirse (a)

allure vt convidar, provocar; atraer; seducir, fascinar

allurement n (snare) añagaza, f; atracción, f; tentación, seducción, f

alluring a atractivo, seductor, tentador; (promising) halagüeño

allusion n alusión, referencia, f; insinuación, f

ally n aliado (-da), allegado (-da); asociado (-da); (state) aliado, m. vt unir. **to become allies**, aliarse

almanac n almanaque, m

almighty a omnipotente

almond n almendra, f; (tree) almendro, m. **bitter a.**, almendra amarga, f. **green a.**, almendruco, m. **milk of almonds**, horchata de almendras, f; (for the hands) loción de almendras, f. **sugar a.**, almendra garapiñada, f. **a.-eyed**, con, or de, ojos rasgados. **a. paste**, pasta de almendras, f. **a.-shaped**, en forma de almendra, almendrado

almoner n limosnero (-ra) mf

almost adv casi; por poco

alms n limosna, f. **to ask a.**, pedir limosna, mendigar. **to give a.**, dar limosna. **a.-box**, cepillo de limosna, m

almsgiving n caridad, f

aloft adv arriba, en alto

alone a solo; solitario. adv a solas, sin compañía; solamente; únicamente. **to leave a.**, dejar solo; dejar en paz

along adv adelante; a lo largo; todo el tiempo. prep a lo largo de; por; al lado (de); en compañía (de). **Come a.!** ¡Ven! **all a.**, todo el tiempo, desde el principio; a lo largo de. **a. with**, junto con; en compañía de

alongside adv al lado; naut al costado. prep junto a, al lado de; naut al costado de. **to bring a.**, naut abarloar. **to come a.**, naut acostarse

aloof adv a distancia; lejos. a altanero, esquivo; reservado. **to keep a.**, mantenerse alejado

aloud adv en alta voz, alto

alpaca n alpaca, f

alphabet n alfabeto, m; abecedario, m

alphabetical a alfabético

Alps, the los Alpes, m

already adv ya; previamente

also adv también, igualmente, además

altar n altar, m. **high a.**, altar mayor, m. **to lead a woman to the a.**, llevar a una mujer a la iglesia. **a.-cloth**, mantel del altar, m. **a.-piece**, retablo, m. **a.-rail**, mesa del altar, f

altar boy n acólito, monaguillo, m

altar girl n acólita, monaguilla, f

altar server n acólito, monaguillo, m (male), acólita, monaguilla, f (female)

alter vt cambiar; alterar; modificar; corregir; transformar; (clothes) arreglar. vi cambiar

alteration n cambio, m, alteración, f; modificación, f; corrección, f; innovación, f; (to buildings, etc.) reforma, f; renovación, f; arreglo, m

alternate a alternativo; (bot and of rhymes) alterno. vt and vi alternar

alternating a alternador. **a. current**, elec corriente alterna, f

alternation n alternación, f; (of time) transcurso, m; turno, m

alternative n alternativa, f, a alternativo, alterno. **to have no a. but**, no poder menos de

alternator n elec alternador, m

although conjunc aunque, bien que; si bien; no obstante, a pesar de

altitude n altitud, elevación, f; altura, f

alto n (voice) contralto, m; (singer) contralto, mf; viola, f

altogether adv completamente; del todo; en conjunto

alto-relievo n alto relieve, m

altruism n altruísmo, m

altruist n altruista, mf

aluminum n aluminio, m

aluminum foil n hoja de aluminio, f

alumnus n Lat. Am. exalumno m.

alumna n Lat. Am. exalumna f

always adv siempre

amalgam n amalgama, f; mezcla, f

amalgamate vt amalgamar; combinar, unir. vi amalgamarse; combinarse, unirse

amalgamation n amalgamación, f; combinación, f; mezcla, f

amass vt acumular, amontonar

amateur a and n aficionado (-da), (sports) no profesional. **a. theatricals,** función de aficionados, f **a. band** Mexico escoleta f

amateurish a no profesional; de aficionado; superficial; (clumsy) torpe

amaze vt asombrar, sorprender; pasmar; confundir

amazed a asombrado; sorprendido; admirado; asustado

amazement n asombro, pasmo, m; sorpresa, f; (wonderment) admiración, f; estupor, m

amazing a asombroso, pasmoso; sorprendente

amazingly adv asombrosamente

Amazon River, the el (Río de las) Amazonas, m

ambassador n embajador, m

ambassadress n embajadora, f

amber n ámbar, m, a ambarino

ambidextrous a ambidextro

ambiguity n ambigüedad, f

ambiguous a ambiguo, equívoco

ambition n ambición, f

ambitious a ambicioso. **to be a. to,** ambicionar

amble n (of a horse) paso de andadura, m; paso lento, m. vi (of a horse) andar a paso de andadura; andar lentamente

ambulance n ambulancia, f. **a. corps,** cuerpo de sanidad, m. **a. man,** sanitario, m

ambulatory n paseo, m; claustro, m, a ambulante

ambush n acecho, m, asechanza, f; mil emboscada, f. vt acechar, asechar; mil emboscar; sorprender. **to be in a.,** emboscarse, estar en acecho

amelioration n mejora, f

amen n amén, m

amenable a sujeto (a); responsable; dócil; fácil de convencer, dispuesto a ser razonable; dispuesto a escuchar. **to make a. to reason,** hacer razonable

amend vt enmendar; modificar. vi reformarse

amendment n enmienda, f; modificación, f

amends n pl reparación, f; satisfacción, f; compensación, f. **to make a.,** dar satisfacción

amenity n amenidad, f

America América, f

American n americano (-na); (U.S.A.) norteamericano (-na). a americano, de América; norteamericano, de los Estados Unidos. **Central A.,** a and n centroamericano (-na). **A. bar,** bar americano, m

Americanize vt americanizar

amethyst n amatista, f

amiability n amabilidad, afabilidad, cordialidad, f

amiable a amable, afable, cordial

amiably adv amablemente, con afabilidad

amicable a amigable, amistoso

amid, amidst prep en medio de; entre; rodeado por

amidships adv en el centro del buque, en medio del navío

amiss adv mal; de más; (ill) indispuesto, enfermo; (inopportunely) inoportunamente, a malo. **It would not come a.,** No vendría mal. **to take a.,** llevar a mal

ammeter n elec amperímetro, m

ammonia n amoníaco, m

ammunition n munición, f. **a. box,** cajón de municiones, m

amnesia n amnesia, f

amnesty n amnistía, f. **to concede an a. to,** amnistiar

amok (to run a.) atacar a ciegas

among prep en medio de; entre; con

amoral a amoral

amorality n amoralidad, f

amorous a amoroso; (tender) tierno

amorousness n erotismo, m; galantería, f

amorphous a amorfo

amortization n amorcización, f

amortize vt amortizar

amount n importe, m, suma, f; cantidad, f, vi (to) subir a, ascender a, llegar a; valer; reducirse a. **gross a.,** importe bruto, m. **net a.,** importe líquido, importe neto, m. **It amounts to the same thing, then,** Es igual entonces, Viene a ser lo mismo pues. **What he says amounts to this,** Lo que dice se reduce a esto

ampere n amper, amperio, m

amphibian n anfibio, m

amphibious a anfibio

amphitheater n anfiteatro, m

amphora n ánfora, f

ample a amplio; abundante; extenso, vasto; (sufficient) bastante, suficiente

amplification n amplificación, f

amplifier n amplificador, m

amplify vt amplificar; aumentar, ampliar

amplitude n amplitud, f; abundancia, f; extensión, f

amply adv ampliamente; abundantemente; suficientemente

amputate vt amputar

amputation n amputación, f

amulet n amuleto, m

amuse vt divertir, entretener, distraer. **to a. oneself**, divertirse; pasarlo bien

amusement n diversión, f, entretenimiento, m; (hobby) pasatiempo, m. **a. park**, parque de atracciones, m

amusing a divertido, entretenido; (of people) salado

amusingly adv de un modo divertido, entretenidamente

an. See **a**.

anachronism n anacronismo, m

anachronistic a anacrónico

anagram n anagrama, m

analgesia n analgesia, f

analgesic a and n analgésico, m.

analogous a análogo

analogy n analogía, f

analyse vt analizar

analysis n análisis, m

analyst n analista, mf

analytical a analítico

anaphrodisiac a anafrodisíaco

anarchic a anárquico

anarchism n anarquismo, m

anarchist n anarquista, mf

anarchy n anarquía, f

anastigmatic a anastigmático

anathema n anatema, mf

anatomically adv anatómicamente; físicamente

anatomist n anatomista, mf

anatomy n anatomía, f

ancestor n antepasado, abuelo, m

ancestral a de sus antepasados; de familia; hereditario. **a. home**, casa solariega, f

ancestry n antepasados, m pl; linaje, abolengo, m; estirpe, f; nacimiento, m; origen, m

anchor n ancla, f. fig áncora, f. vt sujetar con el ancla. vi anclar, echar anclas, fondear. **at a.**, al ancla. **drag a.**, ancla flotante, ancla de arrastre, f. **sheet a.**, ancla de la esperanza, f; fig ancla de salvación, f. **to drop a.**, anclar. **to ride at a.**, estar al ancla. **to weigh a.**, levar el ancla

anchorage n anclaje, m; ancladero, fondeadero, m; derechos de anclaje, m pl

anchovy n anchoa, f, boquerón, m

ancient a anciano; antiguo. n pl an-

cients, los antiguos. **from a. times**, de antiguo. **most a.**, antiquísimo

and conjunc y; (before stressed i or hi) e; (after some verbs and before infin.) de, a; que; (with) con; (often not translated before infins.). **Better and better**, Mejor que mejor. **I shall try and do it**, Trataré de hacerlo. **to come and see**, venir a ver. **We shall try and speak to him**, Procuraremos hablar con él

Andalusia Andalucía, f

Andalusian a andaluz. n andaluz (-za). **A. hat**, sombrero calañés, m

Andean a andino (-na), Argentina, Chile also corderillano (-na)

Andes, the los Andes, f

andiron n morillo, m

Andorran a and n andorrano (-na)

anecdote n anécdota, f

anemia n anemia, f

anemic a anémico

anesthesia n anestesia, f

anesthetic a and n anestésico, m.

anesthetist n anestesiador (-ra)

anesthetize vt anestesiar

aneurism n aneurisma, mf

angel n ángel, m

angelic a angélico

anger n cólera, ira, f, enojo, m, vt enojar, encolerizar; hacer rabiar, Mexico amuinar

angina n angina, f. **a. pectoris**, angina de pecho, f

angle n ángulo, m; rincón, m; esquina, f; (of a roof) caballette, m; fig punto de vista, m, vi pescar con caña. **at an a.**, a un lado. **a.-iron**, hierro angular, m. **to a. for**, pescar; fig procurar obtener

Angle a and n anglo (-la)

angler n pescador (-ra) de caña

Anglican a and n anglicano (-na)

Anglicism n anglicismo, inglesismo, m

angling n pesca con caña, f

Anglo- (in compounds) **anglo-**. **A.-American**, a and n angloamericano (-na). **A.-Indian**, a and n angloindio (-ia). **A.-Saxon**, a and n anglosajón (-ona); (language) anglosajón, m

angora n angora, f. **a. cat**, gato de angora, m. **a. rabbit**, conejo de angora, m

angrily adv airadamente

angry a (of persons) enfadado, enojado, airado; (of waves, etc.) furioso; med inflamado; (red) rojo; (scowling) cenudo; (dark) obscuro. **to be a.**, estar enojado. **to get angry, to grow a.**, enojarse, enfadarse, Lat. Am. entromparse; (of waves) encresparse; (of the sky) obscurecerse. **to make a.**, enojar

anguish n agonía, f, dolor, m; angustia, f. vt angustiar

angular a angular; (of features, etc.) anguloso

animal a and n animal m. **a. fat**, grasa animal, f. **a. kingdom**, reino animal, m.

a. spirits, *phil* espíritus animales, *m pl;* brío, *m,* energía, *f*

animate *vt* animar; inspirar. **a** animado; viviente

animated a animado; vivo, lleno de vida

animation *n* animación, *f;* vivacidad, *f;* calor, fuego, *m*

animosity *n* animosidad, hostilidad, *f*

aniseed *n* anís, *m*

anisette *n* (liqueur) anisete, *m*

ankle *n* tobillo, *m.* **a. bone,** hueso del tobillo, *m.* **a. sock,** calcetín corto, *m*

anklet *n* brazalete para el tobillo, *m;* (support) tobillera, *f*

annals *n pl* anales, *m pl*

annex *vt* unir, juntar; anexar. *n* anexo, *m*

annexation *n* anexión, *f*

annihilate *vt* aniquilar

annihilation *n* aniquilación,

anniversary a and *n* aniversario, *m.*

annotate *vt* anotar, acotar, comentar, hacer anotaciones a

annotation *n* anotación, *f;* nota, *f*

annotator *n* anotador (-ra), comentador (-ra)

announce *vt* proclamar; declarar; publicar; anunciar

announcement *n* proclama, *f;* declaración, *f;* publicación, *f;* anuncio, *m;* (of a betrothal) participación, *f*

announcer *n* anunciador (-ra); (radio or TV) locutor (-ra)

annoy *vt* exasperar, irritar, disgustar; molestar, incomodar, *Lat. Am.* acatarrar, cargosear, engorrar

annoyance *n* disgusto, *m,* exasperación, *f;* molestia, *f,* fastidio, *m*

annoying a enojoso, molesto, fastidioso, *Lat. Am.* cargoso

annual a anual. *n* anuario, *m;* calendario, *m;* planta anual, *f*

annually *adv* anualmente, cada año

annuity *n* anualidad, pensión vitalicia, *f*

annul *vt* anular

annulment *n* anulación, *f*

annunciation *n* anunciación, *f.* **the A.,** la Anunciación

anoint *vt* untar; (before death) olear; (a king, etc.) ungir

anointing *n* unción, *f*

anomalous a anómalo

anomaly *n* anomalía, *f*

anonymity *n* anónimo, *m*

anonymous a anónimo. **a. letter,** anónimo, *m*

another a otro; (different) distinto. *n* otro, *m;* otra, *f.* **For one thing . . . and for a.,** En primer lugar . . . y además (y por otra cosa). **one after a.,** uno después de otro. **They love one a.,** Ellos se aman. **They sent it from one to a.,** Lo mandaron de uno a otro

answer *n* contestación, respuesta, *f;* (refutation) refutación, *f;* (pert reply) réplica, *f;* (solution) solución, *f; math* resultado, *m; law* contestación a la demanda, *f*

answer *vt* responder, contestar; (a letter, etc.) contestar a; (refute) refutar; (reply pertly) replicar; (write) escribir; (return) devolver; (suit) servir; (a bell, etc.) acudir a; (the door) abrir. *vi* contestar; (succeed) tener éxito; dar resultado. **to a. by return,** contestar a vuelta de correo, **to a. back,** replicar. **to a. for,** ser responsable por; ser responsable de; (speak for) hablar por; (guarantee) garantizar, responder de

answerable a responsable; refutable; (adequate) adecuado. **to make a. for,** hacer responsable de

answering machine *n* contestador telefónico, contestador, *m*

ant *n* hormiga, *f.* **ant-eater,** oso hormiguero, *m.* **ant-hill,** hormiguero, *m*

antagonism *n* antagonismo, *m,* hostilidad, oposición, *f*

antagonist *n* antagonista, *mf*

antagonistic a antagónico, hostil

antagonize *vt* contender; hacer hostil (a)

antarctic a antártico, *n* polo antártico, *m*

antecedent a and *n* antecedente, *m.*

antedate *vt* antedatar; anticipar

antelope *n* antílope, *m*

antenna *n* antena, *f*

anterior a anterior

anthem *n* antífona, *f*

anthology *n* antología, floresta, *f*

anthracite *n* antracita, *f,* carbón mineral, *m*

anthropologist *n* antropólogo, *m*

anthropology *n* antropología, *f*

anti-aircraft a antiaéreo. **A.A. gun,** cañón antiaéreo, *m*

antibody *n* anticuerpo, *m*

antic *n* travesura, *f*

anticipate *vt* (foresee) prever; anticipar; adelantarse a; (hope) esperar; (frustrate) frustrar; (enjoy) disfrutar con anticipación de

anticipation *n* anticipación, *f;* adelantamiento, *m;* esperanza, expectación, *f.* **in a. of,** en espera de

anticipatory a anticipador

anticlimax *n* anticlímax, *m*

antidote *n* antídoto, contraveneno, *m*

antifreeze *n* anticongelante, *m*

Antilles, the las Antillas, *f*

antimony *n* antimonio, *m*

antipathetic a antipático

antipathy *n* antipatía, *f*

antipode *n pl* antípodas, *mf pl*

antiquarian a anticuario

antiquary *n* anticuario, *m*

antiquated a anticuado

antique a antiguo. *n* antigüedad, antigualla, *f.* **a. dealer,** anticuario, *m.* **a. shop,** tienda de antigüedades, *f*

antiquity *n* antigüedad, *f*; ancianidad, *f*

anti-Semitic *a* antisemita

anti-Semitism *n* antisemitismo, *m*

antiseptic *a* and *n* antiséptico, *m*

antisocial *a* antisocial

antithesis *n* antítesis, *f*

antithetic *a* antitético

antitoxin *n* antitoxina, *f*

antler *n* asta, *f*

antrum *n* antro, *m*

Antwerp Amberes, *m*

anus *n* ano, *m*

anvil *n* yunque, *m*, bigornia, *f*

anxiety *n* inquietud, intranquilidad, *f*; preocupación, *f*; ansiedad, *f*; curiosidad, *f*; impaciencia, *f*; (wish) deseo, afán, *m*

anxious *a* inquieto, intranquilo; preocupado; ansioso; impaciente; deseoso. **to be a.,** estar inquieto; apurarse. **to be a. to,** ansiar, tener deseos de. **to make a.,** preocupar, inquietar, intranquilizar

anxiously *adv* con inquietud; ansiosamente; impacientemente

any *a* cualquiera; (before the noun only) cualquier; (some) algún, *m*; alguna, *f*; (every) todo; (expressing condition or with interrogatives or negatives, following the noun) alguno, *m*; alguna, *f*, (is often not translated in a partitive sense, e.g. **Have you any butter?** ¿Tienes mantequilla?) *pron* algo; (with the relevant noun) alguno, *m*, and *neut*; la, *pl*; los, *m pl*; las, *f pl*. **He hasn't any pity,** No tiene piedad alguna. **at any rate,** de todos modos; por lo menos. **If there is any,** Si lo (la, etc.) hay. **in any case,** venga lo que venga. **not any,** ninguno, *m*; ninguna, *f*. **Whether any of them . . . ,** Si alguno de ellos . . . **any further,** más lejos. **any longer,** más largo; (of time) más tiempo. **any more,** nada más; nunca más

anybody *n* and *pron* (someone) alguien; cualquiera, *mf*; (everyone) todo el mundo; (with a negative) nadie; (of importance) persona de importancia, *f*. **hardly a.,** casi nadie

anyhow *adv* de cualquier modo; (with a negative) de ningún modo; de cualquier manera; (at least) por lo menos, en todo caso; (carelessly) sin cuidado

anyone *n*. See **anybody**

anything *n* algo, *m*, alguna cosa, *f*; (negative) nada; cualquier cosa, *f*; todo (lo que). **a. but,** todo menos

anyway *adv* de todos modos, con todo; venga lo que venga; (anyhow) de cualquier modo

anywhere *adv* en todas partes, dondequiera; en cualquier parte; (after a negative) en (or a) ninguna parte

aorta *n* aorta, *f*

apart *adv* aparte; a un lado; separadamente; separado (de); apartado (de). **a. from,** aparte de, dejando a un lado. **to keep a.,** mantener aislado; distinguir (entre). **to take a.,** desarmar. **wide a.,** muy distante

apartment *n* cuarto, *m*, habitación, *f*; (flat) piso, *Argentina* departamento, *elsewhere in Lat. Am.* apartamento *m*

apathetic *a* apático; indiferente

apathy *n* apatía, *f*; indiferencia, *f*

ape *n* simio, *m*

aperture *n* abertura, *f*; agujero, *m*; orificio, *m*

apiece *adv* cada uno; por persona

apish *a* simiesco, de simio; (affected) afectado; (foolish) tonto

aplomb *n* confianza en sí, *f*, aplomo, *m*

apocalyptic *a* apocalíptico

Apocrypha *n* libros apócrifos, *m pl*

apocryphal *a* apócrifo

apologetic *a* apologético

apologize *vi* presentar sus excusas; disculparse, excusarse; (regret) sentir

apology *n* excusa, disculpa, *f*; defensa, apología, *f*; (makeshift) substituto, *m*

apoplexy *n* apoplegía, *f*

apostasy *n* apostasía, *f*

apostate *n* apóstata, *mf*, renegado (-da)

apostle *n* apóstol, *m*. **Apostles' Creed,** el Credo de los Apóstoles

apostolic *a* apostólico

apostrophe *n* apóstrofe, *mf*; (punctuation mark) apóstrofo, *m*

Apothecaries' weight peso de boticario, *m*

apothegm *n* apotegma, *m*

appal *vt* horrorizar, espantar, aterrar

appalling *a* espantoso, horrible

apparatus *n* aparato, *m*; máquina, *f*; instrumentos, *m pl*

apparel *n* ropa, *f*; vestiduras, *f pl*; ornamento, *m*. *vt* vestir

apparent *a* aparente; visible; evidente; manifiesto; (of heirs) presunto. **to become a.,** manifestarse

apparently *adv* al parecer, aparentemente

apparition *n* aparición, *f*, fantasma, espectro, *m*

appeal *n* súplica, *f*; llamamiento, *m*; (charm) atracción, *f*, encanto, *m*; *law* apelación, alzada, *f*. *vi* (to) suplicar (a); hacer llamamiento (a); poner por testigo (a); recurrir a; llamar la atención de; interesar (a); (attract) atraer, encantar; *law* apelar. **It doesn't a. to him,** No le atrae, No le gusta. **to allow an a.,** revocar una sentencia apelada. **without a.,** inapelable

appealing *a* suplicante; atrayente

appealingly *adv* de un modo suplicante

appear *vi* (of persons and things) aparecer; (seem) parecer; (before a judge) comparecer, presentarse (ante el juez); (of books) publicarse; (of lawyers) representar; (of the dawn) rayar; (of the sun, etc.) salir; (show itself) manifestarse. **to cause to a.,** hacer presentarse; (show) hacer ver; (prove) demostrar, probar

appearance *n* aparición, *f*; (show, semblance or look, aspect) apariencia, *f*; presencia, *f*; aspecto, *m*; (in court of law) comparecencia, *f*; (of a book) publicación, *f*; (arrival) llegada, *f*; (view) perspectiva, *f*; (ghost) aparición, *f*, fantasma, *m*. **first a.,** (of an actor, etc.) debút, *m*; (of a play) estreno, *m*. **to all appearances,** según las apariencias. **to make one's first a.,** aparecer por primera vez; *theat* debutar. **Appearances are deceptive,** Las apariencias engañan

appease *vt* apaciguar, aplacar, pacificar; satisfacer

appeasement *n* apaciguamiento, aplacamiento, *m*; pacificación, *f*; satisfacción, *f*

appellant *a* and *n law* apelante, *mf*

appellation *n* nombre, *m*; título, *m*

append *vt* añadir; (a seal) poner; (enclose) incluir, anexar

appendage *n* accesorio, *m*; (*bot zool*) apéndice, *m*

appendicitis *n* apendicitis, *f*

appendix *n* apéndice, *m*

appetite *n* apetito, *m*; *fig* hambre, *f*; deseo, *m*. **to have a bad a.,** no tener apetito, estar desganado. **to have a good a.,** tener buen apetito. **to whet the a.,** abrir el apetito

appetizer *n* aperitivo, *Argentina* ingrediente *m*

appetizing *a* apetitoso

applaud *vt* and *vi* aplaudir; aclamar, ovacionar; celebrar

applause *n* aplauso, *m*; ovación, *f*; aprobación, alabanza, *f*

apple *n* manzana, *f*. **the a. of one's eye,** la niña de los ojos. **a. orchard,** manzanar, *m*. **a. sauce,** compota de manzanas, *f*. **a. tart,** pastel de manzanas, *m*. **a. tree,** manzano, *m*

appliance *n* aparato, *m*; instrumento, *m*; utensilio, *m*; máquina, *f*

applicant *n* candidato, *m*; aspirante, *m*, solicitante, *mf*

application *n* aplicación, *f*; solicitud, *f*; petición, *f*; empleo, *m*. **on a.,** a solicitar

appliqué *a* aplicado. *n* aplicación, *f*

apply *vt* aplicar; (use) emplear; (place) poner; (give) dar; (the brakes) frenar; *vi* ser aplicable; ser a propósito; dirigirse (a); acudir (a); (for a post) proponerse para. **a. for,** solicitar, pedir; (a post) proponerse para. **a. for admission (to . . .),** solicitar el ingreso (en . . .). **a. oneself to,** ponerse a; dedicarse a, consagrarse a

appoint *vt* (prescribe) prescribir, ordenar; señalar; asignar; (furnish) amueblar; equipar; (create) crear, establecer; (to a post) nombrar, designar; (manage) gobernar; organizar. **at the appointed hour,** a la hora señalada. **well-appointed,** bien amueblado; bien equipado

appointive *a* por nombramiento

appointment *n* (assignation) cita, *f*; (to a post) nombramiento, *m*; (post, office) cargo, *m*; creación, *f*. **By Royal A.,** Proveedor de la Real Casa. **to make an a. with,** citar

apportion *vt* dividir; distribuir; prorratear; (taxes) derramar

apportionment *n* repartimiento, *m*, distribución, *f*; división, *f*; prorrateo, *m*

apposite *a* a propósito, pertinente, oportuno; justo

appraisal *n* valoración, valuación, *f*; estimación, *f*

appraise *vt* valorar, tasar; estimar

appreciable *a* apreciable, perceptible

appreciably *adv* sensiblemente

appreciate *vt* (understand) darse cuenta de, comprender; estimar; apreciar; (distinguish) distinguir. *vi* encarecer, aumentar en valor; (of shares) subir, estar en alza

appreciation *n* (understanding) comprensión, *f*; apreciación, *f*; (recognition, etc.) aprecio, reconocimiento, *m*; (in value) aumento (en valor), *m*; subida de precio, *f*

appreciatively *adv* con aprecio

apprehend *vt* aprehender, prender; comprender, aprehender; (fear) temer

apprehension *n* aprehensión, comprensión, *f*; (fear) aprensión, *f*; (seizure) aprehensión, presa, *f*

apprehensive *a* aprehensivo; (fearful) aprensivo

apprehensiveness *n* aprehensión, *f*; (fear) aprensión, *f*, temor, *m*

apprentice *n* aprendiz (-za). **to bind a.,** poner de aprendiz

apprenticeship *n* aprendizaje, *m*. **to serve an a.,** hacer el aprendizaje

apprise *vt* dar parte (de), informar (de)

approach *vt* acercarse a; aproximarse a; (pull, etc. nearer) acercar, aproximar; (resemble) parecerse a, ser semejante a; (speak to) hablar con; entablar negociaciones con. *vi* acercarse, aproximarse. *n* acercamiento, *m*; (arrival) llegada, *f*; aproximación, *f*; (of night, etc.) avance, *m*; (entrance) entrada, *f*; avenida, *f*; vía, *f*; (step) paso, *m*; (to a subject) punto de vista (sobre), concepto (de), *m*; (introduction) introducción, *f*; *pl* **approaches,** (environs) alrededores, *m pl*, inmediaciones, *f pl*; (seas) mares, *m pl*; (overtures) avances, *m pl*

approachable *a* accesible

approaching a venidero, próximo, cercano

approbation n asentimiento, m; aprobación, f

appropriate a apropiado; conveniente; vt adueñarse de, tomar posesión de, apropiar

appropriately adv propiamente; convenientemente; justamente

appropriateness n conveniencia, f; justicia, f

appropriation n apropiación, f; aplicación, f; empleo, m

approval n aprobación, f; consentimiento, m. **on a.,** a prueba

approve vt aprobar; confirmar; (sanction) autorizar, sancionar; ratificar; estar contento (de); (oneself) demostrarse. vi aprobar

approved a aprobado; bien visto; (on documents) Visto Bueno (V° B°)

approximate a aproximado. vt acercar. vi aproximarse (a)

approximately adv aproximadamente, poco más o menos

approximation n aproximación, f

apricot n albaricoque, m. **a. tree,** albaricoquero, m

April n abril, m, a abrileño. **A. Fool's Day,** el 1° de abril; (in Spain) el Día de los Inocentes (December 28)

apron n delantal, m; (of artisans and freemasons) mandil, m. **to be tied to a mother's a.-strings,** estar cosido a las faldas de su madre. **a.-stage,** proscenio, m. **a.-string,** cinta del delantal, f

apse n ábside, mf

apt a apto, listo; propenso (a), inclinado (a); expuesto (a); (suitable) apropiado, oportuno

aptitude n aptitud, disposición, facilidad, f

aptly adv apropiadamente; justamente, bien

aquarelle n acuarela, f

aquarium n acuario, m

aquatic a acuático

aqueduct n acueducto, m

aqueous a ácueo, acuoso

aquiline a aguileño

Arab a árabe. n árabe, mf

arabesque n arabesco, m

Arabian a árabe, arábigo. **The A. Nights,** Las Mil y Una Noches

Arabic a arábigo. n (language) arábigo, árabe, m

arable a cultivable, labrantío

arbiter n árbitro (-ra), arbitrador (-ra)

arbitrariness n arbitrariedad, f

arbitrary a arbitrario

arbitrate vi arbitrar, juzgar como árbitro; someter al arbitraje

arbitration n arbitraje, m

arbitrator. See **arbiter**

arbour n glorieta, f, emparrado, m

arc n arco, m. **arc-light,** lámpara de arco, f

arcade n arcada, f; galería, f; pasaje, m

arch n arco, m; (vault) bóveda, f. vt abovedar; arquear; encorvar

arch a (roguish) socarrón; (coy) coquetón

arch- prefix archi-

archaic a arcaico

archangel n arcángel, m

archbishop n arzobispo, m

archenemy n mayor enemigo (-ga); Demonio, m

archeological a arqueológico

archeologist n arqueólogo, m

archeology n arqueología, f

archer n flechero, saltero, m; mil arquero, m

archery n ballestería, f

archery range n campo de tiro con arco, m

archipelago n archipiélago, m

architect n arquitecto, m

architectural n arquitectónico

architecture n arquitectura, f

archive n archivo, m

archivist n archivero, m

archness n coquetería, f; malicia, f

archway n arcada, f, pasaje abovedado, m; arco, m

arctic a ártico; muy frío. **A. Circle,** Círculo ártico, m

ardent a ardiente; apasionado, vehemente; fogoso

ardently adv ardientemente; con vehemencia, apasionadamente

ardor n ardor, m

arduous a arduo, difícil

are pl of present indicative of **be.** See **be.** **There are,** Hay

area n área, f; superficie, f; (extent) extensión, f; espacio, m; región, f; (of a house) patio, m; (of a concert hall, etc.) sala, f

area code n característica, f, (Chile) código territorial (Spain), prefijo (Spain), código interurbano, código (Argentina), m

arena n arena, f

Argentinian a and n argentino (-na)

argonaut n (zool and myth) argonauta, m

argot n jerga, f; (thieves') germanía, f

arguable a discutible

argue vt discutir; persuadir; (prove) demostrar. vi argüir, discutir; sostener. **to a. against,** hablar en contra de, oponer

arguing n razonamiento, m; argumentación, f; discusión, f

argument n argumento, m, Argentina arenga f

argumentative a argumentador; contencioso

arid a árido, seco

aridity n aridez, f

arise vi levantarse; (appear) surgir, aparecer; ofrecerse, presentarse; (of sound) hacerse oír; provenir (de); proceder (de); (result) hacerse sentir; (rebel) sublevarse

aristocracy n aristocracia, f

aristocrat n aristócrata, mf

aristocratic a aristocrático

arithmetic n aritmética, f

arithmetical a aritmético

ark n arca, f. **Noah's ark,** arca de Noé, f. **Ark of the Covenant,** arca de la alianza, f

arm n (anat geog mech of a chair, a cross, and flg) brazo, m; (lever) palanca, f; (of a tree) rama, f, brazo, m; (sleeve) manga, f; naut cabo de una verga, m; (weapon) arma, f; (of army, navy, etc.) ramo, m pl. **arms,** her armas, f pl, escudo, m. **in arms,** en brazos; armado; en oposición. **To arms!** ¡A las armas! **to keep at arm's length,** guardar las distancias; tratar fríamente. **to lay down arms,** rendir las armas. **to present arms,** presentar las armas. **to receive with open arms,** recibir con los brazos abiertos. **to take up arms,** alzarse en armas, empuñar las armas. **under arms,** sobre las armas. **with folded arms,** con los brazos cruzados. **arm in arm,** del bracete, de bracero. **arm of the sea,** brazo de mar, m. **arm-rest,** brazo, m

arm vt armar; proveer (de); (flg fortify) fortificar. vi armarse

armada n armada, f

armament n armamento, m

armchair n sillón, m, silla poltrona, f

armed a armado

armful n brazado, m

armistice n armisticio, m

armor n armadura, f; (for ships, etc.) blindaje, m. vt blindar, acorazar. **(to) a.-plate,** vt blindar. n coraza, plancha blindada, f

armored a blindado, acorazado. **a. car,** carro blindado, m. **a. cruiser,** crucero acorazado, m

armory n armería, f

army n ejército, m; multitud, muchedumbre, f. **to be in the a.,** ser del ejército. **to go into the a.,** alistarse. **a. corps,** cuerpo del ejército, m. **a. estimates,** presupuesto del ejército, m. **a. list,** escalafón del ejército, m. **A. Medical Corps,** Sanidad Militar, f. **A. Supply Corps,** Cuerpo de Intendencia, m

aroma n aroma, m

aromatic a aromático

around prep alrededor de; por todas partes de; cerca de; (with words like corner) a la vuelta de. adv alrededor; a la redonda, en torno; por todas partes; de un lado para otro

arouse vt despertar; excitar. **a. (someone's) suspicions,** despertar las sospechas (de fulano)

arraign vt acusar; law procesar

arraignment n acusación, f; law procesamiento, m

arrange vt arreglar; acomodar; poner en orden, clasificar, Lat. Am. acotejar; (place) colocar; (order) ordenar, disponer; (contrive) agenciar; organizar; preparar; mus adaptar; (of differences) concertar, ajustar. vi convenir, concertarse; arreglar; hacer preparativos

arrangement n arreglo, m; clasificación, f; disposición, f; (agreement) acuerdo, m; mus adaptación, f; pl **arrangements,** preparativos, m pl

array n (of troops) orden de batalla, mf; formación, f; colección, f; (dress) atavío, m, vt poner en orden de batalla; formar (las tropas, etc.); ataviar, adornar

arrears n pl atrasos, m pl. **in a.,** atrasado

arrest vt detener, impedir; (the attention) atraer; (capture) arrestar, prender; (judgment) suspender. n (stop) interrupción, parada, f; (hindrance) estorbo, m; (detention) arresto, m, detención, f; (of a judgment) suspensión, f. **under a.,** bajo arresto

arresting a que llama la atención, notable, muy interesante; asombroso, chocador

arrival n llegada, venida, f, advenimiento, m; naut arribada, f; entrada, f; el, m, (la, f), que llega. **on a.,** al llegar, a la llegada. **the new arrivals,** los recién llegados

arrive vi llegar; aparecer; (happen) suceder; naut arribar; entrar. **to a. at,** (a place or conclusion) llegar a

arrogance n arrogancia altivez, soberbia, f

arrogant a altivo, arrogante, soberbio

arrogate vt arrogar

arrow n saeta, flecha, f. **a.-head,** punta de flecha, f. **a.-shaped,** en forma de flecha, sagital. **a. wound,** flechazo, saetazo, m

arsenal n arsenal, m

arsenic n arsénico, m

arson n incendio premeditado, m

art n arte, mf; (cleverness) habilidad, f; (cunning) artificio, m. **Faculty of Arts,** Facultad de Letras, f. **fine arts,** bellas artes, f pl. **art exhibition,** exposición de pinturas, f. **art gallery,** museo de pinturas, m. **art school,** colegio de arte, m

arterial a arterial; (of roads) de primera clase. **a. forceps,** pinzas hemostáticas, f pl

artery n arteria, f

artful a hábil, ingenioso; (crafty) astuto

artfulness n habilidad, ingeniosidad, f; astucia, maña, f

arthritic a artrítico

arthritis n artritis, f

artichoke n alcachofa, f. **Jerusalem a.,** aguaturma, f

article n artículo, m; (object) objeto, m, cosa, f; pl **articles,** escritura, f; contrato, m; estatutos, m pl. vt escriturar; contratar. **leading a.,** artículo de fondo, m. **articles of apprenticeship,** contrato de aprendizaje, m. **articles of association,** estatutos de asociación, m pl. **articles of war,** código militar, m

articulate vt articular; pronunciar, articular. vi estar unido por articulación; articular. a articulado; claro; expresivo

articulation n articulación, f, (all meanings)

artifice n artificio, m; arte, m, or f, habilidad, f

artificial a artificial; falso, fingido; afectado. **a. flowers,** flores de mano, f pl. **a. silk,** seda artificial, seda vegetal, f

artificiality n artificialidad, f; falsedad, f; afectación, f

artillery n artillería, f. **field a.,** artillería volante (or ligera or montada), f. **a. practice,** ejercicio de cañón, m

artisan n artesano (-na)

artist n artista, mf; (painter) pintor (-ra)

artistic a artístico

artistry n habilidad artística, f, arte, mf

artless a natural; sencillo, cándido, inocente

artlessly adv con naturalidad; con inocencia

artlessness n naturalidad, f; sencillez, candidez, inocencia, f

as adv conjunc rel pron como; así como; (followed by infin.) de; (in comparisons) tan . . . como; (while) mientras, a medida que; (when) cuando, al (followed by infin.); (since) puesto que, visto que; (because) porque; (although) aunque; por; (according to) según; en; (in order that) para (que). **as a rule,** por regla general. **Once as he was walking,** Una vez mientras andaba. **as . . . as,** tan . . . como. **as far as,** hasta; en cuanto a. **as from,** desde. **as good as,** tan bueno como. **as if,** como si. **as it were,** por decirlo así, en cierto modo. **as many,** otros tantos (e.g. **six embassies in as many countries,** seis embajadas en otros tantos países). **as many as,** tanto . . . como; todos los que. **as soon as,** en cuanto, luego que, así que. **as soon as possible,** cuanto antes, Lat. Am. a la mayor brevedad posible. **as sure as can be,** sin duda alguna. **as to,** en cuanto a. **as usual,** como de costumbre. **as well,** también. **as well as,** (besides) además de; tan bien como. **as yet,** todavía.

asbestos n asbesto, amianto, m

ascend vt and vi subir; (on, in) subir a; ascender; (rise) elevarse; (a river) remontar. **to a. the stairs,** subir las escaleras.

to a. the pulpit, subir al púlpito. **to a. the throne,** subir al trono

ascendancy n ascendiente, influjo, m

ascendant n elevación, f. a ascendente; predominante. **to be in the a.,** fig ir en aumento; predominar

ascension n subida, ascension, f; (of the throne) advenimiento (al trono), m. **The A.,** La Ascensión

ascent n subida, f, ascenso, m; elevación, f; (slope) cuesta, pendiente, f

ascertain vt averiguar, descubrir

ascertainable a averiguable, descubrible

ascetic a ascético. n asceta, mf

ascribe vt atribuir, adscribir, imputar

aseptic a aséptico

ash n ceniza, f; cenizas, f pl; (tree and wood) fresno, m; pl **ashes,** cenizas, f pl; restos mortales, m pl. **mountain ash,** serbal, m. **ash-bin,** basurero, m. **ash-coloured,** ceniciento. **ash grove,** fresneda, f. **ashtray,** cenicero, m. **Ash Wednesday,** miércoles de ceniza, m

ashamed a avergonzado. **to be a. (of),** avergonzarse (de), (Mexico) apenarse (de). **to be a. of oneself,** avergonzarse, tener vergüenza de sí mismo

ashore adv a tierra; en tierra. **to go or put a.,** desembarcar

Asiatic a and n asiático (-ca)

aside adv a un lado; aparte. n theat aparte, m. **to set a.,** poner a un lado; (omit) dejar aparte; descontar; abandonar; (a judgment) anular. **to take a.,** llevar aparte

asinine a asnal

ask vt (a question; enquire) preguntar; (request; demand) pedir; (beg) rogar; (invite) invitar. **to ask a question,** hacer una pregunta. **to ask about,** preguntar acerca de. **to ask after,** preguntar por. **to ask down,** invitar a bajar; invitar a visitar (a alguien). **to ask for,** pedir; preguntar por. **ask for the moon,** pedir cotufas en el golfo. **to ask in,** invitar (a alguien) a entrar

askance adv al (or de) soslayo, de reojo; con recelo

askew adv oblicuamente; al lado; a un lado; sesgadamente

aslant prep a través de

asleep a and adv dormido. **to be a.,** estar dormido. **to fall a.,** dormirse

asparagus n espárrago, m. **a. bed,** esparraguera, f

aspect n aspecto, m; vista, f; apariencia, f, semblante, m. **to have a southern a.,** dar (mirar) al sur

asperity n aspereza, f

aspersion n ecc aspersión, f; calumnia, f; insinuación, f

asphalt n asfalto, m, vt asfaltar

asphyxia n asfixia, f

asphyxiate *vt* asfixiar

aspirant *n* aspirante, candidato, *m*

aspiration *n* aspiración, ambición, *f*; deseo, anhelo, *m*

aspire *vi* aspirar (a), pretender, ambicionar; alzarse

aspirin *n* aspirina, *f*

ass *n* asno, *m*

assail *vt* atacar, acometer, arremeter

assailant *n* asaltador (-ra)

assassin *n* asesino, *mf*

assassinate *vt* asesinar

assassination *n* asesinato, *m*

assault *n* asalto, *m*; acometida, embestida, *f*; *fig* ataque, *m*. *vt* asaltar; acometer, embestir; atacar. **to take by a.,** tomar por asalto

assemblage *n* reunión, *f*; (of a machine) montaje, *m*; (of people) muchedumbre, *f*, concurso, *m*; (of things) colección, *f*, grupo, *m*

assemble *vt* (persons) reunir, convocar; (things and persons) juntar; (a machine, etc.) armar, ensamblar. *vi* reunirse, congregarse; acudir

assembly *n* asamblea, *f*; reunión, *f*; *ecc* concilio, *m*. **a. line,** cadena de montaje, línea de montaje, *f*. **a. room,** sala de reuniones, *f*; sala de baile, *f*

assent *n* asentimiento, consentimiento, *m*; aprobación, *f*; (parliamentary, *law*) sanción, *f*. *vi* asentir (a), consentir (en); aprobar

assert *vt* mantener, defender; declarar, afirmar; hacer valer, reclamar. **to a. oneself,** imponerse, hacerse sentir; hacer valer sus derechos

assertion *n* aserción, afirmación, *f*; defensa, *f*; reclamación, *f*

assertive *a* afirmativo; dogmático

assess *vt* tasar, valorar; fijar, señalar; repartir (contribuciones, etc.)

assessment *n* tasación, *f*; fijación, *f*; repartimiento, *m*

assessor *n law* asesor (-ra); (of taxes) repartidor (-ra); (valuer) tasador, *m*. **public a.,** tasador, *m*

asset *n* ventaja, *f*; adquisición, *f*; cualidad, *f*; *pl* **assets,** fondos, *m pl*; *com* activo, *m*, créditos activos, *m pl*

assiduous *a* asiduo

assign *vt law* ceder; señalar, asignar; (appoint) destinar; fijar; atribuir, imputar. *n* cesionario (-ia)

assignation *n* asignación, *f*; cita, *f*; *law* cesión, *f*

assignment *n law* cesión, *f*; escritura de cesión, *f*; atribución, *f*; parte, porción, *f*

assimilate *vt* asimilar; incorporarse. *vi* mezclarse

assist *vt* ayudar; auxiliar, socorrer; (uphold) apoyar; (further) promover, fomentar. *vi* (be present) asistir (a)

assistance *n* ayuda, *f*; auxilio, socorro, *m*;

apoyo, *m*; (furtherance) fomento, *m*. **public a.,** asistencia pública, *f*

assistant *n* ayudante, *m*; *ecc* asistente, *m*; (in a shop) dependiente (-ta); colaborador (-ra); (university) auxiliar, *m*; sub-. **a. secretary,** subsecretario (-ia). **a. secretaryship,** subsecretaría, *f*

associate *n* asociado (-da); miembro, *m*; socio (-ia); compañero (-ra), amigo (-ga); colega, *m*; colaborador (-ra); (confederate) cómplice, *mf a* asociado; auxiliar. *vt* asociar; unir, juntar. **to a. oneself with,** asociarse con; asociarse a. **to a. with,** frecuentar la compañía de, ir con

association *n* asociación, *f*; unión, *f*; sociedad, *f*; compañía, corporación, *f*; (connection) relación, *f*. **a. football,** fútbol, *m*

assort *vt* clasificar; mezclar

assorted *a* surtido, mezclado. **They are a well-a. pair,** Son una pareja bien avenida

assortment *n* clasificación, *f*, arreglo, *m*; surtido, *m*, mezcla, *f*

assuage *vt* mitigar; suavizar; calmar; aliviar

assume *vt* asumir; tomar; apropiarse; (wear) revestir; (suppose) suponer; poner por caso

assumed *a* fingido, falso; supuesto

assumption *n* asunción, *f*; apropiación, arrogación, *f*; suposición, *f*. **Feast of the A.,** Fiesta de la Asunción, *f*

assurance *n* garantía, *f*; promesa, *f*; confianza, seguridad, *f*; (in a good sense) aplomo, *m*, naturalidad, *f*; (in a bad sense) presunción frescura, *f*, descaro, *m*; *com* seguro, *m*

assure *vt* asegurar

assured *a* asegurado; seguro

asterisk *n* asterisco, *m*

asthma *n* asma, *f*

asthmatic *a* asmático

astigmatic *a* astigmático

astir *adv* en movimiento; (out of bed) levantado; excitado

astonish *vt* sorprender, asombrar

astonished *a* atónito, estupefacto

astonishing *a* sorprendente, asómbroso

astonishment *n* asombro, *m*, sorpresa, estupefacción, *f*

astound *vt* aturdir, pasmar. **to be astounded,** *inf* quedarse muerto

astounding *a* asombroso

astray *adv* desviado, extraviado; por el mal camino. **to go a.,** errar el camino, perderse; *fig* descarriarse

astride *adv* a horcajadas. *prep* a horcajadas sobre; a ambos lados de

astringent *a* astringente

astrologer *n* astrólogo (-ga)

astrological *a* astrológico

astrology *n* astrología, *f*

astronaut *n* astronauta, *mf*

astronomer *n* astrónomo, *m*

astronomical a astronómico

astronomy n astronomía, f

astute a astuto, sagaz; (with knave, etc.) redomado, pícaro

astuteness n astucia, sagacidad, f

asunder adv en dos; separadamente; lejos uno de otro

asylum n asilo, m; (for the insane) manicomio, m

asymmetrical a asimétrico

asymmetry n asimetría, f

at prep n en casa de; en; de; con; por; (before) delante de. Sometimes forms part of verb, e.g. **to aim at**, apuntar. **to look at**, mirar. May be translated by using pres. part., e.g. **They were at play**, Estaban jugando. **at a bound**, de un salto. **at peace**, en paz. **at the doctor's**, en casa del médico. **at the crack of dawn**, al rayar el alba, al romper el alba. **at the head**, a la cabeza. **John is at Brighton**, Juan está en Brighton. **at the house of . . . , at . . .'s** en casa de, Lat. Am. also donde (e.g., **My cousin is at my grandmother's** Mi primo está en casa de mi abuela, Mi primo está donde mi abuela) **at first**, al principio. **at last**, por fin. **at no time**, jamás. **at once**, en seguida. **at most**, a lo más. **at one go** Lat. Am. de una leída. **at all events**, en todo caso. **What is he getting at?** ¿Qué quiere saber? **at home**, en casa. **at home day**, día de recibo, m

atheism n ateísmo, m

atheist n ateo (-ea)

atheistic a ateo

Athens Atenas, f

athlete n atleta, m

athletic a atlético

athletics n atletismo, m

Atlantic a and n atlántico m. **A. Charter**, Carta del Atlántico, f. **A. liner**, transatlántico, m

Atlantis Atlántida, f

atlas n atlas, m

atmosphere n aire, m; atmósfera, f; fig ambiente, m

atmospheric a atmosférico

atoll n atolón, m

atom n átomo, m. **splitting of the a.**, escisión del átomo, f

atomic a atómico. **a. bomb**, bomba atómica, f. **a. pile**, pila atómica, f. **a. theory**, teoría atómica, f

atomize vt pulverizar

atomizer n pulverizador, m

atone vi (for) expiar

atonement n expiación, f

atrocious a atroz; horrible

atrocity n atrocidad, f

atrophy n atrofia, f, vi atrofiarse

attach vt (law of goods) embargar; (law of persons) arrestar; (fix) fijar; (tie) atar; (join) juntar; (stick) pegar; (connect) co-

nectar; (hook) enganchar; (with a brooch, etc.) prender; (blame, etc.) imputar; (importance, etc.) dar, conceder; (assign) asignar; (attract) atraer; (enclose) adjuntar, incluir. vi pertenecer (a), ser indivisible (de). **to a. oneself to**, pegarse a; adherirse a, asociarse con; acompañar; hacerse inseparable de

attaché n agregado, m. **a. case**, maletín, m

attachment n (law of goods) embargo, m, vía ejecutiva, f; (law of persons) arresto, m; unión, f; conexión, f; (hooking) enganche, m; (with a brooch, etc.) prendimiento, m; (tying) atadura, f; (fixing) fijación, f; (affection) apego, cariño, m; (friendship) amistad, f

attack n ataque, m; mil ofensiva, f; (access) acceso, m. vt atacar

attacker n atacador (-ra), asaltador (-ra)

attain vt alcanzar, conseguir, lograr. vi llegar a; alcanzar

attainable a asequible, realizable; accesible

attainment n consecución, obtención, f; logro, m; pl **attainments**, prendas, dotes, f pl

attempt vt (try) procurar, tratar de, intentar; ensayar; querer; law hacer una tentativa (de), atentar. n tentativa, prueba, f; esfuerzo, ensayo, m; (criminal) atentado, m, tentativa, f

attend vi prestar atención (a); escuchar; (look after) cuidar (de); (serve) servir; (accompany) acompañar; (await) esperar. vt (be present) asistir (a); (of a doctor) visitar; (accompany) acompañar; (bring) acarrear, traer; (follow) seguir. **to be attended with**, traer consigo, acarrear

attendance n asistencia, presencia, f; (those present) público, m, concurrencia, f; servicio, m; (train) acompañamiento, m; med asistencia, f, tratamiento médico, m. **to be in a.**, acompañar (a)

attendant a que acompaña; que sigue; concomitante. n criado (-da); (keeper) guardián (-ana); (nurse) enfermero (-ra); (in a cloakroom) guardarropa, f; (in a theater) acomodador (-ra); (on a train) mozo, m; (waiter) camarero, m; (at baths) bañero (-ra)

attention n atención, f; cuidado, m. **A.!** ¡Atención!; mil ¡Firmes! **to pay a.**, prestar atención. **to stand to a.**, cuadrarse, permanecer en posición de firmes

attentive a atento; solícito; cortés, obsequioso

attentively adv con atención, atentamente; solícitamente

attentiveness n cuidado, m; cortesía, f

attenuate vt atenuar

attenuating a atenuante. **a. circumstance**, circunstancia atenuante, f

attest vt atestar. vi atestiguar, deponer, dar fe

attestation n atestación, deposición, f; (certificate) certificado, m, fe, f

attic n buhardilla, guardilla, f, desván, sotabanco, m

attire n atavío, m; (dress) traje, m; (finery) galas, f pl, vt ataviar, vestir; engalanar

attitude n actitud, f; postura, f; posición, f

attorney n (solicitor) abogado (-da); (agent) apoderado (-da); (public) procurador, m. **power of a.,** poderes, m pl procuración, f. **A.-general,** fiscal, m

attract vt atraer; (charm) seducir, cautivar, apetecer; (invite) convidar; (goodwill, etc.) captar

attraction n atracción, f; atractivo, aliciente, encanto, m

attractive a atrayente; atractivo, seductivo; apetecible; encantador

attributable a imputable, atribuible

attribute vt atribuir (a), achacar (a), imputar (a). n atributo, m

attribution n atribución, imputación, f; atributo, m

attrition n atrición, f

auburn a castaño, rojizo

auction n subasta, almoneda, f; venta pública, pública subasta, f, vt subastar. **to put up to a.,** sacar a pública subasta

auctioneer n subastador (-ra), Lat. Am. also licitador (-ra)

audacious a atrevido, audaz, osado, temerario; (shameless) descarado, impudente

audaciously adv osadamente; descaradamente

audacity n audacia, osadía, temeridad, f, atrevimiento, m; (shamelessness) descaro, m, desvergüenza, f

audible a audible, oíble

audibly adv en forma audible, perceptiblemente, en alta voz

audience n (interview and law) audiencia, f; oyentes, m pl, auditorio, público, m. **to give a.,** dar audiencia. **a. chamber,** sala de recepción, f

audit vt intervenir, examinar (cuentas). n intervención, f, ajuste de (cuentas), m

audition n audición, f

auditor n (hearer) oyente, mf; interventor, contador, m

auditorium n sala de espectáculos, f

aught n algo. **For a. I know,** Por lo que yo sepa

augment vt aumentar, acrecentar. vi aumentarse, acrecentarse

augmentation n aumento, acrecentamiento, m; añadidura, f

augur n agorero (-ra). vt and vi presagiar, anunciar; pronosticar, agorar

augury n predicción, f; agüero, presagio, pronóstico, m

August n agosto, m

aunt n tía, f. **great-a.,** tía abuela, f. **A. Sally,** el pim, pam, pum

aura n exhalación, f; influencia psíquica, f; med aura, f

auricle n (of the heart) aurícula, ala del corazón, f; oreja, f, pabellón de la oreja, m

auspicious a propicio, favorable, feliz

austere a severo, austero, adusto; ascético; (of style) desnudo

austerity n austeridad, severidad, f; ascetismo, m; (of style) desnudez, f

Australian a and n australiano (-na)

Austrian a and n austríaco (-ca)

authentic a auténtico

authenticate vt autenticar

authenticity n autenticidad, f

author n autor, m

authoritarian a autoritario

authoritative a autoritario

authority n autoridad, f; poder, m. **to have on the best a.,** tener de muy buena fuente

authorization n autorización, f

authorize vt autorizar

auto n =automobile

autobiographical a autobiográfico

autobiography n autobiografía, f

autocracy n autocracia, f

autocrat n autócrata, mf

autocratic a autocrático

autograph n autógrafo, m

automatic a automático. **a. gate,** (at level crossings, etc.) barrera de golpe, f. **a. machine,** máquina automática, f; inf tragaperras, m. **a. pencil,** lapicero, m

automobile n automóvil, coche, Lat. Am. carro m

autonomous a autónomo

autonomy n autonomía, f

autopsy n autopsia, f

autumn n otoño, m

autumnal a otoñal, de otoño

auxiliary a auxiliar. n auxiliador, m

avail vi servir; valer; importar. vt aprovechar. **to a. oneself of,** valerse de, aprovecharse de. **to no a.,** en balde

availability n utilidad, f; disponibilidad, f; provecho, m; (validity) validez, f

available a útil; disponible; aprovechable; válido

avalanche n alud, lurte, m

avarice n avaricia, f

avaricious a avaro, avaricioso

avenge vt vengar; vindicar. **to a. oneself for,** vengarse de

avenger n vengador (-ra)

avenging a vengador

avenue n avenida, f

aver vt afirmar, asegurar

average n promedio, término medio, m; (marine insurance) avería, f, a de promedio; típico; corriente; normal. *vt* hallar el término medio (de); prorratear, proporcionar; ser por término medio. **general a.,** (marine insurance) avería gruesa, *f.* **on the a.,** por término medio

averse *a* opuesto (a); desinclinado (a); enemigo (de); repugnante. **to be a. to,** no gustar de; oponerse a; estar desinclinado a; ser enemigo de; repugnar

aversion *n* aversión, *f*; repugnancia, *f*

avert *vt* apartar; (avoid) evitar

aviary *n* avería, pajarera, *f*

aviation *n* aviación, *f*

aviator *n* aviador (-ra)

avid *a* ávido

avocation *n* pasatiempo, *m*, distracción, *f*; ocupación, *f*; profesión, *f*

avoid *vt* evitar; (pursuit) evadir, eludir; guardarse (de), rehuir; *law* anular

avoidable *a* evitable, eludible

avow *vt* confesar; declarar

avowal *n* confesión, admisión, *f*

avowedly *adv* por confesión propia

await *vt* aguardar, esperar

awake *vt* despertar. *vi* despertarse. a despierto; vigilante; consciente (de); atento (a)

awakening *n* despertamiento, *m*

award *n* sentencia, decisión, *f*; adjudicación, *f*; (prize) premio, *m*. *vt* adjudicar; otorgar, conceder. **She was awarded a professorship in Greek,** Ganó unas oposiciones para una cátedra de griego

aware *a* consciente, sabedor. **to be well a. of,** saber muy bien. **to make a. of,** hacer saber

awash *adv* a flor de agua

away *adv* a distancia, a lo lejos, lejos; (absent) ausente; (out) fuera; (unceasingly) sin parar, continuamente; (wholly) completamente; (visibly) a ojos vistas. In verbs of motion a. is rendered by the reflexive, e.g. **to go a.,** marcharse. Sometimes not translated, e.g. **to take a.,** quitar. *interj* ¡fuera de aquí! ¡márchese Vd.!; ¡vámonos! ¡adelante! **nine miles a.,** a nueve millas de distancia. **a. in the distance,** allá a lo lejos. **She sang a.,** Ella seguía cantando

awe *n* temor reverente, *m*; horror, *m*; respeto, *m*; reverencia, *f*, *vt* intimidar, aterrar; infundir respeto (a). **to stand in awe of,** tener respeto (a), reverenciar

awesome *a* pavoroso, temible, aterrador; terrible; (august) augusto; (imposing) imponente

awestruck *a* espantado, aterrado

awful *a* terrible, pavoroso; horrible; temible; atroz; *inf* enorme. **How a.!** *inf* ¡Qué barbaridad!

awfully *adv* terriblemente; horriblemente; *inf* muy

awfulness *n* lo terrible; lo horrible; atrocidad, *f*; (of a crime, etc.) enormidad, *f*

awkward *a* difícil; peligroso; delicado; embarazoso; (of time, etc.) inconveniente, inoportuno; (of things) incómodo; (clumsy) torpe, desmañado; desagradable; (ungraceful) sin gracia. **the a. age,** la edad difícil

awkwardly *adv* torpemente; incómodamente; mal; con dificultad; sin gracia. **He is a. placed,** Se encuentra en una situación difícil

awkwardness *n* dificultad, *f*; peligro, *m*; delicadeza, *f*; inconveniencia, inoportunidad, *f*; (clumsiness) torpeza, desmaña, *f*; (ungracefulness) falta de gracia, *f*

awl *n* lezna, *f*, punzón, *m*

awning *n* toldo, palio, *m*, *Lat. Am.* carpa *f*; *naut* toldilla, *f*

awry *adv* a un lado; oblicuamente; *fig* mal. a torcido; *fig* descarriado

ax *n* hacha, *f*

axiom *n* axioma, *m*

axiomatic *a* axiomático

axis *n* eje, *m*; *zool* axis, *m*. **A. power,** nación del Eje

axle *n* eje, *m*; peón, árbol (de una rueda), *m*. **back a.,** eje trasero, *m*. **differential a.,** eje diferencial, *m*. **front a.,** eje delantero, *m*

ay *interj* sí. *n* voto afirmativo, *m*

Aztec *a* and *n* azteca, *mf*

azure *n* azul celeste, *m*

b *n* (letter) be, *f; mus* si, *m*

babble *n* (chatter) charla, *f;* (of a child) gorjeo, *m;* (confused sound) vocinglería, barbulla, *f,* rumor, *m;* (of water) murmullo, susurro, *m. vi* charlar; (of children) gorjearse; (incoherently) balbucir; (water) murmurar, susurrar; (a secret) descubrir

babbling *n* garrulería, locuacidad, *f;* (incoherent speech) balbuceo, *m.* (of water) murmullo, *m.* **a** gárrulo, locuaz; balbuciente; murmurante

baboon *n* babuino, *m*

baby *n* bebé, crío, *m;* niño (-ña) de pecho; *fig* gran bebé, *m;* niño mimado, *m,* a infantil. **b. blue,** azul claro, *m.* **b. doll,** muñeca bebé, *f.* **b. girl** *Argentina* beba *f* **b. grand piano,** piano de media cola, *m.* **b. of the family** *Venezuela* cuneco (-ca) *mf*

baby carriage *n* coche de niños, *m*

babyish *a* infantil, aniñado, pueril

babysitter *n* cuidaniños, *mf*

baccalaureate *n* bachillerato, *m*

bachelor *n* soltero, célibe, *m;* (of a university) licenciado, bachiller, *m;* (as a title) caballero, *m.* **confirmed b.,** solterón, *m.* **degree of b.,** licenciatura, *f.* **to receive the degree of b.,** licenciarse, bachillerarse

back *n anat* espalda, *f;* (of an animal) lomo, espinazo, *m;* (reins, loins) riñones, *m pl;* (of chairs, sofas) respaldo, *m;* (of a book) lomo, *m;* (back, bottom) fondo, *m,* parte posterior, parte de atrás, *f;* (of a hand, brush and many other things) dorso, *m;* (of a coin) reverso, *m,* el otro lado de alguna cosa; (in football, hockey) defensa, *m; theat* foro, *m;* (of fire-arms) culata, *f;* (of a knife) canto, *m;* (upper portion) parte superior, *f.* **a** posterior, trasero; de atrás; (remote) alejado, apartado; inferior; (overdue; past; out of date) atrasado; (earlier) anterior; *anat* dorsal. **at the b.,** detrás; en el fondo; en la última fila. **at the b. of one's mind,** por sus adentros, en el fondo del pensamiento. **behind one's b.,** a espaldas de uno, en ausencia de uno. **half-b.,** medio, *m.* **on one's b.,** boca arriba; a cuestas. **to see the b. of,** *inf* ver por última vez, desembarazarse de. **to turn one's b. on,** volver la espalda (a). **with one's b. to the engine,** de espaldas a la máquina. **b. to b.,** espalda con espalda

back *vt* empujar hacia atrás; (a vehicle) dar marcha atrás; hacer retroceder; (line) reforzar; (support) apoyar; (sign) endosar; (bind) forrar; (bet on) apostar a; (a sail) fachear. *vi* retroceder; dar marcha atrás; (of the wind) girar; (with on to) dar sobre, dominar; (with down) abandonar (una pretensión), etc.) **to b. out,** salir, marcharse; volverse atrás; (retract) desdecirse

back *adv* detrás; atrás; otra vez, de nuevo; (returned) de vuelta; a alguna distancia; (at home) en casa. *interj* ¡atrás! **A few**

weeks b., Hace unas semanas, Unas semanas atrás. **It stands b. from the road,** Está a alguna distancia del camino. **to go b. to,** (of families, etc.) remontar a. **to come b.,** regresar. **to come b. again,** regresar de nuevo, regresar por segunda vez

back axle *n* eje trasero, *m*

backbite *vt* cortar (a uno) un sayo, desollarle (a uno) vivo, murmurar de

backbone *n* espinazo, *m,* columna vertebral, *f.* **to the b.,** hasta la médula

backed *a* (lined) forrado; (in compounds; of persons) de espalda; (of chairs) de respaldo

backfire *n* contrafuego *m,* falsa explosión, *f*

background *n* fondo, *m; art* último término, *m.* **in the b.,** en el fondo; *art* en último término; *fig* en las sombras; alejado, a distancia

backhanded *a* de revés, dado con el revés de la mano; (of persons) equívoco

backing *n* forro, *m;* (lining) refuerzo, *m;* (of a vehicle) marcha atrás, *f;* retroceso, *m;* (betting) el apostar (a); (wagers) apuestas, *f pl;* (fig support) apoyo, *m,* ayuda, *f;* garantía, *f*

backlog *n com* rezago de pedidos, *m*

backroom *n* cuarto interior, *m,* habitación trasera, *f.* **b. boy,** investigador ocupado en trabajos secretos para el gobierno, *m*

back seat *n* asiento trasero, *m;* fondo, *m.* **to take a b.-s.,** permanecer en el fondo, ceder el paso

backside *n* trasero, *m,* posaderas, nalgas, *f pl*

backslide *vi* recaer, reincidir

backstage *n* foro, fondo del escenario, *m, adv* hacia el foro; detrás de bastidores

backstaircase *n* escalera de servicio, *f;* escalera secreta, *f*

backstairs *n* escalera de servicio, *f; fig* vías secretas, *f pl,* a de cocina; *fig* secreto

backstitch *n sew* pespunte, *m, vt* and *vi* pespuntar

backstroke *n* reculada, *f; sport* revés, *m*

backward *a* hacia atrás; vuelto hacia atrás; (in development) atrasado, poco avanzado; lento; negligente; (shy) modesto; (late) tardío; atrasado; retrógrado; (dull) torpe; retrospectivo. *adv* hacia atrás; atrás; al revés; (of falling) de espaldas; (of time) al pasado. **to go b. and forward,** ir y venir. **b. and forward,** de acá para allá

backwardness *n* atraso, *m;* lentitud, *f;* negligencia, *f;* modestia, *f;* (lateness) tardanza, *f*; atraso, *m*; (dullness) torpeza, *f*; falta de progreso, *f*

backwards *adv*. See **backward**

backwater *n* remanso, *m*

backwoods *n* monte, *m*, selva, *f*

bacon *n* tocino, *m*

bacteria *n* bacteria, *f*

bacteriologist *n* bacteriólogo, *m*

bacteriology *n* bacteriología, *f*

bad *a* malo; (wicked) perverso; (ill) enfermo, malo (with estar); (naughty; undutiful) malo (with ser); (of coins) falso; (of debts) incobrable; (rotten) podrido; (harmful) nocivo; (dangerous) peligroso; (of pains, a cold) fuerte; intenso; (of a shot) errado; (mistaken) equivocado; (unfortunate) desgraciado. *n* el mal, lo malo; (persons) los malos. **extremely bad**, pésimo. **from bad to worse**, de mal en peor. **It's too bad!** ¡Esto es demasiado! **to go bad**, (fruit) macarse; (food) estropearse. **bad habit**, mala costumbre, *f*, vicio, *m*. **to have the bad habit of**, tener el vicio de. **bad temper**, malhumor, mal genio, *Lat. Am.* catoche m. **bad-tempered**, malhumorado, *Argentina* cabrero. **bad turn**, flaco servicio, *m*, mala pasada, *f*

badge *n* insignia, *f*; (decoration) condecoración, *f*; símbolo, emblema, *m*; (mark) marca, *f*

badger *n* tejón, *m*, *vt* cansar, molestar

Bad Lands (of Nebraska and South Dakota) Tierras malas *f pl*; (of Argentina) la Travesía, *f*

badly *adv* mal. **extremely b.**, pésimamente. **to want something b.**, necesitar algo con urgencia. **b. done**, mal hecho. **b. disposed**, malintencionado

badminton *n* el juego del volante, *m*

badness *n* maldad, *f*; mala calidad, *f*; lo malo

bad-smelling *a* maloliente

baffle *vt* desconcertar; (bewilder) tener perplejo (a); contrariar, frustrar; (obstruct) impedir; (avoid) evitar. **to b. description**, no haber palabras para describir

baffling *a* desconcertante; difícil; confuso; perturbador; (of people) enigmático

bag *n* saco, *m*; talega, *f*; (hand) bolsa, *f*, saco (de mano), *m*; (for tools) capacho, *m*; (for sewing) costurero, *m*; (of bagpipes) fuelle, *m*; (saddle) alforja, *f*; (briefcase) cartera, *f*; (suitcase) maleta, *f*; (under the eye) ojera, *f*; (game shot) caza, *f*. *vt* entalegar; coger, cazar; matar; tomar. *vi* (of garments) arrugarse. **to clear out bag and baggage**, liar el petate. **a bag of bones**, (person) un manojo de huesos. **bag wig**, peluquín, *m*

bagatelle *n* bagatela, friolera, *f*; (game) billar romano, *m*

bagful *n* saco, *m*; bolsa, *f*

baggage *n* equipaje, *m*; *mil* bagaje, *m*; (madcap) pícara, *f*; (jade) mujerzuela, *f*. **b. master**, (railway) factor, *m*. **b. car**, furgón de equipajes, *m*

baggage rack *n* (of automobile) portaequipajes, *m*

baggy *a* (creased, of trousers) con rodilleras, arrugado; (wide) bombacho

bagpipe *n* gaita, *f*

bagpiper *n* gaitero, *m*

Bahamas, the las Islas Bahamas, las Islas Lucayas, *f*

bail *n law* fianza, caución, *f*; (person) fiador (-ra); (cricket) travesaño, *m*, barra, *f*. *vt law* poner en libertad bajo fianza; salir fiador (por); (a boat) achicar. **on b.**, en fiado. **to go b.**, dar fianza, fiar.

bailiff *n law* agente ejecutivo, *m*; alguacil, *m*; mayordomo, *m*; capataz, *m*

bait *n* cebo, *m*; anzuelo, *m*; (fodder) pienso, *m*, *vt* cebar; (feed) dar pienso (a); azuzar; atormentar; (attract) atraer

baiting *n* cebadura, *f*; combate, *m*; tormenta, *f*

bake *vt* cocer; hacer (pan, etc.). **I like to bake cakes**, Me gusta hacer pasteles; *fig* endurecer. *vi* cocerse

bakelite *n* bakelita, *f*

baker *n* panadero, hornero, *m*. **a baker's dozen**, la docena del fraile

bakery *n* panadería, *f*

baking *n* cocimiento, *m*, cocción, *f*; (batch) hornada, *f*; el hacer (pan, etc.) a *inf* abrasador. **b.-dish**, tortera, *f*. **b.-powder**, levadura química, *f*

balance *n* balanza, *f*; equilibrio, *m*; *com* balance, saldo, *m*; (in a bank) saldo (a favor del cuentacorrentista), *m*; *math* resto, *m*; *ast* Libra, *f*; (pendulum) péndola, *f*; (counterweight) contrapeso, *m*. **credit b.**, saldo acreedor, *m*. **debit b.**, saldo deudor, *m*. **net b.**, saldo líquido, *m*. **to lose one's b.**, perder el equilibrio. **to strike a b.**, hacer balance. **b. of power**, equilibrio político, *m*. **b. of trade**, balanza de comercio, *f*. **b.-sheet**, balance, avanzo, *m*. *Lat. Am.* balance de situación, *m*. **b. wheel**, (of watches) volante, *m*

balance *vt* balancear, abalanzar; contrapesar; (accounts) saldar; equilibrar; comparar; considerar; examinar. *vi* balancearse; ser de igual peso; equilibrarse; (accounts) saldarse

balancing *n* balanceo, *m*; *com* balance, *m*. **b.-pole**, balancín, *m*

balcony *n* balcón, *m*; galería, *f*; *theat* anfiteatro, *m*

bald *a* calvo; (of style) seco, pobre; *fig* desnudo, árido, pelado; sin adorno; (simple) sencillo. **to grow b.**, ponerse calvo, encalvecer

baldly *adv* secamente; sencillamente

baldness *n* calvicie, *f*; (of style) sequedad, pobreza, *f*; (bareness) desnudez, aridez, *f*

bale n (bundle) fardo, m; (of cotton, paper, etc.) bala, f

Balearic Islands, the las Islas Baleares, f

baleful a malicioso, siniestro, maligno

balk n obstáculo, m; (beam) viga, f; (billiards) cabaña, f. vt frustrar; impedir. vi resistirse, rehusar

Balkans, the los Balcanes, m

ball n globo, m, esfera, f; (plaything) pelota, f; (as in billiards, cricket, croquet) bola, f; (in football, basket-ball) balón, m; (shot) bala, f; (of wool, etc.) ovillo, m; (of the eye) globo (del ojo), m; (of the thumb) yema (del pulgar), f; (of the foot) planta (del pie), f; (dance) baile, m. vi apelotonarse. **red b.,** (in billiards) mingo, m. **to play b.,** jugar a la pelota. **to roll oneself into a b.,** aovillarse, hacerse un ovillo. **b.-and-socket joint,** articulación esférica, f. **b.-bearing,** cojinete de bolas, m

ballad n romance, m; (song) balada, f

ballast n (naut and fig) lastre, m; rw balasto, m. vt lastrar; llenar de balasto

ballerina n bailarina, f

ballet n baile ruso, ballet, m; baile, m. **b. master,** director de ballet, m

balloon n globo aerostático, m; chem balón, m; (toy) globo, m; arch bola, f. **captive b.,** globo cautivo, m. **b. barrage,** cortina de globos de intercepción, f. **b.-tyre,** neumático balón, m

ballot n votación, f; papeleta para votar, cédula de votación, f. vi votar, balotar. **b. box,** urna electoral, f

ballpoint, ballpoint pen n biro m (Argentina), birome m (Argentina, Uruguay), bolígrafo m (Spain), bolilápiz m (Mexico), esfero m (Colombia), esferográfica f (Colombia), estenógrafo m (Cuba), lapicera f (Argentina), lapicero m (Central America, Colombia), lápiz de bolilla m (Paraguay, Peru), lápiz de pasta m (Chile), pluma esférica f (Spain), pluma esferográfica f (Spain), plumilla f (Venezuela), polígrafo m (Spain), punto bola, punto-bola, puntobola f (Bolivia), pluma de bola f, pluma atómica f

ballroom n salón de baile, m; salón de fiestas, m

balm n bálsamo, m; fig ungüento, m

balminess n fragancia, f; aroma, f; (gentleness) suavidad, f

balmy a balsámico; fragante; aromático; (soft) suave; (soothing) calmante

Baltic, the el (Mar) Báltico, m

balustrade n balaustrada, barandilla, f, antepecho, m

bamboo n bambú, m

bamboozle vt engatusar, embaucar

ban n interdicción, f; prohibición, f; bando, m. vt prohibir; proscribir

banal a banal, vulgar, trivial

banality n banalidad, vulgaridad, trivialidad, f

banana n (tree and fruit) plátano, m; (fruit) banana, f, Venezuela cambur m **b. plantation,** platanar, m

band n lista, tira, f; zona, f; (black mourning) tira de gasa, f; (sash) faja, f; (ribbon) banda; cinta, f; (bandage) venda, f; mech correa, f; arch listón, m; mus banda, f; (group) pandilla, f, grupo, m. vt congregar, reunir. vi reunirse, asociarse. **b.-saw,** sierra de cinta, f

bandage n venda, f, vendaje, m, vt vendar, poner un vendaje en (limbs, etc. or persons)

bandit n bandido, bandolero, m

bandmaster n músico mayor, m; director de orquesta, m

bandsman n músico, m

bandstand n quiosco de música, m

bandy vt cambiar, trocar; pasar de uno a otro

bandy-legged a estevado zanquituerto

bane n (poison) veneno, m; perdición, ruina, f; (nuisance) plaga, f

baneful a pernicioso, funesto; dañino; maligno

bang n golpe, golpazo, m; (of an explosive, fire-arm) estallido, m, detonación, f; (of a firework) traque, m; (of a door) portazo, m; (with the fist) puñetazo, m; (noise) ruido, m; (fringe) flequillo, m. vt golpear; (beat) sacudir; (throw) lanzar, arrojar con violencia; (a door, etc.) cerrar de golpe, cerrar con violencia. vi golpear; estallar; (thunder) retronar; (in the wind) cencerrear. interj ¡pum! ¡zas!

banging n golpeadura, f; sacudidura, f; detonación, f; ruido, m

bangle n (slave b.) esclava, f; pulsera, f; brazalete, m; (for ankles) ajorca, f

banish vt desterrar; apartar; (from the mind) despedir, ahuyentar; (suppress) suprimir

banishment n destierro, m; expulsión, f; relegación, f; (suppression) supresión, f

banister n baranda, f, pasamano, m

banjo n banjo, m

bank n (of rivers, etc.) ribera, orilla, f; margen, m; (of clouds) banda, capa, f; (of sand, fog, snow) banco, m; (embankment) terraplén, m; com banco, m; (gaming) banca, f; (for foreign exchange) casa de cambio, f. **b. account,** cuenta corriente, f. **b. book,** libreta de banco, f. **b. clerk,** empleado del banco, m. **b. holiday,** fiesta oficial, f, **b.-note,** billete de banco, m. **b. stock,** acciones de un banco, f pl

bank vt estancar, represar; amontonar; poner (dinero) en un banco, depositar en un banco. vi tener cuenta corriente en un banco; (gaming) tener la banca; ser banquero; aer inclinarse al virar

banker n banquero, m, (also at cards); (money-changer) cambista, mf

banking n com banca, f; aer vuelo inclinado, *m*, a com bancario. **b. house,** casa de banca, *f*

bankrupt *a* insolvente, quebrado. *n* quebrado (-da). **to go b.,** declararse en quiebra, hacer bancarrota

bankruptcy *n* bancarrota, quiebra, *f*; *flg* pobreza, decadencia, *f*. **fraudulent b.,** quiebra fraudulenta, *f*. **b. court,** tribunal de quiebras, *m*

banner *n* bandera, *f*

banquet *n* banquete, *m*, *vt and vi* banquetear

banqueting *a* de banquetes. **b. hall,** sala de banquetes, *f*

bantam *n* gallina enana, *f*. **b. weight,** (*sport*) a de peso gallo. *n* peso gallo, *m*

banter *vt and vi* tomar el pelo (a). *n* chistes, *m pl*, burlas, *f pl*

baptism *n* bautismo, *m*; *flg* bautizo, *m*

baptist *n* bautista, *m*. **St. John the B.,** San Juan Bautista

baptize *vt* bautizar

bar *n* barra, *f*; (of chocolate, soap) pastilla, *f*; *her* banda, *f*; (on a window) reja, *f*; (of a door) tranca, *f*, barrote, *m*; (bar lever) palanca, *f*; (of a balance) astil, *m*; *mus* barra, *f*; (in the sea, etc.) banco, *m*, alfaque, *m*; (barrier) barrera, *f*; (barrister's profession) foro, *m*, curia, *f*; *flg* tribunal, *m*; (in a court) barra, *f*; *flg* impedimento, *m*; (of light) rayo, *m*; (stripe) raya, *f*; (for refreshments) bar, *m*, *Lat. Am.* chingana *f* mostrador del bar, *m*. *vt* atrancar, abarrotar; impedir, obstruir; prohibir; exceptuar, excluir; (streak) rayar. **the b.,** el cuerpo de abogados. **to be called to the b.,** ser recibido como abogado en los tribunales. **b.-tender,** camarero del bar, *m*

bar association *n* colegio de abogados, *m*

barb *n* púa, *f*; (of an arrow, fish-hook, etc.) lengüeta, *f*; (of a lance) roquete, *m*; (of fish) barbilla, *f*; (of a feather) barba, *f*; (horse) caballo berberisco, *m*. *vt* proveer de púas; armar de lengüetas

barbarian *a* bárbaro, barbárico. *n* bárbaro (-ra)

barbaric *a* barbárico, salvaje

barbarism *n* barbarismo, salvajismo, *m*; crueldad, *f*; (of style) barbarismo, *m*

barbarous *a* feroz, cruel, salvaje; inculto

barbecue *n* barbacoa, *f*

barbed wire *n* alambre de púas, alambre espinoso, *m*

barber *n* barbero, *m*. **barber shop,** barbería, *f*

bard *n* bardo, vate, *m*

bare *a* desnudo; descubierto; vacío; (mere) mero, solo; (worn) raído; pelado, raso; (unadorned) sencillo; (unsheathed) desnudo; (arid) árido; (curt) seco; (unprotected) desabrigado; pobre. *vt* desnudar; descubrir; revelar. **He bared his head,** Se descubrió. **to lay b.,** dejar al desnudo; revelar

bareback a que monta en pelo. *adv* en pelo

barefaced *a* descarado, desvergonzado, cínico

barefoot *a* descalzo

bareheaded *a* sin sombrero, descubierto

barelegged *a* en pernetas, en piernas

barely *adv* apenas; escasamente; meramente, solamente

bareness *n* desnudez, *f*; desadorno, *m*; (aridity) aridez, *f*; pobreza, *f*

bargain *n* contrato, *m*; pacto, acuerdo, *m*; (purchase) ganga, *f*. *vi* negociar; (haggle) regatear; (expect) esperar. **into the b.,** de añadidura, también. **It is a b.,** Es una ganga; Trato hecho. **to get the best of the b.,** salir ganando. **to strike a b.,** cerrar un trato. **b. counter,** sección de saldos, *f*. **b. sale,** venta de saldos, *Mexico* barata *f*

bargainer *n* negociador (-ra); regatón (-ona)

bargaining *n* negociación, gestión, *f*; (haggling) regateo, *m*

barge *n* (for freight) barcaza, gabarra, *f*; falúa, *f*; lancha, *f*. *vi* (into) tropezar con; dar empujones

baritone *n* barítono, *m*

bark *n* (of a tree) corteza, *f*; (quinine) quina, *f*; (boat, *poet*) barca, *f*; *naut* buque de tres palos, *m*; (of a dog) ladrido, *m*; (of a fox) aullido, *m*; (of a gun) ruido, *m*. *vi* (of a dog) ladrar; (of a fox) aullar; (of a gun) tronar

barking *n* ladrido, *m*; (of stags) rebramo, *m*; (of foxes) aullidos, *m pl*; (of guns) trueno, *m*

barley *n* cebada, *f*, a de cebada. **pearl b.,** cebada perlada, *f*. **b.-bin,** cebadera, *f*. **b. dealer,** cebadero, *m*. **b. field,** cebadal, *m*. **b.-water,** hordiate, *m*

barm *n* (froth on beer) giste, *m*; (leaven) levadura, *f*

barmaid *n* moza de bar, camarera, *f*

barn *n* pajar, granero, hórreo, *m*. **b.-owl,** lechuza, *f*

barometer *n* barómetro, *m*

baroque *a* barroco. **the b.,** lo barroco

barracks *n* *mil* cuartel, *m*, caserna, *Lat. Am.* barraca *f*, *vt* acuartelar

barrage *n* presa de contención, *f*; *mil* cortina de fuego, *f*; (barrier) barrera, *f*; (of questions) lluvia, *f*. **b. balloon,** globo de intercepción, *m*

barrel *n* barril, *m*; tonel, *m*, cuba, *f*; (of a gun) cañón, *m*; *mech* cilindro, *m*; (of an animal) cuerpo, *m*. *vt* embarrilar, entonelar. **b.-organ,** organillo, órgano de manubrio, *m*

barrelled *a* embarrilado; (of guns, generally in compounds) de . . . cañones. **double-b. gun,** escopeta de dos cañones, *f*

barren *a* estéril; (of ground) árido; (fruitless) infructuoso

barrenness n esterilidad, f; aridez, sequedad, f; (fruitlessness) inutilidad, f

barricade n barricada, f; barrera, f, vt cerrar con barricadas; obstruir

barricading n el cerrar con barricadas; la defensa con barricadas (de)

barrier n barrera, f; impedimento, m; (for customs duties) portazgo, m

barring prep salvo, excepto, con la excepción de, menos

barrister n abogado (-da)

barter n cambio, trueque, m; tráfico, m, vt and vi cambiar, trocar; traficar

barterer n traficante, mf

base a bajo, vil, ruin; soez; indigno; impuro; (of metals) de mala ley. n base, f; fundamento, m; pie, m; arch pedestal, m; (mil chem geom) base, f; (of a vase) asiento, m, vt basar; fundar. **b. action,** bajeza, f. **b. line,** sport línea de base, f. **b. metal,** metal común, m

baseball n pelota base, f

baseless a sin base; sin fundamento; insostenible

basement n sótano, m

baseness n bajeza, vileza, ruindad, f

bashful a vergonzoso, ruboroso; tímido, corto; (unsociable) huraño, esquivo

bashfulness n vergüenza, f, rubor, m; encogimiento, m, timidez, cortedad, f; (unsociableness) huraña, esquivez, f

basic a básico; fundamental

basic commodity n artículo básico, producto primario, m

basil (sweet) n bot albahaca, f

basilica n basílica, f

basilisk n basilisco, m

basin n vasija, f; (for washing) jofaina, f; (barber's) bacía, f; (of a fountain) taza, f; anat bacinete, m; (of a harbor) concha, f; (of a river) cuenca, f; (in the earth) hoya, f; (dock) dársena, f

basis n base, f; fundamento, m; elemento principal, m

bask vi calentarse; (in the sun) tomar el sol

basket n cesta, f; canasta, capacha, Lat. Am. jaba f; (frail) espuerta, f. **flat b.,** azafate, m. **large b.,** banasta, f. **b. with a lid,** excusabaraja, f. **b. ball,** baloncesto, m. **b. maker** or **dealer,** banastero, cestero, m. **b. work** or **shop** or **factory,** cestería, f. **b. work chair,** sillón de mimbres, m

basketful n cesta, cestada, f

Basque a and n vasco (-ca), vascongado (-da). n (language) vascuence, m

bas-relief n bajo relieve, m

bass n mus bajo, m; (for tying) esparto, m, a mus bajo. **double b.,** contrabajo, m. **figured b.,** bajo cifrado, m. **b. clef,** clave de fa, f. **b. string,** bordón, m. **b. voice,** voz baja, f

bassinet n cochecito de niño, m

bastard n bastardo (-da), hijo (-ja) natural. a bastardo, ilegítimo; espurio

baste vt sew bastear, hilvanar, embastar; cul enlardar, lardear

basting n sew embaste, m; cul lardeamiento, m. **b. spoon,** cacillo, m. **b. stitch,** pasillo, m

bastion n bastión, baluarte, m. **to fortify with bastions,** abastionar

bat n zool murciélago, m; (in cricket) paleta, f; (in table tennis) pala, f. vi (cricket) golpear con la paleta. See **without**

batch n (of loaves, etc.) hornada, f; lote, m; (of recruits) promoción, f

bath n baño, m; (room) cuarto de baño, m; (vat) bañador, m; (for swimming) piscina cubierta, f; (in the open air) piscina al aire libre, f; phot baño, m, solución, f. vt bañar, lavar. **hot mineral baths,** termas, f pl. **Order of the B.,** Orden del Baño, f. **public baths,** casa de baños, f. **reinforcing b.,** phot reforzador, m. **to take a b.,** bañarse, tomar un baño. **b.-chair,** cochecillo de inválido, m. **b.-robe,** bata de baño, f, albornoz, m. **b. room,** cuarto de baño, m. **b. towel,** toalla del baño, f. **b. tub,** bañera, f, baño, m, Argentina bañadera f

bathe vt bañar, lavar; (of light, etc.) bañar, envolver. vi bañarse. n baño, m. **to go for a b.,** ir a bañarse

bather n bañista, mf; bañador (-ra)

bathing a de baño; balneario, n baño, m. **b. cap,** gorro de baño, m. **b. dress,** traje de baño, m. **b. gown,** albornoz, m, bata de baño, f. **b. machine,** caseta de baños, f. **b.-pool,** piscina, f. **b.-resort,** estación balnearia, f. **b.-shoes,** calzado de baño, m

bathos n paso de lo sublime a lo ridículo, m; anticlímax, m

baton n bastón de mando, m; mus batuta, f; (policeman's) porra, f

batten vi engordar (de); medrar, prosperar. **to b. down,** cerrar las escotillas

batter n cul batido, m; pasta, f; sport lanzador, m. vt apalear, golpear; (demolish) derribar, demoler; (with artillery) cañonear; batir. **to coat with b.,** rebozar. **to b. down,** derribar

battery n (mil nav) batería, f; elec pila, batería, f; law agresión, f. **dry b.,** batería de pilas, f. **storage b.,** acumulador, m. **b. cell,** pila de batería eléctrica, f

battle n batalla, f; pelea, f, combate, m; (struggle) lucha, f. vi batallar, pelear; luchar. **b.-array,** orden de batalla, f. **b.-axe,** hacha de combate, f. **b.-cruiser,** acorazado, m. **b.-field,** campo de batalla, m. **b.-front,** frente de combate, m. **b.-piece,** art batalla, f. **b.-ship,** buque de guerra, m

bauble n (trifle) chuchería, fruslería, f; (fool's) cetro de bufón, m

bawdy a obsceno, indecente, escabroso

bawl *vi* chillar, vocear

bay *n geog* bahía, *f;* (small) abra, *f; bot* laurel, *m;* (horse) bayo, *m;* (howl) aullido, *m; arch* abertura, *f; rw* andén, *m.* a (of horses) bayo, isabelino. *vi* aullar. **at bay,** en jaque, acorralado. **sick-bay,** enfermería, *f.* **to keep at bay,** tener a distancia; tener alejado; entretener. **bay rum,** ron de malagueta, *m.* **bay window,** ventana saediza, *f*

bayonet *n* bayoneta, *f, vt* herir o matar con bayoneta.

bazaar *n* bazar, *m*

be *vi* ser; (of position, place, state, temporariness) estar; (exist) existir; (in impersonal expressions) haber; (of expressions concerning the weather and time) hacer; (remain) quedar; (leave alone) dejar; (do) hacer; (of one's health) estar; (of feeling cold, hot, afraid, etc. and of years of one's age) tener; (live) vivir; (belong) ser (de), pertenecer (a); (matter, concern) importar (a); (happen) ocurrir, suceder; (find oneself) hallarse, encontrarse, estar; (arrive) llegar (a); (cost) costar; (be worth) valer; (celebrate, hold) celebrarse, tener lugar; (forming continuous tense with present participle active or passive) estar; (with past participle forming passive) ser (this construction is often replaced by reflexive form when no ambiguity is entailed); (with infinitive expressing duty, intention) haber de; (must) tener que. **He is a soldier (doctor, etc.),** Es soldado (médico, etc.). **He is on guard,** Está de guardia. **They were at the door (in the house, etc.),** Estaban a la puerta (en la casa, etc.). **I am writing a letter,** Estoy escribiendo una carta (but this form is often replaced by a simple tense, e.g. escribo . . .). **It remains to be written,** Queda por escribir. **What is to be done?** ¿Qué hay que hacer? **Woe is me!** ¡Ay de mí! **to be hot (cold),** (of things) estar caliente (frío); (of weather) hacer calor (frío); (of persons) tener calor (frío). **How is John?** He is well, ¿Cómo está Juan? Está bien de salud. **It is daylight,** Es de día. **It is cloudy,** Está nublado. **She is 10,** Tiene diez años. **They are afraid,** Tienen miedo. **I am to go there tomorrow,** He de ir allí mañana. **What is to be will be,** Lo que tiene que ser será. **If John were to come we could go into the country,** Si viniera Juan podríamos ir al campo. **Be that as it may,** Sea como sea. **It is seven years since we saw him,** Hace siete años que no le vemos. **We have been here for three years,** Hace tres años que estamos aquí, Llevamos tres años aquí. **There is** or **there are,** Hay. **There will be many people,** Habrá mucha gente. **There were many people,** Había mucha gente. **There are many people,** Hay mucha gente. **It is three miles to the next village,** Estamos a tres millas del pueblo próximo. **So be it!** ¡Así sea. **Your pen is

not to be seen,** Tu pluma no se ve. **It is to be hoped that . . . ,** Se espera que . . . ; ¡Ojalá que . . . ! **The door is open,** La puerta está abierta. **The door was opened by Mary,** La puerta fue abierta por María. **He was accused of being a fascist,** Lo acusaron de fascista. **to be about to,** estar por; (of a more imminent action) estar para, estar a punto de. **to be in,** estar dentro; estar en casa. **to be off,** marcharse, irse. **Be off!** ¡Márchate! ¡Vete! ¡Fuera! **to be out,** estar fuera; haber salido; no estar en casa; (of a light, etc.) estar apagado. **to be up,** estar levantado. **to be up to,** proyectar, traer entre manos; urdir, maquinar

beach *n* playa, *f;* costa, *f. vt* (a boat) encallar en la costa. **b. shoes,** playeras, *f pl.* **b. suit,** vestido de playa, *m*

beach club *n* club de playa, *m*

beacon *n* (lighthouse) faro, *m;* (buoy) baliza, *f,* fanal, *m;* (watch-tower) atalaya, *f; fig* guía, *f. vt* iluminar. **b. fire,** almenara, *f*

bead *n* cuenta, *f;* (of glass) abalorio, *m;* (drop) gota, *f; arch* perla, *f;* (bubble) burbuja, *f;* (foam) espuma, *f; pl* **beads,** rosario, *m, vt* adornar con abalorios. **to tell one's beads,** rezar el rosario. **b. work,** abalorio, *m*

beak *n* pico, *m;* punta, *f; naut* espolón, *m.* **to tap with the b.,** picotear

beaker *n* copa, *f; chem* vaso de precipitado, *m*

beam *n arch* madero, *m,* viga, *f;* (width of a ship) manga, *f;* (of a balance) palanca, *f;* (of a plough) cama, *f;* (of light) rayo, destello, *m; phys* rayo, *m;* (smile) sonrisa brillante, *f; pl* **beams,** (of a building) envigado, *m;* (of a ship) baos, *m pl.* **main b.,** *arch* viga maestra, *f.* **on her b.-ends,** de costado; *fig* arruinado; en la miseria. **b. feather,** astil, *m.* **b. of light,** rayo de luz, haz de luz, *m*

beam *vt* lanzar, emitir; difundir. *vi* brillar, fulgurar, destellar; estar radiante, estar rebosando de alegría

beaming *a* brillante; radiante

bean *n* haba, *f;* judía, alubia, *f;* (of coffee) grano, *m.* **broad b.,** haba, *f.* **French, haricot, kidney b.,** judía, *f.* **string b.,** judía verde, *f.* **b. field,** habar, *m*

bear *n zool* oso, *m;* (she-bear) osa, *f;* (Stock Exchange) bajista, *mf.* **Great B.,** *ast* Osa Mayor, *f,* Septentrión, *m.*

bear *vt* and *vi* (carry) llevar; (show) ostentar; (company, etc.) hacer; (profess) profesar; (of spite, etc. and of relation) guardar; (have) tener; (fruit) dar; (give birth to) parir; (support) sostener; (endure) aguantar; (suffer) padecer, sufrir; (tolerate) tolerar, sufrir; (a strain, an operation, etc.) resistir; (lean on) apoyarse en; (experience) experimentar; (produce) producir, dar; (enjoy) disfrutar de; (use) usar; (impel) empujar; (occupy, hold) ocupar; (go) dirigirse. **It was suddenly**

borne in on them that . . . , De pronto vieron claro que . . . **I cannot b. any more,** No puedo más. **We cannot b. him,** No le aguantamos, No le sufrimos. **His language won't b. repeating,** Su lenguaje no puede repetirse. **to bring to b.,** ejercer (presión, etc.). **to b. a grudge,** guardar rencor (a), tener ojeriza (a). **to b. arms,** llevar armas; servir en el ejército o la milicia. **to b. company,** hacer compañía (a), acompañar (a). **to b. in mind,** tener en cuenta, tener presente; acordarse de. **to b. oneself,** conducirse, portarse. **to b. to the right,** ir hacia la derecha. **to b. witness,** atestiguar. **to b. false witness,** levantar falso testimonio. **to b. away,** llevarse; ganar. **to b. down,** hundir; derribar; bajar. **to b. down on,** avanzar rápidamente hacia; correr hacia; *naut* arribar sobre; (attack) caer sobre. **to b. in,** llevar adentro. **to b. off,** llevarse; ganar; *naut* apartarse de la costa. **to b. on, upon,** apoyarse en; (refer to) referirse a. **to b. out,** llevar fuera; confirmar; apoyar; justificar. **to b. up,** llevar arriba; llevar a la cumbre (de); sostener; (recover) cobrar ánimo; (against) resistir; hacer frente a. **to b. with,** soportar; sufrir; aguantar; llevar con paciencia; ser indulgente con

bearable a soportable; aguantable; tolerable

beard n barba, f; (of cereals) raspa, arista, f, vt desafiar. **thick b.,** barba bien poblada, f

beardless a barbilampiño, desbarbado, imberbe, lampiño

bearer n llevador (-ra), portador (-ra); (of a bier) andero, m; com dador, portador, m. **good b.,** agr árbol fructífero, m. **to b.,** com al portador

bearing n porte, m; postura, f; presencia, f; conducta, f; aspecto, m; relación, f; (meaning) significación, f; naut demora, orientación, f; mech cojinete, soporte, m; (endurance) tolerancia, f; pl **bearings,** (way) camino, m; her escudo de armas, m. **to get one's bearings,** orientarse; encontrar el camino. **to lose one's bearings,** desorientarse; perderse. **to have a b. on,** tener relación con; tener que ver con; influir en

beast n animal, bruto, m; cuadrúpedo, m; (cattle) res, f; bestia, f. **wild b.,** fiera, f. **b. of burden,** acémila, bestia de carga, f. **b. of prey,** animal de rapiña, m

beastly a bestial, brutal; obsceno; inf horrible

beat n latido, m, pulsación, f; golpe, m; (of a drum) toque (de tambor), m; (of a clock) tictac, m; sonido repetido, m; vibración, f

beat vt and vi batir; golpear; (thrash) pegar, dar una paliza (a), Lat. Am. humear; (to remove dust, etc.) sacudir; (shake) agitar; (the wings) aletear; (hunting) batir; (excel) exceder, superar;

ganar; (defeat) vencer; (of the rain, etc.) azotar; (a drum) tocar; (of the sun) batir, dar (en); (throb) latir, palpitar, pulsar. **to b. about the bush,** andarse por las ramas. **to stop beating about the bush,** dejarse de historias. **to b. a retreat,** mil emprender la retirada; huir. **to b. black and blue,** moler a palos. **to b. hollow,** vencer completamente; ganar fácilmente; aventajar con mucho. **to b. it,** inf escaparse corriendo. **to b. time,** mus llevar el compás; triunfar sobre la vejez. **to b. to it,** inf tomar la delantera. **to b. against,** golpear contra; chocar contra. **to b. back,** rechazar; (sobs, etc.) ahogar; reprimir. **to b. down,** (prices) regatear; (of the sun) caer de plomo, caer de plano; reducir; suprimir; destruir. **to b. off,** rechazar; echar a un lado. **to b. out,** hacer salir; (metals) batir; (a tune) llevar el compás (de). **to b. up,** cul batir; (a mattress) mullir; asaltar; maltratar

beaten a (of paths) trillado; (conquered) vencido; (of metals) batido; (dejected) deprimido; (trite) trivial, vulgar

beater n batidor, m; (for carpets) sacudidor (de alfombras), m; cul batidor, m

beating n batimiento, m; vencimiento, m; (thrashing) paliza, f; (of the heart, etc.) palpitación, f; latido, m; (of metals, Lat. Am. also azotera) batida, f; (of a drum) rataplán, toque de tambor, m; (of waves) embate, m; (of wings) aleteo, aletazo, m

beau n galán, m; (fop) petimetre, m

beautiful a bello, lindo, hermoso; magnífico; excelente; exquisito; elegante; encantador, delicioso

beautify vt embellecer; hermosear; adornar. **to b. oneself,** arreglarse, ponerse elegante

beauty n belleza, hermosura, lindeza, f; magnificencia, f; excelencia, f; elegancia, f; encanto, m; (belle) beldad, Venus, f. **to lose one's b.,** desmejorarse, perder su hermosura. **b. contest,** concurso de belleza, m. **b. parlor,** salón de belleza, instituto de belleza, m. **b. sleep,** el primer sueño de la noche. **b. spot,** lunar, m; lunar postizo, m; (place) sitio hermoso, m. **b. treatment,** masaje facial, m

beaver n castor, m; (hat) sombrero de copa, m; (of helmet) babera, f

because conjunc porque. **b. of,** debido a, a causa de

beckon vt and vi hacer señas (a); llamar por señas, llamar con la mano

become vi volverse; llegar a ser, venir a ser; convertirse en; ponerse; hacerse; (befit) convenir; (suit) ir bien (a), favorecer. **He became red,** Se enrojeció. **The hat becomes you,** El sombrero te va bien. **He became king,** Llegó a ser rey. **What has b. of her?** ¿Qué es de ella?; (Where is she?) ¿Qué se ha hecho de ella? **b. binding,** adquirir carácter de compromiso

becoming a propio; correcto; decoroso;

(suitable) conveniente; (of dress) que favorece, que va bien. **This dress is b. to you,** Este vestido te favorece

bed n cama, f, lecho, m; (of sea) fondo, m; (of river) cauce, m; geol yacimiento, m; (in a garden) cuadro, macizo (de jardín), m; (of a machine) asiento, m; (of a building) cimiento, m; fig fundamento, m, base, f, vt (plants) plantar; (fix) fijar, poner. **double bed,** cama de matrimonio, f. **single bed,** cama de monja, f. **in bed,** en cama. **to be gone to bed,** haber ido a la cama. **to be in bed,** estar acostado. **to get into bed,** meterse en cama. **to get out of bed,** levantarse de la cama. **to go to bed,** acostarse, ir a la cama. **to make the beds,** hacer las camas. **to put to bed,** acostar. **to stay in bed,** quedarse en cama, guardar cama. **bed-bug,** chinche, f. **bed-clothes,** ropa de cama, f. **bed-cover,** cubrecama, colcha, f. **bed-head,** cabecera, f. **bed-pan,** silleta, f. **bed-sore,** úlcera de decúbito, f

bedaub, bedazzle. See daub, dazzle

bedchamber n dormitorio, m, alcoba, f

bedded a con . . . cama(s). **a double-b. room,** un cuarto con dos camas; un cuarto con cama de matrimonio

bedding n ropa de cama, f; cama para el ganado, f

bedeck vt embellecer, adornar, engalanar

bedlam n belén, manicomio, m; fig babel, m

bedraggled a mojado y sucio

bedridden a postrado en cama, inválido

bedrock n lecho de roca, m; fig principios fundamentales, fundamentos, m pl

bedroom n cuarto de dormir, dormitorio, m, habitación, f

bedside n lado de cama, m; cabecera, f. **b. manner,** mano izquierda, diplomacia, f. **b.-table,** mesa de noche, f

bedspread n colcha, cubrecama, sobrecama, f

bedstead n cama, f

bedtime n hora de acostarse, f

bee n abeja, f; (meeting) reunión, f, a abejuno. **queen bee,** rey, m, abeja maestra, f. **to have a bee in one's bonnet,** tener una manía (o idea fija). **to make a bee-line for,** ir directamente a. **bee-eater,** orn abejaruco, m. **bee hive,** colmena, f; abejar, m. **bee-keeper,** apicultor (-ra), colmenero (-ra), abejero (-ra). **bee's wax,** cera de abeja, f

beech n haya, f. **plantation of b. trees,** hayal, m. **b.-nut,** hayuco, m

beef n carne de vaca, f; (flesh) carne, f; (strength) fuerza, f. **roast b.,** rosbif, m. **b.-tea,** caldo, m

beefsteak n biftec, bistec, Argentina bife m

beer n cerveza, f. **b. barrel,** barril de cerveza, m. **b.-house,** cervecería, f. **b. mug,** jarro para la cerveza, m

beet n remolacha, f. Mexico betabel m **b. sugar,** azúcar de remolacha, Mexico azúcar de betabel m

beetle n escarabajo, m. **b.-browed,** cejijunto

beetroot n remolacha, f, Mexico betabel m

befall vi acontecer, suceder, ocurrir. vt ocurrir (a), acontecer (a)

befit vt convenir (a), ser digno de

befitting a conveniente, apropiado; digno; oportuno

before adv delante; al frente; (of time), antes, anteriormente; (of order) antes; (already) ya. prep delante de; en frente de; (of time, order) ante; (in the presence of) ante, en presencia de; (rather than) antes de. **b. going,** antes de marcharse. **B. I did it,** Antes de que lo hiciera; Antes de hacerlo. **as never b.,** como nunca. **b. long,** en breve, dentro de poco. **b.-mentioned,** antes citado. **b. the mast,** al pie del mástil, e.g. **two years b. the mast,** dos años al pie del mástil.

beforehand adv previamente, de antemano

befoul vt ensuciar; fig manchar, difamar

befriend vt proteger, ayudar, favorecer, amparar

beg vt pedir, implorar, suplicar. vi mendigar, pordiosear; vivir de limosna. **I beg to propose,** Me permito proponer; Tengo el gusto de proponer; (the health of) Brindo a la salud de. **I beg your pardon!** ¡Vd. dispense!; (when passing in front of anyone, etc.) Con permiso; (in conversation for repetition of a word) ¿Cómo? **to beg the question,** dar por sentado lo mismo que se trata de probar. **His conduct begs description,** No hay palabras para su comportamiento

beget vt procrear, engendrar; causar; suscitar

beggar n mendigo (-ga), pordiosero (-ra), Lat. Am. also limosnero (-ra). **beggars can't be choosers,** a falta de pan, se conforma con tortillas (Mexico); vt empobrecer; arruinar. **to b. description,** no haber palabras para describir

beggarly a miserable, pobre

begging a mendicante, pordiosero. n mendicidad, f, pordioseo, m. **to go b.,** andar mendigando. **b. letter,** carta pidiendo dinero, f

begin vt and vi empezar; comenzar; iniciar; (a conversation) entablar; (open) abrir; inaugurar; tener su principio; nacer. **to b. to,** empezar a; (start on) ponerse a; (with laughing, etc.) romper a. **to b. with,** empezar por; para empezar, en primer lugar

beginner n principiante (-ta); (novice) novato (-ta); iniciador (-ra); autor (-ra)

beginning n principio, comienzo, Lat.

Am. empleo. *m;* origen, *m.* **at the b.,** al principio; (of the month) a principios (de). **from the b. to the end,** desde el principio hasta el fin, *inf* de pe a pa. **in the b.,** al principio. **to make a b.,** comenzar, empezar

begone *interj* ¡fuera! ¡márchate! ¡vete!

begrudge *vt* envidiar

beguile *vt* engañar; defraudar; (time) entretener; (charm) encantar, embelesar

beguilement *n* engaño, *m;* (of time) entretenimiento, *m;* (charm) encanto, *m*

behave *vi* (oneself) conducirse, portarse; (act) obrar, proceder. **to b. badly,** portarse mal; obrar mal. **B.i** ¡Pórtate bien!

behavior *n* conducta, *f;* comportamiento, *m;* proceder, *m;* (manner) modales, *m pl; biol* reacción, *f*

behead *vt* decapitar, descabezar

behest *n* precepto, mandato, *m*

behind *adv* detrás; por detrás; atrás; hacia atrás; en pos; (of time and order) después; (late and in arrears) con retraso; (old-fashioned) atrasado. *prep* detrás de; por detrás de; inferior a; menos aventajado que. *n inf* trasero, *m.* **from b.,** por detrás. **to be b. time,** retrasarse; llegar tarde. **b. the back of,** a espaldas de. **b. the scenes,** entre bastidores. **b. the times,** *fig* atrasado de noticias; pasado de moda. **the ideology b. the French Revolution,** la ideología que informó la Revolución Francesa.

behold *vt* ver, mirar, contemplar; presenciar. *interj* ¡he aquí! ¡mira!

beholden *a* obligado; agradecido

beholder *n* espectador (-ra). **the beholders,** los que lo presenciaban

behove *vt* incumbir, tocar, corresponder

beige *n* beige, color arena, *m*

being *n* existencia, *f;* operación, *f;* ser, *m;* (spirit) alma, *f,* espíritu, *m;* esencia, *f.* **human b.,** ser humano, *m,* alma viviente, *f.* **for the time b.,** por ahora, por el momento

bejewel *vt* enjoyar, adornar con joyas

belabor *vt* apalear, golpear

belated *a* tardío

belay *vt* amarrar

belch *n* eructo, *m;* detonación, *f;* (of a volcano) erupción, *f. vi* eructar. *vt* vomitar; (curses, etc.) escupir; despedir, arrojar

belching *n* eructación, *f;* (of smoke, etc.) vómito, *m,* emisión, *f*

beleaguer *vt* sitiar

Belgium *n* Bélgica, *f*

belie *vt* desmentir, contradecir; defraudar

belief *n* creencia, *f;* fe, *f;* opinión, *f,* parecer, *m;* (trust) confianza, *f.* **in the b. that,** creyendo que, en la creencia de que

believable *a* creíble

believe *vt* and *vi* creer; opinar, ser de la opinión, parecer (a uno); confiar, tener confianza. **I b. not,** Creo que no, Me parece que no. **I b. so,** Creo que sí, Me parece que sí. **to make (a person) b.,** hacer (a uno) creer. **to b. in,** creer en; confiar en, tener confianza en

believer *n* persona que cree, *f;* creyente, *mf*

belittle *vt* achicar; conceder poca importancia a

bell *n* campana, *f;* (hand-bell) campanilla, *f;* (small, round) cascabel, *m;* (on cows, etc.) cencerro, *m,* esquila, *f;* (electric, push, or bicycle) timbre, *m;* (jester's) cascabeles, *m pl;* (cry of stag) bramido, *m. vt* poner un cascabel (a). *vi* (stags) bramar, roncar. **To bear away the b.,** *fig* llevarse la palma. **to ring the b.,** tocar el timbre; agitar la campanilla. **to ring the bells,** tocar las campanas. **to b. the cat,** ponerle el cascabel al gato, ponerle el collar al gato. **b.-boy,** botones, mozo de hotel, *m.* **b.-clapper,** badajo, *m.* **b.-flower,** campanilla, *f.* **b.-founder,** campanero, *m.* **b.-mouthed,** abocinado. **b.-pull,** tirador de campanilla, *m.* **b.-ringer,** campanero, *m.* **b.-shaped,** campanudo. **b.-tent,** pabellón, *m.* **b. tower,** campanario, *m*

belle *n* beldad, *f*

belles-lettres *n pl* bellas letras, *f pl*

bellicose *a* belicoso, agresivo

belligerent *a* beligerante; belicoso, guerrero. *n* beligerante, *mf*

bellow *n* (shout) grito, *m;* rugido, bramido, *m;* (of guns) trueno, *m. vi* gritar, vociferar; rugir, bramar; tronar

bellows *n* fuelle, *m*

belly *n* vientre, *m,* barriga, *f;* (of a jug, etc.) panza, *f;* estómago, *m;* (womb) seno, *m. vt* hinchar. *vi* hincharse

belong *vi* pertenecer (a); tocar (a), incumbir (a); (to a place) ser de; residir en

belongings *n pl* efectos, *m pl;* posesiones, *f pl;* (luggage) equipaje, *m*

beloved *a* muy amado, muy querido. *n* querido (-da)

below *adv* abajo; (under) debajo; (further on) más abajo; (in hell) en el infierno; (in this world) en este mundo, aquí abajo. *prep* bajo; (underneath) debajo de; (after) después de; (unworthy of) indigno de. inferior a. **The valley lay b. us,** El valle se extendía a nuestros pies. **b. zero,** bajo cero

belt *n* cinturón, *m;* (of a horse) cincha, *f;* (corset) faja, *f; geog* zona, *f;* (of a machine) correa (de transmisión), *f*

beltway *n* anillo periférico, *m*

bemoan *vt* deplorar, lamentar

bemuse *vt* confundir, desconcertar

bench *n* banco, *m;* (with a back) escaño, *m;* mesa de trabajo, *f;* (carpenter's, shoemaker's, in a boat, in parliament) banco, *m;* (judges) tribunal, *m*

bend n corvadura, curva, vuelta, f; (in a river, street) recodo, m; (on a road) codo viraje, m; (of the knee) corva, f; (in a pipe) codo, m; naut nudo, m; her banda, f. **sheet b.**, (knot) nudo de tejedor, m

bend vt encorvar; doblegar; torcer; (the head) bajar; (the body) inclinar; (steps) dirigir, encaminar; (the mind) aplicarse, dedicarse. vi encorvarse; doblegarse; torcerse; (arch) arquear; inclinarse. **to b. the knee**, arrodillarse. **on bended knee**, de rodillas. **to b. back**, vt redoblar. vi redoblarse; inclinarse hacia atrás. **to b. down**, agacharse; inclinarse. **to b. forward**, inclinarse hacia delante. **to b. over**, inclinarse encima de

bendable a que puede doblarse; plegadizo; flexible

bending n doblamiento, m; flexión, f; inclinación, f. a doblado; inclinado

beneath adv abajo; debajo; (at one's feet) a los pies de uno. prep bajo; debajo de; al pie de; (unworthy, inferior) indigno. **He married b. him**, Se casó fuera de su clase

benediction n bendición, f; gracia divina, merced, f

benefaction n beneficiación, f; buena obra, f; beneficio, favor, m

benefactor n bienhechor, m; protector, m; patrono, m; fundador, m

beneficence n beneficiencia, caridad, f, buenas obras, f pl

beneficial a beneficioso; provechoso, útil

beneficiary n beneficiado (-da), beneficiario (-ia)

benefit n beneficio, bien, m; provecho, m, utilidad, f; (favor) favor, m; theat beneficio, m; (help) ayuda, f, servicio, m. vt beneficiar; aprovechar; (improve) mejorar. vi (with by) sacar provecho de; ganar. **for the b. of**, para; en pro de, a favor de. **b. society**, sociedad benéfica, f

benevolence n benevolencia, bondad, f; liberalidad, f; caridad, f; favor, m

benevolent a benévolo; bondadoso; caritativo. **b. society**, sociedad de beneficencia, f

benighted a sorprendido por la noche; fig ignorante

benign, benignant a benigno

bent n talento, m; inclinación, afición, f, a torcido, Mexico chueco; encorvado; resuelto

benumb. See **numb**

benzine n bencina, f

bequeath vt legar, dejar (en el testamento); transmitir

bequest n legado, m

bereave vt privar (de), quitar; arrebatar; afligir. **the bereaved parents**, los padres afligidos

bereavement n privación, f; (by death) pérdida, f; aflicción, f

bereft a privado (de); desamparado; indefenso. **utterly b.**, completamente solo

beret n boina, f

berry n baya, f; (of coffee, etc.) fruto, m, vi dar bayas; coger bayas

berth n (bed) litera, m; (cabin) camarote, m; (anchorage) anclaje, fondeadero, m; (job) empleo, m, vt (a ship) fondear. **to give a wide b. to**, naut ponerse a resguardo de; apartarse mucho de; evitar

beseech vt suplicar, rogar, implorar; (ask for) pedir con ahínco

beseeching a suplicante, implorante. n súplica, f; ruego, m

beseechingly adv suplicantemente

beset vt atacar, acosar; aquejar, acosar, perseguir. **beset by personal misfortune**, acosado por las desgracias personales; (block) obstruir; (surround) rodear, cercar

beside, besides prep al lado de; cerca de; (compared with) en comparación de, comparado con; (in addition) además de; aparte de; excepto. adv además, también. **to be beside oneself**, estar fuera de sí

besiege vt sitiar; (assail) asaltar, asediar; (surround) rodear; importunar

besieging a sitiador. n sitio, asalto, m; asedio, m, importunación, f

besmear vt embadurnar, ensuciar

besotted a estúpido; embrutecido; atontado

bespatter vt manchar; derramar; salpicar

bespeak vt reservar; (goods) encargar; (signify) demostrar, indicar; significar; poet hablar

best a sup of **good** and **well**, mejor; el (la) mejor, m, f., los (las) mejores, m pl, f pl. adv mejor; el mejor; (most) más. **as b. I can**, como mejor pueda. **at the b.**, cuando más, en el mejor caso. **He did it for the b.**, Lo hizo con la mejor intención. **the b.**, lo mejor. **to be at one's b.**, brillar; lucirse. **to do one's b.**, hacer todo lo posible. **to get the b. of**, llevar la mejor parte de; triunfar de (or sobre). **to make the b. of**, sacar el mayor provecho de. **The next b. thing to do is . . . ,** Lo mejor que queda ahora por hacer es . . . **b. man**, padrino de boda, m. **to be b. man**, apadrinar, ser padrino de. **b. seller**, libro que se vende más, libro favorito, m

bestial a bestial

bestiality n bestialidad, f

bestir (oneself) vr menearse, moverse; preocuparse; (hurry) darse prisa

bestow vt (place) poner; (with upon) conferir, conceder, otorgar; (a present) regalar

bestowal n puesta, f; otorgamiento, m; concesión, f; (of a present) regalo, m, dádiva, f

bestride vt montar a horcajadas en; poner una pierna en cada lado de; cruzar de un tranco

bestseller n campeón de venta, éxito editorial, triunfo de librería, m

bet n apuesta, postura, f, vi apostar; (gamble) jugar. **What do you bet?** ¿Qué apuesta Vd.?

betake (oneself) vr acudir (a); darse (a); marcharse

bethink (oneself) vr pensar, reflexionar; (remember) recordar, hacer memoria; ocurrirse

Bethlehem Belén, m

betimes adv pronto; de buena hora, temprano; con tiempo

betoken vt presagiar, prometer; indicar

betray vt traicionar; revelar, descubrir; (a woman) seducir; (show) dejar ver

betrayal n traición, f; (of confidence) abuso (de confianza), m; (of a woman) seducción, f

betrayer n traidor (-ra)

betroth vt desposar(se) con, prometer(se). **to be betrothed to,** estar desposado con

betrothal n desposorio, m, esponsales, m pl; (duration) noviazgo, m

betrothed n desposado (-da), futuro (-ra)

better a comp of **good,** mejor; superior. adv mejor; más. vt mejorar; exceder. n apostador (-ra). **He has bettered himself,** Ha mejorado su situación. **It is b. to . . . ,** Es mejor . . . , Vale más . . . (followed by infin.). **little b.,** poco mejor; algo mejor; poco más. **much b.,** mucho mejor. **our betters,** nuestros superiores. **so much the b.,** tanto mejor. **the b. to,** para mejor. **to be b.,** ser mejor; (of health) estar mejor. **to get b.,** mejorar. **to get the b. of,** triunfar sobre, vencer. **b. half,** inf media naranja, f. **b. off,** mejor situado, más acomodado

betterment n mejora, f, mejoramiento, m; adelantamiento, avance, m

betting n apuesta, f

bettor n apostador (-ra)

between prep entre; en medio de; de. **the break b. Mr. X and Mrs. Y,** el rompimiento del Sr. X y la Sra. Y. adv en medio; entre los dos. **far b.,** a grandes intervalos. **b. now and then,** desde ahora hasta entonces. **b. one thing and another,** entre una cosa y otra. **b. ourselves,** entre nosotros

beverage n brebaje, m, bebida, f

bevy n grupo, m; (of birds) bandada, f; (of roes) manada, f

bewail vt lamentar, llorar

beware vi guardarse (de); cuidar (de); desconfiar (de). interj ¡cuidado! ¡atención! **B. of imitations!** ¡Desconfiad de las imitaciones!

bewilder vt aturdir, abobar; dejar perplejo (a); confundir

bewildered a aturdido, abobado; perplejo; confuso

bewildering a incomprensible; complicado

bewilderment n aturdimiento, m; perplejidad, f; confusión, f

bewitch vt hechizar; fascinar, encantar

bewitching a encantador, hechicero, fascinante. n embrujamiento, encantamiento, m

beyond prep más allá de; más lejos que; (behind) tras, detrás de; (of time) después de; fig fuera del alcance de; (without) fuera de; (above) encima de; (not including) aparte. adv más allá; más lejos; detrás. **b. doubt,** fuera de duda. **b. question,** indiscutible. **b. the sea,** allende el mar. **That is b. me,** Eso es demasiado para mí; Eso no está en mi mano; Eso está fuera de mi alcance. **the back of b.,** donde Cristo dio las tres voces, las quimbambas. **the B.,** la otra vida

bias n sesgo, bies, través, m; fig prejuicio, m; parcialidad, f, vt influir; predisponer. **to cut on the b.,** cortar al sesgo

biassed a parcial; tendencioso

bib n babero, m; pechera, f, vi beber mucho, empinar el codo

Bible n Biblia, f

biblical a bíblico. **b. history,** historia sagrada, f

bibliography n bibliografía, f

bibulous a bebedor, borrachín

bicarbonate n bicarbonato, m

bicentenary n segundo centenario, m

biceps n bíceps, m

bicker vi disputar, altercar; (of stream, etc.) murmurar, susurrar; (of flame) bailar, centellear

bickering n altercado, argumento, m

bicycle n bicicleta, f, vi andar en bicicleta, ir de bicicleta

bicycle pump Lat. Am. inflador m

bicycling n ciclismo, m

bicyclist n biciclista, mf

bid n (at auction) postura, f; (bridge) puja, f; oferta, f, vt mandar, ordenar, invitar a; (at an auction) pujar, licitar. **to make a bid for,** (attempt) hacer un esfuerzo para; procurar. **to bid fair,** prometer; dar indicios de; dar esperanzas de. **to bid goodbye to,** decir adiós (a), despedirse de. **to bid welcome,** dar la bienvenida (a)

biddable a obediente, dócil; manso

bidder n postor, m, pujador (-ra). **the highest b.,** el mejor postor

bidding n (order) orden, f; instrucción, f; invitación, f; (at an auction) postura, licitación, f. **to do a person's b.,** hacer lo que se le manda

bide vt aguardar, esperar. **to b. by,** (fulfil) cumplir con

bidet n bidé, m

biennial a bianual, bienal

bier n andas, f pl; féretro, ataúd, m
bifocal a bifocal
bifurcate vt and vi bifurcar(se)
big a grande; grueso; (grown up) mayor; (tall) alto; voluminoso; (vast) extenso, vasto; (full) lleno (de); (with young) preñada; importante. **to talk big,** echarla de importante. **big-boned,** huesudo. **big-end,** aut biela, f. **big game,** caza mayor, f. **big gun,** inf pájaro gordo, m
bigamist n bígamo (-ma)
bight n (in a rope) vuelta (de un cabo), f; (bay) ensenada, f
bigness n grandor, m; gran tamaño, m; altura, f; (tallness of a person) gran talle, m; (vastness) extensión, f; importancia, f
bigot n fanático (-ca)
bigoted a fanático, intolerante
bigotry n fanatismo, m, intolerancia, f
bikini n bikini, m
bile n bilis, hiel, f; mal humor, m, cólera, f
bilingual a bilingüe
bilious a bilioso
bill n (parliamentary) proyecto de ley, m; law escrito, m; com cuenta, f; (poster) cartel, m; (program) programa, m; (cast) repertorio, m; (bank note) billete de banco, m; (of a bird) pico, m; (for pruning) podadera, f. **due b.,** com abonaré, m. **Post no bills!** Se prohíbe fijar carteles. **b. of exchange,** letra de cambio, f. **b. of fare,** lista de platos, f; fig programa, m. **b. of health,** patente de sanidad, f. **b. of lading,** conocimiento de embarque, m. **b. of rights,** declaración de derechos, f. **b. of sale,** contrato de venta, m, carta de venta, f. **b.-broker,** agente de bolsa, agente de cambio, m. **b.-poster,** fijador de carteles, cartelero, m
bill vt anunciar; publicar; poner en el programa; fijar carteles en. **to b. and coo,** (doves) arrullar; inf besuquearse
billboard, n tablero publicitario, m
billed a (in compounds) de pico
billet n alojamiento, m; (of wood) pedazo (de leña), m; (job) empleo, destino, m, vt alojar (en or con)
billiards n pl billar, m. **billiard ball,** bola de billar, f. **billiard cue,** taco, m. **billiard cushion,** baranda dc la mesa de billar, f. **billiard marker,** marcador, m. **billiard match,** partida de billar, f. **billiard player,** jugador (-ra) de billar. **billiard pocket** Lat. Am. bucbaca f. **billiard room,** sala de billar, f. **billiard table,** mesa de billar, f
billing n facturación, f
billion n billón, m; (U.S.A. and France) mil millones, m pl
bill of particulars n relación detallada, f
billow n oleada, f; poet ola, f; fig onda, f. vi hincharse, encresparse; ondular

billowy a ondulante, ondeante
bimonthly a bimestral
bin n hucha, f, arcón, m; recipiente, m; depósito, m; cajón, m; (for wine) estante, m
binary a binario
bind vt atar; unir, ligar; amarrar; (in sheaves) agavillar; (bandage) vendar; sujetar; fijar; aprisionar; (a book) encuadernar; sew ribetear; (oblige) obligar; comprometer; (constipate) estreñir; contratar (como aprendiz). **I feel bound to,** Me siento obligado a. **to b. over,** obligar a comparecer ante el juez
binder n encuadernador (-ra); agr agavilladora, f
binding a válido, valedero; obligatorio; **become b.,** adquirir carácter de compromiso; med constrictivo. n atadura, ligación, f; (of books) encuadernación, f; sew ribete, m
binge n parranda, juerga, f. **to go on the b.,** ir de parranda, ir de picos pardos, ir de juerga
binocular a binocular. n pl **binoculars,** binóculos, gemelos, m pl
biography n biografía, vida, f
biologist n biólogo, m
biology n biología, f
biped n bípedo, m, a bípedo, bípede
birch n bot abedul, m; (rod) vara, f. a de abedul. vt pegar con una vara, dar una paliza (a)
bird n pájaro, m; ave, f. **Birds of a feather flock together,** Cada cual se arrima a su cada cual. **hen b.,** pájara, f. **b.-call,** voz del pájaro, f, canto del ave, m. **b. catcher or vendor,** pajarero, m. **bird's-eye view,** vista de pájaro, perspectiva aérea, f. **b.-fancier,** aficionado (-da) a las aves; criador (-ra) de pájaros. **b.-like,** como un pájaro; de pájaro. **b.-lime,** liga, f. **to go b.-nesting,** ir a coger nidos de pájaros. **b. of paradise,** ave del paraíso, f. **b. of passage,** ave de paso, f. **b. of prey,** ave rapaz, f. **b.-seed,** alpiste, m
birth n nacimiento, m; (act of) parto, m; origen, m; (childhood) infancia, f; (family) linaje, m, familia, f; fig creación, f. **from b.,** de nacimiento. **to give b. to,** dar a luz, echar al mundo, parir. **b. certificate,** partida de nacimiento, certificación de nacimiento, f. **b. control,** anticoncepcionismo, m, regulación de la fecundidad, f. **b.-mark,** antojos, m pl. **b.-place,** lugar de nacimiento, m. **b.-rate,** natalidad, f
birthday n cumpleaños, m
birthright n derecho de nacimiento, m; herencia, f
Biscay, the Bay of el Golfo de Vizcaya, m
biscuit n galleta, f; bizcocho, m. **b. box or maker,** galletero, m. **b.-like,** abizcochado

bisect *vt* dividir en dos partes iguales; *geom* bisecar

bishop *n* obispo, *m*; (in chess) alfil, *m*. **bishop's crozier,** báculo episcopal, cayado, *m*

bison *n* bisonte, *m*

bit *n* pedazo, *m*; (of grass, etc.) brizna, *f*; (moment) instante, *m*; (quantity) cantidad, *f*; (of a drill) mecha, *f*; (part) parte, *f*; (passage) trozo, *m*; (horse's) bocado, *m*; *inf* miga, *f*. **a bit,** un tanto, algo, un poco. **in bits,** en pedazos. **Not a bit!** ¡Nada! ¡Ni pizca!; ¡Claro que no! **bit by bit,** poco a poco, gradualmente. **to give someone a bit of one's mind,** contarle cuatro verdades. **to take the bit between one's teeth,** desbocarse; *fig* rebelarse. **Wait a bit!** ¡Espera un momento!

bitch *n* (female dog) perra, *f*; (fox) zorra, *f*; (wolf) loba, *f*

bite *n* mordedura, *f*; mordisco, *m*; (mouthful, snack) bocado, *m*, *Lat. Am.* botana *f* (of fish and insects) picada, *f*; (hold) asimiento, *m*; (sting, pain) picadura, *f*; (pungency) resquemor, *m*; (offer) oferta, *f*; (*fig* mordancy) mordacidad, acritud, *f*. *vt* and *vi* morder; (gnaw) roer; (of fish, insects) picar; (of hot dishes) resquemar; (of acids) corroer; (deceive) engañar, defraudar; (of wheels, etc.) agarrar; (hurt, wound) herir. **to b. one's tongue,** morderse la lengua. **to b. the dust,** caer al suelo

biting *a* (stinging) picante; (mordant) mordaz, acre; (of winds, etc.) penetrante; satírico. *n* mordedura, *f*; roedura, *f*

bitter *a* amargo; (sour) agrio, ácido; (of winds) penetrante; (of cold) intenso; cruel. **to the b. end,** hasta la muerte; hasta el último extremo. **b.-sweet,** agridulce

bitterness *n* amargura, *f*; (sourness) acidez, *f*; (of cold) intensidad, *f*; crueldad, *f*

bitters *n pl* (drink) bíter, *m*, angostura, *f*

bitumen *n* betún, *m*

bizarre *a* raro, extravagante; grotesco

black *a* negro; obscuro; (sad) triste, melancólico; funesto; (wicked) malo, perverso; (sullen) malhumorado. *n* (color) negro, *m*; (mourning) luto, *m*; (negro) negro, *m*; (negress) negra, *f*; (stain) mancha, *f*; (dirt) tizne, *m*. *vt* ennegrecer; tiznar. **in b. and white,** por escrito. **to look on the b. side,** verlo todo negro. **b. art,** nigromancia, *f*. **b.-currant,** grosella negra, *f*. **b.-eyed,** ojinegro, con ojos negros. **b.-haired,** pelinegro, de pelo negro. **b.-lead,** plombagina, *f*. **b.-list,** lista negra, *f*. **b.-market,** estraperlo, mercado negro, *m*. **b.-marketeer,** estraperlista, *mf* **b.-out,** oscurecimiento, apagamiento, *m*. **b.-pudding,** morcilla, *f*. **b. sheep,** oveja negra, *f*; *fig* oveja descarriada, *f*; (of a family) garbanzo negro, *m*. **b.-water fever,** melanuria, *f*

blackberry *n* mora, zarzamora, *f*; (bush) zarza, *f*, moral, *m*

blackbird *n* mirlo, *m*

blackboard *n* encerado, *m*, pizarra, *f*

black coffee *Spain* café solo, *Colombia* café tinto, *elsewhere in Lat. Am.* café negro *m*

blacken *vt* ennegrecer; tiznar; *fig* manchar, desacreditar. *vi* ennegrecerse

black eye *n* ojo como un tomate, ojo morado, *m*

blackguard *n* tipo de cuidado, perdido, *m*

blackhead *n* espinilla, *f*

blackmail *n* chantaje, *m*, *vt* hacer víctima de un chantaje; arrancar dinero por chantaje (a)

blackmailer *n* chantajista, *mf*

blackness *n* negrura, *f*; obscuridad, *f*; (wickedness) maldad, perversidad, *f*

blacksmith *n* herrero (-ra) *mf*, *Lat. Am.* also encasquillador (-ra) *mf*. **blacksmith's forge,** herrería, *f*

bladder *n anat* vejiga, *f*; ampolla, *f*; (of sea-plants) vesícula, *f*; (of fish) vejiga natatoria, *f*

blade *n* (leaf) hoja, *f*; (of grass, etc.) brizna, *f*; (of sharp instruments) hoja, *f*; (of oar) pala, *f*; (of propeller) paleta, ala, *f*

bladed *a* de . . . hojas. **a two-b. knife,** un cuchillo de dos hojas

blame *n* culpa, *f*; responsabilidad, *f*; censura, *f*. *vt* culpar, echar la culpa (a); tachar, censurar, criticar; acusar. **You are to b. for this,** Vd. tiene la culpa de esto

blameless *a* inculpable; inocente; intachable; elegante

blamelessness *n* inculpabilidad, inocencia, *f*; elegancia, *f*

blameworthy *a* culpable, digno de censura, vituperable

blanch *vt cul* mondar; hacer palidecer. *vi* palidecer, perder el color

bland *a* afable, cortés; dulce, agradable

blandish *vt* adular, halagar, acariciar

blank *a* en blanco; (empty) vacío; desocupado; pálido; (confused) confuso, desconcertado; (expressionless) sin expresión; (of verse) suelto; sin adorno. *n* blanco, hueco, *m*; papel en blanco, *m*; laguna, *f*; (form to be filled out) hoja *f*, *Mexico* esqueleto *m* **b. cartridge,** cartucho para salvas, cartucho de fogueo, *m*. **b. verse,** verso suelto, *m*

blanket *n* manta, frazada, *Lat. Am.* cobija *f*; (of a horse) sudadero, *Lat. Am.* mandil *m*; *fig* capa, *f*. *vt* cubrir con una manta. **to toss in a b.,** mantear. **wet b.,** aguafiestas, *mf*. **b. maker or seller,** mantero, *m*. **b. vote,** voto colectivo, *m*

blankly *adv* con indiferencia; sin comprender; (flatly) categóricamente

blankness *n* confusión, *f*, desconcierto, *m*; (emptiness) vaciedad, *f*; indiferencia, *f*; incomprensión, *f*

blare n sonido de la trompeta o del clarín, poet clangor, m; (of a car horn) ruido, m. vi sonar

blarney n labia, f. vt lisonjear

blaspheme vi blasfemar. vt renegar de, maldecir

blasphemous a blasfemo, blasfematorio

blasphemy n blasfemia, f

blast n (of wind) ráfaga (de viento), f; (of a trumpet, etc.) trompetazo, son, m; (of a whistle) pitido, m; (draft) soplo, m; explosión, f; fig influencia maligna, f. vt (rock) barrenar, hacer saltar; (wither) marchitar, secar; fig destruir; (curse) maldecir. in full b., en plena marcha. b.-furnace, alto horno, horno de cuba, m. b. hole, barreno, m

blasting n (of rock) voladura, f; (withering) marchitamiento, m; fig destrucción, ruina, f; (cursing) maldiciones, f pl. a. destructor; fig funesto. b. charge, carga explosiva, f

blatant a ruidoso; agresivo; llamativo; (boastful) fanfarrón

blaze n llama, f; fuego, m; conflagración, f; luz brillante, f; (of anger, etc.) acceso, m. vi llamear, encenderse en llamas; brillar, resplandecer. a b. of colour, una masa de color. Go to blazes! ¡Vete al infierno!

blazon n her blasón, m; fig proclamación, f, vt blasonar; adornar; proclamar

bleach n lejía, f. vt blanquear; descolorar. vi ponerse blanco; descolorarse

bleaching n blanqueo, m. b. powder, hipoclorito de cal, m

bleak a yermo, desierto; frío; expuesto; (sad) triste; severo

bleakness n situación expuesta, f; desnudez, f; frío, m; (sadness) tristeza, f; severidad, f

bleary-eyed a legañoso, cegajoso

bleat n balido, m, vt and vi balar, dar balidos

bleed vi sangrar, echar sangre; sufrir. vt sangrar; arrancar dinero a

bleeding n hemorragia, f; sangría, f, Lat. Am. desangre m

blemish n imperfección, f, defecto, m; (on fruit) maca, f; (stain) mancha, f; deshonra, f

blend n mezcla, mixtura, f; combinación, f; fusión, f. vt mezclar; combinar. vi mezclarse; combinarse

bless vt bendecir; consagrar; (praise) alabar, glorificar; hacer feliz (a). B. me! ¡Válgame Dios!

blessed a bendito; ecc beato, bienaventurado; (dear) querido; feliz; inf maldito

blessing n bendición, f; (grace) bendición de la mesa, f; (mercy) merced, gracia, f; favor, m; (good) bien, m. He gave them his b., Les echó su bendición

Bless you! (to someone who has sneezed) ¡Jesús!

blight n agr tizne, tizón, m; (of cereals) añublo, m; (mould) roña, f; (greenfly) pulgón, m; fig influencia maligna, f; (frustration) desengaño, m; (spoil-sport) aguafiestas, mf vt atizonar; anublar; (wither) marchitar, secar; fig frustrar, destruir; malograr

blind a ciego; (secret) secreto; (of a door, etc.) falso; (closed) cerrado, sin salida; (unaware) ignorante; sin apreciación (de). to be b., ser ciego; fig tener una venda en los ojos. to be b. in one eye, ser tuerto. to turn a b. eye, hacer la vista gorda. b. alley, callejón sin salida, m. b. as a bat, más ciego que un topo. b. flying, aer vuelo a ciegas, m. b. man, ciego, hombre ciego, m. b. obedience, obediencia ciega, f. b. side, (of persons) lado débil, m. b. woman, ciega, mujer ciega, f

blind vt cegar; poner una venda en los ojos (de); (dazzle) deslumbrar; hacer cerrar los ojos a; hacer ignorar

blind n persiana, f; (Venetian) celosía, f; (deception) pretexto, m; velo, m

blindfold vt vendar los ojos (a); fig poner una venda en los ojos (de). a and adv con los ojos vendados; a ciegas; con los ojos cerrados

blindman's buff n gallina ciega, f

blindness n ceguedad, f; ofuscación, f; ignorancia, f

blink n parpadeo, m, guiñada, f; (of light) destello, m; reflejo, m; vi parpadear, pestañear; (of lights) destellar

bliss n felicidad, f; deleite, placer, m; ecc gloria, f

blissful a feliz

blithe a alegre

blizzard n ventisca, nevasca, f

bloated a abotagado, hinchado; orgulloso; indecente

blob n masa, f; mancha, f; gota, f

block n bloque, m; (log) leño, m; naut polea, f; (for beheading and of a butcher) tajo, m; (for mounting) apeadero, m; (of shares, etc.) lote, m; (of houses) manzana, Lat. Am. cuadra; (jam) atasco, m; (obstruction) obstrucción, f; (for hats) forma, f. A chip off the old b., De tal palo tal astilla. b. and tackle, naut polea con aparejo. b.-hook, grapa, f. b.-house, mil blocao, m

block vt bloquear; cerrar (el paso); (stop up) atarugar, atascar; (a wheel) calzar; (a bill, etc.) obstruir; (hats) poner en forma. to b. the way, cerrar el paso.

blockade n bloqueo, m, vt bloquear. to run the b., violar el bloqueo

blockhead n leño, zoquete, imbécil, m

blond(e) a (of hair) rubio; (of complexion) de tez blanca. n hombre rubio, m; (woman) rubia, mujer rubia, f. peroxide b., rubia oxigenada, f. b. lace, blondina, f

blood n sangre, f; (relationship) parentesco, *m*; (family) linaje, *m*, prosapia, *f*; (life) vida, *f*; (sap) savia, *f*; jugo, *m*; (horse) caballo de pura raza, *m*; (dandy) galán, *m*. *vt* sangrar. **bad b.**, mala sangre, *f*; odio, *m*; mala leche, *f*. **blue b.**, sangre azul, *f*. **in cold b.**, a sangre fría, *f*. **My b. is up**, Se me enciende la sangre. **My b. runs cold**, Se me hiela la sangre. **to be in the b.**, llevar en la sangre. **b.-bank**, banco de sangre, *m*. **b.-bath**, matanza, *f*. **b.-colored**, de color de sangre, sanguíneo. **b.-feud**, venganza de sangre, *f*. **b.-guilt**, culpabilidad de homicidio, *m*. **b.-heat**, calor de sangre, *m*. **b.-letting**, sangría, *f*. **b. orange**, naranja dulce, *f*. **b.-plasma**, plasma sanguíneo, *m*. **b.-poisoning**, septicemia, *f*; infección, *f*. **b.-pressure**, presión sanguínea, *f*. **b. purity**, limpieza de sangre, *f*. **b.-red**, rojo como la sangre. **b.-relation**, pariente (-ta) consanguíneo(a). **b.-relationship**, consanguinidad, *f*. **b.-stain**, mancha de sangre, *f*. **b.-stained**, ensangrentado, manchado de sangre. **b.-stone**, sanguinaria, *f*. **b.-sucker**, sanguijuela, *f*; *fig* vampiro, *m*; (usurer) avaro (-ra). **b.-vessel**, vaso sanguíneo, *m*.

bloodhound *n* sabueso, *m*

bloodiness *n* estado sangriento, *m*; crueldad, ferocidad, *f*

bloodless *a* exangüe; pálido; incruento; anémico; indiferente

bloodshed *n* efusión de sangre, *f*; matanza, carnicería, *f*

bloodshot *a* (of the eye) inyectado

bloodthirsty *a* sanguinario, carnicero

bloody *a* sangriento; (of battles) encarnizado; (cruel) sanguinario, cruel

bloom *n* flor, *f*; florecimiento, *m*; (on fruit) flor, *f*; (prime) lozanía, *f*; (on the cheeks) color sano, *m*. *vi* florecer. **in b.**, en flor

blooming *a* florido; en flor; fresco; lozano; brillante

blossom *n* flor, *f*. *vi* florecer. **to b. out into**, hacerse, llegar a ser; (wear) lucir; (buy) comprarse

blot *n* borrón, *m*; mancha, *f*. *vt* manchar; (erase) tachar; (dry) secar. **to b. out**, borrar; destruir; secar con papel secante

blotch *n* (on the skin, or stain) mancha, *f*

blotter *n* com libro borrador, *m*; teleta, *f*

blouse *n* blusa, *f*

blow *n* golpe, *m*; bofetada, *f*; (with the fist) puñetazo, *m*; (with the elbow) codazo, *m*; (with a club) porrazo, *m*; (with a whip) latigazo, *m*; (blossoming) floración, *f*; (disaster) desastre, *m*, tragedia, *f*. **to come to blows**, venirse a las manos. **at a b.**, con un solo golpe; de una vez. **We are going for a b.**, Vamos a tomar el fresco. **b. below the belt**, golpe bajo, *m*. **b. in the air**, golpe en vago, *m*. **b. of fate**, latigazo de la fortuna, *m*

blow *vi* (of wind) soplar (el viento), hacer viento, correr aire; (pant) jadear, echar resoplidos; (of fuses) fundirse. *vt* (wind

instruments) tocar; soplar; (inflate) inflar; (swell) hinchar. **to b. a kiss**, tirar un beso. **to b. one's nose**, sonarse las narices. **to b. away**, disipar; ahuyentar; llevar (el viento). **to b. down**, echar por tierra, derribar (el viento). **to b. in**, llevar adentro, hacer entrar (el viento); (windows, etc.) quebrar (el viento). **to b. off**, quitar (el viento). **to b. open**, abrir (el viento). **to b. out**, hacer salir (el viento); llevar afuera (el viento); (a light) matar de un soplo, apagar soplando. **to b. over**, pasar por (el viento); soplar por; disiparse; olvidarse. **to b. up**, (inflate) inflar; (the fire) avivar (el fuego) (explode) volar; (swell) hinchar

blowing *n* soplo *m*; violencia, *f*; (blossoming) florecimiento, *m*. **b. up**, voleo, *m*; explosión, *f*

blow-up *n* (photograph) fotografía ampliada, *f*

blubber *vi* gimotear; berrear. *n* (of the whale) grasa de ballena, *f*. **b.-lip**, bezo, *m*. **b.-lipped**, bezudo

bludgeon *n* cachiporra, porra, *f*; garrote, *m*; estaca, *f*. *vt* golpear con una porra, dar garrotazos (a)

blue *a* azul; (with bruises) amoratado; (sad) deprimido, melancólico; (obscene) verde; (dark) sombrío; (traditionalist) conservador. *n* azul, *m*; (sky) cielo, *m*; (for clothes) añil de lavandera, *m*; *pl* **blues**, melancolía, depresión, *f*; (homesickness) morriña, *f*. *vt* (laundry) añilar. **to look b.**, parecer deprimido; (of prospects, etc.) ser poco halagüeño. **b. black**, azul negro, *m*; (of hair) azabache, *m*. **b.-bottle**, *ent* moscón, *m*. **b.-eyed**, con ojos azules. **b. gum**, eucalipto, *m*. **B. Peter**, bandera de salida, *f*. **b. print**, fotocopia, *f*; plan, *m*

bluestocking *n* marisabidilla, doctora, *f*

bluff *a* (of cliffs, etc.) escarpado; (of persons) franco, campechano, brusco

bluffer *n* Lat. Am. blofista *mf*

bluish *a* azulado

blunder *n* desacierto, desatino, *m*; equivocación, *f*; (in a translation, etc.) falta, *f*. *vi* tropezar (con); desacertar; equivocarse; *inf* meter la pata. *vt* manejar mal; estropear

blundering *a* desacertado; equivocado; imprudente *n*. See **blunder**

blunt *a* romo, embotado; obtuso; (abrupt) brusco; franco; descortés; (plain) claro. *vt* enromar, embotar; (the point) despuntar; *fig* hacer indiferente; (pain) mitigar

bluntly *adv* sin filo; sin punta; bruscamente, francamente; claramente

bluntness *n* embotamiento, *m*; *fig* brusquedad, franqueza, *f*; claridad, *f*

blur *n* borrón, *m*; mancha, *f*; imagen indistinta, *f*. *vt* borrar; manchar; *phot* velar

blurred *a* borroso; indistinto; turbio

blurt (out) vt proferir bruscamente; revelar sin querer

blush n rubor, m; rojo, m. vi enrojecerse, ruborizarse, ponerse colorado; avergonzarse (por)

blushing a ruboroso; púdico

bluster vi (of the wind) soplar con furia; (of waves) encresparse, embravecerse; (of persons) bravear, fanfarronear. n furia, violencia, f; tumulto, m; fanfarronería, f

blustering a (of wind) violento, fuerte; (of waves) tumultuoso; (of people) fanfarrón, valentón

board n tabla, f; (for notices) tablón, m; (b. residence) pensión, f; (table) mesa, f; (food) comida, f; (for chess, checkers) tablero, m; (sign) letrero, m; (of instruments) cuadro, m; (bookbinding) cartón, m; naut bordo, m; (committee) junta, dirección, f; tribunal, m; pl boards theat tablas, f pl. **above b.**, abiertamente, sin disimulo. **free on b.**, (f.o.b.) franco a bordo. **in boards**, (of books) encartonado. **managerial b.**, junta directiva, f. **on b.**, a bordo. **on the boards**, theat en las tablas. **to go on b.**, ir a bordo. **b. and lodging**, pensión completa, casa y comida, f. **b. of directors**, consejo de administración, m. **b. of examiners**, tribunal de exámenes, m. **b. of trade**, junta de comercio, f; ministerio de comercio, m

board vt carp entablar, enmaderar; embarcar en; (nav a ship) abordar; (lodge) alojar, tomar a pensión

boarder n huésped (-da); (at school) pensionista, mf alumno (-na) interno (-na)

boarding n entablado, m; (planking) tablazón, f; (of a ship) abordaje, m; (of a train) subida (al tren), f. **b.-house**, casa de huéspedes, pensión, f. **b.-school**, pensionado, m

boarding gate n puerta de embarque, f

boast n jactancia, f; ostentación, f; (honor) gloria, f. vi jactarse, vanagloriarse, Lat. Am. dragonear, Argentina faramallear; alabarse; ostentar. **to b. about**, jactarse de; hacer gala de; gloriarse en

boaster n vanaglorioso (-sa), jactancioso (-sa)

boastful a vanaglorioso, jactancioso; ostentador

boastfulness n vanagloria, jactancia, f; fanfarronería, f; ostentación, f

boat n barco, m; bote, m; (in a fun fair) columpio, m, lancha, f; (for sauce or gravy) salsera, f. vi ir en barco; (row) remar, navegar. **to b. down**, bajar en barco. **to b. up**, subir en barco. **b. building**, construcción de barcos, f. **b. club**, club náutico, m. **b. crew**, tripulación de un barco, f. **b.-hook**, bichero, garabato, m. **b.-house**, cobertizo de las lanchas, m. **b.-load**, barcada, f. **b.-race**, regata, f.

b.-scoop, achicador, m. **b.-shaped**, en forma de barco. **b.-train**, tren que enlaza con un vapor, m

boating n pasear en bote, m; manejo de un bote, m; (rowing) remo, m. **b.-pole**, botador, m

boatswain n contramaestre, m. **boatswain's mate**, segundo contramaestre, m

bob n (curtsey) reverencia, f; (woman's hair) pelo a la romana, m; (of bells) toque (de campana), m. vi saltar; moverse. bt cortar corto. **long bob**, (hair) melena, f. **to bob up**, ponerse de pie; surgir. **to bob up and down**, subir y bajar; bailar. **bob-tail**, rabo corto, m. **bob-tailed**, rabón

bobbin n carrete, huso, m; (of wool, etc.) ovillo, m; (of looms, sewing machines) bobina, f; (in lace-making) bolillo, palillo, m

bode vt presagiar, prometer. **to b. ill**, prometer mal. **to b. well**, prometer bien

bodily a del cuerpo; físico; corpóreo; real; material; (of fear) de su persona. adv corporalmente; en persona, personalmente; en conjunto, enteramente; en una pieza

boding a ominoso, amenazador. n presagio, m; agüero, m

body n anat cuerpo, m; (trunk) tronco, m; (corpse) cadáver, m; (of a vehicle) caja, f; (of a motor-car) carrocería, f; (of a ship) casco, m; (of a church) nave, f; (centre) centro, m; (of a book, persons, consistency and ast) cuerpo, m; (person) persona, f; corporación, f; grupo, m; (of an army) grueso (de ejército), m; organismo, m. **in a b.**, en masa, juntos (juntas); en corporación. **to have enough to keep b. and soul together**, tener de que vivir. **b.-snatcher**, junta cadáveres mf ladrón de cadáveres, m. **b.-snatching**, robo de cadáveres, m

bodyguard n guardia de corps, f; guardia, f; (escort) escolta, f

body language n el lenguaje del cuerpo, m

bog n pantano, marjal, m, marisma, f, Central America chagüe m

bogey n duende, m; (to frighten children) coco, m; (nightmare) pesadilla, f

bogus a postizo, falso

boil vi bullir, hervir; (cook) cocer. vt hervir; cocer. n ebullición, f; med divieso, m. **to b. away**, consumirse hirviendo; chem evaporar a seco. **to b. over**, rebosar

boiler n cul marmita, olla, f; (of a furnace) caldera, f. **double-b.**, baño de María, m. **steam-b.**, caldera de vapor, f. **b.-maker**, calderero, m. **b. room**, cámara de la caldera, f. **b.-suit**, mono, m

boiling n ebullición, f, hervor, m; (cooking) cocción, f, a hirviente. **b. point**, punto de ebullición, m

boisterous a (of persons) exuberante,

impetuoso; (stormy) tempestuoso, borrascoso; violento

boisterously *adv* impetuosamente, ruidosamente; tempestuosamente; con violencia

boisterousness *n* exuberancia, impetuosidad, *f*; violencia, *f*; tempestuosidad, borrascosidad, *f*

bold *a* intrépido, audaz, *Argentina* agulludo (determined) resuelto; (forward) atrevido; (showy) llamativo; (clear) claro. **b.-faced,** descarado, desvergonzado. **b.-faced type,** letra negra, *f*

boldly *adv* intrépidamente; descaradamente; resueltamente; claramente

boldness *n* intrepidez, valentía, *f*; resolución, *f*; (forwardness) osadia, *f*, descaro, atrevimiento, *m*; claridad, *f*

Bolivian *a* and *n* boliviano (-na)

bolster *n* travesaño, *m*. *vt* apuntalar; *fig* apoyar

bolt *n* pasador, cerrojo, *m*; (pin) perno, *m*; (knocker) aldaba, *f*; (roll) rollo, *m*; (flight) huida, *f*; (of a crossbow) flecha, *f*; (from the blue) rayo, *m*. *adv* (upright) recto una flecha; enhiesto; rígido. **b. and nut,** perno y tuerca, *m*

bolt *vt* echar el cerrojo (a); empernar; (*fam* eat) zampar. *vi* huir; (horses) desbocarse, dispararse; (plants) cerner. **to b. down,** cerrar con cerrojo. **to b. in,** entrar corriendo, entrar de repente. **to b. off,** marcharse corriendo. **to b. out,** *vi* salir de golpe. *vt* cerrar fuera

bomb *n* bomba, *f*, *vt* bombardear. **to be a b.-shell,** *fig* caer como una bomba. **b.-carrier,** portabombas, *m*. **b. crater,** bombazo, *m*. **b.-release,** (*aer nav*) lanzabombas, *m*. **b.-sight,** mira de avión de bombardeo, *f*

bombard *vt* bombardear, bombear; *fig* llover (preguntas, etc.) sobre

bombardment *n* bombardeo, *m*

bombast *n* ampulosidad, pomposidad, *f*

bombastic *a* bombástico, altisonante, pomposo

bomber *n* avión de bombardeo, bombardero, *m*. **dive b.,** bombardero en picado, *m*. **heavy b.,** bombardero pesado, *m*. **light b.,** bombardero ligero, *m*. **b. command,** servicio de bombardero, *m*

bonafide *a* fidedigno

bond *n* lazo, vínculo, *m*; *chem* enlace, *m*; (financial) obligación, *f*; (security) fianza, *f*; (Customs) depósito, *m*; *pl* **bonds,** cadenas, *f pl*, a esclavo. **in b.,** en depósito. **bonds of interest,** intereses creados, *m pl*. **b.-holder,** obligacionista, *mf*

bondage *n* esclavitud, *f*; servidumbre, *f*; cautiverio, *m*; prisión, *f*

bone *n* hueso, *m*; (of fish) espina (de pez), *f*; (whale b.) ballena, *f*; *pl* **bones,** cuerpo, *m*, *vt* deshuesar; poner ballenas (a o en). **to be all skin and bones,** estar en los

huesos. **to have a b. to pick with,** tener que arreglar las cuentas con. **b.-ash,** cendra, *f*

boner *n* gazapo, *m*, patochada, plancha, *f*

bonfire *n* fogata, hoguera, *f*

bonnet *n* capota, *f*; (of babies) gorra, *f*; (of men) boina, *f*; (of chimney and of machines) sombrerete, *m*

bonus *n* paga extraordinaria, bonificación, *f*; sobresueldo, *m*; (of food, etc.) ración extraordinaria, *f*

bon vivant *n* alegre, vividor, *m*

bony *a* huesudo; (of fish-bones) lleno de espinas; óseo

booby *n* pazguato, bobo, *m*. **b.-prize,** último premio, *m*. **b.-trap,** trampa, *f*; *mil* mina, *f*

book *n* libro, *m*; volumen, tomo, *m*; (of an opera) libreto, *m*, *vt* anotar en un libro; apuntar; (seats) tomar (localidades); (tickets) sacar (billetes); (of the issuing clerk) dar; (reserve) reservar; inscribir; consignar (a suspect); (engage) contratar; (invite) comprometer. **to turn the pages of a b.,** hojear un libro. **b.-ends,** sostén para libros, sujetalibros, *m*. **b.-keeper,** tenedor de libros, *m*. **b.-keeping,** teneduría de libros, *f*. **b.-maker,** apostador de profesión, *m*. **b. of reference,** libro de consulta, *m*. **b.-plate,** exlibris, *m*. **b.-post,** tarifa de impresos, *f*. **b.-shop,** librería, *f*. **b.-trade,** venta de libros, *f*; comercio de libros, *m*

bookbinder *n* encuadernador (-ra) de libros

bookbinding *n* encuadernación de libros, *f*

bookcase *n* armario de libros, *Lat. Am.* librero *m*

booking *n* (of rooms, etc.) reservación, *f*; (of tickets) toma, *f*; *com* asiento, *m*; (engagement) contratación, *f*. **b.-clerk,** vendedor (-ra) de billetes. **b.-office,** despacho de billetes, *m*; taquilla, *f*

bookish *a* aficionado a los libros; docto, erudito

bookmark *n* marcador, *m*

bookseller *n* librero, *m*

bookshelf *n* estante para libros, *m*

bookworm *n* polilla que roe los libros, *f*; *fig* ratón de biblioteca, *m*

boom *n* *naut* botavara, *f*; (of a crane) aguilón, *m*; (noise) ruido, *m*; (of the sea) bramido, *m*; (thunder) trueno, *m*; (in a port) cadena de puerto, *f*; *com* actividad, *f*; (*fig* peak) auge, *m*, *vi* sonar; bramar; tronar; *com* subir; ser famoso. **b. sail,** vela de cangreja, *f*

boomerang *n* bumerang, *m*

boon *n* favor, *m*, merced, *f*; bien, *m*, ventaja, *f*; don, *m*; privilegio, *m*, a (of friends) intimo

boor *n* monigote, patán, palurdo, *m*

boorish a rudo, zafio, rústico, cerril

boost vt elec aumentar la fuerza de; inf empujar; subir; (advertise) dar bombo (a)

boot n bota, f; (of a car) compartimiento para equipaje, m. **button-boots,** botas de botones, f pl. **riding-boots,** botas de montar, f pl. **to b.,** además, de añadidura. **b.-maker,** zapatero, m. **b.-tag,** tirador de bota, m. **b.-tree,** horma de bota, f

bootblack n limpiabotas, Mexico bolero (-ra), elsewhere in Lat. Am. embolador (-ra), lustrador (-ra) mf

booth n puesto, m; barraca, f

bootlegger n contrabandista de alcohol, m

booze vi emborracharse. **b. up** Argentina acatarrarse n alcohol, m; borrachera, f

boozed up Lat. Am. apimplado (-da), Argentina acatarrado (-da), Central America azurumbado (-da)

boozer n borracho (-cha)

boracic a bórico. n ácido bórico, m

borax n bórax, m

bordello n burdel, m

border n borde, m; (of a lake, etc.) orilla, f; (edge) margen, m; (of a diploma, etc.) orla, f; sew ribete, m, orla, f; (fringe) franja, f; (garden) arriate, m; (territory) frontera, f; límite, confín, m. vt sew orlar, ribetear; ornar (de); (of land) lindar con. **to b. on,** (of land) tocar, lindar con; (approach) rayar en. **b. country,** región fronteriza, f

borderland n zona fronteriza, f; lindes, m pl

borderline n frontera, f; límite, m; margen, m, a fronterizo; lindero; (uncertain) dudoso, incierto

bore n taladro, barreno, m; perforación, f; (hole) agujero, m; (of guns) calibre, m; (wave) oleada, f; (nuisance) fastidio, m; (dullness) aburrimiento, tedio, m; (person) pelmazo, m, machaca, mf vt taladrar, barrenar, horadar; perforar; hacer un agujero (en); (exhaust) aburrir; fastidiar. **It's a b.,** Es una lata. **to be bored,** aburrirse, fastidiarse

boredom n aburrimiento, m; tedio, hastío, m

boring a aburrido, pesado, tedioso; molesto, fastidioso. n taladro, m; horadación, f; sondeo, m; perforación, f

born a nacido; (by birth) de nacimiento; (b. to be) destinado a; natural (de). **He was b. in 1870.** Nació en 1870. **to be b. again,** renacer, volver a nacer. **well-b.,** bien nacido. **b. with a silver spoon in one's mouth,** Nacido de pie, Nacido en domingo

borough n burgo, m; villa, f; ciudad, f. **b. surveyor,** arquitecto municipal, m

borrow vt pedir prestado; apropiarse, adoptar; copiar; (arithmetic) restar; (a book from a library) tomar prestado. **May I b. your pencil?** ¿Quieres prestarme tu lápiz?

borrower n el (la) que pide o toma prestado

borrowing n el pedir prestado, acto de pedir prestado, m

Bosnian a bosnio

bosom n pecho, m; (heart) corazón, m; (of the earth, etc.) seno, m. **b. friend,** amigo (-ga) del alma, amigo (-ga) íntimo (-ma)

boss n (of a shield) corcova saliente, f; tachón, m; arch pinjante, m. inf amo, m; jefe, m. vt mandar; dominar. **political b.,** cacique, m

bossism n caudillaje, m

bossy a mandón, autoritario. **b. person** Lat. Am. mandarín m

botanical a botánico. **b. garden,** jardín botánico, m

botany n botánica, f

botch n (clumsy work) chapucería, f; remiendo, m. vt chapucear, chafallar; (patch) remendar

both a and pron ambos, m pl; ambas, f pl; los dos, m pl; las dos, f pl, adv tan(to) . . . como; (and) y; a la vez, al mismo tiempo. **It appealed both to the young and the old,** Gustó tanto a los jóvenes como a los viejos. **b. of you,** ustedes dos, vosotros dos, vosotras dos. **b. pretty and useful,** bonito y útil a la vez

bother n molestia, f, fastidio, m; (worry) preocupación, f; dificultad, f; (fuss) alboroto, m, Lat. Am. fregada f, vt molestar, fastidiar, Lat. Am. acatarrar; preocupar. vi preocuparse

bottle n botella, f; (smaller) frasco, m; (babies) biberón, m; (for water) cantimplora, f, vt embotellar, envasar, enfrascar. **to b. up,** (liquids, capital, armies, navies) embotellar; (feelings) refrenar. **to bring up on the b.,** criar con biberón. **b.-green,** verde botella, m. **b.-neck,** (in an industry) embotellado, m; (in traffic) atascadero, m. **b.-washer,** fregaplatos, mf; (machine) máquina para limpiar botellas, f

bottle cap n corchalata, f

bottled a en botella; (of fruit, vegetables) conservado

bottling n embotellado, m; envase, m. **b. outfit,** embotelladora, f; (for fruit, etc.) aparato para conservar frutas o legumbres, m

bottom n base, f; (deepest part) fondo, m; (last place) último lugar, m; fundamento, m; (of a chair) asiento, m; (of a page, table, mountain, etc.) pie, m; (posterior) culo, m; (of a river) lecho, m; (of the sea) fondo, m; (of a ship) casco, m; (of a skirt) orilla, f; (truth) realidad, verdad, f; (basis) origen, m, causa, f. **at b.,** en realidad. **at the b.,** en el fondo. **false b.,** fondo doble, fondo secreto, m. **to be at**

the b. of, ocupar el último lugar en; ser el causante de. to get to the b. of, descubrir la verdad de; profundizar en, analizar. to sink to the b., (of ships) irse a pique

bottomless a sin fondo; (of chairs, etc.) sin asiento; (unfathomable) insondable

bough n rama, f, brazo (de un árbol) m

boulder n roca, peña, f; canto rodado, m; bloque de roca, m

boulevard n bulevar, m

bounce n bote, rebote, m; salto, m; (boasting) fanfarronería, f, vi rebotar; saltar, brincar. vt hacer botar o saltar

bound n límite, m; (jump) salto, brinco, m, vt limitar, confinar. vi saltar, brincar; (bounce) botar. within bounds, dentro del límite. b. for, con destino a; (of ships) con rumbo a

boundary n límite, lindero, término, m; frontera, f; raya, f. b. stone, mojón, m

boundless a sin límites, infinito; inmenso

bounteous, bountiful a dadivoso, generoso; bondadoso

bounty n generosidad, munificencia, f; don, m; (subsidy) subvención, f

bouquet n ramo, ramillete (de flores), m, Lat. Am. also maceta f; perfume, m; (of wine) nariz, f

bourgeois a and n burgués (-esa)

bourgeoisie n burguesía, mesocracia, f

bout n turno, m; (in fencing, boxing, wrestling) asalto, m; (of illness, coughing) ataque, m; (fight) lucha, f, combate, m; (of drinking) borrachera, f

bovine a bovino, vacuno

bow n (weapon) arco, m; (of a saddle) arzón (de silla), m; mus arco, m; (knot) lazo, m; (greeting) saludo, m; reverencia, inclinación, f; (of a boat) proa, f. to tie a bow, hacer un lazo. bow and arrows, arco y flechas, m. bow-legged, patizambo, Central America corveta, f, bow window, ventana saliente, f

bow vi inclinarse; hacer una reverencia, saludar; (remove the hat) descubrirse; fig inclinarse (ante); (submit) someterse (a), reconocer; agobiarse; mus manejar el arco. vt (usher in) introducir en, conducir a; doblar; inclinar. to bow down (to), humillarse ante; obedecer; (worship) reverenciar, adorar. to bow out, despedir con una inclinación del cuerpo

bowel n intestino, m; pl bowels, fig seno, m, entrañas, f pl

bower n (arbor) enramada, f; glorieta, f; (boudoir) tocador de señora, m

bowing n mus arqueada, f; saludo, m, a (of acquaintance) superficial

bowl n receptáculo, m; (of a fountain) taza, f; (of a pipe) cazoleta, f; (barber's) bacía, f; (for washing) jofaina, f; (for punch) ponchera, f; (goblet) copa, f; (for soup) escudilla, f; (for fruit) frutero, m; (for a spoon) paleta, f; (ball) boliche, m. vt

tirar; (in cricket) sacar; (a hoop) jugar con; (in ninepins) tumbar con una bola. to b. along, recorrer; ir en coche o carruaje (por). to b. over, fig dejar consternado (a), desconcertar

bowler n (in cricket) servidor, m; (hat) sombrero hongo, m; (skittle player) jugador de bolos, m

bowling n (in cricket) saque, m; (skittles) (juego de) bolos, m; (juego de) boliche, m. b. alley, bolera, pista de bolos, f, salón de boliche, m. b.-green, bolera en cesped, f

bow tie n pajarita, f

box n caja, f; (case) estuche, m; (luggage) baúl, m, maleta, f; (for a hat) sombrerera, f; bot boj, m; theat palco, m, Mexico lumbrera, f; (for a sentry, signalman, etc.) garita, casilla, f; (on a carriage) pescante, m; (blow) cachete, m, bofetada, f; (for a horse) vagón, m. post office box, apartado de correos, m. box-kite, cometa celular, f. box-maker, cajero, m. box office, taquilla, f, Lat. Am. boletería f. box-pleat, sew tabla, f

box vt encajonar, meter en una caja. vi boxear. to box the ears of, calentar las orejas de. to box up, encerrar

boxer n sport boxeador, pugilista, m

boxing n encajonamiento, m; envase, m; sport boxeo, pugilato, m, b.-gloves, guantes de boxeo, m pl. b.-ring, cuadrilátero de boxeo, m

box-office success n éxito de taquilla, m

boy n muchacho, niño, rapaz, m; (older) chico, joven, m. new boy, nuevo alumno, m. old boy, (of a school) antiguo alumno, m; (fam address) chico. small boy, chiquillo, pequeño, crío, m. b. doll, muñeco, m. boy scout, muchacho explorador, m

boycott vt boicotear. n boicot, m

boyhood n muchachez, mocedad, f; (childhood) niñez, f

boyish a muchachil; pueril; de niñez

brace n (prop) puntal, barrote, m; abrazadera, f; carp berbiquí, m; viento, tirante, m; freno (for the teeth), m, (pair) par, m; pl braces, tirantes, m pl. vt apuntalar; asegurar; carp ensamblar; naut bracear; (trousers) tirar; fig fortalecer, refrescar

bracelet n pulsera, f, brazalete, m, ajorca, f

bracing a (of air, etc.) fortificante, tónico; estimulador

bracket n consola, f; arch repisa, f; soporte, m; (on furniture, etc.) cantonera, f; print paréntesis angular, m; (for a light) brazo (de alumbrado), m. vt print poner entre paréntesis; juntar. In brackets, entre paréntesis. They were bracketed equal, Fueron juzgados iguales

brackish a salobre

brag vi jactarse, fanfarronear, Lat. Am.

dragonear, *Argentina* faramallear *n* jactancia, *f.* **to b. about,** hacer alarde de

braggart a baladrón, jactancioso. *n* jactancioso, fanfarrón, *m*

braid *n* trencilla, *f*, cordoncillo, *m*; (for trimming) galón, *m*; (plait) trenza, *f. vt* (hair) trenzar; (trim) galonear; acordonar, trencillar

brain *n* cerebro, *m*; entendimiento, *m*, inteligencia, *f*; talento, *m*; (common sense) sentido común, *m*; *pl* **brains,** sesos, *m pl,* (animal and human); cacumen, *m. vt* romper la crisma (a). **to blow one's brains out,** levantarse la tapa de los sesos. **to rack one's brains,** devanarse los sesos. **Brains Trust,** masa cefálica, *f*; consorcio de inteligencias, *m.* **b.-box,** cráneo, *m.* **b.-fever,** fiebre cerebral, *f.* **b.-storm,** crisis nerviosa, *f.* **b.-wave,** idea luminosa, *f.* **b.-work,** trabajo intelectual, *m*

brainchild *n* engendro, *m*

brain drain *n* fuga de cerebros, *f*

brainless a sin seso; tonto

brainy a sesudo, inteligente, talentudo

braise *vt cul* asar

brake *n* (of vehicles and *fig*) freno, *m, Chile, Peru* alitranca *f* (flax and hemp) caballete, *m*; (carriage) break, *m*; (thicket) matorral, *m. vt* (vehicles) frenar; (hemp, etc.) rastrillar. **foot-b.,** freno de pedal, *m.* **hand-b.,** freno de mano, *m.* **to b. hard,** frenar de repente. **to release the b.,** quitar el freno

bran *n* salvado, *m*

branch *n* (of a tree, a family) rama, *f*; (of flowers, of learning) ramo, *m*; (of a river) tributario, afluente, *m*; (of roads, railways) ramal, *m*; (of a firm) sucursal, dependencia, *f.* a sucursal, dependiente; (of roads, railways) secundario. *vi* echar ramas; bifurcarse, dividirse; ramificarse. **to b. off,** bifurcarse, ramificarse. **to b. out,** extenderse; emprender cosas nuevas

branching *n* ramificación, *f*; división, *f.* **off,** bifurcación, *f*

brand *n* (torch) tea, *f*; (on cattle, etc.) hierro, *m*; (trademark) marca de fábrica, *f*; marca, *f*; (stigma) estigma, *m. vt* marcar con el hierro, herrar; marcar; estigmatizar, tildar. **b.-new,** flamante

branding *n* (of livestock) herradero, *m*; (of slaves, criminals) estigmatización, *f*; difamación, *f.* **b.-iron,** hierro de marcar, *m*

brandish *vt* blandir

brandy *n* coñac, *m*

brass *n* latón, *m*; *mus* metal, *m*; (tablet) placa conmemorativa, *f*; *inf* dinero, *m.* **the b.,** *mus* el metal. **b. band,** banda de instrumentos de viento, *f.* **b.-neck,** *inf* cara dura, *f.* **b. works** or **shop,** latonería, *f*

brassiere *n* sostén, *m*

brat *n* crío, *m*

bravado *n* bravata, *f*

brave a valiente, animoso, intrépido; espléndido, magnífico; bizarro. *n* valiente, *m. vt* desafiar, provocar; arrostrar

bravery *n* valentía, *f*, valor, *m*, intrepidez, *f*, coraje, *m*; esplendidez, suntuosidad, *f*; bizarría, *f*

bravo *n* bandido, *m*; asesino pagado, *m, interj* ¡bravo! ¡ole!

brawl *n* camorra, reyerta, pelotera, *Lat. Am.* follisca *f. vi* alborotar; (of streams) murmurar. **to start a b.,** armar camorra

brawler *n* camorrista, *mf*

brawn *n cul* embutido, *m*; músculo, *m*; (strength) fuerza, *f*

brawny a membrudo, musculoso, forzudo

brazen a de latón; (of voice) bronca; desvergonzado, descarado

brazier *n* (fire) brasero, *m*; latonero, *m*

Brazil el Brasil

Brazilian a and *n* brasileño (-ña)

breach *n* violación, contravención, *f*; (gap) abertura, *f. vt mil* hacer brecha (en); (in a line of defence) hacer mella (en). **b. of confidence,** abuso de confianza, *m.* **b. of promise,** incumplimiento de la palabra de casamiento, *m.* **b. of the peace,** alteración del orden público, *f*, quebrantamiento de la paz, *m*

bread *n* pan, *m.* **to earn one's b. and butter,** ganarse el pan. **brown b.,** pan moreno, *m.* **unleavened b.,** pan ázimo, *m.* **b. and butter,** pan con mantequilla, *m*; *fig* sustento diario, *m.* **b.-basket,** cesta de pan, *f*; *inf* estómago, *m.* **b.-bin,** caja del pan, *f.* **b.-crumb,** miga, *f*; migaja, *f.* **b.-knife,** cuchillo para cortar el pan, *m.* **b. poultice,** cataplasma de miga de pan, *f.* **b.-winner,** ganador (-ra) de pan, trabajador (-ra)

breadth *n* anchura, *f*; latitud, *f*; liberalidad, *f*; *sew* ancho de una tela, *m*

break *n* rotura, *f*; (opening) abertura, *f*; *geol* rajadura, *f*; (fissure) grieta, *f*; (solución de continuidad, interrupción, *f*; (billiards) serie, *f*; (change) cambio, *m*; (in a boy's voice) muda (de la voz), *f*; (blank) vacío, *m*; (in the market) baja, *f*; intervalo, *m*; descanso, *m*; pausa, *f*; (truce) tregua, *f*; (clearing) clara, *f*; mus quiebra (de la voz), *f*; (carriage) break, *m*; (fam folly) disparate, *m.* **with a b. in one's voice,** con voz entrecortada. **b. of day,** aurora, alba, *f.* **at the b. of day,** al despuntar el alba

break *vt* romper; quebrar; quebrantar, fracturar; (breach) abrir brecha en; (in two) partir, dividir; (into pieces) hacer pedazos, despedazar; (into small pieces) desmenuzar; (into crumbs) desmigajar; (destroy) destrozar; (a blow) parar; (a law) infringir, violar; (the bank in gambling) quebrar; (a journey, etc.) interrumpir; (of a habit) desacostumbrar, hacer perder el vicio de; (a promise) no cumplir, faltar a;

(a record) superar; (plow ground) roturar; (spoil) estropear; arruinar; *com* ir a la quiebra; (an official) degradar; (an animal) domar, amansar; *(fig* crush) subyugar; (betray) traicionar; *(fig* of silence, a spell, a lance, peace, the ranks) romper; (cushion) amortiguar; (lessen) mitigar; (disclose) revelar; *elec* interrumpir. **to b. one's promise,** faltar a su palabra. **to b. the ice,** *fig* romper el hielo. **to b. asunder,** romper en dos (partes); dividir. **to b. down,** derribar; echar abajo; destruir; (suppress) suprimir; subyugar; abolir; disolver. **to b. in,** (animals) domar, amaestrar; (persons) disciplinar; (new shoes) ahormar, romper. **to b. in two,** partir; dividir en dos; (split) hender. **to b. off,** separar, quitar; (a branch) desgajar; *fig* romper; interrumpir; cesar. **to b. open,** forzar, abrir a la fuerza. **to b. up,** hacer pedazos; (scatter) poner en fuga, dispersar; hacer levantar la sesión; (the ground) roturar; (parliament) disolver; (a ship) desguazar, deshacer (un buque)

break *vi* romperse; quebrarse; quebrantarse; (of beads) desgranarse; (burst) reventar, estallar; (of abscesses) abrirse; (of a boy's voice) mudar; *(fig* and of clouds, etc.) romperse; desaparecer; (of the dawn) despuntar (el alba), amanecer; (sprout) brotar; (of a ball) torcerse; (of fine weather) terminar; (change) cambiar; (of a storm) estallar. **to b. loose,** desasirse; *fig* desencadenarse. **to b. away,** escaparse, fugarse; (from a habit) romper con, independizarse de (another country); disiparse. **to b. down,** (of machinery, cars) averiarse; (fail) frustrarse, malograrse; (weep) deshacerse en lágrimas; (lose one's grip) perder la confianza en sí; (in health) sufrir una crisis de salud. **The car broke down,** El auto tuvo una avería. **to b. in,** (of burglars) forzar la entrada; irrumpir (en), penetrar (en); exclamar. **to b. in on,** sorprender; entrar de sopetón; invadir; interrumpir; caer sobre; molestar. **to b. into,** (force) forzar; (utter) romper a, prorrumpir en; empezar (a); pasar de repente a; (of time, etc.) ocupar; hacer perder. **to b. off,** (of speech) interrumpirse; cesar; (detach) desprenderse, separarse; (of branches) desgajarse. **to b. out,** huir, escaparse; *fig* estallar; aparecer; declararse; (of fire) tomar fuego; derramarse; (of an eruption) salir. **to b. over,** derramarse por; bañar. **to b. through,** abrirse paso (por); abrirse salida (por); atravesar; *fig* penetrar; (of the sun, etc.) romper (por). **to b. up,** (depart) separarse; (of meetings) levantarse la sesión; dispersarse; (smash) hacerse pedazos; disolverse; (of a school) cerrarse, empezar las vacaciones; (melt) fundir; desbandarse (of a camp) levantar (el campo); (grow old) hacerse viejo; (be ill) estar agotado. **to b. with,** romper con; cesar; reñir con

breakable *a* quebradizo, frágil

breakage *n* rompimiento, quebrantamiento, *m*; cosa rota, *f*; fractura, *f*

breakdown *n* accidente, *m*; (of a machine) avería, *f*; *aut* pane, *f*; (failure) fracaso, *m*, falta de éxito, *f*; deterioración, *f*; (in health) crisis de salud, *f*. **b. gang,** pelotón de reparaciones, *m*

breaker *n* oleada, *f*

breakfast *n* desayuno, *m*. *vi* desayunar(se), tomar el desayuno. **to have a good b.,** desayunar bien. **b.-cup,** tazón, *m*. **b.-time,** hora del desayuno, *f*

breaking *n* rompimiento, *m*; quebrantamiento, *m*; fractura, *f*; ruptura, *f*; (in two) división, *f*; (into pieces) despedazamiento, *m*; (into small pieces) desmenuzamiento, *m*; (destruction) destrozo, *m*; (of a blow) parada, *f*; (of a law, etc.) violación, *f*; (of one's word) no cumplimiento, *m*; (of a journey, of sleep, etc.) interrupción, *f*; (escape) escape, *m*, huida, *f*; (of an animal) domadura, *f*; (of a boy's voice) muda (de la voz), *f*; (of news) revelación, *f*. **b. down,** demolición, *f* (of negotiations) suspensión, *f*. **b. in,** irrupción, *f*; (of an animal) domadura, *f*; (training) entrenamiento, *m*. **b. open,** forzamiento, *m*; quebranto, *m*. **b. out,** huida, *f*, escape, *m*; *fig* estallido, *m*; aparición, *f*; declaración, *f*; (scattering) derramamiento, *m*; (of a rash) erupción, *f*. **b. up,** dispersión, *f*; disolución, *f*; fin, *m*; ruina, *f*; (of a school) cierre, *m*; (change in weather) cambio, *m*; (of a meeting) levantamiento (de una sesión), *m*; (of the earth) roturación, *f*

breakneck *a* rápido, veloz, precipitado

bream *n icht* sargo, *m*. **sea-b.,** besugo, *m*

breast *n* pecho, *m*; (of birds) pechuga, *f*; (of female animals) teta, mama, *f*; (heart) corazón, *m*, *vt* (the waves) cortar (las olas); luchar con; *fig* arrostrar, hacer frente a. **b.-bone,** esternón, *m*. **b. high,** alto hasta el pecho. **b.-pin,** alfiler de pecho, *m*. **b.-pocket,** bolsillo de pecho, *m*. **b.-stroke,** estilo pecho, *m*

breast cancer *n* el cáncer del seno, *m*

breath *n* aliento, *m*; suspiro, *m*; (phonetics) aspiración, *f*; (breeze) soplo (de aire), *m*; (of scandal, etc.) murmurio, *m*; (fragrance) perfume, *m*, fragancia, *f*; (life) vida, *f*. **in a b.,** de un aliento. **in the same b.,** sin respirar. **out of b.,** sin aliento. **under one's b.,** por lo bajo, entre dientes. **to draw b.,** tomar aliento. **to get one's b. back,** cobrar aliento. **to hold one's b.,** contener el aliento. **to take one's b. away,** *fig* dejar consternado a

breathe *vi* respirar; vivir; (of air, etc.) soplar; (take the air) tomar el fresco; (rest) tomar aliento. *vt* respirar; exhalar; dar aire (a); (whisper) murmurar; (convey) expresar, revelar; (infuse) infundir. **to b. forth fury,** echar rayos. **to b. hard,** jadear. **to b. one's last,** exhalar el último suspiro. **to b. in,** inspirar

breathing n respiración, f; (of the air, etc.) soplo, m; (phonetics) aspiración, f. a que respira; viviente. **hard** or **heavy b.**, jadeo, resuello, resoplido, m. **b.-space,** fig respiro, m

breathless a jadeante, sin aliento; (dead) muerto; (sultry) sin un soplo de aire; intenso, profundo; (of haste) precipitado

breathlessness n falta de aliento, f; respiración difícil, f; (death) muerte, f; (of weather) falta de aire, f

bred a criado. **ill (well) b.,** mal (bien) criado. **pure-b.,** de raza

breeches n calzones, m pl; pantalones, m pl. **riding-b.,** pantalones de montar, m pl. **to wear the b.,** fig ponerse los calzones

breed n casta, raza, f; tipo, m; clase, f, vt procrear; engendrar, crear; (bring up) educar; criar. vi reproducirse; sacar cría; multiplicarse. **to b. in-and-in,** procrear sin mezclar razas

breeding n reproducción, f; cría, f; (upbringing) crianza, f; educación, f; instrucción, f; producción, f; creación, f, a de cría; (of male animals) semental; prolífico. **bad b.,** mala crianza, f. **good b.,** buena crianza, f. **cross b.,** cruzamiento de razas, m. **B. will out,** Aunque la mona se vista de seda, mona se queda. **b. farm,** criadero, m

breeze n brisa, f, vientecillo m, soplo de aire m, Lat. Am. airecito m; (argument) altercación, f, argumento, m; (of coke) cisco de coque, m. **fresh b.,** brisa fresca, f. **light b.,** brisa floja, f. **strong b.,** viento fuerte, viento muy fresco, m

breezy a con brisa, fresco; expuesto a la brisa; oreado; (of manner) animado, jovial

brethren n pl hermanos, m pl

brevet n mil graduación honoraria, f; nombramiento honorario, m. vt mil graduar

brevity n brevedad, f; concisión, f

brew n mezcla, f; brebaje, m. vt hacer (cerveza, té, etc.); preparar, mezclar; flg urdir, tramar. vi prepararse; urdirse; (storm) gestarse.

brewer n cervecero (-ra)

brewery n cervecería, fábrica de cerveza, f

bribe n soborno, cohecho, m, Lat. Am. coima f vt sobornar, cohechar. **to take bribes,** dejarse sobornar

bribery n soborno, m

brick n ladrillo, m; (for children) piedra de construcción, f; bloque, m; inf buen chico, m, joya, f, a de ladrillo. vt enladrillar. **b.-floor,** ladrillado, m; **b.-kiln,** horno de ladrillo, m. **b.-maker,** ladrillero, m. **b.-yard,** ladrillar, m

bricklayer n albañil, m

bridal a nupcial; de la boda; de la novia. **b. bed,** tálamo, m. **b. cake,** torta de la boda, f. **b. shop,** tienda para novias, f. **b.**

shower, despedida de soltera, despedida de soltería, f. **b. song,** epitalamio, m. **b. veil,** velo de la novia, velo nupcial, m. **b. wreath,** corona de azahar, f

bride n novia, desposada, f; (after marriage) recién casada, f

bridegroom n novio, m; (after marriage) recién casado, m

bridesmaid n madrina de boda, f; niña encargada de sostener la cola de la novia, f

bridge n (engineering, mus naut) puente, m; lomo (de la nariz), m; (game) bridge, m, vt construir un puente (sobre), pontear; (obstacles) salvar; evitar; (fill in) ocupar, llenar. **auction b.,** bridge por subasta, m. **contract b.,** bridge por contrato, m. **suspension-b.,** puente colgante, m. **b. toll,** pontazgo, m

bridle n brida, f; freno, m. vt embridar, enfrenar; fig reprimir. vi (of horses) levantar la cabeza; (of persons) erguirse; hacer un gesto despreciativo. **snaffle b.,** bridón, m. **b. path,** camino de herradura, m

brief a breve, corto; conciso; lacónico, seco; rápido; fugaz, pasajero. n (papal) breve, m; law relación, f; escrito, m. vt (a barrister) instruir. **to hold a b. for,** defender, abogar por. **b.-case,** portapapeles, m; cartera (grande), f

briefly adv brevemente; en pocas palabras; sucintamente; (tersely) secamente

brigand n bandolero, bandido, m

bright a brillante, reluciente; vivo; cristalino; subido; claro; optimista; alegre; inteligente; (quick-witted) agudo; ilustre; (smiling) risueño; (of future, etc.) halagüeño. **to be as b. as a new pin,** estar como una ascua de oro. **b. blue,** azul subido, m. **b.-eyed,** con ojos vivos, con ojos chispeantes, ojialegre

Bright's disease n enfermedad de Bright, glomerulonefritis, f

brighten vt hacer brillar; (polish) pulir; (make happy) alegrar; (improve) mejorar. vi (of the weather) aclarar, despejarse (el cielo); sentirse más feliz; mejorar

brightness n brillo, m; claridad, f; esplendor, m; (of colors) brillantez, f; vivacidad, f; inteligencia, f; agudeza de ingenio, f

brilliance n fulgor, brillo, m; refulgencia, f; esplendor, m; lustre, m; talento, m; brillantez, gloria, f

brilliant a brillante. n (gem) brillante, m. **to be b.,** (in conversation, etc.) brillar; (be clever) ser brillante

brilliantine n brillantina, f

brim n (of a glass, etc.) borde, m; (of a hat) ala, f; margen, m, orilla, f. **to be full to the b.,** estar lleno hasta los bordes; flg rebosar. **eyes brimming with tears,** ojos arrasados de lágrimas

brine n salmuera, f; mar, m; poet lágrimas, f pl

bring vt traer; llevar; transportar; (take a

person or drive a vehicle) conducir; *fig* acarrear, traer; causar, ocasionar; producir; crear; (induce) persuadir; hacer (ver, etc.); (be worth) valer; (sell for) vender por; *law* entablar (un pleito, etc.): (before a judge) hacer comparecer (ante); (present) presentar; (attract) atraer; (place) poner. **to b. home,** llevar a casa; *fig* hacer ver, hacer sentir; demostrar; (a crime) probar contra. **to b. near,** acercar. **to b. about,** efectuar, poner por obra; causar, ocasionar; (achieve) lograr, conseguir. **to b. again,** traer otra vez, llevar de nuevo. **to b. away,** lievarse. **to b. back,** devolver; traer; (of memories) recordar. **to b. down,** llevar abajo, bajar; (of persons) hacer bajar; (humble) humillar; hacer caer; (of prices) hacer bajar; arruinar; destruir. **to b. down the house,** *theat* hacer venirse el teatro abajo. **to b. forth,** (give birth to) dar a luz; producir; causar; sacar a luz. **to b. forward,** hacer adelantarse; empujar hacia adelante; *fig* avanzar; (allege) alegar; *com* llevar a nueva cuenta; presentar; producir. **brought forward,** *com* suma y sigue. **to b. in,** (things) llevar adentro; (persons) hacer entrar; introducir; aparecer con; presentarse con; (meals) servir; producir; declarar; (a verdict) dictar (sentencia de). fallar. **to b. into being,** poner en práctica; dar origen (a). **to b. off,** (a ship) poner a flote; (rescue) salvar, rescatar; (carry out) efectuar, poner en práctica; (achieve) conseguir, lograr. **B. me the glass off the table,** Tráeme el vaso que hay en la mesa. **to b. on,** causar, inducir; acarrear; iniciar. **He brought a book on to the stage,** Entró en escena llevando un libro (o con un libro). **to b. out,** sacar; poner afuera; (a person) hacer salir; publicar; (a play) poner en escena; sacar a luz; (an idea, jewels, etc.) sacar a relucir; revelar; demostrar; hacer aparecer; (a girl in society) poner de largo (a). **to b. over,** llevar al otro lado; hacer venir; traer; conducir; hacer cruzar; (convert) convertir. **to b. round,** traer; llevar; (from a swoon) sacar de un desmayo; curar; persuadir; conciliar. **to b. through,** hacer atravesar; llevar a través de; ayudar a salir (de un apuro); (an illness) curar de. **to b. to,** traer a; llevar a; (from a swoon) hacer volver en sí; *naut* ponerse a la capa. **He cannot b. himself to,** No puede persuadirse a. **to b. together,** reunir; (things) juntar, amontonar; reconciliar, poner en paz. **to b. under,** someter; sojuzgar; incluir. **to b. up,** llevar arriba, subir; (a person) hacer subir; hacer avanzar; (a price) hacer subir; ir (a); andar; (breed) criar; (educate) educar, criar; (in a discussion) hacer notar; vomitar. **to b. up the rear,** ir al fin (de); *mil* ir a la retaguardia. **well** (or **badly) brought up,** bien (o mal) educado. **to b. upon oneself,** buscarse, incurrir (en). **to b. up-to-date,** poner al día; refrescar; rejuvenecer

bringing *n* acción de llevar o traer, *f*; conducción, *f*; transporte, *m*. **b. forth,** producción, *f*. **b. in,** introducción, *f*. **b. out,** producción, *f*; publicación, *f*; (of a girl in society) puesta de largo, *f*. **b. under,** reducción, *f*; subyugación, *f*. **b. up,** educación, crianza, *f*

brink *n* borde, margen, *m*; (of water) orilla, *f*; *fig* margen, *m*. **on the b.,** al margen; a la orilla. **to be on the b. of,** (doing something) estar para, estar a punto de

briny *a* salado

briquette *n* briqueta, *f*, aglomerado de carbón, *m*

brisk *a* activo; vivo; animado; rápido, acelerado; enérgico

briskness *n* actividad, *f*; viveza, *f*; animación, *f*; rapidez, *f*; energía, *f*

bristle *n* cerda, seda, *f*, *vi* erizarse

bristly *a* erizado, cerdoso; espinoso; hirsuto

British *a* británico. **the B.,** el pueblo británico; los ingleses

brittle *a* frágil, quebradizo, deleznable, friable

broach *n* *cul* espetón, asador, *m*. *vt* espitar (un barril); abrir; *fig* introducir

broad *a* ancho; grande; (extensive) vasto, extenso; **a b. confession,** una confesión amplia; (full) pleno; (of accents) marcado; (of words) lato; (clear) claro; (of the mind) liberal, tolerante; (of humor, etc.) grosero; (general) general, comprensivo. **in b. daylight,** en pleno día. **b.-brimmed,** de ala ancha. **b.-faced,** cariancho. **b.-minded,** tolerante, liberal, ancho de conciencia, abierto al mundo. **b.-mindedness,** tolerancia, liberalidad, *f*. **to be b.-minded,** ser tolerante, tener manga ancha. **b.-shouldered,** ancho de espaldas

broadcast *n* *agr* siembra al vuelo; *f*; *rad* radiodifusión, radiotransmisión, emisión, *f*, a radiado. *adv* por todas partes; extensamente. *vt* *agr* sembrar a vuelo; *rad* radiodifundir, radiar, transmitir por radio; (news, etc.) diseminar

broadcaster *n* (lecturer) conferenciante, *mf*; radiodifusor (-ra); (announcer) locutor (-ra)

broadcasting *n* radiación, radiodifusión, *f*; radio, *f*. **b.-station,** estación de radio, emisora, *f*. **b.-studio,** estudio de emisión, *m*

broaden *vt* ampliar, ensanchar. *vi* ampliarse, ensancharse

broadly *adv* anchamente; con marcado acento dialectal; de una manera general

broadness *n* anchura, *f*; extensión, vastedad, *f*; tolerancia, *f*; liberalidad, *f*; grosería, *f*; (of accent) acento marcado, *m*

broadside *n* (of a ship) costado, *m*; (of guns) andanada, *f*; *fig* batería, *f*; *print* cara de un pliego, *f*. **to be b. on,** dar el costado

brocade a and n brocado m.. vt decorar con brocado.

brocaded a decorado con brocado; de brocado

broccoli n bróculi, brécol, m

brochure n folleto, m

broil vt emparrillar, asar. vi asarse

broke a quebrado; (penniless) Peru calato

broken a roto; quebrado; (spiritless) abatido, desalentado; (infirm) agotado, debilitado; (ruined) arruinado; (of ground) desigual, escabroso; (of a language) chapucero; (spoilt) estropeado; imperfecto; incompleto; (loose) suelto; (of a horse, etc.) domado; (of the weather) variable; (of sleep) interrumpido; (of the heart, of shoes, etc.) roto; (of the voice, sobs, sighs) entrecortado; (of the voice through old age, etc.) cascada; (incoherent) incoherente. **b.-down,** (tired) rendido, agotado; arruinado; (not working) estropeado. **b.-hearted,** roto el corazón, angustiado. **b.-winged,** aliquebrado. **I speak broken Spanish,** Hablo el español chapuceramente

broker n corredor, m; (stock) corredor de bolsa, m

brokerage n corretaje, m

bronchi n pl bronquios, m pl

bronchitis n bronquitis, f

broncopneumonia n bronconeumonía, f

bronze n bronce, m; objeto de bronce, m, a de bronce. vt broncear. **B. Age,** Edad de Bronce, f

brooch n broche, m; alfiler de pecho, m

brood n (of birds) nidada, f; (of chickens) pollada, f; (other animals) cría, f; prole, f, vi empollar. **to b. over,** meditar sobre, rumiar; (of mountains, etc.) dominar

brook n arroyo, riachuelo, m, vt tolerar, sufrir, permitir

broom n escoba, f; bot retama, f; hiniesta, f. **common b.,** retama de escobas, f. **Spanish b.,** retama común, retama de olor, hiniesta, f. **b.-handle,** palo de escoba, m

broth n caldo, m

brothel n burdel, lupanar, m, casa de trato, f

brother n hermano, m; (colleague) colega, m; inf compañero, m. **foster-b.,** hermano de leche, m. **half-b.,** medio hermano, m. **step-b.,** hermanastro, m. **b.-in-law,** hermano político, cuñado, m. **b.-officer,** compañero de promoción, m

brotherhood n fraternidad, f; ecc cofradía, f; hermandad, f

brotherliness n fraternidad, f

brotherly a fraterno

brow n frente, f; ceja, f; (of a hill) cresta, cumbre, f; (edge) borde, m. **to knit one's b.,** fruncir el ceño

browbeat vt intimidar, amenazar

brown a castaño; (gallicism often used of shoes, etc.) marrón; pardo; (of complexion, eyes, hair) moreno; (dark brown) bruno; (blackish) negruzco; (toasted) tostado; (burnt) quemado. n color moreno, m; color pardo, m; castaño, m; (from the sun) bronce, m. vt (toast) tostar; (a person) volver moreno, broncear; (meat) asar. vi tostarse; volverse moreno, broncearse; asarse. **b. bear,** oso pardo, m. **b. owl,** autillo, m. **b. paper,** papel de estraza, m. **b. study,** ensimismamiento, m, meditación, f. **b. sugar,** azúcar moreno (or quebrado), m

brownish a morenucho; que tira a castaño o a bruno; parduzco; trigueño

browse vi pacer; (through a publication) hojear (un libro)

browsing n apacentamiento, m; hojeo (de un libro), m; lectura, f, estudio, m

bruise n cardenal m. Lat. Am. magullón m; abolladura, f; (in metal) bollo, m; (on fruit) maca, f, vt acardenalar, magullar; abollar; (fruit) macar

bruising n magullamiento, m; (of metal) abolladura, f; (crushing) machacadura, f; (boxing) boxeo, pugilato, m

brunette n trigueña, morena, f

brunt n peso, m; golpe, m; choque, m; esfuerzo, m. **to bear the b.,** soportar el peso; sufrir el choque; inf pagar el pato

brush n cepillo, m; (broom) escoba, f; (for whitewashing, etc.) brocha, f; (for painting) pincel, m; (of a fox) cola (de zorro), f; (undergrowth) breñal, matorral, m; (fight) escaramuza, f; (argument) altercación, f. **scrubbing-b.,** cepillo para fregar, m. **shoe-b.,** cepillo para limpiar los zapatos, m. **stroke of the b.,** brochada, f; pincelada, f. **whitewash-b.,** brochón, m. **b. maker** or **seller,** escobero (-ra); pincelero (-ra)

brush vt cepillar; (sweep) barrer; frotar; (touch) rozar; (touch lightly) acariciar. **to b. against,** rozar, tocar. **to b. aside,** echar a un lado; fig no hacer caso de; ignorar. **to b. off,** sacudir(se); quitar(se); (sweep) barrer. **to b. up,** cepillar; (wool) cardar; (tidy) asear; (a subject) refrescar, repasar

brushing n acepilladura, f; (sweeping) barredura, f; (touching) roce, rozamiento, m; (of hair) peinadura, f

brushwood n enjutos, m pl, chamarasca, f; matorral, m

brusque a brusco, seco

brusqueness n brusquedad, f

Brussels a bruselense; de Bruselas. **B. lace,** encaje de Bruselas, m

Brussels sprouts n pl bretones, m pl

brutal a bestial, brutal; salvaje, inhumano

brutality n brutalidad, bestialidad, f; barbaridad, ferocidad, f

brutalize vt embrutecer

brute n bruto, animal, m; salvaje, bárbaro, m. **b. force,** la fuerza bruta

brutish a bruto; sensual, bestial; grosero; salvaje; estúpido; ignorante. **to become b.,** embrutecerse

bubble n burbuja, f; borbollón, m, vi burbujear; borbollar, bullir, hervir

bubbling n burbujeo, m; hervidero, m; (of brooks) murmullo, m, a burbujeante; hirviente; (of brooks) parlero; (of wine) espumoso, efervescente

bubonic a bubónico. **b. plague,** peste bubónica, f

buccaneer n corsario, m; aventurero, m

buck n zool gamo, m; (male) macho, m; (fop) galán, petimetre, m, vi (of a horse) caracolear; fanfarronear. **to pass the b.,** inf echarle a uno el muerto. **b.-rabbit,** conejo, m. **to b. up,** hacer de tripas corazón

bucket n cubo, balde, m, cubeta, f

buckle n hebilla, f. vt enhebillar, abrochar con hebilla. vi doblarse. **to b. to,** ponerse a hacer algo con ahinco

buckskin n ante, m

buckwheat n alforfón, trigo sarraceno, m

bucolic a bucólico, pastoril

bud n brote, m; botón, capullo, m; (of vines) bollón, m; (of vegetables) gema, f. vi brotar, germinar. vt injertar de escudete

Buddhism n budismo, m

Buddhist n budista, mf

budding n brotadura, f; (of roses, etc) injerto de escudete, m; fig germen, m

budge vi moverse, menearse. vt mover

budget n presupuesto, m; (of news, etc.) colección, f. vi presuponer

buffalo n búfalo, f

buffer n (railway) parachoques, m; (of cars) amortiguador, m. **b. state,** estado tapón, m

buffet n bofetón, m; bofetada, f; bar, m. vt abofetear; golpear; luchar con las olas

buffoon n bufón, m

bug n chinche, f. **bugs** Lat. Am. bicherío, m

bugle n corneta, trompeta, f; (bead) abalorio, m. **b. blast,** trompetazo, m

bugler n trompetero, m

build vt edificar; (engines, ships, organs, etc.) construir; (a nest and fig) hacer; (have built) hacer, edificar; crear; formar; fundar. n estructura, f; (of the body) hechura, f; talle, m. **to b. castles in Spain,** hacer castillos en el aire. **built-up area,** zona urbana, f. **to b. up,** construir, levantar; (block) tapar; (business, reputation) establecer, crear. **to b. upon,** fig contar con, confiar en; esperar de

builder n constructor, m; maestro de obras, m; (laborer) albañil, m; creador (-ra), fundador (-ra) arquitecto, m

building n edificación, f; construcción, f; edificio, m; fundación, f; creación, f. **b. contractor,** maestro de obras, m. **b. ma-** terial, material de construcción, m. **b. site,** solar, terreno, m. **b. timber,** madera de construcción, f

built-in a empotrado. **b. closet,** armario empotrado, m

bulb n bot bulbo, m; (elec phys) bombilla, f; (of an oil lamp) cebolla, f

bulge n bulto, m; hinchazón, f; protuberancia, f; mil bolsa (en el frente), f. vi hincharse; estar lleno (de)

bulging a lleno (de); con bultos; hinchado (de)

bulk n volumen, tamaño, m; bulto, m; (larger part) grueso, m; mayor parte, f; (of people) mayoría, f; (of a ship) capacidad, f. **in b.,** com en bruto, en grueso. **to b. large,** tener mucha importancia

bulkhead n naut mamparo, m

bulkiness n abultamiento, m; volumen, tamaño, m

bulky a voluminoso, grande, grueso

bull n toro, m; ast Tauro, m; (of some animals) macho, m; (Stock Exchange) alcista, mf; (of the Pope) bula (del Papa), f. **a b. in a china shop,** un caballo loco en una cacharrería. **to fight bulls,** torear. **b.-calf,** ternero, m; acierto, m. **b. fight,** corrida de toros, f. **b. fighter's gala uniform,** traje de luces, m. **b.-ring,** plaza de toros, f

bulldog n perro dogo, perro de presa, m

bulldozer n (excavator) tozodora, f

bullet n bala, f. **spent b.,** bala fría, f. **stray b.,** bala perdida, f. **b.-proof,** a prueba de bala, blindado

bulletin n boletín, m

bulletin board n tablero de anuncios, tablero de avisos, tablón, m

bulletproof vest n chaleco blindado, m

bullfighter n torero, m (on foot), toreador, m (on horseback)

bullion n com metálico, m; oro (or plata) en barras, m, f

bullpen n toril, m (bullfighting); calentador, m (baseball)

bully n valentón, perdonavidas, gallito, m; rufián, Argentina compadre m. vt intimidar; tratar mal. **b. beef,** vaca en lata, f

bulwark n baluarte, m; naut antepecho, m

bumblebee n abejorro, m

bump n golpe, m; ruido, m; choque, m; (bruise) chichón, m, roncha, f; aer sacudida, f, meneo, m. vi (into, against) tropezar con; (along) saltar en. vt chocar (contra)

bumper n copa llena hasta los bordes, m; vaso lleno, m; (of a car) parachoques, m. **a b. harvest,** una cosecha abundante

bumpkin n patán, villano, m

bumptious a fatuo, presuntuoso, presumido

bumpy n (of surface) desigual, escabroso; (of a vehicle) incómodo, con mala suspensión

bun n buñuelo, bollo, m; (hair) moño, m

bunch n (of fruit) racimo, m; manojo, m; (of flowers) ramo, m; Lat. Am. also maceta f; (tuft) penacho, m; (gang) pandilla, f, vi arracimarse, agruparse

bundle n atado, lío, m; (of papers) legajo, m; (of sticks) haz, m; (sheaf) fajo, m; (package) paquete, m; fardo, hatillo, m; (roll) rollo, m, vt atar, liar; envolver; empaquetar; (stuff) meter, introducir. **to b. in,** meter dentro (de). **to b. out,** despachar sin ceremonia, poner de patitas en la calle

bungalow n casa de un solo piso, f

bungle vt estropear; hacer mal. n equivocación, f, yerro, m; cosa (o obra) mal hecha, f.

bungling a chapucero, torpe

bunion n juanete (del pie), m

bunk n litera, f, vi inf poner pies en polvorosa, pirarse

bunker n naut pañol, m; (for coal) carbonera, f; (golf) hoya de arena, f

bunkum n patrañas, f pl

bunting n gallardete, m

buoy n boya, baliza, f, vt boyar; abalizar; fig sostener. **light b.,** boya luminosa, f

buoyancy n flotación, f; fig optimismo, m, alegría, f

buoyant a boyante; ligero

burden n carga, f, peso, m; (of a ship) tonelaje, m, capacidad, f; (of a song) estribillo, m; (gist) esencia, f. vt cargar. **to be a b. on,** pesar sobre

burdensome a pesado, oneroso, gravoso; abrumador

bureau n buró, secreter, m; escritorio, m; (office) dirección, oficina, f; departamento, m

bureaucracy n burocracia, f

bureaucrat n burócrata, mf; inf mandarín, m

bureaucratic a burocrático

burglar n ladrón de casas, escalador, m. **cat b.,** gato, m. **b. alarm,** alarma contra ladrones, f. **b. insurance,** seguro contra robo, m

burglary n robo nocturno de una casa, m

burgle vi robar una casa de noche. vt robar

burial n entierro, m. **b.-ground,** campo santo, cementerio, m. **b. service,** misa de difuntos, f. **b. society,** sociedad de entierros, m

burlap n arpillera, f

burlesque a burlesco. n parodia. f. vt parodiar

burly a corpulento, fornido

burn vt quemar; calcinar; (bricks) cocer; cauterizar; (the tongue) picar; (dry up) secar; (the skin by sun or wind) tostar. vi quemar; arder; fig abrasarse (en). **b. at**

the stake, vt quemar en la hoguera. **to b. to ashes,** reducir a cenizas. **to b. away,** consumir(se). **to b. oneself,** quemarse. **to b. the midnight oil** Chile cranearse **to b. up,** quemar del todo, consumir. **to b. with,** fig abrasarse en

burn n quemadura, f; (stream) arroyo, m

burner n quemador (-ra); mechero, m

burning n quema; incendio, m; fuego, m; (inflammation) inflamación, f; (pain) quemazón, f; abrasamiento, m. a en llamas; ardiente; intenso; (notorious) notorio, escandaloso; abrasador; palpitante. **b. question,** cuestión palpitante, f

burnish n bruñido, m; lustre, brillo, m, vt bruñir; pulir, pulimentar, dar brillo a; (weapons) acicalar. vi tomar lustre

burr n bot cáliz de flor con espinas, m; mech rebaba, f; sonido fuerte de la erre, m

burrow n madriguera, f, vivar, m; (for rabbits) conejera, f. vt amadrigar; minar

bursar n tesorero, m; becario, m

burst n estallido, m, explosión, f; (in a pipe) avería, f, (fit) acceso, m; transporte, m; (effort) esfuerzo, m; (expanse) extensión, f, panorama, m. **b. of applause,** salva de aplausos, f

burst vi estallar; reventar; quebrarse; romperse; (overflow) desbordar; (of seams) nacerse; derramarse (por); (into laughter) romper a; (into tears) deshacerse en. vt quebrar; romper; hacer estallar. **to b. upon the view,** aparecer de pronto. **to b. into,** irrumpir en; (exclamations, etc.) prorrumpir en. **to b. into tears,** romper a llorar, deshacerse en lágrimas. **to b. open,** abrir con violencia; forzar

bursting n estallido, m; quebrantamiento, m; (overflowing) desbordamiento, m

bury vt enterrar, sepultar; sumergir; (hide) esconder, ocultar; (forget) echar tierra a

bus n (regular city bus) autobús m (Columbia, Spain, Venezuela), camión m (Mexico), camioneta f (Guatemala), casadoro m (Costa Rica), chiva f (Columbia, Panama, informal), colectivo m (Argentina, Bolivia), flota f (Columbia, informal), góndola f (Chile), guagua f (Canary Islands, Cuba), micro m (Chile), ómnibus m (Peru), omnibús m (Uruguay); (interurban bus), aerobús m (Venezuela), autobús (Argentina, Chile, Spain, Uruguay), camión, camión de primera clase m (Mexico), interprovincial m (Peru), pullmán m (Mexico; (interurban jitney bus) colectivo m (Colombia); (minibus) micro m (Columbia, Peru), liebre (Chile, informal) **double-decker bus,** ómnibus de dos pisos, m **to travel by bus,** ir en autobús. **bus station,** estación de autobuses, Mexico camionera f

bush n arbusto, matojo, m; (undergrowth)

maleza, *f;* tierra virgen, *f; mech* man-guito, *m*

bushel *n* medida de áridos, *f,* (In England 8 gallons or 36.37 liters)

bushy *a* lleno de arbustos; denso; espeso; grueso; (eyebrows, etc.) poblado

busily *adv* diligentemente, solícitamente; afanosamente, laboriosamente. **He was b. occupied in . . .** , Estaba muy ocupado en . . .

business *n* ocupación, *f;* quehaceres, *m pl;* (matter) asunto, *m,* cosa, *f;* empleo, oficio, *m; com* negocio(s), *m, pl.;* casa comercial, *f;* (trade) comercio, *m;* (clients, connection) clientela, *f;* (right) derecho, *m; theat* juego escénico, *m,* pantomima, *f.* **He had no b. to do that,** No tenía derecho a hacer eso. **Mind your own b.!** iNo te metas donde no te llaman! **on b.,** por negocios. **to be in b. for oneself,** tener negocios por su propia cuenta. **to mean b.,** hacer algo en serio; estar resuelto. **to send about his b.,** mandar a paseo (a). **to set up in b.,** establecer un negocio. **b. affairs,** negocios, *m pl.* **b. agent,** agente de negocios, *m.* **b. hours,** horas de trabajo, *f pl.* **b.-like,** formal, práctico, sistemático. **b. man,** hombre de negocios, negociante, *m*

business administration *n* administración de empresas, *f*

bust *n art* busto, bulto, *m;* pecho, *m.* **b. bodice,** sostén, *m*

bustle *n* actividad, animación, *f;* confusión, *f;* (of a dress) polizón, tontillo, *m. vi* menearse, darse prisa. *vt* dar prisa (a)

bustling *a* activo; ocupado, atareado; animado; bullicioso, ruidoso

busy *a* ocupado; atareado; activo, diligente; (of places) animado, bullicioso; (of streets) de gran circulación; (officious) entremetido. **to b. oneself,** ocuparse (en, con); dedicarse (a), entregarse (a); (interfere) entremeterse (con). **to be b.,** estar ocupado; estar atareado, tener mucho que hacer. **b.-body,** bullebulle, *mf,* entremetido (-da), chismoso (-sa), *Argentina* huregute *mf*

but *conjunc prep adv* pero; sino; (only) solamente; (except) menos; excepto; (almost) casi; que no; si no; (that) que; (nevertheless) sin embargo, empero, no obstante; (without) sin, sin que; (of time recently passed) no más que, tan recientemente. *n* pero, *m.* **He cannot choose but go,** No puede hacer otra cosa que marcharse. **to do nothing but . . . ,** hacer únicamente . . . , no hacer más que . . . **but for,** a no ser por. **but yesterday,** solamente ayer. **but then (or but yet),** pero

butcher *n* carnicero, *m. vt* matar reses; hacer una carnicería en. **butcher's boy,** mozo del carnicero, *m.* **butcher's shop,** carnicería, *f*

butchery *n* carnicería, *f;* matanza, *f*

butler *n* mayordomo, *m.* **butler's pantry,** despensa, repostería, *f*

butt *n* (cask) tonel, *m,* pipa, *f;* (for water) barril, *m;* (of a cigarette, etc.) colilla, *f;* (of fire-arms) culata, *f;* (handle) mango, cabo, *m;* (billiards) mocho, *m;* (earthwork) terrero, *m;* (fig object) objeto (de), *m;* (of bulls, etc.) topetada, *f; pl* **butts,** campo de tiro, *m;* (target) blanco, *m. vt* (toss) topar, acornear; (meet) tropezar (con). **to b. in,** *inf* entrometerse, meter baza; encajarse

butter *n* mantequilla, *f, vt* untar con mantequilla. **b.-dish,** mantequera, *f.* **b.-fingers,** torpe, *m.* **b.-knife,** cuchillo para mantequilla, *m.* **b.-milk,** suero de mantequilla, *m.* **b.-print,** molde para mantequilla, *m.* **b.-sauce,** mantequilla fundida, *f*

butterfly *n* mariposa, *f*

butterscotch *n* dulce de azúcar y mantequilla, *m*

buttocks *n pl* nalgas, posaderas, *f pl*

button *n* botón, *m; pl* **buttons,** botones, paje, *m. vt* abotonar, abrochar. *vi* abotonarse, abrocharse. **to press the b.,** apretar el botón. **b.-hook,** abotonador, *m*

buttonhole *n* ojal, *m;* flor que se lleva en el ojal, *f. vt sew* hacer ojales; (embroidery) hacer el festón; *inf* importunar

buttress *n* estribo, macho, contrafuerte, *m; fig* apoyo, sostén, *m. vt* afianzar, estribar; *fig* apoyar, sostener. **flying-b.,** arbotante, *m*

buxom *a* (of a woman) fresca, guapetona, frescachona

buy *vt* comprar; obtener; (achieve) lograr; (bribe) sobornar. **to buy on credit,** comprar al fiado. **to buy back,** comprar de nuevo; redimir; (ransom) rescatar. **to buy for,** (a price) comprar por; (purpose or destination) comprar para. **to buy in,** (at an auction) comprar por cuenta del dueño. **to buy off,** librarse de uno con dinero. **to buy out,** (of a business) comprar la parte de un socio. **to buy up,** comprar todo, acaparar

buyer *n* comprador (-ra)

buying *n* compra, *f.* **b. back,** rescate, *m.* **b. up,** acaparamiento, *m*

buying power *n* capacidad de compra, *f,* valor adquisitivo, *m*

buzz *n* zumbido, *m;* (whisper) susurro, murmullo, *m;* (of a bell) sonido (del timbre), *m. vi* zumbar; susurrar

buzzer *n* zumbador, *m;* sirena, *f;* (bell) timbre, *m*

by *prep* por; de; en; a; con; (of place) cerca de, al lado de; (according to) según, de acuerdo con; (in front of, past) delante (de); (at the latest) antes de, al más tardar; (expressing agency) por; (by means of) mediante; (through, along) por; (upon) sobre; (for) para; (under) bajo. **He**

will be here by Wednesday, Estará aquí para el miércoles; (not later than) Estará aquí antes del miércoles (or el miércoles al más tardar). **How did he come by it?** ¿Cómo llegó a su poder? **He will come by train,** Vendrá en tren. **I know her by sight,** La conozco de vista. **There are three children by the first marriage,** Hay tres niños del primer matrimonio. **He goes by the name of Pérez,** Se le conoce por (or bajo) el nombre de Pérez. **six feet by eight,** seis pies por ocho. **They called her by her name,** La llamaron por su nombre. **two by two,** dos por dos. **The picture was painted by Cézanne,** El cuadro fue pintado por Cézanne. **drop by drop,** gota a gota. **by a great deal,** con mucho. **by all means,** naturalmente; de todos modos; cueste lo que cueste. **by chance,** por ventura. **by day (night),** de día (noche). **by daylight,** a la luz del día. **by doing it,** con hacerlo. **by myself,** solo; sin ayuda. **"By Appointment"** «Cita Previa». **by chance or by mischance,** por ventura o por desdicha. **an hour away by car,** a una hora de automóvil. **music by Brahms,** música de Brahms. **pull by the hair,** tirar por el pelo. **take by the hand,** llevar de la mano.

by adv (near) cerca; (before) delante; al lado; a un lado; aparte; (of time) pasado. **to put by,** (keep) guardar; (throw away) desechar; (accumulate) acumular; (put out of the way) arrinconar. **to pass by,** pasar; pasar delante (de). **by and by,** luego, pronto; más tarde. **by now,** ya, antes de ahora. **by the way,** entre paréntesis, a propósito; de paso; al lado del camino. **by-election,** elección parcial, f. **by-law,** reglamento, m. **by-pass,** ruta de evitación, f, desvío, m; (mech elec) derivación, f. vi desviarse de; mil rebasar. **by-product,** derivado, m; chem producto derivado, m; fig consecuencia, f; resultado, m

bye n (in cricket) meta, f. **by the bye,** a propósito, entre paréntesis

bye! interj. Argentina, Chile ¡chao!

bygone a pasado. **Let bygones be bygones,** Lo pasado pasado

bystander n espectador (-ra); pl bystanders, los circunstantes

byway n camino desviado, m; fig senda indirecta, f; pl byways, andurriales, m pl

byword n proverbio, m; objeto de burla o escándalo, m

Byzantium Bizancio, m

c n (letter) c, f; mus do, m

cab n (horse-drawn) simón, m; (taxi) coche de alquiler, m; (of a locomotive) cabina del conductor, f. **cab-rank,** punto de coches, m

cabaret n cabaret, m; taberna, f

cabbage n col, berza, f. **red c.,** lombarda, f. **c. butterfly,** mariposa de col, f

cabin n cabaña, choza, f; naut camarote, m; (railway) garita, f; aer cabina, f. **c. boy,** grumete, galopín, mozo de cámara, m. **c. trunk,** baúl mundo, m

cabinet n (piece of furniture) vitrina, f; colección, exposición, f; pol gabinete, m; (of a radio) cónsola, f. **c.-maker,** ebanista, m. **c.-making,** ebanistería, f. **c. meeting,** consejo de ministros, m. **c. minister,** ministro, m

cable n amarra, maroma, f; cable, m; cable(grama), m, vt cablegrafiar. **electric c.,** cable eléctrico, m. **overhead c.,** cable aéreo, m

cabman n cochero de punto, simón, m

cache n escondite, escondrijo, m

cackle vi (of a hen) cacarear; (of a goose) graznar; (of humans) chacharear. n cacareo, m; graznido, m; cháchara, f

cacophony n cacofonía, f

cactus n cacto, m

cad n sinvergüenza, m; tipo de cuidado, m

caddish a mal educado, grosero

caddy n (for tea) cajita para té, f; (golf) cadi, mf

cadger n sablista, mf; mendigo, m; (loafer) golfo, m

cadmium n cadmio, m

café n café, m

cafeteria n bar automático, m

caffeine n cafeína, f

cage n (animal's, bird's) jaula, f; (of a lift) camarín, m; (for transporting miners) jaula, f, vt enjaular, encerrar

Cain, to raise armar lo de Dios es Cristo

cajole vt lisonjear; engatusar, embromar; instar

cake n cul pastel, m, torta, f; (of chocolate, etc.) pastilla, f. vt and vi cuajar; formar costra; (with mud) enlodar. **to sell like hot cakes,** venderse como pan bendito. **to take the c.,** llevarse la palma. **c. of soap,** pastilla de jabón, f. **c.-shop,** pastelería, f

calamine n calamina, f

calamitous a calamitoso, desastroso

calamity n calamidad, f; desastre, m, Mexico also funestidad f

calcium n calcio, m

calculate vt calcular; adaptar. **to c. on,** contar con

calculated a premeditado. **to be c. to,** conducir a; ser a propósito para

calculating n cálculo, m, a calculador; (of persons) interesado; (shrewd) perspicaz;

C

atento. **c. machine,** máquina de calcular, f, calculador, m

calculation n cálculo, m; calculación, f

calculus n cálculo, m

calendar n calendario, m; almanaque, m; (university, etc.) programa, m

calf n becerro (-rra), ternero (-ra); (young of other animals) hijuelo, m; (of the leg) pantorrilla, f; (leather) cuero de becerro, m; piel, f. **calf's-foot,** pie de ternera, m. **c. love,** amor de muchachos, m

calibrate vt calibrar

calibre n calibre, m

calico n indiana, f; percal, m. **c.-printer,** fabricante de estampados, m

Californian a californio. n californio (-ia)

calk. See **caulk.**

call n llamada, f; (shout) grito, m; (of a bird) canto, m; (signal) señal, f; (visit) visita, f; (by a ship) escala, f; mil toque, m; (need) necesidad, f; (of religion, etc.) vocación, f; invitación, f; (demand) demanda, f; exigencia, f. **They came at my c.,** Acudieron a mi llamada. **c. to arms,** llamada, llamada a filas, f. **port of c.,** puerto de escala, m. **telephone c.,** llamada telefónica, f. **to pay a c.,** hacer una visita. **within c.,** al alcance de la voz. **c.-box,** cabina del teléfono, f. **c.-boy,** ayudante del traspunte, m

call vi llamar; gritar, dar voces; (visit) visitar, hacer una visita (a); venir; (stop) parar; (of a ship) hacer escala. vt llamar; (a meeting, etc.) convocar; (awaken) despertar, llamar; (say) decir; (appoint) nombrar; (at cards) declarar. **She is called Dorothy,** Se llama Dorotea. **Madrid calling!** ¡Aquí Radio Madrid! **Will you c. me at eight o'clock, please?** Haga el favor de despertarme (llamarme) a las ocho. **to c. at a port,** hacer escala en un puerto. **to c. a halt,** hacer alto. **to c. a strike,** declarar una huelga. **to c. names,** vituperar, injuriar. **to c. to account,** pedir cuentas (a). **to c. to arms,** tocar al arma; alarmar. **to c. to mind,** acordarse (de), recordar. **to c. to witness,** hacer testigo (de). **to c. back,** vt llamar; hacer volver; (unsay) desdecir. vi (return) volver; venir a buscar; ir a buscar. **I called back for the parcel,** Volví a buscar el paquete. **to c. for,** pedir a gritos; llamar; (demand) pedir; exigir; (collect a person) pasar a buscar; (parcels, etc.) ir (or venir) a recoger. **He called for help,** Pidió socorro a gritos. **to c. forth,** producir; provocar; inspirar; revelar; (bring together) reunir. **to c. in,** hacer entrar; invitar; (a specialist, etc.) llamar; (worn coin) retirar de la circulación; recoger. **to c. in question,** poner en duda. **to c. off,** (dogs, etc.) llamar; (a strike) cancelar;

parar; terminar; (a person) disuadir (de); (postpone) aplazar; suspender; (refrain) desistir (de). **to c. on,** (visit) hacer una visita (a), ir a ver, visitar; (of a doctor) visitar; (a person to do something) recurrir (a); (for a speech) invitar a hablar); (invoke) invocar. **I shall now c. on Mr. Martínez,** Doy la palabra al señor Martínez. **to c. out,** vt hacer salir; provocar; inspirar; (challenge) desafiar, retar. vi gritar a. **c. the roll,** pasar lista. **to c. over,** (names) pasar lista (de). **to c. up,** hacer subir; (to the army) llamar a filas (a); (telephone) llamar por teléfono (a); (memories) evocar. **to c. upon.** See **to c. on**

caller n visita, f

calligraphist n calígrafo, m

calling n llamamiento, m; (occupation) profesión, f; empleo, m; vocación, f; (of a meeting) convocación, f

callisthenics n pl calistenia, f

callous a (of skin) calloso; fig insensible, duro, inhumano

callousness n falta de piedad, inhumanidad, dureza, f

callow a (of birds) implume; (inexperienced) bisoño, inexperto, novato

callus n callo, m

calm n calma, f; paz, tranquilidad, f; sosiego, m; serenidad, f. a (of the sea) en calma; tranquilo; sereno; sosegado. vt calmar; tranquilizar; apaciguar. vi calmarse; tranquilizarse; sosegarse. **dead c.,** calma chicha, f

calming a calmante

calmness n calma, tranquilidad, f; ecuanimidad, serenidad, f

calorie n caloría, f

calumny n calumnia, f

calve vi (of a cow, etc.) parir

cam n mech leva, f. **camshaft,** árbol de levas, m

camaraderie n compañerismo, m

camel n camello (-lla). **c.-driver,** camellero, m. **camel's hair,** pelo de camello, m

cameo n camafeo, m

camera n phot máquina fotográfica, f. **folding c.,** máquina fotográfica plegable, f. **in c.,** a puerta cerrada. **c. obscura,** cámara obscura, f

camouflage n camuflaje, m, vt camuflar

camp n campamento, m; campo, m; fig vida de cuartel, f; (for school children, etc.) colonia, f; (party) partido, m. vi acampar; vivir en tiendas de campaña. **to break c.,** levantar el campo. **c.-bed,** cama de campaña, f. **c.-stool,** silla de campaña, f

campaign n campaña, f. vi hacer una campaña

campaigner n veterano, m; propagandista, mf

campaigning n campañas, f pl

camphor n alcanfor, m

camphorated a alcanforado

campus n recinto, m (Puerto Rico), ciudad universitaria, f

can v auxil poder; (know how to) saber. **You can go to the village when you like,** Puedes ir al pueblo cuando quieras. **I cannot allow that,** No puedo permitir eso. **What can they mean?** ¿Qué quieren decir? **If only things could have been different!** ¡Si solamente las cosas hubiesen sido distintas! **Can you come to dinner on Saturday?** ¿Puede Vd. venir a cenar el sábado? **I can come later if you like,** Puedo (or Podría) venir más tarde si Vd. quiere. **Mary can** (knows how to) **play the piano,** María sabe tocar el piano **You can't eat your cake and have it too.** No hay rosa sin espinas

can n lata, f; (for carrying sandwiches, etc.) fiambrera, f. vt conservar en latas. **canopener,** abrelatas, m

Canada el Canadá, m

Canadian a canadiense. n canadiense, mf

canaille n gentualla, gentuza, f

canal n canal, m

canalization n canalización, f

canalize vt canalizar

canary n canario (-ia); color de canario, m; vino de Canarias, m. **roller c.,** canario de raza flauta, m. **c.-seed,** alpiste, m

Canary Islands, the las Islas Canarias, m

cancel vt cancelar; revocar; borrar; anular. **to c. out,** math anular

cancellation n cancelación, f; revocación, f; anulación, f

cancer n med cáncer, m; ast Cáncer, m

cancerous a canceroso. **to become c.,** cancerarse

candelabrum n candelabro, m

candid a franco; sincero. **If I am to be c.,** Si he de decir la verdad, Si he de ser franco

candidate n candidato (-ta); aspirante, m

candidature n candidatura, f

candidness n franqueza, f; sinceridad, f

candied a (of peel, etc.) almibarado, garapiñado

candle n vela, candela, f. **wax c.,** cirio, m. **You cannot hold a c. to him,** No llegas a la suela de su zapato, Ni llegas a sus pies, Ni le llegas a los pies. **The game is not worth the c.,** La cosa no vale la pena. **to burn the c. at both ends,** consumir la vida. **c.-grease,** sebo, m. **c.-light,** luz de las velas, f; luz artificial, f. **c.-maker,** candelero, m. **c.-power,** elec potencia luminosa, bujía, f. **c.-snuffer,** apagavelas, matacandelas, m

candlestick n candelero, m, palmatoria, f; (processional) cirial, m

candor n franqueza, f; sinceridad, f; candor, m

candy n caramelo, bombón, m, vt garapiñar, almibarar

cane n bot caña, f; (for chair seats, etc.) rejilla, f; (walking stick) bastón, m; (for punishment) vara; f. vt apalear, pegar. **sugar-c.,** caña de azúcar, f. **c.-break,** cañaveral, m. **c. chair,** sillón de mimbres, m. **c.-sugar,** azúcar de caña, m. **c.-syrup,** miel de caña, f

canine a canino. n (tooth) diente canino, m

canister n bote, m, cajita, f

canker n úlcera, f; (in trees) cancro, m; fig cáncer, m, vt roer; fig corromper

canned a en lata

cannibal n caníbal, mf antropófago (-ga). a caníbal, antropófago

cannibalism n canibalismo, m, antropofagía, f

canning n conservación en latas, f. **c. factory,** fábrica de conservas alimenticias, f

cannon n (fire-arm) cañón, m; (billiards) carambola, f, vi carambolear. **to c. into,** chocar con. **c.-ball,** bala de cañón, f. **c.-shot,** cañonazo, m

canny a cuerdo, sagaz

canoe n canoa, f; piragua, f, vi ir en canoa

canoeist n canoero (-ra)

canon n (ecc mus print) canón, m; (dignitary) canónigo, m; (criterion) criterio, m. **c. law,** derecho canónico, m

canonize vt canonizar

canopy n dosel, toldo, m; palio, m; fig capa, bóveda, f. **the c. of heaven,** la capa (o bóveda) del cielo

cant vt inclinar; ladear. vi inclinarse; (be a hypocrite) camandulear. n (slope) inclinación, f, sesgo, desplomo, m; (hypocrisy) gazmoñería, f

cantankerous a irritable, intratable, malhumorado, Argentina cabrero

cantata n cantata, f

canteen n cantina, f; (water bottle) cantimplora, f. **c. of cutlery,** juego de cubiertos, m

canter n medio galope, m, vi andar a galope corto

canting a hipócrita

canto n canto, m

canton n (province and her) cantón, m, vt (of soldiers) acantonar

cantor n ecc chantre, m

canvas n lona, f; art lienzo, m; naut vela, f, paño, m. **under c.,** en tiendas de campaña; (of ships) a toda vela

canvass vt (votes, etc.) solicitar

canvasser n solicitador (-ra) (de votos, etc.)

canvassing n solicitación (de votos, etc.), f

canyon n cañón, m

cap n gorra, f; (with a peak) montera, f; (type of military headgear with brim at front) quépis, m; (cardinal's) birrete, m; univ bonete, m; (pointed) caperuza, f; (woman's old-fashioned) cofia, f; (jester's) gorro de bufón, m; (on a bottle) cápsula, tapa, f. vt univ conferir el grado (a). **cap and bells,** gorro de bufón, m. **cap and gown,** birrete y muceta, toga y birrete, toga y bonete. **to throw one's cap over the windmill,** echar la capa al toro. **to cap it all,** ser el colmo

capability n capacidad, f; aptitud, f

capable a capaz; competente; (of improvement) susceptible; (full of initiative) emprendedor

capably adv competentemente

capacious a espacioso; grande; extenso

capacitate vt capacitar

capacity n capacidad, f; calidad, f; aptitud, f. **in one's c. as,** en calidad de. **seating c.,** número de asientos, m; (in aircraft) número de plazas, m

caparison n caparazón, m

cape n (cloak) capa, f; (short) capotillo, m, capeta, f; (fur) cuello, m; geog cabo, promontorio, m. **c. coat,** capote, m

Cape Horn Cabo de Hornos, m

caper vi (gambol) brincar, saltar; cabriolar, corcovear; (play) juguetear. n travesura, f; zapateta, f; cabriola, f; (whim) capricho, m; bot alcaparra, f. **to c. about,** dar saltos, brincar; juguetear

capillary a capilar. n vaso capilar, m

capital a capital; mortal; de muerte; de vida; principal; (of letters) mayúscula; (very good) excelente; (of the capital city) Lat. Am. capitalino n (city) capital, f; (letter) mayúscula, f; com capital, m; arch capitel, chapitel, m. **floating c.,** capital fluctuante, m. **idle c.,** fondos inactivos, m pl. **c. punishment,** pena de muerte, pena capital, pena de la vida, f. **C.!** ¡Estupendo! ¡Excelente! **to make c. out of,** aprovecharse de, sacar ventaja de

capitalism n capitalismo, m

capitalist n capitalista, mf

capitalistic a capitalista

capitalization n capitalización, f

capitalize vt capitalizar

Capitol n Capitolio, m

capitulate vi capitular

capitulation n capitulación, f

capon n capón, m

caprice n capricho, m

capricious a caprichoso

capriciousness n carácter inconstante, m; lo caprichoso

capsize vt naut hacer zozobrar; volcar. vi naut zozobrar; volcarse

capsule n (bot med chem zool) cápsula, f

captain n (mil nav aer and sport) capitán, m, vt capitanear. **to c. a team,** ser el capitán de un equipo. **group c.,** aer capitán de aviación, m

captaincy n capitanía, f

caption n (arrest) arresto, m; (heading)

encabezamiento, título, pie, *m*; (cinema) subtítulo, *m*

captious a capcioso, caviloso

captivate *vt* cautivar, seducir

captivating a encantador, seductor

captive a cautivo, *n* cautivo (-va), prisionero (-ra), preso (-sa). **c. balloon,** globo cautivo, globo de observación, *m*

captivity *n* cautiverio, *m*

captor *n* el, *m*, (*f*, la) que hace prisionero (-ra)

capture *n* captura, *f*; presa, toma, *f*; *law* captura, *f*. *vt* prender, capturar; tomar

car *n* (chariot) carro, *m*; (tram) tranvía, *m*; (motor) automóvil, coche, *Lat. Am.* carro *m*; (on a train) coche vagón, *m*. **sleeping car,** coche camas, *m*. **car park,** parque de automóviles, *m*

carafe *n* garrafa, *f*

caramel *n* caramelo, *m*; azúcar quemado, *m*

carat *n* quilate, *m*

caravan *n* caravana, *f*; coche de gitanos, *m*; coche habitación, *m*

caraway *n* alcaravea, *f*

carbarn *n* encierro, *m* (Mexico), cochera, cochera de tranvías, *f*, cobertizo, cobertizo para tranvías, *m*

carbohydrate *n* hidrato de carbono, *m*

carbolic a carbólico. **c. acid,** ácido fénico, *m*

carbon *n* carbono, *m*. **c. copy,** copia en papel carbón, *f*. **c. dioxide,** anhídrido carbónico, *m*. **c. monoxide,** óxide de carbono, *m*. **c. paper,** papel carbón, papel de calcar, *m*

carbonated a (beverage) carbónico (formal), con gas (informal)

carbonize *vt* carbonizar

carboy *n* damajuana, garrafa, *f*

carbuncle *n med* carbunco, *m*; (stone) carbúnculo, *m*

carburetor *n* carburador, *m*

carcass *n* (animal) res muerta, *f*; (corpse) cadáver, *m*; (body) cuerpo, *m*; (of a ship) casco, *m*

card *n* (playing) naipe, *m*; (pasteboard) cartulina, *f*; (visiting, postal, etc.) tarjeta, *f*; (index) ficha, *f*; (for wool, etc.) carda, *f*, *vt* (wool, etc.) cardar. **I still have a c. up my sleeve,** Me queda todavía un recurso. **to lay one's cards on the table,** poner las cartas boca arriba. **to play one's cards well,** *fig* jugar el lance. **admission c.,** billete de entrada, *m*. **post c.,** tarjeta postal, *f*. **visiting c.,** tarjeta de visita, *f*. **c.-case,** tarjetero, *m*. **c.-index,** fichero, *m*. *vt* poner en el fichero. **c.-sharper,** fullero, *m*. **c.-table,** mesa de juego, *f*. **c. trick,** juego de manos con cartas, *m*

cardboard *n* cartón, *m*, a de cartón

cardiac a cardíaco

cardigan *n* rebeca, chaqueta de punto, *f*

number, número cardinal, *m*. **c. points,** puntos cardinales, *m pl*

carding *n* (of wool, etc.) cardadura, *f*. **c. machine,** carda mecánica, *f*

cardiogram *n* cardiograma, *m*

care *n* cuidado, *m*; atención, *f*; inquietud, ansia, *f*; (charge) cargo, *m*. *vi* preocuparse; tener interés; .(suffer) sufrir. **I don't c.,** Me es igual; No me importa. **I don't c. a straw,** No se me da un bledo. **They don't c. for eggs,** No les gustan los huevos. **We don't c. what his opinion is,** Su opinión nos tiene sin cuidado (or no nos importa). **to c. for,** cuidar, mirar por; (love) querer (a); (like) gustar. **Take c.!** ¡Cuidado! ¡Ojo! **Take c. not to spoil it!** ¡Ten cuidado que no lo estropees! **Would you c. to . . . ?** ¿Le gustaría . . . ? ¿Tendría inconveniente en . . . ? **c. of,** (on a letter, etc.) en casa de. **c.-free,** a libre de cuidados

careen *vt* carenar. *vi* dar a la banda

career *n* carrera, *f*; curso, *m*. *vi* correr a carrera tendida; galopar

careful a cuidadoso (de); atento (a); prudente. **Careful!, Be careful!** ¡Cuidado! **to be c.,** tener cuidado

carefully *adv* con cuidado. **drive c.,** manejar con cuidado; cuidadosamente; prudentemente; atentamente

carefulness *n* cuidado, *m*; atención, *f*; prudencia, *f*

careless a sin cuidado, indiferente (a); insensible (a); negligente; (of mistakes, etc.) de (or por) negligencia

carelessly *adv* indiferentemente; negligentemente; descuidadamente

carelessness *n* indiferencia, *f*; negligencia, *f*; descuido, *m*; omisión, *f*

caress *n* caricia, *f*, *vt* acariciar

caretaker *n* (of museums, etc.) guardián (-ana); (of flats, etc.) portero (-ra)

careworn a devorado de inquietud, ansioso

cargo *n* cargamento, *m*, carga, *f*. **c.-boat,** barco de carga, *m*

Caribbean Sea, the el Mar Caribe, *m*

caricature *n* caricatura, *f*, *vt* caricaturizar

caricaturist *n* caricaturista, *mf*

caries *n* caries, *f*

carious a cariado. **to become c.,** cariarse

carnage *n* carnicería, *f*

carnal a carnal; sensual

carnation *n* clavel, *m*

carnival *n* carnaval, *m*, a de carnaval, carnavalesco

carnivore *n* carnívoro, *m*

carnivorous a carnívoro

carol *n* villancico *m*; canto, *m*. *vi* cantar alegremente; (of birds) trinar, gorjear

carotid *n* carótida, *f*

carousal *n* borrachera, *f*; holgorio, *m*, jarana, *f*

carouse vi emborracharse. n borrachera, orgía, f

carp n carpa, f, vi criticar, censurar

carpenter n carpintero, m, vi carpintear. **carpenter's bench,** banco de carpintero, m. **carpenter's shop,** carpintería, f

carpentry n carpintería, f

carpet n alfombra, f; flg tapete, m. vt cubrir de una alfombra, alfombrar; entapizar. **to be on the c.,** estar sobre el tapete. **c.-beater,** sacudidor de alfombras, m. **c. merchant,** alfombrista, m. **c. slippers,** zapatillas de fieltro, f pl. **c.-sweeper,** aspirador de polvo, m

carpeting n alfombrado, m

carping a capcioso, criticón

carriage n (carrying) transporte, porte, m; (deportment) porte, continente, m, presencia, f; (vehicle) carruaje, m; carroza, f; coche, m; (railway) departamento, m; (chassis) chasis, bastidor, m; (of a typewriter, etc.) carro, m. **hackney c.,** coche de plaza, m. **c. and pair,** carroza de dos caballos, f. **c. door,** portezuela, f. **c.-forward,** porte debido. **c.-free,** franco de porte. **c.-paid,** porte pagado

carrier n el, m, (f, la) que lleva; portador (-ra); com mensajero, m; (on a car, bicycle) portaequipajes, m; (of a disease) vector, m; (aircraft) porta-aviones, m. **c.-pigeon,** paloma mensajera, f

carrion n carroña, f. **c.-crow,** chova, f

carrot n zanahoria, f

carry vt llevar; transportar; traer; conducir; (mil of arms) portar; (have with one) tener consigo; (an enemy position) tomar, ganar; (a motion) aprobar; (oneself) portarse; (one's point, etc.) ganar; (in the mind) retener; (conviction) convencer; (involve) implicar; (influence) influir; (send) despachar, enviar; (contain) incluir, comprender. vi (of the voice, etc.) alcanzar, llegar. **The noise of the guns carried a long way,** El ruido de los cañones se oía desde muy lejos. **to fetch and c.,** traer y llevar. **to c. all before one,** vencer todos los obstáculos. **to c. into effect,** poner en efecto. **to c. one's audience with one,** captar (or cautivar) su auditorio. **to c. oneself well,** tener buena presencia. **to c. on one's back,** llevar a cuestas. **to c. the day,** quedar victorioso, quedar señor del campo. **to c. weight,** ser de peso. **to c. along,** llevar; (drag) arrastrar; conducir; acarrear. **to c. away,** llevar; llevarse, llevar consigo; (kidnap) robar, secuestrar; (of emotions) dominar; (by enthusiasm) entusiasmar; (inspire) inspirar. **to c. forward,** llevar a cabo; avanzar; fomentar; (bookkeeping) pasar a cuenta nueva. **to c. off,** (things) llevarse; (persons) llevar consigo (a); (abduct or steal) robar; (kill) matar; (a prize) ganar. **to c. (a thing) off well,** llevar la mejor parte, salir vencedor. **to c. on,** vt (a discussion, etc.) seguir, continuar. **c. on a conversation,** llevar una conversación; mantener; (a business, etc.) tener; dirigir. vi ir tirando; seguir trabajando. **to c. out,** realizar, llevar a cabo; hacer, ejecutar, efectuar; (a promise) cumplir. **to c. through,** llevar a cabo

cart n carro, m. vt acarrear; llevar. **c.-horse,** caballo de tiro, m. **c.-load,** carretada, f, carro, m. **c.-wheel,** rueda de carro, f; (somersault) voltereta, f

carte blanche n carta blanca, f

cartel n cartel, m

cartilage n cartílago, m

carton n caja de cartón, f

cartoon n (design for tapestry, etc.) cartón, m; caricatura, f

cartoonist n caricaturista, mf

cartridge n cartucho, m. **blank c.,** cartucho sin bala, m. **c.-belt,** cartuchera, canana, f. **c.-case,** cápsula de proyectil, f

carve vt tallar; labrar; grabar; cortar; (meat, etc.) trinchar; (a career, etc.) hacer, forjarse

carver n tallador, m; (at table) trinchador, m; (implement) trinchante, m

carving n talla, f; (design) tallado, m. **c.-knife,** trinchante, m

cascade n cascada, catarata, f, salto de agua, m; flg chorro, m. vi chorrear

case n caso, m; law proceso, m, causa, f; gram caso, m; med caso, m; enfermo (-ma); (box) caja, f; (for scissors, etc.) vaina, f; (for a cushion, etc.) funda, f; (for jewels, manicure implements, etc.) estuche, m; (of a piano, watch and print) caja, f; (for documents) carpeta, f; (glass) vitrina, f; (for a book) sobrecubierta, f; (dressing) neceser, m. vt cubrir; forrar; resguardar. **packing-c.,** caja de embalaje, f. **c. of goods,** caja de mercancías, f; bulto, m. **in any c.,** en todo caso; venga lo que venga. **in c.,** por si acaso. **in c. of emergency,** en caso de urgencia. **in such a c.,** en tal caso. **in the c. of,** en el caso de; respecto a. **lower c.,** print caja baja, f. **upper c.,** print caja alta, f. **c.-hardened,** (of iron) templado; flg endurecido, indiferente

case closed! ¡asunto concluido!

cash n efectivo, metálico, m; dinero contante, m; inf dinero, m; com caja, f. vt cobrar; pagar, hacer efectivo. **hard or ready c.,** dinero contante, m. **to pay c.,** pagar al contado. **c. on delivery,** (C.O.D.) contra reembolso. **c. on hand,** efectivo en caja, m. **c.-book,** libro de caja, m. **c.-box,** caja, f. **c.-desk,** caja, f. **c. down,** pago al contado, m. **c. prize,** premio en metálico, m. **c.-register,** caja registradora, f

cashew n anacardo, m

cashier n cajero (-ra). vt degradar. **cashier's desk,** caja, f

cash machine n cajero automático, m

cashmere n cachemira, f

casino n casino, m

cask *n* pipa, barrica, *f*, tonel, *m*; cuba, *f*

casket *n* cajita, arquilla, *f*, cofrecito, *m*

casserole *n* cacerola, *f*

cast *vt* arrojar, tirar; (in fishing, the anchor, dice, darts, lots, a net, glances, blame, etc.) echar; (skin) mudar; (lose) perder; (a shadow, etc.) proyectar; (a vote) dar; (mold) vaciar; (accounts) echar, calcular; (a horoscope) hacer; (the parts in a play) repartir; (an actor for a part) dar el papel de; (metals) colar, fundir. **the shadow c. by the wall,** la sombra proyectada por el muro. **to c. anchor,** echar anclas, anclar. **to c. in one's lot with,** compartir la suerte de. **to c. something in a person's teeth,** echar en cara (a). **to c. lots,** echar suertes. **to c. about,** meditar, considerar; imaginar; (devise) inventar. **to c. aside,** desechar; poner a un lado; abandonar. **to c. away,** tirar lejos; desechar; (money) derrochar, malgastar. **to be c. away,** *naut* naufragar. **to c. down,** (overthrow) derribar, destruir; (eyes) bajar; (depress) desanimar, deprimir; (humiliate) humillar. **to be c. down,** estar deprimido. **c. iron,** *n* hierro colado, hierro fundido, *m.* **c.-iron,** a de hierro colado; *fig* inflexible. **to c. off,** quitarse; desechar; (a wife) repudiar; (desert) abandonar; (free oneself) librarse (de). **c.-off,** *n* desecho, *m.* **c.-off clothing,** ropa de desecho, *f.* **to c. out,** echar fuera; hacer salir; excluir. **to c. up,** echar; vomitar; (a sum) sumar; (something at a person) reprochar

cast *n* (of dice, fishing-line) echada, *f*; (of a net) redada, *f*; (worm) molde, *m*; (of a play) reparto, *Lat. Am.* elenco *m*; (of mind) inclinación, *f*; (in the eye) defecto en la mirada, *m*; (of colour) matiz, tinte, *m.* **c. of features,** facciones, *f pl*, fisonomía, *f.* **plaster c.,** vaciado, *m*

castanets *n pl* castañuelas, *f pl*

castaway *n* náufrago (-ga), *fig* perdido (-da)

caste *n* casta, *f*; clase social, *f.* **to lose c.,** desprestigiarse

castigate *vt* castigar

Castile Castilla, *f*

Castilian a castellano. *n* castellano (-na); (language) castellano, *m*

casting *n* lanzamiento, *m*; (of metals) fundición, colada, *f*; obra de fundición, *f.* **c.-net,** esparavel, *m.* **c.-vote,** voto de calidad, *m*

castle *n* castillo, *m*; (in chess) torre, *f*, roque, *m.* **to build castles in Spain,** hacer castillos en el aire

castor *n* *zool* castor, *m*; (for sugar) azucarero, *m*; (cruet) convoy, *m*; (on chairs, etc.) ruedecilla, roldana, *f.* **c.-oil,** aceite de ricino, *m.* **c.-sugar,** azúcar en polvo, *m*

castrate *vt* castrar, capar

casual a fortuito, accidental; ligero, superficial; *inf* despreocupado. **c. worker,** jornalero, *m*

casually *adv* por casualidad; de paso; negligentemente

casualness *n* *inf* negligencia, despreocupación, *f*

casualty *n* víctima, *f*; herido, *m*; *mil* baja, *f*; *pl* **casualties,** heridos, *m pl*; muertos, *m pl.* **c.-list,** lista de víctimas, *f*; *mil* lista de bajas, *f*

cat *n* gato (-ta). **She is an old cat,** Ella es una vieja chismosa. **to be like a cat on hot bricks,** estar como en brasas. **to let the cat out of the bag,** tirar de la manta. **to lead a cat-and-dog life,** vivir como perros y gatos. **cat's-cradle,** (game) cunas, *f pl.* **cat's paw,** (person) hombre de paja, *m*; *naut* bocanada de viento, *f.* **cat o' nine tails,** gato de siete colas, *m*, penca, *f.* **catwhisker,** *rad* detector, *m*

cataclysm *n* cataclismo, *m*

catacombs *n pl* catacumbas, *f pl*

Catalan a catalán (-ana). *n* catalán; (language) catalán, *m*

catalogue *n* catálogo, *m*, *vt* catalogar

catalysis *n* catálisis, *f*

cat-and-mouse *n* el juego de ratón, *m*

catapult *n* *mil* catapulta (para lanzar aviones), *f*; (toy) tirador de gomas, *m.* *vt* tirar con una catapulta (or con un tirador de gomas); (throw) lanzar

cataract *n* catarata, cascada, *f*, salto de agua, *m*; (of the eye) catarata, *f*

catarrh *n* catarro, *m*; constipado, resfriado, *m*

catastrophe *n* catástrofe, *f*, desastre, *m*, *Mexico also* funestidad; (in drama) desenlace, *m*

catastrophic a catastrófico

catch *vt* coger; agarrar, asir; (capture) prender, haber; (a disease) contraer; (habit) tomar; (on a hook, etc.) enganchar; (surprise) sorprender; (understand) comprender; (hear) oír; (with blows, etc.) dar. *vi* (of a lock) encajarse; (become entangled) engancharse; (of a fire) encenderse. **to c. a glimpse of,** ver por un instante (a); alcanzar a ver, entrever. **to c. at,** asir; agarrarse (a); echar mano de; procurar asir; alargar la mano hacia; (an idea, etc.) adoptar con entusiasmo. **to c. on,** (be popular) tener éxito; (understand) comprender. **to c. out,** coger en el acto; coger en un error; *sport* coger. **to c. up,** coger; interrumpir. **to c. up with,** (a person) alcanzar; (news) ponerse al corriente de

catch *n* presa, *f*; (of fish) redada, pesca, *f*; (of a window, etc.) cerradura, *f*; (latch) pestillo, *m*; (trick) trampa, *f*; *mus* canon, *m.* **a good c.,** (matrimonial) un buen partido. **to have a c. in one's voice,** hablar con voz entrecortada. **c.-as-c.-can,** lucha libre, *f*

catching a contagioso

catchment *n* desagüe, *m*

catchword n reclamo, m; (theater cue) pie, apunte, m; (slogan) mote, m

catchy a atractivo. **It's a c. tune,** Es una canción que se pega

catechism n catequismo, m

categorical a categórico

category n categoría, f

cater vi proveer, abastecer. **to c. for all tastes,** atender a todos los gustos

caterer n despensero (-ra)

catering n provisión, f

caterpillar n oruga, Argentina isoca f. **c. tractor,** tractor de orugas, m

caterwaul vi (of a cat) maullar

catharsis n med purga, f; fig catarsis, f

cathedral n catedral, f

catheter n catéter, m

cathode n cátodo, m. **c. rays,** rayos catódicos, m pl. **c. ray tube,** tubo de rayos catódicos, m

catholic a católico

Catholicism n catolicismo, m

cattle n ganado vacuno, m; ganado, m; animales, m pl. **c.-dealer,** ganadero, m. **c.-lifter,** hurtador de ganado, m. **c.-pen,** corral, m. **c.-raiser,** criador de ganado, m. **c.-raising,** ganadería, f. **c.-ranch,** hacienda de ganado, estancia, Argentina cabaña f. **c.-show,** exposición de ganado, f. **c.-truck,** vagón de ferrocarril para ganado, m

cattle rustler n abigeo, cuatrero, ladrón de ganado, m

cattle rustling n abigeato, m

catty a gatuno; malicioso, chismoso

Caucasian a and n caucáseo (-ea)

cauldron n caldera, f

cauliflower n coliflor, f

caulk vt calafatear

causality n causalidad, f

cause n causa, f; (reason) motivo, m, razón, f; (lawsuit) proceso, m. vt causar; ocasionar, suscitar; (oblige) hacer, obligar (a). **final c.,** phil causa final, f. **to have good c. for,** tener buen motivo para

causeway n dique, m; acera, f

caustic a cáustico; fig mordaz. **c. soda,** sosa cáustica, f

cauterization n cauterización, f

cauterize vt cauterizar

cautery n cauterio, m

caution n prudencia, cautela, f; (warning) amonestación, f; aviso, m. vt amonestar. **to proceed with c.,** ir con prudencia; ir despacio

"Caution" (road sign) «Precaución»

cautionary a (of tales) de escarmiento

cautious a cauteloso, cauto; prudente, circunspecto

cautiously adv cautamente; prudentemente. **to go c.,** inf ir con pies de plomo

cavalcade n cabalgata, f

cavalier n jinete, m; caballero, m; galán, m, a arrogante, altanero

cavalry n caballería, f. **c.-man,** jinete, soldado de a caballo, m

cave n cueva, caverna, f. **to c. in,** hundirse; desplomarse; fig rendirse. **c.-man,** hombre cavernícola, m

cavern n caverna, f

cavernous a cavernoso

caviar n caviar, m

cavil vi cavilar

cavity n cavidad, f; hoyo, m; hueco, m; (in a lung) caverna, f

cavy n cobayo (-ya), conejillo (-lla) de las Indias

caw n graznido, m, vi graznar, grajear

cayenne n pimentón, m

cease vi cesar (de), dejar de; parar. vt cesar de; parar de; (payments, etc.) suspender; discontinuar. **C. fire!** ¡Cesar fuego!

ceaseless a incesante, continuo, sin cesar

ceaselessly adv sin cesar, incesantemente

ceasing n cesación, f. **without c.,** sin cesar

cedar n (tree and wood) cedro, m. **red c.,** cedro dulce, m

cede vt ceder, traspasar; (admit) conceder

cedilla n zedilla, f

ceiling n techo, m; aer altura máxima, f. **c. price,** máximo precio, m

celebrate vt celebrar; solemnizar. **Their marriage was celebrated in the autumn,** Su casamiento se solemnizó en el otoño

celebrated a célebre, famoso

celebration n celebración, f; festividad, f

celebrity n celebridad, f

celerity n celeridad, f

celery n apio, m

celestial a celestial

celibacy n celibato, m

celibate a célibe. n célibe, mf

cell n celda, f; (bot biol) célula, f; (bees, wasps) celdilla, f; elec elemento, m

cellar n sótano, m; (wine) bodega, f

cellist n violoncelista, mf

cello n violoncelo, m

cellophane n (papel) celofán, m

cellular a celular, celuloso

celluloid n celuloide, f

cellulose n celulosa, f

Celt n celta, mf

Celtic a celta

cement n cemento, m, vt cementar

cemetery n cementerio, m

censor n censor, m, vt censurar. **banned by the c.,** prohibido por la censura

censorious a severo; crítico

censorship n censura, f

censure vt censurar, culpar, criticar

census n censo, m. **to take the c.,** formar el censo, levantar el censo, tomar el censo, empadronar

census-taking n la formación del censo, la formación de los censos, f, el levantamiento del censo, el levantamientos de los censos, m

cent n (coin) centavo, Lat. Am. cobre (of copper) m. **per c.,** por ciento. **not to have a c., not to have a c. to one's name,** no tener donde caer muerto

centavo n centavo, Lat. Am. cobre (of copper) m

centenarian a and n centenario (-ia)

centenary n centenario, m, a centenario

center n centro, m; medio, m. a central; centro. vt centrar; concentrar (en). **nervous centers,** centros nerviosos, m pl. **c.-forward,** sport delantero centro, m. **c.-half,** sport medio centro, m. **c. of gravity,** centro de gravedad, m. **c.-piece,** centro, m

centerfold n páginas centrales, f pl

centigrade a centígrado

centigram n centigramo, m

centiliter n centilitro, m

centimeter n centímetro, m. **cubic c.,** centímetro cúbico, m

centipede n ciempiés, m

central a central; céntrico. **The house is very c.,** La casa es muy céntrica. **C. America** n Centroamérica f **C. American,** a and n centroamericano (-na). **c. depot,** central, f. **c. heating,** calefacción central, f

centralize vt centralizar

centrifugal a centrífugo

centripetal a centrípeto

century n siglo, m, centuria, f

ceramic a cerámico

ceramics n cerámica, f

cereal a cereal. n cereal, m

cerebellum n cerebelo, m

cerebral a cerebral

cerebrum n cerebro, m

ceremonial a ceremonial; de ceremonia. n ceremonial, m

ceremonially adv ceremonialmente; con ceremonia

ceremonious a ceremonioso

ceremoniousness n ceremonia, formalidad, f

ceremony n ceremonia, f. **to stand on c.,** gastar cumplidos. **without c.,** sin cumplidos

cerise a de color cereza

certain a (sure) seguro; cierto; (unerring) certero. **a c. man,** cierto hombre. **I am c. that . . . ,** Estoy seguro de que . . . **to know for c.,** saber con toda seguridad, saber a ciencia cierta. **to make c. of,** asegurarse de

certainly adv seguramente; ciertamente;

(as a reply) sin duda; naturalmente. **c. not,** no, por cierto; claro que no

certainty n certidumbre, f; seguridad, f; convicción, f. **of a c.,** seguramente

certificate n certificado, m; fe, f; partida, f; com bono, título, m; diploma, m. vt certificar. **birth c.,** partida de nacimiento, f. **death c.,** partida de defunción, f. **marriage c.,** partida de casamiento, f

certify vt certificar; atestiguar; declarar

certitude n certeza, certidumbre, f

Cervantine a cervantino

cervix n anat cerviz, f

Cesarean a cesáreo

cessation n cesación, f

cession n cesión, f

cesspool n sumidero, m

cf. cfr.

chafe vt (rub) frotar; (make sore) escocer, rozar. vi raerse, desgastarse; escocerse; fig impacientarse; fig irritarse, enojarse

chaff n (of grain) ahechadura, f; (in a general sense and fig) paja, f; tomadura de pelo, burla, f. vt (a person) tomar el pelo (a), burlarse de

chafing n frotación, f; (soreness) excoriación, f; fig impaciencia, f. **c.-dish,** escalfador, m

chagrin n mortificación, decepción, f, disgusto, m, vt mortificar

chain n cadena, f, vt encadenar. **c. of mountains,** cadena de montañas, cordillera, f. **c.-gang,** cadena de presidiarios, f. **c.-mail,** cota de malla, f. **c.-stitch,** cadeneta, f. **c.-stores,** empresa con sucursales, f. **in chains,** cargado de cadenas (e.g., **prisoners in chains,** prisioneros cargados de cadenas)

chair n silla, f; univ cátedra, f; (of a meeting) presidencia, f. vt llevar en hombros (a). **C.!** ¡Orden! **easy-c.,** (silla) poltrona, f. **to be in the c.,** ocupar la presidencia; presidir. **to take a c.,** sentarse, tomar asiento. **to take the c.,** presidir. **swivel-c.,** silla giratoria, f. **wheel-c.,** silla de ruedas, f. **c.-back,** respaldo de una silla, m

chairman n presidente (-ta). **to act as c.,** presidir

chairmanship n presidencia, f

chaise longue n meridiana, tumbona, f

chalet n chalet, m

chalice n cáliz, m

chalk n creta, f; (for writing, etc.) tiza, f, yeso, m. vt marcar con tiza; dibujar con tiza. **to c. up,** apuntar. **not by a long c.,** no con mucho

chalky a cretáceo; cubierto de yeso; (of the complexion) pálido

challenge n provocación, f; (of a sentry) quién vive, m; (to a duel, etc.) desafío, reto, m; law recusación, f; concurso, m. vt (of a sentry) dar el quién vive (a); desafiar; provocar; law recusar

challenger n desafiador (-ra)

challenging a desafiador, provocador

chamber n cuarto, m; sala, f; (bed-) dormitorio, m, alcoba, f; cámara, f; mech cilindro, m; (in a gun) cámara, f. **c. concert**, concierto de música de cámara, m. **c.-maid**, camarera, f. **c. music**, música de cámara, f. **c. of commerce**, cámara de comercio, f. **c.-pot**, orinal, m

chameleon n camaleón, m

chamois n gamuza, f, rebeco, m. **c. leather**, piel de gamuza, f

chamomile n camomila, manzanilla, f

champ vt mascar; morder. vi fig impacientarse

champagne n (vino de) champaña, m

champion n campeón, m; defensor (-ra)

championship n campeonato, m; (of a cause) defensa, f

chance n casualidad, f; suerte, fortuna, f; posibilidad, f; probabilidad, f; esperanza, f; (opportunity) ocasión, oportunidad, f. a fortuito; accidental. vi impers suceder, acontecer. vt inf arriesgar; probar. **by c.**, por casualidad; por ventura. **if by c.**, si acaso. **If it chances that . . . ,** Si sucede que; Si a mano viene que . . . **The chances are that . . . ,** Las probabilidades son que . . . **There is no c.,** No hay posibilidad; No hay esperanza. **to let the c. slip**, perder la ocasión. **to take a c.,** aventurarse, arriesgarse. **to c. to do**, hacer algo por casualidad. **to c. upon**, encontrar por casualidad.

chancellor n canciller, m; univ cancelario, m. **C. of the Exchequer**, Ministro de Hacienda, m

chandelier n araña de luces, f

chandler n velero, m

change vt cambiar; transformar; modificar; (clothes) mudarse (de); (one thing for another) trocar; sustituir (por). vi cambiar; (clothes) mudarse. **All c.!** ¡Cambio de tren! **to c. a check**, cambiar un cheque. **to c. color**, cambiar de color; (of persons) mudar de color. **to c. countenance**, demudarse. **to c. front**, fig cambiar de frente. **to c. hands**, (of shops, etc.) cambiar de dueño. **to c. one's clothes**, cambiar de ropa, mudarse de ropa. **to c. one's mind**, cambiar de opinión. **to c. one's tune**, cambiar de tono. **to c. the subject**, cambiar de conversación. **to c. trains**, cambiar de trenes

change n cambio, m; transformación, f; modificación, f; variedad, f; (of clothes, feathers) muda, f; (theat of scene) mutación, f; (money) cambio, m; (small coins) suelto, m; (stock) bolsa, f; lonja, f; vicisitud, f; (of bells) toque (de campanas), m. **for a c.**, para cambiar, como un cambio; para variar. **small c.**, suelto, m, moneda suelta, f. **c. for the better**, cambio para mejor, m. **c. for the worse**, cambio para peor, m. **c. of clothes**, cambio de ropa, m; **c. of front**, fig cambio de frente, m. **c.**

of heart, cambio de sentimientos, m; conversión, f. **c. of life**, menopausia, f. **c.-over**, cambio, m

changeability n mutabilidad, f; inconstancia, volubilidad, f

changeable a voluble; variable; cambiable

changeless a immutable; constante

changeling n niño (-ña) cambiado (-da) por otro

changing a cambiante. **c.-room**, vestuario, m

channel n (of a river, etc.) cauce, m; canal, m; (irrigation) acequia, f; (strait) estrecho, m; fig conducto, m; (furrow) surco, m, estría, f; (of information, etc.) medio, m. vt acanalar; (furrow) surcar; (conduct) encauzar

chant n canto llano, m; salmo, m. vt salmodiar; cantar; recitar

chaos n caos, m

chaotic a caótico, desordenado

chap vt agrietar. vi agrietarse. n inf chico, m

chapbook n librito de cordel, m

chapel n capilla, f; templo disidente, m

chaperon n dama de compañía, señora de compañía, dueña, f, vt acompañar

chaplain n capellán, m

chaplet n guirnalda, f; rosario, m; (necklace) collar, m

chapter n (in a book) capítulo, m; ecc cabildo, capítulo, m. **a c. of accidents**, una serie de desgracias. **c. house**, sala capitular, f

char vt (a house, etc.) fregar, hacer la limpieza de; (of fire) carbonizar. n inf fregona, asistenta, f

character n carácter, m; (of a play) personaje, m; (role) papel, m; (eccentric) tipo, m. **Gothic characters**, caracteres góticos, m pl. **in c.**, característico; apropiado. **in the c. of**, en el papel de. **out of c.**, nada característico; no apropiado. **principal c.**, protagonista, mf. **c. actor**, actor de carácter, m. **c. actress**, actriz de carácter

characteristic a característico, típico. n característica, peculiaridad, f, rasgo, m

characterize vt caracterizar

characterless a sin carácter; insípido, soso

charade n charada, f

charcoal n carbón de leña, m; (for blacking the face, etc.) tizne, m; art carboncillo, m. **c. burner**, carbonero, f. **c. crayon**, carboncillo, m. **c. drawing**, dibujo al carbón, m

charge vt cargar; (enjoin) encargar; (accuse) acusar (de); (with price) cobrar; (with a mission, etc.) encomendar, confiar; mil acometer, atacar. vi mil atacar; (a price) cobrar, pedir. **How much do you c.?** ¿Cuánto cobra Vd.? **to c. with a crime**, acusar de un crimen

charge n (load) carga, f; (price) precio, m; gasto, m; (on an estate, etc.) derechos, m pl; (task) encargo, m; (office or responsibility) cargo, m; (guardianship) tutela, f; (care) cuidado, m; exhortación, f; law acusación, f; mil ataque, m. **He is in c. of . . .**, Está encargado de . . . ; Es responsable de . . . **The diamonds are in the c. of . . .**, Los diamantes están a cargo de. **depth c.**, carga de profundidad, f. **extra c.**, gasto suplementario, m; (on a train) suplemento, m. **free of c.**, gratis. **c. for admittance**, entrada, f. **to bring a c. against**, acusar de. **to give (someone) in c.**, entregar (una persona) a la policía. **to take c. of**, encargarse de

chargé d'affaires n encargado de negocios, m

charger n caballo de guerra, corcel, m

chariness n cautela, f

chariot n carro, m

charioteer n auriga, m

charitable a caritativo, limosnero; benéfico

charitableness n caridad, f

charity n caridad, f; beneficencia, f; (alms) limosna, f. **c. child**, niño (-ña) de la doctrina

charlatan n charlatán (-ana); (quack) curandero, m

charlatanism n charlatanismo, m; curanderismo, m

charm n hechizo, m; ensalmo, m; (amulet) amuleto, m; (trinket) dije, m; (general sense) encanto, atractivo, m. vt encantar, hechizar, fascinar

charming a encantador; atractivo, seductor, fascinador

charm school n academia de buenos modales, f

chart n naut carta de marear, f; (graph) gráfica, f. vt poner en una carta

charter n carta, f; (of a city, etc.) fuero, m; cédula, f. vt (a ship) fletar; (hire) alquilar. **royal c.**, cédula real, f

charwoman n fregona, asistenta; mujer de hacer faenas, Mexico fregandera f

chary a cauteloso; desinclinado; frugal

chase n caza, f; seguimiento, m. vt cazar; dar caza (a); perseguir; (drive off) ahuyentar; fig disipar, hacer desaparecer; (engrave) cincelar. **to give c. to**, dar caza (a). **to go on a wild goose c.**, buscar pan de trastrigo

chasm n sima, f, precipicio, m; fig abismo, m

chassis n chasis, m

chaste a casto

chasten vt castigar; corregir; humillar, mortificar

chastened a sumiso, dócil

chastise vt castigar

chastisement n castigo, m

chastity n castidad, f

chat vi charlar, conversar. n conversación, charla, f. **They are having a c.**, Están charlando. Están de palique

chattels n pl bienes muebles, efectos, m pl

chatter vi charlar; hablar por los codos, chacharear; (of water) murmurar; (of birds) piar; (of monkeys, etc.) chillar; (of teeth) rechinar; (of a person's teeth) dar diente con diente. n charla, f; cháchara, parla, f; (of water) murmurio, m; (of birds) gorjeo, m; (of monkeys, etc.) chillidos, m pl

chatterbox n badajo, m, cotorra, f

chatterer n hablador (-ra)

chattering n charla, cháchara, f; (of teeth) rechinamiento, m, a gárrulo, chacharero, locuaz

chauffeur n chófer, m

cheap a barato; (of works of art) cursi. adv barato. **dirt c.**, baratísimo. **to be dirt c.**, estar por los suelos. **to hold** (something) **c.**, tener en poco, estimar en poco

cheapen vt disminuir el valor de; reducir el precio de

cheaply adv barato; a bajo precio

cheapness n baratura, f; precio módico, m; mal gusto, m, vulgaridad, f

cheat n engaño, fraude, m; estafa, f; (person) fullero (-ra), trampista, mf embustero (-ra). vt engañar; estafar; (at cards) hacer trampas. **He cheated me out of my property**, Me defraudó de mi propiedad

cheating n engaño, m; fraude, m; (at cards) fullerías, f pl

check n (chess) jaque, m; revés, m; impedimento, m; contratiempo, m; (of a bridle) cama, f; (control) freno, m; control, m; (checking) verificación, f; (ticket) papeleta, f; (counterfoil) talón, m; (square) cuadro, m; (bill) cuenta, f; Argentina adición f; (bank) cheque, m. vt (chess) jaquear; (hamper) refrenar; detener; contrarrestar; (test) verificar. vi detenerse. **to c. off**, marcar. **to c. oneself**, detenerse; contenerse. **to c. up**, comprobar. **crossed c.**, cheque cruzado, m. **c. book**, libro de cheques, m

checked a (cloth) a cuadros

checker vt escaquear; (variegate) motear, salpicar; diversificar. **a checkered career**, una vida accidentada

checking n represión, f; control, m; verificación, f; comprobación, f

checkmate n mate, jaque, mate, m. vt dar mate (a); (plans, etc.) frustrar

checks and balances n pl frenos y contrapesos, m pl

cheek n mejilla, f; inf descaro, m; insolencia, Lat. Am. impavidez f. **They have plenty of c.**, Tienen mucha cara dura. **c. by jowl**, cara a cara; al lado de. **c.-bone**, pómulo, m

cheekiness n cara dura, insolencia, *Lat. Am.* impavidez f

cheeky a insolente, descarado, *Lat. Am.* impávido, *Peru* lisurero; (pert) respondón

cheer n alegría, f, regocijo, m; vítor, m; aplauso, m. *vt* animar; alegrar, regocijar; vitorear, aplaudir. **to be of good c.,** estar alegre; ser feliz. **C. up!** ¡Ánimo! **to c. up,** animarse, cobrar ánimo

cheerful a alegre; jovial; de buen humor. **It is a c. room,** Es un cuarto alegre

cheerfully adv alegremente; (willingly) con mucho gusto, de buena gana

cheerfulness n alegría, f; jovialidad, f; buen humor, m

cheering n vítores, m pl, aclamaciones, f pl, a animador

cheerleader n porro, m

cheerless a triste; sin alegría; (dank) obscuro, lóbrego

cheese n queso, m. **cream c.,** queso de nata, m. **grated c.,** queso rallado, m. **c.-dish,** quesera, f. **c.-mite,** cresa, f. **c.-paring,** n corteza de queso, f. a inf tacaño. **c.-vat,** quesera, f

cheesecake n *Lat. Am.* alfandoque m

cheesy a caseoso

chemical a químico. **c. warfare,** defensa química, f

chemicals n pl productos químicos, m pl

chemise n camisa (de mujer), f

chemist n químico, m. **chemist's shop,** farmacia, f; droguería, f

chemistry n química, f

cherish vt amar, querer; (a hope, etc.) abrigar, acariciar

cherry n (fruit) cereza, f; (tree and wood) cerezo, m. **c. brandy,** aguardiente de cerezas, m. **c. orchard,** cerezal, m

cherub n querub(e), querubín, m

chess n ajedrez, m. **c.-board,** tablero de ajedrez, m

chessman n pieza de ajedrez, f

chest n arca, f, cofre, m; cajón, m; anat pecho, m. **to throw out one's c.,** inflar el pecho. **c.-expander,** extensor, m. **c. of drawers,** cómoda, f

chestnut n (tree) castaño, m; (fruit) castaña, f; (color) castaño, color castaño, m; (horse) caballo castaño, m; (joke) chiste del tiempo de Maricastaña, m, a castaño. **horse-c. tree,** castaño de Indias, m

chew vt mascar, masticar; (ponder) masticar

chewing n masticación, f. **c.-gum,** chicle, m

chianti n (wine) quianti, m

chiaroscuro n claroscuro, m

chic n chic, m, elegancia, f

chicanery n sofistería, f

chicken n pollo, m. **c.-hearted,** medroso, cobarde, timorato. **c.-pox,** varicela, f

chickenwire n alambrillo, m

chickpea n garbanzo, m

chickweed n pamplina, f

chicory n achicoria, f

chide vt reprender, reñir

chidingly adv en tono de represión

chief n jefe, m, a principal; primero; en jefe; mayor. **c.-of-staff,** jefe de estado mayor, m

chiefly adv principalmente; sobre todo

chieftain n caudillo, m; (of a clan) cabeza, jefe, m

chiffon n chifón, m, gasa, f

chiffonier n cómoda, f

chignon n moño, m

child n niño (-ña), hijo (-ja). *Mexico* escuincle mf desde niño, a niño, desde la niñez. **with c.,** encinta, embarazada. **How many children have you?** ¿Cuántos hijos tiene Vd.? **child's play,** juegos infantiles, m pl; fig niñerías, f pl. **c. welfare,** puericultura, f

childbirth n parto, m

childhood n niñez, infancia, f. **from his c.,** desde su niñez, desde niño

childish a de niño; aniñado; pueril; fútil. **to grow c.,** chochear

childishly adv como un niño

childishness n puerilidad, f; futilidad, f

child labor n trabajo de menores, trabajo infantil, m

childless a sin hijos; sin niños

childlike a de niño, aniñado; pueril

children. See **child**

Chilean a and n chileno (-na)

chili n chile, pimento de cornetilla, *Lat. Am.* ají m. **c. sauce** *Lat. Am.* ají m

chill n frío, m; (of fear, etc.) estremecimiento, m; (illness) resfriado, m; (unfriendliness) frialdad, frigidez, f, a frío; (unfriendly) frígido. vt enfriar; helar; (with fear, etc.) dar escalofríos (de); (discourage) desalentar. vi tener frío; tener escalofríos. **to take the c. off,** templar, calentar un poco

chilliness n frío, m; (unfriendliness) frialdad, frigidez, f

chilly a frío; (sensitive to cold) friolero; (of politeness, etc.) glacial, frígido

chime n juego de campanas, m; repique, campaneo, m; armonía, f. vi (of bells) repicar; fig armonizar. **to c. the hour,** dar la hora

chimera n quimera, f

chimerical a quimérico

chimney n chimenea, f; (of a lamp) tubo (de lámpara), m. **c.-corner,** rincón de chimenea, m. **c.-pot,** sombrerete de chimenea, m. **c.-stack,** chimenea, f. **c.-sweep,** limpiador de chimeneas, deshollinador, m

chimpanzee n chimpancé, m

chin n barbilla, barba, f, mentón, m. **c.-rest,** mentonera, f. **c.-strap,** barboquejo, m; venda para la barbilla, f

china n china, porcelana, f; loza, f. a de
porcelana; de loza. **c. cabinet,** chinero,
m

chinchilla n (animal and fur) chinchilla, f

Chinese a and n chino (-na): (language)
chino, m. **C. lantern,** farolillo de papel,
m. **C. white,** óxido blanco de cinc, m

chink n resquicio, m, grieta, hendidura, f;
(clink) retintín, tintineo, m. vi tintinar

chintz n zaraza, f

chip n astilla, f; (counter) ficha, f. vt picar;
cincelar. **a c. off the old block,** de tal
palo tal astilla. **c. potatoes,** patatas
fritas, f pl

chiropodist n pedicuro, m, callista, mf

chiropractor n quiropráctico, m

chirp vi piar, gorjear. n pío, gorjeo, m

chirping n píada, f, a gárrulo, piante

chisel n escoplo, cincel, m, vt cincelar.
cold c., cortafrío, m

chitchat n charla, f

chivalrous a caballeroso

chivalry n caballería, f; caballerosidad, f.
novel of c., novela de caballería, f

chive n bot cebollana, f, cebollino, m

chlorine n cloro, m

chloroform n cloroformo, m, vt cloroformizar

chock-full a lleno de bote en bote

chocolate n chocolate, m, a de chocolate. **thick drinking-c.,** chocolate a la
española, m. **thin drinking-c.,** chocolate a la francesa, m. **c. shop,** chocolat-
ería, f

choice n selección, f; preferencia, f; elección, f; opción, f; alternativa, f; lo más escogido. a escogido, selecto; excelente.
for c., con preferencia

choir n coro, m. **c.-boy,** niño del coro, m.
c.-master, maestro de capilla, m

choke vi ahogarse; atragantarse; obstruirse. vt ahogar; estrangular. **to c.
with laughter,** ahogarse de risa. **to c.
back,** (words) tragar. **to c. off,** (a person)
disuadir (de); quitarse de encima(a). **to c.
up,** obstruir, cerrar, obturar; (hide) cubrir, tapar

choking a asfixiante, sofocante. n ahogamiento, m, sofocación, f

cholera n cólera, m

cholesterol n colesterina, f

choose vt escoger; elegir; optar por;
(wish) querer, gustar. **They will do it
when they c.,** Lo harán cuando les
parezca bien. **If you c.,** Si Vd. quiere; Si
Vd. gusta. **He was chosen as Mayor,** Fue
elegido alcalde. **There is nothing to c.
between them,** No hay diferencia entre
ellos; Tanto vale el uno como el otro. **You
cannot c. but love her,** No puedes
menos de quererla

choosing n selección, f; (for an office,
etc.) elección, f

chop vt cortar; (mince) picar; (split) hen-

der, partir. n (meat) chuleta, f; (jaw)
quijada, f. **to c. about, round,** (of the
wind) girar, virar. **to c. down,** (trees)
talar. **to c. off,** separar; cortar; tajar. **to c.
up,** cortar en pedazos

choppy a picado, agitado

chopstick n palillo chino, m

choral a coral

chord n cuerda, f; mus acorde, m; **the
right c.,** fig la cuerda sensible

choreographer n coreógrafo, m

chorus n coro, m; (in revues) comparsa, f,
acompañamiento, m; (of a song) refrán,
m. **to sing in c.,** cantar a coro. **c. girl,**
corista, f

chosen a escogido; elegido. **the c.,** los
elegidos

Christ n Cristo, Jesucristo, m

christen vt bautizar

christening n bautizo, m, a bautismal,
de bautizo

christian a cristiano. n cristiano (-na). **c.
name,** nombre de pila, m

christianity n cristianismo, m

Christmas n Navidad, f. **A Merry C.!** ¡Fe-
lices Pascuas (de Navidad)! **Father C.,**
Padre Noel, m; (Sp. equivalent) Los Reyes
Magos. **C. box,** regalo de Navidad, m. **C.
card,** felicitación de Navidad, f. **C. carol,**
villancico de Navidad, m. **C. Day,** día de
Navidad, m. **C. Eve,** Nochebuena, f.
C.-tide, Navidades, f pl. **C. tree,** árbol de
Navidad, m

Christopher Columbus Cristóbal
Colón, m

chrome n cromo, m. **c. yellow,** amarillo
de cromo, m

chromosome n cromosoma, m

chronic a crónico; inveterado

chronicle n crónica, f, vt narrar

chronicler n cronista, mf

chronological a cronológico. **in c.
order,** por orden cronológico

chronology n cronología, f

chrysanthemum n crisantemo, m

chubbiness n gordura, f

chubby a regordete, gordito.
c.-cheeked, mofletudo

chuck vt (throw) lanzar, arrojar; (discontinue) abandonar, dejar. n (in a lathe)
mandril, m. **to c. under the chin,**
acariciar la barbilla (a). **to c. away,** derrochar; malgastar, perder. **to c. out,** echar,
poner en la calle

chuckle vi reír entre dientes. n risa
ahogada, f; risita, f

chum n compinche, camarada, mf. **to c.
up with,** ser camarada de

chunk n pedazo, trozo, m

church n iglesia, f; (Protestant) templo,
m, vt (a woman) purificar. **poor as a c.
mouse,** más pobre que las ratas. **the C.
of England,** la iglesia anglicana. **to go**

to c., ir a misa; ir al templo. **c. music,** música sagrada, *f*

churchyard *n* cementerio, *m*

churl *n* patán, *m*

churlish a grosero, cazurro; (mean) tacaño, ruin

churn *n* mantequera, *f*. *vt* (cream) batir; *fig* azotar, agitar

chute *n* (for grain, etc.) manga de tolva, *f*; vertedor, *m*; (in flats and fun fairs) tobogán, deslizadero, *m*

cicada *n* cigarra, *f*

cicatrize *vt* cicatrizar. *vi* cicatrizarse

cider *n* sidra, *f*

cigar *n* cigarro, *m*. **c.-box,** cigarrera, *f*. **c.-case,** petaca, cigarrera, *f*. **c.-cutter,** corta-puros, *m*

cigarette *n* cigarrillo, pitillo, *Lat. Am.* cigarro *m*. **c.-butt,** colilla, *f*. **c.-case,** pitillera, *f*. **c.-holder,** boquilla, *f*. **c.-lighter,** encendedor de cigarrillos, *m*. **c.-paper,** papel de fumar, *m*

cinch *n* (of a saddle) cincha, *f*; *inf* ganga, *f*; *inf* seguridad, *f*. **c.-strap,** látigo, *m*

cinder *n* ceniza, *f*; carbonilla, *f*. **red-hot c.,** rescoldo, *m*. **c.-track,** pista de ceniza, *f*

cinema, cinematograph *n* cine, cinematógrafo, *m*

cinematography *n* cinematografía, *f*

cinnamon *n* (spice) canela, *f*; (tree) canelo, *m*; color de canela, *m*

cipher *n* math cero, *m*; *fig* nulidad, *f*; (code) cifra, *f*; monograma, *m*. **to be a mere c.,** ser un cero

circle *n* círculo, *m*; (revolution) vuelta, *f*; (group) grupo; *m*; (club, etc.) centro, *m*; (cycle) ciclo, *m*. *vt* dar vueltas alrededor de; rodear; ceñir; (on an application, examination, etc.) encerrar en un círculo. *vi* dar vueltas; (aircraft) volar en círculo; (of a hawk, etc.) cernerse. **dress-c.,** *theat* anfiteatro, *m*. **the family c.,** el círculo de la familia. **to come full c.,** dar la vuelta. **upper c.,** *theat* segundo piso, *m*. **vicious c.,** círculo vicioso, *m*

circuit *n* circuito, *m*; (tour) gira, *f*; (revolution) vuelta, *f*; (radius) radio, *m*. **short c.,** corto circuito, *m*. **c.-breaker,** corta-circuitos, *m*

circuit court of appeals *n* tribunal colegial de circuito, *m*

circuitous a indirecto; tortuoso

circular a circular; redondo. *n* carta circular, *f*; circular, *f*. **c. tour,** viaje redondo, *m*

circularize *vt* enviar circulares (a)

circulate *vi* circular. *vt* hacer circular; poner en circulación; (news, etc.) divulgar, diseminar

circulating library *n* biblioteca por subscripción, *f*

circulation *n* circulación, *f*; (of a newspaper, etc.) tirada, circulación, *f*. **c. of the blood,** circulación de la sangre, *f*

circulatory a circulatorio

circumcise *vt* circuncidar

circumcised a circunciso

circumcision *n* circuncisión, *f*

circumference *n* circunferencia, *f*

circumlocution *n* circumlocución, *f*

circumnavigate *vt* circunnavegar

circumscribe *vt* circunscribir; *fig* limitar

circumscribed a circunscripto; *fig* limitado

circumscription *n* circunscripción, *f*; *fig* limitación, restricción, *f*

circumspect a circunspecto; discreto, correcto; prudente

circumspection *n* circunspección, *f*; prudencia, *f*

circumspectly adv con circunspección; prudentemente

circumstance *n* circunstancia, *f*; detalle, *m*. **aggravating c.,** circunstancia agravante, *f*. **attenuating c.,** circunstancia atenuante, *f*. **in the circumstances,** en las circunstancias. **in easy circumstances,** en buena posición, acomodado. **Do you know what his circumstances are?** ¿Sabes cuál es su situación económica? **under the circumstances,** bajo las circunstancias

circumstantial a circunstancial; detallado. **c. evidence,** prueba de indicios, *f*

circumvent *vt* frustrar; impedir

circumvention *n* frustración, *f*

circus *n* circo, *m*; plaza redonda, *f*; (traffic) redondel, *m*

cirrhosis *n* cirrosis, *f*

cistern *n* tanque, *m*; cisterna, *f*, aljibe, *m*

citation *n* *law* citación, *f*; cita, *f*

cite *vt* citar

citizen *n* ciudadano (-na); vecino (-na); natural, *mf*. **fellow c.,** conciudadano, *m*; compatriota, *mf*

citizenship *n* ciudadanía, *f*

citric a cítrico

citron *n* (fruit) cidra, *f*; (tree) cidro, *m*

city *n* ciudad, *f*, a municipal

civic a cívico; municipal

civics *n* civismo, *m*

civil a civil; doméstico; (polite) cortés, atento; (obliging) servicial. **C. Aeronautics Board,** Dirección general de aeronáutica civil, *f*. **c. defense,** defensa pasiva, *f*. **c. engineer,** ingeniero de caminos, canales y puertos, *m*. **C. Service,** cuerpo de empleados del Estado, *m*

civilian a civil. *n* ciudadano (-na). **c. dress,** traje paisano, *m*

civility *n* civilidad, cortesía, *f*

civilization *n* civilización, *f*

civilize *vt* civilizar

civilly adv civilmente, cortésmente

clad a vestido

claim *vt* reclamar; pretender exigir; *law* demandar; (assert) afirmar. *vi* *law* pedir en juicio. *n* reclamación, *f*; pretensión, *f*;

law demanda, *f*; (in a gold-field, etc.) concesión, *f*; (right) derecho, *m*. **to lay c. to,** pretender a; exigir. **to put in a c. for,** reclamar

claimant *n law* demandante, *mf*; pretendiente (-ta); *com* acreedor (-ra)

clairvoyance *n* doble vista, *f*

clairvoyant *n* vidente, *m*

clam *n* almeja, chirla, *f*

clamber *vi* trepar, encaramarse. *n* subida difícil, *f*

clamminess *n* viscosidad, humedad, *f*

clammy *a* viscoso; húmedo, mojado

clamor *n* clamor, estruendo, *m*; gritería, vocería, *f. vi* gritar, vociferar. **to c. against,** protestar contra. **to c. for,** pedir a voces

clamorous *a* clamoroso, ruidoso, estrepitoso

clamp *n* grapa, *f*; abrazadera, *f*; *carp* tornillo, *m*; (pile) montón, *m. vt* empalmar; sujetar, lañar

clan *n* clan, *m*; familia, *f*; partido, grupo, *m*

clandestine *a* clandestino, furtivo

clang *vi* sonar; (of a gate, etc.) rechinar. *vt* hacer sonar. *n* sonido metálico, *m*; estruendo, *m*

clank *vi* dar un ruido metálico; crujir. *vt* hacer sonar; (glasses) hacer chocar. *n* ruido metálico, *m*; el crujir

clannish *a* exclusivista

clap *vt* (hands) batir; (spurs, etc.) poner rápidamente; (one's hat on) encasquetarse (el sombrero); (shut) cerrar apresuradamente. *vi* aplaudir. *n* (of the hands) palmada, *f*; (of thunder) trueno, *m*; (noise) ruido, *m*. **to c. eyes on,** echar la vista encima de. **to c. someone on the back,** dar una palmada en la espalda (a). **to c. the hands,** batir las palmas

clapper *n* (of a bell) badajo, *m*

clapping *n* aplausos, *m pl*

claret *n* clarete, *m*

clarification *n* clarificación, *f*; elucidación, *f*

clarify *vt* clarificar; elucidar, aclarar

clarinet *n* clarinete, *m*

clarinettist *n* clarinete, *m*

clarity *n* claridad, *f*; lucidez, *f*

clash *vi* chocar; encontrarse; (of events) coincidir; (of opinions, etc.) oponerse, estar en desacuerdo; (of colors) desentonar, chocar. *n* estruendo, fragor, *m*; choque, *m*; *mil* encuentro, *m*; (of opinions, etc.) desacuerdo, *m*; disputa, *f*

clasp *vt* (a brooch, etc.) abrochar, enganchar; (embrace) abrazar; (of plants, etc.) ceñir. *n* (brooch) broche, *m*; (of a belt) hebilla, *f*; (of a necklace, handbag, book) cierre, *m*; (for the hair) pasador, *m*. **to c. someone in one's arms,** tomar en los brazos (a), abrazar. **c.-knife,** navaja, *f*

class *n* clase, *f*; (kind) especie, *f*; (of exhib-

its, etc.) categoría, *f. vt* clasificar. **in a c. by itself,** único en su línea. **the lower classes,** las clases bajas. **the middle classes,** la clase media. **the upper classes,** la clase alta. **c.-mate,** condiscípulo (-la). **c.-room,** sala de clase, *f*, salón de clase, *f*. **c. war,** lucha de clases, *f*

classic *a* clásico. *n* clásico, *m*

classical *a* clásico

classifiable *a* clasificable

classification *n* clasificación, *f*

classified *a* (secreto) reservado, secreto; (advertisement) por palabras

classified advertisement *n* anuncio por palabras, *m*

classify *vt* clasificar

clatter *vi* hacer ruido; (knock) golpear; (of loose horseshoes) chacolotear. *vt* hacer ruido con; chocar (una cosa contra otra). *n* ruido, *m*; (hammering) martilleo, *m*; (of horseshoes) chacoloteo, *m*; (of a crowd) estruendo, *m*, bulla, *f*. **John clattered along the street,** Los pasos de Juan resonaban por la calle

clause *n gram* cláusula, *f*; *law* condición, estipulación, cláusula, *f*

claustrophobia *n* claustrofobia, *f*

clavicle *n* clavícula, *f*

claw *n* garra, *f*; (of a lobster, etc.) tenaza, *f*; (hook) garfio, gancho, *m. vt* arañar, clavar las uñas en; (tear) desgarrar. **c.-hammer,** martillo de orejas, *m*

clay *n* arcilla, *f*; barro, *m*; (pipe) pipa de barro, *f*. **c.-pit,** barrizal, *m*

clean *a* limpio; puro, casto. *adv* limpio; completamente; exactamente. **to make a c. sweep (of),** no dejar títere con cabeza. **to make a c. breast of,** confesar sin tormento, no quedarse con nada en el pecho. **to show a c. pair of heels,** tomar las de Villadiego. **c. bill of health,** patente de sanidad, *m*. **c.-cut,** bien definido; claro. **c.-limbed,** bien proporcionado, gallardo. **c.-shaven,** lampiño; sin barba, bien afeitado

clean *vt* limpiar; (streets) barrer; (a floor) fregar; (dryclean) lavar al seco. **to c. one's hands (teeth),** limpiarse las manos (los dientes). **to c. up,** limpiar; (tidy) asear; poner en orden

cleaner *n* limpiador (-ra); (charwoman) fregona, *f*; (stain remover) sacamanchas, *m*; (drycleaner, person) tintorero (-ra)

cleaning *n* limpieza, *f*, a de *f*. limpiar. **dry-c.,** lavado al seco, *m*. **c. rag,** trapo de limpiar, *m*. **c. woman** *Mexico* fregandera

cleanliness *n* limpieza, *f*; aseo, *m*

cleanse *vt* limpiar; lavar; purgar; purificar

cleansing *n* limpieza, *f*; lavamiento, *m*; purgación, *f*; purificación, *f*

clear *a* claro; (of the sky) sereno, despejado; transparente; (free (from)) libre (de); (open) abierto; (of profit, etc.) neto; (of thoughts, etc.) lúcido; (apparent) evidente; explícito; (of images) distinto; absoluto; (whole) entero, completo. **c. majority,** mayoría absoluta, f. **c. profit,** beneficio neto, m. **c.-cut,** bien definido. **c.-headed,** perspicaz; inteligente. **c.-sighted,** clarividente

clear vt aclarar; despejar; limpiar; librar (de); quitar; (one's throat) carraspear; (com stock) liquidar; (of a charge) absolver; (one's character) vindicar; (avoid, miss) evitar; (jump) salvar, saltar; (a court, etc.) desocupar; (a debt) satisfacer; (an account) saldar; (a mortgage) cancelar; (win) ganar; hacer un beneficio de; (through customs) despachar en la aduana. vi (of sky, etc.) serenarse; escampar; (of wine, etc.) aclararse; despacharse en la aduana. **to c. the table,** levantar la mesa, levantar los manteles. **to c. the underbrush from** Lat. Am. desmalezar. **to c. the way,** abrir calle; fig abrir paso. **to c. away,** vt quitar; disipar. vi disiparse. **to c. off,** vt (finish) terminar; (debts) pagar; (discharge) despedir. vi (of rain) despejarse, escampar; marcharse. **to c. out,** vt limpiar; (a drain, etc.) desatascar; vaciar; echar. vi marcharse, escabullirse. **C. out!** ¡Fuera! **c. the decks,** hacer zafarrancho. **c. the decks for action,** hacer zafarrancho. **to c. up,** vt poner en orden; (a mystery, etc.) aclarar, resolver, vi (of weather) serenarse, escampar, despejarse

clearance n (of trees, etc.) desmonte, m; eliminación, f; expulsión, f; mech espacio muerto, m; despacho de aduana, m. **to make a c. of,** deshacerse de. **c. sale,** liquidación, venta de saldos, f

clearing n (in a wood) claro, m, Argentina abra f; desmonte, m; (com of goods) liquidación, f; (of one's character) vindicación, f. **c.-house,** casa de compensación, f

cleavage n hendimiento, m; (in views, etc.) escisión, f

cleave vt partir; abrir; (air, water, etc.) surcar, hender. vi partirse; (stick) pegarse, adherirse

cleaver n partidor, m; hacha, f

cleft n hendedura, fisura, rendija, abertura, f. **c.-palate,** paladar hendido, m

clemency n (of weather) benignidad, f; (of character, etc.) clemencia, f

clement a (of weather) benigno; (of character, etc.) clemente, benévolo

clench vt agarrar; (teeth, etc.) apretar; (a bargain) cerrar, concluir

clergy n clero, m, clérigos, m pl

clergyman n clérigo, m

cleric n eclesiástico, m

clerical a clerical; de oficina. **c. error,** error de oficina, m. **c. work,** trabajo de oficina, m

clerk n (clergyman) clérigo, m; (in an office) oficinista, escribiente, m; oficial, m; secretario, m

clever a listo, inteligente; ingenioso; hábil; (dexterous) diestro

cleverly adv hábilmente; diestramente, con destreza

cleverness n talento, m; inteligencia, f; habilidad, f; (dexterity) destreza, f

cliché n frase hecha, frase de cajón, f

click vi (of the tongue) dar un chasquido; (of a bolt, etc.) cerrarse a golpe; hacer tic-tac. vt (one's tongue) chascar; (a bolt, etc.) cerrar a golpe. n golpe seco, m; tic-tac, m; (of the tongue) chasquido, m. **to c. one's heels together,** hacer chocar los talones

client n cliente, mf; (customer) parroquiano (-na), Lat. Am. also marchante (-ta) mf

clientele n clientela, f

cliff n acantilado, m, roca, escarpa, f

climate n clima, m

climax n culminación, f; (rhetoric) clímax, m; gradación, f; punto más alto, apogeo, cenit, m; (of a play, etc.) desenlace, m

climb vt and vi trepar; escalar; montar; subir; ascender. **rate of c.,** aer velocidad ascensional, f. **to c. down,** bajar; fig echar el pie atrás. **to c. over,** (obstacles) salvar. **to c. up,** encaramarse por; subir por; montar

climber n alpinista, mf; (plant) trepadera, enredadera, f; (social) arribista, mf

clinch vt (nails, etc.) remachar, rebotar; (a bargain, etc.) cerrar; (an argument, etc.) remachar. n (wrestling) cuerpo a cuerpo, m

cling vi pegarse (a); agarrarse (a); (of scents) pegarse; (follow) seguir. **They clung together for an instant,** Quedaron abrazados un instante

clinging a tenaz; (of plants, etc.) trepador; (of persons) manso, dócil. **to be a c. vine,** inf ser una malva

clinic n clínica, f

clink vi retiñir; (of glasses) chocarse. vt hacer sonar; (glasses) chocar. n retintín, m; (of a hammer) martilleo, m; sonido metálico, m; (of glasses) choque, m; (jail) Argentina, Chile capacha f

clip vt (grasp) agarrar; (sheep, etc.) esquilar; (trim) recortar, cercenar; (prune) podar; (a ticket) taladrar. n pinza, f; (paper-clip) sujetapapeles, Central America ataché, elsewhere in Lat. Am. broche m; mech grapa, escarpia, f; (for ornament) sujetador, m. **to c. a person's wings,** fig cortar (or quebrar) las alas (a)

clipper n (person) esquilador (-ra); (naut and aer) clíper, m; pl **clippers,** tenazas de cortar, f pl; (for pruning) podaderas, f pl; (punch) taladro, m

clipping n (of sheep, etc.) esquileo, m; (of a newspaper, etc.) recorte, m

clique n camarilla, f

cloak n capa, f; manto, m; fig velo, m. vt encapotar; embozar; (conceal) ocultar, encubrir. **c. and sword play,** comedia de capa y espada, *f.* **c.-room,** guardarropa, *m;* (ladies') tocador, *m;* (on a station) consigna, *f*

clock *n* reloj, *m;* (of a stocking) cuadrado, *m.* **It is six o'clock,** Son las seis. **c.-face,** esfera de reloj, *f.* **c.-maker,** relojero, *m.* **c.-making,** relojería, *f.* **c.-work,** aparato de relojería, *m.* **to go like c.-work,** ir como un reloj. **c.-work train,** tren de cuerda, *m*

clockwise *a* and *adv* en el sentido de las agujas del reloj; de derecha a izquierda

clod *n* (of earth) terrón, *m;* (corpse) tierra, *f;* (person) zoquete, *m.* **c.-hopper,** patán, *m*

clog *n* (shoe) zueco, zoclo, *m;* (obstacle) estorbo, obstáculo, *m.* *vt* embarazar; estorbar, impedir; (block) obturar, cerrar; *fig* paralizar

cloister *n* claustro, *m;* convento, *m.* *vt* enclaustrar

close *a* estrecho; (of a prisoner) incomunicado; (reticent) reservado; (niggardly) tacaño, avaro; (scarce) escaso; (of friends) íntimo; (equal) igual; (lacking space) apretado; (dense) denso; (thick) tupido; compacto; (of a copy, etc.) fiel, exacto; (thorough) concienzudo; (careful) cuidadoso; (attentive) atento; (to the roots) a raíz; (of shaving) bueno; (of weather) pesado, sofocante; (of rooms) mal ventilado. **at c. quarters,** de cerca. **It is c. to eight o'clock,** Son casi las ocho. **to press c.,** perseguir de cerca; fatigar. **c. at hand,** cerca; al lado; a mano. **c.-cropped,** (of hair) al rape. **c. fight,** lucha igualada, *f.* **c.-fisted,** tacaño, apretado. **c.-fitting,** ajustado, ceñido al cuerpo; pequeño. **c. season,** veda, *f.* **c.-up,** *n* (cinema) primer plano, *m*

close *n* (end) fin, *m,* conclusión, *f;* (of day) caída, *f; mus* cadencia, *f;* (enclosure) cercado, *m;* (square) plazoleta, *f;* (alley) callejón, *m;* (of a cathedral) patio, *m.* **at the c. of day,** a la caída de la tarde. **to bring to a c.,** terminar; llevar a cabo. **to draw to a c.,** tocar a su fin; estar terminando

close *vt* cerrar; (end) concluir, terminar; poner fin a. *vi* cerrar(se); (of a wound) cicatrizarse, cerrarse; (end) terminar(se), acabar, concluir. **to c. the ranks,** cerrar filas. **to c. about,** (surround) rodear, cercar; (envelop) envolver. **to c. down,** *vt* cerrar. *vi* cerrar; *rad* cerrarse. **to c. halfway** entrecerrar **to c. in,** (surround) cercar; (of night) cerrar; caer; (envelop) envolver; (of length of days) acortarse. **to c. in on,** cercar. **to c. round,** envolver; (of water) tragar. **to c. up,** *vt* cerrar; cerrar completamente; obstruir. *vi* (of persons) acercarse; (of a wound) cicatrizarse; cerrarse

closed *a* cerrado. "**Road C.,**" Paso Cerrado. **to have a c. mind,** ser cerrado de mollera; sufrir de estrechez de miras

closely *adv* estrechamente; de cerca; (carefully) cuidadosamente; (exactly) exactamente; (attentively) con atención, atentamente

closeness *n* estrechez, *f;* densidad, *f;* (nearness) proximidad, *f;* (of a copy, etc.) fidelidad, exactitud, *f;* (stuffiness) falta de aire, *f;* (of friendship) intimidad, *f;* (stinginess) tacañería, *f;* (reserve) reserva.

closet *n* camarín, *m;* (cupboard) alacena, *f;* (water) excusado, *m*

closing *n* cerramiento, *m;* (of an account) saldo, *m.* **c. time,** cierre, *m,* hora de cerrar, *f*

clot *n* coágulo, grumo, *m.* *vt* coagular. *vi* coagularse, cuajarse

cloth *n* tela, *f;* paño, *m;* (table) mantel, *m;* (clergy) clero, *m.* **She cleaned the books with a c.,** Ella limpió los libros con un paño. **in c.,** (of books) en tela

clothe *vt* vestir; cubrir; (with authority, etc.) revestir. **to c. oneself,** vestirse

clothes *n pl* vestidos, *m pl,* ropa, *f.* **a suit of c.,** un traje. **old c. shop,** ropavejería, *f.* **c.-basket,** cesta de la colada, *f.* **c.-brush,** cepillo para ropa, *m.* **c.-hanger,** percha, *f.* **c.-horse,** enjugador, *m.* **c.-line,** cuerda de la ropa, *f.* **c.-peg,** pinza de la ropa, *f.* **c.-prop,** palo para sostener la cuerda de la colada, *m*

clothing *n* vestidos, *m pl,* ropa, *f.* **article of c.,** prenda de vestir, *f*

cloud *n* nube, *f.* *vt* anublar, oscurecer; empañar; (blot out) borrar. *vi* anublarse. **to be under a c.,** estar bajo sospecha. **summer c.,** nube de verano, *f.* **storm-c.,** nubarrón, *m.* **c.-burst,** nubada, *f,* chaparrón, *m.* **c.-capped,** coronado de nubes

cloudiness *n* nebulosidad, *f;* obscuridad, *f;* (of liquids) turbiedad, *f*

cloudless *a* sin nubes, despejado; sereno, claro

cloudy *a* nublado, nubloso; obscuro; (of liquids) turbio

clout *n Central America, Mexico* arranque *m*

clove *n* clavo de especia, *m;* (of garlic) diente de ajo, *m.* **c.-tree,** clavero, *m*

cloven *a* hendido. **to show the c. hoof,** enseñar la oreja. **c. hoof,** pezuña, *f*

clover *n* trébol, *m.* **to be in c.,** nadar en la abundancia

clown *n* patán, *m;* bufón, tonto, *m;* (in a circus) payaso, *m.* *vi* hacer el tonto, hacer el payaso

cloying *a* empalagoso

club *n* porra, cachiporra, clava, *f;* (gymnastic) maza, *f;* (hockey) bastón de hockey, *m;* (golf) palo de golf, *m;* (in cards) basto, *m;* (social) club, *m.* *vt* golpear. **to c. together,** asociarse, unirse. **We clubbed together to buy him a present,** Entre todos le compramos un regalo. **c.-house,** club, *m*

clubfoot n pie calcáneo, pie contrahecho, pie de piña, pie equino, pie talo, pie zambo, m

clue n indicio, m; (to a problem) clave, f; (of a crossword) indicación, f; idea, f

clump n bloque, pedazo, m; (of trees) grupo, m; (of feet) ruido, m

clumsiness n torpeza, f; falta de maña, f; pesadez, f

clumsy a torpe; desmañado; chapucero, sin arte; (lumbering) pesado; (in shape) disforme

cluster n (of currants, etc.) racimo, m; (of flowers) ramillete, m; grupo, m. vi arracimarse; agruparse. **They clustered round him,** Se agrupaban a su alrededor

clutch vt agarrar; sujetar, apretar. n mech embrague, m; (of eggs) nidada, f; fig garras, f pl. **to fall into the clutches of,** caer en las garras de. **to make a c. at,** procurar agarrar. **to throw in the c.,** mech embragar. **to throw out the c.,** mech desembragar. **c. pedal,** pedal de embrague, m

clutter n desorden, m, confusión, f, vt desordenar

coach n carroza, f; charabán, m; rw vagón, coche, m; (hackney) coche de alquiler, m; sport entrenador, m; (tutor) profesor particular, m. vt sport entrenar; (teach) preparar, dar lecciones particulares (a). **through c.,** coche directo, m. **c.-box,** pescante, m. **c.-house,** cochera, f

coaching n sport entrenamiento, m; lecciones particulares, f pl

coagulate vi coagularse. vt coagular, cuajar

coal n carbón, m; pedazo de carbón, m; (burning) brasa, f. vi carbonear, hacer carbón. vt proveer de carbón; carbonear. **to carry coals to Newcastle,** llevar leña al monte, elevar agua al mar. **to haul a person over the coals,** reprender a alguien. **c.-barge,** (barco) carbonero, m. **c.-black,** negro como el azabache. **c.-cellar, house,** carbonera, f. **c.-dust,** cisco, m. **c.-field,** yacimiento de carbón, m. **c.-gas,** gas de hulla, m. **c.-heaver,** cargador de carbón, m. **c.-merchant,** carbonero, m. **c.-mine,** mina de carbón, f. **c.-miner,** minero de carbón, m. **c.-scuttle,** carbonera, f. **c.-tar,** alquitrán mineral, m

coalesce vi fundirse; unirse; incorporarse

coalition n coalición, f

coarse a (in texture) basto, burdo; tosco; (gross) grosero; vulgar. **c.-grained,** de fibra gruesa; (of persons) vulgar, poco fino. **c. woolen cloth** Chile litro m

coarsen vt (of persons) embrutecer. vi embrutecerse; (of the skin) curtirse

coarseness n basteza, f; tosquedad, f; (of persons) grosería, indelicadeza, f; vulgaridad, f

coast n costa, f; litoral, m. vi costear; deslizarse en un tobogán; dejar muerto el motor. **The c. is not clear,** Hay moros en la costa. **c.-guard,** guardacostas, m. **c.-line,** litoral, m

coastal a costanero, costero. **c. defences,** defensas costeras, f pl

coat n abrigo, m; gabán, m; chaqueta, f; (animal's) capa, f; (of paint) mano, f. vt recubrir; (with paint, etc.) dar una mano de. **fur c.,** abrigo de pieles, m. **sports c.,** Americana sport, f. **c. of arms,** escudo de armas, m. **c. of mail,** cota de malla, f. **c.-hanger,** percha, f

coating n (of paint, etc.) capa, mano, f

coax vt instar; halagar, engatusar, Lat. Am. also engaratusar; persuadir (a)

coaxing n ruegos, m pl; mimos, m pl, caricias, f pl; persuasión, f. a mimoso, zalamero; persuasivo

cobbler n zapatero remendón, m. **cobbler's last,** horma, f. **cobbler's wax,** cerote, m

cobblestone n guijarro, m, piedra, f

cobweb n telaraña, f

cocaine n cocaína, f

cochlea n caracol (del oído), m

cock n gallo, m; (male) macho, m; (tap) grifo, m, espita, f; (of a gun) martillo, m; (weather-vane) veleta, f; (of hay) montón, m. vt (a gun) amartillar; (a hat) ladear; (raise) erguir, enderezar. **a cocked hat,** un sombrero de tres picos. **at half c.,** (of a gun) desamartillada f.. **He cocked his head,** Erguió la cabeza. **The dog cocked its ears,** El perro aguzó las orejas. **to c. one's eye at,** lanzar una mirada (a). **c.-a-doodle-doo,** quiquiriquí, m. **c.-a-hoop,** triunfante, jubiloso; arrogante. **c.-crow,** canto del gallo, m. **c.-fight,** riña de gallos, f. **c.-of-the-walk,** gallito, m. **c.-sure,** pagado de sí mismo; completamente convencido

cockpit n galleria, f; aer casilla del piloto, f; fig arena, f

cockroach n cucaracha, f

cocktail n (drink) cótel, coctel, m. **to shake a c.,** mezclar un coctel. **c. party,** coctel m. **c. shaker,** cotelera, f

cocky a fatuo, presuntuoso

cocoa n cacao, m

coconut n coco, m; inf cabeza, f. **c. milk,** agua de coco, f. **c. shy,** pim, pam, pum, m. **c. tree,** cocotero, m

cocoon n capullo, m

cod n bacalao, m. **cod-liver oil,** aceite de hígado de bacalao, m

coddle vt criar con mimo, mimar, consentir

code n código, m; clave, f; (secret) cifra, f. vt poner en cifra. **signal c.,** naut código de señales, m. **c. word,** palabra de clave, f

codeine n codeína, f

codex n códice, m

codicil n codicilio, m

codify vt codificar

coefficient n coeficiente, m

coerce vt forzar, obligar; constreñir

coercion n coerción, coacción, f

coercive a coercitivo, coactivo

coeval a coevo

coexist vi coexistir

coexistence n coexistencia, f

coffee n café, m. **black c.**, café solo, m. **white c.**, café con leche, m. **c.-bean**, grano de café, m. **c.-cup**, taza para café, f. **c.-house**, café, m. **c.-mill**, molinillo de café, m. **c.-plantation**, cafetal, m. **c.-pot**, cafetera, f. **c.-set**, juego de café, m. **c.-tree**, cafeto, m

coffer n cofre, m; arca, caja, f

coffin n ataúd, féretro, m; caja, f

cog n mech diente (de rueda), m

cogency n fuerza, f

cogent a convincente, fuerte; urgente

cogitate vi pensar, considerar, meditar

cogitation n reflexión, meditación, consideración, f

cognac n coñac, m

cognate a (of stock) consanguíneo; afín; análogo; semejante

cognizance n conocimiento, m; jurisdicción, f

cogwheel n rueda dentada, f

cohabit vi cohabitar

cohere vi pegarse, adherirse; unirse

coherent a coherente; consecuente

cohesion n cohesión, f; coherencia, f

cohort n cohorte, f

coiffure n peinado, m; tocado, m

coil vt arrollar; (naut of ropes) adujar. vi arrollarse; enroscarse; serpentear. n rollo, m; (of a serpent and ropes) anillo, m; (of hair) trenza, f; elec carrete, m. **coil of smoke**, nube de humo, f. **to c. up**, hacerse un ovillo

coin n moneda, f; inf dinero, m. vt acuñar; (a new word) inventar. **to pay back in the same c.**, pagar en la misma moneda

coinage n acuñación, f; moneda, f; sistema monetario, m; invención, f; (new word) neologismo, m

coincide vi coincidir (con); estar conforme, estar de acuerdo

coincidence n coincidencia, f; (chance) casualidad, f

coiner n acuñador de moneda, m; monedero falso, m; (of phrases, etc.) inventor, m

coitus n coito, m

colander n colador, m

cold a frío, m; med catarro, constipado, m. **I am c.**, Tengo frío. **It is c.**, Está frío; (weather) Hace frío. **to catch a c.**, acatarrarse, resfriarse. **to grow c.**, enfriarse; (of the weather) empezar a hacer frío. **in c. blood**, a sangre fría. **c.-blooded**, (fishes, etc.) de sangre fría;

(chilly, of persons) friolero; (pitiless) insensible, sin piedad; (of actions) a sangre fría, premeditado. **c.-chisel**, cortafrío, m. **c. cream**, crema (para el cutis), f. **c.-hearted**, seco, insensible. **c.-shoulder**, n frialdad, f. vt tratar con frialdad (a). **c.-storage**, conservación refrigerada, f

coldness n frío, m; (of one's reception, etc.) frialdad, f; (of heart) inhumanidad, f

colic n cólico, m

coliseum n coliseo, m

colitis n colitis, f

collaborate vi colaborar (con)

collaborator n colaborador (-ra); (quisling) colaboracionista, mf

collapse n derrumbamiento, m; desplome, m; med colapso, m; (of buildings and flg) hundimiento, m; (of plans) frustración, f; (failure) fracaso, m. vi derrumbarse; (of buildings, etc.) hundirse, venirse abajo; (of persons, fall) desplomarse; med sufrir colapso; (of plans, etc.) frustrarse, venirse abajo. **George came to us after the c. of France**, Jorge vino a quedarse con nosotros después del hundimiento de Francia

collapsible a plegable

collar n (of a garment and of fur) cuello, m; (of a dog, etc., and necklace) collar, m. vt (seize) agarrar. **detachable c.**, cuello suelto, m. **high c.**, alzacuello, m. **c.-bone**, clavícula, f

collate vt cotejar; (to a benefice) colacionar

collateral a colateral

collation n colación, f

colleague n colega, m; compañero (-ra)

collect vt (assemble) reunir; (catch) coger; acumular; (call for) pasar a buscar, ir (o venir) a buscar; (pick up) recoger; (taxes, etc.) recaudar; coleccionar; (one's strength, etc. and debts, etc.) cobrar; (letters) recoger. vi reunirse, congregarse; acumularse. n ecc colecta, f. **to c. oneself**, reponerse

collected a (of persons) seguro de sí.

collection n reunión, f; (of data, etc.) acumulación, f; (of pictures, stamps, etc.) colección, f; (of a debt, etc.) cobranza, f; (of taxes, etc.) recaudación, f; (from a mail box) recogida, f; (of laws, etc.) compilación, f; ecc ofertorio, m; (of donations) colecta, f

collection agency n agencia de cobros de cuentas, f

collective a colectivo. **c. bargaining**, regateo colectivo, trato colectivo, m

collector n (of pictures, etc.) coleccionador (-ra), coleccionista, mf; cobrador, m; elec colector, m

college n colegio, m; escuela, f; universidad,

collegiate a colegial, colegiado. **c. church**, iglesia colegial, f

collide vi chocar (contra), topar (con);

estar en conflicto (con). **c. head-on,** chocar frontalmente

collie n perro de pastor escocés, m

collier n minero de carbón, m; (barco) carbonero, m

collision n choque, m, colisión, f; (of interests, etc.) antagonismo, conflicto, m. **to come into c. with,** chocar con

Cologne Colonia, f

colloquial a familiar

colloquy n coloquio, m

collusion n colusión, f. **to be in c.,** law coludir; conspirar, estar de manga

Colombia Colombia, f

Colombian a colombiano. n colombiano (-na)

colon n anat colon, m; (punctuation) dos puntos, m pl

colonel n coronel, m

colonial a colonial. n habitante de las colonias, m. **c. government** Lat. Am. coloniaje m **C. Office,** Ministerio de Asuntos Coloniales, m. **c. period** Lat. Am. coloniaje m

colonnade n columnata, f

colony n colonia, f

color n color, m; colorido, m; tinta, f; materia colorante, f; pl **colors,** insignia, f; bandera, f, estandarte, m; naut pabellón, m. vt colorar; pintar; iluminar; (influence) influir, afectar. vi colorarse; ruborizarse; encenderse. **fast c.,** color estable, color sólido, m. **regimental colors,** bandera del regimiento, f. **with colors flying,** con tambor batiente, a banderas desplegadas. **to be off c.,** estar malucho, estar indispuesto. **to change c.,** (of persons) mudar de color, mudar de semblante. **to give c. to,** (a story, etc.) hacer verosímil. **to lay the colors on too thick,** recargar las tintas. **to pass with flying colors,** salir triunfante. **under c. of,** so color de, a pretexto de. **c.-blind,** daltoniano. **c.-blindness,** daltonismo, m

colored a colorado; de color

coloring n (substance) colorante, m; (act of) coloración, f; art colorido, m; (of complexion) colores, m pl

colorist n colorista, mf

colorless a sin color, incoloro; fig insípido

colossal a colosal, gigantesco; enorme; inf estupendo

colossus n coloso, m

colt n potro, m; (boy) muchacho alegre, m

colter n reja, reja del arado, f

column n columna, f. **Fifth c.,** quinta columna, f

columned a con columnas

columnist n periodista, m

coma n coma, m

comatose a comatoso

comb n peine, m; (for flax) carda, f; (curry) almohaza, f; (of cock) cresta, carúncula, f;

(of a wave) cima, cresta, f; (honey) panal, m, vt (hair) peinar; (flax) rastrillar, cardar. **c. and brush,** cepillo y peine. **high c.,** peineta, f. **to c. one's hair,** peinarse

combat vt luchar contra, combatir, resistir. vi combatir, pelear. n combate, m; lucha, batalla, f. **in single c.,** cuerpo a cuerpo

combatant n combatiente, m, a combatiente

combative a belicoso, pugnaz

combination n combinación, f; mezcla, f; unión, f; asociación, f; pl **combinations.** camisa pantalón, f. **c. lock,** cerradura de combinación, f

combine vt combinar; reunir, juntar; chem combinar. vi combinarse; asociarse (con); com fusionarse. n asociación, f; com monopolio, m

combustible a combustible. n combustible, m

combustion n combustión, f. **rapid c.,** combustión rápida, f. **spontaneous c.,** combustión espontánea, f

come vi venir; llegar; avanzar; acercarse; (happen) suceder, acontecer; (result) resultar; (find oneself) encontrarse, hallarse; (become) llegar a ser; (begin to) ponerse (a), empezar (a). **Come!** ¡Voy! ¡Allá voy! **C., c.!** ¡Vamos! ¡No es para tanto! ¡Ánimo! **I am ready whatever comes,** Estoy preparado venga lo que venga. **He comes of a good family,** Es (Viene) de buena familia. **I came to know him well,** Llegué a conocerle bien. **I don't know what came over me,** No sé lo que me pasó. **When I came to consider it,** Cuando me puse a considerarlo. **The bill comes to six thousand pesetas,** La cuenta sale a seis mil pesetas. **He comes up before the judge tomorrow,** Ha de comparecer ante el juez mañana. **What you say comes to this,** Lo que dice Vd. se reduce a esto. **What is the world coming to?** ¿A dónde va parar el mundo? **It does not c. within my scope,** No está dentro de mi alcance. **to c. apart,** deshacerse; romperse; dividirse. **to c. home to,** fig impresionar mucho, tocar en lo más íntimo; hacer comprender (a). **to c. into bloom,** empezar a tener flores, florecer. **to c. into one's head,** venir a las mientes. **to c. into the world,** venir al mundo. **to c. near,** acercarse; aproximarse, estar próximo. **to c. next,** venir después; suceder luego. **to c. to an end,** terminar, acabarse. **to c. to blows,** venir a las manos. **to c. to grief,** salir mal parado; (of schemes, etc.) malograrse. **to c. to hand,** venir a mano; (of letters) llegar a las manos (de). **to c. to life,** despertar; animarse; resucitar. **to c. to nothing,** frustrarse; no quedar en nada. **to c. to pass,** suceder; realizarse. **to c. to terms,** ponerse de acuerdo. **to c. true,** cumplirse, verificarse. **to c. about,** suceder, acontecer, tener lugar; (of the wind) girar. **to c. across,** dar con, encontrar por casualidad; tropezar con. **to c. after,** (a situation) solicitar; (follow) seguir (a); venir más tarde (que); (succeed) suceder. **to c. again,** volver. **to c. along,** caminar (por); andar (por); (arrive) llegar. **C. along!** ¡Ven! ¡Vamos! ¡Andamos! **to c. at,** alcanzar; (attack) embestir, atacar; (gain) obtener, adquirir. **to c. away,** irse, marcharse; (break) deshacerse. **to c. back,** volver, regresar, *Lat. Am.* devolverse **c.-back,** *n inf* respuesta, *f*; contraataque, *m*. **to c. before,** llegar antes; preceder (a). **to c. between,** interponerse (entre), intervenir. **to c. by,** pasar por, pasar junto a; (acquire) obtener, adquirir; (achieve) conseguir. **to c. down,** bajar, descender; (in the world) venir a menos; (be demolished) demolerse; (collapse) derrumbarse, hundirse; (of prices) bajar; (of traditions, etc.) llegar e.g. **This work has c. down to us in two fifteenth-century manuscripts** Esta obra nos ha llegado en dos manuscritos del siglo quince; (fall) caer. **c.-down,** *n* caída, *f*; frustración, *f*; desengaño, *m*; desprestigio, *m*; pérdida de posición, *f*. **to c. down on a person,** cantar la cartilla (a). **to c. down with altitude sickness** *Peru* asorocharse **to c. forward,** avanzar, adelantarse; (offer) ofrecerse; presentarse. **to c. in,** entrar; (of money) ingresar; (of trains, etc.) llegar; (of the tide) crecer; (of the new year) empezar; (of fashion) ponerse de moda; (be useful) servir (para). **C. in!** ¡Adelante! ¡Pase Vd.! **to c. into,** (a scheme) asociarse con; (property) heredar; (the mind) presentarse a la imaginación, ocurrirse (a). **to c. off,** (happen) tener lugar; realizarse, efectuarse; (be successful) tener éxito; (break off) separarse (de); romperse. **to c. off well,** tener éxito; (of persons) salir bien. **c. off the press,** salir de prensas (en, avanzar; (of actors) salir a la escena; (progress) hacer progresos; (develop) desarrollarse; (of pain, etc.) acometer (a); (arrive) llegar; (of a lawsuit) verse. **C. on!** ¡Vamos! ¡En marcha! **to c. out,** salir; (of stars) nacer; (of buds, etc.) brotar; (of the moon, etc.) asomarse; (of stains) borrarse, salir; (of a book) ver la luz, publicarse; (of secrets) divulgarse, saberse; (of a girl, in society) ponerse de largo; (on strike) declararse en huelga; (of fashions, etc.) aparecer. **to c. out with,** (a remark) soltar; (oaths, etc.) prorrumpir (en); (disclose) revelar, hacer público. **to c. round,** (to see someone) venir a ver (a); (coax) engatusar; (after a faint, etc.) volver en sí; (after illness) reponerse; (to another's point of view) aceptar, compartir. **to c. through,** pasar por; (trials, etc.) subir; salir de; (of liquids) salirse. **to c. to,** volver en sí. **to c. together,** reunirse, juntarse; venir juntos; unirse. **to c. under,** venir (or estar) bajo la jurisdicción de; (the influence of) estar dominado por;

(figure among) figurar entre, estar comprendido en. **to c. up,** subir; (of sun, moon) salir; (of plants) brotar; (of problems, etc.) surgir; (in conversation) discutirse; (before a court) comparecer. **to c. up to,** (equal) igualar, ser igual (a); rivalizar con; (in height) llegar hasta. **He came up to them in the street,** Les abordó (or se les acercó) en la calle. **We have c. up against many difficulties,** Hemos tropezado con muchas dificultades. **This novel does not c. up to his last,** Esta última novela no es tan buena como la anterior. **The party did not c. up to their expectations,** La reunión no fue tan divertida como esperaban. **to c. up with,** (a person) alcanzar (a). **to c. upon,** encontrar, hallar; tropezar con; encontrar por casualidad. **to c. upon evil days,** venir a menos

comedian *n* actor cómico, comediante, *m*

comedy *n* comedia, *f*. **c. of manners,** comedia de costumbres, *f*

comeliness *n* hermosura, *f*

comely *a* hermoso

comer *n* el, *m*, (*f*, la) que viene. **all comers,** todo el mundo. **first c.,** primer (-ra) venido (-da)

comet *n* cometa, *m*

comfort *vt* consolar, confortar; (encourage) animar; (reassure) alegrar. *n* consuelo, *m*; satisfacción, *f*; comodidad, *f*; bienestar, *m*. **He lives in great c.,** Vive con mucha comodidad. **c.-loving,** comodón

comfortable *a* cómodo; (with income) suficiente; (consoling) consolador. **to make oneself c.,** ponerse cómodo

comfortably *adv* cómodamente; suficientemente; fácilmente; con facilidad; (well) bien. **He is c. off,** Está bien de dinero

comforter *n* consolador (-ra); (baby's) chupador, *m*; (scarf) bufanda, *f*

comforting *a* consolador

comfortless *a* incómodo, sin comodidad; desconsolador; (of persons) inconsolable, desconsolado

comic *a* cómico; bufo; satírico. *n* cómico, *m*; *pl* **comics,** (printed) historietas cómicas, *f pl*. **c. opera,** ópera cómicas, *f*. **c. paper,** periódico satírico, *m*

comical *a* cómico; divertido, gracioso

coming *a* (with year, etc.) próximo, que viene; (promising) de porvenir; (approaching) que se acerca. *n* venida, *f*; llegada, *f*; advenimiento, *m*. **c.-out party,** puesta de largo, *f*. **comings and goings,** entradas y salidas, *f pl*

comma *n* coma, *f*. **inverted commas,** comillas, *f pl*

command *vt* mandar, ordenar; (silence, respect, etc.) imponer; (an army, fleet, etc.) comandar; capitanear; (one's emotions) dominar; (have at one's disposal) disponer de; (a military position, view) dominar; (sympathy, etc.) despertar, merecer; (of price) venderse por. *vi* mandar. *n* orden, *f*; (*mil nav*) mando, *m*; (of an army, etc.) comandancia, *f*; (of one's emotions, etc.) dominio, *m*; (of a military position, etc.) dominación, *f*; disposición, *f*. **By Royal C.,** Por Real Orden; (of shops, etc.) Proveedor de la Real Casa. **The house commands lovely views of the mountains,** La casa tiene hermosas vistas de las montañas. **word of c.,** orden, *f*. **Yours to c.,** A la disposición de Vd.

commandant *n* comandante, *m*

commandeer *vt* (conscript) reclutar; *mil* requisar; expropiar

commander *n mil* comandante, *m*; *nav* capitán de fragata, *m*; (of order of Knighthood) comendador, *m*. **c.-in-chief,** generalísimo, *m*. **C. of the Faithful,** Comendador de los creyentes, *m*

commanding *a mil* comandante; imponente; (of manner) imperioso; dominante. **c. officer,** comandante en jefe, *m*

commandment *n* precepto, mandamiento, *m*. **the Ten Commandments,** los diez mandamientos

commando *n mil* comando, *m*

commemorate *vt* conmemorar

commence *vt* comenzar, empezar, principiar. *vi* comenzar. **He commenced to eat,** Empezó a comer

commencement *n* principio, comienzo, *m*

commend *vt* (entrust) encomendar; recomendar; alabar

commendable *a* loable; recomendable

commendation *n* aprobación, alabanza, *f*, aplauso, *m*

commensurable *a* conmensurable

commensurate *a* proporcionado (a); conforme (a)

comment *n* observación, *f*; (on a work) comento, *m*; explicación, nota, *f*. *vi* hacer una observación (sobre); (a work) comentar, anotar. **to c. unfavorably on,** criticar

commentary *n* comentario, *m*; (on a person, etc.) comentos, *m pl*, observaciones, *f pl*

commentator *n* comentador (-ra); (of a work) comentarista, *mf*

commerce *n* comercio, *m*; negocios, *m pl*; (social) trato, *m*

commercial *a* comercial; mercantil. **c. traveler,** viajante, *m*

commercialism *n* mercantilismo, *m*

commercialize *vt* hacer objeto de comercio

commingle *vt* mezclar. *vi* mezclarse

commiserate *vi* compadecerse (de), apiadarse (de)

commiseration *n* conmiseración, compasión, *f*

commission *n* comisión, *f*; *mil* graduación de oficial, *f*. *vt* comisionar; (a ship) poner en servicio activo, armar; (appoint) nombrar. **in c.,** en servicio, activo. **out of c.,** (of ships) inutilizado; inservible. **c. agent,** comisionista, *mf* **to gain one's c.,** *mil* graduarse de oficial. **to put out of c.,** retirar del servicio; poner fuera de combate; estropear

commissioner *n* comisario, *m*. **High C.,** alto comisario, *m*. **c. for oaths,** notario, *m*. **c. of police,** jefe de policía, *m*

commit *vt* entregar (a); (a crime) cometer; (to prison) encarcelar; (for trial) remitir. **to c. oneself,** comprometerse. **to c. to memory,** aprender de memoria. **to c. to writing,** poner por escrito

commitment *n* (financial, etc.) obligación, responsabilidad, *f*; compromiso, *m*

committal *n* (of an offence) comisión, *f*; (placing, entrusting) entrega, *f*; (to prison) encarcelamiento, *m*; (legal procedure) auto de prisión, *m*

committee *n* comité, *m*; comisión, junta, *f*; consejo, *m*. **They decided in c.,** Tomaron la resolución en comité. **c. of management,** consejo de administración, *m*

commodious *a* espacioso, grande

commodity *n* artículo, *m*, mercancía, *f*

common *a* común; general, corriente; universal; vulgar; (disparaging) cursi; (elementary) elemental. *n* pastos comunes, *m pl*. **He is not a c. man,** No es un hombre cualquiera; No es un hombre vulgar. **in c.,** en común. **the c. man,** el hombre medio. **the c. people,** el pueblo. **c. sense,** sentido común, *m*. **c. soldier,** soldado raso, *m*. **c. speech,** lenguaje vulgar, *m*. **c. usage,** uso corriente, *m*

commoner *n* plebeyo (-ya)

commonly *adv* comúnmente, por lo general

commonness *n* frecuencia, *f*; vulgaridad, *f*

commonplace *n* lugar común, *m*; trivialidad, *f*. *a* trivial

commons *n* el pueblo; (House of) Cámara de los Comunes, *f*; (food) provisiones, *f pl*. **to be on short c.,** comer mal, estar mal alimentado

Commonwealth *n* estado, *m*; república, *f*; comunidad (de naciones), *f*; mancomunidad, *f*. **the Commonwealth of Puerto Rico,** el Estado Libre Asociado de Puerto Rico, *m*

commotion *n* confusión, *f*; conmoción, perturbación, *f*; tumulto, *m*

communal *a* comunal

commune *n* comuna, *f*; comunión, *f*, *vi* conversar (con). **to c. with oneself,** hablar consigo

communicant *n ecc* comulgante, *mf*; (of information) informante, *mf*

communicate *vt* comunicar; (diseases) transmitir. *vi* comunicarse (con); *ecc* comulgar

communication · n comunicación, f. **lines of c.**, comunicaciones, f pl. **to get into c. with**, ponerse en comunicación con. **c.-cord**, (in a railway carriage) timbre de alarma, m

communicative a comunicativo; expansivo

communicativeness n carácter expansivo, m; locuacidad, f

communion n comunión, f. **Holy c.**, comunión, f. **to take c.**, comulgar. **c. card**, cédula de comunión, f. **c. cup**, cáliz, f. **c. table**, sagrada mesa, f; altar, m

communiqué n comunicación, parte, f. **to issue a c.**, dar parte

communism n comunismo, m

communist n comunista, mf a comunista

community n comunidad, f. **the c.**, la nación; el público. **c. center**, centro social, m

commute vt conmutar; reducir

compact n (pact) acuerdo, pacto, m; (powder) polvorera, f. a compacto; firme; sólido; apretado, cerrado; (of persons) bien hecho; (of style) conciso, sucinto

compactness n compacidad, f; (of style) concisión, f

companion n compañero (-ra); camarada, mf; (of an Order) caballero, m, (or dama, f). vt acompañar. **lady c.**, señora de compañía, f. **c.-hatch**, cubierta de escotilla, f. **c.-ladder**, escala de toldilla, f

companionable a sociable, amistoso

companionship n compañía, f; compañerismo, m

company n (com mil etc.) compañía, f; (ship's) tripulación, f. **I will keep you c.**, Te haré compañía. **to part c. with**, separarse de. **Present c. excepted!** ¡Mejorando lo presente! **They are not very good c.**, No son muy divertidos

compare vt comparar. vi compararse; poder compararse. ser comparable. **beyond c.**, sin comparación; sin igual. **to c. favorably with**, no perder por comparación con. **to c. notes**, cambiar impresiones

comparison n comparación, f. **in c. with**, comparado con

compartment n compartimiento, m; rw departamento, m

compass n circuito, m; límites, m pl; alcance, m; (of a voice) gama, f; naut brújula, f; pl **compasses**, compás, m. vt (achieve) conseguir; (plan) idear, **mariner's c.**, compás de mar. m, rosa de los vientos, f. **pocket c.**, brújula de bolsillo, f. **to c. about**, cercar, rodear

compassion n compasión, f. **to have c. on**, apiadarse de, compadecerse de

compassionate a compasivo, piadoso. **c. leave**, permiso, m

compatriot n compatriota, mf

compel vt obligar (a), forzar (a); exigir;

imponer. **His attitude compels respect**, Su actitud impone el respeto

compelling a compulsivo

compendious a compendioso, sucinto

compendium n compendio, m; resumen, m

compensate vt compensar; (reward) recompensar; (for loss, etc.) indemnizar. **to c. for**, compensar; indemnizar contra

compensation n compensación, f; (reward) recompensa, f; (for loss, etc.) indemnización, f

compensatory a compensatorio

compete vi competir (con); rivalizar; ser rivales; (in a competition) concurrir

competence n aptitud, f; capacidad, f; competencia, f

competent a competente; capaz

competition n competencia, competición, rivalidad, f; emulación, f; (contest, etc.) concurso, m. **spirit of c.**, espíritu de competencia, m

competitive a competidor; de competición. **c. examination**, oposición, f

competitor n competidor (-ra)

compilation n compilación, f

compile vt compilar

complacence n complacencia, satisfacción, f; contento de sí mismo, m

complacent a satisfecho; pagado de sí mismo

complain vi quejarse; lamentarse; law querellarse. **He complains about everything**, Se queja de todo

complaint n queja, f; lamento, m; law demanda, f; (illness) enfermedad, f. **to lodge a c. (against)**, quejarse (de)

complaisant a complaciente, cortés, afable; (of husbands) consentido, sufrido

complement n complemento, m; total, número completo, m. vt completar

complementary a complementario

complete a entero; completo; perfecto; acabado. vt completar; acabar; (happiness, etc.) coronar, poner el último toque (a); (years) cumplir; (forms) llenar

completion n terminación, f, fin, m

complex a complejo. n complejo, m. **inferiority c.**, complejo de inferioridad, m

complexion n tez, f, cutis, m; fig carácter, m

complexity n complejidad, f

compliance n condescendencia, f; (subservience) sumisión, f; obediencia, f. **in c. with**, de acuerdo con, en conformidad con

compliant a condescendiente; sumiso, dócil; obediente

complicate vt complicar

complicated a complejo; complicado; enredado

complicity n complicidad, f. **c. in a crime**, complicidad en un crimen

compliment n cumplido, m, cortesía, f;

requiebro, *inf* piropo, *m*; favor, *m*; honor, *m*; (greeting) saludo, *m*; (congratulation) felicitación, *f*. *vt* cumplimentar; requebrar; (flatter) adular, lisonjear; (congratulate) felicitar. **They did him the c. of reading his book,** Le hicieron el honor de leer su libro. **to pay compliments,** hacer cumplidos; *inf* echar piropos

complimentary *a* lisonjero; galante. **c. ticket,** billete gratuito, *m*

comply *vi* (with) cumplir, obedecer; conformarse (con); consentir

component *a* componente. *n* componente, *m*

comport *vt* (oneself), comportarse

comportment *n* comportamiento, *m*, conducta, *f*

compose *vt* (all meanings) componer. **to c. oneself,** serenarse, calmarse. **to c. one's features,** componer el semblante

composed *a* sereno, tranquilo, sosegado

composite *a* compuesto; mixto. *n* compuesto, *m*; *bot* planta compuesta, *f*

composition *n* (all meanings) composición, *f*

composure *n* tranquilidad, serenidad, calma, *f*; sangre fría, *f*, aplomo, *m*

compote *n* compota, *f*

compound *vt* mezclar, componer; concertar. *a* compuesto. *n* compuesto, *m*; mixtura, *f*. **c. interest,** interés compuesto, *m*

comprehend *vt* comprender

comprehensible *a* comprensible

comprehension *n* comprensión, *f*

comprehensive *a* comprensivo

compress *vt* comprimir; condensar; reducir, abreviar. *n* compresa, *f*

compression *n* compresión, *f*

compressor *n* compresor, *m*

comprise *vt* comprender, abarcar, incluir

compromise *n* compromiso, *m*, transacción, *f*; componenda, *f*. *vt* (settle) componer, arreglar; (jeopardize) arriesgar; comprometer. *vi* transigir. **to c. oneself,** comprometerse

compromising *a* comprometedor

compulsion *n* compulsión, fuerza, *f*. **under c.,** a la fuerza

compulsory *a* obligatorio. **c. measures,** medidas obligatorias, *f pl*. **c. powers,** poderes absolutos, *m pl*

compunction *n* compunción, *f*, remordimiento, *m*; escrúpulo, *m*. **without c.,** sin escrúpulo

computation *n* computación, *f*, cómputo, *m*

compute *vt* computar, calcular.

computer *m* computador, *m* (Western Hemisphere), ordenador, *m* (Spain)

computer center *n* centro calculador, centro de computación, *m*

comrade *n* camarada, *mf* compañero (-ra)

con *vt* estudiar; leer con atención; *naut* gobernar (el buque)

concave *a* cóncavo

conceal *vt* esconder, ocultar; (the truth, etc.) encubrir, callar; disimular

concealed *a* oculto; escondido; disimulado. **c. lighting,** iluminación indirecta, *f*. **c. turning,** (on a road) viraje oculto, *m*

concealment *n* ocultación, *f*; encubrimiento, *m*; (place of) escondite, *m*; secreto, *m*

concede *vt* conceder

conceit *n* presunción, vanidad, fatuidad, *f*, envanecimiento, *m*. **to have a good c. of oneself,** estar pagado de sí mismo

conceited *a* presumido, fatuo, vanidoso. **to become c.** *Lat. Am.* ensimismarse

conceivable *a* concebible, imaginable

conceive *vt* concebir; (affection, etc.) tomar; (an idea, etc.) formar; (plan) formular, idear. *vi* concebir; (understand) comprender; (suppose) imaginar, suponer

concentrate *vt* concentrar. *vi* concentrarse; (on, upon) dedicarse (a), entregarse (a); prestar atención (a), concentrar atención (en)

concentration *n* concentración, *f*. **c. camp,** campo de concentración, *m*

concentric *a* concéntrico

concept *n* concepto, *m*

conception *n* concepción, *f*; conocimiento, *m*; idea, *f*, concepto, *m*. **to have not the remotest c. of,** no tener la menor idea de

concern *vt* tocar, tener que ver con, importar, concernir; interesar; referirse (a); tratar (de); (trouble) preocupar, inquietar; (take part in) ocuparse (de or con). *n* asunto, *m*, cosa, *f*; (share) interés, *m*; (anxiety) inquietud, *f*; solicitud, *f*; (business) casa comercial, firma, *f*. **as concerns . . . ,** en cuanto a . . . , respecto a . . . **It concerns the date of the next meeting,** Es cuestión de la fecha de la próxima reunión. **It is no c. of yours,** No tiene nada que ver contigo. **The book is concerned with the adventures of two boys,** El libro trata de las aventuras de dos muchachos

concerned *a* ocupado (en); afectado; (in a crime) implicado (en); (troubled) preocupado; inquieto, agitado

concerning *prep* tocante a, con respecto a, referente a, sobre

concert *n* acuerdo, concierto, *m*, armonía, *f*; *mus* concierto, *m*, *vt* concertar, acordar. **in c. with,** de acuerdo con. **c. hall,** sala de conciertos, *f*

concerted *a* concertado

concerto *n* concierto, *m*

concession *n* concesión, *f*; privilegio, *m*

concessionaire *n* concesionario, *m*

conciliate *vt* conciliar

conciliatory a conciliador

concise a conciso, breve, sucinto

conclude vt concluir. vi concluirse

conclusion n conclusión, f. **in c.**, en conclusión, para terminar. **to come to the c. that . . .**, concluir que . . .

conclusive a conclusivo, concluyente, decisivo

concoct vt confeccionar; inventar

concomitant a concomitante. n concomitante, m

concord n concordia, buena inteligencia, armonía, f; (mus gram) concordancia, f; (of sounds) armonía, f

concordance n concordia, armonía, f; (book) concordancias, f pl

concrete a concreto; de hormigón. n hormigón, m. vt concretar; cubrir de hormigón. **reinforced c.**, hormigón armado, m

concur vi coincidir, concurrir; estar de acuerdo, convenir (en)

concurrence n (agreement) acuerdo, consentimiento, m, aprobación, f

concurrent a concurrente; unánime; coincidente

concussion n concusión, f; med concusión cerebral, f

condemn vt condenar; censurar, culpar; (forfeit) confiscar. **condemned cell,** celda de los condenados a muerte, f

condemnation n condenación, f; censura, f

condense vt condensar. vi condensarse

condenser n (elec mech chem) condensador, m

condescend vi dignarse; (in a bad sense) consentir (en); (with affability) condescender

condescending a condescendiente

condescendingly adv con condescendencia

condescension n condescendencia, f; afabilidad, f

condign a condigno

condiment n condimento, m

condition n condición, f; estado, m; pl **conditions,** condiciones, f pl; circunstancias, f pl. **on c. that,** con tal que; siempre que, dado que. **to be in no c. to,** no estar en condiciones de. **to change one's c.,** cambiar de estado. **to keep oneself in c.,** mantenerse en buena forma

conditional a condicional. **to be c. on,** depender de

conditioned a acondicionado. **c. reflex,** reflejo acondicionado, m

condole vi condolerse (de); (on a bereavement) dar el pésame

condolence n condolencia, f. **to present one's condolences,** dar el pésame

condom n condón, m; Argentina forro m

condone vt condonar, perdonar

conduce vi contribuir, conducir

conducive a que contribuye, conducente; favorable

conduct n conducta, f. vt conducir; guiar; mus dirigir; (oneself) portarse, conducirse; phys conducir. vi mus dirigir (una orquesta, etc.); phys ser conductor. **conducted tour,** excursión acompañada, f; viaje acompañado, m

conductor n (guide) guía, mf; (of an orchestra) director, m; (on a tram, etc.) cobrador, m; phys conductor, m

conduit n conducto, m; cañería, f; canal, m

cone n (bot geom etc.) cono, m

confection n confección, f. vt confeccionar

confectioner n confitero (-ra); pastelero (-ra)

confectionery n confitería, pastelería, repostería, f

confederate a confederado; aliado. n confederado, m; (in crime) cómplice, mf. vt confederar. vi confederarse; aliarse

confer vt conceder, conferir; (an honor, etc.) otorgar, investir (con). vi consultar (con); deliberar, considerar

conference n conferencia, consulta, f; conversación, f

conferment n otorgamiento, m; concesión, f

confess vt confesar, reconocer; inf admitir; (of a priest) confesar; (of a penitent) confesarse. vi hacer una confesión; (one's sins) confesarse. **I c. that I was surprised,** No puedo negar que me sorprendió

confessed a confesado, declarado

confession n confesión, f; reconocimiento, m; declaración, f; religión, f; (creed) credo, m. **to go to c.,** confesarse. **to hear a c.,** confesar (a)

confessional n confesionario, m

confessor n confesor, m

confetti n pl confeti, papel picado m, serpentina, f

confidant n confidente, m

confidante n confidenta, f

confide vi confiar (a or en). vt confiar

confidence n confianza, f; seguridad, f; (revelation) confidencia, f. **in c.,** en confianza. **over-c.,** presunción, f. **to have c. in,** tener confianza en. **c. man,** caballero de industria, estafador, m. **c. trick,** timo, m

confident a confiado; seguro; (conceited) presumido

confidential a confidencial; de confianza. **c. clerk,** empleado (-da) de confianza. **c. letter,** carta confidencial, f

confidentially adv en confianza, confidencialmente

confidently adv confiadamente

confiding a confiado

confine *vt* limitar; (imprison) encerrar. **confined space,** espacio limitado, *m.* **to be confined,** (of a woman) estar de parto, parir. **to be confined to one's room,** no poder dejar su cuarto. **to c. oneself to,** limitarse a

confinement *n* encierro, *m*, prisión, *f*; reclusión, *f*; (of a woman) parto, *m.* **to suffer solitary c.,** estar incomunicado

confines *n pl* límites, *m pl*; confines, *m pl*; fronteras, *f pl*

confirm *vt* confirmar; corroborar; *ecc* confirmar

confirmation *n* confirmación, *f*; (of a treaty) ratificación, *f*; *ecc* confirmación, *f*

confirmed *a* inveterado

confiscate *vt* confiscar

conflagration *n* conflagración, *f*, incendio, *m*

conflict *n* conflicto, *m*; lucha, *f*. *vi* estar opuesto (a), estar en contradicción (con)

conflicting *a* opuesto; incompatible; (of evidence) contradictorio

conform *vt* ajustar, conformar. *vi* ajustarse (a), amoldarse (a); conformarse (a); adaptarse (a)

conformity *n* conformidad, *f*. **in c. with,** en conformidad con, con arreglo a

confound *vt* confundir. **C. it!** ¡Demonio!

confounded *a* perplejo; *inf* maldito

confront *vt* hacer frente (a), afrontar; salir al paso; confrontar

confuse *vt* turbar, aturdir; confundir (con); (the issue) obscurecer; (disconcert) desconcertar, dejar confuso (a); dejar perplejo (a). **You have confused one thing with another,** Has confundido una cosa con otra. **My mind was confused,** Mis ideas eran confusas; Tenía la cabeza trastornada

confused *a* confuso

confusing *a* turbador; desconcertante. **It is all very c.,** Todo ello es muy difícil de comprender

confusion *n* confusión, *f*. **covered with c.,** confuso, avergonzado. **to be in c.,** estar confuso; estar en desorden

confute *vt* (a person) confundir; (by evidence) refutar, confutar

congeal *vt* congelar; (blood) coagular. *vi* congelarse, helarse; coagularse

congenial *a* (of persons) simpático; propicio, favorable; agradable

congenital *a* congénito

congest *vt* atestar; amontonar; *med* congestionar

congested *a med* congestionado; (of places) atestado de gente; de mayor población; concurrido. **c. area,** área de mayor densidad de población, *f*

congestion *n med* congestión, *f*; densidad del tráfico, *f*; mayor densidad de población, *f*

congratulate *vt* felicitar, dar la enhorabuena (a); congratular

congratulation *n* felicitación, enhorabuena, *f*; congratulación, *f*

congratulatory *a* de felicitación, congratulatorio

congregate *vi* congregarse, reunirse, juntarse

congregation *n* congregación, *f*; asamblea, reunión, *f*; (in a church) fieles, *m pl*; (parishioners) feligreses, *m pl*

congress *n* congreso, *m.* **C.-man,** miembro del Congreso, *m*

conjecture *n* conjetura, *f*, *vt* conjeturar

conjoint *a* asociado, conjunto

conjugal *a* conyugal

conjugate *vt* conjugar. *vi* conjugarse

conjugation *n* conjugación, *f*

conjunction *n* conjunción, *f*. **in c. with,** de acuerdo con

conjunctivitis *n* conjuntivitis, *f*

conjure *vt* (implore) rogar, suplicar. *vi* (juggle) hacer juegos de manos. **a name to c. with,** un nombre todopoderoso. **to c. up,** (spirits) conjurar; *fig* evocar

conjurer, conjuror *n* (magician) nigromante, *m*; prestidigitador, *m.* **conjuror's wand,** varilla de virtudes, *f*

conjuring *n* prestidigitación, *f*, juegos de manos, *m pl.* **c. trick,** juego de manos, *m.* **c. up,** evocación, *f*

connect *vt* juntar, unir; (relate) relacionar; asociar; (*elec* and *mech*) conectar. *vi* juntarse, unirse; relacionarse; asociarse; (of events) encadenarse; (of trains) enlazar. **This train connects with the Madrid express,** Este tren enlaza con el expreso de Madrid. **They are connected with the Borgia family,** Están emparentados con los Borgia, Son parientes de los Borgia

connected *a* conexo; (coherent) coherente; relacionado; asociado; (in a crime) implicado; (by marriage, etc.) emparentado

connecting *a* que une; (*mech* and *elec*) conectivo; (of doors, etc.) comunicante. **c.-link,** *mech* varilla de conexión, *f*; *fig* lazo, *m.* **c.-rod,** biela, *f*

connection, connexion *n* conexión, *f*; unión, *f*; (of ideas) relación, *f*; (junction) empalme, *m*; (of trains, boats) enlace, *m*; (intimacy) intimidad, *f*; (relative) pariente, *m*; (of a firm, etc.) clientela, *f*; *elec* conexión, *f*. **in c. with,** con referencia a; en asociación con. **in this c.,** respecto a esto

connivance *n* consentimiento, *m*; complicidad, *f*

connive (at) *vi* hacer la vista gorda, ser cómplice (en)

connotation *n* connotación, *f*

connote *vt* connotar

conquer *vt* conquistar; vencer. *vi* triunfar

conquering *a* conquistador, vencedor; triunfante, victorioso

conqueror *n* conquistador, *m*; vencedor, *m*

conquest n conquista, f. **to make a c. of,** conquistar

conscience n conciencia, f. **in all c.,** en verdad. **with a clear c.,** con la conciencia limpia. **c.-stricken,** lleno de remordimientos

conscienceless a desalmado, falto de conciencia

conscientious a concienzudo; diligente. **c. objector,** objetor de conciencia, m

conscientiously adv concienzudamente

conscientiousness n conciencia, diligencia, f; rectitud, f

conscious a consciente. n psy consciente, m. **to become c.,** (after unconsciousness) volver en sí. **to become c. of,** darse cuenta de

consciously adv conscientemente, a sabiendas

consciousness n conciencia, f; conocimiento, sentido, m. **to lose c.,** perder el conocimiento, perder el sentido. **to recover c.,** recobrar el sentido, volver en sí

consecrate vt consagrar; bendecir

consecration n consagración, f; dedicación, f

consecutive a consecutivo

consensus n consenso, m, unanimidad, f. **c. of opinion,** opinión general, f

consent vi consentir. n consentimiento, m; permiso, m, aquiescencia, f. **by common c.,** de común acuerdo

consequence n consecuencia, f; resultado, m; importancia, f, **in c.,** por consiguiente. **in c. of,** de resultas de. **of no c.,** sin importancia

consequent a consecuente, consiguiente

consequential a consecuente; (of persons) fatuo, engreído

consequently adv por consiguiente, en consecuencia

conservation n conservación, f. **c. of energy,** conservación de energía, f

conservative a preservativo; conservador. n conservador (-ra). **c. party,** partido conservador, m

conservatoire n conservatorio de música, m

conservatory n invernáculo, invernadero, m

conserve vt conservar

consider vt considerar, pensar meditar; tomar en cuenta; examinar; (deem) juzgar; (believe) creer, estar convencido de (que); (of persons) considerar. **all things considered,** considerando todos los puntos, después de considerarlo todo

considerable a considerable

considerate a considerado, solícito

considerately adv con consideración, solícitamente

consideration n consideración, f; reflexión, deliberación, f; remuneración, f. **out**

of c. for, en consideración de; por consideración a. **to take into c.,** tomar en cuenta, tomar en consideración

considered a considerado

considering prep en consideración de, considerando, en vista de

consign vt consignar; fig enviar. **to c. to oblivion,** sepultar en el olvido

consignee n consignatario, m

consignment n consignación, f; envío, m

consist vi consistir (en); ser compatible (con). **to c. of,** componerse de, consistir de

consistence, consistency n consistencia, f; compatibilidad, f; lógica, f; (of persons) consecuencia, f

consistent a compatible; lógico; (of persons) consecuente

consistently adv conformemente (a); consecuentemente

consolation n consuelo, m, consolación, f

console vt consolar; confortar. n arch cartela, f. **c. table,** consola, f

consolidate vt consolidar. vi consolidarse

consoling a consolador; confortador

consonant a consonante

consort n consorte, mf. **to c. with,** frecuentar la compañía de; ir con; acompañar (a). **prince c.,** príncipe consorte, m

conspicuous a conspicuo; prominente; notable. **to be c.,** destacarse; llamar la atención. **to make oneself c.,** ponerse en evidencia, llamar la atención

conspicuously adv visiblemente; muy en evidencia

conspiracy n conspiración, f; complot, m

conspirator n conspirador (-ra)

conspire vi conspirar

constancy n constancia, f

constant a constante; incesante. n constante, m

constellation n constelación, f

consternation n consternación, f; espanto, terror, m

constipate vt estreñir

constipation n estreñimiento, m, constipación de vientre, f

constituency n distrito electoral, m

constituent a constituyente. n constituyente, m; componente, m; elector (-ra)

constitute vt constituir; nombrar; autorizar

constitution n constitución, f

constitutional a constitucional

constrain vt obligar, forzar. **I felt constrained to help them,** Me sentí obligado a ayudarles

constrained a (of smiles, etc.) forzado;

(of silences) violento; (of persons) avergonzado

constraint *n* fuerza, compulsión, *f*; (of atmosphere) tensión, *f*; (reserve) reserva, *f*; vergüenza, *f*

constrict *vt* apretar, estrechar

construct *vt* edificar; construir

construction *n* construcción, *f*; interpretación, *f*. **to put a wrong c. on,** interpretar mal

constructive *a* constructor

constructor *n* constructor, *m*

construe *vt* construir; (translate) traducir; *fig* interpretar

consul *n* cónsul, *m*

consular fees *n pl* derechos consulares, *m pl*

consulate *n* consulado, *m*. **c. general,** consulado general, *m*

consult *vt* consultar. *vi* consultar (con), aconsejarse (con)

consultant *n* (*med* and other uses) especialista, *m*

consultation *n* consulta, *f*

consulting *a* consultor. **c. hours,** horas de consulta, *f pl.* **c. rooms,** consultorio, *m*

consume *vt* consumir; (eat) comerse, tragarse. *vi* consumirse. **to be consumed by envy,** estar consumido por la envidia. **to be consumed by thirst,** estar muerto de sed

consumer *n* consumidor (-ra)

consummate *a* consumido, perfecto. *vt* consumar

consumption *n* consumo, *m*; gasto, *m*; *med* tuberculosis, *f*. **fuel c.,** consumo de combustible, *m*

consumptive *a* destructivo; *med* tísico, hético. *n* tísico (-ca)

contact *n* contacto, *m*, *vt* ponerse en contacto con. **to be in c. with,** estar en contacto con

contagious *a* contagioso

contain *vt* contener; incluir; *geom* encerrar; (arithmetic) ser divisible por; (oneself) dominarse. **I could not c. myself,** No pude dominarme

container *n* recipiente, *m*; envase, *m*; (box) caja, *f*

contaminate *vt* contaminar; corromper

contemplate *vt* contemplar; meditar, considerar; (plan) tener intención de, pensar, proponerse

contemplation *n* contemplación, *f*; meditación, *f*; expectación, esperanza, *f*; (plan) proyecto, *m*. **to have something in c.,** proyectar algo

contemplative *a* contemplativo

contemporary *a* contemporáneo; (of persons) coetáneo; (of events, etc.) actual. *n* contemporáneo (-ea)

contempt *n* desprecio, menosprecio, *m*;

desdén, *m*. **c. of court,** falta de respeto a la sala, *f*

contempt of court *n* rebeldía a la corte, *f*

contemptible *a* menospreciable, despreciable; vil

contemptuous *a* desdeñoso; despectivo; de desprecio. **to be c. of,** desdeñar; menospreciar, tener en poco (a)

contemptuously *adv* con desprecio, desdeñosamente

contend *vi* contender; (affirm) sostener, mantener. **He contended that . . . ,** Sostuvo que . . . ; **contending party,** *law* parte litigante, *f*

content *n* contenido, *m*; capacidad, *f*; (emotion) contento, *m*; satisfacción, *f*. **a contento; satisfecho (de).** *vt* contentar; satisfacer. **to one's heart's c.,** a pedir de boca; a gusto de uno; cuanto quisiera

contented *a* satisfecho, contento

contention *n* disputa, controversia, discusión, *f*; argumento, *m*, opinión, *f*

contentious *a* contencioso

contentment *n* contentamiento, *m*; contento, *m*

contest *vt* disputar; (a suit) defender; (a match, an election, etc.) disputar. *n* disputa, *f*; combate, *m*, lucha, *f*; (competition) concurso, *m*

contestant *n* contendiente, *mf*

context *n* contexto, *m*

contiguous *a* contiguo, lindero, adyacente

continence *n* continencia, *f*

continent *a* continente. *n* continente, *m*

continental *a* continental

continental shelf *n* plataforma continental, *f*

contingency *n* contingencia, *f*

contingent *a* contingente. *n mil* contingente, *m*. **to be c. on,** (of events) depender de

continual *a* continuo

continuation *n* continuación, *f*; prolongación, *f*

continue *vi* continuar; seguir; prolongarse; durar. *vt* continuar; seguir; proseguir; perpetuar; (in an office) retener. **to be continued,** se continuará, continuará, seguirá

continuity *n* continuidad, *f*

continuous *a* continuo. **c. performance,** sesión continua, *f*

continuously *adv* de continuo, continuamente

contort *vt* retorcer

contortion *n* contorsión, *f*

contour *n* contorno, *m*; curva de nivel, *f*. **c. map,** mapa con curvas de nivel, *m*

contraband *n* contrabando, *m*

contraception *n* anticoncepción, *f*

contraceptive *n* anticonceptivo, *m*

contract *n* pacto, *m*; (com and law) contrato, *m*; (betrothal) esponsales, *m pl*; (marriage) capitulaciones, *f pl*; (cards) "Bridge," *m*. *vt* contraer; (acquire) adquirir, contraer; (a marriage, etc.) contraer; (be betrothed to) desposarse con; (by formal contract) contratar; pactar. *vi* (shrink) contraerse, encogerse; comprometerse por contrato. **breach of c.,** no cumplimiento de contrato, *m*. **c. party,** (of matrimony) contrayente, *mf*

contraction *n* contracción, *f* (act or process); forma contracta, *f* (like *isn't* or *can't*)

contractor *n* contratista, *mf*

contradict *vt* contradecir; desmentir

contradiction *n* contradicción, *f*; negación, *f*

contradictory *a* contradictorio; opuesto (a), contrario (a)

contraption *n* *inf* artefacto, *m*

contrariness *n* *inf* testarudez, terquedad, *f*

contrariwise *adv* al contrario; al revés

contrary *a* contrario; opuesto (a); desfavorable, poco propicio; (of persons) difícil, terco. *n* contraria, *f*; (logic) contrario, *m*, *adv* en contra, contrariamente. **on the c.,** al contrario. **to be c.,** (of persons) llevar la contraria

contrast *n* contraste, *m*. *vt* contrastar (con). *vi* contrastar (con), hacer contraste (con)

contravene *vt* contravenir; atacar, oponerse (a)

contribute *vt* contribuir; (an article) escribir

contribution *n* contribución, *f*; (to a review, etc.) artículo, *m*

contributor *n* contribuyente, *mf*; (to a journal) colaborador (-ra)

contrite *a* penitente, arrepentido, contrito

contrition *n* contrición, penitencia, *f*, arrepentimiento, *m*

contrivance *n* invención, *f*; (scheme) treta, idea, estratagema, *f*; (machine) aparato, mecanismo, artefacto, *m*

contrive *vt* inventar; idear, proyectar. *vi* (succeed in) lograr, conseguir; (manage) arreglárselas

control *n* autoridad, *f*; dominio, *m*; gobierno, *m*; dirección, *f*; regulación, *f*; (restraint) freno, *m*; (biol and spirit) control, *m*; (of a vehicle) conducción, *f*; manejo, *m*, manipulación, *f*; *pl* **controls,** *mech* mando, *m*. *vt* dirigir, regir; regular; usar, manejar, manipular; controlar; (dominate) dominar; (curb) refrenar, reprimir; (command) mandar. **He lost c. of the car,** Perdió el mando (or control) del automóvil. **out of c.,** fuera de mando, fuera de control. **remote c.,** mando a distancia, *m*. **to c. oneself,** dominarse, contenerse. **to lose c. of oneself,** no lograr dominarse, perder el control. **c. stick,**

aer palanca de mando, *f*. **c. tower,** aer torre de mando, *f*

controller *n* interventor, *m*; (device) regulador, *m*

controlling *n* See **control.** *a* regulador

controversial *a* debatible, discutible

controversy *n* controversia, *f*; argumento, *m*; altercación, disputa, *f*

contumacious *a* contumaz

contumely *n* contumelia, *f*

contusion *n* herida contusa, *f*

conundrum *n* acertijo, rompecabezas, *m*; problema, *m*

convalesce *vi* convalecer, estar convaleciente

convalescence *n* convalecencia, *f*

convalescent *a* convaleciente. *n* convaleciente, *mf*. **c. home,** casa de convalecencia, *f*

convene *vt* (a meeting) convocar; (person) citar. *vi* reunirse

convenience *n* conveniencia, *f*; (comfort) comodidad, *f*; utilidad, *f*; (advantage) ventaja, *f*; (public) retretes, *m pl*. **at one's c.,** cuando le sea conveniente a uno. **to make a c. of,** abusar de. **with all modern conveniences,** con todo el confort moderno

convenient *a* conveniente; apropiado; cómodo. **I shall make it c. to see him at 6 p.m.,** Arreglaré mis asuntos para verle a las seis

conveniently *adv* cómodamente; oportunamente; sin inconveniente

convent *n* convento, *m*

convention *n* convención, *f*

conventional *a* convencional

conventual *a* conventual. *n* conventual, *m*

converge *vi* convergir

convergence *n* convergencia, *f*

convergent *a* convergente

conversance *n* familiaridad, *f*, conocimiento, *m*

conversant *a* familiar, versado, conocedor. **c. with,** versado en

conversation *n* conversación, *f*. **to engage in c. with,** entablar conversación con

conversational *a* de conversación; (talkative) locuaz

converse *vi* conversar. **to c. by signs,** hablar por señas

conversion *n* conversión, *f*

convert *vt* convertir; transformar. *n* converso (-sa). **to become a c.,** convertirse

convertible *a* convertible; transformable

convex *a* convexo

convey *vt* transportar; conducir, llevar; (a meaning, etc.) comunicar, dar a entender; expresar; law traspasar

conveyance *n* transporte, *m*; conducción, *f*; medio de transporte, *m*; vehículo, *m*; carruaje, *m*; (of property) traspaso, *m*; (document) escritura de traspaso, *f*. **public c.,** coche de alquiler, *m*; ómnibus, *m*

convict *n* convicto, *m*; presidiario, *m*. *vt law* condenar; culpar. **c. settlement,** colonia penal, *f*

conviction *n* (of a prisoner) condenación, *f*; (belief) convencimiento, *m*, convicción, *f*

convince *vt* convencer

convincing *a* convincente

conviviality *n* jovialidad, *f*

convocation *n* convocación, *f*

convoke *vt* convocar

convolution *n* circunvolución, *f*; espira, *f*

convoy *vt* convoyar, escoltar. *n* convoy, *m*. **to sail in a c.,** navegar en convoy

convulse *vt* agitar; sacudir; estremecer. **to be convulsed with laughter,** desternillarse de risa, morirse de risa

convulsion *n* convulsión, *f*; conmoción, *f*

convulsive *a* convulsivo

cook *n* cocinero (-ra). *vt* guisar, cocer, cocinar; (falsify) falsear

cooker *n* cocina, *f*. **gas c.,** cocina de gas, *f*

cooking *n* arte de guisar, *m*, or *f*; cocina, *f*; (of accounts, etc.) falsificación, *f*. **c. range,** cocina económica, *f*. **c.-stove,** cocina, *f*. **c. utensils,** batería de cocina, *f*

cool *a* fresco; bastante frío; (not ardent and of receptions, etc.) frío; (calm) sereno, imperturbable. *n* fresco, *m*. *vi* enfriarse; (of love, etc.) resfriarse; (of the weather) refrescar; (of persons) refrescarse. *vt* refrescar; enfriar. **to grow cooler,** (of weather) refrescarse; (of persons) tener menos calor. **It is c.,** Hace fresco. **to be as c. as a cucumber,** tener sangre fría. **c. drink,** bebida fría, *f*. **c.-headed,** sereno, imperturbable

cooling *n* enfriamiento, *m*, a refrescante

coolly *adv* frescamente; fríamente, con frialdad; imperturbablemente; (impudently) descaradamente

coolness *n* frescura, *f*; (of a welcome, etc.) frialdad, *f*; (sangfroid) sangre fría, serenidad, *f*; aplomo, *m*

coop *n* gallinero, *m*; caponera, *f*, *vt* enjaular; encerrar. **to keep** (someone) **cooped up,** tener encerrado *m*

cooper *n* tonelero, barrilero, *m*, *vt* hacer barriles

cooperate *vi* cooperar; colaborar

cooperation *n* cooperación, *f*

cooperative *a* cooperativo. **c. society,** cooperativa, *f*

coopt *vt* elegir por votación

coordinate *vt* coordinar. *n math* coordenada, *f*. *a* coordenado

coordination *n* coordinación, *f*

cop *n* (police officer) chapa *Ecuador*, polizonte, *Mexico* cuico (-ca) *mf*

cope *n* *ecc* capa, *f*; (of heaven) dosel, *m*, bóveda, *f*. **to c. with,** contender con; (a difficulty) hacer cara a, arrostrar

Copenhagen Copenhague, *m*

copier *n* copiador (-ra)

coping *n arch* albardilla, *f*. **c.-stone,** teja cumbrera, *f*; *fig* coronamiento, *m*

copious *a* copioso, abundante

copiously *adv* en abundancia

copper *n* cobre, *m*; (coin) calderilla, *f*; (vessel) caldera, *f*. *a* de cobre. **c.-colored,** cobrizo. **c.-smith,** calderero, *m*. **c.-sulphate,** sulfato de cobre, *m*

copulate *vi* copularse

copy *n* copia, *f*; (of a book) ejemplar, *m*; (of a paper) número, *m*; manuscrito, *m*; (subject-matter) material, *m*. *vt* copiar; imitar; tomar como modelo (a). **rough c.,** borrador, *m*. **c.-book,** cuaderno de escritura, *m*

copying *n* imitación, *f*; transcripción, *f*. **c. ink,** tinta de copiar, *f*

copyist *n* copiador (-ra); (plagiarist) copiante, *mf*

copyright *n* derechos de autor, *m pl*; propiedad literaria, *f*. *a* protegido por los derechos de autor. *vt* registrar como propiedad literaria. **C. reserved,** Derechos reservados, Queda hecho el depósito que marca la ley

copywriter *n* escritor de anuncios, *m*

coquetry *n* coquetería, *f*

coquette *n* coqueta, *f*

coquettish *a* coquetón; atractivo

coral *n* coral, *m*; (polyp) coralina, *f*. *a* de coral, coralino. **white c.,** madrépora, *f*. **c. beads,** corales, *m pl*. **c.-island,** atalón, *m*. **c.-reef,** escollo de coral, *m*. **c. snake,** coral, *f*

cord *n* cuerda, *f*; cordel, *m*; cordón, *m*. *vt* encordelar. **spinal c.,** médula espinal, *f*. **umbilical c.,** cordón umbilical, *m*

cordial *a* cordial; sincero, fervoroso. *n* cordial, *m*

cordiality *n* cordialidad, *f*

cordon *n* cordón, *m*; cinto, *m*. **to c. off,** acordonar

cordovan *a* cordobés. *n* (leather) cordobán, *m*

corduroy *n* pana de cordoncillo, *f*

core *n* (of a fruit) corazón, *m*; (of a rope) alma, *f*, centro, *m*; (of an abscess) foco, *m*; (of a corn) ojo, *m*; *fig* núcleo, *m*; esencia, *f*; lo esencial

coreligionist *n* correligionario (-ia)

cork *n* corcho, *m*; (of a bottle) tapón, *m*, a de corcho. *vt* tapar con corcho, taponar; (wine) encorchar; (the face) tiznar con corcho quemado. **pop of a c.,** taponazo, *m*. **to draw a c.,** descorchar. **c.-jacket,** chaleco salvavidas, *m*. **c. tree,** alcornoque, *m*

corkscrew *n* sacacorchos, *m*

corn *n* grano, cereal, *m*; (wheat) trigo, *m*;

(maize) maíz, m; (single seed) grano, m; (on the foot, etc.) callo, m. **Indian c.,** maíz, m. **c. cure,** callicida, m. **c.-exchange,** bolsa de granos, f. **c.-field,** campo de trigo, m. **c.-flower,** aciano, m. **c. liquor** Lat. Am. chicha f

cornea n córnea, f

corner n ángulo, m; (of a street or building) esquina, f; (of a room) rincón, Mexico ancón m; aut viraje, m; com monopolio, m; (of the eye) rabo, m; (Assoc. football) "corner," m. vt arrinconar; acorralar; com acaparar. **the four corners of the earth,** las cinco partes del mundo. **a tight c.,** un lance apretado, un apuro. **to drive into a c.,** fig poner entre la espada y la pared. **to look out of the c. of the eye,** mirar de reojo. **to turn the c.,** doblar la esquina; fig pasar la crisis. **c.-cupboard,** rinconera, f. **c. seat,** asiento del rincón, m. **c. shop** Lat. Am. esquina f **c.-stone,** piedra angular, f.

cornered a (of a person) acorralado, en aprieto; (of hats) de . . . picos. **three-c. hat,** sombrero de tres picos, m

cornet n (musical instrument) corneta, f; mil corneta, m; (paper) cucurucho, m. **c. player,** cornetín, m

cornflour n harina de maíz, f

cornucopia n cornucopia, f

corollary n corolario, m

coronation n coronación, f

coroner n juez de guardia, mf, médico forense, m

corporal a corporal, n mil cabo, m; (altarcloth) corporal, m. **c. punishment,** castigo corporal, m

corporation n corporación, f; concejo, cabildo municipal, m; (com U.S.A.) sociedad anónima, f

corporeal a corpóreo

corps n cuerpo, m

corpse n cadáver, m

corpulence n gordura, obesidad, f

corpulent a corpulento, grueso, gordo

corpus n cuerpo, m. **C. Christi,** Corpus, m. **c. delicti,** cuerpo del delito, m

corpuscle n corpúsculo, m

correct a correcto; exacto, justo. vt corregir; rectificar; amonestar, reprender

correction n corrección, f; rectificación, f

corrective n correctivo, n correctivo, m

correctness n corrección, f; exactitud, f; justicia, f

correlate vt poner en correlación. vi tener correlación

correlation n correlación, f

correspond vi corresponder (a); (by letter) escribirse, corresponderse

correspondence n correspondencia, f; com correo, m. **c. course,** curso por correspondencia, m

correspondent n correspondiente, mf; (com and journalist) corresponsal, mf.

special c., corresponsal extraordinario, m

corresponding a correspondiente. **c. member,** miembro correspondiente, m

corridor n corredor, pasillo, m; (railway) pasillo, m; pol corredor, m. **c. train,** tren con coches corridos, m

corroborate vt corroborar, confirmar

corroboration n corroboración, confirmación, f

corroborative a corroborativo, confirmatorio

corrode vt corroer, morder; fig roer

corrosion n corrosión, f

corrosive a corrosivo; mordaz

corrugate vt arrugar. vi arrugarse

corrugated a arrugado; ondulado. **c. iron,** chapa canaleta, f

corrugation n corrugación, f, arrugamiento, m

corrupt a corrompido; vicioso, desmoralizado. vt corromper. vi corromperse

corruption n corrupción, f

corsage n corpiño, m

corset n corsé, m, vt encorsetar. **c. shop,** corsetería, f

cortege n séquito, acompañamiento, m; desfile, m.

cortex n bot anat corteza, f

cortisone n (drug) cortisona, f

coruscation n brillo, m

cosignatory n cosignatario (-ia)

cosine n coseno, m

cosiness n comodidad, f

cosmetic a cosmético. n afeite, cosmético, m

cosmic a cósmico

cosmopolitanism n cosmopolitismo, m

cosmos n cosmos, universo, m

Cossack a cosaco. n cosaco (-ca)

cosset vt mimar, consentir

cost vi costar. n costa, f, coste, precio, m; fig costa, f; pl **costs,** law costas, f pl. **at all costs,** cueste lo que cueste, a toda costa. **to my c.,** a mi costa. **c. of living,** coste de la vida, m. **to c. a fortune,** costar un sentido

Costa-Rican a costarriqueño. n costarriqueño (-ña)

coster n vendedor (-ra) ambulante

costliness n alto precio, m; suntuosidad, f

costly a costoso; suntuoso, magnífico

costume n traje, m; (fancy-dress) disfraz, m; (tailored) traje sastre, m; "Costume," (among credits in films and plays) «Vestuario»

cot n (hut) choza, cabaña, f; (child's) camita, f

coterie n círculo, grupo, m; (clique) camarilla, f

cotillion n cotillón, m

cottage n cabaña, choza, f; casita, f, hotelito, m; torre, villa, f **c. cheese** *Mexico* asadero m

cotton n algodón, m, a de algodón. **I don't c. to the idea at all,** No me gusta nada la idea; La idea no me seduce. **sewing-c.,** hilo de coser, m. **c. goods,** géneros de algodón, m pl. **c. mill,** hilandería de algodón, algodonería, f. **c. plantation,** algodonal, m. **c.-seed oil,** aceite de semilla de algodón, m. **c.-spinner,** hilandero (-ra) de algodón. **c.-wool,** algodón en rama, m. **c.-yarn,** hilo de algodón, m

couch n sofá, canapé, m; (bed) lecho, m; (lair) cama, f. vt (lay down) acostar, echar; (a lance) enristrar; (express) expresar, redactar. vi acostarse; (crouch) agacharse; estar en acecho

cough vi toser. n tos, f. **to c. up,** escupir, expectorar. **c.-drop,** pastilla para la tos, f

coughing n tos, f

could. See can

council n consejo, m; junta, f; ecc concilio, m. **Privy C.,** consejo privado, m. **C. of the Realm,** Concejo del Reino, m. **to hold c.,** celebrar un consejo; aconsejarse (con); consultarse. **town c.,** ayuntamiento, m. **c. chamber,** sala consistorial, f; sala de actos, f. **c. houses,** casas baratas, f pl. **c. of war,** consejo de guerra, m

councilor n concejal, m; miembro de la junta, m

counsel n consultación, f; deliberación, f; consejo, m; law abogado, m. vt aconsejar. **a c. of perfection,** un ideal imposible. **to keep one's own c.,** no decir nada, callarse, guardar silencio. **to take c. with,** consultar (a), aconsejarse con

counselor n consejero, m. **c. of state,** consejero de estado, m

count vt contar; calcular; (consider) creer, considerar. vi contar. n cuenta, f; (of votes) escrutinio, m; law capítulo, m. **John simply doesn't c.,** Juan no cuenta para nada. **Erudition alone counts for very little,** La mera erudición sirve para muy poco. **to keep c. of,** tener cuenta de. **to lose c. of,** perder cuenta de. **to c. on,** contar con; (doing something) esperar. **to c. up,** contar

count n (title) conde, m

countenance n semblante, m; expresión de la cara, f; aspecto, m; (favor) apoyo, m, ayuda, f. vt autorizar; aprobar; apoyar, ayudar. **to put (a person) out of c.,** desconcertar (a)

counter n (in a bank) contador, m; (in a shop) mostrador, m; (in games) ficha, f, adv contra, al contrario; al revés. a opuesto (a), contrario (a). vt parar; contestar. **to run c. to my inclinations,** oponerse a mis deseos. **to c. with the left,** (boxing) contestar con la izquierda. **c.-attack,** contraataque, m. **c.-attraction,** atracción contraria, f. **c.-offensive,** con-

traofensiva, f. **c.-reformation,** contrarreforma, f. **c.-revolution,** contrarevolución, f

counteract vt neutralizar; frustrar

counterbalance n contrapeso, m, vt contrabalancear; compensar, igualar

counterblast n denunciación, f; respuesta, f

countercharge n recriminación, f. vt recriminar; law reconvenir

counterfeit a falso, espurio; fingido. n falsificación, f; imitación, f; moneda falsa, f; (person) impostor (-ra). vt imitar; (pretend) fingir; (coins, handwriting, etc.) falsificar

counterfeiter n falsario (-ia)

counterfoil n talón, m

countermand vt contramandar; (an order) revocar, cancelar. n contraorden, f; revocación, f

countermarch n contramarcha, f

countermeasure n contramedida, f

counterpart n contraparte, f; (of a document) duplicado, m

counterplot n contratreta, f

counterpoint n mus contrapunto, m

counterpoise n equilibrio, m; vt contrabalancear, contrapesar

countersign n contraseña, f, vt refrendar

counting n cuenta, f; numeración, f; (of votes) escrutinio, m. **c.-house,** contaduría, f

countless a innumerable. **a c. number,** un sinfín, un sinnúmero

countrified a rústico, campesino

country n país, m; (fatherland) patria, f; región, campiña, tierra, f; (as opposed to town) campo, m. a del campo; campesino, campestre, rústico. **He lives in the c.,** Vive en el campo. **c. club,** club campestre, m. **c. cousin,** provinciano (-na). **c.-dance,** baile campestre, m. **c. gentleman,** hacendado, m. **c. girl,** campesina, f; aldeana, f. **c.-house,** finca, f; casa de campo, f. **c. life,** vida del campo, f. **c.-seat,** finca, f

countryman n campesino, m; hombre del campo, m; compatriota, m

countryside n campo, m; campiña, f

countrywoman n campesina, f; compatriota, f

county n condado, m; provincia, f. **c. council,** diputación provincial, f. **c. town,** cabeza de partido, f; ciudad provincial, f

county seat n cabecera municipal, cabeza de partido, f

coup n golpe, m. **c. d'état,** golpe de estado, m

coupe n cupé, m

couple n par, m; (in a dance, etc.) pareja, f. vt enganchar, acoplar; (in marriage) casar; (animals) aparear; (ideas) asociar;

(names) juntar. **the young (married) c.,** el matrimonio joven

couplet n copla, f

coupling n enganche, acoplamiento, m; (of railway carriages) enganche, m; (of ideas) asociación, f

coupon n talón, m; cupón, m

courage n valor, m. **C.!** ¡Ánimo! **to muster up c.,** cobrar ánimo

courageous a valiente

courier n correo, m, estafeta, f; (guide) guía, m; (newspaper) estafeta, f

course n curso, m; (of time) transcurso, m; (of events) marcha, f; (of a river, etc.) cauce, m; (of stars) carrera, f, curso, m; (of a ship) derrota, f, rumbo, m; (way) camino, m, ruta, f; (of conduct) línea de conducta, f; actitud, f; (of study) curso, m; (of a meal) plato, m; (of an illness) desarrollo, m; med tratamiento, m. **He took it as a matter of c.,** Lo tomó sin darle importancia. **in due c.,** a su tiempo debido. **in the c. of time,** andando el tiempo, en el transcurso de los años. **of c.,** claro está; naturalmente. **Are you coming tomorrow? Of c.!** ¿Vienes mañana? ¡Ya lo creo! **the best c. to take,** lo mejor que se puede hacer, el mejor plantamiento, m

course vt cazar, perseguir; poet correr por, cruzar. vi (of blood, etc.) correr; cazar

court n (yard) patio, m; (tennis) campo de tenis, m; (fives, racquets) cancha, f; (royal) corte, f; (of justice) tribunal, m; (following) séquito, acompañamiento, m. vt hacer la corte (a); cortejar, pretender; solicitar; (sleep) conciliar. **to pay c. to,** (a woman) galantear, pretender; (a person) hacer la rueda (a), Lat. Am. afilar. **to respect the c.,** law guardar sala. **c. of appeal,** sala de apelación, f. **c. of justice,** sala de justicia, f; tribunal de justicia, m. **supreme c.,** tribunal supremo, m. **c.-card,** figura, f. **c.-dress,** traje de corte, m. **c. house,** palacio de justicia, m. **c. jester,** bufón, m. **c.-martial,** tribunal militar, m. **c.-plaster,** tafetán inglés, tafetán de heridas, m. **c.-room,** sala de justicia, f

courteous a cortés

courtesy n cortesía, f; favor, m, merced, f; permiso, m

courtier n cortesano, palaciego, m

courtliness n cortesía, urbanidad, f; dignidad, f; elegancia, f

courtly a cortés, galante; digno; elegante

courtship n noviazgo, m; galanteo, m

courtyard n patio, m

cousin n primo (-ma). **first c.,** primo (-ma) carnal. **second c.,** primo (-ma) segundo (-da)

cove n cala, abra, ensenada, f, ancón m

covenant n contrato, m; estipulación, f; pacto, m; alianza, f. vt prometer; estipular

Coventry, to send to, hacer el vacío (a)

cover vt cubrir; abrigar; (dissemble) disimular; (at distance) recorrer; (comprise) comprender, abarcar; (with confusion, etc.) llenar (de); (with a revolver, etc.) amenazar (con); (an overdraft, etc.) garantizar; (of stallions) cubrir; (of a hen and eggs) empollar; (a story, journalism) investigar. n cubierta, f; (for a chair, umbrella, etc.) funda, f; (of a saucepan, jar, etc.) tapa, f; (dish-cover) tapadera, f; (of a book) cubierta, tapa, f; (of a letter) sobre, m; (shelter) abrigo, m; protección, f; (undergrowth) maleza, f; fig velo, manto, m; (pretence) pretexto, m; com garantía, f. **outer c.,** (of tire) cubierta de neumático, f. **to c. oneself with glory,** cubrirse de gloria. **to c. up,** cubrir completamente; (with clothes) arropar; (wrap up) envolver. **to c. with a revolver,** amenazar con un revólver. **to read a book from c. to c.,** leer un libro del principio al fin. **to take c.,** refugiarse, tomar abrigo. **under c.,** bajo tejado; al abrigo

cover charge n consumo mínimo, precio del cubierto, m

covering n cubrimiento, m; cubierta, f; envoltura, f; capa, f, abrigo, m. **c. letter,** carta adjunta, f

covert n guarida, f. a oculto; furtivo

covertly adv secretamente, furtivamente

covet vt codiciar; ambicionar, suspirar por

covetous a codicioso; ávido; ambicioso

covetousness n codicia, avaricia, f; avidez, f; ambición, f

cow vt intimidar, acobardar

cow n vaca, Lat. Am. also lechera f; (of other animals) hembra, f. **c.-bell,** cencerro, m, zumba, f. **c.-catcher,** aut salvavidas, m. **c.-hide,** cuero, cuero de vaca, zurriago, m; penca, f. **c.-house,** establo, m, boyera, f. **c.-pox,** vacuna, f

coward n cobarde, m, a cobarde

cowardice n cobardía, f, Argentina canillera f

cowardly a cobarde, Mexico, Venezuela correlón

cowboy n vaquero, m; gaucho, "cowboy," m

cower vi no saber dónde meterse; temblar, acobardarse

cowl n capucha, f; (of a chimney) sombrerete, m

coworker n colaborador (-ra)

cowshed n establo, m

coxcomb n (of a jester) gorra de bufón, f; mequetrefe, m

coy a modoso, tímido; coquetón

coyness n timidez, modestia, f; coquetería, f

cozy a cómodo; agradable; caliente. **You are very c. here,** Estás muy bien aquí

crab n (sea) cangrejo de mar, cámbaro, m, Lat. Am. also jaiba m; (river) cangrejo, *m; ast* Cáncer, *m. vt* (thwart) frustrar.

hermit c., cangrejo ermitaño, *m.*
c.-apple, manzana silvestre, *f.* **c.-louse,**
ladilla, *f*

crabbed *a* áspero, hosco, desabrido,
arisco; (of handwriting) apretado, metido

crack *vt* hender; quebrantar, romper;
(nuts) cascar; (a whip and fingers) chasquear; (a bottle of wine) abrir. *vi* (of earth,
skin, etc.) agrietarse; romperse, quebrarse; (of the voice) romper; (of the male
voice) mudar. *n* hendedura, rendija, *f;*
quebraja, *f;* (of a whip) chasquido, *m;* (of
a rifle) estallido, *m;* (blow) golpe, garrotazo, *m,* a excelente, de primera categoría; estupendo. **to c. a joke,** decir un
chiste. **to c. up,** *vt* dar bombo (a), alabar.
vi (in health) quebrantarse; (airplane)
cuartearse, estrellarse. **c.-brained,** chiflado; estúpido, loco

cracked *a* agrietado; (of a bell, etc.) hendido; (of the voice) cascada; (of a person)
chiflado

cracker *n* (firework) petardo, *m;* buscapiés, *m*

crackle *vi* (of burning wood, etc.) crepitar;
(rustle) crujir; (of rifle fire) tirotear. *n*
crepitación, *f;* crujido, *m;* (of rifle fire) tiroteo, *m*

crackling *n.* See **crackle;** *cul* chicharrón,
m

Cracow Cracovia, *f*

cradle *n* cuna, *f; fig* niñez, infancia, *f;* (for
a limb) arco de protección, *m;* (for wine-
bottle) cesta, *f. vt* mecer. **c.-song,** canción de cuna, *f*

craft *n* (guile) astucia, *f;* (skill) habilidad,
f; arte, *mf;* (occupation) oficio manual, *m;*
profesión, *f;* (guild) gremio, *m;* (boat)
barco, *m,* embarcación, *f*

craftiness *n* astucia, *f*

craftsman *n* artífice, *m;* arte sano, *m;* artista, *m*

craftsmanship *n* arte, *m,* or *f;* habilidad,
f; artificio, *m*

crafty *a* astuto, taimado, *Lat. Am.*
macuco. **c. person** *Mexico* fistol *m*

crag *n* peña, *f,* risco, despeñadero, *m*

craggy *a* escabroso, escarpado, peñascoso, riscoso

cram *vt* henchir; atestar; (one's mouth)
llenar (de); (poultry) cebar; (a pupil)
preparar para un examen; (a subject) empollar. *vi* (with food) atracarse. **The room
was crammed with people,** La sala estaba atestada de gente

cramp *n med* calambre, *m;* (numbness)
entumecimiento, *m;* (rivet) grapa, *f. vt* dar
calambre (a); (numb) entumecer; (fasten)
lañar; (*fig* hamper) estorbar. **to c. someone's style,** cortar los vuelos (a).
writer's c., calambre del escribiente, *m*

cramped *a* (of space) apretado, estrecho;
(of writing) menuda

cranberry *n* arándano, *m*

crane *n orn* grulla, *f;* (machine) grúa, *f.* **jib
c.,** grúa de pescante, *f.* **travelling c.,**
grúa móvil, *f.* **to c. one's neck,** estirar el
cuello. **crane's bill,** pico de cigüeña, *m*

cranium *n* cráneo, *m*

crank *n* (handle) manivela, *f;* (person)
maniático (-ca). *vt* poner en marcha (un
motor) con la manivela

crankiness *n* (crossness) irritabilidad, *f,*
mal humor, *m;* (eccentricity) excentricidad, *f*

cranky *a* (cross) irritable, malhumorado;
(eccentric) chiflado, maniático, excéntrico

cranny *n* hendedura, grieta, *f*

crape *n* crespón, *m*

crash *vi* caer estrepitosamente; romperse; estallarse; (of aircraft, cars) estrellarse; *fig* hundirse, arruinarse. *n* estrépito, estruendo, *m;* estallido, *m;* (of
aircraft) accidente de aviación, *m;* (car)
accidente, *m,* (or choque, *m* de automóviles; (financial) ruina, *f; fig* hundimiento,
m. **to c. into,** estrellarse contra, chocar
con. **c. helmet,** casco, *m.* **c.-landing,**
aterrizaje violento, *m*

crass *a* craso

crate *n* (box) caja de embalaje, *f;* (basket)
canasto, *m,* banasta, *Mexico* jaba *f*

crater *n* cráter, *m*

cravat *n* corbata, *f*

crave *vt* suplicar, implorar. **to c. for,** perecer por, suspirar por, anhelar

craven *a* cobarde, pusilánime. *n* poltrón,
cobarde, *m*

craving *n* deseo vehemente, *m,* sed, *f*

crawfish *n* cangrejo de río, *m;* cigala, *f*

crawl *vi* arrastrarse; andar a gatas; andar
a paso de tortuga; (abase oneself) humillarse; (be full of) abundar (en). *n* paso de
tortuga, *m;* (swimming) arrastre *m*

crayfish *n* cangrejo de río, *m;* cigala, *f*

crayon *n* carbón, *m;* pastel, *m;* (pencil)
lápiz de color, *m. vt* dibujar con pastel,
etc. **c. drawing,** dibujo al carbón, *m*

craze *vt* enloquecer, volver loco (a). *n*
manía, *f,* capricho, entusiasmo, *m;* (fashion) moda, *f*

craziness *n* locura, *f*

crazy *a* loco; chiflado; (of structure)
dilapidado. **He is c. about music,** Está
loco por la música. **to be completely c.,**
(of persons) ser un loco de atar; ser completamente loco. **to drive c.,** volver loco
(a)

creak *vi* (of shoes, chairs, etc.) crujir; (of
gates, etc.) rechinar, chirriar. *n* crujido,
m; chirrido, *m*

creaky *a* crujiente, que cruje; chirriador

cream *n* crema, *f;* nata, *f; fig* flor, nata, *f.*
a de nata. **whipped c.,** nata batida, *f.* **c.
cake,** pastel de nata, *m.* **c.-cheese,**
queso de nata, *m.* **c.-colored,** de color
crema. **c.-jug,** jarro para crema, *m.* **c. of
tartar,** cremor, tártaro, *m*

creamy a cremoso

crease n (wrinkle) arruga, f; (fold) pliegue, m; (in trousers) raya, f; (in cricket) línea de la meta, f. vt (wrinkle) arrugar; (fold) plegar; (trousers) poner la raya en. vi arrugarse

create vt crear; (appoint) nombrar; (produce) suscitar, producir

creation n creación, f; establecimiento, m; (appointment) nombramiento, m

creative a creador; de la creación

creativeness n facultad creativa, inventiva, f

creator n creador (-ra)

creature n criatura, f; animal, m. c. **comforts**, bienestar material, m

credence n crédito, m, fe, creencia, f; ecc credencia, f. **to give c. to**, dar crédito (a), creer

credentials n pl credenciales, f pl

credibility n credibilidad, verosimilitud, f

credible a creíble, verosímil; (of persons) digno de confianza

credit n crédito, m; reputación, f; honor, m; (com and banking) crédito, m; (in bookkeeping) data, f. vt dar fe (a), dar crédito (a); creer; atribuir; (bookkeeping) acreditar. **It does them c.**, Les hace honor. **on c.**, a crédito, al fiado. **open c.**, com letra abierta, f. **to give on c.**, dar fiado. c. **balance**, haber, m

creditable a loable, honroso, digno de alabanza

creditor n acreedor (-ra); (bookkeeping) haber, m

credulous a crédulo, Lat. Am. creído

credulously adv con credulidad, crédulamente

creed n credo, m

creek n caleta, abra, f

creep vi arrastrarse; (of plants and birds) trepar; (of infants) andar a gatas; (totter) hacer pinitos; (slip) deslizarse; (cringe) lisonjear, rebajarse; (of one's flesh) sentir hormigueo. **to c. about on tiptoe**, andar de puntillas. **to c. into a person's favor**, insinuarse en el favor de. **to c. in**, entrar sin ser notado (en); deslizarse en. **to c. on**, (of time) avanzar lentamente; (of old age, etc.) acercarse insensiblemente. **to c. out**, salir sin hacer ruido; escurrirse. **to c. up**, trepar por; subir a gatas

cremate vt incinerar

cremation n cremación, f

creole a criollo. n criollo (-lla)

crescent n media luna, f; her creciente, m; calle en forma de semicírculo, f. a en forma de media luna; poet creciente

cress n bot berro, m

crest n (of a cock, etc.) cresta, f; (plume) penacho, m; (of a helmet) cimera, f; (of a hill) cumbre, cima, f; (of a wave) cresta, f. **family c.**, blasón, escudo, m

crested a Lat. Am. copetudo (-da)

crestfallen a cabizbajo, cariacontecido

crevice n intersticio, m, rendija, grieta, f

crew n (of ships, boats, aircraft) tripulación, f; (of a gun) servidores de una ametralladora, m pl; (gang) pandilla, cuadrilla, f

crib n pesebre, m; (child's) camita de niño, f; (plagiary) plagio, m. vt (plagiarize) plagiar; (steal) hurtar

crick n (in the neck) tortícolis, m

cricket n ent grillo, m; (game) cricquet, m. c. **ball**, pelota de cricquet, f. c. **bat**, paleta de cricquet, f. c. **ground**, campo de cricquet, m. c. **match**, partido de cricquet, m

crime n crimen, m; ofensa, f, delito, m

criminal a criminal. n criminal, m; reo, mf **C. Investigation Department**, (nearest equivalent) policía secreta, f. c. **laws**, código penal, m

criminologist n criminalista, m

criminology n criminología, f

crimp vt (hair) rizar

crimson n carmesí, m. a de carmesí. vt teñir de carmesí. vi enrojecerse

cringe vi temblar; asustarse, acobardarse; inclinarse (ante)

cringing a servil, humilde; adulador, Mexico also lambioche

crinkle vi arrugarse; rizarse. vt arrugar. n arruga, f

cripple n tullido (-da); cojo (-ja). vt lisiar, tullir, estropear; fig paralizar

crisis n crisis, f

crisp a (of hair and of leaves) crespo; (fresh) fresco; (stiff) tieso; (of style) nervioso, vigoroso; (of manner) decidido; (of repartee) chispeante; (of tone) incisivo

crisscross vt (a body of water or land) surcar

criterion n criterio, m

critic n crítico, m; censor, m

critical a crítico

criticism n crítica, f

criticize vt criticar; censurar

critique n crítica, f

croak vi (of frogs) croar; (of ravens) graznar; (of persons) lamentarse, gruñir

Croat a croata. n croata, mf

Croatia Crocia, f

crochet n ganchillo, m, vi hacer ganchillo. vt hacer (algo) de ganchillo. c. **hook**, aguja de gancho, f, ganchillo, m. c. **work**, croché, ganchillo, m

crockery n loza, f, cacharros, m pl. c. **store**, cacharrería, f

crocodile n cocodrilo, m. c. **tears**, lágrimas de cocodrilo, f pl

crony n compinche, mf

crook n curva, f; (staff) cayado, m; (swindler) caballero de industria, estafador, m, vt doblar, encorvar

crooked a curvo; encorvado; torcido,

Mexico chueco; ladeado; (deformed) contrahecho; (of paths, etc.) tortuoso; (dishonest) torcido, tortuoso

crookedly *adv* torcidamente; de través

crookedness *n* encorvadura, *f*; tortuosidad, *f*

croon *vt* and *vi* canturrear; cantar

crooner *n* cantante, *mf*

crop *n* (of birds) buche, *m*; (whip) látigo, *m*, fusta, *f*; (handle) mango, *m*; (harvest) cosecha, *f*; (of the hair) cortadura, *f*. *vt* cortar; (nibble) rozar; (hair) rapar. **Eton c.**, pelo a la garçonne, *m*. **to c. up**, aparecer, surgir

crop rotation *n* la rotación de cultivos, *f*

croquette *n cul* croqueta, *f*

cross *n* cruz, *f*; *biol* cruzamiento, *m*; (sew bias) bies, *m*. **in the shape of a c.**, en cruz. **the Red C.**, la Cruz Roja. **c.-bearer**, *ecc* crucero, *m*

cross *vt* cruzar; atravesar; pasar por; (a check and animals) cruzar; (thwart) contrariar. **It did not c. my mind**, No se me ocurrió. **Our letters must have crossed**, Nuestras cartas deben haberse cruzado. **to c. oneself**, *ecc* persignarse. **to c. out**, tachar, rayar. **to c. over**, *vt* atravesar, cruzar. *vi* ir al otro lado

cross *a* transversal; cruzado; oblicuo; (contrary) opuesto (a); (bad-tempered) malhumorado. **c.-breed**, *a* mestizo, atravesado. **c.-country**, *a* a campo travieso. **c.-examination**, *law* repregunta, *f*, contrainterrogatorio, *m*. **c.-examine**, *vt law* repreguntar; interrogar. **c.-eyed**, bizco. **c.-fire**, *mil* fuego cruzado, *m sing* fuegos cruzados, *m pl*; *fig* tiroteo, *m*. **c.-grained**, (of wood) vetisesgado; (of persons) áspero, intratable, desabrido. **c.-legged**, con las piernas cruzadas. **c.-purpose**, despropósito, *m*. **at c.-purposes**, a despropósito. **c.-question**, *vt law* repreguntar; interrogar. **c. reference**, contrarreferencia, *f*. **c. section**, sección transversal, *f*. **c.-stitch**, punto cruzado, *m*. **c.-word puzzle**, crucigrama, *m*

crossbred *a* cruzado, mestizo; híbrido

crossbreed *n* mestizo (-za); híbrido, *m*

crossing *n* cruzamiento, *m*; (of the sea) travesía, *f*; (intersection) cruce, *m*; paso, *m*. **level c.**, paso a nivel, *m*. **pedestrian c.**, paso para peatones, *m*. **c.-sweeper**, barrendero, *m*

crossly *adv* con mal humor, con displicencia, irritablemente

crossroad *n* travesía, *f*; cruce, *m*; *pl* **crossroads**, cruce, cruce de caminos, *m sing* encrucijada, *f sing*

crosswise *adv* en cruz; a través

crotch *n* (of a tree) bifurcación, *f*; *anat* horcajadura, *f*; (of breeches) entrepiernas, *f pl*

crotchet *n mus* semínima, *f*; (fad) capricho, *m*; extravagancia, excentricidad, *f*

crotchety *a* caprichoso; raro, excéntrico; difícil

crouch *vi* acurrucarse, agacharse, acuclillarse

croup *n* (disease) crup, garrotillo, *m*; (of a horse) grupa, anca, *f*

croupier *n* coime, crupié, *m*

crow *n orn* cuervo, *m*; *orn* grajo, *m*; (of a cock) canto del gallo, cacareo, *m*; (of an infant) gorjeo, *m*. *vi* (of a cock) cantar, cacarear; (of an infant) gorjearse. **as the c. flies**, en línea recta. **to c. over**, gallear, cantar victoria. **crow's-foot**, pata de gallo, *f*. **crow's-nest**, *naut* gavias, *f pl*

crowbar *n* alzaprima, palanca, *f*

crowd *n* multitud, muchedumbre, *f*; concurso, *m*; vulgo, *m*; (majority) mayoría, *f*; *theat* acompañamiento, *m*. *vi* reunirse, congregarse; agolparse, remolinarse, apiñarse. *vt* (fill) llenar; atestar. **in a c.**, en tropel. **So many ideas crowded in on me**, Se me ocurrieron tantas ideas a la vez. **to follow the c.**, seguir la multitud; *flg* ir con la mayoría. **to c. in**, entrar en tropel. **to c. round**, cercar, agruparse alrededor de. **to c. together**, apiñarse. **to c. up**, subir en masa, subir en tropel

crowded *a* lleno; atestado, apiñado; (weighed down) agobiado; (of hours, etc.) lleno

crowing *n* cacareo, canto del gallo, *m*; (of an infant) gorjeos, *m pl*; (boasting) jactancia, *f*

crown *n* corona, *f*; (of the head) coronilla, corona, *f*; (of a hat) copa, *f*; *arch* coronamiento, *m*. *vt* coronar.

crowning *n* coronamiento, *m*; *arch* remate, *m*, a final; supremo

crucial *a* decisivo, crítico; difícil

crucible *n* crisol, *m*

crucifix *n* crucifijo, *m*

crucifixion *n* crucifixión, *f*

crude *a* crudo; (of colors) chillón, llamativo; (uncivilized) cerril, inculto; (vulgar) cursi; (of truth, etc.) desnudo

crudity *n* crudeza, *f*

cruel *a* cruel

cruelty *n* crueldad, *f*

cruet *n* ánfora, vinagrera, *f*; (stand) angarillas, *f pl*, convoy, *m*

cruise *vi* cruzar, navegar; (of cars) correr. *n* viaje por mar, *m*

cruiser *n* crucero, *m*

crumb *n* miga, *f*; (spongy part of bread) migaja, *f*. *vt* (bread) desmigajar; desmenuzar. **c. brush**, recogemigas, *m*

crumble *vt* desmigajar, desmenuzar. *vi* desmoronarse, desmigajarse; *flg* hundirse, derrumbarse; *flg* desaparecer

crumbling *n* (of buildings, etc.) desmoronamiento, *m*; *flg* destrucción, *f*

crumple *vt* arrugar, ajar. *vi* arrugarse. **to c. up**, *vt* (crush) estrujar; (persons) dejar aplastado. *vi* (collapse) hundirse, derrumbarse; (of persons) desplomarse; (despair) desalentarse

crunch vt mascar; hacer crujir. vi crujir

crusade n cruzada, f

crusader n cruzado, m

crush vt aplastar; (to powder) moler, triturar; (grapes, etc.) exprimir; (crease) arrugar; (opposition, etc.) vencer; (annihilate) aniquilar, destruir; (abash) humillar, confundir; (hope, etc.) matar; (of sorrow, etc.) agobiar. **We all crushed into his dining-room,** Fuimos en tropel a su comedor. **to c. up,** machacar, moler; (paper, etc.) estrujar

crushing a (of defeats and replies) aplastante; (of sorrow, etc.) abrumador

crust n (of bread, pie) corteza, f; (scab) costra, f; (of the earth, snow) capa, f. vt encostrar. vi encostrarse. **c. of bread,** mendrugo de pan, m

crusty a costroso; (of persons) malhumorado, irritable; áspero

crutch n muleta, f; (fork) horquilla, f; (crotch) horcajadura, f

crux n problema, m; (knotty point) nudo, m

cry vi (weep) llorar; (shout) gritar; (exclaim) exclamar. vt (one's wares) pregonar. n grito, m. **to cry for help,** pedir socorro a voces. **to cry to high heaven,** poner el grito en el cielo. **to cry one's eyes out,** llorar a mares. **to cry down,** desacreditar. **to cry off,** desdecirse; volverse atrás. **to cry out,** vt gritar. vi dar gritos; gritar; fig clamar. **cry-baby,** niño (-ña) llorón (-ona)

crying a urgente; notorio. n gritos, m pl; (weeping) llanto, m, lamentaciones, f pl; (tears) lágrimas, f pl

crypt n cripta, f

cryptic a secreto, oculto

crystal n cristal, m. **c. set,** rad receptor de galena, m

cub n cachorro (-rra)

Cuban a cubano. n cubano (-na)

cubbyhole n refugio, m; garita, f; cuarto pequeño, m; chiribitil, m

cube n cubo, m; (of sugar) terrón, m. vt cubicar. **c. root,** raíz cúbica, f

cubic a cúbico

cubicle n cubículo, m

cuckold n cornudo, m

cuckoo n cuclillo, m; (cry) cucú, m. **c.-clock,** reloj de cuclillo, m

cucumber n cohombro m

cuddle vt abrazar. n abrazo, m. **to c. up together,** estar abrazados

cudgel n porra, estaca, tranca, f, vt aporrear, apalear. **to c. one's brains,** devanarse los sesos. **to take up the cudgels for,** salir en defensa de

cue n theat pie, m; (lead) táctica, f; (hint) indicación, f; (of hair) coleta, f; (billiard) taco (de billar), m. **to take one's cue**

from, tomar como modelo (a); seguir el ejemplo de

cueca n cueca f

cuff vt abofetear. n (blow) bofetón, m; (of sleeve) puño, m, bocamanga, valenciana, f.

cufflink n gemelo m, Central America mancuerna, mancuernilla f, Chile collera f, Colombia mancorna f

cuisine n cocina, f

culinary a culinario

culminate vi culminar (en), terminar (en). **culminating point,** punto culminante, m

culmination n culminación, f; fig apogeo, punto culminante, m

culprit n culpado (-da)

cult n culto, m

cultivable a cultivable, labradero

cultivate vt cultivar

cultivated a cultivado; (of persons) culto, fino

cultivation n cultivación, f; (of the land) cultivo, m; (of persons, etc.) cultura, f

cultivator n cultivador (-ra); (machine) cultivador, m

cultural a cultural

culture n cultura, f; (bacteriology) cultivo, m, vt (bacteriology) cultivar

cultured a culto

cumbersome a pesado; incómodo

cumulative a cumulativo

cunning a astuto, taimado, Lat. Am. macuco n (skill) habilidad, f; astucia, f

cup n taza, f; (ecc and bot) cáliz, m; sport copa, f; (hollow) hoyo, m. **c.-final,** sport final de la copa, m. **c.-tie,** sport partido eliminatorio, m

cupboard n armario, m; (in the wall) alacena, f. **c. love,** amor interesado, m

cupful n taza, f

cupidity n avaricia, codicia, f

cup of sorrow n ramito de amargura, m

cupola n cúpula, f

cur n perro mestizo, m; canalla, m

curable a curable

curative a curativo, terapéutico

curator n (of a museum) director, m; (Scots law) curador, m

curb n (of a bridle) barbada, f; fig freno, m; (stone) bordillo, m, guarnición, f. vt (a horse) enfrenar; fig refrenar, reprimir; (limit) limitar

curd n requesón, m; cuajada, f

curdle vi coagularse; (of blood) helarse. vt coagular; (blood) helar

cure n cura, f; ecc curato, m. vt curar; (salt) salar; fig remediar. **to take a c.,** tomar una cura. **c.-all,** panacea, f. **c. of souls,** cura de almas, f

curer n (of fish, etc.) salador, m; (of evils, etc.) remediador, m

curfew n toque de queda, m

curio n curiosidad, antigüedad, f

curiosity n curiosidad, f

curious a (all meanings) curioso

curl n (of hair) rizo, bucle, m; (of smoke) penacho, m. vt rizar. vi rizarse; sport jugar al curling. **in c.**, rizado. **to c. one's lip**, hacer una mueca de desdén. **to c. up**, vt arrollar; fig dejar fuera de combate (a). vi hacerse un ovillo, enroscarse; (of leaves) abarquillarse; fig desplomarse; desanimarse. **c.-paper**, papillote, m

curling n (game) curling, m, a rizado. **c.-tongs**, encrespador, m

curly a rizado, crespo

currant n (dry) pasa de Corinto, f; (fresh) grosella, f. **black c.**, grosella negra, f; (bush) grosellero negro, m. **c.-bush**, grosellero, m

currency n uso corriente, m; moneda corriente, f, dinero, m; dinero en circulación, m; valor corriente, m; estimación, f

current a corriente; presente, de actualidad; (of money) en circulación. n (of water, elec, fig elec) corriente, f. **alternating c.**, elec corriente alterna, f. **direct c.**, elec corriente continua, f. **the c. number of a magazine**, el último número de una revista. **c. events**, actualidades, f pl

curriculum n plan de estudios, m; curso, m

curriculum vitae n hoja de vida, f

curry vt (leather) zurrar; (a horse) almohazar; cul condimentar con cari. **to c. favor with**, insinuarse en el favor de. **c.-comb**, almohaza, f

curse n maldición, f; blasfemia, f; (ruin) azote, castigo, m. vt maldecir; (afflict) castigar. vi blasfemar, echar pestes

cursed a maldito; abominable, odioso

cursing n maldición, f; blasfemias, f pl

cursorily adv rápidamente; de prisa; superficialmente

cursory a rápido; apresurado; superficial

curt a seco, brusco; corto

curtail vt abreviar; reducir; disminuir

curtailment n abreviación, f; reducción, f; disminución, f

curtain n cortina, f; theat telón, m. vt poner cortinas (a) **drop c.**, telón de boca, m. **iron c.**, pol telón de acero, m. **to c. off**, separar por cortinas. **c.-lecture**, reprimenda conyugal, f. **c.-raiser**, entremés, m. **c.-ring**, anilla, f

curtness n brusquedad, sequedad, f

curtsey n reverencia, cortesía, f, vi hacer una reverencia

curve n curva, f; mech codo, m; (aut of a road) viraje, m. vt encorvar, torcer. vi encorvarse, torcerse; (of a road) hacer un viraje.

curved a curvo

curvet n corveta, cabriola, f, vi corvetear, corcovear, cabriolar

cushion n almohada, f; cojín, m; (billiards) banda, f; (of fingers, etc.) pulpejo,

m. vt proveer de almohadas; (a shock) amortiguar; suavizar

custard n flan, m, natillas, f pl

custodian n custodio, m; guardián, m; (of a museum, etc.) director, m

custody n custodia, f; guarda, f; prisión, f. **in safe c.**, en lugar seguro. **to take** (a person) **into c.**, arrestar

custom n costumbre, f; uso, m; com parroquia, clientela, f; (sales) ventas, f pl; pl **Customs**, aduana, f. **to go through the Customs**, pasar por la aduana. **Customs duty**, derechos de aduana, m pl. **Customs officer**, aduanero, m. **c.-house**, aduana, f

customarily adv habitualmente, por lo general

customary a acostumbrado, usual, habitual

customer n cliente, mf parroquiano (-na), Lat. Am. also. marchante (-ta). **He is a queer c.**, Es un tipo raro

cut vt cortar; (diamonds) tallar; (hay, etc.) segar; (carve) labrar, tallar; (engrave) grabar; (a lecture, etc.) no asistir a; (cards) destajar, cortar; (fig wound) herir; (reduce) reducir; abreviar; (teeth) echar; (of lines) cruzar. vi cortar; cortar bien; (fam go) marcharse a prisa y corriendo. **I must get my hair cut**, He de hacerme cortar el pelo. **That cuts both ways**, Es una arma de dos filos. **His opinion cuts no ice**, Su opinión no cuenta. **Mary cut him dead**, María hizo como si no le reconociera. **to cut a caper**, dar saltos; hacer cabriolas. **to cut a person short**, echar el tablacho (a). **to cut and run**, poner los pies en polvorosa. **to cut for deal**, (cards) cortar para ver quién da las cartas. **to cut short**, (a career) terminar. **to cut to the quick**, herir en lo más vivo. **to cut across**, cortar al través; (fields, etc.) atravesar; tomar por un atajo. **to cut away**, vt quitar. vi inf poner pies en polvorosa. **to cut down**, derribar; (by the sword) acuchillar; (by death, etc.) segar, malograr; (expenses, etc.) reducir; (abbreviate) cortar, abreviar. **to cut off**, cortar, separar; amputar; (on a telephone) cortar la comunicación; (gas, water, etc.) cortar; (supply of food, etc.) interrumpir; (of death) llevarse. **to cut off with a shilling**, desheredar (a). **to cut out**, (dresses, etc.) cortar; (oust) suplantar. **He is not cut out for medicine**, No tiene la disposición para la medicina. **to cut up**, trinchar, cortar en pequeños trozos, Lat. Am. destajar; (afflict) entristecer, afligir. **to cut up rough**, inf ponerse furioso

cut a cortado. **well-cut features**, facciones regulares, f pl. **cut and dried opinion**, opinión hecha, idea fija, f; ideas cerradas, f pl. **cut glass**, cristal tallado, m

cut n corte, m; (with a whip) latigazo, m; (with a sword) cuchillada, f; (with a sharp instrument) tajo, m; cortadura, f; (in prices, etc.) reducción, f; (engraving)

grabado, *m*; clisé, *m*; (of cards) corte, *m*.
short cut, atajo, *m*. **the cut of a coat,** el
corte de un abrigo. **to give** (someone)
the cut direct, pasar cerca de (una persona) sin saludarle. **cut-out,** *n* (paper)
recortado, *m*; *elec* cortacircuitos, *m*. **cut-
throat,** *n* asesino, *m*

cut *n* corte, *m*; (with a whip) latigazo, *m*;
(with a sword) cuchillada, *f*; (with a sharp
instrument) tajo, *m*; cortadura, *f*; (in
prices, etc.) reducción, *f*; (engraving)
grabado, *m*; clisé, *m*; (of cards) corte, *m*.
short cut, atajo, *m*. **the cut of a coat,** el
corte de un abrigo. **to give** (someone)
the cut direct, pasar cerca de (una persona) sin saludarle. **cut-out,** *n* (paper)
recortado, *m*; *elec* cortacircuitos, *m*. **cut-
throat,** *n* asesino, *m*

cute *a* cuco, listo; mono
cuticle *n* cutícula, *f*
cutlass *n* alfanje *m*
cutlery *n* cuchillería, *f*
cutlet *n* chuleta, *f*
cutting *n* corte, *m*; (of diamonds) talla, *f*;
(in a mountain, etc.) tajo, *m*; *agr* plantón,
m; (of cloth) retazo, *m*; (newspaper) recorte, *m*. a cortante; (of remarks) mordaz.

newspaper c., recorte de periódico. **c.
down,** (of trees) tala, *f*; reducción, *f*
cycle *n* ciclo, *m*; período, *m*; (bicycle) bicicleta, *f*. *vi* ir en bicicleta
cyclic *a* cíclico
cycling *n* ciclismo, *m*
cyclist *n* ciclista, *mf*
cyclone *n* ciclón, *m*
Cyclopean task *n* obra ciclópea, *f*
cylinder *n* cilindro, *m*; *mech* tambor, *m*.
c. head, culata, *f*
cylindrical *a* cilíndrico
cymbal *n* címbalo, platillo, *m*
cymbalist *n* cimbalero (-ra)
cynic *n* cínico, *m*
cynical *a* cínico
cynicism *n* cinismo, *m*
cynosure *n* *ast* Osa Menor, *f*; blanco, *m*
cypress *n* (tree and wood) ciprés, *m*. **c.
grove,** cipresal, *m*
Cypriot *a* chipriota. *n* chipriota, *mf*
Cyprus Isla de Chipre, *f*
cyst *n* quiste, *m*
Czech *a* checo. *n* checo (-ca); (language)
checo, *m*

d *n* (letter) de, *f*; *mus* re, *m*

dab *vt* golpéar suavemente, tocar; (sponge) esponjar; (moisten) mojar. *n* golpecito, golpe blando, *m*; (small piece) pedazo pequeño, *m*; (blob) borrón, *m*; (peck) picotazo, *m*; *inf* experto (-ta). **to dab at one's eyes,** secarse los ojos

dabble *vt* mojar (en). *vi* chapotear; (engage in) entretenerse en; (meddle in) meterse en; (speculate in) especular en. **to d. in politics,** meterse en política

dabbler *n* aficionado (-da)

daddy *n* papaíto, *m*. **d.-longlegs,** típula, *f*

daft *a* bobo, tonto, chiflado; loco

dagger *n* daga, *f*, puñal, *m*; *print* cruz, *f*. **to be at daggers drawn,** estar a matar. **to look daggers (at),** lanzar miradas de odio (hacia), mirar echando chispas. **d. thrust,** puñalada, *f*

daily *a* diario, de todos los días; cotidiano. *adv* diariamente, cada día, todos los días; cotidianamente. *n* (paper) diario, *m*. **d. bread,** pan cotidiano, pan de cada día, *m*. **d. help,** (person) asistenta, *f*. **d. pay,** jornal, *m*; *mil* pre, *m*

daintiness *n* delicadeza, *f*; elegancia, *f*; (beauty) primor, *m*

dainty *a* delicado; elegante; primoroso, exquisito; (fastidious) melindroso, difícil. *n* bocado exquisito, *m*, golosina, *f*

dairy *n* lechería, *f*. **d. cattle,** vacas lecheras, *f pl*. **d.-farm,** granja, *f*. **d.-farmer,** granjero (-ra). **d.-farming,** industria lechera, *f*

dairyman *n* lechero, *m*

dais *n* estrado, *m*

daisy *n* margarita, *f*

dale *n* valle, *m*

dalliance *n* (delay) tardanza, *f*; (play) jugueteo, *m*; diversiones, *f pl*; (caresses) caricias, *f pl*, abrazos, *m pl*

dally *vi* tardar, perder el tiempo; entretenerse, divertirse; (make love) holgar (con); (with an idea) entretenerse con, jugar con

dam *n* (of animals) madre, *f*; (of a river, etc.) presa, *f*, embalse, *m*; (mole) dique, *m*; pared de retención, *f*. *vt* represar, embalsar; cerrar; (restrain) contener, reprimir

damage *n* daño, perjuicio, *m*; mal, *m*; avería, *f*; pérdida, *f*; (*fam* price) precio, *m*; *pl* **damages,** *law* daños y perjuicios, *m pl*. *vt* dañar, perjudicar, *Lat. Am.* afectar; estropear; deteriorar; (reputation, etc.) comprometer

damaging *a* perjudicial; comprometedor

Damascus Damasio, *m*

damask *n* (cloth) damasco, *m*; (steel) acero damasquino, *m*. *a* de damasco; damasquino. *vt* (metals) damasquinar; (cloth) adamascar. **d.-like,** adamascado. **d. rose,** rosa de Damasco, *f*

dame *n* dama, señora, *f*; *inf* madre, *f*; (schoolmistress) amiga, *f*. **to attend a d. school,** ir a la amiga

damming *n* embalse, *m*, represa, *f*; retención, *f*; represión, *f*

damn *vt* condenar al infierno; maldecir; vituperar. **D. it!** ¡Maldito sea!

damnable *a* detestable, infame; *inf* horrible

damnation *n* condenación, perdición, *f*; maldición, *f*; vituperación, *f*

damned *a* condenado; maldito; detestable, odioso

damning *a* que condena; irresistible

damp *a* húmedo. *n* humedad, *f*; (mist) niebla, *f*; exhalación, *f*; (gas) mofeta, *f*; *fig* tristeza, depresión, *f*. *vt* humedecer, mojar; apagar, amortiguar; (depress) deprimir, entristecer; (stifle) ahogar; (lessen) moderar; (trouble) turbar. **d.-proof,** impermeable

damper *n* (of a chimney) registro de humos, *m*; (of a piano) batiente, *m*; (for stamps) mojador, *m*; (gloom) depresión, tristeza, *f*; (restraint) freno, *m*

dampness *n* humedad, *f*

damsel *n* chica, muchacha, *f*; damisela, *f*

damson *n* ciruela damascena, *f*. **d. tree,** ciruelo damasceno, *m*

dance *n* danza, *f*; baile, *m*. *vi* bailar, danzar; saltar, brincar. *vt* bailar; hacer saltar. **to d. attendance on,** servir humildemente; hacer la rueda (a). **to lead someone a d.,** hacer bailar. **d. band,** orquestina, *f*; orquesta de jazz. **d. floor,** pista de baile, *f*. **d. hall,** salón de baile, *m*. **d. music,** música bailable, *f*. **d.-number,** (in a theater) bailable, *m*. **d. of death,** danza de la muerte, *f*

dancer *n* bailarín (-ina); danzador (-ra), bailador (-ra); *pl* **dancers,** (partners) parejas de baile, *f pl*

dancing *n* baile, *m*, danza, *f*. **d.-girl,** bailarina, *f*; (Indian) bayadera, *f*. **d.-master,** maestro de baile, *m*. **d. school,** academia de baile, *f*. **d. slipper,** zapatilla de baile, *f*

dandle *vt* mecer, hacer saltar sobre las rodillas, hacer bailar

dandruff *n* caspa, *f*

dandy *n* dandi, petimetre, barbilindo, *m*

Dane *n* danés (-esa). **Great D.,** perro danés, *m*

danger *n* peligro, *m*; riesgo, *m*. **out of d.,** fuera de peligro. **to be in d.,** correr peligro, peligrar, estar en peligro

dangerous *a* peligroso; arriesgado; nocivo

dangle *vi* colgar, pender. *vt* dejar colgar; oscilar; (show) mostrar

Danish a danés, de Dinamarca. n (language) danés, m

dank a húmedo

Danube, the el (Río) Danubio, m

dapper a apuesto, aseado; activo, vivaz

dapple vt motear, salpicar, manchar. **d.-grey,** a rucio

dare vi atreverse, osar. vt arriesgar; desafiar, provocar; hacer frente a, arrostrar. n reto, m. **I d. say!** ¡Ya lo creo! ¡No lo dudo! **I d. say that . . . ,** No me sorprendería que . . . ; Supongo que . . . **d.-devil,** calavera, m; atrevido (-da), valeroso (-sa)

daring a intrépido, audaz; atrevido, _Argentina_ agalludo (dangerous) arriesgado, peligroso. n audacia, osadía, f, atrevimiento, m; peligro, m

dark a oscuro; (of complexion, etc.) moreno; negro; lóbrego; (of colours) oscuro; misterioso; enigmático; secreto, escondido; (sad) funesto, triste; (evil) malo, malévolo; (ignorant) ignorante, supersticioso. n oscuridad, f; (shade) sombra, f; ignorancia, f. **after d.,** a nocturno. adv después del anochecer. **in the d.,** a oscuras; de noche; flg **be in the d.,** quedarse en la luna. **to become d.,** oscurecerse; (cloud over) anublarse; (become night) anochecer. **to keep d.,** vt tener secreto. vi esconderse. **d. ages,** los siglos de la ignorancia y de la superstición. **d.-eyed,** de ojos negros, ojinegro. **d. horse,** caballo desconocido, m; pol batacazo, m. **d. lantern,** linterna sorda, f. **d. room,** cuarto oscuro, m; phot laboratorio fotográfico, m; (optics) cámara oscura, f

darken vt obscurecer; sombrear; (of color) hacer más oscuro; (sadden) entristecer. vi obscurecerse; (of the sky) anublarse; (of the face with emotion) inmutarse.

darkly adv oscuramente; misteriosamente; con malevolencia, secretamente; (archaic) indistintamente

darkness n oscuridad, f, tinieblas, f pl; sombra, f; (of color) oscuro, m; (of the complexion) color moreno, m; (of eyes, hair) negrura, f; (night) noche, f; (ignorance) ignorancia, f; (privacy) secreto, m. **Prince of d.,** el príncipe de las tinieblas

darling a querido, amado; (greatest) mayor. n querido (-da); (favorite) el predilecto, la predilecta, el favorito, la favorita. **My d.!** ¡Amor mío! ¡Vida mía! ¡Pichoncito mío!

darn vt zurcir, remendar. n zurcido, remiendo, m

darner n zurcidor (-ra); (implement) huevo de zurcir, m

darning n zurcidura, f; zurcido, recosido, m. **d.-needle,** aguja de zurcir, f. **d. wool,** lana de zurcir, f

dart n dardo, m; movimiento rápido, m; avance rápido, m; sew sisa, f. vi lanzarse, abalanzarse (sobre); volar; correr, avan-

zar rápidamente. vt lanzar, arrojar; dirigir. **to make darts in,** sew sisar

dash n (spirit) fogosidad, f, brío, m; energía, f; (impact) choque, golpe, m; (mixture) mezcla, f; (of a liquid) gota, f; (of the pen) rasgo, m; (attack) ataque, m; avance rápido, m; (a little) algo, un poco (de); gram raya, f; (show) ostentación, f. **He made a d. for the door,** Se precipitó a la puerta, Corrió hacia la puerta. **to cut a d.,** hacer gran papel. **d.-board,** tablero de instrumentos, m

dash vt arrojar con violencia; (break) quebrar, estrellar; (sprinkle) rociar (con), salpicar (con); (mix) mezclar; (knock) golpear; (disappoint) frustrar, destruir; (confound) confundir; (depress) desanimar. vi (rush) precipitarse; quebrarse, estrellarse; chocar (contra); (of waves) romperse. **to d. to pieces,** hacer añicos, estrellar. **to d. along,** avanzar rápidamente; correr. **to d. away,** vi marcharse apresuradamente. vt apartar bruscamente. **to d. down,** vi bajar aprisa. vt derribar; (overturn) volcar; (throw) tirar. **to d. off,** vi marcharse rápidamente. vt hacer apresuradamente; (a letter, etc.) escribir de prisa; (sketch) bosquejar rápidamente. **to d. out,** vi salir precipitadamente; lanzarse a la calle. vt (erase) borrar; hacer saltar. **to d. through,** atravesar rápidamente; hacer de prisa. **to d. up,** llegar a prisa; (sprout) saltar

dashing a valiente; (spirited) fogoso, gallardo; majo, brillante. n choque, m; (breaking) quebrantamiento, m; (of the waves) embate, m

dastardly a cobarde

data n pl datos, m pl

data processing n elaboración electrónica de datos, f, recuento de datos, m

date n fecha, f; (period) época, f; (term) plazo, m; (duration) duración, f; (appointment) cita, f; bot dátil, m. vt fechar, datar; poner fecha a; asignar. vi datar (de), remontar (a). **out of d.,** anticuado; pasado de moda; (of persons) atrasado de noticias. **to be up to d.,** ser nuevo; ser de última moda; (of persons) estar al día. **to bring up to d.,** renovar; (of persons) poner al corriente. **to fix the d.,** señalar el día; (chronologically) ajustar los tiempos. **to d.,** hasta la fecha. **under d. (of),** con fecha (de). **up to d.,** hasta hoy, hasta ahora. **What is the d.?** ¿Qué fecha es? ¿A cómo estamos hoy? ¿A cuántos estamos hoy? **d. palm,** datilera, f

date of expiry n fecha de caducidad, f

daub vt barrar, embadurnar; manchar, ensuciar; untar; (paint) pintorrear. n embadurnamiento, m; (picture) aleluya, f

daughter n hija, f. **adopted d.,** hija adoptiva, f. **little d.,** hijuela, f. **d.-in-law,** nuera, f

daunt vt intimidar, acobardar; dar miedo (a), espantar; (dishearten) desanimar

dauntless a impávido, intrépido

dawdle vi perder el tiempo; haraganear, gandulear

dawdler n gandul (-la)

dawn n alba, madrugada, primera luz, f; fig aurora, f. vi amanecer, alborear, romper el día; (appear) mostrarse, asomar. **at d.,** a primera luz, al amanecer, de madrugada, al alba. **It had not dawned on me,** No me había ocurrido

day n día, m; luz del día, f; (day's work) jornada, f; (battle) batalla, f; (victory) victoria, f; pl **days,** (time) tiempos, m pl, época, f; (life) vida, f; (years) años, m pl, a diario. **all day long,** durante todo el día. **any day,** cualquier día. **by day,** de día. **by the day,** al día. **every day,** todos los días, cada día. **every other day,** un día sí y otro no, cada dos días. **from this day forward,** desde hoy en adelante. **from day to day,** de día en día. **Good day!** ¡Buenos días! **in these days,** en estos días. **in olden days,** en la antigüedad; inf en tiempos de Maricastaña. **in the days of,** en los tiempos de; durante los años de; durante la vida de. **next day,** el día siguiente. **(on) the next day,** al día siguiente, al otro día. **one of these days,** un día de éstos. **some fine day,** el mejor día, de un día a otro. **the day after tomorrow,** pasado mañana. **the day before yesterday,** anteayer. **the day before,** la víspera. **to win the day,** ganar el día, salir victorioso. **day after day,** cada día, día tras día. **day by day,** día por día. **day in, day out,** sin cesar, día tras día. **day-book,** com libro diario, m. **day's holiday,** día de asueto, m; día libre, m. **day laborer,** jornalero, m. **day nursery,** guardería de niños, f. **day-pupil,** alumno (-na) externo (-na). **day-school,** externado, m. **day shift,** turno de día, m. **day-star,** lucero del alba, m. **day ticket,** billete de excursión, m

daybreak n alba, f, amanecer, m. **at d.,** al romper el día, al amanecer

daydream n ensueño, m; ilusión, f; fantasía, visión, f. vi lit soñar despierto, dejar volar sus pensamientos; fig hacerse ilusiones

daydreamer n soñador (-ra); visionario (-ia)

daylight n luz del día, f, día, m; (contrasted with artificial light) luz natural, f. **in broad d.,** a plena calle, a plena luz, en plena luz del día. **It's d. robbery!** ¡Es un desuello! **d.-saving,** hora de verano, f

daytime n día, m. **in the d.,** durante el día

daze vt aturdir, confundir; (dazzle) deslumbrar. n aturdimiento, m, confusión, f; perplejidad, f

dazzle vt (camouflage) disfrazar; deslumbrar, ofuscar. n deslumbramiento, m; brillo, m, refulgencia, f

dazzling a deslumbrador; brillante

dead a and past part muerto; inanimado; (withered) marchito; (deep) profundo; (unconscious) inerte; inmóvil; insensible; (numb) entumecido; (complete) absoluto, completo; (sure) certero, excelente; (useless) inútil; (of color and human character) apagado; sin espíritu; inactivo; (of eyes) mortecino; (of sound) sordo, opaco; (of villages, etc.) desierto, despoblado; (quiet) silencioso; (empty) vacío; (monotonous) monótono; (of fire) apagado; (with weight, language) muerto; elec interrumpido; law muerto civilmente. adv completamente, enteramente; del todo; directamente; exactamente; profundamente. **the d.,** los muertos. **in the d. of night,** en las altas horas de la noche. **to be d.,** estar muerto; haber muerto. **to be d. against,** estar completamente opuesto a. **to drop d.,** caer muerto; morir de repente. **to go d. slow,** ir muy lentamente. **to rise from the d.,** resucitar. **to sham d.,** hacer la mortecina, fingirse muerto. **to speak ill of the d.,** hablar mal de los muertos; inf desenterrar los muertos. **d. ball,** pelota fuera de juego, f. **d.-beat,** muerto de cansancio. **d. body,** cadáver, cuerpo muerto, m. **d. calm,** calma profunda, f; naut calma chicha, f. **d. certainty,** seguridad completa, f. **d.-drunk,** hecho una uva. **d. end,** callejón sin salida, m. **d. heat,** empate, m. **d. language,** lengua muerta, f. **d.-letter,** letra muerta, f; carta devuelta o no reclamada, f. **d.-lock,** punto muerto, m. **to reach a d.-lock,** llegar a un punto muerto. **d. march,** marcha fúnebre, f. **d. season,** temporada de calma, f. **d. set,** empeñado (en). **d. shot,** (person) tirador (-ra) certero (-ra) (shot) tiro certero, m. **d. silence,** silencio profundo, m. **d. stop,** parada en seco, f. **d. tired,** rendido. **d. weight,** peso muerto, m. **d. wood,** leña seca, f; material inútil, m

deaden vt amortiguar; (of pain) calmar; (remove) quitar; (of colours) apagar

deadening n amortiguamiento, m

deadly a mortal; implacable; inf insoportable. adv mortalmente. **He was d. pale,** Estaba pálido como un muerto. **the seven d. sins,** los siete pecados mortales. **d. nightshade,** belladona, f

deadness n falta de vida, f; inercia, f; marchitez, f; (numbness) entumecimiento, m; desanimación, f; parálisis, f

Dead Sea, the el mar Muerto, m

deaf a sordo. **d. people,** los sordos. **to be d.,** ser sordo; padecer sordera. **to be as d. as a post,** ser más sordo que una tapia. **to become d.,** ensordecer, volverse sordo. **to fall on d. ears,** caer en saco roto. **to turn a d. ear,** hacerse el sordo. **d. aid**, audífono, m. **d.-and-dumb**, sordomudo. **d.-and-dumb alphabet**, alfabeto manual, abecedario manual, m. **d.-mute**, sordomudo (-da). **d.-mutism**, sordomudez, f

deafen vt asordar, ensordecer

deafening a ensordecedor

deafness n sordera, f

deal n (transaction) negocio, trato, m; (at cards) reparto, m; (wood) pino, m; (plank) tablón de pino, m. **a d., a great d.**, mucho. **a very great d.**, muchísimo. **to conclude a d.**, cerrar un trato

deal vt repartir; (a blow) asestar, dar; (cards) dar; (justice) dispensar. **to d. a blow at**, asestar un golpe; fig herir (en); fig destruir de un golpe. **to d. in**, comerciar en, traficar en; ocuparse en; meterse en. **to d. out**, dispensar. **to d. with**, (buy from) comprar de; tener relaciones con, tratar; entenderse con; portarse con; (of affairs) ocuparse en, arreglar, dirigir; (contend) luchar con; (discuss) discutir, tratar de; (of books) versar sobre. **d. regularly with** Lat. Am. amarchantarse con

dealer n traficante, mf mercader, m; Lat. Am. marchante (-ta) (at cards) el que da las cartas

dealing n conducta, f; proceder, m; trato, m; tráfico, m; pl **dealings**, relaciones, f pl; transacciones, f pl

dean n ecc deán, m; univ decano, m

dear a (beloved) querido, amado; (charming) encantador, simpático; (in letters) estimado, querido; (favorite) predilecto; (expensive) caro. n querido (-da); persona querida, f, bien amado (-da). adv caro. **Oh d.!** ¡Dios mío! ¡Ay!

dearly adv tiernamente, entrañablemente; caro

dearness n cariño, afecto, m, ternura, f; (of price) precio alto, m

dearth n carestía, f; (of news, etc.) escasez, f

death n muerte, f; (law and in announcements) fallecimiento, m, defunción, f. **to be at death's door**, estar a la muerte. **to put to d.**, ajusticiar. **to the d.**, a muerte. **untimely d.**, muerte repentina, f; malogro, m. **death's head**, calavera, f. **d. certificate**, partida de defunción, f. **d.-duties**, derechos de herencia, m pl. **d.-like**, cadavérico. **d.-mask**, mascarilla, f. **d. penalty**, pena de muerte, f. **d.-rate**, mortalidad, f. **d.-rattle**, sarrillo, m. **d.-trap**, lugar peligroso, m; fig trampa, f. **d.-warrant**, sentencia de muerte, f. **d.-watch bettle**, reloj de la muerte, m

deathbed n lecho mortuorio, lecho de muerte, m. **on one's d.**, en su lecho de muerte

deathblow n golpe mortal, m

deathly a mortal

death toll n (of a bell) doble, toque de difuntos, m; (casualties) número de muertos, saldo de muertos, m

debacle n fig ruina, f

debar vt excluir, privar

debase vt degradar, humillar, envilecer; (the coinage) alterar (la moneda)

debasement n degradación, humillación, f, envilecimiento, m; (of the coinage) alteración (de la moneda), f

debasing a degradante, humillante

debatable a discutible

debate n debate, m; discusión, f; disputa, f. vt and vi debatir; discutir; disputar; considerar

debating n discusión, f; argumentación, f

debauch vt corromper, pervertir; (a woman) seducir, violar. n libertinaje, m; borrachera, f

debauched a vicioso, licencioso

debauchery n libertinaje, mal vivir, m, viciosidad, licencia, f

debenture n obligación, f. **d. holder**, obligacionista, mf

debilitate vt debilitar

debit n débito, cargo, m; saldo deudor, m; "debe" de una cuenta, m. vt adeudar. **d. and credit**, el cargo y la data. **d. balance**, saldo deudor, m

debonair a gallardo, gentil, donairoso; alegre

débris n escombros, desechos, m pl; ruinas, f pl; geol despojos, m pl

debt n deuda, Lat. Am. also dita f. **a bad d.**, una deuda incobrable. **to be in the d. of**, ser en cargo a; deber dinero a; fig sentirse bajo una obligación. **to get into d.**, adeudarse, contraer deudas, Mexico endrogarse, elsewhere in Lat. Am. enditarse

debtor n deudor (-ra); com debe, m

debunk vt demoler

debut n (of a debutante) puesta de largo, f; (of a play, etc.) estreno, m. **to make one's d.**, ponerse de largo, presentarse en sociedad

debutante n debutante, f

decade n década, f, decenio, m; (of the rosary) decena, f

decadence n decadencia, f

decadent a decadente

decamp vi mil decampar; escaparse, fugarse

decant vt decantar

decanter n garrafa, f

decapitate vt decapitar, descabezar

decay vi (rot) pudrirse; degenerar; marchitarse; (of teeth) cariarse; (crumble) desmoronarse, caer en ruinas; decaer, declinar; (come down in the world) venir a menos, arruinarse. n pudrición, putrefacción, f; (of teeth) caries, f; (withering) marchitez, f; degeneración, f; desmoronamiento, m; ruina, f; (oldness) vejez, *f*; decadencia, declinación, *f*; (fall) caída, *f*

decease *n* fallecimiento, *m*, defunción, *f*, *vi* fallecer

deceased *n* finado (-da), difunto (-ta). *a* difunto

deceit *n* engaño, fraude, *m*; duplicidad, *f*

deceitful *a* engañoso, falso; embustero, mentiroso; ilusorio

deceitfulness *n* falsedad, duplicidad, *f*

deceivable *a* fácil a engañar, engañadizo

deceive *vt* engañar; (disappoint) decepcionar, desilusionar; frustrar. **If my memory does not d. me**, Si la memoria no me engaña, Si mal no me acuerdo

deceiver *n* engañador (-ra); seductor, *m*

deceiving *a* engañador

December *n* diciembre, *m*

decency *n* decoro, *m*, decencia, *f*; pudor, *m*, modestia, *f*; conveniencias, *f pl*; *inf* bondad, *f*; (manners) cortesía, *f*, buenos modales, *m pl*

decent *a* decente; decoroso, honesto; púdico; (likable) simpático; (of things) bastante bueno; (honorable) honrado

decentralize *vt* descentralizar

deception *n* engaño, *m*; ilusión, *f*

deceptive *a* engañoso, mentiroso, ilusorio

decide *vt* decidir; *law* determinar. *vi* decidir, resolver; acordar, quedar en; juzgar; *law* dictar sentencia, fallar

decided *a* decidido; (downright) categórico, inequívoco; resuelto; positivo; definitivo

decidedly *adv* decididamente; categóricamente; definitivamente

decimal *a* decimal. **d. fraction**, fracción decimal, *f*. **d. point**, punto decimal, *m*. **d. system**, sistema métrico, *m*

decimate *vt* diezmar

decipher *vt* descifrar; deletrear

decision *n* decisión, determinación, *f*; *law* sentencia, *f*, fallo, *m*; (agreement) acuerdo, *m*; (of character) firmeza, resolución, *f*

decisive *a* decisivo; terminante, conclusivo; crítico

decisiveness *n* carácter decisivo, *m*; firmeza, resolución, *f*; decisión, *f*

deck *n* cubierta, *f*; (of cards) baraja (de naipes), *f*. *vt* adornar, ataviar; decorar. **between decks**, entrecubiertas, *f pl*. **lower d.**, cubierta, *f*. **promenade d.**, cubierta de paseo, *f*. **upper d.**, cubierta superior, *f*. **d.-cabin**, camarote de cubierta, *m*. **d.-chair**, silla de cubierta, silla de tijera, silla extensible, *f*. **d.-hand**, marinero, estibador, *m*

declaim *vt* recitar. *vi* perorar, declamar

declamation *n* declamación, *f*

declamatory *a* declamatorio

declaration *n* declaración, *f*; manifiesto, *m*; proclamación, *f*

declaratory *a* declaratorio, declarativo

declare *vt* declarar; proclamar; afirmar; manifestar; confesar. *vi* declarar; *law* deponer, testificar. **to d. war (on)** declarar la guerra (a)

declaredly *adv* declaradamente, explícitamente, abiertamente

decline *n* declinación, decadencia, *f*; disminución, *f*; debilitación, *f*; (of the day) caída, *f*; (of stocks, shares) depresión, *f*; (illness) consunción, *f*; (fig setting) ocaso, *m*, *vi* declinar; inclinarse; decaer; disminuir; debilitarse; (refuse) negarse (a). *vt* (refuse) rechazar, rehusar; *gram* declinar; (avoid) evitar

declining *a* declinante. **in one's d. years**, en sus últimos años

declutch *vi* desembragar

decode *vt* descifrar

décolletee *a* escotado

decompose *vt* descomponer. *vi* descomponerse

decontaminate *vt* descontaminar

decontrol *vt* suprimir las restricciones sobre

decorate *vt* adornar (con), embellecer; (by painting, etc.) decorar, pintar; (honor) investir (con), condecorar

decoration *n* decoración, *f*; *theat* decorado, *m*; (honor) condecoración, *f*; ornamento, *m*

decorative *a* decorativo

decorator *n* decorador, *m*; (interior) adornista, *m*

decorous *a* decoroso, decente; correcto

decorum *n* decoro, *m*; corrección, *f*

decoy *n* señuelo, *m*; añagaza, *f*; (trap) lazo, *m*, trampa, *f*; *fig* añagaza, *f*. *vt* (birds) reclamar, atraer con señuelo; *fig* tentar (con), seducir (con). **d. bird**, pájaro de reclamo, *m*

decrease *n* disminución, *f*; baja, *f*; reducción, *f*; (of the moon, waters) mengua, *f*, *vi* decrecer, disminuir; bajar; menguar. *vt* disminuir; reducir

decreasingly *adv* de menos en menos

decree *n* decreto, *m*; edicto. *m*. *vi* and *vt* decretar, mandar

decrepit *a* decrépito

decry *vt* desacreditar, rebajar

dedicate *vt* dedicar; consagrar; destinar; aplicar; (a book, etc.) dedicar. **to d. oneself to**, dedicarse a, consagrarse a, entregarse a

dedication *n* dedicación, *f*; consagración, *f*; (of a book, etc.) dedicatoria, *f*

deduce *vt* derivar; deducir, inferir

deduct *vt* deducir; descontar

deduction *n* deducción, *f*; descuento, *m*

deed *n* acción, *f*; hecho, acto, *m*; hazaña, *f*; (reality) realidad, *f*; *law* escritura, *f*; *law* contrato, *m*. **d. of gift**, escritura de donación, *f*

deem *vt* juzgar, creer, estimar

deep a profundo; (wide) ancho; (low) bajo; (thick) espeso; (of colours) subido; (of sounds) grave, profundo; (immersed (in)) absorto (en); (of the mind) penetrante; (secret) secreto; (intense) intenso, hondo; (cunning) astuto, artero; (dark) oscuro; (of mourning) riguroso. *n poet* piélago, mar, *m*; profundidad, *f*; abismo, *m*, *adv* profundamente; a una gran profundidad. **to be in d. waters,** *fig* estar con el agua al cuello. **to be three feet d.,** tener tres pies de profundidad. **to be d. in,** estar absorto en; (of debt) estar cargado de. **three d.,** tres de fondo. **d. into the night,** hasta las altas horas de la noche. **d.-felt,** hondamente sentido. **d. mourning,** luto riguroso, *m*. **d.-rooted,** arraigado. **d.-sea fishing,** pesca mayor, *f*. **d.-sea lead,** escandallo, *m*. **d.-seated,** íntimo, profundo; arraigado. **d.-set,** hundido

deepen *vt* profundizar, ahondar; (broaden) ensanchar; (intensify) intensificar; (increase) aumentar; (of colors) aumentar el tono de, intensificar. *vi* hacerse más profundo, hacerse más hondo; intensificarse; aumentarse; (of sound) hacerse más grave

deeply *adv* profundamente; intensamente; fuertemente

deer *n* ciervo (-va), venado, *m*, a cervuno. **d.-hound,** galgo de cazar venados, *m*. **d.-skin,** piel de venado, *f*. **d.-stalking,** caza del ciervo, *f*

deface *vt* desfigurar, mutilar; estropear; (erase) borrar

defamation *n* difamación, denigración, *f*

defamatory *a* difamatorio, denigrante

defame *vt* difamar, denigrar, calumniar

default *n* omisión, *f*; descuido, *m*; falta, *f*; ausencia, *f*; *law* rebeldía, *f*. *vi* dejar de cumplir; faltar; no pagar. *vt law* condenar en rebeldía. **in d. of,** en la ausencia de

defaulter *n* el, *m*, (*f*, la) que no cumple sus obligaciones; delincuente, *mf*; desfalcador (-ra); *law* rebelde, *mf*

defeat *vt* vencer, derrotar; frustrar; (reject) rechazar; (elude) evitar; *fig* vencer, triunfar sobre. *n* derrota, *f*; vencimiento, *m*; frustración, *f*; rechazamiento, *m*. **to d. one's own ends,** defraudar sus intenciones

defeatist *n* derrotista, *mf*

defecate *vt* defecar

defect *n* defecto, *m*; imperfección, *f*; falta, *f*

defection *n* defección, *f*; deserción, *f*; (from a religion) apostasía, *f*

defective *a* defectuoso; *gram* defectivo; falto; imperfecto; (mentally) anormal. *n* persona anormal, *f*, anormal, *m*

defend *vt* defender; proteger; preservar; sostener; (a thesis) sustentar

defendant *n* *law* acusado (-da), procesado (-da), demandado (-da)

defender *n* defensor (-ra); (of a thesis) sustentante, *mf*

defense *n* defensa, *f*; justificación, *f*; *pl* **defenses,** defensas, *f pl*; obras de fortificación, *f pl*. **for the d.,** (of witnesses) de descargo; (of counsel) para la defensa. **in d. of,** en defensa de. **in one's own d.,** en su propia defensa. **d. in depth,** *mil* defensa en fondo, *f*

defenseless *a* indefenso, sin defensa

defensible *a* defendible; justificable

defensive *a* defensivo. *n* defensiva, *f*. **to be on the d.,** estar a la defensiva

defer *vt* (postpone) diferir, aplazar; suspender. *vi* (yield) deferir, ceder; (delay) tardar, aguardar. **deferred payment,** pago a plazos, *m*

deference *n* deferencia, *f*, respeto, *m*; consideración, *f*

deferential *a* deferente, respetuoso

deferment *n* aplazamiento, *m*; suspensión, *f*

defiance *n* desafío, *m*; provocación, *f*; oposición, *f*; insolencia, *f*. **in d. of,** en contra de

defiant *a* provocativo; insolente

defiantly *adv* de un aire provocativo; insolentemente

deficiency *n* falta, deficiencia, *f*; imperfección, *f*; defecto, *m*; omisión, *f*; (scarcity) carestía, *f*; (in accounts) déficit, *m*

deficient *a* deficiente; falto, incompleto; imperfecto; pobre; defectuoso; (not clever at) débil (en); (mentally) anormal. **to be d. in,** carecer de; ser pobre en

deficit *n* déficit, *m*; descubierto, *m*

defile *n* desfiladero, *m*. *vt* contaminar; profanar; manchar; deshonrar. *vi mil* desfilar

define *vt* definir; (throw into relief) destacar; fijar; *law* determinar

definite *a* definido; positivo; categórico; exacto; concreto. **d. article,** artículo definido, *m*

definitely *adv* positivamente; claramente. **definitely not!** ¡definitivamente no!

definition *n* definición, *f*

definitive *a* definitivo

deflate *vt* desinflar. *vi* desinflarse, deshincharse

deflation *n* desinflación, *f*

deflect *vt* desviar; apartar. *vi* desviarse; apartarse

deforestation *n* desforestación, desmontadura, despoblación forestal, *f*

deform *vt* deformar, desfigurar; afear

deformation *n* deformación, *f*

deformity *n* deformidad, *f*

defraud *vt* defraudar

defrauder *n* defraudador (-ra)

defray *vt* sufragar, costear, pagar

defrayal *n* pago, *m*

defrost *vt* deshelar

deft *a* diestro; hábil

deftly *adv* con destreza; hábilmente

defunct *a* and *n* difunto (-ta)

defy *vt* desafiar; (face) arrostrar; (violate) contravenir

degeneracy *n* degeneración, *f*; depravación, degradación, *f*

degenerate *a* and *n* degenerado (-da). *vi* degenerar

degeneration *n* degeneración, *f*

degradation *n* degradación, *f*; abyección, *f*

degrade *vt* degradar; envilecer, deshonrar

degrading *a* degradante

degree *n* grado, *m*; punto, *m*; clase social, *f*. **by degrees**, poco a poco, gradualmente, **five degrees below zero**, cinco grados bajo cero. **in the highest d.**, en sumo grado, en grado superlativo. **to a certain d.**, hasta cierto punto. **to receive a d.**, graduarse

degree-granting institution *n* plantel habilitado para expedir títulos, *m*

dehydrate *vt* deshidratar

de-ice *vt* deshelar

deify *vt* deificar, endiosar

deign *vi* dignarse. *vt* conceder

deity *n* deidad, divinidad, *f*; dios, *m*

dejected *a* abatido, desanimado, deprimido

dejection *n* abatimiento, desaliento, *m*; melancolía, *f*

delay *n* retraso, *m*, dilación, tardanza, demora, *f*. *vt* retrasar, demorar; (a person) entretener; (postpone) aplazar; (obstruct) impedir. *vi* tardar; entretenerse. **without more d.**, sin más tardar

delectable *a* deleitoso, delicioso

delegacy *n* delegación, *f*

delegate *n* delegado (-da). *vt* delegar, diputar

delegation *n* delegación, *f*

delete *vt* suprimir, borrar

deleterious *a* deletéreo

deletion *n* supresión, borradura, *f*

deliberate *a* premeditado, intencionado; (slow) pausado, lento. *vi* and *vt* deliberar, discurrir, considerar

deliberately *adv* (intentionally) con premeditación, a sabiendas, *Central America* adifés; (slowly) pausadamente, lentamente

deliberation *n* reflexión, deliberación, consideración, *f*; (slowness) lentitud, pausa, *f*

deliberative *a* deliberativo, de liberante

delicacy *n* delicadeza, *f*; fragilidad, *f*; suavidad, *f*; sensibilidad, *f*; escrupulosidad, *f*; (of health) debilidad, delicadez, *f*; (difficulty) dificultad, *f*; (food) manjar exquisito, *m*, golosina, *f*

delicate *a* delicado; fino; frágil; suave; exquisito; delicado (de salud); (of situations) difícil

delicatessen *n* (store) fiambrería, *f*

delicious *a* delicioso

deliciousness *n* deleite, *m*, lo delicioso; excelencia, *f*; delicias, *f pl*

delight *n* deleite, regocijo, *m*; encanto, *m*, delicia, *f*; placer, gozo, *m*. *vt* deleitar, encantar; halagar. *vi* deleitarse, complacerse. **to be delighted with**, estar encantado con. **to d. in**, deleitarse en, complacerse en; tomar placer en

delightful *a* delicioso, precioso, encantador

delimit *vt* delimitar

delimitation *n* delimitación, *f*

delineate *vt* delinear, diseñar; *fig* pintar, describir

delinquency *n* delincuencia, *f*; criminalidad, *f*; culpa, *f*; delito, *m*

delinquent *a* delincuente. *n* delincuente, *mf*

delirious *a* delirante; desvariado; *inf* loco. **to be d.**, delirar, desvariar

delirium *n* delirio, desvarío, *m*. **d. tremens**, delírium tremens, *m*

deliver *vt* librar (de); salvar (de); (distribute) repartir; (hand over) entregar; (recite) recitar, decir; (a speech) pronunciar; comunicar; (send) despachar, expedir; (a blow) asestar; (give) dar; (bring) traer; (battle, a lecture) dar; (a woman, of a doctor) asistir en el parto (a); (a child) traer al mundo; (a judgment) pronunciar. **to be delivered (of a child)**, dar a luz. **to d. oneself up**, entregarse. **delivered free**, porte pagado.

deliverance *n* libramiento, rescate, *m*; redención, salvación, *f*; (of a judgment) pronuncia, *f*

deliverer *n* libertador (-ra); salvador (-ra); (distributor) repartidor (-ra); entregador (-ra)

delivery *n* (distribution) reparto, *m*, distribución, *f*; entrega, *f*; *law* cesión, *f*; (of a judgment) pronuncia, *f*; (of a speech) pronunciación, *f*; (manner of speaking) declamación, *f*; dicción, *f*; (of a child) parto, *m*. **on d.**, al entregarse. **The letter came by the first d.**, La carta llegó en el primer reparto. **d. man**, mozo de reparto, *m*. **d. note**, nota de entrega, *f*. **d. van**, camión de reparto, *m*

delivery truck *n* camioneta de reparto, furgoneta, *f*, sedán de reparto, *m*

dell *n* hondonada, *f*; pequeño valle, *m*

delouse *vt* despiojar, espulgar

delta *n* (Greek letter) delta, *f*; (of a river) delta, *m*

delude *vt* engañar; ilusionar. **to d. oneself**, engañarse

deluded *a* iluso, engañado, ciego

deluge *n* diluvio, *m*. *vt* diluviar; inundar (con)

delusion n engaño, m, ceguedad, f; error, m; ilusión, f

delve vt and vi cavar; fig ahondar (en), penetrar (en), investigar

demagogic a demagógico

demagogue n demagogo (-ga)

demagogy n demagogia, f

demand n exigencia, f; com demanda, f; petición, f; pol econ consumo, m. vt exigir; requerir; pedir; (claim) reclamar. **in d.,** en demanda. **on d.,** al solicitarse. **to be in d.,** ser popular. **d. note,** apremio, m

demanding a exigente

demarcate vt demarcar

demean (oneself) vr degradarse, rebajarse

demeanor n conducta, f; continente, porte, aire, m; (manners) modales, m pl

demented a demente, loco

demerit n demérito, m

demi prefix semi; casi. **d.-tasse,** taza cafetera, jícara, f

demijohn n damajuana, f

demilitarize vt desmilitarizar

demise n law traslación de dominio, f; sucesión de la corona, f; (death) óbito, fallecimiento, m

demobilization n desmovilización, f

demobilize vt desmovilizar

democracy n democracia, f

democrat n demócrata, mf

democratic a democrático. **to make d.,** democratizar

demolish vt demoler, derribar; fig destruir; (eat) engullir, devorar

demolisher n demoledor, m; fig destructor (-ra)

demolition n demolición, f; derribo, m, a demoledor; de demolición. **d. squad,** pelotón de demolición, m

demon n demonio, diablo, m

demoniacal a demoníaco

demonstrate vt demostrar; mostrar; probar. vi hacer una demostración

demonstration n demostración, f; manifestación, f

demonstrative a demostrativo; (of persons) expresivo, mimoso. **d. pronoun,** pronombre demostrativo, m

demoralization n desmoralización, f

demoralize vt desmoralizar

demoralizing a desmoralizador

demur vi dudar, vacilar; objetar, protestar; poner dificultades. n objeción, protesta, f

demure a serio, modoso recatado; púdico; de una coquetería disimulada

demurely adv modestamente; con recato; con coquetería disimulada

demureness n seriedad, f, recato, m; modestia fingida, coquetería disimulada, f

demy n papel marquilla, m; becario de Magdalen College, Oxford, m

den n madriguera, guardia, f; (of thieves) cueva, f; (in a zoo) cercado, recinto, m; (study) gabinete, m; (squalid room) cuartucho, m

denaturalize vt desnaturalizar

denial n negación, f; rechazo, m; contradicción, f; negativa, f

denizen n habitante, m; ciudadano (-na)

Denmark Dinamarca, f

denominate vt denominar, nombrar

denomination n denominación, f; secta, f; clase, f

denominational a sectario

denominator n math denominador, m

denote vt denotar, indicar; significar

dénouement n desenlace, desenredo, m; solución, f

denounce vt denunciar; delatar, acusar

denouncer n denunciante, mf delator (-ra)

dense a denso; espeso, compacto; tupido; impenetrable; inf estúpido

densely adv densamente; espesamente. **d. populated,** con gran densidad de población

density n densidad, f; espesor, m; consistencia, f; inf estupidez, f

dent n mella, f; (in metal) abolladura, f, vt mellar; abollar

dental a dental. n letra dental, f. **d. forceps,** gatillo, m. **d. mechanic,** mecánico dentista, m. **d. surgeon,** odontólogo, m

dental floss n seda dental, f

dentist n dentista, mf; odontólogo, m

dentistry n odontología, f

denture n dentadura, f

denude vt denudar, despojar, privar (de)

denunciation n denuncia, f; acusación, delación, f

denunciatory a denunciatorio

Denver boot n cepo, m

deny vt negar; desmentir; rehusar; rechazar; renegar (de); (give up) renunciar, sacrificar. **to d. oneself,** privarse (de); sacrificar; negarse

deodorant a and n desodorante m.

deodorize vt desinfectar, destruir el olor de

depart vi marcharse, irse, partir; (of trains, etc., and meaning go out) salir; (deviate) desviarse (de), apartarse (de); (go away) alejarse; (leave) dejar; (disappear) desaparecer; (alter) cambiar; (die) morir

departed a (past) pasado; desaparecido; (dead) difunto, muerto. n difunto (-ta)

department n departamento, m; sección, f; (of learning) ramo, m; (in France) distrito administrativo, m. **d. store,** grandes tiendas, f pl, (Argentina), grandes almacenes, m pl

departmental a departamental

departure n partida, ida, f Lat. Am. egreso m; (going out, and of trains, etc.) salida, f; (deviation) desviación, el apartarse. **d. from the rules,** el apartarse de las reglas, f; (disappearance) desaparición, f; (change) cambio, m; (giving up) renuncia, f; (death) muerte, f. **to take one's d.,** marcharse

depend vi depender. **to d. on,** depender de; (rest on) apoyarse en; (count on) contar con; (trust) fiarse de; tener confianza en, estar seguro de. **That depends!** ¡Eso depende!

dependable a digno de confianza; seguro

dependence, dependency n dependencia, f; subordinación, f; (trust) confianza, f

dependent a dependiente; subordinado; condicional. n dependiente, m. **to be d. on,** depender de

depict vt representar; pintar; dibujar; fig describir, retratar

depiction n representación, f; pintura, f; dibujo, m; fig descripción, f

depilate vt depilar

depilatory a and n depilatorio m.

deplete vt agotar; disipar

depletion n agotamiento, m

deplorable a lamentable, deplorable

deplore vt deplorar, lamentar

deploy vt desplegar. vi desplegarse. n despliegue, m

deployment n despliegue, m

depopulate vt despoblar

deport vt deportar

deportation n deportación, f

deportment n comportamiento, m; porte, aire, m; conducta, f

depose vt destronar; (give evidence) testificar, declarar

deposit n depósito, m; geol yacimiento, filón, m; sedimento, m. vt depositar. **to leave a d.,** dejar un depósito. **d. account,** cuenta corriente, f

deposition n deposición, f; law testimonio, m, declaración, Lat. Am. contancia f; (from the Cross) descendimiento, m, (de la Cruz)

depositor n depositador (-ra)

depository n depositaría, f, almacén, m; (of knowledge, etc.) pozo, m

depot n almacén, m; (military headquarters) depósito, m; (for army vehicles, etc.) parque, m; (for buses, etc.) estación, f

depravation n depravación, f

depraved a depravado, perverso, vicioso

depravity n corrupción, maldad, perversión, f

deprecate vt desaprobar, criticar; lamentar, deplorar

deprecatingly adv con desaprobación, críticamente

deprecation n deprecación, f; desaprobación, crítica, f

deprecatory a deprecativo; de desaprobación, de crítica

depreciate vt depreciar, rebajar; fig tener en poco, menospreciar. vi depreciarse, deteriorarse; bajar de precio

depreciation n (in value) amortización, depreciación, f; fig desprecio, m

depredation n depredación, f

depress vt deprimir; (weaken) debilitar; (humble) humillar; (dispirit) abatir, entristecer; (trade) desanimar, paralizar

depressed a deprimido, desalentado, melancólico, triste; (of an area) necesitado

depressing a melancólico, triste; pesimista

depression n depresión, f; (hollow) hoyo, m; (sadness) desaliento, abatimiento, m, melancolía, f; (in prices) baja, f; (in trade) desanimación, parálisis, f; ast depresión, f

deprivation n privación, f; pérdida, f

deprive vt privar (de), despojar (de); defraudar (de); ecc destituir (de)

depth n profundidad, f; (thickness) espesor, m; fondo, m; (of night, winter, the country) medio, m; (of sound) gravedad, f; (of colour, feeling) intensidad, f; (abstruseness) dificultad, f; (sagacity) sagacidad, f; pl **depths,** profundidades, f pl; abismo, m; lo más hondo; lo más íntimo. **to be 4 feet in d.,** tener cuatro pies de profundidad. **to the depths of one's being,** hasta lo más íntimo de su ser; hasta los tuétanos. **d. charge,** carga de profundidad, f

deputize (for) vi desempeñar las funciones de, substituir

deputy n (substitute) lugarteniente, m; (agent) representante, m; apoderado, m; (parliamentary) diputado, m; (in compounds) sub, vice. **d.-governor,** subgobernador, m. **d.-head,** subjefe, m; (of a school) subdirector (-ra)

derail vt (hacer) descarrilar, Lat. Am. desrielar

derailment n descarrilamiento, m

derange vt desordenar; desorganizar; turbar; (mentally) trastornar, hacer perder el juicio (a)

derangement n desorden, m; turbación, f; (mental) trastorno, m, locura, f

derby n carrera del Derby, f; (hat) sombrero hongo, m

deregulate vt desregular

derelict a abandonado, derrelicto. n derrelicto, m

dereliction n abandono, m; omisión, negligencia, f; descuido, m

deride vt burlarse de, mofarse de; ridiculizar

derision n irrisión, f, menosprecio, m

derisive a irrisorio; irónico

derivation n derivación, f

derivative a derivativo. n derivado, m

derive vt derivar; obtener; extraer; fig sacar, hallar. vi (from) derivar de; proceder de; remontar a

dermatologist n dermatólogo, m

derogatory a despectivo, despreciativo; deshonroso

derrick n grúa, machina, f; abanico, m

descant n mus discante, m. vi mus discantar; discurrir (sobre), disertar (sobre)

descend vi descender, bajar; (be inherited) pasar a; (fall) caer; (of the sun) ponerse. vt bajar. **to d. from,** descender de. **to d. to,** (lower oneself) rebajarse; (consider) venir a, considerar. **to d. upon,** caer sobre; (arrive unexpectedly) llegar inesperadamente, invadir

descendant n descendiente, mf; pl **descendants,** descendencia, f

descent n descenso, m; bajada, f; (slope) pendiente, cuesta, f; (attack) invasión, f, ataque, m; (lineage) descendencia, alcurnia, procedencia, f; (inheritance) herencia, f; transmisión, f. **D. from the Cross,** Descendimiento de la Cruz, m

describe vt describir; pintar

description n descripción, f

descriptive a descriptivo

descry vt divisar, descubrir; poet ver

desecrate vt profanar

desert vt abandonar; dejar; (mil etc.) desertar. vi desertar. a solitario; inhabitado; desierto; fig árido. n desierto, m; soledad, f; (merit) mérito, m. **to receive one's deserts,** llevar su merecido

deserted a abandonado; desierto; solitario; inhabitado, despoblado

deserter n desertor, m

desertion n abandono, m, deserción, f; (mil etc.) deserción, f

deserve vt and vi merecer

deserving a merecedor; meritorio. **to be d. of,** merecer

desiccate vt desecar. vi desecarse

design n proyecto, m; plan, m; intención, f, propósito, m; objeto, m; modelo, m; (pattern) diseño, dibujo, m; arte del dibujo, mf. vt idear; proyectar; (destine) destinar, dedicar; diseñar, dibujar, delinear; planear. **by d.,** expresamente, intencionalmente

designate vt señalar; designar; (appoint) nombrar. a electo

designation n designación, f; nombramiento, m

designer n inventor (-ra), autor (-ra); delineador (-ra); dibujante, mf; (of public works, etc.) proyectista, mf

designing a intrigante, astuto

desirability n lo deseable; conveniencia, f; ventaja, f

desirable a deseable; conveniente; ventajoso; agradable; apetecible

desire vt desear; querer; ansiar, ambicionar; (request) rogar, pedir; (order) mandar. n deseo, m; ansia, aspiración, f; ambición, f; impulso, m; (will) voluntad, f. **to d. ardently,** perecerse por; suspirar por

desirous a deseoso (de); ambicioso (de); ansioso (de); impaciente (a); curioso (de)

desist vi desistir; dejar (de)

desk n pupitre, m; escritorio, buró, m; mesa de trabajo, f; (cashier's) caja, f; (teacher's, lecturer's; pulpit) cátedra, f

desolate a solitario; desierto; deshabitado; abandonado; arruinado; árido; (afflicted) desolado, angustiado. vt desolar; despoblar

desolation n desolación, f; aflicción, angustia, f, desconsuelo, m

despair n desesperación, f, vi perder toda esperanza. **His life is despaired of,** Se ha perdido la esperanza de salvarle (la vida). **to be in d.,** estar desesperado

despairing a desesperado

despairingly adv sin esperanza

desperate a desesperado; sin esperanza; irremediable; furioso; violento; (dangerous) arriesgado, peligroso; terrible

desperately adv desesperadamente; furiosamente; terriblemente

desperation n desesperación, f; furia, violencia, f

despicable a vil, despreciable; insignificante

despise vt despreciar; desdeñar

despite prep a pesar de

despoil vt despojar, desnudar

despoliation n despojo, m

despondency n abatimiento, desaliento, m, desesperación, f

despondent a abatido, desanimado, deprimido

despot n déspota, m

despotic a despótico .

dessert n postre, m, a de postre. **d. plate,** plato para postre, m. **d.-spoon,** cuchara de postre, f

destination n destinación, f

destine vt destinar; dedicar; predestinar

destiny n destino, m

destitute a indigente, menesteroso; desnudo (de); privado (de); desprovisto (de), falto (de); desamparado

destitution n destitución, indigencia, miseria, f; privación, falta, f; desamparo, m

destroy vt destruir; demoler; deshacer; (kill) matar; exterminar; (finish) acabar con

destroyer n destructor (-ra); nav destructor, cazatorpedero, m

destruction n destrucción, f; demolición,

f; ruina, *f*; pérdida, *f*; muerte, *f*; exterminio, *m*; perdición, *f*

destructive *a* destructivo, destructor; (of animals) dañino. **d. animal,** animal dañino, *m*, alimaña, *f*

destructiveness *n* destructividad, *f*; instinto destructor, *m*

desultory *a* inconexo; sin método, descosido; irregular

detach *vt* separar, desprender; (unstick) despegar; *mil* destacar

detachable *a* separable, de quita y pon

detached *a* suelto, separado; (*fig* with outlook, etc.) imparcial; indiferente, despegado. **d. house,** hotelito, *m*

detachment *n* separación, *f*; *mil* destacamento, *m*; (*fig* of mind) imparcialidad, *f*; independencia (de espíritu, etc.), *f*; indiferencia, *f*

detail *n* detalle, *m*; pormenor, *m*, particularidad, *f*; circunstancia, *f*; *mil* destacamento, *m*. *vt* detallar; particularizar, referir con pormenores; *mil* destacar. **in d.,** detalladamente; al por menor; *inf* ce por be. **to go into details,** entrar en detalles

detain *vt* detener; (arrest) arrestar, prender; (withhold) retener; (prevent) impedir

detect *vt* descubrir; averiguar; (discern) discernir, percibir; *elec* detectar

detection *n* descubrimiento, *m*; averiguación, *f*; percepción, *f*

detective *n* detective, *m*, a de detectives, policíaco. **d. novel,** novela policíaca, *f*

detector *n* descubridor, *m*; *elec* detector, *m*; *mech* indicador, *m*

detention *n* detención, *f*; (arrest) arresto, *m*; (confinement) encierro, *m*

deter *vt* desanimar, desalentar; acobardar; (dissuade) disuadir; (prevent) impedir

detergent *a* detersorio. *n* detersorio, *m*

deteriorate *vt* deteriorar. *vi* deteriorarse; empeorar

deterioration *n* deterioración, *f*; empeoramiento, *m*

determination *n* determinación, *f*; definición, *f*; resolución, decisión, *f*; *law* fallo, *m*; *med* congestión, *f*

determine *vt* determinar; definir; decidir, resolver; concluir; (fix) señalar; *law* sentenciar. *vi* resolverse, decidirse; (insist (on)) empeñarse en, insistir en

determined *a* determinado; resuelto, decidido; (of price) fijo

deterrent *a* disuasivo. *n* freno, *m*. **to act as a d.,** servir como un freno

deterrent capability *n* poder de disuasión, *m*

detest *vt* detestar, abominar, aborrecer

detestable *a* detestable, aborrecible, abominable

detestation *n* detestación, abominación, *f*, aborrecimiento, *m*

detonate *vt* hacer detonar. *vi* detonar, estallar

detonation *n* detonación, *f*

detour *n* rodeo, *m*; desvío, *m*, desviación, *f*

detract *vt* quitar; (diminish) disminuir; (slander) detraer, denigrar

detriment *n* detrimento, *m*; perjuicio, *m*; daño, *m*

detrimental *a* perjudicial

Deuteronomy *n* Deuteronomio, *m*

devaluation *n* desvalorización, *f*

devalue *vt* rebajar el valor de

devastate *vt* devastar, asolar

devastation *n* devastación, *f*

develop *vt* desarrollar; (make progress) avanzar, fomentar; perfeccionar; *phot* revelar. *vi* desarrollarse; crecer; avanzar, progresar; evolucionar

developer *n* *phot* revelador, *m*

development *n* desarrollo, *m*; evolución, *f*; progreso, avance, *m*; (encouragement) fomento, *m*; (event) acontecimiento, suceso, *m*; (product) producto, *m*; (working) explotación, *f*; *phot* revelación, *f*

deviate *vi* desviarse (de); (disagree) disentir (de)

deviation *n* desviación, *f*

device *n* (contrivance) aparato, artefacto, mecanismo, *m*; (invention) invento, *m*; (trick) expediente, artificio, *m*; (scheme) proyecto, *m*; (design) dibujo, emblema, *m*; (motto) divisa, leyenda, *f*; *pl* **devices,** placeres, caprichos, *m*

devil *n* diablo, Satanás, *m*; demonio, *m*; (printer's) aprendiz de impresor, *m*. **Go to the d.!** ¡Vete enhoramala! **He is a poor d.,** Es un pobre diablo. **little d.,** diablillo, *m*. **The devil's abroad,** Anda el diablo suelto. **The d. take it!** ¡Lléveselo el diablo! **to play the d. with,** arruinar por completo. **What the d.!** ¡Qué diablos! **d.-possessed,** endemoniado

devilish *a* diabólico, demoníaco; infernal

devious *a* desviado; tortuoso

deviousness *n* tortuosidad, *f*

devise *vt* idear, inventar; fabricar; *law* legar

deviser *n* inventor (-ra)

devitalize *vt* restar vitalidad, privar de vitalidad

devoid *a* desprovisto (de), privado (de); libre (de), exento (de)

devolve *vt* traspasar, transmitir. *vi* (on, upon) incumbir (a), corresponder (a), tocar (a)

devote *vt* dedicar; consagrar. **to d. oneself to,** darse a, dedicarse a; consagrarse a

devoted *a* fervoroso, apasionado; (faithful) fiel, leal

devotedly adv con devoción

devotee n devoto (-ta), admirador (-ra); aficionado (-da)

devotion n devoción, f; dedicación, f; (zeal) celo, m; afición, f; (loyalty) lealtad, f; pl **devotions**, rezos, m pl, oraciones, f pl

devotional a devoto, religioso, de devoción.

devour vt devorar; consumir

devouring a devorador; absorbente

devout a devoto, piadoso, practicante (e.g., **a d. Catholic,** un católico practicante)

devoutly adv piadosamente

dew n rocío, sereno, relente, m; fig rocío, m, vt rociar; humedecer; (refresh) refrescar. **d.-drop,** aljófar, m, gota de rocío, f

dexterity n destreza, f

dextrine n dextrina, f

dextrose n dextrosa, glucosa, f

dextrous a diestro; hábil, listo

diabetes n diabetes, f

diabetic a diabético

diabolical a diabólico

diagnose vt diagnosticar

diagnosis n diagnóstico, m, diagnosis, f

diagnostician n diagnóstico, m

diagonal n diagonal, f

diagram n diagrama, m; esquema, f; gráfico, m

dial n (sundial) reloj de sol, m; (of clocks, gas-meter) esfera, f; (of machines) indicador, m; (of a wireless set) cuadrante graduado, m; (of a telephone) marcador, disco, m. vt (a telephone number) marcar. **d. telephone,** teléfono automático, m

dialect n dialecto, m, habla, f, a dialectal

dialogue n diálogo, m. **to hold a d.,** dialogar

dialysis n diálisis, f

diameter n diámetro, m

diametrical a diametral

diamond n diamante, m; brillante, m; (tool) cortavidrios, m; (cards) oros (de baraja), m pl. **rough d.,** diamante bruto, m. **d.-bearing,** diamantífero. **d. cutter,** diamantista, mf **d. cutting,** talla de diamantes, f. **d. edition,** edición diamante, f. **d.-like,** adiamantado. **d. wedding,** bodas de diamante, f pl

diaper n lienzo adamascado, m; (baby's) pañal, m; (woman's) servilleta higiénica, f

diaphanous a diáfano, transparente

diaphragm n diafragma, m

diarrhea n diarrea, f

diary n diario, m

diastole n diástole, f

diatribe n diatriba, denunciación violenta, f

dice n pl dados, m pl. **to load the d.,** cargar los dados

dicky n (front) pechera postiza, f; (seat) trasera, f; (apron) delantal, m. **d. seat,** inf ahí te pudras, m

dictaphone n dictáfono, m

dictate vt dictar; mandar. n (order) dictamen, m; fig dictado, m

dictation n dictado, m. **to write from d.,** escribir al dictado

dictator n dictador, m

dictatorial a dictatorial, dictatorio, imperioso

dictatorship n dictadura, f

diction n dicción, f

dictionary n diccionario, m

didactic a didáctico

die vi morir; fallecer, finar; (wither) marchitarse; (disappear) desvanecerse, desaparecer; (of light) palidecer; extinguirse; (end) cesar; (desire) ansiar, perecerse (por). **Never say die!** ¡Mientras hay vida, hay esperanza! **to die early,** morir temprano; malograrse. **to die a violent death,** tener una muerte violenta, inf morir vestido. **to die from natural causes,** morir por causas naturales; inf morir en la cama. **to die hard,** luchar contra la muerte; tardar en morir; tardar en desaparecer. **to die of a broken heart,** morir con el corazón destrozado, morir de pena. **to die away,** desaparecer gradualmente; extinguirse poco a poco; dejar de oírse poco a poco; cesar; pasar. **to die down,** extinguirse gradualmente; palidecer; dejar de oírse; desaparecer; (of the wind) amainar; perder su fuerza. **to die out,** desaparecer; olvidarse; dejar de existir; pasarse de moda

die n dado, m; fig suerte, f; (stamp) cuño, troquel, m; arch cubo, m. **The die is cast,** La suerte está echada. **die-sinker,** grabador en hueco, m

diehard n valiente, m; tradicionalista empedernido, m; partidario (-ia) entusiasta

diesel a Diesel. **d. engine,** motor Diesel, m

diet n dieta, f, régimen dietario, m; (assembly) dieta, f. vi estar a dieta, hacer régimen

dietetic a dietético

dietician n dietista, mf

differ vi diferenciarse; (contradict) contradecir; (disagree) no estar de acuerdo; disentir

difference n diferencia, f; disparidad, f; contraste, m; (of opinion) disensión, f; controversia, disputa, f. **to make no d.,** no hacer diferencia alguna; no afectar; dar lo mismo, no importar

different a distinto; diferente; vario, diverso

differential a diferencial. **d. calculus,** cálculo diferencial, m

differentiate vt diferenciar, distinguir. vi diferenciarse, distinguirse

differentiation n diferenciación, f

difficult a difícil. **to make d.,** dificultar

difficulty n dificultad, f. **d. in breathing,** opresión de pecho, f

diffidence n modestia, timidez, f; huraña, f; falta de confianza en sí mismo, f

diffident a modesto, tímido; huraño; sin confianza en sí mismo

diffract vt difractar

diffuse vt difundir. a difuso; (long-winded) prolijo

diffusion n difusión, f; esparcimiento, m; diseminación, f

dig vt and vi cavar; excavar; (of animals) escarbar; (mine) zapar, minar; (into a subject) ahondar (en); (with the spurs) aguijonear, dar con las espuelas; (poke) clavar. **to dig one's heels in** Lat. Am. encabestrarse **to dig in,** enterrarse; mil abrir trincheras; inf arreglarse las cosas. **to dig out,** excavar; sacar cavando, sacar con azadón; extraer. **to dig up,** desenterrar; descubrir

digest vt clasificar; codificar; (food, also chem. and fig. tolerate and think over) digerir; (of knowledge and territory) asimilar. vi digerir. n compendio, resumen, m; law digesto, m; recopilación, f. **This food is easy to d.,** Este alimento es fácil de digerir; Este alimento es muy ligero

digestible a digerible, digestible

digestion n digestión, f; (of ideas) asimilación, f; chem digestión, f

digestive a digestivo

digger n cavador (-ra)

digging n cavadura, f; excavación, f; pl **diggings,** minas, f pl; excavaciones, f pl; inf alojamiento, m, posada, f

digit n dígito, m

digital a digital, dígito

digitalin n digitalina, f

digitalis n digital, f

dignified a serio, grave; majestuoso; (worthy) digno; solemne; altivo; noble

dignify vt dignificar, honrar; exaltar; dar dignidad (a); ennoblecer

dignitary n dignatario, m; dignidad, f

dignity n dignidad, f; (rank) rango, m; (post) cargo, puesto, m; (honor) honra, f; (stateliness) majestad, f; mesura, seriedad, f; (haughtiness) altivez, f; (nobility) nobleza, f. **to stand on one's d.,** darse importancia

digress vi divagar

digression n digresión, divagación, f

dike n dique, m; (ditch) acequia, f; canal, m; (embankment) zanja, f, vt represar

dilapidated a arruinado, destartalado; (of fortune) dilapidado; (of persons, families) venido a menos; (shabby) raído

dilate vt dilatar; ensanchar. vi dilatarse. **to d. upon,** extenderse sobre, dilatarse en

dilatory a dilatorio, tardo; (slow) lento

dilemma n dilema, m

dilettante n diletante, m; aficionado (-da)

dilettantism n diletantismo, m

diligence n diligencia, f; asiduidad, f; (care) cuidado, m; (coach) diligencia, f

diligent a diligente, asiduo, aplicado, industrioso; (painstaking) concienzudo

dilute vt diluir; fig adulterar. a diluido

dilution n dilución, f; fig adulteración, f

dim a (of light) apagado, débil, tenue; (of sight) turbio; (dark) sombrío, oscuro; (blurred, etc.) empañado; indistinto, confuso. vt obscurecer; empañar; (dazzle) ofuscar; (eclipse) eclipsar; reducir la intensidad (de una luz); (of memories) borrar. **dim intelligence,** de brumoso seso

dimension n dimensión, f; (size) tamaño, m; (scope) extensión, f, alcance, m

diminish vt disminuir; reducir; debilitar, atenuar. vi disminuir; reducirse; debilitarse, atenuarse

diminishing a menguante

diminution n disminución, f; reducción, f; atenuación, f

diminutive a diminutivo. n diminutivo, m

dimly adv obscuramente; vagamente; indistintamente. **dimly lit,** apenas alumbrado

dimness n oscuridad, f; deslustre, m; (of light) tenuidad (de la luz), f; confusión, f

dimple n hoyuelo, m

dimpled a con hoyuelos, que tiene hoyuelos

din n estrépito, estruendo, ruido, m; algarabía, barahúnda, f, vt ensordecer

dine vi (in the evening) cenar; (at midday) comer. vt convidar a cenar or a comer. **to d. out,** cenar or comer fuera

diner n (on a train) coche comedor, coche restaurante, m; cenador, m; comedor, m

dinghy n lancha, f; canoa, f, bote, m. **rubber d.,** canoa de goma, f

dingy a deslucido, empañado; sucio; oscuro; (of persons) desaseado

dining car n coche comedor, vagón restaurante, m

dining room n comedor, m; refectorio, m

dining table n mesa del comedor, f

dinner n (in the evening) cena, f; (at midday) comida, f. **over the d. table,** de sobremesa. **d.-jacket,** smoking, m. **d. party,** cena, f. **d. plate,** plato, m. **d. roll,** panecillo, m. **d. service,** vajilla, f

dinosaur n dinosauro, m

dint (by d. of) a fuerza de, a costa de

diocese n diócesis, f

dip n inmersión, f; baño, m; (in the ground) declive, m; (in the road) columpio, m, depresión, f; (slope) pendiente, f; (candle) vela de sebo, f; (of the horizon) depresión (del horizonte), f; (of the needle) inclinación (de la aguja), *f*. *vt* sumergir; bañar; (put) poner. *vi* inclinarse hacia abajo. **to dip into a book,** hojear un libro. **to dip the colors,** saludar con la bandera. **to dip the headlights,** bajar los faros

diphtheria *n* difteria, *f*

diploma *n* diploma, *m*

diplomacy *n* diplomacia, *f*; tacto, *m*

diploma mill *n* fábrica de títulos académicos, *f*

diplomat *n* diplomático, *m*

diplomatic *a* diplomático. **d. bag,** valija diplomática, *f*. **d. corps,** cuerpo diplomático, *m*

dipper *n* (ladle) cazo, *m*; *ast* Osa Mayor, *f*

dipsomaniac *n* dipsómano (-na) ·

dire *a* espantoso, horrible; cruel; funesto

direct *a* directo; claro, inequívoco; (of descent) recto; (of electric current) continuo; exacto. *adv* directamente. *vt* dirigir; (command) ordenar, encargar; dar instrucciones. **d. action,** acción directa, *f*. **d. current,** corriente continua, *f*. **d. line,** línea directa, *f*; (of descent) línea recta, *f*. **d. object,** acusativo, *m*. **d. speech,** oración directa, *f*

direct dialing *n* discado directo, *m*

direction *n* dirección, *f*; rumbo, *m*; instrucción, *f*; (on a letter) sobrescrito, *m*; señas, *f pl*. **in the d. of,** en la dirección de; hacia; *naut* con rumbo a. **in all directions,** por todas partes; a los cuatro vientos. **to go in the d. of,** ir en la dirección de; tomar por. **Directions for use,** Direcciones para el uso. **d. indicator, d. signal,** (on car) indicador de dirección, *m*

directive *a* directivo, director

directness *n* derechura, *f*

director *n* director (-triz, -ora), **managing d.,** director gerente, *m*

directory *n* directorio, *m*, guía, *f*. **telephone d.,** guía de teléfonos, *f*

dirge *n* endecha, *f*, lamento, *m*; canto fúnebre, *m*

dirt *n* mugre, suciedad, *f*; (mud) lodo, *m*; (earth) tierra, *f*; (dust) polvo, *m*; *fig* inmundicia, *f*. **d.-cheap,** sumamente barato. **to be d. cheap,** (of goods) estar por los suelos. **d.-track,** pista de ceniza, *f*. **d.-track racing,** carreras en pista de ceniza, *f pl*

dirtiness *n* suciedad, *f*; (untidiness) desaseo, *m*; sordidez, *f*; (meanness) bajeza, *f*

dirty *a* sucio, *Central America* descacharrado; (untidy) desaseado; (muddy) enlodado; (dusty) polvoriento; (of weather) borrascoso; (sordid) sórdido; (base, mean) vil; (indecent) indecente, verde, obsceno. *vt* ensuciar. **d. trick,** mala pasada, *Lat. Am.* chancada *f*

disability *n* incapacidad, *f*; impotencia, *f*; desventaja, *f*

disable *vt* (cripple) estropear, tullir; hacer

incapaz (de), incapacitar; imposibilitar; (destroy) destruir; *law* incapacitar legalmente

disabled *a* inválido; impedido, lisiado; (in the hand) manco; incapacitado; (of ships, etc.) fuera de servicio, estropeado. **d. soldier,** inválido, *m*

disablement *n* (physical) invalidez, *f*; inhabilitación, *f*; *law* impedimento, *m*

disabuse *vt* desengañar, sacar de un error

disadvantage *n* desventaja, *f*. **to be under the d. of,** sufrir la desventaja de

disadvantaged *a* (financially) de escasos recursos

disadvantageous *a* desventajoso

disaffection *n* desafecto, descontento, *m*

disagree *vi* no estar de acuerdo; diferir; (quarrel) reñir; (not share the opinion of) no estar de la opinión (de); (of food, etc.) sentar mal; no probar. **The meat disagreed with me,** La carne me sentó mal

disagreeable *a* desagradable; repugnante; (of persons) antipático, displicente

disagreeableness *n* lo desagradable; (of persons) displicencia, *f*

disagreement *n* desacuerdo, *m*; diferencia, *f*; desavenencia, *f*; discordia, *f*; (quarrel) riña, disputa, *f*; discrepancia, *f*

disallow *vt* negar; rechazar

disappear *vi* desaparecer. **to cause to d.,** hacer desaparecer

disappearance *n* desaparición, *f*

disappoint *vt* desilusionar; frustrar; (hopes) defraudar; (deprive) privar de; (annoy) contrariar; (break a promise) faltar (a la palabra)

disappointing *a* desengañador; pobre; triste; poco halagüeño

disappointment *n* desengaño, *m*, decepción, *f*; frustración, *f*; desilusión, *f*; (vexation) contrariedad, *f*; contratiempo, *m*. **to suffer a d.,** sufrir un desengaño; *inf* llevarse un chasco

disapproval *n* desaprobación, *f*

disapprove *vt* desaprobar

disapproving *a* de desaprobación, severo

disarm *vt* desarmar. *vi* desarmarse; deponer las armas

disarmament *n* desarme, *m*

disarrange *vt* desarreglar; descomponer, desajustar; (hair) despeinar

disarrangement *n* desarreglo, *m*; desajuste, *m*; desorden, *m*

disarray *n* desorden, desarreglo, *m*; confusión, *f*. *vt* desordenar, desarreglar

disaster *n* desastre, *m*; catástrofe, *m*; infortunio, *m*

disastrous *a* desastroso; funesto, trágico

disavow *vt* repudiar; retractar

disavowal *n* repudiación, *f*

disband *vt* licenciar. *vi* desbandarse, dispersarse

disbelief *n* incredulidad, *f*; desconfianza, *f*

disbelieve *vt* and *vi* descreer, no creer; desconfiar (de)

disburse *vt* desembolsar, pagar

disbursement *n* desembolso, *m*

disc *n* disco, *m*

discard *vt* desechar, arrinconar, *Lat. Am.* botar; despedir; (at cards) descartar. *n* (at cards) descarte, *m*

discern *vt* discernir, distinguir, percibir

discernible *a* distinguible, perceptible

discerning *a* perspicaz, discernidor

discernment *n* discernimiento, *m*

discharge *vt* descargar; (a gun) disparar, tirar; (an arrow) lanzar; *elec* descargar; emitir; (dismiss) destituir, despedir; arrojar; *mil* licenciar; (exempt) dispensar (de); (exonerate) absolver, exonerar; (free) dar libertad (a); (from hospital) dar de baja (a); *law* revocar; (perform) cumplir, ejecutar; (pay) pagar, saldar; (of an abscess, etc.) supurar.

discharge *n* (of firearms) disparo, tiro, *m*; (of artillery) descarga, *f*; (of goods, cargo) descargue, *m*; *elec* descarga, *f*; (from a wound, etc.) pus, *m*, supuración, *f*; (from the intestine) flujo, *m*; (of a debt) pago, *m*.; *com* descargo, *m*; (receipt) carta de pago, quitanza, *f*; *mil* licencia absoluta, *f*; (dismissal) despedida, destitución, *f*; (exoneration) exoneración, *f*; (freeing) liberación, *f*; (from hospital) baja, *f*; (performance) cumplimiento, *m*; ejecución, *f*

disciple *n* discípulo (-la)

disciplinarian *n* disciplinario (-ia)

disciplinary *a* disciplinario

discipline *n* disciplina, *f*, *vt* disciplinar

disclaim *vt* renunciar (a); (repudiate) rechazar, repudiar

disclaimer *n* *law* renunciación, *f*; repudiación, *f*

disclose *vt* descubrir, revelar

disclosure *n* descubrimiento, *m*, revelación, *f*

discolor *vt* descolorar. *vi* descolorarse

discoloration *n* descoloramiento, *m*

discomfit *vt* desconcertar

discomfort *n* falta de comodidades, *f*; incomodidad, *f*; malestar, *m*; molestia, *f*; inquietud, *f*; dolor, *m*

discomposure *n* confusión, agitación, inquietud, *f*

disconcert *vt* desconcertar, turbar; (of plans, etc.) frustrar

disconnect *vt* separar; (of railway engines, etc.) desacoplar; desconectar; (of electric plugs) desenchufar

disconnected *a* inconexo; incoherente, deshilvanado

disconsolate *a* desconsolado, triste

disconsolately *adv* desconsoladamente, tristemente

discontent *n* descontento, disgusto, *m*, *vt* descontentar, desagradar

discontented *a* descontentadizo, descontento, disgustado

discontinuance *n* descontinuación, cesación, *f*; interrupción, *f*

discontinue *vt* descontinuar; cesar; interrumpir; (of payments, etc.) suspender. *vi* cesar

discontinuous *a* descontinuo; interrumpido; intermitente

discord *n* discordia, *f*; *mus* disonancia, *f*, desentono, *m*

discordant *a* discorde, poco armonioso; incongruo; *mus* disonante, desentonado. **to be d.,** discordar; ser incongruo; *mus* disonar

discount *n* descuento, *m*; rebaja, *f*. *vt* descontar; rebajar; balancear; (disconsider) desechar. **at a d.,** al descuento; bajo la par; fácil de desechar; superfluo; *fig* en disfavor, en descrédito. **rate of d.,** tipo de descuento, *m*. **d. for cash,** descuento por venta al contado, *m*.

discourage *vt* desalentar, desanimar; oponerse a; disuadir; frustrar

discouragement *n* desaliento, *m*; desaprobación, oposición, *f*; disuasión, *f*; (obstacle) estorbo, *m*

discouraging *a* poco animador, que ofrece pocas esperanzas; (with prospect, etc.) nada halagüeño

discourse *n* discurso, *m*; plática, *f*; (treatise) disertación, *f*. *vi* (converse) platicar, conversar; (with on, upon) disertar sobre, discurrir sobre; tratar de

discourteous *a* descortés, desconsiderado

discover *vt* descubrir; (see) ver; (realize) darse cuenta de; (show) manifestar; revelar

discoverer *n* descubridor (-ra); revelador (-ra)

discovery *n* descubrimiento, *m*; revelación, *f*

discredit *n* descrédito, *m*; des honra, *f*; duda, *f*. *vt* dudar (de), no creer (en); desacreditar; deshonrar

discreditable *a* deshonroso, ignominioso, vergonzoso

discreet *a* discreto; prudente, circunspecto

discreetly *adv* discretamente; prudentemente

discrepancy *n* discrepancia, diferencia, *f*; contradicción, *f*

discretion *n* discreción, *f*; prudencia, circunspección, *f*; juicio, *m*; voluntad, *f*. **at d.,** a discreción. **at one's own d.,** a voluntad (de uno). **years of d.,** edad de discreción, *f*

discriminate *vi* distinguir (entre); hacer

una distinción (en favor de or en perjuicio de). *vt* distinguir

discriminating *a* discerniente, que sabe distinguir, juicioso; culto; diferencial

discrimination *n* discernimiento, *m*; gusto, *m*; distinción, *f*; discriminación, *f*

discursive *a* discursivo; digresivo

discus *n* disco, *m*. **d. thrower,** discóbolo, *m*

discuss *vt* discutir; hablar de; debatir; (deal with) tratar; (*fam* a dish) probar; (a bottle of wine) vaciar

discussion *n* discusión, *f*; debate, *m*

disdain *n* desdén, *m*; altivez, *f*. *vt* desdeñar, desairar, despreciar. **to d. to,** desdeñarse de

disdainful *a* desdeñoso; altivo

disease *n* enfermedad, *f*; *fig* mal, *m*. **infectious d.,** enfermedad contagiosa, *f*

diseased *a* enfermo; (of fruit, etc.) malo

disembark *vt* and *vi* desembarcar

disembarkation *n* desembarque, *m*; *mil* desembarco (de tropas), *m*

disembodied *a* incorpóreo

disembowel *vt* desentrañar, destripar

disenchant *vt* desencantar; deschechizar; desilusionar

disenchantment *n* desencanto, *m*; desilusión, *f*

disengage *vt* desasir; soltar; (gears) desembragar; (uncouple) desacoplar; (free) librar

disentangle *vt* (undo) desatar, desanudar; separar; (of threads, etc., and *fig*) desenredar, desenmarañar. *vi* desenredarse

disfavor *n* disfavor, *m*; (disapproval) desaprobación, *f*. *vt* desaprobar

disfigure *vt* desfigurar, afear; deformar; (mar) estropear

disfigurement *n* desfiguración, *f*; deformidad, *f*; defecto, *m*

disfranchise *vt* privar de los derechos civiles (a)

disgorge *vt* and *vi* vomitar; (of a river) desembocar (en); hacer restitución (de lo robado)

disgrace *n* vergüenza, ignominia, *f*; deshonra, *f*; (insult) afrenta, *f*; (scandal) escándalo, *m*; disfavor, *m*. *vt* deshonrar; despedir con ignominia. **in d.,** fuera de favor; desacreditado; (of children and animals) castigado

disgraceful *a* deshonroso; ignominioso; escandaloso

disgruntled *a* refunfuñador, enfurruñado, malhumorado

disguise *n* disfraz, *m*; (mask) máscara, *f*. *vt* disfrazar; cubrir, tapar; (*fig* conceal) ocultar. **in d.,** disfrazado

disgust *n* repugnancia, aversión, *f*; aborrecimiento, *m*; asco, *m*. *vt* repugnar, inspirar aversión; disgustar; dar asco (a)

disgusted *a* asqueado; disgustado; furioso; (bored) aburrido

disgusting *a* repugnante; odioso, horrible; asqueroso

dish *n* (for meat, vegetables, fruit, etc.) fuente, *f*; (food) plato, *m*; *pl* **dishes,** platos, *m pl*, vajilla, *f*. *vt* servir; *inf* frustrar. **cooked d.,** guiso, *m*. **special d. for today,** plato del día, *m*. **to wash the dishes,** fregar los platos. **d.-cloth,** (for washing) fregador, *m*; (for drying) paño de los platos, *m*. **d.-cover,** cubre-platos, *m*. **d.-rack,** escurre-platos, *m*. **d.-washer,** lavaplatos, lavavajillas, *m*. **d.-water,** agua de lavar los platos, *f*

disharmony *n* falta de armonía, *f*; (disagreement) discordia, desavenencia, *f*; incongruencia, *f*; *mus* disonancia, *f*

dishearten *vt* desalentar, desanimar; desesperar; disuadir (de)

disheveled *a* despeinado, desgreñado; (untidy) desaseado

dishonest *a* falto de honradez, tramposo; fraudulento; falso, desleal, *Lat. Am. also* flequetero

dishonestly *adv* de mala fe, sin honradez; fraudulentamente; deslealmente

dishonesty *n* falta de honradez, falta de integridad, *f*; fraude, *m*; falsedad, deslealtad, *f*

dishonor *n* deshonra, *f*. *vt* deshonrar; *com* no pagar, o no aceptar, un giro

dishonorable *a* deshonroso

disillusion *vt* desengañar, desilusionar

disillusionment *n* desilusión, *f*, desengaño, desencanto, *m*

disinfect *vt* desinfectar

disinfectant *a* and *n* desinfectante *m*.

disingenuous *a* tortuoso, doble, falso, insincero

disinherit *vt* desheredar

disintegrate *vt* despedazar, disgregar. *vi* disgregarse; desmoronarse

disintegration *n* disgregación, *f*; disolución, *f*; desmoronamiento, *m*

disinter *vt* desenterrar

disinterested *a* desinteresado

disinterment *n* desenterramiento, *m*

disjointed *a* dislocado; desarticulado; incoherente, inconexo; (of a speech, etc.) descosido

disk *n* disco, *m*

dislike *n* aversión, *f*; antipatía, *f*; (hostility) animosidad, *f*. *vt* desagradar, no gustar; repugnar. **I d. the house,** No me gusta la casa. **I d. them,** No me gustan

dislocate *vt* dislocar, descoyuntar; *fig* interrumpir

dislocation *n* dislocación, *f*, descoyuntamiento, *m*; *fig* interrupción, *f*

dislodge *vt* desalojar

disloyal *a* desleal, infiel, falso

disloyalty *n* deslealtad, infidelidad, falsedad, *f*

dismal a lóbrego, sombrío; lúgubre; funesto; triste

dismantle vt (a ship or fort) desmantelar; (a machine) desmontar; (a house, etc.) desamueblar

dismay n desmayo, desaliento, m; consternación, f; espanto, terror, m. vt desanimar; consternar; espantar, horrorizar

dismember vt desmembrar

dismemberment n desmembración, f

dismiss vt (from a job) despedir (de); (from an official position) destituir (de) Chile desahuciar (de); (bid good-bye to) despedirse de; (after military parade) dar la orden de romper filas; (thoughts) apartar de sí; ahuyentar; (discard) desechar, descartar; (omit) pasar por alto de; (disregard) rechazar; (a parliament, etc.) disolver; (a law case) absolver de la instancia. **to d. in a few words,** tratar someramente; hablar brevemente de

dismissal n despedida, f; (from an official post) destitución, f, Chile desahúcio m; apartamiento, m; (discard) descarte, m; (of a parliament, etc.) disolución, f

dismount vi apearse, desmontar, echar pie a tierra; bajar. vt desmontar; (dismantle) desarmar

disobedience n desobediencia, f

disobedient a desobediente

disobey vt and vi desobedecer

disorder n desorden, m; confusión, f; (unrest) perturbación del orden público, f, motín, m; (disease) enfermedad, f; (mental) enajenación mental, f; trastorno, m. vt desordenar, desarreglar; (of health) perjudicar; (the mind) trastornar. **in d.,** en desorden, desarreglado; (helter-skelter) atropelladamente

disordered a en desorden; irregular, desordenado; (of the mind and bodily organs) trastornado; (ill) enfermo; (confused) confuso

disorganization n desorganización, f

disorganize vt desorganizar

disorientate vt desorientar

disown vt repudiar; negar; renegar de

disparage vt menospreciar; desacreditar; denigrar; (spoil) perjudicar; (scorn) despreciar

disparagement n menosprecio, m; denigración, f; desprecio, m

disparagingly adv con desprecio

disparity n disparidad, f

dispassionate a desapasionado, sereno; imparcial; moderado

dispatch n despacho, m; com envío, m; (message) mensaje, m; (communiqué) parte, f; (cable) telegrama, m; (promptness) prontitud, presteza, f; (execution) ejecución, muerte, f. vt despachar; enviar, remitir; (fam kill) despachar. **d.-case,** cartera, f. **d.-rider,** mensajero motociclista, m

dispel vt disipar

dispensary n dispensario, m

dispensation n dispensación, f; (of the Pope, etc.) dispensa, f; (decree) ley, f, decreto, m; (of justice) administración, f

dispense vt dispensar; (of justice) administrar. **to d. with,** pasar sin, prescindir de

dispersal n dispersión, f; disipación, f; esparcimiento, m

disperse vt dispersar; disipar; esparcir. vi dispersarse disiparse

dispirited a abatido, desanimado, deprimido; lánguido

displace vt desalojar; cambiar de situación; (of liquids) desplazar; (oust) quitar el puesto (a), destituir

displacement n desalojamiento, m; cambio de situación, m; (of liquid) desplazamiento, m; (from a post) destitución, f

display n exhibición, f; ostentación, f; presentación, f; (development) desarrollo, m; manifestación, f; (naval or military) maniobras, f pl; espectáculo, m; (pomp) pompa, f; fausto, m. vt exhibir; mostrar, manifestar; ostentar; (unfold) desplegar, extender; (develop) desarrollar. **d. cabinet,** vitrina, f

displease vt desagradar; ofender; enojar

displeasing a desagradable

displeasure n desagrado, m; disgusto, m; disfavor, m; indignación, f; enojo, m; (grief) angustia, f

disport vi (**oneself**), divertirse, entretenerse, recrearse; retozar; jugar

disposal n disposición, f; (transfer) cesión, enajenación, f; (sale) venta, f; (gift) donación, f. **I am at your d.,** Estoy a la disposición de Vd. **the d. of the troops,** la disposición de las tropas

dispose vt disponer; inclinar. vi disponer. **to d. of,** disponer de; (finish) terminar, concluir; (get rid of) deshacerse de; (give away) regalar; (sell) vender; (transfer) ceder; (of houses, etc.) traspasar; (kill) matar; (send) enviar; (use) servirse de; (refute) refutar. **"To be disposed of,"** (a business, etc.) «Se traspasa»

disposed a (in compounds) intencionado, dispuesto. **well-d.,** bien intencionado

disposition n disposición, f; (temperament) naturaleza, índole, f, temperamento, carácter, m; (humor) humor, m

dispossess vt desposeer (de); privar (de); desahuciar

dispossession n desposeimiento, m; desahúcio, m

disproportion n desproporción, f

disproportionate a desproporcionado

disprove vt refutar

disputable a disputable; discutible

dispute n disputa, controversia, f; altercación, f; discusión, f; debate, m. vt and vi disputar. **beyond d.**, a incontestable. adv incontestablemente; fuera de duda

disqualification n incapacidad, f; inhabilitación, f; impedimento, m; sport descalificación, f

disqualify vt incapacitar; inhabilitar; sport descalificar

disquiet n desasosiego, m; intranquilidad, inquietud, agitación, f. vt desasosegar, intranquilizar, perturbar, agitar

disquieting a intranquilizador, perturbador

disquisition n disquisición, f

disregard n indiferencia, f; omisión, f; descuido, m; (scorn) desdén, m. vt no hacer caso de, desatender; omitir; desconocer; descuidar; despreciar

disregardful a indiferente; negligente; desatento; desdeñoso

disrepair n deterioro, mal estado, m

disreputable a de mala fama; (shameful) vergonzoso, vil; (compromising) comprometedor; de mal aspecto, horrible; ruin

disreputably adv ruinmente; vergonzosamente

disrepute n disfavor, m; mala fama, f; deshonra, f; descrédito, m. **to come into d.**, caer en disfavor; perder su reputación

disrespect n falta de respeto, f; irreverencia, f

disrespectful a irrespetuoso, irreverente

disrobe vt desnudar. vi desnudarse

disrupt vt quebrar; desorganizar; interrumpir; separar

disruption n quebrantamiento, m; desorganización, f; interrupción, f; separación, f

dissatisfaction n descontento, desagrado, disgusto, m

dissatisfied a descontentado, malcontento, no satisfecho

dissect vt disecar; fig analizar

dissection n disección, f; análisis, m

dissemble vt and vi disimular, fingir

dissembler n hipócrita, mf; disimulador (-ra)

disseminate vt diseminar; propagar, sembrar

dissension n disensión, f; disidencia, f

dissent n disentimiento, m, vi disentir, disidir

dissentient a disidente, divergente. **without one d. voice,** unánimemente

dissertation n disertación, f

disservice n deservicio, m

dissimilar a disímil, desemejante, diferente

dissimilarity n desemejanza, diferencia, disparidad, f

dissimulation n disimulación, f, disimulo, m

dissipate vt disipar; dispersar; (waste) derrochar, desperdiciar. vi disiparse; dispersarse; (vanish) desvanecerse; (of persons) ser disoluto

dissipated a (of persons) disipado, disoluto, vicioso

dissipation n disipación, f; (waste) derroche, m; libertinaje, m

dissociate vt disociar

dissociation n disociación, f

dissolute a disoluto, vicioso, licencioso

dissolution n disolución, f; separación, f; muerte, f

dissolvable a soluble

dissolve vt disolver; derretir; (of parliament) prorrogar; (a marriage, etc.) anular; fig disipar. vi disolverse; derretirse; (vanish) desvanecerse, disiparse, evaporarse. **to d. into tears,** deshacerse en lágrimas

dissolvent a disolutivo. n disolvente, m

dissonance n disonancia, f; fig discordia, falta de armonía, f

dissonant n disonancia, f, a disonante

dissuade vt disuadir (de), apartar (de)

distaff n rueca, f

distance n distancia, f; lontananza, f; lejanía, f; trecho, m; (of time) intervalo, m; (difference) diferencia, f. **at a d.,** a alguna distancia; lejos; (from afar) desde lejos. **from a d.,** desde (or de) lejos. **in the d.,** a lo lejos, en lontananza. **to keep at a d.,** mantener lejos; guardar las distancias (con). **to keep one's d.,** mantenerse a distancia; no intimarse, guardar las distancias. **What is the d. from London to Madrid?** ¿Qué distancia hay desde Londres a Madrid?

distant a distante; lejano; remoto; (of manner) frío, reservado; (slight) ligero; (of references, etc.) indirecto. **He is a d. relation,** Es un pariente lejano. **They are always rather d. with her,** La tratan siempre con bastante frialdad

distantly adv a distancia; a lo lejos; desde lejos; remotamente; (of manner) con frialdad; (slightly) ligeramente

distaste n aversión, repugnancia, f; disgusto, hastío, m

distasteful a desagradable

distemper n enfermedad, f; (in animals) moquillo, m; fig mal, m; (for walls) pintura al temple, f. vt desordenar, perturbar; (walls) pintar al temple

distend vt ensanchar; dilatar; inflar, henchir; med distender. vi ensancharse, etc.

distension n dilatación, f; inflación, f; henchimiento, m; med distensión, f

distil vt destilar; extraer. vi destilar; exudar

distillation n destilación, f; extracción, f; exudación, f

distiller n destilador (-ra)

distillery n destilería, f, destilatorio, m

distinct a distinto; diferente; claro; notable, evidente

distinction n distinción, f

distinctive a distintivo; característico

distinctly adv claramente; distintamente

distinctness n claridad, f; distinción, f; carácter distintivo, m

distinguish vt distinguir; discernir; caracterizar; (honor) honrar. vi distinguir, diferenciar

distinguishable a distinguible; perceptible, discernible

distinguished a distinguido; eminente; famoso, ilustre, egregio

distort vt (twist) torcer; deformar; falsear; pervertir

distortion n deformación, f; torcimiento, m; contorsión, f; perversión, f; rad deformación, f

distract vt distraer; interrumpir; perturbar; (turn aside) desviar, apartar; (madden) enloquecer; volver loco (a)

distracted a aturdido; demente, loco

distraction n distracción, f; (amusement) diversión, f, pasatiempo, m; (bewilderment) confusión, f, aturdimiento, m; (madness) locura, f; frenesí, m. **to drive to d.,** trastornar, sacar de quicio

distrain vi embargar

distraint n embargo, m

distraught a aturdido; desesperado; enloquecido

distress n dolor, m, aflicción, f; pena, f; miseria, penuria, f; (exhaustion) fatiga, f; cansancio, m; (pain) dolor, m; (misfortune) desdicha, f; apuro, m; (danger) peligro, m; law embargo, m. vt afligir, dar pena (a), llenar de angustia; cansar, fatigar; (pain) doler

distressed a afligido; necesitado, pobre

distressing a congojoso, doloroso, penoso

distribute vt (of justice, etc.) administrar; distribuir; repartir

distribution n (of justice) administración, f; distribución, f; reparto, m

district n distrito, m; comarca, f; (of a town) barrio, m; (judicial) partido judicial, m, Lat. Am. comuna f; jurisdicción, f; región, zona, f

distrust n desconfianza, f; recelo, m, sospecha, f. vt desconfiar de, sospechar

distrustful a desconfiado, receloso, suspicaz

disturb vt perturbar; interrumpir; incomodar; (make anxious) inquietar; (alter) cambiar; (disarrange) desordenar, desarreglar. **to d. the peace,** perturbar el orden público

disturbance n perturbación, f; disturbio, m, conmoción, f; incomodidad, f; agitación, f; confusión, f; tumulto, m; desorden, m; rad parásitos, m pl

disturbing a perturbador; inquietador;

conmovedor, impresionante, emocionante

disunion n desunión, f; discordia, f

disunite vt desunir; separar, dividir. vi separarse

disuse n desuso, m. vt desusar; desacostumbrar. **to fall into d.,** caer en desuso

ditch n zanja, f; (for defense, etc.) foso, m; (irrigation) acequia, f. vt zanjar; abarrancar. **to die in the last d.,** morir en la brecha

ditto adv ídem; también

diuretic a diurético

dive n buceo, m; aer picada, f, vi bucear; sumergirse (en); aer volar en picado; penetrar (en); (into a book) enfrascarse en. **to d. out,** salir precipitadamente. **to d.-bomb,** bombardear en picado. **d.-bomber,** avión en picado, m. **d.-bombing,** bombardeo en picado, m

diver n buceador, m; buzo, m; (bird) somorgujo, m

diverge vi divergir

divergence n divergencia, f

divergent a divergente

diverse a diverso, vario

diversify vt diversificar

diversion n diversión, f; entretenimiento, m, recreación, f; pasatiempo, m; placer, m; mil diversión, f

diversity n diversidad, variedad, f

divert vt desviar; (amuse) divertir, entretener

diverting a divertido, entretenido

divide vt dividir; partir; separar; (cut) cortar; (share) repartir, distribuir; (hair) hacer la raya (del pelo); (of voting) provocar una votación. vi dividirse; separarse; (of roads, etc.) bifurcarse; (of voting) votar. **divided skirt,** n falda pantalón, f

dividend n dividendo, m. **d. warrant,** cupón de dividendo, m

divine a divino; sublime; inf estupendo. n teólogo, m. vt (foretell) vaticinar, pronosticar; presentir; (guess) adivinar

diving n buceo, m; aer picado, m. **d.-bell,** campana de bucear, f. **f. d.-board,** (low) trampolín, m; (high) palanca, f. **d.-suit,** escafandra, f

divinity n divinidad, f; teología, f

division n división, f; separación, f; (distribution) repartimiento, m; (mil math) división, f; sección, f; grupo, m; (voting) votación, f; (discord) discordia, desunión, f. **without a d.,** por unanimidad, sin votar

divorce n divorcio, m. vt divorciarse de; fig divorciar, separar. **to file a petition of d.,** poner una petición de divorcio

divorcee n (wife) divorciada, f; (husband) divorciado, m

divulge vt divulgar, revelar

dizziness n vértigo, m; mareo, m; (bewilderment) aturdimiento, m, confusión, f

dizzy a vertiginoso; mareado; confuso, perplejo, aturdido

do vt hacer; ejecutar; (one's duty, etc.) cumplir con; concluir; (cause) causar; (homage) rendir; (commit) cometer; (arrange) arreglar; (cook) cocer, guisar; (roast) asar; (fam cheat) engañar; (suit) convenir; (suffice) bastar; (act) hacer el papel (de); (fam treat) tratar (bien o mal); (learn) aprender; (exhaust) agotar; (walk) andar; (travel, journey) recorrer; (translate) traducir; (prepare) preparar. vi hacer; (behave) conducirse; (of health) estar (bien o mal); (act) obrar; (get on) ir; (be suitable, suit) convenir; (suffice) bastar; (of plants) florecer; (cook) cocerse; (last) durar. **Don't!** ¡No lo hagas! ¡Quieto! ¡Calla! **How do you do?** ¿Cómo está Vd.? ¡Buenos días! **Have done!** ¡Acaba de una vez! **It will do you good,** Te conviene; Te hará bien; Te sentará bien. **It will do you no harm,** No te perjudicará; No te hará daño. **I could do with one,** Me gustaría (tener) uno; (of drinks) Me bebería uno con mucho gusto. **That will do,** Eso basta; Se puede servirse de eso; Está bien así; (leave it alone) ¡Déjate de eso! (be quiet!) ¡No digas más! ¡Cállate! **That won't do,** Eso no es bastante; Eso no sirve; Eso no se hace así; Eso no se hace. **That will never do,** Eso no servirá; Eso no puede ser. **This will do,** (when buying an article) Me quedaré con éste; Me serviré de éste; Esto basta; Esto será suficiente; (is all right) Está bien así. **Thy will be done!** ¡Hágase tu voluntad! **to be doing,** estar haciendo; estar ocupado en (or con) hacer; (of food) estar cocinando. **to be done for,** estar perdido; estar muerto. **to do better,** hacer mejor (que); (mend one's ways) enmendarse, corregirse; (improve) mejorar, hacer progresos; (in health) encontrarse mejor. **to do business with** *Lat. Am.* amancharse con. **to do nothing,** no hacer nada. **to do reverence,** rendir homenaje; inclinarse. **to do to death,** matar; asesinar; ejecutar. **to do violence to,** *fig* hacer fuerza a. **to do well,** hacer bien; obrar bien; (be successful) tener éxito; hacer buena impresión; (prosperous) tener una buena posición. **to do wonders,** hacer maravillas. **to have done with,** renunciar (a); dejar de usar; dejar de hacer, cesar; concluir, terminar; no tener más que ver con; (forsake) abandonar; (a person) romper con. **to have nothing to do,** no tener nada que hacer. **to have nothing to do with,** no tener nada que ver con; (of people) no tratar; (end a friendship) romper su amistad con, dejar de ver. **well done,** bien hecho; (of food) bien guisado; (of meat) bien asado. **What is to be done?** ¿Qué hay que hacer? ¿Qué se puede hacer? **What is to do?** ¿Qué pasa? ¿Qué hay? **When he had done speaking,** Cuando hubo terminado de hablar. **to do again,** hacer de nuevo, volver a hacer, rehacer; repetir. **He will not do it again,** No lo hará más. **to do away with,** quitar; eliminar; suprimir; hacer desaparecer; poner fin a; hacer cesar; destruir; matar. **to do by,** tratar (a), portarse con. **to do for,** arruinar; matar; (suffice) bastar para; ser a propósito para, servir para; (look after) cuidar; (as a housekeeper) dirigir la casa para. **to do out,** (a room) limpiar. **to do out of,** quitar; privar de; (steal) robar. **to do up,** (tie) atar; (fold) enrollar, plegar; envolver; (parcel) empaquetar; (arrange) arreglar; decorar; poner en orden; poner como nuevo; (iron) planchar; (launder) lavar y planchar; (tire) fatigar. **to do with,** (of people) tratar; (of things) tener que ver con; (put up with) poder con; poder sufrir. **to do without,** prescindir de; pasarse sin

do as an auxiliary verb is not translated in Spanish, e.g. **I do believe,** creo. **Do not do that,** no hagas eso. **I did not know,** no sabía

When it is used for emphasis, **do** is translated by **sí, ciertamente, claro** and similar words, e.g.:

She did not know, but he did, Ella no lo sabía pero él sí

You do paint well, Pintas muy bien por cierto

Do come this time, No dejes de venir esta vez

docile a dócil

dock n dique, m, dársena, f; (wharf) muelle, m; (in a law court) banquillo de los acusados, m; bot romaza, f. vt (a tail) descolar; cortar, cercenar; reducir; (money) descontar; (a ship) poner en dique. vi entrar en dársena, entrar en dique, entrar en muelle. **dry-d.,** dique seco, m. **floating-d.,** dique flotante, m. **d.-dues,** muellaje, m. **d. rat,** (thief) raquero, m

docket n (bundle) legajo, m; extracto, m; minuta, f; (label) etiqueta, f, marbete, m

dockyard n arsenal, astillero, m

doctor n doctor (-ra); (medical practitioner) médico (-ca), asistir; (repair) reparar, componer; adulterar; mezclar drogas con; falsificar. vi ejercer la medicina. **family d.,** médico de cabecera, m. **to graduate as a d.,** doctorarse. **d. of divinity, laws, medicine,** doctor (-ra) en teología, en derecho, en medicina, m

doctorate n doctorado, m

doctrinaire a and n doctrinario (-ia)

doctrine n doctrina, f

document n documento, m. vt documentar; probar con documentos. **d.-case,** carpeta, f

documentary a documental; escrito, auténtico. **d. film,** película documental, f

documentation n documentación, f

dodge n esguince, regate, m; evasiva, f; (trick) estratagema, m, maniobra, f; artefacto, m. vt esquivar, evadir

doeskin n ante, m, piel de gama, f

doff vt quitar; (of hats, etc.) quitarse; desnudarse de

dog n perro, m; (male) macho, m; (andiron) morillo, m; ast Can Mayor (or Menor), Sirio, m. vt perseguir; seguir los pasos de; espiar. **You can't deceive an old dog,** A perro viejo no hay tus tus. **to go to the dogs,** ir a las carreras de galgos; fig ir cuesta abajo. **mongrel dog,** perro mestizo, m. **thoroughbred dog,** perro de raza pura, m. **dog-collar,** collar de perro, m; ecc alzacuello, m. **dog-days,** días caniculares, m pl, canícula, f. **dog-eared** (of books) con las puntas de las hojas dobladas. **dog-fight,** lucha de perros, f; combate aéreo, m. **dog-fish,** lija, f, cazón, m. **dog in the manger,** el perro del hortelano. **dog-kennel,** perrera, f. **dog-latin,** bajo latín, m. **dog license,** matrícula de perros, f. **dog-racing,** carrera de galgos, f. **dog-rose,** escaramujo, m. **dog show,** exposición canina, f. **dog-tooth,** arch diente de perro, m. **dog-vane,** naut cataviento, m

dogged a persistente, tenaz, pertinaz, obstinado

doggerel n malos versos, m pl; aleluyas, coplas de ciego, f pl, a malo, irregular

dogma n dogma, m

dogmatic a dogmático

doily n carpeta, f, pañito de adorno, m

doings n pl acciones, f pl; (deeds) hechos, m pl; (behavior) conducta, f; (happenings) acontecimientos, m pl; (works) obras, f pl; (things) cosas, f pl

doldrums n pl calmas ecuatoriales, f pl

dole n limosna, f; porción, f. **to d. out,** repartir; distribuir en porciones pequeñas; racionar; dar contra la voluntad de uno.

doleful a triste, lúgubre, melancólico; doloroso

doll n muñeca, f

dollar n dólar, m

dolly n muñeca, f; (for clothes) moza, f. **d.-tub,** cubo para la colada, m

dolphin n delfín, m

dolt n cabeza de alcornoque, mf, zamacuco, m

domain n territorio, m; heredad, posesión, propiedad, f; (empire) dominio, m

dome n cúpula, f; bóveda, f; (palace) palacio, m

domestic a doméstico; familiar; (home-loving) casero; (of animals) doméstico; (national) interior, nacional. n doméstico, sirviente, m; criada, f. **d. economy,** economía doméstica, f

domesticate vt domesticar

domesticated a (of animals) domesticado; (of persons) casero

domicile n domicilio, m, vt domiciliar

dominant a dominante; imperante. n mus dominante, f. **to be d.,** prevalecer

dominate vt and vi dominar

domination n dominación, f

domineer vi dominar, tiranizar. **to d. over,** mandar en

domineering a dominante, mandón, tiránico. **d. person** Lat. Am. mandarín m

Dominican Republic, the la República Dominicana, f

dominion n dominio, m; autoridad, soberanía, f; imperio, m; pl **dominions,** ecc dominaciones, f pl

domino n dominó, m. **to go d.,** nacer domino

don n (Spanish and Italian title) don, m; señor, m. vt ponerse, vestirse

donation n donación, dádiva, f; contribución, f

done a and past part hecho; (of food) cocido; (roasted) asado; (tired) rendido; (fam deceived) engañado. **Well d.!** ¡Bien hecho! **d. for,** arruinado; muerto; perdido; vencido; (spoilt) estropeado

donkey n borrico (-ca), burro (-rra). **d.-engine,** máquina auxiliar, f

donor n donador (-ra); dador (-ra)

doodle v borrajear, garabatear, hacer garabatos

doom n condena, f; (fate) suerte, f; (judgment) destino, m; ruina, f; juicio, m. vt sentenciar; condenar

doomsday n día del juicio final, m

door n puerta, f; entrada, f. **front d.,** puerta de entrada, f. **next d.,** la casa vecina; la puerta al lado, la puerta vecina. **next d. neighbor,** vecino (-na) de al lado. **out of doors,** al aire libre; en la calle. **to knock at the d.,** llamar a la puerta. **to slam the d. in a person's face,** dar con la puerta en las narices de alguien. **d.-bell,** timbre (non-electric, campanilla, f) de llamada, m. **d.-jamb,** quicial, m. **d. keeper,** portero, m. **d.-knob,** tirador, m. **d.-knocker,** manija, f; picaporte, m, aldaba, f. **d.-plate,** placa, f. **d.-shutter,** cierre metálico, m. **d.-step,** peldaño de la puerta, m; umbral, m. **d.-way,** portal, m

dope n drogas, f pl, narcóticos, m pl; (news) información, f. **d. fiend,** morfinómano (-na)

dope-pusher n narcotraficante, mf

dormant a durmiente; latente; secreto; inactivo. **to go d.,** dormirse

dormitory n dormitorio, m

dory n (fish) dorado, m

dose, dosage n; dosis, f

dossier n documentación, f

dot n punto, m; mus puntillo, m; pl **dots,** gram puntos suspensivos, m pl. vt poner punto (a una letra); (scatter) salpicar. **on the dot,** (of time) en punto. **to dot one's i's,** poner los puntos sobre las íes

dotage n senectud, chochera, f

dotard n viejo chocho, m; vieja chocha, f; inf carcamal, m

dote vi chochear. **to d. on,** adorar en, idolatrar

doting a chocho

double a and adv doble; dos veces; (in a pair) en par; en dos; doblemente; (deceitful) doble, de dos caras, falso; ambiguo. n doble, m; duplicado, m; theat contrafigura, f; pl **doubles,** (tennis) dobles, m pl, juego doble, m. vt doblar; duplicar; (fold) doblegar; (the fist) cerrar (el puño); (theat and naut) doblar. vi doblarse; (dodge) volverse atrás, hacer un rodeo, dar una vuelta; esquivarse. **to d. up,** vt envolver; arrollar; (a person) doblar. vi doblegarse; arrollarse; (collapse) desplomarse. **at the d.,** corriendo. **He was doubled up with pain,** El dolor le hacía retorcerse. **mixed doubles,** parejas mixtas, f pl; dobles mixtos, m pl. **double two,** (telephone) dos dos. **with a d. meaning,** con segunda intención. **d.-barrelled,** de dos cañones. **d.-bass,** contrabajo, m. **d. bed,** cama de matrimonio, f. **d.-bedded,** con cama de matrimonio; con dos camas. **d.-breasted,** cruzado. **d.-chin,** papada, f. **d.-dealing,** duplicidad, f. **d.-edged,** de doble filo. **d.-entry,** con partida doble, f. **d.-faced,** de dos caras. **d.-jointed,** con articulaciones dobles

double room Mexico cuarto doble m

double-spaced a a doble espacio, a dos espacios

doubling n doblamiento, m; doblez, f; plegadura, f; duplicación, f; (dodging) evasiva, f, esguince, m

doubt n duda, f; incertidumbre, f; sospecha, f. vt and vi dudar; sospechar; titubear, hesitar; temer. **beyond all d.,** fuera de duda. **no d.,** sin duda. **There is no d. that,** No hay duda de que, No cabe duda de que. **When in d. . . . ,** En caso de duda

doubtful a dudoso; incierto; perplejo; ambiguo; (of places) sospechoso

doubtfully adv dudosamente; inciertamente; irresolutamente; ambiguamente

doubtless adv sin duda, por supuesto; probablemente

douche n ducha, f, vt duchar

dough n pasta, masa, f; (money) lana, f

dour a huraño, adusto, austero

douse vt zambullir; (a sail) recoger; inf apagar

dove n paloma, f. **d.-cote,** palomar, m

dovetail n carp cola de milano, f, vt carp machihembrar, empalmar; fig encajar

dowager n viuda, f; matrona, f. **d. countess,** condesa viuda, f

dowdy a desaliñado, desaseado; poco elegante. n mujer poco elegante, f

dowel n espiga, clavija, f, zoquete, m, vt enclavijar

down n (of a bird) plumón, m; (on a peach, etc.) pelusilla, f; (hair) vello, m; (before the beard) bozo, m; (of a thistle, etc.) vilano, m. **ups and downs,** vicisitudes, f pl

down a pendiente; (of trains, etc.) descendente. adv abajo; hacia abajo; (lowered) bajado; (of the eyes) bajos; (on the ground) en tierra, por tierra; (stretched out) tendido a lo largo; (depressed) triste, abatido; (ill) enfermo; (fallen) caído; (of the wind) cesado; (closed) cerrado; (exhausted) agotado; com al contado; (of temperature) más bajo. prep abajo de; abajo; en la dirección de; (along) a lo largo de; por. "**Down**" (on elevators) «Para bajar». interj ¡Abajo!; ¡A tierra! **He went d. the hill,** Bajaba la colina. **He is d. now,** Ha bajado ahora; Está abajo ahora; Está derribado ahora. **The sun has gone d.,** Se ha puesto el sol. **His stock has gone d.,** fig inf Ha caído en disfavor. **Prices have come d.,** Los precios han bajado. **Their numbers have gone d.,** Sus números han disminuido. **to be d. and out,** estar completamente arruinado, ser pobre de solemnidad. **to boil d.,** reducir hirviendo. **to come d. in the world,** venir a menos. **while I was going d. the river,** mientras iba río abajo, mientras bajaba al río. **d. below,** allá abajo; abajo; en el piso de abajo. **D. on your knees!** ¡De rodillas! **d. to,** hasta. **d. spout,** tubo de bajada, m. **D. with!** ¡Abajo! ¡Muera! **d.-stream,** agua abajo. **d. train,** tren descendente, m

down vt derribar; vencer. **to d. tools,** declararse en huelga

downcast a bajo; cabizbajo, deprimido, abatido

downfall n caída, f; derrumbamiento, m; (failure) fracaso, m; (fig ruin) decadencia, ruina, f

downhearted a descorazonado, alicaído, desalentado

downhill adv cuesta abajo, hacia abajo. a en declive, inclinado. **to go d.,** ir cuesta abajo

downpayment n Mexico enganche m

downpour n chubasco (Mexico), aguacero, chaparrón, m

downright a franco, sincero; categórico, terminante; absoluto. adv muy; completamente

downstairs adv escalera abajo; al piso de abajo; en el piso bajo; abajo. a del piso de abajo. n planta baja, f; piso de abajo, m. **to go d.,** bajar la escalera; ir al piso de abajo

downtrodden a oprimido, esclavizado

downward a descendente; inclinado. adv hacia abajo

downy a velloso; (*fam* of persons) con más conchas que un galápago

dowry n dote, mf. **to give as a d.,** dotar

dowse vt. See **douse**

doze vi dormitar. n sueño ligero, m

dozen n docena, f

drab a pardo, parduzco, grisáceo; *fig* gris, monótono. n (slut) pazpuerca, f; (prostitute) ramera, f

draft n (detachment) destacamento, m; *com* giro, m, letra de cambio, f; (for the army, navy) conscripción, leva, f; (outline) bosquejo, m; proyecto, m; borrador, m. vt (detach) destacar; (recruit) reclutar; (outline) bosquejar, delinear; (draw up) redactar; proyectar

draft card n cartilla (Mexico), libreta de enrolamiento (Argentina), m

draft dodger n emboscado, prófugo, m

drafting n (*mil nav*) reclutamiento, m; (of a bill, etc.) redacción, f; (wording) términos, m pl

draftsman n dibujante, m; delineante, m; redactor, m

drag n (for dredging) draga, f; (harrow) rastrillo, m; (break) freno, m; (obstacle) estorbo, m; *aer* sonda, f. vt arrastrar; (fishing nets) rastrear; (harrow) rastrillar. vi (of the anchor) garrar; arrastrarse por el suelo; (of time) pasar lentamente; ir más despacio (que); (of interest) decaer, disminuir. **d.-hook,** garfio, m. **d.-net,** brancada, f

draggled a mojado y sucio

dragon n dragón, m. **d.-fly,** libélula, f, caballito del diablo, m

dragoon n *mil* dragón, m, vt someter a una disciplina rigurosa; obligar a la fuerza (a)

drain n desaguadero, m; (sewer) cloaca, alcantarilla, f; sumidero, m; *agr* acequia, f. vt desaguar; sanear; (lakes, etc.) desangrar; secar; (bail) achicar; (empty and drink) vaciar; (swallow) tragar; (*fig* of sorrow, etc.) apurar; (despoil) despojar; (deprive) privar (de); (impoverish) empobrecer; (exhaust) agotar. vi desaguarse; vaciarse; (with off) escurrirse. **to be well drained,** tener buen drenaje. **to d. the sump,** vaciar la culata. **to d. away,** vaciar. **d.-pipe,** tubo de desagüe, m

drainage n (of land) drenaje, m; desagüe, m; (of wounds) drenaje, m; (sewage) aguas del alcantarillado, f pl. **main d.,** drenaje municipal, m

draining n de desagüe; de drenaje. **d.-board,** escurridor, m

drake n ánade macho, m

drama n drama, m

dramatic a dramático

dramatis personae n pl personajes, m pl

dramatist n dramaturgo, m

dramatization n versión escénica, f; descripción dramática, f; (of emotions) dramatización, f

drape vt colgar, cubrir; vestir

drapery n colgaduras, f pl; ropaje, m, ropas, f pl; pañería, f

drastic a drástico; enérgico, fuerte; **a drastic measure,** una medida avanzada, f

draught n (act of drawing) tiro, m; (of liquid) trago, m; (glass) vaso, m; (of a ship) calado, m; (of air) corriente de aire, f, *Lat. Am.* chiflón, m; (party) destacamento, m; n pl **draughts,** (game) damas, f pl. vt see **draft. on d.,** (of beer, etc.) por vaso. **d. horse,** caballo de tiro, m. **d. screen,** cancel, m

draughtsman n dibujante, m; delineante, m; redactor, m; (piece in game) peón, m

draughtsmanship n arte del dibujo lineal, mf; redacción (de un proyecto de ley), f

draughty a que tiene corriente de aire; expuesto a los vientos. **This room is d.,** Hay corriente de aire en esta habitación

draw vt tirar; arrastrar; traer; (pluck) arrancar; (attract) atraer; (extract) extraer; sacar; hacer salir; (unsheath) desenvainar; (a bow-string) tender; (cards, dominoes) tomar, robar; (threads) deshilar; (disembowel) destripar; (a check, etc.) girar, librar; (of a ship) calar; (of lines) hacer (rayas); (curtains) correr; (to draw curtains back) descorrer; (salary, money) cobrar, percibir; (obtain) obtener; (persuade) persuadir, inducir; (inhale) respirar; (a sigh) dar; (win) ganar; (a conclusion) deducir, inferir; (a distinction) hacer formular; *sport* empatar; (a number, etc.) sortear; (suck) chupar; (tighten) estirar; (lengthen) alargar; (comfort, etc.) tomar; (inspiration) inspirarse en; (obtain money) procurarse (recursos); (withdraw funds) retirar; (write) escribir; (draw) dibujar; (trace) trazar; (provoke) provocar. **to be drawn,** (of tickets in a lottery and cards) salir. **to d. lots,** echar suertes. **to d. water,** sacar agua. **to d. along,** arrastrar; conducir. **to d. aside,** tomar a un lado, tomar aparte; quitar de en medio, poner a un lado; (curtains) descorrer. **to d. away,** (remove) quitar; (a person) llevarse (a); apartar. **to d. back,** hacer recular; hacer retirarse; hacer volverse atrás; (curtains) descorrer. **to d. down,** hacer bajar; tirar a lo largo de (or por); bajar; (attract) atraer. **to d. forth,** hacer salir; hacer avanzar; tirar hacia adelante; conducir; (develop) desarrollar; sacar; hacer aparecer; (comment, etc.) suscitar. **to d. in,** tirar hacia adentro; sacar; acercar; atraer. **to d. off,** sacar; retirar; quitar; (water from pipes, etc.) vaciar; *print* tirar; (turn aside) desviar. **to d. on,** (of apparel) ponerse; (boots) calzarse; (occasion) ocasionar. **to d. out,** sacar fuera; hacer salir; tirar (de); (extract) extraer; (trace) trazar;

(a person) hacer hablar. **to d. over,** poner encima de; arrastrar por; hacer acercarse (a), tirar hacia; atraer; persuadir. **d. prestige (from),** cobrar prestigio (de). **to d. round,** poner alrededor de. **to d. together,** reunir; acercar. **to d. up,** tirar hacia arriba; subir; sacar; extraer; (raise) levantar, alzar; (bring) traer; (bring near) acercar; (order) ordenar; *mil* formar; (a document) redactar; formular. **to d. oneself up,** erguirse

draw *vi* tirar; (shrink) encogerse; (wrinkle) arrugarse; (of chimneys, etc.) tirar; (a picture) dibujar; *sport* empatar; (move) moverse; avanzar, adelantarse; (of a ship) calar; (a sword) desnudar (la espada); (lots) echar suertes; (attract people) atraer gente; *com* girar. **to d. aside,** ponerse a un lado; retirarse. **to d. back,** retroceder, recular; retirarse; vacilar. **to d. in,** retirarse; (of days) hacerse corto; (of dusk) caer. **to d. off,** alejarse; apartarse, retirarse. **to d. on,** (approach) acercarse; avanzar; *com* girar contra; inspirarse en. **to d. out,** hacerse largo; (of a vehicle) ponerse en marcha, empezar a andar. **to d. round,** ponerse alrededor; reunirse alrededor. **to d. together,** reunirse. **to d. up,** parar.

draw *n* tirada, *f*; (of lotteries) sorteo, *m*; *sport* empate, *m*; atracción, *f*; (*fig* feeler) tanteo, *m*. **to be a big d.,** ser una gran atracción

drawback *n* desventaja, *f*, inconveniente, *m*

drawee *n com* girado, *m*

drawer *n* tirador (-ra); (of water) aguador (-ra); (extractor (-ra); (in a public-house) mozo de taberna, *m*; (designer) diseñador, *m*; (sketcher) dibujante, *mf*; *com* girador, *m*; (receptacle) cajón, *m*; *pl* **drawers,** (men's) calzoncillos, *m pl*; (women's) pantalones, *m pl*

drawing *n* (pulling) tiro, *m*; atracción, *f*; (extraction) extracción, *f*; saca, *f*; (in raffles, etc. and of lots) sorteo, *m*; (of money) percibo, *m*; *com* giro, *m*; (sketch) dibujo, *m*; (plan) esquema, *f*. **free-hand d.,** dibujo a pulso, *m*. **d. from life,** dibujo del natural, *m*. **d.-board,** tablero de dibujo, *m*. **d.-paper,** papel para dibujar, *m*. **d.-pin,** chinche, *f*. **d.-room,** salón, *m*

drawl *vi* hablar arrastrando las palabras

drawn *past part* See **draw.** a (tired) ojeroso, con ojeras, con un aspecto de cansancio; (with pain) desencajado. **long d. out,** demasiado largo. **d. sword,** espada desnuda, *f*. **d.-thread work,** deshilados, *m pl*

dread *n* pavor, temor, terror, espanto, *m*; trepidación, *f*, miedo, *m*. a temible, espantoso, terrible; augusto. *vt* temer. *vi* tener miedo, temer. **in d. of,** con miedo de, con terror de

dreadful a terrible, pavoroso, espantoso, horroroso; formidable; augusto

dream *n* sueño, *m*; ilusión, *f*; ensueño, *m*; fantasía, *f*. *vt* and *vi* soñar; imaginar. **He dreamed away the hours,** Pasaba las horas soñando. **I wouldn't d. of it!** ¡Ni por sueño! **in a d.,** en sueños; (waking) como en sueños; mecánicamente. **Sweet dreams!** ¡Duerme bien! **to d. of,** soñar con

dreamily *adv* como en sueños; soñolientamente; vagamente

dreaming *n* sueños, *m pl*

dreamland *n* reino de los sueños, *m*

dreamy a soñador; soñoliento; fantástico; (empty) vació

dreary a triste; melancólico; lóbrego

dredge *vt* dragar; (with sugar, etc.) espolvorear

dregs *n pl* heces, *f pl*, posos, *m pl*, *Lat. Am.* concho *m* **to drain to the d.,** vaciar hasta las heces

drench *vt* mojar, calar. **He is drenched to the skin,** Está calado hasta los huesos

dress *vt* (with clothes) vestir; (arrange) arreglar; (the hair) peinar(se); (a wound) curar; (hides) adobar; (cloth) aprestar; (flax) rastrillar; (stone) labrar; (wood) desbastar; (prune) podar; (a garden) cultivar; (manure) abonar; *cul* aderezar; preparar; (season) condimentar; (a table) poner; (adorn) ataviar, adornar; revestir; (a dead body) amortajar. *vi* vestirse; ataviarse; (of troops) alinearse. **all dressed up and nowhere to go,** compuesta y sin novio. **dress to kill, dress to the nines** *Lat. Am.* arriscarse, *Central America* empavonarse **dressed up to the nines,** vestido de veinticinco alfileres. **Left (Right) d.!** ¡A la izquierda (A la derecha) alinearse! **to d. down,** (scold) poner como un trapo (a), dar una calada (a). **to d. up,** *vt* ataviar; (disguise) disfrazar. *vi* ponerse muy elegante; disfrazarse

dress *n* (in general) el vestir; (clothes) ropa, *f*; (frock) vestido, traje, *m*; (uniform) uniforme, *m*; (*fig* covering) hábitos, *m pl*; (appearance) aspecto, *m*; forma, *f*. **full d.,** (uniform) uniforme de gala, *m*; (civilian, man's) traje de etiqueta, *m*; (woman's) traje de gala, *m*. **morning d.,** (man's) traje de paisano, *m*; (woman's) vestido de todos los días, *m*; (man's formal dress) chaqué, *m*. **ready-made d.,** traje hecho, *m*. **d. allowance,** alfileres *m pl*. **d.-circle,** anfiteatro, *m*. **d.-coat,** frac, *m*. **d. protector,** sobaquera, *f*. **d. rehearsal,** ensayo general, *m*. **d. shirt,** camisa de pechera dura, *f*. **d. suit,** (with white tie) traje de frac, *m*; (with black tie) smoking, *m*. **d. sword,** espada de gala, *f*. **d. tie,** corbata de smoking (or de frac), *f*

dresser *n* el que adereza; (of wounds) practicante (de hospital), *m*; (valet) ayuda de cámara, *m*; (maid) doncella, *f*; (of skins) adobador de pieles, *m*; (furniture) aparador, *m*; (in the kitchen) armario de la cocina, *m*

dressing n el vestir(se); aderezamiento, m; (for cloth) apresto, m; (of leather) adobo, m; (of wood) desbaste, m; (of stone) labrado, m; (manuring) estercoladura, f; (sauce) salsa, f; (seasoning) condimentación, f; (of a wound) cura, f; (bandage) apósito, m, vendaje, m. **d.-case,** neceser, saco de noche, m. **d.-down,** inf rapapolvo, m. **d.-gown,** (woman's) salto de cama, quimono, m; (man's) batín, m. **d.-jacket,** chambra, f, peinador, m. **d.-room,** theat camarín, m; (in a house) trasalcoba, recámara, f. **d.-station,** puesto de socorro, m. **d.-table,** tocador, m, mesa de tocador, f

dressmaker n modista, mf

dressmaking n confección de vestidos, f; arte de la modista, mf

dribble vi gotear; (slaver) babear. vt (in football) regatear. n (in football) regate, m

dried a seco; (of fruit) paso. **d. up,** (withered) marchito; (of people) enjuto. **d. fish,** cecial, m. **d. meat,** cecina, f

drift n (in a ship or airplane's course) deriva, f; (of a current) velocidad, f; (tendency) tendencia, f; (meaning) significación, f; (heap) montón, m; (aim) objeto, propósito, fin, m; min galería, f; (of dust, etc.) nube, f; (shower) lluvia, f; (impulsion) impulso, m; violencia, f. vi flotar, ir arrastrado por la corriente; amontonarse; naut derivar; aer abatir. vt llevar; amontonar. **drifts of sand,** arena movediza, f. **to d. into,** (war, etc.) entrar sin querer en; (habits) dar en la flor de; (a room, etc.) deslizarse en. **d.-wood,** madera de deriva, f

drill n (instrument) taladro, perforador, m, barrena, f; ejercicio, m, educación física, f; mil instrucción militar, f; (cloth) dril, m; agr sembradora mecánica, f; (for seeds) hilera, f; (discipline) disciplina, f; (teaching) instrucción, f. vt taladrar, barrenar; enseñar el ejercicio (a); enseñar la instrucción; disciplinar; (seed) sembrar en hileras. vi hacer el ejercicio; hacer la instrucción militar. **d. ground,** (in a barracks) patio de un cuartel, m; (in a school) patio de recreo, m. **d.-sergeant,** sargento instructor, m

drilling n (boring) perforación, f, barrenamiento, m; (of seeds) sembradura en hileras, f; ejercicios, m pl; (maneuvers) maniobras, f pl

drink n bebida, f; (glass of wine, etc.) copita, f; (of water, etc.) vaso, m. vt beber; tomar; (empty) vaciar. vi beber. **to d. the health of,** beber a la salud de, brindar por. **to give someone a d.,** dar a beber. **Would you like a d.?** ¿Quieres tomar algo? **to d. in,** absorber. **to d. off, up,** beber de un trago

drinkable a potable, bebedero

drinker n bebedor (-ra)

drinking n acción de beber, f; el beber,

m; (alcoholism) bebida, f. **a que bebe;** aficionado a la bebida; (of things) para beber; (drinkable) potable; (tavern) de taberna. **d.-fountain,** fuente pública para beber agua, f. **d. place,** bebedero, m; bar, m. **d.-song,** canción de taberna, f. **d.-trough,** abrevadero, m; **d.-water,** agua potable, f

drip vi and vt chorrear, gotear; caer gota a gota; escurrir; destilar; chorrear. n goteo, m; gota, f; arch goterón, m

dripping n goteo, m; chorreo, m; (fat) grasa, f, a que gotea; mojado; que chorrea agua. **d.-pan,** grasera, f

drive vt empujar; arrojar; conducir; (grouse, etc.) batir; (a ball) golpear; (a nail, etc.) clavar; (dog) compeler, forzar a; (a horse, plough, etc.) manejar; (mech work) mover; (cause to work, of machines) hacer funcionar; (a tunnel, etc.) abrir, construir; (a bargain, etc.) hacer; (cause) impulsar, hacer; (mad, etc.) volver. vi lanzarse; (of rain) azotar; (a vehicle) conducir; (in a vehicle) ir en (coche, etc.). **to let d. at,** (aim) asestar. **to a wedge,** hacer mella. **to d. home an argument,** convencer; hacer convincente. **What is he driving at?** ¿Qué se propone?; ¿Qué quiere?; ¿Qué quiere decir con sus indirectas? ¿A dónde quiere llegar con esto? **to d. along,** ir en coche o carruaje por; pasearse en coche o carruaje; conducir un auto, etc., por. **to d. away,** vt echar; (chase) cazar; (flies, etc.) sacudirse, espantar; (care, etc.) ahuyentar; (of persons) apartar, alejar. vi (depart) marcharse (en coche, etc.). **to d. back,** vt rechazar; (a ball) devolver. vi volver en auto, etc.); (arrive) llegar. **to d. crazy, d. insane** enloquecer, Lat. Am. also idiotizar; **to d. down,** hacer bajar; arrojar hacia abajo; (in a vehicle) bajar (por). **to d. in, into,** vt hacer entrar; (of teeth, etc.) hincar; (nails) clavar; fig introducir. vt entrar (en coche, carruaje); llegar (en coche, etc.). **to d. off,** See **away. to d. off the stage,** hacer dejar la escena, silbar. **to d. on,** vt empujar; hacer avanzar; (attack) atacar. vi seguir su marcha; seguir avanzando; emprender la marcha. **to d. out,** vt expulsar; hacer salir; (chase) cazar. vi salir (en coche, etc.); parar. **to d. up,** vi llegar (en coche, etc.); parar. **to d. up to,** avanzar hasta, llegar hasta; conducir (el coche, etc.) hasta

drive n paseo (en coche, etc.), m; (avenue) avenida, f; (distance) trayecto, m; (journey) viaje, m; mech acción, f; conducción, f; m; mil ataque, m; (of a person) energía, f; campaña vigorosa, f; impulso, m. **left (right) hand d.,** conducción a la izquierda (derecha). **to take a d.,** dar un paseo en auto, etc. **to take for a d.,** llevar a paseo en (auto, etc.)

drive-in n autocine, autocinema, m

drivel n vaciedades, patrañas, f pl, disparates, m pl, vi decir disparates, chochear

driver n conductor (-ra); chófer, m; (of an engine) maquinista, m; (of a cart) carretero, m; (of a coach, carriage) cochero, m; (of cattle, etc.) ganadero, m; (golf) conductor, m

driver's license Spain carné de chofer, Argentina carné de conductor m, elsewhere in Lat. Am. licencia de manejar f

"Driveway" «Vado Permante», «Paso de Carruajes»

driving n conducción, f; modo de conducir, m; paseo (en coche, etc.), m; impulsión, f. a de conducir; de chófer; para choferes; motor; propulsor; impulsor; de transmisión; fig impulsor; (violent) violento, impetuoso. **to go d.,** ir de paseo (en auto o carruaje). **d. mirror,** espejo retrovisor, m. **d. seat,** asiento del conductor, m; (of an old-fashioned coach, etc.) pescante, m. **d.-shaft,** mech árbol motor, m. **d. test,** examen para choferes, m. **d.-wheel,** volante, m; rueda motriz, f. **d.-whip,** látigo, m

drizzle n llovizna, f, vi lloviznar, Lat. Am. briznar

droll a chusco, gracioso. n bufón, m

drone n abejón, m; fig zángano, m; (hum) zumbido, m; (of a song, voice) salmodia, f, vt and vi (hum) zumbar; (of a song, voice) salmodiar; (idle) zanganear

droop vi inclinarse; colgar; caer; (wither) marchitarse; (fade) consumirse; (pine) desanimarse. vt bajar; dejar caer. n caída, f; inclinación, f

drooping a caído; debilitado; lánguido; (of ears) gacho; (depressed) alicaído, deprimido

drop n gota, f; (tear) lágrima, f; (for the ear) pendiente, m; (sweet) pastilla, f; (of a chandelier) almendra, f; (fall) caída, f; (in price, etc.) baja, f; (slope) pendiente, cuesta, f. **by drops,** a gotas. **d. bottle,** frasco cuentagotas, m. **d.-curtain,** telón de boca, m. **d.-hammer,** martinete, m. **d.-head coupé,** cupé descapotable, m. **d.-scene,** telón de foro, m

drop vt verter a gotas; destilar; (sprinkle) salpicar, rociar; dejar caer; soltar; (lower) bajar; (of clothes, etc.) desprenderse de, quitar; (lose) perder; (a letter in a mailbox) echar; (leave) dejar; (give up) renunciar (a); desistir (de); abandonar; (kill) tumbar; (a hint) soltar; (a curtsey) hacer. vi gotear, caer en gotas, destilar; (descend) bajar, descender; caer muerto; caer desmayado; (sleep) dormirse; (fall) caer; (of the wind) amainar; (of prices, temperature) bajar. **to let the matter d.,** poner fin a una cuestión. **to d. a line,** poner unas líneas. **to d. anchor,** echar el ancla. **to d. behind,** quedarse atrás. **to d. down,** caer (a tierra). **to d. in,** entrar al pasar. **d. in on somebody,** pasarse por casa de fulano, pasarse por el despacho de (etc.). **to d. off,** separarse (de); disminuir; (sleep) quedar dormido; (die) morir de repente. **to d. out,** separarse; (from a race, etc.) retirarse (de); quedarse atrás; desaparecer; ausentarse, apartarse; (decrease) disminuir; decaer. **He has dropped out of my life,** Le he perdido de vista. **to d. through,** caer por; frustrarse; no dar resultado

dropping n gotera, f; gotas, f pl; (fall) caída, f; pl **droppings** (of a candle) moco, m; (dung) cagadas, f pl. **Constant d. wears away the stone,** La gotera cava la piedra

dropsy n hidropesía, f

dross n escoria, f; (rubbish) basura, f

drought n aridez, f; (thirst) sed, f; (dry season) sequía, f

drove n manada, f, hato, m; (of sheep) rebaño, m; (crowd) muchedumbre, f

drown vi ahogarse. vt ahogar; sumergir; inundar; (fig of cries, sorrow, etc.) ahogar

drowse vi adormecerse

drowsiness n somnolencia, f; sueño, m; (laziness) indolencia, pereza, f

drowsy a soñoliento; adormecedor, soporífero; (heavy) amodorrado. **to grow d.,** adormecerse. **to make d.,** adormecer

drudgery n trabajo arduo, m, faena monótona, f

drug n droga, f; medicamento, m; narcótico, m. vt mezclar con drogas; administrar drogas (a); narcotizar. vi tomar drogas. **d. trade,** comercio de drogas, m. **d. traffic,** contrabando de drogas, narcotráfico m

drug addict n toxicómano, Lat. Am. adicto m

drug addiction n toxicomanía, f

druggist n droguero (-ra)

drum n tambor, m; (of the ear) tímpano (del oído), m; (cylinder) cilindro, m; (box) caja, f; arch cuerpo de columna, m. **bass d.,** bombo, m. **with drums beating,** con tambor batiente. **d.-head,** parche (del tambor), m. **d.-head service,** misa de campaña, f. **d.-major,** tambor mayor, m

drum vt and vi tocar el tambor; (with the fingers) tabalear, teclear; (with the heels) zapatear; (into a person's head) machacar. **to d. out,** mil expulsar a tambor batiente

drummer n tambor, m

drumstick n palillo (de tambor), m

drunk a borracho, ebrio, Lat. Am. also iluminado, Central America azunumbaso n borracho, m. **to be d.,** estar borracho. **to get d.,** emborracharse, Lat. Am. also iluminarse; inf pillar un lobo, (on wine) Mexico envinarse. **to make d.,** emborrachar

drunkard n borracho (-cha)

drunken a borracho, ebrio

dry vi secarse. vt secar; desaguar; (wipe) enjugar. **to dry one's tears,** enjugarse las lágrimas; *fig* secarse las lágrimas. **to dry up,** secarse; (of persons) acecinarse; (with old age) apergaminarse; (of ideas, etc.) agotarse; (be quiet) callarse

dry *a* seco; árido; estéril; (thirsty) sediento; (of wine) seco; (U.S.A.) prohibicionista; (squeezed) exprimido; (of toast) sin mantequilla; (*fig* chilly) aburrido; (sarcastic) sarcástico; (of humour) agudo. **on dry land,** en seco. **dry battery,** pila seca, *f.* **to dry-clean,** lavar al seco. **dry-cleaner,** tintorero (-ra). **dry-cleaning,** lavado al seco, *m.* **dry-cleaning shop,** tintorería, *f.* **dry goods,** lencería, *f.* **dry land,** tierra firme, *f.* **dry measure,** medida para áridos, *f.* **dry-nurse,** ama seca, *f.* **dry-point,** punta seca, *f.* **dry-rot,** carcoma, *f.* **dry-shod,** con los pies secos

drying *n* secamiento, *m;* desecación, *f,* a secante; seco; para secar. **d. ground,** tendedero, *m.* **d. machine,** secadora, *f.* (for the hair) secadora de cabello, *f.* **d. room,** secadero, *m*

dual *a* doble; *gram* dual. **d. control,** mandos gemelos, *m pl.* **d. personality,** conciencia doble, *f*

dub *vt* (a knight) armar caballero; (call) apellidar; (nickname) motejar, apodar

dubbing *n* (of films) doblaje, *m*

dubious *a* dudoso, incierto; indeciso; problemático; ambiguo

dubiousness *n* carácter dudoso, *m;* incertidumbre, *f;* ambigüedad, *f*

duck *n* pato (-ta), ánade, *mf; sport* cero, *m;* (darling) vida mía, querida, *f;* (jerk) agachada, *f;* (under the water) chapuz, *m;* (material) dril, *m; mil* auto anfibio, *m; pl* **ducks,** pantalones de dril, *m pl. vi* agacharse; (under water) chapuzarse. *vt* zabullir, sumergir; bajar, inclinar

ducking *n* chapuz, *m.* **d.-stool,** silla de chapuzar, *f*

duckling *n* anadino (-na)

duct *n* conducto, canal, *m; bot* tubo, *m*

ductless *a* sin tubos

due *a* debido; (payable) pagadero; (fallen due) vencido; (fitting) propio, (expected) esperado; *m* impuesto; *m,* derecho, *m.* **in due form,** en regla. **in its due time,** a su tiempo debido. **to fall due,** vencerse. **due bill,** *com* abonaré, *m.* **due west,** poniente derecho, *m*

duel *n* duelo, lance de honor, *m; fig* lucha, *f.* **to fight a d.,** batirse en duelo

duelist *n* duelista, *m*

duet *n* dúo, *m*

duffer *n* estúpido (-da); ganso, *m;* (at games, etc.) maleta, *m*

dug *n* teta, *f*

dugout *n* trinchera, *f*

duke *n* duque, *m*

dull *a* (stupid) lerdo, estúpido, obtuso; (boring, tedious) aburrido; (of pain, sounds) sordo; (of colors and eyes) apagado; (of light, beams, etc.) sombrío;

(not polished) mate; (pale) pálido; (insipid) insípido, insulso; (of people) soso, poco interesante; (dreary, sad) triste; (gray) gris; (of mirrors, etc.) empañado; (of weather) anublado; (of hearing) duro; (slow) lento; lánguido; insensible; (blunt) romo; *com* encalmado, inactivo. **to find life d.,** encontrar la vida aburrida. **d. of hearing,** duro de oído, algo sordo. **d. pain,** dolor sordo, *m.* **d. season,** temporada de calma, *f.* **d.-eyed,** con ojos apagados. **d.-witted,** lerdo

dull *vt* (make stupid) entontecer; (lessen) mitigar; (weaken) debilitar; (pain) calmar, aliviar; (sadden) entristecer; (blunt) embotar; (spoil) estropear; (a mirror, etc.) empañar; (a polished surface) hacer mate, deslustrar; (of enthusiasm, etc.) enfriar; (tire) fatigar; (obstruct) impedir

dullness *n* (stupidity) estupidez, *f;* (boredom) aburrimiento, *m;* (heaviness) pesadez, *f;* (drowsiness) somnolencia, *f;* (insipidity) insipidez, insulsez, *f;* (of literary style) prosaísmo, *m;* (of persons) sosería, *f;* (of a surface) deslustre, *m;* (laziness) pereza, languidez, *f;* (slowness) lentitud, *f;* (tiredness) cansancio, *m;* (sadness) tristeza, *f;* (bluntness) embotamiento, *m;* (of hearing) dureza, *f; com* desanimación, *f*

dully *adv* (stupidly) estúpidamente; sin comprender; (insipidly) insípidamente; (not brightly) sin brillo; (slowly) lentamente; (sadly) tristemente; (tiredly) con cansancio; (of sound) sordamente

duly *adv* debidamente; puntualmente

dumb *a* mudo; callado; silencioso; *inf* tonto, estúpido, *Lat. Am. also* baboso, *Central America* azurumbado. **to become d.,** enmudecer. **to strike d.,** dejar sin habla. **d.-bell,** barra con pesas, *f.* **d. show,** pantomima, *f.* **d. waiter,** bufete, *m*

dumbfound *vt* dejar sin habla; confundir; pasmar

dumbness *n* mudez, *f,* mutismo, *m;* silencio, *m*

dummy *n* (tailor's, etc.) maniquí, *m;* (puppet) títere, *m;* cabeza para pelucas, *f;* (figurehead) hombre de paja, testaferro, *m;* (baby's) chupador, *m;* (at cards) el muerto. *a* fingido. **to be d.,** (at cards) ser el muerto

dump *n* depósito, *m;* vaciadero, *m. vt* depositar; (goods on a market) inundar (con)

dumping *n* depósito, *m;* vaciamiento, *m;* (of goods on a market) inundación, *f.* **"D. prohibited,"** «Se prohíbe arrojar la basura»

dumps *n* murria, *f*

dun *vt* apremiar, importunar

dun-colored *a* pardo

dunce *n* asno, bobo, zoquete, *m.* **dunce's cap,** coroza, *f*

dunderhead *n* cabeza de alcornoque, zoquete, *m*

dune *n* duna, *f*

dung *n* estiércol, *m*; (of rabbits, mice, deer, sheep, goats) cagarruta, *f*; (of cows) boñiga, *f*; (of hens) gallinaza, *f*. **d.-cart,** carro de basura, *m*

dungarees *n* mono, *m*, pantalones-vaquero, *m pl*

dungeon *n* mazmorra, *f*, calabozo, *m*

dupe *n* víctima, *f*; tonto (-ta). *vt* embelecar, engañar. **to be a d.,** *inf* hacer el primo

duplicate *a* duplicado, doble. *n* duplicado, *m*; copia, *f*, *vt* duplicar

durability *n* duración, *f*. **This is a cloth of great d.,** Este es un paño que dura mucho, Este es un paño muy duradero

durable *a* duradero

duration *n* duración, *f*

duress *n* compulsión, *f*; (prison) prisión, *f*

during *prep* durante

dusk *n* atardecer, anochecer, *m*; (twilight) crepúsculo, *m*; (darkness) oscuridad, *f*. **at d.,** al atardecer, a la caída de la tarde

dusky *a* (swarthy) moreno; (black) negro; (dim, dark) oscuro; (of colors) sucio

dust *n* polvo, *m*; (cloud of dust) polvareda, *f*; (ashes) cenizas, *f pl*; (of coal) cisco, *m*; (sweepings) barreduras, *f pl*; (of grain) tamo, *m*. *vt* desempolvar, quitar (or sacudir) el polvo de; (cover with dust) polvorear; (scatter) salpicar; (sweep) barrer; (clean) limpiar. **d.-bin,** basurero, *m*. **d.-cart,** carro de la basura, *m*. **d. cloud,** polvareda, *f*. **d. jacket,** (books) sobrecubierta, *f*. **d.-pan,** recogedor de basura, *m*. **d.-sheet,** guardapolvo, *m*. **d. storm,** vendaval de polvo, *m*

duster *n* el, *m*, que quita el polvo; paño (para quitar el polvo), *m*; (of feathers) plumero, *m*

dustiness *n* empolvoramiento, *m*; estado polvoriento, *m*

dusting *n* limpieza, *f*; (sweeping) barredura, *f*; (powder) polvos antisépticos, *m pl*

dusty *a* polvoriento, polvoroso, empolvado; del color del polvo; (of colours) sucio. **It is very d.,** Hay mucho polvo. **to get d.,** llenarse (or cubrirse) de polvo

Dutch *a* holandés. **the D.,** los holandeses. **double D.,** griego, galimatías, *m*. **D. cheese,** queso de bola, *m*. **D. courage,** coraje falso, *m*. **D. woman,** holandesa, *f*

Dutchman *n* holandés, *m*

dutiable *a* sujeto a derechos de aduana

dutiful *a* que cumple con sus deberes; obediente, sumiso; respetuoso; excelente, muy bueno

dutifully *adv* obedientemente; respetuosamente

duty *n* deber, *m*; obligación, *f*; (greetings) respetos, *m pl*; (charge, burden) carga, *f*; (tax) derecho, impuesto, *m*; *mil* servicio, *m*; (guard) guardia, *f*. **off d.,** libre. **on d.,** de servicio. **to be on sentry d.,** estar de guardia. **to do d. as,** servir como. **to do one's d.,** hacer (or cumplir con) su deber. **to pay d. on,** pagar derechos de aduana sobre. **d.-free,** franco de derechos

dwarf *a* enano. *n* enano (-na). *vt* impedir el crecimiento de; empequeñecer

dwarfish *a* enano

dwell *vi* vivir, habitar; (with on, upon) (think about) meditar sobre, pensar en; (deal with) tratar de; hablar largamente de; (insist on) insistir en; apoyarse en, hacer hincapié en; (pause over) detenerse en

dweller *n* habitante, *mf*; (more poetic) morador (-ra)

dwelling *n* vivienda, *f*; (abode) morada, habitación, *f*; residencia, *f*; casa, *f*; (domicile) domicilio, *m*. **d.-house,** casa, *f*

dwindle *vi* disminuirse; consumirse; (decay) decaer; (degenerate) degenerar. **to d. to,** reducirse a

dwindling *n* disminución, *f*

dye *vt* teñir, colorar. *vi* teñirse. *n* tinte, *m*; (colour) color, *m*. **fast dye,** tinte estable, *m*. **dye-house,** tintorería, *f*. **dye-stuff,** materia colorante, *f*. **dye-works,** tintorería, *f*

dyed-in-the-wool *a* de pies a cabeza

dyeing *n* teñidura, tintura, *f*; (as a trade) tintorería, *f*. **d. and dry-cleaning shop,** tintorería, *f*

dyer *n* tintorero (-ra)

dyestuff *n* materia colorante, materia de tinte, materia tintórea, *f*

dying *a* moribundo, agonizante; de la muerte; (of light) mortecino; (last) último; supremo; (languishing) lánguido; (deathbed) hecho en su lecho mortuorio. **to be d.,** estar agonizando; (of light) fenecer. **to be d. for,** estar muerto por

dynamic *a* dinámico

dynamite *n* dinamita, *f*

dynastic *a* dinástico

dynasty *n* dinastía, *f*

dysentery *n* disentería, *f*

dyspepsia *n* dispepsia, *f*

e *n* (letter) e, *f*; *mus* mi, *m*

each *a* cada (invariable), todo. *pron* cada uno, *m*; cada una, *f*. **e. of them,** cada uno de ellos. **They help e. other,** Se ayudan mutuamente, Se ayudan entre sí. **to love e. other,** amarse

eager *a* impaciente; ansioso, deseoso; ambicioso

eagerly *adv* con impaciencia; con ansia; ambiciosamente

eagerness *n* impaciencia, *f*; ansia, *f*, deseo, *m*; (promptness) alacridad, *f*; (zeal) fervor, *m*

eagle *n* águila, *f*. **e. royal e.,** águila caudal, águila real, *f*. **e.-eyed,** con ojos de lince, de ojo avizor. **have the eyes of an e.,** tener ojos de lince, tener vista de lince

ear *n* (outer ear) oreja, *f*; (inner ear and sense of hearing) oído, *m*; *bot* espiga, panoja, *f*. **to begin to show the ear,** (grain) espigar. **to be all ears,** ser todo oídos. **to give ear,** dar oído. **to have a good ear,** tener buen oído. **to play by ear,** tocar de oído. **to turn a deaf ear,** hacerse el sordo. **ear-ache,** dolor de oídos, *m*. **ear-drum,** tímpano (del oído), *m*. **ear-flap,** orejera, *f*. **ear-phone, ear-piece,** auricular, *m*. **ear-piercing,** penetrante, agudo. **ear-shot,** alcance del oído, *m*. **to be within ear-shot,** estar al alcance del oído. **ear-trumpet,** trompetilla, *f*. **ear wax,** cerilla, *f*

earl *n* conde, *m*

earlier, earliest *a comp* and *sup* más temprano; más primitivo; más antiguo; (first, of time) primero. *adv* más temprano; más pronto; antes

earliness *n* lo temprano; antigüedad, *f*, lo primitivo; (precocity) precocidad, *f*. **The e. of his arrival,** Su llegada de buena hora

early *a* temprano; primitivo; (of fruit, etc.) temprano, adelantado; (movement) primero (e.g. **early Romanticism,** el primer romanticismo); (person) de la primera época (e.g. **the early Cervantes,** Cervantes de la primera época); (work) un primer (e.g. **an early work of Unamuno's,** una primera obra de Unamuno); (advanced) avanzado; (precocious) precoz; (first, of time) primero; (in the morning) matutino; (near) próximo; cercano; (premature) prematuro; (of child's age) tierno; joven. **in the e. hours,** en las primeras horas; en las altas horas (de la noche). **e. age,** edad temprana, tierna edad, *f*. **e.-fruiting,** *agr* tempranal. **e. riser,** madrugador (-ra). **e.-rising,** *a* madrugador. **e. years,** primeros años, años de la niñez, *m pl*

early *adv* temprano; al principio (de); en los primeros días (de); desde los primeros días (de); (in the month, year) a principios (de); (in time) a tiempo; (in the day) de buena hora; (soon) pronto; (among the first) entre los primeros (de). **as e. as possible,** lo más temprano posible; lo

más pronto posible. **to be e.,** llegar antes de tiempo; llegar de buena hora. **to get up e.,** madrugar. **to go to bed e.,** acostarse temprano. **too e.,** demasiado temprano. **e. in the morning,** de madrugada

earmark *vt* marcar; *fig* destinar, reservar

earn *vt* ganar; obtener, adquirir; (deserve) merecer

earnest *a* serio; fervoroso; diligente; sincero. **to be in e. about something,** tomarlo en serio; ser sincero (en). **e. money,** arras, *f pl*

earnestly *adv* seriamente; fervorosamente; con diligencia; sinceramente, de buena fe

earnings *n pl com* ingresos, *m pl*; (salary) salario, *m*; estipendio, *m*; (of a workman) jornal, *m*

earring *n* pendiente, arete, *Lat. Am. also* aro *m*

earth *n* tierra, *f*; (of a badger, etc.) madriguera, *f*; *rad* tierra, *f*. *vt* cubrir con tierra; *rad* conectar con tierra. **clod of e.,** terrón, *m*. **half the e.,** *inf* medio mundo, *m*. **on e.,** en este mundo, sobre la tierra

earthen *a* terrizo, terroso; (of mud) de barro

earthenware *n* alfar, *m*, a de loza, de barro

earthiness *n* terrosidad, *f*

earthly *a* terrestre, terrenal; de la tierra; (fleshly) carnal; (worldly) mundano; material. **There is not an e. chance,** No hay la más mínima posibilidad

earthquake *n* terremoto, temblor de tierra, *m*

earthy *a* térreo, terroso

ease *n* bienestar, *m*; tranquilidad, *f*; descanso, *m*; (leisure) ocio, *m*; (comfortableness) comodidad, *f*; (freedom from embarrassment) naturalidad, *f*, desembarazo, desenfado, *m*; (from pain) alivio, *m*; (simplicity) facilidad, *f*. *vt* (widen) ensanchar; aflojar; (pain) aliviar; (lighten) aligerar; (moderate) moderar; (soften) suavizar; (free) librar; (one's mind) tranquilizar. **in my moments of e.,** en mis ocios, en mis momentos de ocio. **Stand at e.!** *mil* ¡En su lugar descansen! **to be at e.,** estar a sus anchas; encontrarse bien; comportarse con toda naturalidad. **with e.,** fácilmente. **to e. off,** *vt* (naut cables, sails) arriar. *vi* sentirse menos, cesar

easel *n* caballete (de pintor) *m*

east *n* este, *m*; oriente, *m*, (of countries) Oriente, *m*; Levante, *m*. a del este; del oriente; (of countries) de Oriente, oriental; levantino. **e. North e.,** estenordeste, *m*. **e. South e.,** estesudeste, *m*. **e. wind,** viento del este, *m*

Easter n Pascua de Resurrección, f. **E. egg,** huevo de Pascua, m. **E. Saturday,** sábado de gloria, m. **E. Sunday,** domingo de Pascua, m

eastern a del este; de Oriente; oriental. n oriental, mf

eastward adv hacia el este, hacia oriente

easy a fácil; sencillo; (comfortable) cómodo; (free from pain) aliviado; com flojo; (well-off) acomodado, holgado; (calm) tranquilo; tolerante; natural; afable, condescendiente; (of virtue, women) fácil. adv con calma; despacio. **I must make myself e. about,** he de tranquilizarme sobre. **Stand e.!** iEn su lugar descansen! **to take it e.,** tomarlo con calma. **e.-chair,** (silla) poltrona, f. **easy come, easy go,** lo que por agua, agua (Mexico and Colombia), los dineros del sacristán cantando vienen y cantando se van (Spain). **e.-going,** acomodadizo; indolente; (morally) de manga ancha; (casual) descuidado

eat vt comer; (meals, soup, refreshments) tomar; (with a good, bad appetite) hacer; consumir; (corrode) corroer; desgastar. vi comer; (fam of food) ser de buen (or mal) comer. **to eat one's breakfast (lunch),** tomar el desayuno, desayunar (almorzar). **to eat one's words,** retractarse. **to eat away,** comer; consumir; corroer. **to eat into,** (of chemicals) morder; (a fortune) consumir; gastar. **eat out of s.b.'s hand,** comer de la mano de fulano, comer en la mano de fulano. **to eat up,** devorar (also fig)

eating n el comer; comida, f. **e. and drinking,** el comer y beber. **e.-house,** casa de comidas, f

eau de cologne n agua de Colonia, f

eaves n rafe, alero, m. **under the e.,** debajo del alero

eavesdrop vi escuchar a las puertas; fisgonear, espiar

eavesdropper n fisgón (-ona)

ebb n (of the tide) reflujo, m; menguante, f; fig declinación, f; fig decadencia, f; (of life) vejez, f. vi (of tide) menguar; declinar; decaer. **to ebb and flow,** fluir y refluir. **to ebb away from,** dejar; dejar aislado. **ebb-tide,** marea menguante, f

ebony n ébano, m

ebullient a efervescente, exuberante

eccentric a geom excéntrico; raro, original; extravagante, excéntrico, Lat. Am. ideático. n persona excéntrica, f, original, m

eccentricity n geom excentricidad, f; rareza, extravagancia, excentricidad, f

echo n eco, m; reverberación, resonancia, f. vt repercutir; fig repetir. vi resonar, retumbar, reverberar

eclectic a and n ecléctico (-ca)

eclipse n ast eclipse, m, vt eclipsar, hacer eclipse a. **to be in e.,** estar en eclipse

economic a económico

economical a económico

economics n economía política, f

economist n economista, mf

economize vt economizar, ahorrar. vi hacer economías

economy n economía, f. **domestic e.,** economía doméstica, f. **political e.,** economía política, f

ecstasy n éxtasis, arrebato, m; transporte, m. **to be in e.,** estar en éxtasis

ecstatic a extático

Ecuador el Ecuador

Ecuadorian a and n ecuatoriano (-na)

ecumenical a ecuménico

eczema n eczema, f

eddy n remolino, m, vi remolinar; fig remolinear

edema n med edema, m

edge n (of sharp instruments) filo, m; (of a skate) cuchilla, f; margen, mf; (shore) orilla, f; (of two surfaces) arista, f; (of books) borde, m; (of a coin) canto, m; (of a chair, a precipice, a forest, a curb, etc.) borde, m; (extreme) extremidad, f. **on e.,** de canto; fig ansioso. **to be on e.,** fig tener los nervios en punta. **to set on e.,** poner de canto; (of teeth) dar dentera

edge vt (sharpen) afilar; sew ribetear; orlar; poner un borde (a); (cut) cortar. **to e. away,** escurrirse. **to e. into,** vt insinuarse. vi deslizarse en. **to e. out,** salir poco a poco

edged a afilado, cortante; (in compounds) de . . . filos; (bordered) bordeado; (of books) de bordes . . .

edgeways adv de lado; de canto. **He couldn't get a word in e.,** No pudo meter baza en la conversación

edging n borde, m; ribete, m

edible a comestible

edict n edicto, m

edifice n edificio, m

edify vt edificar

edifying a edificante, edificador, de edificación

edit vt editar; (a newspaper, journal) ser director de; (prepare for press) redactar; (correct) corregir

edition n edición, f; print tirada, f. **first e.,** edición príncipe, f. **miniature e.,** edición diamante, f

editor n (of a book) editor, m; (of a newspaper, journal) director, m

editorial a de redacción; editorial. n editorial, artículo de fondo, m. **e. staff,** redacción, f

educate vt educar; formar; (accustom) acostumbrar

educated a culto

education n educación, f; enseñanza, f; pedagogía, f. **chair of e.,** cátedra de pedagogía, f. **early e.,** primeras letras, f pl. **higher e.,** enseñanza superior, f

educational *a* educativo; pedagógico; instructivo

educationalist *n* pedagogo, *m*

educe *vt* educir; deducir; *chem* extraer

eduction *n* educción, *f*

eel *n* anguila, *f*. **electric eel**, gimnoto, *m*.

eerie *a* misterioso, fantástico; sobrenatural; lúgubre

efface *vt* borrar, destruir; quitar. **to e. oneself**, retirarse; permanecer en el fondo

effect *n* efecto, *m*; impresión, *f*; (result) resultado, *m*, consecuencia, *f*, (meaning) substancia, *f*, significado, *m*; *pl* **effects**, efectos, bienes, *m pl. vt* efectuar; producir. **in e.**, en efecto, efectivamente. **of no e.**, inútil. **striving after e.**, efectismŏ, *m*. **to feel the effects of**, sentir los efectos de; padecer las consecuencias de. **to put into e.**, poner en práctica; hacer efectivo. **to take e.**, producir efecto; ponerse en vigor

effective *a* eficaz; (striking) de mucho efecto, poderoso, vistoso. **to make e.**, llevar a efecto

effectively *adv* eficazmente; (strikingly) con gran efecto; efectivamente, en efecto

effectiveness *n* eficacia, *f*; efecto, *m*

effectuate *vt* efectuar

effeminate *a* afeminado, adamado. **to make e.**, afeminar

effervesce *vi* estar efervescente, hervir

effervescence *n* efervescencia, *f*

effervescent *a* efervescente

effete *a* gastado; estéril; decadente

efficacious *a* eficaz

efficacy *n* eficacia, *f*

efficiency *n* eficiencia, *f*; buen estado, *m*; habilidad, *f*; *mech* rendimiento, *m*

efficient *a* (e.g. medicine) eficaz; eficiente; (person) competente, capaz

effigy *n* efigie, imagen, *f*

effort *n* esfuerzo, *m*. **to make an e.**, hacer un esfuerzo. **make every effort to**, hacer lo posible por + *inf*; empeñar sus máximos esfuerzos en el sentido de + *inf*

effortless *a* sin esfuerzo

effrontery *n* descaro, *m*, insolencia, *f*

effulgent *a* fulgente, resplandeciente

effusive *a* efusivo, expansivo

egg *n* huevo, *m*. **to egg on**, incitar (a). **boiled egg**, huevo cocido, *m*. **fried egg**, huevo frito, *m*. **hard egg**, huevo duro, *m*. **poached egg**, huevo escalfado, *m*. **scrambled egg**, huevos revueltos, *m pl*. **soft egg**, huevo pasado por agua, *m*. **to lay eggs**, poner huevos. **to put all one's eggs in one basket**, *fig* poner toda la carne en el asador. **egg-cup**, huevera, *f*. **egg dealer**, vendedor (-ra) de huevos. **egg flip**, huevo batido con ron, *m*. **egg-plant**, berenjena, *f*. **egg-shaped**, aovado. **egg-shell**, cascarón, *m*, cáscara de huevo, *f*. **egg-shell china**, loza muy fina, *f*. **egg-spoon**, cucharita para comer huevos, *f*. **egg-whisk**, batidor de huevos, *m*

ego *n* yo

egoism *n* egoísmo, *m*

egoist *n* egoísta, *mf*

egoistic *a* egoísta

egregious *a* notorio

egress *n* salida, *f*

Egypt Egipto, *m*

Egyptian *a* egipcio. *n* egipcio (-ia); cigarrillo egipcio, *m*

eh? *interj* ¿eh? ¿qué?

eiderdown edredón, *m*

eight *a* and *n* ocho *m*. **He is e. years old**, Tiene ocho años. **It is e. o'clock**, Son las ocho. **e.-day clock**, reloj con cuerda para ocho días, *m*. **e. hundred**, *a* and *n* ochocientos *m.*. **e.-syllabled**, octosílabico

eighteen *a* and *n* diez y ocho, *m*.

eighteenth *a* décimoctavo; (of the month) (el) diez y ocho, dieciocho; (of monarchs) diez y ocho. *n* décimoctava parte, *f*. **Louis the E.**, Luis diez y ocho

eighth *a* octavo, *m*; (of the month) (el) ocho; (of monarchs) octavo. *n* octavo, *m*

eightieth *a* octogésimo

eighty *a* and *n* ochenta, *m*.

either *a* and *pron* uno u otro, cualquiera de los dos; ambos (-as). *conjunc* o (becomes **u** before words beginning with **o** or **ho**). *adv* tampoco. **I do not like e.**, No me gusta ni el uno ni el otro (ni la una ni la otra). **e. . . . or**, o . . . o

ejaculate *vt* exclamar, lanzar; *med* eyacular

ejaculation *n* exclamación, *f*; *med* eyaculación, *f*

ejaculatory *a* jaculatorio

eject *vt* echar, expulsar; *law* desahuciar; (emit) despedir, emitir

ejection *n* echamiento, *m*, expulsión, *f*; *law* desahúcio, *m*; (emission) emisión, *f*

eke (out) *vt* aumentar, añadir a

elaborate *a* elaborado; primoroso; elegante; complicado; (detailed) detallado; (of meals) de muchos platos; (of courtesy, etc.) estudiado. *vt* elaborar; amplificar

elaborately *adv* primorosamente; elegantemente; complicadamente; con muchos detalles

elaboration *n* elaboración, *f*

elapse *vi* transcurrir, andar, pasar

elastic *a* elástico. *n* elástico, *m*. **e. band**, anillo de goma, *m*; cinta de goma, *f*. **e. girdle**, faja elástica, *f*

elate *vt* alegrar; animar

elation *n* alegría, *f*, júbilo, *m*; triunfo, *m*

elbow *n* codo, *m*; ángulo, *m*; (of a chair) brazo, *m*. *vt* codear, dar codazos (a). **at one's e.**, a la mano. **nudge with the e.**, codazo, *m*. **to be out at e.**, enseñar los codos, tener los codos raídos; ser harapiento. **to e. one's way,** abrirse paso a codazos. **e.-chair,** silla de brazos, f. **e.-grease,** jugo de muñeca, m. **e.-piece** or **patch,** codera, f. **e. room,** libertad de movimiento, f

elder a comp mayor. n persona mayor, f; señor mayor, m; (among Jews and in early Christian Church) anciano, m; bot saúco, m

elderly a mayor

eldest a sup old (el, la, etc.) mayor. **e. daughter,** hija mayor, f. **e. son,** hijo mayor, m

elect vt elegir. a elegido; predestinado. n electo, m; elegido, m

election n theol predestinación, f; elección, f. **by-e.,** elección parcial, f

electioneer vi solicitar votos; distribuir propaganda electoral

electioneering n solicitación de votos, f; propaganda electoral, f

elective a electivo. n (subject at school) materia optativa, f

elector n elector (-ra); (prince) elector, m

electoral a electoral. **e. register,** lista electoral, f

electoral college colegio de compromisarios, m

electorate n electorado, m

electric, electrical a eléctrico; fig vivo, instantáneo. **e. arc,** arco voltaico, m. **e. engineer,** ingeniero electricista, m. **electric fan,** (Spain) ventilador, (Western Hemisphere) ventilador eléctrico, m. **e. fire,** estufa eléctrica, f. **e. immersion heater,** calentador de agua eléctrico, m. **e. light,** luz eléctrica, f. **e. pad,** alfombrilla eléctrica, f. **e. shock,** conmoción eléctrica, f. **e. washing-machine,** lavadora eléctrica, f. **e. wire** or **cable,** conductor eléctrico, m

electrician n electricista, mf

electricity n electricidad, f

electrify vt electrificar; fig electrizar

electro prefix (in compounds) electro. **e.-chemistry,** electroquímica, f. **e.-dynamics,** electrodinámica, f. **e.-magnet,** electroimán, m. **e.-magnetic,** electromagnético. **e.-plate,** vt galvanizar, platear. n artículo galvanizado, m. **e.-therapy,** electroterapia, f

electrocute vt electrocutar

electrocution n electrocución, f

electrolysis n electrólisis, f

electron n electrón, m

elegance n elegancia, f

elegant a elegante; bello

elegy n elegía, f

element n elemento, m; factor, m; ingrediente, m; elec par, elemento, m; chem, phys cuerpo simple, m; pl **elements,** rudimentos, m pl, nociones, f pl; (weather) intemperie, f; (Eucharist) el pan y el vino. **to be in one's e.,** estar en su elemento

elemental a elemental; rudimentario, lo elemental

elementary a elemental; rudimentario; primario. **e. education,** enseñanza primaria, f

elephant n elefante (-ta). **e. keeper** or **trainer,** naire, m

elevate vt (the Host) alzar; elevar; (the eyes, the voice) levantar; (honor) enaltecer

elevated a noble, elevado, sublime; edificante; (drunk) achispado

elevation n elevación, f; enaltecimiento, m; (of style, thought) nobleza, sublimidad, f; (hill) eminencia, altura, f

elevator n (lift) ascensor, m; (for grain, etc.) montacargas, m

elevator shaft caja, f, hueco pozo, m

eleven a once. n once, m. **It is e. o'-clock,** Son las once

eleventh a onceno, undécimo; (of month) (el) once; (of monarchs) once. n onzavo, m; undécima parte, f. **at the e. hour,** fig a última hora. **Louis the E.,** Luis once (XI)

elf n elfo, duende, m; (child) trasgo, m; (dwarf) enano, m

elicit vt sacar; hacer contestar; hacer confesar; descubrir

elicitation n descubrimiento, m

elide vt elidir

eligibility n elegibilidad, f

eligible a elegible; deseable

eliminate vt eliminar; quitar

elimination n eliminación, f

eliminatory a eliminador

elite n nata, flor, f

elk n ante, m

ellipse n geom elipse, f; óvalo, m

elm n olmo, m. **e. grove,** olmeda, f

elocution n elocución, f; (art of elocution) declamación, f

elongate vt alargar; extender. vi alargarse; extenderse. a alargado; (of face) perfilado

elongation n alargamiento, m; prolongación, f; extensión, f

elope vi evadirse, huir; fugarse (con un amante)

elopement n fuga, f

eloquence n elocuencia, f

eloquent a elocuente

else adv (besides) más; (instead) otra cosa, más; (otherwise) si no, de otro modo. **anyone e.,** (cualquier) otra persona; alguien más. **Anything e.?** ¿Algo más? **everyone e.,** todos los demás. **everything e.,** todo lo demás. **nobody e.,** ningún otro, nadie más. **nothing e.,** nada más. **or e.,** o bien, de otro modo; si no. **someone e.,** otra persona, otro más. **somewhere e.,** en otra parte. **There's nothing e. to do,** No hay nada más que hacer; No hay más remedio

elsewhere adv a, or en, otra parte

elucidate vt elucidar, aclarar

elucidation n elucidación, aclaración, f

elude vt eludir, evitar

elusive a (of persons) esquivo; fugaz; difícil de comprender

emaciate vt extenuar, demacrar, enflaquecer

emaciated a extenuado, demacrado. **to become e.,** demacrarse

emaciation n demacración, emaciación, f; med depauperación, f

emanate vi emanar (de), proceder (de)

emanation n emanación, f; exhalación, f

emancipate vt emancipar

emancipation n emancipación, f

emasculate a afeminado. vt emascular; fig afeminar; mutilar

embalm vt embalsamar; fig conservar el recuerdo de; perfumar

embalmer n embalsamador, m

embalmment n embalsamamiento, m

embankment n declive, m; ribera, f; terraplén, m; dique, m; (quay) muelle, m

embargo n embargo, m, vt embargar. **to put an e. on,** embargar. **to remove an e.,** sacar de embargo

embark vi embarcarse; lanzarse (a). vt embarcar

embarkation n (of persons) embarcación, f; (of goods) embarque, m

embarrass vt impedir; (financially) apurar; (perplex) tener perplejo; (worry) preocupar; (confuse) desconcertar, turbar; (annoy) molestar

embarrassed a turbado

embarrassing a embarazoso; desconcertante; molesto

embarrassment n impedimento, m; (financial) apuro, m; (obligation) compromiso, m; (perplexity) perplejidad, f; (worry) preocupación, f; (confusion) turbación, f

embassy n embajada, f

embattled a en orden de batalla; her almenado

embed vt empotrar, enclavar; fijar

embellish vt embellecer; adornar

embellishment n embellecimiento, m; adorno, m

ember n rescoldo, m. **E. days,** témporas, f pl

embezzle vt desfalcar

embezzlement n desfalco, m

embezzler n desfalcador (-ra)

embitter vt fig amargar; envenenar

emblem n emblema, m

embodiment n incarnación, f; expresión, f; personificación, f; símbolo, m; síntesis, f

embody vt encarnar; expresar; personificar; incorporar; contener; formular; sintetizar. **to be embodied in,** quedar plasmado en

embolden vt animar, dar valor (a)

embolism n med embolia, f

emboss vt repujar, abollonar; estampar en relieve

embrace n abrazo, m. vt abrazar, dar un abrazo (a); (fig. seize) aprovechar; (accept) aceptar; adoptar; (engage in) dedicarse a; (comprise) incluir, abarcar; (comprehend) comprender. **They embraced,** Se abrazaron

embroider vt bordar; embellecer; (a tale, etc.) exagerar; vi hacer bordado

embroiderer n bordador (-ra)

embroidery n bordado, m; labor, f. **e.-frame,** bastidor, m. **e. silk,** hilo de bordar, m

embroil vt enredar, embrollar; desordenar

embryo n embrión, m; fig germen, m. **a embrionario**

emend vt enmendar; corregir

emendation n enmienda, f; corrección, f

emerald n esmeralda, f, a de color de esmeralda. **e. green,** verde esmeralda, m

emerge vt emerger; surgir; fig salir; aparecer

emergence n emergencia, f; salida, f; aparición, f

emergency n urgencia, f; necesidad, f; emergencia, f; aprieto, m. **e. exit,** salida de urgencia, f. **e. port,** naut puerto de arribada, m

emergent a emergente; que sale; naciente

emery n esmeril, m. **to polish with e.,** esmerilar. **e.-paper,** papel de lija, m

emetic a and n emético, vomitivo, m.

emigrant a emigrante. n emigrante, mf emigrado, m

emigrate vi emigrar; inf trasladarse

emigration n emigración, f. **e. officer,** oficial de emigración, m

eminence n (hill) elevación, prominencia, f; eminencia (also as title), f; distinción, f

eminent a distinguido, eminente; famoso, ilustre; notable; conspicuo

emissary n emisario (-ia); embajador (-ra); agente, m

emission n emisión, f

emit vt despedir; exhalar; emitir

emollient a emoliente, lenitivo. n emoliente, m

emolument n emolumento, m

emotion n emoción, f. **to cause e.,** emocionar

emotional a emocional, sentimental; emocionante

emotionless a sin emoción

emotive a emotivo

emperor n emperador, m

emphasis (on) n énfasis (en), mf; insistencia especial (en), especial atención (a), f; accentuación, f

emphasize vt subrayar, dar énfasis a, poner de relieve, hacer resaltar, dar importancia a; acentuar; insistir en, hacer hincapié (en)

emphatic a enfático

emphatically adv con énfasis

empire n imperio, m

empiric a empírico

employ n empleo, m; servicio, m. vt emplear; ocupar; tomar; servirse de, usar. **How do you e. yourself?** ¿Cómo te ocupas? ¿Cómo pasas el tiempo?

employable a empleable; utilizable

employee n empleado (-da)

employer n el, m, (f, la) que emplea; dueño (-ña), amo (-a); patrón (-ona)

employment n empleo, m; uso, m; ocupación, f; aprovechamiento, m; (post) puesto, cargo, m; (situation) colocación, f. **e. exchange,** bolsa de trabajo, f

emporium n emporio, m; (store) almacén, m

empower vt autorizar; permitir; ayudar (a); dar el poder (para)

empress n emperatriz, f

emptiness n vaciedad, f; futilidad, f; vacuidad, f; (verbosity) palabrería, f

empty a vacío, m; (of a house, etc.) deshabitado, desocupado; (deserted) desierto; (vain) vano, inútil; frívolo; (hungry) hambriento. e envase vacío, m. vt vaciar; descargar. vi vaciarse; (river, etc.) desembocar, venir a morir en. **e.-handed,** con las manos vacías. **e.-headed,** casquivano

emptying n vaciamiento, m; abandono, m; pl **emptyings,** heces de la cerveza, f pl

emu n emu, m

emulate vt emular

emulation n emulación, f

emulsify vt emulsionar

emulsion n emulsión, f

enable vt (to) hacer capaz (de); ayudar (a); autorizar (para); permitir (de)

enact vt law promulgar; decretar; (a part) hacer, desempeñar (un papel); (a play) representar; (happen) ocurrir, tener lugar

enaction n law promulgación, f

enamel n esmalte, m, vt esmaltar

enameling n esmaltadura, f

enamor vt enamorar. **to be enamored of,** estar enamorado de; estar aficionado a

encamp vt and vi acampar

encase vt encajar; encerrar; (line) forrar

encasement n encaje, m; encierro, m

encephalitis n encefalitis, f. **e. lethargica,** encefalitis letárgica, f

enchant vt encantar, hechizar; fascinar; embelesar, deleitar

enchanting a encantador, fascinador

enchantment n encantamiento, m; fascinación, f, encanto, deleite, m

encircle vt cercar; rodear; dar la vuelta (a)

enclose vt cercar; meter dentro de; encerrar; (with a letter, etc.) incluir, adjuntar

enclosed a (of letters) adjunto

enclosure n cercamiento, m; cercado, m; recinto, m; (wall) tapia, cerca, f; (with a letter) contenido adjunto, m

encomium n encomio, m

encompass vt cercar, rodear

encore n repetición, f, interj ibis!

encounter n encuentro, m; combate, m; conflicto, m; lucha, f. vt encontrar; atacar; tropezar con

encourage vt animar, alentar; estimular; incitar; ayudar; (approve) aprobar; (foster) fomentar

encouragement n ánimos, m pl; estímulo, incentivo, m; ayuda, f; (approval) aprobación, f; (promotion) fomento, m

encourager n instigador (-ra); ayudador (-ra); aprobador (-ra); fomentador (-ra)

encouraging a alentador; estimulante; fomentador; (favorable) halagüeño, favorable

encroach vi usurpar; abusar (de); invadir; robar; (of sea, river) hurtar

encroachment n usurpación, f; abuso, m; invasión, f

encrust vt encostrar; incrustar

encumber vt impedir, estorbar; llenar; (burden) cargar; (mortgage) hipotecar; (overwhelm) agobiar

encumbrance n impedimento, estorbo, m; gravamen, m; carga, f; (mortgage) hipoteca, f

encyclical n encíclica, f

encyclopedia n enciclopedia, f

end n fin, m; extremidad, f; extremo, m; conclusión, f; (point) punta, f; cabo, m; (district) barrio, m; cabeza, f; (death) muerte, f; (aim) objeto, intento, m; (purpose) propósito, m; (issue) resultado, m; (bit) fragmento, pedazo, m; (of a word) terminación, f. vi terminar; acabar; concluir; cesar; (in) terminar en; resultar en; (with) terminar con. vt terminar; acabar; dar fin a. **at an end,** terminado. **at the end,** al cabo (de); al extremo (de). **end of quotation,** fin de cita, final de la cita, m. **from end to end,** de un extremo a otro; de un cabo a otro. **in the end,** por fin, finalmente. **on end,** de pie, de cabeza, derecho; de punta; (of hair) erizado. **no end of,** un sinnúmero de. **to make both ends meet,** pasar con lo que se tiene. **to make an end of,** acabar con. **to put an end to,** poner fin a. **to the end that,** a fin de que, para que; con objeto de. **toward the end of,** (months, years, etc.) a fines de, a últimos de; hacia el fin de. **two hours on end,** dos horas seguidas. **end-paper,** guarda, f

endanger vt arriesgar; poner en peligro

endear vt hacer querer

endearing a que inspira cariño; atrayente; cariñoso

endearment n cariño, amor, m; caricia, terneza, f; palabra de cariño, f

endeavor vi procurar, intentar, hacer un esfuerzo. n esfuerzo, m, tentativa, f

endemic a med endémico

ending n fin, m; conclusión, f; gram terminación, f; cesación, f; (climax) desenlace, m

endive n bot escarola, f

endless a eterno; inacabable; infinito; sin fin; interminable; incesante

endlessly adv sin fin; incesantemente; sin parar

endocrine a endocrino. n secreción interna, f

end-of-season a por final de temporada (e.g., **end-of-season reductions**, rebajos por final de temporada, m pl. **end-of-season sale**, liquidación por final de temporada, f)

endorse vt com endosar; garantizar; (uphold) apoyar; confirmar

endorsee n endosatario (-ia)

endorsement n com endoso, m; aval, m, garantía, f; corroboración, confirmación, f

endorser n com endosante, m

endow vt dotar; fundar; crear

endowment n dotación, f; fundación, f; creación, f; (mental) inteligencia, f; cualidad, f, don, m. **e. policy**, póliza dotal, f

endurance n aguante, m; resistencia, f; sufrimiento, m; tolerancia, f; paciencia, f; (lastingness) duración, continuación, f. **beyond e.**, intolerable, inaguantable. **e. test**, prueba de resistencia, f

endure vt soportar; tolerar, aguantar; sufrir; resistir. vi sufrir; (last) durar, continuar

enduring a permanente, perdurable; continuo; constante

enema n lavativa, enema, f

enemy n enemigo (-ga); adversario (-ia); (in war) enemigo, m. a del enemigo, enemigo. **to be one's own e.**, ser enemigo de sí mismo. **to become an e. of**, enemistarse con; hacerse enemigo de', volverse hostil a

energetic a enérgico

energy n energía, fuerza, f, vigor, m

enervate vt enervar; debilitar. a enervado

enfeeble vt debilitar

enforce vt (a law) poner en vigor; (impose) imponer a la fuerza; hacer cumplir; conseguir por fuerza; (demonstrate) demostrar

enforcement n (of a law) ejecución (de una ley), f; imposición a la fuerza, f; observación forzosa, f

enfranchise vt emancipar; conceder derechos civiles (a)

engage vt empeñar; contratar; tomar en alquiler; tomar a su servicio; (seats, etc.) reservar; (occupy) ocupar; (attention) atraer; (in) aplicarse a, dedicarse a; mil combatir con, librar batalla con; atacar; (of wheels) endentar con. vi obligarse; dedicarse (a); tomar parte (en); (bet) apostar; mil librar batalla; (fight) venir a las manos. **to be engaged in**, traer entre manos, ocuparse en. **to become engaged**, prometerse. **Number engaged!** (telephone) ¡Están comunicando!

engaged a ocupado; (betrothed) prometido; reservado

engagement n obligación, f; compromiso, m; (date) cita, f; (betrothal) palabra de casamiento, f; (battle) combate, m, batalla, f. **I have an e. at two o'clock.** Tengo una cita a las dos

engagement gift regalo de esponsales, m

engaging a simpático, atractivo

engender vt fig engendrar; excitar

engine n máquina, f; motor, m; (locomotive) locomotora, f; (pump) bomba, f. **to sit with one's back to the e.**, estar sentado de espaldas a la máquina (or locomotora). **e. builder**, constructor de máquinas, m. **e. driver**, maquinista, mf. **e. room**, cuarto de máquinas, m. **e. works**, taller de maquinaria, m

engineer n ingeniero, m; mecánico, m. vt fig gestionar, arreglar. **civil e.**, ingeniero de caminos, canales y puertos, m. **Royal Engineers**, Cuerpo de Ingenieros, m

engineering n ingeniería, f; fig manejo, m. a de ingeniería

England Inglaterra, f

English a inglés. n (language) inglés, m. **in E. fashion**, a la inglesa. **to speak E.**, hablar inglés. **to speak plain E.**, hablar sin rodeos; hablar en cristiano. **E. Church**, iglesia anglicana, f. **E.-teacher**, maestro (-ra) de inglés. **English-translator**, traductor al inglés, m

English Channel, the el Canal de la Mancha

Englishman n inglés, m

Englishwoman n inglesa, f

engrain vt inculcar

engrave vt grabar; esculpir, cincelar; fig grabar

engraver n grabador (-ra); (tool) cincel, m

engraving n grabadura, f; (picture) grabado, m. **e. needle**, punta seca, f

engross vt (a document) poner en limpio; redactar; (absorb) absorber

engrossing a absorbente

engulf vt hundir, sumir, sumergir

enhance vt realzar; intensificar; aumentar; mejorar

enhancement n realce, m; intensificación, f; aumento, m; mejoría, f

enigma n enigma, m

enigmatic a enigmático

enjoin vt imponer; ordenar, mandar; encargar

enjoy vt disfrutar; gustar de; gozar de; poseer, tener. **to e. oneself,** recrearse, regocijarse; (amuse oneself) divertirse; entretenerse; pasarlo bien. **Did you e. yourself?** ¿Lo pasaste bien?

enjoyable a agradable; divertido, entretenido

enjoyment n posesión, f; goce, disfruto, m; (pleasure) placer, m; (aprovechamiento, m; utilización, f; (satisfaction) satisfacción, f

enlarge vt agrandar; aumentar; ensanchar; extender; phot ampliar; dilatar; (the mind, etc.) ensanchar. vi agrandarse; ensancharse; aumentarse; extenderse. **an enlarged heart,** dilatación del corazón, f. **to e. upon,** tratar detalladamente, explayarse en

enlargement n engrandecimiento, m; ensanchamiento, m; phot ampliación, f; med dilatación, f; aumento, m; amplificación, f; (of a town, etc.) ensanche, m

enlighten vt iluminar; aclarar; informar

enlightened a culto; ilustrado; inteligente

enlightening a instructivo

enlightenment n ilustración, f; cultura, civilización, f

enlist vt mil reclutar; alistar; obtener, conseguir. vi mil sentar plaza, sentar plaza de soldado; engancharse; alistarse

enlistment n mil enganche, m; reclutamiento, m; alistamiento, m

enliven vt animar; avivar; alegrar

enmity n enemistad, enemiga, hostilidad, f

enormity n enormidad, f; gravedad, f; atrocidad, f

enormous a enorme, colosal

enough a bastante, suficiente. n lo bastante, lo suficiente. adv bastante; suficientemente. interj ¡bastante! ¡basta! **to be e.,** ser suficiente; bastar. **two are enough,** con dos tenemos bastante, con dos tengo bastante

enquire. See inquire

enrage vt enfurecer, hacer furioso; inf hacer rabiar

enraged a furioso

enrapture vt entusiasmar, extasiar; (intoxicate) embriagar; (charm) encantar, deleitar

enrich vt enriquecer; (adorn) adornar, embellecer; (the land) fertilizar

enrichment n enriquecimiento, m; embellecimiento, m; (of the land) abono, m

enroll vt alistar; matricular; inscribir; (perpetuate) inmortalizar

ensconce vt acomodar, colocar; ocultar

ensemble n conjunto, m

enshrine vt poner en sagrario; guardar con cuidado; fig guardar como una reliquia

enshroud vt amortajar; envolver; esconder

ensign n (badge) insignia, f; (flag) enseña, bandera, f; pabellón, m; bandera de popa, f; mil alférez, m; (U.S.A. navy) subteniente, m

enslave vt esclavizar; fig dominar

ensue vt conseguir. vi resultar; suceder, sobrevenir

ensuing a (next) próximo; (resulting) resultante

ensure vt asegurar; estar seguro de que; garantizar

entail vt traer consigo, acarrear; law vincular; n law vinculación, f; herencia, f

entangle vt enredar; coger; fig embrollar

entanglement n enredo, m; complicación, f; intriga, f; (mil of wire) alambrada, f

enter vt entrar en; penetrar; (of thoughts) ocurrirse; (join) ingresar en; entrar en; (become a member of) hacerse miembro de; (enroll) alistarse; (a university) matricularse; (inscribe) inscribir, poner en la lista; (note) anotar, apuntar; (a protest) hacer constar; (make) hacer; formular. vi entrar; theat salir (a la escena); penetrar; com anotarse. **to e. for,** vt inscribir. vi inscribirse, tomar parte en. **to e. into,** entrar en; formar parte de; (conversation) entablar (conversación); (negotiations) iniciar; considerar; (another's emotion) acompañar en; (an agreement, etc.) hacer; (sign) firmar; (bind oneself) obligarse a, comprometerse a; tomar parte en; (undertake) emprender; empezar; adoptar. **to e. up,** anotar; poner en la lista; registrar. **to e. upon,** comenzar, emprender; tomar posesión de; encargarse de, asumir; inaugurar, dar principio a

enterprise n empresa, f; aventura, f; (spirit) iniciativa, f, empuje, m

enterprising a emprendedor, acometedor; de mucha iniciativa

entertain vt (an idea, etc.) acariciar, abrigar; considerar; (as a guest) agasajar, obsequiar; recibir en casa; (amuse) divertir, entretener. vi ser hospitalario; tener invitados en casa; dar fiestas

entertaining a entretenido, divertido

entertainment n convite, m; fiesta, f; reunión, f; banquete, m; (hospitality) hospitalidad, f; (amusement) diversión, f, entretenimiento, m; espectáculo, m; función, f; concierto, m

enthrall vt seducir, atraer, encantar; absorber, captar la atención

enthralling a absorbente; atrayente, halagüeño

enthusiasm n entusiasmo, m

enthusiast n entusiasta, mf

enthusiastic a entusiasta. **to make e.,** entusiasmar. **to be e.,** entusiasmarse

entice vt tentar, inducir; atraer, seducir

enticement n tentación, f; atractivo, m

enticing a seduciente, atrayente; halagüeño

entire a entero; completo; intacto; absoluto; perfecto; íntegro; total

entirely adv enteramente; completamente; integralmente; totalmente

entirety n totalidad, f; integridad, f; todo, m

entitle vt (designate) intitular; dar derecho (a); autorizar. **to be entitled to,** tener derecho a

entity n entidad, f; ente, ser, m

entourage n séquito, m; (environment) medio ambiente, m

entrails n entrañas, tripas, f pl, intestinos, m pl

entrain vi tomar el tren, subir al tren

entrance n entrada, f; theat salida (a la escena), f; (into a profession, etc.) ingreso, m; alistamiento, m; (beginning) principio, m; (door) puerta, f; (porch) portal, m; (of a cave) boca, f. **e. fee,** cuota de entrada, f. **e. hall,** zaguán, m. **e. money,** entrada, f

entrance vt fig encantar, fascinar; ecstasiar

entrancing a encantador

entreat vt suplicar, implorar, rogar

entreating a suplicante, implorante

entreaty n súplica, instancia, f, ruego, m

entree n entrada, f

entrench vt atrincherar

entrust vt confiar a (or en), encomendar a; encargar

entry n entrada, f; (passage) callejuela, f; (note) inscripción, apuntación, f; com partida, f; (registration) registro, m. **double e.,** com partida doble, f. **single e.,** com partida simple, f

entwine vt entrelazar, entretejer

enumerate vt enumerar

enumeration n enumeración, f

enunciate vt enunciar; articular

enunciation n enunciación, f; articulación, f

envelop vt envolver, cubrir

envelope n sobre, m

envelopment n envolvimiento, m; cubierta, f

enviable a envidiable

envious a envidioso. **an e. look,** una mirada de envidia

enviously adv con envidia

environment n medio ambiente, m

environs n inmediaciones, f pl, alrededores, m pl

envisage vt hacer frente a; contemplar; imaginar

envoy n enviado, m; mensajero (-ra)

envy n envidia, f, vt envidiar

enzyme n fermento, m, enzima, f

eon n eón, m

ephemeral a efímero; flg fugaz, pasajero

epic a épico. n epopeya, f

epicenter n epicentro, m

epicure n epicúreo (-ea)

epicurean a epicúreo

epidemic n epidemia, f; plaga, f, a epidémico

epidermis n epidermis, f

epiglottis n epiglotis, f

epigram n epigrama, m

epigrammatic a epigramático

epigraph n epígrafe, m

epilepsy n epilepsia, alferecía, f

epileptic a and n epiléptico (-ca). **e. fit,** ataque epiléptico, m. **e. aura,** aura epiléptica, f

epilog n epílogo, m

epiphany n epifanía, f

episcopacy n episcopado, m

episcopalianism n episcopalismo, m

episode n suceso, incidente, m; lit episodio, m

epistle n epístola, f

epistolary a epistolar

epitaph n epitafio, m

epithet n epíteto, m

epitome n epítome, m

epitomize vt resumir, abreviar

epoch n época, edad, f

Epsom salts n sal de la Higuera, f

equability n igualdad (de ánimo), ecuanimidad, f; uniformidad, f

equable a igual, ecuánime; uniforme

equably adv con ecuanimidad; igualmente; uniformemente

equal a igual; uniforme; imparcial; equitativo, justo. n igual, mf. vt ser igual a; equivaler a; igualar; sport empatar. **to be e. to,** (of persons) ser capaz de; servir para; atreverse a; (circumstances) estar al nivel de; sentirse con fuerzas para. **without e.,** sin igual; (of beauty, etc.) sin par. **e. sign,** math igual, m

equality n igualdad, f; uniformidad, f

equalization n igualación, f

equalize vt igualar

equalizing a igualador; compensador

equally adv igualmente; imparcialmente

equanimity n ecuanimidad, f

equation n ecuación, f

equator n ecuador, m

equatorial a ecuatorial

equerry n caballerizo del rey, m

equestrian a ecuestre

equiangular a equiángulo

equidistance n equidistancia, f

equidistant a equidistante

equilateral a equilátero

equilibrium n equilibrio, m

equine a equino; hípico; de caballo

equinox n equinoccio, m

equip vt proveer; pertrechar; equipar

equipage n (train) séquito, tren, m; (carriage) carruaje, m

equipment n habilitación, f; equipo, m; pertrechos, m pl; material, m; aparatos, m pl; armamento, m

equitable a equitativo, justo

equitably adv equitativamente, con justicia

equity n equidad, f; imparcialidad, justicia, f

equivalence n equivalencia, f

equivalent a and n equivalente, m. **to be e. to,** equivaler a

equivocal a equívoco, ambiguo

equivocally adv equivocadamente

equivocate vi usar frases equívocas, emplear equívocos, tergiversar

equivocation n equívoco, m

era n época, era, f

eradiation n irradiación, f

eradicable a erradicable

eradicate vt erradicar; destruir, extirpar; suprimir

eradication n erradicación, f; destrucción, f; supresión, f

erasable a borrable

erase vt borrar; tachar

eraser n goma de borrar, f. **ink e.,** goma para tinta, f

erasure n borradura, f; tachón, m

ere conjunc antes de (que), antes de. prep antes de

erect a (upright) derecho; erguido; vertical; (uplifted) levantado; (standing) de pie; (firm) firme, resuelto; (alert) vigilante. vt (build) edificar, construir; instalar; (raise) alzar; convertir

erection n erección, f; construcción, edificación, f; (building) edificio, m; (structure) estructura, f; instalación, f; (assembling) montaje, m

erectly adv derecho

ermine n armiño, m, a de armiño

erode vt corroer; comer; geol denudar

erosion n erosión, f

erotic a erótico

err vi desviarse; errar; desacertar; pecar

errand n mensaje, recado, m; encargo, m; misión, f. **e.-boy,** mandadero, mensajero, motril, mozo, recadero, m

errant a errante; (of knights) andante

erratic a (of conduct) excéntrico, irresponsable; (of thoughts, etc.) errante; med errático

erratum n errata, f

erring a extraviado; pecaminoso

erroneous a erróneo; falso; injusto

error n error, m; equivocación, f, desacierto, m; (sin) pecado, m. **in e.,** por equivocación

erudite a erudito; sabio

erudition n erudición, f

erupt vi entrar en erupción, estar en erupción; fig salir con fuerza

eruption n erupción, f

erysipelas n erisipela, f

escalade n escalada, f, vt escalar

escalator n escalera automática, escalera eléctrica, escalera mecánica, escalera móvil, escalera rodante, f

escapable a evitable, eludible

escapade n escapada, f; aventura, f

escape n huida, fuga, f; evasión, evitación, f; (leak) escape, m; fig salida, f. vt eludir, evitar; (of cries, groans, etc.) dar, salir de. vi huir, fugarse, escapar; (slip away) escurrirse; librarse; salvarse; (leak) escaparse. **His name escapes me,** Se me escapa (or se me olvida) su nombre. **to e. notice,** pasar inadvertido. **to have a narrow e.,** salvarse en una tabla. **to e. from,** escaparse de; librarse de; huir de

escape clause n cláusula de salvaguardia, f

escaping a fugitivo

escarpment n escarpa, f

eschew vt evitar

eschewal n evitación, f

escort n mil escolta, f; (of ships) convoy, m; acompañamiento, m; acompañante, m. vt mil escoltar; (of ships) convoyar; acompañar

escritoire n escritorio, m

Eskimo a and n esquimal mf

esoteric a esotérico

especial a especial; particular

especially adv especialmente; ante todo; en particular

Esperanto n esperanto, m

espionage n espionaje, m

esplanade n mil explanada, f; bulevar, paseo, m

espousal n desposorio, m; fig adhesión (a una causa), f

espouse vt desposar; (a cause) abrazar; defender

espy vt divisar, ver, observar

esquire n escudero, m; (landowner) hacendado, m; (as a title) don (before given name)

essay n tentativa, f; lit ensayo, m, vt probar; procurar; (on an examination) tema, m. **essay question,** tema, m

essayist n ensayista, mf

essence n esencia, f

essential a esencial; indispensable, imprescindible; intrínseco. n artículo de primera necesidad, m; elemento necesario, m

establish vt establecer; fundar; crear; erigir, Lat. Am. also instaurar; (constitute) constituir; (order) disponer; (prove) demostrar, probar; (take root, settle) arraigarse

established a establecido; arraigado; (proved) demostrado; bien conocido; (author) consagrado; (of churches) oficial

establishment n establecimiento, m; fundación, f; creación, f, Lat. Am. also instauración; institución, f; (building) erección, f; arraigo, m; (house) casa, f; (church) iglesia oficial, f; demostración, f; reconocimiento, m

estate n estado, m; clase, f; condición, f; (land) propiedad, finca, f; fortuna, f; (inheritance) heredad, f, patrimonio, m; law bienes, m pl. **personal e.,** bienes muebles, m pl; fortuna personal, f. **third e.,** estado llano, m. **e. agent,** agente de fincas, m; agente de casas, m

esteem n estima, f, aprecio, m; consideración, f, vt estimar, apreciar; creer, juzgar

esthete n estético, m

esthetic a estético

esthetics n estética, f

estimable a apreciable, estimable

estimate n estimación, tasa, f; cálculos, m pl; apreciación, f; opinión, f; pl **estimates,** presupuesto, m. vt (value) avalorar, tasar; calcular, computar; considerar. vi hacer un presupuesto

estimation n opinión, f; cálculo, cómputo, m; (esteem) aprecio, m, estima, f

estrange vt enajenar; ofender

estrangement n enajenación, alienación, f

estuary n estuario, m, ría, f

etcetera etcétera. (Used as noun, f)

etch vt grabar al agua fuerte

etcher n grabador (-ra) al agua fuerte

etching n aguafuerte, f; grabado al agua fuerte, m. **e. needle,** punta seca, aguja de grabador, f

eternal a eterno; incesante. n (E.) el Eterno

eternity n eternidad, f

ether n éter, m

ethereal a etéreo; vaporoso, aéreo

ethical a ético, moral; n droga de ordenanza, f

ethics n ética, f; (filosofía) moral, f

Ethiopia Etiopia, f

ethnic a étnico

ethyl n chem etilo, m

ethylene n chem etileno, m

etiquette n etiqueta, f

Etruscan a and n etrusco (-ca)

eucalyptus n eucalipto, m

Eucharist n Eucaristía, f

eugenic a eugenésico

eugenics n eugenesia, f

eulogist n elogiador (-ra), loador (-ra)

eulogistic a elogiador

eulogize vt elogiar, alabar, encomiar

eulogy n elogio, encomio, m; alabanza, f; panegírico, m

eunuch n eunuco, m

euphemism n eufemismo, m

euphonious a eufónico

euphony n eufonía, f

eurhythmic a eurítmico

eurhythmics n euritmia, f

European a and n europeo (-ea)

europeanize vt europeanizar

euthanasia n eutanasia, f

evacuate vt evacuar

evacuation n evacuación, f

evade vt evadir, eludir; evitar, esquivar; rehuir

evaluate vt evaluar, estimar; calcular

evaluation n evaluación, estimación, f

evanescent a transitorio, fugaz, pasajero

evangelical a evangélico

evangelicalism n evangelismo, m

evangelist n evangelista, m

evangelize vt evangelizar

evaporate vi evaporarse; desvanecerse. vt evaporar

evaporation n evaporación, f; desvanecimiento, m

evaporative a evaporatorio

evasion n (escape) fuga, f; evasión, f; evasiva, f, efugio, m, Lat. Am. esquivada, f

evasive a evasivo, ambiguo

evasively adv evasivamente

evasiveness n carácter evasivo, m

eve n víspera, f; ecc vigilia, f. **on the eve of,** la víspera de; fig en vísperas de

even a (flat) llano; (smooth) liso; igual; (level with) al mismo nivel (de); uniforme; (of numbers) par; (approximate, of sums) redondo; rítmico; invariable, constante; (of temper) apacible; (just) imparcial; (monotonous) monótono, igual; (paid) pagado; (com of date) mismo. **to get e. with,** pagar en la misma moneda, vengarse de. **to be e. (with . . .)** (be quits) Lat. Am. estar a mano (con . . .)

even adv siquiera; aun; hasta; (also) también. **not e.,** ni siquiera. **e. as,** así como, del mismo modo que. **e. if,** aun cuando, si bien. **e. now,** aun ahora; ahora mismo. **e. so,** aun así; (nevertheless) sin embargo. **e. though,** aunque; suponiendo que

even vt igualar; (level) allanar, nivelar; (accounts) desquitar; compensar; hacer uniforme

evening n tarde, f, atardecer, m; noche, f; fig fin, m, a vespertino, de la tarde. **Good e.!** ¡Buenas tardes! ¡Buenas noches! **in the e.,** al atardecer. **tomorrow e.,** mañana por la tarde. **yesterday**

e., ayer por la tarde. **e. class,** clase nocturna, *f.* **e. dress,** (women) traje de noche, *m*; (men) traje de etiqueta, *m.* **e. meal,** cena, *f.* **e. paper,** periódico (or diario) de la noche, *m.* **evening primrose,** hierba del asno, onagra, *f.* **e. star,** estrella vespertina, estrella de la tarde, *f.* (Venus) lucero de la tarde, *m*

evenly *adv* igualmente; (on a level) a nivel; uniformemente; imparcialmente; (of speech) con suavidad

evenness *n* igualdad, *f*; (smoothness) lisura, *f*; uniformidad, *f*; imparcialidad, *f*; (of temper) ecuanimidad, serenidad, *f*

evensong *n* vísperas, *f pl*

event *n* incidente, suceso, acontecimiento, *m*; (result) consecuencia, *f*; resultado, *m*; caso, *m*; (athletics) prueba, *f*; (race) carrera, *f.* **at all events,** de todas maneras. **in such an e.,** en tal caso. **in the e. of,** en el caso de

eventful *a* lleno de acontecimientos; accidentado; memorable

eventual *a* eventual; final, último

eventuality *n* eventualidad, *f*

eventually *adv* a la larga, al fin

ever *adv* siempre; (at any time) jamás; alguna vez; nunca; (even) siquiera; (very) muy; (in any way) en modo alguno. **As fast as e. he can,** Lo más aprisa que pueda. **Be it e. so big,** Por grande que sea. **Did you e.!** ¡Hábrase visto! ¡Qué cosa! **for e.,** para siempre. **for e. and e.,** para siempre jamás; (mostly ecclesiastical) por los siglos de los siglos; eternamente. **He is e. so nice,** Es muy simpático. **Hardly e.,** casi nunca. **I don't think I have e. been there,** No creo que haya estado nunca allí. **if e.,** si alguna vez; (rarely) raramente. **nor . . . e.,** ni nunca. **not . . . e.,** nunca. **e. after,** desde entonces; (afterward) después. **e. and anon,** de vez en cuando. **e. so little,** siquiera un poco; muy poco

evergreen *a* siempre verde. *n* planta vivaz, *f.* **e. oak,** encina, *f*

everlasting *a* eterno, perpetuo; (of colors) estable; incesante. **e. flower,** perpetua, *f*

evermore *adv* eternamente

every *a* todo; cada (invariable); todos los, *m pl*; todas las, *f pl.* **e. day,** todos los días, cada día. **e. now and then,** de cuando en cuando. **e. other day,** cada dos días

everybody *n* todo el mundo, *m*; todos, *m pl*; todas, *f pl*; cada uno, *m*; cada una, *f*

everyday *a* diario, cotidiano; corriente, de cada día, usual

everything *n* todo, *m*; (e. that, which) todo lo (que). **e. possible,** todo lo posible

everywhere *adv* por todas partes

evict *vt* desahuciar; expulsar

eviction *n* evicción, *f*, desahúcio, *m*; expulsión, *f*

evidence *n law* testimonio, *m*, deposición, *f*; indicios, *m pl*; evidencia, *f*; prueba, *f*; hecho, *m*, *vt* patentizar, probar. **to give e.,** dar testimonio, deponer

evident *a* evidente, patente, manifiesto; claro. **to be e.,** ser patente, estar a la vista

evidently *adv* evidentemente; claramente

evil *a* malo; malvado, perverso; de maldad; (unfortunate) aciago; de infortunio; (of spirits) diabólico, malo. *n* mal, *m*; maldad, perversidad, *f*; (misfortune) desgracia, *f.* **the E. one,** el Malo. **e.-doer,** malhechor (-ra). **e. eye,** mal de ojo, aojo, *m.* **e.-minded,** mal pensado; malintencionado. **e.-speaking,** maledicencia, calumnia, *f.* **e. spirit,** demonio, espíritu malo, *m*

evince *vt* evidenciar; mostrar

eviscerate *vt* destripar, desentrañar

evocation *n* evocación, *f*

evocative *a* evocador

evoke *vt* evocar

evolution *n* evolución, *f*; desarrollo, *m*; (nav, mil) maniobra, *f*; *math* extracción de una raíz, *f*; (revolution) revolución, vuelta, *f*

evolutionism *n* evolucionismo, *m*

evolutive *a* evolutivo

evolve *vi* evolucionar; desarrollarse. *vt* producir por evolución; desarrollar; pensar

ewe *n* oveja, *f.* **ewe lamb,** cordera, *f*

ewer *n* aguamanil, *m*

exacerbate *vt* exacerbar; agravar, empeorar

exacerbation *n* exacerbación, *f*; agravación, *f*

exact *vt* exacto; fiel; metódico; estricto. *vt* exigir

exacting *a* exigente; severo, estricto; (hard) agotador, arduo

exaction *n* exigencia, *f*; extorsión, exacción, *f*

exactness *n* exactitud, *f*

exaggerate *vt* exagerar; acentuar. *vi* exagerar

exaggerated *a* exagerado

exaggeration *n* exageración, *f*

exaggerator *n* exagerador (-ra)

exalt *vt* exaltar; enaltecer, elevar; (praise) glorificar, magnificar; (intensify) realzar, intensificar

exaltation *n* exaltación, elevación, *f*; alegría, *f*, júbilo, *m*; (ecstasy) éxtasis, arrobamiento, *m*; (of the Cross) exaltación, *f*

exalted *a* exaltado, eminente

examination *n* examen, *m*; inspección, *f*; investigación, *f*; *law* interrogatorio, *m*; prueba, *f.* **to sit an e.,** examinarse. **written e.,** prueba escrita, *f*

examine *vt* examinar; inspeccionar; investigar; *law* interrogar; (search) reconocer; (by touch) tentar; observar; analizar. **to e. into,** examinar; considerar detenidamente; ahondar en

examinee *n* examinando (-da)

examiner *n* examinador (-ra); inspector (-ra)

examining *a* que examina; de examen; *law* interrogante

example *n* ejemplo, *m*; ilustración, *f*; (parallel) ejemplar, *m*; (warning) escarmiento, *m*. **for e.,** por ejemplo. **to set an e.,** dar ejemplo, dar el ejemplo.

exasperate *vt* exasperar, irritar; (increase) aumentar; (worsen) agravar

exasperating *a* exasperante, irritante, provocador

exasperation *n* exasperación, irritación, *f*; (worsening) agravación, *f*; enojo, *m*

excavate *vt* excavar; (hollow) vaciar

excavation *n* excavación, *f*; *arch* vaciado, *m*

excavator *n* excavador (-ra); (machine) excavadora, *f*

exceed *vt* exceder; (excel) superar, aventajar; (one's hopes, etc.) sobrepujar. *vi* excederse. **e. all expectations,** exceder a toda ponderación. **to e. one's rights,** abusar de sus derechos, ir demasiado lejos

exceedingly *adv* sumamente, extremadamente; sobre manera

excel *vt* aventajar, superar; vencer. *vi* sobresalir; distinguirse, señalarse; ser superior

excellence *n* excelencia, *f*; superioridad, *f*; perfección, *f*; mérito, *m*; buena calidad, *f*

excellency *n* (title) Excelencia, *f*. **Your E.,** Su Excelencia

excellent *a* excelente; superior; perfecto; magnífico; (in examinations) sobresaliente

except *vt* exceptuar; omitir

except, excepting *prep* excepto, con excepción de; exceptuando; menos; salvo; fuera de. *conjunc* a menos que. **except for,** si no fuese por; con excepción de; fuera de

exception *n* excepción, *f*; objeción, protesta, *f*. **to make an e.,** hacer una excepción. **to take e. to,** protestar contra; tachar, criticar; desaprobar

excerpt *n* excerpta, *f*, extracto, *m*, *vt* extraer

excess *n* exceso, *m*; superabundancia, *f*; demasía, *f*; *com* superávit, *m*. **in e.,** en exceso, de sobra. **in e. of,** en exceso de; arriba de. **to e.,** excesivamente, demasiado. **e. fare,** suplemento, *m*. **e. luggage,** exceso de equipaje, *m*; (overweight) exceso de peso, *m*

excessive *a* excesivo; superabundante; inmoderado, desmesurado; exagerado

exchange *n* cambio, trueque, *m*; (of pris-

oners) canje, *m*; (financial) cambio, *m*; (building) bolsa, lonja, *f*; (telephone) oficina central de teléfonos, *f*. *vt* cambiar (for, por); trocar; (replace) reemplazar; (prisoners) canjear; (of blows) darse; (pass from, into) pasar de . . . a. *vi* hacer un cambio. **in e. for,** en cambio de, a trueque de; por. **to e. greetings,** saludarse; cambiar saludos. **They exchanged looks,** Se miraron. **What is the rate of e.?** ¿Cuál es el tipo de cambio? **e. of prisoners,** canje de prisioneros, *m*

exchangeable *a* cambiable; trocable

exchequer *n* (public finance) Hacienda pública, *f*; tesorería, *f*; (funds) fondos, *m pl*. **Chancellor of the E.,** Ministro de Hacienda, *m*

excise *n* contribución indirecta, *f*; (customs and e.) Aduana, *f*. *vt* (cut) cortar, extirpar; imponer una contribución indirecta. **e. duty,** derecho de aduana, *m*

excision *n* excisión, *f*; extirpación, *f*

excite *vt* emocionar; conmover; agitar; excitar; suscitar, provocar; incitar, instigar; (attention, interest) despertar; estimular. **to become excited,** emocionarse; exaltarse; (annoyed) acalorarse; (upset) agitarse

excitedly *adv* con emoción; acaloradamente; agitadamente

excitement *n* conmoción, *f*; agitación, *f*, *Central America* embullo *m*; (annoyance) acaloramiento, *m*; emoción, *f*; estímulo, *m*; instigación, *f*, fomento, *m*; (amusement) placer, *m*

exciting *a* emocionante; conmovedor; agitador; muy interesante

exclaim *vt* and *vi* exclamar. **to e. against,** clamar contra

exclamation *n* exclamación, *f*. **e. mark,** punto de exclamación, *m*

exclude *vt* excluir; exceptuar; evitar; (refuse) rechazar

exclusion *n* exclusión, *f*; exceptuación, *f*; eliminación, *f*

exclusive *a* exclusivo; (snobbish) exclusivista. **e. of,** no incluido; aparte de

exclusively *adv* exclusivamente; únicamente

excommunicate *vt* excomulgar. *a* excomulgado

excommunication *n* excomunión, *f*

excrement *n* excremento, *m*

excrescence *n* excrecencia, *f*

excrescent *a* que forma excrecencia; superfluo

excrete *vt* excretar

excretion *n* excreción, *f*

excruciating *a* atormentador, angustioso; (of pain) agudísimo

excursion *n* excursión, *f*; expedición, *f*; (digression) digresión, *f*. **e. ticket,** billete de excursión, *m*. **e. train,** tren de excursionistas, *m*

excursionist n excursionista, mf; turista, mf

excusable a disculpable, excusable

excuse n excusa, f; disculpa, f; pretexto, m; justificación, defensa, f. **to give as an e.**, pretextar

excuse vt disculpar, excusar; dispensar (de); librar (de); (forgive) perdonar; (defend) justificar, defender; (minimize) paiar; (oneself) disculparse. **E. me!** ¡Con permiso! ¡Perdone Vd.! ¡Dispense Vd.!

execrate vt execrar, abominar. vi maldecir

execute vt (perform) ejecutar, poner en efecto, realizar; (art, mus) ejecutar; (part in a play) hacer, desempeñar; (fulfil) cumplir; law otorgar (un documento); (kill) ajusticiar

execution n efectuación, realización, f; (art, mus) ejecución, f; (of part in a play) desempeño (de un papel), m; (fulfilment) cumplimiento, m; law otorgamiento (de un documento), m; (killing) suplicio, m, ejecución de la pena de muerte, f; (law seizure) ejecución, f

executioner n verdugo, m

executive a ejecutivo; administrativo. n poder ejecutivo, m

executor n administrador testamentario, m

executrix n administradora testamentaria, f

exegesis n exégesis, f

exemplary a ejemplar

exemplify vt ejemplificar; ilustrar, demostrar

exempt vt exentar, eximir; librar; dispensar, excusar. a exento; libre; excusado; inmune

exemption n exención, f; libertad, f; inmunidad, f

exercise n ejercicio, m; uso, m; (essay) ensayo, m; pl **exercises**, (on land or sea) maniobras, f pl. vt ejercer; usar, emplear; (train) ejercitar, entrenar; adiestrar; pasear, dar un paseo; (worry) preocupar. vi hacer ejercicio; ejercitarse; adiestrarse. **spiritual exercises**, ejercicios espirituales, m pl. **to take e. in the open air**, tomar ejercicio al aire libre. **to write an e.**, escribir un ejercicio. **e. book**, cuaderno de ejercicios, m

exert vt hacer uso de, emplear, ejercer, poner en juego; (deploy) desplegar. **to e. oneself**, hacer un esfuerzo (para); esforzarse (de); trabajar mucho; tratar (de); apurarse, tomarse mucha molestia; preocuparse

exertion n esfuerzo, m; uso, m; (exercise) ejercicio, m; (good offices) diligencias, gestiones, f pl; buenos oficios, m pl

exhalation n exhalación, f; efluvio, m; vapor, m; humo, m

exhale vt exhalar; emitir, despedir. vi evaporarse; disiparse

exhaust vt agotar; (empty) vaciar; (end) acabar; apurar; consumir; (tire) rendir, cansar mucho; (weaken) debilitar; (a subject) tratar detalladamente. n mech escape, m; emisión de vapor, f; vapor de escape, m. **e. pipe**, tubo de escape, m

exhausting a cansado, agotador

exhaustion n agotamiento, m; rendimiento, cansancio, m; lasitud, f; postración, f

exhaustive a completo; minucioso

exhaustively adv detenidamente; detalladamente; minuciosamente

exhibit vt exhibir; manifestar, ostentar; revelar, descubrir; presentar. vi exhibir, ser expositor. n objeto exhibido, m; law prueba, f

exhibition n exposición, f; (performance) función, f; espectáculo, m; exhibición, f; (showing) manifestación, f; (grant) bolsa de estudio, beca, f

exhibitionist n exhibicionista, mf

exhibitor n expositor (-ra)

exhilarate vt alegrar, alborozar

exhilarating a alegre; estimulador; vigorizador, tonificante

exhilaration n alegría, f, alborozo, regocijo, m

exhort vt and vi exhortar

exhumation n exhumación, f

exhume vt exhumar

exigence n exigencia, f; urgencia, f; (need) necesidad, f

exigent a exigente; urgente

exiguous a exiguo

exile n destierro, m; (person) desterrado (-da), Lat. Am. exiliado (-da) mf vt desterrar, Lat. Am. exiliar

exist vi existir

existence n existencia, f; (being) ser, m; (life) vida, f. **to bring into e.**, causar; producir

existing a existente

exit n salida, f; partida, f; (death) muerte, f; theat mutis, m. vi theat hacer mutis. **to make one's e.**, salir; marcharse; irse; morir; theat hacer mutis

exodus n éxodo, m; salida, f; emigración, f; (Old Testament) Éxodo, m

exonerate vt exonerar

exorbitant a exorbitante

exorcize vt exorcizar, conjurar

exotic a exótico. n planta exótica, f; fig flor de estufa, f

expand vt extender; abrir; (wings, etc.) desplegar; (the chest, etc.) expandir; dilatar; (amplify) ampliar; (an edition) ampliar, aumentar; (develop) desarrollar; fig ensanchar; (increase) aumentar. vi dilatarse; hincharse; abrirse; extenderse; ensancharse; (increase) aumentarse

expanse n extensión, f

expansible a *phys* expansible; dilatable

expansion n expansión, f; extensión, f; dilatación, f; (amplification) ampliación, f; (development) desarrollo, m; *fig* ensanchamiento, m; (increase) aumento, m

expansionism n expansionismo, m

expansive a expansivo; (of persons) efusivo, expresivo, comunicativo, afable

expansiveness n expansibilidad, f; (of persons) afabilidad, f

expatiate (upon) vi extenderse en

expatiation n discurso, m; digresión, f

expect vt esperar; (await) aguardar; (suppose) suponer; (demand) exigir; (count on) contar con. vi creer

expectant a expectante; (hopeful) esperanzudo; (pregnant) embarazada

expectantly adv con expectación

expectation n expectación, f; (hope) esperanza, expectativa, f; probabilidad, f

expectorate vi expectorar. vi escupir

expedience n conveniencia, f; oportunidad, f; aptitud, f; (self-interest) egoísmo, m

expedient a conveniente; oportuno; apto; prudente; político. n expediente, recurso, medio, m

expedite vt acelerar; facilitar; (send off) despachar

expedition n expedición, f; (haste) celeridad, diligencia, f

expeditionary a expedicionario. **e. force,** fuerza expedicionaria, f

expeditious a expedito, pronto

expel vt expeler, expulsar; echar, arrojar; despedir

expend vt gastar, expender; (time) perder

expenditure n gasto, desembolso, m, Lat. Am. erogación f; (of time) pérdida, f

expense n gasto, m; pérdida, f; costa, f; pl **expenses,** expensas, f pl, gastos, m pl. **at the e. of,** a costa de. **to be put to great e.,** tener que gastar mucho. **to pay one's expenses,** pagar sus gastos

expensive a costoso; caro

experience n experiencia, f. vt experimentar; sentir; sufrir. **by e.,** por experiencia

experienced a experimentado; experto; hábil; (lived) vivido

experiment n experimento, m; prueba, f; ensayo, m, tentativa, f, vi experimentar; hacer una prueba

experimental a experimental; tentativo

expert a experto; perito; hábil; (finished) acabado. n experto, m, especialista, f

expertness n pericia, f; maestría, f; habilidad, f; (knowledge) conocimiento, m

expiate vt expiar; reparar

expiration n (breathing out) espiración, f; (ending) expiración, f; terminación, f; *com* vencimiento, m; (death) muerte, f

expiration date fecha de caducidad, f

expire vi (exhale) espirar; (die) morir, dar el último suspiro; (of fire, light) extinguirse; (end) expirar; terminar; *com* vencer

explain vt explicar; aclarar; demostrar; exponer; (justify) justificar, defender. vi explicarse. **to e. away,** explicar; justificar

explanation n explicación, f; aclaración, f

explanatory a explicativo; aclaratorio

expletive a expletivo. n interjección, f

explicit a explícito

explode vi estallar; detonar; reventar. vt hacer estallar; (a mine) hacer saltar; (a belief, etc.) hacer abandonar; desechar

exploit n hazaña, proeza, f; aventura, f. vt explotar

exploitation n explotación, f

exploiter n explotador (-ra)

exploration n exploración, f

exploratory a exploratorio

explore vt explorar; examinar; averiguar; investigar; (med surg) explorar

explorer n explorador (-ra)

explosion n explosión, f; estallido, m, detonación, f

explosive a and n explosivo, m. **high e.,** explosivo violento, m. **explosives chamber,** recámara, f

export n exportación, f, vt exportar. **e. licence,** permiso de exportación, m. **e. trade,** comercio de exportación, m

exportation n exportación, f

exporter n exportador (-ra)

expose vt exponer; arriesgar; (exhibit) exhibir, (unmask) desenmascarar; descubrir; revelar; *phot* exponer; (ridicule) ridiculizar

exposed a descubierto; no abrigado; expuesto, peligroso

exposition n explicación, interpretación, f; declaración, f; (exhibition) exposición, f

expostulate vi protestar, **to e. with,** reprochar; reconvenir

expostulation n protesta, f; reconvención, f

exposure n exposición, f; (aspect) orientación, f; (scandal) revelación, f, escándalo, m; peligro, m; exposición al frío o al calor, f

expound vt exponer, explicar; comentar

expounder n intérprete, mf; comentador (-ra)

express a (clear) categórico, explícito, claro; expreso; (exact) exacto; (quick) rápido. n (messenger, post) expreso, m; (train) (tren) expreso, (tren) rápido, m; (goods) exprés, m. vt expresar; (a letter, etc.) mandar por expreso

expression n expresión, f

expressionless a sin expresión

expressive a expresivo; que expresa

expropriate vt expropiar

expropriation n expropiación, f

expulsion n expulsión, f

expunge vt borrar; testar; omitir

expurgate vt expurgar

exquisite a exquisito, precioso, primoroso; excelente; (acute) agudo, intenso; (keen) vivo. n elegante, petimetre, m

exquisitely adv primorosamente, pulcramente; a la perfección

exquisiteness n primor. m; pulcritud, perfección, f; excelencia, f; (of pain) intensidad, f; (keenness) viveza, f

ex-serviceman n excombatiente, antiguo soldado, m

extant a estante; existente; viviente

extempore a improvisado

extemporize vt and vi improvisar

extend vt extender; (hold out) tender, alargar; (lengthen) prolongar; (a period of time) prorrogar, diferir; (make larger) ensanchar; (increase) aumentar; dilatar; ampliar; (offer) ofrecer; vi extenderse; dilatarse; continuar; (give) dar de sí, estirarse; (last) prolongarse, durar; (become known) propagarse

extension n extensión, f; expansión, f; (increase) aumento, m; prolongación, f; ampliación, f; com prórroga, f; (telephone number) extensión, f, interno, m

extension cord n cordón de extensión, m; ladrón a, (Mexico; slang)

extensive a extenso, ancho, vasto; grande, considerable; (comprehensive) comprensivo

extent n extensión, f; (degree) punto, m; (limit) límite, m. **to a great e.**, en gran parte; considerablemente. **to some e.**, hasta cierto punto. **to the full e.**, en toda su extensión; completamente. **to what e.?** ¿hasta qué punto?

extenuate vt atenuar, desminuir, mitigar, paliar

extenuating a atenuante

extenuation n atenuación, mitigación, f

exterior a exterior, externo; de fuera; (foreign) extranjero. n exterior, m; aspecto, m; forma, f

exterminate vt exterminar

extermination n exterminio, m

exterminator n exterminador (-ra)

external a externo, exterior; (foreign) extranjero. n pl **externals**, apariencias, f pl; aspecto exterior, m; comportamiento, m

extinct a extinto; (of light, fire) extinguido; suprimido

extinction n extinción, f

extinguish vt extinguir; apagar; fig eclipsar

extinguisher n apagador (-ra); (for fires) extintor, m; (snuffer) matacandelas, m

extinguishment n apagamiento, m; extinción, f; abolición, f; (destruction) aniquilamiento, m

extirpate vt extirpar

extol vt elogiar, encomiar, alabar; cantar

extort vt arrancar, sacar por fuerza; exigir por amenazas

extortion n extorsión, f; exacción, f

extortionate a injusto; opresivo; (of price) exorbitante, excesivo

extra a and adv adicional; extraordinario; suplementario; (spare) de repuesto. prefix (in compounds) extra. n extra, m; suplemento, m; (of a paper) hoja extraordinaria, f; (actor) supernumerario (-ia). **e. charge,** gasto suplementario, m; (on the railway, etc.) suplemento, m. **e.-mural,** a de extramuros.

extract vt sacar; (chem math) extraer; extractar; (obtain) obtener. n chem extracto, m; (excerpt) cita, f

extraction n saca, f; extracción, f; obtención, f

extradite vt entregar por extradición

extraneous a extraño; (irrelevant) ajeno (a)

extraordinarily adv extraordinariamente, singularmente

extraordinariness n lo extraordinario; singularidad, f; (queerness) rareza, f

extraordinary a extraordinario; singular; (queer) raro, excéntrico; (incredible) increíble

extraterrestrial a Lat. Am. extraterrenal

extravagance n (in spending) prodigalidad, f, derroche, m; (of dress, speech) extravagancia, f; (foolishness) disparate, m; (luxury) lujo, m

extravagant a extravagante; (queer) extraño, raro; (wasteful) pródigo; (of persons) gastador, manirroto; (of price) exorbitante; excesivo

extravagantly adv extravagantemente; de un modo extraño; pródigamente; profusamente; excesivamente

extreme a extremo. n extremo, m. **in e.**, extremamente, en extremo, en sumo grado. **to carry to extremes,** llevar a extremos; **E. Unction,** Extremaunción, f

extremely adv sumamente; inf muy

extremism n extremismo, m

extremist a and n extremista, mf

extremity n extremidad, f; (point) punta, f; necesidad, f; pl **extremities,** anat extremidades, f pl; (measures) medidas extremas, f pl

extricate vt desenredar; librar; sacar

extrovert n psy extravertido, m

exuberance n exuberancia, f

exuberant a exuberante

exude vt exudar; rezumar; sudar. vi exudar; rezumarse

exult vi exultar; alegrarse

exultant a exultante, triunfante

exultantly adv con exultación; triunfalmente

exultation n exultación, f; triunfo, m

eye *n* ojo, *m*; (sight) vista, *f*; (look) mirada, *f*; atención, *f*; (opinion) opinión, *f*, juicio, *m*; (of a needle, of cheese) ojo, *m*; (of a hook) corcheta, *f*; *bot* yema, *f*; (of a potato) grillo, *m. vt* ojear; fijar los ojos en; examinar, mirar detenidamente. **bright eyes,** ojos vivos, *m pl.* **prominent eyes,** ojos saltones, *m pl.* **He couldn't keep his eyes off Mary,** Se le fueron los ojos tras María. **as far as the eye can reach,** hasta donde alcanza la vista. **before one's eyes,** a la vista de uno, ante los ojos de uno. **in my (etc.) eyes,** *fig* según creo yo, en mi opinión. **in the twinkling of an eye,** en un abrir y cerrar de ojos. **with an eye to,** pensando en. **with my own eyes,** con mis propios ojos. **with the naked eye,** con la simple vista. **to keep an eye on,** vigilar. **to make eyes at,** guiñar el ojo; mirar con ojos de enamorado. **to have one's eyes opened,** *fig* caérsele la venda. **eye-bath,** ojera, *f.* **eye-opener,** revelación, sorpresa, *f.* **eye-pencil,** pincel para las cejas, *m.* **eye-piece,** objetivo, ocular, *m.* **eye-shade,** visera, *f.* **eye-tooth,** colmillo, *m.* **eye-witness,** testigo ocular, testigo de vista, testigo presencial, *mf*

éyeball *n* globo ocular, *m*

eyebrow *n* ceja, *f*

eye care atención de la vista, *f*

eyed *a* que tiene ojos; (in compounds) de ojos . . ., con ojos . . .; con los ojos; (of a needle) con el ojo . . . **She is a blue-eyed child,** Es una niña de ojos azules

eyeglass *n* lente, *m*

eyelash *n* pestaña, *f*

eyelet *n* ojete, *m*

eyelid *n* párpado, *m*

eyesight *n* vista, *f*

eyewash *n* colirio, *m; inf* camelo, *m.* **That's all e.!** ¡Eso es un camelo!

eyrie *n* nido (of any bird of prey), nido de águila (eagle's) *m*

F

f *n* (letter) efe, *f*; *mus* fa, *m*. **f sharp,** fa sostenido, *m*

fa *n mus* fa, *m*

fable *n* fábula, leyenda, historia, *f*, apólogo, cuento, *m*; (untruth) invención, mentira, *f*

fabled *a* celebrado, famoso

fabric *n* obra, fábrica, *f*; estructura, construcción, *f*; (making) manufactura, *f*; (cloth) tejido, paño, *m*; textura, *f*

fabricate *vt* fabricar, construir; (invent) fingir, inventar

fabrication *n* fabricación, manufactura, *f*; construcción, *f*; (lie) invención, ficción, *f*

fabulous *a* fabuloso

façade *n* fachada, frente, *f*

face *n* superficie, *f*; (of persons) cara, *f*, rostro, *m*; (look) semblante, aire, *m*; (of coins) anverso, *m*; (grimace) mueca, *f*, gesto, *m*; (dial) esfera, *f*; (of gems) faceta, *f*; (of a wall) paramento, *m*; (front) fachada, frente, *f*; (effrontery) cara dura, *f*, descaro, *m*. **in the f. of,** ante; en presencia de. *mil* **Left f.!** ¡zquierda! **on the f. of it,** juzgando por las apariencias. **to bring f. to f.,** confrontar (con). **to laugh in a person's f.,** reírse a la cara (de). **to make a f.,** hacer muecas. **to my f.,** en mi cara, en mis barbas. **to put a good f. on,** *fig* poner (or hacer) buena cara a. **to set one's f. against,** oponerse resueltamente a. **to straighten one's f.,** componer el semblante. **to throw in one's f.,** *fig* dar en rostro, dar en cara. **to wash one's f.,** lavarse la cara. **f. card,** figura (de la baraja), *f*. **f.-cloth,** paño para lavar la cara, *m*. **f. downward,** boca abajo. **f. lift,** operación estética facial, *f*. **f. of the waters,** faz de las aguas, *f*. **f. powder,** polvos de arroz, *m pl*. **f. to f.,** cara a cara, de persona a persona; frente a frente. **f. value,** significado literal, *m*; *com* valor nominal, *m*

face *vt* mirar hacia; confrontar, hacer cara (a); (of buildings, etc.) mirar a, caer a (or hacia); *fig* arrostrar, enfrentarse con; *sew* guarnecer, aforrar. *vi* estar orientado. **to f. the facts,** enfrentarse con la realidad. **to f. the music,** *fig* arrostrar las consecuencias. **to f. about,** volver la espalda; *mil* dar una vuelta, cambiar de frente. **to f. up to,** *fig* hacer cara a

faced *a* con cara . . . , de cara . . . ; *sew* forrado (de). **to be two-f.,** *fig* ser de dos haces

facer *n* puñetazo en la cara, *m*; *fig* dificultad insuperable, *f*, problema muy grande, *m*

facet *n* faceta, *f*

facetious *a* chancero, chistoso, jocoso

facetiousness *n* jocosidad, festividad, *f*

facial *a* facial. **f. expression,** expresión de la cara, *f*, semblante, *m*

facile *a* (frivolous) ligero (e.g., a deduction or inference)

facilitate *vt* facilitar

facility *n* facilidad, *f*; habilidad, destreza, *f*

facing *n sew* vuelta, *f*; (of a building) paramento, *m*; (of lumber) chapa *f*; encaramiento, *m*

facsimile *n* facsímile, *m*

fact *n* (event) hecho, suceso, *m*; (datum) dato, *m*; realidad, verdad, *f*. **as a matter of f.,** en realidad. **In f.,** en efecto, en realidad. **I know as a f.,** Tengo por cierto. **The f. is . . . ,** La verdad es (que) . . . **the f. that,** el hecho de que

fact-finding informador (e.g. send s.b. on a fact-finding mission, enviar a fulano en misión informadora)

faction *n* facción, *f*, partido, bando, *m*; (tumult) alboroto, *m*

factional *a* partidario

factious *a* faccioso, sedicioso

factor *n* (fact) factor, elemento, *m*; consideración, *f*; *math* factor, *m*; *com* agente, factor, *m*

factory *n* fábrica, manufactura, *f*; taller, *m*. **F. Act,** ley de trabajadores industriales, *f*. **f. hand,** operario (-ia)

factual *a* basado en hechos, objetivo

faculty *n* facultad, *f*; (talent) habilidad, *f*, talento, *m*; (university division) facultad, *f*; (teachers as a group) claustro de profesores, claustro, profesorado, *m*; (authorization) privilegio, *m*, autoridad, *f*

fad *n* capricho, *m*, chifladura, *f*, dengue, *m*

fade *vi* (of plants) marchitarse, secarse; (of color) palidecer, descolorarse; (vanish) disiparse, desaparecer; (of persons) desmejorarse; (of stains) salir. *vt* descolorar. **to f. away,** desvanecer; (of persons) consumirse. **f.-out,** *n* (cinema) desaparecimiento gradual, *m*

faded *a* (of plants) seco, marchito, mustio; (of colors) descolorado, pálido; (of people) desmejorado

fading *a* que palidece; (of flowers) medio marchito; (of light) mortecino, pálido; decadente. *n* desaparecimiento, *m*, marchitez, *f*; decadencia, *f*

fag *n inf* pitillo, *m*. **f.-end,** fin, *m*; restos, *m pl*, sobras, *f pl*; (of a cigarette) colilla, *f*; (offensive) maricón. *vi* trabajar mucho. *vt* fatigar mucho; hacer trabajar

faience *n* fayenza, *f*

fail *vi* faltar; fracasar, malograrse; no tener éxito, salir mal; (of strength) decaer, acabarse; (be short of) carecer (de); *com* hacer bancarrota, suspender pagos. *vt* abandonar; (disappoint) decepcionar, engañar; (in exams) suspender. **Do not f. to see her,** No dejes de verla.

He failed to do his duty, Faltó a su deber

fail *n* **without f.,** sin falta

failing *n* falta, *f*; (shortcoming) vicio, flaco, *m*, debilidad, *f*; malogro, fracaso, *m*; decadencia, *f*

failure *n* fracaso, *m*; falta de éxito, *f*; (in exams) suspensión, *f*; (of power) no funcionamiento, *m*; omisión, *f*, descuido, *m*; com quiebra, bancarrota, *f*; (decay) decadencia, *f*. **on f. of,** al fracasar; bajo pena de

fain *a* deseoso, muy contento. **He was f. to . . .,** Se sintió obligado a . . . ; Quería

faint *a* débil; (dim) indistinto, vago, borroso; (of colors) pálido, desmayado; (weak) lánguido, desfallecido; (slight) superficial, rudimentario. *vi* perder el sentido, desmayarse. *n* desmayo, *m*. **to be f. with hunger,** estar muerto de hambre. **to cause to f.,** hacer desmayar. **f.-hearted,** pusilánime, medroso. **f.-heartedness,** pusilanimidad, *f*

fair *n* feria, *f*; (sale) mercado, *m*; (exhibition) exposición, *f*

fair *a* (beautiful) hermoso, lindo, bello; (of hair) rubio; (of skin) blanco; (clear, fresh) limpio, claro; (good) bueno; (favorable) favorable, propicio, próspero; (of weather) despejado, sereno; (just) imparcial; (straightforward) honrado, recto, justo; (passable) regular, mediano; (of writing) legible; (proper) conveniente. *adv* honradamente; (politely) cortésmente; exactamente. **by f. means,** por medios honrados. **It's not f.!** ¡No hay derecho! **to become f.,** (of weather) serenarse. **to give a f. trial,** juzgar imparcialmente; dar una buena oportunidad; *law* procesar imparcialmente. **to make a f. copy,** poner en limpio. **f.-haired,** de pelo rubio, rubio. **f. one,** una beldad, *f*. **f. play,** *sport* juego limpio, *m*; proceder leal, *m*. **f.-skinned,** de tez blanca, rubio. **f.-weather,** buen tiempo, *m*, bonanza, *f*. **f.-weather friends,** amigos de los días prósperos, *m pl*

fairly *adv* (justly) con imparcialidad; (moderately) bastante; totalmente, enteramente. **f. good,** bastante bueno; regular

fairness *n* belleza, hermosura, *f*; (of skin) blancura, *f*; (justness) imparcialidad, *f*; (reasonableness) justicia, equidad, *f*; (of hair) color rubio, oro, *m*

fairy *n* hada, *f*, duende, *m*, a de hada, de duendes; *fig* delicado. **f.-gold,** tesoro de duendes, *m*; **f.-light,** lucecillo, *m*; luminaria, *f*. **f.-like,** aduendado, como una hada. **f.-ring,** círculo mágico, *m*. **f.-tale,** cuento de hadas, *m*; patraña, *f*, cuento de viejas, *m*

faith *n* fe, *f*; confianza, *f*; (doctrine) creencia, religión, filosofía, *f*; (honor) palabra, *f*. **in good f.,** de buena fe. **to break f.,** faltar a la palabra dada. **f.-healing,** curanderismo, *m*

faithful *a* fiel, leal; (accurate) exacto; (trustworthy) veraz. **the f.,** los creyentes

faithfully *adv* fielmente, lealmente; (accurately) con exactitud. **Yours f.,** Queda de Vd. su att. s.s.

faithfulness *n* fidelidad, lealtad, *f*; (accuracy) exactitud, *f*

faithless *a* infiel, desleal, pérfido.

fake *vt* imitar, falsificar. *n* imitación, falsificación, *f*. **to f. up,** inventar

Falkland Islands, the *pl* las Malvinas *fpl*

fall *n* caída, *f*; (of temperature, mercury) baja, *f*; (of water) salto de agua, *m*, catarata, cascada, *f*; (in value) depreciación, *f*; (in price and Stock Exchange) baja, *f*; (descent) bajada, *f*; (autumn) otoño, *m*; (declivity) declinación, *f*, declive, desnivel, *m*; (ruin) ruina, *f*; (destruction, *f*; (of night, etc.) caída (de la noche), *f*; (of snow) nevada, *f*; (of rain) golpe, *m*; (*theat* of curtain) caída, bajada, *f*; (surrender) capitulación, rendición, *f*; (of earth) desprendimiento de tierras, *m*; (of the tide) reflujo, *m*

fall *vi* caer; (of mercury, temperature) bajar; (collapse) desplomarse, hundirse, derrumbarse; (die) caer muerto; (descend) descender; (*theat* of the curtain) bajar, caer; (of a river into the sea, etc.) desembocar, desaguar; (of hair, draperies) caer; (decrease) disminuir; (of spirits) ponerse triste, sentirse deprimido; (sin) caer; (come upon) sobrevenir; (of dusk, etc.) caer, llegar; (strike, touch) tocar; (as a share) tocar en suerte; (as a duty, responsibility) tocar, corresponder; (of seasons) caer en; (of words from the lips) caer de (los labios); (say) decir, pronunciar palabras; (of exclamations) escaparse; (become) venir a ser; (happen) suceder; (be) ser. **fallen upon evil days,** venido a menos. **His face fell,** Puso una cara de desengaño. **Christmas falls on a Thursday this year,** Navidad cae en jueves este año. **to let f.,** dejar caer. **to f. a-** (followed by verb) empezar a. **He fell a-crying,** Empezó a llorar. **to f. again,** volver a caer, recaer. **to f. among,** caer entre. **to f. astern,** quedarse atrás. **to f. away,** (leave) abandonar, dejar; (grow thin) enflaquecer; marchitarse; (crumble) desmoronarse. **to f. back,** retroceder, volver hacia atrás. **to f. back upon,** recurrir a; *mil* replegarse hacia. **to f. backward,** caer de espaldas, caer hacia atrás. **to f. behind,** quedarse atrás. **to f. down,** venirse a tierra; venirse abajo, dar consigo en el suelo, caer. **to f. due,** vencer. **to f. flat,** caer de bruces; (be unsuccessful) no tener éxito. **to f. in,** caer en; (collapse) desplomarse; *mil* alinearse; (expire) vencer. **to f. into,** caer en. **to f. in with,** tropezar con; reunirse con, juntarse con; (agree) convenir en; **to f. off,** caer de; (of leaves, etc.) desprenderse de, separarse de; (abandon) abandonar; (diminish) disminuir. **to f. on,**

caer de (e.g. **to f. on one's back,** caer de espaldas); (of seasons) caer en; (attack) echarse encima de, atacar. **to f. out,** (of a window, etc.) caer por; (happen) acontecer, suceder; (quarrel) pelearse, reñir; *mil* romper filas. **to f. out with,** reñir con. **to f. over,** volcar, caer; (stumble) tropezar con. **to f. short,** faltar; carecer, ser deficiente; (fail) malograrse, no llegar a sus expectaciones; (of shooting) errar el tiro. **to f. through,** caer por; (fail) malograrse, fracasar. **to f. to,** empezar a, ponerse a; (be incumbent on) tocar a, corresponder a; (attack) atacar. **to f. under,** caer debajo; caer bajo; sucumbir, perecer; (incur) incurrir en, merecer. **to f. upon,** (attack) caer sobre, acometer; acaecer, tener lugar; (be incumbent) tocar a

fallacious a falaz, engañoso, ilusorio

fallacy *n* error, *m*, ilusión, *f*

fallen a caído; arruinado; degradado. **f. angel,** ángel caído, *m*. **f. woman,** perdida, mujer caída, *f*

fallible a falible

falling a que cae, cayente. *n* caída, *f*; (of mercury, temperature) baja, *f*; (crumbling) desmoronamiento, *m*; (collapse) hundimiento, derrumbamiento, *m*; (of tide) reflujo, *m*; (of waterlevel) bajada, *f*; (in value) depreciación, *f*; (of prices and Stock Exchange) baja, *f*; (diminishment) disminución, *f*; (in level of earth) declinación, *f*; (*com* expiry) vencimiento, *m*; (*theat* of curtain) bajada, caída, *f*. **f. away,** (crumbling) desmoronamiento, *m*; desprendimiento de tierras, *m*; (desertion) deserción, *f*, abandono, *m*. **f. back,** retirada, *f*, retroceso, *m*. **f. down,** caída, *f*; derrumbamiento, *m*. **f. due,** vencimiento, *m*. **f. in,** hundimiento, *m*; (crumbling) desmoronamiento, *m*. **f. off,** caída de, *f*; (disappearance) desaparición, *f*; (diminution) disminución, *f*; (deterioration) deterioración, *f*. **f. out,** caída por, *f*; disensión, *f*. **f. short,** falta, *f*; carácter inferior, *m*; frustración, *f*. **f. star,** estrella fugaz, *f*

fallout caída radiactiva, llovizna radiactiva, precipitación radiactiva, *f*

fallow a (of color) leonado; *agr* barbechado; descuidado. *n* barbecho, *m*. *vt* barbechar. **to leave f.,** dejar en barbecho. **f. deer,** corzo (-za)

false a incorrecto, erróneo, equivocado; falso; (unfounded) infundado; (disloyal) infiel, traidor, desleal; (not real) postizo; artificial; de imitación; *mus* desafinado; (pretended) fingido; engañoso, mentiroso. **to play a person f.,** traicionar (a). **f. bottom,** fondo doble, *m*; **f. claim,** pretensión infundada, *f*. **f. door,** surtida, *f*. **f.-hearted,** pérfido, desleal. **f. teeth,** dientes postizos, *m pl*, dentadura postiza, *f*

falsehood *n* mentira, *f*

falsetto *n* falsete, *m*, voz de cabeza, *f*

falsification *n* falsificación, *f*; (of texts) corrupción, *f*

falsify *vt* falsear, falsificar; (disappoint) defraudar, frustrar, contrariar

falter *vi* (physically) titubear; (of speech) balbucir, tartamudear; (of action) vacilar. **to f. out,** balbucir; hablar con voz entrecortada; decir con vacilación

faltering a titubeante; (of speech) entrecortado; vacilante. *n* temblor, *m*; vacilación, *f*

fame *n* fama, *f*; reputación, *f*; (renown) celebridad, *f*, renombre, *m*. **of ill f.,** de mala fama

famed a reputado; renombrado, célebre, famoso

familiar a íntimo, familiar; afable, amistoso; (ill-bred) insolente, demasiado familiar; (usual) corriente, usual, común; conocido. *n* amigo (-ga) íntimo (-ma); *ecc* familiar, *m*; demonio familiar, *m*. **to be f. with,** (a subject) estar versado en, conocer muy bien; (a person) tratar con familiaridad. **to become f. with,** acostumbrarse a; familiarizarse con; (a person) hacerse íntimo de

familiarity *n* intimidad, familiaridad, confianza, *f*; (friendliness) afabilidad, *f*; (over-familiarity) insolencia, demasiada familiaridad, *f*; (with a subject) conocimiento (de), *m*, experiencia (de), *f*

familiarize *vt* familiarizar, acostumbrar, habituar *vr* familiarizarse

family *n* familia, *f*; (lineage) linaje, abolengo, *m*; (*bot zool*) familia, *f*; (of languages) grupo, *m*. a de familia; familiar; casero. **f. doctor,** médico de cabecera, *m*. **f. life,** vida de familia, *f*; hogar, *m*. **f. man,** padre de familia, *m*. **f. name,** apellido, *m*. **f. seat,** casa solar, *f*. **f. tree,** árbol genealógico, *m*

famine *n* hambre, *f*; carestía, escasez, *f*

famish *vt* matar de hambre. *vi* morirse de hambre

famished a hambriento

famous a famoso, célebre, renombrado; insigne, distinguido; *inf* excelente

famously adv *inf* muy bien, excelentemente

fan *n* abanico, *m*; *agr* aventador, *m*; *mech* ventilador, *m*; (on a windmill) volante, *m*; (amateur) aficionado (-da); (admirer) admirador (-ra); *arch* abanico, *m*. *vt* abanicar; *agr* aventar; ventilar. **fan oneself,** hacerse viento. **tap with a f.,** abanicazo, golpecito con el abanico, *m*. **f.-belt,** *mech* correa de transmisión del ventilador, *f*. **f.-light,** tragaluz, *m*. **f. maker** or **seller,** abaniquero (-ra). **f.-shaped,** en abanico, abanicado, en forma de abanico

fanatic a and *n* fanático (-ca)

fanaticism *n* fanatismo, *m*

fancied a imaginario

fancier *n* aficionado (-da); (of animals) criador (-ra)

fanciful a romántico, caprichoso; fantástico

fancifulness n extravagancia, f; romanticismo, m

fancy n fantasía, imaginación, f; (idea) idea, f, ensueño, m; (caprice) capricho, antojo, m; (liking) afecto, cariño, m; gusto, m, afición, f; (wish) deseo, m; (fantasy) quimera, f, a imaginario; elegante, ornado; com de capricho, de fantasía; fantástico, extravagante. vt imaginar, figurarse; (like) gustar de; aficionarse a; antojarse. **I have a f. for . . . ,** Se me antoja. . . . **Just f.!** ¡Toma! ¡Quia! ¡Parece mentira! **to take a f. to,** (things) tomar afición a; (people) tomar cariño (a). **f.-dress,** disfraz, m. **f.-dress ball,** baile de trajes, m

fancy goods n pl artículos suntuarios m pl

fanfare n tocata de trompetas, f

fang n colmillo, m; raíz de un diente, f

fangless a sin colmillos

fantastic a fantástico; extravagante

fantasy n imaginación, f; fantasía, quimera, visión, f; creación imaginativa, f

far adv lejos; a lo lejos; (much, greatly) mucho, en alto grado; (very) muy; (mostly) en gran parte. a lejano, distante; (farther) ulterior. **as far as,** tan lejos como; (up to, until) hasta; en cuanto, por lo que, según que. (e.g. **As far as we know,** Por lo que nosotros sepamos. **as far as we are concerned,** En cuanto a nosotros toca). **by far,** con mucho. **from far and near,** de todas partes. **from far off,** desde lejos. **He read far into the night,** Leyó hasta las altas horas de la noche. **how far?** ¿a qué distancia?; (to what extent) ¿hasta qué punto? ¿hasta dónde? **How far is it to . . . ?** ¿Qué distancia hay a . . . ? **in so far as,** en tanto que. **on the far side,** al lado opuesto; al otro extremo. **so far,** tan lejos; (till now) hasta ahora. **to go far,** ir lejos. **far away,** a distante, remoto, lejano, f; fig abstraído. adv muy lejos. **far beyond,** mucho más allá. **far-fetched,** increíble, improbable. **far-off,** a distante. adv a lo lejos, en lontananza. **far-reaching,** de gran alcance. **far-sighted,** sagaz, presciente, previsor. **far-sightedness,** sagacidad, previsión, f

farce n farsa, f. vt cul embutir, rellenar

farcical a burlesco, cómico, sainetesco; absurdo, grotesco, ridículo

fare n (price) pasaje, precio del billete, m; (traveler) viajero (-ra), pasajero (-ra); (food) comida, f. vi pasarlo (e.g. **to f. well,** pasarlo bien). **bill of f.,** menú, m. **full f.,** billete entero, m. **f. stage,** trayecto, m

farewell n despedida, f, adiós, m. a de despedida. interj ¡adiós! ¡quede Vd. con Dios! **to bid f. to,** despedirse de

farflung de gran alcance, extenso, vasto; (empire) dilatado

farina n harina (de cereales), f; chem fécula, f, almidón, m; bot polen, m

farm n granja, hacienda, quintería, finca, chacra, f, cortijo, m. vt cultivar, labrar (la tierra); (taxes) arrendar. vi ser granjero. **to f. out,** (taxes) dar en arriendo. **f. girl,** labradora, f. **f. house,** alquería, casa de labranza, granja, f. **f. laborer,** labriego, peón, m. **f. yard,** corral de una granja, m

farmer n granjero, hacendado, quintero, m, agrícola, mf; (small) colono, labrador, m; (of taxes) arrendatario, m

farmers' movement Mexico agrarismo m

farmhand gañán, mozo, mozo de granja, peón m

farming n labranza, f, cultivo, m; agricultura, labor agrícola, f; (of taxes) arriendo, m. a de labranza, labradoril; agrícola

farrago n fárrago, m, mezcla, f

farther adv más lejos; (beyond) más adelante; (besides) además. a ulterior; más distante. **at the f. end,** al otro extremo; en el fondo. **f. on,** más adelante; más allá

farthest adv más lejos. a más lejano, más distante; extremo

fascinate vt fascinar; encantar, hechizar, seducir

fascinating a fascinador; encantador, seductor

fascination n fascinación, f; encanto, hechizo, m

Fascism n fascismo, m

Fascist a and n fascista mf

fashion n (form) forma, hechura, f; (way) modo, m; (custom) costumbre, f, uso, m; (vogue) moda, f; (high life) alta sociedad, f; (tone) buen tono, m. vt hacer, labrar; inventar. **in Spanish f.,** a la española, al uso de España. **the latest f.,** la última moda. **to be in f.,** estar de moda. **to go out of f.,** dejar de ser de moda, perder la popularidad. **f. book,** revista de modas, f. **f. plate,** figurín, m

fashionable a de moda; elegante; de buen tono. **to be f.,** estar en boga, ser de moda. **f. world,** mundo elegante, mundo de sociedad, m

fashion show desfile de modas, m, exhibición de modas, f

fast a (firm) firme; (secure) seguro; (strong) fuerte; (fixed) fijo; (closed) cerrado; (of boats) amarrado; (tight) apretado; (of colors) estable; (of trains) rápido; (of sleep) profundo; (of friends) leal, seguro; (quick) rápido, veloz; (of a watch) adelantado; (dissipated) disoluto. adv firmemente, seguramente; (quickly) rápidamente; (of sleep) profundamente; (tightly) estrechamente, apretadamente; (of rain) (llover) a cántaros; (ceaselessly) continuamente; (often) frecuentemente; (entirely) completamente. **to be f.,** (clocks) adelantar. **to make f.,** naut amarrar, trincar. **f. asleep,** profundamente dormido. **f. color,** color estable, color sólido, *m*

fast *n* ayuno, *m*, *vi* ayunar. **to break one's f.,** romper el ayuno. **f.-day,** día de ayuno, día de vigilia, *m*

fasten *vt* (tie) atar; (fix) fijar; sujetar; (stick) pegar; (a door) cerrar; (bolt) echar el cerrojo; *naut* trincar; (together) juntar, unir; (with buttons, hooks, etc.) abrochar; (on, upon) fijar en; *fig* imputar (a). *vi* fijarse; pegarse; (upon) agarrarse a, asir. **to f. one's eyes on,** fijar los ojos en. **to f. up,** cerrar; atar; (nail) clavar

fastener *n* (bolt) pasador, *m*; (for bags, jewelery, etc.) cierre, *m*; (buckle) hebilla, *f*; (of a coat, etc.) tiador, *m*; (of a book, file) sujetador, *m*; (lock) cerrojo, *m*. **paper-f.,** sujetador de papeles, *m*. **patent-f.,** botón automático, *m*

fastening *n* atadura, *f*; sujeción, *f*, afianzamiento, *m*; (together) union, *f*; (of a garment) brochadura, *f*; (of a handbag) cierre, *m*

fastidious *a* dengoso, melindroso, desdeñoso; (sensitive) sensitivo, delicado; (critical) discerniente, crítico

fasting *n* ayuno, *m*. *a* and *part* de ayuno; en ayunas

fastness *n* firmeza, solidez, *f*; (stronghold) fortaleza, *f*; (retreat) refugio, *m*; (speed) velocidad, rapidez, *f*; (dissipation) disipación, *f*, libertinaje, *m*

fat *a* (stout) gordo, grueso; (greasy) graso, seboso; (greasy) grasiento; (rich) fértil, pingüe; (productive) lucrativo. *n* (stoutness) gordura, *f*; (for cooking) manteca, *f*; (lard) lardo, *m*; (of animal or meat) grasa, *f*; sebo, saín, *m*; *fig* riqueza, *f*; *fig* fertilidad, *f*. **to grow fat,** engordarse, ponerse grueso

fatal *a* fatal, mortal; funesto

fatality *n* fatalidad, *f*; infortunio, *m*, calamidad, *f*; muerte, *f*

fate *n* destino, sino, hado, *m*, providencia, *f*; fortuna, suerte, *f*; destrucción, ruina, *f*; muerte, *f*. **the Three Fates,** las Parcas

fated *a* fatal, destinado; predestinado

fateful *a* decisivo, fatal; aciago, ominoso

father *n* padre, *m*. *vt* prohijar, adoptar; (on or upon) atribuir (a), imputar (a). **Eternal F.,** Padre Eterno, *m*. **Holy F.,** Padre Santo, *m*. **indulgent f.,** padre indulgente, padrazo, *m*. **Like f. like son,** De tal palo tal astilla. **f. confessor,** *ecc* director espiritual, *m*. **f.-in-law,** suegro, *m*

fatherhood *n* paternidad, *f*

fatherland *n* patria, madre patria, *f*

fatherless *a* sin padre, huérfano de padre

fatherly *a* paternal, de padre

fathom *n* *naut* braza, *f*. *vt* sondear; *fig* profundizar, tantear; (a mystery) desentrañar

fathomless *a* insondable; *fig* incomprensible, impenetrable

fatigue *n* fatiga, *f*, cansancio, *m*; *mil* faena, *f*; *mech* pérdida de resistencia, *f*. *vt* fatigar, cansar. **to be fatigued,** estar cansado, cansarse, fatigarse. **f. party,** *mil* pelotón de castigo, *m*

fatiguing *a* fatigoso

fatness *n* (stoutness) gordura, carnosidad, *f*; grasa, *f*, gordo, *m*; (richness) fertilidad, *f*; lo lucrativo

fatten *vt* engordar; (animals) cebar, sainar; (land) abonar, fertilizar. *vi* ponerse grueso, echar carnes

fatty *a* untoso, grasiento; *chem* graso. **f. acid,** ácido graso, *m*. **f. degeneration,** degeneración grasienta, *f*

fatuous *a* fatuo, necio, lelo

faucet *n* canilla, llave, *f*, grifo, *m*

fault *n* defecto, *m*, imperfección, *f*; (blame) culpa, *f*; (mistake) falta, *f*, error, *m*; (in cloth) canilla, barra, *f*; *geol* falla, quiebra, *f*; *elec* avería, *f*; *sport* falta, *f*, *in sport* cometer una falta. **to a f.,** excesivamente. **to be at f.,** (to blame) tener la culpa; (mistaken) estar equivocado; (puzzled) estar perplejo; (of dogs) perder el rastro. **To find f.,** tachar, culpar, criticar. **Whose f. is it?** ¿Quién tiene la culpa?

faultfinder *n* criticón (-ona)

faultless *a* sin faltas; perfecto, sin tacha; impecable

faulty *a* defectuoso, imperfecto

fauna *n* fauna, *f*

favor *n* favor, *m*; (protection) amistad, protección, *f*, amparo, *m*; (permission) permiso, *m*, licencia, *f*; (kindness) merced, gracia, *f*; (gift) obsequio, *m*; (favoritism) favoritismo, *m*, preferencia, *f*; (benefit) beneficio, *m*; (badge) colores, *m pl*; *com* grata, atenta, *f*. *vt* favorecer, apoyar; mirar con favor, mostrar parcialidad (hacia); (suit) favorecer; (be advantageous) ser propicio, *m*; (contribute to) contribuir a, ayudar; (resemble) parecerse (a). **Circumstances f. the idea,** Las circunstancias son propicias a la idea, Las circunstancias militan en pro de la idea. **I f. the teaching of modern languages,** Soy partidario de la enseñanza de lenguas vivas. **in f. of,** a favor de, en pro de. **in the f. of,** en el favor de. **out of f.,** fuera de favor; (not fashionable) fuera de moda. **to count on the f. of,** tener de su parte (a), contar con el apoyo de. **to do a f.,** hacer un favor. **to enjoy the f. of,** gozar del favor de. **to fall out of f.,** caer en desgracia; (go out of fashion) pasar de moda. **to grow in f.,** aumentar en favor

favorable *a* favorable; propicio, próspero

favored *a* favorecido; predilecto; (in compounds) parecido, encarado

favorite *a* favorito; predilecto, preferido. *n* favorito (-ta). **court f.,** valido, privado, *m*; (mistress) querida (de un rey), *f*; (lover) amante (de una reina), *m*. **to be a f.**, ser favorito

fawn *n zool* cervato, *m*; (color) color de cervato, color de ante, *m*. **a de color de** cervato, anteado, pardo; (of animals) rucio, pardo. *vt and vi* parir la cierva. *vi* acariciar; (on, upon) adular, lisonjear

fawning *n* adulación, *Lat. Am.* adulonería *f*, a adulador, lisonjero, *Lat. Am. also* incondicional, *Mexico* lambioche

fear *n* miedo, temor, *m*; *Argentina* canillaera *f* (apprehension) ansiedad, aprensión, *f*, recelo, *m*; (respect) veneración, *f*. *vt* temer; recelar; (respect) reverenciar. *vi* tener miedo; estar receloso, estar con cuidado. **for f. of**, por miedo de. **for f. that**, por temor de que, por miedo de que. **from f.**, por miedo. **There is no f. of . . .**, No hay miedo de (que) . . .

fearful *a* miedoso, aprensivo, receloso; (cowardly) tímido, pusilánime; (terrible) horrible, espantoso, pavoroso; *inf* tremendo, enorme

fearfully *adv* con miedo; tímidamente (terribly) horriblemente; *inf* enormemente

fearless *a* sin miedo, intrépido, audaz

fearsome *a* temible, horrible, espantoso

feasibility *n* practicabilidad, posibilidad, *f*

feasible *a* factible, hacedero, practicable, ejecutable

feast *n ecc* fiesta, *f*; banquete, *m*; *fig* abundancia, *f*, *vi* regalarse. *vt* festejar, agasajar; (delight) recrear, deleitar. **immovable f.**, *ecc* fiesta fija, *f*. **movable f.**, fiesta movible, *f*. **f. day**, día de fiesta, *m*, festividad *f*

feat *n* hazaña, proeza, *f*, hecho, *m*

feather *n* pluma, *f*; (of the tail) pena, *f*; *pl* **feathers**, plumaje, *m*; plumas, *f pl*. *vt* emplumar; adornar con plumas; (rowing) poner casi horizontal la pala del remo. **to f. one's nest**, *inf* hacer su agosto. **f.-bed**, plumón, colchón de plumas, *m*. **f.-brained**, casquivano, alocado, aturdido. **f.-duster**, plumero, *m*. **f.-stitch**, *sew* diente de perro, *m*. **f. weight**, (boxing) peso pluma, *m*

feature *n* rasgo, *m*, característica, *f*; (cinema) número de programa, *m*; *pl* **features** (of the face) facciones, *f pl*. *vt* dar importancia (a); (cinema) presentar. **f. film**, documentaria, *f*

February *n* febrero, *m*

feces *n* heces, *f pl*; excremento, *m*

fecund *a* fecundo, fértil

fecundate *vt* fecundar

fecundity *n* fecundidad, fertilidad, *f*

federal *a* federal, federalista

federate *vt* confederar. *vi* confederarse. **a** confederado

federation *n* confederación, federación, *f*; liga, unión, asociación, *f*

fed up *a Argentina, Chile* incomódo

fee *n* (feudal law) feudo, *m*; (homage) homenaje, *m*; (duty) derecho, *m*; (professional) honorario, estipendio, *m*; (to a servant) gratificación, *f*; (entrance, university, etc.) cuota, *f*; (payment) paga, *f*

feeble *a* débil; lánguido; enfermizo; (of light, etc.) tenue; *fig* flojo. **to grow f.**, debilitarse; disminuir. **f.-minded**, anormal

feed *n* alimento, *m*; (meal) comida, *f*; (of animals) pienso, forraje, *m*; *mech* alimentación, *f*. *vt* alimentar; dar de comer (a); (animals) cebar; *mech* alimentar; mantener; *fig* nutrir. *vi* comer, alimentarse; (graze) pastar. **to be fed up**, *inf* estar hasta la coronilla, estar harto. **to f. on**, alimentarse de; *fig* nutrirse de. **f. pipe**, tubo de alimentación, *m*

feedback retrocomunicación, *f*

feeder *n* el, *m*, (*f*, la) que da de comer a; (eater) comedor (-ra); (of a river) tributario, afluente, *m*; (bib) babero, *m*; *mech* alimentador, *m*; (cup for invalids) pistero, *m*

feeding *n* alimentación, *f*, a alimenticio, de alimentación. **f.-bottle**, biberón, *m*. **f.-cup**, pistero, *m*. **f.-trough**, pesebre, *m*

feel *n* (touch) tacto, *m*; (feeling) sensación, *f*; (instinct) instinto, *m*, percepción innata, *f*

feel *vt* (touch) tocar, tentar, palpar; (experience) sentir, experimentar; (understand) comprender; (believe) creer; (be conscious of) estar consciente de; (the pulse) tomar; examinar. *vi* sentir, ser sensible; sentirse, encontrarse; (to the touch) ser . . . al tacto, estar. **How do you f.?** ¿Cómo se siente Vd.? **I f. cold**, Tengo frío. **I f. for you**, Lo siento en el alma; Estoy muy consciente de ello. **I f. strongly that . . .**, Estoy convencido de que . . . **I f. that it is a difficult question**, Me parece una cuestión difícil. **It feels like rain**, Creo que va a llover. **to f. at home**, sentirse a sus anchas, sentirse como en su casa. **to f. hungry (thirsty)**, tener hambre (sed). **to f. one's way**, andar a tientas; *fig* medir el terreno. **to f. soft**, ser blando al tacto. **to make itself felt**, hacerse sentir. **Your hands f. cold**, Tus manos están frías

feeler *n* (of insects) palpo, *m*, antena, *f*; tentáculo, *m*; *fig* tentativa, *f*, balón de ensayo, *m*

feeling *n* (touch) tacto, *m*; (sensation) sensación, *f*; (sentiment) sentimiento, *m*; emoción, *f*; (premonition) corazonada, intuición, premonición, *f*; (tenderness) ternura, *f*; (perception) sensibilidad, percepción, *f*; (passion) pasión, *f*; (belief) opinión, *f*, sentir, *m*. **a** sensible; tierno; (compassionate) compasivo; apasionado; (moving) conmovedor

feelingly *adv* con emoción; (strongly) enérgicamente, vivamente; (understandingly) comprensivamente

feign *vt* fingir; (invent) inventar, imaginar; simular; (allege) pretextar; (dissemble) disimular. *vi* disimular

feint *n* artificio, engaño, *m*; (in fencing) treta, finta, *f*. *vi* hacer finta

felicitation *n* felicitación, *f*, parabién, *m*

felicitous a feliz, dichoso, afortunado; (of phrases, etc.) feliz, acertado; oportuno

felicity *n* felicidad, dicha, *f*

feline a felino, gatuno, de gato. *n* felino, *m*

fell *n* (skin) piel, *f*; (upland) altura, cuesta de montaña, *f*. a cruel, feroz; (unhappy) aciago, funesto. *vt* talar, cortar; (knock down) derribar; *sew* sobrecoser

fellow *n* compañero (-ra); (equal) igual, *mf*; (in crime) cómplice, *mf*; (man) hombre, *m*; (boy, youth) chico, *m*; (colleague) colega, *m*; (of a society) miembro, *m*; (of a pair of objects) pareja, *f*; *inf* tipo, chico, *m*. **He's a good f.,** Es un buen chico. **How are you, old f.?** ¡Hombre! ¿Cómo estás? **f.-citizen,** conciudadano (-na). **f.-countryman,** compatriota, *m*; paisano (-na). **f.-creature,** semejante, *mf* **f.-feeling,** simpatía, comprensión mutua, *f*. **f.-member,** compañero (-ra); colega, *m*. **f.-passenger,** compañero (-ra) de viaje. **f.-prisoner,** compañero (-ra) de prisión. **f.-student,** condiscípulo (-la). **f.-worker,** compañero (-ra) de trabajo; (collaborator) colaborador (-ra); (colleague) colega, *m*

fellowship *n* coparticipación, *f*; (companionship) compañerismo, *m*; (brotherhood) comunidad, confraternidad, *f*; (society) asociación, *f*; (grant) beca, *f*; (of a university) colegiatura, *f*

felon *n* reo, criminal, *mf*; felón (-ona); malvado (-da); (swelling) panadizo, *m*

felonious a criminal; pérfido, traidor

felony *n* felonía, *f*

felt *n* fieltro, *m*. **a f. hat,** un sombrero de fieltro

female *n* hembra, *f*, a femenino. (**f.** is often rendered in Sp. by the feminine ending of the noun, e.g. **a f. cat,** una gata; **a f. friend,** una amiga.) **This is a f. animal,** Este animal es una hembra. **f. screw,** hembra de tornillo, tuerca, *f*

feminine a femenino; mujeril, afeminado. **in the f. gender,** en el género femenino

feminism *n* feminismo, *m*

feminist *n* feminista, *mf*

femur *n* *anat* fémur, *m*

fen *n* marjal, pantano, *m*

fence *n* cerca, *f*; (of stakes) estacada, palizada, *f*; (hedge) seto, *m*; (fencing) esgrima, *f*; *mech* guía, *f*; *inf* comprador (-ra) de efectos robados. *vi* esgrimir; *fig* defenderse; *inf* recibir efectos robados. *vt* cercar; estacar; *fig* defender; proteger. **to sit on the f.,** *fig* estar a ver venir

fencer *n* esgrimidor, *m*

fencing *n* esgrima, *f*; palizada, empalizada, *f*. **f. mask,** careta, *f*. **f. master,** maestro de esgrima, maestro de armas, *m*. **f. match,** asalto de esgrima, *m*

fencesitter bailarín de la cuerda flaja, *m*

fend (off) *vt* parar; defenderse de, guardarse de. *vi* (for) mantener, cuidar de. **to f. for oneself,** ganarse la vida; defenderse

fender *n* (round hearth) guardafuegos, *m*; *naut* espolón, *m*, defensas, *f pl*; *aut* parachoques, *m*

ferment *n* fermento, *m*; fermentación, *f*; *fig* agitación, conmoción, efervescencia *f*. *vt* hacer fermentar; *fig* agitar, excitar. *vi* fermentar, estar en fermentación; *fig* hervirse, agitarse, excitarse

fermentation *n* fermentación, *f*

fern *n* helecho, *m*

ferocious a feroz, bravo, salvaje

ferocity *n* ferocidad, braveza, fiereza, *f*

ferret *n* *zool* hurón (-ona); **to f. out,** cazar con hurones; (discover) husmear, descubrir

Ferris wheel *n* estrella giratoria, gran rueda, novia, rueda de feria, *f*

ferry *n* barca de transporte, *f*; barca de pasaje, *f*, transbordador, *m*. *vt* transportar de una a otra orilla, llevar en barca. *vi* cruzar un río en barca. **ferry across** *vt* transbordar. **F.-Command,** servicio de entrega y transporte de aeroplanos, *m*

ferryman *n* barquero, *m*

fertile a fértil, fecundo; (rich) pingüe; *fig* prolífico, abundante

fertility *n* fertilidad, fecundidad, *f*

fertilization *n* *biol* fecundación, *f*; *agr* fertilización, *f*, abono, *m*

fertilize *vt* *biol* fecundar; *agr* fertilizar, abonar

fertilizer *n* abono, *m*

fervent a ardiente; fervoroso, intenso; (enthusiastic) entusiasta, apasionado

fervor *n* ardor, fervor, *m*, pasión, *f*; (enthusiasm) entusiasmo, celo, *m*; vehemencia, *f*

fester *vi* ulcerarse, enconarse; *fig* inflamarse, amargarse. *vt* ulcerar

festival a de fiesta. *n* festividad, *f*; *ecc* fiesta, *f*; (musical, etc.) festival, *m*

festive a de fiesta; festivo, alegre

festivity *n* festividad, fiesta, *f*; (merriment) alegría, *f*, júbilo, *m*

festoon *n* festón, *m*, guirnalda, *f*. *vt* festonear

fetal a fetal

fetch *vt* traer; ir a buscar; ir por; llevar; (conduct) conducir; (of tears) hacer derramar lágrimas, hacer saltársele las lágrimas; (blood) hacer correr la sangre; (produce, draw) sacar; (a blow, a sigh) dar; (acquire) conseguir; (charm) fascinar; (of price) venderse por. **to go and f.,** ir a buscar. **to f. and carry,** *vt* (news) divulgar, publicar. *vi* estar ocupado en oficios humildes, trajinar. **to f. away,** llevarse; ir a buscar; venir a buscar. **to f. back,** devolver; (of persons) traer (a casa, etc.); traer otra vez. **to f. down,** bajar, llevar abajo; hacer bajar. **to f. in,** hacer entrar; (place inside) poner adentro; (persons and things) llevar adentro. **to f. out,** hacer salir; (bring out things) sacar; (put out) poner afuera; (an idea, etc.) sacar a relucir. **to f. up,** (a parcel, etc.) subir; (a person) hacer subir; llevar arriba

fete n fiesta, f

fetid a fétido, hediondo

fetish n fetiche, m

fetishism n fetichismo, m

fetter n grillete, m; pl **fetters,** grillos, m pl; cadenas, f pl; prisión, cárcel, f. vt encadenar, atar

fetus n feto, m

feud n enemistad, riña, f; (feudal law) feudo, m

feudal a feudal. **f. lord,** señor feudal, señor de horca y cuchillo, m

feudalism n feudalismo, m

fever n fiebre, f; calentura, f; (enthusiasm) pasión, afición, f. **to be in a f.,** tener fiebre; (agitated) estar muy agitado. **to be in a f. to,** estar muy impaciente de. **puerperal f.,** fiebre puerperal, f. **tertian f.,** fiebre terciana, f. **yellow f.,** fiebre amarilla, f

feverish a febril; fig ardiente, febril, vehemente. **to grow f.,** empezar a tener fiebre, acalenturarse

few a n pocos, m pl; pocas, f pl; algunos, m pl; algunas, f pl; (few in number) número pequeño (de), m. **a good f.,** bastantes, mf pl. **not a f.,** no pocos, m pl, (pocas, f pl). **the f.,** la minoría, f. **f. and far between,** raramente, en raras ocasiones; pocos y contados

fewer a comp menos. **The f. the better,** Cuantos menos mejor

fewest a sup (el) menos, m; el menor número (de), m; (el) menos posible de, m

fiancé(e) n novio (-ia); desposado (-da), prometido (-da)

fiasco n fiasco, mal éxito, fracaso, malogro, m

fiat n fiat, mandato, m, orden, f

fib n mentirilla, f, Peru bacho m vt, decir mentirillas, mentir

fibber n embustero (-ra), mentiroso (-sa)

fiber n fibra, f; filamento, m, hebra, f; (of grass, etc.) brizna, f; fig naturaleza, f

fickle a inconstante; mudable; (of persons) liviano, ligero, voluble

fiction n ficción, f; invención, f; literatura narrativa, f; novelas, f pl. **legal f.,** ficción legal, ficción de derecho, f

fictitious a ficticio; imaginario; fingido

fiddle n violín, m. vt tocar . . . en el violín. vi tocar el violín; (fidget) jugar; perder el tiempo. **to play second f.,** tocar el

segundo violín; fig ser plato de segunda mesa

fiddler n violinista, mf

fiddling a insignificante, trivial, frívolo

fidelity n fidelidad, f

fidget vi estar nervioso, estar inquieto; impacientarse; trajinar; (with) jugar con. vt molestar; impacientar

fidgety a inquieto, nervioso. **to be f.,** tener hormiguillo

field n campo, m; (meadow) prado, m, pradera, f; (sown field) sembrado, m; (phys, her) campo, m; (of ice) banco, m; min yacimiento, m; (background) fondo, m; (campaign) campaña, f; (battle) batalla, lucha, f; (space) espacio, m; (of knowledge, etc.) especialidad, esfera, f; (hunting) caza, f; sport campo, m; (competitors) todos los competidores en una carrera, etc.; (horses in a race) el campo. a campal, pradeño; de campo; de los campos. vt sport parar y devolver la pelota. **in the f.,** mil en el campo de batalla, en campaña. **magnetic f.,** campo magnético, m. **to take the f.,** entrar en campaña. **f.-artillery,** artillería ligera, artillería montada, f. **f.-day,** (holiday) día de asueto, m; (day out) día en el campo, m; mil día de maniobras, m. **f.-glasses,** anteojos, gemelos, m pl. **f.-hospital,** hospital de sangre, m; ambulancia fija, f. **f.-kitchen,** cocina de campaña, f. **f.-marshal,** capitán general de ejército, m. **f.-mouse,** ratón silvestre, m. **f. of battle,** campo de batalla, m. **f. of vision,** campo visual, m. **f.-telegraph,** telégrafo de campaña, m

fielder n (baseball) jardinero (-ra)

field work prácticas de campo, f pl

fiend n diablo, demonio, m; malvado (-da); (addict) adicto (-ta). **morphia f.,** morfinónamo (-ma)

fiendish a diabólico, infernal; malvado, cruel, malévolo

fierce a salvaje, feroz, cruel; (of the elements) violento, furioso; (intense) intenso, vehemente

fiercely adv ferozmente; violentamente, con furia; intensamente, con vehemencia

fierceness n ferocidad, fiereza, f; violencia, furia, f; intensidad, vehemencia, f

fieriness n ardor, m; (flames) las llamas, f pl; (redness) rojez, f; (irritability) ferocidad, irritabilidad, f; (vehemence) pasión, vehemencia, f; (of horses) fogosidad, f

fiery a ardiente; (red) rojo; (irritable) feroz, colérico, irritable; (vehement) apasionado, vehemente; (of horses) fogoso

fifteen a and n quince m.; (of age) quince años, m pl

fifteenth a and n décimoquinto m.; (part) quinzavo, m, décimaquinta parte, f; (of the month) (el) quince, m; (of monarchs) quince; mus quincena, f

fifth a quinto; (of monarchs) quinto; (of

the month) (el) cinco. *n* quinto, *m*; (part) quinto, *m*, quinta parte, *f*; *mus* quinta, *f*, **Charles V,** Carlos quinto. **f. column,** quinta columna, *f*

fiftieth *a* quincuagésimo; (part) quincuagésima parte, *f*, cincuentavo, *m*

fifty *a* and *n* cincuenta *m.*; (of age) cincuenta años, *m pl*

fiftyfold *a* and *adv* cincuenta veces

fig *n* higo, *m*; (tree) higuera, *f*; *fig* bledo, ardite, *m*. **green fig,** higo, *m*, breva, *f*. **I don't care a fig,** No se me da un higo. **to be not worth a fig,** no valer un ardite. **fig-leaf,** hoja de higuera, *f*; *fig* hoja de parra, *f*

fight *n* lucha, pelea, *f*, combate, *m*; batalla, *f*; (struggle) lucha, *f*; (quarrel) riña, pelea, *Argentina* arenga *f*; (conflict) conflicto, *m*; (valor) coraje, brío, *m*. **hand-to-hand** *f*, cachetina, *f*. **in fair f.,** en buena lid. **to have a f.,** tener una pelea. **to show f.,** mostrarse agresivo

fight *vt* luchar contra, batirse con; (a battle) dar (batalla); (oppose) oponer, *Mexico* desafiar; (defend) defender, pelear por; hacer batirse. *vi* luchar, batirse, pelear; (with words) disputar; (struggle) luchar; (make war) hacer la guerra; (in a tournament) tornear. **to f. one's way,** abrirse paso con las armas. **to f. against,** luchar contra. **to f. off,** librarse de; sacudirse. **to f. with,** luchar con; pelear con; reñir con

fighter *n* luchador (rα); combatiente, *m*; guerrero, *m*; duelista, *m*; (boxer) boxeador, *m*; *aer* (avión de) caza, *m*. **night f.,** *aer* (avión de) caza nocturno, *m*. **f.-bomber,** *aer* caza bombardero, *m*. **F. Command,** *aer* servicio de aviones de caza, *m*

fighting *n* lucha, *f*, combate, *m*; el pelear; (boxing) boxeo, *m*, a combatiente; (bellicose) agresivo, belicoso

figment *n* ficción, invención, *f*

figurative *a* figurado, metafórico; figurativo; simbólico

figuratively *adv* en sentido figurativo; metafóricamente

figure *n* figura, *f*; forma, *f*; (statue) estatua, figura, *f*; (of a person) silueta, *f*; talle, *m* (number) cifra, *f*, número, *m*; (quantity) cantidad, *f*; (price) precio, *m*; *geom, gram, dance* (skating) figura, *f*; (appearance) presencia, *f*, aire, *m*; (picture) imagen, *m*; (on fabric) diseño, *m*; *mus* cifra, *f*; *pl* **figures,** aritmética, *f*, matemáticas, *f pl. vt* figurar; (imagine) figurarse, imaginar; *mus* cifrar. *vi* figurar, hacer un papel; (calculate) calcular, hacer cuentas. **to f. out,** calcular; (a problem, etc.) resolver. **a fine f. of a woman,** *inf* una real hembra. **lay f.,** maniquí, *m*. **to be good at figures,** estar fuerte en matemáticas. **to cut a f.,** *fig* hacer figura. **to have a good f.,** tener buen talle. **f. of speech,** figura retórica, figura de dicción *f*; (manner of speaking) metáfora *f*. **f.**

dance, baile de figuras, *m*, contradanza, *f*. **f.-head,** *naut* mascarón, *m*, (or figura, *f*) de proa; *fig* figura decorativa, *f*

figurine *n* figurilla, *f*

filament *n* filamento, *m*; hebra, *f*

filbert *n* avellana, *f*; (tree) avellano, *m*

filch *vt* sisar, ratear

file *n* (line) fila, hilera, sarta, línea, *f*; *mil* fila, *f*; (tool) lima, *f*; (rasp) escofina, *f*; (list) lista, *f*, catálogo, *m*; (for documents) carpeta, *f*, cartapacio, *m*; (bundle of papers) legajo, *m*; (for bills, letters, etc.) clasificador, *m*; archivo, *m*; (in an archives) expediente *m*. **in a f.,** en fila; en cola

file *vt* hacer marchar en fila; (smooth) limar; (literary work) pulir; (classify) clasificar; (note particulars) fichar; (keep) guardar; (a petition, etc.) presentar, registrar. *vi* marchar en fila. **to f. in,** entrar en fila. **to f. off,** desfilar. **to f. a brief,** presentar un escrito. **to f. letters,** clasificar correspondencia. **to f. past,** *mil* desfilar

filibuster *n* filibustero, pirata, *m*

filigree *n* filigrana, *f*, a afiligranado

filing *n* (with a tool) limadura, *f*; clasificación, *f*; (of a petition, etc.) presentación, *f*, registro, *m*; *pl* **filings,** limaduras, *f pl*, retales, *m pl.* **f.-cabinet,** fichero, *m*. **f.-card,** ficha, *f*

fill *vt* llenar; (stuff) rellenar; (appoint to a post) proveer; (occupy a post) desempeñar; (imbue) henchir; (saturate) saturar; (occupy) ocupar; (a tooth) empastar, *Argentina* emplomar; (fulfil) cumplir; (charge, fuel) cargar; (with food) hartar. *vi* llenarse. **fill an order,** servir un pedido. **fill a prescription,** surtir una receta. **to f. the chair,** ocupar la presidencia; (university) ocupar la cátedra. **to f. the place of,** ocupar el lugar de; substituir; suplir. **It will be difficult to find someone to f. his place,** Será difícil de encontrar uno que haga lo que hizo él. **to f. to the brim,** llenar hasta los bordes. **to f. in, out,** (a form) llenar (or completar) (una hoja); (insert) insertar, añadir; (a hollow) terraplenar. **to f. out,** *vt* hinchar. *vi* hincharse; echar carnes; (of the face) redondearse. **to f. up,** colmar, llenar hasta los bordes; (an office) proveer; (block) macizar; (a form) completar, llenar

fillet *n* venda, cinta, *f*; (of meat or fish) filete, *m*; (of meat) solomillo, *m*; *arch* filete, *m. vt* atar con una venda o cinta; *cul* cortar en filetes

filling *n* envase, *m*; (swelling) henchimiento, *m*; (of a tooth) empastadura, *f*; (in or up, of forms, etc.) llenar, *m*. **f. station,** depósito de gasolina, *m*

fillip *n* capirotazo, *m*; (stimulus) estímulo, *m*; (trifle) bagatela, *f. vt* and *vi* dar un capirotazo (a); *vt* estimular, incitar

filly *n* jaca, potra, *f*

film *n* (on liquids) tela, *f*; membrana, *f*; (coating) capa ligera, *f*; (on eyes) tela, *f*;

(cinema) película, cinta, *f; phot* película, *f; fig* velo, *m;* nube, *f, vi* cubrirse de un velo, etc. *vt* cubrir de un velo, etc.; filmar, fotografiar para el cine. **roll f.,** película fotográfica, *f.* **silent f.,** película muda, *f.* **talking f.,** película sonora, *f.* **to shoot a f.,** hacer una película. **to take part in a f.,** actuar, or tomar parte, en una película. **f. pack,** película en paquetes *f.* **f. star,** estrella de la pantalla (or del cine), *f*

film industry industria fílmica, *f*

filmy a transparente, diáfano

filter *n* filtro, *m. vt* filtrar. *vi* infiltrarse; *(fig* of news) trascender, divulgarse. **f.-bed,** filtro, *m.* **f.-paper,** papel filtro, *m*

filth *n* inmundicia, suciedad, *f; fig* corrupción, *f; fig* obscenidad, *f*

filthy a inmundo, sucio; escuálido, *Argentina* cascarriento, *Central America* descacharrado; *fig* asqueroso; *fig* obsceno

fin *n* (of fish) aleta, ala, *f;* (of whale) barba, *f; aer* aleta, *f*

final a último, final; (conclusive) conclusivo, decisivo, terminante. *n sport* finales, *m pl; univ* último examen, *m.* **f. blow,** *fig* golpe decisivo, *m.* **f. cause,** *phil* causa final, *f*

finale *n* final, *m*

finalist *n* finalista, *mf*

finality *n* finalidad, *f;* (decision) determinación, resolución, decisión, *f*

finally *adv* por fin, finalmente, por último, a la postre; (irrevocably) irrevocablemente

finance *n* hacienda pública, *f,* asuntos económicos, *m pl;* finanzas, *f pl. vt* financiar

financial a financiero, monetario. **f. year,** año económico, *m*

financially *adv* del punto de vista financiero

financier *n* financiero, *m*

find *vt* encontrar, hallar; (discover) descubrir, dar con; (invent) inventar, crear; (supply) facilitar, proporcionar; (provide) proveer; (instruct) instruir; *law* declarar. *vi law* fallar, dar sentencia. *n* hallazgo, *m;* descubrimiento, *m.* **I found him out a long time ago,** *fig* Hace tiempo que me di cuenta de cómo era él. **I found it possible to go out,** Me fue posible salir. **The judge found them guilty,** El juez les declaró culpables. **to f. a verdict,** *law* dar sentencia, fallar. **to f. one's way,** encontrar el camino. **to f. oneself,** hallarse, verse, encontrarse. **to f. out,** averiguar, descubrir. **to f. out about,** informarse sobre (or de)

finder *n* hallador (-ra); (inventor) inventor (-ra), descubridor (-ra); (telescope, camera) buscador, *m*

finding *n* hallazgo, *m;* (discovery) descubrimiento, *m; law* fallo, *m,* sentencia, *f*

fine *n* multa, *f;* (end) fin, *m.* **in f.,** en fin, en resumen

fine *vt* multar, cargar una multa de

fine a (thin) delgado; (sharp) agudo; (delicate) fino, delicado; (minute) menudo; (refined) refinado, puro; (healthy) saludable; (of weather) bueno; magnífico; (beautiful) hermoso, lindo; excelente; (perfect) perfecto; (good) bueno; elegante; (showy) ostentoso, vistoso; (handsome) guapo; (subtle) sutil; (acute) agudo; (noble) noble; (eminent, accomplished) distinguido, eminente; (polished) pulido; (affected) afectado; (clear) claro; (transparent) transparente, diáfano. *adv* muy bien. **a f. upstanding young man,** un buen mozo. **a f. upstanding young woman,** una real moza. **He's a f. fellow,** (ironically) Es una buena pieza. **That is all very f. but . . . ,** Todo eso está muy bien pero. . . . **to become f.,** (weather) mejorar

finely *adv* finamente; menudamente; elegantemente; (ironically) lindamente

fineness *n* (thinness) delgadez, *f;* (excellence) excelencia, *f;* delicadeza, *f;* (softness) suavidad, *f;* elegancia, *f;* (subtlety) sutileza, *f;* (acuteness) agudeza, *f;* (perfection) perfección, *f;* (nobility) nobleza, *f;* (beauty) hermosura, *f*

finery *n* galas, *f pl,* atavíos magníficos, *m pl;* adornos, *m pl;* primor, *m,* belleza, *f*

finesse *n* sutileza, diplomacia, *f;* estratagema, artificio, *m;* (cunning) astucia, *f, vi* valerse de estratagemas y artificios

finger *n* dedo, *m;* (of a clock, etc.) manecilla, *f;* (measurement) dedada, *f; fig* mano, *f. vt* manosear, tocar; (soil) ensuciar con los dedos; (steal) sisar; *(mus* a keyed instrument) teclear, (a stringed instrument) tocar. **first f.,** dedo índice, *m.* **fourth f.,** dedo anular, *m.* **little f.,** dedo meñique, *m.* **second f.,** dedo de en medio, dedo del corazón, *m.* **to burn one's fingers,** quemarse los dedos; *fig* cogerse los dedos. **to have at one's f.-tips,** *fig* saber al dedillo. **f.-board,** (of piano) teclado, *m;* (of stringed instruments) diapasón, *m.* **f.-bowl,** lavadedos, lavafrutas, *m.* **finger's breadth,** dedo, *m.* **f.-mark,** huella digital, *f.* **f.-nail,** uña del dedo, *f.* **f.-print,** impresión digital, *f.* **f.-stall,** dedil, *m.* **f.-tip,** punta del dedo, yema del dedo, *f.* **f.-wave,** peinado al agua, *m*

fingering *n* (touching) manoseo, *m; mus* digitación, *f; (mus* the keys) tecleo, *m;* (wool) estambre, *m*

finial *n* pináculo, *m*

finicky a (of persons) dengoso, remilgado; (of things) nimio

finish *n* fin, *m,* conclusión, terminación, *f;* (final touch) última mano, *f;* perfección, *f;* (of an article) acabado, *m; sport* llegada, *(horse race)* meta, *f. vt* terminar, acabar, concluir; llevar a cabo, poner fin a; (perfect) perfeccionar; (put finishing touch to) dar la última mano a; (kill) matar; (exhaust) agotar, rendir; (overcome) vencer.

vi acabar; concluirse. **to f. off,** acabar, terminar; (kill) matar, acabar con; (destroy) destruir. **to f. up,** acabar; (eat) comer; (drink) beber

finished goods *n pl* bienes terminados, *m pl*

finisher *n* terminador (-ra), acabador (-ra); pulidor (-ra); (final blow) golpe de gracia, *m*

finishing *a* concluyente. *n* terminación, *f*, fin, *m*; perfección, *f*; (last touch) última mano, *f*. **to put the f. touch,** dar la última pincelada

finite *a* finito

Finland Finlandia, *f*

Finn *n* finlandés (-esa)

Finnish *a* finlandés. *n* (language) finlandés, *m*

fir *n* abeto, sapino, pino, *m*. **red fir,** pino silvestre, *m*. **fir-cone,** piña de abeto, *f*. **fir grove,** abetal, *m*

fire *n* fuego, *m*; (conflagration) incendio, *m*; (on the hearth) lumbre, *f*, fuego, *m*; *fig* ardor, *m*, pasión, *f*; (shooting) fuego, tiro, *m*. **by f. and sword,** a sangre y fuego. **by the f.,** cerca del fuego; (in a house) al lado de la chimenea. **long-range f.,** *mil* fuego de largo alcance, *m*. **short-range f.,** *mil* fuego de corto alcance, *m*. **on f.,** en fuego, ardiendo, en llamas; *fig* impaciente; *fig* lleno de pasión. **to be between two fires,** *fig* estar entre dos aguas. **to make a f.,** encender un fuego. **to miss f.,** no dar en el blanco, errar el tiro. **to open f.,** *mil* hacer una descarga. **to set on f.,** prender fuego a, incendiar. **to take f.,** encenderse. **under f.,** bajo fuego. **f.-alarm,** alarma de incendios, *f*. **f.-arm,** arma de fuego, *f*. **f.-box,** hogar, *m*. **f.-brand,** tea, *f*. **f.-brigade,** cuerpo de bomberos, *m*. **f.-damp,** aire detonante, grisú, *m*, mofeta, *f*. **f.-dog,** morillo, *m*. **f.-drill,** (firefighters') instrucción de bomberos, *f*, (others') simulacro de incendio, *m*. **f.-engine,** autobomba, bomba, de incendios, *f*. **f.-escape,** escalera de incendios, *f*. **f.-extinguisher,** apagador de incendios, extintor, matafuego, *m*. **f.-guard,** vigilante de incendios, *m*; alambrera, *f*. **f.-hose,** manguera de incendios, *f*. **f.-insurance,** seguro contra incendios, *m*. **f.-irons,** badil *m*. y tenazas *f pl*. **f.-lighter,** encendedor, *m*. **f.-screen,** pantalla, *f*. **f.-ship,** brulote, *m*. **f.-shovel,** badil, *m*, paleta, *f*. **f.-spotter,** vigilante de incendios, *m*. **f.-sprite,** salamandra, *f*. **f.-watching,** servicio de vigilancia de incendios, *m*

fire *vt* incendiar, prender (or pegar) fuego a; quemar; (bricks) cocer; (fire-arms) disparar; (cauterize) cauterizar; *fig* stimulate) estimular, excitar; (inspire) inspirar; (*inf* of questions) disparar; (*inf* sack) despedir. *vi* encenderse; (shoot) hacer fuego, disparar (un tiro); (*inf* away) disparar; (up) enojarse. **to f a salute,** disparar un saludo. *mil* **F.!** ¡Fuego!

firecracker *n* buscapiés *m*

fire department *n* parque de bomberos, servicis de bomberos, servicio de incendios, parque de bombas (Puerto Rico), *m*

firefly *n* cocuyo, *m*

fireman *n* bombero, *m*; (of an engine, etc.) fogonero, *m*. **fireman's lift,** silleta, *f*

fireplace *n* chimenea francesa, chimenea, *f*, *Mexico* brasero *m*; (hearth) hogar, *m*

fireproof *a* a prueba de incendios; incombustible

firewood *n* leña, *Lat. Am.* charamusca *f*. **f. dealer,** leñador (-ra), vendedor (-ra) de leña

firework *n* fuego artificial, *m*

firing *n* (of fire-arms) disparo, *m*; (burning) incendio, *m*, quema, *f*; (of bricks, etc.) cocimiento, *m*; (of pottery) cocción, *f*; (cauterization) cauterización, *f*; (fuel) combustible, *m*; (*inf* sacking) despedida, *f*. **within f. range,** a tiro. **f.-line,** línea de fuego, *f*. **f.-oven,** (pottery) horno alfarero, *m*. **f.-squad,** pelotón de ejecución, *m*

firm *a* firme; (strong) fuerte; (secure) seguro; sólido; (resolute) inflexible, resoluto; severo; (steady) constante; (persistent) tenaz. *n* *com* casa (de comercio), empresa, *f*; razón social, *f*

firmament *n* firmamento, *m*

firmness *n* firmeza, *f*; solidez, *f*; inflexibilidad, resolución, *f*; severidad, *f*; constancia, *f*; tenacidad, *f*

first *a* primero (primer before *m sing* nouns); (of monarchs) primero; (of dates) (el) primero. *n* primero, *m*; (beginning) principio, *m*. *adv* primero, en primer lugar; (before, of time) antes; (for the first time) por primera vez; (at the beginning) al principio; (ahead) adelante. **at f.,** al principio. **from the very f.,** desde el primer momento. **to appear for the f. time,** aparecer (or presentarse) por primera vez; *theat* debutar. **to go f.,** ir delante de todos, ir a la cabeza; ir adelante. **f. and foremost,** en primer lugar; ante todo. **f.-aid,** primera cura, *f*. **f.-aid post,** casa de socorro, *f*. **f.-aider,** practicante, *m*. **f.-born,** *a* and *n* primogénito (-ta). **f.-class,** de primera clase; *fig* excelente. **f.-cousin,** primo (-ma) carnal, primo (-ma) hermano (-na). **f. edition,** edición príncipe, *f*. **f.-floor,** primer piso, *m*. **f. fruits,** frutos primerizos, *m pl*; *fig* primicias, *f pl*. **f.-hand,** *a* original, de primera mano. **f. letters,** primeras letras, *f pl*. **f. night,** *theat* estreno, *m*. **f. of all,** primero, ante todo. **f.-rate,** a de primera clase

fiscal *a* and *n* fiscal *m.*. **f. year,** año económico, *m*

fish *n* pez, *m*; (out of the water) pescado, *m*; *inf* tipo, indivíduo, *m*. *vt* pescar; (out) sacar. *vi* pescar; *fig* buscar. **fried f.,** pescado frito, *m*. **He is a queer f.,** Es un tipo muy raro. **to be neither f. nor fowl,** no ser ni carne ni pescado. **to feel like a f. out of water,** sentirse fuera de su ambiente. **to f. in troubled waters,** A río revuelto ganancia de pescadores. **f.-eating,** *a* ictiófago. **f.-fork,** tenedor de pescado, *m*. **f.-glue,** cola de pescado, *f*. **f.-hook,** anzuelo, *m*. **f.-knife,** cuchillo de pescado, *m*. **f.-like,** de pez; como un pez, parecido a un pez. **f. roe,** hueva, *f*. **f.-server,** pala para pescado, *f*

fishbone *n* espina de pescado, raspa de pescado, *f*

fisherman *n* pescador, *m*

fishery *n* pesquería, *f*

fishing *n* pesca, *f*, a de pescar. **to go f.,** ir de pesca. **f.-boat,** bote de pesca, *m*. **f.-floats,** levas, *f pl*. **f.-line,** sedal, *m*. **f.-net,** red de pesca, *f*. **f.-reel,** carretel, carrete, *m*. **f.-rod,** caña de pescar, *f*. **f.-tackle,** aparejo de pesca, *m*. **f. village,** pueblo de pescadores, *m*

fishmeal harina de pescado, *f*

fishy de pescado; (of eyes, etc.) de pez, como un pez; (in smell) que huele a pescado; *inf* sospechoso; (of stories) inverosímil

fissure *n* grieta, hendidura, rendija, *f*; (*anat, geol*) fisura, *f*

fist *n* puño, *m*; *print* manecilla, *f*; (handwriting) letra, *f*. **with clenched fists,** a puño cerrado

fisticuff *n* puñetazo, *m*; *pl* **fisticuffs,** agarrada, riña, *f*

fit *n* espasmo, paroxismo, *m*; ataque, *m*; (impulse) acceso, arranque, *m*; (whim) capricho, *m*; (of a garment) corte, *m*; (adjustment) ajuste, encaje, *m*. **by fits and starts,** a tropezones, espasmódicamente. **fit of fainting** *Argentina, Venezuela* insulto *m*

fit a propósito (para), bueno (para); (opportune) oportuno; (proper) conveniente; apto; (decent) decente; (worthy) digno; (ready) preparado, listo; (adequate) adecuado; (capable) capaz, en estado (de); (appropriate) apropiado; (just) justo. **It is not in a fit state to be used,** No está en condiciones para usarse. **to be not fit for,** no servir para; (through ill-health) no tener bastante salud para. **to think fit,** creer (or juzgar) conveniente. **fit for use,** usable. **fit to eat,** comestible

fit *vt* ajustar, acomodar, encajar; adaptar (a); (furnish) proveer (de), surtir (con); (of tailor, dressmaker) entallar, probar; (of shoemaker) calzar; (of garments, shoes) ir (bien o mal); (prepare) preparar; (go with) ser apropiado (a); (adapt itself to) adaptarse a. *vi* ajustarse, acomodarse, encajarse; adaptarse; (clothes) ir (bien o mal). **to fit in,** *vt* encajar; incluir. *vi* encajarse; caber; adaptarse. **to fit out,** equipar; proveer (de); preparar. **to fit up,** montar, instalar; proveer (de). **to fit with,** proveer de

fitful a intermitente; espasmódico; caprichoso

fitfully *adv* por intervalos, a ratos; caprichosamente

fitment *n* equipo, *m*; instalación, *f*; (of bookcase, etc.) sección, *f*; (furniture) pieza, *f*, mueble, *m*

fitness *n* conveniencia, *f*; aptitud, capacidad, *f*; oportunidad, *f*; salud, *f*; (good health) vigor, *m*

fitted a (of clothes) ajustado

fitter *n* ajustador, *m*; (mechanic) armador, mecánico, *m*; (tailoring) cortador, *m*; (dressmaking) probador (-ra)

fitting *n* encaje, ajuste, *m*; adaptación, *f*; (of a garment) prueba, *f*; (size) medida, *f*; (installation) instalación, *f*; *pl.* **fittings,** guarniciones, *f pl*; instalaciones, *f pl*; accesorios, *m pl*. a conveniente, justo; apropiado; adecuado; (worthy) digno; (of coats, etc.) ajustado. **f. room,** cuarto de pruebas, *m*. **f. in,** encaje, *m*. **f. out,** equipo, *m*. **f. up,** arreglo, *m*; (of machines) montaje, *m*; (of a house) mueblaje, *m*

five a and *n* cinco *m*.; (of the clock) las cinco, *f pl*; (of age) cinco años, *m pl*. **to be f.,** tener cinco años. **f. feet deep,** de cinco pies de profundidad. **f. feet high,** cinco pies de altura. **f.-finger exercises,** ejercicios de piano, *m pl*. **F.-Year Plan,** Plan Quinquenal, *m*

fix *n* aprieto, apuro, *m*; callejón sin salida, *m*. *vt* fijar; sujetar, afianzar; (bayonets) calar; (with nails) clavar; (*phot, chem, med*) fijar; (decide) establecer; (a date) señalar; (eyes, attention) clavar; (on the mind) grabar, estampar; (one's hopes) poner; (base) basar, fundar; (*inf* put right) arreglar, componer. *vi* fijarse; establecerse; determinarse. **to get in a fix,** hacerse un lío. **to fix a price,** fijar un precio. **to fix on, upon,** elegir, escoger; decidir, determinar. **to fix up,** arreglar; decidir; organizar; (differences) olvidar (sus disensiones)

fixation *n* obsesión, idea fija, *f*; (scientific) fijación, *f*

fixative *n* (*med, phot*) fijador, *m*; (dyeing) mordiente, *m*. a que fija

fixed a fijo; inmóvil; permanente; (of ideas) inflexible. **f. bayonet,** bayoneta calada, *f*. **f. price,** precio fijo, *m*. **f. star,** estrella fija, *f*

fixing *n* fijación, *f*; afianzamiento, *m*; arreglo, *m*; (of a date) señalamiento, *m*. **f. bath,** *phot* baño fijador, *m*

fixture *n* instalación, *f*; accesorio fijo, *m*; *sport* partido, *m*; *inf* permanencia, *f*. **f. card,** *sport* calendario deportivo, *m*

fizz *n* espuma, *f*; chisporroteo, *m*. *inf* champaña, *m*. *vi* (liquids) espumear; (sputter) chisporrotear

fizzle *n* (failure) fiasco, fracaso, *m*. *vi* chisporrotear; (out) apagarse; (fail) fracasar, no tener éxito

fjord n fiordo, m

flabbergast vt dejar con la boca abierta, dejar de una pieza

flabby, flaccid a fláccido, flojo; fig débil

flag n bandera, f; pabellón, estandarte, m; (small) banderola, f; (iris) (yellow) cala, f, (purple) lirio cárdeno, m; (stone) losa, f. **to dip the f.**, saludar con la bandera. **to hoist the f.**, izar la bandera. **to strike the f.**, bajar la bandera; (in defeat) rendir la bandera. **f. bearer**, portaestandarte, abanderado, m. **f.-day**, día de la banderita, m; (in U.S.A.) día de la bandera, m. **f.-officer**, vicealmirante, m; vicealmirante, m; jefe de escuadra, m. **f. of truce**, bandera blanca, bandera de paz, f

flag vi flaquear, debilitarse; languidecer; (wither) marchitarse; decaer, disminuir. vt adornar con banderas; (signal) hacer señales con una bandera; (for a race, etc.) marcar con banderas; (with stones) enlosar, embaldosar.

flagrant a escandaloso, notorio

flagship n capitana, f

flagstaff n asta de bandera, f

flagstone n losa, lancha, Lat. Am. laja f

flair n instinto natural, m, comprensión innata, f; habilidad natural, f

flak n cortina (or barrera) antiaérea, f

flake n escama, f; laminilla, hojuela, f; (of snow) copo, m; (of fire) chispa, f. vt cubrir con escamas, etc.; exfoliar; (crumble) hacer migas de, desmigajar. vi escamarse; (off) exfoliarse; caer en copos

flaky a escamoso; en laminillas; (of pastry) hojaldrado. **f. pastry**, hojaldre, f

flamboyance n extravagancia, f, lit ampulosidad, f

flamboyant a arch flamígero; extravagante, llamativo, rimbombante; (of style) ampuloso. **f. gothic**, gótico florido, m

flame n llama, f; fig fuego, m. inf amorío, m, vi flamear, llamear; arder, abrasarse; (shine) brillar; (up, fig) inflamarse; acalorarse. **f.-colored**, de color de llama, anaranjado. **f.-thrower**, lanzallamas, m

flaming a llameante; abrasador; (of colors) llamativo, chillón; (of feelings) ardiente, fervoroso, apasionado

flamingo n orn flamenco, m

flange n mech reborde, m, vt rebordear

flank n (of animal) ijada, f; (human) costado, m; (of hill, etc.) lado, m, falda, f; mil flanco, m. a (mil nav) por el flanco. vt lindar con, estar contiguo a; (mil, nav) flanquear. vi estar al lado de; tocar a, lindar con.

flannel n franela, f, a de franela

flannelette n moletón, m

flap n golpe, m; (of a sail) zapatazo, m, sacudida, f; (of a pocket) cartera, tapa, f; (of skin) colgajo, m; (of a shoe, etc.) oreja, f; (of a shirt, etc.) falda, f; (of a hat) ala, f; (of trousers) bragueta, f; (rever) solapa, f;

(of a counter) trampa, f; (of a table) hoja plegadiza, f; (of the wings) aletazo, m; (of w.c.) tapa, f. vt sacudir, golpear, batir; agitar; (the tail) menear. vi agitarse; (of wings) aletear; (of sails) zapatear, sacudirse; colgar. **f.-eared**, de orejas grandes y gachas

flapjack n cul torta de sartén, f; (for powder) polvorera, f

flapping n batimiento, m; (waving) ondulación, f; (of sails) zapatazo, m; (of wings) aleteo, m

flare n fulgor, m, llama, f; hacha, f; aer cohete de señales, m; sew vuelo, m. vi relampaguear, fulgurar; brillar; (of a lamp) llamear; (up) encolerizarse, salirse de tino; (of epidemic) declararse; (war, etc.) desencadenarse

flash n relámpago, centelleo, m, ráfaga de luz, f; brillo, m; (from a gun) fuego, fogonazo, m; (of wit, genius) rasgo, m; (of joy, etc.) acceso, m. vi relampaguear, fulgurar, centellear; brillar; cruzar rápidamente, pasar como un relámpago. vt hacer relampaguear; hacer brillar; (a look, etc.) dar; lanzar; (light) encender; (powder) quemar; transmitir señales por heliógrafo; inf sacar a relucir, enseñar. **shoulder-f.**, mil emblema, m. **to be gone like a f.**, desaparecer como un relámpago. **to f. out**, brillar, centellear. **f. of lightning**, relámpago, rayo, m. **f. of wit**, agudeza, f, rasgo de ingenio, m

flashback n episodio intercalado, m, retrospección, f

flashlight n luz de magnesio, f; (torch) lamparilla eléctrica, f, rayo, m (Mexico); **f. photograph**, magnesio, m

flashy a llamativo, de mal gusto, charro, Lat. Am. figuroso; frívolo, superficial

flask n frasco, m, redoma, botella, f; (for powder) frasco, m; (vacuum) termos, m

flat a llano; (smooth) liso; (lying) tendido, tumbado; (flattened) aplastado; (destroyed) arrasado; (stretched out) extendido; (of nose, face) chato, romo; (of tire) desinflado; (uniform) uniforme; (depressed) desanimado; (uninteresting) monótono; (boring) aburrido; com paralizado; (downright) categórico; absoluto; (net) neto; mus bemol; (of boats) de fondo plano. adv See **flatly**. n planicie, f; (of a sword) hoja, f; (of the hand) palma, f; (land) llanura, f; (apartment) piso, m; mus bemol, m. **to fall f.**, caer de bruces, fig no tener éxito. **to make f.**, allanar. **to sing f.**, desafinar. **f. boat**, barco de fondo plano, m. **f.-footed**, de pies achatados; fig pedestre. **f.-iron**, plancha, f. **f. roof**, azotea, f

flatly adv de plano; a nivel; (plainly) llanamente, netamente; (dully) indiferentemente; (categorically) categóricamente

flatness n planicie, f; llanura, f; (smoothness) lisura, f; (evenness) igualdad, f; (uninterestingness) insulsez, insipidez, f;

aburrimiento, *m*; (depression) desaliento, abatimiento, *m*

flatten *vt* aplanar, allanar; aplastar; (smooth) alisar; (even) igualar; (destroy) derribar, arrasar, destruir; (dismay) desconcertar; (out) extender. *vi* aplanarse, allanarse; aplastarse

flatter *vt* adular, lisonjear, halagar, engatusar, *Lat. Am.* also afilar, engaratusar; (of a dress, photograph, etc.) favorecer, (please the senses) regalar, deleitar; (oneself) felicitarse

flatterer *n* adulador (-ra), lisonjero (-ra), *Guatemala* barbero (-ra) *mf*

flattering a adulador, lisonjero; (promising) halagüeño; favoreciente; deleitoso

flattery *n* adulación, *Lat. Am.* adulonería *f*

flat tire llanta desinflada, *f*

flatulence *n* flatulencia, *f*

flaunt *vi* (flutter) ondear; pavonearse. *vt* desplegar; ostentar, sacar a relucir; enseñar

flaunting *n* ostentación, *f*; alarde, *m*. a ostentoso; magnífico; (fluttering) ondeante

flautist *n* flautista, *mf*

flavor *n* sabor, gusto, *m*; *cul* condimento, *m*; *fig* dejo, *m*. *vt cul* sazonar, condimentar; dar un gusto (de), hacer saborear (a); *fig* dar un dejo (de)

flavoring *n cul* condimento, *m*; *fig* sabor, dejo, *m*

flaw *n* desperfecto, *m*, imperfección, *f*; (crack) grieta, hendedura, *f*; (in wood, metals) quebraja, *f*; (in gems) pelo, *m*; (in fruit) maca, *f*; (in cloth) gabarro, *m*; *fig* defecto, error, *m*; (wind) ráfaga de viento, *f*

flawless a sin defecto; perfecto; impecable

flax *n* lino, *m*. **to dress f.**, rastrillar lino. **f.-comb**, rastrillo, *m*. **f. field**, linar, *m*

flaxen a de lino; (fair) rubio, blondo. **f.-haired**, de pelo rubio

flay *vt* desollar; (criticize) despellejar

flea *n* pulga, *f*. **f. bite**, picada de pulga, *f*

fleck *n* pinta, mancha, *f*, lunar, *m*; (of sun) mota, *f*; (speck) partícula, *f*; (freckle) peca, *f*. *vt* abigarrar; manchar; (dapple) salpicar, motear

fledgeling *n* volantón, *m*; *fig* niño (-ña); *fig* novato (-ta)

flee *vi* huir, fugarse, escapar; (vanish) desaparecer; (avoid) evitar, huir de. *vt* abandonar

fleece *n* vellón, *m*; lana, *f*; toisón, *m*. *vt* esquilar; *fig inf* pelar. **Order of the Golden F.**, Orden del Toisón de Oro, *f*

fleecy a lanudo, lanar; (white) blanquecino; (of clouds) borreguero. **f. clouds**, borregos, *m pl*

fleet *n* (navy) armada, *f*; escuadra, flota, *f*; *fig* serie, *f*, a alado, rápido, veloz. **F. Air Arm**, Aviación Naval, *f*. **f.-footed**, ligero de pies

fleeting a fugaz, momentáneo, efímero, pasajero

flesh *n* carne, *f*; (mankind) género humano, *m*, humanidad, *f*; (of fruit) pulpa, *f*. **a man of f. and blood**, un hombre de carne y hueso. **of one's own f. and blood**, de la misma sangre de uno. **to make one's f. creep**, dar carne de gallina (a). **f.-coloured**, encarnado, de color de carne. **f.-eating**, carnívoro. **f. wound**, herida superficial, *f*

fleshpot *n* marmita, *f*; *fig* olla, *f*. **the fleshpots of Egypt**, las ollas de Egipto

fleshy a carnoso, grueso; (of fruit) pulposo; suculento

flex *n elec* flexible, *m*, *vt* doblar. *vi* doblarse

flexibility *n* flexibilidad, *f*; (of style) plasticidad, *f*; docilidad, *f*

flexible a flexible; dúctil, maleable; (of style) plástico; of) voice) quebradizo; adaptable; dócil

flick *n* golpecito, toque, *m*; (of the finger) capirotazo, *m*; *inf* cine, *m*, *vt* dar un golpecito a; dar ligeramente con un látigo; sacudir. **flick one's wrist** hacer girar la muñeca to **f. over the pages of,** hojear

flicker *n* estremecimiento, temblor, *m*; fluctuación, *f*; (of bird) aleteo, *m*; (of flame) onda de una llama), *f*; (of eyelashes) pestañeo, *m*; (of a smile) indicio, *f*, *vi* agitarse; (of flags) ondear; vacilar

flickering a tenue; vacilante

flier *n* volador (-ra); aviador (-ra); piloto, *m*; fugitivo (-va)

flight *n* vuelo, *m*; (of bird of prey) colada, *f*; (flock of birds) bandada, *f*; (migration) migración, *f*; (of time) transcurso, *m*; (of imagination, etc.) arranque, *m*; (volley) lluvia, *f*; (of aeroplanes) escuadrilla de aviones, *f*; (of stairs) tramo, tiro, *m*; (staircase) escalera, *f*; (of locks on canal, etc.) ramal, *m*; (escape) huida, fuga, *f*. **long-distance f.,** aer vuelo de distancia, *m*. **non-stop f.,** aer vuelo sin parar, *m*. **reconnaissance f.,** aer vuelo de reconocimiento, vuelo de patrulla, *m*. **test f.,** aer vuelo de pruebas, *m*. **to put to f.,** ahuyentar, poner en fuga. **to take f.,** alzar el vuelo. **f.-lieutenant,** teniente aviador, *m*. **f.-sergeant,** sargento aviador, *m*

flight attendant sobrecarbo, *Lat. Am.* aeromozo (-za), cabinero (-ra) *mf*

flighty a frívolo, inconstante, veleidoso

flimsy a endeble; frágil, fútil, insubstancial

flinch *vi* echarse atrás, retirarse (ante); vacilar, titubear. **without flinching,** sin vacilar; sin quejarse

fling *vt* arrojar, echar, tirar; lanzar; (scatter) derramar; (oneself) echarse; (oneself upon) echarse encima; *fig* confiar en. *vi* lanzarse; marcharse precipitadamente; saltar. *n* tiro, *m*; (of dice, etc.) echada, *f*; (gibe) sarcasmo, *m*, burla, chufleta, *f*; (of horse) respingo, brinco, *m*; baile escocés, *m*. **in full f.**, en plena operación; en progreso. **to have one's f.,** darse un verde, correrla. **to f. away,** *vt* desechar; (waste) desperdiciar, malgastar, perder. *vi* marcharse enfadado; marcharse rápidamente. **to f. back,** (a ball) devolver; (the head) echar atrás. **to f. down,** tirar al suelo; arrojar; derribar. **to f. off,** *vt* rechazar; apartar; (a garment, etc.) quitar. *vi* marcharse sin más ni más. **to f. oneself down,** tumbarse, echarse; despeñarse (por). **to f. oneself headlong,** despeñarse. **to f. open,** abrir violentamente, abrir de repente. **to f. out,** *vt* echar a la fuerza; (a hand) alargar, extender. *vi* salir apresuradamente. **to f. over,** (upset) volcar; arrojar por; abandonar. **to f. up,** lanzar al aire; levantar, erguir; renunciar (a), abandonar; dejar

flint *n* pedernal, *m*; (for producing fire) piedra de encendedor, *f*

flippant *a* poco serio, ligero; frívolo; impertinente

flipper *n* aleta, *f*

flirt *n* (man) coquetón, castigador, *m*; (woman) coqueta, castigadora, *f*. *vt* (shake) sacudir; (move) agitar; (wave) menear. *vi* flirtear, coquetear; (toy with) jugar con; divertirse con

flirtation *n* flirteo, amorío, *m*

flirtatious *a* (of men) galanteador, castigador; (of women) coqueta

flit *vi* revolotear, mariposear; (move silently) deslizarse, pasar silenciosamente; (depart) irse, marcharse; mudarse por los aires. **to f. about,** ir y venir silenciosamente. **to f. past,** pasar como una sombra

float *n* masa flotante, *f*; (raft) balsa, *f*; *mech* flotador, *m*; (of fishing rod or net) corcho, *m*; (of fish) vejiga natatoria, *f*; (for swimming) nadadera, calabaza, *f*; (for tableaux) carroza, *f*; *pl* **floats,** *theat* candilejas, *f pl*. *vi* flotar; (flags, hair, etc.) ondear; (wander) vagar; *naut* boyar. *vt* poner a flote; hacer flotar; (a grounded ship) desencallar; (com a company) fundar; (a loan, etc.) emitir, poner en circulación; (launch a ship) botar; (flood) inundar

floating *n* flotación, *f*, flote, *m*; com fundación (de una compañía), *f*; (of a loan) emisión, *f*; (of a ship) botadura, *f*. *a* flotante; boyante; *com* en circulación, flotante; fluctuante, variable. **f. capital,** capital fluctuante, *m*. **f. debt,** deuda flotante, *f*. **f. dock,** dique flotante, *m*. **f. light,** buque faro, *m*. **f. population,** población flotante, *f*. **f. rib,** costilla flotante, *f*

flock *n* rebaño, *m*, manada, *f*; (of birds) bandada, *f*; *fig* grey, *f*; (crowd) multitud, muchedumbre, *f*; (parishioners) con-

gregación, *f*; (of wool or cotton) vedija (de lana or de algodón), *f*; *pl* **flocks,** (for stuffing) borra, *f*. *vi* concurrirse, reunirse, congregarse; ir en tropel, acudir; (birds) volar en bandada. **f.-bed,** colchón de borra, *m*

floe *n* banco de hielo, *m*

flog *vt* azotar; castigar

flood *n* inundación, *f*; (Bible) diluvio, *m*; (of the tide) flujo, *m*; *fig* torrente, *m*; (abundance) copia, abundancia, *f*; (fit) paroxismo, *m*. *vt* inundar; sumergir; (of tears) mojar. *vi* desbordar. **f. lighting,** iluminación intensiva, *f*

floor *n* suelo, piso, *m*; (wooden) entarimado, *m*; (story) piso, *m*; (of a cart) cama, *f*; *agr* era, *f*. *vt* entablar; echar al suelo, derribar; *fig* desconcertar, confundir. **on the f.,** en el suelo. **on the ground f.,** en el piso bajo. **to take the f.,** *fig* tener la palabra. **f. mop** *Lat. Am.* lampazo *m*. **f.-polisher,** lustrador de piso, *m*

flop *n* golpe, *m*; ruido sordo, *m*; (splash) chapoteo, *m*; *inf* fiasco, *m*. *vi* dejarse caer

flora *n* flora, *f*

florid *a* florido; demasiado ornado, cursi, llamativo; (of complexion) rubicundo

florist *n* florista, *mf*

floss *n* seda floja, filoseda, *f*; (of maize) penacho, *m*; (of a cocoon) cadarzo, *m*. **f. silk,** seda floja, *f*

flotsam *n* pecio, *m*

flounce *n* volante, *m*, *vi* saltar de impaciencia. **to f. out,** salir airadamente

flounder *n* (nearest equivalent) *icht* platija, *f*; tumbo, *m*. *vi* tropezar; revolcarse; andar dificultosamente

flour *n* harina, *f*, *vt* enharinar. **f.-bin,** tina, *f*, harinero, *m*. **f. merchant,** harinero, *m*

flourish *n* movimiento, *m*; gesto, saludo, *m*; (of a pen) plumada, *f*; (on the guitar, in fencing) floreo, *m*; preludio, *m*; (fanfare) tocata (de trompetas), *f*; (of a signature) rúbrica, *f*; (in rhetoric) floreo, *m*. *vi* (of plants) vegetar; (prosper) prosperar, medrar; florecer; (of the guitar, in fencing) florear; *mus* preludiar; (with a pen) hacer plumadas (or rasgos de pluma); (of a signature) firmar con rúbrica; (sound a fanfare) hacer una tocata (de trompetas). *vt* agitar en el aire, blandir

flourishing *a* (of plants) lozano; floreciente; (prosperous) próspero; (happy) feliz

flout *vt* burlarse de; despreciar, no hacer caso de

flow *n* flujo, *m*; corriente, *f*; chorro, *m*; (of water) caudal, *m*; (output) producción total, cantidad, *f*; (of the tide) flujo (de la marea), *m*; (of words) facilidad, *f*. *vi* fluir; manar; correr; (of the tide) crecer (la marea); (pass) pasar, correr; (result) resultar (de), provenir (de); (of hair, drapery) caer, ondular; (abound) abundar (en). **to f. away,** escaparse, salir. **to f. back,** refluir. **to f. down,** descender, fluir hacia abajo; (of tears) correr por. **to f. from,** dimanar de; manar de; *fig* provenir de. **to f. in,** llegar en abundancia. **to f. into,** (rivers) desaguar en, desembocar en. **to f. over,** derramarse por. **to f. through,** fluir por; atravesar; (water) regar. **to f. together,** (rivers) confluir

flower n flor, f; (best) flor y nata, crema, f. *vi* florecer. **in f.,** en flor. **No flowers by request,** (for a funeral) No flores por deseo del finado. **f.-bud,** capullo, m. **f.-garden,** jardín, m. **f. girl,** florista, vendedora de flores, f. **f. market,** mercado de flores, m. **f.-piece,** florero, m. **f. pot,** tiesto, m, maceta, f, *Lat. Am.* macetero m. **f. show,** exposición de flores, f. **f. vase,** florero, m

flowerbed n cuadro, macizo, m

flowering n florecimiento, m. a floreciente; con flores; (of shrubs) de adorno. **f. season,** época de la floración, f

flowery a florido

flowing n flujo, m; derrame, m. a fluente, corriente; (of tide) creciente; (waving) ondeante; suelto; (of style) flúido

flow of capital corriente de capital, f

fluctuate vi fluctuar, vacilar; variar

fluctuation n fluctuación, f; cambio, m, variación, f; (hesitancy) indecisión, vacilación, f

fluency n fluidez, f

fluent a flúido; fácil

fluently adv corrientemente, con facilidad, de corrido

fluff n borra, pelusa, f, tamo, m

fluffy a velloso; (feathered) plumoso; (woolly) lanudo; (of hair) encrespado

fluid n flúido, líquido, m, a flúido

fluke n (in billiards) chiripa, f; *naut* uña, f; *inf* carambola, chiripa, chambonada, f. **by a f.,** de carambola, por suerte. **f.-worm,** duela del hígado, f

flunkey n lacayo, m; *fig* adulador, m

fluorescence n fluorescencia, f

flurry n (of wind) ráfaga, f; (squall) chubasco, m; agitación, f; conmoción, f. vt agitar

flush n rubor, m; (in the sky) arrebol, rojo, color de rosa, m; emoción, f, acceso, m; sensación, f; (at cards) flux, m; vigor, m; (flowering) floración, f; abundancia, f; (of youth, etc.) frescura, f. a (level) igual, parejo; abundante; (generous) pródigo, liberal; (rich) adinerado. vi ruborizarse, enrojecerse, ponerse colorado; (flood) inundarse, llenarse (de agua, etc.); (of sky) arrebolarse. vt inundar, limpiar con un chorro de agua, etc., lavar; (of blood) circular por; (redden) enrojecer; (make blush) hacer ruborizarse; (exhilarate) excitar, animar; (inflame) inflamar, encender; (make level) igualar, nivelar. **f. with,** a ras de

flushing n rojez, f; (cleansing) limpieza, lavadura, f; (flooding) inundación, f

fluster n agitación, confusión, f, aturdimiento, m. vt agitar, poner nervioso (a), aturdir; (oneself) preocuparse. vi agitarse; estar nervioso, estar perplejo; (with drink) estar entre dos velas

flute n flauta, f; *arch* estría, f; (organstop) flautado, m. vi tocar la flauta, flautear; tener la voz flauteada. vt tocar (una pieza) en la flauta; (groove) encanutar, acanalar, estriar. **f. player,** flautista, mf

flutter n (of wings) aleteo, m; (of leaves, etc.) murmurio, m; (of eyelashes) pestañeo, m; (of flags, etc.) ondeo, m, ondulación, f; (excitement) agitación, f; (stir) sensación, f; (gamble) jugada, f. vi (of birds) aletear; revolotear; (of butterflies) mariposear; (of flags) ondear; palpitar; (of persons) estar agitado. vt agitar; (the eyelashes) pestañear; (agitate) agitar, alarmar

fluttering n mariposeo, m; revoloteo, m; (of birds) aleteo, m; (of leaves, etc.) murmurio, m; (of flags, etc.) ondeo, m, ondulación, f; (of eyelashes) pestañeo, m

flux n flujo, m

fly n (insect) mosca, f; (on a fishhook) mosca artificial, f; (carriage) calesín, m; (of breeches) bragueta, f; *theat* bambalina, f; (of a tent) toldo, m; (flight) vuelo, m; (of a flag) vuelo, m. **fly-blown,** manchado por las moscas. **fly-by-night,** trasnochador (-ra). **fly-catcher,** *orn* papamoscas, m; matamoscas, m. **fly-fishing,** pesca con moscas artificiales, f. **fly-leaf,** guarda (de un libro), f. **fly-paper,** papel matamoscas, m. **fly-swatter,** matamoscas, m. **fly-wheel,** *mech* volante, m

fly vi volar; (flutter) ondear; (jump) saltar; (rush) lanzarse, precipitarse; (pass away) pasar volando, volar; (run off) marcharse a todo correr; (escape) huir, escapar; (seek refuge) refugiarse; (to the head, of intoxicants) subirse; (vanish) desaparecer. vt hacer volar; hacer ondear, enarbolar; (an airplane) pilotar, dirigir; (flee from) huir de; evitar. **to let fly (at),** descargar, tirar; *fig* saltar la sinhueso. **to fly about,** volar en torno de; revolotear. **to fly at,** lanzarse sobre; acometer, asaltar. **to fly away,** emprender el vuelo. **to fly back,** volar hacia el punto de partida; (of doors, etc.) abrir, or cerrar, de repente. **to fly down,** volar abajo. **to fly in,** volar dentro de; volar adentro; (of airplanes) llegar (el avión). **to fly in pieces,** hacerse pedazos. **to fly into a rage,** montarse en cólera. **to fly low,** rastrear; *aer* volar a poca altura. **to fly off,** emprender el vuelo; (hasten) marcharse volando; (of buttons, etc.) saltar (de), separarse (de). **to fly open,** abrirse de repente. **to fly over,** volar por, volar por encima de. **to fly upwards,** volar hacia arriba; subir

flying n vuelo, m. a volante, volador; que vuela; de volar; volátil; (hasty) rápido; (flowing) ondeante, ondulante. **to shoot**

f., tirar al vuelo. **with f. colors,** con banderas desplegadas, triunfante. **f.-boat,** hidroavión, m. **f.-buttress,** botarel, arbotante, m. **f.-column,** mil cuerpo volante, m. **f.-fish,** (pez) volador, m. **f.-fortress,** aer fortaleza volante, f. **f.-officer,** oficial de aviación, m. **f.-sickness,** mal de altura, m. **f.-squad,** escuadra ligera, f. **f.-test,** aer examen de pilotaje, m

foam n espuma, f. vi espumar; (of horses, etc.) echar espumarajos. **to f. and froth,** (of the sea) hervir. **f. at the mouth,** echar espuma por la boca.

foam rubber n caucho esponjoso, m, espuma de caucho, f, espuma sintética, f

foamy a espumoso

fob n bolsillo del reloj, m; faltriquera pequeña, f. vt (off) engañar con

focus n foco, m; centro, m. vt enfocar; concentrar. vi convergir. **in f.,** en foco

fodder n agr pienso, forraje, m. vt dar forraje (a)

foe n enemigo, m

fog n neblina, niebla, f; fig confusión, f; fig perplejidad, f, vt obscurecer; phot velar; fig ofuscar. vi hacerse nebuloso; fig velarse. **fog-signal,** señal de niebla, f

fogey n obscurantista, m. **He is an old f.,** Es un señor chapado a la antigua

fogginess n oscuridad, neblina, f

foggy a nebuloso; phot velado. **It is f.,** Hay niebla

foghorn n sirena, f; bocina, f

foible n flaco, m, debilidad, f

foil n (sword) florete, m; (coat) hoja, f; (of a mirror) azogado, m. vt frustrar. **f. a plot,** desbaratar un complot. **She makes a good f. for her sister's beauty,** Hace resaltar la belleza de su hermana

foist vt imponer; insertar, incluir; engañar (con)

fold n doblez, f, pliegue, m; arruga, f; sew cogido, m; (for sheep) redil, aprisco, m; fig iglesia, congregación de los fieles, f; (in compounds) vez, f. vt doblar, plegar, doblegar; (the arms) cruzar (los brazos); (embrace) abrazar; (wrap) envolver; (clasp) entrelazar; (sheep) meter en redil, encerrar. vi doblarse, plegarse; cerrarse

folding n plegadura, f, doblamiento, m; (of sheep) encerramiento, m, a plegadizo. **f.-door,** puerta plegadiza, f. **f.-machine,** plegador, m. **f.-seat,** aut traspuntín, m. **f.-table,** mesa de tijeras, f; mesa plegadiza, f

foliage n follaje, m, frondas, f pl. **thick f.,** frondosidad, f

folio n folio, m; (a volume) infolio, m. a de infolio. vt foliar

folk n (nation) pueblo, m, nación, f; gente, f; pl **folks,** inf familia, f; parientes, m pl. **f.-dance,** danza popular, f

folklore n folclore, m, tradiciones folclóricas, f pl

folksong n canción popular, f; romance, m; copla, f

folktale n conseja, f, cuento popular, m

follicle n (anat, bot) folículo, m

follow vt seguir; (pursue) perseguir; (hunt) cazar; (adopt) adoptar; (understand) comprender; (notice) observar. vi ir, or venir, detrás; (of time) venir después; (gen. impers.) seguir, resultar; seguirse. **as follows,** como sigue. **I shall f. your advice,** Seguiré tus consejos. **to f. on the heels of,** fig pisar los talones (a). **to f. suit,** (at cards) asistir, jugar el mismo palo; fig imitar. **to f. up,** proseguir; continuar; (pursue) perseguir; (enhance) reforzar. **f.-me-lads,** inf sigueme-pollo, m

follower n seguidor (-ra); adherente, secuaz, mf; (imitator) imitador (-ra); (lover) novio, m; pl **followers,** acompañamiento, séquito, m

following n séquito, acompañamiento, m, comitiva, f; partidarios, m pl, adherentes, mf pl. a siguiente; próximo. **f. wind,** viento en popa, m

folly n locura, extravagancia, absurdidad, tontería, f, disparate, m

foment vt (poultice) fomentar; provocar, incitar, instigar; (assist) fomentar, proteger, promover

fond a (credulous) vano, crédulo, vacío; (doting) demasiado indulgente; (loving) cariñoso, tierno, afectuoso; (addicted to) aficionado a, adicto a, amigo de. **to be f. of,** (things) tener afición a, estar aficionado de; (people) tener cariño (a). **to grow f. of,** (things) aficionarse a; (people) tomar cariño (a)

fondle vt mimar, acariciar; jugar (con).

fondness n cariño, afecto, m; (for things) afición, inclinación, f; gusto, m

font n pila bautismal, f; poet fuente, f; print fundición, f

food n alimento, m; comida, f, el comer; (of animals) pasto, m; fig pábulo, m; materia, f. **She gave him f.** Le dio de comer. **You have given me f. for thought,** Me has dado en qué pensar. **f.-card,** cartilla de racionamiento, f. **food, clothing, and shelter** comida, abrigo y vivienda, f. **F. Ministry,** Ministerio de Alimentación, m. **f. value,** valor nutritivo, m. **food poisoning,** intoxicación alimenticia, f

foodstuffs n pl comestibles, víveres, m pl

fool n tonto (-ta), mentecato (-ta), majadero (ra) necio (-ia); (jester) bufón, m; (butt of jest) hazmerreír, m; víctima, f; cul compota de frutas con crema, f, vi tontear, hacer tonterías. vt poner en ridículo (a); (deceive) engañar, embaucar; (with) jugar con. **to make a f. of oneself,** ponerse en ridículo. **to f. about,** vi perder el tiempo, vagabundear. **to f. away,** malgastar, malbaratar. **fool's**

bauble, cetro de bufón, *m.* **fool's cap,** gorro de bufón, *m*

foolhardy a temerario, atrevido

foolish a imprudente; estúpido, tonto; ridículo, absurdo; imbécil

foolproof a (of utensils, etc.) con garantía absoluta

foot *n* pie, *m*; (of animals, furniture) pata, *f*; (of bed, sofa, grave, ladder, page, etc.) pie, *m*; (hoof) pezuña, *f*; (metric unit and measure) pie, *m*; *mil* infantería, *f*; (base) base, *f*; (step) paso, *m*. a *mil* de a pie; a pie. *vi* ir a pie; venir a pie; bailar. *vt* hollar; (account) pagar (una cuenta); (stockings) poner pie (a). **on f.,** a pie; (of soldiers) de a pie; (in progress) en marcha. **to go ón f.,** ir a pie, andar. **to put one's best f. forward,** apretar el paso; *fig* hacer de su mejor. **to put one's f. down,** poner pies en pared, pararle fulano el alto. **to put one's f. in it,** meter la pata. **to rise to one's feet,** ponerse de pie. **to set f. on,** pisar, hollar. **to set on f.,** poner en pie; *fig* poner en marcha. **to trample under f.,** pisotear. **f.-and-mouth disease,** glosopeda, *f*. **f.-brake,** freno de pedal, *m*. **f.-pump,** fuelle de pie, *m*. **f.-rule,** (nearest equivalent) doble decímetro, *m*. **f.-soldier,** soldado de a pie, infante, *m*

football *n* (game) fútbol, *m*; (ball) pelota de fútbol, *f*. **f. field,** campo de fútbol, *m*. **f. match,** partida de fútbol, *f*. **f. pools,** apuestas de fútbol, *f pl*; (in Spain) apuestas benéficas de fútbol, *f pl*

footbridge *n* puente para peatones, *m*

foothills *n pl* faldas de la montaña, *f pl*

foothold *n* hincapié, *m*; posición establecida, *f*

footing *n* hincapié, *m*; posición firme, *f*; condiciones, *f pl*; relaciones, *f pl*. **on a peacetime f.,** en pie de paz. **to be on an equal f.,** estar en pie de igualdad, estar en iguales condiciones. **to miss one's f.,** resbalar

footlights *n pl* canilejas, candilejas, *f pl*. **to get across the f.,** hacer contacto con el público

footnote *n* llamada a pie de página, nota a pie de página, *f*

footpath *n* senda, vereda, *f*, sendero, *m*

footprint *n* huella, pisada, *f*, vestigio, *m*

footstep *n* paso, *m*; (trace) pisada, huella, *f*. **to follow in the footsteps of,** *fig* seguir las pisadas de

footwear *n* calzado, *m*

fop *n* petimetre, *m*

foppish a presumido, afectado; elegante

for *prep* (expressing exchange, price or penalty of, instead of, in support or favor of, on account of) por; (expressing destination, purpose, result) para; (during) durante, por; (for the sake of) para; (because of) a causa de; (in spite of) a pesar de; (as) como; (with) de; (in favor of) en favor de; (in election campaign) con (e.g., "Ecuadorians for Martínez!" ¡Ecuatorianos con Martínez!) (toward) hacia; (that) que, para que (with *subjunc*); a, (before) antes de; (searching for) en busca de; (bound for) con rumbo a; (regarding) en cuanto a; (until) hasta. What's for dinner? ¿Qué hay de comida? **center for . . .** centro de . . . (e.g., **Center for Applied Linguistics,** Centro de Lingüística Aplicada). **He is in business for himself,** Tiene negocios por su propia cuenta. **It is raining too hard for you to go there,** Llueve demasiado para que vayas allí. **It is not for him to decide,** No le toca a él decidirlo. **Were it not for . . . ,** Si no fuese por . . . **She has not been to see me for a week,** Hace una semana que no viene a verme. **It is impossible for them to go out,** Les es imposible salir. **for all that,** pero con todo. **for ever,** por (or para) siempre. **for fear that,** por miedo de que. **for myself,** en cuanto a mí, personalmente. **for the present,** por ahora. **for what reason?** ¿para qué? ¿por cuál motivo? **for brevity's sake, for the sake of brevity,** por causa de la brevedad

for *conjunc* porque; visto que, pues, puesto que, en efecto, ya que

forage *n* forraje, *m*. *vt* and *vi* forrajear. **to f. for,** buscar. **f. cap,** gorra de cuartel, *f*

foray *n* correría, cabalgada, *f*; saqueo, *m*

forbear *vt* and *vi* dejar (de), guardarse (de); abstenerse de; evitar; reprimirse (de); rehusarse (de); (cease) cesar (de); (be patient) ser paciente; ser tolerante

forbearance *n* abstención, *f*; tolerancia, transigencia, *f*; indulgencia, *f*; paciencia, *f*

forbearing a tolerance, transigente; generoso, magnánimo; paciente

forbid *vt* prohibir, defender (de); impedir. **I f. you to do it,** Te prohibo hacerlo. **The game is forbidden,** El juego está prohibido. **They have forbidden me to . . . ,** Me han defendido de . . . **Heaven f.!** ¡Dios no lo quiera!

forbidden a prohibido; ilícito. **f. fruit,** fruto prohibido, *m*

forbidding a repugnante, horrible; antipático, desagradable; (dismal) lúgubre; (threatening) amenazador. *n* prohibición, *f*

force *n* fuerza, *f*; violencia, *f*; vigor, *m*; (efficacy) eficacia, *f*; (validity) validez, *f*; (power) poder, *m*; (motive) motivo, *m*, razón, *f*; (weight) peso, *m*, importancia, *f*; (police) policía, *f*; *pl* **forces,** *mil* fuerzas, tropas, *f pl*. **by main f.,** por fuerza mayor. **in f.,** vigente, en vigor. **to be in f.,** estar vigente

force *vt* forzar; (compel) obligar, constreñir, precisar; (ravish) violar; *cul* rellenar; (impose) imponer; (plants) forzar; (the pace) apresurar; (cause) hacer; (a lock, etc.) forzar. **to f. oneself into,** entrar a la fuerza en; (a garment) ponerse con dificultad; imponerse a la fuerza. **to f. oneself to,** esforzarse a. **to f. the pace,**

forzar el paso. **to f. away,** ahuyentar. **to f. back,** hacer retroceder; rechazar; (a sigh, etc.) ahogar. **to f. down,** hacer bajar, obligar a bajar; (make swallow) hacer tragar; (of airplanes) hacer tomar tierra. **to f. in,** introducir a la fuerza; obligar a entrar. **to f. into,** meter a la fuerza; obligar a entrar (en). **to f. on, upon,** imponer. **to f. open,** abrir a la fuerza; (a lock) romper, forzar. **to f. out,** hacer salir; empujar hacia fuera; (words) pronunciar con dificultad. **to f. up,** obligar a subir; hacer subir; hacer vomitar

forced a forzado; forzoso; afectado. **f. landing,** aer aterrizaje forzoso, m. **f. march,** mil marcha forzada, f

forceful a See **forcible**

forcemeat n picadillo, m; relleno, m. **f. ball,** albóndiga, f

forceps n pl fórceps, m pl; pinzas, f pl. **arterial f.,** pinzas hemostáticas, f pl

forcible a fuerte; a la fuerza; violento; enérgico, vigoroso; poderoso; lit vívido, gráfico, vehemente. **f. feeding,** alimentación forzosa, f

forcibly adv a la fuerza

forcing n forzamiento, m; compulsión, f. **f. frame,** semillero, m, especie de invernadero, f

ford n esguazo, vado, m. vt esguazar, vadear

fore a delantero; naut de proa. adv delante; naut de proa. **f.-and-aft,** naut de popa a proa.

forearm n antebrazo, m. vt armar de antemano; preparar

forebear n antecesor, m, ascendiente, mf

forebode vt presagiar, augurar, anunciar; presentir

foreboding n presagio, augurio, m; presentimiento, m, corazonada, f

forecast n pronóstico, m; proyecto, plan, m, vt pronosticar; proyectar. **weather f.,** pronóstico del tiempo, m

foreclose vt excluir; impedir; vender por orden judicial; anticipar el resultado de; decidir de antemano

foreclosure n venta por orden judicial, f; juicio hipotecario, m

forefather n antepasado, antecesor, m

forefinger n índice, dedo índice, m

forefront n delantera, primera línea, f; frente, m; vanguardia, f. **in the f.,** en la vanguardia; en el frente

foregoing a precedente, anterior

foregone a decidido de antemano; previsto

foreground n primer plano, primer término, frente, m. **in the f.,** art en primer término

forehand a derecho. **f. stroke,** golpe derecho, m

forehead n frente, f

foreign a extranjero; extraño; exótico; exterior; (alien) ajeno. **f. affairs,** asuntos extranjeros, m pl. **f. body,** cuerpo extraño, m. **f. debt,** deuda exterior, f. **F. Legion,** tercio extranjero, m. **F. Office,** Ministerio de Relaciones Extranjeras, m. **f. parts,** extranjero, m. **f. policy,** política internacional, f. **F. Secretary,** Secretario de Asuntos Extranjeros, Secretario de Asuntos Exteriores, Ministro de Relaciones Extranjeras, m. **f. trade,** comercio con el extranjero, m

foreigner n extranjero (-ra), Argentina, Chile also cuico (-ca), Mexico also fuereño (-ña) mf

foreknowledge n presciencia, precognición, f

forelock n guedeja, vedeja, f; (of a horse) copete, tupé, m. **to take time by the f.,** asir la ocasión por la melena

foreman n (of jury) presidente (del jurado), m; (of a farm) mayoral, m; (in a works) capataz, m

foremost a delantero; de primera fila; más importante. adv en primer lugar; en primera fila

forensic a forense, legal. **f. medicine,** medicina legal, f

foreordained a predestinado

forerunner n precursor (-ra), predecesor (-ra); (presage) anuncio, presagio, m

foresee vt prever, anticipar

foreshadow vt anunciar, prefigurar; simbolizar; hacer sentir

foreshorten vt art escorzar

foresight n presciencia, f; previsión, prudencia, f; (of gun) punto de mira, m; (optical) croquis de nivel, m

forest n bosque, m, selva, f, vt arbolar

forestall vt anticipar, saltear; prevenir; com acaparar

forestation n repoblación forestal, f

forester n silvicultor, guardamonte, ingeniero forestal, m; habitante de los bosques, m

forest fire incendio forestal, m

forestry n silvicultura, f

foretaste n muestra, f; presagio, m. vt gustar con anticipación

foretell vt predecir, profetizar; anunciar, presagiar

forethought n presciencia, previsión, f; prevención, f

forewarn vt prevenir

foreword n prefacio, m, introducción, f

forfeit n pérdida, f; (fine) multa, f; (in games) prenda, f; (of rights, goods, etc.) confiscación, f. a confiscado. vt perder; perder el derecho o el título de

forfeiture n pérdida, f; confiscación, f; secuestro, m

forge n fragua, f; (smithy) herrería, f. vt and vi fraguar, forjar; (fabricate) inventar, fabricar; falsificar; (advance) avanzar lentamente. **to f. ahead,** abrirse camino; avanzar

forged a (of iron) forjado; (of checks, etc.) falso, falsificado

forger n falsificador (-ra), falsario (-ia); (creator) artífice, mf

forgery n falsificación, f

forget vt olvidar; descuidar. vi olvidarse. **to f. about,** olvidarse de, desacordarse de. **to f. oneself,** olvidarse de sí mismo; propasarse; (in anger) perder los estribos

forgetful a olvidadizo; descuidado, negligente

forgive vt perdonar, disculpar, condonar; (debts) remitir

forgiveness n perdón, m; condonación, f; (remission) remisión, f

forgiving a misericordioso, clemente, dispuesto a perdonar

forgo vt renunciar, sacrificar, privarse de; abandonar, ceder

forgoing n renunciación, f, sacrificio, m; cesión, f

"For Immediate Occupancy" «De Ocupación Inmediata»

fork n agr horca, horquilla, f; (table fork) tenedor, m; bifurcación, f; (of rivers) confluencia, f; (of branches) horcadura, f; (of legs) horcajadura, f; (for supporting trees, etc.) horca, f; mus diapasón normal, m. vt hacinar con horca. vi bifurcarse; ramificarse

forlorn a abandonado, desamparado, desesperado. **f. hope,** aventura desesperada, f

form n forma, f; figura, f; (shadowy) bulto, m; (formality) formalidad, f; ceremonia, f; ecc rito, m; método, m; regla, f; (in a school) clase, f; (lair) cama, f; (seat) banco, m; (system) sistema, m; (ghost) espectro, m; aparición, f; (to fill out) documento, m; hoja, f, Mexico esqueleto m; (state) condición, f; lit construcción, forma, f. **It is a matter of f.,** Es una pura formalidad. **in due f.,** en debida forma, en regla. **in the usual f.,** com al usado. **It is not good f.,** No es de buena educación

form vt formar; (a habit) contraer; (an idea) hacerse (una idea). vi formarse. **to f. fours,** mil formar a cuatro

formal a esencial; formal; ceremonioso, solemne; (of person) etiquetero, formalista. **f. call,** visita de cumplido, f

formality n formalidad, f; ceremonia, solemnidad, f

format n formato, m

formation n formación, f; disposición, f; arreglo, m; organización, f; (mil, geol) formación, f

forme n print forma, f, molde, m

former a primero; antiguo; anterior; pasado. **in f. times,** antes, antiguamente. **the f.,** ése, aquél, m; ésa, aquélla, f; aquéllos, m pl; aquéllas, f pl

formerly adv antiguamente, antes

formidable a formidable; terrible, espantoso

formless a informe

formula n fórmula, f. **standard f.,** (math, chem) fórmula clásica, f

formulate vt formular

fornicate vi fornicar

forsake vt dejar, desertar; abandonar, desamparar; separarse de; (of birds, the nest) aborrecer; (one's faith) renegar de

"For Sale" «Se Vende»

forsooth adv ciertamente, claro está

forswear vt abjurar; renunciar a. **to f. oneself,** perjurarse

fort n fortaleza, f, fuerte, m

forte n fuerte, m. a mús fuerte

forth adv (on) adelante, hacia adelante; (out) fuera; (in time) en adelante, en lo consecutivo; (show) a la vista. **and so f.,** y así en lo sucesivo; etcétera

forthcoming a próximo; futuro; en preparación

forthwith adv en seguida, sin tardanza

fortieth a cuadragésimo; cuarenta. n cuarentavo, m

fortify vt fortificar; fortalecer; confirmar; fig proveer (de)

fortitude n aguante, m, fortaleza, f, estoicismo, m

fortnight n quince días, m pl, dos semanas, f pl; quincena, f. **a f. ago,** hace quince días. **a f. tomorrow,** mañana en quince. **in a f.,** dentro de quince días; al cabo de quince días. **once a f.,** cada quince días

fortnightly a quincenal. adv cada dos semanas, dos veces al mes. n revista quincenal, f

fortress n fortaleza, plaza fuerte, f

fortuitous a fortuito, accidental

fortuity n casualidad, f; accidente, m

fortunate a dichoso, feliz; afortunado; próspero. **to be f.,** (of persons) tener suerte

fortunately adv afortunadamente, por dicha, felizmente

fortune n suerte, fortuna, f, destino, m; (money) caudal, m, fortuna, f; bienes, m pl; buena ventura, f. **good f.,** buena fortuna, dicha, f. **ill f.,** mala suerte, f. **to cost a f.,** costar un sentido. **to make one's f.,** enriquecerse; inf hacer su pacotilla. **to tell fortunes,** echar las cartas. **f. hunter,** buscador de dotes, cazador de dotes, cazador de fortunas, aventurero, m. **f.-teller,** adivinadora, f; echadora de cartas, f. **f.-telling,** buenaventura, f

forty a and n cuarenta, m. **He is turned f.,** Ha cumplido los cuarenta. **person of f.,** cuarentón (-ona). **She is f.,** Tiene cuarenta años

forum n foro, tribuna f, (e.g., **to serve as a forum for discussion,** servir de tribuna de discusión)

forward a avanzado; adelantado; (of position) delantero; (ready) preparado; (eager) pronto, listo, impaciente; activo, emprendedor; (of persons, fruit, etc.) precoz; (pert) insolente, desenvuelto, atrevido. *adv* adelante; hacia adelante; (of time) en adelante; (farther on) más allá; hacia el frente; en primera línea. *vt* ayudar, promover; adelantar; (letters) hacer seguir; *com* expedir, remitir; (a parcel) despachar; (hasten) apresurar; (plants) hacer crecer. *n* sport delantero, *m*. **center-f.,** sport delantero centro, *m*. **from this time f.,** de hoy en adelante. **Please f.,** ¡Haga seguir! **putting f. of the clock,** el adelanto de la hora. **to carry f.,** *com* pasar a cuenta nueva. **to go f.,** adelantarse; estar en marcha, estar en preparación. **f. line,** sport delantera, *f*. **F.!** ¡Adelante!

forwarding *n* fomento, *m*, promoción, *f*; *com* expedición, *f*, envío, *m*

forwardness *n* progreso, adelantamiento, *m*; (haste) apresuramiento, *m*; (of persons, fruit, etc.) precocidad, *f*; (pertness) desenvoltura, insolencia, frescura, *f*, descaro, *m*; (eagerness) impaciencia, *f*

fossil a and *n* fósil, *m*.

fossilize *vt* fosilizar; petrificar. *vi* fosilizarse

foster *vt* provocar, promover, suscitar; (favor) favorecer, ser propicio a. **f.-brother,** hermano de leche, *m*. **f.-child,** hijo (-ja) de leche. **f.-father,** padre adoptivo, *m*. **f.-mother,** ama de leche, *f*. **f.-sister,** hermana de leche, *f*

foul a sucio, asqueroso, puerco; (evil-smelling) hediondo, fétido; (of air) viciado; impuro; (language) ofensivo; (coarse) indecente, obsceno; (harmful) nocivo, dañino; (wicked) malvado; infame; vil; (unfair) injusto; *sport* sucio; (ugly) feo; (entangled) enredado; (with corrections) lleno de erratas; (choked) atascado; (of weather) borrascoso, tempestuoso; malo, desagradable; (repulsive) repugnante. *n* sport juego sucio, *Lat. Am.* faul *m*. *vt* ensuciar; *naut* chocar, abordar; (block) atascar; (the anchor) enredar; *Lat. Am.* sports faulear; (dishonor) deshonrar. *vi* atascarse; (anchor) enredarse; *naut* chocar. **to fall f. of,** *naut* abordar (un buque); *fig* habérselas con. **by fair means or f.,** a las buenas o a las malas. **f. breath,** aliento fétido, aliento corrompido, *m*. **f. brood,** peste de las abejas, *f*. **f. language,** palabras ofensivas, *f pl*; lenguaje obsceno, *m*. **f. play,** juego sucio, *m*. **f. weather,** mal tiempo, tiempo borrascoso, *m*

found *vt* fundar; (metal, glass) fundir; (create, etc.) establecer

foundation *n* fundación, *f*; establecimiento, *m*; creación, *f*; *arch* cimiento, embasamiento, *m*; (basis) base, *f*; (cause) causa, *f*, origen, principio, *m*;

(endowment) dotación, *f*; *sew* refuerzo, *m*. **to lay the f.,** poner las fundaciones. **f. stone,** piedra angular, *f*; *fig* primera piedra, *f*. **to lay the f. stone,** poner la piedra angular

founder *n* fundador (-ra); (of metals) fundidor, *m*. *vt* (a ship) hacer zozobrar. *vi* zozobrar, irse a pique; *fig* fracasar

founding *n* fundación, *f*; establecimiento, *m*; (of metals) fundición, *f*

foundling *n* hijo (-ja) de la cuna, expósito (-ta). **f. hospital** or **home,** casa de cuna, casa de expósitos, inclusa, *f*

foundry *n* fundición, *f*

fountain *n* fuente, *f*; (spring) manantial, *m*; (jet) chorro, *m*; (artificial) fuente, *f*, surtidero, *m*; (source) origen, principio, *m*. **f.-head,** fuente, *f*. **Fountain of Youth,** Fuente de la juventud, Fuente de Juvencio, *f*. **f. pen,** pluma estilográfica, *f*

four a and *n* cuatro, *m*. **It is f. o'clock,** Son las cuatro. **She is f.,** Tiene cuatro años. **on all fours,** a gatas. **f.-course,** (of meals) de cuatro platos. **f.-engined,** cuadrimotor. **f.-engined plane,** cuadrimotor, *m*. **f.-footed,** cuadrúpedo. **f.-horse,** de cuatro caballos. **f. hundred,** cuatrocientos. **f.-inhand,** tiro par, *m*. **f.-part,** (of a song) a cuatro voces. **f.-wheel brakes,** freno en las cuatro ruedas, *m*

fourfold a cuádruple

fourscore a and *n* ochenta, *m*.

fourteen a and *n* catorce, *m*. **He is f.,** Tiene catorce años

fourteenth a and *n* décimocuarto *m*.; (of the month) (el) catorce, *m*; (of monarchs) catorce. **April f.,** El 14 (catorce) de abril

fourth a cuarto; (of the month) el cuatro; (of monarchs) cuarto. *n* (fourth part) cuarta parte, *f*; *mus* cuarta, *f*. **f. dimension,** cuarta dimensión, *f*. **f. term,** (U.S.A. *pol*) cuarto mandato, *m*

fowl *n* gallo, *m*; gallina, *f*; (chicken) pollo, *m*; (bird) ave, *f*; (barndoor f.) ave de corral, *f*. *vi* cazar aves. **f.-house** or **run,** gallinero, *m*

fox *n* zorro, *m*; (vixen) zorra, raposa, *Argentina* chilla *f*; *fig* zorro, taimado, *m*. *vi* disimular. *vt* (books) descolorar. **f.-brush,** cola de raposa, *f*. **f.-earth,** zorrera, *f*. **f.-hunting,** caza de zorras, *f*. **f. terrier,** fox-térrier, *m*

foxy a de zorro; zorrero, astuto

foyer *n* foyer, salón de descanso, *m*

fraction *n* math fracción, *f*, número quebrado, *m*; pequeña parte, *f*; fragmento, *m*. **improper f.,** math fracción impropia, *f*. **proper f.,** math fracción propia, *f*

fractional a fraccionario

fractious a malhumorado, enojadizo

fracture *n* surg fractura, *f*. *vt* fracturar. **compound f.,** fractura conminuta, *f*

fragile a frágil, quebradizo; (of persons) delicado

fragment n fragmento, m; trozo, pedazo, m. **to break into fragments,** hacer pedazos, hacer añicos

fragmentary a fragmentario

fragrance n fragancia, f, buen olor, perfume, aroma, m

fragrant a fragante, oloroso. **to make f.,** perfumar

frail a frágil, quebradizo; débil, endeble. n capacho, m, espuerta, f

frailty n fragilidad, f; debilidad, f

frame n constitución, f; sistema, m; organización, f; (of the body) figura, f, talle, m; (of window, picture) marco, m; (of machine, building) armadura, f; (of a bicycle) cuadro (de bicicleta), m; agr cajonera, f; (embroidery) bastidor (para bordar), m; (skeleton) esqueleto, m; lit composición, construcción, f; (of spectacles) armadura, f; (of mind) disposición (de ánimo), f; humor, m. vt formar; construir; arreglar; ajustar; (a picture) enmarcar; componer, hacer; (draw up) redactar; (think up) idear, inventar; (words) articular, pronunciar. **f. a constitution,** elaborar una constitución

framework n armadura, armazón, f, esqueleto, m; organización, f; (basis) base, f

franc n (coin) franco, m

franchise n (exemption) franquicia, f; privilegio, m; (vote) derecho de sufragio, m; (citizenship) derecho político, m

France Francia, f

frank a franco, cándido, sincero; abierto. vt franquear

frankly adv francamente; sinceramente; cara a cara; sin rodeos, claramente; abiertamente. **to speak f.,** hablar claro, hablar sin rodeos

frankness n franqueza, f; sinceridad, f; candor, m

frantic a frenético, furioso, loco. **He drives me f.,** Me vuelve loco

fraternal a fraterno, fraternal

fraternity n fraternidad, hermandad, f

fraternization n fraternización, f

fraternize vi fraternizar

fratricidal a fratricida

fratricide n (person) fratricida, mf; (action) fratricidio, m

fraud n fraude, m; engaño, embuste, Argentina also forro m; (person) farsante, m, embustero (-ra)

fraudulence n fraudulencia, fraude, f

fraudulent a fraudulento

fraught a (with) cargado de; lleno de, preñado de

fray n refriega, riña, f; combate, m, batalla, f; (rubbing) raedura, f. vt raer, tazar. vi tazarse, deshilarse

frayed a raído

fraying n raedura, deshiladura, f

freak n monstruo, m; fenómeno, m; (whim) capricho, m

freakish a monstruoso; caprichoso; extravagante; raro, singular

freakishness n carácter caprichoso, m; extravagancia, f; rareza, extrañeza, f

freckle n peca, f. vi tener pecas; salir pecas (a la cara, etc.)

freckled a pecoso, con pecas

free a (in most senses) libre; independiente; emancipado; desembarazado; abierto; limpio (de); franco; (voluntary) voluntario; (self-governing) autónomo, independiente; accesible; (disengaged) desocupado; (vacant) vacío; (exempt) exento (de); (immune) immune (de); ajeno; gratuito; (loose) suelto; (generous) generoso, liberal; (vicious) disoluto, licencioso; (bold) atrevido; (impudent) insolente, demasiado familiar. adv gratis, gratuitamente. **There are two f. seats in the train,** Hay dos asientos libres en el tren. **to get f.,** libertarse. **to make f. with,** tomarse libertades con; usar como si fuera suyo. **to set f.,** poner en libertad. **f. agent,** libre albedrío, m. **f. and easy,** familiar, sin ceremonia. **f. gift,** com objeto de reclamo, m. **f.-hand drawing,** dibujo a pulso, m. **f. kick,** sport golpe franco, m. **f. love,** amor libre, m. **f. play,** rienda suelta, f; mech holgura, f. **f. port,** puerto franco, m. **f. speech,** libertad de palabra, f. **f. thought,** libre pensamiento, m. **f. ticket,** theat billete de favor, m. **f. trade,** la librecambista. n librecambio, m. **f. trader,** librecambista, mf. **f. verse,** verso libre, verso suelto, m. **f.-wheeling,** desenfrenado, libre. **f. will,** propia voluntad, f; (theology) libre albedrío, m

free vt libertar, poner en libertad (a); librar (de); (slave) salvar; emancipar; exentar; (of obstacles, difficulties) desembarazar; **to f. from,** libertar de; librar de; (clean) limpiar de

freedom n libertad, f; independencia, f; exención, f; inmunidad, f; soltura, facilidad, f, franqueza, f; (over-familiarity) insolencia, f; (boldness) audacia, intrepidez, f; (of customs) licencia, f. **to receive the f. of a city,** ser recibido como ciudadano de honor. **f. of speech,** libertad de palabra, f. **f. of the press,** libertad de la prensa, f. **f. of worship,** libertad de cultos, f

freeing n liberación, f; emancipación, f; salvación, f; (from obstruction) desembarazo, m; limpieza, f

freelance n mil soldado libre, m; pol independiente, m; aventurero (-ra). **f. journalist,** periodista libre, m

freethinker n librepensador (-ra)

freeze vt helar; (meat, etc.) congelar; fig helar. vi helarse; congelarse; (impers, of the weather) helar. **to f. to death,** morir de frío

freezing n hielo, m; congelación, f. a glacial; congelante, frigorífico. **f. mixture,** mezcla frigorífica, *f*. **f. of assets,** bloqueo de los depósitos bancarios, *m*. **f.-point,** punto de congelación, *m*. **above f.-point,** sobre cero. **below f.-point,** bajo cero

freight *n* flete, *m*; porte, *m*. *vt* fletar

freighter *n* fletador, *m*; (ship) buque de carga, *m*

French *a* francés. *n* (language) francés, *m*; (people) los franceses, *m pl*. **in F. fashion,** a la francesa. **to take F. leave,** despedirse a la inglesa. **What is the F. for "hat"?** ¿Cómo se dice «sombrero» en francés? **F. spoken,** Se habla francés. **F. bean,** judía, *f*. **F. chalk,** jabón de sastre, *m*. **F. horn,** trompa, *f*. **F. lesson,** lección de francés, *f*. **F. marigold,** flor del estudiante, *f*. **F. polish,** barniz de muebles, *m*. **F. poodle,** perro (-rra) de aguas. **F. roll,** panecillo, *m*. **F. window,** puerta ventana, *f*

Frenchman *n* francés, *m*. **a young F.,** un joven francés

Frenchwoman *n* francesa, mujer francesa, *f*. **a young F.,** una joven francesa, una muchacha francesa, *f*

frenzied *a* frenético

frenzy *n* frenesí, delirio, paroxismo, *m*

frequency *n* frecuencia, *f*. **high f.,** alta frecuencia, *f*. **low f.,** baja frecuencia, *f*

frequent *a* frecuente; (usual) común, corriente. *vt* frecuentar

frequently *adv* frecuentemente, con frecuencia, muchas veces; comúnmente

fresco *n art* fresco, *m*, pintura al fresco, *f*. *vt* pintar al fresco

fresh *a* fresco; nuevo; reciente; (newly arrived) recién llegado; (inexperienced) inexperto, bisoño; (of water, not salt) dulce; puro; (healthy) sano; (brisk) vigoroso, enérgico; (vivid) vivo, vívido; (bright) brillante; (cheeky) fresco, *Lat. Am.* impávido. *adv* nuevamente, recién (with past participle). **He came to us f. from school,** Vino a nosotros recién salido de su colegio. **We are going to take the f. air,** Vamos a tomar el fresco. **The milk is not f.,** La leche no está fresca. **f.-complexioned,** de buenos colores. **f. news,** noticias nuevas, *f pl*. **f. troops,** tropas nuevas, *f pl*, (reinforcements) tropas de refuerzo, *f pl*. **f. water,** agua fresca, *f*; (not salt) agua dulce, *f*. **f.-water shrimp** *Mexico* acocil *m*. **f. wind,** viento fresco, *m*

freshen *vt* refrescar; (remove salt) desalar. *vi* (wind) refrescar. **to f. up,** renovar; refrescar; (of dress, etc.) arreglar

freshly *adv* nuevamente; recientemente

freshness *n* frescura, *f*; (newness) novedad, *f*; (vividness, brightness) intensidad, *f*; pureza, *f*; (beauty) lozanía, hermosura, *f*; (cheek) frescura, *f*, descaro, *m*

freshwater *n* agua dulce, *f*. **f. sailor,** marinero de agua dulce, *m*

fret *n* agitación, *f*; ansiedad, preocupación, *f*; *arch* greca, *f*; (of stringed instrument) traste, *m*. *vt* roer; (of a horse) bocezar; (corrode) desgastar, corroer; (of the wind, etc.) rizar; (worry) tener preocupado (a); irritar, enojar; (lose) perder; (oneself) apurarse, consumirse; *arch* calar. *vi* torturarse, preocuparse, inquietarse; (complain) quejarse; (mourn) lamentarse, estar triste

fretful *a* mal humorado, mohíno, quejoso, irritable

fretwork *n* calado, *m*

Freudian *a* freudiano

friar *n* fraile, *m*. **Black f.,** dominicano, *m*. **Gray f.,** franciscano, *m*. **White f.,** carmelita, *m*. **f.-like,** frailesco

friction *n* frote, frotamiento, roce, *m*; *phys* rozamiento, *m*; fricción, *f*. **to give a f.,** friccionar, dar fricciones (a). **f. gearing,** engranaje de fricción, *m*. **f. glove,** guante de fricciones, *m*

Friday *n* viernes, *m*. **Good F.,** Viernes Santo, *m*

fried *a* frito. **f. egg,** huevo frito, *m*

friend *n* amigo (-ga); (acquaintance) conocido (-da); (Quaker) cuáquero (-ra); (follower) adherente, *mf*; partidario (-ia); (ally) aliado (-da); *pl* **friends,** amistades, *f pl*; amigos, *m pl*. **a f. of yours,** un amigo tuyo, uno de tus amigos. **to make friends,** hacer amigos; (become friends) hacerse amigos; (after a quarrel) hacer las paces. **Friends!** (to sentinel) ¡Gente de paz!

friendless *a* sin amigos; desamparado

friendliness *n* amabilidad, afabilidad, cordialidad, amigabilidad, *f*

friendly *a* amistoso, amigable, amigo; afable, acogedor, simpático; propicio, favorable. **to be f. with,** ser amigo de. **f. society,** sociedad de socorros, *f*

friendship *n* amistad, intimidad, *f*

fright *n* terror, susto, *m*; (guy) espantajo, *m*. *vt* asustar. **to have a f.,** tener un susto. **to take f.,** asustarse

frighten *vt* espantar, dar un susto (a), alarmar, asustar; horrorizar; (overawe) acobardar. **to be frightened out of one's wits,** estar muerto de miedo. **to f. away,** ahuyentar, espantar

frightened *a* miedoso, tímido, medroso, nervioso

frightening *a* que da miedo; alarmante, amedrentador; horrible

frightful *a* horrible, espantoso, horroroso; *inf* tremendo, enorme

frightfully *adv* horrorosamente, *inf* enormemente

frigid *a* frío; helado; *med* impotente

frigidity *n* frialdad, frigidez, *f*; *med* impotencia, *f*

frill *n sew* volante, *m*; (jabot) chorrera, *f*; (round a bird's neck) collarín de plumas, m; (of paper) frunce, m. vt alechugar; fruncir

fringe n fleco, m, franja, f, Lat. Am. cerquillo f; (of hair) flequillo, m; (edge) borde, m, margen, mf. vt guarnecer con fleco, franjar; adornar; (grow by) crecer al margen (de)

frisk vi retozar, brincar

frisky a retozón, juguetón

fritter n cul fruta de sartén, f. vt (away) malgastar, desperdiciar; perder

frivolity n frivolidad, ligereza, f; futilidad, f

frivolous a frívolo, ligero, liviano; (futile) trivial, fútil

frizzy a (of hair) crespo, rizado

fro adv hacia atrás. **movement to and fro,** vaivén, m. **to and fro,** de un lado a otro. **to go to and fro,** ir y venir

frog n rana, f. **to have a f. in the throat,** padecer carraspera

frolic n (play) juego, m; (mischief) travesura, f; (folly) locura, extravagancia, f; (joke) chanza, f; (amusement) diversión, f; (wild party) holgorio, m, parranda, f. vi retozar, juguetear; divertirse

frolicsome a retozón, juguetón

from prep de; desde; (according to) según; (in the name of, on behalf of) de parte de; (through, by) por; (beginning on) a contar de; (with) con; **F.** (on envelope) Remite, Remitente. **He is coming here f. the dentist's,** Vendrá aquí desde casa del dentista. **Give him this message f. me,** Dale este recado de mi parte. **Judging f. his appearance,** Juzgando por su apariencia. **prices f. five hundred pesetas upward,** precios desde quinientos pesetas en adelante. **f. what I hear,** según mi información, según lo que oigo. **f. above,** desde arriba. **f. among,** de entre. **f. afar,** de lejos, desde lejos. **f. time to time,** de cuando en cuando, de vez en cuando

front n frente, f; cara, f; mil frente, m; (battle line) línea de combate, f; (of a building) fachada, f; (of shirt) pechera, f; (at the seaside) playa, f; (promenade) paseo de la playa, m; (forefront) primera línea, f; (forepart) parte delantera, f; theat auditorio, m; (organization) organización de fachada, f; (impudence) descaro, m, a delantero; anterior; de frente; primero. adv hacia delante. vi mirar a, dar a; hacer frente a. **in f.,** en frente. **in f. of,** en frente de; (in the presence of) delante de, en la presencia de. **to face f.,** hacer frente. **to put on a bold f.,** hacer de tripas corazón. **f. door,** puerta de entrada, puerta principal, f. **f. line,** mil línea del frente, f; primera línea, f. **f. seat,** (at an entertainment, etc.) delantera, f. **f. organization,** organización de fachada f. **f. tooth,** diente incisivo, m. **f. view,** vista de frente, f; vista de cerca, f

frontage n (of a building) fachada, f; (site) terreno de . . . metros de fachada, m

frontal a mil de frente; anat frontal

frontier n frontera, f; fig límite, m. a fronterizo

frost n escarcha, f; helada, f. vt helar; cul escarchar; (glass) deslustrar; fig escarchar. vi helar. **f.-bitten,** helado

frostbite n efectos del frío, m pl

frosted a escarchado; helado; (of glass) deslustrado, opaco; cul escarchado

frosting n escarcha, f; (of glass) deslustre, m; cul cobertura, escarcha, f

frosty a helado; de hielo; (of hair) canoso; fig glacial, frío. **It was f. last night,** Anoche heló

froth n espuma, f; fig frivolidad, vanidad, f, vi espumar, hacer espuma; echar espuma. vt hacer espumar; hacer echar espuma

frothy a espumoso, espumajoso; fig frívolo, superficial

frown n ceño, m; cara de juez, expresión severa, f; desaprobación, f; (of fortune) revés, golpe, m. vi fruncir el ceño. **to f. at, on, upon,** mirar con desaprobación, ver con malos ojos; ser enemigo de; desaprobar

frowning a ceñudo; severo; amenazador

frowsy a fétido; mal oliente; mal ventilado; (dirty) sucio; (untidy) desaliñado, desaseado

frozen a helado; cubierto de hielo; congelado; (geog and fig) glacial. **to be f. up,** estar helado. **f. meat,** carne congelada, f

frugal a económico; frugal; sobrio

frugality n economía, f; frugalidad, sobriedad, f

fruit n (in general sense) fruto, m; (off a tree or bush) fruta, f; fig fruto, m; resultado, m, consecuencia, f. vi frutar, dar fruto. **bottled f.,** fruta en almíbar, f. **candied f.,** fruta azucarada, f. **dried f.,** fruta seca, f. **first fruits,** primicias, f pl. **soft f.,** frutas blandas, f pl. **stone f.,** fruta de hueso, f. **f.-bearing,** frutal. **f.-cake,** pastel de fruta, m. **f.-dish,** frutero, m. **f. farming,** fruticultura, f. **f.-knife,** cuchillo de postres, m. **f. shop,** frutería, f. **f. tree,** frutal, m

fruiterer n frutero (-ra)

fruitful a fructuoso, fértil; prolífico, fecundo; provechoso

fruitfulness n fertilidad, f; fecundidad, f; provecho, m

fruition n fruición, f

fruitless a infructuoso, estéril; inútil

fruity a de fruta; (wines) vinoso; (of voice) melodioso

frump n estantigua, f

frumpish a estrafalario; fuera de moda

frustrate vt frustrar; defraudar; malograr; destruir; anular

frustration n frustración, f; defraudación, *f*; malogro, *m*; destrucción, *f*; desengaño, *m*

fry *n cul* fritada, *f*, *vt* freír. *vi* freírse. **small fry,** *inf* gente menuda, *f*

frying *n* fritura, *f*, el freír. **to fall out of the f.-pan into the fire,** ir de mal en peor, andar de zocos en colodros, ir de Guatemala en Guatepeor. **f.-pan,** sartén, *f*

fuddle *vt* atontar, aturdir; embriagar, emborrachar

fudge *n* patraña, tontería, *f*, disparate, *m*; (food) *Lat. Am.* manjar *m. interj* ¡qué disparate! ¡qué va!

fuel *n* combustible, *m; fig* cebo, pábulo, *m. vt* cebar, echar combustible en. *vi* tomar combustible. **to add f. to the flame,** echar leña al fuego. **f. consumption,** consumo de combustible, *m.* **f.-oil,** aceite combustible, aceite de quemar, *m.* **f.-tank,** depósito de combustible, *m*

fugitive *a* fugitivo; pasajero, perecedero; transitorio, efímero, fugaz. *n* fugitivo (-va); (from justice) prófugo (-ga); *mil* desertor, *m*; (refugee) refugiado (-da)

fugue *n mus* fuga, *f*

fulcrum *n mech* fulcro, *m*

fulfil *vt* cumplir; (satisfy) satisfacer; (observe) observar; guardar. **to be fulfilled,** cumplirse, realizarse

fulfilment *n* cumplimiento, *m*; desempeño, ejercicio, *m*; (satisfaction) satisfacción, realización, *f*; (observance) observancia, *f*

full *a* lleno; colmado; todo; pleno; (crowded) atestado; (replete) harto; abundante; (intent on) preocupado con, pensando en; (loose) amplio; (plentiful) copioso; (occupied) ocupado; completo; (resonant) sonoro; (mature) maduro; puro; perfecto; (satiated) saciado (de); (of the moon, sails) lleno; (weighed down) agobiado, abrumado; (detailed) detallado; (with uniform, etc.) de gala; (with years, etc.) cumplido. *n* colmo, *m*;.totalidad, *f. adv* muy; completamente, totalmente. **f. many a flower,** muchas flores. **at f. gallop,** a galope tendido. **at f. speed,** a todo correr; a toda velocidad. **His hands are f.,** Sus manos están llenas. **The moon was at the f.,** La luna estaba llena. **in f.,** por completo; sin abreviaciones; integralmente. **in f. swing,** en plena actividad. **in f. vigor,** en pleno vigor. **to the f.,** completamente; hasta la última gota; a la perfección. **to be f. to the brim,** estar lleno hasta el tope. **f.-blooded,** sanguíneo; de pura raza; *fig* viril, vigoroso; *fig* apasionado. **f.-blown,** en plena flor, abierto. **f. dress,** *a* de gala. *n* traje de etiqueta, traje de ceremonia, *m.* **f.-face,** de cara. **f.-flavored,** (wine) abocado. **f.-grown,** adulto; completamente desarrollado. **f.-length,** de cuerpo entero. **f. moon,** luna llena, *f*; plenilunio, *m.* **f. name,** nombre y apellidos, *m.* **f. powers,** plenos poderes, *m*

pl. **f. scale,** tamaño natural, *m.* **f. scope,** carta blanca, *f*; toda clase de facilidades. **f. steam ahead,** a todo vapor. **f. stop,** *gram* punto final, *m*

full-color *a* a todo color. **full-color plates,** láminas a todo color

fullness *n* abundancia, *f*; plenitud, *f*; (repletion) hartura, *f*; (of clothes) amplitud, *f*; (stoutness) gordura, *f*; (swelling) hinchazón, *f.* **She wrote with great f. of all that she had seen,** Describía muy detalladamente todo lo que había visto. **in the f. of time,** andando el tiempo

full-page *a* a toda plana. **full-page advertisement,** anuncio a toda plana.

full-time *a* de tiempo completo

fully *adv* plenamente; enteramente. **It is f. six years since . . . ,** Hace seis años bien cumplidos que . . . **It is f. 9 o'clock,** Son las nueve bien sonadas. **f. dressed,** completamente vestido

fulminous *a* fulmíneo, fulminoso

fulsome *a* servil; insincero, hipócrita; asqueroso, repugnante

fumble *vi* (grope) ir a tientas; procurar hacer algo; chapucear (con); (for a word) titubear

fumbling *n* hesitación, *f*; tacto incierto, *m.* *a* incierto; vacilante

fume *n* vaho, humo, gas, *m*; emanación, *f*; mal olor, *m*, fetidez, *f*; *fig* vapor, *m*; (state of mind) agitación, *f*; frenesí, *m. vi* humear; refunfuñar, echar pestes, *Lat. Am.* estar hecho unají

fumigate *vt* fumigar, *Lat. Am.* also humear; sahumar, perfumar; desinfectar

fumigation *n* fumigación, *f*; sahumerio, *m*

fumigator *n* fumigador (-ra); (apparatus) fumigador, *m*

fuming *n* refunfuño, *m.* a refunfuñador

fun *n* diversión, *f*, entretenimiento, *m*; (joke) chanza, broma, *f.* **for fun,** para divertirse; en chanza. **in fun,** de burlas. **to have fun,** divertirse. **to poke fun at,** burlarse de, mofarse de, ridiculizar

function *n* función, *f. vi* funcionar

functional *a* funcional

functionary *n* funcionario, *m.* a funcional

functioning *n* funcionamiento, *m*

fund *n* fondo, *m; pl* **funds,** fondos, *m pl; inf* dinero, *m.* **public funds,** fondos públicos, *m pl.* **sinking f.,** fondo de amortización, *m*

fundamental *a* fundamental, básico; esencial. *n* fundamento, *m*

funeral *a* funeral, fúnebre, funerario. *n* funerales, *m pl.* **to attend the f. (of),** asistir a los funerales (de). **f. feast,** banquetes fúnebres, *m pl.* **f. director, f. furnisher,** director de pompas fúnebres, *m.* **f. procession,** cortejo fúnebre, *m*. **f. pyre,** pira funeraria, *f*. **f. service,** misa de difuntos, *f*

funereal *a* fúnebre, lúgubre

fungicide *n* anticriptógamo, *m*

fungous *a* fungoso

fungus *n* hongo, *m*

funicular *a* funicular. **f. railway,** ferrocarril funicular, *m*

funnel *n chem* embudo, *m*; *naut* chimenea, *f*; (of a chimney) cañón (de chimenea), *m*. **f.-shaped,** en forma de embudo

funny *a* cómico, gracioso; divertido; (strange) extraño, raro; (mysterious) misterioso. **It struck me as f.,** (amused me) Me hizo gracia; (seemed strange) Me pareció raro. **f.-bone,** hueso de la alegría, *m*

fur *n* piel, *f*; depósito, sarro, *m*; (on tongue) saburra, *f*. **a hecho de pieles**. *vt* forrar, or adornar, or cubrir, con pieles; depositar sarro sobre; (the tongue) ensuciarse la lengua. *vi* estar forrado, or adornado, or cubierto, con pieles; formarse incrustaciones; (of the tongue) tener la lengua sucia. **fur cap,** gorra de pieles, *f*. **fur cape,** cuello de piel, *m*; capa de pieles, *f*. **fur trade,** peletería, *f*

furbish *vt* pulir; renovar; limpiar

furious *a* furioso. **to become f.,** ponerse furioso, enfurecerse

furl *vt* plegar; enrollar; *naut* aferrar

furlough *n mil* permiso, *m*. *vt* conceder un permiso (a). **on f.,** de permiso

furnace *n* horno, *m*; (of steam boiler) fogón, *m*; (for central heating) caldera de calefacción central, *f*; (for smelting) cubilote, *m*

furnish *vt* proveer (de), equipar (de), suplir (de); amueblar; (an opportunity) proporcionar; producir

furnished *a* amueblado, con muebles. **f. house,** casa amueblada, *f*

furnishing *n* provisión, *f*, equipo, *m*; *pl* **furnishings,** accesorios, *m pl*; mobiliario, mueblaje, *m*

furniture *n* mobiliario, mueblaje, *Central America, Mexico* amoblado *m*; ajuar, equipo, *m*; avíos, *m pl*; *naut* aparejo, *m*. **a piece of f.,** un mueble. **to empty of f.,** desamueblar, quitar los muebles (de). **f. dealer** or **maker,** mueblista, *mf*. **f. factory,** mueblería, *f*. **f. polish,** crema para muebles, *f*. **f. mover,** transportador de muebles, *m*; (packer) embalador, *m*. **f. repository,** guardamuebles, *m*. **f. van,** carro de mudanzas, *m*

furor *n* furor, *m*

furred *a* forrado or cubierto or adornado de piel; (of the tongue) sucia

furrier *n* peletero, *m*. **furrier's shop,** peletería, *f*

furrow *n* surco, *m*; *carp* muesca, *f*; *arch* estría, *f*; (wrinkle) arruga, *f*. *vt* surcar

furry *a* cubierto de piel; parecido a una piel; hecho de pieles

further *a* ulterior, más distante; (other) otro; opuesto; adicional, más. *adv* más lejos; más allá; además; también; por añadidura. *vt* promover, fomentar; ayudar. **on the f. side,** al otro lado. **till f. orders,** hasta nueva orden. **f. on,** más adelante; más allá

furtherance *n* fomento, *m*, promoción, *f*; progreso, avance, *m*

furthermore *adv* además, por añadidura

furthest *a* (el, la, lo) más lejano or más distante; extremo. *adv* más lejos

furtive *a* furtivo

furtively *adv* furtivamente, a hurtadillas. **to look at f.,** mirar de reojo

fury *n* furor, enfurecimiento, *m*, rabia, *f*; violencia, *f*; frenesí, arrebato, *m*; furia, *f*. **like a f.,** hecho una furia. **to breathe forth f.,** echar rayos

fuse *n* (of explosives) espoleta, mecha, *f*; *elec* fusible, *m*. *vt* (metals) fundir; fusionar, mezclar. *vi* (metals) fundirse; mezclarse. **safety-f.,** espoleta de seguridad, *f*. **time-f.,** espoleta de tiempo, *f*. **to blow a f.,** fundir un fusible. **f. box,** caja de fusibles, *f*. **f. wire,** fusible, *m*

fuselage *n aer* fuselaje, *m*

fusion *n* fusión, *f*; unión, *f*; (melting) fundición, *f*

fuss *n* agitación, *f*; (bustle) conmoción, bulla, *f*; bullicio, *m*. *vi* agitarse, preocuparse. *vt* poner nervioso. **There's no need to make such a f.,** No es para tanto. **to make a f. of,** (a person) hacer la rueda (a), ser muy atento (a); (spoil) mimar mucho (a). **to f. about,** andar de acá para allá

fussy *a* meticuloso, nimio; nervioso; (of style) florido, hinchado; (of dress) demasiado adornado

fustigate *vt* fustigar

fusty *a* (moldy) mohoso; mal ventilado; mal oliente; (of views, etc.) pasado de moda

futile *a* fútil, superficial, frívolo; inútil

futility *n* futilidad, superficialidad, frivolidad, *f*; (action) tontería, estupidez, *f*

future *a* futuro, venidero. *n* futuro, porvenir, *m*. **in the f.,** en adelante, en lo venidero, en lo sucesivo. **for f. reference,** para información futura. **f. perfect tense,** *gram* futuro perfecto, *m*. **f. tense,** *gram* futuro, *m*

fuzz *n* tamo, *m*, pelusa, *f*. **f.-ball,** *bot* bejín, *m*

fuzzy *a* crespo rizado; velloso

G

g *n* (letter) ge, *f*; *mus* sol, *m*. **G clef,** clave de sol, *f*

gab *n inf* labia, *f*. **to have the gift of the gab,** tener mucha labia

gabble *vi* chacharear, garlar; hablar indistintamente; (of goose and some birds) graznar. *vt* decir indistintamente; decir rápidamente; (a language) chapurrear; mascullar. *n* cháchara, *f*; vocerío, *m*; (of goose and some birds) graznido, *m*

gabbler *n* charlatán (-ana), chacharero (-ra)

gad *vi* corretear, callejear. **to gad about,** correr por todos lados; divertirse.

gadabout *n* azotacalles, *mf*; gandul (-la), vagabundo (-da)

gadding *a* callejero; vagabundo. *n* vagancia, *f*; vida errante, *f*; gandulería, *f*

gadfly *n ent* tábano, *m*; *inf* moscardón, *m*

gadget *n* accesorio, *m*; aparato, *m*; chuchería, *f*

Gadsden Purchase la Venta de la Meseta, *f*

gaff *n* (hook) garfio, *m*; *naut* pico de cangrejo, *m*; *theat* teatrucho, *m*

gag *n* mordaza, *f*; *theat* morcilla, *f*. *vt* amordazar; *fig* hacer callar. *vi theat* meter morcillas

gage *n* prenda, fianza, *f*; (symbol of challenge) guante, *m*; (challenge) desafío, *m*. See **gauge**

gaggle *n* (cry) graznido, *m*; (of geese) manada (de ocas), *f*. *vi* graznar; cacarear

gaiety *n* alegría, *f*; animación, vivacidad, *f*; (entertainment) diversión, festividad, *f*

gain *n* ganancia, *f*; provecho, beneficio, *m*; (increase) aumento, *m*; (riches) riqueza, *f*. *vt* ganar; (acquire) conseguir; adquirir; obtener; conquistar; captar; (friends) hacerse; (reach) llegar a, alcanzar. *vi* ganar; (improve) mejorar; (of a watch) adelantarse. **What have they gained by going to Canada?** ¿Qué han logrado con marcharse al Canadá? **to g. ground,** *fig* ganar terreno. **to g. momentum** adquirir velocidad **to g. time,** ganar tiempo. **to g. on, upon,** acercarse a; (overtake) alcanzar; (outstrip) dejar atrás, pasar; (of sea) invadir; (of habits) imponerse

gainful *a* ganancioso, lucrativo; ventajoso

gainfully *adv* ventajosamente; lucrativamente

gainsay *vt* contradecir; oponer; negar

gait *n* porte, andar, *m*; paso, *m*, andadura, *f*

gala *n* gala, fiesta, *f*. **g.-day.** día de fiesta, *m*. **g.-dress,** traje de gala, *m*

galaxy *n ast* vía láctea, *f*; *fig* constelación, *f*; grupo brillante, *m*

gale *n* vendaval, ventarrón, *m*; (storm) temporal, *m*; tempestad, *f*

Galician *a* and *n* gallego (-ga).

Galilean *a* and *n* galileo (-ea)

Galilee Galilea, *f*

gall *n* (on horses) matadura, *f*; (abrasion) rozadura, *f*; hiel, bilis, *f*; *fig* hiel, amargura, *f*; rencor, *m*; (American slang) descaro, *m*, impertinencia, *f*; *bot* agalla, *f*. *vt* rozar; *fig* mortificar, herir. **g.-apple,** agalla, *f*. **g.-bladder,** vejiga de la hiel, *f*. **g.-stone,** cálculo hepático, *m*

gallant *a* hermoso; (imposing) imponente, majestuoso; (brave) valiente, gallardo, valeroso, intrépido; (chivalrous) caballeroso; noble; (attentive to ladies, or amorous) galante. *n* galán, *m*. *vt* galantear, cortejar

gallantly *adv* (bravely) valientemente; caballerosamente; cortésmente; galantemente

gallantry *n* (bravery) valentía, *f*, valor, *m*; heroísmo, *m*, proeza, *f*; (chivalry) caballerosidad, *f*; (toward women, or amorousness) galantería, *f*

gallery *n* galería, *f*; pasillo, *m*; (of a cloister) tránsito, *m*; (cloister) claustro, *m*; (for spectators) tribuna, *f*; *theat* paraíso, gallinero, *m*; (theater audience) galería, *f*; (of portraits, etc.) galería, colección, *f*; (min, mil) galería, *f*; (building) museo, *m*. **art g.,** museo de pinturas, *m*

galley *n* (naut, print) galera, *f*; (kitchen) cocina, *f*; (rowboat) falúa de capitán, *f*. **to condemn to the galleys,** echar a galeras. **wooden g.,** *print* galerín, *m*. **g.-proof,** galerada, *f*. **g.-slave,** galeote, *m*

galling *a fig* irritante; mortificante

gallivant *vi* callejear, corretear; divertirse; ir de parranda

gallon *n* galón, *m*

gallop *n* galope, *m*. *vi* galopar; ir aprisa. *vt* hacer galopar, **at full g.,** a rienda suelta, a galope tendido. **to g. back,** volver a galope. **to g. down,** bajar a galope. **to g. off,** marcharse galopando; alejarse corriendo. **to g. past,** desfilar a galope ante. **to g. through,** cruzar a galope. **to g. up,** *vt* subir a galope. *vi* llegar a galope

gallopade *n* (dance) galop, *m*

galloping *n* galope, *m*; galopada, *f*. *a* que va a galope; *med* galopante. **g. consumption,** tisis galopante, *f*

gallows *n* patíbulo, *m*, horca, *f*; (framework) montante, *m*. **g.-bird,** criminal digno de la horca, *f*

galop *n* galop, *m*

galore *adv* a granel, en abundancia (e.g. **sunshine galore,** sol a granel)

galosh *n* chanclo, *m*

gambit n (chess) gambito, m; fig táctica, f

gamble n juego de azar, m; jugada, f; aventura, f; com especulación, f. vi jugar por dinero; especular; (with) fig aventurar, arriesgar. **to g. on the Stock Exchange,** jugar en la bolsa. **to g. away,** perder al juego

gambler n jugador (-ra), Mexico dadista mf

gambling n juego, m. a jugador; de juego. **g.-den,** casa de juego, f, garito, m

gambol n salto, brinco, retozo, m; cabriola, f; juego, m. vi saltar, brincar, retozar; juguetear

game n juego, m; (match) partido, m; (jest) chanza, f; (trick) trampa, f; (birds, hares, etc.) caza menor, f; (tigers, lions, etc.) caza mayor, f; (flesh of game) caza, f; pl **games,** deportes, m pl. a caza; (courageous) valiente, animoso, brioso; resuelto. vi jugar por dinero. **He is g. for anything,** Se atreve a todo. **big g. hunting,** caza mayor, f. **head of g.,** pieza de caza, f. **It is a g. at which two can play,** Donde las dan las toman. **The g. is not worth the candle,** La cosa no vale la pena. **The g. is up,** fig El proyecto se ha frustrado. **to make g. of,** (things) burlarse de; (persons) tomar el pelo a; mofarse de. **to play the g.,** fig jugar limpio. **to g. away,** perder al juego. **g. of cards,** juego de naipes, m. **g. of chance,** juego de azar, m. **g.-bag,** morral, m. **g. drive,** batida de caza, f. **g.-laws,** leyes de caza, f pl. **g.-licence,** licencia de caza, f. **g.-pie,** tortada, f. **g. preserve,** coto de caza, m

gamely adv valientemente

gaming n juego, m, a de juego. **g.-house,** garito, m. **g.-table,** mesa de juego, f; fig juego, m

gamut n gama, f

gander n ganso, m

gang n cuadrilla, pandilla, Mexico carpanta f; (squad) pelotón, m; (of workers) brigada, cuadrilla, f; group, m. **g.-plank,** plancha, f

ganglion n ganglio, m; fig centro, m

gangrene n gangrena, f. vt gangrenar. vi gangrenarse

gangster n pistolero, gángster, m

gangway n pasillo, m; naut plancha, f, pasamano, m; (opening in ship's side) portalón, m. **midship g.,** crujía, f

gap n brecha, f; abertura, f; (hole) boquete, m; (pass) desfiladero, paso, m; (ravine) hondonada, barranca, f; (blank) laguna, f, vacío, m; (crack) intersticio, m, hendedura, f, resquicio, m. **to fill a gap,** llenar un boquete; llenar un vacío

gape vi estar con la boca abierta, papar moscas. **to g. at,** mirar con la boca abierta

gaping n huelgo, m; abertura, f, a que bosteza; boquiabierto; abierto

garage n garaje, m. vt poner (un coche, etc.) en un garaje. **g. owner,** garajista, mf

garb n traje, vestido, m; uniforme, m; her espiga, f. vt vestir, ataviar

garbage n basura, inmundicia, f

garbage can basurero, tarro de la basura, m

garbage dump Lat. Am. basural m

garble vt falsear, mutilar, pervertir

garden n jardín, m; huerto, m; (fertile region) huerta, f. a de jardín. vi trabajar en el jardín, cultivar un huerto. **g. city,** ciudad jardín, f. **g.-frame,** semillero, m. **g. mold,** tierra vegetal, f. **g.-party,** fiesta de jardín, f. **g.-plot,** parterre, m. **g. produce,** hortalizas, legumbres, f pl. **g. roller,** rodillo, m. **g.-seat,** banco de jardín, m. **g. urn,** jarrón, m

gardener n jardinero, m

gardening n jardinería, f; horticultura, f. a de jardinería

gargantuan a gargantuesco; tremendo, enorme

gargle n (liquid) gargarismo, m; gárgaras, f pl. vi hacer gárgaras, gargarizar

garish a cursi, llamativo, charro, chillón

garishness n cursería, ostentación, f, lo llamativo

garland n guirnalda, f; corona, f; (anthology) florilegio, m; arch festón, m. vt enguirnaldar

garlic n ajo, m

garment n prenda de vestir, f; traje, vestido, m; fig vestidura, f; (fig cloak) capa, f

garner n granero, m; tesoro, m; colección, f. vt atesorar, guardar

garnet n granate, m

garnish n cul aderezo, m; adorno, m. vt cul aderezar; embellecer, adornar

garret n guardilla, buhardilla, f, desván, m

garrison n guarnición, f, presidio, m. vt guarnecer, presidiar. **g. town,** plaza de armas, f

garrulous a gárrulo, locuaz, charlatán

garter n liga, f; (G.) Jarretera, f, vt atar con liga; investir con la Jarretera. **Order of the G.,** Orden de la Jarretera, f

gas n gas, m; fig, inf palabrería, f; (petrol) bencina, f, a de gas; con gas; para gases. vt asfixiar con gas; mil atacar con gas; saturar de gas. **gas attack,** ataque con gases asfixiantes, m. **gas-bag,** bolsa de gas, f; inf charlatán (-ana). **gas-burner,** mechero de gas, m. **gas-chamber,** cámara de gas, f. **gas detector,** detector de gases, m. **gas-fire,** estufa de gas, f. **gas-fitter,** gasista, m. **gas-fittings,** lámparas de gas, f pl. **gas-light,** luz de gas, f; mechero de gas, m. **gas-main,** cañería maestra de gas, f. **gas-man,** gasista, m. **gas-mantle,** camiseta incandescente, f. **gas-mask,** máscara para gases, f. **gas-meter,** contador de gas, m. **gas-pipes,** cañerías (or tuberías) de gas, *f pl.* **gas-ring,** fogón de gas, *m.* **gas-shell,** obús de gases asfixiantes, *m.* **gas-stove,** cocina de gas, *f.* **gas warfare,** guerra química, *f.* **gas-works,** fábrica de gas, *f*

gaseous *a* gaseoso

gash *n* cuchillada, *f*; herida extensa, *f. vt* acuchillar; herir extensamente

gasket *n* aro de empaquetadura, *m*

gasoline *n* gasolina, *f*; bencina *f*

gasp *n* boqueada, *f. vi* boquear. **to be at the last g.,** estar agonizando. **to g. for breath,** luchar por respirar. **to g. out,** decir anhelante, decir con voz entrecortada

gastritis *n* gastritis, *f*

gate *n* puerta, *f*; cancela, verja, *f*; entrada, *f*; (of a lode, etc.) compuerta, *f*; (across a road, etc.) barrera, *f*; (money) entrada, *f*; *flg* puerta, *f.* **automatic g.,** (at level crossings, etc.) barrera de golpe, *f.* **to g.-crash,** asistir sin invitación. **g.-keeper,** portero, *m*; guardabarrera, *mf* **g.-money,** entrada, *f.* **g.-post,** soporte de la puerta, *m*

gateway *n* entrada, *f*; puerta; paso, *m*; vestíbulo, *m*; *flg* puerta, *f*

gather *vt* (assemble) reunir; (amass) acumular, amontonar; (acquire) obtener, adquirir; hacer una colección (de); cobrar; (harvest) cosechar, recolectar; (pick up) recoger; (pluck) coger; (infer) sacar en limpio, aprender; *sew* fruncir; (the brows) fruncir (el ceño). *vi* reunirse, congregarse; amontonarse; (threaten) amenazar; (sadden) amargar; *flg* hover over) cernerse (sobre); (increase) aumentar, crecer; (be covered) cubrirse; (fester) supurar. *n sew* frunce, pliegue, *m.* **to g. breath,** tomar aliento. **to g. speed,** ganar velocidad. **to g. strength,** cobrar fuerzas. **I g. from Mary that they are going abroad,** Según lo que me ha dicho María, van al extranjero. **to g. in,** juntar; reunir; (harvest) cosechar; coger. **to g. together,** *vt* reunir. *vi* reunirse. **to g. up,** recoger; coger; tomar; (one's limbs) encoger. **to g. up the threads,** *fig* recoger los hilos.

gatherer *n* cogedor, colector, *m*; (harvester) segador, *m*; (of grapes) vendimiador (-ra); (of taxes) recaudador, *m*

gathering *n* cogedura, *f*; (fruit, etc.) recolección, *f*; (of taxes) recaudación, *f*; amontonamiento, *m*; colección, *f*; *med* absceso, *m*; *sew* fruncimiento, *m*; (assembly) reunión, asamblea, *f*; (crowd) concurrencia, muchedumbre, *f*

gathers *n sew* fruncidos, pliegues, *m pl*

gauche *a* torpe, huraño

gaudily *adv* ostentosamente; brillantemente

gaudy *a* llamativo, vistoso, brillante, ostentoso

gauge *n* (of gun) calibre, *m*; (railway) entrevía, *f*; (for measuring) indicador, *m*; regla de medir, *f*; *naut* calado, *m*; *flg* medida, *f*; (test) indicación, *f*; (model) norma, *f. vt* calibrar; medir; estimar; (ship's capacity) arquear; (judge) juzgar; (size up) tomar la medida (de); *flg* interpretar; *sew* fruncir; (liquor) aforar. **broad (narrow) g. railway,** ferrocarril de vía ancha (estrecha), *m.* **pressure g.,** manómetro, *m.* **water g.,** indicador del nivel de agua, *m*

gauging *n* medida, *f*; (of ship's capacity) arqueo, *m*; (of liquor) aforamiento, *m*; *flg* apreciación, *f*; interpretación, *f*

gaunt *a* anguloso, huesudo, desvaído; (of houses, etc.) lúgubre

gauntlet *n* guante de manopla, *m*; (part of armor) manopla, *f*; guantelete, *m.* **to throw down the g.,** echar el guante, desafiar

gauze *n* gasa, *f*; (mist) bruma, *f.* **wire-g.,** tela metálica, *f*

gauzy *a* diáfano; de gasa

gawky *a* anguloso, desgarbado, torpe

gay *a* alegre; festivo, animado; ligero de cascos, disipado; homosexual; (of colors) brillante, llamativo

Gaza Strip la franja de Gaza, *f*

gaze *n* mirada, *f*; mirada fija, *f. vi* mirar; mirar fijamente, contemplar

gazing *n* contemplación, *f*, a contemplador; que presencia, que asiste a

gear *n* (apparel) atavíos, *m pl*; (harness) guarniciones, *f pl*, arneses, *m pl*; (tackle) utensilios, *m pl*, herramientas, *f pl*; *naut* aparejo, *m*; *mech* engranaje, *m*; juego, *m*, marcha, *f. vt* aparejar, enjaezar; *mech* poner en marcha, hacer funcionar. *vi* *mech* engranar, endentar. **low g.,** pimera velocidad, *f.* **neutral g.,** punto muerto, *m.* **reverse g.,** marcha atrás, *f.* **second g.,** segunda velocidad, *f.* **three-speed g.,** cambio de marchas de tres velocidades, *m.* **top g.,** tercera (or cuarta—according to gear-box) velocidad, *f.* **to change g.,** cambiar de marcha, cambiar de velocidad. **to throw out of g.,** *flg* desquiciar. **g.-box,** caja de velocidades, *f.* **g.-changing,** cambio de velocidad, *m.* **g.-changing lever,** palanca de cambio de velocidad, palanca de cambio de marchas, *f*

gehenna *n* gehena, *m*

gelatine *n* gelatina, *f.* **cooking g.,** gelatina seca, *f*

geld *vt* capar, castrar

gelding *n* castración, capadura, *f*; caballo castrado, *m*; animal castrado, *m*

gelid *a* gélido, helado; *flg* frío, frígido

gem *n* piedra preciosa, *f*; joya, alhaja, *f*; *flg* joya, *f. vt* adornar con piedras preciosos; enjoyar

gender *n gram* género, *m*; sexo, *m*

gene *n biol* gene, *m*

genealogical *a* genealógico. **g. tree,** árbol genealógico, *m*

general a general; universal; común; corriente; (usual) acostumbrado, usual; del público, público. *n* lo general; (*mil*, *ecc*) general, *m*; *inf* criada para todo, *f*. **in g.,** por lo general, en general, generalmente. **to become g.,** generalizarse. **to make g.,** generalizar, hacer general. **g. average,** (marine insurance) avería gruesa, *f*. **g. election,** elección general, *f*. **g. meeting,** pleno, mitin general, *m*. **g. opinion,** voz general, opinión general, *f*. **G. Post Office,** Oficina Central de Correos, *f*. **g. practitioner,** médico (-ca) general. **g. public,** público, *m*. **the general reader** el lector de tipo general *m*

generality *n* generalidad, *f*

generalization *n* generalización, *f*

generalize *vt* and *vi* generalizar

generally *adv* en general, por regla general, por lo general, generalmente; comúnmente, por lo común

generalship *n* mil generalato, *m*; (strategy) táctica, estrategia, *f*; dirección, jefatura, *f*

generate *vt* (beget) engendrar, procrear; (*phys*, *chem*) generar; *fig* producir, crear

generation *n* procreación, *f*; generación, *f*; *fig* producción, creación, *f*. **the younger g.,** los jóvenes

generative a generador

generator *n* *mech* generador, *m*; dínamo, *f*

generic a genérico

generosity *n* generosidad, *f*; liberalidad, *f*

generous a generoso; liberal, dadivoso, limosnero, *Lat. Am.* maniabierto; magnánimo; (plentiful) abundante; (of wines) generoso

generously *adv* generosamente; abundantemente

genesis *n* principio, origen, *m*; (G.) Génesis, *m*

genetic a genético

genetics *n* genética, *f*

Geneva Ginebra *f*

genial a (of climate) agradable, bueno; (of persons) afable, bondadoso; de buen humor, bonachón

geniality *n* afabilidad, bondad, *f*; buen humor, *m*

genially *adv* afablemente

genie *n* genio, *m*

genital a genital, sexual. *n pl* **genitals,** genitales, *m pl*

genius *n* genio, *m*; carácter, *m*, índole, *f*; ingenio, *m*; *inf* talento, *m*

Genoa Genova, *f*

Genoese a and *n* genovés (-esa)

genre *n* género, *m*. **g. painting,** cuadro de género, *m*

genteel a fino; (affected) remilgado, melindroso; de buen tono; de buena educación

gentile a and *n* gentil *mf*

gentility *n* aristocracia, *f*; respetabilidad, *f*

gentle a noble, bien nacido, de buena familia; amable; suave; ligero; dulce; (docile) manso, dócil; (affectionate) cariñoso; bondadoso; sufrido, paciente; cortés; pacífico, tolerante. **He was a man of g. birth,** Era un hombre bien nacido. **"G. reader,"** «Querido lector». **g. wind** *Lat. Am.* airecito *m*

gentlefolk *n pl* gente de bien, gente fina, *f*; gente de buena familia, *f*

gentleman *n* caballero, señor, *m*; gentilhombre, *m*. **Ladies and gentlemen,** Señoras y caballeros, Señores. **young g.,** señorito, *m*. **to be a perfect g.,** ser un caballero perfecto. **g.-inwaiting,** gentilhombre de la cámara, *m*

gentlemanliness *n* caballerosidad, *f*

gentlemanly a caballeroso

gentleness *n* amabilidad, *f*; suavidad, *f*; dulzura, *f*; mansedumbre, docilidad, *f*; bondad, *f*; paciencia, *f*; cortesía, *f*; tolerancia, *f*

gentlewoman *n* dama, *f*; dama de servicio, *f*

gently *adv* suavemente; dulcemente; silenciosamente, sin ruido; (slowly) despacio, poco a poco. **g. born,** bien nacido

gentry *n* pequeña aristocracia, alta clase media, *f*; (disparaging) gentle, *f*

genuflect *vi* doblar la rodilla

genuine a puro; genuino; verdadero; real; sincero; auténtico

genuinely *adv* genuinamente; verdaderamente; realmente; sinceramente

genus *n* género, *m*

geographer *n* geógrafo, *m*

geographical a geográfico

geography *n* geografía, *f*

geologist *n* geólogo, *m*

geology *n* geología, *f*

geometric a geométrico

geometry *n* geometría, *f*

geranium *n* geranio, *m*

germ *n* embrión, germen, *m*; microbio, bacilo, *m*; *fig* germen, *m*. **g.-cell,** célula germinal, *f*

German a alemán; germánico. *n* alemán (-ana); (language) alemán, *m*; germano (-na), germánico (-ca). **Sudeten G.,** alemán (-ana) sudete. **G. measles,** rubeola, *f*. **G. silver** alpaca, *f*, melchor·*m*, plata alemana *f*

germane a pertinente (a), a propósito (a)

Germanic a germánico. *n* (language) germánico, *m*

Germanize *vt* germanizar. *vi* germanizarse

Germany Alemania, *f*

germicidal a bactericida

germicide *n* desinfectante, *m*

germinal *a* germinal. *n* (G.) germinal, *m*

germinate *vi* germinar, brotar. *vt* hacer germinar

germination *n* germinación, *f*

germinative *a* germinativo

gerund *n* gerundio, *m*

gerundive *n* gerundio adjetivado, *m*

Gestapo *n* Gestapo, *f*

gestation *n* gestación, *f*

gesticulate *vi* gesticular, hacer gestos; accionar. *vt* expresar por gestos

gesticulation *n* gesticulación, *f*

gesticulatory *a* gesticular

gesture *n* movimiento, *m*; gesticulación, *f*; (of the face) gesto, *m*, mueca, *f*; ademán, *m*, acción, *f*. *vi* gesticular. *vt* decir por gestos; acompañar con gestos

get *vt* (obtain) obtener; (acquire) adquirir; (buy) comprar; (take) tomar; (receive) recibir; (gain, win) ganar; (hit) acertar, dar; (place) poner; (achieve) alcanzar, lograr; (make) hacer; (call) llamar; (understand) comprender; (catch) coger; (procreate) procrear, engendrar; (induce) persuadir; (invite) convidar, invitar; (cause) hacer; (with have and past part.) tener; (with have and past part. followed by infin.) tener que; (followed by noun and past part.) hacer; (fetch) buscar, ir a buscar; (order) mandar, disponer; (procure) procurar; (bring) traer; (money) hacer; (a reputation, etc.) hacerse; (a prize, an advantage) llevar, (learn) aprender; (be) ser. *vi* (become) hacerse; ponerse; venir a ser; (old) envejecerse; (angry) montar (en cólera), enojarse; (arrive) llegar a; (attain) alcanzar; (accomplish) conseguir, lograr; (drunk) emborracharse; (hurt) hacerse daño; (wet) mojarse; (cool) enfriarse; (money) hacer (dinero); (of health) ponerse; (find oneself) hallarse, encontrarse; (late) hacerse (tarde); (dark) empezar a caer (la noche), empezar a oscurecer; (put oneself) meterse; (grow, be) estar; (on to or on top of) montar sobre, subir a. **He has got run over,** Ha sido atropellado. **It gets on my nerves,** Se me pone los nervios en punta. **Let's get it over!** ¡Vamos a concluir de una vez! **How do you get on with her?** ¿Cómo te va con ella? **She must be getting on for twenty,** Tendrá alrededor de veinte años. **to get a suit made,** mandar hacerse un traje. **to get altitude sickness** *Peru* asorocharse **to get better,** (in health) mejorar de salud; hacer progresos adelantar. **to get dark,** obscurecer. **to get depressed** *Lat. Am.* amurrarse **to get into conversation with,** trabar conversación con. **to get into bad company,** frecuentar malas compañías. **to get into the habit of,** acostumbrarse a. **to get married,** casarse. **to get near,** acercarse. **to get one's own way,** salir con la suya. **to get oneself up as,** disfrazarse

de. **to get out in a hurry,** salir apresuradamente; marcharse rápidamente, *inf* salir pitando. **to get out of the way,** quitarse de en medio, apartarse. **to get rid of,** desembarazarse de, librarse de; salir de; perder. **to have got,** poseer; tener; padecer. **Get on!** ¡Adelante!; (to a horse) ¡Arre!; (continue) ¡Sigue! **Get out!** ¡Fuera! ¡Largo de aquí! ¡Sal! **to get the blues -to get depressed Get up!** ¡Levántate!; (to a horse) ¡Arre! **to get about,** moverse mucho; andar mucho; (attend to business affairs) ir a sus negocios; (travel) viajar; (get up from sick bed) levantarse; (go out) salir; (be known) saberse, divulgarse, hacerse público. **to get above,** subir a un nivel más alto (de). ¿Cómo le va? **I am getting along?** ¿Cómo le va? **I am getting along all right, thank you,** Voy tirando, gracias. **to get along without,** pasarse sin. **to get angry** *vi Central America* empurrarse **to get at,** (remove) sacar; (find) encontrar; (reach) llegar a; alcanzar; (discover) descubrir; (allude to) aludir a; (understand) comprender. **to get away,** *vi* dejar (un lugar); marcharse, irse; (escape) escaparse. *vt* ayudar a marcharse; ayudar a escaparse. **to get away with,** llevarse, marcharse con; *inf* salir con la suya. **to get back,** *vi* regresar, volver; (get home) volver a casa; (be back) estar de vuelta. *vt* (recover) recobrar; (receive) recibir; (find again) hallar de nuevo. **to get depressed** *Central America* acuilmarse **to get down,** *vi* bajar, descender. *vt* bajar; (take off a hook) descolgar; (swallow) tragar; (note) anotar; escribir. **to get down on all fours,** ponerse en cuatro patas. **to get down to,** ponerse a (estudiar, trabajar, etc.). **to get in,** *vi* entrar en; lograr entrar en; (slip in) colarse en; (of political party) entrar en el poder; (of a club) hacerse socio de; (return) regresar; (home) volver a casa; (find oneself) hallarse, estar; (a habit) adquirir. *vt* hacer entrar en; (a club, etc.) hacer socio de; (a word) decir. **to get in line** *Mexico* formarse **to get into.** See **to get in. to get off,** *vt* apearse de; bajar de; (send) enviar; (from punishment) librar; (bid goodbye) despedirse de; (remove) quitar, sacar. *vi* apearse; bajar; (from punishment) librarse; (leave) ponerse en camino, marcharse. **to get on,** *vi* (wear) tener puesto; (progress) hacer progresos, adelantar; (prosper) medrar, prosperar; (succeed) tener éxito; avanzar; seguir el camino; (agree) avenirse. *vt* (push) empujar; (place) poner; (cause) hacer; (clothes) ponerse; (mount) subir a. **to get open,** abrir. **to get out,** *vt* hacer salir; sacar; (publish) publicar; divulgar. *vi* salir; escapar; **to get out of a jam,** salir de un paso; (descend) bajar (de). **to get over,** (cross) atravesar, cruzar; (an illness, grief, etc.) reponerse, reponerse de; (excuse) perdonar; (surmount) superar; (ground) recorrer. **to get round,** (a person) persuadir; (surround) rodear; (avoid) evitar; (difficulties) superar, vencer. **to g. one's degree** *Lat. Am.* diplomarse. **to get through,** pasar por; (time) pasar, entretener; (money) gastar; (finish) terminar, acabar; (pierce or enter) penetrar; (communicate) comunicar (con); (difficulties) vencer; (an exam) aprobar. **to get the blues** *Central America* acuilmarse **to get to,** llegar a; encontrar; (begin) empezar. **to get together,** *vt* reunir, juntar. *vi* reunirse, juntarse. **to get under,** ponerse debajo de; (control) dominar. **to get up,** *vt* (raise) alzar, levantar; (carry up things) subir; hacer subir; organizar; preparar; (learn) aprender; (linen) blanquear, colar; (ascend) subir; hacer; (dress) ataviar; (steam) generar; (a play) ensayar, poner en escena. *vi* levantarse; (on a horse) montar a caballo; (of the wind) refrescarse; (of the fire) avivarse; (of the sea) embravecerse. **to get up to,** llegar a; alcanzar

get-at-able *a* accesible

getting *n* adquisición, *f*; (of money) ganancia, *f*. **g. up,** preparación, *f*; organización, *f*; (of a play) representación (de una comedia), puesta en escena, *f*

get-up *n* atavío, *m*; (of a book, etc.) aspecto, *m*

gewgaw *n* chuchería, *f*

geyser *n* géiser, *m*; (for heating water) calentador (de agua), *m*

ghastly *a* horrible; de una palidez mortal; cadavérico; (boring) aburrido; muy desagradable

ghetto *n* gueto *m*

ghost *n* fantasma, espectro, aparecido, *m*; (spirit) alma, *f*, espíritu, *m*; (shadow) sombra, *f*; (writer) mercenario, *m*. **Holy G.,** Espíritu Santo, *m*. **to give up the g.,** entregar el alma; perder la esperanza, desesperarse. **to look like a g.,** parecer un fantasma

ghostly *a* espiritual; espectral; misterioso; pálido; vaporoso, tenue; indistinto

ghost town *n* pueblo-fantasma, *m*

ghoul *n* vampiro, *m*

ghoulish *a* insano; cruel; sádico

giant *n* gigante, *m*; *fig* coloso, *m*, a gigantesco; de gigantes; de los gigantes. **g.-killer,** matador de gigantes, *m*. **g.-stride,** (gymnastics) paso volante, *m*

gibber *vi* hablar incoherentemente, hablar entre dientes; farfullar, hablar atropelladamente; decir disparates

gibberish *n* galimatías, *m*; jerigonza, *f*, griego, *m*

gibbet *n* horca, *f*, patíbulo, *m*. **to die on the g.,** morir ahorcado

gibe *n* improperio, escarnio, *m*, burla, mofa, *f*. *vi* criticar. **to g. at,** burlarse de, ridiculizar, mofarse de

giblets *n* menudillos, *m pl*

giddily *adv* vertiginosamente; frívolamente, atolondradamente

giddiness *n* vértigo, *m*; atolondramiento, *m*; inconstancia, *f*; frivolidad, ligereza de cascos, *f*

giddy *a* vertiginoso; mareado; atolondrado, casquivano, frívolo; inconstante. **She felt very g.,** Se sintió muy mareada. **to make g.,** dar vértigo (a), marear

gift *n* regalo, *m*, dádiva, *f*; (quality) don, talento, *m*; prenda, *f*; poder, *m*; *law* donación, *f*; (offering) ofrenda, oblación, *f*. *vt* dotar. **deed of g.,** *law* escritura de donación, *f*. **in the g. of,** en el poder de, en las manos de. **I wouldn't have it as a g.,** No lo tomaría ni regalado. **Never look a g. horse in the mouth,** A caballo regalado no se le mira el diente. **g. of tongues,** don de las lenguas, genio de las lenguas, *m*

gifted *a* talentoso

gig *n* (carriage) carrocín, *m*; (boat) falúa, lancha, *f*; (for wool) máquina de cardar paño, *f*; (harpoon) arpón, *m*

gigantic *a* gigantesco; colosal, enorme

giggle *vi* reírse sin motivo; reírse disimuladamente. *n* risa disimulada, *f*

giggling *n* risa estúpida, *f*; risa nerviosa, *f*

gigolo *n* gigolo, mantenido, jinetero (Cuba), *m*

gild *vt* dorar; (metals) sobredorar; embellecer. **to g. the pill,** dorar la píldora

gill *n* (of fish) agalla, branquia, *f*; (ravine) barranco, *m*; (measure) cierta medida de líquidos, *f*, ($\frac{1}{4}$ litro)

gilt *n* dorado, *m*; pan de oro, *m*; relumbrón, *m*; *fig* encanto, *m*, a dorado, áureo. **g.-edged,** (of books) con los bordes dorados. **g.-edged security,** papel del Estado, *m*; valores de toda confianza, *m pl*

gimcrack *n* chuchería, *f*. a de baratillo, cursi; mal hecho

gimlet *n* barrena, *f*, taladro, *m*

gin *n* (drink) ginebra, *f*; (snare) trampa, *f*. *vt* (snare) coger con trampa. **g. block,** *mech* garrucha, *f*

ginger *n* jengibre, *m*; *inf* energía, *f*, brío, *m*, a rojo. *vt* sazonar con jengibre; *inf* animar, estimular. **g.-beer,** gaseosa, *f*

gingerly *adv* con gran cuidado; delicadamente

gingham *n* guinga, *f*

gingivitis *n* gingivitis, *f*

gipsy *n*. See **gypsy**

giraffe *n* jirafa, *f*

gird *vt* ceñir; (invest) investir; (surround) cercar, rodear; (put on) revestir. **to g.**

oneself for the fray, prepararse para la lucha

girder n viga, jácena, f. **main g.,** viga maestra, f

girdle n (belt) cinturón, m; (corset) faja, f; circunferencia, f; zona, f. vt ceñir; fig cercar, rodear

girl n niña, f; chica, muchacha, f; (maidservant) criada, muchacha, f; (young lady) señorita, f. **a young g.,** una jovencita; (a little older) una joven. **old g.,** (of a school) antigua alumna, f; inf vieja, f; (inf affectionate) chica, f. **g. friend,** amiguita, f. **g. guide, girl scout,** exploradora, f. **girls' school,** colegio de niñas, colegio de señoritas, m

girlhood n niñez, f; juventud, f

girlish a de niña, de muchacha; (of boys) afeminado; joven

girth n (of horse, etc.) cincha, f; circunferencia, f; (of person) talle, m; (obesity) corpulencia, obesidad, f

gist n esencia, substancia, f, importe, m

give vt dar; (a present) regalar; (infect) contagiar; (impart) comunicar; (grant) otorgar; (allow, concede) conceder; (assign) asignar, señalar; (appoint) nombrar; (a toast) brindar (a la salud de); (a party, ball, etc.) dar; (a bill) presentar; (wish) desear; (punish) castigar; (pay) pagar; (hand over) entregar; (names at baptism) imponer; (produce) producir; dar; (cause) causar; (of judicial sentences) condenar a; (evoke) proporcionar; (provoke) provocar; (devote) dedicar, consagrar; (sacrifice) sacrificar; (evidence, an account, orders, a lesson, a performance, a concert) dar; (a cry, shout) lanzar, proferir; (a laugh) soltar; (describe) describir; (paint) pintar; (write) escribir; (offer) ofrecer; (show) mostrar; (transmit) transmitir; (heed, pain) hacer; (a speech) pronunciar, hacer; (award, adjudge) adjudicar; (ear) prestar (oído (a)). vi dar; ser dadivoso, mostrarse generoso; (give in) ceder; (be elastic) dar de sí; ablandarse; (collapse) hundirse. **G. them my best wishes!** ¡Dales mis mejores recuerdos! **G. us a song!** ¡Cántanos algo! **I can g. him a lift in my car,** Puedo ofrecerle un asiento en mi auto. **I g. you my word,** Os doy mi palabra. **to g. a good account of oneself,** defenderse bien; hacer bien; salir bien. **to g. a person a piece of one's mind,** contarle cuatro verdades. **to g. chase** (to) dar caza (a). **to g. it to a person,** poner a uno como nuevo; reprender; (beat) pegar, dar de palos. **to g. of itself,** dar de sí. **to g. rise to,** dar lugar a, ocasionar, causar. **to g. way,** no poder resistir; (break) romperse; (yield) ceder; (collapse) hundirse; (retreat) retroceder. **to g. way to,** (retreat before) retirarse ante; (abandon oneself to) entregarse a, abandonarse a. **to g. away,** enajenar; dar; regalar; (sell cheaply) vender a un precio muy bajo;

(get rid of) deshacerse de; (sacrifice) sacrificar; (a secret) revelar; (betray) traicionar; (expose) descubrir; (tell) contar; (a bride) conducir al altar. **He gave himself away,** Reveló su pensamiento sin querer. **to g. back,** vt devolver; restituir. vi retirarse, cejar. **to g. forth,** divulgar, publicar; (scatter) derramar; (emit) emitir, despedir; (smoke, rays) echar. **to g. in,** vt entregar; presentar. vi darse por vencido. **to g. in to,** (agree with) asentir en, consentir en; rendirse ante. **Mary always gives in to George,** María hace siempre lo que Jorge quiere. **to g. off,** (of odors, etc.) emitir, exhalar, despedir. **to g. out,** vt (distribute) distribuir, repartir; (allocate) asignar; (publish) publicar; (announce) anunciar; (reveal) divulgar; (allege) afirmar, hacer saber; (emit) emitir. vi (be exhausted) agotarse; (end) acabarse; (be lacking) faltar. **to g. over,** vt entregar; (transfer) traspasar; cesar de. vi cesar. **to g. up,** entregar; ceder; (renounce) renunciar (a); (sacrifice) sacrificar; (abandon) abandonar; (cease) dejar de; (as lost) dar por perdido; (of a patient) desahuciar; (a post) dimitir de; (return) devolver, restituir; (a problem) renunciar (a resolver un problema); (lose hope) perder la esperanza; (give in) darse por vencido. **I had given my up,** (didn't expect you) Creí que no ibas a venir. **to g. oneself up to,** entregarse a; dedicarse a; mil rendirse a. **to g. up one's seat,** ceder su sitio (or asiento). **to g. upon,** (overlook) dar sobre

give n elasticidad, f; el dar de sí; (concession) concesión, f. **g. and take,** concesiones mutuas, fpl. **g. away,** inf revelación indiscreta, f

given a dado; especificado; convenido; (with to) dado a, adicto a. **in a g. time,** en un tiempo dado. **g. that,** dado que

giving a = **generous**

gizzard n molleja, f. **It sticks in my g.,** inf No lo puedo tragar

glacial a glacial

glacier n glaciar, m

glad a feliz, alegre; contento, satisfecho; inf elegante. **to be g.,** alegrarse, estar contento; estar satisfecho. **to give the g. eye,** hacer ojos

gladden vt alegrar, regocijar

glade n claro, m; rasa, f

gladiator n gladiador, m

gladly adv alegremente; con mucho gusto, gustoso, de buena gana

glamorous a exótico; garboso

glamour n encanto, m, fascinación, f; garbo, m. **g. girl,** belleza exótica, f

glance n (of a projectile) desviación, f; (of light) vislumbre, m; relumbrón, centelleo, m; (look) vistazo, m, ojeada, f; mirada, f, vi desviar; relumbrar, centellear, brillar; (with at) ojear, echar un vistazo a, lanzar miradas a; (a book) hojear;

mirar; mirar de reojo; *fig* indicar brevemente. **at a g.,** con un vistazo; en
seguida. **at the first g.,** a primera vista.
to g. off, desviarse (al chocar). **to g.
over,** repasar, echar un vistazo a; (a
book) hojear

glancing a (of a blow) que roza

gland n (anat, bot) glándula, f; (in the
neck) ganglio, m. **to have swollen
glands,** tener inflamación de los
ganglios

glandular a glandular

glare n brillo, fulgor, m; luminosidad, f;
reflejo, m; (look) mirada feroz, f. *vi* relumbrar, centellear; (stare) mirar con ferocidad, mirar fijamente

glaring a deslumbrante, brillante; (of colors) chillón, llamativo; (of looks) de
mirada feroz; (flagrant) notorio, evidente

glaringly adv brillantemente; con mirada
feroz; notoriamente

glass n vidrio, m; cristal, m; (glassware)
artículos de vidrio, m pl; cristalería, f; (for
drinking) vaso, m, copa, f; (pane) cristal,
m; (mirror) espejo, m; (telescope) telescopio, m; catalejo, m; (barometer)
barómetro, m; (hour-glass) reloj de
arena, m; (of a watch) vidrio (de reloj), m;
pl **glasses,** (binoculars) anteojos, m pl;
(spectacles) gafas, lentes, m pl; (opera
glasses) gemelos de teatro, m pl, a de
vidrio; de cristal. *vt* vidriar; **John wears
glasses,** Juan lleva gafas. **The g. is falling (rising),** El barómetro baja (sube). **to
clink glasses,** trincar las copas. **to look
in the g.,** mirarse en el espejo. **clear g.,**
vidrio trasparente, m. **cut g.,** cristal tallado, m. **frosted g.,** vidrio jaspeado, m.
plate-g., vidrio plano, m; **safety g.,**
vidrio inastillable, m. **stained g.,** vidrio
de color, vidrio pintado, m. **under g.,**
bajo vidrio; en invernáculo. **g. bead,**
abalorio, m; cuenta de vidrio, f.
g.-blower, soplador de vidrio, m.
g.-blowing, el soplar de vidrio. **g. case,**
escaparate, m. **g.-cloth,** paño para
vasos, m. **g. eye,** ojo de cristal, m. **g.
paper,** papel de vidrio, m. **g. roof,** techo
de cristal, m. **g. window,** vidriera, f

glassful n contenido de un vaso, m; vaso,
vaso lleno, m, copa, f

glassware n cristalería, f

glaucous a de color verdemar; bot
glauco

glaze n barniz, m: lustre, brillo, m. vt
poner vidrios (a); vidriar; barnizar;
(paper, leather, etc.) satinar. *vi* (of eyes)
vidriarse, ponerse vidrioso

glazier n vidriero, m

gleam n rayo, destello, m; (of color) viso,
m, mancha, f; fig rayo, m; (in the eye)
chispa, f. *vi* relucir, centellear, resplandecer; brillar; reflejar la luz; fig brillar. **g.
of hope,** rayo de esperanza, m

gleaming a reluciente, centelleante; brillante. n see **gleam**

glean vt espigar, rebuscar; recoger. vi espigar

gleaning n espigueo, m; rebusca, recolección, f; pl **gleanings,** fragmentos, m
pl

glee n alegría, f, júbilo, alborozo, m; mus
canción para voces solas, f

gleeful a alegre, jubiloso, gozoso

glen n cañada, f, cañón, m, hondonada, f

glib a locuaz, voluble; (easy) fácil

glide n deslizamiento, m; aer planeo, m.
vi deslizarse; resbalar; aer planear. **to g.
away,** escurrirse; desaparecer silenciosamente

glider n aer deslizador, planeador, m

gliding n aer vuelo sin motor, m

glimmer n luz trémula, luz débil, f, tenue
resplandor, m; vislumbre, f. vi brillar
con luz trémula, rielar fig; tener vislum-
bres (de)

glimpse n vistazo, m; vislumbre, m; indicio, m; impresión, f; vista, f. vt entrever,
divisar; tener una vista (de); ver por un
instante; vislumbrar

glint n tenue resplandor, m; lustre, m;
centelleo, m; reflejo, m; (in the eye)
chispa, f. vi relucir, destellar, rutilar; reflejar

glisten vi brillar, relucir

glistening a coruscante; brillante, reluciente

glitter n brillo, resplandor, m, rutilación,
f. vi brillar, resplandecer, relucir; rutilar.
All that glitters is not gold, Todo lo
que reluce no es oro

glittering a reluciente, resplandeciente;
fig brillante

gloat (over) vi recrearse en, gozarse en,
deleitarse en

globe n globo, m; esfera, f; (for fish) pecera, f; (for gas, electric light) globo, m.
geographical g., globo terrestre, m.
g.-trotter, trotamundos, mf

gloom n obscuridad, f; lobreguez, f, tinieblas, f pl; fig melancolía, tristeza, f; taciturnidad, f. vi fig ponerse melancólico;
ser taciturno

gloomy a obscuro; sombrío, lóbrego;
melancólico, triste; taciturno; (of prospects, etc.) poco halagüeño, nada
atrayente

glorify vt glorificar; exaltar; alabar

glorious a glorioso; espléndido, magnífico; insigne; inf estupendo

glory n gloria, f; esplendor, m, magnificencia, f; art gloria, f. vi recrearse, gozarse; glorificarse, jactarse. **to be in
one's g.,** estar en la gloria. **to g. in,**
hacer gala de, glorificarse en

gloss n (sheen) lustre, brillo, m; fig apariencia, f; (note) glose, m; (excuse) disculpa, f. vt pulir; glosar. **to g. over,**
(faults) disculpar, excusar

glossary n glosario, m

glossy a lustroso, terso; brillante; (of hair) liso

glove n guante. **evening gloves,** guantes largos, m pl. **to be hand in g. with,** juntar diestra con diestra. **to fit like a g.,** sentar como un guante. **to put on one's gloves,** ponerse los guantes. **g. shop,** guantería, f. **g.-stretcher,** ensanchador (-ra) de guantes, abridor (-ra) de guantes mf

glove compartment gaveta, **guantera,** f, guantero, portaguantes m

glow n incandescencia, f; claridad, f; luz difusa, f; (heat) calor, m; (of color) intensidad, f; color vivo, m; (enthusiasm) ardor, entusiasmo, m; (redness) rojez, f; (in the sky) arrebol, m; (of pleasure, etc.) sentimiento de placer, m; sensación de bienestar, f. vi estar incandescente; arder; abrasarse; sentir entusiasmo; mostrarse rojo; experimentar un sentimiento de placer o una sensación de bienestar. **to g. with health,** estar rebosando de salud. **g.-worm,** luciérnaga, f

glower n ceño, m; mirada amenazadora, f. vi poner cara de pocos amigos, mirar airadamente; tener los ojos puestos (en)

glowing a candente, incandescente; ardiente; entusiasta; satisfecho; intenso; (bright) vivo; (red) encendido; (with health) rebosante de salud. n see **glow**

glue n engrudo, m, cola, f. vt encolar, engrudar; pegar; fig fijar, poner. **He kept his eyes glued on them,** Tenía los ojos fijados (or pegados) en ellos. **g.-pot,** pote de cola, m

gluey a gomoso; pegajoso; viscoso

glum a deprimido, taciturno, sombrío

glut n superabundancia, f, exceso, m. vt (satiate) hartar; fig saciar; (the market) inundar

glutton n glotón (-ona); fig ávido (-da)

gluttonous a glotón, comilón

gnarled a nudoso; (of human beings) curtido

gnash vt rechinar, crujir (los dientes)

gnat n mosquito, m

gnaw vt roer; morder; (of wood by worms) carcomer; fig roer

go vi ir; (depart) irse, marcharse; (go toward) dirigirse a, encaminarse a; (lead to, of roads, etc.) conducir a, ir a; (vanish) desaparecer; (leave) dejar, salir de; (lose) perder; (pass) pasar; (of time) transcurrir, pasar; (be removed) quitarse; (be prohibited) prohibirse; (fall) caer; (collapse) hundirse; (be torn off) desprenderse; desgajarse; mech funcionar, trabajar, andar; (sound) sonar; (of the heart) palpitar, latir; (follow) seguir; (gesture) hacer un gesto; (be stated) decirse, afirmarse; (live) vivir; (wear) llevar; (turn out) salir, resultar; (improve) mejorar; (prosper) prosperar; (turn, become) ponerse; volverse; (to sleep) dormirse; (into a faint) desmayarse; (decay) echarse a perder;

estropearse; (turn sour) agriarse; (become, adopt views, etc.) hacerse; (be sold) venderse; (be decided) decidirse, ser decidido; (have) tener; (by will) pasar; (belong) pertenecer; (receive) recibir; (have its place) estar; (put) ponerse; (going plus infin.) ir a; (die) morir, irse; (do a journey, a given distance) hacer; (a pace, step) dar; (take) tomar; (escape) escaparse, (contribute) contribuir a; (harmonize) armonizar (con); (be current) ser válido; (be) ser; (of a document, etc., run) rezar, decir; (attend) asistir a; (be broken) estar roto; (be worn) estar raído; (be granted) darse, otorgarse. **It's gone five,** Ya dieron las cinco. **It's time to be going,** Es hora de marcharse. **Let's go!** ¡Vamos! **These two colours go well together,** Estos colores armonizan bien. **Well, how goes it?** Bueno, ¿qué tal? ¿Cómo te va? **Who goes there?** mil ¿Quién va? **to go and fetch,** ir a buscar. **to let go,** soltar; dejar ir. **to go one's way,** seguir su camino. **to go wrong,** salir mal, fracasar; (sin) descarriarse. "**Go!**" (traffic sign) «¡Siga!» **Go on!** ¡Adelante! (continue) ¡Siga! inf ¡Qué va! **to go about,** dar la vuelta a; rodear; recorrer; (undertake) emprender, hacer; intentar; (of news, etc.) circular; naut virar de bordo. **Go about your business!** ¡Métete en lo que te importa! **to go abroad,** ir al extranjero; salir a la calle; publicarse, divulgarse. **to go across,** cruzar, atravesar; pasar. **to go after,** andar tras; seguir; (seek) ir a buscar; (persecute) perseguir. **to go again,** ir de nuevo; (be present) asistir otra vez; volver. **to go against,** ir contra; militar contra; oponerse a; ser desfavorable a. **to go ahead,** adelantar, avanzar; progresar; prosperar; (lead) ir a la cabeza de; conducir; naut marchar hacia adelante. **to go along,** andar por; recorrer; (depart) irse, marcharse. **go apartment-hunting,** ir en busca de piso. **to go along with,** acompañar (a). **to go aside,** quitarse de en medio; apartarse, retirarse. **to go astray,** perderse; extraviarse, descarriarse. **to go at,** atacar, acometer; (undertake) emprender; empezar a. **to go at it again,** inf volver a la carga. **to go away,** irse, marcharse; ausentarse; alejarse; desaparecer. **to go away with,** marcharse con; (an object) llevarse. **to go back,** volver, regresar, Lat. Am. devolverse; (retreat) retroceder, volverse atrás; (in history) remontarse a. **to go back on,** (a promise, etc.) faltar a; (retract) retractarse; (betray) traicionar. **to go backwards,** retroceder, cejar; desandar lo andado; fig deteriorar, empeorar. **to go backwards and forwards,** ir y venir; oscilar. **to go before,** (lead) ir a la cabeza de, conducir; anteceder; proceder; (a judge, etc.) comparecer ante. **to go behind,** ir detrás de; esconderse detrás de; seguir; (evidence, etc.) mirar más allá de. **to go between,** ponerse entre; interponerse; (as a mediator) mediar; (insert) intercalarse; (travel) ir entre; llevar cartas entre, ser mensajero de. **to go beyond,** ir más allá; exceder. **to go by,** pasar por; pasar cerca de, pasar junto a; ir por; (of time) transcurrir, pasar; (follow) seguir; guiarse por, atenerse a; (judge by) juzgar por; (a name) pasar por; tomar el nombre de. **to go down,** bajar, descender; (of the sun) ponerse; (sink) hundirse; sumergirse; (fall) caer; (be remembered) ser recordado; (believe) tragar; ser creído. **to go down again,** bajar de nuevo; volver a caer. **go Dutch,** ir a escote, ir a la gringa, ir a la par, ir a limón. **to go far,** ir lejos; influir mucho (en); impresionar mucho; (contribute) contribuir (a). **to go for,** (seek) ir en busca de; procurar tener; (attack) echarse encima de, atacar. **to go for a ride (by car, bicycle, on horseback),** dar un paseo (en coche, en bicicleta, a caballo). **to go forth,** salir; publicarse. **to go forward,** adelantar, avanzar; progresar; continuar; (happen) tener lugar. **to go from,** dejar, abandonar; separarse de, apartarse de; marcharse de. **to go in,** entrar en; (a railway carriage, etc.) subir a; (compete) concurrir. **to go in again,** volver a entrar en, entrar de nuevo en. **to go in and out,** entrar y salir; ir y venir. **to go in for,** entrar a buscar; dedicarse a, entregarse a; (buy) comprarse; tomar parte en; (an examination) tomar (un examen); (for a competition) entrar en (un concurso); (try) ensayar; arriesgar. **to go into,** entrar en; examinar; investigar; ocuparse con. **to go native** *Lat. Am.* acriollarse. **to go near,** acercarse a. **to go off,** marcharse; (explode) estallar; (of fire-arms) dispararse; (of the voice, etc.) perder (la voz, etc.); (run away) huir, fugarse. **to go off badly,** salir mal, fracasar, no tener éxito. **to go off well,** salir bien, tener éxito. **to go on,** subirse a; continuar; durar; avanzar; proseguir su marcha; progresar; prosperar; *theat.* entrar en escena; (of clothes) ponerse; (rely on) apoyarse en. **to go on an excursion, go on an outing, go on a trip** *Lat. Am.* excursionarse. **Don't go on like that,** No seas así, No te pongas así. **This glove will not go on me,** No puedo ponerme este guante. **to be gone on a person,** *inf* estar loco por. **I went on to say . . . ,** Después dije; Continuando mi discurso dije . . . **It was going on for six o'clock when . . .** Serían alrededor de las seis cuando . . . **He is going on for fifty,** Raya en los cincuenta años. **to go on foot,** ir a pie. **to go on with,** continuar con; empezar. **to go out,** salir; (descend) bajar; (of fires, lights) extinguirse, apagarse; (of fashion, etc.) pasar (de); (the tide) menguar; (retire) retirarse; (in society) frecuentar la alta sociedad; (die) morir; (arouse) excitar. **to go out of** salir de, *Lat. Am. also* egresar de. **to go out of fashion,** pasar

de moda. **to go out of one's way (to),** dejar su camino (para); (lose oneself) perder el camino, extraviarse; (take trouble) desvivirse (por), tomarse molestia (para). **to go over,** cruzar; pasar por encima; (to another party or .to the other side) pasarse a; (read) repasar; examinar. **to go past,** pasar; pasar en frente de. **to go round,** dar la vuelta a; (revolve) girar; (surround) rodear; (of news, etc.) divulgarse; (be enough) ser suficiente para todos. **to go through,** ir por, pasar por; recorrer; (pierce) penetrar, atravesar; (examine) examinar; (suffer) padecer, sufrir; (experience) experimentar; (live) vivir; (of time) pasar; (of money) malgastar, derrochar. **to go through with,** llevar a cabo; terminar. **to go to,** ir a, encaminarse a; (a person) acercarse a, dirigirse a; (help, be useful) servir para; (be meant for) destinarse a; (rise of price) subir a; (find) encontrar; (of a bid) subir una apuesta hasta. **to go to war,** declarar la guerra. **to go together,** ir juntos (juntas). **to go toward,** encaminarse hacia; ir hacia; (help) ayudar a. **to go under,** pasar por debajo de; (sink) hundirse; (fail) fracasar; (be bankrupt) arruinarse, declararse en quiebra; (the name of) hacerse pasar por. **to go up,** subir; ir arriba; (a tree) trepar; (a ladder, etc.) subir; (a river) ir río arriba; (to town) ir a; (explode) estallar. **to go up and down,** subir y bajar; oscilar; ir de una parte a otra. **to go upon,** subirse a; (rely on) apoyarse en; obrar según; emprender. **to go upstairs,** ir arriba; (to another story, as in a flat) subir al otro piso; subir la escalera. **to go up to,** acercarse a; (of a bid) subir una apuesta hasta. **to go with,** acompañar; (agree with) estar de acuerdo con; (of principles) seguir, ser fiel a; (harmonize) armonizar con; (be suitable to) ir bien con; convenir a; (*inf* get along) ir. **to go without,** marcharse sin; (lack) pasarse sin. **It goes without saying that . . . ,** Huelga decir que **Where are you going with this?** (What do you mean?) ¿A dónde quieres llegar con esto?

go *n* (fashion) moda, boga, *f*; (happening) suceso, *m*; (fix) apuro, *m*; (energy) energía, *f*, empuje, brío, *m*; (turn) turno, *m*; (attempt) tentativa, *f*; (action) movimiento, *m*, acción, *f*; (bargain) acuerdo, *m*. **It's a go!** (agreed) ¡Trato hecho! ¡Acordado! ¡Entendido! ¡Entendidas! **It is all the go,** Hace furor, Es la gran moda. **It is no go,** No puede ser, Es imposible. **Now it's my go,** Ahora me toca a mí, Ahora es mi turno. **on the go,** en movimiento; entre manos; ocupado. **to have a go,** probar suerte; procurar, tratar de; tener un turno

goad *n* garrocha, aguijada, *f*, aguijón, *m*, *Lat. Am.* lanceta *f*; *fig* acicate, estímulo, *m*. *vt* aguijar, picar; *fig* incitar, estimular, empujar. **prick with a g.,** aguijonazo, *m*

go-ahead *a* emprendedor; progresivo

goal n (posts in football, etc.) meta, portería, f; Lat. Am. arco m; (score) gol, m; (in racing) meta, f; (destination) destinación, f; fig ambición, f; (purpose, objective) fin, objeto, m. **to score a g.,** marcar un gol. **g.-keeper,** guardameta, m, portero (-ra). **g.-post,** palo de la portería, m

goat n cabra, f; ast capricornio, m. **he-g.,** cabrón, m. **young g.,** cabrito, m, chivo (-va). **g.-herd,** cabrero, m. **g. skin,** piel de cabra, f; (wineskin) odre, m

goatee n pera, perilla, f

gobble vt and vi engullir, tragar. vi (of turkey) gluglutear. n glugluteo, m, voz del pavo, f

go-between n trotaconventos, f; alcahuete, m; (mediator) medianero (-ra)

goblet n copa, f

goblin n trasgo, duende, m

go-by, to give the evitar; pasar por alto de; omitir

go-cart n andaderas, f pl; pollera, f; cochecito de niño, m

god n dios, m; pl gods, dioses, m pl; (in a theater) público del paraíso, m; paraíso, m. **By God!** ¡Vive Dios! **For God's sake,** ¡Por el amor de Dios!; ¡Por Dios! **Please God,** ¡Plegue a Dios! **Thank God!** ¡Gracias a Dios! **God Bless You!** (to someone who has sneezed) ¡Jesús! **God forbid!** ¡No lo quiera Dios! **God grant it!** ¡Dios lo quiera! **God keep you!** ¡Dios le guarde! ¡Vaya Vd. con Dios! **God willing,** Dios mediante. **My father, God rest his soul, was . . .,** Mi padre, que Dios perdone, era . . .

godchild n ahijado (-da)

goddess n diosa, f; poet dea, f

godfather n padrino, m. **to be a g. to,** ser padrino de, sacar de pila (a)

godfearing a timorato, temeroso de Dios; religioso

godforsaken a dejado de la mano de Dios; (of places) remoto, solitario

Godhead n divinidad, f

godless a impío, irreligioso; sin Dios

godlessness n impiedad, irreligiosidad, f

godlike a divino

godliness n piedad, f; santidad, f

godly a devoto, piadoso, religioso

godmother n madrina, f. **fairy g.,** hada madrina, f. **to be a g. to,** ser madrina de

godparent n padrino, m; madrina, f pl. **godparents,** padrinos, m pl

godsend n bien, m; buena suerte, f; fortuna, f

go-getter n buscavidas, mf

goggle n mirada fija, f; pl **goggles,** anteojos, m pl, gafas, f pl; (of a horse) anteojeras, f pl. vi mirar fijamente; salirse a uno los ojos de la cabeza. **g.-eyed,** de ojos saltones. **g.-eyes,** ojos saltones, m pl

going n ida, f; (departure) partida, marcha, f; salida, f; (pace) paso, m; (speed) velocidad, f. **It was heavy g.,** El avance era lento; El progreso era lento; (of parties, etc.) Era aburrido. **The g. was difficult on those mountainous roads,** El conducir (or el ir o el andar) era difícil en aquellos caminos de montaña. **g. back,** vuelta, f, regreso, m. **g. down,** bajada, f, descenso, m; (of the sun, etc.) puesta, f. **g. forward,** avance, m; progreso, m. **g. in,** entrada, f. **g. in and out,** idas y venidas, f pl. **g. out,** salida, f; (of a fire, light) apagamiento, m

going a and pres part que va, yendo; que funciona. **G., g., gone** (at an auction) A la una, a las dos, a las tres. **goings-on,** (tricks) trapujos, m pl; (conduct) conducta, f. **g. concern,** empresa próspera, f. **g. to,** con destino a

going-away present n regalo de despedida, m

goiter n bocio, m

gold n oro, m; color de oro, m. a de oro; áureo. **All that glitters is not g.,** No es oro todo lo que reluce. **cloth of g.,** tela de oro, f. **dull g.,** oro mate, m. **light g.,** oro pálido, m. **old g.,** oro viejo, m. **g.-beater,** batidor de oro, m. **g.-digger,** minero de oro, m; (woman) aventurera, f. **g. dust,** oro en polvo, m. **g.-fever,** fiebre de oro, f. **g. lace,** galón de oro, m. **g. lacquer,** sisa dorada, f. **g. leaf,** pan de oro, oro batido, m. **g.-mine,** mina de oro, f. **g. piece,** moneda de oro, f. **g. plate,** vajilla de oro, f. **g. standard,** patrón oro, m. **g.-thread,** hilo de oro, m. **g.-yielding,** a aurífero

golden a de oro; dorado; áureo; amarillo; fig feliz; excelente. **to become g.,** dorarse. **g. age,** edad de oro, f. **g.-crested wren,** abadejo, m. **g. hair,** cabellos dorados (or de oro), m pl. **g. Legend,** leyenda áurea, f. **g. mean,** justo medio, m. **g. rose,** rosa de oro, f. **g. rule,** regla áurea, f. **g. syrup,** jarabe de arce, m. **g. voice,** voz de oro, f. **g. wedding,** bodas de oro, f pl

goldfish n carpa dorada, f. **g. bowl,** pecera, f

goldsmith n orfebre, oribe, orífice, m

golf n golf, m. **g.-club,** (stick) palo de golf, m; (organization) club de golf, m. **g.-course,** campo de golf, m

golfer n jugador (-ra) de golf

gone a and past part ido; (lost) perdido; (ruined) arruinado; (dead) muerto; (past) pasado; (disappeared) desaparecido; (fainted) desmayado; (suppressed) suprimido; (pregnant) encinta; (drunk) borracho; (ended) terminado; (exhausted) agotado; (ill) enfermo. **far g.,** avanzado; (in years) de edad avanzada; (of illness) cerca de la muerte, avanzado; (in love) loco de amor; (drunk) muy borracho. **It is all g.,** No hay más. **It is g. seven o'clock,** Son las siete y pico, Son las siete ya

gonorrhea n gonorrea, f

good a bueno (before m sing nouns) buen; agradable; afortunado; (appropriate) apropiado, oportuno; (beneficial) provechoso, ventajoso; (wholesome) sano, saludable; (suitable) apto; (useful) útil; (kind) bondadoso; (much) mucho; (obliging) amable; (virtuous) virtuoso; (skilled) experto; (fresh) fresco; (genuine) genuino, legítimo; verdadero. adv bien. interj ¡bueno! ¡bien! **a g. deal,** mucho. **a g. many,** bastantes. **a g. turn,** un favor. **a g. way,** (distance) un buen trecho; mucho. **a g. while,** un buen rato. **as g. as,** tan bueno como. **Be so g. as to . . .** Haga el favor de, Tenga Vd. la bondad de (followed by infin.). **fairly g.,** a bastante bueno. adv bastante bien. **I'm g. for another five miles,** Tengo fuerzas para cinco millas más. **It was g. of you to do it,** Vd. fue muy amable de hacerlo, Vd. tuvo mucha bondad de hacerlo. **to be no g. at this sort of thing,** no servir para tales cosas. **to have a g. time,** pasarlo bien. **to make g.,** reparar; indemnizar; (accomplish) llevar a cabo, poner en práctica; justificar; (a promise) cumplir. **very g.,** a muy bueno. adv muy bien. **g.-feeling,** buena voluntad, f. **g.-fellowship,** compañerismo, m; buena compañía, f. **g.-for-nothing,** n papanatas, badulaque, m. **to be g.-for-nothing,** no servir para nada. **g. luck,** buena suerte, Lat. Am. also derechura, leche f. **g. manners,** buenos modales, m pl; buena crianza, educación, f. **g. nature,** buen natural, m; buen humor, m. **g.-natured,** de buen natural; de buen humor, bonachón. **g. offices,** buenos oficios, m pl. **g.-tempered,** de buen humor

good n bien, m; provecho, m; utilidad, f; pl **goods.** See separate entry. **I am saying this for your g.,** Lo digo para tu bien. **Much g. may it do you!** ¡Buen provecho te haga! **for g. and all,** para siempre jamás. **It is no g.,** Es inútil; No vale la pena. **the g.,** el bien; (people) los buenos. **They have gone for g.,** Se han marchado para no volver. **to do one g.,** hacer bien a uno; mejorar; ser provechoso a (uno); (suit) sentar bien a (uno). **What is the g. of . . . ?** ¿Para qué sirve . . . ?; ¿Qué vale . . . ? **g. and evil,** el bien y el mal

good-bye interj ¡adiós! n! adiós, m, despedida, f. **to bid g.-b.,** decir adiós. **G.-b. for the present!** ¡Hasta la vista! ¡Hasta luego! **G.-b. until tomorrow, then,** Hasta mañana pues, adiós, Hasta mañana entonces

goodness n bondad, f; (of quality) buena calidad, f; (of persons) amabilidad, benevolencia, f; (essence) esencia, sustancia, f; bien, m; excelencia, f; interj ¡Jesús! ¡Dios mío! **For g. sake!** ¡Por Dios! **I wish to g. that,** ¡Ojalá que . . . !

goods n pl bienes, efectos, m pl; artículos, m pl; com mercancías, f pl, géneros, m pl. **by g.-train,** en pequeña velocidad. **stolen g.,** objetos robados, m pl. **g. lift,** montacargas, m. **g. office,** depósito de mercancías, m. **g. station,** estación de carga, f. **g.-train,** tren de mercancías, m. **g. van,** furgón, m. **g. wagon,** vagon de mercancías, m

goodwill n benevolencia, f; buena voluntad, f; (of a business) clientela, f

goose n oca, f, ganso (-sa); (sastre) plancha de sastre, f. a de oca. **g.-flesh,** fig carne de gallina, f. **g. girl,** ansarera, f. **g.-step,** paso de oca, m

gooseberry n uva espina, f

gore n sangre, f; sew sesga, nesga, f. vt acornear; desgarrar; herir (con arma blanca)

gorge n (valley) cañón, barranco, m; (heavy meal) comilona, f, atracón, m. vt engullir, tragar. vi hartarse, atracarse

gorgeous a magnífico, espléndido, suntuoso; inf maravilloso, estupendo

gorilla n gorila, m

gormandize vi glotonear

gory a ensangrentado; sangriento

gosh interj ¡caray! ¡caramba!

gospel n evangelio, m; doctrina, f. **The G. according to St. Mark,** El Evangelio según San Marcos. **to believe as g. truth,** creer como si fuese el evangelio. **to preach the G.,** predicar el evangelio

gossamer n hilo de araña, m, red de araña, telaraña, f; (filmy material) gasa, f; hilo finísimo, m, a de gasa; sutil, delgado, fino

gossip n murmurador '(-ra), chismoso (-sa), hablador (-ra); (scandal) chisme, m, Lat. Am. also lengüeterías fpl; habladuría, murmuración, f; (obsolete, of a woman) comadre, f; (talk) charla, f. vi charlar, conversar; (in bad sense) murmurar, chismear; criticar. **to g. about,** charlar de; poner lenguas en, cortar un sayo (a); hablar mal de. **g. column,** gacetilla, f

gouge n gubia, f. vt escoplear. **to g. out,** vaciar; sacar

gourd n calabaza, f

gourmand n glotón, m

gourmet n gastrónomo, m

gout n med gota, f

govern vt gobernar; regir; (guide) guiar; dominar; domar, refrenar; gram regir; (regulate) regular

governess n institutriz, f; (in a school) maestra, f

governing a gubernante; director; (with principle, etc.) directivo. n See **government**

government n gobierno, m; dirección, f; autoridad, f. **g. bond,** bono del gobierno, m. **g. house,** palacio del gobernador, m. **g. office,** oficina del gobierno, f. **g. stock,** papel del Estado, m

governmental a gubernamental, gubernativo.

Government Printing Office Talleres Gráficos de la Nación, *m pl*

governor n gobernador (-ra); vocal de la junta de gobierno, *mf*; (of a prison) director (-ra) (de una prisión); *mech* regulador, *m*. **g.-general,** gobernador general, *m*

gown n toga, *f*; (cassock) sotana, *f*; (dressing-g.) bata, *f*; (for sleeping) camisa de noche, *f*; (bathing-wrap) albornoz, *m*; (dress) vestido, traje, *m*

grab n asimiento, *m*, presa, *f*; *mech* gancho, *m*. *vt* arrebatar, asir, agarrar; *fig* alzarse con, tomar

grace n elegancia, *f*; simetría, armonía, *f*; gracia, gentileza, *f*, donaire, *m*, encanto, *m*; (goodness) bondad, *f*; gracia, *f*, merced, *f*, favor, *m*; (period of time) plazo, *m*; (privilege) privilegio, *m*; *theol* gracia divina, *f*; (at table) bendición de la mesa, *f*; (as a title) excelentísimo, (to an archbishop) Ilustrísimo. *vt* adornar; favorecer; honrar. **airs and graces,** humos, *m pl.* **the Three Graces,** las Gracias. **three days' g.,** plazo de tres días, *m*. **to get into a person's good graces,** congraciarse con; caer en gracia con. **to say g.,** bendecir la mesa. **with a bad g.,** a regañadientes. **with a good g.,** de buena gana. **g.-note,** *mus* nota de adorno, *f*

graceful a airoso, gentil, gracioso; elegante; bonito

graceless a réprobo; dejado de la mano de Dios; sin gracia

gracious a (merciful) piadoso, clemente; (urbane) afable, condescendiente, agradable. **Good g.!** ¡Vamos!, ¡Dios mío!

graciously adv afablemente; con benevolencia. **to be g. pleased,** tener a bien

graciousness n amabilidad, afabilidad, condescendencia, *f*

gradation n graduación, *f*; *mus* gradación, *f*; paso gradual, *m*; serie, *f*

grade n grado, *m*; (quality) calidad, clase, *f*; (in a school) clase, *f*; (gradient) pendiente, declive, *m*. *vt* graduar, clasificar; (cattle breeding) cruzar. **down g.,** cuesta abajo. **up g.,** cuesta arriba. **highest g.,** n primera clase, *f*. de primera clase; de calidad excelente

gradient n declive, *m*. cuesta, pendiente, *f*

gradual a gradual. n ecc gradual, *m*

gradually adv gradualmente; poco a poco

graduate n licenciado (-da), *Lat. Am.* ex-alumno (na) *mf* a graduado. *vt* graduar. *vi* graduarse; (as a doctor) doctorarse. **to g. as,** recibirse de. **be graduated from . . .** *Lat. Am.* egresar de . . .

graduation n graduación, *f*, *Lat. Am.* egreso *m*

graft n bot injerto, *m*; *surg* injerto de piel, *m*. *vt bot* injertar; *surg* injertar un trozo de piel; *fig* injerir

grain n (corn) grano, *m*; (cereal) cereal, *m*, or *f*; (seed, weight) grano, *m*; (trace) pizca, *f*; (of wood, etc.) hila, *m*, fibra, hebra, veta, *f*; (of leather) flor, *f*; (texture) textura, *f*. *vt* granear; granular; (wood, marble, etc.) vetear. **g. against the g.,** a contrapelo. **g. lands,** mieses, *f pl*

gram n gramo, *m*

grammar n gramática, *f*. **g. school,** instituto de segunda enseñanza, *m*

grammatically adv gramaticalmente, como la gramática lo quiere. (e.g., **She now speaks Catalan g.,** Ahora habla el catalán como la gramática lo quiere)

granary n granero, hórreo, *m*, troj, *f*, *Mexico* espiguero *m*. **g. keeper,** trojero, *m*

grand a magnífico, soberbio; imponente; (of dress) espléndido, vistoso; (of people) distinguido, importante; aristocrático; (proud) orgulloso; (of style) elevado, sublime; (morally) noble; augusto; (main) principal; (full) completo, *inf* estupendo, magnífico; (with duke, etc.) gran. n piano de cola, *m*. **g.-aunt,** tía abuela, *f*. **g. cross,** gran cruz, *f*. **g. duchess,** gran duquesa, *f*. **g. duke,** gran duque, *m*. **g. lodge,** (of freemasons) Gran Oriente, *m*. **g. master,** gran maestre, *m*. **g.-nephew,** resobrino, *m*. **g.-niece,** resobrina, *f*. **g. opera,** ópera, *f*. **g. piano,** piano de cola, *m*. **g.-stand,** tribuna, *f*. **g.-uncle,** tío abuelo, *m*. **g. vizier,** gran visir, *m*

grandchild n nieto (-ta). **great-g.,** bisnieto (-ta). **great-great-g.,** tataranieto (-ta)

granddaughter n nieta, *f*. **great-g.,** bisnieta, *f*. **great-great-g.,** tataranieta, *f*

grandeur n magnificencia, *f*; grandiosidad, *f*; magnitud, grandeza, *f*; (pomp) pompa, *f*, fausto, *m*

grandfather n abuelo, *m*. **great-g.,** bisabuelo, *m*. **great-great-g.,** tatarabuelo, *m*

grandiloquent a grandílocuo

grandiose a grandioso, sublime; impresionante; imponente; (in a bad sense) extravagante; (of style) bombástico, hinchado

grand jury n jurado de acusación, jurado de juicio, *m*

grandmother n abuela, *f*. **great-g.,** bisabuela, *f*. **great-great-g.,** tatarabuela, *f*

grandness n magnificencia, *f*; aristocracia, *f*; (pride) orgullo, *m*; grandiosidad, *f*; (of style) sublimidad, *f*; (of character) nobleza, *f*

grandparent n abuelo, *m*; abuela, *f*; *pl* **grandparents,** abuelos, *m pl.* **great-grand-parents,** bisabuelos, *m pl.* **great-great-grandparents,** tatarabuelos, *m pl*

grandson n nieto, m. **great-g.**, bisnieto, m. **great-great-g.**, tataranieto, m

granny n abuelita, nana, f; abuela, f. **g. knot**, nudo al revés, m

grant n concesión, f; otorgamiento, m; donación, f; privilegio, m; (for study) beca, bolsa de estudio, f; (transfer) traspaso, m, cesión, f. vt conceder; (bestow) otorgar, dar; donar; (agree to) acceder a, asentir en; permitir; (transfer) traspasar; (assume) suponer. **to g. a degree,** expedir un título. **to g. a motion,** dar por entrada a una moción. **to take for granted,** descontar; dar por hecho, dar por sentado. **God g. it!** ¡Dios lo quiera! **granted that,** dado que

granulated a granulado

grape n uva, f. **bunch of grapes,** racimo de uvas, m. **muscatel g.,** uva moscatel, f. **sour grapes,** uvas agrias, f pl; (phrase) ¡están verdes! **g.-fruit**, toronja, f. **g. gatherer,** vendimiador (-ra). **g. harvest,** vendimia, f. **g. juice,** mosto, m. **g.-shot,** metralla, f. **g. stone,** granuja, f. **g.-sugar,** glucosa, f. **g.-vine,** vid, parra, f

graph n gráfica, f; diagrama, m

graphic a gráfico

grapple n naut rezón, arpeo, m; lucha a brazo partido, f. vt naut aferrar; asir, agarrar. vi naut aferrarse. **to g. with,** luchar a brazo partido (con); fig luchar con

grasp n agarro, m; (reach) alcance, m; (of a hand) apretón, m; (power) garras, f pl, poder, m; (understanding) comprensión, f; inteligencia, capacidad intelectual, f. vt agarrar, asir; empuñar; abrazar; fig comprender, alcanzar; (a hand) estrechar. vi agarrarse. **within one's g.,** al alcance de uno. **to g. at,** asirse de

grasping n asimiento, m; (understanding) comprensión, f, a codicioso, tacaño, mezquino

grass n hierba, f; (pasture) pasto, herbaje, m; (sward) césped, m. vt cubrir de hierba; sembrar de hierba; apacentar. **to hear the g. grow,** sentir crecer la hierba. **to let the g. grow,** fig dejar crecer la hierba. **to turn out to g.,** echar al pasto. **g.-blade,** brizna de hierba, f. **g.-green,** a and n verde como la hierba m.. **g.-grown,** cubierto de hierba. **g.-land,** pradera, f. **g.-snake,** culebra, f. **g. widow,** mujer cuyo marido está ausente

grasshopper n saltamontes, m. **grasshopper's chirp,** chirrido (del saltamontes), m

grassy a parecido a la hierba, como la hierba; cubierto de hierba; de hierba

grate n parrilla, f; (grating) reja, f. vt raspar, raer; cul rallar; (make a noise) hacer rechinar. vi raspar; rechinar, chirriar. **to g. on, upon,** (of sounds) irritar, molestar; chocar con. **to g. on the ear,** herir el oído

grateful a agradecido, reconocido; (pleasant) agradable, grato

gratefulness n agradecimiento, m, gratitud, f; (pleasantness) agrado, m

grater n cul rallador, m

gratification n satisfacción, f; (pleasure) placer, gusto, m

gratified a satisfecho, contento

gratify vt satisfacer; (please) gratificar, agradar

gratifying a satisfactorio, agradable

grating n reja, f; rejilla, f; naut jareta, f; (optics) retículo, m; (sound) rechinamiento, chirrido, m. a rechinante, chirriador; áspero

gratis a and adv gratis

gratitude n agradecimiento, m, gratitud, f

gratuitous a gratuito

gratuity n gratificación, propina, f

grave n (hole) sepultura, fosa, f; (monument) tumba, f, sepulcro, m; fig muerte, f. **g.-digger,** enterrador, sepulturero, m

grave a grave; importante; serio; sobrio; (anxious) preocupado; (of accent) grave. n (grave accent) acento grave, m

gravel n grava, f; cascajo, casquijo, m; med arenillas, f pl, cálculo, m

Graves' disease n bocio exoftálmico, m

gravitate vi gravitar; tender

gravitation n gravitación, f; tendencia, f

gravitational a de gravitación, gravitacional, gravitatorio

gravitational pull n atracción gravitatoria, f

gravity n phys gravedad, f; seriedad, f; solemnidad, f; gravedad, f; (weight) peso, m; importancia, f; (enormity) enormidad, f; (danger) peligro, m. **center of g.,** centro de gravedad, m. **law of g.,** ley de la gravedad, f. **specific g.,** peso específico, m

gravy n salsa, f; jugo (de la carne), m. **g.-boat,** salsera, f

gray a gris; (of animals) rucio. n color gris, gris, m; caballo gris, m. **His hair is turning g.,** El pelo se le vuelve gris. **g.-haired,** de pelo gris. **g. matter,** materia gris, f; cacumen, m. **g. mullet,** icht mújol, m. **g. squirrel,** gris, m. **g. wolf,** lobo gris, m

grayish a grisáceo, agrisado; (of hair) entrecano

graze n abrasión, f; (brush) roce, m, vi pacer, apacentarse. vt pastorear, apacentar; (brush) rozar

grazing n agr apacentamiento, pastoreo, m; (brushing) rozadura, f, a que pace, herbívoro; (of land) pacedero. **g. land,** pasto, m

grease n grasa, f; (dirt) mugre, f; (of a candle) sebo, m, cera, f. vt engrasar; manchar con grasa; fig inf untar. **to g. the wheels,** fig untar el carro. **g.-box**

mech caja de sebo, *f.* **g.-gun,** engrasador de compresión, *m.* **g.-paint,** afeites de actor (or de actriz), *m pl.* **g.-proof paper,** papel impermeable, *m.* **g. spot,** lámpara, mancha de grasa, *f.* saín, *m*

greasy *a* grasiento; (oily) aceitoso; (grubby) mugriento, bisunto, *Argentina* cascarriento; *fig* lisonjero. **g. pole,** cucaña, *f*

great *a* gran; grande; enorme; vasto; (much) mucho; (famous) famoso, ilustre; noble, sublime; (intimate) íntimo; importante; principal; poderoso; magnífico, impresionante; *inf* famoso, estupendo; (of time) largo; (clever) fuerte. **Alexander the G.,** Alejandro Magno. **the G. Mogul,** el Gran Mogol. **a g. deal,** mucho. **a g. man,** un grande hombre, un hombre famoso. **a g. many,** muchos (muchas). **He lived to a g. age,** Vivió hasta una edad avanzada. **so g.,** tan grande, tamaño. **the g.,** los grandes hombres. **g. on,** aficionado a. **g.-aunt,** tía abuela, *f.* **g.-grandchild,** etc. See **grandchild,** etc. **g.-hearted,** valeroso; magnánimo, generoso. **g. power,** gran poder, *m.* **G. War,** Gran Guerra, *f.* **the Great Schism,** el Gran Cisma, *m*

greater *a comp. of* **great,** mayor; más grande. **to make g.,** agrandar. **G. London,** el Gran Londres, *m*

greatest *a sup. of* **great,** más grande; mayor; máximo; más famoso; sumo

greatly *adv* mucho; con mucho; (very) muy; noblemente

greatness *n* grandeza, *f.* grandiosidad, *f.* extensión, vastedad, *f.* importancia, *f.* poder, *m.* majestad, *f.* esplendor, *m.* (intensity) intensidad, *f.* (enormity) enormidad, *f*

greed *n* (cupidity) codicia, rapacidad, avaricia, *f.* avidez, ansia, *f.* (of food) gula, glotonería, *f*

greedy *a* (for food) glotón; codicioso; ambicioso; ávido; deseoso

Greece Grecia, *f*

Greek *a* and *n* griego (-ga); (language) griego, *m.* **It's all G. to me,** Para mí es como si fuese en latín, Me es chino. **G. tunic,** peplo, *m*

green *a* verde; (inexpert) inexperto, bisoño; (recent) nuevo, reciente; (fresh) fresco; (of complexion) pálido, descolorido; (flowery) floreciente; (vigorous) lozano; (young) joven; (unripe) verde; (credulous) crédulo; (raw) crudo; (of wood, vegetables) verde. *n* verde, color verde, *m;* (vegetables) verdura, *f;* (meadow) prado, *m;* (turf) césped, *m;* (grass) hierba, *f;* (bowling) campo de juego, *m.* *vt* teñir (or pintar) de verde. **bright g.,** *n* verdegay, verde claro, *m.* **dark g.,** *n* verdinegro, *m.* **light g.,** *n* verde pálido, *m.* **to grow** or **look g.,** verdear. **g.-eyed,** de ojos verdes. **g. peas,** guisantes, *m pl.* **g. table,** tapete verde, *m*

greenery *n* follaje, *m;* verdura, *f*

greenhorn *n* bisoño (-ña); papanatas, *m*

greenhouse *n* invernáculo, invernadero, *m. Lat. Am.* conservatorio *m*

greenish *a* verdoso. **g.-yellow,** cetrino

greet *vt* saludar; recibir; (express pleasure) dar la bienvenida (a)

greeting *n* salutación, *f.* saludo, *m;* recepción, *f;* (welcome) bienvenida, *f; pl* **greetings,** recuerdos, *m pl*

gregarious *a* gregario

grenade *n* granada, bomba, *f.* **hand-g.,** bomba de mano, *f*

grey See **gray**

greyhound *n* galgo, lebrel, *m.* **g. bitch,** galga, *f;* **g. racing,** carreras de galgos, *f pl*

grid *n* (of electric power) red, *f;* rejilla, *f;* (for water, etc.) alcantarilla, *f*

gridiron *n cul* parrilla, *f;* (of electric power) red, *f; theat* telar, *m*

grief *n* angustia, pena, aflicción, *f;* dolor, suplicio, *m.* **to come to g.,** pasarlo mal, tener un desastre

grievance *n* injusticia, *f;* motivo de queja, *m*

grieve *vt* entristecer, afligir, angustiar; atormentar. *vi* entristecerse, afligirse, acongojarse. **to g. for,** lamentar: echar de menos

grievous *a* (heavy) oneroso, gravoso, opresivo; doloroso, penoso; lamentable; cruel. **g. error,** error lamentable

grill *n cul* parrilla, *f;* (grating) rejilla, *f;* (before a window) reja, *f;* (food) asado a la parrilla, *m. vt cul* asar a la parrilla; (burn) quemar; (question) interrogar; (torture) torturar. *vi cul* asarse a la parrilla; (be burnt) quemarse. **g.-room,** parrilla, *f*

grille *n* reja, *f;* rejilla, *f;* (screen) verja, *f*

griller *n cul* parrilla, *f*

grim *a* (fierce) feroz, salvaje; (severe) severo, ceñudo, adusto; inflexible; (frightful) horrible

grimace *n* mueca, *f,* gesto, mohín, visaje, *m, vi* hacer muecas

grime *n* mugre, *f;* suciedad, *f.* **to cover with g.,** enmugrecer

grimly *adv* severamente; sin sonreír; inflexiblemente; (without retreating) sin cejar; (frightfully) horriblemente; de un modo espantoso

grimy *a* mugriento, sucio

grin *n* sonrisa grande, *f;* sonrisa burlona, *f;* (grimace) mueca, *f. vi* sonreír mostrando los dientes; sonreír bonachonamente; sonreír de un modo burlón

grind *vt* (to powder) pulverizar; moler; (break up) quebrantar; (oppress) agobiar, oprimir; (sharpen) afilar, amolar; (a barrel-organ) tocar (un manubrio); (the teeth) crujir, rechinar (los dientes); (into) reducir a; (*inf* teach) empollar. *vi* moler; *fig inf* trabajar laboriosamente. *n fig inf* trabajo pesado, *m*; *n fig inf* estudiantón, *m*

grinder *n* (of scissors, etc.) afilador, *m*; (of an organ) organillero; (mill-stone) piedra de moler, *f*; (molar) muela, *f*

grinding a (tedious) cansado, aburrido; opresivo; (of pain) incesante. *n* pulverización, *f*; amoladura, *f*; (of grain) molienda, *f*; (polishing) pulimento, bruñido, *m*; (oppression) opresión, *f*; (of teeth) rechinamiento, *m*

grindstone *n* amoladera, afiladera, piedra de amolar, *f*. **to have one's nose to the g.,** batir el yunque

grinning a sonriente; riente; (mocking) burlón

grip *n* asimiento, agarro, *m*; (claws, clutches) garras, *f pl*; (hand) mano, *f*; (of shaking hands) apretón de manos, *m*; (of a weapon, etc.) empuñadura, *f*; (reach) alcance, *m*; (understanding) comprensión, *f*; (control) dominio, *m*; (bag) portamanteo, *m*; maleta, *f. vt* asir, agarrar; (of wheels) agarrarse; *mech* morder; (a sword, etc.) empuñar; (pinch) pellizcar; (surround) cercar; (understand) comprender; (press; to grip the hand and *flg* the heart) apretar; (fill) llenar; (the attention) atraer, llamar; (sway, hold) dominar

gripe *n* (*inf* pain) retortijón (de tripas), *m*

grisly a espantoso; repugnante

grist *n* molienda, *f*. **Everything is g. to their mill,** Sacan partido de todo

gristle *n* cartílago, *m*, ternilla, *f*

grit *n* cascajo, *m*; polvo, *m*; *fig* firmeza (de carácter), *f*; (courage) valor, *m*; (endurance) aguante, *m*

gritty a arenoso, arenisco

groan *n* gemido, *m. vi* gemir; (creak) crujir. **to g. out,** decir (or contar) entre gemidos. **to g. under,** sufrir bajo, gemir bajo; (of weight) crujir bajo

groaning *n* gemidos, *m pl*. a que gime, gemidor; (under a weight) crujiente

grocer *n* abacero *, f* vendedor (-ra) de comestibles, *Lat. Am.* abarrotero (-ra). **grocer's shop,** tienda de comestibles, bodega, *f, Mexico* abarrotería, *f*

grocery *n* tienda de comestibles, tienda de ultramarinos, abarrotería, lonja, bodega, *f*, negocio de comestibles, *m*; *pl* **groceries,** provisiones, *f pl*, comestibles, *m pl, Lat. Am.* abarrotes *mpl*

groin *n anat* ingle, *f*

groom *n* (in a royal household) gentilhombre, *m*; lacayo, *m*; mozo de caballos, *m*; (of a bride) novio, *m. vt* (a horse) cuidar; (oneself) arreglarse. **She is always well groomed,** Está siempre muy bien arreglada

groove *n* ranura, muesca, *f*; estría, *f*; surco, *m*; *fig* rutina, *f. vt* entallar; estriar

grope *vi* andar a tientas; (with for) buscar a tientas; procurar, encontrar, buscar. **to**

g. one's way toward, avanzar a tientas hacia; *fig* avanzar poco a poco hacia

gropingly adv a tientas; irresolutamente

gross *n com* gruesa, *f*; totalidad, *f*, a grueso; denso, espeso; (unrefined) grosero; (great) grande; (crass) craso; total; *com* bruto; (tremendous) enorme. **in g.,** en grueso. **g. amount,** total, *m*; *com* importe bruto, *m*. **g. weight,** peso bruto, *m*

grotesque a grotesco; extravagante, estrambótico; ridículo. *n* grotesco, *m*

grotto *n* gruta, *f*

ground *n* suelo, *m*; (of water and *naut*) fondo, *m*; (earth) tierra, *f*; *fig* terreno, *m*; (strata) capa, *f*; *sport* campo, *m*; (parade) plaza (de armas), *f*; (background) fondo, *m*; (basis) base, *f*, fundamento, *m*; (reason) causa, *f*; motivo, *m*; (excuse) pretexto, *m*; *pl* **grounds,** jardines, *m pl*, parque, *m*; (sediment) sedimento, *m*, heces, *f pl*; (reason) causa, *f. vi naut* varar, encallar. *vt* poner en tierra; *naut* hacer varar; *elec* conectar con tierra; (base) fundar (en), basar (en); (teach) enseñar los rudimentos (de). a molido; en polvo; (of floors, stories) bajo; (of glass) deslustrado; *bot* terrestre. **common g.,** tierra comunal, *f*; *fig* tierra común, *f*. **He is on his own g.,** Está en terreno propio. **It fell to the g.,** Cayó al suelo; *fig* Fracasó. **It is on the g.,** Está en el suelo. **It suits me to the g.,** Me viene de perilla. **to break fresh g.,** *fig* tratar problemas nuevos. **to be well grounded in,** conocer bien los elementos (or rudimentos) de. **to cover g.,** cubrir terreno; recorrer; (in discussion) tocar muchos puntos. **to cut the g. from beneath one's feet,** hacer perder la iniciativa (a). **to give g.,** retroceder; perder terreno. **to raze to the g.,** echar por tierra, arrasar. **to stand one's g.,** resistir el ataque; no darse por vencido; *fig* mantenerse firme, mantenerse en sus trece. **to win g.,** ganar terreno. **g. coffee,** café molido, *m*. **g.-color,** (of paint) primera capa, *f*; (color de) fondo, *m*; **g.-floor,** piso bajo, *m*. **g. glass,** vidrio deslustrado, *m*. **g.-ivy,** hiedra terrestre, *f*. **g. nut,** cacahuete, *m*. **g.-plan,** *arch* planta, *f*. **g.-rent,** censo, *m*. **g.-sheet,** tela impermeable, *f*; **g. staff,** *aer* personal del aeropuerto, *m*. **g.-swell,** mar de fondo, *m*

grounded a fundado. **The airplanes are g.,** Los aviones están sin volar. **His suspicions are well g.,** Tiene motivos para sus sospechas

groundless a sin fundamento, inmotivado, sin causa, sin motivo

groundwork *n* fundamento, *m*; base, *f*; principio, *m*

group *n* grupo, *m. vt* agrupar. *vi* agruparse. **g. captain,** coronel de aviación, *m*

grove *n* soto, boscaje, *m*; arboleda, *f*

grovel *vi* arrastrarse; *fig* humillarse

groveling *a fig* servil; ruin

grow *vi* crecer; (increase) aumentar; (become) hacerse; empezar a; llegar a; (turn) volverse, ponerse; (flourish) progresar, adelantar; (develop) desarrollarse; (extend) extenderse. *vt* cultivar; dejar crecer. **I grew to fear it,** Llegué a temerlo. **to g. cold,** ponerse frío; enfriarse; (of weather) empezar a hacer frío. **to g. fat,** engordar. **to g. hard,** ponerse duro; *fig* endurecerse. **to g. hot,** ponerse caliente; calentarse; (of weather) empezar a hacer calor. **to g. like Topsy,** crecer a la buena de Dios. **to g. old,** envejecer. **to g. tall,** crecer mucho; ser alto. **to g. again,** crecer de nuevo. **to g. into,** hacerse, llegar a ser; venir a ser. **to g. out of,** brotar de; originarse en; (a habit) desacostumbrarse poco a poco. **He is growing out of his clothes,** La ropa se le hace pequeña. **to g. up,** (of persons) hacerse hombre (mujer); desarrollarse; (of a custom, etc.) imponerse. **to g. on, upon,** crecer sobre; llegar a dominar; (make think) hacer creer, empezar a pensar; (of a habit) arraigar en

grower *n* cultivador (-ra)

growing *n* crecimiento, *m*; desarrollo, *m*; (increase) aumento, *m*; (of flowers, etc.) cultivación, *f*, *a* creciente

growing pains *n pl* crisis de desarrollo, *f*

growl *n* gruñido, *m*; reverberación, *f*; trueno, *m*. *vi* gruñir; (of guns) tronar; (of thunder) reverberar. **to g. out,** decir gruñendo

grown *a* crecido; maduro; adulto. **a g. up,** una persona mayor. **to be full-g.,** estar completamente desarrollado; haber llegado a la madurez. **g. over with,** cubierto de

growth *n* crecimiento, *m*; (development) desarrollo, *m*; (progress) progreso, adelanto, *m*; (increase) aumento, *m*; (cultivation) cultivo, *m*; (vegetation) vegetación, *f*; *med* tumor, *m*. **He has a week's g. on his chin,** Tiene una barba de una semana

grub *n* larva, *f*, gusano, *m*. *vt* (with up, out) desarraigar; cavar; desmalezar; *fig* *inf* buscar

grubby *a* lleno de gusanos; sucio; bisunto; desaliñado

grudge *n* motivo de rencor, *m*; rencor, resentimiento, *m*, ojeriza, *f*; mala voluntad, *f*; aversión, *f*. *vt* envidiar. **to bear a g.,** tener ojeriza

grudging *a* (niggardly) mezquino; envidioso; poco generoso; de mala gana; nada afable

grudgingly *adv* de mala gana, contra su voluntad; con rencor; a regañadientes

gruel *n* gachas, *f pl*

gruesome *a* pavoroso, horrible; macabro

gruff *a* (of the voice) bronco, grave, áspero; (of manner) brusco, malhumorado

gruffly *adv* en una voz bronca (or áspera); bruscamente, con impaciencia, malhumoradamente

grumble *n* ruido sordo, trueno, *m*; estruendo, *m*; (complaint) refunfuño, rezongo, *m*. *vi* tronar; refunfuñar, rezongar; hablar entre dientes; quejarse; protestar (contra). *vt* decir refunfuñando

grumbling *a* gruñón, refunfuñador; regañón; descontento. *n* See **grumble**

grumpy *a* malhumorado, irritable

grunt *n* gruñido, *m*. *vi* gruñir

guarantee *n law* persona de quien otra sale fiadora, *f*; garantía, *f*; abono, *m*. *vt* garantizar; responder de; abonar; (assure) asegurar, acreditar

guarantor *n* garante, *mf*

guard *n* (watchfulness) vigilancia, *f*; (in fencing) guardia, *f*; (of a sword) guarnición, *f*; (sentry) centinela, *m*; (soldier) guardia, *m*; (body of soldiers) guardia, *f*; (escort) escolta, *f*; (keeper) guardián, *m*; (protection) protección, defensa, *f*; (of a train) jefe de tren, *m*. *vt* guardar; proteger, defender; vigilar; (escort) escoltar. **to g. against,** guardarse de. **the changing of the g.,** el relevo de la guardia. **to be on g.,** *mil* estar de guardia; (in fencing) estar en guardia. **to be on one's g.,** estar prevenido, estar alerta. **to be off one's g.,** estar desprevenido. **to mount g.,** *mil* montar la guardia; vigilar. **guard's van,** furgón de equipajes, *m*. **g.-house,** cuerpo de guardia, *m*; prisión militar, *f*

guarded *a* (reticent) reservado, circunspecto, prudente, discreto

guardedly *adv* prudentemente, con circunspección, discretamente

guardian *n* protector (-ra); guardián (-ana); *law* tutor, *m*. *a* que guarda; tutelar. **g. angel,** ángel de la guarda, ángel custodio, *m*; deidad tutelar, *f*

guardianship *n* protección, *f*; patronato, *m*; *law* curaduría, tutela, *f*

guardsman *n* guardia, *m*

Guatemalan *a* and *n* guatemalteco (-ca)

guava *n bot* guayaba, *f*

guerrilla *n* guerrilla, *f*; (soldier) guerrillero, *m*. *a* de guerrilla. **g. warfare,** guerra de guerrillas, *f*

guess *n* adivinación, *f*; estimación, *f*; conjetura, *f*; sospecha, *f*. *vt* and *vi* adivinar; conjeturar; sospechar; imaginar; (suppose) suponer, creer; calcular. **to g. at,** formar una opinión sobre; imaginar. **a rough g.,** estimación aproximada, *f*. **at a g.,** a poco más o menos, a ojo de buen cubero. **g.-work,** conjeturas, suposiciones, *f pl*

guest *n* (at a meal) convidado (-da), invitado (-da); (at a hotel, etc.) cliente (-da); (houseguest) *Lat. Am.* alojado *biol* parásito, *m*. **g.-room,** alcoba de respeto, alcoba de honor, alcoba de huéspedes, *f*, cuarto de amigos, cuarto para invitados, *m*

guffaw *n* carcajada, *f*. *vi* reírse a carcajadas, soltar el trapo

guidance *n* dirección, *f*; gobierno, *m*; (advice) consejos, *m pl*; inspiración, *f*

guide *n* (person) guía, *mf*; (girl g.) exploradora, *f*; (book and *fig*) guía, *f*; mentor, *m*; modelo, *m*; (inspiration) norte, *m*; *mech* guía, *f*. *vt* guiar; conducir; encaminar; dirigir; (govern) gobernar. **g.-book,** guía (de turistas), *f*. **g.-post,** poste indicador, *m*

guided tour *n* visita explicada, visita programada, *f*

guideline *lit* falsarregla, falsilla, *f*; *fig* pauta, *f*

guile *n* astucia, superchería, maña, *f*

guileless *a* cándido, sin malicia, inocente

guilt *n* culpabilidad, *f*; crimen, *m*; (sin) pecado, *m*

guilt complex complejo de culpa, *m*

guiltily *adv* culpablemente; como si fuese culpable

guiltless *a* libre de culpa, inocente; puro; ignorante

guilty *a* culpable; delincuente; criminal. **to find g.,** encontrar culpable. **to plead g.,** confesarse culpable. **g. party,** culpable, *m*

guise *n* manera, guisa, *f*; (garb) traje, *m*; máscara, *f*; *fig* pretexto, *m*. **under the g. of,** bajo el pretexto de; bajo la apariencia de

guitar *n* guitarra, *f*

guitarist *n* guitarrista, *mf*

gulf *n* golfo, *m*; abismo, *m*

Gulf Stream, the la Corriente del Golfo

gullet *n* esófago, *m*; garganta, *f*

gullible *a* crédulo

gully *n* hondonada, barranca, *f*; (gutter) arroyo, *m*

gulp *n* trago, sorbo, *m*. *vt* engullir, tragar; (repress) ahogar; (believe) tragar. **to g. up,** vomitar

gum *n* (of the mouth) encía, *f*; goma, *f*. *vt* engomar; pegar con goma. **gum arabic,** goma arábiga, *f*. **gum boots,** botas de goma, *f*. **gum-resin,** gomorresina, *f*. **gum starch,** aderezo, *m*. **gum tree,** eucalipto, *m*

gummy *a* gomoso

gumption *n* sentido común, seso, *m*

gun *n* arma de fuego, *f*; (handgun) fusil, *m*; (sporting g.) escopeta, *f*; (pistol) pistola, *f*, revólver, *m*; (cannon) cañón, *m*; (firing) cañonazo, *m*. **big gun,** *inf* pájaro gordo, *m*. **heavy gun,** cañón de grueso calibre, *m*. **gun-barrel,** cañón de escopeta, *m*. **gun-carriage,** cureña, *f*. **gun-cotton,** pólvora de algodón, *f*. **gun-fire,** cañonazos, *m pl*, fuego, *m*. **gun-metal,** bronce de cañón, *m*; pavón, *m*. **gun-room,** armería, *f*; (on a ship) polvorín, *m*. **gun-running,** contrabanda de armas, *f*. **gun-turret,** torre, *f*. **gun wound,** balazo, *m*

gunman *n* escopetero, armero, *m*; bandido armado, *m*; gángster, apache, *m*

gunner *n* artillero, *m*; escopetero, *m*

gun permit *n* licencia de armas, *f*, permiso de armas, *m*

gunpowder *n* pólvora, *f*

gunshot *n* escopetazo, *m*; tiro de fusil, *m*

gurgle *n* murmullo, murmurio, gorgoteo, *m*; gluglú, *m*; (of a baby) gorjeo, *m*. *vi* murmurar; hacer gluglú; (of babies) gorjear

gurgling *a* murmurante; (of babies) gorjeador. *n* See **gurgle**

gush *n* chorro, *m*; (of words) torrente, *m*; (of emotion) efusión, *f*. *vi* chorrear, borbotar; surtir, surgir. **to g. out,** brotar a borbotones, salir a borbollones, salira borbotones. **to g. over,** *fig* hablar con efusión de

gushing *a* hirviente; (of people) efusivo, extremoso, empalagoso

gusset *n sew* escudete, *m*

gust *n* (of wind) ráfaga, bocanada (de aire), *f*; *fig* arrebato, acceso, *m*

gusto *n* brío, *m*; entusiasmo, *m*

gut *n* intestino, *m*, tripa, *f*; (catgut) cuerda de tripa, *f*; *naut* estrecho, *m*; *pl* **guts,** tripas, *f pl*; (content) meollo, *m*, substancia, *f*; (stamina) aguante, espíritu, *m*. *vt* (of fish, etc.) destripar; (plunder) saquear; destruir por completo; quemar completamente

gutter *n* canal, *m*; (of a street) arroyo (de la calle), *m*; (ditch) zanja, *f*; *fig* hampa, *f*. *vt* surcar. *vi* gotear; (of a candle) cerotear, gotear la cera. **g. spout,** canalón, *m*

guy *n* (rope) viento, *m*; *naut* guía, *f*; (effigy) mamarracho, *m*; (scarecrow) espantajo, *m*, *vt* sujetar con vientos o guías; burlarse de

guzzle *vt* tragar, engullir. *vi* atracarse, engullir; emborracharse. *n* comilón, *m*; borrachera, *f*

guzzler *n* tragador (-ra); borracho (-cha)

gymnasium *n* gimnasio, *m*

gymnast *n* gimnasta, *mf*

gymnastic *a* gimnástico. **g. rings,** anillas, *f pl*

gymnastics *n* gimnasia, *f*

gynecological *a* ginecológico

gynecology *n* ginecología, *f*

gypsum *n* yeso, *m*

gypsy *n* gitano (-na). *a* gitano, gitanesco; (music) flamenco

gyrate *vi* girar, rodar

H

h *n* (letter) hache, *f*

ha *interj* ¡ah!

haberdasher *n* mercero, *m*

haberdashery *n* mercería, *f*

habiliment *n* vestidura, *f*; *pl* **habiliments,** indumentaria, *f*

habit *n* costumbre, *f*, hábito, *m*; (temperament) temperamento, carácter, *m*; (use) uso, *m*; (of body) complexión, constitución, *f*; *ecc* hábito, *m*. **to be in the h. of,** soler, acostumbrar, estar acostumbrado a. **to have bad habits,** estar malacostumbrado. **to have the bad h. of,** tener el vicio (or la mala costumbre) de. **to contract the h. of,** contraer la costumbre de. **h. maker,** sastre de trajes de montar, *m*

habitable *a* habitable, vividero

habitat *n* (bot, zool) medio, *m*, habitación, *f*

habitation *n* habitación, *f*

habit-forming *a* enviciador, que crea vicio

habitual *a* habitual, acostumbrado, usual; constante; común

habitually *adv* habitualmente; constantemente; comúnmente

habituate *vt* habituar, acostumbrar

habitué *n* parroquiano (-na); veterano (-na)

hack *n* caballo de alquiler, *m*; rocín, jaco, *m*; (writer) escritor mercenario, *m*. *vt* acuchillar; tajar, cortar. *vi* cortar. **to h. to pieces,** cortar en pedazos; pasar a cuchillo

hacking *a* (of coughs) seco

hackle *n* (for flax, hemp) rastrillo, *m*

hackneyed *a* gastado, trillado, muy usado, repetido, resobado

hacksaw *n* sierra de cerrajero, sierra para metal, *f*

hackwork *n* trabajo de rutina, *m*

haddock *n* merlango, *m*, pescadilla, *f*

hag *n* bruja, *f*

haggard *a* ojeroso, trasnochado, trasojado

haggle *vi* regatear; vacilar

haggling *n* regateo, *m*, a regatón

ha, ha! *interj* ¡ja, ja!

hail *n* (salutation) saludo, *m*; (shout) grito, *m*; aclamación, *f*; (frozen rain) granizo, *m*; (of blows) lluvia, *f*. *interj* ¡salve! *vt* saludar; llamar; aclamar; *fig* lanzar, echar. *vi* (hailstones) granizar; (blows, etc.) llover. **to h. from,** proceder de, ser natural de. **within h.,** al habla. **H. Mary,** Salve Regina, Avemaría, *f*

hailstone *n* granizo, pedrisco, *m*

hailstorm *n* granizada, *f*

hair *n* (single h.) cabello, *m*; (zool, bot) pelo, *m*; (of horse's mane) crin, *f*; (head of h.) cabellera, mata de pelo, *f*, pelo, *m*; (superfluous) vello, *m*; (fiber) fibra, *f*, filamento, *m*; (on the pen) raspa, *f*, pelo, *m*; *fig* pelo, *m*. **lock of h.,** bucle, rizo, *m*; mecha, *f*. **to dress one's h.,** peinarse. **to have one's h. cut,** hacerse cortar el pelo. **to part the h.,** hacer(se) la raya del pelo. **to put up one's h.,** hacerse el moño; (to "come out") ponerse de largo. **to tear one's h.,** mesarse los cabellos. **h. combings,** peinaduras, *f pl*. **h.-curler,** tirabuzón, *m*. **h. dryer,** secadora de cabello, *f*. **h. dye,** tinte para el pelo, *m*. **h.-net,** redecilla, *f*, *Mexico* invisible *m*. **h.-oil,** brillantina, *f*. **h.-raising,** horripilante, espeluznante. **h.-ribbon,** cinta para el pelo, *f*. **h.-shirt,** cilicio, *m*. **h. slide,** pasador, *m*. **h.-splitting,** sofistería, argucia, *f*; mez quinas argucias, quis quillas, *f pl*. **h.-spring,** muelle del volante, *m*. **h.-switch,** añadido, *m*. **h.-trigger,** pelo de una pistola, *m*

hairband *m Lat. Am.* bincha *f*

hairbreadth *n* pelo, *m*. **to have a h. escape,** escapar por un pelo.

hairbrush *n* cepillo para el cabello, *m*

hairdresser *n* peluquero (-ra), peinadora, *f*

hairdressing *n* peinado, *m*. **h. establishment** or **trade,** peluquería, *f*

hairless *a* sin pelo; calvo

hairpin *n* horquilla, *f*, *Argentina* invisible *m*. **h. bend,** viraje en horquilla, *m*

hairsplitting arguments *Lat. Am.* abogaderas, abogaderías *fpl*

hairy *a* peludo; velloso; *bot* hirsuto

Haiti Haití, *m*

Haitian *a* and *n* haitiano (-na)

hake *n* merluza, *f*

halcyon *n* alción, martín pescador, *m*. *fig* feliz, sereno, tranquilo

hale *a* fuerte, sano, robusto. *vt* hacer comparecer

half *n* mitad, *f*; (school term) trimestre, *m*. *a* medio; semi. *adv* a medias; mitad; (almost) casi; insuficientemente; imperfectamente. **I don't h. like it,** No me gusta nada. **It is h.-past two,** Son las dos y media. **an hour and a h.,** una hora y media. **better h.,** *inf* media naranja, cara mitad, *f*. **by halves,** a medias. **in h.,** en dos mitades. **one h.,** la mitad. **to go halves,** ir a medias. **to h. close,** entornar. **to h. open,** entreabrir. **h. a bottle,** media botella, *f*. **h. a crown,** media corona, *f*. **h.-alive,** semivivo. **h. an hour,** media hora, *f*. **h.-and-h.,** mitad y mitad; en partes iguales. **h.-asleep,** semidormido, medio dormido. **h.-awake,** medio despierto, entre duerme y vela. **h.-back,** *sport* medio, *m*. **h.-baked,** medio cocido, crudo; *fig* poco maduro. **h.-binding,** encuadernación en media pasta, *f*. **h.-breed,** a mestizo. *n* cruce, *m*.

h.-brother, hermanastro, hermano de padre, hermano de madre, *m.* **h.-caste,** mestizo. **h. circle,** semicírculo, *m.* **h.-closed,** entreabierto; medio cerrado. **h.-dead,** medio muerto; más muerto que vivo. **h.-done,** hecho a medias, sin acabar. **h.-dozen,** media docena, *f.* **h.-dressed,** medio desnudo. **h. fare,** medio billete, *m.* **h.-full,** medio lleno. **h.-hearted,** débil, poco eficaz, lánguido; indiferente, sin entusiasmo. **h.-heartedness,** debilidad, *f;* indiferencia, *f.* **h.-holiday,** media fiesta, *f.* **h.-hourly,** cada media hora. **h.-length,** (portrait) de medio cuerpo. **h.-length coat,** abrigo de tres cuartos, *m.* **h.-light,** media luz, *f.* **h.-mast,** a media asta. **h.-measure,** medida poco eficaz, *f.* **h.-moon,** *n* media luna, *f; ast* semilunio, *m;* (of a nail) blanco (de la uña), *m.* **h.-mourning,** medio luto, *m.* **h.-pay,** media paga, *f.* **h.-price,** a mitad de precio. **h.-seas-over,** *inf* entre dos velas. **h.-sister,** hermanastra, hermana de padre, hermana de madre, *f.* **h.-time,** *sport* media parte, *f,* medio tiempo, *m.* **h.-tone,** de medio tono. **h.-tone illustration,** fotograbado a media tinta, *m.* **h.-truth,** verdad a medias, *f.* **h.-turn,** media vuelta, *f.* **h.-way,** a medio camino; medio. **h.-witted,** medio loco, tonto, imbécil. **h.-year,** medio año, *m.* **h.-yearly,** semestral

half close *vt* entrecerrar

halibut *n* halibut, *m;* (genus) hipogloso, *m*

halitosis *n* halitosis, *f*

hall *n* (mansion) mansión, casa de campo, *f,* caserón, *m;* (public building) edificio, *m,* casa (de); (town h.) casa del ayuntamiento, *f;* (room) sala, *f;* (entrance) vestíbulo, *m;* (dining room) comedor, *m;* (of residence for students) residencia, *f.* **h. door,** portón, *m,* puerta del vestíbulo, *f.* **h. porter,** conserje, *m.* **h.-stand,** perchero, *m*

hallelujah *n* aleluya, *f*

hallmark *n* marca de ley, *f; fig* señal, *f;* indicio, *m. vt* poner la marca de ley sobre; *fig* sellar

hallow *vt* santificar; reverenciar; (consecrate) consagrar

Halloween *n* la víspera de Todos los Santos, *f*

hallucination *n* alucinación, ilusión, *f;* visión, *f;* fantasma, *m*

hallucinatory *a* alucinador

halo *n* halo, nimbo, *m*

halogen *n chem* halógeno, *m*

halt *n mil* alto, *m;* cesación, *f;* interrupción, *f;* (on a railway) apeadero, *m;* (for trams, buses) parada, *f. vt* parar, detener. *vi* pararse, detenerse; *mil* hacer alto; cesar; interrumpirse; (in speech) titubear; (of verse) estar cojo; (doubt) dudar; (limp) cojear. **H.!** *mil* ¡Alto!

halter *n* ronzal, cabestro, *m;* (for hanging) dogal, *m. vt* encabestrar, cabestrar

halting *n* parada, *f;* interrupción, *f. a* (of gait) cojo; incierto; vacilante; (of speech) titubeante

halve *vt* partir (or dividir) en dos mitades

ham *n* jamón, *m; anat* pernil, *m;* (radiooperator) radioaficionado, *m*

hamlet *n* aldea, *f,* pueblecito, *m*

hammer *n* martillo, *m;* (stone cutter's) maceta, *f;* (mason's) piqueta, *f;* (of firearms) percusor, *m;* (of piano) macillo, *m. vt* amartillar, martillar, batir. **to throw the h.,** lanzar el martillo. **under the h.,** en subasta, al remate. **h. blow,** martillazo, *m*

hammock *n* hamaca, *f; naut* coy, *m*

hamper *n* banasta, canasta, *f,* cesto grande, *m. vt* estorbar, dificultar, impedir; *fig* embarazar

hamster *n zool* hámster, *m,* marmota de Alemania, rata del trigo, *f*

hand *n mano, f;* (of animal) pata, mano, *f;* (worker) operario (-ia); obrero (-ra); (skill) habilidad, *f;* (side) mano, *f,* lado, *m;* (measure) palmo, *m;* (of a clock) manecilla, *f;* (of instruments) aguja, *f;* (applause) aplauso, *m;* (power) poder, *m;* las manos; (at cards) mano, *f;* (card player) jugador, *m;* (signature) firma, *f;* (handwriting) letra, escritura, *f;* (influence) influencia, parte, mano, *f.* **old h.,** veterano; perro viejo. **at h.,** a mano, al lado, cerca. **have at hand,** tener a la mano. **at the hands of,** de manos de. **by h.,** a mano; (on the bottle) con biberón. **from h. to h.,** de mano a mano. **in h.,** entre manos; (of money) de contado. **in the hands of,** *fig* en el poder de. **"Hands wanted,"** «Se desean trabajadores.» **h. over h.,** mano sobre mano. **hand's breadth,** palmo, *m.* **Hands off!** ¡Fuera las manos! **Hands up!** ¡Manos arriba! **lost with all hands,** (of a ship) perdido con toda su tripulación. **off one's hands,** despachado; (of a daughter) casada. **on all hands,** por todas partes. **on h.,** entre manos; (of goods) existente; (present) presente. **on one's hands,** a cargo de uno. **on the one h.,** por un lado; a un lado. **on the other h.,** por otra parte; en cambio. **out of h.,** luego, inmediatamente; revoltoso. **to come to h.,** venir a mano; (of letters) llegar a las manos (or a las de). **to get one's h. in,** ejercitarse. **to have a h. in,** tener parte en; intervenir en. **to have no h. in,** no tener arte ni parte en. **to have on h.,** traer entre manos. **to have the upper h.,** tener la sartén por el mango, llevar la ventaja. **to hold one's h.,** abstenerse; detenerse. **to join hands,** cogerse de las manos. **to lay hands on,** tocar; poner mano en; echar manos a. **to set one's h. to,** emprender; (sign) firmar. **to shake hands,** estrechar la mano. **to stretch out one's hands,** tender las manos. **to take one's hands off,** no tocar. **with**

folded hands, mano sobre mano. **with his hands behind his back,** con las manos en la espalda. **h.-in-h.,** cogidos (cogidas) de las manos. **h.-lever,** manija, *f.* **h.-loom,** telar de mano, *m.* **h. luggage,** equipaje de mano, *m.* **h.-made,** hecho a mano. **h.-mill,** molinillo, *m.* **h.-pump,** *n naut* sacabuche, *m.* **h. rail,** pasamano, *m,* baranda, balustrada, *f.* **h.-sewn,** cosido a mano. **h.-to-h.,** de mano en mano; (of a fight) a brazo partido, cuerpo a cuerpo. **h.-to-h. fight,** cachetina, *f.* **h.-to-mouth,** precario. **to live from h.-to-mouth,** vivir de día en día

hand *vt* dar; entregar; alargar. **to h. down,** bajar; (a person) ayudar a bajar; transmitir. **to h. in,** entregar; (a person) ayudar a entrar; (one's resignation) dimitir; (send) mandar, enviar. **to h. on,** transmitir. **to h. out,** *vt* distribuir; (a person) ayudar a salir; (from a vehicle) ayudar a bajar. *vi inf* pagar. **to h. over,** *vt* entregar. *vi mil* traspasar los poderes (a). **to h. round,** pasar de mano en mano; pasar; ofrecer. **to h. up,** subir; (a person) ayudar a subir

handbag *n* bolso, saco, monedero, *m*

handbill *n* anuncio, *m*

handbook *n* manual, compendio, tratado, *m;* anuario, *m;* (guide) guía, *f*

handcuff *n* esposa, *f,* grillo, *m,* (gen. *pl*). *vt* poner las esposas (a), maniatar

handful *n* puño, puñado, manojo, *m.* **to be a h.,** *inf* tener el diablo en el cuerpo. **in handfuls,** a manojos

handicap *n* desventaja, *f;* obstáculo, *m; sport* handicap, *m;* ventaja, *f. vt fig* perjudicar, impedir, dificultar. **the handicapped,** los lisiados, *m pl*

handicraft *n* mano de obra, *f;* (skill) destreza manual, *f,*

handiwork *n* mano de obra, *f;* trabajo manual, *m;* obra, *f;* (deed) acción, *f,* hecho, *m*

handkerchief *n* pañuelo, *m*

handle *n* mango, puño, *m, Lat. Am. also* manivela *f;* (lever) palanca, *f;* (of baskets, dishes, jugs) asa, *f;* (of doors, windows, drawers) pomo, *m,* (of a car door) picaporte *m;* (to one's name) designación, *f;* título, *m;* (excuse) pretexto, *m. vt* (touch) tocar; manejar, manipular; (treat) tratar; **h. with kid gloves,** tratar con guantes de seda; (deal in) comerciar en; tomar; (paw) manosear; (direct) dirigir; (control) gobernar; (pilot) pilotar; (a theme) explicar, tratar de. **h.-bar grip,** puño de un manillar, *m*

handlebars *npl Spain* guía *fsg,* manillar *msg, Lat. Am.* manubrio *msg*

handling *n* manejo, *m;* manipulación, *f;* (treatment) trato, *m,* relaciones (con), *f pl;* (thumbing) manoseo, *m;* interpretación, *f; art* tratamiento, *m,* técnica, *f*

handshake *n* apretón de manos, *m*

handsome *a* (generous) generoso; mag-

nánimo; considerable; hermoso, bello; elegante; (of people) guapo, distinguido; excelente; (flattering) halagüeño. **He was a very h. man,** Era un hombre muy guapo

handsomely *adv* generosamente; con magnanimidad; elegantemente; bien

handspring *n* voltereta sobre las manos, *f*

handwork *n* obra hecha a mano, *f,* trabajo a mano, *m;* (needlework) labor de aguja, *f*

handworked *a* hecho a mano; (embroidered) bordado

handwriting *n* caligrafía, letra, escritura, *f.* **the h. on the wall,** la mano que escribía en la pared, *f*

handy *a* (of persons) diestro, mañoso, hábil; (of things) conveniente; útil; (near) cercano, a mano. *adv* cerca. **h.-man,** hombre de muchos oficios, *m;* factótum, *m*

hang *vt* colgar; suspender; (execute) ahorcar; (the head) bajar; dejar caer; (upholster) entapizar; (with wallpaper) empapelar; (drape) poner colgaduras en; (place) poner; (cover) cubrir. *vi* colgar, pender; estar suspendido; (be executed) ser ahorcado; (of garments) caer. *n* (of garments) caída, *f;* (of a machine) mecanismo, *m;* (meaning) sentido, *m,* significación, *f.* **to h. by a thread,** pender de un hilo. **to h. in the balance,** estar en la balanza. **to h. fire,** estar (una cosa) en suspenso. **to h. loose,** caer suelto; (clothes) venir ancho. **to h. about,** (surround) rodear, pegarse a; (frequent) frecuentar; (haunt) rondar; (be imminent) ser inminente, amenazar; (embrace) abrazar. **to h. back,** retroceder; quedarse atrás; *fig* vacilar, titubear. **to h. down,** colgar, pender; estar caído; caerse. **to h. on,** seguir agarrado (a); apoyarse en; *fig* persistir; (a person's words) estar pendiente de, beber; (remain) quedarse. **to h. out,** *vt* tender. *vi* (lean out) asomarse (por); (*inf* live) habitar. **to h. over,** colgar por encima; (brood) cernerse sobre; (lean over) inclinarse sobre; quedarse cerca de; (overhang) sobresalir; (overarch) abovedar; (threaten) amenazar. **to h. together,** (of persons) permanecer unidos; (of things) tener cohesión; (be consistent) ser lógico, ser consistente. **to h. up,** colgar; suspender; *fig* dejar pendiente, interrumpir. **to h. upon,** apoyarse en; (a person's words) beber las palabras de uno

hangar *n* cobertizo, *m;* *aer* hangar, *m*

hanger *n* colgadero, *m;* percha *f.* **h.-on,** parásito, *m;* dependiente, *m*

hanging *n* colgamiento, *m;* (killing) ahorcamiento, *m; pl* **hangings,** colgaduras *f pl,* cortinajes, *m pl..* a pendiente colgante; péndulo; (of gardens) pensil. **It's not a h. matter,** No es una cuestión de vida y muerte. **h. bridge,** puente colgante, *m.*

h. committee, junta (de una exposición,) *f.* **h. lamp,** lámpara de techo, *f*

hangman *n* verdugo, *m*

hangnail *n* padrastro, *m*

hangover *n* (after drinking) resaca, cruda (Mexico), *f*

hanker *vi* (with after) ansiar, ambicionar; (with for) anhelar, suspirar por, desear con vehemencia

hanky-panky *n* superchería, *f*; engaño, *m*

haphazard *n* casualidad, *f.* a fortuito, casual

hapless *a* desgraciado, desdichado

happen *vi* suceder, acontecer, ocurrir, pasar; (to be found, be) hallarse por casualidad; (take place) tener lugar, verificarse; (arise) sobrevenir. **Do you know what has happened to . . .?** ¿Sabes qué se ha hecho de . . .? **as if nothing had happened,** como si no hubiese pasado nada. **He turned up as if nothing had happened,** Se presentó como si tal cosa. **How did it h.?** ¿Cómo fue esto? **If they h. to see you,** Si acaso te ven. **I happened to be in London,** Me hallaba por casualidad en Londres. **It won't h. again,** No volverá a suceder. whatever happens, venga lo que venga

happening *n* suceso, acontecimiento, hecho, *m*, ocurrencia, *f*

happiness *n* felicidad, dicha, *f*; alegría, *f*, regocijo, *m*

happy *a* (lucky) afortunado; (felicitous) feliz, oportuno; feliz, dichoso; alegre, regocijado. **to be h.,** estar contento, ser feliz. **to be h. about,** alegrarse de. **to make h.,** hacer feliz, alegrar. **h.-go-lucky,** irresponsable, descuidado

harangue *n* arenga, *f. vt* arengar. *vi* pronunciar una arenga

harass *vt* hostigar, acosar; atormentar; preocupar; *mil* picar. **to h. the rearguard,** picar la retaguardia

harbinger *n fig* precursor, heraldo, *m*; presagio, anuncio, *m. vt* anunciar, presagiar

harbor *n* puerto, *m*; (bay) bahía, *f*; (haven) asilo, refugio, *m. vt* dar refugio (a), albergar, acoger; (cherish) abrigar; acariciar; (conceal) esconder. **inner h.,** puerto, *m.* **outer h.,** rada del puerto, *f.* **to put into h.,** entrar en el puerto. **h. bar,** barra del puerto, *f.* **h.-dues,** derechos de puerto, *m pl.* **h.-master,** capitán de puerto, contramaestre de puerto, *m*

hard *a* duro; (firm) firme; difícil; laborioso, agotador; violento; poderoso; arduo; fuerte, recio; vigoroso, robusto; insensible, inflexible; cruel; (of weather) inclemente, severo; (unjust) injusto, opresivo; (stiff) tieso; (of water) cruda; (of wood) brava. *adv* duro; duramente; con ahínco; con fuerza; de firme; difícilmente; (of gazing) fijamente; severamente; (firmly) firmemente; vigorosamente; (of

raining) a cántaros, mucho; (quickly) rápidamente; excesivamente; (much) mucho; (of bearing misfortune) a pechos; (attentively) atentamente; (heavily) pesadamente; (badly) mal; (closely) de cerca, inmediatamente. **It was a h. blow,** Fue un golpe recio. **to be h. put to,** encontrar difícil. **to go h.,** endurecerse. **to go h. with,** irle mal a uno. **to have a h. time,** pasar apuros, pasarlo mal. **to look h. at,** mirar atentamente, examinar detenidamente; mirar fijamente. **to be a h. drinker,** ser un bebedor empedernido. **h. and fast rule,** regla inalterable, *f.* **h.-bitten,** de carácter duro. **a h.-boiled egg,** un huevo duro. **h. breathing,** resuello, *m.* **h. by,** muy cerca. **h. cash,** efectivo, *m.* **h.-earned,** difícilmente conseguido; ganado con el sudor de la frente. **h.-featured,** de facciones duras. **h.-fisted,** tacaño. **h.-fought,** arduo, reñido. **h.-headed,** práctico, perspicaz. **h.-hearted,** duro de corazón, insensible. **h.-heartedness,** insensibilidad, *f.* **h. labor,** *law* trabajos forzados, *m pl,* presidio, *m.* **h.-mouthed,** (of horses) boquiduro. **h. of hearing,** duro de oído. **h.-up,** apurado. **to be very h.-up,** ser muy pobre; *inf* estar a la cuarta pregunta. **h.-wearing,** duradero; sufrido. **h.-won,** See **h.-earned. h.-working,** trabajador, hacendoso, diligente

harden *vt* endurecer; (metal) templar; robustecer; (to war) aguerrir; (make callous) hacer insensible. *vi* endurecérse; hacerse duro; templarse; robustecerse; (of shares) entonarse

hardening *n* endurecimiento, *m*; (of metal) temple, *m.* **h. of the arteries,** arteriosclerosis, *f*

hardly *adv* duramente; difícilmente; (badly) mal; severamente; (scarcely) apenas, casi. **h. ever,** casi nunca

hardness *n* dureza, *f*; severidad, *f*; inhumanidad, insensibilidad, *f*; (stiffness) tiesura, *f*; (difficulty) dificultad, *f*; (of water) crudeza, *f*; (of hearing) dureza de oído, *f*

hardship *n* penas, *f pl*, trabajos, *m pl*; infortunio, *m*, desdicha, *f*; (suffering) sufrimiento, *m*; (affliction) aflicción, *f*; (privation) privación, *f.* **to undergo h.,** pasar trabajos

hardware *n* ferretería, *f*

hardy *a* audaz, intrépido; (strong) fuerte, robusto; *bot* resistente

hare *n* liebre, *f.* **young h.,** lebrato, *m.* **h. and hounds,** rally paper, *m*, caza de papelitos, *f.* **h.-brained,** casquivano, atronado, con cabeza de chorlito. **hare's foot,** mano de gato, *f pl*, **h.-lip,** labio leporino, *m.* **h.-lipped,** labihendido

haricot *n* (green bean) judía, *f*; (dried bean) alubia, *f*

hark *vt* escuchar; oír. **to h. back,** volver al punto de partida; volver a la misma canción

harlot *n* ramera, prostituta, meretriz, *f*

harm *n* mal, *m*; daño, *m*; perjuicio, *m*; (danger) peligro, *m*; (detriment) menoscabo, *m*; (misfortune) desgracia, *f*, *vt* hacer mal (a); dañar, hacer daño (a); perjudicar. **And there's no h. in that,** Y en eso no hay mal. **to keep out of harm's way,** evitar el peligro; guardarse del mal

harmful *a* malo; dañino, perjudicial, nocivo; (dangerous) peligroso. **to be h.,** (of food, etc.) hacer mal (a); (of pests) ser dañino; (of behavior, etc.) perjudicar

harmless *a* innocuo; inofensivo; inocente

harmonic *n* (*phys math*) harmónica, *f*; *mus* armónico, *m*, *a mus* armónico

harmonica *n* armónica, *f*

harmonious *a* armonioso

harmonize *vt* armonizar. *vi* armonizarse, estar en armonía

harmony *n* armonía, *f*; *fig* paz, *f*, buenas relaciones, *f pl*; música, *f*. **to live in h.,** vivir en paz

harness *n* guarniciones, *f pl*, jaeces, *m pl*; (armor) arnés, *m*. *vt* enjaezar; (yoke) enganchar; (water) represar. **to die in h.,** *fig* morir en la brecha. **h. maker,** guarnicionero, *m*. **h. room,** guadarnés, *m*

harp *n* arpa, *f*. **to h. on,** volver a la misma canción, volver a repetir

harpist *n* arpista, *mf*

harpoon *n* arpón, *m*. *vt* arponear

harpsichord *n* arpicordio, *m*

harrow *n agr* rastra, *f*, escarificador, *m*. *vt agr* escarificar; *fig* lastimar, atormentar

harrowing *a* patibulario, conmovedor, atormentador, angustioso

harry *vt* devastar, asolar; (persons) robar; perseguir; (worry) atormentar; (annoy) molestar

harsh *a* áspero; (of voice) ronco; (of sound) discordante; (of colors) áspero; duro; chillón; severo, duro; (of features) duro; (of taste) ácido, acerbo

harshness *n* (roughness) aspereza, *f*; (of voice) ronquedad, aspereza, *f*; (of sound) disonancia, *f*; (of colors) aspereza, *f*; severidad, *f*; dureza, *f*; (of taste) acidez, *f*

harum-scarum *n* tronera, saltabarrancos, *mf* molino

harvest *n* cosecha, siega, *f*; recolección, *f*; *fig* producto, fruto, *m*. *vt* cosechar; recoger. **h. festival,** fiesta de la cosecha, *f*

harvester *n* segador, *m*, cosechero (-ra); (machine) segadora, *f*

hash *n cul* picado, *m*. *vt cul* picar

hashish *n* hachich, hachís, quif, *m*

hasp *n* pasador, *m*; sujetador, *m*

hassock *n* cojín, *m*

hassle *n* Lat. Am. fregada *f*

haste *n* prisa, rapidez, *f*; precipitación, *f*; urgencia, *f*. *vt* dar prisa (a); acelerar; precipitar. *vi* darse prisa; acelerarse; precipitarse. **in h.,** de prisa, aprisa. **to be**

in h., estar de prisa, llevar prisa. **in great h.,** muy aprisa, aprisa y corriendo, precipitadamente; con mucha prisa. **More h. less speed,** (Spanish equivalent. Words said by Charles III of Spain to his valet) ¡Vísteme despacio que voy de prisa!

hasten *vt* acelerar, apresurar; precipitar. *vi* darse prisa, apresurarse; moverse con rapidez; correr. **to h. one's steps,** apretar el paso. **to h. away,** marcharse rápidamente. **to h. back,** regresar apresuradamente. **to h. down,** bajar rápidamente. **to h. on,** seguir el camino sin descansar; seguir rápidamente. **to h. out,** salir rápidamente. **to h. towards,** ir rápidamente hacia; correr hacia. **to h. up,** subir aprisa, correr hacia arriba; darse prisa

hastily *adv* de prisa, rápidamente; con precipitación, precipitadamente; (angrily) impacientemente, airadamente; (thoughtlessly) sin reflexión

hastiness *n* rapidez, *f*; precipitación, *f*; (anger) impaciencia, irritación, *f*

hasty *a* rápido, apresurado; precipitado; (superficial) superficial, ligero; (ill-considered) desconsiderado, imprudente; (angry) impaciente, irritable; violento, apasionado

hat *n* sombrero, *m*. **to pass round the h.,** pasar el platillo. **Andalusian h.,** sombrero calañés, *m*. **bowler h.,** sombrero hongo, *m*. **broad-brimmed h.,** sombrero chambergo, *m*. **Panama h.,** sombrero de jipijapa, *m*. **picture h.,** pamela, *f*. **shovel h.,** sombrero de teja, *m*. **soft felt h.,** sombrero flexible, *m*. **straw h.,** sombrero de paja, *m*. **three-cornered h.,** sombrero de tres picos, *m*. **top-h.,** sombrero de copa, *m*. **h. shop or trade,** sombrerería, *f*

hatch *n* (wicket) compuerta, *f*; (trap-door) puerta caediza, *f*; *naut* escotilla, *f*; compuerta de esclusa, *f*; (of chickens) pollada, *f*; (of birds) nidada, *f*. *vt* (birds) empollar; incubar, encobar; *fig* tramar, urdir. *vi* empollarse, salir del cascarón; incubarse; *fig* madurarse. **to h. a plot,** urdir un complot, conspirar. **to h. chickens,** sacar pollos

hatchet *n* hacha pequeña, *f*, machado, *m*. **to bury the h.,** hacer la paz. **h.-faced,** de cara de cuchillo

hate *n* odio, aborrecimiento, *m*, aversión, *f*; abominación, *f*. *vt* odiar, aborrecer; detestar; repugnar; saber mal, sentir. **I h. to trouble you,** Me sabe mal molestarle, Siento mucho molestarle. **to h. the sight of,** *inf* no poder ver (a)

hateful *a* odioso, aborrecible; repugnante

hater *n* aborrecedor (-ra). **to be a good h.,** saber odiar

hatred *n* odio, aborrecimiento, *m*, detestación, *f*; aversión, enemistad, *f*

hatter *n* sombrerero, *m*. **as mad as a h.,** loco como una cabra

haughtiness *n* altanería, arrogancia, altivez, soberbia, *f*, orgullo, *m*

haughty *a* altanero, arrogante, altivo, orgulloso *Lat. Am.* copetudo, *Mexico also* alzado

haul *n* (pull) tirón, *m*; (of fish) redada, *f*; (booty) botín, *m*. *vt* arrastrar, tirar de; *naut* halar, *m*. **to h. at, upon,** (ropes, etc.) aflojar, soltar, arriar. **to h. down,** (flags, sails) arriar

haunch *n* anca, culata, *f*; (of meat) pierna, *f*. **h.-bone,** hueso ilíaco, *m*

haunt *n* punto de reunión, lugar frecuentado (por), *m*; (lair) cubil, nido, *m*, guarida, *f*. *vt* frecuentar; rondar; (of ideas) perseguir; (of ghosts) aparecer, visitar. **It is a h. of thieves,** Es una cueva de ladrones

haunted *a* (by spirits) encantado

hauteur *n* altivez, *f*

Havana la Habana, *f*. *n* (cigar) habano, *m*. (native) habanero (-ra), habano (-na)

have *vt* tener; poseer; (suffer) padecer; (spend) pasar; (eat or drink) tomar; (eat) comer; (a cigarette) fumar; (a bath, etc.) tomar; (a walk, a ride) dar; (cause to be done) mandar (hacer), hacer (hacer); (deceive) engañar; (defeat) vencer; (catch) coger; (say) decir; (allow) permitir; (tolerate) tolerar, sufrir; (obtain) lograr, conseguir; (wish) querer; (know) saber; (realize) realizar, (buy) comprar; (acquire) adquirir. As an auxiliary verb, haber (e.g. **I h. done it,** Lo he hecho, etc.). **As fate would h. it,** Según quiso la suerte. **Do you h. to go?** ¿Tiene Vd. que marcharse? **H. him come here,** Hazle venir aquí. **I h. been had,** Me han engañado. **I h. a good mind to . . . ,** Tengo ganas de . . . **I had all my books stolen,** Me robaron todos mis libros. **You had better go,** Es mejor que te vayas. **I had rather,** Preferiría, Me gustaría más bien. **I h. had a suit made,** Mandé hacerme un traje, Hice hacerme un traje. **I would not h. had it otherwise,** No lo hubiese querido de otra manera. **I will not h. it,** No lo quiero; No quiero tomarlo; (object) No lo permitiré. **If we had known,** Si lo hubiésemos sabido. **It has to do with the sun,** Está relacionado con el sol, Tiene que ver con el sol. **Have a good trip!** ¡Buen viaje!, ¡Feliz viaje! **What are you going to h.?** ¿Qué quiere Vd. tomar? **Will you h. some jam?** ¿Quiere Vd. mermelada? **to h. breakfast,** desayunar. **to h. dinner, supper,** cenar. **to h. lunch,** almorzar. **to h. for tea,** invitar a tomar el té; (of food) merendar. **to h. tea,** tomar el té. **to h. it out with,** habérselas con. **to h. just,** acabar de. **I h. just done it,** Acabo de hacerlo. **to h. on hand,** traer entre manos. **to h. one's eye on,** no perder de vista (a), vigilar. **to h. one's tail between one's legs,** ir rabo entre piernas.

to h. to, tener que; deber. **It has to be so,** Tiene que ser así. **to h. too much of,** sobrar, tener demasiado de. **He has too much time,** Le sobra tiempo. **to h. about one,** tener (or llevar) consigo. **to h. back,** aceptar; recibir. **to h. down,** hacer bajar. **She had her hair down,** El pelo le caía por las espaldas. **to h. in,** hacer entrar. **to h. on,** vestir, llevar puesto; (engagements) tener (compromisos). **to h. out,** hacer salir; llevar a paseo; llevar fuera; (have removed) hacerse sacar; quitar. **to h. up,** (persons) hacer subir; (things) subir; llevar a (ante) los tribunales. **to h. with one,** tener consigo. **I h. her with me,** La tengo conmigo, Ella me acompaña

haven *n* puerto, *m*, abra, *f*; *fig* oasis, abrigo, refugio, *m*

havoc *n* destrucción, ruina, *f*; *fig* estrago, *m*. **to wreak h. among,** destruir; *fig* hacer estragos entre (or en)

Hawaii Hawai, *m*

hawk *n* halcón, *m*; gavilán, milano, *m*. *vi* cazar con halcón. *vt* vender mercancías por las calles; *fig* difundir. **h.-eyed,** de ojos de lince. **h.-nosed,** de nariz aguileña

hawker *n* halconero, *m*; (vendor) buhonero, *m*, vendedor (-ra) ambulante

hay *n* heno, *m*. **to make hay while the sun shines,** hacer su agosto. **hay fever,** fiebre del heno, *f*. **hay-fork,** horca, *f*

haystack *n* almiar, *m*, niara, *f*

hazard *n* azar, *m*, suerte, *f*; riesgo, peligro, *m*; (game) juego de azar, *m*. *vt* arriesgar, aventurar. **at all hazards,** a todo riesgo

hazardous *a* azaroso, arriesgado, peligroso

haze *n* bruma, *f*; confusión, *f*

hazel *n* avellano, *m*. **h.-nut,** avellana, *f*

hazy *a* brumoso, calinoso; confuso

he *pers. pron* él. *n* (of humans) varón, *m*; (of animals) macho, *m*. **he who,** el que, quien. **he-goat,** macho cabrío, *m*. **he-man,** todo un hombre, hombre cabal, *m*

head *vt* golpear con la cabeza; encabezar; (lead) capitanear; (direct) dirigir, guiar; (wine) cabecear. *vi* estar a la cabeza de; dirigirse a. **headed for,** con rumbo a, en dirección a. **to h. off,** interceptar; desviar; *fig* distraer

head *n anat* cabeza, *f*; (upper portion) parte superior, *f*; (of a coin) cara, *f*; (hair) cabellera, *f*; (individual) persona, *f*; (of cattle) res, *f*; (of a mountain) cumbre, *f*; (of a ladder) último peldaño, *m*; (of toadstools) sombrero, *m*; (of trees) copa, *f*; (of a stick) puño, *m*; (of a cylinder) culata, *f*; (of a river, etc.) manantial, origen, *m*; (of a bed) cabecera, *f*; (of nails, pins) cabeza, *f*; (froth) espuma, *f*; (flower) flor, *f*; (leaves) hojas, *f pl*; (first place) primer puesto, *m*; (of game, fish) pieza, *f*; (of a page, column) cabeza, *f*; (cape) cabo, *m*;

(of an arrow, dart, lance) punta, *f*; (front) frente, *m*; (leader) jefe, cabeza, *m*; (chief) director (-ra), superior (-ra); presidente (-ta); (of a school) director (-ra); (of a cask) fondo, *m*; *mech* cabezal, *m*; (of an ax) filo, *m*; (of a bridge) cabeza, *f*; (of a jetty, pier) punta, *f*; (of a ship) proa, *f*; (of a flower) cabezuela, *f*; (of asparagus) punta, *f*; (of a table) cabeza, *f*; (of the family) jefe, cabeza, *m*; (seat of honor) cabecera, *f*; (title) título, *m*; (aspect) punto de vista, *m*; (division) capítulo, *m*; (management, direction) dirección, *f*; (talent) talento, *m*, cabeza, *f*; (intelligence) inteligencia, *f*. **a principal; primero; en jefe. at the h. of,** a la cabeza de. **crowned h.,** testa coronada, *f*. **from h. to foot,** de pies a cabeza; de hito en hito; de arriba abajo. **He took it into his h. to . . . ,** Se le ocurrió de . . . **This story has neither h. nor tail,** Este cuento no tiene pies ni cabeza. **with h. held high,** con la frente levantada. **to come to a h.,** llegar a la crisis; llegar al punto decisivo. **to get an idea out of a person's h.,** quitar una idea a uno de la cabeza. **to keep one's h.,** *fig* conservar la sangre fría, no perder la cabeza. **to lose one's h.,** *fig* perder la cabeza. **to put into a person's h.,** *fig* meter (a uno) en la cabeza. **to run one's h. against,** golpear la cabeza contra. **h. first,** de cabeza. **h. of cattle,** res, *f*. **h. office,** central, *f*. **h. of hair,** cabellera, *f*; mata de pelo, *f*. **h.-on,** de cabeza. **h.-on collision,** choque de frente, *m*. **h. opening,** (of a garment) cabezón, *m*. **heads or tails,** cara o cruz (Spain), águila o sol (Mexico), cruz o sello (Argentina, Chile). **h. over heels,** de patas arriba. **h. over heels in love,** calado hasta los huesos. **h.-dress,** tocado, *m*; peinado, *m*; sombrero, *m*. **h. voice,** voz de cabeza, *f*. **h. waiter,** encargado de comedor, jefe de camareros, *m*

headache *n* dolor de cabeza, *m*; *fig* quebradero de cabeza, *m*

headboard *n* cabecera (de una cama), *f*

headed *a* con cabeza . . .; que tiene la cabeza . . .; de cabeza . . .; (of an article) intitulado. **large h.,** cabezudo

header *n* caída de cabeza, *f*; salto de cabeza, *m*

headgear *n* tocado, *m*; sombrero, gorro, *m*

heading *n naut* el poner la proa en dirección (a); el guiar en dirección (a); (of a book, etc.) título, encabezamiento, *m*; (soccer) golpe de cabeza, *m*. **to come under the h. of,** estar incluido entre; clasificarse bajo

headlight *n aut* faro, *m*; (rw, naut) farol, *m*. **to dip the headlights,** bajar los faros. **to switch on the headlights,** encender los faros (or los faroles)

headline *n* (of a newspaper) titular, *m*; (to a chapter) título de la columna, *m*

headlong *a* precipitado; despeñado. *adv*

de cabeza; precipitadamente. **to fall h., caer de cabeza**

headman *n* cacique, cabecilla, *m*; (foreman) capataz, contramaestre, *m*

headmaster *n* director de colegio, rector, *m*

headmistress *n* directora de colegio, rectora, *f*

head-on collision *n* choque frontal, *m*

head nurse enfermero-jefe, *m*

headphones *n pl* auriculares, *m pl*

headquarters *n mil* cuartel general, *m*; oficina central, *f*; jefatura, *f*; centro, *m*

headrest *n* respaldo, *m*; apoyo para la cabeza, *m*

headstrong *a* impetuoso, terco, testarudo

headway *n* marcha, *f*; *fig* progreso, avance, *m*. **to make h.,** avanzar; *fig* hacer progresos; *fig* prosperar

heady *a* apasionado, violento; impetuoso, precipitado; (obstinate) terco; (of alcohol) encabezado; *fig* embriagador

heal *vt* curar, sanar; (flesh) cicatrizar. *vi* curar, sanar; cicatrizarse; (superficially) sobresanar

healer *n* sanador (-ra), curador (-ra); curandero, *m*

health *n* salud, *f*; higiene, sanidad, *f*. **Here's to your very good h.!** ¡Salud y pesetas! **He is in good h.,** Disfruta de buena salud. **to drink a person's h.,** beber a la salud de. **to enjoy good h.,** gozar de buena salud. **to look full of h.,** vender salud. **h.-giving,** saludable. **h. inspection,** visita de sanidad, *f*. **h. officer,** inspector de sanidad, *m*. **h. resort,** balneario, *m*

healthy *a* sano; con buena salud; (healthful) saludable. **to be h.,** tener buena salud

heap *n* montón, *m*; rima, pila, *f*, acervo, *m*; (of people) muchedumbre, *f*, tropel, *m*. *vt* amontonar; apilar; colmar. **in heaps,** a montones. **We have heaps of time,** Nos sobra tiempo, Tenemos tiempo de sobra. **to h. together,** juntar, mezclar. **to h. up,** amontonar; colmar; amontonar; *agr* hacinar; *fig* acumular

hear *vt* oír; (listen) escuchar; (attend) asistir a; (give audience) dar audiencia (a); (a lawsuit) ver (un pleito); (speak) hablar; (be aware of, feel) sentir. *vi* oír; tener noticias; (learn) enterarse de; (allow) permitir. **H.! H.!** ¡Muy bien! ¡Bravo! **I have heard it said that . . .** He oído decir que . . . **Let me h. from you!** ¡Mándame noticias tuyas! **They were never heard of again,** No se volvió a saber de ellos, No se supo más de ellos. **to h. about,** oír de; (know) saber de, tener noticias de; recibir información sobre. **to h. from,** ser informado por; tener noticias de: recibir carta de. **to h. of,** enterarse de, saber; recibir información sobre; (allow) permitir

hearing *n* (sense of) oído, *m*; alcance del

oído, m; presencia, f; audición, f; law
vista (de una causa) f. **It was said in my
h.,** Fue dicho en mi presencia. **out of h.,**
fuera del alcance del oído. **within h.,** al
alcance del oído. **have a h. problem,** ser
parcialmente sordo

hearing aid acústica, aparato auditivo,
aparato acústico, audífono, m

hearsay n fama, f, rumor, m. **by h.,** de
oídas

hearse n coche fúnebre, m

heart n corazón, m; (feelings) entrañas, f
pl; (of the earth, etc.) seno, corazón, m;
(of lettuce, etc.) cogollo, repollo, m; (suit
in cards) copas, f pl; bot médula, f; (soul)
alma, f; (courage) valor, m; ánimo, m. **at
h.,** en el fondo, esencialmente. **by h.,** de
memoria. **from the h.,** con toda sinceridad, de todo corazón. **He is a man
after my own h.,** Es un hombre de los
que me gustan. **I have no h. to do it,** No
tengo valor de hacerlo. **in the h. of the
country,** en medio del campo. **to break
one's h.,** partirse el corazón. **to have
one's h. in one's mouth,** tener el alma
en un hilo, estar muerto de miedo. **to
have no h.,** fig no tener entrañas. **to lose
h.,** desanimarse, descorazonarse. **to set
one's h. on,** poner el corazón en. **to
take h.,** cobrar ánimo; inf hacer de tripas
corazón. **to take to h.,** tomar a pechos.
to wear one's h. on one's sleeve, tener
el corazón en la mano. **with all my h.,**
con toda el alma. **h.-ache,** angustia,
pena, f; **h.-beat,** latido del corazón, m.
h.-breaker, (woman) coqueta, f; (man)
ladrón de corazones, m. **h. disease,** enfermedad del corazón, enfermedad car-
díaca, f. **h. failure,** colapso cardíaco, m.
h.-rending, desgarrador, angustioso.
h.-searching, examen de conciencia, m.
h.-shaped, acorazonado, en forma de
corazón. **h.-strings,** fibras del corazón, f
pl. **h.-to-h. talk,** conversación íntima, f.
h.-whole, libre de afectos

heartbreaking a desgarrador, angustioso, doloroso, lastimoso

heartbroken a acongojado, afligido,
transido de dolor

heartburn n acidez del estómago,
acedia, pirosis, rescoldera, f

hearten vt alentar, animar

heartfelt a hondo; de todo corazón, sincero; más expresivo

hearth n hogar, m; chimenea, f; fig
hogar, m

heartily adv cordialmente; sinceramente; enérgicamente; con entusiasmo; (of eating) con buen apetito;
(very) muy, completamente. **I am h. sick
of it all,** inf Estoy harto hasta los dientes

heartless a sin corazón, sin piedad, despiadado, inhumano, cruel

hearty a cordial; sincero; enérgico;
vigoroso, robusto; (frank) campechano;
(of appetite) voraz; bueno; (big) grande

heat n calor, m; (in animals) celo, m; (of
an action) calor, m; fig vehemencia,
fogosidad, f; fig fuego, m; (passion)
ardor, m, pasión, f; (of a race) carrera
eliminatoria, f. vt calentar; (excite) conmover, acalorar, excitar; (annoy) irritar. vi
calentarse. **dead h.,** empate, m. **in h.,** en
celo. **in the h. of the moment,** en el
calor del momento. **to become heated,**
fig acalorarse, exaltarse. **white h.,** candencia, incandescencia, f. **h. lightning,**
fucilazo, m. **h. spot,** pápula, f; terminación sensible, f. **h. stroke,** insolación, f.
h. wave, onda de calor, f

heater n calentador, m; calorífero, m;
(stove) estufa, f; (for plates) calientaplatos, m. **water-h.,** calentador de agua,
m

heath n brezal, m; yermo, páramo, m; bot
brezo, m

heathen n pagano (-na); idólatra, mf;
ateo (-ea), descreído (-da). a pagano;
ateo; bárbaro

heating n calefacción, f, a calentador; (of
drinks) fortificante. **central h.,** calefacción central, f

heave vt alzar, levantar; naut izar; (the
anchor, etc.) virar; (throw) arrojar, lanzar;
elevar; (extract) extraer; (emit) dar, exhalar. vi subir y bajar; palpitar; agitarse. n
tirón, m; (of the sea) vaivén, m. **to h. in
sight,** aparecer, surgir. **to h. out sail,**
naut desenvergar. **to h. the lead,** naut
escandallar. **to h. to,** naut estarse a la
capa

heaven n cielo, m; firmamento, m;
paraíso, m. **Heavens!** ¡Cielos! ¡Por Dios!
Thank H.! ¡Gracias a Dios! **h.-born,** celeste. **h.-sent,** fig providencial

heavenly a celeste, celestial; divino; fig
delicioso. **h. body,** astro, m

heavily adv pesadamente; torpemente;
penosamente; (slowly) lentamente;
severamente; excesivamente; (of sighing)
hondamente; (sadly) tristemente; (of rain,
etc.) reciamente, fuertemente; (of wind)
con violencia. **He fell h.,** Cayó de plomo.
to lie h. upon, pesar mucho sobre. **to
rain h.,** llover mucho, diluviar

heaviness n peso, m; (lethargy) torpor,
letargo, m; sueño, m, languidez, f; (clumsiness) torpeza, f; (severity) severidad, f;
importancia, responsabilidad, f; dificultad, f; (gravity) gravedad, f; tristeza,
melancolía, f; (boredom) sosería, insulsez, f; (of style) monotonía, pon-
derosidad, f

heaving n levantamiento, m; (of the anchor, etc.) virada, f; (of the sea) vaivén, m;
(of the breast) palpitación, f

heavy a pesado; torpe; sin gracia; (slow)
lento; (thick) grueso; (strong) fuerte;
(hard) duro; grave; difícil; oneroso; responsable, importante; (oppressive)
opresivo, penoso; grande; (sad) triste,
melancólico; (of the sky) anublado; (of
food) indigesto; (tedious) aburrido, soso;

(pompous) pomposo; (of roads) malo; (of scents) fuerte, penetrante; (of sleep, weather) pesado; (weary) rendido; (charged with) cargado de; (of a meal) grande, abundante; (violent) violento; (of a cold, etc.) malo; (drowsy) soñoliento; (torpid) tórpido; (of rain, snow, hail) fuerte, recio; (of firing) intenso; (of sighs) profundo; (of soil) recio, de mucha miga; (phys chem) pesado. **to be h.,** pesar mucho. **How h. are you?** ¿Cuánto pesa Vd.? **h.-armed,** pesado; armado hasta los dientes. **h.-eyed,** con ojeras. **h. guns,** artillería pesada, f. **h.-handed,** de manos torpes; fig tiránico, opresivo. **h.-hearted,** triste, apesadumbrado. **h. industry,** la gran industria, la industria pesada, f. **h.-laden,** muy cargado. **h. losses,** mil pérdidas cuantiosas, f pl. **h.weight,** sport peso pesado, m

Hebrew n hebreo (-ea), judío (-ía): (language) hebreo, m

heckle vt fig interrumpir, importunar con preguntas

heckler n perturbador (-ra)

hectare n hectárea, f

hectic a (consumptive) hético; (feverish) febril; fig inf agitado

hector vt intimidar, amenazar

hectoring a imperioso; amenazador

hedge n seto, m; barrera, f. vt cercar con un seto; rodear. vi fig titubear, vacilar. **h.-hopping,** aer vuelo a ras de tierra, m. **h.-sparrow,** acentor de bosque, m

hedgehog n erizo, m. **h. position,** mil puesto fuerte, m

hedonism n hedonismo, m

heed n atención, f, cuidado, m. vt atender; observar, considerar; escuchar. vi hacer caso

heedful a atento; cuidadoso

heedless a desatento; descuidado, negligente; distraído

heel n anat talón, calcañar, m; (of shoe) tacón, m; (of a violin, etc., bow) talón, m; (remains) restos, m pl. vt poner tacón a; poner talón a; naut hacer zozobrar. vi naut zozobrar. **rubber h.,** tacón de goma, m. **She let him cool his heels for half an hour,** le dio un plantón de media hora. **to follow on a person's heels,** pisarle (a uno) los talones. **to be down at h.,** (of shoes) estar gastados los tacones; estar desaseado. **to take to one's heels,** apretar a correr, poner pies en polvorosa. **to turn on one's h.,** dar media vuelta. **h.-bone,** zancajo, m. **h.-piece,** talón, m

heft vt sopesar, tomar al peso

hegemony n hegemonía, f

heifer n ternera, vaquilla, f

heigh interj (calling attention) ioye! iloiga! **h.-ho!** iay!

height n altura, f; elevación, f; altitud, f; (stature) estatura, f; (high ground) cerro, m, colina, f; (sublimity) sublimidad, ex-

celencia, f; colmo, m; (zenith) auge, m, cumbre, f

heighten vt hacer más alto; (enhance) realzar; (exaggerate) exagerar; (perfect) perfeccionar; (intensify) intensificar

heightening n elevación, f; (enhancement) realce, m; (exaggeration) exageración, f; (perfection) perfección, f; (intensification) intensificación, f

heinous a atroz, nefando, horrible.

heir n heredero, Lat. Am. asignatario m. **h. apparent,** heredero aparente, m. **h.-at-law,** heredero forzoso, m. **h. presumptive,** presunto heredero, m

heiress n heredera, Lat. Am. asignataria f

heirloom n reliquia de familia, f; fig herencia, f

helicopter n helicóptero, m

helium n chem helio, m

hell n infierno, m. **h.-fire,** fuego del infierno, m, llamas del infierno, f pl

hellish a infernal; inf horrible, detestable

hello interj ihola!; (on telephoning someone) ioiga! ialo!; (answering telephone) Spain idiga!, ialo!, Colombia ia ver!, Mexico ibueno!

helm n caña del timón, f; timón, gobernalle, m. **to obey the h.,** obedecer el timón. **to take the h.,** gobernar el timón; ponerse a pilotar

helmet n casco, m; (in olden days) yelmo, capacete, m; (sun) casco colonial, m

help n ayuda, f; auxilio, socorro, m; (protection) favor, m, protección, f; (remedy) remedio, m; (cooperation) cooperación, f, concurso, m; (domestic) criada, f. **A little h. is worth a lot of sympathy,** Más vale un toma que dos te daré. **There's no h. for it,** No hay más remedio. **to call for h.,** pedir socorro a gritos. **without h.,** a solas, sin la ayuda de nadie

help vt ayudar; socorrer, auxiliar; (favor) favorecer; (mitigate) aliviar; (contribute to) contribuir a, facilitar; (avoid) evitar. vi ayudar. **He cannot h. worrying,** No puede menos de preocuparse. **God h. you!** iDios te ampare! **So h. me God!** iAsí Dios me salve! **to h. one another,** ayudarse mutuamente, ayudarse los unos a los otros. **to h. oneself,** (to food) servirse. **to h. down, off,** ayudar a bajar; ayudar a apearse. **to h. in,** ayudar a entrar. **to h. along, forward, on,** avanzar, fomentar, promover; contribuir a. **Shall I h. you on with the dress?** ¿Quieres que te ayude a ponerte el vestido? **to h. out,** ayudar a salir; (from a vehicle) ayudar a bajar; (of a difficulty, etc.) sacar; suplir la falta de; ayudar. **to h. over,** ayudar a cruzar; (a difficulty) ayudar a salir de (an apuro); ayudar a vencer (un obstáculo, etc.); (a period) ayudar a pasar. **to h. to,** contribuir a, ayudar en; (food) servir. **to h. up,** ayudar a subir; ayudar a levantarse, levantar

helper n auxiliador (-ra); asistente (-ta);

(protector) favorecedor (-ra); bienhechor (-ra), *Argentina also* ladero *m*; (colleague) colega, *m*; (co-worker) colaborador (-ra). **He thanked all his helpers,** Dio las gracias a todos los que le habían ayudado

helpful *a* útil, provechoso; (obliging) servicial, atento, *Lat. Am.* acomedido; (favorable) favorable; (healthy) saludable

helping *n* ayuda, *f*; (of food) porción, ración, *f*, plato, *m*. **Won't you have a second h.?** ¿No quiere usted servirse más (or otra vez)? ¿No quiere usted repetir? **to lend a h. hand (to),** prestar ayuda (a)

helpless *a* desamparado, abandonado; (through infirmity) imposibilitado; impotente, sin fuerzas (para); (shiftless) incompetente, inútil

helter-skelter *adv* atropelladamente; en desorden. *n* barahunda, *f*

hem *n sew* dobladillo, filete, *m*, bastilla, *f*; (edge) orilla, *f*. *interj* ¡ejem! *vt* hacer dobladillo en, dobladillar. *vi* (cough) fingir toser. **false hem,** *sew* dobladillo falso, *m*. **running hem,** *sew* jareta, *f*. **to hem and haw,** tartamudear; vacilar. **to hem in,** cercar, sitiar

hemisphere *n* hemisferio, *m*

hemlock *n bot* cicuta, *f*

hemoglobin *n chem* hemoglobina, *f*

hemophilia *n med* hemofilia, *f*

hemorrhage *n* hemorragia, *f*, flujo de sangre, *m*

hemorrhoids *n pl med* hemorroides, *f*

hemp *n* cáñamo, *m*. **h. cloth,** lienzo, *m*. **h.-seed,** cañamón, *m*

hemstitch *n* vainica, *f*. *vt* hacer vainica en

hen *n* gallina, *f*; (female bird) hembra, *f*. **the hen pheasant,** la hembra del faisán. **hen bird,** pájara, *f*. **hen-coop** or **house,** gallinero, *m*. **hen party,** *inf* reunión de mujeres, *f*. **hen-roost,** nidal, ponedero, *m*

hence *adv* (of place) de aquí; (of time) de ahora, de aquí a, al cabo de, en; (therefore) por eso, por lo tanto, por consiguiente. *interj* ¡fuera! ¡fuera de aquí! **I shall come to see you a month h.,** Vendré a verte en un mes (or al cabo de un mes). **ten years h.,** de aquí a diez años. **h. the fact that . . . ,** de aquí que. . . . **H. it happens that . . . ,** Por eso sucede que . . .

henceforth *adv* desde aquí en adelante, de hoy en adelante

henchman *n* escudero, *m*; satélite, secuaz, *m*

henpecked *a* gobernado por su mujer, que se deja mandar por su mujer

her *pers pron direct object* la; (with prepositions) ella. *pers. pron indirect object* le, a ella. *poss a su, mf*; sus, *mf pl*, de ella. **I saw her on Wednesday,** La vi el miércoles. **The message is for her,** El recado es para ella. **It is her book,** Es su libro, Es el libro de ella

herald *n* heraldo, *m*; presagio, anuncio, *m*. *vt* proclamar; anunciar, presagiar

herb *n* hierba, *f*

herby *a* herbáceo

Herculean *a* hercúleo

herd *n* manada, *f*; (of cattle) hato, *m*; (race) raza, *f*; (*fig* contemptuous) populacho, *m*, masa, *f*. *vt* reunir en manadas; reunir en hatos; (sheep) reunir en rebaños; guiar las manadas, etc. *vi* ir en manadas, hatos o rebaños; asociarse, reunirse. **h.-instinct,** instinto gregario, *m*; instinto de las masas, *m*

herdsman *n* ganadero, pastor, manadero, *m*; (head herdsman) rabadán, *m*

here *adv* aquí; (at roll-call) ¡presente!; acá; an este punto; ahora. *n* presente, *m*. **And h. he looked at me,** Y a este punto me miró. **Come h.!** ¡Ven acá! **in h.,** aquí dentro. **h. below,** aquí abajo, en la tierra. **h. and there,** aquí y allá. **h., there and everywhere,** en todas partes. **H. I am,** Heme aquí. **h. is . . . ,** he aquí. . . . **H. they are,** Aquí los tienes, Aquí están. **Here's to you!** (on drinking) ¡Salud y pesetas! ¡A tu salud!

hereabouts *adv* por aquí cerca

hereafter *adv* en lo futuro; desde ahora; en adelante. *n* futuro, *m*. **the H.,** la otra vida

hereby *adv* por esto, por las presentes

hereditarily *adv* hereditariamente, por herencia

hereditary *a* hereditario

heredity *n* herencia, *f*

herein *adv* en esto; aquí dentro; incluso

hereinafter *adv* después, más abajo, más adelante, en adelante, en lo sucesivo

heresy *n* herejía, *f*

heretic *n* hereje, *mf*

heretical *a* herético

hereunder *adv* abajo

hereupon *adv* en esto, en seguida

herewith *adv* junto con esto, con esto; ahora, en esta ocasión

heritage *n* herencia, *f*

hermaphrodite *a and n* hermafrodita, *mf*

hermetic *a* hermético

hermit *n* ermitaño, *m*. **h. crab,** paguro, cangrejo ermitaño, *m*

hernia *n* hernia, *f*

hero *n* héroe, *m*. **h.-worship,** culto a los héroes, *m*

heroic *a* heroico, épico

heroin *n chem* heroína, *f*

heroine *n* heroína, *f*

heroism *n* heroísmo, *m*

herpes *n pl* herpes, *mf pl*

herring *n* arenque, *m*

hers *poss pron 3rd sing* (el) suyo, *m*; (la) suya, *f*; (los) suyos, *m pl*; (las) suyas, *f pl*;

de ella. **This book is h.,** Este libro es suyo, Este libro es de ella. **This book is h., not mine,** Este libro es el suyo no el mío. **a sister of h.,** una de sus hermanas, una hermana suya

herself *pron* sí misma, sí; ella misma; (with reflexive verb) se. **She has done it by h.,** Lo ha hecho por sí misma. **She h. told me so,** Ella misma me lo dijo. **She is by h.,** Está a solas, Está sola

hesitancy. See **hesitation**

hesitant *a* indeciso, vacilante, irresoluto. **to be h.,** mostrarse irresoluto

hesitate *vi* vacilar, dudar; titubear. **I do not h. to say . . . ,** No vacilo en decir . . . **He hesitated over his reply,** Tardaba en dar su respuesta

hesitatingly *adv* irresolutamente; titubeando

hesitation *n* vacilación, hesitación, *f;* irresolución, indecisión, *f;* (reluctance) aversión, repugnancia, *f;* titubeo, *m*

heterogeneous *a* heterógeneo

hew *vt* cortar, tajar; (trees) talar; (a career, etc.) hacerse

hewer *n* partidor, talador, *m*

hey *interj* ¡he! ¡oye!

heyday *n* apogeo, colmo, *m;* buenos tiempos, *m pl;* reinado, *m;* pleno vigor, *m*

hi *interj* ¡oye! ¡hola!

hiatus *n* hiato, *m;* laguna, *f,* vacío, *m*

hibernate *vi* invernar

hibernation *n* invernada, *f*

hiccough *n* hipo, *m. vi* hipar. *vt* decir con hipo

hidden *a* escondido, secreto, oculto

hide *n* piel, *f;* pellejo, cuero, *m*

hide *vt* esconder, ocultar; (cover) cubrir, tapar; (dissemble) disimular; (meaning) obscurecer. *vi* esconderse; ocultarse, *Mexico* atejonarse; refugiarse. **to h. from each other,** esconderse el, uno del otro. **h.-and-seek,** escondite, dormirlas, *m*

hidebound *a* *fig* muy conservador, reaccionario, de ideas muy tradicionales

hideous *a* horrible, repulsivo, horroroso; repugnante, odioso

hideously *adv* horriblemente. **to be h. ugly,** (of people) ser más feo que Picio

hiding *n* ocultación, *f;* encubrimiento, *m;* refugio, *m; inf* paliza, tunda, *f.* **h.-place,** escondite, escondrijo, *m*

hie *vi* apresurarse, ir a prisa

hierarchical *a* jerárquico

hierarchy *n* jerarquía, *f*

hieroglyph *n* jeroglífico, *m*

higgledy-piggledy *adv* revueltamente, en confusión; en montón, en desorden

high *a* alto; elevado; (with altar, Mass, street, festival) mayor; grande; eminente; aristocrático; (of shooting) fijante; (of quality) superior; excelente; (haughty) orgulloso; (solemn) solemne; (good) bueno; noble; supremo; sumo; (of price)

subido; *mus* agudo; (of the sea) tempestuoso, borrascoso; (of wind and explosives) violento, fuerte; (of polish) brillante; (with speed) grande; (with tension, frequency) alto; (with number, etc.) importante, grande; (with colors) subido; (of food) pasado; (angry) enojado, airado; (of cheek bones) saliente, prominente; (well-seasoned) picante; (flattering) lisonjero. *adv* alto; hacia arriba; arriba; (deeply) profundamente; fuertemente; con violencia; (of price) a un precio elevado; (luxuriously) lujosamente; *mus* agudo. **a room 12 ft. h.,** un cuarto de doce pies de altura. **I knew her when she was so h.,** La conocí tamaña. **It is h. time he came,** Ya es hora de que viniese. **on h.,** en alto, arriba; en los cielos. **h. altar,** altar mayor, *m.* **h. and dry,** en la playa, varado; *fig* en seco. **h. and low,** de arriba abajo; por todas partes. **h.-born,** aristocrático, de alta alcurnia. **h.-bred,** (of people) de buena familia; (of animals) de buena raza. **h.-class,** de buena clase; de alta calidad. **h. collar,** alzacuello, *m.* **h. colored,** de colores vivos; *fig* exagerado. **h. command,** (*mil, nav*) alto mando, *m.* **h. court,** tribunal supremo, *m.* **h. day,** día festivo, *m.* **h. explosive,** explosivo violento, *m.* **h.-flown,** hinchado, retumbante, altisonante. **h. frequency,** alta frecuencia, *f.* **h.-handed,** arbitrario, dominador, despótico. **h.-heeled,** a de tacón alto. **h. jump,** salto de altura, *m.* **h. land,** tierras altas, *f pl;* eminencia, *f.* **h. life** *Lat. Am.* jáilaif *m.* **h. light,** art realce, *m;* acontecimiento de más interés, *m;* momento culminante, *m.* **h. mass,** misa mayor, *f.* **h.-minded,** de nobles pensamientos; arrogante. **h.-necked,** con cuello alto. **h.-pitched,** (of tono alto, agudo. **h.-powered,** de alta potencia. **h.-powered car,** coche de muchos caballos, *m.* **h. precision,** suma precisión, *f.* **h. pressure,** *n* alta presión, *f; fig* urgencia, *f; n* de alta presión; *fig* urgente. **h.-priced,** caro. **h. priest,** sumo pontífice, sumo sacerdote, alto sacerdote, *m.* **h. relief,** alto relieve, *m. f.* **h. road,** carretera mayor, *f.* **h. school,** instituto de segunda enseñanza, instituto, colegio, liceo, *m;* colegio, liceo, instituto, *m,* escuela secundaria, secundaria, *f.* **h. sea,** marejada, *f.* **h. seas,** alta mar, *f.* **h.-seasoned,** picante. **h. society,** alta sociedad, *f.* **h.-sounding,** altisonante, bombástico. **h.-speed,** de alta velocidad. **h.-spirited,** brioso; alegre. **h.-strung,** nervioso, excitable, sensitivo. **h. tension,** alta tensión, *f.* **h. tide,** marea alta, *f.* **h.-toned,** *mus* agudo; *inf* de alto copete; aristocrático. **h. treason,** alta traición, *f.* **h. water,** marea alta, pleamar, *f.* **h.-water mark,** límite de la marea, *m; fig* colmo, *m;* apogeo, *m*

High Andes, the el Altiplano *m*

highball *m Spain* qüisquisoda *f, Lat. Am.* jáibol *m*

highbrow a and n intelectual, mf
higher a comp of **high**, más alto; más elevado; superior. **on a h. plane,** en un nivel más alto. **h. education,** enseñanza superior, f. **h. mathematics,** la alta matemática, f. **h. criticism,** la alta crítica. **h. up,** más arriba. **h. up the river,** río arriba
highest a superl of **high**, el más alto; la más alta; los más altos; las más altas; sumo, supremo; excelente. **h. common factor,** math máximo común divisor, m. **h. references,** (of cook, gardener, etc.) informes inmejorables, m pl; com referencias excelentes, f pl
highland n altiplanicie, f; montañas, f pl, distrito montañoso, m. a montañoso
highlight vtr dar relieve a, destacar
highly adv altamente; mucho; muy; extremadamente; grandemente; bien; favorablemente; con lisonja, lisonjeramente. **h. seasoned,** picante. **h. strung,** nervioso, excitable
highness n altura, f; elevación, f; excelencia, f; nobleza, f; (title) Alteza, f. **His Royal H.,** Her Royal Highness, Su Alteza Real
high-ranking a de alta jerarquía, de alto rango
highway n camino real, m, carretera, f. **h. code,** código de la vía pública (or de la circulación), m. **h. robbery,** salteamiento de caminos, atraco, m
highwayman n salteador de caminos, m
highways and byways caminos y veredas
hike vi ir de excursión. n marcha con equipo, f
hiker n excursionista, mf
hiking n excursionismo, m; marcha con equipo, f
hilarious a alegre
hill n colina, f; cerro, otero, m; monte, m, montaña, f; (pile) montón, m. **h.-side,** falda de montaña, ladera de una colina, f. **h.-top,** cumbre de una colina, f
hilly a montañoso
hilt n puño, m, empuñadura, f
him pers pron 3rd sing direct object le, lo; (with prep.) él; indirect object le, a él; (with a direct obj. in 3rd person) se. **I gave him the magazine,** Le di la revista. **I gave it to him,** Se lo di a él. **This is for him,** Esto es para él
himself pron sí, sí mismo; él mismo; (reflexive) se. **He did it by h.,** Lo hizo por sí mismo. For more examples see **herself**
hind n corza, cierva, f. a trasero, posterior. **h.-quarters,** cuarto trasero, m; (of a horse) ancas, f pl
hinder a trasero, posterior
hinder vt impedir, estorbar; embarazar; dificultar; interrumpir. vi ser un obstáculo; formar un obstáculo
hindmost a posterior, postrero, último

hindrance n obstáculo, estorbo, impedimento, m; perjuicio, m; interrupción, f
hinge n gozne, pernio, m, bisagra, f; articulación, f; fig eje, m. vi moverse (or abrirse) sobre goznes; fig depender (de). vt engoznar
hint n indirecta, insinuación, sugestión, f; (advice) consejo, m. vt dar a entender, decir con medias palabras, insinuar, sugerir. vi insinuar. **to take the h.,** darse por aludido
hinterland n interior (de un país), m
hip n anat cadera, f; bot fruto del rosal silvestre, m. **h.-bath,** baño de asiento, m. **h.-bone,** hueso ilíaco, m. **h.-joint,** articulación de la cadera, f. **h.-pocket,** faltriquera, f
hippopotamus n hipopótamo, m
hire n alquiler, arriendo, m; salario, m. vt alquilar, arrendar; tomar en arriendo; (person) contratar; tomar a su servicio. **to h. out,** alquilar. **for** or **on h.,** de alquiler. **h.-purchase,** compra a plazos, f
hireling n mercenario, m
hirer n alquilador (-ra), arrendador (-ra)
hirsute a hirsuto. **non-h.** bot lampiño
his poss pron 3rd sing (el) suyo, m; (la) suya, f; (los) suyos, m pl; (las) suyas, f pl; de él. poss a su, mf; sus, mf pl; de él. **his handkerchiefs,** sus pañuelos. **his mother,** su madre, la madre de él. **a sister of his,** una de sus hermanas, una hermana suya. See **hers** for more examples.
Hispano-American a hispanoamericano
hiss n silbido, m; (sputter) chisporroteo, m. vi silbar
hissing n silbido, m; chisporroteo, m. a silbante
hist interj ¡chist!
histology n histología, f
historian n historiador (-ra)
historic a histórico
historical a histórico. **h. truth,** verdad histórica, f
history n historia, f. **Biblical h.,** historia sagrada, f. **natural h.,** historia natural, f
histrionic a histriónico
hit n golpe, m; aer impacto, m; (success) éxito, m; (piece of luck) buena suerte, f; (satire) sátira, f. vt golpear; (buffet) abofetear, pegar; (find) dar con, tropezar con; (attain) acertar; (guess) adivinar; (attract) atraer; (deal) lanzar, dar; (wound) herir, hacer daño (a). **The sun hits me right in the eyes,** El sol me da en la cabeza. **direct hit,** aer impacto de lleno, m. **lucky hit,** acierto, m. **to hit a straight left,** (boxing) lanzar un directo con la izquierda. **to hit the mark,** dar en el blanco; fig dar en el clavo. **hit or miss,** acierto o error. **to hit against,** dar contra, estrellar contra. **to hit back,** defen-

derse; devolver golpe por golpe. **to hit off,** imitar; (a likeness) coger. **to hit out,** abofetear; *fig* atacar; golpear (la pelota) fuera. **to hit upon,** dar con; tropezar con; encontrar por casualidad; (remember) acordarse de

hitch *n* (jerk) sacudida, *f*; nudo fácil de soltar, *m*; *fig* obstáculo, *m*; *fig* dificultad, *f*; (lift, ride) *Mexico* aventón *m* **give s.b. a hitch,** levantar a fulano. *vt* sacudir; (a chair, etc.) arrastrar, empujar; amarrar, enganchar; atar. *vi* (along a seat, etc.) correrse (en); (get entangled) enredarse, cogerse; (rub) rascarse. **without a h.,** sin dificultad alguna, viento en popa; (smoothly) a pedir de boca. **to h. up,** sacudir, dar una sacudida (a)

hitchhike *vi* ir a dedo (Argentina), pedir aventón (Mexico), pedir botella (Cuba), hacer autostop, ir por autostop (Spain)

hither *adv* acá, hacia acá; a citerior, más cercano. **h. and thither,** acá y aculla allá

hitherto *adv* hasta ahora, hasta el presente

hive *n* (for bees) colmena, *f*; (swarm) enjambre, *m*; *fig* centro, *m*. *vt* (bees) enjambrar. **h. of industry,** centro de industria

hoard *n* acumulación, *f*; provisión, *f*; tesoro, *m*. *vt* acumular, amasar, amontonar; guardar

hoarding *n* amontonamiento, *m*; acaparamiento, *m*; (fence) empalizada, cerca, *f*; palizada de tablas, *f*

hoarfrost *n* escarcha, helada blanca, *f*

hoarse *a* ronco; discordante. **to be h.,** tener la voz ronca. **to grow h.,** enronquecerse

hoarseness *n* ronquera, *f*; *inf* carraspera, *f*

hoary *a* (of the hair) canoso; blanco; (old) vetusto, antiguo, viejo

hoax *n* estafa, *f*, engaño, *m*; broma pesada, *f*; burla, *f*. *vt* estafar, engañar; burlar

hob *n* repisa interior del hogar, *f*

hobble *n* (gait) cojera, *f*; traba, maniota, *f*. *vi* cojear. *vt* manear. **h. skirt,** falda muy estrecha, *f*

hobby *n* pasatiempo, *m*, recreación, *f*; manía, afición, *f*. **h.-horse,** caballo de cartón, *m*; *fig* caballo de batalla, *m*

hobgoblin *n* trasgo, duende, *m*

hobnail *n* clavo de herradura, clavo de botas, *m*

hobnailed *a* (of boots) con clavos

hobnob *vi* codearse, tratar con familiaridad

hock *n* *anat* pernil, *m*; (wine) vino del Rin, *m*

hockey *n* chueca, *m*. **h. ball,** bola, pelota de chueca, *f*. **h. stick,** bastón de chueca, *m*

hocus-pocus *n* juego de pasa pasa, *m*; engaño, *m*, treta, *f*

hodgepodge See **hotchpotch**

hoe *n* azadón, *m*, *Chile, Peru* lampa. *f*. *vt* azadonar; sachar

hog *n* cerdo, puerco, *Peru* cuchí *m*. **to go the whole hog,** ir al extremo. **hogskin,** piel de cerdo, *f*

hoggish *a* porcuno; (greedy) comilón, tragón; (selfish) egoísta

hoist *n* levantamiento, *m*; (lift) montacargas, *m*; (winch) cabria, *f*; (crane) grúa, *f*. *vt* levantar, alzar; (flags) enarbolar; suspender; *naut* izar

hoity-toity *a* picajoso, quisquilloso; presuntuoso

hold *n* asimiento, agarro, *m*, presa, *f*; asidero, *m*; *fig* autoridad, *f*, poder, *m*; *fig* comprensión, *f*; (of a ship) cala, bodega, *f*. **to loose one's h.,** aflojar su presa. **to lose one's h.,** perder su presa. **to seize h. of,** asirse de, echar mano de. **h.-all,** funda, *f*. **h.-up,** (robbery) atraco, robo a mano armada, *m*; (in traffic) atasco (or obstáculo) en el tráfico, *m*; (in work) parada, cesación (de trabajo), *f*

hold *vt* tener; asir, agarrar; coger; retener; (embrace) abrazar; (a post) ocupar; (a meeting, etc.) celebrar; (weight of) aguantar, soportar; (own) poseer; *mil* ocupar, defender; (contain) contener; (have in store) reservar; tener capacidad para; (retain) retener; (believe) creer, sostener; (consider) opinar, tener para (mí, etc.); juzgar; (restrain) detener; contener; (of attention, etc.) mantener; (maneuvers) hacer; (observe) guardar. *vi* resistir, aguantar; (be valid) ser válido; regir; (apply) aplicarse; (last) continuar, seguir. *interj* ¡tente! ¡para! **The room won't h. more,** En este cuarto no caben más. **They h. him in great respect,** Le tienen mucho respeto. **The theory does not h. water,** La teoría es falsa, La teoría no es lógica. **to h. one's own,** defenderse, mantenerse en sus trece. **to h. one's breath,** contener la respiración. **to h. one's tongue,** callarse. **to h. sway,** mandar; reinar. **to h. tightly,** agarrar fuertemente; (clasp) estrechar. **H. the line!** (telephone) ¡Aguarde un momento! **to h. back,** *vt* detener; contener; retener; esconder; abstenerse de entregar. *vi* quedarse atrás; vacilar, dudar; tardar en. **to h. by,** seguir; basarse en, apoyarse en. **to h. down,** sujetar; (oppress) oprimir. **to h. fast,** *vt* sujetar fuertemente. *vi* mantenerse firme; *fig* estar agarrado (a). **to h. forth,** *vt* ofrecer; expresar. *vi* hacer un discurso, perorar. **to h. in,** *vt* contener; retener. *vi* contenerse. **to h. off,** *vt* apartar, alejar. *vi* apartarse, alejarse. mantenerse alejado. **to h. on,** seguir, persistir en; aguantar. **to h. out,** *vt* alargar, extender; ofrecer. *vi* aguantar; durar, resistir. **to h. over,** tener suspendido sobre; (postpone) aplazar; *fig* amenazar con. **to h. to,** agarrarse a; atenerse a. **to h. together,** *vt* unir; juntar. *vi* mantenerse juntos. **to h. up,** *vt* (display) mostrar, enseñar; levantar; sostener, soportar; (rob) atracar, saltear; (delay) atrasar; (stop) interrumpir, parar. *vi* mantenerse en pie; (of weather) seguir bueno. **The train has been held up by fog,** El tren viene con retraso a causa de la niebla

hólder n el m, (f, la) que tiene; poseedor (-ra); *com* tenedor (-ra); inquilino (-na); propietario (-ia); (support) soporte, m; mango, m; asa, f; (in compounds) porta . . .

holding n tención, f; posesión, f; propiedad, f; (leasing) arrendamiento, m; (celebration) solemnización, f; (of a meeting) el celebrar, el tener; *pl* **holdings,** com valores habidos, m pl

holding company n compañía de cartera, f

hole n hoyo, m; *Lat. Am. also* foramen m; boquete, m; agujero, m; cavidad, f; (hollow) depresión, f, hueco, m; orificio, m; (tear) roto, desgarro, m; (eyelet) punto, m; (in cheese) ojo, m; (in stocking) rotura, f, punto, m; (lair) madriguera, f; (nest) nido, m; (golf) hoyo, m; (fix) aprieto, m. *vt* agujerear; excavar; (bore) taladrar; *sport* meter la pelota (en). **to h. out,** (golf) meter la pelota en el hoyo. **h.-and-corner,** a *inf* bajo mano, secreto

hole-puncher n agujereadora, f

holiday n día feriado, m; día de fiesta, día festivo, m; vacación, f. a festivo, alegre; de vacación; de vacaciones; de excursión; (summer) veraniego. **day's h.,** día de asueto, m. **to take a h.,** tomar una vacación; hacer fiesta. **h. camp,** colonia veraniega, f. **h.-maker,** excursionista, turista, mf; (in the summer) veraneante, mf **holidays with pay,** vacaciones retribuidas, f pl

holiness n santidad, f

Holland Holanda, f

hollow a hueco; cóncavo; (empty) vacío; (of eyes, etc.) hundido; (of sound) sordo; (of a cough) cavernoso; (echoing) retumbante; (*fig* unreal) vacío, falso; insincero. *adv* vacío; *inf* completamente. n hueco, m; concavidad, f; (hole) hoyo, m; cavidad, f; (valley) hondanada, f, barranco, m; (groove) ranura, f; (depression) depresión, f; (in the back) curvadura, f. *vt* excavar, ahuecar; vaciar. **h.-cheeked,** con las mejillas hundidas. **h.-eyed,** con los ojos hundidos, de ojos hundidos

holocaust n holocausto, m

holster n pistolera, f

holy a santo; sagrado; (blessed) bendito. **most h.,** a santísimo. **to make h.,** santificar. **H. Father,** Padre Santo, el Papa, m. **H. Ghost,** Espíritu Santo, m. **H. Office,** Santo Oficio, m, Inquisición, f. **H. Orders,** órdenes sagradas, f pl. **h. places,** santos lugares, m pl. **H. Scripture,** Sagrada Escritura, f. **H. See,** Cátedra de San Pedro, f, **h. water,** agua bendita, f. **H. Souls,** las Ánimas Benditas. **h. water stoup,** acetre, m. **H. Week,** Semana Santa, f

Holy Land, the la Tierra Santa, f

homage n homenaje, m; culto, m; reverencia, f. **to pay h.,** rendir homenaje

home n casa, f; hogar, m; domicilio, m, residencia, f; (institution) asilo, m; (haven) refugio, m; (habitation) morada, f; (country of origin) país de origen, m; (native land) patria, f; (environment) ambiente natural, m; *sport* meta, f. a casero, doméstico; nativo; nacional, del país; indígena. *adv* a casa, hacia casa; (in one's country) en su patria; (returned) de vuelta; (of the feelings) al corazón, al alma; (to the limit) al límite. **at h.,** en casa; *fig* en su elemento; (of games) en campo propio; de recibo. **at-h. day,** día de recibo, m. **He shot the bolt h.,** Echó el cerrojo. **one's long h.,** su última morada. **to be at h.,** estar en casa; estar de recibo. **to be away from h.,** estar fuera de casa; estar ausente. **to bring h.,** traer (or llevar) a casa; hacer ver; convencer; llegar al alma; (a crime) probar (contra). **to go h.,** volver a casa; volver a la patria; (be effective) hacer su efecto; (move) herir en lo más vivo. **to make oneself at h.,** ponerse a sus anchas, sentirse como en casa de uno. **Please make yourself at home!** ¡Ha tomado posesión de su casa! **to strike h.,** dar en el blanco; herir; (hit) golpear; herir en lo más vivo; hacerse sentir. **h. affairs,** asuntos domésticos, m pl, (Ministry of) Gobernación, f. **h.-bred,** criado en el país. **h.-brewed,** fermentado en el país; fermentado en casa. **h.-coming,** regreso al hogar, m. **h. counties,** condados alrededor de Londres, m pl. **H. Defense,** defensa nacional, f. **h. farm,** residencia del propietario de una finca, f. **h. for the aged,** asilo de ancianos, m. **h. front,** frente doméstico, m. **H. Guard,** milicia nacional, f. **h. life,** vida de familia, f. **h.-made** casero, de fabricación casera, hecho en casa. **H. Office,** Ministerio de Gobernación, m. **H. Rule,** autonomía, f. **H. Secretary,** Ministro de Gobernación, m. **h. stretch,** último trecho (de una carrera), m. **h. truth,** verdad, mf fresca, f. **to tell someone a few h. truths,** contarle cuatro verdades

homeless a sin casa; sin hogar. **the h.,** los sin techo

homely a doméstico; familiar; (unpretentious) sencillo; llano; (ugly) feo; desabrido

homeopath n homeópata, mf

homeopathic a homeópata

homeopathy n homeopatía, f

homesick a nostálgico. **to be h.,** tener morriña

homesickness n nostalgia, añoranza, morriña, f

homespun a tejido en casa; hecho en casa; basto, grueso

homestead n hacienda, f; casa solariega, f; casa, f

homeward *adv* hacia casa, en dirección

al hogar; de vuelta; hacia la patria.
h.-bound, en dirección a casa; (of ships)
con rumbo al puerto de origen; (of other
traffic) de vuelta

homicidal a homicida

homicide n (act) homicidio, m; (person)
homicida, mf

homogeneous a homogéneo

homosexual a and n homosexual, mf

Honduran a and n hondureño (-ña)

hone n piedra de afilar, f. vt afilar, vaciar

honest a honrado; decente, honesto;
(chaste) casto; (loyal) sincero, leal; (frank)
franco; imparcial. **an h. man,** un hombre
de buena fe, un hombre honrado, un
hombre decente

honesty n honradez, f; honestidad, f;
(chastity) castidad, f; sinceridad, f; rectitud, imparcialidad, f

honey n miel, f. **h.-bee,** abeja obrera, f.
h.-colored, h.-pot, jarro de
miel, m. **h.-tongued,** melifluo; de pico
de oro

honeydew n mielada, f; fig ambrosia, f

honeyed a de miel; fig meloso, adulador

honeymoon n luna de miel, f; viaje de
novios, viaje nupcial, m. vi hacer un viaje
nupcial

honor n honor, m; honra, f; honradez,
rectitud, integridad, f; pl honors,
honores, m pl; condecoraciones, f pl;
(last h.) honras, pompas fúnebres, f pl. vt
honrar; (God) glorificar; (decorate) condecorar, laurear; (respect) respetar; reverenciar; com aceptar; (a toast) beber. **On
my h.,** A fe mía. **point of h.,** punto de
honor, pundonor, m. **word of h.,** palabra
de honor, f. **Your H.,** (to a judge) Excelentísimo Señor Juez

honorable a honorable; glorioso; digno;
ilustre; (sensitive of honor) pundonoroso

honorable mention n accésit, m

honorarium n honorario, m

honorary a honorario, honorífico. **h.
member,** socio (-ia) honorario (-ia). **h.
mention,** mención honorífica, f

hood n capucha, caperuza, f; (folding, of
vehicles) capota, cubierta, cubierta del
motor f; (of a carriage) caparazón, fuelle,
m; (of a car) capó, m, (university) muceta,
f; (of a fireplace) campana (de hogar), f;
(cowl of chimney) sombrerete (de chimenea), m. vt cubrir con capucha; cubrir;
(the eyes) ocultar, cubrir, velar

hoodwink vt vendar (los ojos); fig engañar, embaucar, burlar

hoof n casco, m; (cloven) pezuña, f

hoof it ir a golpe de calcetín

hook n gancho, garfio, m; (boat-) bichero,
m; (fish-) anzuelo, m; (on a dress) corchete, m; (hanger) colgadero, m; (claw)
garra, f. vt enganchar; (a dress) abrochar;
(fish) pescar, coger; (nab) atrapar, pescar. **by h. or by crook,** a tuertas o a derechas. **left h.,** (boxing) izquierdo, m. **right**

h., (boxing) derecho, m. **to catch oneself on a h.,** engancharse. **h. and eye,**
los corchetes. **h.-nosed,** con nariz de
gancho, con nariz aguileña. **h.-up,** rad
circuito, m; transmisión en circuito, f

hookworm n anquilostoma, m

hooligan n rufián, m

hoop n aro, arco, m; (of a skirt) miriñaque, m; (croquet) argolla, f; (toy) aro,
m; círculo, m. vt poner aros a; fig rodear

hoot n (of owls) ululación, f, grito, m;
(whistle) silbido, m; ruido, clamor, m. vi
(of owls) ular, gritar; silbar; aut avisar
con la bocina. **to h. off the stage,** hacer
abandonar la escena. **to h. down,** silbar

hop n salto, brinco, m; bot lúpulo, m; bot
flores de oblón, f pl; (dance) baile, m. vi
saltar con un pie; andar dando brincos;
saltar; (limp) cojear; recoger lúpulo; (of
plant) dar lúpulo. vt saltar. **hop-garden,**
huerto de lúpulo, m. **hop-kiln,** horno
para secar lúpulo, m. **hop-picker,** reco-
lector (-ra) de lúpulo. **hop-picking,** recolección de lúpulos, f

hope n esperanza, f; (faith) confianza, f;
(expectation) anticipación, expectación, f;
(probability) probabilidad, f; (illusion) ilusión, f; sueño, m. vi esperar. **to live in h.
that,** vivir con la esperanza de que. **to
lose h.,** desesperarse. **to h. against h.,**
esperar sin motivo, esperar lo imposible.
to h. for, desear. **to h. in,** confiar en

hopeful a lleno de esperanzas, confiado;
optimista; (fig) risueño. n inf la esperanza
de la casa. **to look h.,** fig prometer bien

hopeless a desesperado, sin esperanza;
irremediable; (of situations) imposible;
(of disease) incurable. **to be h.,** (lose
hope) desesperarse; (have no remedy)
ser irremediable; (of disease) no tener
cura. **to make h.,** hacer perder la esperanza, desesperar; dejar sin remedio;
(a situation) hacer imposible; (an illness)
hacer imposible de curar

hopelessly adv sin esperanza; sin remedio; imposiblemente; incurablemente

hopping mad Lat. Am. hecho un ají

hopscotch n infernáculo, m, rayuela, f

horizon n horizonte, m

horizontal a horizontal. **h. suspension,**
(gymnastics) plancha, f

hormone n hormona, f

horn n (of bull, etc.) cuerno, m; (antler)
asta, f; (of an insect) antena, f; (of a snail)
tentáculo, m; mus cuerno, m; trompa, f;
(of motor and phonograph) bocina, f,
Mexico kláxon m; (of moon) cuerno (de la
luna), m. **article made of h.,** objeto de
cuerno, m. **on the horns of a dilemma,**
entre la espada y la pared. **h. of plenty,**
cuerno de abundancia, m; cornucopia, f.
h.-rimmed spectacles, anteojos de
concha, m pl. **h. thrust,** cornada, f

hornet n avispón, abejón, m

horny a córneo; calloso; duro.
h.-handed, con manos callosas

horoscope n horóscopo, m

horrible a horrible, repugnante, espantoso; (of price) enorme; inf horrible

horrid a horroroso; desagradable

horrific a horrífico, horrendo

horrify vt horrorizar; escandalizar

horrifying a horroroso, horripilante

horror n horror, m. **h.-stricken**, horrorizado

hors d'œuvres n pl entremeses, m pl

horse n caballo, m; Lat. Am. cuaco m; (cavalry) caballería, f; (frame) caballete, m; (gymnastics and as punishment) potro, m. a caballar, caballuno. vt montar a caballo. **pack of horses**, caballada, f. **to ride a h.**, cabalgar, montar a caballo. **H. Artillery**, artillería montada, f. **h. blanket**, manta para caballos, f; sudadero, m; Lat. Am. mandil m. **h.-block**, montador, m. **h.-box**, vagón para caballos, m. **h.-breaker**, domador de caballos, m. **h.-cab**, simón, m. **h.-chestnut**, castaña pilonga, f. **h.-chestnut flower**, candela, f. **h.-collar**, collera, f, collerón m. **h.-dealer**, chalán, m. **h.-doctor**, veterinario, m. **h.-flesh**, carne de caballo, f. **h.-fly**, tábano, m. **H. Guards**, guardias montadas, f pl. **h.-latitudes**, calmas de Cáncer, f pl. **h.-laugh**, carcajada, f. **h.-master**, maestro de equitación, m. **h. meat**, carne de caballo, f. **h. pistol**, pistola de arzón, f. **h.-play**, payasada, f. **h.-power**, caballo de vapor, m; potencia, f. **a twelve-h.p. car**, un coche de doce caballos. **h.-race**, carrera de caballos, f. **h.-radish**, rábano picante, raíz amarga, m. **h.-sense**, sentido común, m; gramática parda, f. **h. show**, exposición de caballos, feria equina f; concurso de caballos, m. **h.-trainer**, entrenador de caballos, m. **h. tram**, tranvía de sangre, m. **h. trappings**, monturas, f pl. **That's a horse of a different color** Es harina de otro costal, Argentina, Peru Esas son otras cuarenta

horseback n lomo de caballo, m. **on h.**, a caballo. **to ride on h.**, ir a caballo

horseman n jinete, cabalgador, m

horsemanship n equitación, f, manejo del caballo, m

horseshoe n herradura, f. **h. arch**, arco de herradura, arco morisco, m

horsewoman n amazona, f

horticultural a horticultural. **h. show**, exposición de flores, f

hose n (tube) manga, f; (breeches) calzón, m; (stockings) medias, f pl; (socks) calcetines, m pl. **h. man**, manguero, m. **h.-pipe**, manga de riego, manguera, f

hosier n calcetero (-ra)

hosiery n calcetería, f. **h. trade**, calcetería, f

hospice n hospicio, m; asilo, refugio, m

hospitable a hospitalario

hospital n hospital, m; (school) colegio,

m. **h. nurse**, enfermera, f. **h. ship**, buque hospital, m

hospital bed cama hospitalaria, f

hospitality n hospitalidad, f

host n huésped, convidado, (of radio or tv program) presentador, m; (at an inn) patrón, mesonero, m; (army) ejército, m; (crowd) multitud, muchedumbre, f; ecc hostia, f; pl **hosts**, huestes, f pl. **h.-plant**, planta huésped, f

hostage n rehén, m; fig prenda, f

host country n (of an organization) país-sede, m

hostel n hostería, f; club, m; residencia de estudiantes, f

hostelry n hospedería, f; parador, mesón, m

hostess n ama de la casa, f; la que recibe a los invitados; la que convida; (of an inn) patrona, mesonera, f

hostile a enemigo; hostil, contrario (a); (of circumstances, etc.) desfavorable

hostility n enemistad, f; antagonismo, m, mala voluntad, f; hostilidad, guerra, f. **suspension of hostilities**, suspensión de hostilidades, f

hot a caliente; (of a day, etc.) caluroso; (piquant) picante; ardiente; vehemente, impetuoso; violento; impaciente; colérico; entusiasta; lleno de deseo; art intenso; (great) grande, mucho; (vigorous) enérgico. **You are getting very hot now**, inf (in a game, etc.) Te estás quemando. **It is hot**, Está caliente; (of weather) Hace calor. **to grow hot**, calentarse; fig acalorarse; (of weather) empezar a hacer calor. **to make hot**, calentar; dar calor (a); inf dar vergüenza. **hot-blooded**, de sangre caliente; apasionado; colérico. **hot-foot**, aprisa, apresuradamente. **hot-headed**, impetuoso. **hot-plate**, elec calientaplatos, m. **hot springs**, termas, f pl. **hot-tempered**, colérico, irascible. **hot water**, agua caliente, f. **hot-water bottle**, bolsa de goma, f. **hot-water pipes**, las cañerías del agua caliente

hotbed n semillero, vivero, m; fig semillero, foco, m

hotchpotch n potaje, m; fig mezcolanza, f, fárrago, m

hotel n hotel, m. **h.-keeper**, hotelero (-ra)

hothead n exaltado (-da), fanático (-ca)

hothouse n invernáculo, m, estufa, f. **h. plant**, fig planta de estufa, f

hound n perro de caza, sabueso de artois, m; perro, m; inf canalla, m. vt cazar con perros; fig perseguir; fig incitar. **master of hounds**, montero, m. **pack of hounds**, jauría, f

hour n hora, f; momento, m; ocasión, oportunidad, f pl. **hours**, horas, f pl. **after hours**, fuera de horas. **at the eleventh h.**, en el último minuto. **by the h.**, por horas; horas enteras. **small hours**,

altas horas de la noche, *inf* las tantas, *f pl.*
to keep late hours, acostarse tarde. **to
strike the h.,** dar la hora. **h.-glass,** reloj
de arena, *m.* **h.-hand,** horario, *m.* **h. of
death,** hora suprema, hora de la muerte,
f

hourly a cada hora; por hora; continuo.
adv a cada hora; de un momento a otro

house *n* casa, *f;* (home) hogar, *m;* (lineage) familia, *f,* abolengo, *m;* (threat.)
sala, *f,* teatro, *m; com* casa comercial, *f;*
(takings) entrada, *f;* (audience) público,
m; (of Lords, Commons) cámara, *f;* (college) colegio, *m;* (parliament) parlamento, *m;* (building) edificio, *m. a* de
casa; de la casa; doméstico. *vt* dar vivienda (a); alojar, recibir (or tener) en
casa de uno; (store) poner, guardar. **The
cottage will not h. them all,** No habrá
bastante lugar para todos ellos en la
cabaña, No cabrán todos en la cabaña.
country-h., finca, *f;* casa de campo, *f.*
full h., casa llena, *f; theat* lleno, *m.* **to
bring down the h.,** *theat* hacer venirse el
teatro abajo. **to keep h.,** llevar la casa;
ser ama de casa. **to keep open h.,** tener
mesa puesta, ser hospitalario. **to set up
h.,** poner casa. **h. of cards,** castillo de
naipes, *m.* **H. of Commons,** Cámara de
los Comunes, *f.* **H. of Lords,** Cámara de
los Lores, *f.* **h.-agent,** agente de casas,
m. **h.-boat,** barco-habitación, *m.* casa
flotante, *f.* **h.-dog,** perro de guardia, *m;*
perro de casa, *m.* **h.-fly,** mosca doméstica, *f.* **h. furnisher,** mueblista, *mf.* **h.
painter,** pintor de brocha gorda, *m.* **h.
party,** reunión en una casa de campo, *f.*
h.-physician, médico (-ca) interno (-na).
h. porter, portero, *m.* **h. property,**
propiedad inmueble, *f.* **h.-room,** capacidad de una casa, *f.* **h. slipper,** zapatilla,
f, pantuflo, *m.* **h.-surgeon,** cirujano interno, *m.* **h.-to-h.,** de casa en casa.
h.-warming, reunión para colgar la cremallera, *f*

housebreaker *n* ladrón de casas, *m*

housebreaking *n* robo de una casa, *m*

houseful *n* casa, *f*

house furnishings *n pl* artefactos para
el hogar, accesorios caseros, aparatos
electrodomésticos, *m pl*

household *n* casa, *f;* familia, *f;* hogar, *m.
a* de la casa; doméstico; del hogar. **to be
a h. word,** andar en lenguas. **h. accounts,** cuentas de la casa, *f pl.* **h. duties,** labores de la casa, *f pl.* **h. gods,** penates, *m pl.* **h. goods,** ajuar, mobiliario,
m. **h. management,** gobierno de la casa,
m

householder *n* padre de familia, *m;*
dueño (-ña) (or inquilino (-na)) de una
casa

house of ill repute *n* burdel, *m,* casa de
citas, casa de zorras, casa pública, *f;*
lupanar, *m*

housekeeper *n* ama de llaves, *f;* mujer
de su casa, *f*

housekeeping *n* gobierno de la casa, *m;*
economía doméstica, *f. a* doméstico. **to
set up h.,** poner casa

housemaid *n* camarera, sirvienta, *f.*
housemaid's knee, rodilla de fregona, *f*

housemaker *n* ama de casa, *f*

housetops *n* tejado, *m;* (flat roof) azotea,
f. **to shout from the h.,** pregonar a los
cuatro vientos

housewife *n* madre de familia, mujer de
su casa, *f;* (sewing-bag) neceser de costura, *m*

housing *n* provisión de vivienda, *f;* (storage) almacenaje, *m;* *inf* alojamiento, *m; inf*
casa, vivienda, *f.* **h. scheme,** urbanización, *f.* **h. shortage,** crisis de vivienda, *f,*
déficit habitacional, *m*

hovel *n* casucha, *f*

hover *vi* revolotear; (of hawks, etc.) cernerse; estar suspendido; rondar; seguir
de cerca, estar al lado (de); *fig* vacilar,
dudar

how *adv* cómo; (by what means, in what
manner) de qué modo; (at what price) a
qué precio; qué; cuánto. *n* el cómo. **to
know how,** saber. **For how long?** ¿Por
cuánto tiempo? **How are you?** ¿Cómo
está Vd.? *inf* ¿Qué tal? *inf* ¿Cómo va do!
¡Mucho gusto (en conocerlo/conocerla/
conocerlos/conocerlas)! **How do you do!**
How old are you? ¿Qué edad tiene Vd.? **How beautiful!** ¡Qué hermoso! **How big!** ¡Cuán
grande! **How early?** ¿Cuán temprano?;
¿Cuándo a más tardar? **How far?** ¿A qué
distancia? ¿Hasta qué punto? ¿Hasta
dónde? **How fast?** ¿A qué velocidad?
How few! ¡Qué pocos! **How little!** ¡Qué
pequeño!; ¡Qué poco! **How long?**
¿Cuánto tiempo? **How many?** ¿Cuántos?
m pl; ¿Cuántas? *f pl.* **How much is it?**
¿Cuánto vale? **How much cloth do you
want?** ¿Cuánta tela quieres? **How
often?** ¿Cuán a menudo? ¿Cuántas
veces? **How would you like to go for a
walk?** ¿Te gustaría pasearte? **How are
you going to Lisbon?** ¿En qué vas a Lisboa?

however *adv* como quiera (que) (followed by subjunctive); por más que (followed by subjunctive); por . . . que (followed by subjunctive). *conjunc*
(nevertheless) sin embargo, no obstante.
h. good it is, por bueno que sea. **h. he
does it,** como quiera que lo haga. **h. it
may be,** sea como sea. **h. much,** por
mucho que

howl *n* aullido, *m;* (groan) gemido, *m;*
(cry) grito, *m;* (roar) rugido, bramido, *m;*
lamento, *m. vi* aullar; gemir; gritar; rugir,
bramar. *vt* chillar. **Each time he opened
his mouth he was howled down,** Cada
vez que abrió la boca se armó una bronca

howler *n* aullador (-ra); *zool* mono (-na)
chillón (-ona); (blunder) coladura, plancha, *f.* **h. monkey** *Lat. Am.* araguato *m*

howling *a* aullante; gemidor; (crying)
que llora; bramante, rugiente. *n* los aul-

lidos; (groaning) el gemir, los gemidos; (crying) los gritos; (weeping) el lloro; (roaring) los bramidos, el rugir; los lamentos

hub n (of a wheel) cubo (de rueda) m; fig centro, m. **hub cap,** tapa de cubo, f

hubbub n algarada, barahúnda, f

huckster n revendedor (-ra). vi revender; (haggle) regatear

huddle n (heap) montón, m; colección, f; (group) corrillo, grupo, m; (mixture) mezcla, f. vt arrebujar, amontonar; acurrucar, arrebujar; (throw on) echarse. vi amontonarse; apiñarse; acurrucarse, arrebujarse

hue n color, m; matiz, tono, m; (of opinion) matiz, m; (clamor) clamor, m, gritería, f. **hue and cry,** alarma, f

huff n acceso de cólera, m

hug n abrazo, m. vt abrazar, apretujar; fig acariciar; naut navegar muy cerca de. **to hug oneself,** fig congratularse

huge a enorme, inmenso; gigante; vasto

hugely adv inmensamente, enormemente

hulk n barco viejo, m; pontón, m

hulking a pesado, desgarbado

hull n naut casco (de un buque), m; (shell) cáscara, f; (pod) vaina, f, vt mondar

hullabaloo n alboroto, tumulto, m; vocerío, m

hullo interj See **hallo**

hum n zumbido, m; ruido confuso, m. vi (sing) canturrear; zumbar; (confused sound) zurrir; (hesitate) vacilar. vt (a tune) tararear

human a humano. **the h. touch,** el don de gentes. **h. being,** ser humano, hombre, m

humane a humanitario, humano

humanitarian a humanitario

humanity n humanidad, f; raza humana, f. **the humanities,** las humanidades

humanize vt humanizar; (milk) maternizar. vi humanizarse

humble a humilde; modesto; (cringing) servil; sumiso; pobre. vt humillar; mortificar. **to h. oneself,** humillarse

humbleness n humildad, f; modestia, f; (abjectness) servilismo, m; sumisión, f; pobreza, f; (of birth, etc.) obscuridad, f

humbling n humillación, f; mortificación, f

humbly adv humildemente; modestamente; servilmente

humbug n (fraud) embuste, engaño, m; (nonsense) disparate, m, tontería, f; mentira, f; (person) farsante, charlatán, m; (sweetmeat) caramelo de menta, m. vt engañar, embaucar; burlarse de

humdrum a monótono; aburrido

humid a húmedo

humidity n humedad, f

humiliate vt humillar, mortificar. **to h. oneself,** humillarse

humiliating a humillante; degradante

humiliation n humillación, mortificación, f; degradación, f

humility n humildad, f; modestia, f

humming n zumbido, m; (of a tune) tarareo, m. a zumbador. **h.-bird,** pájaro mosca, colibrí, m. **h.-top,** trompa, f

humorist n humorista, mf

humorous a humorístico; cómico, risible

humor n humor, m; humorismo, m; (temperament) disposición, f, carácter, m; (whim) capricho, m. vt seguir el humor (a), complacer; satisfacer, consentir en; (a lock, etc.) manejar. **in a good (bad) h.,** de buen (mal) humor. **I am not in the h. to . . .** No estoy de humor para . . . **sense of h.,** sentido de humor, m

humored a (in compounds) de humor . . . **good-h.,** de buen humor. **ill-h.,** malhumorado, de mal humor

humorless a sin sentido humorístico, sin sentido de humor

hump n joroba, giba, f; (hillock) montecillo, m; inf depresión, f

humpback n giba, joroba, f; (person) jorobado (-da), giboso (-sa)

humpbacked a jorobado, giboso, corcovado

humph interj iqué va!; ¡patrañas!

humus n humus, mantillo, m

hunch n: **I have a hunch that . . .** Mexico Me late que . . .

hunchback n joroba, giba, f; (person) jorobado (-da), corcovado (-da), giboso (-sa)

hunchbacked a jorobado, giboso, corcovado

hundred n ciento, m; centenar, m, centena, f. a ciento; (before nouns and adjectives, excluding numerals, with the exception of mil and millón) cien. **a h. thousand,** cien mil. **one h. and one,** ciento uno. **by the h.,** a centenares. **hundreds of people,** centenares de personas, m pl. **h.-millionth,** a and n cienmillonésimo m. **h.-thousandth,** a and n cienmilésimo m.

hundredth a centésimo, céntimo. n centésimo, m, centésima parte, f

Hungary Hungría, f

Hungarian a and n húngaro (-ra); (language) húngaro, m

hunger n hambre, f; apetito, m; (craving) deseo, m, ansia, f. vi estar hambriento, tener hambre. **to h. for,** desear, ansiar. **h.-strike,** huelga de hambre, f

hungry a hambriento; (of land) pobre; (anxious) deseoso. **to be h.,** tener hambre. **to make h.,** dar hambre

hunk n rebanada, f, pedazo, m

hunt n caza, cacería, montería, f; grupo de cazadores, m; (search) busca, f; (pursuit) persecución, f. vt cazar; cazar a caballo; (search) buscar; rebuscar, explorar; (pursue) perseguir. **to h. down,** perseguir. **to h. for,** buscar. **to h. out,** buscar; descubrir, desenterrar

hunter n cazador, m; caballo de caza, m; (watch) saboneta, f

hunting n caza, f; caza a caballo, f; persecución, f. a cazador, de caza. **to go h.,** ir a cazar. **h.-box,** pabellón de caza, m. **h.-cap,** gorra de montar, f. **h.-crop,** látigo para cazar, m. **h.-ground,** coto de caza, terreno de caza, m. **h.-horn,** cuerno de caza, m, corneta de monte, f. **h. party,** partido de caza, m, cacería, f

huntsman n cazador, montero, m

hurdle n valla, f; zarzo, m. **h.-race,** carrera de obstáculos, f; carrera de vallas, f

hurdy-gurdy n organillo, m

hurl vt lanzar, tirar, arrojar, echar. **to h. oneself,** lanzarse. **to h. oneself against,** arrojarse a (o contra). **to h. oneself upon,** abalanzarse sobre

hurly-burly n alboroto, tumulto, m

hurrah interj ¡hurra! ¡viva! n vítor, m. **H. for . . . !** ¡Viva . . . !, ¡Vivan . . . ! **to shout h.,** vitorear

hurricane n huracán, m. **h.-lamp,** lámpara sorda, f

hurried a apresurado, precipitado; hecho a prisa; superficial

hurriedly adv apresuradamente, precipitadamente, con prisa; superficialmente; (of writing) a vuela pluma

hurry n prisa, f; precipitación, f; urgencia, f; confusión, f; alboroto, m. **in a h.,** aprisa. **in a great h.,** aprisa y corriendo. **to be in a h.,** llevar prisa, estar de prisa. **There is no h.,** No corre prisa, No háy prisa

hurry vt apresurar, dar prisa, Lat. Am. apurar (a); llevar aprisa; hacer andar aprisa; enviar apresuradamente; precipitar; acelerar. vi darse prisa; apresurarse. **to h. after,** correr detrás de, seguir apresuradamente. **to h. away,** vi marcharse aprisa, marcharse corriendo; huir; salir precipitadamente. vt hacer marcharse aprisa; llevar con prisa. **to h. back,** vi volver aprisa, apresurarse a volver. vt hacer volver aprisa. **to h. in,** vi entrar aprisa, entrar corriendo. vt hacer entrar aprisa. **to h. off.** See **to h. away. to h. on,** vi apresurarse. vt apresurar, precipitar. **to h. out,** salir rápidamente. **to h. over,** hacer rápidamente; concluir aprisa; despachar rápidamente; (travel over) atravesar aprisa; pasar rápidamente por. **to h. toward,** llevar rápidamente hacia; arrastrar hacia; impeler hacia. **to h. up,** vi darse prisa. vt apresurar, precipitar, Lat. Am. apurar; estimular

hurt n herida, f; (harm) daño, mal, m; perjuicio, m. vt (wound) herir; (cause pain) doler; hacer daño (a); hacer mal (a); (damage) perjudicar, estropear, Lat. Am. afectar; (offend) ofender; (the feelings)

mortificar, lastimar, herir. vi doler; hacer mal; perjudicarse, estropearse. **I haven't h. myself,** No me he hecho daño. **Does it still h. you?** ¿Te duele todavía? **to h. deeply,** fig herir en el alma. **to h. a person's feelings,** herirle (a uno) el amor propio, lastimar, ofender

hurtful a nocivo, dañino; injurioso, pernicioso

hurtle vt lanzar. vi lanzarse; volar; caer

husband n esposo, marido, m. vt economizar, ahorrar. **h. and wife,** los esposos, los cónyuges

husbandry n labor de los campos, agricultura, f; (thrift) frugalidad, parsimonia, f

hush n silencio, m; tranquilidad, f. interj ¡chitón! ¡calla! ¡silencio! vt silenciar, hacer callar, imponer silencio (a); (a baby) adormecer; fig sosegar, calmar. vi callarse, enmudecer. **to h. up,** mantener secreto, ocultar. **h.-h.,** secreto. **h. money,** so-borno, chantaje, m

husk n (of grain) cascabillo, m; zurrón, m; cáscara, f; (of chestnut) erizo, m; vt Lat. Am. deshojar (corn)

husky a (of voice) ronco; bot cascarudo; (Eskimo) esquimal; inf robusto, fuerte. n perro esquimal, m

hustle vt empujar, codear; fig precipitar; inf acelerar. vi codearse; andarse de prisa

hut n choza, cabaña, barraca, f, Mexico jacal, elsewhere in Lat. Am. bohío m

hutch n (chest) arca, f, cofre, m; (cage) jaula, f; (for rabbits) conejera, f; (for rats) ratonera, f; inf choza, f

hyacinth n jacinto, m

hybrid a híbrido; mestizo, mixto. n híbrido, m

hydrant n boca de riego, f

hydraulic a hidráulico. **h. engineering,** hidrotecnia, f

hydrochloric a clorhídrico. **h. acid,** ácido clorhídrico, m

hydrogen n hidrógeno, m. **h. peroxide,** agua oxigenada, f

hydropathic a hidropático. **h. establishment,** balneario, m

hydrophobia n hidrofobia, rabia, f

hydroplane n hidroplano, m

hyena n hiena, f

hygiene n higiene, f. **personal h.,** higiene privada, f

hygienic a higiénico

hymen n anat himen, m; himeneo, m

hymn n himno, m. **h.-book,** himnario, m

hyperbole n hipérbole, f

hyperbolical a hiperbólico

hypercritic n hipercrítico, m

hypercritical a hipercrítico, criticón

hypersensitive a vidrioso, quisquilloso

hypertrophy n hipertrofia, f. vi hipertrofiarse

hyphen *n* guión, *m*

hypnosis *n* hipnosis, *f*

hypnotic *a* hipnótico. *n* (person) hipnótico (-ca); (drug) hipnótico, narcótico, *m*

hypnotism *n* hipnotismo, *m*

hypnotist *n* hipnotizador (-ra)

hypnotize *vt* hipnotizar

hypo *n* (sodium hyposulphite) hiposulfito sólido, *m*

hypochondria *n* hipocondria, *f*

hypochondriac *n* hipocondríaco (-ca)

hypocrisy *n* hipocresía, *f*; mojigatería, gazmoñería, *f*

hypocrite *n* hipócrita, *mf*; mojigato (-ta). **to be a h.,** ser hipócrita

hypocritical *a* hipócrita; mojigato, gazmoño

hypodermic *a* hipodérmico. **h. syringe,** jeringa de inyecciones, *f*

hypothesis *n* hipótesis, *f*

hypothetical *a* hipotético

hysterectomy *n surg* histerectomía, *f*

hysteria *n med* histerismo, *m*; histeria, *f*, ataque de nervios, *m*

hysterical *a* histérico. **to become h.,** tener un ataque de nervios. **hysterics,** *n pl* ataque de nervios, *m*

I

i *n* (letter) i. *1st pers pron* yo. **It is I,** Soy yo. Normally omitted, the verb alone being used except when **yo** is needed for emphasis, e.g. **Hablo a María,** I speak to Mary, *but* **Yo toco el violín, pero Juan toca el piano,** I play the violin, but *John* plays the piano

Iberian Peninsula, the la Península Ibérica

ice *n* hielo, *m*; (ice cream) helado, *m. vt* helar; cubrir de hielo; congelar, cuajar; (a cake, etc.) garapiñar, escarchar, alcorzar. **to ice up,** (*aer*, *aut*) helarse. **to be as cold as ice,** *inf* estar hecho un hielo. **His words cut no ice,** Sus palabras ni pinchan ni cortan. **ice-age,** edad del hielo, *f*. **ice-ax,** piolet, *m*. **ice-box,** nevera, *f*. **ice-cream,** helado, mantecado, *m*. **ice-cream cone,** cucurucho de helado, *m*. **ice-cream freezer,** heladora, *f*. **ice-cream vendor,** mantequero (-ra). **ice-field,** campo de hielo, *m*. **ice-floe,** témpano de hielo flotante, *m*. **ice hockey,** hockey sobre patines, *m*. **ice-pack,** bolsa para hielo, *f*. **ice-skates,** patines de cuchilla, *m pl*. **ice water,** agua helada, *f*

iceberg *n* iceberg, témpano de hielo, banco de hielo, *m*

icebound *a* aprisionado por el hielo; atascado en el hielo; (of roads, etc.) helado

iced *a* helado; congelado, cuajado; (cakes) garapiñado, escarchado; (of drinks) con hielo. **i. drink,** sorbete, *m*

Iceland Islandia, *f*

Icelander *n* islandés (-esa)

icicle *n* carámbano, canelón, cerrión, *m*

icily *adv* fríamente, *fig* frígidamente, con indiferencia, con frialdad

icing *n* helada, *f*, hielo, *m*; (on a cake, etc.) alcorza, capa de azúcar, *f*

icon *n* icono, *m*

iconoclast *n* iconoclasta, *mf*

icy *a* helado; glacial, frío; *med* álgido; *fig* indiferente, desabrido; *poet* frígido, gélido

idea *n* idea, *f*, concepto, *m*; (opinion) juicio, *m*, opinión, *f*; (notion) impresión, noción, *f*; (plan) proyecto, plan, designio, *m*. **to form an i. of,** hacerse una idea de, formar un concepto de. **to have an i. of,** tener una idea de; tener nociones de. **An i. struck me,** Se me ocurrió una idea. **full of ideas,** preñado (or lleno) de ideas. **I had no i. that . . .** No tenía la menor idea de que . . . No sabía que . . . **What an i.!** ¡Qué idea!

ideal *a* ideal; excelente, perfecto; (utopian) utópico; (imaginary) imaginario, irreal, ficticio. *n* ideal, *m*; modelo, prototipo, *m*

idealism *n* idealismo, *m*

idealist *n* idealista, *mf*

idealistic *a* idealista

idealize *vt* idealizar

idem *adv* ídem

identical *a* idéntico, mismo, igual; muy parecido, semejante

identifiable *a* identificable

identification *n* identificación, *f*. **i. number,** placa de identidad, *f*

identify *vt* identificar. **to i. oneself with,** identificarse con

identity *n* identidad, *f*. **i. card,** cédula personal, *f*; carnet de identidad, *m*. **i. disc,** disco de identidad, *m*

ideological *a* ideológico

ideology *n* ideología, *f*

idiocy *n* idiotez, imbecilidad, *f*; (foolishness) necedad, tontería, sandez, *f*

idiom *n* idiotismo, *m*; modismo, *m*, locución, *f*; (language) habla, *f*; lenguaje, *m*

idiomatic *a* idiomático

idiosyncrasy *n* idiosincrasia, *f*

idiosyncratic *a* idiosincrásico

idiot *n* idiota, imbécil, *mf*; (fool) necio (-ia), tonto (-ta), mentecato (-ta)

idiotic *a* idiota, imbécil; (foolish) necio, tonto, sandío

idle *a* desocupado; indolente, ocioso; (unemployed) cesante, sin empleo; (lazy) perezoso, holgazán; (of machines) parado, inactivo; (useless) vano, inútil, sin efecto; (false) falso, mentiroso, infundado; (stupid) fútil, frívolo. *vi* holgar, estar ocioso; holgazanear, haraganear, gandulear. **to i. away,** malgastar, perder. **to i. away the time,** pasar el rato, matar el tiempo. **i. efforts,** vanos esfuerzos, *m pl*. **i. fancies,** ilusiones, fantasías, *f pl*, sueños, *m pl*. **i. hours,** horas desocupadas, *f pl*, ratos perdidos, *m pl*. **i. question,** pregunta ociosa, *f*. **i. tale,** cuento de viejas, *m*. **i. threat,** reto vacuo, *m*

idleness *n* ociosidad, indolencia, inacción, *f*; pereza, holgazanería, gandulería, *f*; (uselessness) inutilidad, futilidad, *f*

idler *n* ocioso (-sa); haragán (-ana); perezoso (-sa), holgazán (-ana), gandul (-la), *Lat. Am.* aplanacalles *mf*

idly *adv* ociosamente, perezosamente; (uselessly) vanamente

idol *n* ídolo, *m*. **a popular i.,** el ídolo de las masas, *m*

idolater *n* idólatra, *mf*; (admirer) amante, *mf* esclavo (-va), admirador (-ra)

idolatrous *a* idólatra, idolátrico

idolatry *n* idolatría, *f*; (devotion) adoración, pasión, *f*

idolize *vt* idolatrar, adorar

idyll *n* idilio, *m*

idyllic *a* idílico

if *conjunc* si; (even if) aunque, aun cuando; (whenever) cuando, en caso de que; (whether) si. **as if,** como si (foll. by subjunc.). **If he comes, we shall tell him,** Si viene se lo diremos. **If he had not killed the tiger, she would be dead,** Si él no hubiera matado al tigre, ella estaría muerta. **If ever there was one,** Si alguna vez lo hubiera. **if necessary,** si fuese necesario. **if not,** si no, si no es que (e.g., **Poet and philosopher are twins, if not one and the same,** Poeta y filósofo son hermanos gemelos, si no es que la misma cosa). **If only!** ¡Ojalá que! (foll. by subjunc.)

igloo n iglú, m

ignite vt encender, pegar fuego (a), incendiar. vi prender fuego, incendiarse; arder

ignition n ignición, f; aut encendido, m. **i. coil,** aut carrete de inducción del encendido, m. **i. key,** aut llave del contacto, f

ignoble a innoble, vil, indigno

ignominious a ignominioso

ignominy n ignominia, deshonra, afrenta, f

ignoramus n ignorante, mf

ignorance n ignorancia, f; (unawareness) desconocimiento, m. **to plead i.,** pretender ignorancia

ignorant a ignorante; inculto. **He is an i. fellow,** Es un ignorante. **to be i. of,** no saber, ignorar. **to be very i.,** ser muy ignorante, inf ser muy burro

ignorantly adv ignorantemente, por ignorancia; neciamente

ignore vt no hacer caso de, desatender; (omit) pasar por alto de; law rechazar; (pretend not to recognize) hacer semblante de no reconocer; (not recognize) no reconocer

ileac a anat ilíaco

ileum n anat íleon, m

ilium n anat ilion, m

ill n mal, m. a (sick) enfermo, malo; (bad) malo; (unfortunate) desdichado, funesto. adv mal. **to be ill,** estar malo. **to be taken ill,** caer enfermo. **ill-advised,** mal aconsejado; desacertado, imprudente. **ill-advisedly,** imprudentemente. **ill at ease,** incómodo. **ill-bred,** mal criado, mal educado, mal nacido. **ill-breeding,** mala crianza, mala educación, f. **ill-disposed,** malintencionado. **ill fame,** mala fama, f. **ill-fated,** malhadado, malaventurado, aciago, fatal. **ill-favored,** mal parecido, feúcho. **ill-feeling,** hostilidad, f, rencor, m. **ill-gotten,** maladquirido. **ill-humor,** mal humor, m. **ill-humored,** de mal humor, malhumorado. **ill-luck,** desdicha, mala suerte, malaventura, f; infortunio, m. **ill-mannered,** mal educado. **ill-natured,** malévolo, perverso. **ill-naturedly,** malignamente. **ill-omened,** nefasto. **ill-spent,** malgastado, perdido. **ill-spoken,** mal hablado. **ill-suited,** malavenido. **ill-timed,** inoportuno, intempestivo. **ill-treat,** maltratar, malpa-

rar, tratar mal. **ill-treated,** que ha sido tratado mal; maltrecho. **ill-treatment,** maltratamiento, m, crueldad, f. **ill-turn,** mala jugada, f. **to do an ill-turn,** hacer un flaco servicio. **ill will,** mala voluntad, f; rencor, m, ojeriza, f. **to bear a person ill will,** guardarle rencor

illegal a ilegal; indebido, ilícito

illegible a ilegible, indescifrable

illegibly adv de un modo ilegible

illegitimacy n ilegitimidad, f; falsedad, f

illegitimate a ilegítimo, bastardo; falso; ilícito, desautorizado

illiberal a iliberal; intolerante, estrecho de miras; (mean) avaro, tacaño, ruin

illicit a ilícito, indebido, ilegal

illicitly adv ilícitamente, ilegalmente

illicitness n ilicitud, ilegalidad, f

illimitable a ilimitado, sin límites, infinito

illiteracy n analfabetismo, m

illiterate a and n analfabeto (-ta), iliterato (-ta)

illness n enfermedad, dolencia, f, mal, m

illogical a ilógico; absurdo, irracional

illuminant a iluminador, alumbrador

illuminate vt iluminar, alumbrar; art iluminar; (explain) aclarar, ilustrar

illuminated a iluminado, encendido; art iluminado. **i. sign,** letrero luminoso, m

illuminating a iluminador; (explanatory) aclaratorio. n art iluminadora, f

illumination n iluminación, f, alumbrado, m; (for decoration) luminaria, f; art iluminación, f; flg inspiración, f

illuminator n art iluminador (-ra)

illusion n ilusión, f, engaño, m; (dream) esperanza, ilusión, f, ensueño, m. **to harbor illusions,** tener ilusiones

illusive a ilusivo, engañoso, falso

illusory a ilusorio, deceptivo, falso, irreal

illustrate vt ilustrar, aclarar, explicar, elucidar; art ilustrar; (prove) probar, demostrar

illustration n ejemplo, m; ilustración, f; art grabado, m; estampa, f; (explanation) elucidación, aclaración, f

illustrative a ilustrativo, ilustrador, explicativo, aclaratorio

illustrator n ilustrador (-ra), grabador (-ra)

illustrious a ilustre, famoso, renombrado, distinguido

image n (optics) imagen, f; efigie, imagen, f; (religious) imagen, estatua, f; art figura, f; (metaphor) metáfora, expresión, f; (of a person) retrato, m. **to be the i. of,** ser el retrato de. **sharp i.,** imagen nítida, f. **i. breaker,** iconoclasta, mf. **i. vendor,** vendedor (-ra) de imágenes

imagery n art imaginería, f; (style) metáforas, f pl

imaginary a imaginario; fantástico, de ensueño

imagination *n* imaginación, *f*; imaginativa, fantasía, inventiva, *f*, ingenio, *m*

imaginative *a* imaginativo; fantástico

imagine *vt* imaginar, concebir; idear, proyectar, inventar; figurarse, suponer. **Just i.!** ¡Imagínese usted!

imam *n* imán, *m*

imbecile *a* imbécil; (foolish) necio, estúpido, tonto. *n* imbécil, *mf*; (fool) necio (-ia), tonto (-ta), estúpido (-da)

imbecility *n* imbecilidad, *f*; (folly) necedad, sandez, *f*

imbibe *vt* embeber, absorber; (drink) sorber, chupar; empaparse de

imbibing *n* imbibición, absorción, *f*

imbroglio *n* embrollo, lío, *m*

imbue *vt* imbuir, calar, empapar; teñir. **to i. with**, infundir de

imitable *a* imitable

imitate *vt* imitar; copiar, reproducir; (counterfeit) contrahacer

imitation *n* imitación, *f*; copia, *f*; remedo, traslado, *m*. **a imitado**; falso, artificial

imitative *a* imitativo; imitador

imitativeness *n* facultad imitativa (or de imitación), *f*

imitator *n* imitador (-ra); contrahacedor (-ra), falsificador (-ra)

immaculate *a* inmaculado, puro; (of dress) elegante. **I. Conception,** la Purísima Concepción

immaculately *adv* inmaculadamente; elegantemente

immanence *n* inmanencia, inherencia, *f*

immanent *a* inmanente; inherente

immaterial *a* inmaterial, incorpóreo; sin importancia. **It is i. to me,** Me es indiferente, No me importa, Me da lo mismo, Me da igual

immateriality *n* inmaterialidad, *f*

immature *a* inmaturo; precoz; (of fruit) verde

immaturity *n* falta de madurez, *f*; precocidad, *f*

immeasurable *a* inmensurable, inmenso, imponderable

immeasurably *adv* inmensamente, enormemente

immediate *a* (of place) inmediato, cercano, contiguo; (of time) próximo, inmediato, directo; (of action) inmediato, perentorio; (on letters) urgente. **to take i. action,** tomar acción inmediata

immediately *adv* (of place) próximamente, contiguamente; (of time) luego, seguidamente, en el acto, ahora mismo, enseguida; directamente; (as soon as) así que

immemorial *a* inmemorial, inmemorable

immemorially *adv* desde tiempo inmemorial

immense *a* inmenso, enorme; vasto, extenso; infinito

immensely *adv* inmensamente, enormemente

immensity *n* inmensidad, *f*; extensión, vastedad, *f*

immerse *vt* sumergir, hundir en, zambullir; bautizar por sumersión. *fig* **to be immersed in,** estar absorto en

immersion *n* sumersión, *f*, hundimiento, *m*; ast inmersión, *f*

immigrant *a and n* inmigrante, *mf*

immigrate *vi* inmigrar

immigration *n* inmigración, *f*

imminence *n* inminencia, *f*

imminent *a* inminente

immobile *a* inmóvil, inmoble; impasible, imperturbable

immobility *n* inmovilidad, *f*; impasibilidad, imperturbabilidad, *f*

immobilization *n* inmovilización, *f*

immobilize *vt* inmovilizar

immoderate *a* inmoderado, excesivo, indebido

immoderately *adv* inmoderadamente, excesivamente

immoderateness *n* inmoderación, *f*, exceso, *m*

immodest *a* inmodesto; indecente, deshonesto; (pert) atrevido, descarado

immodestly *adv* impúdicamente, inmodestamente

immodesty *n* inmodestia, impudicia, *f*; deshonestidad, licencia, *f*; (forwardness) descaro, atrevimiento, *m*

immolate *vt* inmolar, sacrificar

immolation *n* inmolación, *f*, sacrificio, *m*

immolator *n* inmolador (-ra)

immoral *a* inmoral; licencioso, vicioso; incontinente

immorality *n* inmoralidad, *f*

immortal *a* inmortal; perenne, eterno, imperecedero. *n* inmortal, *mf*

immortality *n* inmortalidad, *f*; fama inmortal, *f*

immortalize *vt* inmortalizar, perpetuar

immovable *a* inmoble, fijo, inmóvil; (of purpose) inconmovible, inalterable, constante. *n pl.* **immovables** *law* bienes inmuebles, *m pl*. *ecc* **i. feast,** fiesta fija, *f*

immune *a* inmune, libre; *med* inmune. **i. from,** exento de; libre de

immunity *n* inmunidad, libertad, *f*; exención, *f*; *med* inmunidad, *f*

immunization *n med* inmunización, *f*

immunize *vt* inmunizar

immure *vt* emparedar, recluir, encerrar

immutable *a* inmutable, inalterable, constante

imp *n* trasgo, diablillo, duende, *m*; (child) picaruelo (-la)

impact *n* impacto, *m*, impacción, *f*; choque, *m*, colisión, *f*

impair *vt* perjudicar, echar a perder, deteriorar, empeorar, desmejorar. **to be impaired,** deteriorarse, perjudicarse

impairment *n* deterioración, perjuicio, empeoramiento, *m*

impale *vt* (punishment) empalar; (with a sword) atravesar, espetar

impalement *n* (punishment) empalamiento, *m*; atravesamiento, *m*, transfixión, *f*

impalpable *a* impalpable, intangible; incorpóreo

impart *vt* comunicar, dar parte (de); conferir

impartial *a* imparcial, ecuánime

impartiality *n* imparcialidad, ecuanimidad, entereza, *f*, desinterés, *m*

impartially *adv* imparcialmente, con desinterés

impassable *a* intransitable, impracticable; (of water) invadeable

impasse *n* callejón sin salida, *m*

impassible *a* impasible, insensible; indiferente, imperturbable

impassion *vt* apasionar, conmover

impassioned *a* apasionado, vehemente, ardiente

impassive *a* impasible, insensible; indiferente, imperturbable; apático

impassively *adv* indiferentemente

impassivity *n* impasibilidad, *f*; indiferencia, *f*; apatía, *f*

impatience *n* impaciencia, *f*

impatient *a* impaciente; intolerante. **to make i.,** impacientar. **to grow i.,** impacientarse, perder la paciencia. **to grow i. at,** impacientarse ante. **to grow i. to,** impacientarse a or por. **to grow i. under,** impacientarse bajo

impatiently *adv* con impaciencia, impacientemente

impeach *vt law* denunciar, delatar, acusar, hacer juicio político (Argentina); censurar, criticar, tachar

impeachable *a law* delatable, denunciable, acusable; censurable

impeacher *n* acusador (-ra), denunciador (-ra), delator (-ra)

impeachment *n law* acusación, denuncia, *f*; reproche, *m*, queja, *f*

impeccable *a* impecable, intachable, perfecto; elegante

impeccably *adv* perfectamente; elegantemente

impecunious *a* indigente, pobre

impede *vt* impedir, obstruir, estorbar; *fig* dificultar, embarazar

impediment *n* obstáculo, estorbo, *m*; *fig* dificultad, *f*; *law* impedimento, *m*. **to have an i. in one's speech,** tener una dificultad en el hablar

impel *vt* impulsar, impeler; *fig* estimular, obligar, mover, constreñir. **I felt impelled (to),** Me sentí obligado (a)

impend *vi* ser inminente, amenazar

impending *a* inminente, pendiente

impenetrable *a* impenetrable; intransitable; denso, espeso; *flg* enigmático, insondable, secreto

impenetrably *adv* impenetrablemente, densamente

impenitence *n* impenitencia, *f*

impenitent *a* impenitente, incorregible

impenitently *adv* sin penitencia

imperative *a* imperioso, perentorio; *gram* imperativo; (necessary) esencial, urgente. *n* mandato, *m*, orden, *f*; *gram* imperativo, *m*. **in the i.,** en el imperativo

imperativeness *n* perentoriedad, *f*; urgencia, importancia, *f*

imperceptible *a* imperceptible, insensible

imperceptive *a* insensible

imperfect *a* imperfecto; incompleto, defectuoso. *a and n gram* imperfecto *m*

imperfection *n* imperfección, *f*; defecto, desperfecto, *m*; falta, tacha, *f*

imperial *a* imperial, imperatorio. *n* (beard) pera, *f*. **i. preference,** preferencia dentro del Imperio, *f*

imperialism *n* imperialismo, *m*

imperialist *n* imperialista, *mf*

imperialistic *a* imperialista

imperial *vt* arriesgar, poner en peligro, aventurar

imperious *a* imperioso, altivo, arrogante; (pressing) urgente, apremiante

imperiously *adv* imperiosamente, con arrogancia

imperiousness *n* autoridad, arrogancia, altivez, *f*; necesidad, urgencia, *f*, apremio, *m*

imperishability *n* (immortality) inmortalidad, perennidad, *f*

imperishable *a* imperecedero, inmarchitable, perenne, eterno

impermanence *n* inestabilidad, interinidad, *f*; brevedad, fugacidad, *f*

impermanent *a* interino, no permanente

impermeability *n* impermeabilidad, *f*

impermeable *a* impermeable

impersonal *a* impersonal, objetivo; *gram* impersonal

impersonality *n* objetividad, *f*

impersonate *vt* personificar, simbolizar; *theat* representar

impersonation *n* personificación, simbolización, *f*; *theat* representación, *f*

impertinence *n* impertinencia, majadería, insolencia, *f*; inoportunidad, *f*; despropósito, *m*

impertinent *a* impertinente, insolente; (unseasonable) intempestivo, inoportuno; (irrelevant) fuera de propósito

impertinently *adv* con insolencia, impertinentemente

imperturbability n imperturbabilidad, serenidad, impasibilidad, f; impavidez, f

imperturbable a imperturbable, impasible, sereno; impávido

imperturbably adv con serenidad, imperturbablemente

impervious a impermeable, impenetrable; fig insensible. **He is i. to arguments,** No hace caso de argumentos

imperviousness n impermeabilidad, impenetrabilidad, f; fig insensibilidad, f

impetigo n med impétigo, m

impetuosity n impetuosidad, temeridad, irreflexión, f

impetuous a impetuoso, temerario, irreflexivo; violento, vehemente

impetus n mech ímpetu, m, impulsión, f; fig incentivo, estímulo, impulso, m

impiety n impiedad, irreligión, irreligiosidad, f

impinge (upon) vi chocar con, tropezar con

impious a impío, irreligioso, sacrílego; (wicked) malvado, perverso, malo

impish a travieso, revoltoso, enredador

implacable a implacable, inexorable, inflexible, riguroso

implant vt fig implantar, inculcar, instilar

implantation n fig implantación, instilación, inculcación, f

implement n instrumento, utensilio, m, herramienta, f; (of war) elemento, m. vt cumplir, hacer efectivo; llevar a cabo

implicate vt enredar, envolver; (imply) implicar, contener, llevar en sí; (in a crime) comprometer. **to be implicated in a crime,** estar implicado en un crimen.

implication n implicación, inferencia, repercusión, sugestión, f; (in a crime) complicidad, f

implicit a implícito, virtual, tácito; (absolute) ciego, absoluto, implícito. **with i. faith,** con fe ciega

implied a tácito, implícito

implore vt implorar, suplicar

imploring a suplicante, implorante

imply vt implicar, indicar, presuponer; (mean) querer decir, significar; (hint) insinuar, sugerir

impolite a descortés, mal educado

impolitely adv con descortesía

impolitic a impolítico

imponderable a imponderable

import vt com importar; (mean) significar, querer decir. a com importado, de importación. n com importación, f; (meaning) significado, sentido, m; (value) importe, valor, m; (contents) contenido, tenor, m; importancia, f. **i. duty,** derechos de importación derechos de entrada, m pl, gravamen a la importación, m. **i. licence,** permiso de importación, m. **i. trade,** negocios de importación, m pl

importance n importancia, f; valor, alcance, m, magnitud, f; consideración, eminencia, f. **to be fully conscious of one's i.,** tener plena conciencia de su importancia

important a importante; distinguido; presuntuoso, vanidoso. **to be i.,** importar, ser importante. **i. person,** personaje, m, persona importante, f

importation n importación, f; com introducción (or importación) de géneros extranjeros, f

importer n importador (-ra)

importunate a (of a demand) insistente, importuno; (of persons) impertinente, pesado

importune vt importunar, asediar, perseguir

importuning n persecución, importunación, f

importunity n importunidad, insistencia, impertinencia, f

impose vt (on, upon) imponer, infligir, cargar; print imponer. vi (on, upon) (deceive) engañar, embaucar

imposing a imponente, impresionante; (of persons) majestuoso, importante

imposition n imposición, f; (burden) impuesto, tributo, m, carga, f; (print, etc.) imposición, f; (trick) fraude, engaño, m, decepción, f

impossibility n imposibilidad, f

impossible a imposible. **Nothing is i.,** No hay nada imposible, inf De menos nos hizo Dios. **to do the i.,** hacer lo imposible

impostor n impostor (-ra), bribón (-ona), embustero (-ra)

impotence n impotencia, f

impotent a impotente

impound vt acorralar; (water) embalsar; (goods) confiscar

impoverish vt empobrecer, depauperar, arruinar; (health) debilitar; (land) agotar

impoverished a indigente, necesitado; (of land) agotado

impoverishment n empobrecimiento, m, ruina, f; (of land) agotamiento, m

impracticable a impracticable, no factible, imposible

imprecation n imprecación, maldición, f

impregnable a inexpugnable, inconquistable

impregnate vt impregnar, empapar; biol fecundar. **to become impregnated,** impregnarse

impregnation n impregnación, f; biol fecundación, fertilización, f; fig inculcación, f

impresario n empresario, m

impress vt imprimir; (on the mind) impresionar; inculcar, imbuir; (with respect) imponer; mil reclutar; (of goods) confiscar. n impresión, marca, señal, huella, f

impression n impresión, f; marca, señal, huella, f; *print* impresión, f; efecto, m; idea, noción, f. **He has the i. that they do not like him,** Sospecha que no les es simpático. **to be under the i.,** tener la impresión

impressionable a susceptible, impresionable, sensitivo

impressionism n impresionismo, m

impressionist n impresionista, mf

impressionistic a impresionista

impressive a impresionante; emocionante; imponente, majestuoso; enfático

impressively adv solemnemente, de modo impresionante; enfáticamente

imprint n impresión, señal, marca, huella, f; *print* pie de imprenta, m. vt imprimir; (on the mind) grabar, fijar

imprison vt encerrar, encarcelar, aprisionar

imprisonment n encarcelación, prisión, f, encierro, m

improbability n improbabilidad, f; inverosimilitud, f

improbable a improbable; inverosímil

improbity n improbidad, f

impromptu a indeliberado, impremeditado, espontáneo. adv de improviso, in promptu. n improvisación, f

improper a impropio, inadecuado; incorrecto; indebido; indecente, indecoroso. **i. fraction,** *math* quebrado impropio, m

improperly adv impropiamente, incorrectamente; indecorosamente

impropriety n inconveniencia, f; incorrección, f; (style) impropiedad, f; falta de decoro, f

improve vt mejorar; perfeccionar; (beautify) embellecer, hermosear; (land) bonificar; *lit* corregir, enmendar; (cultivate) cultivar; (increase) aumentar; (an opportunity) aprovechar; (strengthen) fortificar; (business) sacar provecho de, explotar. vi mejorar; perfeccionarse; (progress) hacer progresos, progresar, adelantarse; com subir; (become beautiful) hacerse hermoso, embellecerse; (increase) aumentarse. **to i. upon,** mejorar, perfeccionar; pulir

improvement n mejora, f; perfeccionamiento, m; aumento, m; adelantamiento, progreso, m; (in health) mejoría, f; embellecimiento, m; cultivación, f; (of land) abono, m

improver n aprendiz (-za)

improvidence n imprevisión, f; improvidencia, f

improvident a impróvido, desprevenido

improvisation n improvisación, f

improvise vt improvisar

imprudence n imprudencia, f; desacierto, m, indiscreción, f

imprudent a imprudente; desacertado, indiscreto, mal avisado, irreflexivo

impudence n impudencia, f, descaro, m, insolencia, desvergüenza, f, atrevimiento, m

impudent a impudente, descarado, insolente, desvergonzado, atrevido, *Peru* lisurero

impugn vt impugnar, contradecir, atacar

impugnment n impugnación, f

impulse n ímpetu, m, impulsión, f; impulso, estímulo, m; incitación, instigación, f; motivo, m; (fit) arranque, arrebato, acceso, m

impulsion n ímpetu, m, impulsión, f; empuje, m, arranque, m

impulsive a impelente; irreflexivo, impulsivo

impulsively adv por impulso

impulsiveness n irreflexión, f; carácter impulsivo, m

impunity n impunidad, f. **with i.,** impunemente

impure a impuro; adulterado, mezclado; (indecent) deshonesto, indecente; (dirty) turbio, sucio

impurity n impureza, f; adulteración, mezcla, f; deshonestidad, liviandad, f; suciedad, turbiedad, f

imputation n imputación, atribución, f; (in a bad sense) acusación, f, reproche, m

impute vt imputar, achacar, atribuir; acusar, reprochar

imputer n imputador (-ra); recriminador (-ra), acusador (-ra)

in prep en; a; (of duration) durante, mientras; (with) con; (through) por; dentro de; (under) bajo; (following a superlative) de; (of specified time) dentro de, de aquí a; (with afternoon, etc.) por; (out of) sobre. **course in medieval Catalan literature,** curso de literatura catalana medioeval. **dressed in black,** vestido de negro. **in London,** en Londres. **in the morning,** por la mañana; (in the course of) durante la mañana. **in time,** a tiempo; dentro de algún tiempo. **in a week,** dentro de una semana. **in the best way,** del mejor modo. **in writing,** por escrito. **in anger,** con enojo. **in one's hand,** en la mano. **in addition to,** además de, a más de. **in case,** por si acaso, en caso de que. **in order to,** a fin de, para (foll. by infin.). **in order that,** para que (foll. by subjunc.). **in so far as,** en cuanto. **in spite of,** a pesar de. **in the distance,** a lo lejos, en lontananza. **in the meantime,** entre tanto. **in the middle of,** en el medio de; a la mitad de. **in the style of,** al modo de; a la manera de, a la (francesa, etc.)

in adv adentro, dentro; (at home) en casa; (of sun) escondido; (of fire) alumbrado; (in power) en el poder; (of harvest) cosechado; (of boats) entrado (with haber); (of trains) llegado (with haber). **to be in,** estar dentro; haber llegado; estar en casa. **to be in for,** estar expuesto a, correr el riesgo de. **to be in with a person,**

ser muy amigo de, estar muy metido con. **Come in!** ¡Adelante!; ¡Pase usted! **ins and outs,** sinuosidades, *f pl*; (of river) meandros, *m pl*; (of an affair) pormenores, detalles, *m pl.* **in less time than you can say Jack Robinson,** en menos de Jesús, en un credo, en menos que canta un gallo, en menos que se persigna un cura loco. **in the middle of nowhere,** donde Cristo dio las tres voces, (Western Hemisphere) donde el diablo perdió el poncho.

in a interno. **in-law** (of relations) político. **in-patient,** enfermo (-ma) de hospital

inability *n* incapacidad, inhabilidad, ineptitud, incompetencia, *f*; impotencia, *f*

inaccessible a inaccesible

inaccuracy *n* inexactitud, incorrección, *f*

inaccurate a inexacto, incorrecto

inaccurately adv inexactamente, erróneamente

inaction *n* inacción, *f*

inactive a inactivo, pasivo; (of things) inerte; (lazy) perezoso, indolente; (machinery) parado; (motionless) inmóvil; (at leisure) desocupado, sin empleo

inactivity *n* inactividad, pasividad, *f*; (of things) inercia, *f*; pereza, indolencia, *f*; (of machinery) paro, *m*; inmovilidad, *f*; (leisure) desocupación, *f*

inadequacy *n* insuficiencia, escasez, *f*; imperfección, *f*, defecto, *m*

inadequate a inadecuado, insuficiente, escaso; imperfecto, defectuoso

inadvertence *n* inadvertencia, *f*; equivocación, *f*, descuido, *m*

inadvertent a inadvertido, accidental, casual; negligente

inalienable a inajenable, inalienable

inalterable a inalterable

inane a lelo, fatuo, vacío, necio

inanimate a (of matter) inanimado; sin vida, exánime, muerto

inanition *n* inanición, *f*

inanity *n* vacuidad, fatuidad, necedad, *f*

inappeasable a implacable, riguroso

inapposite a fuera de propósito, no pertinente, inoportuno

inappreciable a inapreciable, imperceptible

inappreciative a desagradecido, ingrato. **i. of,** insensible a, indiferente a

inapproachable a inaccesible, huraño, adusto

inappropriate a impropio, inconveniente, inadecuado, incongruente; inoportuno

inappropriately adv impropiamente; inoportunamente

inapt a inepto, inhábil; impropio

inaptitude *n* ineptitud, inhabilidad, *f*; impropiedad, *f*

inarticulate a (of speech) inarticulado;

(reticent) inexpresivo, reservado; indistinto; *anat* inarticulado

inarticulately adv indistintamente, de un modo inarticulado

inarticulateness *n* tartamudez, *f*; inexpresión, reserva, *f*; silencio, *m*

inartistic a antiartístico, antiestético

inasmuch (as) adv puesto que, visto que, dado que

inattention *n* desatención, inaplicación, abstracción, *f*; falta de solicitud, *f*

inattentive a desatento, distraído; poco solícito, no atento

inattentively adv sin atención, distraídamente

inaudibility *n* imposibilidad de oír, *f*

inaudible a inaudible, no audible, ininteligible

inaudibly adv indistintamente, de modo inaudible

inaugurate *vt* inaugurar; (open) estrenar, abrir, dedicar; (install) investir, instalar; (initiate) originar, iniciar, dar lugar (a)

inauguration *n* inauguración, *f*; (opening) estreno, *m*, apertura, *f*; (investiture) instalación, investidura, *f*

inauspicious a poco propicio, desfavorable; ominoso, triste, infeliz

inborn a innato, instintivo, inherente

inbred a innato, inherente, instintivo

Inca a incaico, de los incas, *Lat. Am. also* incásico. *n* inca, *m*

incalculable a incalculable, innumerable; (of persons) voluble, veleidoso, caprichoso; infinito, immenso

incandescence *n* incandescencia, candencia, *f*

incandescent a incandescente, candente. **i. light,** luz incandescente, *f.* **to make i.,** encandecer

incantation *n* hechizo, *m*, encantación, *f*, ensalmo, *m*

incapable a incapaz; inhábil, incompetente; (physically) imposibilitado

incapacitate *vt* imposibilitar, incapacitar, inutilizar; (disqualify) inhabilitar, incapacitar

incarcerate *vt* encarcelar

incarceration *n* encarcelación, prisión, *f*

incarnate a encarnado. *vt* encarnar

incarnation *n* encarnación, *f*

incautious a incauto, imprudente

incautiousness *n* imprudencia, negligencia, falta de cautela, *f*

incendiary a incendiario. **i. bomb,** incendiaria, *f*

incense *n* incienso, *m*; *fig* adulación, *f. vt ecc* incensar; (annoy) irritar, exasperar, enojar. **i. burner,** incensario, *m*

incentive *n* incentivo, estímulo, motivo, *m.* a estimulador, incitativo

inception *n* comienzo, principio, *m*; inauguración, *f*

incertitude *n* incertidumbre, *f*

incessant *a* incesante, continuo, constante

incessantly *adv* incesantemente, sin cesar

incest *n* incesto, *m*

incestuous *a* incestuoso

inch *n* pulgada, *f*. **every i. a man,** hombre hecho y derecho. **Not an i.!** ¡Ni pizca! **within an i. of,** a dos dedos de. **i. by i.,** palmo a palmo, paso a paso. **i. tape,** cinta métrica, *f*

inchoate *a* rudimentario; imperfecto, incompleto

incidence *n* incidencia, *f*

incident *a* propio, característico, incidental. *n* incidente, acontecimiento, *m*, ocurrencia, *f*

incidental *a* incidente, incidental; accidental, accesorio, no esencial. **i. expense,** gasto imprevisto, *m*

incidentally *adv* (secondarily) incidentalmente; (by the way) de propósito

incinerate *vt* incinerar

incineration *n* incineración, cremación, *f*

incinerator *n* incinerador, *m*

incipient *a* incipiente, naciente, rudimentario

incision *n* incisión, *f*; corte, tajo, *m*; *med* abscisión, *f*

incisive *a* (of mind) agudo, penetrante; (of words) mordaz, incisivo, punzante

incisively *adv* en pocas palabras; mordazmente, incisivamente

incisiveness *n* (of mind) agudeza, penetración, *f*; (of words) mordacidad, *f*, sarcasmo, *m*

incisor *n* diente incisivo, *m*

incite *vt* incitar, estimular, animar; provocar, tentar. **to i. to,** mover a, incitar a

incitement *n* incitación, instigación, *f*; estímulo, *m*; tentación, *f*; aliciente, *m*

incivility *n* incivilidad, descortesía, *f*

inclemency *n* inclemencia, *f*, rigor, *m*

inclement *a* inclemente, riguroso, borrascoso

inclination *n* inclinación, *f*; (slope) declive, *m*, pendiente, cuesta, *f*; (tendency) propensión, tendencia, *f*; (liking) afición, *f*; amor, *m*; (bow) reverencia, *f*; *geom* inclinación, *f*

incline *vt* inclinar, torcer; doblar; (cause) inclinar (a), hacer. *vi* inclinarse, torcerse; (tend) tender, propender, inclinarse; (colors) tirar (a). *n* declive, *m*, pendiente, cuesta, inclinación, *f*. **I am inclined to believe it,** Me inclino a creerlo. **I am inclined to do it,** Estoy por hacerlo. Creo que lo haré

inclined *a* torcido, inclinado, doblado; *fig* propenso, adicto. **i. plane,** plano inclinado, *m*

include *vt* incluir, contener, encerrar; comprender, abrazar

including *present part* incluso, inclusive. **not i.,** no comprendido

inclusion *n* inclusión, *f*

inclusive *a* inclusivo. **January 2 to January 12 i.,** del 2 al 12 de enero, ambos inclusivos. **not i. of,** sin contar, exclusivo de. **i. of,** que incluye. **i. terms,** todo incluido, todos los gastos incluidos

incognito *a* and *adv* and *n* incógnito, *m*.

incoherence *n* incoherencia, inconsecuencia, *f*

incoherent *a* incoherente, inconexo, inconsecuente. **an i. piece of writing,** un escrito sin pies ni cabeza

incoherently *adv* con incoherencia

incombustible *a* incombustible

income *n* renta, *f*, ingreso, *m*; *com* rédito, *m*. **i.-tax,** impuesto de utilidades, *m*. **i.-tax commissioners,** inspectores de impuestos de utilidades, *m pl*. **i.-tax return,** declaración de utilidades, *f*

incoming *a* entrante; nuevo. *n* entrada, llegada, *f*. *n pl* **incomings,** ingresos, *m pl*

incommensurable *a* inconmensurable, no conmensurable

incommensurate *a* desproporcionado, desmedido

incommode *vt* incomodar, molestar, fastidiar

incommodious *a* estrecho; incómodo, inconveniente

incommunicable *a* incommunicable, indecible, inexplicable

incommunicative *a* insociable, intratable, adusto, huraño

incomparable *a* incomparable; sin par, sin igual, excelente

incomparably *adv* incomparablemente, con mucho

incompatible *a* incompatible

incompetence *n* incompetencia, ineptitud, inhabilidad, *f*; *law* incapacidad, *f*

incompetent *a* incompetente, incapaz, inepto, inhábil; *law* incapaz

incompetently *adv* inhábilmente

incomplete *a* incompleto; imperfecto, defectuoso; (unfinished) sin terminar, inacabado, inconcluso. **incomplete sentence,** frase que queda colgando, *f*

incompletely *adv* incompletamente; imperfectamente

incompleteness *n* estado incompleto, *m*; imperfección, *f*; inconclusión, *f*

incomprehensible *a* incomprensible

incomprehension *n* incomprensión, falta de comprensión, *f*

inconceivable *a* inconcebible, inimaginable

inconclusive *a* inconcluyente, cuestionable, dudoso, no convincente

incongruity *n* incongruencia, desproporción, disonancia, *f*

incongruous a incongruente, incongruo; chocante, desproporcionado, disonante

inconsequence n inconsecuencia, f

inconsequent, inconsequential a inconsecuente, ilógico; inconsistente

inconsiderable a insignificante

inconsiderate a desconsiderado, irreflexivo, irrespetuoso

inconsiderately adv sin consideración, desconsideradamente

inconsistency n inconsistencia, inconsecuencia, incompatibilidad, contradicción, anomalía, f

inconsistent a inconsistente, inconsiguiente, incompatible, contradictorio, anómalo

inconsolable a inconsolable, desconsolado. **to be i.,** estar inconsolable, (inf of a woman) estar hecha una Magdalena

inconspicuous a que no llama la atención; insignificante, humilde, modesto

inconspicuously adv humildemente, modestamente

inconstancy n inconstancia, movilidad, f; mudanza, veleidad, f

inconstant a inconstante, mudable, variable; veleidoso, volátil, voluble

incontinence n incontinencia, f

incontinent a incontinente

incontrollable a ingobernable, indomable

incontrovertible a incontrovertible, incontrastable

inconvenience n incomodidad, inconveniencia, f; (of time) inoportunidad, f. vt incomodar, causar inconvenientes (a)

inconvenient a incómodo, inconveniente, molesto, embarazoso; (of time) inoportuno. **at an i. time,** a deshora

incorporate vt incorporar, agregar; comprender, incluir, encerrar. vi asociarse, incorporarse. a incorpóreo, inmaterial; incorporado, asociado

incorporation n incorporación, agregación, f; asociación, f

incorrect a incorrecto; inexacto, erróneo, falso

incorrigible a incorregible, empecatado

incorrigibly adv incorregiblemente, obstinadamente

incorrupt a incorrupto; recto, honrado

incorruptibility n incorruptibilidad, f; honradez, probidad, f

incorruptible a incorrupto; honrado, incorruptible

increase vt aumentar, acrecentar; (in numbers) multiplicar; (extend) ampliar, extender; (of price) encarecer, aumentar. vi aumentar, crecer; multiplicarse; extenderse; encarecerse, aumentar. n aumento, crecimiento, m; multiplicación, f; (in price) encarecimiento, m, alza, f; (of water) crecida, f; (of moon) creciente, f. **It**

is on the i., Va en aumento. **to i. and multiply,** crecer y multiplicar

increasingly adv más y más; en creciente, en aumento

incredible a increíble; fabuloso, extraordinario. **It seems i.,** Es increíble, inf Parece mentira

incredibly adv increíblemente

incredulity n incredulidad, f, escepticismo, m

incredulous a incrédulo, escéptico

incredulously adv con incredulidad, escépticamente

increment n aumento, incremento, m; adición, añadidura, f; math incremento, m. **unearned i.,** plusvalía, mayor valía, f

incriminate vt incriminar

incriminating a incriminante, acriminador

incrust vt incrustar, encostrar

incrustation n incrustación, f; (scab) costra, f

incubate vt empollar; med incubar

incubation n empolladura, incubación, f; med incubación, f

incubator n incubadora, f

incubus n íncubo, m; (burden) carga, f

inculcate vt inculcar, implantar, instilar

inculcation n inculcación, implantación, instilación, f

incumbency n posesión, duración de, posesión, duración (de cualquier puesto), f

incumbent a obligatorio. n ecc beneficiado, m. **to be i. on,** incumbir a, ser de su obligación

incur vi incurrir (en), incidir (en). **to i. an obligation,** contraer una obligación

incurable a incurable, insanable; fig sin solución, irremediable. n incurable, mf

incurably adv incurablemente, irremediablemente

incurious a indiferente, sin interés; incurioso, negligente, descuidado

incursion n incursión, invasión, irrupción, f, acometimiento, m

indebted a empeñado, adeudado; (obliged) reconocido

indebtedness n deuda, f; (gratitude) obligación, f; agradecimiento, m

indecency n indecencia, f

indecent a indecente; obsceno, deshonesto

indecently adv torpemente, indecentemente

indecision n indecisión, vacilación, irresolución, f

indecisive a indeciso, irresoluto, vacilante

indecorous a indecoroso, indecente, indigno

indecorum n indecoro, m, indecencia, f; incorrección, f

indeed adv en efecto, de veras, a la verdad, realmente, por cierto, claro está. interr ¿de veras? ¿es posible? **I shall be very glad i.,** Estaré contento de veras. **It is i. an excellent book,** Es en efecto un libro excelente. **There are differences i. between this house and the other,** Hay diferencias, claro está, entre esta casa y la otra

indefatigability n resistencia, f, aguante, m, tenacidad, f

indefatigable a incansable, infatigable, resistente

indefatigably adv infatigablemente

indefensible a indefendible, insostenible

indefinable a indefinible

indefinite a indefinido, incierto; (delicate) sutil, delicado; gram indefinido; (vague) vago. gram **i. article,** artículo indefinido, m

indefinitely adv indefinidamente

indefiniteness n lo indefinido, el carácter indefinido, m; vaguedad, f

indelibility n resistencia, f, lo indeleble; fig duración, tenacidad, f

indelible a indeleble, imborrable; fig inolvidable

indelibly adv indeleblemente

indelicacy n falta de buen gusto, grosería, f; (tactlessness) indiscreción, falta de tacto, f

indelicate a grosero, descortés; indecoroso, inmodesto; (tactless) inoportuno, indiscreto

indemnification n indemnización, compensación, f

indemnify vt indemnizar, compensar

indemnity n indemnización, reparación, f

indent vt endentar, mellar; print sangrar

indentation n impresión, depresión, f; corte, m, mella, f; línea quebrada, f, zigzag, m

indenture n escritura, f, instrumento, m. vt escriturar

independence n independencia, libertad, f; (autonomy) autonomía, f. **I. Day,** Fiesta de la Independencia, f. **i. movement,** movimiento en favor de la independencia, m

independent a independiente; libre; (autonomous) autónomo; **i. of,** libre de; aparte de. **a person of i. means,** una persona acomodada

independently adv independientemente

indescribable a indescriptible; indefinible, indecible, inexplicable; incalificable

indestructible a indestructible

indeterminable a indeterminable

indeterminate a indeterminado, indefinido, vago; math indeterminado

indetermination n irresolución, indecisión, duda, vacilación, f

index n (forefinger) dedo índice, m; (of book) tabla de materias, f, índice, m; (on instruments) manecilla, aguja, f; math índice, m; (sign) señal, indicación, f. vt poner índice (a); poner en el índice. **i. card,** ficha, f.

India n la India, f. **I. paper,** papel de China, m. **i.-rubber,** bot caucho, m; (eraser) goma de borrar, f. **i.-rubber tree,** yacio, m

Indian a and n indio (-ia). **I. chief,** cacique, m. **I. club,** maza, f. **I. corn,** maíz, m. **I. ink,** tinta china, f. **I. summer,** veranillo, veranillo de San Martín, m

Indian Ocean, the el Océano Índico, m

indicate vt indicar, señalar; (show) denotar, mostrar, anunciar

indication n indicación, f; señal, f, indicio, síntoma, m; prueba, f

indicative a indicador, indicativo, demostrativo; gram indicativo. n gram indicativo, m. **to be i. of,** indicar, señalar

indicator n indicador, señalador, m

indict vt acusar; law demandar, enjuiciar

indictable a procesable, denunciable, enjuiciable

indictment n acusación, f; law procesamiento, m

indifference n indiferencia, apatía, f, desinterés, desapego, m; imparcialidad, neutralidad, f; (coldness) frialdad, tibieza, f

indifferent a indiferente, apático; imparcial, neutral; frío; (ordinary) regular, ordinario, ni bien ni mal

indifferently adv con indiferencia; imparcialmente; friamente

indigence n indigencia, necesidad, penuria, f

indigenous a indígena, nativo, natural

indigent a indigente, necesitado, menesteroso

indigestible a indigesto

indigestion n indigestión, f, Mexico insulto m; fig empacho, ahíto, m

indignant a indignado. **to make i.,** indignar

indignantly adv con indignación

indignation n indignación, cólera, f

indignity n indignidad, f; ultraje, m

indigo n añil, índigo, m

indirect a indirecto; oblicuo; tortuoso; gram **i. case,** caso oblicuo, m

indirectness n (of route) rodeo, m, desviación, f; oblicuidad, f; (falsity) tortuosidad, f

indiscernible a imperceptible

indiscipline n indisciplina, falta de disciplina, f

indiscreet a indiscreto, imprudente, impolítico

indiscretion n indiscreción, imprudencia, f; (slip) desliz, m

indiscriminate a general, universal; indistinto, promiscuo

indiscriminately adv promiscuamente

indiscrimination n universalidad, indistinción, f

indispensable a imprescindible, indispensable, insustituible

indispensably adv forzosamente, indispensablemente

indispose vt indisponer. **to be indisposed,** estar indispuesto, indisponerse

indisposed a indispuesto, enfermo, destemplado; (reluctant) maldispuesto

indisposition n indisposición, enfermedad, f

indisputability n verdad manifiesta, certeza, evidencia, f

indisputable a innegable, incontestable; irrefutable, evidente

indisputably adv indisputablemente

indissoluble a indisoluble

indistinct a indistinto; indeterminado, confuso, vago

indistinctly adv indistintamente; confusamente, vagamente

indistinguishable a indistinguible

individual a (single) solo, único; individual, individuo, particular, propio; personal. n individuo, m, particular, mf

individualism n individualismo, m

individualist n individualist, mf

individualistic a individualista

individuality n individualidad, personalidad, f; carácter, m, naturaleza, f

individualize vt particularizar, individuar

individually adv individualmente, particularmente

indivisible a incompartible, impartible, indivisible

indivisibly adv indivisiblemente

indocile a indócil, desobediente, rebelde

indolence n indolencia, pereza, desidia, f

indolent a indolente, perezoso, holgazán; med indoloro

indomitable a indomable, indómito

indoor a de casa; de puertas adentro, interno. **i. swimming pool,** piscina bajo techo, f. **i. tennis,** tenis en pistas cubiertas, tenis bajo techo, m

indoors adv en casa; adentro, bajo techo

indorsee n endosatario (-ia)

indubitable a indudable

induce vt inducir, mover; instigar, incitar; producir, ocasionar; elec inducir. **Nothing would i. me to do it,** Nada me induciría a hacerlo

inducement n incitamiento, m; estímulo, m; aliciente, atractivo, m; tentación, f

induct vt instalar; introducir, iniciar

induction n instalación, f; iniciación, introducción, f; phys inducción, f. **i. coil,** carrete de inducción, m

inductive a (of reasoning) inductivo; phys inductor

indulge vt (children) consentir, mimar; (a desire) satisfacer, dar rienda suelta a; (with a gift) agasajar (con), dar gusto (con). **to i. in,** vt consentir en. vi entregarse a, permitirse, gustar de

indulgence n (of children) mimo, cariño excesivo, m; (of a desire) propensión (a), afición (a), f; (toward others) tolerancia, transigencia, f; ecc indulgencia, f

indulgent a indulgente; tolerante, transigente

industrial a industrial. **i. alcohol,** alcohol desnaturalizado, m. **i. school,** escuela de artes y oficios, f, com **i. shares,** valores industriales, m pl

industrialist n industrial, m

industrialize vt industrializar

industrious a industrioso, aplicado, diligente

industriousness n industria, laboriosidad, f

industry n diligencia, aplicación, f; (work) trabajo, m, labor, f; com industria, f

inebriate a borracho, ebrio. n borracho (-cha). vt embriagar, emborrachar

inedible a incomible, no comestible

ineffable a indecible, inefable

ineffective a ineficaz; vano, fútil. **to be i.,** (of persons) no pinchar ni cortar. **to prove i.,** quedar sin efecto; no tener influencia

ineffectiveness n ineficacia, f; futilidad, f

inefficiency n ineficacia, incompetencia, ineptitud, f

inefficient a ineficaz, incapaz

inelastic a inelástico

inelegance n inelegancia, fealdad, vulgaridad, f

inelegant a inelegante, ordinario, de mal gusto

inelegantly adv sin elegancia

ineligible a inelegible

inept a inepto, inoportuno; absurdo, ridículo; (of persons) incompetente, ineficaz

ineptitude n ineptitud, f; necedad, f; (of persons) incapacidad, incompetencia, f

ineptly adv ineptamente, neciamente

inequality n desigualdad, desemejanza, disparidad, f; (of surface) escabrosidad, aspereza, f; flg injusticia, f; (of opportunity) diferencia, f

inequitable a desigual, injusto

inequity n injusticia, desigualdad, f

ineradicable a indeleble, imborrable

inert a inerte, inactivo, pasivo; ocioso, flojo, perezoso

inertia *n* inercia, inacción, *f*; abulia, pereza, *f*; *phys* inercia, *f*

inertly *adv* indolentemente, sin mover, pasivamente

inescapable *a* ineludible, inevitable

inestimable *a* inestimable

inevitability *n* fatalidad, necesidad, *f*; lo inevitable

inevitable *a* inevitable, necesario, fatal, forzoso, ineludible

inevitably *adv* inevitablemente, necesariamente, forzosamente

inexact *a* inexacto, incorrecto

inexcusable *a* imperdonable, inexcusable, irremisible

inexcusableness *n* enormidad, *f*; lo inexcusable

inexcusably *adv* inexcusablemente

inexhaustible *a* inagotable, inexhausto

inexorable *a* inexorable, inflexible, duro

inexorably *adv* inexorablemente, implacablemente

inexpediency *n* inoportunidad, inconveniencia, imprudencia, *f*

inexpedient *a* inoportuno; inconveniente; impolítico, imprudente. **to deem i.,** creer inoportuno

inexpensive *a* poco costoso, barato

inexperience *n* inexperiencia, falta de experiencia, *f*

inexperienced *a* inexperto, novato

inexpert *a* inexperto, imperito

inexpertly *adv* sin habilidad

inexpertness *n* impericia, torpeza, *f*

inexpiable *a* inexpiable

inexplicable *a* inexplicable

inexplicit *a* no explícito

inexplosive *a* inexplosible

inexpressible *a* inexplicable, indecible, inefable

inexpressive *a* inexpresivo; (of persons) reservado, callado, poco expresivo, retraído

inexpugnable *a* inexpugnable

inextinguishable *a* inapagable, inextinguible

inextricable *a* inextricable, intrincado, enmarañado

infallible *a* infalible

infamous *a* infame, torpe, vil, ignominioso; odioso, repugnante

infamously *adv* infamemente

infamy *n* infamia, torpeza, vileza, ignominia, *f*; deshonra, *f*

infancy *n* infancia, niñez, *f*; *law* minoridad, *f*

infant *n* criatura, *f*; crío (-ía), niño (-ña); *law* menor, *mf* **i. school,** escuela de párvulos, *f*

infanticide *n* (act) infanticidio, *m*; (person) infanticida, *mf*

infantile *a* infantil. **i. paralysis,** parálisis infantil, *f*

infantry *n* *mil* infantería, *f*

infantryman *n* *mil* infante, peón, *m*

infatuate *vt* infatuar, embobar

infatuation *n* infatuación, *f*, encaprichamiento, *m*

infect *vt* infectar, contagiar; *fig* pegar, influir; (*fig* in a bad sense) corromper, pervertir, inficionar. **to become infected,** infectarse

infected *a* infecto

infection *n* infección, *f*, contagio, *m*; *fig* influencia, *f*; (*fig* in a bad sense) corrupción, perversión, *f*

infectious *a* infeccioso, contagioso; (*fig* in a bad sense) corruptor; *fig* contagioso

infectiousness *n* contagiosidad, *f*

infelicitous *a* poco apropiado, desacertado

infelicity *n* infelicidad, desdicha, *f*, infortunio, *m*; desacierto, *m*, inoportunidad, *f*

infer *vt* inferir, concluir, educir, deducir, implicar

inferable *a* deducible, demostrable

inference *n* inferencia, deducción, conclusión, *f*

inferior *a* inferior; (in rank) subordinado, subalterno; (of position) secundario. *n* inferior, *mf* subordinado (-da). **to be not i.,** no ser inferior, *inf* no quedarse en zaga

inferiority *n* inferioridad, *f*. **i. complex,** complejo de inferioridad, *m*

infernal *a* infernal; *poet* inferno, tartáreo

inferno *n* infierno, *m*

infertile *a* infértil, infecundo, estéril

infertility *n* infertilidad, infecundidad, esterilidad, *f*

infest *vt* infestar. **to be infested with,** plagarse de

infestation *n* infestación, *f*

infidel *n* infiel, gentil, *mf* pagano (-na); (atheist) descreído (-da), ateo (-ea). *a* pagano; infiel, descreído, ateo

infidelity *n* infidelidad, alevosía, perfidia, *f*

infiltrate *vt* infiltrar. *vi* infiltrarse

infiltration *n* infiltración, *f*

infinite *a* infinito, ilimitado; inmenso, enorme; (of number) innumerable, infinito. *n* infinito, *m*

infinitesimal *a* infinitesimal. **i. calculus,** cálculo infinitesimal, *m*

infinitive *a* and *n* *gram* infinitivo, *m*.

infinitude, infinity *n* infinidad, infinitud, *f*; (extent) inmensidad, *f*; (of number) sinfín, *m*; *math* infinito, *m*

infirm *a* achacoso, enfermizo, enclenque; (shaky) inestable, inseguro; (of purpose) irresoluto, vacilante

infirmary *n* enfermería, *f*, hospital, *m*

infirmity *n* achaque, *m*, enfermedad, dolencia, *f*; (fault) flaqueza, falta, *f*

inflame *vt* encender; (excite) acalorar, irritar, provocar; *med* inflamar. *vi* encenderse, arder; acalorarse, irritarse; *med* inflamarse

inflammable a inflamable

inflammation n inflamación, *f*

inflammatory a inflamador; *med* inflamatorio

inflate *vt* inflar, hinchar; (with pride) engreír, ensoberbecer

inflation n inflación, hinchazón, *f*; *com* inflación, *f*

inflect *vt* torcer; (voice) modular; *gram* conjugar, declinar

inflection n dobladura, *f*; (of voice) tono, acento, m, modulación, *f*; *gram* conjugación, declinación, *f*

inflexibility n inflexibilidad, dureza, rigidez, *f*

inflexible a inflexible, rígido; *fig* inexorable, inalterable

inflict *vt* infligir, imponer

infliction n imposición, *f*; castigo, m

inflow n afluencia, *f*, flujo, m

influence n influencia, *f*, influjo, m; ascendiente, m; (importance) influencia, importancia, *f*. *vt* influir, afectar; persuadir, inducir. **to have i. over,** (a person) tener ascendiente sobre. *law* **undue i.,** influencia indebida, *f*

influential a influyente; (of person) prestigioso, importante

influenza n *med* gripe, *f*, trancazo, m

influx n influjo, m; (of rivers) desembocadura, afluencia, *f*

inform *vt* (fill) infundir, llenar; (tell) informar, enterar, advertir; instruir; (with about) poner al corriente de, participar. *vi* (with against) delatar (a), denunciar. **to i. oneself,** informarse, enterarse. **to be informed about,** estar al corriente de

informal a irregular; sin ceremonia, de confianza; (meeting) no oficial, extraoficial

informality n irregularidad, *f*; falta de ceremonia, sencillez, *f*; intimidad, *f*

informally *adv* sin ceremonia

informant n informante, *mf*; informador (-ra)

information n información, instrucción, *f*; noticia, *f*, aviso, m; *law* denuncia, delación, *f*. **piece of i.,** información, *f*. **i. bureau,** oficina de información, *f*

informative a informativo

informer n delator (-ra), denunciador (-ra)

infrared a *phys* infrarrojo, ultrarrojo

infraction n contravención, infracción, transgresión, *f*

infrequency n infrecuencia, rareza, irregularidad, *f*

infrequent a infrecuente, raro, irregular

infrequently *adv* rara vez, infrecuentemente

infringe *vt* infringir, violar, contravenir, quebrantar

infringement n contravención, violación, infracción, *f*

infringer n infractor (-ra), contraventor (-ra), violador (-ra), transgresor (-ra)

infuriate *vt* enfurecer, enloquecer, enojar. **to be infuriated,** estar furioso

infuse *vt* vaciar, infiltrar; *fig* infundir, inculcar, instilar

infusion n infusión, *f*; *fig* instilación, inculcación, *f*

ingathering n cosecha, recolección, *f*

ingenious a ingenioso; mañoso, hábil

ingenuity n ingeniosidad, inventiva, listeza, habilidad, *f*

ingenuous a ingenuo, franco, sincero, cándido, sencillo, inocente

ingest *vt* ingerir

ingestion n ingestión, *f*

inglorious a vergonzoso, ignominioso, deshonroso; desconocido, obscuro

ingoing a entrante, que entra. *n* ingreso, m, entrada, *f*; *com* **i. and outgoing,** entradas y salidas, *f pl*

ingot n pepita, *f*, lingote, m; (of any metal) barra, *f*

ingrained a innato, natural

ingratiate *vt* (oneself with) congraciarse con, captarse la buena voluntad de, insinuarse en el favor de

ingratiating a obsequioso

ingratitude n ingratitud, *f*, desagradecimiento, m

ingredient n ingrediente, m

ingress n ingreso, m; derecho de entrada, m

ingrowing a que crece hacia adentro. **i. nail,** uñero, m

inhabit *vt* habitar, ocupar, vivir en, residir en

inhabitable a habitable, vividero

inhabitant n habitante, residente, m; vecino (-na)

inhabited a habitado, poblado

inhalation n inspiración, *f*; *med* inhalación, *f*

inhale *vt* aspirar; *med* inhalar

inharmonious a *mus* disonante, inarmónico; desavenido, discorde, desconforme. **to be i.,** disonar; (of people) llevarse mal

inhere *vi* ser inherente; pertenecer (a), residir (en)

inherence n inherencia, *f*

inherent a inherente; innato, intrínseco, natural

inherently *adv* intrínsecamente

inherit *vt* heredar

inheritance n herencia, *f*; patrimonio, abolengo, m

inhibit *vt* inhibir, impedir; *ecc* prohibir. **be inhibited, became inhibited,** cohibirse

inhibition n inhibición, *f*

inhibitory a inhibitorio
inhospitable a inhospitalario
inhospitably adv desabridamente
inhuman a inhumano; cruel, bárbaro
inhumanity n inhumanidad, crueldad, f
inhumanly adv inhumanamente, cruelmente
inhume vt inhumar, sepultar
inimical a enemigo, hostil, opuesto, contrario
inimically adv hostilmente
inimitable a inimitable
iniquitous a inicuo, malvado, perverso, nefando; inf diabólico
iniquity n iniquidad, maldad, injusticia, f
initial a inicial. n inicial, letra inicial, f. vt firmar con las iniciales
initially adv al principio, en primer lugar
initiate a iniciado. vt iniciar, poner en pie, empezar, entablar; (a person) admitir
initiation n principio, m; (of a person) iniciación, admisión, f
initiative n iniciativa, f. **to take the i.,** tomar la iniciativa
inject vt inyectar
injection n inyección, f. **i. syringe,** jeringa de inyecciones, f
injudicious a imprudente, indiscreto
injunction n precepto, mandato, m; law embargo, m
injure vt perjudicar, dañar, Lat. Am. afectar; menoscabar, deteriorar; (hurt) lastimar, lisiar. **to i. oneself,** hacerse daño
injured a (physically) lisiado; (morally) ofendido
injurer n perjudicador (-ra)
injurious a dañoso, perjudicial, malo; ofensivo, injurioso
injury n perjuicio, daño, m; (physical) lesión, Lat. Am. also lastimadura f; (insult) agravio, insulto, m
injustice n injusticia, desigualdad, f. **You do him an i.,** Le juzgas mal
ink n tinta, f. vt entintar. **copying-ink,** tinta de copiar, f. **marking-ink,** tinta indeleble, f. **printer's ink,** tinta de imprenta, f. **ink-stand** or **ink-well,** tintero, m
inkling n sospecha, noción, f
inky a manchado de tinta. **i. black,** negro como el betún
inland n el interior de un país, a interior, mediterráneo; del país, regional. adv tierra adentro. **to go i.,** internarse en un país. **I. Revenue,** delegación de contribuciones, f. **i. town,** ciudad del interior, f
inlay vt taracear, ataracear, embutir; incrustar. n taracea, f, embutido, m
inlet n entrada, admisión, f; geog ensenada, f. **i. valve,** válvula de admisión, f
inmate n residente, habitante, m; (of

hospital) paciente, mf; enfermo (-ma); (of prison) prisionero
inmost. See **innermost**
inn n posada, fonda, venta, f, mesón, m. **Inns of Court,** Colegio de Abogados, m
innate a innato, inherente, instintivo, nativo
innately adv naturalmente, instintivamente
innavigable a innavegable
inner a interior, interno. **i. tube** aut cámara de neumatico, cámara de aire, f
innermost a más adentro; fig más íntimo, más hondo
innings n (sport) turno, m
innkeeper n fondista, mf; tabernero (-ra), mesonero (-ra), posadero (-ra)
innocence n inocencia, f; pureza, f; (guilelessness) simplicidad, f, candor, m
innocent a inocente, puro; (guiltless) inocente, inculpable; (foolish) simple, tonto, candoroso, inocentón; (harmless) innocuo. n inocente, mf **Holy Innocents,** Santos Inocentes, m pl
innocuous a innocuo, inofensivo
innovate vt innovar
innovation n innovación, f
innovator n innovador (-ra)
innuendo n indirecta, insinuación, f
innumerable a innumerable, incalculable. **i. things,** un sinfín de cosas
inobservance n inobservancia, f, incumplimiento, m
inoculate vt inocular
inoculation n inoculación, f
inoffensive a inofensivo, innocuo; (of people) pacífico, apacible, manso
inoperable a inoperable
inoperative a ineficaz, impracticable, inútil
inopportune a inoportuno, intempestivo, inconveniente
inopportunely adv inoportunamente, a destiempo
inordinate a desordenado, excesivo
inordinately adv desmedidamente
inorganic a inorgánico
inoxidizable a inoxidable
input n capacidad instalada, f, insumo, m
inquest n law indagación, investigación, f
inquietude n inquietud, f, desasosiego, m, agitación, preocupación, f
inquire vt and vi preguntar, averiguar, indagar. **to i. about,** (persons) preguntar por; (things) hacer preguntas sobre. **to i. into,** investigar, examinar, averiguar. **to i. of,** preguntar a. "**I. within,**" «Se dan informaciones»
inquirer n indagador (-ra), inquiridor (-ra)
inquiring a indagador, inquiridor
inquiry n interrogación, pregunta, f; in-

dagación, pesquisa, investigación, f; examen, m. **i. office,** oficina de informaciones, f. **on i.,** al preguntar

inquisition n investigación, indagación, f; inquisición, f. **Holy I.,** Santo Oficio, m, Inquisición, f

inquisitive a curioso, inquiridor; preguntador, impertinente, mirón

inquisitively adv con curiosidad, impertinentemente

inquisitiveness n curiosidad, f; impertinencia, f

Inquisitor n ecc inquisidor, m

inquisitorial a inquisitorial, inquisidor

inroad n incursión, f

insalubrious a malsano, insalubre

insane a loco, demente, insano; (senseless) insensato, ridículo. **to become i.,** enloquecer, volverse loco, perder la razón. **to drive i.,** volver a uno el juicio, enloquecer, trastornar. **i. person,** demente, mf, loco (-ca)

insanitary a antihigiénico, malsano

insanity n demencia, locura, f; enloquecimiento, m; (folly) insensatez, ridiculez, f

insatiable a insaciable

inscribe vt inscribir

inscription n inscripción, f; letrero, m; (of a book) dedicatoria, f; com inscripción, anotación, f, asiento, m

inscrutable a enigmático, insondable, incomprensible, inescrutable

inscrutably adv incomprensiblemente, enigmáticamente

insect n insecto, m. **insects** Lat. Am. bicherío m. **i. powder,** polvos insecticidas, m pl

insecticide a and n insecticida m.

insecure a inseguro, precario

insecurity n inseguridad, f; incertidumbre, inestabilidad, f

inseminate vt fig implantar; med fecundar

insemination n fig implantación, f; med fecundación, f

insensate a (unfeeling) insensible, insensitivo; (stupid) insensato, sin sentido, necio

insensibility n insensibilidad, inconsciencia, f; (stupor) sopor, letargo, m; impasibilidad, indiferencia, f

insensible a insensible, inconsciente; indiferente, impasible, duro de corazón; (scarcely noticeable) imperceptible. **to make i.,** (to sensations) hacer indiferente (a); insensibilizar

insensibly adv insensiblemente, imperceptiblemente

insensitive a insensible, insensitivo; (person) hecho un tronco, hecho un leño

insentient a insensible

inseparable a inseparable

insert vt insertar, intercalar; (introduce)

meter dentro, introducir, encajar; (in a newspaper) publicar

insertion n inserción, intercalación, f; (introduction) introducción, f; metimiento, encaje, m; sew entredós, m; (in a newspaper) publicación, f

inshore a cercano a la orilla. adv cerca de la orilla. **i. fishing,** pesca de arrastre, f

inside a interior, interno. n interior, m; (contents) contenido, m; (lining) forro, m; (inf stomach) entrañas, f pl. **to turn i. out,** volver al revés. **to walk on the i. of the pavement,** andar a la derecha de la acera. **from the i.,** desde el interior; por dentro. **on the i.,** por dentro, en el interior. **i. information,** información confidencial, f. **i. out,** al revés, de dentro afuera

insidious a insidioso, engañoso, traidor

insight n percepción, perspicacia, intuición, f, atisbo, m

insignia n pl insignias, f pl

insignificance n insignificancia, futilidad, pequeñez, f

insignificant a insignificante; fútil, trivial

insincere a insincero, hipócrita, falso

insincerity n insinceridad, hipocresía, falsedad, falta de sinceridad, doblez, f

insinuate vt insinuar, introducir; (hint) soltar una indirecta, sugerir; (oneself) insinuarse, introducirse con habilidad

insinuation n insinuación, introducción, f; (hint) indirecta, f

insipid a insípido, insulso; (dull) soso

insist vi insistir; persistir, obstinarse. **to i. on,** insistir en; obstinarse en, hacer hincapié en, aferrarse en (or a)

insistence n insistencia, f; obstinación, pertinacia, f

insistent a insistente; porfiado, obstinaz

insistently adv con insistencia; porfiadamente

insobriety n falta de sobriedad, f; embriaguez, ebriedad, f

insole n (of shoes) plantilla, f

insolence n insolencia, altanería, majadería, frescura, f, atrevimiento, descaro, m

insolent a insolente, arrogante, atrevido, descarado, desmesurado, fresco

insoluble a insoluble

insolvency n insolvencia, f

insolvent a insolvente

insomnia n insomnio, m

insomuch adv (gen. with as or that) de modo (que), así (que), de suerte (que)

inspect vt examinar, investigar, inspeccionar; (officially) registrar, reconocer

inspection n inspección, investigación, f; examen, m; (official) reconocimiento, registro, m

inspector n inspector, m, veedor, interventor, m

inspiration n (of breath) inspiración, aspiración, f; numen, m, inspiración, vena, f. **to find i. in,** inspirarse en.

inspire vt (inhale) aspirar, inspirar; (stimulate) animar, alentar, iluminar; (suggest) sugerir, inspirar; infundir. **to i. enthusiasm,** entusiasmar. **to i. hope,** dar esperanza, esperanzar

inspired a inspirado, intuitivo, iluminado; (of genius) genial

inspiring a alentador, animador; inspirador

inspirit vt alentar, inspirar, estimular, animar

inspiriting a alentador, estimulador

instability n inestabilidad, mutabilidad, inconstancia, f

install vt (all meanings) instalar. **to i. oneself,** instalarse, establecerse

installation n (all meanings) instalación, f

installment n (of a story) entrega, f; com plazo, m, cuota, f. **by installments,** com a plazos. **i. plan,** pago a plazos, pago por cuotas, m

instance n ejemplo, caso, m; (request) solicitación, f, ruego, m; law instancia, f. vt citar como ejemplo, mencionar; demostrar, probar. **for i.,** por ejemplo, verbigracia. **in that i. . . .,** en el caso . . . **in the first i.,** en primer lugar, primero

instant a immediato, urgente; com corriente, actual. n instante, momento, m; inf tris, santiamén, m. com **the 2nd i.,** el 2º (segundo) del corriente. **this i.,** (immediately) en seguida

instantaneous a instantáneo. phot **i. exposure,** instantánea, f

instantly adv en seguida, al instante, inmediatamente

instead adv en cambio; (with of) en vez de, en lugar de

instep n empeine, m

instigate vt instigar, incitar, aguijar, animar, provocar; fomentar

instigating a instigador, provocador, fomentador

instigation n instigación, incitación, f; estímulo, m

instigator n instigador (-ra), provocador (-ra), fomentador (-ra)

instil vt instilar; (ideas) inculcar, infundir

instilment n inculcación, implantación, insinuación, f

instinct n instinto, m. **i. with,** imbuido de, lleno de. **by i.,** por instinto, movido por instinto

instinctive a instintivo, espontáneo

instinctively adv por instinto

institute vt instituir, fundar, establecer; (an inquiry) iniciar, empezar. n instituto, m; pl **institutes,** law instituta, f

institution n (creation) fundación, creación, f; institución, f, instituto, m; (beginning) comienzo, m, iniciación, f; (charitable) asilo, m; (custom) uso, m, costumbre, tradición, f

institutional a institucional

instruct vt (teach) instruir, enseñar; (order) mandar, dar orden (a)

instruction n (teaching) instrucción, enseñanza, f; pl **instructions,** (orders) instrucciones, f pl orden, f, mandato, m

instructive a instructivo, instructor, informativo

instructor n instructor, preceptor, m

instrument n instrumento, m; (tool) herramienta, f, utensilio, aparato, m; (agent) órgano, agente, medio, m; law instrumento, m, escritura, f. vt mus instrumentar. **percussion i.,** instrumento de percusión, m. **scientific i.,** instrumento científico, m. **stringed i.,** instrumento de cuerda, m. **wind i.,** instrumento de viento, m

instrumental a instrumental; influyente. **to be i. in,** contribuir a

instrumentality n mediación, intervención, agencia, f, buenos oficios, m pl

instrumentation n mus instrumentación, f; mediación, f

insubordinate a insubordinado, rebelde, desobediente, refractario

insubordination n insubordinación, rebeldía, desobediencia, f

insubstantial a irreal; insubstancial

insufferable. See intolerable

insufficiency n insuficiencia, falta, carestía, f

insufficient a insuficiente, falto. "**I. Postage,**" «Falta de franqueo»

insular a isleño, insular; (narrow-minded) intolerante, iliberal

insularity n carácter isleño, m; (narrow-mindedness) iliberalidad, intolerancia, f

insulate vt aislar

insulating a aislador. **i. tape,** elec cinta aisladora, f

insulation n aislamiento, m

insulator n elec aislador, m

insulin n med insulina, f

insult n insulto, agravio, ultraje, m, afrenta, ofensa, f. vt insultar, ofender, afrentar. **He was insulted,** Fue insultado; Se mostró ofendido

insulting a insultante, injurioso, ofensivo. **He was very i. to them,** Les insultó, Les trató con menosprecio

insuperable a insuperable, invencible

insupportable a insoportable, inaguantable, intolerable, insufrible

insurable a asegurable

insurance n aseguramiento, m; com seguro, m; aseguración, f. **accident i.,** seguro contra accidentes, m. **fire-i.,** seguro contra incendio, m. **life i.,** seguro sobre la vida, m. **maritime i.,** seguro marítimo, m. **National I. Act,** Ley del Seguro Nacional Obligatorio, f. **i. broker,**

corredor de seguros, *m*. **i. company,** compañía de seguros, *f*. **i. policy,** póliza de seguros, *f*. **i. premium,** prima de seguros, *f*

insure *vt com* asegurar. **to i. oneself,** asegurarse. **the insured,** (person) el asegurado

insurer *n* asegurador (-ra)

insurgent *a* insurgente, rebelde; (of sea) invasor. *n* rebelde, *mf* insurrecto (-ta)

insurmountable *a* insalvable, insuperable, invencible, intransitable

insurrection *n* insurrección, sublevación, *f*, levantamiento, *m*

intact *a* intacto, íntegro, indemne

intake *n* (of a stocking) menguado, *m*; *mech* aspiración, *f*; válvula de admisión, *f*; *aer* admisión, toma, *f*; orificio de entrada, *m*

intangible *a* intangible; incomprensible

integer *n math* número entero, *m*

integral *a* íntegro, intrínseco, inherente; *math* entero. *n math* integral, *f*. **i. calculus,** cálculo integral, *m*

integrate *vt* integrar, completar; formar en un todo; *math* integrar

integrity *n* integridad, honradez, rectitud, entereza, *f*

intellect *n* intelecto, entendimiento, *m*

intellectual *a* intelectual, mental. *n* intelectual

intelligence *n* inteligencia, comprensión, mente, *f*; (quickness of mind) agudeza, perspicacia, *f*; (news) noticia, *f*, conocimiento, informe, *m*. **the latest i.,** las últimas noticias. **i. quotient,** cociente de inteligencia, *m*. **I. Service,** Inteligencia, *f*; policía secreta, *f*. **i. test,** prueba de inteligencia, *f*

intelligent *a* inteligente

intelligentsia *n* clase intelectual, intelectualidad, *f*, *inf* masa cefálica, *f*

intelligible *a* inteligible, comprensible

intemperance *n* intemperancia, inmoderación, *f*; exceso en la bebida, *m*

intemperate *a* intemperante, destemplado, descomedido; inmoderado; bebedor en exceso

intend *vt* intentar, proponerse, pensar; destinar, dedicar; (mean) querer decir. **to be intended,** estar destinado; tener por fin; querer decir

intended *a* pensado, deseado. *n inf* novio (-ia), futuro (-ra), prometido (-da)

intense *a* intenso, vivo, fuerte; (of emotions) profundo, hondo, vehemente; (of colors) subido, intenso; (great) extremado, sumo, muy grande

intensification *n* intensificación, *f*; aumento, *m*

intensify *vt* intensar, intensificar; aumentar

intensity *n* intensidad, fuerza, *f*; (of emotions) profundidad, vehemencia, violencia, *f*; (of colors) intensidad, *f*

intensive *a* intensivo

intensive-care unit *n* sala de terapia intensiva, unidad de cuidados intensivos, unidad de vigilancia intensiva, *f*

intent *n* intento, propósito, deseo, *m*. *a* atento; (absorbed) absorto, interesado; (on doing) resuelto a, decidido a. **to all intents and purposes,** en efecto, en realidad. **to be i. on,** (reading, etc.) estar absorto en, entregarse a. **with i. to defraud,** con el propósito deliberado de defraudar

intention *n* intención, voluntad, *f*, propósito, pensamiento, proyecto, *m*

intentional *a* intencional, deliberado, premeditado

intentionally *adv* a propósito, intencionalmente, de pensado

intentioned *a* intencionado

intently *adv* atentamente

inter *vt* enterrar, sepultar

inter *pref* inter, entre. **i.-allied,** interaliado, de los aliados. **i.-denominational,** intersectario. **i.-university,** interuniversitario. **i.-urban,** interurbano

interaction *n* interacción, acción recíproca, acción mutua, *f*

intercede *vi* interceder, mediar. **to i. for,** hablar por

intercept *vt* interceptar, detener; entrecoger, atajar

interception *n* interceptación, detención, *f*

intercession *n* mediación, intercesión, *f*

intercessor *n* intercesor (-ra), mediador (-ra)

interchangeable *a* intercambiable

intercom *n* teléfono interior, *m*

intercostal *a anat* intercostal

intercourse *n* (social) trato, *m*, relaciones, *f pl*; *com* comercio, tráfico, *m*; (of ideas) intercambio, *m*; (sexual) coito, trato sexual, *m*

interdependence *n* dependencia mutua, mutualidad, *f*

interdependent *a* mutuo

interdict *n* interdicto, veto, *m*, prohibición, *f*; *ecc* entredicho, *m*. *vt* interdecir, prohibir, privar; *ecc* poner entredicho

interdiction *n* interdicción, prohibición, *f*

interest *n* interés, *m*; provecho, *m*; *com* premio, rédito, interés, *m*; (in a firm) participación, *f*; (curiosity) interés, *m*; curiosidad, *f*; simpatía, *f*; (influence) influencia, *f*. *n pl* **interests,** (commercial undertakings) empresas, *f pl*, intereses, negocios, *m pl*. *vt* interesar. **to be interested in,** interesarse en, (on behalf of) por. **to be in one's own i.,** ser en provecho de uno, ser en su propio interés. **to bear eight per cent. i.,** dar interés del ocho por ciento. **to pay with i.,** pagar con creces. **to put out at i.,** dar interés. **in the interests of,** en interés de. **com**

pound i., interés compuesto, m. **simple i.,** interés sencillo, m. **vested interests,** intereses creados, m pl

interesting a interesante, curioso, atractivo

interestingly adv amenamente, de modo interesante

interfere vi intervenir, meterse, entremeterse, mezclarse; inf mangonear, meter las narices; (with) meterse con; (impede) estorbar, impedir

interference n intervención, f, entrometimiento, m; (obstacle) estorbo, obstáculo, m; phys interferencia, f; rad parásitos, m pl

interim n ínterin, intermedio, Lat. Am. also interregno m. a interino, provisional. **in the i.,** entre tanto, en el ínterin. com **i. dividend,** dividendo interino, m

interior a interior, interno; doméstico. n interior, m

interject vt interponer

interjection n exclamación, interjección, f; interposición, f

interlace vt entrelazar, entretejer

interleave vt interfoliar, interpaginar

interline vt entrerrenglonar, interlinear

interlining n entretela, f

interlock vt (of wheels, etc.). endentar; trabar; cerrar. vi endentarse; entrelazarse, unirse; cerrar

interlocutor n interlocutor (-ra)

interloper n intruso (-sa); com intérlope, m

interloping a intérlope

interlude n intervalo, intermedio, m; mus interludio, m; theat entremés, m

intermarriage n casamiento entre parientes próximos, entre razas distintas, o entre grupos étnicos distintos, m

intermarry vi contraer matrimonio entre parientes próximos, entre personas de razas distintas, o entre grupos étnicos distintos

intermediary a and n intermediario (-ia)

intermediate a intermedio, medio, medianero. n sustancia intermedia, f. vi intervenir, mediar

interment n entierro, m

interminable a interminable, inacabable

intermingle vt entremezclar, entreverar. vi mezclarse

intermission n intermisión, interrupción, pausa, f; theat entreacto, m. **without i.,** sin pausa, sin tregua

intermittence n intermitencia, alternación, f

intermittent a intermitente, discontinuo; (of fever) intermitente

intermittently adv a intervalos, a ratos, a pausas

intern n med practicante de hospital m, interno (-na), interno de hospital, alumno interno, m. vt confinar, encerrar

internal a interno, interior; (of affairs) doméstico, civil; intrínseco; íntimo. **i.-combustion engine,** motor de combustión interna, m

international a internacional. n sport un partido internacional. **i. law,** derecho internacional, m

internecine a sanguinario, feroz

internee n internado (-da)

internment n internamiento, m. **i. camp,** campo de internamiento, m

interpolate vt interpolar, intercalar, interponer

interpolation n interpolación, inserción, añadidura, f

interpose vt interponer; (a remark) interpolar. vi interponerse, intervenir; (interfere) entrometerse; interrumpir

interpret vt interpretar; (translate) traducir; (explain) explicar, descifrar. vi interpretar.

interpretation n interpretación, f; (translation) traducción, f; (explanation) explicación, f

interpretative a interpretativo, interpretador

interpreter n intérprete, mf

interrelation n relación mutua, f

interrogate vt interrogar, examinar, preguntar

interrogating a interrogante

interrogation n interrogación, f, examen, m; pregunta, f. **mark of i.,** punto de interrogación, m

interrogative a interrogativo. n palabra interrogativa, f

interrogator n examinador (-ra), interrogador (-ra)

interrogatory a interrogativo. n interrogatorio, m

interrupt vt interrumpir

interrupter n interruptor (-ra); elec interruptor, m

interruption n interrupción, f

intersect vt cruzar. vi cruzarse, intersecarse

intersection n intersección, f; cruce, m, (of streets) bocacalle, Lat. Am. cruza f

intersperse vt diseminar, esparcir; interpolar, entremezclar

interstice n intervalo, intermedio, m; (chink) intersticio, m, hendedura, f

intertwine vt entretejer, entrelazar. vi entrelazarse

interval n intervalo, intermedio, m, pausa, f; theat entreacto, m, intermisión, f; (in schools) recreo, m. **at intervals,** a trechos, de vez en cuando. **lucid i.,** intervalo claro, intervalo lúcido, m

intervene vi intervenir, tomar parte (en); mediar; (occur) sobrevenir, acaecer; law interponerse

intervening a intermedio; interventor

intervention n intervención, mediación, f

interview n entrevista, f, interviev, m. vt entrevistarse con

interviewer n interrogador (-ra); (reporter) reportero, periodista, m

interweave vt entretejer, entrelazar

intestate a and n intestado (-da)

intestinal a intestinal, intestino. **i. worm**, lombriz intestinal, f

intestine n intestino, m. **large i.**, intestino grueso, m. **small i.**, intestino delgado, m

intimacy n intimidad, f, familiaridad, f; (of nobility and others) privanza, f

intimate a íntimo; (of relations) entrañable, estrecho; intrínseco, esencial; (of knowledge) profundo, completo, detallado. n amigo (-ga) de confianza. vt intimar, dar a entender, indicar. **to become i.**, intimarse. **to be on i. terms with**, tratar de tú (a), ser amigo íntimo de

intimation n intimación, indicación, f; (hint) insinuación, indirecta, f

intimidate vt intimidar, aterrar, infundir miedo (a), espantar, acobardar, amedrentar

intimidation n intimidación, f

into prep en; a, al, a la; dentro, adentro; (of transforming, forming, etc.) en. **Throw it i. the fire**, Échalo al (or en el) fuego. **She went i. the house**, Entró en la casa. **to look i.**, mirar dentro de; mirar hacia el interior de (de); investigar

intolerable a intolerable, insufrible, inaguantable, insoportable, inllevable

intolerably adv intolerablemente, insufriblemente

intolerance n intolerancia, intransigencia, f

intolerant a intolerante, intransigente; med intolerante

intonation n entonación, f

intone vt entonar; ecc salmodiar

intoxicant a embriagador. n bebida alcohólica, f

intoxicate vt emborrachar, embriagar; med intoxicar, envenenar; (excite) embriagar, embelesar

intoxicated a borracho; (excited) ebrio, embriagado; med intoxicado

intoxicating a embriagador

intoxication n borrachera, embriaguez, f; med intoxicación, f, envenenamiento, m; (excitement) entusiasmo, m, ebriedad, f

intractability n insociabilidad, hurañería, f

intractable a intratable, insociable, huraño

intransigence n intransigencia, intolerancia, f

intransigent a intransigente, intolerante

intransitive a intransitivo, neutro

intrauterine a med intrauterino

intravenous a med intravenoso

intrepid a intrépido, osado, audaz

intrepidity n intrepidez, osadía, audacia, f

intricacy n intrincación, complejidad, f

intricate a intrincado, complejo

intricately adv intrincadamente

intrigue n intriga, maquinación, f, enredo, m; (amorous) lío, m. vi intrigar, enredar; (amorous) tener un lío. vt (interest) atraer, interesar; (with) intrigar con. **to be intrigued** Lat. Am. intrigarse

intriguer n intrigante, mf, urdemalas, m, enredador (-ra)

intriguing a enredador; (attractive) atrayente, interesante, seductor

intrinsic a intrínseco, innato, inherente, esencial

introduce vt introducir; hacer entrar; insertar, injerir; (a person) presentar; poner de moda, introducir; (a bill) presentar; (a person to a thing) llamar la atención sobre. **Permit me to i. my friend**, Permítame que le presente mi amigo

introduction n introducción, f; (of a book) prefacio, prólogo, m, advertencia, f; (of a person) presentación, f; inserción, f

introductory a introductor, preliminar, preparatorio

introspection n introspección, f

introspective a introspectivo

introvert a and n psy introverso (-sa)

intrude vt introducir, imponer. vi entremeterse, inmiscuirse. **Do I i.?** ¿Estorbo?

intruder n intruso (-sa)

intrusion n intrusión, f; geol intromisión, f

intrusive a intruso

intuition n intuición, f. **to know by i.**, intuir, saber por intuición

intuitive a intuitivo

inundate vt inundar, anegar; fig abrumar

inundation n inundación, anegación, f; fig diluvio, m, abundancia, f

inure vt endurecer, habituar

invade vt invadir, irrumpir, asaltar; med invadir

invader n invasor (-ra), acometedor (-ra), agresor (-ra)

invading a invasor, irruptor

invalid a inválido, nulo. **to become i.**, caducar

invalid n inválido (-da), enfermo (-ma). **to become an i.**, quedarse inválido. **to i. out of the army**, licenciar por invalidez. **i. carriage**, cochecillo de inválido, m

invalidate vt invalidar, anular

invalidity n invalidez, nulidad, f

invaluable n inestimable

invariability n invariabilidad, invariación, inalterabilidad, inmutabilidad, f

invariable a invariable, inmutable, inalterable

invasion n invasión, irrupción, f; med invasión, f

invective n invectiva, diatriba, f

inveigh (against) vi desencadenarse (contra), prorrumpir en invectivas (contra)

inveigle vt seducir, engatusar, persuadir

invent vt inventar, descubrir, originar; (a falsehood) fingir; (create) idear, componer

invention n invención, f, invento, descubrimiento, m; (imagination) ingeniosidad, inventiva, f; (falsehood) ficción, mentira, f; (finding) invención, f, hallazgo, m

inventive a inventor, inventivo; ingenioso, despejado

inventiveness n inventiva, f

inventor n inventor (-ra), autor (-ra)

inventory n inventario, m; descripción, f. vt inventariar

inverse a inverso. **i. proportion,** razón inversa, f

inversion n inversión, f, trastrocamiento, m; gram hipérbaton, m

invert vt invertir, trastornar, trastrocar. **inverted commas,** comilla, f

invest vt com invertir; mil sitiar, cercar; (foll. by with) poner, cubrir con; (of qualities) conferir, otorgar, dar. vi (with in) poner dinero en, echar caudal en; inf comprar

investigable a averiguable

investigate vt investigar, estudiar; examinar, averiguar; explorar. **to i. closely** Lat. Am. interiorizar

investigation n investigación, f, estudio, m; examen, m, averiguación, f; encuesta, pesquisa, f

investigator n investigador (-ra); averiguador (-ra)

investigatory a investigador

investment n (com of money) inversión, f, empleo, m; mil cerco, m; (investiture) instalación, f; pl **investments,** com acciones, f pl, fondos, m pl

investor n inversionista, m; accionista, mf, Lat. Am. investor (-ra) mf

inveterate a inveterado, antiguo, arraigado, incurable

invidious a odioso, repugnante, injusto

invigorate vt vigorizar, dar fuerza (a), avivar

invigorating a fortaleciente, fortificador, vigorizador

invincible a invencible, indomable; fig insuperable

inviolable a inviolable

inviolate a inviolado

invisible a invisible. **i. ink,** tinta simpática, f. **i. mending,** zurcido invisible, m

invitation n invitación, f; convite, m; (card) tarjeta de invitación, f

invite vt invitar, convidar; (request) pedir, rogar; (of things) incitar, tentar

inviting a atrayente, incitante; (of food) apetitoso; (of looks) provocativo

invocation n invocación, f

invoice n com factura, f. vt facturar. **proforma i.,** factura simulada, f. **shipping i.,** factura de expedición, f. **i. book,** libro de facturas, m

invoke vt invocar; suplicar, implorar; (laws) acogerse (a)

involuntarily adv sin querer, involuntariamente

involuntary a involuntario; instintivo, inconsciente

involve vt (entangle) enredar, embrollar, enmarañar; (implicate) comprometer; (imply) implicar, ocasionar, suponer, traer consigo

involved a complejo, intrincado; (of style) confuso, obscuro

invulnerable a invulnerable

inward a interior, interno; íntimo, espiritual. adv adentro

inwardly adv interiormente; para sí, entre sí

inwards adv hacia dentro; adentro

iodine n yodo, m. **i. poisoning,** yodismo, m

ion n chem ion, m

Ionic a jónico. **i. foot** poet jónico, m

iota n (letter) iota, f; jota, pizca, f, ápice, m. **not an i.,** ni pizca

I.O.U. n com abonaré, m

ipecacuanha n ipecacuana, f

Iranian a and n iranio (-ia)

irascibility n irascibilidad, iracundia, irritabilidad, f

irascible a irascible, iracundo, irritable

irate a airado, colérico, enojado

ire n ira, cólera, furia, f

Ireland Irlanda, f

iridescence n iridiscencia, f

iridescent a iridiscente. **to look i.,** irisar, tornasolarse

iridium n chem iridio, m

iris n anat iris, m; bot irídea, f

Irish a and n irlandés (-esa). **the I.,** los irlandeses

irksome a fastidioso, tedioso, aburrido

iron n hierro, m; (for clothes) plancha, f; (tool) utensilio, m, herramienta, f; (golf) hierro, m; pl **irons,** grillos, m pl, cadenas, f pl. a de hierro, férreo; fig duro, severo. vt (linen) planchar; (with out) allanar. **to have too many irons in the fire,** tener demasiados asuntos entre manos. **to put in irons,** echar grillos (a). **to strike while the i. is hot,** A hierro caliente batir

de repente. **cast-i.,** hierro colado, *m.*
scrap i., hierro viejo, *m.* **sheet i.,** hierro
en planchas, *m.* **wrought i.,** hierro dulce,
m. **i. age,** edad de hierro, *f.* **i.-foundry,**
fundición de hierro, *f.* **i. lung,** *med*
pulmón de hierro, pulmón de acero, *m.*
i.-mold, mancha de orín, *f.* **i. smelting
furnace,** alto horno, *m.* **i. tonic,** *med*
reconstituyente ferruginoso, *m.* **i. will,**
voluntad de hierro, *f*

ironclad *a* blindado, acorazado. *n* buque
de guerra blindado, acorazado, *m*

ironer *n* planchador (-ra)

ironical *a* irónico

ironing *n* planchado, *m;* ropa por planchar, *f.* a de planchar. **i. board,** tabla de
planchar, *f*

ironwork *n* herraje, *m;* obra de hierro, *f*

ironworks *n* herrería, *f*

irony *n* ironía, *f.* a (like iron) ferruginoso

Iroquois a and *n* iroqués (-esa)

irradiate *vt* irradiar; *fig* iluminar, aclarar

irradiation *n* irradiación, *f; fig* iluminación, *f*

irrational *a* ilógico, ridículo, irracional

irreclaimable *a* irrecuperable, irredimible; (of land) inservible, improductivo; irreformable

irreconcilable *a* irreconciliable

irrecoverable *a* irrecuperable, incobrable

irredeemable *a* irredimible, perdido. **i.
government loan,** deuda perpetua, *f*

irreducible *a* irreducible

irrefutable *a* irrefutable, indisputable,
innegable, irrebatible

irregular *a* irregular; anormal; (of shape)
disforme; desordenado; *gram* irregular;
(of surface) desigual, escabroso

irregularity *n* irregularidad, *f;* anormalidad, *f;* (of shape) desproporción, irregularidad, *f;* (of surface) escabrosidad,
desigualdad, *f;* exceso, *m,* demasía, *f*

irrelevance *n* inconexión, *f;* inoportunidad, *f;* futilidad, poca importancia, *f;*
(stupidity) desatino, *m,* impertinencia, *f*

irrelevant *a* inaplicable, fuera de
propósito; inoportuno; sin importancia,
fútil; (stupid) impertinente

irreligion *n* irreligión, impiedad, *f*

irreligious *a* irreligioso, impío

irremediable *a* irremediable, irreparable

irremediably *adv* sin remedio, irremediablemente

irreparable *a* irreparable

irreplaceable *a* irreemplazable

irrepressible *a* incontrolable, indomable

irreproachable *a* irreprochable, intachable

irresistible *a* irresistible

irresolute *a* irresoluto, indeciso, vacilante

irrespective *a* (with of) independiente
de, aparte de, sin distinción de

irresponsible *a* irresponsable

irretrievable *a* irrecuperable

irreverence *n* irreverencia, *f*

irreverent *a* irreverente, irrespetuoso

irrevocable *a* irrevocable; inquebrantable

irrigable *a* regadío

irrigate *vt agr* poner en regadío, regar;
med irrigar

irrigation *n agr* riego, *m; med* irrigación,
f. **i. channel,** cacera, acequia, *f,* canal de
riego, *m*

irritability *n* irritabilidad, iracundia, *f*

irritable *a* irritable, irascible, iracundo

irritably *adv* con irritación, airadamente

irritant *a* irritante, irritador. *n* irritador,
m; med medicamento irritante, *m*

irritate *vt* provocar, estimular; irritar,
molestar, exasperar; *med* irritar

irritating *a* irritador, irritante

irritatingly *adv* de un modo irritante

irritation *n* irritación, *f,* enojo, *m; physiol*
picazón, *f,* picor, *m*

irruption *n* irrupción, invasión, *f*

isinglass *n* cola de pescado, *f*

Islamic *a* islámico

island *n* isla, *f,* a isleño

islander *n* isleño (-ña)

islet *n* isleta, *f;* islote, *m*

isobaric *a* isobárico

isolate *vt* aislar, apartar

isolated *a* aislado, apartado, solitario;
único, solo

isolation *n* aislamiento, apartamiento,
m, soledad, *f*

isolationism *n pol* aislacionismo, ais-
lamientismo, *m*

isolationist *a* and *n pol* aislacionista, ais-
lamientista, *mf*

isomerism *n chem* isomería, *f*

isometric *a* isométrico

isosceles *a* isósceles

isotope *n* isotope, isotopo, *m*

Israelite *a* and *n* israelita *mf*

issue *n* salida, *f;* (result) resultado, *m,*
consecuencia, *f;* (of a periodical) número,
m; print edición, tirada, *f;* (offspring)
prole, sucesión, *f;* (of notes, bonds) emisión, *f; med* flujo, *m;* cuestión, *f,* problema, *m. vi* salir, fluir, manar; nacer,
originarse; resultar, terminarse. *vt* (an
order) expedir, emitir, dictar; publicar,
dar a luz; (of notes, bonds) poner en circulación, librar. **at i.,** en disputa, en cuestión. **to join i.,** llevar la contraria, oponer

isthmian *a* ístmico

isthmus *n* istmo, *m*

it *pron* (as subject) él, *m;* ella, *f;* (gen.
omitted with all verbs in Sp.); (as object)
lo, *m;* la, *f;* (as indirect object) le (se with
an object in 3rd pers.); (meaning that

thing, that affair) eso, ello. Sometimes omitted in other cases, e.g. **He has thought it necessary to stay at home,** Ha creído necesario de quedarse en casa. **We heard it said that . . .,** Oímos decir que . . . **to make it perfectly clear that . . .,** dejar bien claro que . . . *n* (slang) garbo, aquél, *m*; atractivos, *m pl.* **Is it not so?** ¿No es así? **That is it,** Eso es. **It's me,** Soy yo

Italy Italia, *f*

Italian *a* and *n* italiano (-na) (language) italiano, *m. art* **I. School,** escuela italiana, *f*

italic *a* (of Italy) itálico; *print* itálico, bastardillo. *n* letra bastardilla, bastardilla, letra itálica, *f.* **italics mine,** el subrayado es mío, los subrayados son míos

italicize *vt* imprimir en bastardilla; dar énfasis (a)

itch *n* sarna, *f*; *fig* picazón, *f*; prurito, capricho, *m. vi* picar; *fig* sentir picazón; (with to) rabiar por, suspirar por.

itching *n* picazón, *f*, picor, *m.* *a* sarnoso, picante; *med* pruriginoso. **to have an i. palm,** *fig* ser de la virgen del puño

item *n* ítem, artículo, *m*; *com* partida, *f*; punto, detalle, *m*; (of a program) número, *m*; asunto, *m. adv* ítem

iterative *a* iterativo

itinerant *a* nómada, errante

itinerary *n* itinerario, *m*, ruta, *f*

its *poss a* su (with pl. obj.) sus. **a book and its pages,** un libro y sus páginas.

itself *pron* él mismo, *m*; ella misma, *f*; (with prep.) sí; (with reflex. verb) se; (with noun) el mismo, la misma; (meaning alone) solo. **in i.,** en sí

ivory *n* marfil, *m.* *a* ebúrneo, de marfil, marfileño. **vegetable i.,** marfil vegetal, *m.* **i. carving,** talla de marfil, *f*

ivory tower *n* torre de marfil, *f*

ivy *n* hiedra, *f*

J

j *n* (letter) jota, *f*

jab *vt* (with a hypodermic needle, etc.) pinchar; introducir (en); clavar (con); (scrape) hurgar; (place) poner. *n* pinchazo, *m*; golpe, *m*. **He jabbed his pistol in my ribs,** Me puso la pistola en las costillas

jabber *vt* and *vi* chapurrear; (of monkeys) chillar

jabbering *n* chapurreo, *m*; (of monkeys) chillidos, *m pl*

Jack *n* Juan, *m*; (man) hombre, *m*; (sailor) marinero, *m*; (in cards) sota, *f*; (for raising weights) gato, *m*; (of a spit) torno, *m*; (of some animals) macho, *m*; (bowls) boliche, *m*. *vt* (with up) solevantar con gatos. **Union J.,** pabellón británico, *m*. **j.-boot,** bota de montar, *f*. **J.-in-office,** mandarín, funcionario impertinente, *m*. **J.-in-the-box,** faca, *f*. **j.-knife,** navaja, *f*. **J. of all trades,** hombre de muchos oficios, *m*. **jack of all trades, master of none,** aprendiz de todo, oficial de nada. **j.-rabbit,** liebre americana, *f*. **J.-tar,** marinero, *m*

jackal *n* chacal, adive, *m*

jackass *n* asno, *m*; (fool) tonto, asno, *m*. **laughing j.,** martín pescador, *m*

jacket *n* chaqueta, *f*; americana, *f*; (for boilers, etc.) camisa, *f*; (of a book) forro, *m*, sobrecubierta, *f*. **strait j.,** camisa de fuerza, *f*

jacks *n* (game) matatenas, *f pl*, cantillos, *m pl*

jade *n min* jade, *m*; (horse) rocín, *m*; (woman) mala pécora, *f*; (saucy wench) mozuela, picaruela, *f*

jaded *a* fatigado, agotado, rendido; (of the palate) saciado

jagged *a* dentado

jaguar *n* jaguar, *m*

jai alai *n Mexico* frontón, *m*

jail cárcel, prisión, *f*; encierro, *m*. *vt* encarcelar. *a* carcelario, carcelero.

jailbird malhechor; presidiario, *m*

jailer *n* carcelero (-ra)

jalopy carcacho, *m*, (Mexico), cafetera rusa, *f*, (Spain)

jalousie *n* celosía, *f*

jam *vt* (ram) apretar; apiñar; estrujar; (a machine) atascar; (radio) causar interferencia (a); (preserve) hacer confitura de. *vi* atascarse. *n* (of people) agolpamiento, *m*; (traffic) atasco, *m*; (preserve) confitura, mermelada, compota, *f*. **He jammed his hat on,** Se encasquetó el sombrero. **She suddenly jammed down on the brakes,** Frenó de repente. **jam-dish,** compotera, *f*. **jam-jar,** pote para confitura, *m*

Jamaican *a* jamaicano, *n* jamaicano (-na)

jamboree campamento, *m*

jangle *vi* cencerrear; chocar; rechinar. *n* cencerreo, *m*; choque, *m*; rechinamiento, *m*

janitor *n* portero, *m*; (in a university, etc.) bedel, *m*

January *n* enero, *m*

Japan el Japón, *m*

Japanese *a* japonés. *n* japonés (-esa); (language) japonés, *m*

jar *n* chirrido, *m*; choque, *m*; sacudida, *f*; vibración, trepidación, *f*; (quarrel) riña, *f*; (receptacle) jarra, *f*; (for tobacco, honey, cosmetics, etc.) pote, *m*; (Leyden) botella (de Leyden), *f*. *vi* chirriar; vibrar, trepidar; chocar; (of sounds) ser discorde; (of colors) chillar. *vt* sacudir; hacer vibrar. **It jarred on my nerves,** Me atacaba los nervios. **It gave me a nasty jar,** *fig* Me hizo una impresión desagradable. **on the jar,** entreabierto

jargon *n* jerga, jerigonza, *f*; monserga, *f*; (technical) lenguaje especial, *m*

jarring *a* discorde, disonante; en conflicto, opuesto; (to the nerves) que ataca a los nervios

jasmine *n* jazmín, *m*. **yellow j.,** jazmín amarillo, *m*

jaundice *n* ictericia, *f*

jaundiced *a* envidioso; desengañado, desilusionado

jaunt *n* excursión, *f*, *vi* ir de excursión

jauntily *adv* airosamente, con garbo

jaunty *a* garboso, airoso

javelin *n* jabalina, *f*. **j. throwing,** lanzamiento de la jabalina, *m*

jaw *n* quijada, *f*; maxilar, *m*; *pl* **jaws,** boca, *f*; (of death, etc.) garras, *f pl*; *mech* quijada, *f*; (narrow entrance) boca, abertura, *f*. **j.-bone,** mandíbula, *f*; *anat* hueso maxilar, *m*

jay *n* arrendajo, *m*

jazz *n* jazz, *m*. el bailar el jazz. **j. band,** orquesta de jazz, *f*

jealous *a* celoso; envidioso. **to be j. of,** tener celos de. **to make j.,** dar celos (a)

jealousy *n* celos, *m pl*

jeans *n* vaqueros, *m pl*

jeep *n mil* yip, *m*

jeer *n* burla, mofa, *f*; insulto, *m*, *vi* burlarse; (with at) mofarse de

jeering *a* mofador. *n* burlas, *f pl*; insultos, *m pl*

jellied *a* en gelatina

jelly *n* jalea, *f*; gelatina, *f*, *vi* solidificarse. **j.-bag,** manga, *f*. **j.-fish,** aguamala, aguaviva, malagua, medusa, *f*

jeopardize *vt* arriesgar, poner en juego; comprometer

jeopardy *n* peligro, *m*

jerk *n* sacudida, *f*. *vt* sacudir, dar una sacudida (a); lanzar bruscamente; (pull) tirar de; (push) empujar. *vi* moverse a sacudidas. **I jerked myself free,** Me libré de una sacudida

jerkily *adv* con sacudidas; espasmódicamente; nerviosamente

jerky *a* espasmódico; nervioso (also of style)

jerry-built *a* mal construido, de pacotilla

jersey *n* jersey, *m.* a de jersey; de Jersey. **football j.,** camiseta de fútbol, *f,* jersey de fútbol, *m.* **J. cow,** vaca jerseysa, *f*

Jerusalem Jerusalén, *m*

jest *n* broma, chanza, *f;* (joke) chiste, *m;* (laughingstock) hazmerreír, *m. vi* bromear; burlarse (de). **in j.,** en broma, de guasa

jester *n* burlón (-ona) (practical joker, etc.) bromista, *mf;* (at a royal court) bufón, *m*

jesting *n* bromas, *f pl;* chistes, *m pl;* burlas, *f pl.* a de broma; burlón

jestingly *adv* en broma

Jesuit *n* Jesuita, *m.*

jet *n min* azabache, *m;* (stream) chorro, *m;* (pipe) surtidero, *m;* (burner) mechero, *m, vi* chorrear. **jet-black,** negro como el azabache, de azabache. **jet-propelled engine,** motor de retroacción, *m.* **jet-propelled plane,** aeroplano de reacción, *m*

jetsam *n* echazón, *f; fig* víctima, *f*

jettison *n* echazón, *f. vt* echar (mercancías) al mar; *fig* librarse de, abandonar

jetty *n* dique, malecón, *m;* (landing pier) embarcadero, muelle, *m*

Jew *n* judío, *m.* **Jew's harp,** birimbao, *m*

jewel *n* joya, alhaja, *f;* (of a watch) rubí, *m; fig* alhaja, *f. vt* enjoyar, adornar con piedras preciosas. **j.-box, -case,** joyero, *m*

jeweled *a* adornado con piedras preciosas, enjoyado; (of a watch) con rubíes

jeweler *n* joyero (-ra). **jeweler's shop,** joyería, *f*

jewelry *n* joyas, *f pl;* artículos de joyería, *m pl*

Jewess *n* judía, *f*

Jewish *a* judío

Jewry *n* judería, *f*

jib *n naut* foque, *m. vi* (of a horse) plantarse; (refuse) rehusar. **to jib at,** vacilar en; mostrarse desinclinado. **jib-boom,** *naut* botalón de foque, *m*

jiffy *n* instante, credo, *m.* **in a j.,** en un decir Jesús, en un credo, en un santiamén

jig *n* (dance) jiga, *f. vi* bailar una jiga; bailar, agitarse, sacudirse. *vt* agitar, sacudir; (sieve) cribar

jigsaw puzzle *n* rompecabezas, *m*

jilt *vt* dar calabazas (a)

jingle *n* tintineo, *m;* ruido, *m;* verso, *m;* estribillo, *m. vi* tintinar; sonar; rimar

jitters, to have the no tenerlas todas consigo, no saber dónde meterse

job *n* tarea, *f;* trabajo, *m;* empleo, *m;* (affair) asunto, *m;* (thing) cosa, *f;* (unscrupulous transaction) intriga, *f.* **It is a good (bad) job that . . . ,** Es una buena (mala) cosa que . . . **He has done a good job,** Ha hecho un buen trabajo. **He has lost his job,** Ha perdido su empleo, Le han declarado cesante. **odd-job man,** factótum, *m.* **job-lot,** colección miscelánea, *f;* com saldo de mercancías, *m*

jobber *n* (workman) destajista, *m;* (in stocks) agiotista, *m; com* corredor, *m*

jobless *a* sin trabajo

jockey *n* jockey, *m. vt* engañar; (with into) persuadir, hacer; (with out of) quitar, robar. **j. cap,** gorra de jockey, *f.* **J. Club,** jockey-club, *m*

jocose *a* jocoso, gracioso, guasón

jocular *a* gracioso, alegre; chistoso, zumbón

jocularly *adv* en broma; alegremente

jocund *a* alegre, jovial; jocundo

jog *vt* empujar; (the memory) refrescar. *vi* ir despacio; andar a trote corto. *n* empujón, *m.* **He jogged me with his elbow,** Me dio con el codo. **jog-trot,** trote corto, *m*

joie de vivre *n* goce de vivir, arregosto de vivir, *m*

join *vt* juntar; unir; añadir; (railway lines) empalmar; juntarse con; (meet) encontrarse (con); reunirse (con); (a club, etc.) hacerse miembro (de); (share) acompañar; (regiments, ships) volver (a). *vi* juntarse; unirse; asociarse. *n* unión, *f;* (railway) empalme, *m;* (roads) bifurcación, *f.* **At what time will you j. me?** ¿A qué hora me vendrás a buscar? **He has joined his ship,** Ha vuelto a su buque. **Will you j. me in a drink?** ¿Me quieres acompañar en una bebida? **to j. battle,** librar batalla. **to j. forces,** combinar; *inf* juntar meriendas. **to j. in,** tomar parte en, participar en. **to j. together,** *vt* unir, juntar. *vi* juntarse; asociarse. **to j. up,** alistarse

joiner *n* carpintero, ensamblador, *m,*

joining *n* juntura, conjunción, *f;* (carp etc.) ensambladura, *f; fig* unión, *f*

joint *n* juntura, junta, *f; anat* coyuntura, articulación, *f;* (knuckle) nudillo, *m;* (of meat) cuarto, *m;* (hinge) bisagra, *f; bot* nudo, *m,* a unido; combinado; colectivo; mixto; mutuo; (in compounds) co. *vt* juntar; (meat) descuartizar. **out of j.,** dislocado; (of the times) fuera de compás. **j. account,** cuenta corriente mutua, *f.* **j.-heir,** coheredero, *m.* **j. stock company,** compañía por acciones, sociedad anónima, *f*

jointly *adv* juntamente, en común, colectivamente

joist *n* sopanda, viga, *f*

joke *n* chiste, *m;* burla, broma, *f. vi* bromear, chancearse. *vt* burlarse (de). **Can he take a j.?** ¿Sabe aguantar una broma? **practical j.**, broma pesada, f. **to play a j.**, gastar una broma, hacer una burla

joker n bromista, *Argentina* also fomista, mf; (in cards) comodín, m

joking n chistes, m pl, bromas, f pl. **a chistoso**; cómico

jokingly adv en broma, de guasa

jollity n alegría, f, regocijo, m

jolly a alegre, jovial; (tipsy) achispado; (amusing) divertido; (nice) agradable. adv muy. **He is a j. good fellow,** Es un hombre estupendo. **I am j. glad,** Estoy contentísimo, Me alegro mucho

jolt n sacudida, f. vt sacudir. vi (of a vehicle) traquetear

jolting n sacudidas, f pl, sacudimiento, m; (of a vehicle) traqueteo, m

Jordan Jordania, f

jostle vt empujar, empellar. vi dar empujones, codear

jot n jota, pizca, f. vt (down) apuntar. **not a jot,** ni jota, ni pizca. **to be not worth a jot,** no valer un comino

jotter n taco para notas, m; (exercise book) cuaderno, m

journal n (diary) diario, m; (ship's) diario de navegación, m; (newspaper) periódico, m; (review) revista, m

journalese n lenguaje periodístico, m

journalism n periodismo, *Lat. Am.* also diarismo, m

journalist n periodista, mf

journey n viaje, m; expedición, f; trayecto, m; camino, m. vi viajar. **j. by sea,** viaje por mar. **Pleasant j.!** ¡Buen viaje! **¡Feliz viaje! outward j.,** viaje de ida, m. **return j.,** viaje de regreso, m

jovial a jovial

jowl n (cheek) carrillo, m; (of cattle, etc.) papada, f; (jaw) quijada, f

joy n alegría, f; felicidad, f; deleite, placer, m, vi alegrarse. **I wish you joy,** Te deseo la felicidad. **joy-ride,** excursión en coche, f; vuelo en avión, m. **joy-stick,** (of an airplane) palanca de gobierno, f

joyful a alegre

joyless a sin alegría, triste

joyous. See joyful

jubilant a jubiloso; triunfante

jubilantly adv con júbilo, alegremente; triunfalmente

jubilation n júbilo, m, alegría, f; ruido triunfal, m

jubilee n jubileo, m

Judaic a judaico

Judaism n judaísmo, m

Judas n (traitor and hole) judas, m

Judezmo el judesmo, m

judge n juez, m; (connoisseur) conocedor (-ra) (de); (umpire) árbitro, m. vt juzgar; considerar, tener por. vi servir como juez; juzgar. **judging by,** a juzgar por. **to be a**

good j. of, ser buen juez de. **to j. for oneself,** formar su propia opinión

judgment, judgement n law fallo, m; sentencia, f; juicio, m; (understanding) entendimiento, discernimiento, m; (opinion) opinión, f, parecer, m. **In my j. . . . ,** Según mi parecer, . . . Según creo yo . . . **Last J.,** Juicio Final, m. **to pass j. on,** law pronunciar sentencia (en or sobre); dictaminar sobre; juzgar. **to sit in j. on,** ser juez de; juzgar. **j.-day,** Día del Juicio, m. **j.-seat,** tribunal, m

judicature n judicatura, f; (court) juzgado, m

judicial a judicial; legal; (of the mind) juicioso. **j. inquiry,** investigación judicial, f. **j. separation,** separación legal, f

judiciary a judicial. n judicatura, f

judicious a juicioso, prudente.

judiciously adv prudentemente, juiciosamente

judo n yudo, m

judoka n yudoca, mf

jug n jarro, m; cántaro, m; pote, m; (jail) *Argentina, Chile* capacha f. vt cul estofar. vi (of nightingale) trinar, cantar. **jugged hare,** n liebre en estofado, f

juggle vi hacer juegos malabares. **to j. out of,** (money, etc.) quitar con engaño, estafar. **to j. with,** fig (facts, etc.) tergiversar, falsificar; (person) engañar

juggler n malabarista, mf; (deceiver) estafador (-ra)

jugular a anat yugular. **j. vein,** yugular, m

juice n jugo, m; fig zumo, m. **digestive j.,** jugo digestivo, m

juiciness n jugosidad, f; suculencia, f

juicy a jugoso; suculento

jujube n pastilla, f

jukebox n tocadiscos, vitrola, sinfonola, f

July n julio, m

jumble vt mezclar, confundir. n mezcla confusa, colección miscelánea, confusión, f. **j. sale,** tómbola, f

jump n salto, m; (in prices, etc.) aumento, m. **at one j.,** de un salto. **high j.,** salto de altura, m. **long j.,** salto de longitud, m. **to be on the j.,** inf estar nervioso, tener los nervios en punta

jump vi saltar; dar un salto; brincar; (of tea-cups, etc.) bailar; (throb) pulsar. vt saltar; hacer saltar; (a child) brincar; (omit) pasar por alto de, omitir. **The train jumped the rails,** El tren se descarriló. **to j. out of bed,** saltar de la cama. **to j. to the conclusion that . . . ,** darse prisa a concluir que . . . **to j. about,** dar saltos, brincar; revolverse, moverse de un lado para otro. **to j. at,** saltar sobre; precipitarse sobre, abalanzarse hacia; (an offer) apresurarse a aceptar; (seize) coger con entusiasmo. **to j. down,** bajar de un salto. **to j. over,** saltar; saltar por encima de. **to j. up,** saltar; (on to a horse, etc.)

montar rápidamente; levantarse apresuradamente. **to j. with,** (agree) convenir en, estar conforme con

jumper n saltador (-ra); (sailor's) blusa, f; jersey, suéter m, Lat. Am. chompa, f

jumping n saltos, m pl. a saltador. **j.-off place,** base avanzada, f; fig trampolín, m. **j.-pole,** pértiga, f

jumpy a nervioso, agitado

junction n unión, f; (of roads) bifurcación, f; (railway) empalme, m; (connection) conexión, f

juncture n coyuntura, f; momento, m; crisis, f, momento crítico, m; (joint) junta, f

June n junio, m

jungle n selva, f. **j.-fever,** fiebre de los grandes bosques, f

junior a joven; hijo; más joven; menos antiguo; subordinado, segundo. n joven, mf **Carmen is my j. by three years,** Carmen es tres años más joven que yo. **James Thomson, Jr.,** James Thomson, hijo. **the j. school,** los pequeños. **j. partner,** socio menor, m

juniper n bot enebro, m

junk n trastos viejos, m pl; (nonsense) patrañas, f pl; naut junco, m; (salt meat) tasajo, m. **j.-shop,** tienda de trastos viejos, f

junk bond bono-basura, m

juridical a jurídico

jurisdiction n jurisdicción, f; competencia, f

jurisprudence n jurisprudencia, f

jurist n jurista, legista, mf

juror n (miembro del) jurado, m

jury n jurado, m. **to be on the j.,** formar parte del jurado. **j.-box,** tribuna del jurado, f

juryman n miembro del jurado, m

just a justo; justiciero; exacto; fiel.

just adv justamente, exactamente; precisamente; (scarcely) apenas; (almost) casi; (entirely) completamente; (simply)

meramente, solamente, tan sólo; (newly) recién (followed by past part.), recientemente. **He only j. missed being run over,** Por poco le atropellan. **It is j. near,** Está muy cerca. **It is j. the same to me,** Me es completamente igual. **J. as he was leaving,** Cuando estaba a punto de marcharse, En el momento de marcharse. **Just as you arrive in Spain, you must . . .** Nada más llegar a España, tienes que **. . . That's j. it!** ¡Eso es! ¡Exactamente! **to have j.,** acabar de. **They have j. dined,** Acaban de cenar. **J. as you wish,** Como Vd. quiera. **j. at that moment,** precisamente en aquel momento. **j. by,** muy cerca; al lado. **j. now,** ahora mismo; hace poco; pronto, dentro de poco. **j. yet,** todavía. **They will not come j. yet,** No vendrán todavía. **Just looking** (browser to shopkeeper) Estoy viendo, Estamos viendo

justice n justicia, f; (judge) juez, m; (magistrate) juez municipal, m. **to bring to j.,** llevar ante el juez (a). **to do j. to,** (a person) hacer justicia (a); (a meal) hacer honor (a). **to do oneself j.,** quedar bien

justifiable a justificable

justifiably adv con justicia, justificadamente

justification n justificación, f

justify vt justificar, vindicar; (excuse) disculpar; print justificar. **to be justified (in),** tener derecho (a), tener motivo (para), tener razón (en)

justly adv justamente; con justicia; con derecho; con razón; exactamente; debidamente

justness n justicia, f; exactitud, f

jut (out) vi salir, proyectar; sobresalir

jute n yute, m

juvenile a juvenil; de la juventud; para la juventud; joven; de niños; para niños. n joven, mf. **j. court,** tribunal de menores, m. **j. lead,** theat galancete, galán joven, m. **j. offender,** delincuente infantil, m

juxtapose vt yuxtaponer

K

k *n* (letter) ka, *f*

kaleidoscope *n* calidoscopio, *m*

kangaroo *n* canguro, *m*

keel *n* quilla, *f. vt* carenar. **to k. over,** volcar; caer; *naut* zozobrar

keen *a* (of edges) afilado; agudo; penetrante; vivo; sutil; ardiente; celoso, entusiasta; mordaz; (desirous) ansioso; (of appetite) grande, bueno. **He is a k. tennis player,** Es tenista entusiasta. **Joan has a very k. ear,** Juana tiene un oído muy agudo. **I'm not very k. on apples,** No me gustan mucho las manzanas

keenly *adv* agudamente; vivamente; (of feeling) hondamente; (of looking) atentamente

keep *vt* guardar; tener; que darse con; retener; conservar; mantener; (a shop, hotel, etc.) dirigir, tener; (a school) ser director de; (a promise, etc.) cumplir; (the law, etc.) observar, guardar; (celebrate) solemnizar; (a secret) guardar; (books, accounts, a house, in step) llevar; (sheep, etc., one's bed) guardar; (a city, etc.) defender; (domestic animals, cars, etc.) tener; (lodge) alojar; (detain) detener; (reserve) reservar; (cause) hacer. **They had kept this room for me,** Me habían reservado este cuarto. **Dorothy has kept the blue dress,** Dorotea se ha quedado con el vestido azul. **The government could not k. order,** El gobierno no sabía mantener el orden. **I did not know how to k. their attention,** No sabía retener su atención. **Carmen kept quiet,** Carmen guardó silencio, Carmen se calló. **Can you k. a secret?** ¿Sabes guardar un secreto? **to k. an appointment,** acudir a una cita. **to k. in repair,** conservar en buen estado. **to k. someone from doing something,** evitar que uno haga algo. **to k. someone waiting,** hacer que espere uno. **to k. something from someone,** ocultar algo de uno. **We were kept at it night and day,** Nos hacían trabajar día y noche. **I always k. it by me,** Lo tengo siempre a mi lado (or conmigo). **to k. away,** alejar; mantener a distancia; no dejar venir. **to k. back,** (a crowd, etc.) detener; cortar el paso (a); no dejar avanzar; (retain) guardar, retener; reservar; (tears, words) reprimir, contener; (evidence, etc.) callar, suprimir. **to k. down,** no dejar subir (a); sujetar; (a nation, etc.) oprimir, subyugar; (emotions) dominar; (prices, expenses) mantener bajo; (check) moderar, reprimir. **to k. in,** (feelings) contener; reprimir; (the house) hacer quedarse en casa, no dejar salir; (imprison) encerrar; (school) hacer quedar en la escuela. **to k. off,** alejar; tener a distancia (a); cerrar el paso (a), no dejar avanzar; no andar sobre; no tocar;

(a subject) no tratar de, no discutir, no tocar. **K. your hands off!** ¡No toques! **to k. on,** guardar; retener; (eyes) fijar en, poner en. **to k. out,** no dejar entrar; excluir. **It is difficult to k. him out of trouble,** Es difícil de evitar que se meta en líos. **to k. to,** seguir; limitarse a; adherirse a; **K. to the Left,** «Tome su izquierda», **K. to the right,** «Tome su derecha»; (a path, etc.) seguir por; (one's bed) (fulfil) cumplir; (oblige) hacer, obligar. **to k. under,** subyugar, oprimir; dominar; controlar. **to k. up,** mantener; (appearances) guardar; conservar; persistir en; (prices) sostener; (in good repair) conservar en buen estado; (go on doing) continuar. **He kept me up late last night,** Anoche me entretuvo hasta muy tarde; Ayer me hizo trasnochar; Anoche me hizo velar. **to k. one's end up,** volver por sí, hacerse fuerte. **to k. up one's spirits,** no desanimarse

keep *vi* quedar; (be) estar; (continue) seguir, continuar; mantenerse; (at home, etc.) quedarse, permanecer; (be accustomed) acostumbrar, soler; (persist) perseverar; (of food) conservarse fresco. **How is he keeping?** ¿Cómo está? **to k. in with someone,** cultivar a alguien. **to k. up with the times,** mantenerse al corriente. **to k. at,** seguir; persistir; perseverar; (pester) importunar. **John keeps at it,** Juan trabaja sin descansar. **to k. away,** mantenerse apartado; mantenerse a distancia; no acudir. **to k. back,** hacerse a un lado, apartarse, alejarse. **to k. down,** quedarse tumbado; seguir acurrucado; no levantarse; esconderse. **to k. from,** (doing something) guardarse de. **to k. off,** mantenerse a distancia. **If the storm keeps off,** Si no estalla una tempestad. **If the rain keeps off,** Si no empieza a llover, Si no hay lluvia. **to k. on,** continuar; seguir. **to k. straight on,** seguir derecho. **I'm tired, but I still k. on,** Estoy cansado, pero sigo trabajando. **to k. out,** quedarse fuera. **to k. out of,** (quarrels, trouble, etc.) no meterse en, evitar. **to k. out of sight,** no dejarse ver, no mostrarse, mantenerse oculto. **to k. together,** quedarse juntos; reunirse

keep *n* (of a castle) mazmorra, *f*; (maintenance) subsistencia, *f*; comida, *f*. **for keeps,** para siempre jamás

keeper *n* guarda, *mf*; (in a park, zoo, of a lunatic) guardián, *m*; (of a museum, etc.) director, *m*; (of animals) criador (-ra); (gamekeeper) guardabosque, *m*; (of a boardinghouse, shop, etc.) dueño (-ña); (of accounts, books) tenedor, *m*. **Am I my brother's k.?** ¿Soy yo responsable por mi hermano?

keeping *n* guarda, *f*; conservación, *f*; protección, *f*; (of a rule) observación, *f*; (of an anniversary, etc.) celebración, *f*; (of a person) mantenimiento, *m*. **in k. with,** en armonía con; de acuerdo con. **out of k.**

with, en desacuerdo con. **to be in safe k.,** estar en buenas manos; estar en un lugar seguro. **k. back,** retención, f

keepsake n recuerdo, m

keg n barrilete, m

ken n alcance de la vista, m; vista, f; comprensión, f

kennel n (of a dog) perrera, f; (of hounds) jauría, f; (dwelling) cuchitril, m; (gutter) arroyo, m. **k. man,** perrero, m

kerchief n pañuelo, m; pañoleta, f. **brightly-colored k.,** pañuelo de hierbas, m

kernel n almendra, semilla, f; fig meollo, m, esencia, f

kerosene n petróleo de lámpara, m; kerosén, m

ketchup n salsa de tomate y setas, f

kettle n caldero, m, Mexico marmita, f, **pretty k. of fish,** olla de grillos, f. **k.-drum,** timbal, m. **k.-drum player,** timbalero, m

key n llave, f; (fig arch, mus) clave, f; (tone) tono, m; (of a piano, typewriter, etc.) tecla, f; mech chaveta, f; (of a wind instrument) pistón, m; (winged fruit) sámara, f; elec conmutador, m. **major (minor) key,** tono mayor (menor), m. **latch-key,** llave de la puerta, f; (Yale) llavín, m. **master key,** llave maestra, f. **skeleton key,** ganzúa, f. **He is all keyed up,** Tiene los nervios en punta. **key industry,** industria clave, f. **key man,** hombre indispensable, m. **key point,** punto estratégico, m. **key-ring,** llavero, m. **key signature,** mus clave, f. **key word,** palabra clave, f

keyboard n teclado, m

keyhole n ojo de la cerradura, m. **through the k.,** por el ojo de la cerradura

keynote n mus tónica, f; fig piedra clave, idea fundamental, f

khaki n caqui, m

kick vt dar un puntapié (a); golpear; (a goal) chutar. vi (of horses, etc.) dar coces, cocear; (of guns) recular. **to k. one's heels,** hacer tiempo. **to kick the bucket,** palmarla, Lat. Am. arrancarse. **to k. up a row,** hacer un ruido de mil diablos; (quarrel) armar camorra. **to k. about,** dar patadas (a). **to k. away,** quitar con el pie; lanzar con el pie. **to k. off,** quitar con el pie; lanzar; sacudirse. **k.-off,** n golpe de salida, puntapié inicial, saque, m. **to k. out,** echar a puntapiés

kick n puntapié, m; golpe, m; coz, f; (of guns) culatazo, m. **free k.,** golpe franco, m

kicking n coces, f pl; acoceamiento, m; pataleo, m; golpeamiento, m

kid n cabrito, m, chivo (-va); carne de cabrito, f; (leather) cabritilla, f; inf crío, m. **kid gloves,** guantes de cabritilla, m pl

kidnap vt secuestrar

kidnapper n secuestrador (-ra); ladrón (-ona) de niños

kidnapping n secuestro, m

kidney n riñón, m; fig especie, índole, f. **k.-bean,** (plant) judía, f; (fruit) habichuela, judía, f, fréjol, Mexico calamaco, m

Kidron Cedrón, m

kill vt matar; destruir; suprimir. **to k. off,** exterminar. **to k. time,** entretener el tiempo, pasarse las horas muertas. **to k. two birds with one stone,** matar dos pájaros de un tiro. **k.-joy,** aguafiestas, mf

killer n matador (-ra); (murderer) asesino, mf

killing n matanza, f; (murder) asesinato, m. a matador; destructivo; (comic) cómico; ridículo, absurdo; (ravishing) irresistible

kiln n horno de cerámica, horno, m

kilo n kilo, m

kilogram n kilogramo, m

kilometer n kilómetro, m

kilowatt n elec kilovatio, m

kin n parientes, m pl; familia, f; clase, especie, f. **the next of kin,** los parientes próximos, la familia

kind n género, m, clase, f; especie, f; inf tipo, m. **He is a queer k. of person,** Es un tipo muy raro. **What k. of cloth is it?** ¿Qué clase de tela es? **Nothing of the k!** ¡Nada de eso! **payment in k.,** pago en especie, m

kind a bondadoso, bueno; cariñoso, tierno; amable; favorable, propicio. **Will you be so k. as to . . .** Tenga Vd. la bondad de . . . **With k. regards,** Con un saludo afectuoso. **You have been very k. to her,** Vd. ha sido muy bueno para ella. **k.-hearted,** bondadoso. **k.-heartedness,** bondad, benevolencia, f

kindergarten n jardín de la infancia, kindergarten, m

kindle vt encender; hacer arder; fig avivar. vi prender, empezar a arder; encenderse; fig inflamarse

kindling n encendimiento (del fuego), m; (wood) leña menuda, Lat. Am. charamusca, f

kindly a bondadoso; bueno; benévolo; propicio, favorable; (of climate) benigno. adv con bondad, bondadosamente; fácilmente. **K. sit down,** Haga el favor de sentarse

kindness n bondad, f; benevolencia, f; amabilidad, f; cariño, m; favor, m, atención, f

kindred n parentesco, m; parientes, m pl; familia, f; afinidad, f, a emparentado; hermano

king n (ruler, important person, chess, cards) rey, m; (in draughts) dama, f. **king's evil,** escrófula, f. **k.-bolt,** perno real, m. **k.-craft,** arte de reinar, m, or f. **k.-cup,** bot botón de oro, m. **K.-of-**

Arms, rey de armas, *m.* **k.-post,** pendolón, *m*

kingdom *n* reino, *m.* **animal k.,** reino animal, *m*

kink *n* nudo, *m;* pliegue, *m;* (curl) rizo, *m; fig* peculiaridad, *f*

kinsfolk *n* parientes, *m pl,* familia, *f*

kinship *n* parentesco, *m;* afinidad, *f*

kinsman *n* pariente, deudo, *m*

kinswoman *n* parienta, *f*

kiosk *n* quiosco, *m*

kipper *n* arenque ahumado, *m. vt* ahumar

kiss *n* beso, *m;* (in billiards) pelo, *m. vt* besar; dar un beso (a); (of billiard balls) tocar. **to k. each other,** besarse. **k.-curl,** rizo de la sien, *m,* sortijilla, *f*

kit *n* (tub) cubo *m;* (for tools, etc.) cajita, caja, *f;* (soldier's) equipo, *m.* **kit-bag,** mochila, *f*

kitchen *n* cocina, *f.* **k.-boy,** pinche (de cocina), *m.* **k.-garden,** huerta, *f.* **k.-maid,** fregona, *f.* **k.-range,** cocina económica, *f.* **k.-sink,** fregadero, *Chile, Mexico, also* lavaplatos *m.* **k.-stove,** horno de cocina, *m.* **k. utensils,** batería de cocina, *f*

kitchenette *n* cocinilla, *f*

kite *n orn* milano, *m;* cometa, pájara, *f.* **to fly a k.,** hacer volar una cometa. **box-k.,** cometa celular, *f*

kith and kin *n pl* parientes y amigos, *m pl*

kitten *n* gatito (-ta). *vi* (of a cat) parir

kitty *n* michito, *m;* (in card games) platillo, *m*

kleptomania *n* cleptomanía, *f*

kleptomaniac *a* cleptómano. *n* cleptómano (-na)

knack *n* destreza, *f;* talento, *m;* (trick) truco, *m*

knapsack *n* mochila, *f; mil* alforja, *f*

knave *n* bellaco, truhán, tunante, *m;* (at cards) sota, *f*

knavish *a* de bribón; taimado, truhanesco

knead *vt* amasar; (massage) sobar; *fig* formar

kneading *n* amasijo, *m;* (massaging) soba, *f.* **k.-trough,** amasadera artesa *f*

knee *n* rodilla, *f; fig* ángulo, codillo, *m.* **on bended k.,** de hinojos. **on one's knees,** de rodillas, arrodillado. **to go down on one's knees,** arrodillarse, ponerse de rodillas. **k.-breeches,** calzón corto, *m;* calzón ceñido, *m;* (Elizabethan) gregüescos, *m pl.* **k.-cap,** rótula, *f.* **k.-deep,** hasta las rodillas. **k.-joint,** articulación de la rodilla, *f; mech* junta de codillo, *f.* **k.-pad,** rodillera, *f*

kneel (down) *vi* arrodillarse, hincarse de rodillas, ponerse de rodillas

kneeling *a* arrodillado, de rodillas

knell *n* toque de difuntos, tañido fúnebre,

m; toque de campanas, *m; fig* muerte, *f. vi* tocar a muerto. *vt fig* anunciar, presagiar

knickerbockers *n pl* bragas, *f pl;* calzón corto, *m;* (women's) pantalones, *m pl*

knickknack *n* chuchería, *f*

knife *n* cuchillo, *m.* **to have one's k. in someone,** tener enemiga (a), querer mal (a). **war to the k.,** guerra a muerte, *f.* **k.-edge,** filo de cuchillo, *m;* fiel de soporte, *m.* **k. grinder,** amolador, *m.* **k.-handle,** mango de cuchillo, *m.* **k. thrust,** cuchillada, *f*

knight *n* caballero, *m;* (chess) caballo, *m. vt* armar caballero, calzar la espuela; (in modern usage) dar el título de caballero. **untried k.,** caballero novel, *m.* **k. commander,** comendador, *m.* **k.-errant,** caballero andante, *m.* **k.-errantry,** caballería andante, *f.* **Knight of Labor,** Caballero del Trabajo *m.* **k. of the rueful countenance,** el caballero de la triste figura

knit *vt and vi* hacer calceta, hacer media; juntar, ligar; unir. **Isabel is knitting me a jumper,** Isabel me hace un jersey de punto de media. **to k. one's brows,** fruncir el ceño

knitted *a* de punto. **k. goods,** géneros de punto, *m pl*

knitter *n* calcetero (-ra); (machine) máquina de hacer calceta, *f*

knitting *n* acción de hacer calceta, *f;* trabajo de punto, *m,* labor de calceta, *f;* unión, *f.* **k.-machine,** máquina de hacer calceta, *f.* **k.-needle,** aguja de media, *f.* **k.-needle,** aguja de hacer calceta, *f*

knob *n* protuberancia, *f;* (of a door, etc.) perilla, borlita, *f;* (ornamental) bellota, *f;* (of sugar) terrón, *m;* (of a stick) puño, *m*

knock *n* golpe, *m;* choque, *m;* (with a knocker) aldabada, *f*

knock *vt* golpear; chocar (contra). *vi* llamar a la puerta; (of an engine) picar. **to k. one's head against,** chocar con la cabeza contra, dar con la cabeza contra. **to k. about,** *vt* pegar; aporrear. *vi* viajar; vagar, rodar; callejear. **to k. against,** golpear contra; chocar contra. **to k. down,** derribar; (of vehicles) atropellar, *Mexico* antellevar; (houses, etc.) demoler; (an argument, etc.) destruir; (a tender, etc.) rebajar; (of an auctioneer) rematar al mejor postor. **to k. in,** (nails, etc.) clavar. **to k. into one another,** toparse. **to k. off,** hacer caer; sacudir; quitar; (from price) descontar; (from speed, etc.) reducir; (finish) terminar pronto; (runs in cricket) hacer. **to k. out,** (remove) quitar; (boxing) dejar fuera de combate, noquear; (*fig* stun) atontar; (an idea, etc.) bosquejar. **to k. over,** volcar. **to k. up,** hacer saltar; (call) llamar; (runs at cricket) hacer; (tire) agotar, rendir; (building) construir toscamente. **to k. up against,** chocar contra; tropezar con.

k.-kneed, a patiabierto. **k.-out,** "knock-out," m

knoll n altillo, otero, m

knot n nudo, m; (bow) lazo, m; (of hair) moño, m; naut nudo, m, milla náutica, f; (of people) corrillo, grupo, m; (on timber) nudo, m. vt anudar. vi hacer nudos; enmarañarse. **to tie a k.,** hacer un nudo

knotty a nudoso; fig intrincado, difícil, complicado. **a k. problem,** problema espinoso

know vt conocer; saber; (understand) comprender; (recognize) reconocer. **I k. her very well by sight,** La conozco muy bien de vista. **John knows Latin,** Juan sabe latín. **How can I k.?** ¿Cómo lo voy a saber yo? **I knew you at once,** Te reconocí en seguida. **They always k. best,** Siempre tienen razón. **Did you k. about Philip?** ¿Has oído lo de Felipe? **to be in the k.,** estar bien informado, saber de buena tinta. **to get to k.,** (a person) llegar a conocer, trabar amistad con. **to make known,** dar a conocer; manifestar. **Who knows?** ¿Quién sabe? **to k. by heart,** saber de coro. **to k. how,** (to do something) saber. **to k. oneself,** conocerse a sí mismo. **k.-it-all,** sabelotodo, mf, marisabidilla, f

knowing a inteligente; malicioso; (of animals) sabio. **There is no k.,** No hay modo de saberlo. **worth k.,** digno de saberse

knowingly adv a sabiendas, de intento; conscientemente; (cleverly) hábilmente; (with look, etc.) de un aire malicioso

knowledge n conocimiento, m. **To the best of my k. the book does not exist,** El libro no existe que yo sepa. **He has a thorough k. of . . .,** Conoce a fondo . . . **lack of k.,** ignorancia, f. **He did it without my k.,** Lo hizo sin que lo supiera yo. **It is a matter of common k. that . . .** Es notorio que . . .

knowledgeable a sabedor

knuckle n (of a finger) nudillo, m, articulación del dedo, f; (of meat) jarrete, m. **He knuckled down to his work,** Se puso a trabajar con ahínco. **to k. under,** someterse. **k.-duster,** rompecabezas, m

Korea Corea, f

kosher a cosher; (slang) genuino

kowtow vi saludar humildemente; fig bajar la cerviz

kudos n prestigio, m, gloria, f

L

l n (letter) ele, f

la n mus la, m

label n etiqueta, (on a garment), rótula, m; (on a can), f; (on a museum specimen, etc.) letrero, m; fig calificación, f. vt poner etiqueta en; marcar, rotular; fig calificar, designar, clasificar

labor n trabajo, m; labor, f; fatiga, pena, f; clase obrera, f; (manual workers) mano de obra, f; (effort) esfuerzo, m; (of childbirth) dolores de parto, m pl. vi trabajar; (strive) esforzarse, afanarse; (struggle) forcejear, luchar; (try) procurar, tratar de; avanzar con dificultad; (in childbirth) estar de parto. vt elaborar; pulir, perfeccionar. **to l. under,** sufrir; tener que luchar contra. **hard l.,** trabajo arduo, m; law trabajos forzosos, m pl, presidio, m. **Ministry of L.,** Ministerio de Trabajo, m. **to be in l.,** estar de parto. **to l. in vain,** trabajar en balde, arar en el mar. **to l. under a delusion,** estar en el error, estar equivocado. **L. Exchange,** Bolsa de Trabajo, f. **l. leader,** dirigente sindical, m. **L. party,** partido laborista, partido obrero, m. **l. question,** cuestión obrera, f; (domestic) problema del servicio, m. **l.-saving,** a que ahorra trabajo. **l. union,** sindicato, m

laboratory n laboratorio, m

labored a (of style) premioso, artificial; forzado; (of breathing) fatigoso; (slow) torpe, lento

laborer n obrero, m; (on the land) labrador, labriego, m; (on the roads, etc.) peón, m; (by the day) jornalero, m

laborious a laborioso; arduo, difícil, penoso

labyrinth n laberinto, m

lace n (of shoes, corsets, etc.) cordón, m; (tape) cinta, f; encaje, m; (narrow, for trimming) puntilla, f; (of gold or silver) galón, m. vt and vi (shoes, etc.) atarse los cordones; (trim) guarnecer con encajes, etc.; fig ornar; (a drink) echar (coñac, etc.) en. **blond l.,** blonda, f. **gold l.,** galón de oro, m. **point l.,** encaje de aguja, m. **l. curtain,** cortina de encaje, f; (of net) visillo, m. **l. maker** or **seller,** encajero (-ra), mf. **l. making,** obra de encaje, f. **l.-pillow,** almohadilla para encajes, f. **l. shoes,** zapatos con cordones, m pl

lacerate vt lacerar

lack n falta, f. **l. of evidence,** falta de pruebas, f; carestía, escasez, f; (absence) ausencia, f; (need) necesidad, f. vt carecer de; no tener; necesitar. vi hacer falta; necesitarse. **to l. confidence in oneself,** no tener confianza en sí mismo, carecer de confianza en sí mismo. **l.-luster,** (of eyes) apagado, mortecino. **l. of evidence,** falta de pruebas, f

lackadaisical a lánguido; indiferente; (dreamy) ensimismado, distraído

lackey n lacayo, m

laconic a lacónico

lacquer n laca, f, vt dar laca (a), barnizar con laca. **gold l.,** sisa dorada, f. **l. work,** laca, f

lactate n lactato, m, vi lactar

lactose n lactosa, f

lacuna n laguna, f

lacy a de encaje; parecido a encaje; fig transparente, etéreo

lad n muchacho, joven, mozalbete, m; zagal, m; (stable, etc.) mozo, m. **He's some l.!** ¡Qué tío que es! **l. of the village,** chulo, m

ladder n escalera de mano, f; naut escala, f; (in a stocking, etc.) carrera, f. **companion l.,** escala de toldilla, f. **to l. one's stocking,** escurrirse un punto de las medias

Ladies and gentlemen n. pl Señoras y señores, Señoras y caballeros. **ladies' man,** hombre de salón, Perico entre ellas, mujeriego, m

ladle n cucharón, cazo, m. vt servir con cucharón; (a boat) achicar; inf distribuir, repartir

lady n dama, f; señora, f; (English title) milady, f; (woman) mujer, f. **to be a l.,** ser una señora. **leading l.,** theat dama primera, f. **Our L.,** Nuestra Señora. **young l.,** señorita, f; inf novia, f. **lady's maid,** doncella, f. **l. of the house,** señora de la casa, f. **l. bug,** ent catalina mariquita, vaca de San Antonio, f. **L. Chapel,** capilla de la Virgen, f. **L. Day,** día de la Anunciación (de Nuestra Señora), m. **l.-help,** asistenta, f. **l.-in-waiting,** dama de servicio, f. **l.-killer,** ladrón de corazones, castigador, tenorio, m. **l.-love,** querida, amada, f. **l. mayoress,** alcaldesa, f

ladylike a de dama; elegante; distinguido; bien educado; delicado; (of men) afeminado

lag vt recubrir; aislar. vi retrasarse; quedarse atrás; ir (or andar) despacio; rezagarse; naut roncear. n retraso, m; mech retardación de movimiento, f

laggard n holgazán (-ana), haragán (-ana)

lagoon n laguna, f

laid past part of verb **to lay. l. up,** (ill) enfermo; naut inactivo; (of cars, etc.) fuera de circulación

lair n cubil, m; guarida, madriguera, f

laity n legos, m pl

lake n lago, m; (pigment) laca, f. **small l.,** laguna, f. **l. dwelling,** vivienda palustre, f

lamb n cordero (-ra). vi parir corderos. **lamb's wool,** lana de cordero. f

lambskin n corderina, piel de cordero, f

lame a estropeado, lisiado; (in the feet) cojo; (of meter) que cojea, malo; (of arguments) poco convincente; frívolo, flojo. *vt* lisiar; hacer cojo. **l. excuse,** pretexto frívolo. **to be l.,** (in the feet) (permanently) ser cojo; (temporarily) estar cojo

lament *n* lamento, *m*; queja, lamentación, *f*. *vi* lamentarse; quejarse. *vt* lamentar, deplorar, llorar

lamentable *a* lamentable, deplorable; lastimero

lamentation *n* lamentación, *f*, lamento, *m*. **Book of Lamentations,** Libro de los lamentos, *m*

lamenting *n* lamentación, *f*

laminate *a* laminado, *m*. *vt* laminar

lamp *n* lámpara, *f*; (on vehicles, trains, ships and in the street) farol, *m*; luz, *f*; (oil) candil, *m*, lámpara de aceite, *f*. **safety-l.,** lámpara de seguridad, lámpara de los mineros, *f*. **street l.,** farol (de las calles), *m*. **l.-black,** negro de humo, *m*. **l.-chimney,** tubo de una lámpara, *m*. **l. factory** or **shop,** lamparería, *f*. **l.-holder,** portalámpara, *f*. **l.-lighter,** farolero, lamparero, *m*. **l.-post,** farola, *f*. **l.-shade,** pantalla (de lámpara,) *f*. **l. stand,** pie de lámpara, *m*

lamplight *n* luz de la lámpara, *f*; luz artificial, *f*. **in the l.,** a la luz de la lámpara; en luz artificial

lampoon *n* pasquinada, *f*, pasquín, *m*, *vt* pasquinar, satirizar

lance *n* lanza, *f*; (soldier) lancero, *m*. *vt* alancear; *med* lancinar. **l. in rest,** lanza en ristre, *f*.

land *n* tierra, *f*; terreno, *m*; (country) país, *m*; (region) región, *f*; territorio, *m*; (estate) bienes raíces, *m pl*, tierras, fincas, *f pl*. *vt* desembarcar; echar en tierra; (fig place) poner; *inf* dejar plantado (con); (obtain) obtener; (a fish) sacar del agua; (a blow) dar (un golpe); (leave) dejar. *vi* desembarcar; saltar en tierra; (of a plane) aterrizar; (arrive) llegar; (fall) caer. **to l. on water** *Lat. Am.* acuatizar. **cultivated l.,** tierras cultivadas, *f pl*. **dry l.,** (not sea) tierra firme, *f*. **native l.,** patria, *f*; suelo natal, *m*. **on l.,** en tierra. **to see how the l. lies,** *fig* tantear el terreno. **l. of milk and honey,** jauja, *f*, paraíso, *m*. **l. of promise,** tierra de promisión, *f*. **l. agent,** procurador de fincas, *m*. **l. breeze,** brisa de tierra, *f*. **l. forces,** fuerzas terrestres, *f pl*. **l. law,** leyes agrarias, *f pl*. **l.-locked,** cercado de tierra, mediterráneo **l.-lubber,** marinero de agua dulce, *m*. **l. mine,** mina terrestre, *f*. **l. surveying,** agrimensura, *f*. **l. surveyor,** agrimensor, *m*. **l. tax,** contribución territorial, *f*

landed *a* hacendado. **l. gentry,** hacendados, terratenientes, *m pl*. **l. property,** bienes raíces, *m pl*

landing *n* desembarque, desembarco, *m*; (landing place) desembarcadero, *m*; *aer* aterrizaje, *m*; (of steps) descanso, rellano, *m*, mesa, mesilla, *f*. **forced l.,** aterrizaje forzoso, *m*. **l. certificate,** com

tornaguía, *f*. **l. craft,** barcaza de desembarco, *f*. **l. field,** campo de aterrizaje, *m*, pista de vuelo, *f*. **l.-net,** salabardo, *m*. **l. party,** trozo de abordaje, *m*. **l. signal,** *aer* señal de aterrizaje, *f*. **l.-stage,** desembarcadero, *m*; (jetty) atracadero, *m*

landlady *n* patrona, huéspeda, *f*

landlord *n* (of houses, land) propietario, *m*; hotelero, patrón, *m*

landmark *n* (of a hill or mountain) punto destacado, *m*; lugar conocido, *m*; característica, *f*; *fig* monumento, *m*

landowner *n* hacendado, terrateniente, *m*

landscape *n* paisaje, *m*; perspectiva, *f*. **l. gardener,** arquitecto de jardines, *m*. **l. painter,** paisajista, *mf*

landslide *n* desprendimiento de tierras, *m*; *fig* cambio brusco de la opinión pública, *m*

lane *n* vereda, senda, *f*; (of traffic) carril, *m*, *Argentina, Spain,* línea, *f*

language *n* lenguaje, *m*; lengua, *f*, idioma, *m*. **modern l.,** lengua viva, *f*. **strong l.,** palabras mayores, *f pl*

languid *a* lánguido

languish *vi* languidecer

languor *n* languidez, *f*

languorous *a* lánguido

lank *a* flaco, descarnado, alto y delgado; (of hair) lacio

lanky *a* larguirucho, descarnado, *Lat. Am.* largucho

lanoline *n* lanolina, *f*

lantern *n* linterna, *f*; (naut and of a lighthouse) farol, *m*; *arch* linterna, *f*; (small) farolillo, *m*. **dark l.,** linterna sorda, *f*. **magic l.,** linterna mágica, *f*. **l.-jawed,** carilargo. **l. maker,** farolero, *m*. **l. slide,** diapositiva, *f*

lap *n* regazo, *m*; falda, *f*; (knees) rodillas, *f pl*; (lick) lamedura, *f*; (of water) murmurio, susurro, *m*; (in a race) vuelta, *f*; (stage) etapa, *f*. *vt* (wrap) envolver; (cover) cubrir; (fold) plegar; (lick) lamer; (swallow) tragar. *vi* (overlap) traslaparse; estar replegado; (lick) lamer; (of water) murmurar, susurrar, besar. **l.-dog,** perro faldero, perro faldero, *m*

lapel *n* solapa, *f*

lapidary *a* lapidario

lapping *n* (licking) lamedura, *f*; (of water) murmurio, susurro, chapaleteo, *m*

lapse *n* lapso, *m*; (fault) desliz, *m*, falta, *f*; (of time) transcurso, intervalo, *m*; (fall) caída, *f*; (law termination) caducidad, *f*. **lapse (into),** *vi* caer (en), recaer (en), reincidir (en); volver a, caer de nuevo (en); (law cease) caducar; (law pass to) pasar (a); dejar de existir, desaparecer. **after the l. of three days,** después de tres días, al cabo de tres días. **with the l. of years,** en el transcurso de los años

larceny *n* latrocinio, *m*

lard n manteca, f; lardo, m. vt cul lardear, mechar; fig sembrar (con), adornar (con)

large a grande; grueso; amplio; vasto, extenso; (wide) ancho; considerable; (in number) numeroso; (main, chief) principal; liberal; magnánimo. **at l.,** en libertad, suelto. **on the l. side,** algo grande. **l.-headed,** cabezudo. **l.-hearted,** que tiene un gran corazón, magnánimo. **l. mouth,** boca grande, boca rasgada, f. **l.-nosed,** narigudo. **l. scale,** en gran escala. **l.-sized,** de gran tamaño. **l.-toothed,** dentudo, que tiene dientes grandes. **l. type,** letras grandes, f pl

largely adv grandemente; en gran manera; en so mayor parte, considerablemente; muy; ampliamente; liberalmente; extensamente

largeness n gran tamaño, m; (of persons) gran talle, m; amplitud, f; vastedad, extensión, f; (width) anchura, f; liberalidad, f; (generosity) magnanimidad, f; grandeza de ánimo, f

larger a comp más grande, etc. See **large. to grow l.,** crecer, aumentarse. **to make l.,** hacer más grande; aumentar

largesse n liberalidad, f

lariat n lazo, m

lark n alondra, f; (spree) juerga, f; (joke) risa, f. **to rise with the l.,** levantarse con las gallinas

larva n larva, f

laryngitis n laringitis, f

larynx n laringe, f

lascivious a lascivo, lujurioso

lash n (thong) tralla, f; (whip) látigo, m; (blow) latigazo, m; azote, m; (of the eye) pestaña, f. vt dar latigazos (a); azotar; (of waves) romper contra; (of hail, rain) azotar; (excite) provocar; (the tail) agitar (la cola); (scold) fustigar; (fasten) sujetar, atar; naut trincar. **to l. out,** (of horses, etc.) dar coces; (in words) prorrumpir (en)

lass n muchacha, chica, mozuela, f; zagala, f; niña, f

lassitude n lasitud, f

lasso n lazo, m, mangana, Argentina armada, f, vt lazar, manganear, Lat. Am. lacear

last vi durar; subsistir, conservarse; continuar

last a último; (with month, week, etc.) pasado; (supreme) extremo, (el) mayor. adv al fin; finalmente; por último; después de todos; por última vez; la última vez. n el, m, (f, la) último (-ma); los últimos, m pl, (f pl, las últimas); (end) fin, m; (for shoes) horma, f. **at l.,** en fin; por fin, a la postre. **at the l. moment,** a última hora. **I have not been there these l. five years,** Hace cinco años que no voy allá. **John spoke l.,** Juan habló el último. **She came at l.,** Por fin llegó. **to the l.,** hasta el fin. **l. but one,** penúltimo (-ma). **l. hope,** última esperanza, f; último

recurso, m. **l. kick,** inf último suspiro, m. **l. night,** anoche. **l. week,** la semana pasada

lasting a permanente, perdurable; duradero; constante; (of colours) sólido

lastly adv en conclusión, por fin, finalmente, por último

latch n pestillo, m, vt cerrar con pestillo. **l.-key,** llave de la puerta, f; (Yale) llavín, m

late a tarde; tardío; (advanced) avanzado; (last) último; reciente; (dead) difunto; (former) antiguo, ex . . . ; (new) nuevo. adv tarde. **Better l. than never,** Más vale tarde que nunca. **Helen arrived l.,** Elena llegó tarde. **The train arrived five minutes l.,** El tren llegó con cinco minutos de retraso. **He keeps l. hours,** Se acuesta muy tarde, Se acuesta a las altas horas de la noche (inf a las tantas). **of l.,** últimamente. **to grow l.,** hacerse tarde. **l.-eighteenth-century poetry,** la poesía de fines del siglo diez y ocho; llorado, malogrado (e.g. **the l. Mrs. Smith,** la llorada Sra. Smith, la malograda Sra. Smith);

lately adv recientemente; últimamente, hace poco

lateness n lo tarde; lo avanzado; retraso, m. **the l. of the hour,** la hora avanzada

latent a latente

later a más tarde; posterior; más reciente. adv más tarde; (afterwards) luego, después; posteriormente. **sooner or l.,** tarde o temprano. **l. on,** más tarde

lateral a lateral, ladero

late registration n matrícula tardía, f

latest a and adv sup último; más reciente, etc. See **late. at the l.,** a lo más tarde, a más tardar. **l. fashion,** última moda, f. **l. news,** últimas noticias, f pl; novedad, f

latex n (bot chem) látex, m

lath n listón, m. **to be as thin as a l.,** no tener más que el pellejo, estar en los huesos

lathe n torno, m

lather n espuma de jabón, f, jabonaduras, f pl; (of sweat) espuma, f. vt enjabonar; inf zurrar. vi hacer espuma

Latin n latín, m, a latino. **Low L.,** bajo latín, m. **L.-American,** a latinoamericano n latinoamericano (-na)

latitude n latitud, f; libertad, f

latrine n letrina, f

latter a más reciente; último, posterior; moderno. **the l.,** éste, m; ésta, f; esto, neut; éstos, m pl; éstas, f pl. **the l. half,** la segunda mitad. **toward the l. end of the year,** hacia fines del año. **L.-Day Saint,** santo de los últimos días m, santa de los últimos días, f

latterly adv recientemente, últimamente; en los últimos tiempos; hacia el fin

lattice n rejilla, f; celosía, reja, f. vt poner

celosía (a); entrelazar. **l.-work,** enrejado, *m*

latticed *a* (of windows, etc.) con reja

Latvia Latvia, Letonia, *f*

Latvian *a* latvio. *n* latvio (-ia)

laud *n* alabanza, *f*; *pl.* **lauds,** *ecc* laudes, *f pl. vt* alabar, elogiar

laudable *a* loable, meritorio

laugh *n* risa, *f*; carcajada, *f*, *vi* reír; (smile) sonreír; reírse. **loud l.,** risa estrepitosa, *f*. **to l. in a person's face,** reírsele a uno en las barbas. **to l. loudly,** reírse a carcajadas. **to l. to oneself,** reírse interiormente. **to l. to scorn,** poner en ridículo. **to l. at,** reírse de; burlarse de, ridiculizar

laughable *a* risible, irrisible, ridículo, absurdo

laughing *a* risueño, alegre; (absurd) risible, *n* risa, *f*. **to burst out l.,** reírse a carcajadas. **l.-gas,** gas hilarante, *m*. **l.-stock,** hazmerreír, *m*

laughter *n* risa, *f*; (in a report) risas, *f pl.* **burst of l.,** carcajada, *f*. **to burst into l.,** soltar el trapo, reírse a carcajadas, desternillarse de risa

launch *n* botadura (de un buque), *f*; lancha, *f*; bote, *m*; canoa, *f. vt* (throw) lanzar; (a blow) asestar; (a vessel) botar, echar al agua; (begin) iniciar, dar principio a; (make) hacer. **to l. an offensive,** *mil* emprender una ofensiva. **to l. into,** arrojarse en; entregarse a. **motor l.,** canoa automóvil, *f*. **steam l.,** bote de vapor, *m*

launching *n* botadura (de un buque), *f*; (throwing) lanzamiento, *m*; (beginning) iniciación, *f*; inauguración, *f*; (of a loan, etc.) emisión, *f*. **l. site,** rampa, *f*

launder *vt* lavar y planchar (ropa)

laundress *n* lavandera *f*

laundromat *n* lavandería automática, *f*

laundry *n* lavadero, *m*, lavandería, *f*; (washing) colada, *f*; *inf* ropa lavada or ropa para lavar, *f*. **l.-man,** lavandero, *m*

laurel *n* laurel, cerezo, *m*, a láureo. **to crown with l.,** laurear. **l. wreath,** lauréola, *f*

lava *n* lava, *f*

lavatory *n* lavabo, *m*; retrete, excusado, *m*

lavender *n* espliego, *m*, lavanda, *f*. **l.-water,** agua de lavanda, *f*

lavish *a* pródigo; profuso, abundante; (spender) derrochador. *vt* prodigar

law *n* ley, *f*; derecho, *m*; jurisprudencia, *f*; código de leyes, *m*. **according to law,** según derecho. **canon law,** derecho civil, *m*. **constitutional law,** derecho político, *m*. **criminal law,** derecho penal, *m*. **in law,** por derecho, de acuerdo con la ley; desde el punto de vista legal. **international law,** derecho internacional, *m*. **maritime law,** código marítimo, *m*. **sumptuary law,** ley suntuaria, *f*. **to be the law,** ser la ley. **to go to law,** pleitear (sobre). **to sue at law,** pedir en juicio,

poner pleito. **to take the law into one's own hands,** tomar la ley por su propia mano. **law-abiding,** observante de la ley; amigo del orden. **law-breaker,** transgresor (-ra). **law court,** tribunal de justicia, *m*; palacio de justicia, *m*. **law of nature,** ley natural, *f*. **law report,** revista de tribunales, *f*. **law school,** escuela de derecho, *f*. **law student,** estudiante de derecho, *mf*

lawful *a* legítimo; legal; lícito; válido

lawfully *adv* legalmente; legítimamente, lícitamente

lawfulness *n* legalidad, *f*; legitimidad, *f*

lawless *a* ilegal; desordenado; ingobernable, rebelde

lawn *n* césped, prado, *m*; (cloth) estopilla, *f*. **l.-mower,** cortacésped *m*, tundidora de césped, *f*, máquina segadora del césped, *f*. **l.-tennis,** tenis (en pista de hierba), *m*

lawsuit *n* pleito, litigio, *m*, causa, acción, *f*

lawyer *n* abogado (-da). **lawyer's office or practice,** bufete, *m*

lax *a* laxo; indisciplinado; vago; descuidado

laxative *n* laxante, *m*, purga, *f*, a laxativo

lay *a* laico, seglar, lego; profano. *n* poema, *m*, trova, *f*; romance, *m*; (song) canción, *f*. **the lay of the land,** la configuración del terreno. **lay brother,** confeso, monigote, *m*. **lay figure,** maniquí, *m*. **lay sister,** (hermana) lega, *f*

lay *vt* and *vi* poner; colocar; dejar; (strike) tumbar; (demolish) derribar; (the dust) matar; (pipes, etc.) instalar; (hands on) asentar (la mano en); (deposit) depositar; (beat down corn, etc.) encamar, abatir; (eggs, keel) poner; (the table) cubrir, poner; (stretch) extender(se); (bury) depositar en el sepulcro; (a bet) hacer; (wager) apostar; (an accusation) acusar; (the wind, etc.) sosegar, amainar; (a ghost) exorcizar; (impute) atribuir, imputar; (impose) imponer; (prepare) prepara; (make) hacer; (open) abrir; (blame, etc.) echar; (claim) reclamar; (reveal) revelar. **Don't lay the blame on me!** ¡No me eches la culpa! **We laid our plans,** Hicimos nuestros planes; Hicimos nuestros preparativos. **to lay siege to,** asediar. **to lay the colors on too thick,** *fig* recargar las tintas. **to lay the foundations,** abrir los cimientos; *fig* crear, establecer; fundar. **to lay about one,** dar garrotazos de ciego. **to lay aside,** poner a un lado; arrinconar; (save) ahorrar; (cast away) desechar; abandonar; (reserve) reservar; (a person) apartar de sí; (incapacitate) incapacitar. **lay something at somebody's feet,** embutir algo en el guante de fulano. **to lay before,** mostrar; presentar; poner a la vista; revelar. **to lay by,** See to lay aside. **to lay down,** acostar; depositar; (a burden) posar; (arms) rendir; (one's life); entregar; (give up) renunciar (a); (sketchout) trazar, dibujar; (plan) proyectar; (keep) guardar; (as a principle) establecer, sentar; (the law) dictar. **to lay oneself down**, echarse, tumbarse. **to lay in**, (a stock) proveerse de, hacer provisión de; (hoard) ahorrar; (buy) compara. **to lay off**, *naut* virar de bordo; *inf* quitarse de encima. **to lay on**, *vt* colocar sobre; (thrash) pegar; (blows) descargar; (paint, etc.) dar; (water, etc.) instalar; (impose) imponer; (exaggerate) exagerar. *vi* atacar. **to lay open**, abrir; descubrir, revelar; manifestar; exponer. **to lay oneself open to attack**, exponerse a ser atacado. **to lay out**, poner; arreglar; (the dead) amortajar; (one's money) invertir, emplear; (at interest) poner a rédito; (plan) planear; (knock down) derribar. **to lay oneself out to**, esforzarse a; tomarse la molestia de. **to lay over**, cubrir; sobreponer; extender sobre. **to lay to**, *vi naut* estar a la capa. **to lay up**, guardar, acumular, atesorar; poner a un lado; (a ship) desarmar; (a car) poner fuera de circulación; (a person) obligar a guardar cama, incapacitar

layabout = lazybones

layer *n* capa, *f*; *geol* estrato, *m*; *min* manto, *m*; (bird) gallina (pata, etc.) ponedera, *f*; (one who bets) apostador (-ra); *agr* acodo, *m*. *vt* (of plants) acodar

layette *n* canastilla, *f*

laying *n* colocación, *f*; puesta, *f*; (of an egg) postura, *f*. **l. down**, depósito, *m*; conservación, *f*; (explanation) exposición, *f*. **l. on of hands**, imposición de manos, *f*. **l. out**, tendedura, *f*; (of money) empleo, *m*; inversión, *f*; (arrangement) arreglo, *m*

layman *n* seglar, *mf*; profano (-na)

layout *n* plan, *m*; diagramación, disposición, *f*; distribución, *f*; esquema, *m*

laze *vi* holgazanear, gandulear, no hacer nada; encontrarse a sus anchas

laziness *n* pereza, holgazanería, *f*; indolencia, *f*; lentitud, *f*

lazy *a* perezoso, holgazán; indolente. **l.bones**, gandul (-la), *Lat. Am.* aplanacalles *mf*

lead *n* (metal) plomo, *m*; (in a pencil) mina, *f*; (plummet) sonda, *f*; *print* interlínea, *f*; *pl* **leads**, (roofs) tejados, *m pl*. *vt* emplomar; guarnecer con plomo; *print* interlinear. **black-l.**, grafito, *m*. **deep-sea l.**, *naut* escandallo, *m*. **white l.**, albayalde, *m*. **to heave the l.**, echar el escandallo, sondar. **l.-colored**, de color de plomo, plomizo. **l. mine**, mina de plomo, *f*. **l. poisoning**, saturnismo, *m*

lead *n* delantera, *f*; primer lugar, *m*; dirección, *f*, mando, *m*; (suggestion) indicación, *f*; (influence) influencia, *f*; (dog's) traílla, *f*; *theat* protagonista, *mf*; *theat* papel principal, *m*; (at cards) mano, *f*

lead *vt* and *vi* (conduct) conducir, llevar; guiar; (induce) mover, persuadir, inducir;

inclinar; (cause) hacer, causar; (captain) capitanear, encabezar; dirigir; (channel) encauzar; (with life) llevar; (give) dar; (head) ir a la cabeza de; *mil* mandar; (at cards) salir; (at games) jugar en primer lugar; tomar la delantera; *fig* superar a los demás; (of roads) conducir. **to take the l.**, ir delante; ir a la cabeza, tomar la delantera; tomar la iniciativa. **to l. one to think**, hacer pensar. **to l. the way**, mostrar el camino; ir adelante. **to l. along**, llevar (por la mano, etc.), conducir; conducir por; guiar. **to l. astray**, descarriar; desviar (de), seducir (de). **to l. away**, conducir (a otra parte); llevarse (a). **to l. back**, conducir de nuevo; hacer volver. **This path leads back to the village**, Por esta senda se vuelve al pueblo. **to l. in, into**, conducir a (or ante); introducir en, hacer entrar en; invitar a entrar en; (of rooms) comunicarse con; (sin, etc.) inducir a. **to l. off**, *vi* ir adelante; (begin) empezar; (of rooms) comunicarse con. *vt* hacer marcharse, llevarse (a). **to l. on**, *vt* conducir; guiar; hacer pensar en; (make talk) dar cuerda (a). *vi* ir a la cabeza; tomar la delantera. **to l. out**, conducir afuera; (to dance) sacar. **to l. to**, conducir a; desembocar en, salir a; (cause) dar lugar a, causar; (make) hacer; (incline) inclinar. **This street leads to the square**, Por esta calle se va a la plaza, Esta calle conduce a la plaza. **to l. up to**, conducir a; (in conversation, etc.) preparar el terreno para; preparar; tener lugar antes de, ocurrir antes de

leaden *a* hecho de plomo, plúmbeo; (of skies, etc.) plomizo, de color de plomo, aplomado. **l.-footed**, pesado; lento

leader *n* conductor (-ra); guía, *mf*; jefe (-fa); general, *m*; director (-ra); (in a journal) artículo de fondo, *m*; (of an orchestra) primer violín, *m*. **follow-the-l.**, (game) juego de seguir la fila, *m*

leadership *n* dirección, *f*; jefatura, *f*; *mil* mando, *m*

leading *n* (guidance) dirección, *f*. *a* principal; primero; importante; eminente. **l. article**, artículo de fondo, *m*; editorial, *m*. **l. card**, primer naipe, *m*. **l. counsel**, abogado (-da) principal. **l. lady**, *theat* dama primera, primera actriz, *f*; (cinema) estrella (de la pantalla), *f*. **l. man**, *theat* primer galán, *m*. **l. question**, pregunta que sugiere la respuesta, *f*; cuestión importante, *f*. **l. strings**, andadores, *m pl*; *fig* tutelaje, *m*

leaf *n* (bot and of a page, door, window, table, screen, etc.) hoja, *f*; (petal) pétalo, *m*; *vi* echar hojas. **gold l.**, pan de oro, *m*. **to turn over a new l.**, volver la hoja, hacer libro nuevo, hacer vida nueva. **to turn over the leaves of a book**, hojear (un libro). **l.-bud**, yema, *f*. **l.-mold**, abono verde, *m*. **l. tobacco**, tabaco en hoja, *m*

leaflet *n* hojuela, *f*; (pamphlet) folleto, *m*

league n (measure) legua, f; liga, federación, sociedad, f; (football) liga, f. vt aliar; asociar. vi aliarse; asociarse, confederarse. **to be in l.,** inf estar de manga. **L. of Nations,** Sociedad de las Naciones, f

leak n (hole) agujero, m, grieta, f; naut vía de agua, f; (of gas, liquids, etc.) escape, m; (in a roof, etc.) gotera, f; elec resistencia de escape, f. vi naut hacer agua; (gas, liquids, etc.) escaparse, salirse; (drip) gotear. **to l. out,** (of news, etc.) trascender, saberse. **to spring a l.,** aparecer una vía de agua, hacer agua

leaky a naut que hace agua; agujereado; poroso; que tiene goteras

lean a magro, seco, enjuto, delgado; (of meat) magro; fig pobre, estéril. n carne magra, f, magro, m. **to grow l.,** enflaquecer

lean vi inclinarse; apoyarse (en). vt apoyar (en); dejar arrimado (en). **to l. out of the window,** asomarse a la ventana. **to l. against,** apoyarse en, recostarse en (or contra). **to l. back,** echarse hacia atrás; recostarse. **to l. over,** inclinarse. **to l. upon,** apoyarse en; descansar sobre

leaning n inclinación, tendencia, f; predilección, afición, f

leap n salto, m; brinco, m; (caper) zapateta, f; fig salto, m. vi saltar, dar un salto; brincar. vt saltar; hacer saltar. **at one l.,** en un salto. **by leaps and bounds,** en saltos. **My heart leaped,** Mi corazón dio un salto. **to l. to the conclusion that . . . ,** saltar a la conclusión de que . . . **to l. to the eye,** saltar a la vista. **l. frog,** salto, salto de la muerte, m, pídola f. **l. year,** año bisiesto, m, salta cabrillas, f pl

learn vt and vi aprender; instruirse; enterarse de. **to l. by heart,** aprender de memoria. **to l. from a reliable source,** saber de buena tinta. **to l. from experience,** aprender por experiencia

learned a sabio, docto; erudito; (of professions) liberal; versado (en), entendido (en). **a l. society,** una sociedad erudita

learning n saber, m; conocimientos, m pl; erudición, f; estudio, m; (literature) literatura, f

lease n arrendamiento, arriendo, m; contrato de arrendamiento, m. vt dar en arriendo, arrendar. **on l.,** en arriendo. **to take a new l. on life,** recobrar su vigor. **Lend L. Act,** ley de préstamo y arriendo, f

leash n (of a dog) traílla, f

least a sup little, mínimo; el (la, etc.) menor; más pequeño. adv menos. n lo menos. **at l.,** siquiera; por lo menos, al menos. **at the very l.,** a lo menos. **not in the l.,** de ninguna manera, nada. **to say the l. of,** sin exagerar, para no decir más

leather n cuero, m; piel, f, a de cuero; de piel. **patent l.,** charol, m. **Spanish l.,** cordobán, m. **tanned l.,** curtido, m. **l. apron,** mandil, m. **l. bag,** saco de cuero, m. **l. bottle,** bota, f. **l. breeches,** pantalón de montar, m. **l. jerkin,** coleto, m. **l. shield,** adarga, f. **l. strap,** correa, f. **l. trade,** comercio en cueros, m

leatherette n cartón cuero, m

leave n (permission) permiso, m; (mil etc.) licencia, f; (farewell) despedida, f. vt and vi dejar; abandonar; salir (de), quitar, marcharse (de), Lat. Am. egresar (de . . .); (as surety) empeñar; (by will) legar, mandar; (an employment) darse de baja (de), dejar; (give into the keeping of) entregar; (bid farewell) despedirse (de). **By your l.,** Con permiso de Vd. (Vds.). Con la venia de Vd. (Vds.). **on l.,** de permiso. **l.-taking,** despedidas, f pl. **to be left,** quedar. **to be left over,** quedar; sobrar. **Two from four leaves two,** De cuatro a dos van dos. **to take French l.,** despedirse a la inglesa. **to take l. of,** despedirse de. **to take one's l.,** marcharse; despedirse. **to l. a deep impression,** fig impresionar mucho; quedar grabado (en). **to l. undone,** dejar de hacer, no hacer; dejar sin terminar. **to l. about,** vt dejar por todas partes. vi (of time) marcharse a eso de . . . **to l. ajar,** entreabrir, (when opening), entrecerrar (when closing), entornar. **to l. alone,** dejar a solas; dejar en paz; no molestar, no meterse con. **to l. aside,** omitir; prescindir de; olvidar. **to l. behind,** dejar atrás; olvidar. **l. much to be desired,** tener mucho que desear. **to l. off,** vt dejar de; abandonar; (garments) no ponerse, quitarse. vi terminar. **to l. out,** dejar fuera; dejar a un lado, descontar; omitir; pasar por; (be silent about) callar; suprimir. **to l. to,** dejar para; dejar hacer

leaven n levadura, f, fermento, m, vt fermentar; (fig permeate) penetrar (en), infiltrar en, imbuir; (a speech) salpimentar (con)

leaving n salida, partida, marcha, f, Lat. Am. egreso, m; pl **leavings,** sobras, f pl; desechos, m pl

lecherous a lascivo, lujurioso

lectern n atril, m; (in a church) facistol, m

lecture n conferencia, f; (in a university) lección, clase, f; discurso, m; (inf scolding) sermoneo, m. vi dar una conferencia; (in a university) dar clase. vt (inf scold) predicar, sermonear. **l. room,** sala de conferencias, f; (in a university) sala de clase, aula, f

lecturer n conferenciante, Lat. Am. conferencista, mf; (in a university) auxiliar, m; (professor) catedrático (-ca), profesor (-ra)

ledge n borde, m; capa, f; (of a window) alféizar, m; (shelf) ánaquel, m

ledger n libro mayor, m

leech n sanguijuela, f

leek n puerro, m

leer *vi* mirar de soslayo; guiñar el ojo; mirar con los ojos llenos de deseo. *n* mirada de soslayo, *f*; mirada de lascivia, *f*

leeway *n naut* deriva, *f*; *fig* amplitud, margen de holgura, márgenes de maniobra, *f pl*

left *past part* dejado, etc. See **leave.** *a* izquierdo. *adv* a la izquierda; hacia la izquierda. *n* izquierda, *f*. **on the l.,** a la izquierda. **the L.,** *pol* las izquierdas. **the Left Bank (of Paris)** la Ribera izquierda, la Orilla izquierda. **L. face!** ¡Izquierda! **l.-hand,** mano izquierda, *f*; izquierda, *f*. **l.-hand drive,** conducción a la izquierda, *f*. **l.-handed,** zurdo. **l. luggage office,** consigna, *f*. **l.-overs,** sobras, *f pl*, desperdicios, *m pl*

leg *n* pierna, *f*; (of animals, birds, furniture) pata, *f*; (of a triangle) cateto, *m*; (of a pair of compasses, trousers, lamb, veal) pierna, *f*; (of boots, stockings) caña, *f*; (of pork) pernil, *m*; (support) pie, *m*; (stage) etapa, *f*. **to be on one's last legs,** estar en las últimas; estar acabándose; estar sin recursos. **to pull a person's leg,** tomar el pelo (a). **leg-pull,** tomadura de pelo, *f*. **leg-of-mutton sleeve,** manga de pernil, *f*

legacy *n* legado, *m*, manda, *f*; herencia, *f*

legal *a* legal; de derecho; jurídico; (lawful, permissible) legítimo, lícito; (of a lawyer) de abogado. **l. expenses,** litisexpensas, *f pl*. **l. inquiry,** investigación jurídica, *f*

legalistic *n. Lat. Am.* abogaderas, abogaderías, *f pl*

legalize *vt* legalizar; autorizar, legitimar

legally *adv* según la ley; según derecho; legalmente

legal tender *n* moneda de curso liberatorio, *f*

legend *n* leyenda, *f*

legendary *a* legendario

legerdemain *n* juegos de manos, *m pl*

leggings *n pl* polainas, *f pl*

legible *a* legible

legion *n* legión, *f*. **L. of Honor,** Legión de Honor, *f*

legislate *vt* legislar

legislation *n* legislación, *f*

legislator *n* legislador (-ra)

legislature *n* legislatura, *f*

legitimacy *n* legitimidad, *f*; justicia, *f*

legitimate *a* legítimo; justo

leisure *n* ocio, *m*, desocupación, *f*; tiempo libre, *m*. **at one's l.,** con sosiego, despacio. **You can do it at your l.,** Puedes hacerlo cuando tengas tiempo. **to be at l.,** estar desocupado, no tener nada que hacer. **l. moments,** ratos perdidos, momentos de ocio, *m pl*

leisured *a* desocupado, libre; sin ocupación; (wealthy) acomodado

leisurely *a* pausado, lento, deliberado; tardo

lemon *n* limón, *m*; (tree) limonero, *m*, a limonado, de color de limón; hecho o sazonado con limón. **l. drop,** pastilla de limón, *f*. **l.-grove,** limonar, *m*. **l.-squash,** limonada natural, *f*. **l.-squeezer,** exprime limones, *m*, exprimidera, *f*

lemonade *n* limonada, *f*. **l. powder,** limonada seca, *f*

lend *vt* prestar. **to l. an ear to,** prestar atención a. **It does not l. itself to . . . ,** No se presta a . . . **to l. a hand,** echar una mano, dar una mano

lender *n* el, *m*, (*f*, la) que presta; prestador (-ra); (of money) prestamista, *mf*; *com* mutuante, *mf*

lending *n* prestación, *f*, préstamo, *m*. **l.-library,** biblioteca circulante, *f*

length *n* largo, *m*; longitud, *f*; (of fabric) corte, *m*; (of a ship) eslora, *f*; (in racing) largo, *m*; distancia, *f*; (in time) duración, *f*; alcance, *m*. **at l.,** por fin, finalmente; (in full) extensamente, largamente. **by a l.,** por un largo. **full-l.,** de cuerpo entero. **three feet in l.,** tres pies de largo. **to go the l. of . . . ,** llegar al extremo de . . .

lengthen *vt* alargar; prolongar; extender. *vi* alargarse; prolongarse; extenderse; (of days) crecer

lengthening *n* alargamiento, *m*; prolongación, *f*; crecimiento, *m*

lengthy *a* largo; demasiado largo, larguísimo; (of speech) prolijo; verboso

lenience, leniency *n* lenidad, *f*; indulgencia, *f*

lenient *a* indulgente; poco severo

lens *n* lente, *m*; (of the eye) cristalino, *m*

Lent *n* Cuaresma, *f*

lentil *n* lenteja, *f*

leopard *n* leopardo, *m*

leper *n* leproso (-sa). **l. colony,** colonia de leprosos, *f*

leprosy *n* lepra, *f*

lesbian *a* and *n* lesbiana

lesion *n* lesión, *f*

less *a* menor; más pequeño; menos; inferior. *adv* menos; sin. **l. than,** menos de (que). **more or l.,** poco más o menos. **no l.,** nada menos. **none the l.,** sin embargo. **to grow l.,** disminuir. **l. and l.,** cada vez menos

lessee *n* arrendatario (-ia); inquilino (-na)

lessen *vi* disminuir; reducirse. *vt* disminuir; reducir; (lower) rebajar; (disparage) menospreciar

lessening *n* disminución, *f*; reducción, *f*

lesser *a comp* menor; más pequeño. See **little**

lesson *n* lección, *f*. **to give a l.,** dar lección, dar clase; *fig* dar una lección (a). **to hear a l.,** tomar la lección

lessor *n* arrendador (-ra)

lest *conjunc* para que no; por miedo de (que), no sea que. **I did not do it l. they**

should not like it, No lo hice por miedo de que no les gustase

let *vt* dejar, permitir; (lease) arrendar. *vi* alquilarse, ser alquilado. **Let** as an expression of the imperative is rendered in Spanish by the subjunctive or the imperative, e.g. **Let them go!** ¡Que se vayan! ¡Déjalos marchar! **He let them go,** Les dejó marchar. **to let fall,** dejar caer. **to let go,** dejar marchar; soltar; poner en libertad (a). **to let loose,** dar suelta a; *flg* desencadenar. **to let one know,** hacer saber, comunicar. **to let the cat out of the bag,** tirar de la manta. **to let th chance slip,** perder la ocasión. **to let alone,** (a thing) no tocar; (a person) dejar en paz, dejar tranquilo; (an affair) no meterse (en or con); (omit) no mencionar, omitir toda mención de. **to let down,** bajar; (by a rope) descolgar; (hair, etc.) dejar caer; (a dress, etc.) alargar; *naut* calar; (disappoint) dejar plantado. **to let in,** dejar entrar; hacer entrar; invitar a entrar; recibir; (insert) insertar. **to let into,** (initiate) iniciar en, admitir en; (a secret) revelar. Other meanings, see **to let in. to let off,** dejar salir; dejar en libertad; exonerar; perdonar; (a gun) disparar; (fireworks, etc.) hacer estallar. **to let out,** dejar salir; poner en libertad; (from a house) acompañar a la puerta; abrir la puerta; *sew* ensanchar; (hire) alquilar; (the fire, etc.) dejar extinguirse. **to let up,** dejar subir; (decrease) disminuir; (end) terminar

let *n* estorbo, impedimento, obstáculo, *m*. **without let or hindrance,** sin estorbo ni obstáculo

lethal *a* letal. **l. weapon,** instrumento de muerte, *m*

lethargic *a* aletargado; letárgico

letter *n* (of the alphabet) letra, *f*; (epistle) carta, *f*; *print* carácter, *m*; (lessor) arrendador (-ra); *pl* **letters,** letras, *f pl*; (correspondence) correo, *m*; correspondencia, *f*. *vt* inscribir; imprimir. **capital l.,** letra mayúscula, *f*. **first letters,** *flg* primeras letras, *f pl*. **registered l.,** carta certificada, *f*, certificado, *m*. **small l.,** letra minúscula, *f*. **the l. of the law,** la ley escrita. **to be l.-perfect,** saber de memoria. **to the l.,** *flg* a la letra. **letters patent,** patente, *f*; título de privilegio, *m*. **l.-balance,** pesacartas, *m*. **l.-book,** *com* libro copiador, *m*. **l.-box,** buzón de correos, *m*. **l.-card,** tarjeta postal del gobierno, *f*. **l. of credit,** carta de crédito, *f*. **l. of introduction,** carta de presentación, *f*. **l.-writer,** escritor (-ra) de cartas

lettering *n* inscripción, *f*; letrero, rótulo, *m*

lettuce *n* lechuga, *f*. **l. plant,** lechuguino, *m*. **l. seller,** lechuguero (-ra)

level *n* nivel, *m*; ras, *m*, flor, *f*; llano, *m*; (plain) llanura, *f*; (instrument) nivel, *m*, *a* llano; igual; al nivel (de); uniforme; imparcial. *adv* a nivel; igualmente. *vt* nive-lar; igualar; allanar; (a blow) asestar; (a gun) apuntar; (raze) arrasar, derribar; adaptar; hacer uniforme. **on the l.,** a nivel; *flg* de buena fe. **spirit l.,** nivel de burbuja, *m*. **to make l. again,** rellanar. **l. country,** campaña, llanura, *f*. **l. with the ground,** a ras de la tierra. **l. with the water,** a flor de agua. **l. crossing,** paso a nivel, *m*. **l.-headed,** sensato, cuerdo. **l. stretch,** rellano, *m*; llanura, *f*

leveling *a* a nivelador; de nivelación; igualador. *n* nivelación, *f*; allanamiento, *m*; (to the ground) arrasamiento, *m*; igualación, *f*

lever *n* palanca, *f*; (handle) manivela, *f*; escape de reloj, *m*; (excuse) pretexto, *m*; (means) modo, *m*. *vt* sopalancar. **control l.,** *aer* palanca de mando, *f*. **hand-l.,** palanca de mano, *f*

leverage *n* sistema de palancas, *m*; acción de palanca, *f*; *flg* influencia, fuerza, *f*, poder, *m*

Leviticus *n* Levítico, *m*

levity *n* levedad, frivolidad, ligereza, *f*

levy *n* exacción (de tributos), *f*; impuesto, *m*; (of a fine) imposición, *f*; *mil* leva, *f*. *vt* (taxes) exigir; (a fine) imponer; (troops) reclutar, enganchar

levying *n* (of a tax) exacción (de tributos), *f*; (of a fine) imposición, *f*; (of troops) leva, *f*

lewd *a* lascivo, lujurioso, impúdico

lewdness *n* lascivia, lujuria, impudicia, *f*

liability *n* responsabilidad, obligación, *f*; tendencia, *f*; riesgo, *m*; *pl* **liabilities,** obligaciones, *f pl*; *com* pasivo, *m*

liable *a* responsable; propenso (a); expuesto (a); sujeto (a)

liaison *n* lío, *m*; coordinación, *f*. **l. officer,** oficial de coordinación, *m*

liar *n* mentiroso (-sa)

libel *n* libelo, *m*; difamación, *f*, *vt* difamar, calumniar

libelous *a* difamatorio

liberal *a* liberal; generoso; abundante, *n* liberal, *mf* **l. profession,** carrera liberal, *f*. **l.-minded,** tolerante. **l.-mindedness,** tolerancia, *f*

liberalism *n* liberalismo, *m*

liberality *n* liberalidad, *f*; generosidad, *f*

liberalize *vt* liberalizar

liberate *vt* (a prisoner) poner en libertad; librar (de); (a gas, etc.) dejar escapar

liberation *n* liberación, *f*; (of a captive) redención, *f*; (of a slave) manumisión, *f*

liberator *n* libertador (-ra)

libertine *n* libertino, *m*

liberty *n* libertad, *f*; (familiarity) familiaridad, *f*; (right) privilegio, *m*, prerrogativa, *f*; (leave) permiso, *m*. **at l.,** en libertad; desocupado, libre. **I have taken the l. of giving them your name,** Me he tomado la libertad de darles su nombre. **to set at l.,** poner en libertad (a). **to take liberties**

with, tratar con familiaridad; (a text) tergiversar. **l. of speech,** libertad de palabra, libertad de expresión, *f.* **l. of thought,** libertad de pensamiento, *f*

libidinous *a* libidinoso

librarian *n* bibliotecario (-ia)

library *n* biblioteca, *f;* (book shop) librería, *f.* **l. catalog,** catálogo de la biblioteca, *m*

license *n* licencia, *f*, permiso, *m;* autorización, *f;* (driving) carnet de chófer, permiso de conducción, *m;* (of a car) permiso de circulación, *m;* (for a wireless, etc.) licencia, *f;* (marriage) licencia de casamiento, *f;* (excess) libertinaje, desenfreno, *m.* **import l.,** permiso de importación, *m.* **poetic l.,** licencia poética, *f.* **l. number,** (of a car) número de matriculación, *m. vt* licenciar; autorizar; (a car) sacar la licencia del automóvil

licensee *n* concesionario (-ia)

licentious *a* licencioso, disoluto

licit *a* lícito

lick *vt* lamer; (of waves) besar; (of flames) bailar; (thrash) azotar; (defeat) vencer. **to l. one's lips,** relamerse los labios, chuparse los dedos. **to l. the dust,** morder el polvo

licking *n* lamedura, *f;* (beating) paliza, tunda, *f;* (defeat) derrota, *f*

lid *n* cobertera, *f;* tapa, *f;* (of the eye) párpado, *m*

lie *n* mentira, *f;* invención, falsedad, *f;* mentís, *m, vi* mentir. **to give the lie to,** desmentir, dar el mentís. **to lie barefacedly,** mentir por la mitad de la barba. **white lie,** mentira oficiosa, *f*

lie *vi* estar tumbado, estar echado; estar recostado; descansar, reposar; (in the grave) yacer; (be) estar; (be situated) hallarse, estar situado; (stretch) extenderse; (sleep) dormir; (depend) depender; (consist) consistir, estribar; (as an obligation) incumbir. **Here lies . . . ,** Aquí descansa . . . , Aquí yace . . . **It does not lie in my power,** No depende de mí. **to let lie,** dejar; dejar en paz. **to lie at anchor,** estar anclado. **to lie fallow,** estar en barbecho; *fig* descansar. **to lie about,** estar esparcido por todas partes; estar en desorden. **to lie along,** estar tendido a lo largo de; *naut* dar a la banda. **to lie back,** recostarse; apoyarse (en). **to lie by,** estar acostado al lado de; (of things, places) estar cerca (de); descansar. **to lie down,** tenderse, tumbarse, echarse, acostarse; reposar. **Lie down!** (to a dog) ¡Échate! **to lie down under,** tenderse bajo; (an insult) tragar, sufrir. **to lie in,** consistir en; depender de; (of childbirth) estar de parto. **to lie open,** estar abierto; estar expuesto (a); estar al descubierto, estar a la vista. **to lie over,** (be postponed) quedar aplazado. **to lie to,** *naut* estarse a la capa, ponerse en facha. **to lie under,** estar bajo, hallarse bajo; estar bajo el

peso de; (be exposed to) estar expuesto a. **to lie with,** dormir con; (concern) tocar (a); corresponder (a)

lie *n* configuración, *f;* disposición, *f;* posición, *f.* **the lie of the land,** la configuración del terreno

lieu *n* lugar, *m.* **in l. of,** en lugar de, en vez de

lieutenant *n* teniente, lugarteniente, *m;* (naval) alférez, *m.* **first l.,** (in the army) primer teniente, teniente, *m;* (in the navy) alférez de navío, *m.* **naval l.,** teniente de navío, *m.* **second l.,** (in the army) segundo teniente, *m;* (in the navy) alférez de fragata, *m.* **l.-colonel,** teniente coronel

life *n* vida, *f;* (being) ser, *m;* (society) mundo, *m*, sociedad, *f;* (vitality) vitalidad, *f;* vigor, *m*, a de vida; (of annuities, etc.) vitalicio; (life-saving) de salvamento. **for l.,** de por vida. **from l.,** del natural. **high l.,** gran mundo, *m*, alta sociedad, *f.* **low l.,** vida del hampa, vida de los barrios bajos, *f.* **to the l.,** al vivo. **to lay down one's l.,** entregar la vida. **to take one's l. in one's hands,** jugarse la vida. **l. annuity,** fondo vitalicio, *m.* **l.-belt,** (cinturón) salvavidas, *m.* **l.-blood,** sangre vital, *f; fig* nervio, *m;* vigor, *m.* **l.-boat,** (on a ship) bote salvavidas, *m;* (on the coast) lancha de salvamento, *f.* **l.-boat station,** estación de salvamento, *f.* **l.-giving,** vivificante, que da vida; tonificante. **l.-guard,** (soldier) guardia militar, *f;* Guardia de Corps, *f*, (at beach or swimming pool) guardavivas, *mf.* **l.-insurance,** seguro sobre la vida, *m.* **l.-interest,** usufructo, *m.* **l.-jacket,** chaleco salvavidas, *m.* **l.-like,** natural. **l.-line,** cable de salvamento, *m.* **l.-saving,** a de salvamento; curativo. **l.-saving apparatus,** aparato salvavidas, *m.* **l.-sized,** de tamaño natural

life cycle *n* ciclo vital, *m*

life imprisonment *n* reclusión perpetua, *f*

life jacket *n* chaleco salvavidas, *f*

lifeless *a* sin vida, muerto; inanimado; *fig* desanimado

lifelong *a* de toda la vida

lifetime *n* vida, *f*

lift *n* esfuerzo para levantar, *m;* acción de levantar, *f;* alza, *f;* (blow) golpe, *m;* (help) ayuda, *f;* (hitch, ride) *Mexico* aventón, *m;* (elevator) ascensor, *m;* (for goods) montacargas, *m; pl* lifts, *naut* balancines, *m pl.* **to give a l. to,** (help) ayudar; (hitchhiker etc.) dar un aventón. **l. attendant,** ascensorista, *mf*

lift *vt* levantar; alzar, elevar; (pick up) coger; (one's hat) quitarse; (steal) hurtar; exaltar. *vi* (of mist) disiparse; desaparecer. **to l. the elbow,** empinar el codo. **to l. down,** quitar (de); (a person) bajar en brazos. **to l. up,** alzar; erguir; levantar; levantar en brazos

ligament n ligamento, m

light a (not dark) claro, con mucha luz, bañado de luz; (of colors) claro; (not heavy, and of sleep, food, troops, movements) ligero; (of reading) de entretenimiento; (irresponsible) frívolo; (easy) fácil; (slight) leve; (of hair) rubio; (happy) alegre; (fickle) inconstante, liviano; (of complexion) blanco. adv ligero. **to be l.**, no pesar mucho; estar de día. **to grow l.**, (dawn) clarear; iluminarse. **to make l. of**, no tomar en serio; no preocuparse de; (suffering) sufrir sin quejarse. **l.-colored**, (de color) claro. **l.-fingeredness**, sutileza de manos, f. **l.-footed**, ligero de pies. **l.-haired**, de pelo rubio. **l.-headed**, casquivano, ligero de cascos; delirante. **l.-headedness**, ligereza de cascos, frivolidad, f; delirio, m. **l.-hearted**, alegre (de corazón). **l.-heartedness**, alegría, f. **l. horse**, mil caballería ligera, f. **l. troops**, tropas ligeras, f pl. **l.-weight**, n (boxing) peso ligero, m, a de peso ligero

light n luz, f; (day) día, m; (match) cerilla, f; (of a cigarette, etc.) fuego, m; (of a window) cristal, vidrio, m; (point of view) punto de vista, m; (in a picture) toque de luz, m; pl **lights**, (offal) bofes, m pl. **against the l.**, al trasluz. **by the l. of**, a la luz de; según. **half-l.**, media luz, f. **high light(s)**, art claros, m pl; fig momento culminante, m; acontecimiento de más interés, m. **to come to l.**, descubrirse. **to put a l. to the fire**, encender el fuego. **l.-year**, año de luz, m

light vt (a lamp, fire, etc.) encender; iluminar. vi encenderse; iluminarse; fig animarse; brillar. **to l. upon**, encontrar por casualidad; tropezar con

lighten vt (illuminate) iluminar; (of weight) aligerar; (cheer) alegrar; (mitigate) aliviar. vi (grow light) clarear; (of lightning) relampaguear; (become less heavy) disminuir de peso, aligerarse; volverse más alegre

lightening n aligeramiento, m; (easing) alivio, m; luz, f

lighter n (boat) lancha, barcaza, gabarra, f; (device) encendedor, m. **pocket l.**, encendedor de bolsillo, m. **l. man**, gabarrero, m

lighthouse n faro, m. **l.-keeper**, guardafaro, m

lighting n iluminación, f; alumbrado, m. **flood l.**, iluminación intensiva, f. **l.-up time**, hora de encender los faros, f

lightly adv ligeramente; fácilmente; (slightly) levemente; ágilmente; sin seriedad. **l. wounded**, levemente herido

lightning n relámpago, rayo, m. **as quick as l.**, como un relámpago. **to be struck by l.**, ser herido por un relámpago. **l.-rod**, pararrayos, m

likable a simpático

like a semejante; parecido; igual, mismo; (characteristic) típico, característico; (likely) probable; (equivalent) equivalente. adv como; igual (que); del mismo modo (que). n semejante, igual, mf; tal cosa, f; cosas semejantes, f pl. **Don't speak to me l. that**, No me hables así. **He was l. a fury**, Estaba hecho una furia. **They are very l. each other**, Se parecen mucho. **to be l.**, parecerse (a); semejar. **to look l.**, parecer ser (que); tener el aspecto de; (of persons) parecerse (a). **to return l. for l.**, pagar en la misma moneda

like vt gustar, agradar; estar aficionado (a), gustar de; (wish) querer. **As you l.**, Como te parezca bien, Como quieras. **If you l.**, Si quieres. **James likes painting**, Jaime está aficionado a la pintura. **Judith does not l. the north of England**, A Judit no le gusta el norte de Inglaterra. **I don't l. to do it**, No me gusta hacerlo. **I should l. him to go to Madrid**, Me gustaría que fuese a Madrid

likelihood n posibilidad, f; probabilidad, f

likely a probable; verosímil, creíble, plausible; posible; (suitable) satisfactorio, apropiado; (handsome) bien parecido. adv probablemente. **They are not l. to come**, No es probable que vengan

liken vt comparar

likeness n parecido, m, semejanza, f; (portrait) retrato, m

likewise adv igualmente, asimismo, también. conjunc además

liking n (for persons) simpatía, f, cariño, m; (for things) gusto, m, afición, f; (appreciation) aprecio, m. **I have a l. for old cities**, Me gustan (or me atraen) las viejas ciudades. **to take a l. to**, (things) aficionarse a; (persons) prendarse de, tomar cariño (a)

lilac n lila, f, a. **l. color**, color de lila, m

lilt n canción, f; ritmo, m; armonía, f

lily n lirio, m, azucena, f; (of France) flor de lis, f. **l. of the valley**, lirio de los valles, muguete, m. **l.-white**, blanco como la azucena

limb n anat miembro, m; (of a tree) rama, f

limbo n limbo, m

lime n chem cal, f; (for catching birds) liga, hisca, f; (linden tree) tilo, m; (tree like a lemon) limero, m; (fruit) lima, f. vt (whiten) encalar; agr abonar con cal. **slaked l.**, cal muerta, f. **l.-flower**, flor del tilo, tila, f; flor del limero, f. **l.-juice**, jugo de lima, m. **l.-kiln**, calera, f. **l.-pit**, pozo de cal, m. **l. tree** Lat. Am. limo, m

limelight n luz de calcio, f; fig centro de atención, m; publicidad, f. **to be in the l.**, ser el centro de atención, estar a la vista (de público)

limestone n piedra caliza, f. **l. deposit**, calar, m

limit n límite, m; confín, m; linde, m, or f;

limitación, f, vt limitar; fijar; (restrict) restringir. **This is the l.!** ¡Este es el colmo! ¡No faltaba más!

limitation n limitación f; restricción, f

limousine n limusina, f, coche cerrado, m

limp a flojo; débil; fláccido; lánguido. n cojera, f. vi cojear. **to l. off,** marcharse cojeando. **to l. up,** acercarse cojeando; subir cojeando

limpid a límpido, cristalino, puro

linchpin n pezonera, f

line vt (furrow) surcar; (troops, etc.) poner en fila; alinear; (clothes, nests, etc.) forrar; (building) revestir; (one's pocket) llenar. vi estar en línea, alinearse

line n (most meanings) línea, f; (cord) cuerda, f; naut cordel, m; (fishing) sedal, m; (railway) vía, f; (wrinkle) surco, m; arruga, f; (row) hilera, ringlera, fila, f; (of verse) verso, m; print renglón, m; (of business) ramo, m; profesión, f; (interest) especialidad, f. **bowling** or **serving l.,** línea de saque, f; **hard lines,** mala suerte, f; apuro, m, situación difícil, f. **in a l.,** en fila; en cola. **in direct l.,** (of descent) en línea recta. **It is not in my l.,** No es una especialidad mía; No es uno de mis intereses. **on the lines of,** conforme a; parecido a. **to cross the l.,** (equator) pasar la línea; (railway) cruzar la vía. **to drop a l.,** escribir unas líneas, poner unas líneas. **to read between the lines,** leer entre líneas. **l.-drawing,** dibujo de líneas, m. **l. of battle,** línea de batalla, f

lineage n linaje, m, familia, raza, f

lineament n lineamento, m; (of the face) facciones, f pl

linear a lineal. **l. equation,** ecuación de primer grado, f

lined a rayado, con líneas; (of the face) surcado, arrugado; (of gloves, etc.) forrado. **lined paper,** papel rayado, m

linen n lino, m; inf ropa blanca, f; a de lino. **clean l.,** ropa limpia, f. **dirty l.,** ropa sucia, f; ropa para lavar, f. **table-l.,** mantelería, f. **l. cupboard,** armario para ropa blanca, m. **l. draper,** lencero (-ra). **l.-draper's shop,** lencería, f. **l. room,** lencería, f. **l. tape,** trenzadera, f. **l. thread,** hilo de lino, m

liner n (ship) transatlántico, m; buque de vapor, m; aer avión de pasaje, m

linger vi (remain) quedarse; tardar en marcharse; ir lentamente; hacer algo despacio

lingerie n ropa blanca, f

lingering a lento; largo, prolongado; melancólico, triste

liniment n linimento, m

lining n (of a garment, etc.) forro, m; (building) revestimiento, m

link n (in a chain) eslabón, m; (of beads) sarta, f; fig enlace, m, cadena, f; conexión, f; mech corredera, f; (torch) hacha de

viento, f. vt enlazar, unir; fig encadenar. **missing l.,** fig estabón perdido, m. **to l. arms,** cogerse del brazo

links n pl campo de golf, m

linoleum n linóleo, m

linseed n linaza, f. **l. cake,** bagazo, m. **l.-oil,** aceite de linaza, m

lint n med hilas, f pl; (fluff) borra, f

lion n león, m; fig celebridad, f. **l. cage** or **den,** leonera, f. **l.-hearted,** valeroso. **l.-hunter,** cazador (-ra) de leones. **l.-keeper,** leonero (-ra). **lion's mane,** melena, f. **l.-tamer,** domador (-ra) de leones

lionize vt dar bombo (a), hacer la rueda (a), tratar como a una celebridad (a)

lion's share n parte del león, tajada del león, f

lip n labio, m; (of a vessel) pico, m; (of a crater) borde, m; fig boca, f. **to open one's lips,** abrir la boca. **to smack one's lips,** chuparse los dedos. **lip reading,** lectura labial, f. **lip-service,** amor fingido, m; promesas hipócritas, f pl. **lip stick,** lápiz para los labios, m

liquefaction n licuefacción, f

liquefy vt liquidar. vi liquidarse

liqueur n licor, m. **l.-glass,** copita de licor, f. **l.-set,** licorera, f

liquid n líquido, m, a líquido; límpido. **l. air,** aire líquido, m. **l. measure,** medida para líquidos, f

liquidate vt liquidar; saldar (cuentas); mil soldar

liquidation n liquidación, f

liquor n licor, m. **l. shop,** aguardentería, f. **l. traffic,** negocio de vinos y licores, m; contrabando, m

liquorice n regaliz, m

Lisbon Lisboa, f

lisp n ceceo, m; balbuceo, m, vi cecear; balbucir

lissom a flexible; ágil

list n lista, f; catálogo, m; matrícula, f; naut recalcada, f; inclinación, f; (tournament) liza, f. vt hacer una lista de; catalogar; matricular, inscribir. vi naut recalcar; inclinarse a un lado. **to enter the lists,** entrar en liza. **l. of wines,** lista de vinos, f

listen vi escuchar; (attend) atender. **Don't you want to l. to the music?** ¿No quieres escuchar la música? **to l. in,** (to the radio) escuchar la radio; (eavesdrop) escuchar a hurtadillas

listener n oyente, mf; (to radio) radiooyente, mf

listless a lánguido, apático, indiferente

litany n letanía, f

liter n litro, m

literal a literal. **l.-minded,** sin imaginación

literary a literario

literate a and n literato (-ta)

literature *n* literatura, *f*

lithe *a* flexible; sinuoso y delgado; ágil

Lithuania Lituania, *f*

Lithuanian *a* lituano, *n* lituano (-na); (language) lituano, *m*

litigant *n* litigante, *mf*

litigate *vi* and *vt* litigar, pleitear

litigation *n* litigación, *f*

litmus *n* tornasol, *m*. **l. paper,** papel de tornasol, *m*

litter *n* litera, *f*; (stretcher) camilla, *f*; (bed) lecho, *m*; cama de paja, *f*; (brood) camada, cría, *f*; (rubbish) cosas en desorden, *f pl*; (papers) papeletas, *f pl*; (untidiness) desarreglo, desorden, *m*, confusión, *f*, *vt* poner en desorden

little *a* pequeño; poco; (scanty) escaso; insignificante; bajo, mezquino. *adv* poco. **a l.,** un poco (de); un tanto. **in l.,** en pequeño. **not a l.,** no poco; bastante. **l. by l.,** poco a poco. **l. or no,** poco o nada. **however l.,** por pequeño que. **as l. as possible,** lo menos posible. **to make l. of,** no dar importancia a; no poder en claro de; no comprender bien; no hacer caso de; (persons) acoger mal. **l. by l.,** poco a poco. **l. finger,** dedo meñique, *m*. **l. one,** pequeñuela, *f*, pequeñito, *m*

liturgical *a* litúrgico. **l. calendar,** calendario litúrgico, *m*

liturgical vestment *n* paramento litúrgico, *m*

liturgy *n* liturgia, *f*

live *a* vivo, viviente; (alight) encendido; (of a wire, etc.) cargado de electricidad. **l. cartridge,** cartucho con bala, *m*. **l. coal,** ascua, *f*. **l.-stock,** ganadería, *f*. **l. wire,** conductor eléctrico, *m*; *fig* fuerza viva, *f*

live *vi* vivir; residir, habitar; (of ships) mantenerse a flote; salvarse; subsistir. *vt* (one's life) llevar, pasar. **Long l.!** ¡Viva! **to have enough to l. on,** tener de que vivir. **to l. together,** convivir. **to l. again,** volver a vivir. **to l. at,** vivir en, habitar. **to l. down,** sobrevivir a; (a fault) lograr borrar. **to l. on,** vivir de. **to l. up to,** vivir con arreglo a, vivir en conformidad con; estar al nivel de, merecer. **to l. up to one's income,** vivir al día, gastarse toda la renta

live broadcast *n* emisión en directo, *f*

livelihood *n* vida, subsistencia, *f*. **to make a l.,** ganarse la vida

livelong *a* entero, todo; eterno. **all the l. day,** todo el santo día

lively *a* vivo; vivaracho; brioso, enérgico; alegre; bullicioso; animado; (fresh) fresco; (of colours) brillante; intenso

liver *n* vividor (-ra), el, *m*, (*f*, la) que vive; habitante, *m*; *anat* hígado, *m*. **l. cancer,** cáncer del hígado, *m*. **l. complaint,** mal de hígado, *m*. **l. extract,** extracto de hígado, *m*

livery *n* librea, *f*; uniforme, *m*; *poet* ves-

---

tiduras, *f pl*. **l. stables,** pensión de caballos, *f*; cochería de alquiler, *f*

livid *a* lívido; cárdeno, amoratado

living *a* viviente; vivo, vital. *n* vida, *f*; modo de vivir, *m*; beneficio eclesiástico, *m*. **the l.,** los vivos. **to make one's l.,** ganarse la vida. **l. memory,** memoria de personas vivientes, memoria de los que aún viven, *f*. **l.-room,** sala de estar, *f*. **l. soul,** ser viviente; *inf* bicho viviente, *m*. **l. wage,** jornal básico, *m*

lizard *n* lagarto (-ta). **giant l.,** dragón, *m*. **wall l.,** lagartija, *f*. **l. hole,** lagartera, *f*

load *n* carga, *f*; peso, *m*; (cart) carretada, *f*; *elec* carga, *f*; (quantity) cantidad, *f*. *vt* cargar (con); (with honors) llenar (de); (*fig* weigh down) agobiar (con); (a stick with lead) emplomar; (*elec* and of dice) cargar; (wine) mezclar vino con un narcótico. **to be loaded with fruit,** estar cargado de fruta. **to l. oneself with,** cargarse de. **to l. the dice,** cargar los dados. **to l. again,** recargar

loading *n* carga, *f*. **l. depot,** cargadero, *m*

loaf *n* pan, *m*; (French) barra de pan, *f*. *vi* golfear, vagabundear, gandulear. **l. sugar,** azúcar de pilón, *m*

loafer *n* vago (-ga); azotacalles, *mf*; gandul (-la); golfo (-fa)

loam *n* marga, *f*

loan *n* empréstito, *m*; (lending) prestación, *f*; préstamo, *m*. *vt* prestar. **l. fund,** caja de empréstitos, *f*. **l. company office,** casa de préstamos, *f*

loath *a* desinclinado, poco dispuesto

loathe *vt* abominar, detestar, odiar, aborrecer; repugnar

loathsome *a* odioso, aborrecible; asqueroso; repugnante

lobby *n* pasillo, *m*; antecámara, *f*; (in a hotel, house) vestíbulo, recibidor, *m*; (waiting-room) sala de espera, *f*; (in Parliament) sala de los pasos perdidos, *f*. *vt* and *vi* cabildear

lobe *n bot* lobo, *m*; (*anat arch*) lóbulo, *m*

lobster *n* langosta, *f*; bogavante, *m*. **l.-pot,** cambín, *m*, nasa, *f*

local *a* local; de la localidad. **l. anesthetic,** anestésico local, *m*. **l. color,** color local, *m*

locale *n* local, *m*

locality *n* localidad, *f*; situación, *f*

localize *vt* localizar

locate *vt* situar; colocar; localizar. **to be located,** situarse; hallarse

location *n* colocación, *f*; emplazamiento, *m*, localidad, *f*; situación, posición, *f*

loch *n* lago, *m*

lock *n* cerradura (of a door, including a vehicle); (of a gun) cerrojo, *m*; (in wrestling) llave, *m*; (on rivers, canals) presa, *f*; (at a dock) esclusa, *f*; (of hair) mechón, *m*, guedeja, *f*; (ringlet) bucle, *m*; *pl* **locks,** (hair) cabellos, *m pl*, pelo, *m*. **spring l.,**

cerradura de golpe, f. **to put a l. on,** poner cerradura a. **under l. and key,** bajo cuatro llaves. **l.-jaw,** trismo, m. **l. keeper,** esclusero (-ra) mf. **l.-out strike,** huelga patronal, f

lock vt cerrar con llave; fig encerrar; (embrace) abrazar estrechamente; (of wheels, etc.) trabar; (twine) entrelazar. vi cerrarse con llave. **to l. in,** cerrar con llave; encerrar. **to l. out,** cerrar la puerta (a); dejar en la calle (a). **to l. up,** encerrar; (imprison) encarcelar

locker n (drawer) cajón, m; (cupboard) armario, m; naut cajonada, f

locket n guardapelo, m; medallón, m

locksmith n cerrajero, m. **locksmith's trade,** cerrajería, f

locomotive a locomotor. n locomotora, f

locum tenens n interino (-na)

locust n langosta migratoria, f

lode n filón, m

lodge n casita, garita, f; casa de guarda, f; (freemason's) logia, f; (porter's) portería, f, vi hospedarse, alojarse, vivir, parar; penetrar; entrar (en); fijarse (en). vt hospedar, alojar; albergar; (a blow) asestar; (a complaint) hacer, dar; (money, etc.) depositar. **to l. an accusation against,** querellarse contra, quejarse de. **l.-keeper,** conserje, m

lodger n huésped (-eda), Lat. Am. alojado (-da)

lodging n hospedaje, alojamiento, m; (inn) posada, f; residencia, f; casa, f. **l.-house,** casa de huéspedes, f

loft n desván, sotabanco, m; pajar, m

lofty a alto; sublime; noble; eminente; (haughty) altanero, soberbio

log n madero, tronco, m; palo, m; leño, m; naut, diario de a bordo m, barquilla, f. **to lie like a log,** estar hecho un tronco. **log-book,** naut cuaderno de bitácora, m. **log-cabin,** cabañas de troncos, m. **log-wood,** palo campeche, m

logarithm n logaritmo, m

logic n lógica, f

logical a lógico

loin n ijar, m; (of meat) falda, f; pl **loins,** lomos, riñones m pl. **to gird up one's loins,** fig arremangarse los faldones. **l.-cloth,** taparrabo, m

loiter vi vagabundear, vagar, errar; haraganear; rezagarse

loiterer n haragán (-ana); vago (-ga); rezagado (-da)

loll vi recostarse (en), apoyarse (en). vt (the tongue) sacar

London Londres, m

Londoner n londinense, mf

lone. See lonely

loneliness n soledad, f; aislamiento, m

lonely a solitario; solo; aislado, remoto; desierto

lonesome a solo, solitario

long a largo; prolongado; de largo; (extensive) extenso; (big) grande; (much) mucho. **a l. time,** mucho tiempo. **It is five feet l.,** Tiene cinco pies de largo. **l.-armed,** que tiene los brazos largos. **l.-boat,** falúa, f. **l. clothes,** (infant's) mantillas, f pl. **l.-distance call,** conferencia telefónica, f. **l.-distance race,** carrera de fondo, f. **l.-eared,** de orejas largas. **l.-faced,** de cara larga, carilargo. **l.-forgotten,** olvidado hace mucho tiempo. **l.-haired,** que tiene el pelo largo. **l.-headed,** dolicocéfalo; fig astuto, sagaz. **l.-legged,** zanquilargo, zancudo. **l.-lived,** que vive hasta una edad avanzada; longevo; duradero. **l.-lost,** perdido hace mucho tiempo. **l.-sighted,** présbita; previsor; sagaz. **l.-standing,** viejo, de muchos años. **l.-suffering,** sufrido, paciente. **l.-tailed,** de cola larga. **l.-waisted,** de talle largo. **l.-winded,** prolijo

long adv mucho tiempo; mucho; durante mucho tiempo. **as l. as,** mientras (que). **before l.,** dentro de poco. **the l. and the short of it,** en resumidas cuentas. **How l. has she been here?** ¿Cuánto tiempo hace que está aquí? **not l. before,** poco tiempo antes. **l. ago,** tiempo ha, muchos años ha

long vi anhelar, suspirar (por), desear con vehemencia

longer a comp más largo. adv comp más tiempo. **How much l. must we wait?** ¿Cuánto tiempo más hemos de esperar? **He can no l. walk as he used,** Ya no puede andar como antes

longevity n longevidad, f

longing a anheloso, ansioso; de envidia. n anhelo, m, ansia, f; deseo vehemente, m; envidia, f

longitude n longitud, f

look n mirada, f; (glance) vistazo, m, ojeada, f; (air) semblante, aire, porte, m; (appearance) aspecto, m; apariencia, f. **good looks,** buen parecer, m; guapeza, f. **the new l.,** la nueva línea, la nueva silueta, la nueva moda. **to be on the l.-out,** andar a la mira

look vi and vt mirar; considerar, contemplar; (appear, seem) parecer; tener aire (de); tener aspecto (de); hacer el efecto (de); (show oneself) mostrarse; (of buildings, etc.) caer (a), dar (a); mirar (a).; (seem to be) revelar (e.g., **You don't l. thirty,** No revelas treinta años) **to l. alike,** parecerse. **to l. hopeful,** fig prometer bien. **to l. out of the corner of the eye,** mirar de reojo. **to l. (a person) up and down,** mirar de hito en hito. **to l. about one,** mirar a su alrededor; observar. **to l. after,** tener la mirada puesta en, mirar; (care for) cuidar; (watch) vigilar; mirar por. **to l. at,** mirar; considerar; examinar. **He looked at his watch,** Miró su reloj. **He looked at her,** La miró. **to l.**

away, desviar los ojos, apartar la mirada. **to l. back,** mirar hacia atrás, volver la cabeza; (in thought) pensar en el pasado. **to l. down,** bajar los ojos; mirar el suelo; mirar hacia abajo. **to l. down upon,** dominar, mirar a; (scorn) despreciar; mirar de arriba para abajo. **to l. for,** buscar; buscar con los ojos; (await) aguardar; (expect) esperar. **to l. forward,** mirar hacia el porvenir; pensar en el futuro; esperar con ilusión. **to l. in,** entrar por un instante, hacer una visita corta. **to l. into,** mirar dentro de; mirar hacia el interior de; estudiar, investigar, *Lat. Am. also* interiorizar. **to l. on,** *vt* mirar; considerar; (of buildings, etc.) dar a. *vi* ser espectador. **to l. on to,** dar a, mirar a. **to l. out,** *vi* (be careful) tener cuidado; (look through) mirar por; asomarse a. *vt* (search) buscar; (find) hallar; (choose) escoger, elegir. **L. out!** ¡Atención! ¡Ojo!, *Mexico* ¡abusado! **to l. out for,** buscar; (await) aguardar, esperar; (be careful) tener cuidado con. **to l. out of,** mirar por; asomarse a. **to l. over,** mirar bien; (persons) mirar de hito en hito; examinar; visitar; (a house) inspeccionar; (a book) hojear; mirar superficialmente. **to l. round,** *vt* (a place) visitar. *vi* volver la cabeza, volverse; mirar hacia atrás. **to l. round for,** buscar con los ojos; buscar por todas partes. **to l. through,** mirar por; mirar a través de; examinar; (search) registrar; (understand) registrar. **to l. to,** (be careful of) tener cuidado de; (attend to) atender a; (care for) cuidar de; (count on) contar con; (resort to) acudir a; (await) esperar. **to l. toward,** mirar hacia, mirar en la dirección de; caer a. **to l. up,** *vi* mirar hacia arriba; (aspire) aspirar; (improve) mejorar. *vt* visitar, ir (o venir) a ver; (turn up) buscar; averiguar. **to l. upon,** mirar. Other meanings see **to l. on.** **They l. upon her as their daughter,** La miran como a una hija suya. **to l. up to,** *fig* respetar

looking *a* (in compounds) de . . . aspecto, de . . . apariencia. **dirty-l.,** de aspecto sucio. **l.-glass,** espejo, *m*

lookout vigilancia, observación, *f;* (view) vista, *f,* panorama, *m;* (viewpoint) miradero, *m; mil* atalaya, *f; naut* gaviero, *m;* (*fig* prospect) perspectiva, *f*

loom *n* telar, *m, vi* asomar, aparecer

loop *n* (turn) vuelta, *f;* (in rivers, etc.) recodo, *m,* curva, *f;* (fold) pliegue, *m;* bucle, *m;* (fastening) fiador, *m,* presilla, *f; aer* rizo, *m;* (knot) nudo corredizo, *m.* **to l. the l.,** *aer* hacer el rizo, hacer rizos. **l.-line,** empalme de ferrocarril, *m*

loophole *n* saetera, aspillera, *f; fig* escapatoria, *f;* pretexto, *m,* excusa, *f*

loose *a* suelto; (free) libre; (slack) flojo; (of garments) holgado; (untied) desatado; (unfastened) desprendido; movible; (unchained) desencadenado; en libertad; (of the bowels) suelto (de vientre); (pendu-lous) colgante; (of a nail, tooth, etc.) inseguro; poco firme; que se mueve; (of knots, etc.) flojo; (of the mind, etc.) incoherente, ilógico; poco exacto; (of style, etc.) vago, impreciso; (of conduct) disoluto, vicioso; (careless) negligente, descuidado. *vt* (untie) desatar; desprender; soltar; aflojar; (of a priest) absolver; *fig* desencadenar. **to break l.,** desprenderse; soltarse; libertarse; escapar; *fig* desencadenarse. **to let l.,** desatar; aflojar; poner en libertad; soltar; *fig* desencadenar; (interject) lanzar. **to turn l.,** poner en libertad; dar salida (a); echar de casa, poner en la calle. **to work l.,** desprenderse; aflojarse; desencijarse. **l.-box,** caballeriza, *f.* **l. change,** suelto, *m.* **l.-leaf notebook,** libreta de hojas sueltas, *f*

loosely *adv* flojamente; sueltamente; (vaguely) vagamente; incorrectamente; incoherentemente; (carelessly) negligentemente; (viciously) disolutamente

loosen *vt* (untie) desatar; aflojar; soltar; desasir; (the tongue) desatar; *fig* hacer menos riguroso, ablandar

loot *n* botín, *m, vt* saquear

looter *n* saqueador (-ra)

looting *n* saqueo, pillaje, *m,* a saqueador

lop *vt* mochar; podar; destroncar; cortar de un golpe. *a* (of ears) gacho. **to lop off the ends,** cercenar. **to lop off the top,** desmochar. **lop-sided,** desproporcionado; desequilibrado

loquacious *a* locuaz, gárrulo

lord *n* señor, *m;* (husband) esposo, *m;* (English title) lord, *m,* (*pl* lores); (Christ) Señor, *m.* **feudal l.,** señor de horca y cuchillo, *m.* **my l.,** milord. **my lords,** milores. **Our L.,** Nuestro Señor. **the Lord's Prayer,** el Padrenuestro. **to l. it over,** mandar como señor, mandar a la baqueta. **L. Chamberlain,** camarero mayor, *m.* **L. Chancellor,** gran canciller, *m.* **L. Chief Justice,** presidente del tribunal supremo, *m.* **L.-Lieutenant,** virrey, *m.* **L. Mayor,** alcalde, *m.* **L. Privy Seal,** guardasellos del rey, *m*

lordly *a* señorial, señoril; altivo, arrogante

lore *n* saber, *m;* erudición, *f;* tradiciones, *f pl*

lose *vt* perder; hacer perder, quitar; (forget) olvidar. *vi* perder; (of clocks) atrasar. **to be lost in thought,** estar ensimismado, estar absorto. **to l. oneself (in)** perderse (en); abstraerse (en); entregarse (a). **to l. one's footing,** resbalar. **to l. one's way,** extraviarse, perder el camino. **to l. one's self-control,** perder el tino. **to l. one's head,** perder la cabeza. **to l. ground,** perder terreno. **to l. one's voice,** perder la voz. **to l. patience,** perder la paciencia, perder los estribos

loser *n* perdedor (-ra)

losing *a* perdedor. *n* pérdida, *f*

loss n pérdida, f. **at a l.**, com con pérdida; perplejo, dudoso. **heavy losses,** mil pérdidas cuantiosas, f pl. **loss of blood** Lat. Am. desangre m. **We are at a l. for words . . . ,** No tenemos palabras para . . .

lot n suerte, f; fortuna, f; lote, m; parte, porción, cuota, f; (for building) solar, m. **a lot of people,** muchas personas. **Our lot would have been very different,** Nuestra suerte hubiera sido muy distinta, Otro gallo nos cantara. **to draw lots,** echar suertes, sortear. **to take the lot,** inf alzarse con el santo y la limosna

lotion n loción, f

lottery n lotería, f. **l. ticket,** billete de la lotería, m

loud a fuerte; (noisy) ruidoso, estrepitoso; alto; (gaudy) chillón, llamativo, cursi, Lat. Am. also figuroso. adv ruidosamente. **l.-speaker,** rad altavoz, Mexico magnavoz, m

loudly adv en alta voz; fuertemente; ruidosamente, con estrépito

loudness n (noise) ruido, m; sonoridad, f; (force) fuerza, f; (of colors, etc.) mal gusto, m, vulgaridad, f

lounge n sala de estar, f; salón, m, vi reclinarse, ponerse a sus anchas; apoyarse (en); gandulear; vagar. **l. chair,** poltrona, f. **l.-lizard,** inf pollo pera, m. **l.-suit,** traje americano, m

lounger n holgazán (-ana); golfo (-fa), azotacalles, mf

louse n piojo, m

lousy a piojoso

lout n patán, zamacuco, m

loutish a rústico

lovable a amable; simpático

love n amor, m; (friendship) amistad, f; (enthusiasm, liking) afición, f; (in tennis) cero, m, vt querer, amar; gustar mucho; tener afición (a). vi estar enamorado. **I should l. to dine with you,** Me gustaría mucho cenar con Vds. **to be in l. with,** estar enamorado de. **to fall in l. with,** enamorarse de. **They l. each other,** Se quieren. **to make l. to,** hacer el amor (a), galantear. **l. affair,** amorío, lance de amor, m. **l.-bird,** periquito, m. **l.-letter,** carta amatoria, carta de amor, f. **l.-making,** galanteo, m. **l.-philtre,** filtro, m. **l.-song,** canción de amor, f. **l.-story,** historia de amor, f. **l.-token,** prenda de amor, f

lovely a hermoso, bello; delicioso; amable; inf estupendo

lover n amante, mf; aficionado (-da)

lovesick a enfermo de amor, enamorado

loving a amoroso; cariñoso; (friendly) amistoso; de amor

low a bajo; de poca altura; (of dresses, etc.) escotado; (of musical notes) grave; (soft) suave; (feeble) débil; (depressed) deprimido, triste, abatido; (plain) sen-

cillo; (of a fever) lento; (of a bow) profundo; pequeño; inferior; humilde; (ill) enfermo; (vile) vil, ruin; obsceno, escabroso. adv bajo; cerca de la tierra; en voz baja; (cheaply) barato, a bajo precio. **in a low voice,** en voz baja, paso. **to lay low,** (kill) tumbar; (knock down) derribar; incapacitar. **to lie low,** descansar; estar muerto; esconderse, agacharse; callar. **to run low,** escasear. **low-born,** de humilde cuna. **low-brow,** nada intelectual. **low comedy,** farsa, f. **low flying,** n bajo vuelo, m, a que vuela bajo; terrero, rastrero; que vuela a ras de tierra. **low frequency,** baja frecuencia, f. **low Latin,** bajo latín, m. **Low Mass,** misa rezada, f. **low neck,** escote, m. **low-necked,** escotado. **low-pitched,** grave. **low-spirited,** deprimido. **Low Sunday,** domingo de Cuasimodo, m. **low tension,** baja tensión, f. **low trick,** mala pasada, f. **low water,** marea baja, bajamar, f; (of rivers) estiaje, m

low vi berrear, mugir. n berrido, mugido, m

lower vt bajar; descolgar; disminuir; (price) rebajar; (a boat, sails) arriar. vi (of persons) fruncir el ceño, mostrarse malhumorado; (of the sky) encapotarse, cargarse; (menace) amenazar. **to l. a boat,** arriar un bote. **to l. oneself,** (by a rope, etc.) descolgarse. **to l. the flag,** abatir la bandera

lower a comp más bajo; menos alto; bajo; inferior. **l. classes,** clase obrera, f, clases bajas, f pl. **l. down,** más abajo. **L. House,** Cámara de los Comunes, f; cámara baja, f. **l. jaw,** mandíbula inferior, f. **l. storey,** piso bajo, m; piso de abajo, m

Lower California Baja California, f

lowest a sup el (la, etc.) más bajo; el (la, etc.) más profundo; ínfimo

lowland n tierra baja, f. **the Lowlands,** las tierras bajas de Escocia

lowly a humilde

lowness n poca altura, f; situación poco elevada, f; pequeñez, f; (of musical notes) gravedad, f; (softness) suavidad, f; (feebleness) debilidad, f; (sadness) tristeza, f; abatimiento, m; (of price) baratura, f; ferioridad, f; humildad, f; (vileness) bajeza, f; obscenidad, f

loyal a leal, fiel

loyalist n realista, mf; defensor (-ra) del gobierno legítimo

loyalty n lealtad, fidelidad, f

lozenge n pastilla, f

lubricant a and n lubricante m

lubricate vt lubricar, engrasar

lubricating oil n aceite lubricante, m

lubrication n lubricación, f, engrasado, m

lucid a lúcido; claro

luck *n* destino, azar, *m*; (good) buenaventura, suerte, *f*. **to bring bad l.,** traer mala suerte. **to try one's l.,** probar fortuna

luckily *adv* por fortuna, afortunadamente, felizmente

luckless *a* desdichado

lucky *a* afortunado; dichoso, venturoso, *Lat. Am. also* lechudo; feliz. **to be l.,** tener buena suerte

lucrative *a* lucrativo

lucre *n* lucro, *m*

lucubration *n* lucubración, *f*

ludicrous *a* absurdo, risible, ridículo

lug *n* tirón, *m*; (ear and projection) oreja, *f*, *vt* tirar (de); arrastrar. **to lug about,** arrastrar (por); llevar con dificultad. **to lug in,** arrastrar adentro; introducir; hacer entrar. **to lug out,** arrastrar afuera; hacer salir

luggage *n* equipaje, *m*. **excess l.,** exceso de equipaje, *m*. **piece of l.,** bulto, *m*. **to register one's l.,** facturar el equipaje. **l. carrier,** (on buses, etc.) baca, *f*; (on a car) portaequipajes, *m*. **l. porter,** mozo de equipajes, *m*. **l. rack,** (on a car) portaequipajes, *m*; (in a train) rejilla para el equipaje, *f*. **l. receipt,** talón de equipaje, *m*. **l. room,** consigna, *f*. **l. van,** furgón de equipajes, *m*

lugubrious *a* lúgubre

lukewarm *a* tibio, templado; *fig* indiferente, frío

lull *n* momento de calma, *m*; tregua, *f*; silencio, *m*, *vt* (a child) arrullar, adormecer; (soothe) sosegar, calmar; disminuir, mitigar

lullaby *n* canción de cuna, *f*

lumbago *n* lumbago, *m*

lumber *n* (wood) maderas de sierra, *f pl*; (rubbish) trastos viejos, *m pl*. *vt* amontonar trastos viejos; obstruir. *vi* andar pesadamente; avanzar ruidosamente, avanzar con ruido sordo. **l.-jack,** maderero, ganchero, *m*. **l.-room,** leonera, *f*. **l.-yard,** maderería, *f*, depósito de maderas, *m*

lumbering *a* pesado

luminary *n* lumbrera, *f*

luminous *a* luminoso

lump *n* masa, *f*; bulto, *m*; pedazo, *m*; (of sugar) terrón *m*; (swelling) hinchazón, *f*; protuberancia, *f*. *vt* amontonar. **to l. together,** mezclar; incluir. **in the l.,** en la masa; en grueso. **Let him l. it!** ¡Que se rasque! **l. in one's throat,** nudo en la garganta, *m*. **l. of sugar,** terrón de azúcar, *m*. **l. sum,** cantidad gruesa, *f*

lunacy *n* locura, *f*

lunar *a* lunar

lunatic *n* loco (-ca); demente, *mf* *a* de locos; loco. **l. asylum,** manicomio, *m*

lunch, luncheon *n* almuerzo, *m*, *Mexico* fajina, *f*; (snack) merienda, *f*. *vi* almorzar. **l. basket** or **pail,** fiambrera, *f*

lunch counter, luncheonette *Mexico* almuercería, *elsewhere in Lat. Am.* lonchería, *f*

lung *n* pulmón, *m*

lunge *n* (fencing) estocada, *f*; embestida, *f*, *vi* dar una estocada; abalanzarse sobre

lurch *n* sacudida, *f*; *naut* guiñada, *f*; tambaleo, *m*; movimiento brusco, *m*. *vi naut* guiñar; tambalearse; andar haciendo eses. **to leave in the l.,** dejar plantado

lure *n* añagaza, *f*; reclamo, *m*; aliciente, atractivo, *m*; seducción, *f*. *vt* atraer, tentar

lurid *a* misterioso, fantástico; cárdeno; ominoso; funesto, triste; (orange) anaranjado; (vicissitudinous) accidentado

lurk *vi* acechar, espiar; esconderse

lurking *a* (in ambush) en acecho; (of fear, etc.) vago

luscious *a* delicioso; suculento; meloso; atractivo, apetitoso; sensual

lush *a* jugoso; fresco y lozano; maduro

lust *n* lujuria, lascivia, *f*; codicia, *f*; deseo, *m*. **l. for revenge,** deseo de venganza, *m*

lustful *a* lujurioso, lúbrico, lascivo

luster *n* lustre, brillo, *m*; brillantez, *f*

lustrous *a* lustroso

lusty *a* vigoroso, fuerte, lozano

lute *n* laúd, *m*, vihuela, *f*. **l.-player,** vihuelista, *mf*

Lutheran *a* luterano. *n* luterano (-na)

luxuriance *n* lozanía, *f*; exuberancia, superabundancia, *f*

luxuriant *a* lozano; fértil; exuberante

luxuriate *vi* crecer con exuberancia; complacerse (en); disfrutar (de), gozar (de)

luxurious *a* lujoso

luxuriously *adv* lujosamente, con lujo

luxury *n* lujo, *m*. **l. goods,** artículos de lujo, *m pl*

lyceum *n* liceo, *m*

lye *n* lejía, *f*

lying *a* (recumbent) recostado; (untrue) mentiroso, falso. *n* mentiras, *f pl*. **l.-in,** parto, *m*

lymph *n* linfa, *f*; vacuna, *f*

lymphatic *a* linfático; flemático

lynch *vt* linchar

lynching *n* linchamiento, *m*

lynx *n* lince, *m*. **l.-eyed,** de ojos de lince

lyre *n* lira, *f*. **l.-bird,** pájaro lira, *m*

lyric *n* poesía lírica, *f*; poema lírico, *m*; letra (de una canción,) *f*

lyrical *a* lírico

lyricism *n* lirismo, *m*

M

m *n* (letter) eme, *f*
ma'am *n* señora, *f*
macabre *a* macabro
macadam *n* macadán, *m*, a de macadán
macadamize *vt* macadanizar
macaroni *n* macarrones, *m pl*
macaronic *a* macarrónico
macaroon *n* macarrón de almendras, *m*
macaw *n* macagua, *f*, guacamayo, *m*
mace *n* maza, *f*; *cul* macis, *f*. **m.-bearer,** macero, *m*
Macedonian *a* macedón, macedonio. *n* macedonio (-ia)
macerate *vt* macerar. *vi* macerarse
machete *n* Mexico alfanje, *elsewhere* machete, *m*
Machiavellian *a* maquiavélico
machination *n* maquinación, *f*
machine *n* máquina, *f*; mecanismo, *m*; aparato, *m*; instrumento, *m*; organización, *f*, *vt* trabajar a máquina; *sew* coser a máquina. **m.-gun,** *n* ametralladora, *f*. *vt* ametrallar. **m.-gun carrier,** portametralladoras, *m*. **m.-gunner,** ametrallador, *m*. **m.-made,** hecho a máquina. **m.-oil,** aceite de motores, *m*. **m.-shop,** taller de maquinaria, *m*, *Lat. Am.* maestranza, *f*. **m.-tool,** máquina herramienta, *f*
machinery *n* maquinaria, *f*; mecanismo, *m*; organización, *f*; sistema, *m*
mackerel *n* caballa, *f*. **m. sky,** cielo aborregado, *m*
mad *a* loco; fuera de sí; (of a dog, etc.) rabioso; furioso. **as mad as a hatter,** loco como una cabra. **to drive mad,** volver loco (a). **to go mad,** volverse loco, enloquecer, perder el seso. **mad with joy (pain),** loco de alegría (dolor). **mad dog,** perro rabioso, *m*
madam *n* señora, *f*; (French form) madama, *f*. **Yes, m.,** Sí señora
madcap *n* locuelo (-la), *f*, botarate, *m*; tarambana, *mf*
madden *vt* enloquecer; enfurecer, exasperar
maddening *a* exasperante, irritador
made *past part* and *a* hecho; formado. **self-m. man,** un hombre hecho y derecho. **m.-to-measure,** hecho a la medida. **m.-up,** compuesto; (of clothes) confeccionado, ya hecho; (of the face) pintado; (fictitious) inventado, ficticio; artificial
madhouse *n* casa de locos, *f*, manicomio, *m*
madman *n* loco, *m*
madness *n* locura, *f*; (of a dog, etc.) rabia, *f*; furia, *f*
Madonna *n* Madona, *f*
madrigal *n* madrigal, *m*

Madrilenian *a* madrileño, matritense. *n* madrileño (-ña)
madwoman *n* loca, *f*
Maecenas *n* mecenas, *m*
maelstrom *n* remolino, vórtice, *m*
magazine *n* (store) almacén, *m*; (for explosives) polvorín, *m*, santabárbara, *f*; (periodical) revista, *f*. **m. rifle,** rifle de repetición, *m*
maggot *n* gusano, *m*, cresa, *f*; *fig* manía, *f*, capricho, *m*
Magi, the *n pl* los reyes magos
magic *n* magia, *f*; mágica, *f*; *fig* encanto, *m*, a mágico. **as if by m.,** por ensalmo. **m. lantern,** linterna mágica, *f*
magically *adv* por encanto
magician *n* mago, mágico, brujo, *m*; (conjurer) jugador de manos, *m*
magisterial *a* magistral
magistracy *n* magistratura, *f*
magistrate *n* magistrado, *m*; juez municipal, *m*
Magna Charta *n* Carta Magna, *f*
magnanimity *n* magnanimidad, generosidad, *f*
magnanimous *a* magnánimo, generoso
magnate *n* magnate, *m*
magnesia *n* magnesia, *f*
magnet *n* imán, *m*
magnetic *a* magnético; *fig* atractivo. **m. field,** campo magnético, *m*. **m. needle,** brújula, *f*
magnetize *vt* magnetizar, imanar; (hypnotize) magnetizar; *fig* atraer
magnification *n* (by a lens, etc.) aumento, *m*; exageración, *f*
magnificence *n* magnificencia, *f*
magnificent *a* magnífico
magnify *vt* (by lens) aumentar; exagerar; (praise) magnificar
magnifying *a* de aumento, vidrio de aumento. **m. glass,** lente de aumento, *m*
magniloquent *a* grandílocuo
magnitude *n* magnitud, *f*
magnolia *n* magnolia, *f*
magnum *n* botella de dos litros, *f*
magpie *n* marica, picaza, *f*
mahogany *n* caoba, *f*, a de caoba
maid *n* doncella, muchacha, *f*; virgen, *f*; soltera, *f*; (servant) criada, *f*; (daily) asistenta, *f*. **old m.,** solterona, *f*. **m.-of-all-work,** criada para todo, *f*. **m.-of-honor,** dama de honor, *f*
maiden *n* doncella, joven, soltera, *f*; virgen, *f*; zagala, *f*. a de soltera; soltera *f*; virginal; (of speeches, voyages, etc.) primero. **m. lady,** dama soltera, *f*. **m.-name,** apellido de soltera, *m*. **m. speech,** primer discurso, *m*
maidenhood *n* doncellez, virginidad, *f*
maidenly *a* virginal; modesto, modoso; tímido
maidservant *n* criada, sirvienta, *f*

mail n mala, f; (bag) valija, f; correo, m; correspondencia, f; (armour) cota de malla, f. vt mandar por correo; armar con cota de malla. **coat of m.,** cota de malla, f. **royal m.,** malla real, f. **m.-bag,** valija de correo, f; portacartas, m. **m.-boat,** buque correo, m. **m.-cart,** ambulancia de correos, f. **m.-clad,** vestido de cota de malla; armado. **m.-coach,** coche correo, m, diligencia, f. **m.-order,** pedido postal, m. **m.-order business,** negocio de ventas por correo, m. **m.-plane,** avión postal, m. **m. service,** servicio de correos, m. **m. steamer,** vapor correo, m. **m. train,** tren correo, m. **m. van,** (on a train) furgón postal, m

mailed a de malla; armado. **m. fist,** fig puño de hierro, m

maim vt mancar; mutilar, tullir; estropear

maimed a manco; tullido, mutilado

main a mayor; principal; más importante, esencial; maestro. n (mainland) continente, m; (sea) océano, m; (pipe) cañería maestra, f. **by m. force,** por fuerza mayor. **in the m.,** en general, generalmente; en su mayoría. **m. beam,** viga maestra, f. **m. body,** (of a building) ala principal, f; (of a church) cuerpo (de iglesia), m; (of an army) cuerpo (del ejército), m; mayor parte, mayoría, f. **m. line,** línea principal, f. **m. mast,** palo mayor, m. **m. thing,** cosa principal, f, lo más importante. **m. wall,** pared maestra, f

mainland n continente, m; tierra firme, f

mainly adv principalmente; en su mayoría; generalmente

mainspring n (of a watch) muelle real, m; motivo principal, m; origen, m

mainstay n estay mayor, m; fig sostén principal, m

maintain vt mantener; sostener; tener; guardar; afirmar

maintenance n mantenimiento, m; manutención, f; sustento, m; conservación, f, subsistencia, f

maize n maíz, m. **m. field,** maizal, m

majestic a majestuoso

majesty n majestad, f; majestuosidad, f. **His** or **Her M.,** Su Majestad

majolica n mayólica, f

major a mayor; principal. n mayor de edad, m; mil comandante. **anthropology major,** alumno con la especialidad en antropología m. **m.-domo,** mayordomo, m. **m.-general,** general de división, m. **m. road,** carretera, f; ruta de prioridad, f. **m. scale,** escala mayor, f

Majorca Mallorca, f

majority n mayoría, f; mayor número, m; generalidad, f. **to have attained one's m.,** ser mayor de edad

make vt hacer; crear, formar; (manufacture) fabricar, confeccionar; construir; (produce) producir; causar; (prepare) preparar; (a bed, a fire, a remark, poetry, friends, enemies, war, a curtsey) hacer; (earn, win) ganar; (a speech) pronunciar; (compel) obligar (a), forzar (a); inclinar (a); (arrive at) alcanzar, llegar (a); (calculate) calcular; (arrange) arreglar; deducir; (be) ser; (equal) ser igual a; (think) creer; (appoint as) constituir (en), hacer; (behave) portarse (como). vi (begin) ir (a), empezar (a); (make as though) hacer (como si); (of the tide) crecer; contribuir (a); tender (a). **He made as if to go,** Hizo como si de marcharse. **to m. as though . . . ,** aparentar, fingir. **It made me ill,** Me hizo sentir mal. **They have made it up,** Han hecho las paces. **They m. a great deal of money,** Hacen (o ganan) mucho dinero. **You cannot m. me believe it,** No puedes hacerme creerlo. **He is making himself ridiculous,** Se está poniendo en ridículo. **to m. ready,** preparar. **to m. the tea,** hacer el té; preparar el té. **Two and two m. four,** Dos y dos son cuatro. **to m. oneself known,** darse a conocer. **to m. one of . . . ,** ser uno de . . . **to m. after,** seguir; correr detrás de. **to m. again,** hacer de nuevo, rehacer. **to m. angry** Mexico. amuinar. **to m. away with,** quitar; suprimir; destruir; (kill) matar; (squander) derrochar; (steal) llevarse; hurtar. **to m. away with oneself,** quitarse la vida, suicidarse. **to m. for,** encaminarse a, dirigirse a; (attack) abalanzarse sobre, atacar; (tend to) contribuir a, tender a. **to m. off,** marcharse corriendo, largarse; huir, escaparse. **to m. out,** (discern) distinguir; descifrar; (understand) comprender; (prove) probar, justificar; (draw up) redactar; (fill in a form) completar, llenar; (a check, etc.) extender; (an account) hacer; (get on, succeed or otherwise) ir (with bien o mal); (convey) dar la impresión de que; sugerir. **I cannot m. it out,** No lo puedo comprender. **How did you m. out** (get on)? ¿Cómo te fue? **to m. over,** hacer de nuevo, rehacer; (transfer) ceder, traspasar. **to m. up,** hacer; acabar; concluir; (clothes) confeccionar; fabricar; (the face) pintarse, maquillarse; (the fire) echar carbón, etc. a; print compaginar; (invent) inventar; (lies) fabricar; (compose) formar; (package) empaquetar; reparar; indemnizar; compensar; (an account) ajustar; preparar; arreglar; (conciliate) conciliar; enumerar; theat caracterizarse. **to m. up for,** reemplazar; compensar; (lost time, etc.) recobrar. **to m. up to,** compensar; indemnizar; (flatter) adular, halagar; procurar congraciarse con, procurar obtener el favor de; (court) galantear (con). **m. an impression (on),** dejar(le a fulano) una impresión

make n forma, f; hechura, f; estructura, f; confección, f; manufactura, f; producto, m; (trade name) marca, f; (character) carácter, temperamento, m. **m.-believe,** n artificio, pretexto, m, a fingido, vi fingir. **land of m.-believe,** reino de los sueños, m. **m.-up,** (for the face, etc.) maquillaje, m; theat caracterización, f; print imposi-

ción, f; (whole) conjunto, m; (character) carácter, modo de ser, m

maker n creador, m; autor (-ra); artífice, mf; (manufacturer) fabricante, m; constructor, m; (of clothes, etc.) confeccionador (-ra); (worker) obrero (-ra)

makeshift n expediente, m, a provisional

makeweight n añadidura (de peso), f, contrapeso, m; fig suplente, m

making n creación, f; hechura, f; (manufacture) fabricación, f; construcción, f; (of clothes, etc.) confección, f; formación, f; preparación, f; estructura, f; composición, f; pl **makings**, (profits) ganancias, f pl; (elements) elementos, m pl; germen, m; rasgos esenciales, m pl, características, f pl **m.-up**, (of clothes) confección, f; print ajuste, m; (of the face) maquillaje, m; (invention) invención, f; fabricación, f

maladjustment n mal ajuste, m; inadaptación, f

maladministration n desgobierno, m, mala administración, f; (of funds) malversación, f

maladroit a torpe

malady n enfermedad, f; mal, m

malaria n paludismo, m

malarial a palúdico. **m. fever**, fiebre palúdica, f

malcontent n malcontento (-ta). a descontento

male a macho; masculino. n macho, m; varón, m. **m. child**, niño, m; niño varón, m; (son) hijo varón, m. **m. flower**, flor masculina, f. **m. issue**, sucesión masculina, f. **m. nurse**, enfermero, m. **m. sex**, sexo masculino, m

malediction n maldición, f

malefic a maléfico

malevolence n malevolencia, f

malevolent a malévolo, maligno

malformation n formación anormal, deformidad, deformación congénita, f

malice n malicia, f; law alevosía, f. **to bear m.**, guardar rencor

malicious a malicioso; maligno, rencoroso

malign vt calumniar, difamar. a maligno; malévolo

malignant a maligno; malévolo; med maligno

malinger vi fingirse enfermo

malingerer n enfermo (-ma) fingido (-da)

mallard n pato (-ta), silvestre

malleable a maleable

mallet n mazo, m; (in croquet) pala, f, mazo, m; (in polo) maza (de polo), f

mallow n malva, f

malnutrition n desnutrición, alimentación deficiente, f

malodorous a de mal olor, hediondo, fétido

malpractice n (wrongdoing) maleficencia, f; (by a doctor) tratamiento equivocado, perjudicial o ilegal, m; (malversation) malversación, f; inmoralidad, f

malt n malta, m. vt preparar el malta. **m.-house**, fábrica de malta, f. **m. vinegar**, vinagre de malta, m

malted milk n leche malteada, f

maltreat vt maltratar

mamma n anat mama, f; (mother) mamá, f

mammal n mamífero, m

mammalian a mamífero

mammary a mamario. **m. gland**, mama, teta, f

mammoth n mamut, m, a gigantesco, enorme

man n hombre, m; varón, m; persona, f; (servant) criado, m; (workman) obrero, m; (soldier) soldado, m; (sailor) marinero, m; (humanity) raza humana, f; (husband) marido, m; (chess) peón, m; (checkers) dama, f; (a ship) buque, m. **no man**, nadie; ningún hombre. **young man**, joven, m. **to a man**, como un solo hombre. **to come to man's estate**, llegar a la edad viril. **Man overboard!** ¡Hombre al agua! **man and wife**, marido y mujer, m, cónyuges, esposos, m pl. **man about town**, hombre de mundo, señorito, m. **man-at-arms**, hombre de armas, m. **man-eater**, caníbal, mf; tigre, m. **man-eating**, a antropófago. **man hater**, misántropo, m; mujer que odia a los hombres, f. **man-hole**, pozo, m. **man-hunter**, caníbal, mf; (woman) castigadora, f. **man in charge**, encargado, m. **man in the moon**, mujer de la luna, f. **man in the street**, hombre de la calle, m. **man of letters**, hombre de letras, literato, m; **man of straw**, bausán, m; (figure-head) testaferro, m. **man of the world**, hombre del mundo, m. **man of war**, buque de guerra, m. **man-power**, mano de obra, f, brazos, m pl, (e.g. **lack of manpower**, falta de brazos, f). **man servant**, criado, m

man vt armar; mil poner guarnición (a); ocupar; naut tripular; dirigir; fig fortificar

manacle n manilla, f; pl **manacles**, esposas, f pl; grillos, m pl. vt poner esposas (a)

manage vt manejar; (animals) domar; dirigir; gobernar; administrar; (arrange) agenciar, arreglar; (work) explotar; (do) hacer; (eat) comer. vi arreglárselas (para); (get along) ir tirando; (know how) saber hacer; (succeed in) lograr; (do) hacer

manageable a manejable; flexible; (of persons, animals) dócil

management n manejo, m; dirección, f; gobierno, m; administración, f; arreglo, m; (working) explotación, f; com gerencia, f; theat empresa, f; conducta, f; (economy) economía, f; (skill) habilidad, f; prudencia, f. **the m.**, la dirección, el cuerpo de directores. **domestic m.,** economía doméstica, *f*

manager *n* director, *m*; administrador, *m*; jefe, *m*; *theat* empresario, *m*; *com* gerente, *m*; regente, *m*. **She is not much of a m.,** No es muy mujer de su casa. **manager's office,** dirección, *f*

managerial *a* directivo; administrativo. **m. board,** junta directiva, *f*

managership *n* puesto de director, *m*; jefatura, *f*

managing *a* directivo; (officious) mandón, dominante; (niggardly) tacaño

mandarin *n* mandarín, *m*; (language) mandarina, *f*. **m. orange,** mandarina, *f*

mandate *n* mandato, *m*. **mandated territory,** territorios bajo mandato, *m pl*

mandatory *a* obligatorio

mandible *n* mandíbula, *f*

mandolin *n* bandolín, *m*, bandurria, *f*

mane *n* melena, *f*; (of a horse) crines, *f pl*

maneuver *n* maniobra, *f*. *vi* maniobrar, hacer maniobras. *vt* hacer maniobrar; manipular

maneuvering *n* maniobras, *f pl*; maquinaciones, intrigas, *f pl*

manfully *adv* valientemente; vigorosamente

mange *n* sarna, *f*; (in sheep) roña, *f*

manger *n* pesebre, *m*

mangle *n* (for clothes) exprimidor de la ropa, *m*. *vt* pasar por el exprimidor; (mutilate) mutilar, lacerar, magullar; (a text) mutilar

mango *n* mango, *m*

mangy *a* sarnoso

manhandle *vt* maltratar

manhood *n* virilidad, *f*; edad viril, *f*; masculinidad, *f*; los hombres; (manliness) hombradía, *f*, valor, *m*

mania *n* manía, *f*; obsesión, *f*; capricho, *m*, chifladura, *f, Lat. Am.* barreno *m*

maniac *n* maníaco (-ca). *a* maníaco, maniático

manicure *n* manicura, *f*. *vt* arreglar las uñas. **m.-set,** estuche de manicura, *m*

manicurist *n* manicuro (-ra)

manifest *n naut* manifiesto, *m*. *vt* mostrar; hacer patente, probar; manifestarse. *vi* publicar un manifiesto; (of spirits) manifestarse. *a* manifiesto, evidente, claro, patente. **to make m.,** poner de manifiesto

manifestation *n* manifestación, *f*

manifestly *adv* evidentemente, manifiestamente

manifesto *n* manifiesto, *m*

manifold *a* múltiple; numeroso; diverso, vario

manikin *n* enano, *m*; muñeco, *m*; *art* maniquí, *m*

manipulate *vt* manipular

manipulative *a* manipulador

mankind *n* humanidad, raza humana, *f*, género humano, *m*

manlike *a* de hombre, masculino; varonil; (of a woman) hombruno

manliness *n* masculinidad, hombradía, *f*; virilidad, *f*; valor, *m*; (of a woman) aire hombruno, *m*

manly *a* masculino, de hombre; varonil, viril; valiente; fuerte. **to be very m.,** ser muy hombre, ser todo un hombre

manna *n* maná, *m*

mannequin *n* maniquín, modelo, *f*. **m. parade,** exposición de modelos, *f*

manner *n* manera, *f*, modo, *m*; aire, porte, *m*; conducta, *f*; (style) estilo, *m*; (sort) clase, *f*; *gram* modo, *m*; *pl* **manners,** modales, *m pl*, crianza, educación, *f*; (customs) costumbres, *f pl*. **after the m. of,** en (or según) el estilo de. **in a m. of speaking,** en cierto modo, para decirlo así. **in this m.,** de este modo. **to have bad (good) manners,** tener malos (buenos) modales, ser mal (bien) criado. **the novel of manners,** la novela de costumbres

mannered *a* amanerado; (in compounds) . . . educado, de . . . modales; de costumbres . . . **well-m.,** bien educado, de buenos modales

mannerism *n* amaneramiento, *m*; afectación, *f*; *theat* latiguillo, *m*. **to acquire mannerisms,** amanerarse

mannerly *a* cortés, bien educado, atento

mannish *a* (of a woman) hombruno; de hombre, masculino

manor *n* feudo, *m*; finca, hacienda, *f*; casa solariega, *f*; señorío, *m*

manorial *a* señorial

mansion *n* mansión, *f*; casa solariega, *f*; hotel, *m*. **m.-house,** casa solariega, *f*; residencia del alcalde de Londres, *f*

manslaughter *n* homicidio, *m*; *law* homicidio sin premeditación, *m*

mantelpiece *n* repisa de chimenea, *f*

mantilla *n* mantilla, *f*

mantle *n* capa, *f*, manto, *m*; *fig* cobertura, *f*; (gas) camiseta, *f*, manguito, *mf*; *zool* manto, *m*. *vt* cubrir; envolver; ocultar. *vi* extenderse; (of blushes) inundar, subirse (a las mejillas)

manual *a* manual. *n* manual, *m*; *mus* teclado de órgano, *m*. **m. work,** trabajo manual, *m*

manufactory *n* fábrica, *f*, taller, *m*

manufacture *n* fabricación, *f*; manufactura, *f*. *vt* manufacturar, fabricar

manufacturer *n* fabricante, industrial, *m*. **manufacturer's price,** precio de fábrica, *m*

manufacturing *a* manufacturero, fabril. *n* fabricación, *f*

manure *n* estiércol, abono, *m*. *vt* estercolar, abonar. **m. heap,** estercolero, *m*

manuring *n* estercoladura, *f*

manuscript n manuscrito, m, a manuscrito

many a muchos (-as); numeroso; diversos (-as); varios (-as). n muchos (-as); la mayoría; las masas; muchedumbre, multitud, f. **a great m.,** muchísimos, m pl, muchísimas, f pl; un gran número. **as m. as . . . ,** tantos como . . . **How m. are there?** ¿Cuántos hay? ¿Cuántas hay? **m. a time,** muchas veces. **three too m.,** tres de más. **for m. long years,** por largos años. **m.-colored,** multicolor. **m.-headed,** con muchas cabezas. **m.-sided,** multilátero; polifacético; complicado

map n mapa, m; plano, m; (chart) carta, f, vt hacer un mapa (or plano) de. **to map out,** surv apear; trazar; (plan) proyectar. **ordnance map,** mapa del estado mayor, m. **map of the world,** mapamundi, mapa del mundo, m. **map-making,** cartografía, f

maple n (tree) arce, m; (wood) madera de arce, f. **m.-syrup,** jarabe de arce, m

mapping n cartografía, f

maquiladora n maquiladora, f

mar vt estropear; desfigurar; (happiness) destruir, aguar; frustrar

maraca n Lat. Am. alfandoque, m

marauder n merodeador, m

marauding a merodeador, n merodeo, m

marble n mármol, m; (for playing with) canica, f, a de marmol, marmóreo; fig insensible; (of paper, etc.) jaspeado. vt jaspear. **m. cutter,** marmolista, m. **m. works,** marmolería, f

March n marzo, m. **as mad as a M. hare,** loco como una cabra, loco de atar

march n marcha, f; (step) paso, m; fig marcha, f, progreso, m. **forced m.,** marcha forzada, f. **quick m.,** paso doble, m. **to steal a m. on,** tomar la delantera (a), ganar por la mano (a). **to strike up a m.,** batir la marcha. **m.-past,** desfile, m

march vi marchar; (of properties) lindar (con). vt hacer marchar, poner en marcha (a). **to m. back,** vi regresar (or volver) a pie. vt hacer volver a pie. **to m. in,** entrar (a pie) en. **to m. off,** marcharse. **to m. on,** seguir marchando; seguir adelante; avanzar. **to m. past,** desfilar ante

marching n marcha, f. a en marcha; de marcha. **to receive one's m. orders,** recibir la orden de marchar; inf ser despedido. **m. order,** orden de marcha, m. **m. song,** canción de marcha, f

mardi gras n martes de carnaval, m

mare n yegua, f

margarine n margarina, f

margin n borde, lado, m, orilla, f; (of a page) margen, mf; reserva, f; sobrante, m. **in the m.,** al margen

marginal a marginal. **m. note,** acotación, nota marginal, f

marihuana n marijuana, f. Lat. Am. cáñamo m

marine a marino, de mar; marítimo; naval. n (fleet) marina, f; (soldier) soldado de marina, m. **Tell that to the marines!** ¡Cuéntaselo a tu tía! **mercantile m.,** marina mercante, f. **m. forces,** infantería de marina, f. **m. insurance,** seguro marítimo, m

mariner n marinero, marino, m. **mariner's compass,** aguja de marear, brújula, f

marionette n marioneta, f, títere, m

marital a marital

maritime a marítimo

mark n marca, f; señal, f; mancha, f; impresión, f; (target) blanco, m; (standard) norma, f; (level) nivel, m; (distinction) importancia, distinción, f; (in examinations) nota, f; calificación, f; (signature) cruz, f; (coin) marco, m. vt marcar; señalar; (price) poner precio (a); (notice) observar, darse cuenta (de); (characterize) caracterizar. **trade-m.,** marca de fábrica, f. **to be beside the m.,** no dar en el blanco; errar el tiro; fig no tener nada que ver con; equivocarse. **to hit the m.,** dar en el blanco; fig dar en el clavo. **to make one's m.,** firmar con una cruz; distinguirse. **to m. time,** marcar el paso; fig hacer tiempo. **to m. down,** (a person) señalar; escoger; (in price) rebajar. **to m. out,** marcar; trazar; definir; (erase) borrar; (a person) escoger; destinar **m. somebody absent,** ponerle a fulano su ausencia. **m. somebody present,** ponerle a fulano su asistencia.

marked a marcado; señalado; notable; acentuado; particular, especial. **He speaks with a m. Galician accent,** Habla con marcado acento gallego

markedly adv marcadamente; notablemente; especialmente, particularmente

marker n (billiards) marcador, m; (football, etc.) tanteador, m

market n mercado, m; tráfico, m; venta, f; (price) precio, m; (shop) bazar, emporio, m. vt and vi comprar en un mercado; vender en un mercado. **black m.,** mercado negro, estraperlo, m. **open m.,** mercado al aire libre, m; fig mercado libre, m. **m. day,** día de mercado, m. **m. garden,** huerto, m, huerta, f. **m. gardener,** hortelano, m. **m.-place,** plaza de mercado, f; fig mercado, m. **m. price,** precio corriente, m. **m. stall,** tabanco, puesto de mercado, m. **m.-woman,** verdulera, f

marketable a comerciable, vendible; corriente

marketing n venta, f; compra en un mercado, f; mercado, m. **to go m.,** ir al mercado

marking n marca, f; (spot on animals, etc.) pinta, f. **m.-ink,** tinta de marcar, f. **m.-iron,** ferrete, hierro de marcar, m

marksman *n* tirador (-ra)

marksmanship *n* puntería, *f*

marmalade *n* mermelada de naranjas amargas, *f*

marmoset *n* tití, *m*

maroon *n* (color) marrón, *m*; (slave) cimarrón (-ona); (firework) petardo, *m*. **a de** marrón. *vt* abandonar, dejar

marquee *n* marquesina, *f*

marriage *n* matrimonio, *m*; unión, *f*; (wedding) boda, *f*, casamiento, *m*. **by m.,** (of relationship) político. **She is an aunt by m.,** tía política. **m. articles,** capitulaciones (matrimoniales), *f pl.* **m. contract,** contrato matrimonial, *m*. **m. license,** licencia de casamiento, *f*. **m. portion,** dote, *mf*. **m. rate,** nupcialidad, *f*. **m. register,** acta matrimonial, *f*. **m. song,** epitalamio, *m*

marriageable *a* casadero

married *past part* and *a* casado; matrimonial, conyugal. **newly-m. couple,** los recién casados. **to get m. to,** casarse con. **m. couple,** matrimonio, *m*, cónyuges, *m pl.* **m. life,** vida conyugal, *f*

married name *n* nombre de casada, *f*

marrow *n* tuétano, *m*, médula, *f*; *fig* meollo, *m*. **to the m. of one's bones,** hasta los tuétanos.

marrowbone *n* hueso medular, *m*. **on one's marrowbones,** de rodillas

marry *vt* casarse con, contraer matrimonio con; casar; (of a priest) unir en matrimonio; *fig* juntar, unir. *vi* casarse. **to m. again,** volver a casarse

marsh *n* marjal, pantano, *Central America* chagüe, *m*. **m.-mallow,** *bot* malvavisco, *m*. **m. marigold,** calta, *f*

marshal *n* mariscal, *m*, *vt* poner en orden, arreglar; dirigir. **field-m.,** capitán general de ejército, *m*

mart *n poet* plaza de mercado, *f*; mercado, *m*; emporio, *m*; (auction rooms) martillo, *m*

martial *a* militar; marcial, belicoso. **m. array,** orden de batalla, *m*. **m. law,** derecho militar, *m*; estado de guerra, *m*. **m. spirit,** marcialidad, *f*, espíritu belicoso, *m*

martinet *n mil* ordenancista, *m*; rigorista, *mf*

Martinique Martinica, *f*

martyr *n* mártir, *mf vt* martirizar

martyrdom *n* martirio, *m*

marvel *n* maravilla, *f*. **to m. at,** maravillarse de, admirarse de

marvelous *a* maravilloso

marvelousness *n* maravilla, *f*, carácter maravilloso, *m*, lo maravilloso

marzipan *n* mazapán, *m*

mascot *n* mascota, *f*

masculine *a* masculino; varonil, macho; de hombre; (of a woman) hombruno. *n* masculino, *m*

masculinity *n* masculinidad, *f*

mash *n* mezcla, *f*; amasijo, *m*; pasta, *f*, puré, *m*. *vt* mezclar; amasar. **mashed potatoes,** puré de patatas (de papas), *m*

mask *n* máscara, *f*; antifaz, *m*; (death) mascarilla, *f*; (person) máscara, *mf*. *vt* enmascarar; *fig* encubrir, disimular. *vi* ponerse una máscara; disfrazarse. **masked ball,** *n* baile de máscaras, *m*

masochism *n* masoquismo, *m*

mason *n* albañil, *m*; (freemason) francmasón, masón, *m*

masonic *a* masónico. **m. lodge,** logia de francmasones, *f*

masonry *n* (trade) albañilería, *f*; mampostería, *f*

masque *n* mascarada, *f*

masquerade *n* mascarada, *f*

masquerader *n* máscara, *mf*

mass *n* misa, *f*. **to hear m.,** oír misa. **to say m.,** celebrar misa. **high m.,** misa mayor, *f*. **low m.,** misa rezada, *f*. **m. book,** libro de misa, *m*

mass *n* masa, *f*; (shape) bulto, *m*; (heap) montón, *m*; (great number) muchedumbre, *f*; (cloud of steam, etc.) nube, *f*. *vt* amasar; *mil* concentrar. *vi* congregarse en masa. **in a m.,** en masa; en conjunto. **the m. (of) . . . ,** la mayoría (de) **. . . the masses,** las masas, el vulgo, el pueblo. **m. formation,** columna cerrada, *f*. **m.-meeting,** mitin, mitin popular, *m*. **m.-production,** fabricación en serie, *f*

massacre *n* matanza, carnicería, *f*, *vt* hacer una carnicería (de)

massage *n* masaje, *m*; (friction) fricción, *f*. *vt* dar un masaje (a)

masseur, masseuse *n* masajista, *mf*

massive *a* macizo; sólido

mast *n naut* palo, árbol, *m*; (for wireless) mástil, *m*; poste, *m*; (beech) hayuco, *m*; (oak) bellota, *f*. *vt naut* arbolar. **at half-m.,** a media asta. **m.-head,** calcés, tope, *m*

masted *a* arbolado; (in compounds) de **. . .** palos

master *n* (of the house, etc.) señor, amo, *m*; maestro, *m*; *naut* patrón, *m*; (owner) dueño, *m*; (teacher) profesor, maestro, *m*; (young master and as address) señorito, *m*; director, *m*; jefe, *m*; (expert) perito, *m*; (of a military order) maestre, *m*, a maestro; superior. *vt* dominar; ser maestro en; dominar, conocer a fondo. **This picture is by an old m.,** Este cuadro es de un gran maestro antiguo. **to be m. of oneself,** ser dueño de sí. **to be one's own m.,** ser dueño de sí mismo; trabajar por su propia cuenta; ser independiente; estar libre. **m. builder,** maestro de obras, *m*. **m. hand,** mano maestra, *f*. **M. of Arts,** maestro (-tra) en artes. **M. of Ceremonies,** maestro de ceremonias, *m*. **M. of Foxhounds,** cazador mayor, *m*. **M. of the Horse,** caballerizo mayor del rey, *m*. **M. of the Rolls,**

archivero mayor, *m.* **m.-key,** llave maestra, *f.* **m. mind,** águila, *f,* ingenio, *m.* **m. stroke,** golpe maestro, *m*

masterful *a* imperioso, dominante; autoritario, arbitrario

masterliness *n* maestría, *f;* excelencia, *f;* perfección, *f*

masterly *a* maestro; excelente; perfecto. **m. performance,** obra maestra, *f; theat* representación perfecta, *f;* ejecución excelente, *f*

masterpiece *n* obra maestra, *f*

master plan *n* plan regulador, *m*

masterstroke *n* golpe magistral, golpe de maestro, *m*

mastery *n* dominio, *m;* autoridad, *f;* poder, *m;* ventaja, *f;* superioridad, maestría, *f;* conocimiento profundo, *m.* **to gain the m. of,** hacerse el señor de; llegar a dominar

mastic *n* masilla, almáciga, *f*

masticate *vt* masticar, mascar

mastiff *n* mastín, alano, *m*

mastoid *a* mastoides. *n* apófisis mastoides, *f*

masturbate *vi* masturbarse

masturbation *n* masturbación, *f*

mat *n* esterilla, *f;* alfombrilla, *f;* (on the table) tapete individual, *m. vt* (tangle) enmarañar, desgreñar. *vi* enmarañarse

match *n sport* partido, *m;* (wrestling, boxing) lucha, *f;* (fencing) asalto, *m;* (race) carrera, *f;* (contest) concurso, *m;* (equal) igual, *mf;* (pair) pareja, *f;* compañero (-ra); (marriage) boda, *f,* casamiento, *m;* (for lighting) cerilla, *f,* fósforo, *Mexico* cerillo, *m;* (for guns) mecha, *f. vt* competir con; (equal) igualar; ser igual (a); hacer juego con; emparejar, aparear; armonizar. *vi* ser igual; hacer juego; armonizarse. **good m.,** *inf* buen partido, *m.* **as thin as a m.,** más delgado que una cerilla. **to meet one's m.,** dar con la horma de su zapato. **to play a m.,** jugar un partido. **m.-box,** cajita de cerillas, fosforera, *f.* **m.-seller,** fosforero (-ra)

matchless *a* incomparable, sin igual, sin par

mate *n* compañero, camarada, *m;* (spouse) compañero (-ra), pareja, *f;* (on merchant ships) piloto, *m;* (at chess) mate, *m. vt* (marry) casar, desposar; (animals, birds) aparear, acoplar; (chess) dar jaque mate (a). *vi* casarse; aparearse, acoplarse

maté *n* maté, té del Paraguay, *m*

material *a* material; importante, esencial; considerable; sensible, notable; grave. *n* material, *m;* materia, *f;* (fabric) tela, *f;* tejido, *m.* **raw materials,** materias primas, *f pl.* **writing materials,** utensilios de escritorio, *m pl;* papel de escribir, *m*

materiality *n* materialidad, *f;* importancia, *f*

materialize *vt* materializar

maternal *a* materno, maternal. **m. grandparents,** abuelos maternos; *m pl*

maternity *n* maternidad, *f.* **m. center,** centro de maternidad, *m.* **m. hospital,** casa de maternidad, *f*

mathematical *a* matemático

mathematician *n* matemático, *m*

mathematics *n pl;* matemáticas, *f pl.* **applied m.,** matemáticas prácticas, *f pl.* **higher m.,** matemáticas superiores, *f pl.* **pure m.,** matemáticas teóricas, *f pl*

matinee *n* función de tarde, *f*

mating *n* (of animals) apareamiento, acoplamiento, *m;* unión, *f;* casamiento, *m*

matins *n pl ecc* maitines, *m pl*

matriarch *n* matriarca, *f*

matriculate *vt* matricular. *vi* matricularse

matrimonial *a* matrimonial, de matrimonio; marital. **m. agency,** agencia de matrimonios, *f*

matrimony *n* matrimonio, *m*

matrix *n* matriz, *f*

matron *n* matrona, mujer casada, madre de familia, *f;* (of a hospital) matrona, *f;* (of a school) ama de llaves, *f;* directora, *f.* **m. of honor,** (at a wedding) madrina, *f*

matted *a* enmarañado, enredado

matter *n* materia, *f;* substancia, *f;* caso, *m;* cuestión, *f;* asunto, *m;* causa, *f;* (distance) distancia, *f;* (amount) cantidad, *f;* (duration) espacio de tiempo, *m;* (importance) importancia, *f; med* pus, *m; pl* **matters,** asuntos, *m pl,* etc.; situación, *f.* **as if nothing were the m.,** como si no hubiese pasado nada. **for that m.,** en cuanto a eso. **grey m.,** substancia gris, *f.* **in the m. of,** en el caso de. **It is a m. of taste,** Es cuestión de gusto. **printed m.,** impresos, *m pl.* **What is the m.?** ¿Qué pasa? ¿Qué hay? **What is the m. with him?** ¿Qué tiene? ¿Qué le pasa? **m.-of-course,** cosa natural, *f.* **m.-of-fact,** práctico; sin imaginación; positivista. **m. of fact,** *n* hecho positivo, *m,* realidad, *f.* **As a m. of fact . . . ,** En realidad . . . , El caso es que . . . **m. of form,** cuestión de fórmula, *f;* pura formalidad, *f*

matter *vi* importar; (discharge) supurar. **What does it m.?** ¿Qué importa? **It doesn't m.,** Es igual, No importa, Da lo mismo

mattress *n* colchón, *m.* **spring-m.,** colchón de muelles, *m.* **m.-maker,** colchonero, *m*

mature *a* maduro; *com* vencido. *vt* madurar. *vi* madurarse; *com* vencer

maturity *n* madurez, *f;* edad madura, *f;* (com of a bill) vencimiento, *m*

maudlin *a* sensiblero; lacrimoso; (tipsy) calamocano

maul *vt* maltratar; herir

mausoleum *n* mausoleo, *m*

mauve n color purpúreo delicado, color de malva, m, a de color de malva

maw n (of a ruminant) cuajar, m; (of a bird) buche, m; fig abismo, m

mawkish a insípido, insulso; sensiblero; asqueroso

maxim n máxima, f

maximum a máximo. n máximo, m

may v aux poder; ser posible; (expressing wish, hope) ojalá que . . . , Dios quiera que . . . , or the present subjunctive may be used, e.g. **May you live many years!** i(qué) Viva Vd. muchos años! (to denote uncertainty, the future tense of the verb is often used, e.g. **You may perhaps remember the date,** Vd. quizás se acordará de la fecha. **Who may he be?** ¿Quién será?) **May God grant it!** i(que) Dios lo quiera! **It may be that . . . ,** Puede ser que . . . , Es posible que . . . , Quizás . . . **He may come on Saturday,** Es posible que venga el sábado; Puede venir el sábado. **May I come in?** ¿Puedo entrar? ¿Se puede entrar? **May I come and see you?** ¿Me das permiso para hacerte una visita? ¿Me dejas venir a verte? **May I go then?** ¿Puedo irme pues? ¿Tengo permiso para marcharme entonces?

May n mayo, m; fig abril, m; bot espina blanca, f. **May Day,** primero de mayo, m. **mayflower,** flor del cuclillo, f. **mayfly,** cachipolla, f. **May queen,** maya, f

maybe adv quizás, tal vez

mayonnaise n mayonesa, f. **m. sauce,** salsa mayonesa, f

mayor n alcalde, Argentina intendente, m

mayoral a de alcalde

mayoralty n Argentina intendencia f

mayoress n alcaldesa, f

maze n laberinto, m; fig perplejidad, f. vt dejar perplejo, aturdir

me pron me; (after a preposition only) mí. **They sent it for me,** Lo mandaron para mí. **Dear me!** iAy de mí!

meadow n prado, m, pradera, f. **m.-sweet,** rêina de los prados, f

meager a magro, enjuto, flaco; (scanty) exiguo, escaso, insuficiente; pobre; fig árido

meal n comida, f; (flour) harina, f. **to have a good m.,** comer bien. **test m.,** med comida de prueba, f. **m.-time,** hora de comida, f

mealy a harinoso; (of the complexion) pastoso

mean a (middle) medianero; (average) mediano; (humble) humilde; pobre; inferior; bajo, vil, ruin; (avaricious) tacaño, mezquino, Argentina agalludo, Chile, Peru coñete, **m.-spirited,** vil, de alma ruin

mean n medio, m; medianía, f; pl **means,** medio, m; expediente, m; medios, m pl; (financial) recursos, m pl; modo, m, manera, f. **by all means,** por todos los me-

dios; (certainly) iya lo creo! ino faltaba más! inaturalmente! **by means of,** mediante, por medio de; con la ayuda de. **by no means,** de ningún modo; nada. **by some means,** de algún modo, de alguna manera

mean vt destinar (para); pretender, proponerse; intentar, pensar; querer decir, significar; importar; (wish) querer; (concern, speak about) tratarse (de). vi tener el propósito, tener la intención. **I did not m. to do it,** Lo hice sin querer. **What does this word m.?** ¿Qué significa esta palabra? **What do you m. by that?** ¿Qué quieres decir con eso? **This portrait is meant to be Joan,** Este retrato quiere ser Juana. **What do they m. to do?** ¿Qué piensan (or se proponen) hacer? **Do you really m. it?** ¿Lo dices en serio? **Charles always means well,** Carlos siempre tiene buenas intenciones

meander n meandro, serpenteo, m; camino tortuoso, m, vi serpentear; errar, vagar; (in talk) divagar

meandering n meandros, m pl, serpenteo, m; (in talk) divagaciones, f pl, a serpentino, tortuoso

meaning n intención, voluntad, f; significación, f, significado, m; (of words) acepción, f; (sense) sentido, m; (thought) pensamiento, m. a significante. **double m.,** doble intención, f. **He gave me a m. look,** Me miró con intención. **What is the m. of it?** ¿Qué significa? ¿Qué quiere decir?

meaningful a significante

meaningless a sin sentido; insensato; insignificante

meaningly adv significativamente; con intención

meanness n pobreza, f; inferioridad, f; mediocridad, f; bajeza, ruindad, f; (stinginess) mezquindad, tacañería, Lat. Am. also lechería, f

meantime, meanwhile n ínterin, m, adv entre tanto, mientras tanto, a todo esto. **in the m.,** mientras tanto, en el ínterin

measles n sarampión, m. **German m.,** rubéola, f

measurable a mensurable

measure n medida, f; capacidad, f; (for measuring) regla, f; número, m; proporción, f; (limit) límite, m; (fig step) medida, f; (metre) metro, m; mus compás, m; (degree) grado, m; manera, f; (parliamentary) proyecto (de ley), m. vt medir; proporcionar, distribuir; (water) aforar; (land) apear; (height of persons) tallar; (for clothes) tomar las medidas (a); (judge) juzgar; (test) probar; (poet traverse) recorrer. **a suit made to m.,** un traje hecho a medida. **in great m.,** en gran parte, en alto grado. **in some m.,** hasta cierto punto. **to m. one's length,** caer tendido. **to take a person's m.,** fig tomar las medidas (a). **to m. up to,** fig estar al nivel de, ser igual a

measured a mesurado, moderado; uniforme; limitado. **to walk with m. tread,** andar a pasos contados

measurement n medición, f; medida, f; dimensión, f

meat n carne, f; (food) alimento, m; (meal) comida, f; fig substancia, f. **to sit at m.,** estar a la mesa. **cold meats,** fiambres, m pl. **m.-ball,** albóndiga, f. **m.-chopper,** picador, m. **m.-dish,** fuente, f. **m.-eater,** comedor (-ra) de carne. **m. extract,** carne concentrada, f. **m.-market,** carnicería, f. **m.-pie,** pastel de carne, m. **m.-safe,** fresquera, f

meaty a carnoso; fig substancial

mechanic n mecánico, m

mechanical a mecánico; maquinal

mechanical pencil n lapicero, m

mechanics n mecánica, f

mechanism n mecanismo, m; (philosophy) mecanicismo, m

mechanize vt convertir en máquina; (gen. mil) mecanizar; motorizar

medal n medalla, f

medallion n medallón, m

meddle vi tocar; meterse (con or en); entremeterse, inmiscuirse; intrigar

meddler n entremetido (-da); intrigante, mf

meddlesome a entremetido; oficioso; impertinente; enredador, intrigante. **to be very m.,** meterse en todo

media, the los medios informativos, m pl

median a del medio

mediate vi intervenir, mediar, arbitrar; abogar (por). a medio; interpuesto

mediation n mediación, intervención, f; intercesión, f; interposición, f

mediator n mediador (-ra); arbitrador, m; intercesor (-ra)

medical a médico; de medicina; de médico. n inf estudiante de medicina, m. **Army M. Service,** Servicio de Sanidad Militar, m. **m. books,** libros de medicina, m pl. **m. examination,** examen médico, m, exploración médica, f. **m. jurisprudence,** medicina legal, f. **m. knowledge,** conocimientos médicos, m pl. **m. practitioner,** médico (-ca). **m. school,** escuela de medicina, f

medicament n medicamento, m

medicate vt medicar; medicinar

medication n medicación, f

medicinal a medicinal

medicine n medicina, f; medicamento, m; (charm) ensalmo, hechizo, m. **patent m.,** específico farmacéutico, m. **m. ball,** balón medical, m. **m. chest,** botiquín, m. **m. man,** hechizador, m

medieval a medieval

mediocre a mediocre

meditate vt idear, proyectar, meditar. vi meditar, reflexionar; pensar, intentar

meditation n meditación, f

meditative a meditabundo, contemplativo; de meditación

Mediterranean a mediterráneo. n Mar Mediterráneo, m

medium n medio, m; (cooking) término medio, a medio cocer, a medio asar, m; (environment) medio ambiente, m; (agency) intermediario, m; (spiritualism) médium, m; art medio, m, a mediano; regular; mediocre. **through the m. of,** por medio de. **m.-sized,** de tamaño regular

medlar n (fruit) níspola, f; (tree) níspero, m

medley n mezcla, f; miscelánea, f, a mezclado, mixto

medulla n medula, f

meek a dulce, manso; humilde; modesto; pacífico

meekly adv mansamente; humildemente; modestamente

meet vt encontrar; encontrarse con; tropezar con; (by arrangement) reunirse con; (make the acquaintance of) conocer (a); (satisfy) satisfacer; cumplir (con); (a bill) pagar, saldar; (refute) refutar; (fight) batirse (con); (confront) hacer frente (a). vi juntarse; encontrarse; reunirse; verse; (of rivers) confluir. n montería, f, a conveniente. **I shall m. you at the station,** Te esperaré en la estación. **Until we m. again!** ¡Hasta la vista! **to go to m.,** ir al encuentro de. **to m. half-way,** encontrar a la mitad del camino; partir la diferencia con; hacer concesiones (a). **to m. the eye,** saltar a la vista. **to m. with,** encontrar; experimentar; sufrir

meeting n encuentro, m; reunión, f; (interview) entrevista, f; (of rivers, etc.) confluencia, f; (public, etc.) mitin, m; (council) concilio, m; concurso, m; (race) concurso de carreras de caballos, m. **creditors' m.,** concurso de acreedores, m. **m.-house,** templo de los Cuáqueros, m. **m.-place,** lugar de reunión, m; lugar de cita, m; centro, m. **to adjourn the m.,** levantar la sesión. **to call a m.,** convocar una sesión. **to open the m.,** abrir la sesión

megalomania n megalomanía, monomanía de grandezas, f

megalomaniac n megalómano (-na)

megaphone n megáfono, portavoz, m

melancholia n melancolía, f

melancholy a melancólico. n melancolía, f

mellifluous a melifluo; dulce

mellow a maduro; dulce; (of wine) rancio; blando; suave; (of sound) melodioso; (slang) alegre; (tipsy) entre dos luces. vt madurar; ablandar; suavizar. vi madurarse

mellowing n maduración, f

melodic a melódico

melodious a melodioso

melodrama n melodrama, m

melodramatic a melodramático

melody n melodía, f

melon n melón, m; sandía, f. **slice of m.,** raja de melón, f. **m. bed,** sandiar, m. **m.-shaped,** amelonado

melt vi derretirse; deshacerse; disolverse; evaporarse; desaparecer; (of money, etc.) hacerse sal y agua; (relent) enternecerse, ablandarse. vt fundir; (snow, etc.) derretir; (fig soften) ablandar. **He melted away,** inf Se escurrió. **to m. into tears,** deshacerse en lágrimas. **to m. down,** fundir

melting a fundente; (forgiving) indulgente; (tender) de ternura; lánguido; dulce. n fusión, f; derretimiento, m. **m. point,** punto de fusión, m. **m. pot,** met crisol, m; fig caldera de razas, f, m

member n miembro, m; (of a club, etc.) socio (-ia). **M. of Parliament,** diputado a Cortes, m

membership n calidad de miembro, socio(-ia); número de miembros (or socios), m, composición, integración, f

membrane n membrana, f

memento n recuerdo, m

memoir n memoria, f

memorable a memorable

memorandum n memorándum, m

memorial a conmemorativo. n monumento conmemorativo, m; memorial, m

memorize vt aprender de memoria

memory n memoria, f; recuerdo, m. **from m.,** de memoria. **If my m. does not deceive me,** Si mal no me acuerdo. **in m. of,** en conmemoración de; en recuerdo de

memory span n retentiva memorística, f

menace n amenaza, f, vt amenazar

menacing a amenazador

menacingly adv con amenazas

menagerie n colección de fieras, f; casa de fieras, f

mend vt remendar; componer; reparar; (darn) zurcir; (rectify) remediar; reformar; enmendar; (a fire) echar carbón (or leña, etc.) a; (one's pace) avivar. vi (in health and of the weather) mejorar. n remiendo, m; (darn) zurcido, m. **to be on the m.,** ir mejorando. **to m. one's ways,** reformarse, enmendarse

mendacious a mendaz

mender n componedor (-ra); (darner) zurcidor (-ra); reparador (-ra); (cobbler and tailor) remendón, m

mendicant a mendicante. n mendicante, mf. **m. friar,** fraile mendicante, m

mending n compostura, f; reparación, f; (darning) zurcidura, f; ropa por zurcir, f

menial a doméstico; servil; bajo, ruin. n criado (-da); lacayo, m

meningitis n meningitis, f

menopause n menopausia, f

menses n menstruación, f

menstrual a menstrual

menstruate vi menstruar

menstruation n menstruación, f,

mental a mental; intelectual. **m. derangement,** enajenación mental, f. **m. hospital,** manicomio, m

mentality n mentalidad, f

mention n mención, f; alusión, f. vt hacer mención (de), mencionar, mentar, hablar (de); aludir (a); (quote) citar; (in dispatches) nombrar. **Don't m. it!** (keep silent) ¡No digas nada!; (you're welcome) ¡No hay de qué!

mentor n mentor, m

menu n menú, m; lista de platos, f

meow vi maullar. n maullido, m

mercantile a mercantil; mercante. **m. law,** derecho mercantil, m. **m. marine,** marina mercante, f

mercenary a mercenario. n (soldier) mercenario, m

merchandise n mercancía, f

merchant n traficante (en), mf, negociante (en), m; comerciante, Lat. Am. marchante (-ta) mf mercader, m. a mercante. **The M. of Venice,** El Mercader de Venecia. **m. navy, service,** marina mercante, f. **m. ship,** buque mercante, m

merchantman n buque mercante, m

merciful a misericordioso, piadoso; compasivo; clemente; indulgente

mercifully adv misericordiosamente; compasivamente; con indulgencia

merciless a despiadado, inhumano

mercilessly adv sin piedad

mercurial a mercurial; (changeable) volátil; (lively) vivo

mercury n mercurio, m; (ast and myth) Mercurio, m. **Mercury's wand,** caduceo, m

mercy n misericordia, f; compasión, f; clemencia, f; indulgencia, f; merced, f. **at the m. of the elements,** a la intemperie. **to be at the m. of,** estar a la merced de

mere a mero; simple; no más que, solo. n lago, m

merely adv meramente, solamente; simplemente, sencillamente

meretricious a (archaic) meretricio; (flashy) de oropel; llamativo, charro

merge vt fundir; com fusionar; mezclar. vi fundirse; com fusionarse; mezclarse

merger n combinación, f; com fusión, f

meridian n (geog ast) meridiano, m; (noon) mediodía, m; (peak) apogeo, m

meringue n merengue, m, Lat. Am. espumilla, f

merino a de merino; merino. n (fabric and sheep) merino, m

merit n mérito, m, vt merecer, ser digno de

meritorious a meritorio

merlon n merlón, m, almena, f

mermaid n sirena, f

merrily adv alegremente

merriment n alegría, f; júbilo, m; regocijo, m; diversión, f; juego, m

merriness n alegría, f; regocijo, m; inf ebriedad, f

merry a alegre; jovial; feliz; regocijado, divertido; (tipsy) calamocano. **to make m.**, divertirse. **to make m. over,** reírse de. **M. Christmas!** ¡Felices Navidades! **m.-andrew**, bufón, m. **m.-go-round**, caballitos, m pl, tiovivo, m, Lat. Am. calesita, f. **m.-making**, festividades, fiestas, f pl

meseta n meseta, f

mesh n malla, f; mech engranaje, m; (network) red, f; (snare) lazo, m. vt coger con red; mech endentar

mesmerism n mesmerismo, m

mesmerize vt hipnotizar

mess n (of food) plato de comida, m; porción, ración, f; rancho, m; (mixture) mezcla, f; (disorder) desorden, m; suciedad, f; (failure) fracaso, m. vt (dirty) ensuciar; desordenar; (mismanage) echar a perder. **to be in a m.**, inf estar aviado. **to get in a m.**, inf hacerse un lío. **to make a m. of**, ensuciar; desordenar; (spoil) echarlo todo a rodar

message n mensaje, m; recado, m; (telegraphic) parte, m. **I have to take a m.**, Tengo que hacer un recado

messenger n mensajero (-ra); (of telegrams) repartidor, m; heraldo, m; anuncio, m

Messiah n Mesías, m

Messianic a mesiánico

messrs. n pl (abbreviation) sres. (from señores), m pl

metabolism n metabolismo, m

metabolize va metabolizar

metal n metal, m; vidrio en fusión, m; (road) grava, f; her metal, m; (mettle) temple, temperamento, m; brío, fuego, m; pl metals, (of a railway) rieles, m pl. m. **engraver**, grabador en metal, m. **m. polish**, limpiametales, m. **m. shavings**, cizallas, f pl. **m. work**, metalistería, f. **m. worker**, metalario, m

metallic a metálico

metalloid n metaloide, m

metallurgic a metalúrgico

metamorphosis n metamorfosis, f

metaphor n metáfora, f

metaphorical a metafórico

mete (out) vt repartir, distribuir

meteor n meteoro, m

meteoric a meteórico

meteorite n meteorito, m

meteorological a meteorológico

meteorologist n meteorologista, mf

meteorology n meteorología, f

meter n (for gas, etc.) contador, m; (verse and measure) metro, m

methane n metano, m

method n método, m; técnica, f; táctica, f

methodical a metódico; ordenado, sistemático

methyl n metilo, m. **m. alcohol**, alcohol metílico, m

methylated spirit n alcohol desnaturalizado, m

meticulous a meticuloso; minucioso

meticulously adv con meticulosidad

meticulousness n meticulosidad, f; minuciosidad, f

metric a métrico. **m. system**, sistema métrico, m

metrics n métrica, f

metronome n metrónomo, m

metropolis n metrópoli, f; capital, f

metropolitan a metropolitano; de la capital. n ecc metropolitano, m

mettle n temple, temperamento, m; fuego, brío, m; valor, m. **You have put him on his m.**, Le ha picado en el amor propio

mew n (gull) gaviota, f; (of a cat) maullido, m; (of sea-birds) alarido, m. vi (of a cat) maullar; (of sea-birds) dar alaridos. **to mew up**, encerrar

Mexican a mejicano. n mejicano (-na)

Mexico n Méjico, m

mezzanine n entresuelo, m

mezzosoprano n mezzo-soprano

mi n mus mi, m

miasma n miasma, m

mica n mica, f

microbe n microbio, m

microbiologist n microbiólogo, m

microbiology n microbiología, f

microcosm n microcosmo, m

microphone n micrófono, m

microscope n microscopio, m

microscopic a microscópico

microwave n microonda, f

mid a medio. prep entre; en medio de; a mediados de. **from mid May to August,** desde mediados de mayo hasta agosto. **a mid-fourteenth century castle**, un castillo de mediados del siglo catorce. **in mid air**, en medio del aire. **in mid channel**, en medio del canal. **in mid winter**, en medio del invierno

midday n mediodía, m, a del mediodía, meridional. **at m.**, a mediodía

middle a medio; en medio de; del centro; intermedio; (average) mediano. n medio, m; mitad, f; centro, m; (waist) cintura, f. **in the m. of**, en medio de. **in the m. of nowhere**, donde Cristo dio las tres voces. **toward the m. of the month**, a mediados del mes. **m. age**, edad madura, f. **m.-aged**, de edad madura, de cierta edad. **M. Ages,** edad media, f. **m. class,** clase media, burguesía, f, a de la clase media, burgués. **m. distance,** término medio, m. **m. ear,** oído medio, m. **m. finger,** dedo de en medio (or del corazón), m. **m. way,** fig término medio, m. **m. weight,** peso medio, m

Middle East, the el Oriente Medio, el Levante, m

middleman n agente de negocios, m; (retailer) revendedor, m; intermediario, m

middling a mediano; mediocre; regular, así, así

midge n mosquito, m, mosca de agua, f

midget n enano (-na). **m. submarine,** submarino de bolsillo, m

midnight n medianoche, f. a de medianoche; nocturno. **at m.,** a medianoche. **to burn the m. oil,** quemarse las cejas. **m. mass,** misa del gallo, f

midriff n diafragma, m

midship a maestro. n medio del buque, m. **m. beam,** bao maestro, m. **m. gangway,** crujía, f

midshipman n guardiamarina, m

midst n medio, m; seno, m, prep entre. **in the m. of,** en medio de. **There is a traitor in our m.,** Hay un traidor entre nosotros (or en nuestra compañía)

midstream, n **in m.** m. en medio de la corriente

midsummer n pleno verano, m; solsticio estival, m; fiesta de San Juan, f. **A M. Night's Dream,** El Sueño de la Noche de San Juan

midway a and adv situado a medio camino; a medio camino, a la mitad del camino; entre. n mitad del camino, f; medio, m. **m. between . . . ,** equidistante de . . . , entre

midwife n comadrona, partera, f

midwifery n obstetricia, f

midwinter n medio del invierno, m

mien n aire, m; porte, semblante, m

might vi poder. **It m. or m. not be true,** Podría o no podría ser verdad. **How happy Mary m. have been!** ¡Qué feliz pudo haber sido María! **I thought that you m. have seen him in the theater,** Creí que pudieras haberle visto en el teatro. **That I m . . . !** ¡Que yo pudiese . . . ! **This m. have been avoided if . . .** Esto podía haberse evitado si . . .

might n fuerza, f; poder, m. **with m. and main,** con todas sus fuerzas

mightily adv fuertemente; poderosamente; inf muchísimo, sumamente

mighty a fuerte, vigoroso; poderoso; grande; inf enorme; (proud) arrogante. adv inf enormemente, muy

migraine n migraña, jaqueca, f

migrant a migratorio, de paso. n ave migratoria, ave de paso, f

migrate vi emigrar

migration n migración, f

migratory a migratorio, de paso; (of people) nómada, pasajero

migratory worker n trabajador golondrino, m

milch a f, (of cows) lechera

mild a apacible, pacífico; manso; dulce; suave; (of the weather) blando; med benigno; (light) leve; (of drinks) ligero; (weak) débil

mildew n mildiu, añublo, m; moho, m. vt anublar; enmohecer. vi anublarse; enmohecerse

mildly adv suavemente; dulcemente; con indulgencia

mile n milla, f

mileage n distancia en millas, f; kilometraje, m

milestone n hito, m, piedra miliaria, f; mojón kilométrico, m

militancy n carácter militante, m; belicosidad, f

militant a militante, combatiente; belicoso; agresivo. n combatiente, mf

militarism n militarismo, m

militarist n militarista, mf

militarize vt militarizar

military a militar; de guerra. **the m.,** los militares. **m. academy,** colegio militar, m. **m. camp,** campo militar, m. **m. law,** código militar, m. **m. man,** militar, m. **m. police,** policía militar, f. **m. service,** servicio militar, m

militate (against) vi militar contra

militia n milicia, f

militiaman n miliciano, m

milk n leche, f. a de leche; lácteo. vt ordeñar. vi dar leche. **to have m. and water in one's veins,** tener sangre de horchata. **condensed m.,** leche condensada, leche en lata, f. **m.-can,** lechera, f. **m.-cart,** carro de la leche, m. **m. chocolate,** chocolate con leche, m. **m. of magnesia,** leche de magnesia, f. **m.-pail,** ordeñadero, m. **m.-tooth,** diente de leche, m. **m.-white,** blanco como la leche

milking n ordeño, m. **m.-machine,** máquina ordeñadora, f. **m.-stool,** taburete, banquillo, m

milkmaid n lechera, f

milkman n lechero, m

milksop n marica, m

milky a lechero; de leche; lechoso, como leche; ast lácteo. **the Milky Way** la Vía láctea, f

mill n molino, m; (for coffee, etc.) molinillo, m; (factory) fábrica, f; taller, m; (textile) hilandería, f; fábrica de tejidos, f; (fight) riña a puñetazos, f; pugilato, m. vt (grind) moler; (coins) acordonar; (cloth) abatanar; (chocolate) batir. **cotton m.,** hilandería de algodón, f. **hand-m.,** molinillo, m. **paper-m.,** fábrica de papel, f. **saw-m.,** serrería, f. **spinning m.,** hilandería, f. **water m.,** molino de agua, m.

m.-course, saetín, canal de molino, *m.*
m.-dam, esclusa de molino, *f.* **m.-hand,**
obrero (-ra). **m.-pond,** cubo, *m.* **m.-race,**
caz, *m.* **m.-wheel,** rueda de molino, *f*

millennial a milenario

millennium *n* milenario, *m*

miller *n* molinero, *m.* **miller's wife,** mo-
linera

millet *n* mijo, *m*

milligram *n* miligramo, *m*

millimeter *n* milímetro, *m*

milliner *n* sombrerero (-ra), modista, *mf*
milliner's shop, sombrerería, tienda de
modista, *f*

millinery *n* sombreros, *m pl*; modas, *f pl*;
tienda de modista, *f*

milling *n* molienda, *f*; acuñación, *f*; (edge
of coin) cordoncillo, *m.* **m. machine,**
fresadora, *f*

million *n* millón, *m.* **the m.,** las masas

millionaire *n* millonario. *n* millonario, *m*

millionth a millonésimo

millstone *n* piedra de moler, muela, *f*

mime *n* (Greek farce and actor) mimo, *m*;
(mimicry) mímica, *f*; pantomima, *f.* *vi*
hacer en pantomima

mimetic a mímico, imitativo

mimic a mímico; (pretended) fingido. *n*
imitador (-ra). *vt* imitar, contrahacer; *biol*
imitar, adaptarse a

mimicry *n* mímica, imitación, *f*; *biol*
mimetismo, *m*

minaret *n* minarete, *m*; (of a mosque) alminar, *m*

minatory a amenazador

mince *vt* desmenuzar; (meat) picar;
(words) medir (las palabras). *vi* andar con
pasos menuditos; andar o moverse con
afectación; hacer remilgos. **m.-meat,**
carne picada, *f*; (sweet) conserva de fruta
y especias, *f*

mincing a afectado. *n* acción de picar
carne, *f.* **m. machine,** máquina de picar
carne, *f*

mind *n* inteligencia, *f*; espíritu ánimo, *m*;
imaginación, *f*; alma, *f*; (memory) memoria, *f*, recuerdo, *m*; (understanding) entendimiento, *m*; (genius) ingenio, *m*;
(cast of mind) mentalidad, *f*; (opinion)
opinión, *f*; (liking) gusto, *m*; (thoughts)
pensamiento, *m*; (intention) propósito,
m, intención, *f*; (tendency) propensión,
inclinación, *f.* **I have a good m. to go
away,** Por poco me marcho; Tengo ganas
de marcharme. **I have changed my m.,**
He cambiado de opinión. **out of m.,** olvidado. **I shall give him a piece of my
m.,** Le diré cuatro verdades. **It had quite
gone out of my m.,** Lo había olvidado
completamente. **I can see it in my
mind's eye,** Está presente a mi imaginación. **I shall bear it in m.,** Lo tendré en
cuenta. **I thought in my own m. that
. . . ,** Pensé por mis adentros que . . . **We
are both of the same m.,** Ambos somos

de la misma opinión. **to be out of one's
m.,** estar fuera de juicio. **to call to m.,**
acordarse de. **to have something on
one's m.,** estar preocupado. **to make up
one's m. (to),** resolverse (a), decidirse
(a), determinar; animarse (a). **m.-reader,**
adivinador (-ra) del pensamiento

mind *vt* (remember) recordar, no olvidar;
(heed) atender a; hacer caso de; tener
cuidado de; (fear) tener miedo de; (obey)
obedecer; preocuparse de; (object to)
molestar; importar; (care for) cuidar. *vi*
tener cuidado; molestar; (feel) sentir;
(fear) tener miedo; (be the same thing)
ser igual. **Do you m. being quiet a moment?** ¿Quieres hacer el favor de callarte
un momento? **Do you m. if I smoke?**
¿Le molesta si fumo? **They don't m.,** No
les importa, Les da igual. **Never m.!** ¡No
se moleste! ¡No se preocupe! ¡No importa! ¡Vaya! **M. what you are doing!**
¡Cuidado con lo que haces! **M. your own
business!** ¡No te metas donde no te llaman!

mindful a atento (a), cuidadoso (de); que
se acuerda (de)

mine a poss mío, *m,* (mía, *f*; míos, *m pl*;
mías, *f pl*); el mío, *m,* (la mía, *f*; lo mío,
neut; los míos, *m pl*; las mías, *f pl*); mi (*pl*
mis). **a friend of m.,** un amigo mío; uno
de mis amigos

mine *n* mina, *f. vt* minar; extraer; sembrar
minas en, colocar minas en. *vi* minar;
hacer una mina; dedicarse a la minería.
drifting m., mina a la deriva, *f.* **land m.,**
mina terrestre, *f.* **magnetic m.,** mina
magnética, *f.* **to lay mines,** colocar (or
sembrar) minas. **m.-sweeper,** dragaminas, buque barreminas, *m*

minefield *n* campo de minas, *m*; barrera
de minas, *f*

minelayer *n* barca plantaminas, *f*, barco
siembraminas, lanzaminas, *m*

miner *n* minero, *m*; *mil* zapador minador,
m

mineral *n* mineral, *m,* a mineral. **m.
baths,** baños, *m pl.* **m. water,** agua mineral, *f*; gaseosa, *f*

mingle *vt* mezclar; confundir. *vi* mezclarse; confundirse

mingling *n* mezcla, *f*

miniature *n* miniatura, *f.* a en miniatura.
m. edition, edición diamante, *f*

miniature golf *n* minigolf, *m*

miniaturist *n* miniaturista, *mf*

minibus *n* micro, microbús, *Mexico*
combi, *m*

minimize *vt* aminorar, reducir al mínimo;
mitigar; (underrate) tener en menos, despreciar

minimum *n* mínimo, *m,* a mínimo

mining *n* minería, *f,* a minero; de mina;
de minas; de minero. **m. engineer,** ingeniero de minas, *m*

minion *n* favorito (-ta); satélite, *m*; *print*
miñona, *f*

minister *n* ministro, *m*. *vi* servir; suministrar, proveer de; (contribute) contribuir (a). **m. of health,** ministro de sanidad, *m*. **m. of war,** ministro de la guerra, *m*

ministry *n* ministerio, *m*. **m. of food,** Ministerio de Abastecimientos, *m*

mink *n* visón, *m*

minor *a* menor. *n* menor de edad, *m*; (logic) menor, *f*; *mus* tono menor, *m*; *ecc* menor, *m*. **to be a m.,** ser menor de edad. **m. key,** tono menor, *m*. **m. orders,** *ecc* órdenes menores, *f pl.* **m. scale,** escala menor, *f*

minority *n* minoría, *f*; (of age) minoridad, *f*. **in the m.,** en la minoría

minster *n* catedral, *f*; monasterio, *m*

minstrel *n* trovador, juglar, *m*; músico, *m*; cantante, *m*

mint *n bot* menta, hierbabuena, *f*; casa de moneda, casa de la moneda, ceca, *f*; *fig* mina, *f*; (source) origen, *m*. *vt* (money) acuñar; *fig* inventar, a (postage stamp) en estado nuevo

minus *a* menos; negativo; desprovisto de; sin. *n* signo menos, *m*; cantidad negativa, *f*

minute *a* menudo, diminuto; insignificante; minucioso

minute *n* minuto, *m*; momento, *m*; instante, *m*; (note) minuta, *f*; *pl* **minutes,** actas, *f pl.* **in a m.,** en un instante. **m.-book,** libro de actas, minutario, *m*. **m.-hand,** minutero, *m*

minutely *adv* minuciosamente; en detalle; exactamente

minx *n* picaruela, *f*; coqueta, *f*

miracle *n* milagro, *m*. **m.-monger,** milagrero (-ra). **m. play,** milagro, *m*

miraculous *a* milagroso

mirage *n* espejismo, *m*

mire *n* fango, lodo, *m*; (miry place) lodazal, *m*

mirror *n* espejo, *m*. *vt* reflejar. **to look in the m.,** mirarse al espejo. **full-length m.,** espejo de cuerpo entero, *m*. **small m.,** espejuelo, *m*

mirth *n* alegría, *f*, júbilo, *m*; risa, *f*; hilaridad, *f*

mirthful *a* alegre

miry *a* lodoso, fangoso, cenagoso

misadventure *n* desgracia, *f*; accidente, *m*

misanthrope *n* misántropo, *m*

misanthropic *a* misantrópico

misapply *vt* aplicar mal; hacer mal uso de; abusar de

misapprehend *vt* comprender mal; equivocarse sobre

misapprehension *n* concepto erróneo, *m*; equivocación, *f*, error, *m*

misappropriate *vt* malversar

misbehave *vi* portarse mal; (of a child) ser malo

misbehavior *n* mala conducta, *f*

miscalculate *vt* calcular mal; engañarse (sobre)

miscalculation *n* mal cálculo, error, *m*; desacierto, *m*

miscall *vt* mal nombrar; llamar equivocadamente; (abuse) insultar

miscarriage *n med* aborto, *m*; (failure) malogro, fracaso, *m*; (of goods) extravío, *m*

miscarriage of justice *n* yerro en la administración de la justicia, *m*

miscarry *vi med* abortar, malparir; (fail) malograrse, frustrarse; (of goods) extraviarse

miscellaneous *a* misceláneo; vario, diverso

mischance *n* mala suerte, *f*; infortunio, *m*, desgracia, *f*; accidente, *m*

mischief *n* daño; mal, *m*; (wilfulness) travesura, *f*; (person) diablillo, *m*. **m.-maker,** enredador (-ra), chismoso (-sa); alborotador, *m*; malicioso (-sa). **m.-making,** *a* enredador; chismoso; malicioso; alborotador

mischievous *a* dañino, perjudicial, malo; malicioso; chismoso; (wilful) travieso, juguetón; (of glances, etc.) malicioso

misconceive *vt* formar un concepto erróneo de; concebir mal, juzgar mal

misconception *n* concepto erróneo, *m*, idea falsa, *f*; error, *m*, equivocación, *f*; engaño, *m*

misconduct *n* mala conducta, *f*. **to m. oneself,** portarse mal

misconstruction *n* mala interpretación, *f*; falsa interpretación, *f*; tergiversación, *f*; mala traducción, *f*

misconstrue *vt* interpretar mal; entender mal; tergiversar; traducir mal

miscount *vt* contar mal, equivocarse en la cuenta de; calcular mal. *n* error, *m*; yerro de cuenta, *m*

miscreant *n* malandrín, *m*; bribón, *m*, a vil, malandrín

misdeed *n* delito, malhecho, crimen, *m*

misdemeanor *n* mala conducta, *f*; *law* delito, *m*; ofensa, *f*, malhecho, *m*

misdirect *vt* informar mal (acerca del camino); (a letter) dirigir mal, poner unas señas incorrectas a

miser *n* avaro (-ra)

miserable *a* infeliz, desgraciado; miserable; despreciable; sin valor

miserably *adv* miserablemente

miserly *a* avaro, tacaño

misery *n* miseria, *f*; sufrimiento, *m*; dolor, tormento, *m*

misfire *vi* no dar fuego; (of a motor-car, etc.) hacer falsas explosiones, errar el encendido

misfit *n* traje que no cae bien, *m*; zapato que no va bien, *m*; (person) inadaptado, *m*

misfortune *n* infortunio, *m*, mala suerte,

adversidad, f; desdicha, desgracia, f; mal, m

misgive vt hacer temer; llenar de duda; hacer recelar; hacer presentir

misgiving n temor, m; duda, f; recelo, m; presentimiento, m

misgovern vt gobernar mal; administrar mal; dirigir mal

misgovernment n desgobierno, m; mala administración, f

misguided a mal dirigido; extraviado; engañado; (blind) ciego

mishap n desgracia, f; contratiempo, accidente, m. **to have a m.,** sufrir una desgracia; tener un accidente

misinform vt informar mal; dar informes erróneos (a)

misinformation n noticia falsa, f; información errónea, f

misinterpret vt interpretar mal; entender mal; torcer; tergiversar; traducir mal

misinterpretation n mala interpretación, f; interpretación falsa, f; tergiversación, f; mala traducción, f

misjudge vt juzgar mal; equivocarse (en or sobre); tener una idea falsa de

misjudgment n juicio errado, m; idea falsa, f; juicio injusto, m

mislay vt extraviar, perder

mislead vt extraviar; llevar a conclusiones erróneas, despistar; engañar

misleading a de falsas apariencias; erróneo, falso; engañoso

mismanage vt administrar mal; dirigir mal; echar a perder

misname vt mal nombrar; llamar equivocadamente

misnomer n nombre equivocado, m; nombre inapropiado, m

misogynist n misógino, m

misogyny n misoginia, f

misplace vt colocar mal; poner fuera de lugar

misplaced a mal puesto; inoportuno; equivocado

misprint n error de imprenta, m, errata, f, vt imprimir con erratas

mispronounce vt pronunciar mal

mispronunciation n mala pronunciación, f

misquote vt citar mal, citar erróneamente

misrepresent vt desfigurar; tergiversar; falsificar

misrepresentation n desfiguración, f; tergiversación, f; falsificación, f

misrule vt gobernar mal. n mal gobierno, desgobierno, m; confusión, f

miss n señorita, f

miss vt (one's aim) errar (el tiro, etc.); no acertar (a); (let fall) dejar caer; (lose a train, the post, etc., one's footing, an opportunity, etc.) perder; (fall short of) dejar

de; no ver; no notar; pasar por alto de; omitir; echar de menos; notar la falta de; no encontrar. vi errar; (fail) salir mal, fracasar. **I m. you,** Te echo de menos. **to be missing,** faltar; estar ausente; haberse marchado; haber desaparecido. **to m. one's mark,** errar el blanco. **to m. out,** omitir, pasar por alto de. **She doesn't miss a beat,** (fig.) No se le escapa nada

missal n misal, m

misshapen a deforme

missile n arma arrojadiza, f; proyectil, m

missing a que falta; perdido; ausente; mil desaparecido

mission n misión, f

missionary n misionero, m

missive n misiva, f

misspend vt malgastar; desperdiciar; perder

mist n bruma, neblina, f; vapor, m; (drizzle) llovizna, f; fig nube, f. vt anublar, empañar. vi llovizna r

mistake vt comprender mal; equivocarse sobre; errar; (with for) confundir con, equivocarse con. n equivocación, f; error, m; inadvertencia, f; (in an exercise, etc.) falta, f. **And no m.!** inf Sin duda alguna. **by m.,** por equivocación; (involuntarily) sin querer. **If I am not mistaken,** Si no me engaño, Si no estoy equivocado. **to make a m.,** equivocarse

mistaken a (of persons and things) equivocado; (of things) erróneo; incorrecto

mistakenly adv equivocadamente; injustamente, falsamente

mister n señor, m

mistimed a intempestivo; inoportuno

mistletoe n muérdago, m

mistranslate vt traducir mal; interpretar mal

mistranslation n mala traducción, f; traducción inexacta, f

mistress n señora, f; maestra, f; (fiancée) prometida, f; (beloved) amada, dulce dueña, f; (concubine) amiga, querida, f. **M. (Mrs.) Gómez,** Sra Gómez. **m. of the robes,** camarera mayor, f

mistrust vt desconfiar de, no tener confianza en; dudar de. n desconfianza, f; recelo, m, suspicacia, f; aprensión, f

mistrustful a desconfiado; receloso, suspicaz. **to be m. of,** recelarse de

misty a brumoso, nebuloso; vaporoso; (of the eyes) anublado; (of windows, etc.) empañado

misunderstand vt comprender mal; tomar en sentido erróneo; interpretar mal

misunderstanding n concepto erróneo, error, m; equivocación, f; (disagreement) desavenencia, f

misuse vt emplear mal; abusar de;

(funds) malversar; (ill-treat) tratar mal. *n* abuso, *m*; (of funds) malversación, *f*

mite *n* (coin) ardite, *m*; (trifle) pizca, *f*; óbolo, *m*; *ent* ácaro, *m*

mitigate *vt* (pain) aliviar; mitigar; suavizar

mitigation *n* (of pain) alivio, *m*; mitigación, *f*

mitten *n* mitón, *m*

mix *vt* mezclar; (salad) aderezar; (concrete, etc.) amasar; combinar, unir; (sociably) alternar (con); (confuse) confundir. *vi* mezclarse; frecuentar la compañía (de); frecuentar; (get on well) llevarse bien

mixed *a* mezclado; vario, surtido; mixto; (confused) confuso. **m. doubles,** parejas mixtas, *f pl*. **m. up,** (in disorder) revuelto; confuso. **m. up with,** implicado en; asociado con

mixer *n* mezclador, *m*; (person) mezclador (-ra); *inf* persona sociable, *f*. **electric m.,** mezclador eléctrico, *m*

mixture *n* mezcla, *f*; (medicine) poción, medicina, *f*

mnemonics *n* mnemotecnia, *f*

moan *vt* lamentar; llorar. *vi* gemir; quejarse, lamentarse. *n* gemido, *m*; lamento, *m*; quejido, *m*

moaning *n* gemidos, *m pl*

moat *n* foso, *m*

mob *n* (crowd) muchedumbre, multitud, *f*; (rabble) populacho, *m*, gentuza, *f*. *vt* atropellar; atacar. **mob-cap,** cofia, *f*

mobile *a* móvil; ambulante; (fickle) voluble. **m. canteen,** cantina ambulante, *f*

mobility *n* movilidad, *f*

mobilization *n* movilización, *f*

mobilize *vt* movilizar. *vi* movilizarse

moccasin *n* mocasín, *m*

mocha *n* café de Moca, *m*

mock *vt* ridiculizar; burlarse (de), mofarse (de); (cause to fail) frustrar; (mimic) imitar; (delude) engañar. *vi* mofarse, burlarse, reírse. *a* cómico, burlesco; falso; fingido; imitado. **to make a m. of,** poner en ridículo; hacer absurdo; burlarse de. **m.-heroic,** heroico-cómico. **m.-orange,** *bot* jeringuilla, *f*. **m.-turtle soup,** sopa hecha con cabeza de ternera a imitación de tortuga, *f*

mocker *n* mofador (-ra); el, *m*, (*f*, la) que se burla de

mockery *n* mofa, burla, *f*; ridículo, *m*; ilusión, apariencia, *f*. **to make a m. of,** mofarse de; hacer ridículo

mocking *a* burlón. **m. bird,** pájaro burlón, *m*

mode *n* modo, *m*; manera, *f*; (fashion) moda, *f*; uso, *m*, costumbre, *f*

model *n* modelo, *m*; (artist's) modelo vivo, *m*, a modelo; en miniatura. *vt* modelar; moldear; formar; hacer; planear. **m. display,** (hats, etc.) exposición de modelos, *f*. **m. railway,** ferrocarril en miniatura, *m*

modeling *n* modelado, *m*; modelo, *m*. **m. wax,** cera para moldear, *f*

moderate *a* moderado; (of prices, etc.) módico; (fair, medium) regular, mediano; razonable; mediocre. *n* moderado, *m*. *vt* moderar; modificar; calmar. *vi* moderarse; calmarse

moderately *adv* moderadamente; módicamente; medianamente; bastante; razonablemente; mediocremente

moderation *n* moderación, *f*. **in m.,** en moderación

modern *a* moderno. *n* modernista, *mf*. **in the m. way,** a la moderna. **m. language,** lengua viva, *f*

modernize *vt* modernizar

modest *a* modesto; (of a woman) púdico

modesty *n* modestia, *f*; (of a woman) pudor, *m*

modicum *n* porción pequeña, *f*; poco, *m*

modifiable *a* modificable

modification *n* modificación, *f*

modify *vt* modificar. **It has been much modified,** Se ha modificado mucho; Se han hecho muchas modificaciones

modifying *a* modificante, modificador

modish *a* de moda en boga; elegante

modiste *n* modista, *mf*

modulate *vt* and *vi* modular

modulation *n* modulación, *f*

modus vivendi *n* modo de conveniencia, *m*

moiré *n* muaré, *m*

moist *a* húmedo

moisten *vt* humedecer, mojar

moisture *n* humedad, *f*

molar *n* muela, *f*, a molar

molasses *n pl* melaza, *f*

mold *n* (fungus) moho, *m*; (humus) mantillo, *m*; (iron-mould) mancha de orín, *f*; (matrix) molde, *m*, matriz, *f*; *cul* cubilete, *m*; *naut* gálibo, *m*; (for jelly, etc.) molde, *m*; *arch* moldura, *f*; (temperament) temple, *m*, disposición, *f*. *vt* moldear; (cast) vaciar; *carp* moldurar; *naut* galibar; *fig* amoldar, formar; *agr* cubrir con mantillo. **to m. oneself on,** modelarse sobre. **m.-board,** (of a plough) orejera, *f*

molder *n* moldeador, *m*; *fig* amolador (-ra); creador (-ra). *vi* desmoronarse, convertirse en polvo; *fig* decaer, desmoronarse; vegetar

molding *n* amoldamiento, *m*; vaciado, *m*; *arch* moldura, *f*; *fig* formación,

moldy *a* mohoso, enmohecido; *fig* anticuado

mole *n* (animal) topo, *m*; (spot) lunar, *m*; (breakwater) dique, malecón, *m*; muelle, *m*

molecular *a* molecular

molecule *n* molécula, *f*

molehill *n* topera, *f*

moleskin n piel de topo, f

molest vt molestar; perseguir, importunar; faltar al respeto (a)

molestation n importunidad, persecución, f; molestia, incomodidad, f

mollification n apaciguamiento, m; mitigación, f

mollify vt apaciguar, calmar; mitigar

mollusk n molusco, m

mollycoddle n alfeñique, mírame y no me toques, m; niño (-ña), mimado (-da)

Moloch n Moloc, m

molt vi mudar. n muda, f

molten a fundido; derretido

moment n momento, m; instante m; (importance) importancia, f. **at this m.**, en este momento. **Do it this m.!** ¡Hazlo al instante (or en seguida)!

momentarily adv momentáneamente; cada momento

momentary a momentáneo

momentous a de suma importancia; crítico; grave

momentum n momento, m, velocidad adquirida f; fig ímpetu, m. **to gather m.**, cobrar velocidad, acelerar

monarch n monarca, m

monarchy n monarquía, f

monastery n monasterio, m

monastic a monástico. **m. life**, vida de clausura, f

monasticism n vida monástica, f

Monday n lunes, m

monetary a monetario

money n dinero, m; (coin) moneda, f; sistema monetario, m. **paper m.**, papel moneda, m. **ready m.**, dinero contante, m. **to make m.**, ganar (or hacer) dinero; enriquecerse. **M. talks**, Poderoso caballero es Don Dinero. **m.-bag**, talega, f; (person) ricacho (-cha). **m.-bags**, riqueza, f. **m.-box**, alcancía, hucha, f. **m.-changer**, cambista, mf **m.-lender**, prestamista, mf **m.-making**, n el hacer dinero; prosperidad, ganancia, f. **a** lucrativo, Lat. Am. libranza de correos, f. branza postal, f. **m.-order**, giro postal, m (postal)

moneyed a adinerado; acomodado

mongoose n mangosta, f

mongrel a mestizo, atravesado. n perro mestizo, m; (in contempt) mestizo. m

monitor n monitor, m

monitory a monitorio. n ecc monitorio, m

monk n monje, m. **to become a m.**, hacerse monje, tomar el hábito. **monk's-hood**, acónito, m

monkey n mono (-na); (imp) diablillo, m; (of a pile-driver) pilón de martinete, m; (in glass-making) crisol, m. **to m. with**, meterse con; entremeterse. **m. nut**, cacahuete, m. **m.-puzzle**, (tree) araucaria, f.

m. tricks, monadas, travesuras, diabluras, m pl. **m.-wrench**, llave inglesa, f

monochromatic a monocromo

monocle n monóculo, m

monogamous a monógamo

monogamy n monogamia, f

monogram n monograma, m

monograph n monografía, f, opúsculo, m

monolithic a monolítico

monologue n monólogo, m

monomania n monomanía, f

monoplane n monoplano, m

monopolization n monopolio, m

monopolize vt monopolizar

monopoly n monopolio, m

monotheism n monoteísmo, m

monotheist n monoteísta, mf

monotone n monotonía, f

monotonous a monótono

monotony n monotonía, f

Monroe doctrine n monroísmo, m

monsoon n monzón, mf

monster n monstruo, m

monstrosity n monstruosidad, f

monstrous a monstruoso; horrible, atroz; enorme

montage n montaje, m

month n mes, m. **He arrived a m. ago**, Llegó hace un mes. **a m. later** Lat. Am. al mes

monthly a mensual. adv mensualmente, cada mes. n revista (or publicación) mensual, f; pl **monthlies**, menstruación, regla, f. **m. salary** or **payment**, mensualidad, f

monument n monumento, m

monumental a monumental

moo vi (of cattle) mugir. n mugido, m

mood n humor, m; espíritu, m; gram modo, m

moodily adv taciturnamente; tristemente, pensativamente

moodiness n mal humor, m, taciturnidad, f; melancolía, tristeza, f

moody a taciturno, de mal humor; triste, melancólico, pensativo

moon n luna, f; satélite, m; mes lunar, m; luz de la luna, f. **full m.**, plenilunio, m; luna llena, f. **new m.**, novilunio, m, luna nueva, f

moonless a sin luna

moonlight n luz de la luna, f. **in the m.**, a la luz de la luna. **to do a m. flit**, inf mudarse por el aire

moonlighting n el pluriempleo, m

moonlit a iluminado por la luna. **moonlit night**, noche de luna, f

moonshine n claridad de la luna, f; fig música celestial, ilusión, f

moonstone n adularia, f

moonstruck a lunático

Moor n moro (-ra)

moor n páramo, brezal, m; (marsh) pantano, m; (for game) coto, m. vt amarrar, aferrar; afirmar con anclas o cables. **m.-hen,** polla de agua, f

mooring n amarre, m. **m.-mast,** aer poste de amarre, m

moorings n pl amarradero, m

Moorish a moro; árabe. **M. architecture,** arquitectura árabe, f. **M. girl,** mora, f

moorland n páramo, brezal, m

moose n anta, f

moot n junta, f; ayuntamiento, m. a discutible. vt (bring up) suscitar; (discuss) discutir, debatir

mop n (implement) trapeador, m Ecuador, escoba con fleco, f, elsewhere in Lat. Am. lampazo m; (of hair) mata (de pelo), f. vt trapear Ecuador; (dry) enjugar, secar. **to mop up,** inf limpiar; mil acabar con (el enemigo)

mope vi replace by tristear. **to m. about,** vagar tristemente

moral a moral; (chaste) casto, virtuoso; honrado. n (maxim) moraleja, f; pl **morals,** moralidad, f; ética, f; moral, f; (conduct) costumbres, f pl. **m. philosophy,** filosofía moral, f. **m. support,** apoyo moral, m. **m. tale,** apólogo, m

morale n moral, f

moralist n moralista, m

morality n moralidad, f; virtud, f; castidad, f. **m. play,** moralidad, f, drama alegórico, m

moralize vt and vi moralizar

morals. See **moral**

morass n marisma, ciénaga, f

moratorium n moratoria, f

morbid a mórbido, mórboso; (of the mind, etc.) insano

morbidity n morbidez, f

mordant a mordaz; (of acid) mordiente. n mordiente, m

more a and adv más. **The m. he earns, the less he saves,** Cuanto más gana, menos ahorra. **the m. the better,** cuanto más, tanto mejor. **without m. ado,** sin más ni más; sin decir nada. **Would you like some m.?** ¿Quiere Vd. más? (of food) ¿Quiere Vd. repetir? **no m.,** no más; (never) nunca más; (finished) se acabó. **once m.,** otra vez, una vez más. **m. and m.,** cada vez más, más y más. **m. or less,** más o menos; (about) poco más o menos

moreover adv además, también; por otra parte

morgue n depósito de cadáveres, m

moribund a moribundo

Mormon a mormónico. n mormón (-ona)

Mormonism n mormonismo, m

morning n mañana, f, a matutino, de la mañana. **Good m.!** ¡Buenos días! **the**

next m., la mañana siguiente. **very early in the m.,** muy de mañana. **m. coat,** chaqué, m. **m. dew,** rocío de la mañana, m. **m. paper,** periódico de la mañana, m. **m. star,** lucero del alba, m. **m. suit,** chaqué, m

Moroccan a marroquí, marrueco. n marrueco (-ca), marroquí, mf

Morocco Marruecos, m

morocco n (leather) marroquí, tafilete, m

morose a sombrío, taciturno, malhumorado

morphia, morphine n morfina, f. **m. addict,** morfinómano (-na)

morrow n mañana, f; día siguiente, m

morsel n pedazo, m; (mouthful) bocado, m

mortal a mortal. n mortal, mf. **m. sin,** pecado mortal, pecado capital, m

mortality n mortalidad, f

mortally wounded adv herido de muerte

mortar n (for building) argamasa, f; (for mixing and mil) mortero, m. **m. and pestle,** mortero y majador, m. **m.-board,** (in building) cuezo, m; (academic cap) birrete, m

mortgage n hipoteca, f. vt hipotecar. a hipotecario. **to pay off a m.,** redimir una hipoteca

mortgageable a hipotecable

mortgaged debt n deuda garantizada con una hipoteca, f

mortgagee n acreedor (-ra) hipotecario (-ia)

mortgagor n deudor (-ra) hipotecario (-ia)

mortification n mortificación, f; humillación, f; med gangrena, f

mortify vt mortificar; humillar. vi med gangrenarse

mortifying a humillante

mortise n muesca, f. vt hacer muescas (en); ensamblar

mortuary a mortuorio. n depósito de cadáveres, m

Mosaic a mosaico

mosaic n mosaico, m

Moscow Moscú, m

mosque n mezquita, f

mosquito n mosquito, m. **m. net,** mosquitero, m

moss n musgo, m; moho, m; (swamp) marjal, m

mossiness n estado musgoso, m

mossy a musgoso

most a el (la, los, etc.) más; la mayor parte de; la mayoría de; (el, etc.) mayor. adv más; el (la, etc.) más; (extremely) sumamente; (very) muy; (before adjectives sometimes expressed by superlative, e.g. **m. reverend,** reverendísimo, **m. holy,** santísimo, etc.). n (highest price) el mayor precio; la mayor parte; el mayor número; lo más. **m. of all,** sobre todo. **m. people,** la mayoría de la gente. **at the m.,** a lo más, a lo sumo. **for the m. part,** en su mayor parte; casi todos; generalmente, casi siempre. **to make the m. of,** sacar el mayor partido posible de; aprovechar bien; exagerar

mostly *adv* principalmente; en su mayoría; en su mayor parte; casi siempre; en general, generalmente

mote *n* átomo, *m*; mota, *f*. **to see the m. in our neighbor's eye and not the beam in our own,** ver la paja en el ojo del vecino y no la viga en el nuestro

moth *n* mariposa nocturna, *f*; polilla, *f*. **m.ball,** bola de naftalina, *f*. **m.-eaten,** apolillado

mother *n* madre, *f*; madre de familia, *f*; (of alcoholic beverages) madre, *f*. *vt* cuidar como una madre (a); servir de madre (a); (animals) ahijar. **M. Church,** madre iglesia, *f*; iglesia metropolitana, *f*. **m.-in-law,** suegra, *f*. **m. land,** (madre) patria, *f*. **m.-of-pearl,** *n* madreperla, *f*. nácar, *m*. a nacarado, nacáreo. **M. Superior,** (madre) superiora, *f*. **m. tongue,** lengua materna, *f*

motherhood *n* maternidad, *f*

motherless *a* huérfano de madre, sin madre

motherlike *a* de madre, como una madre

motherliness *n* cariño maternal, *m*

motherly *a* maternal

motif *n* motivo, *m*; tema, *m*; *sew* adorno, *m*

motion *n* movimiento, *m*; *mech* marcha, operación, *f*; mecanismo, *m*; (sign) seña, señal, *f*; (gesture) ademán, gesto, *m*; (carriage) aire, porte, *m*; (of the bowels) movimiento del vientre, *m*, deyección, *f*; (will) voluntad, *f*, deseo, *m*; (proposal in an assembly or debate) proposición, moción, *f*; *law* pedimento, *m*. *vt* hacer una señal (a). *vi* hacer señas. **to set in m.,** poner en marcha. **m. picture,** fotografía cinematográfica, película, *f*. **m.-picture theater,** cine, *m*

motionless *a* inmóvil

motivate *vt* motivar

motive *n* motivo, *m*. a motor; motivo. **with no m.,** sin motivo. **m. power,** fuerza motriz, *f*

motley *a* abigarrado, multicolor; (mixed) diverso, vario. *n* traje de colores, *m*, botarga, *f*

motor *n* motor, *m*; automóvil, *m*, a motor; movido por motor; con motor; (traveling) de viaje. *vi* ir en automóvil. *vt* llevar en automóvil (a). **m.boat,** lancha automóvil, *f*. **m.bus,** autobús, ómnibus, *m*. **m.car,** automóvil, *m*. **m.-coach,** autobús, *m*. **m.cycle,** motocicleta, *f*. **m.cyclist,** motociclista, *mf* **m.-launch,** canoa automóvil, *f*. **m.oil,** aceite para motores, *m*. **m.-road,** autopista, *f*. **m.-rug,** manta

de viaje, *f*. **m.-scooter,** bicicleta con motor, *f*. **m.-spirit,** bencina, *f*

motoring *n* automovilismo, *m*

motorist *n* automovilista, motorista, *mf*

mottled *a* abigarrado; (of marble, etc.) jaspeado, esquizado; manchado (con), con manchas (de); pintado (con)

motto *n her* divisa, *f*; mote, *m*; (in a book, etc.) lema, *m*

mound *n* montón, *m*; (knoll) altozano, *m*; (for defence) baluarte, *m*; (for burial) túmulo, *m*

mount *n* (hill, and in palmistry) monte, *m*; (for riding) caballería, *f*; montadura, *f*; (for a picture) borde, *m*. *vt* subir; (machines, etc.) montar; (jewels) engastar; (a picture) poner un borde a; (a play) poner en escena; poner a caballo; proveer de caballo. *vi* montar; subir; (increase) aumentar. **to m. a horse,** subir a caballo, montar. **to m. guard,** *mil* montar la guardia. **to m. the throne,** subir al trono

mountain *n* montaña, *f*; (mound) montón, *m*. a de montaña(s); montañés; alpino, alpestre. **to make a m. out of a molehill,** convertir un grano de arena en una montaña. hacer de una pulga un camello, hacer de una pulga un elefante. **m.-chain,** cadena de montañas, *f*. **m. climber** *Lat. Am.* andinista *mf*. **m. climbing** *Lat. Am.* andinismo, *m*. **m. dweller,** montañés (-esa). **m. railway,** ferrocarril de cremallera, *m*. **m.-side,** falda de una montaña, *f*

mountaineer *n* (inhabitant) montañés (-esa); (climber) alpinista, *mf*. *vi* hacer alpinismo

mountaineering *n* alpinismo, *m*

mountainous *a* montañoso; (huge) enorme

mountebank *n* saltabanco, *m*; charlatán, *m*

mounting *n* (ascent) subida, *f*; ascensión, *f*; (of machinery, etc.) armadura, *f*; montadura, *f*; (of a precious stone) engaste, *m*. **m.-block,** subidero, *m*

mourn *vi* afligirse, lamentarse; (wear mourning) estar de luto. *vt* llorar; lamentar; llevar luto por

mourner *n* lamentador (-ra); (paid) plañidera, *f*; el, *m*, (*f*, la) que acompaña al féretro

mournful *a* triste, acongojado; funesto, lúgubre; fúnebre; lamentable

mourning *n* aflicción, *f*; lamentación, *f*; luto, *m*. **deep m.,** luto riguroso, *m*. **half m.,** medio luto, *m*. **to be in m.,** estar de luto. **to be in m. for,** llevar luto por. **to come out of m.,** dejar el luto. **m.-band,** (on the hat) lazo de gasa, *f*; (on the arm) brazal de luto, *m*. **m.-coach,** coche fúnebre, *m*

mouse *n* ratón (-na); *naut* barrilete, *m*. *vi* cazar ratones. **m.-coloured,** de color de rata. **m.-hole, m.-trap,** ratonera, *f*

moustache *n* bigote, mostacho, *m*

mousy a ratonesco, ratonil

mouth n (anat human being, of a bottle, cave) boca, f; entrada, f; (of a river) desembocadura, f; (of a channel) embocadero, m; (of a wind-instrument) boquilla, f. vt pronunciar con afectación; (chew) mascar. vi clamar a gritos, vociferar. **down in the m.,** inf con las orejas caídas. **It makes my m. water,** Se me hace la boca agua. **large m.,** boca rasgada, f. **m.-gag,** abrebocas, m. **m.-organ,** armónica, f. **m.-wash,** antiséptico bucal, m (Argentina), enjuague, m

mouthed a que tiene boca . . . ; de boca . . . **open-m.,** boquiabierto

mouthful n bocado, m; (of smoke, air) bocanada, f

mouthpiece n (of wind-instruments, tobacco-pipe, waterpipe) boquilla, f; (of a wineskin) brocal, m; (spokesman) portavoz, m; intérprete, mf

movable a movible; (of goods) mobiliario. **m. feast,** fiesta movible, f

move n movimiento, m; (of household effects) mudanza, f; (motion) marcha, f; (in a game) jugada, f; (fig step) paso, m; (device) maniobra, f. **Whose m. is it?** ¿A quién le toca jugar? **to be on the m.,** estar en movimiento; estar de viaje. **to be always on the m.,** inf parecer una lanzadera

move vt mover; poner en marcha; (furniture) trasladar; cambiar de lugar; (stir) remover; (shake) agitar, hacer temblar; (transport) transportar; (a piece in chess, etc.) jugar; (pull) arrancar; (impel) impulsar; (incline) inclinar, disponer; (affect emotionally) conmover, emocionar, enternecer; impresionar. vi moverse; ponerse en marcha; (walk) andar; ir; avanzar; (a step forward, etc.) dar; (move house) trasladarse; (act) entrar en acción; (in games) hacer una jugada; (progress) progresar; (shake) agitarse, temblar; removerse; (propose in an assembly) hacer una proposición; (in a court of law) hacer un pedimento; (grow) crecer. **to m. about,** pasearse; ir y venir; (of traffic) circular; (remove) trasladarse; (stir, tremble) agitarse. **to m. along,** caminar por; avanzar por. **to m. aside,** vt apartar; poner a un lado; (curtains) descorrer. vi ponerse a un lado; quitarse de en medio. **to m. away,** vt alejar. vi alejarse; marcharse; trasladarse; mudar de casa. **to m. back,** retroceder, volver hacia atrás. **to m. down,** bajar, descender. **to m. forward,** adelantarse; avanzar; progresar. **to m. in,** entrar (en); tomar posesión de una casa. **to m. off,** vt quitar. vi marcharse; ponerse en marcha; alejarse, apartarse. **to m. on,** avanzar; ponerse en marcha; circular; (time) pasar, correr. **to m. out,** vt sacar, quitar. vi salir; (from a house) mudarse, abandonar (una casa, etc.). **to m. round,** dar vueltas; girar; (turn round) volverse. **to m. to,** (make) hacer, animar (a); causar. **to m. up,** vt montar, subir. vi montar; avanzar

movement n movimiento, m; mech mecanismo, m; (Stock Exchange) actividad, f. **encircling m.,** mil movimiento envolvente, m

mover n motor, m; móvil, m; promotor (-ra); (of a motion, proposer) autor (-ra) de una moción

movie n inf cine, m. **m. camera,** máquina de impresionar, f. **m. star,** estrella de la pantalla, f

moving a móvil; motor; (affecting) emocionante, conmovedor; impresionante; patético. n movimiento, m; traslado, m; cambio de domicilio, m. **m. picture,** fotografía cinematográfica, f. **m. staircase,** escalera móvil, f

movingly adv con emoción; patéticamente

mow vt segar. vi (grimace) hacer muecas

mowing n siega, f. **m.-machine,** segadora, f

Mr. See **mister**

Mrs. See **mistress**

much a mucho. adv mucho; (by far) con mucho; (with past part.) muy; (pretty nearly) casi, más o menos. **m. of a size,** más o menos del mismo tamaño. **I was m. angered,** Estuve muy enfadado. **as m. as,** tanto como. **as m. more,** otro tanto. **How m. is it?** ¿Cuánto es? ¿Cuánto cuesta? **however m. . . . ,** por mucho que . . . **not m.,** no mucho. **not to think m. of,** tener en poco (a). **so m. so that,** tanto que. **too m.,** demasiado. **to make m. of,** dar grande importancia a; (a person) apreciar, querer; agasajar; (a child) mimar, acariciar

mucilage n mucílago, m

muck n (dung) estiércol, m; (filth) porquería, inmundicia, f; suciedad, f; (rubbish, of a literary work, etc.) porquería, m. **to m. up,** ensuciar; (spoil) estropear por completo

mucous a mucoso. **m. membrane,** mucosa, f

mucus n mucosidad, f; (from the nose) moco, m

mud n lodo, barro, fango, m. **to stick in the mud,** (of a ship, etc.) embarrancarse. **mudbath,** baño de barro, m. **mud wall,** tapia, f

muddle vt (bewilder) dejar perplejo, aturdir; (intoxicate) emborrachar; (stupefy) entontecer; (spoil) estropear; embarullar, dejar en desorden; hacer un lío de. n desorden, m; confusión, f; lío, embrollo, m. **in a m.,** en desorden; en confusión. **to make a m.,** armar un lío. **to m. away,** derrochar sin ton ni son

muddled a desordenado; confuso; estúpido; torpe; (drunk) borracho

muddy a fangoso, lodoso, barroso; cubierto de lodo; (of liquids, etc.) turbio; (of the complexion) cetrino. *vt* enlodar, cubrir de lodo; ensuciar; (liquids) enturbiar

mudguard *n* guardabarro, *m*

muezzin *n* almuecín, almuédano, *m*

muff *n* manguito, *m*; (for a car radiator) cubierta para radiador, *f*; (*inf* at games, etc.) maleta, *m*. *vt* dejar escapar (una pelota); (an opportunity) perder

muffin *n* mollete, *m*.

muffle *vt* embozar, arrebozar; envolver; encubrir, ocultar, tapar; (stifle sound of) apagar; (oars, bells) envolver con tela para no hacer ruido; *fig* ahogar. **to m. oneself up,** embozarse

muffled a (of sound) sordo; confuso; apagado. **m. drum,** tambor enlutado, *m*

muffler *n* bufanda, tapaboca, *f*; (furnace) mufla, *f*; (of a car radiator) cubierta para radiador, *f*; (silencer) silencioso, *m*

mug *n* vaso, *m*; (tankard) pichel, tarro, *m*; (face) jeta, *f*; (dupe) primo, *m*; (at games, etc.) maleta, *m*

mulatto a mulato. *n* mulato (-ta). **m.-like,** amulatado

mulberry *n* (fruit) mora, *f*; (bush) morera, *f*. **m. plantation,** moreral, *m*

mule *n* mulo (-la); (slipper) mula, chinela, *f*; (spinning-jenny) huso mecánico, *m*

mulish a mular; terco como una mula

mullet *n* (red) salmonete, *m*, trilla, *f*; (grey) mújol, *m*

multicolored a multicolor

multifarious a numeroso, mucho; diverso, vario

multiform a multiforme

multilateral a multilátero

multimillionaire a archimillonario, multimillonario, *n* multimillonario, *m*

multiple a múltiple, múltiplo. *n* múltiplo, *m*

multiple-choice question *n* pregunta optativa, *f*

multiplicand *n* multiplicando, *m*

multiplication *n* multiplicación, *f*. **m. table,** tabla de multiplicación, *f*

multiplier *n* math multiplicador, *m*; máquina de multiplicar, *f*

multiply *vt* multiplicar. *vi* multiplicarse

multitude *n* multitud, *f*. **the m.,** las masas

multitudinous a muy numeroso

mumble *vi* and *vt* musitar, hablar entre dientes; refunfuñar; (chew) mascullar

mummify *vt* momificar. *vi* momificarse

mummy *n* momia, *f*; carne de momia, *f*; (*inf* mother) mama, *f*. **m. case,** sarcófago, *m*

mumps *n pl* parotiditis, papera, *f*

munch *vt* masticar, mascullar, mascar

mundane a mundano

municipal a municipal. **m. charter,** fuero municipal, *m*. **m. government,** gobierno municipal, *m*

municipality *n* municipio, *m*

munificent a munífico, generoso

munition *n* munición, *f*. *vt* municionar. **m. dump,** depósito de municiones, *m*. **m. factory,** fábrica de municiones, *f*. **m. worker,** obrero (-ra) de una fábrica de municiones

mural a mural. *n* pintura mural, *f*

murder *n* asesinato, *m*. *vt* asesinar; dar muerte (a), matar; (a work, etc.) degollar. **He was murdered,** Fue asesinado. **willful m.,** homicidio premeditado, *m*

murderer *n* asesino, *m*

murderous a homicida; cruel, sanguinario; fatal; imposible, intolerable

murky a lóbrego, negro, obscuro; (of one's past, etc.) negro, accidentado

murmur *n* murmullo, *m*; rumor, *m*; susurro, *m*; (grumble) murmurio, *m*. *vi* murmurar, susurrar; (complain) murmurar, quejarse. *vt* murmurar, decir en voz baja

murmuring *n* murmurio, *m*, a que murmura, susurrante

muscatel a moscatel. *n* moscatel, *m*. **m. grape,** uva moscatel, *f*

muscle *n* músculo, *m*

muscular a muscular, musculoso; (brawny) membrudo, fornido. **m. pains,** (in the legs, etc.) agujetas, *f pl*

musculature *n* musculatura, *f*

Muse *n* musa, *f*

muse *n* meditación, *f*. *vi* meditar, reflexionar, rumiar; mirar las musarañas, estar distraído. **to m. on,** meditar en (or sobre)

museum *n* museo, *m*

mushroom *n* seta, *f*. a de setas; de forma de seta; (upstart) advenedizo; (ephemeral) efímero, de un día. **m.-bed,** setal, *m*. **m.-spawn,** esporas de setas, *f pl*

music *n* música, *f*; armonía, *f*; melodía, *f*. a de música. **to set to m.,** poner en música. **m.-hall,** teatro de variedades, *m*; salón de conciertos, *m*. **m. master,** profesor de música, *m*. **m. publisher,** editor de obras musicales, *m*. **m. stand,** atril, *m*; tablado para una orquesta, *m*. **m. stool,** taburete de piano, *m*

musical a musical; de música; armonioso, melodioso. **She is very m.,** Es muy aficionada a la música; Tiene mucho talento para la música. **m.-box,** caja de música, *f*. **m. comedy,** zarzuela, *f*. **m. instrument,** instrumento de música, *m*

musical chairs *n* escobas, *f pl*, el juego de sillas, *m sg*

musician *n* músico (-ca)

musing *n* meditación, *f*; ensueños, *m pl*, a pensativo, meditabundo

musk *n* (substance) almizcle, *m*; perfume de almizcle, *m*. a de almizcle; almizcleño. (of scents) almizcle, *m*. **m.-deer,** almizclero, *m*. **m.-rat,** rata almizclera, *f*

Muslim a musulmán, mahometano. *n* musulmán (-ana)

muslin n muselina, f, a de muselina

mussel n mejillón, m. **m.-bed,** criadero de mejillones, m

must vi haber de; tener que; deber; (expressing probability) deber de, ser. **This question m. be settled without delay,** Esta cuestión debe ser resuelta sin demora. **You m. do it at once,** Tienes que hacerlo en seguida. **I m. have seen him in the street sometime,** Debo haberle visto en la calle alguna vez. **One m. eat to live,** Se ha de comer para vivir. **Well, go if you m.,** Bueno, vete si no hay más remedio. **It m. be a difficult decision for him,** Debe ser una decisión difícil para él. **It m. have been about twelve o'clock when . . . ,** Serían las doce cuando . . .

must n mosto, zumo de la uva, m; (mould) moho, m

mustard n mostaza, f. **m. gas,** iperita, f. **m. plaster,** sinapismo, m. **m. pot,** mostacera, f. **m. spoon,** cucharita para la mostaza, f

muster n lista, f, rol, m; revista, f; reunión, f, vt pasar lista (de); pasar revista (a); reunir. vi juntarse, reunirse. **to m. out,** (from the army) dar de baja (a). **to m. up sufficient courage,** cobrar ánimos suficientes. **to pass m.,** pasar revista; ser aceptado. **m.-roll,** rol muestra, f; naut rol de la tripulación, m

mustiness n moho, m; ranciedad, f; (of a room, etc.) olor de humedad, m

musty a mohoso; rancio; que huele a humedad. **to go m.,** enmohecerse

mutable a mudable; inconstante, inestable

mutation n mutación, f

mute a mudo; silencioso. n mudo (-da); mus sordina, f; (phonetics) letra muda, f. **deaf m.,** sordomudo (-da)

muted a (of sounds) sordo, apagado

mutilate vt mutilar; estropear

mutineer n amotinador, rebelde, m

mutinous a amotinado; rebelde, sedicioso; turbulento

mutiny n motín, m; sublevación, insurrección, f, vi amotinarse, sublevarse

mutt n chucho, m

mutter vt and vi murmurar, musitar; mascullar, decir (or hablar) entre dientes; gruñir, refunfuñar; (of thunder, etc.) tronar, retumbar. n murmurio, m; rumor, m; retumbo, m

mutton n carnero, m, a de carnero. **m.-chop,** chuleta, f

mutual a mutuo, recíproco; común. **by m. consent,** de común acuerdo. **m. aid society,** sociedad de socorros mutuos, f. **m. insurance company,** sociedad de seguros mutuos, f

mutual fund n fondo de inversiones rentables, m

muzzle n (snout) hocico, m; (for a dog) bozal, m; (of a gun) boca, f. vt abozalar, poner un bozal (a); imponer silencio (a)

muzzling n acción de abozalar, f; (fig gagging) amordazamiento, m

my a poss mi, mf; mis, mf pl **my relatives,** mis parientes. **My goodness!** ¡Dios mío!

myelitis n mielitis, f

myopia n miopía, f

myopic a miope

myriad n miríada, f

myrrh n mirra, f

myrtle n mirto, arrayán, m

myself pron yo mismo; (as a reflexive with a preposition) mí; (with a reflexive verb) me. **I m. sent it,** yo mismo (-ma) lo mandé

mysterious a misterioso

mystery n misterio, m. **m. play,** (religious) misterio, drama litúrgico, m; (thriller) comedia de detectives, f. **m. story,** novela policíaca, f; novela de aventuras, f

mystic a místico

mysticism n misticismo, m

mystify vt mistificar

myth n mito, m

mythical a mítico

mythology n mitología, f

N

n *n* (letter) ene, *f*

nab *vt inf* atrapar, apresar, agazapar

nacre *n* nácar, *m*, madreperla, *f*

nadir *n* nadir, *m*

nag *n* jaca, *f*; (wretched hack) rocín, jamelgo, penco, *m*. *vt* zaherir, echar en cara, regañar; (of one's conscience) remorder; *Lat. Am.* majaderear (pester) *vi* criticar, regañar

nagging *n* zaherimiento, *m*. *a* zaheridor, criticón; (pain) continuo, incesante, constante

nail *vt* clavar, enclavar; (for ornament) clavetear, tachonar, adornar con clavos. *n* uña, *f*; *mech* clavo, *m*; (animal's) garra, *f*. **to n. down,** sujetar (or cerrar) con clavos. **to n. to (on to),** clavar en. **to n. together,** fijar con clavos. *inf* **on the n.,** en el acto, en seguida. *inf* **to hit the n. on the head,** dar en el clavo. **brass-headed n.,** tachón, *m*. **French n.,** punta de París, *f*. **headless n.,** puntilla, *f*. **hob-n.,** clavo de herradura, *m*. **hook n.,** gancho, *m*. **round-headed n.,** bellota, *f*. **n.-brush,** cepillo para las (or de) uñas, *m*. **n.-file,** lima para las uñas, *f*. **n. head,** cabeza de un clavo, *f*. **n.-puller,** sacaclavos, arrancaclavos, botador, *m*. **n.-scissors,** tijeras para las uñas, *f pl*. **n. trade,** ferretería, *f*. **n. varnish,** barniz para las uñas, *m*

naive *a* ingenuo, candoroso, espontáneo

naively *adv* ingenuamente, espontáneamente

naiveté *n* ingenuidad, naturalidad, franqueza, *f*; candor, *m*

naked *a* desnudo, nudo, *Peru* calato, *elsewhere in Lat. Am.* encuerado; desabrigado, indefenso, desamparado; (birds) implume; calvo; (truth) simple, sencillo, puro; evidente, patente. **stark n.,** en cueros vivos, tal como le parió su madre. **with the n. sword,** con la espada desnuda. **n. eye,** simple vista, *f*. **n. light,** llama descubierta, *f*

nakedly *adv* nudamente; desabrigadamente; abiertamente, claramente

nakedness *n* desnudez, *f*; *fig* desabrigo, *m*, aridez, *f*; *fig* claridad, *f*. **the truth in all its n.,** la verdad desnuda

namby-pamby *a* soso, insípido, ñoño

name *n* nombre, *m*; título, *m*; fama, opinión, *f*; renombre, crédito, *m*; autoridad, *f*; apodo, mal nombre, *m*. *vt* nombrar, llamar, imponer el nombre de, apellidar; mencionar, señalar; (appoint) designar, elegir; (ships) bautizar. **by n.,** por nombre. **Christian n.,** nombre de pila, *m*. **in his n.,** en nombre de él, en nombre suyo; de parte de él. **in n. only,** nada más que en nombre. **to be named,** llamarse. **to call** (a person) **names,** poner como un trapo (a). **to go under the n. of,** vivir

bajo el nombre de. **to have a good n.,** tener buena fama. **What is her n.?** ¿Cómo se llama? **n. day,** santo, *m*. **n. plate,** (machinery) placa de fábrica, *f*; (streets) rótulo, *m*; (professional) placa profesional, *f*

nameless *a* anónimo; desconocido; (inexpressible) vago, indecible

namely *adv* a saber, es decir

namesake *n* tocayo (-ya)

nap *n* (cloth) pelusa, *f*, pelo, tamo, *m*; (plants) vello, *m*, pelusilla, *f*; (sleep) siesta, *f*, sueño, *m*; (cards) napolitana, *f*. **to take a nap,** *vi* dormitar, echar un sueño, echar una siesta. **to take an afternoon nap,** dormir la siesta. **to be caught napping,** estar desprevenido

nape *n* nuca, *f*, cogote, *m*; (animal's) testuz, *m*

naphtha *n chem* nafta, *f*. **wood n.,** alcohol metílico, *m*

naphthalene *n chem* naftalina, *f*

napkin *n* (table) servilleta, *f*; (babies') pañal, *m*. **n.-ring,** servilletero, *m*

Naples Nápoles, *m*

narcotic *a med* narcótico, calmante, soporífero. *n med* narcótico, *m*, opiata, *f*

narrate *vt* narrar, contar; referir, relatar

narration *n* narración, narrativa; relación, descripción, *f*, relato, *m*

narrative *a* narrador, narrativo, narratorio. *n* narrativa, *f*; descripción, *f*

narrow *vt* estrechar, angostar; reducir, limitar. *vi* reducirse, hacerse más estrecho; (eyes) entornarse; (knitting) menguar. *a* estrecho, angosto; limitado, estringido, reducido, corto; (avaricious) ruin, avaro, mezquino; (ideas) intolerante, intransigente. **"Narrow Road,"** «Camino Estrecho». *n pl* **narrows,** *naut* estrecho, *m*; desfiladero, paso estrecho, *m*. **to have a n. escape,** escapar en una tabla. **n.-brimmed** (hats), de ala estrecha. **n. circumstances,** estrechez, escasez de medios, *f*. **n.-gauge railway,** ferrocarril de vía estrecha (or de vía angosta), *m*. **n. life,** vida de horizontes estrechos, *f*. **n. majority,** escasa mayoría, *f*. **n.-minded,** cerrado de mundo, intolerante, intransigente. **n.-mindedness,** intolerancia, intransigencia, estrechez de miras, *f*

narrowly *adv* estrechamente; por poco, con dificultad; atentamente, cuidadosamente. **I n. escaped being run over,** Por poco me atropellan

nascent *a* naciente

nastiness *n* suciedad, inmundicia, porquería, *f*; (indecency) obscenidad, indecencia, *f*; (rudeness) insolencia, impertinencia, grosería, *f*; (difficulty) dificultad, *f*, lo malo

nasty *a* nauseabundo, repugnante; asqueroso, inmundo, sucio; (obscene) indecente, obsceno; desagradable, malo;

(malicious) rencoroso, malicioso; violento; malévolo, amenazador; peligroso; difícil. *fig* **to be in a n. mess,** tener el agua al cuello. **to turn n.,** *inf* ponerse desagradable

nation *n* nación, *f*, estado, país, *m*; (people) pueblo, *m*

national *a* nacional; público; patriótico. *n* nacional, *mf.* **n. anthem,** himno nacional, *m.* **n. debt,** deuda pública, *f.* **n. schools,** escuelas públicas, *f pl.* **n. socialism,** nacionalsocialismo, *m.* **n. socialist,** *a* and *n* nacionalsocialista *mf.* **n. syndicalism,** *pol* nacionalsindicalismo, *m.* **n. syndicalist,** *a* and *n* *pol* nacionalsindicalista, *mf*

nationalism *n* nacionalismo, patriotismo, *m*

nationalist *a* and *n* nacionalista, *mf*

nationality *n* nacionalidad, *f*; nación, *f*

nationalization *n* nacionalización, *f*

nationalize *vt* nacionalizar, *Lat. Am. also* estatizar

National Labor Relations Board *n* Junta Nacional de Relaciones Laborales

nationally *adv* nacionalmente, como nación; del punto de vista nacional

native *a* (of a place) nativo, natal, oriundo; indígena; nacional, típico, del país; (vocabulary) patrimonial (as opposed to borrowed vocabulary); (of genius) natural, innato, instintivo; *min* nativo; (language) vernáculo. *n* nacional, *mf*; natural, *mf*; ciudadano (-na) indígena, aborigen (gen. pl.), *mf*; producto nacional, *m*. **He is a n. of Madrid,** Nació en Madrid, Es natural de Madrid, Es madrileño. **Native American commune** (in Peru) ayllu, *m*. **native informant,** sujeto, *m*. **n. land,** patria, tierra. **n. of the capital** *Lat. Am.* capitalino, *n*. **n. of Rio de Janeiro** carioca, *mf*. **n. place,** lugar natal, *m*. **n. region,** patria chica, *f*. **n. soil,** terruño, *m*. **n. tongue,** lengua materna, *f*

Native American *movement Lat. Am.* indigenismo, *m*

nativity *n* navidad, natividad, *f*; (manger) nacimiento, *m*

natty *a inf* chulo, majo; coquetón

natural *a* natural; (wild) virgen, salvaje; nativo; (of products) crudo; normal; (usual) acostumbrado, corriente, natural; (of likeness) fiel, verdadero; (illegitimate) ilegítimo, bastardo; (of qualities) innato, instintivo; físico; característico, propio; (of people) inafectado, sencillo, genuino; *mus* natural. *n mus* becuadro, *m*; *mus* nota natural, *f*; imbécil, *mf* **n. features,** geografía física, *f*. **n. history,** historia natural, *f*. **n. philosophy,** filosofía natural, *f*. **n. science,** ciencias naturales, *f pl.* **n. selection,** selección natural, *f*. **n. state,** estado virgen, *m*

natural child *n* hijo ilegítimo, *m*

naturalism *n* naturalismo, *m*

naturalist *n* (*lit* and *science*) naturalista, *mf*

naturalistic *a* naturalista

naturalization *n* naturalización, *f*; aclimatación, *f*. **n. papers,** carta de naturaleza, *f*

naturalize *vt* naturalizar; aclimatar. **to become naturalized,** naturalizarse

naturally *adv* naturalmente, por naturaleza; normalmente; sin afectación; instintivamente, por instinto; (without art) al natural. **n. curly hair** *Guatemala* colocho, *m*

nature *n* naturaleza, *f*; (of people) carácter, fondo, temperamento, genio, natural, modo de ser, *m*; (kind) género, *m*, especie, *f*; (essence) condición, esencia, cualidad, *f*, *art* **from n.,** del natural. **good n.,** bondad natural, afabilidad, *f*. **ill n.,** mala índole, *f*. **nature cure,** naturismo, *m*. **n. curist,** naturista, *mf*. **n. study,** historia natural, *f*. **n. worship,** panteísmo, culto de la naturaleza, *m*

natured *a* de carácter, de índole, con un modo de ser, de condición

naught *n* nada, *f*; cero, *m*. *a* inútil, sin valor. **all for n.,** todo en balde. **to come to n.,** malograrse. **to set at n.,** tener en menos; despreciar

naughty *a* travieso, pícaro, revoltoso, malo; salado, escabroso, verde (stories, etc.). **to be n.,** (children) ser malo

nausea *n* náusea, *f*, bascas, *f pl*, mareo, *m*; *fig* asco, *m*; repugnancia, *f*

nauseate *vt* dar náuseas; *fig* repugnar, dar asco

nauseating *a* repugnante, horrible; asqueroso

nauseous *a* nauseabundo, asqueroso; *fig* repugnante

nauseousness *n* náusea, asquerosidad, *f*; *fig* repugnancia, *f*, asco, *m*

nautical *a* náutico, marítimo. **n. day, twenty-four hours,** singladura, *f*

naval *a* naval; de marina, marítimo. **n. base,** base naval, *f*. **n. engagement,** batalla naval, *f*. **n. hospital,** hospital de marina, *m*. **n. law,** código naval, *m*. **n. officer,** oficial de marina, *m*. **n. power,** poder marítimo, *m*. **n. reservist,** marinero de reserva, *m*. **n. yard,** arsenal, *m*

nave *n arch* nave, *f*; (of wheels) cubo, *m*

navel *n* ombligo, *m*. **n. string,** cordón umbilical, *m*

navigable *a* navegable, practicable

navigate *vt* navegar, marear, dirigir (un buque); *fig* conducir, guiar. *vi* navegar

navigation *n* navegación, *f*; (science of) náutica, marina, *f*. **n. company,** empresa naviera, *f*. **n. laws,** derecho marítimo, *m*. **n. lights,** luces de navegación, *f pl*

navigator *n* navegador, navegante, *m*; piloto, *m*

navvy *n* peón, bracero, jornalero, *m*;

mech máquina, excavadora, *f.* **road n.**, peón caminero, *m.* **to work like a n.**, estar hecho un azacán, sudar la gota gorda

navy *n* marina, *f;* armada, *f;* (color) azul marino, *m.* **n. board,** consejo de la armada, *m.* **n. department** ministerio de marina, *m.* **n. estimates,** presupuesto de marina, *m.* **n. list,** escalafón de marina, *m*

nay *adv* no; al contrario, más bien, mejor dicho. **n** negativa, *f,* voto contrario, *m*

Nazi *a* and *n* nacionalsocialista, naci, *mf*

Nazism *n* nacismo, *m*

n.d. (no date) *s.f.* (sin fecha)

near *vi* acercarse, aproximarse. **a** cercano, immediato, contiguo; (of time) inminente, próximo; (relationship) cercano, consanguíneo; (of friends) íntimo, entrañable; (mean) tacaño, avariento

near *prep* cerca de, junto a; hacia, en la dirección de; (of time) cerca de, casi. *adv* cerca, *Central America, Chile, Mexico* lueguito; (time) cerca, próximamente. **to be n. to,** estar cerca de. **to bring n.,** acercar, aproximar. **It was a n. thing,** Escapamos por un pelo. **n. at hand,** a la mano; (time) cerca, inminente. **n.-by,** a cercano, inmediato, *Central America, Chile, Mexico* lueguito. *adv* cerca. **n. side,** (of vehicles) lado de la acera, *m.* **n.-sighted,** corto de vista, miope. **n.-sightedness,** miopía, cortedad de vista, *f*

nearest *a comp* and *sup* más cercano, más cerca; más corto. **the n. way,** el camino más corto, el camino directo

nearly *adv* casi; cerca de, aproximadamente; estrechamente; íntimamente. **It touches me n.,** Me toca de cerca, Es de sumo interés para mí. **They n. killed me,** Por poco me matan. **to be n.,** (of age) frisar en, rayar en

nearness *n* (of place) cercanía, proximidad, contigüidad, *Argentina* adyacencia, *f;* (of time) inminencia, proximidad, *f;* (relationship) consanguinidad, *f;* (avarice) avaricia, tacañería, *f;* (dearness) intimidad, amistad estrecha, *f*

neat *a zool* vacuno; elegante, sencillo, de buen gusto; (of the body) bien hecho, airoso, esbelto; (clean) limpio, aseado; (of handwriting) legible, bien proporcionado; pulido, esmerado, acabado; hábil, astuto, diestro; (of liquor, spirits) puro, solo. **to make a n. job of,** hacer (algo) bien

neatly *adv* sencillamente, con elegancia, con primor; con aseo, limpiamente; bien (proporcionado); diestramente, hábilmente

neatness *n* aseo, *m,* limpieza, *f;* elegancia, sencillez, *f;* buen gusto, *m;* destreza, habilidad, *f;* (aptness) pertinencia, *f*

nebula *n ast* nebulosa, *f*

nebulous *a* nebuloso; vago, impreciso, confuso

necessarily *adv* necesariamente; inevitablemente, sin duda

necessary *a* necesario, inevitable; imprescindible, preciso, indispensable, esencial; obligatorio, debido, forzoso. *n* requisito esencial, *m.* **if n.,** en caso de necesidad; si fuera necesario. **to be n.,** hacer falta; necesitarse

necessitate *vt* necesitar, exigir, requerir, obligar

necessitous *a* pobre, indigente, miserable, necesitado

necessity *n* necesidad, *f;* menester, *m,* (e.g., **an indispensable n.,** un menester imprescindible); consecuencia, *f,* resultado, efecto, *m;* inevitabilidad, fatalidad, *f;* (poverty) indigencia, pobreza, *f.* **Fire and clothing are necessities,** El fuego y el vestir son cosas necesarias. **from n.,** por necesidad. **in case of n.,** si fuese necesario, en caso de necesidad. **of n.,** de necesidad, sin remedio. **physical necessities,** menesteres físicos, *m pl.* **prime n.,** artículo de primera necesidad, *m.* **to be under the n. of,** tener que, tener la necesidad de

Necessity is the mother of invention La necesidad es una gran inventora, La necesidad aguza el ingenio

neck *n* cuello, *m,* garganta, *f;* (of bottles) gollete, cuello, *m;* (of animals) pescuezo, *m; geog* istmo, *m,* lengua de tierra, *f;* (of musical instruments) clavijero, mástil, *m; sew* escote, *m.* **low-necked,** (of dresses) escotado. **She fell on his n.,** Se colgó de su cuello. **He won by a n.,** Ganó por un cuello; *fig* Ganó por un tris. **to break anyone's n.,** romperle el pescuezo. **to wring the n. of,** torcer el pescuezo (a). **n. and n.,** parejos. **n. or nothing,** todo o nada, perdiz o no comerla. **n. stock,** alzacuello, *m*

necklace *n* collar, *m*

necktie *n* corbata, *f*

nectar *n* néctar, *m*

nectarine *n bot* variedad de melocotón, *f*

need *vt* necesitar, haber menester, requerir, exigir. *vi* ser necesario, hacer falta, carecer; haber (de). **N. I obey?** ¿He de obedecer? **You need to write carefully,** Hay que escribir con cuidado. **The work n. not be done for tomorrow,** No es preciso hacer el trabajo para mañana

need *n* necesidad, *f;* cosa necesaria, *f;* falta; (poverty) indigencia, pobreza, *f;* urgencia, *f;* (shortage) escasez, carestía, *f.* **in case of n.,** en caso de necesidad, en caso de urgencia. **I have n. of two more books,** Me hacen falta dos libros más

needful *a* necesario, preciso; indispensable, esencial. **the n.,** lo necesario

neediness *n* pobreza, penuria, miseria, estrechez, *f*

needle *n sew* aguja, *f*; (of compass) brújula, aguja imanada, *f*; (monument) obelisco, *m*; (of scales) field, *m*, lengüeta, *f*; (of phonograph) pría, *f*, (of measuring instruments) índice, *m*; *med* aguja de inyecciones, *f*. *inf* **to be as sharp as a n.,** no tener pelo de tonto. **pack n.,** aguja espartera, *f*. **n.-case,** alfiletero, agujero, *m*. **n. maker,** fabricante de agujas, *m*. **n.-shaped,** en forma de aguja, acicular. *vt Lat.* Am. engorrar

needle and thread hilo y aguja

needless *a* innecesario, superfluo. **n. to say,** claro está que . . ., huelga decir que . . .

needlessly *adv* innecesaria, inútilmente; en vano, de balde

needlework *n* labor de aguja, labor blanca, costura, *f*; bordado, *m*. **to do n.,** hacer costura

needs *adv* necesariamente, sin remedio *n pl* necesidades, *f pl*. **if n. must,** si hace falta. **N. must when the devil drives,** A la fuerza ahorcan

needy *a* necesitado, menesteroso, corto de medios, pobre, apurado

ne'er-do-well *n* calavera, perdido, *m*. **to be a n.,** ser de mala madera

nefarious *a* nefario, vil, nefando

negative *vt* negar, denegar; votar en contra (de), oponerse a; (prevent) impedir, imposibilitar. *a* negativo. *n* negativa, negación, *f*; repulsa, denegación, *f*; *phot* negativo, *m*, prueba negativa, *f*; *elec* electricidad negativa, *f*. **to reply in the n.,** dar una respuesta negativa

neglect *vt* descuidar, desatender; abandonar, dejar; (ignore) despreciar, no hacer caso (de); omitir, olvidar. *n* descuido, *m*, desatención, *f*; inobservancia, *f*; abandono, olvido, *m*; desdén, *m*, frialdad, *f*. **to fall into n.,** caer en desuso. **to n. one's obligations,** descuidar sus obligaciones

neglectful *a* negligente, descuidado, omiso

negligee *n* salto de cama, quimono, *m*, bata, *f*

negligence *n* negligencia, *f*, descuido, *m*; flojedad, pereza, *f*; (of dress) desaliño, *m*

negligent *a* negligente, descuidado; remiso, flojo, perezoso

negligible *a* insignificante, escaso, insuficiente; sin importancia, desdeñable

negotiable *a* negociable; (of a road) practicable, transitable

negotiate *vt* gestionar, agenciar, tratar; (a bend) tomar; (an obstacle) salvar, franquear; *vi* negociar. **to n. a bill of exchange,** descontar una letra de cambio. **to n. for a contract,** tratar un contrato

negotiation *n* negociación, *f*; com gestión, transacción, *f*; (of a bend) toma, *f*; (of an obstacle) salto, *m*

neigh *vi* relinchar. *n* relincho, relinchido, *m*

neighbor *n* vecino (-na); (biblical) prójimo (-ma)

neighborhood *n* vecindad, *f*, vecindario, *m*; cercanía, *f*, afueras, *f pl*, alrededores, *m pl*; a de barrio (e.g. **neighborhood moviehouse,** cine del barrio)

neighboring *a* vecino; cercano, inmediato, adyacente

neighborliness *n* buena vecindad, *f*

neighborly *a* amistoso, sociable, bondadoso. **to be n.,** ser de buena vecindad

neither *a* ningún; ninguno de los dos, e.g. **N. explanation is right,** Ninguna de las dos explicaciones es correcta. *conjunc* ni, tampoco, e.g. **N. Mary nor John,** Ni María ni Juan. **N. will he give it to her,** Tampoco se lo dará. *pron* ni uno ni otro, ninguno, e.g. **N. of them heard it,** Ni uno ni otro lo oyó.

nemesis *n* némesis, *f*; justicia, *f*

neon *n chem* neón, *m*

neon sign anuncio luminoso, *m*

neophyte *n* neófito (-ta); aspirante, *mf*

nephew *n* sobrino, *m*

nephritis *n med* nefritis, *f*

nepotism *n* nepotismo, *m*

nerve *n* (anat bot) nervio, *m*; valor, ánimo, *m*; vitalidad, *f*; *inf* descaro, *m*, desvergüenza, frescura, *f*. *vt* animar, alentar, envalentonar; esforzar; dar fuerza (a). *vi* animarse, esforzarse (a). **My nerves are all on edge,** Se me crispan los nervios. **n.-cell,** neurona, *f*. **to lose one's n.,** perder la cabeza; perder los nervios. **to strain every n.,** hacer un esfuerzo supremo. **n. center,** centro nervioso, *m*. **n.-racking,** espantoso, horripilante. **n. strain,** tensión nerviosa, *f*

nerveless *a* sin nervio; enervado

nervous *a* nervioso, asustadizo, tímido; agitado, excitado; (of style) vigoroso. **n. breakdown,** crisis nerviosa, *f*. **n. system,** sistema nervioso, *m*

nervousness *n* nerviosidad, timidez, *f*; agitación, *f*; (of style) vigor, *m*; energía, *f*

nervy *a* nervioso

nest *vi* anidar, hacerse un nido. *n* (bird's) nido, *m*; (animal's) madriguera, *f*; (of drawers) juego, *m*, serie, *f*; (of thieves) cueva, guarida, *f*; *inf* casita, *f*, hogar, *m*. **to feather one's n.,** hacer su agosto. **n.-egg,** *fig* nidal, *m*. **n. of eggs,** nidada de huevos, *f*

nestle *vt* apoyar. *vi* apiñarse, hacerse un ovillo. **to n. up to a person,** apretarse contra

nestling *n* pichón, pollo, *m*; pajarito, *m*

net *vt* coger con redes; obtener, coger; cubrir con redes. *vi* hacer redes. *n* red, *f*; (mesh) malla, *f*; (fabric) tul, *m*. **net making,** manufactura de redes, *f*

net *a com* líquido, neto, limpio; (of fabric) de tul. **net amount,** importe líquido, importe neto, *m.* **net balance,** saldo líquido, *m.* **net cost,** precio neto, *m.* **net profit,** beneficio neto (or líquido), *m*

nether a inferior, bajero, más bajo. **n. regions,** infierno, *m*

Netherlander *n* neerlandés (-esa), holandés (-esa)

Netherlands, the los Países Bajos *m pl*

nethermost a lo más bajo, ínfimo, más hondo

netting *n* red, (obra de) malla, *f; naut* jareta, *f;* manufactura de redes, *f;* pesca con redes, *f.* **wire-n.,** tela metálica, malla de alambre, *f*

nettle *vt* picar; *fig* irritar, picar, fastidiar, disgustar. *n* ortiga, *f.* **n.-rash,** urticaria, *f*

network *n* red, malla, randa, *f;* (of communications) sistema, *m*, red, *f*

neuralgia *n* neuralgia, *f*

neuralgic a neurálgico

neurasthenia *n* neurastenia, *f*

neurasthenic a and *n* neurasténico (-ca)

neurologist *n* neurólogo, *m*

neurosurgeon *n* neurocirujano, *m*

neurotic a and *n* neurótico (-ca)

neuter a neutro; (of verbs) intransitivo; (*zool bot*) sin sexo

neutral a neutral; (*chem mech*) neutro; (of colors) indeciso, indeterminado; (of persons) imparcial, indiferente. *n* neutral, *mf mech* **to go into n.,** pasar a marcha neutra

neutrality *n* neutralidad, *f;* indiferencia, *f;* imparcialidad, *f*

neutralize *vt* neutralizar

never *adv* nunca, jamás; de ningún modo, no; ni aun, ni siquiera. **Better late than n.,** Más vale tarde que nunca. **Never look a gift horse in the mouth,** A caballo regalado no se le mira el diente. **Were the hour n. so late,** Por más tarde que fuese la hora. **n. again,** nunca jamás. **n. a one,** ni siquiera uno. **n. a whit,** ni pizca. **N. mind!** ¡No importa! ¡No te preocupes! ¡No hagas caso! **n.-ceasing,** continuo, incesante. **n.-ending,** inacabable, eterno, sin fin. **n.-failing,** infalible. **n.-to-be-forgotten,** inolvidable

nevermore *adv* nunca jamás

nevertheless *adv* sin embargo, no obstante, con todo

new a nuevo; novel, fresco; distinto, diferente; moderno; (inexperienced) novato, no habituado; reciente. *adv* (in compounds) recién. **as good as new,** como nuevo. **brand-new,** flamante, nuevecito. **new-born,** recién nacido. **new-comer,** recién llegado (-da). **new-fashioned,** de última moda. **new-found,** recién hallado. **new-laid egg,** huevo fresco, *m.* **new moon,** luna nueva, *f,* novilunio, *m.* **new rich,** ricacho (-cha); indio, *m.* **new student,** alumno de nuevo ingreso. **New Testament,** Nuevo Testamento, *m.* **New World,** Nuevo Mundo, *m.* **New York (er),**

a and *n* neoyorquino (-na). **New Zealand(er),** a and *n* neozelandés (-esa)

newest a *sup* novísimo; más reciente

Newfoundland Terranova, *f.* **N. dog,** perro de Terranova, *m*

newish a bastante nuevo

newly *adv* nuevamente; hace poco, recientemente. The abb. form **recién** is used only with past part, e.g. **the n. painted door,** la puerta recién pintada. **the n.-weds,** los desposados, los recién casados

newness *n* novedad, *f;* inexperiencia, falta de práctica, *f;* innovación, *f*

New Orleans Nueva Orleans, *f*

news *n pl* noticias, *f pl;* nueva, *f;* reporte, aviso, *m;* novedad, *f.* **No n. is good n.,** Falta de noticias, buena señal. **piece of n.,** noticia, *f.* **What's the n.?** ¿Qué hay de nuevo? **n. agency,** agencia de noticias, agencia periodística, *f.* **n.-agent,** agente de la prensa, *m;* vendedor (-ra) de periódicos. **n. bulletin,** *rad* boletín de noticias, *m. inf* **n.-hound,** gacetillero (-ra). **n. item,** noticia de actualidad, *f.* **n.-print,** papel para periódicos, *m.* **n.-room,** gabinete de lectura, *m.* **n. reel,** película noticiera, revista cinematográfica, *f,* noticiario cinematográfico, noticiero *m,* actualidades, *f pl.* **n.-stand,** puesto de periódicos, quiosco de periódicos, *m.* **n. theater,** cine de actualidades, *m*

newsboy *n Lat. Am.* canillito, *m*

newscast *n* noticiario, *m*

newsgirl *n Lat. Am.* canillita, *f*

newspaper *n* periódico, diario, noticiero, *m.* **n. clipping, n. cutting,** recorte de periódico, *m.* **n. paragraph,** suelto, *m.* **n. reporter,** reportero (-ra); periodista, *mf* **n. reporting,** reporterismo, *m.* **n. serial,** folletín, *m,* novela por entregas, *f.* **n. vendor,** vendedor (-ra) de periódicos, *n*

news report *n* reportaje, *m*

New York Nueva York, *f*

New Zealand Nueva Zelandia, *f*

next a (of place) siguiente, vecino, contiguo; (of time) próximo, siguiente. **on the n. page,** en la página siguiente. **the n. day,** el día siguiente. **the n.-door house,** la casa vecina. **the n. life,** la otra vida. **n. month (year),** el mes (año) próximo (or que viene). **n. time,** otra vez, la próxima vez

next *adv* (of time) luego, en seguida; (of place) inmediatamente después. **I come n.,** Ahora me toca a mí. **It is n. to a certainty that . . . ,** Es casi seguro que . . . **the n. best,** el segundo. **the n. of kin,** los pariente más cercarro, *m,* parientes más cercanos, *m pl.* **to wear n. to the skin,** llevar sobre la piel. **n. to,** al lado de, junto a; primero después de; casi. **n. to nothing,** casi nada, muy poco. **What n.?** ¿Qué más?; ¿Y ahora qué?

nibble *vt* mordiscar, mordisquear, roer;

(horses) rozar; (fish) picar; *fig* considerar, tantear; *vi* picar. *n* mordisco, *m*; roedura, *f*

Nicaraguan a and *n* nicaragüeño (-ña)

nice a escrupuloso, minucioso, exacto; (of persons) simpático, afable, amable; fino; (of things) agradable, bonito; bueno; sutil, delicado; (*inf iron*) bonito. **a n. point,** un punto delicado. **a n. view,** una vista agradable (or bonita). **n.-looking,** guapo. **n. people,** gente fina, *f*; gente simpática, *f*

nicely *adv* muy bien; con elegancia; primorosamente; con amabilidad, gentilmente; agradablemente

niceness *n* exactitud, minuciosidad, *f*; (of persons) bondad, amabilidad, *f*; amenidad, hermosura, *f*; lo bonito; sutileza, *f*; refinamiento, *m*

nicety *n* exactitud, *f*; sutileza, *f*, refinamiento, *m*. **niceties,** *n pl* detalles, *m pl*. **to a n.,** con la mayor precisión; a la perfección

niche *n* nicho, templete, *m*; (vaulted) hornacina, *f*, *fig* **to find a n. for oneself,** encontrar una buena posición; situarse

nick *vt* cortar en muescas, mellar, tarjar. *n* mella, muesca, *f*. **in the n. of time,** en el momento oportuno, a tiempo

nickel *n* níquel, *m*; *com* moneda de níquel, *f*. **n.-plated,** niquelado

nickname *vt* apodar, motejar, apellidar. *n* apodo, sobrenombre, mote, mal nombre, *m*

nicotine *n* nicotina, *f*

niece *n* sobrina, *f*

niggardly a tacaño, avaricioso, mezquino, ruin, miserable

niggling a nimio, meticuloso; escrupuloso, minucioso

nigh. See **near**

night *n* noche, *f*; *fig* oscuridad, *f*, tinieblas, *f pl*. **all n.,** toda la noche, la noche entera. **all n. service,** servicio nocturno permanente, *m*. **at** or **by n.,** de noche. **every n.,** todas las noches, cada noche. **Good n.!** ¡Buenas noches! **last n.,** ayer por la noche, anoche, la noche pasada. **restless n.,** noche mala, noche toledana, *f*. **the n. before last,** anteayer por la noche, *m*. **to-n.,** esta noche. **tomorrow n.,** mañana por la noche. **to be n.,** ser de noche. **to spend the n.,** pernoctar, pasar la noche. **n.-bird,** pájaro nocturno, *m*; *inf* trasnochador (-ra). **n.-blindness,** nictalopia, *f*. **n.-cap,** gorro de dormir, *m*. **n. clothes,** traje de dormir, *m*. **n. club,** cabaré *m*. **n. dew,** relente, sereno, *m*. **n. flying,** vuelo nocturno, *m*. **n.-jar,** *orn* chotacabras, *m*. **n.-light,** mariposa, lamparilla, *f*. **n. mail,** último correo, *m*; tren correo de la noche, *m*. **n. school,** escuela nocturna, *f*. **n. shift,** turno de noche, *m*. **n. table** *Mexico* buró, *m*. **n. watch,** ronda de noche, *f*; *naut* sonochada, *f*. **n.**

watchman, (in the street) sereno, *m*; (of a building) vigilante nocturno, *m*

nightfall *n* anochecer, crepúsculo, atardecer, *m*

nightgown *n* camisa de noche, *f*

nightingale *n* ruiseñor, *m*

nightly a de noche; nocturno, nocturnal. *adv* todas las noches, cada noche

nightmare *n* pesadilla, *f*

Nile, the el Nilo, *m*

nimble a ágil, activo, *Mexico* alacre; vivo, listo. **n.-fingered,** ligero de dedos. **n.-witted,** despierto, vivo

nimbly *adv* ágilmente, ligeramente

nincompoop *n* papirote, *m*, papanatas, *mf* tonto (-ta)

nine a and *n* nueve, *m*. **He is n.,** Tiene nueve años. **the N.,** las nueve Musas. **n. o'clock,** las nueve. **to be dressed up to the nines,** estar hecho un brazo de mar

ninefold a and *adv* nueve veces

nineteen a and *n* diez y nueve, diecinueve *m*

nineteenth a décimonono. *n* (of month) el diez y nueve; (of monarchs) diez y nueve. **the n. century,** el siglo diez y nueve

ninetieth a nonagésimo, noventa

ninety a and *n* noventa *m*. **n.-one,** noventa y uno. **n.-two,** noventa y dos. **the n.-first chapter,** el capítulo noventa y uno

ninny *n* parapoco, chancleta, *mf*; mentecato (-ta)

ninth a noveno, nono. *n* nueve, *m*; (of the month) el nueve (of sovereigns) nono. **one n.,** un noveno

nip *vt* pellizcar, pinchar; mordiscar, morder; (wither) marchitar; (freeze) helar; (run) correr. *vi* pinchar; picar (el viento). *n* pellizco, pinchazo, *m*; mordisco, *m*; (of spirits) trago, *m*; copita, *f*; (in the air) viento frío, hielo, *m*. **to nip in,** colarse dentro, deslizarse en. **to nip off,** pirarse, mudarse. *fig* **to nip in the bud,** cortar en flor

nippers *n pl* alicates, *m pl*; tenacillas, pinzas, *f pl*

nipple *n* pezón, *m*; pezón artificial, *m*

nit *n ent* liendre, *f*

nitre *n* salitre, *m*

nitrogen *n chem* nitrógeno, *m*

no a ningún, ninguno, ninguna, e.g. **by no means,** de ningún modo. **No** is often not translated in Sp., e.g. **I have no time,** No tengo tiempo. *adv* no. *n* voto negativo, no, *m*. **to be of no account,** no tener importancia; no significar nada. **to be no good for,** no servir para. **to be of no use,** ser inútil. **to have no connection with,** no tener nada que ver con. **for no reason,** sin motivo alguno. **"No Admittance,"** «Entrada Prohibida.» **no, indeed,** Cierto que no. **no-man's land,** tierra de nadie, *f*. **no more,** no más. **No**

more of this! ¡No hablemos más de eso!
no one, nadie, ninguno. **no sooner,** no
bien, tan pronto (como). **no such thing,**
no tal. **"No Thoroughfare,"** «Prohibido
el Paso.» **whether or not,** sea o no sea
Noah's Ark *n* arca de Noé, *f*

nobility *n* nobleza, *f*; (of rank) aristocracia, nobleza, *f*; (of conduct) caballerosidad, hidalguía, generosidad, bondad, *f*; (grandeur) grandeza, sublimidad,
f. **the higher n.,** los nobles de primera
clase

noble *a* noble; (in rank) aristocrático,
noble, linajudo; (of conduct) caballeroso,
generoso; (of buildings) sublime, magnífico. *n* noble, *m*, aristócrata, *mf* **to
make n.,** ennoblecer. **n.-mindedness,**
generosidad, grandeza de alma, *f*. **n.
title,** título de nobleza, título del reino, *m*

noblewoman *n* dama noble, mujer
noble, aristócrata, *f*

nobly *adv* noblemente, generosamente.
n. born, noble de nacimiento

nobody *n* nadie, ninguno. **There was n.
there,** No había nadie allí. *inf* **a n.,** un
(una) cualquiera, una persona insignificante. **n. else,** nadie más, ningún otro

nocturnal *a* nocturno, nocherniego, nocturnal

nocturne *n mus* nocturno, *m*

nod *vt* inclinar la cabeza; hacer una señal
(or señas) con la cabeza; *vi* dar cabezadas; cabecear; (of trees) mecerse, inclinarse; inclinar la cabeza. *n* señal (or
seña) con la cabeza, *f*; inclinación de la
cabeza, *f*; cabeceo, *m*, cabezada, *Lat. Am.*
cabeceada, *f*. **A nod is as good as a
wink,** A buen entendedor pocas palabras. **He nodded to me as he passed,**
Me saludó con la cabeza al pasar. **He
signed to me with a nod,** Me hizo una
señal con la cabeza

nodding *a* que cabecea; *bot* colgante, inclinado; temblante. *n* cabeceo, *m*; saludo
con la cabeza, *m*

noddle *n* mollera, *f*

node *n* (*bot med*) nudo, *m*

nodule *n* nódulo, *m*; nudillo, *m*

noise *n* ruido, son, *m*; tumulto, clamor,
estruendo, alboroto, *Central America*
embullo, *m*. **to make a n.,** hacer ruido.
to n. abroad, divulgar, publicar

noiseless *a* silencioso, callado, sin ruido

noisily *adv* ruidosamente

noisiness *n* ruido, estrépito, tumulto,
clamor, *m*; (of voices) gritería, *f*

noisome *a* ofensivo; fétido, apestoso

noisy *a* ruidoso; estruendoso; estrepitoso, clamoroso

nomad *a* nómada, errante; (of flocks) tra-
shumante. *n* nómada, *mf*

nomenclature *n* nomenclatura, *f*

nominal *a* nominal; titular; insignificante, de poca importancia. **the n.
head,** el director en nombre

nominally *adv* nominalmente, en nombre

nominate *vt* nombrar, designar, elegir;
fijar, señalar

nominating *a* nominador

nomination *n* nombramiento, *m*,
nominación, *f*; señalamiento, *m*

nominee *n* nómino propuesto, *m*

non *adv* non; des-; in-; falta de. **non-ac-
ceptance,** rechazo, *m*. **non-acquaint-
ance,** ignorancia, *f*. **non-admission,** no
admisión, *f*; denegación, *f*, rechazo, *m*.
non-aggression, no agresión, *f*. **non-al-
coholic,** no alcohólico. **non-appear-
ance,** ausencia, *f*; *law* no comparecencia, contumacia, *f*. **non-arrival,**
ausencia, *f*; falta de recibo, *f*. **non-at-
tendance,** falta de asistencia, ausencia,
f. **non-carbonated,** sin gas. **non-com-
batant,** no combatiente. **non-commissioned officer,** oficial subalterno, *m*.
non-committal, evasivo, equívoco, ambiguo. **non-compliance,** falta de obediencia, *f*. **non-concurrence,** falta de
acuerdo, *f*. **non-conducting,** no conductivo. **non-conductor,** mal conductor, *m*;
elec aislador, *m*. **non-contagious,** no
contagioso. **non-coöperation,** *pol* resistencia pasiva, *f*; no cooperación, *f*. **non-
delivery,** falta de entrega, *f*. **non-essen-
tial,** no esencial, prescindible.
non-execution, no cumplimiento, *m*.
non-existence, no existencia, *f*. **non-ex-
istent,** inexistente, no existente. **non-in-
tervention,** no intervención, *f*. **non-
manufacturing,** no industrial.
non-member, visitante, *mf* **non-observ-
ance,** incumplimiento, *m*; violación, *f*.
non-payment, falta de pago, *f*. **non-per-
formance,** falta de ejecución, *f*. **non-
poisonous,** no venenoso, innocuo. **non-
resistance,** falta de resistencia, *f*;
obediencia pasiva, *f*. **non-skid,** antides-
lizante, antirresbaladizo. **non-smok-
ing,** que no fuma; (of a railway compartment, etc.) para no fumadores.
non-stop, continuo, incesante; directo,
sin parar; *aer* sin escalas

non-aligned *a* no abanderado

non-alignment *n* no abanderamiento *m*

nonchalance *n* aplomo, *m*, indiferencia,
frialdad, calma, *f*

nonchalant *a* indiferente, frío, impasible

nonchalantly *adv* con indiferencia

nonconformist *a* and *n* disidente *mf*; *a*
inconforme, *n*, inconformista, *mf*

nondescript *a* indeterminado, indefinido, indeciso, mediocre

none *pron* nadie, ninguno; nada. *a* and *n*
ninguno (-na). *adv* no; de ningún modo,
de ninguna manera. **I have n.,** No lo
tengo, No tengo ninguno. **We have n. of
your things,** No tenemos ninguna de tus
cosas. **I was n. the worse,** No me hallaba
peor. **N. can read his account with
pleasure,** Nadie puede leer su narración

con gusto. **n. the less,** no menos; sin embargo

nonentity *n* persona sin importancia, medianía, *f*, cero, *m*

nonplussed *a* cortado, perplejo, confuso

non-profit *a* sin fines de lucro, sin fines lucrativos

nonsense *n* disparate, despropósito, desatino, *m*, absurdidad, *f*; *inf* galimatías, *m*; pamplina, patraña, *f*. **to talk n.,** hablar sin ton ni son. **N.I** IA otro perro con este hueso! ¡Patrañas!

nonsensical *a* absurdo, ridículo, disparatado

noodle *n cul* tallarín, *m*; *inf* mentecato (-ta), bobo (-ba)

nook *n* escondrijo, lugar retirado, rincón, *m*

noon *n* mediodía, *m*; *fig* punto culminante, apogeo, *m*, a de mediodía, meridional. **at n.,** a mediodía

noose *vt* coger con lazos. *n* lazo corredizo, dogal, *m*

nopal *n bot* nopal, *m*

No Parking «Se Prohíbe Estacionar,» «Se Prohíbe Estacionarse»

nor *conjunc* ni, no, tampoco. **He removed neither his coat nor his hat,** No se quitó ni el gabán ni el sombrero. **Nor was this the first time,** Y no fue ésta la primera vez. **Nor I,** Ni yo tampoco

norm *n* modelo, *m*, norma, regla, pauta, *f*; (of size) marca, *f*; (*bot zool*) tipo, *m*

normal *a* normal; común, natural, corriente, regular; *math* perpendicular. *normal. n* condición normal, *f*, estado normal, *m*; *math* normal, *f*. **to become n.,** normalizarse, hacerse normal. **to make n.,** normalizar. **n. school,** escuela normal, *f*

normalize *vt* normalizar

north *n* norte, *m*. a del norte, septentrional. **n. by west,** norte, cuarta noroeste. **n. of the city,** al norte de la ciudad. **N.-American,** a and *n* norte-americano (-na). **n.-east,** a and *n* nordeste *m*. **n.-easter,** viento del nordeste, *m*. **n.-easterly,** del nordeste (winds). **n.-eastern,** del nordeste (places). **n.-eastward,** hacia el nordeste. **n.-n.-east,** nornordeste, *m*. **n.-n.-west,** nornorueste, *m*. **n.-polar,** ártico. **N. Star,** estrella del norte, estrella polar, *f*. **n.-west,** noroeste, *m*. **n.-wester,** viento del noroeste, *m*. **n.-westerly,** del noroeste (winds). **n.-westerly gale,** temporal del noroeste, *m*. **n.-western,** del noroeste; situado al noroeste. **n.-westwards,** hacia el noroeste. **n. wind,** el viento del norte, el cierzo

North America, Norteamérica, América del Norte, *f*

northern *a* del norte, septentrional, norteño; (of races) nórdico. **N. Cross,** crucero, *m*. **n. lights,** aurora boreal, *f*

northerner *n* hombre del norte, *m*, habitante del norte, *mf*

northernmost *a sup* al extremo norte, más septentrional

northwards *adv* hacia el norte

Norway Noruega, *f*

Norwegian a and *n* noruego (-ga); (language) noruego, *m*

nose *n* nariz, *f*; (of animals) hocico, *m*; (sense of smell) olfato, *m*; (of ships) proa, *f*; (of jug) pico, *m*, boca, *f*; (projecting piece) cuerno, *m*, nariz, *f*; (of airplane) cabeza, *f*, *vt* acariciar con la nariz; avanzar lentamente. *vi* husmear, olfatear. **to n. into,** *inf* meter las narices, poner baza. **to n. out,** descubrir, averiguar. **to bleed at the n.,** echar sangre de las narices. **to blow one's n.,** sonar (or limpiarse) las narices. **to keep one's n. to the grindstone,** estar sobre el yunque, batir el cobre. *fig* **to lead by the n.,** tener a uno agarrado por las narices. **to pay through the n.,** costar un ojo de la cara. **to speak through the n.,** ganguear. **to turn up one's n.,** *fig* hacer gestos (a), volver la cara. **flat n.,** nariz chata, *f*. **snub n.,** nariz respingona, *f*. **well-shaped n.,** nariz perfilada, *f*. **under one's n.,** bajo las narices de uno. **n.-bag,** cebadera, mochila, *f*; morral, *m*. **n.-bleeding,** *med* epistaxis, *f*; hemorragia de las narices, *f*. **n.-dive,** *aer* descenso de cabeza, picado, *m*. *vi* picar. **n.-piece,** (of microscope) ocular, *m*. **n.-ring,** (of a bull, etc.) narigón, *m*

-nosed a de nariz . . . , con la nariz . . .

nosegay *n* ramillete, *m*

nosey Parker *n inf* mequetrefe, *m*; cócora, *Lat. Am.* averigüetas, *Argentina* hurguete, *mf*

No Smoking «Prohibido Fumar», Se Prohíbe Fumar

nostalgia *n* nostalgia, añoranza, *f*

nostalgic *a* nostálgico

nostril *n* ventana de la nariz, *f*, *n pl* **nostrils,** narices, *f pl*

nostrum *n* panacea, *f*, curalotodo, *m*; medicina patentada, *f*

not *adv* no; sin; ni, ni siquiera. **Is it not true? We think not,** ¿No es verdad? No lo creemos. **You have seen Mary, have you not?** Vd. ha visto a María, ¿verdad? **not caring whether he came or not,** sin preocuparse de que viniese o no. **not that he will come,** no es decir que venga. **not at all,** de ningún modo; (courtesy) ¡de nada! **not even,** ni siquiera. **not guilty,** no culpable. **not one,** ni uno. **not so much as,** no tanto como; ni siquiera. **It is not so much that, as it is . . .** No es tanto eso, cuanto que . . . **not to say,** por no decir

notable a notable, señalado, memorable; digno de atención. *n* persona eminente, *f*, notable, *mf*

notary *n* notario, escribano, *m*

notation *n* notación, *f*

notch vt cortar muescas (en); mellar, ranurar, entallar. n muesca, mella, ranura, entalladura, f

note vt notar, observar; anotar, apuntar; advertir, hacerse cuenta de. n mus nota, f; son, acento, m; (letter) recado, billete, m; anotación, glosa, f; apuntación, f, apunte, m, nota, f; (importance) importancia, distinción, f; com vale, abonaré, m; (sign) marca, señal, f. **to n. down,** anotar. **worthy of note,** digno de atención. **n.-book,** libro de apuntes, cuaderno, m, libreta, f. **n.-case,** cartera, f, com **n. of hand,** pagaré, m. **n.-paper,** papel de escribir, m. **n.-taker,** apuntador (-ra)

noted a célebre, famoso, ilustre, eminente, insigne

noteworthy a digno de nota, notable, digno de atención

nothing n nada, f; la nada; cero, m. adv en nada. **to come to n.,** anonadarse, fracasar. **to do n.,** no hacer nada. **to do n. but,** no hacer más que. **to have n. to do with,** no tener nada que ver con; inf no tener arte ni parte en. **There is n. else to do,** No hay nada más que hacer; No hay más remedio. **There is n. to fear,** No hay de que tener miedo. **We could make n. of the book,** No llegamos a comprender el libro. **for n.,** de balde, en vano; gratis. **next to n.,** casi nada. **n. else or more,** nada más. **n. like,** ni con mucho. **n. much,** poca cosa. **n. new,** nada nuevo. **n. similar,** nada semejante. **n. to speak of,** poca cosa

notice vt observar, reparar en, darse cuenta de; marcar, caer en la cuenta (de), fijarse (en). n observación, atención, f; aviso, m, notificación, f; anuncio, m; (term) plazo, m; (review) crítica, f. **at short n.,** a corto aviso. **until further n.,** hasta nuevo aviso (or orden). **to attract n.,** atraer la atención. **I hadn't noticed,** No me había fijado. **to be beneath one's n.,** no merecer su atención. **to be under n.,** estar dimitido. **to bring to the n. of,** dar noticia de. **to escape n.,** pasar desapercibido. **to give n.,** hacer saber, informar; (of employer) despedir (a); (of employee) dimitir, dar la dimisión. **to take n. of,** notar, darse cuenta de; hacer caso, atender (a). **n. board,** letrero, tablero de anuncios, m. **n. to quit,** desahúcio, m

noticeable a perceptible, evidente; digno de observación, notable

noticeably adv perceptiblemente; notablemente

notification n notificación, intimación, advertencia, f, aviso, m

notify vt notificar, comunicar, avisar, intimar, hacer saber

notion n noción, idea, f, concepto, m; (view) opinión, f, parecer, m; (novelty) novedad, f; artículo de fantasía, m. **I have a n. that . . . ,** Tengo la idea de que . . . ,

Sospecho que . . . **I haven't a n.,** No tengo idea

No Tipping «No Se Admiten Propinas»

notoriety n notoriedad, publicidad, f; escándalo, m; persona notoria, f

notorious a notorio, famoso, conocido; escandaloso, sensacional

notwithstanding prep a pesar de. adv sin embargo, no obstante. conjunc aunque, bien que, por más que

nougat n turrón, m

nought n math cero, m; nada, f

noun n substantivo, nombre, m

nourish vt sustentar, alimentar, nutrir; fig fomentar, favorecer

nourishing a nutritivo, alimenticio, nutricio

nourishment n nutrición, f; sustento, m; alimento, m; fig fomento, pasto, m

Nova Scotia Nueva Escocia, f

novel a nuevo, original, inacostumbrado. n novela, f. **n. of roguery,** novela picaresca, f

novelette n novela corta, f

novelist n novelista, mf

novelty n novedad, f; innovación, f; cambio, m

November n noviembre, m

novice n ecc novicio (-ia); comenzante, principiante, mf, aspirante, m. Lat. Am. advenedizo (-za)

novocain n med novocaína, f

now adv ahora, actualmente, al presente, a la fecha; en seguida, ahora, inmediatamente; poco ha, hace poco; pues bien. interj ¡A ver! ¡Vamos! conjunc pero, mas. n presente, m, actualidad, f. **before now,** antes, en otras ocasiones, ya, previamente. **just now,** ahora mismo, hace poco. **now . . . now,** ya . . . ya; sucesivamente, en turno. **now and then,** de vez en cuando, de tarde en tarde. **now that,** ya que, ahora que, dado que. **until now,** hasta el presente, hasta aquí, hasta ahora

nowadays adv hoy en día, actualmente, en nuestros días

nowhere adv en ninguna parte. **in the middle of n.,** donde Cristo dio las tres voces. **n. else,** en ninguna otra parte. inf **n. near,** ni con mucho; muy lejos (de)

nowise adv de ningún modo, en modo alguno, de ninguna manera

noxious a dañoso, nocivo; pestífero

nozzle n (of a hose-pipe) boquilla, f; mech gollete, m; tubo de salida, m, tobera, f; inyector, m

n.p. (no place) s.l. (sin lugar)

nuance n matiz, m, gradación, sombra, f

nubile a núbil

nuclear a nuclear

nucleus n núcleo, m; centro, foco, m

nude a desnudo, nudo, Peru calato, elsewhere in Lat. Am. encuerado

nudge *vt* dar un codazo (a). *n* codazo, *m*

nudism *n* nudismo, *m*

nudist *n* nudista, *mf*

nudity *n* desnudez, *f*

nugget *n* *min* pepita, *f*

nuisance *n* molestia, incomodidad, *f*, fastidio, *m*; *inf* tostón, *m*, lata, *Lat. Am.* fregada, *Colombia* vaina, *f*. **to make a n. of oneself**, meterse donde no le llaman, ser un pelmazo. **What a n.!** ¡Qué lata! ¡Qué fastidio!, *Colombia* ¡Qué vaina!

null a nulo, inválido, sin fuerza legal. **n. and void**, nulo, írrito

nullification *n* anulación, invalidación, *f*

nullity *n* nulidad, *f*

numb *vt* entumecer, entorpecer. a entumecido; torpe, dormido; paralizado; *fig* insensible, pasmado. **n. with cold**, entumecido de frío

number *vt* numerar, contar; poner número (a); (pages of a book) foliar; ascender a. *n* número, *m*; (figure) cifra, *f*; (crowd) multitud, muchedumbre, *f*; cantidad, *f*; (of a periodical) ejemplar, *m*; *gram* número, *m*; *pl* versos, *m pl*. **Numbers**, (Bible) Números, *m pl*; **to be numbered among**, figurar entre. **among the n. of**, entre la muchedumbre de. **a n. of**, varios, muchos, una cantidad de. **in great n.**, en gran número; en su mayoría. **6 Peace Street**, Calle de la Paz nᵒ (número) 6. **one of their n.**, uno entre ellos. **n. board**, (racing) indicador, *m*. **n. plate**, *aut* chapa de identidad, placa de número, *f*

numbering *n* numeración, *f*

numberless a innumerable, sin número, sin fin, infinito

numbness *n* entumecimiento, entorpecimiento, *m*; *fig* insensibilidad, *f*

numeral a numeral. *n* número, *m*, cifra, *f*; *gram* nombre o adjetivo numeral, *m*

numerical a numérico

numerous a numeroso; nutrido, grande; muchos (-as)

numismatic a numismático. *n pl* **numismatics**, numismática, *f*

numskull *n* zote, topo, *m*

nun *n* monja, religiosa, *f*. **to become a nun**, profesar, tomar el hábito, meterse monja

nuptial a nupcial. *n pl* **nuptials**, nupcias, *f pl*, enlace, *m*. **n. mass**, *ecc* misa de velaciones, *f*. **n. song**, epitalamio, *m*

nurse *vt* criar; dar de mamar (a), amamantar; (the sick) cuidar, asistir; (fondle) acariciar, mecer; *fig* fomentar, promover. *vi* trabajar como enfermera. *n* (of the sick) enfermera, *f*; (wet) nodriza, ama de leche, *Lat. Am.* criandera, *f*; (children's) niñera, *f*; *fig* fomentador, *m*. **male n.**, enfermero, *m*

nursery *n* *agr* plantel, vivero semillero, criadero, *m*; (children's room) cuarto de los niños, *m*; *fig* sementera, *f*; semillero, *m*. **n. governess**, aya, *f*. **n. rhyme**, canción infantil, *f*

nurseryman *n* horticultor, *m*; jardinero, *m*

nursing *n* lactancia, crianza, *f*; (of the sick) asistencia, *f*, cuido, *m*. **n. home**, clínica, *f*. **n. mother**, madre lactante, *f*

nurture *vt* alimentar; criar, educar. *n* nutrición, alimentación, *f*; crianza, educación, *f*

nut *vi* coger nueces. *n* *bot* nuez, *f*; *mech* tuerca, hembra de tornillo, *f*, *inf* **to be a tough nut to crack**, ser un tío de cuidado. **to crack nuts**, cascar nueces. **to go nutting**, coger nueces. **cashew nut**, anacardo, *m*. **loose nut**, *mech* tuerca aflojada, *f*. **nut-brown**, castaño. **nut tree**, nogal, *m*

nutcrackers *n pl* cascanueces, quebrantanueces, *m*

nutmeg *n* nuez moscada, nuez de especia, *f*

nutrition *n* nutrición, alimentación, *f*

nutritious, nutritive a nutritivo, alimenticio, alible

nutshell *n* cáscara de nuez, *f*. **to put in a n.**, decir en resumidas cuentas, decir en forma apastillada

nutty a de nuez

nuzzle *vt* acariciar con la nariz

nylon *n* nilón, nylon, *m*. **n. stockings**, medias de cristal (or de nilón), *f pl*

nymph *n* ninfa, *f*; *ent* crisálida, *f*. **n.-like**, como una ninfa; de ninfa

nymphomania *n* ninfomanía, *f*, furor uterino, *m*

O

o *n* (letter) o, *f*, *interj* ¡o! **O that . . . !** ¡Ojalá que!

oaf *n* zoquete, zamacuco, *m*

oafish *a* lerdo, torpe

oak *n* (tree and wood) roble, *m*, a de roble. **carved oak**, roble tallado, *m*. **holm-oak**, encina, *f*. **oak-apple**, agalla, *f*. **oak grove**, robledo, *m*

oar *n* remo, *m*. **to lie on the oars**, cesar de remar. **to pull at the oars**, bogar, remar. **to put in one's oar**, *inf* meter baza. **to ship the oars**, armar los remos. **to unship the oars**, desarmar los remos. **oar-stroke**, palada, *f*

oarsman *n* remero, bogador, *m*

OAS (Organization of American States) OEA (Organización de los Estados Americanos)

oasis *n* oasis, *m*

oat *n bot* avena, *f*. **wild oat**, avena silvestre, *f*. **to sow one's wild oats**, correrla, andarse a la flor del berro. **oat field**, avenal, *m*

oath *n* juramento, *m*; (curse) blasfemia, *f*, reniego, *m*. **on o.**, bajo juramento. **to break an o.**, violar el juramento. **to put on o.**, tomar juramento, hacer prestar juramento. **to take an o.**, prestar (or hacer) juramento. **to take the o. of allegiance**, jurar la bandera

oatmeal *n* harina de avena, *f*

obdurate *a* obstinado, terco, porfiado. **He is o. to our requests**, Es sordo a nuestros ruegos

obedience *n* obediencia, sumisión, docilidad, *f*. **blind o.**, obediencia ciega, *f*. **in o. to**, conforme a, de acuerdo con

obedient *a* obediente, sumiso, dócil. **to be o. to**, ser obediente (a), obedecer (a)

obeisance *n* reverencia, cortesía, *f*, saludo, *m*; (homage) homenaje, *m*

obese *a* obeso, corpulento, grueso, gordo

obesity *n* obesidad, gordura, corpulencia, *f*

obey *vt and vi* obedecer. *vt* (carry out) cumplir, observar. **to be obeyed**, ser obedecido

obfuscate *vt* ofuscar, cegar

obituary *a* mortuorio, necrológico. *n* obituario, *m*, necrología, *f*. **o. column**, (in newspaper) sección necrológica, *f*. **o. notice**, esquela de defunción, *f*

object *n* objeto, artículo, *m*, cosa, *f*; (purpose) propósito, intento, *m*; (aim) fin, término, *m*; *gram* complemento, *m*; *inf* individuo, *m*. *vt* objetar, poner reparos a. *vi* oponerse, poner objeciones. **to o. to that remark**, Protesto contra esa observación. **If you don't o.**, Si Vd. no tiene inconveniente. **o. finder**, objetivo, *m*. **o.**

lesson, lección de cosas, *f*; lección práctica, *f*

objection *n* objeción, protesta, *f*, reparo, *m*; (obstacle) dificultad, *f*, inconveniente, *m*. **to have no o.**, no tener inconveniente. **to raise an o.**, hacer constar una protesta, poner una objeción

objectionable *a* censurable, reprensible; desagradable, molesto

objective *a* objetivo; *gram* acusativo. *n* objeto, propósito, *m*; destinación, *f*; *mil* objetivo, *m*, *gram* **o. case**, caso acusativo, *m*,

objector *n* objetante, *mf*, impugnador (-ra). **conscientious o.**, (dissident) el, m, (*f*, la) que protesta contra; (pacifist) pacifista, *mf*

obligation *n* obligación, *f*; deber, *m*, precisión, *f*; compromiso, *m*. **of o.**, de deber; de precepto. **to be under an o.**, estar bajo una obligación; deber un favor. **to place under an o.**, poner bajo una obligación

obligatory *a* obligatorio, forzoso

oblige *vt* (insist on) obligar, hacer, forzar; (gratify) hacer un favor (a), complacer. **He obliged me with a match**, Me hizo el favor de una cerilla. **They are much obliged to you**, Le están muy reconocidos. **Much obliged!** ¡Se agradece!

obliging *a* atento, condescendiente, complaciente, servicial, *Lat. Am.* acomedido

obligingly *adv* cortésmente

oblique *a* oblicuo, sesgado; (indirect) indirecto, evasivo; *gram* oblicuo

obliquely *adv* oblicuamente, al sesgo, sesgadamente; indirectamente. **to place o.**, poner al sesgo

obliterate *vt* borrar; destruir, aniquilar. **to be obliterated**, borrarse; quedar destruido

obliteration *n* testación, *f*; destrucción, *f*. **o. raid**, bombardeo de saturación, *m*

oblivion *n* olvido, *m*. **to cast into o.**, echar al olvido

oblivious *a* olvidadizo, descuidado

oblong *a* oblongo, cuadrilongo, rectangular. *n* rectángulo, cuadrilongo, *m*

obloquy *n* infamia, maledicencia, deshonra, *f*

obnoxious *a* odioso, ofensivo, aborrecible

oboe *n mus* oboe, *m*. **o. player**, oboe, *m*

obscene *a* indecente, obsceno, escabroso

obscenity *n* indecencia, obscenidad, *f*

obscure *a* (indistinct) obscuro, indistinto; (dark) lóbrego, tenebroso; (remote) retirado, apartado; (puzzling) confuso; (unknown) desconocido; humilde; (difficult to understand) abstruso, obscuro; (vague) vago. *vt* obscurecer; (hide) esconder; (eclipse) eclipsar. **to o. the issue**, hacer perder de vista el problema

obscurity *n* (darkness) obscuridad, lobreguez, *f*; (difficulty of meaning) ambigüedad, confusión, vaguedad, *f*; humildad, *f*

obsequious *a* servil, empalagoso, zalamero

observable *a* observable, perceptible, visible; notable

observance *n* observancia, *f*, cumplimiento, *m*; práctica, costumbre, *f*; (religious) rito, *m*

observant *a* observador; obediente, atento. **o. of**, observador de; atento a

observation *n* observación, *f*, examen, escrutinio, *m*; (experience) experiencia, *f*; (remark) advertencia, *f*, comento, *m*. **to escape o.**, no ser advertido. **o. car.**, vagón-mirador, *m*, **o. post**, puesto de observación, *m*

observatory *n* observatorio, *m*

observe *vt* (laws) cumplir; (holy days, etc.) guardar; (notice) observar, mirar, notar, ver, reparar en; (remark) decir, advertir; (examine) vigilar, atisbar, examinar; *ast* observar. *vi* ser observador. **to o. silence**, guardar silencio

observer *n* observador (-ra)

obsess *vt* obsesionar, obcecar

obsessed *a* obseso

obsession *n* obsesión, obcecación, idea fija, manía, *f*

obsolescent *a* que se hace antiguo, que cae en desuso

obsolete *a* obsoleto, anticuado; *biol* rudimentario, atrofiado

obstacle *n* obstáculo, impedimento, *m*; dificultad, *f*, inconveniente, *m*. **to put obstacles in the way of**, *fig* dificultar, hacer difícil. **o. race**, carrera de obstáculos, *f*

obstetrician *n* obstétrico (-ea), médico (-ca) partero (-ra)

obstetrics *n* obstetricia, tocología, *f*

obstinacy *n* obstinación, terquedad, tenacidad, porfía, *f*, tesón, *m*; persistencia, *f*

obstinate *a* terco, porfiado, obstinado, tenaz; refractario; persistente, pertinaz. **to be o.**, ser terco; porfiar. **to be o. about**, obstinarse en.

obstreperous *a* turbulento, ruidoso

obstruct *vt* obstruir: impedir; cerrar; (thwart) estorbar; (hinder) dificultar, embarazar; (the traffic) obstruir, atascar. *vi* estorbar. **to become obstructed**, obstruirse, cerrarse

obstruction *n* obstrucción, *f*; estorbo, obstáculo, *m*. **to cause a street o.**, obstruir el tráfico

obtain *vt* obtener, conseguir, lograr; recibir; (by threats) arrancar. *vi* estar en boga, estar en vigor, predominar. **to o. on false pretences**, conseguir por engaño

obtainable *a* asequible, alcanzable. **easily o.**, fácil a obtener

obtrude *vt* imponer

obtrusion *n* imposición, *f*; importunidad, *f*

obtrusive *a* importuno; entremetido; pretencioso

obtuse *a* (blunt) obtuso, romo; (stupid) estúpido, torpe, lerdo. **o. angle**, obtusángulo, *m*

obtuseness *n* (bluntness) embotamiento, *m*; (stupidity) estupidez, torpeza, *f*

obverse *a* del anverso. *n* anverso, *m*

obviate *vt* obviar, evitar

obvious *a* evidente, manifiesto, patente, obvio, aparente, transparente; poco sutil

obviously *adv* evidentemente, patentemente

occasion *n* ocasión, *f*; oportunidad, *f*, momento oportuno, tiempo propicio, *m*; (reason) motivo, origen, *m*, causa, razón, *f*; (need) necesidad, *f*. *vt* ocasionar, causar, producir. **as o. demands**, cuando las circunstancias lo exigen, en caso necesario. **for the o.**, para la ocasión. **on one o.**, una vez. **on the o. of**, en la ocasión de. **on that o.**, en tal ocasión, en aquella ocasión. **He has given me no o. to say so**, No me ha dado motivos de decirlo. **There is no o. for it**, No hay necesidad para ello. **to have o. to**, haber de, tener que, necesitar. **to lose no o.**, no perder ripio (or oportunidad). **to rise to the o.**, estar al nivel de las circunstancias. **to take this o.**, aprovechar esta oportunidad

occasional *a* (occurring at times) de vez en cuando, intermitente; poco frecuente, infrecuente; (of verse) de ocasión. **o. table**, mesilla, *f*

occasionally *adv* de vez en cuando

occlude *vt* obstruir, cerrar; *med* ocluir; *chem* absorber

occlusion *n* cerramiento, *m*; *med* oclusión, *f*; *chem* absorción de gases, *f*

occult *a* oculto, escondido, misterioso; mágico. **o. sciences**, creencias ocultas, *f pl*

occupancy *n* ocupación, posesión, *f*; (tenancy) tenencia, *f*

occupant *n* habitante, *mf*; ocupante, *mf*; (tenant) inquilino (-na)

occupation *n* ocupación *f*; (tenure) inquilinato, *m*, tenencia, *f*; (work) trabajo, quehacer, *m*, labor, *f*; (employment) empleo, oficio, *m*; profesión, *f*

occupational *a* de oficio. **o. disease**, enfermedad profesional, *f*

occupier *n* ocupante, *mf*, inquilino (-na)

occupy *vt* ocupar; (live in) vivir en, habitar; (time) emplear, pasar; (take over) apoderarse de, ocupar. **to o. oneself in or with**, ocuparse en, ocuparse con. **to**

be **occupied in** or **with**, estar ocupado con, ocuparse en

occur *vi* (happen) suceder, tener lugar, acaecer; (exist) encontrarse, existir; (of ideas) ocurrirse, venirse. **to o. to one's mind**, venírsele a las mientes. **to o. again**, volver a suceder, ocurrir de nuevo. **An idea occurred to her**, Se le ocurrió una idea

occurrence *n* ocurrencia, *f*; incidente, suceso, acontecimiento, *m*. **to be of frequent o.**, ocurrir con frecuencia, acontecer a menudo

ocean *n* océano, *m*; *fig* mar, abundancia, *f*. **o.-going vessel**, buque de alta mar, *m*

Oceania el Mundo Novísmo, *m*

octagon *n* octágono, *m*

octave *n* (ecc metrics, mus) octava, *f*

octavo *n* print libro, etc. en octavo (8°), *m*. **in o.**, en octavo. **large o.**, octavo mayor, *m*. **small o.**, octavo menor, *m*

octet *n* mus octeto, *m*

October *n* octubre, *m*, 2 October 1996, el segundo (2°) de octubre de mil novecientos noventa y seis

octogenarian *a* and *n* octogenario (-ia)

octopus *n* pulpo, *m*

ocular *a* ocular, visual. *n* ocular, *m*

oculist *n* oculista, *mf*

odd *a* (of numbers) impar; (of volumes, etc.) suelto; (strange) raro, curioso, extraño, extravagante; (casual) casual, accidental; (extra) y pico, y tantos, sobrante; (of gloves, etc.) sin pareja. **at odd moments**, en momentos de ocio. **at odd times**, de vez en cuando. **thirty odd**, treinta y pico. **odd number**, número impare, *m*. **odd or even**, pares o impares. **odd trick**, (at cards) una baza más

oddity *n* excentricidad, rareza, extravagancia, *f*; (person) ente singular, *m*; (curio) objeto curioso, *m*, antigüedad, *f*

oddly *adv* singularmente

odds *n pl* diferencia, desigualdad, *f*; (superiority) ventaja, superioridad, *f*; (quarrel) disputa, riña, *f*. **The o. are that . . .**, Lo más probable es que . . . **to fight against dreadful o.**, luchar contra fuerzas muy superiores. **o. and ends**, (remains) sobras y trozas, *f pl*; (trifles) ñaques, *m pl*, chucherías, *f pl*

odious *a* odioso, detestable, aborrecible, repugnante

odium *n* odio, *m*

odor *n* olor, *m*, (fragrance) perfume, aroma, *m*, fragancia, *f*; *fig* sospecha, *f*. **in bad o.**, *fig* en disfavor. **o. of sanctity**, olor de santidad, *m*

odorless *a* inodoro

odorous *a* fragante, oloroso

odyssey *n* odisea, *f*

of *prep* de. **of** has many idiomatic translations which are given as far as possible under the heading of the word concerned. It is also not translated. **I robbed him of his reward**, Le robé su recompensa. **I was thinking of you**, Pensaba en tí. **It was very good of you to . . .**, Vd. ha tenido mucha bondad de . . . **Your naming of the child Mary**, El que Vd. haya dado el nombre de María al niño. **29th of Sept., 1936**, el 29 de septiembre de 1936. **Of course!** ¡Claro está! ¡Ya lo creo! ¡Naturalmente! **of late**, últimamente. **of the** (before *m*, *sing*) del; (before *f*, *sing*) de la; (before *m pl*) de los; (before *f pl*) de las. **to dream of**, soñar con. **to smell of**, oler a tener olor de. **to taste of, etc.**, saber a, tener gusto de.

off *prep* de; fuera de; cerca de; desde; *naut* a la altura de. **from off**, de. **Take your gloves off the table!** ¡Quítate los guantes de la mesa! **The wheel was off the car**, La rueda se había desprendido del coche. **to be off duty**, no estar de servicio; *mil* no estar de guardia. **to lunch off cold meat**, almorzar de carne fría. **off one's head**, chiflado

off *a* (contrasted with near) de la derecha, derecho; (unlikely) improbable, remoto. *adv* (with intransitive verbs of motion) se (e.g. **He has gone off**, Se ha marchado); (contrasted with on) de (e.g. **He has fallen off the horse**, Ha caído del caballo); (of place at a distance) lejos, a distancia (of time) generally a verb is used (e.g. **The wedding is three months off**, Faltan tres meses para la boda); (completely) enteramente. **Off** is often not translated in Sp. (e.g. **to put off**, aplazar, **to cut off**, cortar). **day off**, día libre, día de asueto, *m*. **How far off is the house from here? The house is five miles off**, ¿Cuántas millas está la casa de aquí? La casa está a cinco millas de aquí. **His hat is off**, Está sin sombrero, Se ha quitado el sombrero. **The cover is off**, La cubierta está quitada. **The party is off**, Se ha anulado la reunión. **6% off**, un descuento de seis por ciento. *interj* **Off with you!** ¡Márchate! ¡Fuera! **off and on**, de vez en cuando, espasmódicamente. **off color**, (ill) malucho; (of jokes) verde. **off season**, estación muerta, *f*. **off-shore**, a vista de tierra. **off-stage**, entre bastidores

offal *n* (butchers') menudencias, *f pl*, asadura, *f*, menudos, despojos, *m pl*; desperdicio, *m*

offend *vt* ofender; agraviar, insultar; herir; desagradar, disgustar; *vi* ofender, pecar. **to be offended**, resentirse, insultarse. **This offends my sense of justice**, Esto ofende mi sentimiento de justicia. **to o. against**, pecar contra; violar

offender *n* delincuente, *mf*; agraviador (-ra), pecador (-ra), transgresor (-ra). **old o.**, law criminal inveterado, *m*

offense *n* ofensa, transgresión, violación, *f*; pecado, *m*; law delito, crimen, *m*; (insult) agravio, *m*, afrenta, *f*. **the first o.**, el primer delito, *m*. **fresh o.**, nuevo delito, *m*. **political o.**, crimen político, *m.* **technical o.,** *law* cuasidelito, *m.* **to commit an o. against,** ofender contra. **to take o.,** resentirse, darse por ofendido

offensive *a* ofensivo, desagradable, repugnante; (insulting) injurioso, agraviador, agresivo. *n mil* ofensiva, *f.* **to take the o.,** tomar la ofensiva

offer *n* oferta, *f;* ofrecimiento, *m;* (of help) promesa, *f;* proposición, *f; com* oferta, *f. vt* ofrecer; prometer; (opportunities, etc.) deparar, brindar; tributar. *vi* ofrecerse, ocurrir, surgir. **to o. up,** ofrecer; inmolar, sacrificar. **He did not offer to go,** No hizo ademán de marcharse. **to o. resistance,** oponer resistencia. **o. of marriage,** oferta de matrimonio, *f*

offhand *a* sin preparación, de repente; (casual) casual, despreocupado; (discourteous) brusco, descortés

offhandedly *adv* sin preparación, espontáneamente; negligentemente; bruscamente

office *n* oficina, *m;* (post) cargo, puesto, destino, *m;* (state department) ministerio, *m;* (of a Cabinet minister) cartera, *f;* (room) oficina, *f;* despacho, escritorio, *m;* (of a newspaper) redacción, *f;* (lawyer's) bufete, *m;* departamento, *m; ecc* oficio, *m pl.* **offices,** negocio, *m;* oficinas, *f pl;* (prayers) rezos, *m pl; ecc* oficios, *m pl.* **domestic offices,** dependencias, *f pl.* **good offices,** *fig* buenos oficios, *m pl.* **head o.,** casa central, oficina principal, *f.* **private o.,** despacho particular, *m.* **to be in o.,** estar en el poder. **o.-bearer,** miembro de la junta, *m;* funcionario, *m.* **o.-boy,** mozo de oficina, *m.* **o. employee,** oficinista, *mf.* **o. hours,** horas de oficina, *f pl;* (professions) horas de consulta, *f pl.* **o.-seeker,** aspirante, *m;* pretendiente, *m.* **o. work,** trabajo de oficina, *m*

officer *n* oficial, funcionario, *m;* (police) agente de policía, *m;* (of the Church) dignatario, *m;* (mil nav aer) oficial, *m. vt* mandar. **commissioned o.,** oficial, *m.* **non-commissioned o.,** oficial subalterno, *m.* **to be well officered,** tener buena oficialidad. **Officers' Training Corps,** Escuela de Oficiales, *f*

office worker *n* oficinista, *mf*

official *a* oficial; autorizado; ceremonioso, grave. *n* funcionario, *m;* oficial público, *m.* **high o.,** funcionario importante. **m. o. mourning,** duelo oficial, *m.* **o. receiver,** fiscal de quiebras, *m*

officiate *vi* celebrar; oficiar, funcionar

officious *a* oficioso, entremetido

offing *n naut* mar afuera, *m.* **in the o.,** cerca

off season fuera de temporada

offset *n* compensación, *f, vt* compensar, neutralizar

offshoot *n* renuevo, vástago, *m*

offside *a* (of a car) del lado derecho (or izquierda); *sport* fuera de juego

offspring *n* vástago, *m;* descendiente, *mf;* prole, *f;* hijos, *m pl*

often *adv* a menudo, mucho, con frecuencia, frecuentemente, muchas veces. **as o. as,** tan a menudo como, siempre que. **as o. as not,** no pocas veces. **How o.?** ¿Cuántas veces? **It is not o. that . . . ,** No ocurre con frecuencia que . . . **so o.,** tantas veces, con frecuencia. **Do you go there o.?** ¿Va Vd. allí con frecuencia (or frecuentemente)? **Not o.,** Voy rara vez allá

ogle *vt* and *vi* comer(se) con los ojos (a), ojear, guiñar el ojo (a). *n* ojeada, *f,* guiño, *m*

ogling *n* guiño, *m,* ojeada, *f*

ogre *n* ogro, *m*

oh! *interj* ¡o! **O no!** ¡Ca! ¡Claro que no!

oil *n* aceite, *m;* petróleo, *m;* óleo, *m. vt* aceitar, engrasar, *Argentina* enaceitar; olear, ungir, untar; (bribe) sobornar, untar la mano; *fig* suavizar. a aceitero; petrolero. **to pour oil on troubled waters,** echar aceite sobre aguas turbulentas. **to strike oil,** encontrar un pozo de petróleo; *fig* encontrar un filón. **crude oil,** petróleo bruto, m. **heavy oil,** aceite pesado, m. **thin oil,** aceite ligero, m. art **in oils,** al óleo. **oil-bearing,** petrolífero. **oil-box,** engrasador, m. **oil-burner,** quemador de petróleo, m. **oil-can,** aceitera, f. **oil-colors,** pinturas al óleo, f pl. **oil field,** yacimiento petrolífero, campo de petróleo, m. **oil-filter,** separador de aceite, m. **oil-gauge,** nivel de aceite, m. **oil lamp,** velón, candil, quinqué, m. **oil of turpentine,** aceite de trementina, aguarrás, m. esencia de trementina, f. **oil-painting,** pintura al óleo, f. **oil pipeline,** oleoducto, m. **oil shop,** aceitería, f. **oil-silk,** encerado, m. **oil stove,** estufa de petróleo, f. **oil tanker,** naut petrolero, m. **oil-well,** pozo de petróleo, m

oilcloth *n* hule, *m;* linóleo, *m*

oilskin *n* encerado, *m*

oily *a* aceitoso, grasiento

ointment *n* ungüento, *m,* pomada, *f*

old *a* viejo; antiguo, anciano; (of wines, etc.) añejo; (worn out) usado, gastado; (inveterate) arraigado, inveterado. **How old are you?** ¿Cuántos años tiene usted? **to be sixteen years old,** tener dieciséis años. **He is old enough to know his own mind,** Tiene bastante edad para saber lo que quiere. **to grow old,** envejecer. **to remain an old maid,** quedar soltera, *inf* quedarse para vestir imágenes. **of old,** antiguamente. **prematurely old,** revejido averiado. **old age,** vejez, senectud, f. **old bachelor,** solterón, m. **old clothes,** ropa vieja (or usada), ropa de segunda mano, f. **old-clothes dealer,** ropavejero (-ra). **old-clothes shop,** ropavejería, f. **old-established,** viejo. **old-fashioned,** pasado de moda, viejo; (of people) chapado a la antigua. **old lady,** anciana, dama vieja, *f.* **old-looking,** de aspecto viejo, avejentado. **old maid,** solterona, *f.* **old-maidish,** remilgado. **old man,** viejo, *m; theat* barba, *m.* **old salt,** lobo de mar, *m.* **Old Testament,** Antiguo Testamento, *m.* **old wives' tale,** cuento de viejas, *m.* **old woman,** vieja, *f.* **Old World,** Viejo Mundo, mundo antiguo, *m*

old-age home *n* asilo de ancianos, *m*

olden *a* antiguo. **o. days,** días pasados, *m pl*

older *a comp* más viejo, mayor. **The older the madder,** A la vejez viruelas

old hat *n* viejo conocido

oldish *a* bastante viejo, de cierta edad

olfactory *a* olfatorio, olfativo

olive *n* (tree) olivo, *m;* (fruit) aceituna, oliva, *f,* a aceitunado, *Lat. Am.* aceituno. **wild o. tree,** acebuche, *m.* **o.-complexioned,** con tez aceitunada. **o. green,** verde oliva, *m.* **o. grove,** olivar, *m.* **o. oil,** aceite de oliva, *m*

olympian *a* olímpico

olympic *a* olímpico. **o. games,** juegos olímpicos, *m pl*

olympus *n* olimpo, *m*

omelet *n* tortilla, *f.* **sweet o.,** tortilla dulce, *f*

omen *n* pronóstico, presagio, agüero, *m, vt* agorar, anunciar

ominous *a* ominoso, azaroso, siniestro, amenazante

omission *n* omisión, *f;* olvido, descuido, *m;* supresión, *f*

omit *vt* omitir; olvidar, descuidar; (suppress) suprimir, excluir, callar, dejar a un lado

omitting *pres part* salvo, excepto

omnibus *n* ómnibus, autobús, *m.* **o. conductor,** cobrador de autobús, *m.* **o. driver,** conductor de autobús, *m.* **o. route,** trayecto de autobús, *m.* **o. service,** servicio de autobuses, *m.* **o. volume,** volumen de obras coleccionadas, *m*

omnipotent *a* omnipotente, todopoderoso

omniscience *n* omnisciencia, *f*

omniscient *a* omniscio, omnisciente

omnivorous *a* omnívoro

on *prep* (upon) sobre, en, encima de; (concerning) de, acerca de, sobre; (against) contra; (after) después; (according to) según; (with gerund) en; (with infin.) al; (at) a; (connected with, employed in) de; (by means of) por, mediante; (near to) cerca de, sobre; (into) en. Untranslated before days of week, dates of month or time of day (e.g. **on Monday,** el lunes. **on Friday afternoons,** los viernes por la tarde). **She has a bracelet on her wrist,** Tiene una pulsera en la muñeca. **He will retire on a**

good income, Se jubilará con una buena renta. **on my uncle's death,** después de la muerte (or a la muerte) de mi tío, al morir. **On seeing them, he stopped,** Al verles se paró. **on leave,** con licencia, en uso de licencia. **on the next page,** en la página siguiente. **on this occasion,** en esta ocasión. **on the other hand,** en cambio. **on second thoughts,** luego de pensarlo bien. **on the way,** en camino. **on one side,** a un lado. **on the left,** a la izquierda. **on time,** a tiempo. **on my honor,** bajo palabra de honor. **on pain of death,** so pena de muerte, bajo pena de muerte. **on an average,** por término medio. **on his part,** por su parte. **on and after,** desde, a partir de. **on credit,** de fiado. **on fire,** ardiendo, en llamas. **on foot,** a pie. **on purpose,** a propósito; con intención. **on,** *adv* puesto (e.g. **She has her gloves on,** Tiene los guantes puestos); (forward) adelante, hacia adelante; (continue, with a verb) seguir, continuar (e.g. **He went on talking,** Siguió hablando). Often **on** is included in Sp. verb (e.g. **The new play is on,** Se ha estrenado la nueva comedia. **The fight is on,** Ya ha empezado la lucha. **On!** *interj* ¡Adelante! **and so on,** y así sucesivamente. **to have on,** llevar puesto. **on and off,** de vez en cuando. **on and on,** sin cesar

once *adv* una vez; (formerly) en otro tiempo, antiguamente; *conjunc* si (e.g. **O. you give him the opportunity,** Si le das la oportunidad). **all at o.,** todo junto, a un mismo tiempo; simultáneamente; (suddenly) súbitamente, de repente. **at o.,** en seguida, inmediatamente, *Lat. Am. also* lueguito. **for o.,** por una vez. **more than o.,** más de una vez. **not o.,** ni siquiera una vez. **o. before,** una vez antes. **o. and for all,** una vez para siempre; por última vez. **o. in a while,** de vez en cuando. **o. more,** otra vez. **o. or twice,** una vez o dos, algunas veces. **o. too often,** una vez demasiado. **O. upon a time,** En tiempos pasados, En tiempos de Maricastaña; (as beginning of a story) Érase una vez, Había una vez, Hubo una vez

once in a blue moon a cada muerte de un obispo

one *a* un, uno, una; (first) primero; (single) único, solo; (indifferent) igual, indiferente; (some, certain) algún, cierto, un (e.g. **one day,** cierto día). *n* uno; (hour) la una; (of age) un año. Often not translated in Sp. (e.g. **I shall take the blue one,** Tomaré el azul). *pron se;* uno. **one's,** su, de uno (e.g. **one's work,** el trabajo de uno). **I for one do not think so,** Yo por uno no lo creo. **It is all one,** Es igual, No hace diferencia alguna. **only one,** un solo. **that one,** ése, *m,* ésa, *f,* eso, *neut.* **this one,** éste, *m,* ésta, *f,* esto, *neut.* **these ones,** éstos, etc. **those ones,** ésos, etc. **the one,** el (que), *m,* la (que), f. **with one accord,** unánimemente. **one and all,** todos. **one another,** se, uno a otro, mutuamente. **one by one,** uno a uno. **one day,** un día; un día de éstos, algún día. **one-eyed,** tuerto. **one-handed,** manco. **one-sided,** parcial. **one-way street,** *Spain* calle de dirección única, *Argentina* calle de una sola mano, *Mexico* calle de un sentido, calle de una corrida, f. **one-way traffic,** tráfico en una sola dirección, m

onerous a oneroso, pesado, molesto, gravoso

oneself *pron* se, uno mismo (una misma); (after prep.) sí mismo, sí. **It must be done by o.,** Uno mismo ha de hacerlo

onion n cebolla, f. **string of onions,** ristra de cebollas, f. **young o.,** babosa, f. **o. bed,** cebollar, m. **o. seed,** cebollino, m. **o. seller,** cebollero (-ra)

on-line a *computers* lineal

onlooker n espectado (-ra), observador (-ra); testigo, mf

only a único, solo. *adv* únicamente, sólo; no . . . más (que), tan sólo; con la excepción de, salvo. *conjunc* pero, salvo (que), si no fuera (que). **I shall o. give you three,** No te daré más de tres. **The o. thing one can do,** Lo único que se puede hacer. **I o. wished to see her,** Quería verla nada más. **if o.,** ¡ojalá (que)! **not o. . . . ,** no sólo . . . **o.-begotten,** a unigénito. **o. child,** hijo (-ja) único (-ca)

onrush n asalto, ataque, acometimiento, m; acometida, embestida, f; (of water, etc.) acceso, m; torrente, m, corriente, f

onset n ataque, m, acometida, f; (beginning) principio, m. **at the first o.,** al primer ímpetu

onslaught n asalto, ataque, m

onus n responsabilidad, f. **o. of proof,** obligación de probar, f

onward a progresivo. *adv* adelante, hacia adelante; (as a command) ¡Adelante!

onyx n ónice, m

ooze n légamo, limo, fango, m, lama, f. *vi* exudar, rezumarse; manar; *vt* sudar. **to o. satisfaction,** caérsele (a uno) la baba. **to o. away,** (of money, etc.) desaparecer, volar. **to o. out,** (news) divulgarse

opacity n opacidad, f

opal n ópalo, m

opaque a opaco

op. cit. (opere citato) obra cit. (obra citada)

open *vt* abrir; (a package) desempaquetar, desenvolver; (remove lid) destapar; *Lat. Am.* desenlatar (canned food); (unfold) desplegar; (inaugurate) inaugurar; iniciar, empezar; establecer; (an abscess) cortar; (with arms, heart, eyes) abrir; (with mind, thought) descubrir, revelar; (make accessible) franquear, hacer accesible; (tear) romper; *vi* abrirse; empezar, comenzar; (of a view, etc.) aparecer, exten-

derse; inaugurarse; (of a career, etc.) prepararse. **to o. fire against,** abrir el fuego contra. **to o. into,** comunicar con, salir a. **to o. into each other,** (of rooms) comunicarse. **to o. on,** mirar a, dar a, caer a. **to o. out,** *vt* abrir; desplegar; revelar. *vi* extenderse; revelarse. **to o. the eyes of,** *fig* desengañar, desilusionar. **to o. up,** abrir; exponer; hacer accesible; revelar; *fig inf* desabrocharse. **to o. with** or **by,** empezar con

open a abierto; descubierto; expuesto; (unfenced) descercado; (not private) público; libre; (unfolded) desplegado, extendido; (persuasible) receptivo; no resuelto, pendiente; (frank) franco, candoroso; (with sea) alto; (liberal) generoso; hospitalario; sin prejuicios; *com* abierto, pendiente; sin defensa; (of weather) despejado; (of a letter) sin sellar; (without a lid) destapado; (well-known) manifiesto, bien conocido. **in the o.,** al descubierto. **in the o. air,** al aire libre, al raso, a cielo abierto. **to break o.,** forzar. **to cut o.,** abrir de un tajo, cortar. **to leave o.,** dejar abierto. **wide o.,** muy abierto; (of doors) de par en par. **o. boat,** barco descubierto, m. **o. car,** coche abierto, m. **o. carriage,** carruaje descubierto, m. **o. cast,** *min* roza abierta, f. **o.-eyed,** con los ojos abiertos. **o.-handed,** generoso, dadivoso, *Lat. Am.* also maniabierto. **o. letter,** carta abierta, f. **o.-minded,** imparcial. **o.-mouthed,** con la boca abierta, boquiabierto. **o. question,** cuestión por decidir, cuestión discutible, f. **o. secret,** secreto a voces, m. **o. sea,** alta mar, f. **o. town,** ciudad abierta, f. **o. tramcar,** jardinera, f. **o. truck,** vagoneta, f. **o.-work,** *sew* calado, enrejado, m

opener n abridor, m

opening n abertura, brecha, f; orificio, m; inauguración, apertura, f; principio, m; (chance) oportunidad, f; (employment) puesto, m. **o. price,** *com* (on Exchange) precio de apertura, m, primer curso m

opera n ópera, f. **o. comic** o., zarzuela, f. **o.-cloak,** abrigo de noche, m. **o.-glasses,** gemelos de teatro, m pl. **o.-hat,** clac, m. **o.-house,** teatro de la ópera, m. **o. singer,** cantante de ópera, operista, mf

operate *vi* funcionar, trabajar; obrar; (with on, upon) producir efecto sobre; influir; *surg* operar; (on Exchange) especular, jugar a la bolsa; *vt* hacer funcionar, manejar; mover, impulsar; dirigir

operatic a de ópera, operístico

operating a (of surgeons) operante; de operación. **o. table,** mesa de operaciones, f. **o. theater,** anfiteatro, m; sala de operaciones, f

operation n funcionamiento, m, acción, f; *surg* intervención quirúrgica, operación, f; (mil naut) maniobra, f; manipulación, f. **to come into o.,** ponerse en práctica; hacerse efectivo. **to continue in o.,** (laws) seguir en vigor. **to perform an o.,** surg operar, praticar una intervención quirúrgica; hacer una maniobra. **to put into o.,** poner en práctica

operative a operativo, activo. n operario (-ia), obrero (-ra). **to become o.,** tener efecto

operator n operario (-ia); (telephone) telefonista, mf; (machines, engines) maquinista, mf; surg operador, m

operetta n opereta, f

ophthalmologist n oftalmólogo, m

ophthalmology n oftalmología, f

opine vi and vt opinar, creer

opinion n opinión, f, parecer, juicio, m; concepto, m, idea, f. **in my o.,** según mi parecer. **to be of the o. that,** ser de la opinión que, opinar que. **to be of the same o.,** estar de acuerdo, concurrir. **public o.,** opinión (or voz) pública, f

opinionated a terco, obstinado

opium n opio, m. **o. addict,** opiónamo (-ma). **o. den,** fumadero de opio, m.

opponent n antagonista, mf, enemigo (-ga); contrario (-ia), adversario (-ia), competidor (-ra)

opportune a oportuno, tempestivo, conveniente, a propósito. **to be o.,** venir al caso. **o. moment,** momento oportuno, m; hora propicia, f

opportunist n oportunista, Lat. Am. also maromero (-ra), mf

opportunity n oportunidad, ocasión, posibilidad, f. **to give an o. for,** dar margen para. **to open new opportunities,** abrir nuevos horizontes. **to take the o.,** tomar la oportunidad

oppose vt (counterbalance) oponer, contrarrestar; combatir; hacer frente (a), contrariar, pugnar contra, oponerse (a)

opposed (to) a opuesto a, enemigo de, contra

opposing a opuesto; enemigo, contrario

opposite a (facing) de cara a, frente a, del otro lado de; opuesto; (antagonistic) contrario, antagónico; otro, diferente. n contraria, f, lo opuesto; antagonista, mf; adversario (-ia). **the o. sex,** el otro sexo. **o. leaves,** bot hojas opuestas, f pl. **o. to,** frente a; distinto de

opposition n oposición, f; (obstacle) estorbo, impedimento, m, dificultad, f; resistencia, hostilidad, f; (ast pol) oposición, f; (difference) contraste, m, diferencia, f. a de la oposición. **in o.,** en oposición; pol en la oposición. **to be in o.,** estar en oposición; pol ser de la oposición, estar en la oposición

oppress vt oprimir, tiranizar, sojuzgar, apremiar; (of moral causes) abrumar, agobiar, desanimar; (of heat, etc.) ahogar

oppression n opresión, tiranía, crueldad, f; (moral) agobio, sufrimiento, m, ansia, f;

(difficulty in breathing) sofocación, f, ahogo, m

oppressive a opresivo, tiránico, cruel; (taxes, etc.) gravoso; (of heat) sofocante, asfixiante; agobiador, abrumador

oppressor n opresor (-ra), sojuzgador (-ra), tirano (-na)

opprobrious a oprobioso, vituperioso; infame

opt vi optar, escoger, elegir

optic, optical a óptico. **o. illusion,** ilusión óptica, f; engaño a la vista, trampantojo, m. **o. nerve,** nervio óptico, m

optician n óptico, m

optics n óptica, f

optimist n optimista, mf

optimistic a optimista

optimum n lo óptimo; (used as adjective) óptimo

option n opción, f, (all meanings)

optional a discrecional, facultativo

opulence n opulencia, riqueza, magnificencia, f; (abundance) abundancia, copia, f

opulent a opulento, rico, acaudalado; abundante

opus n obra, composición, f

or conjunc o; (before a word beginning with o or ho) u; (negative) ni. n her oro, m. **an hour or so,** una hora más o menos, alrededor de una hora. **either . . . or,** o . . . o. **or else,** o bien. **whether . . . or,** que . . . que, siquiera . . . siquiera, ya . . . ya. **without . . . or,** sin . . . ni

oracle n oráculo, m

oracular a profético, vatídico; ambiguo, misterioso, sibilino; dogmático, magistral

oral a verbal, hablado; anat oral, bucal

oral cavity n cavidad bucal, f

orange n (tree) naranjo, m; (fruit) naranja, f; **bitter o.,** naranja amarga, f. **blood o.,** naranja dulce, f. **tangerine o.,** naranja mandarina, f. **o. blossom,** azahar, m. **o. color,** color de naranja, m. **o.-colored,** de color de naranja, anaranjado. **o.-flower water,** agua de azahar, f. **o. grove,** naranjal, m. **o. grower** (seller), naranjero (-ra). **o. peel,** piel de naranja, f. **o.-stick,** (for nails) limpiauñas, m

orangeade n naranjada, f; (mineral water) gaseosa, f

oration n oración, declamación, f, discurso, m

orator n orador (-ra), declamador (-ra)

oratorical a oratorio, declamatorio, retórico

oratorio n mus oratorio, m

oratory n oratoria, elocuencia, f; ecc oratorio, m, capilla, f

orb n orbe, m; esfera, f, globo, m; astro, m; poet ojo, m

orbit *n ast* órbita, *f*; *anat* órbita, cuenca del ojo, *f*

orchard *n* huerto, vergel, *m*; (especially of apples) pomar, *m*

orchestra *n* orquesta, *f*. **with full o.**, con gran orquesta. *theat* **o. seat**, **o. stall**, butaca de piatea, *f*

orchestral *a* orquestal, instrumental

orchestrate *vt* orquestar, instrumentar

orchid *n* orquídea, *f*

ordain *vt* mandar, disponer, decretar; *ecc* ordenar. **to be ordained as**, *ecc* ordenarse de

ordeal *n hist* ordalías, *f pl*; prueba severa, *f*

order *n* (most meanings) orden, *m*; (command) precepto, mandamiento, decreto, *m*; orden, *f*; (rule) regla, *f*; (for money) libranza postal, *f*; (for goods) pedido, encargo, *m*; (arrangement) método, arreglo, *m*, clasificación, *f*; (condition) estado, *m*; *arch* estilo, *m*; (*zool bot*) orden, *m*; (sort) clase, especie, *f*; (rank) clase social, *f*; *ecc* orden, *f*; (badge) condecoración, insignia, *f*; (association) sociedad, asociación, compañía, *f*; (to view a house, etc.) permiso, *m*; (series) serie, *f*. **His liver is out of o.**, No está bién del hígado. **in good o.**, en buen estado; arreglado. **in o.**, (alphabetical, etc.) en orden; arreglado; (parliamentary) en regla. **in o. that**, para que, a fin de que. **in o. to**, a fin de, para. **out of o.**, estropeado, descompuesto; (on a notice) No funciona; (parliamentary) fuera del orden del día. **till further o.**, hasta nueva orden. **to o.**, com por encargo especial. **to give an o.**, dar una orden; *com* poner un pedido. **to go out of o.**, descomponerse. **to keep in o.**, mantener en orden. **to put in o.**, poner en orden, arreglar. **to take holy orders**, tomar órdenes sagradas. **O.!** ¡Orden! **O. in Council**, orden real, *f*. **o. of knighthood**, orden de caballería, *f*. **o. of the day**, orden del día, *f*. **o. paper**, orden del día, *f*; reglamento, *m*

order *vt* disponer; arreglar; (command) mandar, ordenar; (request) rogar, pedir; (direct) dirigir, gobernar; *com* encargar, cometer; (a meal, a taxi) encargar. **I ordered them to do it**, Les mandé hacerlo. **to o. about**, mandar. **to o. back**, hacer volver, mandar que vuelva. **to o. down**, hacer bajar, pedir (a uno) que baje. **to o. in**, mandar entrar. **to o. off**, despedir, decir (a uno) que se vaya. **to o. out**, mandar salir; (the troops) hacer salir la tropa; echar. **to o. up**, mandar subir, hacer subir

orderly *a* bien arreglado, metódico; aseado, en orden; (of behaviour) formal, bien disciplinado. *n mil* ordenanza, *m*; ayudante de hospital *m*

ordinal *a and n* ordinal *m*

ordinance *n* ordenanza, *f*, reglamento, *m*; *arch* ordenación, *f*; *ecc* rito, *m*

ordinarily *adv* de ordinario, ordinariamente, comúnmente

ordinary *a* (usual) corriente, común, usual, ordinario, normal; (average) mediano, mediocre; (somewhat vulgar) ordinario, vulgar. *n ecc* ordinario, *m*. **out of the o.**, excepcional; poco común. **o. seaman**, marinero, *m*. **o. share**, *com* acción ordinaria, *f*

ore *n min* mena, *f*, quijo, *Lat. Am.* llampo, *m*

organ *n* (all meanings) órgano, *m*. **barrel-o.**, organillo, órgano de manubrio, *m*. **o.-blower**, entonador (-ra). **o.-grinder**, organillero (-ra). **o.-loft**, tribuna del órgano, *f*. **o.-pipe**, cañón de órgano, *m*. **o.-stop**, registro de órgano, *m*

organdie *n* organdí, *m*

organic *a* orgánico. **o. chemistry**, química orgánica, *f*

organism *n* organismo, *m*

organist *n* organista, *mf*

organization *n* organización, *f*; grupo, *m*, asociación, sociedad, *f*; organismo, *m*

organize *vt* organizar; arreglar. *vi* organizarse; asociarse, constituirse

orgasm *n med* orgasmo, *m*

orgy *n* orgía, *f*

orient *a poet* naciente, oriental. *n* Oriente, Este, *m*. **pearl of fine o.**, perla de hermoso oriente, *f*

oriental *a and n* oriental, *mf*

orientate *vt* orientar; dirigir, guiar. *vi* mirar (or caer) hacia el este; orientarse

orifice *n* orificio, *m*; abertura, boca, *f*

origin *n* origen, génesis, *m*; raíz, causa, *f*; principio, comienzo, *m*; (extraction) descendencia, procedencia, familia, *f*, nacimiento, *m*

original *a* original; primitivo, primero; ingenioso. *n* original, *m*; prototipo, modelo, *m*. **o. sin**, pecado original, *m*

originality *n* originalidad, *f*

originally *adv* originalmente; al principio; antiguamente

originate *vt* (produce) ocasionar, producir, suscitar, iniciar, engendrar; (create) inventar, crear. *vi* originarse, surgir, nacer. **to o. in**, tener su origen en, surgir de, emanar de, venir de

originator *n* iniciador (-ra), fundador (-ra); autor (-ra), creador (-ra)

ornament *n* adorno, *m*; decoración, *f*; *fig* ornamento, *m*; (trinket) chuchería, *f*, *n pl*. **ornaments**, *ecc* ornamentos, *m pl*. *vt* ornar, adornar, decorar, embellecer

ornamental *a* ornamental, decorativo

ornamentation *n* ornamentación, decoración, *f*

ornate *a* vistoso, ornado en demasía, barroco

orphan *a and n* huérfano (-na)

orphanage *n* orfanato, hospicio, *m*

orthodox a ortodoxo

orthodoxy n ortodoxia, f

orthographic a ortográfico

orthography n ortografía, f

orthopedic a ortopédico

orthopedics n ortopedia, f

orthopedist n ortopedista, mf ortopédico (-ca)

oscillate vi oscilar, fluctuar; (hesitate) dudar, vacilar. vt hacer oscilar

oscillation n oscilación, fluctuación, vibración, f; elec oscilación, f

oscillator n oscilador, m

osculation n ósculo, m

osier n bot mimbre, m, or f. **o. bed,** mimbrera, f

osmic a chem ósmico

osmosis n (phys chem) ósmosis, f

osseous a óseo

ossify vt osificar; vi osificarse

osteitis n med osteítis, f

ostensible a ostensible; aparente, engañoso, ilusorio

ostensibly adv en apariencia, ostensiblemente

ostentation n ostentación, f; aparato, fausto, boato, alarde, m, soberbia, f

ostentatious a ostentoso; aparatoso, fastuoso, rumboso

ostentatiously adv con ostentación

osteomyelitis n med osteomielitis, f

osteopath n osteópata, m

osteopathy n osteopatía, f

ostracize vt desterrar; excluir del trato, echar de la sociedad

ostrich n avestruz, m. **o. farm,** criadero de avestruces, m

otalgia n med otalgia, f, dolor de oídos, m

other a otro. pron el otro, m; la otra, f; lo otro, neut adv (with than) de otra manera que, de otro modo que; otra cosa que. **this hand, not the o.,** esta mano, no la otra. **every o. day,** un día sí y otro no, cada dos días. **no o.,** ningún otro, m; otra ninguna, f. **someone or o.,** alguien. **the others,** los (las) demás, m, f pl; los otros, m pl; las otras, f pl. **o. people,** otros, m pl, los demás

otherwise adv de otra manera, de otro modo, otramente; (in other respects) por lo demás, por otra parte; (if not) si no

otitis n med otitis, f

otologist n otólogo, m

otter n zool nutria, f. **o. hound,** perro para cazar la nutria

ottoman a otomano, turco. n otomana, f

ouch! interj ¡ax!, ¡huy!

ought v aux deber, tener la obligación (de); ser conveniente, convenir; ser necesario (que), tener que. **I o. to have done it yesterday,** Debía haberlo hecho ayer. **She o. not to come,** No debe (debiera, debería) venir. **He o. to see them tomorrow,** (should) Conviene que les vea mañana; Tiene la obligación de verles mañana; (must) Es necesario que les vea mañana, Tiene que verles mañana.

ounce n (animal and weight) onza, f. **He hasn't an o. of common sense,** No tiene pizca de sentido común

our a nuestro

ours pron nuestro, m; nuestra, f; nuestros, m pl; nuestras, f pl; de nosotros, m pl; de nosotras, f pl; el nuestro, m; la nuestra, f; lo nuestro, neut; los nuestros, m pl; las nuestras, f pl. **This book is ours,** Este libro es nuestro (or el nuestro)

ourselves pron pl nosotros mismos, m pl; nosotras mismas, f pl

oust vt despedir, desahuciar, expulsar, echar

out adv afuera; hacia fuera; (gone out) fuera, salido, ausente; (invested) puesto; (published) publicado, salido; (discovered) conocido, descubierto; (on strike) en huelga; (mistaken) en error, equivocado; (of journeys) de ida, (on ships) de navegación (e.g. **on the second day out,** al segundo día de navegación); (of fire, etc.) extinguido; (at sea) en el mar; (of girls in society) puesta de largo, que ha entrado en sociedad; (of fashion) fuera de moda; (of office) fuera del poder; (in holes) roto, agujereado, andrajoso; (exhausted) agotado; (expired) vencido; (of a watch) llevar . . . minutos (horas) de atraso or de adelanto; (unfriendly) reñido; (way out) salida, f; (sport) fuera de juego; (of flowers) abierto; (of chickens) empollado. **a scene out of one of Shakespeare's plays,** una escena de una de las comedias de Shakespeare. **I am out $6,** He perdido seis dólares. **I am out of tea,** Se me ha acabado el té. **to drink out of a glass,** beber de un vaso. **to read out of a book,** leer en un libro. **to speak out,** hablar claro. **Murder will out,** El asesinato se descubrirá. **out-and-out,** completo; (with rogue, etc.) redomado. **out of,** fuera de; (beyond) más allá de; (through, by) por; (with) con; (without) sin; (from among) entre; (in) en; (with a negative sense) no. **out of breath,** jadeante, sin aliento. **out of character,** impropio. **out of commission,** fuera de servicio. **out of danger,** fuera de peligro. **out of date,** anticuado. **out of hand,** en seguida; indisciplinado. **out of money,** sin dinero. **out of necessity,** por necesidad. **out of one's mind,** loco, demente. **out of order.** See **order. out of print,** agotado. **out of reach,** fuera de alcance, inasequible. **out of season,** fuera de temporada. **out of sight,** fuera del alcance de la vista; invisible. **Out of sight, out of mind,** Ojos que no ven, corazón que no siente. **out of sorts,** indispuesto. **out of temper,** de mal genio. **out of the question,** imposible. **out of the way,** adv (of work) terminado, hecho; (remote) fuera del camino; (put aside) arrinconado; donde no estorbe. **out-of-the-way,** a remoto, aislado; (unusual) extraordinario, singular. **out of this world,** lo máximo, lo último. **out of touch with,** alejado de; sin relaciones con; sin simpatía con. **out of work,** sin empleo, sin trabajo, en paro forzoso. **out-patient,** enfermo (-ma) de un dispensario. **Out!** interj ¡Fuera! ¡Fuera de aquí! ¡Márchate! **Out with it!** ¡Hable Vd.! ¡sin rodeos! ¡Hablen claro!

outbalance vt exceder, sobrepujar

outbid vt pujar, mejorar

outbidding n puja, mejora, f

outbreak n (of war) declaración, f; comienzo, m; (of disease) epidemia, f; (of crimes, etc.) serie, f

outbuilding n dependencia, f, edificio accesorio, anexo, m

outburst n acceso, arranque, m, explosión, f

outcast n paria, mf; desterrado (-da), proscripto (-ta)

outclass vt aventajar, ser superior (a), exceder

outcome n consecuencia, f, resultado, m

outcry n clamor, grito, m; protesta, f

outdistance vt dejar atrás

outdo vt eclipsar, aventajar, sobrepujar

outdoor a externo; (of activities) al aire libre; fuera de casa

outdoors adv fuera de casa; al aire libre

outer a externo, exterior

outer space espacio extraatmosférico, espacio extraterreste, espacio exterior, espacio sideral, espacio sidéreo, espacio ultraterrestre, m

outermost a sup (el, etc.) más externo, más exterior; extremo, de más allá

outfit n equipo, m; (of clothes) traje, m; (of furniture or trousseau) ajuar, m; (gear) pertrechos, avíos, m pl. vt aviar equipar

outflank vt mil flanquear; ser más listo (que)

outgoing a saliente, que sale; cesante. **outgoings,** n pl gastos, m pl

outgrow vt hacerse demasiado grande para; crecer más que; (ideas) perder; (illness) curarse de, curarse con la edad; pasar de la edad de, ser ya viejo para. **to o. one's clothes,** quedársele a uno chica la ropa. **to o. one's strength,** estar demasiado crecido para su edad

outgrowth n excrecencia, f; resultado, fruto, m, consecuencia, f

outhouse n edificio accesorio, m

outing n excursión, vuelta, f, paseo, m

outlandish a extraño, singular, raro; absurdo, ridículo

outlast vt durar más que; (outlive) sobrevivir a

outlaw n bandido, proscrito, m, vt proscribir

outlay n gasto, desembolso, m

outlet n salida, f; orificio de salida, m; (of drains, etc.) desagüe, m; (of streets, rivers) desembocadura, f; fig escape, m, válvula de seguridad, f

outline n perfil, contorno, m; (drawing) esbozo, bosquejo, m; idea general, f; plan general, m, vt esbozar, bosquejar. **in o.,** en esbozo; en perfil. **to be outlined** (against), dibujarse (contra), destacarse (contra)

outlive vt sobrevivir (a); (live down) hacer olvidar

outlook n (view) perspectiva, vista, f; (opinion) actitud, f, punto de vista, m; aspecto, m, apariencia, f; (for trade, etc.) perspectiva, f, posibilidades, f pl. **o. tower,** atalaya, f

outlying a remoto, lejano, distante

outmaneuver vt superar en estrategia

outmatch vt aventajar, superar

outmoded a anticuado, pasado de moda

outnumber vt ser más numerosos que, exceder en número

out-of-court settlement n arreglo pacífico, m

out-of-town a de las provincias

outpost n mil avanzada, f, puesto avanzado, m

outpouring n derramamiento, m; efusión, f

output n producción, f. **o. capacity,** capacidad de producción, f

outrage n barbaridad infamia, atrocidad, f; rapto, m, violación, f. vt ultrajar; violar; violentar

outrageous a atroz, terrible; desaforado, monstruoso; injurioso; ridículo

outré a cursi, extravagante

outride vt cabalgar más a prisa que

outright adv (frankly) de plano (e.g. **to reject outright,** rechazar de plano), francamente, sin reserva; (immediately) en seguida, immediatamente. a categórico; completo; franco

outrival vt vencer, superar

outrun vt correr más que

outset n principio, comienzo, m

outshine vt brillar más que, eclipsar en brillantez; superar, eclipsar

outside adv afuera, fuera. prep fuera de, al otro lado de, al exterior de; (besides) aparte de, fuera de. a externo, exterior; (of labor, etc.) desde fuera; máximo; ajeno. n exterior, m; superficie, f; aspecto, m, apariencia, f. **at the o.,** a lo sumo, cuando más. **from the o.,** de (or desde) fuera. **on the o.,** (externally) por fuera. **o. the door,** a la puerta

outsider n forastero (-ra); desconocido (-da), Argentina, Chile also cuico (-ca); caballo desconocido, m; persona poco deseable, f

outsize *n* artículo de talla mayor que las corrientes, *m*

outskirts *n pl* alrededores, *m pl*, afueras, immediaciones, cercanías, *f pl*

outspoken *a* franco. **to be o.,** decir lo que se piensa, no tener pelos en la lengua

outspread *a* extendido; (of wings) desplegadas

outstanding *a* excelente; sobresaliente, conspicuo; *com* pendiente, sin pagar. **to be o.,** *com* estar pendiente; *fig* sobresalir. **o. account,** *com* cuenta pendiente, *f*

outstay *vt* quedarse más tiempo que. **to o. one's welcome,** pegársele la silla

outstretched *a* extendido

outstrip *vt* dejar atrás, pasar; aventajar, superar

outvote *vt* emitir más votos que; rechazar por votación

outward *a* exterior, externo; aparente, visible. *adv* exteriormente; hacia fuera; superficialmente. **o. bound,** con rumbo a . . . **o. voyage,** el viaje de ida

outwardly *adv* exteriormente; hacia fuera; en apariencia

outwear *vt* durar más que; gastar

outweigh *vt* exceder, valer más que

outwit *vt* ser más listo que; vencer

outworn *a* anticuado, ya viejo

oval *n* óvalo, *m*, a oval, ovalado, aovado

ovarian *a* (*bot zool*) ovárico

ovary *n* ovario, *m*

ovation *n* ovación, recepción entusiasta, *f*

oven *n* horno, *m*. **o. peel,** pala de horno, *f*. **o. rake,** hurgón, *m*

over *prep* (above, upon, over) sobre, encima de; (on the other side) al otro lado de; (across) allende, a través de; (more than) más de; (beyond) más allá de; (of rank) superior a; (during) durante; (in addition) además de; (through) por. *n* (cricket) serie de saques, *f*, *adv* encima; en; por encima; al otro lado; de un lado a otro; enfrente; al lado contrario; de un extremo a otro; (finished) terminado; (ruined) arruinado, perdido; (more) más; (excessively) demasiado, excesivamente; (covered) cubierto (de); (extra) en exceso; (completely) enteramente; (from head to foot) de pies a cabeza, de hito en hito; (of time) pasado. **over** is also used as a prefix. Indicating excess, it is generally translated by demasiado or excesivamente. In other meanings, it is either not translated or its meaning forms part of the verb, being translated as re-, super-, trans-, ultra. Very often a less literal translation is more successful than the employment of the above prefixes. **all o.,** (everywhere) en todas partes; (finished) todo acabado; (covered) cubierto (de); (up and down) de pies a cabeza. **all the world o.,** en todo

el mundo. **embroidered all o.,** todo bordado. **He is o. in Germany,** Está en Alemania. **He trembled all o.,** Estaba todo tembloroso. **that which is o.,** el exceso, lo que queda. **to read o.,** leer, repasar. **o. again,** de nuevo. **o. and above,** por encima de, fuera de, en exceso de. **o. and o.,** repetidamente, muchas veces. **o. my signature,** bajo mi firma. **o. six months since . . . ,** más de seis meses desde que . . .

overabundant *a* sobreabundante

overact *vt* exagerar (un papel)

overall *n* bata, *f*; guardapolvo, *m*; a deconjunto (e.g., **overall assessment,** evaluación de conjunto) *pl* **overalls,** mono, *m*

overanxious *a* demasiado ansioso; demasiado inquieto. **to be o.-a.,** preocuparse demasiado

overarch *vt* abovedar

overawe *vt* intimidar, acobardar

overbalance *vt* hacer perder el equilibrio. hacer caer; preponderar. *vi* perder el equilibrio, caer

overbalancing *n* pérdida del equilibrio, caída, *f*; preponderancia, *f*

overbearing *a* dominante, autoritario, imperioso

overboard *adv* al agua, al mar.

overburden *vt* sobrecargar, agobiar

overcast *a* anublado, cerrado, encapotado. *vt sew* sobrehilar. **to become o.,** anublarse

overcharge *n* recargo, *m*; (price) recargo de precio, precio excesivo, *m*. *vt* recargar, cobrar un precio excesivo; *elec* sobrecargar. *vi* cobrar demasiado

overcoat *n* abrigo, sobretodo, gabán, *m*

overcome *vt* vencer, rendir, subyugar; (difficulties) triunfar de, allanar, dominar. *vi* saber vencer. *a* (by sleep, etc.) rendido; (at a loss) turbado, confundido; (by kindness) agradecidísimo

overconfidence *n* confianza excesiva, *f*

overcooked *a* recocido, demasiado cocido

overcrowd *vt* atestar, llenar de bote en bote; (over-populate) sobrepoblar

overcrowding *n* sobrepoblación, *f*

overdo *vt* exagerar; ir demasiado lejos, hacer demasiado; *cul* recocer; (overtire) fatigarse demasiado

overdose *n* dosis excesiva, *f*

overdraft *n com* giro en descubierto, *m*

overdraw *vt* and *vi com* girar en descubierto

over-dressed *a* que viste demasiado; cursi

overdue *a* atrasado; *com* vencido y no pagado

overeat *vi* comer demasiado, atracarse, *Lat. Am.* jambarse

overestimate *vt* estimar en valor excesivo; exagerar, sobreestimar, n presupuesto excesivo, m; estimación excesiva, f

overexcite vt sobreexcitar

overexposure n phot exceso deexposición, m

overfatigue vt fatigar demasiado. n cansancio excesivo, m

overflow vt inundar, derramarse por; fig cubrir, llenar; desbordarse. vi (with) rebosar de. n inundación, f, desbordamiento, derrame, m; fig residuo, resto, exceso, m; (plumbing) sumidero, vertedero, m, descarga, f. **The river overflowed its banks,** El río se desbordó, El río salió de cauce

overflowing a rebosante; superabundante; (its banks) Lat. Am. desbocado. **filled to o.,** lleno hasta los bordes. **o. with health,** rebosante de salud, vendiendo salud

overgrown a (gawky) talludo; (plants) exuberante, vicioso; frondoso, cubierto de verdura

overhang vt caer a, mirar a; colgar; fig amenazar. vi colgar, sobresalir; fig amenazar

overhanging a saledizo, sobresaliente; colgante, pendiente

overhaul vt examinar, investigar; componer, hacer una inspección general de; (of boats overtaking) alcanzar. n examen, m, investigación, f; med exploración general, f

overhead adv arriba, en lo alto, encima de la cabeza. a aéreo, elevado; general, fijo. **o. cable,** cable eléctrico, m. **o. expenses,** gastos generales, m pl. **o. railway,** ferrocarril aéreo (or elevado), m

overhear vt (accidentally) oír por casualidad, oír sin querer; (on purpose) alcanzar a oír, lograr oír

overheat vt acalorar, hacer demasiado caliente, recalentar. vi (in argument) acalorarse; hacerse demasiado caliente

overheating n recalentamiento, m

overindulge vt mimar demasiado; dedicarse a algo con exceso; tomar algo con exceso. vi darse demasiada buena vida

overjoyed a contentísimo, lleno de alegría, encantado

overland adv por tierra. a terrestre, transcontinental

overlap vi traslaparse; coincidir. n traslapo, m

overlay vt cubrir, dar una capa; (with silver) platear; (with gold) dorar. n capa, f; cubierta, f

overload vt sobrecargar, recargar. n sobrecarga, f

overlook vt (face) dar a, mirar a, dominar; (supervise) vigilar, examinar, inspeccionar; (not notice) no notar, pasar por alto, no hacer, caso de, no fijarse en; (neglect) desdeñar; (ignore) no darse cuenta de, ignorar; (excuse) perdonar, tolerar, hacer la vista gorda

overlord n señor de horca y cuchillo, señor, jefe, m

overnight adv la noche pasada, durante la noche; toda la noche. a de la víspera, nocturno. **to stay o. with,** pasar la noche con

overpass n pasaje elevado, viaducto, m

overpay vt pagar demasiado

overpayment n pago excesivo, m

overpopulate vt sobrepoblar, become overpopulated recargarse de habitantes (with people), recargarse de animales (with animals)

overpower vt vencer, subyugar; (of scents, etc.) trastornar; rendir, dominar

overpowering a irresistible

overproduce vt and vi sobreproducir

overrate vt exagerar el valor de; (of property) sobrevalorar

overreach vt sobrealcanzar. **to o. oneself,** sobrepasarse, ir demasiado lejos

override vt (trample) pasar por encima (de); fig rechazar, poner a un lado; (bully) dominar; (a horse) fatigar, reventar

overripe a demasiado maduro

overrule vt law denegar, no admitir; vencer

overrun vt (flood) inundar; (ravage) invadir; (infest) plagar, infestar; desbordarse, derramarse

oversea a ultramarino, de ultramar. adv en ultramar, allende los mares

oversee vt vigilar, inspeccionar

overseer n capataz, mayoral, sobrestante, contramaestre, m; inspector (-ra), veedor (-ra)

oversensitive a demasiado sensitivo; vidrioso; susceptible

overshadow vt sombrear; fig eclipsar, obscurecer; (sadden) entristecer

overshoe n chanclo, m; (for snow) galocha, f

overshoot vt tirar más allá del blanco; fig exceder, rebasar el límite conveniente, **overshoot the target** (fig.) ir más allá del blanco, ir más allá de lo razonable. **to o. oneself,** exagerar; propasarse, descomedirse

oversight n inadvertencia, omisión, equivocación, f; descuido, m

oversimplify vt simplificar en exceso

oversleep vi dormir demasiado; inf pegársele a uno las sábanas, levantarse demasiado tarde

overspend vt and vi gastar demasiado

overspread vt desparramar, salpicar, esparcir, sembrar; cubrir

overstate vt exagerar, encarecer, ponderar

overstatement n exageración, ponderación, f

overstep vt exceder, pasar, violar; rebasar, pasar más allá (de)

overstrain vt fatigar demasiado, agotar. n fatiga, f. **to o. oneself,** esforzarse demasiado, cansarse demasiado

overstrung a nervioso, excitable; (piano) de cuerdas cruzadas

overt a abierto, público; manifiesto, evidente

overtake vt alcanzar, pasar, dejar atrás; adelantarse (a); (surprise) coger, sorprender; (overwhelm) vencer, dominar

overtax vt oprimir de tributos; agobiar, cansar demasiado

overthrow vt volcar, echar por tierra, derribar; fig vencer, destruir, destronar. n vuelco, derribo, m; fig destrucción, ruina, f

overtime adv fuera de las horas estipuladas. n horas extraordinarias de trabajo, f pl. **to work o.,** trabajar horas extraordinarias

overture n mus obertura, f

overturn vt volcar, derribar, echar a rodar, echar abajo; (upset) revolver, desordenar. vi volcar, venirse abajo, allanarse; estar revuelto

overweening a arrogante, insolente, altivo

overweight n sobrepeso, exceso en el peso, m. **to be o.,** pesar más de lo debido

overwhelm vt (conquer) vencer, aplastar, derrotar; (of waves, etc.) sumergir, hundir, inundar, engolfar; (in argument) confundir, dejar confuso, avergonzar; (of grief, etc.) vencer, postrar, dominar; (of work) inundar

overwhelming a irresistible, invencible, abrumador, apabullante

overwind vt (a watch) dar demasiada cuerda a; romper la cuerda de

overwork vt hacer trabajar demasiado (or con exceso); esclavizar. vi trabajar demasiado. n exceso de trabajo, demasiado trabajo, m

overwrought a (overworked) agotado por el trabajo, rendido, muy cansado; nerviosísimo, sobreexcitado, exaltado, muy agitado

ovulation n med ovulación, f

owe vt deber, tener deudas (de); deber, estar agradecido (por), estar obligado (a). vi estar en deuda, estar endeudado, tener deudas. **He owes his tailor $30,** Le debe treinta dólares a su sastre. **I owe him thanks for his help,** Le estoy agradecido por su ayuda (or Le debo las gracias por . . .). **He owes his success to good fortune,** Su éxito se debe a la suerte

owing a sin pagar. **o. to,** debido a, a causa de, por. **We had to stay in o. to the rain,** Tuvimos que quedarnos en casa a causa de la lluvia. **What is o. to you now?** ¿Cuánto se le debe ahora?

owl n búho, mochuelo, Peru carancho, m. **barn** or **screech owl,** lechuza, f. **brown owl,** autillo, m

owlish a parecido a un búho, de búho

own a propio. n (dearest) bien, m. vt poseer, tener, ser dueño de; (recognize) reconocer; (admit) confesar. vi confesar. **my (thy, his, our, your) own,** mi (tu, su, nuestro, vuestro) propio, m, (f, propia); mis (tus, sus, nuestros, vuestros) propios, m pl, (f pl, propias); (when not placed before a noun) el mío (tuyo, suyo, nuestro, vuestro), la mía (tuya, etc.), los míos (tuyos, etc.), las mías (tuyas, etc.); (relations) los suyos. **in his own house,** en su propia casa. **my (thy, his, etc.) own self,** yo (tú, él) mismo, m, (f, misma, m pl, mismos, f pl, mismas). **a room of one's own,** un cuarto para sí (or para uno mismo). **to be on one's own,** ser independiente; estar a solas. **to hold one's own,** mantenerse en sus trece. **to own up,** confesar

owner n dueño (-ña), propietario (-ia), posesor (-ra)

ownership n posesión, f, dominio, m; propiedad, f

ox n buey (pl bueyes), m.

oxygen n oxígeno, m. **o. mask,** máscara de oxígeno, f. **o. tent,** tienda de oxígeno, f

oyster n ostra, f. **o. bed,** pescadero (or criadero) de ostras, m. **o. culture,** ostricultura, f

ozone n ozono, m

p n (letter) pe, f. **to mind one's p's and q's,** poner los puntos sobre las íes; ir con pies de plomo

pabulum n pábulo, m; sustento, m

pace n paso, m; (gait) andar, m, marcha, f; (of a horse) andadura, f; (speed) velocidad, f, vi pasear(se), andar; (of a horse) amblar. vt recorrer, andar por; marcar el paso para; (with out) medir a pasos. **at a good p.,** a un buen paso. **to keep p. with,** ajustarse al paso de, ir al mismo paso que; andar al paso de; (events) mantenerse al corriente de. **to p. up and down,** pasearse, dar vueltas. **p.-maker,** el que marca el paso

paced a de andar . . . ; (of a horse) de andadura . . . ; de paso . . .

Pacific, the el (Océano) Pacífico, m

pacific a geog pacífico; sosegado, tranquilo, pacífico. **He is of a p. disposition,** Es amigo de la paz

pacifier n pacificador (-ra)

pacifist a pacifista. n pacifista, mf

pacify vt pacificar; calmar, tranquilizar; aplacar, conciliar

pack n (bundle) fardo, lío, m; paquete, m; (load) carga, f; (of hounds) jauría, f; (herd) hato, m; (of seals) manada, f; (of cards) baraja (de naipes), f; (of rogues) cuadrilla, f; (of lies, etc.) colección, f; masa, f; (of ice) témpanos flotantes, m pl; (Rugby football) delanteros, m pl; (for the face) compresa, f. **p.-horse,** caballo de carga, m. **p.-needle,** aguja espartera, f. **p.-saddle,** albarda, f. **p.-thread,** bramante, m

pack vt embalar; empaquetar; envasar; encajonar; (a suit-case, etc.) hacer; (cram) apretar; (crowd) atestar, llenar; (a pipe joint, etc.) empaquetar; (an animal) cargar. vi llenar; (one's luggage) hacer el equipaje, hacer el baúl, arreglar el equipaje. **packed like sardines,** como sardinas en banasta. **The train was packed,** El tren estababa lleno de bote en bote. **to p. off,** (a person) despachar; poner de partitas en la calle. **to p. up,** hacer el equipaje; empaquetar; embalar; inf liar el hato

package n paquete, m; bulto, m; (bundle) fardo, m

packer n embalador, m; envasador (-ra)

packet n paquete, m; (of cigarettes, etc.) cajetilla, f; (boat) paquebote, m. **to make one's p.,** inf hacer su pacotilla

packing n embalaje, m; envoltura, f; envase, m; (on a pipe, etc.) guarnición, f. **I must do my p.,** Tengo que hacer las maletas. **p.-case,** caja de embalaje, f. **p.-needle,** aguja espartera, f

pact n pacto, convenio, m. **to make a p.,** pactar

pad n almohadilla, f, cojinete, m; (on a bed, chair) colchoneta, f; (on a wound) cabezal, m; (for polishing) muñeca, f; (hockey) defensa, f; (cricket) espinillera, f; (writing) bloque, m; (of a calendar) taco, m; (blotting) secafirmas, m; (of a quadruped's foot) pulpejo, m; (of fox, hare) pata, f; (leaf) hoja grande, f, vt almohadillar; acolchar; rellenar, forrar; (out, a book, etc.) meter paja en. **inking-pad,** almohadilla de entintar, f. **padded cell,** celda acolchonada, f. **shoulder-pad,** (in a garment) hombrera, f

padding n relleno, m, almohadilla, f; (material) borra, f, algodón, m; fig paja, f, ripio, m,

paddle n (oar) canalete, zagual, m; paleta, f; (flipper) aleta, f, vt and vi remar con canalete; (dabble) chapotear. **double p.,** remo doble, m. **p.-steamer,** vapor de ruedas, vapor de paleta, m. **p.-wheel,** rueda de paletas, f

padlock n candado, m, vt cerrar con candado, acerrojar

pagan a and n pagano (-na)

page n (boy) paje, m; (squire) escudero, m; (of a book, etc.) página, f; fig hoja, f. vt compaginar; (a person) vocear. **on p. nine,** en la página nueve. **to turn the p.,** fig volver la hoja

pageant n espectáculo, m; (procession) desfile, m; representación teatral, f; fiesta, f; fig pompa, f, aparato, m

pageantry n pompa, f, aparato, m, magnificencia, f

paid a pagado; (on a parcel) porte pagado. **p. mourner,** plañidera, f. **p.-up share,** acción liberada, f

pail n cubo, pozal, m, cubeta, f

pain n dolor, m; sufrimiento, m; (mental) tormento, m, angustia, f; law pena, f; pl **pains,** (effort) trabajo, esfuerzo, m. vt doler; atormentar, afligir. **dull p.,** dolor sordo, m. **I have a p. in my head,** Me duele la cabeza. **on p. of death,** so pena de muerte. **to be in great p.,** sufrir mucho. **to take pains,** tomarse trabajo, esforzarse, esmerarse

painful a doloroso; angustioso; fatigoso; (troublesome) molesto; (embarrassing) embarazoso; difícil; (laborious) arduo

painless a sin dolor, indoloro

painstaking a concienzudo, diligente, industrioso; cuidadoso. n trabajo, m; diligencia, industria, f; cuidado, m

paint n pintura, f; (for preserving metal) pavón, m; (rouge) colorete, m. vt pintar. vi pintar; pintarse. **The door is painted blue,** La puerta está pintada de azul. **p.-box,** caja de pinturas, f. **p.-brush,** pincel, m; (for house painting) brocha, f

painter n pintor (-ra); (house) pintor de brocha gorda, pintor de casas, m; (of a boat) boza, f. **sign-p.,** pintor de muestras, m

painting n pintura, f; (picture) cuadro, m, pintura, f

pair n par, m; (of people) pareja, f; (of oxen) yunta, f. vt parear, emparejar; (persons) unir, casar; (animals) aparear. vi parearse; casarse; aparearse. **a carriage and p.,** un landó con dos caballos. **a p. of steps,** una escalera de mano. **a p. of pants a p. of** trousers, unos pantalones. **in pairs,** de dos en dos; por parejas. **to p. off,** vi formar pareja; inf casarse

pal n camarada, compinche, mf; amigote, m

palace n palacio, m

palatable a sabroso, apetitoso; fig agradable, aceptable

palate n paladar, m. **hard p.,** paladar, m. **soft p.,** velo del paladar, m

palatial a (of a palace) palaciego; (sumptuous) magnífico, suntuoso

pale n (stake) estaca, f; límite, m; her palo, m, a pálido; (wan) descolorido, Lat. Am. also lívido; (of colours) claro, desmayado; (of light) tenue, mortecino; (lustreless) sin brillo, muerto. vi palidecer, perder el color; fig eclipsarse

palette n paleta, f. **p.-knife,** espátula, f

palisade n palenque, m, tranquera, palizada, f; mil estacada, f

pall n (on a coffin) paño mortuorio, m; (fig covering) manto, m, capa, f; ecc palio, m; (over a chalice) palia, f. vi perder el sabor, hacerse insípido; saciarse (de); aburrirse (de), cansarse (de). **The music of Bach never palls on me,** No me canso nunca de la música de Bach

palliate vt (pain) paliar, aliviar; mitigar; (excuse) disculpar, excusar

palliative a paliativo; (extenuating) atenuante. n paliativo, m

pallid a pálido, Lat. Am. also lívido

pallor n palidez, f

palm n (of the hand, and fig., victory) palma, f; (measurement) ancho de la mano, m; (tree) palmera, f. vt (a card, etc.) empalmar; (with off) defraudar (con); dar gato por liebre (a). **to bear away the p.,** llevar la palma. **p. branch,** palma, f. **p. grove,** palmar, m. **p.-oil,** aceite de palma, m; (bribe) soborno, m. **P. Sunday,** Domingo de Ramos, m. **p. tree,** palmera, Lat. Am. chonta, f

palmy a palmar; (flourishing) floreciente; (happy) dichoso, feliz; (prosperous) próspero; triunfante

palp n palpo, m

palpable a palpable

palpate vt palpar

palpitate vi palpitar

palpitation n palpitación, f

palsy n parálisis, f, vt paralizar

paltry a mezquino, insignificante, pobre

pampas n pampa, f

pamper vt mimar, consentir demasiado;

criar con mimos, regalar; alimentar demasiado bien

pampered a mimado, consentido; demasiado bien alimentado

pamphlet n folleto, m

pan n (vessel) cazuela, f; cacerola, f; (brain) cráneo, m; (of a balance) platillo, m; (of a firelock) cazoleta, f, cinem toma panorámica, f, prefix pan-. **to pan off,** separar el oro en una gamella. **to pan out,** dar oro; fig suceder. **Pan-Americanism,** panamericanismo, m

panacea n panacea, f

panache n penacho, m

panada n cul panetela, f

Panama el Panamá, m

Panama a panameño. (-ña). **P. hat,** sombrero de jipijapa, panamá m

pancake n fruta de sartén, hojuela, f. **p. landing,** aer aterrizaje brusco, m. **P. Tuesday,** martes de Carnaval, m

pancreas n páncreas, m

panda n zool panda, mf

pandemic a pandémico

pandemonium n pandemonio

pander n alcahuete, m, vi alcahuetear. **to p. to,** prestarse a; favorecer, ayudar

pane n hoja de vidrio, hoja de cristal, f; cuadro, m

panegyric a panegírico. n panegírico, m

panel n panel, entrepaño, m; art tabla, f; (in a dress) paño, m; (list) lista, f, registro, m; (jury) jurado, m; lista de jurados, f. vt labrar a entrepaños; artesonar. **p. doctor,** médico (-ca) de seguros

paneled a entrepañado; (of ceilings) artesonado. **p. ceiling,** artesonado, m

paneling n entrepaños, m pl; artesonado, m

panful n cazolada, f

pang n punzada (de dolor), f, dolor agudo, m; dolor, m; (anguish of mind) angustia, f, tormento, m; (of conscience) remordimiento, m

panic n pánico, m; pavor, espanto, m; terror súbito, m, a pánico. vi espantarse. **p.-monger,** alarmista, mf **p.-stricken,** aterrorizado, despavorido

panicky a inf lleno de pánico; nervioso

panoply n panoplia, f

panorama n panorama, m

panoramic a panorámico

pansy n pensamiento, m, trinitaria, f

pant vi jadear; (of dogs) hipar; resollar; (of the heart) palpitar. n jadeo, m; palpitación, f. **to p. after,** suspirar por

pantaloon n (trouser) pantalón, m; (Pantaloon) Pantalón, m

pantechnicon n almacén de muebles, m; (van) carro de mudanzas, m

pantheon n panteón, m

panther n pantera, f

panties n pl pantalones, m pl

panting a jadeante, sin aliento. n jadeo, m; resuello, m, respiración difícil, f; palpitación, f

pantomime n pantomima, f; revista, f. **in p.**, en pantomima; por gestos

pantry n despensa, f

pants n pl calzoncillos, m pl; (trousers) pantalones, m pl. **p. buttoned down the sides** Mexico calzoneras, fpl

pap n (nipple) pezón, m; (soft food) papilla, f

papa n papá, m

papacy n papado, pontificado, m

papal a papal, pontificio. **p. bull**, bula pontificia, f. **p. nuncio**, nuncio del Papa, nuncio apostólico, m. **p. see**, sede apostólica, f

papaya n Cuba fruta bomba, f

paper n papel, m; hoja de papel, f; documento, m; (lecture) comunicación, f; (newspaper) periódico, m; (journal) revista, f; (exam.) examen escrito, trabajo, m; ejercicio, m; pl **papers**, (credentials) documentación, f, credenciales, f pl; com valores negociables, m pl; (packet) paquete, m, a de papel; para papeles; parecido al papel. vt (a room) empapelar; (a parcel) envolver. **daily p.**, diario, m. **in p. covers**, (of books) en rústica. **slip of p.**, papeleta, f. **to send in one's papers**, entregar su dimisión. **p. bag**, saco de papel, m. **p.-chase**, rallypaper, m. **p. clip**, prendedero de oficina, **sujetapapeles**, Central America ataché, ~~elsewhere in Lat. Am.~~ broche, m. **p.-cutting machine**, guillotina, f. **p.-folder**, plegadera, f. **p.-hanger**, empapelador, m. **p.-hanging**, empapelado, m. **p.-knife**, cortapapel, m. **p.-maker**, fabricante de papel, m. **p.-making**, manufactura de papel, f. **p.-mill**, fábrica de papel, f. **p.-money**, papel moneda, m. **p.-pulp**, pasta, f. **p.-streamer**, serpentina, f. **p.-weight**, pisapapeles, m

papering n (of a room) empapelado, m

papier-mâché n cartón piedra, m

papillary a papilar

paprika n pimienta húngara, f

papyrus n papiro, m

par n par, f, al par, com a la par. **above (below) par**, com por encima (or debajo) de la par. **He is a little below par**, No está muy bien de salud. **to be on par with**, ser el equivalente de; ser igual a. **par excellence**, por excelencia

parable n parábola, f

parachute n paracaídas, m; bot vilano, m. **to p. down**, lanzarse en paracaídas. **p. troops**, cuerpo de paracaidistas, m

parachutist n paracaidista, mf

parade n alarde, m; mil parada, revista, f; (procession) desfile, m, procesión, f; (promenade) paseo, m. vt (display) hacer alarde de, hacer gala de, ostentar; (troops) formar en parada; pasar revista (a); (patrol) recorrer. vi mil tomar parte en una parada; desfilar. **to p. up and down**, pasearse. **p.-ground**, campo de instrucción, m; plaza de armas, f

paradigm n paradigma, m

paradise n paraíso, edén, m; fig jauja, f. **bird of p.**, ave del paraíso, f

paradox n paradoja, f

paradoxical a paradójico

paraffin n parafina, f. vt parafinar. **p.-oil**, parafina líquida, f

paragon n modelo perfecto, dechado, m

paragraph n párrafo, m; (in a newspaper) suelto, m, vt dividir en párrafos; escribir un suelto sobre. **new p.**, párrafo aparte, m

Paraguay el Paraguay, m

Paraguayan a and n paraguayo (-ya)

parakeet n orn perico, m

parallel a paralelo; igual; semejante, análogo. n línea paralela, f; paralelo, m; mil paralela, f; geog paralelo, m; print pleca, f. vt poner en paralelo; cotejar, comparar; igualar. **to run p. to**, ser paralelo a; ser conforme a. **p. bars**, paralelas, f pl

paralyse vt paralizar

paralysis n parálisis, f

paralytic a and n paralítico (-ca)

paramount a supremo, sumo

paramour n amante, querido, m; querida, amiga, f

paranoia n paranoia, f

~~paranoiac n paranoico, m~~

parapet n (arch and mil) parapeto, m

paraphernalia n law bienes parafernales, m, p; (finery) atavíos, adornos, m pl; equipo, m; arreos, m pl; insignias, f pl

paraphrase n paráfrasis, f, vt parafrasear

parasite n parásito, m; inf zángano, m, gorrista, mf, Mexico arrimado, m

parasitic a parásito, parasitario; med parasítico

parasol n parasol, quitasol, m

parboil vt sancochar

parcel n paquete, m; fardo, m; (of land) parcela, f. **to p. out**, repartir, distribuir; dividir. **to p. up**, envolver, empaquetar. **p. post**, servicio de paquetes, m

parch vt secar; abrasar, quemar; (roast) tostar. vi secarse; quemarse, abrasarse

parched a seco, sediento. **p. with thirst**, muerto de sed

parchment n pergamino, m; (of a drum) parche, m. **p.-like**, apergaminado

pardon n perdón, m; ecc indulgencia, f. vt perdonar; indultar, amnistiar. **a general p.**, una amnistía. **I beg your p.!** ¡Vd. dispense! ¡Perdone Vd.! **to beg p.**, pedir perdón; disculparse. **P.?** ¿Cómo?

pardonable a perdonable, disculpable, excusable

pardonableness n disculpabilidad, f

pardonably adv disculpablemente, excusablemente

pardoner n vendedor de indulgencias, m; perdonador (-ra)

pardoning n perdón, m; remisión, f

pare vt (one's nails) cortar; (fruit) mondar; (potatoes, etc.) pelar; (remove) quitar; (reduce) reducir

parent n padre, m; madre, f; (ancestor) antepasado, m; (origin) origen, m, fuente, f; (cause) causa, f; (author) autor, m; autora, f; pl **parents,** padres, m pl. a madre, materno; principal

parentage n parentela, f; linaje, m, familia, alcurnia, f; procedencia, f, nacimiento, origen, m

parental a paternal; maternal, de madre

parentally adv como un padre; como una madre

parenthesis n paréntesis, m

parenthetical a entre paréntesis; de paréntesis

parenthood n paternidad, f; maternidad, f

pariah n paria, mf

parietal a parietal

paring n (act) raedura, f; peladura, mondadura, f; (shred) brizna, f; (refuse) desecho, desperdicio, m. **p.-knife,** trinchete, m

Paris París, m

parish n parroquia, f; feligresía, f, a parroquial. **p. church,** parroquia, f. **p. clerk,** sacristán de parroquia, m. **p. priest,** párroco, m. **p. register,** registro de la parroquia, m

parishioner n parroquiano (-na); feligrés (-esa)

Parisian a parisiense. n parisiense, mf

parity n paridad, f

park n parque, m; jardín, m. vt (vehicles) estacionar; (dump) depositar. **car p.,** parque de automóviles, m. **p.-keeper,** guardián del parque, m

parking n (of vehicles) estacionamiento, m; (dumping) depósito, m. **p. lights,** aut luces de estacionamiento, m f pl. **p. place,** parque de estacionamiento, m

parking meter n estacionómetro, m Mexico, parquímetro m Argentina, Spain, parcómetro m elsewhere in Latin America, reloj de estacionamiento m Spain

parlance n lenguaje, m. **in common p.,** en lenguaje vulgar

parley n plática, conversación, f; discusión, f; mil parlamento, m. vi mil parlamentar; discutir; conversar. vt hablar

parliament n parlamento, m; cortes, f pl; cuerpo legislativo, m

parliamentarian a and n parlamentario; (of an academy) censor, m

parliamentary a parlamentario. **p. immunity,** inviolabilidad parlamentaria, f

parlor n salón, gabinete, m; sala de

recibo, f; (in a convent) locutorio, m. **p. games,** diversión de salón, f, juego de sociedad, m. **p.-maid,** camarera, f

parlous a crítico, malo. adv sumamente, muy

Parmesan a parmesano, de Parma. n parmesano (-na). **P. cheese,** queso de Parma, m

parochial a parroquial, parroquiano; fig provincial

parochialism n provincialismo, m

parodist n parodista, mf

parody n parodia, f; vt parodiar

parole n (of convict) libertad vigilada, f

paroxysm n paroxismo, m; ataque, acceso, m

parquet (floor) entarimado m; (of theater) platea, f

parrot n papagayo, loro, m, Lat. Am. cata, f

parry vt (a blow, and in fencing) parar; rechazar; evitar. n parada, f; (in fencing) quite, m, parada, f

parse vt analizar

parsimonious a parsimonioso

parsimoniously adv con parsimonia

parsimony n parsimonia, f

parsley n perejil, m

parsnip n chirivía, f

part n parte, f; porción, f; trozo, m; mech pieza, f; (gram and of a literary work) parte, f; (of a living organism) miembro, m; (duty) deber, m, obligación, f; theat papel, m; mus voz, f; pl **parts,** (region) partes, f pl, lugar, m; (talents) partes, dotes, f pl. **foreign parts,** países extranjeros, m pl, el extranjero. **For my p. . . . ,** Por lo que a mí toca, Por mi parte. **for the most p.,** en su mayoría. **from all parts,** de todas partes. **in p.,** en parte; parcialmente. **spare p.,** pieza de recambio, f. **The funny p. of it is . . . ,** Lo cómico del asunto es . . . **the latter p. of the month,** los últimos días del mes, la segunda quincena del mes. **to form p. of,** formar parte de. **to play a p.,** hacer un papel. **to take a person's p.,** apoyar a alguien, ser partidario de alguien. **to take in good p.,** tomar bien. **to take p. in,** tomar parte en, participar en. **p. of speech,** parte de la oración, f. **p.-owner,** copropietario (-ia). **p.-time job,** trabajo de unas cuantas horas, m

part vt distribuir, repartir; dividir; separar (de); (open) abrir. vi partir, marcharse; despedirse; (of roads, etc.) bifurcarse; dividirse; (open) abrirse. **to p. one's hair,** hacerse la raya. **to p. from,** (things) separarse de; (people) despedirse de. **to p. with,** separarse de; deshacerse de; perder; (dismiss) despedir (a)

partake vt participar de, compartir; tomar parte en. vi tomar algo (de comer, de beber). **to p. of,** comer (beber) de; tener rasgos de

Parthian a parto. n parto (-ta). **P. shot,** la flecha del parto

partial a parcial; (fond of) aficionado (a). **p. eclipse,** eclipse parcial, m

participant a participante. n partícipe, mf

participate vi participar (de), compartir; tomar parte (en)

participation n participación, f

particle n partícula, f; fig átomo, grano, m, pizca, f; gram partícula, f

parti-colored a bicolor

particular a particular; especial; individual; singular; cierto; exacto; escrupuloso; difícil, exigente. n detalle, pormenor, m; circunstancia, f; caso particular, m; pl **particulars,** informes, detalles, m pl. **further particulars,** más detalles. **in p.,** en particular; sobre todo. **He is very p. about . . . ,** Es muy exigente en cuanto a . . . ; Le es muy importante . . . , Le importa mucho . . .

particularize vt particularizar, detallar; especificar

particularly adv en particular; particularmente; sobre todo

parting n despedida, f; partida, f; separación, f; (of the hair) raya, crencha, f; (cross roads) bifurcación, f. a de despedida. **at p.,** al despedirse. **to reach the p. of the ways,** fig llegar al punto decisivo

partisan n partidario (-ia); (fighter) guerrillero, m, a partidario; de guerrilleros

partisanship n partidarismo, m

partition n partición, f; división, f; (wall) pared, f, tabique, m. **the p. of Ireland,** la división de Irlanda. vt **to p. off** Lat. Am. entabicar

partly adv en parte

partner n asociado (-da); com socio (-ia); (dancing) pareja, f; (in games, and companion) compañero (-ra); (spouse) consorte, mf; (in crime) codelincuente, mf **sleeping p.,** socio comanditario, m. **working p.,** socio industrial, m

partnership n asociación, f; com sociedad, compañía, f. **deed of p.,** artículos de sociedad, m pl. **to take into p.,** tomar como socio (a). **to form a p.,** asociarse

partridge n orn perdiz, f. **young p.,** perdigón, m

parturition n parto, m

party n partido, m; grupo, m; (of pleasure, etc.) partida, f; reunión, fiesta, f; mil pelotón, destacamento, m; law parte, f; (person) interesado (-da); (accessory) cómplice, mf. **rescue p.,** pelotón de salvamento, m. **to be a p. to,** prestarse a; ser cómplice en. **to give a p.,** dar una fiesta, dar una reunión. **p.-spirit,** espíritu del partido, m. **p.-wall,** pared medianera, f

parvenu n advenedizo (-za)

pass n (in an exam.) aprobación, f; (crisis) crisis, situación crítica, f; estado, m; (with

the hands) pase, m; (permit) permiso, m; mil licencia, f; (safe-conduct) salvoconducto, m; (in football, etc.) pase, m; (membership card) carnet, m; (defile) desfiladero, paso, puerto, m; naut rebasadero, m; (fencing) estocada, f. **free p.,** billete de favor, m. **p.-book,** libreta de banco, f. **p. certificate,** (in exams.) aprobado, m. **p.-key,** llave maestra, f

pass vi pasar; (of time) correr, pasar, transcurrir; (happen) occurrir; tomar lugar; (end) cesar, desaparecer; (die) morir. vt pasar; hacer pasar; (the butter, etc.) dar, alargar; (in football, hockey) pasar; (excel) aventajar, exceder; (a Bill, an examination) aprobar; (sentence) fallar, pronunciar; (a remark) hacer; (transfer) traspasar; (tolerate) sufrir, tolerar; evacuar. **He passed in psychology,** Aprobó sicología. **to allow to p.,** ceder el paso (a). **to bring to p.,** ocasionar. **to come to p.,** suceder. **to let p.,** (put up with) dejar pasar; no hacer caso de; (forgive) perdonar. **to p. a vote of confidence,** votar una proposición de confianza. **to p. the buck,** inf echarle a uno el muerto. **pass the hat, pass the plate,** pasar la gorra. **to p. along,** pasar por; pasar. **to p. away,** pasar; desaparecer; (die) morir, fallecer; (of time) transcurrir. **to p. by,** pasar por, pasar delante de, pasar al lado de; (omit) pasar por alto de, omitir; (ignore) pasar sin hacer caso de. **to p. for,** pasar por. **to p. in,** entrar. **to p. in and out,** entrar y salir. **to p. off,** vi pasar; cesar, acabarse; desaparecer; evaporarse, disiparse; (of events) tener lugar. vt (oneself) darse por; dar por, hacer pasar por. **to p. a cat off as hare,** dar gato por liebre. **to p. on,** vi pasar; seguir su camino, continuar su marcha. vt pasar algo de uno a otro. **to p. out,** salir. **to p. over,** pasar por encima de; pasar; cruzar, atravesar; (transfer) traspasar; (disregard) pasar por alto de, dejar a un lado; omitir. **to p. over in silence,** pasar en silencio (por). **to p. round,** circular. **to p. through,** cruzar, atravesar, pasar por; (pierce) traspasar; fig experimentar

passable a transitable, pasadero (fairly good) regular, mediano; tolerable

passably adv medianamente, pasaderamente, tolerablemente

passage n pasaje, m; paso, tránsito, m; (voyage) viaje, m, travesía, f; (corridor) pasillo, m; (entrance) entrada, f; (way) camino, m; (alley) callejón, m; (in a mine) galería, f; (of time) transcurso, m; (of birds) pasa, f; (in a book, and mus) pasaje, m; (occurrence) episodio, incidente, m; (of a Bill) aprobación, f. **p. money,** pasaje, m. **p. of arms,** lucha, f, combate, m; disputa, f

passenger n viajero (-ra); (on foot) peatón, m. **by p. train,** en gran velocidad

passerby n transeúnte, paseante, mf

passing a pasajero; fugitivo; momentáneo. *adv* sumamente, extremadamente. *n* pasada, *f;* paso, *m;* (death) muerte, *f;* (disappearance) desaparición, *f;* (of a law) aprobación, *f.* **in p.,** de paso. **p.-bell,** toque de difuntos, *m*

passing grade *n* calificación mínima aprobatoria, *f*

passion *n* pasión, *f;* (Christ's) Pasión, *f;* (anger) cólera, *f.* **to fly into a p.,** montar en cólera. **p.-flower,** pasionaria, granadilla, *f.* **P. play,** drama de la Pasión, *m.* **P. Sunday,** Domingo de Pasión, *m.* **P. Week,** Semana Santa, *f*

passionate *a* apasionado; (quick-tempered) irascible, colérico; (fervid) vehemente, intenso, ardiente

passive *a* pasivo. *n gram* pasiva, *f.* **p. resistance,** resistencia pasiva, *f*

Passover *n* Pascua de los judíos, *f*

passport *n* pasaporte, *m*

password *n* contraseña, *f*

past *a* pasado; último; (expert) consumado; (former) antiguo, ex-. *n* pasado, *m;* historia, *f,* antecedentes, *m pl, prep* después de; (in front of) delante de; (next to) al lado de; (beyond) más allá de; (without) sin; fuera de; (of age) más de; (no longer able to) incapaz de. *adv* más allá. (The translation of **past** as an adverb is often either omitted, or included in the verb, e.g. **The years flew p.,** Los años transcurrieron. **for centuries p.,** durante siglos.) **I am p.** caring, Nada me importa ya. **It is a quarter p. ten,** Son las diez y cuarto. **It is p. four o'clock,** Son las siete pasadas, Son después de las cuatro. **what's p. is p.,** lo pasado, pasado. **p. doubt,** fuera de duda. **p. endurance,** insoportable. **p. help,** sin remedio, irremediable. **p. hope,** sin esperanza. **p.-master,** maestro, consumado, experto, *m.* **p. participle,** participio pasado, *m.* **p. president,** ex-presidente, *m.* **p. tense,** (tiempo) pasado, *m*

paste *n* pasta, *f;* (gloy) engrudo, *m. vt* (affix) pegar; (glue) engomar, engrudar

pastel *n art* pastel, *m.* **p. drawing,** pintura al pastel, *f*

pasteurize *vt* pasteurizar

pastime *n* pasatiempo, entretenimiento, *m,* diversión, recreación, *f*

pastor *n* pastor, *m*

pastoral *a* pastoril; *ecc* pastoral. *n ecc* pastoral, *f;* (*poet mus*) pastorela, *f*

pastry *n* (dough) pasta, *f;* pastel, *m,* torta, *f;* pastelería, *f.* **p.-cook,** repostero, *m,* pastelero (-ra)

pasture *n* (grass, etc.) pasto, herbaje, *m;* pasturaje, *m;* (field) prado, *m,* pradera, dehesa, *f. vi* pacer; pastar. *vt* apacentar, pastar, *Argentina* costear

pasty *a* pastoso; (pale) pálido. *n* empanada, *f*

pat *n* toque, *m;* caricia, *f;* (for butter) molde (de mantequilla), *m. vt* tocar;

acariciar, pasar la mano (sobre). *adv* a propósito; oportunamente; fácilmente. **pat of butter,** pedacito de mantequilla, *m.* **pat on the back,** golpe en la espalda, *m; fig* elogio, *m*

Patagonian *a* and *n* patagón (-ona)

patch *n* (mend) remiendo, *m;* (piece) pedazo, *m;* (plaster and *aut.,* etc.) parche, *m;* (beauty spot) lunar postizo, *m;* (of ground) parcela, *f;* (of flowers, etc.) masa, *f;* (stain, and flag) mancha, *f. vt* (mend) remendar; poner remiendo (a); pegar; (roughly) chafallar; (the face) ponerse lunares postizos. **p. of blue sky,** pedazo de cielo azul. **patch of green grass,** mancha de hierba verde. **to be not a p. on,** no ser de la misma clase que; (of persons) no llegarle a los zancajos de. **to p. up a quarrel,** hacer las paces

patchwork *n* labor de retazos, obra de retacitos, *f; flg* mezcla, mezcolanza, *f.* **p. quilt,** centón, *m*

patchy *a* desigual; manchado

patent *a* evidente, patente; patentado. *n* patente, *f. vt* patentar. **p. of nobility,** carta de hidalguía, ejecutoria, *f.* **"P. Applied For,"** «Patente Solicitada.» **Patent Pending** marca en trámite. **p. leather,** *n* charol, *m. a* de charol. **p. medicine,** específico farmacéutico, *m*

patentee *n* el, *m,* (*f,* la) que obtiene una patente; inventor (-ra)

patently *adv* evidentemente, claramente

paternal *a* paterno, paternal

paternity *n* paternidad, *f*

path *n* senda, vereda, *f,* sendero, *m;* camino, *m;* (track) pista, *f;* (traject) trayectoria, *f.* **the beaten p.,** el camino trillado

pathetic *a* patético

pathology *n* patología, *f*

pathos *n* lo patético

patience *n* paciencia, *f.* **He tries my p. very much,** Me cuesta mucho no impacientarme con él. **to lose p.,** perder la paciencia; (grow angry) perder los estribos. **to play p.,** hacer solitarios

patient *a* paciente. *n* paciente, *mf;* (ill person) enfermo (-ma); (of a physician) cliente, *mf*

patiently *adv* con paciencia, pacientemente

patina *n* pátina, *f*

patriarch *n* patriarca, *m*

patrician *a* and *n* patricio (-ia)

patrimony *n* patrimonio, *m*

patriot *n* patriota, *mf*

patriotic *a* patriótico

patriotism *n* patriotismo, *m*

patrol *n* patrulla, *f; f,* ronda, *f, vi* and *vt* patrullar; rondar; recorrer. **p. boat,** lancha escampavía, *f.* **p. flight,** vuelo de patrulla, *m*

patron *n* (of a freed slave) patrono, *m;* (of the arts, etc.) mecenas, protector, *m;*

(customer) parroquiano (-na), cliente, *mf.*
p. saint, santo (-ta) patrón (-ona)

patronage *n* (protection) patrocinio, *m;* protección, *f; ecc* patronato, *m;* (regular custom) clientela, *f;* (of manner) superioridad, *f*

patronize *vt* patrocinar; proteger, favorecer; (a shop) ser parroquiano de; (treat arrogantly) tratar con superioridad

patronizing *a* (with air, behavior, etc.) de superioridad, de altivez

patter *n* (jargon) jerga, *f;* charla, *f;* (of rain) azotes, *m pl;* (of feet) son, *m;* golpecitos, *m pl. vt* (repeat) decir mecánicamente. *vi* (chatter) charlar; (of rain) azotar, bailar; correr ligeramente

pattern *n* modelo, *m;* (sew and dressmaking) patrón, *m;* (in founding) molde, *m;* (templet) escantillón, *m;* (of cloth, etc.) muestra, *f;* (design) dibujo, diseño, *m;* (example) ejemplar, *m. vt* diseñar; estampar. **p. book,** libro de muestras, *m*

patty *n* empanada, *f,* pastelillo, *m*

paucity *n* poquedad, *f;* corto número, *m;* insuficiencia, escasez, *f*

paunch *n* panza, barriga, *f*

pauper *n* pobre, *mf*

pauperism *n* pauperismo, *m*

pauperize *vt* empobrecer, reducir a la miseria

pause *n* pausa, *f;* intervalo, *m;* silencio, *m;* interrupción, *f; mus* pausa, *f. vi* pausar, hacer una pausa; detenerse, interrumpirse; vacilar. **to give p. to,** hacer vacilar (a)

pave *vt* empedrar, enlosar. **to p. the way for,** facilitar el paso de, preparar el terreno para, abrir el camino de

pavement *n* pavimento, *m, Mexico* escarpa, *f;* (sidewalk) acera, *f.* **p.-artist,** pintor callejero, *m*

pavilion *n* pabellón, *m;* (for a band, etc.) quiosco, *m;* (tent) tienda de campaña, *f*

paving *n* pavimentación, *f;* empedrado, *m;* see **pavement.** **p.-stone,** losa, *f*

paw *n* pata, *f;* (with claws) garra, *f; inf* manaza, *f. vt* tocar con la pata; (scratch) arañar; (handle) manosear. *vi* (of a horse) piafar

pawn *n* (chess) peón (de ajedrez), *m;* empeño, *m; flg* prenda, *f. vt* empeñar, pignorar; dar en prenda. **p.-ticket,** papeleta de empeño, *f*

pawnbroker *n* prestamista, *mf*

pawnshop *n* casa de préstamos, casa de empeño, *f,* monte de piedad, *m*

pay *n* paga, *f; (mil nav)* soldada, *f;* salario, *m;* (of a workman) jornal, *m;* (reward) recompensa, compensación, *f;* (profit) beneficio, provecho, *m.* **pay-day,** día de paga, *m.* **pay-office,** pagaduría, *f.* **pay list, pay-sheet,** nómina, *Mexico* lista de raya, *f*

pay *vt* pagar; (a debt) satisfacer; (spend) gastar; (recompense) remunerar, recom-

pensar; (hand over) entregar; (yield) producir; (a visit) hacer; (attention) prestar; (homage) rendir; (one's respects) presentar. *vi* pagar; producir ganancia; sacar provecho; ser una ventaja, ser provechoso. **It would not pay him to do it,** No le saldría a cuenta hacerlo. **This job doesn't pay,** Este trabajo no da dinero. **to pay a compliment (to),** cumplimentar, decir alabanzas (a), echar una flor (a). **to pay attention,** prestar atención; hacer caso. **to pay cash,** pagar al contado. **to pay in advance,** pagar adelantado, *Lat. Am.* aprontar. **to pay in full,** saldar. **to pay off old scores,** ajustar cuentas viejas. **to pay one's addresses to,** hacer la corte (a), pretender en matrimonio (a). **to pay the penalty,** sufrir el castigo, hacer penitencia. **to pay with interest,** *flg* pagar con creces. **to pay again,** volver a pagar, pagar de nuevo. **to pay back,** devolver, restituir; (money only) reembolsar; *flg* pagar en la misma moneda, vengarse (de). **to pay down,** pagar al contado. **to pay for,** pagar, costear; satisfacer. **to pay in,** ingresar. **to pay off,** (persons) despedir; (a debt) saldar; (a mortgage) cancelar, redimir. **to pay out,** (persons) vengarse de; (money) pagar; (ropes, etc.) arriar. **to pay up,** pagar; pagar por completo; (shares, etc.) redimir

payable *a* pagadero; a pagar; que puede ser pagado

payee *n* tenedor, *m*

paymaster *n* pagador, *m;* tesorero, *m.* **P.-General,** ordenador general de pagos, *m*

payment *n* pago, *m,* paga, *f, Lat. Am.* also entero, *m;* remuneración, *f; flg* recompensa, satisfacción, *f; flg* premio, *m.* **in p. of,** en pago de. **on p. of,** mediante el pago de. **p. in advance,** pago adelantado, anticipo, *m*

pea *n* guisante, *m, Lat. Am.* alverjana, arveja, *f.* **dry or split pea,** guisante seco, *m.* **sweet pea,** guisante de olor, *m.* **peaflour,** harina de guisantes, *f.* **pea-green,** verde claro, *m.* **pea-jacket,** chaquetón de piloto, *m.* **pea-shooter,** cerbatana, *f*

peace *n* paz, *f;* tranquilidad, quietud, *f,* sosiego, *m; law* orden público, *m.* **P.!** ¡Silencio! **to hold one's p.,** callarse, guardar silencio. **to make p.,** hacer las paces. **P. be upon this house!** ¡Paz sea en esta casa! **p.-footing,** pie de paz, *m.* **p.-loving,** pacífico. **p.-offering,** sacrificio propiciatorio, *m;* satisfacción, oferta de paz, *f*

peaceable *a* pacífico; apacible; tranquilo, sosegado

peaceful *a* pacífico; tranquilo; silencioso. **to come with p. intentions,** venir de paz

peacefully *adv* en paz; pacíficamente; tranquilamente

peacemaker n pacificador (-ra); conciliador (-ra)

peach n (fruit) melocotón, m; (tree) melocotonero, melocotón, m; (girl) breva, f. **p.-colour,** color de melocotón, m

peacock n pavo real, pavón, m. vi pavonearse; darse humos. **The p. spread its tail,** El pavo real hizo la rueda

peak n punta, f; (of a cap) visera, f; (of a mountain) peñasco, m, cumbre, cima, f; (mountain itself) pico, m; (naut of a hull) pico, m; fig auge, apogeo, m; punto más alto, m. vi consumirse, enflaquecer. **p. hours,** horas de mayor tráfico, f pl

peaked a en punta; puntiagudo; picudo; (of a cap) con visera; (wan) ojeroso; (thin) delgaducho, macilento, consumido

peal n toque (or repique) de campanas, m; campanillazo, m; carillón, m; (noise) estruendo, ruido, m; (of thunder) trueno, m; (of an organ) sonido, m. vi repicar; sonar. vt tañer, echar a vuelo (las campanas); (of a bell that one presses) hacer sonar, tocar. **a p. of laughter,** una carcajada

peanut n cacahuete, m. **p. butter,** mantequilla de cacahuete, f

pear n pera, f. **p.-shaped,** piriforme, de figura de pera. **p. tree,** peral, m

pearl n perla, f; (mother-of-pearl) nácar, m, a de perla; perlero. vt (dew) rociar, aljofarar. vi pescar perlas; formar perlas. **seed p.,** aljófar, m. **p.-ash,** carbonato potásico, m. **p.-barley,** cebada perlada, f. **p.-button,** botón de nácar, m. **p.-fisher,** pescador de perlas, m. **p.-fishery,** pescadería de perlas, f. **p.-grey,** gris de perla, m

peasant a campesino (-na), labrador (-ra). a campesino

peasant movement Mexico agrarismo, m

peasantry n campesinos, m pl, gente del campo, f

peat n turba, f. **p.-bog,** turbera, f

pebble n guijarro, m, pedrezuela, guija, f; (gravel) guijo, m; cristal de roca, m; lente de cristal de roca, m

peccadillo n pecadillo, m

peck n (of a bird) picotazo, m, picada, f; (kiss) besito, m; (large amount) montón, m; multitud, f. vt (of a bird) picotear; sacar (or coger) con el pico; (kiss) besar rápidamente. vi (with at) picotear; picar

peculiar a particular, peculiar, individual; propio, característico; (marked) especial; (unusual) extraño, raro, extraordinario

peculiarity n peculiaridad, particularidad, f; singularidad, f; (eccentricity) excentricidad, rareza, f

peculiarly adv particularmente, peculiarmente; especialmente; extrañamente

pecuniary a pecuniario

pedagogic a pedagógico

pedagogy n pedagogía, f

pedal a zool del pie. n pedal, m. vi pedalear

pedant n pedante, mf

pedantic a pedante

pedantry n pedantería, f

peddle vi ser buhonero. vt revender

pedestal n pedestal, m; fig fundamento, m, base, f. **to put on a p.,** fig poner sobre un pedestal

pedestrian n peatón, peón, m, a pedestre; fig patoso. **p. traffic,** circulación de los peatones, f

pedestrian crosswalk, cruce peatonal Argentina, cruce de peatones, m

pediatrician n pediatra, mf

pedigree n genealogía, f; raza, f; (of words) etimología, f. a (of animals) de raza, de casta. **p. dog,** perro de casta, m

pedlar n buhonero (-ra), Lat. Am. marchante (-ta) mf

pedometer n pedómetro, cuentapasos, m

peel n (baker's) pala, f; (of fruit, etc.) piel, f, hollejo, m. vt pelar, mondar; (bark) descortezar; Lat. Am. deshojar (fruit). vi descascararse, desconcharse; (of the bark of a tree) descortezarse

peeling n (of fruit, etc.) peladura, monda, f; (of bark) descortezadura, f; (of paint, etc.) desconchadura, f

peep vi (of birds) piar; (of mice) chillar; (peer) atisbar, mirar a hurtadillas; (appear) asomar; mostrarse; (of the dawn) despuntar. n (of birds) pío, m; (of mice) chillido, m; (glimpse) vista, f; (glance) ojeada, mirada furtiva, f; **at the p. of day,** al despuntar el día. **p.-hole,** mirilla, f, atisbadero, m; escucha, f. **p.-show,** óptica, f

peer n par, m; igual, mf. vi atisbar; escudriñar; fig asomar, aparecer

peerless a sin par, incomparable, sin igual

peevish a displicente, malhumorado; picajoso, vidrioso, enojadizo

peg n clavija, f; (of a tent) estaca, f; (of a barrel) estaquilla, f; (of a violin, etc.) clavija, f; (for coats, etc.) colgadero, m; (of whisky, etc.) trago, m; fig pretexto, m. vt clavar, enclavijar, empernar. **to take down a peg,** bajar los humos (a). **to peg away,** batirse el cobre. **to peg down,** fijar con clavijas; (a tent) sujetar con estacas; (prices) fijar

pekinese n perro (-rra) pequinés (-esa)

pelican n pelícano, m

pellagra n med pelagra, f

pellet n bolita, f; (pill) píldora, f; (shot) perdigón, m

pellmell adv a trochemoche; atropelladamente

pellucid a diáfano

pelota n pelota vasca, f. **p. player,** pelotari, m

pelt n pellejo, m; cuero, m; (fur) piel, f; (blow) golpe, m. vt llover (piedras, etc.) sobre, arrojar . . . sobre; (questions) disparar; (throw) tirar. vi (of rrain) azotar, diluviar

pelvis n pelvis, f

pen n (for sheep, etc.) aprisco, m; corral, m; (paddock) parque, m; (for hens) pollera, f; (for writing and fig., author, etc.) pluma, f. vt (shut up) acorralar; encerrar; (write) escribir (con pluma). **pen-and-ink drawing**, dibujo a la pluma, m. **pen-holder**, portaplumas, m. **pen-name**, seudónimo, m. **pen-wiper**, limpia-plumas, m

penal a penal. **p. code**, código penal, m. **p. colony**, colonia penal, f. **p. servitude**, trabajos forzados (or forzosos), m pl. **p. servitude for life**, cadena perpetua, f

penalize vt penar, imponer pena (a); castigar

penalty n law penalidad, f; castigo, m; (fine) multa, f; (risk) riesgo, m; sport sanción, m. **the p. of**, la desventaja de. **under p. of**, so pena de. **p. kick**, (football) penalty, m

penance n penitencia, f. **to do p.**, hacer penitencia

penchant n tendencia, f; inclinación, f

pencil n lápiz, m; (automatic) lapicero, m. vt escribir (or dibujar or marcar) con lápiz. **p.-case**, estuche para lápices, m. **p.-holder**, lapicero, m. **p.-sharpener**, cortalápices, afilalápices, m

pendant n (jewel) pendiente, m, arch culo de lámpara, m; (naut rope) amantillo, m; (flag) gallardete, m

pending a pendiente. prep durante. **to be p.**, pender; amenazar

pendulous a péndulo; colgante; oscilante

pendulum n péndola, f, péndulo, m

penetrable a penetrable

penetrate vt and vi penetrar

penetrating a penetrante

penetration n penetración, f

penguin n pingüino, pájaro bobo, m

penicillin n penicilina, f

peninsula n península, f

peninsular a peninsular. **P. War**, Guerra de la Independencia, f

penis n pene, m

penitence n penitencia, f

penitent a penitente. n penitente, mf

penitentiary n ecc penitenciaria, f; casa de corrección, f; penitenciaria, f, presidio, m; cárcel modelo, f, a penitenciario

penknife n cortaplumas, m

penmanship n caligrafía, f

pennant n naut gallardete, m; banderola, f; (ensign) insignia, bandera, f

penniless a sin un penique, sin blanca; indigente, pobre de solemnidad, Peru

calato. to leave p., dejar en la miseria; inf dejar sin camisa

penning n escritura, f; (drawing up) redacción, f; (of bulls, etc.) acorralamiento, m

penny n de un centavo, penique, m; perra gorda, f. a de un penique. **p.-a-liner**, gacetillero, m. **p. dreadful**, folletín, m, novela por entregas, f. **p.-in-the-slot machine**, tragaperras, m

pension n pensión, f; mil retiro, m; (grant) beca, f; (boardinghouse) pensión de familia, f. vt pensionar, dar una pensión (a); (with off) jubilar. **old age p.**, pensión para la vejez, f. **retirement p.**, pensión vitalicia, f

pensioner n pensionista, mf; (mil and nav) inválido, m

pensive a pensativo, meditabundo; cabizbajo, triste

pentagon n pentágono, m

Pentateuch n pentateuco, m

Pentecost n Pentecostés, m, Pascua, f

pentecostal a de Pentecostés, pascual

penthouse n cobertizo, tinglado, m, tejavana, f

pent-up a encerrado; enjaulado; (of emotion) reprimido

penurious a pobre; escaso; (stingy) tacaño, avaro

penury n penuria, f

people n pueblo, m; nación, f; gente, f; personas, f pl; (used disparagingly, mob) populacho, vulgo, m; (inhabitants) habitantes, m pl; (subjects) súbditos, m pl; (relations) parientes, m pl; familia, f. vt poblar. **little p.**, (children) gente menuda, f. **respectable p.**, gente de bien, f. **the p. of Burgos**, los habitantes de Burgos. **P. say**, Se dice, La gente dice. **Very few p. think as you do**, Hay muy pocas personas que opinan como Vd. **How are your p.** (family)? ¿Cómo están los de tu casa? ¿Cómo está tu familia? "**People Working**" «Trabajadores»

pep n inf energía, f, ánimo, m. **p. talk**, discurso estimulante, m. **p. up**, animar

pepper n pimienta, f; (plant) pimentero, pimiento, m, vt sazonar con pimienta; (pelt) acribillar; (with questions) disparar; (a literary work with quotations, etc.) salpimentar. **black p.**, pimienta negra, f. **red p.**, pimiento, m; (cayenne) pimentón, m. **p.-castor**, pimentero, m

peppercorn n grano de pimienta, m

peppermint n menta, f. **p. drop**, pastilla de menta, f

peppery a picante; (irascible) colérico, irascible

peptic a péptico

per prep por. **ninety miles per hour**, noventa millas por hora. **ten pesetas per dozen**, diez pesetas la docena. **$60 per annum**, sesenta dólares al año. **per cent.**, por ciento

perambulate *vt* recorrer

perambulator *n* cochecito para niños, *m*

percale *n* percal, *m*

percaline *n* percalina, *f*

perceive *vt* percibir, comprender, darse cuenta de; percibir, discernir

percentage *n* tanto por ciento, *m*; porcentaje, *m*

perceptible *a* perceptible, visible; sensible

perception *n* percepción, *f*; sensibilidad, *f*

perceptive *a* perceptivo

perch *n icht* perca, *f*; (for birds) percha, *f*; (measure) pértiga, *f*. *vi* posarse (en or sobre). *vt* posar (en or sobre)

percolate *vi* filtrar; *fig* penetrar. *vt* filtrar, colar

percolation *n* filtración, *f*

percolator *n* filtro, *m*. **coffee p.,** colador de café, *m*

percussion *n* percusión, *f*; choque, *m*. **p. cap,** fulminante, *m*. **p. instrument,** instrumento de percusión, *m*

perdition *n* perdición, *f*; ruina, *f*

peremptory *a* perentorio; (of manner, etc.) imperioso, autoritario

perennial *a bot* vivaz; perenne; eterno, perpetuo. *n* planta vivaz, *f*

perfect *a* perfecto; (of a work) acabado; completo. *n gram* (tiempo) perfecto, *m*. *vt* perfeccionar; (oneself) perfeccionarse. **to have a p. knowledge of . . . ,** conocer a fondo . . . **They are p. strangers to me,** Me son completamente desconocidos

perfectible *a* perfectible

perfection *n* perfección, *f*; excelencia, *f*. **to p.,** a la perfección, a las mil maravillas

perfectionist *n* perfeccionista, *mf*

perfidious *a* pérfido

perfidy *n* perfidia, *f*

perforate *vt* perforar, agujerear

perforating *a* perforador

perforation *n* perforación, *f*; agujero, *m*

perforce *adv* a la fuerza, forzosamente

perform *vt* hacer; poner por obra, llevar a cabo; desempeñar, cumplir; ejercer; (a piece of music, etc.) ejecutar; realizar; (a play) representar, dar; (a part in a play) desempeñar (el papel de . . .); (Divine Service) oficiar. *vi theat* trabajar, representar un papel; (a musical instrument) tocar; (sing) cantar; (of animals) hacer trucos

performable *a* hacedero, practicable, ejecutable; *theat* que puede representarse; *mus* tocable

performance *n* ejecución, realización, *f*; desempeño, ejercicio, *m*; cumplimiento, *m*; acción, *f*; hazaña, *f*; (work) obra, *f*; *theat* función, representación, *f*; (theat acting of a part) interpretación, *f*; *mus* ejecución, *f*; *mech* potencia, *f*. **first p.,** *theat* estreno, *m*

performer *n mus* ejecutante, *mf*; músico, *m*; *theat* actor (-triz), representante, *mf*; artista, *mf*

performing *a* (of animals) sabio. **p. dog,** perro sabio, *m*

perfume *n* perfume, *m*; fragancia, *f*; aroma, *m*. *vt* perfumar; embalsamar, aromatizar, llenar con fragancia. **p. burner,** perfumador, *m*

perfumery *n* perfumería, *f*

perfunctorily *adv* perfunctoriamente, sin cuidado; superficialmente

perfunctory *a* perfunctorio, negligente; superficial; ligero, de cumplido

pergola *n* emparrado, cenador, *m*

perhaps *adv* quizá, quizás; tal vez

peril *n* peligro, *m*; riesgo, *m*. *vt* poner en peligro; arriesgar. **at one's p.,** a su riesgo. **in p.,** en peligro

perilous *a* peligroso, arriesgado

perimeter *n* perímetro, *m*

period *n* período, *m*; época, *f*; edad, *f*; tiempo, *m*; duración, *f*; término, plazo, *m*; *gram* período, *m*; (full stop) punto final, *m*; *med* menstruación, regla, *f*. **p. furniture,** muebles de época, *m pl*

periodic *a* periódico

periodical *a* periódico. *n* publicación periódica, revista, *f*

peripatetic *a* peripatético

peripheral *a* periférico

periphery *n* periferia, *f*

periscope *n* periscopio, *m*

perish *vi* perecer; marchitarse; desaparecer, acabar. **to be perished with cold,** estar muerto de frío

perishable *a* perecedero, frágil

peritonitis *n* peritonitis, *f*

periwinkle *n zool* caracol marino, *m*; *bot* vincapervinca, *f*

perjure *vt* perjurar. **to p. oneself,** perjurarse

perjurer *n* perjuro (-ra); perjurador (-ra)

perjury *n* perjurio, *m*. **to commit p.,** jurar en falso, perjurar

perk (up) *vi* levantar la cabeza; recobrar sus bríos, alzar la cabeza; sacar la cabeza

perky *a* desenvuelto, gallardo; coquetón; atrevido; (gay) alegre

permanence *n* permanencia, *f*; estabilidad, *f*

permanent *a* permanente; estable; (of posts, etc.) fijo. **p. wave,** ondulación permanente, *f*. **p. way,** *rw* vía, *f*

permeable *a* permeable

permeate *vt* penetrar; impregnar; *fig* infiltrar (en)

permissible *a* permisible, admisible; lícito

permission *n* permiso, *m*, licencia *f*

permissive *a* permisivo, tolerado; (optional) facultativo

permit *vt* permitir; dar permiso (a); dejar; tolerar, sufrir; admitir. *n* permiso, *m*; licencia, *f;* pase, *m.* **Will you p. me to smoke?** ¿Me permites fumar?

permutation *n* permutación, *f*

permute *vt* permutar

pernicious *a* pernicioso. **p. anemia,** anemia perniciosa, *f*

pernickety a tiquismiquis

peroration *n* peroración, *f*

peroxide *n* peróxido, *m*

perpendicular *a* perpendicular. *n* perpendicular, *f*

perpetrate *vt law* perpetrar; cometer

perpetrator *n* el, *m,* (*f,* la) que comete; *law* autor (-ra); perpetrador (-ra)

perpetual *a* perpetuo, perdurable, eterno; incesante, constante; (life-long) perpetuo

perpetually *adv* perpetuamente; sin cesar; continuamente; constantemente

perpetuate *vt* perpetuar, eternizar; inmortalizar

perpetuity *n* perpetuidad, *f.* **in p.,** para siempre

perplex *vt* dejar perplejo, aturdir, confundir; embrollar

perplexed *a* perplejo, irresoluto; confuso; (of questions, etc.) complicado, intrincado

perplexing *a* difícil; complicado; confuso

perplexity *n* perplejidad, *f;* confusión, *f*

perquisites *n pl* emolumentos, *m pl;* gajes, percances, *m pl;* (tips) propinas, *f pl*

persecute *vt* perseguir; importunar, molestar

persecution *n* persecución, *f*

persecutor *n* perseguidor (-ra)

perseverance *n* perseverancia, *f*

persevere *vi* perseverar

persevering *a* perseverante

perseveringly *adv* con perseverancia, perseverantemente

Persia (la) Persia, *f*

Persian *a* persa; de Persia; pérsico. *n* persa, *mf;* (language) persa, *m.* **P. blinds,** persianas, *f pl.* **P. cat,** gato (-ta) de Angora

persist *vi* persistir; persistir (en), empeñarse (en), obstinarse (en)

persistence *n* persistencia, *f*

persistent *a* persistente

persistently *adv* con persistencia, persistentemente

person *n* persona, *f.* **first p.,** *gram* primera persona, *f.* **in p.,** en persona. **no p.,** nadie

personable *a* bien parecido

personage *n* personaje, *m*

personal *a* personal; íntimo; particular; en persona; (movable) mueble, *m.* **He is to make a p. appearance,** Va a estar presente en persona. **p. column,** (in a newspaper) columna de los suspiros, *f.* **p.**

equation, ecuación personal, *f.* **p. estate,** (goods) bienes muebles, *m pl*

personality *n* personalidad, *f;* (insult) personalismo, *m.* **dual p.,** conciencia doble, *f*

personate *vt* (in a play) hacer el papel de; (impersonate) hacerse pasar por

personification *n* personificación, *f*

personify *vt* personificar

personnel *n* personal, *m*

perspective *n* perspectiva, *f,* a en perspectiva

perspicacious *a* perspicaz, clarividente, sagaz

perspicacity *n* perspicacia, clarividencia, sagacidad, *f*

perspicuity *n* perspicuidad, claridad, lucidez, *f*

perspicuous *a* perspicuo, claro

perspiration *n* sudor, *m*

perspire *vi* sudar, transpirar

persuadable *a* persuasible

persuade *vt* persuadir; inducir (a), instar (a), mover (a), inclinar (a)

persuasion *n* persuasión, *f;* persuasiva, *f;* opinión, *f;* creencia, *f;* religión, *f;* secta, *f*

persuasive *a* persuasivo. *n* persuasión, *f;* aliciente, atractivo, *m*

persuasively *adv* de un modo persuasivo, persuasivamente

persuasiveness *n* persuasiva, *f*

pert *a* petulante; respondón, desparpajado

pertain *vi* pertenecer (a); tocar (a), incumbir (a), convenir (a); estar relacionado (con)

pertinacious *a* pertinaz

pertinaciously *adv* con pertinacia

pertinacity *n* pertinacia, *f*

pertinence *n* pertinencia, *f*

pertinent *a* pertinente, atinado

pertinently *adv* atinadamente

pertly *adv* con petulancia; con descaro

pertness *n* petulancia, *f;* desparpajo, descaro, *m*

perturb *vt* perturbar, agitar, turbar, inquietar

perturbation *n* perturbación, agitación, inquietud, *f;* confusión, *f;* desorden, *m*

perturbed *a* perturbado, agitado, ansioso, intranquilo

perturbing *a* perturbador, inquietador

Peru el Perú

perusal *n* lectura, *f;* examen, *m*

peruse *vt* leer con cuidado, estudiar, examinar

Peruvian *a* and *n* peruano (-na)

pervade *vt* penetrar; llenar, saturar; difundirse por; reinar en

pervasive *a* penetrante

perverse *a* (wicked) perverso, depravado; obstinado; travieso; intratable

perversion n perversión, f.

perversity n (wickedness) perversidad, f; obstinacia, f; travesura, f

perversive a perversivo

pervert vt pervertir; (words, etc.) torcer, tergiversar

pervious a penetrable; permeable

pessimism n pesimismo, m

pessimist n pesimista, mf

pessimistic a pesimista

pessimistically adv con pesimismo

pest n insecto nocivo, m; animal dañino, m; parásito, m; (pestilence) peste, f; flg plaga, f; (person) mosca, f

pester vt importunar, molestar, incomodar, Lat. Am. acatorrar, cargosear, majaderear. **to p. constantly,** inf no dejar a sol ni a sombra

pestering n importunaciones, f pl; a = **annoying**

pestilence n pestilencia, peste, f; plaga, f

pestilential a pestilente, pestífero; pernicioso

pestle n mano de mortero, f, vt pistar, machacar, majar

pet n animal doméstico, m; niño (-ña) mimado (-da), favorito (-ta), m; (dear) querido (-da); (peevishness) despecho, malhumor, m. vt acariciar; (spoil) mimar. **to be a great pet,** ser un gran favorito

petal n pétalo, m, hoja, f

peter (out) vi desaparecer; agotarse

petition n petición, f; súplica, f; instancia, solicitud, f; memorial, m. vt suplicar; pedir, demandar; dirigir un memorial (a). **to file a p.,** elevar una instancia

petitioner n peticionario (-ia)

pet peeve Lat. Am. barreno, m

petrifaction n petrificación, f

petrify vt petrificar; inf dejar seco. **to become petrified,** petrificarse

petrol n bencina, gasolina, f. a de gasolina, de bencina. **to run out of p.,** tener una pana de bencina. **p. gauge,** indicador del nivel de gasolina, m. **p. pump,** surtidor de gasolina, m. **p. station,** puesto de bencina, m, estación de servicio, f. **p. tank,** depósito de bencina, m

petroleum n petróleo, m. a petrolero; de petróleo. **p. works,** refinería de petróleo, f

petrology n petrografía, f

petrous a pétreo

petticoat n enagua, f; pl **petticoats,** (slang) faldas, f pl. a de faldas, de mujeres; de mujer

pettifogger n (lawyer) picapleitos, m, rábula, mf; (quibbler) sofista, mf

pettifogging a charlatán, mezquino, trivial

pettiness n trivialidad, insignificancia, f;

pequeñez, f; mezquindad, f; ruindad, bajeza, f

petty a trivial, sin importancia, insignificante; inferior; pequeño; mezquino; ruin; bajo. **p. cash,** gastos menores de caja, m pl. **p. expense,** gasto menudo, m. **p. officer,** suboficial, m. **p. thief,** ratero (-ra)

petulance n mal humor, m, displicencia, irritabilidad, f

petulant a malhumorado, displicente, enojadizo, irritable

petulantly adv displicentemente, con mal humor

pew n banco (de iglesia), m. **p.-opener,** sacristán, m

pewter n peltre, m, a de peltre

phalanx n falange, f

phallic a fálico

phallus n falo, m

phantasmagoria n fantasmagoria, f

phantasmagoric a fantasmagórico

phantom n fantasma, espectro, m; sombra, ficción, f; visión, f

pharmaceutical a farmacéutico; n producto farmacéutico, m

pharmacist n farmacéutico, m

pharmacologist n farmacólogo, m

pharmacology n farmacología, f

pharmacopeia n farmacopea, f

pharmacy n farmacia, f

pharyngitis n faringitis, f

pharynx n faringe, f

phase n fase, f; aspecto, m; ast fase, f

pheasant n faisán, m. **hen p.,** faisana, f. **p. shooting,** caza de faisanes, f

phenomenal a fenomenal

phenomenon n fenómeno, m

phial n redoma, f

philander vi galantear

philanderer n Tenorio, galanteador, m

philanthropic a filantrópico

philanthropist n filántropo, m

philanthropy n filantropía, f

philatelic a filatélico

philatelist n filatelista, mf

philately n filatelia, f

philharmonic a filarmónico

Philippine a and n filipino (-na)

Philippines, the las (Islas) Filipinas, f pl

Philistine a and n filisteo (-ea)

philological a filológico

philologist n filólogo, m

philology n filología, f

philosopher n filósofo, m. **philosopher's stone,** piedra filosofal, f

philosophic(al) a filosófico

philosophize vi filosofar

philosophy n filosofía, f. **moral p.,** filosofía moral, f. **natural p.,** filosofía natural, f

philter n filtro, m

phlebitis n flebitis, f
phlebotomist n sangrador, flebotomiano, m
phlebotomy n flebotomía, f
phlegm n flema, f, Lat. Am. desgarro, m
phlegmatic a flemático
phoenix n fénix, f
phonetic a fonético
phonetics n fonética, f
phony a falso; espurio. **p. war,** guerra tonta, guerra falsa, f
phosphate n fosfato, m
phosphorescence n fosforescencia, f
phosphorescent a fosforescente
phosphorus n fósforo, m
photo n foto, f
photochemistry n fotoquímica, f
photogenic a fotogénico
photograph n fotografía, f. vt fotografiar, retratar. **to have one's p. taken,** hacerse retratar
photographer n fotógrafo, m
photographic a fotográfico
photography n fotografía, f
photogravure n fotograbado, m
photostat n fotostato, m
photosynthesis n fotosíntesis, f
phrase n frase, f; mus frase musical, f. vt expresar, frasear; redactar. **p.-book,** libro de frases, m
phraseology n fraseología, f
phrasing n (drawing up) redacción, f; (style) estilo, m; mus frases, f pl
phrenetic a frenético
phthisis n tisis, f
phylactery n filactria, f
physical a físico: **p. fitness,** buen estado físico, m. **p. geography,** geografía física, f. **p. jerks,** ejercicios físicos, m pl. **p. sciences,** ciencias físicas, f pl. **p. training,** educación física, f
physician n médico (-ca)
physicist n físico, m
physics n física, f
physiognomy n fisonomía, f
physiological a fisiológico
physiologist n fisiólogo, m
physiology n fisiología, f
physiotherapy n fisioterapia, f
physique n físico, m
pianist n pianista, mf
piano, pianoforte n piano, m. **baby grand p.,** piano de media cola, m. **grand p.,** piano de cola, m. **upright p.,** piano vertical, m. **p. maker,** fabricante de pianos, m. **p. stool,** taburete de piano, m. **p. tuner,** afinador de pianos, m
pianola n piano mecánico, m
picaresque a picaresco
piccolo n flautín, m
pick n (tool) pico, zapapico, m; (mattock) piqueta, f; (choice) selección, f; derecho

de elección, m; (best) lo mejor, lo más escogido; (fig cream) flor, nata, f. **tooth-p.,** mondadientes, m. **p.-a-back,** sobre los hombros, a cuestas. **p.-ax,** zapapico, m, alcotana, f. **p.-me-up,** tónico, m; trago, m
pick vt (with a pick-ax, make a hole) picar; (pluck, pick up) coger; (remove) sacar; (clean) limpiar; (one's teeth) mondarse (los dientes); (one's nose) hurgarse (las narices); (a bone) roer; (a lock) abrir con ganzúa; (a pocket) bolsear, robar del bolsillo; (peck) picotear; (choose) escoger; (a quarrel) buscar. vi (steal) hurtar, robar; (nibble) picar. **I have a bone to p. with you,** Tengo que ajustar unas cuentas contigo. **Take your p.!** ¡Escoja! **to p. and choose,** mostrarse difícil. **to p. to pieces,** fig criticar severamente. **to p. one's way through,** abrirse camino entre; andar con precaución por; andar a tientas por. **to p. off,** coger; arrancar; quitar; (shoot) disparar; fusilar. **to p. out,** entresacar; escoger; (recognize) reconocer; (understand) llegar a comprender; (a tune) tocar de oídas; (a song) cantar de oídas; (of colours) contrastar, resaltar. **to p. up,** vt (ground, etc.) romper con pico; coger; tomar; recoger; (raise) levantar, alzar; (information, etc.) cobrar, adquirir; (a living) ganar; (make friends with) trabar amistad con; (recover) recobrar; (find) encontrar, hallar; (buy) comprar; (learn) aprender; (a wireless message) interceptar; (a radio station) oír, tener. vi recobrar la salud; reponerse; mejorar. n mech recobro, m
picket n estaca, f; (mil and during strikes) piquete, m. vt cercar con estacas; poner piquetes ante (o alrededor de); poner de guardia; estacionar
picking n (gathering) recolección, f; (choosing) selección, f; (pilfering) robo, m; pl **pickings,** desperdicios, m pl; (perquisites) gajes, m pl; ganancias, f pl
pickle n (solution) escabeche, m; (vegetable, etc.) encurtido, m; (plight) apuro, m; (child) diablillo, m. vt encurtir, escabechar
picklock n (thief and instrument) ganzúa, f
pickpocket n carterista, mf ratero (-ra)
picnic n partida de campo, jira, f, picnic, m. vi llevar la merienda al campo, hacer un picnic
pictorial a pictórico; ilustrado. n revista ilustrada, f
picture n cuadro, m; (of a person) retrato, m; imagen, f; (illustration) grabado, m, lámina, f; fotografía, f; (outlook) perspectiva, f; idea, f. vt pintar; describir; imaginar. **to go to the pictures,** ir al cine. **motion p.,** película, f. **talking p.,** película sonora, f. **p. book,** libro con láminas, m. **p. frame,** marco, m. **p. gallery,** museo de pinturas, m; galería de pinturas, f. **p. hat,** pamela, f. **p. palace,**

cine, *m*. **p. postcard**, tarjeta postal, *f*. **p. restorer**, restaurador de cuadros, *m*. **p. writing**, pictografía, *f*

picturesque *a* pintoresco

pie *n* (savoury) empanada, *f*; (sweet) pastel, *m*, torta, *f*; (of meat) pastelón, *m*; *print* pastel, *m*. **apple pie**, torta de manzanas, *f*. **to eat humble pie**, bajar las orejas. **to have a finger in the pie**, meter baza

piebald *a* pío; tordo

piece *n* pedazo, *m*; trozo, *m*; parte, porción, *f*; (literary, artistic work, coin, of fabric, at chess, etc. and slang) pieza, *f*; (of luggage) bulto, *m*; (of paper) hoja, *f*; (of ground) parcela, *f*; (of money) moneda, *f*, *vt* remendar; unir, juntar. **a p. of advice**, un consejo. **a p. of bread**, un pedazo de pan; una rebanada de pan. **a p. of folly**, un acto de locura. **a p. of furniture**, un mueble. **a p. of insolence**, una insolencia. **a p. of news**, una noticia. **a p. of paper**, un papel, una hoja de papel, una cuartilla. **a p. of poetry**, una poesía. **Peter has a five-shilling p.**, Pedro tiene una moneda de cinco chelines. **to break in pieces**, *vt* hacer pedazos, romper. *vi* hacerse pedazos, romperse. **to come or fall to pieces**, deshacerse; (of machines) desarmarse. **to cut in pieces**, cortar en pedazos; (an army) destrozar. **to give a p. of one's mind (to)**, decir cuatro verdades (a), decir cuántas son cinco (a). **to go to pieces**, (of persons) hacerse pedazos. **to take to pieces**, (a machine) desmontar; deshacer. **to tear or pull to pieces**, hacer pedazos, despedazar; desgarrar. **p. goods**, géneros en piezas, *m pl*. **p.-work**, trabajo a destajo, *m*. **to do p.-work**, trabajar a destajo. **p.-worker**, destajista, *mf*

piecemeal *adv* en pedazos; a remiendos; en detalle; poco a poco

piecrust *n* pasta, *f*

pied *a* bicolor; abigarrado, de varios colores

pier *n* (jetty) dique, *m*; embarcadero, *m*; malecón, *m*; (of a bridge) pila, *f*; (pillar) columna, *f*; (between windows, etc.) entrepaño, *m*. **p.-glass**, espejo de cuerpo entero, *m*. **p. head**, punta del dique, *f*. **p. table**, consola, *f*

pierce *vt* penetrar; (of sorrow, etc.) traspasar, herir; (bore) agujerear, taladrar. *vi* penetrar

pierced ear *n* oreja perforada, *f*

piercing *a* penetrante; (of the wind, etc.) cortante; (of the voice, etc.) agudo. *n* penetración, *f*

piety *n* piedad, devoción, *f*

piffle *n* patrañas, tonterías, *f pl*

pig *n* puerco, cerdo, *Lat. Am.* chancho, *m*; *inf* cochino, *m*; (metal) lingote, *m*. **to buy a p. in a poke**, cerrar un trato a ciegas. **p.-eyed**, de ojos de cerdo. **p.-iron**, ar-

rabio; hierro colado en barras, lingote de fundición, *m*

pigeon *n* paloma, *f*, palomo, *m*; *inf* primo, *m*. *vt* embaucar, engañar. **carrier p.**, paloma mensajera, *f*. **clay p.**, pichón de barro, platillo de arcilla, *m*. **male p.**, pichón, *m*. **pouter p.**, paloma buchona, *f*. **young p.**, palomino, *m*. **p. fancier**, palomero, *m*. **p.-hole**, casilla, *f*, *vt* encasillar. **set of p.-holes**, encasillado, *m*. **p.-shooting**, tiro de pichón, *m*. **p.-toed**, patituerto

piggy bank *n* alcancía, *f*

pigheaded *a* terco, testarudo, *Lat. Am.* empecinado

pigment *n* pigmento, *m*

pigskin *n* piel de cerdo, *m*

pigsty *n* pocilga, *f*

pigtail *n* coleta, *f*

pike *n mil* pica, *f*, chuzo, *m*; (peak) pico, *m*

pilaster *n* pilastra, *f*

pile *n* estaca, *f*; poste, *m*; (engineering) pilote, *m*; (heap) pila, *f*, montón, *m*; (pyre) pira, *f*; (building) edificio grande, *m*; *elec* pila, *f*; (hair) pelo, *m*; (nap) pelusa, *f*; *pl* **piles**, *med* almorranas, *f pl. vt* clavar pilotes en; apoyar con pilotes; (heap) amontonar; (load) cargar. **to make one's p.**, *inf* hacer su pacotilla. **to p. arms**, poner los fusiles en pabellón. **to p. on**, (coal, etc.) echar; (increase) aumentar. **to p. it on**, exagerar, intensificar; (a table) cargar. **to p. up**, *vi* amontonarse; acumularse; *vt Lat. Am.* empilonar; (of a ship) encallar. **p.-driver**, machina, *f*; martinete, *m*. **p. dwelling**, vivienda palustre, sostenida por pilares, *f*

pilfer *vt* sisar, sonsacar, hurtar, ratear, *Mexico* chalequear

pilferer *n* sisador (-ra), ratero (-ra)

pilgrim *n* peregrino (-na). **pilgrim's staff**, bordón, *m*

pilgrimage *n* peregrinación, *f*; romería, *f*. **to make a p.**, hacer una peregrinación, peregrinar; ir en romería

piling *n* amontonamiento, *m*; (of buildings) pilotaje, *m*

pill *n* píldora, *f*. **to gild the p.**, *fig* dorar la píldora. **p.-box**, caja de píldoras, *f*; casamata, *f*, *mil* nido de ametralladoras, *m*

pillage *vt* pillar, saquear. *n* saqueo, *m*

pillager *n* saqueador (-ra)

pillar *n* pilar, *m*, columna, *f*; (person) sostén, soporte, *m*. **from p. to post**, de Ceca en Meca. **p. of salt**, estatua de sal, *f*. **the Pillars of Hercules**, las Columnas de Hércules. **to be a p. of strength**, *inf* ser una roca. **p.-box**, buzón, *m*

pillared *a* con columnas, sostenido por columnas; en columnas

pillory *n* picota, argolla, *f*. *vt* empicotar; *fig* poner en ridículo; censurar duramente

pillow *n* almohada, *f*; (for lace-making)

cojín, *m*; (of a machine) cojinete, *m*. *vt*
apoyar; reposar; servir como almohada.
to take counsel of one's p., consultar
con la almohada. **p.-case**, funda de almohada, *f*

pilot *n* piloto, *m*; *naut* práctico, piloto (de
puerto), *m*. *vt* guiar, conducir; (*naut aer*)
pilotar, pilotear. **p. boat**, vaporcito del
práctico, *m*. **p. jacket**, chaquetón de
piloto, *m*. **p. officer**, oficial de aviación,
m

pimento *n* pimiento, *m*

pimp *n* rufián, alcahuete, *m*, *vi* alcahuetear

pimple *n* grano, *m*

pimply *a* con granos

pin *n* alfiler, *m*; prendedor, *m*; clavija, *f*;
clavo, *m*, chaveta, *f*; (bolt) perno, *m*. *vt*
prender con alfileres; (with a peg) enclavijar; fijar; sujetar. **to pin up**, sujetar con
alfileres; (the hair) sujetar con horquillas.
I don't care a pin, No me importa un
bledo. **to be on pins**, estar en ascuas. **to
suffer from pins and needles**, tener
aguijones. **pin-head**, cabeza de alfiler, *f*.
pin-money, alfileres, *m pl*. **pin-oak**, *bot*
pincarrasco, *m*, carrasca, *f*. **pin point**,
punta de alfiler, *f*. **pin-prick**, alfilerazo, *m*

pinafore *n* delantal de niño, *m*

pincers *n pl* pinzas, tenazas, *f pl*, alicates,
m pl; (of crustaceans) pinzas, *f pl*. **p.
movement**, movimiento de pinzas, *m*

pinch *vt* pellizcar; (crush) estrujar; aplastar; apretar; (of the cold) helar; (steal)
hurtar, birlar; (arrest) coger, prender. *n*
pellizco, torniscón, *m*; pulgarada, *f*, (of
snuff) polvo, *m*; (distress) miseria, *f*;
(pain) dolor, *m*, angustia. *f*. **at a p.**, en
caso de apuro. **to know where the shoe
pinches**, saber dónde le aprieta el
zapato

pincushion *n* acerico, *m*

pine *n* *bot* pino, *m*. *vi* languidecer, marchitarse, consumirse. **to p. for**, anhelar,
suspirar por, perecer por. **pitch-p.**, pino
de tea, *m*. **p.-apple**, piña de las Indias, *f*,
ananás, *m*, **p. cone**, piña, *f*. **p. kernel**,
piñón, *m*. **p. needle**, pinocha, *f*. **p.
wood**, pinar, *m*, pineda, *f*

pinion *n* (wing) ala, *f*; (small feather)
piñón, *m*; (in carving) alón, *m*; (wheel)
piñón, *m*. *vt* atar las alas de; cortar un
piñón de; (a person) atar; (the arms of)
trincar, asegurar

pink *n* *bot* clavel, *m*; color de rosa, *m*;
(perfection) modelo, *m*; colmo, *m*; (hunting) color rojo, *m*; levitín rojo de caza, *m*.
a de color de rosa, rosado. *vt* *sew* picar;
(pierce) penecrar, atravesar. *vi* (of an engine) picar

pinking *n* *sew* picadura, *f*

pinnacle *n* pináculo, *m*

pinpoint *vt* precisar

pint *n* (measure) pinta, *f*

pioneer *n* pionero, explorador, *m*; introductor, *m*. **to be a p. in . . . ,** ser el

primero en (or a) . . . **pioneering role,**
papel de iniciador (e.g. **She played a pioneering role,** jugó un papel de
iniciadora)

pious *a* pío, devoto, piadoso

pip *n* (of fruit) pepita, *f*; (on cards, dice)
punto, *m*; (disease) moquillo, *m*; (of an
army, etc., officer) insignia, *f*

pipe *n* (for tobacco) pipa (de fumar) *Argentina* cachimba, *f*; *mus* caramillo, *m*;
(boatswain's) pito, *m*; (of a bird) trino, *m*;
(voice) voz aguda, *f*; tubo, *m*; (for water,
etc.) cañería, *f*; (of a hose) manga, *f*; (of an
organ) cañón, *m*; (of wine) pipa, *f*; *pl*
pipes, *mus* gaita, *f*. *vi* tocar el caramillo
(or la gaita); empezar a cantar; silbar; (of
birds) trinar. *vt* (a tune) tocar; (sing) cantar; (whistle) llamar con pito; conducir
con cañerías; instalar cañerías en. **He
smokes a p.,** Fuma una pipa. **I smoked
a p.** (of tobacco) **before I went to bed,**
Fumé una pipa antes de acostarme. **Put
that in your p. and smoke it!** ¡Chúpate
eso! **p. clay,** blanquizal, *m*. **p. cleaner,**
limpiapipas, *m*. **p. layer,** cañero, fontanero, *m*. **p. laying,** instalación de cañerías, *f*. **p.-line,** cañería, *f*; (oil) oleoducto,
m. **p. tobacco,** tabaco de pipa, *m*

piper *n* (bagpiper) gaitero, *m*; flautista,
mf

pipette *n* *chem* pipeta, *f*

piping *n* sonido del caramillo, *m*; música
de la flauta, etc., *f*; (of birds) trinos, *m pl*;
voz aguda, *f*; (for water, etc.) cañería, tubería, *f*; *sew* cordoncillo, *m*. **p.-hot,** hirviente

pippin *n* (apple) camuesa, *f*

piquant *a* picante

pique *n* (resentment, and score in game)
pique, *m*. **to p. oneself upon,** preciarse
de, jactarse de. **to be piqued,** estar
enojado; *inf* amoscarse

piracy *n* piratería, *f*

pirate *n* pirata, *mf*. *vi* piratear. *vt* publicar
una edición furtiva de. **p. edition,** edición furtiva, *f*

pirouette *n* pirueta, *f*

pistachio *n* pistacho, *m*

pistol *n* pistola, *f*. **p. belt,** charpa, *f*, cinto
de pistolas, *m*. **p. case,** pistolera, *f*. **p.
shot,** pistoletazo, *m*

piston *n* *mech* émbolo, pistón, *m*; *mus*
pistón, *m*, llave, *f*. **p. ring,** anillo de émbolo, segmento de émbolo, *m*. **p. rod,**
biela, *f*. **p. stroke,** carrera del émbolo, *f*

pit *n* hoyo, *m*; foso, *m*; (in a garage) foso
de reparación, *m*; *theat* platea, *f*; (trap)
trampa, *f*; (scar) hoyo, *m*; precipicio, *m*;
(hell) infierno, *m*. *vt* (with smallpox) marcar con viruelas; (against) competir con.
pithead, boca de mina, *f*. **pit of the
stomach,** boca del estómago, *f*. **pit
stall,** butaca de platea, *f*

pitch *n* *chem* pez, brea, *f*, alquitrán, *m*;
(place) puesto, *m*; (throwing) lanzamiento, *m*; (distance thrown) alcance,

m; (for cricket) cancha, *f;* (bowling) saque, *m;* (slope) pendiente, inclinación, *f;* (height) elevación, *f; mus* tono, *m;* (fig degree) grado, extremo, *m; (naut aer)* cabeceo, *m;* (of threads of a screw, etc.) paso, *m. vt* (camp) asentar; (a tent, etc.) colocar, poner; (throw) lanzar, arrojar, tirar; (cricket, etc.) lanzar; (fix in) clavar; *mus* graduar el tono de; (tell) narrar. *vi* (fall) caer; *naut* cabecear, zozobrar; *aer* cabecear. **to paint with p.,** embrear. **to p. into,** (attack) acometer, atacar; (scold) desatarse contra; (food) engullir. **p.-black,** negro como la pez; oscuro como boca de lobo. **p.-pine,** pino de tea, *m.* **p.-pipe,** diapasón vocal, *m.*

pitched battle *n* batalla campal, *f*

pitcher *n* jarro, cántaro, *m;* (in baseball) lanzador de pelota, *m*

pitchfork *n* horquilla, *f,* aventador, *m. vt* levantar con horquilla; *fig* lanzar

pitching *n* (pavement) adoquinado, *m;* (of a ship) socollada, *f;* cabeceo, *m*

piteous a lastimero; triste; plañidero; compasivo; tierno

pitfall *n* trampa, *f; fig* añagaza, *f,* lazo, peligro, *m*

pith *n bot* médula, *f;* médula espinal, *f; fig* meollo, *m;* fuerza, *f,* vigor, *m;* substancia, *f;* quinta esencia, *f;* importancia, *f*

pithiness *n* jugosidad, *f;* fuerza, *f,* vigor, *m*

pithy a meduloso; *fig* jugoso; enérgico, vigoroso

pitiable a lastimoso, digno de compasión; (paltry) despreciable

pitiful a piadoso, compasivo; conmovedor, doloroso, lastimero; (contemptible) miserable

pitifully *adv* lastimosamente

pitiless a sin piedad; despiadado

pittance *n* pitanza, *f;* pequeña porción, *f;* ración de hambre, *f*

pitted a picoso

pituitary a pituitario

pity *n* piedad, compasión, *f;* lástima, *f. vt* compadecerse de, tener lástima (a); compadecer. **It is a p. that . . . ,** Es lástima que . . . **Have p.!** ¡Ten piedad! **to take p. on,** tener lástima (de). **to move to p.,** dar lástima (a), enternecer

pivot *n* pivote, *m;* eje, *m; fig* punto de partida, *m, vi* girar sobre un pivote o eje

pivotal a *fig* cardinal, principal, fundamental

pixy *n* duende, *m.* **p. hood,** caperuza, *f*

pizzicato a pichigato

placable a aplacable, placable

placard *n* cartel, *m. vt* fijar carteles (en); publicar por carteles

placate *vt* aplacar, ablandar, apaciguar

placatory a placativo

place *n* lugar, *m;* sitio, *m;* (position) puesto, *m;* (seat) asiento, *m;* (laid at table) cubierto, *m;* (square) plaza, *f;*

(house) residencia, *f;* (in the country) casa de campo, finca, *f;* (in a book) pasaje, *m;* position, *f,* rango, *m;* situación, *f;* (employment) empleo, *m,* colocación, *f. vt* poner; colocar; (in employment) dar empleo (a); (appoint) nombrar; (an order) dar; (money) invertir; (remember) recordar, traer a la memoria; (size up) fijar; (confidence) poner. **in p.,** en su lugar; apropiado. **in p. of,** en vez de, en lugar de. **in the first p.,** en primer lugar, primero. **in the next p.,** luego, después. **out of p.,** fuera de lugar; inoportuno. **It is not my p. to . . . ,** No me toca a mí de . . . **to give p. to,** ceder el paso (a); ceder (a). **to take p.,** verificarse, tener lugar, ocurrir. **p. of business,** establecimiento, local de negocios, *m.* **p. of worship,** edificio de culto, *m.*

placenta *n* placenta, *f*

placid a plácido, apacible; calmoso; sereno, sosegado; dulce

placing *n* colocación, *f;* posición, *f;* localización, *f*

placket *n* abertura (en una falda), *f*

plagiarism *n* plagio, *m*

plagiarist *n* plagiario (-ia)

plagiarize *vt* plagiar, hurtar

plague *n* plaga, *f;* peste, pestilencia, *f. vt* importunar, atormentar; plagar

plaid *n* manta escocesa, *f;* género de cuadros, *m,* a a cuadros

plain a claro; evidente; (simple) sencillo; llano; sin adorno; (flat) liso, igual; (candid) franco; (with much, etc.) desnudo; mero; puro, sin mezcla; (of words) redondo; (ugly) feo. *adv* claramente; llanamente; sencillamente; francamente. *n* llanura, *f,* llano, *m.* **the p. truth,** la pura verdad. **p. clothes,** traje de paisano, *m.* **p. clothes man,** detective, *m.* **p. cooking,** cocina sencilla, cocina casera, *f.* **p. dealing,** buena fe, sinceridad, *f.* **p. dweller,** llanero (-ra). **p. living,** vida sencilla, *f.* **p. people,** gente sencilla, *f.* **p. sailing,** *fig* camino fácil, *m.* **p. sewing,** costura, *f.* **p.-song,** canto llano, *m.* **p. speaking,** franqueza, *f.* **p.-spoken,** franco. **in p. English,** sin rodeos, en cristiano (e.g. **Speak in p. English!** ¡Habla sin rodeos! Habla en cristiano!)

plainly *adv* claramente; sencillamente; llanamente; francamente; rotundamente

plainsman *n* hombre de las llanuras, *m*

plaint *n* queja, *f,* lamento, *m; law* demanda, querella, *f*

plaintiff *n* demandante, *mf,* actor, *m,* parte actora, actora, *f*

plaintive a quejumbroso, dolorido; patético

plait *n* trenza, *f. vt* trenzar; tejer. **in plaits,** (of hair) en trenzas

plan *n* plan, *m;* (map) plano, *m;* proyecto, *m. vt* planear; proyectar; proponerse. **the Marshall P.,** el Plan Marshall. **to make a**

p. of, trazar un plano de. **to make plans,** hacer planes

plane *n* (tree) plátano, *m*; (tool) cepillo, *m*; *geom* plano, *m*; (level) nivel, *m*; *aer* avión, *m*, plano. *vt carp* acepillar, alisar. *vi aer* planear

planet *n* planeta, *m*

planetarium *n* planetario, *m*

planetary *a* planetario

plank *n* tabla, *f*; *fig* fundamento, principio, *m*; *pl* **planks,** tablazón, *f*. *vt* entablar, enmaderar

plankton *n* plancton, *m*

planned *a* proyectado, planeado; dirigido. **p. economy,** economía dirigida, *f*

planner *n* proyectista, *mf*; autor (-ra) de un plan

planning *n* proyecto, *m*; concepción, *f*

plant *n bot* planta, *f*; instalación, *f*, material, *m*. *vt* plantar; (place) colocar; fijar; (a blow) asestar; (people) establecer; (instil) inculcar, imbuir (con); (conceal) esconder. **p. pot,** florero, *m*. **p. stand,** jardinera, *f*

plantain *n bot* llantén, *m*

plantation *n* plantación, *f*; plantío, *m*; *fig* colonia, *f*; introducción, *f*, establecimiento, *m*

planter *n* plantador, cultivador, *m*

planting *n* plantación, *f*; *fig* colonia, *f*; introducción, *f*. **p. out,** trasplante, *m*

plaque *n* placa, *f*; medalla, *f*

plash *n* (puddle) charco, *m*; (sound) chapaleteo, *m*. *vt* and *vi* chapotear, chapalear

plasma *n* plasma, *m*

plaster *n* (for walls, etc.) argamasa, *f*; yeso, *m*; *med* parche, emplasto, *m*. *vt* (walls, etc.) enlucir, enyesar; poner emplastos (a or en); (daub) embadurnar, manchar; (cover) cubrir. **p. cast,** vaciado, yeso, *m*. **p. of Paris,** escayola, *f*

plasterer *n* yesero, *m*

plastering *n* revoque, enyesado, guarnecido, *m*. **p. trowel,** fratás, *m*

plastic *a* plástico. *n* plástica, *f*; *pl* **plastics,** materias plásticas, *f pl*. **p. surgery,** cirugía plástica, cirugía estética, *f*

plasticine *n* plasticina, *f*

plate *n* plancha, chapa, *f*; (engraving and *phot.,* of a doctor, etc.) placa, *f*; (illustration) lámina, *f*; (cutlery, etc.) vajilla, *f*; (for eating) plato, *m*; (for money) platillo, *m*; electrotipo, *m*; (dental) dentadura postiza, *f*. *vt* (with armor) blindar; (with metal) planchear; (silver) platear; (electro-plate) niquelar. **silver p.,** vajilla de plata, plata, *f*. **p.-armor,** armadura, *f*; (of a ship) blindaje, *m*. **p.-draining rack,** escurreplatos, *m*. **p.-glass,** vidrio plano, *m*. **p.-rack,** escurridero para platos, *m*. **p. warmer,** calientaplatos, *m*

plateau *n* meseta, altiplanicie, *f*, *Lat. Am.* altiplano, *m*

plater *n* plateador, *m*; platero, *m*

platform *n* plataforma, *f*; (railway) andén, *m*. **p. ticket,** billete de andén, *m*

plating *n* niquelado, *m*; electrogalvanización, *f*; (with armor) blindaje, *m*

platinum *n* platino, *m*. **p. blonde,** rubia platino, *f*

platitude *n* perogrullada, *f*, lugar común, *m*; trivialidad, vulgaridad, *f*

platitudinous *a* lleno de perogrulladas; trivial

platonic *a* platónico

platoon *n mil* pelotón, *m*

platter *n* fuente, *f*, trinchero, *m*; plato, *m*

plaudit *n* aplauso, *m*, aclamación, *f*; (praise) elogio, *m*, alabanza, *f*

plausible *a* plausible

play *vi* jugar; (frolic) juguetear, retozar; recrearse, divertirse; *mech* moverse; (on a musical instrument) tocar; (wave) ondear, flotar; *theat* representar; (behave) conducirse. *vt* jugar; (of a searchlight, etc.) enfocar; (direct) dirigir; (a fish) agotar; (a joke, etc.) hacer; (a piece in a game) mover; (a musical instrument or music) tocar; (a string instrument) tañer; (a character in a play) hacer el papel de; (a drama, etc.) representar, poner en escena. **to p. a joke,** gastar una broma, hacer una burla. **to p. fair,** jugar limpio. **to p. false,** jugar sucio, engañar. **to p. the fool,** hacerse el tonto, hacerse el payaso. **to p. at,** jugar a; (pretend) fingir; hacer sin entusiasmo. **to p. off,** confrontar, contraponer. **to p. on.** See **to p. upon. to p. on the . . . ,** (of musical instruments) tocar. **to p. to,** (a person) tocar para. **to p. upon,** (a person's fears, etc.) explotar. **to p. up to,** (a person) adular, hacer la rueda (a). **to p. with,** jugar con; burlarse de; (an idea) acariciar play. *n* juego, *m*; diversión, *f*, recreo, *m*; (reflection) reflejo, *m*; movimiento libre, *m*; (to the imagination, etc.) rienda suelta, *f*; *mech* holgura, *f*; *lit* pieza dramática, comedia, *f*; (performance) función, representación, *f*; (theater) teatro, *m*. **fair p.,** juego limpio, *m*. **foul p.,** juego sucio, *m*; traición, perfidia, *f*. **to bring into p.,** poner en juego. **to come into p.,** entrar en juego. **to give p. to,** dar rienda a. **p. on words,** juego de palabras, *m*. **p.-pen,** cuadro enrejado, *m*

playact *vi* hacer la comedia

playbill *n* cartel, *m*; programa, *m*

played-out *a* agotado; viejo

player *n* jugador (-ra); *theat* actor (-triz), representante, *mf*; *mus* músico (-ca), tocador (-ra)

playfellow *n* camarada, *mf*; compañero (-ra) de juego, compañero de juegos

playful *a* juguetón; travieso; alegre

playfully *adv* en juego, de broma; alegremente

playgoer *n* persona que frecuenta los teatros, *f*; espectador de comedias, *m*

playground *n* patio de recreo, *m*

playing *n* juego, *m*. **p.-cards**, naipes, *m pl*, cartas, *f pl*. **p.-field**, campo de deportes, *m*

playlet *n* comedia corta, *f*

playmate. See **playfellow**

plaything *n* juguete, *m*

playtime *n* recreación, *f*; (in schools) hora de recreo, *f*, recreo, *m*

playwright *n* dramaturgo, *m*, autor (-ra) de comedias

plea *n law* informe, *m*; declaración, *f; law* acción, *f*, proceso, *m*; (excuse) pretexto, *m*, excusa, *f*; (entreaty) súplica, *f*. **under p. of,** bajo pretexto de, con excusa de

plead *vi law* pleitear; *law* declarar; suplicar; (of counsel, etc.) abogar (por); intercede (por). *vt* defender en juicio; aducir, alegar; pretender. **to p. guilty,** confesarse culpable. **to p. not guilty,** negar la acusación. **to p. ignorance,** pretender ignorancia

pleading *n* súplicas, *f pl; law* defensa, *f; pl* **pleadings,** alegatos, *m pl*, a implorante

pleasant *a* agradable; placentero; ameno; encantador; dulce; alegre; (of persons) simpático, amable; bueno; divertido

pleasantly *adv* agradablemente; de un modo muy amable; alegremente

pleasantry *n* jocosidad, *f*; broma, chanza, *f*

please *vi* dar placer, gustar, dar gusto; agradar; parecer bien, querer, servirse; tener a bien, placer. *vt* deleitar, agradar, gustar; halagar; contentar, satisfacer. **I will do what I p.,** Haré lo que me parezca bien. **If you p.,** Si te parece bien; Con tu permiso. **She is very easy to p.,** Es muy fácil de darle placer. **When you p.,** Cuando Vd. quiera, Cuando a Vd. le venga bien Cuando Vd. guste. **"Please Do Not Disturb,"** «No Molesten.» **P. sit down!** ¡Haga el favor de sentarse! ¡Sírvase de sentarse! **P. God!** ¡Plegue a Dios!

pleased *a* contento (de o con); encantado (de); alegre (de); satisfecho (de o con). **I am p. with my new house,** Estoy contento con mi nueva casa. **I'm p. to meet you,** Mucho gusto (en conocerle), Mucho gusto (en conocerla). **to be p.,** estar contento; complacerse en

pleasing *a* agradable, grato; placentero; halagüeño

pleasurable *a* agradable; divertido, entretenido

pleasure *n* placer, *m*; gusto, *m*; satisfacción, *f*; (will) voluntad, *f*; recreo, *m*; diversión, distracción, *f*. **to give p. (to),** dar placer (a); deleitar, agradar; complacer. **to take p. in,** gustar de, disfrutar de; complacerse en. **I shall do it with great p.,** Lo haré con mucho gusto, Lo haré con mucho placer. **p.-boat,** barco de recreo, *m*. **p.-ground,** parque de atracciones, *m*.

p.-seeking, amigo de placeres, frívolo. **p. trip,** viaje de recreo, *m*; excursión, *f*

pleasure craft *n* barco de recreo, *m*. (one vessel); barcas de recreo (collectively), *m pl*

pleat *n* pliegue, *m*, *vt* plegar, hacer pliegues en

pleating *n* plegado, *m*

plebeian *a* plebeyo. *n* plebeyo (-ya)

plebiscite *n* plebiscito, *m*. **to take a p.,** hacer un plebiscito

pledge *n* prenda, *f*; empeño, *m*; garantía, *f*; (hostage) rehén, *m*; (toast) brindis, *m*. *vt* empeñar, dar en prenda; garantizar; brindar por; prometer. **to p. oneself,** comprometerse. **to p. support for,** prometer apoyo para

plenitude *n* plenitud, *f*

plenteous, plentiful *a* copioso, abundante. **to be p.,** abundar

plentifully *adv* en abundancia

plenty *n* abundancia, *f*; en abundancia; de sobra; mucho. *adv inf* bastante. **There is p. of food,** Hay comida en abundancia. **We have p. of time,** Tenemos tiempo de sobra

plethora *n* plétora, *f*

pleurisy *n* pleuresía, *f*

plexus *n* plexo, *m*

pliable, pliant *a* flexible; dócil

pliers *n pl* pinzas, *f pl*; alicates, *m pl*, tenazas, *f pl*

plight *vt* (one's word) empeñar, dar; prometer en matrimonio. *n* (fix) aprieto, apuro, *m*. **to p. one's troth,** dar palabra de matrimonio

plinth *n arch* plinto, *m*

plod *vi* andar despacio, caminar con trabajo; *fig* trabajar con ahínco

plodder *n* trabajador lento y concienzudo, *m*; (student) empollón (-ona)

plot *n* (of land) parcela, *f*; terreno, solar, *m*; (plan) proyecto, *m*; estratagema, *m*; (literary) intriga, trama, *f*; (story) argumento, *m*; (conspiracy) conjuración, *f*, complot, *m*. *vt* trazar (un plano, etc.); urdir, tramar. *vi* conspirar, intrigar

plotter *n* conspirador (-ra conjurado (-da)

plotting *n* trazado (de un plano, una gráfica), *m*; (conspiracy) conspiración, *f*; maquinaciones, *f pl*; (hatching) trama, *f*

pluckily *adv* valientemente

pluckiness *n* coraje, valor, *m*

plucky *a* valiente, esforzado, resuelto, animoso

plug *n* tapón, tarugo, *m*; (in building) nudillo, *m*; (of a switchboard) clave, *f*; *elec* enchufe, *m*; (of a w.c.) tirador, *m*; (of a bath, etc.) tapón, *m*; (of tobacco) rollo, *m*. *vt* atarugar, taponar, obturar; (in building) rellenar. *vi* (with away) batirse el cobre, sudar la gota gorda. **to p. in,** enchufar

plum *n* (tree) ciruelo, *m*; (fruit) ciruela, *f*;

(raisin) pasa, *f*; (*inf* prize) breva, golosina, *f*. **p. cake,** pastel de fruta, *m*

plumage *n* plumaje, *m*

plumb *n* plomada, *f*; (sounding-lead) escandallo, *m*. **a** perpendiculo; recto; completo. *adv* a plomo, verticalmente; exactamente. *vt* aplomar; naut sondar; (*fig* pierce) penetrar; (understand) comprender. *vi* trabajar como plomero. **p.-line,** plomada, *f*

plumber *n* plomero, fontanero, *m*; instalador de cañerías, *m*

plumbing *n* plomería, fontanería, *f*; instalación de cañerías, *f*

plume *n* pluma, *f*; penacho, *m*. *vt* adornar con plumas; desplumar; **to p. itself,** (of a bird) limpiarse las plumas. **to p. oneself on,** echárselas de, hacer alarde de; jactarse de

plummet *n* plomada, *f*; (weight) plomo, *m*; (sounding-lead) sonda, *f*

plump *a* gordito, llenito; rollizo; hinchado. *adv* de golpe; claramente. *vt* (swell) hinchar, rellenar; (make fall) hacer (or dejar) caer. *vi* (swell) hincharse; engordar; (fall) caer a plomo; dejarse caer. **to p. for,** escoger, dar apoyo (a); votar por. **p.-cheeked,** mofletudo

plunder *vt* saquear; pillar; despojar. *n* saqueo, pillaje, *m*; (booty) botín, despojo, *m*

plunderer *n* saqueador (-ra); ladrón (-ona)

plundering *n* saqueo, *m*; despojo, *m*. **a** saqueador

plunge *vt* chapuzar; sumergir; hundir; meter. *vi* sumergirse; (into water) zambullirse; (rush) precipitarse, lanzarse; *naut* zozobrar; (of a horse) encabritarse; (gamble) jugarse el todo. *n* sumersión, *f*; zambullida, *f*; chapuz, *m*; (rush) salto, *m*; (*fig* step) paso, *m*

plunger *n* mech émbolo, *m*

plunging *n* (of a ship) zozobra, *f*; (of a horse) cabriolas, *f pl*; saltos, *m pl*, For other meanings, see **plunge**

plural *a* plural. *n* plural, *m*. **in the p.,** en el plural. **to make p.,** poner en plural

plurality *n* pluralidad, *f*

plus *prep* and a más; (*math elec*) positivo. *n* signo más, *m*; *math* cantidad positiva, *f*. **p. fours,** pantalones de golf, *m pl*

plush *n* felpa, *f*; velludo, *m*

plushy *a* felpudo; de felpa

plutocrat *n* plutócrata, *mf*

ply *n* cabo, *m*. *vt* emplear, usar; manejar; ejercer; ofrecer, servir (con); importunar (con). *vi* hacer el trayecto; hacer el servicio; ir y venir; hacer viajes. **to ply for hire,** tomar viajeros; ofrecerse para ser alquilado

plywood *n* madera contrachapada, *f*

pneumatic *a* neumático. *n* (tire) neumático, *m*. **p. drill,** barreno neumático, *m*

pneumococcus *n* neumococo, *m*

pneumonia *n* pulmonía, *f*. **double p.,** pulmonía doble, *f*

poach *vi* cazar (or pescar) en vedado. *vt* robar caza de un vedado; *fig* invadir; (*fig* steal) hurtar; (eggs) escalfar. **to p. upon another's preserves,** meterse en los asuntos de otro

poacher *n* cazador furtivo, *m*

poaching *n* caza (or pesca) furtiva, *f*

pock *n* pústula, *f*. **p.-mark,** hoyo, *m*. **p.-marked,** picado de viruelas

pocket *n* bolsillo, *m*; bolsillo del reloj, *m*; faltriquera, *f*; *min* bolsa, *f*, depósito, *m*; *fig* bolsa, *f*; (in billiards) tronera, *f*. *vt* meter (or poner) en el bolsillo; (an insult) tragarse; (in billiards) entronerar; (a profit) ganar; apropiarse. **p.-air,** bolsa de aire, *f*. **to be out of p.,** haber perdido, tener una pérdida. **to have a person in one's p.,** calzarse a una persona. **to p. one's pride,** olvidarse de su orgullo. **p. battleship,** acorazado de bolsillo, *m*. **p.-book,** cartera, *f*. **p. dictionary,** diccionario de bolsillo, *m*. **p.-flap,** portezuela, *f*. **p.-handkerchief,** pañuelo (de bolsillo), *m*. **p.-knife,** cortaplumas, *m*. **p.-lighter,** encendedor de bolsillo, *m*. **p.-money,** alfileres, *m pl*, dinero del bolsillo, *m*. **p. picking,** ratería de cartista, *f*

pocketful *n* bolsillo lleno (de), *m*; lo que cabe en un bolsillo

pocket of resistance *n* foco de resistencia, *m*

pod *n bot* vaina, *f*; (of a silkworm) capullo, *m*. *vt* desvainar; mondar. *vi* hincharse, llenarse

podgy *a* gordo, grueso

poem *n* poema, *m*; *pl* **poems,** poesías, *f pl*, versos, *m pl*

poet *n* poeta, *m*. **p. laureate,** poeta laureado, *m*

poetic *a* poético. **p. licence,** licencia poética, *f*

poetics *n* poética, *f*

poetry *n* poesía, *f*; versos, poemas, *m pl*

pogrom *n* pogrom, *m*

poignancy *n* (of emotions) profundidad, violencia, *f*, lo patético; (of a retort, etc.) mordacidad, acerbidad, *f*

poignant *a* (moving) conmovedor, hondo, agudo; patético; (mordant) mordaz, agudo

poignantly *adv* de un modo conmovedor, patéticamente; mordazmente

poinsettia *n* flor de nochebuena, *f*

point *n* (usual meanings and ast., math., in cards, in a speech, etc.) punto, *m*; característica, *f*; cualidad, *f*; (purpose) motivo, fin, *m*; (question) cuestión, *f*; asunto, *m*; (wit) agudeza, *f*; (significance) significación, *f*; (detail) detalle, *m*; (in rationing) cupón, *m*; (sharp end) punta, *f*; (of a shawl, etc.) pico, *m*; (of land) promontorio, cabo, *m*; (engraving) buril, *m*; (railway) aguja, *f*; (of horses) cabo, *m*. **Mary has many good points**, María tiene muchas cualidades buenas. **There is no p. in being angry**, No hay para que enfadarse. **in p.**, en cuestión; a propósito. **in p. of fact**, en efecto, en verdad. **on the p. of**, a punto de. **to be to the p.**, venir al caso; ser apropiado. **to carry one's p.**, salir con la suya. **to come to the p.**, ir al grano, ir al caso, ir al mollo del asunto. **to make a p. of**, insistir en; tener por principio. **to win on points**, (boxing) ganar por puntos. **p. at issue**, cuestión bajo consideración, *f*, punto en cuestión, *m*. **p.-blank**, a boca de jarro. **p.-duty**, regulación de tráfico, *f*. **p. lace**, encaje de aguja, *m*. **p. of honor**, punto de honor, *m*; cuestión de honor, *f*. **p. or order**, cuestión de orden, *f*. **p. of view**, punto de vista, *m*. **What's your p.?** ¿A dónde quieres llegar con esto?

point *vt* sacar punta (a), afilar; (a moral, etc.) inculcar; (in building) rejuntar; *gram* puntuar; (of dogs) mostrar la caza. **He pointed his gun at them**, Les apuntó con su fusil. **The hands of the clock pointed to seven o'clock**, Las agujas del reloj marcaban las siete. **to p. with the finger**, señalar con el dedo. **to p. at**, señalar, indicar; (with a gun) apuntar; dirigir. **to p. out**, señalar, indicar; enseñar, mostrar; advertir

pointed *a* (sharpened) afilado; (in shape) puntiagudo; picudo; *arch* ojival; *fig* mordaz; satírico; (of a remark, etc.) directo; personal; aparente, evidente

pointedly *adv* explícitamente, categóricamente; mordazmente; directamente; satíricamente

pointer *n* (of a clock, weighing-machine, etc.) aguja, *f*; (of a balance) fiel, *m*; (wand) puntero, *m*; *fig* índice, *m*; (dog) perro de muestra, *m*

pointing *n* (in building) rejuntado, *m*; (of a gun) puntería, *f*

pointless *a* sin motivo, innecesario; fútil; sin importancia

poise *vt* balancear; pesar. *vi* balancearse; posar, estar suspendido. *n* equilibrio, *m*; (of mind) serenidad de ánimo, sangre fría, *f*; aplomo, *m*; (bearing) porte, aire, *m*

poison *n* veneno, *m*; *fig* ponzoña, *f*, veneno, *m*. *vt* envenenar; intoxicar; *fig* emponzoñar. **p. gas**, gas asfixiante, *m*

poisoning *n* envenenamiento, *m*; intoxicación, *f*

poisonous *a* venenoso; tóxico; *fig* ponzoñoso, pernicioso. **p. snake**, serpiente venenosa

poke *vt* (thrust) clavar; (make) hacer; (the fire) atizar; hurgar; (push) empujar; (put away) arrinconar. *vi* andar a tientas; meterse. **Don't p. your nose into other people's business!** ¡No te metas donde no te llaman! **They poked his eyes out**, Le saltaron los ojos. **to p. fun at**, bur-

larse de, mofarse de. **to p. the fire**, atizar la lumbre (or el fuego). **to p. about for**, buscar a tientas. **p.-bonnet**, capelina, *f*

poker *n* (game) póker, *m*; (for the fire) hurgón, atizador, *m*. **p. work**, pirograbado, *m*

poky *a* estrecho, ahogado, pequeño; miserable

Poland Polonia, *f*

polar *a* polar. **p. bear**, oso (-sa) blanco (-ca). **p. lights**, aurora boreal, *f*

polarize *vt* polarizar

pole *n* palo largo, *m*; poste, *m*; (of a tent) mástil, *m*; (of a cart) pértiga, *f*; *sport* pértiga, garrocha, *f*; (measurement) percha, *f*; (*ast geog biol math elec*) polo, *m*. *vt* (a punt) impeler con pértiga. **from p. to p.**, de polo a polo. **greasy p.**, cucaña, *f*. **under bare poles**, *naut* a palo seco. **p.-ax**, hachuela de mano, *f*; hacha de marinero, *f*; (butcher's) mazo, *m*. **p. jumping**, salto de pértiga, salto a la garrocha, *m*. **p.-star**, estrella polar, *f*

Pole *n* polaco (-ca)

polemic *n* polémica, *f*

polemical *a* polémico

police *n* policía, *f*. *vt* mantener servicio de policía en; mantener el orden público en; administrar, regular. **mounted p.**, policía montada, *f*. **p. constable**, (agente de) policía, guardia urbano, *m*. **p. court**, tribunal de la policía, *m*. **p. dog**, perro de policía, *m*. **p. force**, cuerpo de policía, *m*, policía, *f*. **p. magistrate**, juez municipal, *m*. **p. station**, comisaría de policía, *f*. **p. trap**, puesto oculto de la policía del tráfico, *m*. **p. woman**, policía, *f*

policeman *n* policía, guardia, *Lat. Am.* cívico, *m*

policy *n* política, *f*; táctica, *f*; sistema, *m*; norma de conducta, *f*; ideas, *f pl*; principios, *m pl*; prudencia, *f*; (insurance) póliza, *f*. **fixed premium p.**, póliza a prima fija, *f*. **p.-holder**, asegurado (-da), tenedor (de una póliza), *m*

poliomyelitis *n* poliomielitis, *f*

polish *vt* (metals and wood) pulir; (furniture and shoes) dar brillo (a); (*lit works*) pulir, limar; (persons) descortezar, civilizar. *n* (shine) brillo, *m*; (furniture) cera para los muebles, *f*; (metal, silver) líquido para limpiar metales, *m*; (for shoes) betún para zapatos, *m*; (varnish) barniz, *m*; (of *lit.* works) pulidez, elegancia, *f*; (of persons) urbanidad, cultura, *f*. **to p. off**, terminar a prisa; (a person) acabar con; (food) engullir

Polish *a* polaco, polonés. *n* (language) polaco, *m*

polished *a* (of verses, etc.) pulido, elegante; (of person) culto, distinguido; (of manners) fino, cortés

polisher *n* (machine) pulidor, *m*; lustrador, *m*. **floor-p.**, lustrador de piso, *m*. **French p.**, barnizador, *m*

polite a cortés, bien educado; atento; elegante

politeness n cortesía, f. **for p. sake,** por cortesía

politic a político

political a político. **p. agent,** agente político, m. **p. economist,** hacendista, mf **p. economy,** economía política, f

politician n político (-ca)

politics n política, f. **to dabble in p.,** meterse en política

polity n forma de gobierno, constitución política, f

polka-dot a con puntos

poll n (head of person) cabeza, f; (voters' register) lista electoral, f; (voting) votación, f; (polling booth) colegio electoral, m; (counting of votes) escrutinio, m. vt (trees) desmochar; (vote) votar, dar su voto (a); (obtain votes) recibir; (count votes) escrutar. **p.-tax,** capitación, f

pollen n polen, m

pollinate vt fecundar con polen

pollination n polinización, f

polling n votación, f. **p. booth,** colegio electoral, m

pollute vt contaminar; ensuciar; profanar; (corrupt morally) corromper

pollution n contaminación, f; profanación, f; corrupción, f

polo n polo, m. **p. mallet,** maza de polo, f. **p. player,** jugador de polo, m, polista, mf

poltroon n cobarde, m

polychrome a policromo

polygamist n polígamo (-ma)

polygamous a polígamo

polygenesis n poligenismo, m

polyglot n poligloto (-ta). **p. Bible,** poliglota, f

polygon n polígono, m

polyp n pólipo, m

polyphonic a polifónico

polyphony n polifonía, f

polytechnic a politécnico

pomade n pomada, f

pomegranate n granada, f

pommel n pomo, m, vt aporrear

pomp n pompa, magnificencia, f, fausto, aparato, m; ostentación, f

Pompeii Pompeya, f

pompom n pompón, m

pomposity n pomposidad, presunción, f; (of language) ampulosidad, f

pompous a pomposo, ostentoso; (of style) ampuloso, hinchado; importante. **to be p.,** (of persons) darse tono

pond n charca, f, estanque, m

ponder vt ponderar, estudiar, considerar. vi meditar (sobre), reflexionar (sobre)

ponderous a pesado; macizo, abultado; grave; (dull) pesado, aburrido

poniard n puñal, m, vt apuñalar

pontiff n pontífice, m

pontifical a pontificio

pontificate n pontificado, m

pontoon n pontón, m. **p. bridge,** puente de pontones, m

pony n jaca, f

poodle n perro (-rra) de aguas, perro de lanas, perro lanudo

pooh-pooh vt despreciar, desdeñar. Pooh! ¡Bah!

pool n (in a river) rebalsa, f; charca, f, estanque, m; (of blood, etc.) charco, m; (swimming) Spain piscina, Lat. Am. alberca, f; (in cards) baceta, f; com asociación, f; fig fuente, f; pl **pools,** (football) apuestas benéficas de fútbol, f pl. vt (resources, etc.) combinar; juntar

poop n popa, f. **p. lantern,** fanal, m

poor a pobre; malo; (insignificant or unfortunate) infeliz, desgraciado. **the p.,** los pobres. **to be in p. health,** estar mal de salud. **to be p. stuff,** ser de pacotilla. **to be poorer than a church mouse,** ser más pobre que las ratas. **to have a p. opinion of,** tener en poco (a). **P. me!** ¡Ay de mí! ¡Pecador de mí! **p.-box,** cepillo, m. **p.-law,** ley de asistencia pública, f. **p.-spirited,** apocado

poorhouse n asilo, m

pop n (of a cork) taponazo, m; (of a gun) detonación, f; (drink) gaseosa, f, adv ¡pum! vi (of a cork) saltar; (of guns) detonar. vt (corks) hacer saltar; (a gun, a question, etc.) disparar. **popgun,** escopeta de aire comprimido, f. **to pop down,** bajar a presuradamente. **to pop in,** (visit) dejarse caer; entrar rápidamente. **to pop off,** marcharse a prisa; (die) estirar la pata, Lat. Am. arrancarse. **to pop up,** subir corriendo; aparecer de pronto

popcorn nsg palomitas (de maíz), rosetas (de maíz) fpl (Spain), cabritos mpl (Chile), alborotos mpl (Argentina, Central America, Peru), cabritas fpl (elsewhere)

pope n Papa, m

poplar n (black) chopo, álamo, m; (white) álamo blanco, m. **p. grove,** alameda, f

poplin n popelina, f

poppy n amapola, adormidera, f

populace n pueblo, m; (scornful) populacho, m

popular a popular; en boga, de moda; común. **He is a p. hero,** Es un héroe popular

popularity n popularidad, f

popularization n vulgarización, f

popularize vt popularizar, vulgarizar

populate vt poblar

population n población, f

populous a populoso; muy poblado

porcelain n porcelana, f

porch n pórtico, m; (of a house) portal, m

porcupine n puerco espín, m

pore n poro, m. **to p. over,** estar absorto en; examinar cuidadosamente

pork n carne de cerdo, f. **salt p.,** tocino, m. **p. butcher,** tocinero, m. **p. pie,** pastel de carne de cerdo, m

pornographic a pornográfico

pornography n pornografía, f

porosity n porosidad, f

porous a poroso

porphyry n pórfido, m

porpoise n marsopa, f, puerco marino, m

porridge n gachas, f pl, m

port n puerto, m; (in a ship) porta, f; (larboard) babor, m; (wine) vino de Oporto, m; (mien) porte, m, presencia, f. vt (the helm) poner a babor; mil llevar un fusil terciado. **to put into p.,** tomar puerto. **to stop at a p.,** hacer escala en un puerto. **p. dues,** derechos de puerto, m pl

portable a portátil; móvil. **p. typewriter,** máquina de escribir portátil (or de viaje), f. **p. wireless,** radio portátil, f

portal n portal, m

portcullis n rastrillo, m

portend vt presagiar, anunciar

portent n augurio, presagio, m; portento, m

portentous a ominoso; portentoso; importante

porter n (messenger) mozo de cordel, m; (of a university, hotel) portero, m; (of a block of flats) conserje, m; (railway) mozo de estación, Argentina changador, m; (drink) cerveza negra, f. **porter's lodge,** portería, f; conserjería, f

portfolio n carpeta, f; (pol of a minister) cartera, f; (pol ministry) ministerio, m

porthole n tronera, f

portico n pórtico, m

portion n porción, f; parte, f; (marriage) dote, mf; (piece) pedazo, m; (in a restaurant) ración, f; (in life) fortuna, f. vt dividir; repartir; (dower) dotar

portly a corpulento, grueso

portmanteau n maleta, f

portrait n retrato, m. **p. painter,** pintor (-ra) de retratos

portraiture n retratos, m pl; descripción, pintura, f

portray vt retratar; pintar, representar; (in words) describir, pintar

portrayal n pintura, f; retrato, m; (in words) descripción, f

portrayer n retratista, mf, pintor (-ra)

Portuguese a portugués, n portugués (-esa); (language) portugués, m

pose vt colocar; (a problem, etc.) plantear; (a question) hacer; vi colocarse; (with as) echárselas de, dárselas de, fingir ser; hacerse pasar por. n actitud, postura, f; (affected) pose, f; (deception) engaño, m

poser n problema difícil, m; (in an examination) pega, f; pregunta embarazosa, f

position n posición, f; situación, f; actitud, postura, f; condición, f, estado, m; (post) puesto, empleo, m. **He is not in a p. to . . . ,** No está en condiciones de . . . , No está para . . . **to place in p.,** poner en posición, colocar

positive a positivo; absoluto; (convinced) convencido, seguro; (downright) categórico; inf completo. n realidad, f; phot (prueba) positiva, f

positively adv positivamente; categóricamente

posse n pelotón, m; multitud, muchedumbre, f

possess vt poseer; gozar (de); (of ideas, etc.) dominar. **to p. oneself of,** apoderarse de, apropiarse. **What possessed you to do it?** ¿Qué te hizo hacerlo?

possession n posesión, f. **to take p. of,** tomar posesión de; hacerse dueño de, apoderarse de; (a house, etc.) entrar en, ocupar

possessor n poseedor (-ra); dueño (-ña); propietario (-ia)

possibility n posibilidad, f

possible a posible. **as soon as p.,** cuanto antes, lo más pronto posible. **to make p.,** hacer posible, posibilitar

possibly adv posiblemente; (perhaps) quizás. **I shall come as soon as I p. can,** Vendré lo más pronto posible

post n (pole) poste, m; (of a sentry, etc.) puesto, m; (employment) empleo, m; (mail) correo, m; mil toque, m. vt (a notice) fijar; anunciar; (to an appointment) destinar; (letters, etc.) echar al correo; com pasar al libro mayor; (inform) tener al corriente. vi viajar en posta. **"P. no bills!"** «Se prohibe fijar carteles.» **registered p.,** correo certificado, m. **p. card,** postal, f. **p.-chaise,** silla de posta, f. **p.-date,** posfecha, f. **p.-free,** franco de porte. **p.-haste,** con gran celeridad. **p.-horse,** caballo de posta, m. **p.-impressionism,** post-impresionismo, m. **p.-mortem,** n autopsia, f. **p.-natal,** postnatal. **p.-nuptial,** postnupcial. **p. office,** correo, m, correos, m pl; (on a train) ambulancia de correos, f. **p. office box,** Spain apartado de correos, m Lat. Am. casilla f, **p. office savings bank,** caja postal de ahorros, f. **p.-paid,** porte pagado; franco. **p.-war,** n postguerra, f. a de la postguerra

postage n porte de correos, franqueo, m. **p. stamp,** sello postal, m, Mexico timbre, m, elsewhere in Lat. Am. estampilla, f

postage meter n franqueadora, f

postal a postal. **p. money order** Spain giro postal, m, Lat. Am. libranza de correos, estampilla postal, f. **p. order,** orden postal de pago, f. **p. packet,** paquete postal, m

poster n cartel, m. vt fijar carteles (a or

en); anunciar por carteles. **bill-p.,** fijador de carteles, *m*

poste restante *n* lista de correos, *f*

posterior *a* posterior. *n* trasero, *m*, asentaderas, *f pl*

posterity *n* posteridad, *f*

postgraduate *n* estudiante graduado que hace estudios avanzados, *m*. *a* avanzado; para estudiantes graduados

posthumous *a* póstumo

posthumously *adv* después de la muerte

postman *n* cartero, *m*

postmark *n* matasellos, *m*, *vt* poner matasellos (a)

postmaster *n* administrador de correos, *m*

postpone *vt* aplazar, diferir; retrasar; (subordinate) postergar

postponement *n* aplazamiento, *m*; tardanza, *f*

postscript *n* posdata, *f*, *Mexico* aumento, *m*

postulate *n* postulado, *m*, *vt* postular

posture *n* postura, actitud, *f*; (of affairs) estado, *m*, situación, *f*. *vi* tomar una postura

pot *n* pote, *m*; tarro, *m*; (flower-) tiesto, *m*; (for cooking) olla marmita, *f*; jarro, *m*. *vt* plantar en tiestos; conservar en potes. **pot-bellied,** panzudo. **pot-boiler,** obra literaria escrita con el sólo propósito de ganar dinero, *f*. **pot-herb,** hierba que se emplea para sazonar, hortaliza, *f*. **pothole,** bache, **pot-luck,** comida ordinaria, *f*. **pot-shot,** tiro fácil, *m*; tiro al azar, *m*

potage *n* potaje, *m*

potash *n* potasa, *f*. **caustic p.,** potasa cáustica, *f*

potassium *n* potasio, *m*

potato *n* patata, *f*. **sweet p.,** batata, *f*. **p. beetle,** coleóptero de la patata, *m*. **p. omelet,** tortilla a la española, *f*. **p. patch,** patatal, *m*. **p. peeler,** pelapatatas, *m*

potency *n* potencia, *f*; fuerza, eficacia, *f*

potent *a* potente, fuerte; eficaz

potentate *n* potentado, *m*

potential *a* potencial; virtual; (*phys gram*) potencial, *n* poder, *m*; *gram* modo potencial, *m*; *phys* energía potencial, *f*; *elec* tensión potencial, *f*

potion *n* poción, *f*,

potpourri *n* popurrí, *m*

potter *n* alfarero, *m*. *vi* gandulear. *vt* perder. **potter's clay,** barro de alfarero, *m*. **potter's wheel,** tabanque, *m*. **potter's workshop,** alfar, *m*

pottery *n* alfarería, *f*; (china) loza, porcelana, *f*

pouch *n* bolsa, *f*; *zool* bolsa marsupial, *f*; (for tobacco) tabaquera, *f*; (for cartridges) cartuchera, *f*. *vt* embolsar. *vi* bolsear

poultice *n* apósito, emplasto, *m*, *vt* poner emplastos (a or en)

poultry *n* volatería, *f*. **p. dealer,** gallinero (-ra) vendedor (-ra) de volatería. **p. manure** *Mexico* cuitla, *f*. **p. yard,** gallinero, *m*

poultry farming *n* avicultura, *f*

pounce *n* (swoop) calada, *f*. *vi* (swoop) calarse; saltar (sobre); agarrar, hacer presa (en); *fig* atacar; descubrir, hacer patente

pound *n* (weight and currency) libra, *f*; (for cattle) corral de concejo, *m*; (thump) golpe, *m*. *vt* (break up) machacar, pistar; (beat) batir; (thump) golpear, aporrear.

pour *vt* vaciar, verter; derramar. *vi* correr; (of rain) diluviar, llover a cántaros; (fill) llenar; (of crowds, words, etc.) derramarse. **to p. out the tea,** servir el té. **The crowd poured in,** La multitud entró en tropel

pouring *a* (of rain) torrencial

pout *vi* torcer el gesto; hacer pucheritos

poverty *n* pobreza, *f*. **p.-stricken,** menesteroso, indigente, necesitado

powder *n* polvo, *m*; (face) polvos de arroz, *m pl*; (gun) pólvora, *f*. *vt* polvorear; (crush) reducir a polvo, pulverizar. *vi* ponerse polvos. **p.-flash,** fogonazo, *m*. **p.-flask,** polvorín, *m*. **p.-magazine,** santabárbara, *f*. **p.-mill,** fábrica de pólvora, *f*. **p.-puff,** polvera, borla de empolvarse, *f*

powdered *a* en polvo

powdery *a* polvoriento; friable

power *n* poder, *m*; facultad, capacidad, *f*; vigor, *m*, fuerza, *f*; (*pol* and *math*) potencia, *f*; *mech* fuerza, *f*; influencia, *f*. **as far as lies within my p.,** en cuanto me sea posible. **It does not lie within my p.,** No está dentro de mis posibilidades, No está en mi poder. **the Great Powers,** las grandes potencias. **the powers that be,** los que mandan. **to be in p.,** estar en el poder. **p.-house, p.-station,** central eléctrica, *f*. **p. of attorney,** poderes, *m pl*, procuración, *f*. **to grant p. of attorney (to),** dar poderes (a)

powerful *a* poderoso; fuerte; eficaz; potente; (of arguments, etc.) convincente

powerless *a* impotente

power steering *n* dirección asistida *f* (Spain), servo dirección *f*

powwow *n* conferencia, *f*; conversación, *f*

pox *n* sífilis, *f*; (smallpox) viruelas, *f pl*; (chicken-pox) viruelas falsas, *f pl*

practicable *a* practicable, factible, posible; viable, transitable

practical *a* (doable) factible; práctico; virtual. **p. joke,** burla de consecuencias

practically *adv* prácticamente; en práctica; virtualmente; (in fact) en efecto. **p. nothing,** casi nada

practice *n* (custom) costumbre, *f*; práctica, *f*; ejercicio, *m*; (of a doctor, etc.) clientela, *f*; profesión, *f*; (religious) rito, *m*, ceremonias, *f pl*; (experience) experiencia, *f*. **It is not his p. to . . . ,** No es su costumbre de . . . **to be out of p.,** estar desentrenado. **to put into p.,** poner en práctica. **P. makes perfect,** El ejercicio hace maestro. *vt* tener la costumbre de; practicar; (a profession) ejercer; (a game) entrenarse en; (work at) estudiar; (a musical instrument) tocar; (accustom) acostumbrar. **to p. what one preaches,** predicar con el ejemplo

practiced *a* experimentado; experto

practitioner *n* médico (-ca). **general p.,** médico (-ca) general

pragmatic *a* pragmatista; (historical) pragmático; práctico

prairie *n* pradera, sabana, pampa, *f*, a de la pradera, etc.

praise *vt* alabar; ensalzar, glorificar; elogiar. *n* alabanza, *f*; elogio, *m*; glorificación, *f*, ensalzamiento, *m*. **to p. to the skies,** poner en los cuernos de la luna poner por las nubes, poner sobre las estrellas hacerse lenguas de

praiseworthy *a* digno de alabanza, laudable

prance *vi* (of a horse) caracolear, encabritarse, cabriolar; saltar; andar airosamente. *n* corveta, cabriola, *f*; salto, *m*

prank *n* travesura, diablura, *f*. **to play pranks,** hacer diabluras

prate, prattle *vi* charlar, chacharear; (lisp) balbucir; (of brooks, etc.) murmurar, susurrar. *vt* divulgar. *n* charla, cháchara, *f*; balbuceo, *m*

prattler *n* parlanchín (-ina) (gossip) chismoso (-sa); (child) niño (-ña)

prattling *n* charla, *f*; (lisping) balbuceo, *m*; (of brooks, etc.) murmullo, susurro, ruido armonioso, *m*. *a* charlatán, gárrulo; balbuciente; (of brooks, etc.) parlero

prawn *n* camarón, *m*

pray *vt* and *vi* suplicar; implorar; rezar, orar. **P. be seated,** Haga el favor de sentarse

prayer *n* rezo, *m*, plegaria, oración, *f*; súplica, *f*; *law* petición, *f*. **p. book,** libro de devociones, devocionario, *m*. **p.-meeting,** reunión para rezar, *f*. **p.-rug,** alfombra de rezo, *f*

praying *n* rezo, *m*; suplicación, *f*

pre- *prefix* de antes de (e.g. **pre-World-War-1 publications,** publicaciones de antes de la Primera Guerra Mundial)

preach *vt* and *vi* predicar

preacher *n* predicador (-ra). **to turn p.,** meterse a predicar

preaching *n* predicación, *f*, a predicador

preamble *n* preámbulo, *m*

prearrange *vt* preparar de antemano, predisponer

precarious *a* precario; inseguro; incierto, arriesgado

precaution *n* precaución, *f*. **to take precautions,** tomar precauciones

precautionary *a* de precaución; preventivo

precede *vt* preceder (a), anteceder (a); tomar precedencia (a), exceder en importancia (a). *vi* ir delante; tener la precedencia

precedence *n* precedencia, *f*; prioridad, *f*; superioridad, *f*. **to take p. over,** tomar precedencia (a), preceder (a)

precedent *n* precedente, *m*, a precedente. **without p.,** sin precedente

preceding *a* anterior, precedente

precept *n* precepto, *m*

precinct *n* (police station) comisaría de sección *Argentina,* delegación *Mexico*, *f*

precincts *n pl* recinto, *m*; ámbito, *m*; distrito, barrio, *m*

preciosity *n* afectación, *f*

precious *a* precioso; de gran valor; hermoso; amado; muy querido; (with rogue, etc.) redomado; completo. **p. little,** muy poco. **p. nearly,** casi, por poco . . . **p. stone,** piedra preciosa, *f*

precipice *n* precipicio, *m*

precipitant *a* precipitado

precipitate *vt* precipitar, despeñar, arrojar; acelerar; *chem* precipitar. *vi* precipitarse. *n* precipitado, *m*. a precipitado, súbito. **to p. oneself,** tirarse, lanzarse

precipitation *n chem* precipitación, *f*; *chem* precipitado, *m*; (rain, etc.) precipitación pluvial, *f*

precipitous *a* precipitoso, escarpado, acantilado

precipitously *adv* en precipicio

precise *a* preciso; exacto; justo; puntual; escrupuloso; formal; claro; pedante, afectado; ceremonioso

precisely *adv* precisamente; exactamente; puntualmente; escrupulosamente; claramente; con afectación; ceremoniosamente. **at six o'clock p.,** a las seis en punto

precision *n* precisión, *f*; exactitud, *f*; puntualidad, *f*; escrupulosidad, *f*; claridad, *f*; afectación, *f*; ceremonia, *f*

preclude *vt* excluir; impedir, hacer imposible

preclusion *n* exclusión, *f*; imposibilidad, *f*

precocious *a* precoz

preconceived *a* preconcebido

preconception *n* idea preconcebida, *f*; (prejudice) prejuicio, *m*

preconcerted *a* concertado de antemano

precursor *n* precursor (-ra)

precursory *a* precursor

predatory *a* rapaz; de rapiña; voraz

predecease *vt* morir antes (de or que); *law* premorir. *n law* premuerto, *m*

predecessor *n* predecesor (-ra); (ancestor) antepasado, *m*

predicament n (logic) predicamento, m; situación, f; (fix) apuro, m; pl **predicaments**, categorías, f pl

predicate vt afirmar. n (logic, gram) predicado, m

predict vt predecir, pronosticar, profetizar

prediction n predicción, f; pronóstico, vaticinio, m, profecía, f

predilection n predilección, f

predispose vt predisponer

predominance n predominio, m

predominant a predominante

predominate vi predominar

preeminence n preeminencia, f; primacia, superioridad, f

preeminent a preeminente; superior; extraordinario

preeminently adv preeminentemente; extraordinariamente; por excelencia; entre todos

preen vt (of birds) limpiarse; (of people) darse humos, jactarse

prefabricated a prefabricado

preface n prólogo, m; ecc prefacio, m; introducción, f; vt dar principio (a), empezar. **He prefaced his remarks by . . . ,** Dijo a modo de introducción

prefatory a preliminar, introductorio; a manera de prólogo

prefer vt preferir, gustar más (a); (promote) ascender, elevar; (a charge, etc.) presentar. **to p. a charge against,** pedir en juicio (a). **I p. oranges to apples,** Me gustan más las naranjas que las manzanas, Prefiero las naranjas a las manzanas

preferable a preferible

preferably adv preferiblemente, con preferencia

preference n preferencia, f; privilegio, m. **p. share,** acción privilegiada, acción preferente, f

preferential a preferente

preferment n promoción, f, ascenso, m; puesto eminente, m

preferred a preferente; favorito, predilecto. **p. share,** acción preferente, f

prefix vt anteponer, prefijar; (to a word) poner prefijo (a). n prefijo, m

pregnancy n embarazo, m, preñez, f

pregnant a embarazada, encinta, preñada, f; fig fértil; fig preñado

prehensile a prensil

prehistoric a prehistórico

prehistory n prehistoria, f

prejudge vt prejuzgar

prejudice n prejuicio, m; law perjuicio, m. vt influir, predisponer; (damage) perjudicar. **without p.,** sin perjuicio

prejudiced a parcial; con prejuicios

prejudicial a perjudicial

preliminary a preliminar. n preliminar, m

prelude (to) n preludio (de) m; presagio (de) m, vt and vi preludiar

premature a prematuro

premeditate vt premeditar

premeditatedly adv premeditadamente, con premeditación

premeditation n premeditación, f

premier a primero, principal. n primer ministro, m; (in Spain) presidente del Consejo de Ministros, m

premiere n estreno, m

premiership n puesto de primer ministro, m; in Spain presidencia del Consejo de Ministros, f

premise n (logic) premisa, f; pl **premises**, local, m; recinto, m; establecimiento, m; propiedad, f; tierras, f pl. **on the premises,** en el local; en el establecimiento

premium n (prize) premio, m, recompensa, f; com prima, f; precio, m. **at a p.,** a premio; a una prima; (of shares) sobre la par; fig en boga, muy solicitado, en gran demanda

premonition n presentimiento, presagio, m

prenatal a prenatal, antenatal

preoccupation n preocupación, f

preoccupied a preocupado; abstraído, absorto

preoccupy vt preocupar

prepaid a porte pagado, franco de porte

preparation n preparación, f; preparativo, m, disposición, f; (patent food) preparado, m. **I have made all my preparations,** He hecho todos mis preparativos. **The book is in p.,** El libro está en preparación

preparative a preparativo. n preparativo, m

preparatory a preparatorio, preparativo; preliminar. **p. school,** escuela preparatoria, f, m. **p. to,** como preparación para; antes de

prepare vt preparar; aparejar, aviar; equipar; (cloth) aprestar. vi prepararse; hacer preparativos

preparedness n estado de preparación, m; preparación, f, apercibimiento, m

prepay vt pagar adelantado, Lat. Am. aprontar; (a letter, etc.) franquear

prepayment n pago adelantado, m; (of a letter, etc.) franqueo, m

preponderance n preponderancia, f

preponderant a preponderante, predominante

preponderate vi preponderar; prevalecer (sobre), predominar (sobre)

preposition n preposición, f

prepossess vt predisponer; causar buena impresión (a)

prepossessing a atractivo

preposterous a ridículo, absurdo
Prep School n preparatoria, f
prepuce n prepucio, m
prerequisite n requisito necesario, esencial, m, a previamente necesario, esencial
prerogative n prerrogativa, f
presage n presagio, m; anuncio, m. vt presagiar; anunciar
Presbyterian a and n presbiteriano (-na)
prescient a presciente
prescind vt prescindir (de); separar (de). vi separarse
prescribe vt and vi prescribir; med recetar; dar leyes; law prescribir
prescription n prescripción, f; med receta, f
presence n presencia, f; (ghost) aparición, f. **in the p. of,** en presencia de, delante; a vista de. **p. of mind,** presencia de ánimo, serenidad de ánimo, f
present a presente; actual; (with month) corriente; gram presente. **at p.,** al presente, actualmente. **at the p. day,** a la fecha, en la actualidad, hoy día. **P. company excepted!** ¡Mejorando lo presente! **the present writer,** el que suscribe, el que esto escribe, el que estas líneas traza. **to be p. at,** presenciar, ser testigo de; asistir a, acudir a; hallarse en. **p.-day,** de hoy, actual. **p. tense,** gram tiempo presente, m
present n (time) presente, m; actualidad, f; gram tiempo presente, m; (gift) regalo, m, dádiva, f. **By these presents . . . ,** law Por estas presentes . . . **to make a p. of,** regalar. **Jane made me a p. of a watch,** Juana me regaló un reloj
present vt presentar; ofrecer; manifestar; (a gift) regalar, dar; (ecc mil) presentar. **New problems presented themselves,** Nuevos problemas surgieron. **to p. arms,** presentar las armas. **He presented himself in the office,** Se presentó en la oficina. **He presented his friend Mr. Moreno to me,** Me presentó a su amigo el Sr. Moreno
presentation n presentación, f; homenaje, m; (exhibition) exposición, f. **on p.,** com a presentación
presentiment n presentimiento, m, corazonada, f. **I had a p. that . . . ,** Tuve el presentimiento de que . . . , Tuve una corazonada que . . . **to have a p. about,** presentir
presently adv pronto; en seguida; dentro de poco
preservation n conservación, f; (from harm) preservación, f
preservative a preservativo. n preservativo, m
preserve vt preservar (de); guardar; proteger; conservar; cul hacer conservas de; (in syrup) almibarar. n cul conserva, f; (of fruit) compota, confitura, f; (covert)

coto, m. **preserved fruit,** dulce de almibar, m. **p. dish,** compotera, f
preserver n conservador (-ra); (saviour) salvador (-ra); (benefactor) bienhechor (-ra)
preserving n (from harm) preservación, f; conservación, f. **p. pan,** cazuela para conservas, f
preside vi (over) presidir; dirigir, gobernar. **He presided at the meeting,** Presidio la reunión
presidency n presidencia, f
president n presidente, m; (of a college) rector, m. **lady p.,** presidenta, f
presidential a presidencial
press vt prensar; (juice out of) exprimir; (clothes) planchar; (a bell, a hand, and of a shoe, etc.) apretar, Mexico apachurrar; (embrace) dar un abrazo (a); (a stamp, a kiss, etc.) imprimir; (an enemy) hostigar, acosar; (in a game) apretar; (crowd upon) oprimir; (emphasize) insistir en; (urge) instar, instigar; (compel) obligar; apremiar; (oppress) abrumar, agobiar; (paper) satinar; (an advantage) aprovecharse de. **Lola pressed his hand,** Lola le apretó la mano. **Time presses,** El tiempo es breve. **I did not p. the point,** No insistí. **to p. against,** pegar(se) contra. **to p. down,** comprimir; fig agobiar. **to p. for,** exigir, reclamar. **to p. forward, on,** avanzar; seguir el camino, continuar la marcha; (hurry) apretar el paso
press n (pressure) apretón, m; (push) golpe, m; (throng) muchedumbre, f; (of business, etc.) urgencia, f; (apparatus) prensa, f; (printing press and publishing firm) imprenta, f; (cupboard) armario, m. **Associated P.,** Prensa Asociada, f. **freedom of the p.,** libertad de la prensa, f. **in p., in the p.,** en prensa. **in the p. of battle,** en lo más reñido de la batalla. **to go to p.,** entrar en prensa. **p.-agent,** agente de publicidad, m. **p.-box,** tribuna de la prensa, f. **p. clipping, p.-cutting,** recorte de prensa, m. **p.-gallery,** tribuna de la prensa, f. **p.-gang,** ronda de enganche, f. **p.-mark,** número de catálogo, m. **p. proof,** prueba de imprenta, f. **p.-room,** taller de imprenta, m. **p.-stud,** botón automático, m. **p. conference,** rueda de prensa, entrevista de prensa, conferencia de pensa, f
pressing a urgente, apremiante; importuno. n prensado, m, prensadura, f; expresión, f; (of a garment) planchado, m
pressure n presión, f; (of the hand) apretón, m; apremio, m; opresión, f; (weight) peso, m; (force) fuerza, f; urgencia, f. **p.-cooker,** cazuela de presión, olla de presión, f, presto, m. **p.-gauge,** manómetro, m
prestidigitation n prestidigitación, f, juegos de manos, m pl
prestige n prestigio, m
prestigious a prestigiado

presume *vt* presumir; suponer, sospechar; (attempt) pretender. *vi* presumir; tomarse libertades; abusar (de)

presumption *n* presunción, *f*; suposición, *f*; (effrontery) atrevimiento, *m*; insolencia, *f*

presumptive *a* presuntivo; (with heir, etc.) presunto

presumptuous *a* presumido, insolente, presuntuoso; atrevido

presuppose *vt* presuponer

presupposition *n* presuposición, *f*

pretence *n* (claim) pretensión, *f*; afectación, *f*; (simulation) fingimiento, *m*; pretexto, *m*. **false pretences**, apariencias fingidas, *f pl*; engaño, *m*, estafa, *f*. **to make a p. of,** fingir. **under p. of,** bajo pretexto de

pretend *vt* dar como pretexto de; aparentar, fingir, simular, hacer el papel (de). *vi* pretender (a); tener pretensiones (de); ser pretendiente (a); fingir

pretended *a* supuesto, fingido; falso

pretender *n* pretendiente, *m*; hipócrita, *mf*

pretension *n* pretensión, *f*; afectación, simulación, *f*

pretentious *a* pretencioso; (of persons) presumido

pretentiousness *n* pretensiones, *f pl*, lo pretencioso

preterite *n* (tiempo) pretérito, *m*, *a* pretérito, pasado

pretext *n* pretexto, *m*. *vt* pretextar. **under p. of,** bajo pretexto de, so color de

pretty *a* bonito; (of women, children) guapo, mono; (of men) lindo; elegante; excelente; *iron* bueno. *adv* bastante; medianamente; (very) muy; (almost) casi. **p. good,** bastante bueno. **p.-p.,** de muñeca; mono. *n* chuchería, *f*, guapos, *m pl*. **p. ways,** monerías, *f pl*

prevail *vi* prevalecer, predominar; ser la costumbre. **to p. against or over,** triunfar de, vencer (a). **to p. on, upon,** inducir, convencer, persuadir. **to be prevailed upon to,** dejarse persuadir a

prevailing *a* prevaleciente; dominante; predominante, reinante; general; común; (fashionable) en boga

prevalence *n* predominio, *m*; existencia, *f*; (habit) costumbre, *f*; (fashion) boga, *f*

prevalent *a* prevaleciente; predominante; general; común; corriente; (fashionable) en boga

prevaricate *vi* tergiversar; *law* prevaricar

prevaricator *n* tergiversador (-ra)

prevent *vt* evitar; (hinder) impedir (a)

prevention *n* prevención, *f*; (preventive) estorbo, obstáculo, *m*

preventive *a* preventivo. *n* preservativo, *m*

preview *n* vista de antemano, *f*; (of a film) avances, *m pl* (Cuba, Mexico), colas, *f pl*

(Argentina), cortos *m pl* (Venezuela), sinopsis, *f* (Uruguay), tráiler, *m* (Spain)

previous *a* previo, anterior. **p. to,** antes de

previously *adv* anteriormente, antes, previamente

prewar *a* de antes de la guerra

prey *n* presa, *f*; *fig* víctima, *f*; (booty) botín, *m*. *vi* (of animals) devorar; (plunder) robar; pillar; (of sorrow, etc.) hacer presa (de); agobiar, consumir; (sponge on) vivir a costa de. **to fall a p. to,** ser víctima de

price *n* precio, *m*; valor, *m*; costa, *f*. *vt* evaluar, tasar; poner precio a; preguntar el precio de; fijar el precio de. **at any p.,** a cualquier precio; (whatever the cost) cueste lo que cueste. **at a reduced p.,** a precio reducido. **fixed p.,** precio fijo, *m*. **p. ceiling,** precio máximo, precio tope, *m*. **p. control,** control de precios, *m*. **price list,** lista de precios, *f*; tarifa, *f*; (of shares, etc.) boletín de cotización, *m*. **Prices are subject to change without notice,** Los precios están sujetos a variación sin previo aviso.

priceless *a* sin precio; (amusing) divertidísimo. **These jewels are p.,** Estas joyas no tienen precio

prick *n* pinchazo, *m*; picadura, *f*; punzada, *f*; (prickle) espina, *f*; (with a goad) aguijonazo, *m*; (with a pin) alfilerazo, *m*; (with a spur) espolada, *f*; (of conscience) remordimiento, escrúpulo, *m*. *vt* pinchar, punzar; picar; (with remorse) atormentar, causar remordimiento (a); (urge on) incitar. **to p. the ears,** aguzar las orejas

prickle *n* espina, *f*; (irritation) escozor, *m*

prickly *a* espinoso; erizado. **p. heat,** salpullido causado por exceso de calor, *m*. **p. pear,** higo chumbo, *m*, chumbera, *f*

pride *n* orgullo, *m*; arrogancia, *f*; (splendour) pompa, *f*, fausto, aparato, *m*; belleza, *f*; vigor, *m*; (of lions) manada, *f*. **to take p. in,** estar orgulloso de. **to p. oneself,** sentirse orgulloso, ufanarse. **to p. oneself upon,** jactarse de, preciarse de

priest *n* sacerdote, *m*; cura, *m*. **high-p.,** sumo sacerdote, *m*. **p.-ridden,** dominado por el clero

prig *n* fatuo (-ua), mojigato (-ta)

priggish *a* fatuo, gazmoño

prim *a* almidonado, etiquetero; peripuesto; afectado

primacy *n* primacía, *f*

prima donna *n* cantatriz, *f*

primarily *adv* en primer lugar principalmente

primary *a* primario; primitivo; principal. **p. education,** enseñanza primaria, *f*. **p. color,** color primario, *m*. **p. school,** escuela primaria, *f*. **p. election,** elección interna (dentro de un partido), *f*

prime *a* primero; principal; excelente; de primera calidad; de primera clase. *n* (spring) primavera, *f*; (of life, etc.) flor, *f*, primer to **proceed**

666

vigor, *m*; (best) nata, crema, *f*; *ecc* prima, *f*; (number) número primo, *m*. *vt* preparar, aprestar; (fire-arms) cebar. **p. the pump**, cebar la bomba; (with paint, etc.) imprimar; (instruct) dar instrucciones (a), informar. **in his p.**, en la flor de su edad. **of p. quality**, de primera calidad. **P. Minister**, Primer Ministro, *m*. **p. necessity**, artículo de primera necesidad, *m*

primer *n* cartilla, *f*, abecedario, *m*; libro de lectura, *m*; (prayer book) devocionario, *m*

primeval *a* primevo, primitivo

priming *n* preparación, *f*; (of fire-arms) cebo, *m*; (of paint, etc.) imprimación, *f*; instrucción, *f*

primitive *a* primitivo; anticuado. *n* primitivo, *m*

primrose *n* primavera, *f*; color amarillo pálido, *m*

prince *n* príncipe, *m*. **P. Consort**, príncipe consorte, *m*. **P. of Wales**, (Britain) príncipe heredero, *m*; (Spanish equivalent) Príncipe de Asturias, *m*. **p. regent**, príncipe regente, *m*. **P. Charming**, el Príncipe Azul, *m*

princely *a* principesco; magnífico; noble

princess *n* princesa, *f*

principal *a* principal; fundamental; mayor. *n* principal, jefe, *m*; (of a university) rector, *m*; (of a school) director (-ra); *law* causante, *m*; *com* capital, *m*

principle *n* principio, *m*. **in p.**, en principio

print *n* (mark) impresión, marca, *f*; (type) letra de molde, *f*, tipo, *m*; (of books) imprenta, *f*; (fabric) estampado, *m*; (picture) grabado, *m*; (photograph) positiva impresa, *f*; (mold) molde, *m*. *vt* marcar; imprimir; (on the mind) grabar; *print* tirar, hacer una tirada (de); (in photography) tirar una prueba (de); (publish) sacar a luz, publicar; (fabrics) estampar. **in p.**, impreso; publicado; **He likes to see his name in print**, Le gusta ver su nombre en letras de molde; (available) existente. **to be out of p.**, estar agotado. **p. dress**, vestido estampado, *m*

printed *a* impreso. **p. fabric**, estampado, *m*. **p. matter**, impresos, *m pl*

printer *n* impresor, *m*; tipógrafo, *m*. **printer's devil**, aprendiz de impresor, *m*. **printer's ink**, tinta de imprenta, tinta tipográfica, *f*. **printer's mark**, pie de imprenta, *m*

printing *n* imprenta, *f*; impresión, *f*; (of fabrics) estampación, *f*; (art of) tipografía, *f*. **p. house**, imprenta, *f*. **p. machine**, máquina de imprimir, *f*. **p. press**, prensa tipográfica, *f*. **p. types**, caracteres de imprenta, *m pl*

prior *n* prior, *m*, a anterior, previo. **p. to**, anterior a, antes de

priority *n* prioridad, *f*

prism *n* prisma, *m*; espectro solar, *m*

prison *n* prisión, cárcel, *f*. **p.-breaking**,

huida de la prisión, *f*. **p. camp**, campo de prisioneros, *m*. **p. van**, coche celular, *m*. **p. yard**, patio de la prisión, *m*

prisoner *n* prisionero (-ra), preso (-sa). **to take p.**, prender, hacer prisionero (a)

pristine *a* pristino, original

privacy *n* soledad, *f*, aislamiento, retiro, *m*; intimidad, *f*; secreto, *m*

private *a* particular; privado; secreto; confidencial; reservado; íntimo; personal; doméstico; (of hearings, etc.) a puertas cerradas, secreto; (own) propio. *n* (soldier) soldado raso, *m*. **in p.**, en secreto; confidencialmente; de persona a persona. **They wish to be p.**, Quieren estar a solas. **p. company**, sociedad en comandita, *f*. **p. hotel**, pensión, *f*. **p. house**, casa particular, *f*. **p. individual**, particular, *mf*. **p. interview**, entrevista privada, *f*. **p. life**, vida privada, *f*. **p. office**, despacho particular, *m*. **p. secretary**, secretario (-ia) particular. **p. viewing, (of a film)** función privada, *f*; **(of an exhibition)** día de inauguración, *m*

privately *adv* privadamente; en secreto; personalmente; confidencialmente; (of hearings) a puertas cerradas

privation *n* privación, *f*; carencia, escasez, *f*

privilege *n* privilegio, *m*; derecho, *m*; inmunidad, *f*. *vt* privilegiar

privy *a* privado; cómplice; enterado; personal, particular. *n* (latrine) retrete, *m*. **p. council**, consejo privado, *m*

prize *n* premio, *m*; recompensa, *f*, galardón, *m*; (capture) presa, *f*. *a* que ha ganado un premio; premiado; (huge) enorme; (complete) de primer orden. *vt* estimar, apreciar. **to p. open**, abrir con una palanca. **to carry off the p.**, ganar el premio. **cash p.**, premio en metálico, *m*. **first p.**, primer premio, *m*; (in a lottery) premio gordo, *m*. **p. court**, tribunal de presas, *m*. **p. fight**, partido de boxeo, *m*. **p. fighter**, boxeador, *m*. **p. giving**, distribución de premios, *f*. **p. money**, premio en metálico, *m*; (boxing) bolsa, *f*

probability *n* probabilidad, *f*

probable *a* probable

probate *n* verificación de un testamento, *f*

probation *n* probación, *f*; *law* libertad vigilada, *f*

probe *n surg* sonda, cala, tienta, *f*. *vt surg* tentar; escudriñar

probity *n* probidad, integridad, *f*

problem *n* problema, *m*; cuestión, *f*. **p. play**, drama de tesis, *m*

problematic *a* problemático

problem child *n* niño problemático, *m* (male), niña problemática, *f* (female)

proboscis *n* (of an elephant) trompa, *f*; (of an insect) trompetilla, *f*

procedure *n* procedimiento, *m*

proceed *vi* seguir el camino, continuar la

marcha; avanzar, seguir adelante; ir; proceder; ponerse (a); empezar (a); (say) proseguir; (come to) llegar a, ir a; (of a play, etc.) desarrollarse. **Before we p. any further . . .** Antes de ir más lejos . . . **to p. to blows,** llegar a las manos. **to p. against,** proceder contra, procesar. **to p. from,** venir de. **to p. with,** proseguir; poner por obra; usar

proceeding n modo de obrar, m; conducta, f; procedimiento, m; transacción, f; pl **proceedings,** (measures) medidas, f pl, actos, m pl; (of a learned society or a conference) actas, f pl. **to take proceedings against,** law procesar

proceeds n pl producto, m; ganancias, f pl; beneficios, m pl. **net p.,** producto neto, m

process n proceso, m; (method) procedimiento, m; (course) curso, m; marcha, f; (law zool) proceso, m. vt beneficiar (ore), trasformar, elaborar. **in p. of,** en curso de. **in the p. of time,** con el tiempo marchando el tiempo

processing industry n industria de trasformación, industria de elaboración, f

procession n desfile, m; cortejo, m; (religious) procesión, f. **funeral p.,** cortejo fúnebre, m. **to walk in p.,** desfilar

proclaim vt proclamar; publicar, pregonar; anunciar; (reveal) revelar; (outlaw) denunciar

proclamation n proclamación, f; proclama, f, anuncio, m; declaración, f

proclivity n proclividad, propensión, f

procrastinate vi tardar (en decidirse), aplazar su decisión; vacilar; perder el tiempo

procrastination n dilación, tardanza, f; vacilación, f; pereza, f

procreate vt procrear

procreation n procreación, f

proctor n procurador, m; univ censor, m

procurable a procurable; asequible

procure vt obtener, conseguir, lograr

procurement n obtención, f, logro, m

procurer n alcahuete, m

prod n (with a bayonet, etc.) punzada, f; fig pinchazo, m. vt punzar; (in the ribs, etc.) clavar; fig pinchar

prodigal a and n pródigo (-ga)

prodigious a prodigioso

prodigy n prodigio, m; portento, m. **child p.,** niño prodigio

produce vt producir; dar frutos; (show) mostrar, presentar; (take out) sacar; (occasion) causar, traer consigo, ocasionar; (goods) fabricar, manufacturar; (of shares, etc.) rendir; geom prolongar; (a play) poner en escena. n producto, m; víveres, comestibles, m pl

producer n productor (-ra); theat director de escena, m

product n producto, m; (result) fruto,

resultado, m, consecuencia, f; math producto, m

production n producción, f; producto, m; geom prolongación, f; (of a play) dirección escénica, f; (performance) producción, f. **p. cost,** coste de producción, m

productive a productivo

profane a profano; sacrílego, blasfemo. vt profanar

profanity n profanidad, f; blasfemia, f

profess vt (assert) afirmar, manifestar; declarar; (a faith, a profession, teach) profesar; (feign) fingir; (pretend) tener pretensiones de. vi (as a monk or nun) tomar estado, entrar en religión. **He professed himself surprised,** Se declaró sorprendido

professed a declarado; ecc profeso; ostensible, fingido

profession n profesión, f; carrera, f; declaración, f. **p. of faith,** profesión de fe, f. **the learned professions,** las carreras liberales

professional a profesional; de la profesión; de profesión; de carrera. **p. diplomat,** diplomático (-ca) de carrera. **p. etiquette,** etiqueta profesional, f. **p. man,** hombre profesional, m; hombre de carrera liberal, m

professor n catedrático (-ca), profesor (-ra)

professorship n cátedra, f

proffer vt proponer; ofrecer. n oferta, f

proficiency n pericia, habilidad, f

proficient a proficiente, experto, adepto, perito

profile n perfil, m. vt perfilar. **in p.,** de perfil

profit n provecho, m; utilidad, f; ventaja, f; com ganancia, f, vt aprovechar. vi ganar; com sacar ganancia. **to p. by,** aprovechar. **gross p.,** ganancia total, f. **p. and loss,** ganancias y pérdidas, f pl. **p. sharing,** participación en las ganancias, participación de utilidades, f

profitable a provechoso, útil, ventajoso; lucrativo. **p. use,** aprovechamiento, m

profitably adv con provecho, provechosamente; lucrativamente

profiteer n estraperlista, mf

profit incentive n acicate del lucro, m

profligate a licencioso, disoluto. n libertino, m

profound a profundo

profundity n profundidad, f

profuse a profuso; pródigo; lujoso

profusion n profusión, abundancia, f; prodigalidad, f; exceso, m

progenitor n progenitor, m; (ancestor) antepasado, m

progeny n prole, f

prognosis n prognosis, f; presagio, m; med pronóstico, m

prognosticate *vt* pronosticar, presagiar

program *n* programa, *m*

progress *n* progreso, *m*; avance, *m*; (betterment) mejora, *f*; (of events) marcha, *f*. *vi* avanzar, marchar; (improve) progresar, adelantar; mejorar. **to make p.,** adelantarse; hacer progresos

progression *n* progresión, *f*

progressive *a* progresivo; avanzado; *pol* progresista. *n pol* progresista, *mf*

prohibit *vt* prohibir; defender; (prevent) impedir, privar. **His health prohibited him from doing it,** Su salud le impidió hacerlo

prohibition *n* prohibición, *f*; interdicción, *f*; (of alcohol) prohibicionismo, *m*

prohibitive *a* prohibitivo, prohibitorio

project *vt* (all meanings) proyectar. *vi* sobresalir; destacarse. *n* proyectil, plan, *m*

projectile *n* proyectil, *m*, a arrojadizo

projecting *a* saliente, (of teeth) saltón

projection *n* (hurling) lanzamiento, *m*; prominencia, protuberancia, *f*; (other meanings) proyección, *f*

projector *n* proyectista, *mf*; proyector, *m*

proletarian *a* proletario

proletariate *n* proletariado, *m*

prolific *a* prolífico; fecundo, fértil

prolix *a* prolijo

prolog *n* prólogo, *m*, *vt* prologar

prolong *vt* prolongar

promenade *n* paseo, *m*; bulevar, *m*; avenida, *f*. *vi* pasearse. *vt* recorrer, andar por, pasearse por. **p. deck,** cubierta de paseo, *f*

prominence *n* prominencia, *f*; protuberancia, *f*; eminencia, *f*; importancia, *f*

prominent *a* prominente, saliente; (of eyes, teeth) saltón; (distinguished) eminente, distinguido. **They placed the vase in a p. position,** Pusieron el florero muy a la vista. **to play a p. part,** desempeñar un papel importante. **p. eyes, ojos** saltones, *m pl*

promiscuous *a* promiscuo

promise *n* promesa, *f*; (hope) esperanza, *f*; (word) palabra, *f*; (future) porvenir, *m*. *vt* and *vi* prometer. **a young man of p.,** un joven de porvenir. **to break one's p.,** faltar a su palabra; no cumplir una promesa. **to keep one's p.,** guardar su palabra; cumplir su promesa. **to p. and do nothing,** apuntar y no dar. **under p. of,** bajo palabra de. **p. of marriage,** palabra de matrimonio, *f*

promised *a* prometido. **P. Land,** Tierra de promisión, *f*

promising *a* que promete bien, que promete mucho; prometedor; (of the future, etc.) halagüeño; (of persons) que llegará

promissory *a* promisorio. **p. note,** pagaré, abonaré, *m*

promontory *n* promontorio, *m*

promote *vt* fomentar, promover; provo-

car; (aid) favorecer, proteger; avanzar; estimular; (to a post) ascender; (an act bill) promover; *com* negociar

promoter *n* promotor (-ra); instigador (-ra); (*theat* etc.) empresario, *m*

promotion *n* (encouragement) fomento, *m*; (furtherance) adelanto, *m*; protección, *f*, favorecimiento, *m*; (in employment, etc.) promoción, *f*, ascenso, *m*; (of a company, etc.) creación, *f*

prompt *a* pronto; diligente; presuroso; puntual; rápido; *com* inmediato. *vt* impulsar, incitar, mover; dictar; insinuar; *theat* apuntar; (remind) recordar. **He came at five o'clock p.,** Vino a las cinco en punto. **p. book,** libro del traspunte, *m*. **p. box,** concha (del apuntador), *f*

prompter *n theat* apuntador, (in the wings) traspunte, *m*

prompting *n* sugestión, *f*; instigación, *f*; *pl* **promptings,** impulso, *m*; (of the heart, etc.) dictados, *m pl*

promptly *adv* inmediatamente, en seguida; con prontitud, con celeridad; puntualmente

promulgate *vt* promulgar; divulgar, diseminar

promulgation *n* promulgación, *f*; divulgación, diseminación, *f*

prone *a* postrado; inclinado, propenso

prong *n* (pitchfork) horquilla, *f*; (of a fork) diente, *m*, púa, *f*

pronged *a* dentado, con púas

pronoun *n* pronombre, *m*

pronounce *vt* pronunciar; declarar; articular

pronounced *a* marcado; perceptible; bien definido

pronunciation *n* pronunciación, *f*; articulación, *f*

proof *n* prueba, *f*; demostración, *f*; ensayo, *m*; *law* testimonio, *m*; (*phot print*) prueba, *f*; *math* comprobación, *f*, a hecho a prueba (de); impenetrable (a); *flg* insensible (a). *vt* (raincoats, etc.) impermeabilizar. **in p. whereof,** en fe de lo cual. **p. against bombs,** a prueba de bombas. **p. reading,** corrección de pruebas, *f*

prop *n* apoyo, puntal, estribadero, *m*; (for a tree) horca, *f*, rodrigón, *m*; *naut* escora, *f*; *flg* báculo, *m*, columna, *f*, apoyo, *m*. *vt* apoyar; apuntalar; (a tree) ahorquillar; (a building) acodalar; *naut* escorar; *flg* sostener. **He propped himself against the wall,** Se apoyó en el muro, Se arrimó al muro

propaganda *n* propaganda, *f*

propagandist *n* propagandista, *mf*

propagate *vt* propagar. *vi* propagarse

propagation *n* propagación, *f*

propel *vt* propulsar, empujar, mover

propeller *n* propulsor, *m*; *mech* hélice, *f*

propensity *n* propensión, tendencia, inclinación, *f*

proper *a* propio; apropiado; correcto; decente; (prim) afectado; serio, formal; (exact) justo, exacto; (suitable (for)) bueno (para), apto (para); (true) verdadero; (characteristic) peculiar; *her* natural; (with rascal, etc.) redomado; (handsome) guapo. **If you think it p.,** Si te parece bien. **p. noun,** nombre propio, *m*

properly *adv* decentemente; correctamente; propiamente; bien. **to do (a thing) p.,** hacer algo bien. **p. speaking,** propiamente dicho, hablando con propiedad

propertied *a* propietario, hacendado; (rich) pudiente, adinerado

property *n* propiedad, *f*; (belongings) bienes, *m pl*; posesiones, *f pl*; (estate) hacienda, *f*; (quality) cualidad, *f*; *pl* **properties,** *theat* accesorios, *m pl.* **personal p.,** bienes muebles, *m pl*; cosas personales, *f pl.* **real p.,** bienes raíces, *m pl.* **p. man,** *theat* encargado de los accesorios, *m.* **p. owner,** propietario (-ia). **p. tax,** contribución sobre la propiedad, *f*

prophecy *n* profecía, *f*; predicción, *f*

prophesy *vt* profetizar; presagiar, predecir. *vi* hacer profecías

prophet *n* profeta, *m*

prophetic *a* profético

prophylactic *a and n* profiláctico, *m*

propinquity *n* propincuidad, proximidad, *f*; (relationship) parentesco, *m*

propitiate *vt* propiciar; apaciguar, conciliar

propitious *a* propicio, favorable

proportion *n* proporción, *f*; parte, *f*; porción, *f*; *pl* **proportions,** proporciones, *f pl*; dimensiones, *f pl. vt* proporcionar; repartir, distribuir. **in p.,** en proporción; conforme (a), según; *com* a prorrata. **in p. as,** a medida que. **out of p.,** desproporcionado. **He has lost all sense of p.,** Ha perdido su equilibrio (mental)

proportional *a* proporcional; en proporción (a); proporcionado (a). **p. representation,** representación proporcional, *f*

proportionate *a* proporcionado; proporcional. *vt* proporcionar

proposal *n* proposición, *f*; oferta, *f*; (plan) propósito, proyecto, *m.* **p. of marriage,** oferta de matrimonio, *f*

propose *vt* proponer; ofrecer; (a toast) dar, brindar. *vi* pretender, intentar, tener la intención de; pensar; (marriage) declararse

proposer *n* proponente, *m*; (of a motion) autor (-ra) de una proposición

proposition *n* proposición, *f*; (plan) proyecto, propósito, *m*

propound *vt* proponer; plantear, presentar

proprietary *a* propietario; de propiedad

proprietor *n* propietario, *m*; dueño, *m*

propriety *n* decoro, *m*; conveniencia, *f*; corrección, *f*

propulsion *n* propulsión, *f*

prorogation *n* prorrogación, *f*

prorogue *vt* prorrogar, suspender (la sesión de una asamblea legislativa)

pros and cons el pro y el contra

prosaic *a* prosaico

proscenium *n* proscenio, *m*

proscribe *vt* proscribir

proscription *n* proscripción, *f*

prose *n* prosa, *f.* **p. writer,** prosista, *mf*

prosecute *vt* proseguir, llevar adelante; (*law* a person) procesar; (*law* a claim) pedir en juicio

prosecution *n* prosecución, *f*; cumplimiento, *m*; *law* acusación, *f*; (*law* party) parte actora, *f.* **in the p. of his duty,** en el cumplimiento de su deber

prosecutor *n* demandante, actor, *m.* **public p.,** fiscal, *m*

proselyte *n* prosélito, *m*

prose writer *n* prosador, *m*

prospect *n* perspectiva, *f*; esperanza, *f*; probabilidad, *f*; (in mining) indicio de filón, *m*; criadero (de oro, etc.), *m. vi* explorar; (of a mine) prometer (bien), dar buenas esperanzas. *vt* explorar, inspeccionar; examinar. **He is a man with good prospects,** Es un hombre de porvenir

prospecting *n* la prospección, *f*

prospective *a* en expectativa, futuro; previsor

prospector *n* explorador, operador, *m*

prospectus *n* prospecto, programa, *m*

prosper *vi* prosperar. *vt* favorecer, prosperar

prosperity *n* prosperidad, *f*

prosperous *a* próspero; favorable

prostate *n* próstata, *f*

prostitute *n* prostituta, *f, vt* prostituir

prostitution *n* prostitución, *f*

prostrate *a* tendido; postrado; abatido. *vt* derribar; arruinar; (by grief, etc.) postrar; (oneself) prosternarse

prostration *n* postración, *f*; abatimiento, *m.* **nervous p.,** neurastenia, *f*

prosy *a* aburrido, árido; pedestre, prosaico; verboso, prolijo

protagonist *n* protagonista, *mf*

protean *a* proteico

protect *vt* proteger

protection *n* protección, *f*; defensa, *f*; garantía, *f*; abrigo, *m*; refugio, *m*; (passport) salvoconducto, *m*; *pol* proteccionismo, *m*

protective *a* protector; *pol* proteccionista

protector *n* protector, *m*

protein *n* proteína, *f*

protest *vt* protestar; *law* hacer el protesto de una letra de cambio. *vi* declarar; insistir (en); hacer una protesta. *n* protesta, *f*; *law* protesto, *m.* **under p.,** bajo protesta. **to p. against,** protestar contra

Protestant a and n protestante, mf

Protestantism n protestantismo, m

protestation n protestación, f

protester n el, m, (f, la) que protesta

protest literature n literatura de denuncia, f

protocol n protocolo, m, vt protocolizar

protoplasm n protoplasma, m

prototype n prototipo, m

protract vt prolongar; dilatar

protracted a prolongado; largo

protraction n prolongación, f

protractor n (geom and surv) transportador, m. **p. muscle,** músculo extensor, m

protrude vt sacar fuera. vi salir fuera; sobresalir

protuberance n protuberancia, f

protuberant a protuberante, prominente

proud a orgulloso; arrogante; noble; glorioso; magnífico; soberbio, Mexico alzado. **to be p.,** enorgullecerse. **to make p.,** enorgullecer; hacer orgulloso. **to be p. of,** ser orgulloso de, pagarse de, gloriarse en. **p. flesh,** carnosidad, f, bezo, m

proudly adv con orgullo, orgullosamente

prove vt probar; demostrar; (experience) experimentar, sufrir; poner a prueba; (a will) verificar; (show) mostrar; confirmar. vi resultar, salir (bien or mal)

provenance n origen, m

proverb n refrán, m; proverbio, m. **collection of proverbs,** refranero, m. **Book of Proverbs,** Proverbios, m pl

proverbial a proverbial

provide vt proporcionar, dar; proveer, surtir, suplir; (stipulate) estipular; preparar (por); tomar precauciones (contra); sufragar los gastos (de); proporcionar medios de vida (a); señalar una pensión (a). **to p. oneself with,** proveerse de

provided (that) conjunc si; a condición de que, siempre que, con tal que

providence n providencia, f

provident a próvido, previsor, prudente; económico

providential a providencial

providently adv próvidamente, prudentemente

provider n proveedor (-ra)

province n provincia, f; esfera, f; función, incumbencia, f

provincial a provincial, de provincia; provinciano. n provinciano (-na); ecc provincial, m

provincialism n provincialismo, m

provision n provisión, f; (stipulation) estipulación, f; pl **provisions,** provisiones, f pl; víveres, comestibles, m pl. vt abastecer, aprovisionar. **to make p. for,** hacer provisión para, proveer de. **to make p. for one's family,** asegurar el porvenir de su familia. **p. merchant,** vendedor (-ra) de comestibles

provisional a provisional, interino

proviso n condición, estipulación, disposición, f

provocation n provocación, f

provocative a provocativo, provocador

provoke vt provocar; suscitar; incitar, excitar; (irritate) sacar de madre (a), indignar

provoker n provocador (-ra); instigador (-ra)

provoking a provocativo; (irritating) enojoso, irritante

provost n preboste, m; (of a college) director, m; (in Scotland) alcalde, m. **p.-marshal,** capitán preboste, m

prow n proa, f

prowess n valor, m, destreza, f; proeza, f

prowl vi and vt rondar; cazar al acecho

prowler n rondador (-ra); ladrón (-ona)

proximity n proximidad, Argentina adyacencia, f

proximo adv en (or del) mes próximo

proxy n poder, m; delegación, f; apoderado, m; delegado (-da); substituto (-ta). **to be married by p.,** casarse por poderes

prude n mojigata, beata, f

prudence n prudencia, f

prudent a prudente

prudently adv con prudencia

prudery n mojigatería, beatería, damería, gazmoñería, f

prudish a mojigato, gazmoño, remilgado

prune n ciruela pasa, f; color de ciruela, m, vt podar; (cut) cortar; reducir

pruning n poda, f; reducción, f. **p. knife,** podadera, f

prurient a lascivo, lujurioso, salaz

pry vi escudriñar; acechar, espiar, fisgonear; (meddle) entremeterse, meterse donde no le llaman. vt See **prize**

prying n fisgoneo, m; curiosidad, f, a fisgón, curioso

psalm n salmo, m. **to sing psalms,** salmodiar

psalmist n salmista, m

pseudo- a seudo. **p.-learned,** erudito a la violeta

pseudonym n seudónimo, m

psychiatrist n siquiatra, m

psychiatry n siquiatría, f

psychic a síquico

psychoanalysis n sicoanálisis, mf

psychoanalyst n sicoanalista, mf

psychoanalyze vt sicoanalizar

psychological a sicológico

psychologist n sicólogo (-ga)

psychology n sicología, f

psychopathic a sicopático

psychosis n sicosis, f

psychotherapy n sicoterapia, f

ptomaine poisoning n intoxicación por tomaínas, f

puberty n pubertad, f

pubescent a púber

pubic a púbico

public a and n público m. **in p.,** en público. **p. assistance,** asistencia pública, f. **p. funds,** hacienda pública, f. **p. health,** higiene pública, f. **p.-house,** taberna, f. **p. opinion,** opinión pública, f. inf el qué dirán. **p.-spirited,** patriótico. **p. thoroughfare,** vía pública, f. **p. works,** obras públicas, f pl

publication n publicación, f

publicist n publicista, mf

publicity n publicidad, f

publicity agent n publicista, mf

publish vt publicar, divulgar, difundir; (a book, etc.) dar a luz, dar a la prensa, publicar; (of a publisher) editar. **to p. abroad,** pregonar a los cuatro vientos. **to p. banns of marriage,** correr las amonestaciones

publisher n publicador (-ra); (of books) editor (-ra)

publishing n publicación, f. **p. house,** casa editorial, f. **the p. world,** el mundo de la edición, m

puck n trasgo, m; diablillo, picaruelo, m

pucker vt (one's brow, etc.) fruncir; (crease) arrugar. vi arrugarse. n frunce, m; arruga, f; (fold) bolsa, f

puckish a travieso

pudding n pudín, budín, m. **black p.,** morcilla, f

puddle n charco, m

puerile a pueril

puerperal a puerperal. **p. fever,** fiebre puerperal, f

Puerto Rican a and n puertorriqueño (-ña), a boricua, n borinqueño (-ña)

puff vt and vi (blow) soplar; (at a pipe, etc.) chupar; (smoke) lanzar bocanadas de humo; (make pant) hacer jadear; (advertise) dar bombo (a); (distend) hinchar; (make conceited) envanecerse; (of a train, etc.) bufar; resoplar. n soplo, m; (of smoke, etc.) bocanada, f; (of an engine, etc.) resoplido, bufido, m; (for powder) borla (para polvos), f; (pastry) bollo, m; (advertisement) bombo, m. **to be puffed up,** fig hincharse, inflarse. **p. of wind,** ráfaga de aire, f. **p.-ball,** bejín, m. **p.-pastry,** hojaldre, m, or f. **p.-sleeve,** manga de bullón, f

puffy a (of the wind) a ráfagas; (panting) jadeante; (swollen) hinchado

pug n (dog) doguino, m. **p.-nosed,** de nariz respingona

pugilist n pugilista, mf, boxeador, m

pugnacious a pugnaz, belicoso

pugnacity n pugnacidad, belicosidad, f

pull n tirón, m; sacudida, f; golpe, m;

(row) paseo en barco, m; (with the oars) golpe (de remos), m; (at a bell) tirón, m; (bell-rope) tirador, m; (at a bottle) trago, m; (strain) fuerza, f; atracción, f; (struggle) lucha, f; (advantage) ventaja, f; (influence) influencia, f, Central America, Mexico arranque m, **to give a p.,** tirar (de), dar un tirón (a). **to have plenty of p.,** inf tener buenas aldabas

pull vt tirar (de); (drag) arrastrar; (extract) sacar; (a boat) remar; (gather) coger; print imprimir. **He pulled the trigger (of his gun),** Apretó el gatillo. **He was sitting by the fire pulling at his pipe,** Estaba sentado cerca del fuego fumando su pipa. **to p. a hat well down on the head,** calarse el sombrero. **to p. a person's leg,** tomar el pelo (a). **to p. oneself together,** componer el semblante, serenarse; recobrar el aplomo; (tidy oneself) arreglarse. **to p. apart,** vt separar; romper en dos. vi separarse; romperse en dos. **to p. away,** vt arrancar; quitar. vi tirar con esfuerzo. **to p. back,** tirar hacia atrás; hacer retroceder (a); retener. **to p. down,** hacer bajar, obligar a bajar; (objects) bajar; (buildings) derribar, demoler; (humble) humillar; degradar; (weaken) debilitar. **to p. in,** tirar hacia dentro; hacer entrar; (a horse) enfrenar; (expenditure) reducir. **to p. off,** arrancar; (clothes) quitarse; (a deal) cerrar (un trato), concluir con éxito; (win) ganar. **to p. on,** vt (gloves, etc.) meterse, ponerse. vi seguir remando. **to p. open,** abrir; abrir rápidamente. **to p. out,** hacer salir; obligar a salir; (teeth, daggers, etc.) sacar; (hair) arrancar. **to p. round, through,** vt ayudar a reponerse (a); sacar de un aprieto. vi restablecerse; reponerse, cobrar la salud, sanar. **to p. together,** obrar de acuerdo; (get on) llevarse (bien or mal). **He pulled himself together very quickly,** Se repuso muy pronto. **to p. up,** vt montar, subir; (a horse) sofrenar; (stop) parar; (by the root) desarraigar, extirpar; (interrupt) interrumpir; (scold) reñir. vi parar(se); (restrain oneself) reprimirse, contenerse

pullet n polla, f

pulley n polea, f; naut garrucha, f. **p. wheel,** roldana, f

pulling n tracción, f; tirada, f; arranque, m

pullover n jersey, m, Lat. Am. chompa, f

pulmonary a pulmonar

pulp n pulpa, f; (of fruit) carne, f; (paper) pasta, f; (of teeth) bulbo dentario, m. vt reducir a pulpa; deshacer (el papel). **to beat to a p.,** inf poner como un pulpo

pulpit n púlpito, m

pulsate vi pulsar, latir

pulsation n pulsación, f, latido, m

pulse n pulso, m; pulsación, f, latido, m; vibración, f; (vegetable) legumbre, f, vi pulsar, latir; vibrar. **to take a person's p.,** tomar el pulso (a)

pulverize vt pulverizar

pumice n piedra pómez, f

pummel vt aporrear

pump n mech bomba, f; (for water, etc.) aguatocha, f; naut pompa, f; (slipper) escarpín, m, vt bombear, extraer por medio de una bomba; (inflate) inflar; (for information) sondear, sonsacar. **hand-p.,** bomba de mano, f. **to work a p.,** darle a la bomba

pumpkin n calabaza, f, Central America ayote, m, Chile zapallo, m; (plant) calabacera, f

pun n retruécano, m

punch n (drink) ponche, m; (blow) puñetazo, golpe, m; mech punzón, m; (for tickets, etc.) taladro, m; inf fuerza, f. vt (perforate) taladrar, punzar; estampar; (hit) dar un puñetazo (a). **p.-ball,** pelota de boxeo, f. **p.-bowl,** ponchera, f

punctilious a formal, puntual, puntilloso

punctual a puntual

punctuate vt puntuar

punctuation n puntuación, f

puncture n pinchazo, m; perforación, f; surg punción, f. vt pinchar; perforar; punzar. **We have a p. in the right tire,** Tenemos un pinchazo en el neumático derecho

pungency n picante, m; acerbidad, mordacidad, f

pungent a picante; acerbo, mordaz

punish vt castigar; maltratar

punishable a punible

punishment n castigo, m; pena, f; maltrato, m

punitive a punitivo

puny a débil, encanijado; insignificante; pequeño

pup n cachorro (-rra). vi parir la perra

pupil n alumno (-na), discípulo (-la); (of the eye) pupila, niña (del ojo), f; law pupilo (-la). a escolar. **day p.,** alumno (-na) externo (-na). **p. teacher,** maestro (-tra) alumno (-na)

puppet n títere, m, marioneta, f; muñeca, f; (person) maniquí, m. **p. show,** función de títeres, f. **p. showman,** titiritero, titerero, m

puppy n perrito (-ta), cachorro (-rra)

purblind a ciego; (short-sighted and fig) miope

purchasable a comprable, que puede comprarse; fig sobornable

purchase vt comprar; adquirir; fig lograr, conseguir. n compra, f; adquisición, f; mech apalancamiento, m; fuerza, f; (lever) palanca, f, aparejo, m; fig influencia, f. **p. tax,** impuesto de lujo, m

purchaser n comprador (-ra)

purchasing n See **purchase. p. power,** poder de adquisición, m

pure a puro. **p.-bred,** de raza

purgative a purgativo. n purga, f

purgatory n purgatorio, m

purge n purgación, f; (laxative) purga, f; pol depuración, f; purificación, f. vt purgar; pol depurar; purificar; expurgar

purging n purgación, f; pol depuración, f; flg purificación, f

purifier n purificador (-ra)

purify vt purificar; (metals) acrisolar; refinar; depurar; (purge) purgar

purist n purista, mf

puritan a and n puritano (-na)

purity n pureza, f

purl vi (of a stream, etc.) murmurar, susurrar. n (of a stream, etc.) susurro, murmullo, m

purlieu n límite, m; pl **purlieus,** alrededores, m pl, inmediaciones, f pl; (slums) barrios bajos, m pl

purling a murmurante, que susurra, parlero. n murmullo, susurro, m

purloin vt hurtar, robar

purple n púrpura, f, a purpúreo. vt purpurar, teñir de púrpura. vi purpurear

purport vt dar a entender, querer decir; significar; indicar; parecer; tener el objeto de; pretender. n importe, m; sentido, significado, m; objeto, m

purpose n objeto, m; propósito, fin, m; intención, f; proyecto, m; designio, m; determinación, voluntad, f; efecto, m; ventaja, utilidad, f, vi and vt proponerse; pensar, tener el propósito (de), intentar. **It will serve my p.,** Servirá para lo que yo quiero. **for the p. of . . . ,** con el propósito de . . . , con el fin de . . . for purposes of . . . para efectos de . . . **on p.,** de propósito, expresamente, Central America adifés. **to no p.,** inútilmente; en vano

purposeful a resuelto; de substancia

purposeless a irresoluto, vacilante, vago; sin objeto; inútil

purposely adv expresamente, de intento

purr vi ronronear. n ronroneo, m

purse n bolsa, f; monedero, portamonedas, m. **to p. one's lips,** apretar los labios

purser n naut contador, sobrecargo, Argentina comisario, m. **purser's office,** contaduría, f

pursuance n cumplimiento, desempeño, m, prosecución, f. **in p. of,** en cumplimiento de; en consecuencia de

pursuant a and adv según; conforme (a), de acuerdo (con); en consecuencia (de)

pursue vt perseguir; seguir; (search) buscar; (hunt) cazar; (a submarine, etc.) dar caza (a); (continue) proseguir, continuar; (an occupation) dedicarse (a), ejercer

pursuer n perseguidor (-ra)

pursuit n perseguimiento, m; (search) busca, f; (hunt) caza, f; (performance) prosecución, f, desempeño, m; (employment) ocupación, f. **in p. of,** en busca de. **p. plane,** avión de caza, m

purulent a purulento

purvey vt proveer, surtir, suministrar; abastecer; procurar

purveyance n suministro, abastecimiento, m; provisión, f

purveyor n suministrador (-ra), proveedor (-ra), bastecedor (-ra)

pus n pus, m

push n empujón, m; empellón, m; impulso, m; ' (of a person) empuje, m, energía, f; (attack) ataque, m; ofensiva, f; (effort) esfuerzo, m; crisis, f, momento crítico, m. **at a push**, inf en caso de necesidad; en un aprieto, si llegara el caso. **to give the p. to**, inf despedir. **p.-bicycle**, bicicleta, f. **p.-button**, botón, m; botón de llamada, m. **p.-cart**, carretilla de mano, f; (child's) cochecito de niño, m

push vt empujar; (jostle) empellar, dar empellones (a); (a finger in one's eye, etc.) clavar; (a button) apretar; (fig a person) proteger, ayudar; dar publicidad (a); (a claim, etc.) insistir en; (compel) obligar. vi empujar; dar empujones, empellar. **I am pushed for time**, Me falta tiempo. **He is pushed for money**, Está apurado por dinero. **I have pushed my finger in my eye**, Me he clavado el dedo en el ojo. **to p. against**, empujar contra; lanzarse contra; empellar, dar empellones (a). **to p. aside, away**, apartar con la mano; rechazar, alejar. **to p. back**, (hair, etc.) echar hacia atrás; (people) hacer retroceder; rechazar. **to p. by**, pasar. **to p. down**, hacer bajar; hacer caer; (demolish) derribar. **to p. forward**, vt empujar hacia delante, hacer avanzar; (a plan, etc.) llevar adelante. vi adelantarse a empujones; avanzar; seguir el camino. **to p. oneself forward**, fig abrirse camino; entremeterse; darse importancia. **to p. in**, vt empujar; hacer entrar; clavar, hincar. vi entrar a la fuerza; entremeterse. **to p. off**, vt apartar con la mano (a); inf quitar de encima (a). vi naut desatracar; inf ponerse en camino. **to p. open**, empujar, abrir. **to p. out**, vt empujar hacia fuera; hacer salir; echar. vi naut zarpar. **to p. through**, vt (business, etc.) despachar rápidamente; (a crowd) abrirse camino por. vi aparecer, mostrarse. **to p. to**, cerrar. **to p. up**, empujar; hacer subir; (windows, etc.) levantar. **be pushing up the daises**, mirar los árboles de raíz

pushing a enérgico, emprendedor; ambicioso; agresivo. **by p. and shoving**, a empellones, a empujones

pusillanimous a pusilánime

pustule n pústula, f

put vt poner; colocar; (pour out) echar; aplicar; emplear; (estimate) calcular; presentar; (ask) preguntar; (say) decir; (express) expresar; (a question) hacer; (a problem) plantear; (the weight) lanzar; (rank) estimar. **As the Spanish put it,**
Como dicen los españoles. **If I may put it so,** Si puedo expresarlo así, Por así decirlo. **hard put to it,** en dificultades, apurado. **How will you put it to her?** ¿Cómo se lo vas a explicar a ella? **to put ashore,** echar en tierra (a). **to put a child to bed,** acostar a un niño. **to put in order,** arreglar; ordenar, Lat. Am. acotejar. **to put out of joint,** dislocar. **to put out of order,** estropear. **to put to death,** matar; (judicially) ajusticiar. **to put about,** vt (a rumor) diseminar, divulgar; (worry) preocupar. vi naut virar, cambiar de rumbo **to put a roof on** = **roof** vt. **to put aside,** poner a un lado; descartar; (omit) omitir, pasar por alto de; (fears, etc.) desechar. **to put away,** quitar; guardar; poner en salvo; arrinconar; (thoughts) desechar, ahuyentar; (save) ahorrar; (banish) despedir, alejar; (a wife) repudiar, divorciar; (food) tragar. **to put back,** vt echar hacia atrás; hacer retroceder; (replace) devolver, restituir; (the clock) retrasar; (retard) retardar, atrasar. vi volver; naut volver a puerto. **to put down,** depositar; poner en el suelo; (the blinds) bajar; (an umbrella) cerrar; (a rebellion) sofocar; (gambling, etc.) suprimir; (humble) abatir, humillar; degradar; (silence) hacer callar; (reduce) reducir, disminuir; (write) apuntar, anotar; (a name) inscribir; (to an account) poner a la cuenta de; (estimate) juzgar, creer; (impute) atribuir. **The book is so interesting that it's hard to put down,** El libro es tan interesante que es difícil dejarlo. **to put forth,** (leaves, flowers, sun's rays) echar; (a book) publicar, dar a luz; (a hand) alargar; (an arm) extender; (show) manifestar, mostrar; (strength, etc.) desplegar; (use) emplear. **to put forward,** avanzar; (a clock) adelantar; (a suggestion, etc.) hacer; (propose) proponer; (a case) presentar. **to put oneself forward,** ponerse en evidencia. **to put in,** poner dentro; (a hand, etc.) introducir; (liquids) echar en; (a government) poner en el poder; (an employment) nombrar, colocar; (insert) insertar; (a claim) presentar; (say) decir. **I shall put in two hours' work before bedtime,** Trabajaré por dos horas antes de acostarme. **He put in a good word for you,** Habló en tu favor. **to put in writing,** poner por escrito. **to put in for,** (an employment) solicitar (un empleo); (as a candidate) presentarse como candidato para. **to put into,** meter dentro (de); (words) expresar; (port) arribar, hacer escala en (un puerto). **to put off,** desechar; (garments) quitarse, despojarse (de); (postpone) diferir, aplazar; (evade) evadir, entretener; quitarse de encima (a), desembarazarse (de); (confuse) desconcertar; (discourage) desanimar; quitar el apetito (a). **to put on,** poner sobre; (clothes) ponerse; (pretend) fingir, afectar; poner; (a play) poner en escena; (the hands of a clock) adelantar; (weight) engordar,

poner carnes; (add) añadir; (*sport* score) hacer; (bet) apostar; (the light) encender; (assume) tomar; (the brake) frenar; (abuse) abusar (de). engañar. **He put the kettle on the fire,** Puso la tetera en el fuego. **to put on airs and graces,** darse humos. **to put on probation,** dar el azul a, poner a prueba a. **to put on more trains,** poner más trenes. **put one's foot down,** ponerle a fulano el alto. **to put out,** *vt* (eject) echar, expulsar; hacer salir; poner en la calle; (a tenant) desahuciar; (one's hand) alargar; (one's arm) extender; (one's tongue) sacar; (eyes) saltar; (fire, light) apagar, extinguir; (leaves, etc.) echar; (horns) sacar; (head) asomar, sacar; (use) emplear; (give) entregar, dar; (at interest) dar a interés; (finish) terminar; (dislocate) dislocar; (worry) desconcertar; turbar; poner los nervios en punta (a); (anger) enojar; (inconvenience) incomodar; (a book) publicar; (a boat) echar al mar. *vi* (of a ship) hacerse a la vela, zarpar. **to put out to grass,** mandar a pacer. **We put out to sea,** Nos hicimos a la mar. **to put the cart before the horse,** poner la carreta por delante de los bueyes. **to put through,** (perform) desempeñar; concluir, terminar; (thrust) meter; (subject to) someter a; (exercise) ejercitar; (on the telephone) poner en comunicación (con). **to put together,** juntar; (a machine, etc.) montar, armar. **to put two and two together,** atar cabos. **to put up,** *vt* (sails, a flag) izar; (raise a window) levantar, cerrar; (open a window, or an umbrella) abrir; (one's hands, etc.) poner en alto; (one's fists) alzar; (a prayer) ofrecer, hacer; (as a candidate) nombrar; (for sale) poner (a la venta); (the price) aumentar; (a prescription) preparar; (food) conser-

var; (pack) empaquetar; (a sword) envainar; (lodge) alojar; (a petition) presentar; (build) construir; *mech* montar; (*inf* plan) arreglar. *vi* alojarse. **to put upon,** abusar (de); oprimir; (accuse) imputar, acusar (de). **to put up to,** incitar (a), instigar (a); dar informaciones sobre; poner al corriente (de). **to put up with,** tolerar, soportar, aguantar; resignarse a; contentarse con, conformarse con

putative *a* supuesto; (of relationship) putativo

putrefy *vt* pudrir. *vt* pudrirse, descomponerse

putrid *a* pútrido; *inf* apestoso

putting *n* acción de poner, *f*; colocación, *f*. **p. forward of the clock,** adelanto de la hora, *m*. **p. off,** tardanza, dilación, *f*. **p. the weight,** lanzamiento del peso, *m*. **p. up,** (for office) candidatura, *f*. **p. green,** pista de golf en miniatura, *f*

putty *n* masilla, *f*, *vt* enmasillar, rellenar con masilla

puzzle *vt* dejar perplejo; desconcertar; confundir; embrollar. *n* problema, *m*; dificultad, *f*; enigma, *m*; (perplexity) perplejidad, *f*; (game) rompecabezas, *m*. **to p. out,** procurar resolver; encontrar la solución de. **to p. over,** pensar en, meditar sobre. **I am puzzled by . . . ,** Me trae (or tiene) perplejo . . . . **to be puzzled** *Lat. Am.* intrigarse

pygmy *a* and *n* pigmeo (-ea)

pyjamas *n* pijama, *m*

pyramid *n* pirámide, *f*

pyre *n* pira, *f*

Pyrenees, the los Pirineos, *m pl*

python *n* pitón, *m*

q *n* (letter) cu, *f*

quack *vi* (of a duck) graznar. *n* (of a duck) graznido, *m*; (charlatan) charlatán, farsante, *m*; curandero, *m*. **q. doctor,** matasanos, medicastro, curandero, *m*. **q. medicine,** curanderismo, *m*

quackery *n* charlatanería, *f*, charlatanismo, *m*

quadrangle *n* cuadrángulo, *m*; (courtyard) patio, *m*

quadratic *a* cuadrático. **q. equation,** cuadrática, ecuación de segundo grado, *f*

quadrilateral *a* and *n* cuadrilátero *m*

quadruped *a* and *n* cuadrúpedo *m*

quadruple *a* cuádruple. *vt* cuadruplicar. *n* cuádruplo, *m*

quadruplet *n* serie de cuatro cosas, *f*; bicicleta de cuatro asientos, *f*; uno (una) de cuatro niños (-as) gemelos (-as)

quaff *vt* beber a grandes tragos, vaciar de un trago

quagmire *n* tremedal, pantano, *m*; *fig* cenagal, *m*

quail *n* codorniz, *f*; (U.S.A.) parpayuela, *f*. *vi* cejar, retroceder; temblar, acobardarse

quaint *a* pintoresco; curioso, raro; (eccentric) excéntrico, extravagante

quaintly *adv* de un modo pintoresco; curiosamente; con extravagancia

quake *vi* estremecerse, vibrar; temblar. *n* estremecimiento, *m*; (of the earth) terremoto, *m*. **to q. with fear,** temblar de miedo

Quaker *n* cuáquero (-ra)

quaking *a* temblón; tembloroso. *n* temblor, *m*; estremecimiento, *m*. **q. ash,** álamo temblón, *m*

qualification *n* calificación, *f*; requisito, *m*; capacidad, aptitud, *f*; (reservation) reservación, salvedad, *f*

qualified *a* apto, competente; (of professions) con título universitario; habilitado; limitado

qualify *vt* habilitar; calificar; modificar; suavizar; *vi* habilitarse; prepararse; llenar los requisitos

qualitative *a* cualitativo

quality *n* cualidad, *f*; calidad, *f*; propiedad, *f*. **This cloth is of good q.,** Esta tela es de buena calidad. **the q.,** la alta sociedad, la aristocracia

qualm *n* náusea, *f*; mareo, desmayo, *m*; (of conscience) escrúpulo, remordimiento, *m*

quandary *n* incertidumbre, perplejidad, *f*; dilema, apuro, *m*. **to be in a q.,** estar perplejo

quantitative *a* cuantitativo

quantity *n* cantidad, *f*; gran cantidad, *f*. **unknown q.,** incógnita, *f*

quarantine *n* cuarentena, *f*, *vt* someter a cuarentena

quarrel *vi* pelear, disputar; (scold) reñir; (find fault) criticar. *n* pelea, disputa, Ar-

---

Q

gentina arenga, *f*; (glazier's) diamante de vidriero, *m*. **to pick a q. with,** armar pleito con, reñir con, *Chile*, *Peru* cruzar. **to q. with,** reñir con, romper con; quejarse de

quarrelling *n* disputas, altercaciones, *f pl*

quarrelsome *a* pendenciero, peleador, belicoso

quarry *n* cantera, *f*; *fig* mina, *f*; (prey) presa, *f*; víctima, *f*. *vt* explotar una cantera; examinar

quart *n* cuarto de galón, *m*

quarter *n* (fourth part) cuarta parte, *f*, cuarto, *m*; (of a year) trimestre, *m*; (of an hour, the moon, an animal, etc.) cuarto, *m*; (of the compass) cuarta, *f*; *naut* cuartelada, *f*; (of a town) barrio, *m*; (mercy) cuartel, *m*; *her* cuartel, *m*; dirección, *f*; origen, *m*, fuente, *f*; *pl* **quarters,** vivienda, *f*; alojamiento, *m*; (barracks) cuartel, *m*. *vt* cuartear; (a body) descuartizar, hacer cuartos (a); (troops) alojar; (in barracks) acuartelar; *her* cuartelar. **a q. of an hour,** un cuarto de hora. **at close quarters,** de cerca. **hind quarters,** cuartos traseros, *m pl*: **It is a q. to four,** Son las cuatro menos cuarto. **It is a q. past four,** Son las cuatro y cuarto. **q.-deck,** alcázar, *m*; cuerpo de oficiales de un buque, *m*. **q.-mile,** cuarto de milla, *m*. **q.-plate,** cuarto de placa, *m*. **q.-sessions,** sesión trimestral de los juzgados municipales, *f*. **q.-staff,** barra, *f*. **q.-tone,** cuarto de tono, *m*

quartering *n* (punishment) descuartizamiento, *m*; *her* cantón, *m*

quarterly *a* trimestral, trimestre. *n* publicación trimestral, *f*, *adv* trimestralmente

quartet *n* cuarteto, *m*

quarto *n* papel en cuarto, *m*; libro en cuarto, *m*. **in q.,** en cuarto

quartz *n* cuarzo, *m*

quash *vt* *law* anular, derogar; *inf* sofocar, reprimir

quasi *a* and *adv* cuasi

quaver *vi* vibrar; temblar; (trill) trinar, hacer quiebros. *vt* decir con voz temblorosa. *n* vibración, *f*; trémolo, *m*; (trill) trino, *m*; (musical note) corchea, *f*

quaveringly *adv* con voz temblorosa

quavery *a* trémulo, tembloroso

quay *n* muelle, *m*

queasiness *n* náusea, *f*; escrupulosidad, *f*

queasy *a* propenso a la náusea; nauseabundo; delicado, escrupuloso

queen *n* reina, *f*; (in a Spanish pack of cards) caballo, *m*; (in a French or English pack and in chess) reina, *f*. **to q. it,** conducirse como una reina; mandar. **q. bee,** maestra, abeja reina, *f.* **q. cell,** maestril, *m.* **q. mother,** reina madre, *f.* **q. regent,** reina regente, *f*

queenly *a* de reina; regio

queer *a* raro; extraño; singular; ridículo; (shady) sospechoso; (ill) malucho, algo enfermo; (mad) chiflado

queerly *adv* extrañamente; ridiculamente

queerness *n* rareza, extrañeza, singularidad, *f*; ridiculez, *f*

quell *vt* subyugar; reprimir; apaciguar, calmar

quench *vt* apagar; calmar; satisfacer. **to q. one's thirst,** apagar la sed

quenching *n* apagamiento, *m*; satisfacción, *f*

querulous *a* quejumbroso

query *n* pregunta, *f*; duda, *f*; punto de interrogación, *m. vt* preguntar; dudar (de); poner en duda. *vi* hacer una pregunta; expresar una duda

quest *n* busca, *f*; (adventure) demanda, *f*. **in q. of,** en busca de

question *n* pregunta, *f*; problema, *m*; asunto, *m*; cuestión, *f*; (discussion) debate, *m*, discusión, *f. vt and vi* interrogar; examinar; poner en duda, dudar de; preguntarse; hacer preguntas. **beyond q.,** fuera de duda. **to ask a q.,** hacer una pregunta. **without q.,** sin duda. **It is out of the q.,** Es completamente imposible. **It is a q. of whether . . . ,** Se trata de si . . . **q.-mark,** punto interrogante, *m*

questionable *a* cuestionable, discutible, dudoso; equívoco, sospechoso

questioner *n* preguntador (-ra); interrogador (-ra)

questioning *n* preguntas, *f pl*; interrogatorio, *m*

questioningly *adv* interrogativamente

questionnaire *n* cuestionario, *m*

quetzal *n* (money and *orn*) quetzal, *m*

queue *n* coleta, *f*; cola, *f*, *vi* formar cola; hacer cola

quibble *n* equívoco, subterfugio, *m*; sutileza, *f*; (pun) retruécano, *m. vi* hacer uso de subterfugios; sutilizar

quibbler *n* sofista, *mf*

quibbling *n* sofistería, *f*, sofismas, *m pl*, sutilezas, *f pl*

quick *a* vivo; agudo; penetrante; sagaz; rápido, veloz; (ready) pronto; ágil, activo; (light) ligero. *adv* rápidamente; (soon) pronto. *n* carne viva, *f; fig* lo vivo. **Be q.!** ¡Date prisa! **He was very q.,** Lo hizo muy aprisa; Volvió (or fue, according to sense) rápidamente. **the q. and the dead,** los vivos y los muertos. **to cut to the q.,** herir en lo más vivo. **q. march,** paso doble, *m.* **q.-sighted,** de vista aguda; perspicaz. **q. step,** paso rápido, *m.* **q.-tempered,** de genio vivo, colérico. **q.**

time, compás rápido, *m; mil* paso doble, *m.* **q.-witted,** de ingenio agudo

quicken *vt* vivificar; animar; acelerar; excitar, avivar. *vi* vivificarse; despertarse; renovarse; acelerarse; (stir) moverse. **to q. one's step,** acelerar el paso

quicklime *n* cal viva, *f*

quickly *adv* rápidamente; (soon) pronto; (immediately) en seguida; (promptly) con presteza; vivamente

quickness *n* viveza, *f*; (of wit, etc.) agudeza, *f*; rapidez, velocidad, *f*; (promptness) prontitud, *f*; agilidad, *f*; (lightness) ligereza, *f*; (understanding) penetración, sagacidad, *f*

quicksand *n* arena movediza, *f; fig* cenagal, *m*

quicksilver *n* azogue, mercurio, *m, vt* azogar

quiescence *n* reposo, *m*; quietud, tranquilidad, *f*; inactividad, *f*; pasividad, *f*

quiescent *a* quieto; inactivo; pasivo

quiet *a* tranquilo; quieto; silencioso; quedo; monótono; inactivo; (informal) sin ceremonia; (simple) sencillo; (of the mind) sereno; (of colours, etc.) suave. *n* tranquilidad, quietud, *f*; silencio, *m*; paz, *f*; (of mind) serenidad, *f. vt* tranquilizar, sosegar; calmar. **to be q.,** callarse; no hacer ruido. **Be q.!** ¡Estate quieto! ¡A callar!

quietly *adv* tranquilamente; en silencio; sin ruido; en calma; (simply) sencillamente; dulcemente

quill *n* pluma de ave, *f*; (of a feather) cañón, *m*; (pen) pluma, *f*; (of a porcupine) púa, *f.* **q.-driver,** cagatintas, *mf*

quilt *n* colcha, *f*, edredón, *m. vt* acolchar. **q. maker,** colchero, *m*

quilting *n* acolchamiento, *m*; colchadura, *f*

quince *n* (tree and fruit) membrillo, *m.* **q. cheese,** carne de membrillo, *f.* **q. jelly,** jalea de membrillo, *f*

quinine *n* quinina, *f*

quinsy *n* angina, *f*

quintessence *n* quinta esencia, *f*

quintessential *a* quintaesenciado

quintet *n* quinteto, *m*

quintuple *a* quíntuplo

quip *n* agudeza, salida, *f*; (hint) indirecta, *f*; donaire, *m*, chanza, burla, *f*

quirk *n* (quip) agudeza, salida, *f*; (quibble) sutileza, evasiva, *f*; (gesture) gesto, *m*

quit *vt* abandonar; dejar; renunciar (a). *vi* marcharse, *inf* tomar las de Villadiego, poner pies en polvorosa; (slang) dejar de, cesar de. **notice to q.,** aviso de desahúcio, *m*

quite *adv* completamente, enteramente; totalmente; del todo; (very) muy; (fairly) bastante. **It is not q. the thing to do,** Esto es algo que no se hace. **Q. so!**

¡Claro!; ¡Eso es! Se comprende. **It is not q. so good as we hoped,** No es tan bueno como esperábamos. **Peter is q. grown-up,** Pedro está hecho un hombre (or es todo un hombre)

quits *adv* quito, descargado. **be q.,** estar en paz

quitter *n* desertor (-ra); cobarde, *mf*

quiver *vi* temblar; vibrar; estremecerse; palpitar; (of light) titilar. *n* (for arrows) aljaba, *f*, carcaj, *m*. See also **quivering**

quivering *a* tremulante; vibrante; palpitante. *n* temblor, *m*; estremecimiento, *m*

quixotic *a* quijotesco

quiz *n* examen parcial, *m*. *vt* tomar el pelo (a); burlarse (de); (stare) mirar de hito en hito (a)

quizzical *a* burlón; cómico; estrafalario

quoin *n* piedra angular, *f*; ángulo, *m*; (wedge) cuña, *f*. *vt* meter cuñas (a)

quoit *n* tejo, *m*; *pl* **quoits,** juego de tejos, *m*

quondam *a* antiguo

quorum *n* quórum, *m*. **to form a q.,** hacer un quórum

quota *n* cuota, *f*

quotable *a* citable; (Stock Exchange) cotizable

quota system *n* tablas diferenciales, *f pl*

quotation *n* citación, *f*; cita, *f*; *com* cotización, *f*. **q. mark,** comilla, *f*

quote *vt* citar; *com* cotizar. *n* *inf* comilla, *f*

quoth *vt* **q. I,** dije yo. **q. he,** dijo él

quotient *n* cociente, *m*. **intelligence q.,** cociente intelectual, *m*

R

r *n* (letter) erre, *f*

rabbi *n* rabí, rabino, *m*. **grand r.**, gran rabino, *m*

rabbinical *a* rabínico

rabbit *n* conejo (-ja). a conejuno, de conejo. *vi* cazar conejos. **young r.**, gazapo, *m*. **r.-hutch**, jaula para conejos, *f*. **r.-warren**, conejera, *f*

rabble *n* populacho, vulgo, *m*, plebe, *f*

rabid *a* rabioso; fanático; furioso, violento

rabies *n* rabia, hidrofobia, *f*

raccoon *n* mapache, *m*

race *n* carrera, *f*; (current) corriente, *f*; (prize) premio, *m*; (breed) raza, *f*; casta, estirpe, *f*; (family) linaje, *m*, familia, *f*; (scornful) ralea, *f*; (struggle) lucha, *f*. *vi* tomar parte en una carrera; correr de prisa; asistir a concursos de carreras de caballos; (of a machine) dispararse. *vt* (hacer) correr; competir en una carrera (con); desafiar a una carrera. **flat r.**, carrera llana, *f*. **mill-r.**, caz, *m*. **to run a r.**, tomar parte en una carrera; *fig* hacer una carrera. **r.-card**, programa de carreras de caballos, *m*. **r. hatred**, odio de razas, *m*. **r.-meeting**, concurso de carreras de caballos, *m*. **r. suicide**, suicidio de la raza, *m*. **r.-track**, pista, *f*

racecourse hipódromo, *m*; estadio, *m*

racehorse *n* caballo de carrera, *m*

racer *n* (horse) caballo de carreras, *m*; (person) carrerista, *mf*; (car) coche de carreras, *m*; (boat) yate de carreras, *m*; (bicycle) bicicleta de carreras, *f*

rachitic *a* raquítico

racial *a* racial, de raza

racialism *n* rivalidad de razas, *f*

raciness *n* sabor, *m*; savia, *f*, picante, *m*

racing *n* carreras, *f pl*; *mech* disparo, *m*, a de carreras; hípico. **r. calendar**, calendario de concursos de carreras de caballos, *m*. **r. car**, coche de carreras, *m*. **r. cycle**, bicicleta de carreras, *f*

rack *n* (for hay) percha (del pesebre), *f*; (in a railway compartment) rejilla, *f*; (for billiard cues) taquera, *f*; (for clothes) percha, *f*; (for torture) potro, *m*; *mech* cremallera, *f*. *vt* poner en el potro, torturar; atormentar. **to be on the r.**, estar en el potro **to r. one's brains**, devanarse los sesos, quebrarse la cabeza. **r. and ruin**, ruina total, *f*. **r. railway**, ferrocarril de cremallera, *m*

racket *n sport* raqueta, *f*; (din) barahúnda, *f*; ruido, estrépito, *m*; confusión, *f*; (bustle) bullicio, *m*, agitación, *f*; (swindle) estafa, *f*; (binge) parranda, *f*. **to play rackets**, jugar a la raqueta

racoon *n* mapache, *m*

racy *a* picante; sabroso

radar *n* radar, *m*

raddled *a* pintado de almagre; mal pintado

radial *a* radial

radiance *n* resplandor, brillo, *m*, luminosidad, *f*

radiant *a* radiante; brillante, luminoso. *n geom* línea radial, *f*. **r. heat**, calor radiante, *m*

radiantly *adv* con resplandor; brillantemente; con alegría

radiate *vi* radiar. *vt* irradiar

radiation *n* irradiación, *f*; *geom* radiación, *f*

radiator *n* (for central heating and of a car) radiador, *m*; (stove) calorífero, *m*

radical *a* radical. *n* (math chem) radical, *m*; *pol* radical, *mf*

radio *n* radio, *f*; radiocomunicación, *f*. **r. amateur, r. enthusiast**, radioaficionado (-da). **r. announcer**, locutor (-ra). **r. broadcast**, radioemisión, radiodifusión, *f*. **r. listener**, radioyente, *mf* **r. receiver**, (technical) radiorreceptor, *m*; (usual word) aparato de radio, *m*. **r. transmitter**, radiotransmisor, *m*

radioactive *a* radioactivo

radioactive fallout *n* caída radiactiva, llovizna radiactiva, precipitación radioactiva, *f*

radiofrequency *n* radiofrecuencia, *f*

radiologist *n* radiólogo, *m*

radiology *n* radiología, *f*

radish *n* rábano, *m*. **horse-r.**, rábano picante, *m*

radium *n* radio, *m*

radius *n* (geom anat) radio, *m*; (of a wheel) rayo, *m*; (scope) alcance, *m*

raffish *a* disoluto, libertino

raffle *n* rifa, *f*, sorteo, *m*; lotería, *f*. *vt* rifar, sortear

raft *n* balsa, *f*; (timber) armadía, *f*. transportar en balsa; cruzar en balsa

rafter *n* (of a roof) viga, traviesa, *f*; (raftsman) balsero, *m*

rag *n* jirón, guiñapo, *m*; (for cleaning) paño, trapo, *m*; (for papermaking) estraza, *f*; (of smoke, etc.) penacho, *m*; (newspaper) papelucho, *m*; *pl* **rags**, harapos, *m pl*; *inf* viejos hábitos, *m pl*; (tease) tomar el pelo (a); burlarse de; hacer una broma pesada (a). **r.-and-bone-man, ragpicker**, andrajero, trapero (Mexico), pepinador, *m*. **r. doll**, muñeca de trapo, *f*

ragamuffin *n* galopín, *m*

rage *n* (anger) cólera, rabia, ira, *f*; (of the elements) furia, violencia, *f*; (ardour) entusiasmo, ardor, *m*; (fashion) boga, moda, *f*; (craze) manía, *f*; (of the poet) furor, *m*. *vi* (be angry) rabiar, estar furioso; (of the sea) encresparse, alborotarse, enfurecerse; (with fire, animals) bramar, rugir; (of pain) rabiar; (be prevalent) prevalecer, desencadenarse. **to r. against**, protestar furiosamente contra; culpar amargamente (de). **to be all the r.,** *inf* ser la ultima moda. **to fly into a r.,** montar en cólera. **to put into a r.,** hacer rabiar

ragged *a* harapiento, andrajoso; roto; (uneven) desigual; (rugged) peñascoso, áspero, escabroso; (serrated) serrado; dentellado; (of a coastline) accidentado; (unfinished) inacabado, sin terminar; (of style) descuidado, sin pulir

raging *a* furioso, rabioso; violento; (roaring) bramante; (of the sea) bravío; intenso. *n* furia, *f*; violencia, *f*; intensidad, *f*

raglan *n* raglán, *m*. **r. sleeve,** manga raglán, *f*

ragout *n* estofado, *m*

ragpicker *n* trapero (-ra)

raid *n* incursión, correría, *f*; asalto, ataque, *m*; (by the police) razzia, *f*; (by aircraft) bombardeo, *m*, *vt* invadir; atacar, asaltar; apoderarse de; hacer una razzia en; (by aircraft) bombear, bombardear; (pillage) pillar, saquear. **obliteration r.,** hombardeo de saturación, *m*

raider *n* corsario, *m*; atacador, asaltador, *m*; (aircraft) avión enemigo, *m*

rail *n* barra, *f*; antepecho, *m*; (of a staircase) barandilla, *f*, pasamano, *m*; (track) riel, *m*; (railway) ferrocarril, *m*; (of a ship) barandilla, *f*; (of a chair) travesaño, *m pl*. **rails,** (fence) cerca, barrera, palizada, *f*. *vt* cercar con una palizada, poner cerca a; mandar por ferrocarril. **by r.,** por ferrocarril. **to run off the rails,** descarrilar. **to r. at,** protestar contra; prorrumpir en invectivas contra, injuriar de palabra (a)

railing *n* barandilla, *f*; antepecho, *m*, enrejado, *m*; (grille) reja, *f*; (jeers) burlas, *f pl*; insultos, *m pl*, injurias, *f pl*; quejas, *f pl*

raillery *n* jocosidad, tomadura de pelo, *f*; sátiras, *f pl*

railway *n* ferrocarril, *m*; vía férrea, *f*, camino de hierro, *m*, a de ferrocarril, ferroviario. **elevated r.,** ferrocarril aéreo, *m*. **narrow gauge r.,** ferrocarril de vía estrecha, *m*. **r. buffet,** fonda, *f*, (or restaurante, *m*) de estación. **r. carriage,** departamento de tren, *m*. **r. company,** compañía de ferrocarriles, *f*. **r. crossing,** paso a nivel, *m*. **r. engine,** locomotora, *f*. **r. guard,** jefe del tren, *m*. **r. guide,** guía de ferrocarriles, *f*. **r. line,** vía férrea, *f*. **r. marshalling yard,** apartadero ferroviario, *m*. **r. passenger,** viajero (-ra) en un tren. **r. platform,** andén, *m*. **r. porter,** mozo de estación, *m*. **r. siding,** vía muerta, *f*. **r. signal,** disco de señales, *m*. **r. station,** estación (de ferrocarril), *f*. **r. system,** sistema ferroviario, *m*. **r. ticket,** billete de tren, *m*

railwayman *n* ferroviario, empleado de los ferrocarriles, *m*

raiment *n* ropa, *f*; *poet* hábitos, *m pl*

rain *n* lluvia, *f*. *vi* and *vt* llover. **a r. of arrows,** una lluvia de flechas. **fine r.,** llovizna, *f*. **to r. cats and dogs,** llover a cán-

taros. **to r. hard,** diluviar. **r. cloud,** nubarrón, *m*. **r.-gauge,** pluviómetro, *m*

rainbow *n* arco iris, arco de San Martín, *m*

raincoat *n* abrigo impermeable, *m*

raindrop *n* gota de lluvia, *f*

rainfall *n* cantidad llovida, *f*; (shower) aguacero, *m*

rainy *a* lluvioso. **r. day,** día de lluvia, *m*; *fig* tiempo de escasez, *m*

raise *vt* levantar; alzar; (the hat) quitar; solevantar; (dough) fermentar; (erect) erigir, edificar; (dust) levantar; elevar; (promote) ascender; (increase) aumentar; hacer subir; (spirits, memories) evocar; (the dead) resucitar; (cause) causar; dar lugar (a); hacer concebir; (a question, a point) hacer; plantear; (breed or educate) criar; (a crop) cultivar; (an army) alistar; (gather together) juntar; (a subscription) hacer; (money, etc.) obtener, hallar; (a siege, etc.) levantar, alzar; (a laugh, a protest, etc.) suscitar, provocar; (utter) poner, dar; (a fund) abrir. **to r. oneself,** incorporarse. **He succeeded in raising himself,** Logró alzarse; Logró mejorar su posición. **He raised their hopes unduly,** Les hizo concebir esperanzas desmesuradas. **to r. an objection (to),** poner objeción (a). **to r. an outcry,** armar un alboroto. **to r. a point,** hacer una observación; plantear una cuestión. **to r. a siege,** levantar un sitio. **to r. Cain,** armar lo de Dios es Cristo. **to r. one's voice,** alzar la voz

raisin *n* pasa, *f*

raising *n* levantamiento, *m*; alzamiento, *m*; (of a building, monument) erección, *f*; elevación, *f*; (increase) aumento, *m*; provocación, *f*; fundación, *f*; (breeding or education) crianza, *f*; (of spirits) evocación, *f*; (of the dead) resucitación, *f*; producción, *f*; (of crops) cultivo, *m*

rake *n agr* rastrillo, *m*, rastra, *f*; (for the fire) hurgón, *m*; (croupier's) raqueta, *f*; (of a mast, funnel) inclinación, *f*; (person) tenorio, calavera, *m*. *vt agr* rastrillar; (a fire, etc.) hurgar; (sweep) barrer; recoger; (ransack) buscar (en); (with fire) enfilar, tirar a lo largo de; (scan) escudriñar. *vi* trabajar con el rastrillo; (slope) inclinarse. **r. off,** tajada, *f*. **to r. together,** juntar con el rastrillo; amontonar; ahorrar. **to r. up,** (revive) resucitar, desenterrar

rakish *a* (of a ship) de palos muy inclinados, (dissolute) disoluto, libertino; (dashing) elegante

rally *vt* reunir; *mil* rehacer; (faculties) concentrar; (tease) tomar el pelo (a). *vi* reunirse; *mil* rehacerse; (revive) mejorar, recobrar las fuerzas; (of markets, etc.) mejorar *n* reunión, *f*

rallying *n* reunión, *f*; (of faculties, etc.) concentración, *f*; (recovery) mejora, *f*. **r. point,** punto de reunión, *m*

ram *n zool* carnero, morueco, *m*; *ast* Aries, Carnero, *m*; (*mil* etc.) ariete, *m*;

(tool) pisón, *m*; *nav* espolón, *m*, *vt* golpear con ariete o espolón; (of a gun) atacar; apisonar; meter a la fuerza; hacer tragar a la fuerza; (squeeze) apretar; (crowd) atestar

ramble *vi* vagar, vagabundear; hacer una excursión. *vt* errar por

rambler *n* excursionista, *mf*; paseante, *mf*; *bot* rosa trepante, *f*

rambling *a* (of houses) encantado; laberíntico; (straggly) disperso; (of thought, etc.) incoherente, inconexo. *n* vagabundeo, *m*; excursiones, *f pl*; paseo, *m*; (digression) digresiones, *f pl*; (delirium) desvaríos, *m pl*

ramification *n* ramificación, *f*

ramify *vi* ramificarse, tener ramificaciones. *vt* ramificar; dividir en ramales

ramp *n* rampa, *f*; (swindle) estafa, *f*; (storm, commotion) tormenta, *f*

rampage *vi* alborotarse; bramar

rampant *a* salvaje; *her* rampante; (of persons) impaciente, furioso; (of plants, growth) lozano, exuberante; desenfrenado; (rife) prevaleciente, predominante

rampart *n* muralla, *f*; terraplén, *m*; *fig* baluarte, *m*. *vt* abaluartar, abastionar

ramshackle *a* destartalado, ruinoso; desvencijado; (badly made) mal hecho

ranch *n* rancho, *m*, hacienda (de ganado), *Lat. Am.* estancia, *f*

rancher *n* ranchero (-ra), *Lat. Am.* estanciero (-ra) *mf*

rancid *a* rancio

rancor *n* rencor, encono, *m*

random *n* azar, *m*, a fortuito, al azar; sin orden ni concierto. **at r.,** a la ventura, al azar; sin pensar; (of shooting) sin apuntar. **to talk at r.,** hablar a trochemoche

range *n* línea, hilera, *f*; (of mountains) cadena, *f*; serie, *f*; clase, *f*; variedad, *f*; (of goods) surtido, *m*; (of a gun, voice, vision, etc.) alcance, *m*; (area) extensión, área, *f*; esfera de actividad, *f*; (scope) alcance, *m*; (of voice, musical instrument) compás, *m*; (of colors) gama, *f*; (for shooting) campo de tiro, *m*; (for cooking) cocina económica, *f*. **at close r.,** de cerca. **out of r.,** fuera de alcance. **within r.,** al alcance. **r.-finder,** (of guns, cameras) telémetro, *m*. **r. of mountains,** cadena de montañas, *f*; sierra, *f*

range *vt poet* arreglar; alinear; ordenar; clasificar; (a gun, etc.) apuntar; (place oneself) ponerse; sumarse (a); (roam) recorrer; (scan) escudriñar. *vi* extenderse; (roam) vagar; (of plants) crecer (en); variar, fluctuar; oscilar, vacilar; (of guns, etc.) alcanzar; (of the mind) pasar (por); (include) incluir

ranger *n* (wanderer) vagabundo, *m*; (keeper) guardabosque, *m*; *mil* batidor, *m*

rank *n* línea, *f*; fila, *f*; grado, *m*; clase, *f*; rango, *m*; categoría, *f*; posición, *f*; cali-

dad, *f*; distinción, *f*. *vt* ordenar; clasificar; (estimate) estimar; poner (entre). *vi* ocupar un puesto; tener un grado, rango, etc.; estar al nivel (de); ser igual (a); contarse (entre). *a* (luxuriant) lozano, exuberante; fértil; (thick) espeso; (rancid) rancio; (complete) consumado; completo; (foul-smelling) fétido; *fig* repugnante, aborrecible; (very) muy. **of the first r.,** de primera calidad; de primera clase; de distinción. **the r. and file,** los soldados, la tropa; las masas, hombres de filas, *m pl*, mujeres de fila, *f pl*, la mayoría; los socios ordinarios (de un club, etc.). **to break ranks,** *mil* romper filas. **to rise from the ranks,** ascender de las filas. **to r. high,** ocupar alta posición; ser de los mejores (de). **to r. with,** estar al nivel de; (be numbered among) contarse entre, figurar entre

rankle *vi fig* irritar, molestar; envenenarse la vida, hacerse odioso

ransack *vt* (search) registrar; (pillage) saquear; *fig* buscar en

ransacking *n* (searching) registro, *m*; (sacking) saqueo, *m*

ransom *n* rescate, *m*, redención, *f*; liberación, *f*. *vt* rescatar, redimir

ransomer *n* rescatador (-ra)

ransoming *n* redención, *f*; liberación, *f*

rant *vi* declamar a gritos, vociferar; despotricar (contra); desvariar; hablar por hablar, hablar sin ton ni son. *n* declamación, vociferación, *f*; desvarío, *m*

ranter *n* declamador (-ra); agitador populachero, *m*; predicador chillón, *m*

rap *n* golpecito, *m*; toque, *m*; (with the knocker) aldabada, *f*; (worthless trifle) ardite, maravedí, *m*. *vt* and *vi* golpear; tocar. **He doesn't care a rap,** No le importa un ardite. **to rap at the door,** tocar a la puerta. **to rap with the knuckles,** golpear con los nudillos. **to rap out an oath,** proferir una blasfemia

rapacious *a* rapaz

rapacity *n* rapacidad, *f*

rape *n* (carrying off) rapto, *m*. **the Rape of the Sabine Women,** el Rapto de las Sabinas, *m*; *law* estupro, *m*; violación, *f*; *bot* nabo silvestre, *m*. *vt* (carry off) raptar, robar; violar, forzar

rapid *a* rápido. *n* rápido, *m*. **r. combustion,** combustión activa, *f*

rapidity *n* rapidez, *f*

rapidly *adv* rápidamente, con rapidez

rapids *npl Argentina* correntada, *fsg*

rapier *n* estoque, *m*; espadín, *m*

rapine *n* rapiña, *f*

rapping *n* golpecitos, *m pl*; golpeo, *m*; toques, *m pl*; (of the knocker) aldabeo, *m*

rapscallion *n* bribón, *m*

rapt *past part* and *a* arrebatado; absorto; extático, extasiado

rapture *n* arrebato, *m*; éxtasis, *m*; transporte, *m*; embriaguez, *f*; entusiasmo, *m*

rapturous a embelesado; extático; entusiasta

rare a raro; extraordinario; exótico; infrecuente

rarefy vt rarefacer. vi rarefacerse

rareness n rareza, f; singularidad, f; infrecuencia, f

rarity n raridad, f; (uncommonness and rare object) rareza, f

rascal n sinvergüenza, m; truhán, bribón, pícaro, m; (affectionately) picaruelo, m

rascality n bellaquería, truhanería, f

rash a temerario, precipitado; imprudente. n erupción, f, salpullido, m

rasher n magra, f; (of bacon) torrezno, m

rashly adv temerariamente, precipitadamente; imprudentemente, con imprudencia

rasp n escofina, f, rallo, m; sonido áspero, m. vt raspar, escofinar; (get on one's nerves) poner los nervios en punta (a)

raspberry n frambuesa, f. **r.-cane**, frambueso, m. **r. jam**, mermelada de frambuesa, f

rasping a (of the voice) áspero, estridente

rat n rata, f; desertor, m; (black leg) esquirol, m. vi cazar ratas; ser desertor; ser esquirol. **rat-catcher**, cazador de ratas, m. **rat poison**, matarratas, m, raticida, f. **rat-trap**, ratonera, f

ratchet n mech trinquete, m; (of a watch) disparador, m. **r.-drill**, carraca, f. **r.-wheel**, rueda dentada con trinquete, f

rate n velocidad, f; razón, proporción, f; (of exchange) tipo, m; tanto, m; precio, m; clase, f; modo, m, manera, f; naut clasificación, f; (tax) contribución, f, impuesto, m; pl **rates**, (of a house) inquilinato, m. vt tasar; estimar; fijar el precio (a); naut clasificar; imponer una contribución (de); (scold) reñir. **at a great r.**, rápidamente, velozmente. **at a r. of**, a razón de; a una velocidad de. **at any r.**, de todos modos; por lo menos; sea como fuere. **at this r.**, de este modo; a este paso; a esa cuenta; en esta proporción; (with seguir) así. **first-r.**, de primera clase. **rates and taxes**, contribuciones e impuestos, f pl. **r. of climb**, aer velocidad ascensional, f. **r. of exchange**, tipo de cambio, m. **r.-payer**, contribuyente, mf

rather adv más bien; antes; (more willingly) de mejor gana; (somewhat) algo, un poco; (perhaps) quizás; mejor dicho; (fairly) bastante; (very) muy; mucho; al contrario. **R.!** ¡Ya lo creo! **or r.**, o más bien. **anything r. than . . .**, todo menos . . . **He had r.**, Preferiría. **r. than**, antes que, en vez de

ratification n ratificación, f; (of a bill) aprobación, f

ratify vt ratificar

rating n tasación, f; valuación, f; clasificación, f; impuesto, m, contribución, f; repartición de impuestos, f; (of a ship's

company) graduación, f; (scolding) reprensión, f

ratio n razón, f; proporción, f. **in direct r.**, en razón directa

ratiocination n raciocinación, f

ration n ración, f. vt racionar. **r.-book**, cartilla de racionamiento, f

rational a racional; razonable, juicioso. n ser racional, m

rationalist n racionalista, mf

rationalistic a racionalista

rationality n racionalidad, f; justicia, f

rationalization n racionalización, f; justificación, f

rationalize vt hacer racional; concebir racionalmente; math quitar los radicales (a); justificar

rationing n racionamiento, m

rattan n rota, f, bejuco, m; junquillo, m

ratteen n ratina, f

rattle vi hacer ruido; rechinar, crujir; (of loose windows, etc.) zangolotearse; (knock) golpear; tocar; (patter) bailar; sonar; (of the dying) dar un estertor. vt (shake) sacudir; hacer vibrar; (jolt) traquetear; (do rapidly) acabar rápidamente; (confuse) aturdir, hacer perder la cabeza (a); desconcertar. **to r. along**, deslizarse (or correr) rápidamente. **to r. off**, (repeat) decir rápidamente; terminar apresuradamente. **to r. on about**, charlar mucho de, hablar sin cesar sobre

rattle n rechinamiento, crujido, m; zangoloteo, m; ruido, m; son (de la lluvia, etc.), m; (in the throat) estertor, m; (of a rattlesnake) cascabel, m; (child's) sonajero, m; matraca, f; carraca, f; (chatter) charla, f. **r.-headed**, de cabeza de chorlito, casquivano

rattlesnake n serpiente de cascabel, f, crótalo, m

raucous a ronco, estridente

ravage vt devastar; (pillage) saquear; destruir; (spoil) estropear. n devastación, f; destrucción, f; estrago, m

ravager n devastador (-ra); saqueador (-ra)

rave vi desvariar, delirar; (of the elements) bramar, rugir. **to r. about**, hablar con entusiasmo de; delirar por. **to r. against**, vociferar contra, despotricarse contra

ravel vt deshilar, destejer; fig enredar. **to r. out**, deshilarse; fig desenredarse, desenmarañarse

raven n cuervo, m, a negro como el azabache

ravening a rapaz, salvaje

ravenous a voraz

ravine n cañada, f, barranco, cañón, m

raving n delirio, m, desvaríos, m pl. a delirante; violento; bravío

ravioli n pl ravioles, m pl

ravish vt (carry off) arrebatar, raptar; extasiar, encantar; (rape) violar, forzar

ravisher n raptador, m; violador, m

ravishing n violación, f, a encantador

ravishment n violación, f; arrobamiento, m; transporte, éxtasis, m

raw a (of meat, etc., silk, leather, weather) crudo; bruto; (inexpert) bisoño; (of flesh) vivo; com en bruto. **raw-boned,** huesudo. **raw hand,** novato (-ta). **raw material,** primera materia, f. **raw materials,** materias primas, f pl. **raw score,** puntuación bruta, f. **raw silk,** seda cruda, seda en rama, f. **raw sugar,** azúcar bruto, m

rawhide a de cuero crudo

rawness n crudeza, f; inexperiencia, f; (of weather) humedad, f

ray n rayo, m; (line) raya, f; (radius) radio, m; (fish) raya, f. **cathode rays,** rayos catódicos, m pl

rayon n rayón, m

raze vt arrasar, asolar; demoler; (erase) borrar, tachar

razor n navaja, f. **electric r.,** máquina de afeitar eléctrica, f. **safety r.,** máquina de afeitar, f. **slash with a r.,** navajada, f. **r. blade,** hoja de afeitar, f. **r. case,** navajero, m. **r. strop,** suavizador, m

re n mus re, m; prep law causa, f; com concerniente a

re prefix (attached to verb) re-; (after the verb) de nuevo; (followed by infin.) volver a . . . to **re-count,** volver a contar, contar de nuevo, recontar

reabsorb vt resorber

reabsorption n reabsorción, resorción, f

reach vt (stretch out) alargar; extender; alcanzar; llegar hasta; (arrive at) llegar a; (achieve) lograr, obtener. vi extenderse; alcanzar; penetrar. n alcance, m; extensión, f; poder, m; capacidad, f; (of a river) tabla, f. **as far as the eye could r.,** hasta donde alcanzaba la vista. **He reached home very soon,** Llegó muy pronto a casa. **out of r.,** fuera de alcance. **to r. a deadlock,** llegar a un punto muerto. **within r.,** al alcance. **within easy r.,** de fácil acceso; a corta distancia. **to r. after,** procurar alcanzar; hacer esfuerzos para obtener. **to r. back,** (of time) remontarse. **to r. down,** bajar. **r.-me-downs,** ropa hecha, f

react vi reaccionar. vt hacer de nuevo; theat volver a representar

reaction n reacción, f

reactionary a and n reaccionario (-ia)

read vt leer; (a riddle, etc.) adivinar; descifrar; interpretar; (study) estudiar; (the Burial Service, etc.) decir; (correct) corregir; (of thermometers, etc.) marcar. vi leer; estudiar; (be written) estar escrito, decir. **The play acts better than it reads,** La comedia es mejor representada que leída. **to r. aloud,** leer en voz alta. **to r. between the lines,** leer entre líneas. **to r. proofs,** corregir pruebas. **to r. to oneself,** leer para sí. **to r. about,** leer; (learn) enterarse de. **to r. again,** volver a leer, leer otra vez. **to r. on,** continuar leyendo. **to r. out,** leer en alta voz. **to r. over,** leer; leerlo todo. **to r. over and over again,** leer muchas veces, leer y releer.

read past part leído, etc. **well-r.,** releído; instruido, culto

readable a legible; interesante

reader n lector (-ra); ecc lector, m; (proof) corrector de pruebas, m; (citation collector for a dictionary) cedulista, mf; (university) profesor (-ra) auxiliar a cátedra; (book) libro de lectura, m. **to be a great r.,** leer mucho. **the Spanish r.** (reader of Spanish books) el lector de español

readily adv fácilmente; en seguida, inmediatamente; de buena gana, con placer

readiness n prontitud, expedición, f; buena voluntad, f; (of speech, etc.) facilidad, f. **in r.,** preparado. **r. of wit,** viveza de ingenio, f

reading n lectura, Lat. Am. also leída, f; (erudition) conocimientos, m pl; (recital) declamación, f; (lecture) conferencia, f; (study) estudio, m; interpretación, f; (of a thermometer, etc.) registro, m; (of a will) apertura, f. **at one reading** Lat. Am. de una leída. **r.-book,** libro de lectura, m. **r.-desk,** atril, m. **r.-glass,** lente para leer, m, carlita, f. **r.-lamp,** lámpara de sobremesa, f. **r.-matter,** material de lectura, m. **r.-room,** gabinete de lectura, m, sala de lectura, f

readjourn vt (a meeting) suspender (la sesión) de nuevo

readjust vt reajustar, reacomdar; vi reacomodarse

readjustment n reajuste, m, reacomodación, f

readmission n readmisión, f

ready a listo, preparado; dispuesto; pronto; (on the point of) a punto de; (easy) fácil; (near at hand) a la mano; (with money) contante; (with wit, etc.) vivo; (available) disponible; (nimble) ágil, ligero. **I am r. to do it,** Estoy dispuesto a hacerlo. **in r. cash,** en dinero contante. **to get r.,** prepararse; (dress) vestirse. **to make r.,** vt preparar; aprestar; print imponer. vi prepararse, disponerse. **r.-made,** hecho; confeccionado. **r.-made clothing,** ropa hecha, f. **r. money,** dinero contante, m. **r.-witted,** de ingenio vivo

reaffirm vt afirmar de nuevo; reiterar, volver a repetir

reaffirmation n reiteración, f

reafforestation n nuevas plantaciones, f pl

real a real; verdadero; efectivo; (with silk, etc.) puro; sincero. **r. estate, r. property,** bienes raíces, m pl

realism n realismo, m

realist n realista, mf

realistic a realista

reality n realidad, f; verdad, f

realize vt (understand) darse cuenta de, hacerse cargo de; realizar; (make real) dar vida (a); (accomplish) llevar a cabo; com realizar; (gain) adquirir

really adv realmente; en verdad; en realidad; en efecto; (frankly) francamente. **R.?** ¿De veras?

realm n reino, m, dominios, m pl; fig esfera, f

realty n bienes raíces, m pl

reanimate vt reanimar

reap vt segar; fig cosechar, recoger

reaper n segador (-ra); (machine) segadora mecánica, f

reaping n siega, f; fig cosecha, f. **r.-machine**, segadora mecánica, f

reappear vi reaparecer

reappearance n reaparición, f

reapplication n nueva aplicación, f; (of paint, etc.) otra capa, f; (for a post, etc.) neuva solicitud, f

reapply vt aplicar de nuevo; (paint, etc.) dar otra capa (de); (for a post, etc.) mandar una nueva solicitud

reappoint vt designar de nuevo

rear vt (lift) alzar, levantar; (breed, educate) criar; (build) erigir, construir. vi (of horses) encabritarse, corcovear

rear n cola, f; parte de atrás, f; parte posterior, f; última fila, f; (background) fondo, m; inf trasera, f; mil retaguardia, f. a de atrás; trasero; último; posterior; de última fila; mil de retaguardia. **in the r.**, por detrás; a la cola; a retaguardia. **to bring up the r.**, cerrar la marcha. **r.-admiral**, contra almirante, m. **r.-axle**, eje trasero, m. **r.-guard**, retaguardia, f. **r. lamp**, faro trasero, m. **r. rank**, última fila, f. **r. view**, vista por detrás, f; vista posterior, f

rearm vt rearmar. vi rearmarse

rearmament n rearmamento, m

rearrange vt volver a arreglar; arreglar de otra manera; (a literary work) refundir, adaptar

rearrangement n nuevo arroglo, m; (of a literary work) refundición, adaptación, f

reason n razón, f. **I have plenty of r. to . . .** No me faltarían motivos para . . . vi and vt razonar. **to r. out of**, disuadir de. **by r. of**, a causa de, con motivo de; en virtud de. **for this r.**, por esto, por esta razón. **out of all r.**, fuera de razón. **to stand to r.**, ser lógico, estar puesto en razón. **with r.**, con razón. **r. of state**, razón de estado, f

reasonable a razonable; racional

reasoning n razonamiento, m

reassemble vt reunir otra vez. vi juntarse de nuevo

reassess vt tasar de nuevo; repartir de nuevo; (a work of art) hacer una nueva apreciación (de)

reassessment n nueva tasación, f; nuevo repartimiento, m; (of a work of art) nueva estimación, f

reassume vt reasumir

reassure vt asegurar de nuevo; tranquilizar, confortar

reassuring a tranquilizador, consolador

rebate n rebaja, f, descuento, m; reducción, f. vt rebajar, descontar; reducir. **to r. pro rata**, ratear

rebel n rebelde, mf, insurrecto (-ta). vi rebelarse, sublevarse. **r. leader**, cabecilla, m

rebellion n rebelión, f

rebellious a rebelde; revoltoso; refractario

rebirth n renacimiento, m

rebound a (of books) reencuadernado. vi rebotar; repercutir; (revive) reavivarse. n rebote, resalto, m; reacción, f, rechazo, m

rebuff n repulsa, f, desaire, m; contrariedad, f. vt rechazar; contrariar

rebuild vt reedificar

rebuke n reconvención, reprensión, censura, f, reproche, m, vt reprender, censurar, reprochar

rebukingly adv en tono de censura; con reprensión, con reprobación

rebut vt refutar

rebuttal n refutación, f

recalcitrance n terquedad, obstinacia, f; rebeldía, f

recalcitrant a reacio, recalcitrante

recall vt llamar; hacer volver; (dismiss) destituir; (ambassador, etc.) retirar; (remind or remember) recordar; (revoke) revocar. n llamada, f; mil toque de llamada, m; (of ambassadors, etc.) retirada, f; (dismissal) destitución, f. **beyond r.**, irrevocable; (forgotten) olvidado

recant vt retractar, retirar. vi desdecirse (de), retractarse

recantation n recantación, f

recapitulate vt recapitular, resumir

recapture vt volver a prender, hacer prisionero nuevamente; (a place) volver a tomar; (a ship) represar

recast vt (metals, a literary work) refundir; (alter) cambiar; (reckon) volver a calcular

recede vi retroceder; alejarse (de), separarse (de); desviarse (de); retirarse; desaparecer; (diminish) disminuir; (of prices) bajar

receding a que retrocede, etc.

receipt n recibo, m; (for money) recibí, m; (recipe) receta, f; pl **receipts**, ingresos, m pl. vt firmar (or extender) recibo. **on r. of**, al recibir. **to acknowledge the r. of**, acusar recibo de. **r. book**, libro talonario, m

receive *vt* and *vi* recibir; admitir, aceptar; acoger; (money) percibir, cobrar; (lodge) hospedar, alojar; (contain) contener. **to r. one's degree** *Lat. Am.* diplomarse. **to be well received,** tener buena acogida

receiver *n* recibidor (-ra); (of stolen goods) receptador (-ra); (in bankruptcies) síndico, *m*; (for other legal business) receptor, *m*; (of a telephone) auricular, *m*; *elec* receptor, *m*; *rad* radiorreceptor, *m*. **to hang up the r.),** colgar (el auricular)

receivership *n* sindicatura, *f*; receptoría, *f*

receiving *n* recibimiento, *m*; (of money, etc.) cobranza, *f*, percibo, *m*; (of stolen goods) encubrimiento, *m.* a que recibe; recipiente; de recepción. **r. set,** aparato de radio, *m*

recent *a* reciente; nuevo. **in r. years,** en estos últimos años

recently *adv* recientemente; (before past participles) recién. **until r.,** hasta hace poco. **r. painted,** recién pintado

receptacle *n* receptáculo, recipiente, *m*; *bot* receptáculo, *m*

reception *n* recepción, *f*; recibo, *m*; (welcome) acogida, *f*; (of evidence) recepción, *f.* **r. room,** pieza de recibo, *f*, gabinete, *m*

receptive *a* receptivo; susceptible

recess *n* (holiday) vacaciones, *f pl*; (during school hours) hora de receso, *f*; (fig heart) seno, *m*, entrañas, *f pl*; (of the soul, heart) hondón, *m*; (in a coastline, etc.) depresión, *f*; (in a wall) nicho, *m*; (alcove) alcoba, *f*. **parliamentary r.,** interregno parlamentario, *m*

recharge *vt* (a gun, etc.) recargar; acusar de nuevo

recipe *n* receta, *f*

recipient *n* recibidor (-ra); el, *m*, (f, la) que recibe. **a** recipiente; receptivo

reciprocal *a* recíproco

reciprocate *vt* reciprocar; *mech* producir movimiento de vaivén. *vi mech* oscilar, tener movimiento alternativo; corresponder; ser recíproco

reciprocity *n* reciprocidad, *f*

recital *n* narración, relación, *f*; enumeración, *f*; recitación, *f*; *mus* recital, *m*

recitation *n* recitación, *f*

recitative *n* recitado, *m*

recite *vt* recitar, repetir; narrar; declamar. *vi* decir una recitación

reciter *n* recitador (-ra); declamador (-ra)

reckless *a* temerario, audaz; precipitado; descuidado (de); indiferente (a); excesivo; imprudente

recklessly *adv* temerariamente; descuidadamente; imprudentemente

reckon *vt* calcular, computar; contar; enumerar; (believe) considerar, juzgar; (attribute) atribuir; (think) creer (que). **to r. up,** echar cuentas, calcular. **to r. with,** contar con; tomar en serio

reckoner *n* calculador (-ra). **ready r.,** tablas matemáticas, *f pl*

reckoning *n* cálculo, *m*, calculación, *f*; cuenta, *f*; *fig* retribución, *f*, castigo, *m*; *naut* estima, *f*. **the day of r.,** el día de ajuste de cuentas; el día del juicio final. **to be out in one's r.,** equivocarse en el cálculo; engañarse en el juicio

reclaim *vt* (land) entarquinar; (reform) reformar; (tame) domesticar; (claim) reclamar; (restore) restaurar

reclamation *n* (of land) entarquinamiento, *f*; cultivo, *m*; (reform) reformación, *f*; (restoration) restauración, *f*; (claiming) reclamación, *f*

recline *vt* apoyar; recostar; reclinar; descansar, reposar. *vi* recostarse, reclinarse; estar tumbado; apoyarse; descansar

reclining *n* reclinación, *f.* **a** inclinado; acostado; (of statues) yacente

recluse *a* solitario, *n* recluso (-sa); solitario (-ia); ermitaño, *m*, anacoreta, *mf*

recognition *n* reconocimiento, *m*

recognizance *n* reconocimiento, *m*; *law* obligación, *f*

recognize *vt* reconocer; confesar

recoil *n* reculada, *f*; (of a gun) culatazo, *m*; (refusal) rechazo, *m*; (result) repercusión, *f*; (repugnance) aversión, repugnancia, *f*. *vi* recular; retroceder; repercutir; sentir repugnancia

recollect *vt* acordarse de, recordar. **to r. oneself,** reponerse, recobrarse

recollection *n* recuerdo, *m*, memoria, *f*

recommence *vt* and *vi* empezar de nuevo

recommend *vt* recomendar; aconsejar; encargar

recommendation *n* recomendación, *f*

recommendatory *a* recomendatorio

recompense *n* recompensa, *f*, *vt* recompensar

reconcilable *a* reconciliable; compatible; conciliable

reconcile *vt* reconciliar; (quarrels) componer, ajustar; (opposing theories, etc.) conciliar. **to r. oneself (to),** aceptar; acostumbrarse (a); resignarse (a)

reconciliation *n* reconciliación, *f*; (of theories, etc.) conciliación, *f*

reconciliatory *a* reconciliador

recondite *a* recóndito

reconnaissance *n* reconocimiento, *m*; exploración, *f.* **r. flight,** vuelo de reconocimiento, *m.* **r. plane,** avión de reconocimiento, *m*

reconnoiter *vt mil* reconocer; explorar. *vi mil* practicar un reconocimiento; correr la campaña

reconnoitering *n* reconocimiento, *m*, a de reconocimiento

reconquest *n* reconquista, *f*

reconsider *vt* considerar de nuevo, volver a considerar; volver a discutir

reconstitute *vt* reconstituir

reconstruct *vt* reconstruir

reconstruction *n* reconstrucción, *f*

recopy *vt* copiar de nuevo

record *vt* apuntar; inscribir; (recount) contar, escribir; recordar; registrar; (of thermometers, etc.) marcar, registrar; hacer un disco de gramófono de; (radio, cinema) impresionar. *n* relación, *f*; crónica, *f*; historia, *f*; (soldier's) hoja de servicios, *f*; (past) antecedentes, *m pl*; documento, *m*; inscripción, *f*; (entry) partida, *f*; testimonio, *m*; (memory) recuerdo, *m*; registro, *m*; (gramophone) disco de gramófono, *m*; *sport* record, *m*, plusmarca, *f*; *pl* **records**, *m pl*; (notes) notas, *f pl*; (facts) datos, *m pl*; anales, *m pl*. **keeper of the records**, archivero, *m*. **off the r.**, confidencialmente. **on r.**, escrito; registrado; inscrito en los anales de la historia. **to break a r.**, supremar precedentes. **r.-holder**, plusmarquista, *mf*

recorder *n* registrador, *m*; archivero, *m*; *law* juez, *m*; (historian) historiador, *m*; *mus* caramillo, *m*; *mech* contador, indicador, *m*; (scientific) aparato registrador, *m*

recording *a* registrador. **r. apparatus**, (cinema, radio, gramophone) máquina de impresionar, *f*; (scientific) aparato registrador, *m*. **r. van**, carro de sonido, *m*

recount *vt* contar de nuevo; (tell) referir, narrar, contar

recoup *vt* compensar, indemnizar; recobrar, desquitarse de

recourse *n* recurso, *m*. **to have r. to**, recurrir, *a*

recover *vt* (regain) recobrar; *fig* reconquistar; (retrieve) rescatar; *law* reivindicar. *vi* reponerse; (in health) recobrar la salud, sanar, curarse; *law* ganar un pleito. **to r. consciousness**, volver en sí

recoverable *a* recuperable

recovery *n* (regaining) recobro, *m*, recuperación, *f*; (of money) cobranza, *f*; (retrieval) rescate, *m*; *fig* reconquista, *f*; (from illness) mejoría, convalecencia, *f*; restablecimiento, *m*; *law* reivindicación, *f*

recreant *a* traidor, falso, desleal. *n* apóstata, *mf* traidor (-ra)

recreate *vt* recrear

recreation *n* recreación, *f*; (break in schools) recreo, *m*. **r. hall**, sala de recreo, *f*

recreative *a* recreativo

recriminate *vi* recriminar

recrimination *n* recriminación, reconvención, *f*

recriminatory *a* recriminador

recross *vt* volver a cruzar, cruzar de nuevo

recrudesce *vi* recrudecer

recrudescent *a* recrudescente

recruit *n* recluta, *m*. *vt* reclutar; (restore) reponer

recruiting *n* reclutamiento, *m*. **r. office**, caja de reclutamiento, *f*

rectal *a* rectal

rectangle *n* rectángulo, *m*

rectangular *a* rectangular

rectifiable *a* rectificable

rectification *n* rectificación, *f*

rectify *vt* rectificar

rectilinear *a* rectilíneo

rectitude *n* rectitud, *f*

rector *n* (of a university or school) rector, *m*; (priest) párroco, *m*

rectum *n* recto, *m*

recumbent *a* recostado, reclinado; (of a statue) yacente

recuperable *a* recuperable

recuperate *vt* recuperar, recobrar. *vi* restablecerse, reponerse; recuperarse

recuperation *n* recuperación, *f*

recuperative *a* recuperativo

recur *vi* presentarse a la imaginación; volver (sobre); presentarse de nuevo, aparecer otra vez; repetirse; reproducirse

recurrence *n* reaparición, *f*; repetición, *f*

recurrent *a* periódico; *med* recurrente

red *a* rojo; (of wine) tinto. *n* color rojo, *m*; (in billiards) mingo, *m*, bola roja, *f*; *pol* rojo, *m*. **to catch red-handed**, coger con el hurto en las manos; coger con las manos en la masa; coger en el acto. **to grow red**, enrojecerse, ponerse rojo; volverse rojo. **red-berried**, con bayas rojas. **red cabbage**, lombarda, *f*. **red cedar**, cedro dulce, *m*. **red corpuscle**, glóbulo rojo, *m*. **Red Cross**, Cruz Roja, *f*. **red currant**, grosella, *f*. **red currant bush**, grosellero, *m*. **red-eyed**, con los ojos inyectados. **red fir**, pino silvestre, *m*. **red flush**, (in the sky) arrebol, *m*. **red-gold**, bermejo; (of hair, etc.) rojo. **red-haired**, pelirrojo, de pelo rojo. **red-handed**, con las manos ensangrentadas; *fig* en el acto. **red-head** (person) pelirrojo (-ja). **red-heat**, incandescencia, *f*. **red-hot**, candente. *m*. **red-lead**, minio, *m*. **red-letter**, de fiesta; extraordinario. **red-letter day**, día de fiesta, *m*; día extraordinario, *m*. **red mullet**, salmonete, *m*, trilla, *f*. **red ocher**, almagre, *m*. **red pepper**, pimiento, *m*; (cayenne) pimentón, *Lat. Am.* ají, *m*. **Red Sea**, mar Rojo, mar Bermejo, *m*. **red tape**, balduque, *m*; formulismo, *m*; burocracia, *f*. **red wine**, vino tinto, *m*

redden *vt* rojear, enrojecer; pintar de rojo. *vi* enrojecerse, ponerse rojo; volverse rojo

reddish *a* rojizo

redeem *vt* (a mortgage, bonds, etc.) amortizar; (from pawn) desempeñar; (a promise, etc.) cumplir; libertar; redimir; compensar; (a fault) expiar; (reform) reformar; (rescue) rescatar

redeemable *a* redimible; amortizable

redeemer n rescatador (-ra); salvador (-ra); *theol* Redentor, m

redeeming a redentor; compensatorio. **r. feature**, compensación, f; rasgo bueno, m. **There is no r. feature in his work,** No hay nada bueno en su obra

redemption n (of a mortgage, etc.) amortización, f; (from pawn) desempeño, m; (of a promise, etc.) cumplimiento, m; (ransom, etc.) rescate, m; *theol* redención, f; compensación, f; (of a fault) expiación, f; reformación, f

redemptive a redentor

redescend vi bajar de nuevo

rediscovery n nuevo descubrimiento, m

redistribute vt distribuir de nuevo, volver a distribuir

redistribution n nueva distribución, f

redolent a fragante, oloroso; *fig* evocador (de)

redouble vt redoblar. vi redoblarse

redoubling n redoblamiento, m

redoubt n reducto, m

redoubtable a formidable, terrible; valiente

redound vi redundar (en)

redress vt rectificar; reparar; remediar; hacer justicia (a); corregir

reduce vt reducir; disminuir; (in price) rebajar; abreviar; (exhaust, weaken) agotar; (impoverish) empobrecer; (degrade) degradar. **to r. to the ranks,** *mil* volver a las filas; degradar. **to be in reduced circumstances,** estar en la indigencia

reduction n reducción, f; (in price) rebaja, f

redundance n redundancia, f

redundant a redundante; superfluo, excesivo

reduplicate vt reduplicar

reecho vt repetir; devolver el son de, hacer reverberar. vi repercutirse, reverberar

reed n *bot* caña, f; (arrow) saeta, f; (pipe) caramillo, m; (in wind-instruments) lengüeta, f; *arch* junquillo, m; (in a loom) peine, m; (pastoral poetry) poesía bucólica, f. vt (thatch) bardar con cañas

reef n arrecife, escollo, encalladero, m; *min* filón, m; *naut* rizo, m. vt *naut* arrizar. **to take in reefs,** *naut* hacer el rizo. **r.-knot,** nudo de marino, m

reek n humo, m; olor, m. vi humear; oler (de); *fig* recordar, hacer pensar (en)

reel n carrete, m; devanadera, f; (of a fishing rod) carrete, carretel, m; (cinema) cinta, f; (dance) baile escocés, m. vt devanar. vi tambalear, titubear; (of ships, etc.) cabecear; temblar; oscilar. **to r. about drunkenly,** (of persons) andar haciendo eses, arrimarse a las paredes. **to r. off,** recitar; enumerar; decir rápidamente

reelect vt reelegir

reeling n tambaleo, m; andar vacilante,

m; (of a ship, etc.) cabeceo, m; oscilación, f

reembarcation n reembarque, m

reembark vt reembarcar. vi reembarcarse

reemerge vi reaparecer

reenact vt revalidar (una ley); decretar de nuevo

reenactment n revalidación (de una ley), f; nuevo decreto, m

reengage vt contratar de nuevo

reenlist vt and vi alistar(se) de nuevo

reenlistment n reenganche, m

reenter vt volver a entrar (en); reingresar (en)

reentry n segunda entrada, f, reingreso, m

reequip vt equipar de nuevo

reestablish vt restablecer; restaurar

reestablishment n restablecimiento, m; restauración, f

reexamination n reexaminación, f; nuevo examen, m; *law* nuevo interrogatorio, m

reexamine vt reexaminar; *law* interrogar de nuevo

reexport vt reexportar

reexportation n reexportación, f

refashion vt volver a hacer; formar de nuevo

refectory n refectorio, m

refer vt atribuir (a); (send) enviar, remitir; (assign) referir (a), relacionar (con). vi referirse (a); aludir (a); hablar (de)

referee n árbitro, m; *law* juez arbitrador, m; (reference) garante, mf fiador (-ra). vi servir de árbitro

reference n referencia, f; consulta, f; mención, f; alusión, f; (relation) relación, f; pl **references,** com referencias, f pl. **for r.,** para consulta, m. **in r. to,** referencia a, respecto a, en cuanto a. **terms of r.,** puntos de consulta, m pl. **work of r.,** libro de consulta, m

reference book n libro de consulta, m

referendum n referéndum, m

refill vt rellenar; rehenchir; (pen) llenar de nuevo con tinta. n (for a pencil) mina de recambio, f

refine vt refinar; (metals) acrisolar; (fats) clarificar; *fig* perfeccionar, pulir, refinar

refined a refinado; fino; culto; cortés; elegante; delicado; (subtle) sutil; (affected) afectado

refinement n refinamiento, m; finura, f; cultura, f; cortesía, f; elegancia, f; delicadeza, f; (subtlety) sutileza, f; (affectation) afectación, f

refinery n refinería, f

refit vt reparar; *naut* embonar

refitting n reparación, f; *naut* embonada, f

reflect vt reflejar; reflexionar. vi reflejar; reflexionar (sobre), pensar (en), meditar (sobre). **This offer reflects credit on him,** Esta oferta le hace honor. **to r. on, upon,** reflexionar sobre; (disparage) desacreditar; (affect unfavorably) perjudicar

reflection n *phys* reflexión, f; reflejo, m; consideración, f, pensamiento, m; (aspersion) censura, f, reproche, m. **upon mature r.,** después de pensarlo bien

reflective a *phys* reflector; reflexivo, pensativo, meditabundo

reflex a reflejo. n reflejo, m; acción refleja, f. **r. action,** acción refleja, f

refloat vt (a ship) poner otra vez a flote, desvarar

reflux n reflujo, m

reform n reforma, f. a de reforma; reformista. vt reformar; formar de nuevo. vi reformarse

reformation n reformación, f; **Reformation,** Reforma, f

reformatory a reformatorio, reformador. n reformatorio, m, casa de corrección, f

reformer n reformador (-ra), reformista, mf

refract vt refractar

refractive a refringente

refractoriness n terquedad, obstinacia, f; rebeldía, indocilidad, f

refractory a (of substances) refractario; recalcitrante, intratable, rebelde

refrain n estribillo, estrambote, m

refrain vi abstenerse (de), evitar

refresh vt refrescar

refreshing a refrescante; atractivo; estimulante; interesante

refreshment n (solace) solaz, reposo, m; recreación, f, deleite, m; (food and (or) drink) refresco, m. **r.-room,** (at a station) fonda, f. **r. stand** *Mexico* fresquería, f

refrigerate vt refrigerar; enfriar; refrescar

refrigeration n refrigeración, f; enfriamiento, m. **r. chamber,** cámara frigorífica, f

refrigerator n refrigerador, m, nevera, f

refuel vt (a furnace) cargar con carbón, etc.; (of a ship) tomar carbón; (of an airplane, motor vehicle) tomar bencina

refuge n refugio, m; asilo, m; (resort) recurso, m; subterfugio, m; (traffic island) refugio para peatones, m. **to take r.,** refugiarse; resguardarse (de)

refugee a refugiado. n refugiado (-da)

refulgent a refulgente

refund vt reembolsar; devolver

refunding n reembolso, m; devolución, f

refurbish vt restaurar; renovar; (a literary work) refundir

refurnish vt amueblar de nuevo

refusal n negativa, f; (rejection) rechazo, m; (option) opción, f; preferencia, f

refuse vt negar; (reject) rechazar. vi negarse (a), rehusar; (of a horse) resistirse a saltar

refuse n desecho, m; desperdicios, m pl; residuo, m; basura, f. a de desecho. **r. dump,** muladar, m

refute vt refutar

regain vt recobrar, recuperar; cobrar; ganar de nuevo; *fig* reconquistar. **to r. one's breath,** cobrar aliento. **to r. consciousness,** volver en sí

regal a regio, real

regale vt regalar, agasajar; recrear, deleitar

regard vt mirar; observar; considerar; (respect) respetar; (concern) importar, concernir; relacionarse con. n mirada, f; atención, f; (esteem) aprecio, m, estimación, f; respeto, m; veneración, f; (relation) referencia, f; pl **regards,** recuerdos, saludos, m pl. **He has little r. for their feelings,** Le importan poco sus susceptibilidades. **With kindest regards,** Con mis saludos más afectuosos. **as regards, with r. to,** con referencia a, respecto a, en cuanto a

regardful a atento (a), cuidadoso (de); que se preocupa (de)

regarding prep tocante a, en cuanto a, respecto de

regardless a negligente (de); indiferente (a), insensible (a); que no se interesa (en); que no se inquieta (por); sin preocuparse (de)

regatta n regata, f

regenerate vt regenerar. a regenerado

regenerative a regenerador

regent n regente, mf

régime n régimen, m

regimen n (*gram med*) régimen, m,

regiment n regimiento, m. vt regimentar. **r. of the line,** tropa de línea, f

regimentation n regimentación, f

region n región, f

regional a regional

regionalist n regionalista, mf

register n (record and *mech mus print*) registro, m; (of ships, etc.) matrícula, f; lista, f. vt registrar; matricular; (a ship) abanderar; inscribir; (one's child in a school) anotar (Argentina), inscribir; (of thermometers, etc.) marcar; (letters) certificar; (luggage) facturar; (in one's mind) grabar; (emotion) mostrar, manifestar. vi (at a hotel, etc.) registrarse; *print* estar en registro. **cash r.,** caja registradora, f. **r. of births, marriages and deaths,** registro civil, m

registered letter n carta certificada, f

registrar n registrador, m; archivero, m; secretario, m; (of a school) jefe de inscripciones, secretario general (the latter has many more duties). **r. of births, marriages and deaths,** secretario del registro civil, m. **registrar's office,** oficina del registro civil, f

registration n registro, m; inscripción, f; (of a vehicle, etc.) matrícula, f; naut abanderamiento, m; (of a letter, etc.) certificación, f. **r. number,** número de matrícula, m

registry n registro, m; inscripción, f; matrícula, f. **r. office,** oficina del registro civil, f; (for servants) agencia doméstica, f

regression n regresión, f, retroceso, m

regret vt sentir; lamentar, pesar; arrepentirse (de); (miss) echar de menos (a). n sentimiento, pesar, m; (remorse) remordimiento, m. **I r. very much that . . . ,** Me pesa mucho que . . . , Siento mucho que . . . **to send one's regrets,** mandar sus excusas

regretful a lleno de pesar; arrepentido; lamentable, deplorable. **He was most r. that . . . ,** Lamentaba mucho que . . .

regretfully adv con pesar

regrettable a lamentable, deplorable; doloroso; (with loss, etc.) sensible

regrettably adv lamentablemente; sensiblemente

regroup vt arreglar de nuevo; formar de nuevo; reorganizar

regular a regular; normal; (ordinary) corriente, común; (in order) en regla; (gram bot ecc mil geom) regular. n ecc regular, m; (soldier) soldado de línea, m; (officer) militar de carrera, m; (client) parroquiano habitual, m

regularize vt regularizar

regulate vt regular; ajustar, arreglar; (direct) dirigir; reglamentar

regulation n regulación, f; arreglo, m; (rule) reglamento, m, a de reglamento; normal

regulative a regulador

regurgitate vt and vi regurgitar

rehabilitate vt rehabilitar

rehash vt (a literary work, etc.) refundir

rehearing n nueva audición, f, (of a case) revisión, f

rehearsal n theat ensayo, m; recitación, f; relación, narración, f. **dress r.,** ensayo general, m

rehearse vt theat ensayar; recitar; (narrate) narrar; enumerar

reheat vt recalentar

reign n reinado, m. vi reinar; predominar

reigning a reinante; predominante

reimburse vt reembolsar

reimbursement n reembolso, m

reimport vt importar de nuevo, reimportar, n reimporte, m

reimpose vt reimponer

reimprison vt encarcelar de nuevo, reencarcelar

rein n rienda, f, vt llevar las riendas (de); (hold back) refrenar. **to give r. to,** fig dar rienda suelta (a)

reincarnation n reencarnación, f

reincorporate vt reincorporar

reindeer n reno, m

reinforce vt reforzar; (concrete) armar; fortalecer. **reinforced concrete,** n hormigón armado, m

reinforcement n reforzamiento, m; (mil nav fig) refuerzo, m

reinsert vt volver a insertar

reinstall vt reinstalar; rehabilitar

reinstalment n reinstalación, f; rehabilitación, f; restablecimiento, m

reinstate vt reponer, restablecer; reinstalar; rehabilitar

reinstatement n restablecimiento, m; rehabilitación, f

reinsurance n reaseguro, m

reinsure vt reasegurar

reintegrate vt reintegrar

reintegration n reintegración, f

reinter vt enterrar de nuevo

reinvest vt reinvertir

reinvestment n reinversión, f

reinvigorate vt reanimar, dar nuevo vigor (a)

reinvite vt invitar de nuevo (a)

reissue n nueva emisión, f; (of a book, etc.) nueva edición, reimpresión, f. vt hacer una nueva emisión (de); reeditar, publicar de nuevo

reiterate vt reiterar, repetir

reject vt rechazar, rehusar; repudiar; repulsar; desechar

rejection n rechazamiento, m; repudiación, refutación, f; repulsa, f

rejoice vt alegrar, regocijar. vi alegrarse (de), regocijarse (de), gloriarse (en)

rejoicing n regocijo, júbilo, m, alegría, f; algazara, f, fiestas, f pl

rejoin vt and vi juntar de nuevo; volver a; reunirse con; (reply) contestar, replicar

rejoinder n contestación, respuesta, f

rejuvenate vt rejuvenecer

rekindle vt encender de nuevo; despertar, reavivar. vi encenderse de nuevo; reavivarse

relapse n reincidencia, recaída, f; med recidiva, f. vi reincidir (en); med recaer

relapsed a relapso

relate vt (recount) relatar, narrar; relacionar; unir; (of kinship) emparentar. vi ajustarse (a); referirse (a). **The first fact is not related to the second,** El primer hecho no tiene nada que ver con el segundo

related a relacionado; (by kinship) emparentado. **John is well-r.,** Juan es de buena familia; Juan es de familia influyente; Juan tiene buenas relaciones

relation n (narrative) relación, narración, f; conexión, f; relación, f; (kinship) parentesco, m; (person) pariente (-ta). **in r. to,** con relación a, en cuanto a

relationship n parentesco, m; conexión, relación, Lat. Am. atingencia, f

relative a relativo. n pariente (-ta); pl **relatives,** parientes, m pl, parentela, f

relax vt relajar; aflojar; soltar; (make less severe) ablandar; (decrease) mitigar. vi relajarse; aflojar; (rest) descansar

relaxation n relajación, f; aflojamiento, m; ablandamiento, m; mitigación, f; (rest) descanso, reposo, m; (pastime) pasatiempo, m; (amusement) diversión, f

relaxing a relajante; (of climate) enervante

relay n (of horses) parada, f; (shift) tanda, f; relevo, m; elec relais, m; rad redifusión, f. vt enviar por posta; elec reemitir; rad retransmitir; (lay again) colocar de nuevo. **r. race,** carrera de equipo, carrera de relevos, f

release vt soltar; (hurl) lanzar; (set free) poner en libertad (a); librar (de); absolver; (surrender) renunciar (a); dar al público, poner en circulación; (lease again) realquilar. n soltura, f; lanzamiento, m; liberación, f; (from pain) alivio, m; remisión, f; exoneración, f; publicación, f; (of films) representación, f; law soltura, f

relegate vt relegar

relent vi ablandarse, enternecerse; ceder

relenting n enternecimiento, desenojo, m

relentless a implacable, inexorable; despiadado

relentlessly adv inexorablemente; sin piedad

relet vt realquilar

relevance n conexión, f; pertinencia, f; aplicabilidad, f

relevant a relativo; pertinente, a propósito, oportuno; aplicable

reliability n seguridad, f; formalidad, f; confianza, f; exactitud, f; veracidad, f

reliable a seguro; formal; digno de crédito, de confianza, solvente digno de confianza; exacto; veraz

reliably adv seguramente; de una manera digna de confianza; exactamente

reliance n confianza, f. **to place r. on,** tener confianza en

reliant a confiado

relic n vestigio, rastro, m; ecc reliquia, f

relief n (alleviation) alivio, m; desahogo, m; (help) socorro, m, ayuda, f; beneficencia, f; mil relevo, m; (pleasure) placer, m, satisfacción, f; (consolation) consuelo, m; law remisión, f; art relieve, m. **high r.,** alto relieve, m. **low r.,** bajo relieve, m. **r. map,** mapa en relieve, m. **r. train,** tren de socorro, m

relieve vt aliviar; aligerar, suavizar; mitigar; (one's feelings, etc.) desahogar; (mil and to take the place of) relevar; (free) librar; (dismiss) destituir; (remove) quitar; (rob) robar; (help) socorrer, remediar; (redeem) redimir; (ornament) adornar; (from a wrong) hacer justicia (a)

relieving n alivio, m; aligeramiento, m;

mitigación, f; (of the feelings) desahogo, m; mil relevo, m; (help) socorro, m. **r. arch,** sobrearco, m

relight vt volver a encender. vi encenderse de nuevo

religion n religión, f

religiosity n religiosidad, f

religious a religioso; en religión; piadoso, crevente; devoto. n religioso (-sa). **r. orders,** órdenes religiosas, f pl. **r. toleration,** libertad de cultos, f

relinquish vt abandonar; (one's grip) soltar; renunciar; desistir (de), dejar (de); (a post) dimitir (de)

relinquishment n abandono, m; renuncia, f; dejamiento, m; (of a post) dimisión, f

relish n gusto, m; sabor, m; (touch, smack) dejo, m; condimento, m; apetito, m, gana, f. vt gustar de; comer con apetito; saborear, paladear; fig seducir, atraer, gustar. vi tener gusto (de). **I do not much r. the idea,** No me seduce la idea

relishing n saboreo, m; (enjoyment) goce, m, fruición, f; consideración, f

relive vt vivir de nuevo, volver a vivir

reload vt recargar

reluctance n repugnancia, desgana, f. **with r.,** a regañadientes, de mala gana

reluctant a poco dispuesto (a), que tiene repugnancia a (hacer algo), sin gana; (forced) forzado; artificial; (hesitating) vacilante

reluctantly adv de mala gana, con repugnancia, a disgusto

rely on vi contar con, confiar en, depender de

remain vi quedar; permanecer; (be left over) sobrar; continuar. **I r. yours faithfully . . . ,** (in a letter) Queda de Vd. su att. s.s. . . . **It remains to be written,** Queda por escribir

remainder n resto, m; restos, m pl, sobras, f pl; residuo, m. **The r. of the people went away,** Los demás se marcharon

remaining pres. part and a que queda; sobrante. **r. to be paid** Lat. Am. impago

remains n pl restos, m pl; sobras, f pl; desperdicios, m pl; ruinas, f pl

remake vt rehacer; reformar

remand vt law reencarcelar. n law reencarcelamiento, m

remark n observación, f; nota, f; comentario, m. vt and vi observar; notar. **to r. on,** comentar, hacer una observación sobre

remarkable a notable, singular, extraordinario

remarriage n segundas nupcias, f pl, segundo casamiento, m

remarry vt volver a casar (a). vi casarse en segundas nupcias; volver a casarse

remedial a remediador; curativo, terapéutico

remedy n remedio, m; recurso, m, vt remediar; curar

remember vt recordar; tener presente; acordarse de. vi acordarse; no olvidarse. **R. me to your mother,** Dale recuerdos míos a tu madre. **If I r. rightly . . . ,** Si bien me acuerdo . . . **And r. that I shall do no more!** ¡Y no olvides que no haré más!

remembrance n recuerdo, m; memoria, f; pl **remembrances,** recuerdos, m pl

remind vt recordar

reminder n recuerdo, m; (warning) advertencia, f. **a gentle r.,** una indirecta, una insinuación

reminisce vi inf recordar viejas historias

reminiscence n reminiscencia, f, recuerdo, m

reminiscent a evocador, que recuerda; de reminiscencia; que piensa en el pasado. **to be r. of,** recordar; inf oler a

remiss a negligente, descuidado

remission n remisión, f

remit vt remitir; com remesar, enviar. vi (pay) pagar

remittance n remesa, f, envío, m

remitter n remitente, mf

remnant n resto, m; (of fabric) retal, retazo, m; (relic) vestigio, m, reliquia, f. **r. sale,** saldo, m

remodel vt rehacer; reformar; modelar de nuevo; (a play, etc.) refundir

remodeling n reformación, f; (of a play, etc.) refundición, f

remonstrance n protesta, f; reconvención, f

remonstrate vi protestar, objetar. **to r. with,** reprochar, reconvenir

remorse n remordimiento, m

remorseful a lleno de remordimientos; penitente, arrepentido

remorsefully adv con remordimiento

remorseless a sin conciencia, sin remordimientos; despiadado, inflexible

remote a distante, lejano; remoto; aislado; ajeno; (slight) leve, vago. **r. control,** mando a distancia, m

remoteness n distancia, f; aislamiento, m; alejamiento, m; (vagueness) vaguedad, f

remount vt subir de nuevo, montar de nuevo; mil remontar. vi (go back to) remontar (a), derivarse (de). n mil remonta, f

removable a que puede quitarse; (of collars, etc.) de quita y pon; transportable; (of officials, etc.) amovible

removal n acción de quitar o levantar, f; sacamiento, m; separación, f; eliminación, f; alejamiento, m; traslado, m; (from office, etc.) deposición, f; supresión, f; asesinato, m. **r. van,** carro de mudanzas, m

remove vt quitar; retirar; levantar; sacar;

apartar; separar; eliminar; trasladar; (from office) destituir; suprimir; asesinar. vi trasladarse. n grado, m; distancia, f; (departure) partida, f. **to r. oneself,** quitarse de en medio. **to r. one's hat,** descubrirse. **first cousin once removed,** hijo de primo carnal, primo hermano del padre, primo hermano de la madre, m

remunerate vt remunerar

remuneration n remuneración, f

remunerative a remunerador

renaissance n renacimiento, m, a renacentista

renal a renal

rename vt poner otro nombre (a)

renascent a renaciente, que renace

rend vt desgarrar, rasgar; fig lacerar; (split) hender; fig dividir. **to r. from,** arrancar (a). **to r. the air,** (with cries, etc.) llenar el aire

render vt (return) devolver; dar; rendir; (make) hacer; (help, service) prestar; interpretar; (translate) traducir; (fat) derretir y clarificar

rendering n versión, f; interpretación, f

rendezvous n cita, f; lugar de cita, m; reunión, f. vi reunirse

renegade a renegado. n renegado (-da)

renew vt renovar; (resume) reanudar; (a lease, etc.) prorrogar

renewal n renovación, f; (resumption) reanudación, f; (of a lease, etc.) prorrogación, f

renewed a renovado; nuevo

rennet n cuajo, m

renounce vt renunciar; (a throne) abdicar; renegar (de), repudiar; abandonar. vi law desistir; (cards) renunciar

renouncement n renuncia, f; (of a throne) abdicación, f; repudiación, f

renovate vt renovar; limpiar; restaurar

renovation n renovación, f; limpiadura, f; restauración, f

renovator n renovador (-ra)

renown n renombre, m, fama, f

renowned a renombrado, famoso

rent n (tear) rasgadura, f; desgarro, m; abertura, f; raja hendedura, f; (discord) división, f; (hire) alquiler, m; arrendamiento, m. vt arrendar, alquilar. **r.-free,** sin pagar alquiler

rentable a alquilable, arrendable

renter n arrendador (-ra)

renunciation n renunciación, renuncia, f

reoccupy vt volver a ocupar, ocupar otra vez

reopen vt abrir de nuevo, volver a abrir. vi abrirse nuevamente, abrirse otra vez

reopening n reapertura, f

reorder vt ordenar de nuevo, com volver a pedir. n com nuevo pedido, m

reorganize vt reorganizar

reorganizing a reorganizador

repack *vt* reembalar; reenvasar; volver a hacer (una maleta)

repaint *vt* pintar de nuevo

repair *vt* arreglar (e.g. a machine) componer, remendar; reparar; restaurar; rehacer. *vi* (with to) dirigirse a, ir a; acudir a. *n* arreglo *m*, reparación, *f*; compostura, *f*; restauración, *f*. **to keep in r.**, conservar en buen estado

repairer *n* componedor (-ra); restaurador (-ra)

repairing *a* reparador

repartee *n* respuestas, agudezas, *f pl*; *inf* dimes y diretes, *m pl*

repast *n* comida, *f*; (light) colación, *f*

repatriate *vt* repatriar

repay *vt* reembolsar; recompensar; pagar; pagar en la misma moneda. *vi* pagar. **It well repays a visit,** Vale la pena de visitarse

repayable *a* reembolsable

repayment *n* reembolso, *m*; pago, retorno, *m*

repeal *n* abrogación, revocación, *f*, *vt* abrogar, rescindir, revocar

repeat *vt* repetir; reiterar; (renew) renovar; duplicar. *n* repetición, *f*

repeated *a* reiterado; redoblado

repeater *n* repetidor (-ra); reloj de repetición, *m*; arma de repetición, *f*

repel *vt* repeler; ahuyentar; (spurn) rechazar; *phys* resistir; repugnar

repellent *a* repulsivo

repent *vt* arrepentirse de. *vi* arrepentirse

repentance *n* arrepentimiento, *m*, penitencia, *f*

repentant *a* arrepentido, penitente, contrito

repeople *vt* repoblar

repercussion *n* repercusión, *f*

repertory *n* repertorio, *m*

repetition *n* repetición, *f*; recitación, *f*

repetitive *a* iterativo

repine *vi* afligirse (de); quejarse (de); padecer nostalgia

repining *n* pesares, *m pl*; quejas, *f pl*, descontento, *m*; nostalgia, *f*

replace *vt* (put back) reponer, colocar de nuevo; restituir, devolver; (renew) renovar; (in a post, etc.) reemplazar, substituir

replaceable *a* restituible; renovable; reemplazable

replacement *n* reposición, *f*; restitución, devolución, *f*; renovación, *f*; reemplazo, *m*

replant *vt* replantar

replenish *vt* rellenar

replete *a* repleto

replica *n* réplica, *f*

reply *n* respuesta, contestación, *f*, *vi* responder, contestar. **Awaiting your r.,** En espera de sus noticias. **in his r.,** en su respuesta

repopulate *vt* repoblar

repopulation *n* repoblación, *f*

report *n* (rumor) voz, *f*, rumor, *m*; (reputation) fama, *f*; (news) noticia, *f*; (journalistic) reportaje, *m*; (*mil nav* and from school) parte, *f*; (weather) boletín, *m*; (proceedings) actas, *f pl*; (statement) informe, *m*; relación, *f*; (of a gun, etc.) detonación, *f*; explosión, *f*. *vt* dar cuenta de, relatar; informar; (measure) registrar; (*mil nav*) dar parte de; comunicar; (journalistic) hacer un reportaje de; (transcribe) transcribir; (accuse) denunciar; quejarse de. *vi* presentar informe; ser reportero; (present oneself) presentarse, comparecer. **It is reported that . . . ,** Se informa que . . .

report card *n* boletín de calificaciones, *m*

reporter *n* reportero (-ra); *law* relator, *m*

reporting *n* reporterismo, *m*

repose *n* reposo, *m*; quietud, *f*; tranquilidad, serenidad, *f*. *vt* reposar, descansar; reclinar; (place) poner. *vi* reposar; tener confianza (en); basarse (en)

repository *n* repositorio, depósito, *m*; almacén, *m*; (furniture) guardamuebles, *m*; (person) depositario (-ia)

repoussé (work) *n* repujado, *m*. **to work in r.,** repujar

reprehend *vt* reprender, reprobar

reprehensible *a* reprensible

represent *vt* representar; significar

representation *n* representación, *f*

representative *a* que representa; representativo. *n* representante, *mf*

repress *vt* reprimir

repression *n* represión, *f*

repressive *a* represivo

reprieve *vt* *law* aplazar la ejecución (de); *fig* dar una tregua (a)

reprimand *n* reprimenda, *f*, *vt* reprender

reprint *n* reimpresión, tirada aparte, separata, *f*, *vt* reimprimir

reprinting *n* reimpresión, *f*

reprisal *n* represalia, *f*. **to take reprisals,** tomar represalias

reproach *n* reproche, *m*; censura, *f*; (shame) vergüenza, *f*. *vt* reprochar; censurar, echar en cara, afear

reproachful *a* severo; lleno de reproches; de censura; (shameful) vergonzoso

reproachfully *adv* con reprobación, con reprensión, severamente

reprobate *n* réprobo (-ba)

reproduce *vt* reproducir. *vi* reproducirse

reproducible *a* reproductible

reproductive *a* reproductor; de reproducción

reproof *n* reconvención, *f*

reprove *vt* censurar, culpar; reprender

reptile *a* and *n* reptil, *m*

republic *n* república, *f*. **the r. of letters,** la república de las letras

republican *a* and *n* republicano (-na)

republish *vt* publicar de nuevo; volver a editar

repudiate *vt* repudiar; negar, rechazar

repudiation *n* repudiación, *f*

repugnance *n* repugnancia, *f*

repugnant *a* repugnante; contrario; opuesto. **to be r. to,** repugnar (a)

repulse *vt* repulsar, repeler; rebatir, refutar; (refuse) rechazar, *n* repulsa, *f*; refutación, *f*; rechazo, *m*

repulsion *n phys* repulsión, *f*; repugnancia, aversión, *f*

repulsive *a* repulsivo, repugnante, repelente

reputable *a* honrado, respetable, formal

reputation *n* reputación, *f*; fama, *f*, renombre, *m*. **to have the r. of,** ser reputado como, pasar por

reputed *a* supuesto; putativo

reputedly *adv* según la opinión común, según dice la gente

request *n* ruego, *m*, petición, *f*; instancia, *f*; solicitud, *f*; *com* demanda, *f*. *vt* pedir, rogar; suplicar; solicitar. **in r.,** en boga; solicitado; en demanda, **on r.,** a solicitud. **r. stop,** (for buses) parada discrecional, *f*

requiem *n* réquiem, *m*. **r. mass,** misa de difuntos, *f*

require *vt* exigir, requerir; necesitar; (wish) desear; invitar. *vi* ser necesario

required *a* necesario; obligatorio

requirement *n* deseo, *m*; requisito, *m*; formalidad, *f*; estipulación, *f*; necesidad, *f*

requisite *n* requisito, *m*. *a* necesario, requisito, preciso. **to be r.,** ser necesario, ser menester hacer falta

requisition *vt mil* requisar

requital *n* recompensa, *f*; compensación, satisfacción, *f*

requite *vt* pagar, recompensar; (affection) corresponder a

resale *n* reventa, *f*

rescind *vt* rescindir

rescission *n* rescisión, *f*

rescue *vt* salvar; librar; *mil* rescatar. *n* socorro, *m*; salvamento, *m*; *mil* rescate, *m*. **to go to the r. of,** ir al socorro de. **r. party,** expedición de salvamento, *f*; *mil* expedición de rescate, *f*

rescuer *n* salvador (-ra)

research *n* investigación, *f*, *vt* investigar

researcher *n* investigador (-ra)

resell *vt* revender

resemblance *n* parecido, *m*, semejanza, *f*. **The two sisters bear a strong r. to each other,** Las dos hermanas se parecen mucho

resemble *vt* parecerse (a). **Mary doesn't r. her mother,** María no se parece a su madre

resent *vt* resentirse de; ofenderse por, indignarse por; tomar a mal

resentful *a* resentido; ofendido, indignado, agraviado; vengativo

resentfully *adv* con resentimiento; con indignación

resentment *n* resentimiento, *m*

reservation *n* reservación, *f*; reserva, *f*; territorio reservado, *m*; santuario, *m*. **mental r.,** reserva mental, *f*

reserve *n* reserva, *f*. *vt* reservar. **a de reserva. without r.,** sin reserva

reserved *a* reservado; callado, taciturno. **r. compartment,** reservado, *m*. **r. list,** (*mil nav*) sección de reserva, *f*

reservedly *adv* con reserva

reservist *n* reservista, *mf*

reservoir *n* depósito, *m*; cisterna, *f*, aljibe, tanque, *m*

reset *vt* montar de nuevo

resettle *vt* repoblar; rehabilitar; (a dispute) llegar a un nuevo acuerdo sobre

resettlement *n* repoblación, *f*; rehabilitación, *f*; (of a dispute) nuevo acuerdo, *m*

reshape *vt* reformar

reship *vt* reembarcar

reshipment *n* reembarque, *m*

reshuffle *vt* volver a barajar; *fig* cambiar

reside *vi* residir, habitar; vivir

residence *n* residencia, *f*; permanencia, estada, *f*; domicilio, *m*

resident *a* residente; (of a servant) que duerme en casa; interno. *n* residente, *mf*; (diplomacy) residente, *m*. **r. of the capital** *Lat. Am.* capitalino (-na) *mf*. **r. of Rio de Janeiro** carioca, *mf*

residential *a* residencial

residue *n* resto, *m*; (*law, chem*) residuo, *m*

residuum *n* residuo, *m*

resign *vt* renunciar (a); ceder; resignar. *vi* dimitir. **to r. oneself,** resignarse

resignation *n* resignación, *f*; (from a post) dimisión, *f*. **to send in one's r.,** dimitir

resigned *a* resignado

resilient *a* elástico

resin *n* resina, *f*, *Central America, Mexico* copal, *m*; (solid, for violin bows, etc.) colofonia, *f*

resist *vt* and *vi* (bear) aguantar; (impede) impedir; (repel, ward off) resistir; rechazar; hacer frente (a); oponerse (a); negarse (a)

resistance *n* resistencia, *f*; aguante, *m*, tenacidad, *f*; oposición, *f*; repugnancia, *f*. **passive r.,** resistencia pasiva, *f*. **r. coil,** *elec* resistencia, *f*. **r. movement,** movimiento de resistencia, *m*

resistant *a* resistente

resister *n* el, *m*, (*f*, la) que resiste

resole *vt* remontar

resolute *a* resuelto, decidido

resolution *n* resolución, *f*; (proposal

placed before a legislative body, etc.) proposición, *f*; propósito, *m*

resolve *vt* resolver; desarrollar, deshacer (an abbreviation, acronym, or initialism). *vi* resolverse. *n* propósito, *m*; (of character) resolución, firmeza, *f*

resonance *n* resonancia, *f*; sonoridad, *f*

resonant *a* resonante; reverberante, sonoro

resort *n* recurso, *m*; punto de reunión, *m*; (frequentation) frecuentación, *f*; (gathering) concurrencia, *f*; reunión, *f*. *vi* acudir (a), acogerse (a); hacer uso (de); pasar (a); (frequent) frecuentar, concurrir. **health r.,** balneario, *m*. **holiday r.,** playa de verano, *f*; pueblo de veraneo, *m*. **in the last r.,** en último recurso

resound *vi* resonar, retumbar, retronar; *fig* tener fama, ser celebrado. *vt* hacer reverberar; *fig* celebrar

resounding *a* retumbante, resonante

resource *n* recurso, *m*; (of character) inventiva, *f*; *pl* **resources:** recursos, fondos, *m pl*

resourceful *a* ingenioso

respect *n* respeto, *m*; consideración, *f*; (reference, regard) respecto, *m*; *pl* **respects,** (greetings) saludos, *m pl*; homenaje, *m*. *vt* respetar; honrar; (concern, regard) concernir, tocar (a). **in other respects,** por lo demás. **in r. of,** tocante a, respecto a. **in some respects,** desde algunos puntos de vista. **out of r. for,** por consideración a

respectable *a* respetable; pasable; considerable

respected *a* and *part* respetado; apreciado, estimado; digno de respeto, honrado

respectful *a* respetuoso

respectfully *adv* respetuosamente

respecting *prep* con respecto a, en cuanto a, tocante a; a propósito de

respective *a* respectivo; relativo

respectively *adv* respectivamente

respiration *n* respiración, *f*

respirator *n* respirador, *m*

respiratory *a* respiratorio

respire *vt* and *vi* respirar; exhalar; descansar

respite *n* tregua, pausa, *f*; respiro, *m*; *law* espera, *f*. *vt* dar tregua (a); (postpone) aplazar; (relieve) aliviar

resplendence *n* resplandor, *m*, refulgencia, *f*, esplendor, fulgor, *m*

resplendent *a* resplandeciente, refulgente, relumbrante. **He was r. in a new uniform,** Lucía (or Ostentaba) un nuevo uniforme. **to be r.,** ser resplandeciente; relumbrar, refulgir

respond *vi* responder; contestar; (obey) obedecer; reaccionar

respondent *n* (in a suit) demandado (-da)

response *n* respuesta, *f*; *ecc* responso, *m*

responsibility *n* responsabilidad, *f*

responsible *a* responsable

responsive *a* simpático; sensible, sensitivo

rest *n* descanso, *m*; reposo, *m*; (the grave) última morada, *f*; tranquilidad, paz, *f*; inacción, *f*; (prop) soporte, apoyo, *m*; base, *f*; (for a lance) ristre, *m*; (for a rifle) apoyo, *m*; *mus* silencio, *m*, pausa, *f*; (in verse) cesura, *f*. **in r.,** en ristre. **the r.,** el resto; los demás, los otros. **to set at r.,** calmar, tranquilizar; (remove) quitar. **r.-cure,** cura de reposo, *f*. **r.-house,** hospedería, *f*; refugio, *m*. **r.-room, lounge,** sala de descanso, *f*; (toilet) excusado, retrete, *m*; (in theaters) saloncillo, *m*

rest *vi* reposar, descansar; (lie down) acostarse, echarse; (stop) cesar, parar; estar en paz; apoyarse (en); descansar (sobre); posar; depender (de); (remain) quedar. *vt* descansar; dar un descanso (a); (lean) apoyar; basar (en). **It rests with them,** Depende de ellos. **These valuable documents now rest in the Library of Congress,** Estos valiosos documentos han parado en la Biblioteca del Congresso. **May he r. in peace!** ¡Que en paz descanse! **to r. assured,** estar seguro. **to r. on one's oars,** cesar de remar; descansar

restate *vt* repetir, afirmar de nuevo

restaurant *n* restaurante, restorán, *m*. **r.-car,** coche-comedor, *m*

restful *a* descansado; tranquilo, sosegado

resting *n* reposo, *m*. **last r.-place,** última morada, *f*. **r.-place,** descansadero, *m*; refugio, *m*

restitution *n* restitución, *f*

restive *a* (of a horse) repropio, ingobernable; inquieto, agitado; impaciente

restless *a* agitado; inquieto, intranquilo; turbulento; sin reposo; (wakeful) desvelado; (ceaseless) incesante. **r. night,** noche desvelada, noche intranquila, *inf* noche toledana, *f*

restlessly *adv* agitadamente; con inquietud; turbulentamente; incesantemente

restock *vt* (with goods) surtir de nuevo; proveer de nuevo; restablecer; repoblar

restoration *n* restauración, *f*; renovación, *f*; restablecimiento, *m*; (returning) restitución, *f*

restore *vt* restaurar; restituir; devolver; restablecer; reponer; (repair) reformar, reparar; reconstruir; (to former rank, etc.) rehabilitar. **He restored the book to its place,** Devolvió el libro a su sitio

restrain *vt* refrenar; reprimir; (restrict) limitar, restringir; (prevent) impedir; desviar; (detain) recluir. **to r. oneself,** contenerse

restrained *a* moderado, mesurado; sobrio; (of emotion) contenido

restraining a restrictivo; moderador, calmante

restraint n freno, m; restricción, f; limitación, f; prohibición, f; compulsión, f; (reserve) reserva, f; moderación, f

restrict vt restringir; limitar

restriction n restricción, f; limitación, f

restrictive a restrictivo

result n resultado, m; consecuencia, resulta, f; solución, f. vi resultar. **as the r. of,** de resultas de

resultant a resultante; consecuente. n resultado, m; mech resultante, f

resume vt reasumir; (continue) reanudar, continuar; (summarize) resumir

résumé n resumen, m, recapitulación, f

resumption n (renewal) reanudación, f; reasunción, f

resurgence n resurgimiento, m

resurrect vt inf desenterrar; resucitar

resurrection n resurrección, f

resuscitate vt and vi resucitar

resuscitation n resurrección, f; renovación, f; renacimiento, m

retail n venta al por menor, reventa, f. adv al por menor. vt (goods) vender al por menor, revender; (tell) contar; repetir. **r. trade,** comercio al por menor, m

retailer n vendedor (-ra) al por menor; (of a story) narrador (-ra); el, m, (f, la) que cuenta algo

retain vt retener; guardar; conservar; (a barrister) ajustar; (hire) contratar

retainer n (dependent) criado, dependiente, m; partidario, adherente, m; (fee) honorario, m; pl **retainers,** séquito, m, adherentes, m pl; gente, f

retaining wall n muro de contención, m

retake vt volver a tomar; reconquistar

retaliate vt vengarse de, desquitarse de. vi vengarse, tomar represalias

retaliation n represalias, f pl; desquite, m, satisfacción, f. **law of r.,** talión, m,

retard vt retardar

retch vi tener náuseas, procurar vomitar

retention n retención, f; conservación, f

retentive a retentivo

reticence n reticencia, reserva, f

reticent a reservado, inexpresivo, taciturno

retina n retina, f

retinue n séquito, acompañamiento, m, comitiva, f

retire vi retirarse; (to bed) recogerse, acostarse; (from a post) jubilarse. vt retirar; jubilar. **to r. from a post,** mil rendir el puesto

retired a retirado; (remote) apartado, aislado; (hidden) escondido; (former) antiguo; (from employment, etc.) jubilado; (of an officer) retirado. **to place on the r. list,** jubilar; (mil nav) dar el retiro (a)

retirement n retirada, f; (solitude) apartamiento, aislamiento, m; retiro, m; (superannuation) jubilación, f

retiring a que se retira; (from a post) dimitente; (with pension, etc.) de jubilación; (reserved) reservado; modesto

retort vi replicar. vt retorcer; devolver (una acusación, etc.). n réplica, f; contestación, f; chem retorta, f

retouch vt retocar

retrace vt volver a trazar; volver a andar (un camino); (one's steps) volver sobre sus pasos, volver atrás; (in memory) rememorar, recordar; buscar el origen (de); (recount) narrar, contar

retract vt retractar, retirar; (draw back) retraer. vi retractarse

retread vt pisar de nuevo; (tires) recauchetear

retreat n retirada, f; (mil signal) retreta, f; (refuge and ecc) retiro, m. vi retirarse; retroceder; refugiarse

retreating a que se retira; que retrocede; mil que se bate en retirada

retrench vt reducir; disminuir; vi economizar, hacer economías

retrial n (of a person) nuevo proceso, m; (of a case) revisión, f

retribution n retribución, f; justo castigo, m, pena merecida, f

retrieval n recuperación, f; reparación, f; (of game) cobra, f; (of one's character) rehabilitación, f

retrieve vt (game, of dogs) cobrar; (regain) recobrar, recuperar; restaurar; reparar; restablecer; (one's character) rehabilitar. vi cobrar la caza

retroactive a retroactivo

retrocede vi retroceder

retrograde a retrógrado

retrogression n retrogradación, regresión, f; med retroceso, m

retrogressive a retrógrado

retrospect n mirada retrospectiva, f, examen del pasado, m. **in r.,** retrospectivamente

retrospection n retrospección, f

retry vt (a case) rever; (a person) procesar de nuevo

return vi regresar, Lat. Am. devolverse; volver; reaparecer; presentarse de nuevo; law revertir; (answer) contestar, responder. vt (give back or put back) devolver; (a ball) restar; (a kindness, visit) pagar; restituir; (reciprocate) corresponder (a); recompensar; contestar (a); dar; rendir; (yield) producir; (a verdict) fallar, pronunciar; (report) dar parte de; anunciar; (exchange) cambiar; (elect) elegir. n regreso, m; vuelta, f; (giving or putting back) devolución, f; pago, m; restitución, f; correspondencia, f; recompensa, f; (reply) respuesta, f; (reappearance) reaparición, f; reinstalación, f; repetición, f; (gain) ganancia, f, provecho, m; rendimiento, m; (exchange) cambio, m; (report) parte oficial, *f;* informe, *m;* lista, *f;* (election) elección, *f; pl* **returns,** tablas estadísticas, *f pl;* (of an election) resultados, *m pl.* **Many happy returns!** ¡feliz cumpleaños! **by return mail,** a vuelta de correo. **on my (his, etc.) r.,** a la vuelta, cuando vuelva. **to r. like for like,** pagar en la misma moneda. **r. journey, r. trip,** viaje de vuelta, *m.* **r. match,** partido de vuelta, *m.* **r. ticket,** billete de ida y vuelta, *m;* billete de vuelta, *m*

returnable a restituible; susceptible a ser devuelto; (on approval) a prueba; *law* devolutivo

"Return to Sender" «Al remitente»

reunion *n* reunión, *f*

reunite *vt* reunir. *vi* reunirse

revaccinate *vt* revacunar

revaccination *n* revacunación, *f*

reveal *vt* revelar; descubrir

revealing a revelador. *n* revelación; *f;* descubrimiento, *m*

reveille *n mil* diana, *f*

revel *vi* divertirse; regocijarse (en), gozarse (en); entregarse (a); (carouse) ir de parranda; emborracharse. *n* algazara, jarana, *f; pl* **revels,** fiestas, festividades, *f pl*

revelation *n* revelación, *f;* descubrimiento, *m;* (in the Bible) Apocalipsis, *m*

reveler *n* convidado alegre, *m;* (at night) trasnochador (-ra); (drunk) borracho (-cha); (masked) máscara, *mf*

revelry *n* festividades, *f pl;* regocijo, *m;* orgías, *f pl, Central America* embullo, *m*

revenge *n* venganza, *f. vt* vengarse de; desquitarse de

revengeful a vengativo

revenue *n* rentas públicas, *f pl;* (treasury) fisco, *m; com* rédito, *m,* ingresos, *m pl;* beneficio, *m.* **Inland R.,** delegación de contribuciones, *f.* **r. officer,** agente fiscal, *m*

reverberate *vt and vi* (of sound) retumbar, resonar; (of light, etc.) reverberar

reverberation *n* (reflection) reverberación, *f;* (of sound) retumbo, eco, *m*

revere *vt* reverenciar, venerar, honrar

reverence *n* reverencia, *f, vt* reverenciar

reverend a reverendo

reverent a reverente

reverie *n* ensueño, *m*

reversal *n* inversión, *f;* (of a verdict) revocación, *f*

reverse *vt* invertir; (a steam engine) dar contra vapor (a); (a vehicle) poner en marcha atrás; (arms) llevar a la funerala; (a judgment, etc.) revocar, derogar. *vi* (dancing) dar vueltas al revés. *n* lo contrario, lo opuesto; (back) dorso, revés, *m;* (change) cambio, *m;* (check) revés, *m,* vicisitud, *f;* (loss) pérdida, *f;* (defeat) derrota, *f; mech* marcha atrás, *f,* a inverso; contrario, opuesto. **quite the r.,** todo el

contrario. **r. turn,** (of an engine) cambio de dirección, *m;* (in dancing) vuelta al revés, *f*

reversion *n* reversión, *f; biol* atavismo, *m;* (of offices) futura, *f;* (of property) reversión, *f*

revert *vi law* revertir; volver (a)

review *n* examen, análisis, *m;* juicio crítico, *m;* (journal and *mil*) revista, *f;* (criticism) revista, reseña, *f; law* revisión, *f. vt* examinar, analizar; (*mil* etc.) pasar revista (a); revisar; repasar; (a book, etc.) reseñar; *law* revisar. *vi* escribir revistas

revile *vt* injuriar, maldecir, difamar

reviling *n* insultos, *m pl,* injurias, *f pl*

revisal *n* revisión, *f*

revise *vt* revisar; repasar; corregir; (change) cambiar

reviser *n* revisor, *m;* corrector de pruebas, *m*

revision *n* revisión, *f;* repaso, *m;* corrección de pruebas, *f*

revival *n* resurgimiento, *m;* renovación, *f;* (awakening) despertamiento, *m;* restablecimiento, *m;* resurrección, *f;* (of learning) renacimiento, *m; theat* reposición, *f;* (religious) despertar religioso, *m*

revive *vi* reponerse; restablecerse; resucitar; renovarse; renacer; cobrar fuerzas; (recover consciousness) volver en sí. *vt* hacer revivir; resucitar; restablecer; renovar; restaurar; despertar; (fire, colours) avivar

revivify *vt* revivificar

revocation *n* revocación, *f*

revoke *vt* revocar, anular, derogar; (wills) quebrantar. *vi* revocar, anular; (at cards) renunciar. *n* (cards) renuncio, *m*

revolt *n* rebelión, *f, vi* rebelarse, sublevarse. *vt* repugnar, indignar, dar asco (a)

revolting a repugnante, asqueroso; (rebellious) rebelde

revolution *n* revolución, *f;* (turn) vuelta, *f,* giro, *m*

revolutionary a and *n* revolucionario (-ia)

revolutionize *vt* revolucionar

revolve *vi* dar vueltas, girar; suceder periódicamente. *vt* hacer girar; (ponder) revolver, discurrir

revolver *n* revólver, *m*

revolving a giratorio; que vuelve; periódico. **r. chair,** silla giratoria, *f.* **r. door,** puerta giratoria, *f.* **r. stage,** escenario giratorio, *m*

revue *n theat* revista, *f*

revulsion *n* revulsión, *f*

rev up *vt* (an engine) calentar

reward *n* recompensa, *f;* retribución, *f. vt* recompensar; satisfacer, premiar

rewarding a premiador; que recompensa. *n* recompensación, *f.* **a rewarding**

experience, una experiencia compensadora, *f*

rewrite *vt* escribir de nuevo; volver a escribir; redactar otra vez

rhapsody *n* rapsodia, *f*

rhetoric *n* retórica, *f*

rhetorical a retórico; declamatorio

rheumatic a reumático. **r. fever,** reumatismo poliarticular agudo, *m*

rheumatism *n* reumatismo, reuma, *m*

rheumy a catarroso; (of the eyes) legañoso

Rhine, the, el Rin, *m*

rhinestone circón, *m*

rhinoceros *n* rinoceronte, *m*

rhubarb *n* ruibarbo, *m*

rhyme *n* rima, *f*; verso, *m*. *vi* and *vt* rimar. **without r. or reason,** sin ton ni son; a tontas y a locas

rhyming a rimador

rhythm *n* ritmo, *m*

rhythmic a rítmico

rib *n* (anat, bot, aer, naut, arch) costilla, *f*; (of an umbrella or fan) varilla, *f*; (in cloth) cordoncillo, *m*, lista, *f*

ribald a escabroso, ribaldo, indecente

ribaldry *n* ribaldería, escabrosidad, indecencia, *f*

ribbed a con costillas; (of cloth) listado, con listas

ribbon *n* cinta, *f*; tira, *f*; (tatter) jirón, *m*. **to tear to ribbons,** hacer jirones

rice *n* arroz, *m*. a de arroz; con arroz. **r. field,** arrozal, *m*. **r.-paper,** papel de paja de arroz, *m*. **r.-pudding,** arroz con leche, *m*

rich a rico; opulento; (happy) dichoso; (of land, etc.) fértil; abundante; (of objects) magnífico, suntuoso, hermoso; precioso; (of food) exquisito; suculento; (highly seasoned) muy sazonado; (creamy) con mucha nata; (of colours) brillante, vivo. **new r.,** ricacho (-cha). **newly-r.,** advenedizo. **to grow r.,** enriquecerse, *Lat. Am. also* fondearse

riches *n* riqueza, *f*

richness *n* riqueza, *f*; opulencia, *f*; (of land, etc.) fertilidad, *f*; abundancia, *f*; (of objects) magnificencia, suntuosidad, hermosura, *f*; preciosidad, *f*; (of food) gusto exquisito, *m*; suculencia, *f*; (piquancy) gusto picante, *m*; (of colours) viveza, *f*

rickets *n* raquitismo, *m*

rickety a med raquítico; destartalado, desvencijado; (unsteady) tambaleante; cojo

ricochet *n* rebote, *m*, *vi* rebotar

rid *vt* librar (de). **to get rid of,** librarse de; quitarse de encima (a); perder, quitarse; (dismiss) despedir. **to rid oneself of,** librarse de, deshacerse de

riddance *n* libramiento, *m*

riddle *n* acertijo, *m*; enigma, problema, *m*; misterio, *m*; (sieve) tamiz de alambre,

m; *vt* (guess) adivinar; (sift) cribar; (with holes) acribillar

ride *vi* (a horse) montar a caballo, cabalgar; pasear a caballo; (a mule, a bicycle) montar en, pasear en; (a vehicle, train) ir en; (a carriage, car) andar en, pasear en; (float) flotar; (on the wind) dejarse llevar por el viento; ser llevado por el viento; (go) ir; (come) venir; (a distance) hacer . . . a caballo, en coche, etc.; *naut* estar a ancla; *mech* tener juego. *vt* (a horse, mule, bicycle) montar; ir montado sobre; manejar; (a race) hacer; (float) flotar en; (cleave, the sea, etc.) surcar. *n* paseo (a caballo, en bicicleta, en coche, etc.), *m*; viaje (en un autobús, de tren, etc.), *m*; (bridle path) camino de herradura, *m*; cabalgata, *f*, desfile a caballo, *m*; (hitch, lift) *Mexico* aventón, *m*. **a r. on horseback,** un paseo a caballo. **They gave me a r. in their car,** (e.g. to see the sights) Me llevaron a paseo en su auto, (a a certain place) Me dieron un aventón. **ride at anchor,** estar fondeado. **to r. a bicycle,** montar en bicicleta. **to r. roughshod over,** mandar a la baqueta (a), mandar a puntapiés (a). **to r. sidesaddle,** cabalgar a mujeriegas. **to r. at,** embestir con. **to r. away,** marcharse, alejarse; marcharse a caballo, etc. **to r. back,** volver; volver a caballo, en bicicleta, etc. **to r. behind,** seguir a caballo; ir inmediatamente detrás (de); (on the back seat) ocupar el asiento de atrás; (on the same animal) cabalgar en la grupa. **to r. down,** atropellar; (trample) pisotear, pasar por encima de. **to r. on,** seguir su camino. **to r. out,** salir a paseo en caballo, etc.; irse a paseo en coche, etc.; (a storm) hacer frente a, luchar con. **to r. over,** pasar por encima de; recorrer. **to r. up,** *vi* llegar, acercarse; (of a tie, etc.) subir. *vt* montar

rider *n* cabalgador (-ra); jinete, *m*; persona que va en coche, etc., *f*; (on a bicycle) ciclista, *mf*; (on a motorcycle) motociclista, *mf*; (horsebreaker) domador de caballos, *m*; (clause) añadidura, *f*; corolario, *m*

ridge *n* cumbre, cima, *f*; (of mountains) cordillera, sierra, *f*; (of a roof, of a nose) caballete, *m*; agr lomo, caballón, *m*; (wrinkle) arruga, *f*; (on coins) cordoncillo, *m*. *vt* surcar; formar lomos (en); (wrinkle) arrugar

ridicule *n* ridículo, *m*, *vt* poner en ridículo, ridiculizar, burlarse (de), mofarse (de)

ridiculous a ridículo, absurdo

riding a cabalgante; que va a caballo; montado (a, en, sobre); *naut* al ancla; (in compounds) de equitación; de montar. *n* equitación, *f*; paseo a caballo; en bicicleta, etc., *m*; acción de ir a caballo, etc., *f*; (district) comarca, *f*. **r.-boots,** botas de montar, *f pl*. **r.-habit,** traje de montar, *m*; (woman's) amazona, *f*. **r.-master,** profesor de equitación, *m*. **r.-saddle,** silla de montar, f. **r.-school,** escuela de equitación, f

rife a común; corriente; frecuente; prevalente; abundante; general. **r. with,** abundante en; lleno de

riffraff n desperdicios, m pl; (rabble) gentuza, canalla, f

rifle n rifle, fusil rayado, m. vt robar; (a suitcase, etc.) desvalijar; (a gun) rayar. **r.-case,** Mexico carcaj, m. **r.-range,** campo de tiro, m. **r.-sling,** portafusil, m. **r.-shot,** fusilazo, m

rifleman n fusilero, m

rift n hendedura, abertura, f; grieta, f

rig n naut aparejo, m; inf atavío, m. vt (a ship) aparejar; equipar; (elections) falsificar. **to rig out,** proveer de; equipar con; ataviar. **to rig up,** arreglar; armar, construir

rigging n (of a ship) aparejo, m

right a recto; correcto; conveniente; debido; apropiado; exacto; (opposite of left hand) derecho; (straight) directo; en línea recta; razonable; (true) verdadero, genuino, legítimo; (just) justo; (prudent) prudente; (in health) sano. **All r.!** ¡Está bien! **I feel all r.,** Me siento perfectamente bien, Estoy bien. **He is the r. man for the job,** Él es el hombre que hace falta para el puesto. **It is the r. word,** Es la palabra apropiada. **on the r.,** a la derecha. **to be r.,** (of persons) tener razón. **to make r.,** poner en orden; arreglar. **r.-angle,** ángulo recto, m. **r.-angled,** rectangular. **r.-angled triangle,** triángulo rectángulo, m. **the R. Bank (of Paris),** la Orilla derecha, la Ribera derecha, f. **r. hand,** n (mano) derecha, diestra, f; derecha, f; (person) brazo derecho, m. a de la mano derecha; de la derecha; a la derecha. **r.-handed,** derecho; diestro; hábil. **r. mind,** entero juicio, m. **r.-minded,** juicioso, prudente; honrado. **r.-of-way,** derecho a la vía, m

right adv directamente; inmediatamente; derechamente; correctamente; debidamente; exactamente; bien; (quite, thoroughly) completamente; honradamente; (very) muy. **r. on,** adelante; en frente. **R. about face!** ¡Media vuelta a la derecha! **r. at the bottom,** al fondo; al final; **r. at the end of his speech,** al fin de su discurso. **r. away,** en seguida, inmediatamente, Mexico ahorita, elsewhere in Lat. Am. lueguito

right n razón, f; verdad, f; justicia, f; (good) bien, m; derecho, m; (not left side) derecha, f; (of political parties) derechas, f pl. **r. and wrong,** el bien y el mal. "All rights reserved," «Derechos reservados.» **by rights,** por derecho. **It is on the r.,** Está a la derecha. **to exercise one's r.,** usar de su derecho. **r. of association,** derecho de asociación, m. **r. of way,** derecho de paso, m. **to be in the r.,** tener razón; estar en su derecho

right vt enderezar; rectificar; corregir; poner en orden; naut enderezar; hacer justicia (a). **to r. wrongs,** deshacer agravios

righteous a recto, virtuoso, justo; justificado

righteousness n rectitud, integridad, virtud, f; justicia, f

rightful a justo; legítimo; verdadero

rightfully adv justamente; legítimamente; verdaderamente

rightly adv rectamente; debidamente; correctamente; bien. **r. or wrongly,** mal que bien

rightness n rectitud, f; derechura, f; justicia, f; exactitud, f

rigid a rígido; inflexible; severo, riguroso

rigidity n rigidez, f; inflexibilidad, f; severidad, f

rigmarole n monserga, f, galimatías, m, jerigonza, f

rigor n rigor, m

rigorous a riguroso

rigour n rigor, m

rile vt inf irritar, sacar de tino (a)

rim n borde, m; orilla, f; (of a wheel) llanta, f, aro, m

rime n escarcha, f, vt cubrir con escarcha. See also **rhyme**

rind n (of fruit) cáscara, corteza, f; (of cheese) costra, f; (of bacon) piel, f

ring n círculo, m; (round the eyes) ojera, f; (for curtains, etc.) anilla, f; (for the finger) anillo, m, sortija, f; (for children's games, etc.) corro, m; (for the ears) arete, m; (of smoke and for the nose) anillo, m; (for hitching, etc.) argolla, f; (for boxing) cuadrilátero, m; (on a racecourse) picadero, m; (at a circus, bull-fight) ruedo, redondel, m; fig arena, f; (group) camarilla, f, grupo, m; (metallic sound) sonido metálico, m; resonancia, f; (tinkle) tintín, m; (of a bell) repique, tañido, son (de la campana), m; (of bells) juego de campanas, m; (of laughter, etc.) ruido, m; (of truth, etc.) apariencia, f. **r.-bolt,** naut cáncamo, m. **r. finger,** dedo anular, m. **r.-master,** director de circo, m

ring vt (surround) cercar, rodear; (a bull, etc.) poner un anillo (a); (sound) hacer sonar; sonar; (a door bell, etc.) tocar, apretar; (bells) echar a vuelo; (announce by pealing the bells) anunciar, proclamar; sonar, tañer. vi (of bells) sonar; (re-echo) resonar; (of the ears) zumbar; (tinkle) tintinar. **to r. the bell,** tocar la campana; tocar el timbre. **to r. off,** colgar el teléfono. **to r. up,** llamar por teléfono, telefonear

ringing n acción de tocar las campanas o el timbre, f; toque, m; repique, m; campanilleo, m; (in the ears) zumbido, m. a resonante, sonoro. **r. signal,** señal de llamada, f. **the r. of the bells,** el son de las campanas

ringleader n cabecilla, m

ringlet n rizo, bucle, m

ringworm n tiña, f

rink n pista, f. **skating-r.**, sala de patinar, f; pista de patinar, f

rinse n enjuague, m; enjuagadura, f; (of clothes) aclarado, m. vt enjuagar; (clothes) aclarar; lavar

Rio de Janeiro n Rio de Janeiro, f; a carioca, formal fluminense, mf

riot n motín, m; tumulto, m; desorden, m; exceso, m; orgía, f; disipación, f. vi amotinarse; alborotarse; entregarse a la disipación (or al placer); (enjoy) gozar, disfrutar. **to run r.**, hacer excesos; perder el freno; desmandarse; fig extenderse por todas partes; crecer en abundancia, cubrir todo

rioter n amotinador (-ra); alborotador (-ra)

riotous a sedicioso; bullicioso; disoluto; desordenado; desenfrenado

rip vt rasgar; (unsew) descoser; (wood, etc.) partir; (make) hacer. vi rasgarse. n rasgón, m; rasgadura, f; desgarro, m; (libertine) calavera, m. **to rip off**, arrancar; quitar. **to rip open**, abrir; (an animal) abrir en canal

ripe a maduro; preparado; perfecto, acabado

ripen vt and vi madurar

ripeness n madurez, f

ripple n rizo, m; onda, f; (of sound) murmullo, m. vt rizar. vi rizarse; murmurar

rise vi ascender; subir; levantarse; ponerse de pie; (of a meeting) suspenderse; (from the dead) resucitar; (grow) crecer; (swell) hincharse; (of sun, moon) salir; (of sound, gradient, price, stock exchange quotations) subir; (of river source) nacer; (in revolt) sublevarse, rebelarse; (to the mind) presentarse, surgir; (appear) aparecer; (of buildings, etc.) elevarse, alzarse; (in the world) mejorar de posición; (originate) originarse (en), proceder (de); (of mercury) alzarse; (of fish) picar. **He has risen in my estimation,** Ha ganado en mi estimación. **She rose early,** Se levantó temprano. **The color rose in her cheeks,** Se le subieron los colores a la cara. **to r. to the occasion,** estar al nivel de las circunstancias. **to r. to one's feet,** ponerse de pie. **to r. to the bait,** morder el anzuelo. **to r. again,** levantarse de nuevo; resucitar; renovarse; suscitarse otra vez. **to r. above,** alzarse por encima de; mostrarse superior a

rise n ascensión, f; subida, f; levantamiento, m; (in price, temperature) alza, f; (increase) aumento, m; (of the sun, moon) salida, f; (of a river) nacimiento, m; (origin) origen, m; (growth, development) desarrollo, crecimiento, m; (promotion) ascenso, m; (slope) cuesta, f; pendiente, f; (high ground) eminencia, altura, f. **to give r. to,** dar lugar a, causar. **r. and fall,**

subida y baja, f; (of the voice) ritmo, m; (of music) cadencia, f; (of institutions) grandeza y decadencia, f. **r. to power,** subida al poder, f

riser n el, m, (f, la) que se levanta; (of a step) contrahuella, f. **early r.,** madrugador (-ra). **late r.,** el, m, (f, la) que se levanta tarde

risibility n risibilidad, f

rising n subida, f; (of the source of rivers) nacimiento, m; (overflowing of rivers) crecimiento, m; (of sun, moon) salida, f; (from the dead) resurrección, f; (rebellion) sublevación, insurrección, f; (of the tide) crecida, f; (of bread) levadura, f; (of an assembly) suspensión, f; (of a theater curtain) subida, f; (literary) renacimiento, m, a creciente; naciente; saliente; (promising) de porvenir; (young) joven. **the r. generation,** los jóvenes, la generación joven. **He is r. forty,** Raya en los cuarenta. **He likes early r.,** Le gusta madrugar. **On the r. of the curtain . . . ,** Al levantarse el telón . . . **the r. of the moon,** la salida de la luna, f. **the r. tide,** la marea creciente

risk n riesgo, m; peligro, m. vt arriesgar; atreverse (a), osar. **at the r. of,** al riesgo de. **to take a r.,** tomar un riesgo; correr peligro. **to r. everything on the outcome,** jugar el todo por el todo

risk capital n capital-riesgo, m

riskiness n peligro, m

risky a arriesgado, peligroso

rissole n risol, m, (pl risoles)

rite n rito, m

ritual a ritual. n rito, m, ceremonia, f

rival n rival, mf a competidor; rival. vt rivalizar con, competir con

rivalry n rivalidad, f

river n río, m. a del río; fluvial. **r.-basin,** cuenca de un río, f. **r.-bed,** lecho, cauce (de un río), m. **r. civilization,** civilización fluvial, f. **r.-god,** dios de los ríos, m. **r.-mouth,** ría, f; m. **r. port,** puerto fluvial, m

riverside n ribera, orilla de un río, f. a de la(s) orilla(s) de un río; situado a la orilla de un río; ribereño

rivet n remache, roblón, m. vt remachar; clavar; fig fijar, concentrar; fig cautivar, absorber

road n camino, m; carretera, f; ruta, f; pl **roads,** naut rada, f. **high r.,** camino real, m. **main r.,** carretera, f. **secondary r.,** carretera de segunda clase, f. **on the r. to . . . ,** en el camino de . . . **to get out of the r.,** inf quitarse de en medio. **to go by r.,** ir por carretera. **"R. up!"** «Carretera en reparaciones.» **r.-book,** guía de carreteras, f. **r. house,** albergue de carretera, m. **r. maker,** constructor de caminos, m; (navvy) peón caminero, m. **r. making,** construcción de caminos, f. **r. map,** mapa de carreteras, m. **r. sign,** señal de carretera, señal de tránsito, señal vial, f; poste indicador, m. **The r. to**

hell is paved with good intentions, El camino del infierno está empedrado de buenas intenciones. «**R. Repairs,**» «Camino en Reparación»

roadside n borde del camino, m, a al lado del camino

roadway n calzada, carretera, f

roam vi vagar, vagabundear, andar errante. vt errar por

roar vi rugir; (of a bull, of the wind, of a person in anger) bramar; dar voces; (of the fire) crepitar; (of cannon) retumbar; (of thunder) estallar. vt gritar. n rugido, bramido, m; (shout) grito, m; (of the fire) crepitación, f; (of cannon, thunder) estallido, m; (noise) ruido, m. **to r. with laughter,** reírse a carcajadas

roaring n (of horses) asma de los caballos, f, For other meanings, see under **roar.** a rugiente, bramante; inf magnífico. **to do a r. trade,** hacer un buen negocio

roast n asado, m, carne asada, f. a asado; tostado. vt asar; (coffee and to warm one's feet, etc.) tostar; (metals) calcinar; (scold) desollar vivo (a). vi asarse; tostarse. **r. beef,** rosbif, m

roaster n asador, m; (for coffee or peanuts) tostador, m; (for chestnuts, etc.) tambor, m.

rob vt robar; quitar, privar (de). **They have robbed her of her pocketbook,** Le han robado la cartera

robber n ladrón (-ona); (footpad) salteador de caminos, m; (brigand) bandido, m

robbery n robo, m. **It's daylight r.!** ¡Es un desuello! **to commit a r.,** cometer un robo. **r. with violence,** robo armado, m

robe n traje talar, m, toga, f; (of a monk, nun) hábito, m; (of a priest, etc.) sotana, f; poet manto, m; (infant's) mantillas, f pl; pl **robes,** traje de ceremonia, m. vt vestir; cubrir, revestir (de). vi vestirse. **bath r.,** albornoz, m

robot n hombre mecánico, m; aer piloto mecánico, m. **traffic r.,** torre del tráfico, f, aparato automático, m. **r. plane,** avión sin piloto, m

robust a robusto; fuerte, vigoroso. **to make r.,** robustecer

rock n roca, f; (in the sea) abrojo, escollo, m; peña, f, peñasco, m. **as firm as a r.,** como una roca. **to be on the rocks,** inf estar a la cuarta pregunta. **r. bottom,** n fondo, m. a mínimo, más bajo. **r. crystal,** cuarzo, m. **r.-garden,** jardincito rocoso, jardín alpestre, m. **r.-plant,** planta alpestre, f. **r.-rose,** heliantemo, m. **r.-salt,** sal gema, f

rock vt mecer; (shake) hacer temblar, sacudir; (to sleep) arrullar. vi mecerse, balancearse; tambalearse; agitarse; temblar

rocker n (of a chair, cradle) balancín, m; (chair) mecedora, f

rocket n cohete, volador, m. vi lanzarse

r.-launching aircraft, caza lanzacohetes, f

rocking n balanceo, m; (staggering) tambaleo, m; oscilación, f; (of an infant) arrullo, m. **r.-chair,** mecedora, f. **r.-horse,** caballo balancín, caballo mecedor, m

rocky a rocoso; de roca; roqueño; (rough) fragoso, escabroso; (rugged) peñascoso, escarpado. **the R. Mountains,** las Montañas Rocosas, f pl

rod n vara, f; bastón de mando, m; (for fishing) caña, f; (measure) pértiga, f; (surveying) jalón, m; palo, m; (for punishment) vergajo, m; mech vástago, m. **connecting rod,** biela, f. **to fish with rod and line,** pescar con caña

rodent a and n roedor, m.

roe n (deer) corzo (-za); (of fish) hueva, f. **soft roes,** lechas, f pl

rogue n bribón (-ona), pícaro (-ra), pillo (-lla), Argentina farabute, mf; law vago, m; (affectionate) picaruelo (-la)

roguish a picaresco, bellaco; (mischievous) travieso, juguetón; malicioso

role n papel, m

roll n rollo, m; (list) rol, m, lista, f; (of bread) panecillo, Mexico bolillo, m; (of a drum) redoble, m; (of thunder) tronido, m; (of cloth) pieza, f; (of tobacco) rollo, m; (of meat, etc.) pastel, m; (of a ship) balanceo, m; pl **rolls,** (records) archivos, m pl. **He has a nautical r.,** Tiene un andar de marinero. **to call the r.,** pasar lista. **r. film,** película fotográfica, f. **r. of honour,** lista de honor, f. **r.-on corset,** faja elástica, f, corsé de goma, m. **r.-top desk,** buró de cierre enrollable, m

roll vi rodar; dar vueltas; (wallow) revolcarse; (of a ship) balancearse, bambolearse; (in money, etc.) nadar; (flow) correr, fluir; (fig of time) pasar tranquilamente; (of vehicle) rodar; pasar rodando; (of country) ondular; (of the sea) ondear; (of drums) redoblar; (of thunder) retumbar. vt hacer rodar; arrollar; (a cigarette) liar; (metals) laminar; (move) mover; (the eyes) guiñar (los ojos); (the ground) apisonar; (pastry) aplanar; (of an organ) sonar; (a drum) redoblar. **Mary rolled her eyes heavenwards,** María puso los ojos en blanco. **to r. away,** alejarse; desaparecer; (of time) pasar. **to r. back,** volver, retirarse; desaparecer. **to r. by,** pasar rodando; desaparecer. **to r. down,** bajar rodando, rodar por. **to r. in,** llegar en gran cantidad (or en gran número). **to r. off,** caer de. **to r. on,** seguir su marcha; fluir sin cesar; seguir su curso; (of time) avanzar. **to r. out,** (metal) laminar; (pastry) aplanar; (bring out) sacar; desenrollar. **to r. over,** vt volcar; tumbar; dar la vuelta (a). vi dar la vuelta; volverse al otro lado. **to r. up,** arrollar; envolver; (of hedgehogs, etc.) enroscarse, hacerse un ovillo

roller n rodillo, m; cilindro, m; (wheel, castor) rueda, f; (for flattening the ground) apisonadora, *f*; *print* rodillo, *m*; (wave) ola grande, *f*. **r.-bandage,** venda, *f*. **r. canary,** canario de raza flauta, *m*. **r.-skate,** patín de ruedas, *m*. **r.-skating,** patinaje de ruedas, *m*. **r.-towel,** toalla continua, *f*

rollicking *a* alegre, jovial; juguetón

rolling *a* rodante; (of landscape) ondulante, quebrado. *n* rodadura, *f*; (wallowing) revuelco, *m*; (of metals) laminación, *f*; (of a ship) balanceo, *m*; (rolling up) enrollamiento, *m*. **r.-pin,** rollo, rodillo de pastelero, *m*. **r.-stock,** material móvil ferroviario, *m*

Roman *a* romano, de los romanos; (of noses and *print*) romano. *n* romano (-na). **in R. fashion,** a la romana. **R. Catholic,** a católico; católico apostólico romano. *n* el católico (-ca). **R. Catholicism,** catolicismo, *m*. **R. figures,** números romanos, *m pl*

Romance *a* (of languages) romance. *n* (language) romance, *m*

romance *n* novela de caballería, *f*; romance, *m*; aventura, *f*; cuento, *m*, novela, *f*; romanticismo, *m*; *mus* romanza, *f*. *vi* inventar ficciones; exagerar

romantic *a* and *n* romántico (-ca)

Rome Roma, *f*

romp *vi* juguetear, brincar, retozar, loquear; correr rápidamente. *n* locuelo (-la), saltaparedes, *mf*; (game) retozo, *m*. **The horse romped home easily,** El caballo ganó la carrera fácilmente

rompers *n* mono, *m*

romping *n* juegos, *m pl*, travesuras, *f pl*

roof *n* tejado, techado, *m*; (of a motorcar, bus) tejadillo, *m*; (of coaches, etc.) imperial, *f*; cubierta, *f*; (of the mouth) paladar, *m*; (bower) enramada, *f*; (of heaven) bóveda (del cielo), *f*. *vt* techar, tejar, *Lat. Am.* entechar; (shelter) abrigar. **r.-garden,** azotea, *f*. **r.-gutter,** canalera, *f*

roofer *n* techador, *m*; constructor de tejados, *m*

rook *n* chova, *f*, grajo, *m*; (chess) torre, *f*. *vt* engañar, estafar; (overcharge) desollar vivo (a)

room *n* (in a house) habitación, *f*, cuarto, *m*; sala, *f*, cámara, *f*; (behind a shop) trastienda, *f*; (space) sitio, espacio, *m*; lugar, *m*; (opportunity) oportunidad, *f*; (cause) motivo, *m*, causa, *f*. *vi* alojarse. **bath-r.,** cuarto de baño, *m*. **dining-r.,** comedor, *m*. **drawing-r.,** salón, *m*. **There is no r. for us in this car,** No cabemos en este coche. **There is still r. for improvement,** Se puede mejorar todavía. **There isn't r. for anything else,** No cabe más. **to be r.,** caber, haber sitio. **to make r.,** hacer sitio

rooming house *n* casa de huéspedes, *f*

roommate *n* compañero de cuarto, compañero de pieza, *m*

roomy *a* espacioso, amplio; (of garments) holgado

roost *n* percha de gallinero, *f*, *Lat. Am.* dormidero, *m*. *vi* dormir en una percha; recogerse. **to rule the r.,** ser el amo del cotarro

rooster *n* gallo, *m*,

root *n* raíz, *f*; *gram* radical, *m*; *mus* base, *f*; origen, *m*; explicación, *f*. *vt* arraigar; *fig* fijar, clavar. *vi* echar raíces; *fig* arraigarse; (of pigs, etc.) hozar, escarbar; revolver. **to r. out,** arrancar de raíz; *fig* desarraigar; (destroy) extirpar. **cubed r.,** raíz cúbica, *f*. **from the r.,** (entirely) de raíz. **square r.,** raíz cuadrada, *f*. **to cut close to the r.,** cortar a raíz

rope *n* soga, cuerda, *f*; (hawser) maroma, *f*; *naut* cabo, *m*; (tight-rope) cable, *m*, cuerda de volatinero, *f*; (string) ristra, sarta, *f*; hilo, *m*; *pl* **ropes,** (boxing) cuerdas del cuadrilátero, *f pl*. *vt* encordelar, atar con cuerdas; (a horse) enganchar; (a person) enganchar, coger. **a r. of pearls,** una sarta de perlas. **to give a person plenty of r.,** dar mucha latitud (a). **to know the ropes,** conocer todos los trucos. **r.-ladder,** escala de cuerda, *f*. **r.-maker,** cordelero (-ra), soguero, *m*. **r.-making,** cordelería, soguería, *f*. **r.-trick,** truco de la cuerda, *m*. **r.-walk,** cordelería, *f*. **r.-yarn,** *naut* filástica, *f*

rosary *n* rosario, *m*. **to say the r.,** rezar el rosario

rose *n* rosa, *f*; color de rosa, *m*; (rosette) roseta, *f*; *arch* rosetón, *m*; (of watering-can) pomo, *m*, roseta, *f*. *a* de rosa, rosado. **to see the world through r.-colored spectacles,** ver las cosas en color de rosa. **to turn to r.,** volverse color de rosa, rosear. **r.-bay,** *bot* rododafne, adelfa, *f*. **r.-bush,** rosal, *m*. **r.-color,** color de rosa, rosa, *m*. **r.-colored,** de color de rosa, rosado. **r.-garden,** rosalera, rosaleda, *f*. **r. grower,** cultivador (-ra) de rosas. **r. hip,** escaramujo, *m*. **r. leaf,** hoja de rosa, *f*; pétalo de rosa, *m*. **r.-like,** como una rosa, de rosa. **r.-red,** de color de rosa; como una rosa. **climbing r.-tree,** rosal trepador, *m*. **dwarf r.-tree,** rosal bajo, *m*. **standard r.-tree,** rosal de tallo, *m*. **r.-water,** agua de rosas, *f*. **r.-window,** rosetón, *m*, rosa, *f*. **r.-wood,** palo de rosa, *m*

rosé *a* (of wines) rosado

rosebud *n* capullo de rosa, *m*

rosemary *n* romero, *m*

rosin *n* (solid, for violin-bows, etc.) colofonia, *f*; resina, *f*. *vt* dar con colofonia; dar con resina

roster *n* lista, *f*; registro, *m*, matrícula, *f*

rostrum *n* tribuna, *f*; *zool* pico, *m*; (of a ship) espolón, *m*

rosy *a* róseo, rosado; sonrosado; *fig* de color de rosa, halagüeño; optimista. **r.-cheeked,** con (de) mejillas sonrosadas

rot *n* putrefacción, podredumbre, *f*; (in

trees) caries, f; (in sheep) comalía, f; (slang) patrañas, f pl, disparates, m pl, vi pudrirse; descomponerse; fig echarse a perder; (slang) decir disparates. vt pudrir; fig corromper; (slang) tomar el pelo (a)

rotary a rotativo. **r. printing press,** rotativa, f

rotary telephone n teléfono de discado, m

rotate vi girar, dar vueltas; alternarse. vt hacer girar

rotation n rotación, f; turno, m. **in r.,** por turnos. **r. of crops,** rotación de cultivos, f

rote, to learn by vt aprender de memoria, aprender por repetición, aprender de cotorra

rotogravure n rotograbado, m

rotten a putrefacto; podrido; (of bones, teeth) cariado; dañado, echado a perder; fig corrompido; (slang) pésimo. **to smell r.,** oler a podredumbre; apestar

rotting n pudrición, f, a que se pudre

rotund a rotundo

rotunda n rotonda, f

roué n calavera, libertino, m

rouge n colorete, m, vt and vi pintar de rojo, poner(se) colorete

rough a áspero; duro; (of country) fragoso, escabroso; (uneven) desigual; (stormy) borrascoso, tempestuoso; (of the sea) encrespado, bravo; (of movement) violento; (bristling) erizado; (of the hair) despeinado; (unpolished) tosco; basto; (unskilled, clumsy) torpe; (of sounds, tastes) áspero; (of persons) rudo, inculto; (severe) severo; (of behavior) brutal; (of manners) brusco; (rude) grosero; (approximate) aproximado. adv duramente, mal. n estado tosco, m; (person) matón, m. **in the r.,** en bruto; (roughed out) bosquejado. **to grow r.,** (of the sea) encresparse, embravecerse. **to take the r. with the smooth,** fig aceptar la realidad; tomar lo bueno con lo malo. **to r. it,** luchar contra las dificultades, pasar apuros; llevar una vida sencilla; vivir mal. **to r. out,** bosquejar. **r. and ready,** improvisado; provisional. **r. and tumble,** n camorra, pendencia, f. **r.-cast,** vt dar una primera capa de mezcla gruesa (a); bosquejar. **r. diamond,** diamante bruto (or en bruto), m. **r.-draft,** borrador, m; bosquejo, m. **r.-haired,** (of a dog) de pelo crespo. **r.-hewn,** modelado toscamente; desbastado; fig cerril, tosco. **r.-house,** jarana, f. **r.-rider,** domador (de caballos), m. **r. sketch,** bosquejo, esbozo, m. **r.-spoken,** malhablado

roughen vt poner áspero. vi ponerse áspero

roughly adv rudamente, toscamente; duramente; brutalmente; bruscamente; (of tastes, sounds) ásperamente; (approximately) aproximadamente, más o menos

roughness n aspereza, f; dureza, f; tosquedad, f; rudeza. f; (of the sea, wind) braveza, f; violencia, f; (of manner) brusquedad, f; brutalidad, f; (vulgarity) grosería, f. **the r. of the way,** la aspereza del camino

roulette n ruleta, f

round a redondo; (plump) rollizo; rotundo, categórico; sonoro. **a r. sum,** una cantidad redonda; un número redondo. **to walk at a r. pace,** andar a un buen paso. **r. dance,** baile en ruedo, m. **r.-faced,** carilleno, de cara redonda. **r.-house,** cuerpo de guardia, m; naut tumbadillo, m. **r.-shouldered,** cargado de espaldas. **r. table,** mesa redonda, f; (of King Arthur) Tabla Redonda, f. **r. trip,** viaje redondo, viaje de ida y vuelta, m. **r.-up,** rodeo de ganado, m; arresto, m

round n círculo, m; esfera, f; redondez, f; (slice) rodaja, f; (of a ladder) peldaño, m; (patrol and mil) ronda, f; circuito, m; vuelta, f, giro, m; serie, f; rutina, f; (of ammunition) andanada, descarga, f; (of cartridge) cartucho con bala, m; (of applause, etc.) salva, f; (of golf) partido, m; (in a fight) asalto, m; sport vuelta, f; (of drinks) ronda, f; (doctor's) visitas, f pl

round vt redondear; (fig complete) acabar, perfeccionar; (go round, e.g. a corner) dar vuleta (a), doblar, trasponer; rodear, cercar; (of a ship) doblar. vi redondearse. **to r. off,** redondear; terminar; coronar. **to r. up,** (cattle) rodear. **to r. upon,** volverse contra

round adv alrededor, en derredor; por todos lados; a la redonda, en torno; en circunferencia; en conjunto (r. is not translated in Spanish, e.g. **I shall come r. to your house,** Vendré a tu casa). prep alrededor de. **all the year r.,** todo el año, el año entero. **r. about,** a la redonda de, al derredor de; (nearly) cerca de; (of time by the clock) a eso de. **The road is closed and we shall have to go r.,** El camino está cerrado y tendremos que dar una vuelta. **to come r.,** volver; dejarse persuadir; recobrar su buen humor. **to go r.,** (spin) dar vueltas; (of the wind) cambiar. **There is enough to go r.,** Hay bastante para todos

roundabout a indirecto; desviado; vago. n tiovivo, m; (traffic) redondel, m. **He spoke in a r. way,** Hablaba con circunloquios. **We went there by a r. way,** Fuimos dando un rodeo

roundly adv en redondo; rotundamente, claramente

rouse vt despertar; animar; excitar; suscitar, provocar. **to r. oneself,** despertarse; animarse (a hacer algo)

rousing a que despierta; (moving) emocionante; (enthusiastic) entusiasta; grande, bueno

rout n (rabble) chusma, f; (party) sarao,

m; (defeat) derrota, *f*; (meeting) reunión, *f*. *vt* derrotar, poner en fuga; vencer

route *n* ruta, *f*; camino, *m*; itinerario, *m*. **r. march,** marcha de maniobras, *f*

routine *n* rutina, *f*, a rutinario, de rutina

rove *vi* vagar, errar

roving a vagabundo, errante; ambulante

row *n* (line) hilera, fila, hila, *f*; (in a theater, etc.) fila, *f*; (string) ristra, *f*; (in a boat) paseo en bote, *m*; (commotion) alboroto, *m*; (noise) ruido, *m*; (shindy) gresca, camorra, *f*; (scolding) regaño, *m*, *vi* (a boat) remar, bogar. *vt* conducir remando; (scold) regañar. **to be a row,** (shindy) haber la de San Quintín. **to start a row,** (shindy) armar camorra.

rowboat *n* bote de remos, *m*

rowdy a alborotador. *n* trafalmejas, *mf* rufián, *m*. **rowdy party** *Lat. Am.* fandango, *m*

rower *n* remero (-ra), bogador (-ra)

rowing a que rema; de remos. *n* deporte del remo, *m*; paseo en bote, *m*. **r.-boat,** bote de remos, *m*. **r.-club,** club náutico, *m*. **r.-seat,** bancada, *f*. **r.-stroke,** bogada, *f*

royal a real; regio. *n* naut sobrejuanete, *m*. **r. academy,** real academia, *f*. **r. eagle,** águila real, *f*. **R. Highness,** Alteza Real, *f*. **r. letters patent,** cédula real, *f*. **R. Mail,** mala real, *f*. **R. Standard,** estandarte real, *m*

royalty *n* realeza, *f*; miembro de la familia real, *m*; tanto por ciento de los ingresos, *m*; derechos de autor, *m pl*

R.R. (abbrev. of *railroad*) F.R. (abbrev. of *ferrocarril*)

rub *vt* frotar, estregar; fregar; rozar; friccionar; (make sore) raspar. **to rub one's hands together,** frotarse las manos. **to rub the wrong way,** frotar a contrapelo. **to rub against,** rozar. **to rub along,** *inf* ir tirando. **to rub down,** (a horse) bruzar; limpiar; (dry) secar; (wear down) desgastar. **to rub in,** dar fricciones con; frotar con; (an idea, etc.) machacar. **to rub off,** *vt* quitar (frotando); borrar. *vi* borrarse; separarse (de). **to rub out,** *vt* borrar. *vi* borrarse. **to rub up,** (polish) limpiar; *fig* refrescar

rub *n* frotación, *f*; roce, *m*; fricción, *f*; *fig* obstáculo, *m*; dificultad, *f*. **to give a rub,** frotar, etc. **rub-a-dub,** rataplán, *m*

rubber a de caucho, de goma. *n* caucho, *m*, goma, *f*; (for erasing) goma de borrar, *f*; (masseur) masajista, *mf*; (at whist, etc.) partida, *f*; *pl* **rubbers,** zapatos de goma, chanclos, *m pl.* **synthetic r.,** caucho artificial, *m*. **r. band,** goma, banda de goma, *f*. **r. belt,** *mech* correa de transmisión de caucho, *f*. **r.-plant, tree,** cauchera, *f*, *Central America, Mexico* hule, *m*. **r. plantation,** cauchal, *m*. **r.-plantation worker** cauchero (-a) *mf*. **r. planter,** cauchero, *m*. **r. stamp,** estampilla, *f*

rubbing *n* frotación, *f*; fricción, *f*; roce, *m*; (of floors, dishes, etc.) fregado, *m*

rubbish *n* basura, *f*; desperdicios, *m pl*, desecho, *m*; (of goods) pacotilla, *f*; (nonsense) pamplinas, patrañas, *f pl*, disparates, *m pl*. **r. cart,** carro del basurero, *m*

rubble *n* escombros, *m pl*; cascote, *m*; piedra bruta, *f*

rubicund a rubicundo

rubric *n* rúbrica, *f*

ruby *n* rubí, *m*. a de rubíes; de rubí. **r. lips,** labios de rubí, *m pl*

rucksack *n* mochila, *f*

rudder *n* timón, gobernalle, *m*

ruddy a rubicundo; rojo; frescote; (of animals) barcino

rude a rudo; tosco; vigoroso; grosero, descortés

rudeness *n* rudeza, *f*; tosquedad, *f*; grosería, incivilidad, descortesía, *f*

rudiment *n* rudimento, *m*

rudimentary a rudimentario

rue *vt* lamentar, llorar. *n* *bot* ruda, *f*

rueful a triste, melancólico; lamentable

ruff *n* golilla, lechuguilla, *f*; (of a bird) collarín de plumas, *m*; (of an animal) collarín de pelo, *m*

ruffian *n* rufián, *m*

ruffle *n* *sew* volante fruncido, *m*; (of a bird) collarín de plumas, *m*; (of an animal) collarín de pelo, *m*; (ripple) rizo, *m*; (annoyance) irritación, *f*. *vt* (ripple) rizar; (pleat) fruncir; (feathers) erizar; (hair) despeinar; agitar; (annoy) irritar, incomodar

ruffling *n* (rippling) rizado, *m*; (pleating) fruncido, *m*; (of the temper) irritación, *f*

rug *n* (floor) alfombra, *f*; manta de viaje, *f*. **rug strap,** portamantas, *m*

rugged a áspero, escabroso; escarpado, abrupto; (wrinkled) arrugado; tosco; (harsh) duro, severo; inculto; rudo; mal acabado; vigoroso

ruggedness *n* aspereza, escabrosidad, *f*; lo escarpado; dureza, severidad, *f*; rudeza, *f*; vigor, *m*

ruin *n* ruina, *f*. *vt* arruinar; echar a perder, estropear por completo; (a woman) perder

ruination *n* ruina, perdición, *f*

ruined a arruinado; en ruinas

ruinous a ruinoso; en ruinas

rule *n* regla, *f*; gobierno, *m*; autoridad, *f*, mando, *m*; administración, *f*; (reign) reinado, *m*; (of a court, etc.) orden, *f*; (for measuring) regla, *f*; *print* regleta, *f*; *pl* **rules,** reglas, *f pl*; reglamento, *m*. *vt* gobernar; regentar, regir; (control) dominar; (of a chairman, etc.) disponer, decidir; (guide) guiar; (lines) reglar. *vi* gobernar; (of a monarch) reinar; (of prices) mantenerse; estar en boga, prevalecer. **as a r.,** por regla general, en general. **slide-r.,** regla de cálculo, *f*. **to make it a r.,** tener por regla; tener por costumbre; tener por máxima. **to r. out,** excluir;

law no admitir. **to r. over,** (of a king, etc.) reinar sobre. **r. of the road,** reglamento del tráfico, *m*. **r. of thumb,** regla empírica, *f*; rutina, *f*

ruler *n* gobernador (-ra); soberano (-na); (master) amo (ama); (for ruling lines) regla, *f*

ruling *a* regente; dominante; (current) vigente. *n* gobierno, *m*; *law* decisión, *f*, fallo, *m*; (with lines) rayado, *m*. **r. pen,** tiralíneas, *m*

rum *n* ron, *m*

Rumanian *a* rumano. *n* rumano (-na); (language) rumano, *m*

rumble *vi* retumbar, tronar; (of vehicles) rugir; crujir. *n* retumbo, trueno, *m*; rugido, *m*; ruido sordo, *m*; rumor, *m*; crujido, *m*

rumbling *a* que retumba, etc. *n* ruido sordo, *m*; retumbo, *m*; crujido, *m*; (in the bowels) rugido, *m*

ruminant *a and n* rumiante, *mf*

ruminate *vi and vt* rumiar

rumination *n* rumia, *f*; meditación, reflexión, *f*

rummage *vt* revolver, desordenar, trastornar; explorar. **to r. out,** desenterrar

rumor *n* rumor, *m*, fama, *f*. **It is rumored that . . . ,** Hay rumores de que . . . , La voz corre que . . . , Se dice que . . .

rump *n* (of an animal) nalgas, ancas, *f pl*; cuarto trasero, *m*; (of a bird) rabadilla, *f*; (scornful) culo, *m*, posaderas, *f pl*. **r.-steak,** solomillo, *m*

rumple *vt* arrugar; desordenar

run *vi* correr; acudir; (flee) huir; (rush) precipitarse, lanzarse; (in a race) tomar parte en una carrera; competir; (pass over) deslizarse (por); (of machines) andar, marchar; (of traffic) circular; (leave, of trains, ships, etc.) salir; (ply between) hacer el trayecto entre . . . y . . . ; (flow) fluir, correr; (into the sea, of rivers) desembocar (en); (spurt) chorrear, manar; (drip) gotear; (leak) dejar fugar (el agua, etc.); (of colors) correrse; caer; (of tears) correr; derramarse; (of eyes) llorar; (melt) derretirse; (of a sore) supurar; (travel or go) ir; moverse; (work) trabajar; funcionar; (of editions of a book) agotarse; (of a play) representarse; (cross) cruzar; (elapse) correr; transcurrir, pasar; (become) hacerse; (of wording) decir; (be current) correr; (for parliament, etc.) hacerse candidato; (navigate) navegar; (spread) extenderse; (be) estar; ser; (of thoughts) pasar; (last) durar; (tend) tender (a). *vt* (a race, a horse) correr; (drive) conducir; (a business, etc.) administrar; dirigir; (govern) gobernar, regir; (hunt) cazar; perseguir; (water, etc.) hacer correr; (pierce) clavar; introducir; (push) empujar; (one's hand, eye, etc.) pasar; (risks, etc.) correr; (possess) tener; establecer un servicio de (autobuses, etc.); (smuggle) hacer contrabando de. **The ship ran**

aground, El barco encalló. **to run dry,** secarse; agotarse. **to run in the family,** estar en la familia. **to run into debt,** endeudarse, contraer deudas. **to run to seed,** granar; agotarse. **Steamers run daily between Barcelona and Mallorca,** Hay servicio diario de vapores entre Barcelona y Mallorca. **A stab of pain ran up his leg,** Sintió un dolor agudo en la pierna. **Feeling was running high,** Los ánimos estaban excitados. **My arrangements ran smoothly,** Mis planes marchaban bien. **Funds are running low,** El dinero escasea. **The tune runs in my head,** Tengo la canción metida en la cabeza. **The message runs like this,** El mensaje reza así, El mensaje dice así. **He ran his fingers through his hair,** Se mesaba los cabellos. **to run about,** andar de un lado a otro, correr por todas partes; (gad) corretear. **to run across,** cruzar corriendo; (meet) topar con, tropezar con. **to run after,** correr detrás (de); perseguir; buscar. **to run against,** (collide with) dar contra; (meet) tropezar con. **to run at,** abalanzarse hacia, precipitarse sobre; atacar. **to run away,** huir, escaparse; (slip away) escurrirse; (of a horse) dispararse, desbocarse. **to run away with,** huir con, fugarse con; (carry off) arrebatar; (steal) llevarse; (imagine) imaginarse, figurarse; (of temper, etc.) dominar, poseer. **to run back,** volver corriendo; llegar corriendo; retroceder rápidamente, correr hacia atrás. **to run backwards,** correr hacia atrás; **to run backwards and forwards,** ir y venir. **to run behind,** correr detrás (de); quedarse atrás; (be late) estar atrasado. **to run down,** *vi* bajar corriendo; descender, bajar; (of a clock) parar; (of a battery) gastarse; (of liquids) correr; fluir; (drop by drop) destilar. *vt* (capture) coger; alcanzar; (a person by a vehicle) atropellar; (a ship) echar a pique; (disparage) hablar mal de. **run-down,** (in health) agotado; (of a clock) parado. **to run for,** buscar corriendo; correr para coger el autobús, etc.); (president, etc.) ser candidato para. **to run in,** *vi* entrar corriendo. *vt* arrestar; hacer prisionero; *print* encerrar. **to run into,** tropezar con; chocar con; (plunge into) meterse de cabeza en; (of sums of money, etc.) ascender a; (of streets, rivers, etc.) desembocar en. **to run off,** *vi* escaparse corriendo; marcharse corriendo. *vt* deslizarse por; (drain) vaciar; *print* imprimir; (compose) componer. **to run off with,** huir con. **to run on,** correr delante; continuar; (of the mind) pensar en, entregarse a; hablar sin cesar; *print* recorrer. **to run out,** *vi* salir corriendo; (of liquids) derramarse; salir; (end) acabarse; agotarse; (project) sobresalir. *vt* (cricket) coger al lanzador fuera de la línea de saque. **to run out of,** no tener más de, haber terminado. **to run over,** *vi* rebosar; derramarse. *vt* (of a vehicle) atropellar, pasar por encima de, *Mexico* antellevar; (peruse) repasar; revis. **run pell-mell**, salir pitando, salir volando, salvarse por pies. **to run through**, correr por; pasar por; recorrer; (go directly) ir directamente (a); (pierce) traspasar, pasar de parte a parte; (squander) derrochar, malbaratar; (read) hojear, leer por encima. **to run up**, *vt* (hoist) izar; hacer de prisa; construir rápidamente; (incur) incurrir. *vi* subir corriendo; (of plants) trepar (por); (shrink) encogerse; (of expenses) aumentar. **to run up to time**, llegar a su hora. **to run up against**, tropezar con; (opposition, etc.) encontrar.

run *n* carrera, corrida, *f*; (excursion) visita, excursión, *f*; (cricket) carrera, *f*; (walk) paseo, *m*; (by train or sea) viaje, *m*; (by bus, tram) trayecto, *m*; (sea crossing) travesía, *f*; (distance run) recorrido, *m*; (of events, etc.) curso, *m*; marcha, *f*; (of markets, etc.) tendencia, *f*; (rhythm) ritmo, *m*; dirección, *f*; distancia, *f*; *mus* serie de notas, *f*; serie, *f*; duración, *f*; *theat* serie de representaciones, *f*; (freedom to use) libre uso, *m*; (majority) mayoría, *f*; (on a bank) asedio, *m*; (on a book, etc.) demanda, *f*; (for sheep, etc.) terreno de pasto, *m*; (for fowls) gallinero, *m*; (in a stocking) *Lat. Am.* acarraladura, *f*, *m*. **a run of bad luck**, una temporada de mala suerte. **at a run**, corriendo. **in the long run**, a la larga, al fin y al cabo. **on the run**, en fuga; ocupado. **Prices came down with a run**, Los precios bajaron de golpe. **take-off run**, *aer* recorrido de despegue, *m*

runaway *a* fugitivo; (of a horse) desbocado

rung *n* (of a ladder) peldaño, *m*; (of a chair) travesaño, *m*; (lath) listón, *m*

runner *n* corredor (-ra); (carrier of sedan chair, etc.) silletero, *mf*; (smuggler) contrabandista, *m*; (courier) estafeta, *f*; (messenger) mensajero, *m*; (ring) anillo movible, pasador corredizo, *m*; rueda móvil, *f*; (of a sledge) patín, *m*; *bot* tallo rastrero, *m*. **r.-up**, el segundo

running *a* corredor; (of water, bank accounts) corriente; (of a knot) corredizo; (of a sore) supurante; (continuous) continuo; (consecutive) consecutivo. *n* carrera, *f*; marcha, *f*; funcionamiento, *m*; administración, *f*; gobierno, *m*; dirección, *f*; (flowing) derrame, *m*; (of trains, buses, etc.) servicio, *m*; (smuggling) contrabando, *m*; (of a sore) supuración, *f*. **six times r.**, seis veces consecutivas. **The car is in r. order**, El auto está en buen estado. **r. away**, fuga, *f*. **r.-board**, (of a car, etc.) estribo, *m*; (of a locomotive) plataforma, *f*. **r. costs**, gastos de mantenimiento, *m pl*; (railway) gastos de tracción, *m pl*. **r. fight**, acción de retirada, *f*.

r.-knot, lazo corredizo, *m*. **r. title**, *print* título de la columna, *m*

run-off match *n* desempate, *m*

runway *n* (for launching a ship) grada, *f*; (of an airfield) pista de aterrizaje, *f*

rupture *n* rompimiento, *m*, rotura, *f*; ruptura, *f*; *med* hernia, *f*

ruptured *a med* herniado, quebrado

rural *a* rural, campestre, del campo; agrario

ruse *n* artimaña, treta, ardid, *f*

rush *n bot* junco, *m*; acometida, *f*; ataque, *m*; (of water) torrente, *m*; (bustle) bullicio, *m*; (speed) prisa, *f*; precipitación, *f*; acceso, *m*; (crowd) tropel, *m*, masa, *f*; (struggle) lucha, *f*; furia, *f*. *vi* precipitarse, lanzarse; agolparse. *vt* llevar rápidamente (a); despachar rápidamente; precipitar; (attack) asaltar, atacar; (capture) tomar, capturar; hacer de prisa; (a bill) hacer aprobar de prisa. **to r. upon**, abalanzarse hacia; embestir. **in a r.**, en tropel, en masa; de prisa. **to r. to a conclusion**, precipitarse a una conclusión. **r.-bottomed**, con asiento de enea. **r. hour**, hora de mayor circulación, *f*, hora de aglomeración, hora-pico (Argentina), hora brava (Argentina, informal). **r. order**, pedido urgente, *m*

russet *a* rojizo; rojo. **r. apple**, manzana asperiega, *f*

Russia Rusia, *f*

Russian *a* ruso. *n* ruso (-sa); (language) ruso, *m*. **R. leather**, piel de Rusia, *f*

rust *n* herrumbre, *f*, orín, *m*; moho, *m*; (disease) añublo, tizón, *m*. *vt* aherrumbrar; enmohecer. *vi* aherrumbrarse; enmohecerse

rustic *a* rústico; campesino, aldeano; (scornful) palurdo, grosero. *n* aldeano, *m*; (scornful) patán, *m*

rusticate *vi* rusticar, vivir en el campo. *vt* enviar al campo

rustiness *n* herrumbre, *f*; enmohecimiento, *m*; color rojizo, *m*; *fig* falta de práctica, *f*

rustle *n* susurro, *m*; murmurio, *m*; (of silk, a dress, etc.) frufrú, *m*; (of paper, etc.) crujido, *m*. *vi* susurrar; murmurar; crujir. *vt* (a paper) hacer crujir

rusty *a* herrumbroso; enmohecido, mohoso; (red) rojizo, (worn out) usado, viejo; (out of practice) desacostumbrado; (forgotten) empolvorado, oxidado (e.g. **My Portuguese is rusty**, Mi portugués está empolvorado)

rut *n* rodera, *f*, bache, surco, *m*; *fig* sendero trillado, *m*; *fig* rutina, *f*; (sexual appetite) celo, *m*, *vi* estar en celo

ruthless *a* inhumano, insensible, despiadado; inexorable, inflexible

rye *n* centeno, *m*. **rye field**, centenar, *m*

s n (letter) ese, f

Sabbath n (Jewish) sábado, m; (Christian) domingo, m

sabbatical a sabático

sable n (animal and fur) marta, f; her sable, m. a her sable; poet negro

sabotage n sabotaje, m, vt cometer un acto de sabotaje en

saboteur n saboteador, m

sabre n sable, m; (soldier) jinete, m. vt dar sablazos (a), acuchillar. **s. cut, thrust,** sablazo, m

sac n biol saco, m

saccharin n sacarina, f

sachet n sachet, m; bolsa, f. **handkerchief s.,** bolsa para pañuelos, f

sack n (bag) saco, m; mil saqueo, saqueamiento, saco, m. vt meter en sacos; (dismiss) dar pasaporte (a), despedir; mil saquear. **to get the s.,** recibir el pasaporte. **to give the s.,** dar el pasaporte (a), poner de patitas en la calle (a). **s. coat,** saco, m

sackcloth n harpillera, f. **tc repent in s. and ashes,** ponerse cenizas en la cabeza

sacrament n sacramento, m; Eucaristía, f. **the Blessed S.,** el Santísimo Sacramento. **to receive the Holy S.,** comulgar. **to receive the last sacraments,** recibir los sacramentos, recibir la Extremaunción

sacred a sagrado; sacro, santo; consagrado. **Nothing is s. to them,** No hay nada sagrado para ellos, No respetan nada. **the S. Heart of Jesus,** el Sagrado Corazón (de Jesús). **S. to the memory of . . .** Consagrado a la memoria de . . . **s. music,** música sagrada, f

sacrifice n sacrificio, m. vt and vi sacrificar. **s. of the mass,** sacrificio del altar, m

sacrilege n sacrilegio, m

sacrilegious a sacrílego

sacrosanct a sacrosanto

sad a triste; melancólico; (of a mistake) deplorable, funesto; inf redomado; (pensive) pensativo. **How s.!** ¡Qué lástima! ¡Qué triste! **It made me s.,** Me entristecó

sadden vt entristecer, acongojar, afligir

saddle n (riding) silla de montar, Lat. Am. albarda, f; (of a bicycle, etc.) sillín, m; mech silla, f; anat espalda, f. vt ensillar. **to s. with the responsibility of (a).** responsabilidad de (a). **s. of mutton,** lomo de carnero, m. **s.-bag,** alforja, Lat. Am. buchaca, f. **s.-cloth,** mantilla de silla, f. **s.-tree,** arzón, m

sadism n sadismo, m

sadist n sadista, mf

sadistic a sadístico

sadness n tristeza, melancolía, f

safe a al abrigo de; seguro; salvo; (certain) cierto; prudente; digno de confianza. n caja de caudales, f; (for food) alacena, f. **I stood beneath a tree s. from the rain,** Estaba de pie bajo un

árbol, al abrigo de la lluvia. **to put something in a s. place,** poner algo en salvo; poner algo en un lugar seguro. **s. and sound,** sano y salvo. **s.-conduct,** salvoconducto, m. **s.-keeping,** lugar seguro, m; (of a person) buenas manos, f pl

safeguard n protección, garantía, f; precaución, f. vt proteger, guardar; tomar precauciones (contra)

safely adv seguramente; sin accidente, sin novedad, sano y salvo; sin peligro. **You may s. tell him,** Puedes decírselo con toda seguridad. **to put (something) away s.,** poner (algo) en un lugar seguro

safety n seguridad, f. a de seguridad; (of locks) de golpe. **a place of s.,** un lugar seguro. **in s.,** en salvo, en seguro; con seguridad. **to believe in s. first,** poner la seguridad en primer lugar. **to play for s.,** jugar seguro. **with complete s.,** con toda seguridad. **s.-belt,** (cinto) salvavidas, m. **s.-catch,** fiador, m. **s.-curtain,** telón de seguridad, telón contra incendios, m. **s.-fuse,** espoleta de seguridad, f. **s.-glass,** vidrio inastillable, m. **s.-island,** refugio para peatones, m. **s.-lamp,** lámpara de seguridad, f. **s.-latch,** pestillo de golpe, m. **s.-lock,** (of fire-arms) seguro, m; (of doors, etc.) cerradura de seguridad, f. **s.-pin,** imperdible, m. **s.-razor,** máquina de afeitar, f. **s.-valve,** válvula de seguridad, f

saffron n azafrán, m, a azafranado, de color de azafrán.

sag vi doblegarse, ceder; inclinarse; naut caer a sotavento; (of prices) bajar; (of spirits, etc.) flaquear

saga n saga, f; epopeya, f

sagacious a sagaz, perspicaz; (of animals) sabio

sagacity n sagacidad, perspicacia, f; (of animals) sagacidad, f

sage n sabio, m; bot salvia, f. a sabio; sagaz; cuerdo

said a antedicho; tal dicho. **No sooner s. than done,** Dicho y hecho. **the s. Mr. Martínez,** el tal Sr. Martínez

sail n (of a ship) vela, f; (sailing-ship) velero, m; (of a windmill) aspa, f; mech ala, f; (trip) paseo en barco, m. vi navegar; ir en barco; dar un paseo en barco; (leave) salir en barco; zarpar; (of swans, etc.) deslizarse; (of clouds, etc.) flotar. vt (a ship) gobernar; (the sea) navegar por. **She sailed into the room,** Entró majestuosamente en la sala. **The ship sailed at eight knots,** El buque navegaba a ocho nudos. **to go for a s.,** dar un paseo en barco. **to s. round the world,** dar la vuelta al mundo. **to s. the seas,** navegar por los mares. **to set s.,** darse a la vel zarpar. **to take in the sails,** amainar. **s.-maker,** velero, *m*. **to s. into,** entrar en. **to s. round,** (the Cape, etc.) doblar. **to s. up,** subir en barco; (of a boat) ir río arriba

sailing *n* navegación, *f*; (departure) salida, *f*. **It's all plain s.,** Todo va viento en popa. **s.-boat,** bote de vela, *m*. **s.-ship,** buque de vela, velero, *m*

sailor *n* marinero, *m*. **John is a bad s.,** Juan se marea fácilmente. **to be a good s.,** no marearse. **s.-blouse,** marinera, *f*. **s.-suit,** traje de marinero, *m*

saint *n* santo (-ta); (before masculine names of Sts., excluding Sts. Dominic and Thomas) San; *inf* ángel, *m*. **All Saints' Day,** el día de Todos los Santos. **saint's day,** fiesta de un santo (or de una santa), *f*; (of a person) santo, *m*. **St. Bernard dog,** perro de San Bernardo, *m*. **St. John the Baptist,** San Juan Bautista. **St. Martin's summer,** el veranillo de San Martín. **St. Vitus's dance,** el baile de San Vito

sainthood *n* santidad, *f*

saintly *a* de santo; de santa; santo; *inf* angélical

sake *n* amor, *m*; causa, *f*. **for God's s.,** por el amor de Dios. **for the s. of,** para; por amor de. **to talk for talking's s.,** hablar por hablar

salable *a* vendible

salad *n* ensalada, *f*; (lettuce) lechuga, *f*. **fruit s.,** macedonia de frutas, *f*. **s.-bowl,** ensaladera, *f*. **s.-dressing,** aderezo, aliño, *m*, salsa para ensalada, *f*. **s.-oil,** aceite para ensaladas, *m*

salamander *n* salamandra, *f*

salary *n* sueldo, salario, *m*

sale *n* venta, *f*; (auction) almoneda, subasta pública, *f*. **(clearance) s.,** liquidación, *f*, saldo, *m*, *Mexico* barata, *f*. **to be on s.,** estar de venta. **"Piano for s.,"** «Se vende un piano.» **s. price,** precio de venta, *m*; precio de saldo, *m*

salesman *n* dependiente de tienda, *m*; (traveller) viajante, *m*

salesroom *n* salón de ventas, *m*

salient *a* saliente; *fig* prominente, conspicuo, notable, *n* saliente, *m*. **s. angle,** ángulo saliente, *m*

saliva *n* saliva, *f*

sallow *a* cetrino, oliváceo, lívido

sally *n* (*mil* etc.) salida, *f*; (quip) ocurrencia, salida, *f*. *vi* hacer una salida, salir. **to s. forth,** ponerse en camino

salmon *n* salmón, *m*; color de salmón, *m*. **s.-net,** salmonera, *f*. **s. trout,** trucha asalmonada, *f*

salon *n* salón, *m*

saloon *n* sala, *f*; (of a steamer) cámara, *f*, salón, *m*; (on train, for sleeping) departamento de coche cama, *m*; (on train, for dining) coche comedor, *m*; *aut* coche cerrado, *m*. **s. billiard s.,** salón de billares, *m*

dancing s., salón de baile, *m*. **hairdresser's s.,** salón de peluquero, *m*. **s. bar,** bar, *m*

salt *n* sal, *f*; (spice) sabor, *m*; (wit) sal, agudeza, *f*. **a salobre,** salino; salado; (of land) salitroso. *vt* (season) poner sal en; (cure) salar. **kitchen s.,** sal de cocina, *f*. **old s.,** *inf* lobo de mar, *m*. **rock s.,** sal gema, *f*. **sea s.,** sal marina, *f*. **to be not worth one's s.,** no merecer el pan que se come. **to take with a pinch of salt,** tomar con su grano de sal. **s.-cellar,** salero, *m*. **s. lagoon,** albufera, *f*. **s. lake,** lago salado, *m*. **s. marsh,** saladar, *m*. **s. meat,** carne salada, cecina, *f*. **s. merchant,** salinero, *m*. **s.-mine,** mina de sal, *f*. **s.-spoon,** cucharita de sal, *f*. **s. water,** agua salada, *f*; agua de mar, *f*. **s.-water fish,** pez de mar, *m*. **s.-works,** salinas, *f pl*

salty *a* salado; salobre

salubrious *a* salubre, saludable, sano

salutary *a* saludable, beneficioso

salutation *n* salutación, *f*, saludo, *m*

salute *vt* and *vi* saludar, *n* saludo, *m*; (of guns) salva, *f*. **to fire a s.,** hacer salvas, saludar con . . . salvas. **The soldier saluted them,** El soldado les saludó. **to take the s.,** tomar el saludo. **saluting base,** puesto de mando, *m*

Salvadoran, Salvadorian *a* and *n* salvadoreño (-ña)

salvage *n* salvamento, *m*, *vt* salvar

salvation *n* salvación, *f*. **to work out one's own s.,** salvar el alma. **the S. Army,** el Ejército de la Salvación, *m*

salve *n* pomada, *f*; *fig* bálsamo, *m*. *vt* curar; (overcome) vencer; (soothe) tranquilizar; *naut* salvar. **to s. one's conscience,** tranquilizar la conciencia

salvo *n* (of guns or applause) salva, *f*; (reservation) salvedad, reservación, *f*. **s. of applause,** salva de aplausos, *f*

same *a* mismo; igual; parecido; idéntico. *adv* lo mismo; del mismo modo. **all the s.,** sin embargo; con todo, a pesar de eso. **at the s. time,** al mismo tiempo; a la vez. **just the s.,** igual; (nevertheless) sin embargo. **He bowed deeply and I did the s.,** Él hizo una profunda reverencia y yo hice lo mismo. **They do not look at things the s. as we do,** No ven las cosas del mismo modo que nosotros. **If it is the s. to her,** Si le da igual. **It's all the s.,** Es igual, Lo mismo da, Es todo uno. **Ávila, capital of the province of the s. name,** Ávila, capital de la provincia de su nombre

"Same-Day Service" «En el día» (Argentina)

sample *n* muestra, *f*; prueba, *f*; ejemplo, *m*. *vt* sacar una muestra de; (try) probar. **s. book,** muestrario, *m*

sampler *n* probador, *m*; (of wines) catador, *m*; *sew* dechado, *m*

sanatorium *n* sanatorio, *m*

sanctify vt santificar; consagrar

sanctimonious a santurrón, mojigato, beato

sanction n sanción, f. vt sancionar; autorizar. **to apply sanctions,** pol aplicar sanciones

sanctity n santidad, f; lo sagrado; inviolabilidad, f. **odor of s.,** olor de santidad, f

sanctuary n santuario, m; (historical) sagrado, sagrado asilo, m; refugio, asilo, m. **to take s.,** acogerse a sagrado; refugiarse

sand n arena, f; (for drying writing) arenilla, f; granos de arena, m pl; pl **sands,** playa, f; (of life) horas de la vida, f pl. vt arenar. **to plough the s.,** arar en el mar. **s.-bag,** n saco de arena, m. vt (a building) proteger con sacos de arena; (a person) golpear con un saco de arena. **s.-bank,** banco de arena, m, barra, f. **to run on a s.-bank,** encallar. **s.-colored,** de color de arena. **s.-dune,** médano, m. **s.-paper,** n papel de lija, m. vt pulir con papel de lija, lijar. **s.-pit,** arenal, m. **s. shoes,** alpargatas, f pl

sandal n sandalia, f, Central America caite, m; (rope-soled) alpargata, f. **s.-wood,** sándalo, m

sandstorm n tempestad de arena, f; simún, m

sandwich n emparedado, bocadillo, m. vt insertar. **I found myself sandwiched between two fat men,** Me encontré aplastado entre dos hombres gordos. **s.-man,** hombre sándwich, m

sandy a arenoso; sabuloso; (of hair) rojo, rufo, bermejo. **a s. beach,** una playa arenosa

sane a de juicio sano; razonable, prudente; sesudo. **He is a very s. person,** Es un hombre con mucho sentido común. **to be s.,** estar en su juicio; (of a policy, etc.) ser prudente, ser razonable

sangfroid n sangre fría, f; aplomo, m

sanguine a (of complexion) rubicundo; sanguíneo; optimista, confiado. n (drawing) sanguina, f. **to be s. about the future,** ser optimista acerca del porvenir, tener confianza en el porvenir

sanitary a sanitario; higiénico, **s. inspector,** inspector de sanidad, m. **s. napkin, s. towel,** servilleta higiénica, toalla sanitaria, mf, paño higiénico, m

sanitation n higiene, f; sanidad pública, f; (apparatus) instalación sanitaria, f

sanity n juicio sano, m; prudencia, f; (common sense) sentido común, m, sensatez, f

Santa Claus n (Spanish equivalent) los Reyes Magos, m pl

São Paulo San Pablo, m

sap n (bot and fig) savia, f; mil zapa, f. vt (undermine) debilitar, agotar; mil zapar

sapphire n zafiro, m. a de zafiros; cerúleo, de zafiro

Saragossa Zaragoza, f

sarcasm n sarcasmo, m

sarcastic a sarcástico

sarcophagus n sarcófago, m

sardine n sardina, f. **packed like sardines,** como sardinas en banasta. **s.-net,** sardinal, m

Sardinia Cerdeña, f

Sardinian a and n sardo (-da)

sardonic a sardónico

sash n (with uniform) faja, f; (belt) cinto, cinturón, m; (of a window) cerco, m. **s. window,** ventana de guillotina, f

Satan n Satanás, m

satanic a satánico

satchel n saquito de mano, m, bolsa, f; (school) vademécum, m; cartapacio, m, cartera, f

sate vt saciar, hartar; satisfacer

satellite n satélite, m

satiate vt saciar, hartar; satisfacer. a harto; repleto

satin n raso, m. a de raso; (glossy) lustroso, terso. vt (paper) satinar

satire n sátira, f

satiric a satírico

satirist n escritor (-ra) satírico (-ca)

satirize vt satirizar

satisfaction n satisfacción, f; (contentment) contento, m, satisfacción, f; (for sin) expiación, f; (of a debt) pago, m; desquite, m; recompensa, f. **to demand s.,** pedir satisfacción. **to give** (someone) **s.,** dar contento (a), alegrar

satisfactory a satisfactorio; (for sin) expiatorio

satisfy vt satisfacer; (convince) convencer; (allay) tranquilizar, apaciguar. **I am satisfied with him,** Estoy satisfecho (Estoy contento) con él. **The explanation did not s. me,** La explicación no me convenció. **to s. oneself that . . . ,** asegurarse de que . . . **to s. one's thirst,** apagar la sed

satisfying a que satisface; satisfactorio; (of food) nutritivo

saturate vt saturar (de), empapar (de); chem saturar; flg imbuir; flg empapar. **to s. oneself in,** (a subject) empaparse en

saturation n saturación, f. **s. point,** (chem etc.) punto de saturación, m

Saturday n sábado, m

Saturn n Saturno, m

sauce n salsa, f; (thick fruit) compota, f; inf insolencia, f. **s.-boat,** salsera, f

saucepan n cazuela, cacerola, f. **double s.,** baño de María, m

saucer n platillo, m. **flying s.,** platillo volante, m. **s.-eyed,** con ojos redondos

saucy a respondón, descarado; (cheerful) alegre; (of hats, etc.) coquetón, majo

sauerkraut *n* chucruta, *f*

saunter *vi* pasearse, vagar, *n* paseo, *m*, vuelta, *f*

sausage *n* chorizo, *m*; salchicha, *f*. **s.-balloon,** globo cautivo, *m*. **s.-curl,** bucle, *m*. **s.-machine,** choricera, *f*. **s.-maker,** choricero (-ra)

savage a salvaje; feroz; (cruel) inhumano, cruel; (furious) furioso. *n* salvaje, *mf*

savagery *n* salvajismo, *m*; ferocidad, *f*; brutalidad, crueldad, *f*

savannah *n* sabana, *f*. **s. dweller,** sabanero (-ra)

save *vt* salvar; (keep) guardar; conservar; reservar; (money, one's clothes, etc.) ahorrar; (time) ganar; (avoid) evitar. *vi* salvar; hacer economías; ahorrar. **He saved my life,** Me salvó la vida. **They have saved a room for me,** Me han reservado una habitación. **to s. appearances,** guardar las apariencias. **to s. oneself trouble,** ahorrarse molestias. **to s. the situation,** estar al nivel de las circunstancias

save *prep* salvo, excepto, menos. *conjunc* sino, a menos que; con la excepción de. **all s. one,** todos menos uno. **all the conspirators s. he,** todos los conspiradores con la excepción de él

saving a frugal, económico; (stingy) tacaño, avaricioso; (clause) condicional. *n* salvación, *f*; (of money, time, etc.) ahorro, *m*, economía, *f*; *pl* **savings,** ahorros, *m pl. prep* salvo, excepto, fuera de. *conjunc* con excepción de que, fuera de que. **s. grace,** único mérito, *m*. **savings bank,** caja de ahorros, *f*. **savings fund,** montepío, *m*

savior *n* salvador (-ra). **the S.,** el Salvador, el Redentor

savor *n* sabor, gusto, *m*; (aftertaste) dejo, *m*; (zest) salsa, *f*. *vi* saber (a), tener sabor (de); *fig* oler (a). *vt* saborear, paladear; (flavor) sazonar

savory a sabroso, apetitoso; (not sweet) no dulce; (of places) respetable; (of reputation, etc.) bueno. *n* entremés salado, *m*. **s. omelette,** tortilla, *f*

saw *n* (maxim) sentencia, *f*; (proverb) refrán, decir, *m*; (tool) sierra, *f*. *vt* aserrar, *Lat. Am.* aserruchar; (the air) cortar. *vi* usar una sierra. **two-handled saw,** tronzador, *m*. **saw-fish,** pez sierra, *m*. **saw-mill,** molino de aserrar, *m*. **saw-pit,** aserradero, *m*

sawdust *n* aserrín, *m*

saxophone *n* saxófono, saxofón *m*

say *vt* decir; recitar. *vi* decir. **Let us say that the house is worth $100,000,** Pongamos por ejemplo que la casa vale cien mil dólares. **He has no say in the matter,** No entra ni sale en el asunto. **I have said my say,** He dicho lo que quería. **They say,** Se dice, Dicen, La gente dice. **You don't say!** ¡Calle! ¿De veras? ¡Imposible! **that is to say . . . ,** es

decir . . . ; esto es . . . , a saber . . . **to say one's prayers,** rezar, decir sus oraciones. **to say again,** volver a decir; decir otra vez, repetir. **to say over and over again,** repetir muchas veces, decir repetidamente. **What do you say to that?** ¿Qué dices a esto?

saying *n* decir, *m*; (proverb) refrán, *m*; (maxim) sentencia, *f*. **As the s. is,** Como suele decirse; Según el refrán. **It goes without s.,** Huelga decir. **It's only a s.,** Es un decir, nada más

scab *n* (of a wound) costra, *f*; (disease) escabro, *m*; (blackleg) esquirol, *m*

scabby a costroso; (diseased) roñoso, sarnoso

scabies *n* sarna, *f*. **s. mite,** arador de la sarna, *m*

scaffold *n* (in building) andamio, *m*; (for execution) cadalso, patíbulo, *m*. **to go to the s.,** ir al patíbulo; acabar en el patíbulo

scald *vt* escaldar; quemar; (instruments) esterilizar. *n* quemadura, escaldadura, *f*. **to s. oneself,** escaldarse. **scalding hot,** hirviendo

scale *n* (of a balance) platillo, *m*; *zool* escama, *f*; *bot* bráctea, *f*; *bot* hijuela, *f*; (flake) laminita, *f*; (*mus, math*) escala, *f*; (of charges, etc.) tarifa, *f*; (of salaries) escalafón, *m*; (of a thermometer) escala, *f*. *vt* escalar; (fish) escamar. **major s.,** escala mayor, *f*. **minor s.,** escala menor, *f*. **on a grand s.,** en gran escala. **on a small s.,** en pequeña escala. **pair of scales,** balanza, *f*; (for heavy weights) báscula, *f*. **social s.,** escala social, *f*. **The Scales,** *ast* Libra, *f*. **to draw to s.,** dibujar a escala. **to turn the scales,** pesar; *fig* inclinar la balanza. **to s. down,** (art and of charges) reducir

scaling *n* (of fish) escamadura, *f*; (of buildings) desconchadura, *f*; (ascent) escalamiento, *m*

scallop *n* (*icht* and badge) venera, *f*; concha, *f*; *sew* onda, *f*, festón, *m*. *vt cul* guisar en conchas; *sew* ondear, festonear

scalp *n anat* pericráneo, *m*; cuero cabelludo, *m*; *fig* trofeo, *m*. *vt* escalpar. **s.-hunter,** cazador de cabelleras, *m*

scalpel *n* escalpelo, *m*

scaly a escamoso, conchado; (of boilers) incrustado

scamp *n* bribón, granuja, *m*. *vt* (work) frangollar

scamper *vi* retozar, brincar; correr. *n* carrerita, *f*. **to s. off,** salvarse por los pies, huir; marcharse corriendo

scan *vt* (verse) medir, escandir; (examine) escudriñar, examinar; (glance at) dar un vistazo (a)

scandal *n* escándalo, *m*; maledicencia, *f*; (slander) calumnia, *f*. **to talk s.,** murmurar

scandalize *vt* escandalizar

scandalous a escandaloso; infame; calumnioso

Scandinavia Escandinavia, f

Scandinavian a escandinavo. n escandinavo (-va);

scant a escaso; insuficiente

scantiness n escasez, f; insuficiencia, f

scanty a insuficiente; escaso; (of hair) ralo; (of crops, etc.) pobre

scapegoat n víctima propiciatoria, f; cabeza de turco, f. **to be a s. for,** pagar el pato por

scapegrace n bribón, m.

scapula n anat escápula, f

scar n cicatriz, f; fig señal, f. vt marcar con una cicatriz. **to s. over,** cicatrizarse

scarce a escaso; insuficiente; raro. adv poet apenas. **to make oneself s.,** largarse, pirarse, escabullirse; ausentarse, esconderse

scarcely adv apenas; no bien; casi; (with difficulty) a duras penas, con dificultad. **It is s. likely he said that,** No es muy probable que lo hubiese dicho. **There were s. twenty people in the building,** Había apenas veinte personas en el edificio. **S. anyone likes his pictures,** Sus cuadros no le gustan a casi nadie

scarcity n escasez, insuficiencia, f; (famine) carestía, f; (rarity) rareza, f

scare vt asustar, espantar, llenar de miedo (a), Lat. Am. also julepear; intimidar. n susto, pánico, m; alarma, f. **What a s. I got!** ¡Qué susto me he llevado! **to s. away,** ahuyentar. **to be scared** Lat. Am. julepearse

scarecrow n espantapájaros, m; inf estantigua, f, mamarracho, espantajo, m

scarf n bufanda, f; (tie) corbata, f; mil faja, f

scarlatina n med escarlatina, f

scarlet n escarlata, f. a de color escarlata. **to turn s.,** (of persons) enrojecerse. **s. fever,** escarlatina, f. **s. hat,** ecc capelo (cardenalicio), m. **s. runner,** bot judía verde, f

scathing a mordaz, cáustico

scatter vt esparcir, sembrar con; (benefits, etc.) derramar; (put to flight) derrotar; dispersar; disipar; fig frustrar; (squander) derrochar, desparramar. vi dispersarse. **The crowd scattered,** La muchedumbre se dispersó. **s.-brained,** de cabeza de chorlito, atolondrado

scattered a disperso; esparcido

scattered showers n lluvias aisladas, f pl

scavenge vt (streets) recoger la basura de, barrer

scavenger n (of the streets) barrendero, m; (dustman) basurero, m; zool animal que se alimenta de carne muerta, m; insecto que se alimenta de estiércol, m. vt See **scavenge**

scenario n escenario, m

scene n escena, f; teatro, lugar, m; espectáculo, m; (theat décor) decoración, f; (of a play) escena, f; (view) vista, perspectiva, f. **behind the scenes,** entre bastidores. **The s. is laid . . . ,** La acción pasa . . . **to come on the s.,** entrar en escena. **to make a s.,** hacer una escena. **s.-painter,** n escenógrafo (-fa). **s.-shifter,** tramoyista, mf

scenery n theat decorado, m; (landscape) paisaje, m

scenic a dramático; escénico; pintoresco. **s. railway,** montaña rusa, f

scent vt perfumar; (smell) oler; (out) husmear, olfatear; (suspect) sospechar. n perfume, m; fragancia, f, aroma, m; (smell) olor, m; (of hounds) viento, m; (of game, etc.) rastro, viento, m; (fig of person) nariz, f; (trail) pista, f. **to lose the s.,** perder la pista. **to s. danger,** oler el peligro. **to throw off the s.,** despistar. **s.-bottle,** frasco de perfume, m. **s.-spray,** pulverizador, m

sceptic n escéptico (-ca)

sceptical a escéptico

schedule n lista, m; programa, m; (of taxes) clase, f; (of trains, etc.) horario, m. vt poner en una lista; inventariar

scheme n plan, m; proyecto, m; diagrama, esquema, m; (summary) resumen, m; (of colors, etc.) combinación, f; (plot) intriga, maquinación, f. vt proyectar. vi planear, formar planes; (intrigue) intrigar, conspirar. **color s.,** combinación de colores, f

schemer n (plotter) intrigante, mf

scheming a intrigante; astuto. n planes, proyectos, m pl; intrigas, maquinaciones, f pl

schism n cisma, mf

scholar n (at school) colegial (-la); (disciple) alumno (-na); (student) estudiante, mf; (learned person) erudito (-ta), hombre de letras, m; (scholarship holder) becario, m. **to be a poor s.,** fig ser analfabeto

scholarly a de sabio, de hombre de letras; erudito

scholarship n erudición, f; saber, m; (exhibition) beca, f. **s. holder,** becario, m

scholastic a escolar, escolástico; pedante; (medieval) escolástico. n escolástico, m. **the s. profession,** el magisterio

school n escuela, f; colegio, m; academia, f; univ departamento, m; (faculty) facultad, f; (of fish) banco, m. vt enseñar, instruir; formar; disciplinar. **in s.,** en clase. **day s.,** escuela, f, colegio, m. **the Florentine s.,** (of painting) la escuela florentina. **the lower s.,** los alumnos del preparatorio. **private s.,** colegio particular, m. **s.-bag,** vademécum, m. **s.-book,** libro escolar, m. **s.-days,** los días de escuela; los años de colegio. **in his s.-days,**

cuando él iba a la escuela. **s.-fees,** gastos de la enseñanza, *m pl,* cuota escolar, *f*

schoolboy *n* muchacho de escuela, colegial, *m*

school district *n* sector escolar, *m*

schoolfellow *n* compañero de colegio, condiscípulo, *m*

schoolgirl *n* colegiala, *f*

schooling *n* educación, enseñanza, *f*

schoolmaster *n* maestro de escuela, professor, *Mexico* escuelante, *m*

schoolmistress *n* maestra de escuela, profesora, *f*

school of hard knocks *n* universidad sin tejados, *f*

schoolroom *n* aula, sala de clase, salón de clase, *m*

sciatic *a* ciático

sciatica *n* ciática, *f*

science *n* ciencia, *f*

scientific *a* científico; exacto, sistemático

scientist *n* hombre de ciencia, *m,* científico (-ca)

scintilla *n fig* átomo, vestigio, *m*

scintillate *vi* centellear, lucir, chispear; (of persons) brillar

scion *n* (sucker) acodo, *m;* (shoot) vástago, renuevo, *m;* (human) descendiente, *mf.* **s. of a noble race,** vástago de una raza noble, *m*

scissors *n pl* tijeras, *f pl, Argentina* cortante, *msg.* **s.-sharpener,** amolador, *m*

sclerosis *n med* esclerosis, *f*

sclerotic *n anat* esclerótica, *f*

scoff *n* burla, mofa, *f. vi* burlarse. **to s. at,** burlarse de, mofarse de

scoffer *n* mofador (-ra); (at religion, etc.) incrédulo (-la)

scold *n* virago, *f, vt* reñir, reprender

scolding *n* represión, increpación, *f*

scone *n* bollo, *m*

scoop *n* pala de mano, *f;* cuchara de draga, *f;* (boat) achicador, *m;* (financial) golpe, *m;* (journalistic) éxito periodístico, *m. vt* sacar con pala (de); sacar con cuchara (de); (shares, etc.) comprar, obtener. **to s. out,** vaciar; excavar; (bail) achicar

scooter *n* (child's) patinete, patín del diablo, *m;* monopatín, *m*

scope *n* alcance, *m;* esfera de acción, *f;* lugar, *m.* **to give full s. to,** dar rienda suelta a. **to have full s.,** tener plena oportunidad; tener todas las facilidades. **within the s. of,** dentro del alcance de

scorch *vt* chamuscar; (the skin) tostar; (of the sun) abrasar, quemar; (wither) agostar. **to s. along,** ir como un relámpago. **scorching,** *a* abrasador, ardiente; *fig* mordaz

score *n* (scratch) rasguño, *m;* señal, *f;* (crossing out) raya, *f;* (reckoning) cuenta, *f,* escote, *m;* (notch) muesca, *f; sport*

tanteo, *m,* puntuación, *Lat. Am.* anotación, *f;* (point) punto, tanto, *m;* (twenty) veintena, *f;* (reason) motivo, *m,* causa, *f;* respecto, *m; mus* partitura, *f. vt* marcar; rayar; (erase) tachar, borrar; (cricket runs, etc.) hacer; (goals) marcar; (points) ganar; (reckon) apuntar. **s. a triumph,** apuntarse un triunfo; *mus* instrumentar; (for orchestra) orquestar. *vi* (be fortunate) llevar la ventaja. **to pay off old scores,** ajustar cuentas viejas. **to s. off someone,** ganar un punto (a), triunfar de. **upon that s.,** a ese respecto; por esa causa. **Upon what s.?** ¿Con qué motivo? **s.-board,** marcador, *m*

scorer *n* (of a goal, etc.) tanteador, *m;* (keeper of score) marcador, *m*

scorn *n* desprecio, desdén, *m. vt* despreciar, desdeñar; reírse de. **to s. to do,** no dignarse hacer

scornful *a* desdeñoso, despreciativo

scorpion *n* escorpión, alacrán, *m; ast* Escorpión, *m*

Scot *n* escocés, *m*

scotch *vt* (kill) matar; (thwart) frustrar; (a wheel) calzar

Scotland Escocia, *f*

Scotswoman *n* escocesa, *f*

Scottish *a* escocés

scoundrel *n* canalla, sinvergüenza, *mf*

scour *vt* (traverse) recorrer, batir; (pans, etc.) fregar, estregar; (free from) limpiar (de); (of water) arrastrar

scourge *vt* azotar, flagelar; castigar, mortificar. *n* disciplinas, *f pl; fig* verdugo, *m,* plaga, *f*

scout *n mil* batidor, explorador, *m. vi mil* explorar, reconocer. *vt* (flout) rechazar a mano airada, rechazar con desdén. **boy s.,** muchacho explorador, *m*

scowl *vi* fruncir el ceño. *n* ceño, *m.* **to s. at,** mirar con ceño

scraggy *a* flaco, magro, descarnado

scramble *vi* trepar. *vt* (throw) arrojar; (eggs) revolver. **scrambled eggs,** huevos revueltos, *m pl.* **to s. for,** andar a la rebatiña por; (for coins, etc.) luchar para. **to s. up,** escalar; subir a gatas

scrap *n* pedazo, *m;* fragmento, *m;* pizca, brizna, *f;* (shindy) suiza, camorra, *f;* (boxing) combate de boxeo, *m; pl* **scraps,** desperdicios, *m pl;* (food) restos de la comida, *m pl. vt* desechar; (expunge) borrar; *vi* (fight) armar camorra. **a few scraps of news,** algunas noticias. **Do you mind not coming? Not a s.,** ¿Te importa no venir? Ni pizca. **s.-book,** álbum de recortes, *m;* **s.-heap,** depósito de basura, *m; fig* olvido, *m.* **s. iron,** chatarra, *f,* hierro viejo, *m*

scrape *vt* raspar, rascar, raer; (one's shoes) restregar; (a musical instrument) rascar. *n* rasguño, *m;* ruido de raspar, *m;* (predicament) lío, apuro, *m;* dificultad, *f.* **to s. acquaintance with,** trabar amistad con. **to s. along,** *inf* ir tirando. **to s. away,** rascar; quitar. **to s. through,** (an examination) aprobar justo. **to s. together,** amontonar poco a poco

scrappy *a* escaso; fragmentario; (incoherent) descosido. **a s. meal,** una comida escasa

scratch *vt* arañar; (the earth) escarbar; (rub) rascar; (a hole) hacer; (sketch) dibujar, trazar; (a horse) retirar de una carrera. *vi* arañar; rascar; escarbar; (of a pen) rasguear; (back out) retirarse. *n* arañazo, *m*; (of a pen) rasgueo, *m*; (in a race) línea de salida, *f*; (in games) cero, *m*. **a** improvisado. **The dog scratched at the door,** El perro arañó la puerta. **to come up to s.,** estar al nivel de las circunstancias. **to s. one's head,** rascarse la cabeza. **to s. a person's eyes out,** sacar los ojos con las uñas (a). **to s. the surface of,** (a subject) tratar superficialmente. **to s. out,** tachar

scrawl *vi* hacer garabatos. *vt* garabatear, garrapatear. *n* garabato, *m*

scream *vt* and *vi* chillar. *n* chillido, *m*. **It was a perfect s.** Era para morirse de risa. **to s. with laughter,** reírse a carcajadas, morirse de risa

screaming *n* chillidos, *m pl.* **a** chillador; (piercing) penetrante, agudo; (funny) divertidísimo

screech *vi* chillar; (of owls, etc.) ulular; graznar. *n* chillido, *m*, ululación, *f*; graznido, *m*. **s.-owl,** úlula, *f*

screed *n* arenga, *f*; cita larga, *f*

screen *n* biombo, *m*; (wire) tela metálica, *f*; (nonfolding) mampara, *f*; (eco) cancel, *m*; (cinema, television) pantalla, *f*; (of trees, etc., and *mil*) cortina, *f*; (*fig* protection) abrigo, *m*. *vt* proteger; (shelter) abrigar; (hide) esconder, ocultar; (a light) proteger con pantalla; (a film) proyectar; (sieve) cribar, cerner; (examine) investigar. **to s. from view,** ocultar la vista (de), esconder. **s. star,** estrella de la pantalla, *f*

screw *n* tornillo, *m*; (propeller) hélice, *f*; vuelta de tornillo, *f*; presión, *f*; (miser) tacaño, *m*; (salary) salario, *m*. *vt* atornillar; torcer; apretar, oprimir. **He has a s. loose,** Le falta un tornillo. **to s. down,** sujetar con tornillos. **to s. up,** cerrar con tornillos. **to s. up one's courage,** tomar coraje. **to s. up one's eyes,** desojarse, entornar los ojos. **s.-driver,** destornillador, *Mexico* desarmador, *m*

scribble *vt* escribir de prisa, *vi* garabatear, garrapatear; escribir, ser autor. *n* garabato, garrapato, *m*; mala letra, letra ilegible, *f*; (note) billete, *m*

scribe *n* escribiente, copista, *mf*; (Jewish history) escriba, *m*

scrimmage *n* reyerta, pelea, camorra, *f*; (Rugby) mêlée, *f*

script *n* letra cursiva, *f*; *print* plumilla, *f*;

manuscrito, *m*; *law* escritura, *f*; examen escrito, *m*; (film) escenario, *m*

Scripture *n* Sagrada Escritura, *f*. **Scriptures,** Escrituras, *f pl*; (of non-Christian religions) los libros sagrados

scrofula *n* escrófula, *f*

scroll *n* (of paper, etc.) rollo, *m*; pergamino, *m*; (flourish) rúbrica, *f*; (of an Ionic capital) voluta, *f*. **s. of fame,** lista de la fama, *f*

scrotum *n anat* escroto, *m*

scrounge *vi* sablear. *vt* dar un sablazo (a); hurtar

scrub *vt* fregar; limpiar; restregar. *n* fregado, *m*; limpieza, *f*; fricción, *f*; (brushwood) matorral, breñal, *m*, maleza, *f*

scrubbing *n* fregado, *m*. **s.-brush,** cepillo para el suelo, *m*

scrubby *a* (of plants) anémico; (of persons) insignificante, pobre; (of land) cubierto de maleza

scruff *n* nuca, *f*, pescuezo, *m*

scruple *n* escrúpulo, *m*. *vi* tener escrúpulos. **to have no scruples,** no tener escrúpulos

scrupulous *a* escrupuloso; exacto, meticuloso

scrutinize *vt* escudriñar, examinar, *Lat. Am. also* interiorizar; (votes) escrutar

scrutiny *n* escrutinio, *m*

scud *vi* correr; deslizarse; flotar. **to s. before the wind,** ir viento en popa

scuffle *vi* pelear, forcejear, andar a la rebatiña. *n* refriega, pelea, sarracina, arrebatiña, *f*

scull *n* remo, *m*, *vi* remar

scullery *n* fregadero, *m*. **s. maid,** fregona, *f*

sculptor *n* escultor, *m*, escultora, *f*

sculpture *n* escultura, *f*, *vt* esculpir

scum *n* espuma, *f*; (dregs) heces, *f pl. vt* espumar. **s. of the earth,** las heces de la sociedad

scurrilous *a* grosero, indecente

scurry *vi* echar a correr. *n* fuga precipitada, *f*; (of rain) chaparrón, *m*; (of snow) remolino, *m*. **to s. off,** escabullirse. **to s. through,** hacer de prisa, terminar rápidamente

scurvy *a* tiñoso, vil, ruin. *n* escorbuto, *Mexico* berbén, *m*. **a s. trick,** una mala pasada

scuttle *n* (trap-door) escotillón, *m*; *naut* escotilla, *f*; (for coal) carbonera, *f*; (flight) huida precipitada, *f*. *vt* (a boat) echar a pique, *vi* (run away) escabullirse, apretar a correr

scythe *n* dalle, *m*, guadaña, *f*, *vt* dallar, segar

sea *n* mar, *m*, or *f*; ola, *f*; multitud, *f*. **Black Sea,** Mar Negro. **Mediteranean Sea,** (Mar) Mediterráneo, *m*. **at sea,** en el mar; perplejo. **beyond the seas,** allende los mares. **by sea,** por mar. **by the sea,** a la orilla del mar. **high seas,** alta mar, *f.* **the seven seas,** todos los mares del mundo. **to go to sea,** hacerse marinero. **to put to sea,** hacerse a la mar, hacerse a la vela. **sea-anemone,** anémone de mar, *f.* **sea-bathing,** baños de mar, *m pl.* **sea-breeze,** brisa de mar, *f.* **sea captain,** capitán de mar, *m.* **sea chart,** carta de marear, *f.* **sea-coast,** litoral, *m,* costa marítima, *f.* **sea-cow,** manatí, *m.* **sea dog,** lobo de mar, *m.* **sea-fight,** combate naval, *m.* **sea-foam,** espuma de mar, *f.* **sea-girt,** rodeado por el mar. **sea-going,** de altura; navegante. **sea-going craft,** embarcación de alta mar, *f.* **sea-green,** verdemar, *m.* **sea-gull,** gaviota, *f.* **sea-horse,** caballo marino, *m.* **sea-legs,** piernas de marino, *f pl.* **sea-level,** nivel del mar, *m.* **sea-lion,** león marino, *m.* **sea-mist,** bruma, *f.* **sea-nymph,** nereida, *f.* **sea-power,** potencia naval, *f.* **sea-serpent,** serpiente de mar, *f.* **sea-sick,** mareado. **to be sea-sick,** marearse. **sea-sickness,** mal de mar, *m.* **sea-trip,** viaje por mar, *m.* **sea-urchin,** erizo de mar, *m.* **sea-wall,** dique de mar, *m*

seafarer *n* (traveller) viajero (-ra) por mar; (sailor) marinero, *m*

seal *n zool* foca, *f,* lobo marino, *m;* piel de foca, *f;* sello, *m;* (stamp) estampillo, timbre, *m; vt* sellar; (stamp) estampar; (letters, etc.) cerrar; *vi* cazar focas. **His fate is sealed,** Su suerte está determinada. **His lips were sealed,** Sus labios estaban cerrados. **under my hand and s.,** firmado y sellado por mí. **s.-ring,** sortija de sello, *f*

sealskin *n* piel de foca, *f*

seam *n sew* costura, *f; naut* costura de los tablones, *f; anat* sutura, *f; surg* cicatriz, *f;* (wrinkle) arruga, *f,* surco, *m; geol* capa, *f,* yacimiento, *m; min* vena, *f,* filón, *m. vt* coser; juntar; (a face) surcar, arrugar

seaman *n* marinero, *m;* hombre de mar, *m;* navegante, *m.* **able-bodied s.,** marinero práctico, *m*

seamstress *n* costurera, *f*

seamy *a* con costuras. **the s. side of life,** el lado peor de la vida

seaplane *n* hidroavión, hidroplano, *m*

seaport *n* puerto de mar, *m*

sear *a* marchito. *vt* agostar, secar; (a wound) cauterizar; marchitar, ajar; (a conscience) endurecer

search *vt* registrar; (a wound) explorar; examinar; escudriñar; investigar. *vi* buscar. *n* busca, *f;* (of luggage, etc.) reconocimiento, *m.* **in s. of,** en busca de. **to s. after, for,** buscar; ir al encuentro de. **to s. out,** en busca de; preguntar por. **right of s.,** (international law) derecho de visita, *m.* **s.-party,** pelotón de salvamento, *m.* **s.-warrant,** auto de reconocimiento, auto de registro domicil-

iario, orden de allanamiento, orden de cateo, *m*

searching *a* escrutador; penetrante; minucioso. **a s. look,** una mirada penetrante. **a s. wind,** un viento penetrante. **a s. question,** una pregunta perspicaz

searchlight *n* reflector, proyector, *m*

seashore *n* playa, *f;* orilla del mar, *f*

seaside *n* orilla del mar, *f;* playa, *f.* **to go to the s.,** ir al mar, ir a la playa

season *n* estación, *f;* sazón, *f;* temporada, *f;* tiempo, *m. vt* (food) sazonar; (wood, wine) madurar; (accustom) acostumbrar, aclimatar; (with wit, etc.) salpimentar; (temper) templar, moderar. *vi* madurarse. **at that s.,** a la sazón. **close s.,** veda, *f.* **in s.,** en sazón; a su tiempo. **out of s.,** fuera de sazón; fuera de tiempo, inoportuno. **the dead s.,** la estación muerta. **the autumn s.,** el otoño; (for social functions, etc.) la temporada de otoño. **s.-ticket,** billete de abono, *m*

seasonable *a* de estación; tempestivo; oportuno

seasonably *adv* en sazón; oportunamente

seasonal *a* estacional; de temporada

seasonal worker *n* trabajador por temporada, *m*

seasoned *a* (of food) sazonado; (of wood, etc.) maduro. **highly-s.,** (of a dish) picante, con muchas especies

seasoning *n cul* condimento, *m;* madurez, *f;* aclimatación, *f; fig* salsa, sal, *f*

seat *n* asiento, *m;* (bench) banco, *m;* (chair) silla, *f;* (in a cinema, etc.) localidad, *f;* (theat etc., ticket) entrada, *f;* (of a person) trasero, *m,* asentaderas, *f pl;* (of trousers) fondillos, *m pl;* (of government, etc.) sede, capital, *f;* (of war, etc.) teatro, *m;* (place) sitio, lugar, *m;* (house) casa solar, *f. vt* sentar; poner en una silla (a); encontrar sitio; (of buildings) tener . . . asientos; (a chair) poner asiento (a). **The hall seats a thousand,** La sala tiene mil asientos, Hay mil asientos en la sala. **Please be seated!** ¡Haga el favor de sentarse! **to be seated,** estar sentado; sentarse. **to have a good s.,** (on a horse) caer bien a caballo. **to hold a s. in parliament,** ser diputado a Cortes. **to keep one's s.,** permanecer sentado. **to take a s.,** tomar asiento, sentarse. **s.-back,** respaldo, *m;* **s. belt,** cinturón de seguridad, *m*

seaweed *n* alga marina, *f;* (edible) *Lat. Am.* cochayuyo, *m*

secede *vi* retirarse (de); separarse (de)

seclusion *n* reclusión, *f;* apartamiento, retiro, *m;* soledad, *f*

second *a* segundo; otro; igual. *adv* en segundo lugar; después. *n* segundo, *m;* (in a duel) padrino, *m;* (helper) ayudante, *m;* (boxing) segundo, *m;* (railway compartment) departamento de segunda (clase), *m; mus* segunda, *f;* (of time) segundo, *m*; (moment) instante, momento, *m*. *vt* secundar; (a motion) apoyar; *mil* ayudar. **the s. of May,** el dos de mayo. **James the S.,** Jaime el segundo. **on s. thoughts,** después de pensarlo bien. **every s. day,** cada dos días. **They live on the s. floor,** Viven en el primer piso (since the ground floor is not counted separately in Spanish speaking areas, the American second floor = the Spanish **primer piso**). **the s. largest,** el más grande menos uno. **to be s. to none,** no ser inferior a ninguno; (of persons) no ser inferior a nadie; no ceder a nadie. **to come off s.,** llegar el segundo; ser vencido. **seconds hand,** (of watch) segundero, *m*. **s.-in-command,** segundo, *m*; subjefe, *m*. **s.-best,** segundo. **My s.-best hat,** Mi sombrero número dos. **to come off s.-best,** salir mal parado, ser vencido. **s. class,** segunda clase, *f*. **s.-class,** de segunda clase; de calidad inferior; mediocre. **s. cousin,** primo (-ma) segundo (-a). **s. gear,** segunda velocidad, *f*. **s.-hand,** a usado; de ocasión; no nuevo. *adv* de segunda mano. **s.-hand car,** un coche de segunda mano. **s.-hand clothing,** ropa usada, *f*. **s.-hand shop** *Lat. Am.* cambalache *m*. **s. lieutenant,** *mil* subteniente, segundo teniente, *m*; *nav* alférez de fragata, *m*. **s.-rate,** a inferior, mediocre. **s. sight,** doble vista, *f*

secondary *a* secundario; subordinado; accesorio; poco importante. **s. school** colegio, liceo. **s. education,** enseñanza secundaria, *f*

secrecy *n* secreto, *m*; reserva, *f*, silencio, *m*. **in the s. of one's own heart,** en lo más íntimo de su corazón

secret *a* secreto; clandestino; (of persons) reservado, taciturno; (secluded) remoto, apartado; oculto; misterioso. *n* secreto, *m*; (key) clave, *f*. **a s. code,** un código secreto. **in s.,** en secreto, secretamente. **open s.,** secreto a voces. **to keep a s.,** guardar un secreto. **to keep s.,** tener secreto, ocultar. **s. drawer,** secreto, *m*. **S. Service,** servicio de espionaje, *m*

secretary *n* secretario (-ia). **private s.,** secretario (-ia) particular. **S. of State,** ministro, *m*; Ministro de Estado, *m*

secrete *vt* esconder, ocultar; *med* secretar

secretion *n* escondimiento, *m*; *med* secreción, *f*

secretive *a* reservado, callado

sect *n* secta, *f*

section *n* sección, *f*; porción, *f*; subdivisión, *f*; (of a law) artículo, *m*. *vt* seccionar. **conic s.,** sección cónica, *f*

sectional *a* en secciones. **s. bookcase,** biblioteca desmontable, *f*

sector *n* sector, *m*

secular *a* (very old) secular; (lay) seglar;

laico; profano. **s. music,** música profana, *f*. **s. school,** escuela laica, *f*

secularize *vt* secularizar

secure *a* seguro; (certain) asegurado; (safe) en seguridad; sano y salvo; (firm) firme; fijo; (confident (in)) confiado en. *vt* asegurar; (insure) garantizar; (lock) cerrar; (confine) prender; (acquire) adquirir, obtener; lograr, conseguir

securely *adv* seguramente; en seguridad, sin peligro; con confianza; (firmly) firmemente

security *n* seguridad, *f*; protección, defensa, *f*; garantía, *f*; (faith) confianza, *f*; *com* fianza, *f*; (person) fiador, *m*; *pl* **securities,** valores, títulos, *m pl*. **government securities,** papel del Estado, *m*. **to give s.,** *com* dar fianza. **to stand s. for,** *com* salir fiador de

sedate *a* tranquilo, sosegado; formal, serio, grave

sedative *a* and *n* sedativo, calmante *m*

sedentary *a* sedentario

sediment *n* sedimento, *Lat. Am.* concho, *m*

sedition *n* sedición, *f*

seditious *a* sedicioso

seduce *vt* seducir

seduction *n* seducción, *f*

seductive *a* seductivo, atractivo; persuasivo

sedulous *a* asiduo, diligente

see *n* sede, *f*. **The Holy S.,** la Santa Sede, *f*

see *vt* and *vi* ver; mirar; (understand) comprender; (visit) visitar; (attend to) atender a; ocuparse de. **He sees the matter quite differently,** Él mira el asunto de un modo completamente distinto, Su punto de vista sobre el asunto es completamente distinto. **You are not fit to be seen,** No eres nada presentable. **See you next Tuesday!** ¡Hasta el miércoles que viene! **I see!** ¡Ya! ¡Ahora comprendo! **Let's see!** ¡Vamos a ver! **Shall I see you home?** ¿Quieres que te acompañe a casa? **to go and see,** ir a ver. **to see red,** echar chispas. **to see the sights,** visitar los monumentos. **to see life,** ver mundo. **to see service,** servir (en el ejército, etc.). **to see about,** atender a; pensar en; ocuparse de. **to see after,** cuidar de; atender (a); ocuparse de. **to see again,** volver a ver. **to see into,** investigar, examinar. **to see off,** (at the station, etc.) ir a despedir; acompañar. **to see out,** (a person) acompañar a la puerta; (a play, etc.) quedarse hasta el fin (de); no dejar el puesto. **to see over,** inspeccionar. **to see through,** (a house, etc.) inspeccionar; (a person) calarle las intenciones; (a mystery) penetrar; (a person through trouble) ayudar. **to see it through,** llevarlo al cabo; quedarse hasta el fin. **to see to,** atender a; ocuparse de; encargarse de. **to see to every-thing,** encargarse de todo

seed *n* semilla, *f*; simiente, *f*; (of fruit) pepita, *f*, grano, *m*; *fig* germen, *m*; (off-spring) prole, descendencia, *f*. *vi* granar. *vt* sembrar. **s.-bed,** almáciga, *f*, semillero, *m*. **s.-pearl,** aljófar, *m*. **s.-plot,** sementera, *f*; *fig* semillero, *m*. **s.-time,** tiempo de sembrar, *m*

seedling *n* planta de semilla, *f*

seedy a granado; (of clothes) raído, roto; (of persons) andrajoso, desharrapado; infeliz, desgraciado; (ill) indispuesto, malucho

seeing *n* vista, *f*; visión, *f*. **It is worth s.,** Vale la pena de verse. **s. that . . . ,** visto que, dado que, como que. **S. is believing,** Ver es creer

seek *vt* buscar; solicitar, pretender; (demand) pedir; (investigate) investigar; (to do something) procurar, tratar de. **They are much sought after,** Son muy populares, Están en demanda. **to s. after,** buscar; perseguir. **to s. for,** buscar

seeker *n* el, *m*, (*f*, la) que busca; investigador (-ra)

seem *vi* parecer. **He seemed honest,** Parecía honrado. **It seemed to me,** Me pareció a mí. **It seems that they were both at home last night,** Parece ser que ambos estaban en casa anoche

seeming a aparente; supuesto

seemingly *adv* aparentemente; en apariencia

seemly a decoroso, decente

seep *vi* filtrar; rezumarse

seer *n* profeta, *m*

seesaw *n* columpio, *m*; vaivén, *m*. *vi* columpiarse; balancearse, oscilar. a de vaivén, oscilante

seethe *vi* hervir; *fig* bullir

segment *n* segmento, *m*

segregate *vt* segregar. *vi* segregarse. a segregado

segregation *n* segregación, *f*

Seine, the el Sena, *m*

seize *vt* *law* embargar; apoderarse de; asir; (a person) prender; coger; (a meaning) comprender; (an occasion, etc.) aprovecharse de; (of emotions) dominar; (of illnesses) atacar. *vi* *mech* atascarse. **He was seized by fear,** Le dominó el miedo. **to s. the opportunity,** aprovecharse de la oportunidad. **to s. upon a pretext,** valerse de un pretexto

seizure *n* asimiento, *f*; (of property) embargo, secuestro, *m*; (of a person) captura, *f*; arresto, *m*; *med* ataque, *m*

seldom *adv* rara vez, raramente; pocas veces

select a escogido, selecto; exclusivista. *vt* escoger

selection *n* selección, *f*. **selections from Cervantes,** trozos escogidos de Cervantes, *m pl*. **to make a s. from,** escoger

entre. **s. committee,** comité de selección, *m*

selective a selectivo

self *n* mismo (-a), propio (-a); sí mismo (-a), se; personalidad, *f*; ser, *m*. **all by one's s.,** sin ayuda de nadie; solo; *inf* solito. **my other s.,** mi otro yo. **my better s.,** mi mejor parte. **the s.,** el yo. **s.-abasement,** humillación de sí mismo, *f*. **s.-acting,** automático. **s.-apparent,** evidente, patente. **s.-appointed,** nombrado por uno mismo. **s.-assertion,** presunción, *f*. **s.-assertive,** presumido. **s.-assurance,** confianza en sí mismo, *f*; aplomo, *m*; (impertinence) cara dura, frescura, *f*. **s.-centered,** egocéntrico. **s.-colored,** del mismo color; de su color natural. **s.-command,** dominio de sí mismo, *m*; sangre fría, ecuanimidad, *f*. **s.-complacent,** satisfecho de sí mismo. **s.-conceit,** vanidad, arrogancia, petulancia, *f*. **s.-confidence,** confianza en sí mismo, *f*; aplomo, *m*. **s.-confident,** seguro de sí mismo, lleno de confianza en sí mismo. **s.-conscious,** turbado, confuso, apocado. **s.-consciousness,** turbación, confusión, *f*, apocamiento, azoramiento, *m*. **s.-contained,** (of a person) reservado, poco comunicativo; dueño de sí mismo; (of things) completo; (of flats, etc.) independiente; con entrada independiente. **s.-contradictory,** contradictorio. **s.-control,** dominio de sí mismo, *m*; ecuanimidad, serenidad, sangre fría, *f*. **s.-controlled,** dueño de sí mismo; ecuánime, sereno. **s.-deception,** engaño de sí mismo, *m*; ilusiones, *f pl*. **s.-defense,** defensa propia, *f*. **s.-denial,** abnegación, *f*; renunciación, *f*; frugalidad, *f*. **s.-destruction,** suicidio, *m*. **s.-determination,** libre albedrío, *m*; (of peoples) autonomía, *f*; independencia, *f*. **s.-educating,** autodidacto. **s.-esteem,** respeto para uno mismo, *m*; amor propio, *m*. **s.-evident,** aparente, que salta a la vista. **s.-explanatory,** que se explica a sí mismo; evidente. **s.-generating,** autógeno. **s.-government,** (of a person) dominio de sí mismo, *m*; (of a state) autonomía, *f*. **s.-importance,** presunción, petulancia, *f*. **s.-important,** pagado de sí mismo. **to be s.-important,** darse importancia, darse tono. **s.-indulgence,** indulgencia con sí mismo, *f*; (of food, drink, etc.) excesos, *m pl*, falta de moderación, *f*. **s.-indulgent,** indulgente con sí mismo; dado a los placeres, sibarita. **s.-interest,** propio interés, *m*. **s.-knowledge,** conocimiento de sí mismo, *m*. **s.-love,** egolatría, *f*. **s.-made man,** hombre que ha llegado a su posición actual por sus propios esfuerzos, *m*. **self-medication,** automedicación, *f*. **s.-opinionated,** terco, obstinaz. **s.-portrait,** autorretrato, *m*. **s.-possessed,** dueño de sí mismo; reservado; de sangre fría. **s.-possession,** aplomo, *m*, sangre fría, serenidad, *f*. **s.-preserva-**

tion, protección de sí mismo, f. **s.-reliance**, independencia, f; confianza en sí mismo, f. **s.-reliant**, independiente; confiado en sí mismo. **s.-reproach**, remordimiento, m. **s.-respect**, respeto de sí mismo, m; amor propio, m, dignidad, f. **s.-respecting**, que se respeta; que tiene amor propio **s.-restraint**, dominio de sí mismo, m; moderación, f. **s.-righteous**, farisaico. **s.-sacrifice**, abnegación, f. **s.-sacrificing**, abnegado. **s.-same**, mismo, idéntico. **s.-satisfaction**, satisfacción de sí mismo, f; vanidad, f; (of desires, etc.) satisfacción, indulgencia, f. **s.-satisfied**, satisfecho de sí mismo, pagado de sí mismo. **s.-seeking**, a egoísta, interesado. n egoísmo, m. **s.-starter**, mech arranque automático, m. **s.-styled**, autodenominado, autotitulado, llamado por sí mismo. **s.-sufficiency**, suficiencia, f; presunción, f. **s.-sufficient**, que basta a sí mismo; contento de sí mismo. **s.-supporting**, que vive de su propio trabajo; (of an institution, business) independiente. **s.-taught**, autodidacto. **s.-willed**, voluntarioso

selfish a egoísta, interesado

selfishness n egoísmo, m

sell vt vender. vi vender; venderse. **They sold him to his enemies**, Le vendieron a sus enemigos. **House to s.**, «Se vende una casa.» **to s. at a loss**, malvender, vender con pérdida. **to s. for cash**, vender al contado. **to s. retail**, vender al por menor. **to s. wholesale**, vender al por mayor. **to s. one's life dearly**, vender cara la vida. **They sold the chair for $10**, Vendieron la silla por diez dólares. **to s. off**, (goods) liquidar, saldar. **to s. out**, vender; agotar. **The best edition is sold out**, La mejor edición está agotada. **All the nylons have been sold out**, Se han vendido todas las medias de nilón (de cristal). **to s. up**, vender

seller n vendedor (-ra); comerciante (en), m

selling n venta, f. **s. off**, liquidación, f. **s. price**, precio de venta, m

selvage n (in cloth) orillo, m

semblance n apariencia, f. **to put on a s. of woe**, aparentar ser triste

semen n semen, m, esperma, f

semester n semestre, m

semi prefix semi; medio. **s.-conscious**, medio consciente. **s.-detached house**, casa doble, f

semicircle n semicírculo, m

semicolon n punto y coma, m

semidetached a (house) apartado

seminarist n seminarista, mf

seminary n seminario, m; (for girls) colegio interno, m

semolina n sémola, f

senate n senado, m

senator n senador, m

send vt enviar, mandar; com remitir; (a ball) lanzar; (grant) conceder; permitir; (inflict) afligir (con). **I sent Jane for it**, Envié a Juana a buscarlo. **He sent us word that he could not come**, Nos mandó un recado diciéndonos que no podía venir. **to s. mad**, hacer enloquecer. **to s. packing**, mandar a paseo. **to s. again**, volver a mandar. **to s. away**, vt enviar; (dismiss) destituir; despedir; (scare off) ahuyentar, vi enviar a otra parte. **to s. back**, (goods) devolver; (persons) volver. **to s. down**, hacer bajar; (rain, etc.) mandar, derramar; (a student) suspender, expulsar. **to s. in**, mandar; (persons) hacer entrar, introducir; (food) servir; (a bill) presentar; (one's name) dar. **Please s. him in!** ¡Sírvase de invitarle a entrar! **to s. in one's resignation**, mandar su dimisión. **to s. off**, enviar, mandar; (goods) despachar; (persons) destituir; (scare) ahuyentar. **s.-off**, n despedida. **f. a good s.-off**, una despedida afectuosa. **to s. on**, (a letter) hacer seguir; (instructions) trasmitir. **to s. out**, hacer salir; mandar; (emit) despedir, dar; (new shoots, etc.) echar. **to s. round**, (the hat, etc.) hacer circular. **to s. up**, enviar arriba; mandar subir, hacer subir; mandar, enviar; (a ball) lanzar

sender n remitente, mf; elec transmisor, m

senile a senil

senior a mayor, de mayor edad; más antiguo. **Martinez s.**, Martínez padre. **Charles is Mary's s. by five years**, Carlos es cinco años mayor que María. **s. member**, decano, m

seniority n ancianidad, f; antigüedad, f

sensation n sensación, f; sentimiento, m; impresión, f. **to create a s.**, causar una sensación

sensational a sensacional

sense n sentido, m. vt sentir. **in a s.**, hasta cierto punto; desde un punto de vista. **in the full s. of the word**, en toda la extensión de la palabra. **common s.**, sentido común, m. **He has no s. of smell**, No tiene olfato. **the five senses**, los cinco sentidos. **to be out of one's senses**, estar fuera de sí, estar trastornado. **You must be out of your senses!** ¡Debes de haber perdido el juicio! ¡Estás loco! **to come to one's senses**, (after unconsciousness) volver en sí; (after folly) recobrar el sentido común. **to talk s.**, hablar con sentido común, hablar razonablemente. **s. organ**, órgano de los sentidos, m. **have a good s. of direction**, saber orientarse, tener buena orientación. **have no s. of smell**, ser incapaz de percibir olores. **have no s. of taste**, ser incapaz de distinguir gustos

senseless a (unconscious) sin sentido, insensible; desmayado; (silly) necio, estúpido. **to knock s.,** derribar, tumbar

sensible a sensible; (conscious) consciente (de); sesudo. **to be s. of,** estar consciente de; estar persuadido de

sensitive a sensitivo; susceptible (a); impresionable. **s. plant,** sensitiva, f

sensitivity n sensibilidad, f; susceptibilidad, f; delicadeza, f

sensitize vt phot sensibilizar

sensual a sensual; voluptuoso

sensuous a sensorio

sentence n law sentencia, f; (penalty) pena, f; gram frase, f; (maxim) máxima, sentencia, f. vt sentenciar, condenar. **to pass s.,** pronunciar sentencia, fallar. **under s. of,** bajo pena de

sententious a sentencioso

sentient a sensible

sentiment n sentimiento, m; (sentimentality) sentimentalismo, m; opinión, f

sentimental a sentimental; (mawkish) sensiblero

sentimentalist n romántico (-ca), persona sentimental, f

sentimentality n sentimentalismo, m, sensiblería, f

sentimentalize vt idealizar

sentinel n centinela, mf

sentry n centinela, m. **to be on s. duty,** estar de guardia. **s.-box,** garita de centinela, f

separate a separado; distinto; independiente. vt separar; dividir. vi separarse; (of husband and wife) separarse de bienes y de cuerpos

separately adv separadamente; aparte

separatism n separatismo, m

separatist a and n separatista mf

Sephardic a sefaradí

sepia n (color and fish) sepia, f

September n setiembre, septiembre, m

septic a séptico

septicemia n septicemia, f

septuagenarian n setentón (-ona); septuagenario (-ia)

septum septo, tabique, m

sepulcher n sepulcro, m

sequel n (of a story, etc.) continuación, f; consecuencia, f; resultado, m

sequence n sucesión, f; serie, f; orden, mf; (at cards) serie, f; gram correspondencia, f; (ecc and cinema) secuencia, f. **s. of tenses,** correspondencia de los tiempos, f

sequestered a aislado, remoto

sequestrate vt secuestrar

sequestration n secuestro, m,

sequin n lentejuela, f

Serbia Servia, f

Serbian a servio. n servio (-ia); (language) servio, m

serenade n serenata, f, vt dar una serenata (a)

serene a sereno. **His S. Highness,** Su Alteza Serenísima

serenity n serenidad, f; tranquilidad, f

serf n siervo (-va)

serfdom n servidumbre, f

serge n estameña, f; (silk) sarga, f

sergeant n mil sargento, m; (police) sargento de policía, m. **s.-at-arms,** macero, m. **s.-major,** sargento instructor, m

serial a en serie; (of a story) por entregas. n novela por entregas, f. **s. number,** número de serie, m

series n serie, f; cadena, f; math serie, progresión, f. **in s.,** en serie

serious a serio; sincero; verdadero; (of illness, etc.) grave; importante. **He was s.** (not laughing) **when he said it,** Lo dijo en serio. **He is very s. about it,** Lo toma muy en serio. **to grow s.,** (of persons) ponerse serio; (of events) hacerse grave

seriously adv seriamente; en serio; gravemente. **to take** (something) **s.,** tomar (algo) en serio. **to take oneself s.,** tomarse muy en serio

seriousness n seriedad, f; gravedad, f. **in all s.,** en serio, seriamente

sermon n sermón, m

serpent n serpiente, f; mus serpentón, m

serpentine a serpentino; (of character) tortuoso. n min serpentina, f

serrated a serrado; dentellado

serum n suero, m

servant n servidor (-ra); (domestic) criado (-da); (employee) empleado (-da); (slave and flg) siervo (-va); pl **servants,** (domestic) servidumbre, f, servicio, m. **I remain your obedient s.,** Quedo de Vd. atento y seguro servidor (att. y s.s.s.). **civil s.,** empleado del estado, m. **general s.,** criada para todo, f. **man s.,** criado, m. **the s. problem,** el problema del servicio. **Your s., sir,** Servidor de Vd., señor. **s.-girl,** criada, f

serve vt servir (a); ser útil (a); satisfacer; (in a shop) despachar; (an apprenticeship, etc.) hacer; (a prison sentence) cumplir; (treat) tratar; (of stallion) cubrir; (a warrant, etc.) ejecutar; (a notice) entregar; (a ball) servir; (on a jury, etc.) formar parte de; naut aforrar. vi servir; (mil, nav) hacer el servicio. n sport saque, m. **It serves you right!** ¡Lo tienes merecido! **to s. at table,** servir a la mesa. **to s. as,** servir de. **to s. out,** distribuir; servir. **Serves 8,** (recipe) Da 8 porciones

server n ecc acólito, m; sport saque, m; (tray) bandeja, f; (for fish, etc.) pala, f

service n servicio, m; ecc oficio, m; servicio de mesa, m; (of a writ) entrega, f; sport saque, m. **coffee s.,** juego de café, m. **diplomatic s.,** cuerpo diplomático, m. **At your s.,** Para servir a Vd., A su disposición. **on active s.,** en acto de servicio; en el campo de batalla. **to go into s.,** (of servants) ir a servir. **to render s.,** prestar servicios. **s. tree,** serbal, *m*

serviceable a (of persons) servicial; (of things) servible, utilizable; útil; práctico; (lasting) duradero

service r••d *n* vía de servicio, *f*

servile a servil, *Lat. Am.* also incondicional

serving a sirviente; al servicio (de). **s. maid,** criada, *f*. **s. table,** trinchero, *m*

servitude *n* servidumbre, esclavitud, *f*. **penal s.,** cadena perpetua, *f*

session *n* sesión, *f*; junta, *f*. **petty sessions,** tribunal de primera instancia, *m*

set *vt* poner; colocar; fijar; (seeds, etc.) plantar; (bones) reducir, componer; (gems) engastar, montar; (a clock) regular; (sails) desplegar; (the teeth of a saw) trabar, triscar; (congeal) hacer coagular; (a trap) armar; (a snare) tender; (a razor) afilar; (make ready) preparar; (type) componer; (cause) hacer; *mus* poner en música; *mus* adaptar; (order) mandar; (prescribe) dar, asignar; (estimate) estimar, evaluar; (an example, etc.) dar; (establish) establecer, crear. *vi* (of the sun, etc.) ponerse; (solidify) coagularse; solidificarse; (of tides) fluir; (of the wind) soplar; (of dogs) hacer punta. **The joke set him laughing,** El chiste le hizo reír. **set an example,** dar ejemplo, dar el ejemplo. **to set a precedent,** sentar precedente. **to set a person's mind at rest,** tranquilizar, sosegar. **to set a trap,** armar lazo. **to set at ease,** poner a sus anchas (a), hacer cómodo (a). **to set at naught,** despreciar. **to set eyes on,** poner los ojos en. **to set fire to,** pegar fuego a, incendiar. **to set free,** poner en libertad, librar (de). **to set in motion,** poner en marcha. **to set one's teeth,** apretar los dientes. **to set people talking,** dar que hablar a la gente. **to set the fashion,** fijar la moda; poner de moda. **to set the alarm at seven o'clock,** poner el despertador a las siete. **to set the table,** poner la mesa. **to set to work,** ponerse a trabajar. **to set about,** *vi* (begin) ponerse (a); empezar; (undertake) emprender. *vt* (a rumour, etc.) divulgar. **They set about each other,** Empezaron a golpearse, Vinieron a las manos. **to set against,** indisponer (con), enemistar (con); hacer el enemigo (de); ser hostil (a); (balance) oponer, balancear. **to set oneself against,** oponerse a; atacar, luchar contra. **to set aside,** poner a un lado; apartar; (discard) desechar; (omit) omitir, pasar por alto de; dejar aparte, excluir; (keep) reservar; (money, etc.) ahorrar; (reject) rechazar; (quash) anular. **to set back,** retrasar; hacer retroceder. **set-back,** *n* revés, *m*; contrariedad, *f*. **to set before,** poner ante; (facts) exponer; (introduce) presentar. **to set down,** poner en tierra; deposi-

tar; (of a bus, etc.) dejar; (in writing) poner por escrito; anotar, apuntar; narrar, contar; (attribute) atribuir; (fix) fijar, formular; (believe to be) creer. **Passengers are set down at . . . ,** Los viajeros pueden apearse en . . . **to set forth,** *vt* (one's opinions, etc.) exponer; publicar; (display) exhibir, mostrar; (make) hacer. *vi* ponerse en camino. **to set going,** poner en marcha; echar a andar. **to set in,** empezar; (of the tide) fluir. **A reaction has set in,** Se ha hecho sentir una reacción. **to set off,** *vt* (explode) hacer estallar; (cause) hacer; (heighten) realzar; (counterbalance) contraponer. *vi* partir; ponerse en camino. **set-off,** *n* contraste, *m*, contraposición, *f*. **to set off against,** contraponer. **to set on,** *vt* (a dog) azuzar; (incite) instigar, incitar. *vi* atacar. **to set out,** *vt* (state) exponer, manifestar; (embellish) realzar; (display) arreglar, disponer. *vi* ponerse en camino, partir. **to set over,** (rule) tener autoridad sobre, gobernar. **to set to,** (begin to) ponerse a, empezar a; (work) ponerse a trabajar. **set-to,** *n* lucha, *f*; (boxing) asalto, *m*; (quarrel) pelea, riña, *f*. **to set up,** *vt* (a monument, etc.) erigir, levantar; (fix) fijar; (apparatus, machinery) montar; (exalt) exaltar; (found) establecer, *Lat. Am.* also instaurar; crear; (propound) exponer; (a howl, etc.) dar; (equip with) proveer de; instalar; (make strong) robustecer; fortificar; (type) componer; (raise) alzar. *vi* establecerse; dárselas de. **He sets himself up as a painter,** Se las da de pintor. **to set** (a person) **up as a model,** poner como modelo (a). **to set up house,** poner casa. **to set up a business,** establecer un comercio. **set-up,** *n* establecimiento *m*; arreglo, *m*. **to set upon,** atacar

set *n* (of sun, etc.) puesta, *f*, ocaso, *m*; (of the head, etc.) porte, *m*; (of a garment) corte, *m*; (of the tide, etc.) dirección, *f*; (slant) inclinación, *f*; (fig drift) tendencia, *f*, movimiento, *m*; (of the teeth of a saw) triscamiento, *m*; (of men, houses, etc.) grupo, *m*; (of tools, golf clubs, china, etc.) juego, *m*; (gang) pandilla, camarilla, *f*; clase, *f*; (dance) tanda, *f*; (tennis) partido, *f*; *theat* decoración, *f*; *rad* aparato de radio, *m*, radio, *f*. **coffee set,** juego de café, *m*. **all-mains set,** radio de corriente eléctrica, *f*. **battery set,** radio de batería, *f*. **portable set,** radio portátil, *f*. **the smart set,** el mundo elegante. **to have a shampoo and set,** hacerse lavar y marcar (el pelo). **to make a set,** hacer juego. **to make a dead set at,** hacer un ataque vigoroso (a), atacar resueltamente; procurar insinuarse en el favor de. **set of teeth,** dentadura, *f*

set a fijo; inmóvil; (of a smile) forzado; (of a task) asignado; (of times) señalado, fijo; (prescribed) prescrito, establecido; (firm) firme; (resolved) resuelto; (well-known) consabido; (obstinate) terco, nada adaptable. **well set-up,** apuesto, bien plantado. **He is set on doing it,** Se empeña en hacerlo. **to be dead set against,** estar completamente opuesto a. **set phrase,** frase hecha, *f.* **set-square,** cartabón, *m*

setting *n* (of the sun, etc.) puesta, *f;* (of mortar, etc.) fraguado, *m;* (of a jelly) solidificación, *f;* (of jewels) engaste, *m,* montadura, *f;* (of bones) aliño, *m;* (of teeth of saw) traba, *f;* (of razor) afiladura, *f;* (of a trap) armadura, *f;* (of a machine, etc.) ajuste, *m;* (frame) marco, *m; mus* arreglo, *m; theat* decorado, *m;* (emplacement) lecho, *m.* **the s. sun,** el sol poniente. **s. free,** liberación, *f.* **s. off,** partida, salida, *f.* **s. out,** ida, marcha, *f;* principio, *m.* **s.-up,** creación, institución, *f,* establecimiento, *m;* (of a machine) montaje, *m; print* composición, *f*

settle *vt* colocar; asegurar, afirmar; (a country) colonizar; (live in) establecer (en); (populate) poblar; (in a profession, etc.) dar; (install) instalar; (the imagination, etc.) sosegar, calmar; (resolve) resolver; (arrange) disponer, arreglar; (differences) componer, concertar; (an opponent, etc.) confundir; (a bill) saldar, pagar; (a claim) satisfacer; (clarify) depositar, clarificar; (end) poner fin (a). *vi* establecerse; (of weather) serenarse; (to work, etc.) empezar a, ponerse a; aplicarse a (decide) decidirse; (alight) posarse; (of foundations, etc.) asentarse; (of a ship) zozobrar; (of sediment) depositarse; (of liquid) clarificarse. **to s. accounts with,** *fig* ajustar cuentas con. **to s. down,** establecerse, arraigarse; adaptarse (a); (become calm) sosegarse, calmarse; sentar el juicio; (of foundations) asentarse; (of a ship) zozobrar; (of sediment) depositarse. **to s. in,** *vt* instalar. *vi* instalarse. **to s. on,** (choose) escoger; (decide on) decidirse (a). **to s. a pension on,** señalar pensión (a). **to s. up,** *vt* (one's affairs) poner en orden; (bill) pagar, saldar. *vi* llegar a un acuerdo; pagar cuentas

settled *a* fijo; permanente; invariable; (of countries) colonizado; (of weather) sereno

settlement *n* (of a country) colonización, *f;* (of a dispute) arreglo, ajuste, *m;* (of a question) solución, *f;* decisión, *f;* (of a bill) saldo, pago, *m,* liquidación, *f;* (of an obligation) satisfacción, *f;* (colony) colonia, *f;* (creation) creación, institución, *f;* establecimiento, arraigo, *m.* **deed of s.,** escritura de donación, *f.* **marriage s.,** contrato matrimonial, *m;* **s. out of court,** arreglo pacífico, *m*

settler *n* colono, *m;* colonizador (-ra)

seven *a* and *n* siete *m.* **It is s. o'clock,** Son las siete. **the s. deadly sins,** los siete pecados capitales

seventeen *a* diecisiete, diez y siete. *n*

diecisiete, *m.* **She is just s.,** Acaba de cumplir los diez y siete años

seventeenth *a* décimoséptimo; (of monarchs and of the month) diez y siete, *m* décimoséptimo, *m.* **Louis the S.,** Luis diez y siete. **the s. of June,** el diez y siete de junio

seventh *a* séptimo; (of the month) siete. *n* séptimo, *m;* séptima parte, *f;* mus séptima, *f.* **Edward the S.,** Eduardo séptimo. **the s. of August,** el siete de agosto

seventieth *a* septuagésimo, setentavo. *n* setentavo, *m*

seventy *a* and *n* setenta, *m*

sever *vt* separar; romper; dividir

several *a* distinto, diferente; respectivo; varios, *m pl,* (*f pl,* varias); algunos, *m pl,* (*f pl,* algunas)

severally *adv* separadamente; individualmente; independientemente

severance *n* separación, *f;* (of friendship, etc.) ruptura, *f*

severe *a* severo; riguroso; fuerte; duro; (of style) austero; (of pain) agudo; (of illness) grave

severity *n* severidad, *f;* intensidad, *f;* (of weather) inclemencia, *f;* (of illness) gravedad, *f*

sew *vt* and *vi* coser, Lat. Am. costurar, costurear. **to sew on,** coser, pegar

sewage *n* aguas residuales, *f pl.* **s. system,** alcantarillado, *m*

sewer *n* alcantarilla, cloaca, *f,* albañal, *m*

sewing *n* costura, *f.* **s. bag,** costurero, *m.* **s. cotton,** hilo de coser, *m.* **s.-machine,** máquina de coser, *f.* **s. silk,** torzal, *m*

sex *n* sexo, *m.* **the fair sex,** el bello sexo. **the weaker sex,** el sexo débil. **sex appeal,** atractivo, *m*

sh! *interj* ¡Chitón! ¡Chis!

shabbily *adv* (of dressing) pobremente; (of treatment) mezquinamente

shabby *a* (of persons) desharrapado, andrajoso, Lat. Am. maltraído; (of garments) raído, roto; (of a neighborhood, etc.) pobre; (mean) ruin, mezquino

shack *n* choza, *f, Mexico* jacal, *elsewhere in Lat. Am.* bohío *m*

shackle *n* traba, *f; pl* **shackles,** grillos, *m pl,* esposas, *f pl; fig* cadenas, *f pl. vt* poner esposas (a), encadenar; (a horse) apear; *fig* atar; (impede) estorbar

shad *n* sábalo, *m*

shade *n* sombra, *f;* (in a picture) toque de obscuro, *m;* (for the eyes) visera, *f;* (of a lamp) pantalla, *f;* (ghost) espectro, fantasma, *m;* (of color) matiz, *m;* (tinge) dejo, *m. vt* sombrear, dar sombra (a); (the face, etc.) proteger, resguardar; (a drawing) esfumar. **in the s.,** a la sombra. **80° in the s.,** ochenta grados a la sombra. **to put** (a person) **in the s.,** eclipsar

shadow *n* sombra, *f;* obscuridad, *f;* (in a picture) toque de obscuro, *m. vt* sombrear; obscurecer; (a person) seguir **to**

cast a s., proyectar una sombra. to s. forth, indicar; simbolizar. s. show, sombras chinescas, *f pl*

shadowy *a* umbroso; vago, indistinto, indefinido

shady *a* sombreado, umbrío; sombrío; (of persons, etc.) sospechoso. It was s. in the wood, Hacía sombra en el bosque

shaft *n* fuste, *m*; (arrow) flecha, saeta, *f*, dardo, *m*; (of a golf club, etc.) mango, *m*; (of a cart) vara, *f*; *mech* árbol, eje, *m*; (of a column and a feather) cañón, *m*; (of light) rayo, *m*; (of a mine) pozo, tiro, *m*; (airshaft) conducto de aire, ventilador, *m*. cam-s., árbol de levas, *m*. driving s., árbol motor, *m*

shaggy *a* peludo; lanudo

shake *vt* sacudir; agitar; hacer temblar; (weaken) debilitar, hacer flaquear. *vi* estremecerse; temblar; (trill) trinar. He managed to s. himself free, Consiguió librarse por una sacudida. to s. hands, darse la mano, estrecharse la mano. to s. one's finger at, señalar con el dedo (a). to s. one's fist at, amenazar con el puño (a). to s. one's head, mover la cabeza; negar con la cabeza. to s. one's sides, (with laughter) reírse a carcajadas. to s. with fear, temblar de miedo. to s. down, sacudir, hacer caer. s.-down, *n* cama improvisada, *f*. to s. off, sacudirse (dejar (de), perder; quitar de encima (a). to s. out, (unfurl) desplegar; sacudir. to s. up, agitar; sacudir, remover

shake *n* sacudida, *f*; (of the head) movimiento (de la cabeza), *m*; (of the hand) apretón (de manos), *m*; temblor, *m*; *mus* trino, gorjeo, *m*. in two shakes, *inf* en un periquete. to give a person a good s., sacudir violentamente (a)

shaking *n* sacudimiento, *m*; temblor, *m*; (of windows, etc.) zangoloteo, *m*

shaky *a* inestable; poco firme; (of hands, etc.) tembloroso; (of the voice) trémulo; (of gait) vacilante; dudoso

shall *v aux* (expressing simple future) I s. arrive tomorrow, Llegaré mañana. S. we go to the sea next week? ¿Iremos al mar la semana próxima?; (expressing obligation, compulsion) You s. not go out, No has de salir, No quiero que salgas. He s. see her immediately, Tiene que verla en seguida; (as a polite formula) S. I go? ¿Quiere Vd. que vaya? S. we buy the soap? ¿Quiere Vd. que compremos el jabón? ¿Compraremos el jabón?

shallot *n bot* chalote, *m*, ascalonia, *f*

shallow *a* poco profundo; (of a receptacle) llano; (of persons) superficial, frívolo; (of knowledge, etc.) superficial, ligero, somero. *n* bajío, *m*

sham *vt* fingir, simular. *n* farsa, *f*; imitación, *f*; engaño, *m*; (person) farsante, *m*. *a* fingido; falso; espurio. to s. illness, fingirse enfermo. to s. dead, hacer la mortecina. You're just a s., Eres un farsante

shamble *vi* andar arrastrándose. *n* andar pesado, *m*; *pl* shambles, matadero, *m*; *fig* carnicería, *f*

shame *n* vergüenza, *f*; ignominia, *f*; deshonra, *f*. *vt* avergonzar; deshonrar. For s.! ¡Qué vergüenza! What a s.! ¡Qué lástima! to put to s., avergonzar

shamefaced *a* (bashful) vergonzoso, tímido; (ashamed) avergonzado

shameful *a* vergonzoso, escandaloso; indecente

shameless *a* desvergonzado; impúdico, indecente

shamelessly *adv* desvergonzadamente

shampoo *n* champú, *m*. *vt* dar un champú (a); dar un masaje (a). dry s., champú seco, *m*

shank *n* zanca, *f*; *mech* pierna, *f*; (handle) mango, *m*; (of a button) rabo, *m*, cola, *f*. go on Shank's mare, ride on Shank's mare, caminar en coche de San Francisco, ir en boricua de Villadiego

shanty *n* choza, *f*

shanty town *n* barriada (Peru), callampa, población, población, callampa (Chile), *f*, rancho (Venezuela), *m*, villamiseria (Argentina), *f*

shape *n* forma, *f*; bulto, *m*; fantasma, *m*; (of a garment) corte, *m*; (of a person) talle, *m*; *cul* molde, *m*; (of a hat) forma, *f*. *vt* formar; (a garment) cortar; (ideas) dar forma (a); adaptar; (stone, etc.) labrar; (one's life) dominar. *vi* (of events) desarrollarse. to go out of s., perder la forma. to take s., tomar forma. to s. one's course, dirigirse (hacia, a); *naut* dar un rumbo. to s. well, prometer bien

shapeless *a* informe; disforme

shapely *a* bien formado; simétrico

share *n* porción, *f*; parte, *f*; cuota, *f*; contribución, *f*; (part ownership) interés, *m*; (in a company) acción, *f*. *vt* distribuir; compartir; dividir; tomar parte en. *vi* participar (de); compartir, tomar parte (en). to fall to one's s., tocar, corresponder. to go shares with, dividir con, compartir con. to take a s. in the conversation, tomar parte en la conversación. paid-up s., *com* acción liberada, *f*. to s. out, repartir, distribui

sharecropper *Lat. Am.* agregado (-da), *mf*

shareholder *n* accionista, *mf*

shark *n icht* tiburón, *m*; *inf* caimán, *m*

sharp *a* (of edges) afilado, cortante, *Lat. Am. also* filoso, filudo; (of points) punzante, puntiagudo; (of features, etc.) anguloso; (of bends, etc.) brusco; (of outlines, etc.) definido, distinto; (of pain, sound) agudo; (marked) marcado; (intense) intenso; (of winds, glance, etc.) penetrante; (of hearing) fino; (of appetite) bueno; (of showers) fuerte; (quick) rápido; (clever, etc.) vivo, listo; perspicaz; (of children) despierto, precoz; (unscrupulous) astuto, sin escrúpulos; (of criticism, remarks) mordaz; (of rebukes, sentences, etc.) severo; (of winters, etc.) riguroso; (of fighting) encarnizado; (of taste) picante; (sour) ácido; *mus* sostenido. *adv* en punto; puntualmente. *n mus* sostenido, m. **at five o'clock s.,** a las cinco en punto. **Look s.!** ¡Date prisa! **s.-edged,** afilado. **s.-eyed,** con ojos de lince; de mirada penetrante. **s.-featured,** de facciones angulosas. **s.-nosed,** de nariz puntiaguda. **s.-pointed,** puntiagudo. **s. practice,** procedimientos poco honrados, *m pl*. **s.-tongued,** de lengua áspera. **s. turn,** curva brusca, curva cerrada, *f*. **s.-witted,** de inteligencia viva, listo

sharpen *vt* (knives) afilar, amolar; (pencils, etc.) sacar punta (a); (wits, etc.) despabilar; (appetite) abrir. **This walk has sharpened my appetite,** Este paseo me ha abierto el apetito. **to s. one's claws,** afilarse las uñas

sharper *n inf* caballero de industria, timador, *m*; (at cards) fullero, *m*

sharpshooter *n* franco tirador, *m*

sharpsighted *a* de vista penetrante, listo, perspicaz

shatter *vt* romper, quebrantar; hacer añicos; *fig* destrozar. **You have shattered my illusions,** Has destrozado todas mis ilusiones

shave *vt* afeitar, rasurar; (wood, etc.) acepillar. *vi* afeitarse; (of razors) afeitar. *n* afeitada, *f*. **to have a s.,** hacerse afeitar. **to have a close s.,** *inf* escapar por un pelo

shaving *n* afeitada, *f*; (of wood, etc.) viruta, acepilladura, *f*. **s.-bowl,** bacía, *f*. **s.-brush,** brocha de afeitar, *f*. **s.-glass,** espejo de afeitar, *m*. **s.-soap,** jabón de afeitar, *m*. **s.-stick,** barra de jabón de afeitar, *f*

shawl *n* chal, mantón, rebozo, *m*

she *pron* ella; la; (female) hembra, *f*; (translated by fem. ending in the case of animals, etc., e.g. **she bear,** osa, **she cat,** gata). **It is her,** Es ella. **she who is dancing,** la que baila

sheaf *n* (of corn, etc.) gavilla, garba, *f*; (of arrows) haz, *m*; (of papers, etc.) paquete, atado, *m*. **to bind in sheaves,** agavillar

shear *vt* (sheep) esquilar, trasquilar; tonsurar; cortar; (cloth) tundir

shears *n pl* tijeras grandes, *f pl*, cizalla, *f*

sheath *n* vaina, *f*. **s.-knife,** cuchillo de monte, *m*

shed *vt* derramar; (skin, etc.) mudar; perder; (remove) quitarse, desprenderse de; (get rid of) deshacerse de. *n* cobertizo, sombrajo, *m*; cabaña, *f*. **to s. light on,** echar luz sobre, iluminar

sheen *n* lustre, *m*; brillo, *m*

sheep *n* oveja, *f*; carnero, *m*; ganado lanar, *m*. **He is the black s. of the family,** Es el garbanzo negro de la familia. **to cast sheep's eyes at,** lanzar miradas de carnero degollado. **s. breeder,** ganadero, *m*. **s.-dip,** desinfectante para ganado, *m*. **s.-dog,** perro de pastor, *m*. **s.-like,** ovejuno, de oveja. **s.-shearing,** esquileo, *m*

sheepish *a* tímido, vergonzoso; estúpido

sheepskin *n* piel de carnero, *f*. **s. jacket,** zamarra, *f*

sheer *a* puro; completo, absoluto; (steep) escarpado, acantilado; a pico; (of fabrics) transparente; ligero, fino. *adv* completamente; de un golpe; (perpendicularly) a pico. **to s. off,** desviarse; largarse, marcharse

sheet *n* (bed) sábana, *f*; (shroud) mortaja, *f*; (of paper) hoja, *f*; cuartilla, *f*; (pamphlet) folleto, *m*; (news) periódico, *m*, hoja, *f*; (of metal, etc.) lámina, plancha, *f*; (of water, etc.) extensión, *f*; *naut* escota, *f*. *vt* poner sábanas en; envolver en sábanas; (a corpse) amortajar. **to be as white as a s.,** estar pálido como un muerto. **s. bend,** (knot) nudo de tejedor, *m*. **s. glass,** vidrio en lámina, *m*. **s. iron,** hierro en planchas, *m*

shekel *n* (coin) siclo, *m*; *pl* **shekels,** dinero, *m*

shelf *n* estante, anaquel, *m*; (reef) banco de arena, bajío, *m*; (of rock) escalón, *m*. **to be on the s.,** *inf* quedarse para tía, quedarse para vestir imágenes

shell *n* (of small shellfish) concha, *f*; (of tortoise) coraza, *f*; (of insects, lobsters, etc.) caparazón, *m*; (of a nut) cáscara, *f*; (of an egg) cascarón, *m*; (of peas, beans) vaina, *f*; (com and *mus*) concha, *f*; (of a building) casco, *m*; (outside) exterior, *m*; (empty form) apariencia, *f*; *mil* granada, *f*. *vt* pelar; (nuts) descascarar; (beans, etc.) desvainar; *mil* bombardear. **to be under s.-fire,** sufrir un bombardeo. **s. shock,** neurosis de guerra, *f*

shellfish *n* crustáceo, *m*; (as food) marisco, *m*

shelling *n mil* bombardeo, *m*

shelter *n* abrigo, amparo, *m*; refugio, *m*; asilo, *m*. *vt* dar asilo (a); abrigar; (defend) amparar, proteger; (hide) esconder. *vi* refugiarse; resguardarse; esconderse

shelve *vt* (books) poner en un estante; (persons) destituir; (questions, etc.) aplazar, arrinconar; proveer de estantes. *vi* (slope) inclinarse, formar declive; (of sea bed) formar escalones

shepherd *n* pastor, *m*. *vt* guardar; guiar, conducir. **s. boy,** zagal, *m*. **shepherd's pouch,** zurrón, *m*

sherbet *n* sorbete, *m*

sheriff *n* (in U.K.) sheriff, *m*; (U.S.A.) jefe de la policía, *m*

sherry *n* (vino de) jerez, *m*. **dry s.,** jerez seco, *m*

shield *n* escudo, *m*; (round) rodela, *f*; *her* escudo de armas, *m*; *fig* defensa, *f*, amparo, *m*. *vt* proteger, amparar. **to s. a**

person, proteger a una persona. **to s. one's eyes from the sun,** proteger los ojos del sol. **s.-bearer,** escudero, *m*

shift *vt* mover; trasladar; quitar, librarse de; cambiar. *vi* moverse; (of the wind) girar; cambiar. *n* cambio, *m*; (expedient) recurso, expediente, *m*; (dodge) artificio, *m*, trampa, *f*; (of workmen) tanda, *f*, turno, *m*. **to make s.,** arreglárselas (para hacer algo); procurar (hacer algo); (manage) ir tirando. **to s. for oneself,** componérselas, arreglárselas. **to s. the scenes,** *theat* cambiar de decoración. **to s. the helm,** *naut* cambiar el timón. **to work in shifts,** trabajar por turnos

shifting a (of light, etc.) cambiante; (of sand, etc.) movedizo; (of wind) mudable; (of moods) voluble. **s. sand,** arena movediza, *f*

shiftless a perezoso; sin energía, ineficaz

shifty a (tricky) tramposo, astuto; (dishonest) informal, falso; (of gaze) furtivo. **s.-eyed,** a de mirada furtiva

shilling *n* chelín, *m*. **nine shillings in the £,** nueve chelines por libra. **to cut off with a s.,** desheredar

shilly shally *n* irresolución, vacilación, *f*, *vi* estar irresoluto, titubear, no saber qué hacer

shimmer *vi* rielar; relucir. *n* luz trémula, *f*; resplandor, *m*; viso, *m*

shin *n* espinilla, *f*; (of beef) corvejón, *m*. **to s. up,** trepar

shindy *n* suiza, reyerta, tasquera, *f*. **to kick up a s.,** armar camorra

shine *vi* brillar; resplandecer, relucir, relumbrar. *vt* (shoes) dar lustre (a). *n* brillo, *m*; lustre, *m*; (shoeshine) *Mexico* bola, *f*. **in rain or s.,** en buen o mal tiempo. **to s. with happiness,** radiar felicidad. **to take the s. out of,** eclipsar

shingle *n* (pebbles) guijarros, *m pl*; cascajo, *m*; carp barda, *f*; (hair) pelo a la garçonne, *m*; *pl* **shingles,** *med* zona, *f*, herpe zóster, *m*. *vt* (the hair) cortar a la garçonne

shining a resplandeciente, brillante, reluciente; radiante. **s. with happiness,** radiante de felicidad. **s. example,** ejemplo notable, *m*

shiny a brillante; lustroso, terso; (of trousers, etc.) reluciente; (of paper) glaseado

ship *n* buque, barco, *m*; (sailing) velero, *m*. *vt* embarcar; (oars) armar. *vi* embarcar; (as a member of crew) embarcarse. **on board s.,** a bordo. **to s. a sea,** embarcar agua. **to take s.,** embarcar. **to s. off,** mandar. **ship's boat,** lancha, *f*. **ship's boy,** grumete, *m*. **ship's carpenter,** carpintero de ribera, *m*. **ship's company,** tripulación, *f*. **s.-breaker,** desguazador, *m*. **s.-canal,** canal de navegación, *m*. **s.-load,** cargamento, *m*

shipment *n* embarque, *m*; despacho por mar, *m*; (consignment) remesa, *f*

shipowner *n* naviero, *m*

shipper *n* naviero, *m*; importador, *m*; exportador, *m*

shipping *n* embarque, *m*; buques, barcos, *m pl*; (of a country) marina, *f*. **s. agent,** consignatario de buques, *m*. **s. company,** compañía de navegación, *f*. **s. offices,** oficinas de una compañía de navegación, *f pl*

shipshape a en buen orden; bien arreglado

shipwreck *n* naufragio, *m*, *vt* hacer naufragar, echar a pique

shipwrecked person *n* náufrago (-ga). **to be shipwrecked,** naufragar

shipyard *n* astillero, varadero, *m*

shire *n* condado, *m*

shirk *vt* eludir, esquivar; desentenderse de. *vi* faltar al deber

shirr *vt* fruncir

shirt *n* camisa, *f*. **dress s.,** camisa de pechera dura, *f*. **hair-s.,** cilicio, *m*. **in one's s.-sleeves,** en mangas de camisa. **s.-blouse,** blusa sencilla, *f*. **s.-collar,** cuello de camisa, *m*. **s. factory** or **shop,** camisería, *f*. **shirt-front,** pechera, *f*. **s.-maker,** camisero (-ra)

shirting *n* tela para camisas, *f*

shiver *vi* temblar, tiritar; dar diente con diente; (of a boat) zozobrar. *vt* (break) hacer añicos, romper; (sails) sacudir. *n* temblor, estremecimiento, *m*; escalofrío, *m*; (of glass, etc.) fragmento, *m*, astilla, *f*. **You give me the shivers,** Me das escalofríos

shoal *n* (of fish) banco, *m*; gran cantidad, *f*; (of people) multitud, muchedumbre, *f*; (water) bajo fondo, *m*; (sand-bank) banco, bajío, *m*, a poco profundo. **I know shoals of people in Valencia,** Conozco a muchísima gente de Valencia

shock *n* choque, *m*; *elec* conmoción, *f*; *med* shock, *m*; (med stroke) conmoción cerebral, *f*; (fright) sobresalto, susto, *m*. *vt* sacudir, dar una sacudida (a); chocar; escandalizar, horrorizar. *vi* chocar. **electric s.,** conmoción eléctrica, *f*. **She is easily shocked,** Ella se escandaliza fácilmente. **s. of hair,** mata de pelo, *f*. **s. absorber,** *mech* amortiguador, *m*; *aut* amortiguador (de los muelles), *m*. **s. troops,** tropas de asalto, *f pl*, elementos de choque, *m pl*

shocking a escandaloso; repugnante, horrible; espantoso. **How s.!** ¡Qué horror! **s. bad,** malísimo

shod a calzado; (of horses) herrado

shoddy *n* pacotilla, *f*. a de pacotilla; espurio, falso

shoe *n* zapato, *m*; (horse) herradura, *f*; (naut mech) zapata, *f*. *vt* (horses) herrar. **I should not like to be in his shoes,** No me gustaría estar en su pellejo. **That is quite another pair of shoes,** Eso es harina de otro costal. **to cast a s.,** (of horses) desherrarse, perder una herradura. **to put on one's shoes,** ponerse los zapatos, calzarse. **to remove one's shoes,** quitarse los zapatos, descalzarse. **wooden shoes,** zuecos, *m pl*. **s.-buckle,** hebilla de zapato, *f*. **s.-lace,** cordón de zapato, *m*. **s.-leather,** cuero para zapatos, *m*; calzado, *m*. **s.-scraper,** limpiabarros, *m*, estregadera, *f*. **s.-shop,** zapatería, *f*

shoeblack *n* betún, *m*; (person) limpiabotas, *m*

shoehorn *n* calzador, *m*

shoemaker *n* zapatero (-ra)

shoeshine *n Mexico* bola, *f*

shoo! *interj* ¡fuera!; ¡zape! *vt* ahuyentar

shoot *vt* (throw) lanzar; precipitar; (empty) vaciar; (a rapid) salvar; (rays, etc.) echar; (an arrow, a gun, etc.) disparar; (a person, etc.) pegar un tiro a); *sport* tirar; *mil* fusilar, pasar por las armas, *Lat. Am.* afusilar; (a film) hacer, impresionar. *vi* lanzarse, precipitarse; (of pain) latir; (sprout) brotar; disparar; tirar; (at football) tirar a gol, chutar. **to s. a glance at,** lanzar una mirada a). **I was shot in the foot,** Una bala me hirió en el pie. **to s. the sun,** *naut* tomar el sol. **to s. ahead,** tomar la delantera. **to s. at,** tirar a, *Lat. Am.* abalear. **to s. at** *Central America, Mexico* balacear. **to s. by,** pasar como una bala. **to s. down,** *aer* derribar; matar de un tiro. **to s. up,** (of children) espigarse; (of prices) subir mucho; (of cliffs, etc.) elevarse

shoot *n* partida de caza, *f*; tiro, *m*; *bot* renuevo, retoño, *m*

shooting *n* tiro, *m*; caza con escopeta, *f*; (of guns) tiroteo, *m*; (of an arrow) disparo, *m*; (of a film) rodaje, *m*. **to go s.,** ir a cazar con escopeta. **s.-box,** pabellón de caza, *m*. **s. butts,** tiradero, *m*. **s. dog,** perro de caza, *m*. **s.-gallery,** tiro al blanco, *m*. **s. match,** concurso de tiro, *m*. **s. pain,** punzada de dolor, *f*. **s. party,** partida de caza, *f*. **s. practice,** ejercicios de tiro, *m pl*. **s.-range,** campo de tiro, *m*. **s. star,** estrella fugaz, *f*

shop *n* tienda, *f*; (workshop) taller, *m*. *vi* ir de compras, ir de tiendas; comprar. **to talk s.,** hablar de negocios. **s.-assistant,** dependiente (-ta). **s.-soiled,** deslucido. **s.-steward,** representante de los obreros de una fábrica o taller, *m*. **s. window,** escaparate, *Mexico* aparador, *m*

shopkeeper *n* tendero (-ra), *Chile* despachero (-ra)

shoplifter *n* ladrón (-ona) de tiendas, ratero (-ra) de las tiendas

shopper *n* comprador (-ra)

shopping *n* compra, *f*; compras, *f pl*. **to go s.,** ir de compras. **s. basket,** cesta para compras, *f*. **s. center,** centro comercial, *m*

shopwalker *n* jefe de recepción, *m*

shore *n* orilla, ribera, *f*; costa, *f*; (sands) playa, *f*. **off s.,** en alta mar. **on s.,** en

tierra. **to come on s.,** desembarcar. **to s. up,** apuntalar, acodalar; *fig* apoyar

short *a* corto; (of persons) bajo; breve; (of temper) vivo; insuficiente; distante (de); (brusque) seco; (of money) alcanzado. *adv* súbitamente; brevemente. *n* (vowel) vocal breve, *m*; *pl* **shorts,** calzones cortos, *m pl*. **for s.,** para mayor brevedad. **for a s. time,** por poco tiempo. **in a s. time,** dentro de poco. **in s.,** en breve, en resumen, en pocas palabras. **on s. notice,** con poco tiempo de aviso. **s. of,** con la excepción de, menos. **to be s.,** faltar, ser escaso. **to be s. with someone,** tratar con sequedad (a). **to fall s. of expectations,** no cumplir las esperanzas. **to go s. of,** pasarse sin. **to grow s.,** escasear. **s.-circuit,** corto circuito, *m*. **s. cut,** atajo, *Lat. Am.* desecho, *m*. **s.-haired,** pelicorto. **s.-handed,** falto de mano de obra. **s.-lived,** de vida corta; efímero, fugaz. **to be short-lived,** tener vida corta. **s.-sighted,** corto de vista. **s.-sightedness,** miopía, cortedad de vista, *f*. **s. story,** cuento, *m*. **s.-tempered,** irascible, irritable, de genio vivo. **s.-waisted,** corto de talle. **s.-winded,** corto de resuello; asmático

shortage *n* falta, escasez, *f*; carestía, *f*. **water s.,** carestía de agua, *f*

shortcoming *n* defecto, *m*; imperfección, *f*

shorten *vt* acortar; reducir, disminuir; abreviar. *vi* acortarse

shorthand *n* taquigrafía, estenografía, *f*. *a* taquigráfico, estenográfico

shortly *adv* dentro de poco, pronto; brevemente, en resumen, en pocas palabras; (curtly) bruscamente, secamente

shortness *n* cortedad, *f*; brevedad, *f*; (of a person) pequeñez, *f*; (lack) falta, *f*; (of memory, sight) cortedad, *f*; brusqueness) sequedad, brusquedad, *f*. **s. of breath,** falta de aliento, respiración difícil, *f*

shot *n* perdigón, *m*; *inf* perdigones, *m pl*; bala, *f*; (firing) tiro, *m*; (person) tirador (-ra); (stroke, etc.) golpe, *m*, tirada, *f*; (cinema) fotograma, *m*. *a* (of silk) tornasolado. **at one s.,** de un tiro. **like a s.,** *fig* como una bala. **to exchange shots,** tirotearse. **to fire a s.,** disparar un tiro. **to have a s. at,** probar suerte. **s.-gun,** escopeta, *f*. **s. silk,** seda tornasolada, *f*

should *v aux* (expressing future) **I s. like to go to the sea,** Me gustaría ir al mar; (expressing conditional) **I s. like to see them if I could,** Me gustaría verlos si pudiera; (expressing obligation) **You s. go at once,** Debes ir en seguida; (expressing probability) **They s. arrive tomorrow,** Seguramente llegarán mañana; (expressing doubt) **If the moment s. be opportune,** Si el momento fuera oportuno. **I s. just think so!** ¡Ya lo creo! ¡No lo dudo!

shoulder *n* hombro, *m*; (of mutton) espalda, *f*; (of a hill) falda, *f*. *vt* echar al hombro, echar sobre sí; (a responsibility) cargar con, hacerse responsable para; (jostle) dar codazos (a). **s. to s.,** hombro a hombro. **S. arms!** ¡Armas al hombro! **s.-blade,** omoplato, *m.* **s.-knot,** charretera, *f.* **s.-pad,** hombrera, *f.* **s.-strap,** *mil* dragona, *f;* (of a dress, etc.) tirante, *m;* (of a water carrier, etc.) correón, *m*

shout *vi* gritar, hablar a gritos. *vt* gritar. *n* grito, *m.* **shouts of applause,** aclamaciones, *f pl,* aplausos, *m pl.* **to s. from the housetops,** pregonar a los cuatro vientos. **to s. with laughter,** reírse a carcajadas. **to s. down,** silbar. **to s. out,** gritar

shove *vt* empujar; poner. *n* empujón, *m.* **to s. along,** empujar. **to s. aside,** empujar a un lado; apartar a codazos. **to s. away,** rechazar. **to s. back,** hacer retroceder. **to s. forward,** hacer avanzar, empujar hacia adelante. **to s. off,** (a boat) echar afuera. **to s. out,** empujar hacia fuera

shovel *n* pala, *f. vt* traspalar. **s. hat,** sombrero de teja, *m*

show *vt* mostrar; hacer ver; (disclose) descubrir; revelar; (exhibit) exhibir; (indicate) indicar; (prove) demostrar, probar; (conduct) conducir, llevar, guiar; (explain) explicar; (oneself) presentarse. *vi* mostrarse; verse; parecer. **to s. cause,** mostrar causa. **to s. fight,** ofrecer resistencia. **s. signs of,** dar señales de. **to s. itself,** declararse, asomarse, surgir. **to s. to the door,** acompañar a la puerta. **to s. in,** (a person) hacer entrar, introducir (en). **to s. off,** *vt* exhibir; realzar; (new clothes, etc.) lucir. *vi* darse importancia; pavonearse. **to s. out,** (a person) acompañar a la puerta; (in anger) poner de patitas en la calle. **to s. through,** *vi* trasparentarse. *vt* conducir por. **to s. up,** *vi* invitar a subir; (a fraud, etc.) descubrir; (a swindler) desenmascarar; (defects) revelar. *vi* (stand out) destacarse; (be present) asomarse, asistir

show *n* (exhibition) exposición, *f;* espectáculo, *m;* (sign) indicio, *m,* señal, *f;* (ostentation) pompa, *f,* aparato, *m,* ostentación, *f;* (appearance) apariencia, *f;* (affair) negocio, *m.* **to give the s. away,** echar los títeres a rodar. **to make a s. of,** hacer gala de. **s.-case,** escaparate, *m,* vitrina, *f.* **s. of hands,** votación por manos levantadas, *f.* **s.-room,** salón de muestras, *m*

showdown *n* cartas boca arriba, *m*

shower *n* chaparrón, chubasco, *m;* (of spray, etc.) chorro, *m;* (of stones, arrows, etc.) lluvia, *f;* (of honors) cosecha, *f,* (bridal) despedida de soltera, despedida de soltería, *f. vt* derramar; rociar; mojar; llover. *vi* chaparrear, llover. **shower (bath)** ducha, *f, Argentina* baño de China, *f*

showy a vistoso; ostentoso, *Lat. Am. also* figuroso

shrapnel *n* granada, *m,* granada de metralla, *f*

shred *n* fragmento, *m;* (of cloth) jirón, *m;* brizna, *f; fig* pizca, *f. vt* desmenuzar. **to tear in shreds,** hacer pedazos

shrew *n zool* musaraña, *f;* (woman) fiera, *f*

shrewd a sagaz, perspicaz; prudente; (of the wind) penetrante; (pain) punzante. **to have a s. idea of,** tener una buena idea de. **a s. diplomat,** un fino diplomático

shrewish a regañón

shriek *vi* chillar, gritar. *vt* decir a voces, gritar. *n* chillido, *m;* grito agudo, *m.* **shrieks of laughter,** carcajadas, *f pl*

shrift to give short, enviar normala (a), enviar a paseo (a)

shrill a estridente, agudo

shrimp *n* camarón, *m,* gamba, *f, vi* pescar camarones

shrine *n* relicario, *m;* sepulcro de santo, *m;* templete, *m,* capilla, *f;* santuario, *m*

shrink *vi* encogerse; contraerse; disminuir, reducirse. *vt* encoger; reducir, disminuir; desaparecer; disiparse. **I shrank from doing it,** Me repugnaba hacerlo. **to s. away from,** retroceder ante; recular ante; huir de. **to s. back,** recular (ante)

shrinkage *n* encogimiento, *m;* contracción, *f;* reducción, disminución, *f*

shrivel *vi* avellanarse; (of persons, through old age) acartonarse, apergaminarse; (wither) marchitarse; arrugarse. *vt* arrugar; secar, marchitar

shroud *n* sudario, *m,* mortaja, *f; naut* obenque, *m.* **to wrap in a s.,** amortajar

shrub *n* arbusto, *m;* matajo, *m*

shrubbery *n* arbustos, *m pl,* maleza, *f;* bosquecillo, *m*

shrug *vi* encogerse de hombros. *n* encogimiento de hombros, *m*

shrunken a contraído; acartonado, apergaminado; seco, marchito. **shrunken head,** cabeza reducida, *f*

shudder *vi* estremecerse; vibrar. *n* estremecimiento, *m;* escalofrío, *m;* (of an engine, etc.) vibración, *f*

shuffle *vt* (the feet) arrastrar; (scrape) restregar; (cards) barajar; (papers) mezclar. *vi* arrastrar los pies, arrastrarse; (cards) barajar; *fig* tergiversar. *n* (of the cards) barajadura, *f; fig* evasiva, *f;* embuste, *m.* **to s. along,** andar arrastrando los pies

shun *vt* evitar, rehuir, esquivar

shunt *vt rw* apartar; *elec* shuntar. *vi rw* hacer maniobras

shut *vt* and *vi* cerrar. **to s. again,** volver a cerrar. **to s. down,** *vt* cerrar; (a machine) parar. *vi* (of factories, etc.) cerrar. **to s. in,** encerrar; (surround) cercar, rodear. **to s. off,** (water, etc.) cortar; (isolate) aislar (de). **to s. out,** excluir; obstruir, impedir; negar la entrada (a). **to s. up,** *vt* cerrar;

encerrar; *inf* hacer callar (a); *vi inf* callarse, cerrar la boca. **to s. oneself up,** encerrarse

shutter *n* (window) contraventana, *f*, postigo, *m*; (of a camera) obturador, *m*; (of a fireplace) campana (de hogar), *f*. *vt* poner contraventanas (a); cerrar los postigos de

shuttle *n* (weaver's, and sewing-machine) lanzadera, *f*, (airplane service) puente aéreo, *m*. **s.-cock,** volante, gallito, *m*

shy *a* (of animals) tímido, salvaje; (of persons) huraño, tímido; vergonzoso. *vi* (of a horse) respingar; (of persons) asustarse (de). *vt* (a ball, etc.) lanzar. *n* (of a horse) respingo, *m*; (of a ball) lanzamiento, *m*; (try) prueba, tentativa, *f*. **to fight shy of,** procurar evitar. **to have a shy at,** probar

shyness *n* timidez, *f*; huraña, *f*; vergüenza, *f*

Siamese *a* siamés. *n* siamés (-esa); (language) siamés, *m*. **S. cat,** gato siamés, *m*

sic *vt* atacar; abijar, azuzar (a dog); *adv* así (in academic prose)

sick *a* enfermo; mareado. **the s.,** los enfermos. **to be s.,** vomitar; estar enfermo. **to be s. of,** estar harto de. **to feel s.,** sentirse mareado. **to be on the s.-list,** estar enfermo. **s.-bed,** lecho de dolor, *m*. **s.-headache,** jaqueca, con náuseas, *f*. **s.-leave,** *mil* permiso por enfermedad, *m*. **s.-nurse,** enfermera, *f*

sicken *vi* caer enfermo, enfermar; (feel sick) marearse; (recoil from) repugnar; (weary of) cansarse (de), aburrirse (de). *vt* marear; dar asco (a), repugnar; cansar, aburrir. **It sickens me,** Me da asco. **He is sickening for measles,** Muestra síntomas de sarampión

sickly *a* enfermizo, achacoso, malucho, *Lat. Am.* farruto, *Central America, Mexico* fifiriche; (of places, etc.) malsano; (pale) pálido; débil; (of a smell) nauseabundo; (mawkish) empalagoso

sickness *n* enfermedad, *f*; mal, *m*; náusea, *f*, mareo, *m*

side *n* lado, *m*; (hand) mano, *f*; (of a river, etc.) orilla, *f*, margen, *m*; (of a person) costado, *m*; (of an animal) ijada, *f*; (of a hill) falda, pendiente, ladera, *f*; (of a ship) banda, *f*, costado, *m*; (aspect) aspecto, *m*; punto de vista, *m*; (party) partido, grupo, *m*; (team) equipo, *m*; (of descent) lado, *m*. a lateral, de lado; oblicuo. **on all sides,** por todas partes. **on both sides,** por ambos lados. **s. by s.,** lado a lado. **the other s. of the picture,** el revés de la medalla. **to change sides,** cambiar de partido. **to pick sides,** escoger el equipo. **to put on s.,** darse tono, alzar el gallo. **to split one's sides,** desternillarse de risa, reírse a carcajadas. **to s. with,** declararse por; ponerse al lado de, tomar el partido de. **wrong s. out,** al revés. **s.-car,** sidecar, asiento lateral, *m*. **s.-chain,** *chem* cadena lateral, *f*. **s.-dish,**

entremés, *m*. **s. door,** puerta lateral, *f*. **s.-face,** a de perfil. *n* perfil, *m*. **s.-glance,** mirada de soslayo, *f*. **s.-issue,** cuestión secundaria, *f*. **s.-line,** negocio accesorio, *m*; ocupación secundaria, *f*; *rw* vía secundaria, *f*. **s.-saddle,** silla de señora, silla de montar de lado, *f*. **s.-show,** (at a fair) barraca, *f*, puesto de feria, *m*; exhibición secundaria, *f*; función secundaria, *f*. **s.-table,** trinchero, *m*. **s.-track,** *n rw* apartadero, *m*. *vt* desviar (de), apartar (de). **s.-view,** perfil, *m*. **s.-walk,** acera, *f Mexico* banqueta *f, elsewhere in Lat. Am.* andén *m*, vereda *f*. **s.-whiskers,** patillas, *f pl*

sidelight *n* luz lateral, *f*; (on a ship) ojo de buey, *m*; *fig* información incidental, *f*

side road *n* camino lateral, *m*

sideways *adv* oblicuamente, de lado; (edgewise) de soslayo. a de soslayo

sidle *vi* andar (or ir) de lado. **to s. up to,** acercarse servilmente a; arrimarse (a)

siege *n* asedio, sitio, cerco, *m*. **to lay s. to,** poner cerco (a), sitiar, asediar cercar. **to raise a s.,** levantar un sitio

sieve *n* cedazo, tamiz, *m*, criba, *f*, *Lat. Am.* arnero, *m*, *vt* tamizar, cerner, cribar

sift *vt* (sieve) cerner, cribar; (sugar, etc.) salpicar (con); (a question) escudriñar, examinar minuciosamente

sigh *vi* suspirar; (of the wind) susurrar. *n* suspiro, *m*; (of the wind) susurro, *m*. **to s. for,** suspirar por; lamentar

sight *n* vista, *f*; visión, *f*; espectáculo, *m*; (fright) estantigua, *f*. *vt* ver, divisar; (aim) apuntar. **front s.,** (of guns) alza, *f*. **short s.,** (of eyes) vista corta, *f*. **at first s.,** a primera vista. **in s.,** a la vista. **in s. of,** a vista de. **out of s.,** que no está a la vista; perdido de vista. **Out of s., out of mind,** Ojos que no ven, corazón que no siente. **to be lost to s.,** perderse de vista. **to lose s. of,** perder de vista (a). **to catch a s. of,** vislumbrar. **to come in s.,** aparecer, asomarse. **to know by s.,** conocer de vista (a). **s.-reading,** lectura a primera vista, *f*

sightly *a* hermoso; deleitable

sightseeing *n* turismo, *m*. **to go s.,** visitar los monumentos, ver los puntos de interés

sightseer *n* curioso (-sa); turista, *mf*

sign *n* señal, *f*; seña, *f*; indicio, *m*; (of the zodiac and *mus*) signo, *m*; marca, *f*; *ecc* símbolo, *m*; (of a shop, etc.) muestra, *f*, rótulo, *m*; (symptom) síntoma, *m*. *vt* firmar; indicar; *ecc* persignar. **as a s. of,** en señal de. **to converse by signs,** hablar por señas. **to make the s. of the cross over,** santiguar. **to show signs (of),** dar señas (de); indicar. **s.-painter,** pintor de muestras, *m*

signal *n* señal, *f*. *vt* señalar; hacer señas (a). *vi* hacer señales. a insigne, notable. **fog-s.,** señal de niebla, *f*. **landing s.,** *aer* señal de aterrizaje, *f*. **to give the s. for,**

dar la señal para. **s.-box,** garita de señales, f. **s. code,** naut código de señales, m

signature n firma, f; (mus and print) signatura, f

signboard n letrero, m, muestra, f

significance n significación, f, significado, m; importancia, f

significant a significativo, significante; expresivo; importante

signify vt significar; querer decir; importar. vi significar, tener importancia; importar

signpost n indicador de dirección, m

silence n silencio, m, interj isilencio! vt hacer callar, imponer silencio (a); silenciar. **to keep s.,** guardar silencio, callarse. **to pass over in s.,** pasar en silencio (por), pasar por alto de. **S. gives consent,** Quien calla otorga

silencer n (of fire-arms) silencioso, m; aut silenciador, silencioso, m

silent a silencioso. **to become s.,** enmudecer; callar. **to remain s.,** callarse, guardar silencio; permanecer silencioso. **s. partner,** n socio (-ia) comanditario (-ia)

silent film, silent movie n película muda, f

silhouette n silueta, f. vt representar en silueta; destacar. **in s.,** en silueta. **to be silhouetted against the sky,** destacarse contra el sielo

silica n sílice, f

silk n seda, f, a de seda. **artificial s.,** seda artificial, f. **floss s.,** seda ocal, f. **sewing s.,** seda de coser, f. **twist s.,** seda cordelada, f. **as smooth as s.,** como una seda. **s. growing,** sericultura, f. **s. hat,** sombrero de copa, m. **s. merchandise,** sedería, f. **s. stocking,** media de seda, f

silken a de seda; sedoso

silk-screen process n imprenta por tamiz, imprenta serigráfica, imprenta tamigráfica, impresión con estarcido de seda, f, proceso tamigráfico, m, serigrafía, tamigrafía, f

silkworm n gusano de seda, m

silky a sedoso; (of wine) suave

sill n (of a window) alféizar, antepecho, m; (of a door) umbral, m

silly a tonto, estúpido; imbécil, Central America also azurumbado. n tonto (-ta). **You are a s. ass,** Eres un imbécil

silt n aluvión, m, sedimentación, f. **to s. up,** vt cegar (or obstruir) con aluvión. vi cegarse con aluvión

silver n plata, f, a de plata; argénteo; (of the voice, etc.) argentino. vt platear; (mirrors) azogar; (hair) blanquear. **s. birch,** abedul, m. **s. fox,** zorro plateado, m. **s.-gry,** gris perla, m. **s.-haired,** de pelo entrecano. **s.-paper,** papel de estaño, m. **s.-plate,** n vajilla de plata, f. vt platear.

s.-tongued, de pico de oro; de voz argentina. **s. wedding,** bodas de plata, f pl

silversmith n platero, m. **silversmith's shop,** platería, f

similar a parecido (a), semejante (a); similar; geom semejante. **to be s. to,** asemejarse (a), parecerse (a)

similarity n parecido, m, semejanza, similitud, f

similarly adv de un modo parecido, asimismo

simile n símil, m

simmer vi hervir a fuego lento; fig estar a punto de estallar. **to s. down,** fig moderarse poco a poco. **to s. over,** fig estallar

simper vi sonreírse bobamente

simple a sencillo; simple; ingenuo, inocente; crédulo; (humble) humilde; (mere) mero. **s.-hearted,** inocente, cándido, sin malicia. **s.-minded,** ingenuo; crédulo. **s.-mindedness,** ingenuidad, f; credulidad, f

simpleton n primo (-ma); papanatas, m, tonto (-ta)

simplicity n sencillez, f; simplicidad, candidez, f

simplifiable a simplificable

simplify vt simplificar

simply adv sencillamente; simplemente, meramente; absolutamente

simulate vt fingir, aparentar, simular

simultaneous a simultáneo

sin n pecado, m, vi pecar; faltar (a)

since adv desde entonces, desde (que). prep desde. conjunc desde que; ya que, puesto que. **a long time s.,** hace mucho. **not long s.,** hace poco. **How long is it s. . . . ?** ¿Cuánto tiempo hace que . . . ? **s. then,** desde entonces

sincere a sincero

sincerely adv sinceramente. **Yours s.,** Su afectísimo . . .

sincerity n sinceridad, f

sine n math seno, m

sinecure n canonjía, sinecura, f, empleo de aviador (Mexican slang), m

sinew n tendón, m; pl **sinews,** nervio, m, fuerza, f

sinful a (of persons) pecador; (of thoughts, acts) pecaminoso

sing vi cantar; (of the ears) zumbar; (of wind, water) murmurar, susurrar; (of a cat) ronronear. vt cantar. **to s. a child to sleep,** dormir a un niño cantando. **to s. another song,** inf bajar el tono. **to s. small,** hacerse el chiquito. **to s. the praises of,** hacer las alabanzas de. **to s. out,** vocear, gritar. **s.-song,** n cantoría, f; concierto improvisado, m. a monótono

singe vt chamuscar; (a fowl) aperdigar; (hair) quemar las puntas de los cabellos

singer n cantor (-ra); (professional) cantante, mf; (bird) ave cantora, f

singing n canto, m; (of the ears) zumbido, *m.* a cantante. **s.-bird,** ave cantora, *f.* **s.-master,** maestro de cantar, *m*

single a único; sencillo; solo; simple; (individual) particular; individual; (unmarried) soltero. *n* (tennis) juego sencillo, individual, *m.* **in s. file,** de reata. **to s. out,** escoger; singularizar. **s. bed,** cama de monja, *f.* **s. bedroom,** habitación individual, habitación con una sola cama, *f.* **s.-breasted,** (of coats) recto. **s. combat,** combate singular, *m.* **s. entry,** com partida simple, *f.* **s.-handed,** de una mano; para una sola persona; sin ayuda, solo, en solitario. **s.-minded,** sin doblez, sincero de una sola idea. **s. ticket,** billete sencillo, *m*

singleness *n* celibato, *m*, soltería, *f.* **with s. of purpose,** con un solo objeto

single room *Mexico* cuarto sencillo, *m*

singly *adv* separadamente, uno a uno; a solas, solo; sin ayuda

singular a and *n* singular, *m*

sinister a siniestro

sink *vi* ir al fondo; bajar; hundirse; (of ships) irse a pique, naufragar; sumergirse; disminuir; caer (en); penetrar; (of persons, fires) morir; (of the sun, etc.) ponerse. *vt* (a ship) echar a pique; sumergir; hundir; dejar caer; bajar; (wells) cavar; reducir, disminuir; (invest) invertir; (one's identity, etc.) tener secreto; (differences) olvidar; (engrave) grabar. **My heart sank,** Se me cayeron las alas del corazón. **He sank to his knees,** Cayó de rodillas. **He is sinking fast,** Está en las últimas. **Their words began to s. in,** Sus palabras empezaban a tener efecto (or hacer mella). **I found her sunk in thought,** La encontré ensimismada. **to s. one's voice,** bajar la voz. **to s. down on a chair,** dejarse caer en una silla. **to s. into misery,** caer en la miseria. **to s. under,** (a responsibility) estar agobiado bajo

sink *n* (kitchen) fregadero, *Chile, Mexico also* lavaplatos, *m*; sumidero, *m*, sentina, *f.* **s. of iniquity,** sentina, *f*

sinker *n* (engraver) grabador (-ra); (of a fishing line) plomada, *f*

sinking *n* hundimiento, *m*; (of the sun) puesta, *f*; (of wells) cavadura, *f*; sumergimiento, *m.* **the s. of a boat,** el hundimiento de un buque. **with s. heart,** con la muerte en el alma. **s. fund,** fondo de amortización, *m*

sinner *n* pecador (-ra)

sinuous a sinuoso, tortuoso; flexible, ágil

sinus *n* (anat etc.) seno, *m*

sip *vt* sorber; (wine) saborear, paladear. *n* sorbo, *m*

siphon *n* sifón, *m*, *vt* sacar con sifón

sir *n* señor, *m*; (British title) sir. **Dear s.,** Muy Señor mío

sire *n* (to a monarch) Señor, *m*; (father)

padre, *m*; (stallion) semental, *m. vt* procrear, engendrar

siren *n* sirena, *f.* **s. suit,** mono, *m*

sirloin *n* solomillo, *Mexico* diezmillo, *m*

sister *n* hermana, *f*; (before nun's christian name) Sor; (hospital) hermana del hospital, *f*; enfermera, *f.* **s. language,** lengua hermana, *f.* **s. ship,** buque gemelo, *m.* **s.-in-law,** cuñada, hermana política, *f.* **S. of Mercy,** Hermana de la Caridad, *f*

sisterhood *n* hermandad, *f*; comunidad de monjas, *f*

sisterly a de hermana

sit *vi* sentarse; estar sentado; (of birds) posarse; (of hens) empollar; (in Parliament, etc.) ser diputado; (of a committee, etc.) celebrar sesión; (on a committee, etc.) formar parte de; (function) funcionar; (of garments, food, and *fig*) sentar. **to sit a horse,** mantenerse a caballo; montar a caballo. **to sit oneself,** sentarse, tomar asiento. **to sit by,** (a person) sentarse (or estar sentado) al lado de. **to sit for** (a portrait) servir de modelo para; hacerse retratar. **to sit tight,** no moverse. **to sit down,** sentarse; (besiege) sitiar. **to sit on,** sentarse (en or sobre); (eggs) empollar; (a committee, etc.) formar parte de; (investigate) investigar; (snub) dejar aplastado (a). **to sit out,** quedarse hasta el fin (de). **to sit out a dance,** conversar un baile. **to sit up,** incorporarse en la cama; tenerse derecho; (at night) velar; (of dogs, etc.) pedir. **to sit up and take notice,** abrir los ojos. **to sit up in bed,** incorporarse en la cama. **to sit up late,** estar de pie hasta muy tarde

sit-down strike *n* huelga de brazos caídos, huelga de sentados, *f*

site *n* sitio, local, *m*; (for building) solar, *m*

sitting *n* asentada, *f*; (of Parliament, etc.) sesión, *f*; (for a portrait) estadía, *f*; (of eggs) nidada, *f.* **at a s.,** de una asentada. **s.-room,** sala de estar, *f*

situated a situado. **How is he s.?** ¿Cómo está situado? ¿Cuál es su situación?

situation *n* situación, *f*; (job) empleo, *m*

six a and *n* seis, *m.* **It is six o'clock,** Son las seis. **Everything is at sixes and sevens,** Todo está en desorden. **six-foot,** de seis pies. **six hundred,** seiscientos (-as)

sixteen a and *n* diez y seis, dieciséis, *m.* **John is s.,** Juan tiene dieciséis años

sixteenth a décimosexto; (of the month) (el) diez y seis; (of monarch) diez y seis. *n* dieciseisavo, *m*

sixth a sexto; (of the month) (el) seis; (of monarchs) sexto. *n* seisavo, *m*; sexta parte, *f*; *mus* sexta, *f.* **Henry the S.,** Enrique sexto. **May the s.,** el seis de mayo

sixtieth a sexagésimo. *n* sesentavo, *m*; sexagésima parte, *f*

sixty a and *n* sesenta *m.* **John has turned s.,** Juan ha pasado los sesenta

sizable a bastante grande

size n tamaño, m; dimensión, f; (height) altura, f; (measurement) medida, f; talle, m; (in gloves, etc.) número, m; (glue) cola, f. vt clasificar por tamaños; (glaze, etc.) encolar. **to s. up,** tomar las medidas (a).

sizzle vi chisporrotear, chirriar. n chisporroteo, chirrido, m

skate n patín, m; icht raya, f, vi patinar

skater n patinador (-ra)

skating n patinaje, m. **s. rink,** sala de patinar, f; pista de hielo, pista de patinar, f, patinadero, m

skein n madeja, f

skeleton n esqueleto, m; (of a building) armadura, f; (of a literary work) esquema, m. **s. key,** ganzúa, f

sketch n croquis, apunte, m; (for a literary work) esbozo, esquema, m; (article) cuadro, artículo, m; descripción, f; theat entremés, sainete, m. vt dibujar; esbozar, bosquejar; trazar; describir. **s.-book,** álbum de croquis, m

sketching n arte de dibujar, mf. **He likes s.,** Le gusta dibujar

sketchy a bosquejado; incompleto; escaso

skewer n broqueta, f, vt espetar

ski n esquí, m, vi esquiar

skid n (of a vehicle) patinazo, m, vi patinar

skier n esquiador (-ra), mf

skiing n patinaje sobre la nieve, m, el esquiar. **to go s.,** ir a esquiar

skill n habilidad, f

skilled a hábil; experto

skilled worker n obrero calificado, m

skillful a hábil

skim vt espumar; (milk) desnatar, Lat. Am. descremar; (touch lightly) deslizarse sobre, rozar; (a book) hojear

skimp vt escatimar; escasear; (work) frangollar. vi ser parsimonioso

skimpy a escaso

skin n tez, f, cutis, m; piel, f; (of fruit) pellejo, m, piel, f; (for wine) odre, pellejo, m; (on milk) espuma, f. vt despellejar; pelar, mondar; (graze) hacerse daño (a); inf desollar. **next to one's s.,** sobre la piel. **to s. over,** cicatrizarse. **to have a thin s.,** fig ser muy susceptible. **to save one's s.,** salvar el pellejo. **s.-deep,** superficial. **s.-tight,** escurrido, muy ajustado

skinflint n avaro (-ra)

skinny a flaco, descarnado, magro

skip vi retozar, brincar, saltar; saltar a la comba; (bolt) largarse, escaparse. vt saltar; (a book) hojear; (omit) omitir; pasar por alto de. n brinco, pequeño salto, m

skipper n naut patrón, m; (inf and sport) capitán, m

skirmish vi escaramuzar. n escaramuza, f

skirt n falda, f; (edge) margen, borde, m;

orilla, f; (of a jacket, etc.) faldón, m. vt ladear; (hug) rodear, ceñir

skit n sátira, f; parodia, f

skittish a (of a horse) retozón; (of persons) frívolo; caprichoso

skulk vi estar en acecho; esconderse; rondar

skull n cráneo, m; calavera, f. **s.-cap,** gorro, casquete, m; (for ecclesiastics) solideo, m

skunk n zool mofeta, f, chingue, mapurite, yaguré, zorrillo, zorrino, zorro hediondo, m

sky n cielo, m. **to praise to the skies,** poner en los cuernos de la luna. **s.-blue,** n azul celeste, m. a de color azul celeste, cerúleo. **s.-high,** hasta las nubes, hasta el cielo. **s.-line,** horizonte, m. **s.-scraper,** rascacielos, m. **s.-sign,** anuncio luminoso, m

skylight n claraboya, f, tragaluz, m

slab n bloque, m; losa, f, Lat. Am. also laja; plancha, f

slack a lento; flojo; (lazy) perezoso; negligente, descuidado; com encalmado; débil. vi ser perezoso. **the s. season,** la estación muerta. **to be s. in one's work,** ser negligente en el trabajo. **to s. off,** disminuir sus esfuerzos; dejar de trabajar

slacken vt and vi aflojar; disminuir, reducir. **The wind slackened,** El viento amainaba, El viento aflojaba. **to s. one's efforts,** disminuir sus esfuerzos. **to s. speed,** disminuir la velocidad

slacker n gandul (-la)

slacks n pl pantalones, m pl

slake vt (one's thirst and lime) apagar; satisfacer

slam vt cerrar de golpe; golpear. n (of a door) portazo, m; golpe, m; (cards) capote, m. **He went out and slammed the door,** Salió dando un portazo

slander n calumnia, f, vt calumniar

slanderous a calumnioso

slang n argot, m, jerga, f, vt poner como un trapo (a), llenar de insultos

slant vi estar al sesgo; inclinarse; ser oblicuo. vt inclinar. n inclinación, f; oblicuidad, f. **on the s.,** inclinado; oblicuo

slap vt pegar con la mano. n bofetada, f; palmada, Lat. Am. cachetada, f. **to s. on the back,** golpear en la espalda. **s.-dash,** (of persons) irresponsable, descuidado; (of work) chapucero, sin cuidado

slash vt (gash, also sleeves, etc.) acuchillar; cortar; (with a whip) dar latigazos (a). n cuchillada, f; corte, m; latigazo, m

slat n tablilla, f, vi (of sails) dar zapatazos, zapatear

slate n pizarra, f, esquisto, m; (for roofs and for writing) pizarra, f, vt (a roof) empizarrar; (censure) criticar severamente, censurar. **s.-colored,** apizarrado. **s.**

pencil, pizarrín, *m.* **s. quarry,** pizarrería, *f;* pizarral, *m*

slating *n* empizarrado, *m;* (criticism) crítica ∗ severa, censura, *f;* (scolding) peluca, *f*

slattern *n* pazpuerca, *f*

slaughter *n* matanza, *f;* carnicería, *f. vt* (animals) sacrificar, matar; matar, hacer una carnicería de. **s.-house,** matadero, *m*

slaughterer *n* jifero, carnicero, *m*

Slav a and *n* eslavo (-va)

slave *n* esclavo (-va). *vi* trabajar como un negro. **white s. traffic,** trata de blancas, *f.* **s.-bangle,** esclava, *f.* **s.-driver,** capataz de esclavos, negrero, *m; fig* negrero, sayón de esclavos, *m.* **s.-trade,** trata de esclavos, *f*

slaver *vi* babear. *n* baba, *f*

slavering a baboso

slavery *n* esclavitud, *f;* trabajo muy arduo, *m*

slavish a de esclavo; servil

Slavonic a eslavo. *n* (language) eslavo, *m,* lengua eslava, *f*

slay *vt* matar; asesinar

slaying *n* matanza, *f;* asesinato, *m*

sledge *n* trineo, *m. vi* ir en trineo. *vt* transportar por trineo. **s.-hammer,** acotillo, *m*

sleek a liso, lustroso; (of general appearance) pulcro, bien aseado, elegante; (of manner) obsequioso

sleep *n* sueño, *m. vi* dormir; reposar, descansar. *vt* dormir. **a deep s.,** un sueño pesado. **He walks in his s.,** Es un sonámbulo. **to court s.,** conciliar el sueño. **to go to s.,** dormirse; entumecerse. **My foot has gone to s.,** Se me ha dormido (*or* Se me ha entumecido) el pie. **to send a person to s.,** adormecer. **to s. like a top,** dormir como un lirón. **to s. oneself sober,** dormir la mona. **to s. in,** dormir tarde; dormir en casa. **to s. off,** (a cold, etc.) curarse . . . durmiendo; (drunkenness) dormirla. **to s. on,** *vt* (consider) dormir sobre, consultar con la almohada. *vi* seguir durmiendo. **to s. out,** dormir fuera de casa; dormir al aire libre

sleeper *n* durmiente, *mf; rw* traviesa, *f;* (on a train) coche cama, *m.* **to be a bad s.,** dormir mal. **to be a good s.,** dormir bien.

sleeping a durmiente. *n* el dormir. **between s. and waking,** entre duerme y vela. **s.-bag,** saco-cama, *m.* **s.-car,** coche camas, *m.* **s.-draught,** narcótico, *m.* **s. partner,** *n* socio (-ia) comanditario (-ia). **s. sickness,** enfermedad del sueño, *f*

sleepless a (of persons) insomne, desvelado; (unremitting) incansable; (of the sea, etc.) en perpetuo movimiento. **to spend a s. night,** pasar una noche en

vela, pasar una noche toledana, pasar una noche sin dormir

sleepwalker *n* sonámbulo (-la)

sleepwalking *n* sonambulismo, *m*

sleepy a soñoliento; letárgico. **to be s.,** tener sueño. **s.-head,** lirón, *m,* marmota, *f*

sleet *n* aguanieve, cellisca, nevisca, *f, vi* caer aguanieve, cellisquear, neviscar

sleeve *n* manga, *f;* (of a hose pipe, etc.) manguera, *f; mech* manguito, *m.* **to have something up one's s.,** traer algo en la manga

sleeveless a sin manga. **s. shirt** *Lat. Am.* cusma, *f*

sleigh *n* trineo, *m, vi* ir en trineo

sleight of hand *n* prestidigitación, *f;* juego de manos, *m*

slender a delgado; esbelto; tenue; escaso; pequeño; ligero. **Their means are very s.,** Sus recursos son muy escasos. **It is a very s. hope,** Es una esperanza muy remota

sleuth *n* (dog) sabueso, *m; inf* detective, *m*

slice *n* lonja, tajada, *f;* (of fruit) raja, *f;* (of bread, etc.) rebanada, *f;* (share) parte, porción, *f;* (for fish, etc.) pala, *f. vt* cortar en tajadas, *f;* rajar; cortar

slick a hábil, diestro

slide *vi* deslizarse, resbalar; (over a question) pasar por alto de; (into a habit, etc.) caer (en). *n* resbalón, *m;* pista de hielo, *f;* (chute) tobogán, *m;* (of a microscope) portaobjetos, *m;* (lantern) diapositiva, *f;* (for the hair) pasador, *m;* (of rock, etc.) desprendimiento, *m; mech* guía, *f.* **to let things s.,** dejar rodar la bola. **s.-rule,** regla de cálculo, *f*

sliding a resbaladizo; corredizo; movible. **s.-door,** puerta corrediza, puerta de corredera, *f.* **s.-roof,** techo corredizo, *m.* **s.-scale,** escala graduada, *f.* **s.-seat,** asiento movible, *m;* (in a rowing-boat) bancada corrediza, *f*

slight a delgado; débil, frágil; ligero; (small) pequeño; escaso; (trivial) insignificante, poco importante. *vt* desairar, despreciar, *Mexico* descolar. *n* desaire, desprecio, *m;* falta de respeto, *f*

slighting a despreciativo, de desprecio

slightly *adv* ligeramente; poco. **I only know her s.,** La conozco muy poco. **s. built,** de talle delgado

slim a delgado; escaso. *vi* adelgazarse. **He has very s. chances of success,** Tiene muy pocas posibilidades de conseguir el éxito

slime *n* légamo, limo, lodo, cieno, *m;* (of a snail) limazo, *m; fig* cieno, *m*

slimy a limoso, legamoso; pecinoso, viscoso; (of persons) rastrero, servil

sling *vt* arrojar, lanzar; tirar con honda; (a sword, etc.) suspender; (lift) embragar; (a limb) poner en cabestrillo. *n* (for missiles) honda, *f*; *naut* balso, *m*; (for a limb) cabestrillo, *m*, charpa, *f*

slink *vi* (away, off) escurrirse, escabullirse

slip *vi* resbalar, deslizar; (stumble) resbalar, tropezar; (fall) caer; (out of place) salirse; (become untied) desatarse; (steal away) escabullirse; (glide) deslizarse; (of years) correr, pasar; (skid) patinar. *vt* deslizar; (garments, shoes) ponerse; (dogs, cables) soltar; (an arm round, etc.) pasar; *rw* desacoplar; (escape) escaparse de; (free oneself of) librarse de. *n* resbalón, *m*; (skid) patinazo, *m*; (stumble) tropezón, traspié, *m*; (oversight) inadvertencia, *f*; (mistake) falta, equivocación, *f*; (moral lapse) desliz, *m*; (petticoat) combinación, *f*; (cover) funda, *f*; *bot* vástago, *m*; *print* galerada, *f*; (of paper) papeleta, *f*; *pl* **slips,** *naut* anguilas, *f pl.* **It slipped my memory,** Se me fue de la memoria. **There's many a s. 'twixt the cup and the lip,** Del dicho al hecho hay muy gran trecho, De la mano a la boca desaparece la sopa. **to give** (someone) **the slip,** escaparse de. **You ought not to let the opportunity s.,** No debes perder la oportunidad. **to let s. a secret,** revelar un secreto. **to let s. an exclamation,** soltar (dar) una exclamación. **to s. into,** colarse en, deslizarse en. **to s. into,** colarse en, deslizarse en. **to s. into one's clothes,** vestirse rápidamente. **to s. on,** (a garment) ponerse. **to s. out,** salir a hurtadillas; escaparse; (of information) divulgarse. **s. of a boy,** mozalbete, joven imberbe, *m*. **s. of the tongue,** error de lengua, *m*. **s.-knot,** nudo corredizo, *m*

slipcover *n* cubierta, cubierta para muebles, funda, funda para muebles, *f*

slipper *n* babucha, chinela, *f*, pantuflo, *m*; (heelless) chancleta, *f*; (dancing) zapatilla de baile, *f*. **s.-shaped,** achinelado

slippery *a* resbaladizo; poco firme, inestable; (of persons) informal, sin escrúpulos

slipshod *a* descuidado, negligente; poco correcto

slit *vt* cortar; hender, rajar; (the throat) degollar. *n* cortadura, *f*; resquicio, *m*. **to s. open,** abrir de un tajo

slither *vi* resbalar; deslizarse

sliver *n* raja, *f*; (of wood) astilla, *f*; (of cloth) tira, *f*

slobber *vi* babear; (blubber) gimotear, *n* baba, *f*

slog *vt* golpear duramente. **to s. away,** batirse el cobre, trabajar como un negro

slogan *n* grito de batalla, *m*; reclamo, *m*; frase hecha, *f*; mote, *m*

slop *n* charco, *m*; *pl* **slops,** agua sucia, *f*; alimentos líquidos, *m pl. vi* derramarse, verterse. *vt* verter, derramar

slope *n* inclinación, *f*; pendiente, *f*; (of a mountain, etc.) falda, ladera, cuesta, *f*; vertiente, *mf. vi* inclinarse; estar en declive; bajar (hacia). **to s. down,** declinar

sloping *a* inclinado; en declive; (of shoulders) caídos, *m pl*

sloppy *a* casi líquido; (muddy) lodoso, lleno de barro; (of work) chapucero; (of persons) baboso, sobón. **s. sentiment,** sensiblería, *f*

slot *n* ranura, muesca, *f*. **s.-machine,** máquina expendedora, *f*, expendedor, *m*; (in amusement arcades, etc.) tragaperras, *m*

sloth *n* pereza, indolencia, *f*; *zool* perezoso, *m*

slothful *a* perezoso, indolente

slouch *n* inclinación del cuerpo, *f*. *vi* andar cabizbajo, andar arrastrando los pies. **to s. about,** vagar, golfear. **s.-hat,** sombrero gacho, *m*

slough *n* (bog) cenagal, pantano, *m*, marisma, *f*; (of a snake) camisa, *f*. *vt* (a skin) mudar; (prejudices, etc.) desechar

sloven *n* puerco, *m*; (at work) chapucero, *m*

slovenly *a* desgarbado, desaseado, *Central America* descacharrado, *Lat. Am.* distraído; (careless) descuidado, negligente; (of work) chapucero

slow *a* despacio; lento, *Lat. Am.* demorón; (stupid) torpe; tardo; (of clocks) atrasado; (boring) aburrido; (inactive) flojo. *adv* despacio, lentamente. **I was not s. to . . . ,** No tardé en . . . , *Lat. Am.* No dilaté en . . . **The clock is ten minutes s.,** El reloj lleva diez minutos de atraso. **to s. down,** aflojar el paso; ir más despacio. **s.-motion,** velocidad reducida, *f*. **s. train,** tren ómnibus, *m*. **s.-witted,** lerdo tardo

"Slow Down" «Moderar Su Velocidad»

slow learner *n* alumno de lento aprendizaje, *m*

slowly *adv* despacio, lentamente; poco a poco

slug *n* babosa, *f*

sluggard *n* gandul (-la), perezoso (-a)

sluggish *a* perezoso; (of the market) flojo; (of temperament, etc.) calmoso, flemático; (slow) lento

sluice *n* esclusa, *f*; canal, *m*, acequia, *f*. **to s. down,** lavar; echar agua sobre; (a person) dar una ducha (a), dar un baño (a). **s.-gate,** compuerta de esclusa, *f*; tajaderas, *f pl*, tablacho, *m*

slum *nsg* (inner-city slum) barrio bajo (understood everywhere), arrabales *mpl* (Argentina, Uruguay), banda de miseria *fsg* (Argentina), barracas *fpl* (Mexico), barriada *fsg* (Peru), callampa *fsg* (Chile), cantegriles *mpl* (Spain, Uruguay), chabolas *fpl* (Spain), clandestinos *mpl* (Colombia), morenales *mpl* (Honduras), orillas *fpl* (Mexico), población *fsg* (Chile), pueblo joven *msg* (Peru), ranchos *mpl* (Venezuela), tugurios *mpl* (Colombia), villa-miseria *fsg* (Argentina), ranchería *msg*, ribera *fpl*, villorio *msg* (elsewhere in Lat. Am.); (in Brazil) favelas *fpl*; (slum on the outskirts of an urban area) suburbio *msg*

slumber *vi* dormir; (go to sleep) dormirse, caer dormido; (be latent) estar latente. *n* sueño, *m*

slump *n* com baja repentina, *f*; *fig* baja, racha mala, *f*. *vi* com bajar repentinamente. **the s.,** la crisis económica. **to s. into an armchair,** dejarse caer en un sillón

slur *vt* (words) comerse sílabas o letras (de); (in writing) unir (las palabras); (*mus* of notes) ligar. **to cast a s. on,** difamar, manchar. **to s. over,** pasar por alto de, omitir, suprimir

slush *n* lodo, *m*; agua nieve, *f*; (sentimentality) ñoñería, *f*

sly *a* astuto, taimado, socarrón, *Lat. Am.* macuco; disimulado; (arch) malicioso. **on the sly,** a hurtadillas. **sly person** *Mexico* fistol, *m*

smack *n* (taste) sabor, gusto, *m*; (tinge) dejo, *m*; (blow) golpe, *m*; (with the hand) bofetada, palmada, *f*; (with a whip) latigazo, *m*; (crack of whip) restallido, chasquido, *m*; (kiss) beso sonado, *m*; (boat) lancha de pescar, *f*. *vi* (taste of) tener gusto de, saber a; (be tinged with) oler a. *vt* (a whip) hacer restallar; (slap) pegar con la mano. **to s. one's lips over,** chuparse los dedos

small *a* pequeño; menudo; menor; poco; (petty) mezquino, vulgar. *n* parte estrecha, *f*. **a s. number,** un pequeño número. **to make a person look s.,** humillar. **to make oneself s.,** hacerse chiquito. **s.-arms,** armas portátiles, *f pl*. **s. change,** suelto, *m*. **s. craft,** embarcaciones menores, *f pl*. **s. farm** *Lat. Am.* chacra, *Central America* labor, *f*. **s. fry,** pececillos, *m pl*; (children) gente menuda, *f*; gente sin importancia, *f*. **s. hours,** altas horas de la noche, *f pl*. **s.-minded,** adocenado, de cortos alcances. **s.-talk,** trivialidades, *f pl*, charla frívola, *f*

smallholding *n Lat. Am.* chacra, *f*

smallish *a* bastante pequeño; más bien pequeño que grande

smallpox *n* viruelas, *f pl*

smart *vi* picar; dolerse (de). *n* escozor, *m*; dolor, *m*. *a* severo; vivo; rápido; pronto; (competent) hábil; (clever) listo; (unscrupulous) cuco, astuto; (of personal appearance) majo; elegante, distinguido, *Lat. Am. also* fachoso; (neat) aseado; (fashionable, etc.) de moda; de buen tono. **to s. for,** ser castigado por. **to s. under,** sufrir

smarten *vt* embellecer. *vi* (up) ponerse elegante; mejorar. **I must go and s. myself up a little,** Tengo que arreglarme un poco

smash *vt* romper, quebrar; (a ball, etc.) golpear; (annihilate) destruir; (an oppo-

nent) aplastar. *vi* romperse, quebrarse; hacerse pedazos; (collide) chocar (con, contra); estallarse (contra); (financially) hacer bancarrota. *n* rotura, *f*; quebrantamiento, *m*; estruendo, *m*; (financial) quiebra, ruina, *f*; (car, etc.) accidente, *m*; desastre, *m*, catástrofe, *f*. **to s. to atoms,** hacer trizas. **to s. up,** hacer pedazos. **s. and grab raid,** atraco a mano armada, *m*

smash hit *n* éxito arrollador, éxito rotundo, *m*

smattering *n* conocimiento superficial, *m*, tintura, *f*, barniz, *m*

smear *n* mancha, *f*; *biol* frotis, *m*. *vt* embadurnar (de); manchar (con), ensuciar (con); (oneself) untarse; (blur) borrar

smell *n* (sense of) olfato, *m*; (odor) olor, *m*. *vt* oler. *vi* oler; tener olor; (disagreeably) oler mal, tener mal olor; (stink) apestar. **How good it smells!** ¡Qué bien huele! **to s. of,** oler a. **to s. out,** husmear

smelling *n* olfateo, *m*. **s.-bottle,** frasco de sales, *m*. **s.-salts,** sales (inglesas), *f pl*

smelt *vt* fundir. *n icht* eperlano, *m*

smile *vi* sonreír; reírse. *vt* expresar con una sonrisa. *n* sonrisa, *f*. **Mary smiled her thanks,** María dio las gracias con una sonrisa. **smile at adversity,** ponerse buena cara a mal tiempo. **to s. at threats,** reírse de las amenazas

smirch *vt* manchar. *n* mancha, *f*

smirk *vi* sonreír con afectación; hacer visajes. *n* sonrisa afectada, *f*

smite *vt* golpear; (kill) matar; (punish) castigar; (pain) doler; (of bright light, sounds, etc.) herir; (cause remorse) remorder. **My conscience smites me,** Tengo remordimientos de conciencia. **to be smitten by,** *inf* estar prendado de. **I was smitten by a desire to smoke,** Me entraron deseos de fumar

smith *n* herrero, *m*. **smith's hammer,** destajador, *m*

smithereens *n pl* añicos, *m pl*

smithy *n* herrería, *f*

smock *n* blusa, *f*; (child's) delantal, *m*

smoke *n* humo, *m*. *vi* humear, echar humo; (tobacco) fumar. *vt* ahumar; ennegrecer; (tobacco) fumar. **smoked glasses,** gafas ahumadas, *f pl*. **s. helmet,** casco respiratorio, *m*. **s.-screen,** cortina de humo, *f*. **s. signal,** ahumada, *f*. **s.-stack,** chimenea, *f*

smoker *n* fumador (-ra)

smoking *a* humeante. *n* el fumar. **"S. Prohibited,"** «Se prohíbe fumar.» **non-s. compartment,** *rw* departamento de no fumadores, *m*. **s.-carriage,** *rw* departamento para fumadores, *m*. **s.-room,** fumadero, *m*

smooth *a* liso; igual; (of the skin, etc.) suave; (of water) calmo, tranquilo; (flattering, etc.) lisonjero, zalamero; afable. *vt* allanar; (hair, etc.) alisar; (paths, etc.) igualar. **to s. down,** (a person) tranquilizar, calmar. **to s. over,** (faults) exculpar. **to s. the way for,** allanar el camino para. **s.-faced,** barbilampiño, bien afeitado, todo afeitado; *fig* obsequioso, untuoso. **s.-haired,** de pelo liso. **s.-spoken,** de palabras lisonjeras; obsequioso

smoothly *adv* lisamente; (of speech) afablemente; (of manner) **Everything was going s.,** Todo iba viento en popa

smother *vt* ahogar, sofocar; (a fire) apagar; (cover) envolver, cubrir

smoulder *vi* arder sin llama, arder lentamente; (of passions, etc.) arder; estar latente

smudge *vt* manchar, ensuciar; (blur) borrar. *n* mancha, *f*

smug *a* satisfecho de sí mismo, pagado de sí mismo; fariseico

smuggle *vt* pasar de contrabando. *vi* hacer contrabando

smuggler *n* contrabandista, *mf*

smut *n* copo de hollín, *m*; mancha, *f*; (disease) tizón, *m*

smutty *a* tiznado; ahumado; *inf* verde

snack *n* tentempié, piscolabis, bocado, Lat. Am. botana, *f*. **to take a s.,** tomar un piscolabis

snack bar *n* merendero, *m*, Lat. Am. lonchería, *f*

snag *n* (of a tree) tocón, *m*; (of a tooth) raigón, *m*; (problem) busilis, *m*; obstáculo inesperado, *m*

snail *n* caracol, *m*. **at a snail's pace,** a paso de tortuga

snake *n* serpiente, *f*. **s.-charmer,** encantador de serpientes, *m*

snap *vt* morder; (break) romper; (one's fingers) castañetear; (a whip) chasquear; (down a lid, etc.) cerrar de golpe; (beaks, etc.) cerrar ruidosamente; *phot* sacar una instantánea de. *vi* partirse; quebrarse; hablar bruscamente. *n* (bite) mordedura, *f*; golpe seco, *m*; chasquido, *m*; rotura, *f*; (clasp) cierre, *m*; (of weather) temporada, *f*; (spirit) vigor, brío, *m*; *phot* instantánea, *f*. **to s. at,** procurar morder; (an invitation, etc.) aceptar gustoso. **to s. one's fingers at,** *fig* burlarse de. **to s. up,** coger, agarrar; (a person) cortar la palabra (a), interrumpir. **s.-fastener,** botón de presión, *m*

snapdragon *n* dragón, *m*, becerra, boca de dragón, *f*

snappily *adv* irritablemente

snappy *a* irritable; vigoroso

snapshot *n* instantánea, foto, *f*

snare *n* cepo, lazo, *m*, trampa, *f*; *fig* red, *f*. *vt* coger en el lazo; *fig* enredar

snarl *vi* (of dogs) regañar; (cats, etc.) gruñir. *n* regañamiento, *m*; gruñido, *m*

snarling *n* regañamiento, *m*; gruñidos, *m* *pl*, *a* gruñidor

snatch *vt* asir; agarrar; (enjoy) disfrutar; (an opportunity) tomar, aprovecharse de.

n asimiento, agarro, *m*; (of time) rato, *m*; instante, *m*; (of song) fragmento, *m*. **to make a s. at,** procurar agarrar; alargar la mano hacia. **to s. a hurried meal,** comer aprisa. **to s. away,** arrebatar, quitar; (carry off) robar. **to s. up,** coger rápidamente; coger en brazos

sneak *vi* deslizarse (en), colarse (en); (lurk) rondar; (inform) acusar. *n* mandilón, *m*; (accuser) acusón (-ona). **to s. off,** escabullirse; irse a hurtadillas. **s.-thief,** *n* garduño (-ña)

sneaker *n* (shoe) zapatilla de tenis, *f*

sneaking *a* furtivo, ruin, mezquino; secreto

sneer *vi* sonreír irónicamente; burlarse, mofarse. *n* sonrisa sardónica, sonrisa de desprecio, *f*; burla, mofa, *f*. **to s. at,** mofarse de, burlarse de; hablar con desprecio de

sneering *a* mofador, burlón

sneeringly *adv* con una sonrisa sardónica; burlonamente

sneeze *vi* estornudar. *n* estornudo, *m*. **It's not to be sneezed at,** No es moco de pavo

sniff *vi* respirar fuertemente; resollar. *vt* oler, olfatear; aspirar. **to s. at,** oler. **to s. out,** *inf* husmear

snigger *vi* reírse por lo bajo, reírse disimuladamente. *n* risa disimulada, *f*

snip *vt* cortar con tijeras; cortar, quitar. *n* tijeretada, *f*; (of cloth, etc.) recorte, pedacito, *m*

sniper *n* *mil* paco, *m*

snippet *n* pedacito, fragmento, *m*; (of prose, etc.) trocito, *m*; (of news) noticia, *f*

snivel *vi* lloriquear, gimotear

sniveling *n* lloriqueo, gimoteo, *m*. *a* llorón; mocoso

snob *n* esnob, *mf*

snobbery *n* snobismo, *m*

snobbish *a* esnob

snood *n* (for the hair) redecilla, *f*; (turkey's) moco (de pavo), *m*; (fishing) cendal, *m*

snoop *vi* espiar; entremeterse

snooper *n* Lat. Am. averigüetas, *mf*

snooze *vi* dormitar, echar un sueño. *n* sueñecito, *m*; (afternoon) siesta, *f*

snore *vi* roncar. *n* ronquido, *m*

snoring *n* ronquidos, *m* *pl*

snort *vi* bufar; resoplar. *n* bufido, *m*; resoplido, *m*

snout *n* hocico, *m*; (of a pig) jeta, *f*

snow *n* nieve, *f*. *vi* nevar. *vt* nevar; *fig* inundar. **to s. under** (with), inundar con. **to be snowed up,** estar aprisionado por la nieve. **s.-blindness,** deslumbramiento causado por la nieve, *m*. **s.-boot,** bota para la nieve, *f*. **s.-bound,** aprisionado por la nieve; bloqueado por la nieve. **s.-capped,** coronado de nieve. **s.-clad,** cubierto de nieve. **s.-drift,** acumulación

de nieve, f. **s.-field,** ventisquero, m.
s.-goggles, gafas ahumadas, f pl.
s.-line, límite de las nieves perpetuas, m.
s.-man, figura de nieve, f. **s.-plough,**
quitanieve, m. **s.-shoe,** raqueta de nieve,
f. **s.-white,** blanco como la nieve

snowball n bola de nieves; f; bot bola de
nieve, f

snowfall n nevada, f

snowflake n copo de nieve, m

snowstorm n ventisca, f

snowy a nevoso; de nieve

snub vt repulsar; desairar, tratar con desdén, Mexico descolar. n repulsa, f, desaire, m; (nose) nariz respingona, f.
s.-nosed, de nariz respingona

snuff vt (breathe) oler, olfatear; inhalar;
(a candle) atizar, despabilar. n (of a candle) moco, m, despabiladura, f; (tobacco)
rapé, m. **to take s.,** tomar rapé. **to s.
out,** extinguir. **s.-box,** caja de rapé,
tabaquera, f

snuffle vi hacer ruido con la nariz; respirar fuerte; (in speaking) ganguear

snuffling a mocoso; (of the voice) gangoso

snug a caliente; cómodo; (hidden) escondido, **to have a s. income,** tener el riñón
bien cubierto, ser acomodado

snuggle vi hacerse un ovillo; acomodarse; ponerse cómodo. **to s. up to,** arrimarse a, apretarse contra

so adv así; de este modo, de esta manera;
por lo tanto; tanto; (before adjs. and advs.
but not before **más, mejor, menos,
peor,** where **tanto** is used) tan; (in the
same way) del mismo modo, de igual
modo; (therefore) de modo que, de manera que; (also) también; (approximately)
más o menos, aproximadamente. **Is that
so?** ¿De veras? **if so . . . ,** si así es . . . **He
has not yet done so,** no lo ha hecho
todavía. **I told you so!** ¡Ya te lo dije yo!
So be it! ¡Así sea! **so far,** hasta aquí;
hasta ahora. **so forth,** etcétera. **So long!**
¡Nos vemos! **so much,** tanto. **So much
the worse for them,** Tanto peor para
ellos. **so to speak . . . ,** por decirlo así. **so
as to,** a fin de, para. **so long as,** con tal
que, a condición de que. **so on,** etcétera.
so soon as, tan pronto como. **so that,** de
suerte que, de modo que, para que; con
que. **so-and-so,** n fulano (-na); mengano
(-na). **so-called.** así llamado, supuesto.
so-so, así-así, regular

soak vt remojar; empapar; (skins) abrevar. vi estar en remojo. n remojo, m;
(rain) diluvio, m; (booze) borrachera, f. **to
s. into,** filtrar en; penetrar. **to s.
through,** penetrar; filtrar **so-called,** así
llamado, supuesto. **so-so,** así, regular

soaked a remojado. **He is s. to the skin,**
Está calado hasta los huesos

soap n jabón, m. vt jabonar; (flatter) enjabonar. **a tablet of s.,** una pastilla de
jabón. **soft s.,** jabón blando, m. **toilet s.,**

jabón de tocador, jaboncillo, m. **s.-bub-
ble,** burbuja de jabón, f. **s. dish,** jabonera, f. **s. factory,** jabonería, f. **s.-flakes,**
copos de jabón, m pl

soap box n lit caja de jabón, f; fig tribuna
callejera, f

soap opera n radionovela (on radio),
telenovela (on television), f, serial la-
crimógeno (derogatory), m

soapsuds n pl jabonaduras, f pl

soar vi remontarse; fig elevarse; (of
prices, etc.) subir de golpe

soaring n remonte, vuelo, m; fig aspiración, f; (of prices, etc.) subida repentina,
f

sob vi sollozar. n sollozo, m. **to sob one's
heart out,** llorar a lágrima viva. **to sob
out,** decir sollozando, decir entre sollo-
zos

s.o.b. n (son of a bitch) hache de pe (hijo
de puta)

sober a sobrio; moderado; (of colors) obscuro. **s.-minded,** serio; reflexivo

sobriety n sobriedad, f; moderación, f;
seriedad, f; calma, tranquilidad, f

sobriquet n apodo, m

soccer n fútbol (Asociación), m

sociable a sociable; amistoso

social a social; sociable. n reunión,
velada, f. **s.-democrat,** a and n social-
demócrata, mf. **s. event,** acontecimiento
social, m. **s. insurance,** previsión social,
f. **s. services,** servicios sociales, m pl. **s.
work,** asistencia social, f

socialism n socialismo, m

socialist a socialista, laborista. n socialista, mf

socialize vt socializar

society n sociedad, f; (fashionable)
mundo elegante, m, alta sociedad, f;
compañía, f. **to go into s.,** (of girls) ponerse de largo; entrar en el mundo elegante. **s. hostess,** dama de sociedad, f.
**society for the prevention of cruelty
to animals,** sociedad protectora de animales, f. **s. news,** noticias de sociedad, f
pl

sociologist n sociólogo (-ga)

sociology n sociología, f

sock n calcetín, m; (for a shoe) plantilla, f

socket n mech encaje, cubo, ojo, m; (of a
lamp, and elec) enchufe, m; (of the eye)
órbita, cuenca, f; (of a tooth) alvéolo, m;
(of a joint) fosa, f. **His eyes started out
of their sockets,** Sus ojos estaban fuera
de su órbita

sod n césped, m; (cut) tepe, m

soda n sosa, f. **caustic s.,** sosa cáustica,
f. **s.-ash,** carbonato sódico, m. **s.-foun-
tain,** aparato de aguas gaseosas, m.
s.-water, sifón, m

sodden a saturado, empapado

sodium n sodio, m

sofa n sofá, m

soft a blando; suave; muelle; (flabby) flojo; (of disposition, etc.) dulce; (effeminate) muelle, afeminado; (lenient) indulgente; (easy) fácil; (silly) tonto. **to have a s. spot for,** (a person) tener una debilidad para. **s. coal,** carbón bituminoso, m. **s. drink,** bebida no alcohólica, f. **s. felt hat,** sombrero flexible, m. **s. fruit,** fruta blanda, f. **s.-boiled,** (of eggs) pasado por agua; (of persons) inocente, ingenuo. **s.-hearted,** de buen corazón; compasivo, bondadoso. **s.-heartedness,** buen corazón, m, bondad, f. **s.-spoken,** de voz suave; que habla con dulzura, meloso. **s. water,** agua blanda, f

soften vt ablandar, reblandecer) (weaken) debilitar; (mitigate) mitigar, suavizar; (the heart, etc.) enternecer. vi reblandecerse; enternecerse

softening n reblandecimiento, m; (relenting) enternecimiento, m

softly adv suavemente; dulcemente, tiernamente; sin ruido, silenciosamente

soggy a empapado de agua; saturado

soil n tierra, f; (country) país, m, tierra, f. vt ensuciar; fig manchar. **my native s.,** mi tierra, mi patria

soiled a sucio. **s. linen,** ropa sucia, f

sojourn vi morar, residir, permanecer. n residencia, permanencia, f

solace n consuelo, solaz, m. vt consolar; solazar

solar a solar. **s. plexus,** anat plexo solar, m. **s. system,** sistema solar, m

solder n soldadura, f, vt soldar

soldering n soldadura, f

soldier n soldado, m; militar, m. **He wants to be a s.,** Quiere ser militar

soldierly a militar; marcial

soldiery n soldadesca, f

sole n (of a foot) planta, f; (of a shoe) suela, f; (of a plough) cepa, f; icht lenguado, m, suela, f. vt (shoes) solar, poner suela (a). a solo, único; exclusivo. **s. right,** exclusiva, f, derecho exclusivo, m

solely adv sólo; únicamente, puramente; meramente

solemn a solemne; grave; serio; (sacred) sagrado. **Why do you look so s.?** ¿Por qué estás tan serio?

solemnity n solemnidad, f

solemnize vt solemnizar

solicit vt solicitar; implorar, rogar encarecidamente

solicitor n abogado (-da)

solicitous a ansioso (de), deseoso (de); solícito, atento; (worried) preocupado

solicitude n solicitud, f, cuidado, m; (anxiety) preocupación, f

solid a sólido; macizo; (of persons) serio, formal; (unanimous) unánime. n sólido, m. **a s. meal,** una comida fuerte. **He slept for ten s. hours,** Durmió por diez horas seguidas. **solid-colored mate-** rial, tela lisa, f. **s. food,** alimentos sólidos, m pl. **s. geometry,** geometría del espacio, f. **solid gold,** oro de ley, m. **s. tire,** llanta de goma maciza, f

solidarity n solidaridad, f

solidify vt solidificar. vi solidificarse; congelarse

solidity n solidez, f; unanimidad, f

soliloquize vi soliloquiar, hablar a solas

soliloquy n soliloquio, m

solitaire n (diamond and game) solitario, m

solitary a solitario; solo, aislado, único. **He was in s. confinement for three months,** Estuvo incomunicado durante tres meses. **There is not a s. one,** No hay ni uno

solitude n soledad, f

solo n (performance and cards) solo, m. **to sing a s.,** cantar un solo. **It was his first s. flight,** Era su primer vuelo a solas

soloist n solista, mf

solstice n solsticio, m. **summer s.,** solsticio vernal, m. **winter s.,** solsticio hiemal, m

soluble a soluble

solution n solución, f

solvable a que se puede resolver, soluble

solve vt resolver, hallar la solución de

solvency n solvencia, f

solvent a com solvente; (chem and fig) disolvente. n disolvente, m

somber a sombrío

some a alguno (-a), algunos (-as); (before a masculine sing. noun) algún; unos (-as); un poco de, algo de; (as a partitive, often not translated) e.g. **Give me s. wine,** Dame vino); (approximately) aproximadamente, unos (-as). pron algunos (-as), unos (-as); algo, un poco. **I should like s. strawberries,** Me gustaría comer unas fresas. **s. day,** algún día. **S. say yes, others no,** Algunos dicen que sí, otros que no. **There are s. sixty people in the garden,** Hay unas sesenta personas en el jardín

somebody, someone n alguien, mf. **s. else,** otro (-a), otra persona, f. **S. or other said that the book is worth reading,** No sé quién dijo que el libro vale la pena de leerse. **to be s.,** inf ser un personaje

somehow adv de un modo u otro, de alguna manera. **S. I don't like them,** No sé por qué, pero no me gustan

somersault n salto mortal, m, vi dar un salto mortal

something n algo, m, alguna cosa, f. adv algún tanto. **Would you like s. else?** ¿Quiere Vd. otra cosa? **He left s. like fifty thousand pounds,** Dejó algo así como cincuenta mil libras. **He has s. to live for,** Tiene para que vivir

sometime adv algún día, alguna vez; en

algún tiempo. a ex-. **Come and see me s. soon,** Ven a verme algún día de estos. **He will have to go abroad s. or another,** Tarde o temprano, tiene que ir al extranjero. **s. last month,** durante el mes pasado

sometimes adv algunas veces, a veces. **s. happy, s. sad,** algunas veces feliz y otras triste, ora feliz ora triste

somewhat adv algo; algún tanto, un tanto; un poco. **I am s. busy,** Estoy algo ocupado. **He is s. of a lady-killer,** Tiene sus puntos de castigador, Tiene algo de castigador

somewhere adv en alguna parte. **s. about,** por ahí. **s. else,** en otra parte

somnambulism n somnambulismo, m

somnambulist n somnámbulo (-la)

somnolence n somnolencia, f

somnolent a soñoliento; soporífero

son n hijo, m. **son-in-law,** yerno, hijo político, m

song n canto, m; canción, f; (poem) poema, verso, m. **It's nothing to make a s. about,** No es para tanto. **to break into s.,** ponerse a cantar. **to be not worth an old s.,** no valer un pito. **the S. of Songs,** Cantar de los Cantares, m. **s.-bird,** ave canora, f. **s.-book,** libro de canciones, m. **s.-writer,** compositor (-ra) de canciones

sonic adj sónico. **sonic boom,** estampido sónico, m

sonnet n soneto, m

sonorous a sonoro

soon adv pronto; dentro de poco, luego. **as s. as,** así que, en cuanto, luego que, no bien . . . **as s. as possible,** lo antes posible, lo más pronto posible, con la mayor antelación posible, cuanto antes. **s. after,** poco después (de). **See you s.!** ¡Hasta pronto! **sooner or later,** tarde o temprano. **the sooner the better,** cuanto antes mejor. **No sooner had he left the house, when . . .** Apenas hubo dejado la casa, cuando . . . **Emily would sooner go to London,** Emilia preferiría ir a Londres (A Emilia le gustaría más ir a Londres)

soot n hollín, m, vt cubrir de hollín

soothe vt tranquilizar, calmar, (pain) aliviar, mitigar

soothing a calmante, tranquilizador, sosegador; (of powders, etc.) calmante

soothsaying n adivinanza, f

sooty a cubierto de hollín; negro como el hollín

sop n sopa, f; (bribe) soborno, m

sophist n hist sofista, m; (quibbler) sofista, mf

sophistic a phil sofista; (of persons, arguments) sofístico

sophisticated a nada ingenuo; mundano; (cultured) culto

sophistication n falta de simplicidad, f; mundanería, f; cultura, f

sophistry n sofistería, f

soporific a soporífico

sopping a muy mojado. **s. wet,** hecho una sopa

soprano n (voice and part) soprano, m; (singer) soprano, tiple, mf

sorcerer n encantador, mago, brujo, m

sorcery n sortilegio, m, hechicería, brujería, f; encanto, m

sordid a sórdido; (of motives, etc.) ruin, vil

sore a doloroso, malo; (sad) triste; (annoyed) enojado; (with need, etc.) extremo. n llaga, Lat. Am. also lacra, f; (on horses, etc., caused by girths) matadura, f; flg herida, f; recuerdo doloroso, m. **to open an old s.,** fig renovar la herida. **running s.,** úlcera, f. **s. throat,** dolor de garganta, m

sorely adv grandemente; muy; urgentemente. **He was s. tempted,** Tuvo grandes tentaciones

soreness n dolor, m; (resentment) amargura, f, resentimiento, m; (ill-feeling) rencor, m

sorrow n pesar, m, aflicción, pesadumbre, f; tristeza, f. vi afligirse; entristecerse. **To my great s.,** Con gran pesar mío. **s.-stricken,** afligido, agobiado de pena

sorrowful a afligido, angustiado; triste

sort n especie, f; clase, f; tipo, m. vt separar (de); clasificar. **a s. of hat,** una especie de sombrero. **all sorts of,** toda clase de. **He is a good s.,** Es buen chico. **He is a queer s.,** Es un tipo raro. **in some s.,** hasta cierto punto. **I am out of sorts,** Estoy destemplado. **Nothing of the s.!** ¡Nada de eso!

sorter n oficial de correos, m; clasificador (-ra)

sorting n clasificación, f

sotto voce adv a sovoz, en voz baja

soul n alma, f; espíritu, m; (departed) ánima, f; (being) ser, m; (life) vida, f; (heart) corazón, m. **All Souls' Day,** Día de los Difuntos, m. **He is a good s.!** ¡Es un bendito! **She is a simple s.,** Ella es una alma de Dios. **without seeing a living s.,** sin ver un bicho viviente. **Upon my s.!** ¡Por mi vida! **s. in purgatory,** alma en pena, f. **s.-stirring,** emocionante

soulful a sentimental, emocional; espiritual; romántico

sound n sonido, m; son, m; ruido, m; (strait) estrecho, m. vl sonar; hacer ruido; resonar; (seem) parecer. vt sonar; (the horn, the alarm, musical instrument) tocar; (express) expresar; proclamar; (praise) celebrar; naut hondear; med tentar; (the chest) auscultar; (try to discover) tentar, sondar; (experience) experimentar. **to the s. of,** al son de. **s.-box,** (of a gramophone) diafragma, *m.* **s.-detector,** fonolocalización de aviones, *f.* **s.-film,** película sonora, *f.* **s.-proof,** (of radio studios, etc.) aislado de todo sonido. **s.-track,** guía sonora, banda sonora, *f.* **s.-wave,** onda sonora, *f*

sound *a* sano; (of a person) perspicaz; (reasonable) lógico, razonable; (of a policy, etc.) prudente; (of an argument, etc.) válido; (of an investment) seguro; (solvent) solvente; (good) bueno; (deep) profundo. *adv* profundamente, bien

sounding *n naut* sondeo, *m; pl* **soundings,** sondas, *f pl.* a sonoro. **to take soundings,** sondar, echar la plomada. **s.-board,** tabla de armonía, *f*

soundly *adv* sanamente; juiciosamente, prudentemente; bien; (deeply) profundamente

soup sopa, *f.* **clear s.,** consommé, *m.* **thick s.,** puré, *m.* **to be in the s.,** *inf* estar aviado. **s.-ladle,** cucharón, *m.* **s.-plate,** plato sopero, *m.* **s.-tureen,** sopera, *f*

sour *a* ácido, agrio; (of milk) agrio; (of persons, etc.) agrio, desabrido. *vt* agriar. **to go s.,** volverse agrio. **S. grapes!** ¡Están verdes!

source *n* (of a river, etc.) nacimiento, *m;* fuente, *f;* (of infection) foco, *m.* **to know from a good s.,** saber de buena tinta

south *n* sur, *m;* mediodía, *m.* a del sur. *adv* hacia el sur. **S. African,** a and *n* sudafricano (-na). **S. American,** a and *n* sudamericano (-na). **s.-east,** *n* sudeste, *m.* a del sudeste. *adv* hacia el sudeste. **s.-easter,** viento del sudeste, *m.* **s.-easterly,** a del sudeste; al sudeste. *adv* hacia el sudeste. **s.-eastern,** del sudeste. **s.-s.-east,** *n* sudsudeste, *m.* **s.-s.-west,** sudsudoeste, *m.* **s.-west,** *n* sudoeste, *m.* a del sudoeste. *adv* hacia el sudoeste. **s.-west wind,** viento sudoeste, ábrego, *m.* **s.-westerly,** a del sudoeste. *adv* hacia el sudoeste. **s.-western,** a del sudoeste

South Africa República Sudafricana, *f*

South America América del Sur, *f*

southerly *a* del sur; hacia el sur. **The house has a s. aspect,** La casa está orientada al sur

southern *a* del sur; del mediodía; meridional. **S. Cross,** Cruz, *f,* Crucero, *m.* **s. express,** sudexpreso, *m*

southerner *n* habitante del sur, *m*

southward *a* del sur; al sur. *adv* hacia el sur

souvenir *n* recuerdo, *m*

sovereign *a* soberano. *n* soberano (-na); (coin) soberano, *f*

sovereignty *n* soberanía, *f*

Soviet Union, the la Unión Soviética, *f*

sow *n* cerda, puerca, marrana, *f;* (of a wild boar) jabalina, *f;* (of iron) galápago, *m*

sow *vt* sembrar; esparcir; diseminar

sowing *n* sembradura, siembra, *f.* **s. ma-**

---

chine, sembradera, *f.* **s. time,** tiempo de la siembra, *m*

soya bean *n* soja, *f*

spa *n* balneario, *m;* (spring) manantial mineral, *m,* caldas, *f pl*

space *n* espacio, *m;* (of time) temporada, *f;* intervalo, *m;* (print, mus) espacio, *m. vt* espaciar. **blank s.,** blanco, *m.* **s.-bar,** tecla de espacios, *f,* espaciador, *m*

spacious *a* espacioso; amplio

spade *n* pala, azada, *f;* (cards) espada, *f.* **to call a s. a s.,** llamar al pan pan y al vino vino, llamar a las cosas por su nombre. **s.-work,** trabajo preparatorio, *m,* labor de pala, *f*

spaghetti *n* fideos, macarrones, *m pl*

Spain España, *f*

span *vt* medir a palmos; rodear; medir; (cross) atravesar, cruzar. *n* palmo, *m;* espacio, *m,* duración, *f;* (of a bridge) vano, *m;* (of wing, aer, zool) envergadura, *f;* (distance) distancia, *f.* **single-s. bridge,** puente de vano único. **the brief s. of human life,** la corta duración de la vida humana

spangle *n* lentejuela, *f;* (tinsel) oropel, *m. vt* adornar con lentejuelas; sembrar (de), esparcir (de). **spangled with stars,** sembrado de estrellas

Spaniard *n* español (-la). **a young S.,** un joven español

Spanish a español. *n* (language) español, castellano, *m.* **a S. girl,** una muchacha española. **in S. fashion,** a la española. **S. American,** a and *n* hispanoamericano (-na). **S. broom,** retama de olor, *f.* **S. fly,** cantárida, *f*

Spanish America Hispanoamérica, *f*

spank *vt* pegar con la mano, azotar. *n* azotazo, *m.* **to s. along,** correr rápidamente; (of a horse) galopar

spanking *n* azotamiento, vapuleo, *m*

spanner *n* llave inglesa, llave de tuercas, *f*

spar *n naut* mastel, *m;* *min* espato, *m;* (boxing) boxeo, *m;* (quarrel) disputa, *f. vi* boxear; (argue) disputar

spare *a* (meager) frugal, escaso; (of persons) enjuto, flaco; (available) disponible; (extra) de repuesto. *n* recambio, *m.* **s. part,** pieza de recambio, pieza de repuesto, *f.* **s. room,** cuarto de amigos, *m.* **s. time,** ratos de ocio, *m pl,* tiempo disponible, *m.* **s. tire** *Mexico* llanta de refación, *f.* **s. wheel,** rueda de repuesto, *f*

spare *vt* (expense, etc.) escatimar; ahorrar; (do without) pasarse sin; (give) dar; (a life, etc.) perdonar; (avoid) evitar; dispensar de; (grant) hacer gracia de; (time) dedicar. **I cannot s. her,** No puedo estar sin ella. **They have no money to s.,** No tienen dinero de sobra. **to be sparing of,** ser avaro de

sparingly *adv* frugalmente; escasamente. **to eat s.,** comer con frugalidad

spark n chispa, f; (gallant) pisaverde, m. vi chispear, echar chispas

sparking a chispeante. n emisión de chispas, f. **s.-plug,** bujía de encendido, f

sparkle vi centellear, rutilar, destellar; fig brillar; (of wines) ser espumoso. n centelleo, destello, m; fig brillo, m

sparkling a rutilante, centelleante, reluciente; fig brillante, chispeante; (of wines) espumante

sparse a claro, ralo; esparcido

Spartan a and n espartano (-na)

spasm n espasmo, m; ataque, m; acceso, m

spasmodic a espasmódico; intermitente

spat n (gaiter) polaina de tela, f

spate n crecida, f; fig torrente, m. **in s.,** crecido

spatter vt salpicar; (fig smirch) manchar. vi rociar. n salpicadura, f; rociada, f

spatula n espátula, f

spawn vt and vi desovar; engendrar. n huevas, f pl, freza, f; (offspring) producto, m

speak vi hablar; pronunciar un discurso; (sound) sonar. vt decir; (French, etc.) hablar. **She never spoke to him again,** Nunca volvió a dirigirle la palabra. **roughly speaking,** aproximadamente, más o menos. **Speaking for myself,** En cuanto a mí, Por mi parte. **without speaking,** sin decir nada, sin hablar. **to s. for,** (a person) hablar por. **to s. for itself,** hablar por sí mismo, ser evidente. **to s. one's mind,** decir lo que se piensa. **to s. of,** hablar de. **to s. out,** hablar claro; hablar alto. **to s. up for,** (a person) hablar en favor de (alguien)

speaker n el, m, (f, la) que habla; (public) orador (-ra). **the S.,** el Presidente de la Cámara de los Comunes

speaking a hablante; para hablar; elocuente, expresivo. n habla, f, discurso, m. **They are not on s. terms,** No se hablan. **within s. distance,** al habla. **s.-trumpet,** portavoz, m. **s.-tube,** tubo acústico, m

spear n lanza, f; (javelin) venablo, m; (harpoon) arpón, m. vt herir con lanza, alancear; (fish) arponear. **s.-head,** punta de la lanza, f. **s.-thrust,** lanzada, f

special a especial; particular; extraordinario. n (train) tren extraordinario, m. **s. correspondent,** corresponsal extraordinario, m. **s. friend,** amigo (-ga) del alma, amigo íntimo

specialist n especialista, mf

specialization n especialización, f

specialize vt especializar. vi especializarse

specially adv especialmente; particularmente; sobre todo

species n especie, f; raza, f

specific a específico; explícito. n específico, m. **s. gravity,** peso específico, m, densidad, f

specify vt especificar

specimen n espécimen, m; ejemplo, m; inf tipo, m

specious a especioso. **s. arguments** Lat. Am. abogaderas, abogaderías, fpl

speck n pequeña mancha, f; punto, m; átomo, m; (on fruit) maca, f

speckle vt motear, manchar

spectacle n espectáculo, m; escena, f; pl **spectacles,** gafas, f pl, anteojos, m pl. **s.-case,** cajita para las gafas, f

spectacular a espectacular

spectator n espectador (-ra)

specter n espectro, fantasma, m

spectrum n phys espectro, m

speculate vi especular (sobre, acerca de); com especular (en)

speculative a especulativo

speculator n especulador (-ra)

speech n habla, f; palabra, f; (idiom) lenguaje, m; (language) idioma, m; gram oración, f; (address) discurso, m; disertación, f. **part of s.,** parte de la oración, f. **to make a s.,** pronunciar un discurso. **s.maker,** orador (-ra)

speechless a mudo; sin habla; desconcertado, turbado

speed n prisa, rapidez, f; velocidad, f. vt dar la bienvenida (a); conceder éxito (a); (accelerate) acelerar. vi darse prisa; correr a toda prisa; (of arrows) volar. **at full s.,** a toda prisa; a toda velocidad; a todo correr. **maximum s.,** velocidad máxima, f. **with all s.,** a toda prisa. **s. of impact,** velocidad del choque, f. **s.-boat,** lancha de carrera, f. **s.-limit,** velocidad máxima, f, límite de velocidad, m

speedily adv aprisa, rápidamente; prontamente

speeding n exceso de velocidad, m. **s. up,** aceleración, f

speedometer n cuentakilómetros, m

speedway n autódromo, m, pista de ceniza, f

speedy a rápido; pronto

spell n ensalmo, hechizo, m; encanto, m; (bout) turno, m; (interval) rato, m; temporada, f. vt (a word) deletrear; (mean) significar; (be) ser. **a s. of good weather,** una temporada de buen tiempo. **by spells,** a ratos. **to learn to s.,** aprender la ortografía. **s.-bound,** encantado, fascinado; asombrado

spelling n deletreo, m; ortografía, f. **s.-book,** silabario, m; **s. mistake,** falta de ortografía, f

spelling bee n certamen de deletreo, m

spend vt gastar; (time, etc.) pasar; perder; consumir, agotar. vi gastar, hacer gastos. **to s. lavishly** *Mexico* disparar. **to s. oneself,** agotarse

spendthrift *n* derrochador (-ra), manirroto (-ta). **a** despilfarrado, pródigo

spent *a* agotado, rendido. **The night is far s.,** La noche está avanzada. **s. bullet,** bala fría, *f*

sperm *n biol* esperma, *f*; (whale) cachalote, *m*

spermaceti *n* esperma de ballena, *f*

sphere *n* esfera, *f*. **s. of influence,** zona de influencia, *f*

spice *n* especia, *f*; *fig* sabor, *m*; (trace) dejo, *m*. *vt* especiar. **s. cupboard,** especiero, *m*

spick and span *a* limpio como una patena; (brand-new) flamante; (of persons) muy compuesto

spicy *a* especiado; aromático; *fig* picante

spider *n* araña, *f*. **spider's web,** telaraña, *f*

spigot *n* espiche, *m*

spike *n* punta (de hierro, etc.), *f*; escarpia, *f*; (for boots) clavo, *m*; *bot* espiga, *f*. *vt* clavetear; (a cannon) clavar

spill *vt* derramar. *n* (fall) caída, *f*

spilling *n* derramamiento, derrame, *m*

spin *vt* hilar; (a cocoon) tejer; (a top) bailar; (a ball) tornear; (a coin) lanzar. *vi* hilar; girar, bailar. *n* vuelta, *f*; paseo, *m*. **to send spinning downstairs,** hacer rodar por la escalera (a). **to s. a yarn,** contar un cuento. **to s. out,** prolongar

spinach *n* espinaca, *f*

spinal *a* espinal. **s. anaesthesia,** raquianestesia, *f*. **s. column,** columna vertebral, *f*

spine *n anat* espinazo, *m*, columna vertebral, *f*; *bot* espina, *f*; (of a porcupine, etc.) púa, *f*

spinner *n* hilandero (-ra); máquina de hilar, *f*

spinning *n* hilado, *m*; hilandería, *f*. **s.-machine,** máquina de hilar, *f*. **s.-top,** trompo, *m*, peonza, *f*. **s.-wheel,** rueca, *f*

spinster *n* soltera, *f*. **confirmed s.,** solterona, *f*

spiral *a* espiral; en espiral. *n* espiral, *f*

spire *n* (of a church) aguja, *f*; espira, *f*

spirit *n* espíritu, *m*; alma, *f*; (ghost) aparecido, fantasma, *m*; (outstanding person) ingenio, *m*, inteligencia, *f*; (disposition) ánimo, *m*; (courage) valor, espíritu, *m*; (for a lamp, etc.) alcohol, *m*. **the Holy S.,** El Espíritu Santo. **to be in high spirits,** no caber de contento, saltar de alegría. **to be in low spirits,** estar desalentado, estar deprimido. **to be full of spirits,** ser bullicioso, tener mucha energía. **to keep up one's spirits,** sostener el valor. **to s. away,** quitar secretamente; hacer desaparecer; (kidnap) secuestrar. **s.-level,** nivel de burbuja, *m*. **s.-stove,** cocinilla, *f*

spirited *a* animado, vigoroso; fogoso, animoso, brioso

spiritless *a* sin espíritu, apático; flojo, débil; (depressed) abatido, desalentado; (cowardly) sin valor, cobarde

spiritual *a* espiritual

spirituality *n* espiritualidad, *f*

spirituous *a* espiritoso

spirt *vi*, *vt*, *n*. See **spurt**

spit *n* (for roasting) espetón, asador, *m*; (sand-bank) banco de arena, *m*; (of land) lengua de tierra, *f*; (spittle) saliva, *f*. **the spit of, the spit and image of, the spitting image of,** la imagen viva de, la segunda edición de, *f*. *vt* (skewer) espetar; (saliva, etc.) escupir; (curses, etc.) vomitar. *vi* escupir, expectorar; (of a cat) fufear, decir fu; (sputter) chisporrotear; (rain) lloviznar

spite *n* malevolencia, mala voluntad, hostilidad, *f*; rencor, *m*, ojeriza, *f*. *vt* contrariar, hacer daño (a). **He has a s. against them,** Les tiene rencor. **in s. of,** a pesar de; a despecho de

spiteful *a* rencoroso, malévolo

spitefully *adv* malévolamente; con rencor; por maldad; por despecho

spitfire *n* cascarrabias, *mf*, furia, *f*

spittle *n* saliva, *f*

splash *vt* salpicar (de); manchar (con). *vi* derramarse, esparcirse; chapotear, chapalear. *n* chapoteo, *m*; (of rain, etc.) chapaleteo, *m*; (stain or patch) mancha, *f*. **John was splashing about in the sea,** Juan chapoteaba en el mar. **to make a s.,** *fig* causar una sensación. **s.-board,** alero, *m*

spleen *n anat* bazo, *m*; esplín, *m*

splendid *a* espléndido; magnífico; glorioso; excelente

splendor *n* resplandor, *m*; magnificencia, *f*; (of exploits, etc.) esplendor, brillo, *m*

splice *vt* (ropes, timbers) empalmar; (marry) unir, casar. *n* empalme, *m*

splint *n surg* férula, *f*. **to put in a s.,** entablar

splinter *vt* astillar, hacer astillas. *vi* hacerse astillas

split *vi* henderse; resquebrajarse; (of seams) nacerse; abrirse; dividirse. *vt* hender; partir; dividir; abrir; (the atom) escindir. *n* hendedura, *f*; grieta, *f*; división, *f*; (in fabric) rasgón, *m*; (quarrel) ruptura, *f*. **to s. hairs,** andar en quisquillas, pararse en pelillos, sutilizar. **I have a splitting headache,** Tengo un dolor de cabeza que me trae loco. **to s. one's sides,** reírse a carcajadas, desternillarse de risa. **to s. on a rock,** estrellarse contra una roca. **to s. the difference,** partir la diferencia. **The blow s. his head open,** El golpe le abrió la cabeza. **to s. on,** *inf* delatar, denunciar

splodge *n* mancha, *f*, borrón, *m*

splutter vi chisporrotear; (of a person) balbucir. n chisporroteo, m. **to s. out**, decir tartamudeando

spoil n botín, despojo, m; (of war) trofeo, m. vt estropear; echar a perder; (diminish) mitigar; (a child) mimar; (injure) dañar; (destroy) arruinar, destruir. vi estropearse; echarse a perder. **to be spoiling for a fight**, tener ganas de pelearse. **You have spoilt my fun**, Me has aguado la fiesta. **s.-sport**, aguafiestas, mf

spoilt a (of a child, etc.) mimado, consentido, malacostumbrado

spoke n (of a wheel) rayo, m; (of a ladder) travesaño, peldaño, m; naut cabilla (de la rueda del timón), f

spoken a hablado. **well-s.,** bien hablado; cortés

spokesman n portavoz, m. **to be s.,** llevar la palabra

sponge n esponja, f; (cadger) gorrón (-ona); (cake) bizcocho, m. vt limpiar con esponja. **to s.,** inf vivir de gorra. **s.-holder**, esponjera, f

sponger n gorrón (-ona), vividor, m, sablista, mf

sponging n esponjadura, f; inf sablazo, m

spongy a esponjoso

sponsor n garante, mf; valedor (-ra), patron (-na); (godfather) padrino, m; (godmother) madrina, f, (radio and TV) auspiciador, patrocinador, m

spontaneous a espontáneo. **s. combustion**, combustión espontánea, f

spook n fantasma, espectro, m

spool n (for thread) bobina, f, carrete, m; (in a sewing machine) canilla, f; (of a fishing rod) carrete, m

spoon n cuchara, f. vt sacar con cuchara. vi (slang) besuquearse. **to s.-feed**, dar de comer con cuchara (a); tratar como un niño (a)

spoonful n cucharada, f

spoor n pista, huella de animal, f; rastro, m

sporadic a esporádico

sport n deporte, sport, m; deportismo, m; (jest) broma, f; (game) juego, m; (plaything) juguete, m; (pastime) pasatiempo, m. vi jugar; recrearse, divertirse. vt llevar; ostentar, lucir. **He is a s.,** Es un buen chico. **to make s. of**, burlarse de. **sports car**, coche de deporte, m. **sports ground**, campo de recreo, m. **sports jacket**, chaqueta de deporte, americana, f. **sports shirt**, camisa corta, f

sporting a deportista; caballeroso. **I think there is a s. chance,** Me parece que hay una posibilidad de éxito

sporting goods n artículos de deporte, efectos de deportes, m pl

sportive a juguetón; bromista

sportsman n deportista, m; aficionado al sport, m; flg caballero, señor, m; buen chico, m

sportsmanlike a de deportista; caballeroso

sportsmanship n deportividad, f

spot n mancha, f; pinta, f; (on the face, etc.) peca, f; grano, m; (place) sitio, m; lugar, m; (of liquor) trago, m; (of food) bocado, m; (of rain) gota, f. vt manchar; motear; (recognize) reconocer; (understand) darse cuenta de, comprender. **a tender s.,** flg debilidad, f. **on the s.,** en el acto. **s. ball**, (billiards) pinta, f. **s. cash**, dinero contante, m

spotless a saltando de limpio; sin mancha; inmaculado; puro; virgen

spotlight n luz del proyector, f; proyector, m

spotted a (stained) manchado; (of animals, etc.) con manchas; (of garments, etc.) con pintas

spotty a lleno de manchas; moteado; (pimply) con granos

spouse n esposo, m; esposa, f

spout vi chorrear; inf hablar incesantemente. vt arrojar; vomitar; inf declamar, recitar. n (of a jug, etc.) pico, m; (for water, etc.) tubo, m, cañería, f; canalón, m; (gust) ráfaga, nube, f. **down s.,** tubo de bajada, m

spouting n chorreo, m; inf declamación, f

sprachgefühl n sentido del idioma, m

sprain vt dislocar, torcer. n dislocación, f, esguince, m. **Victoria has sprained her foot**, Victoria se ha torcido el pie

sprat n sardineta, f

sprawl vi recostarse (en); extenderse; (of plants) trepar. **He went sprawling**, Cayó cuan largo era

spray n (branch) ramo, m; (of water, etc.) rocío, m; (of the sea) espuma, f; (mechanical device) pulverizador, m. vt pulverizar; rociar; regar; (the throat) jeringar

spread vt tender; cubrir (de); poner; (stretch out) extender; (open out) desplegar; (of disease, etc.) propagar; diseminar; divulgar; difundir. vi extenderse; propagarse; difundirse; divulgarse; (become general) generalizarse. n extensión, f; expansión, f; propagación, f; divulgación, f; (aer and of birds) envergadura, f. **Carmen s. her hands to the fire**, Carmen extendió las manos al fuego. **The peacock s. its tail**, El pavo real hizo la rueda. **The dove s. its wings**, La paloma desplegó sus alas. **to s. out**, vt extender; desplegar; (scatter) esparcir, vi extenderse. **spread like wildfire**, correr como pólvora en reguero, propagarse como un reguero de pólvora, ser un reguero de pólvora

spreading n (of a disease) propagación, f; (of knowledge, etc.) divulgación, f; expansión, f; extensión, f

spree n juerga, parranda, f; excursión, f. **to go on the s.,** ir de juerga, ir de picos pardos

sprig n ramita, f; (of heather, etc.) espiga, f; (scion) vástago, m

sprightly a vivaracho, despierto; enérgico

spring vi saltar, brincar; (become) hacerse; (seek) buscar; (of plants, water) brotar; (of tears) arrasar, llenar; (from) originarse (en), ser causado (por); inspirarse (en). vt (a mine) volar; (a trap) soltar. **to s. a surprise,** dar una sorpresa. **to s. a surprise on a person,** coger a la imprevista (a). **to s. at a person,** precipitarse sobre. **to s. to one's feet,** ponerse de pie de un salto. **to s. back,** saltar hacia atrás; recular; volver a su sitio. **to s. open,** abrirse súbitamente. **to s. up,** (of plants) brotar, crecer; (of difficulties, etc.) surgir, asomarse

spring n (jump) salto, brinco, m; (of water) fuente, f, manantial, m; (season) primavera, f; (of a watch, etc.) resorte, m; (of a mattress, etc.) muelle, m. a primaveral. vi saltar, brincar. **at one s.,** en un salto. **to give a s.,** dar un salto. **s.-board,** trampolín, m. **s.-mattress,** colchón de muelles, m. **s.-tide,** marea viva, f

sprinkle vt esparcir; salpicar; rociar

sprinkling n salpicadura, f; rociadura, f; pequeño número, m. **a s. of snow,** una nevada ligera

sprint vi sprintar. n sprint, m

sprout vi brotar, despuntar, retoñar, tallecer; germinar. vt salir. n brote, retoño, pimpollo, m; germen, m. **Brussels sprouts,** coles de Bruselas, f pl

spruce a peripuesto, muy aseado, pulido; elegante, n bot pícea, f. **to s. oneself up,** arreglarse, ponerse elegante

spry a activo, ágil

spur n espuela, f; aguijada, f; (of a bird) espolón, m; bot espuela, f; (of a mountain range) espolón, estribo, m; fig estímulo, m. vt espolear, picar con la espuela; calzarse las espuelas; fig estimular, incitar, Lat. Am. espuelar. **on the s. of the moment,** bajo el impulso del momento

spurious a espurio; falso

spurn vt rechazar; tratar con desprecio; menospreciar

spurt vi (gush) chorrear, borbotar; brotar, surgir; (in racing, etc.) hacer un esfuerzo supremo. vt hacer chorrear; lanzar. n (jet) chorro, m; esfuerzo supremo, m

sputter vi chisporrotear; crepitar; (of a pen) escupir; (of a person) balbucir

sputum n esputo, m

spy vt observar, discernir. vi espiar, ser espía. n espía, mf. **to spy out the land,** explorar el terreno. **to spy upon, espiar;** seguir los pasos (a). **spy-glass,** catalejo, m

squabble n disputa, f; riña, f. vi pelearse; disputar

squabbling n riñas, querellas, f pl; disputas, f pl

squad n escuadra, f; pelotón, m

squadron n mil escuadrón, m; nav escuadra, f; aer escuadrilla, f; (of persons) pelotón, m. **s.-leader,** comandante, m

squalid a escuálido; (of quarrels, etc.) sórdido, mezquino

squall vi berrear; chillar. n berrido, m; chillido, m; (storm) chubasco, turbión, m; (storm) chubasco, turbión, m; fig tormenta, tempestad, f

squalor n escualidez, f; sordidez, mezquindad, f

squander vt derrochar, tirar, desperdiciar; (time, etc.) malgastar

square n math cuadrado, m; rectángulo, m; (of a chessboard) escaque, m; (of a draughtboard and of graph paper) casilla, f; (in a town) plaza, f; (of troops) cuadro, m, a cuadrado; justo; igual; (honest) honrado, formal; (unambiguous) redondo, categórico; math cuadrado. **She wore a silk s. on her head,** Llevaba un pañuelo de seda en la cabeza. **five s. feet,** cinco pies cuadrados. **nine feet s.,** nueve pies en cuadro. **on the s.,** honradamente. **a s. dance,** contradanza, f. **a s. meal,** una buena comida. **s. dealing,** trato limpio, m. **The account is s.,** La cuenta está justa. **to get s. with,** desquitarse (de), vengarse de. **s. measure,** medida de superficie, f. **s. root,** raíz cuadrada, f. **s.-shouldered,** de hombros cuadrados

square vt cuadrar; carp escuadrar; (arrange) arreglar; (bribe) sobornar; (reconcile) acomodar; math cuadrar. vi conformarse (con), cuadrar (con). **to s. the circle,** cuadrar el círculo. **to s. one's shoulders,** enderezarse. **to s. accounts with,** saldar cuentas con. **to s. up to,** (a person) avanzar belicosamente hacia

squarely adv en cuadro; directamente; sin ambigüedades, rotundamente; (honestly) de buena fe, honradamente

squash vt aplastar. vi aplastarse; apretarse. n aplastamiento, m; (of fruit, etc.) pulpa, f; (of people) agolpamiento, m; muchedumbre, f; (drink) refresco (de limón, etc.), m, (sport) frontón con raqueta, m

squat vi acuclillarse, agacharse, agazaparse ponerse en cuclillas; estar en cuclillas; (on land, etc.) apropiarse sin derecho. a rechoncho

squatter n intruso (-sa); colono usurpador, m

squawk vi graznar; lanzar gritos agudos. n graznido, m; grito agudo, m

squeak vi (of carts, etc.) chirriar, rechinar; (of shoes) crujir; (of persons, mice, etc.) chillar; (slang) cantar. n chirrido, crujido, m; chillido, m. **to have a narrow s.,** escapar por un pelo

squeal vi lanzar gritos agudos, chillar; (complain) quejarse; (slang) cantar. n grito agudo, chillido, m

squeamish a que se marea fácilmente; mareado; (nauseated) asqueado; delicado; remilgado

squeeze vt apretar; estrujar; (fruit) exprimir; (extort) arrancar; (money from) sangrar. n (of the hand, etc.) apretón, m; estrujón, m; (of fruit juice) algunas gotas (de). **It was a tight s. in the car,** Íbamos muy apretados en el coche. **He was in a tight s.,** Se encontraba en un aprieto. **to s. one's way through the crowd,** abrirse camino a codazos por la muchedumbre. **to s. in,** vt hacer sitio para. vi introducirse con dificultad (en)

squelch vi gorgotear, chapotear. vt aplastar

squib n (firework) rapapiés, buscapiés, m; (lampoon) pasquinada, f

squid n calamar, m

squint n estrabismo, m; mirada furtiva, f; inf vistazo, m, mirada, f. vi ser bizco; bizcar. **to s. at,** mirar de soslayo. **s.-eyed,** bizco. **to be s.-eyed,** mirar contra el gobierno

squire n escudero, m; hacendado, m. vt escoltar, acompañar

squirm vi retorcerse; (with embarrassment) no saber dónde meterse. n retorcimiento, m. **to s. along the ground,** arrastrarse por el suelo

squirrel n ardilla, f

squirt vt (liquids) lanzar. vi chorrear, salir a chorros. n chorro, m; (syringe) jeringa, f

stab vt apuñalar, dar de puñaladas (a); herir. n puñalada, f; herida, f; (of pain, and fig) pinchazo, m. **a s. in the back,** una puñalada por la espalda

stability n estabilidad, f; solidez, firmeza, f

stabilize vt estabilizar

stable a estable; fijo, firme. n cuadra, caballeriza, f; (for cows, etc.) establo, m. vt poner en la cuadra; alojar. **s.-boy,** mozo de cuadra, m

stack n (of hay) niara, f, almiar, m; (heap) montón, m; (of rifles) pabellón, m; (of a chimney) cañón, m. vt agr hacinar; amontonar; mil poner (las armas) en pabellón

stacked a (woman) abultada de pechera

stadium n estadio, m

staff n vara, f; (bishop's, and fig) báculo, m; (pilgrim's) bordón, m; (pole) palo, m; (flagstaff) asta, f; (of an office, etc.) personal, m; (editorial) redacción, f; (corps) cuerpo, m; mil plana mayor, f, estado mayor, m; mus pentagrama, m. vt proveer de personal. **general s.,** estado mayor general, m. **s. officer,** mil oficial de estado mayor, m

stag n ciervo, m. **s.-beetle,** ciervo volante, m. **s.-hunting,** caza del ciervo, f

stage n (for workmen) andamio, m; (of a microscope) portaobjetos, m; theat escena, f, tablas, f pl; teatro, m; (of development, etc.) etapa, f; fase, f. vt theat escenificar, poner en escena; theat representar, (a demonstration, etc.) arreglar. **by easy stages,** poco a poco; (of a journey) a pequeñas etapas. **to come on the s.,** salir a la escena. **to go on the s.,** hacerse actor (actriz), dedicarse al teatro: **s. carpenter,** tramoyista, m. **s.-coach,** diligencia, f. **s.-craft,** arte de escribir para el teatro, f; arte escénica, f. **s.-direction,** acotación, f. **s.-door,** entrada de los artistas, f. **s.-effect,** efecto escénico, m. **s.-fright,** miedo al público, m. **s.-hand,** tramoyista, sacasillas, metesillas y sacamuertos, m. **s. manager,** director de escena, m. **s.-whisper,** aparte, m

stagger vi tambalear; andar haciendo eses; (hesitate) titubear, vacilar. vt desconcertar. n titubeo, tambaleo, m; aer decalaje, m. **staggered working hours,** horas de trabajo escalonadas, f pl

staggering a tambaleante; (surprising) asombroso, sorprendente; (dreadful) espantoso. **a s. blow,** un golpe que derriba

stagnant a estancado; paralizado. **to be s.,** estar estancado. **s. water,** agua estancada, f

stagnate vi estancarse; estar estancado; (of persons) vegetar

stagnation n (of water) estancación, f; estagnación, f; parálisis, f

staid a serio, formal, juicioso

stain vt manchar; (dye) teñir. n mancha, f; colorante, m. **without a s.,** fig sin mancha. **stained glass,** vidrio de color, m. **s.-remover,** quitamanchas, m

stainless a sin mancha; inmaculado, puro

stair n escalón, peldaño, m; escalera, f; pl **stairs,** escalera, f. **a flight of stairs,** una escalera; un tramo de escaleras. **below stairs,** escalera abajo. **s.-carpet,** alfombra de escalera, f. **s.-rod,** varilla para alfombra de escalera, f

staircase n escalera, f. **spiral s.,** escalera de caracol, f

stake n estaca, f; (for plants) rodrigón, m; (gaming) envite, m, apuesta, f; (in an undertaking) interés, m; pl **stakes,** (prize) premio, m; (race) carrera, f. vt estacar; (plants) rodrigar; (bet) jugar. **at s.,** en juego; en peligro. **to be burnt at the s.,** morir en la hoguera. **to s. one's all,** jugarse el todo por el todo. **to s. a claim,** hacer una reclamación. **to s. out,** jalonar

stale a no fresco; (of bread, etc.) duro, seco; (of air) viciado; viejo; pasado de moda; (tired) cansado

stalemate n (chess, checkers) tablas, f pl; fig punto muerto, m. **to reach a s.,** llegar a un punto muerto

stalk n bot tallo, m; bot pedúnculo, m; (of a glass) pie, m. vi andar majestuosamente; fig rondar. vt (game) cazar al acecho; (a person) seguir los pasos a

stall n (in a stable) puesto (individual), m; (stable) establo, m; (choir) silla de coro, f; (in a fair, etc.) barraca, f, puesto, m; theat butaca, f; (finger-stall) dedal, m. vt (an engine) cortar accidentalmente. vi aut pararse de pronto; aer perder velocidad; (of a cart, etc.) atascarse. **pit s.**, theat butaca de platea, f

stallion n semental, m

stalwart a robusto, fornido; leal; valiente

stamina n resistencia, f

stammer vi tartamudear; (hesitate in speaking) titubear, balbucir. n tartamudez, f; titubeo, balbuceo, m

stamp vt estampar; imprimir; (documents) timbrar; pegar el sello de correo (a); (characterize) sellar; (fig engrave) grabar; (coins) acuñar; (press) apisonar; (with the foot) golpear con los pies, patear; (in dancing) zapatear. n (with the foot) patada, f, golpe con los pies, m; (mark, etc.) marca, f; (rubber, etc.) estampilla, f; matasellos, m; cuño, m; (for documents) póliza, f; timbre, m; (for letters) sello, m; Mexico timbre m, elsewhere in Lat. Am. estampilla, f, (machine) punzón, m; mano de mortero, f; (fig sign) sello, m; (kind) temple, m, clase, f. The **events of that day are stamped on my memory,** Los acontecimientos de aquel día están grabados en mi memoria. **to s. out,** (a fire, etc.) extinguir, apagar; (resistance, etc.) vencer; destruir. **postage-s.,** sello de correos, m. **s.-album,** álbum de sellos, m. **s.-duty,** impuesto del timbre, m. **s.-machine,** expendedor automático de sellos de correo, m

stampede n fuga precipitada, f; pánico, m. vi huir precipitadamente; (of animals) salir de estampía; huir en desorden. vt hacer perder la cabeza (a); sembrar el pánico entre

stance n posición de los pies, f; postura, f

stanch vt restañar

stand vi estar de pie; ponerse de pie, incorporarse; estar; hallarse; sostenerse; ser; ponerse; (halt) parar; (remain) permanecer, quedar. vt poner; (endure) resistir; tolerar; sufrir; (entertain) convidar. **S.!** ¡Alto! **as things s.,** tal como están las cosas. **I cannot s. any more,** No puedo más. **I cannot s. him,** No le puedo ver. **Nothing stands between them and ruin,** No hay nada entre ellos y la ruina. **I stood him a drink,** Le convidé a un trago. **How do we s.?** ¿Cómo estamos? **It stands to reason that . . . ,** Es lógico que . . . **Edward stands six feet,** Eduardo tiene seis pies de altura. **to s. accused of,** ser acusado de. **to s. godfather** (or **godmother**) **to,** sacar de pila

(a). **to s. in need (of),** necesitar, tener necesidad (de). **to s. on end,** (of hair) ponerse de punta, despeluzarse, **to s. one in good stead,** ser útil, ser ventajoso. **to s. one's ground,** no ceder, tenerse fuerte. **to s. to attention,** cuadrarse, permanecer en posición de firmes. **to s. well with,** tener buenas relaciones con, ser estimado de. **to s. aside,** tenerse a un lado; apartarse; (in favor of someone) retirarse. **to s. back,** quedarse atrás; recular, retroceder. **to s. by,** estar de pie cerca de; estar al lado de; estar presente (sin intervenir); ser espectador; estar preparado; (one's friends) ayudar, proteger; (a promise, etc.) atenerse (a); ser fiel (a); (of a ship) mantenerse listo. **s.-by,** n recurso, m. **to s. for,** representar; simbolizar; (mean) significar; (Parliament, etc.) presentarse como candidato; (put up with) tolerar, sufrir. **to s. in,** colaborar. **to s. in with,** estar de acuerdo con, ser partidario de; compartir. **to s. off,** mantenerse a distancia. **to s. out,** (in relief, and fig. of persons) destacarse; (be firm) resistir, mantenerse firme; naut gobernar más afuera. **S. out of the way!** ¡Quítate del medio! **to s. over,** (be postponed) quedar aplazado. **to s. up,** estar de pie; ponerse de pie, incorporarse; tenerse derecho. **to s. up against,** resistir; oponerse a. **to s. up for,** defender; volverpor. **to s. up to,** hacer cara a

stand n puesto, m; posición, actitud, f; (for taxis, etc.) punto, m; (in a market, etc.) puesto, m; sport tribuna, f; (for a band) quiosco, m; (of a dish, etc.) pie, m; mech sostén, m; (opposition) resistencia, oposición, f. **to make a s. against,** oponerse resueltamente (a); ofrecer resistencia (a). **to take one's s.,** fundarse (en), apoyarse (en). **to take up one's s. by the fire,** ponerse cerca del fuego

standard n (flag) estandarte, m, bandera, f; (for gold, weights, etc.) marco, m; norma, f; convención, regla, f; (of a lamp) pie, m; (pole) poste, m; columna, f; (level) nivel, m. a corriente; normal; típico; clásico. **It is a s. type,** Es un tipo corriente. **gold s.,** patrón de oro, m. **s. author,** autor clásico, m. **s. formula,** fórmula clásica, f. **s. of living,** nivel de vida, m. **s.-bearer,** abanderado, m. **s.-lamp,** lámpara vertical, f

standardization n (of armaments, etc.) unificación de tipos, f; (of dyestuffs, medicinals, etc.) control, m, estandardización, f

standardize vt hacer uniforme; controlar

standing a de pie, derecho; permanente, fijo; constante. n posición, f; reputación, f; importancia, f; antigüedad, f. **It is a quarrel of long s.,** Es una riña antigua. **s. committee,** comisión permanente, f. **s. room,** sitio para estar de pie, m. **s. water,** agua estancada, f. **standoffish,** frío, etiquetero; altanero. **stand-offish-**

ness, frialdad, *f*; altanería, *f*. **standpoint,** punto de vista, *m*

standstill *n* parada, *f*; pausa, *f*. **at a s.,** parado; (of industry) paralizado

stanza *n* estrofa, estancia, *f*

staple *n* (fastener) grapa, *f*; (of wool, etc.) hebra, fibra, *f*; producto principal (de un país), *m*; (raw material) materia prima, *f*; a principal; más importante; corriente

stapler, (device) cosepapeles, engrapador, *m*, atrochadora (Argentina), *f*

star *n* (all meanings) estrella, *f*; (asterisk) asterisco, *m*. *vt* estrellar, sembrar de estrellas; marcar con asterisco. *vi* (theat cinema) presentar como estrella, ser estrella. **stars and stripes,** las barras y las estrellas. **to be born under a lucky s.,** tener estrella. **to see stars,** ver estrellas. **s.-gazing,** observación de estrellas, *f*; ensimismamiento, *m*. **s.-spangled,** estrellado, tachonado de estrellas, sembrado de estrellas. **s.-turn,** gran atracción, *f*

starboard *n* naut estribor, *m*

starch *n* almidón, *m*, las harinas, *f pl*, *vt* almidonar

stare *vi* mirar fijamente; abrir mucho los ojos. *n* mirada fija, *f*. **stony s.,** mirada dura, *f*. **to s. at,** (a person) clavar la mirada en; mirar de hito en hito (a). **The explanation stares one in the face,** La explicación salta a la vista (o está evidente). **to s. into space,** mirar las telarañas. **to s. out of countenance,** avergonzar con la mirada

stark *a* rígido; *poet* poderoso; absoluto. **s. staring mad,** loco de atar. **s.-naked,** en cueros vivos, en pelota

start *vi* estremecerse, asustarse; saltar; (set out) salir; ponerse en camino; (of a train, a race) arrancar; ponerse en marcha; *aer* despegar; (begin) empezar; (of timbers) combarse. *vt* empezar; (a car, etc.) poner en marcha; (a race) dar la señal de partida; (a hare, etc.) levantar; (cause) provocar, causar; (a discussion, etc.) abrir; iniciar. *n* (fright) susto, *m*; (setting out) partida, salida, *f*; (beginning) principio, comienzo, *m*; (starting-point of a race) arrancadero, *m*; *aer* despegue, *m*; (advantage) ventaja, *f*. **at the s.,** al principio. **for a s.,** para empezar. **from s. to finish,** desde el principio hasta el fin. **She started to cry,** Se puso a llorar. **He has started his journey to Canada,** Ha empezado su viaje al Canadá. **I started up the engine,** Puse el motor en marcha. **to get a s.,** asustarse; tomar la delantera. **to give** (a person) **a s.,** asustar, dar un susto (a); dar la ventaja (a). **to give** (a person) **a s. in life,** ayudar a alguien a situarse en la vida. **to make a fresh s. (in life),** hacer vida nueva, empezar la vida de nuevo. **to s. after,** lanzarse en busca de; salir tras. **to s. back,** retroceder; emprender el viaje de regreso; marcharse. **to s. off,** salir, partir; ponerse en camino.

to s. up, *vi* incorporarse bruscamente, ponerse de pie de un salto; (appear) surgir, aparecer. *vt* (an engine) poner en marcha

starter *n* iniciador (-ra); (for a race) starter, juez de salida, *m*; (competitor in a race) corredor, *m*; (of a car, etc.) arranque, *m*

starting *n* (setting out) salida, partida, *f*; (beginning) principio, *m*; (fear) estremecimiento, *m*; susto, *m*. **s.-gear,** palanca de arranque, *f*. **s.-handle,** manivela de arranque, *f*. **s.-point,** punto de partida, *m*; *fig* arrancadero, punto de arranque, *m*. **s.-post,** puesto de salida, *m*

startle *vt* asustar, sobresaltar, alarmar. **The news startled him out of his indifference,** Las noticias le hicieron salir de su indiferencia

startling *a* alarmante; (of dress, etc.) exagerado; (of colors) chillón

starvation *n* hambre, *f*; *med* inanición, *f*. **s. diet,** régimen de hambre, *m*. **s. wage,** ración de hambre, *f*

starve *vi* morir de hambre; pasar hambre, no tener bastante que comer; no comer. *vt* matar de hambre; privar de alimentos (a). **I am simply starving,** Tengo una hambre canina, Me muero de hambre. **to s. with cold,** *vi* morir de frío. *vt* matar de frío

starved *a* muerto de hambre, hambriento. **s. of affection,** hambriento de cariño

state *n* estado, *m*; condición, *f*; (anxiety) agitación, ansiedad, *f*; (social) rango, *m*; (pomp) magnificencia, pompa, *f*; (government, etc.) Estado, *m*; nación, *f*. a de Estado; de gala, de ceremonia. **the married s.,** el estado matrimonial. **s. of war,** estado de guerra. **in s.,** con gran pompa. **to lie in s.,** (of a body) estar expuesto. **s. apartments,** habitaciones de gala, *f pl*. **s. banquet,** comida de gala, *f*. **s. coach,** coche de gala, *m*. **s. control,** control por el Estado, *m*. **S. Department,** Ministerio de Estado, *m*. **s. education,** instrucción pública, *f*. **State of the Union message,** Mensaje al Congreso, *m*. **s. papers,** documentos de Estado, *m pl*

state *vt* decir, afirmar (que); (one's case, etc.) exponer; explicar; *math* proponer

statecraft *n* arte de gobernar, *m*

stated *a* arreglado, indicado; fijo. **the s. date,** la fecha indicada. **at s. intervals,** a intervalos fijos

statehood *n* estadidad, *f*

stately *a* majestuoso; imponente; noble; digno

statement *n* afirmación, declaración, *f*; resumen, *m*; exposición, *f*; *law* deposición, *f*; *com* estado de cuenta, *m*. **to make a s.,** hacer una declaración

stateroom n sala de recepción, f; (on a ship) camarote, m

statesman n hombre de estado, m

static a estático

station n (place) puesto, sitio, m; (rw and ecc) estación, f; (social) posición social, f; naut apostadero, m; surv punto de marca, m. vt estacionar, colocar, poner. **to s. oneself**, colocarse. **Stations of the Cross**, Estaciones, f pl. **s.-master**, jefe de la estación, m

stationary a estacionario; inmóvil; ast estacional

stationer n papelero (-ra). **stationer's shop**, papelería, f

stationery n papelería, f, efectos de escritorio, m pl; papel de escribir, m

station wagon n pisicorre, coche camioneta, coche rural, m

statistical a estadístico

statistician n estadista, m

statistics n estadística, f

statue n estatua, f; imagen, f

statuesque a escultural

statuette n figurilla, f

stature n estatura, f; (moral, etc.) valor, m

status n (law etc.) estado, m; posición, f; rango, m. **What is his s. as a physicist?** ¿Cómo se le considera entre los físicos? **social s.**, posición social, f; rango social, m

statute n ley, f; acto legislativo, m; estatuto, m; regla, f. **s. book**, código legal, m

statutory a establecido; reglamentario; estatutario

staunch a leal, fiel; firme, constante. vt restañar

stave n (of a barrel, etc.) duela, f; (of a ladder) peldaño, m; (stanza) estrofa, f; mus pentagrama, m. **to s. in**, abrir boquete en; romper a golpes; quebrar. **to s. off**, apartar, alejar; (delay) aplazar, diferir; (avoid) evitar; (thirst, etc.) dominar

stay vt detener; (a judgment, etc.) suspender. vi permanecer; quedarse; detenerse; (of weather, etc.) durar; (lodge) hospedarse, vivir. **to come to s.**, venir a ser permanente. **to s. a person's hand**, detenerle a fulano el brazo. **to s. at home**, quedarse en casa. **s.-at-home**, a casero. n persona casera, f. **to s. the course**, terminar la carrera. **S.! Say no more!** ¡Calle! ¡No diga más! **to s. away**, ausentarse. **to s. up**, no acostarse; velar. **to s. with**, quedarse con; alojarse con; quedarse en casa de, vivir con

stay n estancia, permanencia, f; residencia, f; (restraint) freno, m; law suspensión, f; (endurance) aguante, m, resistencia, f; naut estay, m; (prop) puntal, m; fig apoyo, soporte, m; pl **stays**, corsé, m

stead n lugar, m. **in the s. of**, en el lugar de, como substituto de. **It has stood me in good s.**, Me ha sido muy útil

steadfast a fijo; constante; firme; tenaz. **s. gaze**, mirada fija, f

steadily adv firmemente; (without stopping) sin parar; continuamente; (assiduously) diligentemente; (uniformly) uniformemente. **Prices have gone up s.**, Los precios no han dejado de subir. **He looked at it s.**, Lo miraba sin pestañear (or fijamente)

steady a firme; seguro; fijo; constante; uniforme; continuo; estacionario; (of persons) serio, formal, juicioso; (of workers) diligente, asiduo. vt afirmar; (persons) hacer más serio (a); (nerves, etc.) calmar, fortificar. **a s. job**, un empleo seguro. **S.! ¡Calma! ¡Seguro! He steadied himself against the table**, Se apoyó en la mesa

steak n tajada, f; biftec, Argentina bife, m

steal vt robar, hurtar; tomar. vi robar, ser ladrón; (glide) deslizarse; (overwhelm) dominar, ganar insensiblemente (a). **to s. a kiss**, robar un beso. **to s. a look at**, mirar de soslayo (or de lado). **to s. away**, escurrirse, escabullirse; marcharse a hurtadillas. **to s. in**, deslizarse en, colarse en

stealthy a furtivo; cauteloso

steam n vapor, m. a. de vapor. vi echar vapor. vt cul cocer al vapor; (clothes) mojar; (windows, etc.) empañar. **to have the s. up**, estar bajo presión. **The windows are steamed**, Los cristales están empañados. **s.-boiler**, caldera de vapor, f. **s.-engine**, máquina de vapor, f. **s.-hammer**, maza de fragua, f. **s.-heat**, calefacción por vapor, f. **s.-roller**, lit apisonadora, fig fuerza arrolladora, f

steamship n buque de vapor, piróscafo, m

steel n (metal, and poet sword) acero, m; (for sharpening) afilón, m. a de acero; acerado. vt acerar; fig endurecer. **to be made of s.**, fig ser de bronce. **He cannot s. himself to do it**, No puede persuadirse a hacerlo. **to s. one's heart**, hacerse duro de corazón. **cold s.**, arma blanca, f. **stainless s.**, acero inoxidable, m. **s.-engraving**, grabado en acero, m

steel mill n fábrica de acero, f

steep a acantilado, escarpado; precipitoso; (of stairs, etc.) empinado; (of price) exorbitante. vt (soak) remojar, empapar; fig absorber; (in a subject) empaparse (en). n remojo, m. **It's a bit s.!** inf ¡Es un poco demasiado!

steeple n campanario, m, torre, f; aguja, f

steer vt naut gobernar; (a car, etc.) conducir; fig guiar, conducir. vi naut timonear; naut navegar; aut conducir. n zool novillo, m. **to s. clear of**, evitar. **to s. one's way through the crowd**, abrirse paso entre la muchedumbre

steerage n gobierno, m; (stern) popa, f;

(quarters) entrepuente, *m.* **to go s.**, viajar en tercera clase

steering *n naut* gobierno, *m*; (tiller, etc.) gobernalle, timón, *m*; (of a vehicle) conducción, *f.* **s.-column**, barra de dirección, *f.* **s.-wheel**, *aut* volante de dirección, *m*; *naut* rueda del timón, *f*

stem *n* (of a tree) tronco, *m*; (of a plant) tallo, *m*; (of a glass, etc.) pie, *m*; (*mus* of a note) rabo, *m*; (of a pipe) tubo, *m*; (of a word) radical, *m. vt* (check) contener; (the tide) ir contra; (the current) vencer; (dam) estancar. **from s. to stern**, de proa a popa

stench *n* tufo, hedor, *m*, hediondez, *Lat. Am. also* fortaleza, *f*

stencil *n* patrón para estarcir, *m*; estarcido, *m. vt* estarcir

stenography *n* estenografía, taquigrafía, *f*

step *n* paso, *m*; (footprint) huella, *f*; (measure) medida, *f*; (of a stair, etc.) escalón, peldaño, *m*, grada, *f*; (of a ladder) peldaño, *m*; (of vehicles) estribo, *m*; (grade) escalón, *m*; *mus* intervalo, *m.* **at every s.**, a cada paso. **flight of steps**, escalera, *f*; (before a building, etc.) escalinata, *f.* **in steps**, en escalones. **to bend one's steps towards**, dirigirse hacia. **to keep in s.**, llevar el paso. **to take a s.**, dar un paso. **to take steps**, tomar medidas. **s. by s.**, paso a paso; poco a poco. **s.-dance**, baile típico, *m.* **s.-ladder**, escalera de tijera, *f*

step *vi* dar un paso; pisar; andar. **Please s. in!** Sírvase de entrar. **Will you s. this way, please?** ¡Haga el favor de venir por aquí! **to s. aside**, ponerse a un lado; desviarse; *fig* retirarse (en favor de). **to s. in**, entrar; intervenir (en); (meddle) entrometerse. **He stepped into the train**, Subió al tren. **to s. on**, pisar. **to s. on board**, *naut* ir a bordo. **to s. out**, salir; (from a vehicle) bajar; (a dance) bailar. **He stepped out a moment ago**, Salió hace un instante

stepbrother *n* hermanastro, medio hermano, *m*

stepchild *n* hijastro (-ra)

stepdaughter *n* hijastra, *f*

stepfather *n* padrastro, *m*

stepmother *n* madrastra, *f*

steppingstone *n* pasadera, *f*; *fig* escabel, escalón, *m*

stepsister *n* hermanastra, media hermana, *f*

stepson *n* hijastro, *m*

stereotype *n* estereotipia, *f*, clisé, *m*, *vt* (*print* and *fig*) estereotipar

sterile *a* estéril; árido

sterility *n* esterilidad, *f*; aridez, *f*

sterilize *vt* esterilizar

sterling *a* esterlina *f*; *fig* genuino. **pound s.**, libra esterlina, *f*

stern *a* severo, austero; duro. *n naut* popa, *f*

stevedore *n* estibador, *m*

stew *vt* guisar a la cazuela, estofar; (mutton, etc.) hervir; (fruit) cocer. *n* estofado, *m*; *inf* agitación, *f.* **to be in a s.**, *inf* sudar la gota gorda. **stewed fruit**, compota de frutas, *f.* **s.-pot**, cazuela, olla, *f*, puchero, *m*

steward *n* administrador, *m*; mayordomo, *m*; (provision) despensero, *m*; *naut* camarero, *m*

stewardess *n naut* camarera, *f*

stick *vt* clavar (en), hundir (en); (put) poner; sacar; (stamps, etc.) pegar; fijar; (endure) resistir; tolerar. *vi* clavarse, hundirse; estar clavado; pegarse; (remain) quedar; (in the mud, etc.) atascarse, embarrancarse, (on a reef) encallarse; (in the throat, etc.) atravesarse; (stop) detenerse. **It sticks in my throat**, *inf* No lo puedo tragar. **Friends always s. together**, Los amigos no se abandonan. **The nickname stuck to him**, El apodo se le quedó. **to s. at**, persistir en; desistir (ante); pararse (ante); tener escrúpulos sobre. **to s. at nothing**, no tener escrúpulos. **He stuck at his work**, Siguió trabajando. **to s. down**, pegar. **to s. one's nose into other people's business** *Mexico* entrucharse. **to s. out**, *vi* proyectar; sobresalir. *vt* (one's chest) inflar; (one's tongue) sacar. **His ears s. out**, Tiene las orejas salientes. **to s. to**, (one's job) no dejar; (one's plans) adherirse (a); (one's principles) ser fiel (a); (one's friends) no abandonar; (one's word, etc.) cumplir; atenerse a. **to s. up**, *vi* (of hair) erizarse, ponerse de punta; salirse. *vt* clavar; (a notice) fijar. **to s. up for**, (a person) defender

stick *n* estaca, *f*; (for the fire) leña, *f*; (walking-s.) bastón, *m*; (of office) vara, *f*; (of sealing-wax, etc.) barra, *f*; palo, *m*; (baton) batuta, *f*; (of celery) tallo, *m.* **in a cleft s.**, entre la espada y la pared. **to give** (a person) **the s.**, dar palo (a)

stickler *n* rigorista, *mf.* **to be a s. for etiquette**, ser etiquetero

sticky *a* pegajoso, viscoso; *fig* difícil

stiff *a* rígido; inflexible; tieso; (of paste, etc.) espeso; (of manner) distante; (of a bow, etc.) frío; (of a person) almidonado, etiquetero; severo; (of examinations, etc.) difícil; (strong) fuerte; (of price, etc.) alto, exorbitante; (of a shirt front, etc.) duro. **s. with cold**, aterido de frío. **s. neck**, torticolis, *m.* **s.-necked**, terco, obstinaz

stiffen *vt* reforzar; atiesar; (paste, etc.) hacer más espeso; (*fig* strengthen) robustecer; (make more obstinate) hacer más tenaz. *vi* atiesarse; endurecerse; (straighten oneself) enderezarse; (of manner) volverse menos cordial; (become firmer) robustecerse; (become more obstinate) hacerse más tenaz. **The breeze stiffened**, Refrescó el viento

stifle *vt* ahogar, sofocar; apagar; suprimir

stigma *n* estigma, *m*

stile *n* (nearest equivalent) portilla con escalones, *f*

still *a* tranquilo; inmóvil; quedo; silencioso; (of wine) no espumoso. *n* silencio, *m*. **in the s. of the night,** en el silencio de la noche. **Keep s.!** ¡Estate quieto! **to keep s.,** quedarse inmóvil, no moverse. **s.-birth,** nacimiento de un niño muerto, *m.* **s.-born,** nacido muerto. **s. life,** *art* bodegón, *m*, naturaleza muerta, *f*

still *vt* hacer callar, acallar; calmar, tranquilizar; apaciguar; (pain) aliviar

still *adv* todavía, aún; (nevertheless) sin embargo, no obstante; (always) siempre. **I think she s. visits them every week,** Me parece que sigue visitándoles cada semana. **s. and all,** con todo y eso. **s. more,** aún más. **s. to be paid** *Lat. Am.* impago

still *n* alambique, *m.* **salt water s.,** adrazo, *m*

stillness *n* quietud, tranquilidad, *f*; silencio, *m.* **in the s. of the night,** en el silencio de la noche

stilted *a* ampuloso, campanudo, hinchado

stimulant *a* and *n* estimulante, *m*

stimulate *vt* estimular; incitar (a), excitar (a)

stimulating *a* estimulante; (encouraging) alentador; (inspiring) sugestivo, inspirador

stimulation *n* excitación, *f*; (stimulus) estímulo, *m*

stimulus *n* estímulo, *m*; *med* estimulante, *m*; (incentive) impulso, incentivo, *m*; acicate, aguijón, *m*

sting *vt* picar, pinchar; (of snakes, etc.) morder; (of hot dishes) resquemar; (of hail, etc.) azotar; (pain) atormentar; (provoke) provocar a, incitar (a). *n* (zool organ) aguijón, *m*; *bot* púa, *f*; (of a scorpion) uña, *f*; (of a serpent) colmillo, *m*; (pain and wound) pinchazo, *m*; (serpent's) mordedura, *f*; (stimulus) acicate, estímulo, *m*; (torment) tormento, dolor, *m*

stingy *a* tacaño, avaro, mezquino, *Argentina* agalludo, *Chile, Peru,* coñete

stink *vi* apestar, heder, oler mal. *n* tufo, *m*, hediondez, *Lat. Am. also* fortaleza, *f*

stinking *a* apestoso, hediondo, fétido, mal oliente

stint *vt* escatimar; limitar. *n* límite, *m*, restricción, *f.* **without s.,** sin límite; sin restricción.

stipend *n* estipendio, salario, *m*

stipulate *vi* estipular, poner como condición. *vt* estipular, especificar. **They stipulated for a five-day week,** Pusieron como condición (or Estipularon) que trabajasen cinco días por semana

stir *vt* agitar; revolver; (the fire) atizar;

(move) mover; (emotionally) conmover, impresionar; (the imagination) estimular. *vi* moverse. *n* movimiento, *m*; conmoción, *f*; (bustle) bullicio, *m*; sensación, *f.* **to make a s.,** causar una sensación. **to s. one's coffee,** revolver el café. **to s. up discontent,** fomentar el descontento

stirring *a* conmovedor, emocionante, impresionante; (of times, etc.) turbulento, agitado

stirrup *n* estribo, *m.* **s.-cup,** última copa, *f.* **s.-pump,** bomba de mano (para líquidos), *f*

stitch *n* (action) puntada, *f*; (result) punto, *m*; *surg* punto de sutura, *m*; (pain) punzada, *f*, pinchazo, *m. vt* coser; *surg* suturar

stock *n* (of a tree) tronco, *m*; (of a rifle) culata, *f*; (handle) mango, *m*; (of a horse's tail) nabo, *m*; (stem for grafting etc.) injerto, *m*; (race) raza, *f*; (lineage) linaje, *m*, estirpe, *f*; (supply) provisión, *f*; reserva, *f*; (of merchandise) surtido, *m*; *cul* caldo, *m*; (collar) alzacuello, *m*; *bot* alhelí, *m*; (government) papel del estado, *m*, valores públicos, *m pl*; (financial) valores, *m pl*, (of a company) capital, *m*; *pl* **stocks,** *hist* cepo, *m*; (of goods) existencias, *f pl*, stock, *m*, a corriente; (of the repertorio. **in s.** en existencia. **lives.,** ganado *m.* **rolling-s.,** *rw* materia móvil ferroviario, *m.* **s. phrase** frase hecha, *f.* **s. size,** talla corriente, *f.* **to lay in a s. of,** hacer provisión de, almacenar, **to stand s.-still,** quedarse completamente inmóvil. **to take s.,** *com* hacer inventario. **to take s. of,** inventariar; examinar, considerar. **s.-breeder,** ganadero, *m.* **s.-broker,** corredor de bolsa, bolsista, *m.* **s. exchange,** bolsa, *f.* **s.-in-hand,** *com* existencias, *f pl.* **s.-in-trade** (*com* etc.) capital, *m.* **s.-raising,** cría de ganados, ganadería, *f.* **s.-taking,** *com* inventario, *m*

stock *vt* proveer (de), abastecer (de); (of shops) tener existencia de

stockade *n* estacada, empalizada, *f*, *vt* empalizar

stocking *n* media, *f.* **nylon stockings,** medias de cristal (or de nilón), *f pl*

stocky *a* rechoncho, doblado, achaparrado

stodgy *a* (of food) indigesto; (of style, etc.) pesado, amazacotado

stoic *a* and *n* estoico (-ca)

stoke *vt* (a furnace, etc.) cargar, alimentar; (a fire) echar carbón, etc., en. **s.-hole,** cuarto de fogoneros, *m*; *naut* cámara de calderas, *f*

stole *n* (ecc and of fur, etc.) estola, *f*

stolid *a* impasible, imperturbable

stomach *n* estómago, vientre, *m*; apetito, estómago, *m*; (courage) corazón, valor, *m. vt* digerir; (tolerate) tragar, sufrir. **s.ache,** dolor de estómago, *m*

stone *n* piedra, *f*; (gem) piedra preciosa,

f; (of cherries, etc.) hueso, *m*; (of grapes, etc.) pepita, *f*; *med* cálculo, *m*. **a de piedra.** *vt* apedrear; (a wall, etc.) revestir de piedra; (fruit) deshuesar. **to pave with stones,** empedrar. **to leave no s. unturned,** no dejar piedra sin remover. **within a stone's throw,** a corta distancia, a un paso. **S. Age,** edad de piedra, *f*. **s.-breaker,** cantero, picapedrero, *m*. **s.-cold,** muy frío, completamente frío **s.-deaf,** a completamente sordo. **s.-fruit,** fruta de hueso, *f*. **s.-mason,** mazonero, albañil, *m*; picapedrero, *m*. **s.-quarry,** pedrera, cantera, *f*

stony *a* pedregoso; (of hearts, etc.) duro, insensible, empedernido; (of a stare, etc.) fijo, duro

stool *n* banquillo, taburete, *m*; (feces) excremento, *m*

stoop *vi* inclinarse, doblarse; encorvarse; ser cargado de espaldas; andar encorvado; (demean oneself) rebajarse (a). *vt* inclinar, doblar. *n* inclinación, *f*; cargazón de espaldas, *f*

stop *vt* (a hole) obstruir, atascar; (a leak) cegar, tapar; (a tooth) empastar; (stanch) restañar; (the traffic, etc.) parar; detener; (prevent) evitar; (discontinue) cesar (de), dejarse de; (cut off) cortar; (end) poner fin (a), acabar con; (payment) suspender. *vi* parar; detenerse; cesar; terminar; (stay) quedarse, permanecer. **I stopped myself from saying what I thought,** Me abstuve de decir lo que pensaba, Me mordí la lengua. **They stopped the food-supply,** Cortaron las provisiones. **to s. beating about the bush,** dejarse de historias. **to s. one's ears,** *fig* taparse los oídos. **to s. payments,** suspender pagos

stop *n* parada, *f*; pausa, *f*; interrupción, *f*; cesación, *f*; (of an organ) registro, *m*. "Stop," (road sign) «Alto.» **full s.,** *gram* punto, *m*. **tram s.,** parada de tranvía, *f*. **to come to a full s.,** pararse de golpe; cesar súbitamente. **to put a s. to,** poner fin a, poner coto a, acabar con. *f pl*. **s.-watch,** cronógrafo, *m*

stopgap *n* (person) tapagujeros, *m*; substituto, *m*

stoppage *n* parada, *f*; cesación, *f*; suspensión, *f*; interrupción, *f*; pausa, *f*; (obstruction) impedimento, *m*; obstrucción, *f*. **s. of work,** suspensión de trabajo, *f*

stopper *n* tapón, *m*; obturador, *m*, *vt* cerrar con tapón, taponar

stopping *n* parada, *f*; cesación, *f*; suspensión, *f*; (of a tooth) empaste, *m*. **without s.,** sin parar. **without s. to draw breath,** de un aliento. **s.-place,** paradero, *m*; (of buses, etc.) parada, *f*. **s. train,** tren ómnibus, *m*. **s. up,** obturación, *f*

storage *n* almacenamiento, *m*; (charge) almacenaje, *m*; (place) depósito, *m*. **cold s.,** cámara frigorífica, *f*. **s. battery,** acumulador, *m*

store *n* provisión, *f*; abundancia, *f*; reserva, *f*; (of knowledge, etc.) tesoro, *m*; (for furniture, etc.) depósito, almacén, *m*; *pl* **stores,** (shop) almacenes, *m pl*; (food) provisiones, *f pl*; (mil etc.) pertrechos, *m pl*. *vt* proveer; guardar, acumular; tener en reserva; (furniture, etc.) almacenar; (hold) caber en, tomar. **in s.,** en reserva; en depósito, en almacén. **to set s. by,** estimar en mucho; dar importancia a. **to set little s. by,** estimar en poco; conceder poca importancia a. **s.-room,** despensa, *f*

storehouse *n* almacén, *m*; *fig* mina, *f*, tesoro, *m*

storekeeper = shopkeeper

stork *n* cigüeña, *f*

storm *n* tempestad, tormenta, *f*, temporal, *m*; *fig* tempestad, *f*; *mil* asalto, *m*. *mil* tomar por asalto, asaltar. *vi* (of persons) bramar de cólera. **to take by s.,** tomar por asalto; *fig* cautivar, conquistar. **s. cloud,** nubarrón, *m*. **s.-signal,** señal de temporal, *f*. **s.-tossed,** a sacudido por la tempestad. **s. troops,** tropas de asalto, *f pl*. **s. window,** contravidriera, *f*

stormy *a* tempestuoso; de tormenta; (of life, etc.) borrascoso; (of meetings, etc.) tempestuoso

story *n* historia, *f*; cuento, *m*; anécdota, *f*; (funny) chiste, *m*; (plot) argumento, enredo, *m*; (fib) mentira, *f*; (floor) piso *m*. **It's always the same old s.,** Es siempre la misma canción (or historia). **That is quite another s.,** Eso es harina de otro costal, *Argentina, Peru* esas son otras cuarenta. **short s.,** cuento, *m*. **s. book,** libro de cuentos, *m*. **s. teller,** cuentista, *mf*; (fibber) mentiroso (-sa)

stout *a* fuerte; (brave) intrépido, indómito; (fat) gordo, grueso; (firm) sólido, firme; (decided) resuelto; vigoroso. *n* (drink) cerveza negra, *f*. **s.-hearted,** valiente, intrépido

stove *n* estufa, *f*; (open, for cooking) cocina económica, *f*; (gas, etc., for cooking) cocina, *f*, fogón, *m*. **s. dealer; s. maker** *Argentina* fumista, *mf*; **s. pipe,** tubo de la chimenea, *m*

stow *vt* meter, poner; colocar; (hide) esconder; (cargo) estibar, arrimar

stowaway *n* polizón, llovido, *m*, *vi* embarcarse secretamente

straddle *vi* (*nav* etc.) graduar el tiro. *vt* montar a horcajadas en. **s.-legged,** patiabierto

strafe *vt* bombardear concentradamente; castigar; reñir

straggle *vi* rezagarse; vagar en desorden; dispersarse; estar esparcido; extenderse.

straight *a* derecho; recto; (of hair) lacio; directo; (tidy) en orden; (frank) franco; (honest) honrado. *adv* derecho; en línea recta; directamente. **Keep s. on!** ¡Siga Vd. derecho! **to go s. to the point,** dejarse de rodeos, ir al grano. **to look s. in the eyes,** mirar derecho en los ojos. **s. away,** inmediatamente, en seguida. **s. out,** sin rodeos

straighten vt enderezar; poner derecho; poner en orden; arreglar. vi ponerse derecho; enderezarse. **to s. one's face,** componer el semblante. **to s. the line,** mil rectificar el frente. **to s. out,** poner en orden; fig desenredar. **to s. oneself up,** erguirse

straightforward a honrado, sincero; franco; (simple) sencillo. **s. answer,** respuesta directa, f

straightway adv al instante, inmediatamente

strain vt estirar; forzar; esforzar; (one's eyes) quebrarse; (one's ears) aguzar (el oído); (a muscle, etc.) torcer; (a friendship) pedir demasiado (a), exigir demasiado (de); (a person's patience, etc.) abusar (de); (words) tergiversar; (embrace) abrazar estrechamente (a); (filter) filtrar; cul colar. vi hacer un gran esfuerzo, esforzarse (para). n tirantez, f; tensión, f; (effort) esfuerzo, m; (sprain) torcedura, f; (nervous) tensión nerviosa, f; mech esfuerzo, m; (breed) raza, f; biol cepa, f; (tendency) tendencia, f; (heredity) herencia, f; rasgo, m, vena, f; (style) estilo, m; mus melodía, f; (of mirth, etc.) son, ruido, m; (poetry) poesía, f. **to s. a point,** hacer una excepción. **to s. after effect,** buscar demasiado el efecto

strained a tenso; (of muscles, etc.) torcido; (of smiles, etc.) forzado. **s. relations,** pol estado de tirantez, m

strainer n filtró, m; coladero, m

strait n geog estrecho, m. **to be in great straits,** estar en un apuro. **s. laced,** fig de manga estrecha.

straiten vt estrechar; limitar, **in straitened circumstances,** en la necesidad

Strait of Magellan Estrecho de Magallanes, m

strand n (shore) playa, f; (of a river) ribera, orilla, f; (of rope) cabo, ramal, m; (of thread, etc.) hebra, f; (of hair) trenza, f. vt and vi (a ship) encallar, varar. **to be stranded,** hallarse abandonado; (by missing a train, etc.) quedarse colgado. **to leave stranded,** abandonar, dejar plantado (a)

strange a (unknown) desconocido; nuevo; (exotic, etc.) extraño, singular; extraordinario; raro; exótico. **I felt very s. in a s. country,** Me sentía muy solo en un país desconocido. **He is a very s. person,** Es una persona muy rara

stranger n desconocido (-da); (from a foreign country) extranjéro (-ra); (from another region, etc.) forastero (-ra).

strangle vt estrangular; (a sob, etc.) ahogar

stranglehold n collar de fuerza, m. **to**

have a s. (on), tener asido por la garganta; paralizar

strap n correa, f; tirante de botas, m, vt atar con correas

strapping a rozagante, robusto

stratagem n estratagema, f, ardid, m

strategic a estratégico

strategy n estrategia, f

stratum n geol estrato, m, capa, f; (social, etc.) estrato, m

straw n paja, f. **I don't care a s.,** No se me da un bledo. **to be not worth a s.,** no valer un ardite. **to be the last s.,** ser el colmo. **to drink through a s.,** sorber con una paja. **s. hat,** sombrero de paja, m. **s.-colored,** pajizo

strawberry n (plant and fruit, especially small or wild) fresa, f; (large cultivated) fresón, m. **s. bed,** fresal, m. **s. ice,** helado de fresa, m

stray vi errar, vagar; perderse; (from a path, etc., also fig) descarriarse. n animal perdido, m; niño (-ña) sin hogar. a descarriado, perdido; errante; (sporadic) esporádico

stray bullet n bala perdida, f

streak n raya, f; (in wood and stone) vena, f; (of light) rayo, m; (of humor, etc.) rasgo, m. vt rayar. **like a s. of lightning,** como un relámpago

streaky a rayado; (of bacon) entreverado

stream n arroyo, riachuelo, m; río, m; (current) corriente, f; (of words, etc.) torrente, m. vi correr, fluir; manar, brotar; (float) flotar, ondear. vt (blood, etc.) manar, echar. **The tears streamed down Jean's cheeks,** Las lágrimas corrían por las mejillas de Juana. **s.-lined,** fuselado

stream-of-consciousness n escritura automática, f, fluir de la conciencia, m, flujo de la subconciencia, monólogo interior, m

streamer n gallardete, m, serpentina, f; (on a hat, etc.) cinta colgante, f, siguemepollo, m

street n calle, f. **the man in the s.,** el hombre medio. **at s. level,** a ras de suelo. **s. arab,** golfo, m. **s. cries,** gritos de vendedores ambulantes, m pl. **s. entertainer,** saltabanco, m. **s. brawl, s. fight,** algarada callejera, f. **s. fighting,** luchas en las calles, f pl. **s. musician,** músico ambulante, m. **s.-sweeper,** barrendero, m. **s.-walker,** buscona, prostituta, f

strength n fuerza, f; (of colors, etc.) intensidad, f; (of character) firmeza (de carácter), f; (of will) resolución, decisión, f; mil complemento, m. **The enemy is in s.,** El enemigo está presente en gran número. **by sheer s.,** a viva fuerza. **on the s. of,** confiando en, en razón de

strengthen vt fortificar; consolidar; reforzar. *vi* fortificarse; consolidarse; reforzarse

strenuous *a* activo, enérgico; vigoroso; (arduous) arduo

stress *n* tensión, *f*; impulso, *m*; importancia, *f*, énfasis, *m*; *gram* acento (tónico), *m*; acentuación, *f*; *mech* esfuerzo, *m*. *vt* acentuar; poner énfasis en, insistir en. **under s. of circumstance,** impulsado por las circunstancias. **times of s.,** tiempos turbulentos, *m pl*. **to lay great s. on,** insistir mucho en; dar gran importancia a

stretch *vt* (make bigger) ensanchar; (pull) estirar; (one's hand, etc.) alargar, extender; (knock down) tumbar. *vi* ensancharse; dar de sí; ceder; extenderse. **to s. oneself,** estirarse, desperezarse. **to s. as far as,** llegar hasta, extenderse hasta. **to s. a point,** hacer una concesión. **to s. one's legs,** estirar las piernas

stretch *n* estirón, *m*; tensión, *f*; (of country, etc.) extensión, *f*; (scope) alcance, *m*. **by a s. of the imagination,** con un esfuerzo de imaginación. **He can sleep for hours at a s.,** Puede dormir durante horas enteras

stretcher *n* (for gloves) ensanchador, *m*; dilatador, *m*; (for canvas) bastidor, *m*; (for wounded, etc.) camilla, *f*. **s.-bearer,** camillero, *m*

strew *vt* esparcir; derramar

stricken *a* (wounded) herido; (ill) enfermo; (with grief) afligido, agobiado de dolor. **s. in years,** entrado en años

strict *a* exacto; estricto; escrupuloso; severo

strictly *adv* exactamente; estrictamente; severamente, con severidad. **s. speaking,** en rigor, en realidad

stricture *n* *fig* crítica severa, censura, *f*. **to pass strictures on,** criticar severamente

stride *vi* andar a pasos largos, dar zancadas; cruzar a grandes trancos. *vt* cruzar de un tranco; poner una pierna en cada lado de. *n* zancada, *f*, paso largo, tranco, *m*. **to s. up and down,** dar zancadas

strident *a* estridente; (of colors) chillón

strife *n* lucha, *f*, conflicto, *m*

strike *vt* golpear; pegar, dar una bofetada (a); (wound) herir; (a coin) acuñar; (a light) encender; (of a snake) morder; (a blow) asestar, dar; (of ships, a rock, etc.) chocar contra; estrellarse contra; (flags) bajar, arriar; (a tent) desmontar; (camp) levantar; (come upon) llegar a; (discover) encontrar por casualidad, tropezar con; hallar, descubrir; (seem) parecer; (impress) impresionar; (of ideas) ocurrírse; (an attitude) tomar, adoptar; (of a clock) dar; (a balance) hacer; (a bargain) cerrar, llegar a; (level) nivelar; (cuttings) enraciar. *vi* golpear; (of a clock) dar la hora; (of a ship) encallar; (go) ir; (penetrate) penetrar; (of a cutting) arraigar; (sound)

sonar. **He struck the table with his fist,** Golpeó la mesa con el puño. **I was very much struck by the city's beauty,** La belleza de la ciudad me impresionó mucho. **The news struck fear into their hearts,** La noticia les llenó el corazón de miedo. **The clock struck three,** El reloj dio las tres. **The hour has struck,** *fig* Ha llegado la hora. **How did the house strike you?** ¿Qué te pareció la casa? **to s. a bargain,** cerrar un trato. **to s. a blow,** asestar un golpe. **to s. across country,** ir a campo traviesa. **to s. an attitude,** tomar una actitud. **to s. home,** dar en el blanco; herir; herir en lo más vivo; hacerse sentir. **to s. at,** asestar un golpe (a); acometer, embestir; atacar. **to s. down,** derribar; (of illness) acometer. **to s. off,** (a head, etc.) cortar; (a name) borrar, tachar; (print) imprimir. **to s. out,** *vi* asestar un golpe (a); (of a swimmer) nadar; echarse, lanzarse. *vt* (a word, etc.) borrar, rayar; (begin) iniciar. **to s. through,** (cross out) rayar, tachar; (of the sun's rays, etc.) penetrar. **to s. up,** *vt* tocar; empezar a cantar; (a friendship) trabar. *vi* empezar a tocar. **to s. up a march,** *mil* batir la marcha

strike *n* huelga, *f*. *vi* declararse en huelga. **go-slow s.,** tortuguismo, *m*. **lock-out s.,** huelga patronal, *f*. **sit-down s.,** huelga de brazos caídos, *f*. **to go on s.,** declararse en huelga. **s.-breaker,** esquirol, *m*. **s.-pay,** subsidio de huelga, *m*

striker *n* huelguista, *mf*

striking *a* notable, sorprendente; (impressive) impresionante; que llama la atención; llamativo

string *n* bramante, *m*; cuerda, *f*; (ribbon) cinta, *f*; (of beads, etc.) sarta, *f*; (of onions) ristra, *f*; (of horses, etc.) reata, *f*; hilera, *f*; (of a bridge) cable, *m*; (of oaths, lies) sarta, serie, *f*; (of beans) fibra, *f*. *vt* encordar; (beads, etc.) ensartar; (beans) quitar las fibras (de). **He is all strung up,** Se le crispan los nervios. **the strings,** los instrumentos de cuerda. **a s. of pearls,** un collar de perlas. **for strings,** *mus* para arco. **to pull strings,** *fig* manejar los hilos. **to s. up,** (an instrument) templar; (a person) pender, ahorcar. **s. bean,** judía verde, *f*, *Central America, Mexico* ejote, *m*

stringed *a* (of musical instruments) de cuerda. **s. instrument,** instrumento de cuerda, *m*

stringent *a* estricto, severo

stringy *a* fibroso; filamentoso; correoso; arrugado

strip *vt* desnudar; despojar (de), quitar; robar; (a cow) ordeñar hasta agotar la leche. *vi* desnudarse. *n* (tatter) jirón, *m*; tira, lista, *f*; (of wood) listón, *m*; (of earth) pedazo, *m*; (*geog* of land) zona, *f*. **to s. off,** *vt* quitar; (bark from a tree) descortezar; (one's clothes) despojarse de. *vi* desprenderse, separarse. **to s. the leaves**

from, to s. the petals from *Lat. Am.* deshojar

stripe *n* raya, lista, *f*; (*mil* etc.) galón, *m*; (lash) azote, *m*. *vt* rayar. **the stripes of the tiger,** las rayas del tigre

striped a listado, a rayas; con rayas. **s. trousers,** pantalón de corte, *m*

stripling *n* joven imberbe, pollo, mancebo, *m*

strive *vi* esforzarse (a); pugnar (por, para); trabajar (por); (fight against) luchar contra; pelear con. **He was striving to understand,** Pugnaba por (or Se esforzaba a) comprender

stroke *n* (blow) golpe, *m*; (of the oars) golpe del remo, *m*, remada, *f*; (at billards) tacada, *f*; (in golf) tirada, *f*; (in swimming) braza, *f*; (of a clock) campanada, *f*; (of a pen) rasgo de la pluma, *m*; (of a brush) pincelada, *f*; *mech* golpe de émbolo, *m*; (caress) caricia con la mano, *f*. *vt* acariciar con la mano. **on the s. of six,** al acabar de dar las séis. **to have a s.,** tener un ataque de apoplejía. **s. of genius,** rasgo de ingenio, *m*. **s. of good luck,** racha de buena suerte, *f*

stroll *vi* pasearse, vagar. *n* vuelta, *f*, paseo, *m*. **to go for a s.,** dar una vuelta

stroller *n* paseante, *mf*

strolling a errante; ambulante. **s. player,** *n* cómico (-ca) ambulante

strong a fuerte; vigoroso; robusto; *Argentina* alentado; enérgico; firme; poderoso; (of colours) intenso, vivo; (of tea, coffee) cargado; *gram* fuerte. **The government took s. measures,** El gobierno tomó medidas enérgicas. **They gave very s. reasons,** Alegaron unas razones muy poderosas. **Grammar is not his s. point,** La gramática no es su punto fuerte. **The enemy is s. in numbers,** El enemigo es numéricamente fuerte. **The society is four thousand s.,** La sociedad tiene cuatro mil miembros. **s. box,** caja de caudales, *f*. **s. man,** hombre fuerte, *m*; (in a circus) hércules, *m*. **s.-minded,** de espíritu fuerte; independiente. **s. room,** cámara acorazada, *f*

stronghold *n* fortaleza, *f*; refugio, *m*

structural a estructural

structure *n* estructura, *f*; edificio, *m*; construcción, *f*

struggle *vi* luchar; pelear; disputarse, *Lat. Am.* abrocharse (con . . .); *n* lucha, *f*; combate, *m*; conflicto, *m*. **to s. to one's feet,** luchar por levantarse. **without a s.,** sin luchar

strum *vt* (a stringed instrument) rascar; tocar mal

strut *vi* pavonearse. *vt* (prop) apuntalar. *n* pavonada, *f*; (prop) puntal, *m*. **to s. out,** salir de un paso majestuoso

stub *n* (of a tree) tocón, *m*; (of a pencil, candle, etc.) cabo, *m*; pedazo, fragmento, *m*; (of a cigarette or cigar) colilla, *f*. **s.-book,** talonario, *m*

stubborn a inquebrantable, tenaz; persistente; (pig-headed) terco, testarudo, *Lat. Am.* empecinado

stucco *n* estuco, *m*, *vt* estucar

stuck *past part.* of **stick**. **be stuck** (for an answer) = **be stumped**

stuck-up a = **haughty.**

stud *n* (of horses) caballeriza, *f*; (nail) tachón, *m*; (for collars) pasador para camisas, *m*. *vt* tachonar; sembrar. **dress s.,** botón de la pechera, *m*. **s.-farm,** potrero, *m*

student *n* estudiante, *mf*. a estudiantil. **students** (as a body) *Lat. Am.* estudiantado *msg.*

student body *n Lat. Am.* estudiantado *m*

studied a estudiado; calculado; (of style) cerebral, reflexivo; (intentional) deliberado

studio *n* estudio, *m*. **broadcasting s.,** estudio de emisión, *m*

studious a estudioso, aplicado; (deliberate) intencional, deliberate; (eager) solícito, ansioso

study *n* estudio, *m*; solicitud, *f*, cuidado, *m*; investigación, *f*; (room) gabinete, cuarto de trabajo, *m*. *vt* ocuparse de, cuidar de, atender a; considerar; estudiar; examinar; (the stars) observar; (try) procurar. *vi* estudiar. **in a brown s.,** en Babia. **to make a s. of,** hacer un estudio de, estudiar. **to s. for an examination,** prepararse para un examen

stuff *n* substancia, materia, *f*; (fabric) tela, *f*, paño, *m*; (rubbish) cachivaches, *m pl*, cosas, *f pl*. a de estofa. *vt* henchir; llenar; *cul* rellenar; (with food) ahitar (de); (cram) atestar, apretar; (furniture) rehenchir; (an animal, bird) disecar; (put) meter, poner. **S. and nonsense!** ¡Patrañas! **to be poor s.,** ser de pacotilla; no valer para nada

stuffing *n* (of furniture) rehenchimiento, *m*; *cul* relleno, *m*

stuffy a mal ventilado, poco aireado, ahogado

stumble *vi* tropezar; dar un traspié; (in speaking) tartamudear. *n* tropezón, *m*; traspié, *m*. **to s. through a speech,** pronunciar un discurso a tropezones. **to s. against,** tropezar contra. **to s. upon, across,** tropezar con; encontrar por casualidad

stumblingblock *n* tropiezo, impedimento, *m*

stump *n* (of a tree) tocón, *m*; (of an arm, leg) muñón, *m*; (of a pencil, candle) cabo, *m*; (of a tooth) raigón, *m*; (of a cigar) colilla, *f*; (cricket) poste, montante, *m*; *art* esfumino, *m*; (leg) pata, *f*. *vt* (disconcert) desconcertar; *art* esfumar; recorrer. **to s. up,** *inf* pagar. **be stumped** (for an answer) *Mexico* atrojarse

stun *vt* dejar sin sentido (a); aturdir de un golpe (a); (astound) pasmar

stunning a aturdidor; que pasma; *inf* estupendo

stunt *vt* impedir el crecimiento de; encanijar. *n* (advertising) anuncio de reclamo, *m*; recurso (para conseguir algo), *m*; proeza, *f*

stunted a (of trees, etc.) enano; (of children) encanijado; (of intelligence) inmaduro

stupefy *vt* atontar, embrutecer; causar estupor (a), asombrar

stupendous a asombroso; enorme

stupid a (with sleep, etc.) atontado; (silly) estúpido, tonto, *Lat. Am.* baboso, *Central America* azurumbado. *n* tonto (-ta)

stupidity *n* estupidez, *f*; tontería, *f*

stupor *n* estupor, *m*

sturdy a robusto, vigoroso, fuerte; firme, tenaz

sturgeon *n icht* esturión, *m*

stutter *vi* tartamudear. *vt* balbucir. *n* tartamudeo, *m*

sty *n* (pig) pocilga, *f*; *med* orzuelo, *m*

style *n* (for etching) buril, *m*; (*lit, art, arch,* etc.) estilo, *m*; (fashion) moda, *f*; (model) modelo, *m*; (behavior, etc.) tono, *m*; elegancia, *f*; (kind) especie, clase, *f*; (designation) tratamiento, *m*; *vt* llamar, nombrar. **the latest styles from Madrid,** los últimos modelos de Madrid. **He has a very individual s.,** Su estilo es muy personal. **They live in great s.,** Viven en gran lujo

stylish a elegante

suasive a suasorio, persuasivo

suave a afable, cortés, urbano; (of wine) suave

subaltern *n mil* subalterno, *m*, a subalterno, subordinado

subconscious a subconsciente. **the s.,** la subconsciencia

subcutaneous a subcutáneo

subdivide *vt* subdividir. *vi* subdividirse

subdue *vt* subyugar, sojuzgar, vencer; (one's passions) dominar; (colors, voices) suavizar; (lessen) mitigar; apagar

subdued a (of colors) apagado; (of persons) sumiso; (depressed) deprimido, melancólico. **in a s. voice,** en voz baja

subheading *n* subtítulo, *m*

subhuman a subhumano

subject a sujeto; sometido (a); expuesto (a). *n* (of a country) súbdito (-ta); sujeto, *m*; (of study) asignatura, materia, *f*; (theme) tema, *m*; (*gram, phil*) sujeto, *m*. *vt* subyugar; someter. **It can only be done s. to his consent,** Podrá hacerse únicamente si él lo consiente. **He is a British s.,** Es súbdito británico. **to change the s.,** cambiar de conversación. **to s. to criticism,** criticar (a). **s.-matter,** materia, *f*; (of a letter) contenido, *m*

subjection *n* sujeción, *f*; sometimiento, *m*. **He was in a state of complete s.,**

Estaba completamente sumiso. **to bring into s.,** subyugar

subjective a subjetivo

subjoin *vt* añadir, adjuntar

subjugate *vt* subyugar, someter

subjunctive a and *n* subjuntivo *m*

sublet *vt* subarrendar. *n* subarriendo, *m*

sublimate *vt* sublimar. *n* sublimado, *m*

sublime a sublime; absoluto, completo; extremo. **the s.,** lo sublime

submarine a submarino. *n* submarino, *m*. **midget s.,** submarino enano, submarino de bolsillo, *m*.

submerge *vt* sumergir; inundar. *vi* sumergirse. **The submarine submerged,** El submarino se sumergió

submergence *n* sumergimiento, *m*, sumersión, *f*; hundimiento, *m*

submersible a sumergible

submersion *n* sumersión, *f*; hundimiento, *m*

submission *n* sometimiento, *m*; sumisión, resignación, *f*; docilidad, *f*

submissive a sumiso, dócil, manso

submit *vt* someterse (a); doblarse ante; (a scheme, etc.) someter; presentar; (urge) proponer. *vi* someterse; resignarse; (surrender) rendirse, entregarse. **to s. to arbitration,** someter a arbitraje

subnormal a anormal

subordinate a subordinado; subalterno, inferior; secundario. *n* subordinado (-da). *vt* subordinar

subordination *n* subordinación, *f*

subpena *n* citación, *f*, *vt* citar

subplot *n* intriga secundaria, trama secundaria, *f*

subscribe *vt* and *vi* subscribir; (to a periodical, etc.) abonarse (a)

subscriber *n* subscriptor (-ra); abonado (-da)

subscription *n* subscripción, *f*; (to a periodical, series of concerts, etc.) abono, *m*; (to a club) cuota, *f*

subsequent a subsiguiente, subsecuente; posterior. **s. to,** después de, posterior a. **s. upon,** de resultas de

subsequently *adv* más tarde; subsiguientemente; posteriormente

subservient a servil; subordinado; útil

subside *vi* (of water) bajar; (of ground) hundirse; (of foundations) asentarse; disminuir; (of floods) calmarse; (be quiet) callarse. **to s. into a chair,** dejarse caer en un sillón

subsidence *n* hundimiento, *m*; desplome, derrumbamiento, *m*; (of floods) bajada, *f*; (of anger, etc.) apaciguamiento, *m*

subsidiary a subsidiario

subsidize *vt* subvencionar

subsidy *n* subvención, *f*, subsidio, *m*; prima, *f*

subsist *vi* subsistir

subsoil n subsuelo, m

substance n substancia, f

substantial a substancial; sólido; importante

substantiate vt establecer, verificar; justificar

substantive a real, independiente; gram substantivo. n gram substantivo, m

substitute n substituto (-ta); (material) substituto, m. vt substituir, reemplazar. **to be a s. for,** hacer las veces de

substitution n substitución, f, reemplazo, m

subterfuge n subterfugio, m; evasiva, f

subterranean a subterráneo

subtitle n subtítulo, m; (on films) guión, m

subtle a sutil; delicado; penetrante; (crafty) astuto

subtlety n sutileza, f; delicadeza, f; (craftiness) astucia, f

subtract vt restar, substraer

subtraction n resta, substracción, f

suburb n suburbio, m; pl **suburbs,** las afueras, f pl los arrabales, m pl

suburban a suburbano

subversion n subversión, f

subversive a subversivo

subvert vt subvertir

subway n (passageway) pasaje subterráneo, m; (underground railway) metro (Spain, Puerto Rico), subte (Argentina), m

succeed vt seguir (a); suceder (a); heredar. vi seguir (a); suceder (a); (be successful) tener éxito. **I did not s. in doing it,** No logré hacerlo. **to s. to the throne,** subir al trono

succeeding a subsiguiente; futuro; consecutivo; sucesivo

success n éxito, m; triunfo, m. **to be a s.,** tener éxito. **The film was a great s.,** La película tuvo mucho éxito

successful a que tiene éxito; afortunado, venturoso; próspero, Lat. Am. exitoso

successfully adv con éxito; prósperamente

succession n sucesión, f; (series) serie, f; (inheritance) herencia, f; (descendants) descendencia, f. **in s.,** sucesivamente

successive a sucesivo

successor n sucesor (-ra)

succinct a sucinto, conciso

succor vt socorrer, auxiliar. n socorro, m, ayuda, f

succulent a suculento

succumb vi sucumbir; someterse, ceder

such a tal; parecido, semejante; así; tanto; (before an adjective, adverb) tan. n el, m, (f, la) que, los, m pl, (f pl, las) que; tal. **s. men,** tales hombres. **I have never seen s. magnificence,** Nunca no he visto tanta magnificencia. **s. an important man,** un hombre tan importante. **s. pictures as these,** cuadros como estos. **S. is life!** ¡Así es la vida! **science as s.,** la ciencia como tal. **s.-and-s.,** tal y tal

suchlike a parecido, semejante; de esta clase

suck vt chupar; (the breast) mamar; sorber; (of a vacuum cleaner, etc.) aspirar. n chupada, f; succión, f. **to s. down,** tragar. **to s. up,** aspirar; absorber

sucker n zool ventosa, f; bot acodo, mugrón, m; (greenhorn) primo, m; (pig) lechón, m

suckle vt amamantar, dar el pecho (a)

suction n succión, f; aspiración, f. **s.-pump,** bomba aspirante, f

sudden a súbito; (unexpected) inesperado, impensado; (of bends) brusco. **all of a s.,** de repente; súbitamente

suddenly adv súbitamente; de pronto, de repente

suds n pl jabonaduras, f pl; espuma, f

sue vt law proceder contra, pedir en juicio; law demandar; (beg) suplicar. **to sue for peace,** pedir la paz

suede n ante, m. **s. glove,** guante de ante, m

suet n sebo, m

suffer vt sufrir, padecer; pasar, experimentar; (tolerate) tolerar, sufrir; (allow) permitir. vi sufrir. **She suffers from her environment,** es la víctima de su medio ambiente

sufferance n tolerancia, f. **on s.,** por tolerancia

sufferer n enfermo (-ma); víctima, f

suffering n sufrimiento, padecimiento, m; dolor, m. a sufriente

suffice vi ser suficiente, bastar. vt satisfacer

sufficiency n suficiencia, f; (of money) subsistencia, f

sufficient a suficiente, bastante. **to be s.,** bastar, ser suficiente

sufficiently adv suficientemente, bastante

suffix n gram sufijo, m

suffocate vt ahogar, sofocar, asfixiar. vi sofocarse, asfixiarse

suffocating a sofocante, asfixiante

suffocation n sofocación, asfixia, f; ahogo, m

suffrage n sufragio, m; voto, m. **universal s.,** sufragio universal, m

suffragette n sufragista, f

suffuse vt bañar, inundar, cubrir

sugar n azúcar, m. vt azucarar. **brown s.,** azúcar moreno, m. **loaf s.,** azúcar de pilón, m. **white s.,** azúcar blanco, m. **to s. the pill,** dorar la píldora. **s.-almond,** peladilla, f. **s.-basin,** azucarera, f. **s.-beet,** remolacha, f. **s.-candy,** azúcar candi, m. **s.-cane,** caña de azúcar, f. **s.-cane syrup,** miel de caña, f. **s.-paste,** alfeñique, m, alcorza, f. **s.-refinery,** fábrica de azúcar, f. **s.-tongs,** tenacillas para azúcar, f pl

sugary a azucarado; fig meloso, almibarado

suggest vt implicar; indicar, dar a entender; sugerir; (advise) aconsejar; (hint) insinuar; (evoke) evocar. **I suggested they should go to London,** Les aconsejé que fueran a Londres. **An idea suggested itself to him,** Se le ocurrió una idea

suggestion n sugestión, f; insinuación, f

suggestive a sugestivo; estimulante

suicidal a suicida. **s. tendency,** tendencia suicida, tendencia al suicidio, f

suicide n (act) suicidio, m; (person) suicida, mf. **to commit s.,** darse la muerte, quitarse la vida suicidarse

suit n (request) petición, súplica, f; oferta de matrimonio, f; law pleito, m; (of clothes) traje, Colombia, Venezuela flus, m; (cards) palo, m; (of cards held) serie, f, vt convenir; sentar; ir bien (a); venir bien (a); (adapt) adaptar. **S. yourself!** ¡Haz lo que quieras! **The arrangement suits me very well,** El arreglo me viene muy bien. **The climate doesn't s. me,** El clima no me sienta bien. **The color does not s. you,** El color no te va bien. **to follow s.,** seguir el ejemplo (de); (cards) jugar el mismo palo. **s.-case,** maleta, f

suitable a conveniente; apropiado; apto; a propósito. **Not s. for children,** No apto para menores. **to make s. for,** adaptar a las necesidades de

suite n (of retainers, etc.) séquito, acompañamiento, m; (of furniture, etc.) juego, m; mus suite, f. **private s.,** habitaciones particulares, f pl. **s. of rooms,** apartamiento, m

suitor n law demandante, m; pretendiente, m

sulk vi ponerse malhumorado, ser mohíno

sulky a mohíno, malhumorado

sullen a taciturno, hosco; malhumorado, sombrío; (of a landscape, etc.) triste, sombrío

sully vt desdorar, empañar; manchar

sulphur n azufre, m

sultan n sultán, m

sultry a bochornoso, sofocante

sum n suma, f; total, m; cantidad, f; (in arithmetic) problema (de aritmética), m. vt sumar, calcular. **in sum,** en suma; en resumen. **to sum up,** recapitular; resumir; (a person) tomar las medidas (a)

summarize vt resumir brevemente; compendiar

summary a somero; law sumario. n resumen, sumario, compendio, m. **summary records,** actas resumidas, f pl

summer n verano, estío, m. **to spend the s.,** veranear. **s.-house,** cenador, m. **s.-time,** verano, m; hora de verano, f. **s. wheat,** trigo tremesino, m

summit n cima, cumbre, f; fig apogeo, m

summitry n diplomacia en la cumbre, f

summon vt llamar, hacer venir; mandar, requerir; law citar. **to s. up one's courage,** cobrar ánimos

summons n llamamiento, m; mil intimación, f; law citación, f. vt law citar

sumptuous a suntuoso, lujoso, magnífico

sun n sol, m. **The sun was shining,** Hacía sol, El sol brillaba. **to bask in the sun,** tomar el sol. **sun-bathing,** baños de sol, m pl. **sun-blind,** toldo para el sol, m. **sun-bonnet,** capelina, f. **sun-glasses,** gafas ahumadas, f pl. **sun-helmet,** casco colonial, m. **sun-spot,** ast mancha del sol, f; (freckle) peca, f. **sun-worship,** adoración del sol, f

sunburn n quemadura del sol, f; bronceado, m

sunburnt a quemado por el sol; bronceado, tostado por el sol

sundae n helado de frutas, m

Sunday n domingo, m. **in his S. best,** en su traje dominguero, endomingado. **S. school,** escuela dominical, f

Sunday's child n niño nacido de pies, niño nacido un domingo, niño mimado de la fortuna

sunder vt dividir en dos, hender; separar

sundial n reloj de sol, reloj solar, m

sundown n puesta del sol, f

sundry a varios (-as). n pl **sundries,** artículos diversos, m pl; com varios, m pl. **all and s.,** todo el mundo, todos y cada uno

sunflower n girasol, tornasol, m, trompeta de amor, f

sunken a (of eyes, etc.) hundido

sunlight n luz del sol, f, rayos del sol, m pl. **artificial s.,** sol artificial, m. **in the s.,** al sol

sunny a de sol; bañado de sol; asoleado; expuesto al sol; (face) risueño; (of disposition, etc.) alegre. **to be s.,** hacer sol

sunrise n salida del sol, f. **from s. to sunset,** de sol a sol

sunset n puesta del sol, f. **at s.,** a la caída (or puesta) del sol

sunshade n parasol, quitasol, m, sombrilla, f

sunshine n luz del sol, f. **in the s.,** al sol

sunstroke n insolación, f

sup vt sorber. vi cenar. n sorbo, m

super n (actor) comparsa, mf; (film) superproducción, f; (of a beehive) alza, f

superabundance n superabundancia, sobreabundancia, f

superabundant a superabundante, sobreabundante. **to be s.,** sobreabundar

superannuated a (retired) jubilado; (out-of-date) anticuado

superannuation n (retirement and pension) jubilación, f

superb a magnífico, espléndido

supercargo n naut sobrecargo, m

supercilious a altanero, altivo, orgulloso; desdeñoso

superciliousness n altanería, altivez, f, orgullo, m; desdén, m

superficial a superficial

superficiality n superficialidad, f

superfine a superfino

superfluity n superfluidad, f

superfluous a superfluo. **to be s.,** sobrar

superfortress n aer superfortaleza volante, f

superhuman a sobrehumano

superimpose vt sobreponer

superintend vt superentender, dirigir

superintendent n superintendente, mf; director (-ra); (school) inspector (police) subjefe de la policía, m

superior a superior; (in number) mayor; (smug) desdeñoso. n superior (-ra). **Mother S.,** (madre) superiora, f. **s. to,** superior a; encima de

superiority n superioridad, f

superlative a extremo, supremo; gram superlativo. n gram superlativo, m

superlatively adv en sumo grado, superlativamente

superman n superhombre, m

supernatural a sobrenatural

superscribe vt sobrescribir; poner el sobrescrito (a)

superscription n (on letters, documents) sobrescrito, m; leyenda, f

supersede vt reemplazar; suplantar

superstition n superstición, f

superstitious a supersticioso

supervene vi sobrevenir

supervise vt superentender, vigilar; dirigir

supervision n superintendencia, f; dirección, f

supervisor n superintendente, mf; inspector (-ra); director (-ra)

supine a supino; indolente, negligente. n gram supino, m

supper n cena, f. **the Last S.,** la Última Cena. **to have s.,** cenar. **s.-time,** hora de cenar, f

supplant vt suplantar; usurpar; reemplazar

supple a flexible; dócil, manso; (fawning) adulador, servil, lisonjero

supplement n suplemento, m; (of a book) apéndice, m

supplementary a suplementario; adicional

supplicate vt and vi suplicar

supply vt proveer (de); suministrar; proporcionar, dar; (a deficiency) suplir; (a post) llenar; (a post temporarily) reemplazar. n suministro, surtimiento, m; provisión, f; (of electricity, etc.) suministro, m; com oferta, f; (person) substituto (-ta) pl **supplies,** com existencias, f pl; mil pertrechos, m pl; víveres, m pl, provisiones, f pl. **s. and demand,** oferta y demanda, f

support vt apoyar, sostener; mantener; (endure) soportar; (a cause) apoyar, defender; (corroborate) confirmar, vindicar. n apoyo, m; sostén, m; soporte, m. **to speak in s. of,** defender, abogar por. **to s. oneself,** ganarse la vida, mantenerse

supporter n apoyo, m; defensor (-ra); partidario (-ia)

suppose vt suponer; imaginar(se); creer. **always supposing,** dado que, en el caso de que. **Supposing he had gone out?** ¿Y si hubiera salido? **I don't s. they will go to Spain,** No creo que vayan a España, Tiene fama de listo

supposed a supuesto; que se llama a sí mismo

supposition n suposición, hipótesis, f

suppress vt reprimir; (yawns, etc.) ahogar; contener; (heresies, rebellions, books, etc.) suprimir; (dissemble) disimular, esconder; (a heckler, etc.) hacer callar

suppression n represión, f; supresión, f; disimulación, f

suppurate vi supurar

supremacy n supremacía, f

supreme a supremo; sumo. **with s. indifference,** con suma indiferencia. **s. court,** tribunal supremo, m

surcharge n sobrecarga, f

sure a seguro; cierto. adv seguramente. **Be s. to . . . !** ¡Ten cuidado de . . . ! ¡No dejes de . . . ! **to be s.,** seguramente, sin duda; ¡claro!; (fancy!) ¡no me digas!; ¡qué sorpresa! **I am not so s. of that,** No diría yo tanto. **Come on Thursday for s.,** Venga el jueves sin falta. **It is s. to rain tomorrow,** Seguramente va a llover mañana. **to make s. of,** asegurarse de. **to be (or feel) s.,** estar seguro. **s.-footed,** de pie firme, seguro

surely adv seguramente; sin duda, ciertamente; por supuesto

sureness n seguridad, f; certeza, f

surety n garantía, fianza, f; (person) garante, mf. **to go s. for,** ser fiador (de), salir garante (por)

surf n resaca, f; rompiente, m; oleaje, m. **s.-board,** aquaplano, m. **s.-riding,** patinaje sobre las olas, m

surface n superficie, f; exterior, m. a superficial. vi (of a submarine) salir a la superficie. **on the s.,** en apariencia

surface mail n correo por vía ordinaria, servicio ordinario, servicio per vía de superficie, m

surfeit n exceso, m, superabundancia, f; saciedad, f. vt hartar; saciar

surge vi (of waves) embravecerse, hincharse; (of crowds) agitarse, bullir; (of emotions) despertarse. n (of sea, crowd, blood) oleada, f; (of anger) ola, f. **The blood surged into his face,** La sangre se le subió a las mejillas

surgeon n cirujano, m; (nav, mil) médico, m

surgery n cirugía, f; (doctor's) consultorio, m; (dispensary) dispensario, m

surgical a quirúrgico

surly a taciturno, huraño, malhumorado; brusco

surmise n conjetura, suposición, f. vt conjeturar, adivinar; imaginar, suponer. vi hacer conjeturas

surmount vt superar, vencer; coronar

surname n apellido, m, vt denominar, nombrar

surpass vt superar, exceder; aventajarse (a); eclipsar

surpassing a sin par, incomparable

surplus n exceso, sobrante, m; (com of accounts) superávit, m. **sale of s. stock,** liquidación de saldos, f

surprise n sorpresa, f; asombro, m. vt sorprender; asombrar. **to s.** (someone) **in the act,** coger en el acto. **to take** (a person) **by s.,** sorprender (a). **He was surprised into admitting it,** Cogido a la imprevista, lo confesó

surprising a sorprendente

surrealism n surrealismo, m

surrender vt rendir, entregar; (goods) ceder, renunciar (a). vi rendirse, entregarse; abandonarse. n rendición, capitulación, f; entrega, f; (of goods) cesión, f; (of an insurance policy) rescate, m. **to s. oneself to remorse,** abandonarse (or entregarse) al remordimiento. **to s. unconditionally,** entregarse a discreción

surreptitious a subrepticio

surround vt rodear; cercar; mil asediar, sitiar. n borde, m. **Peter was surrounded by his friends,** Pedro estaba rodeado por sus amigos

surrounding a (que está) alrededor de; vecino. **the s. country,** los alrededores

surroundings n pl cercanías, f pl, alrededores, m pl; (environment) medio, m; (medio) ambiente, m

surtax n impuesto suplementario, m

surveillance n vigilancia, f

survey vt contemplar, mirar; (events, etc.) pasar en revista; estudiar; (land, etc.) apear; (a house, etc.) inspeccionar. n vista general, f; inspección, f; (of facts, etc.) examen, m; estudio, m; (of land, etc.) apeo, m; (of literature, etc.) bosquejo, breve panorama, m

surveying n agrimensura, f

surveyor n agrimensor, m; (superintendent) inspector, m; superintendente, m

survival n supervivencia, f. **s. of the fittest,** supervivencia de los más aptos, f

survive vt sobrevivir a. vi sobrevivir; (of customs) subsistir, durar

survivor n sobreviviente, mf

susceptible a susceptible; impresionable; sensible; (to love) enamoradizo. **He is s. to bronchitis,** Es susceptible a la bronquitis

suspect a and n sospechoso (-sa). vt sospechar; dudar; imaginar, suponer. vi tener sospechas

suspend vt suspender. **suspended animation,** muerte aparente, f

suspender n liga, f; pl **suspenders,** (braces) tirantes del pantalón, m pl. **s.-belt,** faja, f

suspense n incertidumbre, f. **to keep** (a person) **in s.,** dejar en la incertidumbre (a)

suspension n suspensión, f. **s.-bridge,** puente colgante, m. **s. of payments,** suspensión de pagos, f

suspicion n sospecha, f; (touch) dejo, m; cantidad muy pequeña, f. **to be above s.,** estar por encima de toda sospecha. **to be under s.,** estar bajo sospecha. **I had no suspicions . . . ,** No sospechaba . . .

suspicious a (by nature) suspicaz; sospechoso. **to make s.,** hacer sospechar

sustain vt sostener; mantener; sustentar; apoyar; corroborar, confirmar; (a note) prolongar. **to s. injuries,** recibir heridas

sustenance n mantenimiento, m; sustento, m, alimentos, m pl

svelte a esbelto, gentil

swab vt naut lampacear; limpiar con lampazo; surg tamponar. n lampazo, m; surg torunda, f, tampón, m

swaddle vt envolver; (infants) fajar

swaddling clothes n pl pañales, m pl. **to be still in s. clothes,** fig estar en mantillas, estar en pañales

swagger vi fanfarronear, pavonearse; darse importancia. n pavoneo, m; aire importante, m; (coat) tonto, m. a majo; de última moda

swain n zagal, m; enamorado, m; pretendiente, amante, m

swallow vt tragar, engullir. n trago, m; sorbo, m; orn golondrina, f. **to s. an insult (a story),** tragar un insulto (una historia). **to s. one's words,** retractarse. **to s. one's pride,** bajar la cerviz, humillarse. **to s. up,** tragar; absorber. **s.-tailed coat,** frac, m

swamp n pantano, m, marisma, f, Argentina fachinal f, Central America chagüe, m. vt sumergir; (a boat) echar a pique, hundir; (inundate) inundar

swan n cisne, m. **swan's down,** plumón de cisne, m. **s.-song,** canto del cisne, m

swank *n* pretensiones, *f pl*, *vi* darse humos

sward *n* césped, *m*, hierba, *f*

swarm *n* enjambre, *m*; (of people) muchedumbre, multitud, *f*; tropel, *m*. *vi* (of bees) enjambrar; (of other insects) pulular; (of people) hormiguear, bullir, pulular. *vt* (climb) trepar. **to s. with**, estar infestado de

swarthy *a* moreno

swashbuckler *n* perdonavidas, matasiete, *m*

swastika *n* esvástica, cruz gamada, *f*

swathe *vt* envolver; fajar; (with bandages) vendar

sway *vi* balancearse; oscilar; (stagger, of persons) bambolearse; (totter, of things) tambalearse; (of carriages) cabecear; (gracefully, in walking) cimbrarse. *vt* balancear, mecer; oscilar; hacer tambalear; (influence) influir, inclinar; (govern) regir, gobernar. *n* balanceo, *m*; oscilación, *f*; vaivén, *m*; tambaleo, *m*; (influence) ascendiente, dominio, *m*, influencia, *f*; (rule) imperio, poder, *m*. **to hold s. over**, gobernar, regir

swear *vt* jurar; (*law* etc.) declarar bajo juramento. *vi* jurar; (curse) echar pestes, blasfemar. **to s. at**, maldecir. **to s. by**, jurar por; poner fe implícita en. **to be sworn in**, prestar juramento. **to s. in**, tomar juramento (a). **to s. to**, atestiguar

sweat *n* sudor, *m*; *inf* trabajo arduo, *m*. *vi* sudar. *vt* sudar; hacer sudar; (workers) explotar. **by the s. of one's brow**, con el sudor de la frente; con el sudor del rostro. **s.-gland**, glándula sudorípara, *f*

sweater *n* suéter, jersey, *m*

sweating *n* transpiración, *f*; (of workers) explotación, *f*

sweaty *a* sudoroso

Swede *n* sueco (-ca); (vegetable) naba, *f*

Sweden Suecia, *f*

sweep *vi* extenderse (por); (cleave) surcar; pasar rápidamente (por); invadir; dominar; andar majestuosamente; (with a brush) barrer. *vt* barrer; pasar (por); (the strings of a musical instrument) rasguear; (the sea) navegar por; (mines) barrer; (the horizon, etc.) examinar; (a chimney) deshollinar; (with a brush) barrer; (remove) arrebatar; quitar; llevarse; (abolish) suprimir. **to s. along**, *vt* (of the current, crowds, etc.) arrastrar. *vi* pasar majestuosamente; correr rápidamente (por). **to s. aside**, apartar con la mano; abandonar; (a protest) desoír, no hacer caso de. **to s. away**, barrer; (remove) llevarse; destruir; suprimir. **to s. down**, *vt* barrer; (carry) arrastrar. *vi* (of cliffs, etc.) bajar; (of an enemy) abalanzarse (sobre); lanzarse (por). **to s. off**, barrer; (a person) llevarse sin perder tiempo; arrebatar con violencia (a). **to be swept off one's feet**, ser arrastrado (-a); perder el balance; (of emotion) ser dominado por. **to**

s. on, seguir su avance inexorable; seguir su marcha. **to s. up**, recoger, barrer

sweep *n* barredura, *f*; (of a chimney) deshollinador, *m*; (of the tide) curso, *m*; (of a scythe, etc.) golpe, *m*; (range) alcance, *m*; (fold) pliegue, *m*; (curve) curva, *f*; (of water, etc.) extensión, *f*; (of wings) envergadura, *f*. **with a s. of the arm**, con un gesto del brazo. **to make a clean s. of**, hacer tabla rasa de

sweeping *a* completo; comprensivo; demasiado general; radical. **a s. judgment**, un juicio demasiado general. **s. change**, cambio radicale, *m pl*. **s. brush**, escoba, *f*

sweepings *n pl* barreduras, *f pl*; residuos, *m pl*; (of society) heces, *f pl*

sweepstake *n* lotería, *f*

sweet *a* dulce; (of scents) oloroso, fragante; (of sounds) melodioso, dulce; (charming) encantador; amable; (pretty) bonito. *n* bombón, *m*; golosina, *f*; (at a meal) (plato) dulce, *m*; dulzura, *f*; (beloved) amor, *m*, querido (-da). **How s. it smells!** ¡Qué buen olor tiene! **the sweets of life**, las dulzuras de la vida. **s.-pea**, guisante de olor, *m*, haba de las Indias, *f*. **s.-potato**, batata, *f*, *Lat. Am.* boniato, camote, *m*. **s.-scented**, perfumado, fragante. **s.-tempered**, amable, de carácter dulce. **s.-toothed**, goloso. **s.-william**, *bot* clavel de la China, clavel de ramillete, clavel de San Isidro, ramillete de Constantinopla, *m*, minutisa, *f*

sweetbread *n* lechecillas, *f pl*

sweeten *vt* azucarar; endulzar. **Cervantes sweetens one's bitter moments**, Cervantes endulza los momentos ásperos

sweetheart *n* amante, *mf*, amado (-da); (as address) querido (-da)

sweet potato *n* batata, *f*, boniato, buniato, camote, *m*

sweet sixteen *n* (age) los dieciséis abriles, *m pl*; (party) quinceañera (at age fifteen) *f*

sweet turnip *Central America* jícama, *f*

swell *vi* hincharse; (of the sea) entumecerse; crecer; aumentarse. *vt* hinchar; aumentar. *n* (of the sea) oleada, *f*, oleaje, *m*; (of the ground) ondulación, *f*; (of sound) crescendo, *m*; (increase) aumento, *m*; (dandy) pisaverde, elegante, *m*; (important person) pájaro gordo, *m*; (at games, etc.) espada, *m*. *a* estupendo; elegantísimo; de primera, excelente. **to suffer from swelled head**, tener humos, darse importancia. **This foot is swollen**, Este pie está hinchado (or tumefacto). **The refugees have swelled the population**, Los refugiados han aumentado la población. **eyes swollen with tears**, ojos arrasados de lágrimas. **to s. with pride**, hincharse de orgullo

swelling n hinchazón, f; med tumefacción, f; (bruise, etc.) chichón, m

swelter vi abrasarse; arder. n bochorno, calor sofocante, m

swerve vi desviarse; apartarse (de); torcerse. n desvío, m

swift a rápido, veloz; pronto. adv velozmente, rápidamente. n orn vencejo, m. **s.-flowing,** (of rivers, etc.) de corriente rápida. **s.-footed,** de pies ligeros

swim vi nadar; flotar; (glide) deslizarse; (fill) inundarse. vt (a horse) hacer nadar; pasar a nado; nadar. n natación, f. **eyes swimming with tears,** ojos inundados de lágrimas. **He enjoys a s.,** Le gusta nadar. **My head swims,** Se me va la cabeza. **Everything swam before my eyes,** Todo parecía bailar ante mis ojos. **to be in the s.,** formar parte (de), ser (de); (be up to date) estar al corriente. **to s. the Channel,** atravesar el canal de la Mancha a nado. **to s. with the tide,** ir con la corriente

swimmer n nadador (-ra). **He is a bad s.,** Nada mal

swimming n natación, f; (of the head) vértigo, m. **s.-bath,** piscina, f. **s.-costume,** traje de baño, m. **s.-pool,** piscina, f, Lat. Am. alberca, f

swindle vt engañar, estafar; defraudar (de). n estafa, f, timo, m; engaño, m; impostura, f, Lat. Am. cambullón, Argentina forro, m

swindler n estafador (-ra), trampeador (-ra); engañador (-ra)

swine n cerdo, puerco, m; (person) cochino (-na). **a herd of s.,** una manada de cerdos

swing vi balancearse; oscilar; (hang) colgar, pender; 'columpiarse; girar; dar la vuelta; (of a boat) bornear. vt balancear; (hang) colgar; (rock) mecer; (in a swing, etc.) columpiar; hacer oscilar; (raise) subir. n oscilación, f; vaivén, m; balanceo, m; (rhythm) ritmo, m; (seat, etc.) columpio, m; (reach) alcance, m. **The door swung open,** La puerta se abrió silenciosamente. **He swung the car round,** Dio la vuelta al auto. **He swung himself into the saddle,** Montó de un salto. **to be in full s.,** estar a toda marcha. **to go with a s.,** tener mucho éxito. **s.-boat,** columpio, m. **s.-bridge,** puente giratorio, m. **s.-door,** puerta giratoria, f

swinging a oscilante; pendiente; rítmico. n balanceo, m; oscilación, f; vaivén, m; ritmo, m. **s. stride,** andar rítmico, m

swipe vt golpear duro; aplastar; (steal) Mexico chalequear. n golpe fuerte, m

swirl vi arremolinarse. n remolino, m

swish vt (of an animal's tail) agitar, mover, menear; (a cane) blandir; (thrash) azotar. vi silbar; (of water) susurrar; (of a dress, etc.) crujir. n silbo, m; (of water) susurro, murmullo, m; (of a dress, etc.) crujido, m

Swiss a and n suizo (-za)

switch n vara, f; (riding) látigo, m; (of hair) trenza, f; elec interruptor, m; rw aguja, f; (rw siding) desviadero, m. vt azotar; (a train) desviar; elec interrumpir; (transfer) trasladar; (of an animal, its tail) remover, mover rápidamente. **to s. off,** (elec and telephone) cortar; (rad and aut) desconectar. **to s. on,** conectar; (a light) poner (la luz); (a radio) encender

switchboard n cuadro de distribución, m

Switzerland Suiza, f

swivel n torniquete, m; anillo móvil, m; pivote, m. vi girar sobre un eje; dar una vuelta. **s.-chair,** silla giratoria, f. **s.-door,** puerta giratoria, f

swoon vi desvanecerse, desmayarse. n desmayo, desvanecimiento, m

swoop vi calarse, abatirse; (of robbers, etc.) abalanzarse (sobre). n calada, f. **at one fell s.,** de un solo golpe

sword n espada, f; sable, m. **to measure swords with,** cruzar espadas con. **to put to the s.,** pasar a cuchillo (a). **s.-arm,** brazo derecho, m. **s.-belt,** talabarte, m. **s.-cut,** sablazo, m. **s.-dance,** danza de espadas, f. **s.-fish,** pez espada, pez sierra, espadarte, m, jifía, f. **s.-play,** esgrima, f; manejo de la espada, m. **s.-stick,** bastón de estoque, m. **s.-thrust,** golpe de espada, m; estocada, f

sybarite a and n sibarita, mf

sycophant n sicofanta, m

syllable n sílaba, f

syllabus n programa, m; compendio, m

sylvan a selvático, silvestre; rústico

symbiosis n simbiosis, f

symbol n símbolo, emblema, m; math símbolo, m; (of rank, etc.) insignia, f

symbolize vt simbolizar

symmetrical a simétrico

symmetry n simetría, f

sympathetic a simpático; compasivo; (of the public, etc.) bien dispuesto. n anat gran simpático, m. **s. words,** palabras de simpatía, f pl. **s. ink,** tinta simpática, f

sympathize vi simpatizar (con); (understand) comprender; (condole) compadecerse (de), condolerse (de); dar el pésame

sympathizer n partidario (-ia)

sympathy n simpatía, f; compasión, f. **Paul is in s. with their aims,** Pablo está de acuerdo con sus objetos. **Please accept my s.,** (on a bereavement) Le acompaño a Vd. en su sentimiento

symphonic a sinfónico

symphony n sinfonía, f

symposium n colección de artículos, f

symptom n síntoma, m; señal, f, indicio, m. **to show symptoms of,** dar indicios de

symptomatic a sintomático

synagogue n sinagoga, f

synchronize vi coincidir, tener lugar simultáneamente; sincronizarse. vt sincronizar

synchronous a sincrónico

syncopate vt (gram mus) sincopar

syncopation n mus síncopa, f

syncope n (med gram) síncope, m

syndical a sindical

syndicalist n sindicalista, mf

syndicate n sindicato, m, vt sindicar

synod n ecc sínodo, m

synonym n sinónimo, m

synonymous a sinónimo

synopsis n sinopsis, f

syntax n sintaxis, f

synthesis n síntesis, f

synthetic a sintético

synthetize vt sintetizar

syphilis n sífilis, f

Syria Siria, f

Syrian a and n siríaco (-ca), sirio (-ia)

syringe n jeringa, f, vt jeringar

syrup n jarabe, m; (for bottling fruit, etc.) almíbar, m

syrup cake Argentina chancaca, f

system n sistema, m; régimen, m; método, m; (body) organismo, m. **He has no s. in his work,** No tiene método en su trabajo. **the nervous s.,** el sistema nervioso. **the feudal s.,** el feudalismo, el sistema feudal

systematic a sistemático, metódico

systole n med sístole, f

T

t n (letter) te, f. **a** en T, en forma de T. **T bandage,** vendaje en T, m. **T square,** regla T, f

tab n oreja, f

tabernacle n tabernáculo, m; templo, m; arch templete, m; ecc custodia, f

tabes n med tabes, f

table n mesa, f; (food) comida, mesa, f; (of the law, weights, measures, contents, etc.) tabla, f; (of land) meseta, f; (of prices) lista, tarifa, f. vt (parliament) poner sobre la mesa; enumerar, apuntar, hacer una lista de. **to clear the t.,** alzar (or levantar) la mesa. **to lay the t.,** cubrir (or poner) la mesa. **to have a t.-d'hôte meal,** tomar el menú. **to rise from t.,** levantarse de la mesa. **to sit down to t.,** ponerse a la mesa. **The tables are turned,** Se volvió la tortilla. **side t.,** aparador, trinchero, m. **small t.,** mesilla, f. **t. of contents,** tabla de materias, f, índice, índice de materias, índice general, m. **t.-centrepiece,** centro de mesa, m. **t.-cloth,** mantel, m. **t.-companion,** comensal, mf **t.-knife,** cuchillo de mesa, m. **t.-lamp,** quinqué, m; lampara de mesa, f. **t.-land,** meseta, f. **t.-leg,** pata de una mesa, f. **t.-linen,** mantelería, f. **t.-napkin,** servilleta, f. **t.-runner,** camino de mesa, m. **t.-spoon,** cuchara para los legumbres, f. **t.-talk,** conversación de sobremesa, f. **t.-turning,** mesas que dan vueltas, f pl. **t.-ware,** artículos para la mesa, m pl

table d'hôte n Spain el menú m, Mexico comida corrida, f

tableau n cuadro, m. **tableaux vivants,** cuadros vivos, m pl

tablespoonful n cucharada, f

tablet n tabla, f; (with inscription) tarjeta, losa, lápida, f; med comprimido, m, tableta, f; (of soap, chocolate) pastilla, f. **writing t.,** taco de papel, m

tabloid n comprimido, m, pastilla, f

taboo n tabú, m. a prohibido, tabú. vt declarar tabú, prohibir

tabor n mus tamboril, tamborín, m. **t. player,** tamborilero, m

tabulate vt resumir en tablas; hacer una lista de, catalogar

tacit a tácito

taciturn a taciturno, sombrío, reservado, de pocas palabras

tack n (nail) tachuela, puntilla, f; sew hilván, embaste, m; naut amura, f; naut puño de amura, m; naut bordada, f; fig cambio de política, m. vt clavar con tachuelas; sew hilvanar, embastar; fig añadir. vi naut virar; fig cambiar de política, adoptar un nuevo plan de acción. **t. puller,** sacabrocas, m

tackle n aparejo, m; maniobra, f; naut cuaderna, m, jarcia, f; (gear) aparejos, avíos, m pl; (football) carga, f. vt agarrar, asir; fig atacar, abordar; (football) cargar; (undertake) emprender; (a problem) luchar con. **t.-block,** polea, f

tacky a pegajoso, viscoso

tact n tacto, m, discreción, diplomacia, delicadeza, f

tactful a lleno de tacto, diplomático, discreto

tactical a táctico

tactics n pl táctica, f

tactile a táctil; tangible

tactless a que no tiene tacto, sin tacto alguno, indiscreto

tadpole n renacuajo, m

taffeta n tafetán, m

tag n herrete, m; (label) marbete, m, etiqueta, f; (of tail) punta del rabo, f; (of boot) tirador de bota, m; (game) marro, m; (rag) arrapiezo, m; (quotation) cita bien conocida, f; (of song, poem) refrán, m. **to play t.,** jugar al marro

Tagus el Tajo, m

tail n cola, f, rabo, m; (plait) trenza, f; (wisp of hair) mechón, m; (of a comet) cola, cabellera, f; (of a note in music) rabito, m; (of a coat) faldón, m; (of a kite) cola, f; (of the eye) rabo, m; (retinue) séquito, m, banda, f; (of an aeroplane) cola, f; (end) fin, m; (of coin) cruz, f; (line) fila, cola, f. vt seguir de cerca, pisarle (a uno) los talones. **to t. after,** seguir de cerca. **to t. away,** disminuir; desaparecer, perderse de vista. **to t. on,** unir, juntar. **to turn t.,** volver la espalda, poner los pies en polvorosa. **with the t. between the legs,** con el rabo entre piernas. **t.-board,** (of a cart) escalera, f. **t.-coat,** frac, m. **t.-end,** extremo, m; fin, m; lo último. **t.-feather,** pena, f. **t.-fin,** aleta caudal, f; aer timón de dirección, m. **t.-light,** farol trasero, m, Mexico calavera, f. **t.-piece,** (of a violin, etc.) cola, f; print marmosete, culo de lámpara, m. **t. spin** aer barrena de cola, f. **t. wind,** viento de cola, m

tailed a de rabo. **big-t.,** rabudo, de cola grande. **long-t.,** rabilargo. **short-t.,** rabicorto

tailless a rabón, sin rabo

tailor n sastre, m. **t.-made,** n traje sastre, m, a de hechura de sastre. **tailor's shop,** sastrería, f

tailoress n sastra, f

tailoring n sastrería, f; (work) corte, m

taint n corrupción, f; infección, f; (blemish) mancha, f; (tinge) dejo, m. vt corromper, pervertir; inficionar; (meat) corromper. vi corromperse, inficionarse; (meat) corromperse

take vt tomar; (receive) aceptar; (remove) quitar; (pick up) coger; (grab) asir, agarrar; math restar; (carry) llevar; (a person) traer, llevar; (guide) conducir, guiar; (win) ganar; (earn) cobrar, percibir; obtener; (make prisoner) hacer prisionero, prender; (a town, etc.) tomar, rendir, conquistar; (appropriate) apoderarse de, apropiarse; (steal) robar, hurtar; (ensnare) coger, cazar con trampas; (fish) pescar, coger; (a trick, in cards) hacer (una baza); (an illness) contraer, coger; (by surprise) sorprender, coger desprevenido (a); (attract) atraer; (drink) beber; (a meal) tomar; (select) escoger; (hire) alquilar; (suppose) suponer; (a journal) estar abonado a; (use) emplear, usar; (impers., require) necesitarse, hacer falta; (purchase) comprar; (assume) adoptar, asumir; (a leap) dar (un salto); (a walk) dar (un paseo); (a look) echar (un vistazo); (measures) tomar (medidas); (the chair) presidir; (understand) comprender; (a photograph) sacar (una fotografía); (believe) creer; (consider) considerar; (a note) apuntar; (jump over) saltar; (time) tomar, emplear. **I t. size three in shoes,** Calzo el número tres. **to t. to be,** (believe) suponer; (mistake) creer equivocadamente. **to t. (a thing) badly,** tomarlo (or llevarlo) a mal. **The book took me two hours to read,** Necesité dos horas para leer el libro, Leí el libro en dos horas. **And this, I t. it, is Mary?** ¿Y supongo que ésta será María? **to be taken with,** ser entusiasta de; (of persons) estar prendado de. **to t. aback,** desconcertar, coger desprevenido (a). **to t. again,** volver a tomar; llevar otra vez; (a photograph) retratar otra vez. **to t. along,** llevar; traer. **to t. a long time,** tardar, *Lat. Am.* dilatar. **to t. away,** quitar; llevarse. **to t. back,** devolver; (retract) retractar; (receive) recibir (algo) devuelto. **to t. down,** bajar; (a building) derribar; (machinery) desmontar; (hair) deshacerse (el cabello); (swallow) tragar; (in writing) apuntar; (humble) quitar los humos (a), humillar. **to t. for,** creer, imaginar; (a walk, etc.) llevar a; (mistake) creer erróneamente; tomar por. **Whom do you t. me for?** ¿Por quién me tomas? **to t. for granted (assume),** dar por descontado, dar por lecho, dar por sentado, dar por supuesto; (underestimate) no hacer caso de, tratar con indiferencia. **t. the lion's share (of),** llevarse la parte del león (de), llevarse la tajada del león (de). **t. shape,** cobrar perfiles más nítidos, estructurarse con más nitidez, ir adquiriendo consistencia, tomar forma. **t. the law into one's own hands,** tomar la justicia por la mano. **to t. from,** privar, quitar de; (subtract) restar; substraer de. **to t. in,** (believe) tragar, creer; (sail) acortar las velas; (deceive) engañar; (lead in) hacer entrar; (accept) recibir, aceptar. **to t. off,** (surgically) amputar; (one's hat, etc.) quitarse (el sombrero); (eyes) sacar; (take away) llevarse; (mimic) imitar; (ridicule) ridiculizar; (unstick) despegar; (discount) descontar. **to t. on,** emprender; aceptar; (at sports) jugar. **to t.**

on oneself, encargarse de, tomar por su cuenta, asumir. **to t. out,** sacar; extraer; (remove) quitar; (outside) llevar fuera; (for a walk) llevar a paseo; (obtain) obtener, sacar; (tire) agotar, rendir. **to t. over,** tomar posesión de; asumir; (show) mostrar, conducir por. **t. the bull by the horns,** ir al toro por los cuernos. **take seriously,** tomar en serio. **to t. up,** subir; (pick up) recoger; tomar; (a challenge, etc.) aceptar; (a dress, etc.) acortar; (absorb) absorber; (of space) ocupar; (of time) ocupar, hacer perder; (buy) comprar; (adopt) dedicarse a; (arrest) arrestar, prender; (criticize) censurar, criticar; (begin) empezar; (resume) continuar

take *vi* tomar; (be successful) tener éxito; (of vaccination, etc.) prender; (a good (bad) photograph) salir bien (mal). **to t. after,** salir a, parecerse a; (of conduct) seguir el ejemplo de; **to t. off,** salir; *aer* despegar. **to t. on,** *inf* lamentarse. **to t. to,** dedicarse a; darse a; (of persons) tomar cariño a; (grow accustomed) acostumbrarse a. **to t. up with,** hacerse amigo de

take *n* toma, *f*; cogida, *f*; *print* tomada, *f*; *theat* taquilla, *f*. **t.-in,** engaño, *m*. **t.-off,** *aer* (recorrido de) despegue, *m*; caricatura, *f*; sátira, *f*

taking *n* toma, *f*; secuestro, *m*, *n pl* **takings,** ingresos, *m pl*; *theat* taquilla, entrada, *f*. *a* atractivo, encantador; simpático; (of disease) contagioso

talcum powder *n* talco, polvo de talco, *m*

tale *n* (recital) narración, historia, *f*; relato, *m*; cuento, *m*; leyenda, historia, fábula, *f*; (number) cuenta, *f*, número, *m*; (gossip) chisme, *m*. **old wives' t.,** cuento de viejas, *m*. **to tell a t.,** contar una historia. **to tell tales,** contar cuentos; revelar secretos, chismear

talebearer *n* correveidile, *mf*; chismoso (-sa), soplón (-ona)

talent *n* (coin) talento, *m*; (ability) ingenio, *m*; habilidad, *f*. **the best t. in Spain,** la flor de la cultura española

talented *a* talentoso, ingenioso

talisman *n* talismán, *m*

talit taled, *m*

talk *vi and vt* hablar, decir. **to t. business,** hablar de negocios. **to t. for talking's sake,** hablar por hablar. **to t. French,** hablar francés. **to t. nonsense,** decir disparates. **to t. too much,** hablar demasiado; *inf* hablar por los codos; irse (a uno) la lengua. **to t. about,** hablar de; conversar sobre. **to t. at,** decir algo a alguien para que lo entienda otro. **Are you talking at me?** ¿Lo dices por mí? **to t. away,** seguir hablando; disipar. **to t. into,** persuadir, inducir (a). **to t. of,** hablar de; charlar sobre. **to t. on,** (continue) seguir hablando. **to t. out of,** disuadir de. **to t. out of turn,** meterse donde no le llaman, meter la pata. **to t. over,** hablar de; discutir, considerar. **to t. round,** persuadir. **to t. to,** (address) hablar a; (consult) hablar con; (scold) reprender. **to t. to each other,** hablarse. **to t. up,** hablar claro

talk n conversación, f; (informal lecture) charla, f; (empty words) palabras, f pl; (notoriety) escándalo, m; rumor, m. **There is t. of . . . ,** Se dice que . . . ; Se habla de que. **to give a t.,** dar una charla. **to indulge in small t.,** hablar de cosas sin importancia, hablar de naderías

talkative a locuaz, gárrulo, hablador, decidor. **to be very t.,** ser muy locuaz; inf tener mucha lengua

talker n hablador (-ra), conversador (-ra); (lecturer) orador (-ra); (in a derogatory sense) fanfarrón (-ona), charlatán (-ana). **to be a good t.,** hablar bien, ser buen conversacionista

talking a.que habla, hablante; (of birds, dolls, etc.) parlero. **to give a good t. to,** dar una peluca (a). **t.-film,** película sonora, f. **t.-machine,** fonógrafo, m

tall a alto; (of stories) exagerado. **five feet tall,** de cinco pies de altura

tallboy n cómoda alta, f

tallow n sebo, m. **t. candle,** vela de sebo, f. **t. chandler,** velero (-ra). **t.-faced,** con cara de color de cera

tall tale Peru bacho, m

tally n tarja, tara, f; cuenta, f. vt llevar la cuenta (de). vi estar conforme, cuadrar

Talmud n Talmud, m

Talmudic a talmúdico

tambour n mus tambor, m; (for embroidery) tambor (or bastidor) para bordar, m

tambourine n pandereta, f

tame a domesticado, manso; (spiritless) sumiso; (dull) aburrido, soso. vt domar, domesticar; (curb) reprimir, gobernar, domar, suavizar. **to grow t.,** domesticarse

taming n domadura, f. **The T. of the Shrew,** La Fierecilla Domada

tamp vt apisonar; (in blasting) atacar (un barreno)

tamper vi (with) descomponer, estropear; (meddle with) meterse con; (witnesses) sobornar; (documents) falsificar

tampon n surg tampón, tapón, m, vt taponar

tan vt curtir, adobar; (of sun) tostar, quemar; (slang) zurrar. vi tostarse por el sol. n color café claro, m; bronceado, cutis tostado, m. a de color café claro

tandem n tándem, m

tang n (of sword, etc.) espiga, f; (flavor) fuerte sabor, m; (sound) retintín, m

tangent a and n tangente f. **to fly off at a t.,** fig salir por la tangente

tangerine a and n tangerino (-na). **t. orange,** naranja mandarina, f

tangible a tangible; fig real

tangle n embrollo, enredo, nudo, m; (of streets) laberinto, m; fig confusión, f. vt embrollar, enmarañar; (entangle) enredar; fig poner en confusión, complicar. vi enmarañarse

tank n tanque, depósito (de agua, etc.), m; cisterna, f; (as a reservoir) aljibe, estanque, m; mil tanque, carro de asalto, m. **t. up** (get drunk) Argentina acatarrarse

tanker n petrolero, m

tanned a bronceado, quemado por el sol, dorado por el sol

tannery n curtiduría, f

tantalize vt tentar, atormentar, provocar

tantalizing a tentador, atormentador; provocativo

tantamount a equivalente, igual. **to be t. to,** ser equivalente a

tantrum n pataleta, rabieta, f, berrinche, m

tap n (blow) pequeño golpe, toque ligero, m; palmadita, f; (for drawing water, etc.) grifo, m, llave, f; (of a barrel) canilla, f; (brew of liquor) clase de vino, f; (taproom) bar con mostrador, m; (tool) macho de terraja, m; (piece of leather on shoe) tapa, f; pl **taps,** mil toque de apagar las luces, m. vt (strike) golpear ligeramente, dar una palmadita a; (pierce) horadar; (a barrel) decentar; surg hacer una puntura en; (trees) sangrar; elec derivar (una corriente); (of water, current) tomar; (information) descubrir; (telephone) escuchar las conversaciones telefónicas. vi golpear ligeramente. **to tap at the door,** llamar suavemente a la puerta. **on tap,** en tonel. **screw-tap,** terraja, f. **tap-dance,** claqué, m. **tap-root,** raíz pivotante, f

tape n (linen) cinta de hilo, f; (cotton) cinta de algodón, f; (telegraph machine) cinta de papel, f; (surveying) cinta para medir, f. **adhesive t.,** cinta adhesiva, f. **red t.,** balduque, m; fig burocracia, f; formulismo, m. **t.-machine,** telégrafo de cotizaciones, bancarias, m. **t.-measure,** cinta métrica, f

taper n bujía, cerilla, f; ecc cirio, m. vi ahusarse, rematar en punta. vt afilar

tapering a cónico, piramidal; (of fingers) afilado

tapestry n tapiz, m. **t. weaver,** tapicero, m

tapeworm n tenia, lombriz solitaria, f

tapis, to be on the estar sobre el tapete

tar n alquitrán, m, brea, f. vt embrear, alquitranar. **to tar and feather,** emplumar. **coal t.,** alquitrán mineral, m

tarantula n tarántula, f

tardy a (late) tardío; (slow) lento; (reluctant) desinclinado

tare n bot yero, m; (in the Bible) cizaña, f; com tara, f; (of a vehicle) peso en vacío, m

target n blanco (de tiro), m; (shield)

rodela, tarja, *f.* **t. practice**, tiro al blanco, *m*

tariff *n* tarifa, *f.* **to put a t. on**, tarifar

tarmac *n* alquitranado, *m*

tarn *n* lago de montaña, *m*

tarnish *n* deslustre, *m. vt* deslustrar, empañar; *fig* obscurecer, manchar. *vi* deslustrarse

tarpaulin *n* alquitranado, encerado, *m*

tarry *vi* tardar, detenerse

tart *a* ácido, acerbo, agridulce; *fig* áspero. *n* tarta, *f;* pastelillo de fruta, *m*

tartar *n chem* tártaro, *m;* (in teeth) sarro, tártaro, *m;* **cream of t.**, (cremor) tártaro, *m.* **t. emetic**, tártaro emético, *m.* **Tartar**, a and *n* tártaro (-ra)

task *n* tarea, labor, *f;* empresa, *f;* misión, *f.* **to take to t.**, regañar, censurar. **t.-force**, (naval or military) contingente, *m*

taskmaster *n* el que señala una tarea; amo, *m*

tassel *n* borla, *f;* (of corn) panoja, espiga, *f*

taste *n* gusto, *m;* (flavor) sabor, *m;* (specimen) ejemplo, *m,* idea, *f;* (small quantity) un poco, muy poco; (liking) afición, inclinación, *f;* (of drink) sorbo, trago, *m;* (tinge) dejo, *m. vt* (appraise) probar; gustar, percibir el gusto de; (experience) experimentar, conocer. *vi* tener gusto, tener sabor. **a matter of t.**, cuestión de gusto. **Each to his own t.**, Entre gustos no hay disputa. **He had not tasted a bite**, No había probado bocado. **in bad (good) t.**, de mal (buen) gusto; de mal (buen) tono. **to have a t. for**, ser aficionado a, gustar de. **to t.**, *cul* a gusto, a sabor. **to t. of**, tener gusto de, saber a

tasted *a* (in compounds) de sabor . . .

tasteful *a* de buen gusto

tastefully *adv* con buen gusto

tasteless *a* insípido, soso, insulso; de mal gusto

taster *n* catador, *m;* (vessel) catavino, *m*

tasting *n* saboreo, *m,* gustación, *f,* a (in compounds) de sabor . . .

tasty *a* apetitoso, sabroso

tatter *n* andrajo, harapo, *m;* jirón, *m.* **to tear in tatters**, hacer jirones

tattered *a* andrajoso, haraposo

tattoo *n* tatuaje, *m;* mil retreta, *f;* (display) parada militar, *f. vt* tatuar

taunt *n* mofa, *f,* insulto, escarnio, *m. vt* insultar, atormentar. **to t. with**, echar en cara

taunting *a* insultante, burlón, insolente

tauntingly *adv* burlonamente, insolentemente

taut *a* tieso, tirante, tenso; en regla; *naut* **to make t.**, tesar

tauten *vt* tesar; poner tieso

tautological *a* tautológico

tavern *n* taberna, *f;* (inn) mesón, *m,* posada, *f.* **t.-keeper**, tabernero, *m*

tawdrily *adv* llamativamente, de un modo cursi

tawdry *a* chillón, charro, cursi

tawny *a* leonado

tax *n* contribución, gabela, imposición, *f; fig* carga, *f; vt* imponer contribuciones (a); *law* tasar; *fig* cargar, abrumar. **to tax with**, tachar (de), acusar (de). **direct (indirect) tax**, contribución directa (indirecta), *f.* **tax-collector**, recaudador de contribuciones, *m.* **tax-free**, libre de impuestos. **tax-rate**, tarifa de impuestos, *f,* cupo, *m.* **tax-register**, lista de contribuyentes, *f*

taxable *a* imponible, sujeto a impuestos

taxation *n* imposición de contribuciones (or impuestos), *f*

tax evasion *n* evasión tributaria, *f*

taxi *n* taxi, *Mexico* libre, *m. vi* ir en un taxi; *aer* correr por tierra. **t. driver**, chófer de un taxi, taxista, *m.* **t. rank**, taxi stand, parada de taxis, *f*

taxidermist *n* taxidermista, *mf*

taxpayer *n* contribuyente, *mf*

taxpaying *a* tributario, que paga contribuciones

tax reform *n* reforma impositiva, reforma tributaria, *f*

tea *n* (liquid) té, *m;* (meal) merienda, *f.* **to have tea**, tomar el té, merendar. **tea-caddy**, bote para té, *m.* **tea-chest**, caja para té, *f.* **tea-cosy**, cubretetera, *m.* **tea-cup**, taza para té, *f.* **tea-dance**, té baile, *m.* **tea-kettle** or **tea-pot**, tetera, *f.* **tea-leaf**, hoja de té, *f.* **tea-party**, reunión para tomar el té, *f.* **tea-room**, salón de té, *m.* **tea-rose**, rosa de té, *f.* **tea-set**, juego de té, *m.* **tea-strainer**, colador de té, *m.* **tea-time**, hora de té, *f.* **tea-urn**, samowar, *m,* tetera para hacer té, *f.* **tea-waggon**, carrito para el té, *m*

teach *vt* (a person) enseñar, instruir; (a subject) enseñar; (to lecture on) ser profesor de; (a lesson) dar una lección (de). *vi* (be a teacher) dedicarse a la enseñanza. **to teach at . . .**, desempeñar una cátedra en . . . **to t. a person Spanish**, enseñar el castellano a alguien. **to t. how to**, enseñar a (followed by infin.)

teachable *a* educable; dócil

teacher *n* preceptor, *m;* profesor, maestro, *m.* **woman t.**, profesora, maestra, *f*

teaching *n* enseñanza, *f;* (belief) doctrina, *f,* a docente. **t. profession**, magisterio, *m*

teak *n bot* teca, *f;* (wood) madera de teca, *f*

team *n* (of horses) tiro, *m;* (of oxen, mules) par, *m,* pareja, yunta, *f; sport* partido, equipo, *m;* compañía, *f,* grupo, *m. vt* enganchar, uncir. **t.-work**, cooperación, *f*

teamster *n* gañán, *m*

tear *vt* rasgar; romper; lacerar; (in pieces) hacer pedazos, despedazar; (scratch) arañar; *fig* atormentar. **to t. asunder,** romper; desmembrar. **to t. away,** arrancar, quitar violentamente. **to t. down,** derribar, echar abajo. **to t. off,** arrancar; desgajar. **to t. oneself away,** arrancarse, desgarrarse. **to t. one's hair,** arrancarse los pelos, mesarse. **to t. open,** abrir apresuradamente. **to t. up,** hacer pedazos; (uproot) arrancar, desarraigar.

tear *vi* rasgarse; romper; correr precipitadamente. **to t. along,** correr rápidamente (por). **to t. away,** marcharse corriendo. **to t. down,** bajar corriendo. **to t. into,** entrar corriendo en. **to t. off,** irse precipitadamente, marcharse corriendo. **to t. up,** subir corriendo; llegar corriendo; atravesar rápidamente

tear *n* lágrima, *f*; (drop) gota, *f*. **with tears in one's eyes,** con lágrimas en los ojos. **to shed tears,** llorar, lagrimear. **to wipe away one's tears,** secarse las lágrimas. **t.-drop,** lágrima, *f*. **t.-duct,** conductor lacrimal, *m*. **t.-gas,** gas lacrimante, *m*. **t.-stained,** mojado de lágrimas

tear *n* (rent) rasgón, *m*

tearful *a* lloroso, lacrimoso

tearjerker *n* drama lacrimón, *m*

tease *vt* (card) cardar; (annoy) fastidiar, irritar, molestar; (chaff) tomar el pelo (a), embromar; (pester) importunar. *n* bromista, *mf*

teaser *n* (problem) rompecabezas, *m*; (person) bromista, *mf*

teaspoon *n* cucharita, *f*

teaspoonful *n* cucharadita, *f*

teat *n* pezón, *m*; (of animals) teta, *f*

technical *a* técnico. **t. offence,** *law* cuasidelito, *m*. **t. school,** escuela industrial, *f*

technicality *n* carácter técnico, *m*; tecnicismo, *m*; detalle técnico, *m*

technician *n* técnico, *m*

technicolor *n* tecnicolor, *m*

technique *n* técnica, *f*; ejecución, *f*; mecanismo, *m*

technological *a* tecnológico

technology *n* tecnología, *f*

teddy bear *n* osito de trapo, *m*

tedious *a* aburrido, tedioso, pesado

tedium *n* tedio, *m*, monotonía, *f*

tee *n* *sport* meta, *f*; (golf) tee, *m*; (letter) te, *f*; cosa en forma de te, *f*. *vt* (golf) colocar la pelota en el tee

teem *vi* rebosar (de), abundar (en); pulular, hormiguear, estar lleno (de); (with rain) diluviar

teeming *a* prolífico, fecundo. **t. with,** abundante en, lleno de

teens *n pl* números y años desde trece hasta diez y nueve; edad de trece a diez y nueve años de edad. **to be still in one's t.,** no haber cumplido aún los veinte

teeter *vi* balancearse, columpiarse

teethe *vi* endentecer, echar los dientes

teething *n* dentición, *f*. **t.-ring,** chupador, *m*

teetotaller *n* abstemio (-ia)

teetotum *n* perinola, *f*

telecast *vt* telefundir

telecommunication *n* telecomunicación, *f*

telegram *n* telegrama, *m*

telegraph *n* telégrafo, *m*. *vi* telegrafiar; *fig* hacer señas. *vt* telegrafiar, enviar por telégrafo. **t. line,** línea telegráfica, *f*. **t. office,** central de telégrafos, *f*. **t. pole,** poste telegráfico, *m*. **t. wire,** hilo telegráfico, *m*

telegraphic *a* telegráfico

telepathic *a* telepático

telepathy *n* telepatía, *f*

telephone *n* teléfono, *m*. *vi* telefonear. *vt* telefonear, llamar por teléfono. **to be on the t.,** (speaking) estar comunicando; (of subscribers) tener teléfono. **dial t.,** teléfono automático, *m*. **t. call,** comunicación telefónica, *f*; conversación telefónica, *f*. **t. call box,** teléfono público, *m*. **t. directory,** guía de teléfonos, *f*. **t. exchange,** central telefónica, *f*. **t. number,** número de teléfono, *m*. **t. operator,** telefonista, *mf*. **t. receiver,** receptor telefónico, *m*. **t. wire,** hilo telefónico, *m*

telephony *n* telefonía, *f*. **wireless t.,** telefonía sin hilos, *f*

teleprinter *n* teletipo, *m*

telescope *n* telescopio, catalejo, *m*. *vt* enchufar. *vi* enchufarse, meterse una cosa dentro de otra

telescopic *a* telescópico; de enchufe

televise *vt* trasmitir por televisión

television *n* televisión, *f*. **on television,** por televisión. **I saw her on television,** La vi por televisión

television series *n* serie televisiva, *f*

tell *vt* contar, narrar; decir; revelar; expresar; (the time, of clocks) marcar; (inform) comunicar, informar; (show) indicar, manifestar; (explain) explicar; distinguir; (order) mandar; (compute) contar. *vi* decir; (have effect) producir efecto. **We cannot t.,** No sabemos. **Who can t.?** ¿Quién sabe? **T. that to the marines!** ¡Cuéntaselo a tu tía! **to t. its own tale,** hacer ver por sí mismo lo que hay. **to t. again,** volver a decir; contar otra vez. **to t. off,** regañar, reñir; (on a mission) despachar, mandar. **to t. on,** delatar. **to t. upon,** afectar

teller *n* narrador (-ra); (of votes) escrutador (-ra) de votos; (payer) pagador (-ra), *m*; (bank) cajero (-ra), *m*

telling *a* notable, significante. *n* narración, *f*

telltale *n* chismoso (-sa), soplón (-ona) (informer) acusón (-ona); *fig* indicio, *m*, señal, *f*, a revelador

temerity n temeridad, f

temper n (of metals) temple, m; (nature) naturaleza, f, carácter, m; espíritu, m; (mood) humor, m; (anger) mal genio, m. vt (of metals) templar; moderar, mitigar; mezclar. vi templarse. **bad (good) t.,** mal (buen) humor. **to keep one's t.,** no enojarse, no impacientarse. **to lose one's t.,** enojarse, perder la paciencia

temperament n temperamento, m; modo de ser, natural, m, naturaleza, índole, f; mus temple, m

temperamental a natural, innato; caprichoso

temperance n moderación, templanza, f; sobriedad, abstinencia, f

temperate a moderado; sobrio; (of regions) templado. **t. zone,** zona templada, f

temperature n temperatura, f. **to have a t.,** tener fiebre

tempered a de humor . . . , de genio . . . **to be good (bad) t.,** ser de buen (mal) humor

tempering n temperación, f

tempest n tempestad, borrasca, f, temporal, m; fig tormenta, f

tempest in a teapot borrasca en un vaso de agua, m

tempestuous a tempestuoso, borrascoso; fig impetuoso, violento

temple n templo, m; anat sien, f

tempo n mus tiempo, m

temporal a temporal; (transient) transitorio, fugaz; anat temporal. n anat hueso temporal, m

temporarily adv provisionalmente

temporary a provisional, interino

temporize vi ganar tiempo; contemporizar

tempt vt tentar; atraer, seducir

temptation n tentación, f; aliciente, atractivo, m

tempting a tentador, atrayente; seductor

ten a diez; (of the clock) las diez, f pl; (of age) diez años, m pl, n diez, m; (a round number) decena, f; **ten-millionth,** a and n diezmillonésimo m. **ten months old,** diezmesino. **ten syllable,** decasílabo. **ten thousand,** a and n diez mil m. **There are ten thousand soldiers,** Hay diez mil soldados. **ten-thousandth,** a and n diezmilésimo m

tenable a sostenible, defendible

tenacious a tenaz; (stubborn) porfiado, obstinaz, terco; (sticky) adhesivo. **to be t. of life,** estar muy apegado a la vida

tenacity n tenacidad, f; porfía, f; tesón, m

tenant n arrendatario (-ia), inquilino (-na); habitante, m; morador (-ra). **t. farmer** Chile inquilino (-na), mf

tend vt cuidar, atender; guardar; vigilar. vi tender; inclinarse (a), propender (a)

tendency n tendencia, inclinación, propensión, f; proclividad, f

tendentious a tendencioso

tender n guardián, m; com oferta, propuesta, f; naut falúa, f; (of a railway engine) ténder, m. **legal t.,** moneda corriente, f

tender a tierno; delicado; (of conscience) escrupuloso; (of a subject) espinoso; compasivo, afectuoso, sensible; muelle, blando. **t.-hearted,** compasivo, tierno de corazón

tender vt ofrecer; dar; presentar. vi hacer una oferta. **to t. condolences,** dar el pésame. **to t. one's resignation,** presentar la dimisión. **to t. thanks,** dar las gracias

tenderness n ternura, f; sensibilidad, f; delicadeza, f; dulzura, f; indulgencia, f; compasividad, benevolencia, f; escrupulosidad, f; mimo, cariño, m

tendon n anat tendón, m. **t. of Achilles,** tendón de Aquiles, m

tenement n casa de vecindad, f; vivienda, f, Lat. Am. conventillo, m; poet morada, f

tenet n principio, dogma, m, doctrina, f

tenfold a décuplo. adv diez veces

tennis n tenis, m. **to play t.,** jugar al tenis. **t. ball,** pelota de tenis, f. **t. court,** campo de tenis, m, cancha de tenis, pista de tenis, f. **tennis club,** club de tenis, m. **t. racket,** raqueta de tenis, f; **tennis shoe,** zapatilla de tenis, f

tenon n carp espiga, f, vt espigar

tenor n curso, m; tenor, contenido, m; mus tenor, m; mus alto, m; (mus. instrument) viola, f. a mus de tenor

tense n gram tiempo, m. a tirante, estirado, tieso; tenso

tension n tensión, f; elec voltaje, m, tensión, f; (of sewing-machine) tensahílo, m. **state of t.,** (diplomatic) estado de tirantez, m

tent n tienda (de campaña), Lat. Am. carpa, f; (bell) pabellón, m; surg tienda, f. **oxygen t.,** tienda oxígena, f. **to pitch tents,** armar las tiendas de campaña; acamparse. **to strike tents,** plegar tiendas. **t. fly,** toldo de tienda, m. **t. maker,** tendero, m. **t. peg,** clave que sujeta las cuerdas de una tienda, f. **t. pole,** mástil (or montante) de tienda, m

tentacle n tentáculo, m

tentative a tentativo, interino, provisional, de prueba, n tentativa, f, ensayo, m

tentatively adv por vía de ensayo, experimentalmente

tenth a décimo; (of monarchs) diez; (of the month) (el) diez. n décimo, m; (part) décima parte, f; mus decena, f

tenthly adv en décimo lugar

tenuous a tenue; sutil; delgado; fino

tenure n tenencia, posesión, f; (duration) duración, f; (of office) administración, f

tepid a tibio

tercentenary n tercer centenario, m

tercet n terceto, m

term n (limit) límite, fin, m; (period) plazo, tiempo, período, m; (schools, universities) trimestre, m; (math, law, logic) término, m; (word) expresión, palabra, f pl. **terms,** (conditions) condiciones, f pl; (charges) precios, m pl, tarifa, f; (words) términos, m pl, palabras, f pl. vt llamar, calificar. **for a t. of years,** por un plazo de años. **in plain terms,** en palabras claras. **on equal terms,** en condiciones iguales. **to be on bad (good) terms with,** estar en (or tener) malas (buenas) relaciones con. **to come to terms,** llegar a un acuerdo; hacer las paces. **What are your terms?** ¿Cuáles son sus condiciones? (price) ¿Cuáles son sus precios? **terms of sale,** condiciones de venta, f pl

termagant n arpía, fiera, f

terminable a terminable

terminal a terminal, final; (of schools, universities) trimestre. n término, m; elec borne, m; (schools, universities) examen de fin de trimestre, m; (railway) estación terminal, f; (arch and figure) término, m; arch remate, m

terminate vt limitar; terminar, concluir, poner fin (a). vi terminarse, concluirse (por); cesar

termination n terminación, conclusión, f; fin, m; gram terminación, f; cabo, remate, m

terminology n nomenclatura, terminología, f

terminus n (railway) estación terminal, f; (arch and figure) término, m; arch remate, m; myth Término

termite n ent termita, m

term paper n trabajo de examen, m

terrace n terraza, f, vt terraplenar

terracotta n terracota, f

terrain n terreno, campo, m, región, f

terrapin n tortuga de agua dulce, f

terrestrial a terrestre, terrenal

terrible a terrible, pavoroso, espantoso; inf tremendo

terrific a espantoso, terrible; inf atroz, tremendo

terrify vt aterrorizar, espantar, horrorizar, Lat. Am. also julepear: **to be terrified** Lat. Am. julepearse

terrifying a aterrado, espantoso

territorial a territorial. n soldado del ejército territorial, m

territory n región, comarca, f; (state) territorio, m; jurisdicción, f. **mandated territory,** territorio bajo mandato, m pl

terror n terror, pavor, espanto, m. **the Reign of T.,** el Reinado del Terror, m. **t.-stricken,** espantado, muerto de miedo

terrorism n terrorismo, m

terrorist n terrorista, m

terrorize vt aterrorizar

terse a conciso, sucinto; seco, brusco

tertiary a tercero; geol terciario. n ecc terciario, m

test n (proof) prueba, f; examen, m; investigación, f; (standard) criterio, m, piedra de toque, f; chem análisis, m; (trial) ensayo, m; zool concha, f. vt chem ensayar; probar, poner a prueba; examinar; (eyes) graduar (la vista). **to put to the t.,** poner a prueba. **to stand the t.,** soportar la prueba. **t. match,** partido internacional de cricket, m. **t. meal,** med comida de prueba, f. **t. pilot,** aer piloto de pruebas, m. **t. tube,** tubo de ensayo, m

testament n testamento, m. **the New T.,** el Nuevo Testamento, m. **the Old T.,** el Antiguo Testamento, m

testate a testado

testator n testador, m, (**testatrix,** testadora, f)

testicle n testículo, m

testify vt and vi declarar, atestar; law atestiguar, testificar, dar fe

testimonial n recomendación, f; certificado, m; (tribute) homenaje, m

testimony n testimonio, m, declaración, f; (proof) prueba, f. **in t. whereof,** en fe de lo cual. **to bear t.,** atestar

testing grounds n campo de experimentación, campo de pruebas, m

testy a enojadizo, irritable, irascible, quisquilloso

tetanus n tétano, m

tether n traba, atadura, maniota, f. vt atar con una correa. **to be at the end of one's t.,** acabarse la resistencia; acabarse la paciencia

text n texto, m; (subject) tema, m; (motto) lema, m; (of a musical composition) letra, f. **t.-book,** libro de texto, m

textile a textil, de tejer. n textil, m, materia textil, f; tejido, m

texture n (material and biol) tejido, m; textura, f

thalamus n (anat, bot) tálamo, m

Thames, the n el Támesis, m. **to set the T. on fire,** descubrir la pólvora

than conjunc que; (between **more, less,** or **fewer** and a number) de; (in comparisons of inequality) que, but que becomes a del (de la, de los, de las) que if the point of comparison is a noun in the principal clause, which has to be supplied mentally to fill up the ellipsis; (b) de lo que if there is no noun to act as a point of comparison, e.g. **He was older than I thought,** Era más viejo de lo que yo pensaba. **They have less than they deserve,** Tienen menos de lo que merecen. **They lose more money than (the money) they earn,** Pierden más dinero del que ganan. **He will meet with more opposition**

than he thought, Va a encontrar más oposición de la que pensaba. **I have more books than you,** Tengo más libros que tú. **She has fewer than nine and more than five,** Ella tiene menos de nueve y más de cinco

thank vt agradecer, dar las gracias (a). **to t. for,** agradecer. **I will t. you to be more polite,** Le agradecería que fuese más cortés. **He has himself to t. for it,** Él mismo tiene la culpa de ello. **No, t. you,** No, muchas gracias. **T. goodness!** ¡Gracias a Dios!

thank n (now in pl. only, **thanks**) gracias, f pl. **a vote of thanks,** un voto de gracias. **Many thanks!** ¡Muchas gracias! **to return thanks,** dar las gracias. **thanks to,** merced a, debido a. **thanks to you,** gracias a tí. **t.-offering,** ofrecimiento en acción de gracias, m

thankful a agradecido. **I am t. to see,** Me alegro de ver, Me es grato ver

thankfully adv con gratitud, agradecido

thankless a ingrato; desagradecido; desagradable

thanksgiving n acción de gracias, f. **t. service,** servicio de acción de gracias, m. **Thanksgiving (Day),** n día de acción de dar gracias, día de gracias, m

that dem a ese, m; esa, f; aquel, m; aquella, f, dem. pron ése, m; ésa, f; eso, neut; aquél, m; aquélla, f; aquello, neut; (standing for a noun) el, m; la, f; lo, neut **All t. there is,** Todo lo que hay. **His temperament is t. of his mother,** Su temperamento es el de su madre. **We have not come to t. yet,** Todavía no hemos llegado a ese punto. **T. is what I want to know,** Eso es lo que quiero saber. **with t.,** con eso; (thereupon) en eso. **Go t. way,** Vaya Vd. por allí; Tome Vd. aquel camino. **T. is to say . . . ,** Es decir . . . **What do you mean by t.?** ¿Qué quieres decir con eso? **The novel is not as bad as all t.,** La novela no es tan mala como tú piensas (or como dicen, etc.)

that pron. rel que; el cual, m; la cual, f; lo cual, neut; (of persons) a quien, mf; a quienes, mf pl; (with from) de quien, mf; de quienes, mf pl; (of place) donde. **The letter t. I sent you,** la carta que te mandé. **The box t. John put them in,** la caja en la cual los puso Juan. **The last time t. I saw her,** La última vez que la vi

that conjunc que; (of purpose) para que; afin de que; (before infin.) para; (because) porque. **O t. he would come!** ¡Ojalá que viniese! **so t.,** para que; (before infin.) para; (as a result) de manera que; de modo que. **It is better t. he should not come,** Es mejor que no venga. **now t.,** ahora que

thatch n barda, f, vt bardar

thaw n deshielo, m. vt deshelar; derretir. vi deshelarse; derretirse

the def art. el, m; la, f; lo, neut; los, m pl; las, f pl; (before feminine sing. noun be-

ginning with stressed a or ha) el; (untranslated between the name and number of a monarch, pope, ruler, e.g. **Charles the Tenth,** Carlos diez). adv (before a comparative) cuanto, tanto más. **at the** or **to the,** al, m, (also before feminine sing. noun beginning with a or ha); a la, f; a lo, neut; a los, m pl; a las, f pl. **from the** or **of the,** del, m, (also before feminine sing. noun beginning with stressed a or ha); de la, f; de lo, neut; de los, m pl; de las, f pl. **the one,** see **one. The sooner the better,** Cuanto antes mejor. **The room will be all the warmer,** El cuarto estará tanto más caliente

theater n teatro, m; (lecture) anfiteatro, m; (drama) teatro, m, obra dramática, f; (scene) teatro, m, escena, f. **t. attendant,** acomodador (-ra)

theater-in-the-round n teatro circular, teatro en círculo, m

theatrical a teatral. n pl **theatricals,** funciones teatrales, f pl. **amateur theatricals,** función de aficionados, f. **t. company,** compañía de teatro, f. **t. costumier,** mascarero (-ra), alquilador (-ra) de disfraces. **t. manager,** empresario de teatro, m

theatricality n teatralidad, f

thee pers pron te; (after prep.) tí. **with t.,** contigo

theft n robo, hurto, m

their poss a su, mf sing; sus, pl; de ellos, m pl; de ellas, f pl. **They have t. books,** Tienen sus libros. **I have t. books,** Tengo los libros de ellos

theirs poss pron (el) suyo, m; (la) suya, f; (los) suyos, m pl; (las) suyas, f pl; de ellos, m pl; de ellas, f pl. **These hats are t.,** Estos sombreros son los suyos

them pers pron ellos, m pl; ellas, f pl; (as object of a verb) los, m pl; las, f pl; (to them) les

thematic a temático

theme n tema, asunto, m; tesis, f; mus tema, motivo, m

themselves pers pron pl ellos mismos, m pl; ellas mismas, f pl, reflexive pron sí; sí mismos; (with a reflexive verb) se. **They t. told me about it,** Ellos mismos me lo dijeron. **They left it for t.,** Lo dejaron para sí (mismos)

then adv (of future time) entonces; (of past time) a la sazón, en aquella época, entonces; (next, afterwards) luego, después, en seguida; (in that case) en este caso, entonces; (therefore) por consiguiente. a de entonces. n entonces, m. conjunc (moreover) además; pues. **And what t.?** ¿Y qué pasó después?; ¿Y qué pasará ahora?; ¿Y qué más? **by t.,** por entonces. **now and t.,** de vez en cuando. **now . . . t.,** ya . . . ya, ora . . . ora. **since t.,** desde aquel tiempo; desde entonces; desde aquella ocasión. **until t.,** hasta entonces; hasta aquella época. **well t.,**

bien, pues. **t. and there,** en el acto, en seguida; allí mismo

thence *adv* desde allí, de allí; (therefore) por eso, por esa razón, por consiguiente

thenceforth *adv* de allí en adelante, desde entonces

theocracy *n* teocracia, *f*

theologian *n* teólogo, *m*

theological *a* teológico, teologal

theology *n* teología, *f*

theorem *n* teorema, *m*

theoretical *a* teórico

theorist *n* teórico, *m*

theorize *vi* teorizar

theory *n* teoría, *f*

therapeutic *a* terapéutico. *n* **therapeutics,** terapéutica, *f*

therapeutist *n* terapeuta, *mf*

therapy *suffix* terapia, *f*

there *adv* allí; ahí, allá; (at that point) en eso; (used pronominally as subject of verb) haber, e.g. **T. was once a king,** Hubo una vez un rey; **What is t. to do here?** ¿Qué hay que hacer aquí? *interj* ¡vaya!; (I told you so!) ¡ya ves! ¡ya te lo dije yo!; (in surprise) ¡toma! **about t.,** cerca de allí. **down t.,** allí abajo. **in t.,** allí dentro. **out t.,** allí fuera. **over t.,** ahí; allá a lo lejos. **up t.,** allí arriba. **T. came a time when . . . ,** Llegó la hora cuando . . . **T. is!** ¡Allí está! **t. is** or **t. are,** hay. **t. was** or **t. were,** había, hubo. **t. may be,** puede haber, quizás habrá. **t. must be,** tiene que haber. **t. will be,** habrá. **T., t.!** (to a child, etc.) ¡Vamos!

thereabouts *adv* (near to a place) cerca de allí, por ahí, allí cerca; (approximately) approximadamente, cerca de

thereafter *adv* después, después de eso

thereby *adv* (near to that place) por allí cerca; (by that means) con lo cual, de este modo

therefore *adv* por lo tanto, por eso, así, por consiguiente; por esta razón

therein *adv* (inside) allí dentro; (in this, that particular) en estre, en eso, en ese particular

thereinafter *adv* posteriormente, más adelante

thereupon *adv* (in consequence) por consiguiente, por lo tanto; (at that point) luego, en eso; (immediately afterwards) inmediatamente después, en seguida

thermal *a* termal. **t. springs,** aguas termales, termas, *f pl*

thermodynamics *n* termodinámica, *f*

thermoelectric *a* termoeléctrico

thermometer *n* termómetro, *m*

thermos flask *n* termos, *m*

thermostat *n* termostato, *m*

thesaurus *n* tesoro, tesauro, *m*

these *dem pron pl* of **this,** éstos, *m pl*; éstas, *f pl,* *dem a* estos, *m pl*; estas, *f pl.* **Are not t. your flowers?** ¿No son éstas

tus flores? **T. pictures have been sold,** Estos cuadros han se han vendito

thesis *n* tesis, *f*

they *pers pron pl* ellos, *m pl*; ellas, *f pl*; (people) se (followed by sing. verb). **T. say,** Dicen, Se dice

thick *a* espeso; (big) grueso, (wall) grueso, (string, cord) gordo; (vapors) denso; (muddy) turbio; (dense, close) tupido apretado; (numerous) numeroso, repetido, continuo; (full of) lleno (de); (of voice) velado, indistinto; (obtuse) estúpido, lerdo; (friendly) íntimo. *adv* densamente; continuamente, sin cesar. **three feet t.,** de tres pies de espesor. **That's a bit t.!** ¡Eso es un poco demasiado! **to be as t. as thieves,** estar unidos como los dedos de la mano. **t.-lipped,** con labios gruesos, bezudo. **t.-headed,** estúpido, lerdo; **t.-skinned,** de piel gruesa; *zool* paquidermo; *fig* sin vergüenza, insensible. **t. stroke,** (of letters) grueso, *m*

thick *n* espesor, *m*; parte gruesa, *f*; lo más denso; (of a fight) lo más reñido; centro, *m.* **in the t. of,** en el centro (de), en medio de

thicken *vt* espesar; (increase) aumentar, multiplicar; *cul* espesar. *vi* espesarse; condensar; aumentar, multiplicarse; (of a mystery, etc.) complicarse; hacerse más denso; *cul* espesarse

thicket *n* matorral, soto, *m,* maleza, *f*; (grove) boscaje, *m*

thickness *n* espesor, *m*; grueso, *m*; densidad, *f*; (of liquids) consistencia, *f*; (layer) capa, *f*; (of speech) dificultad (en el hablar), *f*

thickset *a* doblado

thief *n* ladrón (-ona); (in a candle) moco de vela, *m.* **Stop t.!** ¡Ladrones! **thieves' den,** *fig* cueva de ladrones, *f*

thieve *vi* hurtar, robar. *vt* robar

thievish *a* ladrón

thigh *n* muslo, *m.* **t.-bone,** fémur, *m*

thimble *n* dedal, *m*

thin *a* delgado; (lean) flaco; (small) pequeño; delicado; fino; (of air, light) tenue, sutil; (clothes) ligero; (sparse) escaso; transparente; (watery) aguado; (of wine) bautizado; (not close) claro; (of arguments) flojo. *vt* adelgazar; aclarar; *agr* limpiar; reducir. *vi* adelgazarse; afilarse; reducirse. **somewhat t.,** (of persons) delgaducho, algo flaco. **to grow t.,** enflaquecer; afilarse. **to make t.,** hacer adelgazar volver flaco. **t.-clad,** ligero de ropa; mal vestido. **t.-faced,** de cara delgada. **t.-lipped,** de labios apretados. **t.-skinned,** de piel fina; *fig* sensitivo, sensible

thine. See **theirs.** *poss pron* (el) tuyo, *m*; (la) tuya, *f*; (los) tuyos, *m pl*; (las) tuyas, *f pl*; tu, *mf*; tus, *mf pl*; de tí. **The fault is t.,** La culpa es tuya, La culpa es de tí

thing *n* cosa, *f*; objeto, artículo, *m*; (affair)

asunto, *m*; (contemptuous) sujeto, tipo, *m*; (creature) ser, *m*, criatura, *f*; *pl* **things,** (belongings) efectos, trastos, *m pl*; (luggage) equipaje, *m*; (clothes) trapitos, *m pl*; (circumstances) circunstancias, condiciones, *f pl.* **above all things,** ante todo, sobre todo. **a very pretty little t.,** (child) una pequeña muy mona. **as things are,** tal como están las cosas. **for one t.,** en primer lugar. **Her behavior is not quite the t.,** La conducta de ella no está bien vista. **It is a bad t. that . . . ,** Lo malo es que . . . **It is a good t. that . . . ,** Lo bueno es que . . . **No such t.!** ¡No hay tal! ¡Nada de eso! **Poor t.!** ¡Pobrecito!; (woman) ¡Pobre mujer!; (man) ¡Pobre hombre! **to be just the t.,** venir al pelo. **with one t. and another,** entre unas cosas y otras. **I like things Spanish,** Me gusta lo español

think *vt* and *vi* pensar; (believe) creer; (deem) considerar, juzgar; imaginar; (suspect) sospechar; (opine) ser de opinión (que). **And to t. that . . . !** ¡Y pensar que . . . ! **As you t. fit,** Como usted quiera, Como a usted le parezca bien. **He thought as much.** Se lo figuraba. **He little thought that . . . !** ¡Cuán lejos estaba de pensar que . . . ! **He thinks nothing of . . . ,** No le importa . . . ; Desprecia, Tiene una opinión bastante mala de. **I don't t. so,** No lo creo. **I should just t. not!** ¡Claro que no! ¡Eso sí que no! **I should just t. so!** ¡Claro! ¡Ya lo creo! **It makes me t. of . . . ,** Me hace pensar en . . . **One might t.,** Podría creerse . . . **to t. better of something,** cambiar de opinión, considerar mejor. **to t. highly (badly) of,** tener buen (mal) concepto sobre. **to t. over carefully,** pensarlo bien, considerar detenidamente; *inf* consultar con la almohada. **to t. proper,** creer conveniente. **to t. to oneself,** pensar para sí (or entre sí). **to t. too much of oneself,** pensar demasiado en sí; tener demasiada buena opinión de sí mismo; tener humos. **What do you t. about it?** ¿Qué te parece? **to t. about,** (of persons) pensar en; (of things) pensar de (or sobre); meditar, considerar, reflexionar sobre. **to t. for,** pensar por. **to t. of,** pensar en; pensar de (or sobre). **What do you t. of this?** ¿Qué te parece esto? **to t. out,** idear, proyectar, hacer planes para; (a problem) resolver. **to t. over,** pensar; reflexionar sobre, meditar sobre. **I shall t. it over,** Lo pensaré.

thinker *n* pensador, *m*

thinking *n* pensamiento, *m*, reflexión, meditación, *f*; juicio, *m*; opinión, *f*, parecer, *m*. a pensador; inteligente; racional; serio. **To my way of t.,** Según pienso yo, A mi parecer. **way of t.,** modo de pensar, *m*

third a tercero (tercer before *m, sing* noun); (of monarchs) tercero; (of the month) (el) tres. *n* tercio, *m*, tercera parte, *f*; *mus* tercera, *f*. **T. time lucky!** ¡A

la tercera va la vencida! **t. class,** *n* tercera clase, *f*. a de tercera clase. **t. party,** tercera persona, *f*. **t.-party insurance,** seguro contra tercera persona, *m*. **t. person,** tercero (-ra); *gram* tercera persona, *f*. **t.-rate,** de tercera clase

thirst *n* sed, *f*; *fig* deseo, *m*, ansia, *f*; entusiasmo, *m*. **to satisfy one's t.,** apagar (or matar) la sed

thirsty a sediento. **to be t.,** tener sed. **to make t.,** dar sed

thirteen a and *n* trece *m*. **t. hundred,** a and *n* mil trescientos *m*

thirteenth a décimotercio; (of monarchs) trece; (of month) (el) trece, *m, n* décimotercio, trezavo, *m*

thirtieth a trigésimo; (of month) (el) treinta, *m*. *n* treintavo, *m*

thirty a and *n* treinta, *m*. **t.-first,** treinta y uno

this *dem* a este, *m*; esta, *f*, *dem pron* éste, *m*; ésta, *f*; esto, *neut* **by t. time,** a esta hora, ya. **like t.,** de este modo, así. **T. is Wednesday,** Hoy es miércoles. **What is all t.?** ¿Qué es todo esto?

thistle *n* cardo, *m*. **t.-down,** papo de cardo, vilano de cardo, *m*

thither *adv* allá, hacia allá; a ese fin. a más remoto

thong *n* correa, tira, *f*

thorax *n* tórax, *m*

thorn *n* espina, *f*; (tree) espino, *m*; *fig* abrojo, *m*, espina, *f*. **to be a t. in the flesh of,** ser una espina en el costado de. **t. brake,** espinar, *m*

thorny a espinoso; *fig* difícil, arduo

thorough a completo; perfecto; (conscientious) concienzudo; (careful) cuidadoso. **t.-bred,** (of animals) de pura raza, de casta; (of persons) bien nacido. **t.-paced,** cabal, consumado

thoroughfare *n* vía pública, *f*. **"No t.,"** «Prohibido el paso!» Calle cerrada

thoroughly *adv* completamente; (of knowing a subject) a fondo; concienzudamente

those *dem a pl* of **that,** esos, *m pl*; esas, *f pl*; aquellos, *m pl*; aquellas, *f pl*, *dem pron* ésos, *m pl*; ésas, *f pl*; aquéllos, *m pl*; aquéllas, *f pl*; (standing for a noun) los, *m pl*; las; *f pl.* **t. who,** quienes, *mf pl*; los que, *m pl*; las que, *f pl.* **t. that** or **which,** los que, *m pl*; las que, *f pl.* **Your eyes are t. of your mother,** Tus ojos son los de tu madre

thou *pers pron* tú

though *conjunc* (followed by subjunc. when doubt is implied or uncertain future time) aunque, bien que; (nevertheless) sin embargo, no obstante; (in spite of) a pesar de que; (but) pero. **as t.,** como si (followed by subjunc.). **even t.,** aunque (followed by subjunc.)

thought *n* pensamiento, *m*; meditación, reflexión, *f.* **some thoughts on . . .** algunas reflexiones sobre . . . ; opinión, *f*; consideración, *f*; idea, *f*, propósito, *m*; (care) cuidado, *m*, solicitud, *f*; *inf* pizca, *f*. **on second thought**, después de pensarlo bien. **The t. struck him**, Se le ocurrió la idea. **to collect one's thoughts**, orientarse; informarse (de). **t.-reading**, adivinación del pensamiento, *f*. **t.-transference**, telepatía, transmisión del pensamiento, *f*

thoughtful *a* pensativo, meditabundo; serio; especulativo; (provident) previsor; (kind) atento, solícito; cuidadoso; (anxious) inquieto, intranquilo

thoughtfully *adv* pensativamente; seriamente; (providently) con previsión; (kindly) atentamente, solícitamente

thoughtless *a* irreflexivo; (careless) descuidado, negligente; (unkind) inconsiderado; (silly) necio, estúpido

thoughtlessly *adv* sin pensar, irreflexivamente; negligentemente

thousand a mil. *n* mil, *m*; millar, *m*. **one t.**, mil, *m*. **one t. three hundred**, a mil trescientos, *m pl*; mil trescientas, *f pl*. a mil trescientos, *m pl*; mil trescientas, *f pl.* **two (three) t.**, dos (tres) mil. **by thousands**, por millares; por miles. **t.-fold**, mil veces más

thrash *vt* azotar, apalear *Mexico* festejar, *Lat. Am.* humear; *agr* trillar, desgranar; *inf* triunfar sobre, derrotar. *vi*, trillar el grano; arrojarse, agitarse. *fig* **to t. out**, ventilar

thread *n* hilo, *m*; (fibre) hebra, fibra, *f*, filamento, *m*; (of a screw) filete, *m*; *fig* hilo, *m*, a de hilo. *vt* (a needle) enhebrar; (beads) ensartar; (make one's way) colarse a través de, atravesar; pasar por. **to hang by a t.**, pender de un hilo. **to lose the t. of**, *fig* perder el hilo de

threadbare *a* raído; muy usado; *fig* trivial, viejo

threadworm *n m*, lombriz intestinal, *f*

threat *n* amenaza, *f*

threaten *vt* and *vi* amenazar. **to t. with**, amenazar con

threatening *a* amenazador. *n* amenazas, *f pl*

three a and *n* tres *m*; (of the clock) las tres, *f pl*; (of one's age) tres años, *m pl.* **t.-color process**, tricromía, *f*. **t.-colored**, tricolor. **t.-cornered**, triangular; (of hats) de tres picos, tricornio. **t.-cornered hat**, sombrero de tres picos, tricornio, *m*. **t. decker**, *naut* navío de tres puentes, *m*; novela larga, *f*. **t. deep**, en tres hileras. **t. hundred**, a and *n* trescientos *m*. **t.-hundredth**, a and *n* tricentésimo *m*. **t.-legged**, de tres patas. **t.-legged stool**, banqueta, *f*. **t.-percents**, acción al tres por ciento (3%), *f*. **t.-phase**, *elec* trifásico. **t.-ply**, (of yarn) triple; (of wood) de tres capas. **t.-quarter**, de tres cuartos. **t. quarters of an hour**, tres cuartos de hora, *m pl*. **t.-sided**, trilátero. **t. speed gear box**, cambio de marcha de tres velocidades,

m. **t.-stringed**, *mus* de tres cuerdos. **t. thousand**, a tres mil, *mf pl*; *n* tres mil, *m*

threefold a triple

Three Musketeers, the los Tres Mosqueteros

threescore a and *n* sesenta, *m pl*

threesome *n* partido de tres, *m*

thresh *vt* trillar, desgranar. *vi* trillar el grano. **to t. out**, ventilar

threshold *n* umbral, *Lat. Am. also* dintel, *m*; *psy* limen, *m*; *fig* comienzo, principio, *m*; (entrance) entrada, *f*. **to cross the t.**, atravesar (or pisar) los umbrales

thrice *adv* tres veces

thrift *n* frugalidad, parsimonia, *f*

thrifty a frugal, económico

thrill *n* estremecimiento, *m*; emoción, *f*. *vt* conmover, emocionar; penetrar. *vi* estremecerse, emocionarse

thriller *n* libro, *m*, (or comedia, *f*) sensacional; (detective novel) novela policíaca, *f*

thrilling a sensacional, espeluznante; (moving) emocionante, conmovedor

thrive *vi* prosperar, medrar; enriquecerse, tener éxito; (grow) desarrollarse, robustecerse; florecer; (of plants) acertar

thriving a próspero; floreciente; robusto, vigoroso

throat *n* garganta, *f*; orificio, *m*; (narrow entry) paso, *m*. **sore t.**, dolor de garganta, *m*. **to cut one's t.**, cortarse la garganta. **to take by the t.**, asir (or agarrar) por la garganta

throat cancer *n* cáncer de la garganta, *m*

throb *n* latido, *m*; pulsación, *f*; vibración, *f*; *fig* estremecimiento, *m*. *vi* palpitar, latir; vibrar

throbbing *n* pulsación, *f*; vibración, *f*. a palpitante; vibrante. **t. pain**, dolor pungente, *m*

throe *n* dolor, *m*, agonía, angustia, *f*. **in the throes of**, en medio de; luchando con; en las garras de. **throes of childbirth**, dolores de parto, *m pl*. **throes of death**, agonía de la muerte, *f*

thrombosis *n med* trombosis, *f*

throne *n* trono, *m*; (royal power) corona, *f*, poder real, *m*. *vt* elevar al trono. **speech from the t.**, el discurso de la corona, *m*

throng *n* muchedumbre, multitud, *f*. *vi* apiñarse remolinarse, acudir. *vt* atestar, llenar de bote en bote

throttle *n mech* regulador, *m*; *aut* estrangulador, *m*; *inf* garganta, *f*. *vt* estrangular; *fig* ahogar, suprimir. **to open (close) the t.**, abrir (cerrar) el estrangulador

through *prep* por; al través de; de un lado a otro de; por medio de; (between) entre; por causa de; gracias a. *adv* al través; de un lado a otro; (whole) entero, todo; (from beginning to end) desde el principio hasta el fin; (to the end) hasta el fin. a (of passages, etc.) que va desde . . . hasta . . . ; (of trains) directo. **to look t. the window,** mirar por la ventana, asomarse a la ventana. **to be wet t.,** estar calado hasta los huesos; estar muy mojado. **to carry t.,** llevar a cabo. **to fall t.,** caer por; (fail) fracasar. **to sleep the whole night t.,** dormir durante toda la noche, dormir la noche entera. **t. and t.,** completamente. **through the length and breadth of,** a lo largo y a lo ancho de, hasta los últimos rincones de. **t. traffic,** tráfico directo, *m.* **t. train,** tren directo, *m*

throughout *prep* por todo; durante todo. *adv* completamente; (from beginning to end) desde el principio hasta el fin; (everywhere) en todas partes

throw *vt* arrojar, lanzar, echar; (fire) disparar; (pottery) plasmar; (knock down) derribar; (slough) mudar (la piel); (cast off) despojarse de; (a rider) desmontar; (a glance) echar, dirigir (una mirada, etc.); (silk) torcer; (dice) echar; (light) dirigir, enfocar. **to t. oneself at the head of,** echarse a la cabeza de. **to t. open,** abrir de par en par; abrir. **to t. overboard,** *naut* echar al mar; desechar; (desert) abandonar. **to t. about,** esparcir, desparramar; derrochar. **to t. aside,** echar a un lado, desechar; abandonar, dejar. **to t. away,** tirar; desechar, *Lat. Am.* botar; (spend) malgastar, derrochar; (waste) sacrificar; (of opportunities) malograr, perder. **to t. back,** devolver; echar hacia atrás. **to t. down,** derribar, dar en el suelo con; echar abajo; (arms) rendir. **to t. down the glove,** arrojar el guante. **to t. oneself down,** tumbarse, echarse; (descend) echarse abajo. **to t. oneself down from,** arrojarse de. **to t. in,** echar dentro; (give extra) añadir; (the clutch) embragar; insertar; (a remark) hacer (una observación). **to t. off,** despojarse de; quitarse; (refuse) rechazar; sacudirse; (get rid of) despedir; (renounce) renunciar; (exhale) emitir, despedir; (verses) improvisar. **to t. on,** echar sobre; (garments) ponerse. **to t. oneself upon,** lanzarse sobre. **to t. out,** expeler; hacer salir; plantar en la calle; (utter) proferir, soltar; (one's chest) inflar; (discard) tirar, desechar, *Lat. Am.* botar; **to t. over,** (desert) abandonar, dejar. **to t. up,** (build) levantar; lanzar en el aire; (a post, etc.) renunciar (a), abandonar; vomitar, *Central America, Mexico* deponer

throw *n* echada, *f;* tiro, *m;* (at dice) lance, *m;* jugada, *f;* (wrestling) derribo, *m.* **within a stone's t.,** a tiro de piedra. **t.-back,** retroceso, *m; biol* atavismo, *m*

thrum *vt* and *vi* tocar mal; (of keyed instruments) teclear; (of stringed instruments) rascar las cuerdas (de)

thrust *n* empujón, *m;* (with a sword) estocada, *f;* (fencing) golpe, *m;* (with a lance) bote, *m;* ataque, *m;* asalto, *m. vt*

empujar; (put) meter; (insert) introducir; (pierce) atravesar; (out, through, of the head, etc.) asomar. *vi* acometer, atacar, embestir; meterse, introducirse; (intrude) entrometerse; (fencing) dar un golpe. **to t. aside,** empujar a un lado; (proposals) rechazar. **to t. back,** hacer retroceder, empujar hacia atrás; (words) tragarse; (thoughts) apartar, rechazar. **to t. down,** empujar hacia abajo; hacer bajar; *fig* reprimir. **to t. forward,** empujar hacia delante; hacer seguir. **to t. oneself forward,** adelantarse; *fig* ponerse delante de los otros, darse importancia. **to t. in,** introducir; (stick) hincar; (insert) intercalar. **to t. on,** hacer seguir; empujar sobre; (garments) ponerse rápidamente. **to t. oneself in,** introducirse; entrometerse. **to t. out,** echar fuera; hacer salir, echar; expulsar; (the tongue) sacar (la lengua); (the head, etc.) asomar. **to t. through,** atravesar; (pierce) traspasar. **to t. one's way through,** abrirse paso por. **to t. upon,** imponer, hacer aceptar

thud *n* sonido sordo, *m;* golpe sordo, *m*

thug *n* asesino, criminal, *m*

thumb *n* pulgar, *m. vt* hojear; ensuciar con los dedos. **under the t. of,** *fig* en el poder de. **t. index,** índice pulgar, *m.* **t.-mark,** huella del dedo, *f.* **t.-screw,** tornillo de orejas, *m.* **t.-stall,** dedil, *m.* **t.-tack,** chinche, *m*

thump *n* golpe, porrazo, *m. vt* and *vi* golpear, aporrear; (the ground, of rabbits) zapatear

thunder *n* trueno, *m;* (of hooves, etc.) estampido, *m;* estruendo, *m. vi* tronar; retumbar; *fig* fulminar. *vt* gritar en una voz de trueno, rugir. **to t. along,** avanzar como el trueno; galopar ruidosamente. **t.-clap,** trueno, *m.* **t.-cloud,** nube de tormenta, *f,* nubarrón, *m.* **t.-storm,** tronada, *f.* **t. struck,** muerto, estupefacto. **to be thunderstruck,** quedarse frío

thunderbolt *n* rayo, *m*

thunderer *n* fulminador, *m.* **the Thunderer,** Júpiter tonante, Júpiter tronante, *m;* el «Times» londinense, *m*

Thursday *n* jueves, *m.* **Holy T.,** Jueves Santo, *m*

thus *adv* así; de este modo; en estos términos; hasta este punto. **t. far,** hasta ahora; hasta este punto; hasta aquí. **Thus it is that . . . ,** Así es que . . .

thwart *vt* frustrar, impedir

thyme *n bot* tomillo, *m*

thymus *n anat* timo, *m*

thyroid *a* tiroideo. **t. gland,** tiroides, *f*

thyself *poss pron* tu mismo, *m;* tu misma, *f;* (with prep.) tí mismo, *m;* tí misma, *f;* (in a reflexive verb) te

Tiberias Tiberíades, *f*

Tibetan *a* and *n* tibetano (-na); (language) tibetano, *m*

tic *n* (twitch) tic nervioso, *m*

tick n ent ácaro, m; (sound) tictac, m; (cover) funda de colchón, f; inf fiado, crédito, m; (mark) marca, f vi hacer tictac. vt poner una marca contra. **on t.,** inf al fiado. **to t. off,** poner una marca contra; inf reñir. **to t. over,** aut andar, marchar

ticket n billete, Lat. Am. boleto, m; (for an entertainment) entrada, localidad, f; (label) etiqueta, f; (pawn) papeleta de empeño, f; (for luggage) talón, m; (pol U.S.A.) candidatura, f, vt marcar. **to take one's t.,** sacar el billete (or for entertainment) la entrada, f). **excursion t.,** billete de excursión, m. **return t.,** billete de ida y vuelta, m. **season t.,** billete de abono, m. **single t.,** billete sencillo, m. **t. agency,** (for travel) agencia de viajes, f; (for entertainments) agencia de teatros, f. **t. collector or inspector,** revisor, m. **t. holder,** tenedor de billete, m; abonado (-da). **t. office,** (railway) despacho de billetes, m; taquilla, Lat. Am. boletería, f. **t.-of-leave,** libertad condicional, f. **t. punch,** sacabocados, m; (on tramcars) clasificador de billetes, m

tickle vt hacer cosquillas (a), cosquillear; irritar; (gratify) halagar; (amuse) divertir. vi tener cosquillas; hacer cosquillas; ser irritante

ticklish a cosquilloso; (of persons) difícil, vidrioso; (of affairs) espinoso, delicado

tidal a de marea. **t. wave,** marejada, f; fig ola popular, f

tidbit n See **titbit**

tide n marea, f; (season) tiempo, m, estación, f; (trend) corriente, f; (progress) curso, m; marcha, f. vi (with over) vencer, superar; aguardar la ocasión. **to go against the t.,** ir contra la corriente. **to go with the t.,** seguir la corriente. **high t.,** marea alta, f. **low t.,** marea baja, f, bajamar, m. **neap t.,** marea muerta, f. **t. mark,** lengua del agua, f

tidings n pl noticias, nuevas, f pl

tidy a aseado; metódico, en orden; pulcro; inf considerable. vt poner en orden, asear; limpiar; (oneself) arreglarse

tie n lazo, m, atadura, f; (knot) nudo, m; (for the neck) corbata, f; sport empate, m; mus ligado, m; arch tirante, m; (spiritual bond) lazo, m; (burden) carga, responsabilidad, f. **tie clasp,** pisa corbata, mf. **tie-pin,** alfiler de corbata, Mexico fistol, m. **tie seller,** corbatero (-ra)

tie vt atar; (bind) ligar; (lace) lacear; (a knot) hacer; (with a knot) anudar; (unite) unir; (fig bind) constreñir, obligar; (limit) limitar, restringir; (occupy) ocupar, entretener; (hamper) estorbar, impedir. vi atarse; sport empatar. **to tie one's tie,** hacer la corbata. **to tie down,** atar a; limitar; obligar. **They tied him down to a chair,** Le ataron a una silla. **to tie together,** enlazar, ligar; unir. **to tie up,** liar, atar; (wrap) envolver; recoger; naut amarrar, atracar; (restrict) limitar, restringir; (invest) invertir

tie-breaker n desempate, m

tier n fila, hilera, f. **in tiers,** en gradas; (of a dress) en volantes

tiff n disgusto, m

tiger n tigre, m. **t.-cat,** gato (-ta) atigrado (-da). **t.-lily,** tigridia, f

tight a apretado; (not leaky) hermético, impermeable; (taut) tieso, tirante; (narrow) estrecho; (trim) compacto; (of clothes) muy ajustado; (shut) bien cerrado; naut estanco; (risky) peligroso, difícil; (miserly) tacaño, Argentina agalludo; (of money, goods) escaso; (tipsy) borracho, Mexico abombado. **become t., get t.** (get tipsy) Mexico abombarse. **to be t.-fisted,** ser como un puño. **to hold t.,** agarrar fuerte. **t. corner,** fig aprieto, lance apretado, m. **t.-rope,** cuerda de volantinero, cuerda floja, Lat. Am. maroma, f. **t.-rope walker,** alambrista, equilibrista, mf; volantinero (-ra), bailarín de la cuerda floja, m, Lat. Am. maromero (-ra), mf. **t.-rope walker's pole,** balancín, m

tighten vt estrechar, apretar, Lat. Am. atesar; (stretch) estirar; (of saddle girths) cinchar. vi estrecharse; estirarse. **t. up** Lat. Am. atesar

tights n pl mallas, f pl

tile n teja, f; (for flooring) baldosa, losa, f; (ornamental) azulejo, m; (hat) chistera, f. vt tejar; embaldosar. **t. floor,** enlosado, embaldosado, m. **t. manufacturer,** tejero, m. **t. works or yard,** tejar, m, (Colombia) galpón m

till n (for money) cajón, m. vt agr cultivar, labrar. prep hasta. conjunc hasta que

tilt n inclinación, f; ladeo, m; (fight) torneo, m, justa, f. vt inclinar; ladear; (a drinking vessel) empinar. vi inclinarse; ladearse; (fight) justar. **to t. against,** fig arremeter contra, atacar. **at full t.,** a todo correr. **t. hammer,** martinete de báscula, m. **t.-yard,** palestra, f

timber n madera de construcción, f; (trees) árboles de monte, m pl; bosque, m; (beam) viga, f; naut cuaderna, f. vt enmaderar. **t. line,** límite del bosque maderable, m. **t. merchant,** maderero, m. **t. wolf,** lobo gris, m. **t. work,** maderaje, m. **t. yard,** maderería, f, corral de madera, m

time n (in general) tiempo, m; (epoch) época, edad, f; tiempos, m pl; (of the year) estación, f; (by the clock) hora, f; (lifetime) vida, f; (particular moment of time) momento, m; (occasion) sazón, ocasión, f; (day) día, m; (time allowed) plazo, m; (in repetition) vez, f; mus compás, m; mil paso, m. vt ajustar al tiempo; hacer con oportunidad; (regulate) regular; calcular el tiempo que se emplea en hacer una cosa; (a blow) calcular. **all the t.,** todo el tiempo; continuamente, sin cesar. **a long t.,** mucho tiempo. **a long t. ago,** mucho tiempo ha, hace mucho tiempo. **at a t.,** a la vez, al mismo tiempo; (of period) en una época. **at any t.,** a cualquier hora; en cualquier momento; (when you like) cuando gustes. **at no t.,** jamás, nunca. **at some t.,** alguna vez; en alguna época. **at some t. or another,** un día u otro; en una u otra ocasión; en alguna época. **at that t.,** en aquella época; en la sazón; en aquel instante. **at the one t.,** de una vez. **at the present t.,** en la actualidad, al presente. **at the proper t.,** a su debido tiempo; a la hora señalada; a la hora conveniente. **at the same t.,** al mismo tiempo. **at the same t. as,** mientras, a medida que; al mismo instante que, **at times,** a veces, en ocasiones. **behind the times,** *fig* atrasado de noticias; pasado de moda. **behind t.,** atrasado. by that t., para entonces. **every t.,** cada vez; siempre. **for some t.,** durante algún tiempo. **for some t. past,** de algún tiempo a esta parte. **for the t. being,** de momento, por ahora, por lo pronto. **from this t.,** desde hoy; desde esta fecha. **from this t. forward,** de hoy en adelante. **from t. to t.,** de vez en cuando, de cuando en cuando, de tarde en tarde. **in a month's t.,** en un mes. **in a short t.,** en breve, dentro de poco. **in good t.,** puntualmente; temprano. **in my t.,** en mis días, en mis tiempos. **in olden times,** antiguamente, en otros tiempos. **in the course of t.,** andando el tiempo, en el transcurso de los años. **in the t. of,** en la época de. **in t.,** (promptly) a tiempo; con el tiempo. **in t. to come,** en el porvenir. It is t. to . . . , Es hora de . . . **many times,** frecuentemente, muchas veces. **Once upon a t.,** Érase una vez, Una vez había, Érase que érase. Érase que se era. **Since t. out of mind,** Desde tiempo inmemorial. **the last (next) t.,** la última (próxima) vez. **this t. of year,** esta estación del año. **T. hangs heavy on his hands,** El tiempo se le hace interminable. **T. flies,** El tiempo vuela. **T. will tell!** ¡El tiempo lo dirá! ¡Veremos lo que veremos! **What t. is it?** ¿Qué hora es? **The t. is . . . ,** La hora es . . . **within a given t.,** dentro de un plazo dado. **to be out of t.,** estar fuera de compás. **to gain t.,** ganar tiempo. **to have a good t.,** pasarlo bien, divertirse. **to have a bad t.,** pasarlo mal; *inf* tener un mal cuarto de hora. **to have no t. to,** no tener tiempo para + noun or pronoun, no tener tiempo de + infinitive. **to keep t.,** guardar el compás. **to kill t.,** engañar (or entretener) el tiempo. **to mark t.,** marcar el paso; *fig* hacer tiempo. **to pass the t.,** pasar el rato; pasar el tiempo. **to pass the t. of day,** saludar. **to serve one's t.,** (to a trade) servir el aprendizaje; (in prison) cumplir su condena; *mil* hacer el servicio militar. **to take t. to,** tomar tiempo para. **to take t. by the forelock,** asir la ocasión por la melena. **to waste t.,** perder el tiempo. **t. exposure,** *phot* f. t. **fuse,** espoleta de tiempo, espoleta graduada, f. **t.-honored,** tradicional, consagrado por el tiempo. **t.-keeper,** capataz, m; reloj, m.

t.-saving, que ahorra el tiempo. **t.-server,** lameculos, *mf* **t.-signal,** señales horarias, *f pl.* **t.-table,** horario, m; itinerario, programa, m; (railway) guía de ferrocarriles, f. **t. to come,** porvenir, m, lo venidero

timed *a* calculado; (**ill-**) intempestivo; (**well-**) oportuno

timeless *a* eterno

timely *a* oportuno

timepiece *n* reloj, m

time zone *n* huso esférico, huso horario, m

timid *a* tímido, asustadizo, medroso; (shy) vergonzoso

timing *n* medida del tiempo, f; *mech* regulación, f; (timetable) horario, m

timorous *a* timorato, apocado, asustadizo

tin *n* (metal) estaño, m; (container) lata, f; (sheet) hojalata, f; (money) plata, f. *vt* estañar; (place in tins) envasar en lata; cubrir con hojalata, hoja de aluminio, f. **tinfoil,** papel de estaño, m. **tin hat,** casco de acero, m. **tin opener,** abrelatas, abridor de latas, m. **tin-plate,** hojalata, f. **tin soldier,** soldado de plomo, m. **tin ware,** hojalatería, f

tincture *n* tintura, f, tinte, m; *med* tintura, f; (trace) dejo, m; (veneer) capa, f. *vt* teñir, tinturar

tinder *n* yesca, f. **t. box,** yescas, lumbres, f pl

tinge *n* tinte, matiz, m; *fig* dejo, toque, m. *vt* matizar, tinturar; *fig* tocar

tingle *n* picazón, comezón, f; (thrill) estremecimiento, m. *vi* picar; (of ears) zumbar; (thrill) estremecerse (de); vibrar

tinker *n* calderero remendón, m. *vt* remendar. *vi* chafallar. **to t. with,** jugar con

tinkle *n* tilín, retintín, m; campanilleo, m; cencerreo, m. *vi* tintinar. *vt* hacer tintinar

tinsel *n* oropel, m; (cloth) lama de oro o plata, f, brocadillo, m; *fig* oropel, m. a de oropel; de brocadillo; *fig* charro. *vt* adornar con oropel

tint *n* tinta, f, color, m; matiz, m; tinte, m. *vt* colorar, teñir; matizar

tiny *a* diminuto, minúsculo, menudo, chiquito

tip *n* punta, f; cabo, m, extremidad, f; (of an umbrella, etc.) regatón, m; (of a lance) borne, m; (of a cigarette) boquilla, f; (of a shoe) puntera, f; (of a finger) yema, f; (for rubbish) depósito de basura, m; (gratuity) propina, f; (information) informe oportuno, m; (tap) golpecito, m. **to have on the tip of one's tongue,** tener en la punta de la lengua. **tip-cart,** volquete, m. **tip-up seat,** asiento plegable, m

tip *vt* inclinar; volcar, voltear; (drinking vessel) empinar; poner regatón, etc. (a); *poet* tocar, golpear ligeramente; (reward) dar propina (a). *vi* inclinarse; (topple) tambalearse; (reward) dar propina. **to tip the wink,** guiñar el ojo (a). **to tip off,**

(liquids) echar; hacer caer; (inform) decir en secreto; informar oportunamente. **to tip over,** *vt* volcar; hacer caer. *vi* volcarse; caer; (of a boat) zozobrar. **to tip up,** *vt* (a seat) levantar; (money) proporcionar (el dinero); (upset) volcar; hacer perder el equilibrio. *vi* volcarse; (of a seat) levantarse; (lose the balance) perder el equilibrio

tipple *n* bebida, *f. vt* beber, sorber. *vi* empinar el codo

tipsy *a* achispado, algo borracho, *Lat. Am.* mamado. **to be t.,** estar entre dos luces, estar entre dos velas

tiptoe (on) *adv* de puntillas; *fig* excitado, ansioso. **to stand on t.,** ponerse de puntillas. empinarse

tirade *n* diatriba, *f*

tire *n* (of a cart, etc.) llanta, *f; aut* neumático, *Lat. Am.* caucho, *m;* (of a perambulator, etc.) rueda de goma, *f.* **balloon t.,** neumático balón, *m.* **pneumatic t.,** neumático, *m.* **slack t.,** neumático desinflado, *m.* **solid t.,** neumático macizo, *m.* **spare t.,** neumático de recambio (or de repuesto), *m.* **t. burst,** estallido de un neumático, *m.* **t. valve,** válvula de cámara (del neumático), *f*

tire *vt* cansar, fatigar; (bore) aburrir. *vi* cansarse, fatigarse; aburrirse. **to be tired of,** estar cansado de. **to grow tired,** empezar a cansarse. **to t. out,** rendir de cansancio

tired *a* cansado, fatigado. **to be sick and t. of,** estar hasta la coronilla (de), (of persons) con. **t. of,** cansado de; disgustado de

tireless *a* infatigable, incansable

tiresome *a* fastidioso, molesto, pesado; (dull) aburrido

tiring *a* fatigoso

tissue *n* (cloth) tisú, *m,* lama, *f;* (paper) pañuelito *m; biol* tejido, *m;* (series) serie, sarta, *f.* **t. paper,** papel de seda, *m*

tit *n orn* paro, *m.* **tit for tat,** tal para cual

titbit *n* golosina, *f*

titillate *vt* titilar, estimular

titivate *vi* arreglarse

title *n* título, *m;* (right) derecho, *m;* documento, *m.* **to give a t. to,** intitular; ennoblecer. **t. deed,** títulos de propiedad, *m.* **t. page,** portada, *f.* **t. role,** papel principal, *m*

titter *vi* reírse disimuladamente. *n* risa disimulada, *f*

tittle *n* adarme, tilde, ápice, *m*

to *prep* a; (as far as) hasta; (in the direction of) en dirección a, hacia; (with indirect object) a; (until) hasta; (compared with) en comparación con, comparado con; (against) contra; (according to) según; (as) como; (in) en; (so that, in order to, for the purpose of) para; (indicating possession) a, de; (of time by the clock) menos; (by) por; (before verbs of motion or which imply motion) a (sometimes para); (before some other verbs) de; en; (before verbs of beginning, inviting, exhorting, obliging) a; (indicating indirect object) a; (before a subjunctive or infinitive indicating future action or obligation) que. **To** is often not translated. With most Spanish infinitives no separate translation is necessary, e.g. leer, decir, to read, to speak. Some verbs are always followed by a preposition (e.g. **to begin to speak,** empezar a hablar, etc.). *adv* (shut) cerrado. **to come to,** volver en sí. **to lie to,** *naut* ponerse a la capa. **to and from,** de un lado a otro. **face to face,** cara a cara. **He has been a good friend to them,** Ha sido un buen amigo para ellos. **That is new to me,** Eso es nuevo para mí. **He went to London,** Se fue a Londres. **to go to France (Canada),** ir a Francia (al Canadá). **the road to Madrid,** la carretera de Madrid. **She kept the secret to herself,** Guardó el secreto para sí. **to go to the dentist,** ir al dentista. **We give it to them,** Se lo damos a ellos. **It belongs to me,** Pertenece a mí. **What does it matter to you?** ¿Qué te importa a tí? **I wish to see him,** Quiero verle. **They did it to help us,** Lo hicieron para ayudarnos. **I have to go to see her,** Tengo que ir a verla. **to this day,** hasta hoy, hasta el presente. **It is a quarter to six,** Son las seis menos cuarto. **to the house of . . ., to . . .'s** casa de, *Lat. Am. also* donde (e.g. **My wife went to her friend's house** Mi mujer fue a casa de su amiga, Mi mujer fue donde su amiga). **to the last shilling,** hasta el último chelín. **the next to me,** el que me sigue. **closed to the public,** cerrado para el público

toad *n* sapo, *m*

toady *n* lameculos, *mf* adulador (-ra). *vt* lamer el culo (a), adular

toast *n cul* tostada, *f;* (drink) brindis, *m. vt* tostar; brindar, beber a la salud de. *vi* brindar. **buttered t.,** mantecada, *f.* **t.-rack,** portatostadas, *m*

toaster *n* (device) tostador, *m;* (person) brindador, *m*

tobacco *n* tabaco, *m.* **a** tabacalero. **black** or **cut t.,** picadura, *f.* **leaf t.,** tabaco de hoja, *m.* **mild t.,** tobaco flojo, *m.* **pipe t.,** tabaco de pipa, *m.* **plug t.,** tabaco para mascar, *m.* **strong t.,** tabaco fuerte, *m.* **Turkish t.,** tabaco turco, *m.* **Virginian t.,** tabaco rubio, *m.* **t.-pipe,** pipa (de tabaco), *f.* **t.-pipe cleaner,** escobillón para limpiar pipas, *m.* **t. plantation,** tabacal, *m.* **t. planter,** tabacalero (-ra). **t. poisoning,** tabaquismo, *m.* **t.-pouch** or **jar,** tabaquera, *f*

toboggan *n* tobogán, *m. vi* ir en tobogán. **t. run,** pista de tobogán, *f*

today *adv* hoy; ahora, actualmente, al presente, hoy día. *n* el día de hoy. **from t.,** desde hoy. **from t. forward,** de hoy en adelante

toddle *vi* hacer pinos, empezar a andar; (stroll) dar una vuelta; (leave) marcharse

toddy *n* ponche, *m*

toe *n* dedo del pie, *m*; (cloven) pezuña, *f*; uña, *f*; (of furniture) base, *f*, pie, *m*; (of stockings, shoes) punta, *f*. **He stepped on my toe,** Me pisó el dedo del pie. **big toe,** dedo pulgar del pie, dedo gordo del pie, *m*. **little toe,** dedo pequeño del pie, *m*. **to toe the line,** ponerse en la raya; *fig* cumplir con su deber. **toe-cap,** puntera, *f*. **toe-dancing,** baile de puntillas, *m*. **toe-nail,** uña del dedo del pie, *f*

toffee *n* caramelo, *m*

together *adv* junto; (uninterruptedly) sin interrupción; (in concert) simultáneamente, a la vez, al mismo tiempo; (consecutively) seguido. **t. with,** con; junto con; en compañía de; (simultaneously) a la vez que

toil *n* labor, *f*, trabajo, *m pl*. **toils,** lazos, *m pl*; *fig* redes, *f pl*. *vi* trabajar, afanarse. **to t. along,** caminar penosamente (por); adelantar con dificultad. **to t. up,** subir penosamente

toilet *n* tocado, *m*; atavío, *m*; vestido, *m*; (w.c.) retrete, excusado, *m*; (for ladies) tocador, *m*. **to make one's t.,** arreglarse. **t. case,** neceser, *m*. **t.-paper,** papel higiénico, *m*. **t.-powder,** polvos de arroz, *m pl*. **t. roll,** rollo de papel higiénico, *m*. **t.-set,** juego de tocador, *m*. **t. soap,** jabón de olor, jabón de tocador, *m*

token *n* señal, muestra, *f*; prueba, *f*; (presage) síntoma, indicio, *m*; (remembrance) recuerdo, *m*. **as a t. of,** en señal de; como recuerdo de

tolerable *a* tolerable, soportable, llevadero; (fairly good) mediano, mediocre, regular

tolerably *adv* bastante

tolerance *n* tolerancia, *f*; paciencia, indulgencia, *f*

tolerant *a* tolerante; indulgente

tolerate *vt* tolerar, sufrir, soportar; permitir

toleration *n* tolerancia, *f*; indulgencia, paciencia, *f*. **religious t.,** libertad de cultos, *f*

toll *n* (of a bell) tañido, doble, *m*; (for passage) peaje, portazgo, *m*; (for grinding) derecho de molienda, *m*. *vt* and *vi* doblar, tañer. **to t. the hour,** dar la hora, *t*. **call,** conferencia telefónica interurbana, llamada a larga distancia, *f*. **t. gate,** barrera de peaje, *f*. **t. house,** oficina de portazgos, *f*

toll booth *n* caseta de pago, *f*

tomahawk *n* hacha de guerra de los indios, *f*

tomato *n* tomate, jitomate (Mexico) *m*. **t. plant,** tomatera, *f*. **t. sauce,** salsa de tomate, *f*

tomb *n* tumba, *f*, sepulcro, *m*

tomboy *n* muchachote, torbellino, *m*

tombstone *n* piedra mortuoria, *f*, monumento funerario, *m*

tome *n* tomo, volumen, *m*

tomfoolery *n* necedad, tontería, *f*; payasada, *f*

tomorrow *adv* and *n* mañana, *f*. **a fortnight t.,** mañana en quince. **the day after t.,** pasado mañana. **t. afternoon (morning),** mañana por la tarde (mañana). **T. is Friday,** Mañana es viernes

ton *n* tonelada, *f*

tone *n* tono, *m*; (mus, med, art) tono, *m*; (of the voice) acento, *m*, entonación, *f*; (of musical instruments) sonido, *m*; (shade) matiz, *m*. *vt* entonar; *phot* virar. **to t. down,** *vt* (art, mus) amortiguar; *fig* suavizar, modificar. *vi* (art, mus) amortiguarse; *fig* suavizarse, modificarse. **to t. in with,** (of colors) *vt* armonizar con. *vi* armonizarse, corresponder en tono o matiz. **to t. up,** *vt* subir de color, intensificar el color de; *med* entonar, robustecer. **t. poem,** poema sinfónico, *m*

tongs *n pl* tenazas, *f pl*; tenacillas, *f pl*. **curling t.,** tenacillas para el pelo, *f pl*. **sugar t.,** tenacillas para azúcar, *f pl*

tongue *n anat* lengua, *f*; (language) idioma, *m*, lengua, *f*; (speech) modo de hablar, *m*, habla, *f*; *mus* lengüeta, *f*; (of buckle) diente, *m*; (of shoe) oreja, *f*; (of land) lengua, *f*; (of a bell) badajo, *m*; (flame) lengua, *f*. **My t. ran away with me,** *inf* Se me fue la mula. **to give t.,** ladrar. **to hold one's t.,** cerrar el pico, tener la boca. **t. of fire,** lengua de fuego, *f*. **t. tied,** con impedimento en el habla; turbado, confuso; mudo. **t.-twister,** trabalenguas, *m*

-tongued *a* de voz . . .

tonic *a* tónico. *n med* tónico, reconstituyente, *m*; *mus* tónica, *f*

tonight *adv* and *n* esta noche

tonnage *n* tonelaje, porte, *m*; (duty) derecho de tonelaje, *m*

tonsil *n* amígdala, *f*

tonsillitis *n* amigdalitis, *f*

too *adv* demasiado; (very) muy; también; además. **too hard,** demasiado difícil, demasiado rígido; (of persons) demasiado duro. **too much,** demasiado. **too often,** con demasiada frecuencia

tool *n* herramienta, *f*; utensilio, *m*; instrumento, *m*; (person) criatura, *f*. *vt* labrar con herramienta; (a book) estampar en seco. **t.-bag,** capacho, *m*. **t. box,** caja de herramientas, *f*

toot *n* sonido de bocina, *m*, *vi* sonar una bocina

tooth *n* diente, *m*; muela, *f*; (of comb) púa, *f*; (taste) gusto, paladar, *m*; (cog) diente de rueda, *m*; (of saw) diente, *m*. *vt* dentar; mellar. *vi mech* engranar. **armed to the teeth,** armado hasta los dientes. **double t.,** muela, *f*. **false teeth,** dentadura postiza, *f*. **set of teeth,** dentadura, f. **to cut one's teeth,** echar los dientes. **to have a sweet t.,** ser muy goloso. **to show one's teeth,** enseñar los dientes. **t.-brush,** cepillo para los dientes, m. **t. drawing,** extracción de un diente, f. **t.-paste,** pasta dentífrica, f

toothache n dolor de muelas, m

toothless a desdentado, sin dientes; (of combs) sin púas

toothpick n mondadientes, m

top n (summit) cima, cumbre, f; (of a tree) copa, f; (of the head) coronilla, f; (of a page) cabeza, f; (crest) copete, m, cresta, f; (surface) superficie, f; (of a wall) coronamiento, m; (tip) punta, f; (point) ápice, m; (of a tram, bus) imperial, baca, f; (of a wave) cresta, f; (acme) auge, m; (of a class) primero (de la clase), m; (highest rank) último grado, m; (of a plant) hojas, f pl; (of a piano) cima, f; naut cofa, f; (head of a bed, etc.) cabeza, f; (lid) tapadera, f; (toy) trompo, peón, m; (humming) trompa, f, a más alto; máximo; (chief) principal, primero. vt (cover) cubrir de; (cut off) desmochar; (come level with) llegar a la cima de; (rise above) elevarse por encima (de), coronar, dominar; (be superior to) exceder, aventajar; (golf) topear. **at the top,** a la cabeza; a la cumbre. **from top to bottom,** de arriba abajo. **on top of,** encima de; (besides) en adición a, además de. **to be top-dog,** ser un gallito. **to sleep like a top,** dormir como un lirón. **top boots,** botas de campaña, f pl. **top-dog,** vencedor, m; poderoso, m. **top-hat,** sombrero de copa, m. **top-heavy,** más pesado por arriba que por abajo

topaz n topacio, jacinto occidental, m

topcoat n sobretodo, gabán, m

top floor n piso alto, m

topic n asunto, tema, m

topical a tópico; actual

topmost a más alto; más importante

topple vi tambalearse, estar al punto de caer. **to t. down,** volcarse; derribarse; caer. **to t. over,** vi venirse abajo; perder el equilibrio. vt derribar, hacer caer

topsyturvy a desordenado. adv en desorden, patas arriba, de arriba abajo

torch n antorcha, hacha, tea, f. **electric t.,** lamparilla eléctrica, f. **t.-bearer,** hachero, m

torchlight n luz de antorcha, f. **by t.,** a la luz de las antorchas

torment n tormento, m, angustia, f; (torture) tortura, f; suplicio, m; mortificación, f; disgusto, m. vt atormentar, martirizar; (torture) torturar; molestar

tornado n tornado, m

torpedo n torpedo, m; icht pez torpedo, m. vt torpedear. **self-propelling t.,** torpedo automóvil, m. **t.-boat,** torpedero, m. **t.-boat destroyer,** cazatorpedero, contratorpedero, m. **t. netting,** red contra torpedos, f. **t. station,** base de tor-

pederos, f. **t. tube,** tubo lanzatorpedos, m

torpid a aletargado, entorpecido; (of the mind) torpe, tardo, apático

torrent n torrente, m

torrential a torrencial

torrid a tórrido. **t. zone,** zona tórrida, f

torso n torso, m

tort n law tuerto, m

tortoise n tortuga, f. **t.-shell,** carey, m. a de carey

tortuous a tortuoso

torture n tortura, f, tormento, m; angustia, f. vt torturar, dar tormento (a); martirizar

torturing a torturador, atormentador; angustioso

toss n sacudimiento, m, sacudidad, f; (of the head) movimiento (de cabeza), m; (bull fighting) cogida, f; (from a horse) caída de caballo, f. vt echar, lanzar; agitar, sacudir; (of bulls) acornear. vi agitarse; (of plumes, etc.) ondear; (in a boat) balancearse a la merced de las olas; jugar a cara o cruz. **to t. a coin** Mexico echar un volado. **to t. in a blanket,** mantear, dar una manta (a). **to t. aside,** echar a un lado; abandonar. **to t. off,** beber de un trago. **to t. up,** jugar a cara o cruz

tot n (child) nene (-na), crío (-ía); (of drink) vaso pequeño, m. **to tot up,** sumar

total a total; absoluto, completo, entero. n total, m, suma, f. vt sumar. vi ascender (a). **t. employment,** ocupación total, f. **t. war,** guerra total, f

totalitarian a totalitario

totality n totalidad, f

totem n tótem, m

totter vi (of persons) bambolearse; tambalear, estar al punto de caer; fig aproximarse a su fin

touch vt tocar; (brush against) rozar; (reach) alcanzar; (musical instruments) tocar; (move) emocionar, enternecer; (spur on) aguijar; (food) tomar; (affect) influir, afectar; (arouse) despertar, estimular; (equal) compararse con, igualar; (consider) tratar ligeramente (de); (money) dar un sablazo (a). vi tocarse; imponer las manos para curar. **I have not touched a bite,** No he probado un bocado. **This touches me nearly,** Esto me toca de cerca. **to t. at,** hacer escala en, tocar en (un puerto). **to t. down on water** Lat. Am. acuatizar. **to t. off,** descargar. **to t. up,** retocar; corregir. **to t. upon,** (a subject) tratar superficialmente de, tratar ligeramente de; hablar de; considerar

touch n (sense of) tacto, m; (contact) toque, contacto, m; (brushing) roce, m; (tap) golpe ligero, m; palmadita, f; (of an illness) ataque ligero, m; mus dedeo, m; (little) dejo, m; (test) prueba, f, toque, m; art toque, m, pincelada, f. **by the t.,** a tiento. **in t. with,** en relaciones con; en comunicación con; al corriente de. **to give the finishing t.,** dar la última pincelada; dar el último toque. **t.-line,** (football) línea de toque, línea lateral, *f.* **t.-menot,** *inf* erizo, *m.* **t.-stone,** piedra de toque, *f*

touched *a* emocionado, conmovido

touching *a* patético, conmovedor. *prep* tocante a, acerca de. *n* tocamiento, *m*

touchy *a* susceptible, quisquilloso, vidrioso

tough *a* (hard) duro; vigoroso, fuerte, robusto; resistente; (of character) tenaz, firme; (of a job) difícil; espinoso. *n* chulo, *m*

toughen *vt* endurecer. *vi* endurecerse

toughness *n* dureza, *f;* vigor, *m,* fuerza, *f;* resistencia, *f;* tenacidad, firmeza, *f;* dificultad, *f*

toupee *n* tupé, *m*

tour *n* viaje, *m,* excursión, *f. vi* viajar. *vt* viajar por. **circular t.,** viaje redondo, *m.* **on t.,** *theat* en tour, de gira

touring *a* de turismo. *n* turismo, *m;* viaje, *m.* **t. car,** coche de turismo, *m*

tourist *n* turista, *mf;* viajero (-ra). *f.* **t. agency,** agencia de turismo, *f,* patronato de turismo, *m.* **t. ticket,** billete kilométrico, *m*

tournament *n* torneo, *m,* justa, *f;* (of games) concurso, *m.*

tourniquet *n* torniquete, *m*

tousle *vt* despeinar; desordenar el pelo

tout *n* buhonero, *m.* **to t. for,** pescar, solicitar

tow *n* remolque, *m;* (rope) estopa, *f. vt* (naut, aut) remolcar. **on tow,** a remolque. **tow-path,** camino de sirga, *m.* **tow rope,** cable de remolque, *m*

towards *prep* hacia, en dirección a; (of time) sobre, cerca de; (concerning) tocante a; (with persons) para, con

towel *n* toalla, *f. Lat. Am. also* limpiamanos, *m.* **roller t.,** toalla continua, *f.* **t. rail,** toallero, *m*

tower *n* torre, *f;* (fortress) fortaleza, *f;* (belfry) campanario, *m;* (large) torreón, *m. vi* elevarse. **to t. above,** destacarse sobre, sobresalir; *fig* sobrepujar, superar

towering *a* elevado; dominante; orgulloso; *fig* violento, terrible

town *n* población, *f,* pueblo, *m;* ciudad, *f.* **t. clerk,** secretario de ayuntamiento, *m.* **t. council,** concejo municipal, *m.* **t. councilor,** concejero municipal, *m.* **t. crier,** pregonero, *m.* **t. hall,** (casa de) ayuntamiento, casa consistorial, *f.* **t. house,** casa de ciudad, *f.* **t. planning,** urbanismo, *m;* reforma urbana, *f.* **t. wall,** muralla, *f*

"Town Ahead" «Poblado Próximo»

town worthy *n* persona principal de la ciudad, *f*

toxic *a* tóxico

toy *n* juguete, *m.* *vi* (with) jugar con;

acariciar. **toy maker,** fabricante de juguetes, *m*

toyshop *n* juguetería, tienda de juguetes, *f*

trace huella, pista, *f,* rastro, *m;* vestigio, *m;* indicio, *m,* evidencia, *f;* (of a harness) tirante, *m;* (touch) dejo, *m;* (of fear, etc.) sombra, *f. vt* trazar; (through transparent paper) calcar; seguir la pista (de); (write) escribir; (discern) distinguir; investigar; descubrir; determinar; (walk) atravesar, recorrer. **to t. back,** (of ancestry, etc.) hacer remontar (a)

tracer *n* trazador (-ra). **t. bullet,** bala luminosa, *f*

trachea *n* anat tráquea, *f*

trachoma *n* med tracoma, *f*

tracing *n* calco, *m;* trazo, *m;* seguimiento, *m.* **t.-paper,** papel de calcar, *m*

track *n* huella, *f,* rastro, *m;* (for racing, etc.) pista, *f;* (of wheels) rodada, *f;* (railway) vía, *f;* (of a boat) estela, *f;* (path) senda, vereda, *f;* (sign) señal, evidencia, *f;* (course) ruta, *f. vt* rastrear, seguir la pista (de); *naut* sirgar. **double t.,** vía doble, *f.* **off the t.,** extraviado; (of a train) descarrilado; *fig* por los cerros de Úbeda. **side t.,** desviadero, *m.* **to keep t. of,** *inf* no perder de vista (a); seguir las fortunas de

tract *n* tracto, *m;* región, *f; anat* vía, *f;* (written) tratado, *m*

tractable *a* dócil

traction *n* tracción, *f.* **t.-engine,** máquina de arrastre (or de tracción), *f*

tractor *n* máquina de arrastre, *f;* tractor, *m*

trade *n* comercio, *m;* tráfico, *m;* negocio, *m;* industria, *f;* (calling) oficio, *m,* profesión, *f;* (dealers) comerciantes, *mf pl. vi* comerciar, traficar. *vt* cambiar. **to t. on,** explotar, aprovecharse de. **by t.,** de oficio, por profesión. **t.-mark,** marca de fábrica, *f.* **t.-name,** razón social, *f.* **t. price,** precio para el comerciante, *m.* **t. union,** sindicato, *m.* **T. Union Congress,** Congreso de Sindicatos, *m.* **t. unionism,** sistema de sindicatos obreros, *m.* **t.-winds,** vientos alisios, *m pl*

trader *n* comerciante, traficante, *mf;* mercader, *m;* (boat) buque mercante, *m*

tradesman *n* tendero, *m.* **tradesmen's entrance,** puerta de servicio, *f*

trading *n* comercio, tráfico, *m.* **a mercantil,** comerciante, mercante. **t. ship,** buque mercante, *m.* **t. station,** factoría, *f*

tradition *n* tradición, *f*

traditional *a* tradicional; del lugar

traduce *vt* calumniar, denigrar, vituperar

traffic *n* comercio, negocio, tráfico, *m;* (in transit) transporte, *m;* (in movement) circulación, *f. vi* comerciar, traficar, negociar. **to cause a block in the t.,** interrumpir la circulación. **t. block,** obstrución del tráfico, *f,* atasco en la circulación, *m*. **t. indicator,** (on a car) indicador de dirección, *m*. **t. island,** refugio para peatones, salvavidas, *m*. **t. light,** disco, *m*, luz (de tráfico), *f*, semáforo, *m*. **t. roundabout,** redondel, *m*

tragedy *n* tragedia, *f*

tragic *a* trágico

tragicomedy *n* tragicomedia, *f*

trail *n* rastro, *m*, pista; huella, *f*; (path) sendero, *m*; (of a comet) cola, cabellera, *f*. *vt* rastrear, seguir el rastro de; (drag) arrastrar; (the anchor) garrar. *vi* arrastrar; (of plants) trepar. **on the t. of,** en busca de; siguiendo el rastro de; **put somebody on the t. of . . .** darle a fulano la pista de . . .

trailer *n* cazador (-ra); perseguidor (-ra); *aut* remolque, *m*; (cinema) anuncio de próximas atracciones, *m*; *bot* talle rastrero, *m*

train *n* (railway) tren, *m*; (of a dress) cola, *f*; (retinue) séquito, *m*; (procession) desfile, *m*, comitiva, *f*; (series) serie, sucesión, *f*; (of gunpowder) reguero de pólvora, *m*. **down t.,** tren descendente, *m*. **excursion t.,** tren de excursionistas, *m*. **express t.,** exprés, tren expreso, *m*. **fast t.,** rápido, *m*. **goods t.,** tren de mercancías, *m*. **mail t.,** tren correo, *m*. **next t.,** próximo tren, *m*. **passenger t.,** tren de pasajeros, *m*. **stopping t.,** tren ómnibus, *m*. **through t.,** tren directo, *m*. **up t.,** tren ascendente, *m*. **t.-bearer,** paje que lleva la cola, *m*; dama de honor, *f*; (of a cardinal, etc.) caudatario, *m*. **t.-ferry,** buque transbordador, *m*. **t.-oil,** aceite de ballena, *m*. **t. service,** servicio de trenes, *m*

train *vt* educar; adiestrar; enseñar; *sport* entrenar; (firearms) apuntar; (plants) guiar; (accustom) habituar, acostumbrar; (a horse for racing) entrenar; (circus) amaestrar. *vi* educarse; adiestrarse; *sport* entrenarse

trainer *n* (of men and racehorses) entrenador, *m*; (of performing animals) domador, *m*

training *n* educación, *f*; enseñanza, instrucción, *f*; *sport* entrenamiento, *m*. **t.-college,** escuela normal, *f*. **t.-ship,** buque escuela, *m*

trait *n* rasgo, *m*, característica, *f*

traitor *n* traidor, *m*

trajectory *n* trayectoria, *f*

tram *n* tranvía, *m*. **a tranviario. t. conductor,** cobrador de tranvía, *m*. **t. depot,** cochera de tranvías, *f*. **t. stop,** parada de tranvía, *f*

trammel *n* (of a horse) traba, *f*; *fig* obstáculo, estorbo, *m*. *vt* travar; *fig* estorbar, impedir

tramp *n* (person) vagabundo (-da); vago (-ga); (walk) caminata, *f*, paseo largo, *m*; ruido de pasos, *m*; *naut* vapor volandero, *m*. *vi* ir a pie; patear; vagabundear. *vt* vagar por

trample *n* pisoteo, *m*; (of feet) ruido de pasos, *m*. *vt* pisotear, pisar, hollar. *vi* pisar fuerte. **to t. on,** *fig* atropellar humillar

trance *n* rapto, arrobamiento, *m*; *med* catalepsia, *f*

tranquil *a* tranquilo, apacible; sereno, sosegado

tranquilizer *n* calmante, *m*

tranquility *n* tranquilidad, paz, quietud, *f*; serenidad, *f*, sosiego, *m*; calma, *f*

tranquilize *vt* tranquilizar, sosegar, calmar

trans *prefix* trans-. **t.-Pyrenean,** a traspirenaico. **to t.-ship,** trasbordar. **t.-shipment,** trasbordo, *m*. **t.-Siberian,** trasiberiano

transact *vt* despachar, hacer. *vi* despachar un negocio

transaction *n* desempeño, *m*; negocio, *m*; transacción, operación, *f*; *pl* **transactions** (of a society) actas, *f pl*

transatlantic *a* transatlántico. **t. liner,** transatlántico, *m*

transcend *vt* exceder, superar, rebasar. *vi* trascender

transcribe *vt* trascribir, copiar; *mus* trascribir, adaptar

transcript *n* traslado, trasunto, *m*; (student's) certificado de estudios, certificado de materias aprobadas, *m*, constancia de estudios, copia del expediente académico, hoja de estudios, *f*

transfer *n* traslado, *m*; trasferencia, *f*, traspaso, *m*; *law* cesión, enajenación, *f*; (picture) calcomanía, *f*. *vt* trasladar; trasferir; pasar; *law* enajenar, ceder; estampar; calcografiar. *vi* trasbordarse. **deed of t.,** escritura de cesión, *f*. **t.-paper,** papel de calcar, *m*

transferable *a* trasferible

transference *n* traslado, *m*; trasferencia, *f*; *law* cesión, enajenación, *f*

transfigure *vt* trasfigurar, trasformar

transfix *vt* traspasar; *fig* paralizar

transform *vt* trasformar; convertir, cambiar. **It is completely transformed,** Está completamente trasformado

transformation *n* trasformación, *f*; conversión, *f*, cambio, *m*

transformer *n* *elec* trasformador, *m*

transfuse *vt* trasfundir

transfusion *n* trasfusión, *f*. **blood t.,** trasfusión de sangre, *f*

transgress *vt* exceder, sobrepasar; (violate) contravenir, violar, pecar contra. *vi* pecar

transgression *n* contravención, trasgresión, *f*; pecado, *m*

transgressor *n* trasgresor (-ra), pecador (-ra)

transient *a* transitorio, fugaz, pasajero; perecedero

transit n tránsito, paso, m; trasporte, m; ast tránsito, m. **in t.,** de tránsito

transition n transición, f; cambio, m; tránsito, paso, m

transitional a de transición, transitorio

transitively adv transitivamente

transitorily adv transitoriamente; provisionalmente

transitory a transitorio, fugaz, pasajero, breve

translatable a traducible

translate vt traducir; interpretar; (transfer) trasladar

translation n traducción, f; versión, f; traslado, m

translator n traductor (-ra)

translucent a traslúcido, trasparente

transmigrate vi trasmigrar

transmissible a trasmisible

transmission n trasmisión, f

transmit vt trasmitir; remitir, dar

transmitter n trasmisor (-ra); rad radiotrasmisor, m; elec trasmisor, m

transmute vt trasmutar

transoceanic a transoceánico

transom n carp travesaño, m; naut yugo de popa, m

transparency n transparencia; diafanidad, f; (picture) trasparente, m

transparent a trasparente; diáfano; (of style) claro, limpio

transpire vi traspirar; rezumarse; hacerse público; inf acontecer. vt exhalar

transplant vt trasplantar

transport n trasporte, m; naut navío de trasporte, m; aer avión de trasporte, m; (fit) acceso, paroxismo, m. vt trasportar; (convicts) deportar; fig (joy) colmar; (rage) llenar

transportation n trasporte, m; (convicts) deportación, f

transpose vt trasponer; mus trasportar

transverse a trasverso, trasversal

trap n trampa, f; cepo, m; (net) lazo, m, red, f; (for mice, rats) ratonera, f; mech sifón de depósito, m; pequeño carruaje de dos ruedas, m; (door) puerta caediza, f; theat escotillón, m; pl **traps**, trastos, m pl; equipaje, m. vt coger con trampa; hacer caer en el lazo; fig tender el lazo. vi armar una trampa; armar lazo. **to fall into a t.,** fig caer en la trampa. **to pack one's traps,** liar el hato

trapeze n trapecio (de gimnasia), m

trapper n cazador de animales de piel, m

trappings n pl arneses, jaeces, m pl; arreos, aderezos, m pl, galas, f pl

trash n paja, hojarasca, f; (of sugar, etc.) bagazo, m; trastos viejos, m pl; cachivaches, m pl; (literary) paja, f

trashy a de ningún valor, inútil, despreciable

traumatic a med traumático

travail n dolores de parto, m pl. vi estar de parto; trabajar

travel n el viajar, viajes, m pl. vi viajar; ver mundo; (of traffic) circular, pasar, ir. vt viajar por; recorrer; (with number of miles) hacer. **to t. over,** viajar por; recorrer. **t. worn,** fatigado por el viaje

travel agent n agente de viajes, mf

traveled a que ha viajado, que ha visto muchas partes

traveler n viajero (-ra); pasajero (-ra). **commercial t.,** viajante, mf **traveler's check,** cheque de viajeros, m. **traveler's joy,** bot clemátide, f

traveling n viajes, m pl. a viajero; para (or de) viajar; (itinerant) ambulante. **t. crane,** grúa móvil, f. **t. expenses,** gastos de viaje, m pl. **t. requisites,** objetos de viaje, m pl. **t. rug,** manta, f. **t. show,** circo ambulante, m

traverse n carp travesaño, m; law negación, f; (mil arch) través, m; (crossing) travesía, f, a transversal. adv transversalmente. vt atravesar, cruzar; law negar

travesty n parodia, f, vt parodiar

trawl vt rastrear. vi pescar a la rastra. **t.-net,** red de arrastre, f

trawler n barco barredero, m; pescador a la rastra, m

tray n bandeja, f; (of a balance) platillo, m; (in a wardrobe, etc.) cajón, m; (trough) artesa, f

treacherous a traidor, falso, pérfido, fementido; (of memory) infiel; engañoso; (of ice, etc.) peligroso

treachery n perfidia, traición, falsedad, f

treacle n melado, m

tread n pisada, f; paso, m; (of a stair) peldaño, m; (of tire) pastilla, f; (walk) andar, porte, m, vi pisar; (trample) pisotear; hollar; (oppress) oprimir. vt hollar; (a path) abrir; recorrer; caminar por; bailar. **to t. the grapes,** pisar las uvas. **to t. the stage,** pisar las tablas. **to t. under foot,** hollar; pisotear. **to t. on,** pisar. **to t. on one's heels,** pisarle los talones a uno; seguir de cerca. **to t. out,** (a measure) bailar

treadle n pedal, m; (of a loom) cárcola, f

treadmill n molino de rueda de escalones, m; fig rueda, f

treason n traición, f. **high t.,** alta traición, lesa majestad, f

treasure n tesoro, m; riqueza, f, caudal, m; fig perla, f. vt atesorar; acumular (or guardar) riquezas; (a memory) guardar. **t. trove,** tesoro hallado, m

treasurer n tesorero (-ra)

treasury n tesorería, f; (government department) Ministerio de Hacienda, m; (anthology) tesoro, m. **t. bench,** banco del Gobierno, m

treat n (pleasure) gusto, placer, m; (present) obsequio, m; (entertainment) fiesta, f. vt tratar; med tratar, curar; (regale) obsequiar. *vi* (stand host) convidar; (of) tratar de, versar sobre; (with) negociar con

treatise *n* tesis, monografía, disertación, *f*, tratado, *m*

treatment *n* tratamiento, *m*; (of persons) conducta hacia, *f*, modo de obrar con, *m*; *med* tratamiento, *m*; (*lit, art*) procedimiento, *m*, técnica, *f*

treaty *n* tratado, pacto, *m*; (bargain) contrato, *m*

treble *n mus* tiple, *m*; voz de tiple, *f. a* triple; *mus* sobreagudo. *vt* triplicar; *vi* triplicarse. **t. clef,** clave de sol, *f*

tree *n* árbol, *m*; (for shoes) horma, *f*; (of a saddle) arzón, *m*. **breadfruit t.,** árbol del pan, *m*. **Judas t.,** árbol de amor, *m*. **t. of knowledge,** árbol de la ciencia, *m*. **t.-covered,** arbolado. **t.-frog,** rana de San Antonio, *f*

trek *vi* caminar, andar

trellis *n* enrejado, *m*; (for plants) espaldera, *f. vt* cercar con un enrejado; construir espalderas

tremble *vi* temblar; estremecerse; trepidar; vibrar; (sway) oscilar; (of flags) ondear; agitarse; ser tembloroso. **His fate trembled in the balance,** Su suerte estaba en la balanza. **to t. all over,** temblar de pies a cabeza

trembling *n* temblor, *m*; estremecimiento, *m*; trepidación, *f*; vibración, *f*; (fear) agitación, ansiedad, *f*; temor, *m. a* tembloroso; trémulo

tremendous *a* terrible, espantoso; formidable; grande; importante; *inf* tremendo; enorme

tremendously *adv* terriblemente; *inf* enormemente

tremor *n* temblor, movimiento sísmico, *m*; (thrill) estremecimiento, *m*; vibración, *f*

tremulous *a* trémulo, tembloroso; vacilante; tímido

trench *n* zanja, *f*, foso, *m*; (for irrigation) acequia, *f*; *mil* trinchera, *f. vt* hacer zanjas (en); acequiar; *mil* atrincherar. **t.-fever,** tifus exantemático, *m*. **t.-foot,** pie de trinchera, *m*. **t.-mortar,** mortero de trinchera, *m*

trenchant *a* mordaz

trencher *n* trinchero, *m*

trend *n* curso, rumbo, *m*; *fig* tendencia, *f*; dirección, *f. vi fig* tender

trepan *vt surg* trepanar

trepanning *n surg* trepanación, *f*

trepidation *n* trepidación, *f*

trespass *n* violación de propiedad, *f*; ofensa, *f*; pecado, *m*; (in the Lord's Prayer) deuda, *f. vi* (on land) entrar sin derecho, violar la propiedad; (upon) entrar sin permiso en; (with patience, etc.) abusar de; (against) pecar contra, infringir

trespasser *n* violador (-ra) de la ley de propiedad. **"Trespassers will be prose-**

cuted," «Entrada prohibida,» «Prohibido el paso»

tress *n* (plait) trenza, *f*; rizo, bucle, *m*; *pl* **tresses,** cabellera, *f*

trestle *n* caballete, *m*; armazón, *m*. **trestle-table,** mesa de caballete, *f*

triad *n* terna, *f*; *mus* acorde, *m*

trial *n* prueba, *f*, ensayo, *m*; examen, *m*; (experiment) tentativa, *f*, experimento, *m*; (misfortune) desgracia, pena, *f*; (nuisance) molestia, *f*; *law* vista de una causa, *f*. **on t.,** a prueba; *law* en proceso. **to bring to t.,** procesar. **to stand one's t.,** ser procesado. **t. run,** marcha de ensayo, *f*. **t. trip,** *naut* viaje de ensayo, *m*

trial and error *n* tanteos, *m*. **by trial and error,** por tanteos

triangle *n* triángulo, *m*. **acute-angled t.,** triángulo acutángulo, *m*. **obtuse-angled t.,** triángulo obtusángulo, *m*. **right-angled t.,** triángulo rectángulo, *m*. **the eternal t.,** el eterno triángulo

triangular *a* triangular, triángulo

triangulation *n* (in surveying) triangulación, *f*

tribal *a* tribal

tribe *n* tribu, *f*

tribesman *n* miembro de una tribu, *m*

tribulation *n* tribulación, *f*; pena, aflicción, desgracia, *f*

tribunal *n* (seat) tribunal, *m*; (court) juzgado, *m*; (confessional) confesionario, *m*

tribune *n* (person) tribuno, *m*; tribuna, *f*

tributary *a* and *n* tributario *m*

tribute *n* tributo, *m*; contribución, imposición, *f*

trice *n* tris, soplo, *m*. **in a t.,** en un periquete, en un avemaría, en dos trancos

tricentennial *a* de trescientos años; *n* tercer centenario, tricentenario, *m*

trick *n* (swindle) estafa, *f*, engaño, *m*; (ruse) truco, *m*, estratagema, ardid, *f*; (mischief) travesura, *f*; burla, *f*; (illusion) ilusión, *f*; (habit) costumbre, *f*; (affectation) afectación, *f*; (jugglery) juego de manos, *m*; (knack) talento, *m*; (at cards) baza, *f. vt* engañar, estafar; (with out) adornar, ataviar; (with into) inducir fraudulentamente. *vi* trampear. **dirty t.,** *inf* mala pasada, perrada, *f*. **His memory plays him tricks,** La memoria le engaña. **to play a t. on,** gastar una broma (a). **to play tricks,** hacer travesuras. **t. riding,** acrobacia ecuestre, *f*

trickery *n* maullería, superchería, *f*; fraude, engaño, *m*

trickle *n* chorrito, hilo (de agua, etc.) *m. vi* gotear. **to t. down,** deslizar por, correr por, escurrir por

trickling *n* goteo, *m*; (sound) murmullo, *m*

trickster *n* embustero (-ra), trampeador (-ra). **to be a t.,** ser buena maula

tricky *a* informal, maullero; (of things)

difícil; complicado; (clever) ingenioso; (person) = **crafty**

tricycle n triciclo, m

tried a probado

trifle n (object) baratija, fruslería, f; pequeñez, tontería, bagatela, f; cul, f; (small amount) pequeña cantidad, f, muy poco (de); (adverbially) algo. vi entretenerse, jugar. vt (away) malgastar. **to t. with,** jugar con

trifler n persona frívola, f; (with affections) seductor (-ra)

trifling a insignificante, sin importancia, trivial

trigger n (of a fire-arm) gatillo, m; mech tirador, m

trigonometry n trigonometría, f

trilingual a trilingüe

trill n trino, m, vi trinar

trillion n trillón, m

trilogy n trilogía, f

trim a aseado; bien arreglado; bien ajustado; elegante; bonito; (of sail) orientado. **She has a t. waist,** inf Tiene un talle juncal. n orden, m; buen estado, m; buena condición, f; (toilet) atavío, m. vt arreglar; (tidy) asear; pulir; (ornament) ornar, adornar; (adapt) ajustar, adaptar; sew guarnecer; (lamps) despabilar; (a fire) atizar; (hair, moustache) atusar, recortar; (trees) mondar, atusar; carp alisar; (sails) templar, orientar; (distribute weight in a boat) equilibrar; (of quill pens) tajar. vi (waver) nadar entre dos aguas. **to t. oneself up,** arreglarse

trimly adv aseadamente; lindamente

trimmer n guarnecedor (-ra); contemporizador (-ra)

trimming n arreglo, m; guarnición, f; (on a dress) pasamanería, f; adorno, m; agr poda, f; adaptación, f, ajuste, m; pl **trimmings,** accesorios, m pl

trimness n aseo, buen orden, m; buen estado, m; elegancia, lindeza, f; (slimness) esbeltez, f

Trinity n Trinidad, f

trinket n joya, alhaja, f; dije, m, chuchería, baratija, f

trinomial a math de tres términos. n math trinomio, m

trio n trío, m

trip n excursión, f; viaje, m; (slip) traspié, tropiezo, m; (in wrestling) zancadilla, f; (mistake) desliz, m. vi (stumble) tropezar, caer; (move nimbly) andar airosamente, ir (o correr) ligeramente; (frolic) bailar, saltar; (wrestling, games) echar la zancadilla; (err) equivocarse; cometer un desliz. vt (up) hacer caer; echar la zancadilla (a); coger en una falta; hacer desdecirse; coger en un desliz; naut levantar (el ancla)

tripartite a tripartito

tripe n callos, m pl

triple a triple. vt triplicar. vi triplicarse

triplet n poet terceto, m; mus tresillo, m; cada uno (una) de tres hermanos (hermanas) gemelos (-as)

triplicate a triplicado. vt triplicar

triplication n triplicación, f

tripod n trípode, m

tripper n turista, excursionista, mf

tripping a ligero, ágil

trite a vulgar, trivial

triteness n trivialidad, vulgaridad, f

triumph n triunfo, m. vi triunfar; (over) triunfar de, vencer

triumphal a triunfal. **t. arch,** arco de triunfo, m

triumphant a triunfante, victorioso

trivet n trébedes, f pl; trípode, m

trivial a trivial, frívolo; insignificante, sin importancia

triviality n trivialidad, frivolidad, f; insignificancia, f

trodden a trillado, batido

Trojan a and n troyano (-na). **the T. War,** la guerra de Troya, f

trolley n elec trole, m; (for children) carretón, m. **t.-bus,** trolebús, m. n **trolley car** tranvía, m. **t.-pole,** trole, m

trollop n tarasca, ramera, f

trombone n trombón, m. **t. player,** trombón, m

troop n banda, muchedumbre, f; theat compañía, f; (of cavalry) escuadrón, m; pl **troops,** mil tropas, f pl; ejército, m. vi ir en tropel, congregarse; (with away) marcharse en tropel, retirarse; (with out) salir en masa. **fresh troops,** tropas frescas, f pl. **storm troops,** tropas de asalto, f pl. **t.-ship,** transporte de guerra, m

trooper n soldado de caballería, m

trope n tropo, m

trophy n trofeo, m

tropic a and n trópico, m

tropical a tropical; (figurative) figurativo

trot n trote, m. vi trotar. vt hacer trotar. **to t. out,** inf sacar a relucir

troth n fe, f; palabra, f. **to plight one's t.,** dar palabra de matrimonio, desposarse

trotting a trotón. n trote, m

troubadour n trovador, m, a trovadoresco

trouble n (grief) aflicción, angustia, f; (difficulty) dificultad, f; (effort) esfuerzo, m; pena, desgracia, f; (annoyance) disgusto, sinsabor, m; (unrest) confusión, f; disturbio, m; (illness) enfermedad, f; mal, m; (disagreement) desavenencia, f. **The t. is . . . ,** Lo malo es; La dificultad está en que . . . **to be in t.,** estar afligido; estar en un apuro, estar entre la espada y la pared. **to be not worth the t.,** no valer la pena. **to stir up t.,** revolver el ajo; armar un lío. **to take the t. to,** tomarse la molestia de.

trouble vt turbar; agitar; afligir, inquietar; (badger) importunar; (annoy) molestar; (cost an effort) costar trabajo (e.g.,

Learning Spanish did not t. him much, No le costó mucho trabajo aprender el castellano. *vi* preocuparse; darse la molestia; inquietarse

troubled a agitado; inquieto; preocupado; (of life) accidentado, borrascoso. **to fish in t. waters,** pescar en agua turbia, pescar en río revuelto

troublemaker n Lat. Am. buscapleitos, *mf*

troublesome a dificultoso; molesto; inconveniente; importuno; fastidioso

trough n gamella, *f*; (for kneading bread) artesa, *f*; (of the waves) seno, *m*; (meteorological) mínimo, *m*. **drinking t.,** abrevadero, *m*. **stone t.,** pila, *f*

trounce *vt* zurrar, apalear; *fig* fustigar

troupe n compañía, *f*

trousers n *pl* pantalones, *m pl*. **plus four t.,** pantalones de golf, *m pl*. **striped t.,** pantalón de corte, *m*. **t. pocket,** bolsillo del pantalón, *m*. **t. press,** prensa para pantalones, *f*

trousseau n ajuar de novia, *m*

trout n trucha, *f*

trowel n *agr* almocafre, *m*; (mason's) paleta, *f*, palustre, *m*

troy weight n peso de joyería, *m*

truant n novillero, *m*; haragán (-ana). a haragán, perezoso. **to play t.,** (from school) hacer novillos; ausentarse

truce n tregua, *f*; suspensión, cesación, *f*

truck n (lorry) camión, *m*; carretilla de mano, *f*; (railway) vagón de carga, *m*; (intercourse) relaciones, *f pl*; (trash) cachivaches, *m pl*, cosas sin valor, *f pl*

truckle *vi* humillarse, no levantar los ojos. **t. bed,** carriola, *f*

truculent a truculento, agresivo

trudge *vi* caminar a pie; andar con dificultad, caminar lentamente, andar trabajosamente, n caminata, *f*

true a verdadero; real; leal, sincero; fiel; exacto; honesto; genuino; auténtico; alineado, a plomo. **That is t. of . . .** Es propio de . . . *adv* realmente; exactamente. **t.-bred,** de casta legítima. **t.-hearted,** leal, fiel, sincero

truffle n trufa, *f*. **to stuff with truffles,** trufar

truism n perogrullada, *f*

truly *adv* lealmente; realmente, verdaderamente; en efecto, por cierto; sinceramente, de buena fe. **Yours t.,** su seguro servidor (su s.s.)

trump n (cards) triunfo, *m*; son de la trompeta, *m*; *inf* gran persona, joya, *f*. *vt* ganar con el triunfo. **to t. up,** inventar. **t.-card,** naipe de triunfo, *m*

trumpet n trompeta, *f*. *vt* trompetear; *fig* pregonar. *vi* (of elephant) barritar. **ear.-t.,** trompetilla (acústica), *f*. **speaking t.,** portavoz, *m*. **t. blast,** trompetazo, *m*. **t. shaped,** en trompeta

trumpeter n trompetero, trompeta, *m*

truncheon n porra (de goma), *f*; bastón de mando, *m*. **blow with a t.,** porrazo, *m*

trunk n (*anat bot*) tronco, *m*; (elephant's) trompa, *f*; (railway) línea principal, *f*; baúl, *m*; cofre, *m*; (of a car) *Lat. Am.* baúl *m*; *pl* **trunks,** (Elizabethan, etc.) trusas, *f pl*; calzoncillos cortos, *m pl*. **wardrobe t.,** baúl mundo, *m*. **t.-call,** conferencia telefónica, *f*. **t.-line,** tronco, *m*. **t.-road,** carretera de primera clase, carretera mayor, *f*

truss n *med* braguero, *m*; (of straw, etc.) haz, *m*; (of blossom) racimo, *m*; (framework) armazón, *f*. *vt* atar; *cul* espetar; (a building) apuntalar

trust n fe, confianza, *f*; deber, *m*; *law* fideicomiso, *m*; (credit) crédito, *m*; esperanza, expectación, *f*; *com* trust, *m*. *vt* tener confianza en; confiar en; esperar; creer; *com* dar crédito (a). *vi* confiar; *com* dar crédito. **in t.,** en confianza; en administración, en depósito. **on t.,** al fiado

trustee n guardián, *m*; *law* fideicomisario, depositario, consignatario, *m*

trustful a confiado

trusting a Lat. Am. creído

trustworthy a digno de confianza, honrado; fidedigno, seguro; exacto

trusty a leal, fiel; firme, seguro

truth n verdad, *f*; realidad, *f*; exactitud, *f*. **the plain t.,** la pura verdad. **to tell the t.,** decir la verdad

truthful a veraz; exacto, verdadero

try *vt* and *vi* procurar, tratar de; (test) probar, ensayar; (a case, *law*) ver (el pleito); (strain) poner a prueba; (tire) cansar, fatigar; (annoy) molestar, exasperar; (afflict) hacer sufrir, afligir; (attempt) intentar; (judge) juzgar; (the weight of) tomar a pulso; (assay) refinar. n tentativa, *f*; (football) tiro, *m*. **Try as he would . . . ,** Por más que hizo . . . **to try hard to,** hacer un gran esfuerzo para. **to try one's luck,** probar fortuna. **to try on,** (clothes) probarse (un vestido, etc.). **to try out,** poner a prueba, probar. **to try to,** tratar de, procurar

trying a molesto; fatigoso; irritante; (painful) angustioso, penoso

tryst n cita, *f*; lugar de cita, *m*. *vt* citar. *vi* citarse

tsar n zar, *m*

tub n cuba, *f*, artesón, *m*; cubeta, *f*. *vi* bañarse. **tub thumper,** *inf* gerundio, *m*

tuba n *mus* tuba, *f*

tube n tubo, *m*; (railway) metro, ferrocarril subterráneo, *m*; tubo, *m*; *anat* trompa, *f*. **Eustachian t.,** *anat* trompa de Eustaquio, *f*. **Fallopian t.,** trompa de Falopio, *f*. **inner t.,** *aut* cámara de aire, *f*. **speaking t.,** tubo acústico, *m*. **test t.,** tubo de ensayo, *m*

tuber n tubérculo, *m*. **kind of tuber resembling a sweet potato** *Central America* malanga, *f*

tuberculosis n tuberculosis, *f*

tuberose n nardo, m, tuberosa, f

tuck n sew alforzar, f; pliegue, m. vt recoger; sew alforzar. vi hacer alforzas. **to t. in**, (in bed) arropar; inf tragar. **to t. under**, poner debajo; doblar. **to t. up**, (in bed) arropar; (skirt) sofaldar; (sleeves) arremangar

Tuesday n martes, m. **Shrove T.**, martes de carnaval, m

tuft n (bunch) manojo, m; (on the head) copete, moño, m, cresta, f; (tassel) borla, f; mechón, m

tufted a Lat. Am. copetudo

tug n tirón, m; sacudida, f; (boat) remolcador, m. vt tirar de; halar; sacudir. vi tirar con fuerza. **to give a tug**, dar una sacudida. **tug of war**, lit lucha de la cuerda, f; fig estira y afloja, msg

tuition n (teaching) instrucción, enseñanza, f; lecciones, f pl; (fee) cuota, f

tulip n tulipán, m. **t. wood**, palo de rosa, m

tulle n tul, m

tumble n caída, f; (somersault) tumbo, m; voltereta, f. vi caer; (acrobats) voltear, dar saltos. vt hacer caer; desarreglar. **to t. down**, venirse abajo; caer por. **t. down**, ruinoso, destartalado. **to t. off**, caer de. **to t. out**, vt hacer salir; arrojar. vi salir apresuradamente. **to t. over**, vt tropezar con. vi volcarse. **to t. to**, inf caer en la cuenta

tumbler n (acrobat) volteador (-ra); vaso para beber, m

tumor n tumor, m

tumult n alboroto, tumulto, m; conmoción, agitación, f; confusión, f

tumultuous a tumultuoso, alborotado; ruidoso; confuso; turbulento, violento

tun n tonel, m, cuba, f, vt entonelar, embarrilar

tune n melodía, f; son, m; armonía, f; fig tono, m; inf suma, f. vt mus afinar, templar; rad sintonizar. (up, an engine) ajustar (un motor). vi (in) sintonizar el receptor; (up, mus) templar (afinar) los instrumentos. **in t.**, mus afinado, templado; fig armonioso; (agreement) de acuerdo, conforme. **out of t.**, mus desafinado, destemplado. **to be out of t.**, desentonar; discordar; fig no armonizar, no estar en armonía. **to go out of t.**, desafinar. **to put out of t.**, destemplar. **to change one's t.**, inf bajar el tono

tuneful a melodioso

tuner n afinador, templador, m; rad sintonizador, m

tunic n túnica, Lat. Am. also cusma, f

tuning n afinación, f; rad sintonización, f. **t. fork**, diapasón normal, m. **t. key**, templador, m

tunnel n túnel, m. vt hacer (or construir) un túnel por. vi hacer un túnel

tunny n atún, m. **striped t.**, bonito, m. **t. fishery**, almadraba, f

turbid a turbio; fig confuso, **to make t.**, enturbiar

turbine n turbina, f

turbulence n turbulencia, f; desorden, m: agitación, f

turbulent a turbulento; alborotado; (stormy) borrascoso; agitado

tureen n sopera, f

turf n césped, m; (fuel) turba, f; (racing) carreras de caballos, f pl

turgid a turgente, hinchado; (of style) pomposo

Turk n turco (-ca). **Turk's head**, (duster) deshollinador, m; naut cabeza de turco, f

Turkey Turquía, f

turkey n (cock) pavo, m; (hen) pava, f; **t. red**, rojo turco, m

Turkish a turco. n (language) turco, idioma turco, m. **T. bath**, baño turco, m. **T. slipper**, babucha, f. **T. towel**, toalla rusa, f

turmoil n alboroto, tumulto, desorden, m

turn n turno, m; (twist) torcimiento, m; (bend) recodo, m, vuelta, f; (in a river) meandro, m; (in a road) viraje, m; (revolution) vuelta, revolución, f; (direction) dirección, f; (in spiral stair) espira, f; theat número, m; (change) cambio, m; vicisitud, f; (appearance) aspecto, m; (service) servicio, m; (nature) índole, naturaleza, f; (of phrase) giro, m, expresión, f; (walk) vuelta, f, paseo, m; (talent) talento, m. **a sharp t.**, (in a road) un viraje rápido. **at every t.**, a cada instante; en todas partes. **bad t.**, flaco servicio, m. **by turns**, por turnos. **good t.**, servicio, favor, m. **in its t.**, a su vez. **in t.**, sucesivamente. **Now it's my t.**, Ahora me toca a mí. **The affair has taken a new t.**, El asunto ha cambiado de aspecto. **turn of the century**, vuelta del siglo, f; **turn of the millenium**, vuelta del milenio, f. **to a t.**, cul a la perfección. **to have a t. for**, tener talento para. **to take turns at**, alternar en. **t.-table**, (railway) plataforma, f; (of a gramophone) disco giratorio, m. **t. up**, barahúnda, conmoción, f; (of trousers) dobladillo (del pantalón), m

turn vt (on a lathe) tornear; (revolve) dar vueltas a, girar; (a key, door handle, etc.) torcer; (the leaves of a book) hojear; (the brain) trastornar; (a screw) enroscar; (the stomach) revolver (el estómago), marear; (go round) doblar, dar la vuelta a; (change) cambiar, mudar; (translate) traducir, verter; (dissuade) disuadir; (deflect) desviar; (apply) adaptar; (direct, move) volver; (concentrate) dirigir; concentrar; (turn over) volver del revés al derecho; (upside-down) volver lo de arriba abajo; (make) hacer, volver; (make sour) volver agrio; (transform) transformar convertir; *mil* envolver. **He has turned thirty,** Ha cumplido los treinta. **He said it without turning a hair,** Lo dijo sin pestañear. **He turned his head,** Volvió la cabeza. **They have turned the corner,** Han doblado la esquina; *fig* Han pasado la crisis. **"Please t. over,"** «A la vuelta (de la página).» **to t. a deaf ear to,** no dar oídos a, no hacer caso de. **to t. one's hand to,** aplicarse a. **to t. to account,** sacar ventaja (de). **to t. adrift,** dejar a la merced de las olas; echar de casa, poner en la calle; abandonar. **to t. against,** causar aversión, hacer hostil. **to t. aside,** desviar. **to t. away,** despedir; rechazar; (the head, etc.) volver; desviar. **to t. back,** hacer volver; enviar de nuevo; (raise) alzar; (fold) doblar; (the clock) retrasar. **to t. down,** doblar; (gas) bajar; (a glass, etc.) poner boca abajo; (reject) rechazar; (a suitor) dar calabazas (a). **to t. from,** alejar de, desviar de. **to t. in,** doblar hacia dentro; entregar. **to t. in one's toes,** ser patizambo. **to t. inside out,** volver al revés. **to t. into,** (enter) entrar en; (change) cambiar en, transformar en; convertir en; (translate) traducir a. **to t. off,** (dismiss) despedir; (from) desviarse de, dejar; (light) apagar; (water) cortar; *mech* cerrar; (disconnect) desconectar; (avoid) evitar; (refuse) rechazar. **to t. off the tap,** (water, gas) cerrar la llave (del agua, del gas). **to t. on,** (light) encender; (water, gas, etc.) abrir la llave (del agua, del gas); (steam) dar (vapor); (electric current) establecer (la corriente eléctrica); (eyes) fijar. **to t. out,** (expel) expeler, echar; (dismiss) despedir; (animals) echar al campo; (produce) producir; (dress) vestir; (equip) equipar, guarnecer; (a light) apagar. **to t. over,** (the page) volver (la hoja); (transfer) ceder, traspasar; revolver; (upset) volcar; considerar, pensar. **to t. round,** dar vuelta (a); girar; (empty) descargar. **to t. up,** levantar; apuntar; hacia arriba; (the earth) labrar, cavar; (a glass) poner boca arriba; (one's sleeves, skirt) arremangar; (fold) doblar. **to t. up one's nose at,** mirar con desprecio. **to t. upon,** atacar, volverse contra, acometer; depender de, estribar en. **to t. upside down,** volver lo de arriba abajo; revolver; revolcar

turn *vi* (in a lathe) tornear; (revolve) girar, dar vueltas; (depend) depender (de); torcer; volverse; dar la vuelta; girar sobre los talones; dirigirse (a, hacia); (move) mudar de posición; (deviate) desviarse (de); (be changed) convertirse (en); (become) hacerse, venir a ser; (begin) meterse (a); (take to) dedicarse a; (seek help) acudir; (change behavior) enmendarse, corregirse; (the stomach) revolver (el estómago); (go sour) agriarse, avinagrarse; (rebel) sublevarse. **He turned to the left,** Dio la vuelta a la izquierda;

Torció hacia la izquierda. **My head turns,** (with giddiness) Se me va la cabeza. **to t. about,** voltearse, dar la vuelta. **to t. against,** coger aversión (a), disgustarse con; volverse hostil (a). **to t. aside,** desviarse; dejar el camino; volver la cabeza; apartarse; alejarse. **to t. away,** volver la cabeza; apartarse; alejarse. **to t. back,** volver atrás; volver de nuevo; retroceder; volver sobre sus pasos. **to t. down,** doblarse; reducirse. **to t. from,** alejarse de; apartarse de, huir de. **to t. in,** doblarse hacia dentro; (retire) acostarse. **to t. into,** transformarse en; convertirse en. **to t. off,** (depart from) desviarse (de); (fork) torcer, bifurcarse. **to t. out,** estar vuelto hacia fuera; (leave home) salir de casa; (rise) levantarse (de la cama); (arrive) llegar, presentarse; (attend) asistir, acudir; (result) resultar. **to t. over,** mudar (or cambiar) de posición, revolverse; (upset) voltearse, volcarse. **to t. round,** girar; volverse; cambiar de frente; cambiar de dirección, dar la vuelta; (*aut, aer*) virar; (change views) cambiar de opinión; (change sides) cambiar de partido. **to t. round and round,** dar vueltas, girar. **to t. to,** (apply to) acudir a; (begin) ponerse a; (become) convertirse en; (face) dirigirse hacia; (address) dirigirse a. **to t. up,** (crop up) surgir, aparecer; (arrive) llegar; (happen) acontecer; (be found again) volver a hallarse, reaparecer; (cards) venir; (of hats) levantar el ala; (of hair, etc.) doblarse. **His nose turns up,** Tiene la nariz respingona

turncoat *n* desertor (-ra), renegado (-da). **to become a t.,** volver la casaca

turning *n* (bend) vuelta, *f*; (turnery) tornería, *f*; (of milk, etc.) agrura, *f*; *pl* **turnings,** *sew* ensanche, *m*. **t.-point,** punto decisivo, *m*, crisis, *f*. **t. yellow** *Lat. Am.* amarilloso

turnip *n* nabo, *m*. **t. field,** nabar, *m*

turnover *n com* ventas, *f pl*; *cul* pastelillo, *m*

turnpike *n* barrera de portazgo, *f*

turnstile *n* torniquete, *m*

turpentine *n* aguarrás, *m*, trementina, *f*

turpitude *n* infamia, maldad, *f*

turquoise *n* turquesa, *f*

turret *n* torrecilla, almenilla, *f*; *naut* torre blindada, *f*

turreted *a* con torres, guarnecido de torres; en forma de torre

turtle *n* (dove) tórtola (-la); (sea) tortuga de mar, *f*. **to turn t.,** voltearse patas arriba; *naut* zozobrar. **t. soup,** sopa de tortuga, *f*

tusk *n* colmillo, *m*

tussle *n* lucha, *f*; agarrada, *f*. *vi* luchar, pelear; tener una agarrada

tutelage *n* tutela, *f*

tutor *n* (private) ayo, *m*; profesor (-ra); (Roman law) tutor, *m*; (supervisor of studies) preceptor. *vt* enseñar, instruir. *vi* ser profesor, dar clases

tutorial *n* (university) seminario, *m*; (private) clase particular, *f*

tutoring *n* enseñanza, instrucción, *f*

TWA la TWA, *f*, (pronounced as if written *túa*)

twaddle *n* disparates, *m pl*, tonterías, patrañas, *f pl*

twain *a* and *n* dos, *m*

twang *n* punteado de una cuerda, *m*; (of a guitar) zumbido, *m*; (in speech) gangueo, *m*. *vt* puntear; (las cuerdas de un instrumento) rasguear. *vi* zumbar. **to speak with a t.,** hablar con una voz gangosa

tweak *n* pellizco, *m*; sacudida, *f*, tirón, *m*. *vt* pellizcar; sacudir, tirar

tweed *n* mezcla, *f*, cheviot, *m*

tweezers *n pl* pinzas, tenacillas, *f pl*

twelfth *a* duodécimo; (of the month) (el) doce; (of monarchs) doce. *n* duodécimo, *m*; (part) dozavo, *m*, duodécima parte, *f*. **T.-night,** Día de Reyes, *m*, Epifanía, *f*

twelve *a* and *n* doce *m*; (of age) doce años, *m pl*. **t. o'clock,** las doce; (midday) mediodía, *m*; (midnight) media noche, *f*, las doce de la noche. **t.-syllabled,** dodecasílabo

twentieth *a* vigésimo; (of the month) (el) veinte; (of monarchs) veinte, *n* vigésimo, *m*; (part) vientavo, *m*, vigésima parte, *f*

twenty *a* veinte; (of age) veinte años, *m pl*, *n* veinte, *m*; (score) veintena, *f*. **t.-first,** vigésimo primero; (of date) (el) veintiuno, *m*. (In modern Spanish the ordinals above *décimo* "tenth" are generally replaced by the cardinals, e.g. **the twenty-ninth chapter,** el capítulo veintinueve.)

twice *adv* dos veces. **t. as many** or **as much,** el doble

twiddle *vt* jugar con; hacer girar. *vi* girar; vibrar. *n* vuelta, *f*. **to t. one's thumbs,** dar vuelta a los pulgares, estar mano sobre mano

twig *n* ramita, pequeña rama, *f*

twilight *n* crepúsculo, *m*; media luz, *f*. *a* crepuscular. **in the t.,** en el crepúsculo; en la media luz. **t. sleep,** parto sin dolor, *m*

twin *a* gemelo, mellizo; doble. *n* gemelo (-la), mellizo (-za); (of objects) pareja, *f*, par, *m*. **t.-engined,** bimotor. **t. screw,** (*naut aer*) de dos hélices

twine *n* bramante, cordel, *m*; guita, *f*. *vt* enroscar; (weave) tejer; (encircle) ceñir; (round, about) abrazar. *vi* (of plants) trepar; entrelazarse; (wind) serpentear

twinge *n* punzada, *f*, dolor agudo, *m*; *fig* remordimiento, tormento, *m*. *vi* causar un dolor agudo

twinkle *vi* centellear, chispear, titilar; (of

eyes) brillar; (of feet) moverse rápidamente, bailar. *n* (in the eye) chispa, *f*

twinkling *n* centelleo, *m*; titilación, *f*; (of the eye) brillo, *m*; (glimpse) vislumbre, *m*; *fig* instante, momento, *m*. a titilante, centelleador. **in a t.,** en un dos por tres. **in the t. of an eye,** en un abrir y cerrar de ojos

twirl *n* rotación, vuelta, *f*; pirueta, *f*. *vi* hacer girar; voltear; torcer; (a stick, etc.) dar vueltas (a). *vi* girar, dar vueltas; dar piruetas

twirp *n inf* renacuajo, *m*

twist *n* (skein) mecha, *f*; trenza, *f*; (yarn) torzal, *m*; (of tobacco) rollo, *m*; (of bread) rosca de pan, *f*; (act of twisting) torcimiento, *m*, torsión, *f*; (in a road, etc.) recodo, *m*, curva, vuelta, *f*; (pull) sacudida, *f*; (contortion) regate, esguince, *m*; (in a winding stair) espira, *f*; (in ball games) efecto, *m*; (in a person's nature) peculiaridad, *f*; falta de franqueza, *f*; (to words) interpretación, *f*. *vt* torcer; enroscar; (plait) trenzar; (wring) estrujar; (weave) tejer; (encircle) ceñir; (a stick, etc.) dar vueltas a; (of hands) crispar; (distort) interpretar mal, torcer. *vi* torcerse; enroscarse; (wind) serpentear; dar vueltas; (coil) ensortijarse; (writhe) undular, retorcerse; (of a stair) dar vueltas

twitch *n* sacudida, *f*, tirón, *m*; (nervous) contracción nerviosa, *f*. *vt* tirar bruscamente, quitar rápidamente; agarrar; (ears, etc.) mover; (hands) crispar, retorcer. *vi* crisparse; (of ears, nose) moverse

twitter *n* piada, *f*, gorjeo, *m*. *vi* piar, gorjear

two *a* and *n* dos, *m*; (of the clock) (las) dos, *f pl*; (of age) dos años, *m pl*. a de dos. **in two,** en dos partes. **in two's,** de dos en dos. **one or two,** uno o dos; algunos, *m pl*; algunas, *f pl*. **two against two,** dos a dos. **two by two,** de dos en dos, a pares. **Two can live as cheaply as two,** Donde come uno comen dos. **to put two and two together,** atar cabos. **two-edged,** de dos filos. **two-faced,** de dos caras; *fig* de dos haces. **to be two-faced,** hacer a dos caras. **two-headed,** de dos cabezas; bicéfalo. **two hundred,** a and *n* doscientos, *m*. **two hundredth,** a ducentésimo. *n* ducentésima parte, *f*; doscientos, *m*. **two-legged,** bípedo. **two-ply,** de dos hilos. **two-seater,** de dos asientos. **two-speed gear box,** cambio de marcha de dos velocidades, *m*. **two-step,** paso doble, *m*. **two of a kind,** (well-matched) tal para cual. **two-way switch,** *elec* interruptor de dos direcciones, *m*

twofold a doble. *adv* doblemente, dos veces

twosome *n* partido de dos, *m*

type *n* tipo, *m*; *print* carácter, *m*, letra de imprenta, *f*, tipo, *m*. *vt* and *vi* escribir a máquina. **t. case,** caja de imprenta, *f*. **t. founder,** fundidor de letras de imprenta,

m. **t. foundry,** fundición de tipos, *f.*
t.-setter, cajista, *mf* **t.-setting,** composición tipográfica, *f*

typewrite *vt* and *vi* escribir a máquina

typewriter *n* máquina de escribir, *f*

typhoid *n* tifoidea, fiebre tifoidea, *f*

typhoon *n* tifón, *m*

typhus *n* tifus, tabardillo pintado, *m*

typical *a* típico, característico; simbólico.
t. Mexican dish (of food) antojito, *m*

typify *vt* simbolizar, representar; ser ejemplo de

typist *n* mecanografista, *mf*; mecanógrafo (-fa)

tyrannical *a* tiránico, despótico

tyrannize *vi* tiranizar

tyranny *n* tiranía, *f*, despotismo, *m*

tyrant *n* déspota, *m*, tirano (-na)

tyro *n* novicio (-cia), tirón (-ona), advenedizo (-za), *mf*

U *n* (letter) u, *f.* **U-boat,** submarino, *m.*
u-shaped, en forma de U

ubiquitous *a* ubicuo, omnipresente

udder *n* ubre, teta, mama, *f*

ugh *interj* iuf!

ugliness *n* fealdad, *f*; (moral) perversidad, *f*; (of a situation) peligro, *m*, lo difícil

ugly *a* feo, *Lat. Am. also* feroz; (morally) repugnante, asqueroso, perverso; (of a situation) peligroso, difícil; (of a wound) grave, profundo; (of a look) amenazador; *inf* desagradable; (of weather) borrascoso. **to make u.,** afear, hacer feo

Ukraine Ucrania, *f*

Ukrainian *a* and *n* ucranio (-ia)

ulcer *n* úlcera, *f, Lat. Am. also* lacra

ulcerate *vt* ulcerar. *vi* ulcerarse

ulterior *a* (of place) ulterior; (of time) posterior, ulterior; (of motives) interesado, oculto; **ulterior motive,** segunda intención, *f*

ultimate *a* último; fundamental, esencial

ultimately *adv* por fin, al final; esencialmente

ultimatum *n* ultimátum, *m*

ultra *a* exagerado, extremo. *prefix* ultra-.
u-red, ultrarrojo. **u.-violet,** ultravioleta

ultramarine *a* ultramarino. *n* azul de ultramar, *m*

umbilicus *n* ombligo, *m*

umbrage *n* *poet* sombra, *f*; resentimiento, enfado, *m*. **to take u.,** ofenderse, resentirse

umbrella *n* paraguas, *m.* **u. maker,** paragüero (-ra). **u. shop,** paragüería, *f.* **u. stand,** paragüero, *m*

umpire *n* *sport* árbitro, *m*; *law* juez arbitrador, tercero en discordia, *m. vt* arbitrar

un- *prefix* Used before adjectives, adverbs, abstract nouns, verbs and translated in Spanish by **in-, des-, nada, no, poco, sin,** as well as in other ways

unabashed *a* desvergonzado, descarado, insolente; (calm) sereno, sosegado

unabashedly *adv* sin rubor

unabated *a* no disminuido; cabal, entero

unabbreviated *a* íntegro, sin abreviar

unable *a* incapaz, impotente; (physical defect) imposibilitado. **to be u. to,** no poder, serle a uno imposible. **to be u. to control,** no poder controlar

unabridged *a.* See **unabbreviated**

unaccented *a* sin acento

unacceptable *a* inaceptable

unaccepted *a* rechazado, no aceptado

unaccommodating *a* poco complaciente, nada servicial

unaccompanied *a* solo, sin compañía; *mus* sin acompañamiento

unaccomplished *a* incompleto, sin terminar, inacabado; (not clever) sin talento

unaccountable *a* inexplicable; irresponsable

unaccountably *adv* inexplicablemente, extrañamente

unaccredited *a* no acreditado, extraoficial

unaccustomed *a* no habituado; (unusual) desacostumbrado, insólito, inusitado

unacknowledged *a* no reconocido; (of letter) sin contestación, por contestar; no correspondido, sin devolver; (of crimes, etc.) inconfeso, no declarado

unacquainted *a* que no conoce; que desconoce, que ignora; no habituado. **to be u. with,** no conocer; ignorar; no estar acostumbrado a

unadaptable *a* inadaptable (also of persons)

unadorned *a* sin adorno sencillo, que no tiene adornos

unadulterated *a* sin mezcla, no adulterado, natural; genuino, verdadero; puro

unadventurous *a* nada aventurero, que no busca aventuras, tímido; tranquilo, sin incidente

unadvisability *n* imprudencia, *f*; inoportunidad, *f*

unadvisable *a* imprudente; inoportuno, no conveniente

unadvisedly *adv* imprudentemente

unesthetic *a* antiestético

unaffected *a* natural, llano, sin melindres; impasible; genuino, sincero. **u. by,** no afectado por

unaffectedly *adv* sin afectación

unaffectedness *n* naturalidad, sencillez, *f*; sinceridad, franqueza, *f*

unaffiliated *a* no afiliado

unafraid *a* sin temor

unaided *a* sin ayuda, solo a solas

unaired *a* sin ventilar, no ventilado; húmedo, sin airear

unalloyed *a* sin mezcla, puro

unalterability *n* lo inalterable; constancia, *f*

unalterable *a* inalterable; invariable, constante

unambiguous *a* no ambiguo, nada dudoso, claro

unambitious *a* sin ambición; modesto

unamusing *a* nada divertido

unanimity *n* unanimidad, *f*

unanimous *a* unánime

unanimously *adv* unánimemente, por unanimidad. **carried u.,** adoptado por unanimidad

unanswerable *a* incontestable, incontrovertible, incontrastable, irrefutable

unanswered a no contestado, sin contestar; (unrequited) no correspondido

unapparent a no aparente

unappealable a inapelable

unappeasable a implacable

unappeased a no satisfecho; implacable

unappetizing a no apetitoso; (unattractive) repugnante, feo

unappreciated a desestimado, no apreciado, tenido en poco; (misunderstood) mal comprendido

unapproachable a inaccesible

unapproved a sin aprobar, no aprobado

unarm vt desarmar. vi desarmarse, quitarse las armas

unarmed a desarmado; indefenso; (zool, bot) inerme

unartistic a no artístico

unashamed a sin vergüenza; tranquilo, sereno; insolente, descarado

unasked a sin pedir; no solicitado; espontáneo; (uninvited) no convidado

unassailable a inexpugnable; irrefutable; incontestable

unassisted a. See **unaided**

unassuming a modesto, sin pretensiones

unattached a suelto; law no embargado; mil de reemplazo; independiente

unattainable a inasequible, irrealizable

unattended a solo, sin acompañamiento; (of ill person) sin tratamiento; (of entertainment, etc.) no concurrido

unattested a sin atestación

unattractive a poco atrayente, desagradable, antipático, feo

unauthentic a no auténtico, sin autenticidad; apócrifo

unauthorized a no autorizado

unavailable a inaprovechable

unavailing a inútil, vano

unavenged a no vengado, sin castigo

unavoidable a inevitable, preciso, necesario. **to be u.,** no poder evitarse, no tener remedio

unavoidably adv irremediablemente

unaware a ignorante; inconsciente. **to be u. of,** ignorar, desconocer; no darse cuenta de

unawareness n ignorancia, f, desconocimiento, m; inconsciencia, f

unawares adv (by mistake) sin querer, inadvertidamente; (unprepared) de sobresalto, de improviso, inopinadamente. **He caught me u.,** Me cogió desprevenido

unbalance vt desequilibrar, hacer perder el equilibrio; fig trastornar

unbalanced a desequilibrado; fig trastornado; com no balanceado

unbar vt desatrancar; fig abrir

unbearable a intolerable, insufrible, inaguantable, inllevable, insoportable

unbeatable a inmejorable

unbeaten a (of paths) no frecuentado, no pisado; (of armies) no derrotado, no batido; invicto

unbecoming a impropio, inapropiado, inconveniente; indecoroso, indigno; indecente; (of clothes) que no va bien, que sienta mal

unbelievable a increíble

unbeloved a no amado

unbend vt desencorvar, enderezar; entretenerse, descansar; (naut of sails) desenvergar; (naut of cables) desamarrar. vi enderezarse; mostrarse afable

unbending a inflexible, rígido, tieso; fig inexorable, inflexible, duro, terco; (amiable) afable, jovial

unbiased a imparcial, ecuánime

unbidden a espontáneo; (uninvited) no convidado, no invitado

unbind vt desligar, desatar; (bandages) desvendar; (books) desencuadernar

unbleached a crudo, sin blanquear

unblemished a no manchado; (pure) sin mancha, inmaculado, puro

unblessed a no bendecido, no consagrado; (accursed) maldito; (unhappy) desdichado

unblushing a desvergonzado, insolente

unbolt vt descerrojar, desempernar

unborn a sin nacer, no nacido todavía; venidero

unbosom vt confesar, declarar. **to u. oneself,** abrir su pecho (a) or (con)

unbought a no comprado; gratuito, libre; (not bribed) no sobornado

unbound a suelto, libre; (of books) en rama, no encuadernado

unbounded a ilimitado, infinito; inmenso

unbowed a erguido; no encorvado; (undefeated) invicto

unbreakable a irrompible, inquebrantable

unbridled a desenfrenado, violento; licencioso

unbroken a no quebrantado, intacto, entero; continuo, incesante; no interrumpido; (of soil) virgen; (of a horse) indomado; inviolado; (of the spirit) indómito; (of a record) no batido

unbuckle vt deshebillar

unburden vt descargar; aliviar. **to u. oneself,** (express one's feelings) desahogarse

unburnt a no quemado; incombusto

unbusinesslike a informal; poco comercial, descuidado

unbutton vt desabrochar, desabotonar

uncalled a no llamado, no invitado. **u.-for,** impertinente; innecesario

uncanny a misterioso, horroroso, pavoroso

uncared-for a abandonado, desatendido, desamparado

unceasing a continuo, incesante, sin cesar, constante

unceasingly adv incesantemente, sin cesar

uncensored a no censurado

unceremonious a sin ceremonia, familiar; descortés, brusco

uncertain a incierto, dudoso; inseguro; precario; (hesitant) indeciso, vacilante, irresoluto

uncertainty n incertidumbre, duda, f; inseguridad, f; irresolución, f

uncertificated a sin certificado (of teachers, etc.) sin título

uncertified a sin garantía; no garantizado; (of lunatics) sin certificar

unchain vt desencadenar

unchallenged a incontestable

unchangeable a invariable, inalterable, inmutable

unchanging a inmutable, invariable

uncharitable a nada caritativo, duro; intolerante, intransigente

uncharitableness n falta de caridad, f; intolerancia, intransigencia

uncharitably adv sin caridad; con intolerancia

unchaste a incasto, incontinente; deshonesto, impuro, lascivo

unchecked a desenfrenado; (unproved) no comprobado; com no confrontado

unchivalrous a nada galante, nada caballeroso

uncircumcised a incircunciso

uncivil a descortés, incivil

uncivilized a no civilizado, bárbaro, salvaje, inculto

unclad a sin vestir; desnudo

unclasp vt (jewelery) desengarzar; desabrochar; (of hands) soltar, separar

unclassifiable a inclasificable

unclassified a sin clasificar

uncle n tío, m; (pawnbroker) prestamista, m

unclean a sucio, puerco, inmundo; desaseado; impuro, obsceno; (ritually) poluto

uncleanliness n suciedad, porquería, f; desaseo, m; falta de limpieza, f

uncleanly a sucio, puerco; desaseado

unclench vt (of hands) abrir

Uncle Tom's Cabin La Cabaña del Tío Tom

uncoil vt desarrollar. vi desovillarse; (of snakes) desanillarse

uncollected a disperso; no cobrado; (in confusion) cônfuso, desordenado

uncolored a incoloro; fig imparcial, objetivo, sencillo

uncombed a despeinado, sin peinar

uncomfortable a incómodo; (anxious) intranquilo, inquieto, desasosegado, preocupado; (awkward) molesto, difícil, desagradable. **to be u.,** (people) estar incómodo; (anxious) estar preocupado; (of things) ser incómodo

uncomfortably adv incómodamente; intranquilamente; desagradablemente

uncomforted a desconsolado, sin consuelo

uncommon a poco común, extraordinario, singular, raro, extraño; infrecuente; insólito

uncommonly adv extraordinariamente, muy; infrecuentemente, raramente

uncommunicative a reservado, poco expresivo

uncommunicativeness n reserva, f

uncomplaining a resignado, que no se queja

uncomplainingly adv con resignación

uncompliant a sordo, inflexible

uncomplicated a sencillo, sin complicaciones

uncomplimentary a descortés, poco halagüeño, ofensivo

uncompromising a inflexible, estricto, intolerante; irreconciliable

unconcealed a no oculto; abierto

unconcern n indiferencia, frialdad, f, desapego, m; (lack of interest) apatía, despreocupación, f; (nonchalance) desenfado, m, frescura, f

unconcerned a indiferente, frío, despegado; apático, despreocupado; desenfadado, fresco

unconcernedly adv con indiferencia; sin preocuparse; con desenfado

unconditional a incondicional, absoluto. **u. surrender,** rendición incondicional, f

unconfined a suelto, libre; ilimitado; sin estorbo

unconfirmed a no confirmado; (report) sin confirmar

uncongenial a incompatible, antipático; desagradable, repugnante

uncongeniality n incompatibilidad, antipatía, f; repugnancia, f; lo desagradable

unconnected a inconexo; mech desconectado; (relationship) sin parentesco; (confused) incoherente

unconquerable a invencible, indomable, inconquistable

unconquered a no vencido

unconscientious a poco concienzudo

unconscionable a excesivo, desmedido; sin conciencia

unconscious a inconsciente; (senseless) insensible, sin sentido; espontáneo; (unaware) ignorante. **to be u. of,** ignorar; perder la consciencia de. **to become u.,** perder el sentido

unconsciously *adv* inconscientemente, involuntariamente

unconsciousness *n* inconsciencia, *f*; (hypnosis, swoon) insensibilidad, *f*; (unawareness) ignorancia, falta de conocimiento, *f*

unconsecrated *a* no consagrado

unconsidered *a* indeliberado; sin importancia, trivial

unconstitutional *a* anticonstitucional, inconstitucional

unconstrained *a* libre; voluntario; sin freno

uncontaminated *a* incontaminado; puro, sin mancha, impoluto

uncontested *a* sin oposición

uncontradicted *a* sin contradicción; incontestable

uncontrollable *a* irrefrenable, incontrolable, inmanejable; (temper) ingobernable; indomable

uncontrolled *a* libre, no controlado; desenfrenado, desgobernado

unconventional *n* poco convencional; bohemio, excéntrico, extravagante; original

unconventionality *a* excentricidad, extravagancia, independencia de ideas, *f*; (of a design) originalidad, *f*

unconversant *a* poco familiar, poco versado (en)

unconverted *a* no convertido; sin transformar

unconvinced *a* no convencido

unconvincing *a* no convincente, poco convincente, que no me (nos, etc.) convence; frívolo

uncooked *a* crudo, no cocido, sin cocer

uncork *vt* destapar, descorchar, quitar el corcho

uncorrected *a* sin corregir, no corregido

uncorroborated *a* no confirmado, sin confirmar

uncorrupted *a* incorrupto; puro, no pervertido; (unbribed) no sobornado, honrado

uncorruptible *a* incorruptible

uncounted *a* no contado, sin cuenta

uncouple *vt* soltar; desenganchar, desconectar

uncouth *a* grosero, chabacano, tosco, patán

uncouthness *n* grosería, tosquedad, patanería, *f*

uncover *vt* descubrir; (remove lid of) destapar; (remove coverings of) desabrigar, desarropar; (leave unprotected) desamparar; (disclose) revelar, dejar al descubierto. *vi* descubrirse, quitar el sombrero

uncovered *a* descubierto; desnudo; sin cubierta

uncreated *a* increado

uncritical *a* sin sentido crítico, poco juicioso

uncross *vt* (of legs) descruzar

uncrossed *a* (of check) sin cruzar

uncrowned *a* antes de ser coronado; sin corona

unction *n* unción, *f*; untadura, *f*, untamiento, *m*; (unguent) ungüento, *m*; (zeal) fervor, *m*; (flattery) insinceridad, hipocresía, *f*; (relish) gusto, entusiasmo, *m*. **extreme u.,** extremaunción, *f*

unctuous *a* untuoso, craso; insincero, zalamero

uncultivable *a* incultivable

uncultivated *a* inculto, yermo; (barbarous) salvaje, bárbaro; (uncultured) inculto, tosco; no cultivado

uncultured *a* inculto, iletrado

uncurbed *a* sin freno; *fig* desenfrenado

uncurl *vt* desrizar *vi* desrizarse; desovillarse

uncut *a* sin cortar, no cortado; (of gems) sin labrar

undamaged *a* indemne, sin daño

undated *a* sin fecha

undaunted *a* intrépido, atrevido

undeceive *vt* desengañar, desilusionar

undecided *a* (of question) pendiente, indeciso; dudoso; vacilante, irresoluto

undefended *a* indefenso

undeferable *a* inaplazable

undefiled *a* impoluto, incontaminado; puro

undefinable *a* indefinible; inefable, vago

undefined *a* indefinido; indeterminado

undelivered *a* no recibido; (speech) no pronunciado; (not sent) no enviado

undemonstrative *a* poco expresivo, reservado

undeniable *a* incontestable, innegable, indudable; excelente; inequívoco, evidente

undeniably *adv* indudablemente

undependable *a* indigno de confianza

under *prep* debajo de; bajo; (in) en; (less than) menos de, menos que; (at the orders of) a las órdenes de, al mando de; (in less time than) en menos de; (under the weight of) bajo el peso de; (at the foot of) al abrigo de; (for less than) por menos de; (at the time of) en la época de, en tiempos de; (according to) según, conforme a, en virtud de (e.g. **under the law,** en virtud de la ley); (of monarchs) bajo (or durante) el reinado de; (of rank) inferior a; (in virtue of) en virtud de; (of age) menor de; (with penalty, pretext, etc.) so; en; a (see below for examples); (agr of fields) plantado de, sembrado de. **u. arms,** bajo las armas. **u. contract,** bajo contrato. **u. cover,** al abrigo, bajo cubierto. **u. cover of,** bajo pretexto de, so color de. **u. fire,** bajo fuego. **u. oath,** bajo juramento. **u. pain of,** so pena de. **u. sail,** a la vela. **u.**

separate cover, bajo cubierta separada, en sobre apartado, por separado. **u. steam,** al vapor. **u. way,** en camino; en marcha; en preparación. **to be u. an obligation,** deber favores; (to) tener obligacion de; estar obligado a

under a inferior; (of rank) subalterno, subordinado; bajo, bajero. *adv* debajo; abajo; más abajo; menos; (for less) para menos; (ill) mal; (insufficient) insuficiente. **to bring u.,** someter. **to keep u.,** dominar, subyugar

underact *vt* hacer un papel sin fogosidad

underarm *n* sobaco, *m.* a sobacal; (of bowling) de debajo del brazo. **to serve u.,** sacar por debajo

underbid *vt* ofrecer menos que

undercharge *vt* cobrar menos de lo debido

underclothes *n* ropa interior, *f,* paños menores, *m pl*

undercurrent *n* corriente submarina, *f; fig* tendencia oculta, *f*

underdeveloped a de desarrollo atrasado; *phot* no revelado lo suficiente

underdog *n* víctima, *f;* débil, paciente, *m.* **underdogs,** los de abajo, *m pl*

underdone a (of meat) crudo, medio asado

underestimate *vt* tasar en menos; desestimar, menospreciar

underfeed *vt* alimentar insuficientemente

underfoot *adv* debajo de los pies, en el suelo

undergo *vt* sufrir, padecer, pasar por. **undergo surgery,** someterse a la cirugía

undergraduate *n* estudiante no graduado, *m*

underground a subterráneo; *fig* oculto, secreto. *adv* bajo tierra, debajo de la tierra; *fig* en secreto, ocultamente. *n* sótano, *m;* metro, ferrocarril subterráneo, *m*

undergrowth *n* maleza, *f*

underhand *adv fig* bajo mano, ocultamente, a escondidas. a *fig* secreto, oculto

underlie *vt* estar debajo de; servir de base a, caracterizar

underline *vt* subrayar

underling *n* subordinado (-da)

underlying a fundamental, básico, esencial

undermine *vt* socavar, excavar, minar, destruir poco a poco

undermining *n* socava, excavación, *f;* destrucción, *f,* a minador

underneath *adv* debajo. *prep* bajo, debajo de

undernourished a mal alimentado

undernourishment *n* desnutrición, *f*

underpaid a insuficientemente retribuido, mal pagado

underpass *n* pasaje por debajo, *m*

underpay *vt* pagar mal, remunerar (or retribuir) deficientemente

underpayment *n* retribución mezquina, *f,* pago insuficiente, *m*

underpin *vt* apuntalar, socalzar

underpopulated a con baja densidad de población

underprivileged a menesteroso, pobre, necesitado

underrate *vt* tasar en menos; tener en poco, desestimar, menospreciar

undersecretary *n* subsecretario (-ia)

undersell *vt* vender a un precio más bajo que

undershirt *n Spain* camiseta, *Lat. Am.* franela, *f*

underside *n* revés, envés, *m*

undersigned a infrascrito, suscrito. **the u.,** el abajo firmado, el infrascrito

undersized a muy pequeño, enclenque, enano

understand *vt* comprender, entender; (know) saber; (be acquainted with) conocer; (hear) oír, tener entendido; (mean) sobrentender. *vi* comprender, entender; oír, tener entendido. **to u. each other,** comprenderse. **It being understood that . . .,** Bien entendido que . . .

understandable a comprensible; inteligible. **It is very u. why he does not wish to come,** Se comprende muy bien por qué no quiere venir

understanding *n* (intelligence) entendimiento, *m,* inteligencia, *f;* (agreement) acuerdo, *m;* (knowledge) conocimiento, *m;* (wisdom) comprensión, sabiduría, *f.* a inteligente; sabio; (sympathetic) comprensivo, simpático. **to come to an u.,** ponerse de acuerdo

understate *vt* decir menos que, rebajar, describir sin énfasis

understudy *n* sobresaliente, *mf. vt* sustituir

undertake *vt* comprometerse a, encargarse de; emprender, abarcar, acometer

undertaker *n* empresario, director de pompas fúnebres, *m*

undertaking *n* empresa, tarea, *f;* garantía, promesa, *f;* (funerals) funeraria, *f*

undertone *n* voz baja, *f; art* color tenue (or apagado), *m.* **in an u.,** en voz baja

undervalue *vt* tasar en menos; tener en poco, despreciar

underwater a subacuático, submarino. **underwater flipper,** aleta de buceo

underweight a de bajo peso, que pesa menos de lo debido, flaco

underworld *n* (hell) infierno, averno, *m;* (slums) hampa, *f,* fondos bajos de la sociedad, *m pl;* heces de la sociedad, *f pl.* **u. slang** *Peru* cantuja *f*

underwrite *vt com* asegurar contra riesgos; reasegurar; obligarse a comprar todas las acciones de una compañía no subscritas por el público, mediante un pago convenido

underwriter n asegurador, m; reasegurador, m

undeserved a inmerecido, no merecido

undeserving a indigno, desmerecedor; que no merece

undesirable a no deseable; nocivo, pernicioso; (unsuitable) inconveniente

undesirous a no deseoso

undestroyed a sin destruir, no destruido, intacto

undetected a no descubierto

undeveloped a no desarrollado; rudimentario; inmaturo; (of a country) no explotado, virgen; phot no revelado; (of land) sin cultivar

undigested a no digerido, indigesto

undignified a sin dignidad; poco serio; indecoroso

undiluted a sin diluir, puro

undiminished a no disminuido, sin disminuir, cabal, íntegro

undiplomatic a impolítico, indiscreto

undirected a sin dirección; (of letters) sin señas

undiscernible a imperceptible, invisible

undiscerning a sin percepción, obtuso, sin discernimiento

undisciplined a indisciplinado

undisclosed a no revelado, secreto

undiscovered a no descubierto, ignoto

undiscriminating a sin distinción; sin sentido crítico

undisguised a sin disfraz; abierto, claro

undismayed a intrépido, impávido; sin desaliento

undisposed a desinclinado; (of property) no enajenado, no invertido

undisputed a incontestable, indisputable

undistinguished a (of writers) poco conocido; indistinto; sin distinción

undisturbed a sin tocar; tranquilo, sereno, impasible

undivided a indiviso, íntegro; junto; completo, entero

undo vt anular; reparar; desatar, deshacer; desasir; abrir

undoing n anulación, f; (reparation) reparación, f; (opening) abrir, m; ruina, f

undomesticated a salvaje, no domesticado; poco casero

undone a and part sin hacer; deshecho; arruinado, perdido. **I am undone!** ¡Estoy perdido! **to come u.,** desatarse. **to leave u.,** dejar sin hacer

undoubted a indudable, evidente, incontestable

undoubtedly adv sin duda

undreamed a no soñado. **u. of,** inopinado, no imaginado

undress vt desnudar, desvestir, Peru

calatear, vi desnudarse. n traje de casa, m; paños menores, m pl; mil traje de cuartel, m

undressed a desnudo; en paños menores; (of wounds) sin curar; com en rama, en bruto

undrinkable a impotable

undue a excesivo, indebido; injusto; impropio; (of a bill of exchange) por vencer

undulant a ondulante. **u. fever,** fiebre mediterránea, fiebre de Malta, f

undulate vi ondular, ondear

undulating a ondulante

undulatory a ondulatorio, undoso

unduly adv excesivamente, demasiado, indebidamente; injustamente

undutiful a desobediente, irrespetuoso

undying a inmortal, imperecedero; eterno

unearned a no ganado; inmerecido

unearth vt desenterrar; fig descubrir, sacar a luz

unearthly a sobrenatural; misterioso, aterrador, espantoso, Lat. Am. also extraterrenal

uneasily adv con dificultad; incómodamente; inquietamente

uneasiness n malestar, m; (discomfort) incomodidad, f_i (anxiety) inquietud, intranquilidad, f, desasosiego, m

uneasy a incómodo; inseguro; inquieto, intranquilo, desasosegado; aturdido, turbado. **to become u.,** inquietarse

uneatable a incomible

uneconomical a poco económico, costoso, caro

unedifying a poco edificante

uneducated a ignorante; ineducado, inculto, indocto

unembarrassed a sereno, tranquilo, imperturbable; (financially) sin deudas, acomodado

unemotional a frío, impasible

unemployable a sin uso, inservible; (of persons) inútil para el trabajo

unemployed a sin empleo; (out of work) sin trabajo, parado; desocupado, ocioso; inactivo. n paro obrero, m. **the u.,** los sin trabajo, los cesantes, los desocupados

unemployment n paro forzoso, m. **u. benefit,** subvención contra el paro obrero, f. **u. insurance,** seguro contra el paro obrero, m.

unencumbered a libre, independiente; (of estates) libre de gravamen; (untaxable) saneado

unending a perpetuo, eterno, sin fin; inacabable, constante, continuo, incesante

unendurable a insoportable, insufrible, intolerable

unenlightened a ignorante

unenterprising a poco emprendedor, tímido

unenthusiastic a sin entusiasmo, tibio

unequal a desigual; inferior; (out of proportion) desproporcionado; injusto; insuficiente; incapaz; (of ground) escabroso. **to be u. to the task,** ser incapaz de la tarea; no tener fuerzas para la tarea

unequalled a sin igual, incomparable, sin par, único

unequally adv desigualmente

unequivocal a inequívoco; redondo, claro, franco

unerring a infalible; seguro

unerringly adv infaliblemente; sin equivocarse

uneven a desigual; (of roads) escabroso, quebrado; (of numbers) impar; irregular

unevenly adv desigualmente

unevenness n desigualdad, f; desnivel, m, irregularidad, f. **the unevenness of the terrain,** lo desigual del terreno, lo accidentado del terreno, m

uneventful a sin incidentes, sin acontecimientos notables; tranquilo

unexampled a sin igual, sin par

unexceptionable a intachable, irreprensible; correcto; impecable, perfecto

unexpected a inesperado, imprevisto, inopinado, impensado; repentino, súbito

unexpectedly adv inesperadamente; de repente

unexpectedness n lo inesperado

unexpired a (of bill of exchange) no vencido; (of lease) no caducado

unexplored a inexplorado

unexpressed a no expresado; tácito, sobrentendido

unexpurgated a sin expurgar, completo

unfading a inmarcesible, inmarchitable; eterno, inmortal

unfailing a inagotable; inexhausto; seguro; indefectible

unfailingly adv siempre, constantemente; sin faltar

unfair a injusto; vil, bajo, soez; de mala fe, engañoso; (of play) sucio

unfairly adv injustamente; de mala fe

unfairness n injusticia, f; mala fe, f

unfaithful a infiel; desleal; inexacto, incorrecto. **to be u. to,** ser infiel a; faltar a

unfaltering a sin vacilar; resuelto, firme

unfamiliar a poco familiar; desconocido. **to be u. with,** ser ignorante de

unfashionable a pasado de moda, fuera de moda; poco elegante

unfashionably adv contra la tendencia de la moda; sin elegancia

unfasten vt desatar; desabrochar, desenganchar; abrir; aflojar; soltar

unfathomable a insondable; impenetrable, inescrutable

unfavorable a desfavorable, adverso, contrario

unfeeling a insensible, impasible, frío; duro, cruel

unfeigned a sincero, natural, verdadero

unfenced a descercado, sin tapia; abierto

unfetter vt desencadenar, destrabar; poner en libertad, librar

unfinished a incompleto, inacabado; sin acabar; imperfecto

unfit a incapaz; incompetente, inepto; (unsuitable) impropio; (useless) inservible, inadecuado; (unworthy) indigno; (ill) enfermo, malo. vt inhabilitar, incapacitar. **u. for human consumption,** impropio para el consumo humano

unfitness n incapacidad, f; incompetencia, ineptitud, f; impropiedad, f; falta de mérito, f; falta de salud, f

unfix vt desprender, despegar, descomponer; soltar. **to come unfixed,** desprenderse

unflagging a incansable, infatigable; persistente, constante

unflattering a poco halagüeño

unflinching a inconmovible, resuelto, firme

unfold vt desplegar, desdoblar; tender; abrir; (plans) revelar, descubrir; contar, manifestar. vi abrirse

unfolding a que se abre. n despliegue, m; revelación, f; narración, f

unforced a libre; espontáneo; fácil; natural

unforeseen a imprevisto, inesperado

unforgettable a inolvidable

unforgivable a inexcusable, imperdonable

unforgiving a implacable, que no perdona, inexorable

unformed a informe; rudimentario; inmaturo; (inexperienced) inexperto, sin experiencia

unfortunate a desdichado, infortunado, desgraciado, desventurado. n desdichado (-da); pobre, mf; (prostitute) perdida, f

unfortunately adv por desdicha, desgraciadamente

unfounded a infundado, inmotivado, sin fundamento, injustificado

unfrequented a poco frecuentado, solitario, retirado, aislado

unfriendliness n hostilidad, falta de amistad, frialdad, f; huraña, insociabilidad, f

unfriendly a hostil, enemigo; (of things, events) perjudicial; huraño, insociable

unfruitful a estéril, infecundo; infructuoso, improductivo, vano

unfulfilled a incumplido, sin cumplir; malogrado

unfurl vt desplegar; naut izar (las velas)

unfurnished a desamueblado, sin muebles; desprovisto (de), sin

ungainliness n falta de gracia, torpeza, f; desgarbo, m

ungainly a desgarbado

ungenerous a poco generoso; avaro, tacaño, mezquino; injusto

ungentlemanly a poco caballeroso, indigno de un caballero

ungodliness n impiedad, f

ungodly a impío, irreligioso

ungovernable a ingobernable, indomable; irrefrenable

ungraceful a desagraciado, desgarbado, sin gracia

ungracious a desagradable, poco cortés, desdeñoso

ungraciousness n descortesía, aspereza, inurbanidad, f

ungrammatical a antigramatical, incorrecto

ungrateful a ingrato, desagradecido; desagradable, odioso

ungratefulness n ingratitud, f; lo desagradable

ungrounded a infundado; sin motivo

ungrudging a no avaro, liberal; generoso, magnánimo

ungrudgingly adv de buena gana

unguarded a indefenso, sin protección; descuidado; indiscreto, imprudente; sin reflexión

unguided a sin guía

unhallowed a impío, profano

unhampered a desembarazado, libre

unhappily adv desafortunadamente, por desgracia

unhappiness n infelicidad, desgracia, desdicha, tristeza, f

unhappy a infeliz, desgraciado, desdichado, triste; (ill-fated) aciago, funesto, malhadado; (remark) inoportuno, inapropiado

unharmed a ileso, sano y salvo; (of things) indemne, sin daño

unharness vt desaparejar; desenganchar; desarmar

unhealthiness n falta de salud, f; (of place) insalubridad, f

unhealthy a enfermizo; malsano, insalubre

unheard a no oído; sin ser escuchado; desconocido. **u.-of**, inaudito, no imaginado

unheeding a distraído; desatento, sin prestar atención (a); descuidado

unhelpful a poco servicial; inútil

unhesitating a resuelto, decidido; pronto, inmediato

unhesitatingly adv sin vacilar

unhitch vt desenganchar; descolgar

unholy a impío, sacrílego

unhook vt desenganchar; desabrochar; descolgar

unhoped-for a inesperado

unhurt a ileso, incólume, sano y salvo; (of things) sin daño

unicorn n unicornio, m

unidentified a no reconocido, no identificado

unification n unificación, f

uniform a uniforme; igual, constante, invariable; homogéneo. n uniforme, m. **in full u.**, de gran uniforme. **to make u.**, uniformar, igualar, hacer uniforme

uniformity n uniformidad, igualdad, f

uniformly adv uniformemente

unify vt unificar; unir

unilateral a unilateral

unimaginable a inimaginable, no imaginable

unimaginative a sin imaginación

unimpaired a no disminuido; sin alteración; intacto, entero; sin menoscabo

unimpeachable a irreprochable, intachable

unimportance n no importancia, insignificancia, trivialidad, f

unimportant a sin importancia, nada importante, insignificante, trivial, Lat. Am. also intrascendente

unimpressive a poco impresionante; nada conmovedor; (of persons) insignificante

uninflammable a no inflamable, incombustible

uninfluenced a no afectado (por), libre (de)

uninformed a ignorante

uninhabitable a inhabitable

uninhabited a deshabitado, inhabitado, vacío, desierto

uninjured a ileso; sin daño

uninspired a sin inspiración; pedestre, mediocre

uninstructive a nada instructivo

uninsured a no asegurado

unintelligent a nada inteligente, corto de alcances, tonto

unintelligible a ininteligible, incomprensible

unintentional a involuntario, inadvertido

unintentionally adv sin querer, involuntariamente

uninterested a no interesado, despreocupado

uninteresting a sin interés, poco interesante, soso

uninterrupted a ininterrum pido, sin interrupción; continuo, incesante

uninvited a no invitado, no convidado, sin invitación; (unlooked-for) no buscado

uninviting a poco atrayente; inhospitalario

union n unión, f; mech manguito de unión, m; conexión, f; (poverty) asociación, f; (of trade) gremio de oficios, m; sindicato (obrero), m; (workhouse) asilo, *m*; (U.S.A.) Estados Unidos de América, *m pl*

unique *a* único, sin igual, sin par

uniqueness *n* unicidad, *f*; lo singular

unison *n* unisonancia, *f*. **in u.**, al unísono

unit *n* unidad, *f*. **u. bookcase**, librería en secciones, *f*

unite *vt* unir, juntar; combinar, incorporar; (of countries) unificar; (of energies, etc.) reunir. *vi* unirse, juntarse; reunirse, concertarse; convenirse

united *a* unido; junto. **the U. Nations**, las Naciones Unidas, *f pl*

United States of America los Estados Unidos de Norteamérica, *m pl*

unity *n* unidad, *f*; *math* la unidad; unión, *f*; conformidad, armonía, *f*. **the three unities**, las tres unidades

universal *a* universal; general; común. **to make u.**, universalizar, generalizar. **u. joint**, junta universal, *f*; *aut* cardán, *m*

universe *n* universo, *m*; creación, *f*, mundo, *m*

university *n* universidad, *f*. **a** universitario. **u. degree**, grado universitario, *m*

unjust *a* injusto

unjustifiable *a* injustificable, indisculpable, inexcusable

unjustifiably *adv* injustificadamente, inexcusablemente

unjustly *adv* injustamente, sin razón

unkempt *a* despeinado; desaseado, sucio

unkind *a* nada bondadoso, nada amable; poco complaciente; duro, cruel; desfavorable, nada propicio

unkindly *adv* sin bondad; con dureza, cruelmente

unkindness *n* falta de bondad, *f*; severidad, crueldad, dureza, *f*, rigor, *m*; acto de crueldad, *m*

unknowable *a* impenetrable, incomprehensible, insondable

unknowingly *adv* sin querer, involuntariamente; sin saberlo; insensiblemente

unknown *a* ignoto, desconocido; *math* incógnito. *n* lo desconocido, misterio, *m*; *math* incógnita, *f*; (person) desconocido (-da), forastero (-ra). *math* **u. quantity**, incógnita, *f*

unlabeled *a* sin etiqueta

unlace *vt* desenlazar; desatar

unladylike *a* indigno (or impropio) de una dama; vulgar, ordinario, cursi

unlamented *a* no llorado, no lamentado

unlatch *vt* alzar el pestillo de, abrir

unlawful *a* ilegal, ilícito

unlawfulness *n* ilegalidad, *f*

unlearn *vt* olvidar, desaprender

unleash *vt* soltar

unleavened *a* ázimo, sin levadura

unless *conjunc* a no ser que, a menos

que, como no, si no (all followed by subjunc.); salvo, excepto, con excepción de

unlicensed *a* no autorizado, sin licencia

unlike *a* disímil, desemejante; distinto, diferente. *prep* a distinción de, a diferencia de, al contrario de. **They are quite u.**, No se parecen nada

unlikely *a* improbable, inverosímil; arriesgado

unlimited *a* ilimitado, infinito, inmenso; sin restricción; excesivo, exagerado. **unlimited telephone**, teléfono no medido (Argentina)

unlined *a* no forrado, sin forro; sin rayas; (of face) sin arrugas

unlit *a* no iluminado, oscuro, sin luz

unload *vt* descargar; aligerar; *naut* hondear; (of shares) deshacerse de. *vi* descargar

unloading *n* descarga, *f*, descargue, *m*

unlock *vt* desencerrar, abrir; *fig* revelar, descubrir

unloose *vt* desatar; soltar; poner en libertad

unlovable *a* indigno del querer; antipático, poco amable; repugnante

unluckily *adv* desafortunadamente, por desgracia

unluckiness *n* mala suerte, *f*; (unsuitability) inoportunidad, *f*; lo nefasto, lo malo

unlucky *a* de mala suerte; desdichado, desgraciado, infeliz; (ill-omened) funesto, nefasto, fatal; inoportuno, inconveniente

unmanageable *a* indomable, indócil; ingobernable, inmanejable; (unwieldy) difícil de manejar, pesado

unmannerly *a* mal educado, descortés

unmarketable *a* invendible

unmarriageable *a* incasable

unmarried *a* soltero, célibe

unmask *vt* desenmascarar; *fig* quitar la careta (a). *vi* quitarse la máscara; *fig* quitarse la careta, descubrirse

unmeaning *a* sin sentido, vacío, sin significación

unmentionable *a* que no se puede mencionar; indigno de mencionarse

unmerciful *a* sin piedad, sin compasión; cruel, despiadado, duro

unmerited *a* inmerecido, desmerecido

unmindful *a* olvidadizo; desatento; negligente. **u. of**, sin pensar en, olvidando

unmistakable *a* inequívoco; manifiesto, evidente, indudable

unmistakably *adv* indudablemente

unmitigated *a* no mitigado; completo, absoluto; (of rogue) redomado

unmixed *a* sin mezcla; puro, sencillo; (free) limpio

unmoor *vt* desamarrar

unmoral *a* amoral, no moral; sin fin didáctico

unmounted *a* desmontado

unmoved a fijo; (unemotional) impasible, frío; (determined) firme, inflexible, inexorable

unmusical a sin afición a la música; sin oído (para la música); inarmónico

unnatural a desnaturalizado; (of vices, etc.) contra natural; innatural; (of style) rebuscado; artificial; inhumano, cruel

unnavigable a innavegable, no navegable

unnecessarily adv inútilmente, innecesariamente, sin necesidad

unnecessary a innecesario, superfluo, inútil

unneighborly a de mala vecindad, impropio de vecinos, poco servicial

unnerve vt acobardar quitar el valor, desanimar

unnoticed a inadvertido, no observado

unobjectionable a Lat. Am. inobjetable

unobliging a nada servicial

unobservable a inobservable

unobservant a inobservante

unobserved a sin ser notado, desapercibido

unobtainable a inalcanzable, inasequible

unobstructed a no obstruido; sin obstáculos; libre

unobtrusive a discreto, modesto

unoccupied a (at leisure) desocupado, ocioso, sin ocupación; vacío, vacante, libre; (untenanted) deshabitado

unofficial a no oficial

unopened a sin abrir, cerrado; (of exhibitions, etc.) no inaugurado

unopposed a sin oposición

unoriginal a poco original

unostentatious a sencillo, modesto, sin ostentación

unostentatiousness n sencillez, modestia, falta de ostentación, f

unpack vt desempaquetar; (trunks) vaciar; (bales) desembalar. vi desempaquetar; deshacer las maletas

unpacking n desembalaje, m

unpaid a sin pagar, no pagado, Lat. Am. also impago

unpalatable a de mal sabor; desagradable

unparalleled a sin paralelo, sin par, sin igual

unpardonable a imperdonable, inexcusable, irremisible

unpatriotic a antipatriótico

unpaved a sin empedrar

unperceived a inadvertido, sin ser notado

unperturbed a impasible, sin alterarse, sereno

unpleasant a desagradable, desapacible; ofensivo; (troublesome) enfadoso, molesto

unpleasantly adv desagradablemente

unpleasantness n lo desagradable; disgusto, sinsabor, m; (disagreement) disputa, riña, f

unpleasing a nada placentero; desagradable, sin atractivos

unplug vt desenchufar

unpolished a sin pulir, tosco, mate; fig inculto, cerril. **u. diamond**, diamante en bruto, m

unpolluted a impoluto, incontaminado; puro, sin pervertir

unpopular a impopular

unpopularity n impopularidad, f

unpractical a impracticable, imposible; (of persons) sin sentido práctico

unpracticed a no practicado; inexperto, inhábil

unpraiseworthy a inmeritorio

unprecedented a sin precedente, inaudito

unprejudiced a sin prejuicios, imparcial

unpremeditated a sin premeditación, indeliberado, impremeditado

unprepared a sin preparación, no preparado; desprevenido; desapercibido (unready)

unpreparedness n falta de preparación, imprevisión, f, desapercibimiento, m

unprepossessing a poco atrayente, antipático

unpresentable a impresentable

unpretentious a sin pretensiones, modesto

unprincipled a sin conciencia, sin escrúpulos

unprocurable a inalcanzable, inasequible

unproductive a improductivo; infructuoso, estéril

unproductiveness n infructuosidad, f; esterilidad, f

unprofessional a sin profesión; contrario a la ética profesional

unprofitable a improductivo, infructuoso; sin provecho; inútil; nada lucrativo

unpromising a poco halagüeño

unpronounceable a impronunciable

unpropitious a desfavorable, nada propicio, nada halagüeño

unprotected a sin protección; (of persons) indefenso, desválido

unproved a no probado, sin demostrar

unprovided a desapercibido, desprovisto. **u. for**, sin provisión (para); sin medios de vida, desamparado

unprovoked a no provocado, sin provocación; sin motivo

unpublished a inédito, no publicado, sin publicar

unpunctual a no puntual, retrasado

unpunished a impune, sin castigo

unqualified a incapaz, incompetente;

(with professions) sin título; (downright) incondicional, absoluto

unquenchable a inextinguible, inapagable; insaciable

unquestionable a indiscutible, indudable, indubitable

unquestionably adv indudablemente

unquiet a inquieto, intranquilo; agitado

unravel vt deshilar; destejer; (a mystery, etc.) desentrañar, desembrollar, descifrar

unraveling n deshiladura, f; aclaración, f

unreadable a ilegible

unreadiness n falta de preparación, f, desapercibimiento, m; lentitud, f

unready a desapercibido, desprevenido; lento

unreal a irreal; falso, imaginario, ilusorio; ficticio; artificial; insincero, hipócrita; ideal; incorpóreo

unreality n irrealidad, f; falsedad, f; artificialidad, f; lo quimérico

unreasonable a irrazonable, irracional; disparatado, extravagante; (with price, etc.) exorbitante, excesivo

unreasonableness n irracionalidad, f; exorbitancia, f

unreasonably adv irracionalmente

unreasoning a irracional; sin motivo, sin causa

unrecognizable a que no puede reconocerse; imposible de reconocer

unrecognized a no reconocido

unreconciled a no resignado, no reconciliado

unrectified a no corregido, sin rectificar

unredeemed a no redimido; no mitigado; (of pledges) sin desempeñar

unrefined a no refinado, impuro; inculto, grosero

unreformed a no reformado

unrefuted a no refutado

unregenerate a no regenerado

unregretted a no llorado, sin lamentar

unrehearsed a sin preparación; theat sin ensayar; (extempore) improvisado

unrelated a inconexo; (of persons) sin parentesco

unrelenting a implacable, inflexible, inexorable

unreliability n incertidumbre, f; el no poder confiar en, informalidad, inestabilidad, f

unreliable a incierto, dudoso, indigno de confianza; (of persons) informal

unrelieved a no aliviado; absoluto, completo, total

unremitting a incansable

unrepealed a vigente

unrepentant a impenitente

unrepresentative a poco representativo

unrepresented a sin representación

unrequited a no correspondido

unreserved a no reservado; expresivo, comunicativo, expansivo, franco

unreservedly adv sin reserva; con toda franqueza

unresisting a sin oponer resistencia

unresolved a sin resolverse, vacilante; incierto, dudoso, inseguro; sin solución

unresponsive a flemático; insensible, sordo

unresponsiveness n flema, f; insensibilidad, f

unrest n desasosiego, m, agitación, inquietud, f

unrestful a agitado, inquieto, intranquilo

unrestrained a desenfrenado; ilimitado, sin límites; sin reserva

unrestricted a sin restricción; ilimitado

unrewarded a sin premio, no recompensado

unrighteous a injusto, malo, perverso

unripe a verde, inmaturo

unrivaled a sin igual, sin par

unroll vt desarrollar. vi desarrollarse; (unfold) desplegarse (a la vista)

unromantic a poco (or nada) romántico

unruffled a sereno, plácido, ecuánime; no arrugado; (of hair) liso

unruliness n turbulencia, indisciplina, f; insubordinación, rebeldía, f

unruly a ingobernable, revoltoso; refractario, rebelde; (of hair) indomable

unsaddle vt desensillar; derribar (del caballo, etc.)

unsafe a inseguro; peligroso; arriesgado; (to eat) nocivo

unsaid a sin decir, no dicho

unsalable a invendible

unsalaried a no asalariado

unsalted a soso, sin sal

unsanitary a antihigiénico

unsatisfactory a poco (or nada) satisfactorio; no aceptable

unsatisfied a no satisfecho; descontento; no convencido; (hungry) no harto; com no saldado

unsatisfying a que no satisface

unsavoriness n insipidez, f, mal sabor, m; lo desagradable; sordidez, suciedad, f

unsavory a insípido, de mal sabor; desagradable; sórdido, sucio

unscathed a sin daño, ileso

unscented a sin perfume, sin olor, no fragante

unscholarly a nada erudito; indigno de un erudito

unscientific a no científico

unscrew vt destornillar, Lat. Am. desenroscar. vi destornillarse

unscrupulous a sin escrúpulos, poco escrupuloso, desaprensivo

unseal vt desellar, romper (or quitar) el sello (de)

unseasonable a intempestivo, fuera de

sazón; inoportuno, inconveniente. **at an u. hour,** a una hora inconveniente, a deshora

unseasonably *adv* intempestivamente; a deshora; inoportunamente

unseasoned a *cul* sin sazonar, soso; (wood) verde; no maduro, sin madurar

unseat *vt* (from horse) tirar, echar al suelo; *pol* desituir

unseaworthy a innavegable

unseemly a indecoroso, indigno; indecente; impropio

unseen a no visto, invisible; inadvertido; secreto, oculto. *n* versión al libro abierto, *f*. **the u.,** lo invisible

unselfish a desinteresado, abnegado, nada egoísta; generoso

unselfishness *n* abnegación, *f*; desinterés, *m*; generosidad, *f*

unsentimental a no sentimental

unserviceable a inservible, inútil, que no sirve para nada, sin utilidad.

unsettle *vt* desarreglar; desorganizar; hacer inseguro; agitar, perturbar

unsettled a inconstante, variable; *com* pendiente, sin pagar; incierto; sin resolver; (of estates) sin solucionar

unshackle *vt* desencadenar

unshakable a inconmovible, firme

unshapely a desproporcionado

unshaven a sin afeitar

unsheathe *vt* desenvainar, sacar

unsheltered a desabrigado, desamparado; no protegido, sin protección; (of places) sin abrigo, expuesto; (from) sin defensa contra

unship *vt* desembarcar; (the oars) desarmar

unshod a descalzo; (of a horse) sin herraduras

unshrinkable a que no se encoge

unshrinking a intrépido; resoluto, sin vacilar

unsightly a feo, horrible, repugnante, antiestético

unsinkable a insumergible

unskilled a inexperto, inhábil, imperito, torpe

unsociability *n* insociabilidad, huraña, esquivez, *f*

unsociable a insociable, huraño, esquivo, arisco

unsocial a insocial, antisocial

unsold a no vendido, sin vender

unsolder *vt* desoldar, desestañar

unsoldierly a indigno de un soldado; poco marcial

unsophisticated a ingenuo, inocente, cándido

unsought a no solicitado; no buscado

unsound a enfermo; defectuoso; (rotten) podrido; (fallacious) erróneo, poco convincente; (of persons) informal, indigno

de confianza; (of religious views) heterodoxo. **of u. mind,** insano

unsparing a severo, implacable; generoso, pródigo

unspeakable a indecible, inefable; que no puede mencionarse, horrible

unspecified a no especificado

unspoilt a intacto; ileso, indemne; no corrompido; no estropeado; (of children) no mimado

unspoken a no pronunciado

unsportsmanlike a indigno de un cazador; indigno de un deportista; nada caballeroso. **to play in an u. way,** jugar sucio

unstable a inestable; variable; inconstante; vacilante, irresoluto

unstained a no manchado; no teñido; inmaculado, sin mancha

unstatesmanlike a impropio (*or* indigno) de un hombre de estado

unsteadiness *n* inestabilidad, falta de firmeza, *f*; inconstancia, *f*

unsteady a inestable, inseguro; inconstante

unstitch *vt* desapuntar

unstudied a no estudiado; natural, espontáneo

unsubstantial a insubstancial; ligero; irreal, imaginario; incorpóreo; aparente

unsuccessful a sin éxito; infructuoso. **to be u.,** no tener éxito

unsuccessfully *adv* en vano, sin éxito

unsuitable a inapropiado; inconveniente; impropio; inservible; incapaz; inoportuno

unsung a no cantado; no celebrado en verso

unsupported a sin apoyo; sin defensa; no favorecido

unsurmountable a insuperable, infranqueable

unsurpassable a inmejorable, insuperable

unsurpassed a sin par

unsuspecting a no suspicaz, confiado, no receloso

unswerving a directo; sin vacilar, constante

unsymmetrical a asimétrico

unsympathetic a indiferente, incompasivo; antipático

unsystematic a sin sistema, asistemático, no metódico

untalented a sin talento

untamed a indomado, cerril, bravío, no domesticado; desenfrenado, violento. **u. horse** *Lat. Am.* bellaco, *m*

untenable a insostenible

untenanted a desalquilado, deshabitado; vacío, desierto

unthankful a ingrato, desagradecido

unthinkable a inconcebible; imposible

unthinking a sin reflexión; desatento; indiscreto

unthinkingly adv sin pensar

untidily adv en desorden, sin aseo

untidy a desarreglado; desaseado; abandonado; en desorden, sin concierto

untie vt desatar, desanudar; (knots) deshacer

until prep hasta. conjunc hasta que. (The subjunc. is required in clauses referring to future time, e.g. **No venga usted hasta que le avise yo,** Don't come until I tell you. In clauses referring to past or present time the indicative is generally used, e.g. **No la reconocí hasta que se volvió,** I didn't recognize her until she turned round)

untimely a inoportuno, intempestivo; prematuro

untiring a incansable, infatigable

unto prep hacia

untold a no revelado; no narrado; sin decir, no dicho; incalculable

untouchable a que no puede tocarse, intangible; (of castes) intocable

untouched a sin tocar; intacto, incólume

untrained a indisciplinado; inexperto; no adiestrado

untranslatable a intraducible

untraveled a no frecuentado; (of persons) provinciano

untried a no experimentado. **u. knight,** caballero novel, m

untrodden a no hollado, no frecuentado; inexplorado, virgen

untroubled a tranquilo, sosegado

untrue a mentiroso, falso, engañoso; ficticio, imaginario; traidor, desleal; infiel

untrustworthiness n incertidumbre, inseguridad, f; (of persons) informalidad, f

untrustworthy a indigno de confianza; incierto, dudoso; desleal

untruth n mentira, falsedad, f; ficción, f

untruthful a mentiroso; falso

unused a no empleado; desacostumbrado; inusitado; (postage stamp) sin sellar

unusual a fuera de lo común, desacostumbrado; extraño, raro, peregrino, extraordinario

unusually adv excepcionalmente; infrecuentemente

unvarnished a sin barnizar; fig sencillo

unvarying a invariable, constante, uniforme

unveil vt quitar el velo; (memorial) descubrir; fig revelar. vi quitarse el velo; revelarse, quitarse la careta

unventilated a sin ventilación; sin aire, ahogado; (of topics) no discutido

unverifiable a que no puede verificarse

unverified a sin verificar

unvisited a no visitado; no frecuentado

unvoiced a no expresado

unwanted a no deseado; superfluo, de más

unwarranted a sin garantía; inexcusable, injustificable

unwary a incauto, imprudente

unwashed a sin lavar; sucio

unwavering a resuelto, firme; inexorable; (gaze) fijo

unwaveringly adv sin vacilar; inexorablemente

unwelcome a mal acogido; inoportuno; desagradable

unwell a indispuesto

unwholesome a malsano, nocivo, insalubre

unwieldy a pesado, abultado, difícil de manejar

unwilling a desinclinado, reluctante

unwillingly adv de mala gana

unwillingness n falta de inclinación, repugnancia, f

unwind vt desenvolver; (thread) desdevanar, desovillar. vi desarrollarse; desdevanarse

unwise a imprudente, indiscreto, incauto; (lacking wisdom) tonto

unwisely adv imprudentemente, indiscretamente

unwitting a inconsciente

unwittingly adv sin darse cuenta

unwomanly a poco femenino

unworkable a impráctico

unworkmanlike a chapucero, charanguero

unworldly a poco, mundano, espiritual

unworn a sin llevar, nuevo

unworthy a indigno

unwounded a no herido, sin herida, ileso

unwrap vt desenvolver, desempapelar

unwritten a no escrito. **u. law,** ley consuetudinaria, f

unyielding a duro, firme; (of persons) inflexible, terco, resuelto, obstinado

up adv (high) arriba, en alto; (higher) hacia arriba; (out of bed) levantado; (standing) de pie; (finished) concluido, terminado; (of time) llegado; (excited) agitado; (rebellious) sublevado; (of sun, etc.) salido; (come or gone up) subido; (of universities) en residencia; (for discussion) bajo consideración; (abreast of) al lado, al nivel; (incapable) incapaz, incompetente; (ill) enfermo, indispuesto. **"Up,"** (on elevators) «Para subir.» (For various idiomatic uses of **up** after verbs, see verbs themselves.) a (in a few expressions only) ascendente. prep en lo alto de; hacia arriba de; a lo largo de; (with country) en el interior de; (with current) contra. **to be up in arms,** sublevarse, rebelarse. **to be very hard up,** ser muy pobre, estar a la cuarta pregunta. **to drink up,**

beberlo todo. **to go** or **come up,** subir. **to lay up,** acumular. **to speak up,** hablar en voz alta. **He has something up his sleeve,** Tiene algo en la manga. **It is all up,** Todo se acabó, Mi gozo en el pozo. **It is not up to much,** Vale muy poco; No es muy fuerte. **It is up to you,** Tú dirás, Tú harás lo que te parezca. **What is he up to?** ¿Qué está tramando? **What's up?** ¿Qué pasa? ¿Qué hay? **up and down,** adv bajando y subiendo, de arriba abajo; de un lado a otro; por todas partes. **up-and-down,** a fluctuante; (of roads) undulante; (of life) accidentado, borrascoso. **ups and downs,** vicisitudes, f pl, altibajos, m pl. **up-grade,** subida, f. **up in,** versado en, perito en. **well up in,** fuerte en. **up North,** al norte; en el norte; hacia el norte. **up there,** allí arriba, allí en lo alto. **up to,** hasta; (aware) al corriente de, informado de. **up to date,** adv hasta la fecha. **up-to-date,** a de última moda; al día. **up to now,** hasta ahora. **up train,** tren ascendente. **Up with . . . !** ¡Arriba! **Up you go!** ¡Upa!

upbraid vt reprender, echar en cara

upbringing n crianza, educación, f

upcountry n tierra adentro, f; lo interior (de un país). a de tierra adentro, del interior. adv tierra adentro, hacia el interior

update vt actualizar, poner al día

upheaval n solevantamiento, m; trastorno, m

uphill a ascendente; penoso, fatigoso, difícil. adv cuesta arriba, pecho arriba

uphold vt sostener, apoyar; (help) ayudar, consolar; (protect) defender; (countenance) aprobar; law confirmar

upholster vt entapizar, tapizar

upholsterer n tapicero, m

upholstery n tapicería, f; (of car) almohadillado, m

upkeep n mantenimiento, m, conservación, f

upland n tierra alta, f, a alto, elevado

uplift vt elevar. n elevación, f; inf fervor, m

upon prep. See **on**

upper a comp superior; alto; de arriba. n (of shoe) pala, f, sport **u.-cut,** golpe de abajo arriba, upper-cut, m. **U. Egypt,** Alto Egipto, m. **u. hand,** dominio, m; superioridad, ventaja, f. **u. house,** cámara alta, f; senado, m. **u. ten,** los diez primeros

upper classes n clases altas, capas altas, f pl

uppermost a más alto, más elevado; predominante, principal; más fuerte. adv en primer lugar; en lo más alto. **to be u.,** predominar

upright a recto, derecho; vertical; (honorable) honrado, digno, recto. n (stanchion) mástil, soporte, palo derecho, montante, m. adv en pie; derecho

uprightly adv rectamente, honradamente

uprising n insurrección, sublevación, f

uproar n alboroto, tumulto, estrépito, m, conmoción, f

uproarious a tumultuoso, estrepitoso

uproot vt desarraigar, Lat. Am. destroncar; fig arrancar; (destroy) extirpar

upset vt volcar; (overthrow) derribar, echar abajo; (frustrate) contrariar; desarreglar; (distress) trastornar, turbar; (of food) hacer mal. vi volcarse. n vuelco, m; trastorno, m. **u. price,** tipo de subasta, m

upshot n resultado, m; consecuencia, f

upside n lado superior, m; parte superior, f; (of trains) andén ascendente, m. **u. down,** al revés, de arriba abajo; en desorden

upstairs adv arriba, en el piso de arriba; (with go or come) al piso de arriba

upstanding a gallardo, guapo. **an u. young man (woman),** un buen mozo (una buena moza)

upstart n arribista, mf; advenedizo (-za), insolente, mf; (presuntuoso (-sa)

upstream a and adv contra la corriente, agua arriba, río arriba

upward a ascendente, hacia arriba

upwards adv hacia arriba; en adelante. **u. of,** más de

uranium n min uranio, m

urban a urbano, ciudadano

urban renewal n renovación urbana, renovación urbanística, f

urbane a cortés, urbano, fino

urbanity n urbanidad, cortesía, finura, f

urchin n galopín, granuja, pilluelo, m

urethra n anat uretra, f

urge vt empujar, impeler; incitar, estimular, azuzar, animar; pedir con urgencia, recomendar con ahínco, instar, insistir (en). n instinto, impulso, m; deseo, m; ambición, f

urgency n urgencia, f; importancia, perentoriedad, f

urgent a urgente; importante, apremiante, perentorio. **to be u.,** urgir

urinal n orinal, urinario, m

urinalysis n análisis de orina, urinálisis, m

urinary tract n conducto urinario, m, vías urinarias, f pl

urinate vi orinar

urine n orín, m

urn n urna, f; (for coffee) cafetera, f; (for tea) tetera, f

urticaria n med urticaria, f

Uruguayan a and n uruguayo (-ya)

us pron nos; (with prep.) nosotros. **He came toward us,** Vino hacia nosotros

usable a aprovechable, servible

usage n (handling) tratamiento, m; uso, m, costumbre, f

use n uso, m; manejo, empleo, m; (custom) costumbre práctica, f; (need) necesidad, *f*; (usefulness) aprovechamiento, *m*; *law* usufructo, *m*. **directions for use,** direcciones para el uso, *f pl*, **for the use of . . .,** para uso de . . . **in use,** en uso. **out of use,** anticuado; fuera de moda. **to be of no use,** no servir; ser inútil. **to have no use for,** no tener necesidad de; *inf* tener en poco. **to make use of,** servirse de, aprovechar; *law* ejercer. **to put to use,** poner en uso, poner en servicio

use *vt* usar; (employ) emplear; (utilize) servirse de, utilizar; (handle) manejar; hacer uso de; (consume) gastar, consumir; (treat) tratar; practicar. **to use up,** agotar, acabar con; consumir. *vi impers* acostumbrar, soler (e.g. **It used to happen that . . . ,** Solía ocurrir que . . .). (**Used to** and the verb which follows are often translated simply by the imperfect tense of the following verb, e.g. **I used to see her every day,** La veía todos los días. Use of the verbs **acostumbrar** or **soler** to translate used to adds emphasis to the statement)

used *a* and *past part* acostumbrado, habituado; empleado; (clothes) usado; (postage stamp) sellado. **to become u. to,** acostumbrarse a

useful *a* útil; provechoso; servicial

usefulness *n* utilidad, *f*; valor, *m*

useless *a* inútil; vano, infructuoso. **to render u.,** inutilizar

user *n* el, *m*, (*f*, la) que usa, comprador (-ra)

usher *n* ujier, *m*; (in a theater) acomodador (-ra). *vt* introducir, anunciar; acomodar

usual *a* usual, acostumbrado, habitual; normal, común. **as u.,** como siempre. **in the u. form,** *com* al usado; como de costumbre. **with their usual courtesy,** con la cortesía que les es característica

usually *adv* por lo general, ordinariamente. **We u. go out on Sundays,** Acostumbramos salir los domingos

usurer *n* usurero (-ra)

usurp *vt* usurpar; asumir, arrogarse

usury *n* usura, *f*. **to practice u.,** usurear, dar (or tomar) a usura

utensil *n* utensilio, instrumento, *m*; herramienta, *f*. **kitchen utensils,** batería de cocina, *f*

uterine *a med* uterino

uterus *n* útero, *m*

utilitarian *a* utilitario

utility *n* utilidad, *f*; ventaja, *f*, beneficio, provecho, *m*. **u. goods,** artículos fabricados bajo la autorización del gobierno, *m pl*

utilizable *a* utilizable, aprovechable

utilization *n* empleo, aprovechamiento, *m*

utilize *vt* utilizar, servirse de; aprovechar

utmost *a* (outermost) extremo; (farthest) más remoto, más distante; (greatest) mayor, más grande. *n* lo más; todo lo posible. **to do one's u.,** hacer todo lo posible, hacer todo lo que uno pueda

utopian *a* utópico

utter *a* completo, total; terminate, absoluto; sumo, extremo. **He is an u. fool,** Es un tonto de capirote

utter *vt* pronunciar, proferir, decir, hablar; (a sigh, cry, etc.) dar; (express) manifestar, expresar, explicar; (coin) poner en circulación; (a libel) publicar; (disclose) revelar, descubrir

utterance *n* expresión, manifestación, *f*; pronunciación, *f*; (style) lenguaje, *m*

utterly *adv* enteramente, completamente

uttermost *a*. See **utmost**

V

v *n* (letter) ve, *f*; pieza en forma de V, *f*

vacancy *n* vacío, *m*; vacancia, *f*; (mental) vacuidad, *f*; (of offices, posts) vacante, *f*; (leisure) desocupación, ociosidad, *f*; (gap, blank) vacío, *m*, laguna, *f*

vacant *a* vacío; despoblado, deshabitado; (free) libre; (of offices, etc.) vacante; (leisured) ocioso; (absent-minded) distraído; (vague) vago; (foolish) estúpido, estólido

vacate *vt* dejar vacío; (a post) dejar; (a throne) renunciar a; dejar vacante; *mil* evacuar; *law* anular, rescindir

vacation *n* (of offices) vacante, *f*; (holiday) vacaciones, *f pl, f*. **the long v.,** las vacaciones de verano. **to be on a v.,** estar de vacaciones

vaccinate *vt* vacunar

vaccination *n* vacunación, *f*

vaccine *n* vacuna, *f*

vacillate *vi* (sway) oscilar; (hesitate) vacilar, titubear, dudar

vacillating *a* vacilante

vacuous *a* desocupado, ocioso; estúpido, vacío

vacuum *n* vacío, *m*. **v. brake,** freno de vacío, *m*. **v. cleaner,** aspirador de polvo, *m*. **v. flask,** termos, *m*. **v. pump,** bomba neumática, *f*. **vacuum-shelf dryer,** secador al vacío, *m*

vagabond *n* vagabundo (-da); vago, *m*; (beggar) mendigo (-ga). *a* vagabundo, errante

vagary *n* (whim) capricho, antojo, *m*, extravagancia, *f*; (of the mind) divagación, *f*

vagina *n* vagina, *f*

vaginal *a* vaginal

vagrancy *n* vagancia, *f*

vagrant *n* vago, *m*, *a* vagabundo, errante

vague *a* vago; indistinto; equívoco, ambiguo; (uncertain) incierto

vagueness *n* vaguedad, *f*

vain *a* vano; (fruitless) infructuoso; (useless) inútil; (unsubstantial) fútil, insubstancial; fantástico; (empty) vacío; (worthless) despreciable; (conceited) vanidoso, presumido. **in v.,** en vano, en balde, inútilmente. **v. about,** orgulloso de

vainglorious *a* vanaglorioso

vainly *adv* vanamente; inútilmente; (conceitedly) vanidosamente, con vanidad

valance *n* cenefa, *f*

vale *n* (valley) valle, *m. interj* ¡adiós! *n* (good-bye) vale, *m*

valediction *n* despedida, *f*; vale, *m*

valedictory *a* de despedida

Valencian *a* and *n* valenciano (-na)

valency *n* *chem* valencia, *f*

valet *n* criado, *m*. **v. de chambre,** ayuda de cámara, *m*

valetudinarian *a* valetudinario

valiant *a* valiente, esforzado, animoso, bravo

valid *a* válido, valedero; (of laws in force) vigente

validate *vt* validar

validity *n* validez, *f*

valise *n* valija, *f*, saco de viaje, *m*

valley *n* valle, *m*

valor *n* valor, *m*, valentía, *f*

valorous *a* valoroso, esforzado, intrépido

valse *n* vals, *m*

valuable *a* valioso; costoso; precioso; estimable; excelente. *n pl* **valuables,** objetos de valor, *m pl*

valuation *n* valuación, tasación, *f*; estimación, *f*

value *n* valor, *m*; precio, *m*; estimación, *f*; importancia, *f*; (gram mus) valor, *m*; *pl* **values,** valores morales, principios, *m pl*. *vt* tasar, valorar; estimar; apreciar; tener en mucho; hacer caso de; considerar. **to be of v.,** ser de valor

valued *a* apreciado, estimado; precioso

valueless *a* sin valor; insignificante

valuer *n* tasador, *m*

valve *n* (elec, mech, anat) válvula, *f*; (bot, zool) valva, *f*

vamp *n* (of a shoe) pala (de zapato), *f*; (patch) remiendo, *m*; *mus* acompañamiento improvisado, *m*; *inf* aventurera, *f*. *vt* (of shoes) poner palas (a); (patch) remendar; *mus* improvisar un acompañamiento; (of a woman) fascinar, engatusar

vampire *n* vampiro, *m*

van *n* (mil, nav, fig) vanguardia, *f*; camión, *m*; (for delivery) camión de reparto, *m*; (for furniture) conductora de muebles, *f*; (removal) carro de mudanzas, *m*; (mail) camión postal, *m*; (for bathing) caseta de baño, *f*; (for guard on trains) furgón de equipajes, *m*; (railroad car) vagón, *m*

vandal *n* a and *n* vándalo (-la); bárbaro (-ra)

vandalism *n* vandalismo, *m*

Vandyke *n* cuadro de Vandyke, *m*. **V. beard,** perilla, *f*. **V. collar,** cuello de encaje, *m*

vane *n* (weathercock) veleta, *f*; (of a windmill) aspa, *f*; (of a propeller) paleta, *f*; (of a feather) barba, *f*; (of a surveying instrument) pínula, *f*

vanguard *n* vanguardia, *f*. **in the v.,** a vanguardia; *fig* en la vanguardia

vanilla *n* vainilla, *f*

vanish *vi* desaparecer; desvanecerse; disiparse

vanishing *n* desaparición, *f*; disipación, *f*. **v. cream,** crema desvanecedora, *f*. **v. point,** punto de la vista, *m*

vanity *n* vanidad, *f*. **v. case,** polvera de bolsillo, *f*

vanquish vt vencer, derrotar

vantage n ventaja (also in tennis), f. **v.-ground,** posición ventajosa, f, sitial de privilegio, m

vapid a insípido, insulso; (of speeches, etc.) soso, aburrido, insípido

vapidity n insipidez, sosería, f

vapor n vapor, m; pl **vapors,** (hysteria) vapores, m pl. vi (boast) jactarse, baladronear; decir disparates. **v. bath,** baño de vapor, m

vaporize vt vaporizar. vi vaporizarse

vaporizer n vaporizador, m

vaporous a vaporoso

variable a variable. n math variable, f

variance n variación, f, cambio, m; desacuerdo, m, disensión, f; diferencia, contradicción, f. **at v.,** en desacuerdo, reñidos; hostil (a), opuesto (a); (of things) distinto (de), en contradicción (con)

variant n variante, f

variation n variación, f; cambio, m; variedad, f; diferencia, f; (mus magnetism) variación, f

varicose a varicoso

varied success **éxito vario,** m

variegate vt abigarrar, matizar, salpicar

variegated a abigarrado; variado; mezclado

variety n variedad, f; diversidad, f; (choice) surtido, m. **v. show,** función de variedades, f

various a vario, diverso; diferente

variously adv diversamente

varnish n barniz, m. vt barnizar; (pottery) vidriar; (conceal) disimular. **copal v.,** barniz copal, m. **japan v.,** charol japonés, m. **lacquer v.,** laca, f. **v. remover,** (for nails) quitaesmalte, m

varnishing n barnizado, m; (of pottery) vidriado, m

vary vt variar; cambiar; diversificar; modificar. vi variar; cambiar; (be different) ser distinto (de); (deviate) desviarse (de); (disagree) estar en desacuerdo, distar, estar en contradicción. **to v. directly (indirectly),** math variar en razón directa (inversa)

varying a variante, cambiante, diverso

vase n vaso, jarrón, m; urna, f

vaseline n vaselina, f

vast a vasto, extenso; enorme; grande. n vastedad, inmensidad, f

vat n cuba, tina, f; alberca, f, estanque, m. **dyeing vat,** cuba de tintoreo, f. **tanning vat,** noque, m. **wine vat,** lagar, m

Vatican a and n Vaticano, m

vaudeville n vodevil, m, zarzuela cómica, f

vault n arch bóveda, f; caverna, f; (for wine) bodega, cueva, f; (in a bank) cámara acorazada, f; (in a church) cripta, f; sepultura, f; (of the sky) bóveda celeste, f; (leap) salto, m; voltereta, f. vi (jump)

saltar; (with a pole) saltar con pértiga; saltar por encima de; voltear. vt arch abovedar; saltar

vaulter n saltador (-ra)

vaulting n construcción de bóvedas, f; bóvedas, f pl; edificio abovedado, m; (jumping) salto, m. **v.-horse,** potro de madera, m

vaunt vi jactarse (de), hacer gala (de); triunfar (sobre). vt ostentar, sacar a relucir; (praise) alabar. n jactancia, f

veal n ternera, f. **v.-cutlet,** chuleta de ternera, f

vegetable n vegetal, m; legumbre, f; pl **vegetables,** (green and generally cooked) verduras, f pl; (raw green) hortalizas, f pl. **v. dish,** fuente de legumbres, f. **v. garden,** huerto de legumbres, m; **v. ivory,** marfil vegetal, m. **v. kingdom,** reino vegetal, m. **v. soup,** sopa de hortelano, f

vegetal a vegetal

vegetarian a and n vegetariano (-na)

vegetate vi vegetar

vehemence n vehemencia, f; violencia, f; impetuosidad, f; pasión, f, ardor, m

vehement a vehemente; violento; impetuoso; apasionado

vehemently adv con vehemencia; violentamente; con impetuosidad; apasionadamente

vehicle n vehículo, m; (means) medio, m; instrumento, m

vehicular a vehicular, de los vehículos; de los coches. **v. traffic,** circulación de los coches, f; los vehículos

veil n velo, m; (curtain) cortina, f; (disguise) disfraz, m; (excuse) pretexto, m; (appearance) apariencia, f. vt velar; cubrir con un velo; (hide) tapar, encubrir; (dissemble) disimular; (disguise) disfrazar. **to take the v.,** tomar el velo, profesar

vein n (anat, bot) vena, f; (geol, min) veta, f, filón, m; (in wood) fibra, hebra, f; (fig streak) rasgo, m; (inspiration) vena, f; (mood) humor, m

velocity n velocidad, f; rapidez, f

velours n terciopelo, m

velvet n terciopelo, m, a hecho de terciopelo; aterciopelado

vendor n vendedor (-ra)

veneer vt chapear, taracear; (conceal) disimular, disfrazar. n taraceado, chapeado, m; (plate) chapa, hoja para chapear, f; (fig gloss) barniz, m, apariencia, f

venerate vt venerar, reverenciar

venereal a venéreo. **v. disease,** enfermedad venérea, f

Venetian a and n veneciano (-na). **v. blinds,** persianas, celosías, f pl

Venezuelan a and n venezolano (-na)

vengeance n venganza, f

vengeful a vengativo

venial a venial

Venice Venecia, f

venom n veneno, m

venomous a venenoso; maligno, malicioso

vent n abertura, f; salida, f; (air-hole) respiradero, m; (in pipes) ventosa, f; (in fire-arms) oído, m; anat ano, m; (fig outlet) desahogo, m; expresión, f. vt dejar escapar; (pierce) agujerear; (discharge) emitir, vomitar; (relieve) desahogar; expresar, dar expresión (a), dar rienda suelta (a)

ventilate vt ventilar; discutir

ventilator n ventilador, m

ventricle n ventrículo, m

ventriloquist n ventrílocuo (-ua)

venture n ventura, f; riesgo, m; aventura, f; especulación, f. vt arriesgar, aventurar; (stake) jugar; (state) expresar. vi aventurarse; (dare) atreverse, osar; permitirse. **at a v.,** a la ventura. **to v. on,** arriesgarse a; probar ventura con; lanzarse a; (a remark) permitirse. **to v. out,** atreverse a salir

venturesome a atrevido, audaz; (dangerous) arriesgado, peligroso

Venus n (planet) Venus, m; (woman) venus, f

veracious a veraz, verídico; verdadero

veracity n veracidad, f; verdad, f

veranda n veranda, f

verb n verbo, m. **auxiliary v.,** verbo auxiliar, m. **intransitive v.,** verbo intransitivo (neutro), m. **reflexive v.,** verbo reflexivo, m. **transitive v.,** verbo transitivo, m

verbal a verbal

verbally adv de palabra, verbalmente

verbatim a textual. adv. textualmente, palabra por palabra

verbiage n verbosidad, palabrería, f

verbose a verboso, prolijo

verdant a verde

verdict n law veredicto, fallo, m, sentencia, f; opinión, f; juicio, m. **to bring in a v.,** fallar sentencia

verdure n verdura, f, verdor, m; fig lozanía, f

verge n (wand) vara, f; (edge) margen, borde, m; (of a lake, etc.) orilla, f; (horizon) horizonte, m; fig víspera, f, punto, m. **on the v. of,** al margen de, a la orilla de. **to be on the v. of,** fig estar a punto de; estar en vísperas de

verifiable a verificable

verify vt verificar, confirmar; probar

verily adv de veras, en verdad

verisimilitude n verosimilitud, f

veritable a verdadero

verity n verdad, f

vermicelli n fideos, m pl

vermilion n bermellón, m

vermin n bichos dañinos, m pl; (insects) parásitos, m pl

vermouth n vermut, m

vernacular a vernáculo; nativo; vulgar. n lengua popular, f; lenguaje vulgar, m

versatile a zool versátil; inconstante, voluble; (clever) de muchos talentos; de muchos intereses; adaptable; completo, cabal

verse n verso, m; (stanza) estrofa, f; (in the Bible) versículo, m; (poetry) poesía, f, versos, m pl. **to make verses,** escribir versos

versed a versado, experimentado

version n versión, f; traducción, f; interpretación, f

versus prep contra

vertebra n vértebra, f

vertebrate n vertebrado, m

vertical a vertical

vertiginous a vertiginoso

vertigo n vértigo, m

verve n brío, m, fogosidad, f

very a mismo; (mere) mero; (true) verdadero; (with adjective and comparative) más grande; inf mismísimo; (complete) perfecto, completo. **The v. thought of it made him laugh,** Sólo con pensarlo se rió (or La mera idea le hizo reír). **this v. minute,** este mismísimo instante. **the v. day,** el mismo día

very adv muy; mucho; demasiado; (exactly) exactamente; completamente; absolutamente. **He is v. worried,** Está muy preocupado. **He is not v. well,** (i.e. rather ill) Está bastante bien. **This cloth is the v. best,** Esta tela es la mejor que hay. **I like it v. much,** Me gusta muchísimo. **He is v. much pleased,** Está muy contento. **so v. little,** tan poco; tan pequeño. **v. well,** muy bien

vesper n estrella vespertina, f, héspero, m; pl **vespers,** ecc vísperas, f pl

vessel n vasija, f, recipiente, m; (boat) barco, buque, m; (anat, bot) vaso, m

vest n camiseta, f; (waistcoat) chaleco, m. vt vestir; (with authority, etc.) revestir de; (property, etc.) hacer entrega de, ceder. vi tener validez; (dress) vestirse. **vested interests,** intereses creados, m pl. **v.-pocket,** bolsillo del chaleco, m. **v.-pocket camera,** cámara de bolsillo, f

vestibule n vestíbulo, m; (anteroom) antecámara, f; (of a theatre box) antepalco, m; anat vestíbulo, m

vestige n vestigio, rastro, m; sombra, f; biol rudimento, m

vestry n vestuario, m, sacristía, f

veteran a veterano; de los veteranos; aguerrido; anciano; experimentado. n veterano (-na)

veterinary a veterinario. **v. science,** veterinaria, f. **v. surgeon,** veterinario, m

veto n veto, m; prohibición, f. vt poner el veto; prohibir

vex vt contrariar, irritar; enojar; (make impatient) impacientar; fastidiar; (afflict) afligir, acongojar; (worry) inquietar

vexation n contrariedad, irritación, f; enojo, enfado, m; (impatience) impaciencia, f; fastidio, m; aflicción, f; inquietud, f; disgusto, m

vexatious a irritante; enojoso, enfadoso; fastidioso, molesto

vexed a discutido; contencioso; (thorny) espinoso, difícil

vexing a irritante; molesto; enfadoso

via n vía, f, prep por, por la vía de

viable a viable

viaduct n viaducto, m

vial n frasco, m, ampolleta, f

vibrant a vibrante

vibrate vi vibrar; (of machines) trepidar; oscilar. vt hacer vibrar, vibrar

vibration n vibración, f; trepidación, f; oscilación, f, Lat. Am. cimbrón, m

vibrator n elec vibrador, m; rad oscilador, m

vicarious a vicario; sufrido por otro; experimentado por otro

vicariously adv por delegación; por substitución. **I know it only vicariously,** Lo conozco sólo por referencia

vice n vicio, m; defecto, m; (in a horse) vicio, resabio, m; (tool) tornillo de banco, m, prefix vice. **v.-admiral,** vicealmirante, m. **v.-chairman,** vice-presidente (-ta). **v.-chancellor,** vicecanciller, m. **v.-consul,** vice-cónsul, m. **v.-consulate,** vice-consulado, m. **v.-president,** vice-presidente (-ta)

viceroy n virrey, m

viceversa adv viceversa

vicinity n vecindad, f; (nearness) cercanía, proximidad, f. **to be in the v. of,** estar en la vecindad de

vicious a vicioso. **v. circle,** círculo vicioso, m

vicissitude n vicisitud, f

victim n víctima, f

victimize vt hacer víctima (de); sacrificar; ser víctima (de), sufrir; (cheat) estafar, engañar

victor n víctor, vencedor, m

victorious a victorioso, triunfante. **to be v.,** triunfar, salir victorioso

victory n victoria, f

victual n vitualla, vianda, f; pl victuals, víveres, m pl, provisiones, f pl. vt avituallar; abastecer. vi tomar provisiones

victualler n abastecedor (-ra), proveedor (-ra)

vide Latin imperative véase, véanse

video, n vídeo, m

videotape n videograbación, videocinta, f

vie vi (with) competir con; rivalizar con; (with a person for) disputar; luchar con

Vienna Viena, f

view n vista, f; perspectiva, f, panorama, m; (landscape) paisaje, m; escena, f; inspección, f; (judgment) opinión, f, parecer, m; consideración, f; (appearance) apariencia, f; aspecto, m; (purpose) propósito, m, intención, f; (sight) alcance de la vista, m; (show) exposición, f. vt examinar; inspeccionar; (look at) mirar; (see) ver, contemplar; considerar. **in v. of,** en vista de. **in my v.,** en mi opinión, según creo yo. **on v.,** a la vista. **to keep in v.,** no perder de vista; fig no olvidar, tener presente. **to take a different v.,** pensar de un modo distinto. **to v. a house,** inspeccionar una casa. **with a v. to,** con el propósito de. **v.-finder,** enfocador, m. **v.-point,** punto de vista, m

viewer n espectador (-ra); examinador (-ra)

vigil n vela, vigilia, f; ecc vigilia, f

vigilance n vigilancia, f, desvelo, m

vigilant a vigilante, desvelado

vignette n viñeta, f

vigorous a vigoroso, enérgico, fuerte; Argentina alentado

vigorously adv con vigor

vigor n vigor, m, fuerza, f

Viking n vikingo, m

vile a vil; bajo; despreciable; infame; inf horrible

vilification n vilipendio, m, difamación, f

vilifier n difamador (-ra)

vilify vt vilipendiar, difamar

villa n villa, torre, casa de campo, f; hotel, m

village n aldea, f, pueblo, m. **v. shop** Lat. Am. esquina, f

villager n aldeano (-na)

villain n hist villano, m; malvado, m

villainous a malvado; infame; vil

villainy n vileza, infamia, maldad, f

vindicate vt vindicar, justificar; defender

vindictive a vengativo; rencoroso

vindictiveness n deseo de venganza, m; rencor, m

vine n vid, parra, f; (twining plant) enredadera, f. **v.-arbor,** emparrado, m. **v.-branch,** sarmiento, m. **v.-clad,** cubierto de parras. **v.-grower,** vinicultor, m. **v.-growing,** vinicultura, f. **v.-leaf,** hoja de parra, f. **v.-pest,** filoxera, f. **v.-stock,** cepa, f

vinegar n vinagre, m. **v.-cruet,** vinagrera, f. **v.-sauce,** vinagreta, f

vineyard n viña, f, viñedo, m. **v.-keeper,** viñador, m

vinous a vinoso

vintage n vendimia, f; (of wine) cosecha (de vino), f

vintner n vinatero, m

violate vt (desecrate) profanar; (infringe) contravenir, infringir; (break) romper; (ravish) violar

violation n profanación, f; (infringement) contravención, f; (rape) violación, f

violence n violencia, f

violent a violento

violently adv con violencia

violet n violeta, f. a violado, **v. color,** violeta, color violado, m

violin n violín, m

violinist n violinista, mf

violoncello n violoncelo, m

viper n víbora, f

virgin n virgen, f; (sign of the zodiac) Virgo, m. a virginal; (untouched) virgen. **the V.,** la Virgen. **v. soil,** tierra virgen, f

virginity n virginidad, f

virile a viril

virility n virilidad, f

virtual a virtual

virtue n virtud, f

virtuosity n virtuosidad, f

virtuoso n virtuoso (-sa)

virtuous a virtuoso

virulent a virulento

virus n virus, m

visa n visado, m

visage n cara, f, rostro, m; semblante, aspecto, m

viscera n víscera, f

viscous a viscoso

visé n visado, m, vt visar

visibility n visibilidad, f. **poor v.,** mala visibilidad, f

visible a visible; aparente, evidente

vision n visión, f; (eyesight) vista, f. **field of v.,** campo visual, m

visionary a and n visionario (-ia)

visit n visita, f; (inspection) inspección, f; (doctor's) visita de médico, f. vt visitar; hacer una visita (a); ir a ver; inspeccionar; (frequent) frecuentar; (Biblical) visitar. **to be visited by an epidemic,** sufrir una epidemia. **to go visiting,** ir de visita. **to pay a v.,** hacer una visita

visitation n visita, f; ecc visitación, f; (inspection) inspección, f; (punishment) castigo, m

visiting a de visita. **v. card,** tarjeta de visita, f. **v. card case,** tarjetero, m. **visiting hours,** horas de visita, f pl

visitor n visita, f; (official) visitador, m

visor n visera, f

vista n vista, perspectiva, f

visual a visual. **the v. arts,** las artes visuales

visualize vt and vi imaginarse, ver mentalmente

vital a vital; esencial; trascendental

vitality n vitalidad, f

vitamin n vitamina, f

vitiate vt viciar; corromper, contaminar

vitriolic a vitriólico

vituperate vt vituperar

vituperation n vituperio, m

vivacious a animado, vivaracho

vivacity n vivacidad, animación, f

viva voce a oral. n examen oral, m

vivid a vivo; brillante; intenso; (of descriptions, etc.) gráfico

vividness n vivacidad, f; intensidad, f; (strength) fuerza, f

vivify vt vivificar, avivar

vivisection n vivisección, f

vixen n raposa, zorra, f; (woman) arpía, f

viz adv a saber

vocabulary n vocabulario, m

vocal a vocal. **v. cords,** cuerdas vocales, f pl

vocalist n cantante, mf, voz, f

vocation n vocación, f; oficio, m; empleo, m; profesión, f

vocational a profesional; práctico. **vocational guidance,** guía vocacional, orientación profesional, f. **v. training,** instrucción práctica, f; enseñanza de oficio, f

vociferate vt gritar. vi vociferar, vocear

vociferous a (noisy) ruidoso; vocinglero, clamoroso

vodka n vodca, m

vogue n moda, f. **in v.,** en boga, de moda

voice n voz, f. vt expresar, interpretar, hacerse eco de; hablar. **in a loud v.,** en voz alta. **in a low v.,** en voz baja

voiced a (in compounds) de voz . . . ; hablado

void a (empty) vacío; (vacant) vacante; deshabitado; (lacking in) privado (de), desprovisto (de); (without) sin; law inválido, nulo; sin valor. n vacío, m. vt evacuar; law anular; invalidar

voile n espumilla, f

volatile a volátil; (light) ligero; (changeable) voluble, inconstante

volatility n volatilidad, f; ligereza, f; volubilidad, f

volcanic a volcánico

volcano n volcán, m. **extinct v.,** volcán extinto, m

volition n volición, f; voluntad, f

volley n (of stones, etc.) lluvia, f; (of firearms) descarga, f; (of cannon, naval guns) andanada, f; sport voleo, m; (of words, etc.) torrente, m; (of applause and as a salute) salva, f. vt sport volear; (abuse, etc.) dirigir. vi lanzar una descarga, hacer una descarga

volt n elec voltio, m; (of a horse and in fencing) vuelta, f. **v.-ampere,** voltamperio, m

voltage n voltaje, m. **v. control,** mando del voltaje, m

voluble a gárrulo, locuaz

volume n (book) tomo, m; (amount, size, space) volumen, m; (of water) caudal (de río), *m*; (mass) masa, *f*; (of smoke) humareda, *f*, nubes de humo, *f pl*

voluminous *a* voluminoso

voluntary *a* voluntario; espontáneo; libre; (charitable) benéfico; (intentional) intencional, deliberado. *n* solo de órgano, *m*

volunteer *n mil* voluntario (-ia). a de voluntarios. *vt* ofrecer; contribuir; expresar. *vi* ofrecerse para hacer algo; *mil* alistarse, ofrecerse a servir como voluntario

voluptuous *a* voluptuoso

vomit *vt* and *vi* vomitar; arrojar, devolver, *Central America, Mexico* deponer. *n* vómito, *m*

voodoo *n* vudú, *m*

voracious *a* voraz

vortex *n* torbellino, *m*, vorágine, *f*; *fig* vórtice, *m*

vote *n* voto, *m*; (voting) votación, *f*; (suffrage) sufragio, *m*; (election) elección, *f*. *vt* votar; asignar; nombrar; elegir; (consider) tener por. *vi* votar, dar el voto. **casting v.,** voto de calidad, *m*. **to put to the v.,** poner a votación. **to v. down,** desechar, rechazar. **v. of confidence,** voto de confianza, *m*. **v. of thanks,** voto de gracias, *m*

voter *n* votante, *mf*, votador (-ra); elector (-ra)

voting *n* votación, *f*; elección, *f*. a de votar; electoral. **v. paper,** papeleta de votación, *f*

votive *a* votivo. **v. offering,** exvoto, *m*

vouch *vi* atestiguar, afirmar; garantizar; responder (de)

voucher *n* (guarantor) fiador (-ra); (guarantee) garantía, *f*; (receipt) recibo, *m*; (proof) prueba, *f*; documento justificativo, *m*; vale, bono, *m*

vouchsafe *vt* conceder, otorgar

vow *n* voto, *m*; promesa solemne, *f*. *vt* hacer voto (de), hacer promesa solemne (de); jurar. **to take a vow,** hacer un voto

vowel *n* vocal, *f*

voyage *n* viaje (por mar), *m*; travesía, *f*. *vi* viajar por mar. **Good v.!** ¡Buen viaje!, Feliz viaje!

voyager *n* viajero (-ra)

vulgar *a* vulgar; (ill-bred) ordinario, cursi; (in bad taste) de mal gusto; trivial; adocenado; (coarse) grosero. *n* vulgo, populacho, *m*. **v. fraction,** fracción común, *f*

vulgarism *n* vulgarismo, *m*; vulgaridad, *f*

vulgarity *n* vulgaridad, *f*; grosería, *f*; mal tono, *m*, cursilería, *f*

Vulgate *n* Vulgata, *f*

vulture *n* buitre, *Argentina* carancho, *m*

W

w *n* ve doble, *f*

wabble *vi.* See **wobble**

wad *n* (of straw, etc.) atado, *m;* (of notes, etc.) rollo, *m;* (in a gun) taco, *m. vt sew* acolchar; (furniture) emborrar; (guns) atacar; (stuff) rellenar

wadding *n* borra, *f;* (lining) entretela, *f;* (for guns) taco, *m;* (stuffing) relleno, *m*

waddle *n* anadeo, *m, vi* anadear

wade *vi* and *vt* andar (en el agua, etc.); vadear; (paddle) chapotear. **to w. in,** entrar en (el agua, etc.); *fig* meterse en. **to w. through,** (a book) leer con dificultad; estudiar detenidamente; ir por

wafer *n* (host) hostia, *f;* (for sealing) oblea, *f;* (for ices) barquillo, *m*

waffle *n cul* fruta de sartén, *f*

waft *vt* llevar por el aire o encima del agua; hacer flotar; (stir) mecer; (of the wind) traer. *n* (fragrance) ráfaga de olor, *f*

wag *n* (of the tail) coleada, *f;* movimiento, *m;* meneo, *m;* (jester) bromista, *mf. vt* mover ligeramente; agitar; (of the tail) menear (la cola), colear. *vi* menearse; moverse; oscilar; (of the world) ir. **And thus the world wags,** Y así va el mundo

wage, wages *n* salario, *m; fig* premio, galardón, *m.* **minimum wage,** salario mínimo, *m.* **wages clerk,** pagador (-ra). **wage-earner,** asalariado (-da); (worker) trabajador (-ra)

wage *vt* emprender; sostener; hacer. **to w. war,** hacer guerra

wager *n* (bet) apuesta, *f;* (test) prueba, *f, vt* (bet) apostar; (pledge) empeñar. **to lay a w.,** hacer una apuesta

wages *n pl.* See **wage**

waggish *a* zumbón, jocoso; cómico

waggle *vt* menear; mover; agitar; oscilar. *vi* menearse; moverse; agitarse; oscilar. *n* meneo, movimiento, *m;* oscilación, *f*

wagon *n* carro, *m;* carreta, *f;* (railway) vagón, *m.* **w.-lit,** coche cama, *m.* **w.-load,** carretada, *f;* vagón, *m*

waif *n* niño (-ña) sin hogar; animal perdido o abandonado, *m;* objeto extraviado, *m;* objeto sin dueño, *m.* **waifs and strays,** niños abandonados, *m pl*

wail *n* lamento, gemido, *m;* (complaint) queja, *f. vi* lamentarse, gemir; quejarse (de). *vt* lamentar, deplorar

wainscot *n* entablado de madera, *m. vt* enmaderar; poner friso de madera (a)

waist *n* cintura, *f;* (blouse) blusa, *f;* (belt) cinturón, *m;* (bodice) corpiño, *m;* (narrowest portion) cuello, *m;* garganta, *f; naut* combés, *m.* **w.-band,** pretina, *f.* **w.-deep,** hasta la cintura. **w.-line,** cintura, *f.* **w. measurement,** medida de la cintura, *f.* **w.-coat,** chaleco, *m.* **w. strap,** trincha, *f*

wait *vi* and *vt* esperar, aguardar; (serve) servir. **to keep waiting,** hacer esperar. **to w. at table,** servir a la mesa. **to w. on oneself,** servirse a sí mismo; cuidarse a sí mismo; hacer las cosas por sí solo. **to w. one's time,** aguardar la ocasión. **to w. for,** (until) esperar hasta que; (of persons) esperar (a), aguardar (a); (in ambush) acechar. **to w. upon,** (serve) servir (a); (visit) visitar; presentar sus respetos (a); (*fig* accompany) acompañar; (follow) seguir a

wait *n* espera, *f;* (pause) pausa, *f,* intervalo, *m;* (ambush) asechanza, *f; pl* **waits,** coro de nochebuena, *m.* **to lie in w. for,** estar en acecho para

waiter *n* camarero, mozo, *m;* (tray) bandeja, *f*

waiting *n* espera, *f.* **a que espera;** de espera; de servicio. **lady-in-w.,** dama de servicio, *f.* **w.-maid,** camarera, doncella, *f.* **w.-room,** (of a bus station, etc.) sala de espera, *f;* (of an office) antesala, *f*

waitress *n* camarera, *f*

waive *vt* renunciar (a); desistir (de)

wake *vi* estar despierto; despertarse; (watch) velar. *vt* despertar; (a corpse) velar (a). *n* vela, *f;* vigilia, *f;* (of a corpse) velatorio, *m;* (holiday) fiesta, *f;* (of a ship) estela, *f.* **in the w. of,** *naut* en la estela de; después de; seguido por

wakeful *a* vigilante; (awake) despierto. **to be w.,** pasar la noche en vela

waken *vi* despertarse. *vt* despertar; (call) llamar

waking *a* despierto; de vela. *n* despertar, *m;* (watching) vela, *f*

wale *n* (weal) verdugo, *m,* huella de azote, *f, vt* azotar

Wales (País de) Gales, *m*

walk *n* (pace) paso, *m;* (modo de) andar, *m;* (journey on foot) paseo, *m,* vuelta, *f;* (long) caminata, *f;* (promenade) paseo, *m,* avenida, *f;* (path) senda, *f;* (rank) clase social, *f;* esfera, *f;* profesión, *f;* ocupación, *f.* **quick w.,** paseo rápido, *m;* (pace) andar rápido, *m.* **to go for a w.,** ir de paseo. **to take a w.,** dar un paseo (or una vuelta), pasear. **to take for a w.,** llevar a paseo, sacar a paseo. **w.-out,** (strike) huelga, *f.* **w.-over,** triunfo, *m,* (or victoria, *f*) fácil. **w. past,** desfile, *m*

walk *vi* andar; caminar; ir a pie; (take a walk) pasear, dar un paseo; (of ghosts) aparecer; (behave) conducirse. *vt* hacer andar; (take for a walk) sacar a paseo; andar de una parte a otra (de), recorrer; (a specified distance) hacer a pie, andar; (a horse) llevar al paso. **to w. abroad,** dar un paseo; salir. **to w. arm in arm,** ir de bracero. **to w. past,** pasar; (in procession) desfilar. **to w. quickly,** andar de prisa. **to w. slowly,** andar despacio, andar lentamente. **to w. the hospitals,** estudiar en los hospitales. **to w. the streets,** recorrer las calles; vagar por las calles. **to w. about,** pasearse; ir y venir. **to w. after,** seguir (a), ir detrás de. **to w. along,** andar por; recorrer. **to w. away,** marcharse, irse. **to w. away with,** (win) ganar, llevarse; (steal) quitar, tomar, alzarse con. **to w. back,** volver; volver a pie, regresar a pie. **to w. down,** bajar; bajar a pie; andar por. **to w. in,** entrar en; entrar a pie en; (walk about) pasearse en. **to w. on,** seguir andando; (step on) pisar. **to w. out,** salir. **to w. over,** andar por; llevar la victoria (a); triunfar fácilmente sobre. **to w. round,** dar la vuelta a. **to w. round and round,** dar vueltas. **to w. up,** subir andando; subir. **to w. up and down,** dar vueltas, ir y venir

walker n (pedestrian) peatón, m; andador (-ra); (promenader) paseante, mf

walking n el andar; (excursion on foot) paseo, m. a andante; de andar; a pie; ambulante. **at a w. pace,** a un paso de andadura. **w. encyclopedia,** enciclopedia ambulante, f. **w. match,** marcha atlética, f. **w.-stick,** bastón, m. **w. tour,** excursión a pie, f

wall n muro, m; (rampart) muralla, f; (fig and of an organ, cavity, etc.) pared, f. **partition w.,** tabique, m. **Walls have ears,** Las paredes oyen. **w. lizard,** lagartija, f. **w. map,** mapa mural, m. **w.-painting,** pintura mural, f. **w.-paper,** papel pintado, m. **w. socket,** elec enchufe, m

wall vt cercar con un muro; amurallar. **to w. in,** murar. **to w. up,** tapiar, tabicar

wallet n cartera, f; bolsa de cuero, f

wallop n golpe, m, vt tundir, zurrar

wallow vi revolcarse; encenagarse; (in riches, etc.) nadar (en). n revuelco, m

walnut n (tree and wood) nogal, m; (nut) nuez de nogal, f

walrus n morsa, f

waltz n vals, m, vi valsar

wan a ojeroso, descolorido; (of the sky, etc.) pálido, sin color

wand n vara, f; (conductor's) batuta, f. **magic w.,** varita mágica, f

wander vi errar, vagar; (deviate) extraviarse; (from the subject) desviarse del asunto; divagar; (be delirious) delirar. vt vagar por, errar por, recorrer

wanderer n vagabundo (-da); hombre, m, (f, mujer) errante; (traveler) viajero (-ra)

wandering a errante; vagabundo; nómada; (traveling) viajero; (delirious) delirante; (of thoughts, the mind) distraído; (of cells, kidneys, etc.) flotante. n vagancia, f; viaje, m; (delirium) delirio, m; (digression) divagación, f; (of a river, etc.) meandro, m. **the w. Jew,** el judío errante

wane vi (of the moon, etc.) menguar; (decrease) disminuir; (fig decay) decaer. n (of the moon) menguante de la luna, f; mengua, f; disminución, f; decadencia, f

waning a menguante

wanly adv pálidamente; fig tristemente

want vt (lack) carecer de, faltar; (need) necesitar, haber menester de; (require or wish) querer, desear; (demand) exigir; (ought) deber; (do without) pasarse sin. vi hacer falta; carecer (de); (be poor) estar necesitado. **I don't w. to,** No quiero, No me da la gana. **to be wanted,** hacer falta; (called) ser llamado. **You are wanted on the telephone,** Te llaman por teléfono

wanted se necesita; (advertisement) demanda, f. **Estelle wants me to write a letter,** Estrella quiere que escriba una carta. **What do you w. me to do?** ¿Qué quiere Vd. que haga?; ¿En qué puedo servirle? **What does Paul w.?** ¿Qué quiere Pablo?; ¿Qué necesita Pablo? **He wants (needs) a holiday,** Le hacen falta unas vacaciones, Necesita unas vacaciones

want n (lack) falta, f; escasez, carestía, f; (need) necesidad, f; (poverty) pobreza, indigencia, f; (absence) ausencia, f; (wish) deseo, m; exigencia, f. **in w. of,** por falta de; en la ausencia de. **to be in w.,** estar en la necesidad, ser indigente

wanting a deficiente (en); falto (de); (scarce) escaso; ausente; (in intelligence) menguado. prep (less) menos; (without) sin. **to be w.,** faltar. **to be w. in,** carecer de

wanton a (playful) juguetón; (wilful) travieso; (loose) suelto, libre; (unrestrained) desenfrenado; extravagante; excesivo; caprichoso; (dishevelled) en desorden; (reckless) indiscreto; (of vegetation) lozano; (purposeless) inútil; imperdonable; frívolo; (unchaste) disoluto; lascivo. n mujer disoluta, f; ramera, f; (child) niño (-ña) juguetón (-ona)

wantonly adv innecesariamente; sin motivo; excesivamente; lascivamente

war n guerra, f. a de guerra; guerrero. vi guerrear. **at war with,** en guerra con. **cold war,** guerra tonta, f. **on a war footing,** en pie de guerra. **We are at war,** Estamos en guerra. **to be on the war-path,** fig inf buscar pendencia, tratar de armarla. **to declare war on,** declarar la guerra (a). **to make war on,** hacer la guerra (a). **war to the death,** guerra a muerte, f. **war correspondent,** corresponsal en el teatro de guerra, m. **war-cry,** alarido de guerra, grito de combate, grito de guerra m. **war-dance,** danza guerrera, f. **war horse,** caballo de batalla, m. **war loan,** empréstito de guerra, m. **war-lord,** adalid, caudillo, jefe militar, m. **war material,** pertrechos de guerra, m pl; municiones, f pl. **war memorial,** monumento a los caídos, m. **war minister,** Ministro de la Guerra, m. **war neurosis,** neurosis de guerra, f. **War Office,** Ministerio de la Guerra, m. **war plane,** avión de guerra, m. **war-ship,** barco (or buque) de guerra, m. **war-wearied,** agotado por la guerra

warble *vt* and *vi* trinar; gorjear; murmurar. *n* trino, *m;* gorjeo, *m;* murmurio, *m*

ward *n* protección, *f;* (of a minor) pupilo (-la); (of locks, keys) guarda, *f;* (of a city) barrio, distrito, *m;* (of a hospital, etc.) sala, *f;* (of a prison) celda, *f;* (fencing) guardia, *f.* **w.-room,** cuarto de los oficiales, *m.* **w. sister,** hermana de una sala de hospital, *f*

ward *vt* proteger, defender. **to w. off,** desviar; eviar

warden *n* guardián, *m;* director (-ra); (of a prison) alcaide, *m;* (of a church) mayordomo de la iglesia, *m;* (of a port) capitán, *m*

wardrobe *n* guardarropa, ropero, *m;* (clothes) ropa, *f; theat* vestuario, *m.* **w. trunk,** baúl mundo, *m*

ware *n* mercadería, *f;* (pottery) loza, *f; pl* **wares,** mercancías, *f pl*

war effort *n* esfuerzo bélico, esfuerzo de guerra, esfuerzo guerrero, *m*

warehouse *n* almacén, *m, vt* almacenar

warfare *n* guerra, *f;* lucha, *f;* arte militar, *m, or f.* **chemical w.,** guerra química, *f*

war head *n* (of torpedo) cabeza de combate, punto de combate, *f;* (of missile) detonante, *m*

war heroe *n* héroe de guerra, *m*

war heroine *n* heroína de guerra, *f*

warily *adv* con cautela, cautelosamente; prudentemente

wariness *n* cautela *f;* prudencia, *f*

warlike *a* belicoso, guerrero; militar, de guerra; marcial. **war-spirit,** espíritu belicoso, *m,* marcialidad, *f*

warm *a* caliente; (lukewarm) tibio; (hot) caluroso; (affectionate) cordial, cariñoso, afectuoso; (angry) acalorado; (enthusiastic) entusiasta, ardiente; (art) cálido; (of coats, etc.) de abrigo; (fresh) fresco, reciente; *inf* adinerado. *vt* calentar; *fig* encender; entusiasmar. *vi* calentarse; *fig* entusiasmarse (con). **to have a w. at the fire,** calentarse al lado del fuego. **to be w.,** (of things) estar caliente; (of coats, etc.) ser de abrigo; (of the weather) hacer calor; (of people) tener calor. **to grow w.,** calentarse; (grow angry) excitarse, agitarse; (of a discussion) hacerse acalorado. **to keep w.,** conservar caliente; calentar. **to keep oneself w.,** estar caliente, no enfriarse. **to w. up,** calentar. **w.-blooded,** de sangre caliente; ardiente. **w.-hearted,** de buen corazón; generoso; afectuoso; cordial. **w.-heartedness,** buen corazón, *m;* generosidad, *f;* cordialidad, *f*

warming *n* calentamiento, *m;* calefacción, *f.* a calentador; para calentar. **w.-pan,** calentador, *m*

warmly *adv* (affectionately) cordialmente, afectuosamente; con entusiasmo; (angrily) acaloradamente. **to be w. wrapped up,** estar bien abrigado

warmonger *n* atizador de guerra, belicista, fautor de guerra, fomentador de guerra, propagador (-ra) de guerra

warmth *n* calor, *m*

warn *vt* advertir; prevenir; amonestar; (inform) avisar

warning *n* advertencia, *f;* aviso, *m;* amonestación, *f;* (lesson) lección, *f,* escarmiento, *m;* alarma, *f.* a amonestador; de alarma. **to give w.,** prevenir, advertir; (dismiss) despedir. **to take w.,** escarmentar

warp *vt* torcer; combar; *naut* espiar; (the mind) pervertir. *vi* torcerse; combarse, bornearse; *naut* espiarse. *n* (in a fabric) urdimbre, *f;* (in wood) comba, *f,* torcimiento, *m; naut* espía, *f.* **w. and woof,** trama y urdimbre, *f*

warping *n* (of wood) combadura, *f;* (weaving) urdidura, *f; naut* espía, *f;* (of the mind) perversión, *f.* **w. frame,** urdidera, *f*

warrant *n* autoridad, *f;* justificación, *f;* autorización, *f;* garantía, *f;* decreto de prisión, *m;* orden, *f; com* orden de pago, *f; mil* nombramiento, *m;* motivo, *m,* razón, *f. vt* justificar; autorizar; garantizar, responder por; asegurar. **pay w.,** boletín de pago, *m*

warranty *n* autorización, *f;* justificación, *f; law* garantía, *f*

warren *n* (for hunting) vedado, *m;* (rabbit) conejera, *f;* vivar, *m,* madriguera, *f*

warrior *n* guerrero, *m;* soldado, *m*

Warsaw Varsovia, *f*

wart *n* verruga, *f*

wary *a* cauto, cauteloso; prudente

wash *vt* lavar; (dishes) fregar; (lave) bañar; (clean) limpiar; (furrow) surcar; (wet) regar, humedecer; (with paint) dar una capa de color o de metal. *vi* lavarse; lavar ropa. **Two of the crew were washed overboard,** El mar arrastró a dos de los tripulantes. **Will this material w.?** ¿Se puede lavar esta tela? ¿Es lavable esta tela? **to w. ashore,** echar a la playa. **w. away,** (remove by washing) quitar lavando; derrubiar; (water or waves) arrastrar, llevarse. **to w. one's hands,** lavarse las manos. **to look washed out,** estar ojeroso. **to w. down,** lavar; limpiar; (remove) llevarse; (accompany with drink) regar. **to w. off,** *vt* quitar lavando; hacer desaparecer; borrar; (of waves, etc.) llevarse; (of color) desteñir. *vi* borrarse; desteñirse. **to w. up,** lavar los platos, fregar la vajilla; (cast up) desechar. **w. one's dirty laundry in public,** sacar los más sucios trapillos a la colada

wash *n* lavadura, *f,* lavado, *m;* baño, *m;* (clothes) ropa para lavar, ropa sucia, *f;* colada, *f;* (of the waves) chapoteo, *m;* (lotion) loción, *f;* (coating) capa, *f;* (silt) aluvión, *m.* **w.-basin,** palangana, *f;* lavabo, *m.* **w.-board,** tabla de lavar, *f.* **w.-house,** lavadero, *m.* **w.-leather,** gamuza, badana, *f.* **w.-out,** fracaso, *m.* **w.-stand,**

aguamanil, lavabo, *m.* **w.-tub,** cuba de lavar, *f*

washable a lavable

washer *n* lavador (-ra); (washerwoman) lavandera, *f*; (machine) lavadora, *f*; *mech* arandela, *f*

washerwoman *n* lavandera, *f*

washing *n* lavamiento, *m*; ropa sucia, ropa para lavar, *f*; ropa limpia, *f*; ropa, *f*; (bleaching) blanqueadura, *f*; (toilet) abluciones, *f pl*; *ecc* lavatorio, *m*; *pl* **washings,** lavazas, *f pl.* **There is a lot of w. to be done,** Hay mucha ropa que lavar. **w.-board,** tabla de lavar, *f.* **w.-day,** día de colada, *m.* **w.-machine,** lavadora, máquina de lavar, *f.* **w.-soda,** carbonato sódico, *m.* **w.-up,** lavado de los platos, *m.* **w.-up machine,** fregador mecánico de platos, *m*

wasp *n* avispa, *f, Lat. Am. also* jicote, *m.* **wasp's nest,** avispero, *m.* **w.-waisted,** (of clothes) ceñido, muy ajustado

waspish a enojadizo, irascible; malicioso; mordaz

waste *vt* desperdiciar, derrochar, malgastar; (time) perder; consumir; corroer; (devastate) asolar, devastar; echar a perder; malograr; disipar; agotar. *vi* gastarse; consumirse; perderse. **to w. time,** perder el tiempo. **to w. away,** (of persons) demacrarse, consumirse

waste *n* (wilderness) yermo, desierto, *m*; (vastness) inmensidad, vastedad, *f*; (loss) pérdida, *f*; (squandering) despilfarro, derroche, *m*; disminución, *f*; (refuse) desechos, *m pl*; (of cotton, etc.) borra, *f*; disipación, *f.* a (of land) sin cultivar; yermo; inútil; desechado, de desecho; superfluo. **to lay w.,** devastar. **w. land,** yermo, *m*; tierras sin cultivar, *f pl.* **w. paper,** papel usado, papel de desecho, *m.* **w.-paper basket,** cesto para papeles, *m.* **w.-pipe,** desaguadero, tubo de desagüe, *m*

wasteful a pródigo, derrochador, manirroto; antieconómico; ruinoso; inútil

waster *n* gastador (-ra); disipador (-ra); (loafer) golfo, *m*

watch *vi* velar; mirar. *vt* mirar; observar; guardar; (await) esperar; (spy upon) espiar, acechar. **to w. for,** buscar aguardar. **to w. over,** vigilar, guardar; (care for) cuidar; proteger. **watch out!** *Mexico* ¡abusado!

watch *n* (at night) vela, *f*; (wakefulness) desvelo, *m*; observación, vigilancia, *f*; (*mil naut*) guardia, *f*; (sentinel) centinela, *m*; (watchman) sereno, vigilante, *m*; (guard) ronda, *f*; (timepiece) reloj de bolsillo, *m.* **to be on the w.,** estar al acecho, estar al alerta, estar a la mira. **to keep w.,** vigilar. **dog w.,** media guardia, *f.* **pocket w.,** reloj de bolsillo, *m.* **wrist w.,** reloj de pulsera, *m.* **w.-case,** caja de reloj, relojera, *f.* **w.-chain,** cadena de reloj, leontina, *f.* **w.-dog,** perro guardián, *m.* **w.-glass,** cristal de reloj, *m.* **w.-making,**

relojería, *f.* **w.-night,** noche vieja, *f.* **w.-spring,** muelle de reloj, *m*, espiral, *f.*

watcher *n* observador (-ra); espectador (-ra); (at a sick bed) el, *m*, (*f,* la) que vela a un enfermo

watchful a vigilante, alerto; observador; atento, cuidadoso

watchfully *adv* vigilantemente; atentamente

watching *n* observación, *f*; (vigil) vela, *f*

watchmaker *n* relojero (-ra). **watchmaker's shop,** relojería, *f*

watchman *n* vigilante, sereno, *m*; guardián, *m*

watchword *n* (password) consigna, contraseña, *f*; (motto) lema, *m*

water *n* agua, *f*; (tide) marea, *f*; (of precious stones) aguas, *f pl*; (urine) orina, *f*; (quality) calidad, clase, *f.* a de agua; por agua; acuático; hidráulico. **fresh w.,** (not salt) agua dulce, *f*; agua fresca, *f.* **hard w.,** agua cruda, *f.* **high w.,** marea alta, *f.* **low w.,** marea baja, *f.* **of the first w.,** de primera clase, **running w.,** agua corriente, *f.* **soft w.,** agua blanda, *f.* **to make w.,** *naut* hacer agua; orinar. **to take the waters,** tomar las aguas. **under w.,** *adv* debajo del agua. a acuático. **w.-bird,** ave acuática, *f.* **w. blister,** ampolla, *f.* **w.-boatman,** chinche de agua, *f.* **w.-borne,** flotante. **w.-bottle,** cantimplora, *f.* **w.-brash,** acedia, *f.* **w.-butt,** barril, *m*, pipa, *f.* **w.-carrier,** aguador (-ra). **w.-cart,** carro de regar, *m.* **w.-closet,** retrete, excusado, *m.* **w.-color,** acuarela, *f.* **w.-color painting,** pintura a la acuarela, *f.* **w.-colorist,** acuarelista, *mf.* **w.-cooled,** enfriado por agua. **w.-cooler,** cantimplora, *f.* **w.-finder,** zahorí, *m.* **w. front,** (wharf) muelle, *m*; puerto, *m*; litoral, *m.* **w.-gauge,** indicador de nivel de agua, *m*, vara de aforar, *f.* **w.-glass,** vidrio soluble, silicato de sosa, *m.* **w. heater,** calentador de agua, *m.* **w.-ice,** helado, *m.* **w.-level,** nivel de las aguas, *m.* **w.-lily,** nenúfar, *m*, azucena de agua, *f.* **w.-line,** lengua de agua, *f*; (of a ship) línea de flotación, *f.* **w.-logged,** anegado en agua. **w.-main,** cañería maestra de agua, *f.* **w. man,** barquero, *m.* **w.-melon,** sandía, *f.* **w. mill,** aceña, *f.* **w.-nymph,** náyade, *f.* **w.-pipe,** cañería del agua, *f.* **w. pitcher,** jarro, *m.* **w. plant,** planta acuática, *f.* **w.-polo,** polo acuático, *m.* **w.-power,** fuerza hidráulica, *f.* **w.-rate,** cupo del consumo de agua, *m.* **w. snake,** culebra de agua, *f.* **w. softener,** generador de agua dulce, *m*; purificador de agua, *m.* **w. spaniel,** perro (-rra) de aguas. **w. sprite,** ondina, *f.* **w.-supply,** abastecimiento de agua, *m*; traída de aguas, *f.* **w. tank,** depósito para agua, *m.* **w. tower,** arca de agua, *f.* **w. wave,** ondulado al agua, *m.* **w.-way,** canal, río, *m*, o vía *f*, navegable. **w.-wheel,** rueda hidráulica, *f*, azud, *m*; (for irrigation) aceña, *f.* **w. wings,** nadaderas, *f pl*

water *vt* (irrigate, sprinkle) regar; (moisten) mojar; (cattle, etc.) abrevar; (wine, etc.) aguar; diluir con agua; (bathe) bañar. *vi* (of animals) beber agua; (of engines, etc.) tomar agua; (of the eyes, mouth) hacerse agua. **My mouth waters,** Se me hace agua la boca

watercourse *n* corriente de agua, *f;* cauce, *m;* lecho de un río, *m*

watered-down *fig* pasado por agua

waterfall *n* salto de agua, *m*, cascada, catarata, *f*

watering *n* riego, *m;* irrigación, *f;* (of eyes) lagrimeo, *m;* (of cattle, etc.) el abrevar (a); *naut* aguada, *f.* **w.-can,** regadera, *f.* **w.-cart,** carro de regar, *m.* **w.-place,** (for animals) aguadero, *m;* (for cattle) abrevadero, *m;* (spa) balneario, *m;* (by the sea) playa de veraneo, *f*

watermark *n* (in paper) filigrana, *f;* nivel del agua, *m. vt* filigranar

waterproof *a* impermeable; a prueba de agua. *n* impermeable, *m. vt* hacer impermeable, impermeabilizar

water-repellent *a* repelente al agua

watershed *n* vertiente, *f;* línea divisoria de las aguas, *f;* (river-basin) cuenca, *f*

watertight *a* impermeable, estanco; a prueba de agua; (of arguments, etc.) irrefutable

waterworks *n* establecimiento para la distribución de las aguas, *m;* obras hidráulicas, *f pl*

watery *a* (wet) húmedo; acuoso; (of the sky) de lluvia; (of eyes) lagrimoso, lloroso; (sodden) mojado; (of soup, etc.) claro; insípido

watt *n* vatio, *m.* **w. hour,** vatio hora, *m.* **w.-meter,** vatímetro, *m*

wave *vi* ondear; ondular; flotar; hacer señales. *vt* (brandish) blandir; agitar; (the hair) ondear; ondular; hacer señales (de). **They waved goodby to him,** Le hicieron adiós con la mano; Le hicieron señas de despedida; Se despidieron de él agitando el pañuelo

wave *n* (of the sea) ola, *f; phys* onda, *f;* (in hair or a surface) ondulación, *f;* (movement) movimiento, *m;* (of anger, etc.) ráfaga, *f.* **long w.,** onda larga, *f.* **medium w.,** onda media, *f.* **short w.,** onda corta, *f.* **sound w.,** onda sonora, *f.* **to have one's hair waved,** hacerse ondular el pelo. **w. band,** franja undosa, escala de longitudes de onda, *f.* **w. crest,** cresta de la ola, cabrilla, *f.* **w.-length,** longitud de onda, *f*

waver *vi* ondear; oscilar; (hesitate) vacilar, titubear; (totter) tambalearse; (weaken) flaquear

waverer *n* irresoluto (-ta), vacilante, *m*

wavering *n* vacilación, irresolución, *f.* a oscilante; vacilante, irresoluto; flotante

waving *n* ondulación, *f;* oscilación, *f;* agitación, *f;* movimiento, *m. a* ondulante; oscilante; que se balancea

wavy *a* ondulado; flotante

wax *n* cera, *f;* (cobblers') cerote, *m;* (in the ear) cerilla, *f.* a de cera. *vt* encerar. *vi* crecer; hacerse; ponerse. **to wax enthusiastic,** entusiasmarse. **waxed paper,** papel encerado, *m.* **wax chandler,** cerero, *m.* **wax doll,** muñeca de cera, *f.* **wax modeling,** modelado en cera, *m,* ceroplástica, *f.* **wax taper,** blandón, *m*

waxen *a* de cera; como la cera; de color de cera

waxing *n* enceramiento, *m;* (of the moon) crecimiento, *m;* aumento, *m*

wax museum *n* museo de cera, *m*

waxwork *n* figura de cera, *f*

waxy *a.* See **waxen**

way *n* camino, *m;* senda, *f;* paso, *m;* ruta, *f;* (railway, etc.) vía, *f;* dirección, *f;* rumbo, *m;* distancia, *f;* (journey) viaje, *m;* (sea crossing) travesía, *f;* avance, progreso, *m;* (naut etc.) marcha, *f;* método, *m;* modo, *m;* (means) medio, *m;* manera, *f;* (habit) costumbre, *f;* (behavior) conducta, *f,* modo de obrar, *f;* (line of business, etc.) ramo, *m;* (state) estado, *m,* condición, *f;* (course) curso, *m;* (respect) punto de vista, *m;* (particular kind) género, *m;* (scale) escala, *f.* **a long way off,** a gran distancia, a lo lejos. **a short way off,** a poca distancia, no muy lejos. **by way of,** pasando por; por vía de; como; por medio de; a modo de. **by the way,** de paso; durante el viaje; durante la travesía; a propósito, entre paréntesis. **in a small way,** en pequeña escala. **in a way,** hasta cierto punto; desde cierto punto de vista. **in many ways,** de muchos modos; por muchas cosas. **in no way,** de ningún modo; nada. **in the way,** en el medio. **in the way of,** en cuanto a, tocante a; en materia de. **I went out of my way to,** Dejé el camino para; Me di la molestia de. **Is this the way to . . . ?** ¿Es este el camino a . . . ? **Make way!** ¡Calle! ¡Vía! **Milky Way,** vía láctea, *f.* **on the way,** en camino; al paso; durante el viaje. **out of the way,** puesto a un lado; arrinconado; apartado, alejado; (imprisoned) en prisión; fuera del camino; remoto; (unusual) original. **over the way,** en frente; al otro lado (de la calle, etc.). **right of w.,** derecho de paso, *m.* **The ship left on its way to . . . ,** El barco zarpó con rumbo a . . . **the Way of the Cross,** vía crucis, *f.* **This way!** ¡Por aquí! De este modo, Así. **this way and that,** en todas direcciones, por todos lados. **"This way to . . . ,"** «Dirección a . . . » A . . . **under way,** en camino; en marcha; en preparación. **to bar the way,** cerrar el paso. **to be in the way,** estorbar. **to be out of the way of doing,** haber perdido la costumbre de hacer (algo). **to clear the way,** abrir paso, abrir calle; *fig* preparar el terreno. **to force one's way through,** abrirse paso por. **to find a way,** encontrar un camino; *fig* encontrar medios. **to find one's way,** hallar el camino; orientarse. **to get into the way of,** contraer la costumbre de. **to get under way,** *naut* zarpar, hacerse a la vela; ponerse en marcha. **to give way,** ceder; (break) romper. **to go a long way,** ir lejos; contribuir mucho (a). **to have one's own way,** salir con la suya. **to keep out of the way,** *vt* and *vi* esconder(se); mantener(se) alejado; mantener(se) apartado. **to lose one's way,** perder el camino; desorientarse; *fig* extraviarse. **to make one's way,** abrirse paso. **to make one's way down,** bajar. **to make one's way round,** dar la vuelta a. **to make one's way up,** subir. **to make way,** hacer lugar; hacer sitio; dar paso (a). **to pay one's way,** ganarse la vida; pagar lo que se debe. **to prepare the way for,** preparar el terreno para. **to put out of the way,** poner a un lado; apartar; (kill) matar; (imprison) poner en la cárcel; hacer cautivo (a). **to see one's way,** poder ver el camino; poder orientarse; ver el modo de hacer algo; ver cómo se puede hacer algo. **ways and means,** medios y arbitrios, *m pl.* **way back,** camino de regreso, *m;* vuelta, *f.* **way down,** bajada, *f.* **way in,** entrada, *f.* **way out,** salida, *f.* **way round,** camino alrededor, *m;* solución, *f;* modo de evitar . . . , *m.* **way through,** paso, *m.* **way up,** subida, *f*

wayfarer *n* transeúnte, *mf;* viajero (-ra)

waylay *vt* asechar, salir al paso (de)

wayside *n* borde del camino, *m.* a (of flowers) silvestre; (by the side of the road) en la carretera

wayward *a* caprichoso; desobediente; voluntarioso; travieso; rebelde

waywardness *n* desobediencia, indocilidad, *f;* voluntariedad, *f;* travesura, *f;* rebeldía, *f*

we *pron* nosotros, *m pl;* nosotras, *f pl,* (Usually omitted except for emphasis or for clarity.) **We are in the garden,** Estamos en el jardín. **We have come, but they are not here,** Nosotros hemos venido pero ellos no están aquí

weak *a* débil; flojo; frágil; delicado; (insecure) inseguro; (of arguments) poco convincente; (of prices, markets, etc.) flojo, en baja; (sickly) *Lat. Am.* farruto, *Central America, Mexico* fifiriche. **w.-eyed,** de vista floja. **w.-kneed,** débil de rodillas; *fig* sin voluntad. **w.-minded,** sin carácter; pusilánime; **w. spot,** debilidad, *f;* flaco, *m;* lado débil, *m;* desventaja, *f*

weaken *vt* debilitar; (diminish) disminuir. *vi* debilitarse; flaquear, desfallecer; (give way) ceder

weakening *n* debilitación, *f.* a debilitante; enervante

weaker *a comp* más débil. **the w. sex,** el sexo débil

weakling *n* ser delicado, *m,* persona débil, *f;* cobarde, *m; inf* alfeñique, *m*

weakly *a* enfermizo, delicado, enclenque. *adv* débilmente

weakness *n* debilidad, *f;* imperfección, *f*

weal *n* bienestar, *m;* prosperidad, *f;* (blow) verdugo, *m*

wealth *n* riqueza, *f;* abundancia, *f;* bienes, *m pl*

wealthy *a* rico, adinerado, acaudalado; abundante (en)

wean *vt* destetar, ablactar; separar (de); privar (de); enajenar el afecto de; (of ideas) desaferrar (de)

weaning *n* ablactación, *f,* destete, *m*

weapon *n* arma, *f;* pl **weapons,** (zool, bot) medios de defensa, *m pl.* **steel w.,** arma blanca, *f*

wear *n* uso, *m;* gasto, *m;* deterioro, *m;* (fashion) moda, boga, *f.* **for hard w.,** para todo uso. **for one's own w.,** para su propio uso. **for evening w.,** para llevar de noche. **for summer w.,** para llevar en verano. **w. and tear,** uso y desgaste, *m;* deterioro natural, *m*

wear *vt* llevar; llevar puesto; traer; usar; (have) tener; (exhibit) mostrar; (be clad in) vestir; (waste) gastar; deteriorar; (make) hacer; (exhaust) agotar, cansar, consumir. *vi* (last) durar; (of persons) conservar(se); (of time) correr; avanzar. **She wears well,** Está bien conservada. **to w. one's heart on one's sleeve,** tener el corazón en la mano. **to w. the trousers,** *fig inf* llevar los pantalones. **to w. well,** durar mucho. **to w. away,** *vt* gastar, roer; (rub out) borrar; consumir. *vi* (of time) pasar lentamente, transcurrir despacio. **to w. down,** gastar; consumir; reducir; agotar las fuerzas de; destruir; (tire) fatigar. **to w. off,** *vt* destruir; borrar. *vi* quitarse; borrarse; *fig* desaparecer, pasar. **to w. on,** (of time) transcurrir, correr, pasar. **to w. out,** *vt* usar; romper con el uso; consumir, acabar con; (exhaust) agotar; (tire) rendir. *vi* usarse; romperse con el uso; consumirse

weariness *n* cansancio, *m,* fatiga, lasitud, *f;* aburrimiento *m;* aversión, repugnancia, *f*

wearing *n* uso, *m;* desgaste, *m.* a (tiring) agotador; cansado. **w. apparel,** ropa, *f*

wearisome *a* cansado; laborioso; aburrido, tedioso, pesado

weary *a* cansado, fatigado; aburrido; hastiado; impaciente; tedioso, enfadoso. *vt* cansar, fatigar; aburrir; hastiar; molestar. *vi* cansarse, fatigarse; aburrirse. **to w. for,** anhelar, suspirar por; (miss) echar de menos (a). **to w. of,** aburrirse de; (things) impacientarse de; (people) impacientarse con

weasel *n* comadreja, *f*

weather *n* tiempo, *m;* intemperie, *f;* (storm) tempestad, *f.* a *naut* del lado del viento; de barlovento. *vt* (of rain, etc.) desgastar; curtir; secar al aire; *naut* pasar a barlovento; (bear) aguantar, capear;

(survive) sobrevivir a; luchar con. *vi* curtirse a la intemperie. **Andrew is a little under the w.,** Andrés está algo destemplado; (with drink) Andrés tiene una mona; (depressed) Andrés está melancólico. **to be bad (good) w.,** hacer mal (buen) tiempo. **What is the w. like?** ¿Qué tiempo hace? ¿Cómo está el tiempo? **w.-beaten,** curtido por la intemperie. **w. chart,** carta meteorológica, *f.* **conditions,** condiciones meteorológicas, *f pl.* **w. forecast,** pronóstico del tiempo, *m.* **w.-hardened,** endurecido a la intemperie. **w. prophet,** meteorologista, *mf.* **w. report,** boletín meteorológico, *m.* **w.-worn,** gastado por la intemperie; curtido por la intemperie

weathercock *n* veleta, *f*

weather-resistant *a* resistente a la intemperie

weave *vt* tejer; trenzar; entrelazar; *fig* tejer. *vi* tejer. *n* tejido, *m*; textura, *f*

weaver *n* tejedor (-ra)

weaving *n* tejido, *m*; tejeduría, *f.* **w. machine,** telar, *m*

web *n* tejido, *m*; tela, *f*; (network) red, *f*; (spider's) telaraña, *f*; (of a feather) barba, *f*; (of birds, etc.) membrana interdigital, *f*; (of intrigue) red, *f*; (snarl) lazo, *m*, trampa, *f.* **web-foot,** pie palmado, *m.* **web-footed,** palmípedo.

wed *vt* casarse con; (join in marriage, cause to marry) casar; *fig* unir. *vi* estar casado; casarse

wedded *a* casado; matrimonial, conyugal; *fig* unido (a); aficionado (a), entusiasta (de), devoto (de); aferrado (a). **to be w. to one's own opinion,** estar aferrado a su propia opinión

wedding *n* boda, *f*, casamiento, *m*; (with golden, etc.) bodas, *f pl*; (union) enlace, *m*, a de boda, nupcial, matrimonial, conyugal; de novios, de la novia. **golden w.,** bodas de oro, *f pl.* **silver w.,** bodas de plata, *f pl.* **w. bouquet,** ramo de la novia, *m.* **w.-breakfast,** banquete de bodas, *m.* **w.-cake,** torta de la boda, *f*, pan de la boda, *m.* **w.-day,** día de la boda, *m.* **w.-march,** marcha nupcial, *f.* **w.-present,** regalo de boda, regalo de la boda, *m.* **w.-ring,** anillo de la boda, *m*, Lat. Am. argolla *f.* **w. trip,** viaje de novios, *m*

wedge *n* cuña, *f*; (under a wheel) calza, alzaprima, *f*; *mil* cuña, mella, *f*; (of cheese) pedazo, *m.* *vt* acuñar, meter cuñas; (a wheel) calzar; (fix) sujetar. **to be the thin end of the w.,** ser el principio, ser el primer paso. **to drive a w.,** *mil* hacer mella, practicar una cuña. **to w. oneself in,** introducirse con dificultad (en). **w.-shaped,** cuneiforme

wedlock *n* matrimonio, *m*

Wednesday *n* miércoles, *m*

wee *a* pequeñito, chiquito. **a wee bit,** un poquito

weed *n* mala hierba, *f*; tabaco, *m*; (cigar)

cigarro, *m*; (person) madeja, *f*; (fig evil) cizaña, *f.* *vt* carpir, desherbar, sachar, sallar, escardar. *Lat. Am.* desmalezar; *fig* extirpar, arrancar. **w.-grown,** cubierto de malas hierbas. **to w. out,** extirpar; quitar

weedy *a* lleno de malas hierbas; *fig* raquítico

week *n* semana, *f.* **in a w.,** de hoy en ocho (días); en una semana; después de una semana. **once a w.,** una vez por semana. **a w. ago,** hace una semana. **a w. later** *Lat. Am.* a la semana. **Michael will come a w. from today,** Miguel llegará hoy en ocho. **w. in, w. out,** semana tras semana. **w.-day,** día de trabajo, día laborable, día de la semana que no sea el domingo. **on weekdays,** entre semana, *m.* **w.-end,** fin de semana, *m.* **w.-end case,** saco de noche, *m*

weekly *a* semanal, semanario; de cada semana. *adv* semanalmente, cada semana. *n* semanario, *m*, revista semanal, *f*

weep *vt and vi* llorar. **to w. for,** (a person) llorar (a); (on account of) llorar por; (with happiness, etc.) llorar de. **They wept for joy,** Lloraron de alegría

weevil *n* gorgojo, *m*

weigh *vt* pesar; (consider) considerar, ponderar, tomar en cuenta; comparar; (the anchor) levar. *vi* pesar; ser de importancia. **to w. anchor,** zarpar, levar el ancla, hacerse a la vela. **to w. down,** pesar sobre; sobrecargar; hacer inclinarse bajo; *fig* agobiar. **to be weighed down,** hundirse por su propio peso; *fig* estar agobiado. **to w. out,** pesar. **to w. with,** influir en; *fig* influir con. **w.-bridge,** báscula, *f*

weight *n* peso, *m*; (heaviness) pesantez, *f*; cargo, *m*; (of a clock and as part of a system) pesa, *f*; *fig* peso, *m*, importancia, *f.* *vt* cargar; (a stick) emplomar; aumentar el peso (de); poner un peso (a). **gross w.,** peso bruto, *m.* **heavy w.,** peso pesado, *m.* **light w.,** peso ligero, *m.* **middle w.,** peso medio, *m.* **net w.,** peso neto, *m.* **to lose w.,** adelgazar. **loss of w.,** (of a person) adelgazamiento, *m.* **to put on w.,** cobrar carnes, hacerse más gordo. **to put the w.,** *sport* lanzar el peso. **to throw one's w. about,** *inf* darse importancia. **to try the w. of,** sopesar. **weights and measures,** pesas y medidas, *f pl.* **weightlifting,** halterofilia, *f*

weighty *a* pesado; (influential) influyente; importante, de peso; grave

weird *a* misterioso, sobrenatural; fantástico; mágico; (queer) raro, extraño. **the W. Sisters,** las Parcas

welcome *a* bienvenido; (pleasant) grato, agradable. *n* bienvenida, *f*; buena acogida, *f*; (reception) acogida, *f.* *vt* dar la bienvenida (a); acoger con alegría, acoger con entusiasmo; agasajar, festejar; (receive) acoger, recibir; recibir con gusto. **W.!** ¡Bienvenido! **to bid w.,** dar la bienvenida (a). **You are w.,** Estás bienvenido. **You are w. to it,** Está a su disposición

welcoming *a* acogedor, cordial, amistoso

weld *vt* soldar; combinar; unificar

welder *n* soldador, *m*

welding *n* soldadura, *f*; unión, fusión, *f*

welfare *n* bienestar, bien, *m*; (health) salud, *f*; prosperidad, *f*; intereses, *m pl.* **w. state,** estado benefactor, estado de beneficencia, estado socializante, *m.* **w. work,** trabajo social, *m*

well *a* bien; bien de salud; bueno; conveniente; (advantageous) provechoso; favorable; (happy) feliz; (healed) curado; (recovered) repuesto. **I am very w.,** Estoy muy bien. **to get w.,** ponerse bien. **to make w.,** curar. **w. enough,** bastante bien

well *adv* bien; (very) muy; favorablemente; convenientemente; (easily) sin dificultad. **as w.,** también. **as w. as,** tan bien como; además de. **That is all very w. but . . . ,** Todo eso está muy bien pero . . . **to be w. up in,** estar versado en. **to get on w. with,** llevarse bien con. **Very w.!** ¡Está bien! Muy bien. **w. and good,** bien está. **w. now,** ahora bien. **w. then,** conque; pues bien. **w.-advised,** bien aconsejado; prudente. **w.-aimed,** certero. **w.-appointed,** bien provisto; (furnished) bien amueblado. **w.-attended,** concurrido. **w.-balanced,** bien equilibrado. **w.-behaved,** bien educado; (of animals) manso. **w.-being,** bienestar, *m*; felicidad, *f*. **w.-born,** bien nacido, de buena familia. **w.-bred,** bien criado, bien educado; (of animals) de pura raza. **w.-chosen,** bien escogido. **w.-defined,** bien definido. **w.-deserved,** bien merecido. **w.-disposed,** bien dispuesto; favorable; bien intencionado. **w.-doing,** *n* el obrar bien; obras de caridad, *f pl*, a bondadoso, caritativo. **w.-done,** a bien hecho. *interj* ¡bravo! **w.-educated,** instruido, culto. **w.-favored,** guapo, de buen parecer. **w.-founded,** bien fundado. **w.-groomed,** elegante. **w.-grounded,** bien fundado; bien instruido. **w.-informed,** instruido; culto, ilustrado. **w.-intentioned,** bien intencionado. **w.-known,** bien conocido, notorio, *Lat. Am.* connotado. **w.-meaning,** bien intencionado. **w.-modulated,** armonioso. **w.-off,** acomodado, adinerado; feliz. **w.-read,** culto, instruido. **w.-shaped,** bien hecho; bien formado. **w.-shaped nose,** nariz perfilada, *f*. **w.-spent,** bien empleado. **w.-spoken,** bien hablado; bien dicho. **w.-stocked,** bien provisto. **w.-suited,** apropiado. **w.-timed,** oportuno. **w.-to-do,** acomodado, rico. **w.-wisher,** amigo (-ga). **w.-worn,** raído; (of paths) trillado

well *n* pozo, *m*; (of a stair) caja, *f*; cañón de escalera, *m*; (fountain) fuente, *f*, ma-

nantial, *m*; (of a fishing boat) vivar, *m*; (of a ship) sentina, *f*. **w.-sinker,** pocero, *m*

well *vi* chorrear, manar, brotar, fluir

Welsh *a* galés, de Gales. *n* (language) galés, *m*. **the W.,** los galeses

Welshman *n* galés, *m*

Welshwoman *n* galesa, *f*

welt *n* (of shoe) vira, *f*, cerquillo, *m*; (in knitting) ribete, *m*; (weal) verdugo, *m*

Weltanschauung *n* cosmovisión, postura de vida, *f*

welter *vi* revolcarse; bañarse (en), nadar (en). *n* confusión, *f*, tumulto, *m*; mezcla, *f*. **w.-weight,** peso welter, *m*

wench *n* mozuela, muchacha, *f*

wend *vt* dirigir, encaminar. *vi* ir. **to w. one's way,** dirigir sus pasos, seguir su camino

west *n* oeste, *m*; poniente, *m*; occidente, *m. a* del oeste; occidental. *adv* hacia el oeste, a poniente; al occidente. **W. Indian,** de las Antillas, de las Indias Occidentales. **w.-north-w.,** oesnorueste, *m.* **w.-south-w.,** oessudueste, *m.* **w. wind,** viento del oeste, poniente, *m*

westerly *a* del oeste; hacia el oeste; occidental

western *a* occidental; del oeste. *n* (novel) novela caballista, *f*; (film) película del oeste, *f*

Western Hemispheric americano

westernized *a* influido por el occidente

westernmost *a* más al oeste

West Indies Indias Occidentales, *f pl*

westward *a* que está al oeste. *adv* hacia el oeste; hacia el occidente

wet *a* mojado; húmedo; (rainy) lluvioso. *vt* mojar; humedecer. *n* (rain) lluvia, *f*. **"Mind the wet paint!"** «¡Cuidado, recién pintado!» **to be wet,** estar mojado; (of the weather) llover. **to get wet,** mojarse. **wet blanket,** *fig* aguafiestas, *mf* **wet through,** (of persons) calado, hecho una sopa. **wet-nurse,** nodriza, *Lat. Am.* criandera, *f*

whack *n* golpe, *m*; (try) tentativa, *f*; (portion) porción, parte, *f*. *vt* golpear, aporrear, pegar

whale *n* ballena, *f*. **sperm w.,** cachalote, *m*. **w.-oil,** aceite de ballena, *m*

wharf *n* muelle, embarcadero, descargadero, *m*, *vt* amarrar al muelle

what *a pron* (interrogative and exclamatory) qué; cómo; (relative) que; el que, la que, *f*; lo que, *neut*; los que, *m pl*; las que, *f pl*; (which) que, cuál, *mf*; cuáles, *mf pl*; (how many) cuantos, *m pl*; cuantas, *f pl*; (interrogative and exclamatory) cuántos, *m pl*; cuántas, *f pl*; (how much, interrogative and exclamatory) cuánto, *m*; cuánta, *f*. **And w. not,** Y qué sé yo qué más. **Make w. changes you will,** Haz los cambios que quieras. **W. confidence he had . . . ,** La confianza que tenía . . . **W. is this called?** ¿Cómo

se llama esto? **W. did they go there for?**
¿Por qué fueron? **W. do you take me
for?** ¿Por quién me tomas? **That was
not w. he said,** No fue eso lo que dijo. **to
know what w.,** saber cuántas son
cinco. **You have heard the latest news,
w.?** Has oído las últimas noticias, ¿verdad? **W. a pity!** ¡Qué lástima! **W., do you
really believe it?** ¿Lo crees de veras? **W.
else?** ¿Qué más? **W. for?** ¿Para qué?
what's-his-name, fulano (-na) de tal, *m.*
W. ho! ¡Hola! **W. if . . . ?** ¿Qué será si
. . . ? **W. is the matter?** ¿Qué pasa? ¿Qué
hay? **w. though . . . ,** aun cuando . . . ;
¿Qué importa qué? **w. with one thing,
w. with another,** entre una cosa y otra.
What's more, . . . Es más, . . .

whatever *a pron* cuanto; todo lo que;
cualquier cosa que; cualquier. **W. sacrifice is necessary,** Cualquier sacrificio
que sea necesario. **W. I have is yours,**
Todo lo que tenga es vuestro. **W. happens,** Venga lo que venga. **It is of no use
w.,** No sirve absolutamente para nada

wheal *n.* See **weal**

wheat *n* trigo, *m.* a. de trigo. **summer w.,**
trigo tremesino, *m.* **whole w.,** a. de trigo
entero. **w.-ear,** espiga de trigo, *f.*
w.-field, trigal, *m.* **w.-sheaf,** gavilla de
trigo, *f.*

wheedle *vt* lagotear, engatusar, *Lat. Am.
also* engaratusar; (flatter) halagar; (with
out) sacar con mimos

wheedling *a* zalamero, mimoso; marrullero. *n* lagotería, *f,* mimos, *m pl;* (flattery)
halagos, *m pl;* marrullería, *f*

wheel *n* rueda, *f;* (bicycle) bicicleta, *f;* (for
steering a ship) timón, *m;* rueda del
timón, *f;* (for steering a car) volante, *m;*
(for spinning) rueca, *f;* (potter's) rueda de
alfarero, *f;* (of birds) vuelo, *m;* (turn)
vuelta, *f; mil* conversión, *f.* **Catherine w.,**
(firework) rueda de Santa Catalina, *f.*
back w., rueda trasera, *f.* **front w.,** rueda
delantera, *f.* **to break on the w.,** enrodar. **to go on wheels,** ir en ruedas; *fig* ir
viento en popa. **to take the w.,** (in a ship)
tomar el timón; tomar el volante. **w. of
fortune,** rueda de la fortuna, *f.* **w.-chair,**
silla de ruedas, *f.* **w.-house,** timonera, *f.*
w.-mark, rodada, *f*

wheel *vt* hacer rodar; (push) empujar;
(drive) conducir; transportar; llevar; pasear; (turn) hacer girar; dar vueltas; ir en bicicleta. **to w. about,** cambiar
de frente; volverse; cambiar de rumbo

wheelbarrow *n* carretilla, *f*

wheeled *a* de . . . ruedas; con ruedas. **w.
chair,** silla de ruedas, *f*

wheeler-dealer *n Lat. Am.* ardilla, *f*

wheeze *vi* ser asmático, jadear, respirar
fatigosamente, resollar

wheezing *n* resuello, jadeo, *m;* respiración fatigada, *f*

whelp *n* cachorro (-rra). *vi* and *vt* parir

when *adv* cuando (interrogative,

cuándo); (as soon as) tan pronto como,
en cuanto; (meaning 'and then') y luego, y
entonces; (although) aunque. **I will see
you w. I return,** Te veré cuando vuelva.
**W. he came to see me he was already
ill,** Cuando vino a verme estaba enfermo
ya. **We returned a week ago, since w. I
have not been out,** Volvimos hace ocho
días y desde entonces no he salido. **Since
w.?** ¿Desde cuándo?

whence *adv* de donde (interrogative, de
dónde); a donde (interrogative a dónde);
por donde, de que; por lo que. **W. does
he come?** ¿De dónde viene? **W. comes
it that?** ¿Cómo es que . . . ?

whenever *adv* cuando quiera que, siempre que; cada vez que, todas las veces
que; cuando

where *adv pron* donde (interrogative,
dónde); en donde; en que (interrogative,
en qué); (to where with verbs of motion) a
donde (interrogative, a dónde); (from
where with verbs of motion) de donde (interrogative, de dónde). **W. are you going
to?** ¿A dónde va Vd.? **This is w. we get
out,** (of a bus, etc.) Nos apeamos aquí

whereabouts *adv* (interrogative) dónde;
(relative) donde. *n* paradero, *m*

whereas *conjunc* (inasmuch as) visto
que, ya que; (although) mientras (que)

whereat *adv* por lo cual; a lo cual

whereby *adv* cómo; por qué; por el cual,
con el cual

wherefore *adv* (why) por qué; por lo
cual. *n* porqué, *m*

wherein *adv* en donde (interrogative, en
dónde); en que (interrogative, en qué)

whereinto *adv* en donde; dentro del
cual; en lo cual

whereof *adv* de que; (whose) cuyo

whereon *adv* sobre que; en qué

whereto *adv* adonde; a lo que

whereupon *adv* dónde; sobre lo cual,
con lo cual; en consecuencia de lo cual

wherever *adv* dondequiera (que), en
cualquier sitio; adondequiera (que). **Sit
w. you like,** Siéntate donde te parezca
bien

wherewith *adv* con que (interrogative,
con qué)

wherewithal *n* lo necesario; dinero
necesario, *m*

whet *vt* (knives, etc.) afilar, amolar, aguzar; (curiosity, etc.) excitar, estimular

whether *conjunc* si; que; sea que, ya
que. **W. he will or no,** Que quiera, que no
quiera. **w. or not,** si o no

whetstone *n* afiladera, amoladera, piedra de amolar, *f*

whey *n* suero (de la leche), *m*

which *a* and *pron* cuál, *mf;* cuáles, *mf pl;*
que (interrogative, qué); el cual, *m;* la
cual, *f;* lo cual, *neut;* los cuales, *m pl;* las
cuales, *f pl;* el que, *m;* la que, *f;* lo que,
neut; los que, *m pl;* las que, *f pl;* (who)

quien. **all of w.**, todo lo cual, etc. **in w.**, en donde, en el que; donde. **the w.**, el cual, la cual, etc. **W. would you like?** ¿Cuál quieres? **The documents w. I have seen**, Los documentos que he visto. **W. way have we to go?** ¿Por dónde hemos de ir?

whichever a and pron cualquiera (que), mf; cualesquiera, mf pl; el que, m; la que, f; (of persons only) quienquiera (que), mf; quienesquiera (que), mf pl **Give me w. you like**, Dame el que quieras. **I shall take w. of you would like to come**, Me llevaré a cualquiera de Vds. que guste de venir

whiff n (of air) soplo, m; vaho, m; fragancia, f

while n rato, m; momento, m; tiempo, m. **after a w.**, al cabo de algún tiempo, después de algún tiempo. **a little w. ago**, hace poco. **all this w.**, en todo este tiempo. **at whiles**, a ratos, de vez en cuando. **between whiles**, de cuando en cuando; entre tanto. **It is worth your w. to do it**, Vale la pena de hacerse. **Mary smiled the w.**, María mientras tanto se sonreía. **once in a w.**, de vez en cuando; en ocasiones

while conjunc mientras (que); al (followed by an infinitive); al mismo tiempo que; a medida que; (although) aunque; si bien. **w. I was walking down the street**, mientras andaba por la calle, al andar yo por la calle. vt to w. (away), pasar, entretener. **to w. away the time**, pasar el rato

whim n capricho, antojo, m; manía, f; extravagancia, f; fantasía, f

whimper n quejido, sollozo, gemido, m, vi lloriquear, quejarse, sollozar, gemir

whimsical a antojadizo, caprichoso; fantástico

whine vi gimotear, lloriquear; quejarse

whining n gimoteo, lloriqueo, m; quejumbres, f pl. a que lloriquea; quejumbroso

whinny n relincho, hin, m, vi relinchar

whip vt azotar; pegar; cul batir; sew sobrecoser; (ropes, etc.) ligar; (defeat) vencer. vi moverse rápidamente. **to w. down**, vi bajar volando, bajar corriendo. vt arrebatar (de). **to w. in**, entrar precipitadamente (en), penetrar apresuradamente (en). **to w. off**, cazar a latigazos, despachar a golpes; (remove) quitar rápidamente; (persons) llevar corriendo, llevar aprisa. **to w. open**, abrir rápidamente. **to w. out**, vt (draw) sacar rápidamente; (utter) saltar diciendo (que); proferir. vi escabullirse, escapar, salir apresuradamente. **to w. round**, volverse de repente. **to w. up**, vt (horses, etc.) avivar con el látigo; (snatch) coger de repente agarrar; (gather) reunir. vi (mount) subir corriendo

whip n azote, zurriago, Lat. Am. chicote, m; (riding) látigo, m. **blow with a w.**, latigazo, m. **to have the w.-hand**, man-

dar, tener la sartén por el mango; tener la ventaja. **w.-cord**, tralla del látigo, f

whipping n paliza, f, vapuleo, azotamiento, m. **w. post**, picota, f. **w. top**, trompo, m, peonza, f

whirl n vuelta, f, giro, m; rotación, f; fig torbellino, m. vi girar; dar vueltas; (dance) bailar, danzar. vt hacer girar; dar vueltas (a); (carry) llevar rápidamente. **to w. along**, volar (por), pasar aprisa (por); dejar atrás los vientos, correr velozmente. **to w. past**, pasar volando (por); pasar como una exhalación. **to w. through**, atravesar rápidamente, cruzar volando

whirligig n perinola, f; (merry-go-round) tiovivo, m

whirlpool n vórtice, remolino, m; fig vorágine, f

whirlwind n torbellino, m, manga de viento, f

whirr n zumbido, m; (of wings) ruido (de las alas), m. vi girar; zumbar

whisk n cepillo, m; cul batidor, m; (movement) movimiento rápido, m. vt cul batir; (wag) menear, mover rápidamente; (with off, away) quitar rápidamente; sacudirse, arrebatar; (take away a person) llevarse (a). vi moverse rápidamente; andar rápidamente

whiskers n pl mostacho, m, patillas, barbas, f pl; (of a feline) bigotes, m pl

whisky n güisqui, m

whisper n cuchicheo, m; (rumour) voz, f; (of leaves, etc.) susurro, murmullo, m. vi and vt cuchichear, hablar al oído; (of leaves, etc.) susurrar; (of rumors) murmurar. **in a w.**, al oído, en un susurro

whisperer n cuchicheador (-ra) (gossip) murmurador (-ra)

whispering n cuchicheo, m; susurro, m; (gossip) murmurio, m. **w. gallery**, galería de los murmullos, f. inf sala de los secretos, f

whistle n (sound) silbido, silbo, m; (instrument) pito, silbato, m; inf gaznate, m. vi and vt silbar. **blast on the w.**, pitido, m. **to w. for**, llamar silbando; inf esperar sentado, buscar en vano

whit n pizca, f, bledo, m. **not a w.**, ni pizca

white a blanco; pálido; puro. n color blanco, blanco, m; (pigment) pintura blanca, f; (whiteness) blancura, f; (of egg) clara (del huevo), f; (person) blanco, m. **Elizabeth went w.**, Isabel se puso pálida. **the w.**, (billiards) la blanca. **the w. of the eye**, lo blanco del ojo. **w. ant**, hormiga blanca, termita, f. **w. cabbage**, repollo, m. **w. caps**, (of waves) cabrillas, f pl; (of mountains) picos blancos, m pl. **w. clover**, trébol blanco, m. **w. corpuscle**, glóbulo blanco, m. **w. currant**, grosella blanca, f. **w. elephant**, elefante (-ta) blanco (-ca). **w. ensign**, pabellón blanco, m. **w.-faced**, de cara pálida. **w. fish**, pescado blanco, *m.* **w. flag,** bandera blanca, *f.* **w.-haired,** de pelo blanco. **w. heat,** calor blanco, *m,* candencia, *f;* ardor, *m.* **w. horses,** cabrillas, palomas, *f pl.* **w.-hot,** incandescente. **W. House, the,** la Casa Blanca, *f.* **w. lead,** albayalde, *m.* **w. lie,** mentira inocente, mentira oficiosa, mentira piadosa, la mentirilla, *f.* **w. man,** blanco, hombre de raza blanca, *m.* **the white man's burden,** la misión sagrada de la civilización blanca, *f.* **w. meat,** carne blanca, pechuga, *f.* **w. paper,** libro blanco, *m.* **w. sauce,** salsa blanca, *f.* **w. slave,** víctima de la trata de blancas, *f.* **w. slavery,** trata de blancas, *f.* **w. sugar,** azúcar blanco, azúcar de flor, *m.* **w. woman,** mujer de raza blanca, *f*

whiten *vt* blanquear. *vi* blanquearse

whitewash *vt* blanquear, jalbegar, encalar; (*fig* of faults) disculpar, justificar

whither *adv* (interrogative) adónde; (with a clause) adonde

whithersoever *adv* adondequiera

whiting *n* blanco de España, *m;* blanco para los zapatos, *m;* (fish) pescadilla, *f,* merlango, *m*

whittle *n* navaja, *f. vt* cercenar, cortar; (sharpen) afilar, sacar punta (a); tallar; *fig* reducir. **to w. away, down,** *fig* reducir a nada

whizz *n* silbido, zumbido, *m, vi* silbar, zumbar

who *pron* (interrogative) quién, *mf;* quiénes, *mf pl;* (relative) quien, *mf;* quienes, *mf pl;* que; (in elliptical constructions the person that, etc.) el que, *m;* la que, *f;* los que, *m pl;* las que, *f pl*

whoa *interj* iso!

whoever *pron* quienquiera (que); cualquiera (que); quien. **Give it to w. you like,** Dáselo a quien te parezca bien

whole *a* (healthy) sano; (uninjured) ileso, entero; todo. *n* todo, *m;* total, *m;* totalidad, *f;* conjunto, *m.* **on the w.,** por regla general, en general; en conjunto. **the w. week,** la semana entera, toda la semana. **w.-hearted,** sincero, genuino; entusiasta. **w.-heartedly,** de todo corazón. **w.-heartedness,** sinceridad, *f;* entusiasmo, *m.* **w. length,** a de cuerpo entero. **w. number,** número entero, *m*

wholemeal *n* harina de trigo entero, *f,* a de trigo entero

wholeness *n* totalidad, *f;* integridad, *f;* todo, *m*

wholesale *a com* al por mayor; en grueso; *fig* general; en masa. *n* venta al por mayor, *f.* **w. price,** precio al por mayor, *m.* **w. trade,** comercio al por mayor, *m*

wholesaler *n* comerciante al por mayor, *mf* mercader de grueso, *m*

wholesome *a* sano; saludable; (edifying) edificante

wholly *adv* completamente, enteramente, totalmente; integralmente; del todo

whom *pron* quien; a quien, *mf;* a quienes, *mf pl;* (interrogative) a quién, *mf;* a quiénes, *mf pl;* al que, *m;* a la que, *f;* a los que, *m pl;* a las que, *f pl.* **from w.,** de quien; (interrogative) de quién. **the man w. you saw,** el hombre a quien viste

whoop *n* alarido, grito, *m;* estertor de la tos ferina, *m. vi* dar gritos, chillar; (whooping-cough) toser

whooping cough *n* tos ferina, coqueluche, *f*

whore *n* puta, ramera, *f, Lat. Am.* also araña, *f*

whorl *n* (of a shell) espira, *f; bot* verticilo, *m;* (of a spindle) tortera, *f*

whose *pron* cuyo, *m;* cuya, *f;* cuyos, *m pl;* cuyas, *f pl;* de quien, *mf;* de quienes, *mf pl;* (interrogative) de quién, de quiénes; **W. daughter is she?** ¿De quién es ella la hija? **This is the writer w. name I always forget,** Este es el autor cuyo nombre siempre olvido

whosoever *pron.* See **whoever**

why *adv* (interrogative) por qué; (on account of which) por el cual, *m;* por la cual, *f;* por lo cual, *neut;* por los cuales, *m pl;* por las cuales, *f pl;* (how) cómo. *n* ni porqué, *m, interj* ¡qué!; ¡cómo!; ¡toma!; si. **not to know the why or wherefore,** no saber ni el porqué ni el cómo, no saber ni el qué ni el por qué. **Why! I have just come,** ¡Si no hago más de llegar! **Why not?** ¿Por qué no? ¡Cómo no!

wick *n* mecha, torcida, *f*

wicked *a* malo; malvado, perverso; pecaminoso; malicioso; (mischievous) travieso

wickedness *n* maldad, *f;* perversidad, *f;* pecado, *m;* (mischievousness) travesura, *f*

wicker *n* mimbre, *m,* a de mimbre

wicket *n* postigo, portillo, *m;* (half-door) media puerta, *f;* (at cricket) meta, *f.* **w.-keeper,** guardameta, *m*

wide *a* ancho; (in measurements) de ancho; vasto; extenso; grande; amplio; (loose) holgado; (distant) lejos; liberal; general, comprensivo. *adv* lejos; completamente. **far and w.,** por todas partes. **to be too w.,** ser muy ancho; estar muy ancho; (of garments) venir muy ancho. **two feet w.,** dos pies de ancho. **w.-awake,** muy despierto; despabilado; vigilante. **w.-eyed,** con los ojos muy abiertos; asombrado. **w.-open,** abierto de par en par

widely *adv* extensamente; generalmente; (very) muy

widen *vt* ensanchar; extender. *vi* ensancharse; extenderse

widespread *a* universal, generalizado; extenso; esparcido. **to become w.,** generalizarse

widow *n* viuda, *f. vt* dejar viuda; dejar

viudo; *fig* privar. **to be a grass w.,** estar viuda. **to become a w.,** enviudar, perder al esposo. **widow's pension,** viudedad, *f.* **widow's weeds,** luto de viuda, *m*

widowed a viudo

widower *n* viudo, *m.* **to become a w.,** perder a la esposa, enviudar

widowerhood, widowhood *n* viudez, *f*

width *n* anchura, *f;* (of cloth) ancho, *m;* (of mind) liberalismo, *m.* **double w.,** (cloth) doble ancho, *m*

wield *vt* (a scepter) empuñar; (power, etc.) ejercer; (a pen, sword) manejar

wife *n* esposa, mujer, *f;* mujer, *f;* comadre, *f.* **husband and w.,** los cónyuges, los esposos. **old wives' tale,** cuento de viejas, *m.* **The Merry Wives of Windsor,** Las alegres comadres de Windsor. **to take to w.,** contraer matrimonio con, tomar como esposa (a)

wig *n* peluca, *f;* (hair) cabellera, *f.* **top wig,** peluquín, *m.* **wigmaker,** peluquero, *m*

wigwam *n* tienda de indios, *f*

wild a (of animals, men, land) salvaje; (barren) desierto, yermo; (mountainous) riscoso, montañoso; (of plants, birds) silvestre; montés; (disarranged) en desorden, desarreglado; (complete) absoluto, completo; (dissipated) disipado, vicioso; (foolish) alocado; (of the sea) bravío; (of weather, etc.) borrascoso; (mad with delight, etc.) loco; (frantic, mad) frenético, loco; (with 'talk,' etc.) extravagante, insensato, desatinado; (shy) arisco; (incoherent) inconexo, incoherente; (frightened) alarmado, espantado; (wilful) travieso, indomable. **in tierra virgen,** *f;* desierto, *m;* soledad, *f.* **It made me w.,** (angry) Me hizo rabiar. **to run w.,** volver al estado silvestre; (of persons) llevar una vida de salvajes; volverse loco. **to shoot w.,** errar el tiro. **to spread like w. fire,** propagarse como el fuego. **w. beast,** fiera, *f.* **w. boar,** jabalí, *m.* **w. cat,** gato montés, *Lat. Am.* lince, *m.* **w. duck,** pato silvestre, *m.* **w. goat,** cabra montesa, *f.* **w.-goose chase,** caza infructuosa, *f;* empresa quimérica, *f.* **w. oats,** avenas locas, *f pl; fig* indiscreciones de la juventud, *f pl.* **to sow one's w. oats,** andarse a la flor del berro

wilderness *n* desierto, *m;* yermo, páramo, despoblado, *m;* soledad, *f;* (jungle) selva, *f;* (maze) laberinto, *m;* infinidad, *f*

wildly *adv* en un estado salvaje; sin cultivo; (rashly) desatinadamente; sin reflexión, sin pensar; (incoherently) incoherentemente; (stupidly) of looking, etc.) tontamente; (in panic) con ojos espantados, con terror en los ojos, alarmado

wildness *n* salvajez, *f;* estado silvestre, *m;* naturaleza silvestre, *f;* (ferocity) ferocidad, *f;* (of the wind, sea) braveza, *f;* (of the wind) violencia, *f;* (impetuosity) im-

petuosidad, *f;* (of statements, etc.) extravagancia, *f;* (incoherence) incoherencia, *f;* (disorder) desorden, *m;* (wilfulness, of children) travesuras, *f pl;* (of the expression) gesto espantado, *m*

wile *n* estratagema, *f,* engaño, *m,* ardid, *f*

will *n* voluntad, *f;* albedrío, *m;* (wish) deseo, *m;* (pleasure) discreción, *f,* placer, *m;* (legal document) testamento, *m.* **against my w.,** contra mi voluntad. **at w.,** a voluntad; a gusto; a discreción. **free w.,** libre albedrío, *m.* **of one's own free w.,** por su propia voluntad. **iron w.,** voluntad de hierro, *f.* **last w. and testament,** última disposición, última voluntad, *f.* **to do with a w.,** hacer con toda el alma, hacer con entusiasmo. **to make one's w.,** otorgar (hacer) su testamento. **w.-power,** fuerza de voluntad, *f*

willing a dispuesto, inclinado; (serviceable) servicial; deseoso; espontáneo; complaciente; gustoso; (willingly) de buena gana. **to be w.,** estar dispuesto (a), querer; consentir (en)

willingly *adv* de buena gana, con gusto

willingness *n* buena voluntad, *f;* deseo de servir, *m;* complacencia, *f;* (consent) consentimiento, *m*

will-o'-the-wisp *n* fuego fatuo, *m*

willow *n* sauce, *m.* **weeping w.,** sauce llorón, *m.* **w.-pattern china,** porcelana de estilo chino, *f.* **w. tree,** sauce, *m*

willy nilly *adv* de buen o mal grado, mal que bien

wilt *vi* (of plants) marchitarse, secarse; *fig* languidecer; ajarse. *vt* marchitar; *fig* ajar; hacer languidecer

wily a astuto, chuzón

win *vt* ganar; (reach) alcanzar, lograr; (a victory, etc.) llevarse; conquistar. *vi* ganar; triunfar, *n* triunfo, *m.* **to win back,** volver a ganar; recobrar

wince *vi* retroceder, recular; (flinch) quejarse; (of a horse) respingar. *n* respingo, *m.* **without wincing,** sin quejarse; estoicamente

winch *n* cabria, *f;* (handle) manubrio, *m*

wind *n* viento, *m;* aire, *m;* (flatulence) flatulencia, *f;* (breath) respiración, *f,* aliento, *m;* (idle talk) paja, *f.* **breath of w.,** soplo de viento, *m.* **following w.,** viento en popa, *m.* **high w.,** viento alto, viento fuerte, *m.* **land w.,** viento terrenal, *m.* **It's an ill w. that blows nobody good,** No hay mal que por bien no venga. **There is something in the w.,** Hay algo en el aire, Se trama algo. **to get w. of,** husmear. **to sail before the w.,** navegar de viento en popa. **The w. stiffened,** Refrescó el viento. **You took the w. out of his sails,** Le deshinchaste las velas. **w.-instrument,** instrumento de viento, *m.* **w.-proof,** a prueba del viento. **w.-swept,** expuesto a todos los vientos. **w. storm,** ventarrón, *m*

wind *vi* serpentear; desfilar lentamente;

torcerse. *vt* (turn) dar vueltas (a); (a handle) manejar, mover; (a watch) dar cuerda (a); (wool, etc.) devanar, ovillar; (wrap) envolver; (of arms, embrace) rodear (con); (a horn) tocar. **to w. off,** devanar; desenrollar. **to w. round,** (wrap) envolver; (skirt) rodear; (embrace) ceñir con (los brazos); (pass by) pasar por; deslizarse por; (of snakes) enroscarse. **to w. up,** (a watch) dar cuerda (a); (thread) devanar; (conclude) concluir; *com* liquidar; (excite) agitar, emocionar

windbag *n* pandero, *m*, sacamuelas, *mf*

windfall *n* fruta caída del árbol, *f*; (good luck) breva, *f*; ganancia inesperada, lotería, *f*

winding *a* tortuoso; (e.g., road) sinuoso; serpentino; en espiral. *n* tortuosidad, *f*; meandro, recoveco, *m*, vuelta, curva, *f*. **w. sheet,** mortaja, *f*, sudario, *m*. **w. stair,** escalera de caracol, *f*. **w.-up,** conclusión, *f*; *com* liquidación, *f*

windmill *n* molino de viento, *m*

window *n* ventana, *f*; (of a shop) escaparate, *Mexico* aparador, *m*; (in a train, car, bank, etc.) ventanilla, *f*; (booking office) taquilla, *f*; (of a church) vidriera, *f*. **casement w.,** ventana, *f*. **sash w.,** ventana de guillotina, *f*. **small w.,** ventanilla, *f*. **stained glass w.,** vidriera, *f*. **to lean out of the w.,** asomarse a la ventana. **to look out of the w.,** mirar por la ventana. **w. blind,** (Venetian) persiana, *f*; transparente, *m*; (against the sun) toldo, *m*. **w.-dresser,** decorador (-ra) de escaparates. **w. frame,** marco de ventana, *m*. **w.-pane,** cristal (de ventana), *m*. **w.-shutter,** contraventana, *f*. **w.-sill,** repisa de la ventana, *f*, alféizar, *m*

windpipe *n* tráquea, *f*

windscreen *n* parabrisas, guardabrisa, *m*. **w.-wiper,** limpiaparabrisas, limpiavidrios, *m*

windward *n* barlovento, *m*. *a* de barlovento. *adv* a barlovento

windy *a* ventoso; expuesto al viento; (of style) hinchado, pomposo. **It is w.,** Hace viento

wine *n* vino, *m*; zumo fermentado (de algunas frutas), *m*. *a* de vino; de vinos; para vino. **in w.,** *cul* en vino; (drunk) ebrio, borracho. **heavy w.,** vino fuerte, *m*. **light w.,** vino ligero, *m*. **local w.,** vino del país, *m*, **matured w.,** vino generoso, *m*. **red w.,** vino tinto, *m*. **thin w.,** vinillo, *m*. **white w.,** vino blanco, *m*. **w.-cellar,** bodega, cueva, *f*. **w.-colored,** de color de vino. **w.-cooler,** cubo para enfriar vinos, *m*. **w. country,** tierra de vino, *f*. **w. decanter,** garrafa para vino, *f*. **w.-grower,** vinicultor (-ra). **w.-growing,** *n* vinicultura, *f*. *a* vinícola. **w. lees,** zupia, *f*. **w. merchant,** comerciante en vinos, *mf*. vinatero, *m*. **w.-press,** lagar, *m*. **w.-taster,** catavinos, *m*. **w. waiter,** bodeguero, *m*

wineskin *n* bota, *f*, odre, pellejo, *m*

wing *n* (of a bird and *zool, arch, aer, mil, bot*) ala, *f*; (flight) vuelo, *m*; *theat* bastidor, *m*; *fig* protección, *f*. *vt* dar alas (a); llevar sobre las alas; (wound) herir en el ala; herir en el brazo; volar por. *vi* volar. **beating of wings,** batir de alas, aleteo, *m*. **in the wings,** *theat* entre bastidores. **on the w.,** al vuelo. **to clip a (person's) wings,** cortar (or quebrar) las alas (a). **under his w.,** bajo su protección. **w.-case,** élitro (de un insecto), *m*. **w.-span,** (*zool* and *aer*) envergadura, *f*. **w.-spread,** extensión del ala, *f*. **w.-tip,** punta del ala, *f*

wink *vi* (blink) pestañear; (as a signal, etc.) guiñar; (of stars, etc.) titilar, parpadear, centellear. *vt* guiñar (el ojo). *n* pestañeo, *m*; guiño, *m*. **not to sleep a w.,** no pegar los ojos. **to take forty winks,** echar una siesta. **to w. at,** guiñar el ojo (a); (ignore) hacer la vista gorda

winner *n* ganador (-ra); vencedor (-ra)

winning *a* ganador; vencedor; (attractive) encantador. *n* ganancia, *f*. **w. number,** número galardonado, número premiado, número vencedor, *m*. **w.-post,** meta, *f*. **w. side,** *sport* equipo vencedor, *m*; (politics, etc.) partido vencedor, *m*

winnings *n* ganancias, *f pl*

winnow *vt* aventar, abalear; *fig* separar

winsome *a* sandunguero; dulce, encantador

winter *n* invierno, *m*. *a* de invierno; hiemal. *vi* pasar el invierno, invernar. *vt* (of cattle, etc.) guardar en invierno. **in w.,** en invierno, durante el invierno. **w. clothes,** ropa de invierno, *f*. **w. palace,** palacio de invierno, *m*. **w. pasture** *Lat. Am.* invernada, *f*. **w. quarters,** invernadero, *m*. **w. season,** invierno, *m*; temporada de invierno, *f*. **w. sleep,** invernada, *f*. **w. solstice,** solsticio hiemal, *m*. **w. sports,** deportes de nieve, *m pl*. **w. wheat,** trigo de invierno, *m*

wintry *a* de invierno; invernal; (of a smile, etc.) glacial

wipe *vt* limpiar; (rub) frotar; (dry) secar; (remove) quitar. *n* limpión, *m*; (blow) golpe de lado, *m*. **to w. one's eyes,** enjugarse las lagrimas. **to w. off, out,** limpiar; (remove) quitar; (erase) borrar; (kill) destruir completamente, exterminar; (a military force) destrozar; (a debt) cancelar

wire *n* alambre, *m*; hilo metálico, *m*; telégrafo (eléctrico), *m*; *inf* telegrama, *m*. *vt* atar con alambre; (fence) alambrar; (snare) coger con lazo de alambre; (of electrical equipment, etc.) instalar; (telegraph) telegrafiar. *vi* (telegraph) telegrafiar. **barbed w.,** alambre espinoso, *m*. **live w.,** alambre cargado (de electricidad), *m*; (person) fuerza viva, *f*. **w.-cutters,** cortaalambres, *m pl*. **w.-entanglement,** *mil* alambrada, *f*. **w. fence,**

alambrera, *f*, cercado de alambre, *m*. **w. gauze,** tela metálica, *f*. **w. nail,** punta de París, *f*. **w.-netting,** malla de alambre, *f*; alambrado, *m*. **w.-pulling,** influencias secretas, *f pl*; intrigas políticas, *f pl*

wireless a sin hilos; (of a message) radiotelegráfico; por radio. *n* telegrafía sin hilos, *f*; radiotelefonía, *f*; (telegram) radiocomunicación, *f*; (broadcasting) radio, *f*. *vt* radiotelegrafiar. **Let's listen to the w.,** Vamos a escuchar la radio. **portable w.,** radio portátil, *f*. **w. engineer,** ingeniero radio-telegrafista, *m*. **w. enthusiast,** radioaficionado (-da). **w. licence,** permiso de radiorreceptor, *m*. **w. operator,** radiotelegrafista, *mf*. **w. room,** cuarto de telegrafía sin hilos, *m*. **w. set,** aparato de radio, *m*. **w. station,** estación de radiotelegrafía, *f*; (broadcasting) radioemisora, *f*. **w. telegraph,** telégrafo sin hilos, *m*. **w. telegraphy,** telegrafía sin hilos, radiotelegrafía, *f*. **w. telephony,** telefonía sin hilos, *f*. **w. transmission,** radioemisión, *f*

wiretap *vi* poner escucha. *vt* poner escucha a

wiring *n* instalación de alambres eléctricos, *f*

wiry *a* semejante a un alambre; (of persons) nervudo

wisdom *n* sabiduría, *f*; (learning) saber, *m*; (judgment) juicio, *m*. **Book of W.,** Libro de la Sabiduría, *m*. **w.-tooth,** muela del juicio, *f*

wise *a* sabio; juicioso, prudente; (informed) enterado, informado. **a w. man,** un sabio. **in no w.,** de ningún modo. the **W. Men of the East,** los magos. **w. guy,** *inf* toro corrido, *m*

wish *n* deseo, *m*. **Best wishes for the New Year,** Los mejores deseos para el Año Nuevo. **w.-bone,** espoleta, *f*

wish *vt* querer; desear; ansiar; (with good morning, etc.) dar. **I w. he were here!** ¡Ojalá que estuviera aquí! **Theresa wishes us to go,** Teresa quiere que vayamos. **I w. it had happened otherwise,** Quisiera que las cosas hubiesen pasado de otra manera. **I w. you would make less noise,** Me gustaría que hicieses menos ruido. **I only w. one thing,** Solamente deseo una cosa. **I w. you good luck,** Te deseo mucha suerte. **I wished him a merry Christmas,** Le deseé unas Pascuas muy felices, Le felicité las Pascuas. **to w. a prosperous New Year,** desear un próspero Año Nuevo. **to w. good-by,** despedirse (de). **to w. good day,** dar los buenos días. **to w. for,** desear

wishful *a* deseoso; ansioso; ávido. **w. thinking,** ilusiones, *f pl*; optimismo injustificado, optimismo exagerado, *m*

wisp *n* mechón, *m*; jirón, *m*; trozo, pedazo, *m*

wistful *a* ansioso; triste; patético; (envious) envidioso; (regretful) de pesar; (re-

morseful) de remordimiento; (thoughtful) pensativo

wit, to *adv* a saber

wit *n* (reason) juicio, *m*; agudeza, gracia, *f*, rasgo de ingenio, *m*; ingenio, *m*; inteligencia, *f*, talento, *m*; (person) hombre de ingenio, *m*; mujer de ingenio, *f*. **my five wits,** mis cinco sentidos. **to be at one's wits' end,** no saber qué hacer. **to live by one's wits,** ser caballero de industria. **to lose one's wits,** perder el juicio

witch *n* bruja, *f*. **witches' sabbath,** aquelarre, *m*. **w.-doctor,** hechizador, mago, *m*. **witch-hazel,** carpe, *m*; loción de carpe, *f*

witchcraft *n* brujería, *f*; sortilegio, encantamiento, *m*

with *prep* con; en compañia de; en casa de; (against) contra; (among) entre; en; (by) por; (towards) hacia; para con; (according to) según; (notwithstanding) a pesar de; a; (concerning) con respecto a; en el caso de. **Rose is w. Antony,** Rosa está con Antonio. **He was w. his dog,** Estaba acompañado por su perro. **He pulled at it w. both hands,** Lo tiró con las dos manos. **filled w. fear,** lleno de miedo. **to shiver w. cold,** temblarse de frío. **the girl w. golden hair,** la muchacha del pelo dorado. **They killed it w. one blow,** Lo mataron de un solo golpe. **It rests w. you to decide,** Tú tienes que decidirlo; Te toca a tí decidirlo. **to begin w.,** *adv* para empezar; *v* empezar por. **w. all speed,** a toda prisa. **to part w.,** desprenderse de. (of people) despedirse de; separarse de. **w. that . . . ,** (at once) en esto . . . (disease and poverty, etc.) **are still with us,** están todavía en el mundo

withal *adv* además; al mismo tiempo. *prep* con

withdraw *vt* retirar; (words) retractar; (remove) quitar, privar (de); (a legal action) apartar. *vi* retirarse; retroceder; apartarse; irse

withdrawal *n* retirada, *f*; (retirement) retiro, *m*; apartamiento, *m*

withdrawn *a* (abstracted) ensimismado, meditabundo

wither *vi* marchitarse, secarse, ajarse. *vt* marchitar, secar, ajar; *fig* hacer languidecer, matar; (snub) avergonzar

withered *a* marchito, mustio; muerto; (of persons) acartonado, seco

withering *a* que marchita; (scorching) abrasador, ardiente; (scornful) despreciativo, desdeñoso; (biting) mordaz, cáustico

withhold *vt* retener; detener; (restrain) refrenar; apartar; (refuse) negar; abstenerse de; (refuse to reveal) ocultar

within *adv* dentro, adentro; en el interior; en casa; *fig* en su interior. **He stayed w.,** Se quedó dentro. **Is Mrs. González w.?** ¿Está en casa la Sra. González?

within *prep* dentro de; el interior de; en; entre; (within range of) al alcance de; a la distancia de; (near) cerca de; a poco de; (of time) en el espacio de, en; dentro de; (almost) por poco, casi. **He was w. an ace of being killed,** Por poco le matan. **to be w. hearing,** estar al alcance de la voz. **seen from w.,** visto desde dentro. **twice w. a fortnight,** dos veces en quince días. **w. himself,** por sus adentros, entre sí. **w. an inch of,** *fig* a dos dedos de. **w. a few miles of Edinburgh,** a unas millas de Edimburgo. **w. a short distance,** en una corta distancia; a poca distancia

without *prep* sin; falto de; (outside) fuera de; (beyond) más allá de. *adv* exteriormente; por fuera; hacia afuera; fuera. It goes w. saying, No hay que decir. **w. more ado,** sin más ni más. **w. my knowledge,** sin que yo lo supiese. **w. regard for,** sin miramientos por. **w. saying more,** sin decir más. **without batting an eyelash,** sin sobresaltos

withstand *vt* resistir, oponerse (a); soportar

witless *a* sin seso, tonto, necio

witness *n* (evidence) testimonio, *m*; (person) testigo, *mf*; espectador (-ra). **in w. whereof,** en fe de lo cual. **to bear w.,** atestiguar, dar testimonio. **to bring forward witnesses,** hacer testigos. **w. my hand,** en fe de lo cual, firmo. **w.-box,** puesto de los testigos, *m*. **w. for the defence,** testigo de descargo, *mf*. **w. for the prosecution,** testigo de cargo, *mf*

witness *vt* (show) mostrar, señalar; (see) ser testigo de, ver, presenciar; *law* atestiguar. *vi* dar testimonio; servir de testigo

witticism *n* rasgo de ingenio, donaire, *m*, agudeza, *f*

wittily *adv* ingeniosamente, donairosamente, agudamente

witty *a* salado, gracioso. **w. sally,** agudeza, *f*

wizard *n* mago, hechicero, *m*

wizened *a* seco, arrugado; (of persons) acartonado

wobble *vi* tambalearse, balancearse; (quiver) temblar; oscilar; *mech* galopar; (stagger) titubear; *fig* vacilar

woe *n* dolor, *m*; congoja, aflicción, *f*; mal, desastre, infortunio, *m*. **Woe is me!** ¡Ay de mí! ¡Desdichado de mí!

woebegone *a* angustiado

woeful *a* triste; doloroso; funesto

wolf *n* lobo (-ba). **a w. in sheep's clothing,** un lobo en piel de cordero. **to cry w.,** gritar «el lobo!» **to keep the w. from the door,** ponerse a cubierto del hambre. **w.-cub,** lobezno, *m*. **w.-hound,** perro lobo, *m*. **w. pack,** manada de lobos, *f*

woman *n* mujer, *f*; hembra, *f*; (lady-in-waiting) dama de servicio, *f*. **a fine figure of a w.,** una real hembra. **w. doctor,** médica, *f*. **w.-hater,** misógino, *m*. **w. of**

the town, mujer de la vida airada, *f*. **w. of the world,** mujer de mundo, *f*

womanish *a* afeminado

womankind *n* el sexo femenino, las mujeres

womanly *a* femenino, de mujer

womb *n* útero, *m*, matriz, *f*; *fig* seno, *m*

wonder *n* maravilla, *f*; prodigio, *m*; portento, milagro, *m*; (surprise) sorpresa, *f*; admiración, *f*; asombro, *m*; (problem) enigma, *m*; misterio, *m*. *vi* admirarse, asombrarse, maravillarse; sorprenderse. *vt* (ask oneself) preguntarse; desear saber. **I wondered what the answer would be,** Me preguntaba qué sería la respuesta. **It is no w. that . . . ,** No es mucho que . . . , No es sorprendente que **. . . It is one of the wonders of the world,** Es una de las maravillas del mundo. **to work wonders,** hacer milagros. **to w. at,** asombrarse de, maravillarse de; sorprenderse de. **w.-working,** milagroso

wonderful *a* maravilloso; magnífico; asombroso; *inf* estupendo

wonderland *n* mundo fantástico, *m*; reino de las hadas, *m*; país de las maravillas, *m*. **"Alice in W.,"** Alicia en el país de las maravillas

wondrous *a* maravilloso. *adv* extraordinariamente

wont *n* costumbre, *f*. *vi* soler. **as he was w.,** Como solía

won't. See will not

woo *vt* galantear; hacer la corte (a), solicitar amores a; cortejar, *Lat. Am.* afilar. *fig* solicitar; perseguir

wood *n* bosque, *m*; madera, *f*; (for the fire, etc.) leña, *f*; (cask) barril, *m*. **a de madera;** (of the woods) selvático. **dead w.,** ramas muertas, *f pl*; *fig* paja, *f*. **w. alcohol,** alcohol metílico, *m*. **w.-anemone,** anémona de los bosques, *f*. **w.-block floor,** entarimado, *m*. **w.-borer,** xiló-fago, *m*. **w.-carver,** tallista, *mf* **w.-carving,** talla en madera, *f*. **w.-craft,** conocimiento del campo, *m*. **w.-cut,** grabado en madera, *m*. **w.-cutter,** leñador, *m*. **w.-engraver,** grabador (-ra) en madera. **w.-engraving,** grabado al boj, *m*. **w.-fibre,** fibra de madera, *f*. **w.-louse,** cochinilla, *f*. **w.-nymph,** ninfa de los bosques, *f*. **w.-pigeon,** paloma torcaz, *f*. **w.-pile,** pila de leña, leñera, *f*. **w.-pulp,** pulpa de madera, *f*. **w.-shaving,** acepilladura, *f*. **w.-splinter,** tasquil, *m*, astilla, *f*. **w.-wind,** *mus* madera, *f*. **w.-worm,** carcoma, *f*

wooded *a* provisto de árboles, plantado de árboles, arbolado

wooden *a* de madera; de palo; (of smiles) mecánico; (stiff) indiferente, sin emoción; (clumsy) torpe; (of character) inflexible. **He has a w. leg,** Tiene una pata de palo. **w. beam,** madero, *m*; viga de madera, *f*.

w. bridge, pontón, *m*. **w. galley,** *print* galerín, *m*

woodland *n* bosques, *m pl*. a de bosque; silvestre

woodpecker *n* pájaro carpintero, picamaderos, *m*

woodshed *n* leñera, *f*

woodwork *n* maderaje, *m*; molduras, *f pl*; carpintería, *f*

woof *n* trama, *f*

wool *n* lana, *f*. a de lana; lanar. **to go w.-gathering,** estar distraído. **to pull the w. over a person's eyes,** engañar como a un chino. **w.-bearing,** lanar. **w.-carding,** cardadura de lana, *f*. **w.-growing,** cría de ganado lanar, *f*. **w. merchant,** comerciante en lanas, *mf*, lanero, *m*. **w.-pack,** fardo de lana, *m*. **w. trade,** comercio de lana, *m*

woollen a de lana; lanar. *n* paño de lana, *m*; género de punta de lana, *m*

woolly a lanudo, lanoso; de lana; *bot* velloso; (of hair) lanoso, crespo. *n* género de punta de lana, *m*; (sweater) jersey, *m*

word *n* palabra, *f*; *gram* vocablo, *m*; *theol* verbo, *m*; (maxim) sentencia, *f*, dicho, *m*; (message) recado, *m*; (news) aviso, *m*, noticias, *f*; (mil command) voz de mando, *f*; (order) orden, *f*; (password) contraseña, *f*; (term) término, *m*. *vt* expresar; formular; (draw up) redactar; escribir. **He was as good as his w.,** Fue hombre de palabra. **I do not know how to w. this letter,** No sé cómo redactar esta carta. **in a w.,** en una palabra; en resumidas cuentas. **by w. of mouth,** de palabra. **I give you my w. for it,** Le doy mi palabra de honor. **in other words,** en otros términos, en efecto. **the W.** (of God), el Verbo (de Dios). **to have a w. with,** hablar con; conversar con; entablar conversación con. **to leave w.,** dejar recado. **to have words with,** tener palabras con. **to keep one's w.,** cumplir su palabra

wording *n* fraseología, *f*; expresión, *f*; estilo, *m*; (terms) términos, *m pl*; (drawing up) redacción, *f*

wordy a verboso, prolijo

work *n* trabajo, *m*; (sewing) labor, *f*; (literary, artistic production and theological) obra, *f*; (behavior) acción, *f*, acto, *m*; (employment) empleo, *m*; (business affairs) negocios, *m pl*; *pl* **works,** obras, fortificaciones, *f, pl*; obras públicas, *f pl*; construcciones, *f pl*; (of a machine) mecanismo, *m*; motor, *m*; (factory) fábrica, *f*, taller, *m*. **w. of art,** obra de arte. **w. accident,** accidente del trabajo, *m*. **w.-bag,** bolsa de costura, *f*, saco de labor, *m*. **w.-box,** (on legs) costurero, *m*; (small) neceser de costura, *m*. **w.-people,** obreros (-as). **w.-room,** taller, *m*; (study) estudio, *m*; (for sewing) cuarto de costura, *m*. **w.-table,** banco de taller, *m*; (for writing) mesa de escribir, *f*

work *vi* trabajar, *Central America also*

laborar; *sew* hacer labor de aguja, coser; (embroider) bordar; *mech* funcionar, marchar; (succeed) tener éxito; ser eficaz; (be busy) estar ocupado; (be employed) tener empleo; (of the face) demudarse, torcerse; (ferment) fermentar; (operate) obrar *vt* trabajar; operar, hacer funcionar; mover; (control) manejar; (a mine) explotar; (embroider) bordar; (wood) tallar; (a problem) resolver; calcular; (iron, etc.) labrar; (the soil) cultivar; (a ship) maniobrar; (do) hacer; (bring about) efectuar; traer consigo; producir; (agitate oneself) agitarse, emocionarse, excitarse. **to w. in repoussé,** repujar. **to w. loose,** desprenderse. **to w. one's passage,** trabajar por el pasaje. **to w. overtime,** trabajar horas extraordinarias. **to w. two ways,** ser espada de dos filos. **to w. at,** trabajar en; ocuparse en; dedicarse a; elaborar. **to w. in,** *vt* introducir; insinuar. *vi* combinarse. **to w. into,** penetrar en. **to w. off,** usar, emplear; (get rid of) deshacerse de, librarse de. **to w. on, upon,** influir en; obrar sobre; estar ocupado en. **to w. out,** *vt* calcular; resolver; (a mine, topic, etc.) agotar; (develop) elaborar, desarrollar; trazar, planear; (find) encontrar. *vi* llegar (a); resultar; venir a ser. **to w. up,** crear; (promote) fomentar; producir; (excite) agitar, excitar; (fashion) dar forma (a), labrar; (finish) terminar

workable a laborable; factible, practicable; (of a mine) explotable

workaday a de todos los días; prosaico

workbench banco de mecánico, *f*, banco de taller, banco de trabajo, *m*, mesa de trabajo, *f*

workday *n* día de trabajo, día laborable, *m*

worker *n* trabajador (-ra); (manual) obrero (-ra); (of a machine) operario (-ia). **w.-ant,** hormiga obrera, *f*. **w.-bee,** abeja obrera, *f*

working a de trabajo; (of capital) de explotación; trabajador, que trabaja; obrero. *n* trabajo, *m*; (of a machine, organism, institution) funcionamiento, *m*; explotación, *f*; (of a mine) laboreo, *m*; (of a ship) maniobra, *f*; (of metal, stone, wood) labra, *f*; operación, *f*; (result) efecto, resultado, *m*; (calculation) cálculo, *m*. "**Not w.,**" «No funciona.» **to be in w. order,** funcionar bien. **w.-class,** clase obrera, *f*; pueblo, *m*. **w.-clothes,** ropa de trabajo, *f*. **w.-day,** día de trabajo, *m*. **w.-hours,** horas de trabajo, horas hábiles, *f pl*. **w. hypothesis,** postulado, *m*. **w.-man,** obrero, *m*; trabajador, *m*. **w.-out,** elaboración, *f*; ensayo, *m*. **w.-plan,** plan de trabajo, *m*. **w.-woman,** obrera, *f*; trabajadora, *f*

workman *n* obrero, *m*; (agricultural) labrador, *m*

workmanlike a bien hecho, bien acabado; (clever) hábil

workmanship *n* trabajo, *m*; manufactura, f; hechura, f; (cleverness) habilidad, f

workshop n taller, m

world n mundo, m. **For all the w. as if . . .,** Exactamente como si . . . **to see the w.,** ver mundo. **to treat the w. as one's oyster,** ponerse el mundo por montera. **w. without end,** por los siglos de los siglos. **w.-power,** potencia mundial, gran potencia, f. **w.-wide,** mundial, universal

worldliness n mundanería, f, conocimiento del mundo, m; frivolidad, vanidad mundana, f; egoísmo, m; prudencia, f

worldly a de este mundo; mundano; humano; profano; frívolo. **to be w.-wise,** tener mucho mundo

worm n gusano, m; lombriz, f; chem serpentín, m; (of a screw) tornillo sinfin, m; (person) gusano, m; fig gusano roedor, remordimiento, m. **intestinal w.,** lombriz intestinal, f, gusano de la conciencia. **w.-eaten,** carcomido. **w.-hole,** picadura de gusano, lombriguera, f. **w.-powder,** polvos antihelmínticos, m pl. **w.-shaped,** vermiforme. **having worms, suffering from worms** Lat. Am. lombriciento

worm vt (a dog) dar un vermífugo (a). vi arrastrarse como un gusano. **to w. one's way into,** deslizarse en; fig insinuarse en, introducirse en. **to w. out,** (secrets, information) sonsacar

wormy a gusanoso, lleno de gusanos

worn a (of garments) raído; estropeado; gastado; (of paths) trillado; (of the face) arrugado, cansado. **w. out,** acabado; muy usado; (tired) rendido; (exhausted) agotado

worry n preocupación, inquietud, ansiedad, f; problema, cuidado, m. vt (prey) zamarrear; preocupar, inquietar; molestar; importunar. vi estar preocupado, estar intranquilo, inquietarse. **Don't worry,** Pierda cuidado, No pase cuidado

worse a comp peor; inferior. adv peor; menos. n lo peor. **so much the w.,** tanto peor. **to be w. off,** estar peor; estar en peores circunstancias; ser menos feliz. **to be the w. for wear,** ser muy usado; estar ajado; ser ya viejo. **to grow w.,** empeorarse; (of an ill person) ponerse peor. **w. and w.,** de mal en peor, peor que peor. **w. than ever,** peor que nunca

worsen vt agravar, hacer peor; exasperar. vi agravarse, empeorarse; exasperarse

worship n culto, m; adoración, f; veneración, f. vt adorar; reverenciar. vi adorar; rezar; dar culto (a). **place of w.,** edificio de culto, m. **Your W.,** vuestra merced

worshipful a venerable, respetable

worshipper n adorador (-ra); pl **worshippers,** (in a church, etc.) fieles, m pl, congregación, f

worst a el (la, etc.) peor; más malo. adv el (la, etc.) peor. n el (la, etc.) peor; lo peor. vt vencer, derrotar; triunfar sobre **If the w. comes to the w.,** En el peor de los casos. **The w. of it is that . . . ,** Lo peor es que . . . **to have the w. of it,** salir perdiendo, llevar la peor parte

worsted n estambre, m, a de estambre

worth n valor, m; precio, m; mérito, m, a (que) vale; de precio de; cuyo valor es de; equivalente a; (que) merece; digno de. **He bought six hundred pesetas w. of sweets,** Compró seiscientas pesetas de dulces. **He sang for all he was w.,** Cantó con toda su alma. **It is w. seeing,** Es digno de verse, Vale la pena de verse. **to be w.,** valer. **to be w. while,** valer la pena, merecer la pena

worthless a sin valor; sin mérito; inútil; malo; (of persons) vil, despreciable, indigno

worthy a digno de respeto, benemérito, respetable; digno, merecedor; meritorio. n varón ilustre, hombre célebre, m; héroe, m; (inf iron) tío, m. **to be w. of,** ser digno de, merecer

would preterite and subjunctive of **will.** (indicating a conditional tense) **They w. come if . . . ,** Vendrían si . . . ; (indicating an imperfect tense) **Often he w. sing,** Muchas veces cantaba, **Now and then a blackbird w. whistle,** De vez en cuando silbó un mirlo; (expressing wish, desire) **What w. they?** ¿Qué quieren? **The place where I w. be,** El lugar donde quisiera estar. **W. I were at home!** ¡Ojalá que estuviese en casa! **I thought that I w. tell you,** Se me ocurrió la idea de decírselo. **It w. seem that . . . ,** Parece ser que . . . , Según parece . . . ; Se diría que . . . **He said that he w. never have done it,** Dijo que no lo hubiera hecho nunca. **They w. have been killed if he had not rescued them,** Habrían sido matados si él no los hubiese salvado. **He w. go,** Se empeñó en ir. **He w. not do it,** Rehusó hacerlo, Se resistió a hacerlo; No quiso hacerlo. **This w. probably be the house,** Sin duda esta sería la casa. **W. you be good enough to . . . ,** Tenga Vd. la bondad de . . . , Haga el favor de . . .

would-be a supuesto; llamado; aspirante (a); en esperanza de (followed by infin.); (frustrated) frustrado, malogrado

wound n herida, lesión, f. Lat. Am. also, lastimadura, f. vt herir; (the feelings) lastimar, lacerar. **deep w.,** herida penetrante, f. **the wounded,** los heridos.

wraith n fantasma, espectro, m, sombra, f

wrangle vi discutir; altercar, disputar acaloradamente; reñir; (bargain) regatear. n argumento, m; disputa, f, altercado, m; riña, f

wrap vt envolver; arrollar; cubrir; abrigar; (conceal) ocultar. n envoltorio, m; abrigo, m; pl **wraps,** abrigos y mantas de viaje, m pl. **W. yourself up well!** ¡Abrígate bien! **to be wrapped up in,** estar envuelto en;

fig estar entregado a, estar absorto en; (a person) estar embelesado con

wrapper *n* envoltura, *f*; embalaje, *m*; (of a newspaper) faja, *f*; (of a book) sobrecubierta, *f*; (dressing-gown) bata, *f*, salto de cama, *m*

wrapping *n* envoltura, cubierta, *f*. **w.-paper**, papel de envolver, *m*

wrath *n* ira, *f*

wrathful *a* airado

wreak *vt* ejecutar; (anger, etc.) descargar. **to w. one's vengeance**, vengarse

wreath *n* guirnalda, *f*; corona, *f*; trenza, *f*. **funeral w.**, corona funeraria, *f*

wreathe *vt* trenzar; (entwine) entrelazar (de); (garland) coronar (de), enguirnaldar (con); (encircle) ceñir, rodear; (a face in smiles) iluminar

wreck *n* naufragio, *m*; buque naufragado, *m*; destrucción, *f*; *fig* ruina, *f*; (remains) restos, *m pl*; (person) sombra, *f*. *vt* hacer naufragar; destruir; *fig* arruinar; hacer fracasar. **I am a complete w.**, *inf* Estoy hecho una ruina. **to be wrecked**, irse a pique, naufragar; *fig* arruinarse; frustrarse

wreckage *n* naufragio, *m*; restos de naufragio, *m pl*; ruinas, *f pl*; (of a car, plane, etc.) restos, *m pl*; accidente, *m*

wrench *n* (jerk) arranque, *m*; (pull) tirón, *m*; (sprain) torcedura, *f*; (tool) llave, *f*; (pain) dolor, *m*. *vt* arrancar; forzar; torcer, dislocar. **He has wrenched his arm**, Se ha torcido el brazo

wrest *vt* arrebatar, arrancar

wrestle *vi* luchar. *n* lucha grecorromana, *f*; *fig* lucha, *f*. **to w. with**, *fig* luchar con; luchar contra, *Lat. Am.* abrocharse (con . . .)

wrestler *n* luchador, *m*

wrestling *n* lucha grecorromana, *f*. **all-in-w.**, lucha libre, *f*. **w.-match**, lucha, *f*

wretch *n* infeliz, *mf*; (ruffian) infame, *m*; (playful) picaruelo (-la). **a poor w.**, un pobre diablo

wretched *a* (unhappy) infeliz, desdichado; miserable; pobre; (ill) enfermo; horrible; malo; mezquino; despreciable; lamentable

wriggle *vi* agitarse, moverse; menearse; serpear, culebrear; retorcerse. *n* See under **wriggling**. **to w. into**, insinuarse en, deslizarse dentro (de). **to w. out**, escaparse. **to w. out of a difficulty**, extricarse de una dificultad

wring *vt* torcer; estrujar; exprimir; arrancar; (force) forzar. **to w. one's hands**, restregarse las manos. **to w. the neck of**, torcer el pescuezo (a). **to w. out**, exprimir; estrujar

wrinkle *n* arruga, *f*; pliegue, *m*; *inf* noción, *f*. *vt* arrugar. *vi* arrugarse. **to w. one's brow**, (frown) fruncir el ceño; (in perplexity) arrugar la frente

wrist *n* muñeca, *f*. **w.-band**, tira del puño de la camisa, *f*. **w. bandage**, pulsera, *f*

writ *n* escritura, *f*; *law* decreto judicial, mandamiento, *m*; orden, *f*; título ejecutorio, *m*; hábeas corpus, *m*. **Holy W.**, la Sagrada Escritura. **to issue a w.**, dar orden. **to serve a w.**, notificar una orden. **w. of privilege**, auto de excarcelación, *m*

write *vt* and *vi* escribir; *fig* mostrar. **He writes a good hand**, Tiene buena letra. **I shall w. to them for a list**, Les escribiré pidiendo una lista. **to w. back**, contestar por escrito; contestar a una carta. **to w. down**, poner por escrito; anotar, apuntar; describir. **to w. for**, escribir para; escribir para pedir algo; escribir algo en vez de otra persona. **to w. off**, escribir; escribir rápidamente; cancelar. **to w. on**, seguir escribiendo; escribir sobre. **to w. out**, copiar; redactar. **to w. over again**, escribir de nuevo, escribir otra vez, volver a escribir. **to w. up**, redactar; *com* poner al día; (praise) escribir alabando

writer *n* escritor (-ra); autor (-ra). **the present w.**, el que, *m*, (*f*, la que) esto escribe. **writer's cramp**, calambre del escribiente, *m*

writhe *vi* retorcerse

writing *n* escritura, *f*; (work) escrito, *m*; inscripción, *f*; documento, *m*; (style) estilo, *m*; (hand) letra, *f*; el arte de escribir; trabajo literario, *m*. **in one's own w.**, de su propia letra. **in w.**, por escrito. **w.-case**, escribanía, *f*. **w.-desk**, escritorio, *m*. **w.-pad**, taco de papel, *m*. **w.-paper**, papel de escribir, *m*. **w.-table**, mesa de escribir, *f*

wrong *a* injusto; mal; equivocado, erróneo; inexacto; falso; incorrecto; desacertado; inoportuno. **It is the w. one**, No es el que hacía falta; No es el que quería. **to be in the w. place**, estar mal situado; estar mal colocado. **to be w.**, estar mal; no tener razón; (mistaken) estar equivocado; (of deeds or things) estar mal hecho; (be unjust) ser injusto; (of clocks) andar mal. **to do w.**, hacer mal; obrar mal. **to get out of bed on the w. side**, levantarse del izquierdo. **to go w.**, (of persons) descarriarse; (of affairs) ir mal; salir mal; frustrarse; (of apparatus) estropearse, no funcionar. **We have taken the w. road**, Nos hemos equivocado de camino. **You were very w. to . . .**, Has hecho muy mal en . . . **w.-headed**, terco, obstinado; disparatado. **w.-headedness**, terquedad, obstinación, *f*. **w. number**, (telephone) número errado, *m*. **w. side**, revés, *m*; lado malo, *m*. **w. side out**, al envés; al revés

wrong *adv* mal; injustamente; sin razón; incorrectamente; equivocadamente; (inside out) al revés. **to get it w.**, (a sum) calcular mal; (misunderstand) comprender mal

wrong n mal, m; injusticia, f; perjuicio, m; ofensa, f, agravio, m; culpa, f; error, m. **to be in the w.,** no tener razon; haber hecho mal. **to put one in the w.,** echar la culpa (a), hacer responsable (de)

wrong vt hacer mal (a); perjudicar; ser injusto con; ofender

wrongdoer n malhechor (-ra); pecador (-ra); perverso (-sa)

wrongdoing n maldad, maleficencia, f; pecado, m; injusticia, f

wrongful a injusto; perjudicial; falso

wrongly adv injustamente; erróneamente, equivocadamente; perversamente; mal

wrought a forjado; labrado; (hammered) batido; trabajado. **w. iron,** hierro dulce, hierro forjado, m. **w. up,** muy excitado, muy agitado, muy nervioso

wry a torcido; tuerto; triste; pesimista; desilusionado; irónico. **wry face,** mueca f, de desengaño, de ironía, de disgusto, etc. **make a wry face,** torcer el gesto, Mexico engestarse. **wry neck,** orn torcecuello, m

x n equis, f

x-ray vt tomar una radiografía (de). **x-ray,** rayo x, m pl. **x-ray examination,** examen con rayos x, m. **x-ray photograph,** radiografía, f

xylophone n xilófono, m

y n (letter) i griega, ye, f

yacht n yate, m. **y. club,** club marítimo, m. **y. race,** regata de yates, f

yam n batata, f, Lat. Am. boniato, camote, m

yank n tirón, m, sacudida, f. vt dar un tirón (a); sacar de un tirón

Yankee a and n yanqui, mf

yap vi ladrar. n ladrido, m

yard n (measure) yarda, f; naut verga, f; corral, m; (courtyard) patio, m. vt acorralar. **goods** y., estación de mercancías, f. **y.-arm,** penol (de la verga), m. **y.-stick,** vara de medir de una yarda, f

yarn n hilaza, f; hilo, m; (story) historia, f, cuento, m. **to spin a y.,** contar una historia

yaw vi naut guiñar; aer serpentear. n naut guiñada, f; aer serpenteo, m

yawn vi bostezar; quedarse con la boca abierta; (of chasms, etc.) abrirse. n bostezo, m. **to stifle a y.,** ahogar un bostezo

yea adv en verdad, ciertamente; y aun . . . no sólo . . . sino. n sí, m

year n año, m; pl years, años, m pl, edad, f. **We are getting on in years,** Nos vamos haciendo viejos. **He is five years old,** Tiene cinco años. **all the y. round,** todo el año, el año entero. **by the y.,** al año. **every other y.,** cada dos años, un año sí y otro no. **in after years,** en años posteriores. **last y.,** el año pasado. **next y.,** el año próximo. el año que viene. **y. after y.,** año tras año. **New Y.,** Año Nuevo, m. **to see the New Y. in,** ver empezar el Año Nuevo. **New Year's Day,** día de Año Nuevo, m. **(A) Happy New Y.!** ¡Feliz Año Nuevo! **y.-book,** anuario, m. **a y. later** Lat. Am. al año

yearly a anual. adv anualmente, cada año; una vez al año

yearn vi anhelar, suspirar (por); desear vivamente

yearning n sed, ansia, f; anhelo, deseo vehemente, m. a ansioso; anhelante; (tender) tierno

yeast n levadura, f

yell vi and vt chillar; gritar. n chillido, m; grito, m

yellow a amarillo; (of hair) rubio; (cowardly) cobarde; (newspaper) amarillista, sensacionalista. **to turn y.,** vi ponerse amarillo; amarillear. vt volver amarillo. **y. fever,** fiebre amarilla, f. **y.-hammer,** orn emberizo, m

yellow pages n páginas amarillas, páginas doradas, f pl

yelp vi gañir. n gañido, m

X, Y, Z

yen n (currency) yen, m; (desire) deseo vivo, m

yes adv sí. Yes? ¿De verdad? ¿Y qué pasó después? ¿Y entonces? **to say yes,** decir que sí; dar el sí. **yes-man,** amenista, sacristán de amén, m

yesterday adv ayer. n ayer, m. **the day before y.,** anteayer

yet adv aún, todavía. **as yet,** hasta ahora; todavía. **He has not come yet,** No ha venido todavía. **yet again,** otra vez

yet conjunc sin embargo, no obstante, con todo; pero. **The book is well written and yet I do not like it,** El libro está bien escrito, y sin embargo no me gusta

Yiddish n yídis, yídish, yídico, m; a yídico

yield vt producir; dar; (grant) otorgar; (afford) ofrecer; (surrender) ceder. vi producir; (submit) rendirse, someterse; (of disease) responder; (give way) flaquear, doblegarse; dar de sí; (consent) consentir (en); (to circumstances, etc.) ceder (a), sucumbir (a). n producción, f, producto, m; com rédito, m; (crop) cosecha, f. **to y. to temptation,** ceder a la tentación. **to y. up,** entregar; devolver

yielding a flexible; (soft) blando; dócil, sumiso; fácil; condescendiente

yogurt n yogur, m

yoke n yugo, m; (of oxen) yunta, f; (for pails) balancín, m; (of a garment) canesú, m; fig férula, f, yugo, m. vt uncir, acoplar. **to throw off the y.,** sacudir el yugo

yokel n patán, rústico, m

yolk n (of an egg) yema, f

yonder a aquel, m; aquella, f; aquellos, m pl; aquellas, f pl. adv allí; allí a lo lejos

yore n **in days of y.,** antaño; en otro tiempo

you pers pron nominative (polite form) usted (Vd.), mf; ustedes (Vds.), mf pl; (familiar form) sing tú, mf; (plural) vosotros, m pl; vosotras, f pl; (one) uno, m; una, f; se (followed by 3rd pers. sing. of verb). pers pron accusative (polite form) le, m; la, f; les, m pl; las, f pl; a usted, a ustedes; (informal form) te, mf, os, mf pl; (after most prepositions) ti, mf; vosotros, m pl; vosotras, f pl. **Are you there?** (telephone) ¡Oiga! **I gave the parcel to you,** Te (os) di el paquete; Di el paquete a usted (a ustedes). **I shall wait for you in the garden,** Te (os) esperaré en el jardín; Esperaré a Vds. (a Vd.) en el jardín. **This present is for you,** Este regalo es para tí (para vosotros, para Vd. (Vds.)). **Away with you!** ¡Vete! ¡Marchaos! **Between you and me,** Entre tú y yo. **you can't eat your cake and have it too,** no hay rosa sin espinas. **You never can tell,** No se sabe nunca, Uno no sabe nunca

young *a* joven; nuevo, reciente; inexperto; poco avanzado. *n* cría, *f*, hijuelos, *m pl.* **y. blood,** *inf* pollo pera, *m.* **y. girl,** jovencita, *f.* **y. man** joven, *m.* **y. people,** jóvenes, *m pl.* **in his y. days,** en su juventud. **The night is y.,** La noche está poca avanzada. **to grow y. again,** rejuvenecer. **with y.,** (of animals) preñada *f*

younger *a* más joven; menor. **Peter is his y. brother,** Pedro es su hermano menor. **to look y.,** parecer más joven

youngster *n* jovencito, chico, muchacho, *m*; niño, *m*

your *a poss* (polite form) su (*pl* sus), de usted (Vd.), (*pl* de ustedes (Vds.)); (familiar form) tu (*pl* vuestro). **I have y. papers,** Tengo tus (vuestros) papeles; Tengo los papeles de Vd. (or de Vds.). **How is y. mother?** ¿Cómo está su (tu) madre? **It is y. turn,** Te toca a ti, Le toca a Vd.

yours *pron poss* (polite form) (el) suyo, *m*; (la) suya, *f*; (los) suyos, *m pl*; (las) suyas, *f pl*; el, *m*; la, *f*; lo, *neut*; los, *m pl*; las, *f pl*; de usted (Vd.), *mf sing* or de ustedes (Vds.), *mf pl*; (familiar form) (el) tuyo, *m*; (la) tuya, *f*; (los) tuyos, *m pl*; (las) tuyas, *f pl*; (el) vuestro, *m*; (la) vuestra, *f*; (los) vuestros, *m pl*; (las) vuestras, *f pl.* **This is a picture of y.,** (addressing one person), Este es uno de los cuadros de usted (Vd.), Este es uno de tus cuadros. **This hat is mine, it is not y.,** Este sombrero es el mío, no es el tuyo. **The horse is y.,** El caballo es tuyo (de Vd.). **Y. affectionately,** Un abrazo de tu amigo . . . **Y. faithfully,** Queda de Vd. su att. (atentísimo) s.s. (seguro servidor). **Y. sincerely,** Queda de Vd. su aff. (afectuoso)

yourself *pron pers* (familiar form *sing*) tú mismo, *m*; tú misma, *f*; (after a preposition) tí, *mf*; (polite form) usted (Vd.) mismo, *m*; usted misma, *f*; *pl* **yourselves,** (familiar form) vosotros mismos, *m pl*; vosotras mismas, *f pl*; (polite form) ustedes (Vds.) mismos, *m pl*; ustedes mismas, *f pl.* **This is for y.,** Esto es para ti; Esto es para Vd.

youth *n* juventud, *f*; (man) joven, chico, mozalbete, *m*; (collectively) jóvenes, *m pl*, juventud, *f*

youthful *a* joven, juvenil; de la juventud

Yucatan *a* yucateco

Yule *n* Navidad, *f.* **y.-log,** leño de Navidad, *m.* **y-tide,** Navidades, *f pl*

z *n* (letter) zeda, zeta, *f*

zeal *n* celo, entusiasmo, *m*; ardor, fervor, *m*

zealot *n* fanático (-ca)

zealous *a* celoso, entusiasta

zebra *n* cebra, *f*

zenith *n* cenit, *m*; *fig* apogeo, punto culminante, *m*

zephyr *n* céfiro, *m*, brisa, *f*

zero *n* cero, *m.* **below z.,** bajo cero. **z. hour,** hora cero, *f*

zest *n* sabor, gusto, *m*; entusiasmo, *m.* **to eat with z.,** comer con buen apetito. **to enter on with z.,** emprender con entusiasmo

zigzag *n* zigzag, *m.* *a* and *adv* en zigzag. *vi* zigzaguear, hacer zigzags, serpentear; (of persons) andar haciendo eses

zinc *n* cinc, *m.* **z. oxide,** óxido de cinc, *m*

Zion *n* Sión, *m*

Zionism *n* sionismo, *m*

Zionist *n* and *a* sionista

zip *n* (of a bullet) silbido, *m*; *inf* energía, *f.* **zip fastener,** cierre de cremallera, *m*

zip code *n* código postal, *m*

zipper *n* cremallera, *f*, cierre relámpago, cierre, cerrador, *m*

zither *n* cítara, *f*

zodiac *n* zodiaco, *m*

zone *n* zona, *f*; faja, *f*

zoo *n* jardín zoológico, *m*

zoological *a* zoológico. **Z. garden,** jardín zoológico, *m*

zoom *n* zumbido, *m.* *vi* zumbar; *aer* empinarse

Numbers/Números

Cardinal/Cardinales

one	1	uno, una
two	2	dos
three	3	tres
four	4	cuatro
five	5	cinco
six	6	seis
seven	7	siete
eight	8	ocho
nine	9	nueve
ten	10	diez
eleven	11	once
twelve	12	doce
thirteen	13	trece
fourteen	14	catorce
fifteen	15	quince
sixteen	16	dieciséis
seventeen	17	diecisiete
eighteen	18	dieciocho
nineteen	19	diecinueve
twenty	20	veinte
twenty-one	21	veintiuno
twenty-two	22	veintidós
thirty	30	treinta
thirty-one	31	treinta y uno
thirty-two	32	treinta y dos
forty	40	cuarenta
fifty	50	cincuenta
sixty	60	sesenta
seventy	70	setenta
eighty	80	ochenta
ninety	90	noventa

one hundred	100	cien
one hundred one	101	ciento uno
one hundred two	102	ciento dos
two hundred	200	doscientos, -as
three hundred	300	trescientos, -as
four hundred	400	cuatrocientos, -as
five hundred	500	quinientos, -as
six hundred	600	seiscientos, -as
seven hundred	700	setecientos, -as
eight hundred	800	ochocientos, -as
nine hundred	900	novecientos, -as
one thousand	1,000	mil
two thousand	2,000	dos mil
one hundred thousand	100,000	cien mil
one million	1,000,000	un millón
two million	2,000,000	dos millones

Ordinal/Ordinales

first	1st /	1°	primero
second	2nd /	2°	segundo
third	3rd /	3°	tercero
fourth	4th /	4°	cuarto
fifth	5th /	5°	quinto
sixth	6th /	6°	sexto
seventh	7th /	7°	séptimo
eighth	8th /	8°	octavo
ninth	9th /	9°	noveno
tenth	10th /	10°	décimo

Spanish ordinal numbers are used as adjectives: el primer hombre, los primeros hombres, la primera mujer, las primeras mujeres, etc.

Weights and Measures/Pesos y Medidas

1 centímetro	=	.3937 inches	1 kilolitro	=	264.18 gallons
1 metro	=	39.37 inches	1 inch	=	2.54 centímetros
1 kilómetro	=	.621 mile	1 foot	=	.305 metros
1 centigramo	=	.1543 grain	1 mile	=	1.61 kilómetros
1 gramo	=	15.432 grains	1 grain	=	.065 gramos
1 kilogramo	=	2.2046 pounds	1 pound	=	.455 kilogramos
1 tonelada	=	2.204 pounds	1 ton	=	.907 toneladas
1 centilitro	=	.338 ounces	1 ounce	=	2.96 centilitros
1 litro	=	1.0567 quart (liquid);	1 quart	=	1.13 litros
		.908 quart (dry)	1 gallon	=	4.52 litros

Signs/Señales

Caution	Precaución	**No smoking**	Prohibido fumar
Danger	Peligro	**No admittance**	Entrada prohibida
Exit	Salida	**One way**	Dirección única
Entrance	Entrada	**No entry**	Dirección prohibida
Stop	Alto	**Women**	Señoras or Mujeres or Damas
Closed	Cerrado	**Men**	Señores or Hombres or Caballeros
Open	Abierto	**Ladies' Room**	Cuarto de Damas
Slow	Despacio	**Men's Room**	Servicio

Days of the Week/Días de la Semana

Sunday	domingo	Thursday	jueves
Monday	lunes	Friday	viernes
Tuesday	martes	Saturday	sábado
Wednesday	miércoles		

Months/Meses

January	enero	July	julio
February	febrero	August	agosto
March	marzo	September	septiembre
April	abril	October	octubre
May	mayo	November	noviembre
June	junio	December	diciembre

Useful Phrases/Locuciones Útiles

Good day or Good morning! ¡Buenos días!

Good afternoon. ¡Buenas tardes!

Good night or Good evening! ¡Buenas noches!

Hello! ¡Hola!

Welcome! ¡Bienvenido!

See you later! ¡Hasta luego!

Goodbye! ¡Adiós!

How are you? ¿Cómo está usted?

I am fine, thank you. Estoy bien, gracias.

I am pleased to meet you. Mucho gusto en conocerle.

May I introduce . . . Quisiera presentar . . .

Thank you very much. Muchas gracias.

You're welcome. De nada or No hay de qué.

Please. Por favor.

Excuse me. Con permiso.

Good luck! ¡Buena suerte!

To your health! ¡Salud!

Please help me. Ayúdeme, por favor.

I don't know. No sé.

I don't understand. No entiendo.

Do you understand? ¿Entiende usted?

I don't speak Spanish. No hablo español.

Do you speak English? ¿Habla usted inglés?

How do you say . . . in Spanish? ¿Cómo se dice . . . en español?

What do you call this? ¿Cómo se llama esto?

Speak slowly, please. Hable despacio, por favor.

Please repeat. Repita, por favor.

I don't like it. No me gusta.

I am lost. Ando perdido or Me he extraviado.

What is your name? ¿Cómo se llama usted?

My name is . . . Me llamo . . .

I am an American. Soy norteamericano.

Where are you from? ¿De dónde es usted?

I'm from . . . Soy de . . .

How is the weather? ¿Qué tiempo hace?

It's cold (hot) today. Hace frío (calor) hoy.

What time is it? ¿Qué hora es?

How much is it? ¿Cuánto es?

It is too much. Es mucho.

What do you wish? ¿Qué desea usted?

I want to buy . . . Quiero comprar . . .

May I see something better? ¿Podría ver algo mejor?

May I see something cheaper? ¿Podría ver algo menos caro?

It is not exactly what I want. No es precisamente lo que quiero.

I am hungry. Tengo hambre.

I am thirsty. Tengo sed.

Where is there a restaurant? ¿Dónde hay restaurante?

I have a reservation. Tengo reservación.

I would like . . . Quisiera . . . ; Me gustaría . . .

Please give me . . . Me da . . .

Please bring me . . . Me trae . . .

May I see the menu? ¿Se puede ver el menú?

The bill, please. La cuenta, por favor.

Is service included in the bill? ¿El servicio está incluido en la cuenta?

Where is there a hotel? ¿Dónde hay hotel?

Where is the post office? ¿Dónde está el correo?

Is there any mail for me? ¿Tengo correo?

Where can I mail this letter? ¿Dónde se puede echar esta carta?

Take me to . . . Lléveme a . . .

I believe I am ill. Creo que estoy enfermo.

Please call a doctor. Por favor, llame al médico.

Please call the police. Por favor, llame a la policía.

I want to send a telegram. Quiero poner telegrama.

As soon as possible. Cuanto antes.

Round trip. Ida y vuelta.

Please help me with my luggage. Por favor, ayúdeme con equipaje.

Where can I get a taxi? ¿Dónde hay taxi?

What is the fare to . . . ¿Cuánto es el pasaje hasta . . . ?

Please take me to this address. Por favor, lléveme a esta dirección.

Where can I change my money? ¿Dónde se puede cambiar dinero?

Where is the nearest bank? ¿Dónde está el banco más cercano?

Can you accept my check? ¿Aceptará cheque?

Do you accept traveler's checks? ¿Aceptan cheques de viaje?

What is the postage? ¿Cuánto es el franqueo?

Where is the nearest drugstore? ¿Dónde está la farmacia más cercana?

Where is the men's (women's) room? ¿Dónde está el servicio de caballeros (de señoras)?

Please let me off at . . . Por favor, déjeme bajar en . . .

Right away! ¡Pronto!

Help! ¡Socorro!

Who is it? ¿Quién es?

Just a minute! ¡Un momento no más!

Come in! ¡Pase usted!

Pardon me. Dispense usted.

Stop! ¡Pare!

Look out! ¡Cuidado!

Hurry! ¡De prisa! or ¡Dése prisa!

Go on! ¡Siga!

To (on, at) the right. A la derecha.

To (on, at) the left. A la izquierda.

Straight ahead. Adelante.

The foundation of any reference library:

RANDOM HOUSE WEBSTER'S DICTIONARY

Now completely revised and updated!

With 60,000 new entries and hundreds of new words and meanings, this fine resource is an up-to-the-minute authority on word definitions.

Includes more than 150 new illustrations, helpful supplements on writing, usage, and metric measurements, and up-to-date computer and business terms!

RANDOM HOUSE WEBSTER'S DICTIONARY
Third Edition

Published by Ballantine Books.
Available in bookstores everywhere.

When you are looking for just the
right word, turn to:

RANDOM HOUSE
ROGET'S THESAURUS

With more than 11,000 main entries and
200,000 synonyms and antonyms, this is
the authoritative, comprehensive, and
easy-to-use thesaurus favored by writers
and students alike!

RANDOM HOUSE
ROGET'S THESAURUS
Third Edition

Published by Ballantine Books.
Available in bookstores everywhere.

Articles, memos, letters, scripts, essays,
fiction—you can improve them all when
you use the

RANDOM HOUSE
GUIDE TO
GOOD WRITING

Featuring exercises and examples from
great writers to help you master style,
usage, grammar, and punctuation.

Clear, concise, effective—it's a must for
anyone who wishes to communicate well
in writing.

RANDOM HOUSE
GUIDE TO GOOD WRITING

by Mitchell Ivers

Published by Ballantine Books.
Available in bookstores everywhere.

Express yourself with precision . . .

RANDOM HOUSE WEBSTER'S POWER VOCABULARY BUILDER

teaches how words work—and how to make them work for you!

- Strengthen your word power and expertise!
- Learn proper pronunciation!
- Try your skill at numerous vocabulary tests and entertaining word puzzles to gauge your mastery of English!

RANDOM HOUSE WEBSTER'S POWER VOCABULARY BUILDER

Published by Ballantine Books.
Available in bookstores everywhere.

The authoritative, comprehensive, and handy reference for writers, students, and businesspeople alike:

RANDOM HOUSE WEBSTER'S SPELL CHECKER & ABBREVIATIONS DICTIONARY

- 50,000 entries spelled and divided
- Preferred hyphenation breaks
- Vocabulary featuring business and computer terms
- More than 10,000 abbreviations for common words and phrases
- Covers all areas of school, business, and science
- Includes acronyms, initialisms, and symbols

RANDOM HOUSE WEBSTER'S SPELL CHECKER & ABBREVIATIONS DICTIONARY

Published by Ballantine Books.
Available in bookstores everywhere.

The finest collection of affordable reference resources available.

RANDOM HOUSE REFERENCE

Tools to help you communicate effectively.